lonely planet

Italy

Damien Simonis
Fiona Adams
Miles Roddis
Sally Webb
Nicola Williams

LONELY PLANET PUBLICATIONS
Melbourne • Oakland • London • Paris

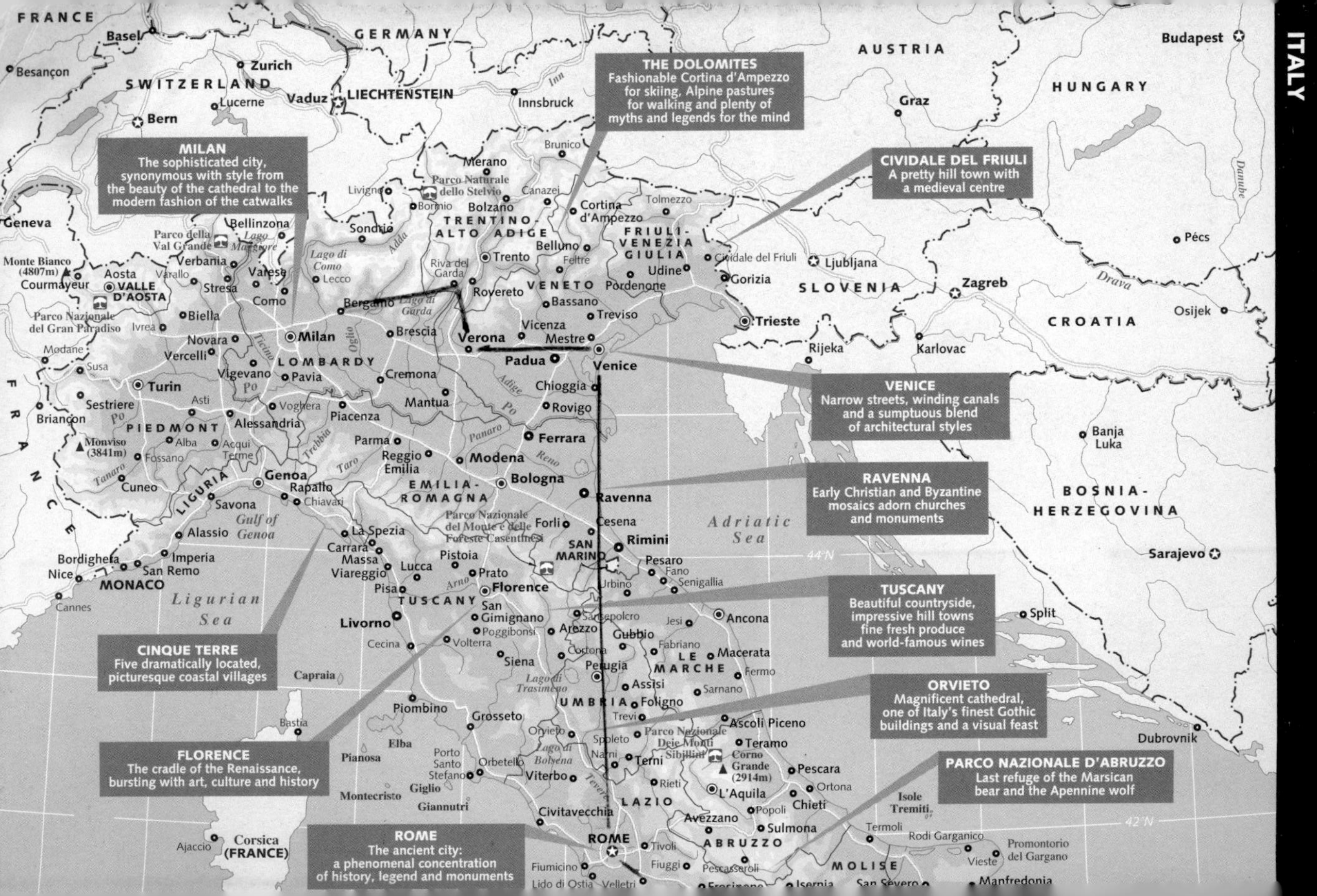

THE DOLOMITES
Fashionable Cortina d'Ampezzo for skiing, Alpine pastures for walking and plenty of myths and legends for the mind
MILAN
The sophisticated city, synonymous with style from the beauty of the cathedral to the modern fashion of the catwalks
CIVIDALE DEL FRIULI
A pretty hill town with a medieval centre
VENICE
Narrow streets, winding canals and a sumptuous blend of architectural styles
RAVENNA
Early Christian and Byzantine mosaics adorn churches and monuments
TUSCANY
Beautiful countryside, impressive hill towns fine fresh produce and world-famous wines
CINQUE TERRE
Five dramatically located, picturesque coastal villages
ORVIETO
Magnificent cathedral, one of Italy's finest Gothic buildings and a visual feast
FLORENCE
The cradle of the Renaissance, bursting with art, culture and history
PARCO NAZIONALE D'ABRUZZO
Last refuge of the Marsican bear and the Apennine wolf
ROME
The ancient city: a phenomenal concentration of history, legend and monuments
FRANCE
SWITZERLAND
GERMANY
LIECHTENSTEIN
AUSTRIA
HUNGARY
SLOVENIA
CROATIA
BOSNIA-HERZEGOVINA
MONACO
SAN MARINO
Adriatic Sea
Ligurian Sea
Corsica (FRANCE)

MATERA
Troglodyte city of 20,000 people until the 1950s and now a UNESCO World Heritage Site

AMALFI COAST
Dramatic cliffs and clear blue water, paths weaving from hillside villages to coastal towns – one of Europe's most beautiful coastlines

SARDINIA
Secluded sandy beaches, ancient archaeological sites, rugged mountains and unique traditions

MT ETNA
One of the world's most active volcanoes and Europe's largest at 3350m

ELEVATION

3000m
2000m
1000m
500m
0

0 50 100km
0 30 60mi

Italy
5th edition – March 2002
First published – September 1993

Published by
Lonely Planet Publications Pty Ltd ABN 36 005 607 983
90 Maribyrnong St, Footscray, Victoria 3011, Australia

Lonely Planet Offices
Australia Locked Bag 1, Footscray, Victoria 3011
USA 150 Linden St, Oakland, CA 94607
UK 10a Spring Place, London NW5 3BH
France 1 rue du Dahomey, 75011 Paris

Photographs
All of the images in this guide are available for licensing from Lonely Planet Images.
email: lpi@lonelyplanet.com.au
Web site: www.lonelyplanetimages.com

Front cover photograph
The gardens of Villa Pisani, Venice (Damien Simonis)

ISBN 1 86450 352 1

Printed by The Bookmaker International Ltd
Printed in China

Contents – Text

THE AUTHORS 9

THIS BOOK 13

FOREWORD 14

INTRODUCTION 15

FACTS ABOUT ITALY 16

History 16
Geography 43
Geology 43
Climate 45
Ecology & Environment 46
Flora & Fauna 46
Government & Politics 48
Economy 49
Population & People 50
Education 51
Science & Philosophy 51
Arts 52
Society & Conduct 60
The Mafia 62
Religion 63
Language 64

ART & ARCHITECTURE 66

The Greeks, The Etruscans & The Latins 66
The Romans 68
Early Christian & Byzantine 70
Romanesque 72
Gothic 74
Renaissance 76
High Renaissance 78
Baroque 80
Neoclassicism 81
The 19th Century to Today 83

FACTS FOR THE VISITOR 85

Suggested Itineraries 85
Planning 86
Responsible Tourism 88
Tourist Offices 89
Visas & Documents 90
Embassies & Consulates 92
Customs 94
Money 94
Post & Communications 99
Digital Resources 103
Books 103
Films 105
Newspapers & Magazines 105
Video Systems 107
Photography & Video 107
Time 107
Electricity 107
Weights & Measures 108
Laundry 108
Toilets 108
Health 108
Women Travellers 114
Gay & Lesbian Travellers 115
Disabled Travellers 115
Senior Travellers 116
Travel with Children 116
Dangers & Annoyances 117
Legal Matters 119
Business Hours 120
Public Holidays 121
Special Events 121
Activities 123
Courses 125
Work 125
Accommodation 127
Food 130
Italian Food 132
Drinks 138
Entertainment 140
Spectator sports 141
Shopping 144

GETTING THERE & AWAY 146

Air 146
Land 151
Sea 157
Organised Tours 157

GETTING AROUND 159

Air 159
Bus 159
Train 160
Car & Motorcycle 162
Bicycle 166
Hitching 167
Boat 167
Local Transport 168
Organised Tours 168

ROME & LAZIO 170

Rome (Roma) 170
History 171
Orientation 172
Information 173
Rome for Children 178
Walking Tour 178
Capitoline Hill 180
Piazza Venezia 182
Imperial Forums 183
Roman Forum & Palatine 184
Colosseum 188
Domus Aurea 189
Esquiline Hill 190
Basilica di San Giovanni in Laterano 191
Caelian Hill 192
Terme di Caracalla 192
Aventine Hill 192
Towards the Jewish Ghetto 209
Trastevere 209
Piazza di Campo de' Fiori & Around 210
Piazza Navona 210
Palazzo Altemps 210
The Pantheon 211
Chiesa di Santa Maria Sopra Minerva 211
Trevi Fountain 211
Piazza di Spagna & the Spanish Steps 212
Piazza del Popolo 212
The Vatican 213
Ara Pacis 223
Villa Borghese & Around 223
Around Via Vittorio Veneto 224
Quirinale 224
Terme di Diocleziano 225
Palazzo Massimo alle Terme 225
San Paolo Fuori-le-Mura 225
San Lorenzo Fuori-le-Mura 225
Via Appia Antica & the Catacombs 226
Gianicolo & Villa Doria Pamphilj 227
EUR 228
Language Courses 228
Organised Tours 228
Special Events 229
Places to Stay 229
Places to Eat 238
Entertainment 248
Spectator Sports 252
Shopping 252
Getting There & Away 254
Getting Around 256
Lazio 259
Ostia Antica 261
Tivoli 261
Etruscan Sites 262
Civitavecchia 264
Viterbo 265
Around Viterbo 268
The Lakes 268
South of Rome 270

LIGURIA, PIEDMONT & VALLE D'AOSTA 274

Liguria 274
Genoa (Genova) 276
Around Genoa 290
Riviera di Levante 291
Riviera di Ponente 301
Piedmont (Piemonte) 310
Turin (Torino) 312
Valle di Susa 325
Southern Piedmont 326
Eastern Piedmont 330
Northern Piedmont 331
Valle d'Aosta 332
Aosta 334
Around Aosta 338
Courmayeur 339
Valtournenche 341
Parco Nazionale del Gran Paradiso 341
Around Monte Rosa 342

LOMBARDY & THE LAKES 343

Milan (Milano) 344
South of Milan 367
Pavia 367
East of Milan 369
Bergamo 369
Around Bergamo 374
Valtellina 374
Brescia 374
Cremona 377
Mantua (Mantova) 380
Around Mantua 383
The Lakes 384
Lago Maggiore 384
Lago d'Orta 388
Lago di Como 389
Lago di Garda 395
Lago d'Iseo & Valle Camonica 399

TRENTINO-ALTO ADIGE 401

Walking in the Dolomites 404
Skiing in the Dolomites 405
Other Activities 406
Trentino 406
Trent (Trento) 406
Brenta Dolomites 409
Val di Non 413
Val di Sole & Valle di Peio 413
San Martino di Castrozza 414
Canazei & Around 415
Gruppo di Sella 416
Alto Adige 417
Bolzano (Bozen) 417
Merano (Meran) 420
Parco Nazionale dello Stelvio 422
Val Gardena 423
Alpe di Siusi & Parco Naturale dello Sciliar 424
Val Badia 425
Cortina d'Ampezzo 427
Valzoldana 430
Val Pusteria & the Sesto Dolomites 431

THE VENETO 433

Venice (Venezia) 433
Around the Veneto 473
The Brenta Riviera 473
Padua (Padova) 473
Around Padua 479
Vicenza 480
Around Vicenza 484
Verona 484
Treviso 490
Belluno 492

FRIULI-VENEZIA GIULIA 494

Trieste 495
Around Trieste 501
Gorizia 502
Aquileia 504
Palmanova 504
Grado 505
Lignano 505
Udine 505
Cividale del Friuli 509
Il Carnia 509

EMILIA-ROMAGNA & SAN MARINO 511

Bologna 513
Porretta 522
West of Bologna 522
Modena 522
Around Modena 527
Reggio Emilia 527
Around Reggio Emilia 529
Parma 530
Around Parma 535
Piacenza 536
Ferrara 538
Po Delta (Foci del Po) 541
Ravenna 542
Around Ravenna 547
Rimini 547
San Marino 551

TUSCANY (TOSCANA) 554

Florence (Firenze) 556
Around Florence 594
Northern & Western Tuscany 596
Prato 596
Pistoia 598
Lucca 600
The Garfagnana 604
Massa & Carrara 604
Pisa 605
Livorno (Leghorn) 610
Elba Island (Isola d'Elba) 613
Central Tuscany 616
Il Chianti 616
Siena 617
San Gimignano 626
Volterra 628
Certaldo 630
Abbazia di San Galgano 630
Le Crete 631
Montalcino 632
Sant'Antimo 632
Montepulciano 633
Southern Tuscany 635
Maremma & Etruscan Sites 635
Monte Argentario 637
Eastern Tuscany 638
Arezzo 638
Sansepolcro 641
Cortona 641

UMBRIA & LE MARCHE 643

Umbria 643
Perugia 645
Lago di Trasimeno 653
Deruta 655
Todi 655
Assisi 656
Spello 662
Around Spello 662
Gubbio 663
Around Gubbio 666
Spoleto 666
The Valnerina 670
Terni 672
Orvieto 672
Around Orvieto 677
Le Marche 677
Ancona 678
Around Ancona 682
Urbino 682
Around Urbino 686
Pesaro 686
Around Pesaro 689
Fano 689
Around Fano 690
Senigallia 690
Grotte di Frasassi 690
Macerata 691
Around Macerata 692
Ascoli Piceno 693
Monti Sibillini 696

ABRUZZO & MOLISE 697

Abruzzo 697
L'Aquila 698
Parco Nazionale del Gran Sasso e Monti della Laga 702
Sulmona 702
Around Sulmona 704
Parco Nazionale d'Abruzzo 705
Pescara 706
Molise 707
Campobasso 707
Around Campobasso 708
Isernia 709
Around Isernia 709
Termoli 709
Albanian Towns 710

CAMPANIA 711

Naples (Napoli) 712
Around Naples....................734
Campi Flegrei......................734
Caserta 736
Around Caserta 737
Benevento 737
Avellino & Around 738
Gulf of Naples (Golfo di Napoli) 738
Ischia 744
Procida................................746
South of Naples 747
Herculaneum & Ercolano 747
Mt Vesuvius (Vesuvio) 749
Pompeii 750
Sorrento..............................754
Amalfi Coast (Costiera Amalfitana) 759
Positano..............................759
Around Positano 762
Amalfi 762
Ravello................................765
From Amalfi to Salerno 766
Paestum..............................769
Parco Nazionale del Cilento e Vallo di Diano 771
Costiera Cilentana (Cilento Coast)...............771

APULIA, BASILICATA & CALABRIA 773

Apulia (Puglia) 773
Foggia 775
Lucera 777
Troia 778
Manfredonia 778
Promontorio del Gargano (Gargano Promontory)......778
Isole Tremiti 783
Trani 784
Around Trani 785
Bari 787
The Trulli Area 792
Brindisi...............................796
Lecce 799
Around Lecce......................803
Otranto 803
Around Otranto...................804
Gallipoli 805
Taranto 805
Around Taranto 808
Basilicata 808
Potenza 808
North of Potenza 810
Matera................................811
Aliano 814
Metaponto..........................815
Around Metaponto 815
Tyrrhenian Coast (Costa Tirrenica)...............816
Calabria 816
Catanzaro 818
Ionian Coast 820
Cosenza.............................822
La Sila 825
Reggio di Calabria 826
Aspromonte Massif 829
Tyrrhenian Coast (Costa Tirrenica)...............830

SICILY (SICILIA) 833

Palermo 838
Around Palermo..................850
Northern Coast 852
Parco Naturale Regionale delle Madonie 852
Cefalù 853
Tindari 854
Milazzo 854
Aeolian Islands (Isole Eolie) 855
Lipari 856
Vulcano 859
Salina.................................861
Panarea 861
Stromboli 862
Filicudi & Alicudi 863
Eastern Coast.....................864
Messina 864
South to Taormina 866
Taormina 866
Around Taormina 870
Catania 870
Mt Etna 875
South-Eastern Sicily 877
Syracuse (Siracusa)............877
Noto 883
Ragusa & Ragusa Ibla 885
Modica 886
Central & South-Western Sicily...............................886
Enna 886
Piazza Armerina 888
Morgantina 889
Agrigento...........................889
Eraclea Minoa 893
Isole Pelagie (Pelagic Islands) 893
Sciacca 894
Selinunte 894
North-Western Sicily 895
Marsala 895
Between Marsala & Trapani 897
Trapani..............................897
Erice..................................901
Segesta 901
Golfo di Castellammare 902
Egadi Islands (Isole Egadi)....903
Pantelleria 904

SARDINIA (SARDEGNA) 905

Cagliari 908
Around Cagliari 913
Southern Sardinia 914
Sant'Antioco & San Pietro ..914
Iglesias..............................916
Around Iglesias 916
Western Sardinia 917
Costa Verde 917
Oristano.............................918
Around Oristano 920
Bosa..................................921
Central Sardinia 922

Around Barumini 922
Northern Sardinia 923
Alghero 923
Around Alghero 925
Sassari 926
Around Sassari 928
Porto Torres 929
Stintino 929
Santa Teresa di Gallura........930
Palau & la Maddalena 931
Costa Smeralda 933
Olbia 933
Golfo Aranci 935
Eastern Sardinia 935
Nuoro 936
Oliena 937
Orgosolo 937
Dorgali, Cala Gonone & Around 939
Baunei, Urzulei & Around....942
Arbatax 943

LANGUAGE **944**

GLOSSARY **950**

ACKNOWLEDGEMENTS **954**

INDEX **963**

Text 963
Boxed Text.........................971

MAP LEGEND **back page**

METRIC CONVERSION **inside back cover**

Contents – Maps

GETTING AROUND

Train Routes 161

ROME & LAZIO

Rome Walking Tour 179
Roman Forum (Foro Romano) 185
Palatine 187
Rome Colour Maps 193
St Peter's Basilica 216
Getting Around Rome 256
Lazio 260
Viterbo 267

LIGURIA, PIEDMONT & VALLE D'AOSTA

Liguria 275
Genoa (Genova) 277
Central Genoa 280–1
La Spezia 298
San Remo 306
Piedmont (Piemonte) 311
Turin (Torino) 314–15
Valle d'Aosta 333
Aosta 335

LOMBARDY & THE LAKES

Lombardy (Lombardia) 344
Greater Milan (Milano) 346
Milan 348–9
Central Milan 350
Golden Quad (Quadilatero d'Oro) 365
Pavia 368
Bergamo 370
Brescia 375
Cremona 378
Mantua (Mantova) 381
Como 391

TRENTINO-ALTO ADIGE

Trentino-Alto Adige 402–3
Trento (Trent) 407
Bolzano (Bolzen) 418

THE VENETO

The Veneto 434
Venice (Venezia) 440–1
San Marco, San Polo & Santa Croce 446–7
Cannaregio 455
Padua (Padova) 475
Vicenza 481
Verona 486

FRIULI-VENEZIA GIULIA

Friuli-Venezia Giulia 495
Trieste 497
Udine 506

EMILIA-ROMAGNA & SAN MARINO

Emilia-Romagna 512
Bologna 514
Modena 524
Reggio Emilia 528
Parma 531
Piacenza 536
Ferrara 539
Ravenna 544
Rimini 549
San Marino 551

TUSCANY (TOSCANA)

Tuscany (Toscana) 555
Greater Florence (Firenze) 558
Florence 562–3
Central Florence 564–5
Around the Cathedral 567
Prato 597
Pistoia 599
Lucca 601
Pisa 606
Livorno (Leghorn) 611
Siena 618
Volterra 629
Arezzo 639

UMBRIA & LE MARCHE

Umbria .... [illegible]
Perugia 646
Assisi 657
Gubbio 664
Spoleto 668
Orvieto 673
Le Marche 678
Ancona .... [illegible]
Urbino 683
Pesaro 688
Macerata 691
Ascoli Piceno 694

ABRUZZO & MOLISE

Abruzzo 698
L'Aquila 700
Molise 708
Campania 712
Naples (Napoli) 716–17
Capri 739
Herculaneum 748
Old Pompeii..............................752
Sorrento..............................755
Positano..............................760
Amalfi 763
Salerno..............................767

APULIA, BASILICATA & CALABRIA

Apulia (Puglia) 774
Bari 788
Brindisi..............................797
Lecce 801
Taranto 807
Basilicata 809
Matera..............................812
Calabria 817
Catanzaro 819
Cosenza..............................823
Reggio di Calabria 827

SICILY (SICILIA)

Sicily (Sicilia) 834
Palermo 839
Catania 871
Syracuse (Siracusa)..............................878
Agrigento..............................891
Trapani..............................898

SARDINIA (SARDEGNA)

Sardinia (Sardegna) 907
Cagliari 909
Oristano..............................918
Sassari 927
Olbia 934

MAP LEGEND – SEE BACK PAGE

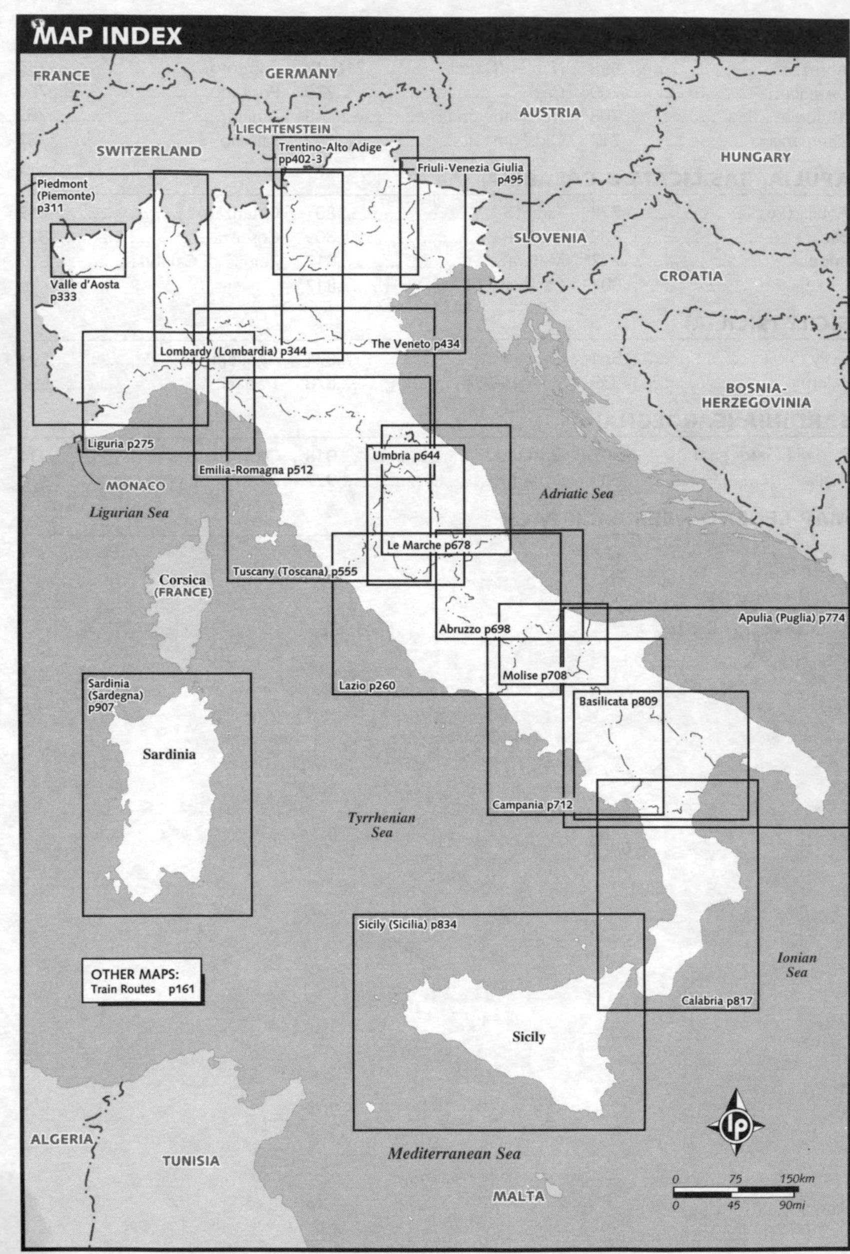
MAP INDEX
FRANCE
GERMANY
AUSTRIA
LIECHTENSTEIN
SWITZERLAND
HUNGARY
SLOVENIA
CROATIA
BOSNIA-HERZEGOVINIA
Trentino-Alto Adige pp402-3
Friuli-Venezia Giulia p495
Piedmont (Piemonte) p311
Valle d'Aosta p333
Lombardy (Lombardia) p344
The Veneto p434
Liguria p275
Emilia-Romagna p512
MONACO
Ligurian Sea
Umbria p644
Adriatic Sea
Le Marche p678
Tuscany (Toscana) p555
Corsica (FRANCE)
Apulia (Puglia) p774
Abruzzo p698
Molise p708
Lazio p260
Sardinia (Sardegna) p907
Basilicata p809
Sardinia
Campania p712
Tyrrhenian Sea
Sicily (Sicilia) p834
Ionian Sea
OTHER MAPS:
Train Routes p161
Calabria p817
Sicily
ALGERIA
TUNISIA
Mediterranean Sea
MALTA
0 75 150km
0 45 90mi

The Authors

Damien Simonis

With a degree in languages and several years' reporting and sub-editing on several newspapers (including the *Australian* and the *Age*), Sydney-born Damien left Australia in 1989. He has lived, worked and travelled extensively throughout Europe, the Middle East and North Africa. Since 1992, Lonely Planet has kept him busy in Jordan, Syria, Egypt, the Sudan, Morocco, North Africa, Italy (including guides on Venice, Florence and Tuscany) and Spain (including titles on Madrid, Barcelona, Catalunya and the Costa Brava and the Canary Islands). As this edition of *Italy* was heading off to the printers, Damien was already rushing back to Spain to update a raft of LP titles there. Damien has also written and snapped for books, newspapers and magazines in Australia, the UK and North America. When not on the road, Damien splits his time between splendid Stoke Newington in deepest north London and the slightly dodgy Raval district of central Barcelona.

Sally Webb

After living and working in Italy for more than five years, Sally swapped the cobblestone streets of Rome for harbour views in Sydney. The end of an era was nigh and she's now in therapy for the absence of fresh *mozzarella di bufala* and centuries-old mosaics in her life. Sally has authored/co-authored many Lonely Planet guides, including the 4th edition of *Italy*, *Rome* (1st and 2nd editions), *Rome Condensed*, *Corfu & the Ionians*, *Western Australia* and *New South Wales*. She has also eaten her way around Sydney and Melbourne for Lonely Planet's *Out to Eat* guides. An art historian by training, journalist by profession, and travel writer by choice, Melbourne-born Sally has contributed to publications in the UK, Italy and Australia, including the *Independent on Sunday*, *Wanted in Rome*, the *Sunday Age*, *Vive*, *Australian Financial Review Magazine*, *Australian Gourmet Traveller*, *Vacations and Travel*, *Qantas Club* and *Vogue Entertaining & Travel*, where she now works as Features Editor.

Nicola Williams

Nicola lives in Lyon, a handy hop from the Alps and the Mediterranean. She graduated from Kent and completed an MA in Islamic Societies & Cultures at London's School of Oriental & African Studies. A journalist by training, Nicola first hit the road in 1990 when she bussed and boated it from Jakarta to East Timor and back again. Following a two-year stint at the *North Wales Weekly News*, she moved to Latvia to bus it around the Baltics as Features Editor of the English-language *Baltic Times* newspaper. Following a happy 12 months exploring the Baltic region as Editor-In-Chief of the *In Your Pocket* city-guide series, she traded in Lithuanian *cepelinai* for Lyonnaise *andouillette*. Nicola authored Lonely Planet's tri-city guide to *Milan, Turin & Genoa* and French regional titles to *Provence & the Côte d'Azur* and *The Loire*, and has worked on several others, including *France*, *Romania & Moldova*, *Russia, Ukraine & Belarus* and *Estonia, Latvia & Lithuania*.

Miles Roddis

With this book, Miles – satisfyingly, and running counterdirection to the spread of the Roman Empire – completes his Latin Mediterranean set, having previously contributed to Lonely Planet's *Spain* and *France* guides. He has also worked on Lonely Planet's *Walking in Britain*, *Walking in France*, *Walking in Spain*, *Canary Islands*, *Mediterranean Europe*, *Europe on a Shoestring*, *Africa on a Shoestring*, *West Africa*, *Read This First: Africa*, *Lonely Planet Unpacked* and, once again beside the Med, Lonely Planet's new *Valencia & the Costa Blanca* title.

Fiona Adams

Fiona has lived in Africa and South America working as a freelance journalist and writer. Prepared to go anywhere in search of an unusual story, some of her more memorable adventures involve piranha-fishing in the Amazon and joining an expedition in search of Atlantis. She has a degree in Archaeology and Anthropology and an MA in Latin American Studies, and has worked on Lonely Planet's latest edition of *South America on a Shoestring*. Fiona presently lives in the Scottish Highlands with her husband Jamie but still fantasises about the Mediterranean sunshine, Italian food and a villa in Tuscany.

FROM THE AUTHORS

Damien Simonis A big thank you to Silvia Mosconi in Florence, who in spite of exam pressure went out of her way to include me back into local life after a long absence. Thanks also for the pleasure of their company to Michela and Fabiana, Silvia's friends Enrico, Paolo and Francesca, as well as Gerard Collon, Kristina Nordahl and Marco of Hotel Dalí.

In Padua, Alberto Stassi provided me with a comfortable base and exceeded all known norms of hospitality for two long weeks. *Mi casa es tu casa*. As always, the crew in Milan had the welcome mat out when the road became a little too much and thoughts turned to a one-time home. Daniela Antongiovanni, Sergio Bosio, Anna Cerutti, Paola Brussa, Lucia Spadaro, Maurizio Gallotti and Sara Bigatti all had a hand in making my time in Italy as pleasurable as it was profitable (indeed more so!).

Many thanks to Sally, Nicola, Miles and Fiona for their efforts to breath new fire into this book. Also to the staff of the tourist offices in Florence, Siena, Prato, Pistoia, Pisa, Volterra, Venice, Verona, Padova, Vicenza, Treviso and Bassano del Grappa. All helped to make my job on the ground that little bit easier. And thanks to Rachel Suddart (UK), Leonie Mugavin (Australia) and Pelin Thornhill (USA) for help with travel information.

As always, LP authors in the same country help each other by trading and pooling information. I owe a particular debt of thanks on this score to Sally Webb.

Sally Webb *Grazie mille* to: Francesco Bongarrà, *ciccio bello*, for his delightful company in Palermo and wealth of information about Sicily; LP walking guide guru Sandra Bardwell, for valuable walking information; Lamberto Prati, from Barilla, for giving up a day to show me why Parma is the food capital of Italy (and to Naomi Menehem in Sydney for the contact); Nancy Hart for hospitality in Rome; and Sari and Alessandro Taddei, my gastronomic comrades-in-arms, for a warm Easter welcome. Once again thanks to Mary, Laura, Sabina, Maggie and Marco at *Wanted in Rome*, to my resident sports expert Nick Rigillo, and to Vezio and Maria for not forgetting how I like my cappuccino. *Mi mancate tanto*.

Thanks also to Damien Simonis for his ridiculous but entertaining troop-rallying missives during research and to Matthew Evans for happily sharing his extensive food knowledge.

Nicola Williams Special thanks in Milan to Beatriz Barro at Armani, Marcello Mosesso at Versace, Maria Pada Tradli at Gucci, Lucilla Castellari at Teatro alla Scala, Maria Cristina Lani at the Camera Nazionale della Moda Italiana for her insights into the fashion industry, and Patrizia Mutti at the Camera di Commercio, Industria e Agricoltura. Also thanks to Florisa Gatti, Maurizio Bettica and Roberto Strocco in Turin and to Annamaria Torre and Patrizia Pesca in Genoa. Closer to home, the wedding of Nicola and Francesca Assetta at the Palazzina di Caccia di Stupingi near Turin proved an unforgettable introduction to Piedmontese cuisine and a fabulous opportunity to meet Claudia Perucchio of Turin-based EDT again. A golden star goes to the APT office in Riva del Garda for being the most efficient, friendly and fun tourist office in northern Italy. And finally, no thanks would be complete without a heartfelt *grazie* to Matthias Lüfkens – unbeatable dining, travel and life companion.

Miles Roddis Special thanks to Irene Volterrani for being such a cheerful fact-chaser, to Paolo Genova, HI warden in San Lazzaro for sharing his enthusiasm for the mountains behind Amalfi; to Igo Punzo, fellow HI warden in Agropoli; John Hiestand for a memorable night out in Naples; Tony Ryan of the British Council,

Naples; ebullient Mario Gallidoro of Friends of the Earth in Bari; Luigi Carruezzo of Hellenic Mediterranean Lines in Brindisi; Simona Melchiorre in Lecce, who communicated so infectiously her passion for her home town; and fellow author Damien Simonis for some hot Apulian restaurant leads.

Tourist office staff were generally helpfulness itself and I'm particularly grateful to Daniela Pipoli (Foggia), fellow writer Matteo di Sabato (Manfredonia), Stefania Tirabassi (Sulmona), Umberto Alfonsetti and Renato Palumbo (L'Aguila), Annabruna Pacilio (Matera), Santo Placanica (Reggio di Calabria), Roberta Aveta (Pozzuoli), Guiseppe Musella (Caserta), Ennio Montagna (Amalfi), Guiseppe Ruggiero (Sorrento), Donatella Guidetti (Capri) and to three particularly charming and helpful ladies: Ivana Brandi, Teresa Incoronato and Daniela di Barnardo from the Piazza del Gesú Nuovo AAST office in Naples.

And, of course, as always thanks to Ingrid, who played Giulietta to my bluff Quinn all the way down the book's long *strada*.

Fiona Adams Firstly, many thanks to the staff in the London LP office for keeping me on the right track and to Damien Simonis, for being such an amusing (and great) c-in-c. In Italy, my warmest thanks go to the staff in all the tourist offices in Tuscany, Umbria and Le Marche who managed to stay so sweet and smiling in spite of my million seemingly asinine questions. A heap of thanks to everyone else, from waiters, hostel workers and bus drivers, who provided a wealth of invaluable information and insider knowledge. Thanks especially to Mario in Cortona, Fiona in Perugia and to Gisella Isidori in Orvieto for all her wonderful foodie advice. I owe a special debt of gratitude to whoever or whatever invented Italian coffee, ice cream and proscuitto.

Special thanks back home to Silviana for the crash course in Italian and, as always, thanks and love to Jamie.

This Book

The 1st edition of *Italy* was written by Helen Gillman and John Gillman. Helen Gillman and Damien Simonis updated the 2nd edition. The 3rd edition was revised and expanded by Helen Gillman, Damien Simonis and Stefano Cavedoni. The 4th edition was updated by Helen Gillman, Damien Simonis, Sally Webb and Stefano Cavedoni. For this 5th edition, Damien and Sally teamed up with Fiona Adams, Miles Roddis and Nicola Williams.

Damien coordinated the project and updated the Facts about Italy, Getting There & Away and The Veneto chapters. He also updated the Florence section of the Tuscany chapter and revised the Art & Architecture special section, based on the work by Ann Moffat and Sally Webb for previous editions. Sally was responsible for updating the Facts for the Visitor, Getting Around, Rome & Lazio, Emilia-Romagna & San Marino, Sicily and Sardinia chapters. Miles updated the Abruzzo & Molise, Campania and Apulia, Basilicata & Calabria chapters while Nicola was responsible for the Liguria, Piedmont & Valle d'Aosta, Lombardy & the Lakes, Trentino-Alto Adige and Friuli-Venezia Giulia chapters. Fiona updated the Umbria & Le Marche and Tuscany (excluding Florence) chapters. The food special section was based on Lonely Planet's *World Food Italy* by Matthew Evans.

From the Publisher

This 5th edition of *Italy* was produced in Lonely Planet's London office by Imogen Franks (editorial) and James Ellis (cartography and design). Imogen was assisted with editing and proofing by a team comprising Susan Grimshaw, Claire Hornshaw, Francesca Parnell, Sally Schafer, Arabella Shepherd, Clare Tomlinson and Sam Trafford. The index was produced by Imogen, and Sam helped with last-minute checks. James was assisted in the mapping by Rachel Beattie, Fiona Christie, Paul Edmunds, Liam Molloy and Angela Watts. The cover was designed by Andrew Weatherill and Annika Roojun, and the back-cover map was drawn by Lachlan Ross. Jane Smith and Asa Andersson supplied the illustrations. Emma Koch compiled the language chapter and Donna Wheeler checked the food special section.

Thanks to Rachel Suddart, Pelin Thornhill and Leonie Mugavin for their help with the Getting There & Away chapter, and to Tom Hall for his useful additions to the Spectator Sports section. Thanks also to Barbara Dombrowski and Brett Pascoe from LPI for their image-selection skills. Thanks are also due to Tim Fitzgerald, Paul Piaia and Tim Ryder for their expert advice, to Sara Yorke for cheerfully stepping in at the last minute and to Amanda Canning for remaining a voice of calm throughout production.

Finally, to Damien, Sally, Miles, Nicola and Fiona for all their hard work and enthusiasm for the country and this book...*grazie mille*.

THANKS
Many thanks to the travellers who used the last edition and wrote to us with helpful hints, advice and interesting anecdotes. Your names appear in the back of this book.

Foreword

ABOUT LONELY PLANET GUIDEBOOKS

The story begins with a classic travel adventure: Tony and Maureen Wheeler's 1972 journey across Europe and Asia to Australia. There was no useful information about the overland trail then, so Tony and Maureen published the first Lonely Planet guidebook to meet a growing need.

From a kitchen table, Lonely Planet has grown to become the largest independent travel publisher in the world, with offices in Melbourne (Australia), Oakland (USA), London (UK) and Paris (France).

Today Lonely Planet guidebooks cover the globe. There is an ever-growing list of books and information in a variety of media. Some things haven't changed. The main aim is still to make it possible for adventurous travellers to get out there – to explore and better understand the world.

At Lonely Planet we believe travellers can make a positive contribution to the countries they visit – if they respect their host communities and spend their money wisely. Since 1986 a percentage of the income from each book has been donated to aid projects and human rights campaigns, and, more recently, to wildlife conservation.

Although inclusion in a guidebook usually implies a recommendation we cannot list every good place. Exclusion does not necessarily imply criticism. In fact there are a number of reasons why we might exclude a place – sometimes it is simply inappropriate to encourage an influx of travellers.

UPDATES & READER FEEDBACK

Things change – prices go up, schedules change, good places go bad and bad places go bankrupt. Nothing stays the same. So, if you find things better or worse, recently opened or long-since closed, please tell us and help make the next edition even more accurate and useful.

Lonely Planet thoroughly updates each guidebook as often as possible – usually every two years, although for some destinations the gap can be longer. Between editions, up-to-date information is available in our free, quarterly *Planet Talk* newsletter and monthly email bulletin *Comet*. The *Upgrades* section of our website (w www.lonelyplanet.com) is also regularly updated by Lonely Planet authors, and the site's *Scoop* section covers news and current affairs relevant to travellers. Lastly, the *Thorn Tree* bulletin board and *Postcards* section carry unverified, but fascinating, reports from travellers.

Tell us about it! We genuinely value your feedback. A well-travelled team at Lonely Planet reads and acknowledges every email and letter we receive and ensures that every morsel of information finds its way to the relevant authors, editors and cartographers.

Everyone who writes to us will find their name listed in the next edition of the appropriate guidebook, and will receive the latest issue of *Comet* or *Planet Talk*. The very best contributions will be rewarded with a free guidebook.

We may edit, reproduce and incorporate your comments in Lonely Planet products such as guidebooks, websites and digital products, so let us know if you don't want your comments reproduced or your name acknowledged.

How to contact Lonely Planet:
Online: e talk2us@lonelyplanet.com.au, w www.lonelyplanet.com
Australia: Locked Bag 1, Footscray, Victoria 3011
UK: 10a Spring Place, London NW5 3BH
USA: 150 Linden St, Oakland, CA 94607

Introduction

Italy is a moveable feast of seemingly endless courses. No matter how much you gorge yourself on its artistic and architectural wonders, its culinary delights, its natural splendours, you always feel you haven't made it past the *antipasti*. Few countries offer such variety and few visitors leave without a fervent desire to come back. There is nothing new in that – Italy has kept travellers spellbound since the earliest days of the Grand Tour.

Italy has been a united country for little more than a century. Its young and troubled national identity barely masks a deeply complex and unevenly woven tapestry. Centuries before the birth of Christ, Rome gathered all the peninsula's tribes under its wing and went on to create one of the greatest empires in history. Upon its collapse, the empire's spiritual successor, the Catholic Church, could not hope to exercise the same kind of central control. A chequer-board of city-states and feudal kingdoms jostled for power, until Rome finally fell in 1870 and the Kingdom of Italy was completed.

From all this chaos emerged the astonishing regional variety we see today. The great *città d'arte* (cities of art) are high on everyone's list and all are intrinsically different. Rome, the eternal capital, bristles with proud reminders of its imperial Roman past; Florence and Venice, two of the most powerful trading city states of medieval and Renaissance Italy, are virtually outdoor museums – compact but high dosage shots of art that leave even the hardiest of art lovers and sightseers gasping for air. Many visitors don't stray from these tried and true options, but the entire country is strewn with artistic jewels, from the Norman-Byzantine wonders of Palermo in Sicily to the Baroque marvels of Lecce in Apulia.

Italy exerts as much fascination beyond the city. From the icy walls of the Alps to the splendid beaches of Sicily, there is something for everyone. Ski with the chic in Cortina or get lost away from the crowds hiking in Tuscany's Apuan Alps. Go island-hopping in the Aeolian and Egadi groups off Sicily, explore the emerald waters of western Sardinia or go hang-gliding above Umbria's extraordinary Piano Grande plateau.

Your taste buds will demand equal attention. Hundreds of types of pasta are served up and down the country in a variety of sauces that has no apparent end. Regional specialities abound, like basil-based pesto in the north, game-meat sauces in the centre, truffles in Piedmont and Umbria and Sicily's spicy sauces that hark back to the days of its one-time Arab masters. And that's just the first course! Some of the world's finest wines are produced in Italy. Adventure beyond the known and reliable reds of Tuscany and try the quality drops of Piedmont, the Veneto, great whites and reds in Trentino and Alto Adige, and some robust reds in the south.

The Italians are not joking when they refer to their own country as the *Belpaese*, the Beautiful Country. Come and see for yourself!

Facts about Italy

HISTORY

Some things don't change. The illegal immigrants who struggle across the Mediterranean from North Africa and over the Adriatic from Albania and the former Yugoslavia are just the latest human wave to break across Italian shores. Their predecessors, from ancient Greece, North Africa, the far-off lands of Troy and beyond, came by sea as well, thousands of years before Christ. Still other peoples came from the north, across the mighty Alps. By the time Rome was founded, the peninsula had been long inhabited by a diverse array of peoples.

Italy's long coastlines and central position in the Mediterranean have made it the focus of migration and invasion repeatedly throughout its history. But it's not all been one-way traffic, for it made an ideal launch pad for the creation of one of the world's greatest empires, Ancient Rome. Over the centuries, Italy (which from the fall of the Roman Empire until the formation of the Kingdom of Italy in 1861 remained a fragmented collection of often squabbling states and city-states) remained a pole of attention.

In better times its more enterprising powers threw wide trade nets across the Mediterranean and beyond. In frequently less happy times, the peninsula (or parts of it) was the object of the covetous attention of a constantly changing crew of foreign powers. In the last century Italy's most telling 'expansion' came in the form of massive emigration to the four corners of the earth, the bombast of Mussolini and his 'new Rome' notwithstanding.

Prehistoric Italy

The Italian peninsula has supported human life for thousands of years. Archaeological finds show that Palaeolithic nomadic hunter-gatherers roamed across Italy as long as 70,000 years ago. By around 4000 BC, the Neolithic humans entering Italy from the east were bringing with them the art of cultivating the land. Agriculture meant staying in one spot and so the first fixed settlements emerged. It appears the Bronze Age reached Italy around 3000 BC (see the boxed text 'The Iceman Cometh').

By 1800 BC Italy had been settled by numerous tribes united by the Indo-European origins of their various Italic languages. Hunters, farmers, fishermen and traders, the people of these tribes travelled overland, by canoe along the rivers and in sailing boats across broad sweeps of the Mediterranean. Trade and cultural exchange, especially with Crete and the Greek mainland, enriched their lives and fostered contact. Inevitably such contact led frequently to conflict.

North of the Apennines the main tribes were the Ligurians (in the north-west), the

The Iceman Cometh

In 1991 tourists in the mountains near the Italo-Austrian border stumbled across the body of a prehistoric hunter, remarkably well preserved in ice, together with weapons, leather clothing and a basket. The hunter subsequently became known as Ötzi, the Iceman.

The body, the oldest frozen mummy yet found, was taken to Innsbruck, in Austria, where scientists dated it to around 3000 BC. This forced a re-evaluation of when the Bronze Age arrived in Italy, which until this discovery had been put at around 1800 BC.

The Austrians were intent on keeping the body until surveyors discovered that the site where it was found is 11m inside the Italian border. After a six-year custody battle, in 1998 the Iceman was transported to the northern Italian city of Bolzano, where museum curators created a refrigerated showcase to keep him in the same frozen state that preserved his body for 5000 years.

Raeti (later over-run by the Etruscans) and the Veneti. In Latium (Lazio today), the dominant tribes were the Latins, who later would come to dominate the entire peninsula. Most of central Italy was inhabited by a group of tribes (including the Marsi, Aequi, Volsci, Sabines, Umbrians and Samnites) often collectively known as the Umbro-Sabellians. The south was dominated by the Oscans, except in Apulia, which was populated by various tribes together known as the Iapygians (later Apulians). Before the arrival of the Greeks, Sicily was dominated by the Siculi, while Sardinia was populated by the descendants of Neolithic tribes.

The Etruscans

Historians differ on the origins of the Etruscan people and when they reached the Italian peninsula, although it is widely agreed that they migrated from the Aegeo-Asian area at the end of the 12th century BC. It is known that the Etruscans created a flourishing civilisation between the Arno and Tiber valleys, with other important settlements in Campania, Lazio and the Po Valley (Pianura Padana).

The earliest evidence of the Etruscan people in Italy dates from the Villanovan culture (around the 9th century BC), centred around present-day Bologna and characterised by the practice of cremating the dead and burying their ashes in urns.

From the 7th to the 6th century BC, Etruscan culture was at its height. Etruria was based on large city-states, among them Caere (Cerveteri), Tarquinii (Tarquinia), Veii (Veio), Volsinii (believed to be either Bolsena or Orvieto), Felsina (Bologna), Perusia (Perugia), Volaterrae (Volterra), Faesulae (Fiesole) and Arretium (Arezzo), which were collectively known as the Etruscan League. The Etruscans were predominantly navigators and traders, competing against the Phoenicians and Greeks for markets in the Mediterranean.

A good deal of what is known about Etruscan culture has been learned from the archaeological evidence unearthed at the sites of their tombs and religious sanctuaries, many of which can be visited today. Their belief in life after death necessitated the burial of the dead with everything they might need in the afterlife. This included such items as food and drink, clothing, ornaments and weapons. Painted tombs depicting scenes of everyday life, notably those discovered at Tarquinia near Rome, provide important information about how the Etruscans lived.

The long period of Etruscan decline began in 535 BC when the Greeks of Campania defeated an Etruscan war fleet in the battle of Cumae. By the 4th century BC they had lost their northern territories to invaders from Gaul and settlements in Campania to the Samnites, confining Etruria to its original territories in central Italy. Etruscan civilisation continued to flourish but its development was increasingly determined by its relationship with the growing power of the Latin city of Rome.

The Romans had long been profoundly influenced by Etruscan culture and three of the seven Roman kings who ruled before the Republic (see Romulus, Kings & the Republic later) were Etruscans, known as the Tarquins.

The Etruscan and Roman civilisations coexisted relatively peacefully until the defeat of Veii and its incorporation into Roman territory in 396 BC. During the ensuing century, Etruscan cities were either defeated or entered into peaceful alliances with the increasingly powerful Romans, However, they maintained a fair degree of autonomy until 90 BC – when the Etruscans (along with all the Italic peoples of the peninsula) were granted Roman citizenship

The separate Etruscan culture and language rapidly disappeared, partly because scholars of the day attached little importance to their preservation and few translations into Latin were made. No Etruscan literature survives and the only remaining examples of the written language are related to religious and funerary customs.

Greek Colonisation

The first Greek settlements in Italy were established in the early 8th century BC, first on the island of Ischia in the Gulf of Naples, then along the peninsula's southern coast and in Sicily. What became known as Magna Graecia (Greater Greece) was really a group of independent city-states, established by colonists from different Greece cities. The founders of the colonies at Ischia and Cuma were from the island of Euboea, the great Sicilian city of Syracuse was founded by the Corinthians, and Spartan exiles founded the wealthy city of Taranto.

The civilisation of Magna Graecia spanned about six centuries, and flourished in Sicily and in the coastal settlements of southern Italy. The ruins of magnificent Doric temples in Italy's south (at Paestum) and on Sicily (Agrigento, Selinunte and Segesta) and other monuments, such as the Greek theatre at Syracuse, stand as testimony to its splendour.

Syracuse's power was such that Athens came to regard the city as a rival and despatched a fleet to tame it. The ill-fated expedition, prompted in part also by Athenian dreams of creating a western empire (after reports of fabulous wealth in the Greek Sicilian cities), resulted in a long siege that ended only in 413 BC when Syracuse routed the Athenian fleet and put its troops on land to flight.

By the end of the 3rd century BC, Magna Graecia had succumbed to the might of the advancing Roman Republic. The Romans in turn had largely succumbed to the sparkle of Hellenistic culture, in philosophy, literature, art, architecture and coinage.

Romulus, Kings & the Republic

Aeneas, a refugee from Troy whose mother was the goddess Venus, is said to have landed in Italy in 1184 BC. Through alliances and warfare, the Trojans established a kingdom based at Alba Longa. The last of this line produced the twins Romulus and Remus, allegedly sired by Mars himself.

The traditional date of the foundation of Rome by Romulus is 753 BC. The next seven kings were elected from the ranks of the nobles. Most notably, Numa Pompilius is credited with the creation of the legal and religious framework of early Roman society. The Etruscan Servius Tullius built the first walls around the city-state and established the basic organisation of the political and military system.

Servius Tullius was assassinated by a rival, Tarquinius Superbus (Tarquin the Proud). It is said the misdeeds of Tarquinius, and those of his son, were sufficient to provoke rebellion and the overthrow of the monarchy. It is more likely that the king had managed to alienate the noble class, anxious for a greater share of power in the administration of the Roman city-state and the adjacent territories it by now controlled. Tarquinius was unseated in 509 BC and replaced by the Roman Republic (see the following section for details of how the Republic was organised). Around the same time the first temple was erected on the Capitoline Hill (Campidoglio).

Initially the Republic ran into problems as in-fighting among the nobles weakened Rome. The city had come to lord it over the Latin League, a loose federation of city-states in Latium, and its other members now sought to challenge that authority. In 496 BC Rome defeated a coalition of them in battle and the city's hegemony was formally recognised. Meanwhile, Rome spent much of the century in firefights to ward off attacks by the land-hungry Aequi and Volsci tribes. Conflict with the Etruscans to the north was also a constant thorn in Rome's side but, in 396 BC, the important Etruscan city of Veii fell to them. Two years later, an invading force of marauding Gauls, who had already inflicted considerable damage on Etruscan towns to the north, assaulted and sacked Rome.

The Romans eventually managed to pay the Gauls (who headed back to the Po Valley) to go away. They then repaired their city and embarked on a policy of expansion that by 265 BC had brought the peninsula south of the River Arno and the Apennines under Roman control.

How the Republic Worked

After ousting their kings, the patricians (noble class) of Rome established a new system of rule: the Republic. The *imperium*, or regal power, was placed into the hands of two consuls (with the right of veto over one another) who acted as political and military leaders. Also known by the general title of 'magistrates' (a term applied to all those who exercised political, military, judicial and religious office), the consuls were elected for nonrenewable one-year terms by an Assembly of the People. The Senate, whose members were appointed for life (by the consuls!), advised (a loose term) the consuls.

For a long time the patricians, less than 10% of the population of Rome, monopolised power. Although from the beginning monuments and the like were emblazoned with the initials SPQR (*Senatus Populusque Romanus*; the Senate and People of Rome), the 'people' had precious little say in affairs. (The initials are still used and many Romans would argue that little has changed.) Known as *plebs* ('the many'), the disenfranchised majority became increasingly restive and wrested considerable concessions from the patrician class in the more than two centuries that followed the founding of the Republic. By the 3rd century BC, Rome's basic laws had been codified and published as the Twelve Tables, a Council of Plebs acquired considerable importance, and, increasingly, plebs were being appointed as consuls and entering the Senate (it was customary for ex-consuls to be enrolled in the Senate upon completion of their term). The magistracy had become more complex, with a variety of offices (quaestors, aediles, praetors and censors) forming part of the executive with the consuls.

The Romans also developed a unique system for dealing with the other peoples in the region (the Sabines and Etruscans to the north and the Oscans, Samnites and Greek colonies to the south). Defeated city-states were not taken over but instead became allies. They were allowed to retain their own government and lands, but they were required to provide troops on demand to serve in the Roman army alongside native soldiers. This naturally increased the Republic's military strength and the protection offered by Roman hegemony induced many cities to become allies voluntarily.

Life under the Republic

For all its military success and the complexity of their political system, the Romans remained a rough and ready lot for much of the life of the Republic. A mostly agrarian society, Rome was slow to take off commercially and did not bother to mint coins until 269 BC, even though the neighbouring (and later conquered/allied) Etruscans and Greeks had long had their own currencies in circulation. The Etruscans and Greeks also brought writing to the attention of Romans, who found it terribly useful for documents and technical affairs but hardly glowed in the literature department at this stage. Even in religion they were rather unoriginal, mixing and matching outside influences with their own animistic beliefs. Eventually the Greek pantheon of gods formed the bedrock of Roman worship.

Wars of Expansion

While Rome consolidated its power on the peninsula, another military and commercial power flourished in the Mediterranean. The Kingdom of Carthage, based in modern Tunisia, had trading colonies and bases flung across the Mediterranean from Spain to Sicily. And it was in the latter that it would come to clash with Rome, for while the island's western cities were under Carthage's sway, those in the east were linked to Rome.

The First Punic (from Phoenicia, the eastern Mediterranean trading power that originally founded Carthage in 814 BC) War (264–241 BC) broke out when squabbling factions in the city of Messina appealed to both the Romans and Carthaginians for help. The grinding conflict brought hard-won victory to Rome, which spread its control to Sicily, Sardinia and Corsica, and taught the Republic the importance of naval power.

In the meantime other conflicts brewed. Illyrian pirates from the eastern Adriatic, allied to the Greek Kingdom of Macedonia, harassed southern Italian cities to the extent that they turned to their federate ally and head, Rome, for help. Rome launched a heavy assault that earned it victory and Macedonia's enmity. Thus Rome entered the vortex of Greek squabbles and a series of complex wars in which Rome's allies and enemies on the Greek mainland and throughout the eastern Mediterranean changed with bewildering rapidity.

In the meantime, the Gauls resident in the Po Valley had become restless. Aided by tribes from Gaul itself, they raided and devastated territory south of the Apennines. The Romans, allied with the Veneti, responded and by the end of their campaign in 218 BC, all of the Italian peninsula south of the Alps, except the north-west, was under Roman control (either directly or by alliance).

In the meantime, Hannibal, son of the Spain-based Hamilcar Barca who was defeated in the First Punic War, inherited command of the army and initiated a violent campaign. This escalated into the Second Punic War (218–202 BC) when the Roman Senate once again declared war on Carthage.

Rome ruled the waves this time around so Hannibal daringly crossed into Italy by leading his army across Spain and southern France and over the Alps. Despite losing up to half his troops and almost all of his war elephants in the crossing, Hannibal inflicted several crushing defeats on the Romans, notably at Lago di Trasimeno (in present-day Umbria) in 217 BC and at Cannae (in Apulia) the following year, when the Romans lost 30,000 soldiers. Stalemate ensued. Hannibal roamed Italy and the Romans avoided direct clashes. With control of the sea, the Romans had no trouble preventing the arrival of reinforcements to Hannibal until 207 BC when his brother Hasdrubal crossed the Alps.

The Romans then discovered a military genius of their own to match Hannibal – Publius Cornelius Scipio. Backed by a strong army, the 25-year-old general struck first at Hannibal's power base in Spain and then, in 204 BC, attacked Africa, forcing the Carthaginians to recall Hannibal to defend the capital. In 202 BC Scipio won the decisive Battle of Zama over Hannibal, who committed suicide in exile some 20 years later. Rome was left the Iberian peninsula, which, apart from the occasional protracted uprising, became a comparatively peaceful Roman territory.

During the following years, the Roman Republic added Macedonian Greece to its provinces after the decisive defeat of Perseus, the son of Philip V of Macedon, in a three-year war. By 146 BC, all of mainland Greece was under Roman control. In 129 BC the Romans extended their control to Asia Minor.

In the meantime Carthage continued to exercise the Roman imagination and in 149 BC Rome sent an invasion to finish off its arch-rival once and for all. After three years of siege the Roman legions finally marched in and erased the city.

From Republic to Empire

The rapid expansion of Roman control from Italy to cover much of the Mediterranean brought far-reaching changes at home. Italy came to depend on the wealth imported from the provinces. Much of this wound up in the pockets of the oligarchs, and a large underclass, increasingly poor and alienated, became a growing source of social discontent. The poor remained poor and the rich wallowed in a new refinement, much of it learned from the older and more developed societies the Romans had subjugated. The need for land reforms caused a deep rift between those who advocated such changes and the conservative Senate.

As the 2nd century BC drew to a close, Rome slipped into a period of factional strife, exacerbated by problems abroad. Germanic tribes moving across northern Europe in search of land challenged Roman authority in client states and attacked Gaul. The emergency persisted and in part explained the repeated nomination of the general Gaius Marius as consul. He reorganised the armed forces and replaced the increasingly unpopular system of conscription with a new system of accepting volunteers from the ranks of the landless urban poor. Roman armies now looked to their individual generals for recompense after a campaign and the commanders realised that conquest and retaining the fidelity of their troops bestowed on them considerable political power.

Meanwhile, Roman politics was increasingly polarised. One of the many questions at stake was the citizenship status of the Italic peoples beyond the city of Rome. The Senate opposed proposals to extend Roman citizenship across the peninsula but, in the face of rebellion by its peninsula allies in what became known as the Social War, eventually caved in on this point. The weight of military men in domestic political affairs grew and resulted ultimately in the proclamation in 82 BC of the dictatorship of Cornelius Sulla, who had been a bitter opponent of Gaius Marius and his faction. A conservative who had returned to Italy at the head of a victorious army from the Middle East, his rise marked a turning point in republican government.

Sulla allowed one of his protégés, Gnaeus Pompeius Magnus (Pompey the Great), to leapfrog up the political ladder. In 77 BC he was sent to Spain to end a revolt by Quintus Sertorius, a talented general and the last of the Marius faction. Rome had to put out several fires at the same time. In Asia Minor war broke out in 74 BC (not for the first time) with a Black Sea ruler, Mithridates, and in 73 BC the last great slave revolt, led by the Thracian gladiator Spartacus, shook Italy. Marcus Licinius Crassus was given an extraordinary appointment to put down the revolt, which he accomplished just as a victorious Pompey was returning home from Spain in 71 BC (see the boxed text 'Spartacus the Dimply One' below).

Crassus and Pompey, by now bitter rivals, together then campaigned (and bribed) their way to the consulships in 70 BC. Pompey later took an army to Syria.

In 59 BC Gaius Julius Caesar became consul with the connivance of Crassus and the newly returned Pompey. In return for their electoral and financial support, Caesar as consul would ensure that his allies' interests would be looked after. The three men became known as the First Triumvirate and their pact was reinforced by Pompey's marriage to Caesar's daughter, Julia.

After his consulship, Caesar left to win military glory in Gaul, which he conquered in the years 58–51 BC. His treatment of the Gauls in defeat was mild and the area became his main power base. At the same time he also made incursions into Germanic territory across the Rhine and into Britain. Crassus meanwhile died while campaigning in Parthia and Pompey became consul again in 52 BC. He and Caesar arranged for the

Spartacus the Dimply One

An obscure warrior about whom we know little except that he led a slave revolt against Rome, in the course of which he died in 71 BC, has a better remembered face than many of the greatest emperors of the Empire. Well, the borrowed and deeply dimpled face of Kirk Douglas at any rate. It is hard for anyone who ever saw the Hollywood classic *Spartacus* (1960) to read about the Thracian slave and not think of Douglas.

The real Spartacus probably didn't have the same sex appeal as Douglas but was a rugged fellow. Initially conscripted as a soldier in the Roman army, it appears he tired of legionary life and absconded, turning his hand to a little brigandage before being captured and sold into slavery.

In 73 BC, he and 70 other slaves escaped from a gladiator training school in Capua and took refuge on Mt Vesuvius. There they were soon joined by other slaves and successfully fought off several Roman armies as they roamed around southern Italy. It is said the rebel force eventually numbered about 90,000! Spartacus and his force battled their way to northern Italy in 72 BC but, rather than push on, his men determined to stay in Italy. This was their undoing. Spartacus traversed the entire peninsula and even tried to cross to Sicily. When Crassus was appointed to put down the rebellion, the game was up. His eight divisions split and defeated Spartacus' force, the remnants of which fled north, only to be intercepted by Pompey, who by chance was returning from a campaign in Spain.

Spartacus himself fell in the field against Crassus. The Roman commander rounded up the 6000 of the slave's followers who did not die in battle and had them crucified along the Appian Way (Via Appia).

latter to stand again for the consulship in 50 BC, but Pompey's growing jealousy of Caesar's success pushed him into the arms of conservative senators who opposed the popularity and power of Caesar. Before too long, civil war between Caesar and Pompey seemed increasingly likely. In 49 BC Pompey was put in command of the army in Italy and Caesar called upon to disband his forces in Gaul or be outlawed. Caesar, knowing he had a good degree of popular support, elected to march on Rome. Pompey and his forces moved to Greece, where they were defeated in 48 BC. In the following two years Caesar campaigned against opponents in Spain and North Africa. Pompey fled to Egypt, where he was assassinated, and in 46 BC Caesar became dictator.

He launched a series of reforms, overhauling the calendar and the Senate. Of his extensive building programme, the Curia (Senate House) and the Basilica Giulia remain. Initially declared dictator for one year, Caesar had this extended to 10 years and then, in 44 BC, was proclaimed dictator for life.

This accumulation of power alienated even those political allies (including his friends and protégés) who had initially supported him and Caesar was assassinated on the Ides of March (15 March) in 44 BC.

All hail Julius Caesar!

The Liberators, as Caesar's assassins called themselves, found they had severely underestimated Caesar's popularity. The people regarded the dead dictator as a new god. Caesar's lieutenant, Mark Antony (Marcus Antonius), took command of the city, aided by troops under the command of Lepidus. Caesar's will had declared the adoption of his 18-year-old great-nephew, Octavian, as his son and heir. Octavian, then studying in Greece, returned to Rome to claim his inheritance. Now calling himself Gaius Julius Caesar Octavianus (Octavian), the young man first sided with the Liberators against Antony, then switched sides and fought with Antony at Philippi when Brutus and Cassius were defeated.

Lepidus was quickly frozen out of the Second Triumvirate and the Roman world was divided in two, with the new Caesar raising troops in the western half while Antony administered the wealthy provinces and client kingdoms of the east. Although initially amicable – Antony married Octavian's sister – the situation deteriorated into another civil war, with Octavian making brilliant propagandistic use of Antony's affair with Cleopatra VII, queen of Egypt.

Octavian's general Marcus Agrippa defeated Antony and Cleopatra in a naval clash off the coast of Actium in 31 BC and the couple committed suicide in Alexandria the following year.

The Empire

Octavian was left as sole ruler of the Roman world but, remembering Caesar's fate, trod carefully. In 27 BC he officially surrendered his extraordinary powers to the Senate, which promptly gave most of them back. Four years later his position was regularised again, with the Senate voting him the unique title of Augustus (Your Eminence). By 19 BC, with all-important control of the army in his hands, Augustus had cemented his position as virtual emperor of all Rome and its possessions.

The new era of political stability that followed allowed the arts to flourish. Augustus was exceptionally lucky in having as his contemporaries the poets Virgil, Horace and

Ovid, as well as the historian Livy. He also encouraged the visual arts, restoring existing buildings and constructing many new ones. Augustus dedicated the Teatro di Marcello (Marcellus Theatre) in honour of his nephew, Marcellus, and commissioned the Ara Pacis (Altar of Peace) explicitly to commemorate his own achievement. During his reign the Pantheon was also raised. He boasted in his memoirs that he 'found Rome in brick and left it in marble'.

Augustus succeeded because, instead of trying to reinvent the political system, he simply made room for himself at the top. He never called himself king or emperor, but rather *princeps* (the leading man). The Republic, although its institutions lost some of their effective power, continued as usual. Augustus died aged 75 after 40 years in the commander's seat.

The reign of his successor Tiberius (AD 14–37) proved stable and the smoothness of his succession helped enshrine the Principate instituted by Augustus. The Republic, even in name, began to slip out of usage.

Gaius Caligula (AD 37–45) had little time for the political niceties that the Senate expected; his increasingly extravagant and bizarre behaviour led to his assassination by an officer of the Praetorian Guard, the imperial bodyguard.

A return to a truly republican form of government was contemplated, but the Praetorians, with an eye on job security and handsomely rewarded for their support, declared Claudius, Gaius' uncle, emperor. The unprepossessing Claudius, much to the surprise of those around him, proved to be a conscientious ruler. He extended the port at Ostia and built a new aqueduct, the Aqua Claudia, to service the growing population of Rome. He also strengthened the Romans' hold on Britain, first invaded by Caesar. Something of an intellectual, he understood and wrote on the Etruscan language – invaluable learning of which only its renown survived its author.

Probably poisoned by his wife, Agrippina, Claudius died in AD 58 and was succeeded by Nero, Agrippina's 17-year-old son by a previous marriage. Nero gradually showed his preference for Gaius Caligula's style of government. In the ultimate act of youthful rebellion, he had his mother assassinated, then began to impose his passion for all things Greek on an increasingly resentful Roman aristocracy. With revolt spreading among the provincial governors, who commanded armies, the Senate declared Nero a public enemy in AD 68 and he committed suicide while on the run. In the Year of the Four Emperors that followed, Galba, Otho and Vitellius came and went in quick succession.

Stability was restored when Vespasian, who had been sent to Judaea to crush the Great Rebellion of AD 66, was proclaimed emperor by his troops. The Senate, unwilling to oppose the will of the troops, sanctioned their choice. A practical man, Vespasian (AD 69–79) made a point of rebuilding the temple on the Capitoline Hill and constructing a huge amphitheatre in the grounds of Nero's Domus Aurea. He also rededicated the enormous statue in front of the Colosseum (originally of Nero and destined for Nero's entrance hall) to Apollo, the sun god. As a parallel to Augustus' Ara Pacis, Vespasian celebrated the return of normality by building the Forum of Peace.

The brief reign of his successor, Titus (AD 79–81), is chiefly remembered for the catastrophic eruption of Mt Vesuvius. He did find time to construct public baths, as well as Arco di Tito (Titus' Arch), which commemorates him as the captor of Jerusalem.

Domitian, Titus' younger brother, built the Forum Transitorio (for which his successor, Nerva, took the credit and the name, calling it the Nerva Forum) and greatly extended the palace complex on the Palatine Hill (he had the corridors lined with highly polished stone to allow him to detect lurking assassins). This paranoia was justified, for he was murdered in a palace plot in AD 96.

Pax Romana

Although written records of the first two centuries AD are poor, it is clear that in this period the enlightened rule (with one or two exceptions) of a series of capable emperors brought about an unprecedented (and, it can fairly safely be asserted, never repeated) degree of prosperity and security to the entire Mediterranean. The Empire reached its maximum extent and was, in the main, wisely administered.

By AD 100, the city of Rome is said to have had more than 1.5 million inhabitants and all the trappings of the capital of an empire – its wealth and prosperity were obvious in the rich mosaics, marble temples, public baths, theatres, circuses and libraries. An extensive network of aqueducts fed the baths and provided private houses with running water and flushing toilets. The Empire extended from the Iberian peninsula, Gaul and Britain to a line that basically followed the Rhine and Danube rivers. All of present-day Yugoslavia, Albania and Greece, along with Dacia, Moesia and Thrace (considerable territories reaching to the Black Sea), were under Roman control. Most of modern-day Turkey, Syria, Lebanon, Palestine and Israel was occupied by Rome's legions and linked up with Egypt. From there a deep strip of Roman territory stretched along the length of North Africa to the Atlantic coast of what is today northern Morocco. The entire Mediterranean was a Roman lake.

After the brief reign of the elderly stopgap emperor Nerva (AD 96–98) came Trajan, an experienced general of Spanish birth. His victories over the Dacians are depicted on the column erected in the forecourt of his forum, which also contained separate Greek and Latin libraries. Other public works constructed during this time included his market, and the Via Traiana (Trajan Way) linking Benevento with Brindisi. Indeed, Trajan was a generous ruler, concerned that the material well-being of the people – as well as the smooth functioning of the Empire – got considerable attention. He repaired old highways and laid new ones, built aqueducts, bridges, canals and ports. He improved the postal system and instituted loans and grants to stimulate agriculture. Trajan was also the first Roman general to conquer Parthia, the traditional eastern enemy, as part of a generally aggressive and expansionist policy abroad. He died in 117 and his ashes were buried in the base of his column in Rome.

Hadrian (AD 117–138), known as a prodigious traveller, was also a keen architect who remodelled the Pantheon to its present form and built an extensive and elaborate holiday villa at Tivoli, outside Rome. An enlightened ruler, he gave priority to the maintenance of a peaceful and prosperous empire, well guarded by disciplined garrisons along its long frontiers. To achieve this he was busy on several fronts. In Britain he built Hadrian's Wall from the mouth of the River Tyne to the Solway Firth (marking more or less what would thereafter be the frontier between England and Scotland). In Germany too he bolstered the imperial defences, while in Palestine he was obliged to suppress a revolt by the Jews – a task he carried out with uncommon violence. His administrative reforms tended to weaken an already ailing Senate.

The reigns of Antonius Pius (138–161) and the philosopher-emperor Marcus Aurelius (161–180) were stable, but the latter did spend 14 years fighting invaders along the Danube and from Parthia. The Empire's resources were stretched to the limit dealing with these two festering sores and, although Aurelius emerged victorious in the short term, the ongoing battles were a taste of what was to come further down the line.

Marcus Aurelius, a stoic and dutiful ruler, was succeeded by the wholly decadent and inept Commodus (180–192). He managed to empty the imperial coffers and presided over a series of crises within the Empire as economic stagnation in Italy and Gaul pushed citizens to revolt. The frontiers were under attack from all sides but the Roman armies in the field managed to keep the enemies at bay.

With the assassination of Commodus, the events of AD 68–69 repeated themselves. Pertinax, Didius Julianus and Pescennius Niger came and went before Septimius Severus (193–211), born in North Africa, defeated other challengers to become emperor. Civil strife with rivals kept Severus busy for four years, but he subsequently brought a steadying hand to the administration of the Empire. In the course of his rule e was obliged to deal with wars in Parthia nd Britain but devoted considerable energy o restoring Rome's treasury, bolstering imerial defences and promoting improved conomic conditions in the provinces.

Under Severus the importance of the rmy in the imperial power structure beame still more important and the Senate's ole was reduced to one of a rubber stamp. t was an inevitable result of a process that vent back at least as far as Augustus. The rmy, moreover, had become a different nimal. Increasingly the legions were loally raised forces designed to defend the Empire's immense frontiers. They were, on he whole, not mobile and frequently incaable of halting a major invasion.

Severus was jointly succeeded by the rothers Caracalla and Geta. The former predictably) had his sibling assassinated. Despite financial problems, his building rogramme included refurbishing roads as vell as building his monumental public aths. Caracalla was above all a military nan and he had his hands full with camaigns in Germany and Parthia.

Decline of the Empire

When Caracalla was throttled in 213, chaos ensued. Some 24 emperors and pretenders violently rose and fell in a period marked by continuous assaults from beyond the Empire (Goths, Franks and Alamanni) and revolts within. Reliance on the military for power and an increasing tax burden weighed on citizens throughout the Empire. Epidemics wrought havoc on the population and commerce declined rapidly.

By the time Diocletian (285–305) became sole emperor, the world had changed. The idea of the principate had disappeared (in all but name) with the Senate, and autocratic rule had become the norm.

Society was also much altered. What had been an insignificant minority religion, Christianity, had become a serious social force, with converts in many parts of the Empire and across most classes of society. Technically considered traitors because of their refusal to worship the pagan deities, the Christians were viewed by the authorities with growing alarm. Some believed the turmoil of the decades before the ascent to power of Diocletian was a manifestation of the gods' wrath at Rome's inadequate defence of the state religion. In earlier days the Romans had taken a generally hands-off approach to the Christians: while they didn't cause trouble the Romans left them alone. In these trying times it became increasingly easy to target them as a cause of the Empire's problems. Although Empire-wide persecution occurred rarely, localised campaigns against Christians were not uncommon.

The energetic Diocletian, faced with war and rebellion across the Empire, developed a system of joint rule under his command, the so-called tetrarchy. He and his joint ruler Maximian ruled as joint Augustuses, each with an army, while two further commanders were named Caesar. Diocletian based himself in Asia Minor and Maximian in Milan (Rome ceased to be the fulcrum of the Empire). In Diocletian's thinking, the two Caesars would be the successors to the two Augustuses.

Diocletian resigned in 305 and chaos again ensued as rivals to imperial power (as many as seven at one stage) all proclaimed themselves Augustus and embarked on fratricidal campaigns. Constantine I (sole emperor 324–337) emerged from the melee victorious. He reversed Diocletian's policy of persecuting Christians and, convinced (he claimed) the Christian god had helped him along, Constantine converted to the monotheistic religion and granted Christians full freedom of worship in the Edict of Milan of 313. Years of rivalry with his co-emperor Licinius ended in defeat of the latter in 324.

Shortly thereafter Constantine founded Constantinople, on the Bosphorus in Byzantium, as a new strategic centre and his home. Over time it would come to overshadow the old and increasingly symbolic capital of Rome. Initially, however, he still lavished attention on the ageing city. His ambitious building programme included churches such as St Peter's, San Lorenzo Fuori le Mura and Santa Croce, Constantine's Basilica in the Roman Forum and his own triumphal arch, Constantine's Arch.

Constantine's successors, with frequently more than one Augustus dividing up the administration, were more or less constantly engaged in military efforts to protect the Empire and arrest what in hindsight was clearly a slow but steady decline in its fortunes. Valentian (364–375) and his brother Valens (364–378) split the administration of the Empire in two, with the elder and more capable Valentian taking the western half. Unity was preserved in name until the death of their successor, Theodosius, in 395. One of his sons, Honorius, ruled the Western Roman Empire, while his other son, Arcadius, ruled the Eastern Roman Empire.

Slow Agony

By the opening of the 5th century, anyone still under any illusion about the Empire's prospects must surely have seen the writing on the wall.

The Western Empire in particular careened quickly down the slippery slope. The main source of pressure came from wave after wave of barbarian invasions. Visigoths, Goths, Vandals, Burgundians, Franks and the fierce Attila's Huns all swept across Gaul, Spain, Italy and even into Africa. Saxons and other north German tribes poured into (by the mid-century) defenceless Britain. In 476 the Germanic Odovacar proclaimed himself king in the Western Empire, a *fait accompli* tacitly accepted by the Eastern Empire. He was later trounced by the Ostrogoth Theodoric in 493, by which time the Western Empire had ceased to exist. Theodoric ruled in Italy until 526.

The story in the Eastern Empire, with its capital in Constantinople, was rather different. Although also engaged in an interminable struggle for survival, its rulers managed to hold this half of the Empire together. By the time Justinian (518–565) came to the imperial throne, the map of the onetime Roman world had changed beyond recognition. The Roman Empire (that is, what was left of its eastern half) stretched from parts of present-day Yugoslavia across to Bulgaria and Greece, Asia Minor, a deep strip of the Mediterranean coast of what is now Syria, Lebanon, Jordan and Israel (facing the Persian Empire and free-wheeling Arab tribes) and down to Egypt and a strip of North Africa as far west as modern Libya.

In the west, Italy and much of what is now Yugoslavia was ruled by the Ostrogoths. Gaul was divided into the kingdoms of the Franks, Burgundians and Visigoths. The latter also controlled all of Iberia (modern Spain and Portugal). The Vandals exercised loose control over a long coastal strip of north-western Africa. Roman and Romanised citizens rubbed along with their new bosses to a greater or lesser degree, in some cases managing to fill an important role as cultured and knowledgeable administrators of territories generally too vast for the newcomers to adequately populate or control alone.

Justinian, however, had a dream. He saw the glory of Rome restored and embarked on a series of wars of reconquest. At the height of his success he had retaken most of Italy (including Sicily, Sardinia and Corsica), extended imperial power in Africa to what is now north-western Algeria and even controlled a coastal slice of southern Spain. At the same time he codified Roman law and attempted to quash growing schismatic tendencies within the Christian church by favouring the western (Roman) branch. It was all a costly, and ultimately futile, exercise. As the early Middle Ages crept up on Europe, forces far beyond the control of Justinian and his Byzantine successors would forever seal the tomb in which lay the once mighty Roman Empire. Within three years of Justinian's death, the Lombard tribes lurking to the north of Italy launched invasions on the peninsula. The Byzantines were left with Ravenna and other pockets along the southeastern coast of Italy.

Meanwhile in Rome, the western Church was asserting itself as a spiritual and secular force. Pope Leo I 'the Great' (440–461) had convinced Attila the Hun not to sack Rome, and Pope Gregory I (590–604) set the pattern of Church administration that was to guide Catholic services and rituals throughout history. Gregory oversaw the Christianisation of Britain and tightened relations with the Church abroad (mainly in Gaul and Spain), mproved conditions for slaves, provided ree bread in Rome and repaired Italy's exensive network of aqueducts. He also left an normous volume of writing on which much Catholic dogma was subsequently based and e elevated the role of music in Catholic iturgy with the Gregorian chant.

ombard Italy & the Papal States (600–800)

Even before Gregory became pope, the ombard invasion of Italy had begun. The ombards were a Swabian people who apear to have originally inhabited the lower asin of the Elbe. As often happened with onquerors of the Italian peninsula, the ombards ended up adopting much of the ocal culture, including language, rather than mposing their own. Their more communal oncept of land and property tenure soon ave way to the Romans' high regard for rivate property, either absolute or leased, nd the Lombards, who settled mainly round Milan, Pavia and Brescia, soon beame city-dwellers, building many churches nd public baths that still grace these cities. They eventually expanded their control farher down the peninsula – taking over the mportant duchies of Spoleto and Benevento - although they were unable to take Rome.

In an effort to unseat the Lombards, the ope invited the Franks to invade Italy, which they duly did in 754 and 756 under he command of their king, Pepin. The opes were, even at this early stage in the ong history of the Church, an incredibly anny lot. The papacy invented the Donaion of Constantine, a document in which he Roman emperor Constantine I purportedly granted the Church temporal control of he city of Rome and surrounding terriories. At this point Rome was technically controlled by the duke of Rome, under the uspices of the Eastern Empire in Constaninople. In return for the papal blessing and n ill-defined say in Roman affairs, Pepin marched into Italy, defeated the Lombards and at the same time declared the creation of the Papal States (ie, territories under the direct political control of the pope), whose number and constitution would change constantly over the centuries. They survived until 1870. Using the Donation of Constantine as his precedent, Pepin issued the Donation of Pepin in 756, under which land still nominally belonging to the Byzantine Empire was awarded to Pope Stephen II.

When Pepin's son and successor, Charlemagne, visited Rome in 774, he confirmed the Donation of Pepin. Charlemagne was crowned emperor by Pope Leo III in St Peter's Basilica on Christmas Day 800 and the concept of the Holy Roman Empire came into being. The bond between the papacy and the Byzantine Empire was thus forever broken and political power in what had been the Western Roman Empire shifted north of the Alps, where it would remain for more than 1000 years. This early collaboration between papacy and Empire would later degenerate into enmity, and the cycle of papal-imperial conflict would mark the history of Italy for centuries to come.

Charlemagne's successors were unable to hold together his vast Carolingian Empire. In 843 the Partition of Verdun divided it between his three nephews, and Italy became a battleground of rival powers and states. The imperial crown was ruthlessly fought over; similarly Rome's aristocratic families engaged in battle for the papacy.

An Oasis of Calm

Meanwhile, momentous events were taking place on the south side of the Mediterranean. The rise in the early decades of the 7th century of a new monotheistic faith, Islam, among the Arab tribes under the guidance of the prophet Mohammed passed unnoticed in Europe. Upon the death of Mohammed in 632 the Muslims, as his followers were called, embarked on an astonishing campaign of conquest, in which they seemingly won the hearts and minds of many of the conquered, across the Middle East and all of North Africa. In 711 they crossed into Spain and their lightning advance was only brought to a halt in Poitiers, western France, in 732.

Given their spectacular progress in the west, it is surprising that the Muslims took so long to try their luck in Italy. The Aghlabid dynasty in Tunisia had launched repeated raids against nearby Sicily since the second half of the 7th century, but only in 827 did they make a serious landing. From then they embarked on a slow campaign of conquest, and one by one the Greek (read Byzantine) cities of the island fell. Palermo went in 831. The last to surrender was Taormina in 902.

The Muslims (who in Italy came to be known as Saracens), a mix of Arabs and Berbers, established a splendid civilisation. The fundamentals of Greek culture were restored and elaborated on by Muslim scholars such as the physician and philosopher Avicenna, the astronomer and geographer Al-Battani and the mathematician Al-Kovarizmi. Cotton, sugar cane, oranges and lemons were introduced in the south, taxes were lower than elsewhere in Italy and the Sicilians lived relatively peacefully under their Arab lords for more than two centuries.

The Muslims were soon on the mainland, largely as mercenaries in the service of rival southern potentates, mostly Byzantine Greek in orientation if not always politically loyal or tied to Constantinople. The Muslims gained a foothold for themselves, too, occupying Taranto and Bari.

Amalfi, which had secured independence from Naples in the 840s, soon became a major trading republic in the western Mediterranean. It also became a centre of great cosmopolitan civilisation and learning – as did the republics of Gaeta and Naples, and Salerno, which was still a Lombard principality. In the 11th century Salerno was famous for its medical school, where Greek, Jewish, Muslim and western Christian teachers worked together.

Papacy Versus Empire

While the south prospered, the rest of Italy was not so calm. Following the demise of the Carolingian Empire in 887, warfare broke out in earnest between local Italian rulers, who were divided in their support of Frankish and Germanic claimants (all of whom were absentee landlords) to the imperial title and throne. Italy became the battleground of Europe, the stage on which rival factions fought for ascendancy, and refugees flooded into the cities from the devastated countryside. Many of Italy's medieval hill towns developed in this period as easily defendable safe havens.

In 962 the Saxon Otto I was crowned Holy Roman Emperor in Rome. His son Otto II, and later his grandson, Otto III, also took the same title, cementing a tradition that was to remain the privilege of Germanic emperors until 1806.

Inevitably, the two protagonists in the creation of this illusory successor to the Roman Empire must end up in conflict. The prestige of the Christian Church based in Rome was doubted by none and its blessing was considered vital by whomever aspired to the Holy Roman throne. Competition between Franks and Germanic candidates was intense. The Church, at least initially, relied on the might of the Holy Roman Empire to help it pursue territorial ambitions in Italy and clearly resented the assumption by the northern emperors that papal anointment gave them pre-eminence in Italy as well.

In the course of the 11th century, a heated contest over who had the right to invest bishops in Germany brought the popes and emperors to a stand-off. After Pope Gregory VII (aided by German aristocrats who, for their own reasons, opposed the emperor) excommunicated Emperor Henry IV, the latter literally had to come to the pope on his knees to beg forgiveness. Victory in this battle established the clear precedent that Rome had sole control over the appointment of bishops throughout the Christian world. Pope Gregory thus not only reinforced the position of the papacy as the supreme seat of the western Church but won enormous political power, since the pope would clearly only nominate bishops friendly to Rome.

This was nevertheless little more than round one. In the following two centuries imperial armies, on one pretext or another, would descend on Italy with monotonous regularity. This conflict formed the focal point of Italian politics in the late Middle Ages and two camps emerged: Guelphs (Guelfi, in support of the pope) and Ghibellines (Ghibellini, in support of the emperor). Dante Alighieri, the great poet and writer whom Italians see as the father of the Italian language, was one of the casualties of the Guelph-Ghibelline struggle. A dedicated Guelph supporter, Dante was exiled from his birthplace, Florence, in 1301 because he belonged to the wrong faction.

Norman Conquest of the South

As popes and emperors duelled in the northern half of the country, Christian Norman zealots, who had embarked on a successful invasion of Britain, arrived in southern Italy in the early stages of the 11th century. They found a highly confusing mix of Muslim Arab rule (in Sicily and sprinkled about the south), Byzantine Greek city-states and independent duchies such as Naples and Lombard enclaves in the interior.

Over the following century, the Normans, ably exploiting local grievances and internecine squabbles, gained control of the south. Roger II was crowned king of Sicily in Palermo in 1130 and thus a unified kingdom of the south was created.

The Normans, well outnumbered by the local populace, tended to assimilate and adapt local culture. The result could be seen in their architecture, in which elements of Romanesque simplicity, Muslim elegance and Byzantine decorative splendour all shone through. The Chiesa di San Giovanni degli Eremiti in Palermo might equally pass as a mosque or a Greek or Norman basilica. King Roger's magnificent Cappella Palatina (in Palermo) and the cathedral at Monreale (just outside Palermo) are excellent examples of the Norman genius for adaptation and fusion.

Norman rule in the south gave way to Germanic claims due to the foresight of Holy Roman Emperor Frederick I (known as Barbarossa), who married off his son Henry to Constance de Hauteville, heir to the Norman throne in Sicily. Barbarossa's grandson, Frederick II, became Holy Roman Emperor in 1220. An enlightened ruler, Frederick, who became known as Stupor Mundi (Wonder of the World), was a warrior and a scholar. A profound admirer of Arabic culture, he allowed freedom of worship to Muslims (as well as to Jews). He studied philosophy and magic, wrote laws and earned a place in Italian history as one of the country's earliest poets. In 1224 Frederick founded the University of Naples, with the idea of educating administrators for his kingdom. As a half-Norman southerner, Frederick rejected the tradition that Holy Roman Emperors lived north of the Alps. He moved his exotic, multicultural court (complete with Saracen guard) between Sicily and southern Italy, where he built several castles, notably the superb octagonal Castel del Monte in Apulia.

Italy of the Comunes

While the south of Italy was thus forged into a single kingdom, albeit frequently shaken by revolt and external attack, the north was heading the opposite way.

Trade centres such as the ports of Genoa, Pisa and especially Venice, along with internal centres such as Florence, Milan, Parma, Bologna, Padua, Verona and Modena, became increasingly insolent towards direct imperial control as they got steadily more prosperous on the back of enterprising commercial expansion in the Mediterranean, banking and small industry.

Their growing independence also brought them into conflict with Rome and the Papal States. In the interminable battles of wits between papacy and Empire, the city-states of the northern half of Italy would align themselves or remain aloof as occasion demanded. Frequently a state would invoke the help of one great power in conflicts against the other, or against other city-states.

Between the 12th and 14th centuries, these city-states also developed new forms of government. Venice, for example, was set apart from the other Italian cities by its Byzantine origins and powerfully independent commercial empire-building. It developed an oligarchic, 'parliamentary' system of government in an imperfect but laudable attempt at limited democracy.

More commonly, the city-state created a town council (or *comune*), a form of republican government dominated at first by aristocrats but then increasingly by the burgeoning middle classes whose commercial nous catapulted the cities to increased wealth. These well-heeled families soon passed from business rivalry to internal political struggles in which each aimed to gain control of the government *(signoria)*. This was the highest level of republican government of the city-states and was particularly prevalent in Florence. The complex electoral systems and inevitable corruption led most of the city-states to dabble with dictatorship in one form or another, and murder and intrigue were never far off. In some of the cities, great dynasties, such as the Medici in Florence and the Visconti and Sforza in Milan, came to dominate their respective stages and embark on frequently costly campaigns of commercial and military expansion. Italian city-state politics were rarely boring.

The Sicilian Vespers

In the south, Germanic rule was ousted by Charles of Anjou, who had defeated and beheaded Conradin, Frederick II's 16-year-old grandson and heir. French dominion brought heavy taxes, particularly on rich landowners, who did not accept such measures graciously. Although always a hated foreigner, Charles supported much-needed road repairs, reformed the coinage, imposed standard weights and measures, improved the equipment of ports and opened silver mines.

Charles of Anjou had the pope's ear and was off conquering and sacking Jerusalem and Constantinople when not in his kingdom. But none of his exploits or alliances could alter the hatred he and his French troops had unleashed among the Sicilians.

They revolted, allegedly because of an assault by French soldiers on a Sicilian woman in Palermo in 1282. The rising came to be known as the Sicilian Vespers. While locals massacred French soldiers, they peacefully accepted the rule of Peter of Aragon, who thus managed to take control of the island for the Kingdom of Aragon (in Spain) without firing a shot. Not until 1423 would the Aragonese take over Naples and so restore unity of the southern kingdom.

Famine & Feast

Fourteenth-century Europe was a continent ripe for disaster. Population growth, mismanaged agriculture and urban overcrowding led to famine and paved the way for the horrors of the plague.

If anything, Italy, with a total population of around nine million at the end of the 13th century, was in a worse position than some of its neighbours. Population density in the cities was greater than in many other parts of Europe and the consequent pressure on the surrounding countryside to feed people was enormous – famines were frequent.

In 1348 the first great wave of plague swept across Italy and much of the rest of western Europe, killing swathes of people in urban centres (Florence is said to have lost three quarters of its populace) and wreaking havoc in the country as well. The Black Death, as the disease came to be known, remained a constant of life in Europe well into the next century, visiting death and suffering on one region or another with frightening frequency.

People starved while unemployed armies and destitute nobles roamed the countryside as bandits. With hunger never far away, peasant and urban revolts (such as that in 1378 of the Ciompi, or artisan class, in Florence) became a frequent occurrence. Farming and business suffered enormously.

In spite of the hardships and uncertainties, some people prospered. The grand traders, speculators and bankers lived in aristocratic opulence while other strata of society suffered. Florence's Medici family was perhaps the clearest example. They built one magnificent mansion after another as they took control of the city's government.

War between the city-states was also a constant and eventually a few emerged as small regional powers while the others, no longer able to pay the high price of independence (especially the payment of mercenary armies to protect them), were absorbed by their more powerful neighbours.

In Florence, prosperity was based on the wool trade, finance and general commerce, allowing craft and trade guilds to become increasingly powerful in the affairs of the city. Abroad, its coinage, the *firenze* (florin), was king. By dint of war and purchase, Florence had managed to acquire control of almost all Tuscany by the 1450s – only

Siena and Lucca remained beyond the city's grasp.

In Milan, the Della Torre family, which represented the popular party of the city-state, came into fierce conflict with the Visconti family, representing the Ghibelline nobility. Ottone Visconti had been made archbishop of Milan in 1262 and his nephew, Matteo, was made imperial vicar by Henry VII. He subsequently destroyed the power of the Della Torre, extending Milanese control over Pavia and Cremona, and later Genoa and Bologna. Giangaleazzo Visconti (1351–1402) would turn Milan from a city-state into a strong European power and, although the Visconti were disliked as dictators, Milan managed to resist French attempts at invasion.

The policies of the Visconti (up to 1450), followed by those of the Sforza family, allowed Milan an economic and territorial development that extended the borders of the Signoria from Genoa to Bologna and from Ticino in Switzerland to Lago di Garda. During those years of tireless labour, the entire area of the Po Valley was transformed. Massive hydraulic and irrigation projects (involving Leonardo da Vinci) converted the plain from a swampy woodland into an extremely productive agricultural collective with some of the most fertile farmland in Italy. Among other things, the cultivation of rice and mulberries was introduced. In the 15th century parmesan cheese, a product of Parma, Reggio Emilia and Lodi, was among the most prized cheeses in Europe and butter from the plains of Lombardy was exported as far as Rome.

The Milanese sphere of influence butted up against that of Venice in the east. By 1450 the lagoon city had reached the height of its territorial greatness. In addition to its possessions in Greece, Dalmatia and beyond – all serving to feed its commercial empire – Venice had expanded inland. The banner of the Lion of St Mark flew across all north-eastern Italy, from Gorizia across to Bergamo.

The other big players were the Papal States, a forever-changing constellation of states and regions under papal control, and the kingdom of the south, with its capital in Naples and by now under Aragonese control.

Humanism

The growth of this handful of regional states necessitated the creation of increasingly complex administration and led inevitably to the growth of courtly life around their rulers. As the 15th century progressed, more universities were founded and growing importance was placed on learning. And so emerged a lively intelligentsia, whose protagonists frequently moved from one court to another, enriching their knowledge and scholarly interchange.

As early as the 12th century, Averroës, a Muslim philosopher born in 1126 in Córdoba (southern Spain), had resurrected Aristotle's doctrine that immortality was gained through individual efforts towards universal reason. This emphasis on the autonomy of human reason, based on the ancient theories of the classical philosophers instead of the increasingly self-serving dogmas of the Church hierarchy, was a revolutionary philosophical position which by the 15th century became known as humanism.

The Church had chosen to embrace only those classical philosophers whose thinking fitted its theological purposes. However, humanist thinkers were discovering ancient Roman and Greek works which had been transcribed by religious orders during the Middle Ages and remained hidden away, often thought lost, in monasteries throughout Europe. Many of these works had been banned as subversive by the Church but now inspired great debate among intellectuals.

Translated into Latin, Averroës' work strongly influenced another interpreter of Aristotelian thought, St Thomas Aquinas, who was educated at Monte Cassino by the Benedictines and at the University of Bologna before joining the Dominicans in 1243. Aquinas bridged the gap between the Christian belief in God and Aristotle's respect for the validity of reason with his *Summa Theologiae*. This resulted in Italian Christianity never losing either its grip on the real world or its respect for good works.

By the early decades of the 15th century, the thirst for classical knowledge had been greatly accelerated by the arrival of Greek scholars from Byzantium, fleeing before the advance of the Turks. Through them, western European scholars were able to rediscover the works of the ancients, especially of those key figures such as Plato and Aristotle. A rigorous scientific approach to learning, frequently flying in the face of Church doctrine, characterised the new *studia humanitatis* (study of the humanities).

This rediscovery of classical learning would inevitably spill over into a rediscovery of classical art and architecture that would lead in turn to the artistic explosion that was the Italian Renaissance (see The Renaissance later). The seats of Italian government increasingly sought the prestige of the presence of scholars in their midst. Venice, Florence, Milan and lesser cities frequently chose to thumb their noses at Rome and shelter scholars considered heretics by the papacy.

The Babylonian Captivity

Malaise in the Church did not come solely from the new learning, which threatened to unseat it from its self-appointed role as sole arbiter of knowledge (a handy position that had greatly encouraged the corruption rampant among the clergy).

The papacy's ongoing crusades against Muslims during the 13th century had turned into campaigns against European heretics in the 14th, campaigns that were thinly disguised grabs for wealth and prosperity by claimants from Italian ruling families and the related nobility of Europe.

Pope Boniface VIII (1294–1303) came from Italian nobility and his efforts were directed at ensuring his family's continuing wealth and power. His papal bull of 1302, *Unam Sanctum*, claimed papal supremacy in worldly and spiritual affairs, an instrument for (among other things) removing opponents by simply branding them as heretics.

In 1309 the French Pope Clement V chose to base the papacy in Avignon. He was perhaps influenced by the fact that real urban power in Rome was wielded by two competing noble families, the Orsini and Colonna, who contested (often violently) the pope's claim to temporal power over the city and the Papal States. Those states began to fall apart during the 70 years the mostly French popes remained in Avignon – what came to be known as the Babylonian Captivity. Rome itself became a festering wasteland as the Orsini and Colonna families battled for control and bled the place dry. Public funding disappeared and soon goats and cows were grazing on the Capitoline Hill.

Seven popes presided in Avignon between 1309 and 1377. After the failed attempt of Cola di Rienzo, a popular leader, to wrest control of Rome from the nobility, Cardinal Egidio d'Albornoz managed to restore the Papal States with his *Egidian Constitutions*, thereby enabling Pope Gregory XI to return to Rome in 1377. Finding a ruined and almost deserted city, Gregory made the Vatican his base because it was fortified and had the formidable Castel Sant'Angelo nearby.

On Gregory's death, a year after he returned to Rome, Roman cardinals moved to retain their power. They elected Urban VI as pope but he proved unpopular. This sparked off a renegade movement of cardinals (mainly French) who, a few months later, elected a second pope, Clement VII, who set up his claim in Avignon. So began the Great Schism, with one pope in Avignon and another in Rome, which divided the papacy until 1417, when the Council of Constance healed the rift and elected one pope, Martin V.

The Renaissance

With the end of the Great Schism in the 15th century, the papacy initiated the transformation of Rome. Reduced during the Middle Ages to a conglomeration of majestic ruins and wretched dwellings, the city assumed a new elegance. In 1455 the sculptor Bernardo Rossellino began construction of Palazzo Venezia and Pope Sixtus IV initiated an urban plan to link the areas that had been cut off from one another during the Middle Ages. Donatello, Sandro Botticelli and Fra Angelico lived and worked in Rome at this time.

The Borgia Family

By today's standards, the popes of 15th-century Italy were a very different breed. They fought wars to maintain their territories, indulged in political assassination, kept mistresses and had children by them. Most were motivated more by the desire for personal gain or by dynastic interest than by any spiritual concerns. They were the ultimate proponents of an Italian *realpolitik* and were no saints.

The Spaniard Rodrigo Borgia, who became Pope Alexander VI in 1492 in what is said to have been the most corrupt election in papal history, probably took the biscuit. He established a notoriously corrupt and licentious court and throughout his papacy he maintained a mistress, Vannozza Catanei, who bore him several infamous offspring – all of whom the pope shamelessly manoeuvred into positions worthy of their descent! It all seemed to make little difference to the Christian pilgrims who flocked to Rome to honour Alexander in the jubilee year of 1500.

Alexander's son Cesare, who killed his own brother, terrorised Italy in a campaign to consolidate and expand the Papal States. Ruthless and brilliant, he was at one point admired by Machiavelli. An all-round nasty fellow (countless of his victims were found floating down the River Tiber in Rome) but a cunning planner, it all went wrong when Pope Julius II – a bitter enemy of the Borgia family – came to the papal throne in 1503. Cesare, stripped of his territories and deported to Spain, died four years later.

His sister, Lucrezia, has gone down in history, perhaps unfairly, as the embodiment of Borgia cruelty, lust and avarice. It is said that Pope Alexander was obsessed with his daughter to the point of incest. He ensured that she lived in incredible luxury and considered no man worthy of her. Nevertheless, Lucrezia married several times – one of her husbands was assassinated by Cesare and another was publicly declared impotent by Alexander. She finally ended up with Alfonso d'Este, the duke of Ferrara. In hindsight it appears she had been, in the main, an instrument of her father's and brother's machinations rather than a willing participant.

At the beginning of the 16th century, Pope Julius II opened Via del Corso and Via Giulia and gave Bramante the task of beginning work on the second St Peter's Basilica, which was to take more than a century to finish. In 1508 Raphael started painting the rooms in the Vatican now known as Le Stanze di Raffaello, while between 1508 and 1512 Michelangelo worked on the vaults of the Sistine Chapel. All the great artists of the epoch were influenced by the increasingly frequent discoveries of marvellous pieces of classical art, such as the *Laocoön*, found in 1506 in the area of Nero's Domus Aurea (the sculpture is now in the Vatican Museums).

Rome had 100,000 inhabitants at the height of the Renaissance and became the major centre for Italian political and cultural life. Pope Julius II was succeeded by Leo X, of the Medici family, and the Roman Curia (or Papal Court) became a meeting place for learned men such as Baldassar Castiglione and Ludovico Ariosto.

With the Renaissance, Italians found they could no longer accept the papal domination of earlier times. A remarkable treatise by the humanist Lorenzo Valla revealed the *Donation of Constantine* to be a forgery. Serious study of the Greek classics and Jewish and Arab scholars influenced the literary works of the later 15th century and the idea of the place of the individual in the universe grew in importance.

The 15th and early 16th centuries showed unparalleled creativity and visionary accomplishments in all aspects of political, cultural and social life. In Florence, Cosimo de' Medici, private citizen and wealthy merchant, took over the Signoria in 1434. His nephew, Lorenzo Il Magnifico (the Magnificent), is remembered as a great politician who laid importance on the economic and financial security of Florence. In his refined diplomacy he focused on building the prestige of the city by enriching it with the presence, and the works, of the greatest artists of the time, thus becoming the greatest art patron of the Renaissance.

Feudal lords such as Federico da Montefeltro in Urbino, a merchant as rich as the Medicis, and Francesco Sforza, military commander of Milan, shifted their allegiance between the pope and the emperor as best suited them. They became wealthy bankers and competed with each other for the services of artists, writers, poets and musicians.

The Venice of the Doges, which had always tended to stand aloof from the rest of Italy, nevertheless got on the Renaissance train and a distinctly northern, slightly melancholy, Venetian branch of the Renaissance took off.

This phenomenal creativity was disrupted in Florence by Savonarola, a Dominican monk turned philosopher, who preached fire and brimstone against humanist thinking and allied himself with the French King Charles VIII to overthrow the Medici family and declare a republic in Florence in 1494. Although the monk eventually met a gruesome end, he wielded tremendous power in Florentine politics in the later 15th century.

The Medicis, briefly reinstated, could not reassert their positive influence over the Florentines, who eventually rejected them, setting up a second democratic republic in 1527. In 1530 this republic was in turn overthrown when Emperor Charles V, who had sacked Rome in 1527, brought back the Medicis, who ruled over Florence for the next 210 years.

The first Florentine Republic produced Niccolò Machiavelli (1469–1527), a public official whose short handbook, *Il Principe* (The Prince), outlined somewhat cynically the prerequisite skills for securing and retaining power. Machiavelli advocated the end of all foreign rule in Italy and urged the people to employ their native wit and cunning to achieve this end.

Not all Italian states experienced the great social blossoming of the Renaissance. In the south, quarrels over power and land between the Visconti family (in league with Alfonso V of Aragon) and the house of Anjou ensured repression of the liberty and freethinking that had inspired the new sense of creativity and productivity in other parts of the country.

The Counter-Reformation

By the third decade of the 16th century, the broad-minded curiosity of the Renaissance had begun to give way to the intolerance of the Counter-Reformation. This was the response of the Church to the Reformation, a collective term for the movement led by Germany's Martin Luther that aimed to reform the Church (and which led to the rise of Protestantism in its many forms).

The transition was epitomised by the reign of Pope Paul III (1534–49), who – in best Renaissance style – promoted the building of the classically elegant Palazzo Farnese in Rome but who also allowed the establishment of Ignatius Loyola's order of the Jesuits in 1540 and the organisation in 1542 of the Holy Office. The Holy Office was the final (and ruthless) court of appeal in the trials of suspected heretics and part of the Inquisition (1232–1820), the notorious judicial arm of the Church whose aim was to suppress heresy.

Pope Paul III's fanatical opposition to Protestantism and his purging of clerical abuse, as he saw it, resulted in a widespread campaign of torture and fear. In 1559 the Church published the *Index Librorum Prohibitorum* (Index of Prohibited Books) and the persecution of intellectuals and freethinkers intensified as part of the Roman Church's strategy to regain papal supremacy over the Protestant churches.

Two of the great Italian intellectuals to suffer during the Counter-Reformation were Giordano Bruno (1548–1600) and Galileo Galilei (1564–1642). Bruno, a Dominican monk, was forced to flee Italy for Calvinist Geneva, from where he travelled extensively throughout Europe before being arrested by the Inquisition in Venice in 1592. In 1870 the Kingdom of Italy erected a statue of Bruno in Rome's Campo de' Fiori, where he had been burned at the stake.

An advocate of Aristotelian science, Galileo was forced by the Church to renounce his approval of the Copernican astronomical system, which held that the earth moved around the sun rather than the reverse. But where Bruno had rejected the Catholic Church, Galileo never deviated from the faith that rejected him.

The latter years of the 16th century were not all counterproductive. Pope Gregory XIII (1572–85) replaced the Julian calendar with the Gregorian one in 1582, fixing the start of the year on 1 January and adjusting the system of leap years to align the 365-day year with the seasons. In addition, the city of Rome was greatly embellished by the architectural and sculptural achievements of Gian Lorenzo Bernini (1598–1680).

However, despite these exceptions, Italy no longer determined European cultural expression. The Age of Exploration that had opened up the Americas and other markets to the Atlantic maritime powers of Spain and Portugal (and later Britain and Holland) meant the decline of Italian ports and trade. Epidemics and wars left Italy divided and dominated by foreign powers, especially Spain and, to a lesser extent, France. Spain's hold was wrenched loose in the wake of the War of the Spanish Succession (1701–14). France's ambitions were also held in check. Instead the Austrians moved in to control Lombardy and much of the north (but not Venice and the Veneto). Tuscany was under the control of the Lorraine dynasty (and closely linked to Austria). The Bourbon dynasty installed in Naples meant the southern kingdom, or what was now known as the Kingdom of the Two Sicilies, had become independent.

The Enlightenment

The Italy of the 18th century, although mainly ruled from abroad, was set to play its part in an era that broke down many of the national barriers of Europe – a development as much due to the intermarriage of its monarchies as to new trading laws necessitated by bad harvests in many areas of the continent. The papacy became less influential, particularly following the expulsion of the Jesuits from Portugal, France and Spain.

The Enlightenment swept away the dark days of the Counter-Reformation, producing great philosophers and writers such as Cesare Beccaria (1738–94), whose masterpiece *Of Crimes & Punishments* attacked torture and capital punishment as barbarism and advocated reform of the criminal code, a proposal taken up by Grand Duke Leopold of Tuscany, who abolished the death sentence.

In the field of economics, ideas advocating the liberalisation of trade laws were put forward by the influential writer Pietro Verri (1728–97) who, along with his brother Alessandro, introduced reforms in schools and universities as well as in the government of Lombardy.

Napoleon

Italy had been the source of many enlightened political ideas but the concept of national sovereignty had not been one of them. However, when the French general 27-year-old Napoleon Bonaparte invaded Italy in 1796 and unilaterally declared himself its dictator, a nationalist movement began in earnest. Inspired by the ideas of Jean-Jacques Rousseau, the French leftist Jacobin movement gained significant support in Italy when, in his first year of occupation, Napoleon used Italy as the base for his expedition into Egypt.

The Jacobin movement established a republic in Rome, renewing the debate about Italy as a nation and the sovereign rights of its people. This movement was dubbed the Risorgimento (Revival) by Italian dramatist Vittorio Alfieri (1749–1803). However, the mainly middle-class movement found itself unable to bring about social reforms quickly

Napolean Bonaparte – small man, big ideas

enough for the peasants, particularly the very poor of Naples. A peasant army sacked the city, littering its streets with dead Jacobins.

Although he had declared himself first consul of Italy in 1799, Napoleon acceded to the calls of Italian deputies in the north to proclaim a republic. For the first time in history, the political entity known as Italy came into being, albeit with Napoleon as its first, self-elected president.

When Napoleon made himself emperor of France in 1804 he established the Kingdom of Italy and made himself its first sovereign, inviting Pope Pius VII to crown him king in Paris. Pius delayed his visit, reluctant to give his endorsement to the power brokers of the French Revolution (which had greatly curtailed the power of the Catholic Church). He was also loath to endorse the marriage of Napoleon to the divorcee Josephine. When the pope finally arrived several days late, Napoleon was not amused. As the pope raised the emperor's crown to his head, Napoleon took it and crowned himself.

Unification

During the final years of Napoleon's domination of Italy, hopes grew that his regime would be replaced with independence and constitutional rule. It was not to be. Following Napoleon's defeat at Waterloo in 1815, all of the peninsula's former rulers were reinstated by the Congress of Vienna. It was a backward step that had terrible consequences for the country but it did encourage the rapid growth of secret societies comprised, in the main, of disaffected middle-class intellectuals. In the south, one of these societies, the republican Carbonari society, pushed hard and often ruthlessly for a valid constitution, leading a revolutionary uprising in Naples in 1820.

One of the leading revolutionary figures of the secret societies of the time was Filippo Buonarroti, who strove for independence from Austria and the establishment of a communist society devoid of private-property interests.

A Genovese, Giuseppe Mazzini (1805–72), emerged as a key proponent of nationhood and political freedom. Having quit the Carbonari movement in 1830, Mazzini founded Young Italy, a society of young men whose aims were the liberation of Italy from foreign and domestic tyranny and its unification under a republican government. This was to be achieved through education and, where necessary, revolt by guerrilla bands.

Exiled from his homeland for his former activities with the Carbonari, Mazzini was responsible for organising a number of abortive uprisings throughout Italy during the 1830s and 1840s. These left many of the young men dead who had flocked to join Young Italy. Twice sentenced to death, Mazzini was to live out his days in England, from where he wrote articles and solicited as much support as he could from influential allies in order to raise the consciousness of Europeans about the Italian question.

In 1848 there were revolutions in almost every major city and town of Europe. In their newspaper, *Il Risorgimento*, one of several publications to have sprung up as the Italian nationalist movement gained ground among citizens of all classes, nationalist writer Cesare Balbo and Count Camillo Benso di Cavour of Turin pressed for a constitution. In 1848 they published their Statuto (Statute) advocating a two-chamber parliament, with the upper chamber to be appointed by the Crown and the lower chamber to be elected by educated taxpayers. In 1861 the Statuto was to become the constitutional basis of the Kingdom of Italy, but not before 13 more years of warring between the various European princes had resulted in the deaths of a great many more Italians.

Returning to Italy in 1848 from his famous exploits in South America, where he is still remembered as one of the founding fathers of Uruguay, Giuseppe Garibaldi (1807–82) was to become the hero Italians needed to lead them towards unification. Garibaldi's personal magnetism, the result of his respect for people, both rich and poor, drew more Italians into the fight for nationhood than ever before.

Despite significant personal animosity, Garibaldi and Cavour fought side by side, each in their chosen arena, to break the stranglehold of foreign domination. The brilliant diplomacy of Cavour, coupled with the independent efforts of Garibaldi and his popular base, finally caught the attention of European communities, particularly the British (who became staunch supporters of a free and united Italy).

When King Carlo Alberto, the sympathetic Piedmontese monarch, granted his people a constitution based on the Statuto in March 1848, Cavour stood for election. In 1850 he was given three ministries – navy, commerce and finance – in the government headed up by Massimo d'Azeglio. When Cavour's centre-left faction joined forces with the centre-right, headed by Urbano Rattazzi, behind d'Azeglio's back, the prime minister resigned and Cavour was asked by the king to take the top government post. As Piedmontese prime minister, Cavour focused on forging an alliance with the French emperor Napoleon III, in a move destined to overthrow Austrian domination of Piedmont.

Meanwhile the unification movement was literally on the move as Garibaldi led his Expedition of One Thousand, which took Sicily and Naples in 1860. The Kingdom of Italy was declared on 17 March 1861 and Vittorio Emanuele II, who had been king of Sardinia-Piedmont from 1849, was proclaimed king. But Italy was not completely united: Venice remained in the hands of the Austrians and Rome was held by France.

Cavour died within six months of leading the first parliament of the Kingdom of Italy. He had been betrayed by his French allies when Napoleon III signed the armistice of Villafranca, ending the Franco-Austrian war (fought in Italy, largely by Italians) without consulting Cavour, who resigned his post. Venice was wrested from the Austrians in 1866 but it wasn't until the Franco-Prussian War of 1870 that Napoleon III's hold over Italy was broken. Needing all available troops elsewhere, he withdrew from Rome, leaving the way clear for the Italian army to claim the capital.

The only resistance to the push on Rome came from the papal soldiers of Pope Pius IX, who refused to recognise the Kingdom of Italy. The pope was eventually stripped of his remaining secular powers as well as his palace, the Quirinale. The papacy would regain some autonomy in the 1920s when the Fascist dictator, Benito Mussolini, restored the independent papal state but, in the interim, the papacy forbade Catholics to participate in governmental elections.

As the 20th century approached, the economic crisis of Europe was reflected by constant fluctuations in Italian politics as socialist democrats and right-wing imperialists in turn gained and lost the support of the populace. In the general elections of 1894, Pope Pius X formally gave Catholics the right to vote (although many had already been doing just that) and there was a widespread backlash against socialism.

Giovanni Giolitti, one of Italy's longest-serving prime ministers (heading five governments between the years 1892 and 1921), managed to bridge the political extremes and was able to embark on parliamentary reforms that gave the vote to all literate men aged 21 or over and all illiterate men who had completed military service or were aged 30 or over. Male suffrage had been achieved but Italian women were denied the right to vote until after WWII.

WWI

When war broke out in Europe in July 1914, Italy chose to remain neutral rather than become caught between old enemies. But senior politicians soon allied themselves with the British, Russians and French, while the papacy spoke out against the 'atheist' French in favour of Catholic Austria.

Italy was, in fact, a member of the Triple Alliance with Austria and Germany. Although Italy had territorial claims to make in Trent, the southern Tyrol, Trieste and even in Dalmatia, the weakness of the new country had compelled it to pursue a policy of appeasement with its powerful Austrian neighbour.

Between July 1914 and May 1915, the government had a change of heart and decided to join the Allies, on the understanding that upon the successful conclusion of hostilities Italy would receive the territories it sought. From then until the end of 1918, Italy and Austria engaged in a wearing war of attrition. The front lines, along the River Isonzo in the east and in the Adige valley in the north, barely changed. In August 1916 the Italians took Gorizia but in October 1917 the Austrians routed the Italians at Caporetto and marched onto the Venetian plain, only to be halted on the Piave. When the Austro-Hungarian forces collapsed in November 1918, the Italians were able to march into Trieste and Trent.

The young country had been manifestly ill-prepared for this gruesome conflict. Not only did Italy lose 600,000 men but the war economy had produced a small concentration of immensely wealthy and powerful industrial barons and left the bulk of the civilian populace in penury. It was an explosive cocktail.

Fascism

In 1919 Benito Mussolini, one-time socialist and journalist, founded the Fascist Party, with its hallmarks of the black shirt and Roman salute. These were to become symbols of violent oppression and aggressive nationalism for the next 23 years. In 1921 the party won 35 of the 135 seats in parliament. In October 1922 the king asked Mussolini to form a government, and thus he began his domination of Italy. With an expedition of 40,000 Fascist militia, he began the famous march on Rome to 'free the nation from the socialists'.

In April 1924, following a political campaign marked by violence and intimidation, the Fascist Party won the national elections and Mussolini created the world's first Fascist regime. By 1925 the term 'totalitarianism' had come into use. By the end of that year Mussolini had expelled opposition parties from parliament, gained control of the press and trade unions and had rescinded the right to vote from two-thirds of the electorate. In 1929 Mussolini and Pope Pius XI signed the Lateran Treaty, whereby Catholicism was declared the sole religion of Italy and the Vatican was recognised as an independent state. In return, the papacy finally acknowledged the united Kingdom of Italy.

The famous facist, Benito Mussolini

In the 1920s Mussolini embarked on an aggressive foreign policy, leading to skirmishes with Greece over the island of Corfu and to military expeditions against nationalist forces in the Italian colony of Libya. In 1935 Italy sought a new colonial conquest through the invasion of Abyssinia (present-day Ethiopia) from the Italian base in Eritrea, but took seven months to capture Addis Ababa. The act was condemned by the League of Nations, which imposed limited sanctions on Italy.

Fearful of international isolation, Mussolini formed the Axis with Hitler in 1936. They were soon joined by Japan and in June 1940 Italy entered WWII as an ally of Germany.

After a series of military disasters and the landing of the Allied armies on Sicily on 10 July 1943, Mussolini was faced not only with increasing discontent among Italians and diminishing support for Fascism but also with Hitler's refusal to assign more troops to defend southern Italy. Two weeks after the Allied landing, the king of Italy, Vittorio Emanuele III, led a coup against Mussolini and had him arrested.

In the confused period that followed, now known as the 45 Days, Italy erupted in a series of massive demonstrations demanding an end to the war. The king signed an armistice with the Allies that amounted to an unconditional surrender and declared war on Germany, but it was too late to prevent the takeover of northern Italy by Nazi troops. As the Allies moved painfully up through the south of the Italian peninsula, the Germans began their campaign of brutal suppression in the north, prompting the formation of the Resistance.

King Vittorio Emanuelle III

The Germans rescued Mussolini from his prison on the Gran Sasso in what is now Abruzzo and installed him as head of the Republic of Salò in the north. By now completely demoralised, Mussolini was nothing more than a German puppet. He was captured and shot along with his mistress, Clara Petacci, by partisans in April 1945 and then hung upside down from the roof of a petrol station in Milan's Piazzale Loreto.

The Resistance

Members of the Resistance, which conservative estimates put at more than 100,000 in early 1945, managed to gain control of small areas of the north and played a significant role in liberating Florence from the Germans in August 1944. The Nazi response to partisan attacks was savage. Whole villages were exterminated; in one of the most notorious reprisals, 1830 men, women and children were murdered by an SS battalion at Marzabotto, south of Bologna, on 1 October 1944. In March of that year urban partisans had blown up 32 military police in Rome. In reprisal, the Germans shot 335 prisoners at the Fosse Ardeatine, just outside the city.

Northern Italy was finally liberated by May 1945 after Allied troops broke through German lines. The Resistance had suffered huge losses and its contribution to the Allied victory did not go unacknowledged. These people had fought not only against German and Fascist oppression but also for an ideal of social and political change – and after the war they wanted to put that ideal into action. The Allies, meanwhile, were wondering how to deal with what amounted to a massive, armed, left-wing movement whose leaders spoke often of insurrection.

The Republic

The Resistance was disarmed, either voluntarily or by force, as Italy's political forces scrambled to regroup. The USA, through the economic largesse of the Marshall Plan, wielded considerable political influence in the country and no doubt used this in attempts to keep the left, of which it was highly suspicious, in check.

Immediately after the war three coalition governments succeeded one another. The third, which came to power in December 1945, was dominated by the newly formed Democrazia Cristiana (DC; Christian Democrats), led by Alcide de Gasperi, who remained prime minister until 1953.

In 1946, following a referendum, the constitutional monarchy was abolished and a republic established, with the DC winning the majority of votes at the first post-war elections. The Partito Comunista Italiano (PCI; Communist Party), led by Palmiro Togliatti, and the Partito Socialista Italiano (PSI; Socialist Party), led by Pietro Nenni, participated in coalition governments until 1947, when de Gasperi formed a government that excluded the left.

Economic Recovery

By the early 1950s the country's economy had begun to show strong signs of recovery, although the more impoverished and less industrialised south lagged behind. To counter this, the government formed the Cassa per il Mezzogiorno (State Fund for the South) in 1950, which would eventually pour trillions of lire into development projects in the southern regions.

In 1958 Italy became a founding member of the European Economic Community (EEC) and this signalled the beginning of the Economic Miracle, a period of significant economic growth that saw unemployment drop as industry expanded. A major feature of this period was the development of Italy's automobile industry and, more particularly, of Fiat in Turin, which sparked a massive migration of peasants from the south to the north in search of work.

Although it was the only major party not to participate in the government of the country, the PCI nevertheless played a crucial role in Italy's social and political development well into the 1980s. The party steadily increased its share of the poll at each election and always had more card-carrying members than the DC, but the spectre of European communism and the Cold War continued to undermine its chances of participating in government.

By the mid-1960s Italy's economic strength was waning and social unrest was becoming commonplace. Togliatti, the long-serving leader of the PCI, died in 1964. His policy of cooperation with the DC in the interests of national unity had played a significant role in avoiding serious social conflict. One year earlier, Aldo Moro had been appointed prime minister, a position he held until 1968. It was Moro who invited the PSI into government in 1963; 15 years later, he was moving towards a historic compromise that would have allowed the communists to enter government for the first time. This prompted his kidnapping and murder by the Brigate Rosse (BR; Red Brigades) terrorist group.

Protest & Terrorism

Influenced by similar events in France, in 1967 and 1968 Italian university students rose up in protest, ostensibly against poor conditions in the universities. However, the protests were really aimed at authority and the perceived impotence of the left. The movement resulted in the formation of many small revolutionary groups that attempted to fill what the students saw as an ideological gap in Italy's political left wing. The uprising was closely followed in 1969 by what has become known as the Autunno Caldo (Hot Autumn), when factory workers embarked on a series of strikes and protests that continued into 1971.

The 1970s, however, were dominated by the new spectre of terrorism. By 1970, a group of young left-wing militants had formed the Brigate Rosse.

Neo-Fascist terrorists had already struck. On 12 December 1969, a bomb was set off in a bank in Milan's Piazza Fontana, killing 16 people. Controversy and mystery shrouded this incident and when its perpetrators, supposedly right-wing extremists directed by forces within the country's secret services, were finally convicted in 2001, there were outcries from the right that the convicting judge was a 'red'. In any event, the bombing formed part of what was known as the Strategy of Tension, which culminated in the 1980 bombing of the Bologna train station by right-wing terrorists, in which 84 people died.

The Brigate Rosse, however, was the most prominent terrorist group operating in the country during the Anni di Piombo (Years of Lead) from 1973 to 1980. While many of the BR's original members were dead or in prison by the mid-1970s, a major recruiting campaign in 1977 gave new life to the movement. That year was also marked by student protests, sparked largely by their opposition to education reforms proposed by the government. As opposed to 1968, this was more an anti-political than an ideological movement. Universities were occupied in Rome, Bologna and Milan and the *centro sociale* – a type of left-wing cultural centre established through the occupation of unused buildings – had its origin in this period.

In 1978 the Brigate Rosse claimed their most important victim – Aldo Moro. During the 54 days Moro was held captive, his colleagues laboured over whether to bargain with the terrorists to save his life or to adopt a position of no compromise. In the end, they took the latter path and the BR killed Moro on 9 May 1978, leaving his body in the boot of a car parked in a central Rome street equidistant from the headquarters of the DC and the PCI.

Finally, the *carabinieri* (military police) general Carlo Alberto dalla Chiesa was appointed to wipe out the terrorist groups. Using a new law that allowed *pentiti* (repentants) much-reduced prison sentences for grassing on their colleagues, he convinced key terrorists to aid his efforts. In 1980 the government appointed Dalla Chiesa to fight the Mafia in Sicily. He and his wife were assassinated in Palermo within months of his taking up the job.

However, the 1970s also produced much positive political and social change. In 1970 the country was divided into administrative regions and regional governments were elected. In the same year divorce became legal and efforts by conservative Catholics to have the law repealed were defeated in a referendum in 1974. In 1978 abortion was legalised, following anti-sexist legislation that allowed women to keep their own names after marriage.

The compromise with the communists was never to come about but in 1983 the DC government was forced by its diminishing share of the electoral vote to hand over the prime ministership to a socialist. Bettino Craxi became the longest-serving prime minister since De Gasperi, holding the post from 1983 to 1989. A skilled politician, Craxi continued to wield considerable power in government until he fled the country in 1993 after being implicated in the Tangentopoli national bribery scandal (see the next section).

A spurt in the 1980s saw Italy become one of the world's leading economies (see Economy later in this chapter) but by the 1990s a new period of crisis had set in. High unemployment and inflation, combined with a huge national debt and an extremely unstable lira, led the government to introduce draconian measures to revive the economy.

During this period the PCI reached a watershed. Internal disagreements led to a split in the party in the early 1990s. The old guard now goes by the title Partito Rifondazione Comunista (PRC; Refounded Communist Party), under the leadership of Fausto Bertinotti. The breakaway, more moderate wing of the party reformed itself and now calls itself – after several name changes along the way – Democratici di Sinistra (DS; Left Democrats).

Tangentopoli

The scandal known as Tangentopoli ('kickback city') broke in Milan in early 1992 when a functionary of the PSI was arrested on charges of accepting bribes in exchange for public works' contracts. Led by Milanese magistrate Antonio di Pietro, dubbed 'the reluctant hero', investigations known as Mani Pulite ('clean hands') eventually implicated thousands of politicians, public officials and businesspeople.

Charges ranged from bribery, making illicit political payments and receiving kickbacks to blatant theft. All of this came as no surprise to ordinary Italians. The corruption went from petty bribery to the highest levels of government and few of the country's top politicians escaped the taint of scandal.

In elections held just after the scandal broke in 1992, voters expressed their discontent and the DC's share of the vote dropped by 5%. In this election Umberto Bossi's Lega Nord (Northern League) made its first appearance as a force to be reckoned with at the national level, winning 7% of the vote on a federalist, anti-corruption platform.

Tangentopoli left two of the traditional parties, the DC and PSI, in tatters and effectively demolished the centre of the Italian political spectrum.

At the 1994 national elections, voters again took the opportunity to express their disgust with the old order. The elections were won by a new right-wing coalition known as the Polo per le Libertà (Freedom Alliance), whose members included the newly formed Forza Italia (Go Italy) and the neo-Fascist Alleanza Nazionale (National Alliance), as well as Umberto Bossi's federalist Lega Nord. The leader of the alliance, billionaire media magnate Silvio Berlusconi, who had entered politics only three months before the elections, was appointed prime minister. After a turbulent nine months in power, Berlusconi's volatile coalition government disintegrated when Bossi withdrew. Berlusconi himself had been notified that he was under investigation by the Milan Mani Pulite judges and various court proceedings against him were still pending in 2001 – the year in which he would be re-elected prime minister.

Steady as She Goes

President Oscar Luigi Scalfaro named an interim government of technocrats to fill the void left by Berlusconi's exit. A largely colourless outfit, it set about dealing with some of the country's economic Gordian knots – the biggest of them being the need to cut public spending.

If Berlusconi represented a new centre-right tendency in Italian politics, it was inevitable that a centre-left grouping should also emerge. Known as the Ulivo (Olive Tree) and led by Bolognese university professor Romano Prodi, it emerged victorious in the April 1996 elections and continued with the task of reducing public debt. Prodi promised that Italy would be in the first wave of EU countries participating in the economic and monetary union in 1999 and ultimately in the single currency, or euro, in 2001. He delivered, but internal bickering in the coalition, especially from the PRC, led to Prodi's fall in September 1998.

Into his shoes stepped the leader of the DS, Massimo d'Alema. For the first time in Italian politics the communists, or rather their softline successors, entered an Italian government. D'Alema continued Prodi's work, although his succession was viewed by some as bordering on treacherous. Prodi gathered around him a new party of the centre-left that made d'Alema's life uncomfortable until Prodi accepted the job as head of the European Commission and abandoned the Italian political stage.

The election in May 1999 of Carlo Azeglio Ciampi, a former Bank of Italy governor, as 10th president was greeted warmly in Italy and abroad. NATO's war with Yugoslavia that year threw Italy into the international spotlight and political squabbling was minimised in the country's attempts to cope with its frontline position. In the end Italy gained brownie points as a competent and faithful ally during the conflict (in which it effectively served as a giant aircraft carrier for NATO air raids on Yugoslavia).

In the meantime, Italy's political game of musical chairs continued. Massimo d'Alema could no better survive the squabbling within the centre-left coalition than Prodi had. He was replaced by the techocrat Giuliano Amato in April 2000 in what was seen as an interim move until the next elections, which were held in May 2001. Amato, although he opted not to stand for prime minister in the elections, proved to be a steadying hand during his short mandate and boasted significant cuts in the country's still gargantuan public debt when he bowed out.

The Return of Il Cavaliere

Plus ça change... Berlusconi (known in the press as Il Cavaliere, 'the Knight') proved to have more political fire in his belly than many had anticipated. After years, as he put it, 'in the desert', the magnate presented a coalition to the 2001 electorate disconcertingly similar to that of 1994. This time it was called the Casa delle Libertà (House of Liberty) and all the main players were back, including Alleanza Nazionale and Bossi's league. Facing him as the Ulivo's representative was the telegenic former Rome mayor Francesco Rutelli. The election campaign was, more than ever, one of personal image in the American presidential style – and one of the nastiest on record. Keep it simple, Berlusconi might well have said, as his eternal suntan and grin were plastered over walls and TV sets, and delivered in election packages to people's homes.

His programme, which in essence seemed to be little more than to run Italy like a giant corporation, obviously appealed to many Italians sick of the rhetoric and comparative inaction typical of other politicians and parties. Berlusconi emerged from the May 2001 national elections with an unexpectedly powerful absolute majority in both houses. Better still from his point of view, his separatist partners under Bossi failed to reach the 4% minimum cut-off to take up seats in the Chamber of Deputies (although they hold the balance of seats in the Senate), while Alleanza Nazionale's vote also dropped off considerably. Berlusconi's Forza Italia party carried almost 30% of the vote – not since the halcyon days of the DC hegemony in the 1950s and '60s had a single Italian political party united such a chunk of the electorate behind it. A month and a half later, his coalition also swept to victory in Sicily's regional elections.

There was an air of expectation mixed with trepidation in the wake of his steamroller victory. Just what could the magnificent magnate achieve in Italy with such a rare electoral gift? Bossi, made minister for devolution, made it clear from the outset he intended to push that issue hard. Berlusconi, the country's 59th prime minister since WWII, ordered his team to get to work, promising 'few words and plenty of action.'

GEOGRAPHY

Italy's boot shape makes it one of the most recognisable countries in the world, with the island of Sicily appearing somewhat like a football at the toe of the boot and Sardinia situated in the middle of the Tyrrhenian Sea to the west of the mainland.

The country is bounded by four seas, all part of the Mediterranean. The Adriatic Sea separates Italy from Slovenia, Croatia, Montenegro, Albania and Greece; the Ionian Sea laps the southern coasts of Apulia, Basilicata and Calabria and the Ligurian Sea and Tyrrhenian Sea are to the west of the country. Coastal areas vary from the cliffs of Liguria and Calabria to the generally flat, low-lying Adriatic coast.

More than 75% of Italy is mountainous, with the Alps stretching from the Gulf of Genoa to the Adriatic Sea north of Trieste and dividing the peninsula from France, Switzerland, Austria and Slovenia. The highest Alpine peak is Mont Blanc (Monte Bianco; 4807m) on the border with France, while the highest mountain in the Italian Alps is Monte Rosa (4633m), on the Swiss border. The highest peak wholly within Italy is the Gran Paradiso at 4061m.

The Alps are divided into three main groups – western, central and eastern – and undoubtedly the most spectacular scenery is found in the Dolomites in the eastern Alps in Trentino-Alto Adige and the Veneto. There are more than 1000 glaciers in the Alps, remnants of the last Ice Age that are in a constant state of retreat. The best known in the Italian Alps is the Marmolada glacier on the border of Trentino and the Veneto, popular for summer skiing.

The Apennine range forms a backbone extending 1220km from near Genoa, in Liguria, to the tip of Calabria and into Sicily. The highest peak is the Corno Grande (2914m) in the Gran Sasso d'Italia group in Abruzzo. Another interesting group of mountains, the Apuane Alps, is in northwestern Tuscany and constitutes a part of the sub-Apennine range. These mountains are composed almost entirely of marble and have been mined almost continuously since Roman times. Michelangelo selected his blocks of perfect white marble at Carrara in the Apuan Alps.

Lowlands make up less than a quarter of Italy's total land area. The largest is the Po Valley, bounded by the Alps, the Apennine range and the Adriatic Sea. The plain is heavily populated and industrialised and through it runs Italy's largest river, the Po (as do the Rivers Reno, Adige, Piave and Tagliamento). Other plains include the Tavoliere di Apulia and the Pianura Campana around Mt Vesuvius.

GEOLOGY

Italy has a complex geological history, characterised by marked environmental and climatic changes. Around 100 million years ago the area now occupied by the peninsula was covered by a tropical sea, the Tethys, which

Rock Varieties

Even though Italy is not a large country, it contains a great variety of rock types. The Alps are largely formed of crystalline rocks, such as granite and porphyry, and there are also sedimentary rocks, such as limestone, dolomite and sandstone, in the eastern Alps. Sedimentary rocks are also found throughout the Apennine range and on Sicily and Sardinia. Crystalline and volcanic rocks predominate in Sardinia. Volcanic rocks are also common on Sicily and along the Tyrrhenian side of the country, consistent with the volcanic activity in these parts of Italy. The country's plains are mainly formed from mixed deposits of gravel, sand and clay.

separated the Euro-Asiatic and African continental plates. As the ocean began to recede, various types of materials were deposited, including limestones, dolomites and sandstones, as well as the extensive coral reefs to the north-east from which the Dolomite mountain range was later formed.

Although earlier volcanic activity had resulted in the formation of the original nucleus of the Alpine chain and other mountains farther south, the crucial moment came around 40 million years ago when the African and European continental plates collided. The collision forced the respective borders of the plates and part of the bed of the Tethys to fold and rise up, beginning the formation of the Alpine and Apennine chains. The Alps rose up relatively quickly, at first forming an archipelago of tropical islands in the Tethys Sea. The curvature of the Alpine and Apennine chains, as well as the transverse orientation of the peninsula itself in the Mediterranean basin, reflect the manner in which the continental plates collided.

Both mountain chains underwent significant erosion, resulting in huge deposits of sand, gravel and clay at their feet and in part preparing the way for the development of land areas including Tuscany. It is interesting to note that around six million years ago, when both the Alps and the Apennine range were still largely submerged, the Straits of Gibraltar closed up completely. As a result, the Mediterranean Sea, which was all that remained of the vast Tethys, began to dry up. The Straits of Gibraltar reopened some two million years ago, allowing the Atlantic Ocean to refill the Mediterranean. Some scholars have suggested that this ancient geological event could have given rise to the Atlantis myth, as well as the biblical story of Noah and the great flood.

By around two million years ago, after the landscape had been shaped and reshaped by the combined forces of continental plate movement and erosion, the Italian peninsula had almost arrived at its present-day form. The level of the sea continued to rise and fall with the alternation of ice ages and periods of warm climate, until the end of the last ice age around 10,000 to 12,000 years ago.

Earthquakes & Volcanoes

A fault line runs through the entire Italian peninsula – from eastern Sicily, following the Apennine range up into the Alps of Friuli-Venezia Giulia in the north-east of the country. It corresponds to the collision point of the European and African continental plates and subjects a good part of the country to seismic activity. Central and southern Italy, including Sicily, are occasionally rocked by sometimes devastating earthquakes. The worst this century was in 1908, when Messina and Reggio di Calabria were destroyed by a seaquake (an earthquake originating under the sea floor) registering seven on the Richter scale. Almost 86,000 people were killed by the quake and subsequent tidal wave. In November 1980 an earthquake south-east of Naples destroyed several villages and killed 2570 people. A more recent earthquake in the Apennine range in September 1997, which affected Umbria and Le Marche, killed 10 people and caused part of the vaulted ceiling of the Basilica di San Francesco d'Assisi, in Assisi, to collapse, destroying important frescoes.

Italy has six active volcanoes: Stromboli and Vulcano (on the Aeolian Islands), Vesuvius, the Campi Flegrei and the island of Ischia (near Naples), and Etna (on Sicily). Stromboli and Etna are among the world's most active volcanoes, while Vesuvius has not erupted since 1944. However, this has become a source of concern for scientists, who estimate that it should erupt every 30 years. Etna's most recent major eruption occurred in 2001, when officials were forced to close a tourist area and scientific monitoring station after lava flowed down the volcano's southern slopes.

Related volcanic activity produces thermal and mud springs, notably at Viterbo in Lazio and on the Aeolian Islands. The Campi Flegrei near Naples is an area of intense volcanic activity, which includes hot springs, gas emissions and steam jets.

CLIMATE

Situated in the temperate zone and jutting deep into the Mediterranean, Italy is regarded by many tourists as a land of sunny, mild weather. However, due to the north-south orientation of the peninsula and the fact that it is largely mountainous, the country's climate is actually quite variable.

In the Alps, temperatures are lower and winters are long and severe. Generally the weather is warm from July to September, although rainfall can be high in September. While the first snowfall is usually in November, light snow sometimes falls in mid-September and the first heavy falls can occur in early October. Freak snowfalls in June are not unknown at high altitudes.

The Alps shield northern Lombardy and the Lakes area, including Milan, from the extremes of the northern European winter and Liguria enjoys a mild, Mediterranean climate similar to southern Italy because it is protected by both the Alps and the Apennine range.

Winters are severe and summers very hot in the Po Valley. Venice can be hot and humid in summer and, although not too cold in winter, it can be unpleasant as the sea level rises and *acqua alta* (literally 'high water') inundates the city.

Farther south in Florence, which is encircled by hills, the weather can be extreme but, as you travel towards the tip of the boot, temperatures and weather conditions become milder. Rome, for instance, has an average July and August temperature in the mid-20°s (Celsius), although the impact of the sirocco (a hot, humid wind blowing from Africa) can produce stiflingly hot weather in August, with temperatures in the high 30°s for days on end. Winters are moderate and snow is very rare in Rome, although winter clothing (or at least a heavy overcoat) is still a requirement.

The south of Italy and the islands of Sicily and Sardinia have a Mediterranean climate. Summers are long, hot and dry, and winter temperatures tend to be quite moderate, averaging around 10°C. These regions are also affected by the humid sirocco in summer.

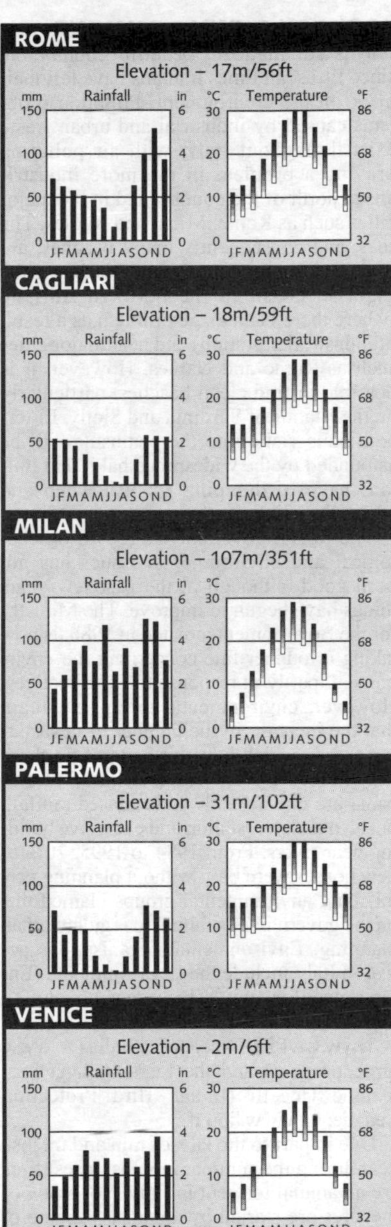

ECOLOGY & ENVIRONMENT

Italy is a dramatically beautiful country, but since Etruscan times humans have left their mark on the environment. Pollution problems caused by industrial and urban waste exist throughout Italy, with air pollution proving a problem in the more industrialised north of the country and in the major cities such as Rome, Milan and Naples. The seas, and consequently many beaches, are fouled to some extent, particularly on the Ligurian coast, in the northern Adriatic (where there is an algae problem as a result of industrial pollution) and near major cities such as Rome and Naples. However, it is possible to find clean beaches, particularly on the islands of Sardinia and Sicily. Litter-conscious visitors to the peninsula will be astounded by the widespread habit that Italians have of dumping rubbish when and where they like.

The Italian government's record on ecological and environmental issues has not been good, although in the past few years things have begun to improve. The Ministry for the Environment, created in 1986, is now taking a tougher line concerning the environment, partly in response to EU directives. However, environmental groups maintain that the increase in the number of devastating floods which have hit parts of northern Italy in recent years and landslides in Campania are due not only to increased rainfall, but also to deforestation and excessive building near rivers. From 1984 to 1995, 20% of new houses were built without planning permits and environmental groups blamed this on the government's failure to regulate urban planning. Environmental organisations active in Italy include the Lega Ambiente (Environment League; **W** www.legambiente.it), the World Wide Fund for Nature (WWF; **W** www.wwf.it), Greenpeace Italia (**W** www.greenpeace.it) and the Lega Italiana Protezione Uccelli (Italian Bird Protection League; **W** www.lipu.it).

Due in part to the lack of rain and intense heat during the summer months, forest fires are an annual torment in Italy. Not a few of the fires are started by arsonists – some of them wanting to clear forest land, others hoping to find work when it's time to replant the trees destroyed by the fire.

FLORA & FAUNA

Flora

The long human presence on the Italian peninsula has had a significant impact on the environment, resulting in the widespread destruction of original forests and vegetation and their replacement with crops and orchards. Aesthetically the result is not always displeasing – much of the beauty of Tuscany, for instance, lies in the interaction of olive groves with vineyards, fallow fields and stands of cypress and pine.

Italy's flora is predominantly Mediterranean. Three broad classifications of evergreen tree dominate – ilex (or evergreen oak), cork and pine. The occasional virgin ilex and oak forest still survives in the more inaccessible reaches of Tuscany, Umbria, Calabria, Apulia and Sardinia. These ancient woods are made up of trees that can reach up to 15m high, and whose thick canopies block out light to the forest floor, preventing most undergrowth. Most common are ilex strands that have been created, or at least interfered with, by humans. They tend to be sparser, with smaller trees and abundant undergrowth.

Next to the ilex, the most common tree is the cork. Cork wood has been prized since ancient times and not a cork tree that stands today is part of virgin forest. Often they are mixed in with ilex and other oaks, although in Sicily and Sardinia it is possible to come across pure cork forests.

There are three types of pine: the Aleppo pine (the hardiest of the three); the domestic pine, especially common in Tuscany and also known as the umbrella pine for the long, flattened appearance of its branches; and the maritime pine, which, in spite of its name, is generally found further inland than the other two!

Ancient imports that are an inevitable part of much of the Italian countryside (especially from Tuscany south) are the olive and cyprus. The former comes in many shapes and sizes, among the most striking being the robust trees of Apulia.

Much of the country is covered by *macchia* (maquis), a broad term that covers all sorts of vegetation ranging from two metres to as much as six metres in height. Herbs such as lavender, rosemary and thyme are typical maquis plants, as are shrubs of the cistus family, gorse, juniper and heather. If the soil is acidic, there may also be broom. Orchids, gladioli and irises may flower beneath these shrubs, which are colourful in spring.

Where the action of humans and nature has been particularly harsh, or the soil is poor, the macchia becomes *gariga*, the very barest of scrub. This is dominated by aromatic herbs such as lavender, rosemary and thyme.

Fauna

The Alps are home to marmots and an increasing number of ibex (mountain goat), chamois and roe deer. In the Parco delle Foreste Casentinesi, in Emilia-Romagna, there are about 1000 deer. Among the native animals on Sardinia are wild boar, the mouflon sheep, deer and a variety of wild cat. You will find evidence of wild boar (and the people who hunt them) throughout the hills and countryside in Italy. Commonly available maps in national parks in the Alps and Apennine range detail the local wildlife and indicate areas where they might be found.

Hunters continue to plunder the countryside for birds. However, enough remain to make bird-watching an interesting pastime. A large variety of falcons and hawks are found throughout Italy, as are many varieties of small birds. The irony is that it is often easier to spot the colourful smaller birds in city parks – among the few refuges they have from the Italian hunter – than in their natural habitats in the countryside. A good place to observe water birds is the Parco Nazionale del Circeo, just south of Rome; huge flocks of flamingos can be seen on Sardinia, just outside Cagliari and near Oristano.

Italy is home to remarkably little dangerous fauna. It has only one poisonous snake, the viper.

Endangered Species

Changes to the environment, combined with the Italians' passion for hunting *(la caccia)*, have led to many native animals and birds becoming extinct, rare or endangered. Hunters constitute a powerful lobby group in Italy and continue to win regular referendums on whether hunting should be banned.

In the 20th century, 13 species became extinct in Italy, including the Alpine lynx, the white-tailed eagle *(aquila di mare)* and the crane. Under laws progressively introduced over the years, many animals and birds are now protected but the World Wide Fund for Nature (WWF) says 60% of Italy's vertebrates are at risk.

Among those slowly making a comeback after being reintroduced in the wild are the brown bear, which survives only in the Brenta area of Trentino, the Marsican bear, which has been reintroduced in Abruzzo, and the lynx, which is extremely rare and found mainly in the area around Tarvisio in Friuli-Venezia Giulia. Efforts are also underway to reintroduce the lynx in Abruzzo. Wolves are slightly more common, although you will still be hard pressed to spot one in the wild. They can be seen in a large enclosure at Civitella Alfedena in the Parco Nazionale d'Abruzzo.

JANE SMITH

There are only about 100 otters left in Italy and most live protected in the Parco Nazionale del Cilento in Campania. Another extremely rare animal is the monk seal: only about 10 are thought to survive in sea caves on the eastern coast of Sardinia. The magnificent golden eagle was almost wiped out by hunters and now numbers about 300 pairs throughout the country. A colony of griffon vultures survives on the western coast of Sardinia, near Bosa. The bearded vulture, known in Italy as the *gipeto*, has been reintroduced in the Alps in the past decade.

The seas around southern Italy and Sicily have been used since ancient times as breeding grounds for blue-fin tuna and swordfish. The Egadi Islands, off the western coast of Sicily, are famous for the bloody netting and killing of tuna that occurs annually between May and June (see the boxed text 'La Mattanza' in the Sicily chapter). While the great white shark is known to exist in the Mediterranean, particularly in the southern waters, attacks are extremely rare. Italians will generally respond with a blank stare if you enquire about the presence of sharks.

National Parks

Italy has 20 national parks, with four more on the way, and well over 400 smaller nature reserves, natural parks and wetlands. The national parks cover just over 1.5 million hectares (5%) of the country. Italy's environmentalists have been campaigning for years to bring the total protected area up to 10% of the land. They have had some success. From 1922 to 1991, only five national parks were created in Italy and their management left a lot to be desired. However, a law passed in 1991 allowed for the creation of 14 new national parks. This goal has been exceeded, although some projects have been slow to come to fruition. For more information, check out **W** www.parks.it, the official Italian national parks Web site.

The five long-standing national parks are Parco Nazionale del Gran Paradiso (Piedmont/Valle d'Aosta); Parco Nazionale d'Abruzzo; Parco Nazionale del Circeo (Lazio); Parco Nazionale dello Stelvio (Lombardy/Trentino/Alto-Adige); and Parco Nazionale della Calabria. The new national parks include Parco della Val Grande (Piedmont); Parco delle Dolomiti Bellunesi (Veneto); Parco delle Foreste Casentinesi (Emilia-Romagna); Parco dei Monti Sibillini (Le Marche/Umbria); Parco del Gran Sasso-Monti della Laga (Abruzzo); Parco della Maiella (Abruzzo); Parco del Vesuvio (Campania); Parco del Cilento e Vallo di Diano (Campania); Parco del Gargano (Apulia); Parco dell'Aspromonte (Calabria); Parco del Pollino (Basilicata/Calabria); Parco dell'Arcipelago Toscano (Tuscany); Parco dell Arcipelago di la Maddalena (Sardinia); Parco delle Cinque Terre (Liguria); Parco di Gennargentu (Sardinia); and Parco dell'Asinaru (Sardinia).

GOVERNMENT & POLITICS

The Italian State

In 1948 a new constitution made Italy a parliamentary republic. Since unification in 1861, Italy had been ruled under a statute of constitutional monarchy that, as thé years passed, took on an increasingly parliamentary tone. This did not, however, signal broader democracy, since it was within this system that Mussolini's Fascists rose to power.

The new post-WWII constitution created a bicameral parliament, consisting of a senate and a chamber of deputies. The differences between the two houses, which have equal legislative power, are relatively minor, calling into question the need for such duplication. From the ranks of the houses, governments and their prime ministers are formed and officially appointed by the president, whose role as impartial guarantor of the constitution is designed to help maintain stability and accountability, although to a large extent the position is symbolic. The president is elected by both houses of parliament and 58 regional representatives for a seven-year term.

Since 1994 deputies and senators have been elected by a mixed voting system, 75% based on the UK-style first-past-the-post system and 25% by proportional representation. The previous system of 100% proportional representation had encouraged the growth of a plethora of minor parties and it was hoped that the reform would move Italy in the direction of other western democracies that tend to be dominated by no more than two or three major political parties or groupings. Although this has not really happened, the many parties now tend to form coalitions. National elections are meant to take place every five years, although frequently they are brought forward.

On average, 88% of Italians go to the polls. Although there has been much talk of major constitutional reform since the Tangentopoli scandal of the 1990s (see History earlier), little of note has been achieved. To the average Italian voter, although some (but by no means all) of the faces have changed, the system has remained largely untouched. Much talk of passing from the 'first' to the 'second' republic is largely hot air as no substantial constitutional change has occurred.

The seat of national government is in Rome. The president resides in Palazzo del Quirinale, the Chamber of Deputies sits in Palazzo Montecitorio and the Senate in Palazzo Madama, near Piazza Navona.

National Government

At the time of writing, Italy's president is Carlo Azeglio Ciampi and the prime minister is the somewhat controversial Silvio Berlusconi (see The Return of Il Cavaliere under History earlier in this chapter), who heads up Italy's 59th government since 1945.

The Regions

For administrative purposes, Italy is divided into 20 regions *(regioni)*, which approximately correspond to the historical regions of the country. The regions are divided into provinces *(province)*, themselves further divided into town councils *(comuni)*.

Five regions (Sicily, Sardinia, Trentino-Alto Adige, Friuli-Venezia Giulia and Valle d'Aosta) are semi-autonomous or autonomous, with special powers granted under the constitution. Their regional assemblies are similar to parliaments and they have a wider range of economic and administrative powers than those of the other 15 Italian regions.

Indeed those remaining regions are the weakest element in the country's political hierarchy. Each is ruled by a *giunta regionale* (regional government) formed in elections (held every four years) to the *consiglio regionale* (regional assembly). These parliaments only came into being in 1970 and the regional governments, with no revenue-raising powers, remain little more than an administrative link between the central state and local government. They receive funds from the state and can legislate on a limited field of issues, such as tourism and the hospitality industry, agriculture and forests, museums and libraries, some areas of professional training, markets and fairs and so on. These regions, so far with minimal results, are pushing for much wider-ranging powers and a more genuine autonomy from the central government. Devolution in some form is high on the current government's agenda.

Local Government

The *consiglio provinciale*, the provincial equivalent of the regional assembly, does the day-to-day work of administration, usually in conjunction with the lowest tier of government, the *comune*, or town council. Local government elections are held every five years.

ECONOMY

Italy's economy lay in ruins at the close of WWII but the country wasted little time in setting about repairing the damage. By the early 1950s Italy had regained prewar levels of production. The boom of the 1950s and early 1960s, known as the Economic Miracle, relied to a great extent on the masses of workers who migrated from the poorer south of the country to the industrial north, providing an ample but low-paid workforce.

Today, services and public administration account for 65.8% of GDP, industry 31.6% and agriculture 2.6%. Most raw materials for industry and more than three-quarters of energy needs are imported. Tourism remains an important source of income. In 1999 estimated takings were about US$28.4 billion and Italy ranked fourth in income from international tourism. Italy's main exports include clothing and textiles (Italy's fashion industry is one of its style flagships around the world), motor vehicles, food, drink, tobacco, engineering products, chemicals and production equipment.

Following its sustained growth of 3% through much of the 1980s, Italy became the fifth-largest economy in the world, made possible largely by a national tendency to produce entrepreneurs. As well as the household names, such as Agnelli (Fiat), De Benedetti (Olivetti) and Berlusconi (media), numerous ordinary Italians run their own businesses. Some 90% of Italian firms have fewer than 100 workers, and many of these firms are family businesses – officially at least. There are those who suggest that many companies artificially divide themselves into smaller units to sidestep tax and labour laws that apply to larger firms.

Some would say that Italian business succeeds in spite of the national government. Massive public debt, widespread corruption and arcane legal and tax systems have always combined to restrain economic progress. As well as this, many of the country's top business people were implicated in the Tangentopoli corruption scandals in the early and mid-1990s. Foreign firms have long found all this, combined with the country's seemingly endless political wrangling, a strong deterrent to investing in Italy.

Although Italy entered the European economic and monetary union with the first wave of members in 1999, it continues to have trouble respecting the economic parameters laid down by the Maastricht Treaty. Reining in government debt financing (the external debt stands at US$45 billion) and waste remain among the most intractable problems facing the country.

That the country is, however, firmly locked into Europe is illustrated by the fact that more than half its exports go to EU partners. Industry slowed in the late 1990s and growth fell as low as 1.4% in 1999 but by 2001 it was tipped to be above 2%, more or less in line with a fairly stagnant Europe.

In spite of all the postwar efforts to promote growth in the poor south, the gap between north and south remains as great as ever. Although the desperate poverty of the past is a memory and regions such as Apulia and Abruzzo have seen real progress, the fact remains that Italy's richest regions (Piedmont, Emilia-Romagna and Lombardy) are all northern and its poorest (Calabria, Campania and Sicily) are all southern. Unemployment in the south is double the national average of 11.5% and three times the level in the north. Infrastructure remains poorer and several attempts to establish industry in the south *(mezzogiorno)* have come to little, in spite of the trillions of lire – in the form of subsidies, tax breaks and loans – spent. As the EU contemplated the enormous task of extending its membership to as many as 12 countries, mostly Eastern European and in need of hefty subsidies, Italy dug in its heels and demanded that EU funds for southern Italy not be affected by the entry of new and poorer member nations.

POPULATION & PEOPLE

The population of Italy is 57.8 million, according to 2000 estimates. The population growth rate is almost imperceptible at 0.09% percent. The slight growth in 2000, some 160,000 people, was due entirely to immigration. The birth rate is less than 1.2 children per woman, the lowest rate in the world. An average of 2.1 children per woman are needed to keep population stable, so Italy's population would be decreasing if it weren't for immigration. More children are born in the south than in the north – the birth rate in Emilia-Romagna is half that of Campania, for instance.

Heavily populated areas include those around Rome, Milan and Naples, Liguria, the Veneto, Friuli-Venezia Giulia, Piedmont and parts of Lombardy. The most densely populated spot in Italy – in fact the most populous in the world after Hong Kong – is Portici, a suburb of Naples, directly under Mt Vesuvius.

There is only a small minority of non-Italian speakers, including those who speak German in the province of Bolzano in Alto Adige and a tiny French-speaking minority in the Valle d'Aosta. Slovene is spoken by some around Trieste and along the border with Slovenia. The south has pockets of Greeks and Albanians, whose ancestors arrived in the 14th and 15th centuries.

Italy has traditionally been a country of emigrants, with Italians leaving to search for work in the USA, Argentina, Brazil, Australia and Canada. Southern Italians have also traditionally moved to the north of the country to work in the factories of Piedmont and Lombardy.

In recent years, however, Italy has become a country of immigration. Long coastlines and a fairly relaxed attitude to the enforcement of immigration laws by the Italian authorities have made Italy an easy point of entry into Europe. Of the estimated 1.9 million immigrants (about 3.5% of the total population), as many as half a million are reckoned to be clandestine. By some reckonings, more than 10% of the Italian population will be made up of immigrants by 2025.

Illegal immigrants, frequently trafficked in by cut-throat rackets operating out of countries such as Albania, the former Yugoslavia and Turkey, are known in Italy as *extracomunitari*. Many of them are in transit for other EU countries and the situation worries not only Italians, who have made repeated calls for an EU-wide police effort to curb the tide, but the rest of the EU as well.

Italians, however, are still more concerned with the traditional hostility of northern Italians towards southerners. Many northerners feel the richer north subsidises the poorer south. A minority of northerners have expressed their resentment by voting for secessionist parties, notably Umberto Bossi's Lega Nord, over the past few years.

EDUCATION

The Italian state-school system is free of charge and consists of several levels. Attendance is compulsory from the ages of six to 14 years, although children can attend a *scuola materna* (nursery school) from the ages of three to five years before starting the *scuola elementare* (primary school) at six. After five years they move on to the *scuola media* (secondary school) until they reach the age of 14.

The next level, the *scuola secondaria superiore* (higher secondary school), is voluntary and lasts a further five years until the student is 19 years old. This level is essential for study at university. At this higher school level there are several options: four types of *liceo* (humanities-based school), four types of technical school and a teacher-training school.

The government is in the process of reforming the state education system. It compares reasonably well with those in other countries but there are problems: teacher-training standards are often deficient and management is poor.

Private schools in Italy are run mainly by religious institutions, notably the Jesuits.

Italy has a long tradition of university education and can claim to have the world's oldest university, established at Bologna in the 11th century. Courses usually last from four to six years, although students are under no obligation to complete them in that time. In fact, students often take many more years to fulfil their quota of exams and submit their final thesis. Attendance at inevitably overcrowded lectures is optional and for scientific courses practical experimentation is rare. Students therefore tend to study at home from books. All state-school and university examinations are oral, rather than written.

Italy produces far fewer graduates per capita than most other countries in the west. Despite that, unemployment among graduates is estimated at higher than 40%.

Officially at least, 2% of Italians over the age of 15 cannot read or write, more or less in line with European averages.

SCIENCE & PHILOSOPHY

Italy is not readily associated with dramatic scientific discovery, especially when most advances seem to emanate from the powerhouse that is the United States. But some of the best-known geniuses in history came from Italy.

Leonardo da Vinci (1452–1519) was perhaps the greatest polymath of his time. He considered himself first and foremost an artist but his curiosity led him into a vast array of fields of knowledge. Painting itself led him to anatomy. Anxious to win greater insight into the human body in order to be better able to portray it, he carried out numerous dissections that in turn resulted in his striking anatomical studies and drawings. For the time they were a unique and insightful medical tool.

An architect and engineer, Leonardo was also at home with mechanics. His biggest contribution to scientific progress was the systematic use of diagrams to illustrate engineering principles. He also let his fantasy

JANE SMITH

A man of many talents: Leonardo da Vinci

loose and envisaged flying machines and even armoured vehicles centuries before they would become reality.

Galileo Galilei (1564–1642), a fellow Tuscan, had more specific interests that he pursued with tenacity in the face of increasing opposition from the Church. Foremost of these was his belief in Copernicus' system that the earth revolved around the sun and not the other way round. Schooled in medicine and mathematics (he is considered the father of experimental physics), he was fascinated by the invention of the telescope and proceeded to make his own. With this and later instruments, he confirmed Copernicus' theory and thus turned thinking about the earth's place in the universe on its head. The Church felt so threatened by theories that might call into question the universal order that lay behind its omnipotence that Galileo was obliged to recant his radical theories in his later years. He never stopped studying and remained convinced of his discoveries until his dying days.

Giambattista Vico (1668–1744), a historical philosopher from Naples, is thought to have influenced the work of such later luminaries as Marx, Goethe and Nietzsche through his opus magnus, *Scienza Nuova* (New Science; 1725).

More than a century later, Alessandro Volta (1745–1827) from Como electrified the world with his invention of the battery. He had been galvanised by his colleague and friend, Luigi Galvani (1737–98) who, in 1780, had discovered that by using a frog's leg as a conductor between two pieces of metal, a small electric current could be created. Volta took this a step further, found the animal conductor was not needed and in 1800 demonstrated the battery – the first ever source of continuous current. The volt, a unit of electric current, was named after Volta in 1881.

Without electricity, the Bolognese Nobel-prize winner Guglielmo Marconi (1874–1937) could never have invented and developed his system of radio-telegraphy, which he presented in 1896 and then later patented in the UK. Over succeeding years he developed means of sending messages on radio waves over increasing distances. His big triumph came in 1901 when he managed to transmit a message between Wales and Newfoundland – silencing critics who had predicted such messages could not be sent over long distances because of the earth's curvature. Marconi kept at it and in 1918 he broadcast the first radio message from the UK to Australia.

ARTS

See the special section Art & Architecture for information on architecture, painting and sculpture.

Literature

Roman The roots of ancient Latin literature lie in simple popular songs, religious rites and official documents. As Latin evolved and the Romans came into contact with the Greek world, the emerging Empire's upper classes began to acquire more sophisticated tastes. Plautus (259–184 BC) adapted classic Greek themes to create his own plays – a step forward from the translations of Greek literature that had come before.

The classical period did not start until well into the 1st century BC. The work of Cicero (106–43 BC) stands out during the early years of this period as the Roman Republic collapsed into civil war and gave way to dictatorial government. Cicero's writing, infused with political commitment, explored new terrain in Latin prose with works such as *Brutus*. More concerned with affairs of the heart, particularly his own, Catullus (c.84–54 BC) devoted his creative power to passionate love poetry. Julius Caesar combined conquest with commentary in recording his campaigns in Gaul and the disintegration of the Republic.

The reign of Augustus (27 BC–AD 14) marked the emergence of a new wave of intellectuals. Among them was Virgil, whose epic poem *The Aeneid* links the founding of Rome with the fall of Troy. Some years later Ovid addressed love in his *Amores* poems, annoyed Emperor Augustus with descriptions of lewd lifestyles in *Ars Amatoria* after the emperor's daughter had been banished for vice, and wrote about transformation myths in *Metamorphoses*. Horace commented on military matters while Livy chronicled the emergence of the new Empire.

Seneca the Younger (4 BC–AD 65), a philosopher from Spain, introduced a more introspective, even existential, note into Latin writing in the early years of the Christian era. Petronius (died AD 66) conveyed the decadence of the Nero era in his *Satyricon*, although only a fragment still exists, and it is to Pliny the Younger (AD 62–113) that we owe first-hand descriptions of the disaster of Pompeii. The years following the downfall of Nero are detailed in the *Histories* of Tacitus (AD 55–120), while his *Annales* reveal the astounding court intrigues of the early emperors. Marcus Aurelius' *Meditations* were the musings of the last philosopher-king of the crumbling Empire.

The Middle Ages From before the final collapse of the Roman Empire until well into the Middle Ages, creative literary production declined, kept barely alive in Western Europe by clerics and the erudite people who debated theology, wrote history, translated or interpreted classical literature and used Latin as their lingua franca. Above all, however, theology and philosophy were what preoccupied the great minds of medieval Italy and Europe.

The most outstanding Italian figure in this field was San Tommaso d'Aquino (St Thomas Aquinas; 1224–1274). He wrestled with Aristotelian thinking and in works such as *De Aeternitate Mundi* (On the Eternity of the World) sought to expound his vision of our existence. He was also a gifted poet.

The Birth of Italian Literature By the time Aquinas was penning his theses, Latin had ceased to be a living language. The genius of Dante Alighieri (1265–1321), probably the greatest figure in Italian literature, confirmed the Italian vernacular (in its Florentine form) as a serious medium for poetic expression – particularly in his *Divina Commedia*, an allegorical masterpiece that takes his protagonist on a search for God through hell, purgatory and paradise. His Latin work *De Monarchia* reflects his desire for a return of imperial power and his vision of a world where the roles of pope and emperor complement each other.

Another master writer of this time was Francesco Petrarca (Petrarch; 1304–74), son of a lawyer exiled from Florence at the same time as Dante. Petrarch was crowned poet laureate in Rome in 1341 after earning a reputation throughout Europe as a classical scholar. His epic poem *Africa* and the sonnets of *Il Canzoniere* are typical of his formidable lyricism, which has permanently influenced Italian poetry.

Completing the triumvirate is Giovanni Boccaccio (1313–75). As the author of *Il Decamerone*, 100 short stories – ranging from the bawdy to the earnest – which chronicle the exodus of 10 young Florentines from their plague-ridden city, Boccaccio is considered the first Italian novelist.

The Renaissance The 15th century produced several treatises on architecture and politics, but perhaps more important was the feverish study and translation of Greek classics along with the work of more recent Jewish and Arab scholars. The advent of the printing press accelerated the spread of knowledge. In Italy, the industry was most highly developed in Venice, where Aldo Manuzio (c.1450–1515) flooded the market with Greek classics from his Aldine Press, and introduced the octavo book size (half the size of a standard quarto page and more suitable for printed books) and italic type (in 1501).

Machiavelli's *Il Principe* (The Prince), although purely political, has proved the most lasting of the Renaissance works. Machiavelli (1469–1527) was also an accomplished playwright and his *Mandragola* is a masterpiece.

Machiavelli's contemporary Ludovico Ariosto (1474–1533) was arguably the star of the Italian Renaissance. His *Orlando Furioso* is a subtle tale of chivalry, told in exquisite verse and laced with subplots.

Torquato Tasso (1544–95) continued a strong tradition of narrative poetry with his *Gerusalemme Liberata*, for which he drew inspiration from Italy's increasingly precarious political situation towards the end of the 16th century.

The 18th & 19th Centuries At a time when French playwrights ruled the stage, the Venetian Carlo Goldoni (1707–93) attempted to bring Italian theatre back into the limelight. He combined realism and a certain literary discipline with a popular feel rooted in the *commedia dell'arte* (the tradition of improvisational theatre based on a core of set characters).

The heady winds of Romanticism that prevailed in Europe in the first half of the 19th century did not leave Italy untouched. In the small town of Recanati in Le Marche, Giacomo Leopardi (1798–1837) penned verses that are heavy with longing and melancholy, but equally erudite (although he was largely self-taught). The best of them, the *Canti*, constitute a classic of Italian verse.

Poetry remained the main avenue of literary expression for much of the century but Milan's Alessandro Manzoni (1785–1873) changed all that with his *I Promessi Sposi* (The Betrothed), a historical novel on a grand scale. Manzoni laboured hard to establish a narrative language accessible to all Italians, lending the manuscript a barely disguised nationalist flavour lost on no-one when it appeared in the 1840s. In 1881 Giovanni Verga (1840–1922) announced the arrival of the realist novel in Italy with *I Malavoglia*, which follows the trials and tribulations of a poor fishing family around the time Italy was unified.

The 20th Century & Today The turbulence of political and social life in Italy throughout most of the 20th century produced a wealth of literature, much of it available in translation for English speakers. Many literary critics lament that the golden days of modern Italian literature are a thing of the past but some bright lights still shine!

Theatre In Sicily, the playwright Luigi Pirandello (1867–1936) began his career writing novels and short stories along realist lines but soon moved to theatre. With such classics as *Sei Personaggi in Cerca d'Autore* (Six Characters in Search of an Author), he threw into question every preconception of what theatre should be. A Nobel-prize winner in 1934, Pirandello's genius continues to assert itself in the west; from Brecht to Beckett, few modern playwrights could claim to have escaped his influence.

Modern Italian theatre is very much the junior member of Italy's literary family. Its most enduring contemporary representative is Dario Fo (born 1926), who has been writing, directing and performing since the 1950s. Often in the form of a one-man show but also in company (most often with Franca Rame), his work is laced with political and social critique. He has had a number of hits in London's West End, including *Accidental Death of an Anarchist* (Morte Accidentale di un Anarchista), *Can't Pay, Won't Pay* (Non Si Paga, Non Si Paga) and *Mistero Buffo*. Much to the consternation of the Italian literary establishment, Fo won the 1997 Nobel Prize for Literature.

Poetry Gabriele d'Annunzio (1863–1938) is in a class of his own. An ardent nationalist, his often virulent poetry is perhaps not of the highest quality but his voice was a prestige tool for Mussolini's Fascists.

Giuseppe Ungaretti (1888–1970), whose creative and personal baptism of fire took place on the battlefields of WWI, produced a robust, spare poetry, far from the wordy complexity of his predecessors. The sum of his work is contained in *Vita d'un Uomo*.

Two other poets stand out, both Nobel-prize winners. The work of Eugenio Montale (1896–1981), who devoted much of his time after WWII to journalism, is less accessible than that of Ungaretti. Sicilian Salvatore Quasimodo (1901–68) reached a high point after WWII, when he believed poetry could and should empathise with human suffering. The myth exploded; his later work is heavy with melancholy and nostalgia.

Fiction Italy's richest contribution to modern literature has been in the novel and short story. Turin especially has produced a wealth of authors. Cesare Pavese, born in a Piedmont farmhouse in 1908, took Walt Whitman as his guiding light. Involved in the anti-Fascist circles of pre-war Turin, his greatest novel, *La Luna e Il Falò* (The Moon and the Bonfire), was published in 1950, the year he took his life.

Like Pavese, Carlo Levi (1902–75), a doctor from Turin, experienced internal exile in southern Italy under the Fascists. The result was a moving account of a world oppressed and forgotten by Rome, *Cristo si è Fermato a Eboli* (Christ Stopped at Eboli).

Primo Levi, a Turin Jew, ended up in Auschwitz during the war. *Se Quest'è Un Uomo* is the dignified account of his survival, while *La Tregua* recounts his long road back home through Eastern Europe. Born in 1919, Levi committed suicide in 1987.

Palermo-born Natalia Ginzburg (1916–90) spent most of her life in Turin. Much of her writing is semi-autobiographical. *Tutti I Nostri Ieri*, *Valentino* and *Le Voci della Sera* are just three novels from her range of fiction, plays and essays. Her particular gift lies in capturing the essence of gestures and moments in everyday life.

A writer of a different ilk is Italo Calvino (1923–85), who was born in Cuba. A Resistance fighter and then Communist Party member until 1957, Calvino's works border on the fantastical, thinly veiling his main preoccupations with human behaviour in society. *I Nostri Antenati* (Our Ancestors), a collection of three such tales, is perhaps his greatest success.

Alberto Moravia (1907–90) describes Rome and its people in his prolific writings. Such novels as *La Romana* (A Woman of Rome) convey the detail of place and the sharp sense of social decay, making his storytelling compelling.

Il Gattopardo (The Leopard) is the only work of lasting importance by Sicily's Giuseppe Tomasi di Lampedusa (1896–1957). Set at the time of Italian unification, it is a moving account of the decline of the virtually feudal order in Sicily, embodied in the slow ruin of Prince Fabrizio Salina (later played by Burt Lancaster in Luchino Visconti's 1963 film of the same name).

Leonardo Sciascia (1921–89) dedicated most of his career to his native Sicily, attacking all facets of its past and present in novels and essays. His first great success was *Il Giorno della Civetta* (The Day of the Owl), a kind of whodunnit illustrating the extent of the Mafia's power.

The novels of Rome's Elsa Morante (1912–85), characterised by a subtle psychological appraisal of her characters, can be seen too as a personal cry of pity for the sufferings of individuals and society. Her 1948 novel *Menzogna e Sortilegio* brought her to prominence. In it she recounts the slow decay of the southern Italian noble family.

Italian literature of the 1980s was briefly dominated by Bologna intellectual Umberto Eco (born 1932), who shot to popularity with his first and best-known work, *Il Nome della Rosa* (The Name of the Rose). It was made into a successful film starring Sean Connery.

Pisa-born Antonio Tabucchi (born 1943) is a writer of some stature, with more than a dozen books to his credit. Possibly one of his most endearing works remains *Sostiene Pereira*, set in pre-war Lisbon and made into a film starring Marcello Mastroianni.

One of the most prolific and respected women writing today is the Rome-based Florentine Dacia Maraini (born 1936), columnist and outstanding feminist novelist. She has also had success as a poet and playwright. Her all-women theatre company,

Teatro della Maddalena, has staged many of her 30-plus plays, some of which, such as the 1978 *Dialogo di una Prostituta con un suo Cliente*, have played in theatres abroad as well. Author of 10 novels and several collections of stories, she sometimes treats some tough subjects. Her latest book, *Buio*, is a collection of 12 stories of children neglected or abused. Drawn from crime reports, she has created hard-hitting narrative. Holding it all together is the central character, a woman detective by the name of Adele Sòfia, who also appeared in an earlier novel, *Voci*.

The 2000 Strega Prize (the Italian equivalent of the UK Booker Prize) went to Ernesto Ferrero for his *N*, an engaging historical novel about Napoleon's exile to the island of Elba, which with characteristically restless energy he converted into a mini-kingdom.

Music

Classical Music & Opera The Italians have played a pivotal role in the history of music: they invented the system of musical notation in use today, a 16th-century Venetian printed the first musical scores, Stradivari (Stradivarius) and others produced violins in Cremona and Italy is the birthplace of the piano.

The 16th century brought a musical revolution with the development of opera, which began as an attempt to recreate the drama of ancient Greece. One of the earliest successful composers in this genre, Claudio Monteverdi (c.1567–1643), drew from a variety of sources.

In the 17th and early 18th centuries, instrumental music became established, helped by the concertos of Arcangelo Corelli (1653–1713) and Antonio Vivaldi (1675–1741). Vivaldi, whose best-known work is *Le Quattro Stagioni* (The Four Seasons), created the concerto in its present form while he was teaching in Venice. Domenico Scarlatti (1685–1757) wrote more than 500 sonatas for harpsichord and Giovanni Battista Sammartini (1700–75) experimented with the symphony.

Verdi (1813–1901), Puccini (1858–1924), Bellini (1801–1835), Donizetti (1797–1848) and Rossini (1792–1868) are all stars of the modern operatic era. Giuseppe Verdi became an icon midway through his life; his achievements include *Aïda* and one of the most popular operas of all, *La Traviata*. Rossini's *Barber of Seville* is an enduring favourite with a lively score and *Madame Butterfly* ensures Puccini a firm place in musical history.

The composer Gian Carlo Menotti (born 1911) is famed for creating the Festival dei Due Mondi (Festival of Two Worlds; see Special Events in the Facts for the Visitor chapter) at Spoleto in Umbria. In addition to his operas, written in English (he has lived most of his life in the USA), he has also written many ballets.

One of the greatest conductors of the past two centuries was, with little doubt, Italy's Arturo Toscanini (1867–1957). See under Western Bank in the Parma section of the Emilia-Romagna chapter for biographical details.

Classical Music & Opera Today The main opera season in Italy runs from December to June. The country's premier opera houses include La Scala in Milan, San Carlo in Naples, the Teatro dell'Opera in Rome and La Fenice (closed at the time of writing) in Venice. With restorations partially completed, Sicily's prestigious Teatro Massimo in Palermo is back in action.

The tenor Luciano Pavarotti (born 1935) is today's luminary of Italian opera, although the remarkable blind tenor Andrea Bocelli (born 1958), who has done some mixing and matching and even managed to make the pop charts, is seen by some critics as Pavarotti's natural successor. Meanwhile Cecilia Bartolli (born 1966) has been making great strides as Italy's latest mezzo-soprano sensation.

Among the country's leading conductors, Naples-born Riccardo Muti (born 1941) has a distinguished career behind him both at home and abroad. Since 1986 he has been musical director at La Scala in Milan and continues to tour widely across Europe and the USA. He is equally at home conducting opera or symphonic music. Claudio Abbado (born 1933) comes from a long line of Milanese musicians. He has been the main conductor for some of the most prestigious orchestras in the world, including the Berlin Philharmonic and the London Symphony Orchestra, and has been musical director of the Vienna State Opera.

Canzone Napoletana If a great many rock and pop greats in the English-speaking world have their roots in the blues tradition, Italian popular music has much the same relation to the *canzone Napoletana* (Neapolitan song).

By the late 18th century, an annual pilgrimage in September to the Chiesa di Santa Maria di Piedigrotta in Pozzuoli had become an occasion for merriment and song. At a time when the Neapolitan dialect had the status of a language in its own right, bands played in impromptu competitions that soon began to produce what could be considered the year's top hits. In 1840 came the first real classic, *Te Voglio Bene Assaje*, a song that remains enshrined in the city's musical imagination. But surely the best-known Neapolitan song is *O Sole Mio*.

Contemporary Music Few modern Italian singers or groups have made any impact outside Italy. Probably the best vocalist to emerge since WWII is Mina, who cut dozens of records during the 1960s. Many of her songs were written by Giulio Rapetti, better known as Mogol, the undisputed king of Italian songwriters.

The 1960s and 1970s produced various *cantautori* (singer-songwriters) who were vaguely reminiscent of some of the greats of the UK and USA. Lucio Dalla, Vasco Rossi and Pino Daniele have been successfully hawking their own versions of protest music since the early 1970s. While they are not of the stature of, say, Bob Dylan, the strength of their music lies in lyrics – occasionally laced with venom – portraying the shortcomings of modern Italian society. Daniele, whose Neapolitan roots are clearly on display, brings an unmistakably bluesy flavour to his music.

Lucio Battisti's material is much softer and less inclined towards social comment but has been highly popular since the end of the 1960s. Some of the early stuff (the classics) may make your hair stand on end (*very* 1970s).

Ivano Fossati is another well-established singer-songwriter but some of his most agreeable material is purely instrumental.

Zucchero (Adelmo Fornaciari) is a phenomenon on the Italian music scene. Starting out as a session musician with the likes of Joe Cocker, he has aimed at both the Italian and international market in a way few other Italians have; he sings many of his songs in Italian *and* English.

Other classic names to look out for include Luca Carboni, Francesco de Gregori, Antonello Venditti and Franco Battiato. A much rockier sound comes from Vasco Rossi, still a big concert draw.

The grand public face of Italian pop is the annual San Remo songfest in February, but most would agree that the veteran performers and new hopefuls who appear at this glitzy spectacle are not always of the best quality.

As well as these die-hard melody-makers, a whole jungle of new bands ranging from rock to punk to hip-hop has thrived in Italy over the past few years. Litfiba is a high-profile indie Florentine duo that has been around since the 1990s. Ligabue is more of a straight rock band with a big following.

Jovanotti's lyrics are thought-provoking and make him the top exponent of rap in Italy – and one of the most fun and challenging of Italy's contemporary musos. For truly demented lyrics (such as the song dedicated to John Holmes, the deceased American porn star renowned for his genitalia), check out the band Elio e Le Storie Tese.

One of the most popular female singers of the moment is the Tuscan Irene Grandi.

Cinema

Born in Turin in 1904, the Italian film industry initially made an impression with silent spectaculars. By 1930 it was virtually bankrupt and Mussolini began moves to nationalise the industry. These culminated in 1940, when Rome's version of Hollywood, Cinecittà, was ceded to the state. Set up in 1937, this huge complex was fitted out with

Stars of the Screen

In his brief six-year career, Rudolph Valentino (actually Rodolfo Pietro Filiberto Guglielmi; 1895–1926) took Hollywood by storm in the silent movie era. His 10 pictures remain classics, just as his own was a classic American success tale. Born in Apulia, he migrated to the USA at 18 in search of fortune; after working as a waiter and professional dance partner he was 'discovered'.

Among Italy's greatest actors since WWII was Marcello Mastroianni (1924–1996), who starred in *La Dolce Vita* and countless other films, including Robert Altman's *Prêt-à-Porter*. Vittorio Gassman (1922–2000) was of similar stature in Italy but less acclaimed outside his homeland. One of his last film appearances was as a New York gangland boss in the American flick *Sleepers* (1996). Other notable Italian thespians include Anna Magnani (1908–73), who won an Academy Award for *The Rose Tattoo*, Gina Lollobrigida (born 1927), best known for *Go Naked in the World* and *Come September*, and, of course, Sophia Loren (born 1934), whose innumerable films include *It Started in Naples*, *Houseboat* and *Boy on a Dolphin*.

Following in the steps of Loren, Isabella Rossellini (born 1952), film director Roberto Rossellini's daughter, has carved out a career for herself in Hollywood. She came to particular attention with her role in David Lynch's disturbing 1986 film, *Blue Velvet*, but has appeared in many other pictures.

For a long time Totò (1898–1967) was the undisputed king of film comedy. Until his death, Totò was for Italy what Chaplin became internationally. That he never achieved similar recognition can perhaps be attributed to the special appeal for Italian audiences of his quick Neapolitan wit, the kind of thing that does not translate well.

Who, however, has not seen at least one spaghetti western with 160kg Bud Spencer and his thin, blue-eyed counterpart Terence Hill? The names are pseudonyms – these cowboys are all-Italian. From 1970, when *They Called Him Trinity* was released, until 1986, they kept Italy and much of the rest of the world in stitches with their version of how the West was won.

The contemporary scene has thrown up few actors of international stature but there are some names to watch. Massimo Troisi (1953–1994) brought a striking human touch to his characters, who were nearly always Neapolitan. His greatest legacy was his starring role in *Il Postino* (The Postman; 1995), the story of Pablo Neruda's exile from Chile to a southern Italian town.

One who has occasionally appeared out of the Italian context is Roberto Benigni (born 1952), a highly popular Tuscan comedian. Long established as one of Italy's favourite comedic actors, he must be the first director to try to get a laugh out of the Holocaust – and succeed. He picked up three Oscars in 1999, including that for best actor – an honour rarely bestowed by Hollywood upon anyone but its own – for his *La Vita è Bella* (Life is Beautiful; 1998). Benigni was already known to cinema-goers outside Italy for his appearances in Jim Jarmusch's *Down by Law* and *Night on Earth*.

Two Mediterranean beauties who started as models before branching into film in the past few years are the Umbrian Monica Bellucci and Sicily's Maria Grazia Cucinotta. Both were born in 1968 and it remains to be seen what acting heights they can scale. Bellucci has appeared in 20-odd films, of which the latest was Giuseppe Tornatore's *Malena*. With barely a line in this uneven movie, she relies heavily on her beauty (to which the picture seems dedicated). Cucinotta's most serious cinematic moment came with her role in *Il Postino*.

Italy's answer to Chaplin: Totò

the latest in film equipment. Half the nation's production took place here – 85 films in 1940 alone.

Abandoned later in the war, Cinecittà only went timidly back into action in 1948 – its absence had not bothered the first of Italy's neo-realist directors anyway (see the following section). In 1950 an American team arrived to make *Quo Vadis?* and for the rest of the 1950s film-makers from Italy and abroad moved in to use the site's huge lots. By the early 1960s, however, this symbol of Italian cinema had again begun to wane as location shooting became more common.

The Italian version of the Oscars, the David awards, were instituted in 1955 and continue to be a barometer for Italian film-making.

Neorealism Even before the fall of Mussolini in 1943, those who were about to launch Italy's most glorious cinematic era were at work. Luchino Visconti (1906–76) came to cinema late, after meeting Jean Renoir, the French film-maker, in France in 1936. His first film, *Ossessione*, based on James M Cain's *The Postman Always Rings Twice*, was one of the earliest examples of the New Wave in cinema – a movement concerned with depicting the lives of the poor in society.

In the three years following the close of hostilities in Europe, Roberto Rossellini (1906–77) produced a trio of neorealist masterpieces. The first, in 1945, was *Roma Città Aperta* (Rome Open City), which was set in German-occupied Rome and starred Anna Magnani. For many cinema-lovers, this film marks the truc beginning of neorealism, uniting simplicity and sincerity in a way peculiar to Italian film-making; often heart-rending without ever succumbing to the bathos to which so many Hollywood products fall victim. *Paisà* (1946) follows the course of war from Sicily to the River Po in a series of powerful vignettes, while *Germania Anno Zero* (Germany Ycar Zero; 1947) pulls no punches in looking at a country left crushed by the war it had launched.

Vittorio de Sica (1901–74) kept the neorealist ball rolling with another classic in 1948, *Ladri di Biciclette* (Bicycle Thieves), the story of a man's frustrated fight to earn enough to keep his family afloat. It is one of 10 films he made between 1939 and 1950.

The 1950s to the 1970s Federico Fellini (1920–94) took the creative baton from the masters of neorealism and carried it into the following decades. His disquieting style is slightly more demanding of audiences, abandoning realistic shots for pointed images at once laden with humour, pathos and double-meaning – all cleverly capturing not only the Italy of the day but also the human foibles of his protagonists. Fellini's greatest international hit was *La Dolce Vita* (1968) with Anita Ekberg and Marcello Mastroianni. Others include *8 1/2* (1963), *Satyricon* (1969), *Roma* (1972) and *Amarcord* (1973). Fellini's wife, Giulietta Masina, starred in many of his pictures.

Luchino Visconti made movies from 1942 until his death in 1976, including the memorable adaptation of Giuseppe Tomasi di Lampedusa's *Il Gattopardo* (The Leopard; 1963).

Michelangelo Antonioni (born 1912) began directing in 1950; his films explore existential themes and individual crises and reached a climax with *Blow-Up* (1967). Pier Paolo Pasolini (1922–75) had some altogether different themes: preoccupied at first with the condition of the subproletariat in films such as *Accattone* (1961) and *Teorema* (1968), he later dealt with human decay and death in such films as *Il Decamerone*, *I Racconti di Canterbury* and *Il Fiore delle Mille e Una Notte*.

In 1974 Lina Wertmüller (born 1928) incurred the wrath of feminists with her work *Swept Away* ('Travolti da un Insolito Destino nell'Azzurro Mare di Agosto' in Italian!). Bernardo Bertolucci (born 1940) first made a splash on the international scene with *Last Tango in Paris* (1972).

On a different notc, Sergio Leone (1929–89) ended up specialising in a particular brand of rough Western in the late 1960s. Critical approval for movies such as *The Good, the Bad and the Ugly* (1968) came late but the films were highly successful at the box office.

1980 to the Present Bertolucci's foreign profile has continued to grow with English-language blockbusters such as *The Last Emperor* (1987), *Little Buddha* (1992) and *Stealing Beauty* (1996). Another Italian director who has worked extensively outside his home country is Franco Zeffirelli (born 1923), among whose better-known films are *Othello* (1986), *Hamlet* (1990) and *Jane Eyre* (1995). His 1999 *Tea with Mussolini*, set in Tuscany, is a comedy following the doings of an art dealer (played by Cher) in Fascist Italy. At the time of writing, Zeffirelli was set to make a film on the life of Maria Callas.

Paolo (born 1931) and Vittorio Taviani (born 1929) got started in the 1960s and in 1976 produced *Padre Padrone*, a heart-rending account of peasant life on Sardinia and one man's escape. Their biggest hits of the 1980s were *Good Morning Babilonia* (1986), an account of the creation of WD Griffiths' *Intolerance*, and *Kaos* (1984), inspired by stories by Luigi Pirandello.

Nuovo Cinema Paradiso (1988), by Giuseppe Tornatore (born 1956), is a wonderful homage to film-making. He was back in 2000 with *Malena*, a nicely shot but somewhat damp film starring Monica Bellucci as a beautiful war widow in a Sicilian town during WWII. Through the eyes of a young adolescent who fantasises about her, the story of her fall into prostitution reflects a broader tale of small-town meanness and double standards.

Nanni Moretti (born 1953), who first came to the silver screen in the late 1970s, has proven to be a highly individualistic actor-director. *Caro Diario* (Dear Diary), his whimsical and self-indulgent autobiographical three-part film, won the prize for best director at Cannes in 1994. Seven years later he took the film festival's top prize, the Palme d'Or, for *La Stanza del Figlio*, in which a family deals (not particularly well) with the trial of losing a son. Moretti again wrote, directed and acted.

Roberto Benigni (see also the boxed text 'Stars of the Screen' earlier) made a big international splash with *La Vita è Bella* (Life is Beautiful; 1998), which he directed and starred in.

Silvio Soldini's (born 1958) *Pane e Tulipani* (Bread and Tulips; 1999) is a charming film that charts a housewife's unlikely escape from urban drudgery to the canals of Venice, where she embroils herself in all manner of odd occurrences.

SOCIETY & CONDUCT

It is difficult to make blanket assertions about Italian culture, if only because Italians have only lived as one nation for a little over 100 years. Prior to unification the peninsula was long subject to a widely varied mix of masters and cultures. This lack of unity contributed to the maintenance of local dialects and customs. Only with the advent of national TV did the spread of a standard Italian language begin. Previously it was not unusual to find farmers and villagers who spoke only their local dialect.

Italians at a World Cup football match may present a patriotic picture but most Italians identify more with their region or even home town – a phenomenon known as *campanilismo* (an attachment to one's local bell tower!). An Italian is first and foremost a Sicilian or Tuscan, or even a Roman, Milanese or Neapolitan, before being Italian.

Confronted with a foreigner, however, Italians will energetically reveal a national pride difficult to detect in the relationships they have with each other.

Stereotypes

Foreigners may think of Italians as passionate, animated people who gesticulate wildly when speaking, love to eat and drive like maniacs. There's a lot more to it than that, however.

Journalist Luigi Barzini has defined his compatriots as a hard-working, resilient and resourceful people who are optimistic and have a good sense of humour. If you really feel that you have to subscribe to a national stereotype, Barzini's description is probably closer to the truth.

Italians are also passionately loyal to their friends and families – all-important qualities, noted Barzini, since 'a happy private life helps people to tolerate an appalling public life'.

Mummy's Boys

The rough charm of the unshaven Italian Lothario mounted jauntily on his Vespa is an inescapable image, one redolent of the Latin lover. The truth is perhaps a little less alluring.

According to figures published in 1997 by Istat (Istituto Centrale di Statistica), the country's main statistics body, Italian men actually constitute an *esercito di mammoni* (army of mummy's boys). Forget Oedipus, these boys know which side their bread is buttered. Perhaps they are not so different from men the world over, but the numbers are certainly telling.

If you can believe Istat, 66.5% of single Italian men remain at home with mum (and dad) at least up to the age of 34. Granted, this is partly caused by problems of unemployment, the cost of housing and so on. Of the remainder who do move out of home, some 42% of those aged up to 65 do not shift more than 1km away and only 20% dare to move more than 50km beyond the maternal home. Of all these 'independent' single men, 56% manage to stop by mum's place every day of the week. The unkind might be led to believe (as was the author of at least one newspaper story on the subject) that, apart from filial devotion, the lads might well bring with them a bag of dirty washing and time the visit to coincide with lunch.

But even if the washing and lunch are taken care of by their wives (not an uncommon situation among Italian couples), those men who are married still find time to pop in to see mamma at least a few times a week. And when marriage fails, a quarter of ex-husbands go home to mother as opposed to 17% of wives. For Luigi Barzini, whose 1964 book *The Italians* remains a classic, the family represented a 'stronghold in a hostile land'. That hostile land is a state that is not so hot on providing unemployment benefits and other aid that makes it easier for young ones in some other countries to fly the nest (and stay out).

Italians have a strong distrust of authority and when confronted with a silly rule, an unjust law or a stupid order (and they are regularly confronted with many of them) they do not complain or try to change rules, but rather try to find the quickest way round them.

Family

The family remains of central importance in the fabric of Italian society, particularly in the south. Most young Italians tend to stay at home until they marry, a situation admittedly partly exacerbated by the lack of affordable housing. Still, modern attitudes have begun to erode the traditions. Statistics show that one in three married couples has no children and one in nine children is born out of wedlock. In Milan, for example, more than one-third of families are headed by a single parent, two-thirds of whom are women.

Dos & Don'ts

Italians tend to be tolerant but – despite an apparent obsession with (mostly female) nakedness, especially in advertising – they are not excessively free and easy.

In some parts of Italy, particularly in the south, women will be harassed if they wear skimpy or see-through clothing. Topless sunbathing, while not uncommon on some Italian beaches, is not always acceptable. Take your cue from other sunbathers. Nude sunbathing is likely to be offensive anywhere but on appropriately designated beaches. Walking the streets near beaches in a bikini or skimpy costume is also not on and on the Venice Lido it'll get you a fine.

It would be nice to see more travellers wandering around with an awareness of local sensibilities. Visitors all too often seem to leave manners and common sense at home. In the main tourist centres, locals are by now used to the sight of men wandering around in little more than a pair of shorts and (maybe) sandals. But you have to ask yourself, if you wouldn't walk around like that in your town, why do so in someone else's? Remember that most people find sunscorched bellies a grim sight, so

Italians, known for their delight in dressing well, will probably be even more repulsed.

In churches you are expected to dress modestly. This means no shorts (for men or women) or short skirts, and shoulders should be covered. Those that are major tourist attractions, such as St Peter's in Rome and San Francesco in Assisi, enforce strict dress codes. Churches are places of worship so if you visit one during a service (which you should refrain from doing), try to be as inconspicuous as possible.

The police and carabinieri (see Police under Legal Matters in the Facts for the Visitor chapter) have the right to arrest you for insulting a state official if they believe you have been rude or offensive, so be diplomatic in your dealings with them!

THE MAFIA

A journalist once noted that 'the Mafia and the establishment are intertwined, and that this marriage is one of the pillars of political life in Italy. The Mafia is not only omnipotent, it is omnipresent.'

The multiple crises that have rocked Italy's political establishment, from the stream of revelations linking Mafia figures to politicians through to Tangentopoli (see History earlier in this chapter), have only served to increase people's awareness of the problem.

The term Mafia can be used to describe five distinct groups of organised criminals: the original Sicilian Mafia, also known as the Cosa Nostra; the Calabrian 'ndrangheta; the Camorra of Naples; and two relatively new organisations, the Sacra Corona Unita (United Holy Crown) and La Rosa (the Rose), in Apulia. These groups operate both separately and together.

Their activities range from contraband to protection rackets and monopolising lucrative contracts in just about every field. Narcotics is another big source of income. By the early 1990s, the combined worth of the Italian Mafia groups was estimated at around €51.65 billion, or about 12% of GNP. It comes as little comfort to the EU to know that similar organisations which have recently emerged in Russia, the former Yugoslavia and Albania appear to match, or even outdo, their Italian counterparts in ruthlessness and the scope of their activities throughout Europe.

Cosa Nostra

The Sicilian Mafia has its roots in the oppression of the Sicilian people and has a history extending back as far as the 13th century. Its complex system of justice is based on the code of silence known as *omertà*.

In the early 1930s, Mussolini moved against the Mafia in a way no-one has attempted since, appointing a proconsul with dictatorial powers and a brief to destroy the Mafia and eliminate it from the Sicilian mentality. A tall order. Mussolini managed to drive the Mafia so far underground that its activities became negligible.

From the devastation of WWII, however, grew the modern version of the organisation, known as Cosa Nostra. This has spread its tentacles worldwide and is far more ruthless and powerful than its predecessor. It is involved in drug-trafficking and arms deals, as well as finance, construction and tourist development, not to forget public-sector projects and politics. Few Italians doubt the claim that the Mafia's influence extends into almost every part of the country, and well beyond.

When, in the early 1990s, the Mafia assassinated two anti-Mafia judges in Palermo in separate bomb blasts, the central government was finally moved to act. The first big success of this operation was the arrest of Salvatore 'Toto' Riina, the Sicilian godfather. Riina, head of the powerful Corleonese clan, had been the world's most wanted man since 1969. More recently, the venerable ex-prime minister Giulio Andreotti, one of the longest-serving and most dominant political figures in post-war Italy, was put on trial in Palermo in the mid-1990s for alleged links with the Mafia. In late 1999 he was cleared of all charges. In June 1997 Pietro Aglieri, widely regarded as Riina's number two, was also finally arrested.

The policy of clemency for *pentiti*, arrested Mafia members who grass, has raised ncomfortable questions. On more than one ccasion the pentiti have been found to be ying. Spilling the beans (or pretending to) oesn't necessarily get them off scot-free: Mafia killer and supergrass Giovanni Brsca was imprisoned for 30 years in 1999.

But however much the judiciary have lamped down, Cosa Nostra is alive and vell – so much so that it is claimed that Riina is running it from inside his jail cell. A spine-chilling reality is the Mafia training oys as young as 10 to become assassins. A raining 'school' in the southern town of Gela apparently teaches the 'baby killers' ll they need to know to become hit-kids. And when they do hit, as minors, they canot be tried and punished as adult killers. ngenious.

ndrangheta

Jntil the late 1980s, the 'ndrangheta was a disorganised group of bandits and kidnapers; today it controls an organised crime etwork specialising in arms, drug-dealing nd construction. In the 1970s, 16-year-old oil heir J Paul Getty III was kidnapped and eld by the 'ndrangheta, having his ear severed before his release. The organisation continues to kidnap for profit. Based in the villages of Calabria, the 'ndrangheta is notorious for its savage violence: in the early 1990s, they carried out an average of one execution per day.

Camorra

This secret society grew to power in Naples n the 19th century. It was all but completely suppressed around the turn of the century but enjoyed a renaissance after WWII, dealing mainly in contraband cigaettes. After the earthquake of 1980, the Camorra diverted hundreds of millions of dollars of the aid money that poured in for econstruction around Naples and built a criminal empire that has since diversified nto drugs, construction, finance and tourist developments. It has worked closely with he Sicilian Mafia.

As the Camorra clans began to fragment n the mid-90s, their internecine squabbles over territory left a trail of death across Naples. In all, it is estimated that Camorra activities and fights cost more than 2700 people their lives from the early 1980s to 2000. In 1997, the then-mayor of Naples, Antonio Bassolino, declared that 'there is not one sector of society that has been spared by the system of corruption in Campania'. A note of hope was struck when, in May 2001, police finally captured Angelo Nuvoletta, considered the last of the Mr Bigs of the Camorra. Strangely he had been living just outside Naples and changed address only once in 17 years!

Sacra Corona Unita & La Rosa

Apulia had managed to escape the clutches of organised crime that had terrorised the rest of the south but by the late 1980s the Mafia had arrived in the form of the Sacra Corona Unita in the south of the region and La Rosa in the north. As a gateway to Eastern Europe through its main ports of Bari and Brindisi, Apulia was a natural target following the collapse of communism. It quickly supplanted Naples as a base for smuggling, chiefly of cigarettes, and an early consequence of large-scale organised drug-running activities has been a massive upsurge in the number of heroin addicts in Bari, Brindisi and Taranto.

RELIGION

Under the terms of the Lateran Treaty of 1929 between Mussolini and the Catholic Church, the city of Rome was recognised as the centre of the Catholic world. The treaty resolved the uncomfortable standoff that had resulted from Italian unification and the effective removal from the Church's hands of secular power: the pope recognised the Italian state with Rome as its capital, the Vatican was declared an independent state and Catholicism was made the state religion of Italy.

Times change and in 1985 the Vatican and the Socialist prime minister Bettino Craxi rencgotiated the treaty. As a result, Catholicism is no longer the state religion and compulsory religious education was dropped.

In a sense, this just reflected reality. Church attendance had fallen from 70%

after the war to 25% and nowadays many children are not baptised. But the Church moves slowly. Since 1978 the Polish Pope John Paul II has been at the helm. An arch-conservative, he is seen as having played a major role in the collapse of the communist bloc in the 1980s and 1990s. On social policy issues he has not been afraid to confront critics and has remained steadfast in his opposition to contraception, abortion, the idea of women priests and a host of other novelties. In Italy especially, he has been quick to criticise hedonism and consumerism, fuelling the impression some have of him as overly puritanical. At the same time, however, he has won the hearts of Catholics around the world with his indefatigable papal tours, taking the faith to the faithful. He continues to undertake this punishing schedule, in spite of his advanced age and concerns over his health.

Religiosity among the Italians appears often to be more a matter of form than a serious belief. First communions, church weddings and religious feast days are an integral part of Italian life. In the same way that the royal family is part of the ritual scenery in the lives of many Britons, so the papacy is a kind of royal family to Italians.

Stray Flock

Most Italians claim to be Catholic, but ask them about the *malocchio* (evil eye) and see what happens. Some will make a simple hand movement (index and little finger pointing down, with the middle and ring fingers folded under the thumb) designed to ward off evil spirits. Others, if pressed, might admit to wearing amulets. A pregnant woman might wear a chicken's neck hanging around her own neck to ensure that her child is not born with the umbilical cord around its neck. Insurance agents can have difficulty discussing life insurance policies with clients, as many of them don't want to discuss their eventual death, or the possibility of suffering serious accidents. This phenomenon is known to sociologists as Catholic paganism.

It is sometimes hard to draw the line between faith and superstition. Busloads of Italians still crisscross the country on pilgrimages to venerate one saint or another. The present pope is big on beatification: the latest to receive the honour is Padre Pio (see San Giovanni Rotondo in the Apulia, Calabria & Basilicata chapter), beatified in May 1999, and at the time of writing a tribunal was considering the beatification of Mother Teresa of Calcutta, who died in 1997. In general, it is hard to escape the conclusion that the majority of people who express their faith in this regard are hoping for a little intervention on earth rather than spiritual improvement.

Some 85% of Italians professed to be Catholic in a census taken in the early 1980s. Of the remaining 15%, there were about 500,000 evangelical Protestants, about 200,000 Jehovah's Witnesses, and other smaller groups, including a Jewish community in Rome and the Valdesi (Waldenses, Swiss-Protestant Baptists) living in small communities in Piedmont. There are also communities of orange-clad followers of the Bhagwan Rajneesh who are known in Italy as the *arancioni*.

The big surprise to emerge from the census is the growth of the Muslim population, estimated at anything from 600,000 to one million and thus the second-largest religious community in Italy after the Catholics. A fitting symbol for this novelty in the heart of Christendom was the inauguration in 1995 of a big Saudi-financed mosque in Rome.

LANGUAGE

For an introduction to the Italian language, some useful words and phrases, and a glossary of common food items, see the Language chapter later.

Many Italians speak some English because they study it in school but it is more widely understood in the north, particularly in major centres such as Milan, Florence and Venice, than in the south. Staff at hotels and restaurants often speak a little English but you will be better received if you at least attempt to communicate in Italian.

Art & Architecture

ART & ARCHITECTURE

Since ancient times Italy has been a fertile ground for artistic creativity. The Romans, admittedly fine architects and engineers, nevertheless did little more than follow the lead of their predecessors the Etruscans and the Greeks. Before the Roman Empire slowly slid into chaos, the artists and architects of the peninsula and its far-flung possessions had scaled enormous heights, leaving behind remarkable testimony to their power and diligence in Rome. What comes down to us today is mainly a mix of monuments, sculpture, mosaics and ceramics.

With the richness that comes from fragmented regionalism, all the great movements in western European art swept across Italy. Romanesque and Gothic, although variously adapted to local tastes, originated north of the Alps. And perhaps the most profound revolution in the history of art, the Renaissance, was born and flourished in Italy.

Since the 17th century, much of the impetus in western art and architecture has come from other centres, but Italy has to this day remained an active, if no longer such a glorious, player in all fields of the arts.

THE GREEKS, THE ETRUSCANS & THE LATINS

The earliest well-preserved Italian art and architecture dates from the 1st millennium BC. It is the product of three cultures: Latin and Roman in Lazio; Etruscan in what is now northern Lazio and southern Tuscany; and Magna Graecia in southern Italy and Sicily, where city-states were founded in the 8th and 7th centuries BC by Greek colonists.

In the main, the Greeks made the running. The Etruscans tended to ape and adapt what they learned from the Hellenistic masters, and the Latins and early Romans owed their comparatively primitive early efforts to the example shown them in turn by the Etruscans.

BETHUNE CARMICHAEL

Tomb decorations discovered at Paestum in Campania, dating mainly from the 6th and 5th centuries BC, are extremely well preserved but are almost the only examples of Greek painting in Italy to have survived.

Title page: Byzantine mosaics in Palazzo dei Normanni, Palermo (Bethune Carmichael)

Left: The ancient Greek city of Selinunte (Sicily)

They represent mythological and narrative scenes, and include the Tomba del Tuffatore (Tomb of the Diver), now in the Museo di Paestum.

While little painting has survived, the Greeks left behind a widespread architectural heritage in southern Italy. By far the greatest concentration is in Sicily. The Valley of the Temples just outside central Agrigento is a remarkable series of temples in varying states of repair. Other important temples include those of Selinunte (in the south-west) and Segesta, high up on hills in the north-west of the island. Syracuse and Taormina both host fine Greek theatres. On the mainland, the aforementioned temples of Paestum are the most impressive, although there are more remains at Metaponto in Calabria. Greek sculpture in stone and bronze also survives – it's on display in several museums, including Florence's and Syracuse's archaeological collections.

SALLY WEBB

Right: Ruins at Metaponto (Basilicata)

Like the Greeks, the early Romans built temples of stone. However, whereas the Greek temples had steps and colonnades on all sides, the Roman variety had a high podium with steps and columns only at the front, forming a deep porch. The Romans also favoured fluted Ionic columns with volute capitals and Corinthian columns with acanthus leaf capitals (rather than the Doric columns with cushion-like capitals used by the Greeks). In any event, the Romans would not come into their own until much later.

Etruscan temples followed the Greek style but were more elaborately decorated. Few Etruscan architectural remains are visible today, except for fragments of temple friezes, unless we include the many tombs and funerary complexes that have survived. The tombs at Tarquinia and Cerveteri (both in Lazio) are among the most engaging Etruscan sites you can visit. The Ara della Regina temple on the Civita hill near Tarquinia is the only significant structure of which anything remains.

A surprising number of Etruscan wall paintings have survived in various tombs. Indeed, most evidence of Etruscan art has come from their tombs, richly furnished with carved stone sarcophagi, fabulous gold jewellery, ceramics and bronzes. Decorated in vibrant colours, the tombs were intended to be a pleasing environment for the dead, who were buried with their favourite worldly goods around them. The earliest subject matter was of a religious nature; representations of the afterlife became more common in later centuries. The best tomb paintings, dating from the 6th to the 1st centuries BC, can be seen at Tarquinia (Lazio). There are others at Chiusi in Tuscany.

The Etruscan artists, like the architects, took Greek artistic techniques and used them to create a unique style of their own. The 7th century BC saw ceramics decorated with geometric and oriental motifs with lions and sphinxes, but by the end of the century there was a growing interest in the human figure. Terracotta and stone sculpture and bronze figurines, whether executed by Etruscans or Romans (it becomes increasingly difficult to tell if certain pieces were done by one group or the other as Roman domination of the Etruscans grew), often followed Greek styles, from the rather stiff figures of the archaic period (6th century BC) to the almost idealised naturalism of the classical period (5th and 4th centuries). Finally, a more naturalistic and even expressive realism surfaced in the Hellenistic period (from 323 BC to 31 BC).

The Etruscans were famous for metalwork, such as the bronze *Lupa Capitolina* (She-Wolf) in the Capitoline Museums in Rome. Such large sculptures are rare. Most of the surviving pieces are smaller figurines or jewellery with intricate filigree work. Rome's Museo Nazionale Etrusco di Villa Giulia and Museo Gregoriano Etrusco (part of the Vatican Museums) and Florence's Museo Archeologico have the richest collections of Etruscan art. The height of creativity and skill that the Etruscan artists reached is demonstrated at Villa Giulia by the beautifully sculpted *Sarcofago degli Sposi* (Sarcophagus of the Married Couple) from a tomb at Cerveteri.

THE ROMANS

In terms of style, the Romans invented little; their great achievement was to perfect existing construction techniques to create aqueducts and arches on a grandiose scale, the likes of which had never been seen before.

From the 1st century BC they used a quick-curing, strong concrete for vaults, arches and domes to roof vast areas such as the Pantheon in Rome. Dry stone masonry was used for some temples, aqueducts and for the supporting vaults of theatres and amphitheatres, such as the Colosseum in Rome and the amphitheatres in Verona, Lucca and Capua.

Marble was used from the 2nd century BC until the 2nd century AD. As Rome's

JON DAVISON

Left: The Colosseum (Rome)

JONATHAN SMITH

power grew, new buildings were needed to reflect the city's status in the Mediterranean world and the Romans started building forums, public baths, colonnaded streets and theatres, and complexes for both commercial and political activities.

From the days of the Republic onwards, sculpture was used above all as a propaganda device – a means of communicating the greatness either of the state or its individual masters. More than any other art form it provides a compelling historical record.

The first Roman sculptures were actually made by Greek artists brought to Rome or were copies of imported classical Greek works. An exception was portrait sculpture, which was derived from the Etruscans. The Romans often had statues made of themselves in the guise of Greek gods or heroes. The most interesting Roman sculpture is that of the 1st and 2nd centuries AD; it commemorated the history of Rome and its citizens or was made for specific architectural settings such as the Villa Adriana at Tivoli.

Emperor Augustus was the first to exploit the possibilities of sculpture as a propaganda tool. One of the most important works of Roman sculpture is the Ara Pacis (13 BC) in Rome, made to celebrate Augustus' victories in Spain and Gaul and the peace that he had established in the Empire. The carved reliefs of scenes from Augustus' reign, exemplified by clarity and classical restraint, mark the point at which Roman sculpture gained its own identity.

Later commemorative works include Colonna di Traiano (Trajan's Column), erected in the early 2nd century AD to celebrate Emperor Trajan's military achievements in the Dacian campaigns, and the Colonna Antonina (AD 180–196), built to commemorate Marcus Aurelius' victories over the Germans and Sarmatians between AD 169 and 176. Both are in Rome.

In the 3rd and 4th centuries little public sculpture was done, although a notable exception was the 4th-century statue of Emperor Constantine, a 10m-high colossus that stood at his basilica in the Roman Forum. Pieces of it (the head, a hand and a foot) are in Rome's Capitoline Museums.

Right: Colonna di Traiano (Rome)

The Romans used painting and mosaics, both legacies from the Greeks, to decorate houses and palaces from at least the 1st century BC.

Although comparatively little survives, there are some magnificent examples (such as the Villa Livia frescoes of an imaginary garden) in the Museo Nazionale Romano collection at Palazzo Massimo alle Terme in Rome and in the Museo Nazionale Archeologico in Naples. Traces of mosaics and frescoes *in situ* can be found at Rome's ancient port of Ostia, as well as at Pompeii and the ancient town of Herculaneum.

EARLY CHRISTIAN & BYZANTINE

The early Christians practised their religion in private houses (many of which later became churches) and catacombs. In the 4th century, under the Christian emperor Constantine, several places of worship were constructed – the architecture based on the buildings of Imperial Rome, in particular the rectangular basilica or public hall. Over time, transepts were added to create the shape of a cross.

The domed baptistry of San Giovanni in Laterano (in Rome), built by Constantine between 315 and 324 and remodelled into its present octagonal shape in the 5th century, became the model for many baptistries throughout the Christian world. The starkly simple Basilica di Santa Sabina in Rome, built in the 5th century, is one of the best preserved churches of this period.

OLIVIER CIRENDINI

In 402, Ravenna became the imperial capital and several churches were built there, some in the basilican style. The Byzantine dome was freely adopted, often supported on a square (rather than round as the Romans had used) base. The innovative plan for the town's Basilica di San Vitale used an octagon within an octagon.

The Byzantine architectural style reached its peak in Venice, with the magnificent St Mark's Basilica (consecrated in 1094). Although the church as you see it today betrays a mix of styles (with some Romanesque and later Renaissance elements), it has a markedly eastern air. The bubbled roof of domes and the inclusion of a narthex, a kind of lobby you pass through before entering the church proper, are just two such distinctive elements.

In the 10th and 11th centuries, the Greeks in the south built several small, cross-shaped and domed churches in the Byzantine style.

Roman painting went into decline from the 2nd century AD, when mosaics and coloured marble veneers became a popular decorative

Left: Mosaics in St Mark Basilica (Venice)

medium. At first, black-and-white mosaic cubes were used for floors in both public and private buildings. Later, coloured stones were employed, as in the villa at Piazza Armerina, south of Enna on Sicily, and in the early churches of Aquileia and Grado, near Trieste.

By the 4th century, glass tesserae (mosaic tiles) were used to splendid effect in the apses of the early Christian churches of Rome (such as the Basilica di Santa Maria Maggiore) and Ravenna (Mausoleo di Galla Placidia, the Basilica di San Vitale and the Basilica di Sant'Apollinare Nuovo).

During the 5th and 6th centuries, art was an instrument for the propagation and maintenance of the faith. At first restricted to depictions of Christ and other holy figures such as the Virgin Mary, saints and angels, the range of images broadened to include more complex themes and scenes from the Old Testament and the Passion of Christ.

In those parts of Italy that continued to be influenced by Byzantium, the art of mosaics continued to develop in splendour. To walk into St Mark's Basilica in Venice is to be swallowed by a shimmering sea of gold and colour. Work first started on these mosaics in the 11th century and continued long after. Some of them were done as late as the 15th century, when other artistic styles and mediums had long taken pre-eminence elsewhere in Italy. The oldest cathedral in the Venetian lagoon, Santa Maria Assunta on the island of Torcello, is home to magnificent mosaics. The one depicting the Last Judgement is extraordinary for its detail and symbolic density.

JON DAVISON

At the other end of the country, Byzantine artists were called in to decorate the interior of the splendid Norman cathedral of Monreale, outside Palermo on Sicily. The result is a splendid Christ Pantocrator dominating a series of Old and New Testament scenes

The early Christian period saw an almost total rejection of sculpture, except for carved decoration on sarcophagi. The carved wooden panels depicting scenes of the Passion of Christ on the doors of the Basilica di Santa Sabina in Rome, dating from the 5th century, are a significant but rare exception. Only with the arrival of a new architectural and decorative style, Romanesque, would sculpture recover its importance.

Above: St Mark's Basilica (Venice)

DAMIEN SIMONIS

ROMANESQUE

The Romanesque period (c.1050–1200) saw a revival of buildings whose size and structure resembled those of the Roman Empire. The origins of this style (which didn't get its name until 1818) are complex but grew out of developments in German and Frankish territory. The collapse of the Roman Empire, the decimation of the population and heightened insecurity, combined with the rise of Christianity, had led religious orders to build robust, defensive monastery complexes. These contained churches, chapels, libraries, sleeping quarters, kitchens and cloisters. In these early monasteries the Romanesque style came to the fore. It was rooted in Roman architecture but allowed diverse influences ranging from Byzantine to Islamic thinking.

In simple terms, the style made a virtue of mass. Thick, plain walls culminated in barrel-vaulted roofs. The main decorative device was the semicircle – used in doorways, windows and between arches. Apses (one or more) at the rear of the church were also semi-circular. The most common edifices were churches, the focal point of the community, but other public buildings, bridges and so on were also built. In Italy the earliest signs of Romanesque, and what is sometimes referred to as pre-Romanesque, came in northern Italy, especially in Lombardy. It spread across the country and with time the style became more diverse. Early Lombard construction tended to be simple and on a small scale, but in its many reincarnations up and down the peninsula, it became increasingly sophisticated.

In Lombard towns today some churches of the period survive (such as the curious Rotonda in Brescia and the Chiesa di Santa Maria Maggiore in Bergamo). Frequently, as churches were replaced or rebuilt in later styles, separate free-standing baptistries were left in their Romanesque condition. A particularly Italian touch seems to have been the use of an octagonal base for them. From the baptistry of Cremona to the magnificent pink marble structure of the baptistry of Parma, the plan was repeated over and over.

In Tuscany, the use of different coloured marbles led local builders to create stunning facades of surprising decorative verve. Examples

Left: Facade of Pisa's cathedral

abound, but the cathedrals of Pisa (along with the Leaning Tower) and Lucca are masterpieces.

Romanesque entered its richest period around 1050 and lasted well into the 13th century. Even as innovative engineering was leading to the creation of grandiose Gothic structures, Romanesque continued to thrive in many areas. The Normans left behind fine examples of Romanesque churches in Apulia (at Bari, Molfetta, Trani, Barletta, Bitonto and Canosa).

In Sicily, and to a lesser extent in Venice, Romanesque design melded with Byzantine to create remarkable hybrids. Romanesque elements are clearly visible in Monreale cathedral outside Palermo and St Mark's Basilica in Venice.

While the use of mosaics flourished in certain parts of Italy and penetrated to areas well beyond the influence of Byzantium (such as Rome and Florence), the use of frescoes to decorate the interior of churches also spread. Although no easy alternative, the fresco was less fiddly than mosaic work. From the mid-12th century, painting on wooden panels also became increasingly important, particularly in Tuscany, as frescoes were expensive to produce and tended to fade over time. As evidence that Byzantine-style mosaics continued to have their fans, the extraordinary mosaic series, dominated by an image of Christ Pantocrator, in the dome of Florence's Baptistry was carried out by Venetian specialists in the late 13th century!

In Rome in the 12th century, the Cosmati (originally a single family of artisans but eventually a name for a whole school) used fragments of coloured glass and marble from ancient ruins to create intricately patterned pavements, altars, paschal candlesticks and pulpits. Their work is referred to as 'cosmatesque' and can be found in churches all over Rome, as well as in other regions.

Below: Chiesa di San Michele in Foro (Lucca)

DAMIEN S MONIS

Romanesque painting and sculpture, with their seemingly infantile slender, two-dimensional portraiture and apparently lifeless execution, served a didactic purpose. Themes were always religious and generally aimed to remind people of the other-worldliness of the Holy Trinity, the angels and the saints. In more complex cases they served to communicate stories from the Bible or illustrate doctrine and matters of faith to an illiterate people.

Sculpture recovered much of its prestige with the spread of Romanesque building, beginning in the north. Church portals in Modena are decorated with intricate bas-reliefs by Wiligelmo and his pupil Nicolo Pisano (c.1220–84), who also carved, among others, the portals of cathedrals in Verona, Ferrara, Piacenza and Cremona. Nicolò created an illusion of space by using different levels of relief, and also carved out voluminous figures. His pulpits in the baptistry in Pisa and in Siena's cathedral have a creative expression not seen in sculpture since Roman times.

GOTHIC

Medieval engineers wanted to build higher and bigger. The fundamental problem lay in calculating load distribution. It was not enough to heap heavy stone blocks one on top of the other, so new forms of vaulting were developed. They opened up whole new architectural panoramas. The first Gothic structures were the mighty churches built in France and later elsewhere in northern Europe. The use of flying buttresses and further technical innovations accelerated the process of daring change. The one element most Gothic churches have in common is their great height. Soaring structures, it was felt, would lift mortal eyes to the heavens and at the same time remind people of their smallness compared with the greatness of God.

These complex structures were perfected using pillars, columns, arches and vaulting of various kinds to support high ceilings. Rather than relying on the solidity of mass and building thick, heavy walls, priority was given to a clear light pouring through tall pointed windows. The whole was topped off by an almost obsessive desire to decorate. Gothic churches are bedecked with pinnacles, statues, gargoyles and all sorts of baubles. In Italy, however, where architecture remained heavily influenced by the cleaner, more simple lines of the buildings of classical antiquity, the fiddly decoration, pointed arches and vaults of Gothic architecture never flourished in the way they did north of the Alps.

JON DAVISON

The most outstanding early Gothic church in Italy is the Basilica di San Francesco in Assisi, begun in the mid-13th century, which combines a heavily vaulted, dark and mysterious lower church with a light-filled upper church.

The Franciscan order, responsible for the construction of the cathedral in Assisi, competed with the rival Dominicans not only in theological matters but also in the building of churches. It was common for both

Left: Milan's cathedral

DAMIEN SIMONIS

orders to raise vast Gothic churches on the outskirts of medieval cities, such as Santa Maria Novella (Dominicans) and Santa Croce (Franciscans) in Florence. That pair is mirrored in Venice by Santa Maria Gloriosa dei Frari (Franciscans) and SS Giovanni e Paolo (Dominicans). The two pairs tell us much about the development of Gothic in Italy. In all cases the buildings are epic in proportion but comparatively unadorned (there are none of the spires and gargoyles that adorn the Gothic cathedrals of France). Regional differences were pronounced. While the Venetians favoured a sober brick exterior, the Tuscans opted for stone and marble facing.

Among the great Italian cathedrals are some outstanding examples of Gothic architecture. Florence's magnificent marble-clad cathedral competes with those of Siena and Orvieto in splendour. Siena's, started in 1196, is arguably one of the most splendid Gothic cathedrals ever built. Milan's cathedral is a late-Gothic fantasy and one of the few in all of Italy to imitate the style favoured north of the Alps. Built using a light-coloured marble and rather squat by northern European standards, it is nevertheless a sumptuous forest of spires, statues and reliefs – not a square centimetre has been left bare.

Many public buildings and private mansions were also raised in the Gothic style (although fewer examples remain). In these cases builders did not necessarily aim to reach great heights, but the same techniques allowed them to create structures of great elegance. With the growth of trade and city government, town halls were built, such as the Palazzo Vecchio in Florence (built 1298–1310) and the imposing Palazzo Pubblico in Siena (built 1298–c.1326), and many patrician families built impressive Gothic mansions.

The Gothic style in Italy lingered longest in Venice. A fine example is the Palazzo Ducale (Doges' Palace) built in the 14th and early 15th centuries, which combines Gothic and Islamic styles in its facade. The elegant Ca' d'Oro (Golden House; built 1420–34) on the Grand Canal was freely based on the Palazzo Ducale.

Right: The delightful dome of Florence's cathedral

These great buildings had to be decorated and the use of frescoes, panel paintings and sculpture all flourished under the influence of the new architectural style. Painting was infused with more colour and expression than before, the figures depicted acquired greater fluidity and humanity. Artists still relied above all on commissions from the Church and hence religious themes remained at the core of Italian artistic production. Nevertheless, depictions of kings and other personalities, as well earthly events, represent a significant breach in the age's artistic repertoire.

One of the most interesting centres of Gothic painting was Siena. The only artist there to hold a candle to Giotto (see Renaissance later) was Duccio di Buoninsegna (c.1255–1318). Although still much attached to the Byzantine school (iconographic and laden with gold), he mixed it in with Gothic ideas and introduced a hitherto rare degree of expressiveness. A variety of his works can be seen in Siena's cathedral and Florence's Uffizi Gallery. Duccio's star pupil was Simone Martini (c.1284–1344). Perhaps his most celebrated work is the *Annunciazione* (Annunciation), done for the cathedral in Siena but now hanging in the Uffizi.

Other artists of note in Siena included the brothers Pietro (c.1290–c.1348) and Ambrogio Lorenzetti (died 1348). Both worked in Siena and elsewhere. Pietro was particularly active in Assisi. Ambrogio's best known work is the startling *Effetti del Buon e del Cattivo Governo* (Allegories of Good and Bad Government) in Siena's Palazzo Pubblico.

Florentine Cimabue (c.1240–1302) had more experimental tendencies and his use of rounded, modelled forms in his frescoes in the Basilica di San Francesco in Assisi (painted 1228–53) were a foretaste of what was to come with the Renaissance.

Giovanni Pisano (1250–1314), Nicolò's son (see Romanesque earlier), was an innovative sculptor. His statues for the facade of the cathedral in Siena broke away from the static figures of Romanesque sculpture used for similar purposes elsewhere. Posed in dramatic ways, they were placed high up on the facade and were designed to be viewed from a distance.

RENAISSANCE

The distinctions between one artistic period and another are always blurred and perhaps never more so than with the Renaissance (c.1400–1600). A combination of humanistic curiosity and economic well-being led the rulers of Florence to be more daring in their artistic tastes. More than ever before, artists could approach lay as well as religious patrons, and so whole new thematic fields could be explored at the same time as techniques were revolutionised.

One of the links between the more static Gothic painters and sculptors and the new wave was Giotto di Bondone (1266–1337). The innovative Giotto cast aside the two-dimensional restrictions of painting and created an illusion of depth. He represented gesture and emotion in a completely new way and was the first artist to come to terms fully with foreshortening, modelling and the effects of light and shade. This is evident in his frescoes in the Cappella degli Scrovegni in Padua (painted 1305). In Florence, Giotto's followers included Taddeo and Agnolo Gaddi.

Experimentation with optics and perspective was a feature of the early Renaissance. This is evident in the work of Masaccio (1401–28), who achieved a perfect sense of depth and perspective in his *Trinity* fresco in the Basilica di Santa Maria Novella in Florence and in his fresco cycle in Santa Maria del Carmine (also in Florence), which uses a single light source and realistic shadows. Also in Florence, the Dominican friar Fra Angelico (c.1400–55) created ethereal and beautifully coloured religious works while his pupil, Benozzo Gozzoli (c.1421–97), painted startling decorative frescoes in the Palazzo Medici-Riccardi.

Classical mythology was of great interest to the Florentine painters, none more so than Sandro Botticelli (1445–1510), whose *Allegoria della Primavera* (Joy of Spring) and *Nascita di Venere* (Birth of Venus) in the Uffizi remain enigmatic to this day.

DAMIEN SIMONIS

Artistic activity elsewhere in Italy came nowhere near the rich style of Florence, although Piero della Francesca (c.1410–92) did produce magnificent fresco cycles in the Chiesa di San Francesco in Arezzo and Urbino, and Luca Signorelli (c.1441–1523) drew on a deep understanding of anatomy for his frescoes in the Orvieto cathedral. In northern Italy, Andrea Mantegna (c.1431–1506) was outstanding. His *Cristo Morto* (Dead Christ) in the Pinacoteca di Brera, Milan, took foreshortening and perspective to a new level. In Venice, the various members of the Bellini family achieved lasting influence, especially Giovanni (c.1430–1516), who employed a uniquely soft mix of colour and an innovative use of picture planes, one behind the other, to create depth and recession.

The architects in no way lagged behind the painters. The first major architectural achievement of the early Renaissance was Filippo Brunelleschi's (1377–1446) bold experiment in 1436 to span Florence's cathedral with a double-skinned, segmented dome. It was followed by other domes: the Tempietto (built c.1504–10) of Donato Bramante beside San Pietro in Montorio (Rome); on the Gianicolo (Rome), and the large, centrally planned Santa Maria della Consolazione (near Todi). The latter was begun in 1508 when Bramante was designing St Peter's Basilica in Rome; originally conceived as centrally planned and domed, the basilica was finally built in the form of a long Latin cross, with a 42m-diameter dome designed by Michelangelo Buonarroti (1475–1564).

Right: Fresco on Orvieto's cathderal

A palazzo in the city was a visible sign of a family's success. In Florence, Michelozzo di Bartolommeo (1396–1472) designed influential urban buildings, including the Palazzo Medici-Riccardi, which features severe facades and rusticated stonework. Leon Battista Alberti (1404–72) wrote treatises on architecture, the harmony of classical forms and the ratio of measurements. He employed his theories in church facades such as Santa Maria Novella in Florence, Sant'Andrea and San Sebastiano in Mantua and the Tempio Malatestiano in Rimini, as well as in the Palazzo Rucellai in Florence. Giuliano da Sangallo (1445–1516) chimed in with the Palazzo Strozzi in Florence, the most ambitious mansion of the century.

Florence was also the heart of sculptural activity during the early Renaissance, with the limelight falling on sculptors such as Lorenzo Ghiberti (1398–1455), responsible for the magnificent cast bronze baptistry doors of the cathedral, and the prolific Donatello (Donato Bardi; 1386–1466), many of whose works are now in the Museo del Bargello in Florence. Donatello's large equestrian statue, the *Gattamelata* (built 1453), in front of the Basilica del Santo in Padua, is considered the first great bronze of the Italian Renaissance.

Three generations of the Della Robbia family produced (from the 15th to the mid-16th centuries) distinctive terracotta sculpture using blue and white enamel glazes, sometimes with the addition of yellow and green.

Michelangelo already had an established reputation as a sculptor when he arrived in Rome from Florence at the end of the 15th century. He was only 25 when he sculpted the staggeringly beautiful *Pietà*, now in St Peter's Basilica. Pope Julius II put him to work immediately on the massive project of creating a tomb, involving 40 sculptures, for the pope. The tomb occupied the artist for his entire career but was never completed.

HIGH RENAISSANCE

With the return of the papacy, Rome became the centre of the High Renaissance (1500–1600). The popes of the 15th century summoned the leading artistic and architectural masters to rebuild the city. The Venetian Pope Paul II (1464–71) commissioned many works, including the Palazzo Venezia, Rome's first great Renaissance palazzo (built 1455–64). Other important buildings in Rome include the Palazzo della Cancelleria, Palazzo Farnese, Palazzo Spada and Villa (Palazzo) Farnesina.

The lengthy construction of St Peter's Basilica occupied most of the other notable architects of the High Renaissance, including Raphael (1483–1520), Giuliano da Sangallo (1443–1516), Baldassarre Peruzzi (1481–1537) and Antonio da Sangallo the Younger (1483–1546).

Jacopo Sansovino (1486–1570) introduced the High Renaissance to Venice, leaving his mark in various public buildings around Piazza San Marco. In the mid-16th century, Andrea Palladio applied Ancient Roman temple design to the facades of his churches in Venice and also to his villas in Vicenza and the Veneto. His La Rotonda (outside Vicenza), a cardinal's party-house, imitates the Pantheon in Rome.

During the Counter-Reformation, both art and architecture were entirely at the service of the Church. In Rome, the Jesuits created massive and impressive places of worship to attract and overawe the faithful. Giacomo della Porta (1539–1602), the last architect of the Renaissance tradition, designed the Mannerist facade of the main Jesuit church in Rome, the Gesù (built 1568–75), with elements creating a play of light and shade. Both the exterior and the interior – a wide nave and side chapels instead of aisles – were extensively copied throughout Italy.

The Tuscan genius Leonardo da Vinci (1452–1519) painted his *Cenacolo* (Last Supper) in the refectory of Santa Maria delle Grazie in Milan at the end of the 15th century. The artist's ability to represent the psychological characteristics of his subjects and create illusions of space marked the beginning of the High Renaissance in painting. By now the canvas was becoming a common base on which to paint.

Between 1481 and 1483 some of the country's greatest painters were employed by Pope Sixtus IV to decorate the walls in his newly rebuilt Sistine Chapel in the Vatican. The frescoes of the lives of Moses and Christ and portraits of popes were done by Perugino (1446–1523), Sandro Botticelli (1444–1510), Domenico Ghirlandaio (1449–94), Cosimo Rosselli (1439–1507) and Luca Signorelli (1450–1523).

The decoration of the official apartments of Pope Julius II (Le Stanze di Raffaello) marked the beginning of the brilliant Roman career of Urbino-born Raphael (Raffaello Sanzio; 1483–1520). In the true spirit of the Renaissance, he absorbed the grand manner of classical Rome and became the most influential painter of his time.

Raphael was also adept at portraiture and mythological paintings, and there are wonderful frescoes in this vein from 1508 to 1511 in Rome's Villa Farnesina. Other leading artists who worked on the villa designed by Baldassarre Peruzzi were Sebastiano del Piombo (c.1485–1547), Sodoma (1477–1549) and Giulio Romano (c.1492–1546), one of the few native Roman artists of the Renaissance.

The greatest artistic achievement of the period (and arguably of all time) was by Raphael's contemporary, Michelangelo Buonarroti (1475–1564), on the Sistine Chapel ceiling (painted 1508–12), which is crammed with dramatically foreshortened statuesque figures. Three decades later Michelangelo returned to adorn the altar wall with the *Giudizio Universale* (Last Judgement) between 1535 and 1541.

A distinct artistic school emerged in mid-16th century Venice. It placed emphasis on colour rather than drawing and line. Titian (Tiziano Vecelli; 1493–1576) painted the huge panel of the *Assumption of the Virgin* (1516–18), in which the composition is built up with colours as much as by form, in the Frari. The artist was sought after as a portraitist and produced sensuous paintings such as the *Venere d'Urbino* (Venus of Urbino; 1538), which is in the Uffizi Gallery in Florence.

Venice's Scuola Grande di San Rocco houses an overwhelming cycle of biblical scenes by Tintoretto (Jacopo Robusti; 1518–94), including the 12m-wide *Crucifixion*, in which a pool of light in the centre is ringed by a crowd of figures.

Another striking canvas of the period is Veronese's (c.1528–88) *Feast in the House of Levi* (1573), in the Gallerie dell'Accademia, Venice. It depicts the Last Supper with Christ seated at a banquet in a lavish palazzo with a crowd in contemporary Venetian dress.

BAROQUE

The Baroque style is synonymous with Rome. The two great architects of this period were the Naples-born Gian Lorenzo Bernini (1598–1680) and Francesco Borromini (1599–1667) from Lombardy.

No other architect before or since has had such an impact on a city as Bernini did on Rome. He was patronised by the Barberini pope, Urban VIII, who in 1629 appointed him official architect of St Peter's, for which he designed the *baldacchino* (altar canopy) above St Peter's grave. Bernini transformed the face of the city and his churches, palaces, piazzas and fountains (such as the Fontana dei Quattro Fiumi in Piazza Navona) are Roman landmarks to this day.

Bernini's great rival was Borromini, who created buildings involving complex shapes and exotic geometry. His most memorable works (both in Rome) are the Chiesa di San Carlo alle Quattro Fontane (built 1641), which has an oval interior, and the Chiesa di Sant'Ivo alla Sapienza, which combines a unique arrangement of convex and concave surfaces and is topped by an innovative spiral campanile.

Bernini was also the period's master sculptor. Baroque sensibilities gave a new importance to exaggerated poses, cascading drapery and primacy of emotions, and Bernini remained unequalled in his capacity to render such swirling emotion and, one might say today, camp movement. His works are not sculptures but rather theatrical and emotional spectacles set in stone that unfold before the viewer's eyes. His *Davide*, *Il Ratto di Proserpina* (The Rape of Proserpine) and *Apollo e Dafne*, all in Rome's Galleria Borghese, are cases in point. Bologna-born Alessandro Algardi (1595–1654) was one of the few sculptors not totally overshadowed by Bernini. His bronzes and marbles grace several Roman churches and palazzos and his white marble monument to Pope Leo XI (1650) is in St Peter's.

Rome may have been the epicentre of this billowing artistic outpouring but the tremors washed over other towns and cities. And again, styles varied from place to place. Florence and Venice, the other two senior stages of the Renaissance, were touched to a far lesser degree by the excesses of Baroque. In Florence relatively few examples of a more restrained version of the style appeared. The most important is the facade of the Chiesa di Ognissanti. In Venice, Baldassare Longhena (1598–1682) directed the Baroque orchestra. His masterstroke is the Basilica di Santa Maria della Salute – without doubt one of the best known images of the Grand Canal.

Far from the grand city states of northern and central Italy, the deep south town of Lecce (Apulia) became a showcase island of Baroque. Quarries near the city yielded a comparatively soft stone that lent itself to decorative manipulation and then hardened with time. As a result, the city is laden with elegant Baroque churches, led by the opulent Basilica della Santa Croce.

In Sicily, following the 1693 earthquake, new churches and public buildings were erected in a derivative late-Baroque style.

The late-16th century saw few highlights in Italian painting, although Annibale Carracci (1560–1609) created magnificent frescoes of mythological subjects in the Palazzo Farnese, Rome, between 1597 and 1603.

Michelangelo Merisi da Caravaggio (1573–1610) heralded a move away from the confines of the High Renaissance towards a new naturalism. His paintings, using street urchins and prostitutes as models for biblical subjects, were often rejected for being too real. However, his innovative sense of light and shade and supreme drawing ability meant that he was courted his contemporaries and was influential for centuries.

More successful in their day, although less highly revered since, were the drily academic painters Guido Reni (1575–1642) and Domenichino (1581–1641), who were considered by their contemporaries and immediate successors to be on a par with Raphael and Michelangelo. Domenichino, a native of Bologna and a pupil of Annibale Carracci, received innumerable commissions from the aristocratic clergy and his best works adorn nine churches in Rome.

Michelangelo had started a fashion for ceiling frescoes that continued for some time into the 17th century. Pietro da Cortona (1596–1669) was one of the most sought-after decorators of Baroque Rome, completing the ceiling frescoes in the Salone Grande of Palazzo Barberini as well as in the Chiesa Nuova and many private palaces.

The Jesuit artist Andrea dal Pozzo (1642–1709) made a name for himself by creating trompe l'oeil perspectives on ceilings and walls in the many Jesuit churches erected in Rome, while serene landscapes were produced by Salvator Rosa (1615–73) and the Italianised French painters Nicolas Poussin (1594–1665) and Claude Lorrain (1600–82).

NEOCLASSICISM

The early 18th century saw a brief flurry of surprisingly creative architecture, such as Rome's Spanish Steps (built 1726) and exuberant Fontana di Trevi (Trevi Fountain), which was designed in 1732 by Nicola Salvi (1697–1751) and completed three decades later.

NEIL SETCHFIELD

Right: Ceiling detail in Palazzo Barberini (Rome)

The neoclassical style is generally considered to have begun in the mid-18th century. It returned to the fundamental principles of classicism and was a direct reaction against the frivolous excesses of Baroque.

In Naples, the ruling Spanish dynasty, the Bourbons, built the Palazzo Reale di Capodimonte and at Caserta, to the north, Luigi Vanvitelli (1700–73) designed another vast royal palace and grounds, the Reggia di Caserta, combining an ornate Baroque interior with a restrained neoclassical exterior. In Milan, Vanvitelli's pupil Giuseppe Piermarini (1734–1808) became the most popular architect, building – among other edifices – La Scala opera house in 1778. Venetian Giorgio Massari (1686–1766), inspired by Palladio, was one of the country's main exponents of neoclassicism. He is remembered above all for the Chiesa dei Gesuati. Venice's opera house, Teatro la Fenice, first built in 1792, was a fine piece of neoclassical design. You wouldn't know that to look at it now, sad and forlorn after being gutted by fire in 1936 and again in 1996.

BETHUNE CARMICHAEL

The neoclassical sculptural style was adopted by many foreign artists who had come to Rome, but among the Italians it was best represented by Antonio Canova (1757–1822). He was an accomplished modeller, but his work is sometimes devoid of emotion. His most famous work is a daring sculpture of Pauline Bonaparte Borghese as a reclining *Venere Vincitrice* (Conquering Venice), in the Galleria Borghese in Rome, which is typical of the slightly erotic sculptures for which the sculptor became known.

Meanwhile, a late offshoot of Baroque, the still more ebullient rococo, took particular hold in Venice with Giambattista Tiepolo (1696–1770) and his son Giandomenico (1727–1804). At much the same time, other painters in Venice were exploring an altogether different genre, that of

Left: Trevi Fountain (Rome)

the *vedutisti*. Led by the prolific Canaletto (1697–1768), they produced remarkable landscapes and urban views. Canaletto is best known for his numerous portraits of Venice, which he tended to sell above all to foreign collectors based in the city and abroad.

The attention of many foreign artists who settled in Italy during the 18th century turned to the antique. The widely disseminated etchings of Rome and its ancient ruins by Giovanni Battista Piranesi (1720–78) attracted Grand Tourists and artists alike.

THE 19TH CENTURY TO TODAY

Architecture in 19th-century Italy was fairly unremarkable, although there were interesting developments in town planning in Turin, Trieste and Milan. The beginning of modern architecture in Italy is epitomised by the late-19th-century shopping galleries in Milan, Naples, Genoa and Turin, with their distinctive iron-and-glass roofs. This fashion never quite made it to Rome, which instead got the massive white marble monument to Vittorio Emanuele II – the so-called wedding cake – built between 1885 and 1911. As the new capital of Italy, Rome got its own dose of urban planning, including massive apartment blocks, monumental public buildings and the River Tiber embankment.

DAMIEN SIMONIS

Right: Naples' Galleria Umberto I

The only notable artistic endeavours of the early 19th century were produced by academic history painters such as Francesco Hayez (1791–1882).

The years from 1855 to 1865 saw the heyday of the *Macchiaioli* (from the Italian for 'stain' or 'blot'), who produced a version of pointillism using thousands of dots of pure colour to build up the picture, and the end of the century saw the rise of the Italian Symbolists. Painting since Italian unification in 1870 is most readily found in Rome's Galleria Nazionale d'Arte Moderna.

In the 20th century Art Nouveau, known in Italy as Lo Stilo Liberty, made a brief appearance before Mussolini and the Fascist era inaugurated massive building schemes such as EUR (Esposizione Universale di Roma), a complete district on the outskirts of Rome. Art Nouveau probably would have died out anyway, much as it did elsewhere in Europe in the course of the 1920s. But the arrival of Mussolini ushered in an era of grandiose, state-sponsored architecture that left no room for the whimsy of Art Nouveau.

The internationally celebrated Pier Luigi Nervi (1891–1979) made reinforced concrete one of his chief materials in his designs for Rome's Olympic Stadium (built 1960) and the papal audience chamber in the Vatican.

The Italian Futurists were inspired by urbanism, industry and the idea of progress. Umberto Boccioni (1882–1916) and Giacomo Balla (1871–1958) aligned themselves with the *Futurist Manifesto* (1909) by writer Emilio Marinetti, while Carlo Carrà (1881–1996) had much in common with Cubists such as Pablo Picasso. Giorgio Morandi (1890–1964) consistently depicted tangible objects such as bottles and jars and made them appear as abstract forms, while the Surrealist Giorgio De Chirico (1888–1978) painted visionary empty streetscapes with elements disconcertingly juxtaposed, often incorporating allusions to classical antiquity.

Amedeo Modigliani (1884–1920) spent most of his adult life in Paris. However, his art – mainly arresting portraits and sensuous reclining female nudes – was firmly rooted in the tradition of the Italian Renaissance and Mannerist masters.

Giacomo Manzù (1908–91) revived the Italian religious tradition in sculpture. His best known work is a bronze door (to the left of the central Holy Door) in St Peter's in Rome.

Italy's two leading contemporary architects are Renzo Piano (born 1937), whose new music auditorium in Rome is almost complete, and Paolo Portoghesi (born 1931), who designed Rome's mosque, but both seem to do more work abroad than in their native country.

Important post-WWII painters and sculptors include Burri, Colla, Manzoni and Pascali, as well as the *Transavanguardia* ('beyond the avant-garde'), whose exponents include Enzo Cucchi, Francesco Clemente, Mimmo Paladino, Alberto Giacometti, Lucio Fontana and Sandro Chia, many of whom have worked and gained success both in Italy and abroad. A good place to get a handle on modern Italian art is Rome's Galleria Nazionale d'Arte Moderna.

Sally Webb, Ann Moffatt & Damien Simonis

Facts for the Visitor

Highlights

The Best

Coming up with a Top 10 hit list for Italy is a little like trying to find the 10 shiniest gold ingots in Fort Knox. Bearing that in mind, we've gone for 11 of the places, sights and experiences that make Italy so special:

- Food, glorious food
- Michelangelo's Sistine Chapel frescoes
- Medieval & Renaissance Florence
- The Aeolian Islands
- The Amalfi Coast
- Siena
- The Cinque Terre
- Ancient ruins in Rome, Pompeii, Paestum and Sicily
- Venice during Carnevale (or not)
- Walking in the Dolomites
- Mosaics in Palermo and Monreale

The Worst

It is just possible that the thought of driving headlong down a Po Valley autostrada in dense fog will turn some people on – obviously you should make of the following what you will.

- Potenza (ugly & boring)
- Italian bureaucracy
- Brindisi (ugly & unpleasant)
- Italian drivers
- *Autostrada* tolls & petrol (both are expensive)
- Italian *papagalli* (men on the make)
- Imperious shop assistants
- Driving through fog in the Po Valley (Emilia-Romagna)
- Tourist crowds in the Vatican Museums & the Uffizi (hard to avoid!)
- Italian beaches in August (so packed you can't breathe)

SUGGESTED ITINERARIES

However you decide to approach the country, and whatever itinerary you map out, remember that the determined monument zealot could spend days (and in some cases weeks) in any one Italian city. No human being can 'do' all of Italy, probably not even in a lifetime dedicated to the project. So do some research before you go and assemble a package of cities, monuments and countryside you particularly wish to see – and build in time for detours, long lunches and the unexpected!

One Week

A week is not a long time to spend in Italy but speedy travellers have been known to arrive in Rome and undertake a whistle-stop tour of the tried and true. After a couple of days in Rome you could make for Florence by train, spend two nights there (allowing time for a quick excursion to Siena or Pisa) and then push on to Venice, where another two days would allow you to sample the place. The ultra-keen might stop en route for a day in Bologna. Such a trip could be a one-way journey or end with a return trip by rail to the point of departure.

Two Weeks

With two weeks the options widen a little. The same route could be used as a basis and further side trips thrown in to suit. Between Rome and Florence, Perugia could be a stop, while Florence itself can be used as a base for a whole range of exploratory touring – why not try the medieval village of San Gimignano? It is one among many in the Tuscan and Umbrian countryside worth poking about in.

Digging Deeper

Those who know Italy or simply want to 'specialise' a little could devote three or four weeks to one or two regions. Sicily, for example, offers plenty. You could do a circuit taking in Palermo then heading east to

Cefalù, the Aeolian Islands (where you could easily chew up a week alone), Taormina, Etna, Siracuse, Ragusa, Agrigento, Trapani (for the Egadi Islands), Erice and the Riserva Naturale dello Zingaro. Speedy travellers can accomplish this in less time and add in the villages and hill country of the interior – a world little observed by foreigners. Another area to consider for a concentrated visit is Campania. Basing yourself in Italy's fascinating southern metropolis, Naples (itself worthy of several days' investigation), you could easily spend a week or two taking in the wonders of Mt Vesuvius; the ancient cities of Pompeii, Herculaneum and, farther south, Paestum; the captivating islands of Capri, Ischia and Procida; the seaside resort of Sorrento and the dazzling Amalfi Coast; and the regal town of Caserta.

A 'Grand Tour'

Those with a month or more have unlimited options. Backpackers often wander into the north of Italy from France and make their way south to Brindisi to catch a boat on to the next obvious destination – the Greek isles. You might begin with some exploration of the Ligurian coast, including chic Portofino and the charming Cinque Terre, then head eastward for Bologna and on to Venice. Or you could simply maintain a straightforward south-easterly course. This would allow you to take in Pisa, Florence, Siena, Perugia, perhaps some excursions in the Tuscan and Umbrian countryside, Rome and Naples, before cutting east across to Brindisi and the ferries for Greece.

PLANNING

When to Go

The best time to visit Italy is from April to June, when prices are lower and competition from other tourists is not as great. Late July and August is the time to avoid Italy – the weather boils, prices are inflated and the whole country swarms with holidaymakers. Most Italians go on holiday in the month of August, abandoning the cities (and leaving many shops, hotels and restaurants closed) and packing out the coastal and mountain resorts.

July and September are the best month for walking in the Alps and Apennines. Lik everywhere else, walking trails and *rifug* (mountain huts) are crowded in August During these months the weather is gener ally good although you should always allov for cold snaps. Rifugi are usually open fron late June to the end of September for walk ers, and at Easter (March/April) for skiers

Italy's southern regions can be mild i winter but you shouldn't bank on it as freez ing conditions, heavy rain and snow ca prevail, especially inland. Your best chanc of mild weather in winter is on Sicily o Sardinia, although even on these island cast-iron guarantees are impossible.

You may prefer to organise your trip o itinerary to coincide with one or more of th many festivals that litter the Italian calenda (see Special Events later in this chapter).

What Kind of Trip

Virtually any kind of trip is possible in Italy and what you decide on will depend on you budget, time, how well you know the country and whether or not you have specific interests. The top tourist cities (such as Rome Venice and Florence) are popular destinations for short excursions from Europe – many travel agencies and companies offe travel-and-accommodation packages fo this kind of weekend break. In winter, you can get some great deals.

The budget traveller could spend months slowly touring around the whole country using local transport and sticking to *ostelli per la gioventù* (youth hostels) and basic pensiones (small hotels). Those with less time might prefer instead to concentrate on a single region (Tuscany or the island of Sicily, for instance) or make up an itinerary taking in some of the great cities. Having your own vehicle is a great advantage, allowing you to explore off-the-beaten-track places – and Italy is great motorcycling country.

Skiers often spend a week or two in the mountains of northern Italy and pretty much ignore the rest of the country.

There is no shortage of possibilities if you fancy an organised tour. They reduce hassle but can be restricting and pricey (see Organised Tours in the Getting There & Away chapter). Some tours are theme-based, such as art tours or cookery courses in rural Italy. Another approach is to undertake language and culture courses in cities such as Perugia and Florence and fit in travel around study (for some ideas see Courses later in this chapter).

Maps

Small-Scale Maps Michelin has a series of good fold-out country maps. No 988 (€6.20) covers the whole country on a scale of 1:1,000,000. You could also consider the series of area maps (€6.20 each) at 1:400,000 – Nos 428 to 431 cover the mainland, 432 covers Sicily and 433 Sardinia. The Touring Club Italiano (TCI) publishes a decent map (€5.20) covering Italy, Switzerland and Slovenia at 1:800,000.

Road Atlases If you are driving around Italy, the AA's *Big Road Atlas – Italy*, available in the UK for UK£9.99, is scaled at 1:250,000 and includes 39 town maps. Pretty much as good is Michelin's *Tourist and Motoring Atlas Italy*, which is scaled at 1:300,000, has 78 town maps and retails for UK£9.95 (available in Italy for about €16).

In Italy, the Istituto Geografico de Agostini publishes a comprehensive *Atlante Turistico Stradale d'Italia* (1:250,000), which includes 145 city maps, for €20.20. TCI publishes an *Atlante Stradale d'Italia* (1:200,000) divided into three parts – Nord, Centro and Sud (€17.55 each). It also publishes *Autoatlante d'Italia* (€20.20), a road/street directory for the whole country which includes 206 city maps on a scale of 1:1,350,000.

City Maps The city maps in this book, combined with tourist office maps, are generally adequate. More detailed maps are available in Italy at good bookshops (such as Feltrinelli, which has branches throughout the country) or newsstands. Excellent city plans and maps are published by de Agostini, TCI and Michelin. Other decent city-map publishers include FMB (with the yellow covers) and Milan's Vincitorio Editore. TCI publishes *200 Piante di Città* (€10.50), a handy book of street plans covering pretty much any city whose layout might otherwise be a source of confusion.

Lonely Planet publish a *Rome City Map* for UK£3.99.

Walking Maps Maps of walking trails in the Alps and Apennines are available in major bookshops in Italy, but the best by far are the TCI bookshops. Otherwise, you can usually locate maps of specific zones once you are in the area.

The best walking maps are the 1:25,000 scale series published by Tabacco (they mainly cover the north). Kompass publishes 1:25,000 scale maps of various parts of Italy, as well as a 1:50,000 series and several in other scales (including one at 1:7500 of Capri). Edizioni Multigraphic Florence produces a series of walking maps concentrating mainly on the Apennines. All of these maps cost from around €5.20 to €6.30.

The series of *Guide dei Monti d'Italia*, grey hardbacks published by the TCI and Club Alpino Italiano, are exhaustive walking guides with maps.

What to Bring

Pack as little as possible. A backpack is an advantage since petty thieves prey on the luggage-laden tourists with no free hands. Backpacks whose straps and openings can be zipped inside a flap are less awkward and more secure than the standard ones.

Suitcases with wheels or trolleys may be fine in airports but otherwise you won't get

JANE SMITH

far on foot with them. If you must carry a suitcase/bag, make sure it's lightweight and not too big. Remember that most everyday necessities can be found easily in Italy.

A small pack (with a lock) for day trips and sightseeing is preferable to a handbag or shoulder bag, especially in the southern cities where motorcycle bandits are particularly active.

Clothes Except in the mountains, Italy is uniformly hot in summer but variable in winter. In most areas, during the months of July and August a light jacket will do for cool evenings. In winter you will need a heavy coat, hat, gloves and scarf for the north, while a lined raincoat will do on Sicily. Rome has a mild climate, so you will need heavy woollens in January/February only.

Italians dress up just to do the daily food shopping, so if you plan to hang around in cafes and bars or enjoy some of the nightlife you'll feel more comfortable with a set of casually dressy clobber.

You'll need a pair of hardy, comfortable walking shoes with rubber soles. Trainers are fine except for going out, so something a little more presentable, though practical, might cover all bases.

People planning to walk in the Alps should bring the necessary clothing and equipment, in particular a pair of walking boots (lightweight and waterproof). Even in mid-summer you will need warm clothing on long walks or if you plan to go to high altitudes on cable cars – even if it's sweltering in the valley, the temperature can drop to below 0°C at 3000m. Inexperienced walkers should check with a local mountaineering group for a list of essentials before leaving home. Otherwise, the list provided in the Walking in the Dolomites section of the Trentino-Alto Adige chapter should be adequate.

Unless you plan to spend large sums in dry-cleaners and laundrettes, it's wise to pack a portable clothesline. Many pensiones and hotels ask guests not to wash clothes in the room, but such rules are rarely enforced.

Useful Items As well as any special personal needs, consider the following:

- under-the-clothes money belt or shoulder wallet, useful for protecting your money and documents in cities
- towel and soap, which aren't always available in cheap accommodation
- small Italian dictionary and/or phrasebook
- Swiss army knife
- medical kit (see Health later in this chapter)
- adapter plug for electrical appliances
- padlock(s) to secure your luggage to racks and to close hostel lockers
- sleeping sheet to save on sheet rental costs if you're using youth hostels (a sleeping bag is unnecessary unless you're camping)
- torch (flashlight)
- alarm clock
- sunglasses and a hat
- universal sink plug

RESPONSIBLE TOURISM

When visiting sites such as Pompeii or the Greek temples at Paestum, Agrigento and Selinunte, every care should be taken to minimise your impact on these precious reminders of the world's ancient heritage. Clambering all over walls and handling objects all help speed decay. By leaving things alone, you do your little bit to help preserve them. The sheer volume of people visiting these places is already problematic – in Venice it has been suggested that some sort of restriction should be placed on the number of visitors entering the city on any one day.

If you plan to climb volcanoes or walk on isolated mountain paths, always stick to designated trails and follow instructions. They are there not only for your own safety but also to preserve the unique natural environment.

Forest fires are an annual problem during the Italian summer. When outdoors, be extremely careful with cigarettes, glass bottles and other potential causes of fire.

Don't use flash when photographing art works in museums, churches and so on. The burst of light can damage the art.

Respect for tradition and religion is deeply rooted in Italy, especially in the south, so be sure to show the proper decorum when visiting churches. If you must talk in churches, do so in a whisper so as not to disturb those who have come to pray.

The moral of the story is treat the monuments and works of art, the towns and their people as you would your own prized possessions. Tread softly and with respect.

TOURIST OFFICES

Local Tourist Offices

The quality of tourist offices in Italy varies dramatically. One office might have enthusiastic staff but no useful printed information, while indifferent and even hostile staff in another might keep a gold mine of brochures hidden under the counter.

Three tiers of tourist office exist: regional, provincial and local. The names of tourist boards are different throughout the country but they all offer roughly the same services.

Regional offices are generally concerned with promotion, planning, budgeting and other projects far removed from the daily concerns of the humble tourist. Provincial offices are known either as the Ente Provinciale per il Turismo (EPT) or, more commonly, as the Azienda di Promozione Turistica (APT), and usually have information on both the province and the town. Local offices generally have information only about the town you're in and go by various names. Increasingly common is Informazioni e Assistenza ai Turisti (IAT) but you may also come across Azienda Autonoma di Soggiorno e Turismo (AAST) offices. These are the places to go if you want specific information about bus routes, museum opening times and so on.

In many small towns and villages, the local tourist office is called a Pro Loco. These are often similar to the IAT or AAST offices but on occasion are little more than a meeting place for the local elderly men.

Most EPT, APT and AAST offices will respond to written and telephone requests for information about hotels, apartments for rent and so on.

Tourist offices are generally open 8.30am to 12.30pm or 1pm and 3pm to around 7pm Monday to Friday. Hours are usually extended in summer, when some offices also open on Saturday or Sunday.

Information booths at most major train stations (and some smaller stations) tend to keep similar hours but in some cases operate only in summer. Staff can usually provide a *pianta della città* (map), *elenco degli alberghi* (list of hotels) and *informazioni sulle attrazioni turistiche* (information on the major sights). Many will help you find a hotel.

English, and sometimes French or German, is spoken at tourist offices in larger towns and major tourist areas. German is, of course, spoken in Alto Adige. Printed information is generally provided in a variety of languages.

If you are arriving in Rome, you can obtain limited information about the major destinations throughout the country from the APT office (☎ 06 488 99 253, fax 06 488 99 228), Via Parigi 11, 00185 Rome, and at the headquarters of Italy's national tourist office, Ente Nazionale Italiano per il Turismo (ENIT; ☎ 06 4 97 11, fax 06 446 33 79, w www.enit.it), Via Marghera 2, 00185 Rome. Both offices are near Rome's central train station.

The addresses and telephone numbers of local, provincial and some useful regional tourist offices are listed under towns and cities throughout this book.

Tourist Offices Abroad

Information on Italy is available from the Italian State Tourist Office in the following countries.

Australia
(☎ 02-9262 1666, e enitour@ihug.com.au) Level 26, 44 Market Street, Sydney 2000

Austria
(☎ 0900-970 228, e enit-wien@aon.at) Kaerntnerring 4, A-1010 Wien

Canada
(☎ 416-925 4882, e enit.canada@on.aibn.com) Suite 907, South Tower, 17 Bloor Street East, Toronto, Ontario M4W 3R8

France
(☎ 01 42 66 03 96, e enit.parigi@wanadoo.fr) 23 Rue de La Paix, 75002 Paris

Germany
Berlin: (☎ 030-247 83 97, e enit-berlin@t-online.de) Karl Liebknecht Strasse 34, 10178 Berlin
Munich: (☎ 089-531 317, e enit-muenchen@t-online.de) Goethestrasse 20, 80336 Munich

Frankfurt: (☎ 069-259 126, ⓔ enit.ffm@t-online.de) Kaiserstrasse 65, 60329 Frankfurt

Netherlands
(☎ 020-616 82 44, ⓔ enitams@wirehub.nl) Stadhouderskade 2, Amsterdam 1054 ES

Spain
(☎ 091-559 97 50, ⓔ italiaturismo@retemail.es) Gran Via 84, Edificio Espagna 1-1, Madrid 28013

Switzerland
(☎ 01-2117917, ⓔ enit@bluewin.ch) Uraniastrasse 32, 8001 Zurich

UK
(☎ 020-7355 1557, ⓔ enitlond@globalnet.co.uk) 1 Princess St, London W1R 9AY

USA
Chicago: (☎ 312-644 0996, ⓔ enitch@italiantourism.com) 500 North Michigan Avenue, Suite 2240, Chicago, IL 60611
Los Angeles: (☎ 310-820 1898, ⓔ enitla@earthlink.net) 12400 Wilshire Blvd, Suite 550, Los Angeles, CA 90025
New York: (☎ 212-245 4822, ⓔ enitny@italiantourism.com) 630 Fifth Avenue, Suite 1565, New York, NY 10111

VISAS & DOCUMENTS

Passport

Citizens of European Union (EU) member states can travel to Italy with their national identity cards alone. People from countries that do not issue ID cards, such as the UK, must carry a valid passport. All non-EU nationals must have a full valid passport.

If you've had the passport for a while, check that the expiry date is at least some months off, otherwise you may not be granted a visa (if you need one). If you travel a lot, keep an eye on the number of pages you have left in the passport. US consulates will generally insert extra pages into your passport if you need them, but others tend to require you to apply for a new passport.

If your passport is stolen or lost while in Italy, notify the police and obtain a statement, and then contact your embassy or consulate as soon as possible.

The only time you are likely to have your passport stamped is when you arrive by air – although even at Rome's airport there's a good chance they won't stamp it. If you are entering Italy for any reason other than tourism or if you plan to remain in the country for an extended period, you should insist on having the entry stamp. Without it you could encounter problems when trying to obtain a *permesso di soggiorno* – in effect, permission to remain in the country for a nominated period – which is essential for everything from enrolling at a language school to applying for residency (see Permesso di Soggiorno later).

Visas

Italy is among the 15 countries that have signed the Schengen Convention, an agreement whereby all EU member countries (except the UK and Ireland) plus Iceland and Norway agreed to abolish checks at common borders. Legal residents of one Schengen country do not require a visa for another Schengen country. Citizens of the UK and Ireland are also exempt from visa requirements for Schengen countries. Nationals of a number of other countries, including Canada, Japan, New Zealand and Switzerland, do not require visas for tourist visits of up to 90 days to any Schengen country.

Various other nationals not covered by the Schengen exemption can also spend up to 90 days in Italy without a visa. These include Australian, Israeli and US citizens. If you are a citizen of a country not mentioned in this section, you should check whether you need a visa with an Italian consulate.

The standard tourist visa issued by Italian consulates is the Schengen visa, valid for up to 90 days. A Schengen visa issued by one Schengen country is generally valid for travel in other Schengen countries. However, individual Schengen countries may impose additional restrictions on certain nationalities. It is therefore worth checking visa regulations with the consulate of each Schengen country you plan to visit.

It's now mandatory that you apply for a Schengen visa in your country of residence. You can apply for no more than two Schengen visas in any 12-month period and they are not renewable inside Italy. If you are going to visit more than one Schengen country, you are supposed to apply for the visa at a consulate of your main destination country or the first country you intend to visit.

EU citizens do not require any permits to live or work in Italy. They are, however, required to register with a *questura* (police station) if they take up residence and obtain a permesso di soggiorno (see the following section).

Permesso di Soggiorno If you plan to stay at the same address for more than one week you are technically obliged to report to the questura to receive a *permesso di soggiorno* (permit to remain in the country). Tourists who are staying in hotels are not required to do this as hotel owners are required to register all guests with the police.

A permesso di soggiorno only becomes a necessity if you plan to study, work (legally) or live in Italy. Obtaining one is never a pleasant experience. It involves enduring long queues and the frustration of finally arriving at the counter to find that you don't have all the necessary documents.

The exact requirements, such as specific documents and official stamps *(marche da bollo)*, can change from year to year. In general, you will need: a valid passport, containing a visa stamp indicating your date of entry into Italy; a special visa issued in your own country if you are planning to study; four passport-style photographs; and proof of your ability to support yourself financially.

It is best to go to the questura to obtain precise information on what is required. Sometimes there is a list posted, otherwise you will need to join a queue at the information counter.

The main Rome questura, in Via Genova, is notorious for delays and best avoided if possible. This problem has been solved by decentralisation: in Rome it is now possible to apply at the *ufficio stranieri* (foreigners' bureau) of the police station closest to where you are staying.

Work Permits Non-EU citizens wishing to work in Italy will need to obtain a *permesso di lavoro* (work permit). If you intend to work for an Italian company, the company must organise the permesso and forward it to the Italian consulate in your country – only then will you be issued an appropriate visa.

If non-EU citizens intend to work for a non-Italian company or will be paid in foreign currency or wish to go freelance, they must organise the visa and permesso in their country of residence through an Italian consulate. This process can take many months, so look into it early.

In any case it's advisable to seek detailed information from an Italian embassy or consulate on the exact requirements before attempting to organise a legitimate job in Italy. Many foreigners don't bother with such formalities, preferring to work 'black' in areas such as teaching English, bar work and seasonal jobs. See Work later in this chapter for details.

Study Visas Non-EU citizens who want to study at a university or language school in Italy must have a study visa. These visas can be obtained from your nearest Italian embassy or consulate. You will normally require confirmation of your enrolment, proof of payment of fees and the adequate funds to support yourself before a visa is issued. The visa will then cover only the period of the enrolment. This type of visa is renewable within Italy but, again, only with confirmation of ongoing enrolment and proof that you are able to support yourself (bank statements are preferred).

Travel Insurance

Don't leave home without it! It will cover you for medical expenses, luggage theft or loss, and for cancellation of and delays in your travel arrangements. Cover depends on your insurance and type of ticket, so ask both your insurer and ticket-issuing agency to explain where you stand. Ticket loss is also covered by travel insurance but keep a separate record of your ticket details (see Copies later). Buy travel insurance as early as possible. If you buy it the week before you fly or hop on the bus, you may find, for example, that you are not covered for delays to your trip caused by industrial action.

Paying for your ticket with a credit card can often provide limited travel accident insurance and you may be able to reclaim the payment if the operator doesn't deliver. Ask your credit card company what it will cover.

Driving Licence & Permits

If you plan to drive while in Italy, you will need to carry your driver's licence. Those driving their own vehicles will need to carry the vehicle's papers and insurance.

See Paperwork & Preparations under Car & Motorcycle in the Getting There & Away chapter for more details.

Hostel Card

A valid HI (Hostelling International) hostelling card is required in all associated youth hostels (Associazione Italiana Alberghi per la Gioventù; AIG) in Italy. You can get this in your home country or at the youth hostel in Rome. In the latter case you apply for the card and must collect six stamps in the card at €2.60 each. You pay for a stamp on each of the first six nights you spend in the hostel. With six stamps you are considered a full international member.

HI has a Web site at Ⓦ www.iyhf.org.

Student & Youth Cards

An ISIC (International Student Identity Card) or similar card will get you discounted admission into some museums and other sights and is an asset for other purposes. It can help for cheap flights out of Italy and can also come in handy for such things as cinemas, theatres and travel discounts. Similar cards are available to teachers (ITIC). They are good for various discounts and also carry a travel insurance component.

If you're aged under 26 but aren't a student, you can apply for a Euro<26 card, which gives much the same discounts as ISIC.

These student cards are issued by student unions, hostelling organisations and some youth travel agencies (such as Usit Campus in the UK). They don't always automatically entitle you to discounts but you won't find out until you flash the card.

In Rome, the office of the Centro Turistico Studentesco e Giovanile (CTS) will issue these (ISIC, ITIC and Euro<26) cards.

Copies

All important documents (passport data page and visa page, credit cards, travel insurance policy, air/bus/train tickets, driving licence and so on) should be photocopied before you leave home. Leave one copy with someone at home and keep another with you, separate from the originals.

It's also a good idea to store details of your vital travel documents in Lonely Planet's free online Travel Vault in case you lose the photocopies. Your password-protected Travel Vault is accessible online anywhere in the world – create it at Ⓦ www.ekno.lonelyplanet.com.

EMBASSIES & CONSULATES

Italian Embassies & Consulates

The following is a selection of Italian diplomatic missions abroad. Bear in mind that Italy maintains consulates in additional cities in many of the countries listed here:

Italian Embassies & Consulates Abroad

Italian diplomatic missions abroad include

Australia

Embassy: (☎ 02-6273 3333, fax 6273 4223, Ⓔ embassy@ambitalia.org.au, Ⓦ www.ambitalia.org.au) 12 Grey St, Deakin, ACT 2600

Consulate: (☎ 02-9392 7900, fax 9252 4830, Ⓔ itconsydn@itconsyd.org) Level 43, The Gateway, 1 Macquarie Place, Sydney, NSW 2000

Consulate: (☎ 03-9867 5744, fax 9866 3932, Ⓔ itconmel@netlink.com.au) 509 St Kilda Rd, Melbourne, VIC 3004

Austria

Embassy: (☎ 01-712 5121, fax 713 9719, Ⓔ ambitalviepress@via.at) Metternichgasse 13, Vienna 1030

Canada

Embassy: (☎ 613-232 2401, fax 233 1484, Ⓦ www.italyincanada.com) 21st Floor, 275 Slater St, Ottawa, Ontario KIP 5H9

Consulate: (☎ 604-684 7288, fax 685 4263, Ⓔ consolato@italianconsulate.bc.ca) Standard Building #1100, 510 West Hastings St, Vancouver, BC V6B 1L8

rance
Embassy: (☎ 01 49 54 03 00, fax 45 49 35 81, e ambasciata@amb-italie.fr) 47 Rue de Varenne, Paris 75007

reland
Embassy: (☎ 01-660 1744, fax 668 2759, e italianembassy@eircom.net, w http://homepage.eircom.net/~italianembassy) 63–65 Northumberland Rd, Dublin

letherlands
Embassy: (☎ 070-302 1030, fax 361 4932, e italemb@worldonline.nl, w www.italy.nl) Alexanderstraat 12, The Hague 2514 JL

lew Zealand
Embassy: (☎ 04-473 53 39, fax 472 72 55, e ambwell@xtra.co.nz) 34 Grant Rd, Thorndon, Wellington

witzerland
Embassy: (☎ 031-352 41 51, fax 351 1026, e ambital.berna@spectraweb.ch, w www3.itu.int/embassy/italy) Elfenstrasse 14, Bern 3006

JK
Embassy: (☎ 020-7312 2200, fax 7312 2230, e emblondon@embitaly.org.uk, w www.embitaly.org.uk) 14 Three Kings Yard, London
Consulate: (☎ 0131-226 3631, fax 226 6260, e consedimb@consedimb.demon.co.uk) 32 Melville Street, Edinburgh EH3 7H

JSA
Embassy: (☎ 202-612 4400, fax 518 2154, e stampa@itwash.org, w www.italyemb.org) 1601 Fuller St, NW Washington DC 20009
Consulate: (☎ 212-7737 9100, fax 249 4945, e italconsulnyc@italconsulnyc.org, w www.italconsulnyc.org) 690 Park Ave, New York 10021
Consulate: (☎ 213-826 6207, fax 820 0727, e cglos@conlang.com, w www.conlang.com) Suite 300, 12400 Wilshire Blvd, Los Angeles 90025

Embassies & Consulates in Italy

t's important to realise what your embassy – the embassy of the country of which you are a citizen – can and cannot do to help you.

Generally speaking, it won't be much help in emergencies if the trouble you're in is even remotely your own fault. Remember that you are bound by the laws of the country you are in. Your embassy will not be sympathetic to your cause if you end up in a foreign jail after committing a crime locally.

In genuine emergencies you might get some assistance but only if other channels have been exhausted. For example, if you need to get home urgently, a free ticket is exceedingly unlikely – the embassy would expect you to have insurance. If you have all your money and documents stolen, it might assist with getting a new passport but not with a loan for onward travel.

The following is a list of embassies (all in Rome) and consulates (in major cities).

Australia
Embassy: (☎ 06 85 27 21) Via Alessandria 215, 00198 Rome
Consulate: (☎ 02 77 70 41, toll free ☎ 800 87 77 80, e australian-consulate-general@austrade.gov.au, MM1 San Babila) 3rd Floor, Via Borgogna 2, 20122 Milan

Austria
Embassy: (☎ 06 844 01 41) Via Pergolesi 3, 00198 Rome
Consulate: (☎ 02 481 20 66) Via Tranquillo Cremona 27, 20145 Milan

Canada
Embassy: (☎ 06 44 59 81) Via G B de Rossi 27, 00161 Rome
Consulate: (☎ 02 6 75 81, e milan-cs@dfait-maeci.gc.ca, w www.canada.it, MM2/3 Centrale FS) Via Vittorio Pisani 19, 20124 Milan

France
Embassy: (☎ 06 68 60 11) Piazza Farnese, 00186 Rome
Consulate: (☎ 06 688 02 152) Via Giulia 251, 00186 Rome
Consulate: (☎ 02 655 91 41) Via C Mangile 1, 20121 Milan
Consulate: (☎ 081 761 22 75) Piazza della Repubblica 2, 80122 Naples
Consulate: (☎ 041 522 43 19) Ramo del Pestrin, Castello 6140, Venice
Consulate: (☎ 010 247 63 27 or 010 247 63 40) Via Garibaldi 20, 16124 Genoa
Consulate: (☎ 011 573 23 11) Via Roma 366, 10123 Turin

Germany
Embassy: (☎ 06 49 21 31) Via San Martino della Battaglia 4, 00185 Rome
Consulate: (☎ 055 29 47 22) Lungarno Amerigo Vespucci 30, 50123 Florence
Consulate: (☎ 02 623 11 01) Via Solferino 40, 20121 Milan
Consulate: (☎ 081 61 33 93) Via Francesco Crispi 69, 80121 Naples
Consulate: (☎ 041 523 76 75) Campo Sant'Angelo 3816, San Marco, Venice

Consulate: (☎ 010 545 19 13) Via San Vincenzo 4/28, 16121 Genoa
Consulate: (☎ 011 53 10 88) Corso Vittorio Emanuele II 98, 10121 Turin

Ireland
Embassy: (☎ 06 697 91 21) Piazza Campitelli 3, 00186 Rome
Consulate: (☎ 02 551 87 569) Piazza F Pietro in Gessate 2, 20122 Milan

Netherlands
Embassy: (☎ 06 322 11 41) Via Michele Mercati 8, 00197 Rome
Consulate: (☎ 081 551 30 03) Via Agostino Depretis 114, 80133 Naples
Consulate: (☎ 091 58 15 21) Via Roma 489, 90139 Palermo
Consulate: (☎ 02 485 58 41, e nlgovmil@iol.it, MM1 Conciliazione) Via San Vittore 45, 20123 Milan
Consulate: (☎ 010 56 68 38) Viale Sauli 4, 16121 Genoa

New Zealand
Embassy: (☎ 06 441 71 71) Via Zara 28, 00198 Rome
Consulate: (☎ 02 480 12 544, fax 02 480 12 577, e milano@tradenz.govt.nz) Via Guido d'Arezzo 6, 20145 Milan

Switzerland
Embassy: (☎ 06 80 95 71) Via Barnarba Oriani 61, 00197 Rome
Consulate: (☎ 055 22 24 34) Piazzale Galileo 5, 50125 Florence
Consulate: (☎ 02 777 91 61) Via Palestro 2, 20121 Milan
Consulate: (☎ 081 761 45 33) Via Pergolesi 1, 80122 Naples

UK
Embassy: (☎ 06 482 54 41) Via XX Settembre 80a, 00187 Rome
Consulate: (☎ 055 28 41 33, fax 055 21 91 12) Lungarno Corsini 2, 50123 Florence
Consulate: (☎ 02 72 30 01, fax 02 720 20 153) Via S Paolo 7, 20121 Milan
Consulate: (☎ 081 66 35 11, fax 081 761 37 20) Via dei Mille 40, 80121 Naples
Consulate: (☎ 041 522 72 07, fax 041 522 26 17) Palazzo Querini, Dorsoduro 1051, 30123 Venice
Consulate: (☎ 011 650 92 02, e timp@teleion.it, w www.grbr.it) Via Saluzzo 60, 10125 Turin
Consulate: (☎ 010 41 68 28) Via di Francia 28, Genoa

USA
Embassy: (☎ 06 467 41, w www.usis.it) Via Vittorio Veneto 119a–121, 00187 Rome
Consulate: (☎ 055 239 82 76) Lungarno Amerigo Vespucci 38, 50123 Florence
Consulate: (☎ 02 29 03 51) Largo Donegani Milan
Consulate: (☎ 081 583 81 11) Piazza della Repubblica, 80122 Naples
Consulate: (☎ 091 30 58 57) Via Vaccarini 90141 Palermo
Consulate: (☎ 010 58 44 92) Via Dante 2/43 16121 Genoa

For other foreign embassies in Rome and consulates in other cities, look under 'Ambasciate' or 'Consolati' in the telephone directory. Alternatively, tourist offices generally have a list.

CUSTOMS

There is no limit on the amount of euros brought into the country. Goods brought in and exported within the EU incur no additional taxes, provided duty has been paid somewhere within the EU and the goods are for personal consumption.

Duty-free sales within the EU no longer exist. Visitors coming into Italy from non-EU countries can import, duty free, 1L of spirits, 2L wine, 60mL perfume, 250mL eau de toilette, 200 cigarettes and other goods up to a total of €175.50; anything over this limit must be declared on arrival and the appropriate duty paid.

MONEY

Currency

On 1 January 2002, the euro became the currency of cash transactions in all of Italy (including the Vatican City and the Republic of San Marino) and throughout the EU (except for the three foot-draggers: Denmark, Sweden and the UK).

Euro coins and notes were introduced into Italy on 1 January 2002. For two months lire and euros will circulate side by side and lire can be exchanged for euros free of charge at banks. From 28 February 2002, the euro will be Italy's sole currency. Banks will still accept lira for ten years beyond that date, but will only issue euros. During the transition period, you can pay for goods and services in either euros or lire, and change will be given in both currencies.

The euro is divided into 100 cents. Coin denominations are one, two, five, 10, 20 and 50 cents, €1 and €2. The notes are €5, €10, €20, €50, €100, €200 and €500.

All euro coins across the EU are identical on the side showing their value, but there are 12 different obverses, each representing one of the 12 euro-zone countries. All euro notes of each denomination are identical on both sides. All euro coins and notes are legal tender throughout the euro zone.

Once euro notes and coins are issued in 2002, you won't need to change money at all when travelling to other single-currency members and prices in the member states will be immediately comparable. Banks may still charge a handling fee (yet to be decided) for travellers cheques but they won't be able to profit by buying the currency from you at one rate and selling it back to you at another. And even EU countries not participating in the single currency may price goods in euros and accept euros over shop counters.

For more information check out the euro section of the European Union Web site at **w** www.europa.eu.int/euro.

Exchange Rates

country	unit		euro
Australia	A$1	=	€0.55
Canada	C$1	=	€0.70
Japan	¥100	=	€0.90
New Zealand	NZ$1	=	€0.45
UK	UK£1	=	€1.60
USA	USA$1	=	€1.10

Exchanging Money

You can change money in banks, at the post office or in a *cambio* (exchange office). Banks are generally the most reliable and tend to offer the best rates. However, you should look around and ask about commission. This can fluctuate considerably and a lot depends on whether you are changing cash or cheques.

While the post office charges a flat rate of €0.60 per cash transaction, banks charge at least €1.55 or more. Travellers cheques attract higher fees. Some banks charge €0.50 per cheque with a €1.55 minimum, while

Prices Quoted

This book was researched during the transition period, when not all prices were available in euros. Prices quoted (for example, by hotels, restaurants and entertainment venues) in the national currency have been converted to euros at the fixed conversion rate (€1 is equal to 1936.27L). These may undergo further change as the euro comes into use.

the post office charges a maximum €2.55 per transaction. Other banks will have different arrangements again, and in all cases you should compare the exchange rates. Exchange booths often advertise 'no commission' but the rate of exchange can often be inferior to that in the banks.

The desire to save on such fees by making occasional large transactions should be balanced against a healthy fear of pickpockets – you don't want to be robbed the day you have exchanged a huge hunk of money to last you weeks!

Cash There is little advantage in bringing foreign cash into Italy. True, exchange commissions are often lower than for travellers cheques but the danger of losing the lot far outweighs such petty gains.

Travellers Cheques These are a safe way to carry money and are easily cashed at banks and exchange offices throughout Italy. Always keep the bank receipt listing the cheque numbers separate from the cheques themselves, and keep a list of the numbers of those you have already cashed – this will reduce problems in the event of loss or theft. Check the conditions applying to such circumstances before buying the cheques.

If you buy your travellers cheques in euros, you should not be charged commission when cashing them. Most hard currencies are widely accepted, although you may have occasional trouble with the New Zealand dollar. Buying cheques in a third currency (such as US dollars if you are not coming from the USA), means you pay commission when you buy the cheques and again when cashing them in Italy. Try to get most of the cheques in largish denominations so you can save on per-cheque exchange charges.

Travellers using the better known travellers cheques (such as Visa, American Express and Thomas Cook) will have little trouble in Italy. American Express, in particular, has offices in all the major Italian cities and agents in many smaller cities. If you lose your American Express cheques, call toll free ☎ 800 872 000 (24 hours). For Thomas Cook or MasterCard cheques call ☎ 800 872 050 and for Visa cheques call ☎ 800 874 155.

Take along your passport when you go to cash travellers cheques.

Credit/Debit Cards & ATMs Carrying plastic (whether a credit or debit card) is the simplest way to organise your holiday funds. You don't have large amounts of cash or cheques to lose, you can get money after hours and on weekends and the exchange rate is better than that offered for travellers cheques or cash exchanges. By arranging for payments to be made into your credit card account while you are travelling, you can avoid paying interest.

Major credit cards, such as Visa, MasterCard, Eurocard, Cirrus and Euro Cheques cards, are accepted throughout Italy. They can be used for many purchases (including in many supermarkets) and in hotels and restaurants (although pensiones and smaller trattorias and pizzerias still tend to accept cash only).

Credit cards can also be used in ATMs *(bancomat)* displaying the appropriate sign or (if you have no PIN number) to obtain cash advances over the counter in many banks – Visa and MasterCard are among the most widely recognised for such transactions. Check what charges you will incur with your bank.

It is possible to use your own ATM debit card in machines throughout Italy to obtain money from your own bank account. This is without doubt the simplest way to handle your money while travelling.

If an ATM rejects your card, don't despair or start wasting money on international calls to your bank. Try a few more ATMs displaying your credit card's logo before assuming the problem lies with your card rather than with the local system. Italian ATMs are notoriously fickle.

If your credit card is lost, stolen or swallowed by an ATM, you can telephone toll free to have an immediate stop put on its use. For MasterCard the number in Italy is ☎ 800 870 866 or make a reverse-charges call to St Louis in the USA on ☎ 314-275 66 90. For Visa, phone ☎ 800 877 232 in Italy.

American Express is also widely accepted (although not as common as Visa or MasterCard). American Express's full-service offices (such as in Rome and Milan) will issue new cards, usually within 24 hours and sometimes immediately, if yours has been lost or stolen. Some American Express offices have ATMs that you can use to obtain cash advances if you have made the necessary arrangements prior to travel.

The toll-free emergency number to report a lost or stolen American Express card varies according to where the card was issued. Check with American Express in your country or contact American Express in Rome on ☎ 06 7 22 82, which itself has a 24-hour cardholders' service.

International Transfers One reliable way to send money to Rome is by TT (Telegraphic Transfer) or swift transfer through the foreign office of a large Italian bank, or through major banks in your own country, to a nominated bank in Rome. It is important to have an exact record of all details associated with the money transfer, particularly the exact address of the Italian bank to where the money has been sent. The money will always be held at the head office of the bank in the town to which it has been sent. Urgent-telex transfers should take only a few days, while other means (such as telegraphic transfer or draft) can take weeks.

It is also possible to transfer money through American Express and Thomas Cook. You will be required to produce identification, usually a passport, in order to

ALAN BENSON

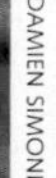

DAMIEN SIMONIS

ALAN BENSON

JOHN HAY

DOUG MCKINLAY

Unified by a strong sense of national pride, the Italians nevertheless remain a varied bunch, with their regional identities firmly rooted in a history that predates the unification of 1861.

BILL WASSMAN

The butchery business is booming in these parts.

ALAN BENSON

The best coffee in the world? Italians think so.

SALLY WEBB

Due cappucini? A cafe on Rome's Piazza Navona

SALLY WEBB

The nation's favourite sport: football Italia

DAMIEN SIMONIS

Quintessentially Italian: the Fiat 500

MARTIN MOOS

When in Rome, eat ice cream as the Romans do.

collect the money. It is also a good idea to take along the details of the transaction.

One of the speedier options is to send money through Western Union (toll free ☎ 800 01 38 39). Call the toll-free number for the address of the outlet (usually only in main cities) closest to you. The sender and receiver have to turn up at a Western Union outlet with passport or other form of ID. Fees charged for the virtually immediate transfer depend on the amount sent.

Security

Petty theft is a problem throughout Italy and tends to get worse the farther south you travel. Keep only a limited amount of your money as cash and the bulk in more easily replaceable forms, such as credit cards or travellers cheques. If your accommodation has a safe, use it. If you must leave money and documents in your room, divide the former into several stashes and hide them in different places. Lockable luggage is a good deterrent.

On the streets, keep as little on you as possible. The safest thing is a shoulder wallet or under-the-clothes money belt or pouch. External money belts tend to attract attention to your belongings rather than deflect it. If you eschew the use of any such device, keep money in your front pockets and watch out for people who seem to brush close to you. Teams of delinquents employ an infinite number of tricks whereby one distracts you and the other deftly empties your pockets. See Theft under Dangers & Annoyances later in this chapter for more advice.

Costs

Italy isn't cheap. Accommodation charges and high admission fees for many museums and monuments keep daily expenditure high. Prices also vary significantly between north and south (they are generally higher in the north), and between cities and provincial or rural areas. A *very* prudent backpacker might scrape by on around €40 to €45 per day, but only by staying in youth hostels, eating one simple meal per day (at the youth hostel), buying a sandwich or pizza slice for lunch, travelling slowly to keep transport costs down and minimising visits to museums and galleries.

One rung up, you can get by on €55 to €60 per day if you stay in the cheaper pensiones or small hotels and keep sit-down meals and museum visits to one per day. Lone travellers may find even this budget hard to maintain since single rooms tend to be pricey.

If money is no object, you'll find your niche in Italy. There's no shortage of luxury hotels, expensive restaurants and pricey shops. Realistically, a traveller wanting to stay in comfortable mid-range hotels, eat two square meals per day, not feel restricted to one museum visit per day and be able to enjoy the odd drink and other minor indulgences should reckon on a minimum daily average of between €100 to €130 – possibly more if you are driving.

A basic breakdown of costs per person during an average day for the budget to mid-range traveller could be: accommodation €13 (youth hostel) to €30 (single in a budget hotel or per person in a comfortable double), breakfast €1.50 to €2 (coffee and croissant), lunch (sandwich or pizza slice and mineral water) €3, bottle of mineral water €0.80, public transport (bus or underground railway in a major town) up to €3.10, entrance fee for one museum up to €6.20, sit-down dinner €8 to €18. On top of that you have to add transport (train/bus/ferry) between destinations.

Accommodation Budget travellers can save by staying in youth hostels (open to people of all ages) or camp sites. If you are travelling in a group and staying in pensiones or hotels, always ask for triples or quads. The cost per person drops the more people you have in a room. Avoid, where possible, pensiones and hotels that charge for a compulsory breakfast. A cappuccino and *cornetto* (croissant) at a bar cost less and are undoubtedly better.

If you plan to ski, it is usually cheaper to organise accommodation as part of a skiing package which offers a ski pass, accommodation and meals.

Food In Italian bars, prices can double (sometimes even triple) if you sit down and are served at the table. Stand at the bar to drink your coffee or eat a sandwich, or buy a slice of pizza and head for the nearest piazza.

Read the fine print on menus (usually posted outside eating establishments) to see if there's a *coperto* (cover charge) and *servizio* (service fee). These can make a big difference to the bill and it is best to avoid restaurants that charge both. Shop in markets and *alimentari* (grocery shops) for picnic lunches and the odd meal in your room. Steer clear of the 'touristy' food-and-drink kiosks in major cities: the 'fresh' food is rarely fresh and the mark-up is extortionate.

Travel If you're travelling by train and have time to spare, take a *regionale* or *diretto*: they are slower but cheaper than the Intercity trains, for which you have to pay a *supplemento* (supplement). It's best to travel overnight, if possible, to save on a night's accommodation. See the Getting Around chapter for information about the different types of trains and various discounts on train travel within Italy.

If you are catching a ferry in summer, travelling *passaggio ponte* (deck class) is cheapest.

In cities, where you need to use public transport a lot, buy a daily transport ticket.

Other Cost-Savers Aerograms (€0.45), on sale only at post offices, are the cheapest way to send international mail.

At museums, never hesitate to ask if there are discounts for students (you will be asked to produce an ISIC card to prove your student status), young people, children, families or the elderly. When sightseeing, where possible buy a *biglietto cumulativo*, a ticket that allows admission to a number of associated sights for less than the combined cost of separate admission fees. Details of such tickets are listed throughout the book; otherwise ask at the local tourist office.

Avoid buying food and drinks at service stations on the *autostrade* (motorways), where they can cost up to 30% more. Petrol also tends to be slightly more expensive on the autostrade.

Tipping & Bargaining

You are not expected to tip on top of restaurant service charges but it is common to leave a small amount, perhaps €0.60 per person. If there is no service charge, the customer might consider leaving a 10% tip but this is by no means obligatory. In bars, Italians often leave any small change as a tip, maybe only €0.05 or €0.10. Tipping taxi drivers is not common practice, but you are expected to tip the porter at top-end hotels.

Bargaining is common throughout Italy in flea markets but not in shops. At the Porta Portese market in Rome, for instance, don't hesitate to offer half the asking price for any given item. Don't be deterred by stallholders who dismiss you with a wave of the arm: the person at the next stall may well accept your offer after a brief (and obligatory) haggle. While bargaining in shops is not acceptable, you might find that the proprietor is disposed to give a discount if you are spending a reasonable amount of money.

It is quite acceptable (and advisable) to ask if there is a special price for a room in a pensione if you plan to stay for more than a few days.

Taxes & Refunds

A value-added tax of around 19%, known as IVA (Imposta di Valore Aggiunto), is slapped onto just about everything in Italy. If you are resident outside the EU and you spend more than €154.95 in the same shop on the same day, you can claim a refund on this tax when you leave the EU. The refund only applies to purchases from affiliated retail outlets which display a 'Tax free for tourists' sign. You have to complete a form at the point of sale, then get it stamped by Italian customs as you leave. At major airports you can then get an immediate cash refund; otherwise it will be refunded to your credit card. For information, pick up a pamphlet on the scheme from participating stores.

Receipts

Laws aimed at tightening controls on the payment of taxes in Italy mean that the onus is on the buyer to ask for and retain receipts for all goods and services. This applies to everything from a litre of milk to a haircut. Although it rarely happens, you could be asked by an officer of the Guardia di Finanza (Fiscal Police) to produce the receipt immediately after you leave a shop. If you don't have it, you may be obliged to pay a fine of up to €154.95.

POST & COMMUNICATIONS

Post

Italy's postal system is notoriously unreliable, although things look better today than they did a decade ago now that there is a more efficient (but also more expensive) *posta prioritaria* (priority mail) service for some domestic and all international mail. Ironically, the introduction of this additional service has reduced the demand on the regular mail system, which in turn is functioning better.

Stamps *(francobolli)* are available at post offices and authorised tobacconists (look for the official *tabacchi* sign: a big 'T', usually white on black). Since letters often need to be weighed, what you get at the tobacconist's for international air mail will occasionally be an approximation of the proper rate. Tobacconists keep regular shop hours.

Information about postal services can be obtained on ☎ 800 22 26 66 or online at W www.poste.it.

Postal Rates The cost of sending a letter air mail *(via aerea)* depends on its weight, destination and method of postage. For regular post, letters up to 20g cost €0.40 within Europe, €0.65 to the USA and €0.75 to Australia and New Zealand. Postcards cost the same.

However, very few people use the regular post anymore, preferring the slightly more expensive posta prioritaria, guaranteed to deliver letters sent to Europe within three days and to the rest of the world within four to eight days. Letters up to 20g sent posta prioritaria cost €0.60 within Europe, €0.75 to the Americas, Africa, Asia, Australia and New Zealand. Letters weighing 21–100g cost €1.25 within Europe, €1.55 to Africa, Asia and the Americas and €1.80 to Australia and New Zealand.

For more important items, use registered mail *(raccomandato)* – €2.60 on top of the normal cost of the letter – or insured mail *(assicurato)*, the cost of which depends on the value of the object being sent (€5.15 for objects up to €51.65 value). Insured mail is not available to the USA.

Sending Mail An air-mail letter can take up to two weeks to reach the UK or the USA, while a letter to Australia will take between two and three weeks. Postcards take even longer because they are classed as low-priority mail. Put them in an envelope and send them as letters.

Express Mail Urgent mail can be sent by *postacelere* (also known as CAI Post), the Italian post office's courier service. Letters up to 500g cost €15.50 in Europe, €23.75 to the USA and €35.10 to Australia. A parcel weighing 1kg will cost €17.55 in Europe, €27.90 to the USA and Canada, and €41.30 to Australia and New Zealand. CAI post is not necessarily as fast as private courier services. It will take one to three days for a parcel to reach European destinations and three to five days to reach the USA, Canada or Australia and. Ask at post offices for addresses of CAI post outlets or check out W www.postacelere.com.

Couriers Several international couriers operate in Italy: DHL ☎ 800 34 53 45 (24-hour toll free), Federal Express ☎ 800 83 30 40 (toll free) and UPS ☎ 800 82 20 54 (toll free). Look in the telephone book for addresses. Note that if you are having articles sent to you by courier in Italy, you might be obliged to pay IVA of up to 20% to retrieve the goods.

Receiving Mail Poste restante (general delivery) is known as *fermo posta* in Italy. Letters marked thus will be held at the counter of the same name in the main post office in the relevant town. Poste restante mail to Verona, for example, should be addressed as follows:

John SMITH,
Fermo Posta,
37100 Verona,
Italy

Postcodes are provided throughout this guide. You will need to pick up your letters in person and you must present your passport as ID.

American Express card or travellers cheque holders can use the free client mail-holding service at American Express offices throughout Italy. You can obtain a list of these from any American Expres office. Take your passport when you go to pick up mail.

Telephone

The state-run Telecom Italia is the largest telecommunications organisation in Italy and its orange public pay phones are liberally scattered about the country. The most common accept only telephone cards *(carte/schede telefoniche)*, although you will still find plenty that accept cards and coins. Some card phones accept credit cards. Among the latest generation of pay phones are those that also send faxes.

Telecom pay phones can be found in the streets, train stations and some big stores as well as in Telecom offices. Some of the latter are staffed and a few have telephone directories for other parts of the country. Where these offices are staffed, it is possible to make international calls and pay at the desk afterwards. Details of Telecom offices are included under Post & Communications throughout this book.

You can buy phonecards at post offices, tobacconists and newsstands and from vending machines in Telecom offices. To avoid the frustration of trying to find (fast-disappearing) coin telephones, always keep a phonecard on hand. They come with a value of €2.60, €5.15 or €25.80. You must break the top left-hand corner of the card before you can use it.

Public phones operated by the private telecommunications companies Infostrada and Albacom can be found in airports and stations. These phones accept Infostrada or Albacom phonecards (available from post offices, tobacconists and newspaper stands), which come with a value of €2.60 or €5.15. The rates are slightly cheaper than Telecom's for long-distance and international calls.

Emergency Numbers

Wherever you are in Italy, these are the numbers to ring in an emergency:

Ambulance (Ambulanza)	☎ 118
Fire Brigade (Vigili del Fuoco)	☎ 115
Highway Rescue (Soccorso Stradale)	☎ 116
Police (Carabinieri)	☎ 112
Police (Polizia)	☎ 113

Costs Rates, particularly for long-distance calls, are among the highest in Europe. The cheapest time for domestic calls is from 10pm to 8am. For international calls, off-peak hours are 10pm to 8am and all of Sunday.

A local call *(comunicazione urbana)* from a public phone will cost €0.10 for three to six minutes, depending on the time of day you call. Peak call times are 8am to 6.30pm Monday to Friday and 8am to 1pm on Saturday.

Rates for long-distance calls within Italy *(comunicazione interurbana)* depend on the time of day and the distance involved. At the worst, one minute will cost about €0.20 in peak periods.

If you need to call overseas, beware of the cost – even a call of less than five minutes to Australia after 10pm will cost around €3.80 from a private phone (more from a public phone). Calls to most European countries cost about €0.25 per minute, and closer to €0.60 from a public phone.

Travellers from countries that offer direct dialling services paid for at home-country rates (such as AT&T in the USA and Telstra in Australia) should think seriously about taking advantage of them.

Domestic Calls Telephone area codes all begin with 0 and consist of up to four digits. The area code is followed by a number of anything from four to eight digits.

Area codes are an integral part of all telephone numbers in Italy – even if you are calling within a single zone. So any number you're calling in Florence will start with 055, in Venice with 041, Naples 081 and Milan 02 regardless of whether you're in that place or in another part of Italy.

Mobile phone numbers begin with a three-digit prefix such as 330, 335, 347, 368 and so on.

Toll-free (free-phone) numbers are known as *numeri verdi* and usually start with 800. National call rate numbers start with 848 or 199.

For directory enquiries, dial ☎ 12.

International Calls Direct international calls can easily be made from public telephones by using a phonecard. Dial ☎ 00 to get out of Italy, then the relevant country and area codes, followed by the telephone number. Useful country codes are: Australia ☎ 61, Canada and the USA ☎ 1, New Zealand ☎ 64, and the UK ☎ 44. Codes for other countries in Europe include France ☎ 33, Germany ☎ 49, Greece ☎ 30, Ireland ☎ 353, and Spain ☎ 34. Other codes are listed in Italian telephone books.

To make a reverse charges (collect) international call from a public telephone, dial ☎ 170. For European countries dial ☎ 15. All operators speak English.

Easier, and often cheaper, is using the Country Direct service for your country. You dial the number and request a reverse charges call through the operator in your country. Numbers for this service include:

Australia (Optus)	☎ 172 11 61
Australia (Telstra)	☎ 172 10 61
Canada	☎ 172 10 01
France	☎ 172 00 33
New Zealand	☎ 172 10 64
UK	☎ 172 00 44
USA (AT&T)	☎ 172 10 11
USA (IDB)	☎ 172 17 77
USA (MCI)	☎ 172 10 22
USA (Sprint)	☎ 172 18 77

For international directory enquiries call ☎ 176.

Mobile Phones Italy has one of the highest levels of mobile phone penetration in Europe, and there are several companies through which you can get a temporary or prepaid account if you already own a GSM, dual- or tri-band cellular phone. You will usually just need your passport to open an account.

Both TIM (Telecom Italia Mobile) and Omnitel offer prepaid *(prepagato)* accounts for GSM phones (frequency 900 mHz), whereby you can buy a SIM card (€51.65) for either network which gives you €25.80 worth of calls. You can then top up the account with multiples of €25.80 (plus a €5.15 service fee) as required. There are TIM and Omnitel retail outlets in virtually every Italian town. Calls on these plans cost around €0.10 per minute.

The dual-band operator Wind works on frequencies of 900 mHz and 1800 mHz and also offers prepaid accounts. You don't pay for Wind's SIM card but calls are more expensive than Telecom and Omnitel – around €0.25 per minute for the first three minutes, then €0.10 per minute. There are Wind retail outlets in most Italian towns.

Always check with your mobile service provider in your home country to ascertain whether your handset allows use of another SIM card.

Taking Your Mobile Phone

Italy uses GSM 900/1800, which is compatible with the rest of Europe and Australia but not with North American GSM 1900 or the totally different system in Japan (although some GSM 1900/900 phones do work here). If you have a GSM phone, check with your service provider about using it in Italy and beware of calls being routed internationally (very expensive for a 'local' call). The alternative is to link up with a local service provider – see Mobile Phones under Telephone for details.

eKno Communication Service Lonely Planet's eKno global communication service provides low-cost international calls – for local calls you're better off with a local phonecard. eKno also offers free messaging services, email, travel information and an online travel vault, where you can securely store all your important documents. You can join online at W www.ekno.lonelyplanet.com, where you will find the local-access numbers for the 24-hour customer-service centre. Once you have joined, always check the eKno Web site for the latest access numbers for each country and updates on new features.

Call Centres There are cut-price call centres all over Italy, especially in the major cities. These are run by various companies and the rates are significantly lower than Telecom payphones for international calls. It's usually a little less noisy than making a call from a payphone in a busy street and you don't need a phonecard – you simply place your call from a private booth inside the centre and pay for it when you've finished.

Calling Italy from Abroad The country code for Italy is ☎ 39. You must always include the initial 0 in area codes. For example to call the number ☎ 02 777 77 77 in Milan you need to dial the international access code followed by ☎ 39 02 777 77 77.

Fax

You can send faxes from post offices and some tobacconists, copy centres and stationers plus some Telecom public phones. To send a fax within Italy, expect to pay €1.55 for the first page and €1 for each page thereafter, plus €0.05 a second for the actual call. International faxes can cost €3.10 for the first page and €2.05 per page thereafter, and €0.05 a second for the call.

Email & Internet Access

Italy was a little slower than some parts of Western Europe to march down the cyber highway but is fast catching up with the rest of the pack.

If you are bringing your laptop to Italy and want access to the Internet you will need to have a server that operates in Italy too. AOL (W www.aol.com), CompuServe (W www.compuserve.com) and IBM Net (W www.ibm.net) have dial-in nodes in Rome and Milan as well as slower-access numbers in other towns. It's best to download a list of the dial-in numbers before you leave home. If you access your Internet email account at home through a smaller ISP or your office or school network, your best option is either to open an account with a global ISP (such as those mentioned above) or to rely on cybercafes and other public access points to collect your mail.

If you do intend to rely on cybercafes, you'll need to carry three pieces of information with you to enable you to access your Internet mail account: your incoming (POP or IMAP) mail server name, your account name and your password. Your ISP or network supervisor will be able to give you these. Armed with this information, you should be able to access your Internet mail account from any net-connected machine in the world, provided it runs some kind of email software (remember that Netscape and Internet Explorer both have mail modules). It pays to become familiar with the process for doing this before you leave home.

Keep in mind that the telephone socket in each country you visit will probably be different from the one at home, so ensure that you have at least a US RJ-11 telephone adapter that works with your modem. Most electronics shops in Rome sell adapters that convert from RJ-11 to the local three-pinned plug variety; more modern phone lines take the RJ-11 jack directly. Consider bringing an extension cord and a female-to-female RJ-11 adapter to make life easier. Also make sure you've got the right AC adapter for your computer, which enables you to plug it in anywhere without frying the innards. For more information on travelling with a portable computer, see W www.teleadapt.com or W www.warrior.com.

Some Italian servers can provide short-term accounts for local Internet access. Agora (☎ 06 699 17 42, W www.agora.stm)

is one of them. Several Italian ISPs offer free Internet connections: check out Tiscalinet (W www.tiscalinet.it), kataweb (W www.kataweb.it and W www.kataweb.com) and Libero (W www.libero.it).

There are cybercafes throughout Italy; we have listed some in the major cities in relevant chapters. You may also find public Internet access in post offices, libraries, hostels, hotels, universities and so on.

DIGITAL RESOURCES

The World Wide Web is a rich resource for travellers. You can research your trip, hunt down bargain air fares, book hotels, check on weather conditions or chat with locals and other travellers about the best places to visit (or avoid!).

There's no better place to start your Web explorations than the Lonely Planet Web site (W www.lonelyplanet.com). Here you'll find succinct summaries on travelling to most places on earth, postcards from other travellers and the Thorn Tree bulletin board, where you can ask questions before you go or dispense advice when you get back. You can also find travel news and updates to many of our most popular guidebooks, and the subWWWay section links you to the most useful travel resources elsewhere on the Web. Other useful sites include:

W **www.cts.it** This is the Web site of Italy's leading student travel organisation, CTS.

W **www.beniculturali.it** If you're planning a few museum visits and want to book tickets, then the culture ministry's site has information on museums and galleries throughout the country and an online reservation service.

W **www.itwg.com** This tourist guide site has useful links for accommodation and transport.

W **www.fs-on-line.com** Information on rail travel throughout Italy is available here.

W **www.mondoweb.it/eyp** This site, the *English Yellow Pages*, is a useful directory of English-speaking professionals, commercial activities, organisations and services in Rome, Milan, Florence, Naples, Genoa and Bologna. The Web site is a good first stop and has lots of useful links.

W **www.vatican.va** The Vatican's official Web site is available in six European languages; among other things, you can have a virtual tour of the Vatican Museums.

W **www.wantedinrome.com** The Web site of the Rome-based fortnightly English-language magazine *Wanted in Rome* has listings and reviews of current exhibitions and cultural events as well as informative articles on aspects of Rome and the surrounding region. It also has classified advertisements on line which are helpful if you're planning a longer stay in the city and want to find a room in a shared flat.

W **www.comune.roma.it** This is the official Web site of Rome's municipal government. The section on tourism and culture provides a good overview of current and forthcoming events, with links to other sites.

CitySync

CitySync Rome is Lonely Planet's digital city guide for Palm OS hand-held devices. With CitySync you can quickly search, sort and bookmark hundreds of Rome's restaurants, hotels, attractions, clubs and more – all pinpointed on scrollable street maps. Sections on activities, transport and local events mean you get the big picture plus all the little details. Purchase or demo CitySync Rome at W www.citysync.com.

BOOKS

Most books are published in different editions by different publishers in different countries. As a result, a book might be a hardcover rarity in one country while it is readily available in paperback in another. Your local bookshop or library is best placed to advise you on the availability of the following recommendations.

For information on Italian literature from the Roman epic poem to the modern novel, see Literature in the Arts section of the Facts about Italy chapter.

Lonely Planet

Europe on a shoestring, *Mediterranean Europe* and *Western Europe* include chapters on Italy and are recommended for those planning further travel in Europe. The *Italian phrasebook* lists all the words and phrases you're likely to need in Italy. *Walking in Italy* is a useful guide for experienced and not-so-experienced walkers who want to explore Italy's great outdoors. If you're intending to limit your travelling to one city or region, look out for Lonely Planet's *Rome*, *Rome Condensed*, *Florence*, *Venice*, *Tuscany*, *Sicily* and *Milan, Turin & Genoa*, which provide in-depth, detailed coverage.

Lonely Planet's *World Food Italy*, by Australia's leading food writer Matthew Evans, is a full-colour book with information on the whole range of Italian food and drink. It includes a useful language section, with the definitive culinary dictionary and a handy quick-reference glossary.

Guidebooks

The paperback Companion Guides are excellent and include *Rome* by Georgina Masson (revised and updated by Tim Jepson) and *Venice* by Hugh Honour. If you can read Italian you can't get better than the excellent red guides published by the Touring Club Italiano.

Rome: An Oxford Archaeological Guide is an extremely detailed guide to the ruins of Rome, with descriptions, maps, plans and photos of more than 150 sites.

Travel

Three 'Grand Tour' classics are Johann Wolfgang von Goethe's *Italian Journey*, Charles Dickens' *Pictures from Italy* and Henry James' *Italian Hours*. DH Lawrence wrote three short travel books while living in Italy, now combined in one volume entitled *DH Lawrence and Italy*.

Other interesting travel books include: *Venice* by James Morris, *The Stones of Florence and Venice Observed* by Mary McCarthy, *On Persephone's Island* by Mary Taylor Simeti, *Old Calabria* by Norman Douglas, *North of Naples, South of Rome* by Paolo Tullio and *A Traveller in Southern Italy* by HV Morton. Although written in the 1960s, the latter remains a valuable guide to the south and its people. See also *A Traveller in Italy* by the same author.

A Small Place in Italy and *Love and War in the Apennines* by Eric Newby make good introductory reading, as do Lisa St Aubin de Terán's *A Valley in Italy*, Frances Maye's chart-topping *Under the Tuscan Sun*, and *Night Letters*, Robert Dessaix's 1990s counterpart to Thomas Mann's *Death in Venice*.

History & Politics

For a simple introduction to the ancient history of the country try *The Oxford History of the Roman World*, edited by John Boardman, Jasper Griffin & Oswyn Murray, or *A History of Rome*, compiled by M Carey & HH Scullard. *Daily Life in Ancient Rome*, by Jerome Carcopino and Robert Graves' classics *I, Claudius* and *Claudius the God* are on the same subject. Other interesting titles include *Italy: A Short History*, by Harry Hearder; *The Horizon Concise History of Italy*, by Vincent Cronin; *History of the Italian People*, by Giuliano Procacci; *The Oxford Dictionary of Popes*, compiled by JND Kelly; and *Rome: Biography of a City*, *Venice: Biography of a City* and *The House of Medici*, all by Christopher Hibbert. *A History of Contemporary Italy: Society and Politics 1943–1988*, by Paul Ginsborg, is an absorbing and very well-written book that will help Italophiles place the country's modern society in perspective.

The Mafia is the subject of a number of titles, including *The Honoured Society*, by Norman Lewis. *Excellent Cadavers: The Mafia and the Death of the First Italian Republic*, by Alexander Stille, is a shocking and absorbing account of the Mafia in Sicily, focusing on the years leading up to the assassinations of anti-Mafia judges Giovanni Falcone and Paolo Borsellino in 1992. *Midnight in Sicily*, by Peter Robb, is also recommended. In 2000, 40 years after his first in-depth examination of Sicily, Norman Lewis followed up his study of the Mafia with *In Sicily*.

Italian Politics Today, by Hilary Partridge (first published 1998), is a clear and accessible guide to the labyrinth of Italian politics. Essential facts on society, business and politics in Italy can be gleaned from *Italy Profiled*, edited by Barry Turner.

Art & Architecture

The Penguin Book of the Renaissance, by JH Plumb, *The Italian Painters of the Renaissance*, by Bernard Berenson, and Giorgio Vasari's *Lives of the Artists* should be more than enough for people interested in the Renaissance. Other useful books include *A Handbook of Roman Art*, edited by Martin Henig, *Roman Architecture*, by Frank Sear, and *Art and Architecture in Italy 1600–1750*, by Rudolf Wittkower.

There is also a series of guides to Italian art and architecture published under the general title World of Art. These include: *Palladio and Palladianism*, by Robert Tavernor, *Michelangelo*, by Linda Murray, *Italian Renaissance Sculpture*, by Roberta JM Olson and *Roman Art and Architecture*, by Mortimer Wheeler.

People

For background on Italian people and their culture there is the classic, *The Italians*, by Luigi Barzini. *Italian Labyrinth* by John Haycraft looks at Italy in the 1980s. *Getting it Right in Italy: Manual for the 1990s* by William Ward aims, with considerable success, to provide accessible, useful information about Italy while also providing a reasonable social profile of the people. *An Italian Education* by Tim Parks is an often hilarious account of the life of an expatriate in Verona.

Food & Drink

The Food of Italy, by Waverly Root, is an acknowledged classic. Mitchell Beazley does a very good guide to Italian wines, *Wines of Italy*, and has also recently published a guide called *The New Italy: A Complete Guide to Contemporary Italian Wines.*

See Lonely Planet earlier for information on *World Food Italy*.

FILMS

If you want to get in the mood before heading off to Italy, here are a few suggestions: *Roman Holiday* (Gregory Peck and Audrey Hepburn scootering round Rome); *Three Coins in the Fountain* (three American women get their men at the Trevi Fountain); *It Started in Naples* (Sophia Loren); *La Dolce Vita* (Fellini's study of Roman society); *Come September* (Rock, Gina, Sandra and Bobby romp around the Amalfi Coast); *The Pink Panther* (set in Cortina and Rome); *The Agony and the Ecstasy* (Charlton Heston as Michelangelo); and *Death in Venice* (Dirk Bogarde).

More recently there's been *A Room with a View* (not a view in the world can beat the one from Fiesole over Florence); *Cinema Paradiso* (the story of a young boy living in a small Sicilian town soon after WWII); *Enchanted April* (two women escape from London to a Tuscan villa); *Stealing Beauty* (a pretty banal film, but a great Tuscan travelogue); *The Wings of the Dove* (Henry James' story of love and betrayal in Venice); and *The Talented Mr Ripley* (filmed on the Amalfi Coast and in Rome).

And who can forget magnificent Italian films such as *Il Postino*, filmed on the Aeolian island of Salina, and *La Vita e Bella* (Life is Beautiful)? The early scenes of the latter were filmed in Arezzo and won Roberto Benigni a best-actor Oscar.

If you want to see what Sicily and Sardinia are like before you go, watch the Lonely Planet video *Corsica, Sicily & Sardinia: Mediterranean Islands.*

NEWSPAPERS & MAGAZINES

English Language

The *International Herald Tribune* (€1.65) is available from Monday to Saturday. It has a daily four-page supplement, *Italy Daily*, covering Italian news.

British papers, including the *Guardian* (€1.85), *The Times* (€2.60), the *Daily Telegraph* (€3), the *Independent* (€2.30) and the *Financial Times* (€1.50), as well as various tabloids, are sent from London. They are available from newsstands towards lunchtime on the day of publication in major cities or the next day in smaller towns.

US newspapers such as *USA Today* (€1.55), the *Wall Street Journal Europe* (€1.80) and the *New York Times* (€6.20) are also available (a day late). The major German, French and Spanish dailies and some Scandinavian papers can also be found in major cities.

News magazines such as *Time* (€2.60), *Newsweek* (€3.10) and *The Economist* (€4.15) are available weekly. *Wanted in Rome* (€0.75) is a fortnightly English-language news and listings magazine directed towards the foreign residents of Rome. It contains informative articles about Italian politics and bureaucracy, city news, history and culture, plus arts and entertainment listings and reviews. It also has hundreds of classified ads useful for those seeking accommodation or jobs.

Italian Language

Italian newspapers, available from all newsstands, can be frustrating, even for fluent Italian readers. Don't expect the Italian press to give you a balanced view of current events as most newspapers reflect the political or business interests of those who control them. The articles tend to be long-winded and the point, if indeed there is one, is usually buried in the final paragraphs. The domestic politics section, which normally occupies the first four or five pages of the newspaper, is difficult to follow even for the most dedicated reader and if you miss an instalment it's almost impossible to catch up on events.

Most Italian daily newspapers cost €0.75 (or €1 if a supplement is included).

Corriere della Sera, based in Milan, is the country's leading daily and has the best foreign news pages and the most comprehensive and comprehensible political coverage.

Il Messaggero is a popular Rome-based broadsheet. It is especially good for news about Rome and the Vatican and has a weekly listings supplement, *Metro*.

The former left-wing mouthpiece, *L'Unità*, was relaunched in March 2001 (after closing in July 2000). A new editorial company has bought the title from the Democratici di Sinistra political party (the former communists) and the new-look paper is now closer to the political centre.

The tabloid-format *La Repubblica*, also a Rome-based paper, usually has great photos but it also has a reputation for sloppy reporting. Its *Trovaroma* supplement on Thursday provides entertainment listings.

The conservative *L'Osservatore Romano* is published daily (with weekly editions in English and other foreign languages) and is the official voice of the Vatican. There are several other daily papers.

All of the above are available nationally from larger newsstands.

RADIO & TV

Radio

You can pick up the BBC World Service on medium wave at 648kHz, short wave at 6195kHz, 9410kHz, 12095kHz and 15575kHz, and on long wave at 198 kHz depending on where you are and the time of day. Voice of America (VOA) can usually be found on short wave at 15205kHz.

Vatican Radio (1530 AM, 93.3 FM and 105 FM) broadcasts the news in English at 7am, 8.30am, 6.15pm and 9.50pm. The reports usually include a run-down on what the pope is up to on any particular day. Pick up a pamphlet at the Vatican information office.

There are three state-owned Italian stations: RAI-1 (1332 AM or 89.7 FM), RAI-2 (846 AM or 91.7 FM) and RAI-3 (93.7 FM). They combine classical and light music with news broadcasts and discussion programs. RAI-2 broadcasts news in English every day from 1am to 5am at three minutes past the hour.

Commercial radio stations are a better bet if you're after contemporary music. Popular stations are Radio Centro Suono (101.3 FM), the Naples-based Radio Kiss Kiss (97.25 FM), and Radio Città Futura (97.7 FM), which broadcasts a listing of the day's events in Rome at 10am daily.

TV

Italian television is so bad that it's compelling. There is an inordinate number of quiz shows and variety programs featuring troupes of scantily clad women prancing and thrusting across the set. The home-bred soap operas are so terrible that it's sometimes embarrassing to watch but they attract a huge following. So, too, do the many imported soaps, mainly from the USA, all of which are dubbed into Italian. Current-release films transfer to the small screen relatively quickly in Italy, but again, they are always dubbed.

The state-run channels are RAI 1, RAI 2 and RAI 3. The main commercial stations are Canale 5, Italia 1, Rete 4 and La 7. The

French-language TV channel, Antenne 2, can sometimes be received on Channel 10.

Most of Rome's mid- to top-range hotels, as well as many bars and restaurants, have satellite TV and can receive BBC World, Sky Channel, CNN and NBC Superchannel.

VIDEO SYSTEMS

Italy uses the PAL video system (the same as Australia and the rest of Europe, except France). This system is not compatible with NTSC (used in the USA, Japan and Latin America) or Secam (used in France and other French-speaking countries). Modern video players are often multi-system and can read all three.

PHOTOGRAPHY & VIDEO

Film & Equipment

The major Italian airports are all fully equipped with modern inspection systems that do not damage film or other photographic material carried in hand luggage.

There are numerous outlets that sell and process films, but beware of poor-quality processing. Many places claim to process films in one hour but you will rarely get your photos back that quickly – count on late the next day if the outlet has its own processing equipment or three to four days if it hasn't.

A roll of film is called a *pellicola* but you will be understood if you ask for 'film'. A 100 ASA Kodak film will cost around €4.15/5.15 for 24/36 exposures. Developing costs around €5.70/7.25 for 24/36 exposures in standard format. A roll of 36 slides *(diapositive)* costs €5.15 to buy and €4.15 to develop.

Tapes for video cameras, including V8, are often available at the same outlets or can be found at stores selling cameras, videos and electrical goods.

Restrictions

Photography is not permitted in many churches, museums and galleries. Look out for crossed-out camera symbols as you go in. These restrictions do not normally apply to archaeological sites.

In military zones you will encounter signs in Italian warning you not to trespass and not to take photographs. Realistically, photography in these areas carries little risk in peace time – although the enforcement of restrictions is left to the discretion of the soldiers.

Photographing People

The standard rules about photographing people apply in Italy. In the south, you need to be particularly sensitive to the fact that people – especially women and the elderly – are traditionally more reserved. Children, on the other hand, will often come running to have their photo taken.

TIME

Italy operates on a 24-hour clock.

It is one hour ahead of GMT/UTC. France, Germany, Austria and Spain are on the same time as Italy. Greece, Egypt and Israel are one hour ahead. When it's noon in Rome, it's 3am in San Francisco, 6am in New York and Toronto, 11am in London, 7pm in Perth, 9pm in Sydney and 11pm in Auckland.

Daylight-saving time, when clocks are moved forward one hour, starts on the last Sunday in March. Clocks are put back an hour on the last Sunday in October. When phoning home, remember to allow for daylight-saving in your own country.

ELECTRICITY

Voltages & Cycles

The electric current in Italy is 220V, 50Hz, but check with the hotel management because some places, especially those in older buildings, may still use 125V.

Plugs & Sockets

Power points have two or three holes and do not have their own switches; plugs have two or three round pins. Some power points have larger holes than others. Italian homes are usually full of plug adapters to cope with this anomaly.

Make sure you bring international plug adapters for your appliances. It is a good idea to buy these *before* leaving home as they are virtually impossible to get in Italy. If you do forget, there is always the option of taking your appliance to an electrical store and having them replace the foreign plug with an Italian one. Travellers from North America need a voltage converter (although many of the more expensive hotels have provision for 110V appliances such as electric razors).

WEIGHTS & MEASURES

Italy uses the metric system. Basic terms for weight include *un etto* (100g) and *un chilo* (1kg). Travellers from the USA (and often the UK) will have to cope with the change from pounds to kilograms, miles to kilometres and gallons to litres. A standard conversion table can be found on the inside back cover of this book.

Note that for numbers, Italians indicate decimals with commas and thousands with points.

LAUNDRY

Coin-operated laundrettes, where you can do your own washing, are catching on in Italy and you'll find them in most of the main cities. A load will cost around €4.

Lavasecco (dry-cleaning) charges range from around €3 for a shirt to €7.50 for a jacket. Be careful, though – the quality can be unreliable.

TOILETS

Public toilets are not exactly widespread in Italy, although coin-operated toilets are becoming increasingly common in major tourist areas. Most people use the toilets in bars and cafes (you might need to buy a coffee first).

HEALTH

Travel health depends on your predeparture preparations, your daily health care while travelling and how you handle any medical problem that does develop. While the potential dangers can seem daunting, in reality few travellers experience anything more than an upset stomach.

Predeparture Planning

Immunisations No vaccinations are required for entry into Italy, though it's recommended that everyone keep up-to-date with diphtheria, tetanus and polio vaccinations. Consider a vaccination against tick-borne encephalitis if you plan to do extensive hiking between May and September in Europe.

You should seek medical advice at least six weeks before travel; some vaccinations require more than one injection, while some should not be given together. Note that some vaccinations should not be given during pregnancy or to people with allergies – discuss the situation with your doctor.

Health Insurance

Make sure that you have adequate health insurance. Some travel insurance policies will cover aspects of health insurance (see Travel Insurance under Visas & Documents earlier in this chapter for details). EU citizens are covered for emergency treatment on presentation of an E111 form. Ask about the E111 at your local health services department or travel agency at least a few weeks before you travel. In the UK you can get the form from post offices. Australia has a reciprocal arrangement with Italy. Medicare in Australia publishes a brochure with the details and it is advisable to carry your Medicare card. Treatment in private hospitals is not covered, and charges are also likely for medication, dental work and secondary examinations, including x-rays and laboratory tests.

Citizens of New Zealand, the US and Canada and other countries have to pay for anything other than emergency treatment.

Travel Health Guides

Travel with Children from Lonely Planet includes advice on travel health for younger children.

There are also a number of excellent travel health sites on the Internet. On the Lonely Planet home page, there are links at **W** www.lonelyplanet.com/weblinks/wlheal.htm to the World Health Organization and the US Centers for Disease Control & Prevention.

Other Preparations

Make sure you are healthy before you leave home. If you are embarking on a long trip,

Medical Kit Check List

Following is a list of items you should consider including in your medical kit – consult your pharmacist for brands available in your country.

- ☐ **Aspirin or paracetamol (acetaminophen in the USA)** – for pain or fever
- ☐ **Antihistamine** – for allergies, eg, hay fever; to ease the itch from insect bites or stings; and to prevent motion sickness
- ☐ **Cold and flu tablets, throat lozenges and nasal decongestant**
- ☐ **Multivitamins** – consider for long trips, when dietary vitamin intake may be inadequate
- ☐ **Antibiotics** – consider including these if you're travelling well off the beaten track; see your doctor, as they must be prescribed, and carry the prescription with you
- ☐ **Loperamide or diphenoxylate** –'blockers' for diarrhoea
- ☐ **Prochlorperazine or metaclopramide** – for nausea and vomiting
- ☐ **Rehydration mixture** – to prevent dehydration, which may occur, for example, during bouts of diarrhoea; particularly important when travelling with children
- ☐ **Insect repellent, sunscreen, lip balm and eye drops**
- ☐ **Calamine lotion, sting relief spray or aloe vera** – to ease irritation from sunburn and insect bites or stings
- ☐ **Antifungal cream or powder** – for fungal skin infections and thrush
- ☐ **Antiseptic (such as povidone-iodine)** – for cuts and grazes
- ☐ **Bandages, Band-Aids (plasters) and other wound dressings**
- ☐ **Water purification tablets or iodine**
- ☐ **Scissors, tweezers and a thermometer** – note that mercury thermometers are prohibited by airlines

make sure your teeth are OK (dental treatment is particularly expensive in Italy).

If you wear glasses, take a spare pair and your prescription. If you lose your glasses, you will be able to have them replaced within a few days (sometimes within a few hours) by an *ottico* (optician).

Travellers who require a particular medication should take an adequate supply as it may not be available locally. Take part of the packaging showing the generic rather than the brand name as this will make getting replacements easier. It's a good idea to have a legible prescription or letter from your doctor to show that you legally use the medication. Basic drugs are widely available and indeed many items requiring prescriptions in countries such as the USA can be obtained over the counter in Italy.

Medical Services

If you need an ambulance anywhere in Italy, call ☎ 118.

The quality of medical treatment in public hospitals varies in Italy. Simply put, the farther north, the better the care.

Private hospitals and clinics throughout the country generally provide excellent services but are expensive for those without medical insurance. That said, certain treatments, tests or referrals to specialists in public hospitals may also have to be paid for and can be equally costly.

Your embassy or consulate in Italy can provide a list of recommended doctors in major cities. If you have a specific health complaint, it would be wise to obtain the necessary information and referrals for treatment before leaving home.

The public health system is administered along provincial lines by centres generally known as Unità Sanitarie Locali (USL). Increasingly they are being reorganised as Aziende Sanitarie Locali (ASL). Through them you find out where your nearest hospital, medical clinics and other services are. Look under 'U' or 'A' in the telephone book (sometimes the USL is under 'A' as Azienda USL).

Under these headings you'll find long lists of offices – look for Poliambulatorio (Polyclinic) and the telephone number for Accetazione Sanitaria. You need to call this number to make an appointment: there is no point in just rolling up. Clinic opening hours vary widely, with the minimum generally being about 8am to 12.30pm Monday to Friday. Some open for a couple of hours in the afternoon and on Saturday mornings too.

Each ASL/USL area has its own Consultorio Familiare (Family Planning Centre) where you can go for contraceptives, pregnancy tests and information about abortion (legal up to the 12th week of pregnancy).

For emergency treatment, go straight to the *pronto soccorso* (casualty) section of a public hospital, where you can also get emergency dental treatment. Sometimes hospitals are listed in the phone book under Aziende Ospedaliere. In major cities you are likely to find English-speaking doctors, or a volunteer translator service. Often, first aid is also available at train stations, airports and ports.

IAMAT (International Association for Medical Assistance to Travellers; ☎ 716-754 4883, fax 519-836 3412), 417 Center Street, Lewiston, NY 14092, a non-profit organisation based in New York, can provide a list of English-speaking doctors in Rome who have been trained in the USA, the UK or Canada.

Basic Rules

Food & Water Stomach upsets are the most likely travel health problem, and the majority of these will be relatively minor and probably due to overindulgence in the local food. Some people take a while to adjust to the regular use of olive oil in the food.

Tap water is drinkable throughout Italy although Italians themselves have taken to drinking the bottled stuff. The sign *acqua non potabile* tells you that water is not drinkable (you may see the sign in trains and at some camp sites). Water from drinking fountains is safe unless there is a sign telling you otherwise.

Everyday Health Normal body temperature is 37°C or 98.6°F; more than 2°C (4°F) higher indicates a 'high' fever. Normal adult pulse rate is 60 to 100 beats per minute (children 80 to 100; babies 100 to 140). As a general rule, the pulse increases by about 20 beats per minute for each °C (2°F) rise in fever.

Environmental Hazards

Heatstroke This serious (and occasionally fatal) condition can occur if the body's heat-regulating mechanism breaks down and body temperature rises to dangerous levels. Long, continuous periods of exposure to high temperatures and insufficient fluids can leave you vulnerable to heatstroke.

The symptoms are feeling unwell, not sweating very much (or at all) and a high body temperature (39° to 41°C or 102° to 106°F). Where sweating has ceased, the skin becomes flushed and red. Severe, throbbing headaches and lack of coordination will also occur, and the sufferer may be confused or aggressive. If untreated, severe cases will eventually become delirious or convulse. Hospitalisation is essential but in the interim get victims out of the sun, remove their clothing, cover them with a wet sheet or towel and then fan them continually. Give them fluids if they are conscious.

Hypothermia Too much cold can be just as dangerous as too much heat. If you are walking at high altitudes, particularly at night, be prepared.

Hypothermia occurs when the body loses heat faster than it can produce it and the core temperature of the body falls. It is surprisingly easy to progress from very cold to dangerously cold due to a combination of wind, wet clothing, fatigue and hunger, even if the air temperature is above freezing. It is best to dress in layers: silk, wool and some of the new artificial fibres are all good insulating materials. A hat is important as a lot of heat is lost through the head. A strong, waterproof outer layer (and a 'space' blanket for emergencies) is essential. Carry basic supplies, including food containing simple sugars to generate heat quickly and fluid to drink.

Symptoms of hypothermia are exhaustion, numb skin (particularly toes and fingers), shivering, slurred speech, irrational or violent behaviour, lethargy, stumbling, dizzy spells, muscle cramps and violent bursts of energy. Irrationality may take the form of sufferers claiming they are warm and trying to take off their clothes.

To treat mild hypothermia, first get the person out of the wind and/or rain, remove their clothing if it's wet and replace it with dry, warm clothing. Give them hot liquids (not alcohol) and some high-kilojoule, easily digestible food. Do not rub victims – allow them to slowly warm themselves. This should be enough to treat the early stages of hypothermia. The early recognition and treatment of mild hypothermia is the only way to prevent severe hypothermia, which is a critical condition.

Heat Exhaustion & Prickly Heat Dehydration and salt deficiency can cause heat exhaustion. Take time to acclimatise to high temperatures, drink sufficient liquids such as tea and drinks rich in mineral salts (such as clear soups and fruit and vegetable juices), and do not do anything too physically demanding. Salt deficiency is characterised by fatigue, lethargy, headaches, giddiness and muscle cramps; salt tablets may help, but adding extra salt to your food is better.

Prickly heat is an itchy rash caused by excessive perspiration trapped under the skin. It usually strikes people who have just arrived in a hot climate. Keeping cool by bathing often, using a mild talcum powder or even resorting to spending time in an air-conditioned environment may help.

Fungal Infections These occur more commonly in hot weather and are usually found on the scalp, between the toes (athlete's foot) or fingers, in the groin and on the body (ringworm). You get ringworm (which is a fungal infection, not a worm) from infected animals or other people. Moisture encourages these infections.

To prevent fungal infections wear loose, comfortable clothes, avoid artificial fibres, wash frequently and dry yourself carefully. If you do get an infection, wash the infected area at least daily with a disinfectant or medicated soap and water, and rinse and dry well. Apply an antifungal cream or powder like tolnaftate. Try to expose the infected area to air or sunlight as much as possible. Wash all towels and underwear in hot water, change them often and let them dry in the sun.

Infectious Diseases

Diarrhoea Simple things such as a change of water, food or climate can all cause a mild bout of diarrhoea, but a few rushed toilet trips with no other symptoms is not indicative of a major problem.

Dehydration is the main danger with any diarrhoea, particularly in children or the elderly where dehydration can occur quite quickly. Under all circumstances *fluid replacement* (at least equal to the volume being lost) is the most important thing to remember. Weak black tea with a little sugar, soda water, or soft drinks allowed to go flat and diluted 50% with clean water are all good. With severe diarrhoea a rehydrating solution is preferable to replace minerals and salts lost. Commercially available oral rehydration salts (ORS) are very useful; add them to boiled or bottled water. In an emergency you can make up a solution of six teaspoons of sugar and a half teaspoon of salt to a litre of boiled or bottled water. Keep drinking small amounts often. Stick to a bland diet as you recover.

Gut-paralysing drugs such as loperamide or diphenoxylate can be used to bring relief from the symptoms, although they do not actually cure the problem. Only use these drugs if you do not have access to toilets, for example if you *must* travel. Note that these drugs are not recommended for children under 12 years.

In certain situations antibiotics may be required: diarrhoea with blood or mucus (dysentery), any diarrhoea with fever, profuse watery diarrhoea, persistent diarrhoea not improving after 48 hours and severe diarrhoea. These suggest a more serious cause of diarrhoea and in these situations gut-paralysing drugs should be avoided.

Hepatitis Hepatitis is a general term for inflammation of the liver. The symptoms are similar in all forms of the illness, and include fever, chills, headache, fatigue, feelings of weakness and aches and pains, followed by loss of appetite, nausea, vomiting, abdominal pain, dark urine, light-coloured faeces, jaundiced (yellow) skin, and the whites of the eyes may turn yellow. People who have had hepatitis should avoid alcohol for some time after the illness, as the liver needs time to recover.

Hepatitis A is transmitted by contaminated food and drinking water. You should seek medical advice but there is not much you can do apart from resting, drinking lots of fluids, eating lightly and avoiding fatty foods. Hepatitis E is transmitted in the same way as hepatitis A; it can be particularly serious in pregnant women.

Hepatitis B is spread through contact with infected blood, blood products or body fluids – for example, through sexual contact, unsterilised needles and blood transfusions or contact with blood via small breaks in the skin. Other risk situations include having a shave, a tattoo or body piercing with contaminated equipment. The symptoms of hepatitis B may be more severe than type A and the disease can lead to long-term problems such as chronic liver damage, liver cancer or a long term carrier state. Hepatitis C and D are spread in the same way as hepatitis B and can also lead to long-term complications.

There are vaccines against hepatitis A and B but there are currently no vaccines against the other types of hepatitis. Following the basic rules about food and water (hepatitis A and E) and avoiding risk situations (hepatitis B, C and D) are important preventative measures.

HIV & AIDS Infection with the human immunodeficiency virus (HIV) may lead to acquired immune deficiency syndrome (AIDS), which is a fatal disease. Any exposure to blood, blood products or body fluids may put the individual at risk. The disease is often transmitted through sexual contact or dirty needles – vaccinations, acupuncture, tattooing and body piercing can be potentially as dangerous as intravenous drug use. HIV/AIDS can also be spread through transfusions using infected blood, but in Italy blood is screened and so transfusions are safe. If you do need an injection, ask to see the syringe unwrapped in front of you, or take a needle and syringe pack with you.

Fear of HIV infection should never preclude treatment for serious medical conditions.

Sexually Transmitted Diseases (STDs)

HIV/AIDS and hepatitis B can be transmitted through sexual contact – see the relevant sections earlier for more details. Other STDs include gonorrhoea, herpes and syphilis; sores, blisters or rashes around the genitals and discharges or pain when urinating are common symptoms. In some STDs, such as wart virus or chlamydia, symptoms may be less marked or not observed at all, especially in women. Chlamydia infection can cause infertility in men and women before any symptoms have been noticed. Syphilis symptoms eventually disappear completely but the disease continues and can cause severe problems in later years. While abstinence from sexual contact is the only 100% effective prevention, using condoms is also effective. The treatment of gonorrhoea and syphilis is with antibiotics. The different sexually transmitted diseases each require specific antibiotics.

Bites & Stings

Bedbugs & Lice Bedbugs live in various places, but particularly in dirty mattresses and bedding, evidenced by spots of blood on bedclothes or on the wall. Bedbugs leave itchy bites in neat rows. Calamine lotion or a sting relief spray may help.

All lice cause itching and discomfort. They make themselves at home in your hair (head lice), your clothing (body lice) or in your pubic hair (crabs). You catch lice through direct contact with infected people or by sharing combs, clothing and the like. Powder or shampoo treatment will kill the lice; infected clothing should then be washed in very hot, soapy water and left in the sun to dry.

Jellyfish Italian beaches are occasionally inundated with jellyfish. Their stings are painful but not dangerous. Dousing in vinegar will de-activate any stingers that have not fired. Calamine lotion, antihistamines and analgesics may reduce the reaction and relieve pain. If in doubt about swimming, ask locals if any jellyfish are in the water.

Snakes Italy's only dangerous snake, the viper, is found throughout the country except on Sardinia. To minimise the possibilities of being bitten, always wear boots, socks and long trousers when walking through undergrowth where snakes may be present. Don't put your hands into holes and crevices and do be careful when collecting firewood.

Viper bites do not cause instantaneous death and an antivenin is widely available in pharmacies. Keep the victim calm and still, wrap the bitten limb tightly, as you would for a sprained ankle, and attach a splint to immobilise it. Seek medical help, if possible with the dead snake for identification. Don't attempt to catch the snake if there is a possibility of being bitten again. Tourniquets and sucking out the poison are now comprehensively discredited.

Ticks Always check all over your body if you have been walking through a potentially tick-infested area as ticks can cause skin infections and other more serious diseases. In recent years there have been several reported deaths on Sardinia related to tick bites. Health authorities have yet to pinpoint the cause.

If a tick is found attached, press down around the tick's head with tweezers, grab the head and gently pull upwards. Avoid pulling the rear of the body as this may squeeze the tick's gut contents through the attached mouth parts into the skin, increasing the risk of infection and disease. Smearing chemicals on the tick will not make it let go and is not recommended.

Less Common Diseases

Rabies Rabies is still found in Italy but only in isolated areas of the Alps. It is transmitted through a bite or scratch by an infected animal. Dogs are noted carriers. Any bite, scratch or even lick from a mammal in an area where rabies does exist should be cleaned immediately and thoroughly. Scrub with soap and running water and then clean with an alcohol solution. Medical help should be sought immediately. A course of injections may then be necessary to prevent the onset of symptoms and death.

Leishmaniasis This is a group of parasitic diseases transmitted by sandflies and found in coastal parts of Italy. Cutaneous leishmaniasis affects the skin tissue and causes ulceration and disfigurement; visceral leishmaniasis affects the internal organs. Avoiding sandfly bites by covering up and using repellent is the best precaution against this disease.

Lyme Disease This disease is an infection transmitted by ticks that can be acquired throughout Europe, including in forested areas of Italy. The illness usually begins with a spreading rash at the site of the tick bite and is accompanied by fever, headache, extreme fatigue, aching joints and muscles and mild neck stiffness. If untreated, these symptoms usually disappear over several weeks but disorders of the nervous system, heart and joints may develop over subsequent weeks or months. Treatment works best early in the illness. Medical help should be sought.

Tick-borne Encephalitis Ticks can carry encephalitis, a virus-borne cerebral inflammation. Tick-borne encephalitis can occur in most forest and rural areas of Europe, especially in eastern Austria, Germany, Hungary and the Czech Republic. Symptoms include blotches around the bite, which is sometimes pale in the middle. Headache, stiffness and other flu-like symptoms, as well as extreme tiredness, appearing a week or two after the bite, can progress to more serious problems. Medical help must be sought.

Women's Health

Women travellers often find that their menstrual periods become irregular or even cease while they're on the road. Remember that a missed period in these circumstances doesn't necessarily indicate pregnancy.

If you use contraceptive pills, don't forget to take time zones into account and do be aware that the pills may not be absorbed if you suffer intestinal problems. Ask your physician about these matters. If you think you've run into problems while in Italy, contact the nearest Consultorio Familiare, attached to each USL or ASL (see Medical Services earlier for details).

Pregnancy Most miscarriages occur during the first three months of pregnancy, so this is the most risky time to travel as far as your own health is concerned. Miscarriage is not uncommon and can occasionally lead to severe bleeding. The last three months of pregnancy should also be spent within reasonable distance of good medical care. A baby born as early as 24 weeks into the pregnancy stands a chance of survival but only in a good, modern hospital. Pregnant women should avoid all unnecessary medication. Additional care should be taken to prevent illness and particular attention should be paid to diet and nutrition. Alcohol and nicotine should be avoided.

Gynaecological Problems Antibiotic use, synthetic underwear, sweating and contraceptive pills can lead to fungal vaginal infections, especially when travelling in hot climates. Fungal infections are characterised by a rash, itch and discharge and can be treated with a highly-diluted vinegar or lemon-juice douche, or with yoghurt. Nystatin, miconazole or clotrimazole pessaries or vaginal cream are the usual treatment. Maintaining good personal hygiene and wearing loose-fitting clothes and cotton underwear may help prevent these infections. Pharmacies can provide creams and pessaries for common fungal infections *(candida)*.

Cystitis is known as *cistiti*; you can buy capsules (called Pipram) to treat it over the counter.

Sexually transmitted diseases are a major cause of vaginal problems. Symptoms include a smelly discharge, painful intercourse and sometimes a burning sensation when urinating. Medical attention should be sought and male sexual partners must also be treated. For more details see the section on Sexually Transmitted Diseases earlier. Besides abstinence, the best thing is to practise safer sex using condoms.

WOMEN TRAVELLERS

Italy is not a dangerous country for women, but women travelling alone will often find themselves plagued by unwanted attention from men. This attention usually involves catcalls, hisses and whistles and, as such, is more annoying than anything else. Get used to being stared at – because it's likely to happen often, especially in smaller towns in the south of Italy and in Sicily and Sardinia.

Lone women will also find it difficult to remain alone: you will have Italian men harassing you as you walk along the street, drink a coffee in a bar or try to read a book in a park. Usually the best response is to ignore them but if that doesn't work, politely tell them that you are waiting for your *marito* (husband) or *fidanzato* (boyfriend) and, if necessary, walk away. Avoid becoming aggressive as this almost always results in an unpleasant confrontation. If all else fails, approach the nearest member of the police or *carabinieri* (military police).

Watch out for men with wandering hands on crowded buses. Either keep your back to the wall or make a loud fuss if someone starts fondling your backside. A loud *che schifo!* (how disgusting!) will usually do the trick. The locals will sympathise with you and the culprit will almost certainly make a hasty exit at the next stop.

Basically, most of the attention falls into the nuisance/harassment category. However, women on their own should use their common sense. Avoid walking alone in deserted and dark streets, and look for hotels that are central and within easy walking distance of places where you can eat at night (unsafe areas for women are noted throughout this book). Women should also avoid hitchhiking alone.

Women will find that the farther south they travel, the more likely they are to be harassed. It is advisable to dress more conservatively in the south, particularly if you are travelling to small towns and villages. Skimpy clothing is a sure attention-earner – take your cue from the Italian women.

In cities where there is a high petty-crime rate, such as Rome, Naples, Palermo, Syracuse and Bari, women on their own are regarded as prime targets for bag-snatchers (on foot or on wheels). Use a backpack if you can (it's harder to pull off) or keep one hand on your bag (preferably carried diagonally across the body with the bag on the side away from the road), and be very careful about walking in deserted streets.

GAY & LESBIAN TRAVELLERS

Homosexuality is legal in Italy and well tolerated in major cities, particularly in the north. Friendships between Italian men tend to involve physical contact so the sight of two men (or two women) walking down a street arm in arm is not unusual. However, overt displays of affection by homosexual couples could attract a negative response in smaller towns. The legal age of consent is 16. A few years ago the gay capitals of Italy were Milan and Bologna, but Rome is now giving both cities some strong competition.

There are gay clubs in Rome, Florence and Milan, which may be listed in newspapers but can be more reliably tracked down through local gay organisations (see the next section) or publications such as *Pride* (€3.10), a national monthly magazine, and *AUT* (free) published by Circolo Mario Mieli in Rome, both available at gay and lesbian organisations and bookshops. The international gay guide *Spartacus International Gay Guide* (which sells for around US$32.95 or UK£19.95 and is available in bookshops worldwide) also has listings of gay venues all over Italy (and the rest of the world). *Places for Women*, published by Ferrari Publications, Phoenix, Arizona, USA, has information for lesbian travellers.

More information about gay and lesbian venues can be found in the Entertainment sections of individual cities in this book.

Organisations

The national organisations for gay men and lesbians are ArciGay and ArciLesbica (☎ 051 644 70 54, fax 051 644 67 22), Piazza di Porta Saragozza 2, 40123 Bologna.

In Rome the main cultural and political organisation is the Circolo Mario Mieli di Cultura Omosessuale, Via Efeso 2/a (☎ 06 541 39 85, e info@mariomieli.it) off Via Ostiense near the Basilica di San Paolo, which organises debates, cultural events and social functions. It also runs a free AIDS/HIV testing and care centre. Mario Mieli organises Rome Pride which takes place every year in June. Its excellent Web site (w www.mariomieli.it) has information and listings of forthcoming events, both social and political.

You'll find any number of Italian gay sites on the Internet, but some are all but useless. However, ArciGay's Web site (w www.gay.it/arcigay) has general information on the gay and lesbian scene in Italy and plenty of useful links to local organisations in other regions.

DISABLED TRAVELLERS

Italy is not an easy country for disabled travellers, who will almost certainly need to depend on other people more than they would in their home countries. Getting around can be a problem for the wheelchair bound. Even a short journey in a city or town can become a major expedition if cobblestoned streets have to be negotiated. Although many buildings have lifts, they are not always wide enough to accommodate a wheelchair.

The Italian State Tourist Office (see Tourist Offices Abroad earlier in this chapter) in your country may be able to provide advice on Italian associations for the disabled and information on what help is available in the country. It may also carry a small brochure, *Services for Disabled Passengers*, published by the Italian railways company, Ferrovie dello Stato, which details facilities at stations and on trains.

Organisations

The UK-based Royal Association for Disability & Rehabilitation (RADAR; ☎ 020-7250 3222, w www.radar.org.uk), Unit 12, City Forum, 250 City Rd, London EC1V 8AS, has some information on travel in Europe for disabled people. Another UK organisation worth contacting is Holiday

Care Service (☎ 01293-774535, W www.holidaycare.org.uk). It produces an information pack on Italy for disabled people and other travellers with special needs and has an excellent Web site.

Mobility International (☎ 02-201 5608, fax 02-201 5763), 18 blvd Baudouin, Brussels, Belgium, organises all sorts of events throughout Europe for the disabled.

In Italy itself, the best point of reference for disabled travellers is the Rome-based Consorzio Cooperative Integrate (COIN) which can provide information about services for the disabled in the capital (including transport and museum access). COIN is also happy to share its contacts throughout Italy with those who ask. It operates a telephone helpline (☎ 06 712 90 11) from 9am to 5pm Monday to Friday. Information is also available online at W www.coinsociale.it or via email at e turismo@coinsociale.it.

COIN publishes a multilingual guide, *Roma Accessibile*, which lists the facilities available at museums, department stores, theatres and metro stations. The guide is available from public offices and by mail order; some tourist offices might have copies.

The Associazione Italiana Assistenza Spastici (☎ 02 550 17 564), Via S Barnaba 29, Milan, operates an information service for disabled travellers called the Sportello Vacanze Disabili. It has information for disabled travellers in Milan and around the country.

Accessible Italy (☎ 011 309 63 63, W www.tour-web.com/accessibleitaly/), Piazza Pitagora 9, 10137 Turin, is a private company which specialises in holiday services for the disabled, ranging from tours to the hiring of adapted transport.

SENIOR TRAVELLERS

Senior citizens are often entitled to public transport discounts in Italian cities but usually only for monthly passes (not daily or weekly tickets). The minimum qualifying age is 65 years.

For rail travel on the Ferrovie dello Stato (FS), seniors (over 60) can get 30% to 40% reductions on full fares by purchasing an annual seniors' pass called the *Carta Argento* for €23.25. However you'll have to be doing a fair bit of train travel to make it worth it. See the boxed text 'Rail Passes & Discount Tickets' in the Getting There & Away chapter for more details.

Admission to most museums in Rome is free for the over-60s but in other cities (such as Florence) often no concessions are made for non-residents.

You should also seek information in your own country on travel packages and discounts for senior travellers, through senior citizens' organisations and travel agents. Consider booking accommodation in advance to avoid inconvenience.

TRAVEL WITH CHILDREN

Successful travel with children can require a special effort. Don't try to overdo things by packing too much into the time available and make sure activities include the kids as well. Remember that visits to museums and galleries can be tiring, even for adults. Children might be more interested in some of the major archaeological sites, such as Pompeii, the Colosseum and the Forum in Rome, and Greek temples in the south and Sicily. If you're travelling in northern Italy, you might want to make a stopover at Gardaland, the amusement park near Lago di Garda in Lombardy, or at Italia in Miniatura at Viserba near Rimini in Emilia-Romagna.

Allow time for the kids to play, either in a park or in the hotel room; taking a toddler to a playground for an hour or so in the morning can make an amazing difference to their tolerance for sightseeing in the afternoon. When travelling long distances by car or public transport, take plenty of books and other activities. Include older children in the planning of the trip – if they have helped to work out where they will be going, they are likely to be much more interested when they get there.

Discounts are available for children (usually aged under 12 but sometimes based on the child's height) on public transport and for admission to museums, galleries and other sites.

When travelling by train, especially in busy periods, make sure to reserve seats on

Intercity or Eurostar trains to avoid finding yourselves and your children standing up for the entire journey.

There are special sections on activities for families in the Rome, Florence and Venice sections of this guide. These include activities that might interest the kids and usually point out where you can find a playground for young children. Always make a point of asking staff at tourist offices if they know of any special family or children's activities and for suggestions on hotels that cater for kids. Book accommodation in advance, where possible, to avoid unnecessary inconvenience.

You can buy baby formula in powder or liquid form, as well as sterilising solutions such as Milton, at *farmacie* (chemists). Disposable nappies (diapers) are widely available at supermarkets, farmacie (where they are more expensive) and sometimes in larger *cartolerie* (stores selling paper goods). A pack of around 30 disposable nappies costs about €9.30. Fresh cow's milk is sold in cartons in bars which have a '*Latteria*' sign and in supermarkets. If it is essential that you have milk, carry an emergency carton of UHT milk, since bars usually close at 8pm. In many out-of-the-way areas in southern Italy, the locals use only UHT milk.

You can hire car seats for infants and children from most car-rental firms, but you should always book them in advance.

For more information, see Lonely Planet's *Travel with Children*.

DANGERS & ANNOYANCES

Theft

This is the main problem for travellers in Italy. Pickpockets and bag-snatchers operate in most major cities and are particularly active in Naples and Rome. The best way to avoid being robbed is to wear a money belt under your clothing. You should keep all important items, such as money, passport, other documents and tickets, in your money belt at all times. If you are carrying a bag or camera, ensure that you wear the strap across your body and have the bag on the side away from the road to deter snatchers, who often operate from motorcycles and scooters. Since the aim of young motorcycle bandits is often fun rather than gain, you are just as likely to find yourself relieved of your sunglasses – or worse, an earring – as something more valuable. Motorcycle bandits are very active in Naples, Rome, Syracuse and Palermo.

You should also watch out for groups of dishevelled-looking women and children. They generally work in groups of four or five and carry paper or cardboard which they use to distract your attention while they swarm around and rifle through your pockets and bag. Never underestimate their skill – they are lightning fast and very adept. Their favourite haunts are in and near major train stations, at tourist sights and in shopping areas. If you notice that you have been targeted by a group, either take evasive action (such as crossing the street) or shout '*Va via!*' (Go away!) in a loud, angry voice.

Pickpockets often hang out on busy buses (the No 64 in Rome, which runs from Stazione Termini to the Vatican, is notorious) and in crowded areas such as markets. There is only one sure way to avoid losing everything to pickpockets: simply *do not* carry any money or valuables in your pockets and be very careful with your bags.

Even the most cautious travellers are still prey to expert thieves but there is no need to be paranoid. By taking a few basic precautions, you can greatly lessen the risk of being robbed.

Be careful even in hotels and don't leave valuables lying around your room. You should also be cautious of sudden friendships, particularly if it turns out that your new-found *amico* or *amica* wants to sell you something.

Parked cars are also prime targets for thieves, particularly those with foreign numberplates or rental-company stickers. Try removing the stickers, or cover them and leave a local newspaper on the seat to make it look like a local car. *Never* leave valuables in your car – in fact, try not to leave anything in the car if you can help it and certainly not overnight. It is a good idea to pay extra to leave your car in supervised car parks, although there is no guarantee it will be completely safe. Throughout Italy, particularly in the south, service stations along the motorways are favourite haunts of thieves who can clean out a car in the time it takes to have a cup of coffee. If possible, park where you can keep an eye your car.

In recent years there have been isolated incidences of armed robberies on the motorways south of Naples, when travellers have been forced off the road or tricked into pulling over and have then been robbed at gunpoint. Fortunately, these incidents are rare.

When driving in cities you also need to beware of thieves when you pull up at traffic lights. Keep the doors locked and, if you have the windows open, ensure that there is nothing valuable on the dashboard. Car theft is a major problem in the regions of Campania and Apulia, particularly in the cities of Naples, Bari, Foggia and Brindisi. It is also a problem in Rome. Beware also of unofficial parking attendants who say you can leave your car double-parked as long as you leave them your keys: you will return to find that both the attendant and your car have disappeared.

Some Italians practise a more insidious form of theft: short-changing. If you are new to euros, take the time to acquaint yourself with the denominations. When paying for goods, tickets, a meal or whatever, keep an eye on the bills you hand over and then count your change carefully. One popular method of short-changing goes something like this: you hand over €50 for a newspaper that costs €1.50; you are handed change for €10 and, while the person who sold you the paper hesitates, you hurry off without counting it. If you'd stayed for another five seconds, the rest of the change probably would have been handed over.

In case of theft or loss, always report the incident at the *questura* (police station) within 24 hours and ask for a statement, otherwise your travel insurance company won't pay out.

Traffic

Italian traffic can at best be described as chaotic, at worst downright dangerous for the unprepared tourist. Drivers are not keen to stop for pedestrians, even at pedestrian crossings, and are more likely to swerve. Italians simply step off the footpath and walk through the (swerving) traffic with determination. It is a practice that seems to work, so if you feel uncertain about crossing a busy road, wait for the next Italian. (Better still, wait for a nun or priest to cross the road – most Italians seem to 'stop for God'.)

In many cities, roads that appear to be for one-way traffic have lanes for buses travelling in the opposite direction – always look both ways before stepping onto the road.

Pollution

Tourists will be affected in a variety of ways by the surprising disregard Italians have for their country (see Ecology & Environment in the Facts about Italy chapter). Noise and air pollution are problems in the major cities, caused mainly by heavy traffic. A headache after a day of sightseeing in Rome is likely to be caused by breathing carbon monoxide and lead, rather than simple tiredness. While cities such as Rome, Florence and Milan have banned normal traffic from their historic centres, there are still more than enough cars, buses and motorcycles in and around the inner city areas to pollute the air.

Particularly in summer, there are periodic pollution alerts. The elderly, children and people who have respiratory problems are warned to stay indoors. If you fit into one of these categories, keep yourself informed through the tourist office or your hotel.

One of the most annoying things about cities such as Rome, Naples, Palermo and Catania is that the pavements are littered with dog pooh – so be careful where you plant your feet or roll your suitcase.

Italy's beaches are generally heavily polluted by industrial waste, sewage and oil spills from the Mediterranean's considerable sea traffic. There are clean beaches on Sardinia, Sicily and in the less populated areas of the south and around Elba.

Annoyances

It requires a lot of patience to deal with the Italian concept of service. What for Italians

A Special Shopping Species

While you shop, look out for a distinctive breed of Italian – the boutique/shop assistant. These curious creatures are imperious, grumpy and rude – they spend hours chatting to colleagues or talking on the phone and have developed a highly skilled art in ignoring customers. Scientists believe that the role of the shop assistant was originally to help shoppers part with their money; in Italy creatures exhibiting these behavioural traits are now virtually extinct.

is simply a way of life can be horrifying for the foreigner. For example, the bank clerk who wanders off to have a cigarette just as it is your turn to be served (after a one-hour wait) or the postal worker who has too much important work to do at a desk to sell stamps to customers. Anyone in a uniform or behind a counter (including police officers, waiters and shop assistants) is likely to regard you with imperious contempt. Long queues are the norm in banks, post offices and any government offices.

It pays to remain calm and patient. Aggressive, demanding and angry customers stand virtually no chance of getting what they want.

As a popular destination for both tourists and immigrants, Italy is used to foreigners and it is very rare for Italians to show any animosity to strangers. However, the recent rise in illegal immigrants, known as *extra comunitari* to the Italians, entering Italy has led to some racial tensions – tensions which do not usually involve tourists.

LEGAL MATTERS

For many Italians, finding ways to get around the law (any law) is a way of life. They are likely to react with surprise, if not annoyance, if you point out that they might be breaking a law. Few people pay attention to speed limits; most motorcyclists and many drivers don't stop at red lights – and certainly not at pedestrian crossings. No-one bats an eyelid about littering or dogs pooping in the middle of the pavement, even though many municipal governments have introduced laws against these things. But these are minor transgressions when measured up against the country's organised crime, the extraordinary levels of tax evasion and the corruption in government and business.

The average tourist will probably have a brush with the law only if they are robbed by a bag-snatcher or pickpocket.

Drugs

Italy's drug laws are relatively lenient on drug users and heavy on pushers. If you're caught with drugs which the police determine are for your personal use, you'll be let off with a warning (and, of course, the drugs will be confiscated). If, instead, it is determined that you intend to sell the drugs in your possession, you could find yourself in prison. It's up to the discretion of the police to determine whether or not you're a pusher, since the law is not specific about quantities. It's best to avoid illicit drugs altogether.

Drink Driving

The legal limit for blood-alcohol level is 0.08% and random breath tests do occur. See Road Rules in the Getting Around chapter for more information on drink driving.

Police

To call the *polizia* (police) dial the toll-free emergency number ☎ 113. To report a non-violent theft or incident that doesn't endanger life, call the *carabinieri* (military police with civic duties) on ☎ 112. Addresses and local telephone numbers of police stations are given in the Emergency sections in this guide.

If you run into trouble in Italy, you're likely to end up dealing with either the polizia or the carabinieri. The polizia are a civil force and take their orders from the Ministry of the Interior, while the carabinieri fall under the Ministry of Defence. There is a considerable duplication of their roles, despite a 1981 reform of the police forces which intended to merge the two. Both forces are responsible for public order and security, which means that you can visit either in the event of a robbery or attack.

The carabinieri wear a black uniform with a red stripe and drive dark-blue cars with a red stripe. They are well trained and tend to be helpful. You are more likely to be pulled over by the carabinieri than the polizia if you are speeding. Their police station is called a *caserma* (barracks), a reflection of their military status.

The polizia wear powder-blue trousers with a fuchsia stripe and a navy-blue jacket. They drive light-blue cars with a white stripe and 'polizia' written on the side. People wanting to get a residence permit will have to deal with them. Their headquarters is called the *questura*.

Other varieties of police in Italy include the *vigili urbani*, who are basically traffic police. You will have to deal with them if you get a parking ticket or your car is towed away. The *guardia di finanza* are responsible for fighting tax evasion and drug smuggling. It's a long shot, but you could be stopped by one of them if you leave a shop without a receipt for your purchase. The *guardia forestale* or *corpo forestale* are responsible for enforcing laws concerning forests and their fauna and flora and the environment in general. Like the carabinieri, their headquarters is called a caserma. They are often found in isolated townships bordering on areas of environmental interest. They are armed and can fine law-breakers.

Your Rights

Italy still has some anti-terrorism laws on its books which could make life very difficult if you happen to be detained by the police – for any alleged offence. You can be held for 48 hours without a magistrate being informed and you can be interrogated without the presence of a lawyer. It is difficult to obtain bail and you can be held legally for up to three years without being brought to trial.

BUSINESS HOURS

Business hours vary from city to city, but generally shops open 9am to 1pm and 3.30pm to 7.30pm (or 4pm to 8pm) Monday to Saturday. In some cities, grocery shops might not reopen until 5pm and, during the warmer months, they could stay open until 9pm. They may close on Saturday afternoon and on Thursday or Monday afternoon (depending on the town). Many other shops and supermarkets also close for a half-day during the week – it varies from city to city but is usually either Monday morning or Thursday afternoon. In major towns, most department stores, such as Coin and Rinascente, and supermarkets now have continuous opening from 9am to 7.30pm Monday to Saturday. Some even open from 9am to 1pm on Sunday.

Banks tend to open (hours can vary) 8.30am to 1.30pm and 3.30pm to 4.30pm Monday to Friday. They are closed at weekends but it is always possible to find a bureau de change open in the larger cities and in major tourist areas.

Major post offices open 8.30am to 5pm or 6pm Monday to Friday and also 8.30am to 1pm or 2pm on Saturday. Smaller post offices are generally open from 8.30am to 1.50pm Monday to Friday, and also 8.30am to 11.50am on Saturday. All post offices close two hours earlier than normal on the last business day of each month (not including Saturday).

Pharmacies are usually open 9am to 12.30pm and 3.30pm to 7.30pm. They are always closed on Sunday and usually on Saturday afternoon. When closed, pharmacies are required to display a list of pharmacies in the area that are open.

Bars (in the Italian sense, coffee and sandwich places) and cafes generally open 7.30am to 8pm, although some stay open after 8pm and turn into pub-style drinking-and-meeting places. Clubs and discos might open around 10pm but often there'll be no-one there until around midnight. Restaurants open noon to 3pm and 7.30pm to 11pm (later in summer and in the south). Restaurants and bars are required to close for one day each week; which day it is varies between establishments.

The opening hours of museums, galleries and archaeological sites vary, although there is a trend towards continuous opening from 9.30am to 7pm. Many close on Monday. Increasingly, the major national museums and galleries remain open until 10pm during the summer.

PUBLIC HOLIDAYS

Most Italians take their annual holiday in August, deserting the cities for the cooler coastal or mountain resorts. This means that many businesses and shops close for at least a part of the month, particularly during the week around Ferragosto (Feast of the Assumption) on 15 August. Larger cities, notably Milan and Rome, are left to the tourists, who may be frustrated that many restaurants and shops are closed until early September. The Settimana Santa (Easter Week) is another busy holiday period for Italians.

National public holidays include the following:

New Year's Day	1 January
Epiphany	6 January
Easter Monday	March/April
Liberation Day	25 April
Labour Day	1 May
Feast of the Assumption	15 August
All Saints' Day	1 November
Feast of the Immaculate Conception	8 December
Christmas Day	25 December
Feast of Santo Stefano	26 December

Individual towns also have public holidays to celebrate the feasts of their patron saints. See the following Special Events section for details.

SPECIAL EVENTS

Italy's calendar bursts with cultural events ranging from colourful traditional celebrations, with a religious and/or historical flavour, through to festivals of the performing arts, including opera, music and theatre.

Many towns celebrate the feasts of their patron saints in eye-catching fashion. These include: the Feast of St Agata from 3 to 5 February in Catania; the Feast of St Mark on 25 April in Venice; the Feast of St John the Baptist on 24 June in Florence, Genoa and Turin; the Feast of Sts Peter and Paul on 29 June in Rome; the Feast of St Gennaro on 19 September in Naples; and the Feast of St Ambrose on 7 December in Milan. Religious festivals are particularly numerous on Sicily and Sardinia, notably Holy Week (Le Feste di Pasqua) on Sicily.

Among the important opera seasons are those at Verona's Arena and at La Scala in Milan. Major music festivals include Umbria Jazz in Perugia and Maggio Musicale Fiorentino in Florence, while the Festival dei Due Mondi (Festival of Two Worlds) in Spoleto is also worth visiting. Venice plays host to an international film festival and the Biennale visual arts festival, the latter held every odd year.

Festivals

The following is a selection of Italy's main festivals:

February/March/April

Carnevale (Carnival) During the period before Ash Wednesday, many towns stage carnivals and enjoy their last opportunity to indulge before Lent. The carnival held in Venice during the 10 days before Ash Wednesday is the most famous, but more traditional and popular carnival celebrations are held at Viareggio, on the northern coast of Tuscany, and at Ivrea, near Turin.

Sartiglia This is the highlight of carnival celebrations at Oristano on Sardinia, held on the Sunday and Tuesday before Lent. It involves a medieval tournament of horsemen in masquerade.

Sagra del Mandorlo in Fiore (Festival of the Almond Blossoms) This traditional festival features a historical pageant and fireworks. It is held in Agrigento, Sicily, in early/mid-February.

Le Feste di Pasqua (Holy Week) Holy Week in Italy is marked by solemn processions and Passion plays. In Taranto in Apulia on Holy Thursday there is the Procession of the Addolorata and on Good Friday there is the Procession of the Mysteries, when statues representing the Passion of Christ are carried around the town. One of Italy's oldest and most evocative Good Friday processions is held at Chieti in Abruzzo. In Sicily, the week is marked by numerous events, including a Procession of the Mysteries at Trapani and the celebration of Easter according to Byzantine rites at Piana degli Albanesi, near Palermo. Women in colourful 15th-century costume give out Easter eggs to the public.

Scoppio del Carro (Explosion of the Cart) Held in Florence on the Piazza del Duomo at noon on Easter Sunday, this event features the explosion of a cart full of fireworks, which is a tradition dating back to the crusades. It is seen as a good omen for the city if it works.

May

Festa di San Nicola On 2 and 3 May, the people of Bari in Apulia process in traditional costume to re-enact the delivery of the bones of their patron saint to Dominican friars. The next day a statue of the saint is taken to sea.

Processione dei Serpari (Snake-Charmers' Procession) Held at Cocullo in Abruzzo on the first Thursday of May, this famous traditional festival honours the village's patron saint, San Domenico. His statue is draped with live snakes and carried in procession.

Festa di San Gennaro Three times a year (the first Sunday in May, 19 September and 16 December), the faithful gather in Naples' cathedral to wait for the blood of San Gennaro to liquefy. If the miracle occurs, it is considered a good omen for the city.

Corsa dei Ceri This exciting, traditional race is held in Gubbio (Umbria) on 15 May. Groups of men carrying huge wooden shrines race uphill to the town's basilica, which is dedicated to the patron saint, Ubaldo.

Cavalcata Sarda (Sardinian Cavalcade) Hundreds of Sardi wearing colourful traditional costume gather at Sassari on Sardinia on the second-last Sunday in May to mark a victory over the Saracens in the year 1000.

Palio della Balestra (Crossbow Contest) Held in Gubbio (Umbria) on the last Sunday in May, this contest is between the men of Gubbio and neighbouring Sansepolcro, who dress in medieval costume and use antique weapons. There is a rematch at Sansepolcro in September.

Maggio Musicale Fiorentino This music festival is held in Florence in May and June.

June

Palio delle Quattro Antiche Repubbliche Marinare (Regatta of the Four Ancient Maritime Republics) This event sees a procession of boats and a race between the four historical maritime rivals – Pisa, Venice, Amalfi and Genoa. The event rotates between the four towns: Pisa in 2002, Venice in 2003, Genoa in 2004, Amalfi in 2005. Although usually held in June, it has been known to be delayed as late as September.

Festa di Sant'Antonio Fans of Sant'Antonio, patron saint of Padua and of lost things, might want to attend the procession of the saint's relics, held annually on 13 June.

Infiorata (Flower Festival) To celebrate Corpus Domini on 21 June, some towns (including Bolsena and Genzano near Rome and Spello in Umbria) decorate a street with colourful designs made with flower petals.

Gioco del Ponte (Game of the Bridge) Two groups in medieval costume contend for the Ponte di Mezzo, a bridge over the River Arno in Pisa.

Festival dei Due Mondi (Festival of Two Worlds) This is an international arts event held in June and July at Spoleto, a beautiful hill town in Umbria. It was created by Gian Carlo Menotti and features music, theatre, dance and art.

July

Il Palio (The Banner) The pride and joy of Siena in Tuscany, this famous traditional event is held twice a year – on 2 July and 16 August – in the town's beautiful Piazza del Campo. It involves a dangerous bareback horse race around the piazza, preceded by a parade of supporters in traditional costume.

Sa Ardia More dangerous than Il Palio, this impressive and chaotic horse race at Sedilo on Sardinia on 6 and 7 July celebrates the victory of the Roman Emperor Constantine over Maxentius in AD 312 (the battle was actually at the Ponte Milvio in Rome). A large number of horsemen race around town while onlookers shoot guns into the ground or air.

Festa del Redentore (Feast of the Redeemer) On the third weekend in July, there are fireworks and a procession over the bridge to the Chiesa del Redentore on Isola della Giudecca in Venice.

Umbria Jazz Held at Perugia in Umbria in July, this week-long festival features performers from around the world. There's also Umbria Jazz Winter held in Orvieto at the end of December/early January.

Festival Internazionale del Balleto (International Ballet Festival) This festival is held at Nervi near Genoa and features international performers.

August

Quintana (Medieval Joust) This historical pageant features a parade of hundreds of people in 15th-century costume, followed by a spectacular jousting tournament. It is held at Ascoli Piceno in Le Marche on the first Sunday in August.

I Candelieri (The Candlesticks) Held on 14 August at Sassari on Sardinia, I Candelieri features town representatives in medieval costume carrying huge wooden columns through the town. The celebrations are held to honour a vow made in 1652 for deliverance from a plague.

Il Palio This repeat of Siena's famous horse race is held on 16 August.

Festa del Redentore Held in Nuoro on Sardinia, this folk festival and parade is attended by thousands of people from all over the island, who dress in traditional regional costume.

Mostra del Cinema di Venezia (Venice International Film Festival) Held at the Lido, Venice, the festival attracts the international film scene.

September

Partita a Scacchi (Living Chess Game) The townspeople of Marostica in the Veneto dress as chess figures and participate in a match on a chessboard marked out in the town square. Games are held in even years on the first weekend in September.

Palio della Balestra A rematch of the crossbow competition between Gubbio and Sansepolcro is held at Sansepolcro on the first Sunday in September.

Regata Storica (Historic Regatta) This gondola race along Venice's Grand Canal is preceded by a parade of boats decorated in 15th-century style. It is held on the first Sunday in September.

Giostra della Quintana (Medieval Joust) This medieval pageant held in Foligno, near Perugia, involves a parade and jousting event with horsemen in traditional costume. It is held on the second Sunday in September.

Festa di San Gennaro On 19 September the faithful of Naples gather for the second time to await the miraculous liquefaction of San Gennaro's blood.

October

Festa di San Francesco Special religious ceremonies are held in the churches of San Francesco and Santa Maria degli Angeli in Assisi on 3 and 4 October.

November

Festa della Madonna della Salute Held in Venice on 21 November, this procession over a bridge of boats across the Grand Canal to the Chiesa di Santa Maria della Salute is to give thanks for the city's deliverance from plague in 1630.

Festa di Santa Cecilia A series of concerts and exhibitions take place in Siena in Tuscany to honour the patron saint of musicians.

December/January

Festa di San Nicola Various religious ceremonies as well as traditional folk celebrations take place at Bari in Apulia on 6 December.

Festa di San Gennaro On 16 December the faithful of Naples gather for a third and final time to await the liquefaction of the blood of San Gennaro.

Natale (Christmas) During the weeks preceding Christmas there are numerous processions and religious events. Many churches set up elaborate cribs or nativity scenes known as *presepi*.

Umbria Jazz Winter The winter version of Umbria's jazz festival is held in Orvieto. It takes place late December/early January.

ACTIVITIES

If the museums, galleries and sights are not enough for you, there are numerous options for getting off the beaten tourist track. From mountaineering to water sports, Italy offers a wide range of outdoor pursuits.

Walking

Italy is a walker's paradise – in the mountains, by the sea, in the gently undulating countryside, there are enough walks to keep you busy for a lifetime. Thousands of kilometres of marked trails *(sentieri)* can make it all relatively easy, but you still need to be able to read a map and use a compass. *Rifugi* (mountain huts) provide far-from-spartan accommodation in mountainous areas, so it's possible to do extended walks without having to carry a tent and supplies. You need to have suitable protective gear for bad weather and for the inevitable sunshine and heat.

The Dolomites is among the best known and most popular areas with multitudes of stunning peaks – see Walking in the Dolomites in the Trentino-Alto Adige chapter for more information. Parco Nazionale Gran Paradiso in Valle d'Aosta has a magnificent network of sentieri over high passes and through beautiful valleys. The Matterhorn (Monte Cervino) and Monte Rosa, two names which resonate for mountaineers, lie generally north of Valle d'Aosta. You can enjoy them from below along paths linking the fringing valleys. For wild and remote mountains, try the Maritime Alps in south-western Piedmont and the Carniche and Giulie Alps in Friuli-Venezia Giulia. The long chain of the Apennines also has a number of higher-level walks, especially in Tuscany's Apuane Alps and Parco Nazionale d'Abruzzo. Both Sicily and Sardinia have mountains in profusion including, most famously, Sicily's Mt Etna. You can also brave the other active volcanoes on foot – Vesuvius near Naples and Stromboli and Vulcano on the Aeolian Islands.

Walking in the mountains and the valleys around the lakes of Garda, Como and Maggiore (mostly in Lombardy) is superb. Tuscany offers incomparable opportunities for combining scenic walks and finding food and wine. If you like to be near the sea, two great areas, apart from the islands, are the Cinque Terre in Liguria and the Amalfi-Sorrento peninsula in Campania where age-old paths follow miraculous routes across precipitous hillsides.

Look out for Lonely Planet's *Walking in Italy* for detailed descriptions of more than 50 walks and outlines of many more. Guided walks are organised in many national parks, though you'd need to speak Italian (enquire at local tourist offices for details). Many companies run organised walking holidays in the major and lesser-known walking areas – *Walking in Italy* has some suggestions.

Skiing

There are numerous excellent ski resorts in the Italian Alps and, again, the Dolomites provide the most dramatic scenery. Options include *lo sci* (downhill skiing) and *sci di fondo* (cross-country skiing), as well as *sci alpinismo* (ski mountaineering). The latter is only for the adventurous and advanced: skiers head well away from the organised runs and combine their mountaineering and skiing skills.

ASA ANDERSSON

Skiing is quite expensive because of the costs of ski lifts and accommodation but a *Settimana Bianca* (White Week) package can reduce the expense. It's not expensive, on the other hand, to hire ski equipment – and this factor should be weighed up against the inconvenience of bringing your own gear. Cross-country skiing costs less because you don't pay for the lifts.

The season in Italy generally runs from December to late March, although at higher altitudes and in particularly good years it can be longer. There is year-round skiing in areas such as the Marmolada glacier in Trentino-Alto Adige and on Mt Blanc (Monte Bianco) and the Matterhorn in the Valle d'Aosta.

The five major (read most fashionable and expensive) ski resorts in Italy are Cortina d'Ampezzo in the Veneto; Madonna di Campiglio, San Martino di Castrozza and Canazei in Trentino; and Courmayeur in the Valle d'Aosta. There are many other, less expensive resorts that also offer excellent facilities (see the northern Italy chapters for details).

Water Sports

Windsurfing and sailing are extremely popular in Italy and at most beach resorts it is possible to hire boats and equipment. There are also various diving schools, but the scenery above water is much more interesting. Information on boat and windsurfing equipment hire at water resorts is given throughout this book.

Cycling

The only problem with cycling in Italy is that more than 75% of the country is mountainous or hilly, so you will need plenty of stamina and a decent bike. A mountain bike is a good idea as it would enable you to tackle some of the Alpine trails as well. Cycling and mountain biking are becoming increasingly popular in Italy and you'll find that most tourist offices will be able to offer information on mountain-bike trails and

ASA ANDERSSON

guided rides. For information on hiring or buying a bike and on travelling around Italy with one, see the Bicycle section in the Getting Around chapter.

The hills of Tuscany are very popular for cycling, particularly around Florence and Siena, from where you can explore the countryside around Fiesole, San Gimignano and Chianti, just to name a few possibilities. A bike would be particularly useful for getting around Sardinia. In Umbria, areas such as the Valnerina and the Piano Grande at Monte Vettore have beautiful trails and quiet country roads to explore. Serious cyclists will know where to go for the most challenging routes – the tortuous, winding road up to the Passo Stelvio is one of the most famous.

COURSES

Many people come to Italy to study the language. Courses are run by private schools and universities throughout the country and are a great way to learn Italian while enjoying the opportunity to live in an Italian city or town.

One of the cheapest options is the Università per Stranieri in Perugia (see Courses in the Perugia section of the Umbria chapter). Individual schools and universities are listed under the relevant towns throughout this book. The schools can usually also arrange accommodation in a student residence or with an Italian family. There are also extracurricular or full-time courses in painting, art history, sculpture and architecture available; however, all these courses can be expensive.

The Istituto Italiano di Cultura (IIC), with branches all over the world, is a government-sponsored organisation aimed at promoting Italian culture and language. It puts on classes in Italian and provide a library and information service. This is a good place to start your search for places to study in Italy. Try the IIC's Web sites at **W** www.iicmelau.org (Melbourne, Australia), **W** www.iicsyd.org (Sydney, Australia), **W** www.iicto-ca.org/istituto.htm (Canada), **W** www.italynet.com/cultura/istcult (France) and **W** www.italcultny.org (USA).

Another option is to check with travel agencies in your country for organised study tours to Italy. In England, ***Anglo-Italian Study Tours*** *(☎/fax 020-7680 1377,* **e** *tours@vallicorte.demon.co.uk,* **W** *www.vallicorte.com, 78 Wapping High St – no 15, London E1W 2NB)* runs courses in cooking, wine, art and architecture, and painting in a farmhouse near Lucca, in Tuscany. Courses run in spring and autumn and cost around €1500 for seven days, including food and accommodation.

Cookery courses are becoming increasingly popular and can be an excellent, if expensive, introduction to the local cuisine. In Rome, published cookery writer ***Diane Seed*** *(☎ 06 679 71 03,* **e** *dianeseed@compuserve.com)* runs seven-day long non-residential courses for around €680, including lessons in shopping and olive-oil tasting.

For the hefty sum of around €3000 you can learn the art of Tuscan cuisine in a 9th-century former monastery in the Chianti area with ***Lorenza de Medici*** *(☎ 0577 74 94 98, fax 0577 74 92 35,* **e** *cuisineint@aol.com)* – and you get to sleep in a monk's cell to boot.

The more adventurous traveller might want to take a course in rock climbing, ski mountaineering or hang-gliding, just to name a few of the possibilities. Mountain-guide groups offering courses are listed in the relevant sections of the northern Italy chapters or you can always get information from local tourist offices in the relevant areas.

WORK

It is illegal for non-EU citizens to work in Italy without a *permesso di lavoro* (work permit), but trying to obtain one can be time-consuming. EU citizens are allowed to work in Italy but they still need to obtain a *permesso di soggiorno* (residence permit) from the main questura in the town, ideally before they look for employment. See Permesso di Soggiorno and Work Permits in the Visas & Documents section earlier in this chapter for more information.

Immigration laws require foreign workers to be 'legalised' through their employers, which can apply even to cleaners and babysitters. The employers then pay pension and health-insurance contributions. This doesn't mean, however, that there aren't employers willing to take people without the right papers.

Work options depend on a number of factors (location, length of stay, nationality and qualifications, for example) but, in the major cities at least, job possibilities for English speakers can be surprisingly plentiful. Go armed with a CV (if possible in Italian) and be persistent. Research potential employers before going to Italy and expect to have to follow up any speculative written applications with a visit once you have arrived.

Jobs are advertised in local newspapers and magazines, such as Rome's *Porta Portese* (published on Tuesday and Friday) and *Wanted in Rome* (fortnightly) or *Secondamano* in Milan, and you can also place an ad yourself.

A very useful guide is *Living, Studying and Working in Italy* by Travis Neighbour & Monica Larner. You could also have a look at *Work Your Way Around the World* by Susan Griffith.

Nannying & Au Pair Work

Babysitting is a good possibility, and in the major cities you can try to pick up a summer job accompanying a family on their annual beach holiday. Look in magazines such as *Wanted in Rome* or place an advertisement. Another option is au pair work, which should be organised before you come to Italy. A useful guide is *The Au Pair and Nanny's Guide to Working Abroad* by S Griffith & S Legg.

Teaching English

The most obvious source of work for foreigners is teaching English but even with full qualifications an American, Australian, Canadian or New Zealander might find it difficult to secure a permanent position. Most of the larger, more reputable language schools will hire only people with a work permit, but their attitude can become more flexible if the demand for teachers is high and they come across someone with good qualifications. The more professional schools will require a TEFL (Teaching English as a Foreign Language) certificate. It is advisable to apply for work early in the calendar year, in order to be considered for positions available in the new academic year (language-school years correspond roughly to the Italian school year: late September to the end of June).

There are numerous schools throughout the country that hire people without a valid permit or qualifications but the pay is usually low (around €7.75 an hour). It is more lucrative to teach private students. Rates, however, can vary hugely: in a large city such as Rome, the average rate is around €15.50, while in smaller provincial towns, where the market is more limited, even qualified and experienced private teachers will have to charge as low as €7.75 to €10.35 in order to attract students. Many people get started by advertising in English-language bookshops and churches, on university notice boards or in the local press.

Bar Work

A good option is to look for employment in a bar, nightclub or restaurant during the tourist season. The Irish pubs that have recently sprung up in Italy are good starting points.

Street Performing

Busking is common in Italy, although theoretically buskers require a municipal permit. Italians tend not to stop and gather around street performers but they are usually quite generous.

Other Work

Freelance translation work is a possibility if you have good Italian and access to a word processor. Advertise in a local paper or contact the local agencies (listed in the phone directory). People with secretarial skills and a good knowledge of Italian sometimes manage to pick up part- or full-time secretarial work with international companies in the major cities. Look in the local papers for advertisements.

There are plenty of markets around the country where you can set up a stall and sell your wares, although you may need to pay a fee. Selling goods on the street is illegal unless you have a municipal permit and it is quite common to see municipal police moving people along. Another option is to head for beach resorts in summer, particularly if you have handicrafts or jewellery you want to sell.

ACCOMMODATION

Prices for accommodation quoted in this book are intended as a guide only. There is generally a fair degree of fluctuation in hotel prices throughout Italy, depending on the season and whether establishments raise prices when they have the opportunity. It is not unusual for prices to remain fixed for years on end (and in some cases they even go down) but it is more common that they rise by around 5% or 10% annually.

In budget hotels it can sometimes be worth bargaining. Try mentioning the names of a few close competitors and see how the owner miraculously finds an identical room at half the original price.

Reservations

It is a good idea to book a room if you're planning to travel during peak tourist times such as summer, Easter or Christmas. Hotels usually require confirmation by fax, email or letter, as well as a deposit. Fax numbers and email addresses for larger hotels in major cities are listed in this book. If you need more choice than we provide, staff at tourist offices will generally send out information about hotels, camping, apartments and so on. Another option is to use one of the local hotel-booking services – you'll find some listed under Places to Stay in Rome and Florence.

Camping

Most camp sites in Italy are major complexes with swimming pools, tennis courts, restaurants and supermarkets. Like hotels, they are graded according to a star system. Prices at even the most basic camp sites can be surprisingly expensive during the peak periods, once you add up the various charges for each person and for a site for your tent or caravan and a car, but they can generally still work out cheaper than a double room in a one-star hotel. Charges range from €4 to €10 per adult, €3 to €8 for children aged under 12, and €5 to €12 for a site.

Locations are usually good, ranging from beach or lakeside to valleys in the Alps. In the major cities, camp sites are often a long way from the historic centres and the inconvenience, plus the additional cost of using public transport, should be weighed up against the price of a hotel room.

Independent camping is generally not permitted in protected areas and you might find yourself moved on by the carabinieri if you attempt it. But, out of the main tourist season, independent campers who choose spots not visible from the road, who don't light fires and who try to be inconspicuous shouldn't have too much trouble. Always get permission from the landowner if you want to camp on private property. Camper vans are very popular in Italy.

Full lists of camp sites in and near cities and towns are usually available from local tourist offices. The tourist boards of Sicily and Sardinia publish annual booklets listing all facilities on the islands. TCI publishes an annual book listing all camp sites in Italy, *Campeggi in Italia* (€18.50), and the Istituto Geografico de Agostini publishes the annual *Guida ai Campeggi in Europa*, sold together with *Guida ai Campeggi in Italia* (€16). These books are available in major bookshops (including all Feltrinelli stores).

Hostels

Ostelli per la gioventù (youth hostels) are run by the Associazione Italiana Alberghi per la Gioventù (AIG), which is affiliated to Hostelling International (HI). An HI card is not always required but it is recommended that you have one. For details on how to get a card see Hostel Card in the Visas & Documents section earlier in this chapter.

Pick up a booklet on Italian hostels, with details of prices, locations and so on, from the AIG national head office (☎ 06 487 11 52, ⓔ aig@uni.net), Via Cavour 44, Rome. Their Web sites at ⓦ www.travel.it/hostels and ⓦ www.hostels-aig.org explain all the facilities on offer.

Many Italian hostels are beautifully located, some in castles and villas. Many have bars and with few exceptions they have restaurants or kitchens or both. Nightly rates vary from €8 to €14, which often includes breakfast. In some hostels there is a small additional charge for use of heating and hot water. A meal will cost from €7.

Accommodation is in segregated dormitories, although many hostels offer doubles or family rooms (at a higher price per person). Hostels will usually have a lock-out period between 9am and 3.30pm, although there are many exceptions. Check-in is from 6pm to 10.30pm, although some hostels will allow you a morning check-in before they close for the day (it is best to find out beforehand). Curfew is usually 10.30pm or 11pm in winter and 11.30pm or midnight in summer. It is usually necessary to pay before 9am on the day of your departure, otherwise you could be charged for another night.

Pensiones & Hotels

It is very important to remember that prices quoted in this book are intended as a guide only. Travellers should always check on prices before committing to stay in a place. Make a complaint to the local tourist office if you believe you're being overcharged. Remember that many proprietors employ various methods of bill-padding, such as charging for showers or making breakfast compulsory.

There is often no difference between a pensione and an *albergo* (hotel); in fact, some hotels use both titles. However, a pensione will generally be of one- to three-star quality, while an albergo can be awarded up to five stars. *Locande* (inns) and *affittacamere* (rooms for rent), also known as *alloggi*, are generally cheaper, but not always. Locande and affittacamere are not included in the star classification system, although in some areas (such as the Aeolian Islands and the Alps) the standard of affittacamere is very high.

While the quality of accommodation can vary a great deal, one-star hotels/pensiones tend to be very basic and usually do not have a private bathroom attached to rooms. Standards at two-star places are often only slightly better but rooms will generally have a private bathroom. Once you arrive at three stars you can assume that standards will be reasonable, although quality still varies dramatically. Four- and five-star hotels are usually part of a chain and offer facilities such as room service, laundry and dry-cleaning.

Overall, prices are highest in Rome, Florence, Milan and Venice, and at other major tourist destinations. They also tend to be higher in northern Italy. Prices can soar in the high season at beach resorts and during the ski season in the Alps.

A single room *(camera singola)* is uniformly expensive in Italy, costing from around €25. A double room with twin beds *(camera doppia)* and a double room with a double bed *(camera matrimoniale)* will cost from around €33. It is much cheaper to share with two or more. Proprietors will usually charge no more than 15% of the cost of a double room for each additional person.

Tourist offices have booklets listing all local pensiones and hotels, including prices (although they might not always be up-to-date). Ask for lists of the locande and affittacamere.

Agriturismo

Agriturismo – a holiday on a working farm – is becoming increasingly popular in Italy. Traditionally, the idea was that families rented out rooms in their farmhouses, and it is still possible to find this type of accommodation. However, more commonly now the term refers to a restaurant in a restored farm complex with rooms available for rent. All agriturismo establishments grow or make some sort of produce and you will usually be able to sample/buy the wares.

JOHN HAY

Lunch on the run: an Italian takeaway

RUSSELL MOUNTFORD

Better than Viagra – let the chillis do the talking.

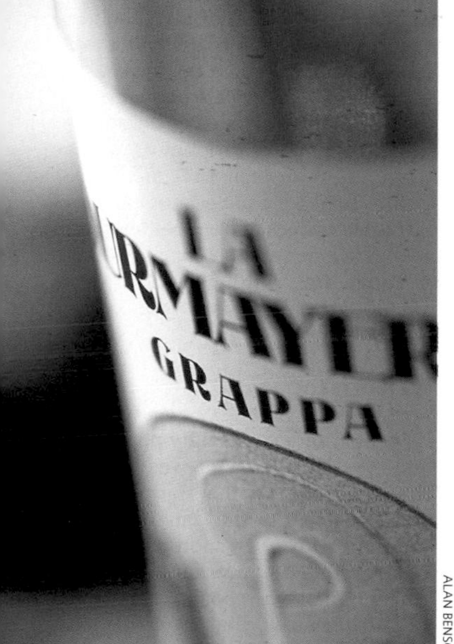

ALAN BENSON

Grappa can make you feel crappa the next day.

ALAN BENSON

Fresh asparagus invades the markets in May.

ALAN BENSON

A creation made from cow's curd: scamorza cheese

JOHN HAY

ALAN BENSON

JOHN HAY

JOHN HAY

Life in its most unadulterated, unbridled form: the Italian market is a chaotic, colourful and lively affair wherever you are in the country and at any time of year.

Agriturismo is quite well organised in Trentino-Alto Adige, Tuscany and Umbria, and increasingly so in parts of Sicily and Sardinia. Local tourist offices usually have lists of operators. For detailed information on all agriturismo facilities in Italy contact Agriturist (☎ 06 685 23 337), Corso Vittorio Emanuele 89, 00186 Rome. It publishes a book with agriturismo listings for the whole country (Agriturist 2002; €22), available at the office and in selected bookshops.

Mountain Refuges

If you are planning to walk in the Alps, Apennines or other mountains in Italy, obtain information on the network of rifugi. The various kinds of refuges are detailed in the relevant sections of the northern Italy chapters. It should be noted that most are only open from July to September.

Accommodation is generally in dormitories but some of the larger refuges have double rooms. The price per person for an overnight stay plus breakfast varies from around €10 to €22 (more if you are staying in a double room). Meals are always available, but a hearty post-walking dinner could set you back another €20. Note that the average price of a bottle of mineral water is around €2 and the beer will be the highest in price that you have ever come across.

The locations of rifugi are marked on good walking maps. Some are close to chair lifts and cable-car stations, which means they are usually expensive and crowded with tourists. Others are at high altitude, involving hours of hard walking or climbing from the nearest village or another refuge. These tend to be a little bit cheaper and, in general, are used by serious walkers and mountaineers. It is important to book a bed in advance otherwise you could end up walking for an unplanned extra few hours to the next one. Additional information, including telephone numbers, can be obtained from local tourist offices.

The Club Alpino Italiano (CAI) owns and runs many of the mountain refuges. Its Web site at W www.cai.it/rifugi is a useful source of information. Members of organisations such as the Australian Alpine Club and British Mountaineering Council can enjoy discounted rates for accommodation and meals by obtaining (for a fee) a reciprocal rights card.

Landmark Trust

If you fancy staying in the building where Keats died, one of Palladio's villas or Browning's house, contact the Landmark Trust in the UK. Established as a charity in 1965, the trust restores and conserves a host of architectural marvels in the UK, as well as three in Italy: the 3rd-floor apartment where Keats died in Piazza di Spagna, Rome; the Casa Guidi in Florence, where Browning lived; and the Villa Saraceno near Vicenza, an early Palladio commission. For more details contact the Landmark Trust (☎ 01628-825925, W www.landmarktrust.co.uk), Shottesbrooke, Maidenhead, Berkshire SL6 3SW, UK.

Religious Institutions

Known as *casa religiosa per l'ospitalità*, these institutions offer accommodation in major cities and in many monasteries in the country. The standard is usually good but prices are no longer low – expect to pay about the same as for a mid-range hotel, if not more. Information can be obtained through local tourist offices or through the archdiocese of the relevant city.

Student Accommodation

People planning to study in Italy can usually organise accommodation through the school or university they will be attending. Options include a room with an Italian family or a share arrangement with other students in an independent apartment. Some Italian universities operate a *casa dello studente*, which houses Italian students throughout the school year and lets out rooms during the summer break (July to the end of September). It can be very difficult to organise a room in one of these institutions – the best way is to attempt to book through your own university or to contact the relevant Italian university directly.

Rental Accommodation

Finding rental accommodation in the major cities can be difficult and time-consuming, but it's not impossible. There are rental agencies that will assist, for a fee. We've listed some under major cities. Rental rates are higher for short-term leases. A small apartment anywhere near the centre of Rome will cost around €930 per month and it is usually necessary to pay a deposit (generally at least one month in advance). Apartments and villas for rent are listed in local publications such as Rome's weekly *Porta Portese* and fortnightly *Wanted in Rome*. You will find that many owners want to rent to foreigners because the let is short term or because they intend to charge a high rent. Another option is to answer an advertisement in a local publication to share an apartment.

In major resort areas, such as the Aeolian Islands and other parts of Sicily, the coastal areas of Sardinia and in the Alps, the tourist offices have lists of local apartments and villas for rent. Most offices will be more than cooperative if you telephone beforehand for information on how to book an apartment.

People wanting to rent a villa in the countryside can seek information from specialist travel agencies in their own country or contact an organisation in Italy directly. One of the major companies in Italy is Cuendet, which has villas in Tuscany, Umbria, the Veneto, Rome, Le Marche, the Amalfi Coast, Apulia, Sicily and Sardinia. This reliable company publishes a booklet listing all the villas in its files, with photographs of most of them. Prices for a villa for four to six people range from around €460 per week in winter up to €1300 per week in August. For details, write to Cuendet & Cie Spa (☎ 0577 57 63 30, fax 0577 30 11 93, e cuede@tin.it, w www.cuendet.com), Strada di Strove 17, 53035 Monteriggioni, Siena. In the UK, you can order Cuendet's catalogues and make reservations by calling ☎ 0800 891573. In the USA, Cuendet bookings are handled by Rentals in Italy (☎ 805-987 5278, fax 482 7976), 1742 Calle Corva, Camarillo, CA 93010.

CIT travel agency offices (also called Sestante or CIT Sestante) throughout the world have lists of villas and apartments available for rent in Italy. Check out their Web site at w www.cittravel.com for details.

In Australia, try an organisation called Cottages & Castles (☎ 03-9853 1142, fax 03-9853 0509, e cottages@vicnet.net.au), 11 Laver St, Kew 3101, Victoria.

Don't expect to land in Italy and find an apartment or villa immediately: unless you are staying for an indefinite period, you might find that your holiday is taken up with flat-hunting.

FOOD

Eating is one of life's great pleasures for Italians. Be adventurous and don't ever be intimidated by eccentric waiters or indecipherable menus and you will find yourself agreeing with the locals that nowhere in the world is the food as good as in Italy – and, more specifically, as in their own town.

For information on the staples of Italian food and regional varieties, see the Food special section later in this chapter. The Language chapter at the back of this book has a glossary of food and culinary terms.

For more information and plenty of full-colour photos to make your mouth water, see Lonely Planet's *World Food Italy*.

Restaurants

These fall into several categories. A *tavola calda* (literally 'hot table') normally offers cheap, pre-prepared food, which showcases local specialities and can include self-service pasta, roast meats, *pizza al taglio* (pizza by the slice) and vegetable dishes. A *pizzeria* will, of course, serve pizza but usually also has a trattoria-style menu. An *osteria* is likely to be either a wine bar offering a small selection of dishes with a verbal menu, or a small trattoria. A *trattoria* is basically a cheaper version of a *ristorante* (restaurant) with less aloof service and simple dishes; a ristorante generally has a wider selection of dishes, printed menus, a higher standard of service and generally higher prices. The problem is that many of the establishments that are in fact restaurants call themselves trattorias and vice versa, usually to capture the spirit of the other establishment – rustic charm or elegance and sophistication. It is best to check the menu, usually posted by the door, for prices.

Don't judge the quality of a restaurant or trattoria by its appearance. You are likely to eat your most memorable meal at a place with plastic tablecloths in a tiny backstreet, a dingy piazza or on a back road in the country. And don't panic if you find yourself in a trattoria that has no printed menu: they are often the ones that offer the best and most authentic food and have menus which change daily to accommodate the availability of fresh produce.

Most eating establishments have a cover charge (*coperto*; usually from around €1 to €1.55) and a service charge *(servizio)* of 10% to 15%. Restaurants usually open for lunch from 12.30pm to 3pm, but many are not keen to take orders after 2pm. In the evening, opening hours vary from north to south. In the north, dinner starts at around 7.30pm but in Sicily you will be hard-pressed to find a restuarant open before 8.30pm.

Bars & Gelaterias

Bars are very popular hangouts, mostly serving coffee, soft drinks, juices and alcohol. They often sell *brioche* (breakfast pastry), *cornetti* (croissants), *panini* (bread roll with simple fillings) and *spuntini* (snacks), such as olives, nuts and potato chips, to have with a drink. You can round off the meal with a *gelato* (ice cream) from a *gelateria* – a crowd outside is always a good sign – followed by a *digestivo* (digestive liqueur) or *caffè* (coffee) at a bar.

Fast Food & Takeaways

There are numerous outlets where you can buy pizza al taglio. You could also try one of the *alimentari* (grocery stores) and ask them to make a *panino* (bread roll) with the filling of your choice.

Fast food is becoming increasingly popular in Italy. There are McDonald's outlets throughout the country, along with other chain restaurants and hamburger joints. But, seriously, why would you bother when Italian fast food – *arancini* (herby, deep-fried rice balls stuffed with meat or cheese) in Sicily, *filetti di baccalà* (dried salted cod) in Rome and pizza all over the country – is so good?

Self-Catering

If you have access to cooking facilities, it is best to buy fruit and vegetables at markets (usually open in the mornings only) and salami, cheese and wine at alimentari or *salumerie* (a cross between a grocery store and a delicatessen). A *rosticceria* sells cooked meats. Fresh bread is available at a *forno* or *panetteria* (bakeries that sell bread, pastries and sometimes groceries) and usually at alimentari. At a *pasticceria* you can buy pastries, cakes and biscuits. There are also supermarkets in most towns and these are listed in the relevant sections throughout this book. Remember that most food shops close for lunch.

Meals

Italians will rarely eat a sit-down *colazione* (breakfast). They tend to drink a cappuccino, usually *tiepido* (warm), and eat a cornetto or other type of pastry while standing at a bar.

Pranzo (lunch) is traditionally the main meal of the day and many shops and businesses close for three to four hours every afternoon to accommodate the meal and the siesta which is traditionally supposed to follow. A full meal will consist of an *antipasto* (starter), which can vary from *bruschetta*, a type of garlic bread with various toppings, to fried vegetables or *prosciutto e melone* (cured ham wrapped around melon). Next comes the *primo piatto* (first course), a pasta or risotto, followed by the *secondo piatto* (second course) of meat or fish. Italians often then eat an *insalata* (salad) or *contorno* (vegetable side dish) and round off the meal with fruit, or occasionally with a *dolce* (dessert) and coffee, often at a bar on the way back to work.

Cena (evening meal) was traditionally a more simple affair but in recent years habits have been changing because of the inconvenience of travelling home for lunch every day.

[continued on page 138]

Italian Food

To eat and drink in Italy is to be thrust into the heart of Italian life. To sit at dinner with an Italian is to understand where their heart is at, what is important to them. Italian food is something to be enjoyed, as part of embracing the moment, as part of life.

Although this is a country that has exported its food culture around the world, Italian cuisine *(cucina italiana)* doesn't exist. Spend any time among the people of, say, Umbria and you'll hear an awful lot about Umbrian cuisine. But Italian cuisine? Well, that's not something they know about. The geography makes for many micro-climates and the history for plenty of micro-cultures. The result is a range of food that is one of the most diverse, unexpected and intriguing imaginable. But, for all their culinary distinctions, Italians are actually united by many of the staples which make up their cooking. Despite the mind-boggling number of variations which exist, the regions of Italy are bound by the common use of bread, pasta, cheese, *salumi* (cured meats), pizza, seafood, *gelati* (ice cream) and *dolci* (sweets), as well as the myriad vegetables and meats Italians draw on to create their favourite dishes.

JANE SMITH

Staples

Bread

Il pane is served at every meal apart from breakfast; you'll be given a basket of it in restaurants and freshly cut chunks in homes. Most of the time it will be white and fairly ordinary, although brilliant speciality breads still exist. Wholemeal bread lovers should look for *pane integrale* (bread made with at least some proportion of wholemeal flour). On restaurant tables you'll see *grissini*, thin sticks of crispy bread made from a yeast-risen dough.

Pizza

One of Italy's biggest exports, pizza is still a firm favourite at home but don't expect it to be the same as the impostors you find around the globe. In Naples, where the modern pizza (round and baked to order) was born, the passion for eating it is only surpassed by its high quality. All over Italy, they've made it the best fast food in the nation by baking it in large rectangular trays and selling it in slices as *pizza a(l) taglio*.

Pasta

Pasta existed in Liguria and Campania long before Marco Polo went east. Although both regions still dispute who made it first, pasta is now synonymous with Italian food the world over. The mainstay of most Italians' diet, pasta is infinitely varied but can be roughly divided into two groups: dry and fresh. Dry pasta *(pastasciutta)* is usually made with *semolino* (durum wheat) and water. Most dried pastas originated in the south (think spaghetti and penne) and suit predominantly vegetable-based (and usually runnier) sauces. Fresh pasta (*pasta fresca*, but also known as *pasta all'uovo*, pasta with eggs, or *fatto a mano*, hand-made) is made with eggs and flour. The heartland of this pasta is Emilia-Romagna, but these days you will find tortellini, ravioli or thin-

Cooking Pasta

Cooking good pasta is no mean feat – it has to be cooked for precisely the correct length of time, so that it is *al dente* (with a bite to it, or literally 'to the teeth'). Italians always add salt to the boiling water before adding the pasta and never rinse it after cooking. No self-respecting restaurant will cook pasta ahead of time, so you can always expect to wait at least the 10 or so minutes it takes to cook.

stripped tagliatelle all over Italy. Egg pasta is usually served with richer, creamier sauces and slow-braised meats but is also often eaten simply with butter or parmesan. The correct match of pasta type and sauce is as important as the quality of the sauce itself.

Grains & Pulses

Grains have always played a fundamental role in Italian cuisine. One of the most popular of all grains is polenta, the cornmeal staple of the north and classic belly-filler in poorer times. Finely ground corn is cooked with stock or milk for up to an hour while being stirred constantly. It's served hot and soft (referred to as wet polenta in English) or left to set and then reheated in slices. Another popular grain is rice. In the north, rice usually means risotto, which is only made with the short-grained *arborio*, *carnaroli* and *vialone nano* rice varieties. The best risottos are made from simple ingredients – chicken stock, mushrooms and wine – and finished with a dollop of butter or mascarpone and, more often than not, freshly grated parmesan *(parmigiano reggiano)*. Italians also love *lenticchie* (lentils), *ceci* (chickpeas) and dried beans such as borlotti and cannellini, which make a frequent appearance in soups.

Fruits & Vegetables

The variety of fresh produce available at any one time is reasonably limited. From north to south, the ingredients you see are often the same: flattish *cipolle* (onions), ropes of *aglio* (garlic), mounds of *carciofi* (artichokes), deep red *pomodori* (tomatoes) sold on the vine and *melanzane* (aubergines). It's what each region does with the ingredients that differs. Apart from cultivated produce, many Italians have a taste for the wild: *finocchio* (fennel), *rucola* (rocket) and other greens – and the national obsession, *funghi* (mushrooms), of which there are over 50 edible species.

JANE SMITH

Olives & Olive Oil

The olive tree *(olivo)* has an almost philosophical importance to the people of Italy and the oil is seen as divine essence. Thousands of hectares of the countryside are given over to growing olives, which are used both as eating and cooking (or 'table') olives, and – more importantly – for making oil. The quality of olive oil depends on the region in which the olives are grown, their variety, the ripeness at which they're picked, how soon they're crushed and the crushing method. The best olive oil is *olio d'oliva extravergine* (extra-virgin olive oil).

Meat & Poultry

Where for generations there was relative poverty in Italy, a new-found prosperity means that meat and poultry is now the focus of many meals. And, as natural feeding techniques are usually employed, it's often very high quality with a more intense flavour than factory-farmed meat. Italians tend to serve most of their meats, including the prime cuts, well-done. Many cheaper cuts are *stracotto* (cooked for a very long time, literally 'overcooked'), such as in a braise or ragu. And then there are Italy's famous cured meats. Salumi is a broad term that takes in all *prosciutto* (cured ham), *salsiccia* (roughly translating as sausages) and related pig products, as well as other meat products, including salami.

Seafood

Seafood *(frutti di mare)*, traditionally a mainstay of the Italian diet, has become a luxury item as pollution, overfishing and the pressures of population growth have taken their toll on fish numbers. But spend any amount of time (and a bit of money) in Italy and you will invariably end up eating seafood, which you know will be fresh (rarely will an Italian be happy to buy fish that is more than a few hours old). Italians favour *polpo* (octopus), *seppia* (cuttlefish) and lots of tiny fish known in some areas as *neonati* or *bianchetti*, usually fried and eaten whole. Imported, preserved fish such as *stoccafisso* (air-dried cod) and *baccalà* (salted cod) are also very popular.

JANE SMITH

Cheese

Italians love their *formaggio* (cheese) and produce nearly 450 different types, using it in every course of a meal. They make cheese from the milk of cows (mainly in the north of the country), goats (Piedmont and Valle d'Aosta), sheep (the centre and south) and even buffalo (around Naples). While parmesan and gorgonzola have gained a name overseas, much of Italy's great cheese is simply known as pecorino. There exists a DOC (Denominazione di Origine Controllata) system for cheese, similar to that for wine, to protect the origin and integrity of cheese styles.

Gelati

No other nation today can boast such consistently good frozen desserts as the Italians. *Gelati* (singular *gelato*) is the most accessible, lickably soft

A Cheese Lexicon

dolce – sweet, signifying a young cheese with a sweetish, often nutty taste
pastorizzato – pasteurised, which not all cheeses are (the best usually aren't but ask the vendor if you are concerned)
piccante – piquant, meaning the cheese is sharp, often aged and sometimes acidic
stagionato – aged
vecchio – old
stravecchio – really old

ice cream in existence. Look for *artigianale* (artisanal or home-made), *produzione propria* (proprietor's production) or *nostra produzione* (our production) and ask for a *cono* (cone) or a *coppa* (cup). Other frozen sweets include *granite*, *sorbetti* (sorbets) and *semifreddi* (semi-frozen). Granite (singular *granita*) are slushy ices that take their name from their granular texture and are served in bars in the south during the summer months; the most popular flavours are *limone* (lemon) and *caffè* (coffee). *Caffè granita con panna* is the classic espresso ice topped with whipped cream and served with a *brioche* (pastry), spoon and straw. Sorbetti are made from fruit and sugar, and are usually water-based. In the streets of Naples, a *sorbetto* can be a refreshing, slushy iced drink made from fresh lemon, while in the north it can resemble the French sorbet, like an icy gelato. A *semifreddo* has a mousse-like texture and is served at least fridge-cold.

JANE SMITH

Dolci

Italian desserts tend to fall into three distinctions: fruit, pastry or frozen. Cakes, while a must at any special occasion, are not often seen in day-to-day life. The end of a family meal will often include fruit or a home-made *crostata* (tart). Other preferences are for *biscotti* (biscuits) and treats from the *pasticceria* (pastry shop). The standard of bought pastries, cakes and biscuits is remarkably high across Italy. The Italians are also champion *cioccolato* (chocolate) makers, with *gianduia* (a hazelnut and chocolate combination) now a speciality. Bars, *alimentari* (food stores) and most *tabacchi* (tobacco shops) all sell mass-produced Italian chocolate, which is well worth trying. The most famous brands are Perugina from Umbria and Ferrero from Piedmont.

Regional Cuisines

The food of Italy is a vast collection of regional dishes. With many years of internal migration and, more recently, internal tourism and mass media, many dishes do cross regional boundaries to a little or great extent. This regional guide is meant as a map to help you find your way through the maze of disparate cuisines.

Lazio

The food in this region sits heavily in the stomach but is no less mouth-watering for it. Traditional pasta dishes include *carbonara* (with egg yolk, cheese and bacon) and *alla matriciana* (with tomato, bacon and a touch of chilli). Offal is popular in Rome – *pasta pajata* is made with the entrails of very young veal, which are considered a delicacy as they contain the mother cow's congealed milk (not for the faint-hearted!).

Liguria

The cuisine of this coastal region makes good use of the products of the Mediterranean: fresh herbs, olive oil and seafood. Culinary specialities include pesto – a delicious uncooked sauce of fresh basil, garlic, oil, pine nuts and pecorino cheese (made from sheep's milk), traditionally ground together with a mortar and pestle – which is served with pasta, green beans and potato or dolloped into the classic *minestrone alla genovese* soup. Also try the *farinata*, a flat tart made with chickpea flour, and focaccia, a chewy, oil-enriched bread.

Piedmont
Often delicate and always flavoursome, the cuisine of Piedmont is influenced to some extent by nearby France. *Tartufo bianco* (white truffle) is used in a wide variety of dishes and the Piedmontese make good use of game birds and animals, including chamois, pheasant, quail and even frogs. Chocolate is another speciality and, as this area is one of the largest rice producers, so is risotto.

Lombardy
Lombardy's dishes favour butter over olive oil. Risotto and polenta are staples, and are both often eaten instead of pasta. The cheeses are some of the most interesting in the country – gorgonzola, *taleggio* and *stracchino*. Milan is the home of *panettone* (a yeast-risen sweet bread eaten at Christmas).

Trentino-Alto Adige
The cuisine in this region has quite a considerable Austrian influence and alongside minestrone and spaghetti you will find *canederli* (a noodle soup), bread dumplings, goulash and Wiener schnitzel. Local specialities include smoked meats and heavy, black-rye bread.

The Veneto
This region is renowned for its *bollito misto* (boiled meats) and the *radicchio trevisano* (bitter red lettuce), which is eaten baked with pasta or in risotto. Risotto comes in many varieties in the Veneto, using ingredients from mushrooms and courgettes to sausage, quail and trout. Don't miss the *risotto nero*, risotto coloured and flavoured with squid ink, or the simpler rice dish of *risi e bisi* (rice and peas). The globally popular sweet *tiramisù* (sponge cakes soaked in coffee and arranged in layers with mascarpone cheese) comes from this region.

Emilia-Romagna
The regional specialities of Emilia-Romagna, including *tagliatelle al ragù* (and its prosaic adaptation, spaghetti bolognese), lasagne and tortellini, are among the best-known Italian dishes abroad. Parma is the home of the best prosciutto and also of parmesan, while Modena is famed for its *aceto balsamico* (balsamic vinegar).

JANE SMITH

Tuscany
Here, as in neighbouring Umbria, the locals use a lot of olive oil and herbs and regional specialities are noted for their simplicity, fine flavour and the use of fresh produce. Try *bistecca alla fiorentina*, a huge T-bone steak (it's quite acceptable, and in fact advisable, to order one steak for two people). Among the staples of Tuscan cuisine are small white cannellini beans, although all types of beans are widely used. There is also a range of soups, from the simple *acquacotta* (literally 'cooked water') and soups thickened with bread to rich *minestrone alla*

fiorentina, flavoured with pork and chicken giblets. Don't miss the incredibly rich *panforte*, Siena's famous Christmas fruitcake.

Umbria

In Umbria both the *tartufo* and *porcini* mushrooms are abundant; they turn up in pasta, rice and much more. While many dishes are based upon vegetables, the locals also love their meat. A speciality is *porchetta*, a whole roast piglet stuffed with rosemary. Cakes and pastries stand out, as do chocolates such as the famous *baci* (chocolate-coated hazelnuts).

Campania

Naples is home to that most famous of Italian dishes, the pizza. Although the Romans hotly contest the supremacy of their own version (thin and crispy), the general consensus is that Neapolitan pizza, softer and cooked to order, is the best. Take note of the basics – *mozzarella di bufala* (literally 'buffalo milk cheese') and the *conserva di pomodoro* (tomato sauce) are unequalled in flavour and appear in many dishes as well as pizza. A favourite sweet in Naples is *sfogliatella*, layers of flaky pastry with a ricotta filling. The lemon liqueur, *limoncello*, is also popular.

Apulia

The cuisine here is simple, often taking a single ingredient, capturing its special qualities and bringing it to the fore. Vegetables and seafood are favourites. Try the *orecchiette* (pasta in the shape of 'little ears'), traditionally served with *cime di rapa* (turnip tops), or broccoli and anchovies. Another traditional dish is *fave a cicoria*, a puree of dried broad beans served with chicory and drizzled with extra-virgin olive oil.

Sicily

The focus on Sicily is on seafood and fresh produce. Try the *pescespada* (swordfish),sliced into thick steaks and cooked on an open grill, or the Palermo speciality, *pasta con le sarde*, with sardines, wild fennel, pine nuts and raisins. Aubergine *(melanzana)* is popular in Sicily, as are capers *(capperi)*, both of which feature in *caponata*, a vegetable starter. And not only do the Sicilians claim credit for inventing gelati but they offer delicious regional specialities as well. Don't leave the island without trying *cassata*, a rich sponge cake filled with a cream of ricotta, liqueur and candied fruits, or *cannoli*, tubes of sweet pastry filled with *creme pasticceria* or sweet ricotta with pieces of candied fruit. Other specialities include an assortment of *paste di mandorle* (almond pastries) and almond-milk granita.

JANE SMITH

Sardinia

One of the island's best-known dishes is *porcheddu*, baby pig roasted on a spit. Try the *carta musica*, a thin, crisp bread eaten warm and sprinkled with salt and oil, and the *bottarga*, dried pressed tuna roe which tops pasta instead of cheese. As for cheese, *pecorino sardo* is a sharp, aged sheep's-milk variety of which the Sardi are justifiably proud.

from Lonely Planet's *World Food Italy* by Matthew Evans

[continued from page 131]

In general, Italians are not big snackers, although it is not uncommon for them to have a quick bite – usually a *tramezzino* (sandwich), slice of pizza or *merendina* (cake or biscuit) – halfway through the morning or afternoon.

Etiquette If you are lucky enough to eat in an Italian home, remember that generosity at a meal is a sign of hospitality so refuse at your own peril! You can, and should, *fare la scarpetta* (make a shoe) with your bread and wipe plates clean of sauces – a sign you've really enjoyed the meal and one that won't go unnoticed.

When eating pasta, don't be afraid to shovel it in. Any bits hanging down are bitten through and not slurped up as is done in parts of Asia. You'll probably never be offered a spoon to eat your pasta with as locals consider this practice quite rude.

As with everywhere, the etiquette when eating out is a little more refined. Italians tend to dress with impeccable style at most meals so try to look smart-casual.

Italians don't like people who eat with their mouth open or talk with their mouth full.

Vegetarians & Vegans

While menus around the country carry a bounty of vegetable-based dishes, vegetarians need to be aware of misleading names and that many Italians don't think a little bit of prosciutto really counts as meat. But most eating establishments serve a good selection of *antipasti* (starters) and *contorni* (vegetables prepared in a variety of ways) and the farther south you go, the more excellent vegetable dishes you will find. Look for the word *magro* (thin or lean) on menus which usually means that the dish is meatless. Vegans are in for a much tougher time. Cheese is used universally, so you have to say '*senza formaggio*' (without cheese) as a matter of course. Also remember that pasta fresca, which may also turn up in soups, is made with eggs. Vegetarian restaurants can be found in larger cities such as Rome and Milan.

DRINKS

Nonalcoholic Drinks

Tea Italians don't drink a lot of *tè* (tea) and generally do so only in the late afternoon when they might take a cup with a few *pasticcini* (small cakes). You can order tea in bars, although it will usually arrive in the form of a cup of warm water with an accompanying tea bag. If this doesn't suit your taste, ask for the water *molto caldo* (very hot) or *bollente* (boiling). The good-quality packaged teas, such as Twinings tea bags and leaves, as well as packaged herbal teas such as camomile are often sold in alimentari and sometimes in bars. You can find a wide range of herbal teas in an *erboristeria* (herbalist's shop), which sometimes also stocks health foods.

Water Despite the fact that tap water is reliable throughout the country, most Italians prefer to drink bottled *acqua minerale* (mineral water). This is available either *frizzante* (sparkling) or *naturale* (still) and you will be asked in restaurants and bars which you would prefer. If you just want a glass of tap water, you should ask for *acqua dal rubinetto*, although simply asking for *acqua naturale* will also suffice.

Alcoholic Drinks

Wine & Spirits *Vino* (wine) is an essential accompaniment to any meal and *digestivi* (liqueurs) are a popular way to end one. Italians are very proud of their wines and find it hard to believe that anyone else in the world could produce wines as good as theirs. Many Italians only drink alcohol with meals and the foreign custom of going out for a drink is still considered unusual, although in some parts of Italy it is common to see men starting their day with a *grappa* (grape-based liqueur) for breakfast and continuing to consume strong drinks throughout the day.

Wine is reasonably priced and you will rarely pay more than €8 for a good bottle of wine, although prices go up to more than €15 for really good quality. There are three main classifications of wine – DOCG *(denominazione d'origine controllata e garantita)*, DOC *(denominazione di origine controllata)*

Caffè Society

An *espresso* is a small amount of very strong black coffee. It is also referred to simply as *un caffè*. You can ask for a *caffè doppio*, which means a double shot, or a *caffè lungo* (literally 'long coffee') or *caffè Americano*, though the last two will usually just be an espresso with extra water run through the grinds and can be bitter.

A *caffè corretto* is an espresso with a dash of grappa or some other spirit, and a *macchiato* ('stained' coffee) is espresso with a dash of milk. You can ask for a *macchiato caldo* (with a dot of hot, foamed milk) or *freddo* (with a spot of cold milk). On the other hand, *latte macchiato* is warmed milk stained with a spot of coffee. *Caffè freddo* is a long glass of cold, black, sweetened coffee. If you want it without sugar, ask for *caffè freddo amaro*.

Then, of course, there is the *cappuccino*, coffee with hot, frothy milk. If you want it without the froth, ask for *a cappuccino senza schiuma*. Italians tend to drink cappuccino only with breakfast and during the morning, never after meals – 'How can you put all that hot milk on a full stomach?' – and, if you order one after dinner, don't be surprised if the waiter checks two or three times, just to make sure that they heard correctly.

JANE SMITH

You will also find it difficult to convince bartenders to make your cappuccino hot rather than *tiepido* (lukewarm) – overheating the milk destroys the natural sweetness and the silkiness of the milk. If you must, ask for it *ben caldo*, *molto caldo* or *bollente* and wait for the same 'tut-tut' response that you attracted when you ordered a cappuccino after dinner.

Variations on the milky coffee menu include a *caffè latte*, a milkier version of the cappuccino with less froth. In summer the *cappuccino freddo*, a bit like an iced coffee, is popular. You will also find *caffè granita*, sweet and strong, which is traditionally served with a dollop of whipped cream.

and *vino da tavola* (table wine) – which will be marked on the label. A DOC wine is produced subject to certain specifications, although the label does not certify quality. DOCG is subject to the same requirements as normal DOC but it is also tested by government inspectors for quality. While there are table wines better left alone, there are also many that are of excellent quality, notably the Sicilian Corvo red and white.

Although some excellent wines are produced in Italy, most trattorias stock only a limited selection of bottled wines and generally only cheaper varieties. Most people will usually order the *vino della casa* (house wine) or the *vino locale* (local wine) when they go out to dinner.

The style of wine varies throughout the country, so make a point of sampling the local produce in your travels. Try the many varieties of the famous Chianti wines produced in Tuscany, the white Vernaccia of San Gimignano, the excellent Brunello of Montalcino, the Vino Nobile of Montepulciano, the Soave in Verona and Valpolicella around Venice. Piedmont and Trentino-Alto Adige both produce excellent wines, notably the Barolo in Piedmont. The wines of Orvieto in Umbria are also noteworthy. In Rome try the local Frascati and other wines of the Castelli Romani. Sicily is the home of sweet Marsala and the fragrant Moscato, but the region also produces feisty dry whites and reds full of sun-ripened fruit (not dissimilar to some Australian and other 'new world' wines).

Before dinner, Italians might drink a Campari and soda or a fruit cocktail, usually pre-prepared and often without alcohol. After dinner, try a shot of grappa (either an acquired taste or a relative of paintstripper, depending on your viewpoint) or an *amaro*, a dark liqueur prepared from herbs. If you prefer a sweeter liqueur, try the almond-flavoured *amaretto* or the sweet aniseed *sambuca*. On the Amalfi Coast and the islands of the Gulf of Naples, the fragrant local lemons are used to produce *limoncello*.

Beer The most common Italian beers are crisp and light Pilsener-style lagers, and younger Italians are happy to guzzle them down with a pizza. The main local labels are Peroni, Dreher and Moretti, all very drinkable and cheaper than the imported varieties. If you want a local beer, ask for a *birra nazionale*, which will be either in a bottle or *alla spina* (on tap). Italy also imports beers from throughout Europe and the rest of the world. All the main German beers are available in bottles or cans, English beers and Guinness are often found on tap in *birrerie* (bars specialising in beer) and you will also find Foster's and Castlemaine XXXX. There's been a proliferation of pubs that specialise in beers from all around the world lately. See Bars & Pubs under Entertainment below.

ENTERTAINMENT

Bars & Pubs

Italians cannot be said to have a 'drinking culture' but, in the bigger cities especially, you'll find plenty of bars. You can get a beer, wine or anything else at practically any bar. They range from workaday grungy through to chic places to be seen in. Those places operating first and foremost as nocturnal drinking establishments can be expected to stay open until about 1am, sometimes later.

The Italian version of an Irish pub has taken off in a big way. Basically places where you can get Guinness on tap or select from a wide range of international beers, they are becoming more numerous by the month in major cities such as Rome, Florence and Milan. Some pubs, in particular those where you are likely to meet up with other young foreigners, are listed under the major cities in this book.

Discos & Clubs

Discos (what Brits think of as clubs, not necessarily some awful retro 1980s scene) are expensive: entrance charges range from

The Italian Bar

Most people hear the word 'bar' and think of beer, wine and cocktails. And while Italian bars do serve alcohol, as well as soft drinks, sandwiches and pastries, what they are really about is coffee, which accounts for over 80% of most bars' takings. Around the country, more than 70 million espressos are downed each day, an average of 600 espressos per person per year (the highest consumption in the world).

Basically, cafes and bars are one and the same, although there some cafes function more like coffee houses or tea rooms, where you can sit down over a leisurely cup of coffee or tea, perhaps accompanied by a small cake or pastry. Few Italians would spend more than five minutes in a typical bar – they enter, order, down their coffee at the counter and leave.

There's a certain etiquette to dealing with the bar. The usual practice is to pay for what you want at the *cassa* (cash desk) first. If the bar is empty you can usually pay afterwards but if it's busy this rule always applies. Place your *scontrino* (receipt) down on the bar and ask for what you want (most Italians add €0.05 or €0.10 to ensure attention). Remember that prices skyrocket in cafes as soon as you sit down, particularly near the major tourist haunts such as Piazza Navona in Rome or Piazza San Marco in Venice, where a cappuccino at a table can cost as much as €6.20. The same cappuccino taken at the bar will cost around €0.85.

ASA ANDERSSON

around €15 up to €55 for hotspots in places such as Rimini during the summer. This usually covers the cost of the first drink; after that you will pay around €3 just for a glass of wine. Venues are usually enormous with big dance floors and the music ranges from mainstream Top 40 fare to hip-hop and so on.

You'll find a wide assortment of smaller clubs and bars too, some of which have live music. Admission fees vary from free to around €10.

Be aware that the word 'nightclub' means something far seedier to Italians – think sex that you pay for and you get the idea.

Rock

The world's major performers are constantly passing through Italy on tour – keep an eye on local newspapers. Information on the important venues and how to book tickets is listed under the major cities throughout the book.

Jazz

Italians love jazz and some of the numerous jazz venues are listed in this book. The country's premier jazz festival is Umbria Jazz, held in Perugia in July and Orvieto in December/January. Rome's Villa Celimontana jazz festival is one of the most popular of the summer events in the capital. See the relevant chapters for details.

Classical Music

The main concert seasons are usually during the winter months, although there are always plenty of classical music concerts included in major summer entertainment festivals, such as Rome's Estate Romana. Details of other classical music venues are included throughout the book.

Cinemas

There is no shortage of cinemas in Italy, but there is quite a dearth of ones showing original-language films. Even in a large city like Milan, only three or four cinemas show films in their original languages with Italian subtitles, and then only once a week. The dubbing industry is justifiably proud in Italy, but that doesn't help foreigners who don't want to hear John Cleese spout Italian! The only other option in larger cities is the foreign cultural centres, which often put on film seasons.

A cinema ticket costs up to €6.70, although this can come down to €3.10 on the cheap day (often Wednesday).

Theatre

If you understand Italian, you'll have plenty of options in all the major cities. Performances in languages other than Italian are hard to come by, although the Agora in Rome has an international season. Tourist offices should be able to help out with information. In summer, there are performances of Greek theatre in Sicily at Siracuse, Taormina and Segesta. A ticket costs from €16 upwards.

Opera

There are opera seasons in the major cities, including Rome, Milan, Palermo, Bologna and Venice. In summer, there are special seasons at the Arena in Verona and, less atmospherically, at the Stadio Olimpico football stadium in Rome. An opera is also usually performed as part of the Festival dei Due Mondi at Spoleto in June and July. A ticket to the opera costs from €27 to more than €60 for better seats. At La Scala, in Milan, the top seats on an opening night can go for up to €800!

SPECTATOR SPORTS

Motor Racing

Italy is one of the homes of prestige motor racing. The Italian Formula One Grand Prix races are held at the Monza race track, just north of Milan, each September. The San Marino Grand Prix (to all intents and purposes, if not technically, an Italian race) is held at the 5km Imola circuit in April or May.

Italy has provided some of the world's greatest driving machines. Ferrari, more than any other manufacturer, continues to dominate the Grand Prix in the popular imagination – even if it has not been in the winner's circle so often in recent years. Alfa Romeo has also been up there. For a while back in the 1950s, Maserati was on top but the company ran into difficulties in 1958. Maserati has continued to contribute motors, as have Lamborghini and Lancia. Bugatti surfaced briefly in the 1950s but never took line honours.

The Autodromo Nazionale Monza (☎ 039 2 48 21, **W** www.monzanet.it), Via Vedano 5, Parco di Monza, 20052 Monza, has been a venue since 1922. Next to the present track is the crumbling reminder of more dangerous days: a circuit with slopes at such a steep gradient that it was the scene of enough accidents to convince all concerned it should be closed – it was last used in 1969. This dinosaur has long been destined for demolition but as yet remains an intact, if overgrown, curio for bicycle riders doing more relaxed circuits of the adjacent Parco di Monza.

Tickets are sold at Automobile Club Italiano (ACI; ☎ 02 7 74 51, fax 02 78 18 44), Corso Venezia 43, 20121 Milan; at ACP & Partners (☎ 02 760 02 574 or 02 774 52 30, fax 02 78 09 38, **e** acp@acpmilano.it, **W** www.autodromodimonaza.com), Piazza Duse 1, 20121 Milan; and from the ticket office at the track (☎ 039 248 22 12, fax 039 32 03 24), Parco di Monza, 20052 Monza. Tickets cost from €56 for a spot on the grass to €362 for the best grandstand seat.

Tickets for the San Marino Grand Prix cost from €36.15 to €335.70 and are available via the Consorzio San Marino (☎ 0549 88 54 31/32/98/99). Full details are available online at **W** www.formula1.sm.

The classic Italian motor race was the long-distance Mille Miglia, which took place annually (interrupted by WWII) from 1927 to 1957. Nowadays it's held as a nostalgic competition in which vintage racing cars career 1000 miles around Italy from Brescia to Rome and back again. In 2001, 836 cars entered the event, which is great fun to watch if you can catch it – usually in the middle of May. See **W** www.millemiglia.it for details.

Football

Italy's national team, the Azzuri (Blues) have long been one of the front-running teams, although ultimate success has been elusive in the past few World Cup contests. In 1998 they failed to make the finals and in the 1994 tussle in the USA they lost 3-2 on penalties to Brazil after an agonising 0-0 draw. Almost as frustratingly in 1990, they managed to come in third by defeating England 2-1. However, Italy has picked up the World Cup three times, in 1934, 1938 and 1982.

Italians adore the beautiful game.

On the home front, 18 teams tough out the Italian football honours in Serie A (the top division). Serie B consists of a further 20 teams, while another 90 teams dispute the medals at Serie C level, itself split up into several more manageable sub-competitions.

Predictably enough, Serie A is dominated by an elite group of *squadre* (teams) that generally take most of the silverware. To provide some idea of how a few teams monopolise the top honours, AC Milan has been champion in five of the last 13 seasons, and runner-up twice. Juventus took the laurels three times and came in second three times. Their closest rivals are Inter, with one *scudetto* (shield) and two second-places. The two Rome-based teams, Lazio and AS Roma, have been dominating the Serie A in the past few years, with Lazio winning the cup in 2000 and local arch-rivals AS Roma taking the honours in the 2001 season.

Of course, not everyone can be top all the time. At the close of the 1998–99 season, Inter had so disappointed its fans that at one stage they were howling for the blood of the then-captain, Brazilian Ronaldo. Genoa's

Gooooooooaaaaaaaaallllllll!

Il calcio (football) excites Italian souls more than politics, religion, good food and dressing up all put together. Football (soccer) is one of the great forces in Italian life, so if you can get to one of the big games you'll be in for a treat. Tempers run high and at times overflow, and not just on the pitch either. Accusations that referees had favoured the 1998 championship winners, Turin-based Juventus, led to parliamentary punch-ups!

Sampdoria did even worse. After 17 years as one of the top league's better teams, it was relegated to Serie B in 1999.

In between the World Cup and national league there is a bewildering array of competitions and cups at both national and European level. The Coppa Italia (Italian Cup) is one of the most well known of these.

Whatever the form or place on the ladder of the various teams, some local derbies make for particularly hot clashes – for instance, when AC Milan and rivals Inter come face to face or when Roma takes on Lazio. Both are traditionally excuses for a little sporting lunacy – with *tifosi* (fans) even more vociferous than usual.

Tickets for games start at around €13 for the lousiest positions and rise to well over €50. They are best purchased through specific ticketing agencies, some of which are listed in this guide; staff at the local tourist office can tell you where to find them if not.

Rugby Union

While football is the dominating sporting passion in Italy, interest in rugby is at an all time high – mainly thanks to Italy's entry into the Six Nations Championship in 2000. Though they won the wooden spoon for finishing bottom in their first tournament, Italy are proving a positive addition to the historic northern hemisphere competition. The team play home international games at the Stadio Flaminio (☎ 06 323 65 39), Viale Tiziano, 00195 Flaminio, Rome. Tickets for games are available from branches of Sestante Travel (☎ 06 687 31 38, fax 06 687 32 40 in Rome).

Cycling

Second only to the Tour de France, the Giro d'Italia is *the* event on the summer cycling calendar. Little wonder, since Italy has a long record of producing world-class riders. The race usually starts in Rome (near the Colosseum) and finishes in Milan.

The race was first held in 1909 and has been staged every year since, interrupted predictably enough by WWI and WWII. It was initially a mostly Italian affair and the 1909 winner, Luigi Ganna, was followed by a long succession of local victors. Only in 1950 did a non-Italian finally break the home side's long winning streak – the Swiss Hugo Koblet took the finishing-line honours. In total, the Giro has been won by non-Italians 24 times and by Italian 58 times.

This event is one of the few things in life that are free: if you want to watch, find out when the race is passing a location convenient to you and wait for the cyclists – it's as simple as that.

Gazetta Dello Sport, one of Italy's daily sports newspapers, covers this event in detail. Check out W www.gazetta.it.

Skiing

Most people would probably rather do it than watch it, but skiing is something of a prestige spectator sport in Italy. Maybe that has something to do with the fact that Italy has had some stars who are particularly good at it.

For a decade, the brash Alberto Tomba ('*Tomba la bomba!*', literally 'The bomb is falling!') dominated the world ski scene, despite (or perhaps because of) his off-piste antics. Before retiring in 1997, he won Olympic gold as well as the World Cup, but his performance was visibly sliding towards the end. Since his exit, Italian skiing has gone, if you'll pardon the expression, downhill.

World champions Deborah Compagnoni and Isolde Kostner held the torch for Italy's downhill skiers at the end of the 20th century;

Stefania Belmondo was the most successful cross-country skier.

Several Italian ski fields host annual World Cup competitions. It doesn't cost anything to watch – just a fortune to find accommodation! Turin will witness world-class skiing in 2006 when it hosts the Winter Olympics.

SHOPPING

Shopping in Italy is probably not what you are used to back home. The vast majority of shops are small businesses: large department stores and supermarkets tend to be very thin on the ground. If you need necessities such as underwear, tights (pantyhose), pyjamas, T-shirts and toiletries, head for one of the large retail stores, such as Standa, Upim, Oviesse or Rinascente. Otherwise, you can pick up underwear, tights and pyjamas in a *merceria* (haberdashery); toiletries and condoms in a farmacia, a supermarket or sometimes in an alimentari; and items such as T-shirts in a normal clothing store. Hardware items can be purchased at a *ferramenta* (ironmonger's) and air-mail paper, notepads, pens and greeting cards at a *cartoleria* (paper-goods shop).

Clothing & Accessories

Italy is synonymous with elegant, fashionable and high-quality clothing. However, fashions tend to be conservative and middle of the range, and cheaper clothing can be downright boring for British, US and Australian visitors accustomed to a wide variety of styles and tastes. You will find that most of the better-quality clothes are very expensive. However, if you can manage to be in the country during the summer sales (July and August) and the winter sales (December and January), you can pick up incredible bargains. By mid-sale, prices are often slashed by up to 60% or 70%. Rome, Florence and Milan have the greatest variety of clothing, shoes and accessories. Main shopping areas are detailed under the relevant cities throughout this book.

The same applies to shoes. Expect to pay dearly (although still considerably less than at home) for the best quality at shops such as Beltrami and Pollini. Again, prices drop dramatically during the sales, but expect to have some difficulty finding shoes to fit if you take a larger size.

Would you strut your stuff on the catwalks?

Italy is particularly noted for the quality of its leather goods, so plan to stock up on bags, wallets, purses, belts and gloves. At markets such as Porta Portese in Rome, you can find some incredible second-hand bargains. The San Lorenzo leather market in Florence has a vast array of goods, including jackets, bags, wallets and belts, although the variety can be limited and you should check carefully for quality before buying.

Glassware & Ceramics

Some might call the famous and expensive Venetian glass grotesque – and it is certainly an acquired taste. Shops all over Venice are full of it but, if you listen to the claims of the shop assistants, most of it (except for the glass in *their* shop) is not the real thing. If you want to buy Venetian glass, shop around and compare prices and quality. The merchandise at the larger factories is generally not cheaper but you can be sure it is authentic. And remember you will probably have to pay customs duty on your purchase when you arrive home. For more information see Shopping in the Venice section of the The Veneto chapter.

Ceramics and pottery are less costly and nore rustic. There is a great diversity of raditional styles associated with villages or reas, where designs have been handed down hrough many centuries. Some of the major entres are: Deruta, near Perugia in Umbria; 'aenza, in Emilia-Romagna; Vietri sul Mare, near Salerno at the start of the Amalfi Coast; nd Grottaglie, near Taranto in Apulia. Sicilan pottery is particularly interesting; Caltagirone and Santo Stefano di Camastra are two f the important ceramic-producing towns.

'ewellery

'opular jewellery tends to be chunky and heap looking, but more expensive gold ewellery can be beautiful. The best-known naunt for tourists wanting to buy gold in taly is the Ponte Vecchio in Florence, which is lined with tiny shops full of both nodern and antique jewellery. Consider arefully the environmental impact on coral communities before purchasing jewellery and ornaments carved from this endangered animal (coral is not in fact a plant) for sale at Torre del Greco and on the western coast of Sardinia. Overharvesting and pollution are severely threatening marine ecosystems here and everywhere.

Souvenirs & Handicrafts

The beautiful Florentine paper goods, with their delicate flower design, and the Venetian equivalent, which have a marbled design, are reasonably priced and make wonderful gifts. Specialist shops are dotted around both Florence and Venice, although it is possible to buy these paper goods in cartolerie throughout the country.

Local handicrafts include lace and embroidery, notably found on the Isola Maggiore in Lago di Trasimeno, Umbria, and the woodcarvings of the Val Gardena in Trentino-Alto Adige.

Getting There & Away

Competition between airlines on intercontinental routes means you should be able to pick up a reasonably priced fare to Italy, even if you are coming from as far away as Australia.

If you live in Europe, you can easily go overland to Italy but don't ignore the flight option, as enticing deals often pop up.

AIR

Airports & Airlines

Italy's main intercontinental gateway is the Leonardo da Vinci (Fiumicino) airport in Rome but regular intercontinental flights also serve Milan. Plenty of flights (scheduled, budget and charter) from other European cities also go direct to regional capitals around the country.

Many European and international airlines compete with the country's national carrier, Alitalia.

Buying Tickets

World aviation has never been so competitive but you have to research all the options carefully to make sure you get the best deal. The Internet is a useful resource for checking air fares.

Full-time students and those under 26 years (under 30 in some countries) have access to better deals than other travellers. You have to show a document proving your date of birth or a valid International Student Identity Card (ISIC) when buying your ticket and boarding the plane.

Generally, there is nothing to be gained by buying a ticket direct from the airline. Discounted tickets are released to selected travel agents and specialist discount agencies, and these are usually the cheapest deals going.

One exception to this rule is the expanding number of 'no-frills' carriers, which mostly only sell direct to travellers. Unlike 'full-service' airlines, no-frills carriers often make one-way tickets available at around half the return fare, meaning that it is easy to put together an open-jaw ticket when yo fly to one place but leave from another.

The other exception is booking on the In ternet. Many airlines, full service and n frills, offer some excellent fares to We surfers. They may sell seats by auction o simply cut prices to reflect the reduced cos of electronic selling.

Many travel agencies around the worl have Web sites, which can make the Interne a quick and easy way to compare prices There is also an increasing number of onlin agents such as **W** www.travelocity.co.uk an **W** www.deckchair.com, which operate onl on the Internet. Online ticket sales work wel if you are doing a simple one-way or retur trip on specified dates. However, the onlin superfast fare generators are no substitut for a travel agent who knows all abou special deals, has strategies for avoidin stopovers and can offer advice on every thing from which airline has the best vege

Warning

The information in this chapter is particularly vulnerable to change. Prices for international travel are volatile, routes are introduced and cancelled, schedules change, special deals come and go, and rules and visa requirements are amended. Airlines and governments seem to take a perverse pleasure in making price structures and regulations as complicated as possible. You should check directly with the airline or a travel agent to make sure you understand how a fare (and ticket you may buy) works. In addition, the travel industry is highly competitive and there are many lurks and perks.

The upshot of this is that you should get opinions, quotes and advice from as many airlines and travel agents as possible before you part with your hard-earned cash. The details given in this chapter should be regarded as pointers and are not a substitute for your own careful, up-to-date research.

rian food to the best travel insurance to undle with your ticket.

You may find the cheapest flights are advertised by obscure agencies. Most such irms are honest and solvent but there are ome rogue fly-by-night outfits around. Payng by credit card generally offers protection s most card issuers provide refunds if you an prove you didn't get what you paid for. imilar protection can be obtained by buying ticket from a bonded agent, such as one overed by the Air Travel Organiser's Licence (ATOL; W www.atol.org.uk) scheme n the UK. Agents who only accept cash hould hand over the tickets straight away nd not tell you to 'come back tomorrow'. After you've made a booking or paid your eposit, call the airline and confirm that the ooking was made. It's generally not advisble to send money (even cheques) through he post unless the agent is very well estabished – some travellers have reported being ipped off by fly-by-night mail-order ticket gents.

Many travellers change their routes alfway through their trips so think carefully before you buy a ticket which is not asily refunded.

Youth Passes

Lufthansa, British Midland and Scandinavian Airlines operate a youth pass (YES) for people aged under 26. You buy a series of coupons (from four to 10) and create an tinerary hopping across European cities, he proviso being you start and end in the UK and/or Ireland. The network includes 120 cities and prices start at UK£45 per light. It is not much use if you intend to ravel in Italy alone but could be worth ooking into if you wish to fly around the continent. Travel agents such as STA Travel (see The UK & Ireland section later) have details.

Travellers with Specific Needs

If they're warned early enough, airlines can often make special arrangements, such as wheelchair assistance at airports or vegetarian meals on the flight, for travellers with specific needs.

Children under two years travel for 10% of the standard fare (or free on some airlines) as long as they don't occupy a seat. They don't get a baggage allowance. 'Skycots', baby food and nappies should be provided by the airline if requested in advance. Children aged between two and 12 can usually occupy a seat for half to two-thirds of the full fare and do get a baggage allowance.

The disability-friendly Web site found at W www.everybody.co.uk has an airline directory that provides useful information on the facilities offered by various airlines.

Departure Tax

The departure tax payable when you leave Italy by air is factored into your airline ticket.

The UK & Ireland

Discount air travel is big business in London. Advertisements for many travel agencies appear in the travel pages of the weekend broadsheet newspapers, such as the *Independent* on a Saturday and the *Sunday Times*, as well as in magazine publications such as *Time Out* and *Exchange & Mart*. Look out for the free magazines, such as *TNT*, which are widely available in London – you can start by looking outside the main train and underground stations.

For students and travellers aged under 26, a popular travel agency in the UK is STA Travel (☎ 0870 160 0599, W www.statravel.com), 86 Old Brompton Rd, London SW7, which has offices throughout the UK.. The agency sells tickets to all travellers but caters especially for young people and students.

Other recommended UK travel agencies include Trailfinders (☎ 020-7937 1234 for European travel, W www.trailfinder.com), 215 Kensington High St, London W8; and Flightbookers (☎ 020-7757 2324), 177–178 Tottenham Court Rd, London W1P. They have an efficient flight-booking Web site at W www.ebookers.com. You can also book hotels, buy insurance and hire cars on this site.

No-frills airlines (see Buying Tickets earlier) are increasingly big business for travel between the UK and Ireland and Italy. They increasingly serve minor airports as well as a couple of the main ones and encourage you to book flights online. Go (☎ 0845 605 4321 in the UK, ☎ 848 88 77 66 in Italy, W www.go-fly.com) flies to Rome, Milan, Venice, Naples and Bologna from London Stansted. Standard returns (no changes, no refunds) start at UK£100, including taxes. Go also runs direct flights between Rome and Bristol and offers connections to Italy from Edinburgh, Glasgow and Belfast via London Stansted.

The Irish airline Ryanair (☎ 0870 156 9569 in the UK, ☎ 199 11 41 14 in Italy, W www.ryanair.ie) flies to Alghero, Ancona, Brescia, Genoa, Pescara, Pisa, Rimini, Trieste, Turin and Venice from London Stansted, with flights to each destination at least once daily. Fares vary wildly according to demand and season. A one-way flight to Genoa in November could cost around UK£25; the same flight in July can be UK£99.50 or more. The airline also operates flights to Pisa and Venice from Brussels.

KLM UK's no-frills airline Buzz (☎ 0870 240 7070 in the UK, ☎ 02 696 8 22 22 in Italy, W www.buzzaway.com) flies to Milan's Linate airport from Stansted. One-way flights typically cost from UK£40 to UK£80, but special offers are sometimes available.

The two national airlines linking the UK and Italy are British Airways (BA; ☎ 0845 773 3377, W www.british-airways.com), 156 Regent St, London W1R, and Alitalia (☎ 0870 544 5259, W www.alitalia.it), 4 Portman Square, London W1H. They both operate regular flights (usually several daily) to Rome, Milan, Venice, Florence, Turin, Naples and Pisa, as well as other cities, including Palermo, during the summer. Standard returns with either airline cost from UK£200. However, both airlines generally have special deals and you shouldn't have to pay the standard fares. With a little luck and forward planning an average ticket to most destinations will cost around UK£140 return.

The Charter Flight Centre (☎ 020-7828 1090), 19 Denbigh St, London SW1, has charter and scheduled flights to several destinations in Italy. A charter to Venice with a two-week limit can cost from UK£13[illegible] return in late June. A similar ticket to Rome will cost around UK£150 and to Florence will be UK£170.

Most British travel agents are registered with ABTA (Association of British Travel Agents). If you have paid for your flight with an ABTA-registered agent who then goes bust, ABTA will guarantee a refund or an alternative.

If you're coming from Ireland, it might be worth comparing the cost of flying direct with the cost of travelling to London first and then flying to Italy.

Continental Europe

Air travel between Italy and other places in continental Europe is worth considering if you are pushed for time. Short hops can be expensive but good deals are available from some major hubs.

Several airlines, including Alitalia, Qantas Airways and Air France, offer cut-rate fares between cities on the European legs of long-haul flights. These are usually cheap but often involve flying at night or early in the morning.

France The student travel agency OTU Voyages (☎ 01 44 41 38 50, W www.otu.fr) has a central Paris office at 39 ave Georges Bernanos and another 36 offices around the country. It's a safe bet for reasonable student and cut-price travel.

Regular flights connect Paris with Rome, Milan and other major cities. The train is generally an easier bet for travel to Milan but to Rome you can occasionally find good air deals. A return flight in June/July with Air Kuwait costs €215.55.

Air Littoral (☎ 0803 83 48 34 in France, ☎ 035 23 30 04 in Italy, W www.air-littoral.fr) operates flights from Nice to Bologna, Florence, Naples, Rome and Venice for high flyers. To Nice there are connections once or twice per day from other destinations within France as well as Barcelona, Madrid, Geneva and Munich. A return flight from Nice can cost €245.

Germany Munich is a haven of discount and budget travel outlets. Council Travel (☎ 089-39 50 22) at Adalbertstrasse 32, near the university, is one of the best.

In Berlin, Kilroy Travel-ARTU Reisen (☎ 030-310 00 40) at Hardenbergstrasse 9, near Berlin Zoo, is good. There is also a branch of STA Travel (☎ 030-311 09 50, fax 313 09 48, W www.statravel.de) at Goethestrasse 73. It is one of three in Berlin. They have branches in cities around the country, including Frankfurt am Main, where you will find a branch (☎ 069 70 30 35) at Bockenheimer Landstrasse 133.

Greece Try ISYTS (☎ 01 323 37 67, fax 01 322 15 31), Upper Floor, 11 Nikis St, Syntagma Square, Athens. Alternatively, you could try the travel agencies in the back streets of Athens between Syntagma and Omonia squares. You can find return tickets from Athens to Rome for around €440.20.

Belgium & The Netherlands Virgin Express (☎ 02 752 05 05 in Belgium, ☎ 800 09 70 97 in Italy, W www.virgin-express.com) flies to Rome from Brussels five times daily and to Milan once or twice daily. Each leg can cost from €61.75 to more than €198.30, depending on offers and the level of flexibility/comfort you choose.

In Amsterdam, a recommended travel agency is Malibu Travel (☎ 020 638 60 59), Damrak 30. There are also plenty of bucket shops along Rokin – shop around before you commit to anything.

If you're searching online, try W www.budgettravel.com or www.airfair.nl.

At the time of writing, a return flight from Amsterdam to Rome in the high season cost around €308.55, but deals can go as low as around €204.20.

Spain Getting cheap flights between Spain and Italy is difficult. Frequently the best value flights are routed through another European city (such as Munich) and involve changing flights. Such tickets can cost around €150.25 return from Madrid or Barcelona. Direct flights from either can easily cost more than €180.30 unless you plan well ahead.

In Madrid, one of the most reliable budget travel agencies is Viajes Zeppelin (☎ 91 547 79 03), Plaza de Santo Domingo 2.

The Italian airline Meridiana has direct flights from Barcelona to Bologna, Milan (Linate), Catania, Florence, Cagliari and Olbia. Enquire at travel agents for route and pricing details.

The USA

The North Atlantic is the world's busiest long-haul air corridor and the flight options are bewildering. Several airlines fly direct to Italy, landing at either Rome or Milan airports. These include Alitalia, Lufthansa, Air France, TWA and Delta Air Lines. If your trip will not be confined to Italy, check for cheaper flights to other European cities.

Discount travel agencies in the USA are known as consolidators (although you won't see a sign on the door saying 'Consolidator'). San Francisco is the ticket consolidator capital of America although some good deals can be found in Los Angeles, New York and other big cities. Consolidators can be found through the phone book or the major daily newspapers. The *New York Times*, the *Los Angeles Times,* the *Chicago Tribune* and the *San Francisco Examiner* all produce weekly travel sections in which you will find a number of travel agency advertisements. Look out for an SOT number: if they have one of these they are probably legitimate.

Council Travel (☎ 800 226 8624, W www.counciltravel.com), the largest student travel organisation in America, has around 75 offices in the USA. STA Travel (☎ 800 781 4040, W www.statravel.com) has offices in Boston, Chicago, Los Angeles, New York, Philadelphia, San Francisco and other major cities.

Fares vary wildly depending on season, availability and a little luck. Low season fares can range from around US$640 to US$800 for a return from Los Angeles to

Rome, Milan, Florence or Venice. If you miss out on such offers you will be looking at more. All involve at least one change and sometimes two (generally New York and again at Milan or another European hub, depending on the airline). In high season you are looking at around US$1250 to US$1500. Prices from New York are predictably lower. In the low season you are looking at around US$550 return to any main Italian destinations but in summer be prepared for fares in excess of US$1100.

Discount and rock-bottom options from the USA include charter, stand-by and courier flights. Stand-by fares are often sold at 60% of the normal price for one-way tickets. Whole Earth Travel (W www.4standby.com) is a company that specialises in stand-by ticketing. Once you purchase a one-way 'flight coupon' you gain access to stand-by flight information and have a year within which to make your trip. The coupon costs between US$139 and US$269, depending on your destination, and is only good for one-way travel.

A courier flight from New York to Rome can cost about US$300 (more from the West Coast) for a return. Now Voyager (☎ 212-431 1616), Suite 307, 74 Varrick St, New York, NY 10013, specialises in these courier flights but you must pay an annual membership fee (around US$50) that entitles you to take as many courier flights as you like. More information can be found on their Web site at W www.nowvoyagertravel.com.

Also worth considering are Europe by Air coupons (☎ 1 888 3872479, W www.eurair.com). You purchase a minimum of three US$99 coupons before leaving North America. Each coupon is valid for a one-way flight within the combined system of more than 30 participating regional airlines in Europe (exclusive of local taxes, which you will be charged when you make the flight). The coupons are valid for 120 days from the day you make your first flight. A few words of caution – using one of these coupons for a one-way flight won't always be better value than local alternatives, so check them out before committing yourself to any given flight. The same company offers two- and three-week unlimited flight passes and sells one-off air fares too.

If you can't find a particularly cheap flight, it is always worth considering a cheap transatlantic hop to London to prowl around the discount travel agencies there. See The UK & Ireland earlier.

Canada

Alitalia has direct flights to Rome and Milan from Toronto and Montreal. Scan the budget travel agencies' advertisements in the *Toronto Globe & Mail*, the *Toronto Star* and the *Vancouver Province*.

Canada's main student travel organisation is Travel CUTS (☎ 800 667 2887, W www.travelcuts.com), which has offices in all major cities. It is known as Voyages Campus in Quebec.

Low-season return fares from Montreal to Rome start from around C$920, while a high season ticket could cost C$1800. From Vancouver you'd be looking at C$1200 and C$2000 respectively.

Australia

Cheap flights from Australia to Europe generally go via South-East Asian capitals, involving a stopover at Kuala Lumpur, Bangkok or Singapore. If a long stopover between connections is necessary, transit accommodation is sometimes included in the price of the ticket. If it's at your own expense, it may be worth considering a more expensive but direct ticket.

Discounted return fares to Italy can be surprisingly cheap. Qantas and Alitalia offer the only direct flights from Melbourne and Sydney to Rome but if you are looking for a bargain fare you will probably end up with another airline such as Thai International or Malaysia Airlines. Many European airlines throw in a return flight to another European city, for example, BA may fly you return to London with a London-Rome-London flight included in the price. Flights from Perth are generally a few hundred dollars cheaper.

Average low-season return fares to Rome, Milan, Florence and Venice start at around A$1600 (although they can go lower). In the high season you could be looking at between A$2100 and A$2500.

Quite a few travel offices specialise in discount air tickets. Some travel agencies, particularly smaller ones, advertise cheap air fares in the travel sections of weekend newspapers, such as the *Age* in Melbourne and the *Sydney Morning Herald*.

STA Travel and Flight Centre are well known for cheap fares. STA Travel (☎ 1300 360 390, **W** www.statravel.com.au) has offices in all major cities and on many university campuses. Flight Centre (☎ 1300 362 665, **W** www.flightcentre.com.au) has dozens of offices throughout Australia. To find your nearest branch call ☎ 131 600.

For courier flights try Jupiter (☎ 02-9317 2113), Unit 3, 55 Kent Rd, Sydney 2020.

New Zealand

Depending on which airline you choose, flights from New Zealand to Europe travel via South-East Asia or the West Coast of America. Low season return fares start from NZ$2199 or NZ$2599 in the high season with Malaysian or Singapore Airlines.

The *New Zealand Herald* has a travel section in which travel agencies advertise fares. Flight Centre (☎ 09-309 6171) has a large central office in Auckland at National Bank Towers (corner of Queen and Darby Sts) and many other branches throughout the country. STA Travel (☎ 0800 874 773, **W** www.statravel.com.au) has offices in Auckland, as well as in Hamilton, Palmerston North, Wellington, Christchurch and Dunedin.

Asia

Although you can find some fairly competitive air-fare deals in most Asian countries, Bangkok, Singapore and Hong Kong are still the best places to shop around for discount tickets.

In Bangkok, try STA Travel (☎ 02-236 0262) at 33 Surawong Rd. In Hong Kong many travellers use the Hong Kong Student Travel Bureau (☎ 2730 3269), 8th Floor, Star House, Tsimshatsui. You could also try Phoenix Services (☎ 2722 7378), 7th Floor, Milton Mansion, 96 Nathan Rd, Tsimshatsui. In Singapore a safe bet is STA Travel (☎ 737 7188), Orchard Parade Hotel, 1 Tanglin Rd.

Africa

Nairobi and Johannesburg are probably the best places in East and South Africa to buy tickets. Flight Centres (☎ 02-21 00 24), Lakhamshi House, Biashara St, in Nairobi has been in business for many years. In Johannesburg, the South African Students' Travel Services (☎ 011-716 30 45) has an office at the University of Witwatersrand. STA Travel (☎ 011-447 55 51) has an office on Tyrwhitt Ave in Rosebank.

LAND

Not quite all roads lead to Rome, but there are plenty of options for entering Italy by train, bus or private vehicle. Bus is generally the cheapest option but services are less frequent and considerably less comfortable than the train.

If you are travelling by bus, train or car to Italy it will be necessary to check whether you require visas to the countries you intend to pass through on your way.

Bus

Eurolines (**W** www.eurolines.com), a consortium of European coach companies, operates across Europe. You can contact them in your own country or in Italy. Ticket offices around Italy include the following.

Florence Autostazione (☎ 055 21 51 55), Piazza Stazione 1, on the corner of Piazza Adua
Milan Autostradale Viaggi (☎ 02 720 01 304), Piazza Castello 1
Rome Lazzi Express (☎ 06 884 08 40), Via Tagliamento 27/r
Rome Agenzia Elios (☎ 06 440 40 09), Circonvallazione Nomentana 574, Lato Stazione Tiburtina
Turin Autostazione Comunale (☎ 011 433 25 25), Corso Inghilterra 3
Venice Agenzia Brusutti (☎ 041 520 30 98), Piazzale Roma 540

Bus Passes Eurolines offers the Eurolines Pass, a useful option for travellers planning to pack in a lot of kilometres touring Europe. A pass valid for 15/30/60 days in high season (June to mid-September) costs UK£120/179/195 for those under 26 (those aged over 26 have only the 30/60 options at UK£222/259). In low season the pass costs about 25% less. It allows unlimited travel between up to 46 European cities, including Florence, Milan, Naples, Rome and Venice.

Another option if you plan to travel a lot beyond Italy is Busabout (☎ 020-7950 1661, fax 7950 1662, W www.busabout.com), 258 Vauxhall Bridge Rd, London SW1V. This company offers passes of varying duration allowing you to use their hop-on hop-off bus network in Western and Central Europe. The frequency of departures and the number of stops available goes up between April and October (when buses pass through each stop once every two days). There are 14 stops in Italy and you can book onward travel and accommodation on the bus or at their Web site. Busabout's passes cost UK£169 (15 days), UK£229 (21 days), UK£309 (one month), UK£479 (two months), UK£589 (three months) and UK£699 (seven-month season pass). Students and young people with appropriate ID (such as ISIC, GO25 and Euro<26) pay UK£149/209/279/429/529/629 respectively.

The UK Eurolines (☎ 0870 514 3219), 52 Grosvenor Gardens, London SW1W, runs buses twice weekly (Wednesday and Saturday) at 9am to Milan (22 hours), Rome (33 hours) and other destinations (which may involve a change in Milan) such as Turin, Florence, Siena, Bologna and Venice. Up to five services run in summer. The lowest youth fares from London to Rome cost around UK£80/110 for a single/return. The full adult fares cost around UK£90/130. From London to Milan, the youth fare costs around UK£70/100 and the adult fare costs UK£80/110. Prices rise in the peak summer season (July and August) and in the week before Christmas.

Austria In Austria, Eurolines buses connect from Vienna with Rome, Milan, Florence, Venice, Verona, Trento, Bolzano and Brescia. Adult one-way/return fares to Rome (15 hours, five departures per week) are €71.95/114.80. Contact Eurolines (☎ 01 712 04 53) at Landstrasser, Hauptstrasse 1b, A1030 Vienna.

France One of several Eurolines offices in Paris is at the bus station (☎ 08 36 69 52 52) at 28 ave du Général de Gaulle. The adult low-season one-way/return fare from Paris to Milan (16 hours, four to seven times per week) costs around €80.05/132.15.

Germany Eurolines has offices all over Germany. The Munich office (☎ 089-5458 7000) is represented (as are many others around the country) by Deutsche Touring GmbH, Arnulfstrasse 3 (Starnberger Bahnhof), 80335 Munich.

Eurolines coaches leave from a plethora of German cities for destinations in Italy. For example, the journey from Frankfurt to Rome costs €92/165.65 (19¾ hours, twice weekly). To Florence it is €83.85/150.85 (16 hours 35 minutes, twice weekly). And from Berlin it's €105.85/190.70 to Florence (18 hours 35 minutes, twice weekly).

Netherlands Eurolines (☎ 020 560 87 87) has an office at Julianaplein 5, 1097 Amsterdam. The adult one-way/return fare from Amsterdam to Rome (twice per week) costs around €106.65/165.65.

Slovenia For buses from Slovenia contact the Ljubljana bus station (☎ 061 134 3838). Buses from Koper (near the border) leave for Trieste (the only destination in Italy) regularly from Monday to Friday and once on Saturday.

Spain Eurolines services connect Madrid and Barcelona with Rome and other destinations in Italy. From Madrid the one-way/return fares are €130.70/235.30 (30¾ hours, Monday to Saturday). The office in Madrid (☎ 91 528 11 05) is at the Estación Sur de Autobuses, Calle de Méndez Alvaro 83.

Switzerland Eurolines' Zurich office (☎ 01 431 57 24) is at Carplatz am Sihlquai, 8005 Zurich. The company operates buses to southern Italy (Campania, Calabria and

Sicily), aimed predominantly at Italian migrants, from Basle, Zurich, Luzern and Chiasso. Departures are a couple of times per week and it's a helluva journey. The most expensive single/return tickets are those for Sicilian destinations at SFR155/279. The train is the preferred option between Switzerland and the northern half of Italy.

Train

If you plan to travel extensively by train in Europe it might be worth getting hold of the *Thomas Cook European Timetable*, which has a complete listing of train schedules. It is updated monthly and available from Thomas Cook offices worldwide. On overnight hauls you can book a couchette for around €15 to €23 on most international trains. In 1st class there are four bunks per cabin and in 2nd class there are six bunks. It is always advisable, and sometimes compulsory, to book seats on international trains to and from Italy. Some of the main international services include transport for private cars – an option worth examining to save wear and tear on your vehicle before it arrives in Italy.

The UK The Channel Tunnel allows for land transport links between Britain and continental Europe. The Eurostar passenger-train service (☎ 0870 518 6186, W www.eurostar.com) travels between London and Paris and London and Brussels. The Eurotunnel vehicle service (☎ 0870 241 2938, W www.eurotunnel.com) travels between terminals in Folkestone and Calais.

Alternatively, you can get a train ticket that includes crossing the Channel by ferry, SeaCat or hovercraft. Once across the channel, you can travel via Paris and southern France or by swinging from Belgium down through Germany and Switzerland.

At the time of writing, the cheapest standard fares were around UK£185 to Rome and around UK£193 to Florence. On some journeys there are slight discounts for people aged under 26.

For the latest fare information on journeys to Italy, including the Eurostar, contact the Rail Europe Travel Centre (☎ 0870 584 8848, W www.raileurope.co.uk). Another source of rail information for all of Europe is Rail Choice (☎ 020-8659 7300).

Continental Europe Regular trains on two lines connect Italy with main cities in Austria and on into Germany, France or Eastern Europe. Those crossing the frontier at the Brenner Pass go to Innsbruck, Stuttgart, Munich and on. Those crossing at Tarvisio in the east proceed to Vienna, Salzburg and Prague. Trains from Milan head for Switzerland and on into France and the Netherlands. The main international train line to Slovenia crosses near Trieste. You can get trains to Ljubljana and onwards to Zagreb, Budapest and as far as Moscow.

Adult single 2nd-class fares from Paris to Rome (12 hours; TGV to Milan and a Eurostar Italia connection from there to Rome) range from around €99.10 to €144.85. The same ticket to Milan (six hours 40 minutes) costs around €83.85.

From Spain, the only direct service is an overnight Barcelona-Milan (12¾ hours) train that runs from three to seven days per week depending on the season. A reclining seat costs €96.75 one way. From Milan you have to organise onward connections. A 2nd-class couchette is €119.60 and a top-class single cabin €299.30.

Cisalpino trains run at speeds of up to 200km/h from major Swiss cities to Milan. One Cisalpino train per day proceeds to Florence and another to Venice.

Car & Motorcycle

Coming from the UK, you can take your car across to France by ferry or via the Channel Tunnel on Eurotunnel (☎ 0870 241 2938). The latter runs around the clock with up to four crossings (35 minutes) an hour between Folkestone and Calais in the high season. You pay for the vehicle only and fares vary according to time of day and season but you can be looking at paying as much as UK£297 return (valid for a year). In low season you can sometimes get much cheaper offers.

The main points of entry to Italy are the Mt Blanc tunnel from France at Chamonix

Rail Passes & Discount Tickets

If you're planning a wider European trip, it may make financial sense to get a rail pass. Remember that, even with a pass, you must still pay for seat and couchette reservations, full fare on the Eurostar and supplements on express trains such as Italy's Eurostar Italia and France's TGV. Treat your pass like gold, as it is virtually impossible to obtain replacements or refunds in the event of loss or theft. If you intend to travel mainly or only within Italy, consider a discount ticket or an Italian domestic rail pass (see Train in the Getting Around chapter).

Rail Passes

The InterRail Pass and Rail Europe Senior Card are available to people who have lived in Europe for six months or more. They can be bought at most major stations and student travel outlets or, within the UK, from the Rail Europe Travel Centre (☎ 0870 584 8848, W www.raileurope.co.uk), 179 Piccadilly, London W1V 0BA.

Eurail passes and Europasses are for those who have lived in Europe for less than six months. These passes are supposed to be bought outside Europe, and are cheaper if you do so. They are available from leading travel agencies. You can review passes and special deals on Eurail International's Web site at W www.eurail.com. In the USA and Canada you can purchase passes over the phone on ☎ 1 888 6679734 and have them sent to your home by courier.

InterRail Pass The InterRail map of Europe is divided into zones, one of which comprises Italy, Greece, Slovenia and Turkey. The pass is designed for people aged under 26 but there is a more expensive version for older folk, the InterRail 26+. Twenty-two days of unlimited 2nd-class travel in one zone costs UK£129/185 respectively. Better value is the one-month ticket for two zones for UK£169/239 (which from the UK would get you across France too). A three-zone pass for one month costs UK£199/275. If you think you can stand careering around virtually all of Europe, you could go for the one month all-in UK£229/319 ticket.

Cardholders get discounts on travel in the country where they purchase the ticket, as well as on a variety of other services, such as ferry travel.

Senior Railcard Seniors can get a Rail Europe Senior Card, which is valid for a year for trips that cross at least one border and which entitles you to 30% off standard fares. In the UK the card costs UK£5 but you must already have a Senior Railcard (UK£18), which is available to anyone who can prove they are aged 60 and over (check W www.senior-railcard.co.uk or call ☎ 0845 748 4950). The

(closed at the time of writing but due to reopen late 2001) which connects with the A5 for Turin and Milan; the Grand St Bernard tunnel from Switzerland, which also connects with the A5; and the Brenner Pass from Austria, which connects with the A22 to Bologna. Mountain passes are often closed in winter and sometimes in autumn and spring, making the tunnels a less scenic but more reliable way to arrive in Italy (although there are safety concerns following the fires in the Mt Blanc and Gotthard tunnels). Make sure you have snow chains in winter.

Italy is made for motorcycle touring and motorcyclists swarm into the country in summer to tour the scenic roads. With a bike you rarely have to book ahead for ferries and can enter restricted traffic areas in cities. Italian traffic police generally turn a blind eye to motorcycles parked on footpaths. Crash helmets are compulsory.

An interesting Web site loaded with advice for people planning to drive in Europe is W www.ideamerge.com/motoeuropa. For help with route-planning check out W www.euroshell.com.

Rail Passes & Discount Tickets

Europe-wide card is known in Italy as Carta Rail Plus and it costs €20 (the equivalent of the UK Senior Railcard in Italy is the Carta d'Argento, which costs €23.25).

Eurail Passes Eurail passes are expensive so look at the options before committing yourself. The cards are good for travel in 17 European countries (not including the UK) but forget it if you intend to travel mainly in Italy. People aged over 26 pay for a 1st-class pass (Eurailpass) and those aged under 26 for a 2nd-class pass (Eurailpass Youth). Passes are valid for 15 or 21 days or for one, two or three months. These cost US$554/718/890/1260/1558 respectively for the Eurailpass. Children aged between four and 11 pay half-price for 1st-class passes. The Eurailpass Youth comes in at US$388/499/623/882/1089. You'll need to cover more than 2400km within two weeks to get value for money.

Eurail also offers Flexi passes, with which the traveller is entitled to 10 or 15 days of train travel over a two-month period. These cost US$458/599 for those under 26 in 2nd class and US£654/862 for those aged over 26 in 1st class.

Eurailpass Saver is for two to five people travelling together and is available for 15 or 21 days or one, two or three months. The price per person is US$470/610/756/1072/1324 respectively.

The Eurailpass Saver Flexi entitles the travellers (up to five on one pass) using the pass to 10 or 15 days of train travel over a two-month period. The pass costs US$556/732 per person (children half-price).

The Eurailpass/Hertz Drive gives the bearer four days of unlimited 1st-class train travel combined with two days of car rental. There are various permutations on this and prices start at US$364 per person (if two are travelling together).

Europass This provides between five and 15 days of unlimited travel within a two-month period in five 'core' countries (France, Spain, Germany, Switzerland and Italy). As with Eurail passes, those aged over 26 pay for a 1st-class pass while those aged under 26 can get a cheaper Europass Youth for travel in 2nd class. The basic five-day pass costs US$348/244 for the adult/youth version. You can add other countries by upping the price. There is also a Europass Saver which works like the Eurailpass Saver (see Eurail Passes earlier). It costs US$296 per person.

Discount Tickets

Always ask about discounts. Students and people under 26 generally pay less for international train journeys. Kids aged four to 11 travel for half the adult fare and toddlers aged under four go for free.

Paperwork & Preparations When driving in Europe always carry proof of ownership of a private vehicle (a Vehicle Registration Document for UK-registered cars). All EU member states' driving licences are fully recognised throughout Europe, regardless of your length of stay. However, if you are coming from the UK and hold an old-style green driving licence, you will need to obtain an International Driving Permit (IDP). Those with a non-EU licence are supposed to obtain an IDP to accompany their national licence. In practice, you will probably be OK with national licences from countries such as Australia, Canada and the USA. If you decide to get an IDP, your national automobile association can issue them. It is valid for 12 months and must be kept with your proper licence. People who have held residency in Italy for one year or more must apply for an Italian driving licence.

Third-party motor insurance is a minimum requirement in Italy and throughout Europe. The Green Card, an internationally recognised proof of insurance obtainable from your insurer, is mandatory. Also ask your insurer for a European Accident Statement form (it can simplify matters in the event of an accident). Never sign statements you can't read or understand – insist on a translation.

A European breakdown assistance policy is a good investment. Outfits in the UK include the AA Five Star Service (☎ 0870 550 0600) or the RAC's Eurocover Motoring Assistance (☎ 0870 572 2722). In Italy, assistance can be obtained through the Automobile Club Italiano (ACI).

See Roadside Assistance under Car & Motorcycle in the Getting Around chapter for details.

Every vehicle travelling across an international border should display a nationality plate of its country of registration (GB for Great Britain, F for France and so on). A warning triangle (to be used in the event of a breakdown) is compulsory throughout Europe. Recommended accessories are a first-aid kit, a spare-bulb kit and a fire extinguisher.

Rental There is a mind-boggling variety of special deals and terms and conditions attached to car rental in Europe. Here are a few pointers to help you through.

Multinational agencies – Hertz, Avis, Budget and Europe's largest rental agency, Europcar – will provide a reliable service and good standard of vehicle. However, if you walk into an office and ask for a car on the spot, you will always pay high rates (even allowing for special weekend deals). National and local firms can sometimes undercut the multinationals but make sure you examine the rental agreement carefully.

Planning ahead and pre-booking a rental car through a multinational agency before leaving home will enable you to find the best deals. Pre-booked and prepaid rates are always cheaper. Fly/drive combinations and other packages are worth looking into. You will simply pick up the vehicle on your arrival in Italy and return it to a nominated point at the end of the rental period. Ask your travel agency for information or contact one of the major rental agencies.

Holiday Autos (☎ 0870 400 0099 in the UK, W www.holidayautos.co.uk) sometimes has good rates for Europe. You nee to pre-book. At the time of writing, the were charging UK£174 (all-inclusive) for small car, such as a Fiat Punto, for on week, with the option of one-way rental Another possibility is Car Rental Direc (☎ 020-7625 7166 in the UK, W www .globcars.com).

If you don't pre-book, you could ad Switzerland to your driving itinerary. Ca hire costs can be much lower than in Italy and generally there is no problem wit cross-border travel in rental cars (confir this before signing on the dotted line).

No matter where you hire your ca make sure you understand what is include in the price (unlimited kilometres, tax, in surance, collision damage waiver and s on) and what your liabilities are. Insuranc can be a vexed issue. Are you covered fo theft, vandalism and fire damage? Since th most common and convenient way to pa for rental is by credit card, check whethe or not you have car insurance with th credit-card provider and what the condi tions are. The extra cover provided ma pick up the slack in any local cover.

See Rental under Car & Motorcycle i the Getting Around chapter for details o hiring cars and motorcycles in Italy.

Purchase The UK is probably the bes place to buy second-hand cars (prices ar not competitive for new cars). Bear in min that you will be getting a left-hand-drive ca (with the steering wheel on the right).

If you want a right-hand-drive car an can afford to buy new, prices are relativel low in Belgium, the Netherlands and Lux embourg. Paperwork can be tricky wher ever you buy.

Note that it is illegal for nonresidents t purchase vehicles in Italy.

Camper Van Travelling in a camper va can kill several birds with one stone, takin care of eating, sleeping and travelling i one package. London is a good place to buy Look in publications such as *TNT* magazin or *Loot* newspaper or go to the van marke on Market Rd, London N7 (near Caledon an Road tube station; generally open summer only). If you want to rent, organise it before you arrive in Italy, as there are few camper-van rental outlets there.

SEA

Ferries connect Italy with other countries around the Mediterranean. Tickets are most expensive in summer and prices for cars, camper vans and motorcycles vary according to the size of the vehicle. Bicycles can sometimes be taken free of charge. Eurail and InterRail pass holders pay only a supplement on the Italy-Greece routes but must travel with approved companies. Ticket prices are competitive on the heavily serviced Brindisi-Greece route.

You can travel to Italy (to the towns listed) from the following countries. See the Getting There & Away sections for each town for more details.

Albania Ancona, Bari, Brindisi
Corsica Genoa, La Spezia, Livorno, Naples, Palau, Porto Torres, Santa Teresa di Gallura, Savona
Croatia Ancona, Pescara, Trieste
Greece Ancona, Bari, Brindisi, Otranto, Trieste, Venice
Malta Catania
Slovenia Trieste, Venice
Spain Genoa
Tunisia Cagliari, Genoa, Naples, Trapani (via Pantelleria)
Turkey Brindisi
Yugoslavia Bari

ORGANISED TOURS

There are many many options for organised travel to Italy. The Italian State Tourist Office (see Tourist Offices Abroad in the Facts for the Visitor chapter) can provide a list of tour operators, noting what each specialises in. Tours can save you hassles but they rob you of independence and generally do not come cheap.

General

A couple of big specialists in the UK are Magic of Italy (☎ 0870 027 0500, W www.magicofitaly.co.uk) and Alitalia's subsidiary, Italiatour (☎ 01883-621900, W www.italiatour.com). Between them they offer a wide range of tours, city breaks and resort-based holidays covering most of the country.

In the USA, Breakaway Adventures (☎ 800 567 62 86, fax 202 293 04 83, W www.breakaway-adventures.com), 1312 18th St, NW, Suite 401, Washington, DC 20036, operates trips to Italy.

In Australia, CIT Travel (☎ 02-9267 1255, fax 9261 4664, W www.cittravel.com.au), Level 2, 263 Clarence St, Sydney, NSW 2000, is a good general operator for trips to Italy. Another with specialist knowledge of Italy is ATI Tours (☎ 02-9798 0588 or toll free ☎ 1800 069 985, fax 02-9716 0891, W www.atitours.com.au), 125 Ramsay St, Haberfield NSW 2045.

Short Breaks

Kirker Travel Ltd (☎ 020-7231 3333) at 3 New Concordia Wharf, Mill St, London SE1, offers pricey short breaks from London in exclusive hotels in the main cities of Italy. Such a trip starts at about UK£400 per person for three nights in twin accommodation with air fare, transfers and breakfast included. Depending on the hotel you choose, the price can rise considerably. Prices also rise in summer.

Self-Catering Holidays

For many people the ideal Italian holiday is to rent a villa or restored farmhouse for a week or longer and take care of the cooking themselves. For more information on this style of accommodation, see Rental Accommodation in the Facts for the Visitor chapter.

Tours for Under-35s

Top Deck Travel (☎ 020-7370 4555), 131–135 Earls Court Rd, London SW5, and Contiki Travel Ltd (☎ 020-7637 0802), c/o Royal National Hotel, Bedford Way, London WC1H, do a range of coach tours across Europe for young people – they are generally aimed at the high-speed, party-minded crowd. Both companies have offices in North America, Australia, New Zealand and South Africa.

Tours for Seniors

For people aged over 60, Saga Holidays offers holidays ranging from cheap coach tours to luxury cruises. Saga has offices in the UK (☎ 0800 300456, W www.holidays.saga.co.uk), Saga Building, Middelburg Square, Folkestone, Kent CT20 1AZ; the USA (toll free ☎ 1 877 265 6862, W www.sagaholidays.com), 222 Berkeley St, Boston, MA 02116; and Australia (☎ 02-9957 4266), 10/17 Paul St, Milson's Point, Sydney 2061.

Cooking & Wine Holidays

There are many tours for those people with specific interests. Tasting Places (☎ 020-7460 0077), Unit 40, Buspace Studios, Conlan St, London W10 5AP, offers one-week trips led by cooking instructors. You cook and eat your way to a better understanding of a chosen region and won't get much change from UK£1100.

Truffle fanatics could enquire about the Alternative Travel Group's (☎ 01865-315678)truffle-hunting trips to Umbria in October. You hunt them and then, best of all, consume them.

If drinking is more your thing, Arblaster and Clarke Wine Tours (☎ 01730-893344) might have something for you. They organise a variety of trips, which will set you back about UK£1000 per person, to different wine regions of Italy. Winetrails (☎ 01306-712111) is a similar option although a little cheaper.

Walking Tours

Several companies offer organised walking tours. Explore Worldwide (☎ 01252-760000, W www.exploreworldwide.com), 1 Frederick St, Aldershot, Hants GU11 1LQ, is one. They have tours of Sicily, for instance, that combine hiking up volcanoes (such as Etna and Stromboli) with city tours of places such as Palermo and Syracuse.

Also in the UK, Alternative Travel Group (☎ 01865-315678) offers a series of escorted and unescorted walking and cycling tours in many parts of Italy. With the unescorted version, accommodation is prebooked and luggage is forwarded while you walk or cycle. Prices for the unescorted tours start at around UK£350 for eight days (excluding flights). Another UK company organising guided walking holidays to Italy is Ramblers Holidays (☎ 01707-331133, W www.ramblersholidays.co.uk).

Walking holidays of varying lengths are offered by Headwater (☎ 01606-813333, W www.headwater.com). Destinations for guided and more independent walking tours include Tuscany, the Dolomites and Sicily. Headwater has branches in the USA and Australia too.

Cycling Tours

The European Bike Express (☎ 01642-251440 in the UK, e bike@bike-express.co.uk) is a coach service for cyclists and their bikes. It runs in summer from north-eastern England to Italy or Spain with pick-up/drop-off points en route. The return fare is up to UK£174 (UK£164 for Cyclists' Touring Club members) depending on where you start and finish.

Language Trips

Although some agents can organise study trips to Italy, it will probably work out more cheaply to contact language schools in Italy directly. There is no shortage of them; for more information see Courses in the Facts for the Visitor chapter (some language schools are also mentioned in the course of the guide).

Getting Around

Domestic air travel is expensive and probably worth it only if you are trying to cover long distances or are really short of time. You can reach almost any destination in Italy by train or bus and services are efficient and relatively cheap (though not always quick). Trains are the most straightforward method of travel and stations are usually in or near the historic centre of towns. Bus travel can be a little more complicated to work out because there are so many different companies but it is a cheap method of transport. Your own wheels give you the most freedom and flexibility and can allow you to stray off the main routes to discover out-of-the-way hill towns or deserted beaches. However, be aware that both petrol and *autostrada* (motorway) tolls are expensive and that the stress of driving and parking your car in a big Italian city could easily ruin your trip.

AIR

The domestic lines are Alitalia (☎ 06 6 56 41 in Rome or ☎ 848 86 56 41, **W** www.alitalia.it), Meridiana (toll free ☎ 800 40 11 60, **W** www.meridiana.it) and Air One (☎ 848 84 88 80, **W** www.flyairone.it).

The main airports are in Rome, Pisa, Milan, Naples, Catania and Cagliari; there are other, smaller airports throughout the country (including Florence, Bari, Bologna, Trieste, Venice, Verona, Turin, Reggio di Calabria, Olbia and Alghero). Domestic flights can be booked through any travel agency, including Sestante CIT (☎ 06 47 86 41, fax 06 478 64 200), Via Barberini 86, Rome, and Centro Turistico Studentesco e Giovanile (CTS; ☎ 06 687 26 72), Corso Vittorio Emanuele II 297, Rome. Travel agents are given under Information in the individual cities throughout this guide.

There are no domestic air passes available in Italy. Alitalia offers a range of discounts for young people, families, seniors and weekend travellers, as well as occasional promotional fares and advance purchase deals. It should be noted that airline fares fluctuate and that special deals have restrictions (for example, tickets must be bought in Italy or deals are for return fares only). Barring special deals, a one-way fare is generally half the cost of the return fare.

Sample fares are Rome-Milan €177.65, Rome-Florence €114.65, Rome-Olbia €117, Rome-Palermo €146.15, Florence-Catania €215, Florence-Olbia €150, Milan-Catania €209.15, Naples-Bologna €176, Naples-Turin €170.45, Palermo-Turin €229.

All applicable airport taxes are factored into the price of your ticket.

BUS

Bus services within Italy are provided by numerous companies and vary from local routes linking small villages to fast and reliable intercity connections. By utilising the local services, it is possible to get to almost any location in the country. Buses can be a cheaper and faster way to get around if your destination is not on a main train line (trains tend to be cheaper on major routes).

It is usually possible to get bus timetables for the provincial and intercity services from local tourist offices. In larger cities, most of the main intercity bus companies have ticket offices or operate through agencies. Buses leave from either an *autostazione* (bus station) or from a particular piazza or street. Details are provided under Getting There & Away in the individual town and city sections of this guide. In some smaller towns and villages, tickets are sold in bars – just ask for *biglietti per il pullman* (tickets for the coach) – or on the bus. Note that buses almost always leave on time.

Major companies that run long-haul services include Marozzi (Rome to Brindisi), SAIS, Segesta and Interbus (Rome to Sicily), and Lazzi and SITA (from Lazio, Tuscany and other regions to the Alps).

Although it is usually not necessary to make reservations on buses, it is advisable in the high season for overnight or long-haul trips. Phone numbers and addresses of major bus companies are listed throughout this book.

TRAIN

Travelling by train in Italy is simple, cheap and generally efficient. The Ferrovie dello Stato (FS) is the partially privatised state train system which runs most, but certainly not all, of the services in Italy; it also runs some bus and ferry services. Other private Italian train lines are noted throughout this book.

For train information throughout Italy, call ☎ 848 88 80 88 (in Italian) from 7am to 9pm or go to the information office at any train station; in larger cities you're sure to find staff who speak English. You can also get information at **W** www.fs-on-line.com (in Italian, English, Spanish, French and German).

There are several types of trains. Some stop at all stations, such as *regionale* or *interregionale* trains. Faster trains, such as the Intercity (IC) or the very fast Eurostar Italia (ES), Italy's answer to France's TGV, stop only at major cities.

Travellers should note that all tickets must be validated *before* you board your train. You simply punch them in the yellow machines installed at the entrance to all train platforms. If you don't validate them, you risk a large fine. This rule does not apply to tickets purchased outside Italy.

There are left-luggage facilities at all train stations. They are usually open 24 hours; those that aren't often close only for a few hours after midnight. They are open daily and charge from €3.10 per day for each piece of luggage. (Note that the left-luggage facilities at Stazione Termini in Rome have become ridiculously expensive.)

Rail Passes

It is not worth buying a Eurail or Inter-Rail pass if you are going to travel only in Italy as train fares are reasonably cheap and the FS offers its own discount passes for travel within the country. These include the Carta Verde for people aged from 12 to 26 years. It costs €20.65, is valid for one year and entitles you to a 20% discount on all train travel, but you'll need to do a fair bit of travelling to get your money's worth. The Carta d'Argento entitles people aged 60 years and over to a 20% discount on 1st and 2nd-class travel for one year. It also costs €20.65. Children aged between four and 12 years are automatically entitled to a 50% discount; those aged under four travel free.

You can buy a *biglietto chilometrico* (kilometric ticket), which is valid for two months and allows you to cover 3000km in a maximum of 20 trips. It costs €110.50 (2nd class) and you must pay the supplement if you catch an Intercity or Eurostar train. Its main attraction is that it can be used by up to five people, either singly or together – the number of kilometres travelled by each person is subtracted from the 3000km total.

Two other useful passes (only for foreign visitors) are the Italy Railcard and Italy Flexi Rail. The Italy Railcard is valid for eight, 15, 21 or 30 days and is available for 1st- or 2nd-class travel. An eight-day pass costs €275/183 for 1st/2nd class; a 21-day pass costs €398/265. Italy Flexi Rail is valid for four, eight or 12 days for travel within one month. A four-day pass costs €216/144 for 1st/2nd class; a 12-day pass costs €389/259. With both passes, prices include supplements for travel on Intercity trains but not for Eurostar trains. You should have your passport for identification when purchasing either pass.

Classes

There are 1st and 2nd classes on all Italian trains; a 1st-class ticket costs just under double the price of a 2nd-class ticket. On Eurostar trains, 2nd class is much like 1st class on other trains.

Reservations

If you don't reserve a seat on a long train trip – particularly if you're travelling at the weekend or during holiday periods – you could find yourself standing in the corridor for the entire journey. Bookings can be made when you buy your ticket, and usually

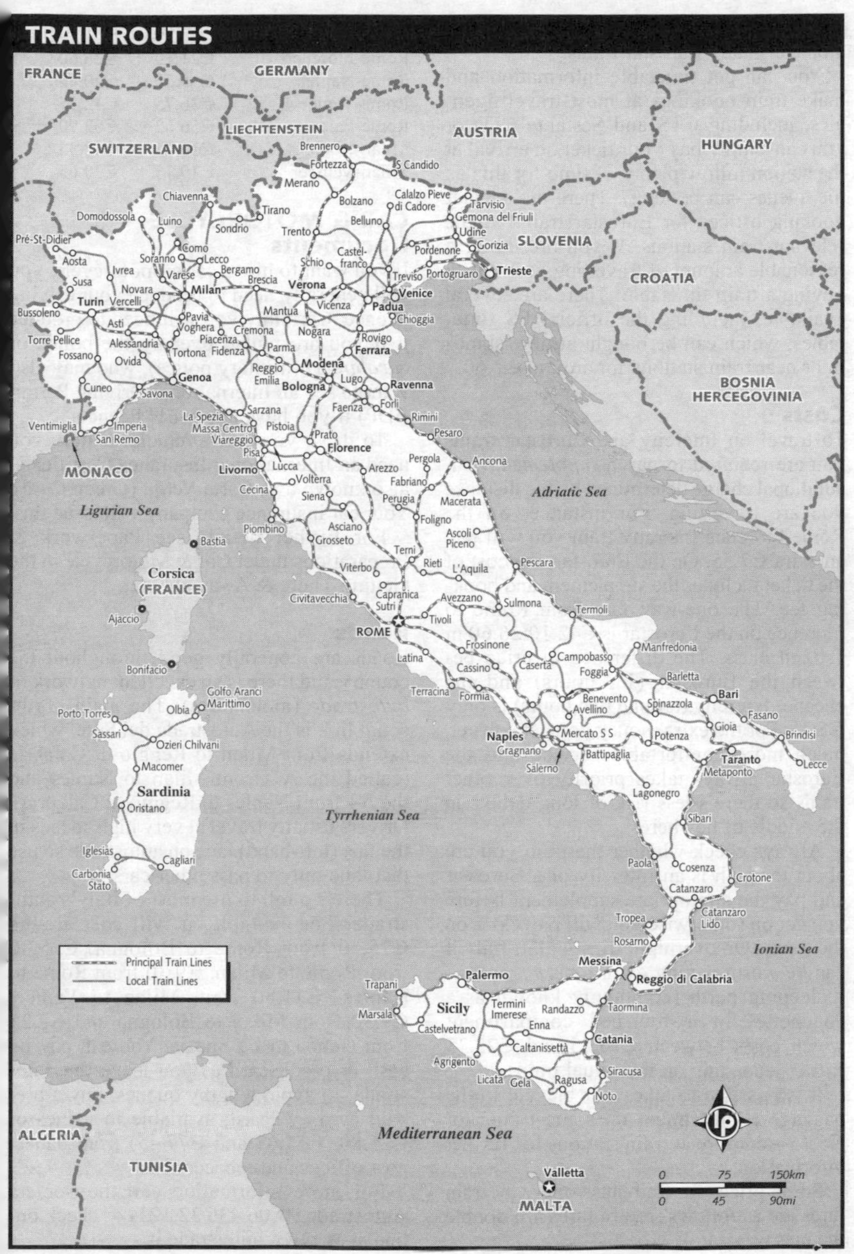
TRAIN ROUTES
FRANCE
GERMANY
LIECHTENSTEIN
AUSTRIA
HUNGARY
SWITZERLAND
SLOVENIA
CROATIA
BOSNIA HERCEGOVINIA
MONACO
Corsica (FRANCE)
Sardinia
Sicily
ALGERIA
TUNISIA
MALTA
Ligurian Sea
Adriatic Sea
Tyrrhenian Sea
Ionian Sea
Mediterranean Sea
Brennero
Fortezza
S Candido
Merano
Bolzano
Calalzo Pieve di Cadore
Tarvisio
Gemona del Friuli
Udine
Gorizia
Trieste
Belluno
Trento
Chiavenna
Tirano
Sondrio
Domodossola
Luino
Pré-St-Didier
Aosta
Como
Lecco
Soranno
Varese
Bergamo
Ivrea
Susa
Novara
Milan
Brescia
Verona
Schio
Castel-franco
Pordenone
Treviso
Portogruaro
Venice
Padua
Vicenza
Chioggia
Turin
Vercelli
Bussoleno
Mantua
Nogara
Rovigo
Ferrara
Pavia
Voghera
Asti
Torre Pellice
Alessandria
Tortona
Cremona
Piacenza
Fidenza
Parma
Reggio Emilia
Modena
Bologna
Lugo
Ravenna
Forlì
Faenza
Rimini
Pesaro
Fossano
Ovida
Genoa
Cuneo
Savona
La Spezia
Sarzana
Massa Centro
Ventimiglia
Imperia
San Remo
Viareggio
Pistoia
Prato
Florence
Pisa
Lucca
Livorno
Volterra
Arezzo
Pergola
Fabriano
Ancona
Cecina
Siena
Perugia
Macerata
Foligno
Piombino
Asciano
Grosseto
Ascoli Piceno
Bastia
Terni
Rieti
Pescara
Viterbo
L'Aquila
Capranica Sutri
Civitavecchia
Avezzano
Sulmona
Termoli
Ajaccio
Tivoli
ROME
Frosinone
Manfredonia
Latina
Campobasso
Caserta
Foggia
Cassino
Barletta
Bonifacio
Terracina
Formia
Benevento
Bari
Spinazzola
Avellino
Fasano
Naples
Mercato S S
Gioia
Brindisi
Gragnano
Potenza
Salerno
Battipaglia
Taranto
Lecce
Metaponto
Lagonegro
Golfo Aranci Marittimo
Olbia
Porto Torres
Sassari
Ozieri Chilvani
Macomer
Oristano
Iglesias
Cagliari
Carbonia Stato
Sibari
Paola
Cosenza
Crotone
Catanzaro
Catanzaro Lido
Tropea
Rosarno
Messina
Reggio di Calabria
Palermo
Trapani
Termini Imerese
Randazzo
Taormina
Marsala
Castelvetrano
Enna
Catania
Caltanissettà
Agrigento
Siracusa
Licata
Gela
Ragusa
Noto
Valletta
Principal Train Lines
Local Train Lines
0 75 150km
0 45 90mi

cost an extra €1.05. Reservations are obligatory for many Eurostar trains.

You can get timetable information and make train bookings at most travel agencies, including CTS and Sestante CIT, or you can simply buy your ticket on arrival at the station (allow plenty of time for this as the queues can be long). There are special booking offices for Eurostar trains at the relevant train stations. If you are doing a reasonable amount of travelling, it is worth buying a train timetable. There are several available, including the official FS timetables, which can be bought at newsstands in or near train stations for around €2.60.

Costs

To travel on Intercity and Eurostar trains you are required to pay a *supplemento*, an additional charge determined by the distance you are travelling. For instance, on the Rome-Florence Intercity train you will pay an extra €7.55. On the Eurostar, the cost of the ticket includes the supplement and booking fee. The one-way fare from Rome to Florence on the Eurostar is €42.10/26.60 in 1st/2nd class. The difference in price between the Eurostar (1½ hours) and the cheaper Intercity (around two hours) is only €5.45. For the extra money you get a faster, much more comfortable service and the Eurostar always takes priority over other trains so there's less risk of long delays in the middle of nowhere.

Always check whether the train you are about to catch is an Intercity or a Eurostar and pay the appropriate supplement before you get on (otherwise you will pay extra on the train). On overnight trips within Italy it can be worth paying extra for a *cuccetta* – a sleeping berth (commonly known as a couchette) in a four-bed compartment which costs between €16.55 and €23.25 extra (depending on the actual train).

It is possible to take your bicycle in the baggage compartment on some trains for €5.15 – enquire at train stations for further information.

Some prices for 2nd-class one-way train fares are as follows (return fares are double the one-way fare):

Route	Intercity	Eurostar
Rome-Florence	€21.10	€26.60
Rome-Naples	€15.50	€20.40
Rome-Venice	€36.75	€42.35
Rome-Palermo	€56.62	€62.90
Milan-Rome	€36.75	€42.35
Milan-Venice	€19.15	€20.65

CAR & MOTORCYCLE

Documents

If you want to hire a car or motorcycle, you will generally need to produce your driving licence. Certainly you will need to produce it if you are pulled over by the police or *carabinieri* (military police), who may also want to see an International Driving Permit (IDP) if you have a non-EU licence.

To drive your own vehicle in Italy you need an International Insurance Certificate, also known as a Carta Verde (Green Card). Your car insurance company will issue this.

For further details see Paperwork & Preparations under Car & Motorcycle in the Getting There & Away chapter.

Roads

Roads are generally good throughout the country and there is an excellent network of *autostrade* (motorways). The main north-south link is the Autostrada del Sole, which extends from Milan to Reggio di Calabria (called the A1 from Milan to Naples and the A3 from Naples to Reggio di Calabria). Drivers usually travel at very high speeds in the fast (left-hand) lane on autostrade so use that lane only to pass other cars.

There's a toll to use most of Italy's autostrade. For example, it will cost around €15.50 from Rome to Bologna, €25.80 from Rome to Milan, €9.30 from Rome to Naples, €11.80 from Milan to Venice, €9.30 from Milan to Bologna and €7.25 from Genoa to La Spezia. You can pay by cash or credit card as you leave the autostrada; to avoid lengthy queues, buy a prepaid card (Viacard; available in values of €25.80, €51.65 and €77.45) from banks, post offices and tobacconists.

For more information call the Società Autostrade (☎ 06 436 32 121) or check online at W www.autostrade.it.

Travellers with time to spare could consider using the system of *strade statali* (state roads), which are often multilane dual carriageways and are toll free. They are represented on maps as 'S' or 'SS'. The *strade provinciali* (provincial roads) are sometimes little more than country lanes but provide access to some of the more beautiful scenery and to the many small towns and villages. They are represented as 'P' or 'SP' on maps.

Road Rules

In Italy, as in the rest of continental Europe, drive on the right side of the road and overtake on the left. Unless otherwise indicated, you must always give way to cars entering an intersection (including a T-junction) from a road on your right. It is compulsory to wear seat belts if fitted to the car (front seat belts on all cars, rear seat belts on cars built after 26 April 1990). If you are caught not wearing a seat belt, you will be required to pay an on-the-spot €29.95 fine – although this doesn't seem to deter Italians, many of whom use them only on the autostrade.

Random breath tests now take place in Italy. If you're involved in an accident while under the influence of alcohol, the penalties can be severe. The blood-alcohol limit is 0.08%.

Speed limits, unless otherwise indicated by local signs, are as follows: on the autostrade 130km/h for cars of 1100cc or more, 110km/h for smaller cars and for motorcycles under 350cc; on all main, non-urban highways 110km/h; on secondary, non-urban highways 90km/h; and in built-up areas 50km/h. Speeding fines follow EU standards and are €30.45 for up to 10km/h over the limit, €121.35 for up to 40km/h, and €303.15 for more than 40km/h. Driving through a red light – and getting caught doing it – will set you back €60.45.

You don't need a licence to ride a moped under 50cc but you should be aged 14 or over; a helmet is compulsory for those aged

Road Distances (km)

Note
Distances between Palermo and mainland towns do not take into account the ferry from Reggio di Calabria to Messina. Add an extra hour to your journey time to allow for this crossing.

	Bari	Bologna	Brindisi	Florence	Genoa	Livorno	Milan	Naples	Palermo	Perugia	Reggio di Calabria	Rome	Siena	Turin	Trento	Trieste	Venice	Verona
Bari	---																	
Bologna	670	---																
Brindisi	114	785	---															
Florence	662	101	776	---														
Genoa	889	291	1004	227	---													
Livorno	742	176	857	84	179	---												
Milan	877	207	992	296	146	296	---											
Naples	253	568	368	466	694	547	762	---										
Palermo	665	1234	669	1132	1360	1213	1429	683	---									
Perugia	565	235	679	150	378	231	447	369	1036	---								
Reggio di Calabria	446	1014	449	912	1140	993	1209	463	220	816	---							
Rome	413	369	527	267	495	305	563	217	884	170	664	---						
Siena	616	168	731	70	275	118	362	420	1087	103	867	221	---					
Turin	995	325	1109	394	168	345	139	860	1527	545	1307	661	460	---				
Trento	890	220	1005	309	354	384	223	775	1442	459	1222	576	375	355	---			
Trieste	891	290	1006	390	536	465	405	857	1523	465	1303	658	457	536	284	---		
Venice	754	154	868	255	400	329	269	721	1388	327	1168	522	321	401	159	153	---	
Verona	808	137	922	226	289	301	158	693	1359	377	1139	494	293	290	97	250	114	---

under 18. You can't carry passengers or ride on autostrade. The speed limit for a moped is 40km/h. To ride a motorcycle or scooter up to 125cc, you must be aged 16 or over and have a licence (a car licence will do). Helmets are compulsory for everyone riding a motorcycle bigger than 50cc. Although this is a rule that Italians have traditionally chosen to ignore, since mid-2000 the police have actively been enforcing the regulations and now it's only in Naples and a few Sicilian towns that helmetless scooter riders can be spotted regularly. For motorcycles over 125cc you will need a motorcycle licence.

You will be able to enter restricted traffic areas in Italian cities on a motorcycle without any problems, and traffic police generally turn a blind eye to motorcycles or scooters parked on footpaths. There is no lights-on requirement for motorcycles during the day.

Motoring in Europe, published in the UK by the RAC, gives an excellent summary of road regulations in each European country, including parking rules. Motoring organisations in other countries have similar publications.

City Driving

Driving in Italian towns and cities is quite an experience and may well present the unprepared with headaches. The Italian attitude to driving bears little similarity to the English concept of traffic in ordered lanes (a normal two-lane road in Italy is likely to carry three or four lanes of traffic) and the farther south you travel, the less drivers seem to pay attention to road rules. Instead, the main factor in determining right of way is whichever driver is more *prepotente* (forceful). If you must drive in an Italian city, particularly in Rome or Naples, remain calm and keep your eyes on the car in front and you should be OK. Once you arrive in a city, follow the *centro* (city centre) signs. Most roads are well signposted.

Parking

Be extremely careful where you park your car, especially in major cities. If you leave it in an area marked with a sign reading *Zona Rimozione* (Removal Zone) and featuring a tow truck, it will almost certainly be towed away and you'll have to pay a heavy fine. A stopover in a medieval hill town will generally mean leaving the car in a car park some distance from the town centre. It is a good idea to leave your car in a supervised car park if you have luggage, but even then it's a risk to leave your belongings in an unattended car. If it can be seen it can be stolen. Be especially vigilant in motorway service areas as extremely professional gangs of thieves can clean out the contents of a locked vehicle in seconds. Where practical, always leave someone watching the car.

Car parks in the major cities are indicated in this book. They are denoted on signs throughout Italy by a white 'P' on a blue background. There are parking meters in most cities and even in the historic centres of small towns. You are likely to have to pay in advance for the number of hours you think you will stay. Per hour, they can cost anything from €0.25 to €1 (all over Rome, for example).

Petrol

The cost of petrol in Italy is very high. You'll pay around €1.10 per litre for leaded petrol, up to €1.20 for unleaded and around €0.85 for diesel.

Petrol is called *benzina*, unleaded petrol is *benzina senza piombo* and diesel is *gasolio*. If you are driving a car that uses LPG (liquid petroleum gas), you will need to buy a special guide to service stations that have *gasauto* or GPL. By law these must be in nonresidential areas and are usually in the the country or on city outskirts, although you'll find plenty on the motorways. GPL costs around €0.55 per litre.

Rental

Rental agencies are listed under the major cities in this book. Most tourist offices and hotels can provide information about car or motorcycle rental; otherwise, look in the local *Pagine Gialle* (Yellow Pages) under *autonoleggio* (car hire).

Car It is cheaper to arrange car rental before leaving your own country, for instance

Free Wheelers

There was something magical about driving into Italy from France for the first time and something rather disturbing about the simultaneous red and green traffic lights at a choked intersection just beyond Ventimiglia. Judging by the irritated honking behind me, red and green meant green for go and red for watch out for what everyone else is doing.

Driving in Italy, especially in the cities, is special. It's a little like a combination of Formula One and bumper cars. Out on the *autostrada* (motorway), it's pretty straightforward: when your rear-view mirror suddenly fills with the flashing headlights of an angry Audi doing 180km/h right up your caboose while you are overtaking a truck at 130km/h, just smile and complete your manoeuvre. Resist the temptation to lightly touch the brakes and have the Audi crumple itself into your rear end. Tailgating is *de rigueur* and speeding a matter of honour (in spite of the occasional fine), so things get a little hairy in dense fog with zero visibility. On the subject of honour, many locals look upon the seat belt with considerable disdain. This, as even most Italians will admit, is foolish in the extreme.

Most other aspects of Italian driving are infectious. You soon realise that what at first seems like clueless indiscipline is, in fact, the height of driving skill. When you begin to see how traffic flows, how drivers seem to have a sixth sense for what is happening around them and so generally proceed without having accidents, you begin to understand that, actually, these guys are good... and masters of entering the impossible parking spot.

The rules of the road are certainly subject to interpretation. For instance, stopping at pedestrian crossings is for pedestrians, not cars. In cities such as Naples, stopping only occurs during gridlock – you can be sure everyone is running red lights. In most other cities red lights are respected but scooters tend to slow rather than stop on a red. Nippy lane crossing, and even lane creation on wide boulevards (and some narrow ones) and roundabouts, is the norm. Decisiveness is the key. Even when you have no clue where you're going, go there with *brio* (liveliness) – otherwise the guy going with brio behind you may wind up in your behind.

Perhaps the spirit of Italian driving is best illustrated by a late-night habit in cities such as Milan and Rome. All traffic lights flash orange in the wee hours, no matter how complex the intersection. Keep your eyes peeled, feet poised over accelerator and brake (you never know which will come in most handy) and go. Get enough of this and you'll never be able to drive in that staid Anglo-Saxon fashion again.

Damien Simonis

through some sort of fly/drive deal. Most of the major car-hire firms, including Hertz, Avis and Budget, can arrange this for you. All you have to do is pick up the vehicle at a nominated point when you arrive in Italy. Foreign offices of Sestante CIT (W www.cittravel.com) can also help to organise car or camper van rental before you leave home.

You have to be aged 21 or over (23 or over for some companies) to hire a car in Italy and you have to have a credit card. Most firms will accept your standard licence, sometimes with an Italian translation (which can usually be provided by the agencies themselves), or IDP.

At the time of writing, Avis offered a special weekend rate for unlimited kilometres which compared well with rates offered by other firms: €150.80 for a Fiat Punto (Group A) or €255.15 for a Fiat Brava (Group B), from 9am Friday to 9am Monday. Maggiore National offered a weekend deal of €119.30 for a Fiat Punto, with a limit of 100km/day. The same car for five to seven days, with a limit of 1400km, costs €307.30. If you pick up or drop off the car at an airport, there is usually a surcharge of around €25.80.

Motorcycle You'll have no trouble hiring a small motorcycle such as a scooter (Vespa) or moped. There are numerous

rental agencies in cities, where you'll also usually be able to hire larger motorcycles for touring, and at tourist destinations such as seaside resorts. The average cost for a 50cc scooter (per person) is around €31/155 per day/week. For a 125cc (for two people) you will pay from around €42/207 per day/week. For a moped you'll pay around €24/114 per day/week.

Most agencies will not rent motorcycles to people aged under 18. Note that many places require a sizeable deposit and that you could be responsible for reimbursing part of the cost of the bike if it is stolen. Always check the fine print in the contract.

See Road Rules earlier in this chapter for more details about age, licence and helmet requirements.

Purchase

Car It's very difficult for foreigners to buy a car in Italy – the law requires that you be a resident to own and register one. You can get round this by asking a friend who is resident in Italy to buy one for you.

It is possible to buy a cheap, small 10-year-old car for as little as €775, though you'll pay up to around €3700 for a reasonable five-year-old Fiat Uno and up to €5200 for a two-year-old Fiat Uno. Look in the classified section of local newspapers to find cars for sale.

Motorcycle The same laws apply to owning and registering a motorcycle as apply to purchasing a car. The cost of a second-hand Vespa ranges from €260 to €780, and a moped will cost from €150 to €520. Prices for more powerful bikes start at around €780.

Roadside Assistance

The Automobile Club Italiano (ACI) will provide free emergency roadside assistance once only to members of foreign automobile associations – but only to get you and the car to the nearest ACI-registered mechanic (which is not always convenient). If you are not a member of a foreign automobile association, you'll pay a minimum fee of €82.70 but again this only gets you and the vehicle to the nearest garage. If you want your car to go to a specialist mechanic or to a more distant destination, you will have to shell out the towing costs – which are both there and back to the pick-up point. To get roadside assistance call ☎ 116.

ACI has offices in Rome (☎ 06 4 99 81) at Via Marsala 8, and in Milan (☎ 02 7 74 51) at Corso Venezia 43.

A European breakdown assistance policy, such as the AA Five Star Service or the RAC Eurocover Motoring Assistance, is a good investment.

BICYCLE

Cycling is a national pastime in Italy and can be a great way to see the countryside as well as get around busy town centres. See Activities in the Facts for the Visitor chapter for suggestions on places to cycle. There are no special road rules for cyclists. Helmets and lights are not obligatory but you would be wise to equip yourself with both. You cannot take bikes onto the autostrade. If you plan to bring your own bike, check with your airline for any additional costs. The bike will need to be disassembled and packed for the journey.

Make sure you include a few tools and spare parts (including a puncture-repair kit and a spare inner tube), a helmet and a very solid bike lock and chain (theft of mountain bikes is a major problem in the big cities).

Bikes can be taken very cheaply on trains for €5.20, although only certain trains will actually carry them. Fast trains (Intercity and Eurostar) will generally not accommodate bikes so they must be sent as registered luggage, which can take a few days. Check with the FS (see Train earlier) for more information. Bikes can be transported for free on ferries to Sicily and Sardinia.

Rental & Purchase

Bikes are available for hire in most Italian towns and many places have both city and mountain bikes. Rental costs for a city bike start at €8/50 per day/week (a good mountain bike will cost more).

If you shop around, bargain prices for bikes range from about €100 for a ladies' bike without gears to €210 for a mountain bike with 16 gears, but you will pay a lot more for a very good bike. A good place to shop for bike bargains is Tacconi Sport, which buys in bulk. It has large outlets near Perugia, Arezzo, Trento and in the Republic of San Marino.

See Getting Around under the individual cities in this guide for more information.

Organisations

There are organisations that can help you plan your bike tour or through which you can organise guided tours. In England, you should contact the Cyclists' Touring Club (☎ 01483-417217, W www.ctc.org.uk) for information on cycling conditions, itineraries and cheap insurance. You will have to become a member first.

HITCHING

Hitching is never safe in any country and we don't recommend it. Travellers who decide to hitchhike should understand they are taking a small but potentially serious risk. People who do choose to hitchhike will be safer if they travel in pairs and let someone know where they are planning to go. A man and a woman travelling together is probably the best combination. Women travelling alone should be extremely cautious about hitching anywhere. Hitchhiking is not a major pastime in Italy, but Italians are friendly people and you will generally find a lift.

It is illegal to hitchhike on Italy's motorways but quite acceptable to stand near the entrance to the toll booths. Never hitchhike where drivers can't stop in good time or without causing an obstruction. You could also approach drivers at petrol stations and truck stops. Look presentable, carry as little luggage as possible and hold a sign in Italian indicating your destination.

It is sometimes possible to arrange lifts in advance – ask around at youth hostels and budget accommodation places. The International Lift Centre (☎ 055 28 06 26) in Florence and Enjoy Rome (see Tourist Offices under Information in the Rome chapter) may be able to help.

BOAT

Navi (large ferries) service the islands of Sicily and Sardinia, and *traghetti* (smaller ferries) and *aliscafi* (hydrofoils) service areas such as the Aeolian Islands, Elba, the Isole Tremiti, the Pontine Islands and the islands in the Gulf of Naples (Capri, Ischia and Procida). The main embarkation points for Sardinia are Genoa, Livorno, Civitavecchia and Naples; for Sicily the main points are Naples and Villa San Giovanni in Calabria. The main points of arrival in Sardinia are Cagliari, Arbatax, Olbia and Porto Torres; in Sicily they are Palermo and Messina.

Tirrenia Navigazione (☎ 199 12 31 99, W www.tirrenia.it) is the major company servicing the Mediterranean and it has offices throughout Italy. The FS (W www.fs-on-line.com) operates ferries to Sicily and Sardinia. Detailed information on ferry companies, prices and times is provided in the Getting There & Away sections of the Sicily and Sardinia chapters and other relevant destinations.

Many ferry services are overnight and travellers can choose between cabin accommodation (men and women are usually segregated in 2nd class, although families will be kept together) or a *poltrona*, an airline-type armchair. Deck class (a ticket with no reserved seat or cabin, which allows you to sit/sleep in the general lounge areas or on deck) is available only in summer and only on some ferries, so ask when making your booking. Restaurant, bar and recreation facilities, including cinemas, are available on the larger, long-haul ferries. All ferries carry vehicles.

LOCAL TRANSPORT

All the major cities have good transport systems, with bus and underground-train networks usually integrated. However, in Venice your only options are by boat or on foot.

Bus & Underground Trains

City bus services are usually frequent and reliable. You must always buy bus tickets before you board the bus and validate them once aboard. It is common practice among Italians and many tourists to ride buses for free by not validating their tickets – just watch how many people rush to punch their tickets when an inspector boards the bus. The introduction in Rome and some other cities of electronic machines that 'read' magnetised tickets is going some way to reduce fare evasion. If you get caught with an unvalidated ticket, you will be fined on the spot (up to €25.80 in most cities, but between €51.65 and €258.25 in Rome).

Efficient provincial and regional buses also operate between towns and villages. Tourist offices will provide information on bus routes and timetables.

There are underground systems in Rome (Metropolitana), Milan (MM) and Naples (Metropolitana). You must buy tickets and validate them before getting on the train. You can get a map of the network from tourist offices in the relevant city.

Tickets Tickets can be bought at most *tabaccheria* (tobacconists), at many newsstands, at ticket booths or dispensing machines at bus stations (for instance, outside Stazione Termini in Rome, where many of the city buses stop), and in underground stations. They are valid both for buses and for the underground systems in Rome, Milan and Naples. Tickets generally cost from €0.75 to €1.10 for one hour to 90 minutes (it varies from city to city). Most cities offer 24-hour or daily tourist tickets which can mean big savings.

Taxi

Taxis in Italy are expensive and it is often possible to catch a bus instead. You can usually find taxis in taxi ranks at train and bus stations or you can telephone (radio-taxi phone numbers are listed in the Getting Around sections of the major cities). If you book a taxi by phone, you will be charged for the trip the driver makes to reach you. Taxis will rarely stop when hailed on the street (it's illegal for them to do so) and generally will not respond to telephone bookings if you are calling from a public phone. The alternative is to head for a taxi rank.

Rates vary from city to city. A good indication of the average is Rome, where the minimum charge is €2.40 (which covers the first 3km), then €0.62 per kilometre. There are supplements of around €2.60 from 10pm to 7am, and €1.10 from 7am to 10pm on Sundays and public holidays. No more than four or five people will be allowed in one taxi, depending on the size of the car. Each piece of luggage also incurs a supplement (around €1).

In Rome, there's a supplement of €7.80 on travel to and from the airports, because they are outside the city limits.

Watch out also for taxi drivers who take advantage of new arrivals and stretch out the length of the trip – and consequently the size of the fare.

ORGANISED TOURS

People wanting to travel around Italy on a fully organised package tour have a wide range of options and it is best to discuss these with your travel agent. A selection of companies that offer tours of Italy can be found in the Organised Tours section of the Getting There & Away chapter.

Once in Italy, it is often less expensive and usually more enjoyable to see the sights independently. If you are in a hurry or prefer guided tours, try a Sestante travel agency (there are offices in all major cities). They organise city tours for an average price of €20. They also offer an eight-day tour of

Sicily for around €650, and a three-day tour which takes in Rome, Assisi, Florence, Pisa, Padova and Venice for €350. The prices include twin-share accommodation, transport and some meals.

CTS, which has offices in all major cities, offers six- or seven-day tours of various destinations, including northern Italy (Rome, Venice, Florence, Siena and much more), southern Italy (Capri, Naples and Pompeii) or Sicily, for around €780. The price includes twin-share accommodation, half-board, transport by bus, and admission to museums and sites.

Tourist offices can generally assist with information on local agencies that offer tours. There are also organisations in Italy that can offer guided bike tours, for example Florence by Bike (see Cycling in the Florence section of the Tuscany chapter).

ROME

Rome & Lazio

Rome (Roma)

postcode 00100 • pop 3.8 million

'Rome, a lifetime is not enough,' goes the popular saying. And it's true. You'd need several lifetimes to come to grips fully with this beautiful, beguiling, chaotic, fascinating, frustrating and romantic city.

The Eternal City has always inspired wonder and awe in its visitors. Its ruined, but still quite imposing, monuments represent a point of reference for a city that, through the imperial, medieval, Renaissance and Baroque periods and beyond, has undergone many transformations and which has produced an archaeological archive of Western culture. And the street level sights are merely the tip of the iceberg. Tourists wandering around the city with their eyes raised to admire its many monuments should know that about 4m under their feet exists another city, with traces of other settlements deeper still.

The phenomenal concentration of history, legend and monuments coexists with an equally phenomenal concentration of people busily going about everyday life. It is easy to pick the tourists because they are the only ones to turn their heads as the bus passes the Colosseum. Modern-day Rome is the vibrant capital of Italy and the centre of national government.

Tourists usually spend their time in the historic centre, thereby avoiding the sprawling and architecturally anonymous suburbs. Realistically, a week is probably a reasonable amount of time to explore the city. Whatever time you devote to Rome, put on your walking shoes, get a good map and plan your time carefully, and the city will seem less overwhelming than it first appears. Be warned that the suffocatingly hot and humid weather in July and August can make sightseeing less than pleasant. The up-side is that most Romans head for the beaches or mountains at this time, leaving

Highlights

- Climb up the dome of St Peter's, from where the view of Rome is unrivalled, before descending to see the splendours of the basilica
- Spend hours, if not days, in the magnificent Vatican Museums and breathtaking Sistine Chapel
- Imagine the glory of ancient Rome while wandering through the Roman Forum, Palatine and the Colosseum
- Stroll along Via Appia Antica on Sunday, when it is closed to traffic, and visit the catacombs
- Enjoy a leisurely afternoon in Villa Borghese park and be wowed by Bernini's magnificent sculptures in the Borghese Museum.
- Throw a coin in the Trevi Fountain to ensure you'll return to Rome

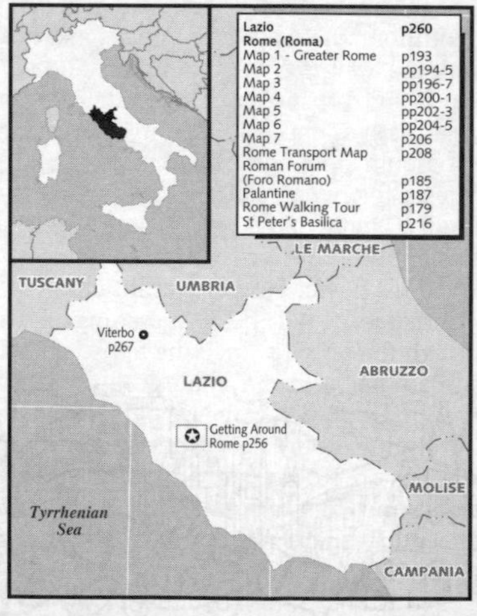

the city relatively empty and therefore quieter and more tolerable.

Whenever you visit, for whatever length of time, just be sure to grab yourself a slice of *dolce vita* and gobble it up. After all, when in Rome...

HISTORY

It is generally agreed that Rome has its origins in a group of Etruscan, Latin and Sabine settlements on the Palatine, Esquiline and Quirinale hills (three of the famous seven hills of Rome). The agreed date of the foundation of the city, when Romulus became its first king, is 21 April 753 BC, and archaeological discoveries have confirmed the existence of a settlement on the Palatine in that period. The city prospered and took shape under the Roman Republic; new temples, forums and buildings plus roads and aqueducts were constructed.

Under the first emperor, Augustus, Rome enjoyed a new era of political stability and artistic achievement. Augustus boasted that 'he found Rome in brick, and left it in marble'; monuments such as the Ara Pacis were built at this time. Much of the city was burnt to the ground in the Great Fire of AD 64 (see the boxed text 'Nero Rules OK?'). But by AD 100, the city of Rome had more than 1.5 million inhabitants, and trades and taxes from the empire's vast domains brought wealth and prosperity. The Roman Forum was an active centre of municipal life and the Colosseum had been hosting gladiatorial contests for two decades. Rome was Caput Mundi (Capital of the World) until 330 when Constantine – the first Christian emperor – moved his power base to Byzantium.

Christianity had been spreading slowly through the empire since the apostles Peter and Paul had joined a small group of Christians in Rome; they were persecuted but the religion flourished. The sites of many churches in Rome can be traced back to clandestine Christian meeting places. In the 5th century, the Goths and Vandals invaded the city but Gregory I's papacy (590–604) rescued Rome from its demise. Four of the city's great basilicas were built during his reign and missionaries were despatched throughout Europe to encourage pilgrimages to Rome. In 774, Rome's place as centre of the Christian world was cemented when Pope Leo III crowned Charlemagne as Holy Roman Emperor.

Rome's fortunes oscillated as the papal states battled with city states throughout the Italian peninsula. Clement V moved the papal court to Avignon in 1309 and, while livestock grazed in the Roman Forum, the city became a battleground between the powerful Colonna and Orsini families. Pope Gregory XI returned to Rome in 1377 but chose to reside in the fortified Vatican area.

The popes of the 15th and early 16th centuries saw that the best way to ensure political power was to rebuild the city. It brought incredible riches to their families – the Barberini, Farnese, Aldobrandini, Boncompagni and Pamphilj among others. The leading artists and architects of the Florentine Renaissance were summoned to Rome to

Nero Rules, OK?

Although Emperor Nero was in Anzio when the Great Fire of Rome broke out in AD 64, the rumour quickly spread that he was responsible. One tale was that he callously used the burning city as a backdrop for a recital on the fall of Troy; even worse was the rumour that he had actually started the fire. The pleasure with which he used a large amount of the ruined city for his new palace, the Domus Aurea, hardly helped calm popular feeling.

Unnerved, Nero looked for scapegoats – and he chose the early Christian community, for whom the rest of the population had little understanding and no sympathy. Some were thrown to the wild animals in the circus and others, in perverse retribution for arson, were burned alive as human torches.

Saints Peter and Paul are said to have been martyred during this period. Peter was crucified (upside down at his own request so as not to imitate the death of Jesus too closely) near Nero's racetrack in the Vatican and Paul, a Roman citizen, was given the privilege of decapitation.

work on the Sistine Chapel, St Peter's and other projects. Power struggles in Europe still affected the papacy and in 1527 Pope Clement VII was forced to take refuge in Castel Sant'Angelo in the Vatican when the troops of Charles V sacked Rome.

The broad-minded curiosity of the Renaissance gave way to the intolerance of the Counter Reformation. The Gesù was the prototype of Rome's great Counter-Reformation churches, built to attract and overawe huge congregations. In the 17th century, under the popes and grand families of Rome, the theatrical exuberance of the Baroque found masterful interpreters in Bernini and Borromini. With their churches, fountains, palazzos and other architectural wonders, these two architects changed the face of the city.

Mass tourism in Rome in the form of the Grand Tour really took off in the 18th century when Italy started to rediscover its ancient past, and it hasn't stopped since. The building boom following the unification of Italy and the declaration of Rome as its capital also profoundly influenced the look of the city, and has only been matched by the post-WWII spree to erect ugly apartment buildings in the growing suburbs.

The Jubilee Year in 2000, during which around 16 million Catholic pilgrims visited the city, gave Rome impetus to clean up her act. Billions were spent preparing the city for the year-long event: cleaning church and palazzo facades, improving roads and transport, and reclaiming public spaces from the car parks they'd become. At the dawn of the new millennium, Rome has never looked more beautiful.

ORIENTATION

Rome is a vast city but the *centro storico* (historic centre) is relatively small, defined by the twisting River Tiber to the west, the sprawling Villa Borghese park to the north, the Roman Forum and the Palatine to the south, and the central train station, Stazione Termini, to the east. The Vatican City and the characteristic area of Trastevere are on the west bank of the Tiber.

In ancient times, the city was enclosed by defensive walls, the Mura Serviane, only traces of which remain. From AD 271, Emperor Aurelian built a second defensive wall for the expanding city, most of which is still standing. Most major sights are located within the historic centre, making sightseeing relatively simple and walking the best way to get around town. Most of Rome's parks, some major churches, and the catacombs lie outside the walls. Rome's best-known geographical features are its seven hills: the Palatine, Capitoline, Aventine, Caelian, Esquiline, Viminal and Quirinal. Two other hills, the Gianicolo (Janiculum), which rises above Trastevere, and the Pincio, above Piazza del Popolo, were never actually part of the ancient city.

Most new arrivals in Rome will end up at Stazione Termini (Map 4), which is the terminal for all international and national trains. The majority of cheap hotels and pensiones are concentrated around Stazione Termini. The main city bus station is on Piazza dei Cinquecento, directly in front of the station. Many intercity buses depart from and arrive at the front of Stazione Tiburtina in the east of the city, accessible from Stazione Termini on the Metropolitana Linea B. (This should not be confused with Piazzale Tiburtino, at the top of Via Tiburtina near Stazione Termini.) Buses serving towns in the region of Lazio depart from various points throughout the city, usually corresponding to stops on Metro lines (see Getting There & Away later in this chapter for details).

The main airport is Leonardo da Vinci (also known as Fiumicino airport) at Fiumicino. From the city centre, it's about 35 minutes by the special airport-Termini train, or 45 minutes to one hour by car. A second airport, Ciampino, south of the city on the Via Appia Nuova, handles most no-frills/charter flights to Rome. Although it's closer to the city than Fiumicino, it is not as easily accessible (see Getting Around later in this chapter).

If you plan to arrive in Rome by car, invest in a good road map of the city beforehand, so as to have an idea of the various routes into the city centre. Rome is encircled by a ring road, called the Grande Raccordo

Anulare (GRA), which is connected to the A1 *autostrada* (motorway), the main north–south route in Italy. The main access routes from the GRA into the city centre include Via Salaria from the north, Via Aurelia from the north-west and Via Cristoforo Colombo from the south.

Maps

Lonely Planet's fold-out *Rome City Map* is perfect for sightseeing. It is plastic-coated and therefore virtually indestructible, and indicates all the major landmarks, museums and shops. There's also a street index.

Editrice Lozzi publishes a street map and bus guide simply entitled *Roma* (€3.10); it is available at any newsstand in Stazione Termini. It lists all streets, with map references, as well as bus/tram routes. Lozzi also publishes the very good *Archaeo Map*, a plan of the Roman Forum, Palatine and Colosseum.

There is a free city map, *Charta Roma*, which has a reasonable map of the city centre with major monuments and sights indicated. It also details the city's public transport routes, including buses, trams and the underground. Information is in English and Italian. Pick it up at tourist offices (see under Information for details) or at the ATAC (public transport company) booth in Piazza dei Cinquecento in front of Stazione Termini.

INFORMATION

Tourist Offices

The Comune di Roma (Rome's municipal government) has an information office at Stazione Termini (Map 4), at the end of Platform 4. It opens 8am to 9pm. Free city maps, transport guides and brochures on museums, festivals and events are available here. There's also an infoline (☎ 06 360 04 399), open 9am to 7pm daily, and 10 Comune di Roma tourist information kiosks dotted around the city, all of which are open 9am to 6pm daily: Piazza dei Cinquecento, outside Stazione Termini (Map 4); Via dei Fori Imperiali, near Largo Ricci (Map 4); Via Nazionale, next to the Palazzo delle Esposizioni (Map 4); Via del Corso, at Via Minghetti (Map 3); Via del Corso, at Largo Goldoni (Map 3); Castel Sant'Angelo, at Piazza Pia (Map 3); Trastevere, at Piazza Sonnino (Map 3); Santa Maria Maggiore, at Via dell'Olmata (Map 4); Piazza Navona, at Piazza delle Cinque Lune (Map 7); Piazza San Giovanni in Laterano, opposite the basilica (Map 6).

The APT office (Map 4; ☎ 06 488 99 253), Via Parigi 5, opens 8.15am to 7.15pm Monday to Friday and 7.15am to 1.45pm Saturday. It's operated by the regional authorities and has information (including brochures, maps and accommodation listings) on destinations outside the city centre. There is another office at Fiumicino airport in the arrivals hall.

Enjoy Rome (Map 4; ☎ 06 445 18 43), Via Marghera 8, is a privately run tourist office a few minutes' walk north-east of the train station. The office (which also provides a complete range of travel agency services including free hotel reservations in Rome and other parts of Italy) is brimming with information about the city, including the free *Rome City Guide* pamphlet, which is packed with practical information for the visitor. There's always someone who speaks English in the office and staff are friendly and helpful. Check out its Web site at W www.enjoyrome.com.

Money

Banks open 8.30am to 1.30pm and, usually, 2.45pm to 3.45pm Monday to Friday. You will find a bank and several currency exchange booths at Stazione Termini. There is also a Banca di Roma exchange booth at Fiumicino airport (to the right as you exit from the customs area). Numerous other exchange booths are scattered throughout the city, including American Express on Piazza di Spagna (Map 3) and Thomas Cook on Piazza Barberini and Piazza della Repubblica (both Map 3).

Most people use *bancomats* (ATMs) to get cash advances on their credit cards and you should have no problems in Rome. It is straightforward and most ATMs give you the option of conducting the transaction in English, French or German.

It is also possible to transfer money through Western Union (toll free ☎ 800 01 38 39). This service functions in Rome through a number of different outlets. See International Transfers under Money in the Facts for the Visitor chapter for details.

Post

See Post & Communications in the Facts for the Visitor chapter for more detailed information about postal services in Italy.

The main post office (Map 3) is at Piazza di San Silvestro 20, just off Via del Tritone, and opens 9am to 6pm Monday to Friday, and 9am to 2pm Saturday. *Fermo posta* (the Italian version of poste restante) is available here. The Vatican post office, on Piazza San Pietro (Map 3), opens 8.30am to 7pm Monday to Friday, and 8.30am to 6pm Saturday.

Telephone

There are Telecom offices at Stazione Termini, from where you can make international calls either direct or through an operator. International calls can also easily be made (with a phonecard) from any public telephone. Phonecards can be purchased at tobacconists *(tabacchi)* and bookstands or from dispensing machines at Telecom offices. See Telephone in the Facts for the Visitor chapter for information about the various telecommunications companies operating in Italy.

Fax

There are public fax services at major post offices. Otherwise, there are numerous private services, which usually also offer photocopying and film processing.

Email & Internet Access

Rome has dozens of Internet cafes and new ones are opening up continually. Costs vary but are usually in the region of €5.15 an hour, with hefty discounts or bonus hours if you take out a subscription, and with discounts for students.

The Netgate (Map 7; ☎ 06 689 34 45), Piazza Firenze 25. In the heart of the historic centre near the Pantheon, The Netgate offers Internet access at €5.15 per hour, including a netgate email account. It opens 10.30am to 9pm daily. There are two other locations: near St Peter's Basilica at Borgo Santo Spirito 17–18 (Map 3; ☎ 06 681 34 082) and in the underground Forum shopping area at Termini station (Map 4; ☎ 06 874 06 008).

Bibli Bookshop (Map 5; ☎ 06 588 40 97), Via dei Fienaroli 28. Conveniently located near Piazza Santa Maria in Trastevere, Bibli Bookshop opens 11am to midnight Tuesday to Saturday and 5.30pm to midnight Monday. Internet access costs €25.80 for 10 hours or €51.65 for 25 hours, including an email account.

Splashnet (Map 4; ☎ 06 493 82 073), Via Varese 33. You can kill two birds with one stone at this Internet-cafe-cum-laundrette near Termini. It costs €3.10 per hour but if you're doing your washing you get 10 minutes free.

Internet Café (Map 3; ☎ 06 445 49 53), Via dei Marrucini 12. In the San Lorenzo area, this imaginatively named cybercafe charges €4.15 per hour or €31 for 10 hours. It opens 9am to 2am Monday to Friday and 5pm to 2am Saturday and Sunday.

Internet Resources

A page is dedicated to Rome on Lonely Planet's Web site at Ⓦ www.lonelyplanet.com. Rome's municipal government has its own site at Ⓦ www.comune.roma.it, which provides information about everything from health and social services, education and rubbish collection to cultural listings. The site is geared towards residents of Rome, although the section on tourism and culture provides a good overview of current and forthcoming major events. The Vatican's official Web site is at Ⓦ www.vatican.va; among other things you can have a virtual tour of the Vatican Museums. The Web site of the fortnightly magazine *Wanted in Rome* (Ⓦ www.wantedinrome.com) has listings and reviews of current exhibitions and cultural events as well as informative articles on aspects of Rome and the surrounding region. It also has classified ads online, which are helpful if you want to find a room in a shared apartment.

Travel Agencies

CTS (Map 3; ☎ 06 687 26 72, Ⓦ www.cts.it), Corso Vittorio Emanuele II 297, Italy's official student travel service, offers discounted air, rail and bus tickets to students and travellers under 30 years old. CTS also issues ISICs (International Student Identity Cards). There are other branches at Via Genova 16 (Map 4; ☎ 06 467 92 71) and at Via degli Ausoni 5 (Map 4; ☎ 06 445 01 41), near La Sapienza university. Note that to take advantage of CTS fares if you are not a student, you have to have a CTS card, which costs around €26 and is valid for a year.

The well-run private tourist office Enjoy Rome (see Tourist Offices earlier) also operates as a travel agency, selling discount tickets for air, bus and rail travel and dealing with everything from car hire to Vatican tours.

Nouvelles Frontières (Map 2; ☎ 06 322 24 63 or 848 88 99 00), Via Angelo Brunetti 25, off Via del Corso near Piazza del Popolo, is another popular travel agency catering for the youth and budget travel markets.

Elsy Viaggi, Via di Torre Argentina 80 (Map 7; ☎ 06 688 01 372) has some of the cheapest fares available for flights to other European cities, but it doesn't accept credit cards.

Bookshops

The Corner Bookshop (Map 5; ☎ 06 583 69 42), Via del Moro 48, Trastevere, has an excellent range of English-language fiction, non-fiction and travel guides. The Anglo-American Bookshop (Map 3; ☎ 06 678 96 57), Via della Vite 102, off Piazza di Spagna, also has an excellent range of literature, travel guides and reference books, and sells the Thomas Cook European train timetable. The Lion Bookshop (Map 3; ☎ 06 326 54 007) is at Via dei Greci 33–36 and stocks a good range of books and magazines.

Feltrinelli International (Map 3; ☎ 06 487 01 71), Via Orlando 84, just off Piazza della Repubblica, stocks- an extensive range of books for adults and children in English, Spanish, French, German and Portuguese, plus lots of guidebooks to Rome, Italy and the rest of the world. There's another Feltrinelli (Map 6; ☎ 06 688 03 248), Largo di Torre Argentina 5/a, which sells mainly Italian-language books and has an excellent selection of travel guides and maps.

The Economy Book & Video Center (Map 3; ☎ 06 474 68 77), Via Torino 136, also has a good selection of books, including some second-hand paperbacks.

For travellers, Libreria del Viaggiatore (Map 6; ☎ 06 688 01 048), Via del Pellegrino 78, is a real find. This intimate bookshop is devoted to travelling and is crammed with travel guides and travel literature (some in English and French). It carries a huge range of maps for countries, regions and towns around the world, as well as walking maps.

Universities

Rome is home to three state universities, La Sapienza, Tor Vergata and Roma Tre. The latter two are in outlying areas of the city and student life tends to centre around the San Lorenzo area close to La Sapienza. None of these universities has facilities useful to the traveller – stick to Internet cafes and English bookshops. There are also about 20 pontifical universities run by different religious orders and a private Italian university, LUISS.

There are a number of private international universities in Rome. Tuition fees and course requirements vary from one institution to another. John Cabot University (Map 3; ☎ 06 681 91 221, **W** www.johncabot.edu) is in Trastevere, at Via della Lungara 233, and offers courses in business administration, international affairs, political science and art history. St John's University (Map 1; ☎ 06 63 69 37, **W** www.stjohns.edu), Via Santa Maria Mediatrice 24 (near the Vatican), offers MBA degrees and MA programs in government and politics. The American University of Rome (Map 5; ☎ 06 583 30 919, **W** www.aur.edu), Via P Roselli 4, offers degree programs in international business, international relations and liberal arts. The European School of Economics (Map 3; ☎ 06 678 05 03, **W** www.uniese.it), Largo del Nazareno 15, has degree programs in international business (including MBAs).

Libraries & Cultural Centres

Rome's main public library is the Biblioteca Nazionale Centrale Vittorio Emanuele II (Map 4; ☎ 06 49 89), Viale Castro Pretorio

105. It is the national repository of books published in Italy, and also has periodicals, newspapers, official acts, drawings, engravings and photographs. It opens 8.30am to 7pm Monday to Friday and 8.30am to 1.30pm Saturday. Readers need an identity document in order to get a day pass.

If it's fiction in English that you are after, try the Santa Susanna Lending Library (Map 4; ☎ 06 482 75 10), Via XX Settembre 15 (1st floor). You have to pay a modest annual fee but you can then borrow all the books you want. Opening hours are irregular so phone to check first.

There is a large number of foreign cultural academies and institutes in Rome, where artists, writers, performing artists and academics come from their home countries to spend several months, creating, researching and absorbing Italian history and culture. The academies organise exhibitions, poetry readings, drama and dance performances, lectures and conferences. Both *Time Out Roma* and *Wanted in Rome* magazines carry regular listings of the events, and they are also sometimes listed in *Roma C'è*.

Laundry

In most cases, laundrettes are open 8am to 10pm daily and a 6–8kg load costs around €3 to wash and €3 to dry. There are several self-service laundrettes in the streets northeast of Stazione Termini (Map 4); Bolle Blu has two outlets, at Via Palestro 59–61 and Via Malazzo 20b, both open 8am to 10pm; Oblo Service is in the same area at Via Vicenza 50. Near the Vatican is Onda Blu (Map 1; Via Vespasiano 50). Wash & Dry Lavarapido has two outlets, one at Via della Chiesa Nuova 15–16, off Corso Vittorio Emanuele II (Map 7), and another in Trastevere at Via della Pellicia (Map 4).

Dry-cleaning *(lavasecco)* costs range from around €3 for a shirt to €6 for a jacket.

Toilets

Public toilets are not exactly widespread in Rome (it is estimated that there are less than 40 of them in the whole city). Most people use the toilets in bars and cafes – although you might need to buy a coffee first. At Stazione Termini there are two sets of public toilets on the lower ground level which charge €0.50. The toilets on the Via Giolitti side also have showers (€7.80).

Left Luggage

There are left-luggage services at Stazione Termini on the lower ground level under platform 24. They open 7am to midnight daily. The rate is an exorbitant €3.10 for the first five hours then €0.50 per hour for each additional hour (so you'll pay €12.90 for 24 hours). There are also self-service luggage lockers at the start of platform 24. They cost €1.55, €2.05 and €2.60 (according to size) for each six-hour period.

At Fiumicino airport there is a left luggage facility, open 24 hours, in the international arrivals area on the ground floor. It costs €2.15 per item per day. For luggage over 160cm long, you pay an extra €2.15 per day. Make sure you have your passport handy as a photocopy will be made when you leave your luggage.

Medical Services

For emergency treatment, go straight to the casualty *(pronto soccorso)* section of a public hospital *(ospedale)*, several of which are listed below. You are likely to find doctors who speak English or a volunteer translator service.

Policlinico Umberto I (Map 4; ☎ 06 4 99 71) Via del Policlinico 155, near Stazione Termini

Ospedale San Giacomo (Map 2; ☎ 06 3 62 61) Via Canova 29, off Via del Corso near Piazza del Popolo

Ospedale Bambino Gesù (Map 3; ☎ 06 685 92 351) Piazza di Sant'Onofrio, on the Gianicolo; Rome's paediatric hospital

Ospedale San Gallicano (Map 4; ☎ 06 588 23 90) Via di San Gallicano, Trastevere; skin problems and venereal diseases

If you chip a tooth or require emergency dental treatment, head to Ospedale di Odontoiatria G Eastman (☎ 84 48 32 32), Viale Regine Elena 287b.

There is a 24-hour pharmacy at Piazza dei Cinquecento 51, just outside Stazione Termini (Map 4; ☎ 06 488 00 19). Within the station a pharmacy on the lower ground floor opens 7.30am to 10pm daily.

Emergency

The *questura* (police station; Map 4; ☎ 06 468 61) is at Via San Vitale 11. The Ufficio Stranieri (Foreigners' Bureau; Map 3; ☎ 06 468 63 216) is around the corner at Via Genova 2. It opens 24 hours and thefts can be reported here. This office can issue you with a *permesso di soggiorno* (see Visas & Documents in the Facts for the Visitor chapter). In case of emergency, call the following numbers.

Police (Polizia)	☎ 113
Police (Carabinieri)	☎ 112
Fire	☎ 115
Ambulance	☎ 118

Dangers & Annoyances

Thieves are very active around Stazione Termini, at major sights such as the Colosseum and in the city's more expensive shopping streets, such as those around Piazza di Spagna. Be careful in crowded shops and watch out for motorcycle-riding bag and camera snatchers. Pickpockets like to work on crowded buses (the No 64 from Stazione Termini to St Peter's is notorious). For more information on how to avoid being robbed, see Dangers & Annoyances in the Facts for the Visitor chapter.

Although Rome's traffic is nowhere near as chaotic as that in Naples, some drivers, particularly motorcyclists, do not stop at red lights. Don't expect them to stop at pedestrian crossings either. The accepted mode of crossing a road is to step into the traffic and walk at a steady pace. If in doubt, follow a Roman.

The heavy traffic also means heavy pollution, which can rise to such high levels in summer that elderly people, children and people with respiratory complaints are warned to stay indoors. Check with your hotel for daily information.

Gay & Lesbian Rome

Rome's main cultural and political organisation is the Circolo Mario Mieli di Cultura Omosessuale (☎ 06 541 39 85, ⓔ info@mariomieli.it, ⓦ www.mariomieli.it, Via Efeso 2/a), off Via Ostiense near the Basilica di San Paolo, which organises debates, cultural events and social functions. It also runs a free AIDS/HIV testing and care centre. Its Web site has information and listings of forthcoming events, both social and political, including Rome Pride, which takes place every year in June. Mario Mieli also publishes a free monthly magazine *AUT* (predominantly in Italian), available from gay bookshops and organisations.

The national organisation for lesbians is Co-ordinamento Lesbiche Italiano (CLI), also known as the Buon Pastore Centre (Map 3; ☎ 06 686 42 01, ⓔ cli_network@iol.it), on the corner of Via San Francesco di Sales and Via della Lungara in Trastevere.

Libreria Babele (Map 2; ☎ 06 687 66 28), Via dei Banchi Vecchi 116, parallel to Corso Vittorio Emanuele near the River Tiber, is an exclusively gay and lesbian bookshop and a good first stop for information about Rome's gay scene. Forthcoming gay and lesbian events are listed on the shop's noticeboard. The Libreria delle Donne: Al Tempo Ritrovato (Map 5; ☎ 06 581 77 24), Via dei Fienaroli 31d, in Trastevere, is a women's bookshop with a well-stocked lesbian section, including material in English, and a noticeboard full of information and events.

Rome has several gay bars and discos and there is even a gay beach. These can be tracked down through local gay organisations and publications such as *Pride* (€3.10), a national monthly magazine, and *AUT* (free), both available at gay and lesbian organisations and in bookshops. The magazine *Time Out Roma* (€1.05), which is published weekly (in Italian) and is available from bookstalls, has good coverage of gay and lesbian venues and events. The international gay guide *Spartacus* also has listings of gay venues in Rome.

The lesbian scene is less active than the gay scene and there is not yet any permanent lesbian nightclub, although there are various associations that organise events.

ROME FOR CHILDREN

Sightseeing in Rome will wear out adults, so imagine how the kids feel! If the weather isn't too hot, children of all ages should appreciate a wander through the Roman Forum and up to the Palatine. Also take them to visit the port city of Ostia Antica (see the Lazio section later in this chapter). Another interesting, if somewhat tiring, experience is the climb to the top of the dome of St Peter's Basilica for a spectacular view of the city. There is a Luna Park at EUR (see that section later in this chapter), as well as a couple of museums which older children might find interesting.

During the Christmas period, Piazza Navona is transformed into a festive marketplace, with stalls selling puppets, figures for nativity scenes and Christmas stockings. Most churches set up nativity scenes, many of them elaborate arrangements, which will fascinate kids and adults alike. The most elaborate of these is a Neapolitan nativity scene *(presepio)* from the 18th-century at the Basilica di SS Cosma e Damiano (see the Roman Forum map).

Fortunately the city has plenty of parks. Take a break for a picnic lunch and an afternoon in the Villa Borghese (Map 2). Near the Porta Pinciana there are bicycles for hire, as well as pony rides, train rides and a merry-go-round. In the Villa Celimontana (Map 3), on the western slopes of the Celio (entrance from Piazza della Navicella), is a lovely public park and a children's playground. See also the Gianicolo & Villa Doria Pamphilj section in this chapter.

WALKING TOUR

This is a short route through the heart of Rome, an area dense with important monuments, where Renaissance buildings and the impressive ruins of classical antiquity coexist. It explores the courtyards of patrician palazzos and the narrow streets of one of the city's more characteristic areas, ending at Piazza del Campidoglio.

Largo di Torre Argentina is well served by public transport, including buses from Piazza Venezia and Stazione Termini (Nos H, 40 & 64), from the Vatican (Nos 40, 64 & 62), from San Giovanni in Laterano and the Colosseum (Nos 87 & J5), and from Via del Corso and Via Vittorio Veneto (No 63). The No 8 tram from Trastevere-Casaletto terminates in Largo di Torre Argentina.

Start on the south-east corner of the large and noisy Largo di Torre Argentina, from where you can admire the Largo Argentino archaeological zone, and walk south. Cross Via delle Botteghe Oscure to Via Paganica, skirting the elegant **Palazzo Mattei di Paganica**, built in 1541. This is one of five palazzos in the area built by the patrician Mattei family, causing it to be renamed L'isola dei Mattei (Mattei Island) in the mid-16th century.

Continue south to the charming Piazza Mattei with its elegant **Fontana delle Tartarughe**. In the piazza at No 10 is the 16th-century **Palazzo Costaguti**, and at Nos 17–19 is **Palazzo di Giacomo Mattei**. The building on the right has a beautiful 15th-century courtyard with a staircase and an open gallery.

Detour to the left along Via dei Funari and enter the **Palazzo Mattei di Giove** at No 3. Built by Carlo Maderno in 1598, today it houses the Centro Italiano di Studi Americani (Italian Centre for American Studies); sections are open to the public. The palazzo, which is adorned with numerous pieces of ancient Roman sculpture, bas-reliefs and stuccoes, is a good example of the taste of the Renaissance noble classes for all things classical. The private courtyards contain ancient Roman bas-reliefs set into the walls, and busts and statues from what remains of the Mattei collection, once one of the most valuable collections of Roman antiquities. The monumental staircase decorated with classical stucco and ancient sculpture leads to a library; the balustrade is decorated with 16th-century busts of numerous emperors. In the **library** *(open 10am-6pm Mon-Thurs, 10am-2pm Fri)*, there is large hall with ceiling frescoes and an interesting Renaissance floor with the family coat of arms at its centre.

From Piazza Mattei, take narrow Via della Reginella, which is lined with artisan workshops, framers and bookshops. The street is a reminder of what the old Jewish ghetto area would have once looked like. A few paces to the right along Via del Portico d'Ottavia bring you to the curious **Casa di Lorenzo Manilio** at Via del Portico d'Ottavia 1. The building was constructed in 1468 or, according to the Latin inscription on its facade, 'AB URB CON MMC CXXII', 2221 years after the traditional founding of Rome in 753 BC. Another Latin inscription on the doors on the ground floor tells us the owner's name: LAUR MANLIUS. There is also an inscription in Greek and fragments of Roman sculpture set into the wall, including a relief depicting a lion killing a fallow-deer, a Greek stela with two dogs and a funereal relief with four busts.

From the Casa di Lorenzo Manilio, walk south-east down Via del Portico d'Ottavia (en route noting the medieval and Renaissance houses) until you reach the ruins of the **Portico d'Ottavia**. In AD 755 this portico was remodelled to incorporate the **Chiesa di Sant'Angelo in Pescheria** (Map 3). A medieval fish market established in the portico was operational until the end of the 19th century.

Beyond the portico is the 14th-century **Casa dei Valati** *(Via del Portico d'Ottavia 29)*, housing the X Circoscrizione of the Comune di Roma, which oversees the city's cultural patrimony. Unusually for this area, the building stands in isolation, since the surrounding buildings were demolished in 1927 during the restoration of the Teatro di Marcello at the rear.

A narrow passage to the left of the portico opens onto the deserted Via Sant'Angelo in Pescheria. Go around the back of the church and then bear right at a water fountain until you come to a dead end. From this isolated spot you get a view of the arches of the **Teatro di Marcello**. Only 12 of the original 41 arches, which are made of large travertine blocks, remain. You can also see the three marble columns with Corinthian capitals and beams of the Tempio di Apollo Sosiano, dedicated in 431 BC and rebuilt in 34 BC.

Retrace your steps out of the dead end street, and take Via della Tribuna Campitelli to the right. On the corner, at No 23, there is a house incorporating a medieval portico with granite columns and Ionian capitals. After a short walk you'll come to Piazza Campitelli. On the west and north-eastern

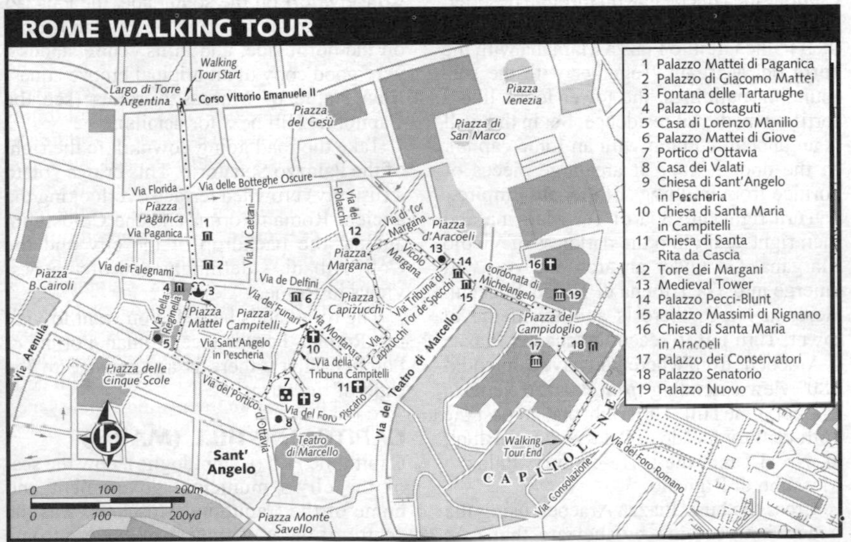

sides of the piazza stand a row of fine palazzos belonging to five noble families: the Gaetani-Lovatelli family at Via della Tribuna Campitelli 16, the Patrizi-Clementi family at Via Cavaletti 2 (16th century), the Cavaletti family at Piazza Campitelli 1 (16th century), the Albertoni family (early 17th century), and the Capizucchi family (late 16th century).

About half-way along the piazza is the **Chiesa di Santa Maria in Campitelli**, built by Carlo Rainaldi and a masterpiece of late Baroque style, with an elegant travertine facade. The church was built in 1662 in honour of the Virgin Mary, who was believed to have halted the plague of 1656. Inside, on the main altar, there is an image of the miraculous Madonna in silver leaf and enamel. In front of the church, on the piazza, there is a pretty fountain designed in 1589 by Giacomo della Porta.

Slightly further on is the **Chiesa di Santa Rita da Cascia** *(Via Montanara)*, now deconsecrated. It was built by Carlo Fontana in 1665 at the foot of the nearby Scalinata dell'Aracoeli and rebuilt on this spot in 1940 to allow for an urban revamp. Take Via Capizucchi to the left off the Piazza Campitelli. This takes you through deserted narrow streets into Piazza Capizucchi, and then to the left into Piazza Margana with the **Torre dei Margani**. Together with the surrounding buildings, the tower looks like a fortified medieval residence. Set in the wall is an ancient column with an Ionic capital. In the door next to it are large pieces of cornice from buildings of the late Empire.

Turn right into Via di Tor Margana and then right again into the darkness of Vicolo Margana. Go under an arch and you will emerge into Via Tribuna di Tor de' Specchi. Here, at No 3, there is another medieval tower. Turn left to reach the chaotic Piazza d'Aracoeli, from where you have a splendid 180° view extending from Palazzo Venezia to Capitoline Hill. Turn right and go past the 16th-century facade of Palazzo Pecci-Blunt, at No 3, and the 17th-century Palazzo Massimo di Rignano.

Cross the busy Piazza Aracoeli using the pedestrian crossing but beware that cars don't always stop! This brings you to the **Cordonata di Michelangelo**, the monumental flight of steps designed by Michelangelo, which lead up to the **Piazza del Campidoglio**. The Cordonata is guarded at the bottom by two Egyptian basalt lions (turned into fountains in 1588), and almost touches the older staircase on the left, which leads up to the **Chiesa di Santa Maria in Aracoeli**, also accessible from Piazza del Campidoglio. Climb the Cordonata, noting the shift in perspective as you approach the colossal Dioscuri, Castor and Pollux, at the top. These statues date from the late Empire and were found in a temple complex dedicated to them near Monte dei Cenci. On the same balustrade in a symmetrical arrangement are the **Trofei di Mario** (Trophies of Mario), representing barbarian weapons that date back to the reign of Domitian, and statues of Constantine and his son Constans, found at the Terme di Costantino. There are also two milestones taken from the Via Appia Antica, which bear inscriptions of Nerva and Vespasian.

Once at the top of the stairs, the piazza, designed by Michelangelo, will take your breath away. It is bordered by the **Palazzo dei Conservatori** on the south side, the **Palazzo Senatorio** at the rear, and the **Palazzo Nuovo** on the north side, and in its centre stands a very good copy of an original bronze equestrian statue of Marcus Aurelius (see the Capitoline Hill next for details).

Take the road going downhill to the right of the Palazzo Senatorio. This brings you to a (usually) crowded terrace overlooking the ancient Roman Forum and the Colosseum against the backdrop of the city and the Colli Albani – definitely one of the best views in Rome.

The route ends here. If you want to visit the **Roman Forum** (see Roman Forum & Palatine later), there is an entrance to the right of the terrace.

CAPITOLINE HILL (MAP 3)

Capitoline Hill (Campidoglio), now the seat of the city's municipal government and home of the Capitoline Museums, was the centre of the government of ancient Rome and where Nelson hoisted the British flag in 1799 before he prevented Napoleon from entering the city.

The elegant Piazza del Campidoglio was designed by Michelangelo in 1538 and is bordered by three palaces: the **Palazzo Nuovo** on the north side, the **Palazzo Senatorio** *(free, but bring identification; open 9am-4pm Sun)* at the rear, and the **Palazzo dei Conservatori** on the south side. Together, Palazzo Nuovo and Palazzo dei Conservatori house the Capitoline Museums (see the next section).

For the greatest visual impact, approach the piazza from the west from Piazza d' Ara Coeli and ascend the Cordonata, a stepped ramp designed by Michelangelo. It is guarded at the bottom by two ancient Egyptian granite lions and at the top by two mammoth statues of Castor and Pollux, which were found in the nearby Ghetto area in the 16th century.

The bronze equestrian statue of Marcus Aurelius in the centre of the piazza is a copy. The original, which dates from the 2nd century AD, was badly damaged by pollution, weather and pigeon poo and was removed in 1981. It has been restored and is now housed behind glass in the Palazzo Nuovo.

In front of the Palazzo Senatorio's double staircase is a fountain displaying a marble and porphyry statue of a sitting **Minerva**, which dates from the time of Domitian. The statue sits uncomfortably on an elevated plinth and is about the only thing in the piazza that seems out of proportion. On either side of it are colossal statues representing the Tiber (on the right) and the Nile (on the left). Martino Longhi il Vecchio's bell tower replaced an old medieval tower in 1578.

To the left of the palazzo is Via di San Pietro in Carcere and (down the stairs) the ancient Roman **Carcere Mamertino** (Mammertine Prison), where prisoners were put through a hole in the floor to starve to death. St Peter was believed to have been imprisoned here and to have created a miraculous stream of water to baptise his jailers. It is now a church, San Pietro in Carcere.

At the bottom of Capitoline Hill, next to the staircase leading up to the Chiesa di Santa Maria in Aracoeli, are the ruins of a Roman apartment block or *insula*. Only the upper storeys are visible; three lower levels are buried below current street level. Buildings of this type were used to house the urban poor, who lived in cramped and squalid conditions.

Chiesa di Santa Maria in Aracoeli *(☎ 06 679 81 55, Piazza Santa Maria in Aracoeli; free; open 7am-noon & 4pm-6.30pm daily)* is between Piazza del Campidoglio and the Vittoriano monument (Il Vittoriano), at the highest point of the hill. Built on the site where legend says the Tiburtine Sybil told Augustus of the coming birth of Christ, it features frescoes by Pinturicchio in the first chapel of the south aisle. The church is noted for a statue of the baby Jesus, said to have been carved from the wood of an olive tree from the garden of Gethsemane. The statue was stolen in 1994 and a replica is on display.

Capitoline Museums

The **Capitoline Museums** *(Musei Capitolini; ☎ 06 399 67 800, Palazzo Nuovo & Palazzo dei Conservatori, Piazza del Campidoglio; admission €6.20; open 10am-9pm Tues-Sun)* collection was started in 1471 with Pope Sixtus IV's donation of bronze sculptures to the city. The Palazzo Nuovo houses many important works, including statues of Roman emperors and other famous personages. Busts of philosophers, poets and politicians, among them Sophocles, Homer, Epicuros and Cicero, line the Sala dei Filosofi. The impressive *Galata Morente* (Dying Gaul) is a Roman copy of a 3rd-century-BC Greek original and the red marble *Satiro Ridente* (a satyr holding a bunch of grapes) is the Marble Faun of Nathaniel Hawthorne's novel.

A tunnel links Palazzo Nuovo to Palazzo dei Conservatori opposite and gives access to the **Tabularium** beneath Palazzo Senatorio, where important inscriptions of the republic and empire were kept.

The inner courtyard of the Palazzo dei Conservatori contains the head, a hand and a foot of a colossal acrolith of Constantine originally in the Basilica di Massenzio in the Roman Forum. The highlight of the Palazzo dei Conservatori is the famous **Lupa Capitolina**, an Etruscan bronze statue of a she-wolf from the 6th century BC. The suckling figures of Romulus and Remus were added by Antonio Pollaiolo around 1509. Also of interest in this wing is the 1st-century-BC **Spinario**, a delicate bronze statue of a boy removing a thorn from his foot.

If the sculpture hasn't worn you out, head up to the **Pinacoteca**. Artists from the Venetian school, including Giovanni Bellini, Paolo Veronese, Titian and Tintoretto, are represented and there are also works by Guido Reni, Federico Zucchari, Salvator Rosa, van Dyck and Rubens. You can view paintings by Domenichino, Poussin, the Carracci, Pietro da Cortona and others. Highlights include Caravaggio's sensual *San Giovanni Battista* in his fully-fledged realist style, and Guercino's immense *Santa Petronilla*, a mosaic of which can be found in St Peter's Basilica. Both are in the Sala di Santa Petronilla.

PIAZZA VENEZIA (MAP 3)

Piazza Venezia is overshadowed by the **Vittoriano** *(☎ 06 699 17 18; free; open 10am-1 hr before sunset Tues-Sun)*. This white, monolithic monument commemorates Vittorio Emanuele II and the united Italy, and is often dubbed the 'typewriter' or the 'wedding cake'. It's the biggest modern building in the centre of Rome, intentionally rivalling St Peter's in scale and visibility. It incorporates the Altare della Patria (Altar of the Fatherland), the tomb of the unknown soldier and some lovely Art Nouveau murals and sculpture.

On the western side of the piazza is the Renaissance-era **Palazzo di Venezia**, which was partially built with materials quarried from the Colosseum. Mussolini used it as his official residence and made some of his famous speeches from the balcony. Major art exhibitions are held here (the only way to get into the palace is by seeing one) and there is also a permanent museum, **Museo del Palazzo di Venezia** *(☎ 06 679 88 65, entrance at Via del Plebiscito 118; adult/reduced €4.15/2.05; open 9am-7pm Tues-Sat)*. This often-overlooked museum has a superb collection of Byzantine and early Renaissance paintings, plus decorative arts from the medieval period to the 18th century: jewellery, tapestries, silver, ivories, ceramics, hundreds of 15th- to 17th-century bronze figurines spread over several rooms, 18th- and 19th-century pastels, carved wooden wedding chests as well as a collection of arms and armour.

Basilica di San Marco *(Piazza di San Marco; free; open 7am-noon & 4pm-6.30pm daily)* was founded in the 4th century in honour of St Mark the Evangelist. After undergoing several major transformations over the centuries, the church has a Renaissance facade, a Romanesque bell tower and a largely Baroque interior. The main attraction is the 9th-century mosaic in the apse, which depicts Christ with saints and Pope Gregory IV.

Galleria Doria Pamphilj (Map 3)

The **Palazzo Doria Pamphili** is just north of Piazza Venezia on the corner of Via del Corso and Via del Plebiscito. Inside is the **Galleria Doria Pamphilj** *(☎ 06 679 73 23, entrance at Piazza del Collegio Romano 2; adult/reduced €7.30/5.70 plus €3.10 for private apartments; open 10am-5pm Fri-Wed)*. This collection was started by Pamphilj Pope Innocent X and is astounding even by Roman standards. Elaborate picture galleries – and the stunning private apartments – are crammed from floor to ceiling with paintings, although Velasquez's portrait of Innocent X dazzles in its own chamber.

Chiesa del Gesù (Map 6)

The **Chiesa del Gesù** *(☎ 06 69 70 01, Piazza del Gesù; free; open 6am-12.30pm & 4pm-7.15pm daily)* was the first Jesuit church in Rome.

Construction of the church began in 1568 and it was consecrated in 1584. With an interior designed by Vignola and a facade by Giacomo della Porta, the Gesù represents the epitome of Counter-Reformation architecture and highlights the

Jesuits' aim to attract worshippers with splendour and breathtaking artworks. In Baciccia's astounding vault fresco, two and three dimensions merge, and the foreshortened figures appear to tumble onto the coffered ceiling. Baciccia also painted the cupola frescoes and designed the stucco decoration. St Ignatius' opulent marble and bronze tomb with lapis-lazuli-encrusted columns is in the north transept.

The church was financed by Cardinal Alessandro Farnese, who was subsequently regarded as being the owner of the three most beautiful things in Rome – his family palazzo, his daughter and the church of the Gesù. This is one church definitely not to be missed.

To the right of the church are the **rooms** *(free; open 4pm-6pm Mon-Sat, 10am-noon Sun)* where St Ignatius, founder of the Jesuits, lived from 1544 until his death in 1556. The rooms have been restored and display paintings and memorabilia, including a masterful trompe l'oeil perspective by Andrea del Pozzo.

IMPERIAL FORUMS

The Imperial Forums (Fori Imperiali) – of Trajan, Augustus, Caesar, Nerva and Vespasian – were built between 42 BC and AD 112. In 1933 Mussolini built a grand thoroughfare as a symbolic link of the Fascist regime with the marvels of ancient Rome and a practical link between Piazza Venezia and the Colosseum. In the process, many 16th-century buildings were destroyed and the Imperial Forums were almost completely covered. Their hidden treasures are only now being fully excavated and evaluated. You cannot enter any of these forums but you can view the excavations from Via dei Fori Imperiali.

The most extensively excavated of the Imperial Forums is **Foro di Traiano** (Trajan's Forum; Map 3). Designed by Apollodorus of Damascus for Emperor Trajan and constructed at the beginning of the 2nd century AD, Trajan's Forum was a vast complex measuring 300m by 185m that extended from what is now Piazza Venezia. It comprised a basilica for the judiciary, two libraries (one Greek and one Latin) a temple, a triumphal arch in honour of the emperor, and the **Colonna di Traiano** (Trajan's Column; Map 3). Restored in the late 1980s, the column was erected to mark Trajan's victories over the Dacians. It was used to house the ashes of the emperor, which were contained in a golden urn placed on a marble slab at the base of the column. The urn and ashes disappeared during one of the Saracen sacks of Rome.

The column is decorated with a series of reliefs depicting the battles between the Roman and Dacian armies. These are regarded as among the finest examples of ancient Roman sculpture. A golden statue of Trajan once topped the column but it was lost during the Middle Ages and replaced with a statue of St Peter. Apart from the column, all that remains of the grand imperial forum are some of the pillars that once formed part of the Basilica Ulpia, the largest basilica built in the ancient city.

Mercati di Traiano *(Trajan's Markets; ☎ 06 679 00 48, entrance IV Novembre 94; admission €6.20; open 9am-7pm Tues-Sun)* were also designed by Apollodorus. This complex, built in the early 2nd century and comprising six floors of shops and offices, was the precursor to the modern shopping mall. Wine, oil, vegetables, flowers, imported silks and spices were sold here. The tall red brick tower above the market buildings, the Torre delle Milizie, was built in the 13th century.

Just to the south-east of Trajan's forum and markets are the **Foro d'Augusto** and the **Foro di Nerva**, although very little remains of either complex. The 30m-high wall behind the Foro d'Augusto was built to protect the area from the fires that frequently swept through the area.

There is a delightful walkway beneath the loggia of the 12th-century Casa dei Cavalieri di Rodi (the ancient seat of the Knights of St John of Jerusalem), which is between the forums of Trajan and Augustus and accessible from either Via dei Fori Imperiali or Piazza del Grillo.

In summer the three forums are illuminated at night.

ROMAN FORUM & PALATINE

Roman Forum

(Roman Forum Map)

The ancient Roman commercial, political and religious centre, the Roman Forum *(Foro Romano; ☎ 06 399 67 700, entrances at Largo Romolo e Remo off Via dei Fori Imperiali, Piazza di Santa Maria Nova near the Arco di Tito, from Capitoline Hill at Via di Monte Tarpeo; free; open 9am-7pm Mon-Sat May-Aug, closes earlier other months)* stands in a valley between the Capitoline and Palatine hills. The forum was constructed over the course of 900 years, with later emperors erecting buildings next to those from the Republican era. Its importance declined along with the Roman Empire after the 4th century, and the temples, monuments and buildings constructed by successive emperors, consuls and senators fell into ruin until eventually the site was used as pasture land. In the Middle Ages the area was known as the Campo Vaccino (literally 'cow field') – ironic, since the valley in which the forum stood had been used as pasture land in the earliest days of the city's development.

During medieval times the area was extensively plundered for its stone and precious marbles. Many temples and buildings were converted to other uses, while other monuments lay half revealed. The physical destruction of Rome's ancient city can be blamed not on invaders or natural disasters but on the Romans themselves. Over the centuries, in the name of what they called progress, the Romans dismantled the city brick by brick and marble block by marble block in order to build their new palaces, churches and monuments.

During the Renaissance, with the renewed appreciation of all things classical, the Forum provided inspiration for artists and architects. The area was systematically excavated in the 18th and 19th centuries, and excavations continue.

As you enter the Forum from Via dei Fori Imperiali, to your left is the **Tempio di Antonino e Faustina**, erected in AD 141 by the Senate and dedicated to the Empress Faustina and later, after his death, to the Emperor Antoninus Pius. It was transformed into the church of San Lorenzo in Miranda in the 8th century. To your right is **Basilica Aemilia**, built in 179 BC. The building was 100m long and its facade was a two-storey portico lined with shops. Destroyed and rebuilt several times, the basilica was almost completely demolished during the Renaissance, when it was plundered for its precious marbles.

The **Via Sacra**, which traverses the Forum from north-west to south-east, runs in front of the basilica. Continuing along Via Sacra in the direction of the Capitoline, you will reach the **Curia**, on the right just after the Basilica Aemilia. Once the meeting place of the Roman Senate, it was rebuilt successively by Julius Caesar, Augustus and Domitian and converted into a Christian church in the Middle Ages. The church was dismantled and the Curia restored in the 1930s. The bronze doors are copies – the Roman originals were moved by Borromini to San Giovanni in Laterano basilica (Map 6).

In front of the Curia is the famous **Lapis Niger**, a large piece of black marble that covered a sacred area that legend says was the tomb of Romulus. Down a short flight of stairs (rarely open to the public) under the Lapis Niger is the oldest known Latin inscription, dating from the 6th century BC.

The **Arco di Settimio Severo** (Arch of Septimus Severus) was erected in AD 203 in honour of the emperor and his sons, and is considered one of Italy's major triumphal arches. A circular base stone, the **umbilicus urbis**, beside the arch, marks the symbolic centre of ancient Rome. To the south is the **Rostrum**, used in ancient times by public speakers.

Just to the north-west of the arch is the **Tempio di Saturno** (Temple of Saturn), inaugurated in 497 BC and one of the most important ancient Roman temples. It was used as the state treasury and during Caesar's rule contained 13 tonnes of gold ingots, 114 tonnes of silver ingots and 30 million silver coins. Eight granite columns are all that remain. Behind the temple and backing onto the Capitoline are (from north to south) the ruins of the **Tempio della**

Concordia (Temple of Concord), the three remaining columns of the **Tempio di Vespasiano** (Temple of Vespasian) and the **Portico degli Dei Consenti**.

The remains of the **Basilica Giulia**, which was the seat of civil justice, are on **Piazza del Foro**. The piazza was the site of the original forum, which served as the main market and meeting place during the Republican era. The **Colonna di Foca** (Column of Phocus), which stands on the piazza and dates from AD 608, was the last monument erected in the Roman Forum. It honoured the Eastern Roman Emperor Phocus, who donated the Pantheon to the Church. At the south-eastern end of the piazza is the **Tempio di Giulio Cesare** (Temple of Julius Caesar), which was erected by Augustus in 29 BC on the site where Caesar's body was burned and Mark Antony read his famous speech. Just to the south-west is the **Tempio di Castore e Polluce** (Temple of Castor and Pollux), built in 489 BC to mark the defeat of the Etruscan Tarquins and in honour of the Dioscuri – or Heavenly Twins – who miraculously appeared to the Roman troops during an important battle. Three elegant Corinthian columns from the temple, which served at times as a banking hall and also housed the city's weights and measures office, survive today.

South of the temple is the **Chiesa di Santa Maria Antiqua**, the oldest Christian church in the Forum. Inside the church are some early Christian frescoes. This area has been closed to the public since 1992. Back towards the Via Sacra is the **Casa delle Vestali** (House of the Vestal Virgins), home of the virgins who tended the sacred flame in the adjoining Tempio di Vesta. The six priestesses were selected from patrician families when aged between six and 10 years. They had to serve in the temple for 30 years and were bound by a vow of chastity during this time. If the flame in the temple went out it was seen as a bad omen

ROMAN FORUM (FORO ROMANO)

and the priestess responsible would be flogged. If a priestess lost her virginity she was buried alive, since her blood could not be spilled. The offending man was flogged to death.

The next major monument is the vast **Basilica di Costantino**, which is also known as Basilica di Massenzio. Emperor Maxentius initiated work on the basilica and it was finished in AD 315 by Constantine. A colossal statue of Constantine was unearthed at the site in 1487. Pieces of this statue – a head, a hand and a foot – are on display in the courtyard of the Palazzo dei Conservatori in the Capitoline Museums (see that section earlier in this chapter).

The **Arco di Tito** (Arch of Titus), at the end of the Roman Forum nearest the Colosseum, was built in AD 81 in honour of the victories of the emperors Titus and Vespasian against Jerusalem. Titus is represented with Victory on one of the reliefs on the inside of the arch. On the other side, the spoils of Jerusalem are paraded in a triumphal procession. In the past, Roman Jews would avoid passing under this arch, the historical symbol of the beginning of the Diaspora.

Basilica di SS Cosma e Damiano & Chiesa di Santa Francesca Romana

To the north of the Forum is the 6th-century Basilica di SS Cosma e Damiano *(☎ 06 699 15 40, Largo Romolo e Remo; free; open 9am-1pm & 4pm-7pm daily)*. The church once incorporated a large hall which formed part of Vespasian's Forum. In the apse are 6th-century mosaics which are among the most beautiful in Rome. In a room off the 17th-century cloisters is a vast Neapolitan presepio, dating from the 18th century.

Past the Basilica di Costantino there is a small stairway leading to the Chiesa di Santa Francesca Romana *(☎ 06 679 55 28, Piazza di Santa Francesca Romana; free; open 9.30am-12.30pm & 3.30pm-7pm daily)*. Built in the 9th century over an earlier oratory, the church incorporates part of the **Tempio di Venere e Roma** (Temple of Venus and Roma). It has a lovely Romanesque bell tower. In the apse is a 12th-century mosaic of the Madonna and child with saints. The skeleton of Francesca Romana, patron saint of motorists, lies beneath the altar of this 9th-century church, holding a book and wearing black leather slippers. On 9 March each year, drivers park their vehicles as close as possible to be blessed. Note the lovely Romanesque bell tower and 12th-century mosaic.

Palatine (Palatine Map)

The Palatine *(Palatino; ☎ 06 399 67 700, entrances at Piazza di Santa Maria Nova & Via di San Gregorio 30; admission €6.20, including entry to Museo Palatino; open 9am-7pm May-Aug, closes earlier other months)* was the mythical founding place of Rome. Wealthy Romans built their homes here during the era of the Republic and it later became the realm of the emperors. Like those of the Roman Forum, the temples and palaces of the Palatine fell into ruin and in the Middle Ages a few churches and castles were built over the remains. During the Renaissance, members of wealthy families established their gardens on the hill, notably Cardinal Alessandro Farnese, who had elaborate gardens laid out over the ruins.

The largest part of the Palatine as it appears today is covered by ruins of a vast complex built for the emperor Domitian, which served as the main imperial palace for 300 years. This was an ambitious project to create an official imperial palace (the Domus Flavia), the emperor's private residence (the Domus Augustana) and a stadium *(stadio)*. The complex was designed by the architect, Rabirius, who levelled a crest of land and demolished many Republican era houses in the process. Some of these buried buildings have since been unearthed and excavations are continuing.

The **Domus Augustana** was built on two levels with rooms leading off a peristyle or garden courtyard on each floor. You can't get down to the lower level but from above you can see the basin of a fountain and beyond it rooms that were paved with coloured marble. The palazzo had an elaborate colonnaded facade to the south overlooking Circo

Iassimo (Map 5), from where you get the learest indication of the grand scale of the omplex. East of the Domus Augustana is ne **stadium**, probably used by the emperors or private games and events. Next to the tadium are the scant remains of baths built y Septimus Severus, the **Terme di Settimio evero**.

The big white building (a former convent) etween the Domus Augustana and the Domus Flavia houses the **Museo Palatino**. t was established in the 1860s and contains rtworks and artefacts found on the Palatine. Note that the museum closes one hour earier than the Palatine itself.

North of the Museo Palatino is the **Domus Flavia,** which was once connected to the Domus Augustana. The palace comprised hree large halls to the north, the central one of which was the emperor's throne room, nd a large banqueting hall, or *triclinium*, to he south, which was paved in coloured marbles that can still be seen. The triclinium looked out onto an oval fountain, the remains of which are clearly visible. The Domus Flavia was constructed over earlier edifices, one of which is the **Casa dei Grifi** (House of the Griffins), so called because of a stucco relief of two griffins in one of the rooms. It is the oldest building on the Palatine and dates from the late 2nd or 1st century BC. It was excavated in the 18th century.

Among the best-preserved buildings on the Palatine is the so-called **Casa di Livia,** west of the Domus Flavia. It is well below current ground level and is reached by steps down to a mosaic-covered courtyard. Livia was the wife of Augustus; she owned this house and also a larger villa at Prima Porta to the north of Rome (see Palazzo Massimo alle Terme later in this chapter). The walls were decorated with frescoes – some of which can still be seen, although they have been detached from the walls in order to preserve them. In front of the Casa di Livia is the **Casa d' Augusto**, the actual residence

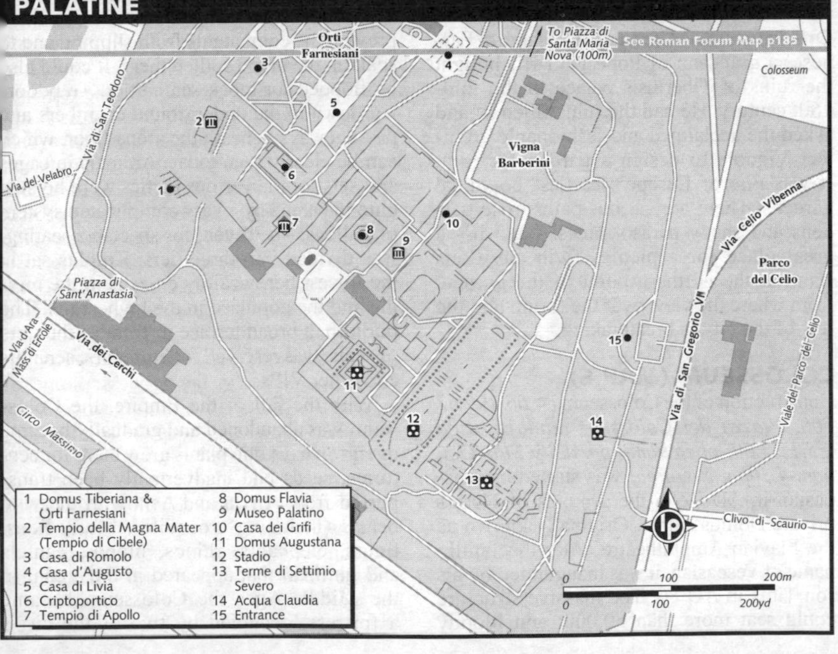

of Augustus – the two constructions were most likely part of the same complex. Both these houses are being restored and can sometimes be visited, depending on what the archaeologists and restorers are up to.

Next to the Casa d'Augusto is the so-called **Casa di Romolo** (House of Romulus), where it is thought Romulus and Remus were brought up after their discovery by the shepherd Faustulus. Excavations carried out in the 1940s revealed evidence of supports for wattle and daub huts dating from the 9th century BC.

North of the Casa di Livia is the **Criptoportico** (Cryptoporticus), a 128m-tunnel built by Nero to connect his Domus Aurea (see that section later in this chapter) with the imperial palaces on the Palatine. Unfortunately you can't walk into it. The tunnel had windows on one side, which provided light and ventilation. Elaborate stucco decorations once lined part of the Criptoportico.

The area west of this was once the **Domus Tiberiana**, Tiberius' palace, which Gaius Caligula extended further north towards the forum. Today it is the site of the **Orti Farnesiani**. Cardinal Alessandro Farnese, a grandson of Pope Paul III, bought the ruins of Tiberius's palace in the mid-16th century. He had the ruins filled in and asked the acclaimed and fashionable architect Vignola to design a garden for him. It was one of Europe's earliest botanical gardens. There are various paths, rose gardens and shady parasol pines – and it's a great place for a picnic. Twin pavilions stand at the northern point of the garden, from where the view over the forum and the rest of the city is breathtaking.

COLOSSEUM (MAP 6)

Construction of the Colosseum *(☎ 06 399 67 700, Piazza del Colosseo; adult/reduced €5.15/2.60; open 9am-7pm daily Mar-Oct, 9am-4.30pm Nov-Feb)* was started by Vespasian in AD 72 in the grounds of Nero's private Domus Aurea. Originally known as the Flavian Amphitheatre, after the family name of Vespasian, it was inaugurated by his son Titus in AD 80. The massive structure could seat more than 50,000, and bloody gladiator combat and wild beast shows were held there (see the boxed text 'Gladiators'). The splendid games held at the inauguration of the Colosseum lasted for 100 days and nights, during which some 5000 animals were slaughtered. Trajan once held games that lasted for 117 days, during which 9000 gladiators fought to the death.

The outer walls of the Colosseum have three levels of arches, which are articulated by columns topped by capitals of the Ionic (at the bottom), Doric and Corinthian (at the top) orders. The external walls were covered in travertine, and marble statues once filled the niches on the second and third storeys. The upper level, punctuated by windows and slender Corinthian pilasters, had supports for 240 masts that held up a canvas awning over the arena, shielding the spectators from sun and rain. The 80 entrance arches allowed the spectators to enter and be seated in a matter of minutes.

The interior of the Colosseum was divided into three parts: the arena, the cavea and the podium. The **arena** originally had a wooden floor, which was covered in sand to prevent the combatants from slipping and to soak up the blood spilled there. It could also be flooded for mock sea battles. Trapdoors led down to the underground chambers and passageways beneath the arena floor, which can be clearly seen today. Animals in cages and sets for the various battles were hoisted onto the arena by a very complicated system of pulleys. The **cavea**, for spectator seating, was divided into three tiers. Knights sat in the lowest tier, wealthy citizens in the middle and the populace in the highest tier. The **podium**, a broad terrace in front of the tiers of seats, was reserved for emperors, senators and other VIPs.

With the fall of the Empire, the Colosseum was abandoned and gradually became overgrown. Exotic plants grew there for centuries; seeds had inadvertently been transported from Africa and Asia with the wild beasts (including crocodiles, bears, lions, tigers, elephants, rhinos, hippos, camels and giraffes) that appeared in the arena. In the Middle Ages the Colosseum became a fortress, occupied by two of the city's

Gladiators

Gladiatorial combat originated as part of Etruscan funerary rites as a form of human sacrifice. By the 1st century BC, gladiatorial games had far outstripped this ritual context; Caesar exhibited 320 pairs of gladiators in 65 BC, while Augustus and Trajan each showed 5000 pairs of gladiators on different occasions.

Gladiators were prisoners of war, slaves sold to gladiatorial schools, or volunteers. Some were equipped with heavy swords and shields, and others were almost naked, armed only with a net and a trident. Pairings were made to match a heavily armed gladiator against a lightly armed one.

Bouts were not necessarily to the death. A defeated gladiator could appeal to the crowd and the presiding magistrate, who could signal that he had fought well and deserved to be spared. Thumbs down, however, meant death, which the defeated man was expected to face with quiet courage.

Although gambling was technically illegal in Rome, vast sums were wagered on gladiatorial combats. Successful gladiators were popular heroes and lived to enjoy a comfortable retirement, with some running their own training schools.

As with the other blood sports held in Rome, gladiatorial games were more than just particularly gruesome entertainment. This state-run public spectacle was a demonstration of empire through the display of exotic beasts and prisoners of war. It also allowed the people to share in the Roman State's judgement of the defeated by sticking their thumbs up or down according to whether the prisoners should live or die.

Inspired as much by award-winner Russell Crowe in the box office hit *Gladiator* as by the history of ancient Rome, the Gruppo Storico Romano, an association of history enthusiasts, has established Rome's first gladiator school on the Via Appia. Romans are enrolling in courses over several months to transform themselves into gladiators under the direction of a *magister*. Short intensive courses have also been introduced to cater for tourists keen to get a grip on gladiatorial combat in three days. For more information see w www.gsr.3000.it or contact e gruppo_storicoromano@libero.it.

ASA ANDERSSON

warrior families: the Frangipani and the Anibaldi. Its reputation as a symbol of Rome, the Eternal City, also dates to the Middle Ages, with Bede writing that 'while the Colosseum stands, Rome shall stand, but when the Colosseum falls, Rome shall fall – and when Rome falls, the world will end'.

Damaged several times by earthquakes, it was later used as a quarry for travertine and marble for other buildings. Pollution and the vibrations caused by traffic and the underground railway have also taken their toll.

Arch di Costantino

On the western side of the Colosseum is the triumphal arch built to honour Constantine following his victory over Maxentius at the battle of the Milvian Bridge (near the Zona Olimpica, north-west of the Villa Borghese) in AD 312.

DOMUS AUREA (MAP 4)

Nero didn't do things by halves. His massive Domus Aurea *(Golden House; ☎ 06 399 67 700, Viale della Domus Aurea; admission €6.20 by accompanied groups only; open 9am-8pm Wed-Mon)*, built after the fire of AD 64, extended over the Palatine, Oppian and Caelian hills. The gold paint that covered the facade gave the Domus Aurea its name. Its banqueting halls, nymphaeums, baths and terraces were decorated with frescoes and mosaics, a few of which remain. The extensive grounds had vineyards, game and an artificial lake.

After Nero's death in 68, his successors were quick to remove all trace of his excesses, razing much of the Domus Aurea to the ground. Vespasian drained the lake and built the Colosseum in its place, Domitian built his palace on the Palatine, and Trajan constructed a baths complex on top of the Colle Oppio ruins (this is this area that has been excavated).

Many of the original loggias and halls were walled when Trajan's baths were built and, significantly, the light which filtered through the Domus Aurea's pavilions was completely lost. It is quite confusing trying to identify the parts of the original complex and the later baths.

The baths and the underlying ruins were abandoned by the 6th century. During the Renaissance, artists (including Ghirlandaio, Perugino and Raphael) lowered themselves into the ruins in order to study the frescoes. Some left their own graffiti – not quite 'Pinturicchio woz 'ere', but not far off – and all copied motifs from the Domus Aurea frescoes in their work in the Vatican and other parts of Rome.

ESQUILINE HILL (MAP 4)

Esquiline Hill (Esquilino) is the largest and highest of Rome's seven hills. It stretches from the Colosseum to Stazione Termini, encompassing Via Cavour (a major traffic artery between Stazione Termini and Via dei Fori Imperiali), the charming residential area of Monti, the Basilica di Santa Maria Maggiore, the market square of Piazza Vittorio Emanuele II and the Colle Oppio (Oppian Hill). The Esquiline originally had four summits. In ancient times the lower slope of the western summit, the Suburra, was occupied by crowded slums, while the area between Via Cavour and the Colle Oppio was a fashionable residential district for wealthier citizens. Much of the hill was covered with vineyards and gardens, many of which remained until the late 19th century, when they were dug up to make way for grandiose apartment blocks.

From the Colle Oppio, follow Via delle Terme di Tito and turn left into Via Monte Oppio to reach the **Basilica di San Pietro in Vincoli** *(☎ 06 488 28 65, Piazza San Pietro in Vincoli 4a; free; open 7am-12.30pm & 3.30pm-7pm daily)*, built in the 5th century by the Empress Eudoxia, wife of Valentinian III, to house the chains of St Peter. Legend has it that when a second part of the chains was returned to Rome from Constantinople, the two pieces miraculously joined together. The church also offers another great treasure – Michelangelo's unfinished tomb of Pope Julius II, with his powerful *Moses* and unfinished statues of *Leah* and *Rachel* on either side. Michelangelo was frustrated for many years by his inability to find time to complete work on the tomb; in the end, Pope Julius was buried in St Peter's Basilica without the great tomb he had envisioned. A flight of steps through a low arch leads down from the church to Via Cavour.

Basilica di Santa Maria Maggiore (Map 4)

One of Rome's four patriarchal basilicas, Santa Maria Maggiore *(☎ 06 48 31 95, Piazza Santa Maria Maggiore; free; open 7am-6.30pm daily)* was built on Esquiline Hill in the 5th century, during the time of Pope Sixtus III. Its main facade was added in the 18th century, although the mosaics of an earlier 13th-century facade were preserved. The interior is Baroque and the bell tower Romanesque. The basilican form of the vast interior, a nave and two aisles, remains intact and the most notable feature is the cycle of mosaics dating from the 5th century that decorate the triumphal arch and nave. They depict biblical scenes; in particular, events in the lives of Abraham, Jacob and Isaac (to the left), and Moses and Joshua (to the right). Note also the Cosmatesque pavement, dating from the 12th century. The sumptuously decorated Cappella Sistina, last on the right, was built in the 16th century and contains the tombs of popes Sixtus V and Pius V. Opposite is the Cappella Borghese (or Cappella Paolina), also full of elaborate decoration, erected in the 17th century by Pope Paul V. The *Madonna and*

Child above the altar is believed to date from the 12th to the 13th century.

Basilica di San Clemente (Map 6)

At the base of Esquiline Hill, near the Colosseum and Caelian Hill, is the **Basilica di San Clemente** (*☎ 06 704 51 018, Via San Giovanni in Laterano; admission free to church, €2.10 to lower levels; open 9am-12.30pm & 3pm-6pm Mon-Sat, 10am-12.30pm & 3pm-6pm Sun*). Dedicated to one of the earliest popes, the church exemplifies how history in Rome exists on many levels. The 12th-century church at street level was built over a 4th-century church which was, in turn, built over a 1st-century Roman house, to which was added a late 2nd-century temple to the pagan god Mithras (imported to Rome by soldiers returning from the east). Furthermore, it is believed that foundations from the era of the Roman Republic lie beneath the house.

It is possible to visit the first three levels. In the medieval church, note the marble choir screen, originally in the older church below, and the early Renaissance frescoes – which depict the life of Santa Caterina of Alexandria – by Masolino in the Cappella di Santa Caterina. The stunning mosaics in the apse date from the 12th century. On the triumphal arch are Christ and the symbols of the four Evangelists. There is also a depiction of the Triumph of the Cross, with 12 doves symbolising the apostles. Figures around the cross include the Madonna and St John, as well as St John the Baptist and other saints, encircled by a vine growing from the foot of the cross.

The church below was mostly destroyed by Norman invaders in 1084 but some Romanesque frescoes remain. Descend farther and you reach the Roman house and temple of Mithras.

BASILICA DI SAN GIOVANNI IN LATERANO (MAP 6)

Founded by Constantine in the 4th century, the Basilica di San Giovanni in Laterano (*☎ 06 698 86 452, Piazza San Giovanni in Laterano 4; admission free to church & baptistry, €2.10 to cloister; church open 7am-7pm summer, 7am-6pm winter; baptistry open 9am-1pm & 4pm-6pm Mon-Thurs, 9am-1pm Fri & Sat; cloister open 9am-6pm daily in summer, 9am-5pm daily in winter)* was the first Christian basilica constructed in Rome. It is Rome's cathedral and the pope's seat as Bishop of Rome. It has been destroyed by fire twice and rebuilt several times. In 1425 Martin V had the floor inlaid with stone and mosaic looted from other derelict Roman churches.

Borromini transformed the interior in the mid-17th century. The **bronze doors** of the eastern facade were moved here from the Curia in the Roman Forum. Alessandro Galilei's **portico** (porch; built 1736) is surmounted by colossal statues representing Christ with Sts John the Baptist and John the Evangelist and the 12 apostles. The Gothic **baldacchino** over the papal altar contains relics that include the heads of Saints Peter and Paul. The apse was rebuilt in the 19th century; its mosaics are copies of the originals.

Fortunately the beautiful 13th-century **cloister** escaped the fires. Built by the Vassalletto family in Cosmati style, the cloister has columns and an architrave that were once completely covered with inlaid marble mosaics. The outer walls are lined with sarcophagi and sculpture, including an inscription of a Papal Bull of Sixtus IV.

The domed **baptistry**, near Domenico Fontana's northern facade, was also built by Constantine, but has been remodelled several times. Sixtus III gave it its present octagonal shape, which became the model for many baptistries throughout the Christian world. The **Cappella di Santa Rufina** is decorated with a stunning 5th-century mosaic of vines and foliage against a deep blue background, while the vault of **Cappella di San Giovanni Evangelista** has a mosaic of the Lamb of God surrounded by birds and flowers. **Cappella di San Venanzio** was added by Pope John IV in the 7th century. It has extremely well-preserved mosaics; in the apse are Christ with angels and the Madonna and saints, and on the triumphal arch are Christian martyrs. Right at the top are views of Jerusalem and Bethlehem.

The **Palazzo Laterano**, which adjoins the basilica, was the papal residence until the popes moved to Avignon early in the 14th century. It was largely destroyed by fire in 1308 and most of what remained was demolished in the 16th century. The present building houses offices of the diocese of Rome.

The building on the eastern side of Piazza di San Giovanni in Laterano contains the **Scala Santa** *(Holy Staircase; free; open 6.15am-noon & 3.30pm-6.45pm daily Apr-Sept, 6.15am-noon & 3pm-6.15pm daily Oct-Mar)* and the **Sancta Sanctorum** *(admission €2.60; open 10.30am-11.30am & 3pm-4pm Tues, Thurs & Sat)*. The Scala Santa is said to come from Pontius Pilate's palace in Jerusalem and people are allowed to climb it only on their knees. The Sancta Sanctorum was the popes' private chapel and contains 13th-century frescoes and mosaics.

East of Piazza di San Giovanni is the **Chiesa di Santa Croce in Gerusalemme** *(☎ 06 701 47 69, Piazza di Santa Croce in Gerusalemme 12; free; open 6.30am-12.30pm & 3.30pm-7.30pm daily)*. This pilgrimage church was founded in AD 320 by St Helena, Constantine's mother, who brought Christian relics, including a piece of the cross on which Christ was crucified, to Rome from Jerusalem. The bell tower was added in 1144, the facade and oval vestibule in 1744.

CAELIAN HILL (MAP 6)

Caelian Hill (Celio) is accessible either from Via di San Gregorio VII to the west or from Via della Navicella to the east. The **Villa Celimontana** *(Via della Navicella; free; open dawn-dusk)* is a large public park on top of the hill, perfect for a quiet picnic. There is also a children's playground. The 4th-century **Chiesa di SS Giovanni e Paolo** *(Piazza SS Giovanni e Paolo)* is dedicated to Sts John and Paul, two Romans who had served in the court of Emperor Constantine II and were beheaded by his anti-Christian successor, Emperor Julian, for refusing to serve as officers in his court. The church was built over their houses. The 8th-century **Chiesa di San Gregorio Magno** was built in honour of Pope Gregory the Great on the site where he dispatched St Augustine to convert the people of Britain to Christianity. The church was remodelled in the Baroque style in the 17th century.

The fascinating circular **Chiesa di Santo Stefano Rotondo** *(☎ 06 704 93 717, Via di S Stefano Rotondo 7; free; open 1.50pm-4.20pm Mon, 9am-1pm & 1.50pm-4.20pm Tues-Sat, 9am-noon on 2nd Sun of each month in summer)*, built between 468 and 483, is one of Rome's earliest churches. Inside are two rings of antique granite and marble columns. The wall is lined with frescoes depicting the various ways in which saints were martyred. The vivid scenes are quite grotesque and you might not make it through all 34 of them.

TERME DI CARACALLA (MAP 6)

These baths *(☎ 06 575 86 26, Via delle Terme di Caracalla 52; admission €4.20, open 9am-6pm Tues-Sat Apr-Oct, 9am-4pm Tues-Sat Nov-Mar, 9am-1pm Sun & Mon year-round)* are south of the Celio, accessible by bus Nos 160 and 628 from Piazza Venezia. Covering 10 hectares, Caracalla's Baths could hold 1600 people and had shops, gardens, libraries and entertainment. Begun by Antonius Caracalla and inaugurated in AD 217, the baths were used until the 6th century AD. Excavations of the baths in the 16th and 17th centuries unearthed important sculptures, which found their way into the Farnese family collection.

AVENTINE HILL (MAP 5)

South of the Circo Massimo is Aventine Hill (Aventino), best reached from Via del Circo Massimo by Via di Valle Murcia or from Clivo de Publici by Via di Santa Sabina. It is also easily accessible by bus No 27 from Stazione Termini and the Colosseum, or on the Metro Linea B, disembarking at Circo Massimo (Map 6). Nearby are the **Roseto Comunale**, a beautiful public rose garden best seen in spring and summer, and the pretty, walled **Parco Savello**, planted with orange trees. There is a stunning view of Rome from the park.

[continued on page 209]

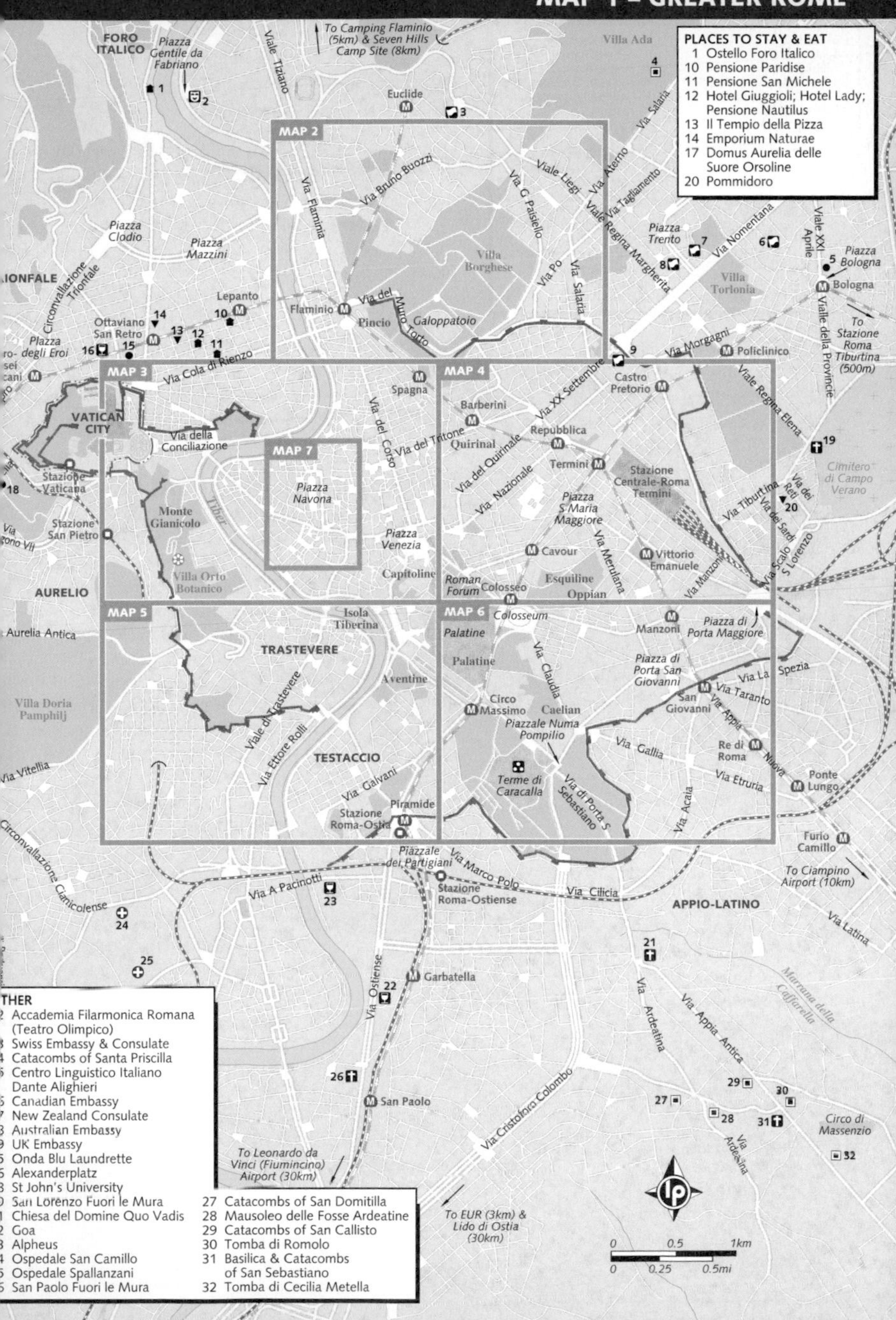
PLACES TO STAY & EAT
1 Ostello Foro Italico
10 Pensione Paridise
11 Pensione San Michele
12 Hotel Giuggioli; Hotel Lady; Pensione Nautilus
13 Il Tempio della Pizza
14 Emporium Naturae
17 Domus Aurelia delle Suore Orsoline
20 Pommidoro
THER
Accademia Filarmonica Romana (Teatro Olimpico)
Swiss Embassy & Consulate
Catacombs of Santa Priscilla
Centro Linguistico Italiano Dante Alighieri
Canadian Embassy
New Zealand Consulate
Australian Embassy
UK Embassy
Onda Blu Laundrette
Alexanderplatz
St John's University
San Lorenzo Fuori le Mura
Chiesa del Domine Quo Vadis
Goa
Alpheus
Ospedale San Camillo
Ospedale Spallanzani
San Paolo Fuori le Mura
27 Catacombs of San Domitilla
28 Mausoleo delle Fosse Ardeatine
29 Catacombs of San Callisto
30 Tomba di Romolo
31 Basilica & Catacombs of San Sebastiano
32 Tomba di Cecilia Metella
FORO ITALICO
Piazza Gentile da Fabriano
Viale Tiziano
To Camping Flaminio (5km) & Seven Hills Camp Site (8km)
Villa Ada
Euclide
MAP 2
Via Flaminia
Via Bruno Buozzi
Viale Liegi
Via G Paisiello
Via Aterno
Via Salaria
Via Tagliamento
Viale Regina Margherita
Villa Borghese
Via Po
Piazza Trento
Via Nomentana
Viale XXI Aprile
Piazza Bologna
Bologna
Villa Torlonia
Viale delle Provincie
To Stazione Roma Tiburtina (500m)
Piazza Clodio
Piazza Mazzini
Circonvallazione Trionfale
Lepanto
Ottaviano San Retro
Piazza degli Eroi
Flaminio
Via del Muro Torto
Pincio
Galoppatoio
Via Morgagni
Policlinico
MAP 3
Via Cola di Rienzo
VATICAN CITY
Via della Conciliazione
Stazione Vaticana
Stazione San Pietro
Monte Gianicolo
Villa Orto Botanico
Tiber
AURELIO
MAP 7
Piazza Navona
Spagna
Via del Corso
Piazza Venezia
Capitoline
MAP 4
Barberini
Via del Tritone
Quirinal
Via del Quirinale
Via Nazionale
Via XX Settembre
Repubblica
Termini
Castro Pretorio
Stazione Centrale-Roma Termini
Piazza S.Maria Maggiore
Via Merulana
Cavour
Vittorio Emanuele
Esquiline
Oppian
Roman Forum
Colosseo
Viale Regina Elena
Cimitero di Campo Verano
Via Tiburtina
Via dei Reti
Via dei Sardi
Via Scalo S Lorenzo
Via Manzoni
MAP 5
Aurelia Antica
Isola Tiberina
TRASTEVERE
Aventine
Villa Doria Pamphilj
Viale di Trastevere
Via Ettore Rolli
TESTACCIO
Via Galvani
Piramide
Stazione Roma-Ostia
Via Vitellia
MAP 6
Colosseum
Palatine
Via Claudia
Circo Massimo
Caelian
Piazzale Numa Pompilio
Terme di Caracalla
Via di Porta S Sebastiano
Manzoni
Piazza di Porta Maggiore
Piazza di Porta San Giovanni
San Giovanni
Via La Spezia
Via Taranto
Via Appia Nuova
Via Gallia
Re di Roma
Via Etruria
Ponte Lungo
Via Acaia
Furio Camillo
To Ciampino Airport (10km)
Circonvallazione Gianicolense
Piazzale dei Partigiani
Via Marco Polo
Via A Pacinotti
Stazione Roma-Ostiense
Via Cilicia
APPIO-LATINO
Via Latina
Garbatella
Via Ostiense
Via Ardeatina
Via Appia Antica
Marrana della Caffarella
San Paolo
Via Cristoforo Colombo
Circo di Massenzio
To Leonardo da Vinci (Fiumincino) Airport (30km)
To EUR (3km) & Lido di Ostia (30km)
0 0.5 1km
0 0.25 0.5mi

MAP 2

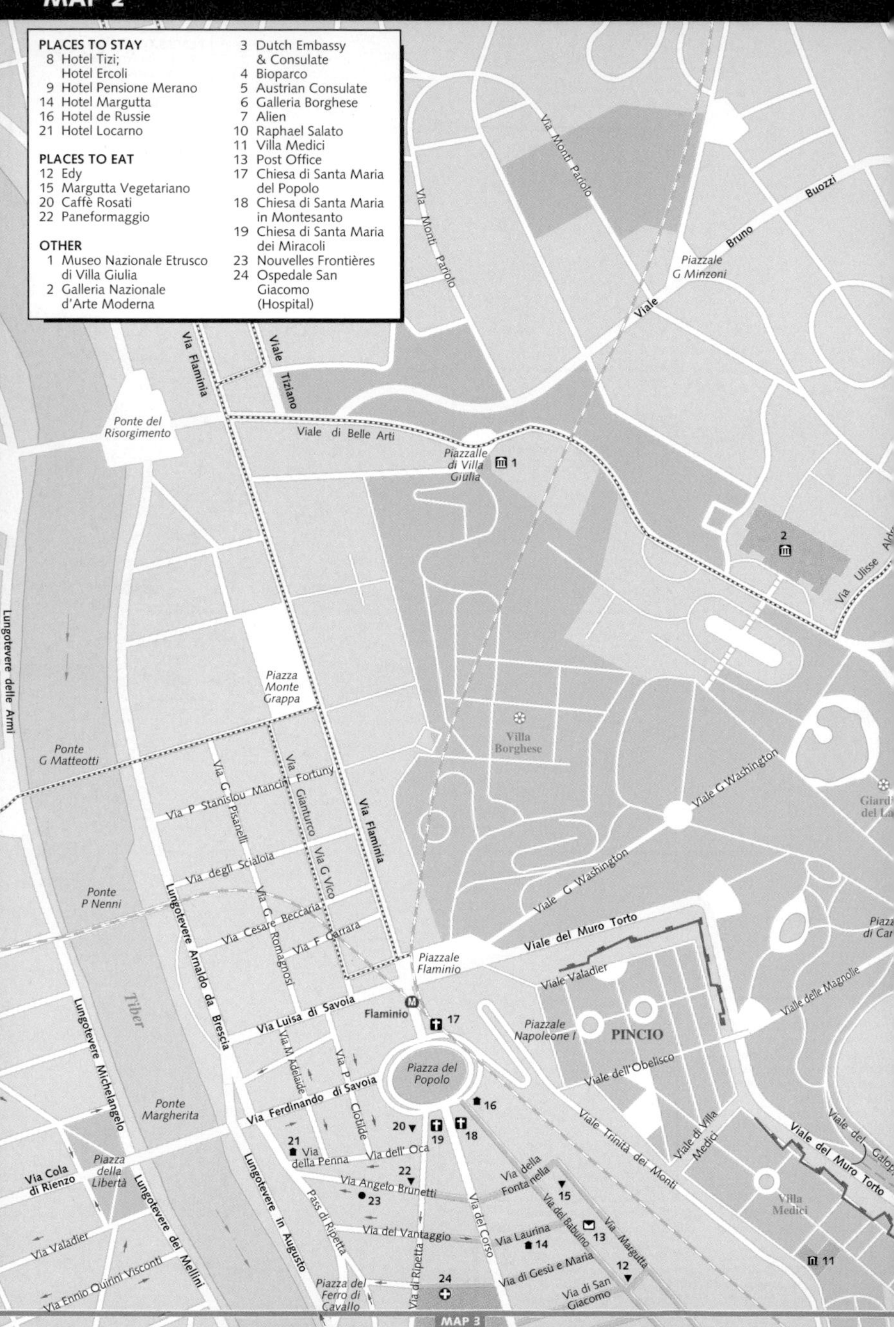

PLACES TO STAY
8 Hotel Tizi; Hotel Ercoli
9 Hotel Pensione Merano
14 Hotel Margutta
16 Hotel de Russie
21 Hotel Locarno
PLACES TO EAT
12 Edy
15 Margutta Vegetariano
20 Caffè Rosati
22 Paneformaggio
OTHER
1 Museo Nazionale Etrusco di Villa Giulia
2 Galleria Nazionale d'Arte Moderna
3 Dutch Embassy & Consulate
4 Bioparco
5 Austrian Consulate
6 Galleria Borghese
7 Alien
10 Raphael Salato
11 Villa Medici
13 Post Office
17 Chiesa di Santa Maria del Popolo
18 Chiesa di Santa Maria in Montesanto
19 Chiesa di Santa Maria dei Miracoli
23 Nouvelles Frontières
24 Ospedale San Giacomo (Hospital)
Via Monti Pariolo
Viale Bruno Buozzi
Piazzale G Minzoni
Via Flaminia
Viale Tiziano
Ponte del Risorgimento
Viale di Belle Arti
Piazzalle di Villa Giulia
Via Ulisse Aldo
Lungotevere delle Armi
Piazza Monte Grappa
Villa Borghese
Ponte G Matteotti
Via G Pisanelli
Via P Stanislou Mancini
Via Fortuny
Via Gianturco
Viale G Washington
Via degli Scialoia
Via G Vico
Ponte P Nenni
Lungotevere Arnaldo da Brescia
Via G Romagnosi
Via Cesare Beccaria
Via F Carrara
Viale del Muro Torto
Piazzale Flaminio
Viale Valadier
Viale delle Magnolie
Tiber
Via Luisa di Savoia
Flaminio
Piazzale Napoleone I
PINCIO
Lungotevere Michelangelo
Via M Adelaide
Via P Clotilde
Piazza del Popolo
Viale dell'Obelisco
Ponte Margherita
Via Ferdinando di Savoia
Viale Trinità dei Monti
Viale di Villa Medici
Viale del Galoppatoio
Piazza della Libertà
Via della Penna
Via dell' Oca
Via Cola di Rienzo
Lungotevere dei Mellini
Lungotevere in Augusto
Pass di Ripetta
Via Angelo Brunetti
Via della Fontanella
Via del Babuino
Via Margutta
Villa Medici
Via del Corso
Via Valadier
Via del Vantaggio
Via Laurina
Via Ennio Quirini Visconti
Via di Gesù e Maria
Piazza del Ferro di Cavallo
Via di Ripetta
Via di San Giacomo
MAP 3

Viale dei Parioli
Viale Romania
Via Panama
Piazza Cuba
Villa Grazioli
Piazza Ungheria
Via A Stoppani
Via F Siacci
Viale Bruno Buozzi
Via Liegi
Viale G Rossini
Via Cavalieri
Via G D'Arezzo
0 150 300m
0 150 300yd
3
Mercati
Via U Aldrovandi
Viale G Rossini
Piazza G Verdi
Via Aterno
V G Carissimi
Via G Paisiello
4
Via N Porpora
Via S Mercadante
Via Metauro
Largo N Spinelli
5
Via Pergolesi
Via Po
Viale del Giardino Zoologico
Piazza Giardino Zoologico
Via Basento
Piazzale di Daini
Viale dell Uccelliera
Viale dei Due Mascheroni
Villa Borghese
Via G Vasanzio
Villa Torlonia (Gi/Æ Albani)
Largo Aqua Felix
Piazza San Borghese
6
Piazza di Sienna
Viale dei Cavalli Marini
Piazza le dei Cavalli Marini
Via Po
Via Salaria
Via di Villa Albani
Via Pinciana
Via Savoia
Via Tevere
Via Isonzo
7
Via Velletri
Via Nizza
Via Wolfango Goethe
Viale del Museo Borghese
Piazzale Sienkiewicz
V G Puccini
Via Teresa
Via Anieni
Viale San Paolo del Brasile
Villa Borghese
Piazza Fiume
Via Bergamo
Via Campania
Via Ripa
Corso d'Italia
Via Pinciana
Corso d'Italia
Via Lucania
Porta Pinciana
Via Romagna
Via Puglie
Via Valenziani
Piazzale Brasile
Via Piemonte
Via Calabria
Viale del Galoppatoio
Largo Federico Fellini
Via Campania
Via Sardegna
Via Abruzzi
Via Toscana
Via Belisario
Via Collina
Via Piave
Porta Pia
Viale del Muro Torto
Via di Porta Pinciana
Via Lazio
Via Vittorio Veneto
9
Via Marche
8
Via Aurora
Via Emilia
10
Via Sicilia
Via Boncompagni
Piazza Sallustio
Via Cadorna
MAP 4

To Entrance to Sistine Chapel, Vatican Museums & Post Office (100m)
Via Germanico
Via Ottaviano
Viale B di Michelangelo
Via Vespasiano
Via Catone
Via dei Gracchi
Piazza dell'Unità
Via Cola di Rienzo
Via Catullo
Via Plinio
Via Orazio
Via Boezio
Via Tacito
Via Giuseppe G Belli
Piazza del Risorgimento
Via Varrone
Via Tibullo
Via Terenzio
Via Cassiodoro
Via Crescenzio
Via Stefano Porcari
Via P Leto
Via Properzio
Via Cancellieri
Via S Pallavicini
Via P Della Valle
Borgo Angelico
Vatican Museums
Via della Posta
Via della Tipografia
Via del Pellegrino
Via di Porta Angelica
Via del Mascherino
Via del Falco
Piazza Americo Capponi
Via Plauto
Via Ombrellari
Via Vitelleschi
Via Alberico II
Castello
Piazza Adriana
Borgo Vittorio
Via del Belvedere
Piazza della Città Leonina
Borgo Pio
Vic Farinone
Vic delle Palline
Vic del Orfeo
Borgo
Largo di Porta Castello
Via P
Largo San Martino
Via dei Corridori
Borgo Sant'Angelo
Sistine Chapel
Largo Colonnato
Via Rusticucci
Via Erba
Piazza Pia
Castel Sant' Angelo
Lungotevere Vaticano
St Peter's Basilica
Piazza San Pietro
Piazza Pio XII
Via della Conciliazione
Piazza Giovanni XXIII
Via Pfeiffer
Via San Pio X
Lgt
Ponte Sant'Angelo
Largo degli Alicorni
Piazza dei P Romani
Borgo Santo Spirito
Largo I Gregore
Ponte Vittorio Emanuele II
Piazza Ponte Sant'Angelo
Lungotevere
Via del Sant'Uffizio
Via Paolo VI
Lgt della Altoviti
Via di Porta Santo Spirito
Lungotevere in Sassia
Via del Banco Santo Spirito
Piazza di Salvatore in
Piazza di Sant'Uffizio
Piazza P Paoli
Via Paola
Piazza dei Coronari
Via di Panico
Largo Porta Cavalleggeri
Galleria Principe Amedeo Savoia Aosta
Lgt della Fiorentini
Corso Vittorio Emanuele II
Ponte
Piazza dell'Oro
Largo O Tassoni
Piazza della Rovere
Ponte Principe Amedeo
Via A De Gasperi
Via del Gianicolo
Vic Sant'Onofrio
Piazza dell' Orologio
Vic delle Palle
Tiber
Via di Sant'Onofrio
Via Giulia
Vic Sugarelli
Piazza Santa Maria alle Fornaci
Via Nicolò III
Viale delle Mura Aurelie
Salita di Sant'Onofrio
Vic del Cefalo
Via della Stazione di San Pietro
Lungotevere Gianicolense
Lungotevere D Sangallo
Via dei Bresciani
Via dei Banchi Vecchi
Piazza di Sant'Onofrio
Via del Lago Terrione
Via D Silveri
Via delle Fornaci
Via Bravaria
Vic delle Prigioni
Piazza Ricci
Largo L Perosi
Via degli Orti d'Alibert
San Pietro
Regola
Via delle Mantellate
Ponte G Mazzini
Lungotevere dei Tebaldi
Via Innocenzo III
Via G Missori
Via Clemente Alessandrino
Via di San Francesco di Sales
Vic della Penitenza
Via della Penitenza
Via della Lungara
Lungotevere della Farnesina
Monte Gianicolo
Via dei Riari
Villa Orto Botanico
Piazzale Anita Garibaldi
Via Nuove delle Fornaci
Piazza San Giovanni della Malva
Via Corsini
Parco Gianicolence
Via S Dorotea
Via della Scala
Villa Abamelek
Piazzale Giuseppe Garibaldi

0 100 200m
0 100 200yd

1, 2, 3, 4, 5, 6, 105, 106, 107, 108, 109, 110, 111, 112, 113, 114, 115, 116, 117, 118, 119, 120, 121, 122, 123, 124, 125, 126, 127, 128, 129, 130, 131, 132

MAP 5

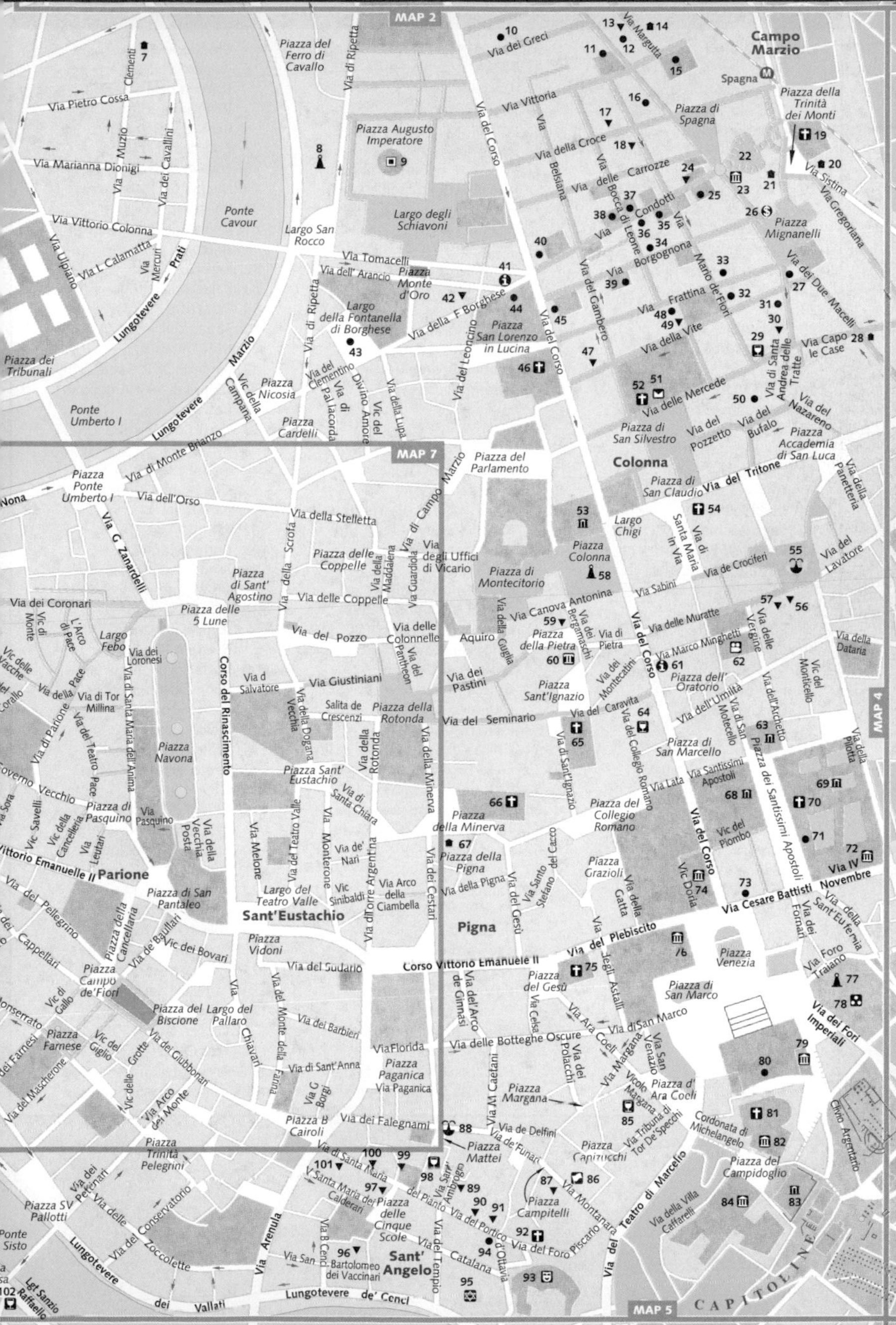

MAP 3

PLACES TO STAY

1 Hotel Amalia
2 Pensione Ottaviano
4 Hotel Joli; Hotel Florida
6 Colors Hotel
7 Hotel Mellini
14 Hotel Forte
20 Hassler Villa Medici
21 Hotel Scalinata di Spagna
28 Casa Howard
67 Minerva
121 Padri Trinitari
123 Hotel Columbus
129 Hotel Bramante
130 Hotel Adriatic

PLACES TO EAT

3 Piazza dell' Unità Market
5 Castroni
13 Osteria Margutta
17 Otello alla Concordia
18 Al 34
24 Caffè Greco
30 Sogo Asahi
42 Pizzeria il Leoncino
47 Naturist Club-L'Islola
49 Mario
56 Antico Forno
57 Pizza a Taglio
59 Osteria dell'Ingegno
87 Vecchia Roma
89 Billo Bottarga
90 Da Giggetto
91 La Dolceroma
96 Piperno
97 Sora Margherita
99 Il Forno del Ghetto
100 Zì Fenizia
101 L'Albero del Pane
103 Surya Mahal
104 Monzù Vladi
110 ATM Sushi Bar
112 Hostaria Giulio

SHOPPING

10 Lion Bookshop
11 Emporio Armani
12 Flos Arteluce
15 Alinari
16 C.U.C.I.N.A
25 Gucci
27 Mandarina Duck
31 Anglo-American Bookshop
32 Sisley
33 La Cicogna
34 Fratelli Rossetti
35 Valentino
36 MaxMara
37 Salvatore Ferragamo (women)
38 Salvatore Ferragamo (men)
39 Fendi
40 Max & Co
43 Market
44 Fendissime
45 Tod's
48 Stefanel
71 Mel Giannino Stoppani
73 Benetton
94 Leone Limentani
116 Libreria Babele

OTHER

8 Ara Pacis
9 Mausoleo di Augusto
19 Trinità dei Monti
22 Spanish Steps; Barcaccia
23 Keats-Shelley House
26 American Express
29 Gilda
41 Tourist Information Kiosk
46 Chiesa di San Lorenzo in Lucina
50 European School of Economics
51 Main Post Office
52 Chiesa di San Silvestro in Capite
53 Palazzo Chigi
54 Chiesa di Santa Maria in Via
55 Trevi Fountain
58 Colonna Antonina
60 Tempio di Adriano
61 Tourist Information Kiosk
62 Quirinetta
63 Palazzo Muti
64 Trinity College
65 Chiesa di Sant'Ignazio di Loyola
66 Chiesa di Santa Maria Sopra Minerva
68 Palazzo Odelscalchi
69 Palazzo Colonna
70 Chiesa di Santi Apostoli
72 Galleria Colonna
74 Palazzo Doria Pamphilj (Galleria Doria Pamphilj)
75 Chiesa del Gesù
76 Palazzo Venezia (Museo del Palazzo di Venezia); Basilica di San Marco
77 Colonna di Traiano
78 Foro di Triano
79 Museo del Risorgimento
80 Il Vittoriano
81 Chiesa di Santa Maria in Aracoeli
82 Palazzo Nuovo
83 Palazzo Senatorio
84 Palazzo dei Conservatori
85 Edoardo II
86 Irish Embassy
88 Fontana delle Tartarughe
92 Chiesa di Sant'Angelo in Pescheria
93 Teatro di Marcello
95 Synagogue (Museo della Communità Ebraica)
98 Bartarnga
102 Friends Art Café
105 Porta Settimiano
106 John Cabot University
107 Villa Farnesina
108 Palazzo Corsini (Galleria Nazionale d'Arte Antica)
109 Garibaldi Monument
111 Buon Pastore Centre (CLI)
113 Palazzo Ricci
114 Il Goccetto
115 Teatro dell'Orologico
117 Bed & Breakfast Italia
118 CTS
119 Chiesa di San Giovanni dei Battista dei Fiorentini
120 Ospedale Bambino Gesù (Hospital)
122 The Netgate
124 Centro Servizi Pellegrini e Turisti (Vatican Tourist Office)
125 Vatican Post Office
126 Farmacia del Vaticano
127 Vatican Museums; Vatican Library
128 Post Office
131 Accademia di Santa Cecilia
132 Tourist Information Kiosk

SALLY WEBB

Bernini's Fontana del Tritone, Piazza Barberini

MARTIN MOOS

If all roads lead to it, it's worth getting a lift.

CHRISTOPHER GROENHOUT

Take a break with the Spanish on their Steps.

MARTIN MOOS

Wherever I rest my helmet, that's my home.

TERESA GAUDIO

The famous Trevi Fountain – throw that coin!

MAP 4

MAP 2
MAP 3
MAP 6
Sallustiano
Trevi
Monti
Cavour
Via Boncompagni
Piazza Sallustio
Via Castelfidardo
Via Goito
Via Q Sella
Via Piemonte
Via Lucullo
Via Sallustiana
Via Friuli
Via Lombardia
Via di Porta Pinciana
Via Ludovisi
Via Aurora
Via Emilia
Via Liguria
Via Vittorio Veneto
Via Leonida Bissolati
Via Umbria
Via G Carducci
Via A Salanda
Via Flavia
Via XX Settembre
Piazza delle Finanze
Via Montebello
Via Calabria
Via Volturno
V Pastrengo
Via Cernaia
Via Francesco Crispi
Via degli Artisti
Via delle Purificazione
Via Molise
Via Versilia
Via di San Basilio
Salita San Nicola da Tolentino
Via di San Nicola da Tolentino
Largo di Santa Susanna
Via Parigi
Via Sistina
Via Zucchelli
Piazza Barberini
Via Barberini
Barberini
Piazza San Bernardo
Via Orlando
Largo del Tritone
Via del Tritone
Via d Avignonesi
Via Rasella
Via dei Giardini
Via delle Quattro Fontane
Via Firenze
Piazza della Repubblica
Via L Einaudi
Via Enrico de Nicola
Via del Traforo
Via Arcione
Via Scuderie
Giardino del Quirinale
Traforo Umberto I
Via Modena
Via Torino
Repubblica
Via delle Terme di Diocleziano
Largo di Villa Peretti
Via Montalto
Termini
Piazza B Gigli
Via Napoli
Via San Vitale
Via Genova
Via Nazionale
Via Agostino de Pretis
Via del Viminale
Piazza del Viminale
Via Massimo D'Azeglio
Via Rosmini
Via Cavour
Via G Amendola
Via Principe Amedeo
Via D Manin
Via Gioberti
Via Farini
Via del Quirinale
Via Piacenza
Via Milano
Piazza del Quirinale
Salita di Montecarlo
Vic Mazzarino
Via Parma
Via della Consulta
Via Palermo
Ministero dell' Interno
Via Cesare Balbo
Via Urbana
Piazza dell' Esquilino
Via dell'Esquilino
Villa Colonna
Via XXIV Maggio
Via de' Serpenti
Via Liberiana
Via di Santa Maria Maggiore
Piazza Santa Maria Maggiore
Via Mazzarino
Via del Boschetto
Via Panisperna
Via Cimarra
Via de Ciancaleoni
Via dei Capocci
Via dei Quattro Cantoni
Via Paolina
Via dell'Olmata
Via Santa Prassede
Largo Magnanapoli
Largo Angelicum
Via di Sant' Agata de Goti
Piazza Zingari
Via Sforza
Via San Martino ai Monti
Casa dei Cavalieri di Rodi
Piazza Madonna dei Monti
Via degli Zingari
Piazza Suburra
Via Giovanni Lanza
Piazza San Martino ai Monti
Largo Brancaccio
Via Alessandrina
Via Tor de' Conti
Via Baccina
Via Leonina
Largo Visconti Venosta
Via in Selci
Via della Madonna de' Monti
Piazza San Francesco di Paola
Parco di Traiano
Largo C Ricci
Via Frangipane
Piazza di San Pietro in Vincoli
Via delle Sette Sale
Via della Salaria Vecchia
Largo Romolo e Remo
Via del Colosseo
Via di Cardello
Via delle Carine
Via Vittorino da Feltre
Via degli Annibaldi
Via del Fagutale
Via della Polveriera
Via Eudosiana
Largo D Polveriera
Viale del Monte Oppio
Via delle Terme di Traiano
Via Mecenate
Roman Forum
Via dei Fori Imperiali
Largo G Agnesi
Via Monte Oppio
Via delle Terme di Tito
Colle Oppio
Parco Oppio
Via C Botta

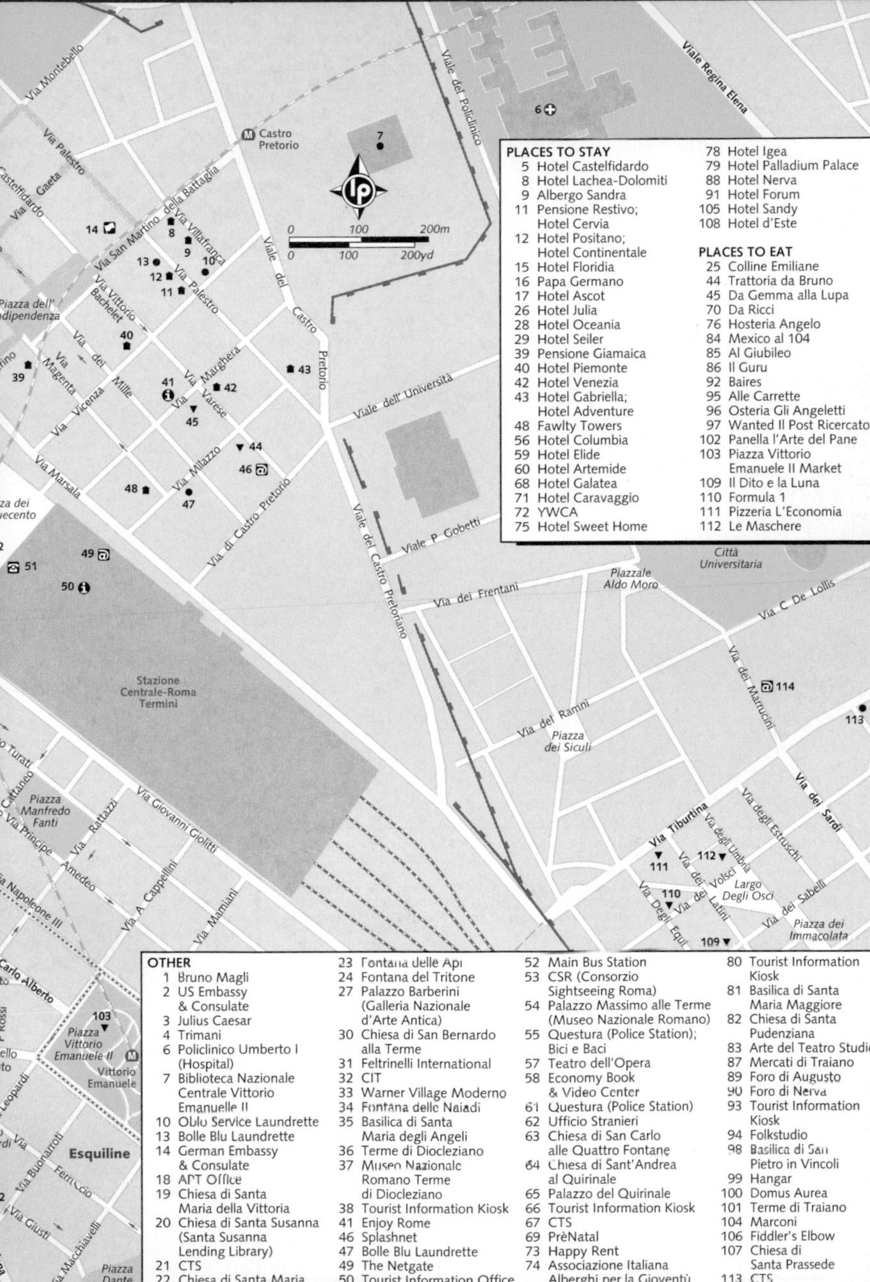
PLACES TO STAY
5 Hotel Castelfidardo
8 Hotel Lachea-Dolomiti
9 Albergo Sandra
11 Pensione Restivo; Hotel Cervia
12 Hotel Positano; Hotel Continentale
15 Hotel Floridia
16 Papa Germano
17 Hotel Ascot
26 Hotel Julia
28 Hotel Oceania
29 Hotel Seiler
39 Pensione Giamaica
40 Hotel Piemonte
42 Hotel Venezia
43 Hotel Gabriella; Hotel Adventure
48 Fawlty Towers
56 Hotel Columbia
59 Hotel Elide
60 Hotel Artemide
68 Hotel Galatea
71 Hotel Caravaggio
72 YWCA
75 Hotel Sweet Home
78 Hotel Igea
79 Hotel Palladium Palace
88 Hotel Nerva
91 Hotel Forum
105 Hotel Sandy
108 Hotel d'Este
PLACES TO EAT
25 Colline Emiliane
44 Trattoria da Bruno
45 Da Gemma alla Lupa
70 Da Ricci
76 Hosteria Angelo
84 Mexico al 104
85 Al Giubileo
86 Il Guru
92 Baires
95 Alle Carrette
96 Osteria Gli Angeletti
97 Wanted Il Post Ricercato
102 Panella l'Arte del Pane
103 Piazza Vittorio Emanuele II Market
109 Il Dito e la Luna
110 Formula 1
111 Pizzeria L'Economia
112 Le Maschere
OTHER
1 Bruno Magli
2 US Embassy & Consulate
3 Julius Caesar
4 Trimani
6 Policlinico Umberto I (Hospital)
7 Biblioteca Nazionale Centrale Vittorio Emanuelle II
10 Oblò Service Laundrette
13 Bolle Blu Laundrette
14 German Embassy & Consulate
18 APT Office
19 Chiesa di Santa Maria della Vittoria
20 Chiesa di Santa Susanna (Santa Susanna Lending Library)
21 CTS
22 Chiesa di Santa Maria della Concezione
23 Fontana delle Api
24 Fontana del Tritone
27 Palazzo Barberini (Galleria Nazionale d'Arte Antica)
30 Chiesa di San Bernardo alla Terme
31 Feltrinelli International
32 CIT
33 Warner Village Moderno
34 Fontana delle Naiadi
35 Basilica di Santa Maria degli Angeli
36 Terme di Diocleziano
37 Museo Nazionale Romano Terme di Diocleziano
38 Tourist Information Kiosk
41 Enjoy Rome
46 Splashnet
47 Bolle Blu Laundrette
49 The Netgate
50 Tourist Information Office
51 Telephone Office
52 Main Bus Station
53 CSR (Consorzio Sightseeing Roma)
54 Palazzo Massimo alle Terme (Museo Nazionale Romano)
55 Questura (Police Station); Bici e Baci
57 Teatro dell'Opera
58 Economy Book & Video Center
61 Questura (Police Station)
62 Ufficio Stranieri
63 Chiesa di San Carlo alle Quattro Fontane
64 Chiesa di Sant'Andrea al Quirinale
65 Palazzo del Quirinale
66 Tourist Information Kiosk
67 CTS
69 PrèNatal
73 Happy Rent
74 Associazione Italiana Alberghi per la Gioventù
77 Ciao Roma
80 Tourist Information Kiosk
81 Basilica di Santa Maria Maggiore
82 Chiesa di Santa Pudenziana
83 Arte del Teatro Studio
87 Mercati di Traiano
89 Foro di Augusto
90 Foro di Nerva
93 Tourist Information Kiosk
94 Folkstudio
98 Basilica di San Pietro in Vincoli
99 Hangar
100 Domus Aurea
101 Terme di Traiano
104 Marconi
106 Fiddler's Elbow
107 Chiesa di Santa Prassede
113 CTS
114 Internet Café
Castro Pretorio
Via Montebello
Via Palestro
Via Gaeta
Via Castelfidardo
Via San Martino della Battaglia
Via Villafranca
Via Vittorio Bachelet
Piazza dell' Indipendenza
Via Magenta
Via dei Mille
Via Marghera
Via Varese
Via Vicenza
Via Milazzo
Via Marsala
Via di Castro Pretorio
Viale del Castro Pretorio
Viale del Policlinico
Viale Regina Elena
Viale dell' Università
Viale P Gobetti
Viale del Castro Pretoriano
Via dei Frentani
Piazzale Aldo Moro
Città Universitaria
Via C De Lollis
Via dei Marrucini
Via dei Ramni
Piazza dei Siculi
Via dei Sardi
Via degli Estruschi
Via Tiburtina
Via degli Umbri
Via dei Volsci
Largo Degli Osci
Via dei Latini
Via Degli Equi
Via dei Sabelli
Piazza dei Immacolata
Stazione Centrale-Roma Termini
Via Giovanni Giolitti
Piazza Manfredo Fanti
Via Rattazzi
Via Principe Amedeo
Via Napoleone III
Via A Cappellini
Via Mamiani
Carlo Alberto
Piazza Vittorio Emanuele II
Vittorio Emanuele
Esquiline
Via Leopardi
Via Buonarroti
Via Ferruccio
Via Giusti
Via Macchiavelli
Piazza Dante
MAP 6
0 100 200m
0 100 200yd

MAP 5

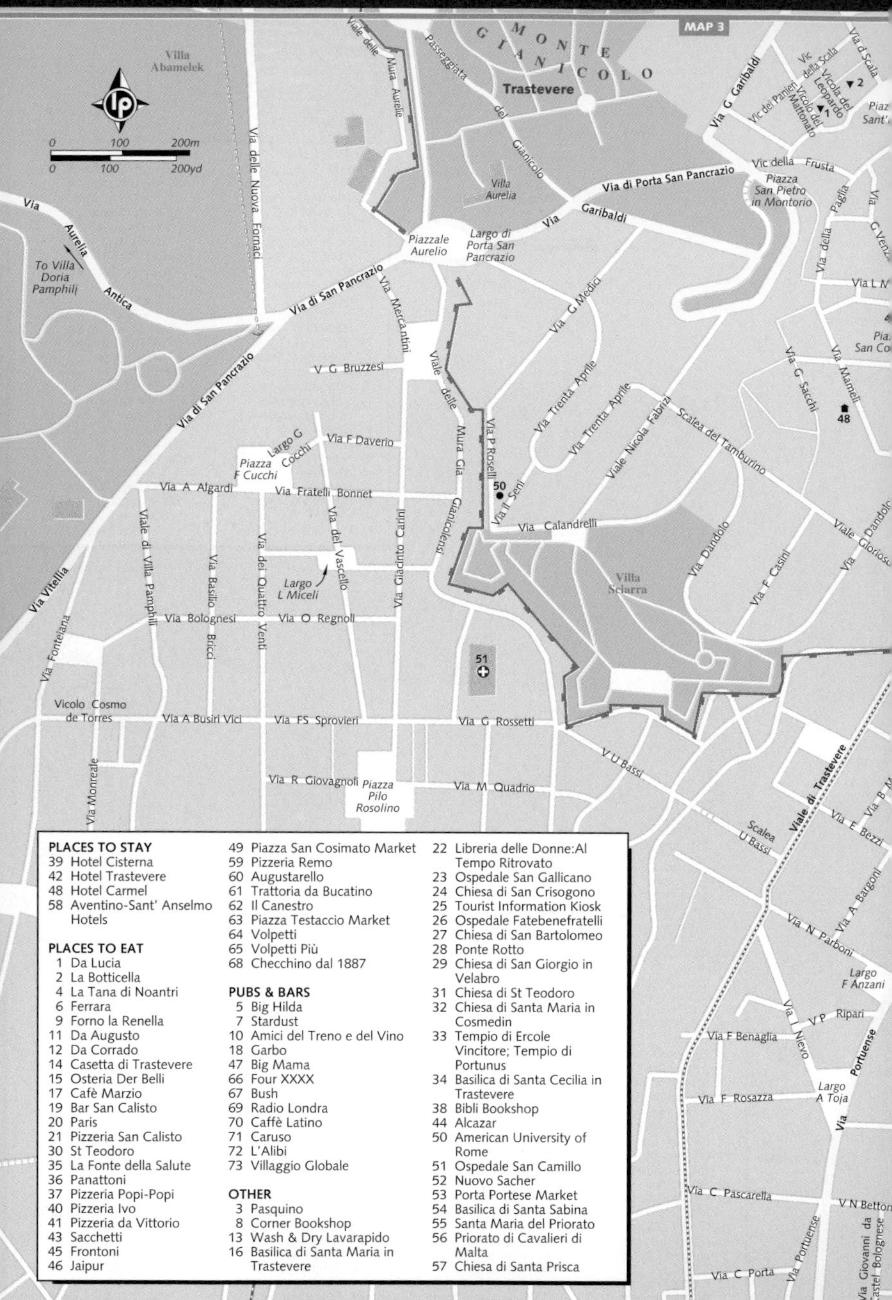
MAP 3
MONTE GIANICOLO
Trastevere
Villa Abamelek
0 100 200m
0 100 200yd
Via Aurelia Antica
To Villa Doria Pamphilj
Viale delle Mura Aurelie
Passeggiata del Gianicolo
Villa Aurelia
Via delle Nuova Fornaci
Piazzale Aurelio
Largo di Porta San Pancrazio
Via di Porta San Pancrazio
Via Garibaldi
Via G Garibaldi
Vic della Frusta
Piazza San Pietro in Montorio
Via di San Pancrazio
Via Mercantini
V G Bruzzesi
Viale delle Mura Gianicolensi
Via G Medici
Via Trenta Aprile
Viale Nicola Fabrizi
Scalea del Tamburino
Via G Sacchi
Via Mameli
48
Via F Daverio
Largo G Cocchi
Piazza F Cucchi
Via A Algardi
Via Fratelli Bonnet
Via P Roselli
Via Il Seni
50
Via Calandrelli
Via Dandolo
Viale Glorioso
Via F Casini
Villa Sciarra
Via Vitellia
Viale di Villa Pamphili
Via Basilio Bricci
Via dei Quattro Venti
Via del Vascello
Largo L Miceli
Via Giacinto Carini
Via Bolognesi
Via O Regnoli
Via Fonteiana
51
Vicolo Cosmo de Torres
Via A Busiri Vici
Via FS Sprovieri
Via G Rossetti
V U Bassi
Via R Giovagnoli
Piazza Pilo Rosolino
Via M Quadrio
Via Monreale
Viale di Trastevere
Scalea U Bassi
Via E Bezzi
Via A Bargoni
Via N Parboni
Largo F Anzani
V P Ripari
Via F Benaglia
Via I Nievo
Via Portuense
Via F Rosazza
Largo A Toja
Via C Pascarella
V N Bettoni
Via C Porta
Via Giovanni da Castel Bolognese
PLACES TO STAY
39 Hotel Cisterna
42 Hotel Trastevere
48 Hotel Carmel
58 Aventino-Sant' Anselmo Hotels
PLACES TO EAT
1 Da Lucia
2 La Botticella
4 La Tana di Noantri
6 Ferrara
9 Forno la Renella
11 Da Augusto
12 Da Corrado
14 Casetta di Trastevere
15 Osteria Der Belli
17 Cafè Marzio
19 Bar San Calisto
20 Paris
21 Pizzeria San Calisto
30 St Teodoro
35 La Fonte della Salute
36 Panattoni
37 Pizzeria Popi-Popi
40 Pizzeria Ivo
41 Pizzeria da Vittorio
43 Sacchetti
45 Frontoni
46 Jaipur
49 Piazza San Cosimato Market
59 Pizzeria Remo
60 Augustarello
61 Trattoria da Bucatino
62 Il Canestro
63 Piazza Testaccio Market
64 Volpetti
65 Volpetti Più
68 Checchino dal 1887
PUBS & BARS
5 Big Hilda
7 Stardust
10 Amici del Treno e del Vino
18 Garbo
47 Big Mama
66 Four XXXX
67 Bush
69 Radio Londra
70 Caffè Latino
71 Caruso
72 L'Alibi
73 Villaggio Globale
OTHER
3 Pasquino
8 Corner Bookshop
13 Wash & Dry Lavarapido
16 Basilica di Santa Maria in Trastevere
22 Libreria delle Donne:Al Tempo Ritrovato
23 Ospedale San Gallicano
24 Chiesa di San Crisogono
25 Tourist Information Kiosk
26 Ospedale Fatebenefratelli
27 Chiesa di San Bartolomeo
28 Ponte Rotto
29 Chiesa di San Giorgio in Velabro
31 Chiesa di St Teodoro
32 Chiesa di Santa Maria in Cosmedin
33 Tempio di Ercole Vincitore; Tempio di Portunus
34 Basilica di Santa Cecilia in Trastevere
38 Bibli Bookshop
44 Alcazar
50 American University of Rome
51 Ospedale San Camillo
52 Nuovo Sacher
53 Porta Portese Market
54 Basilica di Santa Sabina
55 Santa Maria del Priorato
56 Priorato di Cavalieri di Malta
57 Chiesa di Santa Prisca

MAP 3
MAP 6
Ponte Garibaldi
Ponte Fabricio
Isola Tiberina
Piazza di San Bartolomeo all'Isola
Ponte Cestio
Piazza Monte Savello
Via del Foro Olitorio
Vic Jungario
Piazza della Consolazione
Via dei Fienili
Via Bucimazza
Via di San Teodoro
Lungotevere Raphaello Sanzio
Via del Politeama
Via Renella
Via del Moro
Via della Lungaretta
Piazza Santa Maria in Trastevere
Piazza G Tavani Arguati
Via G Modena
Piazza Belli
Lgt degli Anguillara
Vic della Luce
Via Gensola
Lgt dei Pierleoni
Via L Petroselli
Via del Ponte Rotto
Via della Misericordia
Via di San Giovanni Decollato
Via della Lungari
Piazza Santa Rufina
Piazza Sonnino
Via Lungarina
Ponte Palatino
Piazza Bocca della Verità
Via del Velabro
Via dell'Arco di San Calisto
Piazza in Piscinula
Piazza Castellani
Trastevere
Via della Cisterna
Via di San Gallicano
Via della Luce
Via dei Salumi
Lungotevere Ripa
Piazza dei Ponziani
Piazza di Sant'Anastasia
Via San Cosimato
Via dei Genovesi
Via della Greca
Via della Fratte di Trastevere
Viale di Trastevere
Via Cardinal Marmaggi
Via dei Vascerelli
Via d Ara Mass di Ercole
Via dei Cerchi
Piazza di Santa Cecilia
Circo Massimo
Via del Circo Massimo
Natale del Grande
Via di San Francesco a Ripa
Piazza Mastai
Piazza D Mercanti
Via Anicia
Aventine
Morosini
Piazza San Francis d'Assisi
Via di San Michele
Clivio di Rocca Savella
Parco Savello
Piazzale Ugo la Malfa
Via di Valle Murcia
Rosetta di Roma
Via di Santa Sabina
Clivo de Publicii
Via G Indumo
Porta di Ripa Grande
Lungotevere Aventino
Piazza Pietro d'Illiria
Piazza Ponte Portese
Piazza
Piazzale Portuense
Ponte Sublicio
Largo Arrigo VII
Via San Domenica
Piazza Giunone Regina
Via Terme Deciante
Via M Carcani
Piazza D Emporio
Via di Santa Sabina
Piazza dei Cavaleri di Malta
Via di Prisca
Piazza San Prisca
Clivio Putuense
Lungotevere Portuense
Via di Porta Lavernale
Tiber
Via A Cecchi
Via A Vespucci
Via R Gessi
Piazza Sant'Anselmo
Via di San Alessio
Viale Aventino
Via Marmorata
Via Orti di Trastevere
Lungotevere Testaccio
Via G Bianchi
Via Giovanni Branca
Via Querini
Via Rubattino
Via Vanvitelli
Piazza Albania
Via di S Saba
Viale M Gelosimini
Via Florio
Testaccio
Piazza Testaccio
Via Luca della Robbia
Via Ginori
Via Giovan Battista Bodoni
Via Giorgio
Via Franklin
Via Aldo Manuzio
Via A Volta
Largo M Gelsomini
Viale di Piramide Cestia
Via Faustina
Via Torricelli
Via Ghiberti
Via Nicola Zabaglia
Via Pontelli Baccio
Via Ancia
Via Galvani
Viale del Campo Boario
Via di Monte Testaccio
Piazza di Porta San Paolo
Viale Giotto
Largo GB Marzi
Parco Testaccio
Piazzale Ostiense
Viale di Porta Ardeatina
Ponte Testaccio
Via Caio Cestio
Viale del Campo Boario
Piramide
Stazione Roma-Ostia
Viale Marco Polo
1 2 3 4 5 6 7 8 9 10 11 12 13 14 15 17 18 19 20 21 22 23 24 25 26 27 28 29 30 31 32 33 34 35 36 37 38 39 40 41 42 43 44 45 46 47 52 53 54 55 56 57 58 59 60 61 62 63 64 65 66 67 68 69 70 71 72 73

Roman Forum
Colosseo
Via N Salvi
ESQUILINE
MAP 4
OPPIAN
Orti Farnesiani
Viale della Domus Aurea
Parco Oppio
Via Ruggero Bo
Colosseum
Piazza del Colosseo
Via L Murato
Via Crescimbeni
Via dei Normanni
1
2
Via di San Giovanni in Laterano
5
Piazza San Clemente
Via Labica
3
Via dei S Quattro
4
Via Celio Vibenna
Viale del Parco del Celio
Via Ostilia
Via Capo d'Africa
Via Celimontana
Parco del Celio
Via M Aurelio
Via di Querceti
6
Via Claudia
Via Annia
PALATINE
Palatine
Via di San Gregorio VII
15
Piazza di SS Giovanni E Paolo
Clivo di Scaurio
Via di S Stefano Rotondo
Via del Cerchi
Via della Croce
Via di Villa F
Circo Massimo
16
14
Via del Circo Massimo
Via della Navicella
Via di Viale delle Camene
MAP 5
Circo Massimo
Via d Fonte di Fauno
Via di S Erasmo
Villa Celimontana
CAELIAN
Via dell'Amba Aradam
Via de Ferrete in Laterano
Via della Terme di Caracalla
Viale Aventino
Piazza Porta Metronia
Via Ippo
Via Ga
Piazzale Metronia
Parco di Porta Capena
Via P
Via Antonina
Via Druso
Viale Metronio
17
Via B Peruzzi
Via Aventina
Piazzale Numa Pompilio
Via Ligorio Pirro
Viale Guido
Via Flamingo Ponzio
Via E Rosa
Terme di Caracalla
Via di Villa Pepoli
Via delle Terme di Caracalla
Via di Porta Latina
Piazza GL Bernini
Via Bramante
Via A Palladio
Via GD Porta
Viale Guido Baccelli
Via di Porta S Sebastiano
Via Giotto
Via Tata Giovanni
Viale di Porta Ardeatina
Via Fabio L Cilone
Via G Miani

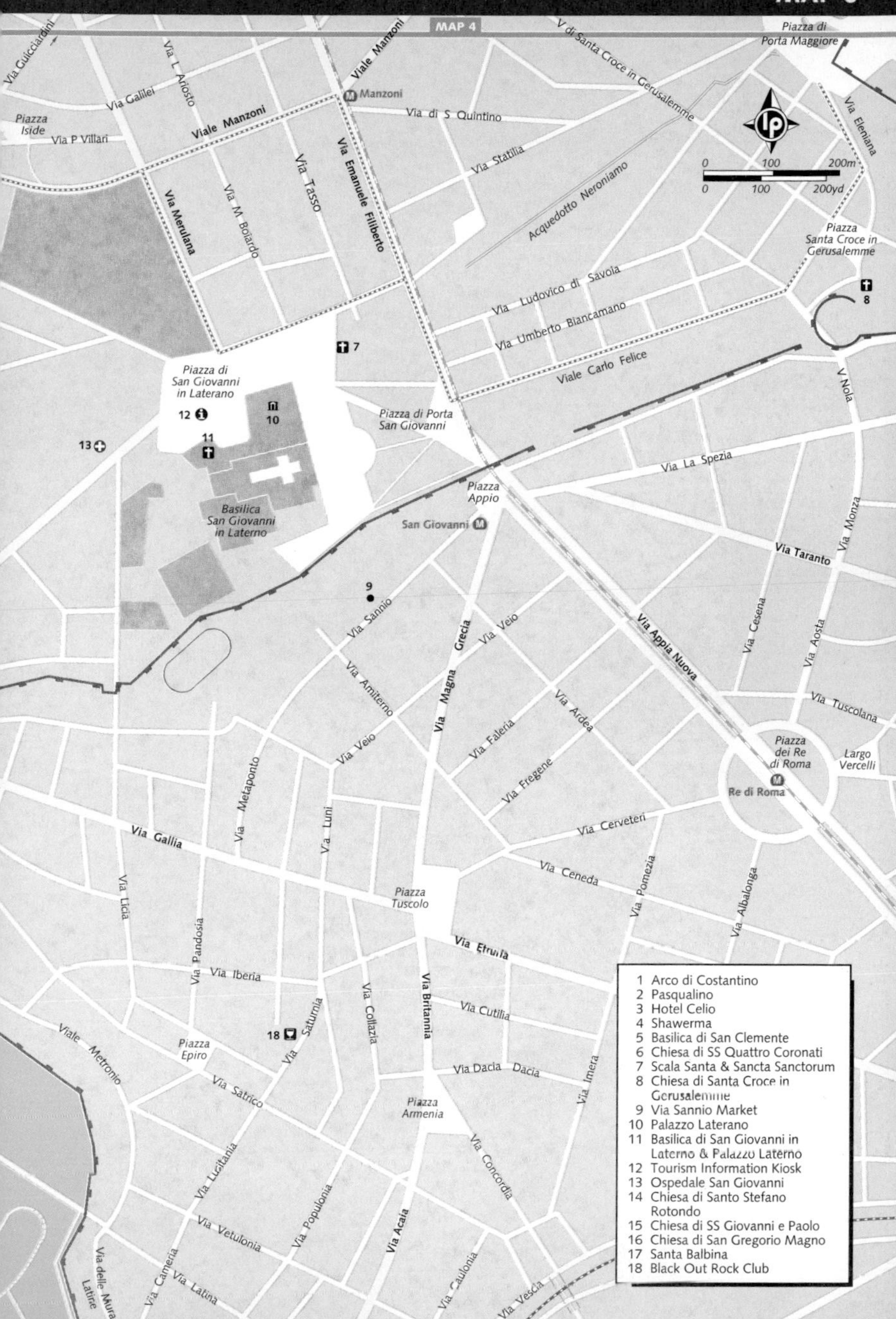
MAP 4
Piazza di Porta Maggiore
V di Santa Croce in Gerusalemme
Via Guicciardini
Via L Ariosto
Viale Manzoni
Manzoni
Via Galilei
Piazza Iside
Via P Villari
Via di S Quintino
Via Statilia
Acquedotto Neroniamo
Via Elenjana
Via Merulana
Via M Boiardo
Via Tasso
Via Emanuele Filiberto
Piazza Santa Croce in Gerusalemme
Via Ludovico di Savoia
Via Umberto Biancamano
Viale Carlo Felice
V Nola
Piazza di San Giovanni in Laterano
Piazza di Porta San Giovanni
Piazza Appio
San Giovanni
Basilica San Giovanni in Laterno
Via La Spezia
Via Monza
Via Taranto
Via Sannio
Via Appia Nuova
Via Cesena
Via Aosta
Via Magna Grecia
Via Veio
Via Amiterno
Via Ardea
Via Tuscolana
Via Faleria
Via Fregene
Piazza dei Re di Roma
Re di Roma
Largo Vercelli
Via Metaponto
Via Luni
Via Gallia
Via Cerveteri
Via Ceneda
Via Licia
Piazza Tuscolo
Via Pomezia
Via Albalonga
Via Etruria
Via Pandosia
Via Iberia
Via Collazia
Via Britannia
Via Cutilia
Viale Metronio
Piazza Epiro
Via Saturnia
Via Satrico
Via Dacia
Dacia
Via Imera
Piazza Armenia
Via Concordia
Via Lucitania
Via Vetulonia
Via Populonia
Via Acaia
Via delle Mura Latine
Via Cameria
Via Latina
Via Caulonia
Via Vescia
1 Arco di Costantino
2 Pasqualino
3 Hotel Celio
4 Shawerma
5 Basilica di San Clemente
6 Chiesa di SS Quattro Coronati
7 Scala Santa & Sancta Sanctorum
8 Chiesa di Santa Croce in Gerusalemme
9 Via Sannio Market
10 Palazzo Laterano
11 Basilica di San Giovanni in Laterno & Palazzo Laterno
12 Tourism Information Kiosk
13 Ospedale San Giovanni
14 Chiesa di Santo Stefano Rotondo
15 Chiesa di SS Giovanni e Paolo
16 Chiesa di San Gregorio Magno
17 Santa Balbina
18 Black Out Rock Club

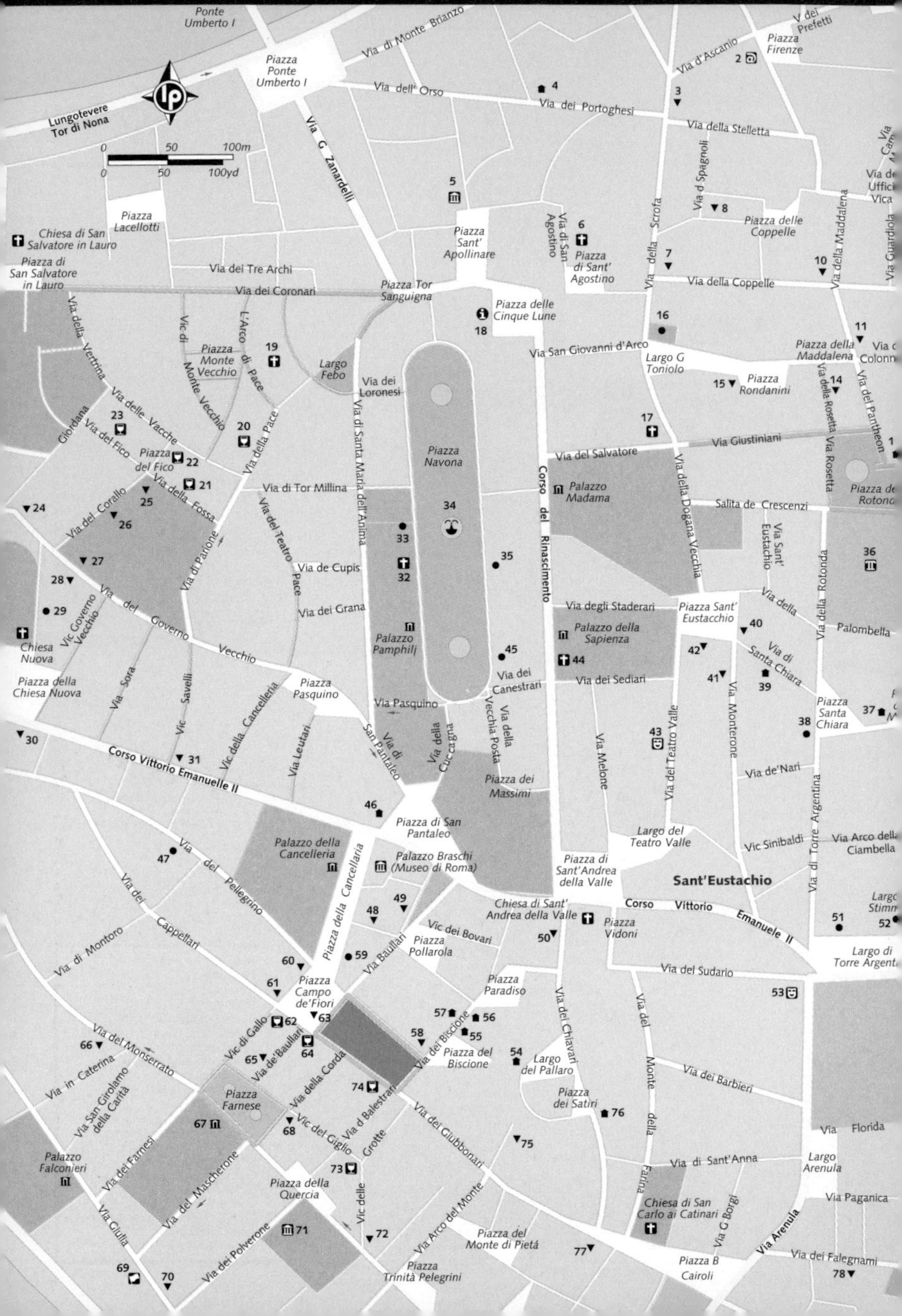

Ponte Umberto I
Via di Monte Brianzo
Piazza Ponte Umberto I
Lungotevere Tor di Nona
Via dell' Orso
Via dei Portoghesi
Via d'Ascanio
V dei Prefetti
Piazza Firenze
Via della Stelletta
Via G Zanardelli
Via d Spagnoli
Via della Scrofa
Piazza delle Coppelle
Via della Coppelle
Via della Maddalena
Via degli Uffici del Vicario
Via Guardiola
Piazza Lacellotti
Chiesa di San Salvatore in Lauro
Piazza di San Salvatore in Lauro
Via dei Tre Archi
Via dei Coronari
Piazza Sant' Apollinare
Via di San Agostino
Piazza di Sant' Agostino
Piazza Tor Sanguigna
Piazza delle Cinque Lune
Via della Vetrina
Vic di Monte Vecchio
L'Arco di Pace
Piazza Monte Vecchio
Largo Febo
Via dei Loronesi
Via San Giovanni d'Arco
Largo G Toniolo
Piazza della Maddalena
Piazza Rondanini
Via della Rosetta
Via del Pantheon
Giordana
Via delle Vacche
Via del Fico
Piazza del Fico
Via della Pace
Via di Santa Maria dell'Anima
Piazza Navona
Via Giustiniani
Via del Salvatore
Via della Dogana Vecchia
Palazzo Madama
Corso del Rinascimento
Salita de Crescenzi
Piazza della Rotonda
Via della Fossa
Via del Corallo
Via di Tor Millina
Via del Teatro Pace
Via di Parione
Via Sant' Eustachio
Via della Rotonda
Via de Cupis
Via dei Grana
Via del Governo Vecchio
Vic Governo Vecchio
Chiesa Nuova
Piazza della Chiesa Nuova
Via della Palombella
Via degli Staderari
Piazza Sant' Eustacchio
Palazzo della Sapienza
Palazzo Pamphilj
Via di Santa Chiara
Via dei Canestrari
Via dei Sediari
Piazza Pasquino
Via Sora
Vic Savelli
Vic della Cancelleria
Via Leutari
Via Pasquino
Via di San Pantaleo
Via della Cuccagna
Via della Vecchia Posta
Via Melone
Via del Teatro Valle
Via Monterone
Piazza Santa Chiara
Corso Vittorio Emanuelle II
Piazza dei Massimi
Via de'Nari
Via di Torre Argentina
Piazza di San Pantaleo
Via del Pellegrino
Palazzo della Cancelleria
Piazza della Cancellaria
Palazzo Braschi (Museo di Roma)
Largo del Teatro Valle
Piazza di Sant'Andrea della Valle
Vic Sinibaldi
Via Arco della Ciambella
Sant'Eustachio
Via dei Cappellari
Chiesa di Sant' Andrea della Valle
Corso Vittorio Emanuele II
Piazza Vidoni
Largo di Torre Stimmate
Via di Montoro
Vic dei Bovari
Piazza Pollarola
Via Baullari
Largo di Torre Argentina
Piazza Campo de' Fiori
Piazza Paradiso
Via del Sudario
Via dei Chiavari
Via del Monte della Farina
Via del Monserrato
Vic di Gallo
Via de'Baullari
Via del Biscione
Piazza del Biscione
Largo del Pallaro
Via dei Barbieri
Via in Caterina
Via San Girolamo della Carità
Piazza Farnese
Via della Corda
Via d Balestrari
Piazza dei Satiri
Via dei Giubbonari
Via Florida
Vic del Giglio
Via delle Grotte
Palazzo Falconieri
Via dei Farnesi
Via del Mascherone
Piazza della Quercia
Vic delle
Via di Sant'Anna
Largo Arenula
Via Paganica
Via Giulia
Via dei Polverone
Via Arco del Monte
Piazza del Monte di Pietà
Chiesa di San Carlo ai Catinari
Via G Borgi
Via Arenula
Piazza B Cairoli
Via dei Falegnami
Piazza Trinità Pelegrini

0 50 100m
0 50 100yd

2 3 4 5 6 7 8 10 11 14 15 16 17 18 19 20 21 22 23 24 25 26 27 28 29 30 31 32 33 34 35 36 37 38 39 40 41 42 43 44 45 46 47 48 49 50 51 52 53 54 55 56 57 58 59 60 61 62 63 64 65 66 67 68 69 70 71 72 73 74 75 76 77 78

MAP 7 – AROUND PIAZZA NAVONA

PLACES TO STAY
- 4 Hotel Portoghesi
- 13 Albergo Abruzzi
- 37 Hotel Santa Chiara
- 39 Hotel Mimosa
- 46 Pensione Primavera
- 54 Albergo Teatro di Pompeo
- 55 Albergo del Sole
- 56 Albergo della Lunetta
- 57 Hotel Campo de' Fiori
- 76 Hotel Pomezia

PLACES TO EAT
- 1 Da Gino
- 3 M & M Volpetti
- 7 Oliphant
- 8 Il Bacaro
- 9 Gelateria Giolitti
- 10 Gelateria della Palma
- 11 Gino Placidi
- 12 La Tazza d'Oro
- 14 La Rosetta
- 15 Le Cornacchie
- 24 Osteria
- 25 Trattoria Pizzeria da Francesco
- 26 Pizzeria Corallo
- 27 Paladini
- 28 Pizzeria da Baffetto
- 30 Bella Napoli
- 31 Pizzeria La Montecarlo
- 40 Camilloni a Sant'Eustachio
- 41 L'Eau Vive
- 42 Caffè Sant'Eustachio
- 48 Ditirambo
- 49 Pizza a Taglio
- 50 Insalata Ricca
- 58 Pizza Rustica
- 60 La Carbonara
- 61 Forno di Campo de' Fiori
- 63 Market
- 65 Caffè Farnese
- 66 Ristorante Monserrato
- 68 Camponeschi
- 70 Thien Kim
- 72 Sergio alla Grotta
- 75 Filetti di Baccalà
- 77 Bernasconi
- 78 Benito

PUBS, BARS & CLUBS
- 20 Bar della Pace
- 21 Jonathan's Angels
- 22 Bar del Fico
- 23 Locale
- 62 The Drunken Ship
- 64 Vineria
- 73 L'Angolo Divino
- 74 Sloppy Sam's

OTHER
- 2 The Netgate
- 5 Palazzo Altemps (Museo Nazionale Romano)
- 6 Chiesa di Sant'Agostino
- 16 Città del Sole
- 17 Chiesa di San Luigidei Francesi
- 18 Tourist Information Kiosk
- 19 Chiesa di Santa Maria della Pace
- 29 Wash & Dry Lavarapido
- 32 Chiesa di Sant'Agnese in Agone
- 33 Nardecchia
- 34 Fontana dei Quattro Fiumi
- 35 Libreria Sorgente
- 36 Pantheon
- 38 Elsy Viaggi
- 43 Teatro Valle
- 44 Chiesa di Sant'Ivo alla Sapienza
- 45 Bertè
- 47 Libreria del Viaggiatore
- 51 Feltrinelli
- 52 Berlitz
- 53 Teatro Argentina
- 59 Italiaidea
- 67 Palazzo Farnese (French Embassy)
- 69 French Consulate
- 71 Palazzo Spada (Galleria Spada)

SALLY WEBB

Piazza Navona boasts a Bernini masterpiece: Fontana dei Quattro Fiumi (Fountain of the Four Rivers).

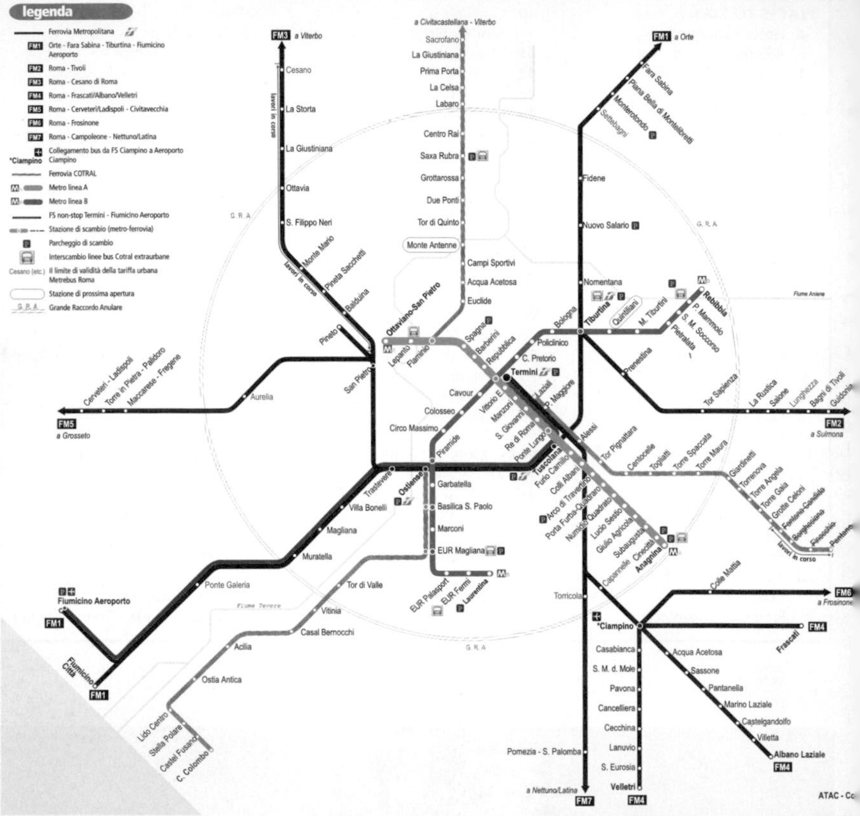

legenda

- Ferrovia Metropolitana
- FM1 Orte - Fara Sabina - Tiburtina - Fiumicino Aeroporto
- FM2 Roma - Tivoli
- FM3 Roma - Cesano di Roma
- FM4 Roma - Frascati/Albano/Velletri
- FM5 Roma - Cerveteri/Ladispoli - Civitavecchia
- FM6 Roma - Frosinone
- FM7 Roma - Campoleone - Nettuno/Latina
- *Ciampino Collegamento bus da FS Ciampino a Aeroporto Ciampino
- Ferrovia COTRAL
- Metro linea A
- Metro linea B
- FS non-stop Termini - Fiumicino Aeroporto
- Stazione di scambio (metro-ferrovia)
- Parcheggio di scambio
- Interscambio linee bus Cotral extraurbane
- Cesano (etc.) Il limite di validità della tariffa urbana Metrebus Roma
- Stazione di prossima apertura
- G.R.A. Grande Raccordo Anulare

ATAC - Co

GRATEFUL ACKNOWLEDGEMENT IS MADE FOR REPRODUCTION PERMISSION: ATAC S.P.A. : ROME METRO MAP 2001

MARTIN MOOS

When in Rome... scoot around as Romans do (but at your own peril).

[continued from page 192]

Next to the park is the 5th-century **Basilica di Santa Sabina**. Of particular note is the carved wooden door to the far left as you stand under the 15th-century portico facing the church. Dating from the 5th century, the door features panels depicting biblical scenes; the crucifixion scene is one of the oldest in existence.

TOWARDS THE JEWISH GHETTO

The refurbished **Chiesa di Santa Maria in Cosmedin (Map 5)** *(☎ 06 678 14 19, Piazza Bocca della Verità 18; free; open 9am-1pm & 2.30pm-6pm daily)* is regarded as one of the finest medieval churches in Rome. It has a 12th-century, seven-storey bell tower and its interior, including the beautiful floor, was heavily decorated with inlaid marble. There are 12th-century frescoes in the aisles. Under the portico is the famous **Bocca della Verità** (Mouth of Truth), a large, round, marble mask that probably served as the cover of an ancient drain. Legend says that if you put your right hand into the mouth while telling a lie, it will snap shut. Opposite the church are two tiny Roman temples: the round Tempio di Ercole Vincitore and the Tempio di Portunus.

Just off the piazza are the **Arco di Giano (Map 5)** *(Arch of Janus)*, a four-sided Roman arch that once covered a crossroads, and the medieval church of **San Giorgio in Velabro**.

From Piazza Bocca della Verità, follow Via L Petroselli to reach the **Teatro di Marcello (Map 3)** *(see the Rome Walking Tour earlier in this chapter)*, built around 13 BC to plans by Julius Caesar and dedicated by Emperor Augustus. It was converted into a fortress and residence during the Middle Ages, and a palace built on the site in the 16th century preserved the original form of the theatre.

From the theatre, head north along Via Montanara to Piazza Campitelli and then take Via dei Funari to Piazza Mattei. In the piazza is the **Fontana delle Tartarughe (Map 3)** *(Fountain of the Tortoises)*.

The area just south of here, around Via del Portico d'Ottavia, is known as the Jewish Ghetto. In the 16th century Pope Paul IV ordered the confinement of Jewish people to this area, marking the beginning of a time of intolerance that continued well into the 19th century. Follow Via del Portico d' Ottavia to the river and the 19th-century **synagogue (Map 3)**. Along the way, note the medieval houses. There is a 15th-century house at No 1 which incorporates pieces of ancient Roman sculpture in its facade. See the Rome Walking Tour earlier in this chapter for more details on the ghetto area.

From here, you can reach the **Isola Tiberina (Map 5)** across the Ponte Fabricio, which was built in 62 BC and is Rome's oldest standing bridge. The island has been associated with healing since the 3rd century BC, when the Romans adopted Aesculapius, the Greek god of healing, as their own and erected a temple to him on the island. Today it is the site of one hospital, the Ospedale Fatebenefratelli. **Chiesa di San Bartolomeo** was built on the island in the 10th century on the ruins of the Roman temple. It has a Romanesque bell tower and a marble well-head, believed to have been built over the same spring that provided healing waters for the temple. The Ponte Cestio, built in 46 BC, connects the island to Trastevere to the south. It was rebuilt in the late 19th century. Also to the south of the island are the remains of part of the **Ponte Rotto** (Broken Bridge), ancient Rome's first stone bridge.

TRASTEVERE (MAP 5)

Separated from the historic centre by the river, Trastevere is one of the most picturesque parts of Rome. The many bars and restaurants tucked into its labyrinthine lanes make it the most popular area of the city for eating and hanging out. Its traditionally proletarian nature is changing as crumbling old palazzos become gentrified and wealthy foreigners move in.

The heart of Trastevere is the lovely **Piazza Santa Maria in Trastevere**. It's a true Roman square – by day it's peopled by mothers with prams, chatting locals and guidebook-toting tourists, by night there are artisans selling their craftwork, young Romans looking for a good time and the odd homeless person looking for a bed.

The **Basilica di Santa Maria in Trastevere** *(☎ 06 581 94 43, Piazza Santa Maria in Trastevere; free; open 7.30am-12.30pm & 3.30pm-7.30pm daily)* is believed to be the oldest place of worship dedicated to the Virgin Mary in Rome. Although the first basilica was built on this site in AD 337, the present structure was built in the 12th century and contains a Romanesque bell tower and facade, with a mosaic of the Virgin from the 12th century. The impressive interior features 21 ancient Roman columns. Of particular interest are the 17th-century wooden ceiling and the vibrant mosaics in the apse (dating from 1140) and on the triumphal arch. Note the richly patterned dress of the Madonna in the apse. A badly deteriorated painting of the Madonna and angels, dating from the Byzantine era, is displayed in a room to the left of the altar.

Also well worth visiting is the **Basilica di Santa Cecilia in Trastevere (Map 4)** *(☎ 06 589 92 89; Piazza di Santa Cecilia; admission free to church, €1.10 to Cavallini fresco; church open 10am-noon & 4pm-5.30pm daily; fresco open for viewing 10am-11.30am Tues & Thur, 11.15am to 11.45am/after Mass Sun)* closer to the River Tiber. There's a magnificent 13th-century fresco of the Last Judgement by Pietro Cavallini in the nuns' choir, entered through the convent.

PIAZZA DI CAMPO DE' FIORI & AROUND (MAP 7)

Piazza di Campo de' Fiori is a lively square with a colourful flower and vegetable market every morning except Sunday. By day the occupants of the piazza are Roman mamas with their market baskets and by night beer-clutching bright young things. The piazza was a place of execution during the Inquisition. In 1600 the monk Giordano Bruno was burned at the stake here for heresy and his statue now stands at the piazza's centre.

Nearby, in Piazza Farnese, is the **Palazzo Farnese** *(not open to the public)*. A magnificent Renaissance building, it was started in 1514 by Antonio da Sangallo and work was continued by Michelangelo and completed by Giacomo della Porta. Built for Cardinal Alessandro Farnese (later Pope Paul III), the palace is now the French embassy. The facade features elegant geometrical decorations, the meaning of which remains a mystery. The piazza contains two fountains, which were enormous granite baths taken from the Terme di Caracalla.

South of Piazza di Campo de' Fiori and Piazza Farnese is the 16th-century **Palazzo Spada** *(☎ 06 686 11 58, Piazza Capodiferro 13; adults/reduced €5.20/2.60; open 9am-7pm Tues-Sat, 9am-6.30pm Sun)*. Rome's prettiest palazzo houses the Galleria Spada, a family art collection (acquired by the state in 1926) with works by Titian, Andrea del Sarto, Guido Reni, Guercino and Titian. The highlight is Borromini's clever trompe l'oeil perspective in the courtyard – which is only a quarter of the length it appears to be.

PIAZZA NAVONA (MAP 7)

Lined with Baroque palazzos, this vast and beautiful piazza was laid out on the ruins of Domitian's stadium and contains three fountains, including Bernini's masterpiece in the centre, the **Fontana dei Quattro Fiumi** (Fountain of the Four Rivers), depicting the Nile, Ganges, Danube and Plata. Facing the piazza is the **Chiesa di Sant'Agnese in Agone**, its facade designed by Bernini's bitter rival, Borromini. It's traditionally held that the statues of Bernini's Fontana dei Quattro Fiumi are shielding their eyes in disgust from Borromini's church, but actually Bernini completed the fountain two years before his contemporary started work on the facade.

PALAZZO ALTEMPS (MAP 7)

The prestigious Ludovisi collection forms the main body of the exhibits in the Renaissance and Baroque **Palazzo Altemps** *(☎ 06 683 35 66, Piazza Sant'Apollinare 46; adults/reduced €5.20/2.60; open 9am-7.30pm Tues-Sun)*. The palazzo was designed by Antonio da Sangallo the Elder, Baldassarre Peruzzi and Martino Longhi for generations of the noble Altemps family.

Cardinal Ludovico Ludovisi, a nephew of Pope Gregory XV, was a ravenous collector of ancient sculpture, which was regularly unearthed in the building boom of Counter-Reformation Rome. He employed leading sculptors – including Bernini and Alessandro Algardi – to repair and 'enhance' the works, replacing missing limbs or sticking a new head on a headless torso.

Baroque frescoes provide a decorative backdrop for the sculpture. Landscapes and hunting scenes are seen through trompe l'oeil windows in the Sala delle Prospettive Dipinte, and a fresco by Melozzo da Forlì (in the Sala della Piattaia, once the main reception room of the palazzo) displays a cupboard full of wedding gifts.

The *Trono Ludovisi*, discovered in the late 19th century, is one of the prize exhibits. Most scholars believe the carved marble throne came from a Greek colony in Italy and dates from the 5th or 6th century BC.

In the Sala del Camino, intricate carvings graphically depict a Roman battle scene on a giant marble sarcophagus. The expression and movement extracted from a lump of stone is astonishing. Equally impressive is the *Galata Suicida*. Blood spurts out of his flesh as the Gaul knifes himself to death.

THE PANTHEON (MAP 7)

The Pantheon *(☎ 06 683 00 230, Piazza della Rotonda; free; open 8.30am-7.30pm Mon-Sat, 9am-6pm Sun)* is the best-preserved building of ancient Rome. The original temple was built by Marcus Agrippa, son-in-law of Augustus, in 27 BC and was dedicated to the planetary gods. Although the temple was rebuilt by Emperor Hadrian around AD 120, Agrippa's name remained inscribed over the entrance, leading historians to believe it was the original building until excavations in the early 19th century revealed traces of the earlier temple.

The dramatic, imposing interior is the kind of place that inspires people to become architects. The height and diameter of the interior both measure 43.3m, and the extraordinary dome – the largest masonry vault ever built – is considered the most important achievement of ancient Roman architecture. Light is provided by the oculus – a 9m opening in the dome – and small holes in the marble floor beneath it allow any rain that enters to drain away. The weight of the dome is supported by brick arches embedded in the structure of the walls – evident from the exterior. Rivets and holes in the brickwork indicate where the original marble veneer panels have been removed. The 16 massive Corinthian columns of the portico are each a single block of stone.

After being abandoned under the first Christian emperors, the temple was given to the Church by the Eastern emperor, Phocus, in AD 608 and dedicated to the Madonna and all martyrs. Over the centuries the temple was consistently plundered and damaged. The gilded bronze roof tiles were removed by an emperor of the Eastern empire and in the 17th century Pope Urban VIII had the bronze ceiling of the portico melted down to make the *baldaccino* (canopy) over the main altar in St Peter's and 80 cannons for Castel Sant'Angelo. The Italian kings Vittorio Emanuele II and Umberto I and the artist Raphael are buried here.

CHIESA DI SANTA MARIA SOPRA MINERVA (MAP 3)

On Piazza della Minerva *(☎ 06 679 39 26, Piazza della Minerva; free; open 7am-7pm daily)*, just east of the Pantheon, this 13th-century Dominican church was built on the site of an ancient temple of Minerva. It was heavily restored in the Gothic style in the 19th century and contains a number of important art treasures, including superb frescoes by Filippino Lippi in the Cappella Carafa (c.1489), which depicts events in the life of St Thomas Aquinas and (left of the high altar) Michelangelo's statue of *Christ Bearing the Cross* (c.1520). The body of Santa Caterina di Siena, minus her head (which is in Siena) lies under the high altar. In the piazza in front of the church is a delightful Bernini statue of an elephant supporting an Egyptian obelisk.

TREVI FOUNTAIN (MAP 3)

This high-Baroque fountain (Fontana di Trevi) is one of Rome's most famous monuments. Completely dominating a tiny piazza, it was designed by Nicola Salvi in

1732. Its water is supplied by one of the city's earliest aqueducts. It is one of Rome's most famous monuments and is where Marcello Mastroianni and Anita Ekberg frolicked in Fellini's film *La Dolce Vita*. Neptune's chariot is led by Tritons with sea horses – one wild, one docile – representing the moods of the sea. The word Trevi refers to the three roads *(tre vie)* which converged at the fountain.

The famous custom is to throw a coin into the water (over your shoulder while facing away) to ensure you return to Rome. Toss a second coin and you'll fall in love with an Italian. Chuck a third coin at your peril – it will have you marrying him or her!

PIAZZA DI SPAGNA & THE SPANISH STEPS (MAP 3)

The piazza, church and famous Spanish Steps (Scalinata della Trinità dei Monti) have long provided a gathering place for foreigners. The piazza was named after the Spanish Embassy to the Holy See, although the staircase, built with a legacy from the French in 1725, leads to the French church, Trinità dei Monti.

To the right as you face the steps is the house where Keats died in 1821, now the **Keats-Shelley House** *(☎ 06 678 42 35, Piazza di Spagna 26; admission €2.60; open 9am-1pm & 2.30pm-5.30pm Mon-Fri)*. In the piazza is a fountain of a sinking boat, the **Barcaccia**, believed to be by Pietro Bernini, father of the famous Gian Lorenzo.

PIAZZA DEL POPOLO (MAP 2)

This vast piazza was laid out in the early 16th century at the point of convergence of the three roads – Via di Ripetta, Via del Corso and Via del Babuino – which form a trident at what was the main entrance to the city from the north. The two Baroque churches between the three roads are Santa Maria dei Miracoli and Santa Maria in Montesanto. The piazza was redesigned in the neoclassical style by Giuseppe Valadier in the early 19th century. In its centre is an obelisk brought by Augustus from Heliopolis, in ancient Greece, and moved here from the Circo Massimo in the mid-16th century. To the east is a ramp leading up to **Pincio Hill**, which affords a stunning view of the city.

The **Chiesa di Santa Maria del Popolo** *(☎ 06 361 08 36, Piazza del Popolo; free; open 7am-noon & 4pm-7pm Mon-Sat, 8am-2pm & 4.30pm-7.30pm Sun)* is next to the Porta del Popolo at the northern side of the piazza. This smorgasbord of art treasures dates from 1099. Bramante designed the apse and the vault frescoes (c.1509) are by Pinturicchio, who also painted the lunettes and the *Adoration* in the Della Rovere chapel. Raphael designed the Cappella Chigi, which features a macabre mosaic of a kneeling skeleton, but it was completed by Bernini 100 years after Raphael's death. Don't miss Caravaggio's *Conversion of St Paul* and *Crucifixion of St Peter* in the Cerasi chapel.

Caravaggio Crawl

Rome has more masterpieces by Caravaggio than any other city in the world. They are spread between museums, churches and private collections. For starters, head for the Capitoline Museums, Galleria Borghese, Galleria Doria Pamphilj, Galleria Nazionale d'Arte Antica, the Pinacoteca at the Vatican Museums, San Luigi dei Francesi, Chiesa di Santa Maria del Popolo and Chiesa di Sant'Agostino.

Trouble with the law was a daily fact of life for Michelangelo Merisi da Caravaggio (1573–1610), who arrived in Rome around 1590. He fled the city in 1606 after killing his opponent in a ball game, spent four years on the run in Naples, Malta and Sicily, and died in Tuscany at the age of 36.

Caravaggio's paintings were as controversial as his behaviour. His innovative and dramatic use of lighting influenced generations of subsequent artists. He used peasants and prostitutes as his models, which gave the Madonnas and saints of his paintings a realism that was not always well received. He often had to repaint commissions for churches because the subjects were deemed to be too lifelike: saints would *not* have had such dirty feet. Several of these rejected works were snapped up by intuitive private collectors, including Cardinal Scipione Borghese.

THE VATICAN (Map 3)

LEE FOSTER

After unification in 1861, the Papal States of central Italy became part of the new Kingdom of Italy, losing much of their former power and causing a considerable rift between the church and the state. In 1929, Mussolini signed the Lateran Treaty (or Concordat) with Pius XI, giving the pope full sovereignty over what is now the Vatican City (Città del Vaticano). The Lateran Treaty also granted extra-territoriality to the basilicas of San Giovanni in Laterano (as well as the Palazzo Laterano), Santa Maria Maggiore and San Paolo Fuori-le-Mura.

The Vatican City is the smallest independent state in existence. It has its own postal service, currency, newspaper, radio station and train station (now used only for freight). It also has its own army of Swiss Guards, responsible for the pope's personal security. The corps was established in 1506 by Julius II to defend the Papal States against invading armies. The guards still wear the traditional eye-catching red, yellow and blue uniform (not, as legend would have it, designed by Michelangelo) and brandish unwieldy 15th-century pikes, but they are in fact highly trained soldiers. The guards are at the pope's side whenever he appears in public and accompany him on all overseas trips.

Dress regulations are stringently enforced at St Peter's Basilica (Basilica di San Pietro) and throughout the Vatican. It is forbidden to enter the church wearing shorts (men included) or a short skirt, or with bare shoulders.

LEE FOSTER

Right: Head busts in the Vatican Museum

Building the Vatican

When Pope Symmachus (498–514) was ousted from the Palazzo Laterano by the Emperor Theodoric the Great, he had a mansion built for himself on the Vatican hill next to St Peter's Basilica. Charlemagne stayed at the Vatican during his visits to Rome in 781 and 800. In 846, after a Saracen fleet sailed up the Tiber and attacked Rome, Pope Leo IV built a protective barrier – the Leonine Walls – around the Vatican area.

The Vatican Palace (Palazzo Vaticano) was restored by Pope Eugenius III in 1150 and Pope Celestine made further improvements in 1191. Under Innocent III (1198–1216) and Nicholas III (1277–1280), the palace was enlarged and fortified; the latter linked Castel Sant'Angelo to the Vatican palaces in 1277 by a wall and passageway, which allowed the popes to escape to the fortress in times of threat.

During the Great Schism, the Palazzo Laterano had become uninhabitable, so on his return to Rome from Avignon in 1377, Gregory XI took up residence in the Vatican. Subsequent centuries saw massive expansion of the Vatican Palace, with many popes overseeing significant additions.

Nicholas V (1447–55) turned the mansion into a palace, which he built around the Cortile dei Pappagalli. Sixtus IV (1471–84) built the Sistine Chapel (Cappella Sistina) in 1473.

The Belvedere pavilion was added under Innocent VIII in the late 15th century. It was built as a summer *casino* (house) on the northern summit of the Vatican hill. Julius II situated his impressive collection of classical sculpture in the Belvedere and had Donato Bramante design a new entrance to the palace, which included a spiral staircase up which horses could be ridden. Under Julius II, Bramante also created the Cortile del Belvedere when he joined the Belvedere to Nicholas V's palace and the Sistine Chapel with long corridors.

The courtyard was subsequently sliced into three smaller sections with the additions of the Biblioteca Apostolica (Vatican Library) under Pope Sixtus V and the Braccio Nuovo under Pope Pius VII. The northern courtyard, the Cortile della Pigna, is named after the colossal bronze pine cone, dating from the 1st or 2nd century, placed there in 1608 by Paul V. As part of the conversion of the Belvedere into a museum in the late 18th century, a monumental staircase (by Michelangelo Simonetti) was added, as well as a new entrance, the Atrio dei Quattro Cancelli.

The 20th century saw more additions. Pius XI unveiled a new *pinacoteca* (art gallery) and a new entrance to the museums in 1932. New galleries of modern religious art in the Borgia apartments were opened in 1973, and in the same year the new Museo Missionario-Ethnologico (Ethnological Missionary Museum) was inaugurated. Under John Paul II, a new entrance to the museums was opened in 2000. The magnificent Simonetti staircase is now the exit.

An Audience with the Pope

On Wednesday the pope meets his flock. For permission to attend an audience, go to the Prefettura della Casa Pontificia (☎ 69 88 46 31), through the bronze doors under the colonnade to the right of St Peter's as you face the church. The office opens 9am to 1pm and you can apply on the Tuesday before the audience (or, at a push, on the morning of the audience). You can also apply in writing to the Prefettura della Casa Pontificia, 00120 Città del Vaticano or fax 06 698 83 865. Specify the date you'd like to attend and the number of tickets required. If you have a hotel in Rome, the office will forward the (free) tickets there.

INFORMATION & SERVICES

The Centro Servizi Pellegrini e Turisti (tourist office; ☎ 06 698 81 662, fax 06 698 81 694) is in Piazza San Pietro to the left of the basilica. It opens 8.30am to 7pm Monday to Saturday and has general information about St Peter's and the Vatican, including times of daily Mass.

The Vatican post office, said to provide a faster and more reliable service than the normal Italian postal system, is a few doors from the tourist office (there is another outlet on the other side of the piazza and one in the Vatican Museums). Letters can be posted in blue Vatican post boxes only if they carry Vatican stamps.

PIAZZA SAN PIETRO

Bernini's piazza is considered a masterpiece. Laid out in the 17th century as a place for the Christians of the world to gather, the immense square is bounded by two semicircular colonnades, each of which is made up of four rows of Doric columns. In the centre of the piazza is an obelisk brought to Rome by Caligula from Heliopolis in ancient Egypt.

ST PETER'S BASILICA (BASILICA DI SAN PIETRO)

In the same area where St Peter's Basilica *(Piazza San Pietro; admission free to basilica, €3.10 to dome; open 7am-7pm daily Apr-Sept, 7am-6pm daily Oct-Mar, dome ascent opens 8am year-round)* now stands, there was once the Circo Vaticano, built by Nero. It was probably in this stadium that St Peter and other Christians were martyred between AD 64 and 67. The body of St Peter was buried in an anonymous grave next to the wall of the circus and his fellow Christians built a humble red wall to mark the site (see the boxed text 'St Peter's Tomb' later). In AD 160, the stadium was abandoned and a small monument erected on the grave. In 315 Emperor Constantine ordered the construction of a basilica on the site of the apostle's tomb, and the first St Peter's was consecrated in 326.

By the mid-15th century, after more than 1000 years, the church was in a poor state of repair and Pope Nicholas V put architects, including Alberti, to work on its reconstruction. But it was not until 1506, when Pope Julius II employed Donato Bramante, that serious work began. Bramante designed a new basilica on a Greek cross plan, with a central dome and four smaller domes. He oversaw the demolition of

ST PETER'S BASILICA

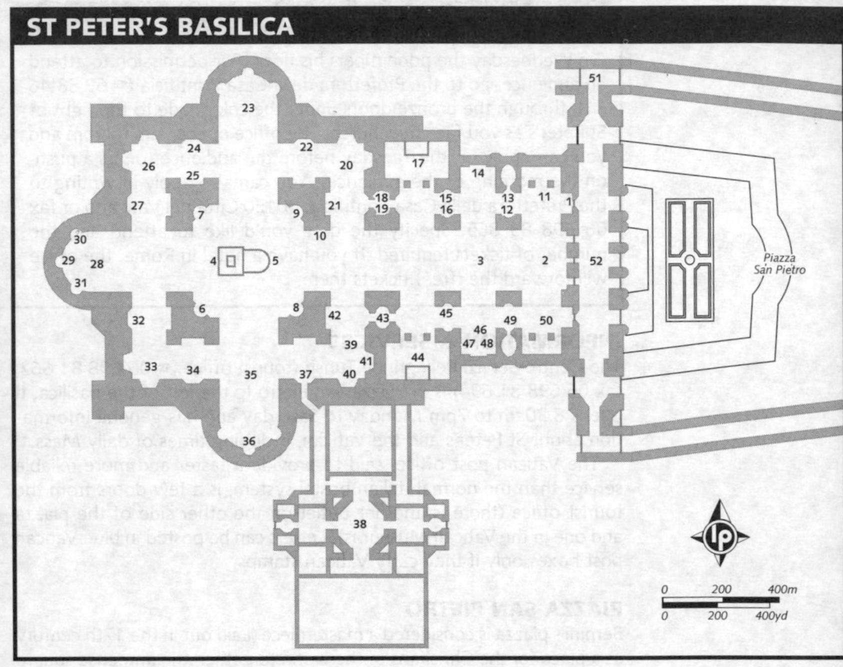

much of the old basilica and attracted great criticism for the unnecessary destruction of many of its precious works of art.

It took more than 150 years to complete the new basilica, with contributions from Bramante, Raphael, Antonio da Sangallo, Michelangelo, Giacomo della Porta and Carlo Maderno. It is generally held that St Peter's owes most to Michelangelo, who took over the project in 1547 at the age of 72 and was responsible for the design of the dome. He died before the church was completed.

The facade and portico were designed by Maderno, who took over the project after Michelangelo's death. He was also instructed to lengthen the nave towards the piazza, effectively altering Bramante's original Greek cross plan to a Latin cross. Restoration work on the facade was carried out between 1997 and 1999. This mainly consisted of cleaning the travertine marble and repairing damage caused by age and pollution.

The cavernous interior, decorated by Bernini and Giacomo della Porta, can hold up to 60,000 people. It contains art treasures, including Michelangelo's superb *Pietà*, sculpted when he was only 25 years old and the only work to carry his signature (on the sash across the breast of the Madonna), at the beginning of the right aisle. It is now protected by bulletproof glass after a hammer-wielding vandal attacked it in 1972. The red porphyry disk just inside the main door marks the spot where Charlemagne and later Holy Roman Emperors were crowned by the pope.

ST PETER'S BASILICA

1 Porta Santa
2 Red Porphyry Disk
3 Bronze Plates
4 Baldacchino
5 Confessione
6 Pier of St Veronica
7 Pier of St Helena
8 Pier of St Andrew
9 Pier of St Longinus; Entrance to Vatican Grottoes
10 Statue of St Peter
11 Pietà
12 Monument to Queen Christina of Sweden
13 Statue of Leo XII; Entrance to Cappella del Crocifisso
14 Cappella di San Sebastiano
15 Monument to Innocent XII
16 Monument to Countess Matilda of Tuscany
17 Cappella del Santissimo Sacramento
18 Monument to Gregory XIII
19 Unfinished Tomb of Gregory XIV
20 Cappella Gregoriana
21 Communion of St Jerome Mosaic
22 Tomb of Benedict XIV
23 South Transept
24 Monument to Clement XIII
25 Altare della Navicella
26 Cappella di San Michele
27 Monument to Clement X
28 Tribune
29 Throne of St Peter
30 Monument to Urban VIII
31 Monument to Paul III
32 Monument to Alexander VIII
33 Cappella della Colonna
34 Monument to Alexander VII
35 North Transept
36 Tomb of Giovanni Pierluigi da Palestrina
37 Entrance to Sacristy
38 Museo Storico Artistico (Treasury)
39 Cappella Clementina
40 Tomb of St Gregory the Great
41 Monument to Pius VII
42 Mosaic of the Transfiguration
43 Monument to Leo XI
44 Cappella del Coro
45 Monument to Innocent VIII
46 Cappella della Presentazione
47 Monument to John XXIII
48 Monument to Benedict XV
49 Stuart Monuments
50 Baptistry
51 Entrance to Dome
52 Portico

Bernini's Baroque *baldacchino* (canopy) stands 29m high in the centre of the church and is an extraordinary work of art. The bronze used to make it was taken from the Pantheon. The high altar, which only the pope can use, stands over the site of St Peter's grave.

To the right as you face the high altar is a famous bronze statue of St Peter, believed to be a 13th-century work by Arnolfo di Cambio. The statue's right foot has been worn down by the kisses and touch of many pilgrims.

Michelangelo's dome, a majestic architectural masterpiece, soars 119m above the high altar. Its balconies are decorated with reliefs depicting the Reliquie Maggiori (Major Relics) – the lance of San Longino, which he used to pierce Christ's side; the cloth of Santa Veronica, which bears a miraculous image of Christ; and a piece of the True Cross, collected by Sant'Elena, the mother of Emperor Constantine. Entry to the dome is to the right as you climb the stairs to the atrium of the basilica. Access to the roof of the church is by elevator or stairs; from there, you ascend the stairs to the base of the dome for a view down into the basilica. A narrow staircase leads eventually to the top of the dome and St Peter's lantern, from where you have an unequalled view of Rome. It is well worth the effort, but bear in mind that it's a long and tiring climb.

The Vatican Grottoes (Sacre Grotte Vaticane) below the church are the resting place of numerous popes. The tombs of many early popes

St Peter's Tomb

The excavations beneath St Peter's, which began in 1940, have uncovered part of the original church, an early Christian cemetery and Roman tombs. Archaeologists believe they have also found the tomb of St Peter; the site of the empty tomb is marked by a shrine and a wall plastered with red. Nearby is another wall, scrawled with the graffiti of pilgrims; in 1942 the bones of an elderly, strongly built man were found in a box placed in a niche behind this wall. In 1976, after many years of forensic examination, Paul VI declared the bones to be those of St Peter. John Paul II had some of the relics transferred to his hospital room when he was recovering from the 1981 assassination attempt. The bones were then returned to the tomb and are kept in hermetically sealed perspex cases designed by NASA.

The excavations can be visited only by appointment, which can be made either in writing or in person at the Ufficio Scavi (☎ 06 698 85 318, fax 06 698 85 518), in Piazza Braschi. Address your letter to Ufficio Scavi, 00120 Città del Vaticano, and stipulate the date you'd like to visit. The office will then contact you to confirm the time and date. You need to book at least one week ahead; tickets cost €5.20. The office opens 9am to 5pm Monday to Friday. Small groups are taken most days between 9am and noon and 2pm to 5pm.

were moved here from the old St Peter's, and more recent popes, including John XXIII, Paul VI and John Paul I, are also buried here. The entrance is next to the pier of San Longino (one of four piers supporting the arches at the base of Michelangelo's cupola), to the right as you approach the papal altar.

VATICAN MUSEUMS

The incredible collection of art and treasures accumulated by the popes can be seen at the Vatican Museums *(Musei Vaticani;* ☎ *06 698 84 341 or 06 698 84 947,* 🅆 *www.vatican.va/museums; adult/reduced €9.30/6.20; open 8.45am-4.45pm (last admission 3.30pm) Mon-Fri, 8.45am-1.45pm (last admission 12.45pm) Sat mid-Mar–late-Oct, 8.45am-1.45pm (last admission 12.45pm) Mon-Sat the rest of the year, closed Sun except last Sun of month 9am-1pm year-round)*. You will need several hours to see the most important areas and museums.

Make sure you pick up a floor-plan leaflet. There are four 'one-way' itineraries, which have been mapped out with the aim of simplifying visits and containing the huge number of visitors. It is basically compulsory that you follow the itineraries (which vary in duration from 1½ to 5 hours) but you can make some deviations if you want. The new entrance (with every facility you could want) leads up to the area known as the Quattro Cancelli, where each of the separate itineraries starts.

Another point to note is that the Sistine Chapel comes towards the end of each itinerary. If you want to spend most of your time in the chapel or you want to get there early to avoid the crowds, it is possible to walk straight there and then walk back to the Quattro Cancelli to pick up one of the itineraries. Most tour groups (and there are many!) head straight to the chapel and it is almost always very crowded. You can also hire CD audio guides.

The museums are well equipped for disabled visitors; there are four suggested itineraries, several lifts and specially fitted toilets. Ask for a folder at the ticket window or information desk or call in advance on ☎ 06 698 84 341. Wheelchairs can be reserved. Parents with young children can take pushchairs into the museums.

The buildings that house the Vatican Museums, known collectively as the Palazzo Apostolico Vaticano, cover an area of 5½ hectares. Their construction has been a work in progress since the 5th century (see the boxed text 'Building the Vatican' earlier). The buildings to the west of the Quattro Cancelli are the most recent and house the Museo Gregoriano Profano (Gregorian Museum of Pagan Antiquities), the Museo Pio-Cristiano (Pio Christian Museum), the Pinacoteca, the Museo Missionario-Etnologico and a carriage museum. These galleries come last on the longer itineraries and are probably the ones to miss if you run out of time.

The **Museo Gregoriano Egizio** (Egyptian Museum) contains pieces taken from Egypt in Roman times. The collection is small but there are fascinating exhibits including the *Throne of Rameses II*, part of a statue of the seated king.

The Vatican's enormous collection of ancient sculpture is contained in a series of galleries. The long corridor that forms the **Museo Chiaramonti** contains hundreds of marble busts, while the **Braccio Nuovo** (New Wing) contains some important works. These include a famous statue of Augustus, and a carving depicting the Nile as a reclining god with 16 babies (which are thought to represent the number of cubits the Nile rose when in flood) playing on him.

The **Museo Pio-Clementino** is in the Belvedere Pavilion. In the Cortile Ottagono (Octagonal Courtyard) is part of the Vatican sculpture collection: the *Apollo Belvedere*, a 2nd-century Roman copy in marble of a 4th-century BC Greek bronze, considered one of the great masterpieces of classical sculpture; and, notably, the *Laocoön*, depicting a Trojan priest of Apollo and his two sons in mortal struggle with two sea serpents. This statue was excavated from the Domus Aurea area.

In the **Sala delle Muse** (Room of the Muses) is the *Belvedere Torso*, a Greek sculpture of the 1st century BC, which was found in the Piazza Campo de' Fiori during the time of Pope Julius II and was much admired by Michelangelo and other Renaissance artists. In the **Sala a Croce Greca** (Greek Cross Room) are the porphyry sarcophagi of Constantine's daughter, Constantia, and his mother, Sant'Elena.

Up one flight of the Simonetti staircase is the **Museo Gregoriano Etrusco** (Etruscan Museum), which contains artefacts from Etruscan tombs in southern Etruria. Of particular interest are those from the Regolini-Galassi tomb, discovered in 1836 south of Cerveteri. Those buried in the tomb included a princess, and among the finds on display are gold jewellery and a funeral carriage with a bronze bed and funeral couch. A collection of Greek vases and Roman antiquities is also displayed in the museum.

Michelangelo in Rome

Michelangelo Buonarotti was born in Caprese near Arezzo in Tuscany in 1475, the son of a Tuscan magistrate. He was a moody and solitary figure, easily offended and irritated. The true Renaissance man, he was a supremely talented architect and painter but he regarded himself as a sculptor above all else.

And it was as a sculptor that Michelangelo achieved his early recognition. One of his greatest early carvings is the *Pietà* in St Peter's Basilica, which he completed when he was 25.

Michelangelo came to work in Rome for Pope Julius II, who wanted a grand marble tomb for himself which would surpass any funerary monument that had ever been built. Although the tomb preoccupied Michelangelo throughout his working life, it was never completed and Julius II lies in an unadorned grave in St Peter's. The original design included 40 statues. The famous figure of Moses as well as statues of Leah and Rachel are in the church of San Pietro in Vincoli (in Rome). Two of the slaves are now in the Louvre and several famous unfinished slaves are in the Accademia in Florence.

Despite claiming to be a reluctant painter, Michelangelo's single greatest artistic achievement – and one of the most awe-inspiring acts of individual creativity in the history of the visual arts – is the ceiling of the Sistine Chapel, painted between 1508 and 1512.

Michelangelo never wanted the commission (also from Julius II) and the project was problematic from the outset. First the artist rejected the scaffolding that Bramante had built for him; then he considered his assistants so incompetent that he dismissed them all, scraped off their work and ended up painting the entire ceiling by himself. The artist was pushed to his physical and emotional limits, and was continually harassed by the pope and his court, who wanted the job finished.

Michelangelo returned to Rome aged 59 at the request of Pope Clement VII to paint the *Last Judgment* on the altar wall of the Sistine Chapel. Once again he accepted the commission against his will, preferring to continue sculpting figures for Julius II's tomb which he did secretly while he prepared the Last Judgment cartoons.

On Clement VII's death, his successor Paul III was determined to have Michelangelo working exclusively for him and have the Sistine Chapel completed; in 1535 he appointed Michelangelo as chief

Through the superb **Galleria delle Carte Geografiche** (Map Gallery) and the **Galleria degli Arazzi** (Tapestry Gallery) are the magnificent **Stanze di Raffaello**, the private apartments of Pope Julius II. Raphael painted the Stanza della Segnatura and the Stanza d'Eliodoro, while the Stanza dell'Incendio was painted by his students to his designs and the ceiling was painted by his master, Perugino. In the Stanza della Segnatura is one of Raphael's masterpieces, *La Scuola d'Atene* (The School of Athens), featuring philosophers and scholars gathered around Plato and Aristotle. Opposite is *La Disputa del Sacramento*

Michelangelo in Rome

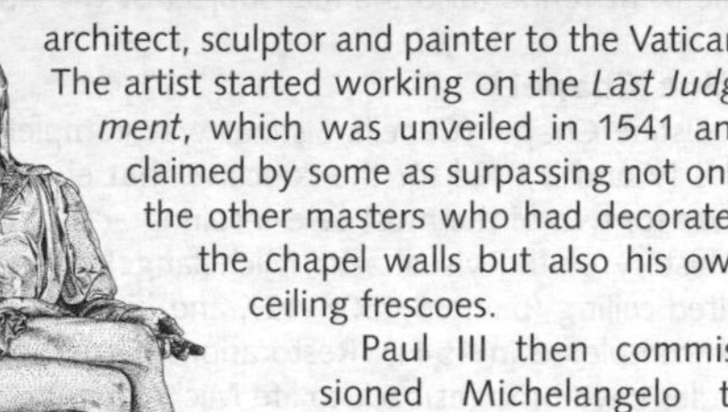
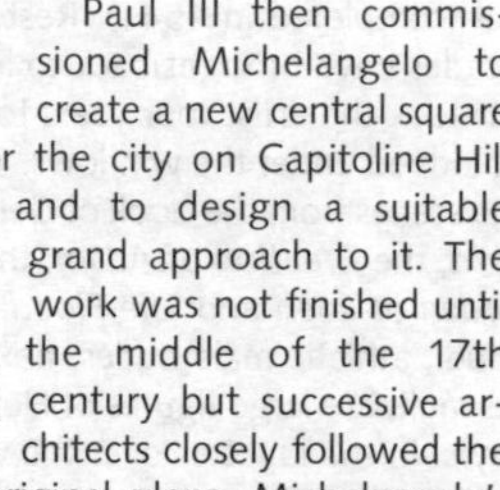

TRUDI CANAVAN

Michelangelo's exquisite *Piéta*.

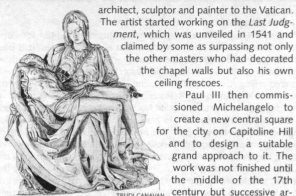

architect, sculptor and painter to the Vatican. The artist started working on the *Last Judgment*, which was unveiled in 1541 and claimed by some as surpassing not only the other masters who had decorated the chapel walls but also his own ceiling frescoes.

Paul III then commissioned Michelangelo to create a new central square for the city on Capitoline Hill and to design a suitable grand approach to it. The work was not finished until the middle of the 17th century but successive architects closely followed the original plans. Michelangelo's design for the upper storey of the Palazzo Farnese was also realised posthumously when Giacomo della Porta completed the building; similarly his design for the city gateway at Porta Pia was not finished until a year after his death.

The artist spent his last years working – unhappily (he felt that it was a penance from God) – on St Peter's Basilica. He disapproved of the plans that had been drawn up by Antonio da Sangallo the Younger before his death, claiming that they deprived the basilica of light, and argued with Sangallo's assistants who wanted to retain their master's designs. Instead Michelangelo created the magnificent light-filled dome based on Brunelleschi's design for the cathedral Florence, and a stately facade.

In his old age, he was said to work with the same strength and concentration as he had as a younger man. He continued to direct the work until his death on 18 February 1564. He was buried in the Chiesa dei Santi Apostoli, although his remains were later moved to Florence. The dome and facade of St Peter's were completed to his designs by Vignola, Giacomo della Porta and Carlo Fontana.

(Disputation on the Sacrament), also by Raphael. In the Stanza d'Eliodoro is another Raphael masterpiece, *Expulsion of Heliodorus from the Temple*, on the main wall (to the right as you enter from the Sala dei Chiaroscuri), which symbolises Julius' military victory over foreign powers. To the left is *Mass of Bolsena*, showing Julius II paying homage to a relic from a 13th-century miracle in that town. Next is *Leone X ferma l'invasione di Attila* (Leo X Repulsing Attila), by Raphael and his school, and on the fourth wall is *Liberazione di San Pietro* (Liberation of St Peter), which depicts the saint being freed from prison but is actually an allusion to Pope Leo's imprisonment after the battle of Ravenna (also the real subject of the Attila fresco).

Sistine Chapel

The Sistine Chapel (Capella Sistina) was completed in 1484 for Pope Sixtus IV and is used for the conclave that elects the popes. It is best known for two of the most awe-inspiring acts of individual creativity in the history of the visual arts: Michelangelo's **frescoes** on the barrel-vaulted ceiling (painted 1508–12), and his **Last Judgment** on the end wall (completed in 1541). Restorations carried out over the past two decades have brought back to life Michelangelo's rich, vibrant colours.

It took the artist four years to paint the ceiling, working on scaffolding lodged under the windows. The frescoes down the middle represent nine scenes from the book of Genesis, including the *Division of Day from Night*, the *Creation of Adam*, the *Expulsion of Adam and Eve from the Garden of Eden* and *The Flood*. These main images are framed by the **Ignudi**, athletic male nudes; next to them, on the lower curved part of the vault, are large figures of Hebrew **Prophets** and androgynous pagan **Sibyls**. In the lunettes over the windows are the ancestors of Christ.

More than 20 years later, Michelangelo was commissioned to paint the Last Judgment. The dramatic, swirling mass of predominantly naked bodies caused a scandal when it was unveiled and Pope Pius IV had Daniele da Volterra (one of Michelangelo's students) do a cover-up job with fig leaves and loin cloths in appropriate places.

The walls of the chapel were painted by important Renaissance artists, including Botticelli, Domenico Ghirlandaio, Pinturicchio and Luca Signorelli. Try to drag your attention away from Michelangelo's frescoes to appreciate these late 15th-century works, depicting events in the lives of Moses and Christ; thanks to a recent restoration, they are as stunning as the ceiling. Botticelli's *Temptation of Christ and the Cleansing of the Leper* (second fresco on the right) is particularly beautiful, with its typical Botticelli maiden in a diaphanous dress. The first frescoes in each cycle, *Finding of Moses* and *Birth of Christ* by Perugino, were destroyed to make way for the *Last Judgment* – a great controversy at the time.

CASTEL SANT'ANGELO

Originally the mausoleum of Emperor Hadrian, this building was converted into a fortress for the popes in the 6th century AD. It was named Castel Sant'Angelo *(☎ 06 681 91 11, Lungotevere Castello; €5.20; open 9am-8pm Tues-Sun)* by Pope Gregory the Great in AD 590, after he saw a vision of an angel above the structure heralding the end of a plague in Rome. The fortress was linked to the Vatican palaces in 1277 by a wall and passageway, often used by the popes to escape to the fortress in times of threat. During the 16th century sacking of Rome by Emperor Charles V, hundreds of people lived in the fortress for months.

Hadrian built the **Ponte Sant'Angelo** across the River Tiber in AD 136 to provide an approach to his mausoleum. It collapsed in 1450 and was subsequently rebuilt, incorporating parts of the ancient bridge. In the 17th century, Bernini and his pupils sculpted the figures of angels which now line the pedestrian-only bridge.

ARA PACIS (MAP 3)

The **Ara Pacis Augustae** *(Altar of Peace; ☎ 06 688 06 848; call for opening hours)* was inaugurated in 13 BC to commemorate the peace that Augustus had established both at home and abroad. The actual altar is enclosed by a marble wall decorated with reliefs – historical scenes on the north and south friezes and mythological scenes at the east and west. It is one of the most important works in the history of ancient Roman sculpture and represents the point at which Roman art emerged as a distinct entity. Panels excavated from the 16th century onwards ended up in the Medici collection, the Vatican and the Louvre; in 1937, under Mussolini, the remaining parts were reassembled in the present location. A new, state-of-the-art museum complex designed by Richard Meier is due to open in 2002.

Just east of the monument is the **Mausoleo d'Augusto** *(Mausoleum of Augustus, not open to public)*, built by the emperor for himself and his family. It was originally faced with marble and was converted into a fortress during the Middle Ages. It then served various purposes until restored to its original state in 1936.

VILLA BORGHESE & AROUND (MAP 2)

This beautiful park, just north-east of the Piazza del Popolo, was once the estate of Cardinal Scipione Borghese. The main entrance is from Piazzale Flaminio but it is also accessible through the park at the top of Pincio Hill. It's a good place to have a picnic or to take children for a break from sightseeing.

Also in the park is the **Bioparco** *(☎ 06 321 65 64; admission €3.10; open 8am-5.45pm daily Apr-Sept, 8am-4.45pm daily Oct-Mar)*, the flashy new name for the former Zoological Gardens, at the northern end of the park in Viale del Giardino Zoologico. There are better ways to spend your money but kids might enjoy it.

Galleria Borghese

The Galleria Borghese *(☎ 06 3 28 10, Piazzale Scipione Borghese; adult/reduced €7.25/4.15, booking advised; open 9am-7pm Tues-Sun)* was formed by Cardinal Scipione Borghese, the most passionate and knowledgeable connoisseur of his day. The collection and the mansion were acquired by the Italian state in 1902; a lengthy restoration took place in the 1990s.

The ground floor contains some important classical statuary, intricate Roman floor mosaics and Antonio Canova's daring sculpture of Paolina Bonaparte Borghese as a reclining *Venere Vincitrice*, her diaphanous drapery leaving little to the imagination. But Bernini's spectacular carvings – flamboyant depictions of pagan myths – are the stars. His precocious talent is evident in works such as *Ratto di Proserpina* (Rape of Persephone) where Pluto's hand presses into Persephone's solid marble thigh and in the swirling *Apollo e Dafne*, which depicts the exact moment when the nymph is transformed into a laurel tree, her fingers becoming leaves, her toes turning into tree roots, while Apollo watches helplessly.

There are six Caravaggio paintings including several early works, as well as masterpieces by Giovanni Bellini, Giorgione, Veronese, Botticelli, Guercino, Domenichino and Rubens, among others. Highlights are Raphael's *Deposizione di Cristo* of 1507 and Titian's early masterpiece *Amor Sacro e Amor Profano*.

Galleria Nazionale d'Arte Moderna

The *belle époque* palazzo housing the **Galleria Nazionale d'Arte Moderna** *(☎ 06 32 29 81, Viale delle Belle Arti 131; adult/reduced €6.20/3.10; open 9am-7.30pm Tues-Sun)* was built for the 1911 Rome international exhibition. It now showcases 19th- and 20th-century painting and sculpture, including work by De Chirico, Carrà, Fontana and Guttuso, the futurists (Boccioni, Balla), and the *Transavanguardia* (Clemente, Paladino, Cucchi). Degas, Cézanne, Kandinsky, Mondrian,

There's also a modern international collection in which works by Henry Moore and Cy Twombly stand out.

Museo Nazionale Etrusco di Villa Giulia (Map 2)

Situated in the 16th-century villa of Pope Julius III, at the top end of the Villa Borghese, this museum *(☎ 06 320 19 51, Piazzale di Villa Giulia 9; admission €4.15; open 9am-7.30pm Tues-Sun)* houses the national collection of Etruscan treasures, many of which were found in tombs at sites throughout Lazio. If you plan to visit Etruscan sites near Rome, a visit to the museum before setting out will give you a good understanding of Etruscan culture. There are thousands of exhibits, including domestic objects, cooking utensils, terracotta vases and amphoras, distinctive black bucchero tableware, bronze mirrors engraved with mythological scenes, and the remains of a horse drawn chariot. An Etruscan tomb has been reconstructed, complete with burial objects and armchairs sculpted into the rock.

Of particular note is the polychrome terracotta statue of Apollo and other pieces found at Veio, dating from the late 6th century or early 5th century BC. Another highlight is the *Sarcofago degli Sposi* made for a husband and wife, from a tomb at Cerveteri.

AROUND VIA VITTORIO VENETO (MAP 4)

The *dolce vita* atmosphere of the 1960s is long dead, but Via Vittorio Veneto still has its attractions.

The **Chiesa di Santa Maria della Concezione** *(☎ 06 487 11 85, Via Vittorio Veneto 27; admission by compulsory donation; open 9am-noon & 3pm-6pm Fri-Wed)* is an austere 17th-century church, but the Capuchin cemetery beneath (access is on the right of the church steps) features a bizarre display of the bones of some 4000 monks, used to decorate the walls of a series of chapels between 1528 and 1870.

In the centre of **Piazza Barberini**, at the southern end of Via Vittorio Veneto, is the spectacular **Fontana del Tritone** (Fountain of the Triton), created by Bernini in 1643 for Pope Urban VIII, patriarch of the Barberini family. It features a Triton blowing a stream of water from a conch shell. In the north-eastern corner of the piazza is another fountain, the **Fontana delle Api** (Fountain of the Bees), created by the same artist for the Barberini family, whose crest, which features three bees, can be seen on many buildings throughout Rome.

The 17th-century Palazzo Barberini is well worth a visit. Carlo Maderno was commissioned to build the palazzo by Urban VIII, and both Bernini and Borromini worked on its construction for the Barberini family. The building houses part of the **Galleria Nazionale d'Arte Antica** *(☎ 06 481 45 91, Palazzo Barberini, Via delle Quattro Fontane, entry at Via Barberini 18; admission €6.20; open 9am-7pm Tues-Sat, 9am-8pm Sun)*, which includes paintings by Raphael, Caravaggio, Guido Reni, Guercino, Bronzino, Bernini, Filippo Lippi and Holbein. A highlight is the ceiling of the main salon, entitled the *Triumph of Divine Providence* and painted by Pietro da Cortona.

QUIRINALE (MAP 4)

The **Palazzo del Quirinale** *(☎ 06 469 92 568, Piazza del Quirinale; admission €5.20; open 8.30am-12.30pm 2nd & 4th Sunday of month)* is the official residence of the president of the Republic. Built and added to from 1574 to the early 18th century, it was the summer residence of the popes until 1870, when it became the royal palace of the kings of Italy.

The obelisk in the centre of the piazza was moved here from the Mausoleo di Augusto in 1786. It is flanked by the large statues of the Dioscuri, Castor and Pollux, which are Imperial-era copies of 5th-century-BC Greek originals.

Along the Via del Quirinale are two excellent examples of Baroque architecture: the churches of **Sant'Andrea al Quirinale** *(☎ 06 489 03 187, Via del Quirinale 29; free; open 9am-noon & 4pm-7pm Mon-Fri, 9am-noon Sat)*, designed by Bernini, and **San Carlo alle Quattro Fontane** *(☎ 06 488 32 61, Via del Quirinale 23; free; open 9.30am-12.30pm daily)*, designed by Borromini. Sant'Andrea is considered one of Bernini's masterpieces. He designed it with an elliptical floor plan and with a series of chapels opening onto the central area. The interior is decorated with polychrome marble, stucco and gilding. Note the cherubs that adorn the lantern of the dome. San Carlo was the first church designed by Borromini in Rome and it was completed in 1641. The small cloister was also designed by Borromini. The church stands at the intersection known as Quattro Fontane, after the late-16th-century fountains at its four corners.

TERME DI DIOCLEZIANO (MAP 4)

The complex of baths, libraries, concert halls and gardens that made up the Terme di Diocleziano (Diocletian's Baths) was completed in the early 4th century. It was the largest of its kind in ancient Rome, covering about 13 hectares and with a capacity of 3000 people. The complex fell into disrepair after the aqueduct that fed the baths was destroyed by invaders in about AD 536.

Michelangelo incorporated the main hall and *tepidarium* of Diocletian's baths into the design of the **Basilica di Santa Maria degli Angeli** *(☎ 06 488 08 12, Piazza della Repubblica; free; open 7.30am-12.30pm & 4pm-6.30pm daily)*, although only the great vaulted ceiling remains from his original plans. The meridian in the transept traces both the polar star and the time of the sun's zenith (visible at noon).

The **Museo Nazionale Romano Terme di Diocleziano** *(☎ 06 481 55 76; Via Enrico di Nicola 78; adult/reduced €4.20/2.10; open 9am-7pm Tues-Sun)* is in part of the baths complex. Ancient epigraphs and artefacts from Italian protohistory are the focus of this section of the Museo Nazionale Romano, although its elegant Renaissance cloister is lined with classical sarcophagi, capitals and (mostly headless) statues.

PALAZZO MASSIMO ALLE TERME (MAP 4)

Palazzo Massimo all Terme *(☎ 06 489 03 500, Largo di Villa Peretti 1; adults/reduced €6.20/3.10; open 9am-7.45pm Tues-Sun)*, part of the Museo Nazionale Romano collection, boasts some of the best examples of Roman art in the city. The commissioned sculptural portraits of emperors, statesmen and their families (in the ground-floor galleries) are idealised representations of the ruling classes. Realism had little to do with these busts and statues; self-glorification was the order of the day.

The highlights of the museum are the sensational Roman paintings and mosaics, including frescoes (dating from at least 20–10 BC) from the excavated Villa Livia, which belonged to the wife of Augustus. These stunning frescoes depict an illusionary garden with cypresses, pines, oleander, myrtle and laurel, and fruit trees abundant with ripe pomegranates and quinces.

SAN PAOLO FUORI-LE-MURA (MAP 1)

The basilica of **San Paolo Fuori-le-Mura** *(St Paul's Outside the Walls, ☎ 06 541 03 41, Via Ostiense 186; Metro Linea B to San Paolo; free; open 7.30am-6.30pm daily)* was built by Constantine on the site of St Paul's burial and was destroyed by fire in 1823. The 5th-century mosaics on the triumphal arch, a Romanesque paschal candlestick, and the marble tabernacle (c.1285) by Arnolfo di Cambio survived. The reconstruction recreates some sense of the huge scale of the original; until the construction of the present-day St Peter's, this was the largest church in the world. The **cloisters** survived the fire and are a masterpiece of Cosmati work, with elaborate mosaic-encrusted columns.

SAN LORENZO FUORI-LE-MURA (MAP 1)

Constantine's 4th-century church, built over the martyred St Laurence's burial place, was joined with another early Christian church nearby; medieval additions and later WW2 bombing raids gave us the basilica of **San Lorenzo Fuori-le-Mura** *(St Lawrence Outside the Walls; ☎ 06 49 15 11, Piazzale del Verano 3; free; open 7.30am-noon & 4pm-6.30pm daily)* we see today, highlights of which are the Cosmatesque floor, 13th-century frescoed portico, and the catacombs of Santa Ciriaca where St Laurence was buried.

VIA APPIA ANTICA & THE CATACOMBS (MAP 1)

Known to ancient Romans as the *regina viarum* (queen of roads), the Via Appia Antica (Appian Way) runs from the Via di Porta San Sebastiano, near the Terme di Caracalla, to Brindisi on the coast of Apulia. It was started around 312 BC by the censor Appius Claudius Caecus, but did not connect with Brindisi until around 190 BC. The first section of the road, which extended 90km to Terracina, was considered revolutionary in its day because it was almost perfectly straight.

Every Sunday a long section of the Via Appia Antica becomes a car-free zone. You can walk or ride a bike for the several kilometres from Via Porta di Sebastiano. To get to Via Appia Antica and the area of the catacombs, catch bus No 218 from Piazza San Giovanni in Laterano or Metro Linea A from Stazione Termini to Colli Albani and then bus No 660 to the Via Appia Antica. On Sunday, ATAC runs a shuttle bus from the Colosseum to the Via Appia Antica.

Monuments along the road include catacombs (see The Catacombs later) and Roman tombs. The **Chiesa del Domine Quo Vadis?** is built at the point where St Peter, while fleeing Rome, is said to have met Jesus. The saint consequently returned to Rome, where he was martyred.

Circo di Massenzio

Archaeologists believe this arena *(☎ 06 780 13 24, Via Appia Antica 153; admission €2.60; open 9am-7pm Tues-Sun)*, built by Maxentius around AD 309, was never actually completed. It is well preserved, and starting stalls for the chariots can still be made out. In front is the **Tomba di Romolo**, a tomb built for Maxentius' son Romulus, and next to it are ruins of an imperial residence.

Tomba di Cecilia Metella

Farther along Via Appia is this famous tomb of a Roman noblewoman *(☎ 06 780 24 65, Via Appia Antica; admission €2.10; open 9am-6pm Tues-Sat, 9am-1pm Sun & Mon Feb-Oct, 9am-4pm Tues-Sat, 9am-1pm Sun & Mon Nov-Mar)*. Money talked in Roman times, and Cecilia Metella's fabulously wealthy in-laws made sure she was buried in style. This grand tomb was used as a fortress by the Caetani family in the early 14th century. Not far past it is a section of the original Via Appia.

Mausoleo delle Fosse Ardeatine (Map 1)

When a brigade of Roman partisans blew up 32 German military police in WWII, the Germans retaliated by taking 335 random prisoners (including 75 Jews) to the Ardeatine Caves, where they were shot. The Germans then used mines to explode sections of the caves and thus bury the bodies. This moving mausoleum *(☎ 06 513 67 42, Via Ardeatina 174; free; open 8.15am-5.15pm Mon-Sat, 8.45am to 5.45pm Sun)* honours the dead.

The Catacombs (Map 1)

There are several catacombs along Via Appia Antica – kilometres of tunnels carved out of the soft tufa rock (see the boxed text 'Roman Underworld'). Corpses were wrapped in simple white sheets and usually placed in rectangular niches carved into the tunnel walls, which were then closed with marble or terracotta slabs.

Catacombs of San Callisto These catacombs *(☎ 06 513 01 580, Via Appia Antica 110; admission €4.20 for guided tours only; open 8.30am-noon & 2.30pm-5.30pm Thurs-Tues Apr-Sept, 8.30am-noon & 2.30pm-5pm Thurs-Tues Oct-Mar)* are the largest and most famous, and contain the tomb of the martyred Santa Cecilia (although her body is now in the Basilica di Santa Cecilia in Trastevere). There is also a crypt containing the tombs of seven popes martyred in the 3rd century. In the 20km of tunnels explored to date, archaeologists have found the sepulchres of some 500,000 people.

Basilica & Catacombs of San Sebastiano These catacombs *(☎ 06 788 70 35, Via Appia Antica 136; admission €4.20; open 8.30am-noon & 2.30pm-5.30pm Mon-Sat Apr-Sept; 8.30am-noon & 2.30pm-5pm*

Mon-Sat Oct-Mar; closed mid-Nov–mid-Dec) were a safe haven for the remains of Saints Peter and Paul during the reign of Vespasian. The first level is now almost completely destroyed but frescoes, stucco-work, epigraphs and three perfectly preserved mausoleums can be seen on the 2nd level. The basilica above them dates from the 4th century and preserves one of the arrows used to kill St Sebastian.

Catacombs of San Domitilla Among the largest and oldest in Rome, these catacombs *(☎ 06 511 03 42, Via delle Sette Chiese 283; admission €4.20; open 8.30am-noon & 2.30pm-5.30pm Wed-Mon, closed late Dec–Jan)* were established on the private burial ground of Flavia Domitilla, niece of the Emperor Domitian and a member of the wealthy Flavian family. They contain Christian wall paintings and the underground church of SS Nereus e Achilleus.

GIANICOLO & VILLA DORIA PAMPHILJ

If you're after a panoramic view of Rome, go to the top of Gianicolo Hill **(Map 3)** between the St Peter's Basilica and Trastevere. At the top of the hill, just off Piazza Giuseppe Garibaldi, there are pony rides and a permanent merry-go-round, as well as a small bar. Puppet shows are often held

Roman Underworld

The catacombs are underground corridors and passageways that were built as communal burial grounds. The best known are the Christian catacombs along the Via Appia Antica, although there are Jewish and pagan ones as well. Scholars are divided as to whether the catacombs were also clandestine meeting places of early Christians in Rome, as well as useful places for secreting important relics from Christian persecutors.

Catacombs were often established in areas where there were existing quarries or underground passages; the soft volcanic earth of the Roman countryside enabled the Christians to dig to a depth of 20m or so.

During the periods of persecution, martyrs were often buried in catacombs beside the fathers of the Church and the first popes. Many Christians wanted to be buried in the same place as the martyrs and consequently a trade in tomb real estate developed, becoming increasingly unethical until Pope Gregory I issued a decree in 597 abolishing the sale of graves. However, Christians had already started to abandon the catacombs as early as in 313, when Constantine issued the Milan decree of religious tolerance.

Increasingly, Christians opted to bury their dead in catacombs near the churches and basilicas that were being built (often above pagan temples). This became common practice under Theodosius, who made Christianity the state religion in 394. The catacombs became sanctuaries for remember Ing the martyrs buried there.

In about 800, the increasingly frequent incursions by invaders necessitated the removal of the saintly bodies of the martyrs and the first popes to the basilicas inside the city walls. The catacombs were thus left abandoned and eventually many were forgotten and filled up with earth. In the Middle Ages only three catacombs were known. Those of San Sebastiano were the most frequented as a place of pilgrimage, since they had earlier been the burial place of Sts Peter and Paul.

The catacombs of Santa Priscilla on Via Salaria were discovered by chance at the end of the 16th century, following the collapse of a tufa quarry. From that time on, groups of curious aristocrats began to lower themselves into the dark underground passages on a regular basis, often risking losing themselves permanently in the underground labyrinths. From the mid-19th century onwards, passionate scholars of Christian archaeology began a program of scientific research and more than 30 catacombs in the Rome area have been uncovered.

here on Sunday. Take bus No 870 from Via Paola at the end of Corso Vittorio Emanuele II where it meets the Lungotevere or alternatively walk up the steps from Via Mameli in Trastevere.

The bus will also take you within easy walking distance of the nearby Villa Doria Pamphilj **(Map 1)** *(open dawn-dusk)*. It is the largest park in Rome and a lovely quiet spot for a walk and a picnic. Built in the 17th century for the Pamphilj family, it is now used for official government functions.

EUR

This acronym, which stands for Esposizione Universale di Roma, has become the name of a peripheral suburb south of Rome, interesting for its many examples of Fascist architecture. These include the **Palazzo della Civiltà del Lavoro** (Palace of the Workers), a square building with arched windows known as the Square Colosseum.

Mussolini ordered the construction of the satellite city for an international exhibition, which was to have been held in 1942. Work was suspended with the outbreak of war and the exhibition never took place; however, many buildings were completed during the 1950s.

The **Museo della Civiltà Romana** *(☎ 06 592 61 35, Piazza G Agnelli; admission €4.20; open 9am-7pm Tues-Sat, 9am-1.30pm Sun)* reconstructs the development of Rome with the use of models. Also of interest is the **Museo Nazionale Preistorico Etnografico Luigi Pigorini** *(☎ 06 54 95 21, Piazza Marconi 14; admission €4.20; open 9am-8pm daily)*. The prehistoric section covers the development of civilisation in the region, while the ethnographical collection includes exhibits from around the world.

LANGUAGE COURSES

Centro Linguistico Italiano Dante Alighieri *(☎ 06 442 31 400, fax 06 442 31 007, e clidar@tin.it, w www.cli dante.it, Piazza Bologna 1)* **Map 1** Four-week courses (four hours per day) cost from €516. Courses run throughout the year.

Berlitz *(☎ 06 683 40 00 or 06 688 06 951, w www.berlitz.com, Via di Torre Argentina 21)* **Map 7** Sixty-lesson courses cost from €300.

Italiaidea *(☎ 06 683 07 620, fax 06 689 29 97, e italiaidea@italiaidea.com, Piazza della Cancelleria 85)* **Map 7** Four-week intensive courses (three hours a day) cost about €415. It is located near Campo de' Fiori.

ORGANISED TOURS

Bus

ATAC (☎ 06 469 52 252, w www.atac.roma.it, Piazza dei Cinquecento) Tickets €7.80. Rome's public transport company operates a good hop-on-hop-off bus tour of the city's major monuments. You've got the flexibility to spend as much (or as little) time as you'd like at each sight. The full loop takes 1½ hours, and tours leave every 30 minutes.

Ciao Roma *(☎ 06 874 06 481, Via Giolitti 34)* **Map 3** Tickets €15.50. Ciao Roma operates buses (some of which are painted to look like old trolley cars) that zip you around Rome. Hop on/off at the Vatican, Colosseum, Piazza Venezia, Piazza Navona, Stazione Termini and Villa Borghese, among other stops.

Walking

Through Eternity Rome *(☎ 06 700 93 36 or 0347 336 52 98, w www.througheternity.com)* Enthusiastic 'storytellers', who are passionate about their subject and native English speakers to boot, make Rome come alive on their walking tours. Twilight tours of Renaissance and Baroque Rome show the city in arguably its best light, and 'Feast of Bacchus' wine sampling tours combine aesthetic pleasures with gastronomic ones.

Enjoy Rome *(see Tourist Offices at the beginning of the chapter)* These tours are designed for the budget traveller. Their three-hour walking tours (€16) cover ancient Rome (by day or night), the Vatican, Trastevere and the Ghetto.

Scala Reale *(☎ 06 447 00 898, w www.scalareale.org)* Scala Reale organises archaeological walks in small groups with knowledgeable guides, often American graduate students specialising in art history and archaeology. Tours are tailor-made and by prior arrangement only.

Cycling

Enjoy Rome *(see Tourist Offices at the beginning of this chapter)* 3½-hour bike tours €18 (everything provided). These tours are a huge hit. The route includes Villa Borghese, the Bocca della Verità and the Colosseum.

SPECIAL EVENTS

Holy Week events include the famous procession of the cross between the Colosseum and the Palatine on Good Friday, and the pope's blessing of the city and the world in Piazza San Pietro on Easter Sunday.

Rome celebrates her birthday on 21 April (she was 2755 in 2002) and bands and standard bearers perform in Piazza del Campidoglio. The area around the Spanish Steps becomes a sea of flowers in April/May during the Spring Festival.

Keep an eye out for Italian Cultural Heritage Week, which in recent years has been held in mid-April. Many museums, galleries, archaeological zones and monuments can be visited free of charge throughout the week, and numerous monuments normally closed to the public open their doors.

Although Romans desert their city in summer, cultural and musical events liven up the place and many performances and festivals are held outdoors. The municipal government coordinates a diverse series of concerts, performances and events throughout summer under the general title of Estate Romana (Roman Summer). Information is published in Rome's daily newspapers and tourist offices have details.

Two of the most popular summer events take place on Caelian Hill: Villa Celimontana Jazz and Massenzio (see Entertainment later in this chapter). The Festa di Noantri is held in Trastevere in the last two weeks of July; locals celebrate over wine and *porchetta* (roast pork stuffed with herbs).

Autumn sees more jazz (indoors this time) with Roma Jazz, and culture (dance, opera and theatre) takes centre stage in the Romaeuropa Festival.

PLACES TO STAY

Rome has a vast number of pensiones and hotels but it is always best to book. While spring and autumn are the peak periods, tourists and pilgrims flock to Rome year-round.

There is a free ***hotel reservation service*** *(☎ 06 699 10 00, Stazione Termini opposite platform 21; open 7.30am to 9pm daily)*. A good alternative is the private tourist office Enjoy Rome (see Tourist Offices at the beginning of this chapter).

Avoid the people at the train station who claim to be tourism officials and offer to find you a room. They usually lead you to pretty seedy accommodation for which you end up paying more than the official rate.

Most of the budget pensiones and larger hotels that cater for tour groups are located near Stazione Termini. The area south-west (to the left as you leave the platforms) can be noisy and unpleasant. The city authorities have gone to some lengths to clean it up in recent years but pickpockets are active in this area and women alone may feel uncomfortable at night. To the north-east of Stazione Termini, you can find accommodation in a quieter and more pleasant residential area and there are several decent hotels in the streets around Via Nazionale, a busy traffic thoroughfare and shopping area. However, the historic centre of Rome is far more appealing and the area around the Vatican is much less chaotic; both of these areas are only a short bus or Metro ride away from Stazione Termini.

You will often find three or four budget pensiones in the same building, although many are small establishments of 12 rooms or less, which fill up quickly in summer. Most hotels will accept bookings in advance, although some demand a deposit/credit card details for the first night.

Although Rome does not have a low season as such, the majority of hotels offer significant discounts in July and August and from November to March (excluding the Christmas/New Year period). A lot of mid-range and top-end hotels also offer special deals for families and discounts for extended stays, so be sure to enquire.

There is a terrible lack of on-site parking facilities in the city centre, but your hotel should be able to direct you to a private garage.

PLACES TO STAY – BUDGET

Unless otherwise stated, the prices quoted for hotels in this section are for rooms without a private shower or bath. Many accept payment in cash only.

Camping

All of Rome's camp sites are a fair distance from the centre.

Seven Hills *(☎ 06 303 10 826, fax 06 303 10 039, Via Cassia 1216)* Sites per person/tent €7.30/5. This camp site is a bit of a hike from Stazione Termini: catch the Metro Linea A to Ottaviano, then take bus No 907 (ask the driver where to get off). From Via Cassia it is a 1km walk to the camping ground.

Camping Flaminio *(☎ 06 333 26 04, fax 06 333 26 04, ⓔ info@villageflaminio.com, Via Flaminia Nuova 821)* Sites per adult/child/tent €9/7/11.50, bungalows from €38. Take Metro Linea A to Flaminio, change to the Roma-Nord train line and get off at Due Ponti station, or take bus No 910 to Piazza Mancini then No 200 to the camp site. At night, catch bus No 24N from Piazzale Flaminio (just north of Piazza del Popolo).

Hostels

The Italian youth hostels association, ***Associazione Italiana Alberghi per la Gioventù*** *(☎ 06 487 11 52, ⓦ www.hostel-aig.org, Via Cavour 44)*, has information about all the youth hostels in Italy and will assist with bookings to stay at universities during summer. You can also join Hostelling International (HI) here.

Ostello Foro Italico *(☎ 06 323 62 67, ⓔ aig@uni.net, Viale delle Olimpiadi 61)* **Map 1** Dorm bed €15. Rome's only official hostel is nothing flash; it has a bar, self-service restaurant and a garden but no kitchen. It accepts bookings a minimum of one month in advance; otherwise you have to turn up at 10am to be assigned a bed. However you cannot enter the dorm until 2pm and there is a midnight curfew. Given its location so far from the action, and these restrictions (hell for someone arriving on an early-morning flight), you will do better heading for the centre of town.

YWCA *(☎ 06 488 04 60, fax 06 487 10 28, Via Cesare Balbo 4)* **Map 3** Singles/doubles without bath €37/62, singles/doubles with bath €47/74, triples/quads €26 per person. The YWCA accepts men, women and couples and is centrally located. This is the place for early risers with a serious sightseeing agenda but is probably best avoided by night-owls as there's a midnight curfew. Prices include breakfast; payment by cash only.

Religious Institutions

A number of religious institutions offer accommodation in Rome, including some near Stazione Termini and the Vatican. However, they have strict curfews. If you want to stay in one, you can apply to the nearest Catholic archdiocese in your home town. If you haven't done so, try one of the options listed below.

Domus Aurelia delle Suore Orsoline *(☎ 06 63 67 84, fax 06 393 76 480, Via Aurelia 218)* **Map 1** Singles/doubles/triples with bath €39/60/78. Clean, simple accommodation, about 1km west of St Peter's. From Stazione Termini catch bus No 64 to Largo Argentina, then No 46 to Via Aurelia. Get off the bus after it has done a steep ascent and made a sharp left turn.

Padri Trinitari *(☎ 06 638 38 88, fax 06 393 66 795, Piazza Santa Maria alle Fornaci 27)* **Map 2** Singles/doubles/triples €42/73/93. Good value (includes breakfast) and well positioned just south of St Peter's.

Bed & Breakfast

B&B is a relatively new concept in Rome. It has taken off thanks to the influx of pilgrims during the Jubilee year 2000 and the overdemand for really good budget accommodation. The bonus of B&B accommodation is that Italian houses are invariably spotlessly clean. The drawback is that you are staying in someone's home and will probably be expected to operate within the family's timetable. Keys are not always provided. A hotel would be more suitable for those who expect to be coming in late at night.

Most of the accommodation is fairly central but when making the booking (which should be done well in advance) make sure you understand fully the location of the accommodation that is being proposed. You don't want to find yourself in an outer suburb with limited public transport if you don't have a car.

Lists of authorised private B&B operators in and around Rome can be obtained from the Comune di Roma and APT tourist information offices (see Tourist Offices at the beginning of this chapter). Private B&B operators are also listed in the magazine *Wanted in Rome* (see Newspapers and Magazines in Facts for the Visitor chapter for details), although not all of these are registered (and therefore insured) by the city authorities.

Bed & Breakfast Italia *(☎ 06 687 86 18, fax 06 687 86 19, ⓔ md4095@mclink.it, Ⓦ www.bbitalia.it, Corso Vittorio Emanuele II 282)* **Map 2** This is the longest established of several B&B networks. It has accommodation throughout Rome in three price categories: singles/doubles/triples without bath €32/52/75, singles/doubles/triples with bath €44/82/109, luxurious singles/doubles/triples with bath €57/98/130. You can view apartments and book online via the Web site.

A useful online accommodation agency which has a large number of very good B&Bs or *affittacamere* (virtually the same thing but without the breakfast) on its books is Cross Pollinate at Ⓦ www.cross-pollinate.com. This sophisticated Web site allows you to view pictures and maps of the accommodation (all of which are in the centre of the city) and tells you if the place is already booked. A credit card deposit reserves the room and you'll have a confirmation in 24 hours. The young American couple who run the site also manage the excellent Beehive hostel (see South-West of Stazione Termini under Pensiones & Hotels later).

Pensiones & Hotels

North-East of Stazione Termini These places can be found on Map 4.

Fawlty Towers *(☎ 06 445 03 74, fax 06 493 82 878, Ⓦ www.fawltytowers.org, Via Magenta 39)* Dorm beds without/with shower €19/24, singles/doubles without bath €39/57, singles/doubles with bath €47/73. As far as budget accommodation goes, this is one of Rome's best options. Added bonuses are the sunny terrace, satellite TV, communal fridge and microwave. Advance bookings are accepted only for the private (non-dorm) rooms. To reserve a dorm bed, you have to call (either in person or by phone) at 9pm the night before you wish to stay there and they'll hold the bed until around 10am the following morning. It's also a good place to go if you've arrived in Rome late at night and the accommodation agencies are all closed, as the staff can usually recommend a pensione with vacancies.

Pensione Giamaica *(☎ 06 49 01 21, fax 06 445 19 63, ⓔ md0991@mclink.it, Via Magenta 13)* Singles/doubles €29/44. The decor's frightful and the rooms looking into the dark and grimy internal courtyard are probably best avoided, but the communal bathrooms are clean and there's no curfew.

Pensione Restivo *(☎ 06 446 21 72, fax 06 445 26 29, Via Palestro 55)* Singles/doubles/triples €37/57/65. This spotlessly clean pensione is run by the friendly and helpful Signor Restivo (a former *carabiniere* officer) who proudly displays thank-you letters from past guests. There is a midnight curfew.

Hotel Cervia *(☎ 06 49 10 57, fax 06 49 10 56, ⓔ hotelcervia@wnt.it, Via Palestro 55)* Dorm beds €19-21 per person, singles/doubles/triples without bath €29/47/55, doubles/triples with bath €68/78. The rooms in this 19th-century building have high vaulted ceilings and seem enormous. A recent addition are the four- and five-bed dorms on the 3rd floor.

Albergo Sandra *(☎ 06 445 26 12, fax 06 446 08 46, Via Villafranca 10)* Singles/doubles €43/75. This medium-sized pensione with clean and pleasant rooms is run by a house-proud Italian *mamma* and her English-speaking son.

North-West of Stazione Termini Unless indicated otherwise, these places can be all be found on Map 4.

Papa Germano *(☎ 06 48 69 19, fax 06 478 25 02, ⓔ info@hotelpapagermano.it, Via Calatafimi 14a)* Dorm beds €19, singles/doubles €47/68. A good budget choice, Papa Germano has a friendly family atmosphere and staff who speak English and French. There is Internet access available, and telephones and TVs in each room.

Hotel Floridia *(☎ 06 481 40 89, fax 06 444 13 77, Via Montebello 45)* Singles/doubles with bath €57/83. The elegant entrance area on the ground floor gives a misleading impression of quality; the rooms are quite small and decorated in pseudo-elegant style but all have telephone and private bath.

Hotel Ascot *(☎ 06 474 16 75, fax 06 474 01 65, Via Montebello 22)* Singles/doubles with bath €47/68. The hotel itself is fine – as long as you're not concerned about the porn cinemas and sex shops in the area. Ask for room No 24, which still has its original parquet floor.

Hotel Castelfidardo *(☎ 06 446 46 38, fax 06 494 13 78, ⓔ castelfidardo@italmarket.it, Via Castelfidardo 31)* Singles/doubles/triples without bath €37/50/62, doubles/triples with bath €57/78. Off Piazza dell'Indipendenza, this is one of Rome's better one-star hotels. The English-speaking staff are friendly and helpful.

Hotel Ercoli *(☎/fax 06 474 54 54, Via Collina 48)* Singles/doubles with bath €68/93. This comfortable hotel is about a 10-minute walk from Stazione Termini. Its quality rooms are at the upper end of the budget scale and have a bath, TV, telephone and hairdryer.

Hotel Tizi *(☎ 06 482 01 28, fax 06 474 32 66, Via Collina 48)* **Map 2** Singles/doubles without bath €37/47, doubles with bath €57. Recently refurbished, this hotel offers light and spacious rooms. Check for discounts in low season and for stays of more than five days. Cash only.

South-West of Stazione Termini These places can be found on Map 4.

The Beehive *(☎ 06 474 07 19, fax 06 478 81 190, ⓔ info@the-beehive.com, Ⓦ www.the-beehive.com, Via Giovanni Lanza 99)* Dorm beds €16, doubles/triples without bath €26/52, doubles/triples with bath €39/78. The Beehive is *the* place for the discerning budget traveller. Well-positioned off Via Cavour near Piazza Esquilino, it has clean, attractive rooms and kitchen use is included. You must book ahead as walk-ins are not accepted and party animals positively discouraged.

Hotel Sandy *(☎ 06 488 45 85, fax 06 445 07 34, Ⓦ www.sandyhostel.com, Via Cavour 136)* Dorm beds €16. Hotel Sandy is probably the closest thing in Rome to a backpackers crash pad. The hotel is on the 5th floor (no lift). There are metal lockers but no keys and the hotel lacks adequate bathroom facilities – so be prepared to queue. Reservations are not accepted and payment is in cash only.

Near Via Nazionale The following places can be found on Map 4.

Hotel Elide *(☎ 06 488 39 77, fax 06 489 04 318, Via Firenze 50)* Singles/doubles/triples with bath €62/88/114. Off Via Nazionale, this place has well-maintained rooms. Ask for No 18, which has an elaborate, gilded ceiling.

Hotel Galatea *(☎ 06 474 30 70, fax 06 489 04 318, Via Genova 24)* Singles/doubles without bath €52/68, singles/doubles with bath €62/78. The well-positioned Galatea has beautifully furnished rooms. It's popular with school groups and often overrun by kids.

City Centre Really economical hotels in Rome's historical centre basically don't exist. But in the areas around Piazza di Spagna, Piazza Navona, the Pantheon and Campo de' Fiori, you do have the convenience and pleasure of staying right in the centre of historic Rome.

Albergo Abruzzi *(☎ 06 679 20 21, Piazza della Rotonda 69)* **Map 7** Singles/doubles €60/88. The Abruzzi wins the prize for position, being directly opposite the Pantheon, but the rooms can be very noisy until late at night when the piazza is finally deserted. There's nothing fancy about the rooms but the chatty management make it a perennial budget favourite. No credit cards.

Hotel Mimosa *(☎ 06 688 01 753, fax 06 683 35 57, ⓔ hotelmimosa@tin.it, Via di Santa Chiara 61)* Singles/doubles/triples without bath €57/78/109, doubles/triples with bath €88/124. Some rooms are a bit pokey but all of them are clean and it's in a great position near Piazza della Minerva – hence it's always full and you have to book weeks in advance. The elderly owners and their son (who speaks English and French) are helpful and friendly.

Albergo della Lunetta *(☎ 06 686 10 80, fax 06 689 20 28, Piazza Paradiso 68)* Singles/doubles/triples without bath €57/78/109, doubles/triples with bath €88/124. Just east of Campo de' Fiori, this is a Roman pensione of the old school, run by three rather cantankerous but somewhat charming *signore* (gentlemen). The labyrinthine corridors and staircases lead to small but spotless rooms. It is popular with young foreign students who stay for months at a time.

Near the Vatican Although there aren't many bargains in this area, it's comparatively quiet and close to the main sights. Bookings are an absolute necessity because rooms are often filled with people attending Vatican conferences. Unless indicated otherwise, the following places can be found on Map 3.

Pensione Ottaviano *(☎ 06 397 37 253, ⓔ gi.costantini@agora.stm.it, Via Ottaviano 6)* Dorm beds €16, doubles/triples €47/62. Though good and dirt cheap, this place has a rather brutal check-in policy, which means that for the dorm beds you have to call by 9pm the night before you want to stay and then check in by noon. You can book doubles and triples in advance, but you need to reconfirm two weeks before and it's best to call the night before to double check. If you're arriving in Rome after noon, they won't hold your room/bed, so it's probably best to go somewhere else.

Colors Hotel *(☎ 06 687 40 30, fax 06 686 79 47, ⓔ fulang@flashnet.it, ⓦ www.colors hotel.com, Via Boezio 31)* Dorm beds €16, doubles without/with bath from €52/73. Run by the people at Enjoy Rome (see Tourist Offices at the beginning of this chapter). Colors offers good quality accommodation, a fully equipped kitchen, mini-gym and Internet access. There is no curfew and no lock-out period.

Hotel Giuggioli *(☎ 06 324 21 13, 1st floor, Via Germanico 198)* **Map 1** Doubles without/with bath €78/104. This small, old-fashioned pensione is run by a delightful Italian-speaking signora. The decor won't win any awards but it is clean.

Pensione Nautilus *(☎ 06 324 21 18, 2nd floor, Via Germanico 198)* **Map 1** Doubles/triples €68/93. This place has clean, simple rooms and a small lounge-TV area.

Hotel Lady *(☎ 06 324 21 12, fax 06 324 34 46, 4th floor, Via Germanico 198)* **Map 1** Doubles without/with bath €83/104. A quiet, old-fashioned pensione with pleasant rooms and spotless bathrooms. Ask for room No 4 or 6, both of which still have the original beamed ceiling. The eccentric owner and his wife do not speak English, but their eager conversation will give you lots of practice in Italian.

Pensione Paradise *(☎ 06 321 31 84, Viale Giulio Cesare 47)* **Map 1** Singles/doubles with bath €47/83. Located near the Lepanto metro stop, this place has simple but bright rooms.

PLACES TO STAY – MID-RANGE

All rooms in this section have a private bathroom unless otherwise stated.

North-East of Stazione Termini (Map 4)

Hotel Adventure *(☎ 06 446 90 26, fax 06 446 00 84, ⓔ hotel.adventure@flashnet.it, Via Palestro 88)* Doubles €93-124, triples/quads €155/233. This hotel has been decorated by someone with a particular predilection for pastel pink, fake stucco and reproduction antiques, and there are more chandeliers in reception than you'd find in a lighting showroom. But it's spotless and safe. One huge room on the top floor has its own terrace. The rooms looking onto the internal courtyard are quieter than those facing onto the street.

Hotel Gabriella *(☎ 06 445 01 20, fax 06 445 02 52, ⓔ gabriel@micanet.it, 1st floor, Via Palestro 88)* Singles/doubles €83/104, air-con €10 per day. This two-star hotel is an unassuming place, family-run and friendly.

Hotel Continentale *(☎ 06 445 03 82, fax 06 445 26 29, ⓦ www.hotel-continentale.com, Via Palestro 49)* Singles/doubles/triples €47/83/109. The owners of this friendly place speak several languages, including English and French. All rooms are clean and most have been renovated (try to get one of these). Separate rooms with shared bathrooms in an apartment on the 5th floor of the same building cost €42/62 double/triple.

Hotel Positano *(☎ 06 49 03 60, fax 06 446 91 01, ⓔ hotposit@tin.it, Via Palestro 49)* Singles/doubles/triples €73/104/145. This family-run hotel is particularly good for families, as they don't charge for children under six. There are also some grim dorm rooms for €17 per person – if mattresses on the floor appeal. All credit cards are accepted.

Hotel Lachea-Dolomiti *(☎ 06 495 72 56, fax 06 445 46 65, ⓔ dolomiti@hotel-dolomiti.it, Via San Martino della Battaglia 11)* Singles/doubles/triples €62/93/109. Two hotels have been turned into one, with elegant and airy rooms (all with private bathroom, mini-bar, TV, telephone, air-conditioning, double glazing, safe and hairdryer). English, French and Spanish are spoken.

Hotel Venezia *(☎ 06 445 71 01, fax 06 495 76 87, Via Varese 18)* Singles/doubles/triples €102/138/186. At the upper end of mid-range, the Venezia is beautifully furnished with antiques and attractive fabrics. The multilingual staff are charming and it is the nicest place to stay in this area. Prices drop by about 10% in the low season.

Hotel Piemonte *(☎ 06 445 22 40, fax 06 445 16 49, ⓔ piemonte@italyhotel.com, Via Vicenza 34)* Singles/doubles €104/145. Well-located for an early train, the pleasant Piemonte is a stone's throw from Stazione Termini. There's double glazing throughout and the bathrooms are particularly nice. One room has disabled access.

South-West of Termini (Map 4)

Hotel Sweet Home *(☎ 06 488 09 54, fax 06 481 76 13, ⓔ homesweet@libero.it, Via Principe Amedeo 47)* Singles/doubles €62/93. The rooms here vary in size and comfort; ask for one facing away from the street as these are larger and quieter.

Hotel Igea *(☎/fax 06 446 69 11, ⓔ igea@igearoma.com, Via Principe Amedeo 97)* Singles/doubles/triples €83/130/150. The fancy entrance suggests a great interior, which in fact isn't the case. The rooms are simple, with basic furniture, but all have satellite TV, double-glazed windows and air-conditioning.

Around Via Nazionale (Map 3)

Hotel Seiler *(☎ 06 488 02 04, fax 06 488 06 88, ⓔ acropoli@rdn.it, Via Firenze 48)* Singles/doubles €83/114, family rooms (up to 5 people) €30 per person. A friendly, helpful management and clean, comfortable rooms are the selling points of this hotel. Ask for room 405, known as *la camera degli angeletti* (room of the angels) for its ceiling fresco of angels dating from 1885.

Hotel Oceania *(☎ 06 482 46 96, fax 06 488 55 86, ⓔ hoceania@tin.it, Via Firenze 38)* Singles/doubles/triples €99/127/161. This small hotel stands out for the unbeatable hospitality offered by the delightful owners, and nice touches such as English newspapers for guest use.

Hotel Columbia *(☎ 06 474 42 89, fax 06 474 02 09, ⓔ info@hotelcolumbia.com, ⓦ www.hotelcolumbia.com, Via del Viminale 15)* Singles/doubles/triples €102/138/186. Rooms in this pleasant hotel are large and bright and there's a nice roof terrace.

City Centre

Albergo del Sole *(☎ 06 687 94 46, fax 06 689 37 87, ⓔ alb.sole@flashnet.it, Via del Biscione 76)* **Map 7** Singles/doubles without bath €57/88, singles/doubles with bath €83/119. Just off Campo de' Fiori, this place dates from 1462 and is claimed by some to be the oldest hotel in Rome. It has comfortable rooms, some with antique furniture. There is lots of communal space, including a TV room, an internal patio and a roof terrace, which is open to guests until 11pm. No credit cards.

Hotel Campo de' Fiori *(☎ 06 688 06 865, fax 06 687 60 03, Via del Biscione 6)* **Map 7** Singles/doubles with bath €104/130. The decor at this quirky establishment – garish blue carpet and clashing floral wallpaper – is not recommended if you have a hangover, and in some cases the 'bathroom' is merely a shower stall plonked unceremoniously in the room. The six-storey, no lift set-up might worry some, but it gets 10 points for position.

Pensione Primavera *(☎ 06 688 03 109, fax 06 686 92 65, Piazza di San Pantaleo 3)* **Map 6** Doubles/triples without bath €83/114, doubles/triples with bath €109/135. Just south of Piazza Navona, this centrally-located hotel has clean and comfortable rooms, all with air-conditioning and double glazing to keep out the (considerable) traffic noise. Bathrooms, added to the rooms as an afterthought, are a bit cramped. No credit cards.

Hotel Pomezia *(☎/fax 06 686 13 71, e hotelpomezia@openaccess.it, Via dei Chiavari 12)* **Map 7** Singles/doubles/triples €78/114/130. A good lower mid-range choice, especially after its recent renovation, with one room equipped for disabled travellers.

Hotel Margutta *(☎ 06 322 36 74, fax 06 320 03 95, Via Laurina 34)* **Map 2** Singles/doubles €88/99, doubles with shared/private terrace €124/135. Near Piazza del Popolo, off Via del Corso, Hotel Margutta has small and dark rooms but they're spotlessly clean. Book well in advance for a terrace room.

Hotel Forte *(☎ 06 320 76 25, fax 06 320 27 07, e forte@venere.it, Via Margutta 61)* **Map 3** Singles €104-145, doubles €130-197. Near Piazza di Spagna, the pleasant Hotel Forte is perfect if you like antiques, as Via Margutta is lined with antique shops and artists' studios.

Hotel Pensione Merano *(☎ 06 482 17 96, fax 06 482 18 10, Via Vittorio Veneto 155)* **Map 2** Singles/doubles/triples €73/101/130. Surprisingly cheap given the upmarket location, this is a quaint old place with dark, heavy furniture. The rooms can get really hot in summer.

Hotel Julia *(☎ 06 488 16 37 or 06 487 34 13, fax 06 481 70 44, e info@hoteljulia.it, Via Rasella 29)* **Map 4** Singles/doubles €104/155. Close to busy Piazza Barberini, Hotel Julia offers simple comfort in a tranquil environment. There's a small bar and all rooms have satellite TV and air-conditioning.

Trastevere (Map 5)

Hotel Trastevere *(☎ 06 581 47 13, fax 06 588 10 16, Via L Manara 24a–25)* Singles/doubles/triples €68/88/109, apartments sleeping four €155. One of the best deals in the area (if not the city), with three-star quality at excellent prices. Most of the spotlessly clean rooms look out over the market square of Piazza San Cosimato.

Hotel Carmel *(☎ 06 580 99 21, fax 06 581 88 53, Via Mameli 11)* Singles/doubles €62/93. A quirky place with a shady roof terrace that can be used by guests.

Hotel Cisterna *(☎ 06 581 72 12, fax 06 581 0091, Via della Cisterna 7–9)* Singles/doubles/triples €97/119/154. Located in a quiet, pretty street around the corner from the busy Piazza Santa Maria in Trastevere, Hotel Cisterna is close to the action. Some of the rooms are larger and airier than others.

Near the Vatican (Map 3)

Hotel Adriatic *(☎ 06 688 08 080, fax 06 689 35 52, e adriatic@ats.it, Via Vitelleschi 25)* Singles/doubles without bath €57/78, with bath €78/99. Hotel Adriatic is on the continuation of Via Stefano Porcari, off Piazza del Risorgimento, and has simple but comfortable rooms. The large terrace is a bonus for guests and makes up for the somewhat unfriendly management

Hotel Joli *(☎ 06 324 18 54, fax 06 324 18 93, 6th floor, Via Cola di Rienzo 243)* Singles/doubles €62/93. This is a family-friendly hotel with pleasant rooms although the bathrooms are small and the hand-held showers are liable to soak everything in the room. Readers have reported that the walls are not well soundproofed.

Hotel Florida *(☎ 06 324 18 72, fax 06 324 18 57, 2nd floor, Via Cola di Rienzo 243)* Singles/doubles/triples €78/104/135. Popular with families, the Florida is small and quiet with pleasantly furnished rooms. There are some cheaper rooms with shared bathroom. Discounts are given in low season.

Hotel Amalia *(☎ 06 397 23 354, fax 06 397 23 365, e hotelamalia@iol.it, Via Germanico 66)* Singles/doubles €119/166. A stone's throw from the Vatican, this is one of the best-value mid-range hotels in the area. There's nothing special about the rooms but they are bright, spacious and spotlessly clean, with fans rather than air-conditioning.

PLACES TO STAY – TOP END

If it's serious luxury you're after then in Rome you'll be spoilt for choice. Just make sure there's plenty of credit left on your card. The following hotels have been selected on the basis of their individual charm, as well as value for money and location. All rooms have bathroom, telephone and TV; most also have a minibar, hairdryer and safe. Breakfast is generally included in the given price but it's wise to check. Unless stated otherwise, all these hotels accept credit cards.

Near Stazione Termini (Map 3)

Hotel Palladium Palace *(☎ 06 446 69 18, fax 06 446 69 37, e nox@iol.it, Via Gioberti 36)* Singles/doubles/triples €161/207/279. This hotel's stylishly refurbished rooms are all individually decorated with parquet floors and gilded ceilings. There are four rooms for disabled travellers and a roof garden with sauna.

Hotel d'Este *(☎ 06 446 56 07, fax 06 446 56 01, e d.este@italyhotel.com, Via Carlo Alberto 4b)* Singles/doubles €135/197. A stone's throw from Piazza Santa Maria Maggiore, this is one of the better hotels in the area, with beautifully furnished rooms and a pleasant roof garden.

Hotel Artemide *(☎ 06 48 99 11, fax 06 489 91 700, e hotel.artemide@tiscalinet.it, Via Nazionale 22)* Singles/doubles €223/300. This elegant, four-star hotel on Via Nazionale has attractive extras, including free mineral water, soft drinks and daily newspapers. There is one twin room with facilities for disabled people. Ask about low-season discounts.

City Centre

Casa Howard *(☎ 06 699 24 555, fax 06 679 46 44, e casahowardroma@yahoo.com, w www.casahoward.com, Via Capo le Case 18)* **Map 3** Doubles €150-186, triples €186-217. More guesthouse than hotel, Casa Howard has only five rooms, each individually decorated with gorgeous fabrics and paintings.

Hotel Scalinata di Spagna *(☎ 06 679 30 06, fax 06 699 40 598, e info@hotelscalinata.com, w www.hotelscalinata.com, Piazza della Trinità dei Monti 17)* **Map 3** Singles/doubles €207/285, suite €465. Magnificently located at the top of the Spanish Steps, with views over the Roman rooftops. Room No 18 has a private terrace and connects with an adjoining room to make a family suite.

Hassler Villa Medici *(☎ 06 69 93 40, fax 06 678 99 91, e hassler roma@mclink.it, w www.hotelhasslerroma.com, Piazza della Trinità' dei Monti 6)* **Map 3** Singles/doubles €367/460. Rome's class act for over a century can claim among its past guests the royal families of Sweden, Greece and Britain, John F. Kennedy and Elizabeth Taylor. If you can't afford to join them then at least go for Sunday brunch.

Hotel Locarno *(☎ 06 361 08 41, fax 06 321 52 49, info@hotellocarno.com, Via della Penna 22)* **Map 2** Singles/doubles €135/205, superior doubles €225. Near Piazza del Popolo, the Locarno is a friendly alternative to some of the more impersonal top-end hotels; popular with both tourists and business travellers. It has an attractive Art Deco lounge-bar.

Hotel de Russie *(☎ 06 32 88 81, fax 06 328 88 888, e hotelderussie@hotelderussie.it, Via del Babuino 9)* **Map 2** Singles from

€305, doubles €439-605, suites €439-605. Rome's newest luxury hotel is opulent, minimal and tasteful. That no expense has been spared is evident from the enormous bathrooms (complete with mosaic tiles) and fine linens. But it is the terraced gardens behind the hotel and the various rooftop spaces that take your breath away.

Minerva *(☎ 06 69 52 01, fax 06 679 41 65, ⓔ minerva@pronet.it, Piazza della Minerva 69)* **Map 3** Singles €336, doubles €414-491, suites €724. Opposite Bernini's *Elefantino* statue near the Pantheon, this deluxe hotel, part of the Crowne Plaza chain, is located in a 17th-century palace redesigned in the 1980s by the Italian architect Paolo Portoghesi. One of his additions was a magnificent Art Deco-style coloured glass ceiling in the lobby.

Hotel Santa Chiara *(☎ 06 687 29 79, fax 06 687 31 44, ⓔ info@albergosantachiara.com, Via Santa Chiara 21)* **Map 7** Singles/doubles/triples €140/202/238. Attractively-positioned behind the Pantheon, the Santa Chiara is a pleasant hotel. Some rooms have small balconies overlooking the street, although the rooms around the internal courtyard are quieter.

Hotel Portoghesi *(☎ 06 686 42 31, fax 06 687 69 76, ⓔ info@hotelportoghesiroma.com, Via dei Portoghesi 1)* **Map 7** Singles/doubles €130/171, suites €186, suite with terrace €310. The delightful Portoghesi is superbly positioned in a quiet street lined with craft shops and jewellers. Prices include breakfast on the delightful roof terrace.

Albergo Teatro di Pompeo *(☎ 06 687 28 12, fax 06 688 05 531, Largo del Pallaro 8)* **Map 7** Singles/doubles €154/199. Parts of this hotel, just off Campo de' Fiori, go back as far as the Roman Republic; guests have breakfast in the remains of Pompey's Theatre (dating from 55 BC).

Hotel Ponte Sisto *(☎ 06 68 63 11, fax 06 686 31 801, ⓔ info@pontesisto.com, Via dei Pettinari 64)* **Map 7** Singles/doubles from €130/207. An extensive renovation has turned this hotel, close to Campo de' Fiori, into a city-centre delight; several of the elegant rooms have their own terraces with unrivalled Roman rooftop views.

Hotel Forum *(☎ 06 679 24 46, fax 678 64 79, ⓔ info@hotelforum.com, ⓦ www.hotelforum.com, Via Tor de' Conti 25)* **Map 4** Singles/doubles €212/305. This former convent near the Roman Forum has an antique-filled lobby area panelled in wood. The hotel's best asset, however, is its delightful roof garden restaurant with views to take your breath away. Over breakfast, you can watch Rome come to life or you can have dinner against the impressive backdrop of the Forum and Palatine.

Hotel Nerva *(☎ 06 678 18 35, fax 06 699 22 204, Via Tor de' Conti)* **Map 4** Singles/doubles €155/217, suites €336. Rooms in this cosy establishment (off Via dei Fori Imperiali and directly behind the forum from which it takes its name) aren't huge but what they lack in size is made up for by the friendly management. Two rooms have facilities for disabled travellers.

Hotel Celio *(☎ 06 704 95 333, fax 06 709 63 77, Via dei Santi Quattro 35c)* **Map 5** Singles/doubles €192/204. Just south-east of the Colosseum is this little slice of heaven in an area with few accommodation options. A small fortune has been spent on meticulous renovations: stunning mosaic floors decorate corridors and guest rooms, and large-screen TVs feature in most rooms, each of which is named after a famous artist.

Near the Vatican (Map 3)

Hotel Bramante *(☎ 06 688 06 426, fax 06 687 98 81, ⓔ bramante@excalhq.it, Via delle Palline 24)* Singles/doubles €130/181. The secret's out – this is one of the most charming hotels in Rome. It has superbly decorated bedrooms and antique furniture and carpets throughout. The Bramante is located in a restored 16th-century building designed and lived in by the Swiss architect, Domenico Fontana, until he was expelled from Rome by Pope Sixtus V.

Hotel Mellini *(☎ 06 32 47 71, fax 06 324 77 881, ⓔ battistini@hotelmellini.com, ⓦ www.hotelmellini.com, Via Muzio Clementi 81)* Singles/doubles €197/248. Near the River Tiber, between the Lepanto and Flaminio metro stops, this hotel has large, comfortable rooms (some equipped for disabled people). There's a roof terrace overlooking the Palazzo della Giustizia and a snack bar serving light meals.

Hotel Columbus *(☎ 06 686 54 35, fax 06 686 48 74, ⓔ hotel.columbus@alfanet.it, Via della Conciliazione 33)* Singles/doubles €192/295. The deluxe Hotel Columbus is in a magnificent 15th-century palace in front of St Peter's. It is a Renaissance curiosity with its splendid halls and frescoes by Pinturicchio.

Aventino (Map 4)

Aventino – Sant'Anselmo Hotels *(☎ 06 574 51 74, fax 06 578 36 04, ⓔ frpiroli@tin.it, ⓦ www.aventinohotels.com, Piazza Sant' Anselmo 2)* Two-star singles/doubles/triples €88/130/140, three-star singles/doubles/triples €109/166/192. Five separate turn-of-the-century villas make up this group of hotels, situated in a predominantly residential area but still only a stone's throw from the historic centre (to the north) and the restaurants of Testaccio (to the south). These hotels offer both two-star and three-star accommodation and are the perfect place if you prefer quieter surroundings or if you have a car, as street parking is fairly easy to find.

RENTAL ACCOMMODATION

Apartments near the centre of Rome are expensive and you can expect to pay a minimum of €780 per month for a studio apartment or small one-bedroom place. A room in a shared apartment will cost at least €310 per month, plus bills. Apartment rentals and shares are advertised in *Wanted in Rome* and *Porta Portese*, both available from newsstands. There are also agencies, known as *agenzie immobiliari*, specialising in short-term rentals in Rome, that charge a fee for their services. They are listed in *Wanted in Rome*.

PLACES TO EAT

Rome offers a pretty good range of places to eat. There are some excellent establishments offering typical Roman fare to suit a range of budgets, as well as some good, but usually fairly expensive, restaurants specialising in international cuisines such as Indian, Vietnamese and Japanese. Generally, the restaurants near Stazione Termini are to be avoided if you want to pay reasonable prices for good-quality food. The side streets of the historic centre around Piazza Navona and Campo de' Fiori harbour many good-quality, low-priced trattorias and pizzerias, and the areas of San Lorenzo (to the east of Stazione Termini, near the university) and Testaccio are popular eating districts with the locals. Trastevere offers an excellent selection of rustic-style places hidden in tiny piazzas and pizzerias where it doesn't cost the earth to sit at a table on the street.

During summer, these areas are lively and atmospheric and most establishments have outside tables. Meal times are generally from 12.30pm to 3pm and 8pm to 11pm, although in summer many restaurants stay open later. If you want to be sure of getting a table (especially one outside), either make a booking or arrive before 8.30pm.

Always remember to check the menu posted outside the establishment for prices and cover and service charges. Expect to pay under €15 per person at a simple trattoria, up

Eating alla Romana

Antipasto dishes in Rome are particularly good and many restaurants allow you to make your own mixed selection. Typical pasta dishes include: *bucatini all'Amatriciana*, with a usually very salty sauce of tomato and *pancetta* (cured bacon), topped with *pecorino romano* (matured sheep's cheese); *penne all'arrabbiata*, which has a spicy sauce of tomatoes and chilli; and *spaghetti carbonara*, with pancetta, eggs and cheese. *Saltimbocca alla romana* (slices of veal and ham) and *abbacchio* (roast lamb seasoned with rosemary) are classic meat dishes, which are followed by a wide variety of vegetables. During winter, try *carciofi* (artichokes) *alla romana* (stuffed with mint or parsley and garlic) or *alla giudia* (deep-fried). Offal is very popular in Rome and a local speciality is the *pajata* (pasta with a sauce of chopped veal intestines).

o €25 at an average restaurant and around €50 or more at Rome's top eating places. These prices are for a full meal including starter, main course, dessert and wine. Eating only pasta and salad and drinking the house wine at a trattoria can keep the bill down. If you order meat or, especially, fish you will push up the bill substantially.

City Centre – Budget

Pizzeria il Leoncino *(☎ 06 687 63 06, Via del Leoncino 28)* **Map 3** Full meals €10.30. Open Thurs-Tues. It's cheap, it's hectic, it's not full of tourists and, best of all, it serves up delicious, thin-crusted pizzas, fast. Cards aren't accepted.

Da Gino *(☎ 06 687 34 34, Vicolo Rosini 4)* **Map 7** Full meals €15.50. Open Mon-Sat. A trattoria of the old school with old-fashioned prices. Off Via Campo Marzio, it's always full and it's popular with politicians and journalists, especially at lunchtime. Try the home-made fettuccine pasta cooked with peas and *guanciale* (bacon made from the pig's cheek), or the *coniglio al vino bianco* (rabbit cooked in white wine).

Pizzeria La Montecarlo *(☎ 06 686 18 77, Vic Savelli 12)* **Map 7** Full meals €10.30. Open daily. This is a very traditional pizzeria, with paper sheets for tablecloths, serving fine pizza and good beer.

Pizzeria da Baffetto *(☎ 06 686 16 17, Via del Governo Vecchio 11)* **Map 7** Pizzas €4.10-6.20. Open for dinner daily. A Roman institution, its large pizzas would feed an army and deserve their reputation as among the best (and best value) in Rome. Expect to join a queue if you arrive after 9pm and don't be surprised if you end up sharing a table.

Osteria *(Via del Governo Vecchio 18)* **Map 7** Full meals €12.90-15.50. Open Mon-Sat. This tiny, nameless osteria, run by Antonio Bassetti, has a name for itself among locals as one of the best cheap eats in town – a step back in time to the days when it was as cheap to eat out as in. There's no menu – you take your pick from the list the owner rattles off.

Trattoria Pizzeria da Francesco *(☎ 06 686 40 09, Piazza del Fico 29)* **Map 7** Pizzas €4.65-7.20, pasta from €4.65, mains around €12.90. Open lunch & dinner Wed-Mon, Tues dinner only. As well as tasty pizza, this restaurant has good pasta and a variety of antipasti and vegetables.

Hostaria Giulio *(☎ 06 688 06 466, Via della Barchetta 19)* **Map 3** Full meals €18.05. Open Mon-Sat. This excellent-value family-run eatery serves consistently good food with traditional fare and a few less common dishes sharing space on the menu. Try the fresh *porcini* mushrooms, celery and parmesan salad or the feather-light gnocchi, a home-made speciality. The building dates from the 16th century, the dining room has a vaulted ceiling, and it's decorated cheerfully, with plenty of tables outdoors in summer.

Insalata Ricca *(☎ 06 856 88 036, Largo dei Chiavari 85)* **Map 7** Full meals €12.90. Open daily. Hearty pasta dishes and meal-in-themselves salads are on offer here. It's good value and has become very popular with young Romans.

Sergio alla Grotta *(☎ 06 686 42 93, Vic delle Grotte 27)* **Map 7** Open Mon-Sat. You don't need to see a menu here; decide what takes your fancy by looking at the pictures on the walls, then enjoy enormous helpings of traditional Roman pasta and sauces – *cacio e pepe* (pecorino cheese and ground black pepper), *carbonara*, *amatriciana* (with pancetta, tomato and chilli) – and good meat and fish dishes. The pizza oven and grill cater to all tastes. It's got a great atmosphere and has tables outside in summer.

Filetti di Baccalà *(☎ 06 686 40 18, Largo dei Librari 88)* **Map 7** Full meals €5.15. Open Mon-Sat. The main item on the menu here is deep-fried *baccalà* (salt cod). The fish fillets, which literally melt in the mouth, are presented wrapped in paper, and you eat them with your fingers rather than with a knife and fork. Various antipasto dishes, salads (including a Roman favourite of *puntarelle*, also known as Catalonian chicory, with an anchovy and garlic dressing) and desserts are also available.

Benito *(☎ 06 686 15 08, Via dei Falegnami 14)* **Map 7** Pasta & salad €5.70. Open lunch only Mon-Sat. Fast food, Roman style. There's a daily choice of two pasta dishes and a good range of meats and vegetables. Turnover is fast and furious so don't eat here if a long, leisurely lunch is what you're after.

Sora Margherita *(☎ 06 686 40 02, Piazza delle Cinque Scole 30)* **Map 3** Full meals €12.90-15.50. Open lunch only Mon-Fri. In the heart of the old Ghetto, Sora's is so well known and popular with the locals that there isn't even a sign over the door. Don't let the formica table tops put you off: you're here for the food – traditional Roman and Jewish fare – and the bargain prices. Get here early to avoid a queue (especially on Thursday if you want the fresh gnocchi).

City Centre – Mid-Range

Otello alla Concordia *(☎ 06 679 11 78, Via della Croce 81)* **Map 3** Pasta €5.15, main courses €15.50. Open Mon-Sat. The faithful following of local artisans and shopkeepers keeps Otello away from the tourist trap tag. Cannelloni and *pollo alla romana* (chicken with capsicums) are among the many dishes they do well. A glassed-in courtyard is used as an attractive winter garden in the colder months.

Mario *(☎ 06 678 38 18, Via della Vite 55)* **Map 3** Full meals €31. Open Mon-Sat. The very popular Mario's offers Tuscan food – fabulous bean soups, grilled meat and game. We've had some reports saying the service was fabulous, others that it was dreadful.

Al 34 *(☎ 06 679 50 91, Via Mario de' Fiori 34)* **Map 3** Full meals around €31. Open Tues-Sun. The menu here combines Roman cooking with regional dishes from throughout Italy. Try the rigatoni with *pajata* (chopped veal intestines) if you can stomach it, or the spaghetti with courgettes if you can't. For those with a really large appetite, a *menu degustazione* (gourmand's menu) is also available.

Osteria Margutta *(☎ 06 323 10 25, Via Margutta 82)* **Map 2** Full meals €25.85. Open Mon-Sat. In pretty Via Margutta, Osteria Margutta has a good selection of vegetable antipasto dishes, and pasta with tasty sauces such as broccoli and sausage.

Edy *(☎ 06 360 01 738, Vic del Babuino 4)* **Map 3** Full meals €23.25. Open Mon-Sat. Residents and shopkeepers of upmarket Via del Babuino make up Edy's regular clientele – they know it's a good bet in an area not known for great value. Try the house speciality, spaghetti *al cartoccio*, a silver-foil parcel of pasta and seafood. Fettucine with artichokes is also worth writing home about.

Colline Emiliane *(☎ 06 481 75 38, Via d'Avignonesi 22)* **Map 4** Full meals around €31. Open Sat-Thurs. A small trattoria near Piazza Barberini serving superb Emilia-Romagnan food. Try the home-made pasta stuffed with pumpkin and the veal *(vitello)* with mashed potatoes – both are delicious.

Osteria dell'Ingegno *(☎ 06 678 06 62, Piazza della Pietra 45)* **Map 3** Pasta from €8.25, full meals around €28. Open Mon-Sat. The modern designer decor of this eatery contrasts strongly with the ancient Hadrian's Temple opposite. The cuisine is central Italian with an international twist. Antipasti include porcini mushroom salad and warm goat's ricotta with grilled vegetables. Pastas range from farfalle with leeks and saffron to crepes stuffed with *scamorza* cheese and chicory *(radicchio)*. Meat mains include turkey, veal and Angas beef, plus a good selection of salads and an excellent wine list.

Il Bacaro *(☎ 06 686 41 10, Via degli Spagnoli 27)* **Map 7** Meals around €31. Open Mon-Sat. Just north of the Pantheon, Il Bacaro is a tiny restaurant where miracles are performed in a minute kitchen. The pasta and risotto dishes are imaginative and delicious, and they do great things with beef and veal. Booking is essential.

Ristorante Monserrato *(☎ 06 687 33 86, Via del Monserrato 96)* **Map 7** Full meals €25.85. An unassuming neighbourhood eatery that does marvellous things with fish and seafood. The spaghetti *alle vongole* (with clams) and risotto *con scampi* (with scampi) are among the best in Rome. Shady outdoor tables and a great wine list (with excellent whites from north-east Italy) encourage long, relaxed summer lunches.

La Carbonara *(☎ 06 686 47 83, Campo de' Fiori 23)* **Map 7** Full meals €31. Open Wed-Mon. La Carbonara is a popular spot, serving consistently good, traditional Roman fare at honest prices. As the name might suggest, it is known for its *spaghetti alla carbonara*.

Ditirambo *(☎ 06 687 16 26, Piazza della Cancelleria 72)* **Map 7** Full meals €20.65. Open Wed-Sun & dinner Mon. Ditirambo has a rustic feel with its wood beamed ceilings and wooden floors. The food is traditional Italian with a dash of innovation (such as tortelli with mint) and a good selection of vegetable-only dishes. The home-made bread and pasta add to its charms.

Da Giggetto *(☎ 06 686 11 05, Via del Portico di Ottavia 21–22)* **Map 3** Full meals €25.85. Open Tues-Sun. Good food and the Ghetto go hand in hand, and Giggetto is a local institution which combines the two well. It has been serving Roman Jewish cooking for years (the deep-fried artichokes are especially good). In the heart of the Ghetto, right next to the ancient Portico d'Ottavia, its location can't be beaten.

City Centre – Top End

Camponeschi *(☎ 06 687 49 27, Piazza Farnese)* **Map 7** Full meals €51.65. Open dinner Mon-Sat. You cannot find a more perfect setting for a restaurant than that of Camponeschi on the beautiful (and, delightfully, car free) Piazza Farnese. It is a favourite with politicians, diplomats and the glitterati.

La Rosetta *(☎ 06 686 10 02, Via della Rosetta 8–9)* **Map 7** Full meals from €67.15. Open Mon-Sat. Near the Pantheon, La Rosetta is without doubt the best seafood restaurant in Rome. The menu features innovative combinations – how about shrimp, grapefruit and raspberry salad or fried *moscardini* (baby octopus) with mint? Owner-chef Massimo Riccioli is regarded as one of the best in Italy. Expensive but memorable. Booking is essential.

Piperno *(☎ 06 688 06 629, Via Monte de' Cenci 9)* **Map 3** Full meals from €41.30. Open Tues-Sat & lunch Sun. In the heart of the Ghetto, Piperno has turned deep frying into an art form; the house special is a mixed platter of deep-fried fillets of baccalà, stuffed courgette flowers, vegetables and mozzarella cheese. Offal eaters will be well satisfied.

Vecchia Roma *(☎ 06 686 46 04, Piazza Campitelli 18)* **Map 3** Full meals €43.90. Open Thurs-Tues. The terrace of Vecchia Roma is one of the prettiest in Rome, and it's an extremely pleasant spot to pass a few hours. The pan-Italian menu is extensive and changes seasonally. In summer there are imaginative salads, in winter lots of dishes based on polenta, and there's good pasta and risotto year-round.

St Teodoro *(☎ 06 678 09 33, Piazza dei Fienili 49–50)* **Map 5** Full meals from €41.30. Open Mon-Sat. Tucked away in a quiet area between the Teatro di Marcello and the Palatine, the upmarket but informal St Teodoro offers an innovative menu combining Roman dishes with regional cuisine (the rich cooking of Emilia-Romagna features) and a strong emphasis on fish. Pasta dishes with seafood are especially good (the pasta is freshly made each day by the owner's mother). Try the *tonarelli St Teodoro*, which is incredibly light pasta with a sauce of juicy prawns, courgette and cherry tomatoes. Save space for *gelatini di frutta* – exquisite fruit flavoured ice creams. There's an interesting selection of wines from all over Italy in addition to good house wine. The gorgeous terrace is *the* place to be in summer, although the attractive modern art works lining the walls also make it very pleasant in winter.

Trastevere – Budget

In Trastevere's maze of tiny streets there are any number of pizzerias and cheap trattorias. The area is beautiful at night and most establishments have outside tables. It is also very popular, so arrive before 9pm unless you want to queue for a table.

Osteria Der Belli *(☎ 06 580 37 82, Piazza Sant'Apollonia 9–11)* **Map 5** Full meals €15.50. Open Tues-Sun. A reliable trattoria with a great antipasto selection and large helpings of pasta, although the main courses are nothing special. They also do pizza.

Da Augusto *(☎ 06 580 37 98, Piazza de' Renzi 15)* **Map 5** Full meals €12.90. Open Mon-Sat, but sometimes closes without notice. One of Trastevere's favourite mamma's kitchens, dishing up honest fare at prices you only read about. Enjoy your home-made fettuccine pasta or *stracciatella* (clear broth with egg and parmesan) at one of the rickety tables that spill out onto the piazza in summer.

Casetta di Trastevere *(☎ 06 580 01 58, Piazza de' Renzi 31a)* **Map 5** Full meals €12.90. Open Tues-Sun. There's nothing fancy about this neighbourhood trattoria just across the piazza – except that it always seems to be serving just what you fancy, such as steaming bowls of *pasta e fagioli* (thick borlotti bean soup) or piquant mounds of *penne amatriciana* (pasta with pancetta, tomato and chilli). When it's warm, the outdoor tables cram up and service gets slow.

Da Corrado *(Via d Pelliccia)* **Map 5** Full meals €10.35. Open Mon-Sat Sept-July. Just off Piazza de' Renzi, hidden behind an anonymous frosted-glass door, this is a no-frills workers' canteen and a favourite haunt of Trastevere's shopkeepers, especially at lunch. Choose from two or three pastas and two or three meat dishes daily.

Pizzeria San Calisto *(☎ 06 581 82 56, Piazza San Calisto 9a)* **Map 5** Pizzas €5.15-7.25. Open Tues-Sun. The enormous pizzas here fall off your plate. Dine at one of the outdoor tables in summer and watch the passing parade.

Pizzeria da Vittorio *(☎ 06 580 03 53, Via di San Cosimato 14)* **Map 5** Full meals €12.90. Neapolitan-style pizzas with a thicker base are on offer here. You'll have to wait for an outside table if you arrive after 9pm but the atmosphere is great. There are all the regular pizzas plus a few house specials such as the *Vittorio* (fresh tomato, basil, mozzarella and parmesan) and the *Imperiale* (fresh tomatoes, lettuce, cured ham and olives).

Pizzeria Popi-Popi *(☎ 06 589 51 67, Via delle Fratte di Trastevere 45)* **Map 5** Pizzas €4.15-6.20. Open Fri-Wed. A popular haunt among the youth of Rome, which is hardly surprising since its pizzas are good, big and cheap. Dodge those garlands of garlic in the cavernous interior. The outdoor tables that spill into the piazza opposite are a big attraction in summer.

Panattoni *(☎ 06 580 09 19, Viale di Trastevere 53)* **Map 5** Meals around €7.75. Open Thurs-Tues Sept-July. Also known as L'Obitorio (The Morgue) on account of its cold hard marble tables, this is one of the more popular pizzeria in Trastevere. It opens late and is always crowded.

Pizzeria Ivo *(☎ 06 581 70 82, Via di San Francesco a Ripa 158)* **Map 5** Pizzas from €4.65. This pizzeria has outdoor tables but the pizza could be bigger for the price. The bruschetta is an excellent start to the meal.

Trastevere – Mid-Range

Da Lucia *(☎ 06 580 36 01, Vicolo del Mattonato 2)* **Map 5** Meals around €18.05. Open Tues-Sun. Excellent antipasto and pasta are on offer here as well as Roman specialities such as *pollo con peperoni* (chicken with peppers) and *trippa all romana* (tripe). Many locals return time and again for the spaghetti *alla gricia* (with pecorino cheese, pancetta and a dash of olive oil). In summer it has outside tables where you sit beneath a cobweb of washing lines.

La Botticella *(☎ 06 581 47 38, Vicolo del Leopardo 39a)* **Map 5** Full meals €18.05. Rome's best *spaghetti all'amatriciana* can be had here, as well as typically Roman tripe, oxtail or lamb, and *fritto alla botticella* – a tempura-like dish of deep-fried vegetables, strangely including delicious apple slices. In summer you'll eat outside beneath the neighbours' washing and probably feel that you're part of their conversations and arguments as well.

La Tana di Noantri *(☎ 06 580 64 04, Via Paglia 1)* **Map 5** Pizzas from €4.15, full meals €25.85. Open Wed-Mon. Tucked between Piazza Santa Maria in Trastevere and Piazza Sant'Egidio, this place has an extensive menu and is a good place to take children, who can tuck into a pizza while their parents enjoy more sophisticated fare. The antipasto and meat and fish dishes are particularly good. In the warmer months tables are set up under huge umbrellas in the small courtyard opposite the restaurant – an excellent spot to watch the passing parade of human (rather than vehicular) traffic.

Ferrara *(☎ 06 580 37 69, Via del Moro 1a)* **Map 5** Full meals €36.15. Open Wed-Mon. Ferrara is a compulsory stop on any foodie itinerary for dishes such as *orecchiette* pasta with courgettes and ginger-scented prawns or warm rabbit salad with spicy couscous. Expert advice is on tap for choosing wine from the encyclopaedic lists – this is one of Rome's best *enoteche* (wine bars) after all – and the vaulted, whitewashed dining room is decorated with old barriques. Book a courtyard table.

Monzù Vladi *(☎ 06 589 56 40, Piazza San Giovanni della Malva 2)* **Map 3** Full meals from €18.05. This attractive restaurant offers Neapolitan cuisine in an elegant setting. The *frittelle* (fired pastry disks) topped with a dollop of tomato sauce and the home-made *cavatelli* pasta with seafood are especially good.

Paris *(☎ 06 581 53 78, Piazza San Calisto 7)* **Map 5** Full meals €41.30. Open Tues-Sat & lunch Sun. Paris is the best place outside the ghetto proper to sample true Roman-Jewish cuisine. The delicate *fritto misto con baccalà* (deep-fried vegetables with salt cod) is memorable, as are simpler dishes such as the *pasta e ceci* (a thick chickpea soup in which the pasta is cooked) and fresh grilled fish.

Testaccio – Budget & Mid-Range

Pizzeria Remo *(☎ 06 574 62 70, Piazza Santa Maria Liberatrice 44)* **Map 5** Meals around €8.25. You won't find a noisier, more popular pizzeria in Rome than Pizzeria Remo in Testaccio. The pizzas are huge but have a very thin crust. You make your order by ticking your choices on a sheet of paper given to you by the waiter.

Augustarello *(☎ 06 574 65 85, Via Giovanni Branca 98)* **Map 5** Pasta €5.70, mains €6.70-7.75. Open Mon-Sat. If sweetbreads and oxtail aren't your thing, then don't come here. Virtually every dish (other than the pasta) in this old-fashioned trattoria has some correlation to the innards of an animal.

Trattoria da Bucatino *(☎ 06 574 68 86, Via Luca della Robbia 84)* **Map 5** Pasta €5.15-6.20, pizzas €5.15-6.20, full meals around €15.50. Open Tues-Sun. This restaurant is a popular Testaccio eating place, with pizza, pasta and Roman fare.

Checchino dal 1887 *(☎ 06 574 63 18, Via di Monte Testaccio 30)* **Map 5** Full meals around €38.75. Open Tues-Sun. This family-run eatery provides constant fodder for travel magazines seeking the best places for traditional Roman dining. Its location near the former abattoir is appropriate, given that offal – from calves' heads to pigs' trotters and sweetbreads – is its trademark. The great wine cellar is a bonus.

Around Stazione Termini & San Lorenzo – Budget & Mid-Range

If you have no option but to eat near Stazione Termini, try to avoid the places offering overpriced tourist menus – the food is never any good. There are many *tavole calde* (self-service eateries with ready-cooked food) in the area, particularly to the west of the train station, which offer *panini* (sandwiches) and pre-prepared dishes for reasonable prices. There are also several bars and self-service places within the station complex.

Moka *(☎ 06 474 22 11, Via Giolitti 34)* **Map 4** Brilliant for train travellers (and others), Moka, next to platform 24 at Stazione Termini, offers really tasty ready-made food – pastas, salads and snacks – and is open 24 hours a day.

Da Gemma alla Lupa *(☎ 06 49 12 30, Via Marghera 39)* **Map 4** Full meals €15.50. A simple trattoria (north-east of the station) with prices to match.

Trattoria da Bruno *(Via Varese 29)* **Map 4** Pasta €4.65, mains €7.75. One of the best places to eat in this (relative) culinary wasteland with good food at reasonable prices. Home-made gnocchi is served on Thursday.

Hosteria Angelo *(Via Principe Amedeo 104)* **Map 4** Pasta €5.15. Hosteria Angelo is a traditional trattoria with very reasonable prices.

As Rome's university district, eating places in San Lorenzo are influenced by the student population.

Pizzeria l'Economia *(Via Tiburtina 44)* **Map 4** Pizzas from €4.15. One of the more popular places, it serves local fare and good pizzas at prices students can afford.

Formula 1 *(☎ 06 445 38 66, Via degli Equi 13)* **Map 4** Pizzas from €4.15, full meals €7.75. A good-value pizzeria in the university area, which is always full.

Le Maschere *(☎ 06 445 38 05, Via degli Umbri 8)* **Map 4** Pizzas from €4.15. Cheap and cheerful, Le Maschere has a huge student clientele.

Il Dito e la Luna *(☎ 06 494 07 26, Via dei Sabelli 47–51)* **Map 4** Meals around €25.85.

Eating Ethnic

Fed up with pasta? Pizza'd out? Well try one of the following for a spicy taste of multicultural Rome.

L'Eau Vive *(☎ 06 688 01 095, Via Monterone 85)* **Map 6** Full meals from €41.95. Open Mon-Sat. L'Eau Vive is quite unique. It is run by the Domus Dei order of nuns – who drop everything to sing a tuneful Ave Maria in the middle of the dinner service. The food is French/international but it's not great.

Sogo Asahi *(☎ 06 678 60 93, Via di Propaganda 22)* **Map 3** Full meals from €36.15. Open Mon-Sat. A separate sushi bar, teppanyaki room and sakura (with tatami mats) preserve the atmosphere and ritual of Japanese dining. Tasting menus are excellent value and sushi lovers shouldn't miss the Saturday evening sushi buffet.

Baires *(☎ 06 692 02 164, Via Cavour 315)* **Map 4** One of a chain of fun, funky Argentinian restaurants, which serves up steaks as big as Sardinia, meat any which way and flavoursome soups based on legumes and pulses. Knock it all back with the excellent organic house wine. It's a good place for a rowdy, hungry group.

Il Guru *(☎ 06 474 41 10, Via Cimarra 4–6)* **Map 4** Full meals from €18.05. Gurus in the know and those who just want a good Indian meal eat here. The menu offers tandooris, curries (of every strength) and great vegetarian choices. The exotic decor will transport you eastwards and the friendly proprietor will steer you clear of curries that are too hot to handle.

Mexico al 104 *(☎ 06 474 27 72, Via Urbana 104)* **Map 4** Set menu €15. It's hardly Acapulco but it's the closest you'll get in the centre of Rome. Tuck into tacos, burritos, chimichanga, flautas, tamales or enchiladas.

Shawerma *(☎ 06 700 81 01, Via Ostilia 24)* **Map 6** Full meals from €15.50. Open Mon-Sat. Half pub, half informal eatery, Shawerma serves Egyptian-style comfort food to soak up the lagers. House specialities are vegetable couscous, vegetable tagine, kebabs, taboule and falafels. Come on Friday or Saturday night for belly-dancing.

Oliphant *(☎ 06 686 14 16, Via della Coppelle 31)* **Map 7** Full meals from €41.95. Rome's first 'Tex-Mex' restaurant is still one of the best and is a good place for a meat fix if that's what you want. Go Tex with hot dogs or buffalo wings or Mex with tortillas and enchiladas. A good range of beers makes it a popular hangout.

Thien Kim *(☎ 06 683 07 832, Via Giulia 201)* **Map 7** Full meals from €23.25. Open Mon-Sat. This place offers an Italian take on Vietnamese cooking, with tasty dishes that are lighter and more strongly flavoured than other Vietnamese restaurants in Rome.

Surya Mahal *(☎ 06 589 45 54, Piazza Trilussa 50)* **Map 3** Full meals around €25.85. This Indian restaurant has a delightful garden terrace right next to the fountain on Piazza Trilussa in Trastevere. Set menus – vegetarian, meat or fish – provide an opportunity to try almost everything.

ATM Sushi Bar *(☎ 06 683 07 053, Via della Penitenza 7)* **Map 3** Full meals from €23.25. This sushi bar is tucked away in the quiet backstreets of Trastevere. Chill out amidst the minimalist decor, soft lighting and relaxed music, and chow down on excellent sushi, sashimi, nori rolls, tempura and other Japanese classics.

Jaipur *(☎ 06 580 39 92, Via San Francesco a Ripa 56)* **Map 5** Full meals €15.50. Open Tues-Sun & dinner Mon. An excellent Indian restaurant in the heart of Trastevere.

The excellent Sicilian-inspired menu serves interesting dishes such as anchovies marinated in orange juice, a savoury tart made with onions and melted parmesan and *caponata* (a sort of Sicilian ratatouille).

Pommidoro *(☎ 06 445 26 92, Piazza dei Sanniti 44)* **Map 1** Full meals €20.65. Open Mon-Sat. This place is one of the area's more famous trattorias, popular with artists and intellectuals. Specialities are grilled meats and, in winter, game.

Monti & Celio – Budget & Mid-Range

This is a good area for cheap eateries. Stroll around Via del Boschetto, Via dei Serpenti, Via Panisperna, Via Urbana and Via Madonna de' Monti and you're bound to find something to whet your appetite. Many of the best ethnic eateries are located here.

Alle Carrette *(☎ 06 679 27 70, Vicolo delle Carrette 14)* **Map 4** Full meals €10.30. A decent pizzeria off Via Cavour near the Roman Forum, well placed to rest weary legs after a hard day's sightseeing.

Al Giubileo *(☎ 06 481 88 79, Via del Boschetto 44)* **Map 4** Full meals €12.90. Open Tues-Sun. Waiters dash around this high-energy pizzeria punching orders into computer handsets, pizza is piled onto wooden slabs, and hungry punters dig in. Neapolitan pizza comes to Rome with Al Giubileo's *pizza verace*. There's plenty of other stuff on the menu, including melt-in-your-mouth *gnocchi alla sorrentina*.

Da Ricci *(☎ 06 488 11 07, Via Genova 32)* **Map 4** Pizzas from €5.70. Open Tues-Sun. Reputed to be the oldest pizzeria in Rome, Da Ricci started up as a wine shop in 1905 and has been run by the same family ever since. The pizzas turned out here have a slightly thicker crust than the normal Roman variety but some say this is the best pizza in town. There are also good salads and home-made desserts.

Osteria Gli Angeletti *(☎ 06 474 33 74, Via dell'Angeletto)* **Map 4** Pasta €5.15-7.25, mains around €8.25. Open Jan-Nov. Consistently good food and outdoor seating on atmospheric Piazza Madonna dei Monti make this an excellent little trattoria. The service can get a bit slow when they're busy but the prices are reasonable. The menu caters well to both carnivores and vegetarians, with a cluster of fail-safe pasta dishes to satisfy the fussiest of eaters.

Vegetarian Restaurants

Vegetarians will have no problems eating in Rome. Most eating establishments serve a good selection of antipasti, *contorni* (vegetable side dishes prepared in a variety of ways) and salads. Most traditional Roman pasta dishes are suitable for vegetarians. Other dishes to look out for are: *pasta e fagioli*, a thick soup made with borlotti beans and pasta; *pasta al pesto*, with basil, parmesan, pine nuts and olive oil; and *orecchiette ai broccoletti*, ear-shaped pasta with a broccoli sauce, often quite spicy. Risotto is usually a good choice, although sometimes it is made with a meat or chicken stock. For a dedicated vegetarian restaurants, try one of the following.

Naturist Club – L'Isola *(☎ 06 679 25 09, 4th floor, Via delle Vite 14)* **Map 4** Full meals from €12.90. Also known as the Centro Macrobiotico Italiano, this place has a double life: at lunch it's a semi-self-service vegetarian eatery serving veggie pies and wholegrain risottos; by night it's a la carte dining with fish as the speciality.

Margutta Vegetariano *(☎ 06 678 60 33, Via Margutta 118)* **Map 2** Full meals from €20.65. Unfortunately the vegetarian specialities here are bland and disappointing; stick with veggie versions of Italian staples – pizza and pasta – and you'll eat well. The bizarre decor features black '70s-style love couches. There's another branch of the same operation near the Pantheon, ***Le Cornacchie*** *(Map 7; ☎ 06 681 34 544, Piazza Rondanini 53)*.

Cafes

Coffee aficionados have a wealth of choice for their daytime tipplings. There are several excellent bars near the Pantheon (Map 7), including ***La Tazza d'Oro*** *(Via degli Orfani 84–86)*, ***Camilloni a Sant'Eustachio*** *(☎ 06 686 49 95, Piazza Sant'Eustachio 54–55)* and ***Caffè Sant' Eustachio*** *(☎ 06 686 13 09,*

Piazza Sant'Eustachio 82). The latter makes *gran caffè*, a wonderful, almost bubbly, coffee made by beating the first drops of espresso and several teaspoons of sugar into a frothy paste, then adding the coffee on top.

Caffè Farnese *(☎ 06 688 02 125, Via dei Baullari 106)* **Map 7** On one corner of the lovely Piazza Farnese, this is a great spot for people watching, especially on Saturday morning when the Campo de' Fiori market is at its busiest.

Caffè Marzio *(Piazza Santa Maria in Trastevere)* **Map 4** You will pay €2.60 for a cappuccino if you sit down outside (compared with €0.75 at the counter inside) but it's worth it as this cafe looks onto one of Rome's most beautiful and atmospheric piazzas.

Bar Vezio *(Via dei Delfini 23)* **Map 6** You won't find a panoramic view or a sun-filled piazza at this bar in the Ghetto but you should find some old *compagni* (companions) without much effort. Vezio's bar, also known as the 'communist bar', is the neighbourhood watering hole for the nearby Democratici di Sinistra party headquarters. It's a veritable archive of Italian communist memorabilia; Stalin competes against Che Guevara for space on the walls and there's even Fidel Castro's visiting card.

Sandwiches & Snacks

Fast food Roman style usually consists of a hearty filled *panino* (sandwich), a slice of piping hot *pizza bianca* (plain focaccia-like bread) or a tasty slice of *pizza a taglio* (also known as *pizza rustica)*.

There are hundreds of bars around the city that are good options for cheap, quick meals. A sandwich taken at the bar *(al banco)* will cost between €1.50 and €3. At a takeaway pizzeria, a slice of freshly cooked pizza, sold by weight, can cost as little as €1.50. There are numerous bakeries in the Campo de' Fiori area which are good for a cheap snack. A piece of pizza bianca costs from around €0.75 cents a slice.

Paladini *(Via del Governo Vecchio 29)* **Map 6** The staff are glum, there's nowhere to sit and you can wait for ages to be served, but the continuous mass of customers affirms its position as Rome's best sandwich shop. Fill your piping-hot door-stopper pizza bianca with cured meats, cheese, artichokes and more.

M & M Volpetti *(Via della Scrofa 31)* **Map 6** Near Piazza Navona, this upmarket sandwich bar-cum-deli-cum-*rosticceria* (restaurant specialising in grilled meats) sells gourmet lunch snacks (and takeaway dinners) for above-average prices.

Antico Forno *(☎ 06 679 28 66, Via delle Muratte 8)* **Map 3** Your wishes won't necessarily come true by throwing a coin into the Trevi Fountain but a few coins spent in this famous bakery opposite will assure you of a delicious slice of pizza or a hearty filled panino.

Forno di Campo de' Fiori *(☎ 06 688 06 662, Campo de' Fiori 22)* **Map 7** People come from all over the city for this bakery's pizza bianca. Drizzled with extra virgin olive oil and sprinkled with crunchy grains of sea salt, it proves the maxim that less is more. Buy it by the metre.

Forno la Renella *(☎ 06 581 72 65, Via del Moro 15–16)* **Map 5** Trastevere's famous bakery has been producing Rome's best bread for decades. As the embers die down in the wood-fired ovens, the bakers turn their hand to slabs of thick, doughy pizza with toppings such as tomato, olives and oregano, or potato and rosemary. This pizza a taglio is worth crossing rivers for.

Frontoni *(Viale di Trastevere)* **Map 4** Among the city's more famous sandwich outlets, Frontoni makes its panini with both pizza bianca and bread, with an enormous range of fillings. Sandwiches are sold by weight. It also has good pizza a taglio.

Volpetti Più *(Via A Volta 8)* **Map 5** It is worth making a special trip to Testaccio to eat lunch at Volpetti Più. It's a tavola calda so you don't pay extra to sit down. The pizza a taglio is extraordinarily good and there are plenty of pasta, vegetable and meat dishes.

Zì Fenizia *(Via di Santa Maria del Pianto 64)* **Map 3** Open Fri-Wed, closed Jewish holidays. Better known as the kosher pizzeria, Zì Fenizia makes, arguably, the city's best pizza a taglio. There's no cheese on this kosher variety but you don't miss it, and the toppings are not the usual suspects either. This is pizza a taglio *par excellence*.

There are numerous pizza-a-taglio outlets all over the city. Usually you can judge the quality of the pizza simply by taking a look. Some good places are around Campo de' Fiori (Map 6): ***Pizza Rustica*** *(Campo de' Fiori)* and ***Pizza a Taglio*** *(Via Baullari)*, between Campo de' Fiori and Corso Vittorio Emanuele II. Just off Piazza di Trevi (Map 3) is ***Pizza a Taglio*** *(Via delle Muratte)*.

Ice Cream

Gelateria Giolitti *(Via degli Uffici del Vicario 40)* **Map 6** Gelateria Giolitti has long been a Roman institution. At one time it regularly delivered tubs of Pope John Paul II's favourite flavour, *marrons glacé* (glacé chestnuts) to his summer residence. The 70-odd flavours on offer are bound to satisfy less pious sweet tooths.

Gelateria della Palma *(Via della Maddalena 20)* **Map 7** You could be forgiven for thinking you'd stumbled into Willy Wonka's factory here, and choosing from the 100 flavours is surprisingly difficult. The house specialities are the extra creamy (and rich) *mousse gelati*, and the *meringata* varieties with bits of meringue dotted through them.

La Fonte della Salute *(Via Cardinal Marmaggi 2–6)* **Map 5** Whether this Trastevere gelateria really is a fountain of health (as its name translates) is debatable, although the soy- and yoghurt-based gelati support the theory. The fruit flavours are superb and the marron glacé so delicious that it *has* to be good for you. Scoops are more generous than at gelaterias in the historic centre.

Bar San Calisto *(☎ 06 583 58 69, Piazza San Calisto)* **Map 5** There's nothing fancy about this neighbourhood bar but our ongoing research suggests that the chocolate gelato – soft and creamy and almost like a mousse – is the best in town.

Cakes & Pastries

Bernasconi *(Piazza B Cairoli 16)* **Map 7** There's always a tempting selection of cakes and pastries at Bernasconi; the *cornetti all crema* (custard-filled pastries) are to die for.

Bella Napoli *(Corso Vittorio Emanuele 246a)* **Map 7** You won't get better Neapolitan-style pastries outside of Naples. Try stopping at just one *sfogliatelle* (ricotta-filled sweet pastry).

La Dolceroma *(Via del Portico d'Ottavia 20)* **Map 3** Right next to the Portico d' Ottavia, La Dolceroma specialises in Austrian cakes and pastries, and American treats such as cheesecake, brownies and chocolate-chip cookies.

Il Forno del Ghetto *(Via del Portico d'Ottavia 2)* **Map 3** You'll lose all self-control when you see what the all-female team in this tiny kosher bakery can produce. People come from all parts of Rome for the ricotta and damson tart. Buy a slice and you'll know why.

Sacchetti *(Piazza San Cosimato 61)* **Map 5** Sacchetti is a Trastevere favourite with shoppers and stallholders at Piazza San Cosimato market. Ignore the grumpy proprietors; these cakes – especially the chestnut and cream confection called *monte bianco* – are something special.

Panella l'Arte del Pane *(Largo Leopardi 2–10)* **Map 4** On Via Merulana, near Stazione Termini, this place has a big variety of pastries and breads.

Self-Catering

For groceries and supplies of cheese, *prosciutto*, salami and wine, shop at *alimentari* (grocery stores). For fresh fruit and vegetables, there are numerous outdoor markets, notably the lively daily markets in Campo de' Fiori, Piazza Testaccio (Map 7), Piazza San Cosimato (Map 5), Piazza Vittorio Emanuele (Map 5) and Via Andrea Doria (north of the Vatican). Supermarkets are few and far between in the centre, although you'll find a few in Trastevere; the rest are in the outer suburbs. The following are some of Rome's better-known gastronomic establishments.

Castroni *(☎ 06 687 43 83, Via Cola di Rienzo 196)* **Map 3** Castroni, in Prati near the Vatican, has a wide selection of gourmet foods, packaged and fresh, including international foods (desperate Aussies will find Vegemite here). There are other outlets around the city.

Gino Placidi *(Via della Maddalena 48)* **Map 7** This place, near the Pantheon, is one of central Rome's best alimentarie.

Volpetti *(☎ 06 574 23 52, Via Marmorata 47)* **Map 5** Volpetti, in Testaccio, is famous for its gastronomic specialities, including a large selection of unusual cheeses from throughout Italy.

Billo Bottarga *(Via Sant'Ambrogio 20)* **Map 3** This store, near Piazza Mattei, specialises in kosher food and is famous for its *bottarga* (roe of tuna or mullet).

Health Foods

Buying muesli, soya milk and the like can be expensive in Italy. The following outlets have a good range of products, including organic fruit and vegetables, at relatively reasonable prices.

L'Albero del Pane *(☎ 06 686 50 16, Via di Santa Maria del Pianto 19)* **Map 3** In the Jewish quarter, this store has a wide range of health foods, both packaged and fresh.

Emporium Naturae *(Viale Angelico 2)* **Map 1** This is a well-stocked health-food supermarket. To get there, take Metro Linea A to Ottaviano San Retro.

Il Canestro *(Via Luca della Robbia 47)* **Map 5** In Testaccio, near the market, this shop has a large selection of health foods, as well as fresh fruit and vegetables and take-away food.

ENTERTAINMENT

You don't have to look far to be entertained in Rome. Whether it's opera or football, dance or drinking, the Eternal City has something for everyone. Most of the activity is in the historic centre. Campo de' Fiori is especially popular with younger crowds, while the alleyways near Piazza Navona hide some interesting late-night hang-outs. Trastevere, Monti and Equiline hills are also full of bars, pubs and gay venues.

The pub and bar scene isn't huge – basically because Romans (and Italians in general) don't consume a lot of alcohol. However the past few years has seen the arrival of dozens of new 'theme' pubs, which cater to the growing numbers of young travellers and students. The clubbing scene is less active in Rome than in other European capitals. Still, there is something for all tastes, with some clubs retaining a certain sophisticated glamour and others priding themselves on being the latest in hip and groovy.

Rome comes alive in summer with the many festivals of dance, music, opera, theatre and cinema. Many of these performances take place under the stars, in parks, gardens and church courtyards, with classical ruins and Renaissance villas as the backdrop. Catch one of these productions and it will undoubtedly be the highlight of your trip. Autumn is also full of cultural activity with specialised festivals dedicated to dance, drama and jazz.

And if you tire of all of the above, follow the lead of the Roman youth, who have made doing nothing into an art form.

Roma C'è is the most comprehensive entertainment guide and has a small section in English. It is published every Thursday. *Wanted in Rome*, published on alternate Wednesdays, contains listings and reviews of the most important festivals, exhibitions, dance, classical music, opera and cinema. Both magazines are available from newsstands. The daily newspapers *Il Messaggero* and *La Repubblica* have listings of theatre, cinema and special events.

Pubs & Bars

Pubs Pubs are not traditionally part of Roman culture but have taken off with a bang since the early 1990s. Most are styled after traditional English or Irish pubs, although there are also places with Australian or American themes. They offer a wide selection of draught and bottled beers and many have Guinness on tap.

The Drunken Ship *(☎ 06 683 00 535, Campo de'Fiori 20)* **Map 7** Foreign students (especially Americans) seem to make The Drunken Ship their second home in Rome. Perhaps it's the welcoming atmosphere or the daily happy hour from 7pm to 9pm.

Trinity College *(☎ 06 678 64 72, Via del Collegio Romano 6)* **Map 3** There's a good selection of imported beers, great food and an easy-going ambience in this stalwart of the pub scene. It gets packed to overflowing on Fridays and at weekends.

Four XXXX *(☎ 06 575 72 96, Via Galvani 29)* **Map 5** This eclectic Testaccio haunt has undergone a bit of 'Latinisation' and has something for everyone: Castlemaine XXXX beer on tap for homesick Aussies, Tequila cocktails if you want something stronger, tasty South American food, and good live jazz or a DJ most nights.

Big Hilda *(☎ 06 580 33 03, Vic del Cinque 33–34)* **Map 5**. Murphy's stout and bitter on tap and a few good wines are the attractions here in this smoky, buzzing, music-filled Trastevere pub.

Marconi *(☎ 06 486 636, Via Santa Prassede 9)* **Map 4** Regulars come here as much for the food as the booze. It's a bit of an international smorgasbord, with Irish breakfasts and stodgy English fish'n'chips alongside Hungarian goulash. Oh, and then there's the beer...

Fiddler's Elbow *(☎ 06 487 21 10, Via dell'Olmata 43)* **Map 3** The Guinness, darts and chips formula has been working well here for over 20 years, so they don't look like they're going to change it. This was one of the first Irish pubs to hit Rome, and it's still popular with foreigners and locals.

Bars If you prefer bars to pubs, try one of the following.

Sloppy Sam's *(☎ 06 688 02 637, Campo de' Fiori 9–10)* **Map 7** A cross between an Italian bar and an English pub, Sloppy Sam's is friendly and relaxed. Settle into a repro antique chair, choose your beer from the selection on tap, grab a plate of nachos and take it from there.

Bar del Fico *(☎ 06 686 52 05, Piazza del Fico 26)* **Map 7** Popular with local actors and artists, this bar buzzes until the early hours, and crowds spill out the door and block the neighbouring streets.

Bar della Pace *(☎ 06 686 12 16, Via della Pace 5)* **Map 7** Drowning in ivy and with a superb wood-panelled interior, this gorgeous corner bar is as good for an early evening aperitif outside in summer as for a leisurely nightcap (or a light meal) inside in winter. Bring some serious attitude with you.

Jonathan's Angels *(☎ 06 689 34 26, Via della Fossa 18)* **Map 7** Rome at its quirky best is on display here. Run by an artist, the whole bar – even the loo – is covered with pictures and decorations. It's a relaxed place for a late night drink.

Bar San Calisto *(☎ 06 583 58 69, Piazza San Calisto)* **Map 5** Seedy and cheap, the perennially popular but decidedly unglamorous Bar San Calisto attracts Trastevere locals, the arty set, people apparently doing drug deals and a few well-known winos. It's famous for its to-die-for hot chocolate in winter and chocolate gelato (the best in town) in summer.

Stardust *(☎ 06 583 20 875, Vicolo dei Renzi 4)* **Map 5** A cross between a pub and a jazz venue, Stardust often has live jazz and jam sessions. It's a real neighbourhood place that tends to close when the last customers fall out the door.

Friends Art Café *(☎ 06 581 61 11, Piazza Trilussa 34)* **Map 3** A fashionable and lively drinking spot that has Internet access and staff with attitude.

Bartaruga *(☎ 06 689 22 99, Piazza Mattei 9)* **Map 3** Named – in a fashion – after the Fontana delle Tartarughe opposite, this combined cocktail bar, tearoom and pub is quirky and original. Decked out in bright colours, with oriental furniture, velvet cushions and a Turkish harem feel, it's the type of place where you can spend hours either sipping tea or scoffing wine.

Wine Bars Wine bars are a feature of most Roman neighbourhoods. They sell wine, spirits and olive oil, and are often frequented by groups of elderly locals enjoying a glass of wine and a chat in much the same manner as they might have a coffee at a bar. In recent years a more sophisticated breed of *enoteca* (wine bar) has been attracting a different crowd from the regular pub-goers. Many of these offer snacks or light meals in addition to an extensive range of wines that you can taste by the glass (ask for it *alla mescita* or *al bicchiere*) or buy by the bottle.

Vineria *(☎ 06 688 03 268, Campo de' Fiori)* **Map 7** Also known as Da Giorgio, this enoteca was once the gathering place of the Roman literati. Today, the crowd that spills out into the piazza is decidedly less bookish but it's still a fun place to drink with a wide selection of wine and beers.

L'Angolo Divino *(☎ 06 686 44 13, Via dei Balestrari)* **Map 7** This charming enoteca, with wooden beams and terracotta floors, is a lovely place for a quiet glass of wine, a nibble of cheese or a light meal.

Il Goccetto *(☎ 06 686 42 68, Via dei Banchi Vecchi 14)* **Map 3** Most of the customers of this club-like wine bar are regulars who drop in for a drink after work. Wines from all over the world share shelf space with the top Italian drops and there's a choice of around 20 wines by the glass.

Amici del Treno e del Vino *(☎ 06 581 66 93, Via del Moro 10)* **Map 7** This tiny Trastevere haunt is done up like a train carriage. Cute but cramped, it has a good selection of wines.

Trimani *(☎ 06 446 96 61, Via Cernaia 37)* **Map 4** Trimani, near Stazione Termini, is Rome's biggest enoteca and has a vast selection of Italian regional wines with excellent soups, pasta and *torta rustica* (quiche) on offer for lunch and dinner.

Clubs & Live Music Venues

In terms of dance clubs – discos to the locals – Rome falls way behind Berlin or London. Still, there's plenty of choice, from grungy clubs with live music or cool DJs to upmarket discos frequented by jet-set types. The latter can be expensive; expect to pay up to €20 to get in, which may or may not include one drink.

Alien *(☎ 06 841 22 12, Via Velletri 13)* **Map 2** The distinctive decor of Alien is like something out of a science fiction film. Dancers on raised platforms groove to the rhythm of house, techno and hip-hop. For the retros among us, one of the two dance areas features 1970s' and '80s revivals.

Gilda *(☎ 06 678 48 38, Via Mario de'Fiori 97)* **Map 3** Appealing to a slightly older, wealthier and – some might say – 'less-than-cool' clientele, Gilda has plush decor, state-of-the-art lighting and a huge dance floor. Despite all this, it has a sterile, formal atmosphere – not helped, perhaps, by the dress code, which requires jackets.

Goa *(☎ 06 574 82 77, Via Libetta 13)* **Map 1** The far-from-central location near San Paolo Fuori-le-Mura hasn't affected the popularity of Goa. It's decked out in ethnic style, with comfy couches to sink into when your feet need a break from the dance floor. The bouncers rule – you might not get in if they don't like the look of you. Tuesday is 'Gorgeous Goa Gay' night.

Black Out Rock Club *(☎ 06 704 96 791, Via Saturnia 18)* **Map 6** Known as *the* club for punk, rock and indie music, Black Out occasionally has gigs by British (and American) punk and rock bands.

Locale *(☎ 06 687 90 75, Via del Fico 3)* **Map 7** Off Via del Governo Vecchio, near Piazza Navona, this live music/dance venue is very popular among young foreigners and Italians. Expect to queue on Friday and Saturday night.

Bush *(☎ 06 572 88 691, Via Galvani 46)* **Map 5** This Testaccio club has a reputation for excellent DJs, especially on Thursday which is hip-hop, R&B and soul night.

Radio Londra *(☎ 06 575 00 44, Via di Monte Testaccio 65b)* **Map 5** Decked out like an air-raid shelter, Radio Londra has live music four nights a week.

Caruso *(☎ 06 574 50 19, Via di Monte Testaccio 36)* **Map 5** There's live music twice a week at Caruso, and good DJs playing Latin, rock and hip-hop the rest of the time.

Caffè Latino *(☎ 06 574 40 20, Via di Monte Testaccio 96)* **Map 5** As you might expect, this venue has live Latin American music most nights, followed by a disco of Latin, acid jazz and funk. There are also cabaret and film screenings.

Villaggio Globale *(☎ 06 573 00 39, Lungotevere Testaccio)* **Map 5** Located in the former slaughterhouse, Villaggio Globale is one of Rome's *centri sociali*, a type of squatters' club frequented by ageing hippies, new-age types and people who are still into punk and 'grunge'. Many big acts perform here.

Jazz & Blues

Alexanderplatz *(☎ 06 397 42 171, Via Ostia 9)* **Map 1** Top international (particularly

American) musicians and well-known Italian artists feature on the programme nightly. In July and August the club moves to the grounds of the Renaissance Villa Celimontana (Map 6) on Caelian Hill for ***Villa Celimontana Jazz*** *(☎ 06 589 78 07)* one of Rome's popular summer festivals.

Folkstudio *(☎ 06 487 10 630, Via Frangipane 42)* **Map 4** This place, near Via Cavour, is an institution in the Roman music scene and provides a stage for folk, jazz and world music as well as young artists just starting out.

Big Mama *(☎ 06 581 25 51, Vic San Francesco a Ripa 18)* **Map 5** Big Mama has branded itself as the 'home of the blues', although it also plays host to rock and jazz artists, both Italian and international.

Classical Music

Accademia di Santa Cecilia *(☎ 06 688 01 044, Via della Conciliazione 4)* **Map 3** World-class international performers join the highly regarded Santa Cecilia Orchestra, directed by Myung-Whun Chung. Short festivals dedicated to a single composer are a feature of the autumn calendar. In June the orchestra and its guest stars move to the beautiful gardens of the Renaissance Villa Giulia (north of the city; also houses the Museo Nazionale Etrusco) for its summer concert series.

Accademia Filarmonica Romana *(☎ 06 323 48 90, Teatro Olimpico, Piazza Gentile da Fabriano 17)* **Map 1** The Filarmonica programme features mainly chamber music, with some contemporary concerts and multimedia events. The academy was founded in 1821 and its members have included Rossini, Donizetti and Verdi.

Free concerts are often held in many of Rome's churches, especially at Easter and around Christmas and New Year. Seats are available on a first-come-first-served basis and the programs are generally excellent. Check newspapers and listings press for programs.

Gay & Lesbian Venues

Details of Rome's gay and lesbian bars and clubs are provided in gay publications and through local gay organisations (see Gay & Lesbian Travellers in the Facts for the Visitor chapter).

Hangar *(☎ 06 488 13 97, Via in Selci 69)* **Map 4** Rome's oldest gay bar, run by an American, is still one of its most popular. The varied clientele – international and Italian, all age groups – includes a significant portion of gym bunnies. Monday is gay video night.

L'Alibi *(☎ 06 574 34 48, Via di Monte Testaccio 44)* **Map 5** L'Alibi is regarded by many as Rome's premier gay venue.

Edoardo II *(☎ 06 699 42 419, Vicolo Margana 14)* **Map 3** There's amusing decor (it's done up like a medieval torture chamber) and a mixed clientele (mostly dressed in black) at this gay club just off Piazza Venezia. There's no dancing – it's just a bar – but it's a good cruising spot.

Garbo *(☎ 06 583 20 782, Vicolo di Santa Margherita 1a)* **Map 4** Rome's first (and not only) gay cafe/bar catering to couples rather than cruisers. The clientele is a mix of Italians and foreigners.

Alpheus *(☎ 06 541 39 58, Via del Commercio 271b)* **Map 1** It's a fair way from the centre but this is where it happens for gays and lesbians on Friday night.

Buon Pastore Centre *(☎ 06 686 42 01, Via San Francesco di Sales 1a)* **Map 3** This place is hardly hip and happening but it's one of the few lesbian spaces in Rome. There's a cafe and a women-only restaurant, ***Le Sorellastre***.

Cinemas

Films are shown regularly in English at the following cinemas.

Pasquino *(☎ 06 580 36 22, Piazza Sant' Egidio)* **Map 3** Films in English daily.

Quirinetta *(☎ 06 679 00 12, Via Marco Minghetti 4)* **Map 3** Films in English daily.

Alcazar *(☎ 06 588 00 99, Via Merry del Val)* **Map 5** Films in English on Monday.

Nuovo Sacher *(☎ 06 581 81 16, Largo Ascianghi 1)* **Map 4** Films in original language Monday and Tuesday.

Warner Village Moderno *(☎ 06 477 79 202, Piazza della Repubblica)* **Map 4** Five cinemas showing Hollywood blockbusters (both in English and dubbed into Italian) and major release Italian films.

A popular form of entertainment in the hot Roman summer is outdoor cinema.

Isola del Cinema *(☎ 06 583 31 13, W www.isoladelcinema.com)* This international film festival takes place on the Isola Tiberina and features independent films.

Massenzio *(☎ 06 428 14 962, W www.massenzio.it)* Massenzio is one of Rome's most popular summer festivals. Several films, both current release and old favourites, are shown each night on a huge screen under the stars on Caelian Hill (Map 6) opposite the Colosseum. Check the listings magazines or the daily press for details of these events.

Theatre

Italian theatre is often more melodramatic than dramatic. There are over 80 theatres in the city, many of them worth visiting as much for the architecture and decoration as for the production itself. Some performances are in English.

Teatro Argentina *(☎ 06 688 04 601, Largo di Torre Argentina 52)* **Map 7** This state-funded theatre, the official home of the Teatro di Roma, stages major theatre and dance productions.

Teatro dell'Orologio *(☎ 06 683 08 735, Via dei Filippini 17a)* **Map 3** Fringe theatre and works by contemporary Italian playwrights are staged here.

Teatro Valle *(☎ 06 688 03 794, Via del Teatro Valle 23a)* **Map 7** This theatre shows English-language works translated into Italian plus some excellent international productions.

Off-Night Repertory Theater *(☎ 06 444 13 75, Arte del Teatro Studio, Via Urbana 107)* **Map 4** An international theatre company that performs a mix of contemporary one-act plays and full-length dramas in English every Friday.

The Miracle Players *(☎ 06 446 98 67, W www.miracleplayers.org)* This group performs classic English drama such as *Everyman* and *Julius Caesar*, usually in abridged form, near the Roman Forum and other atmospheric open-air locations.

Opera

Teatro dell'Opera *(☎ 06 481 60 255 or toll free 800 01 66 65, fax 06 488 17 55, Piazza Beniamino Gigli)* **Map 5** Rome's opera season starts in December and continues until June. Tickets are expensive: the cheapest upper balcony seats (not recommended for vertigo sufferers) start at around €25 and prices go up to €120. First-night performances cost more.

In summer, opera is performed outdoors in the Stadio Olimpico.

Dance

There's an active dance scene in Rome and many of the world's best companies tour Italy although quality home-grown companies are few and far between. See the listings magazines and daily press for details. The Teatro dell'Opera (see the Opera section earlier) includes a few classical ballets in its season. These productions are generally worth seeing only if there are important guest stars, as the opera's corps de ballet has been in a sorry state for many years.

SPECTATOR SPORTS

The city's two football teams, AS Roma and Lazio, play their home matches at ***Stadio Olimpico*** *(Foro Italico)* to the north of the city centre. Tickets cost around €16–70 can be bought from the ticket office (☎ 06 323 73 33) at the ground or from agencies such as Orbis (☎ 06 482 74 03), Piazza Esquilino 36.

SHOPPING

Don't feel bad if you find that Rome's shop windows are competing with its monuments for your attention. Just make sure you allocate plenty of time (as well as funds) for shopping. Rome's main shopping districts include Piazza di Spagna for designer clothing, shoes and leather goods; Via Nazionale and surrounds for a good mix of affordable clothing; Via dei Coronari for antiques; and Via del Governo Vecchio for second-hand and alternative clothing. If you can time your visit to coincide with the sales *(saldi)*, you'll pick up some marvellous bargains. The winter sales run from early January to around mid-February and the summer sales from July to August. Shops open from around 9.30am to 1pm and 3.30pm to 7.30pm (4pm to 8pm in summer). There is a trend towards longer opening hours (9.30am to 7.30pm) but usually only the larger shops or department stores do this.

Clothing, Shoes & Leather Goods

The big designer names need no introduction; all are located around Via Condotti (Map 3 unless otherwise indicated). Good diffusion ranges include ***Emporio Armani*** *(☎ 06 360 02 197, Via del Babuino 140)*, ***MaxMara*** *(☎ 06 679 36 38, Via Frattina 28; also at Via Condotti 17 and Via Nazionale 28)*, ***Fendissime*** *(☎ 06 69 66 61, Via della F Borghese 56/a)* and ***Valentino*** *(☎ 06 360 01 906, Via del Babuino 61)*.

For shoes and leather, try ***Gucci*** *(☎ 06 678 93 40, Via Condotti 8)*, ***Bruno Magli*** *(☎ 06 488 43 55, Via Vittorio Veneto 70)* **(Map 4)**, ***Fratelli Rossetti*** *(☎ 06 678 26 76, Via Borgognona 5a)*, ***Tod's*** *(☎ 06 678 68 28, Via Borgognona 45)* and ***Mandarina Duck*** *(☎ 06 699 40 320, Via di Propaganda 1)*.

For cheaper high-street fashion, head for ***Benetton*** *(☎ 06 699 24 010, Via Cesare Battisti 129)*, ***Sisley*** *(☎ 06 699 41 787, Via Frattina 19a)*, ***Stefanel*** *(☎ 06 679 26 67, Via Frattina 31–32)* and ***Max & Co*** *(☎ 06 678 79 46, Via Condotti 46)*.

Antiques, Design & Homewares

The best antique shops are in and around Via dei Coronari (near Piazza Navona), Via Giulia and Via del Babuino. Bargain furniture is a rare find in Rome but a wander past the artisan workshops on Via del Pellegrino or Via dei Cappellari (near Campo de' Fiori) might unearth a gem.

Alinari *(☎ 06 679 29 23, Via Alibert 16a)* **Map 3** The Alinari brothers were famous Italian photographers in the late 19th century. The photographic prints (mostly views of Rome) on sale here are reproduced from the archives of their work, which contain more than a million glass plate negatives.

Nardecchia *(☎ 06 686 93 18, Piazza Navona 25)* **Map 7** This Roman landmark is only marginally less famous than Bernini's Fontana dei Quattro Fiumi opposite. It sells antique prints, including 18th-century etchings of Rome by Giovanni Battista Piranesi, and less expensive 19th-century views of the city.

Flos Arteluce *(☎ 06 320 76 31, Via del Babuino 84–85)* **Map 3** More like a museum of lighting fixtures than a retail outlet, Flos 'exhibits' minimalist pieces in chrome and steel, and simple colours such as black and white.

C.U.C.I.N.A. *(☎ 06 679 12 75, Via del Babuino 118/a)* **Map 3** Once upon a time C.U.C.I.N.A. was seriously avant-garde, selling groovy chrome everything and innovative modular shelf units on which to store it. The stainless steel look has become ubiquitous, but good quality kitchenware can still be snapped up here.

Leone Limentani *(☎ 06 688 06 686, Via Portico d'Ottavia 47)* **Map 3** This warehouse-style shop has an unbelievable choice of kitchenware and tableware. High-priced fine porcelain and crystal sits alongside bargain basement items. It also stocks plenty of Alessi.

For Children

La Cicogna *(☎ 06 678 69 77, Via Frattina 138)* **Map 3** Italians spend big on kids' clothes, and the La Cicogna chain is a favourite store; it has fashionable children's clothes by top designers as well as its own label.

PrèNatal *(☎ 06 488 14 03, Via Nazionale 45)* **Map 4** This Italy-wide chain sells well-made wardrobe staples for kids (up to 11 years) and expecting mums, as well as equipment such as bottles, strollers, cradles and cots.

Città del Sole *(☎ 06 688 03 805, Via della Scrofa 65)* **Map 7** When only the best quality educational and creative toys will do, this is the place for kids and adults alike.

Bertè *(☎ 06 687 50 11, Piazza Navona)* **Map 7** The patriarch of the family that runs this fabulous toy shop bears a striking resemblance to Pinocchio's Geppetto. So it's rather appropriate that the toys here include beautifully made wooden dolls and puppets, finely crafted scooters in wood and metal, and high-quality educational games.

Mel Giannino Stoppani *(☎ 06 699 41 045, Piazza dei Santissimi Apostoli 59–65)* **Map 3** The best children's bookshop in Rome stocks mainly Italian books but one corner is devoted to French, Spanish, German and English titles.

Markets

Everyone flocks to the ***flea market*** **(Map 5)** at Porta Portese on Sunday morning. A mishmash of new and old, the market has all manner of incredible deals but you have to be prepared to drive a hard bargain. The market extends along the side streets parallel to Viale Trastevere. Be extremely aware of pickpockets and bag snatchers.

The excellent ***market*** **(Map 6)** on Via Sannio, near Porta San Giovanni, sells new and second-hand clothes. It's open to around 1pm Monday to Saturday. For prints, antiques and books, head for the ***market*** **(Map 3)** at Largo della Piazza Fontanella di Borghese , held every morning except Sunday.

GETTING THERE & AWAY

Air

Rome's main airport is Leonardo da Vinci (☎ 06 659 53 640 or 06 659 54 455), also known as Fiumicino after the town nearby. The city's other airport is Ciampino (☎ 06 79 49 41), where many national and some international (including charter) flights arrive. See the Getting Around section in this chapter for details on getting to and from the airports, and the Getting There & Away chapter for information on flights to and from Rome.

All the airlines serving Rome have counters in the departure hall at Fiumicino. Many of the head offices are now based at or near the airport, although most have ticket offices in the area around Via Vittorio Veneto and Via Barberini, north-west of Stazione Termini (Map 4).

Alitalia (☎ 06 6 56 42, Ⓦ www.alitalia.it) Via Bissolati 20
Air France (☎06 48 79 11, Ⓦ www.airfrance.it) Via Sardegna 40
British Airways (☎ 848 81 22 66, Ⓦ www.british-airways.com) Via Bissolati 54
Air Canada (☎ 06 655 15 06, Ⓦ www.aircanada.ca) Via C Veneziani 58
Cathay Pacific (☎ 06 482 09 30, Ⓦ www.cathaypacific.com) Via Barberini 3
Delta (☎ 800 86 41 14, Ⓦ www.delta.com) Via Sardegna 40
Lufthansa (☎ 06 656 84 004, Ⓦ www.lufthansa.com) Via di San Basilio 41
Qantas (☎ 06 524 82 725, Ⓦ www.qantas.com) Via Bissolati 54
Singapore Airlines (☎ 06 47 85 51, Ⓦ www.singaporeair.com) Via Barberini 11
TWA (☎ 800 84 18 43, Ⓦ www.twa.com) Via Barberini 67

Bus

The main station for intercity buses is on Piazzale Tiburtina, in front of Stazione Tiburtina (Map 1). Take Metro Linea B from Stazione Termini to Tiburtina. Various bus lines run services to cities throughout Italy; all depart from the same area and the relevant ticket offices or agents are next to the bus terminus.

Linee Laziali (formerly, but frequently still, referred to as Cotral) buses service the Lazio region and depart from numerous points throughout the city, depending on their destination. The company is linked with Rome's public transport system, which means that you can usually buy one ticket that covers city buses, trams, Metro and train lines, and regional buses and trains. Some useful bus lines include:

ARPA, SIRA, Di Fonzo, Di Febo & Capuani Services to Abruzzo, including L'Aquila, Pescasseroli and Pescara. Information and tickets from ARPA (toll free ☎ 8488 6 54 14), Via Teodorico 24, off Piazzale Tiburtina.
Segesta Services to Sicily (Messina, Palermo & Trapani). Information and tickets from Tiburviaggi (☎ 06 442 90 091), Via Guido Mazzoni 36–38, off Piazzale Tiburtina.
SAIS Services to Sicily. Information from Picarozzi (☎ 06 440 44 95; Ⓦ www.autolinee.it), Via Guido Mazzoni 12–14, off Piazzale Tiburtina.
Interbus Services to Sicily. Information and tickets from Tiburviaggi (☎ 06 442 90 091), Via Guido Mazzoni 36–38, off Piazzale Tiburtina.
Bonelli Services to Emilia-Romagna. Information and tickets from Picarozzi (☎ 06 440 44 95; Ⓦ www.autolinee.it), Via Guido Mazzoni 12–14, off Piazzale Tiburtina.

Lirosi Services to Calabria. Information from Eurojet (☎ 06 474 28 01).

Marozzi Services to Bari and Brindisi, Sorrento, the Amalfi Coast and Pompeii. Information and tickets from Eurolines (☎ 06 440 40 09, W www.eurolines.it), Circonvallazione Nomentana 574, off Piazzale Tiburtina, and Eurojet (☎ 06 474 28 01), Piazza della Repubblica 54.

Sena Services to Siena. Information at Picarozzi (☎ 06 440 44 95), Via Guido Mazzoni, off Piazzale Tiburtina, and Eurojet (☎ 06 474 28 01), Piazza della Repubblica 54.

Sulga Services to Perugia and Assisi, as well as to Leonardo da Vinci airport. Information at Eurojet (☎ 06 474 28 01) or SUGLA Perugia (☎ 075 500 96 41).

Train

Almost all trains arrive at and depart from Stazione Termini. There are regular connections to all the major cities in Italy and Europe. Sample 2nd-class, one-way train fares on Intercity/Eurostar trains (including supplements) are Rome-Milan €37/43, Rome-Venice €37/43 and Rome-Naples €16/21. Return fares are double the one-way fare.

For train information, ring ☎ 848 88 80 88 (Italian only) from 7am to 9pm or go to the information office at the train station, where English is spoken. The office opens 7am to 9.45pm but be aware that there are always lengthy queues. Timetables can be bought at most newsstands in and around Stazione Termini and are particularly useful if you are making multiple train journeys. Remember to validate your train ticket in the yellow machines on the station platforms. If you don't, you may be forced to pay a fine on the train.

Services at Stazione Termini include (very expensive) luggage storage, telephones, Internet cafes and currency exchange booths. Metro and city bus tickets are sold at tobacconists inside the train station.

There are eight other train stations scattered throughout Rome. Some trains depart from or stop at Stazione Ostiense and Stazione Tiburtina.

Car & Motorcycle

The main road connecting Rome to the north and south of Italy is the Autostrada del Sole, which extends from Milan to Reggio di Calabria. On the outskirts of the city it connects with the Grande Raccordo Anulare, the ring road encircling Rome. From here, there are several arteries into the city.

If you are approaching from the north, take the Via Salaria, Via Nomentana or Via Flaminia exits. From the south, Via Appia Nuova, Via Cristoforo Colombo and Via del Mare (which connects Rome to the Lido di Ostia; see South of Rome later in this chapter) all provide reasonably direct routes into the city. The Grande Raccordo Anulare and all arterial roads in Rome are clogged with traffic on weekday evenings from about 5pm to 7.30pm. On Sunday evening, particularly in summer, all approaches to Rome are subject to traffic jams as Romans return home after weekends away.

The A12 goes out to Civitavecchia and then runs north along the coast to Genoa (it also connects the city to Leonardo da Vinci airport).

Signs to the autostrada from the centre of Rome can be vague and confusing so invest in a good road map. It's best to stick to the arterial roads to reach the Grande Raccordo Anulare and then exit at the appropriate point. Main roads out of Rome basically follow the same routes as ancient Roman consular roads. The seven most important are listed below.

Via Aurelia (S1) Starts at the Vatican and leaves the city to the north-east, following the Tyrrhenian coast to Pisa, Genoa and France.

Via Cassia (S2) Starts at the Ponte Milvio and heads north-west to Viterbo, Siena and Florence.

Via Flaminia (S3) Starts at the Ponte Milvio; goes north-west to Terni, Foligno and over the Apennines into Le Marche, ending on the Adriatic coast at Fano.

Via Salaria (S4) Heads north from near Porta Pia in central Rome to Rieti and into Le Marche, ending at Porto d'Ascoli on the Adriatic coast.

Via Tiburtina (S5) Links Rome with Tivoli and Pescara, on the coast of Abruzzo.

Via Casilina (S6) Heads south-east to Anagni and into Campania, terminating at Capua near Naples.

Via Appia Nuova (S7) The most famous of the consular roads, it heads south along the coast of Lazio into Campania and then goes inland across the Apennines into Basilicata, through Potenza and Matera to Taranto in Apulia and on to Brindisi.

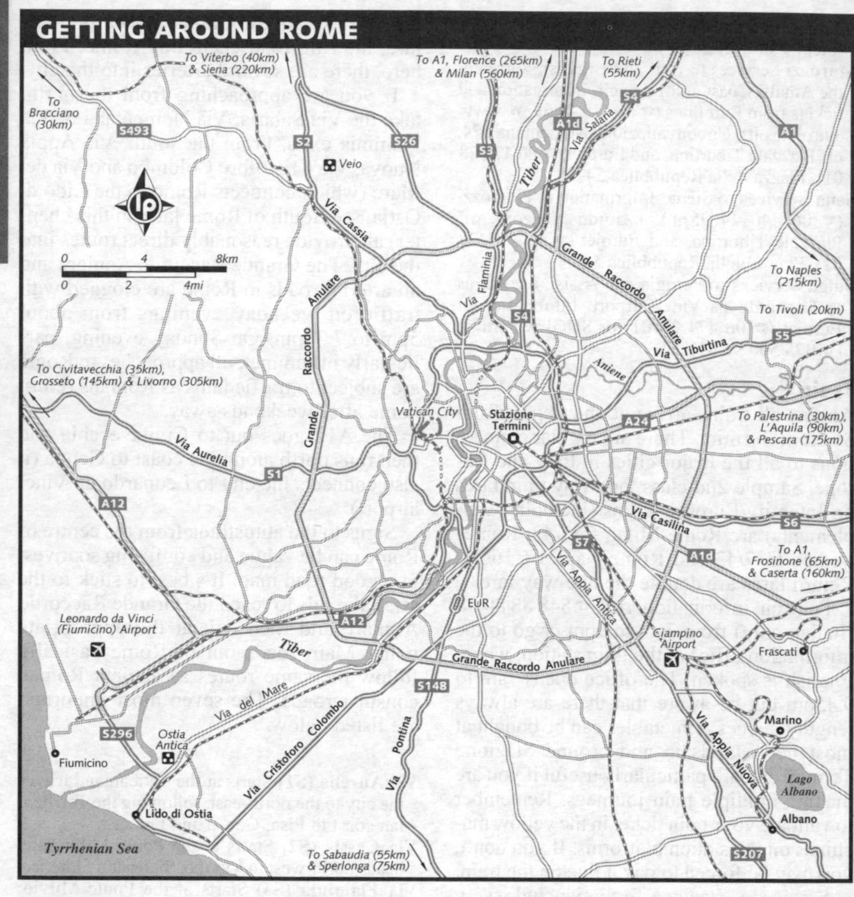

Hitching

It is illegal to hitchhike on the autostrada so you have to wait on main roads near autostrada entrances. To head north on the A1, take bus No 319 from Stazione Termini, get off at Piazza Vescovio and then take bus No 135 to Via Salaria. To go south to Naples on the A1/A2, take the Metro to Anagnina and wait in Via Tuscolana.

There is an International Lift Centre in Florence (☎ 055 28 06 26) that matches people up with drivers, and Enjoy Rome (see Tourist Offices at the beginning of this chapter) might also be able to help. Hitching is not recommended, particularly for women, either alone or in groups. See the Getting Around chapter for more details.

GETTING AROUND

To/From the Airports

Rome's main airport, Leonardo da Vinci (also known as Fiumicino), is about 30km south-west of the city centre. The Leonardo Express, the direct Fiumicino-Stazione Termini train (follow the signs to the train station from the airport arrivals hall), costs €8.80. The train arrives at and leaves from platform Nos 25–29 at Termini (a fair walk from the main concourse) and takes about 30 minutes. The first direct train leaves the airport for Termini at 7.37am, then trains run half-hourly until the last one at 10.37pm. From Termini to the airport, trains start at 6.51am and run half-hourly until the last train at 9.21pm.

Another train from Leonardo da Vinci stops at Trastevere, Ostiense and Tiburtina stations (€4.65). From the airport, trains run about every 20 minutes from 5.57am to 11.27pm, and from Tiburtina from 5.06am until 10.36pm. You should allow more time on Sundays and public holidays when there is a reduced service. This train does not stop at Termini.

From midnight to 5am, an hourly bus runs from Stazione Tiburtina (accessible by bus No 42N from Piazza dei Cinquecento, in front of Termini) to the airport (€4.65).

Taxis leave from outside the arrivals hall, but they are expensive: a taxi to the centre of Rome will cost from €36.15 (including an airport surcharge of €7.75, plus surcharges for luggage, at night and on public holidays).

Several private companies run limousine services which work out about the same price as a taxi but are usually a lot more comfortable. Airport Connection Services (☎ 06 338 32 21) has two deals – a shuttle service in a minivan for €17.05 per person (minimum two passengers) or a chauffeur driven Mercedes for €38.75. Coop Airport (☎ 06 650 88 141 Monday to Saturday or ☎ 06 659 54 910 on Sunday) has offices in the arrivals areas at Leonardo da Vinci and offers a limousine service for €41.35 to central Rome (with a 20% supplement from 11pm to 7am). Both services can be booked for airport pick-ups or drop-offs.

The airport is connected to the city by an autostrada. Follow the signs for Rome out of the complex and exit from the autostrada at EUR. From there, you'll need to follow the centro signs or else ask directions to reach Via Cristoforo Colombo, which will take you directly into the centre.

If you arrive at Ciampino airport, infrequent Cotral buses (operating from 5.45am to 10.30pm) will take you to the Anagnina Metro station, from where you can get to Stazione Termini. If you arrive late or very early, you have little option other than to take a taxi (around €31). Ciampino airport is connected to Rome by the Via Appia Nuova.

Bus & Tram

ATAC (☎ 800 43 17 84 from 8am to 6pm, W www.atac.roma.it) is the city's public transport company. Many of the main bus routes terminate in Piazza dei Cinquecento at Stazione Termini where there's an information booth (on stand C in the centre of the piazza). Largo di Torre Argentina, Piazza Venezia and Piazza San Silvestro are other hubs. Buses generally run from about 6am until midnight, with limited services throughout the night on some routes. Pick up a free transport map from the ATAC information booth at Termini or from any tourist information booth.

Travel on Rome's buses, trams, Metro and suburban railways is part of the same system, and the same Metrebus ticket – also known as *biglietto integrato a tempo* (BIT) – is valid for all modes of transport. You can buy tickets at tobacconists, at newsstands and from vending machines at main bus stops. Single tickets cost €0.77 for 75 minutes. Children up to 1m tall travel free. Daily tickets cost €3.09, weekly tickets €12.40. Tickets must be purchased before you get on the bus or train and then validated in the machine once on the bus or tram (at the entrance gates for the Metro). You risk a €52 fine if you're caught without a valid ticket; being an 'ignorant' tourist won't get you off the hook.

Rome also has a private network of J buses (☎ 800 07 62 87, W www.linee-j.com), which are express services covering a limited number of routes. Tickets cost €1 and last 75 minutes. Day tickets are €2.45, two-day tickets €4.13, three-day tickets €5.90 and weekly tickets €9.30.

Useful routes are listed below.

No 8 (tram) Largo di Torre Argentina to Trastevere, Stazione Trastevere and Monteverde Nuovo.

No 46 Piazza Venezia to St Peter's and the Via Aurelia.

No 64 Stazione Termini to St Peter's.

No 40 Stazione Termini to St Peter's (Express route with fewer stops than No 64).
No 27 Stazione Termini to the Colosseum, Circo Massimo and Aventine Hill.
No 36 Stazione Termini along Via Nomentana (for foreign embassies).
No 116 Via Giulia through the city centre to Villa Borghese park (small electric bus).
No 218 Piazza San Giovanni in Laterano to the Via Appia Antica and the Catacombs.
No 910 Stazione Termini to the Villa Borghese.
No 590 Follows the route of Metro Line A and has special facilities for disabled passengers.
J4 San Paolo Fuori-le-Mura, Circo Massimo, Colosseum, Roman Forum, Castel Sant'Angelo.
J5 Stazione Tiburtina to San Giovanni, Colosseum, Roman Forum, Largo Argentina, Corso Vittorio Emanuele to St Peter's.
J3 Stazione Termini to the catacombs via Santa Maria Maggiore and Terme di Caracalla.

Metropolitana & Train

The Metropolitana (Metro) has two lines, Linea A and Linea B. Both pass through Stazione Termini. It operates from 5.30am to 11.30pm (one hour later on Saturday) and trains run approximately every five to 10 minutes. Useful Metro stations include Spagna (Linea A) for Piazza di Spagna; Flaminio (Linea A) for Villa Borghese; Ottaviano/Cipro-Musei Vaticani (Linea A) for the Vatican; Colosseo (Linea B) for the Colosseum; Circo Massimo (Linea B) for Circo Massimo, Aventino, Celio, Terme di Caracalla; and Piramide (Linea B) for Stazione Ostiense, trains to the airport and Lido di Ostia.

In addition to the underground Metropolitana, Rome has an overground rail network. The rail network is useful only if you are heading out of town to the Castelli Romani, the beaches at Lido di Ostia or the ruins at Ostia Antica (see the Lazio section later in this chapter).

Car & Motorcycle

Negotiating Roman traffic by car is difficult enough, but you may be taking your life in your hands if you ride a motorcycle or moped in the city. The rule in Rome is to look straight ahead to watch the vehicles in front and hope that the vehicles behind are watching you!

Most of the historic centre of Rome is closed to normal traffic. Police control some of the entrances to the centre, while other entrances have electronic gates. Check with your hotel about gaining access – traffic officers *(vigili urbani)* might let you through if they see your car full of luggage but an electronic gate can't make a judgement.

Traffic police are getting very tough on illegally parked cars. At best you'll get a heavy fine (around €105), at worst a wheel clamp or your car towed away. In the event that your car goes missing after it was parked illegally, always check first with the traffic police (☎ 06 6 76 91). You will have to pay about €95 to get it back, plus a hefty fine.

A parking system operates around the periphery of Rome's city centre. Spaces are denoted by a blue line in most areas including the Lungotevere (the roads beside the Tiber; Map 5) and near Stazione Termini (Map 4). You'll need small change to get tickets from machines, otherwise scratch tickets are available from tobacconists.

The major parking area closest to the centre is at the Villa Borghese; entry is from Piazzale Brasile at the top of Via Vittorio Veneto (Map 2). There is also a supervised car park at Stazione Termini. Other car parks are at Piazzale dei Partigiani, just outside Stazione Ostiense and at Stazione Tiburtina, from where you can also catch the metro into the centre.

Car Rental See the Getting Around chapter for details (including sample costs) on renting a car.

The major rental companies have representatives in Rome.

Avis
24-hour Booking ☎ 199 100 133
Ciampino Airport ☎ 06 793 40 195
Leonardo da Vinci Airport ☎ 06 650 11 531
Stazione Termini ☎ 06 481 43 73

Europcar
Central Booking ☎ 06 52 08 11
Leonardo da Vinci Airport ☎ 06 650 10 879
Stazione Termini ☎ 06 488 28 54

Maggiore National
Central Booking ☎ 848 86 70 67
Leonardo da Vinci Airport ☎ 06 650 10 678
Stazione Termini ☎ 06 488 00 49

Allow plenty of time if you're dropping off hire cars at Leonardo da Vinci airport or at a station. There are usually dedicated parking areas for hire cars *(autonoleggio)* but these aren't always easy to find.

Motorcycle & Bicycle Rental Motorcycles (as well as scooters or mopeds) and bicycles can be rented from Happy Rent (Map 4; ☎ 06 481 81 85), Via Farini 3. Motorcycle (600cc) rental costs are around €103 per day and scooters and mopeds (50cc to 125cc) cost from €31 to €68 per day. Bicycle rental is from €2.60 for one hour to €62 for a week. It also rents cars and mini-vans. Baby seats are available for both cars and bicycles.

Another option is Bici e Baci (Map 4; ☎ 06 482 84 43), Via del Viminale 5, near Piazza della Repubblica. Scooter rental starts at €20 per day; a bicycle costs €8 per day. Bicycles are also usually available for hire on Piazza del Popolo and at the Villa Borghese.

Taxi

Rome's taxis are notoriously expensive. Flagfall is €2.30 (for the first 3km), then €0.60 per km with supplements for luggage (€1.05), night travel (€2.60) and to/from the airports. Pick up a cab from a taxi rank as, strictly speaking, they're not allowed to be hailed in the street. If you telephone for a taxi (☎ 06 55 51 or 06 49 94 or 06 35 70) the driver will turn on the meter immediately and you will pay the cost of travel from wherever the driver was.

Lazio

Declared a region in 1934, the Lazio area has, since ancient Roman times, been an extension of Rome. Through the ages, the rich built their villas in the Lazio countryside and many towns developed as the fiefdoms of noble Roman families such as the Orsini, Barberini and Farnese families. Even today, Romans build their weekend and holiday homes in the picturesque areas of the region (the pope, for instance, has his summer residence at Castelgandolfo, south-east of Rome) and Romans continue to migrate from the chaotic and polluted city to live in the Lazio countryside. This means the region is relatively well served by public transport and tourists can take advantage of this to visit places of interest.

While the region isn't exactly packed with major tourist destinations, it does offer some worthwhile day trips from the city. A tour of Etruria, the ancient land of the Etruscans (which extended into northern Lazio) is highly recommended. Visits to the tombs and museums at Cerveteri and Tarquinia provide a fascinating insight into Etruscan civilisation. The ruins of Villa Adriana (Hadrian's Villa), near Tivoli, and of the ancient Roman port at Ostia Antica, are both easily accessible from Rome, as is the medieval town of Viterbo, north of the capital. In summer, tired and overheated tourists can head for the lakes north of Rome, which are somewhat preferable to the polluted beaches near the city, or head south to the relatively clean and sandy beaches of Sabaudia or Sperlonga.

There are some hill-top towns to the south-east of Rome that are worth visiting, such as Anagni (which has remarkable frescoes in its Romanesque cathedral), Alatri and those of the Castelli Romani (see South of Rome later in this chapter) in the hills just past Rome's outskirts. Those interested in Italy's involvement in WWII might want to visit Monte Cassino, the scene of a major battle during the last stages of the war.

If you have your own transport, try to avoid day trips out of Rome on Sunday during summer. On your return in the evening, you are likely to find yourself in traffic jams

Cheap Bus & Train Tickets

If you are travelling in Lazio by Cotral bus and trains, check out the daily BIRG tickets, which allow unlimited use of city and regional transport, including the metro in Rome. The cost depends on the distance travelled but ranges from around €4.50 to €10.

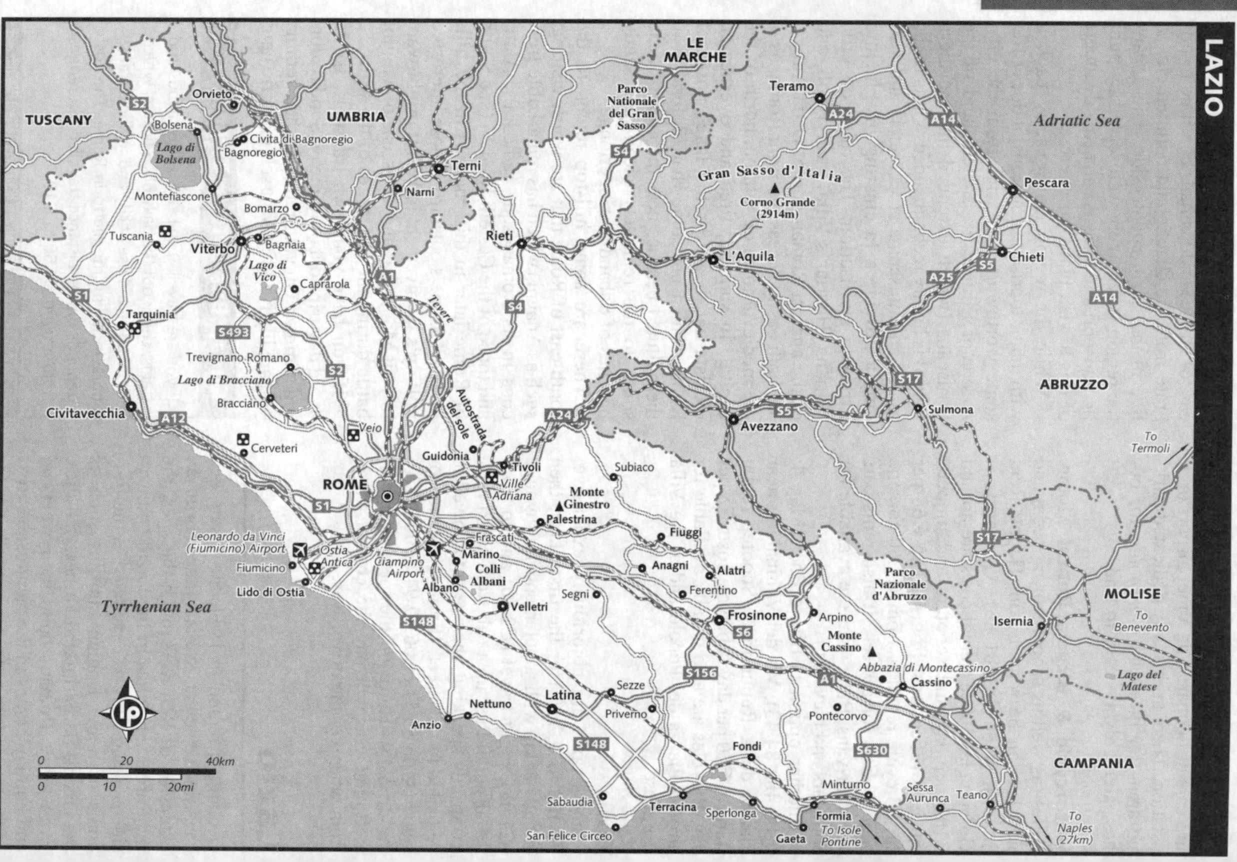
LAZIO
TUSCANY
UMBRIA
LE MARCHE
ABRUZZO
MOLISE
CAMPANIA
Adriatic Sea
Tyrrhenian Sea
Orvieto
Bolsena
Lago di Bolsena
Civita di Bagnoregio
Bagnoregio
Montefiascone
Bomarzo
Tuscania
Viterbo
Bagnaia
Lago di Vico
Caprarola
Tarquinia
Trevignano Romano
Lago di Bracciano
Bracciano
Civitavecchia
Cerveteri
Veio
Terni
Narni
Rieti
Tevere
Autostrada del sole
Guidonia
Tivoli
Villa Adriana
ROME
Leonardo da Vinci (Fiumicino) Airport
Ostia Antica
Fiumicino
Lido di Ostia
Ciampino Airport
Frascati
Marino
Colli Albani
Albano
Velletri
Parco Nationale del Gran Sasso
Teramo
Gran Sasso d'Italia
Corno Grande (2914m)
L'Aquila
Pescara
Chieti
Avezzano
Sulmona
To Termoli
Subiaco
Monte Ginestro
Palestrina
Fiuggi
Anagni
Alatri
Ferentino
Segni
Frosinone
Arpino
Parco Nazionale d'Abruzzo
Monte Cassino
Abbazia di Montecassino
Cassino
Isernia
To Benevento
Lago del Matese
Latina
Sezze
Priverno
Nettuno
Anzio
Pontecorvo
Fondi
Sabaudia
San Felice Circeo
Terracina
Sperlonga
Gaeta
To Isole Pontine
Formia
Minturno
Sessa Aurunca
Teano
To Naples (27km)
A1
A12
A14
A24
A25
S1
S2
S4
S5
S6
S17
S148
S156
S493
S630
0 20 40km
0 10 20mi

extending for many kilometres, including on the autostrada.

OSTIA ANTICA

The Romans founded this port city at the mouth of the River Tiber in the 4th century BC and it became a strategically important centre for defence and trade. It was populated by merchants, sailors and slaves, and the ruins of the city provide a fascinating contrast to the ruins at Pompeii, which was a resort town for the wealthy classes. Barbarian invasions and the outbreak of malaria led to the city's eventual abandonment, and it slowly became buried – up to 2nd-floor level – under river silt, which explains the excellent state of preservation of the remains. Pope Gregory IV re-established the town in the 9th century AD.

Information about the town and ruins is available from the APT office in Rome (see Tourist Offices under Rome at the beginning of this chapter).

There is a good ***cafe/restaurant*** within the complex, but it's also an atmospheric spot for a picnic.

Things to See

The **ruins** *(☎ 06 563 58 099; admission €4.20; 9am-6pm Tues-Sun Feb-Oct, 9am-5pm Tues-Sun Nov-Mar)* are quite spread out and you will need a few hours to see them all.

The clearly discernible ruins of restaurants, laundries, shops, houses and public meeting places give a good impression of everyday life in a working Roman town. The main thoroughfare, the **Decumanus Maximus**, runs over 1km from the city's entrance (the Porta Romana) to the Porta Marina, which originally led to the sea. Behind the restored **theatre**, built by Agrippa and later enlarged to hold 3000 people, is the **Piazzale delle Corporazioni**, the offices of Ostia's merchant guilds, which display well-preserved mosaics depicting the different interests of each business.

The 2nd-century **Casa di Diana** is a pristine example of ancient Rome's high-density housing, built when space was at a premium. Nearby the **Thermopolium** bears a striking resemblance to a modern bar.

Ostia had several baths complexes, including the **Baths of the Forum**, which were also equipped with a roomful of stone toilets – the *forica* – still pretty much intact.

Continue along the Via dei Dipinti to reach the **museum**, which houses statuary and sarcophagi excavated on site.

Getting There & Away

From Rome, take the Metro Linea B to Piramide, then the Ostia Lido train from Stazione Porta San Paolo (next to the Metro station). Trains leave about every 30 minutes and the trip takes approximately 30 minutes. It is covered by the standard BIT tickets (see Getting Around under Rome for details).

The ruins are also easy to reach by car from Rome. Take the Via del Mare, a fast *superstrada* (superhighway), which runs parallel to the Via Ostiense.

TIVOLI

Set on a hill by the Aniene river, Tivoli was a resort town of the Romans and became popular as a summer playground for the rich during the Renaissance. While the majority of tourists are attracted by the terraced gardens and fountains of the Villa d'Este, the ruins of the spectacular Villa Adriana, built by the Roman Emperor Hadrian, are far more interesting.

The IAT office (☎ 0774 31 12 49) is on Largo Garibaldi, near the Cotral bus stop. It opens 8.30am to 2.30pm Tuesday to Saturday, plus 3pm to 6pm on Tuesday and Thursday.

Things to See

Villa Adriana Emperor Hadrian's summer residence, Villa Adriana *(☎ 0774 53 02 03; admission €6.20; open 9am-1hr before sunset daily)* was built between AD 118 and 134. It was one of the largest and most sumptuous villas in the Roman Empire. A model near the entrance gives you some idea of the scale of the massive complex, which you'll need several hours to explore.

Hadrian travelled widely and was a keen architect, and parts of the villa were inspired by buildings he had seen around the world. The massive **Pecile**, through which you enter, was a reproduction of a building in Athens, and the **Canopo** is a copy of the sanctuary of Serapis near Alexandria, with a long canal of water, originally surrounded by Egyptian statues, representing the Nile.

Highlights of the excavations include the fish pond encircled by an underground gallery where Hadrian took his summer walks and the emperor's private retreat, the **Teatro Marittimo**, on an island which could be reached only by a retractable bridge, in an artificial pool. There are also nymphaeums, temples and barracks, and a museum displaying the latest discoveries from ongoing excavations. Archaeologists have found features such as a heated bench with steam pipes under the sand and a network of subterranean service passages for horses and carts.

Villa d'Este There's a sense of faded splendour about Villa d'Este *(☎ 0774 31 20 70, Piazza Trento; admission €4.20; open 9am-7.30pm Tues-Sun Apr-Sept, 9am-5.30pm Tues-Sun Oct-Mar)*. This former Benedictine convent was transformed by Lucrezia Borgia's son, Ippolito d'Este, into a sumptuous pleasure palace with a breathtaking formal garden full of elaborate fountains and pools in 1550. From 1865 to 1886 the villa was home to Franz Liszt and inspired his composition *Fountains of the Villa d'Este.*

The Mannerist frescoes in the villa are worth a fleeting glance but it's the garden you come for – terraces with water-spouting grotesque heads, shady pathways and spectacular fountains powered solely by gravitational force. One fountain once played the organ, another imitated the call of birds. Don't miss the Rometta fountain, has reproductions of the landmarks of Rome.

Getting There & Away

Tivoli is 30km east of Rome and is accessible by Cotral bus from outside the Ponte Mammolo station on Metro Linea B. Buses depart at least every 20 minutes, stopping at Villa Adriana, about 1km from Tivoli, along the way. The trip takes about one hour. Local bus No 4 goes to Villa Adriana from Tivoli's Piazza Garibaldi.

The fastest route by car is on the Rome-L'Aquila autostrada (A24).

ETRUSCAN SITES

Lazio has several important Etruscan archaeological sites, most within easy reach of Rome by car or public transport. These include Tarquinia, Cerveteri, Veio and Tuscania (four of the major city-states in the Etruscan League).

If you have the time, a few days spent touring at least Tarquinia and Cerveteri, combined with visits to their museums (and the Museo Nazionale Etrusco di Villa Giulia in Rome – see Villa Borghese & Around under Rome earlier in this chapter), should constitute one of your most fascinating experiences in Italy. A useful guidebook to the area, *The Etruscans*, is published by the Istituto Geografico de Agostini and has a map. If you really want to lose yourself in a poetic journey, read DH Lawrence's 'Etruscan Places' in *DH Lawrence and Italy* (published by Penguin).

Cerveteri

Cerveteri, ancient Caere, was one of the most important commercial centres in the Mediterranean from the 7th to the 5th century BC. In 358 BC, the city was annexed to Rome and the inhabitants granted Roman citizenship. This colonisation of the city (as of the other cities in the Etruscan league in the same period) resulted in the absorption of the Etruscan culture into Roman culture and its eventual disappearance. After the fall of the Roman Empire, the spread of malaria and repeated Saracen invasions caused further decline. In the 13th century there was a mass exodus from the city to the nearby town of Ceri, further inland and Caere became Caere Vetus ('Old Caere'), from which its current name derives. The first half of the 19th century saw the first tentative archaeological explorations in the area and in 1911 systematic excavations began in earnest.

The main attraction here is the atmospheric **Necropoli di Banditaccia** *(Banditaccia Necropolis; ☎ 06 994 00 01, Via del Necropoli; admission €4.20; open 9am-7pm Tues-Sun in summer, 9am-4pm Tues-Sun in winter)* and its remarkable *tumoli* in which the Etruscans entombed their dead. The tumoli – mounds of earth with carved stone bases – are laid out in the form of a town, with streets, squares and terraces of 'houses'. The best example is the 4th-century-BC **Tomba dei Rilievi**, decorated with painted reliefs of cooking implements and other household items.

Treasures taken from the tombs can be seen in the Vatican Museums and Villa Giulia in Rome, and also at the **Museo Nazionale di Cerveteri** *(☎ 06 994 13 54, Piazza S Maria; free; open 9am-7pm Tues-Sun)* in Cerveteri town centre, which has an interesting display of pottery and sarcophagi.

To get to the main necropolis area, take the (infrequent) local bus from the main square. Otherwise it is a pleasant 2km walk west from the town. There is a Pro Loco tourist office (☎ 06 995 51 971) at Piazza Risorgimento 19.

Many Romans make the trip to Cerveteri just to eat at the ***Antica Locanda Le Ginestre*** *(☎ 06 994 06 72, Piazza Santa Maria 5)*, just near the museum. The *panzerotti in salsa d'ortiche* (stuffed pasta parcels in a creamy, herby sauce) are especially good, and there's a nice outdoor terrace.

Cerveteri is easily accessible from Rome by Cotral bus from outside the Lepanto stop on Metro Linea A. Buses leave about every half hour and the journey takes approximately 75 minutes. Buy a regional ticket (BIRG) for €4.50 covering the return bus journey, public transport in Cerveteri and the metro and buses in Rome. By car take either Via Aurelia (S1) or the Civitavecchia autostrada (A12) and come off at the Cerceteri-Ladispoli exit. The journey takes approximately 40 minutes.

Tarquinia

Believed to have been founded in the 12th century BC, and home of the Tarquin kings who ruled Rome before the creation of the Roman Republic, Tarquinia was an important economic and political centre of the Etruscan League. The town has a small medieval centre with a good Etruscan museum but the major attractions here are the painted tombs of the burial grounds.

Orientation & Information By car or bus you arrive at the Barriera San Giusto, just outside the main entrance to the town (see Getting There & Away later). The APT office (☎ 0766 85 63 84), Piazza Cavour 1, is on your left as you walk through the medieval ramparts and opens 8am to 2pm Monday to Saturday.

It's a long day-trip from Rome to Tarquinia; if you prefer to stay overnight in the medieval town, it is advisable to book accommodation (see Places to Stay & Eat later).

Things to See The 15th-century Palazzo Vitelleschi houses the **Museo Nazionale Tarquiniese** *(☎ 0766 85 60 36, Piazza Cavour; admission €6.20, including the necropolis; open 9am-7pm Tues-Sun)*, a significant collection of Etruscan treasures, including frescoes removed from the tombs. There is a beautiful terracotta frieze of winged horses, taken from the Ara della Regina temple. Numerous sarcophagi found in the tombs are also on display.

The famous painted tombs are at the **necropolis** *(☎ 0766 85 63 08; admission €6.20 including the Museo Nazionale Tarquiniese; open 9am-1hr before sunset Tues-Sun)*, a 15- to 20-minute walk away (get directions from the museum). Almost 6000 tombs have been excavated, of which 60 are painted, but only a handful are open to the public. Excavation of the tombs started in the 15th century and continues today. Unfortunately, exposure to air and human interference has led to serious deterioration in many tombs and they are now enclosed and maintained at constant temperatures. The painted tombs can be seen only through glass partitions.

If you have time, wander through the pleasant medieval town of Tarquinia, where there are several churches worth a look.

And if you have a car, you can get to the remains of the Etruscan acropolis of Tarxuna, on the crest of Civita Hill nearby. There is little evidence of the ancient city, apart from a few limestone blocks that once formed part of the city walls, since the Etruscans generally used wood to build their temples and houses.

However, a large temple, the **Ara della Regina**, has been excavated.

Places to Stay & Eat There are no budget options in the old town and it can be difficult to find a room if you don't book in advance.

Tusca Tirrenia *(☎ 0766 86 42 94, Viale delle Neriedi)* Open Apr-Oct. This camp site, 5km from the medieval town, is by the sea at Tarquinia Lido.

Hotel San Marco *(☎ 0766 84 22 34, Piazza Cavour 10)* Singles/doubles €45/60. This hotel has pleasant rooms and is in the medieval section of town, near the museum.

Hotel all'Olivo *(☎ 0766 85 73 18, fax 0766 84 07 77, Via Togliatti 13/15)* Singles/doubles €48/70. In the newer part of town, Hotel all'Olivo is a 10-minute walk downhill from the medieval centre. Prices include breakfast.

There are few places to eat in Tarquinia but for a good, cheap meal go to ***Trattoria Arcadia*** *(Via Mazzini 6)* or ***Cucina Casareccia*** *(Via Mazzini 5)*.

Getting There & Away Cotral buses leave approximately every hour for Tarquinia from outside the Lepanto stop on Metro Linea A, arriving at Tarquinia at the Barriera San Giusto, a short distance from the tourist office.

By car, take the autostrada for Civitavecchia and then the Via Aurelia (SS1). Tarquinia is about 90km north-west of Rome.

CIVITAVECCHIA

There is little to recommend this busy port and industrial centre to tourists, other than the fact that it is the main point of departure for the daily ferries to Sardinia.

Established by Emperor Trajan in AD 106 as the port town of Centumcellae, it was later conquered by the Saracens, but regained importance as a papal stronghold in the 16th century. The medieval town was almost completely destroyed by bombing during WWII. In 1995, the town hit the headlines when a 43cm-high statue of the Madonna, located in the private garden of a local family (but now in Sant'Agostino church), started crying tears of blood. Tests revealed the tears were in fact human blood and the statue continues to attract crowds of pilgrims, although the Vatican is yet to rule on the authenticity of the miracle.

Orientation & Information

The port is a short walk from the train station. As you leave the station, turn right into Viale Garibaldi and follow it along the seafront. The APT office (☎ 0766 2 53 48), Viale Garibaldi 42, opens 8.30am to 1.30pm and 4pm to 7pm Monday to Friday. There is also an information booth at the port.

Places to Stay & Eat

It's unlikely you'll spend the night in Civitavecchia. It is easily accessible from Rome and if you are travelling to Sardinia a night ferry saves money and time.

Hotel Traghetto *(☎ 0766 2 59 20, fax 0766 2 36 92, Via Braccianese Claudia 2)* Singles/doubles €74.90/92.95. If you get stuck in Civitavecchia, this hotel near the port is worth a try. Rooms are comfortable if a bit pricey; breakfast is included.

Trattoria da Vitale *(☎ 0766 2 36 39, Viale Garibaldi 23)* Full meals from €12.90. Simple, decent fare is on offer here.

Alternatively you can head for one of several ***pizzerias*** along the waterfront.

It's not too expensive to eat on the ferry (restaurant meals and snacks are available) but it is wise to take supplies on board if you want to save money. There's a ***grocery shop*** near the station and a ***market*** every morning except Sunday on Piazza Regina Margherita in the town centre.

Getting There & Away

Cotral buses from Rome to Civitavecchia leave from outside the Lepanto station on Metro Linea A about every 40 minutes.

Civitavecchia is on the main train line between Rome (1½ hours) and Genoa (2½ hours).

By car it is easily reached from Rome on the A12. If arriving from Sardinia with your car, simply follow the A12 signs from Civitavecchia port to reach the autostrada for Rome.

Ferries to/from Sardinia Tirrenia operates ferries to Olbia (eight hours), Arbatax (10 hours) and Cagliari (14 to 17 hours). Departure times and prices change annually and it is best to check with a travel agency or with Tirrenia (☎ 199 12 31 99, W www.tirrenia.it) for up-to-date information. At the time of writing, a high-season one-way fare to Olbia was €23 for a *poltrona* (airline-type seat), €33.50 for a bed in a 2nd-class cabin, €42 for a bed in a 1st-class cabin and €85 to take a small car.

The company operates fast boats (in summer only) from Civitavecchia to Olbia and from Fiumicino to Golfo Aranci (about 20km north of Olbia and accessible by bus or train) in Sardinia. They take only 3½ to 4 hours but are considerably more expensive than the slower ferries. It costs around €45 for 2nd-class ticket and €88 for a small car. Tickets can be purchased at travel agencies, including CIT, and at the Stazione Marittima in Civitavecchia. In high season it is advisable to book well in advance.

The Ferrovie dello Stato (FS) also runs two daily ferries to Sardinia, docking at Golfo Aranci; the fare is only €13 if you are prepared to stand. The downside is that you cannot book in advance and availability cannot be guaranteed. Go to the port at Civitavecchia and try your luck.

VITERBO

postcode 01030 • pop 60,000

Founded by the Etruscans and eventually taken over by Rome, Viterbo developed into an important medieval centre, and in the 13th century became the residence of the popes.

Papal elections were held in the town's Gothic Palazzo Papale and stories abound about the antics of impatient townspeople anxious for a decision. In 1271, when the college of cardinals had failed to elect a new pope after three years of deliberation, the Viterbesi locked them in a turreted hall of the palazzo, removed its roof and put the cardinals on a starvation diet. Only then did they manage to elect Gregory X.

Although badly damaged by bombing during WWII, Viterbo remains Lazio's best-preserved medieval town and is a pleasant base for exploring northern Lazio. For travellers with less time, Viterbo is an easy day trip from Rome.

Apart from its historical appeal, Viterbo is famous for its therapeutic hot springs. The best known is the sulphurous Bulicame pool, mentioned by Dante in his *Divine Comedy*.

Orientation & Information

As is the case with most historic centres in Italy, the town of Viterbo is neatly divided between newer and older sections. Hotels are in the newer part of town; you must walk south and cross the Piazza del Plebiscito, with its palazzos, before reaching medieval Viterbo and the real reason for your visit. There are train stations north (Stazione Porta Fiorentina) and south-east (Stazione Porta Romana) of the town centre; both are just outside the town walls. The intercity bus station is somewhat inconveniently located at Riello, a few kilometres out of town.

The APT office (☎ 0761 30 47 95) is on Piazza San Carluccio, in the medieval quarter, and opens 9am to 1pm Monday to Saturday, with sporadic afternoon openings.

The main post office is on Via F Ascenzi, just off Piazza del Plebiscito. The unstaffed Telecom office is at Via Cavour 28, off the southern side of the piazza.

Things to See

Piazza del Plebiscito The piazza is enclosed by 15th- and 16th-century palaces, the most imposing of which is the **Palazzo dei Priori** *(Piazza del Plebiscito; free; open 9am-1pm & 2pm-7pm daily)*, with an elegant 17th-century fountain in its courtyard. Many rooms are decorated with frescoes, notably the Sala Reggia, which is decorated with a late Renaissance fresco depicting the myths and history of Viterbo.

Cathedral & the Palazzo Papale The 12th-century cathedral *(Cattedrale di San Lorenzo; ☎ 0761 32 54 62, Piazza San Lorenzo; admission €2.60, including the Sala del Conclave in the Palazzo Papale; open 9am-12.30pm & 3.30pm-6pm daily)* was rebuilt in the 14th century to a Gothic design, although the interior has just been restored to its original Romanesque simplicity.

Also on the piazza is the **Palazzo Papale**, built in the 13th century with the aim of enticing the popes away from Rome. Its beautiful, graceful *loggia* (colonnade) is in the early Gothic style. The part facing the valley collapsed in the 14th century but the bases of some of the columns remain. The hall, the **Sala del Conclave**, in which papal conclaves were held, is at the top of the steps. Admission is included with your ticket to the cathedral museum and opening times are the same as the cathedral's.

Chiesa di Santa Maria Nuova This Romanesque church *(Piazza Santa Maria Nuova)* was restored to its original form after bomb damage in WWII. The cloisters, which are believed to date from an earlier period, are worth a visit.

Medieval Quarter Via San Pellegrino takes you through the medieval quarter into **Piazza San Pellegrino**. The extremely well-preserved buildings that enclose this tiny piazza comprise the finest group of medieval buildings in Italy.

Other Things to See Built in the early 13th century, the **Fontana Grande** *(Piazza Fontana Grande)* is the oldest and largest of Viterbo's Gothic fountains.

At the old northern entrance to the town is the **Chiesa di San Francesco** *(Piazza San Francesco; free; open 8am-noon & 3.30pm-7pm daily)*, a Gothic building that was restored after suffering serious bomb damage during WWII. The church contains the tombs of two popes: Clement IV (died 1268) and Adrian V (died 1276). Both are lavishly decorated, notably that of Adrian, which features Cosmati work, a mosaic technique used in the 12th and 13th centuries.

There's no shortage of museums in town. The **Museo della Macchina di Santa Rosa** *(☎ 0761 34 51 57, Via San Pellegrino; admission €1.05; open 10am-1pm & 4pm-8pm Wed-Sun)* documents the history of the festival that takes place on 3 September each year, when the Viterbesi parade a 30m-high tower around the town. The **Museo Civico** *(☎ 0761 34 82 75, Piazza Crispi; admission €3.10; open 9am-7pm Tues-Sun)* is housed in the restored convent of the church of Santa Maria della Verità, just outside the Porta della Verità, on the eastern side of town. Among the works in the museum are Iron age Etruscan artefacts, a lovely *Pietà* by Sebastiano del Piombo and a Roman sarcophagus which is said to be the tomb of Galiana, a beautiful and virtuous woman murdered by a Roman baron after she refused his advances.

Places to Stay & Eat

Hotel Roma *(☎ 0761 22 72 74, fax 0761 30 55 07, Via della Cava 26)* Singles/doubles without bath €30/47, singles/doubles with bath €41/60. Just off Piazza della Rocca, Hotel Roma offers one-step-up-from-budget accommodation in pleasant rooms. Prices include breakfast; there's a restaurant and free parking.

Hotel Tuscia *(☎ 0761 34 44 00, fax 0761 34 59 76, Via Cairoli 41)* Singles/doubles up to €52/83. For more comfortable accommodation, including breakfast, Hotel Tuscia is a good choice.

Pizzeria San Pellegrino *(☎ 0349 778 19 87, Via San Pellegrino 28)* Pizzas from €4.65. Built into the lower level of an old stone building near the tourist office, this popular pizzeria offers thin-crust pizza at both lunch and dinner.

Il Labirinto *(☎ 0761 30 70 26, Via San Lorenzo 46)* Pizzas €4.15-6.20, pasta €4.65-6.20, mains €4.65-8.25. Typical Roman pasta dishes such as carbonara and all' amatriciana are good here, but the pizzas and excellent desserts also draw the crowds.

Il Richiastro *(☎ 0761 22 80 09, Via della Marrocca 18)* Pasta from €5.15, mains from €7.25. This restaurant serves hearty food based on ancient Roman recipes and has outside tables in summer.

Getting There & Away

Direct, if slow, FS trains depart hourly from Rome's Ostiense, Trastevere and San Pietro stations, stopping at both the Porta Romana

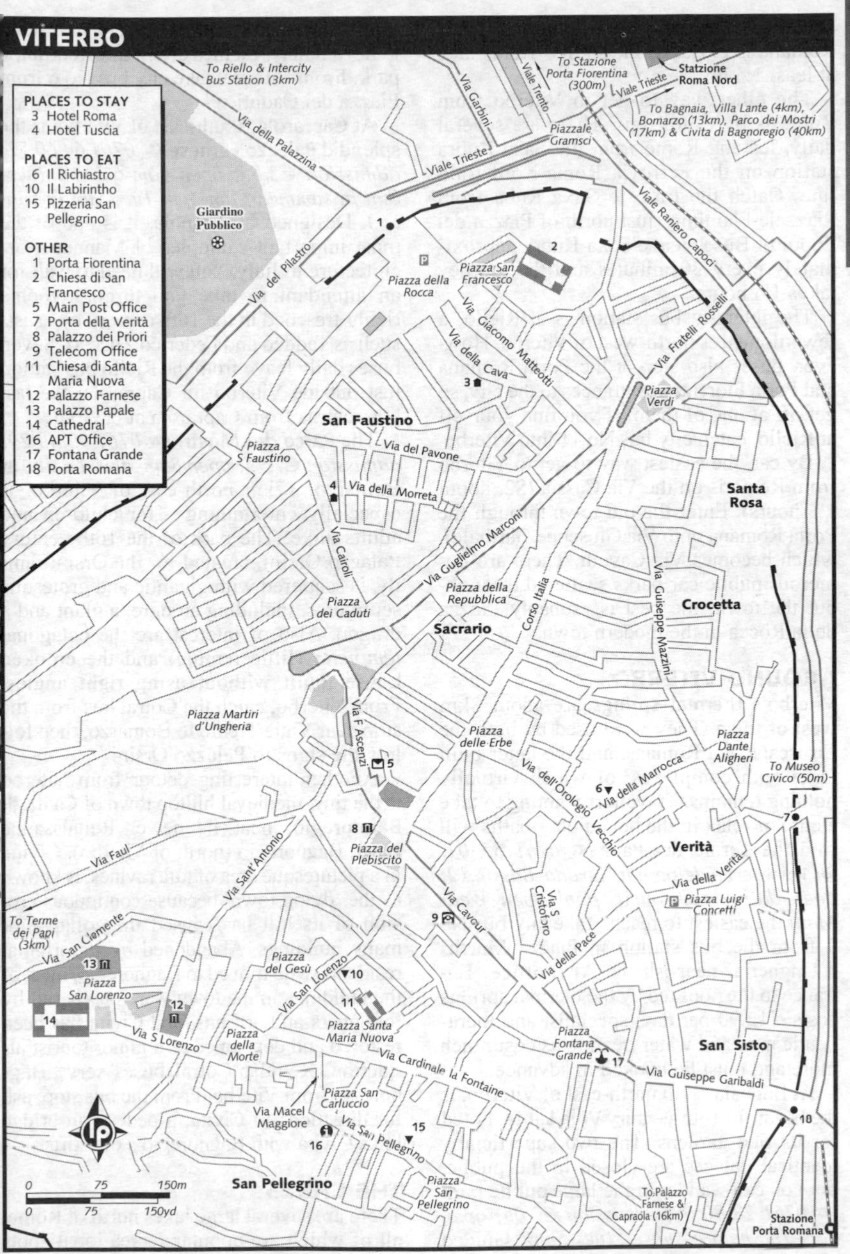

VITERBO
PLACES TO STAY
3 Hotel Roma
4 Hotel Tuscia
PLACES TO EAT
6 Il Richiastro
10 Il Labirintho
15 Pizzeria San Pellegrino
OTHER
1 Porta Fiorentina
2 Chiesa di San Francesco
5 Main Post Office
7 Porta della Verità
8 Palazzo dei Priori
9 Telecom Office
11 Chiesa di Santa Maria Nuova
12 Palazzo Farnese
13 Palazzo Papale
14 Cathedral
16 APT Office
17 Fontana Grande
18 Porta Romana
To Riello & Intercity Bus Station (3km)
To Stazione Porta Fiorentina (300m)
Statzione Roma Nord
To Bagnaia, Villa Lante (4km), Bomarzo (13km), Parco dei Mostri (17km) & Civita di Bagnoregio (40km)
Via Garbini
Viale Trento
Viale Trieste
Piazzale Gramsci
Via della Palazzina
Viale Raniero Capoci
Giardino Pubblico
Via del Pilastro
Piazza San Francesco
Piazza della Rocca
Via Giacomo Matteotti
Via della Cava
Via Fratelli Rosselli
Piazza Verdi
San Faustino
Piazza S Faustino
Via del Pavone
Via della Morreta
Santa Rosa
Via Cairoli
Via Guglielmo Marconi
Corso Italia
Via Giuseppe Mazzini
Piazza della Repubblica
Crocetta
Piazza dei Caduti
Sacrario
Piazza Martiri d'Ungheria
Via F Ascenzi
Piazza delle Erbe
Piazza Dante Aligheri
To Museo Civico (50m)
Via della Marrocca
Via dell'Orologio Vecchio
Piazza del Plebiscito
Via Faul
Via Sant'Antonio
Verità
Via della Verità
Piazza Luigi Concetti
Via S Cristoforo
Via Cavour
To Terme dei Papi (3km)
Via San Clemente
Via della Pace
Piazza del Gesù
Via San Lorenzo
Piazza San Lorenzo
Piazza Santa Maria Nuova
Via S Lorenzo
Piazza della Morte
Via Cardinale la Fontaine
Piazza Fontana Grande
San Sisto
Via Guiseppe Garibaldi
Piazza San Carluccio
Via Macel Maggiore
Via San Pellegrino
San Pellegrino
Piazza San Pellegrino
To Palazzo Farnese & Capraola (16km)
Stazione Porta Romana
0 75 150m
0 75 150yd

and Porta Fiorentina train stations. Porta Romana is closer to the sights. Trains take at least 1½ hrs.

The other way to get to Viterbo from Rome is by Cotral bus. There are several daily, leaving Rome from the Saxa Rubra station on the Ferrovia Roma-Nord train line. Catch the train to Saxa Ruba from Piazzale Flaminio (just north of Piazza del Popolo). Buses leave Saxa Rubra approximately every 30 minutes and the journey takes 1½ hours.

The intercity bus station is at Riello, a few kilometres north-west of Viterbo. However, buses also stop at the Porta Romana and Porta Fiorentina entrances to the city, so get off at one of them. If you find yourself at Riello, catch city bus No 11 into Viterbo.

By car, the easiest way to get to Viterbo from Rome is on the Via Cassia (S2, about 1½ hours). Enter the old town through the Porta Romana onto Via Giuseppe Garibaldi, which becomes Via Cavour. There are numerous public car parks scattered throughout the town; the best is probably Piazza della Rocca in the modern town.

AROUND VITERBO

Viterbo's **thermal springs** are about 3km west of town. They were used by both the Etruscans and Romans, and the latter built large bath complexes, of which virtually nothing remains. Travellers wanting to take a cure or relax in the hot sulphur baths will find the Terme dei Papi *(☎ 0761 35 01, W www.termedeipapi.it, Strada Bagni 12; open daily year-round, pool open Wed-Mon)* the easiest to reach. Take city bus No 2 from the bus station in Piazza Martiri d'Ungheria, near-ish the APT office. Entrance to the pool fed by the thermal springs costs €12.90 per day; specialist and therapeutic mud and water treatments cost much more and must be booked in advance.

At Bagnaia, 4km north-east of Viterbo, is the beautiful 16th-century **Villa Lante**, noted for its fine gardens. The two superficially identical palaces are closed to the public, but you can wander in the large **public park** *(☎ 0761 28 80 08; admission €2.05; open 9am-1hr before sunset Tues-Sun)*. Guided tours of the gardens leave every half hour. Unfortunately, picnics aren't allowed in the park. From Viterbo, take city bus No 6 from Piazza dei Caduti.

At Caprarola, south-east of Viterbo, is the splendid **Palazzo Farnese** *(☎ 0761 64 60 52; admission €2.05; open 9am-6.30pm Tues-Sun in summer, 9am-4pm Tues-Sun in winter)*. Designed by Vignola, it is one of the most important examples of Mannerist architecture in Italy. You will need to wait for an attendant to take you through rooms richly frescoed in the 16th century by artists such as Taddeo and Federico Zuccari. Seven buses daily leave from the Riello bus station just outside Viterbo for Caprarola; the last bus returns from Caprarola at 6.35pm.

The **Parco dei Mostri** *(☎ 0761 92 40 29; admission €7.75; open 8am-sunset daily)* at Bomarzo, 17km north-east of Viterbo, is especially entertaining – for children and adults alike. The park of the 16th-century Palazzo Orsini, created for the Orsini family, is scattered with gigantic and grotesque sculptures, including an ogre, a giant and a dragon. Also of interest are the octagonal *tempietto* (little temple) and the crooked house, built without using right angles. From Viterbo, catch the Cotral bus from the stop near Viale Trento to Bomarzo, then follow the signs to Palazzo Orsini.

Another interesting detour from Viterbo is the tiny, medieval hilltop town of **Civita di Bagnoregio**, near its newer Renaissance sister, Bagnoregio (north of Viterbo). Civita, in a picturesque area of tufa ravines, is known as the 'dying town' because continuous erosion of its hill has caused the collapse of many buildings. Abandoned by its original residents, who moved to Bagnoregio, most of the buildings in the town were purchased by foreigners and artisans, and Civita has been restored and developed as a minor tourist attraction. Regular Cotral buses serve Bagnoregio from Viterbo. From the bus stop, ask for directions to Civita; a pedestrian bridge links Civita with Bagnoregio's outskirts.

THE LAKES

There are several large lakes north of Rome, all of which are popular recreational spots in summer. The lake shores never seem to get as crowded as Lazio's beaches and their hilly, leafy environment makes them more attractive swimming destinations.

Lago di Bracciano

Lago di Bracciano, 40km north of Rome, is easily accessible by public transport. Visit the **Castello Orsini-Odelscalchi** *(☎ 06 998 04 348, Piazza Castello; free; open 10am-noon & 3pm-5pm Tues-Sun)* in the medieval town of Bracciano or head straight for the lake for a swim. On the northern edge of the lake is the picturesque town of Trevignano Romano, with its pretty waterfront and modest beach.

There are a couple of good places to eat in the area.

Trattoria del Castello *(☎ 06 998 04 339, Piazza Castello, near the castle)* This has excellent food; if *funghi porcini* (porcini mushrooms) are on the menu, have them.

La Tavernetta *(☎ 06 999 90 26, Via Garibaldi 62, Trevignano Romano)* Full meals from €15.50. On the shores of the lake, this rustic, family-run restaurant serves simple but tasty fare.

Cotral buses, which depart roughly every hour from outside the Lepanto Metro station in Rome, serve Bracciano directly, arriving in Piazza Roma in the middle of town. By car, take Via Braccianense (S493) for Bracciano, or take Via Cassia (S2) and then follow the signs to Trevignano Romano.

Lago di Bolsena

This elliptical lake, 100km from Rome, is too far to reach in a day but is close to Viterbo (see Viterbo earlier). The town of Bolsena was the scene of a miracle in 1263 – a doubting priest was convinced of transubstantiation when blood dripped from the host he was holding during a mass. To commemorate the event Pope Urban IV founded the festival of Corpus Domini: each June the townspeople hold a 3km procession and decorate the town with flowers.

Castello Monaldeschi *(☎ 0761 79 86 30; open 9.30am-1.30pm & 4pm-8pm Tues-Fri, 10am-1pm & 3pm-6pm Sat & Sun in summer, 9.30am-1.30pm Tues-Fri, 10am-1pm & 3pm-6pm Sat & Sun in winter)* in the medieval quarter has an interesting history. The original structure dates from between the 13th and 16th centuries. However, it was pulled down by the locals in 1815 to prevent it from being taken by Luciano Bonaparte. It now houses a museum and a tourist office (☎ 0761 79 99 23). Also of interest in the medieval quarter are the 11th-century **Chiesa di Santa Cristina** and the **catacombs** beneath it. Just before the entrance to the catacombs is the **altare del miracolo**, where the miracle of Bolsena occurred. The catacombs are noteworthy because they contain tombs that are still sealed.

There are many hotels and camp sites by the lake.

Villaggio Camping Lido *(☎ 0761 79 92 58)* Sites per adult/child/tent €7.75/4.15/5.15. This large camp site 1½km from Bolsena has a bar, restaurant and bungalow facilities.

Hotel Eden *(☎ 0761 79 90 15, fax 0761 79 60 56, Via Cassia)* Singles/doubles €46.50/62. This hotel is by the lake.

If you're touring the area by car, it is worth heading on to **Montefiascone**, which is noted for its white wine, Est, Est, Est. Local history has it that on his travels a monk wrote 'est' (it is) to indicate the places where the wine was good. On arriving at Montefiascone he was so overcome by the quality of the wine that he exclaimed '*Est! Est! Est!*'. Visit the cathedral and the nearby Romanesque church of Sant' Andrea. On the Orvieto road, just outside Montefiascone, in Umbria, is the Romanesque church of **San Flaviano**.

In summer, Cotral runs a direct bus service to Bolsena from the Saxa Rubra stop on Ferrovia Roma-Nord (catch the train from the station in Piazzale Flaminio); otherwise you need to change at Viterbo. There are regular Cotral buses, Monday to Saturday, to Bolsena from Viterbo leaving from the bus station at Riello. On Sunday there is only one bus that leaves around 9am (returning at around 6pm). By car, take the Via Cassia (S2) to Viterbo and follow the signs from the Riello bus station.

SOUTH OF ROME

The Castelli Romani

Just past the periphery of Rome are the Colli Albani (Alban Hills) and the 13 towns of the Castelli Romani. A summer resort area for wealthy Romans since the days of the Roman Empire, its towns were mainly founded by popes and patrician families. Castel Gandolfo and Frascati are perhaps the best known; the former is the summer residence of the pope and the latter is famous for its crisp white wine. The other towns are Monte Porzio Catone, Montecompatri, Rocca Priora, Colonna, Rocca di Papa, Grottaferrata, Marino, Albano Laziale, Ariccia, Genzano and Nemi.

The APT tourist office (☎ 06 942 03 31), Piazzale Marconi 1, opens 8am to 2pm Monday to Saturday, plus 3.30pm to 6.30pm Tuesday to Friday.

The area has numerous villas, including the 16th-century **Villa Aldobrandini** *(Frascati; admission to the gardens only by a permit available from the tourist office)*, designed by Giacomo della Porta and built by Carlo Maderno, which has a beautiful garden. Just outside Frascati is the site of the ancient city of **Tusculum**. Imposing and impregnable, Tusculum remained independent until 380 BC, when it came under Roman domination. Today, scant evidence of the city remains. There is a small amphitheatre, the remains of a villa and a stretch of ancient Roman road leading up to the city.

At Grottaferrata there's a 15th-century **abbey** *(abbazia; ☎ 06 945 93 09, Viale San Nilo; free; open 8.30am-noon & 4.30pm-6pm Tues-Sat, 8.30am-10am & 4.30pm-6pm Sun)*, founded in the 11th century and home to a congregation of Greek monks. There is also a museum.

Nemi is worth a visit to see the pretty **Lago di Nemi** in a volcanic crater. In ancient times there was an important sanctuary beside the lake, where the goddess Diana was worshipped. Today, very little remains of this massive temple complex but it is possible to see the niche walls of what was once an arcade portico. New excavations at the site have just started. The incongruous-looking building at the edge of the lake, near the ruins of the temple, has an interesting story attached to it. It was built by Mussolini to house two ancient Roman boats (one 73m long, the other 71m), which were recovered from the bottom of the lake when it was partly drained between 1927 and 1932. The official story is that retreating German troops burned the ships on 1 June 1944. Locals tell a different story, but you'll have to go there to find out!

In Nemi, the ***Trattoria la Sirena del Lago*** *(☎ 06 936 80 20)* is a delightful trattoria with simple but excellent meals. It is right on the edge of a cliff and overlooks the lake. Signs direct you from the centre of town.

It is really best to tour this area by car: you could see most of the more interesting sights on an easy day trip from Rome. However, most of the towns of the Castelli Romani, including Nemi, are accessible from Rome by Cotral bus from the Anagnina station on Metro Linea A. Access between them, though, is well-nigh impossible. Trains also leave from Stazione Termini for Frascati, Castelgandolfo and Albano Laziale, from where you can catch a bus to Nemi.

Palestrina

The town of Palestrina is dominated by the massive **Santuario della Fortuna Primigenia**. Built by the ancient Romans on a series of terraces on the slope of Monte Ginestro, the sanctuary was topped by a circular temple with a statue of the goddess Palestrina on the top. On a clear day the view from the sanctuary is sensational. The 17th-century **Palazzo Colonna Barberini** was built on the site and houses the **Museo Archeologico Nazionale Prenestino** *(☎ 06 953 81 00, Piazza Santa Maria degli Angeli; admission €4.15; open 9am-8pm daily, shorter hours in winter)*. The museum houses an important collection of Roman artefacts and is one of Lazio's best. Of particular interest is the spectacular **Nile mosaic**, a masterpiece of Hellenistic art, which came from the most sacred part of the temple (where the cathedral with its Romanesque belfry now stands). It depicts the Nile in flood from Ethiopia to Alexandria.

Apart from its historical and archaeological importance, Palestrina is also renowned for being the birthplace of the 16th-century choral composer, Giovanni Pierluigi da Palestrina. His former home, the **Casa di Palestrina**, is now a museum and important music library *(admission €4.15; open 9.30am-12.30pm Tues-Sun)*. Craft-lovers can purchase locally produced beaten copper work in the shape of shells and 'Palestrina point' embroidery.

The tourist office (☎ 06 957 31 76), Piazza Santa Maria degli Angeli 2, is next to the Museo Archeologico Nazionale Prenestino in the town centre. It opens 9.30am to 1pm and 3.30pm to 5.30pm daily.

Palestrina is accessible from Rome by Cotral bus (€2, 30 minutes, every half hour) from the Anagnina stop on Metro Linea A. At Palestrina, you can either walk uphill to the Santuario or save your legs and take the small local bus. By car it is a straightforward 39km along the Via Prenestina (S155).

Anagni & Alatri

These medieval towns are in an area known as the Ciociaria, 40 minutes' drive south of Roma. **Anagni**, birthplace of several medieval popes, is of particular interest for its 11th-century Lombard-Romanesque cathedral. Its pavement was laid in the Middle Ages by Cosmati marble workers. The crypt has an extraordinary series of vibrant frescoes, painted by Benedictine monks in the 13th century. Depicting a wide range of subjects, the frescoes are considered to be a major example of medieval painting at the crucial stage of its transition from the Byzantine tradition to the developments culminating in the achievements of Giotto. The frescoes have been restored and certainly deserve a look. The crypt's pavement was also laid by the Cosmati.

Alatri has a couple of interesting churches, including the 13th-century Santa Maria Maggiore in its main piazza. Its ancient **acropolis** is ringed by huge 6th-century-BC walls, built by the town's original inhabitants, the Ernici.

To get to Anagni by bus you have to change at Colle Ferro. Cotral buses for Colle Ferro leave from the Anagnina stop on the Metro Linea A approximately every half hour. From here take the bus to Anagni. Otherwise take the Frosinone train from Stazione Termini (leaving approximately every hour) and get off at Anagni-Fiuggi. To get to Alatri, catch the train to Anagni and then take the Cotral bus to Alatri.

Along the Coast

Beaches close to Rome include Fregene, the Lido di Ostia and the long stretch of dune-lined beach between Ostia and Anzio. However, they really are not terribly inviting and the water tends to be heavily polluted. You'll need to go further south to Sabaudia and Sperlonga to find cleaner and more attractive spots for a swim. Sabaudia has the added attraction of sand dunes and the **Parco Nazionale del Circeo**, a wetlands nature reserve along the coast. It is accessible by Cotral bus from outside the EUR-Fermi station on Metro Linea B.

Sperlonga The small coastal town of Sperlonga is a good destination for a weekend break, with two long, sandy beaches on either side of a rocky promontory jutting into the sea. The town is divided into two parts. Medieval Sperlonga Alta is on top of the promontory and, with its whitewashed buildings, seems more Greek than Italian. Modern Sperlonga Bassa is at sea level.

Other than the beach, the main attraction is the **Grotta di Tiberio** *(admission €2.60; open 9am-7pm daily summer, 9am-4pm daily winter)*, a cave with a circular pool used by the emperor Tiberius. The remains of his villa are in front of the cave. Statues found in the cave are housed in the nearby museum and include a large group in the style of the *Lacoön* (now in the Vatican Museums).

For a place to stay and somewhere to eat, try one of the places listed below.

Albergo Major *(☎ 0771 54 92 44, Via Romita I 4)* Low season singles/doubles €56.80/67.15, high season half-board per person €77.50. Open year-round. All prices include access to sun loungers and umbrellas on the private beach area.

Lido da Rocco *(☎ 0771 5 44 93, Via Spiaggia Angelo 22)* For a snack on the beach, try Lido da Rocco on the seafront, which does very tasty rolls filled with mozzarella, tomato and basil.

Agli Archi *(☎ 0771 5 43 00, Via Ottaviano 17)* Full meals €20.65-62. In the heart of the medieval town, this restaurant specialises in fish and there are a lot of dishes to choose from.

To get to Sperlonga from Rome, take a *diretto* regional train (not the Intercity) from Stazione Termini towards Naples and get off at Fondi. From here take the connecting Cotral bus (or a taxi) to Sperlonga. The return us leaves from the main piazza at the top of the hill in the centre of Sperlonga Alta.

Sperlonga is 120km from Rome by car. Take Via Pontina (S148) from EUR going south and follow signs to Terracina. From Terracina it is a short drive on the S213.

Isole Pontine

International tourists are only just beginning to discover this group of small islands between Rome and Naples. Only two of the islands – Ponza and Ventotene – are inhabited and both are popular summer holiday spots or Italians; they are especially crowded on summer weekends. Prices are not cheap and budget travellers are best to go out of season when the islands are more affordable – although beware that many services shut down.

The history of the islands goes back a long way. Homer refers to Ponza in the *Odyssey*, attesting to the presence of the ancient Greeks, confirmed by the remains of the tombs on the bluff overlooking Chiaia di Luna. In 313 BC, the archipelago came under Roman rule, and later came the building of sumptuous villas for the emperor and his circle. The collapse of the Empire brought about a period of decline on the islands, during which they sustained violent attacks by Saracens and by groups from mainland Italy and the nearby Aeolian islands. Unfaithful wives, promiscuous daughters and persecuted Christians counted among the large number of people exiled to the islands at this time.

The recent history of the islands begins in 1734, when surrender to the Bourbon ruler Charles III gave rise to a wave of migration to Ponza that was to last the rest of the century. Commerce on the island flourished at the expense of the natural habitat, which was largely destroyed in the rush to build and to cultivate. The island of Ponza is ecologically in pretty poor shape. Almost every inch of the hilly island was terraced and used for farming, and now there's a lot of erosion. Bird hunting is virtually an obsession for the locals; migrating birds pass over on their journeys between Europe and Africa. However, all the islands are now under National Park protection.

There is a Pro Loco tourist information office on Ponza in the main town (☎ 0771 8 00 31), Via Molo Musco, near the port. It opens 9am to 1pm and 4pm to 7.30pm daily in summer, 10am to noon daily in spring and autumn, and 10am to noon on Saturday and Sunday in winter. On Ventotene, go to the private travel agency Bemtilem (☎ 0771 8 53 65) for information.

Places to Stay & Eat Many locals rent out individual rooms to tourists for much less than Hotel Mari (listed below) and you'll find them touting at the port; otherwise go to the tourist information office for an authorised list.

Hotel Mari *(☎ 0771 8 01 01, fax 0771 8 02 39, Corso Pisacane 19)* High season singles/doubles €56.80/103.50, low season singles/doubles €41.30/72.30. Book ahead and ring to check that the hotel is open in low season. Prices include breakfast.

The Pontine Islands are renowned for their fish-based cuisine. Lentil soup is also a local speciality.

Ristorante da Ciro *(☎ 0771 80 83 88, Via Calacaparra)* Open year-round. One kilometre or so past the town of Le Forna on Ponza, this is the place to go for a good seafood meal. The restaurant is open for lunch and dinner, and there is a west-facing terrace with a view of Palmarola.

Getting There & Around Ponza and Ventotene are accessible by car ferry or hydrofoil from Anzio, Terracina or Formia. Timetable information is available from most travel agents. During the summer he timetables are also published in the *Cronaca di Roma* section of the national daily newspapers *Il Messaggero* and *Il Tempo*. There is a hydrofoil that runs between Ponza and Ventotene. In both cases get information from the port or the Pro Loco office.

Cars and large motorbikes are forbidden on Ponza during the high season but there is a good local bus service that covers the main points of interest. Otherwise, you can rent a scooter at the port, either at one of the numerous outlets or from one of the touts who will meet you at the ferry.

Liguria, Piedmont & Valle d'Aosta

The north-western corner of Italy has long been a political, economic and intellectual engine room for the country. It was here that the movement for Italian unity took wing. Piedmont (Piemonte) was the cradle of Italy's industrial success and the birthplace of its labour movements. And for much of the 20th century, the Piedmontese capital, Turin, was a hotbed of intellectual activity. Farther south, Genoa was once a major city port, open to the rest of the world for centuries. Today it is regaining importance.

Turin and Genoa resonate with past glories, but they are only one side of the coin. From the pistes and walking trails of the Valle d'Aosta and northern Piedmont to the Ligurian coast and the magic of the Cinque Terre ('Five Lands'), this corner of the country is a microcosm of the best Italy has to offer.

LIGURIA

Highlights

- Explore the streets of medieval Genoa
- Dodge volleys of oranges at Carnevale in Ivrea
- Contemplate the mystery of the Turin Shroud
- Stroll between the picturesque coastal villages of the Cinque Terre
- Tuck into a plate of *trenette al pesto* and a seafood dish in a Genoese trattoria
- Ski the slopes at Courmayeur or ride the Mt Blanc cable car
- Escape the crowds in the Valle d'Aosta

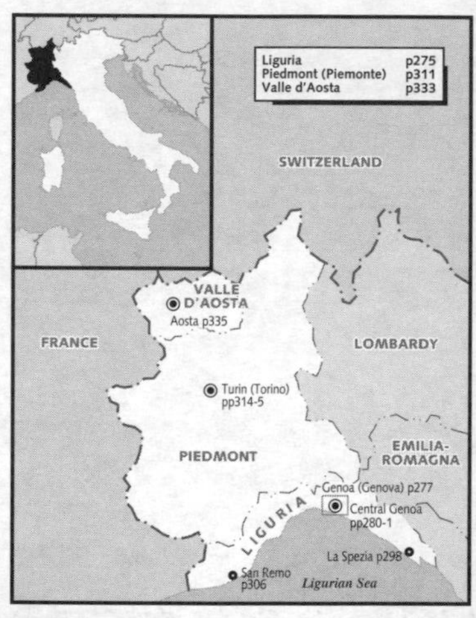

Liguria

The Ligurian coast was inhabited by Neanderthals about one million years ago and many remains have been unearthed. Locals say these early inhabitants were lured by the beaches, which still exert a hold over the hundreds of thousands of tourists who flock to this narrow coastal region each year. There is more to Liguria, however, than just beaches. Stretching from the French border in the west to La Spezia in the east, the coast is dotted with resorts and medieval towns; the mountainous hinterland hides hilltop villages and the occasional piste, and holds plenty of scope for walkers. Genoa, regional capital and one-time sea power, is an important port and much-overlooked attraction in its own right.

Liguria has been ruled by the Greeks, Romans, Saracens, Lombards, Venetians and French, and strong early trade influences from as far afield as Sicily, Northern Africa and Spain are evident.

The cuisine is marked by the products of the Mediterranean climate – fresh herbs, extra virgin olive oil and seafood. Among

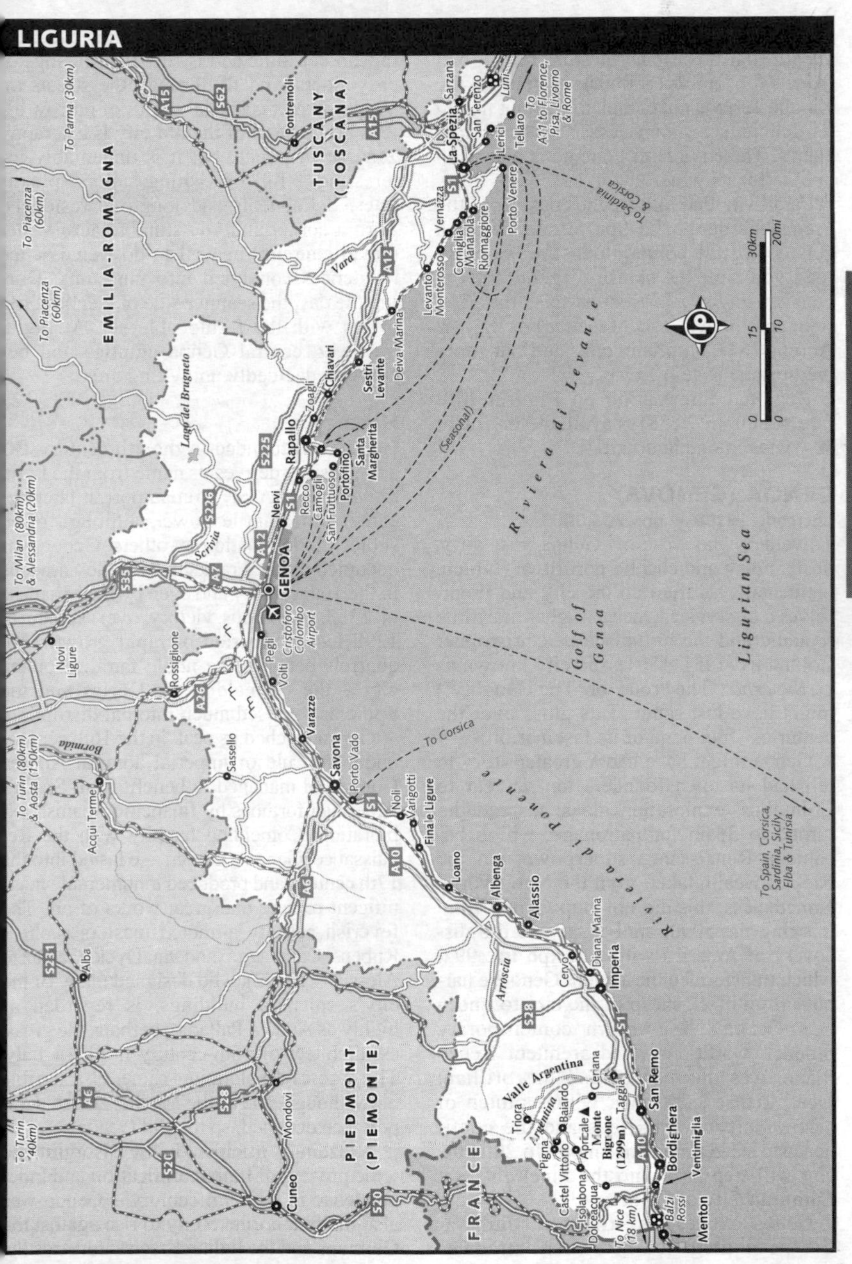
LIGURIA
EMILIA-ROMAGNA
TUSCANY (TOSCANA)
PIEDMONT (PIEMONTE)
FRANCE
To Parma (30km)
To Piacenza (60km)
To Piacenza (60km)
To Milan (80km) & Alessandria (20km)
To Turin (80km) & Aosta (150km)
To Turin (40km)
To Nice (18 km)
To A11 to Florence, Pisa, Livorno & Rome
To Sardinia & Corsica
To Corsica
To Spain, Corsica, Sardinia, Sicily, Elba & Tunisia
(Seasonal)
Riviera di Levante
Riviera di Ponente
Golf of Genoa
Ligurian Sea
Lago del Brugneto
Scrivia
Bormida
Vara
Arroscia
Argentina
Valle Argentina
GENOA
Cristoforo Colombo Airport
Pontremoli
Sarzana
La Spezia
San Terenzo
Lerici
Luni
Tellaro
Porto Venere
Riomaggiore
Manarola
Corniglia
Vernazza
Monterosso
Levanto
Deiva Marina
Sestri Levante
Chiavari
Zoagli
Rapallo
Santa Margherita
Portofino
San Fruttuoso
Camogli
Recco
Nervi
Pegli
Volti
Varazze
Savona
Porto Vado
Noli
Varigotti
Finale Ligure
Loano
Albenga
Alassio
Diana Marina
Cervo
Imperia
San Remo
Taggia
Ceriana
Bajardo
Triora
Pigna
Castel Vittorio
Apricale
Monte Bignone (1299m)
Isolabona
Dolceacqua
Bordighera
Ventimiglia
Balzi Rossi
Menton
Cuneo
Mondovì
Alba
Acqui Terme
Sassello
Rossiglione
Novi Ligure
A15
S62
A12
S1
S225
S226
A7
S35
A26
A10
A6
S28
S231
S20
0 15 30km
0 10 20mi

the region's culinary creations are pesto, *focaccia* (flat bread) and *farinata* (flat bread made with chickpea flour). A visit to the Cinque Terre is not complete without trying its delicious but rare dessert wine, Sciacchetrà. The Riviera di Ponente is also well known for its wine.

A railway line follows the coast from the French border to La Spezia and beyond, connecting all points along the way. By road you have the choice of good but expensive *autostrade* (motorways; the A10 west and the A12 east of Genoa) or the Via Aurelia (S1), an often congested but more picturesque state highway.

Regional information on Liguria (toll free ☎ 800 46 98 38) is available online at W www.regione.liguria.it.

GENOA (GENOVA)

postcode 16100 • pop 706,000

Travellers who write off Genoa as a dirty, dusty, noisy and chaotic port town (which, incidentally, is true) do the city and themselves a disservice. Once a mighty maritime republic and the birthplace of Christopher Columbus (1451–1504), the city known as *La Superba* ('The Proud' or 'The Haughty') might have lost some of its gloss over the centuries – but none of its fascination.

Genoa might have had a greater story to tell had its town founders lent an ear to Columbus' exploration ideas; instead, he turned to Spain for patronage, which became a Renaissance superpower on the back of wealth taken from the New World. Nonetheless, this did not stop Genoa from marking the 500th anniversary of the discovery of America with an Expo in 1992, which transformed the ancient Genoese harbour from black sheep of the city to queen bee. Genoa's best-known contemporary product, world-renowned architect Renzo Piano, was the man behind the brilliant face-lift that left Genoa with a clutch of lasting portside attractions and the confidence to stand proud once more. In 2004 the city will step back into the limelight as a European City of Culture.

Genoa exudes a distinctive southern-European gregariousness – it straddles Italy's most alluring strip of sunny Mediterranean coastline and is filled with gangs of easy riders who fly through the streets on Vespa scooters. The labyrinth of narrow alleys at the heart of the old city is a scrappy zone of ill-repute, but it is undeniably interesting – full of visiting sailors, prostitutes, delinquents and longtime residents. Turn a corner and you stumble across medieval churches or well-to-do Renaissance residences converted into museums. During the day, the seamier side of Genoese life mixes with the fashionable set. At night however, central Genoa empties and becomes a decidedly uninviting area.

History

Genoa was founded in the 4th century BC and possibly derives its name from the Latin *ianua* (door). A key Roman port, it later became a mercantile power, although often subject to domination by others. Genoa was occupied by the Franks in 774, the Saracens in the 10th century and even by the Milanese in 1353. A famous victory over Venice in 1298 led to a period of rapid growth, but quarrels between the noble families of the city – the Grimaldis, the Dorias and the Spinolas – caused much internal disruption.

Genoa reached its peak in the 16th century under the rule of imperial admiral Andrea Doria, and managed to benefit from Spain's American fortunes by financing Spanish exploration. Coinciding happily with the Renaissance, Genoa's golden age lasted into the 17th century and produced innumerable magnificent palaces and great works of art. The feverish activity attracted masters such as Rubens, Caravaggio and van Dyck. Galeazzo Alessi (1512–72), who designed many of the city's splendid buildings, is regarded as highly as Andrea Palladio, perhaps the greatest architect of 16th-century northern Italy. The Age of Exploration came as a terrible blow, though, and as the Mediterranean's importance declined, so too did Genoa's.

A leading participant in the Risorgimento – the process of Italian unification and independence in the 19th century – Genoa was also the first northern city to rise against the Germans and the Italian Fascists towards the

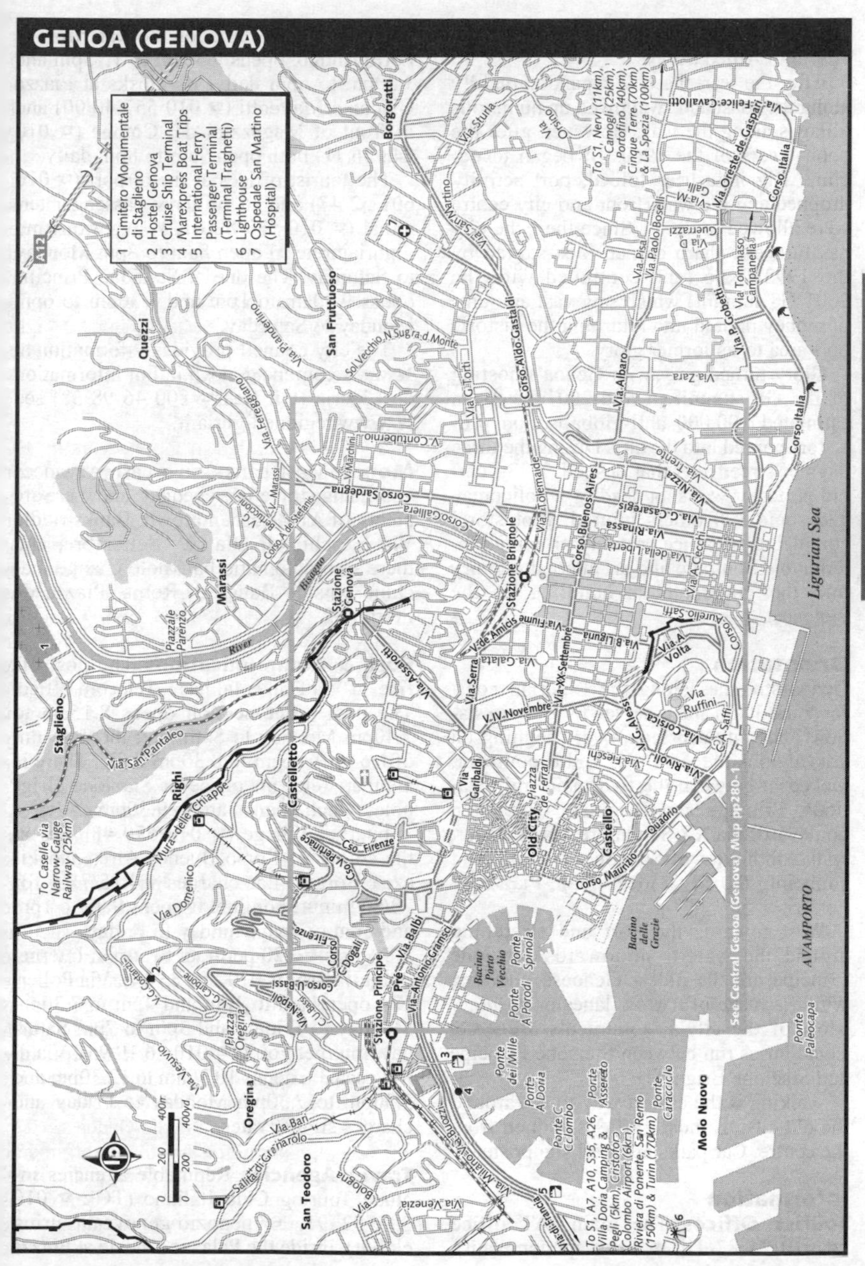
GENOA (GENOVA)
1 Cimitero Monumentale di Staglieno
2 Hostel Genova
3 Cruise Ship Terminal
4 Marexpress Boat Trips
5 International Ferry Passenger Terminal (Terminal Traghetti)
6 Lighthouse
7 Ospedale San Martino (Hospital)
To Caselle via Narrow-Gauge Railway (25km)
To S1, Nervi (11km), Camogli (25km), Portofino (40km), Cinque Terre (70km) & La Spezia (100km)
To S1, A7, A10, S35, A26, Villa Doria Camping & Pegli (5km), Cristoforo Colombo Airport (6km), Riviera di Ponente, San Remo (150km) & Turin (170km)
See Central Genoa (Genova) Map pp280-1
Ligurian Sea
AVAMPORTO
Bacino Porto Vecchio
Bacino delle Grazie
Staglieno
Righi
Castelletto
Marassi
Quezzi
San Fruttuoso
Borgoratti
Oregina
San Teodoro
Molo Nuovo
Old City
Castello
Stazione Genova
Stazione Brignole
Stazione Principe
Bisagno River
Ponte dei Mille
Ponte A Doria
Ponte C Colombo
Ponte Assereto
Ponte Caracciolo
Ponte Paleocapa
Ponte A Porodi
Ponte Spinola
Corso Italia
Via Oreste de Gaspari
Corso Buenos Aires
Corso Sardegna
Corso Aldo Gastaldi
Via Tolemaide
Via XX Settembre
Via Assarotti
Via Balbi
Via Antonio Gramsci
Corso Maurizio Quadrio
Via Garibaldi
Mura delle Chiappe
Via San Pantaleo
Via Albaro
Via Nizza
Via Rivoli
Via Corsica
Via A Volta
Corso Firenze
Corso Ugo Bassi
Piazza de Ferrari
Piazzale Parenzo
Piazza Oregina
0 200 400m
0 200 400yd

LIGURIA

close of WWII, liberating itself before the arrival of Allied troops.

After the war, the city expanded rapidly along the coast and swallowed up numerous villages along the way. However, after the boom years of the 1960s, it began to decline. Big industries folded, port activity dropped and the waterfront and city centre were allowed to decay. Since then, the city has turned a sharp corner, kick-started by the 1992 Expo (and continued with the 2001 G8 summit) which saw vast amounts of money poured into returning the historic port area to its former glory.

Glory turned gory with Genoa's hosting of the G8 summit in mid-2001 when an estimated 100,000 anti-globalisation protestors poured into the city. During the three days of street riots that ensued, a 23-year-old protestor was shot dead by a policeman and some 300 others injured. Protestors' complaints of police brutality prompted international outrage and an internal enquiry into the government's handling of the violence.

Orientation

Genoa stretches along the Ligurian coast for some 30km and is served by 15 train stations. The city can seem overwhelming on arrival, but the centre is quite compact, tucked in-between the two main train stations, Principe and Brignole. The main boulevard, Via XX Settembre, starts a short walk south-west of Stazione Brignole and spills into the city's focal point, Piazza de Ferrari.

West towards the port and stretching around the waterfront towards Stazione Principe are the oldest Genoese quarters, within a maze of narrow lanes or *caruggi*. Most of the city's monuments are here. Local buses run between Stazione Principe and Stazione Brignole.

Walking is the easiest way to get around the old city, as most traffic is banned from the centre. Car parks are well signposted.

Information

Tourist Offices The main IAT office (☎ 010 24 87 11, W www.apt.genova.it), Palazzina Santa Maria, on the waterfront at Porto Antico, opens 9.30am to 1.15pm and 3.30pm to 6pm daily. Its kiosks at Piazza Giacomo Matteotti (☎ 010 557 40 00) and in front of Magazzini del Cotone (☎ 010 248 56 11) both open 9am to 8pm daily.

The tourist offices at the airport (☎ 010 601 52 47) and at the ferry passenger terminal (☎ 010 530 82 01, W www.turismo.liguriainrete.it) open 8am to 8pm Monday to Saturday. The one at Stazione Principe opens 9.30am to 1pm and 3.30pm to 6pm Monday to Saturday.

The city council provides information at W www.comune.genova.it. For information on Liguria (toll free ☎ 800 46 98 38) see W www.regione.liguria.it.

Money Most banks give cash advances and change travellers cheques, and there are plenty of ATMs around town. Banks riddle Via Fieschi, off Via XX Settembre, and there's an automatic banknote change machine outside Banca di Roma, Piazza de Ferrari 32.

Post & Communications The post office, at Via Dante 4a, has a Telecom office. The post office section opens 8.15am to 7.40pm Monday to Saturday; the Telecom office opens 6am to 8.30pm daily. There is another Telecom office at Stazione Brignole, which opens 8am to 9.30pm daily.

Internet Village (☎ 010 570 48 78), on the corner of Corso Buenos Aires and Piazza Borgo Pila, charges €4.15/7.75 for 30/60 minutes online. It opens 9am to 1pm and 3pm to 7pm Monday to Friday.

It costs €6.20 per hour to surf at Internet Point Il Faro (☎ 010 251 83 14), Via Polleri 17r, open 9am to 1pm and 4pm to 7.30pm Monday to Friday, and 3pm to 7pm Saturday. Internet Point (☎ 010 26 19 95), Via di Ravecca 39, opens 10.30am to 12.30pm and 3.30pm to 7.30pm Monday to Friday and charges similar rates.

Travel Agencies Reputable agencies include Touring Club Italiano (TCI: ☎ 010 595 52 91, e negozio.genova@touringclub.it), inside the Palazzo Ducale at Piazza

The Genius of Genoa

Born in 1782, Niccolò Paganini knew just about all there was to know about the violin by his 13th year, thanks in part to his father's tyrannical teaching methods. His concert career took him to every corner of Italy and to all of Europe's great stages.

Paganini played a mean violin, extracting chords, arpeggios and rhythms hitherto undreamed of, and revolutionising violin technique with his use of harmonics and left-handed pizzicato. He was a virtuoso on the guitar as well and a prolific composer, leaving behind six concertos, 24 quartets for violin, viola, guitar and other strings, 12 sonatas for violin and guitar, and a long list of further sonatas. Liszt and Chopin applied much of what they learned from Paganini's genius to the piano.

The combination of Paganini's virtuosity and sickly appearance led some to believe that he was demonically inspired. Such wild stories began to circulate that, in 1828, he felt obliged to publish a long defence of himself in the *Revue Musicale*. These diabolical rumours didn't diminish his popularity, though, and at the height of his fame, he had hats, shawls, food and delicacies named after him and hundreds of adoring fans would follow him from the concert hall back to his hotel.

The virtuoso spent the last days of his restless life a little farther along the coast from his native Genoa in Nice, France, where he died in 1840. He is buried in Parma.

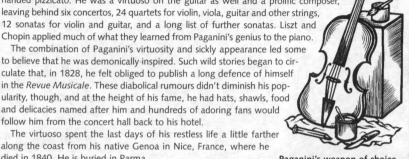

JANE SMITH

Paganini's weapon of choice

Matteotti 62r, and Pesci Viaggi e Turismo (☎ 010 56 49 36, ⓔ pesciros@tin.it), Piazza della Vittoria 94r.

Bookshops Touring Club Italiano bookshop (see Travel Agencies earlier) and Libreria Bozzi (☎ 010 246 17 18, ⓔ bozzi@panet.it), Via Cairoli 2r, stock healthy selections of maps and guides. Feltrinelli (☎ 010 54 08 30, Ⓦ www.feltrinelli.it), Via XX Septembre, sells English-language novels.

Gay & Lesbian Travellers ArciGay (☎ 010 545 02 24) runs a small office at Salita Salvator Viale 15r.

Laundry La Maddalena, Vico della Maddalena 2, opens 8am to 8pm daily. At the Porto Antico, try Lavanderia, Ponte Morosini 26, open 6am to 11pm daily. Both charge about €3.60 to wash 7kg of clothes.

Left Luggage The left-luggage counter at Stazione Principe opens 6am to 10pm daily and charges €2.60 per bag for every 12 hours. At Stazione Brignole there are only small/medium automatic lockers, accessible 24 hours and costing €2.05/2.60 for 24 hours.

Medical Services & Emergency Ospedale San Martino (hospital; ☎ 010 55 51), Largo Rosanna Benci 10, is east of the town centre.

Ghersi (☎ 010 54 16 61), Corso Buenos Aires 18, is an all-night pharmacy.

The *questura* (police station; ☎ 010 5 36 61) is on Via Armando Diaz.

Piazza de Ferrari

With its star-studded cast of the Art Nouveau **Palazzo della Borsa** (the former stock exchange), the neoclassical facade of the WWII-bombed **Teatro Carlo Felice** and the **Palazzo Ducale**, this elegant square is the focal point of Genoa and an obvious starting place for exploration of the city.

Facing Piazza Matteotti is the main entrance to the Palazzo Ducale *(☎ 010 557 40 00, Ⓦ www.palazzoducale.genova.it, Piazza de Ferrari; exhibitions adult/child €6.20/4.65; exhibitions open 9am-9pm Tues-Sun).* Once the seat of the city's rulers, it now houses a small jazz museum, bookshop, cafe

CENTRAL GENOA

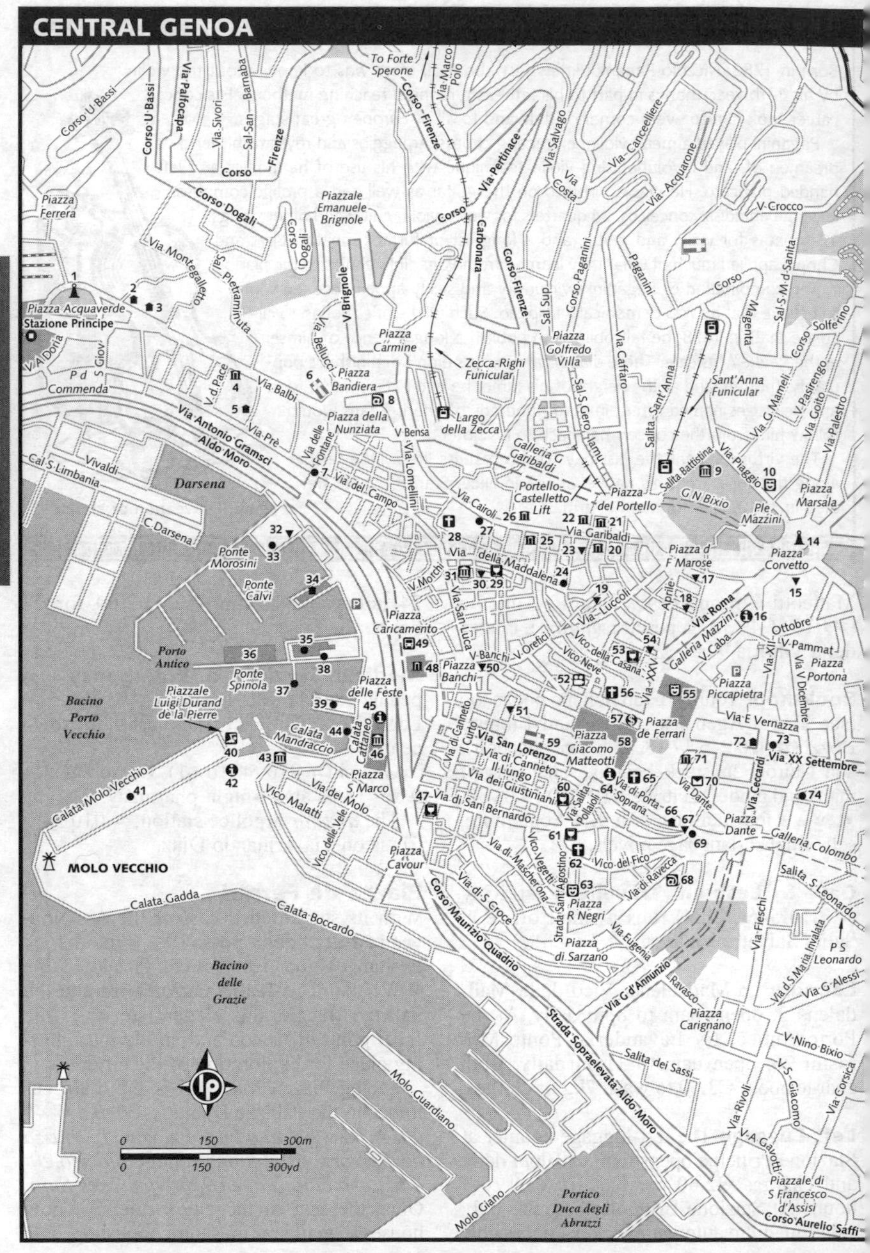

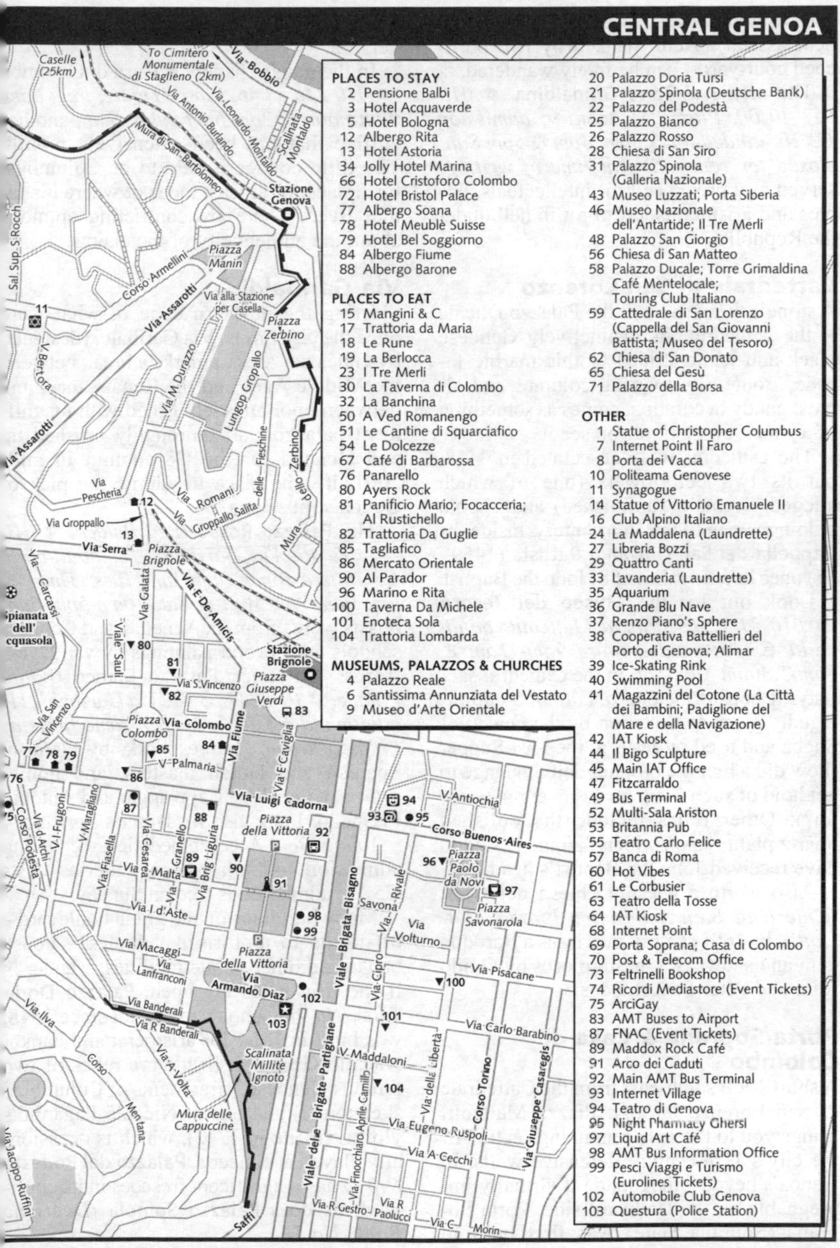
CENTRAL GENOA
PLACES TO STAY
2 Pensione Balbi
3 Hotel Acquaverde
5 Hotel Bologna
12 Albergo Rita
13 Hotel Astoria
34 Jolly Hotel Marina
66 Hotel Cristoforo Colombo
72 Hotel Bristol Palace
77 Albergo Soana
78 Hotel Meublè Suisse
79 Hotel Bel Soggiorno
84 Albergo Fiume
88 Albergo Barone
PLACES TO EAT
15 Mangini & C
17 Trattoria da Maria
18 Le Rune
19 La Berlocca
23 I Tre Merli
30 La Taverna di Colombo
32 La Banchina
50 A Ved Romanengo
51 Le Cantine di Squarciafico
54 Le Dolcezze
67 Café di Barbarossa
76 Panarello
80 Ayers Rock
81 Panificio Mario; Focacceria; Al Rustichello
82 Trattoria Da Guglie
85 Tagliafico
86 Mercato Orientale
90 Al Parador
96 Marino e Rita
100 Taverna Da Michele
101 Enoteca Sola
104 Trattoria Lombarda
MUSEUMS, PALAZZOS & CHURCHES
4 Palazzo Reale
6 Santissima Annunziata del Vestato
9 Museo d'Arte Orientale
20 Palazzo Doria Tursi
21 Palazzo Spinola (Deutsche Bank)
22 Palazzo del Podestà
25 Palazzo Bianco
26 Palazzo Rosso
28 Chiesa di San Siro
31 Palazzo Spinola (Galleria Nazionale)
43 Museo Luzzati; Porta Siberia
46 Museo Nazionale dell'Antartide; Il Tre Merli
48 Palazzo San Giorgio
56 Chiesa di San Matteo
58 Palazzo Ducale; Torre Grimaldina Café Mentelocale; Touring Club Italiano
59 Cattedrale di San Lorenzo (Cappella del San Giovanni Battista; Museo del Tesoro)
62 Chiesa di San Donato
65 Chiesa del Gesù
71 Palazzo della Borsa
OTHER
1 Statue of Christopher Columbus
7 Internet Point Il Faro
8 Porta dei Vacca
10 Politeama Genovese
11 Synagogue
14 Statue of Vittorio Emanuele II
16 Club Alpino Italiano
24 La Maddalena (Laundrette)
27 Libreria Bozzi
29 Quattro Canti
33 Lavanderia (Laundrette)
35 Aquarium
36 Grande Blu Nave
37 Renzo Piano's Sphere
38 Cooperativa Battellieri del Porto di Genova; Alimar
39 Ice-Skating Rink
40 Swimming Pool
41 Magazzini del Cotone (La Città dei Bambini; Padiglione del Mare e della Navigazione)
42 IAT Kiosk
44 Il Bigo Sculpture
45 Main IAT Office
47 Fitzcarraldo
49 Bus Terminal
52 Multi-Sala Ariston
53 Britannia Pub
55 Teatro Carlo Felice
57 Banca di Roma
60 Hot Vibes
61 Le Corbusier
63 Teatro della Tosse
64 IAT Kiosk
68 Internet Point
69 Porta Soprana; Casa di Colombo
70 Post & Telecom Office
73 Feltrinelli Bookshop
74 Ricordi Mediastore (Event Tickets)
75 ArciGay
83 AMT Buses to Airport
87 FNAC (Event Tickets)
89 Maddox Rock Café
91 Arco dei Caduti
92 Main AMT Bus Terminal
93 Internet Village
94 Teatro di Genova
95 Night Pharmacy Ghersi
97 Liquid Art Café
98 AMT Bus Information Office
99 Pesci Viaggi e Turismo (Eurolines Tickets)
102 Automobile Club Genova
103 Questura (Police Station)
Caselle (25km)
To Cimitero Monumentale di Staglieno (2km)
Via Bobbio
Via Antonio Burlando
Via Leonardo Montaldo
Scalinata Montaldo
Mura di San Bartolomeo
Stazione Genova
Piazza Manin
Corso Armellini
Via Assarotti
Via alla Stazione per Casella
Piazza Zerbino
V Bertora
Via M Durazzo
Lungop Gropallo
Via Pescheria
Via Romani
Via Groppallo
Via Serra
Piazza Brignole
Via E De Amicis
Viale Sauli
Stazione Brignole
Piazza Giuseppe Verdi
Via S Vincenzo
Piazza Colombo
Via Colombo
Via Fiume
V Palmaria
Via Luigi Cadorna
V Antiochia
Corso Buenos Aires
Piazza della Vittoria
Piazza Paolo da Novi
Via Malta
Via Cesarea
Via Granello
Via Brig Liguria
Via I d'Aste
Via Macaggi
Via Lanfranconi
Via Armando Diaz
Via Banderali
Via R Banderali
Via A Volta
Via Ilva
Corso Mentana
Scalinata Millite Ignoto
Mura delle Cappuccine
Viale Brigata Bisagno
Viale delle Brigate Partigiane
Via Cipro
Via Rivale
Via Volturno
Piazza Savonarola
Via Pisacane
Via Carlo Barabino
V Maddaloni
Via della Libertà
Corso Torino
Via Giuseppe Casaregis
Via Eugeno Ruspoli
Via A Cecchi
Via Finocchiaro Aprile Camillo
Via R Gestro
Via R Paolucci
Saffi
Via Jacopo Ruffini
Corso Podestà
Via d Archi
V I Frugoni
V Maragliano
Via Fiasella
Via San Vincenzo
Via Galata
Via Carcassi
Spianata dell' Acquasola
Sal Sup S Rocch
Via E Caviglia
Mura dello Zerbino
LIGURIA

and restaurant (see Places to Eat later). Its neoclassical atrium, flanked by two porticoed courtyards, can be freely wandered.

The medieval **Torre Grimaldina** *(☎ 010 557 40 00, Piazza Matteotti 9; admission €3.10; guided tours 3pm, 4pm & 5pm Sun; closed for renovation at time of writing)* served as a prison cell for intellectuals, nobles and aristocrats left to rot in hell under the Republic.

Cattedrale di San Lorenzo

A stone's throw west of the Palazzo Ducale is the cathedral. Its distinctively Genoese black-and-white-striped Gothic marble facade, fronted by twisting columns and almost gaudy decoration, comes as something of a shock every time you see it.

The cathedral was consecrated in 1118, but its two bell towers (one of which allegedly remains unfinished) and cupola didn't go up until the 16th century. Inside, its **Cappella del San Giovanni Battista** (1450–65) once housed relics of St John the Baptist.

Look out for the **Museo del Tesoro** *(☎ 010 31 12 69, Piazza Matteotti; adult/child €5.15; guided tours 9am-11am & 3pm-5.30pm Mon-Sat)* in the cathedral sacristy. It houses the *Sacro Catino*, a cup allegedly given to Solomon by the Queen of Sheba and used by Jesus at the Last Supper (how did a humble prophet/deity manage to get hold of such a cup for his evening nosh-up?). Other relics include the polished quartz platter upon which Salome is said to have received John the Baptist's head.

Also worth a peek is **Chiesa del Gesù** *(Chiesa di Sant'Ambrogio; Piazza Matteotti)*. Its 16th-century interior is a Baroque gem and showcases masterpieces by Guido Reni and Peter Paul Rubens.

Porta Soprana & Casa di Colombo

A short stroll south-east from the Cattedrale di San Lorenzo through Piazza Matteotti brings you to the only remaining section of the city's 12th-century defensive walls. In Genoa's heyday, they made it virtually impregnable on the landward side. Porta Soprana (Soprana Gate) was first built in 1155, but what you see today is a restored version.

In the gate's shadow is Casa di Colombo *(☎ 010 246 53 46, Piazza Dante; free; open 9am-noon & 2pm-6pm Sat & Sun)*, another edifice that has been extensively rebuilt. The little cottage is said to be Columbus' birthplace, or at least the spot where his father lived. There are conflicting opinions about the authenticity of the claims.

Via Garibaldi

Skirting the northern edge of what were once the city limits, Via Garibaldi (designed by Galeazzo Alessi) marks a break between the Middle Ages and the Renaissance, and between poor and rich. Lined with magnificent palazzos, all thoroughly brushed up and cleaned for the G8 summit in mid-2001, it's the place to admire the pick of Genoa's museums.

The **Palazzo Rosso** *(Red Palace; ☎ 010 271 02 36, Via Garibaldi 18; adult/child €3.10/free; open 9am-1pm Tues, Thurs & Fri, 9am-7pm Wed & Sat, 10am-5pm Sun)* boasts works from the Venetian and Genoese schools and several paintings by van Dyck. Across the street, **Palazzo Bianco** *(White Palace; ☎ 010 247 63 77, Via Garibaldi 11; adult/child €3.10/free; open same times as Palazzo Rosso)* features works by Flemish, Spanish and Dutch masters, and home-grown material by Caravaggio and Antonio Pisanello. Look also for Dürer's *Portrait of a Young Boy*. A combined ticket covering admission to both palace galleries costs €5.15; admission is free on Sunday.

Many buildings on the grand boulevard – off-limits to motorised vehicles – house banks and other public facilities; wander in if the iron gates are open. **Palazzo Doria Tursi** *(No 9)*, Genoa's town hall since 1848, was built in 1564 for aristocrat and banker Niccolò Grimaldi. Inside are relics of two famous Genoese – fragments of Columbus' skeleton (!) and one of Niccolò Paganini's violins (made in 1742), which is occasionally played at concerts. **Palazzo del Podestà** *(No 7)* has magnificent frescoes in its courtyard, as does **Palazzo Spinola** *(Deutsche Bank; No 5)*.

A short walk east of Via Garibaldi, a path rom Piazza Corvetto twists up through iered gardens to the **Museo d'Arte Orientale** *(☎ 010 54 22 85, Piazzale Mazzini 1; ıdult/child €3.10/free; open 9am-1pm Tues & Thurs-Sun)*, home to one of the largest collections of Oriental art in Europe. Heading south, elegant **Via Roma** (dating from 1870), with its Art Nouveau boutiques and ıdjacent glass-covered **Galleria Mazzini**, is Genoa's finest shopping street. It links Piazza Corvetto with Piazza de Ferrari.

Old City

Medieval Genoa is famous for its *caruggi* – an historic maze of twisting lanes and dank blind alleys that spills in a bewildering spaghetti formation across the oldest part of Genoa. The best way to explore it is just to wander around. Its core is bounded (in a clockwise direction) by Porta dei Vacca, the waterfront Vias Cairoli, Garibaldi and XXV Aprile, and the Porta Soprana around the inland periphery. Beyond this it straggles along the coast in both directions, especially at the northern end, up the seedy Via Prè.

Most of the old city's lowlife is concentrated in the zone west of **Via San Luca**, itself a hip thoroughfare full of cafes and bars, with Piazza Bianchi at its southern end. East of the piazza is **Via Orefici**, where you'll find market stalls, more cafes and a couple of restaurants and cake shops.

The **Palazzo Reale** *(Royal Palace; ☎ 010 271 02 72, Via Balbi 10; adult/child €4.15/free; open 8.15am-1.45pm Mon & Tues, 8.15am-7.15pm Wed-Sun)* features Renaissance works and is one good reason to venture into Prè. Stop off en route to peer inside the trompe l'oeil dome of **Santissima Annunziata del Vestato** *(Piazza della Nunziata)*, a rich example of 17th-century Genoese architecture, virtually destroyed by bombing in WWII but since restored. Nearby, **Chiesa di San Siro** *(Via San Siro)* dates to the 4th century but was rebuilt in the 16th century.

Not far from Via Garibaldi, as you head south into the old city, is **Palazzo Spinola** *(☎ 010 270 53 00, Piazza Superiore di Pellicceria 1; adult/child €4.15/free; open 9am-8pm Tues-Sat, 2pm-8pm Sun)*, a 16th-century mansion once owned by one of the Republic's most formidable and feared dynasties. The Spinola's ancestral home displays Italian and Flemish Renaissance works of art today, and serves as an awe-inspiring example of the splendour in which Genoese nobility lived in the 16th to 18th centuries.

Dozens of medieval churches and palazzos in the area were built by the ruling families, who staked out pockets of the old city for themselves and their *alberghi* (clan), defying rival families (with death, pillage and so on) to set foot on their patch. The Sarzanos controlled 11th-century **Chiesa di San Donato** *(Strada Sant'Agostino)*, built in pure Romanesque style and enlarged in the 12th and 13th centuries, while the church of the Doria family, **Chiesa di San Matteo** *(Piazza San Matteo)*, was founded in 1125. Andrea Doria's sword is preserved under the altar and his tomb is in the crypt.

Although Genoa's old city is busy in daylight, just about everything shuts at night. Exceptions are some eateries and the 24-hour prostitution and drug trades, which are concentrated in the zone west of Via San Luca.

Porto Antico

The 1992 Expo transformed the old port into Genoa's strongest draw. And as the city gears up for its role as European City of Culture in 2004, rejuvenation of the ancient Greek port continues. Unfortunately, nothing can detract from the Sopraelevata, the horrendously ugly flyover that slashes straight through the old port area. Just back from the waterfront, frescoed **Palazzo San Giorgio** *(Piazza Caricamento)* houses the port authority. Built in 1260, it became a prison in 1298; inmate Marco Polo worked on *Il Milione* within its walls.

Genoa's star attraction is the portside **Acquario** *(Aquarium; ☎ 010 248 12 05, W www.acquario.ge.it, Ponte Spinola; adult/child €11.35/6.70; open 9.30am-7pm/7.30pm Mon-Wed & Fri, 9.30am-11pm Thurs, 9.30am-8pm/8.30pm Sat & Sun in summer; 9.30am-7pm/7.30pm Tues-Fri & 9.30am-8pm/8.30pm Sat & Sun in winter)*. Sharks and dolphins – watch the latter being fed at 10am, 12.30pm, 2.30pm and 4.30pm

LIGURIA

Ocean Blue

Christopher Columbus (Cristoforo Colombo to Italians) exhibited a bad case of the travel bug from an early age. Steeped in Marco Polo's writings and Pliny's *Natural History*, the Genoese adventurer (born 1451) conceived an ambitious project to reach the Orient by sailing west instead of east.

Adventurous as Genoa's rulers might have been, this preposterous idea was too much for them, forcing Columbus to seek other patrons. Spain eventually gave him a sympathetic hearing and backed his journey of a lifetime.

On 3 August 1492, Columbus (Cristóbal Colón to Spaniards) set off with 100 men and three small caravels (two- or three-masted sailing ships), *Niña*, *Pinta* and *Santa Maria*. Two months later, he and his entourage landed in the Bahamas. Over the following eight years, he discovered Cuba, Haiti, Jamaica and some of the Antilles, still convinced he was in Asia.

Sent back to Spain on charges of committing atrocities (although subsequent Spanish colonisers evidently developed a thicker skin in this regard), he was later pardoned. He made one last voyage between 1502 and 1504, tracking the central American coast and reaching Colombia. When Columbus died, forgotten and embittered, two years later in Valladolid, Spain, he still had no idea of the New World that he'd discovered.

Set sail for the new world!

– are among the 5000 marine animals ogled by 1.4 million visitors annually. The **Grande Nave Blu**, the floating barge at the end of the wharf, takes visitors on a whirlwind voyage through the Age of Discovery (Darwin, Columbus et al), then whisks them off to a Madagascan rain forest.

Renzo Piano's breathtaking **Bubble** – a monumental ball of glass filled with a fluttering kaleidoscope of butterflies and tropical plants – was unveiled in July 2001 in front of world leaders attending the G8 Summit in Genoa. Floating by the side of the aquarium, the space will eventually have a multimedia centre aimed at teaching kids about its green micro-botanical environment.

A hundred metres south-west is another fabulous Piano creation, **Il Bigo** *(Calata Cattaneo; adult/child €2.60/2.05; open 11.30am-1pm & 2.30pm-4pm Tues-Fri, 11.30am-1pm & 2.30pm-5pm Sat & Sun)*. The derrick was built for the sole purpose of hoisting a cylindrical container 200m into the air, thereby giving its occupants a bird's-eye view of the Porto Antico. Behind it is a canopy-covered **ice-skating rink** *(☎ 010 246 13 19, Piazza delle Feste; admission €4.15; open 1pm-11.45pm Mon, 8am-11.45pm Tues-Fri, 8am-11pm Sat, 10.30am-11.30pm Sun Oct-Apr)*.

A chilly addition to the waterfront is **Museo Nazionale dell'Antartide** *(☎ 010 254 36 90, W www.mna.it, Calata Cattaneo; adult/child €5.15/4.15; open 10am-7pm Sun-Thurs & 10am-10.30pm Fri & Sat June-Sept, 9.45am-6.15pm Tues-Sat & 10am-7pm Sun Oct-May)*. Multimedia devices encourage visitors to explore the 98% ice-covered white continent of Antarctica and learn about Italy's research programme there, conducted from its base at Terra Nova Bay since 1986. Free audioguides in English are available at reception.

Walking west along Calata Mandraccio you pass **Porta Siberia** (1550), a city gate named after *cibaria*, a derivation of the Italian word for food (alluding to the port's grain warehouses). Inside, exhibitions on controversial Genoese artist and scenographer Emanuele Luzzati (born 1921) are hosted in the **Museo Luzzati** *(☎ 010 253 03 28, W www.museoluzzati.it, Calata Mandraccio* *adult/child €2.60/2.05; open 10am-6pm Tues-Fri & 11am-7pm Sat & Sun Sept-June, 3pm-11pm Tues-Sat July & Aug).*

Farther west still are the **Magazzini del Cotone**, one-time cotton warehouses since converted into an entertainment area with congress centre, nine-screen cinema, shopping centre and two museums. On the 1st floor, **La Città dei Bambini** *(☎ 010 246 55 35, e cdibimbi@split.it, Porto Antico; adult/child €4.15/3.35; open 10am-6pm Tues-Sun)* is an interactive space aimed at showing kids the wonders of 'play, science and technology'. On the 2nd floor, Genoa's proud maritime history is celebrated in the **Padiglione del Mare e della Navigazione** *(☎ 010 246 36 78, Porto Antico; adult/child €5.15/2.60; open 10.30am-6pm Mon-Fri & 10.30am-7pm Sat & Sun Mar-Sept, 10.30am-5.30pm Tues-Fri & 10.30am-6pm Sat & Sun Oct-Feb)*. Life-sized dioramas transport you back to Genoa's busy port days and there's a reconstruction of a 16th-century dockyard and the interior of a transatlantic liner.

A sweeping view of Porto Antico and its **lighthouse** (1543) can be enjoyed from Molo Vecchio, the westernmost tip of the peninsula behind Magazzini del Cotone. The lighthouse can only be visited by guided boat tour; the tourist office has details.

City Walls & Walks

The high country leaning protectively over the city bears a 13km-long scar of city walls, built between 1626 and 1632 to shield the port's landward side. These **Mura Nuove** (New Walls) covered a much larger area than their 12th-century predecessors, stretching west to the lighthouse, east to Piazza della Vittoria and north to **Forte Sperone** (490m), the largest of the remaining defensive forts, where open-air plays and concerts are held in summer. The fortress can only be visited by pre-arranged guided tour; ask at the IAT office for details.

The easiest way to get to the wall and inspect its forts is by the **funicular** from Largo della Zecca to Righi (300m). From Largo Giorgio Caproni (the square in front of Righi funicular station), walking trails indicated by red markers lead to Forte Begato, Forte Sperone, Forte Puin and Forte Diamante. For more details, contact the Club Alpino Italiano *(☎ 010 59 21 22, Galleria Mazzini 7–3)*.

A **narrow-gauge railway** snakes from **Stazione Genova-Piazza Manin** *(☎ 010 83 73 21, e fgc@ferroviagenovacaselle.it, Via alla Stazione per Caselle 15)*, 25km north to Caselle (405m), a tiny village in the Scrivia Valley. The railway has been in operation since 1929 and offers passengers great views of the Cimitero Monumentale di Staglieno (see the boxed text 'Bury the Dead'), the forts of Sperone, Puin and Dimante, and the low-lying Portofino promontory. The journey takes one hour (€1.60, nine to 11 daily).

Bury the Dead

The best of Genoa's dead – including the revolutionary Giuseppe Mazzini (1805–72) and Constance Lloyd (1858–98), who Oscar Wilde wed in 1884 only to later abandon – are buried in the **Cimitero Monumentale di Staglieno**, the city's monumental cemetery tucked in the hills north of town. The sea of graves dates to 1840 and is an extravaganza of ornate marble statues and neoclassical carvings. To get here, take bus No 34 from Stazione Principe to the end of line.

Organised Tours

Information and tickets for boat trips are available from the ***ticket booths*** *(☎ 010 248 57 10 or 010 248 57 50, Ponte Spinola; open 9.30am-6.30pm daily Sept-June, 9am-8pm daily July & Aug)*, next to the aquarium at Porto Antico.

Tours of the port (45 minutes) by ***Cooperativo Battellieri del Porto di Genova*** *(☎ 010 26 57 12, W www.battellierigenova.it, Calata Zingari; €5.15/3.60 per adult/child)* depart at 10am from Ponte Spinola. Between June and September, it runs excursions to San Fruttuoso, Portofino, the Cinque Terre and Porto Venere.

Whale-spotting excursions *(adult/child €33.55/18.10)*, organised by Cooperativo Battellieri del Porto di Genova in conjunction with the Worldwide Fund for Nature, who plant a biologist on board, depart once weekly mid-June to mid-September (three times per week in July and August).

Alimar *(see Boat under Getting There & Away later)* is another boat company running organised boat tours.

Special Events

Genoa is one of the four historical maritime cities that race each other in the Palio delle Quattro Antiche Repubbliche Marinare (Regatta of the Four Ancient Maritime Republics). The hosting of the event rotates amongst the rivals: Pisa in 2002, Venice in 2003, Genoa in 2004 and Amalfi in 2005.

Places to Stay – Budget

Camping Several camp sites and caravan parks are scattered along the coast; ask at the IAT office for details.

Villa Doria *(☎ 010 696 96 00, Via al Campeggio Villa Doria 15)* Sites per person/tent/car €5.15/5.15/2.60. This camp site, on the way to Pegli, opens year-round and can be reached by bus Nos 1, 2 and 3 from Piazza Caricamento.

Hostels ***Hostel Genova*** *(☎/fax 010 242 24 57, Via Costanzi 120)* B&B €12.90, meals €7.25. Open Feb-mid-Dec. Genoa's Hostelling International (HI) hostel is in Righi, north of the city's old centre. Catch bus No 40 from Stazione Brignole to the end of the line or No 35 from Stazione Principe, then connect with No 40.

Hotels Although the old city, Stazione Principe and the port areas have a fair smattering of budget places, you'll get better value and a greater feeling of security near Stazione Brignole and Via XX Settembre.

Pensione Carola *(☎ 010 839 13 40, Via Groppallo 4)* Singles/doubles €28.40/43.90. Carola's clean, well-kept rooms can be found on the 3rd floor of a lovely old building near Stazione Brignole.

Albergo Rita *(☎/fax 010 87 02 07, Via Groppallo 8)* Single/doubles without bath €25.80/38.75, singles/doubles with bath €38.75/49.05. Up the road from Carola, Rita offers a variety of good rooms.

Albergo Fiume *(☎ 010 59 16 91 or 010 570 54 60, fax 010 570 28 33, Via Fiume 9r)* Doubles without bath €23.25, singles/doubles with bath €38.75/43.90. The reek of disinfectant testifies to the squeaky cleanliness of rooms here.

Albergo Barone *(☎/fax 010 58 75 78, Via XX Settembre 2/23)* Singles/doubles/triples/quads without shower €28.40/36.15/51.65/64.55, singles/doubles/triples/quads with shower €36.15/43.90/56.80/69.70, doubles/triples with shower & toilet €43.90/62. A faintly chaotic air fills this appealing 3rd-floor hotel, decked out with large rooms and decorative moulded ceilings in a building dating to 1910.

Hotel Meublè Suisse *(☎ 010 54 11 76, Via XX Settembre 21/6)* Singles/doubles with shower €33.55/43.90. This eclectic seven-room hotel, in a building dating to 1850, overflows with books, vases, photographs and other homely items.

If it's dirt cheap (and, in some instances, dodgy) you want, prey on Prè, the quarter around Stazione Principe.

Pensione Balbi *(☎ 010 247 21 12, Via Balbi 21–23)* Singles/doubles from €36.15/46.50. Several hotels in a similar category are dotted along this street.

Hotel Bologna *(☎ 010 246 57 72, fax 010 246 54 47, Piazza Superiore del Roso 3)* Singles/doubles from €25.80/36.15. Tucked down a narrow alley off Via Balbi, this ratty little one-star place is one of several dirt-cheap set-ups around Stazione Principe.

Hotel Acquaverde *(☎ 010 26 54 27, fax 010 246 48 39, Via Balbi 29)* Singles/doubles €36.15/46.50. Bologna's solo-starred companion stands a tad closer to the railway line.

Places to Stay – Mid-Range

Hotel Cristoforo Colombo *(☎/fax 010 251 36 43, ⓔ colombo@libera.it, Via di Porta Soprana 59r)* Singles/doubles €52/72. Cristoforo Colombo is an extremely charming choice in what is probably the nicest part of the old city. Advance reservations are essential.

Hotel Bel Soggiorno *(☎/fax 010 58 14 18, Via XX Settembre 19)* Singles/doubles from €46.50/72.30. This reliable option puts you to bed in a turn-of-the-century town house smack-bang in the middle of Genoa's busy shopping street.

Albergo Soana *(☎ 010 56 28 14, fax 010 56 14 86, ⓔ soana@hotelsoana.it, Via XX Settembre 23/8)* Singles/doubles/triples €62/77.45/98.15. A stone-faced pair of weary atlantes (columns in the form of male figures) prop up the entrance to this hotel.

Hotel Astoria *(☎ 010 87 33 16, fax 010 831 73 26, ⓦ www.hotelastoria-ge.com, Piazza Brignole 4)* Singles/doubles €82.65/129.10. This restful hotel, with its warm ochre facade on a quiet square, is a popular place with briefcase-carriers seeking peace. Prices include breakfast.

Jolly Hotel Marina *(☎ 010 2 53 91, fax 010 251 13 20, ⓔ genova_marina@jollyhotels.it, Molo Ponte Calvi)* Singles/doubles from €139.45/170.45. Characterless but comfortable rooms recline inside a pink concrete block, across the water from the aquarium at Porto Antico.

Places to Stay – Top End

Hotel Bristol Palace *(☎ 010 59 25 41, fax 010 56 17 56, ⓔ info@hotelbristolpalace.com, ⓦ www.hotelbristolpalace.com, Via XX Settembre 35)* Singles/doubles from €170.45/242.75 Mon-Fri, €111.05/154.95 Sat & Sun. A former 19th-century mansion, Hotel Bristol Palace has a breathtakingly beautiful staircase topped by a fab stained glass ceiling – both dramatically visible from reception.

Places to Eat

The bulk of the good eating is to be done in the old city, although there are exceptions. Don't leave town without eating pasta with *pesto genovese* (a sauce of basil, garlic, parmesan cheese and pine nuts), *torta pasqualina* (made with spinach, ricotta cheese and eggs), *pansotti* (spinach ravioli with a thick, creamy hazelnut sauce), *trenette al pesto* (a spaghetti with pesto and potato) and, of course, focaccia.

Restaurants Via San Vincenzo, near Stazione Brignole, is a short but busy food street offering ample dining and snacking opportunities. ***Panificio Mario*** *(No 61)* and ***Focacceria*** *(No 61a)* dish up slices of farinata to eat on the move. If you prefer to sit down, dine on a cheap and cheerful €5.15 menu (Mon-Fri only) at ***Ayers Rock*** *(☎ 010 58 84 70, Viale Sauli 33n)*, a self-service buffet joint in a side street off Via San Vincenzo.

The following two places are more atmospheric places to dine.

Al Rustichello *(☎ 010 58 85 56, Via San Vincenzo 59r)* 1st/2nd courses €5.15/7.75. This rustic and cosy spot is just the place for hearty Genoese fodder.

Trattoria Da Guglie *(Via San Vincenzo 64)* 1st/2nd courses from €3.10/3.60. As down-to-earth as you'll ever get, Da Guglie stuns diners with its stark interior where food, rather than aesthetic beauty, clearly rules. Its *trippe in umido* (tripe cooked in liquid) is not for the faint-hearted.

Another clutch of locally popular lunchtime spots near Stazione Brignole are an easy stroll south-east of Piazza della Vittoria.

Taverna Da Michele *(☎ 010 59 36 71, Via della Libertà 41r)* Pizzas €4.15-7.75, 1st/2nd courses from €5.15. Enjoy a wholemeal pizza beneath creeping vines at this little-known spot, which sports a peaceful terrace.

Enoteca Sola *(☎ 010 59 45 13, Via Carlo Barabino 120)* 1st/2nd courses €6.20/ 10.35. Dine in style at this fabulous wine shop – if you can get a table, that is.

Trattoria Lombarda *(☎ 010 59 46 29, Via Finocchiaro Aprile Camillo 26)* 1st/2nd courses from €4.15/6.20. A traditional and charming bistro where you can feast on the cheap on *stoccafisso alla genovese* (stockfish) and other typically local delights.

Cheap deals are not to be had at the Porto Antico, although atmosphere ranks high in the flashy sushi bar, lobster house and American-style diner on the 3rd floor of Sul Fronte del Porto, the building behind Il Bigo on Calata Cattaneo. On ground level, ***I Tre Merli*** *(☎ 010 246 44 16, Calata Cattaneo)* offers winers and diners a blackbird's-eye view of the waterfront goings-on.

Genoa's old-city rabbit warren hides some gems.

La Taverna di Colombo *(☎ 010 24 62 447, Vico della Scienza 6)* 1st/2nd courses

€2.85/3.60, menus €6.20 & €7.25. This charming, bistro-style place dishes up simple but delicious cuisine to the hungry clientele that packs out the cosy red cellar.

Trattoria da Maria *(Vico Testa d'Oro 14)* Menu €6.70, including wine. Off Via XXV Aprile, Maria's trattoria exudes a simple charm with its checked tablecloths and handwritten menu.

I Tre Merli *(☎ 010 247 40 95, Vico della Maddalena 26r)* Full meals about €20.65. Just off Via Garibaldi, this charming spot touts an interior of uncovered brick and vaults and is great for a candlelit meal.

Le Cantine di Squarciafico *(☎ 010 247 08 23, Piazza Ivrea 3)* 1st/2nd courses €7.25/9.30. A good-value €6.20 self-service menu (including water or wine) draws a predominantly local crowd to this vaulted cellar. Classical music adds an elegant touch.

La Berlocca *(☎ 010 247 41 62, Via dei Macelli di Soziglia 45r)* Full meals about €23.25. This memorable *enoteca* (wine bar), devoid of any pretension, is renowned for its traditional dishes with a twist – sea bass with apples, pear tart without flour or tiramisu without liqueur! The place only has seven tables so book ahead.

Le Rune *(☎ 010 59 49 51, Vico Domoculta 14r)* 1st/2nd courses €12.90/15.50, menus €23.75 & €36.15. This is the splurging option. Sample tempting creations such as scampi and venus clam gnocchi in tomato sauce or stockfish dressed in Genoese *salsa di noci* (nut sauce).

Cafes & Pasticcerias One of the best places to pull in for a pit stop in the old city is ***Le Dolcezze***, a sandwich shop at Via XXV Aprile 22, stuffed full of equally stuffed *panini* (rolls), quiches, salads and cakes to take away.

Plenty of pasticcerias sell *kranz* (honey-glazed raisin bread baked in a twist and topped with sugar crystals) and traditional Genoese fruit bread, the city's answer to *panettone* (Christmas cake from Milan) – try ***Tagliafico*** *(Via Galata 31)*, ***Panarello*** *(Via XX Settembre 156)*, ***Marino e Rita*** *(Piazza Paolo da Novi 40–42)* or ***Mangini & C*** *(☎ 010 56 40 13, Piazza Corvetto)*, which is renowned as Genoa's finest.

A Ved Romanengo *(☎ 010 247 29 15, Via Orefici 31–33)* This historic shop has been serving pastries, confectionery and sweet chestnuts since 1805. Its cafe – clad with three lace-dressed tables – serves lunch. There's no printed menu; just ask what's cooking.

Café di Barbarossa *(☎ 010 246 50 97, Piano di Sant'Andrea 21–23r)* Open until 2am. This simple but stylish cafe-cum-bar basks in the shade of towering 12th-century Porta Soprana.

La Banchina *(☎ 010 246 10 30, Ponte Morosini 1)* Pizzas €4.65-7.75. Tucked in the shade of a moored galleon, this terrace cafe is one of the few waterside spots where you can escape the chaos of the Porto Antico. It serves pizza, farinata and focaccia.

Al Parador *(☎ 010 58 17 71, Piazza della Vittoria 49)* 1st/2nd courses €4.15/5.15. A modern restaurant-bar, Al Parador serves well-filled panini and full meals on a quiet terrace beneath porticoes.

Café Mentelocale *(☎ 010 595 96 48, W www.mentelocale.it, Piazza Matteotti 5, inside Palazzo Ducale)* Newspapers to read, designer chairs to slouch on and computer terminals to check the latest happenings in town are all part-and-parcel of this ultra-modern cafe. It's run by the cyber team responsible for Genoa's most up-to-date online city guide. It runs a tasty fusion-inspired restaurant on the 2nd floor of the palace.

Self-Catering Self-caterers can stock up on fresh produce at the ***Mercato Orientale*** *(Via XX Settembre)*.

Entertainment

Away from the waterfront, central Genoa all but shuts down in the evening – 'better to go home and sleep' was the advice of one local.

Tickets for cultural and sporting events are sold at box offices inside the ***Ricordi Mediastore*** *(Via alla Porta degli Archi 88–94)* and at ***FNAC*** *(Via XX Settembre 58)*.

A cinema showing English-language films daily is ***Multi-Sala Ariston*** *(☎ 010*

LIGURIA

247 35 49, ⓦ www.cinema-online.net, Vico San Matteo 14–16)

The Genoa Theatre Company performs at ***Politeama Genovese*** *(☎ 010 831 16 21, ⓦ www.politeamagenovese.it, Via Piaggio)* and ***Teatro Di Genova*** *(☎ 010 534 23 00, ⓦ www.teatro-di-genova.it, Piazza Borgo Pila 42)*.

Teatro della Tosse *(☎ 010 247 07 93, ⓦ www.teatrodellatosse.it, Piazza Renato Negri 4)* This theatre dates from 1702 and Casanova walked the boards here. The season runs from January to May.

In summer, plays are sometimes held at Forte Sperone; the IAT office has details.

Teatro Carlo Felice *(☎ 010 538 12 24/7, ⓔ www.carlofelice.it, Piazza de Ferrari)* Genoa's opera house was built on the site of the original opera house, which was heavily bombed in WWII. The four-stage theatre has a year-round programme.

Bars & Clubs Most of the recommendations given here are in the old city.

Quattro Canti *(☎ 010 25 29 97, Via Ai Quattro Canti di San Francesco 28)* This old-town bar dishes up panini, *bruschette* (toasted garlic bread) and good music to a mellow crowd. Bring a beer mat to woo the bar staff.

Le Corbusier *(☎ 010 246 86 52, ⓔ mixersnc@libero.it, Piazza San Donato 36–38)* Despite its name, this cocktail bar and cafe appears to have nothing to do with the architect.

Hot Vibes *(Salita Pollaioli 26)* This alternative club is strictly somewhere for after dark. Posters advertising what's on where in the clubbing scene are plastered outside.

Liquid Art Café *(☎ 347 488 68 25, Piazza Savonarola 28)* This industrial music bar serves breakfast from 6.30am and has a DJ spinning tunes from 10pm.

Maddox Rock Café *(☎ 010 56 58 96, Via Malta 15)* American-style Maddox shakes a mean aperitif, matched by an endless (free) supply of complimentary pizza slices, fries, tortilla chips and olives.

Britannia Pub *(☎ 010 247 45 32, Vico della Casana 76)* Homesick Brits and Irish, or those sick of Italian lager, can down a pint of Guinness or Kilkenny here.

Fitzcarraldo *(Piazza Cavour 35r)* This bar offers live music by the water.

Getting There & Away

Air Regular domestic and international flights use Cristoforo Colombo international airport (☎ 010 601 54 10), 6km west of the centre at Sestri Ponente.

Bus Buses to international cities arrive at/depart from Piazza della Vittoria, as do limited inter-regional services and buses for other points in Liguria. Tickets for most services, including Eurolines buses, are sold at Pesci Viaggi e Turismo (see Travel Agencies under Information earlier).

Train Genoa is linked by train to Turin, Milan, Pisa and Rome and it makes little difference which of the two train stations (Principe or Brignole) you choose, except for trips along the two Rivieras. Going west to San Remo and Ventimiglia, for example, there are more departures from Stazione Principe than from Brignole.

Car & Motorcycle Cars and motorcycles are banned from the pedestrianised old city. Automobile Club Genova (☎ 010 5 39 41, ⓦ www.acigenova.it), Viale Brigate Partigiane 1a, is a handy information source for motorists.

The A12 connects Genoa with Livorno in Tuscany and with the A11 for Florence. The A7 goes to Milan, the A26 to Turin and the A10 to Savona and the French border. Hitchhikers will probably have more luck on the S1 heading in either direction along the coast, or the S35 heading north to Alessandria (and on to Turin).

Boat Genoa is an important embarkation point for ferries to Spain, Sicily, Sardinia, Corsica and Tunisia. Most maritime activity is June to September only. Unless otherwise noted, the ferry operators' contact details listed below are for the ticketing desks at Genoa's passenger terminal (*terminal traghetti*; 24-hour information service ☎ 166 152 39 393, ⓦ www.porto.genova.it), wedged between Ponte C Colombo and

LIGURIA

Ponte Assereto. Only cruise ships use the 1930s terminal on Ponte dei Mille.

Fares listed are for one-way, low/high-season deck-class tickets, unless stated otherwise. Major companies based at the ferry port are:

Corsica Marittima (☎ 010 58 95 95, Ⓦ www.corsica-marittima.com) C/o GSA/Cemar, Via XX Settembre 2–10. A subsidiary of SNCM, this company sails to/from Bastia in Corsica.

Grandi Navi Veloci (Grimaldi group; ☎ 010 2 54 65, Ⓦ www.grimaldi.it) Seasonal luxury ferries to/from Sardinia (Porto Torres and Olbia; €43.40/72.30) and year-round to/from Sicily (Palermo; €74.35/106.40) and Spain (Barcelona; €59.90/88.85).

Moby Lines (☎ 010 254 15 13, ☎ 0565 93 61, Ⓦ www.mobylines.it) Ferries year-round to/from Corsica (Bastia; €18.10/28.90) and Sardinia (Olbia; €23.25/51.15).

SNCM Ferryterranee (☎ 010 58 95 95, Ⓦ www.sncm.fr) C/o GSA/Cemar, Via XX Settembre 2–10. Weekly boats, June to late September, to/from Tunisia (Tunis; high season single deck fare €108.25).

Tirrenia (☎ 199 12 31 99, ☎ 800 82 40 79, Ⓦ www.tirrenia.it) Ferries and high-speed boats to/from Sardinia (Porto Torres, Olbia and Arbatax), with connections to Sicily. Deck passenger/car from €20.90/45.75.

Tris Traghetti (☎ 010 576 24 11, Ⓦ www.tris.it) Ferries and high-speed boats to/from the Sardinian ports of Palau (€29.45/49.05) and Porto Torres (€23.25/48.55).

See the Getting There & Away sections in the Sicily and Sardinia chapters for more details.

Ferries serve towns on the Riviera di Levante, including Camogli, Portofino, Santa Margherita, the Cinque Terre, and San Fruttuoso, June to September. Cooperativa Battellieri del Golfo Paradiso (☎ 0185 77 20 91, Ⓦ www.golfoparadiso.it) sails from a quay in the Mandraccio quarter of Porto Antico. Alimar (☎ 010 25 67 75, ☎ 010 25 59 75, Ⓦ www.alimar.ge.it) runs Marexpress, a summertime catamaran service to Porto Venere and the Cinque Terre. Frequency depends on demand.

Getting Around

To/From the Airport The AMT's Volabus (line No 100; ☎ 010 558 24 14) departs from Piazza Giuseppe Verdi, outside Stazione Brignole (€2.05 one way, 25 minutes, every 30 minutes between 5.30am and 11pm). It stops at Stazione Principe en route to the airport. Day tickets costing €2.60 are available.

Bus AMT (☎ 010 599 74 14) operates buses throughout the city. Main terminals include the two train stations, Piazza della Vittoria and Piazza Caricamento. A ticket valid for 90 minutes costs €0.75; an all-day ticket is €2.60. Tickets can also be used on main-line trains within the city limits (as far as Voltri and Nervi).

Taxi For a cab, call Radiotaxi (☎ 010 59 66).

AROUND GENOA

Any trip out of central Genoa reveals the sheer enormity of this city's unfortunate portside sprawl.

Westwards, the noisy two-lane *autostrada* speeds past abandoned grain stores and through a blinding succession of tunnels to Pegli, distinguishable in this industrial wasteland by the gas storage tanks that scar its rolling green hills. Lavish **Villa Pallavicini**, with its magnificent park (modelled on Genoese gardens of the Renaissance), testifies to the aristocracy lured by the once-fashionable seaside resort in the 19th-century. It houses a **Museo Archeologico** *(☎ 010 698 40 45, Ⓔ archligure@mail.it, Via Pallavicini 11; adult/child €3.10/free; open 8am-7pm Tues-Sat, 8am-1pm Sun)*, dedicated to Ligurian prehistory. Take No 1, 2 or 3 from Genoa's Stazione Brignole or No 30 from Piazza Caricamento to Pegli.

At the eastern edge of Genoa, **Nervi** is a lesser victim of the city's growth. Its pretty-in-pink **Villa Grimaldi Fassio** *(☎ 010 32 23 96, Via Capolungo 9; adult/child €2.60/free; open 9am-7pm Tues-Sat, 9am-1pm Sun)* is a 17th-century mansion surrounded by a rose garden where the Festival Internazionale del Balleto is held in July and outdoor films in August. Inside is a modern art collection. Take bus No 17 from Genoa's Stazione Brignole to Nervi, then bus No 517 to Via Capolungo.

Recco, a little farther east, is ablaze with colour in early September during an enormous firework festival, part of its three-day Festa della Madonna which culminates in a grand religious procession on Sunday. Take a train there, as traffic is so tight you could spend all evening in search of a parking spot.

RIVIERA DI LEVANTE

The coast east of this portside sprawl unfolds in a sprinkling of seaside villages, which, despite their evident popularity (especially the Cinque Terre), promise pretty walking, dramatic scenery and a unique charm.

Camogli

postcode 16032 • pop 5790

Wandering through the alleyways and the long, cobbled streets of Camogli, 25km east of Genoa, it is hard not to be taken aback by the painstaking trompe l'oeil decoration – house after house sports meticulously painted columns, balustrades and windows. This is a feature of many Ligurian towns but Camogli seems to take special pride in this genre of civic art. The esplanade, Via Garibaldi, is a colourful place for a stroll and really comes to life on the second Sunday in May, when local fishermen celebrate the Sagra del Pesce (Fish Festival; W www.sagradelpesce.it), frying hundreds of fish for all and sundry in 3m-wide pans along the waterfront.

Camogli, meaning 'house of wives', takes its name from the days when the women ran the town while their husbands were at sea. The town was also a strong naval base and once boasted a fleet larger than Genoa's.

Information To the right when leaving the train station, the IAT office (☎/fax 0185 77 10 66), Via XX Settembre 33, opens 9am to 12.30pm and 3.30pm to 6pm Monday to Saturday and 9am to 1pm Sunday. Buy tickets here for local buses that run along the coast (see Getting There & Away later).

There is a bank with an ATM outside the train station at Via XX Settembre 19.

Activities For diving courses and gear rental, contact **B&B Diving Centre** *(☎ 0185 7 72 51, Calata Prospero Castelletto)*. Canoes, pedal boats, rowing boats and motorboats can be rented from **Luigi Simonetti Nautica** *(☎ 0185 77 19 21, Via Garibaldi 59)*.

Lounging away a sweltering afternoon on **Punta Chiappi**, a rocky crop south of Camogli on the Portofino promontory, is a fine activity. The traditional fishing hamlet touts a handful of fishing huts, three restaurants and too many tourists to count. You can swim here. Boats yo-yo to/from Camogli (see Getting There & Away later).

Seaside strollers can take a stiff 2½-hour walk to the Abbazia di San Fruttuoso di Capodimonte at San Fruttuoso (see San Fruttuoso later); ask at the IAT office for a map.

LIGURIA

Places to Stay & Eat There are numerous hotels along the waterfront, all costly. Waterfront restaurants likewise charge high prices for far-from-startling food. Piazza Colombo is loaded with bars and cafes. Less expensive trattorias are tucked down the lanes away from the water.

Primula *(☎ 0185 77 03 51, Via Garibaldi 140)* Pasta around €9.30. Camogli's largest terrace dishes up 26 types of panini (from €3.85), some pasta dishes and exotic ice-cream sundaes.

La Moreia *(☎ 0185 77 60 56, Via Garibaldi 103)* 1st/2nd courses from €8.25/12.90. Dine here if you fancy fish at a price.

Getting There & Away Camogli (€1.75, 30 minutes from Stazione Principe) is on the Genoa–La Spezia train line, with hourly services in both directions between 6.30am and 9pm.

Tigullio buses (☎ 0185 23 11 08 in Rapallo) head for Rapallo and Santa Margherita (both €0.70, every 20 minutes), and for Portofino Vetta along a pretty drive known as La Ruta; buses use the stop just past the tourist office on Via XX Settembre.

Year-round ferries operated by Trasporti Marittimi Turistic Golfo Paradiso (☎ 0185 77 20 91, W www.golfoparadiso.it) connect Camogli with Punta Chiappi (€5.20 return, 15 minutes), San Fruttuoso (€7.80 return, 30 minutes), Portofino (€11.90 return, June-Sept), Porto Venere (€19.65 return,

June-Sept) and the Cinque Terre (€18.60 return, June-Sept).

Drivers can reach Camogli from the A12 or the Via Aurelia (S1).

Santa Margherita

postcode 16038 • pop 10,690

Once home to a coral-fishing fleet that roamed as far afield as Africa, Santa Margherita, 32km south-east of Genoa, is known today for its orange blossoms and lace. In a sheltered bay on the eastern side of the Portofino promontory on the Golfo di Tigullio, its waterfront is an eclectic jumble of one-time fishing cottages, elegant four-star hotels with Liberty facades and moored million-dollar yachts.

Orientation & Information From the train station on Via Roma, head downhill to the palm-tree-clad port, then along Corso Doria to Piazza Vittorio Veneto, from where most buses depart. Boat trips use the jetty off the adjoining square, Piazza Martiri della Libertà.

The IAT office (☎ 0185 28 74 85, ⓔ turismo@comune.santa-margherita-ligure.ge.it), Via XXV Aprile 4, opens 9am to noon and 3pm to 6pm daily.

The post office, Via Giunchetto 45 (off Piazzetta Degli Alpini), opens 8am to 6pm Monday to Friday and 8am to 1.15pm Saturday.

For medical help, Ospedale Civile di Rapallo (hospital; ☎ 0185 68 31) is at Rapallo in Piazza Molfino. For an ambulance (Croce Rossa), call ☎ 0185 66 91 60; for a night doctor (Guardia Medica), call ☎ 010 35 40 22.

Activities The IAT office has details on sailing, water-skiing, scuba diving and numerous other activities.

For a green source of information, including a list of **walking trails** from Santa Margherita, go to the headquarters of the **Parco Naturale Regionale di Portofino** *(☎ 0185 28 94 79, ⓔ enteparco.portofino@libero.it, Viale Rainusso 1)*.

Places to Stay Stay in Santa Margherita and pretend you're a millionaire.

Albergo Azalea *(☎/fax 0185 28 81 60, Via Roma 60)* Doubles €51.65. This rock-bottom option sports zero aesthetic appeal but is a pebble's throw from the train station.

Albergo Annabella *(☎ 0185 28 65 31, Via Costasecca 10)* Singles/doubles €38.75/51.65. This is a clean, well-lit place, just off Piazza Mazzini and handy for the centre,

Albergo Fasce *(☎ 0185 28 64 35, fax 0185 28 35 80, ⓦ www.hotelfasce.it, Via Luigi Bozzo 3)* Singles/doubles/triples €76.45/88.85/142.05. Tucked off Corso Matteotti, this Anglo/Italian-run place has ultra-clean modern rooms, a roof terrace for sunbathing, bicycles to borrow and a peaceful bar out back.

Places to Eat Simple but appealing food is the order of the day in these eateries.

Bar Colombo *(☎ 0185 28 70 58, Via Pescino 13)* Do what Burton, Taylor and other Hollywood greats did and while away a few hours at this historic Art Nouveau place on the waterfront.

Caffè del Porto *(☎ 0185 28 70 44, Via Bottaro 32)* 1st/2nd courses €6.20/15.50. Oodles of charm from an era gone by can be found here, making it *the* place to sniff and swill locally produced wines.

Trattoria dei Pescatori *(Via Bottaro 43)* 1st/2nd courses €11.35/18.10. This simple but soulful seafood spot serves rustic cooking with a fervently fishy flavour.

The budget-conscious can shop for fresh pasta, bread and focaccia at ***Da Renato*** *(Largo Amendola 1)*, and everything else along pedestrianised Via Palestro. Haggle for the catch of the day at the ***fresh fish market*** *(Corso Marconi; open 4pm-7pm Mon-Fri)*, in the red-arched building on the seafront.

Getting There & Around Santa Margherita is on the Genoa-La Spezia railway line (Genoa €1.75, La Spezia €3.55).

Bus No 82 to/from Portofino (€0.90, every 20 minutes) and bus Nos 71–73 to/from Camogli (€1.05, every 30 minutes) arrive/depart from Piazza Vittorio Veneto.

In the summer months, Servizio Marittimo del Tigullio (☎ 0185 28 46 70, ⓦ www.traghettiportofino.it) runs ferries to/from Portofino, San Fruttuoso, the Cinque Terre and Porto Venere (see those sections for details). Boats depart from the jetty overlooking Piazza Martiri della Libertà.

For a taxi, call ☎ 0185 28 79 98.

Portofino

postcode 16034 • pop 574

Dubbed the 'richest promontory in Italy', exclusive Portofino, 38km east of Genoa, is home to the rich, powerful and famous. Scholar and poet Petrarch, writers Guy de Maupassant and Truman Capote, and English photographer Cecil Beeton all sojourned here.

A haughty disdain on the part of many residents lends the village a healthy air of restraint, and the huddle of pastel-coloured houses around the portside piazza is a delight. In summer, the square, fronted by expensive cafes and Cartier-et-al designer boutiques, is full of the glitterati, attracted to Liguria's most chichi spot where Europe's movers and shakers come to wheel, deal, play and pose.

In summer, motorists sit in the searing heat waiting to enter the village. A digital clock, 2km north of Portofino in **Paraggi**, flashes how much longer they can expect to sweat. Unlike beachless Portofino, Paraggi boasts one of the area's few slivers of white sand.

Things to See & Do At the port near **Chiesa di San Giorgio**, a flight of stairs marked 'Salita San Giorgio' leads up to the 16th-century **castle** of the same name. Built by the Genoese (under some pressure from their Spanish allies) over an existing fort, the castle occasionally saw action, particularly when occupied by Napoleon and taken by the English in 1814. It offers a great view, but for an even better outlook continue along the same track through olive groves to the **lighthouse**; it's an hour's walk there and back.

Sailing and motorboats can be hired from **Giorgio Mussini & Co** *(☎ 0185 26 93 27, ☎ 0185 26 15 16, Ⓦ www.giorgiomussini.com, Calata Marconi 38)*.

Places to Stay & Eat Accommodation is scarce and expensive.

Eden *(☎ 0185 26 90 91, fax 0185 26 90 47, Ⓔ eden@free.it, Vico Dritto 18)* Singles/doubles €103.30/129.10. The 'cheapest' hotel is the three-star Eden.

Splendido Mare *(☎ 0185 26 78 00, fax 0185 26 78 07, Ⓔ reservations@splendido.net, Via Roma 2)* Singles/doubles from €232.40/413.15. Portofino's priciest place is Splendido Mare.

The waterfront restaurants are horribly overpriced.

Ristorante ö Magazin *(☎ 0185 26 91 78, Calata Marconi 34)* Decked out like a boat cabin, this eatery is as expensive as the rest, but seems the most authentic.

Getting There & Away Portofino is an easy bus ride from Santa Margherita (for details, see that section earlier).

Between April and October, the Servizio Marittimo del Tigullio (☎ 0185 28 46 70) runs daily ferries from Portofino to San Fruttuoso (€5.15/7.75 single/return, 30 minutes) and Santa Margherita (€3.10/5.70, 15 minutes).

Drivers must park at the village entrance and pay €3.60/12.90 per one hour/four hours (cash only). Vehicles are banned farther in.

San Fruttuoso

San Fruttuoso is a fascinating village dominated by the **Abbazia di San Fruttuoso di Capodimonte** *(☎ 0185 77 27 03; adult/child €5.15/3.10; open 10am-6pm Tues-Sun in summer, 10am-4pm Tues-Sun in winter, closed Nov)*, a Benedictine abbey with medieval origins. Built as a final resting place for bishop St Fructuosus of Tarragona, martyred in Spain in 259, it was rebuilt in the mid-13th century with the assistance of the Doria family, who used it as a family crypt. It fell into decay with the decline of the religious community, and in the 19th century it was divided into small living quarters by local fishermen.

Perhaps more fascinating is the bronze statue of Christ, *Il Cristo degli Abissi*, lowered 15m to the sea bed by locals in 1954 as a tribute to divers lost at sea and to bless the waters. Dive to see it – you can even get married while you're down there – or view it from a boat if the waters are calm. A replica, in a fish tank, is on display in the church adjoining the abbey. A religious ceremony is held over the statue each August.

San Fruttuoso is accessible either on foot from Camogli or Portofino (an exhilarating cliffside walk that takes up to 2½ hours each way from either town), or by ferry (summer only from Santa Margherita, Portofino and Rapallo, year-round from Camogli).

Rapallo

postcode 16035 • pop 28,150

The major resort of Rapallo is often overlooked for the more illustrious Santa Margherita and Portofino. A bigger place, it has an air of bustle independent of tourists that the towns farther down the promontory lack – all the more so on Thursday, which is market day on Piazza Cile. Bright blue changing cabins line its sandy beach.

With its Roman origins, Rapallo boasts a bridge supposedly used by Hannibal during the Carthaginian invasion of Italy in 218 BC. More recently, Rapallo enjoyed a brief period of international popularity in the treaty-signing business. In 1920, the Italo-Yugoslav Treaty that defined the borders of the two countries was signed here. In 1922, the Russians and Germans sealed a peace deal that lasted for 19 years, when the German army invaded Soviet territory.

Information The IAT office (☎ 0185 23 03 46, fax 0185 6 30 51), Lungo Vittorio Veneto 7, opens 9.30am to 12.30pm and 2.30pm to 5.30pm Monday to Saturday. Among other things, it stocks a list of boat-hire places and walking maps. Otherwise, contact the Club Alpino Italiano (☎ 0185 5 78 62), Via Venezia 4.

Things to See & Do Since 1933, a cable car has trundled up to **Montallegro** *(☎ 0185 23 90 00; free; open 7.30am-noon & 2.30pm-6pm in summer, 7.30am-noon & 2.30pm-5.30pm in winter)*, a sanctuary built on the spot where, on 2 July 1557, the Virgin Mary was reportedly sighted. Numerous votives fill the sanctuary, which celebrates its biggest feast days during the first three days of July. To get to the cable car *(☎ 0185 27 34 44; single/return €3.85/5.70; open 9am-12.30pm Mon-Fri, 8.30am-12.30pm Sat & Sun, 2pm-6pm daily)* from the train station on Piazza dei Molfino, follow the 'funivia' signs along Corso Assereto – a five-minute walk. Bus No 92 also links the train station with Montallegro, taking a circuitous 11km road that also reaches the site. Walkers can follow an old mule track to the hilltop site (1½ hours).

Just off Lungo Vittoria Veneto, by the waterfront, Rapallo's small 16th-century **castle** *(free; open 10am-noon & 4pm-6pm daily)* hosts occasional exhibitions.

Places to Stay For the camp sites in the hills near Rapallo, take the Savagna bus from the train station.

Albergo Ristorante il Pellegrino *(☎ 0185 23 90 03, Santuario di Montallegro)* B&B €31. Open May-Aug, Easter & Christmas. Stunning views of Rapallo and the coastline are the speciality of this old, highly atmospheric hotel, perched behind Montallegro and popular with walkers. A footpath leads from the hotel to the sanctuary.

Albergo La Vela *(☎/fax 0185 5 05 51, Via Milite Ignoto 21/7)* Doubles without bath €41.30, doubles with bath €51.65. Friendly, simple and soulful are the attributes of La Vela, among Rapallo's most central and cheapest.

Bandoni *(☎ 0185 5 04 23, fax 0185 5 72 06, Via Marsala 24/3–4)* Singles/doubles from €23.25/40.30. The best of the budget hotels in Rapallo, Bandoni is right on the waterfront.

The waterfront is lined with places to eat, drink and snack any time of the day.

Getting There & Away Regular bus services connect Rapallo with Santa Margherita (€0.70, every 20 minutes) and Camogli. The trip is more pleasant by bus than by train.

Chiavari to Levanto

The stretch of coast between the Portofino promontory and the Cinque Terre can come as a bit of a letdown, wedged as it is between two such beauty spots. It does have some of the Riviera di Levante's best beaches, but the resorts of Sestri Levante, Deiva Marina and Levanto become predictably crowded in summer.

The Cinque Terre

If you miss the five villages (Monterosso, Vernazza, Corniglia, Manarola and Riomaggiore) that make up the Cinque Terre (literally 'five lands'), you will have bypassed some of Italy's most extraordinary countryside. But blink as the train zips between tunnels and miss them you will.

The mountains, covered by terraced vineyards, drop precipitously into the Mediterranean, so local wine growers use ingenious monorail mechanisms to ferry themselves up and the grapes down. Olive groves, tinted orange with nets in November when the black fruits fall, embrace the lower slopes, leaving little room for the Cinque Terre villages cluttering coves, tucked into ravines or perched atop sharp ridges. Fishing and viniculture (along with tourism these days) remain the traditional industries.

Prices in the Cinque Terre are neither low nor extortionate. Hotels are scarce, but numerous villagers have rooms to rent: look for signs reading *camere* (rooms) or *affittacamere* (rooms for rent). Equally – if not more – seductive are the Cinque Terre's renowned white and dessert wines Morasca, Chiaretto del Faro, its heavenly, sweet Sciacchetrà and *limoncino*, a lemon liqueur guaranteed to make your heart race.

Getting There & Around The Cinque Terre's greatest asset is its distinct lack of motorised traffic. Cars are not permitted beyond village entrances, meaning a hike of up to 1km.

The most convenient way to get there and around is the local Genoa-La Spezia train service, which trundles along the coast every 15 to 30 minutes between 6.30am and 10pm. A one-day Biglictto Giornaliero Cinque Terre (€2.85) allows unlimited rail travel between Monterosso and La Spezia.

In summer, Cooperativa Battellieri del Golfo Paradiso and Alimar run ferry and catamaran services to the Cinque Terre from Genoa; see Getting There & Away in the Genoa section earlier for details. Boats (adult/child €23.25/16.80 return) depart three to six times daily July to September and weekends only in June.

Between April and 1 November, La Spezia-based Navigazione Golfo dei Poeti (☎ 0187 96 76 76, ☎ 0187 73 29 87, W www.navigazionegolfodeipoeti.it), Viale Mazzini 21, operates daily shuttle boats between all the villages (except Corniglia). A one-day 'village-hopping' ticket costs €10.35/6.20 per adult/child; a single/return fare to one village is €2.60/4.15. It also operates boat excursions to the Cinque Terre from Porto Venere and La Spezia (see those sections later for details).

You can hire bicycles to pedal around in Riomaggiore and Manarola (see those sections for details).

Monterosso

postcode 19016 • pop 1640

Huge statues embedded into the rocks overlook one of the few Cinque Terre beaches, a grey, pebbly affair. In the historic centre, Enoteca Internazionale (☎ 0187 81 72 87), Via Roma 62, is one of the best places in the Cinque Terre to munch on anchovy-topped bruschette and sip sweet Sciacchetrà. Other local specialities such as limoncino (made from Monterosso lemons) can be tasted and bought here.

Vernazza

postcode 19018 • pop 1100

Possibly the most fetching of the villages, Vernazza makes the most of the sea, with a promenade and piazza on the water. Waterfront steps lead to **Castello Doria** *(adult/child €1.05; open 10am-5.30pm daily)*, an 11th-century castle with sweeping views from its tower. Heading inland, the road is choked with vineyards and lemon groves.

Vernazza's main cobbled lane, Via Roma, links seaside Piazza Guglielmo Marconi with the train station. There's a tasty *focacceria* at No 3, a grocers at Nos 23–25, a laundrette at No 49 and public internet access (€0.15/minute) inside ***Blue Marlin***

LIGURIA

(☎ *0187 82 11 49,* ⓔ *bmarlin@tin.it, Via Roma 43)*, Vernazza's busiest cafe and bar. The coastal path (see the boxed text 'Lovers' Lane') can be picked up from steps next to (or opposite for westbound walkers) the pharmacy at Via Roma 4.

Vernazza has a couple of hotels and numerous rooms to let, including ***Albergo Barbara*** *(☎ 0187 81 23 98, Piazza Guglielmo Marconi 30)*, ***Francamaria*** *(☎ 0187 81 20 02, Piazza Guglielmo Marconi 30)*, and ***Da Martina*** *(☎ 0187 81 23 65, Piazza Guglielmo Marconi 36)*. If you dine at ***Trattoria da Sandro*** *(☎ 0187 81 22 23, Via Roma 69)*, don't miss the huge mixed fried fish platters (€12.40) or *insalata di polpo* (octopus salad).

Corniglia Balanced precariously along a ridge high above the sea, charming Corniglia is a picture postcard of four-storey houses, narrow lanes and stairways woven into a hill by **La Torre**, a medieval lookout. Good views

Lovers' Lane

For those with time or romance on their hands, there's the Via dell'Amore (Lovers' Lane), part of a scenic coastal path that links Monterosso with Riomaggiore and the villages in between. The going can get strenuous at times, but reasonably fit walkers can cover the 12km (one way) fairly comfortably in five or so hours. The 4km stretch between Monterosso and Vernazza is the least scenic and most difficult. Farther east, dramatic coastal views and pretty little coves with crystal-clear water (bring your swimming gear) compensate for any sweat and tears.

Fierce storms, torrential rain and high seas in October 2000 wreaked havoc along this stretch of coastline, causing cultivated terraces to collapse and part of the Cinque Terre's lovely Lovers' Lane – the section between Manarola and Riomaggiore – to temporarily close. See Ⓦ www.cinqueterre.it for details in English.

In case of emergency, call Emergenza Soccorso (emergency mountain rescue; ☎ 0336 68 93 16) in Montagna.

of the vines and dry stone walls, distinctive to these terraced parts, can be enjoyed from the central square. From here, Via Fieschi cuts through the village heart to **Belvedere Santa Maria**, another lookout with a coastal panorama. In summer, minibuses shuttle tourists between the station and village.

La Posada *(☎ 0187 82 11 74, Via della Stazione 11)* Doubles about €62. Stay here if you can't face the uphill hike (363 steps) to the village. Its flower-filled garden restaurant dishes up ocean views.

Via Fieschi is sprinkled with homestay options and food shops.

A Cantina de Mananan *(☎ 0187 82 11 66, Via Fieschi 117)* Pasta from €6.20. This is a charming osteria, next to a fine enoteca where you can taste the Cinque Terre wines.

Manarola

postcode 19010

More grapes are grown around Manarola than any other Cinque Terre village. A 13th-century church, a bell tower used as a defensive lookout in the 14th century, and an oratory that once served as a leper hospital line the central square, at the northern end of steep Via Discovolo. Those game for a climb can follow a path off nearby Via Rollandi that leads through vineyards to the top of the mountain.

Ostello 5 Terre *(☎ 0187 92 02 15, fax 0187 92 02 18,* Ⓦ *www.cinqueterre.net/ostello, Via Riccobaldi 21)* B&B €18.10. Open 7am-1pm & 5pm-1am daily May-Sept, 7am-1pm & 4pm-midnight daily Oct-Apr. The Cinque Terre's only hostel rents out mountain bikes, kayaks and snorkelling gear.

Riomaggiore

postcode 19017 • pop 1880

The Via dell'Amore straggles along the cliffside from Manarola to Riomaggiore – a mess of houses slithering down a ravine that forms the main street, with tiny fishing boats lining the shore and stacked in the small square. The older part of town is a few minutes' walk south of the train station, through a long tunnel.

Cinque Terre marine life can be viewed through a mask alongside divers from the

Cooperative Sub 5 Terre *(☎ 0187 92 05 96, Via San Giacomo)*. It also rents out snorkels and canoes/kayaks.

Cyclists can hire wheels from **Mar Mar** *(☎ 0187 92 09 32, Via Colombo 234; €5.15/25.80 per hour/day)*. Walkers with a keen eye for nature should make a beeline for **Torre Guardiola**, a nature observation centre on **Fossola Beach**, immediately south-east of Riomaggiore marina, from where a botanical trail can be followed along the coast. The less energetic can **taste local wine** at D'Uu Scintu, a wine shop at Via Colombo 84.

More than half a dozen affittacamere are available, some along Via Colombo. ***La Dolcevita*** *(☎ 0187 76 00 44, No 122)*, ***Edi*** *(☎ 0187 92 03 25, ⓔ edi-vesigna@iol.it, No 111)* and ***Fazioli*** *(☎/fax 0187 92 09 04, ⓔ robertofazioli@libero.it, No 94)* are agencies that rent out rooms and apartments (€15.50–46.50 per person).

Down at the marina, there are several eating choices.

La Lanterna *(Via San Giacomo 46; open 11am-11pm daily year-round)* The Lighthouse fries up the catch of the day for about €4.15 per 100g.

La Spezia

postcode 19100 • pop 93,300

La Spezia, 100km south-east of Genoa, sits at the head of the gulf of the same name – also known as the Gulf of Poets, in deference to Byron, Dante, DH Lawrence, Shelley, George Sand and others drawn here by its beauty.

The construction from 1860 to 1865 of Italy's largest naval base propelled La Spezia from minor port to provincial capital, its street grid and venerable public buildings largely a product of that time. It's still a navy town, with the ubiquitous blue sailor's uniform a constant reminder.

Orientation The city of La Spezia is sandwiched between the naval base to the west and the commercial port to the east. The main street and scene of the ritual *passeggiata* (evening stroll) is narrow Via del Prione, which runs from the train station to palm-lined Viale Italia on the waterfront.

Information The IAT office (☎ 0187 25 43 11, fax 0187 77 09 08, ⓦ www.aptcinqueterre.sp.it), Viale G Mazzini 47, opens 9am to 1pm and 3pm to 6pm Monday to Saturday and 9am to 1pm Sunday.

The post office, on Piazza di Giuseppe Verdi, opens 8am to 6pm Monday to Friday and 8am to noon Saturday. An unstaffed Telecom office at Via da Passano 40 opens 7am to 10pm daily.

For medical help out of hours, call ☎ 0187 50 77 27. The *questura* (police station; ☎ 0187 53 01) is well away from the centre at Viale Italia 497.

Things to See La Spezia's star attraction is the **Museo Amedeo Lia** *(☎ 0187 73 11 00, ⓦ www.castagna.it/mal, Via Prione 234; adult/child €6.20/3.10; open 10am-6pm Tues-Sun)*, a fine-arts museum in a restored 17th-century convent. The private collection covers the 13th to 18th centuries and contains some 2000 works by masters such as Tintoretto, Tiepolo, Titian, Veronese, Bellini and Sansovino.

Adjoining the Museo Amedeo Lia is the Palazzina delle Arti, dating to the 19th century but designed to match its medieval neighbour. Inside is the **Museo del Sigillo** *(Seal Museum; ☎ 0187 77 85 44, Via Prione 236; adult/child €5.15/3.60; open 10am-noon & 4pm-7pm daily)* – seals, that is, for letters rather than of the breathing variety.

There's a real mixture of booty on display inside the **Castello di San Giorgio** *(☎ 0187 75 11 42, ⓔ sangiorgio@castagna.it, Via XXVII Marzo; adult/child €5.15/3.60; open 9.30am-12.30pm & 2pm-5pm Tues-Sun in winter, 9.30am-12.30pm & 5pm-8pm Tues-Sun in summer)*. A hotchpotch of Bronze Age and Iron Age relics and ancient Ligurian

Money Saver

Museum-goers who love trios – namely the Museo Amedeo Lia, Castello di San Giorgio and Museo del Sigillo – should invest €7.75 in a combination ticket covering admission to all three. It's valid for 48 hours.

LIGURIA

statue-stelae are just some of the archaeological treasures.

Across the canal from Piazza Domenico Chiodo is the **Museo Tecnico Navale** *(Naval Museum; ☎ 0187 78 30 16, Viale Amendola 1; admission €1.55; open 2pm-6pm Mon & Fri, 8.30am-1.15pm Sun, 9am-noon & 2pm-6pm Tues-Thurs & Sat).* Founded in 1870 following the transfer of the Genoese maritime museum to La Spezia, it hosts a phalanx of *polene* (colourful busts or statuettes that graced the prows of vessels) and lots of model ships. The adjoining naval base opens to the public each year on 19 March, the festival of the town's patron saint, Joseph.

A state-of-the-art **Museo di Arte Moderna e Contemporanea** (Modern & Contemporary Art Museum) will open in La Spezia's former courthouse on Piazza Cesare Battisti in October 2001. The IAT office has details.

Places to Stay The town's proximity to the Cinque Terre, Porto Venere and Lerici makes it a perfect base, especially as the limited accommodation in the surrounding area often fills up. There is no camp site in La Spezia, but there are plenty in surrounding towns

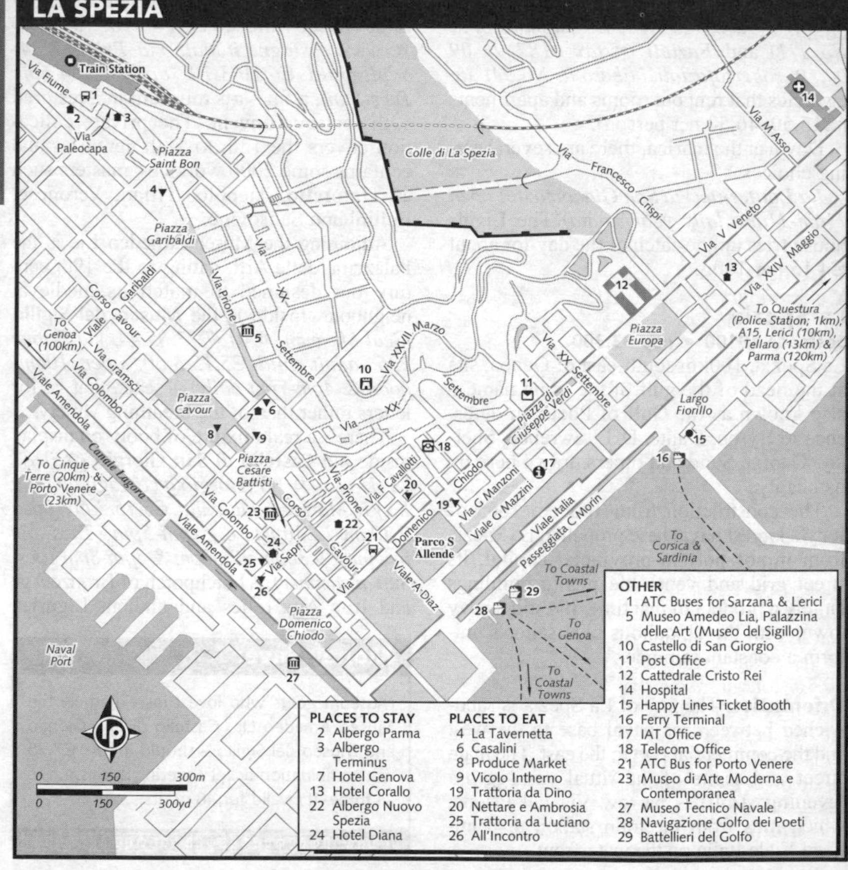

Ask at the IAT office about *agriturismo* (accommodation on a working farm) options.

Albergo Nuovo Spezia *(☎ 0187 73 51 64, fax 0187 73 99 88, ⓔ albergospezia@hotmail.com, Via F Cavallotti 31)* Singles/doubles without bath €21.70/31, singles/doubles with bath €25.80/36.15. This is the place for the budget-conscious.

Albergo Terminus *(☎ 0187 70 34 36, fax 0187 70 00 79, Via Paleocapa 21)* Singles/doubles without bath €20.65/28.40, singles/doubles with bath €28.40/33.55. La Spezia's train-station option was temporarily closed for renovation at the time of writing.

Albergo Parma *(☎ 0187 74 30 10, fax 0187 74 32 40, Via Fiume 143)* Singles/doubles from €41.30/51.65. Up one notch, rooms here come with shower, TV and phone.

Hotel Diana *(☎ 0187 73 40 97, Via Colombo 30)* Doubles without bath €41.30, singles/doubles with bath €41.30/51.65. Diana can be found lurking near the naval base. Some would sum up her choice of furnishings as 'tasteless'.

Hotel Genova *(☎ 0187 73 29 72, fax 0187 73 17 66, ⓔ hgenova@co.it, Via F Rosselli 84)* Singles/doubles €6.20/98.15. A charming renovated exterior dresses a modern interior at this three-star pad, in La Spezia's historic centre.

Hotel Corallo *(☎/fax 0187 73 13 66, Via Francesco Crispi 32)* Singles/doubles from €62/82.65. Handily placed near the port and La Spezia's gobsmackingly large contemporary cathedral, Corallo is a solid mid-range choice.

Places to Eat There are plenty of restaurants, cafes and bars along Via del Prione.

La Tavernetta *(☎ 0187 70 41 47, Via Fiume 57)* Pizzas €4.65-6.20. A tavern is exactly what this cavernous, wooden-clad bar is. 'Pub grub' includes pizza and a €9.30 'tourist menu'.

Trattoria da Luciano *(Via Colombo 27)* 1st/2nd courses €3.60/4.65. 'Cheap' best sums up this ageing place, where you can fill up on copious amounts of food for as little as €10.35.

Trattoria da Dino *(Via Da Passano 17)* 1st/2nd courses from €5.15/6.70. Sample succulent seafood at a reasonable price at Dino's Tuscan-inspired trattoria.

Vicolo Intherno *(☎ 0187 2 39 98, Via della Canonica 16)* Full meals about €15.50. Sit around hefty wooden tables – beneath an even heftier wooden-beamed ceiling – and wash down *torte di verdure* (Ligurian vegetable pie) or stockfish with local vintages.

Nettare e Ambrosia *(☎ 0187 73 72 52, Via Fazio 85)* Full meals €12.90. It might well appear a tad shabby and simple from the outside, but it's *the* place to sample *grand vini* (literally 'great wines') in an authentic La Spezian atmosphere. Its food is equally inspiring.

All'Incontro *(☎ 0187 2 46 89, ⓔ ristorante-incontro@sp.itline.it, Via Sapri 10)* 1st/2nd courses €6.20/9.30. Tuck into a plate of *spaghetti alla chitarra ai 'batti batti' di Monterosso* (chunky spaghetti in a sauce topped with flavoursome local sea critters), followed by a juicy slab of kangaroo or bison. Exotic animals aside, fish is said to be the speciality.

A daily ***produce market*** fills Piazza Cavour. For bread or pastries, try ***Casalini*** *(Via Prione 191)*.

Getting There & Away La Spezia is on the Genoa-Rome railway line, which follows the coast, and is also connected to Milan, Turin and Pisa. The Cinque Terre and other coastal towns are easily accessible by train but other towns close to La Spezia can only be reached by ATC buses (☎ 0187 52 25 22). These include Porto Venere (from Via Domenico Chiodo) and Lerici (from the train station). Buy tickets from the town's tobacconists.

The A12 runs past La Spezia to Genoa and Livorno, and the A15 to Parma also connects with the main north-south route, the A1. Hitchhikers can catch the Lerici bus and get off at Via Valdilocchi in the port area for access to the A12 and A15. The S1 passes through the city and connects with the S62 for Parma and the north.

Ferries depart from La Spezia for Genoa and other coastal towns throughout the summer and occasionally on pleasant weekends during the rest of the year. Navigazione

Golfo dei Poeti (☎ 0187 96 76 76, W www.navigazionegolfodeipoeti.it), which has its office in Lerici, and Battellieri del Golfo (☎ 0187 2 10 10), at Banchina Revel, both run services.

Between April and October, Happy Lines (☎ 0187 56 45 30, W www.happylines.it), Largo Fiorillo, runs daily ferries to Bastia in Corsica, departing at 8.15am. Its ticket kiosk (☎ 0187 56 44 27) at the port opens 6.30am to 9am and 5pm to 9.30pm. Tirrenia operates summer services to Palau and Porto Vecchio (Sardinia) and Tris runs boats to/from Golfo Aranci. Alternatively, contact a travel agency. Giuli Viaggi International (☎ 0187 2 32 89), Via G Manzoni 22, and Apuotour (☎ 0187 3 97 33), Via G Manzoni 9, are two of many in town.

Porto Venere

postcode 19025 • pop 4350

It is worth a trip to Porto Venere – a boat excursion from Genoa or a wiggly drive 12km south from La Spezia – simply for the razor-clam soup it has contributed to Ligurian fare. The Romans built Portus Veneris on the western shore of the Golfo della Spezia as a base on the route from Gaul to Spain. From the brightly coloured houses along the waterfront, narrow steps and cobbled paths lead up the hillside to 12th-century **Chiesa di San Lorenzo**. In the church's shadow lies **Castello Doria**, built in the 16th century as part of the Genoese Republic's defence system and offering magnificent views from its terraced gardens. **A Pasaà** at Piazza Bastreri 2 is the place to shop for wine.

At the end of the quay, a Cinque Terre panorama unfolds from the rocky terraces of **Grotta Arpaia**, a former haunt of Byron, who once swam across the gulf from Porto Venere to Lerici. Traces of a pagan temple believed to date from before 6 BC have been uncovered inside **Chiesa di San Pietro** (1277), built in the typical Genoese Gothic fashion with black-and-white bands of marble.

Just off the promontory lie the tiny islands of **Palmaria**, **Tino** and **Tinetto**, which can be visited by boat. Navigazione Golfo dei Poeti runs three-island boat trips (40 minutes) in summer.

Places to Stay & Eat The IAT office (☎ 0187 79 06 91, W www.portovenere.it), Piazza Bastreri 5, has a list of Porto Venere hotels – all horribly expensive. A half-dozen or so restaurants line Calata Doria, by the sea.

La Piazzetta *(Via Cappellini 56)* This delicious teashop, on Porto Venere's main Genoese-style caruggi, serves warming pots of tea and plates of *cantuccini* (hard almond biscuits) to dunk in your cuppa.

La Pizzaccia *(☎ 0187 79 27 22, Via Cappellini 94)* Feast on pizza, focaccia and farinata at this highly respected takeaway joint.

Antica Osteria del Caruggio *(Via Cappellini 94)* Sample razor-clam soup and other traditional dishes at this old-world place decorated with antique furnishings.

Lerici

postcode 19032 • pop 11,280

At the south-eastern end of the Riviera di Levante, 10km and a short bus ride from La Spezia, Lerici is an exclusive summer refuge for wealthy Italians. It is a town of villas with manicured gardens and equally well-kept swimming pools built into the cliffs along the beach. For outstanding views, make your way up to 12th-century Castello di Lerici, which is home to a ferociously fascinating **Museo Geopaleontologico** *(☎ 0187 96 90 42, W www.museocastello.lerici.sp.it, Piazza San Giorgio 1; adult/child €4.15/2.60; open 9am-1pm & 2.30pm-5.30pm Tues-Fri, 9am-6pm Sat & Sun Nov-Mar, 9am-1pm & 3pm-7pm Tues-Fri, 9am-7pm Sat & Sun Sept, Oct, Apr & June, 10am-1pm & 5pm-midnight Tues-Sun July & Aug)*. Earthquakes, robots and dinosaurs are the stars of this museum's futuristic exhibits.

If you plan to stay in the area, jump off the bus at – or walk from Lerici (½ hour) to – **San Terenzo**, a pleasant village dominated by a Genoese castle. It was a former haunt of the Shelleys, and it was off the coast here that Percy Bysshe's boat sank in 1822 on a return trip from Livorno (Leghorn), costing him his life.

A pleasant 4km walk or bus ride from Lerici along the Fiascherino road takes you past some magnificent little bays towards

Tellaro. The quiet fishing hamlet with pink and orange houses cluttered about narrow lanes and tiny squares was visited by DH Lawrence in the year before WWI broke out. Weave your way to the Chiesa di San Giorgio, sit on the rocks and watch the world go by.

Val di Magra

South-east of La Spezia, the Val di Magra forms the easternmost tongue of Ligurian territory before you reach Tuscany. **Sarzana** (pop 20,000), a short bus or train ride from La Spezia, was once an important outpost of the Genoese republic. In its cathedral you can see the world's oldest crucifix, painted on wood. The phial in the chapel is said to have contained the blood of Christ. Nearby, the fortress of Sarzanello (built by Castruccio Castracani) offers magnificent views. Take a pretty detour to the hillside hamlet of **Castelnuovo Magra**, which has a medieval castle.

Die-hard fans of all things Roman may be interested in **Luni** *(☎ 0187 6 68 11; site & museum adult/child €2.05/free; open 9am-7pm Tues-Sun)*, about 6km south-east of Sarzana (1km off the S1 towards the coast; it's not well signposted). Established as a Roman colony in 177 BC on the site of an Etruscan village, it thrived until the 13th century. Excavations have revealed the amphitheatre, forum, temple and other remnants of a classic Roman town, but the ruins are not in top condition.

RIVIERA DI PONENTE

Stretching south-west from Genoa to France, this part of the Ligurian coast is more heavily developed than the eastern side. However, some of the resorts are not bad; several of Genoa's historical maritime rivals retain the architectural trappings of a more glorious past, and the mountains, hiding a warren of hilltop villages, promise cool air and pretty walking and driving circuits.

Savona

postcode 17100 • pop 63,100

When you approach Savona from the south-west or north-east, it is the sprawl of the port's facilities that strikes you first – a sprawl that scarcely matches the chaos of its longtime rival, Genoa. The two cities were steady opponents from the time of the Punic Wars and the Genoese destroyed the town in 1528, proving their dominance. Now a provincial capital and bishopric, Savona suffered heavy bombing raids during WWII.

The small medieval centre, dominated by the Baroque **Cattedrale di Nostra Signora Assunta**, still survives, as does Savona's lumbering **Fortezza del Priamàr**, built on Piazza Priamàr from 1528 to protect the town against Genoese attacks. Within the fortress's impressive walls is a hostel (see Places to Stay later), an art gallery displaying works from the 16th to the 20th centuries, a couple of sculpture museums and an archaeological museum. Opening hours vary; the IAT office has details.

Orientation The monster of a train station is in a relatively new part of town, south-east of the River Letimbro. Via Collodi, to the right of the train station as you walk out, and Via Don Minzoni, to the left, both lead across the river towards the leafy Piazza del Popolo. From here, Via Paleocapa, Savona's elegant main boulevard, runs to the marina.

The pedestrian old town lies immediately west. From the waterfront foot of Via Paleocapa, turn right along Via Spinola onto Via Pia, the main old-town street adorned with cafes, trattorias and food shops. To get to the beach, turn right along Corso Italia, midway along Via Paleocapa.

Information The IAT office (☎ 019 840 23 21, fax 019 840 36 72, ⓔ iatsavona@infocomm.it), Via Guidobono 23, is near the beach; head three blocks west from Corso Italia. The office opens 9am to 12.30pm and 3pm to 6pm Monday to Saturday.

For ferry tickets, try Lugares travel agency (☎ 019 85 65 36, fax 019 85 65 38, ⓔ lugares@tiscalinet.it), Via Pia 96–98r.

Places to Stay Savona touts the coast's most dramatically located hostel.

Fortezza del Priamar *(☎/fax 019 81 26 53, Corso Mazzini)* B&B €11.35. Open year round. Splendidly placed inside Savona's

LIGURIA

mighty fortress overlooking the beach, this hostel is well worth a night's kip. Take bus No 2 from the train station.

Beyond that, Savona has a mean choice of two- to five-star pads.

Albergo Savona *(☎ 019 82 18 20, fax 019 82 18 21, Piazza del Popolo 53r)* Singles/doubles from €25.80/41.30. This cheapie – a rare breed – sits above a bar.

Albergo Riviera Suisse *(☎ 019 85 08 53, fax 019 85 34 35, Via Paleocapa 24)* Singles/doubles €54.25/77.45. Its inflated three-star rates are known to drop considerably when things get slow.

Places to Eat A smattering of restaurants, trattorias and cafes dot Via Paleocapa.

Vino e Farinata *(Via Pia 15r)* There is no better place along the entire Riviera di Ponente to sample farinata. Stacks of wood waiting to fire the open oven fill the entrance. Wash the food down with 25cl of wine (€1.05).

Malvasia *(☎ 019 82 10 95, Via Pia 118)* Sniff and swill local wines at this authentic, red-brick wine bar, which dishes up cheese platters and salads too.

Buy fresh fish from the ***fish market***, near the marina at Via Pietro Giuria 64.

Getting There & Away Trains run along the coast to Genoa and to San Remo, but SAR (☎ 0182 2 15 44) and ACTS (☎ 019 2 20 11) buses – departing from Piazza del Popolo and the train station – are the best option for reaching points inland.

Corsica Ferries (☎ 019 21 55 11) runs boats from Savona's Porto Vado to Bastia/Calvi in Corsica. A single deck fare is €44.15/36.40. In summer, there are up to three daily departures both ways.

ACTS bus No 6 links Piazza Mameli (a block east of Piazza del Popolo along Via Paleocapa) to the port.

Savonesi Apennines

About a 40-minute bus ride north of Savona, **Sassello** (pop 1800, elevation 386m) is a tranquil mountain resort close to the regional boundary with Piedmont. Among its modest monuments is the Bastia Soprano, a Doria family castle. A pleasant circuit from Savona to Genoa, if you have your own transport, takes you along winding mountain roads to Sassello and past several towns, including **Rossiglione**, near the border with Piedmont. **Acqui Terme** (pop 20,215, elevation 164m), 32km farther north in Piedmont, is an ancient spa built around the ruins of a Roman water system. Enjoy a bath in the natural hot springs.

Noli

postcode 17026 • pop 2800

The small seaside town of Noli has little of the Riviera di Ponente's made-to-measure resort atmosphere. It was an independent republic for 600 years, a history hinted at by the ruined medieval walls, which run up a hill behind the old town and peak in a fort designed to watch for invaders from North Africa. The town sells itself as the original home of a Ligurian culinary singularity, *trofie* (tiny pasta shreds made from potato flour and eaten with pesto sauce). The claim is disputed by Recco, a town east of Genoa. Fishing remains one of Noli's mainstays and the waterfront is often converted into an impromptu seafood market.

The IAT office (☎ 019 740 90 03, fax 019 749 93 00, ⓔ iatnoli@italianriviera.com), on the waterfront at Corso Italia 8, stocks information on accommodation, although don't expect any bargains in high season. One of the cheapest is ***Albergo Rino*** *(☎ 019 74 80 59, Via Cavalieri di Malta 3)*, which has singles/doubles from €43.90/51.65.

Buses run from Finale Ligure and Savona. For even better beaches, stop off at **Varigotti**, just past Noli on the way south-west to Finale Ligure. The IAT office here (☎ 019 69 80 13, fax 019 69 84 88, ⓔ iatvarigotti@italianriviera.com) is on Via Aurelia.

Finale Ligure

postcode 17024 • pop 12,300

With a good beach and affordable accommodation, Finale Ligure is a handy base for exploring the Riviera di Ponente. If climbing rocks is your idea of fun, pack your ropes and head for the hinterland. Many areas offer good free climbing, and well-organised clubs make maps of the best climbs; the tourist office has details.

Finale Ligure is divided into three areas. Finalborgo, the original centre, is away from the coast on the River Pora. A clutter of twisting alleys behind medieval walls, it's the most interesting part of the Finale triad. Equally atmospheric is the waterfront Finale Marina area, where most accommodation and restaurants are found. Finale Pia, towards Genoa, runs along the River Sciusa and is rather suburban. The train station is at Piazza Vittorio Veneto, at Finale Marina's western end. Walk straight down Via Saccone to reach the sea and tourist office.

Information The IAT office (☎ 019 68 10 19, fax 019 68 18 04, ⓔ iatfinale@italianriviera.com), opposite the beach at Via San Pietro 14, opens 9am to 12.30pm and 3pm to 6.30pm Monday to Saturday and 9am to noon Sunday.

Places to Stay To get to the camp sites, take an ACTS bus from the centre.

La Foresta *(☎ 019 69 81 03, fax 019 69 86 98, Via Torre)* Sites per person/tent/car from €3.10/5.15/5.15. La Foresta, 7km north-east of town, is one of two camp sites open year-round.

Albergo San Marco *(☎/fax 019 69 25 33, Via Concezione 22)* Singles/doubles from €28.40/46.50. This is Finale's only one-star hotel to overlook the sea – so get in quick. Numerous three-star places line the same sandy stretch.

Places to Eat The wide promenade lining Via Concezione and Via San Pietro, and Via Roma – the pedestrian street a block inland – are crammed with places to eat. Come aperitif time, head for the cluster of cocktail and ice-cream bars overlooking the beach between Nos 19 and 29 on Via San Pietro.

Patrick *(☎ 019 68 00 07, Via Roma 45)* Pizzas €2.60-7.75. Munch on delicious pizza baked in a wood-stoked fire or twist your tongue around a plate of spaghetti in a bright, modern setting.

La Tavernetta *(☎ 019 69 20 10, ⓦ www.tavernettafinale.com, Via Cristoforo Colombo 37)* This extraordinarily simple yet charming trattoria is the place to fill that craving for a spot of local cuisine.

Getting There & Around SAR (☎ 0182 215 44) buses yo-yo about every 30 minutes along the coast to/from Savona (€2, 50 minutes), stopping en route in Finalborgo (€1.05, five minutes) and Noli (€1.25, 20 minutes). Buses use the stop in front of the train station.

Albenga

postcode 17031 • pop 22,650

Albenga's medieval centre sets it apart from many of the resorts farther west. Settled as far back as the 5th century BC, Albenga grew from its Roman roots to become an independent maritime republic in the Middle Ages, despite being destroyed several times by barbarian invaders. In the 13th century, it threw in its lot with Genoa.

From the train station on Piazza Matteotti, turn left out of the station building, turn left again beneath the railway bridge, and bear east along tree-lined Viale Italia to the sea. To get to the historic centre from Piazza Matteotti, walk straight ahead (west) along Viale Martiri della Libertà. The APT tourist office (☎ 0182 55 84 44, fax 0182 55 87 40, ⓔ iatalbenga@italianriviera.com), Viale Martiri della Libertà 1, stocks information on the entire Riviera delle Palme and opens 9am to 12.30pm and 3pm to 6.30pm Tuesday to Saturday.

Things to See Albenga's **Museo Diocesano di Arte Sacra** *(Museum of Sacred Art; ☎ 0182 5 02 88, Via Episcopio 5; adult/child €2.60/1.55; open 10am-noon & 3pm-6pm Tues-Sun)*, featuring a painting by Caravaggio, is near the 5th-century **baptistry** and Romanesque **cathedral**. The baptistry is somewhat unusual, if only because the 10-sided exterior breaks with the octagonal shape that characterises its counterparts throughout northern Italy.

The **Museo Navale Romano** *(Roman Naval Museum; ☎ 0182 5 12 15, Piazza San Michele 12; adult/child €2.60/1.55; open 10am-12.30pm & 2.30pm-6pm Tues-Sun)* has a collection of 1st-century amphoras (wine urns), recovered in 1950 from the wreck of a Roman cargo vessel found 4km offshore. It is one of the world's oldest discovered shipwrecks.

Places to Stay & Eat There are around 20 camp sites in the area.

Delfino *(☎ 0182 5 19 98, fax 0182 55 50 85, Via Aurelia 22)* Sites per person/tent & car from €2.60/7.75. This camp site is south of the train station, by the sea on the S1.

Albergo Torino *(☎ 0182 5 08 44, Viale Italia 25)* Singles/doubles without bath €20.65/36.15, singles/doubles with bath €25.80/46.50. Rates might rise by €5.15 per night in high season but Hotel Turin still offers an astonishing price-quality ratio. Its flower-filled terrace, a stone's throw from the sea, is welcoming indeed.

Albergo Italia *(☎ 0182 5 04 05, Viale Martiri della Libertà 8)* Singles/doubles €25.80/43.90. Prices include breakfast at this cheap and cheerful, seven-room hotel.

Hotel Sole Mare *(☎ 0182 5 18 17, fax 0182 554 52 12, Lungomare Cristoforo Colombo 15)* Doubles €62-77.45. A light, bright and airy reception decked out like the deck of a ship leads to balconied rooms with sea views.

Don't leave Albenga without sampling a slice of *panciucco al limoncello*, the sweetest, moistest, most succulent lemon cake you're ever likely to taste. ***Pasticceria Fili*** *(Via Venezia 8)*, off Viale Italia, is the place to buy it. Tasty tip: turn your cake upside-down and leave for 30 minutes before devouring. In the old town, Via Palestro is the foodie street to shop.

Da Rosetta *(☎ 0182 5 09 33, Via delle Medaglie d'Oro 60)* 1st/2nd courses from €4.15. Dine well at this chequered-tablecloth trattoria; kick off your dining spree with a wine-tasting session at the next-door bar.

Hosteria Sutta Ca' *(☎ 0182 5 31 98, Via Rolandi Ricci 10)* Full meals about €15.50. Dare to try *ventre* (stomach of tuna fish baked in a pine kernel sauce) at one of medieval Albenga's most traditional eating houses.

Getting There & Around Albenga is served by trains and SAR buses (main stop on Piazza del Popolo) along the coast. Europcar (☎ 0182 55 52 66), Piazza Torlaro 3, also rents out scooters from €6.20 per day.

Alassio

postcode 17021 • pop 11,300

In addition to 3km of white beaches, Alassio boasts its own variety of *baci* (literally 'kisses'), delicious concoctions comprising two biscuit whirls sandwiched together with chocolate cream. Delightfully narrow alleys cut from Via XX Settembre, the *budello* (main pedestrian street in the old centre) to the beach. A couple of streets inland, between the sea and the Art Nouveau train station, is the **Muretto di Alassio**, a 'wall of fame' engraved with visiting celebrities' autographs – Roosevelt, Louis Armstrong and playwright Dario Fo. Hemingway's is stuck on the facade of the building opposite at Corso Dante 312. In the 1930s, this was the legendary Caffè Roma.

Alassio is one of the prettier beach resorts on this mountainous stretch of the Ligurian coast and there is no shortage of hotels should you decide to stay. The IAT office (☎ 0182 64 70 27, fax 0182 64 78 74, e iatalassio@italianriviera.com), Piazza della Libertà 5, can assist you. It opens 9am to 12.30pm and 3pm to 6.30pm Monday to Saturday and 9am to noon Sunday.

The seafront is lined with places to snack or dine in style. ***Bar Spotti*** *(Passeggita dino Drollero 16)* is a hip place to lunch on the cheap. Buy baci or try them with afternoon tea at ***Caffè San Lorenzo*** *(Via Torino 59)*. Expensive and starred ***Ristorante Palma*** *(☎ 0182 64 03 14, Via Cavour 5)* prides itself on its €67.15 specialist menu featuring no butter or cream – simply Ligurian olive oil.

Cervo

Past Capo Cervo on the way south-west to Imperia, this small fishing village, surrounded by a ring of walls and towers around the medieval centre, makes a pretty stop.

Imperia

postcode 18100 • pop 40,350

Dominated by lines of hothouses on the surrounding hillside, Imperia is the main city of the westernmost province of Liguria, commonly known as the Riviera dei Fiori because of the area's flower-growing industry, said to be among the most extensive in Italy. Imperia was founded in 1923 by Mussolini when he bridged the River Impero and unified the towns of Porto Maurizio (to the west) and Oneglia (to the east), although they retain the air of separate towns. Unfortunately, the resort today, with its outlying apartment blocks and smoke stacks, can hardly be described as the coast's most attractive place to holiday. Porto Maurizio, the older of the two towns, dominated by a large neoclassical cathedral, is pleasant enough, however, and merits a pre-lunchtime stroll.

From Porto Maurizio train station, head up the hill to Viale G Matteotti or through an underpass to the waterfront, which eventually leads to Corso Garibaldi. The APT office (☎ 0183 66 01 40, fax 0183 66 65 10), Viale G Matteotti 37, can advise on accommodation options, including the resort's numerous camp sites.

Diana Marina, a train stop north-east of Imperia, has a beautiful sweeping seafront.

Getting There & Away Buses for the coast stop virtually in front of the APT office. Tickets are sold in the cafe next door. Buses connect both train stations and bus No 3 runs through Porto Maurizio. Trains stop at Oneglia and Porto Maurizio stations, but the latter is the handiest.

San Remo

postcode 18038 • pop 59,100

San Remo gained prominence as a resort for Europe's social elite, especially British and Russian, in the mid-to-late 19th century, when the likes of Empress Maria Alexandrovna (mother of Nicholas II, the last tsar) held court there. Today, although a few hotels thrive as luxury resorts, many from that period are long past their prime and are cut off from the beach by the railway line.

Orientation The old centre, La Pigna (literally 'pine cone'), is just north of Corso Matteotti, San Remo's main strip, where the wealthy shop for Armani glad rags and Cavelli shoes by day and take their evening stroll come dusk. Farther east, past Piazza Colombo and Corso G Garibaldi, is the seedier area. Corso Matteotti meets San Remo's other famous strip, Corso Imperatrice, at Piazzale Battisti near the train station.

Information The APT office (☎ 0184 5 90 50), Largo Nuvoloni 1, just near the corner of Corso Imperatrice, opens 8am to 7pm Monday to Saturday and 9am to 1pm Sunday.

A rash of banks lines Via Roma. The post office, Via Roma 156, opens 8am to 6pm Monday to Saturday. There are public telephones at the train station and the APT office has the latest telephone directories for most of Italy.

For medical assistance, head north to the Ospedale Generale (hospital; ☎ 0184 53 61), Via Giovanni Borea 56. The *questura* (police station; ☎ 0184 5 90 81) is at Via del Castillo 5.

Things to See & Do The **Chiesa Russa Ortodossia** *(Russian Orthodox Church; Piazza Nuvoloni; admission €0.50; open 9.30am-noon & 3pm-6.30pm daily)* was built for the Russian community that followed Tsarina Maria Alexandrovna to San Remo. The church – with its onion-shaped domes and simple, candle-scented interior – was designed in 1906 by Alexei Shchusev who, 20 years later, planned Lenin's mausoleum in Moscow.

A stroll along shop-lined Corso Matteotti brings you to the sumptuous **Palazzo Borea d'Olimo** *(☎ 0184 55 19 42, Corso Matteotti 143; open 9am-12.30pm & 3pm-6pm Tues-Sat)*, built in Genoese style in the 15th century. Inside, there are small archaeological, art and local history museums. From here, cut west through the narrow streets to get to **La Pigna**, the old part of town.

Continuing north-east along Corso Matteotti, you reach Italy's principal **flower market** *(Corso Garibaldi; 6am-8am daily June-Oct)* – go to watch the frenetic bidding. Farther east still, Corso Felice Cavallotti leads to a rash of elegant villas and gardens, perfect for romantic picnics in the sun. **Villa Nobel**

LIGURIA

(☎ 0184 50 73 80, Corso Felice Cavallotti 112) is the former home of Alfred Nobel, the Swedish inventor of dynamite after whom the Nobel prize is named. Very occasional art exhibitions are held in **Villa Ormond** *(☎ 0184 50 57 62, Corso Felice Cavallotti 51; free; gardens open 8am-7pm daily)*, best known for its Japanese gardens.

A short drive from the centre or a cable-car ride (if it's working) from Corso degli Inglesi, **Monte Bignone** (elevation 1299m) offers views over San Remo and as far west as Cannes.

Activities Book boat trips with **San Remo Navigazione** *(☎ 0184 50 50 55, W www.rivieraline.it, Corso Nazario Sauro)*, at the old port, who run various day excursions out to sea.

Whale-watching *(€25.80/15.50 per adult child; June-Sept)* 6½-hour trips run three times weekly.

To/from Bordighera *(€10.85/5.15 per adult child; Apr-Oct)* 1½-hour-trips depart from Sa Remo daily at 10am and 3pm.

To/from Monaco *(July & Aug)* Trips run tc Monte Carlo to see the international firework festivals.

In summer, sunbathers lay out their oiled bodies to bake on the rocks around the **Giardini Vittorio Veneto**, the garden dominated by the **Forte di Santa Tecia** (closed tc the public) at the southern end of Corsc Mombello. Kids' merry-go-rounds and other funfair amusements occupy the patch of tarmac here.

The APT office has a list of contacts for many sporting activities, including diving, windsurfing, sailing and fishing. The Libreria della Gente, Via Roma 121, sells walking maps and guides.

Places to Stay San Remo is stuffed with hotels and there are reasonable deals to be

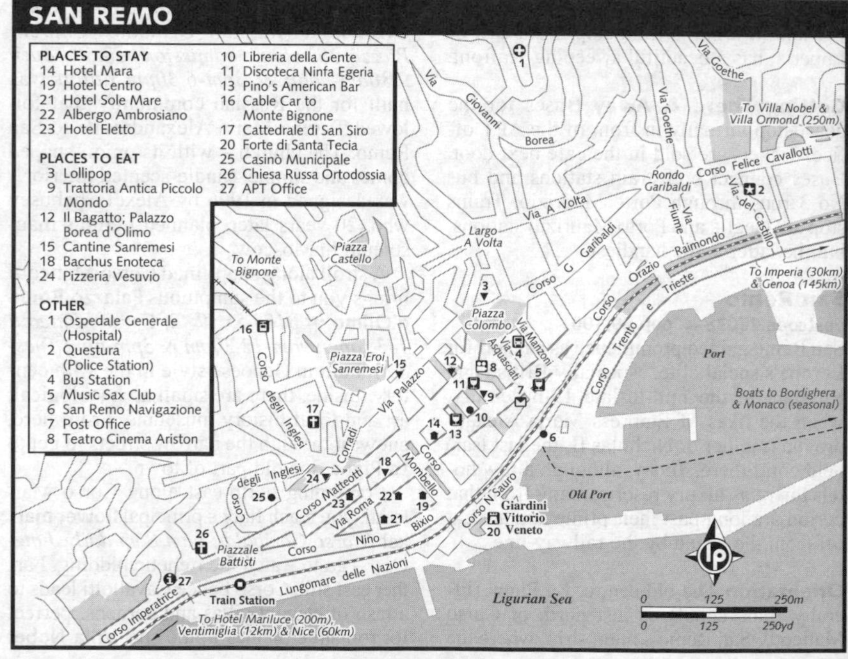

struck. Summer can be difficult, however, while many places shut up shop for holidays in September. Palatial four- and five-star pads are clustered at the more exclusive, western 'seaside' end of the resort.

Hotel Mara *(☎ 0184 53 38 60, Via Roma 93)* Doubles €36.15. This one-star joint on the 3rd floor is best suited to Italian speakers with a penchant for the grey and ageing.

Hotel Centro *(☎ 0184 50 30 86, fax 0184 59 37 25, Corso Mombello 50)* Singles/doubles €20.65/41.30. Similar to Mara, a stay at 11-room Centro is rather like kipping in someone else's (very messy) house.

Albergo Ambrosiano *(☎/fax 0184 57 71 89, Via Roma 36)* Low season singles/doubles €31/46.50, high season singles/doubles €36.15/56.80. This two-star, 4th-floor place is one of the best deals in town. Its eight rooms are clean and spacious; some tout a *frigo-bar*.

Hotel Sole Mare *(☎ 0184 57 71 05, fax 0184 53 27 78, Via Carli 23)* Singles/doubles €41.30/67.15. This is a bright and airy option, painted blue and on the 4th floor.

Hotel Mariluce *(☎ 0184 66 78 05, Corso Matuzia 3)* Doubles without bath €46.50, singles/doubles with bath €31/56.80. A short walk from the centre at the 'seaside' end of San Remo, this excellent-value hotel is an attractive option with a small garden and private parking.

Hotel Eletto *(☎ 0184 53 15 48, fax 0184 50 15 06, Corso Matteotti 44)* Doubles €77.45, half-board per person €67.15. For something a little upmarket, Eletto has a range of good rooms and a pleasing terrace.

Places to Eat Cheap trattorias litter the old-town alleys around Piazza Eroi Sanremesi and open-air snack bars stud the length of Corso N Sauro, the promenade overlooking the old port. ***Lollipop***, next to McDonald's on Piazza Colombo, is San Remo's hot spot for ice cream – two scoops for €1.30.

Pizzeria Vesuvio *(☎ 0184 50 91 27, Via Corradi 5)* Pizzas €4.65-8.80. Eat cheap at the foot of a pedestrian ramp leading from San Remo's glitzy designer shops to its crumbling old-town maze.

Cantine Sanremesi *(☎ 0184 57 20 63, Via Palazzo 7)* Focaccia €6.70, 2nd courses €7.25-10.35. Try the local cuisine at this old tavern, about the only place in San Remo with a time-worn character. The *stoccafisso alla sanremasa* (stockfish with tomato and potatoes) is a delicious steal at €10.35.

Trattoria Antica Piccolo Mondo *(☎ 0184 50 90 12, Via Piave 7)* 1st/2nd courses from €4.90/5.95. Feast on *trippe alla ligure* (Ligurian tripe), *ossobuco* (veal shanks) or *fonduta* (fontina cheese melted with butter and egg yolks, then fried on toast) at San Remo's most traditional dining spot.

Il Bagatto *(☎ 0184 53 19 25, Corso Matteotti 145)* 1st/2nd courses from €10.35/15.50, menu €36.15. Il Bagatto is the place to woo your sweetheart with a feast of fancy fish platters.

Bacchus Enoteca *(☎ 0184 53 09 90, Via Roma 65)* 1st/2nd courses €6.70/9.80. For modestly priced food and a few glasses of tastebud-tickling wine, try this atmospheric wine bar and *grapperia* (serves grappa).

Entertainment With more than 20 clubs and numerous bars, San Remo jumps at night. The San Remese tend to frequent a series of clubs around La Pigna. More sedate cafes and bars line slick Corso Matteotti.

Music Sax Club *(☎ 0184 50 37 43, W www.saxpub.it, Via Roma 160)* This jazzy bar opposite the post office at the north-eastern end of Via Roma is a fun spot to kick-start your drinking spree.

Pino's American Bar *(☎ 0184 57 72 99, Via Roma 105)* Drop in for a beer at this saloon-style bar.

Discoteca Ninfa Egeria *(☎ 0184 59 11 33, W www.ninfaegeria.it, Corso Matteotti 178)* Check what event's on at this mainstream club before shelling out the €10.35 entrance fee.

Teatro Cinema Ariston *(☎ 0184 50 60 60, W www.aristonsanremo.com, Corso Matteotti 212)* San Remo's mainstream cinema is the hub of the night action on Via Matteotti.

Casinò Municipale *(Corso degli Inglesi 18)* The first and foremost place to entertain is San Remo's grand Casinò Municipale, with its 'American Games', cabaret shows, roof garden and nightclub. Bring your gold reserves. The slotties can be played all day; roulette, blackjack and the like operate evenings only.

Getting There & Away San Remo is on the Genoa-Ventimiglia railway line and there are regular trains from both cities.

Riviera Trasporti buses (☎ 0184 59 27 06) leave from the train station and the main bus station at Piazza Colombo 42 for the French border, Imperia (€1.70, 45 minutes, at least hourly) and inland destinations such as Taggia (25 minutes, at least hourly) and Triora (€2.25, 1¼ hours, four daily). Other companies operate from the same bus station to destinations such as Milan (€17.05, 5½ hours, one daily).

By car, you can reach San Remo quickly on the A10 or more scenically (and less expensively) by following the S1 along the coast.

Getting Around Europcar (☎ 0184 59 17 46), Piazza Cesare Battisti 1, inside the train station building, rents out cars, scooters and motorcycles. It opens 9am to 12.30pm and 3pm to 7pm Monday to Friday and 9.30am to noon Saturday. In summer, head down to Giardino Vittorio Veneto to hire bicycles.

For a taxi, call ☎ 0184 54 14 54.

Valle Argentina

The 'Silver Valley' stretches away from **Taggia**, a charming little place a few kilometres inland from the San Remo–Imperia road, into thickly wooded mountains that seem light years from the coastal resorts. Quaint villages abound in this neck of the woods, each seeming even more impossibly perched on a hill crest than the one before.

Buses from San Remo go as far as **Triora** (pop 427, elevation 776m), 33km from San Remo. This haunting medieval village, the scene of celebrated witch trials and executions in the 16th century, dominates the surrounding valleys and the trip is well worth the effort. Gruesome tales of witches being burned alive are vividly portrayed in the local **Museo Etnograifico e della Streganeria** *(Museum of Ethnography & Witchcraft, ☎ 0184 9 44 77, Corso Italia 1; adult/child €1.55/0.50; open 2.30pm-6pm Mon-Fri, 10.30am-noon & 2.30pm-6pm Sat & Sun)*. The IAT tourist office (☎ 0184 9 44 77), Corso Italia 7, has information, including accommodation details, for the entire valley.

Valle Nervia

From Triora, a stunning drive through 25km of wiggles and hairpins brings you to **Pigna** (pop 1150, elevation 280m) in the upper Valle Nervia. Riddled with alleys and narrow streets criss-crossing in all directions, the medieval village is a delight to get lost in. Its fortified neighbour and traditional rival, **Castel Vittorio** (pop 520, elevation 420m), 5km to the south-east, is equally medieval in outlook. It celebrates a sweet pancake *(peti di muneghe)* festival in September.

Isolabona (pop 630, elevation 106m), a former stronghold of the Doria family 10km to the south, is dominated by a half-ruined 15th-century castle where concerts are held in summer. From here, a scenic loop takes you to San Remo on the coast (see the 'Scenic Loop' boxed text).

Monet was a frequent visitor to **Dolceacqua** (pop 1900, elevation 51m) and painted the medieval village's plentiful palazzos several times. The Doria's family castle tops off the old upper part of the village on the left bank of the River Nervia. Theatre performances are held here in July and August. Cross the late-medieval, single span bridge – 33m wide – to get to *il borgo*, Dolceacqua's newer quarters. The tourist office (☎ 0184 22 95 07), Via Patrioti Martiri 22, has a list of places where you can taste and buy the village's well-known Rossese, ruby-red DOC wine. Black olives are its other tasty product.

Buses (four to six daily) link Ventimiglia with Pigna, Castel Vittorio, Apricale, Isolabona and Dolceacqua; the tourist office in Ventimiglia has updated schedules.

Bordighera

postcode 18012 • pop 10,700

A few kilometres west of San Remo is built-up Bordighera. Apart from being a one-time favourite haunt of rich British seaside lovers – the collection of charming and costly hotels attests to this – Bordighera's fame rests on a centuries-old monopoly of the Holy Week palm business. The Vatican selects its branches exclusively from the palms along the promenade, Lungomare Argentina. The APT office (☎ 0184 26 23 22, fax 0184 26 44 55), Via Vittorio Emanuele 172, has accommodation details.

Ventimiglia

postcode 18039 • pop 26,700

If you are coming in from the splendidly rich end of the French Riviera, you may find arrival in Ventimiglia a bit of a letdown. The town is jaded, the grey, pebbly beach is nothing special and the limpid blue water of Nice seems far away. Typically in this frontier area, French seems almost to have equal status with Italian.

Ventimiglia's Roman ruins, which can't be visited, include an amphitheatre dating from the 2nd and 3rd centuries, when the town was known as Albintimulium.

Squatting on a hill on the western bank of the River Roia is the medieval town, crowned with a 12th-century **cathedral** on Via del Capo. There are some breathtaking views of the coast from Corso Giuseppe Verdi.

Scenic Loop

A scenic loop takes Sunday motorists 4km east from Isolabona to **Apricale** (pop 570, elevation 275m), a hilltop village known literally as the 'village of the sun'. A maze of medieval streets wends it way to the 11th-century feudal **Castello della Lucertola** *(Castle of the Lizard; open 4pm-7pm & 8pm-10pm Tues-Sun in summer, 2pm-8pm Tues-Sat, 10.30am-noon & 2pm-7pm Sun in winter)*, where local lore and legend come to life. Artisans' workshops abound in the village and olive groves carpet its surrounding slopes. Eat *pansarole* (fried aniseed pastries) and other regional specialities for lunch at ***La Favorita*** *(☎ 0184 20 81 86, fax 0184 20 82 47, W www.la-favorita-apricale.it, Strada San Pitero 1)*, a delicious trattoria with a handful of rooms above.

Whit Sunday in the hilltop village of **Bajardo** (elevation 896m) sees singing villagers dance in circles around a giant tree in their central square. This is to honour the Count of Bajardo who, so legend says, was sentenced to death with his loved one on Whit Sunday. Immediately east, the **Passo Ghimbegna** loops through chestnut trees and pine groves to the **Valle Intemelia** and beyond, to San Remo. Stock up with olive oil in **Ceriana** (elevation 900m), another pretty medieval village a few kilometres south of the pass.

Orientation & Information The train station is at the head of Via della Stazione, which continues to the waterfront as Corso della Repubblica. Corso Genova, which runs past the Roman ruins, is the main eastern exit from the city, while its continuation to the west, Via Cavour, runs through the centre and heads to France.

The APT office (☎/fax 0184 35 11 83), Via Cavour 61, opens 9am to 12.30pm and 3pm to 7pm Monday to Saturday. There are several banks, ATMs and an exchange booth at the train station. The post office, Corso della Repubblica 8c, opens 8am to 6pm Monday to Saturday.

Places to Stay & Eat Scattered amongst the exclusive hotels are some cheaper options.

Albergo XX Settembre *(☎ 0184 35 12 22, Via Roma 16)* Singles/doubles €25.80/46.50. The nine rooms here are quite cheap, as is the popular restaurant below.

Villa Franca *(☎ 0184 35 18 71, Corso della Repubblica 12)* Singles/doubles/triples €23.75/44.95/63.50. Chaotic, charming and just-like-home sum up this seaside villa, complete with speaking parrot who pipes up in both Italian and French.

Hotel Posta *(☎ 0184 35 12 18, fax 0184 23 16 00, e olivieri@masterweb.it, Via Sottoconvento 15)* Singles/doubles/triples/quads €46.50/67.15/82.65/103.30. Hotel Posta is a three-star step up in quality, near the tourist office.

Stock up on self-catering supplies at the ***Standa*** supermarket at Via Roma 25. A series of pizza restaurants lines the beach on Passeggiata G Oberdan. There are several down-to-earth places around Via Roma and Piazza della Libertà, and along Via Cavour.

Getting There & Around Trains connect the city with Genoa (two to 3½ hours, hourly), Nice (50 minutes, hourly), Cannes (1½ hours, hourly) and Marseilles (3½ to four hours, eight to 10 daily).

By bus, Riviera Trasporti (☎ 0184 35 13 77), next to the APT office, connects the city with towns along the coast and into France; frequency drops out of high season.

The A10 and Via Aurelia (S1) link the town with Genoa and the French border. The S20 heads north into France.

Balzi Rossi

Eight kilometres west of Ventimiglia, on the French border, right by the Ponte San Lodovico, is the Balzi Rossi (Red Rocks) Stone Age site. To enter the grottoes where Cro-Magnon people once lived, you must get a guide and a ticket from the small **Museo Preistorico** *(admission €2.05/1.05; open 9am-7pm daily)*. The museum features a Cro-Magnon triple grave, pots of weapons and animal remains from the period.

The Riviera Trasporti bus (line No 1; €1.15, 15 minutes, eight or nine times daily) to Menton (Garavan) in France that leaves Via Cavour in Ventimiglia drops you right at the site.

Villa Hanbury

Overlooking the coast by the village of Mortola are the **Giardini Botanici Hanbury** *(☎ 0184 22 95 07; adult/child €6.20/free; open 9am-6pm daily in summer, 10am-4pm Thur-Tues in winter)*. Established in the 19th century by Sir Thomas Hanbury, an English noble, the tumbledown gardens surround his Moorish-style mausoleum on the 18-hectare estate. Take the No 1A bus from Via Cavour in Ventimiglia; the bus goes on to the Ponte San Lodovico frontier post, from where you can walk down to the Balzi Rossi.

Piedmont (Piemonte)

The region's position against the French and Swiss Alps has helped forge an identity for Piedmont that is quite separate from that of the rest of Italy. Its neat and tidy northernmost reaches could easily be Swiss, while Turin's grand squares, arcades and sophisticated cafe life owe more to French influence than to anything 'typically' Italian.

The House of Savoy (originally a feudal family from south-east France), which ruled Piedmont in the early 11th century, created one of Europe's grand cities in Turin. Vittorio Emanuele II and the Piedmontese statesman Count Camillo Cavour were instrumental in achieving Italian unification and succeeded in making Turin the capital of Italy, albeit briefly, for three years from 1861.

Much of Italy's industrial boom last century had its roots in the region, particularly in and around Turin where Fiat started making cars. Today, Piedmont is second only to Lombardy in industrial production and is one of the country's wealthiest regions.

Piedmontese cuisine is heavily influenced by French cooking and uses marinated meats and vegetables. *Bagna caoda* (meat dipped in oil, anchovies and garlic) is popular during winter, and the white truffles of Alba are considered Italy's best. The region accounts for two-thirds of Italy's rice production, so it comes as no surprise that risotto is popular in Piedmont. The crisp climate is no hindrance to winemaking and you can find some good reds, notably those from the vineyards of Barolo and Barbera, and sparkling wines from Asti.

Central Turin is an ideal base for exploring the region. The area's main attraction is the Grande Traversata delle Alpi (GTA), a walk of more than 200km through the Alps from the Ligurian border to Lago Maggiore in the north-east of the region.

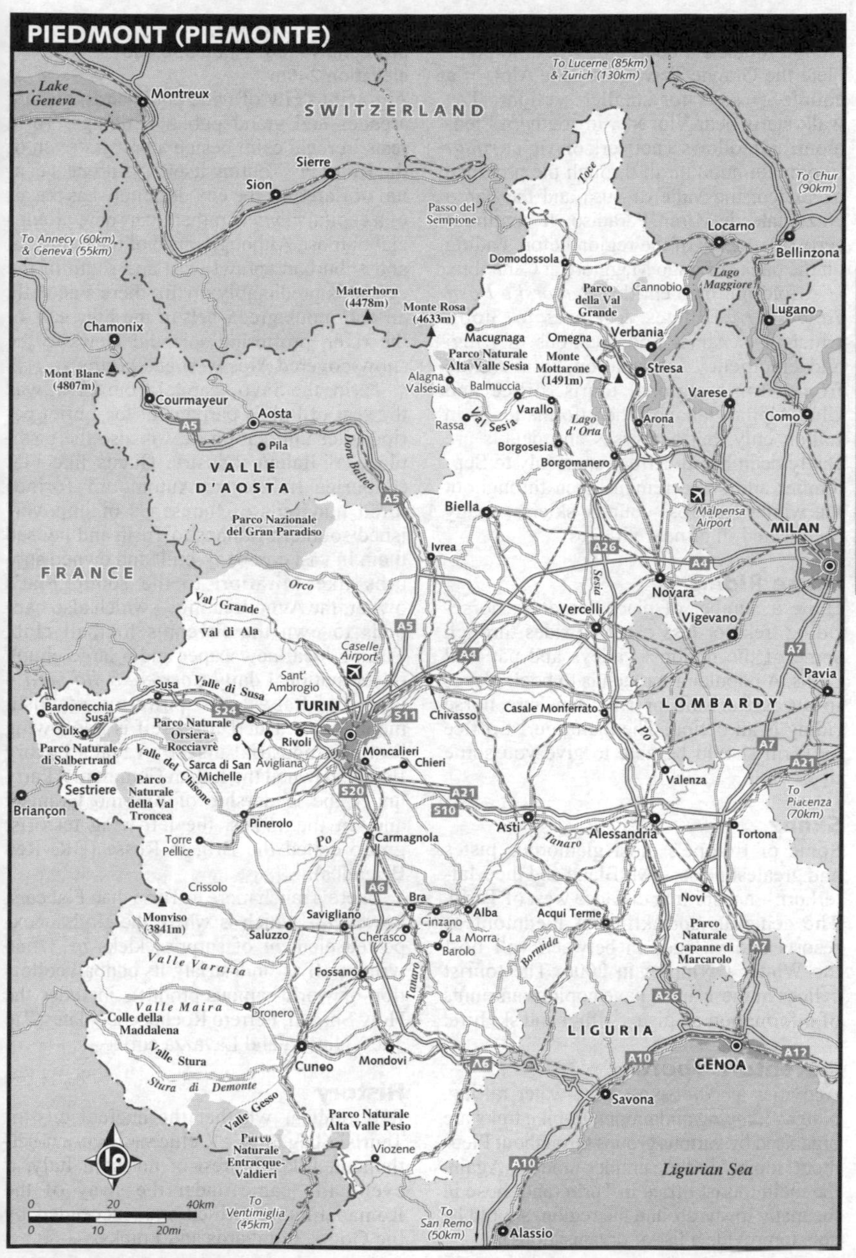
PIEDMONT (PIEMONTE)
To Lucerne (85km) & Zurich (130km)
Lake Geneva
Montreux
SWITZERLAND
Sierre
Sion
Toce
To Chur (90km)
Passo del Sempione
To Annecy (60km) & Geneva (55km)
Locarno
Bellinzona
Domodossola
Lago Maggiore
Cannobio
Parco della Val Grande
Matterhorn (4478m)
Monte Rosa (4633m)
Lugano
Chamonix
Macugnaga
Omegna
Verbania
Parco Naturale Alta Valle Sesia
Monte Mottarone (1491m)
Stresa
Mont Blanc (4807m)
Alagna Valsesia
Balmuccia
Courmayeur
Varallo
Varese
Aosta
Rassa
Val Sesia
Lago d' Orta
Arona
Como
Pila
Dora Baltea
Borgosesia
Borgomanero
VALLE D'AOSTA
Malpensa Airport
Biella
MILAN
Parco Nazionale del Gran Paradiso
Ivrea
FRANCE
Novara
Orco
Sesia
Val Grande
Vercelli
Vigevano
Val di Ala
Caselle Airport
Pavia
Sant' Ambrogio
Susa
Valle di Susa
Bardonecchia
Susa
TURIN
Chivasso
Casale Monferrato
LOMBARDY
Oulx
Parco Naturale Orsiera-Rocciavrè
Rivoli
Parco Naturale di Salbertrand
Valle del Chisone
Moncalieri
Avigliana
Chieri
Sarca di San Michelle
Po
Sestriere
Parco Naturale della Val Troncea
Valenza
Briançon
To Piacenza (70km)
Pinerolo
Asti
Alessandria
Tortona
Torre Pellice
Po
Carmagnola
Tanaro
Crissolo
Monviso (3841m)
Bra
Alba
Novi
Savigliano
Cinzano
Acqui Terme
Saluzzo
Cherasco
La Morra
Barolo
Parco Naturale Capanne di Marcarolo
Valle Varaita
Bormida
Fossano
Tanaro
Valle Maira
Dronero
Colle della Maddalena
LIGURIA
Valle Stura
GENOA
Cuneo
Mondovi
Stura di Demonte
Savona
Valle Gesso
Parco Naturale Alta Valle Pesio
Parco Naturale Entracque-Valdieri
Viozene
Ligurian Sea
0 20 40km
0 10 20mi
To Ventimiglia (45km)
To San Remo (50km)
Alassio
A5
A26
A4
A7
A21
S24
S11
S20
S10
A6
A10
A12
PIEDMONT

Walking

Allow yourself a couple of weeks to complete the Grande Traversata delle Alpi, or a couple of days for smaller sections. The walk starts near Viozene, in southern Piedmont, and follows a network of Alpine *rifugi* (mountain huts) north through the province of Cuneo, the Valle di Susa and the Parco Nazionale del Gran Paradiso. It continues across the north of the region before ending on the banks of Lago Maggiore at Cannobio.

A fold-out map entitled *Percorsi e Posti Tappa GTA* (Routes & Places to Stop), which lists names and locations of rifugi and emergency information, is available from Turin's regional tourist office and Club Alpino Italiano. The information is in Italian only, but addresses and details are easily deciphered. Rifugi open July to September and some remain open throughout the winter for cross-country skiers – many are located in or near villages.

Horse Riding

Quite a number of places organise horse-riding treks or less exacting rides through some of the region's valleys and national parks. A popular approach is to book places in an agriturismo or rifugio where horse riding is an option. The main tourist office in Turin should be able to give you some tips.

Skiing

Some of Europe's most glamorous pistes and greatest peaks – Mt Blanc and the Matterhorn – are spitting distance west of Turin. The generous sprinkling of Piedmontese resorts and villages in between will host the Winter Olympics in 2006. The tourist offices in these areas have copious amounts of information on pistes, rifugi and ski hire.

Adventure Sports

Activities as diverse as white-water rafting, bungee jumping and mountain-bike treks are organised by various groups throughout Piedmont, mostly in the summer months. Again, the main tourist office in Turin (and those in the many towns around the region) should be able to provide a list of organisations.

TURIN (TORINO)

postcode 10100 • pop 950,000
elevation 240m

A gracious city of wide boulevards, elegant arcades and grand public buildings, Turin rests in regal calm beside a pretty stretch of the River Po. Touting itself as Europe's capital of Baroque, the city definitely has the air of a capital *manqué* rather than some provincial outpost. Although much of the industrial and suburban sprawl west and south of the centre is predictably awful, there's actually an enormous green belt in the hills east of the river, proffering splendid views to the snow-covered Alps west and north.

Turin, the Savoy capital from 1574, was the seat of Italy's parliament for a brief period after unification. It was also the birthplace of Italian industry. Giants like Fiat (Fabbrica Italiana di Automobili Torino) lured hundreds of thousands of impoverished southern Italians to Turin and housed them in vast company-built and owned suburbs like Mirafiori to the south. Fiat's owner, the Agnelli family – which also happens to own the Juventus football club, Turin's local newspaper and a large chunk of the national daily *Corriere della Sera* – is one of Italy's most powerful establishment forces. But Turin itself is a left-wing bastion. Industrial unrest on Fiat's factory floors spawned the Italian Communist Party under the leadership of Antonio Gramsci and, in the 1970s, the left-wing terrorist group called the Brigate Rosse (BR; Red Brigades).

There's much more to Turin than Fiat cars, however – which is where the city's unexpected element of surprise kicks in. Often written off as 'industrial', its oddball collection of world-famous products includes the Holy Shroud, Ferrero Rocher chocolates, Tic Tacs, Nutella and Lavazza coffee.

History

It is unclear whether the ancient city of Taurisia began as a Celtic or Ligurian settlement. Like the rest of northern Italy, it eventually came under the sway of the Roman Empire, which was succeeded by the Goths, Lombards and Franks.

When Turin became capital of the House f Savoy, it pretty much shared the dynasty's ortunes thereafter. The Savoys annexed ardinia in 1720, but Napoleon virtually put n end to their power and occupied Turin in 798. Turin suffered Austrian and Russian ccupation before Vittorio Emanuele I restored the House of Savoy and re-entered 'urin in 1814. Nevertheless, Austria remained the true power throughout northern taly until unification, when Turin became he capital, an honour it passed on to Florence hree years later.

Turin adapted quickly to its loss of political significance, becoming first a centre for ndustrial production during the WWI years nd later a hive of trade-union activity. Today, it is Italy's second-largest industrial ity after Milan.

Orientation

The north-east-facing Stazione Porta Nuova s the point of arrival for most travellers. Trams and buses departing from the front of he station connect with most parts of the istoric centre, which is quite spread out. Busy Corso Vittorio Emanuele II is the main oute, running south-east-north-west, and Via Roma links the station (south-west) with Piazza Castello (north-east). Piazza Carlo Felice, the square in front of the station, and Via Nizza, which continues south-west past t, are the main axes of Turin's seedier side of life and can be dodgy at night.

The Mole Antonelliana dominates the orizon to the east, near Via Po (the student rea), Piazza Vittorio Veneto and the mighty River Po.

Information

Tourist Offices Turin's main APT office (☎ 011 53 59 01 or 011 53 51 81, fax 011 53 00 70, W www.turismotorino.org), Piazza Castello 161, opens 9.30am to 7pm Monday to Saturday and 9.30am to 3pm Sunday, as does its booth at Stazione Porta Nuova (☎ 011 53 13 27). Another booth at he airport (☎ 011 567 81 24) opens 8.30am o 11.30pm daily.

For information on events, try the city's cultural information service, Vetrina per Torina (toll free ☎ 800 01 54 75, W www.comune.torino.it/cultura), Piazza San Carlo 159, open 11am to 7pm Monday to Saturday.

Money Stazione Porta Nuova shelters a bank, ATM and exchange booth. Other banks dot Via Roma and Piazza San Carlo. There's a 24-hour automatic banknote change machine outside Banca CRT on Piazza CLN, and another in front of Banca San Paolo at Via Santa Teresa 1g.

Post & Communications The main post office, at Via Alfieri 10, opens 8.30am to 6.30pm Monday to Friday and 8.30am to noon Saturday. Unstaffed Telecom booths at Via Roma 18 and in Stazione Porta Nuova open 8am to 10pm.

Informa Giovani, at Via Assarotti 2, offers 40 minutes of free Internet access per day to its punters (of any age); the youth information centre opens 10.30am to 6.30pm Monday and Wednesday to Saturday. Look for the grey door plastered in posters advertising upcoming gigs around town.

Alternatively, surf the net for €5.15 an hour at American Stars (see Entertainment later). Mailboxes Etc (☎ 011 517 41 40, e mbe239@inwind.it), Via Arsenale 25m/n, opens 9am to 1pm and 2pm to 7pm Monday to Saturday, and charges €7.75 per hour. The hourly rate is €5.15 at @h! (☎ 011 815 40 58), Via Montebello 13, open 10am to 1pm and 2pm to 7pm Monday to Friday.

Bookshops An excellent range of maps and guides is sold athe bookshop in the Touring Club Italiano (☎ 011 562 72 07, e negozio.torino@touringclub.it), Piazza Solferino 3bis, which opens 9am to 1pm and 2pm to 7pm Monday to Friday, and 9am to 1pm Saturday. Libreria Luxemburg, Via Battisti 7, is an Anglo-American bookshop. A stunning choice of art, architecture and design books is stacked high at Libreria Druetto (☎ 561 91 66, e drulib@tin.it), Via Roma 227.

Gay & Lesbian Turin Contact ArciGay Maurice (☎ 011 521 11 16, e maurice@arpnet.it), Via della Basilica 3/5, for gay and lesbian information.

PIEDMONT

TURIN (TORINO)

PLACES TO STAY
- 21 Hotel Dogana Vecchia
- 26 Albergo Canelli
- 28 Albergo Kariba
- 36 Hotel Venezia
- 77 Grand Hotel Sitea
- 84 Hotel Artuá
- 85 Albergo Solferino
- 91 Hotel Montevecchio
- 92 Albergo Magenta
- 95 Turin Palace Hotel
- 97 Hotel Bologna
- 98 Albergo Sila; Hotel Roma
- 106 Albergo Versilia
- 117 Ostello Torino

PLACES TO EAT
- 2 Gennaro Esposito
- 3 Osteria No 1
- 6 Al Bicerin
- 7 Fusion Café
- 8 Hafa Café
- 9 I Tre Galli
- 11 Il Bagatto
- 12 Tre Galline
- 23 La Focacceria
- 24 Olsen
- 27 Express Restaurant
- 41 Baratti & Milano
- 43 Pepino
- 46 Caffè Milassano
- 49 Caffè Fiorio & Gelateria Fiorio
- 53 Mamma Mia
- 60 Caffè San Carlo
- 62 Il Granaio
- 63 Brek
- 66 Caffè Torino
- 70 Neuv Caval 'd Brôns
- 71 Kirkuk Kafè
- 73 Société Lutéce
- 75 Il Punto Verde
- 76 Giolitti Lunch & Tea
- 90 Platti
- 94 Caffè Miretti
- 100 Brek
- 101 Gatsby's
- 103 Balbo
- 104 Stek Self-Service Restaurant
- 105 C'era Una Volta

MUSEUMS & CHURCHES
- 5 Museo della Sindone
- 14 Museo d'Antichità
- 16 Duomo di San Giovanni (Cappella della Santa Sindone)
- 31 Chiesa di San Lorenzo
- 33 Armeria Reale
- 35 Palazzo Madama
- 44 Palazzo Carignano (Museo Nazionale del Risorgimento Italiano)
- 52 Mole Antonelliana (Museo Nazionale del Cinema)
- 56 Palazzo dell' Accademia delle Scienze (Museo Egizio; Galleria Sabauda)
- 61 Museo della Marionetta (Chiesa di Santa Teresa)
- 80 Palazzo Bricherasio (Art Gallery)
- 88 Galleria Civica d'Arte Moderna e Contemporanea
- 102 Palazzo Cavour
- 107 Synagogue
- 115 Chiesa di Gran Madre di Dio
- 116 Chiesa e Conventa di Santa Maria

OTHER
- 1 Questura (Police Station)
- 4 Informa Giovani
- 10 Montagna Viva
- 13 Lava e Asciuga
- 15 Palazzo Reale
- 17 Roman Amphitheatre
- 18 Porta Palatina
- 19 Palazium
- 20 ArciGay Maurice
- 22 Mario Bianchetti Clothing
- 25 La Taverna dei Guitti
- 29 Legatoria Rocchietti Book Binder
- 30 Coronel Tapiocca Mountain Equipment
- 32 APT Office
- 34 State Archives; Prefecture
- 37 Club Alpino Italiano
- 38 American Stars
- 39 Telecom Booth
- 40 Bus Stop for ATM Bus Tours
- 42 Libreria Luxemburg
- 45 Galleria Subalpina
- 47 Teatro Regio & Piccolo Regio
- 48 Roar Roads
- 50 Abrate
- 51 @h!
- 54 Lava e Asciuga
- 55 Cinema Massimo
- 57 Galleria San Frederico
- 58 Theatró
- 59 Banca San Paolo; 24-hour Banknote Exchange
- 64 Touring Club Italiano
- 65 Post Office
- 67 Statue of Emanuele Filiberto
- 68 Stratta Confectioner
- 69 Vetrina per Torina
- 72 Automobile Club Torino
- 74 Barrumba
- 78 La Rinascente Department Store
- 79 Libreria Druetto
- 81 Ricordi Media Store
- 82 Banca CRT & 24-hour Banknote Exchange
- 83 Mailboxes etc
- 86 Gerla Chocolate House
- 87 Statue of Vittorio Emanuele II
- 89 Peyrano Chocolate House
- 93 Farmacia Boniscontro
- 96 Airport Bus Tickets (Un-named Bar-Gelateria)
- 99 Avvignano & Giordano
- 108 Lava e Asciuga
- 109 British Consulate
- 110 Castello del Valentino
- 111 Imbarco Murazzi
- 112 Alcatraz
- 113 Pier
- 114 Doctor Sax Music Club

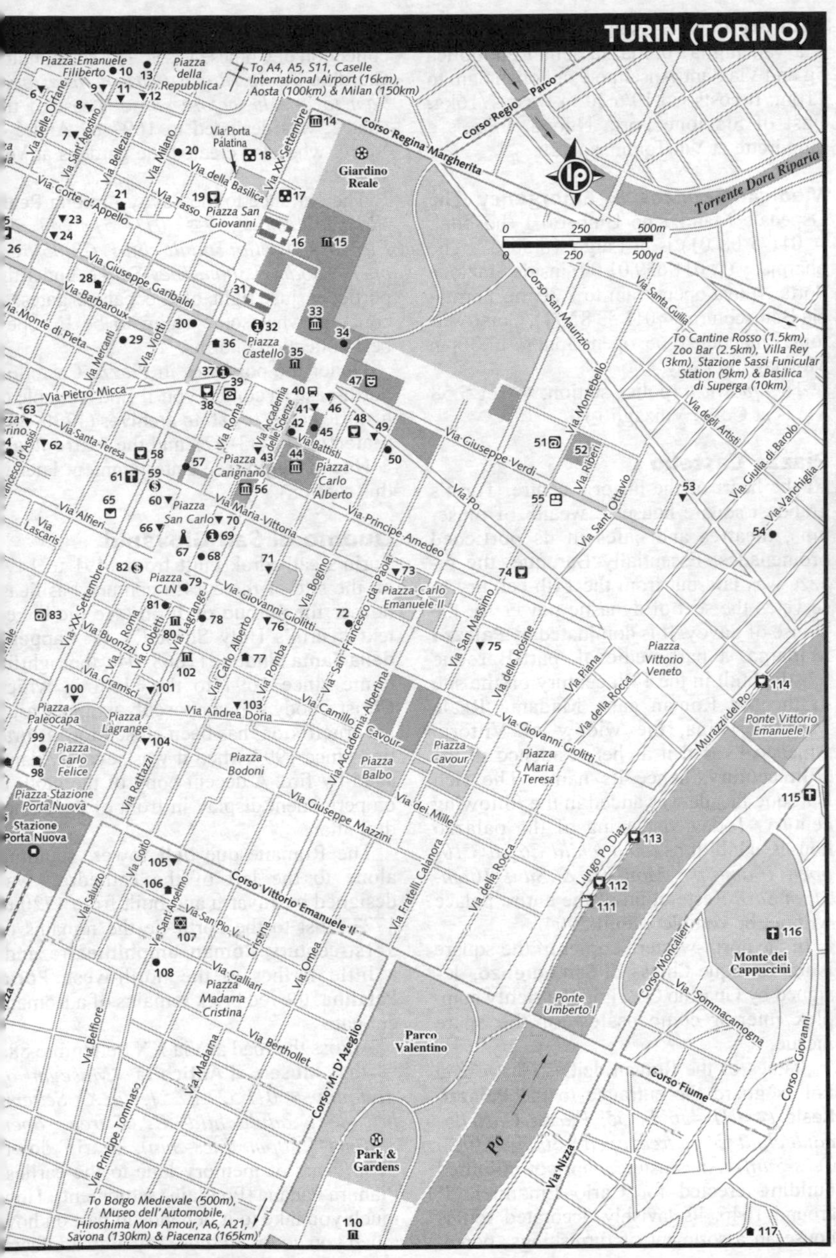
TURIN (TORINO)
To A4, A5, S11, Caselle International Airport (16km), Aosta (100km) & Milan (150km)
To Cantine Rosso (1.5km), Zoo Bar (2.5km), Villa Rey (3km), Stazione Sassi Funicular Station (9km) & Basilica di Superga (10km)
To Borgo Medievale (500m), Museo dell' Automobile, Hiroshima Mon Amour, A6, A21, Savona (130km) & Piacenza (165km)
Giardino Reale
Parco Valentino
Park & Gardens
Monte dei Cappuccini
Stazione Porta Nuova
Piazza Emanuele Filiberto
Piazza della Repubblica
Piazza San Giovanni
Piazza Castello
Piazza Carignano
Piazza Carlo Alberto
Piazza San Carlo
Piazza CLN
Piazza Carlo Emanuele II
Piazza Vittorio Veneto
Piazza Paleocapa
Piazza Lagrange
Piazza Carlo Felice
Piazza Bodoni
Piazza Balbo
Piazza Cavour
Piazza Maria Teresa
Piazza Stazione Porta Nuova
Piazza Madama Cristina
Ponte Vittorio Emanuele I
Ponte Umberto I
Torrente Dora Riparia
Po
Corso Regina Margherita
Corso Regio Parco
Corso San Maurizio
Corso Vittorio Emanuele II
Corso M. D'Azeglio
Corso Moncalieri
Corso Fiume
Corso Giovanni
Via Giuseppe Verdi
Via Po
Via Roma
Via Pietro Micca
Via Giuseppe Garibaldi
Via Maria Vittoria
Via Principe Amedeo
Via Giovanni Giolitti
Via Andrea Doria
Via Camillo Cavour
Via Giuseppe Mazzini
Via dei Mille
Via XX Settembre
Via Accademia Albertina
Via San Francesco da Paola
Via Lagrange
Via Carlo Alberto
Via Pomba
Via Bogino
Via San Massimo
Via delle Rosine
Via della Rocca
Via Piana
Via Montebello
Via Riberi
Via Sant'Ottavio
Via Santa Giulia
Via degli Artisti
Via Giulia di Barolo
Via Vanchiglia
Murazzi del Po
Lungo Po Diaz
Via Sommacampagna
Via Nizza
Via Madama
Via Berthollet
Via Galliari
Via San Pio V
Via Sant'Anselmo
Via Goito
Via Saluzzo
Via Belfiore
Via Principe Tommaso
Via Omea
Via Fratelli Calandra
Cristina
Via Rattazzi
Via Gramsci
Via Buonzzi
Via Gobetti
Via Alfieri
Via Lascaris
Via Santa Teresa
Via Mercanti
Via Viotti
Via Monte di Pieta
Via Barbaroux
Via Corte d'Appello
Via Tasso
Via della Basilica
Via Porta Palatina
Via Milano
Via Bellezia
Via Sant'Agostino
Via delle Orfane
Via Accademia delle Scienze
Via Battisti
0 250 500m
0 250 500yd

Laundry Lava E Asciuga has branches at Via Vanchiglia 10, Piazza della Repubblica 5g and Via Sant'Anselmo 9, all open 8am to 11pm. It costs €3.10/6.20 to wash 7/16kg. East of Stazione Porta Nuova, there's a laundrette at Via Tommaso 12b.

Medical Services & Emergency The Ospedale Mauriziano Umberto I (hospital; ☎ 011 5 08 01) is at Largo Turati 62. The pharmacy (☎ 011 659 01 00) inside Stazione Porta Nuova opens 7am to 7.30pm. Farmacia Boniscontro (☎ 011 53 82 71), Corso Vittorio Emanuele II 66, opens 3pm to 12.30pm Monday to Friday.

The *questura* (police station; ☎ 011 5 58 81) is at Corso Vinzaglio 10.

Piazza Castello

At the heart of the historic centre, Turin's grandest square houses a wealth of museums, theatres and cafes in its porticoed promenades. Essentially Baroque, the piazza was laid out from the 14th century to serve as the seat of dynastic power for the House of Savoy. It is dominated by **Palazzo Madama**, a part-medieval, part-Baroque 'castle' built in the 13th century on the site of the old Roman gate. Madama Reale Maria Cristina, the widow of Vittorio Amedeo I, used it as her residence in the 17th century, hence its name. The rich Baroque facade was added in the following century. Today, one wing of the palazzo houses **exhibitions** *(adult/child €6.20/3.10; open 10am-8pm Mon-Fri & Sun, 10am-11pm Sat)*. Restoration of the entire palace will not be complete until 2004.

In the north-western corner of the square is the Baroque **Chiesa di San Lorenzo**, designed by Guarino Guarini. The richly complex interior compensates for the spare facade.

Statues of the Roman deities Castor and Pollux guard the entrance to the **Palazzo Reale** *(☎ 011 436 14 55, Piazza Castello; adult/child €4.15/free; open 8.30am-7.30pm Tues-Sun)*. An austere, apricot-coloured building erected for Carlo Emanuele II around 1646, its lavishly decorated rooms house an assortment of furnishings, porcelain and other bits and pieces, including collection of Chinese vases. The surroundin **Giardino Reale** *(Royal Garden; free; ope 9am to one hr before sunset)*, east of th palace, was designed in 1697 by André Nôtre, who also created the gardens at Ve sailles.

The entrance to the Savoy **Armeria Real** *(Royal Armoury; ☎ 011 518 43 58 Piazza Castello; adult/child €2.05/free open 8.30am-7.30pm Tues-Sun)* is under th porticoes just right of the palace gates. contains what some claim to be Europe' best collection of arms.

Under the porticoes in Piazza Castello' north-eastern corner, you'll find a couple c historic cafes, the **state archives** (1730–34) **prefecture** (1733–57), and the **Teatro Regi & Nuova Regio** (see Entertainment later i this section).

Duomo di San Giovanni

Turin's cathedral, built from 1491 to 149 on the site of three 14th-century basilicas houses the **Shroud of Turin** (see the boxe text 'Turin's Holy Shroud'). Its **Cappell della Santa Sindone** (1668–94), the rightfu home since 1694 to the cloth in whic Christ's body was supposedly wrapped afte his crucifixion, has been closed for restoration since 1997 when it was severely damaged by fire. A decent copy of the cloth i on permanent display in front of the cathedral altar.

The Romanesque **bell tower**, standing alone to the left of the cathedral, wa designed by Juvarra and built from 1720 t 1723. Just to the north lie the remains o a 1st-century **Roman amphitheatre** and a little farther to the north-west, **Porta Palatina**, the red brick remains of a Roman-era gate.

Across the road at Via XX Settembre 88c is the **Museo d'Antichità** *(Museum o Antiquity; ☎ 011 521 22 51, Via XX Settembre 88c; adult/child €2.05/free; open 8.30am-7.30pm Tues-Sun)*, a trip down 7000 years of memory lane to the earliest Pianura Padana (Po Plain) settlements. How much you take to it depends in part on how much you go for all those itty bitty artefacts.

Museums

Perfect for a typical rainy day in Turin are the museums just south of Piazza Castello.

Baroque **Palazzo Carignano** was the birthplace of Carlo Alberto and Vittorio Emanuele II, and the seat of Italy's first parliament from 1861 to 1864. You can see the parliament as part of the **Museo Nazionale del Risorgimento Italiano** *(☎ 011 562 11 47, Palazzo Carignano, Via Accademia delle Scienze 5; adult/child €4.15/free; open 9am-6.30pm Tues-Sat, 9am-6.30pm Sun)*, which has an extensive display of arms, paintings and documents tracing the turbulent century from the revolts of 1848 to WWII. It's one of the best of this genre in northern Italy (and there are many) but is of limited interest to those who don't read Italian.

On the topic of the Risorgimento, one of its prime architects, Camillo Benso di Cavour, was born and died at **Palazzo Cavour** *(☎ 011 53 06 90, Via Cavour 8; adult/child €6.20/free; open 10am-7.30pm Tues-Sun)*. The Baroque palace dates to 1729 and can be visited during temporary exhibitions held in its grandiose interior.

On the same street as Palazzo Carignano is **Palazzo dell'Accademia delle Scienze**, home to the **Museo Egizio** *(☎ 011 561 77 76, e egizio@multix.it, Via Accademia delle Scienze 6; adult/child €6.20/free; open 8.30am-7.30pm Tues-Sun)*. Established in the late 18th century, it's considered to have one of the best collections of ancient Egyptian art, second only to those in London and Cairo. In the same building is **Galleria Sabauda** *(☎ 011 561 83 91, Via Accademia delle Scienze 6; adult/child €4.15/free; open 8.30am-5.30pm Tues-Sat, 1pm-8pm Sun)*, housing the Savoy collection of art, which includes works by Italian, French and Flemish masters. A combination ticket covering admission to both museums costs €7.75 for adults (free for children).

Shroud fiends should search no farther than the **Museo della Sindone** *(☎ 011 436 58 32, W www.sindone.it, Via San Domenico 28; adult/child €5.15/4.15; open 9am-noon & 3pm-7pm daily)*. Despite its informative displays and unexpected 'shroud' paraphernalia – such as the first camera used to photograph the cloth (1898), and test tubes used to store traces of human blood removed from the shroud in 1978 – the museum does little to

Turin's Holy Shroud

The Holy Shroud (*sindone* in Italian) is Christianity's greatest icon of faith and object of devotion, luring three million pilgrims to Turin when it was publicly displayed in 1978, 2.1 million pilgrims in 1998 and another million in 2000 (with each showing, numbers drop as those who've 'seen it once' fall away). Only the pope and the bishop of Turin can decide when the sacred cloth will next be hauled out.

For centuries, experts and fanatics have argued over the authenticity of the Shroud of Turin, said to be the burial cloth in which Jesus' body was wrapped. Tests in 1981 uncovered traces of human blood (type AB) and pollen from plants known to exist only in and around Jerusalem. Many guessed the shroud as being from AD 1260 to 1390; carbon dating carried out in 1988 seemed to confirm this, tying it to the 13th century and making it far from sacred. Most agree that the white cloth – 4.37m long and 1.10m wide – was woven in the Middle East.

How the image of a human body – with fractured nose, bruised right cheek, lance wound on chest, scourge marks on back, thorn wounds on forehead and nail wounds on both wrists and feet – was formed on the cloth remains the biggest mystery. Antishroudies claim it's neither the blood of Christ nor a medieval fake but, rather, the first ever attempt at photography (using a camera obscura) by Leonardo da Vinci.

Crusaders first brought the shroud to Europe. It belonged to Louis of Savoy from 1453 who folded the cloth into squares and stashed it in a silver treasure trove in Chambéry in France. The 'tie-dye'-style brown patterns visible on it today were caused by a fire in 1532 that saw a drop of hot silver fall into the casket and through the folded layers. Safeguarded in Turin since 1578, the shroud is laid out flat today in a vacuum-sealed box, which in turn is stored in a controlled atmosphere.

unravel the mystery of the Holy Shroud. Guided tours in Italian only; ask for an English-language audioguide.

Farther afield is the **Galleria Civica d'Arte Moderna e Contemporanea** *(☎ 011 562 99 11, Via Magenta 31; adult/child €5.15/2.60; open 9am-7pm Tues-Sun)*, which is dedicated to 19th- and 20th-century artists, including Renoir, Courbet, Klee and Chagall. Other great modern-art exhibitions are held in **Palazzo Bricherasio** *(☎ 011 517 16 60, Via Lagrange 20, W www.palazzobricherasio.it; adult/child €6.20/4.15; open 2.30pm-7.30pm Mon, 9.30am-7.30pm Tues, Wed & Sun, 9.30am-10.30pm Thurs, Fri & Sat)*. The art gallery in this 17th-century palace has hosted surrealist Dali and been 'wrapped' by Christo and Jeanne Claude in its time.

For modern art of a more metallic sheen, head for the **Museo dell'Automobile** *(☎ 011 67 76 66, Corso Unità d'Italia 40; adult/child €5.15/3.60; open 10am-6.30pm Tues-Sun)*. Among its 400 masterpieces is one of the first Fiats, and the Isotta Franchini driven by Gloria Swanson in the film *Sunset Boulevard*. Take bus No 34 from beside Stazione Porta Nuova.

Back in central Turin, the **Museo della Marionetta** *(☎ 011 53 02 38, Via Santa Teresa 5; adult/child €2.60/2.05; open 9am-1pm Mon-Fri, 2pm-6pm Sat)*, tucked in beside the charming **Chiesa di Santa Teresa**, contains puppets and costumes tracing the history of marionette theatre from the 17th century. Visits must be booked in advance. Shows are staged at 3pm on Sundays.

Piazzas

It is the great squares and elegant boulevards that lend Turin its air of reserved majesty. Via Roma, Turin's main shopping thoroughfare since 1615, stretches south from **Piazza Castello** to the grandiose Stazione Porta Nuova, built by Mazzucchetti in 1865.

Walking south from Piazza Castello, you will emerge onto **Piazza San Carlo**. Known as Turin's drawing room, and home to several renowned cafes, the piazza is surrounded by characteristic porticoes (central Turin has some 18km of them) and is capped at its southern end by two Baroque churches, Chiesa di San Carlo and Chiesa di Santa Cristina. Farther down Via Roma, you reach **Piazza Carlo Felice**, at once piazza and garden. Like Via Nizza, which continues south past the train station, it has seen better days.

Now the main axis of Turin's seedier side of life, Via Nizza and the surrounding area is worth exploring but is dodgy territory at night. If you do happen to be wandering around here, head east a few blocks to admire the Oriental strangeness of the 19th-century **synagogue** on Piazzetta Primo Levi.

Another extremely elegant promenade is **Piazza Solferino**, over to the north-west.

> **Money Saver**
>
> Those intent on some serious sightseeing should invest €10.85 in a Torino Card (W www.turismotorino.org). Valid for one adult and one child aged under 12, it gets you into most monuments and museums in town for free or at a reduced rate, and entitles you to free public transport. The card is valid for 48 hours and is sold at the tourist office.

Via Po & Around

The hip young scene, revolving around Turin's university, can be freely enjoyed in the cafes and trattorias along and around Via Po, which connects Piazza Castello with the river by way of Piazza Vittorio Veneto.

Turin's single most remarkable sight is the **Mole Antonelliana**, a couple of blocks north of Via Po. Intended as a synagogue when it was started in 1863, this extraordinary structure – 167m tall – comes as something of a shock when you first see it from the surrounding narrow streets. Capped by an aluminium spire, it is engineering as art form (in a similar vein to the Eiffel Tower) and quite a spectral sight when lit up at night. Inside you'll find the riveting **Museo Nazionale del Cinema** *(☎ 011 812 56 58, Via Montebello 20; adult/child €5.15/free; open 10am-8pm Sun-Fri, 10am-11pm Sat)*. The National Cinema Museum takes visitors on an interactive tour of Italian cinematic history. Its glass **Panoramic Lift** *(adult/child €3.60/2.60, combined lift & museum ticket €6.70/5.15)* silently whisks visitors up to the Mole's stunning roof terrace in 59 seconds.

Walking south-west along the River Po, you come to **Castello del Valentino** (closed to the public), a mock French-style chateau built in the 17th century. The carefully designed French-style park around it opened in 1856 and is one of the most celebrated in Italy – particularly by Rollerbladers, cyclists and smooching young romancers. A little farther south-west is a minor Disney-style medieval **castle** *(adult/child €2.60/1.55; open 9am-7pm Tues-Sun)* and village *(free)*, collectively known as Borgo Medievale. They were built for the Italian General Exhibition in 1884. Free guided tours (one hour) depart at 4pm on Sunday. Along the river banks here, you can hire bicycles and buggies, feed the ducks and stroll through the manicured green gardens with an ice cream in hand.

South-east from Piazza Vittorio Veneto, across the Po, is **Chiesa di Gran Madre di Dio** (usually closed to the public), built between 1818 and 1831 to commemorate the return of Vittorio Emanuele I from exile. Set into the hills, the church's dome is an unmistakable landmark.

Basilica di Superga

In 1706, Vittorio Amedeo II promised to build a basilica to honour the Virgin Mary if Turin was saved from besieging French and Spanish armies. The city was indeed saved, and architect Filippo Juvarra built the church on a hill across the River Po to the north-east of central Turin. It became the final resting place of the Savoys, whose lavish tombs make for interesting viewing. In 1949, a plane carrying the entire Turin football team crashed into the basilica in thick fog. Their tomb lies at the rear of the church.

To get there, take tram No 15 from Piazza Vittorio Veneto to the Sassi-Superga stop on Corso Casale, then walk 20m to Stazione Sassi, the funicular station *(toll free ☎ 800 01 91 52, Strada Communale di Superga 4)*. The line was closed at the time of writing and is not expected to reopen until 2002. Until then, take bus No 79 from the stop on Strada Communale di Superga.

If you have a vehicle, the drive up through the thickly wooded Pino Torinese helps to contradict the belief that Turin is little more than a polluted, industrial town.

La Palazzina di Caccia di Stupinigi

A visit to the Savoys' sprawling hunting lodge, in manicured grounds beyond Mirafiori, is a must. The Juvarra creation, a rococo delight, was designed for Vittorio Amedeo II in 1729. Many parts of the building are in original condition and the rest is slowly being restored with Fiat money. Pieces of art and furniture from Savoy palaces are displayed in the **Museo di Arte e Ammobiliamento Storia** *(☎ 011 358 12 20, e pstorico@mauriziano.it; adult/child €5.15/2.60; open 10am-6pm Tues-Sun)*.

Take bus No 4 from along Via San Secondo (near Stazione Porta Nuova) or along its southbound route from Piazza della Repubblica to Piazza Caio Mario, then bus No 41 to the palace (€1.25).

Castello di Rivoli

The preferred residence of the Savoy family from the 14th century onwards lies just outside central Turin in Rivoli. The 17th-century castle *(☎ 011 956 52 22; adult/child €6.20/free; open 10am-5pm Tues-Fri, 10am-7pm Sat & Sun, 10am-10pm every 1st & 3rd Sat of the month)* now houses a contemporary art gallery filled with daring installations.

Take ATM bus No 36 from Piazza Statuto to Rivoli bus station, then bus No 36n or any No 36 marked 'Castello' up the hill. Journey time is about one hour (€1.25).

Walking

Before donning hiking boots, you might want to contact the Club Alpino Italiano (☎ 011 54 60 31, e cai.torino@iol.it), Via Barbaroux 1, open 2.30pm to 6.30pm Monday to Friday.

Organised Tours

There are city tours of Turin, and buses which run to the castle at nearby Rivoli.

PIEDMONT

ATM Touristibus *(see Bus, Tram & Metro under Getting Around later)* Adult/child €6.20/5.15. 2.30pm daily. Two-hour city tours by Touristibus (which, so the brochure says, 'lead and pet you') depart from the stop on the Via Po side of Piazza Castello. Tickets are valid for the day on public transport.

Centro Guide Torino *(☎/fax 010 562 41 00, ⓔ centroguide@tiscalinet.it, Via Amedeo 8a)* Adult/child €7.75/4.15. Weekends only. These thematic city tours (historical cafes, palace of Savoy and so on) are in Italian only. Reservations can be made at the APT office on Piazza Castello.

ATM Navette Turistiche *(See Bus, Tram & Metro under Getting Around later)* Adult/child €2.60/free. Three to five times on weekends and holidays. For shuttlebus tours to/from Rivoli, buy tickets at ATM offices and tourist offices; these also get you a reduced entrance fee at the castle.

ATM also runs ***Navigazione sul Po*** *(☎ 011 88 80 10 or toll free 800 01 91 52)*, which operates boat trips on the River Po. Boats depart from Imbarco Murazzi, Via Murazzi del Po 65, and there are return trips to Borgo Medievale (€2.05), Italia 61 (€4.15) and Moncalieri (€5.15, summer only). Departures are six times per day Tuesday to Sunday (six times per day weekends only May to mid-June; three times per day Sunday and holidays only October to April).

Places to Stay – Budget

Camping & Hostels Both of these recommendations are located in the hills east of the River Po.

Villa Rey *(☎/fax 011 819 01 17, Strada Val San Martino Superiore 27)* Sites per person/tent/car €3.60/4.65/1.05. Open Mar-Oct. Take bus No 61 from Piazza Stazione Porta Nuova to the end of the line, then bus No 54 from the corner of Corso Casale and Corso Gabetti to the site.

Ostello Torino *(☎ 011 660 29 39, fax 011 660 44 45, Via Alby 1)* B&B €11.35. Turin's youth hostel can be reached by bus No 52 from Stazione Porta Nuova. Ask the driver where to get off.

Hotels Turin offers a pleasant selection of budget hotels.

Albergo Versilia *(☎ 011 65 76 78, Via Sant'Anselmo 4)* Singles/doubles €33.55/43.90. Near Stazione Porta Nuova, opposite a synagogue, Albergo Versilia is basic but not bad value.

Albergo Canelli *(☎ 011 54 70 78, 011 53 71 66, Via San Dalmazzo 5b)* Low season singles/doubles from €12.90/18.10, high season singles/doubles €20.65/28.40. Little motorised traffic passes by this quiet, ageing place, off Via Giuseppe Garibaldi on the fringe of cobbled Turin. Rooms are bare but serviceable.

Albergo Kariba *(☎ 011 53 48 56, Via San Francesco d'Assisi 4)* Singles/doubles/triples €25.80/36.15/51.65. Digs are marginally more comfortable here than at Canelli but equally kitsch.

Hotel Bologna *(☎ 011 562 02 90, fax 011 562 01 93, Corso Vittorio Emanuele II 60)* Singles/doubles €51.65/72.30. Just across from Stazione Porta Nuova, this busy two-star pad is a friendly and smiley place to stay – if you can bag a room, that is.

Albergo Sila *(☎ 011 54 40 86, Piazza Carlo Felice 80)* Singles/doubles with shower €41.30/51.65, singles/doubles with shower and toilet €49.05/62. Decent rooms are found on the 3rd floor of this porticoed building, handy for Stazione Porta Nuova.

Hotel Roma *(☎ 011 561 27 72, fax 011 562 81 37, ⓔ hotel.roma@tin.it, Piazza Carlo Felice 60)* 'Tourist' singles/doubles €41.30/59.40, 'economy' singles/doubles/triples €60.95/72/83.15, renovated singles/doubles/triples €71.80/88.85/97.60. Rates fall by 15% on Friday and Saturday night at neon-lit Roma, a solid budget to mid-range choice.

Albergo Magenta *(☎ 011 54 26 49, fax 011 54 47 55, Corso Vittorio Emanuele II 67)* Singles/doubles about €51.65/67.15. This small 2nd-floor hotel warrants few complaints.

Hotel Montevecchio *(☎ 011 562 00 23, fax 011 562 30 47, Via Montevecchio 13)* Singles/doubles about €56.80/72.30. At the top of this range, this family-run place in a quiet residential area is hard to beat.

Portofino, playground of the rich and famous

RUSSELL MOUNTFORD

Lapping it up on the Cinque Terre coast

JON DAVISON

Hanging out in Vernazza

LAUREN SUNSTEIN

Picturesque Vernazza, one of the Cinque Terre villages, is surrounded by vineyards and olive trees.

DIANA MAYFIELD

ALAN BENSON

The majestic Parco Nazionale del Gran Paradiso

DAMIEN SIMONIS

Lest we forget: war memorial, Piazza Chanoux, Aosta

PAUL PIAIA

A Turin statue sports the latest in designer shrouds.

NEIL SETCHFIELD

Facade on Piazza San Carlo, Turin

TONY WHEELER

Courmayeur's sundial: time to take to the piste?

Places to Stay – Mid-Range & Top End

Hotel Dogana Vecchia *(☎ 011 436 67 52, fax 011 436 71 94, Via Corte d'Appello 4)* Low season singles/doubles €82.65/103.30, high season singles/doubles €92.95/113.60. Mozart and Verdi were among the more distinguished guests to stay at this elegant, three-star pad. If you get lucky, it may have a few cheaper rooms without private bath.

Hotel Venezia *(☎ 011 562 33 84, fax 011 562 37 26, Via XX Settembre 70)* Low season singles/doubles €72.30/92.95, high season singles/doubles €77.45/103.30. Two white china dogs greet guests at the entrance to this chichi spot, waltzing distance from Piazza Castello.

Hotel Artuá *(☎ 011 517 53 01, fax 011 517 51 41, Via Brofferio 1)* Singles/doubles from €62/82.65. Artuá is one of two hotels at this very pleasant address, just off the grand and leafy Corso Umberto I.

Albergo Solferino *(☎ 011 561 34 44, fax 011 562 22 41, Via Brofferio 3)* Singles/doubles from €56.80/72.30. Like Artuá, Solferino occupies the 4th floor of an elegant town house, surrounded down below by plenty of street parking.

Grand Hotel Sitea *(☎ 011 517 01 71, fax 011 54 80 90, W www.thi.it, Via Carlo Alberto 35)* Singles/doubles from €170.45/227.25. This top-notch oasis of calm and sophistication is apparently where the Juventus football team is put up when in town.

Turin Palace Hotel *(☎ 011 562 55 11, fax 011 561 21 87, e palace@thi.it, Via Sacchi 8)* Singles/doubles from €149.75/175.60. Opened in 1872, this is the city's last word in late 19th-century luxury.

Places to Eat

Turin's cuisine is heavily influenced by the French, and the massive migration of southern Italians to the city brought traditions of cooking unmatched anywhere else in the north. Try risotto *alla piemontese* (with butter and cheese) or *zuppa canavesana* (turnip soup), and finish with a Savoy favourite, *panna cotta* (a kind of crème caramel). The wines are largely from the Asti region or the Barolo vineyards.

Restaurants Several budget options are guaranteed to fill the roundest of tummies.

Giolitti Lunch & Tea *(Via Giovanni Giolitti 16)* 1st/2nd courses €2.85/3.35. Munch down a two-course lunch for €5.10 at one of the cheeriest self-service restaurants in town.

Express Restaurant *(☎ 011 54 54 38, Via Barbaroux 37–39)* 1st/2nd courses €2.60/3.85. A self-service joint of the same ilk as Giolitti, Express serves a €5.95 lunchtime menu and free coffee at various times of day.

Stek Self-Service Restaurant *(☎ 011 54 21 26, Via Lagrange 43g)* 1st/2nd courses €2.60/3.35. Those with no more than €5.15 in their pocket can head here for a two-course lunch.

Brek *(Piazza Carlo Felice 22)* Brek, the Italian version of fast food, is a quick stumble from the train station. There's another on Piazza Solferino.

Osteria No 1 *(☎ 011 561 10 28, Via Garibaldi 59)* 1st/2nd courses €3.60/5.15. Consume hearty portions of home-made cooking around wooden tables at this unpretentious enoteca with brick vaulted ceiling.

There are several excellent places to dine around Piazza Carlo Emanuele II.

Il Punto Verde *(☎ 011 88 55 43, Via San Massimo 17)* One course €5.15, two courses €7.75. Dedicated vegetarians should try this cheap veggie place.

Société Lutéce *(☎ 011 88 76 44, Piazza Carlo Emanuele II 21)* A definite *ciao* rather than *arrividecci* place, this trendy bistro sports retro furnishings, a €12.90 weekend brunch and a fab pavement terrace.

Dai Saletta *(☎ 011 668 78 67, Via Belfiore 37)* Full meals about €20.65. Must-tries include truffle-filled ravioli and *brasato al Barolo* (mouth-melting-tender meat braised in Barolo wine). This traditional trattoria is a couple of blocks east of Stazione Porta Nuova.

C'era Una Volta *(☎ 011 65 54 98, Corso Vittorio Emanuele II 41)* Full meals about €23.25. Typical Piedmont cuisine is the fare here. Buzz the buzzer to shift the hefty wooden door.

Il Granaio *(☎ 011 562 10 03, Via San Francesco d'Assisi 87)* Full meals about

€10.35. Walk through the *pastifico* (pasta shop) to uncover the perfect lunchtime spot. Don't miss its melon and ham pie or Tuscan *castagnaccio* (chestnut-flour cake topped with pine kernels and rosemary).

There are some fine spots to savour traditional cuisine in the old-town streets west of Piazza Castello.

Tre Galline *(☎ 011 436 65 53, Via Bellezia 37d)* 1st/2nd courses €8.25/12.40. An old Turinese favourite, Tre Galline serves traditional Piedmont cuisine at prices a smidgen out of the budget range.

I Tre Galli *(☎ 011 521 60 27, Via Sant' Agostino 25)* Full meals about €12.90. This one is spacious, rustic and full of light. It serves food until 12.30am, although wine is the main reason why many come here.

Hafa Café *(☎ 011 436 70 91, Via Sant' Agostino 23c)* Full meals about €12.90. For a taste of Morocco, eat spicy couscous and grilled meats, slumber on floor cushions or sip mint tea (€2.05).

Fusion Café *(☎ 011 436 50 22, W www.fusioncafe.it, Via Sant'Agostino 17f)* 1st/2nd courses from €8.80/13.45. Modernity reaches new heights at this minimalist cafe-cum-restaurant-cum-bar, where the menu flashes up on a digital screen.

Il Bagatto *(☎ 011 436 88 87, Via Sant' Agostino 30a)* 1st/2nd courses from €3.10/4.15. Another late opener (until 2am Tues-Sun), this wine bar serves a €6.70 menu that includes 25cl of wine. Ochre-washed walls add a heart-warming touch.

Kirkuk Kafè *(Via Carlo Alberto 16bis)* Meals about €12.90. For a real change, have a munch at this popular place serving Kurdish, Turkish, Iraqi and Iranian food. Call to book as it's popular, cheap and tiny.

Balbo *(☎ 011 839 57 75, Via Andrea Doria 11)* 1st/2nd courses €23/31. One of Turin's most exclusive spots, best enjoyed on a credit card other than your own. Invest €67/57 in a memorable fish/Piedmontese *menù degustazione*.

Cafes Partly due to Turin's legacy of French and Austrian involvement, the city has a flourishing and chic cafe life.

Olsen *(☎ 011 436 15 73, Via Sant' Agostino 4b)* It's not a historical spot but it's the best place in town for tummy-tickling strudels, muffins, banoffee pie and cherry clafoutis. Tucked down the cobbled maze west of Piazza Castello, down-to-earth Olsen gets jam-packed.

Neuv Caval 'd Brôns *(☎ 011 562 74 83, e ross@cavalbrons.it, W www.cavalbrons.it, Piazza San Carlo 157)* This lavish place, with a vaulted trompe l'oeil ceiling, serves oodles of finger-licking cakes, pastries and imaginatively stuffed panini (from €1.80), and is a winner with hungry tourists.

Caffè San Carlo *(☎ 011 53 25 86, Piazza San Carlo 156)* Host to a gaggle of *Risorg-*

Chocolate

Feasting your way around Turin's fiesta of old-fashioned sweet shops and chocolate makers is undoubtedly the tastiest way to tour the city.

Peyrano *(☎ 011 53 87 65, Corso Vittorio Emanuele II 76; ☎ 011 660 22 02, Corso Moncalieri 47; W www.cioccolato-peyrano.it)* is Turin's most famous chocolate house. Bite into some *Dolci Momenti a Torino* (Sweet Moments in Turin) or *grappini* (chocolates filled with grappa). ***Gerla*** *(Corso Vittorio Emanuele II 88)*, with its exquisite cakes and wood-carved interior, and ***Giordano*** *(Piazza Carlo Felice 69)* are Turin's other well-known chocolate makers.

Turin's best-known confectioner, Leone, has made sweets since 1857. Favourites include fruity bonbons inscribed with the word *allegria* (meaning 'happiness') on the outer wrapper; old-fashioned 'matchboxes' filled with tiny *pastiglie* in mint, mandarin and a myriad of other flavours; and its gold-wrapped *gianduiotti*, chocolates filled with hazelnut cream first concocted in 1875.

Historic shops selling Leone bonbons, chocolates and jellied fruits packaged so beautifully they're too good to eat include ***Stratta*** *(☎ 011 54 79 20, Piazza San Carlo 191)*, founded in 1836; ***Abrate*** *(Via Po 12a)*, with its lovely 1920s shop; and ***Avvignano*** *(Piazza Carlo Felice 50)*, founded in 1883 and known for its *crema di marroni* (sweet chestnut cream) and *sorrisi di Torino* (literally, 'smiles from Turin').

imento nationalists and intellectuals in the 1840s, this sumptuous cafe, dating back to 1822, is where bankers and other suited folk network today. It offers cocktails, toasted snacks and 28 types of coffee.

Caffè Fiorio *(☎ 011 817 32 25, Via Po 8)* Another nationalist haunt favoured by Count Camillo Benso di Cavour and other pro-unification patriots, who, so legend claims, ate ice cream here. Fiorio first opened its doors in 1780.

Caffè Milassano *(☎ 011 54 79 90, Piazza Castello 15)* Milassano (built 1907–09) is an Art Nouveau gem, lined with marble floor, mirrored walls, a coffered ceiling and – yes – four tables. As in days gone by, the theatre mob from nearby Teatro Regio adore this relic.

Baratti & Milano *(☎ 011 561 30 60, Piazza Castello 27)* Elegant Baratti & Milano, with a stunning interior dating to 1858, serves coffee, cakes and a fabulous €13.45 lunchtime menu (main course, dessert, coffee and water or wine). Crowds flock here on Sunday to buy cakes, sweets and biscuits – boxed and ribbon-wrapped – from its old-fashioned shop counter.

Caffè Torino *(☎ 011 54 51 18, Piazza San Carlo 204)* This one has served coffee beneath its chandelier-lit, frescoed ceiling since 1903. Stand with the gaggle of Turinese at the bar or pay a fortune for silver service. When leaving, smear your shoe across the brass bull (embedded in the pavement) to ensure good luck.

Al Bicerin *(☎ 011 436 93 25, Piazza della Consolata 5)* Cavour, Dumas et al came here to drink this cafe's most famous beverage – *bicerin*, a hot mix of coffee, chocolate, milk and cream. The cafe dates to 1763 and has a peaceful summer terrace.

Platti *(☎ 011 506 90 56, ⓔ platti1875@tin.it, Corso Vittorio Emanuele II 72)* 1st/2nd courses average €8.25/12.90. The original Art Nouveau interior (1870) remains firmly intact at this sweet-laden coffee, cake and liquor shop. Skip thc noisy terrace and lunch inside.

Gelaterias Turin contains many an ice-cream legend.

Caffè Miretti *(☎ 011 53 36 87, Corso Giacomo Matteotti 5)* Flavours at this Turin favourite include yoghurt, peach, nougat, chestnut and minty After Eight – licked on the move or on its sunny pavement terrace.

Gatsby's *(☎ 011 562 25 45, Via Soleri 2)* Open 8am-midnight Mon-Sat. Turin's swish modern spot to go suck ice. Come dark, feast on a vanilla and strawberry ice cream doused in champagne (€7.25).

Other places include ***Pepino*** *(Piazza Carignano 8)*, which dates to 1884, and ***Gelateria Fiorio***, part of Caffè Fiorio (see Cafes earlier).

Pizzerias You'll be spoiled for choice at Turin's pizzerias.

Mamma Mia *(☎ 011 88 83 09, Corso San Maurizio 32)* Pizzas €3.60-7.25. Ask any Turinese where to eat pizza and the answer is always the same: Mamma Mia! It has 45 varieties.

Gennaro Esposito *(☎ 011 53 59 05, Via Passalacqua 1g)* Pizzas €5.70-9.30. Open until midnight Mon-Sat. This hot choice dishes up 26 pizza types.

La Focacceria *(Via Sant'Agostina 6)* Farinata costs €1.05 per slice, traditional Ligurian focaccia with one of 13 different toppings is €0.75 per slice, and there are 16 different pizza types (from €12.90).

Entertainment

On Friday, the newspaper *La Stampa* (ⓦ www.lastampa.it) runs an entertainment insert, *Torino Sette*, which lists what's on where. Its daily *Spettacoli Cronaca* includes cinema, theatre and exhibition listings, reviews and a calendar of events. Also worth picking up at the APT office is the free 80-page *News Spettacolo*, a weekly booklet listing several hundred entertainment venues, ranging from straight to gay and innocent to downright naughty (ⓦ www.newspettacolo.com).

Tickets for rock concerts are sold at the box office inside the Ricordi Media Store (☎ 011 562 11 56), Piazza CLN 251, a hip under-18 hang-out come Sunday afternoon. For other events, try Vetrina per Torina (see Tourist Offices under Information earlier).

Bars, Discos & Clubs Music, music everywhere…

La Taverna dei Guitti *(☎ 011 53 31 64, e guitti_lobit@libero.it, Via San Dalmazzo 1)* This quaint taverna hosts live jazz and cafe-theatre most Thursday and Friday evenings from 10pm.

American Stars *(☎ 011 54 89 33, Via Pietro Micca 3a)* On the old town's southern fringe, this 1970s-style American bar packs a punch with its pink cadillac bar, pinball machine, jukebox and wild cocktails.

Roar Roads *(☎ 011 812 01 71, Via Carlo Alberto 3)* This is a good central spot for trying a very un-Italian selection of beers, served on an odd wooden contraption.

Barrumba *(☎ 011 819 43 47, w www.barrumba.com, Via San Massimo 1)* This hip indie-rock club is one of the most central places to dance.

Theatró *(☎ 011 518 71 07, Via Santa Teresa 10)* A clutch of young DJs mix tunes at this artsy venue inside an old cinema.

Things hot up down by the river on Ai Murazzi (also called Lungo Po Murazzi), the arcaded riverside area stretching alongside the Po between Ponte Vittorio Emanuele I and Ponte Umberto I. Hip venues set to reopen after being washed away in the floods of late 2000 include ***Doctor Sax Music Club***, ***Pier*** *(Ai Murazzi 7–11)* and ***Alcatraz*** *(Ai Murazzi 39)*.

Across the water, several music bars are clustered along Corso Casale.

Cantine Rosso *(☎ 011 819 55 31, Corso Casale 79)* This is a rare spot where you can sip wine in a peaceful walled garden. The bar's wine-tasting evenings and other thematic events are hugely popular.

Zoo Bar *(☎ 011 819 43 47, e zoobar@barrumba.com, Corso Casale 127)* This industrial bar hosts bands, DJs and cabarets. From Piazza Vittorio Veneto, take bus No 61 to the Casaborgone stop.

Music also thrives outside the city centre.

Docks Dora *(☎ 011 28 02 51, Via Valprato 68)* The real star of Turin's music scene is set in a converted 1912 warehouse complex.

Magazzino di Gilgamesh *(☎ 011 749 28 01, Piazza Moncensio 13bis)* This big music venue is west of Stazione Porta Susa, with several more places strung the length of Corso Francia.

Hiroshima Mon Amour *(☎ 011 317 54 27, w www.hiroshimamonamour.org, Via Bossoli 83)* The other big name in the dance and music circuit, HMA plays everything from folk and punk to tango and techno.

Palazium *(☎ 011 521 73 40, e palazium@jumpy.it, Via Porto Palatina 23)* Head here for Saturday night hip-hop, reggae, soul and garage.

Cinemas Near the Mole Antonelliana, ***Cinema Massimo*** *(☎ 011 812 56 58, Via Montebello 8)* offers an eclectic mix of films, mainly in English or with subtitles. One of its three screens is run by the Museo Nazionale del Cinema (see Via Po & Around earlier) and only screens classic films.

Theatre, Opera & Ballet These two adjoining theatres are on Piazza Castello.

Teatro Regio Torino *(☎ 011 881 52 41, w www.teatroregio.torino.it, Piazza Castello 215)* Opera season tickets (€12.40–38.75) are sold at the box office.

Teatro Piccolo Regio *(☎ 011 881 52 46, Piazza Castello 215)* It is sometimes possible to watch sold-out performances for free live on TV in this small theatre, where Puccini premiered *La Bohème* in 1896.

Shopping

Every morning until about noon, Piazza della Repubblica, north of the city centre, is filled with the cries and smells of the main food and clothes market. On Saturday, the area north of the same square becomes an antique collector's heaven known as Il Balôn. On the second Sunday of every month it goes one better and becomes Il Gran Balôn, with antique dealers from far and wide. You can buy anything from fine furniture to used old-style petrol pumps.

Porticoed Via Roma is *the* street to shop for designer labels. Many more chic boutiques stud parallel Via Lagrange, home to the city's department store ***La Rinascente*** at No 15. Those into made-to-measure priestwear can try ***Mario Bianchetti*** *(Piazza*

Savoia 0g) for size; it has created cassocks and white-collared shirts since 1916.

Mountain equipment, magic razors, monoculars and gear for thrill- and spill-seekers is sold at ***Coronel Tapiocca*** *(Via Garibaldi,* W *www.coroneltapiocca.com).*

Piedmontese fare (honey, meats, wine) to take home can be sampled and purchased at ***Montagna Viva*** *(☎ 011 521 78 22, Piazza Emanuele Filiberto 3a)*, a tasty shop run by the regional consortium for typical agricultural products.

Via Mercanti is a lovely little cobbled street dotted with craft shops and artisan workshops. ***Legatoria Rocchietti*** *(☎ 011 54 42 66, Via Mercanti 9a)*, in a 15th- to 16th-century house, binds and restores antique books. It also makes albums of hand-crafted paper.

Getting There & Away

Air Turin is served by Caselle international airport (☎ 011 567 63 61 or 011 300 06 11, W www.turin-airport.com), 16km north-west of the city centre, with connections to European and national destinations.

You can also get to Turin from Milan's Malpensa airport.

Bus Most international, national and regional buses terminate at the spanking new bus terminal (☎ 011 433 25 25), next to the Esso garage at the northern end of Corso Castelfidardo. Tickets for Eurolines buses are only sold from 9am to 12.30pm and 3pm to 7pm Monday to Friday and 9am to 12.30 pm Saturday.

You can also get to Milan's Malpensa airport from here.

Train The main train station is Stazione Porta Nuova, Piazza Carlo Felice. Regular trains connect Turin with Milan, Aosta, Venice, Genoa and Rome. Most stop at Stazione Porta Susa as well.

Car & Motorcycle Turin is a major autostrada junction. The A4 connects with Milan, the A5 with Aosta, the A6 with Savona and the Ligurian Coast, and the A21 with Piacenza. If you're heading for Genoa, take the A21 and then the A7 rather than the expensive and sometimes dangerous A6. For hitchhikers, the S10 heads for Asti, the S24 for Susa and the S11 east for Milan.

Getting Around

To/From the Airport Sadem (☎ 011 300 01 66, e sadembus@tin.it) runs buses to the airport from Stazione Porta Nuova (40 minutes), stopping also at Stazione Porta Susa (30 minutes). Buses depart every 30 minutes between 5.15am and 10.30pm (6.30am and 11.30pm from the airport). Single tickets cost €4.15 (free for those less than 1m tall) and are sold at Porta Nuova in the unnamed bar-gelateria at Corso Vittorio Emanuele II 55; buses use the stop on the corner of Corso Vittorio Emanuele II and Via Sacchi.

Buses for Milan's Malpensa airport leave from the bus terminal on Corso Inghilterra.

Bus, Tram & Metro The city boasts a dense network of buses, trams and a funicular run by ATM (toll free ☎ 800 01 91 52, W www.comune.torino.it/atm), which has an information office at Stazione Porta Nuova. Buses and trams run 6am to midnight and tickets cost €0.75 (€2.60 for a day pass). By 2005, Turin will be graced with a metro; one line will link Porta Nuova with Lingotto.

Car & Motorcycle Motoring information, road maps and guides are provided by the Automobile Club Torino (ACT; ☎ 011 5 77 91), Via San Francesco da Paola 20a. Major rental agencies have offices at Stazione Porta Nuova and Caselle airport.

Taxi Call ☎ 011 57 37 or 011 57 30 or 011 33 99 for a cab.

Bicycle Hire a bicycle from the left-luggage desk (signposted 'deposito bagagli'), opposite the tracks at Stazione Porta Nuova. Rental costs €2.60/3.60/6.20 for six/12/24 hours and is available 6am to midnight daily.

VALLE DI SUSA

West of Turin and easily accessible by car, bus and train, the Valle di Susa takes in the old Celtic town of Susa and several ski resorts, including the glamorous but overdeveloped Sestriere. There are some beautiful spots in the valley and a few pleasant mountain villages, all of which heave during the ski season and at weekends when Turin's weekend escapees flee the city.

Sacra di San Michele

Perched on top of Monte Pirchiriano high above the road from Turin, this brooding Gothic-Romanesque abbey *(☎ 011 93 91 30; admission €2.60; open 9.30am-11.30am & 3pm-5pm Tues-Sun)* dates back to the 11th century.

The closest town is Avigliana, a 26km train ride from Turin, connected to the abbey by bus (there are about three daily). An alternative is to continue by train to Sant'Ambrogio, at the foot of the hill, and tackle the steep 90-minute walk. Check opening times with the APT office in Turin or the IAT office in Avigliana (☎/fax 011 932 86 50), Piazza del Popolo 6, before setting out.

Susa & Oulx

On the busiest route between Turin and France, Susa (pop 1475, elevation 205m) started life as a Celtic town (a Druid well remains as testimony) before falling under the sway of the Roman Empire. The modest Roman ruins make it a pleasant stop on the way to the western ski resorts. In addition to the remains of a Roman **aqueduct**, a still-used **amphitheatre** and the **Arco d'Augusto**, the town's early 11th-century **cathedral** is a rare medieval survivor in Piedmont.

Worth a brief look is the forbidding **Forte di Exilles** *(☎ 0122 5 82 70; admission €5.15; open 10.30am-6.30pm Tues-Sun May-Sept)*, overlooking the quiet village of Exilles, 15km west of Susa. Its military role only ended in 1943. Opening hours do vary so check with the tourist office before making a special trip.

Nothing much in itself, Oulx, 21km farther west, is a good place to get information on skiing, walking and other activities throughout the Valle di Susa. Its tourist office (☎ 0122 83 15 96), Piazza Garambois 5, is the main one for the valley and can help with lodgings, Settimana Bianca (White Week Skiing) packages and walking details. Regular trains run from Turin, and Sapar buses connect with destinations along the Susa and Chisone valleys.

Sestriere

postcode 10058 • pop 900
elevation 2033m

Conceived by Mussolini and built by the Agnelli clan (of Fiat fame), Sestriere is a cultural desert that has grown to become one of Europe's most fashionable ski resorts. The mountains here are pleasant indeed and there are several villages (such as Cesana Torinese) on either side of Sestriere that could make more appealing bases, unless of course you feel a need to be seen here in your apres-ski garb.

The IAT office (☎ 0122 75 54 44), Via Pinerolo 14, has information on skiing and accommodation. Summer activities include walking, free-climbing and mountain-bike riding. Out of season, only a couple of three-star hotels remain open.

Buses connect the resort with Oulx, Susa and Turin.

SOUTHERN PIEDMONT

The roads south of Turin to Liguria mark the divide between the low hills and dull plains of most of eastern Piedmont from the slopes that rise in the west to the southern French Alps. It is an area little frequented by foreign tourists, and where numerous valleys slice paths west towards France (although only a few offer access across the border). Not as high as the mountains of the north, the area still provides good walking opportunities and skiing in winter.

Cuneo

postcode 12100 • pop 54,700
elevation 543m

Cuneo is a mildly interesting provincial capital and a transport junction between Turin and Liguria. The old town lies in the northern wedge of the city, presenting a pleasant if faded picture, although there is not too much to delay the sightseer. Cuneo is useful as a base for exploring the southern valleys of Piedmont, especially for those without their own transport. If you have wheels, a better alternative is Saluzzo (see that section later), 33km to the north.

The bus station is located at the northern tip of the old town, which peters out at the vast central square, Piazza di Duccio Galimberti. The train station lies to the south-west on Piazzale Libertà.

The IAT tourist office (☎ 0171 69 32 58, W www.cuneotourism.com), Corso Nizza 17, has extensive information about the province.

Piazza di Duccio Galimberti and Corso Nizza are the best places to look for cafes.

Albergo Cavallo Nero *(☎ 0171 69 20 17, fax 0171 63 08 78, Piazza Seminario 8)* is one of several reasonably priced places to stay.

Getting There & Away Cuneo's big plus is transport. There are regular trains to Saluzzo, Turin, San Remo, Ventimiglia and Nice in France. There is a second train station for the Cuneo-Gesso line, serving small towns in that valley to the south-west.

Various bus companies run services to Saluzzo, Turin, Imperia, Savona and along the Valle Stura.

By car, take the A6 from Turin towards Savona and exit at Fossano, or follow the S20.

Around Cuneo

Among the valleys that radiate westwards from Cuneo, the **Valle Stura** (the longest) leads to the Colle della Maddalena, crossing into France. The surrounding mountains offer skiing when snowfalls are good, and there are several rifugi for walkers. The same can be said of the bare rock mountain slopes that feature along the **Valle Gesso**.

Another attractive option is the **Valle Maira**, which starts to the north-west of Cuneo. **Dronero**, a pretty medieval village with houses topped by precarious-looking grey slate roofs, marks the start of the climb upwards and westwards.

Saluzzo

postcode 12037 • pop 15,720
elevation 395m

About 60km south of Turin, Saluzzo deserves a day trip and is a good base for closer exploration of the valleys and castles of southern Piedmont. Once a feisty medieval stronghold, the town maintained its independence until the Savoys won it in a 1601 treaty with France. One of Saluzzo's better-known sons was General Carlo dalla Chiesa, whose implacable pursuit of the Mafia led to his assassination in 1982. Saturday and Wednesday mornings see Piazza Risorgimento and the surrounding streets filled with a huge outdoor market.

The friendly IAT tourist office (☎ 0175 4 67 10, fax 0175 4 67 18, e iat@comune.saluzzo.it), Via Torino 51a, opens 9am to 12.30pm and 3pm to 6.30pm Tuesday to Sunday. Banks line Corso Italia.

Things to See Cobbled lanes twist upwards to **La Castiglia**, the sombre castle (used as a prison for a time last century) of the Marchesi, Saluzzo's medieval rulers. Rickety old Salita al Castello is lined with medieval houses.

Commanding stunning views over the old town's burnt-red tiled rooftops is the **Torre Civica** *(☎ 0175 4 14 55, Via San Giovanni; admission €1.30; open 9am-12.15pm & 3pm-6.15pm Wed-Sat, 9am-12.15pm & 3pm-6.45pm Sun)*, a restored 15th-century tower that was part of the old *municipio* (town administration).

Pass the contemporary church and convent of San Giovanni on the same square and you reach the **Museo Civico di Casa Cavassa** *(☎ 0175 4 14 55, Via San Giovanni 5; adult/child €2.60/1.30; open 9am-12.15pm & 2pm-5.15pm Wed-Sat & 9am-12.15pm & 2pm-5.45pm Sun Oct-Mar; 9am-12.15pm & 3pm-6.15pm Wed-Sat & 9am-12.15pm & 3pm-6.45pm Sun Apr-Sept)*. This is a fine example of a 16th-century noble's residence. A combined admission ticket covering the museum and tower is €3.10.

Places to Stay & Eat Unwind after a hard day's castle-spotting with grub, beer and bed.

Albergo Persico *(☎ 0175 4 12 13, Vicolo Mercati 10)* Singles/doubles/triples €36.15/51.65/62. This one is tucked down an alleyway and offers mediocre accommodation.

Trattoria Përpôin *(☎ 0175 4 23 83, fax 0175 4 28 00, Via Spielberg 19–27)* Singles/doubles €36.15/67.15. Menus €11.35-20.65. Enjoy hearty homecooking at shared tables in this cheap and cheerful eating and sleeping option.

Osteria dei Mondagli *(☎ 0175 4 63 06, Piazza Mondagli 1a)* Full meals around €25.80. Heading up into the old town, on the tiny piazza of the same name (at the base of Via Muletti), Osteria dei Mondagli is a good bet. Eat outside in summer.

Taverna dell'Artista *(☎ 0175 4 20 31, Via Gualtieri 8)* 1st/2nd courses €4.15/5.15, pizzas €2.60-5.70. Sink your teeth into a plate of *gnocchi al castelmango* (potato dumplings baked in a nutty blue cheese unique to Piedmont).

Bistrot Pub La Drancia *(☎ 0175 4 33 94, Via San Chiara 19)* Reward yourself with a pint of local brew at the top of steep Salita al Castello.

Mushroom Magic

When autumn comes to Piedmont, it's time to *andare a funghi* – go mushroom-picking. Mushrooms, especially the popular *porcini* (boletus) and the harder to find *tartufo* (truffle), also known as *Tuber magnatum*, are considered something of a delicacy.

So prized are mushrooms that the town of Alba celebrates the Fiera del Tartufo (Truffle Fair) for a couple of weeks in mid-October. This is a delightful occasion for the palate, when Alba's best wines and rival vintages from Asti and the Langhe are brought out to accompany mouthwatering mushroom and truffle recipes dating from the 17th century. The markets overflow with great slabs of porcini, known to get as big as 2kg.

Porcini and other specimens sprout in the dark oak and chestnut-forest floors on sunny days immediately following a good burst of rain. Truffles, on the other hand, incubate for several months, and those who know where to look often take specially trained truffle-sniffing dogs. If you head off mushroom-picking yourself, let someone in the know examine them before you gobble them up – many species are poisonous.

Getting There & Away There are hourly bus connections from Turin (from the intersection of Via Nizza and Corso Marconi) to Saluzzo (☎ 0175 4 37 44 for information). Journey time is 1½ hours. Otherwise, trains link the town with Cuneo and Savigliano, from where there are connections for Turin.

By car, Saluzzo is an easy drive via the A6 (get off at the Bra exit) or S20.

Around Saluzzo

A few minutes' drive south of Saluzzo is one of the more easily reached castles in the area, **Castello di Manta** *(☎ 0175 8 78 22, Mantua; adult/child €4.15/2.05; open 10am-1pm & 2pm-5pm daily Oct-Dec, 10am-1pm & 2pm-6pm daily Feb-Sept)*. Free guided tours depart at 3pm on Sunday. Enquire at the Saluzzo tourist office for more information.

The River Po doglegs north a few kilometres west of Saluzzo, and the valley leading westwards to its source, below **Monviso** (3841m), is an enticing excursion. Should you want to walk around the mountain, there are rifugi as well as a few hotels in the nearby town of **Crissolo**. Take your passport in case you want to cross into France.

Alba

postcode 12051 • pop 29,800
elevation 172m

Solid red-brick towers rise above the heart of Alba, a wine town that has kept enough of its medieval past to make it a worthwhile stop. During WWII, citizens proclaimed an independent republic for 23 days after partisans liberated it from the Germans.

Alba was first settled in Neolithic times, but it has a couple of modern claims to fame. Its white truffle crop is celebrated in mid-October with a truffle fair and it is famous for a contest on donkeys. The latter was inaugurated in 1932 as a snub to nearby Asti, its eternal rival in all things, including wine production. Some of Italy's best reds come from the hills of the Langhe around Alba; Barbaresco, Barolo and La Morra – named after the surrounding pin-

Lovely Lumache

Lumache (snails) are an integral part of Langhe cuisine. And nowhere more so than in snail-paced Cherasco (pop 7000, elevation 288m), a village 23km west of Alba, which claims to be Italy's snail capital.

Snails are not actually born and bred in the medieval village – the climate is chilly compared to Italy's hot south, meaning eggs take an age to incubate – rather, the country's molluscs are marketed and sold here. Although the number of snails eaten in Italy has increased four-fold since 1980 (to 130,000 quintals in 1997), only 34% are reared by Italy's 5500 snail breeders – the rest are imported.

Contrary to what the French do, the lumache in this neck of the woods are never served as a starter or, for that matter, curled up in their shells. Rather, the ugly little molluscs are dished up *nudo* (nude). They can be pan-fried, roasted on a spit, dressed in an artichoke sauce or minced inside ravioli. Dishes typical to Piedmont include *lumache al barbera* (snails simmered in Barbera red wine and ground nuts), *lumache alla piemontese* (stewed with onions, nuts, anchovies and parsley in a tomato sauce) and *lumache di bobbio* (fried with leeks then bubbled in wine and herbs).

Cherasco touts two splendid, snail-driven trattorias. In a cellar on the corner of Via San Pietro and Via Cavour, ***La Lumaca*** *(☎ 0172 48 94 21)* dishes up a €25.80 menu comprising three antipasti, a starter, choice of first and second courses (both with snail options), cheese, dessert and coffee. It offers a choice of 700 regional wines and opens Wednesday to Sunday. Nearby ***Osteria della Rosa Rossa*** *(☎ 0172 48 81 33, Via San Pietro 31)* has first/second courses from €4.65/6.20 and a range of snail dishes averaging €6.20. It opens Friday to Tuesday. Advance reservations are essential at both.

Cherasco tourist office (☎/fax 0172 48 93 82 or 0172 48 91 01, W www.cherasco2000.com) is at Via Vittorio Emanuele 79. Everything you ever wanted to know about *elicicoltura* (heliciculture, or 'snail breeding') can be discovered at the Istituto Internazionale di Elicicoltura (☎ 0172 48 93 82, W www.lumache-elici.com), Via Vittorio Emanuele 32. The village celebrates an international snail fair each year in mid-September.

prick villages that produce them – are big names to look for.

The Langhe is equally famous for its hazelnuts, which end up in Gianduiotti chocolates and, more recently, in the chocolate spread Nutella (see the 'Chocolate' boxed text in the Turin section earlier).

Orientation & Information The tumbledown Piazza del Risorgimento, dominated by the 15th-century Cattedrale di San Lorenzo, leads onto Via Vittorio Emanuele II, Alba's main street and a busy pedestrian zone. It, in turn, is capped by the ample Piazza Savona, where chic cafes line porticoed footpaths.

The tourist office (☎ 0173 3 58 33, W www.langheroero.it), Piazza Medford 3, can suggest wineries to seek out in the region and can sometimes offer advice on which of the many privately owned castles and medieval manors in the surrounding Langhe and Roero regions welcome visitors.

Places to Stay & Eat Piazza Savona and Via Vittorio Emanuele II are lined with various cafes and trattorias.

Leon d'Oro *(☎ 0173 44 19 01, Piazza Marconi 2)* Singles/doubles from €41.30/51.65. This is the cheapest place in town.

Getting There & Away Alba is accessible by bus from Turin, Cuneo and Asti (30km to the north-east).

Cinzano

Approximately 80% of Cinzano, one of Italy's best-known drinks, is concocted and bottled in the monstrous distilling plant of United Distillers & Vintners (UDV), 10km west of Alba in Cinzano at the hilltop Santa Vittoria d'Alba area on the busy S231.

Hidden among the company's distillery and warehouses is **Villa Cinzano** and its vast **cellars** *(☎ 0172 47 71 11; pre-arranged museum/cellar tours only, minimum 20 people)*. This former hunting lodge of Carlo Alberto now displays 143 precious glasses, photographs and other artefacts chronicling the history of a company that started as a small distilling operation in Turin's hills in 1757. Sweet-talking individuals can sometimes join tour groups.

The Cinzano family got involved in the vermouth-making business on an industrial scale in the mid-19th century, but it only really took off when the company's representatives started travelling the globe early in the 20th century. Publicity has been the key to worldwide success and, long before you reach Cinzano, you can't fail to notice the name on billboards all over the surrounding countryside.

Barolo

Robust, velvety, truffle-scented with orange reflections and 'wine of kings and king of wine' are some of the compliments piled onto this extraordinary red wine, produced around Barolo, 20km south-west of Alba. The village celebrates wine fairs in mid-September and October, and you can taste and buy wine in its **Enoteca Regionale** (☎ 0173 5 62 77) inside the village castle or in the **Cantina Comunale** (☎ 0173 50 92 04), Via Carlo Alberto 2, in neighbouring La Morra, about 5km north.

No, you aren't that drunk. **Capella Sol LeWitt-David Tremlett** *(☎ 0173 28 25 82)*, a chapel on top of a vine-covered hill between Barolo and La Morra, really is painted all the colours of a rainbow. Built by a farmer in 1914, the ruined church (never consecrated) was restored and painted with symmetrical patterns in red, blue, green, yellow and orange by English and American artists in 1999. Milanese couturier Missoni designed a priest's cassock to match. The chapel is 1.6km south-east of La Morra along a dust track, signposted off Via Roma at the southern end of the village. It can be accessed from Barolo too. You need your own wheels to get here.

EASTERN PIEDMONT

Asti

postcode 14100 • pop 73,300
elevation 123m

Asti has had a rocky history. Its original settlers became part of a Roman colony in 89 BC. Then, after existing as an independent city state in the 13th and 14th centuries, it was passed around between Spain, Austria, Napoleon's France and finally the Savoys, prior to unification. During the late 13th century, the region became one of Italy's wealthiest and some 100 towers of the period stand as reminders of its glorious past. Since the 1850s, the grapes grown on the largely flat plains around it have produced Italy's top sparkling wine – Asti (better known, incorrectly since 1993, as Asti Spumante).

Information The tourist office (☎ 0141 53 03 57, ⓔ atl@axt.it), Piazza Alfieri 29, can assist with itineraries for the wine areas (see Wine Tasting later).

Wine Tasting Asti's sweet white wine is best drunk young and at a chilled 6–8°C, like its less fizzy cousin Moscato d'Asti. In town there are numerous places to sample it.

Tacaband *(☎ 0141 53 09 99, ⓔ osteria.tacaband@tin.it, Via al Teatro Alfieri 5)*, next to the theatre off pedestrian Corso Alfieri, is a wine cellar where you can shop

Martini & Rossi

Martini (an alcohol salesman) and Rossi (a distillery supplier) were two men from Turin who teamed up in the 1850s to create a wine and liqueur distillery of their own in 1879. What happened after that can be discovered at the **Museo Martini di Storia dell'Enologia** *(☎ 011 941 92 17, Piazzale Luigi Rossi 1; free; open 4pm-5pm Tues-Fri, 9am-noon & 2pm-5pm Sat & Sun)*, about 20km south-east of Turin in Pessione. The museum is housed in the cellars of an 18th-century villa. One of Martini's largest production plants is also here but guided tours and tasting sessions have to be arranged in advance.

and taste (its €10.35 *antipasti in degustazione* is superb).

Out of town, 9120 hectares of Asti vineyards are tended by 6800 wine growers, meaning ample tasting opportunities. The ***Consorzio per La Tutela dell'Asti*** *(Consortium for the Promotion of Asti;* ☎ *0141 59 42 15,* e *consorzio@astidocg.it, Piazza Roma 10)* has lists of wineries you can visit (by appointment only).

Special Events September brings a flurry of wine festivals to Asti, notably the 10-day Douja d'Or (a *douja* being a terracotta wine jug unique to Asti), followed by the Delle Sagre food festival on the 2nd Sunday of the month and a medieval Palio on the 3rd, which sees 21 madcap jockeys race their horses around central Piazza Alfieri. In November, the square hosts several truffle fairs.

Getting There & Away Asti is on the Turin-Alessandria-Genoa railway line and is served by regular trains (hourly) in both directions. Journey time to/from Turin is 55 minutes (1¾ hours to/from Genoa).

The A21 – dubbed the 'Autostrada dei Vini' (wine motorway) – links Turin with Asti (60km). It is also an easy drive from Genoa on good roads, starting with the S35.

NORTHERN PIEDMONT

Head north-east from Turin towards Milan and you'll pass through wide plains that largely typify eastern Piedmont – some of it is so flat and wet that it's good for growing rice, as is evident on the approach to Vercelli. Turn left here and aim north; the landscape quickly changes as the lower slopes preceding the Swiss Alps come into view. Skiing, walking and white-water rafting are among the treats on offer among the valleys that spread west and north. To the east, you can strike out for Lago d'Orta and Lago Maggiore, the first two in a string of lakes across northern Italy.

Varallo

postcode 13019 • pop 7500
elevation 451m

Varallo marks the beginning of the Valsesia, one of the less crowded Piedmontese valleys.

Battle of the Oranges

The mildly charming plains town of Ivrea, 55km north-east of Turin, explodes out of its year round torpor in early February to celebrate the Battaglia delle Arance (Battle of the Oranges).

The story goes that, back in medieval times, a miller chose another miller's pretty young daughter for his wife. But the nasty tyrant who ruled at the time, like many feudal overlords, reserved for himself the right to the first round with any local woman who was about to be married. A feisty individual, the miller's daughter was so upset by this that she sparked a revolt by the impoverished townspeople. On foot and armed only with stones, they launched themselves against the tyrant's troops, pelting them as they rode around the town in horse-drawn carts. This desperate uprising went down in the town's folk history and centuries later provided an excuse for rival gangs from different parts of town to stage an annual riot around Carnevale.

When Napoleon occupied this part of Italy at the beginning of the 19th century, his administrators ordered everyone to wear red revolutionary bonnets. They also put a stop to the fatal nature of the brawling, ordering that from then on the re-enactment of the famous uprising was to be carried out with oranges.

And so today, for three consecutive days, teams of 'revolutionaries' wait at four different piazzas for roaming carts laden with helmeted 'soldiers' – and they pound each other with tonnes of oranges imported from Sicily for the occasion. In the midst of the mayhem, a costume procession featuring the miller's daughter, medieval characters and Napoleonic troops slips and slides its way along a slimy carpet of squashed orange (well-mixed with horse manure). *Anyone* on the ground caught not wearing some kind of red headgear is considered fair game for a massive orange assault by the 'rebel' squads.

Ivrea is an easy day trip from Turin, accessible by regular trains and occasional buses. The centre of town, where all the fun takes place, is a few minutes' walk from the train station.

The tourist office (☎ 0163 5 12 80), Corso Roma 38, has plenty of pamphlets on every conceivable aspect of the area.

Varallo is a sensible starting point if only because it's a railhead and bus line junction. A narrow winding road also links the valley directly with the pretty **Lago d'Orta** (see the Lombardy & the Lakes chapter for details).

The Valsesia to Monte Rosa From Varallo, you can follow the valley up towards Monte Rosa and the Swiss frontier, where some peaks exceed 4000m. **Alagna Valsesia** is the last town along the valley; you can get detailed local skiing information there from Monterosa Ski. Some 20 rifugi dot the area, the Capanna Osservatorio Regina Margherita at Punta Gnifetti (4559m) being the highest. A cable car at Alagna Valsesia climbs to Punta Indren (3260m). From here it's possible (in summer at least) to walk to many of the various peaks.

Get expert local advice on what can be safely undertaken before setting out, as some of the trails require expert alpine skills and gear. Some of the toughest skiing in Europe is possible here – you could find yourself abseiling into *couloirs* (canyons) to make it down from the Monte Rosa peak. Off-piste challenges abound. Some 25 Alpine guides are on the books at Alagna – inquire at the IAT tourist office (☎ 0163 92 29 88), Piazza Grober.

Domodossola

postcode 28845 • pop 18,650
elevation 277m

The last main stop before Switzerland, Domodossola may once have been an attractive pre-Alpine town, but suburban sprawl and hotels have ruined the effect. Those intending to explore the surrounding valleys should make haste to do so and leave this place behind them.

The IAT office (☎/fax 0324 24 82 65, ⓔ ufficioiat@libero.it), on Piazza Stazione, stocks detailed information on walking, skiing and accommodation possibilities. It opens 8.30am to noon and 2.30pm to 6.30pm Monday to Saturday.

***Eurossola** (☎ 0324 48 13 26, fax 0324 24 87 48, Piazza Stazione 36)* Singles/doubles €46.50/67.15. It might be opposite the train station, but it's also opposite a small green park.

Getting There & Away Trains regularly run to Milan and Novara (for Turin). You can also board international trains to Switzerland (including the charming run to Locarno) – a trip well worth doing. You can see France, Germany and even the Czech Republic from here (see Stresa under the Lakes section of the Lombardy & the Lakes chapter).

The bus station is in front of the train station. Milan is 125km to the south-east and Turin is 168km to the south-west of Domodossola.

Valle d'Aosta

Covering a mere 3262 sq km and with a population of only 116,000, the Valle d'Aosta is the smallest Italian region but one of the wealthiest. It enjoys self-governing status meaning that 90% of local taxes are spent in the province.

Human settlement in the Valle d'Aosta dates back to 3000 BC and Neolithic and early Bronze Age remains have been discovered. Early Roman sites dot the valley and Aosta is known as the Rome of the Alps. The area's fate was often tied to that of neighbouring French regions. For a century, the Valle d'Aosta was part of the kingdom of Bourgogne, and was later made a part of Republican France, and then of Napoleon's Imperial France. Under Mussolini's regime, massive immigration from other parts of Italy was encouraged in an attempt to bury the region's separate identity.

The Valdostans, as the inhabitants are called, speak a Franco-Provençal patois, and French is afforded equal rights with Italian. Italian was in fact introduced into the region only after it was incorporated into the newly united Italian state in 1861. To the east of the region, the Walser villagers cling to their German dialect, Tich. The valley has always

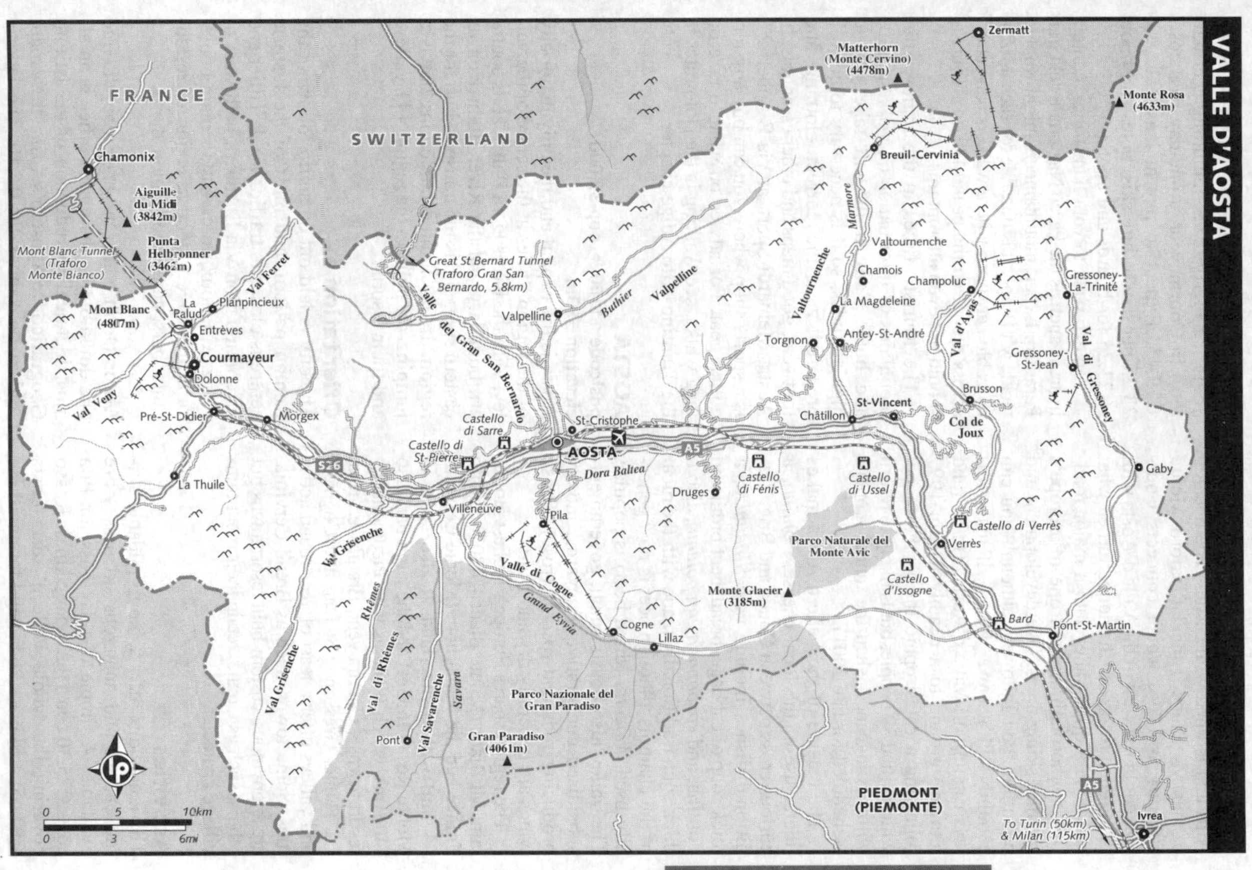

VALLE D'AOSTA

been an important passageway through the Alps and is lined with castles. The opening of the Mt Blanc Tunnel (Traforo Monte Bianco) in 1965, which connects Courmayeur in the west of the Valle d'Aosta with the French resort of Chamonix, turned what had been a quiet valley into a major road-freight thoroughfare and one of Europe's premier skiing areas. Overdevelopment and pollution soon followed, although you can certainly still 'get away from it all' in the valleys running off Valle d'Aosta. Traffic (and tourism) ground to a deathly halt in 1997 following a catastrophic fire in the tunnel which killed 39 people, but is likely to return with a vengeance when the tunnel reopens (scheduled for late 2001).

The cuisine of the Valle d'Aosta makes liberal use of the local cheese, *Fontina*, a curious cross between Gouda and Brie. Traditional dishes include *valpellineuntze*, a thick soup of cabbage, bread, beef broth and Fontina, and *carbonada con polenta*, also a thick soup traditionally made with the meat of the chamois although beef is now generally used. *Mocetta* (dried beef) is popular. The valley also boasts small, government-subsidised cooperative vineyards, mostly producing reds and *rosatos* (rosé). These wines are generally dry and fruity.

The region shares Europe's highest mountain, Mt Blanc (Monte Bianco; 4807m), with France and the Matterhorn (Monte Cervino; 4478m) with Switzerland. It also takes in Monte Rosa (4633m) and the Gran Paradiso (4061m), which it shares with Piedmont. Its resort towns – Courmayeur, Breuil-Cervinia, La Thuile, Gressoney-St-Jean and Cogne – and valleys offer a feast of year-round activities. Some towns, such as Breuil-Cervinia, are anonymous, custom-built resort towns but others, such as Cogne, retain their mountain-village character.

Activities

The mountains offer some formidable skiing options and numerous ski passes are available. A simple one-day pass for Pila costs €25.30 and a three-day Skipass Rosso covering the whole Valle d'Aosta costs €82.65. A Skipass Pool, valid for one/three days in Breuil-Cervinia, costs €28.40/76.45 (€34.10/92.95 including Zermatt too). In Courmayeur, a one-day pass costs €29.45. Expect to pay at least €12.90/23.25 per day to hire skis, poles and boots (€23.25 for boards and boots).

You can walk to your hamstrings' content in areas such as the Parco Nazionale del Gran Paradiso. Expert mountaineers might want to tackle Mt Blanc. It is possible to reach 3462m by cable car, from where walkers can set off across the ice to the peak (4807m). Tourists should not even attempt this.

The tourist offices in the region offer mountains of information on walking trails and huts. Many trails will take you to high altitudes, so it is necessary to be well prepared with the correct clothing and footwear, good maps and other essentials. In Aosta, Meinardi Sport, at Via E Aubert 27, is a sports shop where you can buy any forgotten gear. For advice on what to take on long walks, see Walking in the Dolomites in the Trentino-Alto Adige chapter.

AOSTA

postcode 11100 • pop 39,000
elevation 583m

Aosta is the capital and the only major city of the region. It lies at the centre of the valley, with the River Dora Baltea at its southern boundary and the River Buthier on its eastern side, and is the transport hub for the region. It has limited attractions but is a jumping-off point to the region's 11 valleys and their resorts.

Orientation

The city is laid out on a grid following the Roman pattern, and most of the historic centre is closed to traffic. Via de Tillier and its continuation Via E Aubert, both west of Piazza Chanoux, form Aosta's main boulevard and have a good selection of restaurants, bars, cafes and fashion shops.

Maps Don't bother buying a map; the free one doled out by the tourist office is an almost identical reproduction of the Istituto Geografico De Agostini's *Aosta/Aoste* map, sold in bookshops for €5.10. The latter's regional map, entitled *Valle d'Aosta/Vallée d'Aoste* (1:100,000; €5.10), is worth picking up if you venture farther afield.

Walkers shouldn't set so much as a little toe out of Aosta without buying the relevant walking maps published by the Istituto Geografico Centrale (1:25,000; €6.70). Bookshops sell them.

Information

Tourist Offices The APT office (☎ 0165 23 66 27, fax 0165 3 46 57, Ⓦ www.regione.vda.it/turismo), Piazza Chanoux 8, provides information on the entire region and stocks comprehensive lists of rifugi, hotels and camp sites. It opens 9am to 1pm and 3pm to 8pm daily June to September, 9am to 1pm and 3pm to 8pm Monday to Saturday and 9am to 1pm Sunday the rest of the year.

The Valle d'Aosta APT has an office in Rome (☎ 06 474 41 04, fax 06 482 38 37, Ⓔ vda_vit_roma@tin.it), Via Sistina 9, and the regional government is online at Ⓦ www.aostavalley.com.

The Unione Valdostana Guide Alta Montagna, also known as Cooperativa Interguide, runs a mountain guide and rescue service for the entire valley. It has stations in most resorts

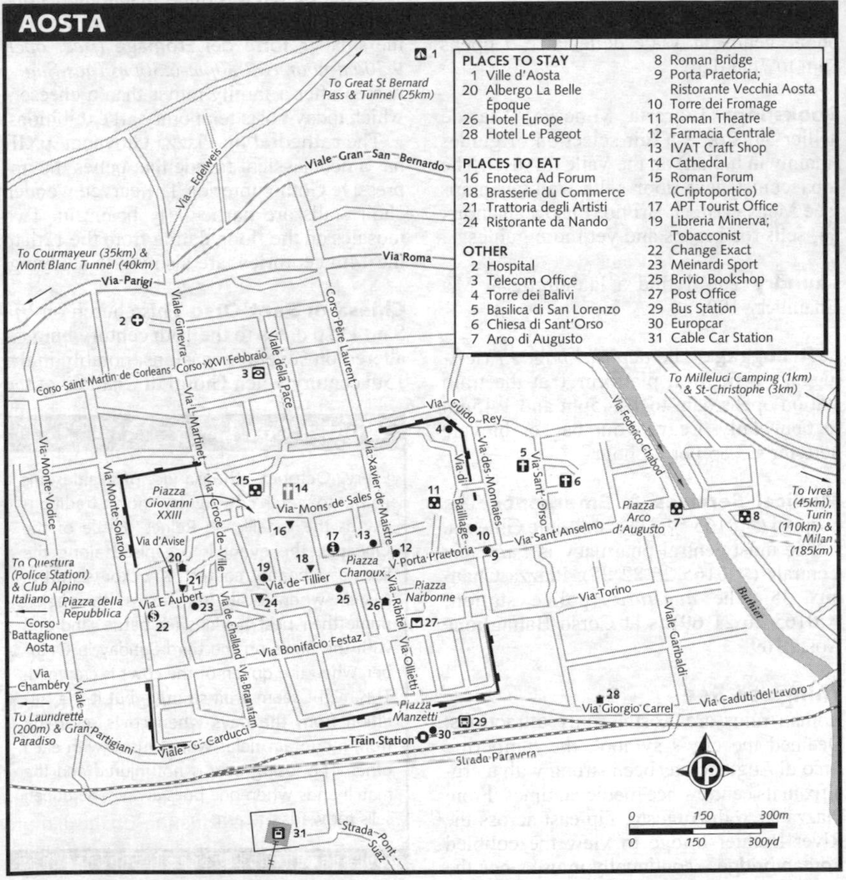

(see Information in the respective sections) and its headquarters in Aosta (☎ 0165 4 09 39 or 0165 3 49 83, fax 0165 4 19 29, W www.interguide.it), Via Monte Emilius 13.

Money Change Exact, Via E Aubert 77, offers a Western Union money transfer service and opens 10am to 1pm and 2.30pm to 6.30pm Monday to Saturday. Banks abound on and around Piazza Chanoux.

Post & Communications The post office, on Piazza Narbonne, opens 8.15am to 6pm Monday to Friday and 8.15am to 1pm Saturday.

The unstaffed section of the Telecom phone centre at Viale della Pace 9 opens 8am to 7pm daily.

Bookshops Libreria Minerva, Via de Tillier 34, stocks a fair selection of guides (mainly in Italian) on the Valle d'Aosta. The tobacconist next door sells walking maps (see Maps earlier). Brivio, Piazza Chanoux 34, sells road maps and yet more guides.

Laundry You'll find a laundrette at Via Chambéry 100.

Left Luggage The *depositi bagagli* (left-luggage office) on platform 1 at the train station opens 6am to 12.45pm and 1.45pm to 6pm daily. Leave your bag or bicycle here for €3.85 per 24 hours.

Medical Services & Emergency The hospital (☎ 0165 54 31) is on Viale Ginevra.

The most central pharmacy is Farmacia Centrale (☎ 0165 26 22 05), Piazza Chanoux 35. The *questura* (police station; ☎ 0165 26 21 69) is at Corso Battaglione Aosta 169.

Things to See

Roman ruins are Aosta's only attractions. Deemed the city's symbol, the lumbering **Arco di Augusto** has been strung with a crucifix in its centre since medieval times. From Piazza Arco di Augusto, nip east across the River Buthier bridge to view the cobbled **Roman bridge** – continually in use since the 1st century – then backtrack west 300m along Via Sant'Anselmo to **Porta Praetoria**. This is the main gate to the Roman city.

North along Via di Bailliage takes you to Aosta's **Roman theatre** *(free; open 9am-6.30pm daily Oct-Mar, 9am-8pm daily Apr-Sept)*. Currently being renovated, part of its 22m-high facade is still intact. In summer, performances are occasionally held in the better-preserved lower section. All that remains of the **Roman forum**, another couple of blocks to the west, beneath Piazza Giovanni XXIII, is a colonnaded walkway known as the **Criptoportico**. The foreboding **Torre dei Balivi**, a former prison, marks one corner of the Roman wall and peers down on the smaller **Torre dei Fromage** *(free; open 9.30am-noon & 2.30pm-6.30pm Tues-Sun)* – named after a family rather than a cheese – which today hosts temporary art exhibitions.

The **cathedral** on Piazza Giovanni XXIII has a neoclassical facade that belies the impressive Gothic interior. The carved wooden choir stalls are particularly beautiful. Two mosaics on the floor, dating from the 12th to the 14th centuries, are also worth studying.

Chiesa di Sant'Orso This church on Via Sant'Orso dates to the 10th century but was altered on several occasions, notably in the 15th century when Giorgi di Challant of the

What a Cow!

Every October, thousands of Valdestans gather to watch cow fights. Known traditionally as the Bataille de Reines (Battle of the Queens), the event is organised along the lines of a beauty contest. Knockouts start in March, when locals from across the region prime their best bovines for battle, and end with the finals on the third Sunday in October, when the queen of the cows is crowned. This might seem a bit strange, but it is a tradition from the days when cows returning from mountain fields would tussle with each other. The losing cow is not injured and the match ends when one pulls away. The queen sells for wads of cash.

ruling family ordered the original frescoes covered and a new roof installed. Remnants of these frescoes can be viewed by clambering up into the cavity between the original and 15th-century ceilings. Ask the church attendant for a tour. The interior and the magnificently carved choir stalls are Gothic, but excavations have unearthed the remains of an earlier church, possibly dating from the 8th century. The Romanesque cloister, with its ornately carved capitals representing biblical scenes, is to the right of the church.

Activities

The small resort of **Pila** (1800m), accessible by cable car from Aosta or 18km south by driving, is quick and easy to reach from the town. Its 70km of runs, served by 13 lifts, form one of the largest ski areas in the valley. The highest slope, in the shadow of Gran Paradiso, reaches 2700m and sports a snow park – complete with half pipe, fun box, jump and slide – for snowboarders. There is a small village in the ski station, but most services, such as the tourist office, police and medical services, are handled from Aosta. For ski-pass details, see Activities at the start of the Valle d'Aosta section.

You can climb on the rocks known as Adrénaline, Polyester and Lipstick. For information, call ***Cooperativa Interguide*** *(see Information earlier)*. ***Aeroclub Valle d'Aosta*** *(☎ 0165 26 24 42)* in St Christophe, just outside Aosta, can set you up for hang-gliding or paragliding.

The lower slopes leading down from Pila into the Dora Baltea valley provide picturesque and easy walks.

The APT office can give advice on walking trails or put you in contact with an Alpine guide if you prefer not to go it alone. Alternatively, contact the ***Club Alpino Italiano*** *(☎/fax 0165 4 01 94, Corso Battaglione Aosta 81)*.

Special Events

The Fiera di Sant'Orso, the annual wood fair held on 30 and 31 January in honour of the town's patron saint, brings together craftspeople from all over the valley to display their carvings and then present an item to the saint at the Chiesa di Sant'Orso. It is held near Porta Praetoria.

Places to Stay

Accommodation in Aosta is generally expensive and difficult to find – and even more expensive and harder to find in Pila. Cheaper and more pleasant lodgings can be found in the hinterland; check with staff at the APT office.

Ville d'Aosta *(☎ 0165 36 13 60, Viale Gran San Bernardo 76)* Sites per person/tent/car €4.15/5.70/5.70. Open June-Sept. This camp site is 1km north of the town centre.

Milleluci *(☎ 0165 23 52 78, fax 0165 23 52 84, W www.hotelmilleluci.com, Roppoz 15)* Sites per person/tent & car €5.15/10.30. Open year-round. Milleluci is about 1km east of Aosta and can be reached by bus No 11.

Albergo La Belle Époque *(☎/fax 0165 26 22 76, Via D'Avise 18)* Singles/doubles from €31/41.30. Basic rooms above a simple pizzeria clock in as Aosta's cheapest.

Hotel Le Pageot *(☎ 0165 3 24 33, fax 0165 3 32 17, Via Giorgio Carrel 31)* Singles/doubles €56.80/87.80. Its proximity to the train and bus stations is about the only saving grace of this concrete block, complete with chain-smoking cleaning lady.

Hotel Europe *(☎ 0165 23 63 63, fax 0165 4 05 66, e hoteleurope@tiscalinet.it, Piazza Narbonne 8)* Doubles from €51.65, high season up to €340.85. Elegant style and service mean that Europe lives up to its four-star reputation.

Places to Eat

Plenty of notable open-air cafe terraces spring up on sun-baked Piazza Chanoux in summer.

Ristorante da Nando *(☎ 0165 4 44 55, Via de Tillier 41)* Menu €16.55. Its *menu turistica* might be a tad overpriced, but the hearty plates of spaghetti (from €6.70), traditional polenta dishes (from €7.25), salads (from €4.65) and pizzas (€3.60-6.20) are guaranteed to please.

Brasserie du Commerce *(☎ 0165 3 56 13, Via de Tillier 10)* 1st/2nd courses €5.15/7.75.

Dip into a steaming fondue, mouth-melting *raclette* (hot, melted cheese scrapped from a block in front of a grill) or hefty *choucroute* (sauerkraut) – all €7.75 – at this busy brasserie.

Enoteca Ad Forum *(Via Mons de Sales)* Menu €18.10. Tickle those tastebuds with a bottle of valley vintage at Aosta's fabulous wine bar, complete with a Roman cellar which you can visit for free. Cheese platters cost upwards of €4.40 and there's a sinful selection of gooey cakes. Bask in the back garden for lunch in the sun.

Trattoria degli Artisti *(☎ 0165 4 09 60, Via Maillet 5–7)* 1st/2nd courses from €6.20/9.30. Antipasti fiends come in droves to tuck into this rustic kitchen's imaginative appetisers. Tucked down an alleyway off Via de Tillier, it serves plenty of traditional regional fodder too.

Ristorante Vecchia Aosta *(☎ 0165 36 11 86, Piazza Porta Praetoriane 4)* 1st/2nd courses from €7.25/10.35. Right inside the arches of Porta Praetoria, is a choice spot to enjoy local Valdotaine cuisine. Big eaters can munch through a four-course *menu Valdotaine* (€23.25).

Shopping

Tradition has it that Sant'Orso gave carved wooden shoes known as *sabi* to the city's poor. Valdestans continue to carve shoes, tiny houses and ceremonial pots, all still widely used. Tacky shops throughout the city, particularly along Via Porte Praetoria, sell these goods, as does ***IVAT*** *(☎ 0165 4 14 62, ⓔ ivat.vda@tin.it, Via Xavier de Maistre 1)*, an upmarket shop run by the Instituto Valdotain de l'Artisanat Typique. Other interesting craft places dot Via Martinet.

Getting There & Away

Air Aosta has a small airport that services commuter flights. The airports at Turin and Geneva (Switzerland) are both about an hour away by car.

Bus Buses to Milan (€11.60, 1½ to 3½ hours, two daily), Turin (€6.50, two hours, eight daily) and Courmayeur (€2.50, 2½ to 4½ hours, five daily) leave from Aosta bus station (☎ 0165 26 20 27), virtually opposite the train station on Via Giorgio Carrel. To get to Breuil-Cervinia, take a bus to Châtillon (30 minutes), then a connecting bus (one hour, seven daily) to the resort.

Train Aosta train station, at Piazza Manzetti, is served by trains from most parts of Italy via Turin (€5.70, two to 2½ hours, more than 10 daily). Travellers to/from Milan must change trains at Chivasso. A limited train service connects Aosta with Pré-St Didier (€2.30, 1¾ hours), some 5km short of Courmayeur.

Car & Motorcycle Aosta is on the A5, which connects Turin with the Mt Blanc tunnel; the last stretch of the highway is still being built. Another exit road north of the city leads to the Great St Bernard tunnel.

Getting Around

Aosta's sites are easily reached on foot. *Navetta* (shuttlebuses) run through town from the train station. Taxis can be booked on ☎ 0165 3 18 31 and you can hire your own wheels from Europcar (☎ 0165 4 14 32) at the train station.

AROUND AOSTA

If you need a break from the slopes, the Aosta valley is peppered with castles, many of them Romanesque and Gothic, just waiting to be explored. Each castle is within view of the next, and messages used to be transferred along the valley by flag signals. From Aosta, follow the scenic S26 that runs parallel to the A5.

East from Aosta is the magnificently restored **Castello di Fénis** *(☎ 0165 76 42 63; adult/child €3.10/1.55; open 9am-7pm daily Mar-June & Sept; 9am-8pm daily July & Aug; 10am-12.30pm & 1.30pm-5pm Wed-Mon & 10am-12.30pm & 1.30pm-6pm Sun rest of the year)*. Formerly owned by the Challant family, it features rich frescoes as well as period graffiti. It was never really used as a defensive post but served as a plush residence.

Past St Vincent is the sober **Castello di Verrès** *(☎ 0125 92 90 67; adult/child €3.10/1.55; open 9am-7pm daily Mar-June*

VALLE D'AOSTA

& Sept; 9am-8pm daily July & Aug; 10am-12.30pm & 1.30pm-5pm Fri-Wed & 10am-12.30pm & 1.30pm-6pm Sun rest of the year). More the real thing, this castle does sentinel duty high on its rocky perch.

About 1km south-west of the River Dora Baltea, below the town of Verrès, is the restored 15th-century **Castello d'Issogne** *(☎ 0125 92 93 73; adult/child €5.15/2.60; open 9am-7pm daily Mar-June & Sept; 9am-8pm daily July & Aug; 10am-12.30pm & 1.30pm-5pm Thur-Tues & 10am-12.30pm & 1.30pm-6pm Sun rest of the year)*. This building was a castle, though you'd hardly know it – it looks for all the world like a stately home.

Farther down the valley still, towards Pont-St-Martin, the fortress of **Bard** (closed) was a no-nonsense military outpost given short shrift by Napoleon on his first campaign into Italy. Once you are at Pont-St-Martin, you could strike north for Gressoney-St-Jean. Just near the town is the fairy-tale **Castel Savoia** *(☎ 0125 35 53 96; adult/child €3.10/1.55; open 9am-7pm daily Mar-June & Sept; 9am-8pm daily July & Aug; 10am-12.30pm & 1.30pm-5pm Fri-Wed & 10am-12.30pm & 1.30pm-6pm Sun rest of the year)*. It was begun in 1900 for the Italian royals.

Heading west towards Mt Blanc from Aosta, you quickly come upon **Castello di Sarre** *(☎ 0165 25 75 39; adult/child €5.15/2.60; open 9am-7pm daily Mar-June & Sept; 9am-8pm daily July & Aug; 10am-12.30pm & 1.30pm-5pm Tues-Sat & 10am-12.30pm & 1.30pm-6pm Sun rest of the year)*. Built in 1710 on the remains of a 13th-century fort, King Vittorio Emanuele II bought it in 1869 to use as a hunting residence. The Savoys sold the castle in 1972 and it now serves as a museum of the royal presence in the region.

Castello di San Pierre *(☎ 0165 90 34 85; adult/child €2.60/1.30; open 9am-7pm daily Apr-Sept)*, which houses a natural science museum, is the last main item of interest on the castle route.

Visitors are sent through the castles at 30 minute intervals. A ceiling of 20 to 50 visitors in any 30 minute period is imposed. The Aosta APT has full timetable information.

Probably the only reason to visit **St Vincent**, Valle d'Aosta's second-biggest city, is for its **casino** *(☎ 0166 52 21, W www.casinodelavallee.it)*. It is also a stopping-off point for the Valle d'Ayas and Valtournenche, which leads to the Matterhorn.

COURMAYEUR

postcode 11013 • pop 3015
elevation 1224m

With much of the original village intact, and set against the backdrop of Mt Blanc, Courmayeur is one of the more picturesque skiing resorts in the Valle d'Aosta. It is also one of the most expensive. Out of season, wealthy Milanese and Turinese women leave their fur coats in a local furrier's vault – minks and ermines are too valuable to be worn in the streets of their home cities.

The resort has more than 140km of downhill and cross-country ski runs and a feast of summer activities, including skiing, horse riding, hang-gliding, canoeing and 280km of mountain walking trails. Year-round, a cable car links La Palud, near Courmayeur, with Punta Helbronner (3462m) on Mt Blanc – an extraordinary 20-minute ride (€27.90 return). From here, another cable car (April to September only) takes you on a breathtaking 5km transglacial ride across the Italian border to the Aiguille du Midi (3842m) in France (from where the world's highest cable car transports you into Chamonix).

Information

Tourist Offices The APT office (☎ 0165 84 20 60, fax 0165 84 20 72, W www.courmayeur.net), at Piazzale Monte Bianco 13, opens 9am to 12.30pm and 3pm to 6.30pm daily.

Next door, the Società delle Guide Alpine di Courmayeur (☎ 0165 84 20 64, W www.guidecourmayeur.com), at Piazzale Monte Bianco 14, can guide those seeking more daring off-piste adventures, including heli skiing. In summer, the Associazione Accompagnatori della Natura Courmayeur-Mt Blanc (☎ 0165 86 21 40), Strada La Palud 1, can help you discover the region's green attractions.

VALLE D'AOSTA

Medical Services For medical attention and ambulance, call ☎ 0165 84 46 84 or go to *pronto soccorso* (casualty) at the Ospedale Regionale d'Aosta (hospital; ☎ 0165 30 42 56, 0165 54 32 90).

Mountain Biking

To hire a bike, try ***Noleggio Ulisse*** *(☎ 0165 84 22 55)*, in front of the Courmayeur chair lift; ***Caraco*** *(☎ 0165 84 41 52)*, Via Roma 150; or ***Club des Sports*** *(☎ 0165 8 95 70)* in Planpincieux, which is about 5km north of Courmayeur.

Walking & Climbing

The APT has a basic map of walking trails in the Valdigne and on Mt Blanc. You would, however, be better off with the IGC 1:25,000 map No 107. If you walk the higher trails on Mt Blanc or you want to walk on the glaciers, go properly equipped and consider hiring a guide. Many people who take the Punta Helbronner cable car are completely unprepared for what awaits them at almost 3500m. Even if it's sweltering in the valley, it can be -10°C at Punta Helbronner. Moral of the story: take heavy winter clothes. Head up early in the morning because by early afternoon heavy weather usually descends onto the summit area.

You can continue from Punta Helbronner down to Chamonix in France (bring your passport and check if you need a visa to enter France). The return fare from La Palud to Punta Helbronner is €27.90.

Many rifugi and huts are located along walking trails in the mountains around Courmayeur. They are marked on all walking maps. Those offering hotel-style service and accommodation are usually only open in summer. Unattended huts, or *bivacchi*, are open year-round. The APT publishes a hut guide.

Skiing

Mt Blanc offers skiing year-round. ***The Ski Club Courmayeur Monte Bianco*** *(☎ 0165 84 24 77)* is at the Centro Sportivo in Plan des Lizzes. You can reach the skiing school on the same number or at Strada Regionale 51. The best bet if you are just skiing is to book a Settimana Bianca package through an agency such as CIT. Most ski runs, chair lifts and ski lifts are reachable by the Courmayeur, Dolonne and Val Veny cable cars. For details, check with the APT or Cableways Monte Bianco in La Palud (☎ 0165 8 99 25).

Adventure Sports

Rafting and Hydrospeed *(☎ 0165 84 40 96)*, based at Courmayeur's Centre Sportif in Plan des Lizzes, can advise on canoeing. If you want to go ballooning, contact the ***Club Aérostatique Mont Blanc*** *(☎ 0165 4 02 05 or 0335 20 71 96)*.

Places to Stay & Eat

Peak-season accommodation in Courmayeur is very expensive if you aren't on a package deal but the towns along the valleys (of La Palud, Dolonne, Entrèves, La Saxe, Plan Ponquet, Val Ferret, Pré-St Didier and Morgex) offer reasonably priced rooms.

Val Veny Cuignon *(☎ 0165 86 90 73)* Sites per person/tent/car €4.15/6.70/5.15. Open July-mid-Sept. This camp site is in the locality of the same name, 4.5km from Courmayeur.

Hotel Vallée Blanche *(☎ 0165 89 70 02, fax 0165 8 92 77, La Palud)* Doubles from €77.45. Family-run White Valley is steps away from the Palud-Helbronner cable car, offering views and peace.

There are good food shops and restaurants along Via Roma, in the old part of Courmayeur.

Getting There & Away

Three trains daily from Aosta terminate at Pré-St Didier, with bus connections to the main bus station at Piazzale Monte Bianco in Courmayeur, outside the APT office. Courmayeur bus station (☎ 0166 84 13 97) is served by long-haul buses from Milan (€15.60, 4½ hours, three to five daily) and Turin (€8.90, 3½ hours, two to four daily). Local buses connect the resort with Aosta and surrounding towns and villages.

By car, take the S26 from Aosta. The journey from Chamonix (France) through the Mt Blanc Tunnel should be possible again following the reopening of the 11.5km-long tunnel late in 2001. Check with the Courmayeur tourist office before setting out.

VALTOURNENCHE

Stretching from the Valle d'Aosta to the Matterhorn, the Valtournenche takes in several smaller and reasonably priced skiing areas – Antey-St-André, Chamois, La Magdeleine and Torgnon – and culminates in the resorts of Valtournenche and Breuil-Cervinia. The latter is the second-largest resort in Valle d'Aosta and is modern, purpose-built, expensive and fairly ugly, although it offers some of the best skiing in Europe.

Information

The Matterhorn Central Valley APT office (☎ 0166 54 82 66, fax 0166 54 83 88, ⓔ antey@netvale.it) is in Antey-St-André and the Breuil-Cervinia APT office (☎ 0166 94 91 36, fax 0166 94 97 31, ⓔ breuil cerviniaq@netvalee.it) is at Via Carrel 29. Online, see Ⓦ www.montecervino.org. In the town of Valtournenche, seek information at the APT office (☎ 0166 9 20 29, fax 0166 9 24 30, ⓔ valtournenche@netvallee.it) at Via Roma 45.

For mountain and Alpine guides, contact the Società Guide del Cervino (☎ 0166 94 81 69), Via Carrel, in Valtournenche.

Walking

Basic walking maps are available at the APT offices, but if you want to tackle the Matterhorn you need to be properly dressed and equipped. Get a 1:25,000 walking map, such as the IGC map No 108 (see Maps in the Aosta section).

Skiing

There are several resorts in the valley, all well equipped with downhill and cross-country runs. From Breuil-Cervinia, 25 cable cars and lifts take skiers into breathtaking terrain. This resort and Pila are the only places in the Valle d'Aosta to tout snowparks aimed specifically at free-style boarders. Summer skiing is also possible as several cableways and lifts continue to operate, taking skiers on to the Plateau Rosa. This resort introduced Valle d'Aosta to night skiing, in the Campetto area. The tourist office has details on ski hire, passes and ski schools.

Places to Stay

Albergo Leonardo Carrel *(☎/fax 0166 94 90 77, Località Avouil, Breuil-Cervinia)* Singles/doubles up to €31/41.30. Leonardo is only one of two one-star joints in Breuil-Cervinia, so get in quick.

Hotel Sporting *(☎ 0166 94 91 12, fax 0166 94 00 68, Via Carrel, Breuil-Cervinia)* Singles €41.30-82.65, doubles €51.65-103.30. Hotel Sporting is another handsome choice.

Getting There & Away

Buses run from Aosta to the resorts and most ski areas in the valley. Savda (☎ 0165 36 12 44) operates services from Châtillon (one hour) to Breuil-Cervinia and on to other resort villages.

PARCO NAZIONALE DEL GRAN PARADISO

Gran Paradiso was Italy's first national park, established in 1922 after Vittorio Emanuele II gave his hunting reserve to the state. This park incorporates the valleys around the Gran Paradiso (4061m), three of which are in the Valle d'Aosta: the Valsavarenche, Val di Rhêmes and the beautiful Valle di Cogne (check out IGC map No 102). On the Piedmont side of the mountain, the park includes the valleys of Soana and Orco. By 1945 the ibex (wild goat) had been almost hunted to extinction and there were only 419 left in the park. Today, as the result of a conservation policy, there are almost 4000 living there.

Excellent cross-country skiing trails line the Valle di Cogne, but the park is really devoted to summer activities. There are numerous well-marked trails and rifugi in this, one of the most picturesque, unspoiled valleys, and there is a good range of accommodation in the village of Cogne. The main point of departure for the Gran Paradiso peak is Pont in the Valsavarenche.

Information

Tourist Offices The Gran Paradiso Mountain Community Tourist Office (☎ 0165 9 50 55, fax 0165 9 59 75, **W** www.granparadiso.org) is at Località Champagne 18 in Villeneuve. Cogne's APT (☎ 0165 7 40 40, fax 0165 74 91 25) is at Piazza Chanoux 36. Both have information about summer and winter activities.

Places to Stay

Al Sole *(☎ 0165 7 42 37, Località Lillaz)* Sites per person/tent €4.65/6.45. This camp site, perched at 1617m in the Lillaz area of the Valle di Cogne, opens year-round.

Camping Pont Breuil *(☎/fax 0165 9 54 58, Valsavarenche)* Sites per person/tent/car €4.15/7.25/5.15. Open June-Sept. This camp site at Pont proudly sits at 2000m.

There are numerous hotels in and around Cogne; ask at the tourist office for more information.

Getting There & Away

Several bus companies operate reliable services between valley towns and Cogne, running on to Aosta and beyond. Cogne can also be reached by cable car from Pila.

AROUND MONTE ROSA

The Val di Gressoney, the first of the Valle d'Aosta's eastern valleys, and the parallel Val d'Ayas are dominated by the massive Monte Rosa. Both valleys are picturesque and popular in summer and winter.

In the Valle di Gressoney, stay in the pretty lakeside mountain village of Gressoney-St-Jean, which retains its traditional atmosphere. Alpine fauna can be discovered in the village's **Museo Regionale della Fauna Alpina** *(☎ 0125 35 54 06)*. Gressoney-La-Trinité, higher up the valley, is closer to the main walking trails and ski runs, but has been largely taken over by anonymous tourist facilities.

In the Valle d'Ayas, the main resort is Champoluc at the head of the valley, but Brusson is a good option too, particularly if you want to do easy half- or one-day walks. Serious walkers may want to invest in the IGC map No 101.

Information

Tourist Offices There are tourist offices in Champoluc (☎ 0125 30 71 13, fax 0125 30 77 85, **e** info@libero.it), at Via Varasc 16; Brusson (☎ 0125 30 02 40, fax 0125 30 06 91, **e** infobrusson@libero.it), at Piazza Municipio 2; Gressoney-La Trinité (☎ 0125 36 61 43, fax 0125 36 63 23), on Piazza Tache; and Gressoney-St Jean (☎ 0125 35 51 85, fax 0125 35 58 95, **e** aptwalser@libero.it), at Villa Margherita 1.

Heli-skiing is but one of the numerous mountain activities arranged by the Gressoney-La Trinité's alpinism school (☎ 0125 36 61 39).

Medical Services & Emergency For an ambulance anywhere in the valley, call ☎ 0125 80 70 67. For police in Brusson, call ☎ 0125 30 01 32; in St Jean, call ☎ 0125 35 59 80; and in Verrès, call ☎ 0125 92 93 24.

Places to Stay

All the following places are in the Valle di Gressoney.

La Pineta *(☎ 0125 35 53 70, Schneke)* Sites per person/tent/car €3.60/6.45/5.15. This camp site is one of two in Gressoney-St-Jean. Both open year-round.

Hotel Grünes Wasser *(☎/fax 0125 35 54 03,* **e** *camisasca@gressoney.it, Strada Regionale 41, No 14, Gressoney-St-Jean)* Singles €25.80-38.75, doubles €51.65-67.15. Rooms are far from upmarket but serve nevertheless to please tired ski legs.

Hotel Lyskamm *(☎ 0125 35 54 36, fax 0125 35 59 17,* **e** *thyman@libero.it, Strada Statale 505 1, Gressoney-St-Jean)* Singles/doubles up to €51.65/123.95. Three stars add a comfortable touch.

Getting There & Away

Trains running through Aosta stop in St Vincent and Verrès, from where you can catch a bus to either valley. Savda operates bus No 33 along the Valle di Gressoney and bus No 35 from Verrès to Champoluc. Bus No 40 connects Aosta with Champoluc, via Col de Joux.

Leave the A5, S26 or Aosta-Turin/Milan train at Pont-St-Martin and swing north for the Valle di Gressoney.

Lombardy & the Lakes

From the Alps to the lush plains of the River Po, Lombardy's (Lombardia) often fractious political history is reflected in its geographical diversity. Beyond the financial metropolis of Milan, the region is peppered with affluent towns that preserve a distinct character inherited from the days of the city-states. Mantua, Cremona, Bergamo, Brescia and Pavia have wealth and style, but the northern clime and a degree of orderly self-satisfaction make them staid in comparison with cities farther south. The hard-working people of Milan have built Italy's economic and fashion capital – a businesslike place that more closely resembles the great cities of northern Europe.

Italy's richest and most developed region offers its populace numerous escape routes. The most popular is the stretch of enchanting lakes from Lago d'Orta to Lago di Garda.

Lombardy formed part of Gallia Cisalpina (Cisalpine Gaul) before it fell to Saracen tribes and later to the Germanic Lombards (Langobards). Interference by the Franks under Barbarossa (Frederick I) in the 12th century ended when the cities united under the Lega Lombarda (Lombard League). After the League collapsed, Lombardy was divided between powerful families – the Viscontis, Sforzas, Gonzagas and Scaligers – and was later invaded by the Venetians, the Austrian Habsburgs and Napoleon.

Lombard cuisine relies heavily on rice and polenta and features butter, cream and cheese from the Alpine pastures. Gorgonzola originated just outside Milan. Pasta is fresh and usually stuffed with squash, meat, cheese or spinach. As a dessert it can contain raisins or candied fruit. Meats are predominantly pork and veal – *cotoletta alla milanese* (fillet of veal fried in breadcrumbs) is famous. Lombardy's sparkling wines are among Italy's best; the Franciacorta red is mellow, while the white is fruity and dry.

Highlights

- Enjoy a hot date at La Scala in Milan for a night at the opera
- Contemplate the Gothic complexity of Milan's cathedral and then climb up to its roof for stunning views
- Have some drinks at a club in Milan's Navigli district
- Visit the magnificent Certosa di Pavia monastery, south of Milan
- Wander around Bergamo's upper town and listen for the strange *bergamasco* dialect
- Listen to the sounds of violins at Cremona's Triennale Internazionale degli Strumenti ad Arco
- Chug along in a boat across Lago di Como with a lunch stop in Bellagio, the 'pearl' of the lake

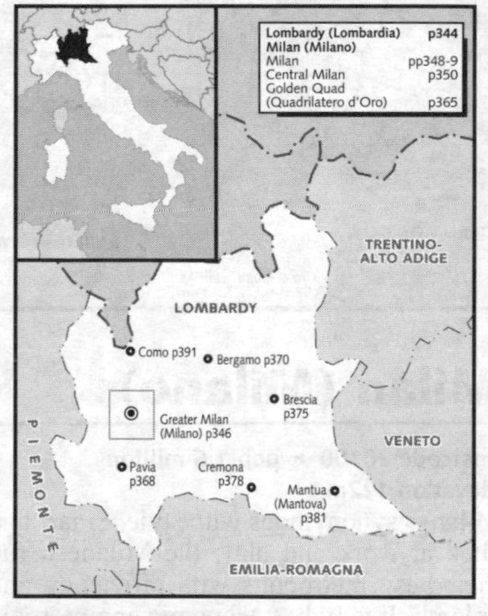

Public transport is excellent in the region and nearly all towns can be reached easily by road or rail.

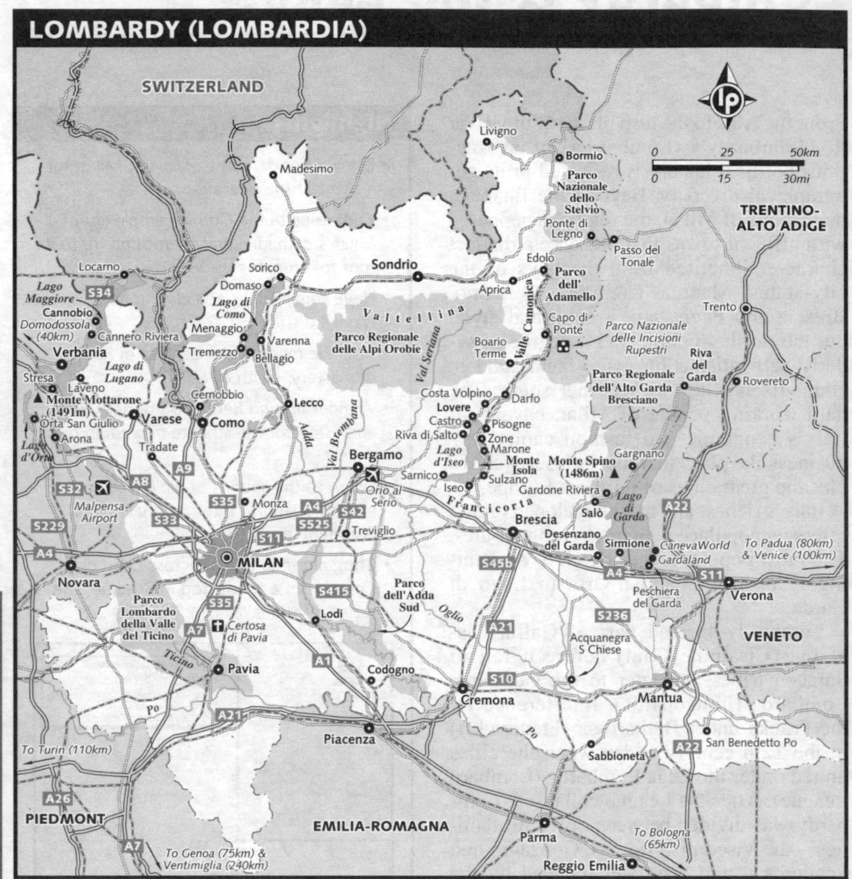

Milan (Milano)

postcode 20100 • pop 1.6 million
elevation 122m

Milan is synonymous with style. Smart and slick at work and play, the Milanese run their busy metropolis with efficiency and aplomb. It is Italy's economic engine room and the world's design capital, and it rivals Paris as a leading fashion centre. Although the city is smaller than Rome, it's Milan – not the ancient imperial capital – that is home to Italy's stock market, most of the country's major corporations and the nation's largest concentration of industry.

Milan is distinctly sophisticated. Shopping, whether of the window variety or – for those who can afford it – the real thing, is of almost religious significance. Theatre and cinema flourish here, the city is top of most international music tour programs and its clubbing scene is hot and busy.

Food is another Milanese joy and historical cafes where Verdi and other eminent composers sank espresso shots are plentiful. Italy's quintessential Christmas cake, *panettone*, is said to be modelled on the lofty domes of a Lombardy cathedral. Milan's, incidentally, is the world's fourth largest.

Milan's business and political leaders have long railed against inefficient and corrupt government in Rome and subsidies directed to the south. This sense of protest spawned a separatist party in the late 1980s, the Lega Nord (Northern League), led by the rather explosive Umberto Bossi – appointed minister without portfolio in Berlusconi's right-wing coalition government in mid-2001.

Milan's smog is almost as legendary as London's. Should you be fortunate enough to see the sun, note that a pair of shades is an essential fashion accessory. Despite many Milanese talking endlessly of escaping Milan and moving to the country, most are staunchly proud of their city and few leave – except in August when city dwellers depart en masse to escape the stifling heat. And you'd do well to stay away then too.

History

Milan is said to have been founded by Celtic tribes who settled along the River Po in the 7th century BC. In 222 BC, Roman legions marched into the territory, defeated the Gallic Insubres and occupied the town, which they knew as Mediolanum ('middle of the plain'). Mediolanum's key position on the trade routes between Rome and north-western Europe ensured its continued prosperity and it was here in AD 313 that Constantine I made his momentous edict granting Christians freedom of worship.

The city endured centuries of chaos, caused by waves of barbarian invasions, to form a *comune* (town council) in the 11th century. The city-state, ruled by a council including members of all classes, entered a period of rapid growth but soon found itself squabbling with neighbouring towns. The Holy Roman emperor, Frederick I (Barbarossa), decided to exploit the local conflicts and besieged Milan in 1162. Milan and its allies formed the Lega Lombarda and exacted revenge in 1176.

From the mid-13th century the city was governed by a succession of important families: the Torrianis, the Viscontis and finally the Sforzas. Under the latter two it enjoyed considerable wealth and power. Milan came under Spanish rule in 1535 and passed to Austria with the Treaty of Utrecht of 1713, signed at the end of the War of the Spanish Succession. Legacies of the reign of Maria Theresa of Austria are still evident, particularly the dull-yellow (her favourite colour) facades of La Scala and the Palazzo Reale.

Napoleon made Milan the capital of his Cisalpine Republic in 1797 and, five years later, of his Italian Republic, crowning himself king of Italy there in 1805. Austria returned in 1814 but this time the occupation was short-lived. Troops under Vittorio Emanuele II and Napoleon III crushed the Austrian forces at the Battle of Magenta in 1859 and Milan was incorporated into the nascent Kingdom of Italy.

Heavily bombed in WWII, the city was subsequently rebuilt and quickly grew to acquire its modern industrial prominence.

Orientation

Milan is a sprawling metropolis, but most of its attractions are concentrated in the centre between the cathedral and Castello Sforzesco. The city is serviced by an efficient underground railway, the Metropolitana Milanese (MM).

Apart from the centre of town, the main areas of interest for tourists are the Brera, which encompasses many galleries and fashionable shopping streets, immediately north of the cathedral, and Navigli to the south.

Exiting from Stazione Centrale, a 1931 classic of the Fascist era, you emerge onto Piazza Duca d'Aosta, a square pierced by a gigantic 'beam of light' sculpture (Map 2; Milan 2001 Symbol of Light) that conducts waves of light in the dark. It was unveiled in 2001 to mark the third millennium. A good orientation point from here is the Pirelli building (Map 2), the 127m-tall skyscraper to your right as you leave the train station. South-east of Stazione Centrale (Map 2), Via Dom Vitruvio leads to the main budget-hotel area. The city centre is a 20-minute walk from Piazza Duca d'Aosta.

Information

Tourist Offices The main APT office (Map 3; ☎ 02 725 24 300, fax 02 725 24 350), overlooking Piazza del Duomo at Via Marconi 1, opens 8.30am to 8pm Monday to Friday, 9am to 1pm and 2pm to 7pm Saturday and 9am to 1pm and 2pm to 5pm Sunday and holidays. Less horribly busy is the APT office (Map 2; ☎ 02 725 24 360) at Stazione Centrale, open 8am to 7pm Monday to Saturday, 9am to noon and 1.30pm to 6pm Sunday. There are also offices at Malpensa (☎ 02 748 67 213) and Linate (☎ 02 702 00 443) airports, both open 9am to 5pm Monday to Friday. Unlike the Piazza del Duomo office, the latter three answer queries by telephone.

The city council provides practical information at W www.comune.milano.it; there's info on the province at W www.provincia.milano.it; and on Lombardy at W www.inlombardia.it.

Books, Newspapers & Magazines Handy references include the visitors listings guide *Milan – Where, What, When* (€1.55), which tourist offices sell, and the bilingual *Milano Time Out* (€1.05), available in

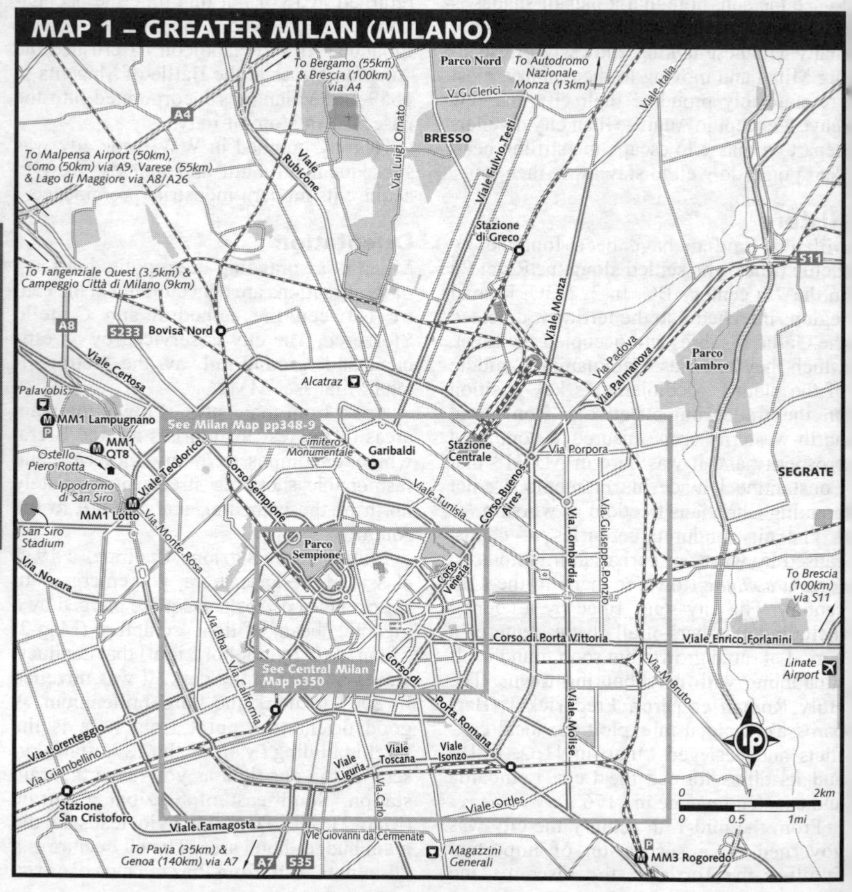

bookshops and useful for entertainment listings. The online edition of *Hello Milan* (W www.hellomilano.it) is much meatier than its monthly print edition (free).

Book-wise, try *A Key to Milan* (€15.50), last updated in 2001 and full of practical facts, and *Milanopass* (€9.80), a hip annual Italian-only listings guide, essential for clubbing fiends. Bookshops sell both; check out *A Key to Milan* on the Internet at W http://users.iol.it/kiwi.milano/keymilan.htm.

Money Change and Money Shop (both Map 3) on the western side of Piazza del Duomo open 9am to 9pm daily. At Stazione Centrale, Exact opens 7am to 10.30pm daily and offers a Western Union money transfer service. There are bureaux de change at both airports.

Banca Commerciale Italiana (Map 3) runs a 24-hour booth with currency exchange machine and ATMs, on the corner of Via Alessandro Manzoni and Piazza della Scala – you need a cash or credit card to get in. There is a 24-hour automatic banknote exchange machine outside Banca Cesare Ponte (Map 3) at Piazza del Duomo 19 and another at Stazione Centrale.

American Express (Map 3; ☎ 02 720 03 694), Via Brera 3, opens 9am to 5.30pm Monday to Friday.

Post & Communications The main post office is on Piazza Cordusio (Map 3), but the offices (and parcel post) at Via Cordusio 4 and Stazione Centrale open longer hours: 8am to 7pm Monday to Friday and 8.30am to noon Saturday.

The unstaffed Telecom office inside Galleria Vittorio Emanuele II (Map 3) and its Stazione Centrale (Map 2) counterpart both open 8am to 9.30pm daily. There are cut-price phone offices in the streets around Stazione Centrale, especially on Via Dom Scarlatti. The annual *English Yellow Pages* (W www.englishyellowpages.it) is a useful directory resource for Milan-based Anglophones.

Log-on for free (after a lengthy queue) at Rizzoli, a bookshop on the western side of Piazza del Duomo, open 10am to 8pm daily; or in the Sony Gallery of Emporio Armani (see the boxed text 'Fashion' later), both on Map 3. Otherwise, pay €7.75 an hour at Mailboxes Etc (Map 2), Corso Sempione 38.

Travel Agencies For student and budget travel, CTS (Map 2; ☎ 02 837 26 74) has an office at Corso di Porta Ticinese 100. CIT (Map 3; ☎ 02 863 70 210) is inside the Galleria Vittorio Emanuele II, and Voyages Wasteels (☎ 02 669 00 20) has a branch at Stazione Centrale (Map 2).

Bookshops The American Bookstore (Map 3; ☎ 02 87 89 20), Via M Camperio 10, has an excellent selection of English books. Alternatively try the English Bookshop (Map 2; ☎ 02 469 44 68, e tmpanton@hotmail.com), Via Mascheroni 12. For French books, visit Île de France (Map 3; ☎ 02 760 01 767), Via San Pietro all'Orto 10. Rizzoli (Map 3; ☎ 02 864 61 071), inside Galleria Vittorio Emanuele II, sells an unbeatable range of translated works by Italian writers and Italy-inspired travel literature in its basement.

For an extensive range of guidebooks and walking maps, shop at Touring Club Italiano (Map 3; ☎ 02 535 99 71), Corso Italia 10.

Cultural Centres Cultural centres in Milan include the British Council (Map 3; ☎ 02 77 22 21, e enquiry.bcmilan@britishcouncil.it), Via Alessandro Manzoni 38; the Goethe Institut (Map 3; ☎ 02 776 91 71, e goethe.mailand.spr@agora.stm.it), Via S Paolo 10; and the Centre Culturel Français (Map 2; ☎ 02 485 91 911), Corso Magenta 63.

Gay & Lesbian Travellers For information on gay activities, call ArciGay (☎ 02 541 22 225, e cigmilano@libero.it or

Information dial-up

Call these local information numbers (Italian only) for location, opening times and anything else you want know about:

Pharmacies	☎ 1100
Cinema & Museums	☎ 1101
Hotels & ATMs	☎ 1102

LOMBARDY

MAP 2 – MILAN
See Central Milan Map p350
0 250 500m
0 250 500yd

MILAN – MAP 2

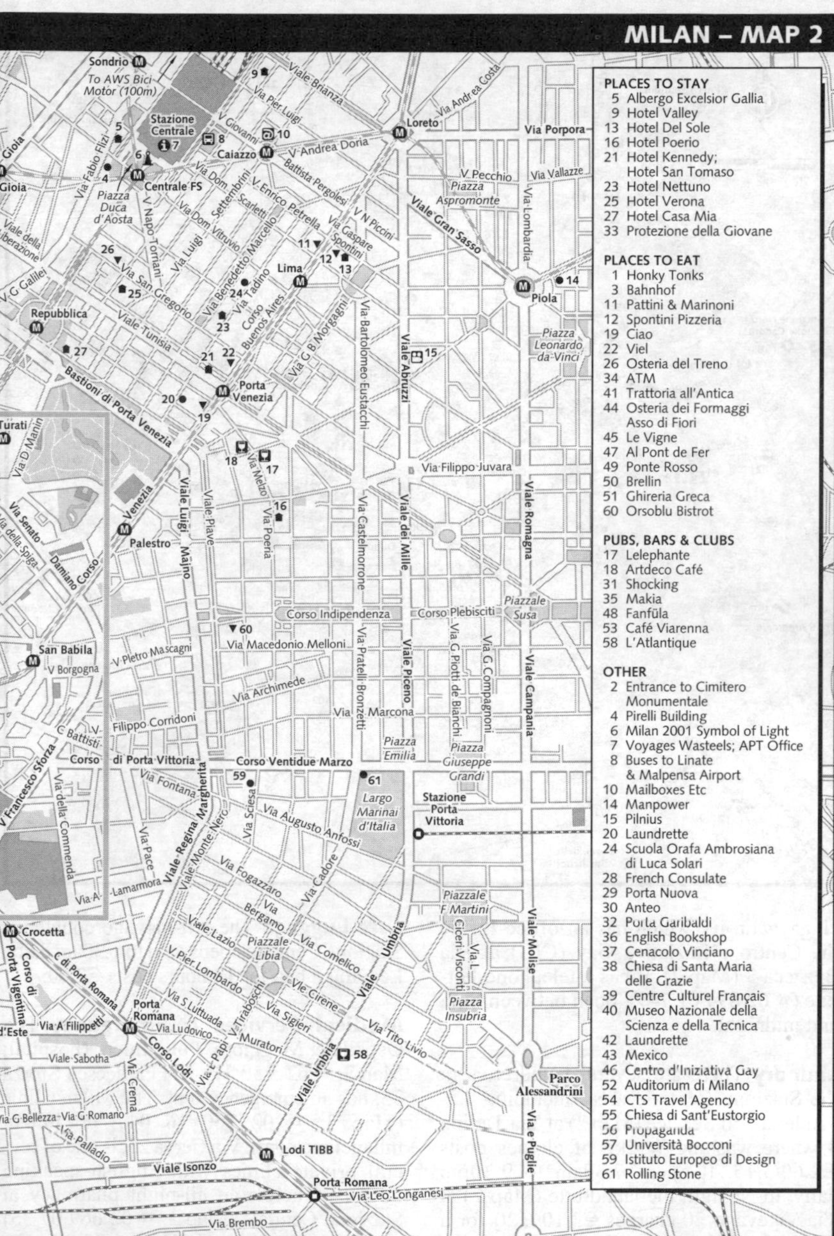
PLACES TO STAY
5 Albergo Excelsior Gallia
9 Hotel Valley
13 Hotel Del Sole
16 Hotel Poerio
21 Hotel Kennedy; Hotel San Tomaso
23 Hotel Nettuno
25 Hotel Verona
27 Hotel Casa Mia
33 Protezione della Giovane
PLACES TO EAT
1 Honky Tonks
3 Bahnhof
11 Pattini & Marinoni
12 Spontini Pizzeria
19 Ciao
22 Viel
26 Osteria del Treno
34 ATM
41 Trattoria all'Antica
44 Osteria dei Formaggi Asso di Fiori
45 Le Vigne
47 Al Pont de Fer
49 Ponte Rosso
50 Brellin
51 Ghireria Greca
60 Orsoblu Bistrot
PUBS, BARS & CLUBS
17 Lelephante
18 Artdeco Café
31 Shocking
35 Makia
48 Fanfüla
53 Café Viarenna
58 L'Atlantique
OTHER
2 Entrance to Cimitero Monumentale
4 Pirelli Building
6 Milan 2001 Symbol of Light
7 Voyages Wasteels; APT Office
8 Buses to Linate & Malpensa Airport
10 Mailboxes Etc
14 Manpower
15 Pilnius
20 Laundrette
24 Scuola Orafa Ambrosiana di Luca Solari
28 French Consulate
29 Porta Nuova
30 Anteo
32 Porta Garibaldi
36 English Bookshop
37 Cenacolo Vinciano
38 Chiesa di Santa Maria delle Grazie
39 Centre Culturel Français
40 Museo Nazionale della Scienza e della Tecnica
42 Laundrette
43 Mexico
46 Centro d'Iniziativa Gay
52 Auditorium di Milano
54 CTS Travel Agency
55 Chiesa di Sant'Eustorgio
56 Propaganda
57 Università Bocconi
59 Istituto Europeo di Design
61 Rolling Stone
Sondrio
To AWS Bici Motor (100m)
Stazione Centrale
Centrale FS
Caiazzo
Loreto
Via Porpora
Viale Brianza
Via Pier Luigi
Viale Andrea Costa
V Andrea Doria
Gioia
Piazza Duca d'Aosta
Viale della Liberazione
V G Galilei
Repubblica
Lima
Piola
Piazza Leonardo da Vinci
Piazza Aspromonte
Viale Gran Sasso
Via Lombardia
Viale Abruzzi
Porta Venezia
Bastioni di Porta Venezia
Turati
Palestro
San Babila
Corso Indipendenza
Corso Plebisciti
Piazzale Susa
Viale Romagna
Viale dei Mille
Viale Piceno
Viale Campania
Corso Ventidue Marzo
Largo Marinai d'Italia
Stazione Porta Vittoria
Piazza Emilia
Piazza Giuseppe Grandi
Piazzale F Martini
Viale Molise
Piazza Insubria
Parco Alessandrini
Crocetta
Porta Romana
Corso Lodi
Viale Umbria
Lodi TIBB
Viale Isonzo
Via Leo Longanesi
Via Brembo
Via Tito Livio
Piazzale Libia
Viale Regina Margherita
Corso di Porta Vittoria
Via Francesco Sforza

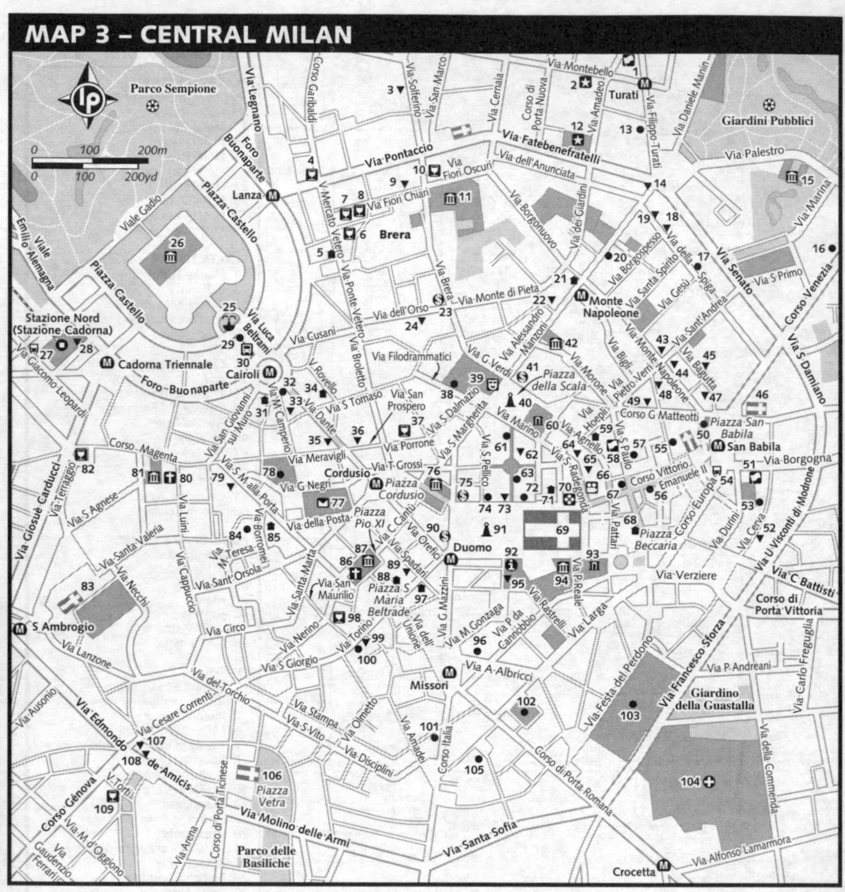

ciggay@tin-it), which has an office inside the Centro d'Iniziativa Gay (CIG) at Via Bezzeca 3 (Map 2). It has a telephone hotline (☎ 02 894 01 749), open between 8pm and midnight.

Laundry There are several laundrettes in the Stazione Centrale area, including Lavanderia Self Service (Map 2) at Via Tadino 4 where washing 7/12kg of clothes costs €2.60/5.15. It opens 7.30am to 9.30pm daily. In Navigli, the laundrette (Map 2) at Via Vigevano 20 charges €3.10/6.20 for a 7/12kg load and opens 8am to 10pm daily.

Left Luggage The left-luggage counter at Stazione Centrale opens 4am to 1.30am daily. Leaving a bag for 12 hours costs €2.60.

Medical Services & Emergency The Ospedale Maggiore Policlinico (hospital; Map 3; ☎ 02 5 50 31), Via Francesco Sforza 35, has an emergency unit. The Milan Clinic (Map 3; ☎ 02 760 16 047, ⓔ info@milanclinic.com), Via Cerva 25, is one of several private clinics with English-speaking doctors. There's an all-night pharmacy at Stazione Centrale (Map 2; ☎ 02 669 07 35) and another at Piazza del Duomo 21 (Map 3).

MAP 3 – CENTRAL MILAN

PLACES TO STAY
5 Albergo Commercio
21 Grand Hotel et de Milan
31 Hotel Cairoli
34 Hotel London
59 Hotel de la Ville
68 Hotel Nuovo
71 Grand Hotel Duomo
85 Hotel Vecchio Milano
88 Hotel Gritti
97 Hotel Speronari; Il Bread & Breakfast

PLACES TO EAT
3 Pottery Café
9 Orient Express
14 Brek
18 Café Rêve
19 Armandola
22 Bar Biffino
24 Il Coriandolo
28 Pattini & Marinoni
33 Antica Osteria Milanese
35 Ciao
36 Coco's
43 Il Salumaio
44 Cova
45 Trattoria Bagutta
47 Paper Moon
48 Sunflower Bar
49 Bar Centro
52 Trattoria da Pino
62 Il Salotto
64 Luini
65 Di Gennaro
73 Zucca in Galleria
79 Marchesi
89 Peck
95 Viel
99 Superfresco Standa
107 Pizzeria Naturale
108 Caffe della Pusteria

PUBS, BARS & CLUBS
4 Le Trottoir
6 Biblos
7 Cajun Louisana Bistro
8 Heaven
10 Jamaica
37 La Banque
82 Bar Magenta
98 Ronchino's
109 Le Biciclette

MUSEUMS & CHURCHES
11 Palazzo di Brera (Pinacoteca di Brera)
15 Civica Galleria d'Arte Moderna & Padiglione d'Arte Contemporanea
26 Castello Sforzesco (Museo d'Arte Antica; Pinacoteca e Raccolte d'Arte; Museo degli Strumenti Musicali)
42 Museo Poldi-Pezzoli
46 Chiesa di San Babila
69 Cathedral
76 Palazzo Affari al Giureconsulti
80 Chiesa di San Maurizio
81 Civico Museo Archeologico
83 Basilica di Sant'Ambrogio
86 Chiesa di San Sepolcro
87 Pinacoteca Ambrosiana
94 Palazzo Reale (Civico Museo d'Arte Contemporanea; Museo del Duomo)
106 Chiesa di San Lorenzo Maggiore

OTHER
1 US Embassy
2 Ufficio Stranieri (Foreigners' Office; Police Station)
12 Questura (Police Station)
13 Kartell
16 Automobile Club Italia
17 Nilufar
20 British Council
23 American Express
25 Fountain
27 Bus Stop for Malpensa Airport
29 Eurolines; Autostradale Viaggi
30 Main Bus Station
32 American Bookstore
38 Teatro alla Scala Box Office
39 Teatro alla Scala; Museo Teatrale alla Scala
40 Statue of Leonardo da Vinci
41 Banca Commerciale Italiana
50 Conservatorio Giuseppe Verdi
51 Australian Consulate
53 Milan Clinic
54 Bus Stop for ATM Buses to Linate Airport
55 Île de France; Milan Point
56 Galleria del Corso (Messaggerie Musicali)
57 Goethe Institut
58 British Consulate
60 Palazzo Marino
61 Rizzoli
63 Galleria Vittorio Emanuele II (CIT; Ricordi Mediastore)
66 Odeon
67 Galleria Mode
70 La Rinascente Department Store
72 Duomo Centre
74 Pharmacy
75 Banca Cesare Ponte
77 Main Post Office
78 Stock Exchange
84 Area Design
90 Change; Money Shop; Rizzoli; Gran Caffé Visconti
91 Equestrian Statue of Vittorio Emanuele II
92 Main APT Office
93 Palazzo Arcivescovile
96 Alitalia
100 FNAC
101 Touring Club Italiano
102 Torre Velasca
103 University of Milan
104 Hospital
105 International House

The *questura* (police station; Map 3; ☎ 02 6 22 61) is at Via Fatebenefratelli 11. Some staff speak English but foreigners will receive better attention at the Uffico Stranieri (Foreigners' Office; Map 3; ☎ 02 6 22 61), Via Montebello 26.

Dangers & Annoyances Pickpockets and thieves haunt Milan's main shopping areas, train stations and busiest public-transport routes.

Beware bird-seed sellers on Piazza del Duomo who flog seeds to unsuspecting tourists by sneakily popping seed in their pockets, prompting pigeons to dive-bomb the victim – and the victim then has to buy seed to escape further bombardment by the ever-greedy pigeons.

LOMBARDY

Cathedral (Map 3)

Milan's impressive navel, Piazza del Duomo *(MM1/3 Duomo)*, has the atmosphere of London's Piccadilly Circus but the latter's statue of Eros hardly compares with Milan's most visible monument, the cathedral. Since medieval times, the square has been Milan's social, geographical and pigeon centre.

Commissioned in 1386 by Gian Galeazzo Visconti, the cathedral can hold a congregation of 40,000. The first glimpse of this late-Gothic wonder is memorable, with its marble facade shaped into pinnacles, statues and pillars, the whole held together by a web of flying buttresses. Some 135 spires and 3200 statues – built between 1397 and 1812 – have somehow been crammed onto the roof and into the facade. The central spire, 108m tall, is capped by a gilded copper statue of the **Madonnina** (literally 'our little Madonna'), the traditional protector of the city. The surrounding forest of spires, statuary and pinnacles distracts observers from an interesting omission – Milan's cathedral has no bell tower.

The huge brass doors at the front bear the marks of bombs that fell near the cathedral during WWII. The inside of the cathedral features 15th-century stained-glass windows on the right and later copies on the left.

High above the altar is a nail, said to have come from Christ's cross and displayed once a year in September. Originally lowered using a device made by Leonardo da Vinci called the *nigola*, the nail is now retrieved by more modern means. The nigola is stored near the roof on the right-hand side as you enter the cathedral by the main entrance off Piazza del Duomo. Next to the main entrance a stairwell leads to an early Christian **baptistry** *(free; open 10am-noon & 3pm-5pm Tues-Sun)* that predates the Gothic church.

The 165-step (some say 158) climb to the roof of the cathedral *(admission €3.10; open 9am-5.30pm daily)* is well worth the effort, if only to view one of Milan's more memorable skyscrapers, the 20-storey **Torre Velasca**, which is topped by a six-storey protruding block and was designed in the late 1950s by Studio BBPR. The lift *(admission €4.65; open 9am-5.30pm daily)* is less fun but kinder on the thigh muscles. The entrances to both are outside the cathedral on the northern flank.

Around the Cathedral (Map 3)

The southern side of Piazza del Duomo is dominated by the **Palazzo Arcivescovile** and **Palazzo Reale**, the traditional seats of Milan's ecclesiastical and civil rulers from the 11th and 12th centuries. Works by Italian Futurists and lesser-known 20th-century Italian artists can be viewed in the **Civico Museo d'Arte Contemporanea** *(☎ 02 439 11 119, Piazza del Duomo 14; adult/child €7.75/free; open 9.30am-5.30pm Tues & Wed, Fri-Sun, 9.30am-10.30pm Thurs)*, the modern art museum inside the Palazzo Reale. At the **Museo del Duomo** *(☎ 02 86 03 58, Piazza del Duomo 14; adult/child €5.15/2.60; open 9.30am-12.30pm & 3pm-6pm daily)*, in the palace's left wing, you can study the cathedral's six centuries of history in more detail.

Virtually destroyed in bombing raids during WWII and rebuilt afterwards, the cruciform **Galleria Vittorio Emanuele II** – known as '*il salotto di Milano*' (Milan's drawing room) thanks to its elegant cafes (see the boxed text 'Historical Cafes' under Places to Eat later) – leads north off Piazza del Duomo. The covered arcade, designed by Giuseppe Mengoni, was one of the first buildings in Europe to employ mainly iron and glass as structural elements. The four mosaics around the central octagon represent Europe, Africa, Asia and North America. Smear the sole of your shoe across the bull's worn-away testicles for good luck.

South-west of Piazza del Duomo, the **Pinacoteca Ambrosiana** *(Ambrose Art Gallery; ☎ 02 806 92 225, **W** www.ambrosiana.it, Piazza Pio XI 2; MM1 Cordusio; adult/child €7.25/3.60; open 10am-5.20pm Tues-Sun)* is one of the city's finest galleries. It contains Italy's first real still life, Caravaggio's *Canestra di Frutta* (Fruit Basket), as well as works by Tiepolo, Titian and Raphael. Also on show is da Vinci's *Musico* (Musician).

Behind the gallery on Piazza San Sepolcro sits **Chiesa di San Sepolcro**, begun in

LOMABARDY

STAEVEN VALLAK

Milan's Castello Sforzesco, for art inside and out

DAMIEN SIMONIS

Reach for the sky at Milan's magnificent cathedral.

JON DAVISON

The sun sets over the sophisticated city.

DAN HERRICK

On top of the world, or at least of Milan's cathedral

JOHN HAY

How things change: the old and the new in Milan

MARTIN MOOS

Milan's striking Galleria Vittorio Emanuele II

ALENA MATTHEWS

Shop till you drop onto the Galleria's mosaic floor.

DAMIEN SIMONIS

The stunning detail on the Galleria's entrance

MARTIN MOOS

Absolutely fabulous: Milanese fashion to die for

MARTIN MOOS

Just one of the ways to motor around Milan

1030. It is dedicated to the Holy Sepulchre and features a Romanesque crypt.

La Scala & Around (Map 3)

Walk north through the Galleria Vittorio Emanuele II from Piazza del Duomo to Piazza della Scala, dominated by a monument dedicated to Leonardo da Vinci, and Milan's legendary opera house, La Scala. Officially called the Teatro alla Scala, the fabulous playhouse opened on 3 August 1778 and was the venue for innumerable operatic first nights throughout the 19th and early 20th centuries. Practically destroyed during WWII, it was rebuilt and reopened in 1946 under the baton of Arturo Toscanini, who returned from New York after a 15-year absence. See Entertainment later for ticket details.

Adjoining the theatre is the **Museo Teatrale alla Scala** *(☎ 02 851 55 831 or 02 851 55 13, ⓔ scala@energy.it, Via Filodrammatici 2; MM1/3 Duomo; adult/child €3.10/1.55; open 9am-12.30pm & 2pm-5.30pm daily Apr-Oct, 9am-12.30pm & 2pm-5.30pm Mon-Sat Nov-Mar)*. When there's no rehearsal on (phone ☎ 02 88 79 473 to check), admission to the museum includes a peep at the theatre's distinctive C-shaped auditorium from one of its many boxes. The museum's musical instrument collection is displayed a short walk south in the **Palazzo Affari al Giureconsulti** *(Piazza Mercanti; MM1/3 Duomo; free; open 9am-noon & 2pm-5pm Mon-Fri)*, Milan's former stock exchange dating to 1823. To get in, ask for an 'invitation' at the Museo Teatrale alla Scala.

Palazzo Marino, between Piazza della Scala and Piazza San Fedele, was begun in 1558 by Galeazzo Alessi and is a masterpiece of 16th-century residential architecture. Milan's municipal council has sat here since 1859. There are more than 60 other grand palazzos scattered about the city centre – a far cry from the several hundred that stood at the end of the 19th century.

North-east along Via Alessandro Manzoni is the **Museo Poldi-Pezzoli** *(☎ 02 79 63 34, Via Alessandro Manzoni 12; MM3 Monte Napoleone; adult/child €5.15/2.60; open 10am-6pm Tues-Sun)* containing a rich collection bequeathed to the city in 1881 by nobleman Gian Giacomo Poldi-Pezzoli. Wandering the two floors of this old mansion is a pleasure; it is filled with collections of jewellery, porcelain, sundials, tapestries, ancient armaments, period furniture and paintings. Of the latter (mostly on the 1st floor), you'll find Botticelli's *Madonna and Child* and contributions from Tiepolo, Giovanni and Jacopo Bellini, Piero della Francesca, Mantegna, Crivelli, Lorenzo Lotto, Il Pinturicchio, Filippo Lippi and others.

Castello Sforzesco (Map 3)

At the northern end of Via Dante looms Castello Sforzesco *(Piazza Castello; MM1/2 Cadorna Triennale or MM1 Cairoli; free; open 9.30am-5.30pm Tues-Sun)*, home to some excellent art museums. Originally a Visconti fortress, it was remodelled by Francesco Sforza in the 15th century and Leonardo da Vinci aided in designing the defences.

A vast collection of Lombard sculptures is displayed in the **Museo d'Arte Antica**, including a fresco by Leonardo da Vinci and Michelangelo's *Pietà Rondanini*. In the **Pinacoteca e Raccolte d'Arte** is an applied arts display and a decent picture gallery, featuring works by Bellini, Tiepolo, Mantegna, Correggio, Titian and van Dyck. Another museum is devoted to prehistoric and ancient Egyptian artefacts, while the **Museo degli Strumenti Musicali** enchants visitors with its collection of musical instruments.

Behind the red-brick castle is **Parco Sempione** *(open 6.30am-8pm daily Nov-Feb, 6.30am-9pm daily Mar, Apr & Oct, 6.30am-10pm daily May, 6.30am-11.30pm daily June-Sept)*, a 47-hectare park featuring a neoclassical arch, a sadly neglected arena inaugurated by Napoleon in 1806 and the rather ugly Palazzo dell'Arte.

Palazzo di Brera (Map 3)

East of Castello Sforzesco, sprawling 17th-century Palazzo di Brera houses the **Pinacoteca di Brera** *(☎ 02 894 21 146, ⓔ info@amicidibrera.milano.it, Via Brera 28; MM2 Lanza; adult/child €4.15/free; open 8.30am-7.15pm Tues-Sun)*. Its extensive treasury of paintings has continued to grow since the gallery was inaugurated at the beginning of the 19th century but it's a somewhat fusty old place and a little disappointing. Taking photos (no flash) costs an extra €3.60.

Andrea Mantegna's masterpiece *The Dead Christ* is one of the better-known works on display. Also represented are Raphael, Bellini (look for his *Madonna and Child*), Tiepolo, Rembrandt, Goya, Caravaggio, van Dyck, El Greco and many more.

Cenacolo Vinciano (Map 2)

Leonardo da Vinci's masterful mural depicting the Last Supper decorates one wall of the Cenacolo Vinciano, the refectory adjoining **Chiesa di Santa Maria delle Grazie** *(Corso Magenta; MM1 Conciliazione, MM1/2 Cadorna; see later in this section for information about booking; open 8.30am-7.30pm Tues-Fri & Sun, 8.30am-11.30pm Sat)*. Painted between 1495 and 1498, Leonardo's work is believed to capture – unusually – the moment when Jesus uttered the words 'One of you will betray me'. The word *cenacolo* means refectory, the place where Christ and the 12 Apostles celebrated the Last Supper, and is also used to refer to any mural depicting this scene.

Painstaking restoration of the *Last Supper* began in 1977 and was finally completed in May 1999. Centuries of damage from floods, bombing and decay had left the mural in a lamentable state. The method employed by restorers in the 19th century caused the most damage – their alcohol and cotton wool removed a layer from the painting. Even so, Leonardo must take some of the blame, as his experimental mix of oil and tempera was not very durable. Vasari, the 16th-century biographer of Italian artists, observed that it was already fading in his time. The Dominicans did not help matters in 1652 by raising the refectory floor, callously chopping off a lower section of da Vinci's scene – including Jesus' feet.

Getting to see the *Last Supper* is a medieval test of faith, with groups of 25 sluiced through every 15 minutes. The real hitch, however, is that you have to book ahead by phone *(☎ 02 894 21 146; adult/child €6.20/free, €1.05 booking fee; open 9am-6pm Mon-Fri, 9am-2pm Sat)*; call at least three or four days in advance if you want to guarantee a ticket. Once through to an operator, you'll be allotted a visiting time and a reservation number which you present, 30 minutes before your visit, at the ticket desk of the Cenacolo Vinciano. Turn up late and your ticket will be sold to someone else.

The ticket desk at the refectory sells English-language audioguides (€2.60/4.15 for one/two people). Guided tours (15 minutes) in English cost an extra €3.10 and depart at 11.15am and 3.30pm Tuesday to Friday, 10.15am and 3.30pm on Saturday and Sunday. Again, places must be booked in advance by telephone.

If luck's on your side, you can turn up at the Cenacolo Vinciano and snag a cancellation or unfilled place for a tour that day. If this happens, you'll be allocated a time, made to pay on the spot (minus the €1.05 booking fee) and told to return 10 minutes before the scheduled visit starts.

South of Castello Sforzesco

Housed in the Monastero Maggiore, a 9th-century Benedictine convent rebuilt in the 1500s, the **Civico Museo Archeologico (Map 3)** *(☎ 02 864 50 011, Corso Magenta 15; MM2 Cadorna; free; open 9.30am-5.30pm Tues-Sun)* has substantial Roman, Greek, Etruscan, Gandhara (ancient northwest Indian) and medieval sections. Adjoining it is the **Chiesa di San Maurizio** with 16th-century frescoes by Bernardino Luini. The classical music concerts that are held here are worth attending (see Entertainment later for details).

A short stroll south is Romanesque **Basilica di Sant'Ambrogio (Map 3)** dedicated to Milan's patron saint, St Ambrose (see the boxed text 'A Saint of the World'). Founded in the 4th century by Ambrose, Bishop of Milan, the church on Piazza Sant'Ambrogio has been repaired, rebuilt and restored several times since and is a bit of a hotchpotch of styles. The shorter of the two bell towers dates to the 9th century, as does the remarkable ciborium (freestanding canopy over the altar) under the dome inside. It is believed that at least parts of the columns inside date back to the time of St Ambrose and the saint himself is buried in the crypt. The attached **museum** *(☎ 02 864 50 895, Basilica di Sant' Ambrogio; closed for renovation at the time of writing)* houses relics dating from the earliest days of the basilica's existence.

For proof that Leonardo da Vinci did far more than paint, check out the fascinating displays at one of the world's largest technical museums, the **Museo Nazionale della Scienza e della Tecnica (Map 2)** *(☎ 02 48 55 51, W www.museoscienza.org, Via San Vittore 21; MM2 Sant'Ambrogio; adult/child €6.20/4.15; open 9.30am-5pm Tues-Fri, 9.30am-6.30pm Sat & Sun).*

Around Piazza Cavour (Map 3)

The **Civica Galleria d'Arte Moderna** *(GAM; ☎ 02 760 02 819, Via Palestro 16; MM1 Palestro; free; open 9.30am-5.30pm Tues-Sun)*, in the 18th-century Villa Reale which Napoleon temporarily called home, has a wide collection of 19th-century works, including many from the Milanese neoclassical period. More recent works can be enjoyed in the neighbouring **Padiglione d'Arte Contemporanea** *(PAC; ☎ 02 79 50 14, W www.pac-milano.org, Via Palestro 14; MM1 Palestro; adult/child €5.15/2.60; open 9.30am-5.30pm Tues-Sun).*

To the south, **Chiesa di San Babila** *(MM1 San Babila)* is said to have been built on the site of a palaeo-Christian church dating from AD 46.

Around Navigli

Chiesa di San Lorenzo Maggiore (Map 3) *(Piazza Vetra; MM3 Missori)*, an early Christian church built between 355 and 372 on the site of a Roman building, features several 3rd-century columns. **Chiesa di Sant' Eustorgio (Map 2)** *(Piazza Sant'Eustorgio; MM3 Missori)* was built in the 9th century and altered in the 11th century. It features a 15th-century Cappella Portinari (Chapel of St Peter Martyr) and a baptistry designed by Donato Bramante.

A block north of the Naviglio Grande canal, an abandoned factory is being transformed by British architect David Chipperfield into a state-of-the-art **Città delle Culture (Map 2)** *(City of Cultures; Via Bergognone 34)*. The complex will house an archaeological museum, a cultural centre displaying world ethnographical exhibits, TV studios, a cinema school, puppet workshops, bookshops and a couple of bars and restaurants. The €14 million project should be completed by 31 December 2005.

Courses

International House *(☎ 02 527 91 24, fax 02 556 00 324, e ih.milan@iname.com, Piazza*

A Saint of the World

When the future St Ambrose (Sant'Ambrogio) was appointed bishop of Milan in 374 his credentials were hardly in order – he hadn't even been baptised. Small matter. This former governor of Liguria had impressed everyone with his skills in umpiring between Catholics and Arians (a Christian sect that denied Christ's oneness with God), so he received all the sacraments and the mitre in an unusually accelerated procedure.

At that time, Milan was the effective capital of the western half of the crumbling Roman Empire and Ambrose became a leading figure in imperial politics. He and the emperor of the Western Roman Empire, Gratian, embarked on a crusade to eradicate paganism and the Arian heresy.

His influence grew to such an extent that he was later able to challenge the authority of Theodosius – the eastern emperor and guarantor of the Western Empire after Gratian's assassination – with impunity. In one incident, the emperor ordered Christians to rebuild a synagogue they'd burned. Ambrogio demanded the order be revoked and, threatening to thump the pulpit and stir popular feeling, convinced the emperor to see things his way.

Ambrogio, the public functionary who had never been a priest, was a powerful and charismatic bishop. He was the incarnation of the triumph of spiritual over secular power. He presaged the Church's future political role in European affairs and inspired the composition of the *Te Deum*. He died in 397.

Erculea 9) **Map 3** €361/155 for a two-/four-week course (15 hours' group tuition per week) plus €51.65 registration fee. This is one of several language schools in Milan to offer individual and group courses in Italian. Ten hours' private tuition costs €413. International House also runs two-week courses (two afternoons per week) in Italian cookery and wine (€129) and Italian opera history (€180).

Istituto Europeo di Design *(☎ 02 579 69 51, fax 02 550 12 613, Via Sciesa 4)* **Map 2** For courses in photography, interior design, fashion design and graphic advertising, this is the place. It runs intensive one-month summer courses and full-time three-year courses.

Scuola Orafa Ambrosiana di Luca Solari *(☎/fax 02 294 05 005, W www.scuolaorafaambrosiana.com, Via Alessandro Tadino 30)* **Map 2** Aspiring jewellers can learn the art of crafting gold at the goldsmith school. It offers 'hobby' goldsmith courses comprising 50 hours' individual tuition (three hours per day) as well as advanced courses in enamel work and waxing.

Università Bocconi *(☎ 02 583 62 018, W www.uni-bocconi.it, Via R Sarfatti 25)* **Map 2** The Università Bocconi offers a fashion and design component in its MBA course (in Italian). Aspiring McQueens can also try the Università Cattolica *(☎ 02 7 23 41, Largo Gemellis 1)*.

LOMBARDY

Work

If you are so taken with Milan that you'd like to live there, one possible source of work is teaching English. There are many schools but competition is stiff and pay unspectacular.

The British Council (Map 3; Via Manzoni 38, ☎ 02 77 22 21, fax 02 78 11 19, W www.britishcouncil.it) can't find you work, but it can provide you with an information sheet on employment in Milan. It directs job-hunters to Manpower (Map 2; ☎ 02 706 08 324, W www.manpower.it, Via d'Ovidio 8), an employment agency which handles work for English speakers.

Otherwise, pick up a copy of *Secondamano* (W www.secondamano.it), a Milan-based newspaper crammed with classifieds and advertisements.

Organised Tours

Autostradale *(☎ 02 339 10 794 or 02 80 11 61, outside the APT office on Piazza del Duomo)* 3-hour bus tour €38.75 at 9.30am daily. Tickets include admission to Da Vinci's *Last Supper* and the Pinacoteca di Brera.

Tourist tram *(☎ 02 720 02 584 for information and reservations)* Tickets €15.50. 11am, 1pm & 3pm daily Apr-Oct; 11am & 1pm Mon-Fri, 11am, 1pm & 3pm Sat & Sun Nov-Mar. Run by ATM's Ciao Milano, this is a vintage piece from the 1920s that runs past the main points of interest. You can get on and off as you please.

You can buy tickets for both the Autostradale and tourist tram tours at the APT office (Map 3).

Between mid-April and the end of July, the APT office runs day trips to Lago di Como (see that section later in this chapter), departing every Sunday at 9am and returning to Milan around 1pm. Trips cost €54.25 per person and include breakfast in Como, a mini cruise on the lake and a visit to a silk mill.

Special Events

The Festa di Sant'Ambrogio, 7 December, is Milan's biggest feast day. Celebrations take place at the Fiera di Milano (MM1 Amendola Fiera), the trade, conference and exhibition centre north-west of the city centre. La Scala marks the solemn occasion by opening its opera season on this day.

The first 10 days of June are devoted to the Festa del Naviglio, a smorgasbord of parades, music and other performances. Milan plays year-round host to fairs of all kinds – the big fashion shows are held in January, February/March, June/July and September/October.

The Milan Jazz Festival rocks through the city in November, the highlight of a jam-packed, year-round calendar of jazz festivals. The APT office has details of others.

Places to Stay

Milan's hotels are among Italy's most expensive and are pricey even by London, Paris or Rome standards. Finding a room (let alone a cheap one) can be literally impossible at times – especially if there's a trade fair on, when hotels hike up their prices even further. However, most mid-range and top-end hotels don't have fixed rates meaning you can negotiate at quieter times.

The APT offices rarely make recommendations and never take bookings but they do distribute *Milano Hotels*, a free 130-page listings guide to Milan's 350-odd hotels.

Places to Stay – Budget

Camping There is one recommended camp site.

Campeggio Città di Milano *(☎ 02 482 00 134, fax 02 482 02 999, Via G Airaghi 61)* **Off Map 1** Sites per person/tent/car €6.20/5.15/1.55. Open Feb-Nov. Take the metro to De Angeli station (MM1), then bus No 72 from Piazza de Angeli to the Di Vittorio stop, from where it is a 400m walk to the camp site. By car, leave the Tangenziale Ovest at San Siro-Via Novara.

Hostels & Religious Institutions The city's hostel is out of the city centre.

Ostello Piero Rotta *(☎ 02 392 67 095, fax 02 330 00 191, Viale Angelo Salmoiraghi 1)* **Map 1** B&B €15.50. To get to this HI hostel, take the metro to QT8, from where it is a two-minute walk south along Viale Angelo Salmoiraghi.

Protezione della Giovane *(☎ 02 290 00 164, Corso Garibaldi 123)* **Map 2** B&B €22.20. East of Parco Sempione, Protezione della Giovane accommodates women aged between 16 and 25.

Hotels – Stazione Centrale & Corso Buenos Aires (Map 2) Many budget places in this area, although handy, double quietly (and sometimes not so quietly!) as brothels. You could easily sleep in one of these places and be blissfully ignorant – or you could be less fortunate.

Hotel Valley *(☎ 02 669 27 77, fax 02 669 87 552, Via Soperga 19)* Singles/doubles without bath €36.15/67.15, with bath €61.95/77.47. Hotel Valley is not in the greatest of spots but the rooms are reasonable and the staff friendly. Reception opens 24 hours; buzz to get in.

Hotel Del Sole *(☎ 02 295 12 971, fax 02 295 13 689, Via Gaspare Spontini 6)* Singles/doubles/triples without bath €31/47/67.15, with bath €47/67.15/77.47. The mirrored walls at this hotel east of Corso Buenos Aires make it a must for voyeurs.

Hotel Nettuno *(☎ 02 294 04 481, fax 02 295 23 819, Via Tadino 27)* Singles/doubles without bath €31/47, with bath €47/61.95. Distinctly dodgy but dirt cheap, these rock-bottom rooms are a 10-minute walk south-east of Stazione Centrale.

Hotel Casa Mia *(☎ 02 657 52 49, fax 02 655 22 28, Viale Vittorio Veneto 30)* Singles/doubles €47/75. Down near Piazza della Repubblica, renovated Hotel Casa Mia has something of a family atmosphere. Rates don't appear to be fixed, so try to bargain.

Hotel Verona *(☎ 02 669 83 091, fax 02 669 87 236, Via Carlo Tenca 12)* Singles/doubles €56.80/82.65. Hotel Verona, close to Piazza della Repubblica, is another place where you can bargain down the price depending on the day of the week and time of year.

Hotel Kennedy *(☎ 02 294 00 934, fax 02 294 01 253, Viale Tunisia 6)* Singles/doubles without bath €36.15/47, doubles with bath €67.15. Rooms at this one-star joint are acceptable (despite being on the 6th floor).

Hotel San Tomaso *(☎/fax 02 295 14 747, Viale Tunisia 3)* Singles/doubles without bath €33.55/54.25, with shower €36.15/61.95, doubles with toilet and shower €77.45. Three floors down from the Kennedy, Hotel San Tomaso touts a friendly English-speaking staff and basic but sleepable-in rooms.

Hotel Poerio *(☎ 02 295 22 872, Via Poerio 32)* Singles/doubles from €41.30/ 56.80. Tucked down a quiet residential street, Hotel Poerio must be Milan's most peaceful budget option.

Hotels – City Centre & Navigli (Map 3) There are fewer budget options in the centre of Milan.

Albergo Commercio *(☎ 02 864 63 880, Via Mercato 1)* Singles/doubles with shower €41.30/51.65. This place is often full. From Piazza Cordusio, walk north up Via Broletto, which later becomes Via Mercato Vetero. The entrance to the hotel is around the corner in Via delle Erbe.

Hotel Speronari *(☎ 02 864 61 125, fax 02 720 03 178, Via Speronari 4)* Singles/doubles without shower €41.30/61.95, with shower €51.65/77.47, doubles with bath €92.95. Rooms with bath are substantially more comfortable than those without. At all costs, avoid the single room 'usually reserved for hotel staff' – unless you have a fetish for windowless rooms with walls so thin you know every time your neighbour pulls the chain.

Hotel Nuovo *(☎ 02 864 64 444, fax 02 864 60 542, Piazza Beccaria 6)* Singles/doubles without bath €31/47, doubles/triples with bath from €61.95/103.30. Strangely flashy from the outside, this one-star pad is just off Corso Vittorio Emanuele II and offers a good deal for your money.

Places to Stay – Mid-Range (Map 3)

Hotel Gritti *(☎ 02 80 10 56, fax 02 890 10 999, Ⓦ www.hotelgritti.com, Piazza Santa Maria Beltrade 4)* Singles/doubles/triples €90.40/129.10/180.75. Midway along Via Torino, this three-star place overlooks a quiet(ish) square and often has rooms available when others don't.

Hotel Vecchio Milano *(☎ 02 87 50 42, fax 02 864 54 292, Via Borromei 4)* Singles/doubles €67.15/103.30. Old-world charm exudes from 'Old Milan', perfectly placed in a quiet cobbled street off Via Torino.

Hotel London *(☎ 02 720 20 166, fax 02 805 70 37, Via Rovello 3)* Singles/doubles without bath €72.30/103.30, with bath €82.65/129.15. Off Via Dante, Hotel London looks swanky but charges reasonable rates. Pay in hard cash and get a 10% discount.

Hotel Cairoli *(☎ 02 80 13 71, fax 02 720 02 243, Via Porlezza 4)* Singles/doubles €103.30/154.95. In a quiet alley close to Castello Sforzesco, Hotel Cairoli is just off Via Camperio.

LOMBARDY

Places to Stay – Top End

Hotel de la Ville *(☎ 02 86 76 51, fax 02 86 66 09, Via Hoepli 6)* **Map 3** Singles/doubles from €211.75/273.70. This large hotel, unattractive from the outside but stunning inside, has long lured a long-legged catwalk set.

Grand Hotel Duomo *(☎ 02 88 33, fax 02 864 62 027, Ⓔ grandduomo@hotmail.com, Via San Raffaele 1)* **Map 3** Singles/doubles from €227.25/320.20. With five golden stars pinned up outside, how can one possibly complain?

Grand Hotel et de Milan *(☎ 02 864 60 861, Ⓦ www.grandhoteletdemilan.it, Via Alessandro Manzoni 29)* **Map 3** Singles/doubles from €300/372. Milan's most prestigious hotel dates to 1863 and was home to Verdi for the last few years of his life.

Albergo Excelsior Gallia *(☎ 02 6 78 51, fax 02 667 13 239, Ⓦ www.excelsiorgallia.it, Piazza Duca d'Aosta 9)* **Map 2** Singles/doubles from €387.35/464.80. Ernest Hemingway and Maria Callas stayed at this elegant Art Nouveau hotel, a stroll back into early 20th-century splendour opposite Stazione Centrale.

Places to Eat

Italians say Lombard cuisine is designed for people who don't have time to waste (because they're always in a hurry for work). The result? The streets around the cathedral and north towards Stazione Centrale are littered with sandwich bars and fast-food outlets – ideal for eaters on a tight budget. At the other end of the scale, you can blow a small fortune on dining, should you wish.

The city has a strong provincial cuisine. Polenta (a cornmeal porridge similar to American grits) is served with almost everything and risotto – traditionally scented with saffron (hence its bold yellow colour) and bone marrow to become risotto *alla milanese* – dominates the first course of many menus. Meaty dishes worth sinking your teeth into include *fritto misto alla milanese* (fried slices of bone marrow, liver and lung), *busecca* (sliced tripe boiled with beans) and *cotoletta alla milanese* (a breaded and fried veal cutlet offering fewer surprises).

Bar snacks are an institution in Milan and most bars lay out their fare from 5pm daily.

Restaurants – Stazione Centrale & Around (Map 2) The area around Stazione Centrale offers plenty of places to grab a bite.

Brek *(Piazza Cavour)* and ***Ciao*** *(Corso Buenos Aires 7, Corso Europa & Via Dante 5)* are canteen-style chains – superior alternatives to hamburger joints – where you can refuel on quality fodder for less than €7.75.

Osteria del Treno *(☎ 02 670 04 79, Via San Gregorio 46–48)* Full meals about €10.35. Open Mon-Sat. This traditional osteria is a wise choice for those seeking a taste of quintessential Milan.

West of Stazione Centrale near the Cimitero Monumentale is a trio of trendy eating places which double as late-night drinking spots.

ATM *(☎ 02 655 23 65, Bastioni di Porta Volta 15)* 1st/2nd courses €5.16/7.75. The ungainly bunker sandwiched between speeding cars on a traffic island was an ATM terminal until Milanese glamour queens transformed it into the chic place it is today.

Bahnhof *(☎ 02 290 01 511, Via Giuseppe Ferrari)* Full meals about €15.50. In the pits overlooking the tracks into Stazione Porta Garibaldi, trendy Bahnhof's stainless-steel interior and moderately priced food are worth the hike.

Honky Tonks *(☎ 02 345 25 62, Via Fratelli Induno 10)* Full meals about €12.90. Looking for the best grub in Wyoming? Go no further than this US-inspired 1940s diner, 'three minutes north of Jackson on the 26/89/189'.

Restaurants – City Centre On the northern side of Piazza del Duomo, ***Autogrill*** houses Burger King, Spizzico and Ciao. It opens 7am to 2am.

Trattoria da Pino *(☎ 02 760 00 532, Via Cerva 14)* **Map 3** Lunch menu €10.85. Open lunchtimes only. Nowhere can beat the cost–quality ratio dished up at this authentic trattoria where strangers dine at shared tables. Its lunchtime menu is built solely from hearty home-made cooking and includes a 25cl jug of wine or 50cl of mineral water.

Armandola *(☎ 02 760 21 657, Via della Spiga 50)* **Map 3** In the Monte Napoleone district, shoppers can indulge in a cheap bowl of pasta standing up. Pick the right day and white Alba truffles might just end up (at a price) on your plate.

Trattoria Bagutta *(☎ 02 760 00 902, Via Bagutta 14–16)* **Map 3** 1st/2nd courses €10.35/15.50. Open Mon-Sat. In the 1950s the infamous Gucci clan frequently dined at this fashionable 1920s trattoria, a scissor-snip away from their Via Monte Napoleone boutique.

Il Coriandolo *(☎ 02 869 32 73, Via dell'Orso 1)* **Map 3** 1st/2nd courses from €8.25/13.45. Dine on delicious *risotto alla vecchia maniera Milanese* (old Milanese risotto) beneath an ornate moulded ceiling on the edge of Brera.

Antica Osteria Milanese *(☎ 02 86 13 67, Via M Camperio 12)* **Map 3** 1st/2nd courses about €10.35/12.90. This traditional, frill-free trattoria fills up with suits (predominantly males) every lunchtime. Don't miss the *meneghina alla griglia al Grand Marnier* (€4.15), Milanese sponge cake soaked in liqueur and baked.

Il Salumaio *(☎ 02 78 46 50, Via Monte Napoleone 12)* **Map 3** 1st/2nd courses €14.45/18.10. A fine delicatessen and restaurant with courtyard terrace in the fashion district, Il Salumaio is the spot to dine – any time of day – between shops.

Orsoblu Bistrot *(☎ 02 78 25 16, Corso Concordia 2)* **Map 2** 1st/2nd courses €10.35/15.50. Open evenings Mon-Sat. With a decor said to represent the five elements, this is the place to impress friends with your knowledge of feng shui – the inspiration behind this oh-so-cool bistro.

In Brera, hip places line Via Fiori Chiari, known for its pavement terraces in summer.

Orient Express *(☎ 02 805 62 27, Via Fiori Chiari 8)* **Map 3** 1st/2nd courses from €8.25/13.95. It might resemble a train, but prices are less than its Vienna-bound equivalent. Sunday sees the chic crowd flock here for brunch or a post antique-browsing drink.

Restaurants – Navigli (Map 3) Options abound in this area, renowned for its innovative cuisine cooked up by a mixed bag of chefs. Canalside Ripa di Porta Ticinese makes for a particularly tasty evening stroll. For good, cheap Greek snacks and meals, you can't beat ***Ghireria Greca*** *(Ripa di Porta Ticinese 13)*.

Al Pont de Fer *(☎ 02 894 06 277, Ripa di Ticinese 55)* 1st/2nd courses €4.65/7.75. Sip wine and discover ecstasy with a sublime slice of caramel-and-honey tart.

Le Vigne *(☎ 02 837 56 17, Ripa di Ticinese 61)* 1st/2nd courses €4.65/5.15. Those seeking nothing more than a feast of local cheese and wine are heartily welcomed here.

Osteria dei Formaggi Asso di Fiori *(☎ 02 894 09 415, Alzaia Naviglio Grande 54)* 1st/2nd courses €7.25/10.35. This traditional osteria is a must for cheese fiends – Italian cheese makes up every dish.

Ponte Rosso *(☎ 02 837 31 32, Ripa di Porta Ticinese 23)* Full meals about €23.25. 'Red Bridge' is run by a wine and balsamic vinegar connoisseur who also collects corkscrews, cocktail shakers and miniature toys. Attempt to order anything less than the four-course dining experience and you'll be severely frowned upon.

Brellin *(☎ 02 581 01 351, Alzaia Naviglio Grande 14)* 1st/2nd courses €6.70/11.90. Brellin's canalside flower-filled garden is unique among Milanese restaurants.

Trattoria all'Antica *(☎ 02 837 28 49, Via Montevideo 4)* Full meals about €15.50. Eat home-made gnocchi here. Most dishes require at least two people; solo diners can ask what their neighbour's ordered.

LOMBARDY

Pizzerias There are plenty of pizzerias to chose from.

Spontini Pizzeria *(☎ 02 204 74 44, Via Gaspare Spontini)* **Map 2** Pizza slices from €0.75. This busy little pizza joint cooks up the best pizza in the Stazione Centrale area. Neighbouring ***Spontini Bar*** is equally popular with snackers.

Luini *(☎ 02 864 61 917, Via Santa Radegonda 16)* **Map 3** One of Milan's oldest fast-food outlets sells *panzerotti* (pizza dough stuffed with tomatoes, garlic and mozzarella).

Di Gennaro *(☎ 02 805 34 54, Via Santa Radegonda 14)* **Map 3** Pizzas €2.30-6.10. Well placed near Galleria Vittorio Emanuele II, Di Gennaro cooked up the first Milanese pizza.

Pizzeria Naturale *(☎ 02 839 57 10, Via Edmondo de Amicis 24)* **Map 3** Pizzas €5.15-10.35. Tea infusions and wholemeal pizzas are among the decidedly non-naughty options offered here for the health-conscious.

Paper Moon *(☎ 02 760 22 297, Via Bagutta 1)* **Map 3** 1st/2nd courses €9.30/12.90. Minimalist Paper Moon lures a chic, well-dressed crowd. Its fresh asparagus (in season) topped with two fried eggs is a must-try.

Cafes & Bars In the Stazione Centrale area, ***Pattini & Marinoni*** *(***Map 2** *Corso Buenos Aires 53;* **Map 3** *Piazza Cadorna 10)* sells delicious breads and pizza slices for about €1.55. As well as the numerous 'in-your-face' tourist options around Piazza del Duomo, there's a handful of less obvious places which lack the pretension and inflated prices of the piazza's terraced cafes.

Bar Biffino *(Via Andegari 15)* **Map 3** Grab a sandwich (€3.60) and extra-frothy cappuccino (€1.20) between sights at this friendly tobacconists (entrance on Via Alessandro Manzoni).

Gran Caffè Visconti *(☎ 02 805 25 56, Piazza del Duomo)* **Map 3** Sit on the western side of Piazza del Duomo and munch on a cake-and-coffee breakfast from 7am.

Café Rêve *(☎ 02 760 01 505, Via della Spiga 42)* **Map 3** 1st/2nd courses €7.75/10.35. 'Absolutely fabulous' sums up this chic spot which serves some of Milan's most creative cafe food.

Caffè della Pusteria *(☎ 02 894 02 146, Via Edmondo de Amicis 22)* **Map 3** Lunch from €10.35. An old-fashioned, jazz-inspired interior and a terrace beneath vines lure a young and trendy lunchtime crowd.

Sunflower Bar *(☎ 02 760 22 754, Via Pietro Verri 8)* **Map 3** This is another haunt of the fashion-conscious with a terrace bar beneath arches.

Bar Centro *(☎ 02 760 01 415, Corso G Matteotti 3)* **Map 3** It might have a boring name but Bar Centro touts an eclectic decor and a cool cocktail-and-cappuccino-quaffing crowd.

Pottery Café *(☎ 02 890 13 660, Via Solferino 3)* **Map 3** Paint your own plate while sipping espresso or munching brunch (€23.25 including pottery piece).

Coco's (☎ *02 454 83 253, Via San Prospero 4)* **Map 3** Italy's first vegetarian chain fries up veggie burgers (€3.05 or €3.35 with cheese) in a soulful wooden interior.

Gelaterias (Map 3) If you are after ice cream, there's one great recommendation.

Viel (☎ *02 295 16 123, Via Alessandro Manzoni 3e & Corso Buenos Aires 15)* Open 8am-2am Wed-Mon. Ice creams and *frullati di frutta* (fruit shakes) here are packed with fruit, as the lush displays waiting to be mushed up testify.

Self-Catering (Map 3) Via Speronari, just off Piazza del Duomo, is the best street around the cathedral for bread, cakes, salami, cheese, fruit and wine. ***Il Bread & Breakfast*** *(Via Speronari 6)* sells pizza slices, cakes, bread and fresh pasta. ***Superfresco Standa*** *(Via Palla 2a)* is a five-minute walk away; its entrance is on Via Torino. ***Peck*** *(W www.peck.it, Via Spadari 7–9)* is a must for gourmet eating. Established in 1883, it is one of Europe's elite food outlets – as tempting as London's Harrods and famous since 1920 for its home-made ravioli, 3200 variations of *parmigiano reggiano* (parmesan) and wine cellar.

Historical Cafes

These institutions (all on Map 3) are fabulous places for breakfast, lunch or an early-evening aperitif in the company of a lavish array of never-ending hors d'oeuvres.

Il Salotto *(Galleria Vittorio Emanuele II)* Milan's 'drawing room' is generally filled with tourists and harassed waiters. An outrageous €3.60 for a cappuccino (sitting down) is the price you pay for its historical location.

Zucca in Galleria (☎ *02 864 64 435, Galleria Vittorio Emanuele II 21)* 1st/2nd courses €9.30/15.50. Milan's most historic cafe overlooks Piazza del Duomo. Its Art-Deco mosaic interior dates to 1867.

Cova (☎ *02 760 05 578, Via Monte Napoleone 8)* Founded in 1817 by a soldier in Napoleon's army who set up shop in front of La Scala, this elegant tearoom has languished in Monte Napoleone since 1950 (the original was destroyed during WWII). Sip champagne amid Japanese tourists.

Marchesi (☎ *02 87 67 30, Via S M alla Porta 11a)* The legendary marchioness has been in the cake-and-coffee business since 1824. Her heavily wood-panelled interior shelters luscious displays of chess and draughtboards made from chocolate.

Entertainment

Milan has some of Italy's top clubs, several cinemas screening English-language films and a fabulous year-round cultural calendar, topped off by La Scala's opera season. The main theatre and concert season opens in October.

Other than those mentioned in this guide, there are at least another 50 active theatres in Milan; check the newspapers and ask at the APT office.

An essential reference for culture buffs is *Milano Mese*, a free monthly entertainment guide (in English) available at APT offices.

For club listings, *Corriere della Sera* (W www.corriere.it) runs a reasonable supplement, *ViviMilano* (W www.vivimilano.it) on Wednesday. *La Repubblica* (W www.repubblica.it) counters on Thursday with *Tutto Milano*. Both papers run cinema listings too.

Bars & Pubs There are two areas in particular to search for a drink, some music and the madding crowd. Otherwise, good bars are sprinkled at distant intervals across the city. Most chic and trendy bars stay open until 2am or 3am.

Brera (Map 3) This is the stamping ground for trendy Milanese who mill through its narrow lanes and swirl in and out of watering holes where a beer costs from €4.15 to €10.35. A clutch of smoke-filled joints are gathered along cobbled Via Fiori Chiari, including ***Cajun Louisana Bistro*** *(Via Fiori Chiari 17)*, a US-style music bar.

Biblos (☎ *02 869 84 517,* e *biblosbiblos@hotmail.com, Via Madonnina 17)* Big hip Biblos is popular with a mixed bag of revellers.

Le Trottoir *(☎ 02 80 10 02, Corso Garibaldi 1)* Aspiring artists hang wild art on the walls of this wacky bar. Its small stage hosts alternative bands (often jazz) and food is served upstairs.

Jamaica *(☎ 02 87 67 23, Via Brera 32)* Artists and intellectuals have lamented the world's woes here since 1921. Lap up Brera street life on its pavement terrace.

Navigli & Porta Ticinese For an alternative to the Brera bars, head south along Corso di Porta Ticinese. Several bars float on moored canal barges alongside Via Ascanio Sforza.

Café Viarenna *(☎ 02 839 22 11, Piazza XXIV Maggio 4)* **Map 2** Happy punters make this music bar throb from 7am to 2am daily. Lunch here (1st/2nd courses €3.60/5.15) overlooking the park.

Le Biciclette *(☎ 02 581 04 325, Via Torti 1)* **Map 3** In a converted bicycle workshop, Le Biciclette is an ode to two wheels, a busy bar and a popular Sunday-brunch spot (€15.50).

Fanfüla *(☎ 02 894 06 749, Ripa di Porta Ticinese 37)* **Map 2** The grungy feel here – a *paninoteca* (sandwich shop), *birreria* (beer hall) and *enoteca* (wine bar) rolled into one – makes a refreshing change. Live music tops off weekend sessions.

How to Buy Tickets

Theatre and concert listings and tickets can be booked through ***Ticket One*** *(☎ 02 39 22 61 or toll free ☎ 840 05 27 20, W www.ticketone.it)* or ***Ticket Web*** *(☎ 02 760 09 131, W www.ticketweb.it)*. ***Milano Concerti*** *(☎ 02 487 02 726, W www.milanoconcerti.it)* handles tickets for international rock concerts.

In Milan itself, try the *biglietteria* (ticket office) inside ***FNAC*** *(☎ 02 87 80 04, e fnac@ticketweb.it, Via Palla 2)*; ***Virgin Megastore*** *(☎ 02 720 03 370, Duomo Centre, Piazza del Duomo)*; ***Messaggerie Musicali*** *(☎ 02 79 55 02, Galleria del Corso 20, entrance on Corso Vittorio Emanuele II)*; and ***Ricordi Mediastore*** *(☎ 02 864 60 272, W www.ricordimediastores.it, Galleria Vittorio Emanuele II)*.

Elsewhere Beyond the main drinking area are plenty of other options.

Bar Magenta *(☎ 02 805 38 08, Via Giosue Carducci 13)* **Map 3** Seekers of that quintessential aperitif and more adventurous Milanese night owls have long sought solace here.

L'Atlantique *(☎ 02 551 93 925, Viale Umbria 42)* **Map 2** Interior design is hi tech and Sunday brunch is served from 12.30pm at this hip bar, oh so *alla moda*.

Ronchino's *(☎ 02 869 98 097, Via San Maurilio 8)* **Map 3** Ronchino's is an unpretentious enoteca, tucked down a narrow street off Via Torino, with live music from Thursday to Saturday.

Lelephante *(☎ 02 295 18 768, Via Melzo 22)* **Map 2** Open 6pm-2am Tues-Sun. A myriad of boldly coloured walls and an even bolder collection of chairs make this a very hip place to hang out.

Artdeco Café *(☎ 02 295 24 720, Via Lambro 7)* **Map 2** On the opposite side of the street to Lelephante, the interior here is the ultimate in interior design. The tables are Milan's snazziest.

Makia *(☎ 02 336 04 012, Corso Sempione 28)* **Map 2** The furnishings at this ultramodern drinks and food bar reflect the very latest in contemporary design – a drawcard with Milan's hobnobbing set.

Discos & Clubs Milan boasts dozens of places to dance the night away, although the 'scene' for Milanese social butterflies revolves around 10 or so clubs, generally open until 3am or 4am daily.

La Banque *(☎ 02 869 96 565, Via Porrone 6)* **Map 3** Among the most central of clubs, this was indeed a bank before the clerks moved out and the clubbers in.

Heaven *(☎ 02 864 62 575, Via Fiori Chiari 17)* **Map 3** Brick meets steel in Brera.

Shocking *(Bastioni di Porta Nuova 12)* **Map 2** Face control rules at Shocking, a highly fashionable place known for its thematic music nights.

Alcatraz *(☎ 02 690 16 352, Via Valtellina 25)* **Map 1** Alcatraz, an excellent venue for live concerts to the north of the city centre, s transformed into one of Milan's biggest lubs at weekends.

I Magazzini Generali (☎ *02 552 11 313, 'ia Pietrasanta 14)* **Map 1** This thumping pace, happily housed in a converted ware-ıouse, is a fair hike south of the city centre.

ᴚock If you are keen on rock, ***Propaganda*** ☎ *02 583 10 682, Via Gian Carlo Castel-›arco 11)* and ***Rolling Stone*** (☎ *02 73 31 '2, Corso XXII Marzo 32)* are live-band 'enues to watch out for. Both are on Map 2.

The biggest names play at ***Palavobis*** ☎ *02 334 00 551, Viale Sant'Elia 33)* **(Map)**, near the San Siro stadium, and ***Filafo-um di Assago*** (☎ *02 48 85 71,* **W** *www filaforum.it)*, farther out of town. To get to he latter, take the MM2 line to Romolo and ›ick up a special shuttle bus put on for :oncerts.

Ɔpera La Scala's main opera season runs rom 7 December through to July but – with he exception of the last two weeks in July ınd all of August – you can see theatre, bal-et and concerts here year-round.

Scoring tickets to the opera requires luck ınd perseverance. Performances sell out nonths before. Your only hope may be the !00 standing-room tickets, which are sold for as little as €5.15) at the entrance to the Auseo Teatrale alla Scala 45 minutes before he scheduled starting time. Rarer still are ickets for unsold seats sold (at half-price) rom noon on the day of the performance. 'eople turn up from 6am to queue.

The ***Teatro alla Scala box office*** (☎ *02 '20 03 744,* **W** *www.lascala.milano.it, Via Filodrammatici; open noon-6pm daily & 30 ninutes before performances start)* **(Map 3)** s tucked in the portico at the side of the ›pera house. Pre-booked tickets carry a !0% surcharge.

Classical Music There are plenty of op-›ortunities to hear classical music in Milan.

Conservatorio Giuseppe Verdi (☎ *02 762 1 101,* **W** *www.verdi-2001.com, Via del Conservatorio 12)* **Map 3** The best of Milan's fat calendar of classical concerts :an usually be enjoyed here.

Auditorium di Milano (☎ *02 833 89 201, Corso San Gottardo 42a)* **Map 2** This prestigious venue is near Ripa di Porta Ticinese.

Chiesa di San Maurizio *(Corso Magenta 15)* **Map 3** Concerts of Baroque and Renaissance pieces by small ensembles are often held in this atmospheric church, inside Monastero Maggiore. Tickets for performances are sold at the APT office.

Cinemas English-language films (☎ 02 657 10 93 for programme information) are shown at these cinemas: ***Anteo*** (☎ *02 659 77 32,* **W** *www.anteospaziocinema.com, Via Milazzo 9)* **(Map 2)**; ***Pilnius*** (☎ *02 295 31 103, Viale Abruzzi 28–30)* **(Map 2)**; and ***Mexico*** (☎ *02 489 51 802, Via Savona 57)* **(Map 2)**. Tickets cost €5.15. Historic ***Odeon*** (☎ *02 87 45 47, Via S Radegonda 8)* **(Map 3)** occasionally shows original-language films too.

Spectator Sports

The Italian Grand Prix tears around the ***Autodromo Nazionale Monza*** (☎ *039 2 48 21,* **W** *www.monzanet.it)* each September. The track, some 20km north of central Milan, can be reached along Viale Monza from Piazzale Loreto. See Motor Racing under Spectator Sports in the Facts for the Visitor chapter for more details.

Milan's two football clubs, AC Milan and FC Internazionale Milano (known simply as Inter) play on alternate Sundays in season at the San Siro stadium, also called Meazza. Take tram No 24, bus No 95, 49 or 72, or the metro to the Lotto metro station (MM1), from where a free shuttle bus runs to the stadium. Tickets are available at the stadium or, for AC Milan matches, from ***Milan Point*** (☎ *02 79 64 81, Via San Pietro all'Orto 8)* **(Map 3)** or branches of the Cariplo bank. For Inter matches, try Banca Popolare di Milano branches or call ☎ 02 7 70 01. See Football under Spectator Sports in the Facts for the Visitor chapter for more details.

Shopping

Anything that money can buy can be snapped up in Milan. Its many design shops sell sought-after pieces, while famous fashion boutiques fill the Golden Quad (see the boxed text 'Fashion'). The streets for more affordable clothing, footwear and accessories are behind the cathedral around Corso Vittorio Emanuele II, and between Piazza della Scala and Piazza San Babila. In the 1960s Giorgio Armani dressed the windows of La Rinascente (Map 3), Milan's department store on the northern side of Piazza del Duomo.

Markets fill the waterfronts around th canals, notably on Viale Papiniano on Tues day and Saturday mornings. There is a fle market in Viale Gabriele d'Annunzio o Saturday and an antique market in Brera a Via Fiori Chiari every third Saturday of th month. A huge market where you can bu anything is held on the last Sunday of eac month on the Alzaia Naviglio Grande an Ripa di Porta Ticinese.

Fashion

Milan's Golden Quad (Quadrilatero d'Oro) – Europe's fashion Mecca where the world's best-known designers showcase the season's creations – is sketched out by Via della Spiga, Via Sant'Andrea, Via Monte Napoleone and Via Alessandro Manzoni. See the Golden Quad (Quadrilatero d'Oro) map.

Big names stud traffic-free Via della Spiga, including glove house ***Semoneta*** *(No 46)*; kids' fashion house ***I Pinco Pallini*** *(No 44)*; Florentine designer ***Robert Cavalli*** *(No 42)*, whose sensuality-driven designs dress Whitney Houston; Madonna's favourite fashion house, ***Dolce & Gabbana***, which has three shops here; and New York's bejewelled ***Tiffany & Co*** *(No 19a)*. Amid the clutch of Milan-bred couturiers, look for ***Krizia*** *(No 23)*; power-dresser ***Gian Franco Ferré*** *(No 11)*; and ***Gio Moretti*** *(Nos 4 and 9)* – shop at No 4 for designs by Elvira Biki (Puccini's Milanese granddaughter) and at No 9 for designer baby grows and other such stuff). Nearby, powerhouse ***Prada*** flaunts its lingerie and shoe collections.

Strutting down Via Sant'Andrea, twirl through ***Chanel*** *(No 10)*, the women's collection at ***Prada*** *(No 21)*, and the men's collection at ***Gian Franco Ferré*** *(No 15)*. Fried eggs for blazer buttons and designs dripping in irony are the trademarks of Milanese wild child ***Moschino*** *(No 12)*. ***Kenzo*** and ***Armani*** sit serenely farther south.

Via Monte Napoleone (or 'Monte Napo' as the 'in' crowd know it) offers ample opportunity to shell out shedloads of cash. ***Prada*** *(Nos 8 and 6)*, with its origins in a 1913 Milanese leatherwear shop, dominates the southern end of this exclusive street with state-of-the-art boutiques. Florence-founded ***Gucci***, another darling of Italy's fashion scene, has been at Via Monte Napoleone 5 since 1951. It has another boutique at No 27. Maurizio, the last Gucci to rule the empire, was shot by his estranged wife outside his office at Via Palestro 20 in 1995.

Mariella Burani *(No 3)* dresses, among others, the larger-sized woman (Piu'donna). Stunning (and stunningly pricey) sportswear fills Florentine fashion house ***Emilio Pucci*** *(No 14)*, next door to ***Louis Vuitton***. Shoe queens can have a ball with ***Bally***, ***Sergio Rossi*** and ***Camper*** *(No 6a)*, ***Salvadore Feragamo*** *(No 3)*, and ***Fausto Santini*** and ***Fratelli Rossetti*** *(No 1)*.

Girls seeking diamonds as a best friend can try police-guarded ***Cartier*** on the corner of Via Monte Napoleone and Via Gesu; or ***Damiani*** *(Via Monte Napoleone 16)*. Glittering gobstoppers aside, its dramatic marble facade makes Italy's leading diamond house, founded in Milan in 1924, impossible to miss – or resist.

Swinging north along Via Monte Napoleone, you come face to face with ***Versace*** *(No 11)*. King of the fashion industry in the 1980s, Gianni Versace was murdered outside his Miami home in 1997 and is buried next to his villa on Lago di Como. Sting, Princess Diana, Elton John and Naomi Campbell attended his funeral in Milan's cathedral.

The northern end of Via Alessandro Manzoni sizes up well with Brit ***Paul Smith*** at No 30 and Armani's revolutionary flagship store, the ***Emporio Armani*** *(No 31)*. Shop on three floors then drop into a sofa in the basement to watch action-packed movies on giant cutting-edge Sony screens.

Getting There & Away

Air Milan has two airports. Most European and other international flights use one of two terminals at Malpensa airport (off Map 1; Ⓦ www.malpensa.com), some 50km north-west of the city. Most (but not all) domestic and a handful of European flights use Linate (Map 1; Ⓦ www.sea-aeroportimilano.it), about 7km east of the city centre.

For flight information for both airports call ☎ 02 748 52 200. For a computerised information service on flight departures only call ☎ 02 585 83 497.

National carrier Alitalia (Map 3; ☎ 02 748 65 194) has an office in town at Via A Albricci 2.

Bus Bus stations are scattered across the city so unless you know exactly where you're going, you're better off travelling by train.

Buses (operated by national and regional companies) to many national and international points leave from Piazza Castello in front of Castello Sforzesco. Autostradale Viaggi (Map 3; ☎ 02 80 11 61), Via Luca Beltrami, sells tickets for destinations in Italy. Eurolines (Map 3; ☎ 02 720 01 304 or 055 35 71 10, Ⓔ posta@eurolines.it) has an office next door.

Train You can catch a train from Stazione Centrale (Map 2) to all major cities in Italy and Europe. The information office (☎ 147 88 80 88) opens 7am to 9pm daily. Daily trains (IC fares quoted) run to/from Venice (€19.15, 3½ hours), Florence (€21.70, 3½ hours), Genoa (€12.85, 1½ hours), Turin (€16.65, 1½ hours), Rome (€38.15, 5¾ hours) and Naples (€48.50, 8 hours). This is also a good point to pick up international connections to/from Switzerland (with the Cisalpino train) and France (with the TGV).

FNM trains from Stazione Nord (also called Stazione Cadorna, MM1/2 Cadorna Triennale), Piazza Luigi Cadorna, connect Milan with Como (€2.85, one hour, hourly) and Desanzano (€5.70, 1¼ hours, hourly). Regional services to many towns north-west of Milan are more frequent from Stazione Porta Garibaldi (metro MM2 Garibaldi FS), Piazza Sigmund Freud.

Car & Motorcycle Milan is the major junction of Italy's motorways – including the Autostrada del Sole (A1) to Reggio di

Calabria in southern Italy; the A4, aka the Milano-Turino, west to Turin; the Serenissima, east to Verona and Venice; the A7, south to Genoa; and the A8 and A9, north to the lakes and the Swiss border. The city is also a hub for smaller national roads, including the S7 (Via Emilia), which runs south through Emilia-Romagna, and the S11, which runs east-west from Brescia to Turin.

All of these roads meet the Milan ring road, known as the Tangenziale Est and the Tangenziale Ovest. From here, follow signs into the city centre. Note that the A4 in particular is an extremely busy road on which accidents can hold up traffic for hours. From October to April all roads in the area become extremely hazardous because of rain, snow and, especially, fog.

Getting Around

To/from Malpensa Airport The Malpensa Express train links Stazione Nord (Stazione Cadorna) with Malpensa airport (€7.75/10.35 single/return, 40 minutes, every 30 minutes). Some early morning and evening services are provided by bus (€6.70 single, 50 minutes) instead; the stop is outside Stazione Nord on Via Leopardi. See W www.malpensaexpress.com for updated schedules.

The airport is also served by Malpensa Shuttle coaches (☎ 02 585 83 185), departing from Piazza Luigi di Savoia, outside Stazione Centrale, every 20 minutes between 4.30am and 10.30pm. This route (50 minutes) is operated by two different companies which charge €4.15 or €5.05 for a one-way ticket. See W www.airpullman.com and W www.malpensa-shuttle.com for current schedules. STAB (☎ 035 31 84 72) runs buses to Orio al Serio airport (€6.70, 60 minutes, nine daily) near Bergamo.

A taxi from Malpensa airport to Milan city centre will cost about €77.45.

To/from Linate Airport From Milan's Piazza Luigi di Savoia, in front of Stazione Centrale, STAM (Map 2; ☎ 02 748 52 757) buses run to Linate airport (€1.80 single, 25 minutes, every 30 minutes between 5.40am and 9.35pm). Tickets are sold on board by the driver. You can also get local ATM bus No 73 from Piazza San Babila (corner Corso Europa; (0.75 single, 20 minutes, about every 15 minutes between 5.30am and 8pm).

A taxi from Linate airport to Milan city centre should cost no more than €15.50.

Metropolitana, Tram & Bus Milan's public transport system, run by ATM (☎ 800 01 68 57, W www.atm-mi.it) is efficient. The MM consists of four underground lines (red MM1, green MM2, yellow MM3 and blue Passante Ferroviario). Travelling on the underground is the most convenient – and easiest – way to get around, although ATM buses and trams are useful too. Trains run from around 6am to midnight.

A Metropolitana ticket costs €0.75, valid for one underground ride or up to 75 minutes travel on buses and trams. You can buy a book of 10 tickets (five double-journey tickets) for €7.25 or unlimited one-/two-day tickets for bus, tram and MM for €2.60/4.65. Tickets are sold at MM stations, tobacconists and newspaper stands.

Free public transport maps are available from the ATM office at the Duomo MM station.

Car & Motorcycle Entering central Milan by car is a major hassle. Street parking costs €1.30 per hour (flat fee of €2.60 after 8pm) and is limited to two hours. To pay, buy a 'scratch-and-park' SostaMilano card from a tobacconist, scratch off the date and hour, and display it on your dashboard. Illegally parked cars attract fines and can be towed away.

When parking in the streets, note that at least once a fortnight the street is cleaned, meaning you have to shift your car between midnight and 6am. Warning signs reading '*divieto di sosta*' are usually displayed the day before. Illegally parked cars risk being towed. Your best bet by far is to dump your vehicle in one of ATM's cheaper out-of-town car parks (€1/1.55 for four/eight hours) and take the MM into town.

Motoring information is provided by the Automobile Club Italia (ACI; Map 3; ☎ 02 7 74 51, W www.aci.it), Corso Venezia 43, open 8.30am to 12.45pm and 2.15pm to

5pm Monday to Friday. If you break down, call ☎ 116.

Hertz, Avis, Maggiore and Europcar have offices at Stazione Centrale and both airports.

Bicycle Cyclists can hire some wheels from AWS Bici Motor (☎ 02 670 72 145), Via Ponte Seveso 33, on the corner of Via Schiaparelli, for €10.35 per day (plus €5.15 deposit).

Taxi Don't bother trying to hail taxis – they generally won't stop. Head for a taxi rank or call one on ☎ 147 81 47 81.

South of Milan

PAVIA

postcode 27100 • pop 85,000
elevation 77m

Virtually a satellite of Milan, Pavia is nonetheless a thriving industrial and agricultural centre on the banks of the River Ticino, perhaps best known for its prestigious university. Originally the Roman Ticinum, Pavia later rivalled Milan as the capital of the Lombard kings until the 11th century. Like many cities of the north, Pavia became a pawn of power politics as the Renaissance dawned. Spain occupied it in the early 16th century and only relinquished control under the Treaty of Utrecht in 1713, when the Austrians promptly replaced the Spanish. Austrian rule, interrupted by a few years of Napoleonic French control from 1796, lasted until 1859.

Less than 30 minutes from Milan by train, Pavia warrants a visit – the nearby Certosa di Pavia, a Carthusian monastery founded by the Visconti family, makes such a trip a must.

The province produces about one-third of Italy's rice, making risotto the thing to eat. Don't leave town without sampling Pavia's culinary speciality, *risotto con le rane* (risotto peppered with small frogs). Top it off with a bite of paradise – a slice of *torta paradiso* (moist sponge cake topped with icing sugar).

Orientation & Information

The town is small and easy enough to get around. SGEA bus Nos 3 and 6 link the train station with the main square, Piazza della Vittoria.

The APT office (☎ 0382 2 21 56, fax 0382 94 45 40, W www.apt.pavia.it), Via Filzi 22, opens 8.30am to 12.30pm and 2pm to 6pm Monday to Saturday.

The post office, Piazza della Posta 2, opens 8am to 5pm Monday to Friday and 8am to noon Saturday. Nearby Banca Nazionale del Lavoro (BNL), Via Mentana, has an ATM.

Farmacia Fapa, the pharmacy at Corso Nuova Strada 100, runs a night service. More serious medical needs are met at Ospedale San Matteo (hospital; ☎ 0382 50 11), Piazza Golgi 2. The *questura* (police station; ☎ 0382 51 21) is at Piazza Italia 5.

Wash your dirty socks at Lavanderia Tintoria, across the tracks from

Castello Visconteo

This forbidding castle (only two of its original four massive towers remain) which watches over the northern end of the medieval city was, in fact, only ever used as a residence. It was built in 1360 for Galeazzo II Visconti and it now houses the **Museo Civico** *(☎ 0382 30 48 16, e museocivici@comune.pv.it, Viale Febbraio; adult/child €4.15/2.60; open 9am-1.30pm Tues-Fri, 10am-7pm Sat & Sun March-June & Sept-Nov, open 9am-1.30pm Tues-Sat & 9am-1pm Sun Dec-Feb, July & Aug)*.

University

The University of Pavia *(☎ 0382 50 41, W www.unipv.it, Corso Strada Nuova 65)* started life as a school in the 9th century and was elevated to university status in 1361. Christopher Columbus was among its notable graduates and the self-taught physicist Alessandro Volta, who discovered the electric volt, lectured here.

Churches & Medieval Towers

The **cathedral** *(Piazza Duomo)* boasts Italy's third largest dome. Work started on the cathedral in 1488 but it wasn't completed until the 19th century. Both Leonardo da Vinci and Donato Bramante contributed to the church's design. In 1989 its bell tower fell over, killing four people.

Basilica di San Michele *(Piazzetta Azzani 1)*, built in the Romanesque style in 1090, was long a preferred location for European coronations. Barbarossa was crowned Holy Roman Emperor here in 1155. Although deteriorated, the soft sandstone facade remains a masterwork of Romanesque. Statues and restrained floral sculptures adorn the arches above the main entrance.

Pavia once boasted some 100 medieval watchtowers – a trio remains on Piazza di Leonardo da Vinci.

Certosa di Pavia

The splendid Certosa di Pavia *(Charterhouse; ☎ 0382 92 56 13, Piazza del Monumento; free; open 9am-11.30am & 2.30pm-4.30pm Tues-Sun Oct-Apr, 9am-11.30am & 2.30pm-6pm May-Sept)*, a Carthusian monastery 10km north of Pavia en route to Milan, is one of the most notable buildings produced during the Italian Renaissance. Founded by Gian Galeazzo Visconti of Milan in 1396 as a private chapel for the Visconti family and a home for 12 monks, the Charterhouse soon became one of the most lavish buildings in northern Italy.

The interior is Gothic, although some Renaissance decoration is evident. Note the trompe l'oeil high on the nave, which gives the impression that people were watching the monks. In the former sacristy is a giant sculpture, dating from 1409 and made from hippopotamus teeth, including 66 small bas-reliefs and 94 statuettes.

The small cloisters to the right offer good photo angles of the church, particularly from behind the Baroque fountain. Behind the 122 arches of the larger cloisters are 24 cells, each a self-contained living area for one monk. Several are open to the public.

To get there by car from Milan, take the S35 to Pavia and turn off at Torre del Mangano (well signposted). SGEA buses depart from Pavia bus station and Viale Bligny in Milan (see Getting There & Away).

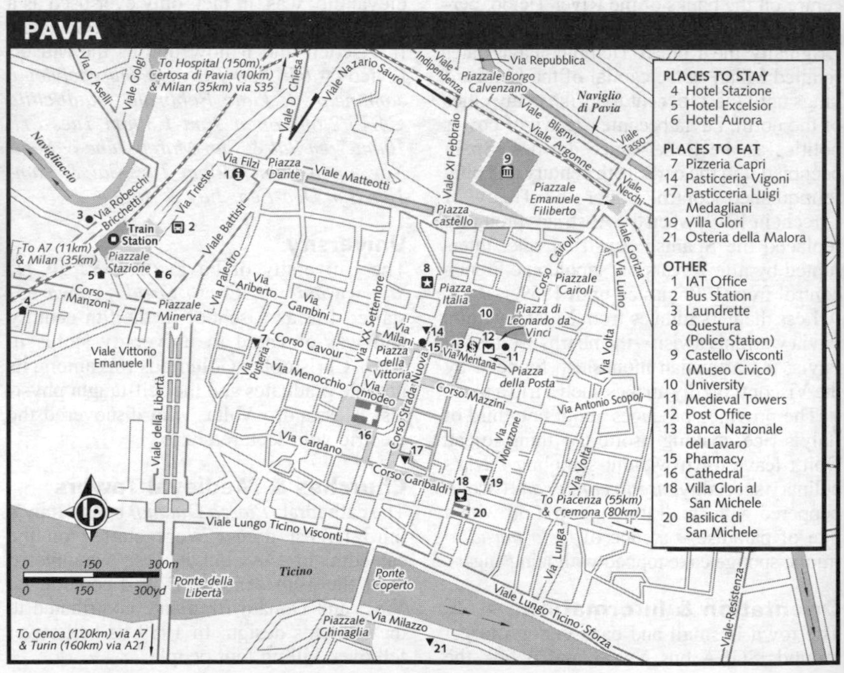

Places to Stay

Accommodation is limited, making a day trip from Milan the easiest option.

***Hotel Stazione** (☎ 0382 3 54 77, Via Bernardino de Rossi 8)* Singles/doubles from €36.15/47. As the name suggests, this best suits train spotters or those who relish the sound of passing locomotives.

***Hotel Aurora** (☎ 0382 2 36 64, fax 0382 2 12 48, Viale Vittorio Emanuele II 25)* Singles/doubles €41.30/64.55. This two-star pad is one of the cheapest options in Pavia.

***Hotel Excelsior** (☎ 0382 93 49 45, fax 0382 93 30 04, Via Togliatti 8)* Singles/doubles €49.05/72.30. Three-star interior comforts make the Excelsior, across from the train station, decidedly more inviting from the inside than out.

Places to Eat

Cafes abound beneath the arches on Piazza della Vittoria. Sample a slice of torta paradiso (€1) at ***Pasticceria Vigoni** (☎ 0382 2 21 03, Corso Strada Nuova 110)*, a cake shop and tearoom dating to 1878 in front of the university, or buy a *torta di polenta* or *torta di cioccolato* to sweeten up granny back home from ***Pasticceria Luigi Medagliani** (☎ 0382 2 32 94, Via Garibaldi 4)*.

***Pizzeria Capri** (☎ 0382 2 00 67, Corso Cavour 32)* Pizzas about €7.75. Fill up on pizza, a simple bowl of pasta or meat.

***Villa Glori** (☎ 0382 2 07 16, Via Villa Glori 10)* Full meals about €20.65. Feast on Pavian culinary pleasures on a charming cobbled terrace. Taste local vintages around the corner at ***Villa Glori al San Michele** (Next to Basilica San Michele)*, a stylish wine bar run by the same team.

***Osteria della Malora** (☎ 0382 3 43 02, Via Milazzo 79)* Full meals €25.80. Dine outside in summer at this lovely osteria, one of several places dishing up hearty local cuisine across Ponte Coperto.

Getting There & Away

Pavia's bus station is on Via Trieste, opposite the train station. SGEA buses (☎ 0382 51 35 11) run hourly to Milan (€2.45, 50 minutes) arriving at Viale Bligny, south of the centre. The same buses stop at Certosa di Pavia (€1.20, 15 minutes).

Direct trains run to Milan (€2.40, 30 minutes), Genoa and beyond.

By car, take the A7 *autostrada* from Milan and exit at the Bereguardo or Gropello C turn-off. The S35 from Milan is a better bet for hitchhikers.

East of Milan

BERGAMO

postcode 24100 • pop 118,000
elevation 249m

Virtually two cities, Bergamo's walled hilltop upper town *(città alta)* is surrounded by the lower town *(città bassa)*, a sprawling modern addition to this magnificent former outpost of the Venetian empire. Although Milan's skyscrapers to the south-west are visible on a clear day, historically Bergamo was more closely associated with Venice, which controlled the city for 350 years until Napoleon arrived at the gates. Although long dominated by outsiders, Bergamo has retained a strong sense of local identity, perhaps demonstrated most colourfully by the local dialect, which is all but incomprehensible to visitors. Despite its wealth of medieval, Renaissance and Baroque architecture, the city is not a big tourist destination.

Orientation

Viale Papa Giovanni XXIII, which becomes Viale Roma and then Viale Vittorio Emanuele II as it continues uphill towards the old town, forms the city's axis. It is capped at the southern end by the train and bus stations. Via XX Settembre, the main shopping street, is strung with pricey and irresistible boutiques.

Viale Vittorio Emanuele II swings east around the old town walls to enter the upper town at Porta di Sant'Agostino. You can also take a funicular up for the last leg.

Information

Tourist Offices In the lower town, the APT office (☎ 035 21 02 04, fax 035 23 01 84, W www.apt.bergamo.it), Viale Vittorio

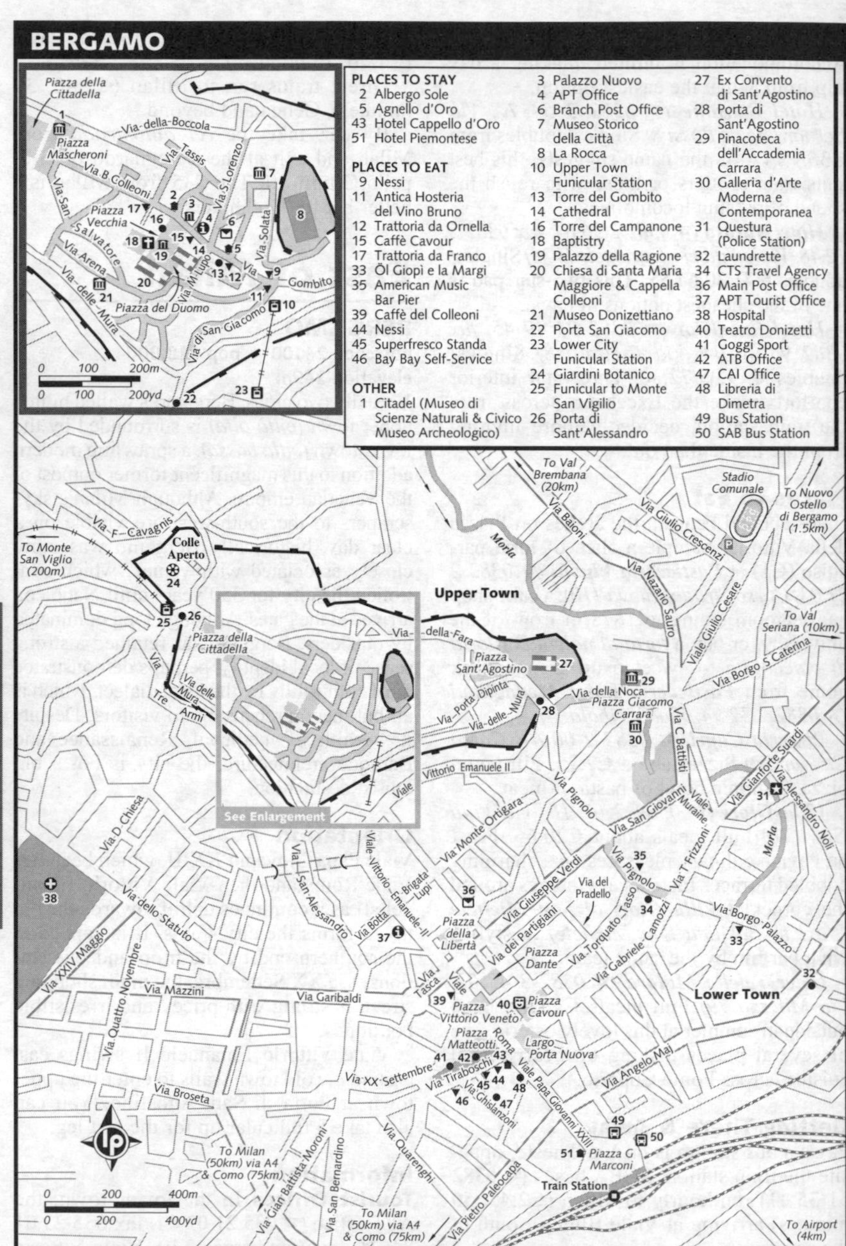
BERGAMO
PLACES TO STAY
2 Albergo Sole
5 Agnello d'Oro
43 Hotel Cappello d'Oro
51 Hotel Piemontese
PLACES TO EAT
9 Nessi
11 Antica Hosteria del Vino Bruno
12 Trattoria da Ornella
15 Caffè Cavour
17 Trattoria da Franco
33 Öl Giopì e la Margi
35 American Music Bar Pier
39 Caffè del Colleoni
44 Nessi
45 Superfresco Standa
46 Bay Bay Self-Service
OTHER
1 Citadel (Museo di Scienze Naturali & Civico Museo Archeologico)
3 Palazzo Nuovo
4 APT Office
6 Branch Post Office
7 Museo Storico della Città
8 La Rocca
10 Upper Town Funicular Station
13 Torre del Gombito
14 Cathedral
16 Torre del Campanone
18 Baptistry
19 Palazzo della Ragione
20 Chiesa di Santa Maria Maggiore & Cappella Colleoni
21 Museo Donizettiano
22 Porta San Giacomo
23 Lower City Funicular Station
24 Giardini Botanico
25 Funicular to Monte San Vigilio
26 Porta di Sant'Alessandro
27 Ex Convento di Sant'Agostino
28 Porta di Sant'Agostino
29 Pinacoteca dell'Accademia Carrara
30 Galleria d'Arte Moderna e Contemporanea
31 Questura (Police Station)
32 Laundrette
34 CTS Travel Agency
36 Main Post Office
37 APT Tourist Office
38 Hospital
40 Teatro Donizetti
41 Goggi Sport
42 ATB Office
47 CAI Office
48 Libreria di Dimetra
49 Bus Station
50 SAB Bus Station
Piazza della Cittadella
Piazza Mascheroni
Via della Boccola
Via Tassis
Via S Lorenzo
Via B Colleoni
Piazza Vecchia
Via San Salvatore
Via Arena
Via delle Mura
Via M Lupo
Via Solata
Via Gombito
Piazza del Duomo
Via di San Giacomo
0 100 200m
0 100 200yd
To Val Brembana (20km)
Stadio Comunale
To Nuovo Ostello di Bergamo (1.5km)
Via Baioni
Via Giulio Crescenzi
Morla
Via Nazario Sauro
Viale Giulio Cesare
To Val Seriana (10km)
Via Borgo S Caterina
Via F Cavagnis
To Monte San Viglio (200m)
Colle Aperto
Upper Town
Via della Fara
Piazza Sant'Agostino
Via Porta Dipinta
Via della Noca
Piazza Giacomo Carrara
Via delle Mura
Via Tre Armi
Viale Vittorio Emanuele II
Via C Battisti
Via Gianforte Suardi
Via Alessandro Noli
See Enlargement
Via D Chiesa
Via Pignolo
Via Monte Ortigara
Via San Giovanni
Viale Muraine
Via T Frizzoni
Via San Alessandro
Viale Vittorio Emanuele II
Via Brigata Lupi
Via Botta
Piazza della Libertà
Via Giuseppe Verdi
Via del Pradello
Via dei Partigiani
Via Torquato Tasso
Via Gabriele Camozzi
Via Borgo Palazzo
Via dello Statuto
Via XXIV Maggio
Via Quattro Novembre
Via Mazzini
Via Garibaldi
Via Tasca
Piazza Vittorio Veneto
Piazza Dante
Piazza Cavour
Lower Town
Piazza Matteotti
Largo Porta Nuova
Via XX Settembre
Via Tiraboschi
Via Ghislanzoni
Viale Roma
Viale Papa Giovanni XXIII
Via Angelo Maj
Via Broseta
To Milan (50km) via A4 & Como (75km)
Via Gian Battista Moroni
Via San Bernardino
Via Quarenghi
Via Pietro Paleocapa
Piazza G Marconi
Train Station
To Airport (4km)
0 200 400m
0 200 400yd

Emanuele II 20, opens 9am to 1pm and 2pm to 5.30pm Monday to Friday. Buzz the buzzer to get through the heavy iron gates. Its counterpart in the upper town (☎ 035 24 22 26 or 035 23 27 30, fax 035 24 29 94) is at Vicolo Aquila Nera 2 and opens 9am to noon and 2pm to 5.30pm daily.

Money You'll find several banks in the lower town and a couple on Via B Colleoni, near the upper town APT office.

Post & Communications The main post office is in the lower town at Via Masone 2a, beyond Piazza della Libertà. It opens 8.15am to 8pm Monday to Friday and 8.30am to 12.30pm Saturday. The branch office on Via S Lorenzo, in the upper town, opens 8.10am to 1.30pm Monday to Friday and 8.10am to 11.40am Saturday.

Travel Agencies In the lower town, the CTS travel agency (☎ 035 24 41 67, fax 035 22 22 49, ⓔ bergamo@cts.it), Via Pignolo 16a, opens 9.30am to 12.30pm and 3pm to 7pm Monday to Friday and 9.30am to 12.30pm Saturday.

Laundry Wash your socks and smocks at the laundrette at Via Angelo Maj 39b, open 7.30am to 8pm daily.

Medical Services & Emergency The Ospedali Riuniti (hospital; ☎ 035 26 91 11) is at the western edge of town, along Via dello Statuto. The *questura* (police station) is on Via Alessandro Noli.

Things to See & Do

Piazza Vecchia Medieval Bergamo's heart is hard to miss. Whichever way you enter the walled hilltop town, you'll soon find yourself in this gracious square. The white porticoed building on Via B Colleoni, which forms the northern side of the piazza, is the 17th-century **Palazzo Nuovo**, now a library and the square's least interesting feature. Turn to the south and you face the imposing arches and columns of the **Palazzo della Ragione**, first built in the 12th century but largely reconstructed four centuries later. The lion of St Mark is a reminder of Venice's long reign. Note the sun clock in the pavement beneath the arches. Next to the palazzo, the **Torre del Campanone** *(adult/child €1.05/0.50; open 10am-8pm Mon-Thurs, 10am-10pm Fri & Sat May-Sept, 10am-8pm Mon-Fri Oct-Apr)* still tolls the 10pm curfew. Scale the tower for wonderful views.

Tucked in behind these secular buildings is the core of Bergamo's spiritual life, the Piazza del Duomo. Oddly enough, the modest Baroque **cathedral** *(open 7.30am-11.45am & 3pm-6.30pm daily)*, dedicated to St Alexander, plays second fiddle to neighbouring **Chiesa di Santa Maria Maggiore** *(open 7.30am-11.45am & 3pm-6.30pm daily)*, an imposing Romanesque church begun in 1137, whose weather-worn exterior hides a lavish Baroque interior. Gaettano Donizetti, a 19th-century composer and son of Bergamo, is buried here. The gaudy Renaissance **Cappella Colleoni** *(Funeral Chapel; open 9am-12.30pm & 2pm-6.30pm Tues-Sun summer, 9am-12.30pm & 2pm-4.30pm Tues-Sun winter)* is an extravagant addition to the church.

The octagonal **baptistry** was built inside the Chiesa di Santa Maria Maggiore in 1340 but moved outside in the late 19th century.

Citadel The upper city's western tip is filled by the defensive hulk of Bergamo's citadel, occupied today by two small museums, the **Museo di Scienze Naturali** *(☎ 035 23 35 13, ⓔ museogeo@cyberg.it, Piazza Citadella 10; free; open 9am-noon & 2.30pm-6pm Tues-Fri, 9am-7pm Sat & Sun Apr-Sept, 9am-12.30pm & 2.30pm-5.30pm Tues-Sun Oct-Mar)* and the **Civico Museo Archeologico** *(☎ 035 24 28 39, Piazza Citadella 12; free; open 9am-12.30pm & 2.30pm-6pm Tues-Fri, 9am-7.30pm Sat & Sun)*. A wander through the citadel's impressive courtyard is as interesting, if not more so, than the science and archaeological museums, which are mediocre.

Museo Storico della Città In the former Convento di San Francesco (founded in the 13th century), this museum *(☎ 035 24 71 16,*

(W www.museostoricobg.org, Piazza Mercato del Fieno 3; free; open 9.30am-1pm & 2pm-5.30pm Tues-Fri, 9am-7pm Sat & Sun) traces the history of the city, with special emphasis on the period from the end of Venetian rule in 1797 to Italian unification in the 1860s.

Museo Donizettiano A small collection of furnishings and objects belonging to the city's favourite musical son, Gaettano Donizetti, can be seen in Bergamo's music institute at the Museo Donizettiano *(☎ 035 39 92 69, Via Arena 9; free; open 10am-1pm Mon-Fri, 10am-1pm & 2.30pm-5pm Sat & Sun)*.

Lookouts A stroll downhill along Via B Colleoni and Via Gombito takes you past **Torre del Gombito**, a 12th-century tower. Carry on along the medieval 'main street' towards the funicular station and then turn left to **La Rocca**, a fortress set in a park. The views from the park are worth the effort.

For more spectacular views, take the **funicular** *(tickets €0.85; open 10am-8pm Mon-Thurs, 10am-1.30am Fri & Sat, 9am-10.45pm Sun)* from Porta di Sant'Alessandro at the north-western end of the upper city to Monte San Vigilio. Alternatively, trudge uphill along Colle Aperto and bear left (following the yellow signs) up a steep flight of stone steps to Bergamo's **Giardini Botanico** *(Botanical Gardens; ☎ 035 39 94 66, e botanico@cyberg.it, Scaletta di Colle Aperto; free; open 9am-noon & 2pm-5pm Mon-Fri, 9am-7pm Sat & Sun Mar-Oct)*.

LOMABARDY

Pinacoteca dell'Accademia Carrara Make time to visit the art gallery of the Accademia Carrara *(☎ 035 39 96 43, W www.accademiacarrara.bergamo.it, Piazza Giacomo Carrara 82a; adult/child €3/1.55; open 9.30am-12.15pm & 2.30pm-5.15pm Tues-Sun)*, reached pleasantly on foot from the upper town through Porta di Sant' Agostino and down cobbled Via della Noca. Founded in 1780, it contains an impressive range of Italian masters, particularly of the Venetian school. An early *St Sebastian* by Raphael is worth looking out for and there are works by Botticelli, Canaletto, Lorenzo Lotto, Andrea Mantegna, Giovanni Tiepolo and Titian.

On the opposite side of the square, and home to some fantastic modern art exhibitions, is the academy's **Galleria d'Arte Moderna e Contemporanea** *(☎ 035 39 95 27, Piazza Giacomo Carrara; permanent exhibitions free, temporary exhibitions adult/child €7.75/6.20; open 9.30am-12.30pm & 3pm-6.30pm Tues-Sun)*.

Lower Town If heading back to the station for a train to Milan, you could do worse than hover about the squares that make up the centre of the lower town. Piazza Matteotti was redesigned in 1924 by Fascist favourite Marcello Piacentini.

The **Teatro Donizetti**, near Piazza Cavour, was built in the shape of a horseshoe in the 18th century and dedicated to the composer in 1897, the centenary of his birth.

Activities

The **Club Alpino Italiano** *(CAI; ☎ 035 23 68 62 or 035 24 42 73, Via Ghislanzoni 15)* has details about winter sports, walking and gentle strolls in the nearby Bergamo Alps. Buy forgotten gear at Goggi Sport, Via XX Settembre 73–77.

The APT office produces maps of walking trails in the Bergamo province. The **Libreria di Dimetra** *(☎ 035 21 00 86, Viale Papa Giovanni XXIII 28)* has a range of walking and cycling guidebooks, in Italian, devoted to the area. It also sells city maps at 1:9000 (€5.15).

Places to Stay

Bergamo is an easy day trip from Milan. If you want to stay, arrive early or telephone ahead as what hotels there are can fill distressingly quickly.

The APT office has a list of camp sites, *rifugi* (mountain huts) and *agriturismo* (accommodation on working farms) rooms throughout the province.

Lower Town A few cheaper hotels, often full of migrant workers from the south, are scattered about the lower town.

Nuovo Ostello di Bergamo *(☎/fax 035 36 17 24, e hostelbg@spm.it, Via Galileo Ferraris 1)* Dorm beds/singles/doubles €13.45/19/36.15. Reception open 7am-midnight daily. Bergamo's hostel is about 4km north from the train station. Take bus No 14 from the station or follow Viale Giulio Cesare north past the stadium and take the fourth turning on the right after crossing the large Circonvallazione Fabriciano intersection.

Hotel Piemontese *(☎ 035 24 26 29, fax 035 23 04 00, Piazza G Marconi 11)* Singles/doubles €67.15/92.95. This place is one of several three-star hotels in the area.

Hotel Cappello d'Oro *(☎ 035 23 25 03, fax 035 24 29 46, e cappello@hotelcappellodoro.it, Viale Papa Giovanni XXIII 12)* Singles/doubles €98.15/139.45. With four stars and a Best Western label, you can't really go wrong here.

Upper Town If your wallet can take the crunch, there are some excellent options up the hill.

Agnello d'Oro *(☎ 035 24 98 83, fax 035 23 56 12, w www.agnello.it, Via Gombito 22)* Singles/doubles €47/80. With the incredible clutter of objects adorning just about every wall, this 17th-century spot could pass for a very full antique shop. Rooms are attractive and it's a short walk from the funicular station.

Albergo Sole *(☎ 035 21 82 38, fax 035 24 00 11, Via B Colleoni 1)* Singles/doubles €47/62. Just off Piazza Vecchia, soulful Sole has lovely rooms and a restaurant with a pretty garden out back for delightful alfresco dining in the summer.

Places to Eat

Like the Pavians and Venetians, the Bergamaschi are passionate about polenta and eat it as a side dish or dessert – *polenta e ösei* are little polenta cakes filled with jam and topped with yellow icing and chocolate birds. Bergamo contributed *casonsei*, a ravioli stuffed with meat, to the Italian table and the area is noted for its fine red wines, including Valcalepio. Taste the latter with some fine slices of *carne solata di cavallo* (salted horse meat), another local delicacy.

Lower Town Schoolkids swarm into ***Nessi*** *(☎ 035 24 74 24, Largo Porta Nuova 5, Entrance on Via Tiraboschi)* to stock up on sweet breads, cakes and pizza slices. Nearby ***Superfresco Standa*** *(Via Tiraboschi)* is the place for supermarket fare and there's an ultra-modern ***gelateria*** to cool down in at Via XX Settembre 58.

Bay Bay Self-Service *(Via Tiraboschi 73)* 1st/2nd courses €2.60/3.35. Open Mon-Fri. Lunch is dished up at this self-service joint, which is ideal for good, cheap bites.

Caffè del Colleoni *(☎ 035 22 55 62, Portici del Sentierone 33–34)* Sink your teeth into a well-filled pastry or sip tea on a lovely people-watching terrace at this elegant cafe-cum-*salon de thé*.

American Music Bar Pier *(☎ 035 24 73 73, Via Pignolo 23)* Open 8am-2am Mon-Sat. Mingle with locals, well away from the tourist pantomime on the top of the hill.

Öl Giopì e la Margì *(☎ 035 24 23 66, Via Borgo Palazzo 25g)* Full meals €25.80. This place is expensive, but handsome young Bergamaschi waiters do run around in traditional costume.

Upper Town Dining is tasty but not cheap in medieval Bergamo.

Nessi *(☎ 035 24 70 73, Via Gombito 34)* Killer-calorie apple strudel, *torta trentino al cioccolato* (a heavy chocolate sponge in pastry) and *crostatine alla nutella* (a sweet and sugary pastry oozing nutella) are among the sweet goodies displayed in Nessi's window. Kids and teens teem in here for pizza and *focaccia* (flatbread), both €6.70/kg.

Caffè Cavour *(Via Gombito 6)* Sandwiches, salads and other light lunchtime dishes are served at this historic tea room.

Trattoria da Ornella *(☎ 035 23 27 36, Via B Gombito 15)* 1st/2nd courses €5.15/12.90. *Polenta taragna* (polenta cooked with butter, cheese and a choice of rabbit, chicken or veal) is the house speciality at Bergamo's most traditional eating house.

Antica Hosteria del Vino Bruno *(☎ 035 24 79 93, Piazza Mercato delle Scarpe)* 1st/2nd courses €6.20/8.75. Opt for a bowl of steaming polenta (€7.75) or splurge on a full-Monty menu (€12.90).

Trattoria da Franco (Via B Colleoni 8) Full meals about €12.90. This is a good spot to dine alfresco and eat something other (read: pizza, bean soup, octopus salad) than Bergamasco dishes.

Getting There & Away

Air The local airport, Orio al Serio (☎ 035 32 63 23, W www.milanoorio-airport.it), is a few kilometres south-east of the train station. A handful of international flights land here.

Bus SAB operates services from Bergamo bus station (☎ 035 24 02 40), Piazzale G Marconi, to the lakes and mountains from its own terminal. Services include Milan's Piazza Castello (€3.80, half-hourly), Como (€4.30, 1¾ hours, seven to 10 daily), Brescia, Cremona and Piacenza, to name a few.

Train The train station is also on Piazzale G Marconi. There are frequent trains for the 50-minute run to Milan and less frequent trains to Brescia and Cremona.

Car & Motorcycle To reach Bergamo by car, take the A4 autostrada from Milan or Venice, the S11 (and then S525) from Milan or the S42 north from Treviglio. On entering Bergamo note that the 'centro' signs refer to the città bassa. If you want to head straight for the old city, follow the 'città alta' signs. Hitchhikers could try the S11.

Getting Around

ATB buses serve the city and you can get free route maps from the office on Via Tirboschi. Bus No 1 connects the train station with the funicular (open 7.15am to 6.45pm Monday to Friday, 7.15am to 11.50pm Saturday and Sunday) to the upper city. Bus No 3 runs from Porta di Sant'Alessandro in the upper city to Via Pietro Paleocapa in the lower city. Buy tickets, valid for an hour's travel on buses and funiculars for €0.85 (all-day ticket €2.30), from machines at the train and funicular stations.

AROUND BERGAMO

There are several small ski resorts in the Bergamo Alps, notably around the **Val Brembana**, reached from Bergamo along Via Nazario Sauro, and **Val Seriana**, reached by way of Via Borgo Santa Caterina from the lower town. Each valley boasts seven or eight Alpine rifugi for summer and winter activities, many walking tracks and reasonably priced accommodation. Details are available from the APT office in Bergamo.

VALTELLINA

Covering the band of Alps across Lombardy's north, the Valtellina is one of Italy's least attractive Alpine regions, although it does have some acceptable skiing and is well set up for walking.

The APT Valtellina has a Web site at W www.valtellinaonline.com and offices in Bormio (☎ 0342 90 33 00, W www.bormio.com), Via Roma 131b; in Sondrio (☎ 0342 51 25 00), Via C Battisti 12; in Aprica (☎ 0342 74 61 13), Corso Roma 178; in Madesimo (☎ 0343 5 30 15), Via Carducci 27; and in Livigno (☎ 0342 99 63 79), Via de la Gesa 65. See Lonely Planet's *Walking in Italy* or pick up a copy of *Trekking in Valtellina*, both of which detail walks and give information on accommodation for the area.

Trains leave Milan for Sondrio, a regional transport hub, and buses connect with the resorts and towns.

BRESCIA

postcode 25100 • pop 197,000
elevation 149m

Brescia is a somewhat scruffy provincial capital, arms production centre and transport hub. Although rough around the edges, its student life gives the place a bit of buzz, which is noticeably lacking in other Lombard towns. There are also a few sights worth stopping for.

When the Romans took control of the Gallic town in 225 BC, Brescia (the name derives from a word meaning hill) already had hundreds of years of now obscure history behind it. Charlemagne and his successors were in the driver's seat in the 9th century, followed for 1000 years by a parade of outside rulers. As revolutionary fervour swept Europe in 1848–49, Brescia was dubbed 'The Lioness' for its 10-day uprising against Austria – an unsuccessful prelude to its participation in the movement towards Italian unification a decade later.

Orientation

From the train and bus stations on the south-western edge, the city centre is a 10-minute walk along Viale della Stazione and Corso dei Martiri della Libertà towards Piazza della Vittoria.

Information

Tourist Offices The APT office (☎ 030 4 34 18, fax 030 29 32 84, W www.asm.brescia.it), Corso Zanardelli 34, opens 9am to 12.30pm and 3pm to 6pm Monday to Friday and 9am to 12.30pm Saturday. The smaller tourist office (☎ 030 240 03 55, fax 030 377 37 73), Piazza della Loggia 6, opens 9.30am to 6.30pm Monday to Saturday.

Money Banca San Paolo di Brescia, on Corso Zanardelli, and Banca Credito Agrario Bresciano, on Piazza Paolo VI, are a couple of commercial banks with ATMs.

Post & Communications The post office, on Piazza della Vittoria, opens 8.15am to

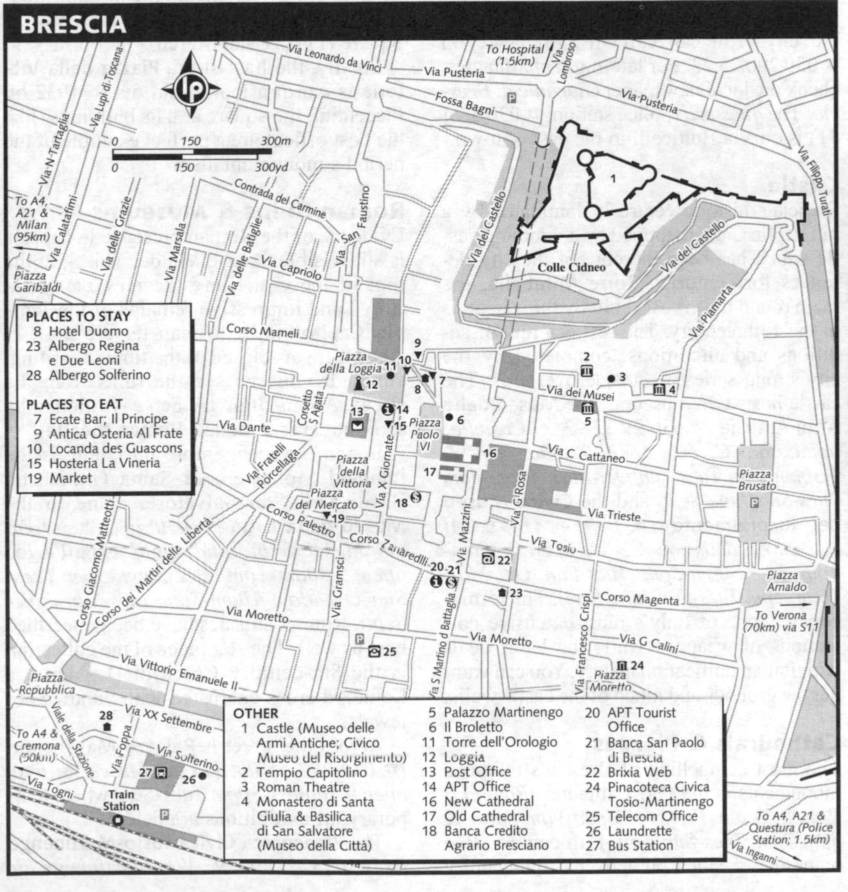

5.30pm Monday to Friday and 8.15am to 1pm Saturday. The Telecom office, Via Moretto 46, opens 8am to 8pm Monday to Saturday.

Brixia Web (☎ 030 375 93 31, W www.brixiaweb.it), Via Antiche Mura 6a, charges surfers €5.15 an hour to use its 'Internet Train' point. It opens 10am to 8pm Monday to Friday, 10am to 7pm Saturday and 2pm to 7pm Sunday.

Laundry Give your clothes a tumble at Onda Blu laundry, Via Solferino 8f.

Medical Services & Emergency The Ospedale Civile (hospital; ☎ 030 3 99 51) is on Piazzale Ospedale at the northern edge of the city. You can call an ambulance on ☎ 030 200 25 22. For late-night pharmacies, check the local newspaper *Giornale di Brescia*. The *questura* (police station; ☎ 030 3 74 41) is on Via Botticelli to the east of town.

Castle

Brescia's historic centre is dominated by a hill, Colle Cidneo, topped by a rambling castle which has been the core of the city defences for centuries. **Torre Mirabella**, the main round tower, was built by the Viscontis in the 13th century. The rest is a mix of additions and alterations, completed by the city's long series of outside overlords. The castle hosts two museums, the **Museo delle Armi Antiche** *(☎ 030 29 32 92, Al Castello; admission €2.60; open 9.30am-1pm & 2.30pm-5pm Tues-Sun Oct-May, 10am-5pm Tues-Sun June-Sept)* and the **Civico Museo del Risorgimento** *(☎ 030 4 41 76, Al Castello; admission €2.60; open 9.30am-1pm & 2.30pm-5pm Tues-Sun Oct-May, 10am-5pm Tues-Sun June-Sept)*. The former contains one of Italy's most extensive collections of weapons while the latter deals with Italian unification history. You can wander the grounds and much of the castle walls.

LOMABARDY

Cathedrals & Piazzas

The most compelling of Brescia's religious monuments is the **Old Cathedral** *(Rotonda; Piazza Paolo VI; free; open 9am-noon & 3pm-7pm Tues-Sun)*, an 11th-century Romanesque basilica built over a 6th-century circular structure. The form of the church is uncommon and there are hints in the mosaics of an even earlier Roman presence here. Next door, the Renaissance **New Cathedral** *(Piazza Paolo VI; free; open 7.30am-noon & 4pm-7.30pm Mon-Sat, 8am-1pm & 4pm-7.30pm Sun)* dwarfs its elderly neighbour but is of less interest. Also on the square is **Il Broletto**, a medieval town hall with an 11th-century tower.

North-west of Piazza Paolo VI is Piazza della Loggia, dominated by the squat 16th-century **loggia** (lodge) in which Palladio had a hand. The **Torre dell'Orologio**, with its exquisite astrological timepiece, is modelled on the one in Venice's St Mark's Square (Piazza San Marco).

Finally, the Fascist-era **Piazza della Vittoria** is worth a look. Laid out in 1932 by Piacentini, the square and its buildings (like the post office) are a perfect example of the period's monumentalism.

Roman Ruins & Museums

Evidence of the Roman presence in Brescia is still visible. Along Via dei Musei, at the foot of the castle, are the now partly restored and impressive remains of the **Tempio Capitolino**, a Roman temple built in AD 73. It was closed at the time of writing, although you can see the ruins from the street. About 50m farther east along the same street is a modest **Roman theatre**.

In some respects more intriguing is the jumbled Monastero di Santa Giulia and Basilica di San Salvatore, home to the **Museo della Città** *(☎ 030 297 78 34, Via dei Musei 81b; adult/child €6.20/4.15; open 9.30am-1pm & 2.30pm-5pm Tues-Sun Oct-May, 10am-5pm Tues-Sun June-Sept)*. Roman mosaics have been unearthed here as well. The star piece of the collection is the 8th-century Croce di Desiderio, a Lombard cross encrusted with hundreds of jewels.

Across the street is **Palazzo Martinengo** *(☎ 030 297 55 08, Via dei Musei 28; free; open 9.30am-7.30pm Tues-Sun)* where temporary art exhibitions are held.

The **Pinacoteca Civica Tosio-Martinengo** *(☎ 030 377 49 99, Via Martinengo da*

Barco; admission €3; open 9.30am-1pm & 2.30pm-5pm Tues-Sun Oct-May, 10am-5pm Tues-Sun June-Sept), overlooking Piazza Moretto, features works by artists of the Brescian school as well as by Raphael.

Special Events

The International Piano Festival, held from early April until June, is staged in conjunction with nearby Bergamo, while the Estate Aperta festival of music occupies the summer months.

Places to Stay

Albergo Solferino *(☎ 030 4 63 00, Via Solferino 1)* Singles €12.90-25.85, doubles €23.25-36.15. Near the tram and bus stations, Solferino touts basic and reasonably cheap rooms.

Hotel Duomo *(☎ 030 377 28 78, fax 030 377 02 79, Via Cesare Beccaria 17)* Singles €28.40-28.75, doubles €46.50-56.80. Singles can be pokey at Brescia's budget choice, just off Piazza Paolo VI.

Albergo Regina e Due Leoni *(☎ 030 375 78 81, fax 030 4 54 00, Corso Magenta 14)* Doubles without bath €31-36.15, with bath €46.50-61.95. Ageing fails to aptly describe this spartan pad, firmly trapped in some strange time warp.

Places to Eat

Risotto, beef dishes and *lumache alla bresciana* (snails cooked up with parmesan cheese and fresh spinach) are common in Brescia and the region offers many good wines, including those from Botticino, Lugana and Riviera del Garda.

The happening area of town is along Corso Mameli and Via dei Musei, where there are plenty of restaurants, cafes and bars. Sandwiches are served amid flowers in pretty gardens at ***Ecate Bar*** and neighbouring ***Il Principe***, two delightful cafes at Via dei Musei 20.

Locanda des Guascons *(Via dei Musei 21)* 1st/2nd courses €6.70/9.30. Munch your way through a €10.85 menu at this atmospheric spot in the trendy part of town.

Antica Osteria Al Frate *(☎ 030 375 14 69, Via dei Musei 25)* Full meals €23.25. Al Frate serves well-presented regional dishes – and is always packed.

Hosteria La Vineria *(Via X Giornate 4)* Full meals about €12.90. La Vineria offers moderately priced meals and doubles as an enoteca.

There's a choice of cheap snack places at the bus station. For fresh produce, head for the ***market*** on Piazza del Mercato.

Getting There & Away

The bus station is across the road from the train station, with regular services to Verona (€6.70, two hours, 10 to 14 daily) via Desenzano del Garda (€2.60, 50 minutes) and Sirmione (€3.35, one hour), and to/from Cremona (€3.60 1¼ hours, hourly).

From Milan, frequent trains take 50 minutes. From Brescia there are trains to Cremona (€3.25, one hour), Bergamo (€2.85, 30 minutes), Venice (€13.55), Ventimiglia (€36.55) and Genoa (€25.35).

By car, the A4 and S11 go west to Milan and east to Lago di Garda and Verona, while the A21 and S45 head south to Cremona.

CREMONA

postcode 26100 • pop 81,000
elevation 45m

Home of the Stradivari violin, Cremona today jealously maintains its centuries-old status as premier exponent of the delicate art of making the perfect string instrument. All of the great violin-making dynasties started here – Amati, Guarneri and Stradivari – and there are plenty of opportunities to get better acquainted with the art of violin making. Not that Cremona is Italy's only centre for violin-makers – rivals in nearby cities will assure you that the only thing better about the Cremonese product is the publicity. For centuries an independent city-state, Cremona boasts a compact but impressive city centre, meriting a stopover, if not necessarily an overnight stay. Cremona is an easy day trip from Milan, Mantua, Brescia and Piacenza.

Information

The APT office (☎ 0372 2 32 33, fax 0372 53 40 80, W www.cremonaturismo.com), Piazza del Comune 5, opens 9.30am to

12.30pm and 3pm to 6pm Monday to Saturday, 10am to 1pm Sunday and holidays.

Banca Popolare di Cremona, on Piazza del Comune, has a 24-hour banknote exchange machine and ATM.

The post office, Via Verdi 1, opens 8.10am to 5.30pm Monday to Friday and 8.10am to 11.40am Saturday. The hospital (☎ 0372 40 51 11) is on Largo Priori. The *questura* (police station; ☎ 0372 48 81) is at Via Tribunali 6.

Piazza del Comune

Medieval Cremona, like most Lombard towns, was an independent comune until the 14th century, when the Viscontis of Milan added it to their growing collection. To keep clear the difference between the secular and the spiritual, the buildings connected with the Church were erected on the eastern side of the square, and those concerned with earthly affairs were constructed across the way. Even if violins don't ring your bell, the rust-red heart of Cremona, the Piazza del Comune, makes at least a brief stop in this quiet town worthwhile.

The **cathedral** on Piazza del Comune started out as a Romanesque basilica but, by the time it was finished in 1190, it had been heavily overtaken by Gothic modishness (best demonstrated by its Latin cross-shaped ground plan). The facade, however, is largely faithful to the original concept. Inside there is plenty of artwork to admire. Perhaps most interesting are the partial frescoes uncovered in the early 1990s – some, including one of a winged harpy, date to the cathedral's first days. Look for work by the Renaissance masters Boccaccino and Bembo.

The adjoining **Torrazzo** *(Piazza del Comune; adult/child €4.15/2.05; open 10.30am-1pm & 2-6pm daily)*, or bell tower, is connected to the cathedral by a Renaissance loggia, the **Bertazzola**. At 111m, the Torrazzo is said to be the tallest tower of its kind in Italy. Its staircase can be scaled by visi-

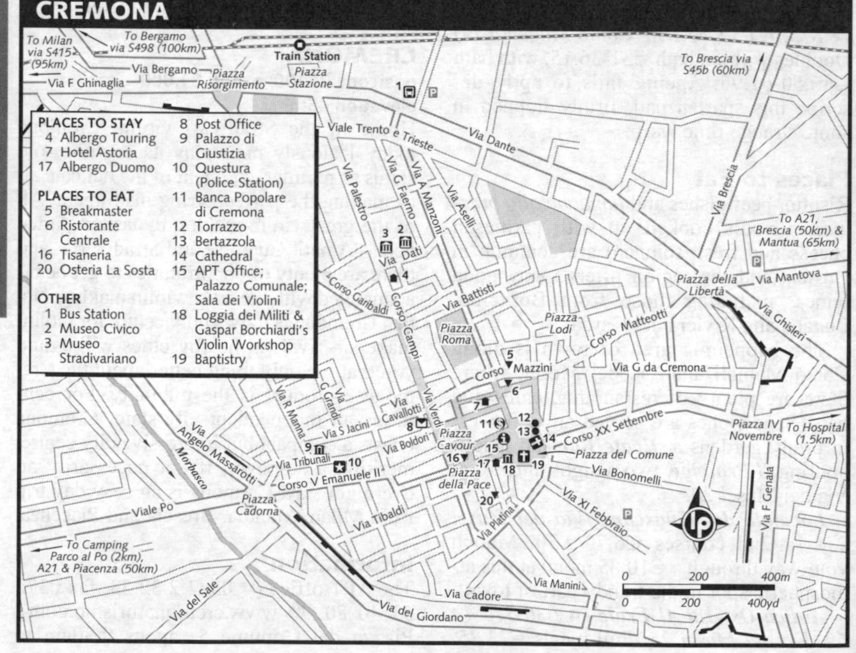

Money Savers

Cremona's *biglietto cumulativo* allows admission to all of the town's museums, costs €7.75/5.15 per adult/child and is valid for three months. Alternatively, invest €6.20 in a City Card which includes admission to key museums, three hours' parking, postcards, city map and bus tickets. The APT office sells both.

tors. To the south is the 12th-century **baptistry** which, like many Italian medieval baptistries, has an octagonal base. Alluding to renewal and hence to baptism and resurrection, the figure eight appears in much religious decoration – its use in this kind of architecture is no coincidence.

Across the square are the **Palazzo Comunale** and, to its south, the smaller porticoed **Loggia dei Militi**. Both date to the 13th century. The former was, and remains, the town hall; the latter housed the town's militia.

Museums & Violins

While you're at the Palazzo Comunale, visit the **Sala dei Violini** *(Piazza del Comune; adult/child €4.15/2.05; open 8.30am-6pm Mon-Sat, 10am-6pm Sun)*. The stars of the small violin collection are two Amatis dating to 1566 and 1658, two Guarneris and a 1715 Stradivari. A local maestro occasionally plays the instruments to keep them in working order.

The **Museo Stradivariano** *(☎ 0372 46 18 86, Via Palestro 17; adult/child €3.10/1.55; open 8.30am-6pm Tues-Sat, 10am-6pm Sun)* features items from the Stradivari workshop. Around the corner, the **Museo Civico** *(☎ 0372 40 77 64, Via Ugolani Dati 4; adult/child €5.15/2.60; open 8.30am-6pm Tues-Sat, 10am-6pm Sun)* has a mixed bag of paintings and other odds and sods.

Gaspar Borchiardi *(☎ 0372 3 19 69, Piazza San Antonio)* is one of several violin- and bow-making workshops sprinkled on the streets around Piazza del Comune. Cremona has some 90-odd in all; the APT office has a list and can help you arrange a guided visit to watch the artisans at work.

Special Events

Violin-lovers flock to Cremona for the Triennale Internazionale degli Strumenti ad Arco (International String Instrument Expo). It's held every third October and the next one will be in 2003. The autumn and winter tend to be rich in music programs and concerts – check with the APT office for details.

Places to Stay

Camping Parco al Po *(☎/fax 0372 2 71 37, Via Lungo Po Europa 12a)* Sites per person/tent & car €8.25/€6.70. Head south-west from Piazza Cavour to reach this site, outside the city centre.

Albergo Touring *(☎ 0372 3 69 76, Via Palestro 3)* Singles/doubles €20.65/46.50. A dusty, dingy, musty feel detracts from its handy location midway between the station and Cremona's cobbled warren-like historical centre.

Albergo Duomo *(☎ 0372 3 52 55, fax 0372 45 83 92, Via Gonfalonieri 13)* Singles/doubles €36.15/56.80. Set in the heart of old Cremona and ablaze with wrought-iron flower boxes in spring, Albergo Duomo is among Cremona's most pleasing places to stay. It runs its own pizzeria, too.

Hotel Astoria (☎ 0372 46 16 16, fax 0372 46 18 10; Via Bordigallo 19) Singles/doubles/triples/quads €38.75/56.80/74.93/82.95. In a small lane near Piazza Cavour, rooms here brandish three-star mod cons.

Places to Eat

Cremona's gifts to Italian cuisine include *bollito* (boiled meats) and *cotechino* (boiled pork sausage) with polenta. *Mostarda*, often served with bollito, consists of fruit in sweet mustardy goo. Sounds unpalatable, but it's really not bad at all.

Tisaneria *(☎ 0372 2 55 27, Via Lombardini 9)* This atmospheric cafe, astride Piazza del Pace, is an idyllic spot for sitting on the cobbled square, sipping a cappuccino and watching the world walk or cycle by.

Breakmaster *(Corso Mazzini 4)* 1st/2nd courses €2.60/4.15. Wallet watchers can head straight to this clean, cheap and bright self-service joint.

Osteria La Sosta *(☎ 0372 45 66 56, Via Sicardo 9)* Full meals about €25.80. Practically surrounded by violin-makers' workshops, just off Piazza del Comune, this is a beautiful place to feast on regional delicacies. Its *lumache gratinate* (oven-baked snails) should be not missed.

Ristorante Centrale *(Via Pertusio 4)* Full meals €20.65. Centrale is a popular spot, oozing history and charm, where you can try cotechino, admire human-size jars of mostarda and drool over huge drums of fresh local cheese.

Open-air market stalls on Piazza del Pace sell fresh fruit and veg every morning.

Getting There & Away

The city can be reached by train from Milan (€9.30, one hour, several daily) via Treviglio, from Mantua, Pavia and Brescia, or from the south by changing at Piacenza.

The most direct road from Milan is the S415 (Paullo exit). The A21 takes you to Brescia, where it joins with the A4.

MANTUA (MANTOVA)

postcode 24100 • pop 52,000

On the shores of Lago Superiore, Lago di Mezzo and Lago Inferiore (a glorified widening of the River Mincio) is Mantua, a serene and beautiful city. However, industrial sprawl from its booming petrochemical industry has scarred the surrounding countryside and left the lakes heavily polluted.

The city can be visited as a day trip from as far afield as Milan but spend the night there to do it justice. Thursday is market day – stalls flogging everything from fruit and flowers to pots, pans, clothes and useless clutter fill Piazzas Sordello, Broletto and Erbe and their surrounding streets.

History

Mantua was settled by the Etruscans in the 10th century BC and later prospered under Roman rule. It passed to the House of Gonzaga in 1328, flourishing under one of the foremost Renaissance dynasties and attracting the likes of Andrea Mantegna, Petrarch, Antonio Pisanello, Giulio Romano and Rubens. The golden days of 'La Gloriosa' came to a mean end when Austria took control in 1708. Vienna's troops stayed in control (aside from the Napoleonic interlude at the end of the 18th century) until 1866.

The Chaste & Royal Poet

Dryden called Virgil 'the chastest and royalest of poets'. Born 70 years before Christ on his parents' farm just outside Mantua, Virgil, the city's favourite son, was one of ancient Rome's greatest poets. Of the three works he left behind, *The Aeneid* is the most exalted. An epic in the great tradition of the ancient Sumerian myth *Gilgamesh*, and Homer's *Iliad* and *Odyssey*, the tale is a fantastic account of the foundation of Rome, loaded with symbolism and told with unsurpassed virtuosity. The inspiration of countless poets since, Virgil comes to life as Dante's 'sweet master' in the *Divine Comedy*, 14 centuries after Virgil's death.

Information

The APT office (☎ 0376 32 82 53, fax 0376 36 32 92, W www.aptmantova.it), Piazza Mantegna 6, opens 8.30am to 12.30pm and 3pm to 6pm Monday to Saturday, and 9.30am to 12.30pm Sunday.

Banks are scattered throughout the city centre and there's a currency exchange and ATM inside the post office, Piazza Martiri di Belfiore, which opens 8.30am to 7pm Monday to Saturday. Online access costs €6.20 an hour at Caffè Borsa (see the Places to Eat section later).

The hospital (☎ 0376 20 14 34) is on Via Albertoni at the southern end of the old town. The *questura* (police station; ☎ 0376 20 51) is at Piazza Sordello 46.

Palazzo Ducale

Also known as the Reggia dei Gonzaga after the longtime rulers of Mantua, the Palazzo Ducale *(☎ 0376 38 21 50, Piazza Sordello 40; adult/child €6.20/3.10; open 8.45am-7.15pm Tues-Sun, 8pm-11pm Sat May-Sept)* occupies a great chunk of the city's north-eastern corner. Its walls hide three piazzas, a park, a basilica and a total of 450 rooms.

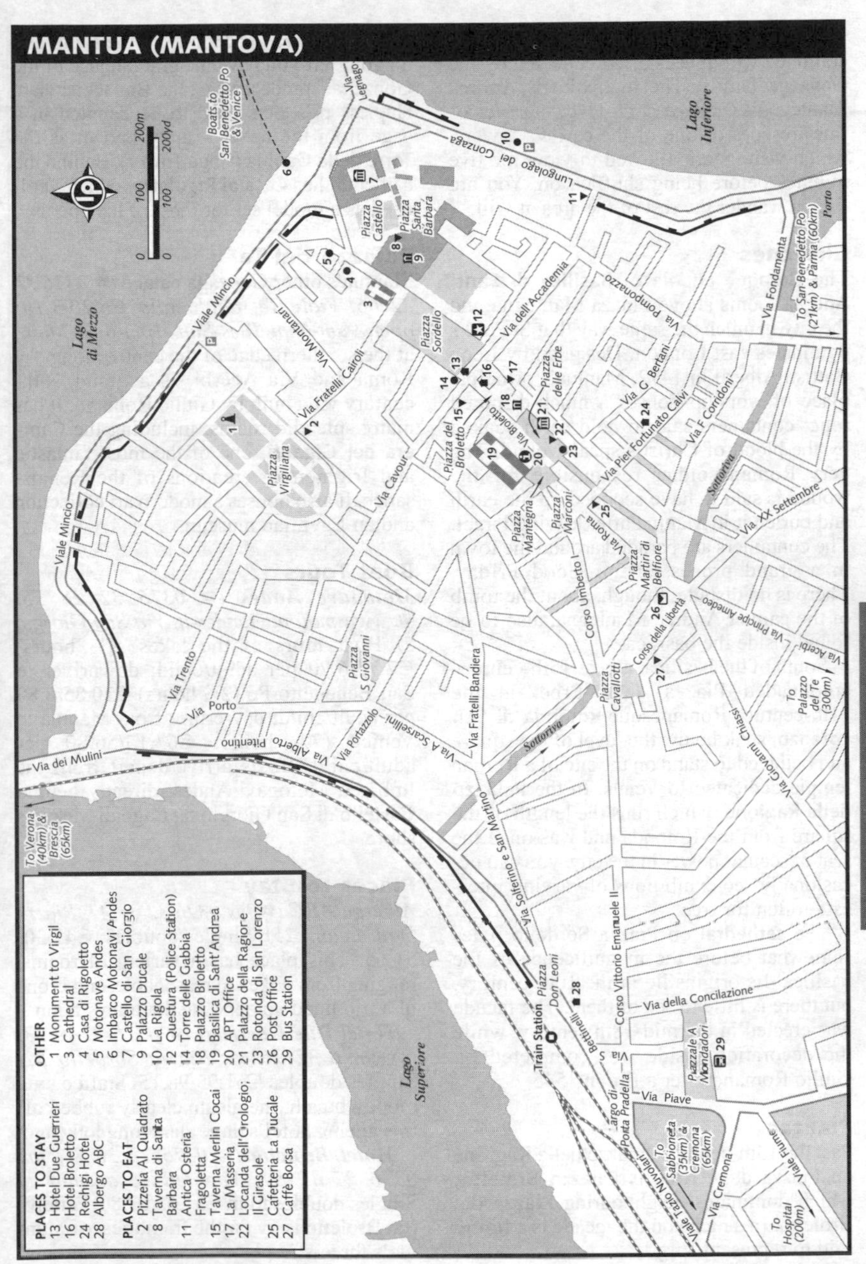
MANTUA (MANTOVA)
PLACES TO STAY
13 Hotel Due Guerrieri
16 Hotel Broletto
24 Rechigi Hotel
28 Albergo ABC
PLACES TO EAT
2 Pizzeria Al Quadrato
8 Taverna di Santa Barbara
11 Antica Osteria Fragoletta
15 Taverna Merlin Cocai
17 La Masseria
22 Locanda dell'Orologio; Il Girasole
25 Cafetteria La Ducale
27 Caffè Borsa
OTHER
1 Monument to Virgil
3 Cathedral
4 Casa di Rigoletto
5 Motonave Andes
6 Imbarco Motonavi Andes
7 Castello di San Giorgio
9 Palazzo Ducale
10 La Rigola
12 Questura (Police Station)
14 Torre delle Gabbia
18 Palazzo Broletto
19 Basilica di Sant'Andrea
20 APT Office
21 Palazzo della Ragione
23 Rotonda di San Lorenzo
26 Post Office
29 Bus Station
Lago di Mezzo
Lago Superiore
Lago Inferiore
Boats to San Benedetto Po & Venice
To Verona (40km) & Brescia (65km)
To San Benedetto Po (21km) & Parma (60km)
To Sabbioneta (35km) & Cremona (65km)
To Palazzo del Te (300m)
To Hospital (200m)
Train Station
Piazza Virgiliana
Piazza Sordello
Piazza Castello
Piazza Santa Barbara
Piazza del Broletto
Piazza delle Erbe
Piazza Mantegna
Piazza Marconi
Piazza Martiri di Belfiore
Piazza Cavallotti
Piazza S Giovanni
Piazza Don Leoni
Piazzale Mondadori
Porto
Sottoriva
Viale Mincio
Via Trento
Via Porto
Via dei Mulini
Via Cavour
Via Fratelli Cairoli
Via Montanari
Lungolago dei Gonzaga
Via dell'Accademia
Via Pomponazzo
Via Broletto
Via Roma
Via Pier Fortunato Calvi
Via F Corridoni
Via XX Settembre
Via Principe Amedeo
Via Acerbi
Via Giovanni Chiassi
Corso Umberto I
Corso della Libertà
Corso Vittorio Emanuele II
Via Fratelli Bandiera
Via Solferino e San Martino
Via A Scarsellini
Via Portazzolo
Via Alberto Pitentino
Via della Conciliazione
Via Piave
Viale Tazio Nuvolari
Via Cremona
Viale Fiume
Via Fondamenta
Via Legnago
Largo di Porta Pradella

LOMBARDY

The centrepiece is **Castello di San Giorgio**, crammed with pieces of art collected by the Gonzaga family. The highpoint is Andrea Mantegna's *Camera degli Sposi*, a series of fine frescoes in one of the castle's towers, which visitors are allowed to view for five minutes before being shuffled on. You are free to wander the rest of the area at will.

Churches

The Baroque cupola of **Basilica di Sant' Andrea** looms above Piazza Mantegna and the city in much the same way that St Paul's dominates east London. Designed by Leon Battisti Alberti in 1472, Mantua's principal place of worship houses a much-disputed relic: containers said to hold earth soaked by the blood of Christ's spear wound. The very Roman soldier responsible for the wound is said to have scooped up the earth and buried it in Mantua after leaving Israel. The containers are paraded around the town in a grand procession on Good Friday. There is no dispute, though, about the tomb of the painter Andrea Mantegna, also to be found inside the basilica.

South of the basilica, across 15th-century colonnaded Piazza delle Erbe, is the 11th-century Romanesque **Rotonda di San Lorenzo**, sunk below the level of the square and believed to stand on the site of a Roman temple dedicated to Venus. In the **Palazzo della Ragione**, which runs the length of the square from the Rotonda and was once the seat of secular power in the city, you can occasionally see exhibitions of varying interest – often for free.

The **cathedral** on Piazza Sordello pales somewhat before the magnificence of the basilica. Its origins lie in the 10th century, but there is little to see of them. The facade was erected in the mid-18th century, while the decoration inside was completed by Giulio Romano after a fire in 1545.

Piazzas

Past the 13th-century Palazzo della Ragione on Piazza delle Erbe is **Palazzo Broletto**, which dominates neighbouring Piazza del Broletto. In a niche on the facade is a figure said to represent Virgil.

Enter Piazza Sordello from the south and on your left you have the grand house of the Gonzagas' predecessors, the Bonacolsi clan. Hapless prisoners used to be dangled in a cage from the tower – aptly known as the **Torre della Gabbia** (Cage Tower). Behind the cathedral lies **Casa di Rigoletto**, which Verdi used as a model set for most of his operas.

Palazzo del Te

Mantua's other Gonzaga palace *(☎ 0376 32 32 66, Viale Te; adult/child €6.20/3.10; open 9am-6pm Tues-Sun, 1pm-6pm Mon)*, at the southern edge of the centre along Via Roma and Via Acerbi, is a grand 16th-century villa built by Giulio Romano. It has many splendid rooms, including the **Camera dei Giganti**, one of the most fantastic and frightening creations of the Renaissance. It also houses a modern art collection and an Egyptian museum.

Boat Tours

Motonave Andes *(☎ 0376 32 28 75, **W** www.motonaviandes.it, Via San Giorgio 2)* Boat tours of the lakes (1½ hours) €7.75/6.70 per adult/child; downriver to San Benedetto Po (2½ hours) €10.85/8.80 per adult/child; day-cruise from Mantua to Venice (7½ hours) €67.15/56.80 per adult/child. Boats arrive/depart from the Imbarco Motonavi Andes, directly behind Castello di San Giorgio on Lago di Mezzo's shore.

Places to Stay

Albergo ABC *(☎/fax 0376 32 33 47, Piazza Don Leoni 25)* Singles/doubles €41.30/51.65. This place has a variety of rooms, ranging from pokey to reasonable, and is one of a trio lined up opposite the train station.

Hotel Due Guerrieri *(☎ 0376 32 15 33, fax 0376 32 96 45, Piazza Sordello 52)* Singles/doubles €61.95/98.15. Staffed by a moody bunch, the gleam clearly rubbed off this ageing hotel's three stars long long ago.

Hotel Broletto *(☎ 0376 22 36 78, fax 0376 22 12 97, Via dell'Accademia 1)* Singles/doubles from €51.65/87.80. Family-run Broletto is by far the friendliest of Mantua's three-star places.

Rechigi Hotel *(☎ 0376 32 07 81, fax 0376 22 02 91, ⓔ info@rechigi.com, ⓦ www.rechigi.com, Via Pier Fortunato Calvi 30)* Singles/doubles/triples €113.60/175.60/191.10. A stark marble interior provides a stunning backdrop for the contemporary art at Mantua's fabulous four-star hotel.

Places to Eat

Over a million pigs a year are reared in the province of Mantua – as local cuisine testifies. Try *salumi* (salt pork), *pancetta* (salt-cured bacon), *prosciutto crudo* (salt-cured ham) or *salamella* (small sausages), or risotto with the locally grown *vialone nano* rice. Wines such as red Rubino dei Morenici Mantovani from the hills around Lago di Garda are equally palatable.

Open-air cafes abound on Piazzas Sordello, Broletto and Erbe.

Caffè Borsa *(☎ 0376 32 60 16, Corsa della Libertà 6)* 1st/2nd lunch courses €3.62/4.15. A tad off the tourist track, this cafe – with its Internet hook-up, funky Kartell chair-clad interior and quiet terrace – is a hit with all ages.

Cafetteria La Ducale *(☎ 0376 32 13 05, Via Pier Fortunato Calvi 25)* Traditional Ducale dates to 1865 and is crammed with sweet treats and three round tables.

Pizzeria Al Quadrato *(☎ 0376 36 88 96, Piazza Virgiliana 49)* Pizzas €4.15-8.80, 1st/2nd courses €4.65/8.80. Fill up on fishy delights at this flower-filled terrace pizzeria, overlooking the city park.

Il Girasole *(☎ 0376 22 58 80, Piazza delle Erbe 15)* Pizzas €3.10-5.15. Sit in the sun, munch on well-topped pizzas and watch the world go by.

Locanda dell'Orologio *(☎ 0376 36 97 57, Piazza delle Erbe 15)* 1st/2nd courses from €5.15/10.35. One of a bunch of tasty places to eat outside on this square, Locanda is known for its designer decor and refreshing use of vegetables.

La Masseria *(☎ 0376 36 53 03, Piazza del Broletto 7)* Pizzas €4.15-7.25, 1st/2nd courses €6.20/8.25. Come dusk, pizza fiends flock here, as do diners wanting to sink their teeth into braised wild boar or a saucy pike.

Antica Osteria Fragoletta *(☎ 0376 32 33 00, Piazza Arche 5a)* 1st/2nd courses €5.15/7.75. This place has dished up generous servings of local food since the 18th century.

Taverna di Santa Barbara *(☎ 0376 32 94 96, Piazza di Santa Barbara 19)* 1st/2nd courses €6.20/7.25. Part of the Palazzo Ducale complex, Santa Barbara cooks up delicious noodles laced in venison sauce, pumpkin-stuffed ravioli, tripe soup and other traditional creations on a peaceful terrace.

Taverna Merlin Cocai *(Via Cavour 98)* This vaulted wine cellar is the place to swill, sniff and swallow local vintages and befriend locals. Sensibly, it serves food too.

Getting There & Away

From the bus station, APAM (☎ 0376 32 72 37) operates buses to/from Sabbioneta and San Benedetto Po (see those sections below).

The easiest way to get to/from Mantua is by train, often with a change of train in Verona, Cremona or Milan.

By road, Mantua is close to the A22 autostrada; take either the Mantova Nord or Sud exit and follow the 'centro' signs. The S236 runs direct to Brescia and the S10 to Cremona.

Getting Around

You can hire a bicycle year-round from La Rigola (☎ 0335 605 49 58), on the banks of Lago Inferiore at Lungolago dei Gonzaga. Rates start at €1.55/7.75 per hour/day for a regular bike and €6.20/25.80 for a tandem. Ask at the APT office for a copy of the free *Cycling along the Po* brochure, which maps out 12 cycling itineraries.

AROUND MANTUA

Sabbioneta

About 35km south-west of Mantua, Sabbioneta was created in the second half of the 16th century by Vespasiano Gonzaga Colonna in a failed attempt to build Utopia. There are five 16th-century monuments, of which you can make a ***grand tour*** *(adult/child €5.70/3.10, with guide adult/child €7.25/3.10, individual monuments €2.60; open 9.30am-12.30pm & 2.30pm-5pm Tues-Sun, 9.30am-12.30pm &*

2.30pm-6pm/7pm Tues-Sun June-Sept). For more information, pop into the local tourist office (☎ 0375 22 10 44, fax 0375 22 21 19), inside Palazzo Giardino at Piazza d'Armi 1.

Other Sabbioneta sights to see include a 19th-century **synagogue** *(adult/child €2.05/1.30; open 10am-12.30pm Tues-Fri, 10am-12.30pm & 2.30pm-5.30pm Sat & Sun)*; and the **Museo di Arte Sacra** *(☎ 0375 22 02 99; adult/child €3.10/1.55; open 9.30am-12.30pm & 2.30pm-5pm Tues-Fri, 9.30am-12.30pm & 2.30pm-6pm Sat & Sun)*, which includes the Sala del Tesoro (with a Golden Fleece found in the tomb of Vespasiano Gonzaga) and an art gallery.

Buses link Sabbioneta with Mantua (€3, one hour, about five daily).

San Benedetto Po

The Benedictine abbey *(☎ 0376 62 30 36, Piazza Matteotti; open 2.30pm-6pm Mon-Fri)* in this small Po Valley (Pianura Padana) town, 21km south-east of Mantua, was founded in 1007. Little remains of the original buildings, although Chiesa di Santa Maria still sports a 12th-century mosaic. The star attraction is the Correggio fresco discovered in the refectory in 1984.

There are buses to the town from Mantua (€2.10, 35 minutes, 11 to 13 daily).

THE LAKES

The Lakes

Where the Lombard plains rise into the Alps, northern Italy is pocked by a series of lakes, among the most beautiful of Italy's natural attractions. Unfortunately, the secret has been out for at least a century – the prices and summer crowds can detract from the pleasure. The lakes are not only the playground of the Milanese rich; tourists from all over northern Europe converge on their favourites. Lago di Garda, Lago di Como and Lago Maggiore are especially busy, although even the minor lakes are hardly immune to tourism.

Most are within easy reach of Milan and provincial centres such as Bergamo and Brescia. There are plenty of camp sites, hostels and hotels to suit all pockets, as well as many rifugi in the mountains.

LAGO MAGGIORE

The most captivating of the lakes, Maggiore (also known as Lago Verbano), is stunning in parts, although its shores are flatter and less spectacular than those of some of its pre-Alpine counterparts. Fed principally by the Rivers Ticino and Tresa, this lovely lake is about 65km long and lures stifling crowds in July and August.

There's a tourist office in Stresa (see the next section) and smaller tourist offices in Arona (☎/fax 0322 24 36 01) at Piazzale Dica d'Aosta; Baveno (☎/fax 0323 92 46 32) at Piazza Dante Alighieri 14; and Verbania (☎/fax 0323 55 76 76) at Corso Zanitello 6–8. Useful online resources include Ⓦ www.stresa.net and Ⓦ www.lagomaggiore.it.

Stresa

postcode 28838 • pop 4885
elevation 205m

Extremely popular with Germans and Brits, Stresa, 80km north-west of Milan on the lake's western shore, is like one great English tearoom – prim and not unattractive, but staid and insipid. It's commonly touted as a base for visiting the Borromean Islands (see that section later), although they can easily be reached from other resorts around the lake too.

Hemingway was among the rash of writers to seek inspiration on Maggiore's shores. He first set foot in Stresa in 1918 to convalesce from a war wound, and part of one of his novels, *A Farewell to Arms*, is set here.

Information The IAT office (☎ 0323 3 01 50, fax 0323 3 13 08, Ⓔ proloco.stresa@libero.it) can be found in its new pride-of-place waterfront location at Piazza Marconi 16 (near the Navigazione Lago Maggiore ticket office). It opens 10am to 12.30pm and 3pm to 6.30pm daily April to September, and 10am to 12.30pm and 3pm to 6.30pm Monday to Friday, 10am to 12.30pm Saturday October to March.

Banks and ATMs abound on Corso Italia, the road running along Stresa's waterfront.

Things to See & Do Apart from visiting the Borromean Islands (see that section later), you can ride a cable car west to the summit of Monte Mottarone (1491m). Some 700 different Alpine species flourish in the **Giardino Alpinia** *(free; open 9am-6pm Tues-Sun Apr-Oct)*, a botanical garden dating to 1934 midway up Mottarone's slopes.

On top of Mottarone, **Parco del Mottarone** offers pleasant **biking** trails and **walking** opportunities. **Mountain bikes** *(☎ 0323 3 03 99 or 338 839 56 92, ⓔ juriol@tin.it; €12.90/18.10 per half/full day)* can be hired inside the Stresa cable-car station. Rental rates include a helmet and a road book detailing a 25km panoramic descent (two to three hours) from Mottarone to Stresa.

Walkers should ask at the cable-car station for a copy of *Trekking on the Slopes of Mont Mottarone*, a free brochure compiled by the Club Alpino Italiano (CAI), which outlines a two-/four-hour walk from Stresa to the Giardino Alpinia/top of Mottarone. Walks farther afield are mapped out in the free multi-lingual *Nature Hikes* brochure, available at tourist offices. In town, Cartolibreria de Mauri, on the central square at Piazza Cadorna 35, sells the *Laghi Maggiore, d'Orta e di Varese* walking map (1:50,000; €6.20), which is published by the Istituto Geografico Centrale and is indispensable for serious walkers.

Most years skiers and boarders can cruise down the gentle slopes of Mottarone from late December to early March. **Skiing** is limited to five green and two blue slopes. All the gear can be hired from the small station at the top of Mottarone. In town, there's a small sports shop at Via de Vit 4.

The **cable car** *(☎ 0323 3 03 99, ⓦ www.paginegialle.it/funistresa, Piazzale Lido; open 9.20am-5pm daily)* departs from next to the Carciano boat station at the northern end of Stresa every 40 minutes. It stops at the Giardino Alpinia (adult/child €5.70/4.15 return; 10 minutes) and Mottarone (adult/child €10.35/5.70 return; 20 minutes), the main access point for the park. A one-day ski pass costs €6.70 and cyclists pay €8.80 (€6.20 for hired bikes) for a one-way trip with bike. Motorists pay €3.60 to use the private road which leads through the park.

Villa Pallavicino *(☎ 0323 3 24 07, ⓦ www.parcozoopallavicino.it; adult/child €6.20/4.65; open 9am-6pm daily Mar-Nov)*, at the southern end of the resort, is a huge garden with a zoo where the animals roam relatively freely. It offers superb views of the lake and the surrounding mountains.

Places to Stay There are some 40 camp sites up and down the lake's western shore; the IAT office in Stresa has a list. Hotels are numerous but must be booked well in advance in summer. For bottomless wallets, several palatial waterfront pads flaunt glittering stars.

Sette Camini Residence *(☎ 0323 2 01 83, fax 0323 2 03 98, Via Pianezza 7)* Sites per person/tent & car €5.40/€8. This is the closest camp site to Stresa, a few kilometres south-west in Gignese.

Hotel Luina *(☎/fax 0323 3 02 85, ⓔ luina@katamail.com, Via Garibaldi 21)* Low season singles/doubles without bath €33.55/46.50, high season €35.65/61.95. In the heart of Stresa's cobbled streets, a block from the waterfront, Hotel Luina is a simple but friendly place with quiet rooms. Some have a lake view.

Hotel Elena *(☎ 0323 3 10 43, fax 0323 3 33 39, ⓦ www.hotelelena.com, Piazza Cadorna)* Low season singles/doubles €46.50/67.15, high season €59.40/92.95. Adjoining a cafe, old-fashioned Hotel Elena is slap-bang on Stresa's pedestrianised central square.

Grand Hotel des Iles Borromees *(☎ 0323 93 89 38, fax 0323 3 24 05, ⓔ borromees@stresa.net, Corso Umberto I)* Singles/doubles from €157.52/235.50. Rockefeller, Bernard Shaw, Hemingway, Clark Gable and Mussolini are among the illustrious guests to have stayed in Stresa's most fabulous hotel, built in 1861 and furnished precisely as it would have been in the 'bella' *belle epoque*.

Places to Eat After a hard day's biking, relax in one of the town's eateries.

Osteria degli Amici *(☎ 0323 3 04 53, Via Anna Maria Bolongaro 33)* Pizzas €3.60-7.75. Dine under vines on one of Stresa's most delightful terraces overlooking Piazza Rossi. Expect to queue as it's always packed.

Chez Osvaldo *(☎ 0323 3 19 48, Via Anna Maria Bolongaro 57)* 1st/2nd courses from €4.65/8.25. A small hotel too, Chez Osvaldo comes through on the eating front. Try the *scaloppine panna e mele* (veal cooked in an apple and cream sauce). It's a short walk from Piazza Rossi.

Ristorante del Pescatore *(☎ 0323 3 19 86, Vicolo del Poncivo 3)* Full meals about €20.65. Spanish dishes (read 'paella') and fish are the house specialities here.

Stock up on picnic fodder at the ***GS Insieme supermarket*** *(Via Roma 11)*. Fresh fish is sold at the nameless ***fishmongers*** *(Via Bolongaro 6)*.

Getting There & Away Stresa lies on the Domodossola-Milan train line. Buses leave from the waterfront for destinations around the lake and elsewhere, including Milan, Novara and Lago d'Orta.

By car, the A8 autostrada connects Milan with Varese, south-east of Lago Maggiore. Exit at Legnano for the S33 road, which passes the lake's western shore and continues to the Simplon Pass. The A8/A26 from Milan has an exit for Lago Maggiore, via Arona.

Ferries and hydrofoils around the lake are operated by Navigazione Lago Maggiore (☎ 0323 3 03 93 or toll free ☎ 800 55 18 01, W www.navlaghi.it), which has its ticket office and landing stage in Stresa at Piazza Marconi 14–16. Boats connect Stresa with Arona (€7.55 return), Angera (€7.55 return), Baveno (€4.55), Cannobio (€12.60), Pallanza (€6.40 return) and the islands (€4.55-6.40 for one island, depending on the island, €8.25 for all three, and €9.30 for all three plus admission to Villa Taranto). Services are reduced in autumn and winter.

A good trip is the circular excursion from Stresa to Domodossola by train, from where you get a charming little train to Locarno (Switzerland – take your passports) and then a ferry back from Locarno to Stresa. The 'Lago Maggiore Express' package deal costs €25.30/12.65; Navigazione Lago Maggiore sells tickets.

Borromean Islands (Isole Borromee)

The Borromean Islands can be reached from various points around the lake but Stresa and Baveno are the best departure points. The four islands – Bella, Madre, Pescatori (or Superiore) and San Giovanni – form the lake's most beautiful corner. San Giovanni is off-limits to tourists.

Bella was named after Charles III's wife, the *bella* Isabella, in the 17th century and has courted a number of famous holiday-makers – Wagner, Stendhal, Byron and Goethe among them. **Palazzo Borromeo** *(adult/child €8.25/3.60; open 9am-12.30pm & 1.30pm-6pm daily)* is its main drawcard. Built in the 17th century for the Borromeo family, the sumptuous palace contains works by Giovanni Tiepolo and Anthony van Dyck as well as Flemish tapestries and sculptures by Canova. Napoleon stayed here with an entourage of 60 in 1797, Mussolini tried to stave off WWII here at the Conference of Stresa in April 1935, and the fossilised boat displayed behind glass in one of the palace grottoes is said to be 3000 years old. The actual grottoes – extravagantly studded by hand with pebbles from the lake bed – took 25 years to complete and were used by the Borromeo family as their cool (literally) hang-out. Plants from around the world grow in the magnificent gardens. What's left of the island (little) swarms with stalls selling ice cream, pizza slices and tacky island souvenirs.

Madre provides fertile ground for Italy's tallest palm trees. The entire island is taken up by the fabulous, 16th- to 18th-century **Palazzo Madre** *(adult/child €7.75/3.60; open 9am-12.30pm & 1.30pm-5.30pm daily)* and its peacock-filled gardens which are even more lavish than those of Palazzo Borromeo. Period furnishings cram the palace interior; highlights include Countess Borromeo's doll collection, a neoclassical theatre designed by a scenographer from

Milan's La Scala and a smaller theatre starring hell.

Beyond an 11th-century apse and a 16th-century fresco in the **Chiesa di San Vittore**, there are no real sights to see on **Isola dei Pescatori**, making it most visitors' port of call for lunch. Despite the many places to eat, there are no snack stalls and the tiny island retains some of its original fishing-village atmosphere. Count on eating (and paying) much the same in whichever waterfront restaurant you plump for – grilled fish 'fresh from the lake' for €12.90. If you want to stay on the island, the romantic ***Albergo Verbano*** *(☎ 0323 3 25 34, fax 0323 3 31 29, W www.hotelverbano.it, Isola dei Pescatori)* will impress your sweetheart with its idyllic terrace and rooms overlooking the water. It's open from March to December and singles/doubles/triples cost €92/134/154.

Western Shore

Stresa is not the only town on Lago Maggiore and it is worth considering the alternatives. The choice depends a little on your taste, but you should remember that you will never really escape the feeling of being in a somewhat artificial environment.

South of Stresa by some 20km, **Arona** (pop 14,750) is a handy accommodation base but there is little of interest save the ruins of the Rocca di Arona, a fortified castle that French novelist Stendhal vividly depicted in prose after witnessing its demolition – clearly a fantastic spectacle – in 1800. Ruins of the 9th-century fortress, an early Romanesque chapel and a couple of storehouses are all that remain in the vast parkland today.

Heading towards Switzerland, **Verbania** (pop 30,300), the biggest town on the lake, offers plenty of accommodation in most classes but it's the least inviting place. The green-fingered might want to make a pit stop here to stroll the grounds of the late 19th-century **Villa Taranto** *(☎ 0323 40 45 55, W www.villataranto.it; adult/child €6.20/5.15; open 8.30am-sunset daily Apr-Oct)*. In 1931 royal archer and Scottish captain Neil McEacharn bought the villa from the Savoy family and planted some 20,000 species over 30 years, creating what are considered today to be among Europe's finest botanical gardens. The villa itself can't be visited.

Cannero Riviera (pop 1150) is a small, tranquil lakeside village. Just off the coast lie some tiny islets that, before being taken over by the Borromeo family in the 15th century, served as a den for thieves who operated in the area during the 12th century.

More interesting is **Cannobio** (pop 5100), 5km short of the Swiss border. The tiny toy town's spotless cobblestone streets retain something of a village flavour, despite the waves of Swiss day-trippers. It has an active sailing and surfing school *(☎ 0323 7 22 14, W www.tomaso.com)* next to a patch of gritty beach at the village's northern end. The IAT office (☎/fax 0323 7 12 12), Viale Vittorio Veneto 4, opens 9am to noon and 4.30pm to 7pm Monday to Saturday and 9am to noon Sunday.

Bold sculptures can be enjoyed at the Galleria Amici dell'Arte *(Via Leoncavallo 7; free; open 10am-11.30am & 3pm-5.30pm Tues-Sat)* in **Brissago**, a tiny village about 8km north of Cannobio along the scenic lakeside S34.

Places to Stay Camp sites are sprinkled along the shore and Cannobio has a handful of lovely hotels.

Ostello Verbania *(☎ 0323 50 16 48, fax 0323 50 78 77, Via alle Rose 7, Verbania)* B&B €12.40. Open Mar-Oct & Christmas. Reception open 7am-11am & 3.30pm-11.30pm daily. Backpackers should make a beeline for Verbania's only hostel.

Hotel Pironi *(☎ 0323 7 21 84, fax 0323 7 01 49, e hotel.pironi@cannobio.net, Via Marconi 35, Cannobio)* Low season singles/doubles €67.15/95.55, high season €74.90/100.70. Languishing in a 15th-century palazzo amid Cannobio's cobbled maze, this is the town's most charming hotel.

Antica Stallera *(☎ 0323 7 15 95, fax 0323 7 22 01, Via Paolo Zaccheo 7, Cannobio)* Singles/doubles €46.50/77.45. This is another safe bet where you can sleep and eat in comfort in Cannobio.

Getting There & Away Navigazione Lago Maggiore (see Getting There & Away under Stresa earlier) runs a car ferry between Intra (Verbania) and Laveno on the eastern shore. Its regular ferry boats, which yo-yo between lake resorts, stop in front of Villa Taranto. All the western shore towns are connected by ferry and bus.

LAGO D'ORTA

Only 15km long and about 2.5km wide, Lago d'Orta is one of the smaller of the Italian lakes. It is actually in the Piedmont region and is separated from its more celebrated eastern neighbour, Lago Maggiore, by Monte Mottarone. Its still waters are surrounded by lush woodlands and, unlike the big lakes, the area is not yet swarming with visitors. It still gets congested at weekends and in summer, though.

Orta San Giulio

postcode 28016 • pop 1100
elevation 293m

Undoubtedly the prettiest of the lake's towns, Orta suffers less than places such as Stresa from the blandness born of 'overtourism'. It is difficult to beat sipping a coffee over the morning paper in one of the cafes on the lakeside square. This idyllic spot makes an obvious choice for a base, not only for Lago d'Orta but for Maggiore as well (if you have a vehicle at any rate), which you can reach via Monte Mottarone.

Orientation & Information From Orta Miasino train station on Piazza Stazione, bear left beneath the railway line and downhill along Via Marconi to the large intersection at the bottom of the hill. Cross the intersection, then bear left immediately after Villa Crespi (the Moorish extravaganza) along Via G Fava for 1.5km. The pleasant stroll from the station to the historic centre should take no more than 20 minutes.

The APT office (☎ 0322 90 56 14, fax 0322 90 58 00, ⓔ ortatl@tin.it), Via Panoramica, is on the right just after the intersection and Via G Fava turn-off. It opens 9am to 1pm and 2pm to 4pm daily and has information on the whole lake. Internet access at La Sibilla Cusiana (see Places to Eat later) costs €7.75 per hour.

Things to See & Do Regular launches make the short trip to the **Isola San Giulio** (€3 return by public motorboat, €1.80 with Navigazione Lago d'Orta), named after a Greek evangelist who earned his saintly status by ridding the island of an assortment of snakes and monsters late in the 4th century. The tiny island, dubbed the 'island of silence', is dominated by the 12th-century **Basilica di San Giulio**. Sunday Mass is celebrated at 11am. A lone path – La Via del Silenzio – encircles the island and there's one museum you can visit, the **Museo del Regio Esercito Italiano** *(☎ 0322 90 52 24, ⓔ museo_regio_esercito@libero.it; adult/child €5.15/2.60; open 9.30am-6pm daily)*, which recounts military history from 1861 to 1945. In summer, sun bathers pack themselves on to the island's pocket-sized patch of pebble beach.

Back on the mainland, Navigazione Lago d'Orta *(☎ 0322 84 48 62, Via Simonotti 35, Borgomanero)* runs boats to numerous other lakeside spots, including north to **Omegna** (€3.10/4.65 single/return), popular for its Thursday market; and to **Pella** (€1.55/2.85 single/return), a village with a factory that churns out taps and valves on the lake's western shore. Departures are less frequent from October to mid-April.

Sacro Monte, behind Orta San Giulio, is dotted with a series of 20 small chapels erected to St Francis of Assisi over a 200-year period from 1591. It makes for a pleasant stroll above the town.

The small village of **Armeno**, at the foot of Monte Mottarone, is worth visiting, not least for its umbrella museum. The narrow road that perilously wiggles from here to the mountain peak (and then down to Stresa on Lago Maggiore) makes for a heart-thumpingly splendid drive.

The cultural association ***Da Orta In Poi*** *(☎ 338 514 31 06 or 339 411 76 73, ⓦ www.orta.net/daortainpoi, Via Albertoletti 37)* promotes Lago d'Orta's historical, cultural and gastronomical traditions through guided

THE LAKES

tours of the island, wine-tasting trips and cookery classes.

Places to Stay The hitch in Orta San Giulio can be finding a place to stay, especially in high season and at weekends. Four camp sites stretch along the coast north of Orta San Giulio and another couple inland. If you have the cash, Orta boasts two of the region's most beautiful hotels (see the boxed text 'Splash Out').

Camping Orta *(☎/fax 0322 9 02 67, Via Domodossola 28)* Low season per person/tent/car €3.85/3.10/3.10, high season €4.90/4.15/3.60. Open year-round. This is one of three sites in Orta.

Piccolo Hotel Olina *(☎ 0322 90 56 56, fax 0322 90 65 45, Via Olina 40)* Doubles with bath/whirlpool €67.15/72.30, overnight attic for two/four people €72.30/108.45. Rooms here are rather cosy, but charming nonetheless. There are self-catering apartments to rent too, plus a tasty restaurant.

Hotel Orta *(☎ 0322 9 02 53, fax 0322 90 56 46, ⓔ hotelorta@iname.com, Piazza Motta 1)* Singles/doubles €38.75/49.05, half-board per person €61.95/72.30. The same family has run this lakeside hotel for the last 100 years.

Hotel Santa Caterina *(☎ 0322 91 58 65, 0322 90 58 77, Via Marconi 10)* Singles/doubles €67.15/82.65. This is the modern choice, midway between the train station and the historic lakeside centre.

Places to Eat Plenty of waterfront places sell pizza slices to eat on the move. All the hotels mentioned under Places to Stay double as restaurants.

Il Buongustaio *(Piazza Ragazzoni 8–10)* This place sells *pane di san giulio* (bread with orange peel, raisins and walnuts) and other sweet, moist fruit loaves.

Enoteca Re Di Coppe *(☎ 0322 91 58 71, Piazza Motta 32)* This is a charming but miniscule wine bar, dishing up oodles of atmosphere and light wine-enhancing snacks.

La Sibilla Cusiana *(☎ 0322 90 51 17, Via Giovanetti 27)* Tuck into a salami platter, gargle on grappa and surf the Internet at this young 'n' fun wine bar.

Splash Out

Giuseppine nuns lived a life of seclusion at Orto San Giulio's 17th-century convent until 1960, when it was transformed into luxurious ***Hotel San Rocco*** *(☎ 0322 91 19 77, fax 0322 91 19 64, ⓦ www.hotelsanrocco.it, Via Gippini 11; singles/doubles from €92.95/144.60)*, an absolutely fabulous place to stay. Moor your motorboat outside and cruise into this pool-filled oasis of luxury.

Secular decadence was lived out to the full by 19th-century Lombard industrialist Benigno Crespi who made a fortune trading cotton – and had the oriental ***Villa Crespi*** *(☎ 0322 91 19 02, fax 0322 91 19 19, ⓔ crespi@slh.com, ⓦ www.slh.com/crespi; singles/doubles from €113.60./165.25)* built in 1879 to prove it. Its lavish gardens and opulent Moorish interior are breathtaking.

Getting There & Away Orta Miasino train station, a short walk from the centre of Orta San Giulio, is just off the Novara-Domodossola train line. In summer there are direct buses to Stresa.

From the south, take the S32 or the S229 from Novara in Piedmont. The second road isn't as interesting but it is much quicker.

LAGO DI COMO

Marie Henri Beyle first set foot on the shores of Lago di Como (also known as Lago Lario) as a 17-year-old conscript under Napoleon. Years later, as Stendhal, he wrote in *La Chartreuse de Parme* that the blue-green waters of the lake and the grandeur of the Alps made it the most beautiful place in the world. Pliny the Elder and Pliny the Younger were born here, but are not known to have gushed about the area to the same degree as Stendhal. In any case, many people would no doubt consider another of Como's famous sons as having achieved quite a deal more for the world: Alessandro Volta, born in 1745, came up with, well, the battery.

This immense body of water, which sprawls for 51km in an upside down 'Y' shape at the foot of the Rhaetian Alps, is enchantingly beautiful, as are its tiny waterside villages, some of which are accessible only by boat. Bathers wanting to wash that city dust right out of their hair should note that Lago di Como's waters are murky. Swimming is inadvisable.

Como

postcode 22100 • pop 90,000
elevation 202m

Como, 50km north of Milan, is the main access town to Lago di Como, sitting at the foot of the lake. On the last Saturday of the month, its streets are filled with a huge antiques market – a fabulous (and the only) excuse for a day trip here. Otherwise, the town has few attractions in its own right but can serve as a good base to explore the fairy-tale lakeside villages around the lake.

Information The main APT office (☎ 031 330 01 11 or 031 26 97 12, fax 031 23 04 52, **W** www.lakecomo.com), Piazza Cavour 17, opens 9am to 1pm and 2.30pm to 6pm Monday to Saturday. The tourist kiosk (☎ 031 26 42 15), on the southern side of the cathedral, opens 10am to 12.30pm and 2.30pm to 6pm Monday to Friday, 10am to 6pm Saturday and Sunday.

Change money at Credito Italiano, just off Piazza Cavour, or nearby Banca d'Italia, Via Boldoni 15. There are ATMs here and elsewhere in the centre.

The post office, Via T Gallio 6, opens 8.15am to 6pm Monday to Saturday. The Telecom office, on a small square off Via Albertolli, opens 8am to 8pm Monday to Saturday.

There's a CTS travel agency branch (☎ 031 26 68 60) at Via Vitani 35. It opens 10am to 1pm and 3pm to 7pm Monday to Saturday.

The hospital, Ospedale Sant'Anna (☎ 031 58 51 11), is at Via Napoleona 60. The *questura* (police station; ☎ 031 31 71) is at Viale Roosevelt 7.

Cathedral From Piazza Cavour, walk along the arcaded Via Plinio to Piazza del Duomo and the marble-faced cathedral, built and repeatedly altered from the 14th to the 18th centuries. The cathedral combines elements of Baroque, Gothic, Romanesque and Renaissance design and is crowned with a high octagonal dome. Next to it is the polychromatic **town hall**, altered in 1435 to make way for the cathedral.

Churches & Museums Named after the saint who brought Christianity to the Como region, the **Basilica di San Fedele** first went up on Via Vittorio Emanuele II in the 6th century. It has undergone various changes since, including those to the bell tower and facade which took place in the 20th century, but the original lines of the basilica have been largely respected.

South along the same street is Como's Palazzo Giovio and Palazzo Olginati. The former, dating from the 18th-century, houses the **Museo Archeologico** *(☎ 031 27 13 43,* **e** *musei.civici@comune.como.it, Piazza Medaglie d'Oro; adult/child €2.60/free; open 9.30am-12.30pm & 2pm-5pm Tues-Sat, 10am-1pm Sun)*, which contains important prehistoric and Roman remains. The latter palace – host to Garibaldi for a time – is closed for renovation and will house further archaeological wonders when complete.

Brunate East of Piazza Cavour along the waterfront is the **Funicoloare Como-Brunate** *(☎ 031 30 36 08, Piazza de Gasperi 4)*, from where a funicular has lurched uphill to Brunate since 1894. Tickets per adult/child cost €2.10/1.40 one way or €3.70/2.30 return. Journey time is seven minutes and trains run every 30 minutes between 6am and midnight daily (less in winter).

The village of Brunate (elevation 720m) overlooks Como and the lake and offers a pleasant walk and excellent views from the small town of **San Maurizio**, a short walk from the Brunate funicular station. For a bird's-eye view, scale the 143 steps to the top of the lighthouse, built here in 1927 to mark the centenary of Alessandro Volta's death and still flashing its three-coloured beam. The more lazily inclined can hop aboard a shuttle bus (€0.75) which links the two hamlets.

Before setting off from Como, serious walkers can pick up a copy of the free *Guida*

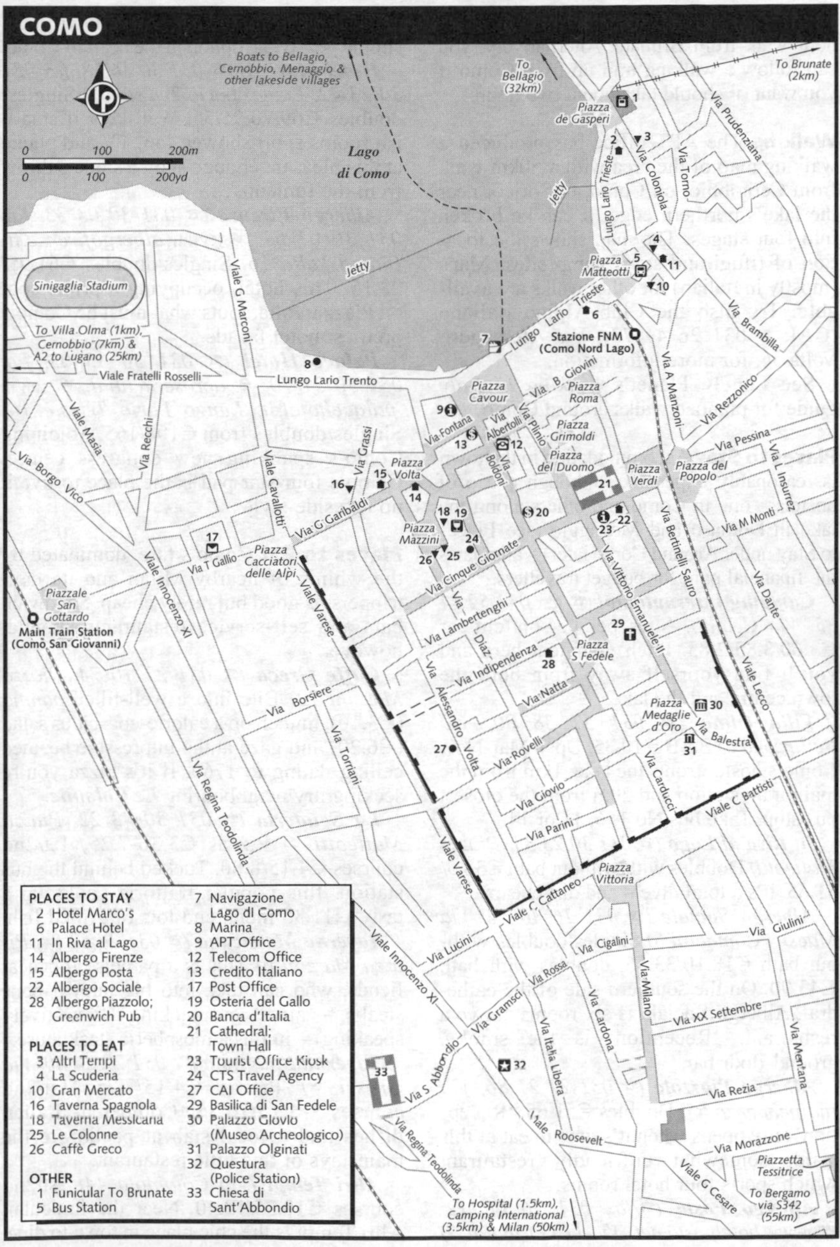
COMO
Boats to Bellagio, Cernobbio, Menaggio & other lakeside villages
To Bellagio (32km)
To Brunate (2km)
Lago di Como
Sinigaglia Stadium
To Villa Olma (1km), Cernobbio (7km) & A2 to Lugano (25km)
Stazione FNM (Como Nord Lago)
Main Train Station (Como San Giovanni)
To Hospital (1.5km), Camping International (3.5km) & Milan (50km)
To Bergamo via S342 (55km)
Piazza de Gasperi
Piazza Matteotti
Piazza Cavour
Piazza Roma
Piazza Grimoldi
Piazza del Duomo
Piazza Verdi
Piazza del Popolo
Piazza Volta
Piazza Mazzini
Piazza Cacciatori delle Alpi
Piazzale San Gottardo
Piazza S Fedele
Piazza Medaglie d'Oro
Piazza Vittoria
Piazzetta Tessitrice
PLACES TO STAY
2 Hotel Marco's
6 Palace Hotel
11 In Riva al Lago
14 Albergo Firenze
15 Albergo Posta
22 Albergo Sociale
28 Albergo Piazzolo; Greenwich Pub
PLACES TO EAT
3 Altri Tempi
4 La Scuderia
10 Gran Mercato
16 Taverna Spagnola
18 Taverna Messicana
25 Le Colonne
26 Caffè Greco
OTHER
1 Funicular To Brunate
5 Bus Station
7 Navigazione Lago di Como
8 Marina
9 APT Office
12 Telecom Office
13 Credito Italiano
17 Post Office
19 Osteria del Gallo
20 Banca d'Italia
21 Cathedral; Town Hall
23 Tourist Office Kiosk
24 CTS Travel Agency
27 CAI Office
29 Basilica di San Fedele
30 Palazzo Giovio (Museo Archeologico)
31 Palazzo Olginati
32 Questura (Police Station)
33 Chiesa di Sant'Abbondio

al Sentieri Trekking, which maps out a six-hour walk from Brunate. Alternatively, you can follow a walking trail up from Como if you want (it should take about two hours).

Walking The APT office has produced a walking map of the area with a 50km walk from Cernobbio, on Como, to Sorico, near the lake's northern edge. It can be broken into four stages. The map shows the location of rifugi and some camp sites. Maps (mostly in Italian) for other walks are available. Try also the Club Alpino Italiano (CAI; ☎ 031 26 41 77), Via Alessandro Volta 56, for more information.

See Lonely Planet's *Walking in Italy* guide for planned walks around Como.

Places to Stay Accommodation in the town is reasonably expensive, although a trio of hostels – one in Como and others along the lake in Domaso and Menaggio (see Places to Stay under Around Como later) – alleviates the financial pain for budget travellers.

Camping International *(☎/fax 031 52 14 35, Via Cecilio)* Sites per person/tent/car €3.60/3.85/2.85. Pitch your tent here and you'll find yourself away from both the town centre and the lake.

Villa Olmo *(☎ 031 57 38 00, Via Bellinzona 6)* B&B €10.35. Open Mar-Nov. Como's hostel fronts the lake, 1km from the main train station and 20m from the closest bus stop. Take bus No 1, 6, 11 or 14.

In Riva al Lago *(☎ 031 30 23 33, Piazza Matteotti)* Doubles with/without bath €38.5/51.65. It's a total dive – and dirt cheap.

Albergo Sociale *(☎ 031 26 40 42, Via Maestri Comacini 8)* Singles/doubles without bath €18.10/33.55, doubles with bath €43.90. On the southern side of the cathedral, Albergo Sociale is six rooms above a restaurant. 'Reception' is the smoky, ground-floor bar.

Albergo Piazzolo *(☎ 031 27 21 86, Via Indipendenza 65)* Doubles €51.65. 'Reception' only opens when it's time to eat at this staid, somewhat unfriendly restaurant which sports four hotel rooms.

Albergo Posta *(☎/fax 031 26 60 12, W www.hotelposta.net, Via G Garibaldi 2)* Singles/doubles €51.65/67.15. Plump for a simple yet stylish option in the heart of Como.

Hotel Marco's *(☎ 031 30 36 28, fax 031 30 23 42, Lungo Lario Trieste 62)* Singles/doubles €69.70/95.55. Well-kept if smallish rooms sport shower, loo, TV and phone at this pleasant enough spot, a stone's throw from the funicular.

Albergo Firenze *(☎ 031 30 03 33, fax 031 30 01 01, W www.albergofirenze.it, Piazza Volta 16)* Singles/doubles €61.95/98.15. This hotel, occupying a prime spot on Piazza Volta, touts what must be Como's prettiest hotel facade.

Palace Hotel *(☎ 031 30 33 03, fax 031 30 31 70, e aproser@tin.it, W www.palacehotel.it, Lungo Lario Trieste 16)* Singles/doubles from €108/165. Adjoining Como's spanking new congress centre, Como's four-star pad is the place to live it up lakeside-style.

Places to Eat Como's fare, dominated by the whims of nearby Milan and its day-trippers, is good but rarely cheap. Sandwich bars and self-service restaurants abound, however.

Caffè Greco *(☎ 031 27 10 74, Piazza Mazzini 13)* Bite into a well-filled *panino* (€3.10), munch on a calorie-conscious salad (€6.20) and gaze at the impressive beamed ceiling dating to 1760. If it's pizza you're seeking, try neighbouring ***Le Colonne***.

La Scuderia *(☎ 031 30 43 22, Piazza Matteotti 4)* Pizzas €3.36-7.25, 1st/2nd courses €4.15/8.80. Tucked behind the bus station, this popular trattoria cooks up a tasty €11.35 menu and lots of grilled fish.

Taverna Messicana *(☎ 031 26 62 04, Piazza Mazzini 6)* This is a paradise for meat fiends, who can tuck into big juicy T-bone steaks – alive and kicking (figuratively speaking) – in this atmospheric steakhouse.

Taverna Spagnola *(☎ 031 27 24 60, Via Grassi 8)* Pizzas €4.15/7.75, 1st/2nd courses €5.15/10.35. Competent Italian dishes and a local stab at paella are the mainstays of this little restaurant.

Altri Tempi *(Via Coloniola 44)* 1st/2nd courses €10.35/12.40. Near the funicular, Altri Tempi is the chic place in town to dine.

Self-caterers and picnic-makers can stock up on supplies at the ***Gran Mercato*** supermarket, opposite the bus station, or at the ***market*** *(Via Mentana 15)*.

Entertainment There are a couple of places to enjoy a drink.

Osteria del Gallo *(☎ 031 27 25 91, Via Vitani 16)* Open 9am-7.30pm Mon-Sat. Osteria del Gallo is a quaint, genteel and cosy den for a lunchtime glass of wine and something delicious to nibble on. They have bottles to go, too.

Greenwich Pub *(☎ 031 26 78 72, Piazzolo Terragni 7–8)* This English-inspired pub dishes up Italian-inspired pub grub, washed down with a pint or three.

Getting There & Away SPT buses (☎ 031 30 47 44) leave from Piazza Matteotti for destinations along the lake, Bergamo (€4.30 single, €5.16 for a day return, two hours, six to eight daily) and other cities in the region.

Trains from Milan's Stazione Centrale arrive at Como's main train station (listed as Como San Giovanni on train timetables) and continue to many Western European cities. Trains from Milan's Stazione Nord (Stazione Cadorna) are more frequent (€2.85, one hour, hourly) and use Como's lakeside Stazione FNM (listed on timetables as Como Nord Lago). They are timed to link with the ferries.

By car, Como is on the A9 autostrada, which connects with the A8 to Milan's ring road. The S35 from Como also connects to the ring road.

Ferries operated by Navigazione Lago di Como (☎ 031 57 92 11 or toll free ☎ 800 55 18 01), Piazza Cavour, criss-cross the lake year-round. Their speedy hydrofoils only sail April to September. A day ticket allowing unlimited trips around the entire lake costs €17.05/8.50 per adult/child. Cheaper, and more realistic given the time it takes to cruise from one town to another, is the €15.50/7.75 day ticket which allows unlimited trips between Como and Bellano. A whole host of other tickets is available, including those for day cruises with lunch and those which include admission to the various lakeside villas.

Around Como

The myriad towns of Lago di Como can easily be explored by boat or bus from Como and are worth at least a two-day visit. Monumental villas stud its central shores. **Isola Comacina**, where Lombard kings took refuge from invaders, is the lake's sole island. The northern lakeside towns are lesser tourist attractions.

Places to Stay Lago di Como touts two hostels, numerous camp sites and many reasonably priced hotels. Check with the APT office in Como for lists of the 50 or so camp sites, hotels and agriturismo facilities along the lake shore.

Ostello La Primula *(☎ 0344 3 23 56, Via IV Novembre 86)* B&B €10.85. Open Mar-Oct. In Menaggio, about halfway up the lake on the western side, this great hostel is close to the bus stop on the route from Como.

Ostello Domaso *(☎ 0344 9 74 49, Via Case Sparse 12, Domaso)* B&B €10.35. Open Mar-Oct. Domaso Hostel is on the same bus route as Ostello La Primula.

Villa d'Este *(☎ 031 34 81, W www.villadeste.it, Via Regina 40, Cernobbio)* Singles/doubles from €245/405. This splendid villa in Cernobbio is ideal for those with a bottomless bank account and a taste for queenly pleasures. It's Lago di Como's most famous hotel.

Tremezzo On the western shore of the lake is Tremezzo (pop 1300). The APT office (☎/fax 0344 4 04 93, e infotremezzo@tiscalinet.it), next to Tremezzo's main boat jetty on waterfront Via Statale Regina, opens 9am to noon and 3.30pm to 6.30pm Wednesday to Monday, April to October. It stocks a particularly plentiful supply of walking information in English.

Pergolas knitted from orange trees, and some of Europe's finest rhododendrons and azaleas (April to May) are among the blooming wonders to be enjoyed in the fabulous botanical gardens of 17th-century **Villa Carlotta** *(0344 4 04 05, W www.unicei.it/villacarlotta, Riva Garibaldi; adult/child €6.20/free; open 9am-6pm daily Apr-Sept, 9am-11.30am & 2pm-4.30pm daily Mar &*

Tremezzo Trivia

A couple of love scenes from *Star Wars Episode II (Attack of the Clones)* were shot in Tremezzo – in the woods at Rogaro and on the flight of marble steps leading up to the town garden.

Nov). The villa itself, with an art-strung interior, can be visited. It takes its name from the Prussian princess who was given the place as a wedding present by her mother in 1847.

Tremezzo's short waterfront is lined with places to sleep, eat, drink and be merry.

Grand Hotel Tremezzo *(☎ 0344 4 24 91, fax 0344 4 02 01, W www.grandhotel tremezzo.com, Via Statale Regina 8)* Low season doubles without/with lake view from €200/240, high season €230/276. A glass lift whisks guests from the lake shore up to one of Lago di Como's most romantic hotels, dating from 1910.

Red & White *(☎ 0344 4 00 95, Via Portici Sampietro 18)* Red & White is an authentic enoteca where you can sample local wines over lunch. Its hot chocolate is thick enough to spoon.

Regular boats plough between Tremezzo, Como and other lakeside towns. Villa Carlotta is a three-minute walk from the Tremezzo jetty. Frequent SPT buses (☎ 0344 3 21 18) link the resort with Menaggio (10 minutes) and Como (one hour).

Bellagio Considered the 'pearl' of the lake, Bellagio (pop 3000) is indeed a pretty little town sitting more or less on the point where the western and eastern arms of the lake split and head south. The 32km drive from Como is itself rewarding, though the trip down the eastern side towards Lecco is less so.

The APT office (☎/fax 031 95 02 04, W www.bellagiolakecomo.com) is at Piazza Chiesa 14 and opens 9am to noon and 3pm to 6pm Monday and Wednesday to Saturday year-round, 10.30am to 12.30pm and 3.30pm to 5.30pm on Tuesday and Sunday May to September. It has mountains of information on water sports, mountain-biking and other activities on and around the lake. The tobacconist at Salita Serbelloni 7 sells a good choice of walking maps. Dry-land surfers can log-on at Il Sorbetto (e ilsorbetto@tiscalinet.it), Salita Serbelloni 34, for €5.15 per hour.

The lavish gardens of **Villa Serbelloni** *(☎ 031 95 51; adult/child €5.15/2.60; open 11am-4pm Tues-Sun Apr-31 Oct, visits by guided tour only)* cover much of the promontory on which Bellagio sits. Tours are limited to 16 people and 'gold-dust' tickets are sold 10 minutes in advance from the small office above the tourist office (see later). Garden lovers can also stroll the grounds of neoclassical **Villa Melzi d'Eril** *(adult/child €5.15/2.60; open 9am-6pm daily Apr-Oct)*, built in 1808 for one of Napoleon's assistants and known in horticultural circles for its springtime azaleas and rhododendrons.

Shopping for silk is the other major pastime of most visitors to Bellagio. Shops selling ties, scarves and other exquisite silky accessories are liberally sprinkled along most of its steep and narrow 'staircase' streets, particularly Via Centrale.

There are a couple of places to stay in Bellagio.

Albergo Roma *(☎ 031 95 04 24, fax 031 95 19 66, e prombell@tin.it, Salita Granda 6)* Singles/doubles without bath €25.80/41.30, with bath €41.30/67.15. Open Mar-Oct. This is as cheap as Bellagio gets.

Grand Hotel Villa Serbelloni *(☎ 031 95 02 16, fax 031 95 15 29, W www.villaserbelloni.com, Via Roma 1)* Low season singles/doubles €199/282, high season €241/326. This richman's villa, dating from 1852, has been a very grand hotel since 1872. Thirteen self-catering apartments lounge in its extensive pool-lined grounds.

The lake's only car ferries, connecting the eastern and western shores in this area, stop at Bellagio.

Varenna A short boat ride away on the lake's eastern shore, Varenna (pop 850) is a pretty village crowned by a castle and studded with extravagant villas. The gardens of two can be visited. **Villa Cipressi** *(☎ 0341 83 01 13, fax 0341 83 04 01, e villacipressi@libero.it, Via IV Novembre 18; adult/child €2.60/2.05;*

open 9am-7pm Mar-Oct), a three-star hotel today, first welcomed guests in 1838. Everything from magnolias and camellias to yucca trees fill its peaceful gardens. Nearby **Villa Monastero** *(☎ 0341 83 12 81, Piazza Venini 1; adult/child €2.60/2.05; open 9am-6pm Mar-Oct)* started life as a monastery.

To get to both villas from Piazzale Martiri Libertà, the square next to the boat jetty by the lake, follow the lakeside promenade around the shore then bear left (inland) up the steep flight of steps to Piazza San Giorgio, the main village square, from where both villas are clearly signposted.

Albergo Milano *(☎/fax 0341 83 02 98, Via XX Settembre 29)* Doubles €103.30. Tucked down a narrow cobbled street by the lake, this hotel is one of Lago di Como's sweetest, prettiest and most charming bets. Every rooms touts a balcony and lake view.

LAGO DI GARDA

The largest and most popular of the Italian lakes, Garda (370 sq km) lies between the Alps and the Po Valley and enjoys a temperate climate. At its northern reaches, the lake is hemmed in by craggy mountains and resembles a fjord. As it broadens towards the south, the lake takes on the appearance of an inland sea.

There are many large villages around the lake but most are heavily developed and unpleasant. The picturesque but Disneyland-like resort of Sirmione is worth visiting, as is Gardone Riviera on the lake's western edge. Both places are popular with elderly visitors. At the northern end, Riva del Garda is a good base for walking in the nearby Alps.

Getting There & Away

Buses leave from Verona, Brescia, Mantua and Milan for the main towns around the lake.

Desenzano del Garda is on the main Milan-Venice train line. A taxi from Desenzano to Sirmione should cost no more than €15.50.

By car, the A4 autostrada and the S11, which connect Milan with Venice, pass the southern edge of the lake and the A22, connecting Verona with Trento, runs parallel to the lake's eastern shore. Riva del Garda can be reached by exiting the A22 at Rovereto Sud.

Getting Around

Navigazione sul Lago di Garda (☎ 030 914 95 11 or toll free ☎ 800 55 18 01), Piazza Matteotti 2, in Desenzano del Garda, operates ferries year-round between most towns on the lake. It has offices or booths in all of the towns it serves. Tourist offices have timetables. Fares range from €1.20 to €11.65, depending on the length of the trip and whether you get the *battello* (ferry) or *aliscafo* (hydrofoil). Bicycles can be taken on board for an extra €3.70 fee.

Sirmione

postcode 25019 • pop 6200
elevation 68m

The Roman poet Catullus celebrated Sirmione – a narrow peninsula jutting out from the southern shore of the lake – in his writings and his name is still invoked in connection with the place. It is a popular bathing spot and generally jammed tight with tourists. In spite of this, Sirmione retains a comparatively relaxed atmosphere. The area of interest (watch for the castle) is an islet attached by a bridge to the rest of the peninsula.

The tourist office (☎ 030 91 61 14, fax 030 91 62 22), Viale Marconi 8, opens 9am to 9pm daily.

Things to See & Do The Roman villa and baths known as the **Grotte di Catullo** *(☎ 030 91 61 57; adult/child €4.15/free; open 8.30am-7pm daily Mar–mid-Oct, 8.30am-5pm daily mid-Oct–Feb)* probably had nothing to do with the Roman poet, although Catullus and his family did have a villa in the area. The extensive ruins – a peaceful 15-minute walk from the centre – occupy a prime position on the northern, quieter end of the Sirmione island. En route, you pass **Lido delle Bionde**, a small beach with deck chairs and pedal boats to rent.

Castello Scaligero *(Rocca Scaligera; ☎ 030 91 64 68; adult/child €4.15/free; open 8.30am-7.30pm Tues-Sun)* was built by Verona's ruling family, the Scaligeri, as a stronghold on the lake in 1250. There's not a lot inside but the views from the tower are good.

You can go for a watery spin around the island. Plenty of boats leave from near the castle (about €15.50 per person). All sorts of vessels will also make any manner of trip around the lake – at a price – and an array of water activities can be arranged in the town. Windsurfers can call ***Centro Surf Lana*** *(☎ 338 624 36 50)* or ***Centro Surf Martini*** *(☎ 330 76 72 36)*.

Massages, saunas and other sensuous delights can be enjoyed at the **Terme di Sirmione** *(☎ 030 9 16 81 or toll free ☎ 800 80 21 25, W www.termedisirmione.com, Piazza Virgilio 1)*. A 25-/55-minute massage typically costs €67.15/92.95.

Places to Stay & Eat It is hard to believe that there are 90-odd hotels crammed in here, many of which slam shut their shutters from the end of October until March. Book ahead or stay away in summer and at long weekends. Four camp sites lie near the town and the APT office can advise on others around the lake.

Campeggio Sirmione *(☎/fax 030 91 90 45, Via Sirmioncino 9)* Sites per person/tent & car €5.15/€8.25. Open Mar-Nov. On the foreshore, this is one of the largest camp sites in the area.

Albergo Al Progresso *(☎ 030 91 61 08, Corso Vittorio Emanuele 16–18)* Doubles €41.30. Al Progresso is as cheap as you'll find in old Sirmione's heart.

Albergo degli Oleandri *(☎ 030 990 57 80, fax 030 91 61 39, e hoteloleandri@libero.it, Via Dante 31)* Singles/doubles €38.75/51.65. Stay near the castle in a shady, pleasant location, in spotlessly clean rooms with TVs.

Hotel Speranza *(☎ 030 91 61 16, fax 030 91 64 03, Via Casello 6)* Singles/doubles €38.75/61.95. Tucked in the maze of tourist shops, Hotel Speranza is a safe two-star bet.

Palace Hotel Villa Cortine *(☎ 030 990 58 90, fax 030 91 63 90, W www.hotelvillacortine.com, Via Grotte 6)* Doubles from €361.50. The five-star neoclassical villa, built in the 1880s, languishes in a fabulous park with statues of Neptune, Narcissus et al.

There are loads of takeaway food outlets to be found, especially around Piazza Carducci, where the bulk of cafes, gelati joints and restaurants are.

Getting Around Save for the crowds, Sirmione is easily navigable on foot. Motorised vehicles are banned from the historic centre. Those keen to venture farther afield can rent a mountain bike/50cc scooter for €10.35/31 per day from Adventure Sprint (☎ 030 91 90 00), Via Brescia 9.

Around Sirmione

Sirmione is about 5km east of **Desenzano del Garda** (pop 23,500), the lake's largest town and a main transport hub – but not really worth a visit. Farther north from Desenzano is **Salò** (pop 9900) which gave its name to Mussolini's puppet republic in 1943, after the dictator was rescued from the south by the Nazis. The APT office in Salò (☎/fax 0365 2 14 23), inside the Palazzo Comunale on Via Pietro da Salò, can help you track down information on walks and rifugi in the mountains.

Heading east, larger-than-life dinosaurs, buddhas and pirate ships are all part of the excitement at Italy's answer to Disneyland – kid-orientated **Gardaland** *(☎ 045 644 97 77, W www.gardaland.it; adult/child €19.65/16.55; open 9.30am-6.30pm daily 31 Mar-30 Sept; 9.30am-midnight daily mid-June–early Sept; 9.30am-6.30pm Sat & Sun Oct)*.

Next door is **CanevaWorld** *(☎ 0457 59 06 22, W www.canevaworld.it, Via Fossalta 1; aqua park adult/child €16.55/13.95, medieval zone adult/child €19.65/12.90; aqua park open 10am-7pm daily mid-May–mid-Sept; medieval zone open mid-Apr–30 Sept)*. At the last count the giant entertainment complex featured a medieval zone, aqua park and ***cafe*** *(open 6pm-2am Jul & Aug)* dedicated to rock music. The nearest train station to both parks is Peschiera del Garda, from where free buses shuttle visitors the remaining 2km.

Gardone Riviera

postcode 25083 • pop 2480
elevation 85m

On the western edge of the lake at the head of a small inlet is the popular resort of

THE LAKES

Gardone Riviera. It retains a hint of its past as the lake's most elegant holiday spot but has succumbed to development and the problems of being a group tourist destination.

The APT office (☎/fax 0365 2 03 47, W www.bresciaholiday.com), Corso Repubblica 8, stocks a wealth of information on accommodation and activities around the lake. It opens 9am to 12.30pm and 3.30pm to 6.30pm daily (closed Thursday afternoon and all day Sunday from October to June).

Buses arrive at/depart from the bus station (☎ 0365 2 10 61) at Corso Zanardelli 12 (the S45b).

Things to See & Do A visit to the town is a must to see **Il Vittoriale** *(☎ 0365 29 65 11, W www.vittoriale.it, Piazza Vittoriale; adult/child €5.15/4.15 to grounds, plus €5.15/3.60 to d'Annunzio's house & €2.60 to war museum; grounds open 8.30am-8pm daily Apr-Sept, 9am-5pm daily Oct-Mar; house & museum open 10am-6pm Tues-Sun Apr-Sept, 9am-1pm & 2pm-5pm Tues-Sun Oct-Mar)*. This absolutely fabulous villa belonged to Italy's controversial 20th-century poet and screeching nationalist, Gabriele d'Annunzio (1863–1938), who moved here in 1922 because, he claimed, he wanted to escape the world, which made him ill.

Visits to d'Annunzio's house are by guided tour only (25 minutes, departures every 10 minutes). The Museo della Guerra (War Museum) records the WWI antics of d'Annunzio and his contemporaries. One of d'Annunzio's most triumphant and more bizarre feats was to capture, with a band of his soldiers, a battleship from the fledgling Yugoslavia shortly after WWI when Italy's territorial claims had been partly frustrated in postwar peace talks. In July and August, classical concerts, ballets, plays and operas are staged in the **open-air theatre** *(box office ☎ 0365 29 65 19, e teatro.vittoriale@tiscalinet.it)* in the villa grounds. Tickets cost €10.35 to €31. The box office is outside the estate entrance.

Sigmund Freud, David Bowie and Peter Gabriel, among others, have strolled through Gardone's **Giardino Botanico Fondazione André Heller** *(☎ 336 41 08 77, Via Roma; adult/child €5.15/3.10; open 9am-3pm daily mid-Mar–mid-Oct)*, which you pass on the road to Il Vittoriale. The innovative, 'ecologically friendly' gardens were first laid out in 1900 and were redesigned 98 years later by multimedia artist André Heller. They include sculptures by Keith Haring, Roy Lichtenstein and other contemporary greats, and some 8000 species grow here.

Some pleasant and easy walks can be undertaken from Gardone, heading inland to the rifugi at **Monte Spino** or **Monte Pizzicolo**. The APT office has details.

Places to Stay & Eat There are plenty of options to chose from.

Hotel Nord *(☎ 0365 2 07 07, fax 0365 2 10 43, Corso Zanardelli 28)* Singles/doubles without bath €25.80/31, with bath €33.60/41.30. Hotel Nord is definitely past its prime but if it's dirt-cheap you want, that's what you get.

La Maison du Relax *(☎ 0365 29 04 84, fax 0365 2 07 77, W www.villaparadiso.com, Corso Zanardelli 126)* Three-/seven-day packages from €1048/1988. Relax – everyone from frogs to princesses does at this lakeside beauty farm.

Villa Fiordaliso *(☎ 0365 2 01 58, fax 0365 29 00 11, e fiordaliso@relaischateaux.fr, Via Zanardelli 150)* Doubles €181-491. Historically furnished rooms are named after flowers at this 1903 waterside palace. D'Annunzio lived here from 1921 to 1923, as did Mussolini's mistress, Clara Petacci, from 1943 to 1945. It has an acclaimed restaurant.

Trattoria Agli Angeli *(☎ 0365 2 08 32, Piazza Garibaldi 2)* Full meals about €18.10. Tucked well away from the waterfront circus en route to Il Vittoriale, this pretty little trattoria with a handful of rooms above (doubles €72.30) overlooks a quintessentially Italian piazza.

The waterfront is lined with plenty more places to eat, drink and be merry.

Bar Milano *(☎ 0365 2 15 19, Lungolago d'Annunzio 18)* Sink your teeth into a well-topped *bruschetta* (toasted seasoned garlic bread; €2.60-3.60) and killer-calorie sundae (€4.65) or wrap your lips around a dusk-time cocktail at this friendly, lakeside cafe-cum-bar. Breakfast here costs €4.90.

Gargnano

postcode 25084 • pop 3000
elevation 98m

Gargnano is really just another lake resort town. Mussolini was based here for the short life of his Repubblica Sociale Italiana (or Repubblica di Salò). He was guarded by German SS units and the republic was, in fact, fictitious, as northern Italy was occupied territory after Italy signed an armistice with the Allies in September 1943. The republic lasted until 25 April 1945 when the last German troops were finally cleared from Italy. Mussolini and Petacci were lynched three days later near Lago di Como.

Mountain-bike and wind-surfing enthusiasts can strut their stuff at ***OK Surf*** *(☎ 0365 79 00 12, ⓔ ok.surf@tin.it)*, an activity centre in Parco Fontanella, by the waterfront at Gargnano's northern end.

Riva del Garda

postcode 38066 • pop 14,359
elevation 70m

The most popular of the resort towns around Lago di Garda is Riva del Garda, at its northern edge. It has a pleasant old centre of cobbled lanes and squares and occupies a nice position on the lake. Links with the Germanic world are evident, not only in the bus and car loads of Germans and Austrians but also in the town's history. Riva was part of Habsburg Austria until it was incorporated into Italy after WWI and was annexed briefly by Nazi Germany in the closing years of WWII. Central European luminaries such as Nietzsche, Kafka and Thomas Mann were wont to put their feet up in Riva.

Information The APT office (☎ 0464 55 44 44, fax 0464 52 03 08, ⓔ info@gardatrentino.com, ⓦ www.gardatrentino.it), Giardini di Porta Orientale 8, opens 9am to noon and 3pm to 6.15pm Monday to Saturday, plus 10am to noon and 6pm to 6.30pm Sunday mid-June to mid-September; and 9am to noon and 2.30pm to 5.15pm Monday to Friday October to March. Between April and October it also operates a kiosk (☎ 0464 55 07 76, fax 0464 56 17 30), Lungolago d'Annunzio 4c, overlooking Piazza Catena where boats dock. It opens 9am to noon and 3pm to 6.15pm daily.

In addition to a hip crowd, trendy Caffè Italia (☎ 0464 55 25 00, ⓔ masterplanet@caffeitalia.it), Piazza Cavour 8, touts two Internet terminals; surf for €7.75 an hour. From Piazza Garibaldi (the square behind the Museo Civico), head uphill along Via Mazzini. The cafe opens 7am to 1am.

Things to See Guarding the waterfront is the **Museo Civico** *(☎ 0464 57 38 69, Piazza Cesare Battisti 3; adult/child €2.10/free; open 9.30am-12.30pm & 2.30pm-6.30pm Tues-Sun)*, a typical city museum inside the Rocca di Riva built in 1124. The castle touts changing photographic exhibitions on the ground floor; an art gallery on the 1st; and various archaeological finds from Arco and Magna Greece on the 2nd.

3km north of town and a pleasant 45-minute stroll is the **Cascata Varone** *(☎ 0464 52 14 21; adult/child €3.60/free; open 9am-7pm daily July & Aug; 9am-6pm daily Sept & Oct; 10am-12.30pm & 2pm-5pm Sat & Sun Nov-Feb; 10am-12.30pm & 2pm-5pm daily Mar-June)*. This 100m waterfall is fed by Lago di Tenno (a tiny lake north-west of Lago di Garda).

Activities The APT office has information on everything in the area from climbing and paragliding to wine tasting and touring flea markets.

Riva is one of Italy's most popular spots for **windsurfing** and has three schools that runs courses, hire equipment and so on. **Nautic Club Riva** *(☎ 0464 55 24 53, ⓦ www.nauticclubriva.com, Lungolago del Pini 7, c/o Hotel du Lac)* and **Surf Segnana Windsurf** *(☎ 0464 50 59 63, ⓦ www.surfsegnana.it, Lungolago del Pini 19, c/o Campeggio Bavaria)* both run sailing classes and organise mountain-bike expeditions. Nautic Club Riva does canyoning too. They both hire out mountain bikes (from €10.35 per day) and city bikes (from €3.10/10.35 per hour/day).

Alternatively, motor into **Fiori e Bike** *(☎ 0464 55 18 30, ⓔ pedre@dnet.it, Viale dei Tigli 24)*, which charges €9.30/7.75 per day for a mountain/road bike.

You can hire two-person paddle boats (€6.20 per hour) from the waterfront in front of the Museo Civico. To the side of the castle, **Speedy Gonzales** *(☎ 0464 55 20 89)* runs speedier boat excursions around the lake from €7.75 per person per hour.

The town is a great starting point for walks around Monte Rocchetta, which dominates the northern end of Lago di Garda. The APT office stocks various English-language brochures detailing walks around Riva.

Places to Stay Hotels are plentiful but book ahead for summer stays. Riva's hotel reservation centre ***Consorzio Garda Trentino Hotel*** *(☎ 0464 55 36 67, fax 0464 55 60 09, W www.gardatrentinohotels.com, Via Bastoni 7)* makes reservations for free for hotels with three or more stars.

Campeggio Bavaria *(☎ 0464 55 25 24, fax 0464 55 91 26, e campingbavaria@yahoo.it, Viale Rovereto 100)* Sites per person/tent/car €8.25/6.20/5.15. One of four camp sites to dot Riva's waterfront, this one sports a biking and surfing centre too (see Activities earlier).

Ostello Riva *(☎ 0464 55 49 11, fax 0464 55 99 66, e ostelloriva@anthesi.com, Piazza Cavour 10)* B&B €11.35. Reception opens 7am-9am & 3pm-midnight daily Mar-Oct. To find this HI hostel, bang in the centre of Riva, follow the same directions as for Caffè Italia (see Information earlier). There's a midnight curfew.

La Montanara *(☎/fax 0464 55 48 57, e enricoevia@dnet.it, Via Montanara 18)* Singles/doubles without bath €15.50/31, doubles with bath €34.10. This one-star pad, down a narrow shop-lined lane in the centre, is one of Riva's cheapest places.

Albergo Ancora *(☎ 0464 52 21 31, fax 0464 55 00 50, e hotelancora@rivadelgarde.com, Via Montanara 2)* Singles/doubles from €38.75/77.45. Ancora is a satisfying mid-range option.

Hotel Sole *(☎ 0464 55 26 86, fax 0464 55 28 11, W www.hotelsole.net, Piazza 3 Novembre 35)* Singles/doubles from €43.90/87.80. Despite its four modern stars, this once-elegant waterfront hotel – where Nietzsche stayed – has clearly seen better days.

Places to Eat The resort has many takeaway places and good delicatessens for picnic supplies, as well as a mind-boggling bonanza of lakeside cafes, pastry shops and ice-cream parlours.

Bella Napoli *(☎ 0464 55 21 39, Via Armandi Diaz 29)* Pizzas €4.90-9.80, 1st/2nd courses €5.70/7.75. For an exceptional wood-cooked pizza – so large that it flops off either side of your plate onto the table – head straight for 'Beautiful Naples'.

Getting There & Away The bus station on Viale Trento, in the newer part of town, is a 10-minute walk from the lake. Regular APT buses (☎ 045 800 41 29) connect Riva with Verona's Porta Nuova station (€4.91, 2¼ hours, about six daily). Atesina buses (☎ 0461 92 10 00) link Riva with Arco (€0.75, 20 minutes, hourly) and Trento (€3.40, 1½ hours, about 10 daily). Other buses serve various stops around the lake.

LAGO D'ISEO & VALLE CAMONICA

The least known of the large Italian lakes, Lago d'Iseo is possibly the least attractive. Although shut in by mountains, it is scarred in the north-east (around Lovere and Castro) by industry and a string of tunnels.

At the southern end of the Valle Camonica, the lake is fed by the River Oglio and marks the boundary between the provinces of Bergamo and Brescia (getting information about one side from tourist offices on the other is not easy). At the southern end of the lake stretches the Franciacorta, a patch of rolling countryside that produces good wine. The mountainous hinterland offers decent walking possibilities. Check with the APT office in the towns around the lake or at Bergamo or Brescia.

Getting There & Around

Buses connect the lake with Brescia and Bergamo. There are also trains from Brescia to Iseo and several other lakeside towns. Navigazione sul Lago d'Iseo (☎ 035 97 14 83), based in Costa Volpino, operates ferries between (south to north) Sarnico, Iseo, Monte Isola, Lovere and Pisogne. Single fares range from €1.40 to €4.90 (€2.30 to €8.30 return) with substantially fewer boats sailing in winter. Gestione Navigazione Laghi (☎ 035 97 14 83, W www.navigazionelaghi.it) operates a handful of boats around Lago d'Iseo, Lago Maggiore, Lago di Como and Lago di Garda and organises night cruises with dinner and dancing aboard (adult/child €15.50/7.75).

Buses also connect towns around the lake.

Iseo

postcode 25049 • pop 8300
elevation 198m

A pleasant, if somewhat dull, spot fronting the southern end of the lake, Iseo boasts the first monument erected to Garibaldi. South of the small town lie 18th-century peat beds, since dug up and filled with water to form a 2 sq km protected wetland. In late spring, the pools are smothered in water lilies.

The APT office (☎ 030 98 02 09, fax 030 98 13 61) is at Lungolago Marconi 2 and has information on the whole lake.

The area is well supplied with accommodation, particularly camp sites. Iseo itself has 16 sites, including ***Belvedere*** *(☎ 030 98 90 48, Via Risorgimento 64)*.

Albergo Milano *(☎ 030 98 04 49, Lungolago Marconi 4)* Singles/doubles €38.75/51.65, with lake view €41.30/56.80. This place is about the cheapest hotel in the centre of town.

THE LAKES

Monte Isola

The best thing to do here is get a boat to Monte Isola – Europe's biggest lake island at 5 sq km. Few vehicles are allowed on the streets – cycling is the preferred means of getting around – so the fishing village is quite peaceful. It has four hotels and a camp site. Grilled sardines and smoked salami are the things to eat here.

Campeggio Monte Isola *(☎ 030 982 52 21, Via Croce 144)* Sites per person/tent €43.30/5.15. Motorists will have to dump their cars on the other side of the water before heading to this island site, open year-round.

Eastern Shore

If Iseo seems a little empty and you want to stay on the mainland, there are a few smaller towns farther north. **Sulzano** (pop 1475) is small and quiet and on the ferry run to Monte Isola. Farther up the road is **Marone**, from where a side road winds up into the mountains to **Zone**. Walking is the attraction here, and there are a few rifugi about if you want accommodation – enquire at the APT office for details.

Western Shore

The northern end of the lake you can forget, although some of the driving through the blasted rock face at the water's edge is enjoyable. **Riva di Solto** (pop 800) is a fairly unspoiled village on the western shore but **Sarnico** (pop 5700), towards the southern end of the lake, is better, with hotels and restaurants.

Valle Camonica

The Valle Camonica weaves its way from the north of Lago d'Iseo to the vast **Parco Naturale Adamello-Brenta** and, farther north, to the **Parco Nazionale dello Stelvio**. The area borders on Trentino-Alto Adige and takes in the better parts of the Lombard Alps. The two national parks offer many walks of varying difficulty and are dotted with Alpine rifugi. See the Trentino-Alto Adige chapter for more details.

About halfway between Darfo and Edolo, lovers of rock-carving will have a field day. The **Parco Nazionale delle Incisioni Rupestri** *(☎ 0364 4 21 40; adult/child €4.15/2.05; open 9am-6.30pm Tues-Sun in summer, 8.30am-4.30pm Mon-Fri & 9am-4.30pm Sat & Sun in winter)*, at Capo di Ponte, is a 30-hectare open-air museum containing a representative array of engravings going as far back as the Bronze Age. The valley is littered with such carvings.

The area from Edolo north offers some reasonable **skiing** in winter, particularly near Ponte di Legno, at the northern end of the valley, and the nearby Passo del Tonale. Brescia's APT is a good place to obtain walking, camping and rifugi information. In the valley there are tourist offices at Darfo Boario Terme (☎ 0364 53 16 09), Piazza Einaudi 2; and Ponte di Legno (☎ 0364 9 11 22), Corso Milano 41.

Gone fishing on Lago di Como

JOHN HAY

Sirmione's Castello Scaligero

JON DAVISON

Certosa di Pavia: one of northern Italy's most lavish buildings

DAMIEN SIMONIS

Taking leisure seriously: Sirmione boats await their customers.

DAMIEN SIMONIS

Detail of Certosa di Pavia

DAMIEN SIMONIS

ANDREW PEACOCK

ANDREW PEACOCK

ANDREW PEACOCK

ANDREW PEACOCK

The Dolomites: walk, ski or climb in this spectacular mountain range and it won't be the exertion of your chosen activity that takes your breath away.

Trentino-Alto Adige

This autonomous Alpine region, incorporating much of the spectacular limestone Dolomite mountain range, is best thought of as two distinct areas. Its provinces, Trentino and Alto Adige, are culturally, linguistically and historically separate.

Alto Adige, or South Tirolo (Südtirol), in the north of the region was part of the Tirolo province of Austria until ceded to Italy in 1918. The people, mostly of Germanic descent, predictably favour the German language (68%) over Italian (28%), although Ladin (4%), an ancient Latin-based language, is also spoken in some zones, mainly the Val Badia (Gadertal) and the Val Gardena (Grödnertal); see the boxed text 'The Ladin Tradition' in the Val Badia section later for more information.

Trentino, to the south of Alto Adige, was a reluctant part of the Austrian and Austro-Hungarian empires for about a century until it was returned to Italy after WWI. The population here has a strong Italian identity, although German is widely spoken too.

The marriage of Trentino to Alto Adige, Italian to Tirolean, has at times created friction, and extreme right-wing political parties have always done well here. Alleanza Nazionale, the descendant of the neo-Fascist Movimento Sociale Italiano (MSI) party, has strong support in the area but, in Alto Adige, the Südtiroler Volkspartei (SVP) is easily the most popular party. One of its primary aims is the preservation and development of German and Ladin ethnic groups, but more extreme elements want to secede from Italy. Bombings of railways, power stations and military installations that shook the region in the 1950s, 1960s and 1980s were attributed to radical secessionists. A long-haggled-over deal covering the area's statutes and privileges was agreed to by Italy and Austria in 1992, with the blessing of the UN. The SVP continues to push for Alto Adige to be made a separate region, however, alarming many people of Trentino who fear being swallowed up by other regions (such as the Veneto) and losing the benefits gained by the Trentino-Alto Adige joint status as an autonomous region.

Politics aside, tourism throughout the region is highly organised and travellers will have little difficulty finding appealing, inexpensive accommodation and extensive information on their chosen activity, be it walking, skiing or horse riding.

Accommodation ranges from hotels and pensiones to *garni* (B&Bs) and *rifugi* (mountain huts), which can be anything

Highlights

- Indulge in some local dishes and convince yourself you're still in Italy
- Ski in the Brenta group, the Val di Fassa or just about anywhere in the Dolomite range
- Visit Cortina d'Ampezzo – a favourite with the jet set
- Go mountain biking in the Alpe di Siusi

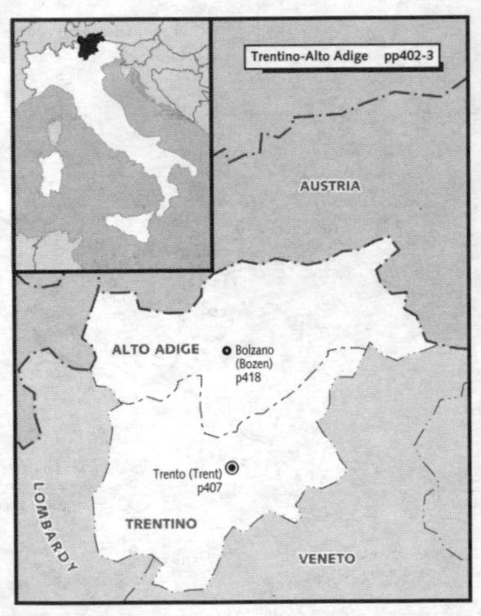

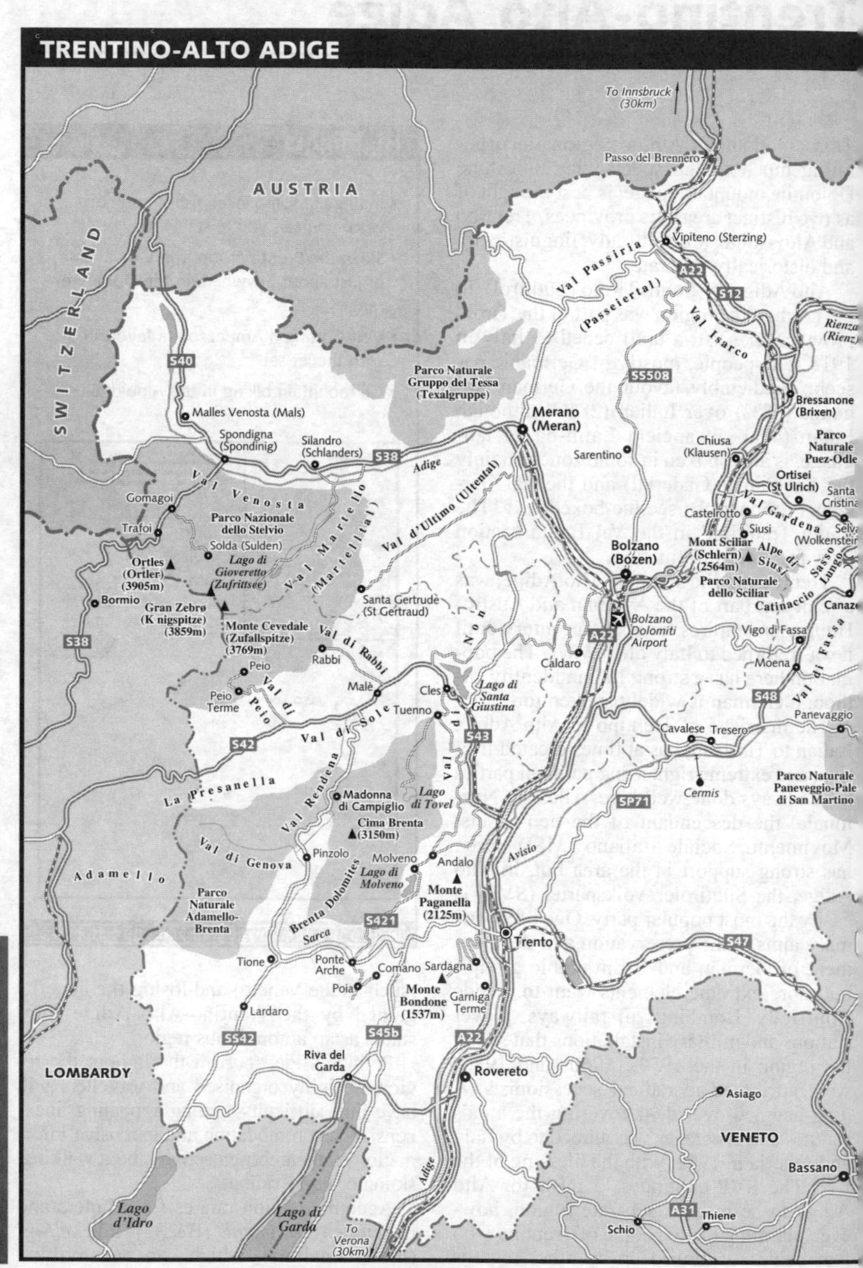
TRENTINO-ALTO ADIGE
To Innsbruck (30km)
Passo del Brennero
AUSTRIA
SWITZERLAND
Vipiteno (Sterzing)
A22
S12
Val Passiria (Passeiertal)
Val Isarco
Rienza (Rienz)
SS508
S40
Parco Naturale Gruppo del Tessa (Texalgruppe)
Bressanone (Brixen)
Malles Venosta (Mals)
Merano (Meran)
Spondigna (Spondinig)
Silandro (Schlanders)
S38
Adige
Sarentino
Chiusa (Klausen)
Parco Naturale Puez-Odle
Ortisei (St Ulrich)
Santa Cristina
Val Venosta
Gomagoi
Parco Nazionale dello Stelvio
Val Martello (Martelltal)
Val d'Ultimo (Ultental)
Castelrotto
Val Gardena
Selva (Wolkenstein)
Trafoi
Solda (Sulden)
Siusi
Ortles (Ortler) (3905m)
Lago di Gioveretto (Zufrittsee)
Bolzano (Bozen)
Mont Sciliar (Schlern) (2564m)
Alpe di Siusi
Sasso Lungo
Parco Naturale dello Sciliar
Bormio
Gran Zebrø (K nigspitze) (3859m)
Santa Gertrude (St Gertraud)
Bolzano Dolomiti Airport
Catinaccio
Canazei
Monte Cevedale (Zufallspitze) (3769m)
Val di Rabbi
Val di Non
A22
Vigo di Fassa
S38
Rabbi
Caldaro
Moena
Val di Fassa
Peio
Peio Terme
Val di Peio
Malè
Cles
Lago di Santa Giustina
S48
Tuenno
Val di Sole
Panevaggio
S42
S43
Cavalese
Tresero
Val di Non
Cermis
La Presanella
Madonna di Campiglio
Lago di Tovel
Parco Naturale Paneveggio-Pale di San Martino
SP71
Val Rendena
Cima Brenta (3150m)
Val di Genova
Pinzolo
Molveno
Andalo
Avisio
Adamello
Lago di Molveno
Monte Paganella (2125m)
Parco Naturale Adamello-Brenta
Brenta Dolomites
S421
Sarca
Trento
S47
Tione
Ponte Arche
Comano
Sardagna
Poia
Monte Bondone (1537m)
Garniga Terme
Lardaro
SS42
S45b
A22
LOMBARDY
Riva del Garda
Rovereto
Asiago
VENETO
Bassano
Adige
Lago d'Idro
Lago di Garda
To Verona (30km)
A31
Schio
Thiene

from expensive hotel-restaurants at the top of chair-lift routes to simple *bivacchi* (spartan mountain shacks). Prices vary greatly according to the season. Most Alpine rifugi open late June to late September and get packed in August (so book well ahead of time). Many hotels in the region's ski resorts are closed from mid-April to late June and again from mid-October to mid-December, transforming many resorts into eerily empty ghost towns.

Information

The provincial tourist offices in Trento and Bolzano (see those sections later) stock reams of practical information, including updated lists of rifugi. The APT del Trentino has other offices in Rome (☎ 06 360 95 842, fax 06 320 24 13), c/o Touring Club Italiano, Via del Babuino 20, and Milan (☎ 02 864 61 251, fax 02 720 02 188), Piazza Diaz 5. Within Italy, there's a 24-hour information service (toll free ☎ 800 01 05 45) you can call. Online, try W www.trentino.to.

Trentino-Alto Adige for Children

Families are well catered for throughout the region, particularly in Alto Adige. Many tourist offices organise special activities for kids in the summer and winter high seasons, and some guide groups offer special courses and walks for youngsters. Most resorts in Alto Adige have sports centres and playgrounds, and many hotels are equipped for children, providing cots, high chairs, special menus, playrooms and so on. A family walk is given in this chapter (see the boxed text 'Family Walk from Rifugio Malga Ra Stua to Forcella Lerosa' later), but contact tourist offices for more details.

Getting There & Around

The nearest airports for high-fliers are Verona and Innsbruck (Austria); Bolzano Dolomiti airport in the region is only served by a couple of European flights. Alternatively, you could land at Munich (Germany), then train it south to Bolzano.

Public transport in Trentino-Alto Adige is excellent. The two main companies are Servizi Autobus Dolomiti (SAD; toll free

☎ 800 84 60 40, W www.sad.it) in Alto Adige, and Atesina in Trentino. The main towns and many ski resorts can be reached directly from major Italian cities – including Rome, Florence, Bologna, Milan and Genoa. Information about these services is available from tourist offices and bus stations throughout Trentino-Alto Adige, or from bus stations in the respective cities.

WALKING IN THE DOLOMITES

The Dolomites, stretching across Trentino-Alto Adige into the Veneto, provide the most spectacular and varied opportunities for walkers in the Italian Alps – from half-day strolls to more demanding routes that require mountaineering skills.

Trails are generally well marked with numbers on red-and-white painted bands (on trees and rocks along the trails) or inside different coloured triangles for the Alte Vie (High Routes). Numerous rifugi offer overnight lodging and refreshments. Tourist offices usually have maps with roughly marked trails, but walkers planning anything more than the most basic itinerary should buy detailed maps to use.

Those wanting to undertake guided walks or tackle more difficult trails that combine mountaineering skills with walking (with or without a guide) can seek information at Guide Alpine (mountain guide) offices in the region – listed in this chapter under Information in the relevant town sections.

For more information on walking the Dolomites, see Lonely Planet's *Walking in Italy* guide.

An Alpine Coral Reef

The Dolomites are, in fact, ancient coral reefs reincarnated as Alpine peaks. Accounting for a vast portion of the eastern Alps, the spiky peaks take their name from French geologist De Dolomieu, the first to identify their composition of sedimentary limestone formed from calcium carbonate and magnesium. During the Triassic period, the entire area was covered with tropical forest and a shallow, warm sea. After millions of years, the sea receded at the same time as the Alps were being formed, raising what had once been the seabed to heights of between 2000 and 3000m. During the Ice Age, the coral reefs and rocks were eroded by glaciers that, together with normal atmospheric erosion, shaped the fantastic and spectacular formations seen today in the Dolomites. It is not unusual to find marine fossils among the pinnacles, towers and dramatic sheer drops of these mountains.

Preparations

The walking season runs from the end of June to the end of September (sometimes into October, depending on the weather). Most rifugi close from mid-September.

The best maps are the Tabacco 1:25,000 maps, which provide extensive details of trails, altitudes and gradients, as well as marking all rifugi and bivacchi. They are widely available in bookshops throughout this mountainous region. An alternative is the Kompass series.

Always check weather predictions before setting out, ensure you're prepared for high-altitude conditions (see the boxed text 'Get the Gear') and set out early: the weather can change suddenly in the Alps, even in hot August when it can dramatically turn cold and wet, especially in the afternoon.

Walking Areas

The best areas for walking in the Dolomites include:

- the Brenta Dolomites (Brenta group), accessible from Molveno or Madonna di Campiglio
- the Val di Genova and the Adamello group, accessible from Madonna di Campiglio (the Brenta and Adamello groups form the Parco Naturale Adamello-Brenta)
- the Sella group, accessible from the Val Gardena, the Val Badia, Pieve di Livinallongo and the Val di Fassa
- the Alpe di Siusi, the Sciliar and the Catinaccio group, accessible from Siusi and Castelrotto
- the Pale di San Martino, accessible from San Martino di Castrozza and Fiera di Primiero
- the area around Cortina that straddles Alto Adige and the Veneto and features the magnificent Parco Naturale di Fanes-Sennes-Braies

Get the Gear

Good walking shoes, a warm jacket, a map and plenty of water are essential items for even the shortest of walks. Tackling a high-altitude walk of more than a day? Pack the following in your knapsack:

- comfortable, waterproof walking boots (already worn in)
- light, comfortable backpack
- anorak (or pile/wind jacket)
- change of T-shirt, underwear and socks (wool and cotton)
- shorts and long trousers
- gloves, wool/pile hat or headband, and scarf
- water bottle containing at least 1L water per person
- hooded raincoat or poncho
- torch (flashlight) and batteries, pocket knife, lightweight thermal blanket (for emergencies), suncream, tissues, sunglasses and, if necessary, a sheet or sleeping bag
- slippers or thongs to wear at rifugi (optional)
- some lightweight, energy-giving food

and, to the south, Monte Pelmo, Monte Civetta and the Val di Zoldo area
- the Sesto Dolomites north of Cortina towards Austria, accessible from San Candido or Sesto in Val Pusteria

There are four Alte Vie in the Dolomites, each taking up to two weeks to complete. Routes link existing trails and, in places, incorporate new trails created to make difficult sections easier to traverse.

Each route links a chain of rifugi, and you can opt to only walk certain sections:

- Alta Via No 1 crosses the Dolomites from north to south, from Lago di Braies to Belluno
- Alta Via No 2 extends from Bressanone to Feltre and is known as the 'High Route of Legends' because it passes through Odle, the mythical kingdom of ancient Ladin fairy tales
- Alta Via No 3 links Villabassa and Longarone
- Alta Via No 4 goes from San Candido to Pieve di Cadore

The Alte Vie are marked by numbers inside triangles – blue for No 1, red for No 2 and orange/brown for No 3; No 4 is marked by normal numbers on red-and-white bands. Booklets mapping out the routes in detail are available at most APT offices in the region.

SKIING IN THE DOLOMITES

The Dolomites boast innumerable excellent ski resorts, including fashionable Cortina d'Ampezzo (for drop-dead gorgeous people and their weighty wallets), Madonna di Campiglio, San Martino di Castrozza and Canazei, as well as the extremely popular resorts of the Val Gardena.

Accommodation and ski facilities are abundant and you have plenty of scope to choose between downhill and cross-country skiing, as well as *sci alpinismo*, which combines skiing and mountaineering skills on longer excursions. Snowboarding and other white-stuff activities are equally well catered for.

High season runs from Christmas to early January and early February to mid-March – Settimana Bianca skiing packages are big money-savers (see Activities in the Facts for the Visitor chapter for details).

Ski passes range from those covering use of lifts in one resort and its immediate neighbours – ideal if you only have one or two days or don't intend venturing far – to the Dolomiti Superski ski pass which allows access to 464 lifts and some 1220km of ski runs across 12 regions. In 2001/02, it cost €96/169 for a three-/six-day pass (€84/149 from 6 January to 2 February and from 17 March to 14 April).

More information is available online at W www.dolomitisuperski.com. Prices for

The Weather

Daily weather and avalanche bulletins (☎ 176 85 00 77 or 0461 49 48 77) are available online at W www.provincia.tn.it/meteo. For the latest information on snow in the area, call ☎ 0461 23 89 39. In case of emergency in the mountains, call ☎ 118 for Soccorso Alpino.

passes covering individual resorts are listed in the respective sections in this chapter.

Ski schools operate at all resorts. A five-day course (three hours' group tuition per day) costs about €100, while private lessons average €25 per hour. The average cost of ski and boot hire ranges from €10.35 to €23.25 per day for downhill skis (from €15.50 for carving skis) and up to €10.35 for cross-country skis and boots. In expensive resorts such as Cortina, however, prices jump to as high as €18.10 to €33.55 per day to hire downhill skis and boots.

Tourist offices abound across the region, but the best for getting general information, including more on ski-pass prices and accommodation packages, are those in Trento and Bolzano (see Information in those sections later in this chapter).

OTHER ACTIVITIES

Summer pastimes include mountain biking, hang-gliding and rock climbing. Tourist offices can help you find trails, bike rental outlets and hang-gliding schools. Gruppi Guide Alpine (Mountain Guide Groups) arrange guided excursions and courses, ranging from family rambles to challenging walks of several days at high altitudes.

Taking Music to New Heights

Every summer the APT del Trentino organises a string of free high-altitude concerts, embracing everything from classical and blues to jazz, ethnic and funk sounds. Performances start at 2pm, allowing audiences ample time to ramble uphill to the respective venue – always a *rifugio* (mountain hut) or mountain pass. Some rifugi are better reached with the aid of the local Gruppo Guide Alpine; most run free guided treks to the concert.

The culturally inclined who prefer a tad more wrist-action can limber up with a spot of wine-tasting in a traditional Trentino wine cellar, followed by an evening concert (☎ 0461 82 28 20; admission €10.35). Local wine can likewise be sampled during the musical events held in a *malghe* – an Alpine hut on a hill where butter and cheese are traditionally made.

For more information call ☎ 0461 83 90 00, look online at W www.trentino.to or contact the APT del Trentino office in Trento or any local APT office.

Trentino

TRENT (TRENTO)

postcode 38100 • pop 103,000
elevation 194m

This calm, well-organised provincial capital is a fine starting point for forays into the province and the neighbouring Parco Naturale Adamello-Brenta. Its tourist offices have extensive information on the town and Trentino, and its public transport network is both efficient and extensive. Castel Toblino, a remote lakeside castle with a restaurant and cafe, some 17km west of town along the S45b, makes for a romantic lunchtime spot for those with wheels at hand.

Known by the ancient Romans as Tridentum, Trento later passed from the Goths to the Lombards, and was eventually annexed by the Holy Roman Empire when it became known as Trento or Trient. From 1027 until the early 19th century, it was an episcopal principality during a period marked by political and territorial conflict with the rulers of Tirolo. The Council of Trent (1545–63) considered the restructuring of the Catholic Church and dreamed up the ideals of the Counter-Reformation here.

Goose races, dunkings, medieval jousts and fireworks are all part and parcel of the merry-makings that fill Trent's pedestrian streets during the Feste Vigiliane, a five-day festival thrown to celebrate the feast of St Vigil (the town's patron saint) in mid-June. Tastier still is the annual Polenta Festival, held on the last weekend of September to celebrate Trento's most traditional culinary dish.

Information

Tourist Offices The APT office (☎ 0461 98 38 80, fax 0461 98 45 08, W www.apt.trento.it), Via Manci 2, opens 9am to 7pm Monday to Saturday. For regional information,

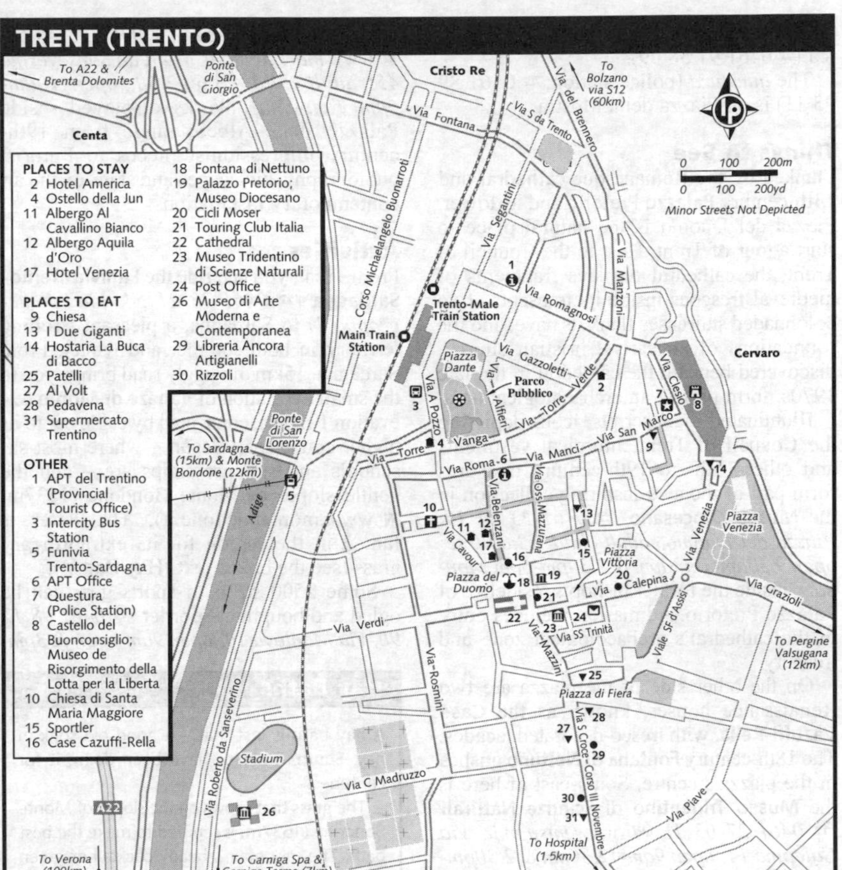

try the provincial tourist office, APT del Trentino (☎ 0461 49 73 53, fax 0461 26 02 77, **W** www.trentino.to or www.provincia.tn.it), Via Romagnosi 11.

Staff at both offices can advise on skiing, walking, climbing and other activities. See the Information section in the introduction to this chapter for details of its offices in Rome and Milan.

Post & Communications The post office, straddling Piazza Vittoria on Via Calepina, opens 8.30am to 6.30pm Monday to Friday, and 8.10am to 12.30pm Saturday.

Bookshops Travel guides abound in the bookshop inside the Touring Club Italia (☎ 0461 22 11 61, fax 0461 22 11 68, **e** negozio.trento@touringclub.it), Via Garibaldi 27. The best place for walking maps and guides is Libreria Ancora Artigianelli, Via Santa Croce 35. Rizzoli, a little farther south at Corso III Novembre, stocks English-language novels in its basement.

Medical Services & Emergency Ospedale Santa Chiara (hospital; ☎ 0461 90 31 11) is on Largo Medaglie d'Oro, south-east of the centre, off Corso III Novembre. In a medical emergency, call the Guardia Medica (☎ 0461 91 58 09).

The *questura* (police station; ☎ 0461 89 95 11) is on Piazza della Mostra.

Things to See

Flanked by the Romanesque **cathedral** and 13th-century **Palazzo Pretorio** and its tower, Piazza del Duomo is the natural place to start a tour of Trent. Host to the Council of Trent, the cathedral displays fragments of medieval frescoes inside its transepts. Two colonnaded staircases flank its nave, and the foundations of an early Christian church, discovered beneath the cathedral in the late 1970s, form part of an archaeological area.

Illuminated manuscripts, icons depicting the Council of Trent, liturgical vestments and other 15th- to 19th-century treasures form part of the awe-inspiring collection in the **Museo Diocesano** *(☎ 0461 23 44 19, Piazza del Duomo; adult/child €2.60/free; open 9.30am-12.30pm & 2.30pm-6pm Mon-Sat)*, inside the former bishop's residence of Palazzo Pretorio. Admission includes entry to the cathedral's archaeological zone and treasury.

On the other side of the piazza are two Renaissance houses, known as the **Case Cazuffi-Rella**, with fresco-decorated facades. The 18th-century **Fontana di Nettuno** gushes in the piazza's centre. South-east of here is the **Museo Tridentino di Scienze Naturali** *(☎ 0461 27 03 11, W www.mtsn.tn.it, Via Calepina 14; open 9am-12.30pm & 2.30pm-6pm Tues-Sun)*. Admission costs vary depending on which temporary exhibition the Natural Science Museum is hosting.

An easy stroll north-east through pedestrianised streets takes you to **Castello del Buonconsiglio** *(☎ 0461 23 37 70, Via Bernardo Clesio 5; adult/child €2.60/1.55; open 9am-noon & 2pm-5pm Tues-Sun Oct-Mar, 10am-5.30pm Tues-Sun Apr-Sept)*, home of the bishop-princes who once ruled Trent. The fortified complex incorporates the 13th-century Castello Vecchio, the Renaissance Magno Palazzo and a **Museo del Risorgimento e della Lotta per la Libertà**.

Impressively showcased in a regal palace is Trento's enjoyable **Museo di Arte Moderna e Contemporanea** *(☎ 0461 23 48 60, W www.mart.trento.it, Via R da Sanseverino 45; adult/child €3.60/2.60; open 10am-6pm Tues-Sun)*. Works displayed inside Palazzo delle Albere range from 19th-century impressionist pieces to Futurist photography, cityscapes and state-of-the art contemporary installations.

Activities

From Trent, you can ride the **Funivia Trento-Sardagna** *(☎ 0461 23 21 54, Via Montegrappa 1)* to Sardagna, a pleasant strolling territory in both summer and winter. From Sardagna, 15km of wiggly road brings you to the small ski station of **Vaneze di Monte** (elevation 1350m), connected by cable car to its higher counterpart **Vasòn** – where most ski schools and ski hire shops are – and the gentle slopes of Monte Bondone (1537m; W www.montebondone.it). The latter is famed in the region for its extraordinary grass (see the boxed text 'Hay Baths').

Some 2500 sq m of sports gear can be ogled and bought at **Sportler** *(☎ 0461 98 12 90, Via Mantova 10; open 9am-noon & 3pm-*

Hay Baths

A hay bath is just that – a good old soak in hay. South Tiroleans have been doing it for centuries.

The grass that grows on the slopes of Monte Bondone (1537m) is reputed to make the best bath. The mountain's heady cocktail of green blades, aromatic plants and medicinal herbs, such as thyme, are cut when damp and left to ferment for several days. Then it's bath time.

Swaddled in a sheet, bathers immerse themselves in a 'trough' of heated fermented hay. As the bath hots up, so bathers sweat. Obesity, backache, gout, rheumatism and lumbago are among the rash of ills a hay bath is said to soothe. Spotty skins likewise benefit.

The ***Garniga Spa*** *(☎ 0461 84 25 86, fax 0461 84 30 98)*, some 7km south of Trento in Garniga Terme, is Trentino's best-known spa, equipped with 130 hay baths where you can dip into one of South Tirol's oldest traditions.

7pm Tues-Sat, 3pm-7pm Mon), an excellent sports shop which also rents **mountain bikes** for €15.50/51.65 a day/week. Road bikes can be hired from **Cicli Moser** *(☎ 0461 23 03 27, Via Calepina 37; €12.90/41.30 per day/week; open 9am-noon & 3pm-7pm Tues-Sat, 3pm-7pm Mon)*.

Places to Stay

Ostello della Jun *(☎ 0461 26 23 84, Via Torre Vanga 9)* Dorm beds €13.95. Open year-round. This hostel – a mere hop, skip and a jump from the bus and train stations – welcomes travellers aged up to 30.

Albergo Al Cavallino Bianco *(☎ 0461 23 15 42, Via Cavour 29)* Singles/doubles without bath €25.80/37.20, with bath €35.10/ 49.05. Rooms at this 1st-floor hotel are simple – predictably so, given their price tag.

Hotel Venezia *(☎/fax 0461 23 41 14, Piazza del Duomo 45)* Singles/doubles from €34.60/47.50. This 1950s-style hotel is split across two buildings; rival Albergo Aquila d'Oro forms the filling in the sandwich.

Albergo Aquila d'Oro *(☎ 0461 98 62 82, Via Belenzani 76)* Singles/doubles €51.65/ 72.30. A quiet, family-run hotel with 20 rooms, Aquila d'Oro warrants no complaints.

Hotel America *(☎ 0461 98 30 10, fax 0461 23 06 03, Via Torre Verde 50)* Singles/doubles €56.80/82.65. This 1920s pad is situated over a busy non-pedestrianised street.

Places to Eat

I Due Giganti *(☎ 0461 23 75 15, Via del Simonino 14)* Locals flock to this cheap self-service joint for lunch and dinner; its eat-till-you're-stuffed, help-yourself pizza and salad buffet is a steal at €5.15.

Al Volt *(☎ 0461 98 37 76, Via Santa Croce 16)* 1st/2nd courses €5.15/7.75. A simple yet soulful place, Al Volt has specialised in typical Trentino dishes, or *piatti tipici trentini* (see the boxed text 'Gastronomic Orgasms' later), since 1894. No wonder – its *strudel della nonna* (Grandma's strudel) is so naughty but nice.

Patelli *(☎ 0461 23 52 36, Via Dietro le Mura 1/5)* 1st/2nd courses from €6.70/8.80. Off Via Mazzini, Patelli serves some fine and unusual Italian dishes, as well as lighter *bruschette* (toasted bread with garlic and seasoning; from €2.05) and salad from a buffet (€2.60/3.10 for small/large plate).

Pedavena *(☎ 0461 98 62 55, Piazza di Fiera 13)* 1st/2nd courses from €4.15/5.15. You can't beat this place for that German beer-hall feeling, complete with stags' heads mounted on the wall, and cheap, hearty food. Better still, it dishes it up non-stop between 9am and midnight.

Hostaria La Buca di Bacco *(☎ 0461 98 31 61, Via dei Ventuno 1)* 1st/2nd courses €6.20/7.75. Tucked in a stone cellar outside the castle walls, this is the place to munch on filling fodder, chink beer glasses and sing along to lively songs into the wee hours.

Chiesa *(☎ 0461 23 87 66, Via Marchetti 9)* 1st/2nd courses €7.75/10.35. With a bird-twittering terrace in Parco San Marco, Chiesa dishes up finely presented and imaginative dishes. Don't miss the several-metres-deep well in the ladies' loo.

Pick up picnic supplies at ***Supermercato Trentino*** *(Corso 3 Novembre 4-6)*.

Getting There & Away

From the bus station on Via Andrea Pozzo, intercity buses leave for destinations including Madonna di Campiglio, San Martino di Castrozza, Molveno, Canazei and Riva di Garda. Timetables are posted at the bus station. You can also pick up a full guide to Trentino's public transport from the APT del Trentino office.

Regular trains connect Trent with Verona, Venice, Bologna and Bolzano. The Trent-Male train line (station next to the main station) connects the city with Cles in the Val di Non.

Trent is well linked with Verona to the south and Bolzano to the north on the A22.

BRENTA DOLOMITES

North-west of Trent and part of the Parco Naturale Adamello-Brenta, this majestic group of jagged peaks is isolated from the main body of the Dolomites and provides dramatic walking opportunities. Best suited to those keen to test their mountaineering skills, less-experienced walkers should check routes very carefully before setting

Gastronomic Orgasms

Tuck into the following for a titillating taste of Trentino-Alto Adige. Remains of the plate can be mopped up with a hunk of bread – often dense, scented with caraway or rye, and almost always brown. Dry palates can be whetted with a mug of Forst, the local beer brewed in Merano.

canederli – Germanic Alto Adige's answer to pasta: large bread dumplings, known as *knödel* by good Germans who, like those in Alto Adige, are reared on platefuls of the hefty tummy-filling balls

cotto e cren – cooked ham with horseradish; *salsa al cren* is a sausage variation; both are antipasti

formaggio grigio – a most bizarre cheese from the Val Pusteria, concocted from unpasteurised milk and guaranteed to thrill the most fanatic of foodies. The Gasthof-Albergo Oberraut near Brunico is one of the few farms where one can still sample it; season with apple vinegar, olive oil and salt 'n' pepper

gulasch – a thinner version of spicy Hungarian goulash, either served as a soup or with canederli as a blood-stirring main course

polenta e crauti – cornflour meal and sauerkraut, two staple ingredients set to stuff the stoutest of stomachs

polenta e coniglio – game is all the rage in Trentino-Alto Adige as this dear little rabbit, cooked up with polenta, would attest

risotto ai funghi – risotto laced with *brisa* mushrooms, locally picked and known for their extraordinarily strong and distinctive flavour

trippe alla parmigiana – tripe with parmesan cheese

spàtzle – little flour and egg dumplings, topped with melted gorgonzola to make a tasty antipasto or dished up alongside meat as a main course

strangolapreti – spinach-flavoured gnocchi

strudel – sliced and cooked apples rolled in a thicker, less-refined pastry than one finds in Vienna.

out. Harnesses and ropes are essential for many high-altitude trails, including one of the group's most famous trails, the Via Bocchetta di Tuckett, which runs from Molveno to Cima Brenta. The trail was opened up by 19th-century climber Francis Fox Tuckett and includes gruelling sections of *vie ferrate* (climbing trails with permanent steel cords).

Lakeside Molveno and Madonna di Campiglio make suitable bases from which to delve into the Brenta Dolomites (Dolomiti di Brenta). The wiggly S421, S237 and S239 linking Molveno to Madonna make for a scenic, if perilous, drive.

Molveno

postcode 38018 • pop 1050
elevation 864m

This pretty village, 38km north-west of Trent by road, languishes in a picturesque position by Lake Molveno, overshadowed by the towering Brenta Dolomites. It became famous in the 19th century as a base for English and German mountaineers who came to open up trails into the group. In winter, skiers and snowboarders fly down the slopes of Monte Paganella (2125m), linked by cable car to Andalo, Molveno's winter playground 4km north.

Information The APT office (☎ 0461 58 69 24, fax 0461 58 62 21, ⓔ info@aptmolveno.com), Piazza Marconi 5, opens 9am to 12.30pm and 3pm to 6.30pm Monday to Friday. Its counterpart in Andalo (☎ 0461 58 58 36, fax 0461 58 55 70, ⓔ info@aptandalo.com), Piazza Dolomiti 1, opens 9am to 12.30pm and 3.30pm to 7pm Monday to Saturday, and 9.30am to 12.30pm Sunday. Staff at either office can advise on walking trails and give free maps; the offices also stock the excellent, English-language booklet entitled *MTB sull'Altopiano Andalo-Molveno Fai della Paganella*, which details (in English) 17 mountain-bike routes in the region, including a less-demanding 15km tour of Lake Molveno. Online, see ⓦ www.apt.dolomitipaganella.com.

Molveno town council (☎ 0461 58 60 45) provides a tourist medical service in the Palazzo Comunale (entrance at the rear).

Birds, Bears & Tree Trunks

The Italian Alps' last remaining brown bears mingle with ibex (wild goats), red deer, marmots (rodents belonging to the squirrel family) and chamois (mountain-dwelling goats) in the Parco Naturale Adamello-Brenta, Trentino's largest protected area, embracing 618 sq km and 50 lakes. The brown beasts can be viewed at relatively close quarters at the **Santuario di San Romedio** *(☎ 0463 53 61 98; 3km east of San Zeno; free; open 9am-1pm & 2pm-6pm July & Aug)*, a remote Alpine church overlooked by a bear-watching area set up by park authorities. The latter runs an information point here in July and August.

Some 82 bird species nest in the Parco Naturale Adamello-Brenta. Spot some around the banks of **Lago di Tovel**, set deep in a forest some 16km south of Cles in the park's heart. An easy walking trail encircles the lake (one hour). The **visitors centre** *(☎ 0463 45 10 33; open 9am-1pm & 2pm-6pm daily July & Aug, Sat & Sun only in Sept)* here has extensive information on other walks in the park. Ask about the numerous nature activities it runs.

Tree trunks are turned into planks of wood at an old Venetian **water-powered saw mill**, on the shore of Lake Molveno in the park's deep south. The restored mill operates July and August.

Detailed park information can be obtained from the **park headquarters** *(☎ 0465 80 46 37, fax 0465 80 46 49, W www.parcoadamellobrenta.tn.it, Via Nazionale 12, Sede di Strembo; open 8.30am-noon & 2pm-7pm daily in high season, 8.30am-noon & 4pm-6pm Mon-Fri in low season)*.

Between 8pm and 8am, call Andalo's Guardia Medica (☎ 0461 58 56 37) instead.

Activities Practise your doggy paddle in Molveno's Olympic-sized, open-air, heated **swimming pool** *(☎ 0461 58 60 15, adult/child €3.10/1.55; Via Lungolago)*, overlooking Lago di Molveno; or hire a racquet (€2.60) to bash some balls about on the neighbouring **tennis courts** *(€6.20/7.25 per hour low/high season)*.

Cyclists and mountain bikers should touch base with Molveno's **Scuola di Mountain Bike** *(☎ 0461 228 65 00)*, inside the office of Molveno's **Gruppo Guide Alpine** *(☎ 0461 58 64 09, fax 0461 58 64 12, e costa.armando_guida@iol.it, Piazza Marconi 3; open 5pm-7pm & 8.30pm-10pm July & Aug)*. At other times contact **Camping Spiaggia** *(see Places to Stay & Eat later)*. The Gruppo Guide Alpine organises **rock-climbing** courses and **guided walks** in summer, and **ski-mountaineering**, frozen waterfall climbing and less strenuous **snow-shoeing excursions** – suitable for all abilities – in the Parco Naturale Adamello-Brenta in winter.

Andalo, the area's winter playground, sports two cross-country trails and some 50 downhill pistes, ranging from beginner-friendly greens to heart-thumping blacks. Plenty of sports shops in Andalo rent gear.

From the top of Molveno village, a two-seater **cable car** *(☎ 0461 58 69 81; €5.15 return)* takes you up to Pradel (elevation 1400m), from where trail No 340 leads to Rifugio Croz dell'Altissimo (1430m; ☎ 0461 58 61 95), a pleasant and easy one-hour walk. Take trail No 340 to Rifugio Selvata (1630m; ☎ 0330 23 92 27), then trail No 319 to Rifugi Tosa and Pedrotti (2491m; about four hours' walk; ☎ 0461 94 81 15). From here most trails are difficult; prepare yourself for vie ferrate and/or glaciers. The APT offices have complete lists of mountain rifugi.

Casual strollers should attempt no more than a walk around the lake from Camping Spiaggia. A complete circuit takes about 3½ hours, although half the route is on the road, meaning you might prefer to double-back when the walking trail ends.

Places to Stay & Eat Visitors to Molveno can rest their heads at camp sites, *agriturismo* (tourist accommodation on farms) or hotels.

Camping Spiaggia *(☎ 0461 58 69 78, fax 0461 58 63 30, W www.molveno.it/camping,*

Via Lungolago 25). Low season sites per person/tent €4.15/5.15, high season €7.75/ 11.90. Reception open 9am-noon & 2pm-7pm. Rates at Molveno's lakeside site include free admission to the neighbouring pool (see Activities earlier), tennis court and table-tennis tables.

There are numerous agriturismo places to stay and eat around Molveno, ideally suited for travellers with wheels wanting to get away from it all.

Azienda Agrituristica Maso-Marocc *(☎/fax 0465 70 20 98, 20km south of Molveno along S421 to Ponte Arche, then 2km along SP213 to Poia, at end of village left towards Comano then immediately right onto dirt track)* Low/high season B&B per person €25.80/36.15. Fabulously perched at the top of a dirt track, this rustic farmhouse offers guests charming rooms with a view, an inspirational summer terrace overlooking the mountains, and hearty home cooking (1st/2nd courses €4.15/6.20).

Albergo Fiore *(☎ 0465 70 14 01, centre of Poia village)*. Low season doubles €31, high season up to €46.50. Stay here if Maso-Marocc is full.

In Molveno, many hotels only offer full board in high season (December to March, July and August).

Albergo Bellariva *(☎ 0461 58 69 52, fax 0461 58 63 38, W www.bellariva.com, Via Lungolago 23)* Low season full board €36.65 per person, high season up to €67.65. Touting two stars and some of Molveno's cheapest rates, Bellariva sits near the lake and swimming pool.

Garni Alpenrose *(☎ 0461 58 61 69, fax 0461 58 60 26, e garni.alpenrose@tin.it, Via Lungolago)* Rooms fill up fast at this cosy, one-star pad near Camping Spiaggia.

Grand Hotel Molveno *(☎ 0461 58 69 34, fax 0461 58 61 76, Via Bettega 18)* Singles/doubles from €64.55/75.90. Open July-Sept. Slightly out of town, this grandiose, ochre-coloured mansion sits astride the lake shores, south of Molveno on the S421.

Getting There & Away From Molveno, FTM (☎ 0461 23 83 50) runs buses to/from Trent (one way €2.85, 3½ hours, two to three daily).

Madonna di Campiglio & Pinzolo

postcode 38084 • elevation 1522m

One of the top ski resorts in the Alps, Madonna di Campiglio (known locally simply as Madonna) sprawls along the Val Rendena on the north-western side of the Brenta Dolomites. Less expensive, family-orientated Pinzolo is located 16km south of the resort. Austrian emperor Franz Joseph and his wife were frequent visitors to Madonna at the end of the 19th century – an era relived in late February when fireworks blaze and costumed pageants waltz through town during the annual Habsburg Carnival. As with most resorts in the region, Madonna and Pinzolo are all but dead out of season.

Information The APT office in Madonna (☎ 0465 44 20 00, fax 0465 44 04 04, W www.campiglio.it or www.aptcampiglio.tn.it), in the centre of the village off Piazza Brenta Alta, advises on accommodation and stocks stacks of information on skiing and walking, as does its counterpart in Pinzolo (☎ 0465 50 10 07, fax 0465 50 27 78, e apt.pinzolo@trentino.to). Both offices open 9am to noon and 3pm to 6.30pm Monday to Saturday, and 9am to noon Sunday.

Madonna's tourist medical service (☎ 0465 44 30 73) operates in season; otherwise, call the Guardia Medica (☎ 0465 44 08 81).

Activities A network of chair lifts and cable cars takes you from Madonna to the numerous **ski runs** or, in summer, to the **walking trails**. A one-/six-day ski pass for Madonna di Campiglio and Pinzola costs €28.90/142 and a six-day Skirama Dolomiti lift pass covering both resorts plus one day's use of lifts in the Dolomiti Superski region is €155; Dolomiti Superski passes are also valid. Up-to-the-minute prices are online at W www.funiviecampiglio.it.

Some 2km north of Madonna at Campo Carlo Magno, a **cable car** *(€7.75/12.90 one way/return)* takes you up, in two stages, to

TRENTINO

the Passo Grostè (2440m), from where walkers can set off into the Brenta Dolomites. The Via delle Bocchette (trail No 305) leaves from the Rifugio Grostè (2438m) at the cable-car station. This is the **via ferrata** for which the Brenta group is famous. Only experienced mountaineers with the correct equipment should attempt it; equipment can be hired locally. Otherwise, take trail No 316 to Rifugio del Tuckett and Q Sella (2271m). From there, take trail No 328 and then No 318 (sentiero Bogani) to the Rifugio Brentei (2182m; four to five hours from Grostè). All trails heading higher into the group from here cross little glaciers and special equipment is needed.

Pinzolo's interesting 16th-century **Chiesa di San Vigilio** merits a visit for its external painting entitled *La Danza Macabra* (The Dance of Death), 20m in length. North of Pinzolo is the entrance to the **Val di Genova**, often described as one of the Alps' most beautiful valleys. A series of spectacular waterfalls along the way enhances its reputation as great walking and picnic country. Four rifugi, strung out along the valley floor, make overnight stays an option: the Rifugio Adamello Collini (1641m) is at the end of the road, from where you can take trail No 212–220 to the Rifugio Città di Trento (2449m), or trail No 241 to the end of the valley (about 2000m) beneath a huge, receding glacier. From here the trail climbs steeply to the Rifugio Caduti dell'Adamello (3020m) at the edge of the glacier.

Descending into the Val Rendena a few kilometres south-west of Madonna brings you to the Valli Giudicarie area near Lardaro, where there is a helpful tourist office (☎ 0465 90 12 17). The area is not served by public transport and you need your own car to explore the spectacular side valleys. The 25km-long Val di Daone road, south-west of Lardaro, brings you to a reservoir. Walk along the edge of the reservoir for about two hours and you arrive at the peaceful Rifugio Val di Fumo (☎ 0465 67 45 25) at the foot of the imposing Carè Alto in the Adamello group. This old-style rifugio recalls the mountain-lovers' paradise of the 1950s before tourists discovered the Dolomites.

Places to Stay & Eat Few places to stay in Madonna suit the pockets of budget travellers. Most require half or full board and in the high season may be reluctant to accept bookings for less than seven days. Prices are given per person per day in the high season unless otherwise stated.

Bucaneve *(☎ 0465 44 12 71, fax 0465 44 16 72)* Doubles €62. This place is south of Madonna, near Piazza Palù.

La Baita *(☎ 0465 44 10 66, fax 0465 44 07 50, Piazza Brenta Alta 17)* Doubles €82.65-98.15, half-board per person €59.40-77.45. Comfort and good value for money are among Baita's three-star attributes.

Getting There & Away Madonna di Campiglio is accessible from Trent's bus station by regular Atesina bus. Autostradale and SIA operate weekend services from Milan, while Lazzi and SITA between them run services from cities including Florence and Bologna.

VAL DI NON

The Val di Non is a picturesque valley of apple orchards and castles accessible from Trent by Trent-Male train or bus. The main town is Cles, dominated by Castel Cles. The local Pro Loco tourist office (☎ 0463 42 13 76) is on Corso Dante, just off the main road through town, and there is an APT office in the nearby village of Fondo (☎ 0463 83 01 33). You may want to stay here on your way north, although accommodation choices are limited.

Antica Trattoria *(☎ 0463 42 16 31, Via Roma 13)* Singles/doubles €37.20/64.55. This place is in Cles. Dine here for about €20.65 or opt for a half-/full-board option.

VAL DI SOLE & VALLE DI PEIO

A scenic drive west from Cles along the scenic S42 thrusts you into the Val di Sole, a pretty valley which traces the course of the River Noce.

The APT office in **Malè** (☎ 0463 90 12 80, fax 0463 90 21 11, e info@valdisole.net, w www.valdisole.net), Piazza Regina Elena 19, has extensive information on the Val di Sole, including accommodation, transport and sporting activities, and can advise on walking trails and ski facilities. It opens 9am to noon and 3.30pm to 6.30pm Monday to Saturday, and 10am to noon Sunday.

Catch forty winks at ***Liberty Hotel Malè*** *(☎ 0463 90 11 05, fax 0463 90 17 40)*, where singles/doubles cost from €38.75/56.80. This is one of a handful of atmospheric, shuttered places to kip in the village heart.

From **Peio Terme** (Pejo Terme; elevation 1393m) in the Valle di Peio, chair lifts operate to the Rifugio Doss dei Cembri (2400m), from where you can pick up trail No 105 to the Rifugio Mantova al Vioz (3535m) at the edge of the Forni glacier. Assuming you've got what it takes, all the necessary equipment for scaling Monte Vioz (3645m) can be hired in Peio Terme.

Ferrovia Trent-Male buses connect Peio Terme with Madonna di Campiglio and with Malè in the Val di Sole. Malè is on the Trent-Malè train line.

SAN MARTINO DI CASTROZZA

postcode 38058 • elevation 1467m

Hopping east across the Brenner motorway (A22), which brutally slices through the region, one comes up against the imposing Pale di San Martino – mountains so stark and grey-white they virtually glow in the dark. Noted for its Alpine vegetation and wildlife, including roe deer, chamois, marmots, wildfowl and birds of prey such as the golden eagle, this impressive mountain range is embraced by the Parco Naturale Paneveggio-Pale di San Martino. At its feet huddles glamorous San Martino, another popular Trentino ski resort and walking spot.

Equally well known, but for less fortunate reasons, is **Cavalese** (elevation 1000m), a small town wedged in the floor of the Val di Fiemme from where skiers cable car up to the Cermis ski area (2229m) and beyond. In 1998 the place made international headlines when a low-flying aircraft slashed straight through the cables of a full cable car, causing the skiers inside to plummet to their deaths. The World Cup ski-jumping championships will fly down its slopes in 2002, and the Nordic World Ski Championships, last held in the Val di Fiemme in 1991, will return to the valley in 2003.

Information

In San Martino, the APT office (☎ 0439 76 88 67, fax 0439 76 88 14, **W** www.sanmartino.com), Via Passo Rolle 165, has mountains of information on walking trails, sports activities and accommodation. It opens 8.30am to 12.30pm and 3pm to 6pm Monday to Saturday and 9.30am to 12.30pm Sunday. Its counterpart in Cavalese (☎ 0462 24 11 11, fax 0465 24 11 99, **W** www.aptfiemme.tn.it), Via Bronzetti 60, opens 9am to 5pm and 3.30pm to 7pm.

The nearest hospital is at Feltre, although a tourist medical service is available during summer and winter at San Martino (☎ 0439 76 87 39) and Fiera di Primiero (☎ 0439 76 20 60).

Activities

San Martino is surrounded by excellent **ski runs** which, together with those in the Val di Fiemme, form part of the extensive Superski Dolomiti region.

During winter a special ski bus connects the valley with the various runs. In summer, a chair lift and cable car from San Martino whisk walkers to the Rifugio Rosetta (2600m), from where several walks (some easy, some requiring mountaineering skills) can be followed.

Maps of the Pale di San Martino's well-marked **walking trails** are available at the APT office. Alternatively, try the Parco Naturale Paneveggio-Pale di San Martino's **visitors centre** *(☎ 0439 76 88 59,* **W** *www.parcopan.org, Via Laghetto, San Martino)*, or head 16km north to **Paneveggio** where the park runs another **visitors centre**. A 1.2km trail leads from the cabin to the **Area Faunistica del Cervofauna**, a nature area where you can watch deer.

The tourist offices act as contact points for the Guide Alpine. The latter organise **mountaineering ascents** (on Pala di San Martino, Cima della Madonna and Sass Maor) and a 120km-long, high-altitude skiing excursion, as well as walks along vie ferrate and rock climbing courses.

Places to Stay & Eat

Hotel Suisse *(☎ 0439 6 80 87, fax 0439 6 80 87, Via Dolomiti 1)* B&B per person €29.95. Hotel Suisse offers one-star glamour.

Biancaneve *(☎ 0439 6 81 35, Via Dolomiti 14)* B&B per person €24.80-35.10. This is a two-star mediocrity on San Martino's main street.

Agritur Darial *(☎ 0462 81 47 05, Via Cavada 61, 4km east of Cavalese in Tresero, W www.agriturdarial.it)* B&B €25.80, half-board €33.55-38.75. Perched high on a hill above the village, this inviting farmhouse dishes up stunning views of the Val di Fiemme and heart-warming local cuisine. Winter warmers include a sauna and roaring fire.

Local food is served at the various malghe around San Martino, since transformed into restaurants.

Malga Venegiota *(☎ 0462 57 60 44)* Try the traditional-style Malga Venegiota at 1824m, accessible from Passo Rolle by a trail from Malga Juribello (three hours return) or by a shorter trail that incorporates the Baita Segantini chair lift (elevation 2170m).

Getting There & Away

Atesina buses run to San Martino from Trent and Canazei (via Predazzo). San Martino is connected with Padova and with Venice (Venezia) by long-haul services run by SITA and Brusutti respectively.

CANAZEI & AROUND

This popular ski resort in the **Val di Fassa** is surrounded by the striking peaks of the Gruppo di Sella to the north, the Catinaccio (Rosengarten; 2981m) to the west and the Marmolada to the south-east. Canazei (pop 1780, elevation 1465m) and a series of other towns along the valley to Vigo di Fassa and Moena are geared to summer and winter tourism, although some locals still make a traditional living from dairy farming. Those who'd rather flee the tourist flock can always head east from Moena, across the Passo San Pellegrino (1918m) into the **Valle del Biois**, where more rural pastures hold a couple of delicious places to stay and eat.

Information

Canazei's APT office (☎ 0462 60 11 13, W www.fassa.com), Via Roma 34, opens 8.30am to 12.15pm and 3pm to 6.30pm Monday to Saturday, and 10am to 12.30pm Sunday. Information on the Valle del Biois is doled out by the tiny tourist offices in Caviola (☎ 0437 59 01 16, fax 0437 59 01 16), Via Lungo Tegosa 8, open 10.30am to 12.30pm and 4pm to 5pm Monday to Friday; and Falcade (☎ 0437 59 92 41, fax 0437 59 92 42, e infofalcade@apt-dolomiti-cortina.it), Piazza Municipio 1, open 9am to 12.30pm and 3.30pm to 6.30pm daily. On the web, see W www.trevalli.com for skiing information.

Things to See & Do

Possibilities for **skiing** include downhill and cross-country runs, as well as challenging Alpine tours and the Sella Ronda network (see Gruppo di Sella later in this chapter). Dolomiti Superski passes are valid, alongside cheaper passes specific to the Val di Fassa (from €70.25/123.45 for a three-/six-day pass). The Tre Valli ski pass (from €76.45/136.35 for a three-/six-day pass) covers the Fassa, Biois and San Pellegrino valleys. In summer, you can ski down the Marmolada glacier. Numerous sports shops along Via Pareda in Canazei rent ski gear.

Walkers can approach the Catinaccio group from Vigo di Fassa, 11km south of Canazei. The best approach to the Gruppo di Sella (see that section later) is from the Passo Pordoi, where a cable car takes you up to almost 3000m. Any forgotten gear can be picked up in Canazei at the Tecnica sports shop, Via Roma 24.

Canazei's green surrounds offer ample rambles for less experienced walkers. Ask at the APT office for a copy of the English-language brochure *Low-level Walks in the Fassa Valley*, which outlines 28 walks in the Val di Fassa ranging in length from 1.5km to 8km. Of particular interest are those incorporating visits to old Ladin landmarks such as the **Molin de Pezol** *(☎ 0462 76 40 89, Via Jumela 6, about 11km south of Canazei in Pera di Fassa)*, a 19th-century mill; the **Botega da Pinter** *(☎ 0462 57 35 74, Via Dolomiti 4, 17km south of Canazei in Moena;*

open 10am-noon & 3pm-7pm Mon-Sat, mid-June–mid-Sept), an authentic reconstruction of a cooper's workshop; and a 16th-century **saw mill** *(☎ 0462 60 23 23, Via Pian Trevisan, about 3km east of Canazei in Penia along the narrow S641; open 10am-noon & 3pm-7pm Mon-Sat, mid-June–mid-Sept)*.

Staff at the APT office can likewise advise on **mountain-bike trails**. In Canazei, **La Zondra** *(☎ 0462 60 11 19, Via Pareda 85)* and **Detomas Fiorenzo** *(☎ 0462 60 24 47, Via Pareda 31)* hire wheels. In Falcade, try **Tarcy Sport** *(☎ 0437 50 70 79, Via Veneto 5)*. Rates average €4.15/15.50 per hour/day.

Places to Stay & Eat – Canazei

Camping Marmolada *(☎ 0462 60 16 60, Via Pareda)* Sites per person/tent & car €7.75/7.75. This site, strategically placed in the town centre almost opposite the cable car to Pecol (elevation 1926m), opens for both the winter and summer seasons.

Hotel Laurin *(☎/fax 0462 60 12 86, Via Dolomiti 105)* Singles/doubles €36.15/51.65. One of the region's few hotels to open year-round, Hotel Laurin is a cosy wooden place with blooming flower boxes and a fun-loving clientele.

Albergo Garni Stella Alpini *(☎ 0462 60 11 27, fax 0462 60 21 72, ⓔ stella.alpina@softcom.it, Via Antermont 4)* B&B per person from €28.40. Stella Alpini is a charming shuttered place, which stares face-to-face at a traditional, Alpine wooden hut for storing hay and at a colourfully painted wooden shop-house. A vaulted cellar made just for tasting wine adjoins the hotel.

Hotel Millenium *(☎ 0462 76 41 55, fax 0462 76 20 91, 10km south of Canazei in San Giovanni)* B&B per person from €33.55. The ornately carved wooden exterior of this lovely hotel, with colourfully tiled turrets and cosy Alpine interior, is one of a handful of romantic choices in a peaceful green setting, 10km south of Canazei.

Ristorante Pizzeria Italia *(☎ 0462 60 13 35, Via Dolomiti 168)* Pizzas €6.20-8.80, 1st/2nd courses €7.25/14.45. It might not be worthy of a postcard home but nothing can beat its hefty portions when that tummy's all of a rumble.

Osteria La Montanara *(☎ 0462 60 13 52, Via Dolomiti 147-151)* Meals around €18.10. As well as full-blown meals, this cosy osteria cooks up a tasty range of well-topped bruschette (€4.40) until 1am.

Canazei touts numerous ***bars***, ***cafes*** and a handy ***supermarket*** *(Via Dolomiti 118-120)*, although there are more substantial eating options on offer.

Places to Stay & Eat – Valle del Biois

There is a trio of three-star hotels on Via Pineta (the S346) just west of Caviola in Falcade, although there are some other options to try.

Camping Eden *(☎ 0437 59 91 38, fax 0437 59 91 38, ⓔ edenk@tin.it, Via Pecol 2, Falcade)*. This pretty Falcade site is tucked in a valley between two rivers.

Pensione Rondinella *(☎ 0437 59 01 22, fax 0437 59 01 22, Via Lungo Tegosa, Fedèr)* Singles/doubles from €20.65/33.55. Open July-Apr. What you see is what you get at this simple, down-to-earth pensione with 11 rooms in the tiny hamlet of Fedèr, 2km from Caviola, signposted west of Canale d'Agordo off the S346. Rooms with balconies tout stunning views.

Tabià *(☎ 0437 59 04 34, Fedèr)* Open Wed-Mon. 1st/2nd courses €5.15/6.45. Authentic, home-made cuisine is cooked up at this fabulous, family-run *tabià* (hay barn) which touts no menu but dishes up wholesome temptations like ravioli stuffed with pear and gorgonzola, mushroom-laced *pansotti* (triangle-shaped ravioli) and fried cheese.

Getting There & Away

Canazei can be reached by Atesina bus from Trent and by SAD bus from Bolzano and the Val Gardena. Buses do not cross the high mountain passes (such as Passo di Sella) in winter.

GRUPPO DI SELLA

The Sella group, in the western Dolomites, straddles the border between Trentino and Alto Adige, close to Cortina d'Ampezzo in the Veneto and the spectacular Parco Naturale di Fanes-Sennes-Braies. To the west is the spiky Sasso Lungo (Langkofel; 3181m), which extends to the Alpe di Siusi in Alto Adige. To the east is the Val Badia and its main town, Corvara, while to the south lies the Val di Fassa.

Skiers can complete the tour of the Sella in a single day on the famous network of runs known as Sella Ronda. The long and challenging route – 23.1km covered by runs and 13.5km by ski lifts – is only suitable for speedier skiers with some experience, a good level of fitness and lots of luck with the weather. Tourist offices can supply a leaflet that describes the clockwise and anticlockwise routes, kicking off from Selva (1565m; see the Val Gardena information section later) no later than 10am; Portavescovo, at 2495m, is the highest point. You'll need a Dolomiti Superski ski pass to complete the circuit.

For serious **walkers**, there is a summer version of the same leaflet, which details the circular route that takes roughly eight hours to complete. Both the Sella and Sasso Lungo walking trails can be reached from Canazei or the Val Gardena resorts by bus to Passo di Sella or Passo di Pordoi. Passo di Sella (2244m) is a mountain pass laced with hairpin bends – a motorcyclist's paradise in summer – topped with the eyesore hotel-restaurant ***Albergo Maria Flora*** *(☎/fax 0462 60 11 16, W www.maria-flora.val-di-fassa.com)*, which dishes up fantastic views and great espressos. From Passo di Pordoi (2239m) a cable car takes you to Sasso Pordoi (2950m) – dubbed the 'panoramic terrace of the Dolomites'. Digest its breathtaking views from the cafe terrace of the Rifugio Maria (☎ 0462 60 11 78), then pick up the Alta Via No 2 trail which crosses the group, heads down to the Passo Gardena and continues into the breathtaking Parco Naturale Puez-Odle.

For more information on the Sella, the Val Gardena and the Val Badia, see the following section on Alto Adige.

Alto Adige

This orderly Alpine fairyland owes more to its largely Austrian heritage than to its recent Italian history. Alto Adige (Südtirol) is a year-round attraction for skiers, climbers, walkers or those folk just looking to appreciate its natural splendour. For local news, views and events, pick up a copy of the local Italian daily, online at W www.altoadige.it); *Dolomitten* (W www.dolomitten.it), published daily in German; or for those culturally inquisitive souls – *La Usc di Ladins* (see the boxed text 'The Ladin Tradition' later in this chapter).

BOLZANO (BOZEN)

postcode 39100 • pop 100,000
elevation 265m

The provincial capital Bolzano is unmistakably Austrian. Forget your cappuccino and brioche and tuck into some *deutscher Kaffee* (German coffee) with *Sachertorte* (chocolate apricot cake). You'll hear Italian and German spoken (both languages are compulsory subjects in school) but, aside from concessions to the former in street, hotel and restaurant signs, there are precious few reminders of Italian rule here. The town's small historic centre, with its engaging Tirolean architecture and arcaded streets, harbours numerous outdoor cafes and restaurants, making it a very pleasant place to spend a few days.

Settled in the Middle Ages, Bolzano was an important market town that became a pawn in the power battles between the bishops of Trent and the counts of Tirolo. During the first decades of the 19th century, it passed, with the rest of the Tirolo, from Bavaria to Austria to Napoleon's kingdom of Italy and, finally, again to Austria. Along with the rest of the Südtirol, Bolzano passed to Italy after WWI and was declared the capital of the province in 1927.

Bolzano is linked by cable car to San Genesio (elevation 1087m), 10km west by road, from where numerous walking and biking trails can be picked up. Stunning views of the Dolomites can be enjoyed on clear days.

Information

Tourist Offices Bolzano's AAST office (☎ 0471 30 70 00, fax 0471 98 01 28, e info@bolzano-bozen.it), Piazza Walther 8, opens 9am to 6.30pm Monday to Friday, and 9am to 12.30pm Saturday. It provides a special Guest Pass to tourists who spend three or more nights in town. The pass covers admission to some sights and museums, a cable-car ride and a guided tour of the town. The office also has information on accommodation, activities, transport and walking possibilities in the Alto Adige region. Online, try **W** www.bolzano-bozen.it.

Club Alpino Italiano (☎ 0471 97 81 72, 0471 98 13 91), Piazza delle Erbe 46, can help you plan Alpine itineraries and organises guided expeditions in Alto Adige.

Money Banks riddle the centre and there's a currency exchange booth at the train station.

Post & Communications The post office, Via della Posta, opens 8am to 6.30pm Monday to Friday and 8am to 1pm Saturday.

Medical Services & Emergency Ospedale Regionale San Maurizio (hospital; ☎ 0471 90 81 11) is on Via Lorenz Böhler, some distance from the town centre off the SS38 to Merano, and accessible on city bus Nos 8 and 10a from the train station.

The *questura* (police station; ☎ 0471 97 60 00 or ☎ 0471 94 76 80) is at Via Marconi 33.

Things to See & Do

While away a few hours at one of the many outdoor cafes on Piazza Walther or along the side streets that lead to Piazza delle Erbe. Otherwise, **hire a bike** for a ride around town from **Sportler Velo** *(☎ 0471 97 77 19, **W** www.sportler.com, Via Grappoli/Weintraubengasse 56)*, or pick one up for free at the open-air stall in front of Via della Stazione 2, open Easter to October. Walkers and cyclists can buy forgotten gear at Sportler Velo or the Giacomelli sports shop, Via Museo 20a.

Start a sightseeing tour with the Gothic **cathedral** on Piazza Parrocchia/Pfarrplatz and nearby **Chiesa di Domenicani**, Piazza Domenicani/Dominikanerplatz, with its

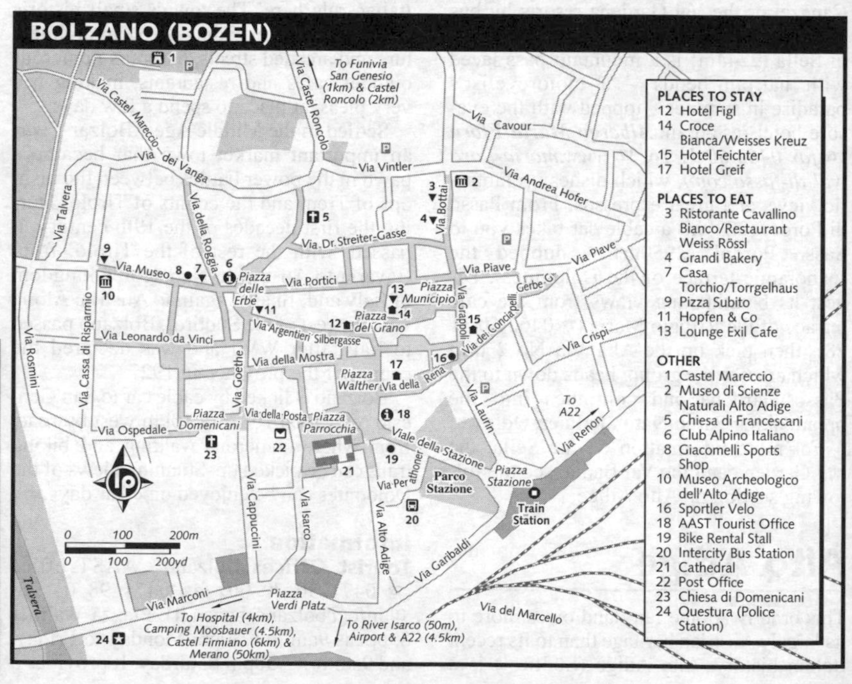

cloisters and chapel featuring 14th-century frescoes of the Giotto school. Take a walk along the arcaded **Via Portici/Laubengasse**, through the charming Piazza delle Erbe (the German name Obstplatz explains what this square is – the daily fresh produce market), to reach the 14th-century **Chiesa di Francescani** on Via dei Francescani/Franziskanergasse. It features beautiful cloisters and a magnificent Gothic altarpiece carved by Hans Klocker in 1500 in the Cappella della Beata Vergine (Virgin's Chapel).

The **Museo Archeologico dell'Alto Adige** *(☎ 0471 98 20 98, Ⓦ www.iceman.it, Via Museo 43; adult/child €6.70/3.60; open 10am-6pm Tues, Wed & Fri-Sun, 10am-8pm Thur)* houses an important collection of regional treasures, including the much-vaunted mummified body of unter-traveller 'Ötzi', discovered by chance in the Similaun glacier in September 1991 and dating back about 5000 years. His equipment is also on display, accompanied by an exhaustive commentary.

The geological wonders of Alto Adige can be unearthed in the **Museo di Scienze Naturali Alto Adige** *(☎ 0471 41 29 61, Ⓔ naturmuseum@provincia.bz.it, Via Bottai; adult/child €4.15/2.60; open 9am-6pm Tues, Wed & Fri-Sun, 9am-8pm Thurs)*.

Bolzano's surrounds sport several castles worth a peek: 13th-century **Castel Mareccio** (Schloss Maretsch), north along Via della Roggia from Piazza delle Erbe; **Castel Roncolo** *(Schloss Runkelstein; ☎ 0471 32 88 44, Ⓔ roncolo@comune.bolzano.it, Via San Antonio 15; open 10am-6pm Tues-Sun Oct-Jun, 10am-8pm Tues-Sun July-Sept)*, out of town on the road to Sarentino (Sarnthein), renowned for its 14th-century frescoes; and **Castel Firmiano** (Schloss Sigmundskron), built on a military site dating back to AD 945. A bike is an invigorating means of getting to/from all three.

Places to Stay

Bolsano offers everything from camp sites to a techy art hotel.

Moosbauer *(☎ 0471 91 84 92, Via San Maurizio 83)* Sites per person/tent/car €5.15/4.65/4.65. This camp site is out of town, towards Merano.

Croce Bianca/Weisses Kreuz *(☎ 0471 97 75 52, fax 0471 97 22 73, Piazza del Grano 3)* Singles/doubles without bath €26.85/45.45, doubles/triples with bath €53.70/68.15. Breakfast is included in the rates charged by this appealing, family-run place off Via dei Portici.

Hotel Feichter *(☎ 0471 97 87 68, fax 0471 97 48 03, Ⓦ www.paginegialle.it/feichter, Via Grappoli 15)* Singles/doubles €46.50/72.30. The restaurant is on the ground floor and hotel reception on the first at this unremarkable but nothing-to-complain-about hotel.

Hotel Figl *(☎/fax 0471 97 84 12, Piazza del Grano 9)* Singles/doubles from €67.15/77.45. Peering out across yet another pretty tourist-riddled square, Figl is a fine mid-range option for those seeking a tad more style and comfort.

Hotel Greif *(☎ 0471 97 31 80 00, fax 0471 31 81 48, Ⓦ www.greif.it, Piazza Walther)* Singles/doubles from €105.85/157.50. Light and spacious with a PC in every room (each designed by a different artist), this highly innovative hotel is an architect's or rich (wo)man's dream. If you've got the dosh, stay here.

Places to Eat

The best Bolzano restaurants specialise in Tirolean-style Austrian dishes such as *speckknödelsuppe* (bacon dumpling soup) washed down with a red Lagrein or St Magdalener wine.

Lounge Exil Cafe *(☎ 0471 97 18 14, Piazza del Grano 2a)* Young, fun and a funky place to hang out, this trendy industrial-style cafe is the place to sip cocktails, drink tea or sink your teeth into a brownie, a salad or a healthy bowl of yoghurt, fruit and muesli.

Ristorante Cavallino Bianco/Restaurant Weiss Rössl *(☎ 0471 97 32 67, Via Bottai 6; open 8am-1am)* 1st/2nd courses €5.15/7.75. Extremely popular and reasonably priced, the White Horse serves a wide choice of traditionally meaty treats (such as *testina di vitello* – lamb intestines) as well as less gruesome dishes for vegetarians.

Pizza Subito *(Via Museo)*. Grab a pizza slice to take away or eat in at this bright and modern fast-food joint.

Hopfen & Co *(☎ 0471 30 07 88, Piazza delle Erbe 17)* 1st/2nd courses from €4.15/7.75. Hearty portions of traditional dishes – including a very memorable *gulasch* (stew) simmered with *canederli* (dumplings) in beer brewed on the premises – are served at this authentic brewery-cum-eating house.

Casa Torchio/Torrgelhaus *(Via Museo 2)* Full meals about €18.10. This restaurant, just off Piazza delle Erbe, is a wonderful place, with antique glass windows and excellent local specialities at reasonable prices.

Pick up fruit, vegetables, bread and cheese from the ***morning market*** which fills Piazza delle Erbe Monday to Saturday. Wholesome breads topped or filled with every grain imaginable are sold at the ***Grandi*** bakery *(Via de Bottai 16a)*.

Getting There & Away

Air Bolzano Dolomiti airport (☎ 0471 25 16 81 or 0471 25 40 70, W www.abd-airport.it) is served by daily flights to/from Frankfurt and Rome. Schedules are online.

Bus Bolzano is a major transport hub for Alto Adige. SAD buses leave from the bus terminal on Via Perathoner, near Piazza Walther, for destinations throughout the province, including Val Gardena, the Alpe di Siusi, Brunico, Val Pusteria and Merano (where you can change for destinations including the valleys leading up into the Parco Nazionale dello Stelvio).

SAD buses also head for resorts outside the province, such as Canazei and Cortina d'Ampezzo in Trentino and Veneto respectively (for the latter you have to change at Dobbiaco). Timetables are available from the bus station (toll free ☎ 800 84 60 47) or the AST office.

Train Regular trains connect Bolzano with Merano, Trent, Verona, Milan, Innsbruck (Austria) and Munich (Germany). You can also catch a train from Bolzano to Brunico and San Candido in the Val Pusteria.

Car & Motorcycle The town is easily accessible from the north and south on the A22.

MERANO (MERAN)

postcode 39012 • pop 33,800
elevation 323m

Merano is a sedate little place, although its typically Tirolean centre – clean and well tended – throngs with tourists in season. Its Terme di Merano, a complex of therapeutic baths and treatments, lures a more elderly set, who flock here to ease their aches, pains and other ills with a dose of self-pampering. The town neighbours the Parco Naturale del Gruppo di Tessa (Texalgruppe), the Parco Nazionale dello Stelvio and the spectacular Ortles (Ortler) mountain range, making Merano – the self-proclaimed 'sunny city' – a handy stopover on your way to higher altitudes.

Orientation & Information

The train and intercity bus stations are on Piazza Stazione/Bahnhofsplatz, a 10-minute stroll from the centre of town. Exit the train station, turn right into Via Europa/Europaallee and at Piazza Mazzini/Mazziniplatz take Corso Libertà/Freiheitsstrasse to reach the historic centre. Pedestrianised Via dei Portici/Laubengasse is the main shopping street. Maps and guides are sold at the Poetzelbercer bookshop on Piazza del Duomo/Pfarrplatz.

The Azienda di Cura, Soggiorno e Turismo (ACST; ☎ 0473 23 52 23, fax 0473 23 55 24, W www.meraninfo.it), Corso Libertà 35, opens 9am to 6.30pm Monday to Friday, and 10am to 12.30pm Saturday and Sunday.

Several banks and ATMs line the stretch of Corso Libertà opposite the tourist office. The post office and Telecom office, Via Roma/Romastrasse 2, are on the other side of the River Passirio from the old town.

Ospedale Civile Tappeiner (☎ 0473 26 33 33) is at Via Rossini 5, off Via Goethe.

Things to See & Do

The historic centre of town surrounds arcaded Via dei Portici and Piazza del Duomo – take any of the streets off Corso Libertà near the ACST office (leading away from the river). The **Terme di Merano** *(Meraner Kurbad; ☎ 0473 23 77 24, Via Piave 9)* are therapeutic baths offering a full range of medical and relaxation treatments, including underwater massages (€34.35), regular massages (€23.25 per 25-minute pound, 10 for €164.30) and healthy radon baths (€18.85) in a small thermal pool. Admission to the sauna/thermal swimming pool costs €12.40/7.75. Serious self-pamperers should ask about the 'relax paket' and other packages available.

The past two centuries are recaptured from a female perspective at the **Museo della Donna** *(Frauenmuseum; ☎ 0473 23 12 16, Via dei Portici 68; adult/child €3.60/2.60; open 9.30am-12.30pm & 2.30pm-6.30pm Mon-Fri, 9.30am-1pm Sat)*. Period costumes are among the exhibits displayed. Those seeking to buy their own traditional Tirolese costume to take home can buy one at Haladi, Via dei Porticiat 85. Local history is the focus of the **Museo Civico** *(Städtisches Museum; ☎ 0473 23 60 15, Via delle Corse 42; adult/child €2.05/1.55; open 10am-5pm Tues-Sat, 10am-1pm Sun Sept-June, also 4pm-7pm Sun July & Aug)*. The third in the museum trio, the **Museo Ebraico** *(Jüdische Museum; ☎ 0473 23 61 27, Via Schiller 14; free; open 3pm-6pm Tues & Wed, 9am-noon Thur, 3pm-5pm Fri)* is housed in Merano's synagogue, dating to 1901. The museum recounts the history of the town's Jewish population from the early 19th century through to WWII.

Castello Principesco *(Landesfürstliche Burg; ☎ 0473 23 01 02; Via Galilei; adult/child €2.05/1.55; 10am-1pm Sun Sept-June, also 4pm-7pm Sun July & Aug)* was home to the Tirol princes from 1470 and is one of Alto Adige's better-maintained castles.

Lush Mediterranean foliage surrounds **Castel Trauttmansdorff** *(Schloss Trauttmansdorff; ☎ 0473 23 57 30; Via San Valentino 51a; admission €6.70; open 9am-6pm mid-Mar–mid-Nov, 9am-9pm June-Aug)*. A guided tour of the botanical gardens – a must for the green-fingered – costs €4.15 per person. Beer-lovers will probably prefer a tour of the **Forst Brewery** *(☎ 0473 26 01 11)* at Forst, just outside Merano; ask at the tourist office.

Activities

Merano 2000 offers limited **skiing**, ideal for beginners. A cable car carries winter sports enthusiasts from the town to the 2000m-high station, which is served by five chair lifts and a couple of buttons (drag lifts). Between October and May, twirl on the ice at the **ice rink** *(☎ 0473 23 69 82, Via Palade 74)* inside the Meranarena sports complex.

The ACST office distributes a free city map, marked up with various parks and walks, including the popular **Passeggiata Tappeiner** which kicks off on Via Laurin, in the Quarazze quarter of town and meanders for 3.5km around Monte Benedetto (514m) before dropping down to the banks of the River Passirio. Another itinerary, the **Passeggiata Gilf** makes for a pleasant riverside stroll. For details of more taxing walks, contact the Scuola di Alpinismo Merano (☎ 0473 23 52 23 or 0348 260 08 13, fax 0473 56 38 45); the tourist office acts as a contact point for the club.

Merano is a pleasant town to cycle around. Pick up a pair of wheels for free (€5.15 deposit) from the open-air stand marked 'Noleggio Biciclette-Fahrradverleih' next to the bus station *(open 9am to 7pm Mon-Sat Mar-Sept)*. More adventurous cyclists can hire **mountain bikes** from **Sportler** *(☎ 0473 21 13 40, Via dei Portici 279)*, a huge sports shop where you can also buy all the gear for walking, cycling and other sports.

Places to Stay

Rest up in this typical Tirolean town before tackling the neighbouring peaks.

Pension Tyrol *(☎ 0473 44 97 19, Via XXX Aprile/30 Aprilstrasse 8)* B&B per person €23.25-25.80. Most establishments in the centre are expensive, although Pension Tyrol, off Corso della Libertà, has reasonable double rooms to let; singles are hard to get.

Villa Pax *(☎ 0473 23 62 90, Via Leichter 3)* B&B €18.10. This place is a religious institution. To reach it from Corso della Libertà, cross the river at Piazza D Rena and follow Via Cavour to Via Dante, turn right and then left into Via Leichter.

Conte di Merano/Graf von Meran *(☎ 0473 23 21 81, fax 0473 21 18 74, Via* *delle Corse/Rennweg 78)* Low season B&B per person €41.32, high season €49, single-room supplement €7.75. This place is near Via dei Portici. It has lovely rooms.

Places to Eat

Café Relais *(Piazza della Rena/Sandplatz 10)* Open Tues-Sun from 7.30am. Breakfast in the early-morning sun on the roof terrace at this charming cafe-cum-ice-cream parlour, overlooking a flower-filled pedestrian square.

Café Wolf *(☎ 0473 23 33 49, Via delle Corse/Rennweg)* The Wolf, with its modern and minimalist interior, peers across at the Conte di Merano hotel. An ideal spot for coffee and cake.

Forsterbräu *(☎ 0473 23 65 35, Corso della Libertà 90)* 1st/2nd courses from €5.15/10.35. Nestled in and around an atmospheric courtyard, this typically Tirolean restaurant cooks up a hot *gulaschsuppe* and a swimming choice of fresh trout dishes.

Rainer *(☎ 0473 23 61 49, Via dei Portici 266)* 1st/2nd courses €7.75/12.90. Rainer is another top spot to sample traditional Tirolese fodder in a wooden interior. The hand-written menu can be a trifle hard to decipher.

Haisrainer *(☎ 0473 23 79 44, Via dei Portici 100)* 1st/2nd courses from €4.40/6.20. Open Mon-Sat. Sink your teeth into a meaty Tirolese platter (€11.35) starring *wurstel* (sausage), *crauti* (sauerkraut) et al at this traditional spot, notable for its cavernous feel.

Alto Adige's famed *speck* (smoked, cured ham) and oodles of other meats and sausages can be ogled at and bought at ***Gögele*** *(Via dei Portici 77-83)*. A stunning array of nutty brown breads riddled with every imaginable grain can be enjoyed at ***Preiss Chritine & Co*** *(☎ 0473 23 73 29, Via delle Corse/Rennweg 118-120)*, a fabulous bakery. Pick up anything else at the ***A&O*** supermarket *(Via dei Portici 188)*.

Getting There & Away

Merano is easily accessible by bus or train from Bolzano (about 40 minutes). SAD buses connect the town with Monte San Caterina (Katharinaberg) and other villages that give access to the Tessa group, as well as to Silandro (Schlanders) and the valleys leading into the Ortles range and the Parco Nazionale dello Stelvio. See the section on the Parco Nazionale dello Stelvio for bus information.

PARCO NAZIONALE DELLO STELVIO

If you can tear yourself away from the Dolomites, this major national park offers more fantastic walking possibilities: at low altitudes in the pretty valleys, Val d'Ultimo (Ultental), Val Martello (Martelltal) and Val di Solda (Suldental), and at high altitudes on spectacular peaks such as the Gran Zebrù (Königsspitze; 3859m), Cevedale (Zufallspitze; 3769m) and the breathtaking Ortles (3905m), all part of the Ortles range. There is a network of well-marked trails, including routes over some of the range's glaciers. The park incorporates one of Europe's largest glaciers, the Ghiacciaio dei Forni.

The glaciers permit year-round skiing and there are well-serviced runs at Solda and the Passo Stelvio (2757m); the latter is the second-highest pass in the Alps and is approached from **Trafoi** on one of Europe's most spectacular roads, a series of tight switchbacks covering 15km with, at times, nerve-wrackingly steep gradients. The road is famous among cyclists, who flock to the park every summer to tackle the ascent.

The park straddles Alto Adige and Trentino and can be approached from Merano (from where you have easy access to the Val d'Ultimo, Val Martello, Val di Solda and the Passo Stelvio), or from the Val di Sole in Trentino, which gives easy access to the Valle di Peio and the Val di Rabbi.

Val di Solda

The village of Solda (Sulden; elevation 1906m), at the head of the Val di Solda, is a small ski resort and a base for walkers and climbers in summer. Challenging trails lead you to high altitudes; these include trail No 28, which crosses the Madriccio pass (3123m) into the Val Martello. The tourist office at Solda (☎ 0473 61 30 15) has information on accommodation and activities. The village virtually closes down from October to Christmas.

SAD buses connect Solda with Merano Monday to Friday during the summer only; you need to change at Spondigna.

Val Martello

This picturesque valley is a good choice for relatively low-altitude walks, with spectacular views of some of the park's high peaks. The real beauty of the valley is that the environment is unspoiled by ski lifts and downhill ski runs. It is a popular base for tackling the glaciers (guided walks can be organised). In winter, there is excellent cross-country skiing, and climbers can crawl up the valley's frozen waterfalls from January to March. In spring, the valley attracts ski mountaineers, since there is no danger of avalanches.

People with children might like to take trail No 20 up into the Val di Peder. It is an easy walk, with some lovely picnic spots along the way and the chance to see animals, including chamois and deer. For accommodation, inquire at the Pro Loco office.

The road into the valley is open year-round, and SAD bus 107 runs to Martello village from Silandro. In summer the bus proceeds to Rifugio Genziana (Enzianhütte).

VAL GARDENA

An enchanting Alpine valley, Val Gardena (Grödnertal) is hemmed in by the towering peaks of the Parco Naturale Puez-Odle (Naturpark Puez-Geisler), the imposing Gruppo di Sella and Sasso Lungo, and the gentle slopes and pastures of the Alpe di Siusi, the largest high plain in the Alps. It is one of the most popular skiing areas in the Alps because of the relatively reasonable prices and excellent facilities proffered by the valley's main towns – Ortisei (St Ulrich; elevation 1236m), Santa Cristina (St Christina; elevation 1428m) and Selva (Wolkenstein; elevation 1563m). Its ski runs throng with snow fiends in winter, while warmer months see walkers flock to trails at both high and low altitudes.

Along with Val Badia (Gadertal), the Val Gardena is an enclave that has managed to preserve the ancient Ladin language and culture, and a rich tradition in colourful legends (for more details see the boxed text 'The Ladin Tradition' later in this chapter). The ancient tradition of woodcarving is likewise nurtured here and the valley's artisans are famed for their statues, figurines, altars and toys. Beware of mass-produced imitations.

Information

There are tourist offices in each of the towns: Ortisei (☎ 0471 79 63 28, fax 0471 79 67 49, ⓔ ortisei@val-gardena.com), Str Rezia 1; Santa Cristina (☎ 0471 79 30 46, fax 0471 79 31 98, ⓔ s.cristina@val-gardena.com), Str Chemun 9; and Selva (☎ 0471 79 51 22, fax 0471 79 42 45, ⓔ selva@val-gardena.com), Str Mëisules 213. All three open 8am to noon and 2.30pm or 3pm to 6.30pm Monday to Saturday, and 9am or 10am to noon and 4.30pm or 5pm to 6.30pm on Sunday, with no lunch break in summer. Comprehensive information is online at ⓦ www.val-gardena.com.

Activities

In addition to its own fine **downhill ski** runs, the valley forms part of the Sella Ronda, a network of runs connecting the Val Gardena, Val Badia, Livinallongo and Val di Fassa (for which you'll need a Dolomiti Superski pass). Ski passes covering the use of 81 lifts in the Val Gardena are cheaper. Areas such as the Vallunga, near Selva, offer good **cross-country skiing**. There are stunning trails around Forcella Pordoi and Val Lasties in the Gruppo di Sella, and on the Sasso Lungo.

This is walkers' paradise, with endless possibilities, from the challenging Alte Vie of the Gruppo di Sella and the magnificent Parco Naturale Puez-Odle, to picturesque family strolls in spots like the Vallunga. Those seeking guidance can contact the **Val Gardena Mountain Guide Association** *(☎ 0471 79 41 33, ⓔ guide-alpine@val-gardena.com; Cultural Centre Oswald von Wolkenstein; open 5.30pm-7pm in summer, 5.30pm-6pm in winter)*. It organises botanical walks as well as climbing courses, glacier excursions and treks.

From Ortisei (elevation 1250m) in the Val Gardena, you can take the **cable car to Seceda** *(€8.25/13.95 one way/return; open*

8.45am-4.45pm) which, at 2456m, offers a memorable view – one of the most spectacular in the Alps – of the Gruppo di Odle, a series of spiky pinnacles. From Seceda, trail No 2a passes through what most people would consider a typical Alpine environment – lush, green sloping pastures dotted with wooden malghe, used by herders as summer shelters.

Just behind Selva, the valley is home to some over-friendly horses who like to harass picnicking tourists. The walk to the end of the valley takes three to four hours. It is possible to continue from the end of the valley along trail No 14 to pick up the Alta Via No 2. From here, you can continue up into Gruppo di Odle, or double back into Gruppo di Puez and on to the Gruppo di Sella.

Places to Stay

Garni Gran Cësa *(☎ 0471 79 74 22, Via Zitadella-Strasse 67, Ortisei)* B&B €23.25-25.80. This is about the cheapest you'll get in Ortisei.

Affittacamera Tyrol *(☎/fax 0471 79 20 58, Via Plesdinaz-Strasse 113, Santa Cristina)* B&B €23.75-25.80. Tyrol is one of several charming, family-run places that offer B&B year-round; the APT offices have lists of other.

Pensione Bellavista *(☎/fax 0471 79 20 39, Via Plesdinaz-Strasse 65, Santa Cristina)* B&B/half-board up to €31.50/43.85. Head 1km north of town for a room with a *bella vista* in a panoramic setting.

Garni Zirmei *(☎ 0471 79 52 12, fax 0471 79 44 54, Via Col da Lech-Strasse 60, Selva)* B&B €20.65-28.90. In Selva, roll out of bed and across the street to the ski bus stop at Zirmei.

Alpenhotel Rainell *(☎ 0471 79 61 45, fax 0471 79 62 79, W www.rainell.com, Via Vidalong-Strasse 19, Ortisei)* Low season half-board €54.25, high season €67.15. Alpenhotel Rainell is, surprisingly, a quintessential Alpine pad surrounded by quintessential Alpine pastures.

Hotel Hell *(☎ 0471 79 67 85, fax 0471 79 81 96, W www.hotelhell.it, Str Promenade 3, Ortisei)*. Half-board €56.80-64. Hotel Hell is run by the Hell family and flashes four stars.

Hotel Adler *(☎ 0471 77 50 00, fax 0471 77 55 55, W www.hotel-adler.com, Str Rezia 7, Ortisei)* Singles/doubles from €72.30 per person. A 'water world' with oriental and Turkish baths, and a Ladin farmstead where you can dip into a hay bath (see the boxed text 'Hay Baths' earlier in this chapter) are among the self-pampering novelties awaiting guests who at this stylish four-star wonder, housed in a frescoed 13th-century building.

Getting There & Away

The Val Gardena is accessible from Bolzano by SAD bus, as well as from Canazei (summer only). Regular buses connect the towns along the valley and you can reach the Alpe di Siusi by either bus or cable car. Full timetables are available at the tourist offices.

Long-distance bus services (Lazzi, SITA and STAT) to major cities throughout Italy are available in July and August and between Christmas and Easter. Information can be obtained at Alpintourdolomit Viaggi (☎ 0471 79 61 35) in Ortisei.

ALPE DI SIUSI & PARCO NATURALE DELLO SCILIAR

There's something magical about the view across the Alpe di Siusi (Seiser Alm) to the Sciliar (Schlern), as the green undulating pastures end dramatically at the foot of these towering peaks. It is a particularly spectacular scene in an area that certainly doesn't lack scenery. The Alpe di Siusi (1700m to 2200m), the largest plateau in Europe, forms part of what is known as the Altipiano dello Sciliar, which also incorporates the villages of Castelrotto (Kastelruth) and Siusi (Seis), lower down at about 1000m.

There is something for walkers of all ages and expertise in this area. The gentle slopes of the Alpe di Siusi are perfect for families with young kids, and you won't need much more than average stamina to make it to the Rifugio Bolzano (Schlernhaus; elevation 2457m; ☎ 0471 61 20 24), just under Monte Pez (2564m), the Sciliar's summit. If you're after more challenging walks, the jagged peaks of the Catinaccio group and the Sasso Lungo are nearby. These mountains are famous among climbers worldwide.

Information

Highly organised tourist offices in the area include those in Castelrotto (☎ 0471 70 63 33), Piazza Kraus 1; Siusi (☎ 0471 70 70 24), Via Sciliar 8; Compaccio (Compatsch; ☎ 0471 72 79 04) in the Alpe di Siusi; and Fie' allo Sciliar (☎ 0471 72 50 47).

For medical assistance call ☎ 0471 70 65 55. The Guardia Medica Turistica (☎ 0471 70 54 44) is based at Telfen, between Castelrotto and Siusi.

Activities

There's no shortage of organised activities or details on how to organise your own. In winter the area offers excellent skiing: downhill, ski-mountaineering and cross-country. It forms part of the Superski Dolomiti network. As in the Val Gardena, the area gets pretty crowded during peak periods. Ask at the tourist offices about walking trails open during the snow season.

In summer the trails in the Alpe di Siusi are crowded with walkers but as soon as you get to higher altitudes they start to thin out. Using a good map and following the tourist office recommendations, you could spend days taking leisurely walks in the Alpe di Siusi, stopping for picnics or planning your walks to ensure that you reach a *malga* (Alpine hut) for a lunch break. The tourist offices organise low-priced guided walks of varying lengths and difficulties. There are also plenty of good trails for mountain bikers. There are plenty of challenging walks, including several vie ferrate. The Catinaccio group can also be approached from the Val di Fassa.

Places to Stay

There are plenty of hotels and pensiones in this area, but bookings are recommended during the summer and winter high seasons. If you're travelling with kids, ask staff at the tourist office for information on hotels equipped, or offering special deals, for children. There's a choice between places in the villages or up on the Alpe di Siusi. If you choose to stay in the Alpe di Siusi, there is a regular bus service; in summer normal traffic is banned from the plateau. For details see Getting There & Around below.

Albergo Zallinger *(☎ 0471 72 79 47, Saltria 74)* Half-board per person up to €51.65. This place is at the foot of the Sassopiatto.

Garni Villa Rosa *(☎ 0471 70 63 27, St Annaweg 3)* B&B per person from €23.25. In Castelrotto, Villa Rosa is about 10 minutes' walk from the centre.

Gasthof zum Wolf *(☎ 0471 70 63 32, Oswald von Wolkensteinstrasse 5)* B&B per person from €36.15. Traditional and comfortable Gasthof zum Wolf is right in the middle of Castelrotto. The management might insist that you take half-board.

Getting There & Around

The Altipiano dello Sciliar is accessible by SAD bus from Bolzano, the Val Gardena and Bressanone. By car, exit the Brenner *autostrada* (A22) at Bolzano Nord or Chiusa.

From May to October the roads of the Alpe di Siusi are closed to normal traffic. Tourists with a booking at a hotel in the zone can obtain a special permit from the tourist office at Compaccio allowing them to drive between 4pm and 10am. It is best to organise your pass before arriving in the area; ask your hotel owner for assistance. A regular bus service operates from Castelrotto and Siusi to Compaccio, and from there on to the Alpe di Siusi. Tourists staying in some hotels in the area are given a special Favorit card that entitles them to free bus travel on the Buxi line. For information about the pass and participating hotels, ask at the tourist offices.

VAL BADIA

Along with the Val Gardena, Val Badia is one of the last strongholds of the ancient Ladin culture and language. Most local kids (as well as adults) are aware of the Ladin legends, richly peopled by giants, kings, witches, fairies and dragons. Many are set on the nearby Fanes high plain, which forms part of the magnificent Parco Naturale di Fanes-Sennes-Braies. This is one of the most evocative places in the Dolomites, and can be reached easily from the Alta Val Badia either on foot or by cable car from Passo Falzarego.

Towns in the valley include Colfosco (Colfosch; elevation 1645m), La Villa (La Ila; elevation 1433m), San Cassiano (San

The Ladin Tradition

Ladin language and culture can be traced back to around 15 BC, when the people of the Central Alps were forcibly united into the Roman province of Rhaetia. The Romans, of course, introduced Latin to the province but the original inhabitants of the area, with their diverse linguistic and cultural backgrounds, modified the language to such an extent that by around AD 450 it had evolved into an independent Romance language, known as raeto-romanic. At one point the entire Tirol was Ladin but today the language and culture are confined to the Val Gardena and the Val Badia where, in the 1981 census, about 90% of locals declared that they belonged to the Ladin language group. Along with German and Italian, Ladin is taught in schools, and the survival of the Ladin cultural and linguistic identity is protected by law. *La Usc di Ladins* is the local Ladin-language newspaper, covering the Val Gardena and Val Badia. It can be found online at Ⓦ www.lauscdiladins.com. The library inside the Union di Ladins de Gherdëina (☎ 0471 79 68 70), Str Rezia 83, in Ortisei opens 4pm to 7pm Monday and Thursday, and from 10am to noon Saturday.

Ladin culture is rich in vibrant poetry and legends, set amid the jagged peaks of the Dolomites and richly peopled by fairies, gnomes, elves, giants, princesses and heroes. Passed on by word-of-mouth for centuries, and often heavily influenced by Germanic myths, many of these legends were in danger of being lost. In the first decade of the 20th century, journalist Carlo Felice Wolff, who had lived most of his life in Bolzano, undertook a major project: he spent 10 years gathering and researching the local legends, listening to the old folk, farmers and shepherds recount the legends and fairy tales. The legends he eventually published were reconstructed from the many different versions and recollections he gathered.

The magic of these many myths is rekindled in Ortisei's **Museo Ladin** *(☎ 0471 79 75 54, Piazza San Antonio; free; open 3pm-6.30pm Tues-Fri June, Sept & Oct, 10am-noon & 3pm-7pm Tues-Sun July & Aug, 3pm-6.30pm Tues & Fri winter)*. The Ladin Museum has particularly good sections on flora and fauna specific to the Ladin lands, and local wood-carving. Ask here or at the APT office for information on wood-carving courses run in the town in July and August. Of a similar ilk is the **Museo di Storia usi Costumi e Tradizioni della Gente Ladina** *(History Museum of Customs & Traditions of the Ladin People; ☎ 0471 79 75 54; open 4pm-7pm Tues-Thurs July & Sept, 4pm-7pm daily Aug)*, hidden on the 3rd floor of an old building perched on the main street (S48) at the western end of Pieve di Livinallongo.

True Ladin fiends should not miss out on the third in the trio, the **Museum Ladin Ciastel de Tor** *(☎ 0474 52 40 20, Ⓦ www.museumladin.it, Via Tor 72)* inside 12th-century Tor Castle, some 15km south of Brunico in San Martino in Badia (S244). South Tirol's largest Ladin museum was set to open in July 2001, although it was still closed in autumn. Phone for further information on reopening times.

Ciascian; elevation 1537m) and Corvara (elevation 1568m). The village of Pieve di Livinallongo, about 15km south-east of Corvara, is home to a museum dedicated to Ladin customs and traditions (see the boxed text 'The Ladin Tradition').

Corvara

postcode 39033 • pop 1280
elevation 1568m

This ski resort is an excellent base for walkers wanting to tackle the peaks enclosing the Alta Badia. The central town of the Ladin tribes, and contemporary host to the 2001 Alpine Ski World Cup, Corvara is a pleasant little place, with a well-organised tourist office and plenty of accommodation.

The tourist office (☎ 0471 83 61 76, fax 0471 83 65 40, Ⓦ www.altabadia-dolomites.com or www.altabadia.org), Str Col Alt 36, opens 8am (9am Saturday) to noon and 3pm to 6pm Monday to Saturday, and 10.30am to 12.30pm Sunday. The Associazione Guide Alpine Val Badia (☎ 0471 83 68 98, e guide.valbadia@rolmail.net) – the people to ask for advice on skiing and walking trails – has an office in the same building.

For medical assistance, go to the Croce Bianca, set back from Corvara's main street near the tourist office. The nearest public hospital is in Brunico (☎ 0474 58 11 11).

Activities Corvara is on the Sella Ronda **ski trail** and is part of the Dolomiti Superski network. The more restrictive Alta Badia ski pass costs €73.85/129.65 for three/six days in low season (€83.65/147.70 in high season).

From Corvara, you can reach the Passo Falzarego by SAD bus and then take the **cable car** up into the Parco Naturale di Fanes-Sennes-Braies; see the Walking in the Dolomites section earlier in this chapter. Alternatively, pick up trail No 12 from near La Villa, or trail No 11, which joins Alta Via No 1 at the Capanna Alpina, a few kilometres off the main road between Passo Valparola and San Cassiano. Either trail takes you up to the Alpe di Fanes and the two rifugi, Lavarella and Fanes.

A combination of cable car and chair lift will take you from Corvara up into the Gruppo di Sella at Vallon (elevation 2550m), where you'll get a spectacular view across to the Marmolada glacier. From Vallon you can traverse the Sella or follow the trail that winds around the valley at the top of the chair lift (about one hour). A good area for family walks is around Prelongià (Prelungé) (elevation 2138m). Catch the cable car from La Villa and then take trail No 4 and trail No 23 to reach Prelongià. Trail No 23 takes you down to Corvara.

Horse riding, mountain biking and **hang-gliding** are other popular activities in the valley; the Centro Volo Libero Alta Badia *(☎ 0471 84 75 92 or 0336 46 64 91, Via Bosc da Plan 315)* in La Villa is one of a handful of gliding schools. The APT office in Corvara has a list of places where you can hire mountains bikes. It also distributes the excellent trilingual map-brochure *Ideas for Mountain Bike Tours* detailing 10 trails in the area, ranging in length from 8.2km to 44.5km.

Places to Stay & Eat Check out these classy Corvaran alternatives.

Ciasa Blancia *(☎ 0471 83 62 96, fax 0471 83 67 60, Via Sassongher 52)* Low season half-board €38.75, high season up to €62. Mountains and lots of fir trees make this something of a Heidi's hide-out, great for kids who like to roam wild.

La Tambra *(☎ 0471 83 62 81, fax 0471 83 66 46,* w *www.latambra.com, Via Sassongher 2)* Full board up to €92.95 per person. La Tambra is a pleasant, family-run choice with three stars and a munchable restaurant next door.

La Perla *(☎ 0471 83 61 32, fax 0471 83 65 68,* e *perla@altabadia.it, Via Col Alt 105)* Low season half-board €97, high season up to €195. Marketing itself as Corvara's 'romantik hotel', this oasis of luxury does indeed live up to its name. Excellent gourmet food and good wine dished up in a traditional, 18th-century Ladin-style restaurant are among the many sensory delights on offer.

Getting There & Away SAD buses link Corvara with Bolzano (1¾ hours, one daily), Merano, Brunico (1¼ hours, six to seven daily), the Val Gardena, the Passo Sella and Passo Pordoi, Canazei and the Passo Falzarego. Buses re-route in winter to avoid crossing high mountain passes.

CORTINA D'AMPEZZO

postcode 32043 • pop 6570
elevation 1224m

Across the Fanes-Conturines range from the Val Badia is the Dolomites' so-called jewel, Cortina d'Ampezzo. Italy's most famous, fashionable and expensive ski resort, Cortina is situated in the Veneto, but has been included here because of its central location. It is one of the best-equipped and most picturesque resorts in the Dolomites. Moreover, there is cheapish accommodation to be found if you know where to look and book well in advance.

Situated in the Ampezzo bowl, Cortina is surrounded by some of the most stunning mountains in the Dolomites, including (in a clockwise direction) Cristallo, the Gruppo di Sorapiss-Marmarole, Antelao, Becco di Mezzodi-Croda da Lago, the Nuvolau-Averau-Cinque Torri and Tofane. To the south are the Pelmo and the Civetta. Facilities for both downhill and cross-country skiing are first class, and the small town's population swells dramatically during the ski season as the rich and famous pour in; equally great walking and climbing possibilities crowd out the town in summer too.

Family Walk from Rifugio Malga Ra Stua to Forcella Lerosa

This is a good walk for families because the climb is not too steep. It's fairly short – around four hours up and back, including a picnic stop – and you'll see lots of animals and birds along the way. The area is easily accessible from the Val Pusteria and Cortina by car or public transport – from Cortina or Dobbiaco take the S51. Use the Tabacco 1:25,000 map of Cortina d'Ampezzo e Dolomiti Ampezzane.

Eight kilometres north of Cortina, take the small road to the left at the first switchback – if you are approaching from Dobbiaco it is the first switchback after Passo Cimabanche. During summer, from mid-June to mid-September, the road up to Ra Stua is closed to normal traffic. You can walk the 3 to 4km from the car park at the switchback (elevation 1420m) to Ra Stua (elevation 1670m), or use the reasonably priced minibus service which operates 8am to 6pm in summer from another large parking area situated to the west of the main road, 900m south of Pensione Fiames, 4km north of the centre of Cortina.

If you decide to walk from the car park, take the track that heads uphill from the eastern side of the switchback and follows the slope of the Croda de R'Ancona. The track doesn't have a number but is marked on the map.

Malga Ra Stua is at the beginning of the Val Salata, a lovely Alpine environment and perfect for a family walk. Before heading off for a walk in the valley, make sure you let the people running the rifugio know where you are going and check on the departure time of the last minibus.

More serious walkers can walk to the end of the Val Salata, ascend to Lago di Sennes (elevation 2116m) and pick up the walk through the Parco Naturale di Fanes-Sennes-Braies, which is detailed earlier in this chapter.

However, those wishing to do the family walk from Ra Stua, head up along the Val Salata for about 150m and take the dirt road to your right; cross two bridges and you'll come to a signpost. Here, leave the dirt road that continues as a shortcut to Forcella Lerosa and turn right to take track No 8 for Forcella Lerosa – Val de Gotres. This former military road, built by the Austrian army during WWI, is a little bit longer but much easier and more scenic. There is a series of switchbacks winding uphill past ancient fir trees, and at certain points there are panoramic views across the Fanes high plain. You will reach a lovely small valley where, if you approach quietly, you might see the resident marmots, chamois and squirrels. Follow the trail around the valley, always keeping to the main track and avoiding the several diversions to the right. The trail will bring you to a little wooden house with a water fountain in a wide valley with a dirt road. From here, Passo Forcella Lerosa (elevation 2020m) is a few minutes' walk to the right. In front of you now is the majestic Croda Rossa (elevation 3146m), one of the most beautiful peaks in the Dolomites.

One option is to turn right on the dirt road, still numbered as trail No 8, to reach the pass. After a picturesque descent of about 4km, you will reach the S51, closer to Dobbiaco and just before Passo Cimabanche.

Alternatively you can turn left at the wooden house and follow the dirt road back down to Ra Stua. This route is the aforementioned shortcut near Ra Stua but is less attractive than the ascent, so there is always the option to return the way you came.

Back at the Malga Ra Stua, try the fantastic hot chocolate topped with fresh cream.

Information

The APT office (☎ 0436 32 31/2/3, fax 0436 32 35, W www.apt-dolomiti-cortina.it), Piazzetta San Francesco 8, opens 9am to 12.30pm and 3.30pm to 6.30pm (4pm to 7pm July and August).

Cortina's Gruppo Guide Alpine (☎/fax 0436 86 85 05), inside the Casa delle Regole at Corso Italia 69/a, opens 8am to noon and 4pm to 8pm. Apart from the usual rock-climbing courses and guided walks for adults, the guides offer historical and naturalistic excursions and courses for kids.

The post office and adjoining telephone centre is at Largo Poste 20.

Dolomiti Multimedia (☎ 0436 86 80 90, W www.sunrise.it/cortina), Largo Poste 58, charges about €7.75 per hour for online access and opens 8.30am to 12.30pm and 3pm to 7.30pm Monday to Friday.

Activities

Expect to pay €77/135 in low season (€87/154 in high season) for a three-/six-day **ski pass** covering Cortina d'Ampezzo; the latter is also included in the pricier Dolomiti Superski ski pass. The APT office has a list of both sports shops, which rent skis, poles and boots, and of ski schools.

Dog sledding, **scaling frozen waterfalls**, and **ice-skating** inside Cortina's Olympic Ice Stadium *(☎ 0436 43 80; admission & skate hire €6.70; open 10.30am-12.30pm & 2.30pm-5.30pm Dec-Apr, 2.30pm-6pm or 6.30pm July–mid-Sept)* are among the other winter sports you can feast your muscles on.

Not far from Cortina, and accessible by Dolomiti Bus in summer, are the Tre Cime di Lavaredo, one of the world's most famous **climbing** locations and a panoramic place to walk. The fact that you can arrive by bus literally at the foot of the Tre Cime means the area is crawling with tourists in the high season.

Cortina offers a network of spectacular **walking trails**. A series of three **cable cars** *(☎ 0436 50 52; €23.25 return; open 9am-5pm)* whisks summer trekkers from Cortina, via Col Druscie, to the Tofana di Mezzo (elevation 3243m). All the trails from here are difficult and incorporate vie ferrate requiring special equipment. You can link up with the Alta Via No 1 either at the Passo Falzarego or at the evocative Passo Giau, with the spiky Croda da Lago to the east and the Cinque Torri to the north-west. To get to the Passo Giau, you can catch a bus from Cortina to Pocol and then take a taxi. A family walk is detailed below.

Mountain bikers can hire bikes from the **Centro Mountain Bike** *(☎ 0436 56 15; upwards of €5.15/25.80 per hour/day; open 8.30am-7pm)* in Fiames. The **Centro Sportivo Cortina** *(☎ 0436 27 08, Via Roma 91c)* in Cortina runs biking, rafting and summer skiing expeditions.

Places to Stay

International Camping Olympia *(☎ 0436 50 57, 3.5km north of Cortina in Fiames)* Sites per person/tent & car from €4.15 & €8.80. Open year-round. Pitch your tent at 1283m at this friendly site or book well ahead and snag one of 25 beds in a bungalow.

Pensione Fiames *(☎ 0436 23 66, fax 0436 75 33, Via Fiames 13)* Low season singles/doubles €23.25/36.15, high season up to €46.50/72.30. This pension, 4km north of Cortina, is about as cheap and basic as it gets.

Hotel Montana *(☎ 0436 86 04 98, fax 0436 86 82 11, e montana@cortina-hotel.com, Corso Italia 94)* Low season singles/doubles €28.40/39.25, high season up to €62/111.55. Bang next to the church, central Montana is an unbeatable two-star deal.

Meuble' Cavallino *(☎ 0436 26 14, fax 0436 87 99 09, Corso Italia 142)* Low season singles/doubles €46.50/71.25, high season up to €112.60/148.75. Another Cortina bargain in the heart of the town, Cavallino touts a cosy wooden interior.

Places to Eat

Villa Sandi *(☎ 0436 51 25, Largo Poste 1).* For a stiff shot or heart-warming tipple of wine, dive into this tiny and authentic wine cellar. Even locals have been known to drink here.

Pizzeria Croda Café *(☎ 0436 86 65 89, Corso Italia 163)* This place has reasonably priced meals; big salads cost €8.80.

El Bronzin *(☎ 0436 86 70 51, Via Roma 47)* Full meals about €18.10. This place is a good pizzeria.

El Zoco *(☎ 0436 86 00 41, Via Cademai 18)* Full meals about €25.80. El Zoco specialises in grills.

Stock up on power snacks to munch on the slopes at the ***Standa*** supermarket *(Via Franchetti)*.

Getting There & Away

Cortina's bus station is on Via Marconi. SAD buses connect Cortina with Dobbiaco, where you can change for Brunico and Bolzano. Dolomiti buses run to Belluno, Pocol and Passo Falzarego. There are also bus services to Venice (4½ hours, one daily), run by ATVO (☎ 0436 86 79 21), which has a Web site at W www.atvo.it. Zani runs services to Bologna and Milan. Local services connect the town with International Camping Olympia at Fiames and Pocol.

As mentioned in the walk to Ra Stua, a minibus service connects Fiames with the Rifugio Malga Ra Stua from 8am to 6pm, mid-July to mid-September.

A special service for mountain bikers and their bikes also runs from Fiames to various locations. Call ☎ 0436 86 70 88 for information.

VALZOLDANA

Valzoldana lies a mere 20km south of Cortina, south of the imposing Civetta (3220m) and Pelmo (3168m) groups, yet it has none of the tourist trappings displayed by its more illustrious neighbour. Until the 19th century, the Zoldani made their living by exploiting the local resources – metal deposits and water – to make nails for the Venetian Republic; until 1890, that is, when a flood destroyed their makeshift smithies. Many people left the region and emigrated to Munich and Vienna, setting up as travelling ice-cream and sorbet salesmen; today many of their descendants run famous ice-cream parlours the world over. Since the 1970s the profits from these commercial activities have fostered the growth of the tourism industry.

Information

For details of summer and winter activities and accommodation, go to the APT Valzoldana office in Forno di Zoldo (☎ 0437 78 73 49) or in Zoldo Alto (☎ 0437 78 91 45). Online, try W www.dolomiti.it.

Activities

Modern **ski runs** hug the Civetta group at Zoldo Alto. Eighty kilometres of runs link the valley to the Dolomiti Superski network, allowing skiers to reach the Sella and Marmolada groups. In the lower valley around Forno di Zoldo, the landscape is unchanged, the prices and crowds have been kept under control and the food is authentic and excellent.

Walkers might like to take advantage of the extensive network of paths in the area. In six days you can do a round trip through unspoiled woodland beneath the peaks of less 'famous' mountains such as Sfornioi, Bosconero and Pramper.

Places to Stay

There are numerous hotels and camp sites in the valley. Walkers can ask at the tourist office about the ***Rifugio Casera di Bosconero***, which has a handful of dorm beds too. At 1457m, in the conifer forest at the foot of the mountain of the same name, it is accessible from Forno on the path marked 490A (three to four hours), or from Lago di Pontesi on paths 490 or 485 (two to three hours).

Hotel Corinna *(☎ 0437 7 85 64, fax 0437 78 75 93, e corinna@dolomiti.it, Via ai Pez 3)* Singles/doubles up to €54/92.95, half-board singles/doubles €64/112. This very friendly hotel run by efficient staff is at Forno di Zoldo (elevation 850m).

Hotel Corona *(☎ 0437 78 92 90, fax 0437 78 94 90, Viale Dolomiti 11)* Half-board about €56.80. This three-star wonder is a pleasant, Alpine option with a terrace offering stunning views.

Getting There & Away

The valley is served by the S251 that descends from the Forcella Staulanza pass (1789m) in the north to Longarone in the south-east. Coming from the south, leave the S51 at Longarone, following signs to Cortina, and then turn left onto the S251.

VAL PUSTERIA & THE SESTO DOLOMITES

On the Dolomites' northern edge, the Val Pusteria (Pustertal) is bordered by the magnificent Parco Naturale di Fanes-Sennes-Braies and, farther north, by the Parco Naturale delle Dolomiti di Sesto, which includes some of the area's most famous peaks – among them the Tre Cime di Lavaredo (Drei Zinnen). The valley is easily reached from the Val Badia and Cortina d'Ampezzo along the spectacular Valle di Landro (Höhlensteintal). Its main centre is Brunico (Bruneck), a pleasant market town, which neighbours the tiny ski resort of Plan de Corones (Kronplatz; elevation 2275m) and sports excellent transport connections for excursions into Fanes-Sennes-Braies. More picturesque options are San Candido (Innichen; pop 3200, elevation 1175m) and Sesto (Sexten; pop 1900, elevation 1311m) at the base of the Sesto Dolomites.

Information

Brunico tourist office (☎ 0474 55 57 22, fax 0474 55 55 44, Ⓦ www.bruneck.com), adjoining the bus station at Via Europa 26, opens 9am to 12.30pm and 3pm to 6pm Monday to Friday, and 9am to noon Saturday. Its counterpart in San Candido (☎ 0474 91 31 49), Piazza del Magistrato, opens 8am to noon and 2pm to 6pm Monday to Saturday, and 10am to noon Sunday. Sesto tourist office (☎ 0474 71 03 10), Via Dolomiti, shares the same hours.

Activities

Easy to get to from the Val Pusteria is beautiful Lago di Braies, a perfect spot for a picnic and a leisurely lakeside stroll. More serious walkers might like to tackle part of the Alta Via No 1, which starts here. The Fanes-Sennes-Braies park is more easily approached from the Val Badia or from Passo Falzarego.

At the other end of the valley, towards Austria, are the Sesto Dolomites, where there are some spectacular trails. The **Valle Campo di Dentro** (Innerfeldtal), near San Candido, and the **Val Fiscalina** (Fischleintal), near Sesto, are criss-crossed with trails – both **walking** and **cross-country skiing**. From the Val Fiscalina, it's a long but easy walk along trail No 102 to Rifugio Locatelli (Drei Zinnen-Hütte; elevation 2405m), from where you will be able to get a great view of the **Tre Cime di Lavaredo**. Most trails around the Tre Cime are easy enough for first-time walkers and families, although they become rather like motorways in July and August when paths get packed with walkers on the tourist trail.

May to October, adventure seekers can take a watery spin on a raft with **Rafting Club Activ** *(☎ 0474 67 84 22, Via Valle Aurina/Ahrntalerstrasse 22)*, some 12km north of Brunico in Campo Tures (Sand in Taufers). River **kayaking**, **canyoning** and **waterfall climbing** are among the wet activities run by the club. Count on paying about €40 per person for a half-day of **white-water rafting**; equivalent trips for kids along the tame River Ahr cost from €15. Alternatively, take to the skies with the paragliding school **Free Sky Paragliding** *(☎ 0474 91 34 88, ⓔ alpinschule@dnet.it, Via Schranzhofer 7, Brunico)*.

Plan de Corones, some 4km south of Brunico, sports ample green and blue runs, making it ideal for beginners. The station is linked by cable car to Brunico. Ski passes cost up to €29.45/57.85 for one/three days, and the Dolomiti Superski pass is also valid. Gear can be hired in Brunico and Plan de Corones. More information is online at Ⓦ www.kronplatz.com.

Sportler *(☎ 0474 55 60 23, Via Centrale/Stadgasse)* in Brunico is an unbeatable sports shop, which sells walking and cycling gear as well as maps and guides.

Places to Stay & Eat

The best places to nap and nosh are located in the peaceful market town of Brunico.

Gasthof-Albergo Oberraut *(☎ 0474 55 99 77, 6km east of Brunico in Perco)* Beds per person €21.70-24.80, including breakfast. Open Fri-Wed. Peace, perfect peace, is what this family-run farmhouse dishes up. Snuggle under huge feather-filled bolsters, feast on deer goulash with polenta (1st/2nd courses €7.25/12.90), breakfast on farm eggs and ham in the *stube* (cosy room with a fireplace) and remind yourself you really are still in Italy.

Berggasthof Amaten-Hotel Amato *(☎/fax 0474 55 99 93, ⓔ g.amaten@jumpy.it, 6km east of Brunico in Perco)* Low season half-board €26.65, high season €35.90. Laze away the day on the flowery terrace of this lovely hotel-restaurant, around the corner from Oberraut and surrounded by green fields.

Blitzburg-Castel Lampo *(☎ 0474 55 57 23, fax 0474 55 57 52, ⓦ www.blitzburg.it, Via Europa 10)* Low season singles/doubles €43.90/46.50, high season up to €49.05/51.65. Castel Lampo is Brunico's travellers' choice, just across from the bus station and flaunting a sunny terrace.

Krone-Corona *(☎ 0474 41 11 08, fax 0474 55 34 25, ⓔ hotel.krone@dnet.it, Via Ragen di Sopra/Oberragen 8)* B&B per person €33.55-49.05. Brunico's old-town choice.

Getting There & Away

By SAD bus you can reach Brunico and San Candido from Bolzano and Merano, the Val Badia and San Vigilio di Marebbe, the Val Gardena (on the Innsbruck bus) and Cortina. Catch a bus from Brunico or San Candido to Dobbiaco, from where you can catch a bus to Lago di Braies. To get to the Rifugio Auronzo at the Tre Cime di Lavaredo, catch the Cortina bus from San Candido or Dobbiaco then, from Cortina, catch the bus for Misurina and the Tre Cime.

The Val Pusteria is reached by train from Bolzano via Fortezza (where a change is necessary). By road, the valley is easily accessible from the Val Badia, from Cortina via the S51 in the Valle di Landro and from the A22.

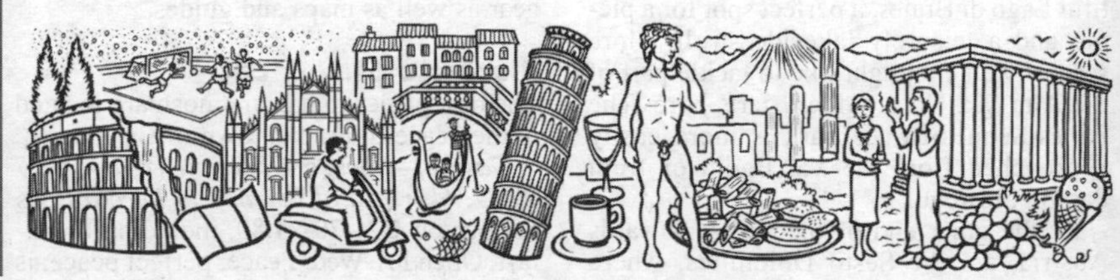

JULIET COOMBE

The colourful, lace-making island of Burano

TONY FANKHAUSER

Dorsoduro, Venice: fancy a room with a view?

DAMIEN SIMONIS

One view of the Santa Croce quarter, Venice

JON DAVISON

Venetian gondaliers find their land legs.

JON DAVISON

Last one to the other side buys the pizzas...

DAMIEN SIMONIS

St Mark's lion flies the Comune di Venezia flag.

JOHN HAY

A painted face mask lights up the Carnevale.

JULIET COOMBE

A lady in red celebrates Carnevale in Venice.

JON DAVISON

Venice: La Serenissima (the Most Serene Republic) lives up to its name.

The Veneto

Most travellers to the Veneto region are so dazzled by Venice that they neglect the rest, which is a shame. You should try to set aside extra days at least to behold Giotto's extraordinary frescoes in Padua and to take in an opera at Verona's Roman Arena.

Vicenza, which was the home town of the architect Palladio, is also well worth a stopover, perhaps on your way to the northern reaches of the Veneto for a visit to Cortina d'Ampezzo, one of the world's most famous ski resorts, and for some walking in the eastern Dolomites.

The region's cuisine is founded on rice and corn. Risotto is cooked with almost everything the countryside and lagoon have to offer – from baby peas to shellfish and game. A local favourite is risotto flavoured with the ink of *seppia* (cuttlefish). The corn-based polenta is fried, served with hearty game stews and included in other main course dishes. One of the Veneto's best-known contributions to the Italian table is *tiramisù*, a rich dessert of mascarpone cheese, coffee, Marsala, sponge and chocolate.

The wine list provides some of Italy's most popular drops, including Soave, a fine white. Bardolino red wines are also widely appreciated. The single most popular local tipple is *prosecco*, a generic bubbly that flows freely in bars across the region. The Bellini, a cocktail of prosecco and fresh peach juice, has come a long way since Giuseppe Cipriani first mixed one at Harry's Bar in Venice in the 1950s.

Getting around is easy. The A4, which runs between Turin and Venice, bisects the region and there is an efficient bus and train network, meaning few parts are out of reach.

Highlights

- Lose yourself in the back lanes and canals of Venice
- Visit the lagoon islands of colourful Burano and peaceful Torcello
- Tuck in to a good seafood meal in one of Venice's osterias
- Marvel at the mosaics of St Mark's Basilica
- Take a tour of Palladio's villas, from the Brenta to Vicenza
- Catch an opera at Verona's Roman Arena
- Walk in the Dolomites or ski at fashionable Cortina d'Ampezzo

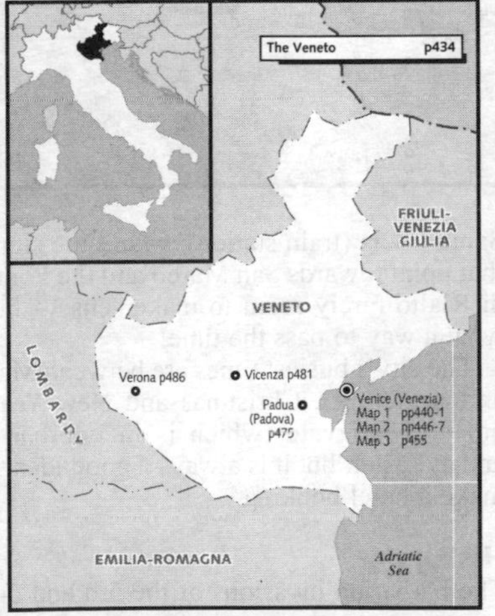

Venice (Venezia)

postcode 30100 • pop 65,909 (274,580 including mainland)

Perhaps no other city in the world has inspired the many superlatives heaped upon Venice by writers and travellers through the centuries.

Forget that Venice is no longer a great maritime republic and that its buildings are in serious decay and constantly threatened by rising tides. Today, Byron might be reluctant to take his daily swim along the now too-dirty Grand Canal (Canal Grande) but

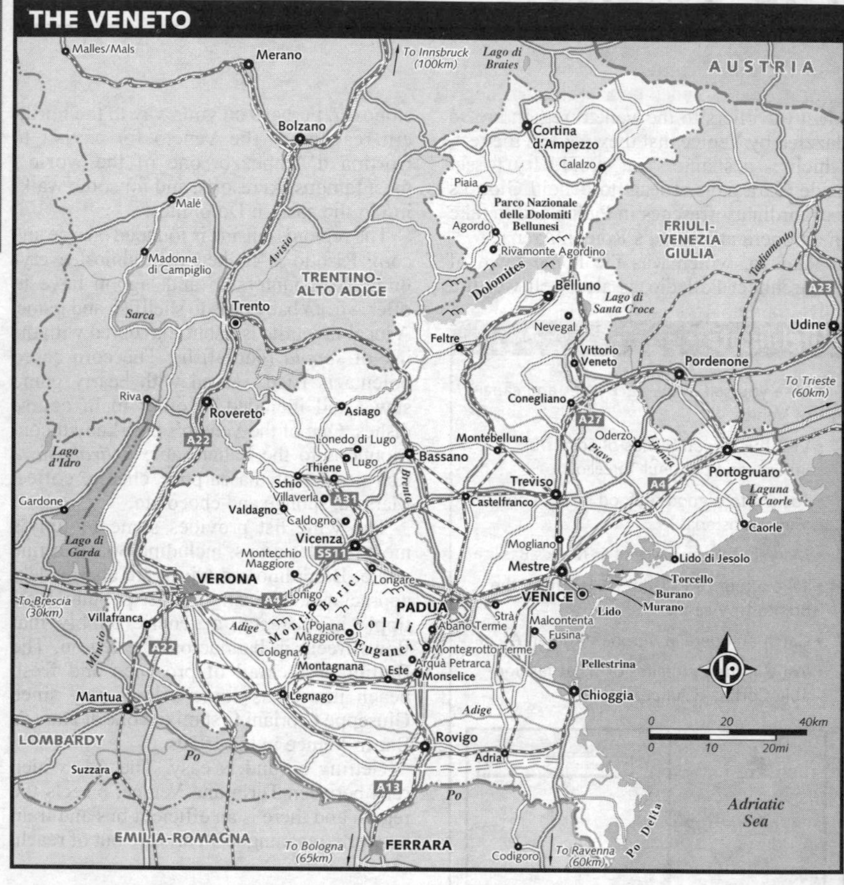

the thoughts of Henry James are as true as they were a century ago: 'Dear old Venice has lost her complexion, her figure, her reputation, her self-respect; and yet, with it all, has so puzzlingly not lost a shred of her distinction.' La Serenissima (Most Serene Republic), remains a singular phenomenon.

The secret to seeing and discovering the real romance and beauty of Venice is to *walk*. Parts of Cannaregio, Dorsoduro and Castello are empty of tourists, even in the high season. You can become lost for hours in the narrow, winding streets between the Ponte dell'Accademia and Stazione di Santa Lucia (train station), where the signs that point towards San Marco and the Ponte di Rialto rarely seem to make sense – but what a way to pass the time!

The city's busiest times are between May and September, Christmas and New Year, during Carnevale (which is in February) and at Easter, but it is always a good idea to make a hotel booking.

History

The barbarian invasions of the 5th and 6th centuries saw the people from the Roman towns of the Veneto and along the Adriatic

Sea flee to the marshy islands of the Venetian lagoon.

In the 6th century the islands began to form a type of federation, with each community electing representatives to a central authority, although its leaders were actually under the control of the Byzantine rulers in Ravenna. Byzantium's hold over Italy weakened in the early 8th century and in AD 726 the people of Venice elected their first *doge*, a type of magistrate, whose successors would lead the city for more than 1000 years.

By the late 10th century, Venice had become an important trading city and a great power in the Mediterranean, prospering out of the chaos caused by the First Crusade launched in 1095. The city continued to profit from the crusades during the 12th century and at the beginning of the 13th century, under Doge Enrico Dandolo, Venice led the Fourth Crusade to Constantinople. Venice not only kept most of the treasures plundered from that great city, it also kept most of the territories won during the crusade, consolidating a maritime might that made it the envy of other powers. In 1271, Venetian merchant and explorer Marco Polo set out on his overland trip to China, returning by sea over 20 years later.

During much of the 13th and 14th centuries, the Venetians struggled with Genoa for maritime supremacy, a tussle that culminated in Genoa's defeat in 1380 during an epic siege at Chioggia. Their maritime power consolidated, the Venetians turned their attentions to dominating the mainland, capturing most of the Veneto and portions of what are now Lombardy and Emilia-Romagna.

However, events beyond Venetian control began to have a telling effect on the lagoon city. The increasing power of the Turks forced the Venetians to deploy forces to protect their Mediterranean interests. The fall of Constantinople in 1453 and the Venetian territory of Morea (Greece) in 1499 gave the Turks control of access to the Adriatic Sea.

At about the same time, the rounding of Africa's Cape of Good Hope in 1498 by the Portuguese explorer Vasco da Gama opened an alternative trade route to Asia, thus allowing European importers to avoid the Mediterranean and the taxes imposed on passing goods through intermediaries such as Venice.

But Venice remained a formidable power. At home, the doges, the Signoria and the much-feared judicial Consiglio dei Dieci (Council of Ten), which was responsible for internal security, ruled with an iron fist. They headed a complex system of councils and government committees, of which the Maggior Consiglio (Great Council) was the equivalent of parliament. The doge, an elected leader, was the figurehead of state and generally the most powerful individual in government, but the complex set of checks and balances put in place over the years limited his power and ensured that Venice was ruled by its aristocracy. A decree of 1297 virtually closed off membership of the Maggior Consiglio to all but the most established of patriarchal families, making Venice a tightly knit oligarchy.

For the security of the state, all Venetians were encouraged to spy on other Venetians in every city, port and country where the Venetian Republic had an interest. Acts considered detrimental to the interests of the state were punished swiftly and brutally. Public trials and executions were rare; a body would just turn up on the street as an example to other potentially wayward citizens.

Venice was remarkably cosmopolitan, its commerce attracting people of all nationalities. And although Venice limited the commercial and social activities of its Jewish community, which it concentrated in one of Europe's earliest ghettos, it did nothing to stifle the Jewish religion. Similarly, the Armenians were permitted religious freedom for centuries and given protection during the Inquisition.

The city's wealth was made all the more conspicuous by the luxury goods traded and produced there. Venice had a European monopoly on the making of what is now known as Murano glass, its merchants had reintroduced the art of making mosaics, and Venetian artisans made fine silks and lace.

But even as her people wallowed in their well-being, Venice was on the wane. The

Turks and the Vatican States made gains at the Republic's expense during the 16th and 17th centuries and in 1669 Venice lost Crete to the Turks after a 25-year battle – its last stronghold in the Mediterranean was gone.

Finally, in 1797 the Maggior Consiglio abolished the constitution and opened the city's gates to Napoleon, who in turn handed Venice to the Austrians. Napoleon returned in 1805, incorporating the city into his Kingdom of Italy, but it reverted to Austria after his fall. The movement for Italian unification spread quickly through the Veneto and, after several rebellions, Venice was united with the Kingdom of Italy in 1866. The city was bombed during WWI but suffered only minor damage during WWII, when most attacks were aimed at the neighbouring industrial zones of Mestre and Porto Marghera.

The city's prestige as a tourist destination grew during the 19th century as it was surpassed as a trade port by Trieste. Today, Venice's modest permanent population (less than half that of the 1950s) is swollen by up to 20 million visitors every year, the majority of them day-trippers.

Orientation

Venice is built on 117 small islands and has some 150 canals and 409 bridges. Only three

Acque Alte

Venice can be flooded by high tides during winter. Known as *acque alte*, these mainly occur between November and April, flooding low-lying areas of the city such as St Mark's Square (Piazza San Marco). The serious floods are announced several hours before they reach their high point by the sounding of 16 sirens throughout the city and islands.

In some areas you can see the water rising up over the canal border, although most of the water actually bubbles up through drains. The best thing to do is buy a pair of *stivali di gomma* (Wellington boots; gumboots) and continue sightseeing. *Passerelle* (raised walkways) are set up in St Mark's Square and other major tourist areas of the city (you can pick up a brochure with a map of the passerelle at the tourist office) and the floods usually last only a few hours. If the flood level exceeds 1.2m, then you can be in trouble as even the walkways are no use at that level.

Venice's flooding problems are compounded by the fact that the city has actually sunk by 23cm in the past hundred years. Another major concern is that the waters of the canals are incredibly polluted. Until 20 years ago, the Adriatic Sea's natural tidal currents flushed the lagoons and kept the canals relatively clean. But the dredging of a 14m-deep canal in the 1960s, to allow tankers access to the giant refinery at Porto Marghera, changed the currents. Work is now underway to clean the sludge from the city canals.

As though all this was not enough, the salt water – even when unpolluted – is corroding the city's foundations. Alarm bells are ringing and the city fathers have warned that if efforts are not made to counteract the corrosion, canalside buildings could start to collapse.

The Mose (Modulo Sperimentale Elettromeccanico) plan to install three massive floodgates at the main entrances to the lagoon was first approved by the Italian government in the 1980s but never seems to get past the starting line. After finally getting approval from various commissions in 1998, the plan was stopped again in December when left-wing and Green politicians in Venice said the US$2.5 billion plan required further study, as its environmental impact on the lagoon was still unknown. The Ministry of the Environment in Rome put its rubber stamp to the doubts (again!) and said no.

Supporters of the project, such as the present mayor and former public works minister, Paolo Costa, claim the city will be submerged by the end of the 21st century if nothing is done. The Greens say the funds for the project (which would require up to US$10 million worth of maintenance annually) would be better spent cleaning up chemical and oil pollution in the lagoon and dredging silted-up canals. The foot dragging goes on apace.

bridges cross the Grand Canal: the Ponte di Rialto, the Ponte dell'Accademia and the Ponte degli Scalzi.

Stretching away to the north and south are the shallow waters of the Laguna Veneta, dotted by what seems a crumbling mosaic of islands, islets and rocks. Among them, Murano, Burano and Torcello are all of interest and lie to the north. Acting as a breakwater to the east, the long and slender Lido di Venezia stretches some 10km south, followed by another similarly narrow island, Pellestrina, which reaches down to the sleepy town of Chioggia. The latter marks where the mainland closes off the lagoon to the south.

The city is divided into six quarters *(sestieri)*: Cannaregio, Castello, San Marco, Dorsoduro, San Polo and Santa Croce. These town divisions date back to 1171. In the east, the islands of San Pietro and Sant' Elena, largely ignored by visitors, are attached to Castello by two and three bridges respectively.

You can drive your car *to* Venice and park it but there is nowhere to drive once you arrive. Ferries also transport cars to the

A Street by Any Other Name

If you have travelled elsewhere in Italy and got to grips with common street terminology, abandon all hope ye who enter here. Why? Well, Venice always thought of itself as something quite apart from the rest of the peninsula and seemingly this applied even to street naming. The names for the types of street in use today go back to the 11th century.

Of course, the waterways are not streets at all. The main ones are called *canale*, while the bulk of them are called *rio*. Where a rio has been filled in it becomes a *rio terrà* or *rio terà*.

What anywhere else in Italy would be called a *via* (street) is, in Venice, a *calle*. A street beside a canal is called a *fondamenta*. A *ruga* or *rughetta* is a smaller street flanked by houses and shops, while those called *salizzada* (sometimes spelled with one 'z') were among the first streets to be paved. A *ramo* is a tiny side lane, often connecting two bigger streets. A *corte* is a small dead-end street or courtyard. A quay is a *riva* and where a street passes under a building (something like an extended archway) it is called a *sotoportego*. A *piscina* is not a swimming pool but a one-time little lake of motionless water later filled in.

The only square in Venice called a *piazza* is San Marco (St Mark's Square), all the others are called *campo* (except for the bus station area, which is called Piazzale Roma). The small version is a *campiello*. Occasionally you come across a *campazzo*. On maps you may see the following abbreviations:

Calle – C, Cl
Campo – Cpo
Corte – Cte
Fondamenta – Fond, Fondam, F
Palazzo – Pal
Salizzada – Sal, Salizz

Street Numbering

Confused? You will be. Venice also has its own style of street numbering. Instead of a system based on individual streets, each *sestiere* (quarter) has a long series of numbers. For instance, a hotel might give its address as San Marco 4687, which doesn't seem to help much. This system of numbering was actually introduced by the Austrians in 1841. Because the *sestieri* are fairly small, wandering around and searching out the number is technically feasible and sometimes doesn't take that long. But there is precious little apparent logic to the run of numbers – frustration is never far away. Most streets are named, so where possible we provide street names as well as the sestiere number throughout the guide.

See also Maps later for other suggestions on navigational aids.

Lido, where they can be driven (although buses are more than adequate there). In Venice itself all public transport is by *vaporetto* (small passenger boat/ferry) along the canals. To cross the Grand Canal between the bridges, use a *traghetto* (ferry), a cheap way to get a short gondola ride. Signs will direct you to the traghetto points.

The alternative is to go *a piedi* (on foot). To walk from the train station to St Mark's Square (Piazza San Marco) will take a good half-hour – follow the signs to San Marco.

From San Marco, the routes to other main areas, such as the Rialto, Accademia and the train station, are well signposted but can be confusing, particularly in the Dorsoduro and San Polo areas.

Maps One of the best maps is the wine-red covered *Venezia* (€5.20), produced by the Touring Club Italiano, which displays the city on a scale of 1:5000. They also produce a cheap paper map (€2.30) of the *Centro Storico* (Historic Centre). Another reasonable one is the yellow FMB map, *Venezia* (€5.20), which lists all street names with map references.

Information

Tourist Offices APT offices have information on the town and the province. There is one central information line in Venice (☎ 041 529 87 11; fax 041 523 03 99).

The main APT office is at Piazza San Marco 71/f (Map 2). Staff will assist with information on hotels, transport and things to see and do in the city. The office opens 9.45am to 3.15pm Monday to Saturday. Another office, or Infopoint (Map 2), opens 9am to 6pm daily in the so-called Venice Pavilion (ex-Palazzina dei Santi) next to the Giardini Ex Reali, a quick walk from St Mark's Square.

The smaller office at the train station (Map 2) opens 8am to 8pm. Next door to the Garage Comunale in Piazzale Roma is

Saving Venice

Floods, neglect, pollution and many other factors have contributed to the degeneration of Venice's monuments and artworks. Since 1969 however, a group of private international organisations, under the aegis of UNESCO, has worked to repair the damage.

The Joint UNESCO-Private Committees Programme for the Safeguarding of Venice has raised millions of dollars for restoration work in the city; between 1969 and 2000 more than 100 monuments and 1000 works of art were restored.

Major restoration projects completed including the Chiesa di Madonna dell'Orto, the facade of the Chiesa di San Zulian, the Chiesa di San Francesco della Vigna, the Chiesa di Santa Maria Formosa and the Chiesa di San Nicolò dei Mendicoli, the Basilica di Santa Maria Assunta on Torcello and, more recently, the old Jewish cemetery on the Lido (opened to the public in 1999).

Funding for the programme comes from 29 private and charitable organisations from Italy and a dozen other countries. Apart from restoration work, the programme also finances specialist courses for trainee restorers in Venice. Among the higher-profile groups involved in the effort are the UK's Venice in Peril Fund, chaired by Lord Norwich, perhaps the greatest historian of Venice writing in English. The sources of their funding are numerous – the UK restaurant chain, Pizza Express, for example, has raised hundreds of thousands of pounds (UK£64,000 in 1999) by adding a discretionary 25p charge to its Veneziana pizzas. For UK£50 a year you can join Venice in Peril (☎ 020-7636 6138, fax 7636 6139, W www.veniceinperil.org), Morley House, 314–322 Regent St, London W1R 5AB. The fund is presently helping to restore the Emiliana chapel on San Michele.

Important though the work of these organisations is in keeping Venice's difficulties in the public eye, more than 90% of the finance for restoration and related projects in Venice since 1966 has come from the Italian government.

another APT office (Map 1) which opens 9am to 6pm daily. There are also offices on the Lido, at Gran Viale Santa Maria Elisabetta 6/a (summer only), and at the airport. In Mestre, there's an office (☎ 041 97 53 57) at Corso del Popolo 65.

The useful monthly booklet *Un Ospite di Venezia* (A Guest of Venice), published by a group of Venetian hoteliers, is sometimes available from tourist offices. If not, you can find it in most of the larger hotels. Similar but a little less informative is *Pocket Venice*, sometimes available from tourist offices.

If you have a complaint to make about services poorly rendered (in hotels, restaurants, water taxis and the like), the APT operates a 24-hour tourist helpline. Call ☎ 800 35 59 20 and follow the instructions.

InformaGiovani can provide information ranging from assistance for the disabled to courses offered in the city. It has a branch in the Assessorato alla Gioventù (see the boxed text 'Discounts on Admission' later).

Money Most of the main banks are in the area around Ponte di Rialto and San Marco. There are numerous bureaux de change across the city and at the train station. Compare rates and commissions before parting with your hard-earned cash.

The American Express office (Map 2; ☎ 041 520 08 44) is on Salizzada San Moisè. The postal address is San Marco 1471. For AmEx cardholders, there's an ATM *(bancomat)*. The office opens 9am to 5.30pm Monday to Friday and 9am to 12.30pm on Saturday. Thomas Cook has two offices, one at Piazza San Marco 142 (Map 2; ☎ 041 522 47 51) and the other at Riva del Ferro 5126 (Map 2; ☎ 041 528 73 58), near Ponte di Rialto. They open 8.45am to 8pm Monday to Saturday and 9am to 6pm on Sunday.

Post & Communications The main post office is on Salizzada del Fondaco dei Tedeschi (Map 2), just near the Ponte di Rialto. It opens 8.10am to 7pm Monday to Saturday. Stamps are available at window Nos 1 to 4 in the central courtyard.

There is an unstaffed Telecom office (Map 2) next to the post office and a bank of telephones nearby on Calle Galeazza (Map 2). Other unstaffed offices can be found on Strada Nuova, on the corner of Corte dei Pali, in Cannaregio (Map 2); Ruga Vecchia San Giovanni 480, in San Polo (Map 2); and Calle San Luca 4585, in San Marco (Map 2). You will also find phones at the train station.

There are numerous Internet cafes in Venice.

Chips & Colors (Map 1; ☎ 041 277 05 83) Via G Garibaldi 1592, Castello. This oddly named place is part Internet cafe and part shop selling all manner of odd bits and pieces. You pay €7.20 per hour. It opens 10am to 2pm and 3.30pm to 10pm Monday to Saturday, 3.30pm to 10pm on Sunday.

Internet Café (Map 2; ☎ 041 524 12 00, fax 041 275 69 34) Ramo Chioverette 664/c, Santa Croce. In spite of the name, there is no coffee. An hour online costs €7.20. It opens 8.30am to 1pm and 3pm to 7.30pm Monday to Friday, 8.30am to 1pm on Saturday.

Internet Point (Map 2; ☎ 041 71 04 70) Ramo de la Donzela 888, San Polo. An hour online costs €6.20. It opens 8.30am to 12.30pm and 3.30pm to 7pm Monday to Friday, 8.30am to 12.30pm on Saturday.

Net House (Map 2; ☎ 041 277 11 90) Campo Santo Stefano 2958–2967, San Marco. You can sip cocktails, eat sandwiches, slug Irish beers and/or go online here, where they (claim to) open 24 hours. It costs a minimum €2.60 for the first 20 minutes and €0.15 for every minute thereafter.

Omniservice Internet Café (Map 2; ☎ 041 71 04 70) Fondamenta dei Tolentini 220, Santa Croce. An hour online costs €5.20. It opens 8am to 10pm daily.

Planet Internet (Map 2; ☎ 041 524 41 88) Rio Terrà San Leonardo 1519, Cannaregio. An hour online costs €8.30. It opens 9am to midnight daily.

The Netgate (Map 2; ☎ 041 244 02 13, W www.thenetgate.it), Calle dei Preti Crosera 3812/a, Dorsoduro. An hour online costs €5.20. It opens 10.15am to 8pm Monday to Friday, 10.15am to 10pm Saturday, 2.15pm to 10pm on Sunday.

Travel Agencies For budget student travel, contact the Centro Turistico Studentesco e Giovanile (CTS; Map 2; ☎ 041 520 56 60, W www.cts.it), Calle Foscari 3252, Dorsoduro.

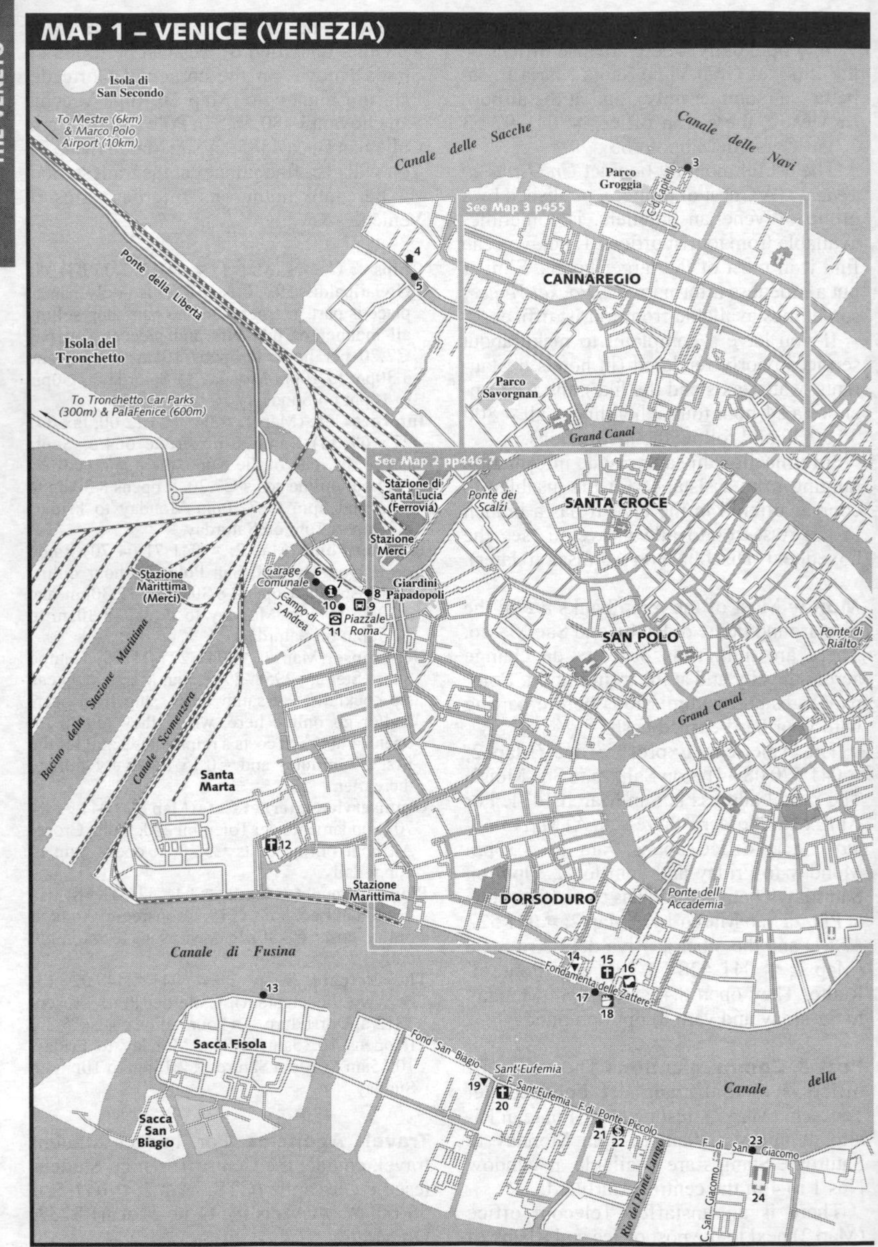
MAP 1 – VENICE (VENEZIA)
Isola di San Secondo
To Mestre (6km) & Marco Polo Airport (10km)
Canale delle Sacche
Canale delle Navi
Parco Groggia
C.d.Capitello
See Map 3 p455
CANNAREGIO
Ponte della Libertà
Isola del Tronchetto
To Tronchetto Car Parks (300m) & PalaFenice (600m)
Parco Savorgnan
Grand Canal
See Map 2 pp446-7
Stazione di Santa Lucia (Ferrovia)
Ponte dei Scalzi
SANTA CROCE
Stazione Merci
Garage Comunale
Giardini Papadopoli
Stazione Marittima (Merci)
Campo di S Andrea
Piazzale Roma
SAN POLO
Ponte di Rialto
Bacino della Stazione Marittima
Canale Scomenzera
Grand Canal
Santa Marta
Stazione Marittima
DORSODURO
Ponte dell' Accademia
Canale di Fusina
Fondamenta delle Zattere
Sacca Fisola
Fond San Biagio
Sant'Eufemia
F. Sant'Eufemia
F. di Ponte Piccolo
Canale della
Sacca San Biagio
Rio del Ponte Lungo
F. di San Giacomo
C. San Giacomo

VENICE (VENEZIA) – MAP 1

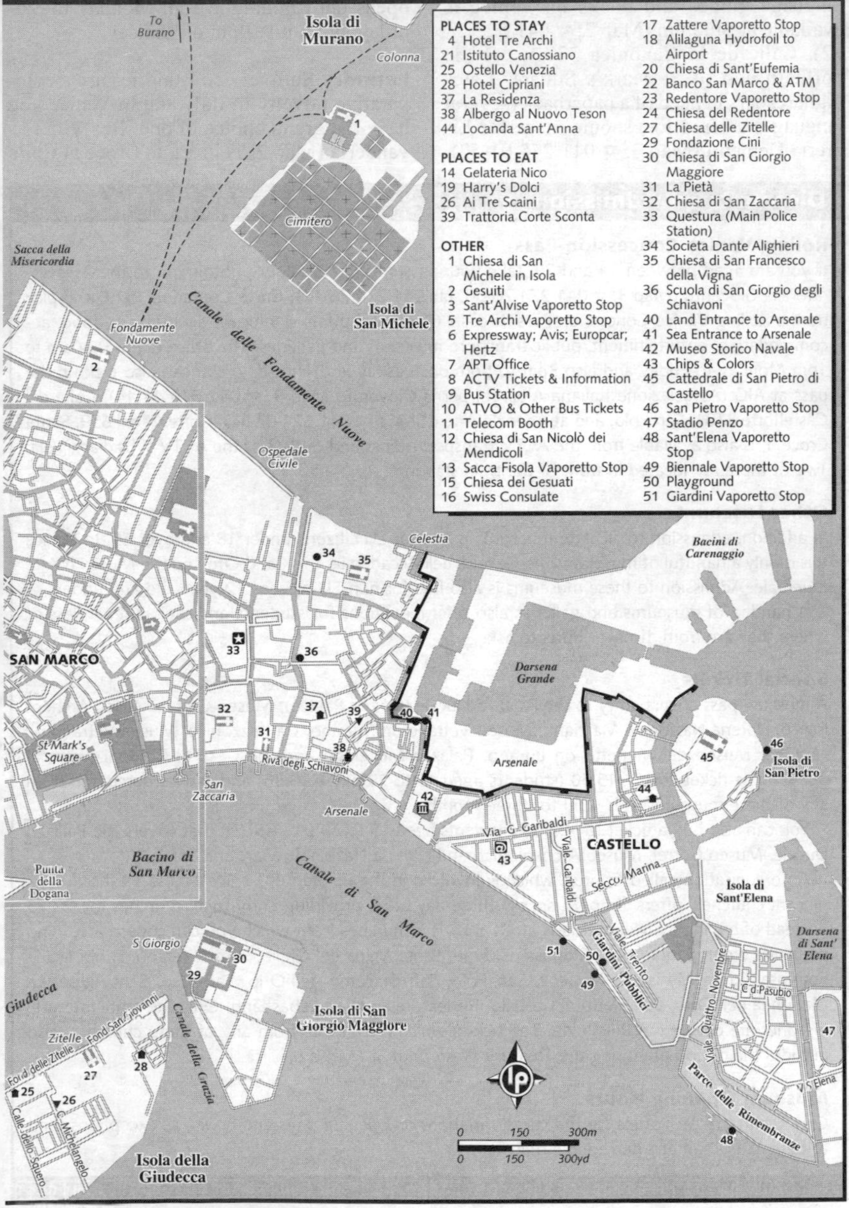

PLACES TO STAY
4 Hotel Tre Archi
21 Istituto Canossiano
25 Ostello Venezia
28 Hotel Cipriani
37 La Residenza
38 Albergo al Nuovo Teson
44 Locanda Sant'Anna

PLACES TO EAT
14 Gelateria Nico
19 Harry's Dolci
26 Ai Tre Scaini
39 Trattoria Corte Sconta

OTHER
1 Chiesa di San Michele in Isola
2 Gesuiti
3 Sant'Alvise Vaporetto Stop
5 Tre Archi Vaporetto Stop
6 Expressway; Avis; Europcar; Hertz
7 APT Office
8 ACTV Tickets & Information
9 Bus Station
10 ATVO & Other Bus Tickets
11 Telecom Booth
12 Chiesa di San Nicolò dei Mendicoli
13 Sacca Fisola Vaporetto Stop
15 Chiesa dei Gesuati
16 Swiss Consulate
17 Zattere Vaporetto Stop
18 Alilaguna Hydrofoil to Airport
20 Chiesa di Sant'Eufemia
22 Banco San Marco & ATM
23 Redentore Vaporetto Stop
24 Chiesa del Redentore
27 Chiesa delle Zitelle
29 Fondazione Cini
30 Chiesa di San Giorgio Maggiore
31 La Pietà
32 Chiesa di San Zaccaria
33 Questura (Main Police Station)
34 Societa Dante Alighieri
35 Chiesa di San Francesco della Vigna
36 Scuola di San Giorgio degli Schiavoni
40 Land Entrance to Arsenale
41 Sea Entrance to Arsenale
42 Museo Storico Navale
43 Chips & Colors
45 Cattedrale di San Pietro di Castello
46 San Pietro Vaporetto Stop
47 Stadio Penzo
48 Sant'Elena Vaporetto Stop
49 Biennale Vaporetto Stop
50 Playground
51 Giardini Vaporetto Stop

To Burano
Isola di Murano
Colonna
Cimitero
Sacca della Misericordia
Isola di San Michele
Fondamente Nuove
Canale delle Fondamente Nuove
Ospedale Civile
Celestia
Bacini di Carenaggio
SAN MARCO
Darsena Grande
St Mark's Square
Riva degli Schiavoni
Arsenale
San Zaccaria
Isola di San Pietro
Via G Garibaldi
CASTELLO
Viale Garibaldi
Secco Marina
Isola di Sant'Elena
Bacino di San Marco
Punta della Dogana
Canale di San Marco
Darsena di Sant' Elena
S Giorgio
Viale Trento
Giardini Pubblici
C d Pasubio
Viale Quattro Novembre
Giudecca
Isola di San Giorgio Maggiore
Fond San Giovanni
Zitelle
Fond delle Zitelle
Canale della Grazia
C Michelangelo
Calle dello Squero
Parco delle Rimembranze
V S Elena
0 150 300m
0 150 300yd
Isola della Giudecca

Bookshops A good selection of English-language guides and books on Venice is available at Studium (Map 2; ☎ 041 522 23 82), Calle de la Canonica 337/a, off the northern end of St Mark's Square. Late-night readers in need of a paperback (several languages catered for) should make for Libreria Demetra (Map 3; ☎ 041 275 01 52), Campo San Geremia 282, Cannaregio. It opens until midnight from Monday to Saturday and until 10pm on Sunday.

Laundry Self-service laundries are a comparative novelty in Italy and in Venice you have the grand choice of one. Bea Vita Lavanderia (Map 2) is in Santa Croce at Calle

Discounts on Admission

Rolling Venice Concession Pass

If you are aged between 14 and 29, take your passport and a colour photograph to the Assessorato alla Gioventù (Map 3; ☎ 041 274 76 50, fax 041 274 76 42), Corte Contarina 1529, and pick up the Rolling Venice Concession Pass. It costs €2.60 and offers significant discounts on food, accommodation, entertainment, public transport, museums and galleries. The office opens 9.30am to 1pm Monday to Friday and also 3pm to 5pm on Tuesday and Thursday. You can also pick up the pass at AIG (Associazione Italiana Alberghi per la Gioventù; Map 3; ☎ 041 520 44 14), Calle del Castelforte 3101, San Polo, and at Agenzia Arte e Storia (☎ 041 524 02 32), Corte Canal 659, Santa Croce. It is also available from the ACTV transport offices and outlets of the ACTV subsidiary, Vela. Two of these are located in front of the train station.

Other Discounts

In addition, admission to all state museums is free for EU citizens under 18 and over 65. In Venice this is only a handful of museums: the Gallerie dell'Accademia, the Ca' d'Oro and the Museo d'Arte Orientale. Admission to these museums is also free for non-EU citizens 12 years old and under.

A handful of museums and galleries also offer reductions for students and seniors regardless of where they are from. It never hurts to ask.

Special Tickets

A museum pass covers entry to the Palazzo Ducale (Doge's Palace), Museo Correr, Museo Archeologico, Libreria Nazionale Marciana, Museo Vetrario on Murano, Ca'Rezzonico, Museo Vetrario on Murano, Museo del Merletto on Burano, Palazzo Mocenigo and the Casa di Goldoni (when it opens). The ticket costs €15.50 (students aged 15 to 29 pay €10.35) and can be purchased from any of these museums. It is valid for three months.

You can also buy a ticket for €9.30 (students aged 15 to 29 pay €5.15) that covers the Palazzo Ducale, Museo Correr, Museo Archeologico and Libreria Nazionale Marciana only.

An organisation called Chorus, which is involved in the upkeep of Venice's most artistically significant churches, offers visitors a special three-day ticket providing entry to all churches for €7.75 (instead of buying individual tickets at €1.55). The churches from which you can choose are, in no particular order: Santa Maria Gloriosa dei Frari, Santa Maria del Giglio, Santo Stefano, Santa Maria Formosa, Santa Maria dei Miracoli, San Polo, San Giacomo dell'Orio, San Stae, Sant'Alvise, La Madonna dell'Orto, San Pietro di Castello, Redentore and San Sebastiano. Only the more interesting ones are covered in this guide. The ticket, which is available from any of these churches, also includes the option of visiting the Treasury (Tesoro) of St Mark's Basilica.

Museum Opening Hours

Check with the APT office for the latest variations on opening days and hours, as exceptions tend to be greater than any perceptible rule.

Chioverette 665/b. You pay €3.10 to wash 8kg and €1.55 for 15 minutes' drying time. It opens 8 am to 10pm daily.

Medical Services & Emergency The Ospedale Civile (hospital; Map 2; ☎ 041 529 41 11) is at Campo SS Giovanni e Paolo. On the mainland, Mestre's modern Ospedale Umberto I (☎ 041 260 71 11) is at Via Circonvallazione 50.

Current information on late-night pharmacies is listed in *Un Ospite di Venezia* and daily newspapers such as *Il Gazzettino* or *La Nuova Venezia*.

The *questura* (police station; ☎ 041 271 57 72) is at Fondamenta di San Lorenzo 5053, Castello.

Lost Property For property lost on trains call ☎ 041 78 52 38. Otherwise call the *vigili urbani* (local police) on ☎ 041 522 45 76.

Grand Canal (Canal Grande)

Described by French writer Philippe de Commines in the 15th century as 'the finest street in the world, with the finest houses', the Grand Canal is a little dilapidated these days but still rivals the world's great boulevards. It weaves for 3.5km through the city like a huge, upside-down 'S', with a depth of about 6m and a width ranging from 40m to 100m. Taking a vaporetto is the only way to see the incredible parade of buildings, including more than 100 palazzos, which date from the 12th to the 18th centuries. Board vaporetto No 1 at Piazzale Roma and try to grab a seat on the deck at the back. For details of the attractions mentioned see later under the relevant areas. Unless otherwise specified you'll find all places mentioned on Map 2.

Not far past the train station and Canale di Cannarcgio (the city's second-largest canal) and just after the Riva di Biasio stop (to the right) is one of the most celebrated Veneto-Byzantine buildings, the **Fondaco dei Turchi**. Once a Turkish warehouse and now the Museo Civico di Storia Naturale (Natural History Museum), it was badly restored in the 19th century. It is recognisable by the three-storey towers on either side of its colonnade.

The canal continues past Rio di San Marcuola to **Palazzo Vendramin-Calergi** (Map 3) on the left. Richard Wagner died here in 1883 and it is now a fine Renaissance winter home for the casino. Farther on and to the right, just after the San Stae stop, is the **Ca' Pesaro**, Baldassare Longhena's Baroque masterpiece (built between 1679 and 1710). Longhena died worrying about the cost and the building was only completed after his death. It houses the Galleria d'Arte Moderna and Museo d'Arte Orientale.

Shortly after, to the left, is the **Ca' d'Oro** (Golden House), acclaimed as the most beautiful Gothic building in Venice. To the right, as the boat turns for the Ponte di Rialto, is the **pescaria** (fish market) on Campo della Pescaria, built in 1907. On the other side of the canal is the **Palazzo Michiel dalle Colonne**, with its distinctive colonnade.

On the right, just after the pescaria, are the **Fabbriche Nuove di Rialto**, built in 1555 by Jacopo Sansovino as a court house. Next door is the city's produce market and then the **Fabbriche Vecchie di Rialto**, built in 1522 to house markets and offices. Just before the Ponte di Rialto, on the left bank, the **Fondaco dei Tedeschi** was once the most important trading house on the canal and now serves as the main post office. It was rebuilt after a fire in 1505 and frescoes by Titian and Giorgione (remnants on view in the Ca' d'Oro) once adorned its facade.

The stone **Ponte di Rialto** was built in the late 16th century by Antonio da Ponte, who won the commission over architects including Palladio in a public competition. The Renaissance **Palazzo Grimani**, on the left after the bridge and just before the Rio di San Luca, was designed by Sanmicheli. Farther along the same bank, the **Palazzo Corner-Spinelli** was designed in the same period by Mauro Cordussi. On the right, as the canal swings sharply to the left, is the late Gothic **Ca' Foscari**, commissioned by Doge Francesco Foscari. One of the finest mansions in the city and seat of the university, it is followed on the left by the 18th century **Palazzo Grassi**. Now owned by Fiat, it is used as a cultural and exhibition centre. Opposite, the massive **Ca' Rezzonico**, designed

Venice in a Nutshell

Uneven alleys turn porticoed corners and end in tiny bridges arched over muddied canals. Others lead nowhere. Still others take you along wider waterways and, often enough, you'll emerge to behold yet another wonder of Venice before you – one of its more than 200 churches or some grand palatial residence. Cheerful osterias are tucked away in the most unlikely spots, colourful markets abound and the bustling main streets throng with crowds of locals and visitors window-shopping, parading or simply racing from A to B.

Venice is unique for many reasons but where else in the world can you immerse yourself in such activity without having your ears assaulted by the roar of cars? Instead, here you are carried along by the tramp of feet, the music of human discourse echoing through the narrow streets and canals, the lap of the water and the hum of the *vaporetti* (small passenger boats/ferries). You could spend months here and never tire of learning your way through the labyrinth. Give yourself as much time as you can.

The main tourist areas are St Mark's Square, the Rialto and the streets of souvenir shops that connect the two, as well as the main thoroughfare linking the train station and St Mark's.

But it is easy enough to escape the crowds – head for the tranquil streets and squares of Dorsoduro and San Polo. While the hordes are cramming into the St Mark's Basilica, you will be virtually alone admiring Tintoretto's paintings in the Scuola Grande di San Rocco or Titian's masterpieces in the adjacent Frari. If you go to the *sestiere* (quarter) of Castello, farther away from San Marco, you'll discover relatively little-visited monuments such as the massive Gothic Chiesa dei SS Giovanni e Paolo. Cannaregio, if you keep away from the main thoroughfare, is also worth exploring.

Before you do anything else, catch the vaporetto No 1 along the Grand Canal, Venice's main 'street' – see the Grand Canal section for a description of the outstanding grand buildings along the waterway.

by Baldassare Longhena, houses the city's collection of 18th-century art.

You are now approaching the last of the canal's three bridges, the wooden **Ponte dell' Accademia**, built in 1930 to replace a metal 19th-century structure. Past it and on the right is the unfinished **Palazzo Venier dei Leoni**, where American heiress Peggy Guggenheim lived until her death in 1979. It is home to her collection of modern art. Two buildings along is the delightful **Palazzo Dario** built in 1487 and recognisable by the multicoloured marble facade and its many chimneys.

On the left bank, at the Santa Maria del Giglio stop, is **Palazzo Corner**, an imposing, ivy-covered residence also known as the Ca' Granda and designed in the mid-16th century by Jacopo Sansovino. On the right, before the canal broadens into the expanse facing San Marco, is Baldassare Longhena's magnificent **Chiesa di Santa Maria della Salute**.

San Marco (Map 2)

St Mark's Square (Piazza San Marco)

Napoleon thought of St Mark's Square as the finest drawing room in Europe. Enclosed by the basilica and the arcaded Procuratie Vecchie and Nuove, the square plays host to competing flocks of pigeons and tourists. Stand and wait for the bronze *Mori* (Moors) to strike the bell of the 15th-century Torre dell'Orologio, which rises (at the time of writing hidden by scaffolding) above the entrance to the Mercerie, the main thoroughfare from San Marco to the Rialto. Or sit and savour a coffee at Florian or Quadri, 18th-century cafes across from each other on the piazza – expect to pay at least €5.20 for a cappuccino (and even more if there is music).

St Mark's Basilica (Basilica di San Marco) The basilica *(☎ 041 522 56 97, Piazza San Marco; open 9.30am-5pm Mon-Sat, 2pm-5pm Sun & holidays)* embodies a magnificent blend of architectural and decorative styles, dominated by the Byzantine and ranging through Romanesque to Renaissance.

Venetian merchants stole the body of St Mark from Alexandria, Egypt, in AD 828 and brought it to Venice for Doge Giustiniano Participazio, who bequeathed a huge sum of money to build a basilica fitting for such an estimable theft. The honourable merchants were doing nothing more than fulfilling a pious portent – for legend had it that an angel once appeared to St Mark and told him he would be laid to rest in Venice.

The original church was destroyed by fire in 932 and rebuilt, but in 1063 Doge Domenico Contarini decided it was poor in comparison to the splendid Romanesque churches being raised in mainland cities and had it demolished.

The new basilica, built on the plan of a Greek cross, with five bulbous domes, was modelled on Constantinople's (later destroyed) Church of the Twelve Apostles and consecrated in 1094. It was actually built as the doges' private chapel and remained so until it became Venice's cathedral in 1807.

For more than 500 years, the doges enlarged and embellished the church, adorning it with an incredible array of treasures plundered from the East, in particular Constantinople, during the crusades.

The arches above the doorways in the **facade** boast fine mosaics. The one on the left, depicting the arrival of St Mark's body in Venice, was completed in 1270. The three arches of the main doorway are decorated with Romanesque carvings, dating from around 1240.

On the *loggia* (balcony) above the main door are copies of four gilded bronze horses; the originals, on display inside, were stolen and brought to Venice when Constantinople was sacked in 1204, during the Fourth Crusade. Napoleon moved them to Paris in 1797 but they were returned following the collapse of the French Empire.

Through the doors is the **narthex**, or vestibule, its domes and arches decorated with mosaics, mainly dating from the 13th century. The oldest mosaics in the basilica, dating from around 1063, are in the niches of the bay in front of the main door from the narthex into the church proper. They feature the Madonna with the Apostles.

The **interior** of the basilica is dazzling; if you can take your eyes off the glitter of the mosaics, take time to admire the 12th-century marble pavement, a geometrical whimsy which has subsided in places, making the floor uneven.

The lower level of the walls is lined with precious eastern marbles and above this decoration the extraordinary feast of gilded **mosaics** begins. Work started on the mosaics in the 11th century and continued until well into the 13th century. Mosaics were added in the 14th and 15th centuries in the baptistry and side chapels and, as late as the 18th century, mosaics were being added or restored.

To the right of the high altar is the entrance to the sanctuary. St Mark's body is contained in a sarcophagus beneath the altar. Behind the altar is the exquisite **Pala d'Oro** *(admission €1.55)*, a gold, enamel and jewel-encrusted altarpiece made in Constantinople for Doge Pietro Orseolo I in 976. It was enriched and reworked in Constantinople in 1105, enlarged by Venetian goldsmiths in 1209 and reset again in the 14th century. Among the almost 2000 precious stones which adorn it are emeralds, rubies, amethysts, sapphires and pearls.

The **Tesoro** *(Treasury; admission €2.10)*, accessible from the right transept, contains most of the booty from the 1204 raid on Constantinople, including a thorn said to be from the crown worn by Christ.

Through a door at the far right end of the narthex is a stairway leading up to the **Galleria** *(aka Museo di San Marco; ☎ 041 522 52 05; admission €1.55; open 9.45am-5pm daily)*, which contains the original gilded bronze horses and the **Loggia dei Cavalli**. The galleria affords wonderful views of the church's interior, while the loggia offers equally splendid vistas of the square.

The mosaics are best seen when illuminated: 11.30am to 12.30pm Monday to Friday and 'all day' at weekends. This 'all day' really means when Mass is said. On Saturday, in particular, there is nothing to say the lights won't go out for a good part of the day when no service is on.

The basilica's 99m-tall **Campanile** *(Bell Tower; admission €5.20; open 9am-9pm daily, late June-Aug; 9am-7pm daily Apr-Jun & Sept-Oct; 9.30am-5.30pm Nov-Mar)*, built in the 10th century, suddenly collapsed on 14 July 1902 and was rebuilt brick by brick.

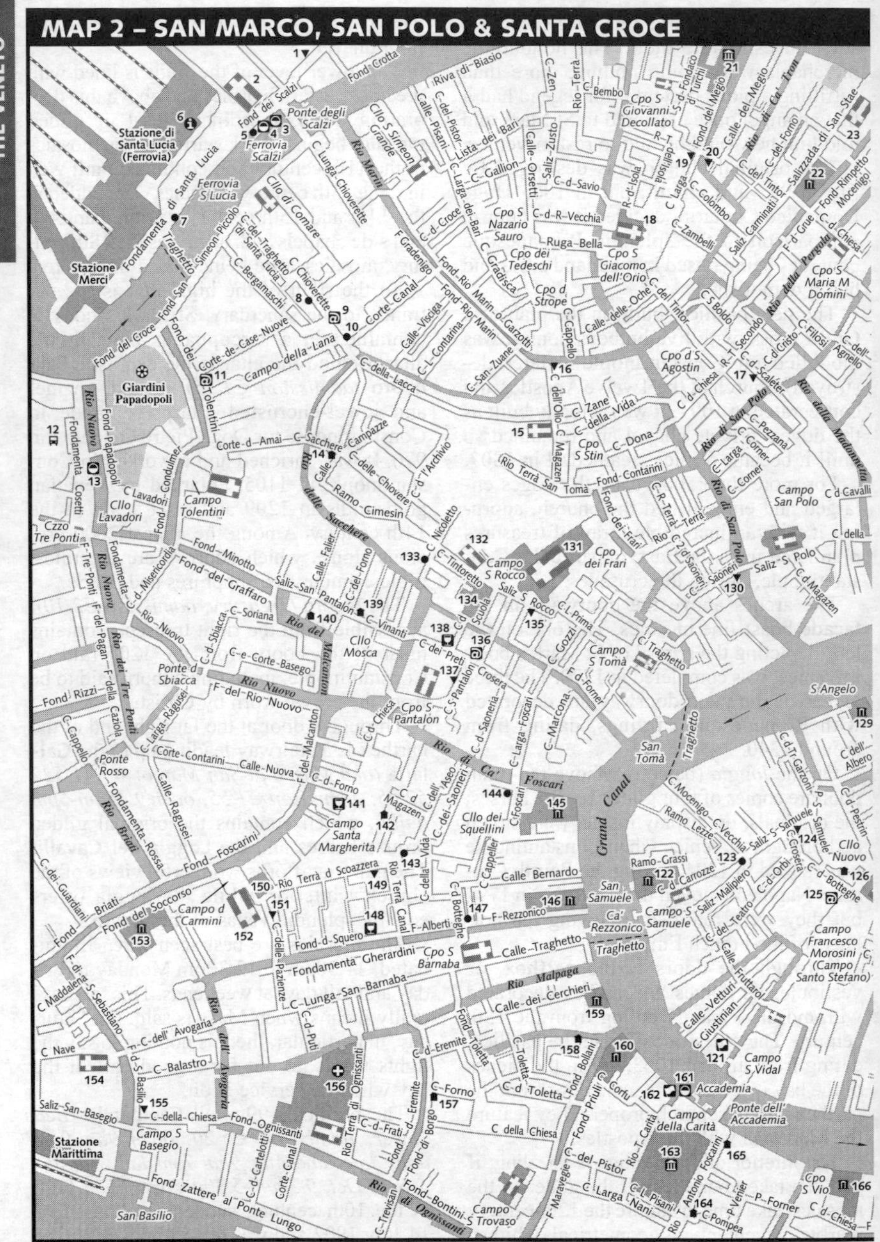
MAP 2 – SAN MARCO, SAN POLO & SANTA CROCE
Stazione di Santa Lucia (Ferrovia)
Ferrovia Scalzi
Ferrovia S Lucia
Ponte degli Scalzi
Fond dei Scalzi
Fond Crotta
Riva di Biasio
Stazione Merci
Fondamenta di Santa Lucia
Giardini Papadopoli
Rio Nuovo
Fond Papadopoli
Campo Tolentini
Tolentini
Campo della Lana
Corte Canal
Corte de Case Nuove
Fond del Croce
Rio Marin
Fond Rio Marin
Fond Rio Marin o Garzotti
F Gradenigo
Cllo S Simeon Grande
Lista dei Bari
C Larga dei Bari
Cpo S Nazario Sauro
Cpo dei Tedeschi
Cpo d Strope
Ruga Bella
Cpo S Giacomo dell'Orio
Calle delle Oche
C del Tintor
Cpo S Giovanni Decollato
Fond del Megio
Calle del Megio
Rio di Ca' Tron
Salizzada di San Stae
Rio della Pergola
Cpo S Maria M Domini
Cpo d S Agostin
Rio di San Polo
Campo San Polo
Rio della Madonnetta
Cpo S Stin
Rio Terà San Tomà
Fond Contarini
Fond dei Frari
Cpo dei Frari
Campo S Rocco
Saliz S Rocco
Campo S Tomà
San Tomà
Traghetto
S Angelo
Rio delle Sacchere
Rio del Malcanton
Saliz San Pantalon
Cllo Mosca
Cpo S Pantalon
Rio di Ca' Foscari
Grand Canal
Cllo dei Squellini
Campo Santa Margherita
Rio Terà Canal
Ponte d Sbiacca
Rio Nuovo
Rio dei Tre Ponti
Czzo Tre Ponti
Fondamenta Cosetti
Cllo Lavadori
Fond Minotto
Fond del Graffaro
Fond Rizzi
Ponte Rosso
Rio Briati
Fondamenta Rossa
Fond Foscarini
Fond del Soccorso
Campo d Carmini
Fond d Squero
Fondamenta Gherardini
Cpo S Barnaba
Calle Traghetto
Rio Malpaga
Calle dei Cerchieri
C Lunga San Barnaba
Rio dell' Avogaria
Ca' Rezzonico
San Samuele
Campo S Samuele
Ramo Grassi
Calle Bernardo
Campo Francesco Morosini (Campo Santo Stefano)
Cllo Nuovo
Campo S Vidal
Accademia
Ponte dell' Accademia
Campo della Carità
Cpo S Vio
Campo S Trovaso
Rio di Ognissanti
Fond Ognissanti
Campo S Basegio
Stazione Marittima
Saliz San Basegio
Fond Zattere al Ponte Lungo
San Basilio
C Maddalena
C Nave
Fond Bontini S Trovaso
C Larga Nani
C Pompea
P Forner

SAN MARCO, SAN POLO & SANTA CROCE – MAP 2

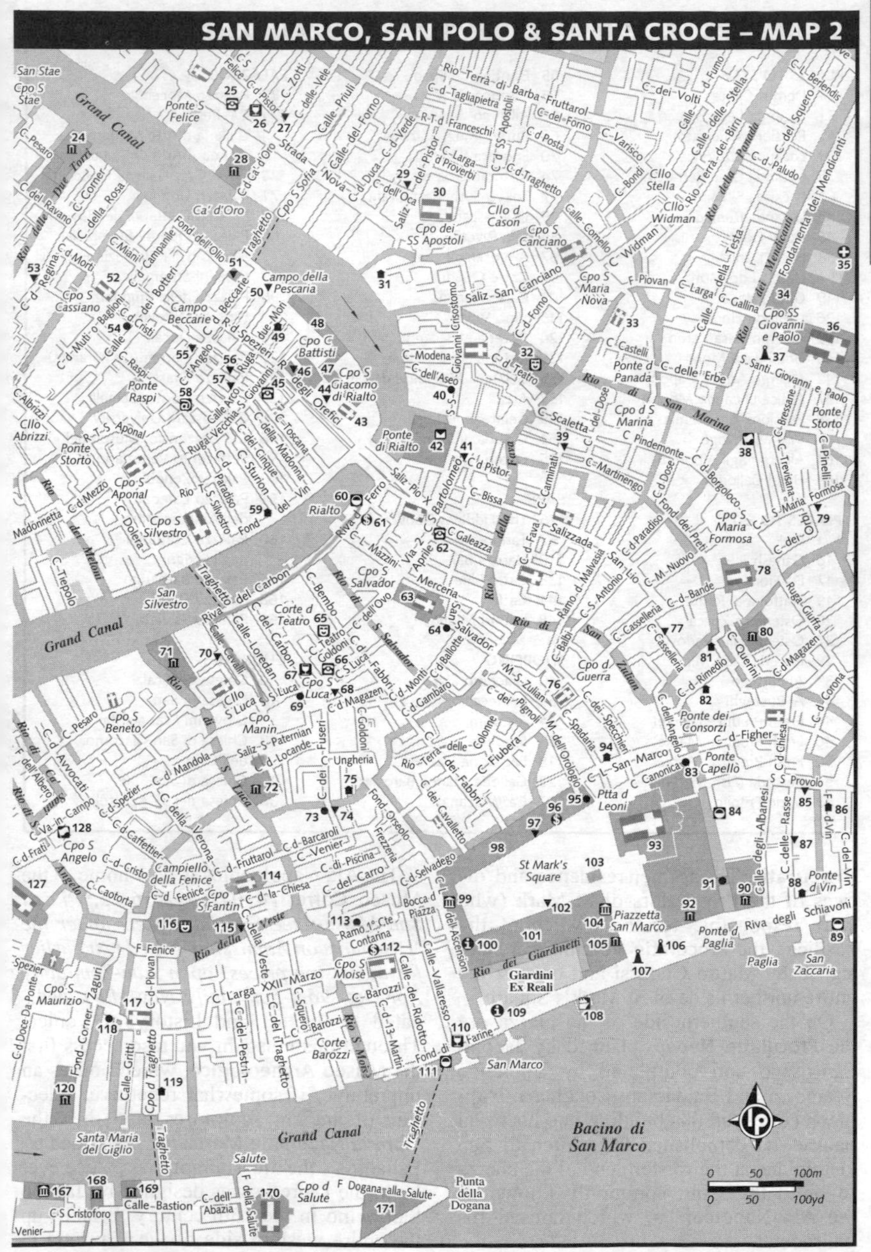

MAP 2 – SAN MARCO, SAN POLO & SANTA CROCE

PLACES TO STAY
14 Domus Civica
31 Locanda Leon Bianco
49 Pensione Guerrato
59 Locanda Sturion
75 Locanda Casa Petrarca
81 Locanda Silva
82 Locanda Remedio
86 Hotel Doni
88 Hotel Danieli
94 Hotel ai do Mori
119 Gritti Palace
126 Locanda Fiorita
139 Albergo Casa Peron
140 Hotel dalla Mora
142 Albergo Antico Capon
157 Antica Locanda Montin
158 Pensione Accademia Villa Maravege
164 Albergo agli Alboretti
165 Hotel Galleria

PLACES TO EAT
1 Brek
16 Ganesh Ji
17 Da Fiore
19 Trattoria al Ponte
20 Osteria La Zucca
27 Osteria dalla Vedova
29 Pizzeria Casa Mia
39 Al Portego
41 Ai Rusteghi
44 Fresh Produce Market
46 Fresh Produce Market
50 Fresh Produce Market
51 Pescaria (Fish Market)
53 Vecio Fritolin
55 Cantina do Spade
56 Cantina do Mori
57 All'Arco
68 Burger King; Spizzico
70 Enoteca Il Volto
74 Ristorante da Ivo
77 Tokyo Sushi Restaurant
79 La Mascareta
85 Alla Rivetta
87 Al Vecchio Penasa
97 Caffè Quadri
102 Caffè Florian
115 Vino Vino
124 Osteria al Bacareto
130 Osteria alla Patatina
135 Gelateria Millefoglie da Tarcisio
137 Arca
149 Gelateria il Doge
151 Osteria ai Carmini
155 Osteria da Toni

BARS
26 The Fiddler's Elbow
67 Torino@Notte
110 Harry's Bar
138 Caffè Blue
141 Caffè
148 Round Midnight

SHOPPING
40 Giacomo Rizzo
54 L'Arlecchino
64 Jesurum
83 Studium
118 Legatoria Piazzesi
123 Galleria Marina Barovier
147 Ca' Macana

PALAZZOS
22 Palazzo Mocenigo
24 Ca' Pesaro; Galleria d'Arte Moderna; Museo d'Arte Orientale
28 Ca' d'Oro; Galleria Franchetti
71 Palazzo Grimani
72 Palazzo Contarini del Bovolo
80 Palazzo Querini-Stampalia; Museo della Fondazione Querini-Stampalia
90 Palazzo delle Prigioni (Prigioni Nuove)
92 Palazzo Ducale
120 Palazzo Corner (Ca' Granda)
122 Palazzo Grassi
129 Palazzo Corner-Spinelli
145 Ca' Foscari; University
146 Ca' Rezzonico; Museo del Settecento Veneziano
153 Palazzo Zenobio
159 Palazzo Loredan dell'Ambasciatore
160 Palazzo Contarini degli Scrigni
166 Palazzo Barbarigo
168 Palazzo Dario
169 Palazzo Salviati

CHURCHES
2 Chiesa dei Scalzi
15 Chiesa di San Giovanni Evangelista
18 Chiesa di San Giacomo dell'Orio
23 Chiesa di San Stae
30 Chiesa dei SS Apostoli

Procuratie The former residence and offices of the Procurators of St Mark (who were responsible for the upkeep of the basilica), the **Procuratie Vecchie** were designed by Mauro Codussi and occupy the entire northern side of St Mark's Square.

On the southern side of the piazza are the **Procuratie Nuove**, planned by Jacopo Sansovino and completed by Vincenzo Scamozzi and Baldassare Longhena. Napoleon converted this building into his royal palace and demolished the church of San Geminiano at the western end of the piazza to build the wing commonly known as the Ala Napoleonica, which housed his ballroom.

The Ala Napoleonica is now home to the **Museo Correr** *(☎ 041 522 56 25, Piazza San Marco; see Special Tickets under the 'Discounts on Admission' boxed text earlier for admission prices; open 9am-7pm daily Apr-Oct, 9am-5pm daily Nov-Mar)*, dedicated to the art and history of Venice. Through this museum you also access first the **Museo Archeologico**, which houses an impressive, if somewhat repetitive, selection of ancient sculptures, and then the **Libreria Nazionale Marciana**. Described by Palladio as the most sumptuous palace ever built, the Libreria was designed by Jacopo Sansovino in the 16th century. It takes up the entire western side of the Piazzetta di

SAN MARCO, SAN POLO & SANTA CROCE – MAP 2

33 Chiesa di Santa Maria dei Miracoli
36 Chiesa dei SS Giovanni e Paolo
43 Chiesa di San Giacomo di Rialto
52 Chiesa di San Cassiano
63 Chiesa di San Salvador
76 Chiesa di San Zulian
78 Chiesa di Santa Maria Formosa
93 St Mark's Basilica
114 Chiesa di San Fantin
117 Chiesa di Santa Maria del Giglio
127 Chiesa di Santo Stefano
131 Chiesa di Santa Maria Gloriosa dei Frari
132 Chiesa di San Rocco
152 Chiesa dei Carmini
154 Chiesa di San Sebastiano
170 Chiesa di Santa Maria della Salute

OTHER

3 Scalzi Gondola Service
4 Water Taxis
5 ACTV/Vela Ticket Point
6 APT Office; Hotel Booking Office
7 ACTV/Vela Ticket Point
8 Bea Vita Lavanderia
9 Internet Café
10 Agenzia Arte e Storia
11 Omniservice Internet Café
12 ACTV Bus for Padua via Malcontenta
13 Gondola Service
21 Fondaco dei Turchi; Museo Civico di Storia Naturale
25 Telecom Office
32 Teatro Malibran
34 Scuola Grande di San Marco; Entrance to Hospital
35 Ospedale Civile (Hospital)
37 Statue of Condottiere Colleoni
38 French Consulate
42 Main Post Office; Fondaco dei Tedeschi; Telecom Office
45 Telecom Office
47 Fabbriche Vecchie di Rialto
48 Fabbriche Nuove di Rialto
58 Internet Point
60 Water Taxi Stand & Rialto Gondola Service
61 Thomas Cook
62 Telephones
65 Teatro Goldoni
66 Telecom Office
69 Cassa di Risparmio di Venezia (Tickets for La Fenice)
73 ACTV Office & Vela Ticket Outlet
84 Gondola Service
89 Gondola Service
91 Ponte dei Sospiri (Bridge of Sighs)
95 Torre dell'Orologio
96 Thomas Cook
98 Procuratie Vecchie
99 Museo Correr (Ala Napoleonica)
100 Main APT Office
101 Procuratie Nuove
103 Campanile
104 Museo Archeologico
105 Libreria Nazionale Marciana
106 Statue of Lion of St Mark
107 Statue of St Theodore
108 Alilaguna Hydrofoil to Airport
109 Venice Pavilion Infopoint; Vela Ticket Outlet
111 Gondola Service
112 American Express & ATM
113 Assessorato alla Gioventù
116 Teatro La Fenice
121 Dutch Consulate
125 Net House
128 German Consulate
133 AIG (Associazione Italiana Alberghi per la Gioventù)
134 Scuola Grande di San Rocco
136 The Netgate
143 Istituto Venezia
144 CTS Travel Agency
150 Scuola Grande dei Carmini
156 Ospedale G B Giustina (Hospital)
161 Accademia Gondola Service
162 UK Consulate
163 Gallerie dell'Accademia
167 Peggy Guggenheim Collection; Palazzo Venier dei Leoni
171 Dogana da Mar

San Marco. See the boxed text 'Discounts on Admission' earlier for details of a multi-entry ticket that includes these museums.

Piazzetta di San Marco Stretching from St Mark's Square to the waterfront, the piazzetta features two columns bearing statues of the Lion of St Mark and St Theodore (San Teodoro), the city's two emblems. Originally a marketplace, the area was also a preferred location for public executions and political meetings.

Palazzo Ducale The Palazzo Ducale *(Doges' Palace; ☎ 041 522 49 51; see Special Tickets under the 'Discounts on Admission' boxed text earlier for admission prices; open 9am-7pm daily Apr-Oct, 9am-5pm daily Nov-Mar; ticket sales cease 1½ hours before closing time)* was not only the doges' official residence, as the name suggests, but was also the seat of the Republic's government, housed bureaucrats and contained the prisons. Established in the 9th century, the building began to assume its present form 500 years later with the decision to build the massive Sala del Maggior Consiglio for the council members, who ranged in number from 1200 to 1700. It was inaugurated in 1419.

The palace's two magnificent Gothic facades in white Istrian stone and pink

Veronese marble face the water and Piazzetta di San Marco. Much of the building was damaged by fire in 1577 but it was successfully restored by Antonio da Ponte (who designed the Ponte di Rialto).

Making his Mark

The story goes that an angel appeared to the Evangelist Mark when his boat put in at Rialto while on his way to Rome from Aquileia. The winged fellow informed the future saint that his body would rest in Venice. When he did die some years later, it was in Alexandria, Egypt. In 828, two Venetian merchants persuaded the guardians of his Alexandrian tomb to let them have the corpse, which they then smuggled down to their ship in port.

You've got to ask yourself why they would bother with such a strange cargo. Well, in those days, any city worthy of the name had a patron saint of stature. Venice had St Theodore (San Teodoro) but poor old Theodore didn't really cut the mustard in the Christian hierarchy. An Evangelist, though, would be something quite different. Did Doge Giustinian Partecipazio order this little body-snatching mission? We will never know. Whatever the truth of this tale, it seems that *someone's* putrid corpse was transported to Venice and that everyone rather liked to think St Mark was now in their midst. St Theodore was unceremoniously demoted and the doge ordered the construction of a chapel to house the newcomer. That church would later become the magnificent St Mark's Basilica. St Mark was symbolised in the Book of Revelation (the Apocalypse) as a winged lion and this image came to be synonymous with La Serenissima (Most Serene Republic).

Legend also has it that, during the rebuilding of the basilica in 1063, the body of St Mark was hidden and then 'lost' when its hiding place was forgotten. In 1094, when the church was consecrated, the corpse (which must have been a picture of frailty by this time) broke through the column in which it had been enclosed. 'It's a miracle!' the Venetians cried. Or was it just incredibly dodgy plasterwork? St Mark had been lost and now was found. A grateful populace buried the remains in the church crypt where they now lie beneath the basilica's high altar.

The former main entrance (and now exit), the 15th-century **Porta della Carta** (Paper Door), to which government decrees were fixed, was carved by Giovanni and Bartolomeo Bon. Leading from the courtyard, the **Scala dei Giganti** (Giants' Staircase) by Antonio Rizzo takes its name from the huge statues of Mars and Neptune, by Jacopo Sansovino, that flank the landing.

Past Sansovino's **Scala d'Oro** (Golden Staircase) are rooms dedicated to the various doges, including the **Sala delle Quattro Porte** on the 3rd floor, where ambassadors would be kindly requested to await their ducal audience. The room's ceiling was designed by Palladio and the frescoes are by Tintoretto. Off this room is the **Anticollegio**, which features four Tintorettos and the *Rape of Europa* by Paolo Veronese. Through here, the ceiling of the splendid **Sala del Collegio** features a series of artworks by Veronese. Next is the **Sala del Senato**, graced by yet more Tintorettos.

The indicated route (you have no choice in the matter) then takes you to the immense **Sala del Maggior Consiglio** on the 2nd floor. It is dominated at one end by Tintoretto's *Paradise*, one of the world's largest oil paintings, measuring 22m by 7m. Among the many other paintings in the hall is a masterpiece, the *Apotheosis of Venice* by Veronese, in one of the central ceiling panels. Note the black space in the frieze on the wall depicting the first 76 doges of Venice. Doge Marin Falier would have appeared there had he not been beheaded for treason in 1355.

Next, you find yourself crossing the small, enclosed **Ponte dei Sospiri** (Bridge of Sighs) to reach the prisons. The bridge is named because of the sighs prisoners tended to make on their way into the dungeons. The poor unfortunates to make this dismal crossing must have been well behaved indeed not to give more vigorous vent to their displeasure than a mere sigh.

The Itinerari Segreti (Secret Itineraries) is a guided tour of lesser-known areas of the palace. The 1½-hour tour is an intriguing look at the underside of the palace. You pass from civil servants' offices to a torture chamber, the Inquisitor's office and upstairs to the **Piombi** (Leads; prison cells beneath the roof of the building). Here prisoners froze in winter and sweltered in summer. Giacomo Casanova got five years but managed to escape. You also get an explanation of the engineering behind the ceiling of the immense Sala del Maggior Consiglio below. Call ☎ 041 522 49 51 in advance to book the tour. From April to October, tours in English run daily at 10am and 11.30am, tours in Italian are at 9.30am and 11am, and tours in French are at 10.30am and noon. From November to March, daily tours in some or all of the above languages are at 10am, 10.30am, 11.30am & noon. Admission costs €12.40.

San Marco to the Rialto The **Mercerie**, a series of streets lined with shops, connects St Mark's Square and the Rialto in a rather tortuous manner. The **Chiesa di San Salvador** *(admission free; open 10am-noon & 3pm-6pm Mon-Sat)*, built on a plan of three Greek crosses laid end to end, features Titian's *Annunciation* and Bellini's *Supper in Emmaus*.

San Marco to the Accademia The area immediately west of St Mark's Square is a rabbit warren of streets and alleys lined with exclusive shops, where – if you search hard enough – you might pick up some interesting gifts and souvenirs, such as watercolours of the city, marbled paper and carnival masks.

On the way to the Ponte dell'Accademia there are a couple of churches of interest. The Renaissance **Chiesa di San Fantin** *(Campo San Fantin)* has a domed sanctuary and apse by Jacopo Sansovino. Also in Campo San Fantin stands what's left of the **Teatro la Fenice**, the opera house that opened in 1792 and was largely gutted by fire in January 1996. Several of Verdi's operas had their opening nights here.

Before you go elsewhere, make sure you duck up just north of the Chiesa di San Fantin to admire the wonderful 15th-century external spiral staircase at the **Palazzo Contarini del Bovolo** *(☎ 041 270 24 64, San Marco 4299; admission €2.10; open 10am-6pm daily)*.

Return to Calle Larga XXII Marzo and turn right for the **Chiesa di Santa Maria del Giglio** *(admission €1.55; open 10am-5pm Mon-Sat, 1pm-5pm Sun)*, also known as Santa Maria Zobenigo. Its Baroque facade features maps of European cities as they were in 1678. Go on to Campo Francesco Morosini (aka Campo Santo Stefano) and the Gothic **Chiesa di Santo Stefano** *(entry on the western side; admission €1.55; open 10am-5pm Mon-Sat, 1pm-5pm Sun)* is on your right. Of note are three paintings by Tintoretto in the little museum: *Ultima Cena* (Last Supper), *Lavanda dei Piedi* (Washing of the Feet) and *Orazione nell'Orto* (Agony in the Garden). Outside, the church's bell tower leans rather worryingly.

Dorsoduro

Gallerie dell'Accademia (Map 2) This is a must for anyone with even a passing interest in art. The former church and convent of Santa Maria della Carità, with additions by Palladio, hosts a collection *(☎ 041 522 22 47; admission €6.20; guided tour €4.15; open 8.15am-2pm Mon, 8.15am-7.15pm Tues-Sun; hours subject to frequent change)* that follows the progression of Venetian art from the 14th to the 18th centuries.

Room 1 contains works by the early 14th-century painter Paolo Veneziano, including the *Incoronazione di Maria* (Coronation of Mary). The main feature of Room 2, which covers the late 15th and early 16th centuries, is Carpaccio's altarpiece *Crocifissione e Apoteosi dei 10,000 Martiri del Monte Ararat* (Crucifixion and Apotheosis of the 10,000 Martyrs of Mt Ararat). It also contains works by Giovanni Bellini. Rooms 4 and 5 feature Andrea Mantegna's *San Giorgio* (St George), several paintings of the Madonna and Child by Giovanni Bellini and Giorgione's fabulous *La Tempesta* (The Storm). Rooms 6 to 10 contain works of the High Renaissance, including Tintoretto and Titian, but one of the highlights is Paolo Veronese's *Convito in Casa di Levi* (Feast in the House of Levi) in Room 10. Originally called *Ultima Cena* (Last Supper), the painting's name was changed because the Inquisition objected to its depiction of characters such as drunkards and dwarfs. The room also contains one of Titian's last works, a *Pietà*. In Room 13 are a number of works by the 18th-century painter Giambattista Tiepolo. Giovanni Bellini and Carpaccio appear again in subsequent rooms and the collection ends in Room 24 with Tiepolo's beautiful *Presentazione di Maria al Tempio* (Presentation of Mary at the Temple).

Peggy Guggenheim Collection (Map 2) Peggy Guggenheim called the unfinished Palazzo Venier dei Leoni home for 30 years until she died in 1979. She left behind a collection *(☎ 041 240 54 11, Dorsoduro 701; admission €6.20; open 10am-6pm Wed-Fri & Sun-Mon, 10am-10pm Sat)* of works by her favourite modern artists, representing most of the major movements of the 20th century. Picasso, Mondrian, Kandinsky, Ernst, Chagall, Klee, Miró, Dalí, Pollock, Brancusi, Magritte and Bacon are all represented. Take a wander around the sculpture garden (which includes works by Moore, Giacometti and Ernst), where Miss Guggenheim and many of her pet dogs are buried.

Chiesa di Santa Maria della Salute (Map 2) Dominating the entrance to the Grand Canal, this beautiful church *(sacristy admission €1; open 9am-noon & 3pm-6pm daily)* was built in the 17th century in honour of the Virgin Mary, who was believed to have delivered the city from an outbreak of plague that had killed more than a third of the population. Inside Baldassare Longhena's octagonal church, Titian and Tintoretto left their mark in the Great Sacristy. Every year, on 21 November, a procession takes place from St Mark's Square to the church to give thanks for the city's good health.

The Zattere (Maps 1 & 2) The Fondamenta delle Zattere runs along the Canale della Giudecca from Punta della Salute to Stazione Marittima. It is a popular *passeggiata* (traditional evening stroll) location. The main sight is the 18th-century Santa Maria del Rosario, or **Chiesa dei Gesuati (Map 1)** *(admission €1.55; open 8am-noon & 5pm-7pm daily)*, designed by Giorgio Massari. Tiepolo's ceiling frescoes tell the story of San Domenico. At the end of the Zattere, over Rio di San Basilio, the **Chiesa di San Sebastiano (Map 2)** *(admission €1.55; open 10am-5pm Mon-Sat)* was the local church of Paolo Veronese, who provided most of the paintings and lies buried in the church.

Ca' Rezzonico (Map 2) This 17th-and 18th-century mansion, which faces the Grand Canal, houses the **Museo del Settecento Veneziano** *(Museum of the 18th Century; ☎ 041 241 01 00, Dorsoduro 3136; admission €6.70 or buy a multi-entry ticket – see Special Tickets under the 'Discounts on Admission' boxed text earlier; open 10am-6pm Wed-Mon)*. Designed by Baldassare Longhena and completed by Massari, it was home to several notables over the years, including the poet Robert Browning, who died there. The museum houses a collection of 18th-century art and furniture and is also worth visiting for the views over the Grand Canal and the fine ceiling frescoes by Tiepolo, notably the *Allegory of Merit* in the Throne Room.

Scuola Grande dei Carmini (Map 2) Tiepolo also had a hand in this 16th-century building *(☎ 041 528 94 20, Dorsoduro 2617; admission €4.15; open 9am-6pm Mon-Sat, 9am-4pm Sun)*, near the church of the same name, just west of Campo Santa Margherita. Of its numerous works of art, the nine ceiling paintings by Tiepolo in the Salone Superiore (upstairs) depict the virtues surrounding the Virgin in Glory. Restored in the late 1980s, they suffered a blow in 2000 when one of the panels collapsed from the ceiling, partly eaten away by woodworm. In 2001 woodworm were found to be at work on at least two other panels.

San Polo (Map 2)

Chiesa di Santa Maria Gloriosa dei Frari This massive Gothic church *(admission €1.55; open 9am-6pm Mon-Sat, 1pm-*

6pm Sun), rich in art treasures, is one of the highlights of a visit to Venice. It was built for the Franciscans in the 14th and 15th centuries and decorated by an illustrious array of artists. Titian, who is buried in the church, is the main attraction of the Frari. His dramatic *Assunta* (Assumption; 1518) over the high altar represents a key moment in his rise as one of the city's greatest artists, praised unreservedly by all and sundry as a work of inspired genius. Another of his masterpieces, the *Madonna di Ca' Pesaro* (Madonna of Ca' Pesaro), hangs above the Pesaro altar (in the left-hand aisle, near the choir stalls).

Scuola Grande di San Rocco Built for the Confraternity of St Roch in the 16th century and decorated with more than 50 paintings by Tintoretto, the Scuola Grande di San Rocco *(☎ 041 523 48 64, Dorsoduro 3052; admission €5.20; open 9am-5.30pm daily Easter-Oct, 10am-4pm daily Nov-Easter)* is one of Venice's great surprises.

After winning a competition (one of the other competitors was Paolo Veronese), Tintoretto went on to devote 23 years of his life to decorating the school. The overwhelming concentration of more than 50 paintings by the master is altogether too much for the average human to digest. Chronologically speaking, you should start upstairs (Scarpagnino designed the staircase) in the Sala Grande Superiore. Here you can pick up mirrors to carry around to avoid getting a sore neck while inspecting the ceiling paintings (which depict Old Testament episodes). Around the walls are scenes from the New Testament. A handful of works by other artists (such as Titian, Giorgione and Tiepolo) can also be seen. To give your eyes a rest from the paintings, inspect the woodwork below them – it is studded with curious designs, including a false book collection.

Downstairs, the walls of the confraternity's assembly hall feature a series on the life of the Virgin Mary, starting on the left wall with the *Annunciazione* (Annunciation) and ending with the *Assunzione* (Assumption) opposite.

Towards Ponte di Rialto Heading for Ponte di Rialto from the Chiesa di Santa Maria Gloriosa dei Frari, you soon arrive in the vast **Campo San Polo**, the city's largest square after St Mark's. Locals bring their children here to play so if you are travelling with small kids they might appreciate some social contact while you take a cappuccino break.

The area around **Ponte di Rialto**, bursting with the life of the daily produce market, was one of the earliest settled locations in Venice. Rialto, or *rivo alto*, means high bank and the spot was considered one of the safest in the lagoon. There has been a market here for almost 1000 years – the **Fabbriche Vecchie** along the Ruga degli Orefici and the **Fabbriche Nuove**, running along the Grand Canal, were built by Scarpagnino after a fire destroyed the old markets in 1514.

Although there has been a bridge at the Rialto since the foundation of the city, the present stone bridge by Antonio da Ponte was completed in 1592.

Virtually in the middle of the market, off the Ruga degli Orefici, is the **Chiesa di San Giacomo di Rialto**. According to local legend it was founded on 25 March 421, the same day as the city.

Towards Stazione di Santa Lucia Tintoretto fans will want to visit the **Chiesa di San Cassiano** *(Campo San Cassiano; open 9am-noon Tues-Sat)*, north-west of the Rialto. The sanctuary is decorated with three of Tintoretto's paintings, *Crucifixion*, *Resurrection* and *Descent into Limbo*.

The Renaissance **Ca' Pesaro**, farther north with its facade facing the Grand Canal, houses the **Galleria d'Arte Moderna** *(☎ 041 524 06 95, Santa Croce 2070)* on the ground floor since 1902. The collection includes works purchased from the Venezia Biennale art festival and is one of the largest collections of modern art in Italy. You can enjoy works by De Chirico, Miró, Chagall, Kandinsky, Klee, Klimt, Moore and others. The gallery is due to open in 2002 after almost 20 years closed.

The **Museo d'Arte Orientale** *(☎ 041 524 11 73, Santa Croce 2070; admission*

€2.05), in the same building on the top floor, features a collection of Asian and Eastern oddments.

Continuing north-west past the Chiesa di San Stae, you'll find the **Fondaco dei Turchi** *(☎ 041 524 08 85, Santa Croce 1730)*, a 12th-century building used as a warehouse by Turkish merchants and now housing the **Museo Civico di Storia Naturale** (Natural History Museum). The museum has been closed for years but is due to reopen in 2003 – if it does take the kids there to see the impressive 12m-long crocodile.

As you head south, the 13th-century **Chiesa di San Giacomo dell'Orio** *(Campo San Giacomo dell'Orio; admission €1.55; open 10am-5pm Mon-Sat, 1pm-5pm Sun)* is worth a visit. It is one of the few good examples of Romanesque architecture (albeit somewhat disguised by later Gothic additions) in Venice. In front of the main altar is a wooden crucifix by Veronese and on the wall at the rear of the central apse a rare work by Lorenzo Lotto, *Madonna col Bambino e Santi* (Madonna with Child and Saints).

Cannaregio

The long pedestrian thoroughfare connecting the train station and St Mark's Square crawls with tourists – few venture off it into the peaceful back lanes.

The Carmelite **Chiesa dei Scalzi (Map 2)** *(literally 'barefoot'; free; open 7am-11.45am & 4pm-6.45pm Mon-Sat, 7.45am-12.30pm & 4pm-7pm Sun & holidays)* is next to the train station. There are damaged frescoes by Tiepolo in the vaults of two of the side chapels.

Along the Rio Terrà Lista di Spagna, the otherwise uninspiring 18th-century **Chiesa di San Geremia (Map 3)** holds the body of Santa Lucia, who was martyred in Syracuse in AD 304. Her body was stolen by Venetian merchants from Constantinople in 1204 and moved to San Geremia after the Palladian church of Santa Lucia was demolished to make way for the train station.

Ghetto Nuovo (Map 3) Most easily accessible from the Fondamenta Pescaria, next to the Canale di Cannaregio, through the Sotoportego del Ghetto, this was the world's original ghetto. The area was once a foundry and it is tempting to think that the Venetian word for foundry *(getto)* gave rise to what would become an unpleasant addition to Europe's cultural vocabulary.

The city's Jews were ordered to move to the small island, which became known as Ghetto Nuovo, in 1516. They were locked in at night by Christian soldiers and forced to follow a set of rules limiting their social and economic activities, but they retained full freedom of religious expression.

Extreme overcrowding combined with building height restrictions means that some apartment blocks have as many as seven storeys but with low ceilings. In 1797, after the fall of the Venetian Republic, Jews were allowed to leave the ghetto to live wherever they chose.

The **Museo Ebraico** *(☎ 041 71 53 59, Campo di Ghetto Nuovo, Cannaregio 2902/b; admission €2.60; open 10am-7pm Sun-Fri except Jewish holidays)* contains a modest collection of Jewish religious silverware. The guided tours of the Ghetto and three of its synagogues *(scholas)* that leave from the museum are highly recommended. Tours cost €6.20 which includes admission to the museum. They run hourly 10.30am to 5.30pm Sunday to Friday (except Jewish holidays). Also enquire at the museum about guided tours to the old Jewish cemetery on the Lido.

Cross the iron bridge from Campo di Ghetto Nuovo to reach the Fondamenta degli Ormesini and turn right. This is a truly peaceful part of Venice, almost completely empty of tourists. There are some interesting bars and a couple of good restaurants along the *fondamenta* (street by a canal).

Chiesa della Madonna dell'Orto (Map 3) This 14th-century church *(admission €1.55; open 10am-5pm Mon-Sat, 1pm-5pm Sun)* was Tintoretto's parish church and contains many of his works. Among them are the *Giudizio Finale* (Last Judgement), *Adorazione del Vitello d'Oro* (Adoration of the Golden Calf) and the *Apparizione della Croce a San Pietro* (Vision of the Cross to

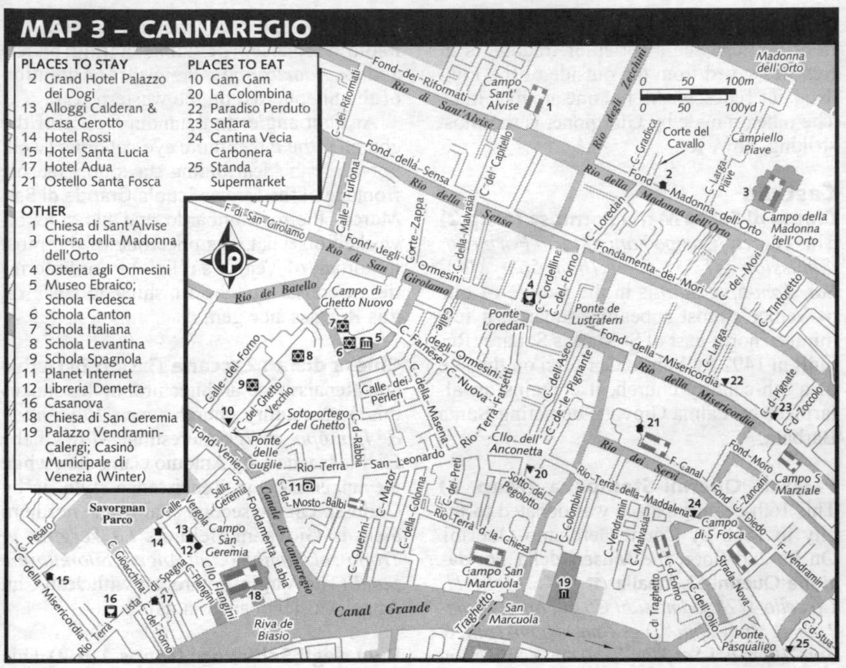

St Peter). On the wall at the end of the right aisle is the *Presentazione di Maria al Tempio* (Presentation of the Virgin Mary in the Temple). Tintoretto is buried with other family members in the church.

Gesuiti (Map 1) This Jesuit church *(proper name: Santa Maria Assunta; open 10am-noon & 4pm-6pm daily)* dates from the early 18th century. Its Baroque interior features walls with inlaid marble in imitation of curtains. Titian's *Martirio di San Lorenzo* (Martyrdom of St Lawrence) is first on the left as you enter the church, balanced by Tintoretto's *Assunzione della Vergine* (Assumption of the Virgin) in the northern transept.

Chiesa di Santa Maria dei Miracoli (Map 2) This particularly beautiful Renaissance church *(admission €1.55; open 10am-5pm Mon-Sat, 1pm-5pm Sun)*, designed by Pietro Lombardo, boasts magnificent sculptures. Pietro and his son Tullio Lombardo executed the carvings on the choir.

Chiesa dei SS Apostoli (Map 2) This church *(open 7.30am-11.30am & 5pm-7pm Mon-Sat, 8.30am-noon & 4pm-6.30pm Sun)*, at the eastern end of the Strada Nova, is worth visiting for the 15th-century Cappella Corner by Mauro Codussi, which features a painting of Santa Lucia by Tiepolo (removed for restoration in 1994).

Ca' d'Oro (Map 2) Built in the 15th century, this magnificent Gothic structure was named Ca' d'Oro *(Golden House; ☎ 041 523 87 90; admission €3.10; open 8.15am-2pm Mon, 8.15am-7.15pm Tues-Sun)* for the gilding that originally decorated the sculptural details of the facade. Visible from the Grand Canal, the facade stands out from the remainder of the edifice, rather drab by comparison. Ca d'Oro houses the **Galleria Franchetti**, an impressive collection of bronzes, tapestries and paintings. On the 2nd floor you can see a series of fragments of frescoes saved from the outside of the Fondaco dei Tedeschi. All but one are by Titian. The other, a nude by Giorgione, is the most striking, however.

Castello

Chiesa di Santa Maria Formosa (Map 2) This church *(Campo Santa Maria Formosa; admission €1.55; open 10am-5pm Mon-Sat, 1pm-5pm Sun)* is in the middle of one of Venice's most appealing squares, a few minutes north-east of St Mark's Square. Rebuilt in 1492 by Mauro Cordussi on the site of a 7th-century church, it contains an altarpiece by Palma Giovane depicting Santa Barbara.

Palazzo Querini-Stampalia (Map 2) This 16th-century palace was donated to the city in 1868 by Count Gerolamo Querini. On its 2nd floor, the **Museo della Fondazione Querini-Stampalia** *(☎ 041 271 14 11, Castello 4778; admission €6.20; open 10am-1pm & 3pm-6pm, Tues-Sun, 10am-1pm & 3pm-10pm Fri-Sat May-Sept)* has a collection of paintings and Venetian furniture.

Chiesa dei SS Giovanni e Paolo (Map 2) This huge Gothic church *(open 7.30am-12.30pm & 3.30pm-7pm Mon-Sat, 3pm-6pm Sun)*, founded by the Dominicans, rivals the Franciscans' Frari in size and grandeur. Work started on the church in 1333, but it was not consecrated until 1430. Its vast interior is divided simply into a nave and two aisles, separated by graceful, soaring arches. The beautiful stained-glass window (the largest in Venice) in the southern transept was made in Murano to designs by various artists, including Bartolomeo Vivarini and Girolamo Mocetto, in the 15th century.

Around the walls, many of the tombs of 25 doges were sculpted by prominent Gothic and Renaissance artists. Look out for Giovanni Bellini's polyptych of San Vincenzo Ferreri (St Vincent Ferrer) over the second altar of the right aisle. In the Cappella del Rosario, off the northern arm of the transept, is a series of paintings by Paolo Veronese, including ceiling panels and an *Adorazione dei Pastori* (Adoration of the Shepherds) on the western wall.

At right angles to the main facade of the church is the rather more eye-catching (well, not while the scaffolding stays up!) marble frontage of the former **Scuola Grande di San Marco**. Pietro Lombardo and his sons all worked on what was once one of the most important of Venice's religious confraternities. Codussi put the finishing touches on this Renaissance gem.

Chiesa di San Zaccaria The mix of Gothic and Renaissance architectural styles makes this 15th-century church *(open 10am-noon & 4pm-6pm daily)* interesting. Most of the Gothic facade is by Antonio Gambello, while the upper part, in Renaissance style, is by Codussi. On the second altar of the northern aisle is Giovanni Bellini's *La Vergine in Trono col Bambino, un Angelo Suonatore e Santi* (The Virgin Enthroned with Jesus, an Angel Musician and Saints).

Riva degli Schiavoni (Maps 1 & 2) This walkway extends along the waterfront from the Palazzo Ducale to the Arsenale ferry point at the far south-eastern end of Castello. The exclusive hotels that line it have long been favourites for Venice's more affluent visitors. About halfway along is Chiesa di Santa Maria della Pietà, known as **La Pietà**, where concerts are regularly held. Vivaldi was concert master here in the early 18th century. Look for the ceiling fresco by Tiepolo.

Scuola di San Giorgio degli Schiavoni (Map 1) The school *(☎ 041 522 88 28, Castello 3259/a; admission €2.60; open 9.30am-12.30pm & 3.30pm-6.30pm Tues-Sat, 9.30am-12.30pm Sun)* was established by Venice's Slavic community in the 15th century and this building was erected in the 16th century. The walls of the ground-floor hall are decorated with a series of superb paintings by Vittore Carpaccio, depicting events in the lives of the three patron saints of Dalmatia: George, Tryphone and Jerome.

Chiesa di San Francesco della Vigna (Map 1) Designed and built by Jacopo Sansovino, this 16th-century Franciscan church *(open 8am-12.30pm & 3pm-7pm daily)* is named for the vineyard that once thrived on the site. Its facade was designed by Palladio and inside, just to the left of the main door, is a triptych of saints by Antonio Vivarini. The Cappella dei Giustiniani, to the left of the main altar, is decorated with reliefs by Pietro Lombardo and his school.

Arsenale (Map 1) The city's huge dockyards were founded in 1104 and at their peak were home to 300 shipping companies and employed up to 16,000 people, capable of turning out a new galley every 100 days. Covering 32 hectares and completely enclosed by fortifications, the Arsenale was a symbol of Venice's maritime supremacy. Napoleon wrecked it in 1797 but it was later rebuilt and remained in use until WWI as a shipyard for the Italian navy.

The Renaissance gateway surmounted by the Lion of St Mark commemorates the Christian victory over the Turkish fleet in the Battle of Lepanto in 1571. You can enter the vestibule and peer through to the interior of the Arsenale. It can be open as early as 7am and is generally shut by 5pm.

The **Museo Storico Navale** *(☎ 041 520 02 76, Castello 2148; admission €1.55; open 8.45am-1pm Mon-Fri, 8.45am-1.30pm Sat)*, towards the Canale di San Marco on the far side of Rio dell'Arsenale, covers the Republic's maritime history with a huge exhibition of paraphernalia, model boats, costumes and weapons. Among the exhibits is Peggy Guggenheim's gondola, one of the oldest remaining in the city.

At the eastern edge of Venice, the residential back lanes of Castello are worth walking through to see how the locals live. Beyond, the islands of **San Pietro** and **Sant'Elena** are pools of peace far removed from the busy heart of Venice.

Islands of the Lagoon

Giudecca (Map 1) Originally known as *spina longa* (long spine) because of its shape, Giudecca's present name probably derives from the word Zudega (from *giudicato*; the judged), which was applied to families of rebellious nobles at one time banished from Venice and later allowed to return. Rich Venetians later came of their own accord to build villas on the island. Its main attraction is the **Chiesa del Redentore** *(admission €1.55; open 10am-5pm Mon-Sat, 1pm-5pm Sun)*, built by Palladio in 1577 after the city was saved from a savage outbreak of plague. On the third Saturday in July the doge would pay a visit to the church, crossing the canal from the Zattere (see The Zattere under Dorsoduro earlier) on a pontoon (the name Zattere means 'rafts'). The Festa del Redentore (Feast of the Redeemer) remains one of the most important on Venice's calendar of events.

San Giorgio Maggiore (Map 1) On the island of the same name, Palladio's **Chiesa di San Giorgio Maggiore** *(bell-tower lift €2.60; church admission free; open 9.30am-12.30pm & 2.30pm-6.30pm daily)* has one of the most prominent positions in Venice and, although it inspired mixed reactions among the architect's contemporaries, it had a significant influence on architecture at the time. Built between 1565 and 1580, the church has an austere interior, an interesting contrast to its bold facade. Its art treasures include works by Tintoretto: an *Ultima Cena* (Last Supper) and the *Raccolta della Manna* (Shower of Manna) on the walls of the high altar, and a *Deposizione* (Deposition) in the Cappella dei Morti. Take the lift to the top of the 60m-high bell tower for an extraordinary view.

San Michele (Map 1) The city's cemetery was established on Isola di San Michele under Napoleon and is maintained by the Franciscans. The **Chiesa di San Michele in Isola**, begun by Codussi in 1469, was among the city's first Renaissance buildings.

Murano The people of Venice have been making crystal and glass (the difference between the two lies in the amount of lead employed) since as early as the 10th century, when the secrets of the art were brought back from the East by merchants. The industry was moved to the island of Murano in the 13th century.

Venice had a virtual monopoly on the production of what is now known as Murano glass and the methods of the craft were such a well-guarded secret that it was considered treason for a glass-worker to leave the city. The incredibly elaborate pieces produced by the artisans can range from the beautiful to the grotesque – but, as the Italians would say, *i gusti son gusti* (each to his own). Watching the glass-workers in action is certainly interesting. You can see them in several outlets along Fondamenta dei Vetrai and a couple on Viale Garibaldi. Look for the sign 'Fornace' (furnace).

The **Museo Vetrario** *(☎ 041 73 95 86, Fondamenta Giustinian 8; admission €5.20 or buy a multi-entry ticket – see Special Tickets under the 'Discounts on Admission' boxed text earlier; open 10am-5pm Thurs-Tues)* contains some exquisite pieces.

The nearby **Chiesa dei SS Maria e Donato** is a fascinating example of Veneto-Byzantine architecture. Founded in the 7th century and rebuilt 500 years later, the church was first dedicated to the Virgin Mary. It was rededicated to San Donato after his bones were brought there from Cephalonia, along with those of a dragon he had supposedly killed (four of the 'dragon' bones are hung behind the altar). The church's magnificent mosaic pavement was laid in the 12th century and the impressive mosaic of the Virgin Mary in the apse dates from the same period.

The island can be reached on vaporetto Nos 12, 13 or 42 (41 the other way) from Fondamente Nuove (No 42 also leaves from San Zaccaria and Piazzale Roma). No 62 (61 the other way) also chugs there from Piazzale Roma.

Burano Famous for its lace industry, Burano is a pretty fishing village, its streets and canals lined with bright, pastel-coloured houses. The **Museo del Merletto di Burano** *(☎ 041 73 00 34. Piazza Galuppi 187; admission €4.15 or buy a multi-entry ticket – see Special Tickets under the 'Discounts on Admission' boxed text earlier; open 10am-5pm Wed-Mon, ticket window shut from 3.30pm)* is a museum of lace making. If you plan to buy lace on the island, choose with care as these days not all of it is locally made.

Take vaporetto No 12 from Fondamente Nuove to get to Burano.

Torcello This delightful little island, with its overgrown main square and sparse, scruffy-looking buildings and monuments, was at its peak from the mid-7th to the 13th century when it was the seat of the Bishop of Altinum and home to some 20,000 people. Rivalry with Venice and a succession of malaria epidemics systematically reduced the island's splendour and its population. Today, fewer than 80 people call the island home.

The island's Veneto-Byzantine cathedral, **Santa Maria Assunta** *(admission €2.60, to climb bell tower €2.10, ticket including admission to Museo di Torcello €5.20; cathedral open 10am-5.30pm)*, shouldn't be missed. Founded in the 7th century, it was Venice's first cathedral. It was rebuilt early in the 11th century and contains magnificent Byzantine mosaics.

On the cathedral's western wall is a vast mosaic depicting the Last Judgement but its great treasure is the mosaic of the Madonna in the semi-dome of the apse. Starkly set on a pure gold background, the figure is one of the most stunning works of Byzantine art you will see in Italy. Admission includes an informative audio tape.

The adjacent tiny **Chiesa di Santa Fosca** was founded in the 11th century to house the body of Santa Fosca. Across the square, in the Palazzo del Consiglio, is the **Museo di Torcello** *(☎ 041 73 07 61; admission €1.55, open 10.30am-5.30pm Tues-Sun)*, which tells the history of the island. Part of the collection is in the adjacent **Palazzo dell'Archivio**. Both buildings date from the 13th century and together formed the nerve centre of temporal power in Torcello.

To reach the island take vaporetto No 12 from Fondamente Nuove.

The Lido The main draw here is the beach but the water can be polluted and the public areas are often unkempt. Some of the beaches at the southern end of the island, such as those at Alberoni, are an exception. If you want to stay closer to the northern end of the island (and the vaporetto stops), you will pay a small fortune (between €10.35 and €41.30) to hire a chair and umbrella in the more easily accessible and clearer areas of the beach.

The Lido forms a land barrier between the lagoon and the Adriatic Sea. For centuries the doges trekked out here to fulfil Venice's Marriage to the Sea ceremony by dropping a ring into the shallows, celebrating Venice's close relationship with the sea.

It became a fashionable seaside resort around the late 19th century and its more glorious days are depicted in Thomas Mann's novel *Death in Venice*. The rows of modern apartments and hotels ensure the beaches are crowded but the Lido is not quite the fashionable place that it once was.

The snappy **Palazzo del Cinema** hosts Venice's international film festival each September (see Special Events later) and the **casino** packs them in during the summer. Apart from that, there is little to attract you here, unless you are passing through on your way to Chioggia. The Lido can be reached by vaporetto No 1, 6, 14, 52 or 82 and the vehicle ferry from Tronchetto (Map 1).

Chioggia

Chioggia lies at the southern end of the lagoon and is the second most important city in it after Venice. Invaded and destroyed by the Venetian Republic's maritime rival, Genoa, in the late 14th century, the medieval core of modern Chioggia is a crumbly but not uninteresting counterpoint to its more illustrious patron to the north. In no way cute like Murano or Burano, Chioggia is a firmly practical town, its big fishing fleet everywhere in evidence. If your time is limited in Venice, you can live without Chioggia – the trip can take about two hours each way. City bus No 1, 2, 6 or 7 connects Chioggia with the Sottomarina, saving you the 15-minute walk.

From the Lido, bus No 11 leaves from Gran Viale Santa Maria Elisabetta, outside the tourist office; it boards the car ferry at Alberoni and then connects with a steamer at Pellestrina that will take you to Chioggia. Or you can take a bus from Piazzale Roma. The APT office (☎ 041 554 04 66) is on the waterfront at the Sottomarina.

Gondola Rides

A gondola ride is the quintessence of romantic Venice, although at €62 for 50 minutes (€77.50 after 8pm) the *official* price is a rather hefty return from the clouds to reality. The rates are for a maximum of six people – less romantic but more affordable. After the first 50 minutes you pay in 25-minute increments (€31, or €38.70 after 8pm). Several travellers have reported successfully negotiating below the official rates, so get your haggling skills in order!

Gondolas are available near main canals all over the city, or can be booked in the following areas: San Marco (☎ 041 520 06 85), Rialto (☎ 041 522 49 04), Piazzale Roma (☎ 041 522 11 51) and the train station (☎ 041 71 85 43).

Venice for Children

Venice isn't for art-lovers and hopeless romantics alone. The city is varied enough to keep even the most recalcitrant juniors interested at least some of the time. Some of the stuff grown-ups like, such as gondola and vaporetto rides, exploring funny corners and watching the passing parade of boats along the canals, will also appeal to kids.

Children will certainly enjoy a trip down the Grand Canal on vaporetto No 1. And if you can't afford a gondola, at least treat them to a short trip across the canal on a traghetto. They will probably also enjoy a trip to the islands, particularly to see the glass-making demonstrations on Murano. Older kids might enjoy watching the big ships pass along the Canale della Giudecca, so take them to Gelati Nico on the Fondamenta Zattere, where you can relax for half an hour or so. Children of all ages will enjoy watching the Mori strike the hour at the Torre dell'Orologio on St Mark's Square.

If you are having a spot of bother, or have been unkind enough to drag the little mites around just a few too many monuments for their liking, you can try a couple of things to mollify them.

The Giardini Pubblici and Parco Savorgnan both have swings and the like. In summer, a trip to the beach – the Lido, Sottomarina (Chioggia) or Lido di Jesolo – should win you a few points. If you are using your own transport, remember to leave early to beat the horrible traffic jams. And forget it at weekends (except on the Lido) – whether you drive or catch buses you'll be stuck on the roads for an eternity either way.

Discounts are available for children (usually aged under 12) on public transport and for admission to museums, galleries and other sights.

Courses

Società Dante Alighieri *(housed in the Istituto Paolo Sarpi;* ☎ *041 528 91 27, fax 041 523 08 57,* **e** *venicedantealighieri@libero.it, Castello 2821)* **Map 1** This place offers courses in Italian at all levels.

Istituto Venezia *(☎ 041 522 43 31, fax 041 528 56 28,* **w** *www.istitutovenezia.com, Campo Santa Margherita, Dorsoduro 3116/a)* **Map 2** The Istituto Venezia offers language and one- to two-week cookery courses. It also does a course in Venetian history and art, involving 12 guided tours of the city.

Fondazione Cini *(☎ 041 528 99 00, Isola di San Giorgio Maggiore)* **Map 1** This organisation runs seminars on subjects relating to the city, in particular music and art.

Organised Tours

You can join free tours for a biblical explanation of the mosaics in St Mark's Basilica. They are arranged by the Patriarcato (the church body in Venice) and take place in Italian at 11am Monday to Saturday, except on Wednesday, when it is at 3pm. English-language tours are at 11am on Monday, Thursday and Friday, and French-language tours are at the same time on Thursday. This timetable seems to be subject to regular change. Call ☎ 041 270 24 21 for details.

Consult *Un Ospite di Venezia* for details of other visits to churches and sights in the city. The APT has an updated list of authorised guides, who will take you on a walking tour of the city.

Travel agencies all over central Venice can put you onto all kinds of city tours, ranging from guided walks for €23.25 to gondola rides with serenade for €31 per person.

Want to do it yourself but without a real person? A popular new option are the My Venice handheld itinerary earpieces. You rent these things (which look like long mobile phones) for anything from an hour (€3.60) to two days (€15.50). With the accompanying map, you can follow itineraries with commentaries to key parts of the city. Want a break? Switch it off (can't do that with human guides!). You can hire the earpieces at the Venice Pavilion tourist office (see under Tourist Offices earlier). Languages catered for are Italian, English, French and German. You need to leave your passport as a guarantee that you'll return the item when you've finished.

Special Events

The major event of the year is Carnevale, when Venetians don spectacular masks and costumes for a 10-day street party in the run up to Ash Wednesday.

The APT publishes a list of annual events, including the many religious festivals staged by almost every church in the city. One is held in July at the Chiesa del Redentore (see Giudecca under Islands of the Lagoon earlier) and another at the Chiesa di Santa Maria della Salute each November (see the earlier Dorsoduro section).

The city next hosts the Regatta of the Four Ancient Maritime Republics in June 2003. The former maritime republics of Genoa, Pisa, Venice and Amalfi take turns to host this colourful event. The annual Regatta del Redentore, held each July on the Grand Canal, is another celebration of the city's former maritime supremacy.

The Regata Storica (Historic Regatta) is a gondola race along the Grand Canal and is preceded by a parade of boats decorated in 15th-century style. It is held on the first Sunday in September.

The Venice Biennale, a major exhibition of international visual arts, started in 189[illegible] and was held every even-numbered year from the early 20th century onwards. However, the 1992 festival was postponed until 1993 so there would be a festival on the Biennale's 100th anniversary in 1995. It is held from June to October in permanent pavilions in the Giardini Pubblici (Map 1), as well as in other locations throughout the city. The next one is in 2003. Major art exhibitions are held at the Palazzo Grassi (see under Grand Canal earlier) and you will find smaller exhibitions in various venues around the city throughout the year.

The Venice International Film Festival, Mostra del Cinema di Venezia, Italy's version of Cannes, is organised by the Biennale and held annually in August/September at the Palazzo del Cinema on the Lido (see The Lido earlier).

Places to Stay

Venice is an expensive place to stay, it's as simple as that. Even in the depths of low season you won't find more than about half a dozen places offering singles/doubles without bathroom for less than €36.15/51.65. A decent budget double with private bathroom can easily cost from €77.45 up in high season. Most places include breakfast (usually unsatisfactory) whether you like it or not.

Budget travellers have the option of the youth hostel on Giudecca and a handful of other dormitory style arrangements, some of them religious institutions. They mostly open in summer only.

Most of the top hotels are around San Marco and along the Grand Canal but it is possible to find bargains tucked away in tiny streets and on side canals in the heart of the city. There are lots of hotels near the train station but it is a good 30-minute walk to San Marco. The Dorsoduro area is quiet and relatively tourist-free.

It's advisable to book well in advance year-round in Venice but particularly in May, September, during Carnevale and other holidays (such as Easter, Christmas and New Year) and at weekends.

The ***Associazione Veneziana Albergatori*** has offices at the train station, in Piazzale Roma and at the Tronchetto car park. Staff here will book you a room but you must leave a small deposit.

By the time you have this guide in your hands, inflation will have sent prices up but in Venice hotel rates also vary wildly for a range of other reasons. Some hotels have the same prices year-round while others drop them when things are slow (as though that happens a lot). Low season for the average Venetian hotelier means November, early December and January. For some there's a dip in July and early August.

Some of the more expensive hotels operate further price differentials: weekend rates can be higher than during the week. Rooms with views (especially of the Grand Canal) are generally dearer than those without. Finally, proprietors' whims can produce all sorts of results.

The prices that follow should, therefore, be regarded as an orientation at best. Where possible, plan ahead and shop around. Remember that, unless you leave a deposit, many smaller hotels won't feel obliged to hold a room for you all day unless you call to confirm.

Consider using Mestre or Padua (see Padua under Around the Veneto later in the chapter) as a base, or at least for a day or two while you get oriented in Venice (Padua is only 37km, or 30 minutes on most trains, away), to give yourself time to find and book a place that suits.

Places to Stay – Budget

Camping There are numerous camp sites, many with bungalows, at Litorale del Cavallino, the coast along the Adriatic Sea, north-east of the city. A handful of sites are located closer to the city. The APT has a full list.

Marina di Venezia *(☎ 041 96 61 46, fax 041 96 60 36, W www.marinadivenezia.it; Via Montello 6, Punta Sabbioni)* Sites per person €7.50, per tent €13.40-18.60. Open late Apr-Sept. This camp site, which is on the Litorale de Cavallino, has just about everything, from a private beach to a shop, cinema and playground. You can get the No 12 vaporetto from Punta Sabbioni to Fondamente Nuove (Cannaregio) via Burano and Murano or the No 14 to San Zaccaria via the Lido.

Hostels The one HI hostel in Venice is complemented by several other hostel-style and dorm options.

Ostello Venezia *(☎ 041 523 82 11, fax 041 523 56 89, Fondamenta delle Zitelle 86)* **Map 1** B&B in dorm beds €15.50. Open 7am-9.30am & 2pm-11.30pm. This HI property is on Giudecca. It's open to members only, although you can buy a card there (see Documents in the Facts for the Visitor chapter for more details). Evening meals are available for €7.75. The hostel is on HI's computerised International Booking Network (IBN). Catch vaporetto No 41, 42 or 82 from the train station or Piazzale Roma to Zitelle.

Istituto Canossiano *(☎/fax 041 522 21 57, Fondamenta di Ponte Piccolo 428)* **Map 1** Singles/doubles €56.80/87.80, beds in triples or quads €38.70. Open June-Sept. Near the Ostello Venezia this place, clearly no longer a budget option but included here because it is run as a hostel, is for women only. Vaporetto No 41, 42 or 82 takes you to Sant'Eufemia on Giudecca.

Ostello Santa Fosca *(☎/fax 041 71 57 75, Fondamenta Canal 2372, Cannaregio)* **Map 3** Dorm beds/doubles per person €18.10/€20.65. This is a fairly no-nonsense hostel for young people but the setting is peaceful and there's a garden. From July to September guests have use of kitchen facilities too.

Domus Civica *(☎ 041 72 11 03, fax 041 522 71 39, Calle Campazze 3082)* **Map 2** Dorm beds/doubles €25.80/46.50. Open mid-Jun–early Sept. This place has student dorm-style beds and doubles, and is not bad for what it is. The location is fine and not too far from the train station.

Pensiones & Hotels – San Marco Despite being the most heavily touristed part of Venice, San Marco contains a few places that offer comparatively good value for money. All are on Map 2.

Hotel ai do Mori *(☎ 041 520 48 17, fax 041 520 53 28, w www.hotelaidomori.com, Calle Larga San Marco 658)* Doubles without/with bath up to €82.60/118.80. This hotel is just off St Mark's Square. It has pleasant rooms, some of which offer views of the basilica. The pick of the crop is without doubt the cosy little double at the top that comes with a terrace attached.

Locanda Casa Petrarca *(☎/fax 041 520 04 30, San Marco 4386)* Singles/doubles without bath €41.30/77.50. Doubles with toilet and shower €98.15. This is one of the nicest places to stay in this area. Breakfast costs an extra €5.20. It's a bit of a family affair and the cheerful owner speaks English.

Locanda Fiorita *(☎ 041 523 47 54, fax 041 522 80 43, e locafior@tin.it, San Marco 3457/a)* Singles without bath up to €72.30, doubles with bath up to €108.45. This old Venetian pile is set on a wonderful little square a spit away from the broad Campo Santo Stefano. The rooms are simple but well maintained.

Pensiones & Hotels – Dorsoduro
You'll find all these on Map 2.

Albergo Antico Capon *(☎/fax 041 528 52 92, e hotelanticocapon@hotmail.com, Campo Santa Margherita 3004/b)* Rooms up to €85.20. This place is right on the liveliest square in Dorsoduro and has a variety of rooms. The beds are wide and firm, the rooms bright and airy.

Hotel Galleria *(☎/fax 041 520 41 72, w www.hotelgalleria.it, Accademia 878/a)* Singles/doubles from €51.65/87.80, largest double €123.95. This is the only one-star hotel right on the Grand Canal. Space is a little tight, but the decor is welcoming. If you can get one of the rooms on the canal, how can you possibly complain?

Pensiones & Hotels – San Polo This pensione is on Map 2.

Pensione Guerrato *(☎ 041 522 71 31, fax 041 528 59 27, e hguerrat@tin.it, Ruga due Mori 240/a)* Doubles without/with bath €87.80/108.45. This pensione, in amid the Rialto markets, is a gem. It is housed in a former convent, which before had served as a hostel for knights heading off on the Third Crusade.

Pensiones & Hotels – Santa Croce These are both on Map 2.

Albergo Casa Peron *(☎ 041 71 00 21, fax 041 71 10 38, Salizzada San Pantalon 85)* Singles/doubles with shower €43.90/67.15. This is a small but characterful place, with rooms tucked around corners and up stairs. You'll pay €20.65 to €25.80 for a room with its own toilet.

Hotel dalla Mora *(☎ 041 71 07 03, fax 041 72 30 06, Santa Croce 42/a)* Singles/doubles with bath up to €56.80/82.65. This hotel is on a small canal just off Salizzada San Pantalon, near the Casa Peron. It has clean, airy rooms, some (like No 5) with lovely canal views, and there is a terrace.

Pensiones & Hotels – Cannaregio There are plenty to choose from here, with many hotels just a stone's throw from the train station. Find these on Map 3.

Hotel Santa Lucia *(☎/fax 041 71 51 80, Calle della Misericordia 358)* Singles without bath €51.65, doubles without/with bath €77.50/98.15. Off the Lista di Spagna, this hotel is in a newish building with clean, spacious and well-kept rooms.

Hotel Adua *(☎ 041 71 61 84, fax 041 244 01 62, Lista di Spagna 233/a)* Doubles without/with bath €72.30/108.45. Renovated in 1999, this place is not a bad deal. The theme is blinding white but it's clean and comfortable. Single occupancy of rooms costs a little less.

Hotel Rossi *(☎ 041 71 51 64, fax 041 71 77 84, Calle delle Procuratie 262)* Singles/doubles without bath up to €46.50/69.70, doubles with bath €85.20. This place is in a tiny lane off the Lista di Spagna. The rooms are pleasant enough, with wood panelling, fans and heating. The location is nice and quiet while still handy for the train station. Prices include breakfast.

Alloggi Calderan and ***Casa Gerotto*** *(☎ 041 71 53 61, Campo San Geremia 283)* Dorm beds about €18.10, doubles without/with bath €67.15/93. This twin family pack is the pick of the crop on this square for a simple, budget deal. They have combined to offer a whole range of rooms. The handful of bright singles are hard to come by as they are generally occupied by long-term residents. The dorms are single sex. Triples are also available and most rooms have pleasing views over the square. Prices can drop by about a third in slow periods.

Pensiones & Hotels – Castello Close to the centre or farther out, Castello offers a range of places to lay your head.

Hotel Doni *(☎/fax 041 522 42 67, Fondamenta del Vin 4656)* **Map 2** Singles/doubles without bath €46.50/72.30, doubles with bath €98.15. A stone's throw east of San Marco, this delightful little establishment, an 18th-century mansion, has been a hotel for more than a century. The 12 rooms are mostly spacious and the ceiling of one is adorned with a fine fresco dating from 1850.

Locanda Silva *(☎ 041 522 76 43, fax 041 528 68 17, e albergosilva@libero.it, Fondamenta del Rimedio 4423)* **Map 2** Singles/doubles without bath €43.90/72.30, singles/doubles with shower & toilet €62/98.15. This place, south of Campo Santa Maria Formosa has modest rooms that are clean and pleasant enough. A few look onto the narrow canal.

Albergo al Nuovo Teson *(☎/fax 041 520 55 55, Ramo Pescaria 3980)* **Map 1** Singles/doubles up to €108.45/118.80. This place is secreted away on a square with a real local flavour. The rooms are elegantly furnished and equipped with shower, TV and phone.

Locanda Sant'Anna *(☎/fax 041 528 64 66, e hsantanna@tin.it, Corte del Bianco 269)* Single/doubles without bath up to €54.20/64.60, doubles with bath €93. The locanda is hidden away right in the east of Castello. You can't get much farther away from the heart of Venice and still be there! Rooms are modest but comfortable.

Pensiones & Hotels – The Lido Hop off to the Lido to be near the beach.

Pensione La Pergola *(☎ 041 526 07 84, Via Cipro 15)* Singles/doubles with bath €38.75/77.50. This pensione, just off Gran Viale Santa Maria Elisabetta, has a range of rooms. Prices can be halved in the low season. The rooms are simple but pleasant enough. It's about as cheap as you'll find on the Lido in summer.

Pensiones & Hotels – Burano For village appeal, check out Burano.

Locanda Al Raspo de Ua *(☎/fax 041 73 00 95, Via Galuppi 560)* Doubles without bath from €96.50. This is a modest place on the island's main drag. It is the only place to stay here and could make your Venetian visit a quite different experience.

Pensiones & Hotels – Mestre Mestre is a drab, if sometimes necessary, alternative to staying in Venice. There are a number of good hotels, as well as plenty of cafes and places to eat around the main square.

Albergo Roberta *(☎ 041 92 93 55, fax 041 93 09 83, Via Sernaglia 21)* Singles without bath €43.90, singles/doubles with bath €62/93. This place has good-sized, clean rooms; breakfast is included.

Giovannina *(☎ 041 92 63 96, fax 041 538 84 42, Ⓦ www.hotelgiovannina.it, Via Dante 113)* Singles without bath €33.55, doubles up to €67.15. This place is a cheaper alternative to the Albergo Roberta and perfectly acceptable. Prices include breakfast.

Places to Stay – Mid-Range

Dorsoduro There are a couple of excellent choices here, both on Map 2.

Pensione Accademia Villa Maravege *(☎ 041 521 01 88, fax 041 523 91 52, Ⓦ www.pensioneaccademia.it, Fondamenta Bollani 1058)* Singles/doubles up to €113.60/216.90. This popular hotel is set in lovely gardens, with views of the Grand Canal.

Albergo agli Alboretti *(☎ 041 523 00 58, fax 041 521 01 58, Ⓔ alborett@gpnet.it, Rio Terrà Antonio Foscarini 884)* Singles/doubles up to €90.40/139.45. This is a charming hotel that almost feels like an inviting mountain chalet when you step inside. In its category, it is one of Venice's star choices. The management is friendly and the rooms tastefully arranged. The restaurant is also of a high standard.

San Polo Find this on Map 2.

Locanda Sturion *(☎ 041 523 62 43, fax 041 522 83 78, Ⓦ www.locandasturion.com, Calle Sturion 679)* Singles/doubles from €108.45/175.60. This inn is two minutes from the Ponte di Rialto. It has been a hotel on and off since the 13th century and has superb rooms.

Cannaregio Head north for more interesting options.

Hotel Tre Archi *(☎ 041 524 43 56, fax 041 71 03 57, Ⓦ www.hoteltrearchi.com, Fondamenta di Cannaregio 923)* **Map 1** Singles/doubles €196.25/206.60. This attractive little hotel of 24 rooms is set away from the tourist rush in a bit of the 'real Venice'. The place is furnished and decorated in classical Venetian style. Many rooms have views over the canal.

Locanda Leon Bianco *(☎ 041 523 35 72, fax 041 241 63 92, Campiello Leon Bianco 5629)* **Map 2** Doubles €144.60. This is a fine option. The best three rooms (of eight) look right onto the Grand Canal. The undulating *terrazzo alla Veneziana* floors and heavy timber doors with their original locks lend the rooms real charm. There are no singles but the price drops to €118.80 in small rooms which do not have canal views.

Castello There are good, historic accommodation options in this range here.

La Residenza *(☎ 041 528 53 15, fax 041 523 88 59, Ⓦ www.venicelaresidenza.com, Campo Bandiera e Moro)* **Map 1** Singles/doubles up to €92.96/144.50. If you can live without watery views, head inland to this delightful 15th-century mansion. The main hall upstairs makes quite an impression with its candelabras, elaborate decoration and distinguished furniture. The rooms are rather more restrained but fine value.

Locanda Remedio *(☎ 041 520 62 32, fax 041 521 04 85, Calle del Rimedio 4412)* **Map 2** Singles/doubles up to €93/154.95. This is indeed something of a remedy... especially after the streaming, screaming masses of visitors thronging around San Marco, just a few minutes away. It's hard to imagine them so close to the tranquil little courtyard in which this inn is hidden. Try for the front double with the 16th-century fresco.

Places to Stay – Top End

San Marco This is marked on Map 2.

Gritti Palace *(☎ 041 79 46 11, fax 041 520 09 42, ⓔ reso73.grittipalace@luxury collection.com, Campo Santa Maria del Giglio 2467)* Doubles up to €981.30. This luxury property, the facade of which fronts the Grand Canal, is one of the most famous hotels in Venice. If you can afford to pay top rates, you'll be mixing with royalty.

Cannaregio This is on Map 3.

Grand Hotel Palazzo dei Dogi *(☎ 041 220 81 11, fax 041 72 22 78, ⓔ grandhotel deidogi@italyhotel.com, Fondamenta Madonna dell'Orto 3500)* Singles/doubles up to €284.05/387.35. A cut above and apart, this hotel stands in splendid isolation right up in the north-west of the city.

Castello This is on Map 2.

Hotel Danieli *(☎ 041 522 64 80, fax 041 520 02 08, ⓔ reso72danieli@starwood hotels.com, Riva degli Schiavoni 4196, Castello)* Singles/doubles up to €413.20/878. Most of the rooms in this top ranking establishment look out over the canal. It opened as a hotel in 1822 in the Palazzo Dandolo.

Giudecca Check out Map 1 for this hotel.

Hotel Cipriani *(☎ 041 520 77 44, fax 041 520 39 30, ⓔ info@hotelcipriani.it, Giudecca 10)* Suites up to €1084.60. This place is set in the one-time villa of the Mocenigo family and surrounded by lavish grounds. Prices drop considerably in the low season.

The Lido Out on the Lido you'll find these top-end options.

Villa Mabapa *(☎ 041 526 05 90, fax 041 526 94 41, ⓦ www.villamabapa.com, Riviera San Nicolò 16)* Singles/doubles up to €181.80/284.05. This is a pleasant hideaway, handy for the vaporetto stop. A grand old residence, it is frequently booked out in summer and for the cinema festival in September.

Grand Hotel Des Bains *(☎ 041 526 59 21, fax 041 526 01 13, ⓦ www.starwood.com/sheraton, Lungomare Guglielmo Marconi 17)* Doubles around €402.85. This is the top address for Thomas Mann fans.

Places to Eat

Venice is about the most expensive city in Italy for eating out, so you may find yourself resorting to *tramezzini* (sandwiches) that cost up to €2.60 for lunch-time snacks.

Search out the little trattorias and osterias tucked away along side lanes and canals or dotted about squares away from the main tourist centres. Many bars serve filling snacks with lunch-time and pre-dinner drinks.

Better areas to look for places to eat include the back streets of Cannaregio and San Polo, as well as around Campo Santa Margherita in Dorsoduro. A few good spots lurk about in Castello and even a few in San Marco if you are prepared to search them out.

San Marco These are all on Map 2.

Ai Rusteghi *(☎ 041 523 22 05, Calletta della Bissa 5529)* Snacks €1.55-2.60. Open 9.30am-3pm & 5pm-8.30pm Mon-Sat. For a great range in mini-*panini* (sandwiches), pop into Ai Rusteghi. They also offer good wines. There's nothing better than an *ombra* (small glass of wine) or two and a couple of panini as a quick lunch-time snack.

Vino Vino *(☎ 041 241 76 88, Ponte delle Veste 2007/a, San Marco)* Pasta or risotto €4.65, mains €8.30. Open Wed-Mon. This is a popular bar/osteria near Teatro La Fenice. The menu changes daily and the pre-prepared food is of a reasonable quality. *Sarde in saor* (fried, marinated pilchards) costs €8.30. There is a good selection of vegetables. Wine is sold by the glass for €1.

Osteria al Bacareto *(☎ 041 528 93 36, San Marco 3447)* Meals around €23. Open Mon-Fri. The search for a good traditional trattoria in this corner of San Marco is over when you reach Osteria al Bacareto. Since it doubles as an osteria, you can opt for a plateful of *cicheti* (snacks) with a glass of wine.

Ristorante da Ivo *(☎ 041 528 50 04, San Marco 1809)* Meals €46.50-51.65. Open Mon-Sat. This dining classic specialises in seafood as well as offering a mix of Venetian and Tuscan meat dishes.

Dorsoduro You'll find all these on Map 2.

Osteria da Toni *(☎ 041 528 68 99, Fondamenta San Basilio 1642)* Meals around €21. Open Tues-Sun. This is a popular workers' haunt. You can eat great seafood at relatively low prices or just sip wine. When the sun shines, take your place by the canal.

Arca *(☎ 041 524 22 36, Calle San Pantalon 3757)* Pizzas & pasta €4.65-7.75. Open Mon-Sat. On Tuesday nights there's live music here, usually of a light jazz variety, to accompany your cheap and cheerful chow.

Osteria ai Carmini *(☎ 041 523 11 15, 2894/a Dorsoduro)* Meals around €31. Open 9.30am-11pm Mon-Sat. For fresh fish and seafood, this one of the best spots around Campo Santa Margherita.

Santa Croce & San Polo These are all on Map 2.

Trattoria al Ponte *(☎ 041 71 97 77, Ponte del Megio 1666)* Meals around €26. Open Mon-Fri & Sat lunch. Arrive early here and try to grab one of the few canalside tables. This simple, rustic little eatery tends to specialise in fish but other options are available. The food is solid and the prices reasonable.

Osteria La Zucca *(☎ 041 524 15 70, Calle del Tintor 1762)* Meals €31. Open Mon-Sat. Just over the bridge, this is an excellent alternative. It seems like just another Venetian trattoria but the menu (which changes daily) is an enticing mix of Mediterranean themes. The vegetable side orders alone are inspired (try the *peperonata alle melanzane*, a cool stew of capsicum and aubergine) while the mains are substantial. You won't need to order pasta as well.

Ganesh Ji *(☎ 041 71 90 84, Rio Marin, San Polo 2426)* Set menu €22.20. Open Thur-Tues. Fancy a quick curry? Forget it. But a good slow one can be had on the pleasant little canalside terrace of this place. Danilo and his charmingly chaotic staff serve up authentic dishes at reasonable prices – particularly pleased guests have scribbled their appreciation on the walls. They even do takeaways.

Da Fiore *(☎ 041 72 13 08, Calle del Scaleter 2202)* Meals from €82.65. Open Tues-Sat. Recipient of a Michelin star, the unprepossessing shop-front appearance belies an Art Deco interior. Traditional dishes, such as *risotto ai scampi* (prawn risotto) and *bigoli in salsa* (thick spaghetti with sauce), are prepared with optimum care. They have a good wine selection. The prices don't deter people and the place can easily be booked out for dinner weeks in advance. It's easier to get in for lunch.

Vecio Fritolin *(☎ 041 522 28 81, Calle della Regina 226)* Set lunch €21.50, pasta €13, mains €18. Open Tues-Sat & Sun lunch. New management has brought a touch of class to dining here. Fresh ingredients are unfailingly used to create a combination of classic and inventive Italian cuisine.

Cannaregio Italian and international food can be found in this area.

La Colombina *(☎ 041 275 06 22, Campiello del Pegolotto 1828)* **Map 3** Meals around €21. Open Tues-Sat. An excellent wine list accompanies a delicious range of dishes and snacks.

Paradiso Perduto *(☎ 041 72 05 81, Fondamenta della Misericordia 2539)* **Map 3** Meals around €21. Open Thurs-Sat & Mon-Tues. Young people will enjoy this restaurant/bar, which has live music and tables outside in summer. The *lasagna ai carciofi* (artichoke lasagne) is great.

Sahara *(☎ 041 72 10 7, Fondamenta della Misericordia 2520)* **Map 3** Mains €9.30. Open Tues-Sun. Sahara serves up good Middle Eastern food and you can even clap along to a not-so-authentic display of belly dancing.

Pizzeria Casa Mia *(☎ 041 28 55 90, Calle dell'Oca 4430)* **Map 2** Pizzas & pasta around €6, mains around €13. Open Wed-Mon. Venice is full of pizzerias but this welcoming little place, hidden just out of sight of the hubbub, is a good spot for pizzas prepared the way they should be.

Gam Gam *(☎ 041 71 52 84, Ghetto Nuovo 2884)* **Map 3** Pasta around €7.75, mains €12.90. Open noon-10pm, Sun-Thurs & Fri lunch. Gam Gam is great for your taste buds if you like Israeli-style falafels and other Middle Eastern delicacies, with the occasional variation on Italian food.

Castello Snacks, seafood or sushi, Castello's got a lot to offer.

Al Vecchio Penasa *(☎ 041 523 72 02, Calle delle Rasse, Castello 4587)* **Map 2** Sandwiches €1.30. Open 6.30am-11.30pm daily. This place is between Riva degli Schiavoni and Campo SS Filippo e Giacomo. It offers an excellent selection of sandwiches and snacks at reasonable prices.

Alla Rivetta *(☎ 041 528 73 02, Ponte San Provolo 4625)* **Map 2** Mains €9.30-11.40. Open Tues-Sun. This is one of the few restaurants near St Mark's Square that can be recommended. It has long been on the tourist list of 'must' places to eat but you can still get edible seafood for not unreasonable prices.

Tokyo Sushi Restaurant *(☎ 041 277 04 20, Calle Casselleria 5281)* **Map 2** Sushi around €10.30. Don't get too excited as this is not the best sushi you will ever eat. It is, however, about the only sushi you'll find in Venice. And that's about all we can say really.

Trattoria Corte Sconta *(☎ 041 522 70 24, Calle Pestrin 3886)* **Map 1** Meals with wine around €46.50. Open Tues-Sat. This trattoria is hidden well away off even the unbeaten track. The chefs prepare almost exclusively seafood, fresh from the market and served up to you in a charming little garden (or indoors). Try the *risotto ai scampi* (€14.50), for instance.

Giudecca Find these on Map 1.

Ai Tre Scaini *(☎ 041 522 47 90, Calle Michelangelo 53/c)* Meals with wine about €23. Open noon-2.30pm & 6pm-1am Mon-Sat. This is *the* popular local eatery. It's a no-nonsense place for seafood and other goodies, and you can dine in the garden out the back.

Harry's Dolci *(☎ 041 522 48 44, Fondamenta San Biagio 773)* Pasta from €17.60, mains from €28.90. Open Wed-Mon Apr-Oct. Run by the Hotel Cipriani, this place has fantastic desserts (which is the main reason for dropping in). Should you want a full meal they can accommodate you (at elevated prices). There's a snack bar too.

Torcello This island offers an enticing lunch-time stop.

Locanda Cipriani *(☎ 041 73 01 50, Piazza Santa Fosca 29)* Meals from €51.65. Open lunch Wed-Mon & dinner Sat. This has been an exclusive culinary hideaway since 1946. Ernest Hemingway, more readily associated with Spain, set down his bags here in 1948 and wrote part of his *Across the River and Into the Trees*. They don't let out rooms in this rustic retreat anymore but it's an enticing place to splash out on your rumbling tum.

Chioggia Make the trip if it's good seafood that you're after.

Osteria Penzo *(☎ 041 40 09 92, Calle Larga Bersaglio 526)* Meals around €26 excluding wine. Open Wed-Mon. This place once offered no more than wine and basic cicheti but now presents local cuisine based entirely on the fleet's catch.

Mestre Head to the mainland to find this osteria.

Osteria La Pergola *(☎ 041 97 49 32, Via Fiume 42)* Meals under €22. Open Mon-Fri & dinner Sat. At this osteria you could be served a delicious plate of *pappardelle all'anatra* (a thick pasta with duck) below the vines of the garden pergola.

Chains Those on a tight budget in particular may want to keep an eye out for these cheaper eateries. Find them on Map 2.

Brek *(☎ 041 244 01 58, Rio Terrà Lista di Spagna 124, Cannaregio)* First/second courses about €3.35/5.20. Open 7.30am-10.30pm (full meals available lunch & dinner) daily. If you have to do cheap fastish food, you could do a lot worse than take a break here.

Spizzico *(Campo San Luca 4475–4476, San Marco)* Pizza slices around €3. Open 9am-11pm daily (sometimes closed Sun). For quick slices of pizza this place isn't bad – the chain is quite popular across northern Italy. If you want burgers instead, a ***Burger King*** is located on the same premises.

Osterias A Venetian osteria is a cross between a bar and a trattoria, where you can sample cicheti, generally washed down with an ombra. Locals often choose to bar-hop from osteria to osteria, a great way to experience a more down-to-earth side of Venice. Some osterias also serve full meals.

La Mascareta *(☎ 041 523 07 44, Calle Lunga Santa Maria Formosa 5138, Castello)* **Map 2** Open Mon-Sat. This 'little mask' is a perfectly genial tavern for the sipping of wine accompanied by a limited but tempting range of cicheti.

Al Portego *(☎ 041 522 90 38, San Lio 6015, Castello)* **Map 2** Open Mon-Sat. Situated beneath the portico that gives this osteria its name, Al Portego is an inviting stop for cicheti and wine, along with some robust meals. Try the *bigoli*, a thick wholemeal flour spaghetti – a Venetian speciality – whatever sauce it comes with.

Osteria dalla Vedova *(☎ 041 528 53 24, Calle del Pistor 3912)* **Map 2** Meals around €23. Open Mon-Wed & Fri-Sat. Off Strada Nova in Cannaregio, the 'Widow's Hostelry' is also called Trattoria Ca d'Or and is one of the oldest osterias in Venice. The food is excellent and modestly priced.

Cantina Vecia Carbonera *(☎ 041 71 03 76, Ponte Sant'Antonio 2329, Cannaregio)* **Map 3** Meals around €21. Open Tues-Sun. You can prop up the bar and treat yourself to an ombra and a few cicheti or sit down for a full meal in this ageless osteria.

Enoteca Il Volto *(☎ 041 522 89 45, Calle Cavalli 4081)* **Map 2** Open Mon-Sat. In the San Marco area, near Campo San Luca, this spot has an excellent wine selection and good snacks.

Cantina do Mori *(☎ 041 522 54 01, Sotoportego dei do Mori 429)* **Map 2** Open Mon-Sat. On the San Polo side of the Ponte di Rialto, this is something of a traditional institution.

Cantina do Spade *(☎ 041 521 05 74, Calle do Spade 860)* Meals €31. Open Mon-Sat. Welcome to Venice's oldest eating house, where the emphasis is more on the full meals than hanging about the bar for snacks.

All'Arco *(☎ 041 520 56 66, Calle Arco, San Polo 436)* **Map 2** Open Mon-Sat. If what you are looking for around here is cicheti and a glass or two of wine, All'Arco is the place for you.

Cafes If you can cope with the idea of paying from €5.20 (some lucky people have reported being charged as much as €10.35!) for a cappuccino, spend an hour or so sitting at an outdoor table at the centuries-old Florian or Quadri and enjoy the atmosphere of St Mark's Square (Map 2).

Caffè Florian *(☎ 041 520 56 41, Piazza San Marco 56/59)* This is the more famous of the two. Lord Byron and Henry James used to take breakfast (separately) here.

Caffè Quadri *(☎ 041 522 21 05, San Marco 120)* Open Wed-Sun. Quadri is in much the same league as Florian, and equally steeped in history.

Gelaterias & Pasticcerias Ice cream prices range from about €1 for a small cup to €2.10 for a big cone. Prices don't vary much but the generosity of serves can.

Gelateria Millefoglie da Tarcisio *(San Polo 3034)* **Map 2** This gelateria, behind the Chiesa di Santa Maria Gloriosa dei Frari, is an excellent ice cream stop.

Gelateria Nico *(Fondamenta delle Zattere 922, Dorsoduro)* **Map 1** Head here for the best ice cream in Venice. The locals take their evening stroll along the fondamenta while eating their gelato.

Gelateria il Doge *(Campo Santa Margherita, Dorsoduro)* **Map 2** This place also has excellent gelato.

Self-Catering Putting your own snacks together is the cheapest way to keep body and soul together. The best markets take place on the San Polo side of the Ponte di Rialto. Grocery shops, where you can buy salami, cheese and bread, are concentrated around Campo Beccarie, which happens to lie next to the city's main fish market.

Standa Supermarket *(Strada Nova, Cannaregio)* **Map 3** Open 9am-7.30pm daily. This supermarket is a reasonably well-stocked option for self-caterers.

Entertainment

The Venice Carnevale (see Special Events earlier) is one of Italy's best-known festivals but exhibitions, theatre and musical events continue throughout the year in Venice. Information is available in *Un Ospite di Venezia* and the APT office also has brochures listing events and performances year-round. The monthly *Venezia News* magazine has extensive listings too.

Bars & Pubs There's a number of places in Venice where you can wet your whistle.

Torino@Notte *(☎ 041 522 39 14, Campo San Luca 459, San Marco)* **Map 2** Open 10pm-2am Tues-Sat. This unlikely looking spot during the day livens up at night as a young student set settles in for mixed drinks, music and occasionally even a live act.

Caffè Blue *(☎ 041 523 72 27, Dorsoduro 3778)* **Map 2** Open 8am-2pm & 5pm-2am Mon-Sat. This is a coolish student bar with live music on Friday. It can be a little quiet on some evenings.

Caffè *(☎ 041 528 79 98, Campo Santa Margherita 2693, Dorsoduro)* **Map 2** Open Mon-Sat. A lively, hip student bar with snacks, it is known to locals as the *caffè rosso* because of the red sign.

Round Midnight *(☎ 041 523 20 56, Fondamenta dei Pugni 3102, Dorsoduro)* **Map 2** Open 7pm-2am Mon-Sat. After you've finished hanging about and soaking up the atmosphere on Campo Santa Margherita, head around to this little drink-and-dance cove on a back canal. You can sip all sorts of cocktails and even get a snack. The music tends to be acid jazz and Latin.

The Fiddler's Elbow *(☎ 041 523 99 30, Corte dei Pali 3847, Cannaregio)* **Map 2** Open 5pm-1am Thurs-Tues. On the Irish scene, this place is representative of the genre.

Osteria agli Ormesini *(☎ 041 71 38 34, Fondamenta degli Ormesini 2710, Cannaregio)* **Map 3** Open to 2am Mon-Sat. Oodles of wine and 120 types of bottled beer in one knockabout little place? Perhaps you should get along to this osteria. It's something of a student haunt and tipplers spill out on to the fondamenta to enjoy their ambers.

Harry's Bar *(☎ 041 528 57 77, Calle Vallaresso 1323, San Marco)* **Map 2** As well as being one of the city's more notable restaurants (a meal will cost more than €77.45), Harry's is, of course, first and foremost known as a bar. Everyone who is anyone and passing through Venice usually ends up here sooner or later. The Aga Khan has lounged around here and other characters as diverse as Orson Welles, Ernest Hemingway and Truman Capote have all sipped on a cocktail or two at Harry's.

Discos & Clubs This place is on Map 3.

Casanova *(☎ 041 275 01 99, Lista di Spagna 158/a, Cannaregio)* Open 6pm-4am Tues & Thurs-Sat. A quick stumble from the train station, this is it, about the only place in Venice that can vaguely call itself a disco.

Most locals go to one of a handful of clubs on the mainland in and around Mestre. In summer, Jesolo and its beach (to the north of the lagoon) is where most of the action takes place.

Cinemas There is no English-language cinema in the city.

Summer Arena *(Campo San Polo)* This is a cinema-under-the-stars during July and August. It often features British and American films but they are generally dubbed.

The time to see cinema in the original language is during the September film festival (see Special Events earlier).

Theatre, Opera & Classical Music There are a number of options for more classical entertainment in Venice.

Teatro La Fenice *(Campo San Fantin 1970, San Marco)* **Map 2** Until it was destroyed by fire in January 1996, this was Venice's premier opera stage. Performances of opera and ballet are still organised but held in alternative venues. The bulk of performances have been held at the hastily erected circus-style big top called the ***PalaFenice*** *(☎ 041 520 40 10, Isola del Tronchetto)*.

Tickets for Fenice performances are available from the ***Cassa di Risparmio di Venezia bank*** *(☎ 041 521 01 61, Campo*

San Luca) **Map 2** Open 8.30am-1.30pm Mon-Fri. Alternatively, you can try at the theatres an hour before the show starts. You can also look up the programme on the Web at **W** www.teatrolafenice.it and book online. At the same online address, you can also find details of booking agents in your country. The cost of ticket ranges up to €31 for a decent seat at the opera.

Teatro Goldoni *(☎ 041 520 75 83, Calle Teatro Goldoni 4650/b, San Marco)* **Map 2** Named after the city's greatest playwright, this is, unsurprisingly, the main theatre in the centre of town. It's not unusual for Goldoni's plays to be performed here – after all, what more appropriate location?

Casinos Gamble away your cash at the itinerant casino.

Casinò Municipale di Venezia *(☎ 041 529 71 11)* In winter the casino is at the Palazzo Vendramin-Calergi (Map 3), on the Grand Canal and in summer it moves to the Palazzo del Casinò on the Lido. Vaporetto No 61 or 62 from San Zaccaria take you to/from the summer residence.

Shopping

You can expect most shops hoping to sell to tourists to open all weekend during the high season (Easter to September).

The main shopping area for clothing, shoes, accessories and jewellery is in the narrow streets between San Marco and the Rialto, particularly the Mercerie and around Campo San Luca (Map 2). The more up-market shopping area is west of St Mark's Square.

Classic gift options include Carnevale masks, *carta marmorizzata* (marbled paper), Murano glass and Burano lace.

You'll find all of the following places on Map 2.

Galleria Marina Barovier *(☎ 041 522 61 02, Calle delle Carrozze 3216, San Marco)* This place is damn expensive but wander down here to see the latest creations in glass of some of the most outstanding artists in Venice.

Ca' Macana *(☎ 041 520 32 29, Calle delle Botteghe 5176, Dorsoduro)* This is one of several places where you can see how Carnevale masks are made. Leonardo di Caprio even popped by, as the autograph in the window clearly testifies!

L'Arlecchino *(☎ 041 71 65 91, Calle dei Cristi 1722–1729, San Polo)* L'Arlecchino claims that their masks are made only with papier-maché to their own designs.

Jesurum *(☎ 041 520 60 85, Merceria del Capitello 4856, San Marco)* Jesurum has been in the lace business since 1860, when Michelangelo Jesurum opened a lace school on the Isola di Burano.

Legatoria Piazzesi *(☎ 041 522 12 02, Campiello della Feltrina 2551/c, San Marco)* This is the oldest shop purveying marbled paper products; they employ time-honoured methods to turn out high-quality (and high-priced) items.

Giacomo Rizzo *(☎ 041 522 28 24, Salizzada S Giovanni Crisostomo 5778, Cannaregio)* This place has been keeping the locals in pasta since 1905. Take a look at the unusual types, for instance Curaçao-blue tagliatelle.

Getting There & Away

Air Marco Polo airport (☎ 041 260 92 60 for flight details) is just east of Mestre and 12km from central Venice. It is served by flights from many major Italian and European cities, and from New York. Some flights, for example, Ryanair flights from the UK and Brussels, also arrive at Treviso's minuscule San Giuseppe airport. It is only about 5km south-west of Treviso and 50km from Venice. Airport bus services link both airports with Venice and Mestre and the Alilaguna hydrofoil runs from Marco Polo airport. See Getting Around later for details.

Bus ACTV local buses (☎ 041 528 78 86) leave from Piazzale Roma (Map 1) for surrounding areas, including Mestre and Chioggia.

ATVO (Azienda Trasporti Veneto Orientale; ☎ 041 520 55 30) operates buses to destinations all over the eastern part of the Veneto. A handful of other companies have the occasional service to more distant locations but to get to most places in Italy the train is an easier option. Tickets and information are available at the ticket office on Piazzale Roma.

Train The train station, Stazione di Santa Lucia (Maps 1 & 3), is directly linked by train to Padua (€2.35, 40 minutes), Verona (€5.75, one hour 35 minutes), Milan (€19.20, 2¾ hours), Trieste and Bologna, and is easily accessible from Florence and Rome. You can also reach Venice from major points in France, Germany, Austria, Switzerland, Slovenia and Croatia.

Orient Express The Venice Simplon Orient Express runs between London and Venice via Paris, Zürich and Verona, twice weekly from March to November. Departures from London are on Thursday and Sunday. The trip in old-world luxury takes about 30 hours and costs UK£1200 one way. You can choose from a couple of alternative routes too. Contact the headquarters in London (☎ 020-7805 5100, W www.orient-expresstrains.com).

Car & Motorcycle The A4 passes through Mestre. It's the fastest way to reach Venice. Take the Venice exit and follow the signs for the city. The A4 connects Trieste with Turin, passing through Milan. From the south, take the A13 from Bologna, which connects with the A4 at Padua. A more interesting route is to take the SS11 from Padua to Venice.

Once you cross the bridge from Mestre, the Ponte della Libertà (Map 1), cars must be left at one of the huge car parks on Piazzale Roma or on the island of Tronchetto. Parking is not cheap and you will pay €15.50 or more for every 24 hours. A cheaper alternative is to leave the car at Fusina near Mestre and catch the vaporetto No 16 to the Zattere (Map 2) and then the No 52 or No 51 to either San Marco or the train station (Map 2). Ask for information at the tourist office just before the bridge to Venice.

In Piazzale Roma (Map 1), you'll find Avis (☎ 199 10 01 33), Europcar (toll free ☎ 800 82 80 50), Hertz (☎ 199 11 22 11) and Expressway (☎ 041 522 30 00). They all have reps at Marco Polo airport too.

Boat Minoan Lines (☎ 041 271 23 45), Porto Venezia, Zona Santa Marta, runs ferries to/from Greece (Corfu, Igoumenitsa and Patras) daily in summer (four times weekly in winter). Passengers pay up to €89.80 one way, depending on the season, for an airline-style seat. Minoan Lines has offices in Athens and elsewhere in Greece but you can pick up tickets from most travel agents.

Strintzis Lines (☎ 041 277 05 59), Stazione Marittima 103, operates up to four ferries weekly in summer to the same destinations in Greece. A simple spot on the deck costs from €42.85 in the lowest season up to €61.35. Airline-style seats cost about the same as with Minoan Lines.

The journey to Igoumenitsa takes about 27 hours with either line. To Patras add another eight.

Getting Around

To/From the Airports The Alilaguna airport hydrofoil costs €9.80 to/from Venice or the Lido and €4.65 to/from Murano. You can pick it up at the Zattere or near St Mark's Square, in front of the Giardini Ex Reali. The official rate for the water-taxi ride between Piazzetta di San Marco and the airport is €44.95. To/from the Lido costs €55.30.

ATVO buses (☎ 041 520 55 30) run to the airport from Piazzale Roma (€2.60, 20 minutes) via Mestre train station. Regular ACTV city bus No 5 also serves the airport from Piazzale Roma (€0.80, 30 minutes). It makes more stops.

Vaporetto The city's mode of public transport are *vaporetti* (small passenger boats/ferries). A car ferry (No 17) transports vehicles from Tronchetto, near Piazzale Roma, to the Lido. From Piazzale Roma, vaporetto No 1 zigzags up the Grand Canal to San Marco and then the Lido. It is a great introduction to Venice but there are faster lines if you are in a hurry.

Single vaporetto tickets cost €3.10 (plus €3.10 for luggage!), even if you only ride to the next station. A 24-hour ticket is good value at €9.30 for unlimited travel. Better still are the three-day (€18.10) and weekly

(€31) tickets. Rolling Venice passholders (see the boxed text 'Discounts on Admission' earlier) can get the three-day ticket for €12.90. Those understandably tempted to ride without paying should note that ticket inspectors do *occasionally* make an appearance and the fine is €20.15.

Tickets can be purchased at the ticket booths at most landing stations and should be validated in the machines at each landing station if they have not already been validated on purchase. They must be used immediately after validation.

Routes and route numbers can change, so the following list should be taken as a guide:

No 1 Piazzale Roma–Ferrovia–Grand Canal–Lido (and back).
No 3 Fast Circular line: Tronchetto–Ferrovia–San Samuele–Accademia–San Marco–Tronchetto (summer only).
No 4 Fast Circular line in reverse direction to No 3 (summer only).
No 6 San Zaccaria-Lido (and back).
No 12 Fondamente Nuove–Murano–Burano–Torcello–Punta Sabbioni (and back).
No 13 Fondamente Nuove–Murano–Vignole–Treporti (and back).
No 14 San Zaccaria–Lido–Litorale del Cavallino (Punta Sabbioni). The one-way trip beyond the Lido costs an extra €2.60.
No 17 Car ferry: Tronchetto–Lido (and back).
No 20 San Zaccaria–San Servolo–San Clemente (and back).
No 41 Circular line: Piazzale Roma–Sacca Fisola–Giudecca–San Zaccaria–San Pietro–Fondamente Nuove–Ferrovia.
No 42 Circular line in reverse direction to No 41.
No 51 Circular line: Piazzale Roma–Zattere–San Zaccaria–Lido–Ferrovia.
No 52 Circular line in reverse direction to No 51.
No 61 Limited-stops circular line: Ferrovia–Piazzale Roma–Zattere–Arsenale–Sant'Elena–Lido (extends to the Casinò in summer).
No 62 Circular line in reverse direction to No 61.
No 71 Fast limited-stops line: San Zaccaria–Murano–Ferrovia–Piazzale Roma–Tronchetto (summer only).
No 72 Fast limited-stops line in reverse direction to No 71 (summer only).
No 82 San Zaccaria–San Marco–Grand Canal–Ferrovia–Piazzale Roma–Tronchetto–Zattere-Giudecca–San Giorgio-Lido (in summer only). A Limitato San Marco or Limitato Piazzale Roma sign means it will not go beyond those stops.
N All-stops night circuit: Lido–Giardini–San Zaccaria–Grand Canal–Ferrovia–Piazzale Roma–Tronchetto–Giudecca–San Giorgio–San Zaccaria.

Traghetto The poor man's gondola, *traghetti* are used by locals to cross the Grand Canal where there is no nearby bridge. There is no particular limit (except common sense) on the number of passengers who stand.

Traghetti operate from about 9am to 6pm between Campo del Traghetto (near Santa Maria del Giglio) and Calle de Lanza; Campo San Samuele, north of the Ponte dell'Accademia, and Calle Traghetto; Calle Mocenigo, farther north, and Calle Traghetto; and Campo Santa Sofia and Campo della Pescaria.

Several other routes operate from 9am to noon only. They include: the train station to Fondamenta San Simeon Piccolo; Campo San Marcuola (Map 3) to Salizzada del Fondaco dei Turchi; Fondamenta del Vin and Riva del Carbon; Calle Vallaresso to Punta della Dogana. Some of these may on occasion not operate at all. The ride costs €0.42 (although some locals round it up to €0.50).

Water Taxis Water taxis are prohibitively expensive, with a set €13.95 charge for a maximum of seven minutes, an extra €4.15 if you order one by telephone, and various surcharges that make a gondola ride seem cheap.

Porters Getting from the vaporetto stop to your hotel can be difficult if you are heavily laden with luggage. There are several stands around the city where porters *(portabagagli)* can be engaged to escort you to your hotel. They charge €10.35 for one item and roughly €5.20 for each extra one. Prices virtually double to transport bags to any of the other islands, including Giudecca.

Points where porters can be found include Ponte dell'Accademia (☎ 041 522 48 91), the train station (☎ 041 71 52 72), Piazzale Roma (☎ 041 522 35 90), Ponte di Rialto (☎ 041 520 53 08) and San Marco (☎ 041 523 23 85).

Around the Veneto

THE BRENTA RIVIERA

Dotted along River Brenta, which passes through Padua and spills into the Venetian lagoon, are more than 100 villas built by wealthy Venetian families as summer homes; most are closed to the public. The most outstanding are the **Villa Foscari** (1571), built by Palladio at Malcontenta, and the **Villa Pisani**, also known as the Villa Nazionale, at Strà, which was built for Doge Alvise Pisani. It was used by Napoleon and was the site of the first meeting between Hitler and Mussolini. ACTV buses running between Padua and Venice stop at or near the villas. Those that open do so with widely varying timetables from May to the end of September. Ask at the tourist offices in Venice for the latest details on opening times and admission costs. See Around Vicenza later for information on other Venetian villas. You can do tours along the River Brenta.

Burchiello *(☎ 049 377 47 12)* Day trips about €62. Mar-Oct. The luxurious *Burchiello* barge plied the Brenta between Venice and Padua in the 17th and 18th centuries. Today, these modern barges bear nothing in common with the original except the name. The price includes lunch and short tours. The trip is one way (either way) between Venice and Strà, with connecting shuttle buses between Strà and Padua. You can also get information from travel agents in Venice.

At least three other companies operate tours along the Brenta, including ***I Batelli del Brenta*** *(☎ 049 876 02 33)*. Ask at the Padua APT office for more details on all four companies.

PADUA (PADOVA)

postcode 35100 • pop 211,985

Although famous as the city of St Anthony and for its university, one of the oldest in Europe, Padua is often seen merely as a convenient and cheap place to stay while visiting Venice. This is a shame as the city offers a rich collection of art treasures, including Giotto's incredible frescoed chapel. There's also many piazzas and arcaded streets which are a pleasure to explore.

Padua's wealth grew during the 13th century when it was controlled by the counts of Carrara, who encouraged cultural and artistic pursuits (when they weren't busy warring with all and sundry neighbours) and established the Studium, the forerunner of the university.

Orientation

From the train station, it's a 10-minute walk across the square and up Corso del Popolo (later Corso Garibaldi) to the centre. Piazza della Frutta and the adjoining Piazza delle Erbe form the lively heart of the old city, bustling with market activity – take some time to drool over all the fine foods. The Basilica del Santo and the vast Prato della Valle (an enormous piazza that has been the site of theatres, fairgrounds and quarries over the past two thousand years) are a good 20-minute walk south from the train station.

Information

Tourist Offices The IAT office at the train station (☎ 049 875 20 77) opens 9.15am to 5.45pm Monday to Saturday and 9am to noon on Sunday.

Another IAT office (☎ 049 876 79 27) operates in Vicolo Pedrocchi. It opens 9am to 12.30pm and 3pm to 7pm Monday to Saturday. A third office (☎ 049 875 30 87) is located in a booth on Piazza del Santo. It opens only in peak season with a variable timetable.

Post & Communications The post office, Corso Garibaldi 33, opens 8.15am to 7pm Monday to Saturday and 8.30am to 6.30pm Sunday. Address poste restante mail to 35100 Padova. Mail Boxes Etc has a branch at Largo Europa 2. Here you can arrange to send parcels and have money wired to you through Western Union.

Telecom has an unstaffed phone office at Riviera Ponti Romani 33, open 7am to 10pm Monday to Saturday.

You can go online at Internet Point In Collegio (☎ 049 65 84 84), Via Petrarca 9. You pay a €0.15 membership fee, then €5.20 for the first hour and €2.60 per hour after that. It opens 9am to 2am daily.

Bookshops Padua is full of bookshops. If you're looking for anything in languages other than Italian, try Feltrinelli International at Via San Francesco 14.

Medical Services & Emergency Medical assistance is provided by the Complesso Clinico Ospedaliero (hospital; ☎ 049 821 11 11), Via Giustiniani 1. The *questura* (police station; ☎ 049 83 31 11) is at Riviera Ruzante 11, on the corner of Via Santa Chiara.

Things to See

A combined ticket, Padova Arte, costs €7.75 (€5.20 for students) and admits you to the main monuments. It's available from the IAT offices and ticket offices at the monuments concerned. (There's a similar ticket at the same price for sights in the surrounding province.)

Cappella degli Scrovegni Many art lovers visit Padua just to see this chapel in the Giardini dell'Arena *(☎ 049 820 45 50; admission €5.20 plus €1.05 booking fee or €1.55 with Padova Arte; closed at the time of writing for restoration)*. Enrico Scrovegni commissioned it in 1303 as a resting place for his father, who had been denied a Christian burial because of his money-lending practices. Giotto's remarkable fresco cycle, probably completed between 1304 and 1306, illustrates the lives of Mary and Christ and is arranged in three bands. You can pick up an adequate guide to the frescoes as you enter. Among the most famous scenes in the cycle is the *Bacio di Giuda* (Kiss of Judas). The series ends with the *Ultima Cena* (Last Supper) on the entrance wall and the Vices and Virtues are depicted around the lower parts of the walls. Keep in mind when the frescoes were done – Giotto was moving well away from the two-dimensional figures of his medieval contemporaries and presaging greater things to come.

The flow of visitors has become such that you can no longer simply turn up and visit. Booking is obligatory. The admission ticket is also valid for the adjacent **Museo Civico** *(Giardini dell'Arena; open 9am-7pm Tues-Sun)*, whose collection of 14th- to 18th-century Veneto art and largely forgettable archaeological artefacts includes a remarkable crucifix by Giotto.

Chiesa Eremitani Completed in the early 14th century, this Augustinian church *(Giardini dell'Arena; open 8.30am-1pm & 4pm-7pm daily)* was painstakingly rebuilt after being almost totally destroyed by bombing in WWII. The remains of frescoes created by Andrea Mantegna during his 20s are displayed in a chapel to the left of the apse. Most were wiped out in the bombing, the greatest single loss to Italian art during the war. The *Martirio di San Jacopo* (Martyrdom of St James), on the left, was pieced together from fragments found in the rubble of the church while the *Martirio di San Cristoforo* (Martyrdom of St Christopher), opposite, was saved because it had been removed before the war.

Historic Centre Via VIII Febbraio leads to the city's **university** *(☎ 049 876 79 27)*, the main part of which is housed in the Palazzo Bò ('ox' in Veneto dialect – it's named after an inn that previously occupied the site). Established in 1222, the university is Italy's oldest after the one in Bologna. Europe's first anatomy theatre was opened here in 1594 and Galileo Galilei taught at the university from 1592 to 1610. The main courtyard and its halls are plastered with the

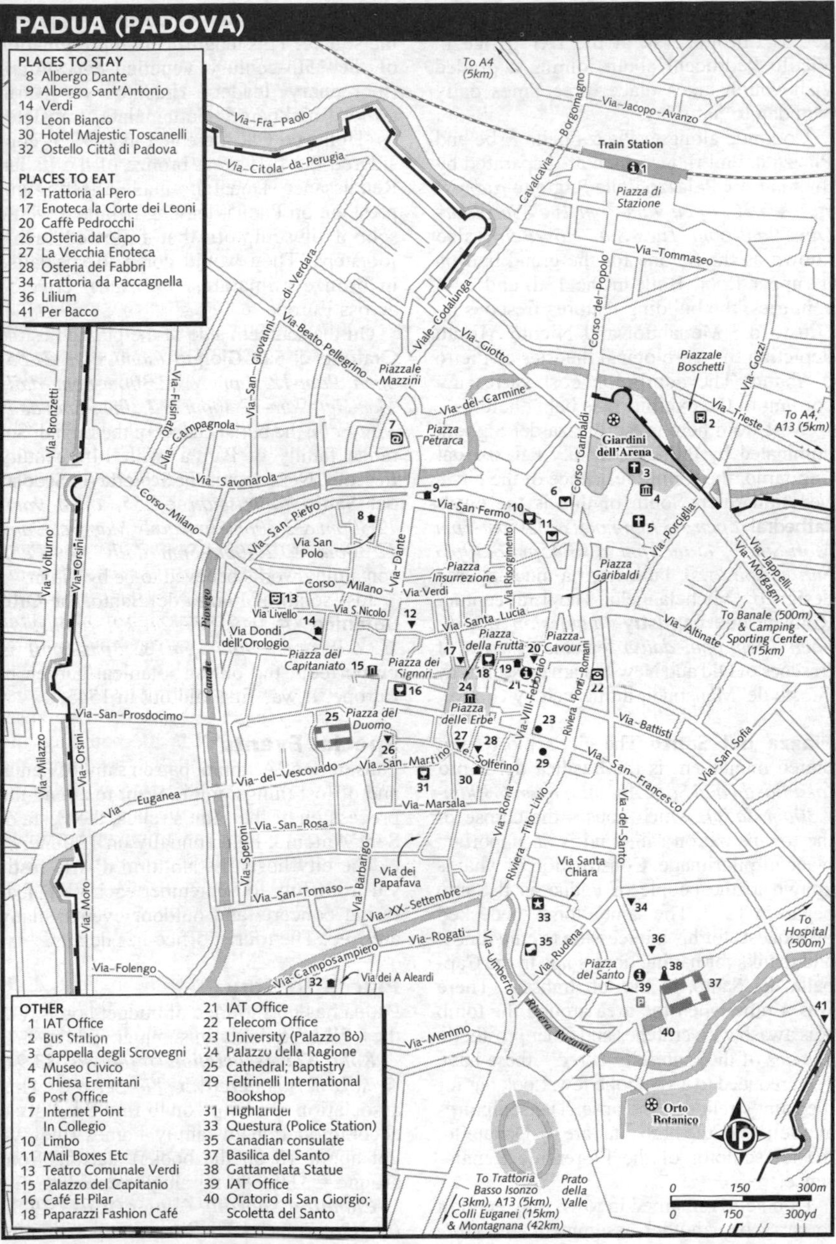
PADUA (PADOVA)
PLACES TO STAY
8 Albergo Dante
9 Albergo Sant'Antonio
14 Verdi
19 Leon Bianco
30 Hotel Majestic Toscanelli
32 Ostello Città di Padova
PLACES TO EAT
12 Trattoria al Pero
17 Enoteca la Corte dei Leoni
20 Caffè Pedrocchi
26 Osteria dal Capo
27 La Vecchia Enoteca
28 Osteria dei Fabbri
34 Trattoria da Paccagnella
36 Lilium
41 Per Bacco
OTHER
1 IAT Office
2 Bus Station
3 Cappella degli Scrovegni
4 Museo Civico
5 Chiesa Eremitani
6 Post Office
7 Internet Point In Collegio
10 Limbo
11 Mail Boxes Etc
13 Teatro Comunale Verdi
15 Palazzo del Capitanio
16 Café El Pilar
18 Paparazzi Fashion Café
21 IAT Office
22 Telecom Office
23 University (Palazzo Bò)
24 Palazzo della Ragione
25 Cathedral; Baptistry
29 Feltrinelli International Bookshop
31 Highlander
33 Questura (Police Station)
35 Canadian consulate
37 Basilica del Santo
38 Gattamelata Statue
39 IAT Office
40 Oratorio di San Giorgio; Scoletta del Santo
To A4 (5km)
Train Station
Piazza di Stazione
Via Jacopo Avanzo
Via Tommaseo
Cavalcavia Borgomagno
Corso del Popolo
Via Fra Paolo
Via Citola da Perugia
Viale Codalunga
Via Beato Pellegrino
Via San Giovanni di Verdara
Via Fusinato
Via Campagnola
Via Bronzetti
Via Savonarola
Corso Milano
Via San Pietro
Via Volturno
Via Orsini
Piazzale Mazzini
Via Giotto
Via del Carmine
Piazza Petrarca
Piazzale Boschetti
Via Gozzi
Via Trieste
To A4, A13 (5km)
Giardini dell'Arena
Corso Garibaldi
Via San Fermo
Via San Polo
Via Dante
Piazza Insurrezione
Via Risorgimento
Piazza Garibaldi
Via Porciglia
Via Jappelli
Via Morgagni
Via Verdi
Via Livello
Via S Nicolo
Via Santa Lucia
Via Altinate
To Banale (500m) & Camping Sporting Center (15km)
Via Dondi dell'Orologio
Piazza del Capitaniato
Piazza dei Signori
Piazza della Frutta
Piazza Cavour
Via VIII Febbraio
Riviera Ponti Romani
Piovego
Canale
Via San Prosdocimo
Piazza del Duomo
Piazza delle Erbe
Via Battisti
Via Milazzo
Via del Vescovado
Via San Martino e Solferino
Via San Francesco
Via San Sofia
Via Euganea
Via Marsala
Via Roma
Riviera Tito Livio
Via del Santo
Via Speroni
Via San Rosa
Via Barbarigo
Via dei Papafava
Via Santa Chiara
Via San Tomaso
Via XX Settembre
Via Moro
To Hospital (500m)
Via Rogati
Via Rudena
Via Folengo
Via Camposampiero
Via dei A Aleardi
Via Umberto
Piazza del Santo
Riviera Ruzante
Via Memmo
Orto Botanico
To Trattoria Basso Isonzo (3km), A13 (5km), Colli Euganei (15km) & Montagnana (42km)
Prato della Valle
0 150 300m
0 150 300yd

coats of arms of the great and learned from across Europe. Ask at the IAT office in Vicolo Pedrocchi about joining a guided visit which takes place three times daily Monday to Saturday.

Continue along to Piazza delle Erbe and Piazza della Frutta, which are separated by the majestic **Palazzo della Ragione** *(admission €5.20; open 9am-7pm Tues-Sun Mar-Oct, 9am-6pm Tues-Sun Nov-Feb)*, also known as the Salone for the grand hall on its upper floor. Built in the 13th and 14th centuries, the building features frescoes by Giusto de' Menabuoi and Nicolò Mireto depicting the astrological theories of Pietro d'Abano. The admission cost varies according to the exhibition is being held.

West from here is the Piazza dei Signori, dominated by the 14th-century **Palazzo del Capitanio**, the former residence of the city's Venetian ruler. South of this is the city's **cathedral** *(open 7.30am-noon & 3.45pm-7pm Mon-Sat, 7.45am-1pm & 3.45pm-8.30pm Sun & holidays)*, built from a much-altered design by Michelangelo. The 13th-century Romanesque **baptistry** *(admission €2.10; open 10am-6pm daily)* features a series of frescoes of Old and New Testament scenes by Giusto de' Menabuoi, influenced by Giotto.

Piazza del Santo The city's most celebrated monument is the **Basilica del Santo** *(aka Basilica di Sant'Antonio; open 6.30am-7.30pm daily)*, which houses the corpse of the town's patron saint and is an important place of pilgrimage. Construction of what is known to the people of Padua as Il Santo began in 1232. The saint's tomb, bedecked by requests for his intercession to cure illness and thanks for having done so, is in the Cappella del Santo, in the left transept. There was a time when the area around the tomb was awash with crutches and other prosthetic devices of the gratefully cured – these have been reduced to a symbolic few. Look out for the saint's relics in the apse. The sculptures and reliefs of the high altar are by Donatello, master sculptor of the Florentine Renaissance.

Donatello remained in town long enough to carry out another assignment, the *Gattamelata* equestrian statue that dominates the square. This magnificent representation of the 15th-century Venetian *condottiero* (mercenary leader) Erasmos da Narni (whose nickname, Gattamelata, translates as 'Honeyed Cat'), created in 1453, is considered the first great bronze of the Italian Renaissance. Donatello made a lasting impression on Padua, leaving behind a whole school of sculptors that followed in his footsteps. They would come to specialise in bronze miniatures *(bronzetti)* coveted across Europe.

On the southern side of the piazza lies the **Oratorio di San Giorgio** *(admission €1.55; open 9am-12.30pm & 2.30pm-6pm daily Mar-Oct, 9am-12.30pm & 2.30pm-5pm daily Nov-Feb)*, the burial chapel of the Lupi di Soranga family of Parma, with 14th-century frescoes. Next door is the **Scoletta** (or **Scuola**) **del Santo** *(admission €1.55; open 9am-12.30pm & 2.30pm-7pm daily Mar-Oct, 9am-12.30pm & 2.30pm-5pm daily Nov-Feb)*, containing works believed to be by Titian.

Just south of Piazza del Santo, the **Orto Botanico** *(☎ 049 827 21 19; admission €2.60; open 9am-1pm & 3pm-6pm)* is purportedly the oldest botanical garden in Europe. It was first laid out in 1545.

Special Events

Fans of Sant'Antonio, patron saint of Padua and of lost things, might want to attend the procession of the saint's relics, the Festa di Sant'Antonio, held annually on 13 June.

The city hosts the Notturni d'Arte festival from July to September each year, featuring concerts and outdoor events; many are free. The tourist office has details.

Places to Stay

Padua has no shortage of budget hotels, but they fill up quickly in summer.

Koko Nor Association *(☎ 049 864 33 94, ⓔ kokonor@intercity.it, Via Selva 5)* This association can help you to find B&B-style accommodation in family homes (they've got about 10 on the books) starting from around €31/56.80 for singles/doubles.

Camping Sporting Center *(☎ 049 79 34 00, Via Roma 123)* Sites per person/tent

€6.70/12.50. This is the nearest camp site to Padua, about 15km out of town at Montegrotto Terme. It's big and boasts a swimming pool, shops and just about anything else your heart might desire. It can be reached by city bus M from the train station.

Ostello Città di Padova *(☎ 049 875 22 19, fax 049 65 42 10, Via dei A Aleardi 30)* B&B in dorm beds €12.40. To get to this place take bus No 3, 8 or 12 from the train station to Prato della Valle and then ask for directions. It's not bad as hostels go and has family rooms too.

Verdi *(☎ 049 875 57 44, Via Dondi dell'Orologio 7)* Singles/doubles up to €22.70/34.60. The rooms are simple but clean and this is one of the cheapest deals in town.

Albergo Sant'Antonio *(☎ 049 875 13 93, Via San Fermo 118)* Singles/doubles without bath €33.60/48.55, with bath €52.70/64.60. The comfortable rooms here are a good deal, all with TV and phone.

Albergo Dante *(☎ 049 876 04 08, Via San Polo 5)* Singles/doubles €25.80/35.10. This is a cheapie tucked away near the Albergo Sant'Antonio. The bathroom is in the corridor and the rooms are a little bare but the prices are hard to argue with. Parking is also available.

Leon Bianco *(☎ 049 875 08 14, fax 049 875 61 84, ⓔ leonbianco@toscanelli.com, Piazzetta Pedrocchi 12)* Singles/doubles €73.85/95.55. This is an immaculately maintained and charming hotel right in the heart of the city. From your flower-box decorated balcony you look right over the elegant Caffè Pedrocchi (see Places to Eat).

Hotel Majestic Toscanelli *(☎ 049 66 32 44, fax 049 876 00 25, ⓔ majestic@toscanelli.com, Via dell'Arco 2)* Singles/doubles up to €111/160.10. Hidden away in a leafy corner of one of the lanes that twist away from Piazza delle Erbe, this hotel boasts stylishly renovated rooms in various styles (ranging from Imperial to what the owners call '19th-century English'), complete with all the usual mod cons.

Places to Eat

Restaurants tend to open from around noon to 2pm and about 7.30pm to 10pm. You will find it hard to be served after this time in the evening.

Restaurants You'll find a good selection of regional cooking and other national cuisine here.

Trattoria al Pero *(☎ 049 875 87 94, Via Santa Lucia 72)* Full meal around €18.10. Open Mon-Sat. The 'Pear Tree' serves tasty regional dishes in a straightforward dining area. You eat well for comparatively little.

Osteria dei Fabbri *(☎ 049 65 03 36, Via dei Fabbri 13)* Full meal around €20.65. Open Mon-Sat. This lively spot is full of atmosphere, although more expensive than the Pero. Try the *ravioloni di magro* – exquisite, light ravioli with a butter and sage sauce.

Osteria dal Capo *(☎ 049 66 31 05, Via degli Obizzi 2, cnr of Via Soncin)* Mains from around €10.35. Open Mon evening-Sat. A busy little eatery, the 'Chief' offers home-style Veneto cooking that is much appreciated by locals.

La Vecchia Enoteca *(☎ 049 875 28 56, Via San Martino e Solferino 32)* Mains start at €13.45. Open Mon evening-Sat. This is an altogether swankier joint where mouthwatering meals can be had but with a greater impact on the wallet. They do a divine *arrosto di salmone* (lightly roasted salmon) with rocket salad and a creamy sauce.

Enoteca la Corte dei Leoni *(☎ 049 875 00 83, Via Pietro d'Abano 1)* Full meal €41.30. Open Tues-Sat. This place, in the heart of Padua, is not only a modern temple of wine but also offers a fine dining experience. In summer especially, book a table in the courtyard (where jazz concerts are also occasionally staged). The food is very good if a little nouvelle in terms of portions and you can taste wine by the glass at the bar from a broad and well-selected wine list.

Trattoria da Paccagnella *(☎ 049 875 05 49, Via del Santo 113)* Full meal around €20.65. Open Mon-Sat. This trattoria is a comfortably elegant setting for fine Veneto cuisine, especially their duck dishes, for which the restaurant is known.

Per Bacco *(☎ 049 802 23 27, Piazzale Pontecorvo 10)*. Full meal around €25.80.

Open Tues-Sun. This is another of the city's better restaurants. Try their *tagliatelle alla norcina con tartufo nero* (tagliatelle with black truffles), a classic of Umbrian cuisine and a standing favourite here. The wine list is also strong.

Trattoria Basso Isonzo *(☎ 049 68 08 13, Via Montepertica 1)* Full meal €15.50. Open Tues-Sun. A local favourite for simple, economically priced home cooking, the trattoria lies a way out of town to the south-west. It's a pain to get to unless you opt for a cab from, say, Prato della Valle, but they do a mean creamy *baccalà* (salt cod). Bus No 22 from Prato della Valle also goes close.

Cafes & Pasticcerias Behind the blunt neoclassical facade of the newly refurbished ***Caffè Pedrocchi***, just off Via VIII Febbraio, lay the meeting place for 19th-century liberals and one of Stendhal's favourite haunts. Today it's more posy than cosy.

Lilium *(☎ 049 875 11 07, Via del Santo 181)* Open 7.30am-8pm Tues-Sun in winter, 7.30am-10pm Tues-Sun in summer. This fine pastry shop offers wonderful gelato and delicious sweet things.

Self-Catering Daily *markets* are held in the piazzas around the Palazzo della Ragione, with fresh produce sold in the Piazza delle Erbe and Piazza della Frutta and bread, cheese and salami sold in the shops under the porticoes.

Entertainment

Padua can offer you theatre, bars and discos.

Teatro Comunale Verdi *(☎ 049 877 70 11, Via Livello 32)* Here you can see opera and theatrical performances.

Highlander *(☎ 049 65 99 97, Via San Martino e Solferino 71)* Open 11am-3pm & 5pm-2am Mon-Sat. Beer-lovers wanting a variation on the Irish theme could strike out for, you guessed it, a 'Scottish' pub. It's mostly full of locals and the beers are tasty. You might like to ignore all the silly Scottish stuff on the walls.

Paparazzi Fashion Café *(☎ 049 875 93 06, Via Marsilio da Padova 17)* Open 6pm-1am Tues-Sun. Far from the fake UK experience (now demised), this place attracts a young cool crowd, all sunglasses at night and designer stubble, low red lights and dark drinking corners.

There are several traditional spots around Piazza delle Erbe for taking the evening *spritz* – the classic early evening aperitif in the Veneto, made of one part prosecco (local sparkling white),one part soda and one part bitters (such as Campari or Aperol).

In summer especially, hundreds of people clutching their favourite tipples spread out across the square in the early evening. Much the same thing happens on a reduced scale on Piazza dei Signori.

Café El Pilar *(☎ 049 65 75 65, Piazza dei Signori 8)* Open 11am-3pm & 6pm-midnight. This is a classic example of a spot where a mix of beautifuls and others converge for the evening spritz. Often by 10pm people have scarpered – off to the disco perhaps? Nearby on Piazza del Duomo, a fair crowd of beautiful people, students and others hang about sipping cocktails and the like later on into the evening.

For some tips on discos, start with the tourist office's *Dove Andiamo Stasera* brochure. Many, as is the Italian custom in smaller cities, are located well outside town.

Limbo *(☎ 049 65 68 82, Via San Fermo 44)* Open 9pm-3am. This is about the only disco in town itself. It is OK but nothing spectacular.

Banale *(☎ 049 807 18 48, Vicolo Ognissanti 1c)* This place is popular with a hip, young student crowd and live rock music is often on the cards.

Getting There & Away

Bus SITA buses (☎ 049 820 68 44) from Venice (€2.75) arrive at Piazzale Boschetti, 200m south of the train station.

From Padua you can get buses to Montegrotto Terme, the Colli Euganei and as far afield as Genoa. Often you are better off with the train. Details for surrounding destinations appear in the course of the chapter.

Train The easiest way to Padua from Venice is by train. The standard regional trains

(€2.30) take 40 minutes. If you want to go a little faster (30 minutes) you can pay almost double (€4.45) on an Intercity train. Regular trains proceed from Padua to Bologna (€9.20, one hour 20 minutes on Intercity), Vicenza, Verona, Milan and beyond.

Car & Motorcycle The A4 (Milan-Venice) passes to the north, while the A13, which connects the city with Bologna, starts at the southern edge of town. The two motorways are connected by a ring road.

Getting Around

ACAP bus No 10 will get you to Piazza Cavour from the train station while No 12 will take you to Prato della Valle. Buy tickets (€0.85 per ride) at tobacconists and stamp them in the machines on the bus. For a taxi, call Radiotaxi on ☎ 049 65 13 33.

AROUND PADUA

Colli Euganei

South-west of Padua, along the A13 or the SS16, the Colli Euganei (Euganean Hills) are dotted with vineyards and good walking trails: ask at the Padua IAT office for information about the trails and accommodation. As you move around, you will encounter numerous curious villages, along with the occasional castle and abbey scattered about the countryside.

If you are driving (which you pretty much have to as public transport is abysmal in the area), follow the signposted Strada dei Vini dei Colli Euganei (Euganean Hills Wine Road), which will take you on a tour of many vineyards. Pick up a map and itinerary from the IAT in Padua. Most of the vineyards are open to the public and some offer accommodation.

The area is also famous for its hot springs or *terme*. The two main centres in this respect are Abano Terme and Montegrotto Terme. The tourist office at the former (☎ 049 866 90 55) is at Via Pietro d'Abano 18 while the one at Montegrotto (☎ 049 79 33 84) is at Viale Stazione 60.

Arquà Petrarca This quiet, hilly medieval village in the southern Colli Euganei was where Italy's great poet Petrarch (Petrarca) chose to spend the last five years of his life. You can visit his **house** *(☎ 0429 71 82 94; admission €3.10; open 9am-noon & 3pm-7pm Tues-Sun Feb-Sept, 9am-12.30pm & 2.30pm-5pm Tues-Sun Oct-Jan)*, which is set in cheerful gardens and contains various bits and bobs that purportedly had something to do with the scribe. Buses run here from Este and Monselice, both a short distance to the south. A handful of buses from Padua (around three daily) run a route to Este that takes them through here.

Monselice

An easy train trip south from Padua, Monselice was once wrapped in no less than five protective layers of fortifications. The main point of interest here is the 11th-century **castle** *(☎ 049 7 29 31; admission €5.20; open 9am-11am & 3pm-5pm daily Apr–mid-Nov)*, which can be visited by guided tour of about an hour only. If you decide to stay, you have the choice of only two places. The train from Padua (€1.90) takes about 20 minutes.

Este

Heading west from Monselice along the road to Mantua (Mantova), this town is yet another in the chain of fortified strongholds in the area. Padua's Carrara clan were assiduous fortress builders – it seems they had a good number of enemies to keep at bay. Although the walls of their castle are in reasonable shape, the inside is pretty much a ruin. On the bumpy lane that climbs northwards behind the castle is the **Villa Kunkler**, where Byron settled in for a year or so in 1817. Shelley also stayed here.

You'll find a couple of hotels here and the town is linked to Monselice (10 minutes) and Padua (€2.30, 30 minutes) by train. Buses also run here but they tend to take longer and are slightly more expensive.

Montagnana

The main attraction in this plains town is the remarkably well-preserved set of medieval defensive walls. Of all the Veneto's walled towns, this is the most impressive – from the outside. Once you get inside there's not an awful lot to see.

Ostello Rocca degli Alberi *(☎/fax 0429 8 10 76, Castello degli Alberi)* €9.30 per person. Open Apr–mid-Oct. This fabulous HI youth hostel is in a former watchtower of the town's extraordinary walls, and is close to the town's train station.

The train from Padua (€2.80, 50 minutes) run via Monselice and Este.

VICENZA

postcode 36100 • pop 108,947

Vicenza is the centre for Italian textile manufacture and a leader in the development and production of computer components, making it one of the country's wealthiest cities. Most tourists come to Vicenza to see the work of Palladio, who was particularly busy here.

Vicenza flourished as the Roman Vicentia. In 1404 it became part of the Venetian Republic. Testimony to the close ties between the lagoon city and Vicenza are the many Venetian Gothic mansions here.

Orientation

From the train station, in the gardens of Campo Marzo, Via Roma heads into Piazzale de Gasperi. From here, the main street, Corso Andrea Palladio, leads to the cathedral and the centre of town.

Information

Tourist Office The APT office (☎ 0444 32 08 54) is at Piazza Matteotti 12. It opens 9am to 1pm and 2.30pm to 6pm Monday to Saturday, 9am to 1pm Sunday.

The office organises free guided tours of the city – enquire for the latest details.

Post & Communications The main post office is at Contrà Garibaldi, near the cathedral. Address poste restante mail to 36100 Vicenza. The small, unstaffed Telecom office, at Contrà Vescovado 2, opens 7am to 10pm daily.

Medical Services & Emergency For urgent medical assistance, go to the Ospedale Civile (hospital; ☎ 0444 99 31 11), Viale Ferdinando Rodolfi 37, north of the city centre from Piazza Matteotti. The *questura* (police station; ☎ 0444 54 33 33) is at Viale Giuseppe Mazzini 24.

Things to See

Piazza Castello contains several grand edifices, including the **Palazzo Porto-Breganze** on the southern side, designed by Palladio and built by Scamozzi, one of the city's leading 16th-century architects. Corso Andrea Palladio runs north-east from the square and is lined with fine buildings.

Piazza dei Signori, nearby, is dominated by the immense **Basilica Palladiana** *(☎ 0444 32 36 81; open 9am-5pm Tues-Sun)*, on which Palladio started work in 1549 over an earlier Gothic building (the slender 12th-century bell tower is all that remains of the original structure). Palladio's **Loggia del Capitaniato**, at the north-western side of the piazza on the corner of Via del Monte, was left unfinished at his death. South-west from the basilica is the **cathedral**, a dull church destroyed during WWII and later rebuilt (some of its works of art were saved).

Contrà Porti, which runs north from Corso Andrea Palladio, is one of the city's most majestic streets. The **Palazzo Thiene** at No 12, by Lorenzo da Bologna, was originally intended to occupy the entire block. Palladio's **Palazzo Barbaran da Porto** *(☎ 0444 32 30 14; admission €5.20; open 10am-6pm Tues-Sun)* at No 11 features a double row of columns. A World Heritage listed building, it is richly decorated and frequently hosts exhibitions. Palladio also built the **Palazzo Isoppo da Porto** at No 21, which remains unfinished. His **Palazzo Valmarana**, at Corso Antonio Fogazzaro 18, is considered one of his more eccentric creations. Across River Bacchiglione is the **Parco Querini**, the city's largest park.

North along Corso Andrea Palladio and left into Contrà di Santa Corona is the **Chiesa di Santa Corona** *(open 8.30am-noon & 3pm-6pm Tues-Sun)*, established in 1261 by the Dominicans to house a relic from Christ's crown of thorns. Inside are the *Battesimo di Gesù* (Baptism of Christ) by Giovanni

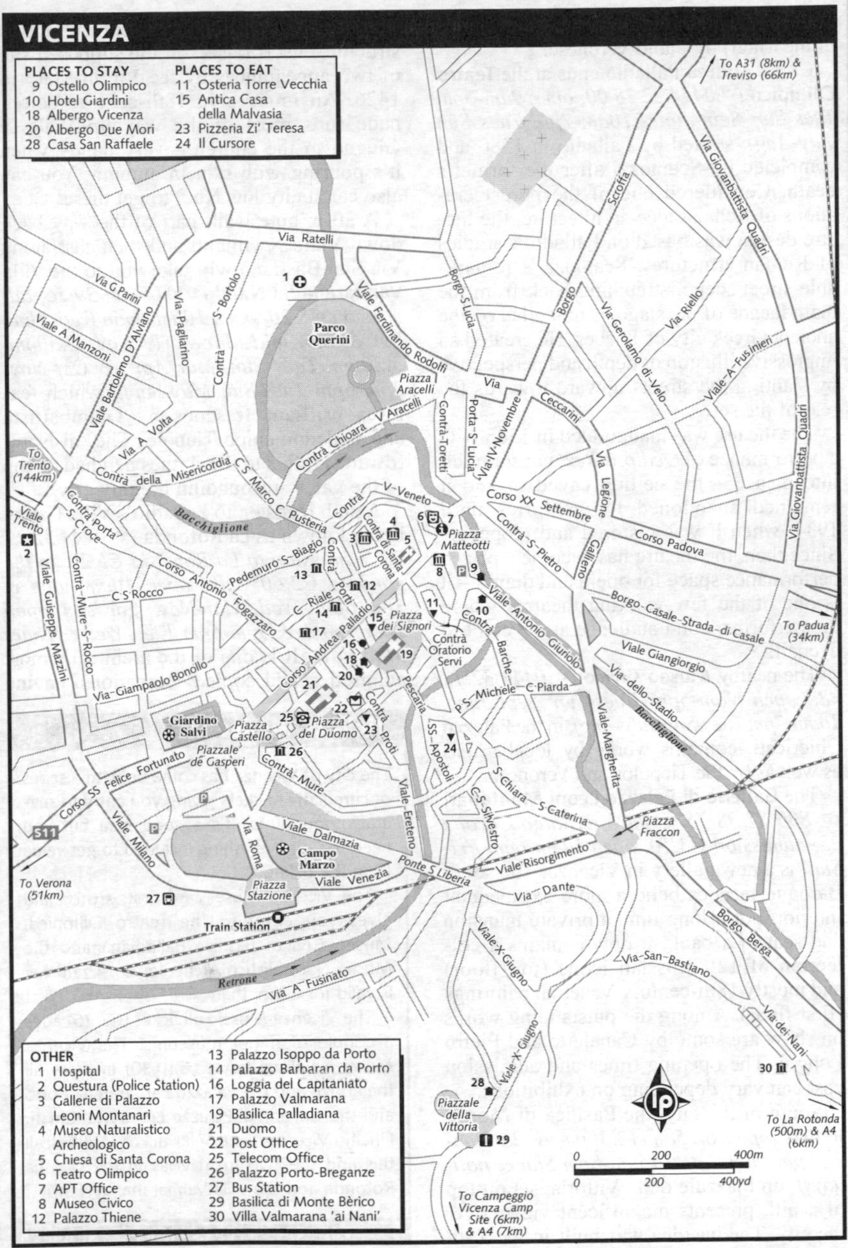
VICENZA
PLACES TO STAY
9 Ostello Olimpico
10 Hotel Giardini
18 Albergo Vicenza
20 Albergo Due Mori
28 Casa San Raffaele
PLACES TO EAT
11 Osteria Torre Vecchia
15 Antica Casa della Malvasia
23 Pizzeria Zi' Teresa
24 Il Cursore
OTHER
1 Hospital
2 Questura (Police Station)
3 Gallerie di Palazzo Leoni Montanari
4 Museo Naturalistico Archeologico
5 Chiesa di Santa Corona
6 Teatro Olimpico
7 APT Office
8 Museo Civico
12 Palazzo Thiene
13 Palazzo Isoppo da Porto
14 Palazzo Barbaran da Porto
16 Loggia del Capitaniato
17 Palazzo Valmarana
19 Basilica Palladiana
21 Duomo
22 Post Office
25 Telecom Office
26 Palazzo Porto-Breganze
27 Bus Station
29 Basilica di Monte Bèrico
30 Villa Valmarana 'ai Nani'
To A31 (8km) & Treviso (66km)
To Trento (144km)
To Padua (34km)
To Verona (51km)
To La Rotonda (500m) & A4 (6km)
To Campeggio Vicenza Camp Site (6km) & A4 (7km)
Parco Querini
Giardino Salvi
Campo Marzo
Train Station
Piazza Aracelli
Piazza Matteotti
Piazza dei Signori
Piazza Castello
Piazza del Duomo
Piazzale de Gasperi
Piazza Stazione
Piazza Fraccon
Piazzale della Vittoria
Bacchiglione
Retrone
Via Ratelli
Via G Parini
Viale A Manzoni
Viale Bartolomeo D'Alviano
Via Pagliarino
Contrà S Bortolo
Viale Ferdinando Rodolfi
Borgo S Lucia
Scroffa
Via Giovanbattista Quadri
Borgo
Via Gerolamo di Velo
Via Riello
Viale A Fusinieri
Via Ceccarini
Contrà Porta S Lucia
Contrà Toretti
Via IV Novembre
Via Legione Gallieno
Corso XX Settembre
Contrà S Pietro
Corso Padova
Borgo Casale Strada di Casale
Viale Giangiorgio
Via dello Stadio
Viale Antonio Giuriolo
Contrà Barche
Contrà Oratorio Servi
P S Michele
C Piarda
Viale Margherita
S Chiara S Caterina
C S Silvestro
SS Apostoli
Viale Risorgimento
Via Dante
Viale X Giugno
Via San Bastiano
Borgo Berga
Via dei Nani
Contrà Chioara
V Aracelli
Via A Volta
Contrà della Misericordia
C S Marco
C Pusteria
Contrà V Veneto
Viale Trento
Contrà Porta S Croce
Contrà Mure S Rocco
Viale Guiseppe Mazzini
Corso Antonio Fogazzaro
Pedemuro S Biagio
C S Rocco
Contrà Porti
C Riale
Contrà di Santa Corona
Corso Andrea Palladio
Via Giampaolo Bonollo
Corso SS Felice Fortunato
Viale Milano
Contrà Mure
Via Roma
Viale Dalmazia
Viale Venezia
Viale Eretenio
Ponte S Liberia
Pescaria
Contrà Proti
Via A Fusinato
S11
0 200 400m
0 200 400yd

Bellini and *Adorazione dei Magi* (Adoration of the Magi) by Paolo Veronese.

Corso Andrea Palladio ends at the **Teatro Olimpico** *(☎ 0444 22 28 00; open 9am-5pm Tues-Sun Sept-June, 10am-7pm Tues-Sun July-Aug)*, started by Palladio in 1580 and completed by Scamozzi after the former's death. Considered one of the purest creations of Renaissance architecture, the theatre design was based on Palladio's studies of Roman structures. Scamozzi's remarkable street scene, stretching back from the main facade of the stage, is modelled on the ancient Greek city of Thebes. He created an impressive illusion of depth and perspective by slanting the streets upward towards the rear of the set.

The theatre was inaugurated in 1585 with a performance of *Oedipus Rex*, but soon fell into disuse – the ceiling caved in and it remained abandoned for centuries until 1934, when it was restored and reopened. Since then, the theatre has become a prized performance space for opera and drama – it is one of the few working theatres where the performers and audience are eyeball to eyeball.

The nearby **Museo Civico** *(☎ 0444 32 13 48; open 9am-5pm Tues-Sun Sept-June, 10am-7pm Tues-Sun July-Aug)*, in the Palazzo Chiericati, contains works by local artists as well as by the Tiepolos and Veronese.

The **Gallerie di Palazzo Leoni Montanari** *(☎ 800 57 88 75, Contrà di Santa Corona 25; admission €3.10; open 10am-6pm Fri-Sun)* is a new gallery in Vicenza. The sober Baroque facades belie a more extravagant interior. For a long time a private mansion and seat of a bank, it now contains a collection of 120 Russian icons (top floor) and mostly 18th-century Venetian paintings (first floor). Among the outstanding works on show are some by Canaletto and Pietro Longhi. The opening times and admission cost can vary depending on exhibitions.

South of the city, the **Basilica di Monte Bèrico** *(open 6.15am-12.30pm & 2.30pm-7.30pm Mon-Sat, 6.15am-8pm Sun & holidays)*, on Piazzale della Vittoria, set on top of a hill, presents magnificent views over the city. The basilica was built in the 18th century to replace a 15th-century Gothic structure, itself raised on the supposed site of two appearances by the Virgin Mary in 1426. An impressive 18th-century colonnade runs most of the way up Viale X Giugno to the church – very handy when it's pouring with rain in autumn. You can also catch city bus No 9 to get there.

A 20-minute walk part of the way back down Viale X Giugno and then east along Via San Bastiano will take you to the **Villa Valmarana 'ai Nani'** *(☎ 0444 54 39 76; admission €5.20; open 10am-noon Wed, Thur, Sat & Sun mid-Mar–early Nov; 2.30pm-5.30pm Tues-Sun Mar-Apr & Oct-Nov; 3pm-6pm Tues-Sun May-Sept)*, which features brilliant frescoes by Giambattista and Giandomenico Tiepolo. The 'ai Nani' (dwarfs) refers to the statues perched on top of the gates surrounding the property.

A path leads on to Palladio's Villa Capra, better known as **La Rotonda** *(☎ 0444 32 17 93; admission to La Rotonda €5.20, to the gardens €2.60; villa open 10am-noon & 3pm-6pm Wed Mar-Nov, gardens open 10am-noon & 3pm-6pm Tues, Wed & Thurs Mar-Nov)*. It is one of the architect's most admired – and copied – creations, having

Tickets Please

The city of Vicenza has come up with a series of cumulative tickets giving you entry to several monuments. It's a good idea but you need to visit everything included to get value from the ticket.

The Vicenza Musei card costs €6.70 and gives you entry to the Teatro Olimpico, Museo Civico, Basilica Palladiana and the Museo Naturalistico Archeologico. The ticket is valid for a month.

The Vicenza Musei Full ticket (€7.75) adds a couple of minor museums. The Vicenza Musei e Palazzi ticket (€10.30) includes all the above and the Palazzo Barbaran da Porto and the Gallerie di Palazzo Leoni Montanari. Finally, Vicenza e Le Ville ticket includes all this and the two main villas in the city, La Rotonda and the Villa Valmarana 'ai Nani'.

served as a model for buildings across Europe and the USA. Groups can book ahead to visit outside the normal opening hours but the price is hiked up to €10.35 per person. Bus No 8 stops nearby.

Places to Stay

Many hotels close during the summer, particularly in August, so book ahead. At other times you should have no problems getting a room.

Campeggio Vicenza *(☎ 0444 58 23 11, fax 0444 58 24 34, Strada Pelosa 239)* Sites per person/tent up to €5.95/13.45. This is the closest camp site to Vicenza and is near the Vicenza Est exit from the A4.

Ostello Olimpico *(☎ 0444 54 02 22, fax 0444 54 77 62, Viale Antonio Giuriolo 7–9)* Dorm beds €13.45. Open 7.30am-9.30am & 3.30pm-11.30pm. This HI youth hostel is in a fine building right by the Teatro Olimpico.

Albergo Vicenza *(☎/fax 0444 32 15 12, Stradella dei Nodari 5–7)* Singles/doubles without bath €36.15/49.10, with bath €41.30/56.80. Located near Piazza dei Signori, this hotel is one of only a few cheapish spots in central Vicenza. The rooms are basic but the place has a little character and it puts you in the thick of things.

Albergo Due Mori *(☎ 0444 32 18 86, fax 0444 32 61 27, Contrà do Rode 26)* Singles/doubles up to €38.75/67.15. Close by the Albergo Vicenza, this place is a slight step up in quality but in much the same league.

Casa San Raffaele *(☎ 0444 54 57 67, fax 0444 55 22 59, Viale X Giugno 10)* Singles/doubles with bath €41.30/56.80. Located in a former convent behind the colonnade leading to Monte Bèrico, this is a charming spot to spend the night and the best choice in the lower budget range. The hotel has parking space and prices include breakfast.

Hotel Giardini *(☎/fax 0444 32 64 58, Viale Antonio Giuriolo 10)* Singles/doubles €82.65/113.65. A rather modern hotel (with decidedly little in the way of gardens), this is nevertheless a perfectly comfortable and handy choice for the heart of the town. They have parking and prices here also include breakfast.

Places to Eat

A large ***produce market*** takes place each Tuesday and Thursday in Piazza delle Erbe.

Pizzeria Zi' Teresa *(☎ 0444 32 14 11, Contrà San Antonio 1)* Pizzas €4.15-6.20. Open Tues-Sun. This is a handy place for a pizza. If you want a full meal you are better off trying one of the places listed below.

Antica Casa della Malvasia *(☎ 0444 54 37 04, Contrà delle Morette 5)* Mains €7.75. Open Tues-Sat. This den has been around since 1200. In those days, it was the local sales point for Malvasia wine imported from Greece by Venetian merchants, who usually gathered here in the evenings to sample the goods. Drinking is still a primary occupation in a locale that has changed little in all those centuries – on offer is an array of 80 types of wine (especially Malvasia varieties) and around a hundred types of *grappa* (a grape-based liqueur)!

Il Cursore *(☎ 0444 32 35 04, Stradella Pozzetto 10)* Full meal around €18.10. Open Wed-Mon. They've been serving up food in here since the 19th century and although it's been given a face-lift, it's a great little spot for some local dishes, such as *spaghetti col baccalà mantecato* (spaghetti with salted cod prepared in garlic and parsley).

Osteria Torre Vecchia *(☎ 0444 32 00 50, Contrà Oratorio Servi 23)* Full meal around €23.25. Open 7pm-2am Mon-Sat. This elegant old house with wooden ceilings offers fine eating at a highish price. The menu changes constantly and occasionally contains *sorprese* (surprises) – clearly for the adventurous diner!

Entertainment

Concerts are held in summer at the Villa Valmarana 'ai Nani'; check at the APT office for details. For information about performances at the ***Teatro Olimpico*** *(☎ 0444 22 21 11)*, contact the theatre or the APT. The APT can also give you some initial clues on bars and clubs, although there are few of the latter and they are well out of the centre. On summer afternoons and evenings the central squares fill with people who gather for the *aperitivo*, that lingering evening tipple, and to chat.

Getting There & Away

Bus FTV buses (☎ 0444 22 31 15) leave from the bus station, just near the train station, for Thiene, Asiago (in the hilly north of the province), Bassano and towns throughout the nearby Monti Berici (Berici Hills).

Train Regular trains arrive from Venice (€3.60, 50 minutes) and Padua (€2.30, 27 minutes). You can speed things up by paying more for an Intercity. Other trains connect Vicenza with Milan, Verona, Treviso and smaller towns in the north.

Car & Motorcycle By car, the city is on the A4 connecting Milan with Venice. The SS11 connects Vicenza with Verona and Padua, and this is the best route if you choose to hitchhike. There is a large car park near Piazza Castello and the train station.

Getting Around

Bus Nos 1, 2, 3 and 7 link the train station with the centre but it's best to explore on foot.

AROUND VICENZA

As Venice's maritime power waned in the 16th century, the city's wealthy inhabitants turned their attention inland, acquiring land to build sumptuous villas (see also The Brenta Riviera earlier). Forbidden from building castles by the Venetian senate, which feared a landscape dotted with well-defended forts, Vicenza's patricians were among those to join the villa construction spree. Many of the thousands that were built still remain, although most are inaccessible to the public and run down.

The APT in Vicenza can provide reams of information about the villas, including an illustrated map *Ville dal 1400 al 1800*.

Drivers should have little trouble planning an itinerary. If you don't have a car, take the FTV bus north from Vicenza to Thiene, passing through Caldogno and Villaverla, and then continue on to Lugo. The Villa Godi-Valmarana, now known as the **Malinverni**, at Lonedo di Lugo, was Palladio's first villa.

A good driving itinerary is to take the SS11 south to Montecchio Maggiore and continue south to Lonigo and Pojana Maggiore before heading north for Longare and back to Vicenza. A round trip of 100km, the route takes in about a dozen villas.

Check with the APT in Vicenza for details of the Concerti in Villa Estate, a series of classical concerts held in villas around Vicenza each summer (usually July). You will need your own transport to get to the concerts and back. You can also ask about accommodation, which is available in some villas.

VERONA

postcode 37100 • pop 254,748

Wander the quiet streets of Verona on a winter's night and you might almost be forgiven for believing the tragic love story of Romeo and Juliet to be true. Get past that Shakespearean hyperbole, however, and you'll find plenty to keep you occupied in what is one of Italy's most beautiful cities. Known as *piccola Roma* (little Rome) for its importance in the days of the Roman Empire, its truly golden era came during the 13th and 14th centuries under the Della Scala family (also known as the Scaligeri). The period was noted for the savage family feuding which Shakespeare wrote about in his play.

Orientation

Old Verona is small and easy to find your way around. There is a lot to see and it is a popular base for exploring surrounding towns. Buses leave for the centre from outside the train station (see Getting Around later); otherwise, walk to the right, past the bus station, cross the river and walk along Corso Porta Nuova to Piazza Brà, 15 minutes away. From the piazza, walk along Via G Mazzini and turn left at Via Cappello to reach Piazza delle Erbe.

Information

Tourist Offices The main tourist office (☎ 045 806 86 80, Ⓦ www.tourism.verona.it), Via degli Alpini 9 (virtually on Piazza Brà), opens 9am to 7pm Tuesday to Saturday, 9am to 3pm Sunday and 1pm to 7pm Monday.

The other office (☎ 045 800 08 61), inside the train station (the eastern end), opens 9am to 6pm Monday to Saturday.

Both have reams of information on the city and surrounding province.

A third office (☎ 045 861 91 63) operates at the airport to meet flights.

Money Banks dot the town centre, including the Banca Popolare di Bergamo on Piazza Brà, one of several with a currency exchange machine.

Post & Communications The main post office, Piazza Viviani 7, opens 8am to 7pm Monday to Saturday. Address poste restante mail to 37100 Verona. You'll find telephones at the train station, as well as an unstaffed Telecom office on Via Leoncino, just behind the Arena.

You can get onto the Internet at a spot by platform 1 at the train station or at Diesis, Via Sottoriva 15. It generally open 11am to between 10pm and midnight. You can also try Internet Train (☎ 045 801 33 94, **W** www.internettrain.it) at Via Roma 19.

Laundry There is an Onda Blu laundrette at Via XX Settembre 62a. It opens 8am to 10pm daily. It costs €5.20 to wash a 16kg load, and the same to dry.

Medical Services & Emergency The Ospedale Civile Maggiore (hospital; ☎ 045 807 11 11) is at Piazza A Stefani, north-west from Ponte Vittoria. Otherwise, the city's Guardia Medica (☎ 045 807 56 27) provides medical services from 8pm to 8am daily and usually comes to you.

The *questura* (police station; ☎ 045 809 04 11) is at Lungadige Porta Vittoria, near Ponte Navi.

Things to See

Remember that just about everything is closed on Monday – if you plan to spend one day here only, make it any other day.

There is a joint ticket for getting into all the main sights called the Verona Card. It is great value at €11.40. With it you can enter all the main monuments and churches, and get reduced admission on a few places of lesser importance. The card also allows you to get around town on the buses. It is valid for a year (at the time of writing from April 2001 to March 2002).

On the first Sunday of the month, admission to Juliet's Tomb, the Museo Lapidario Maffeiano (which shows stone fragments from Greek and Roman times), the Castelvecchio museum and the Roman theatre is free. Admission to the Roman Arena on the same day is reduced to €1.05.

Roman Arena This pink marble Roman amphitheatre *(☎ 045 800 32 04, Piazza Brà; admission €3.10; open 9am-6.30pm Tues-Sun, 8am-3.30pm during opera season)* was built in the 1st century AD and is now Verona's opera house. The third-largest Roman amphitheatre in existence, it could seat around 20,000 people. It is remarkably well preserved, despite a 12th-century earthquake that destroyed most of its outer wall. See the Entertainment section for information about opera and plays performed here. A joint ticket with the Museo Lapidario Maffeiano costs €3.60.

Casa di Giulietta Just off Via G Mazzini, Verona's main shopping street, is Casa di Giulietta *(Juliet's House; ☎ 045 803 43 03, Via Cappello 23; admission €3.10; open 9am-6.30pm Tues-Sun)*. Romeo and Juliet may have been fictional but here you can swoon beneath what popular myth says was her balcony or, if in need of a new lover, approach a bronze statue of Juliet and rub her right breast for good luck. Others have made their eternal mark by adding to the slew of scribbled love graffiti on the walls of the house. It is, by the way, doubtful there was ever a feud between the Cappello and Montecchi families, on whom Shakespeare based the play.

If the theme excites you sufficiently, you could also search out the **Tomba di Giulietta** *(Juliet's Tomb; ☎ 045 800 03 61, Via del Pontiere 5; admission €2.60; open 9am-6.30pm Tues-Sun)*. Also housed here is the **Museo degli Affreschi**, with a collection of frescoes of minor interest.

Piazza delle Erbe Originally the site of a Roman forum, this piazza remains the lively

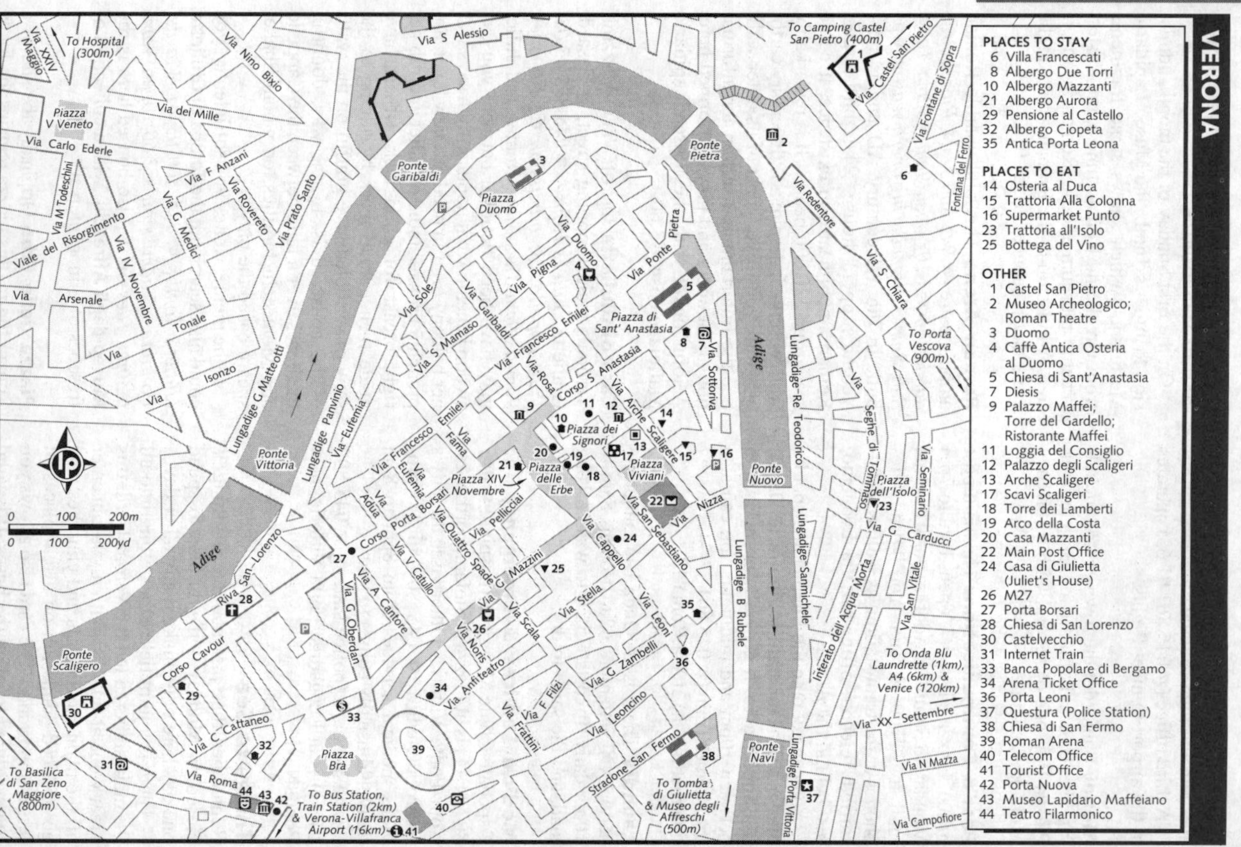

VERONA
PLACES TO STAY
6 Villa Francescati
8 Albergo Due Torri
10 Albergo Mazzanti
21 Albergo Aurora
29 Pensione al Castello
32 Albergo Ciopeta
35 Antica Porta Leona
PLACES TO EAT
14 Osteria al Duca
15 Trattoria Alla Colonna
16 Supermarket Punto
23 Trattoria all'Isolo
25 Bottega del Vino
OTHER
1 Castel San Pietro
2 Museo Archeologico; Roman Theatre
3 Duomo
4 Caffè Antica Osteria al Duomo
5 Chiesa di Sant'Anastasia
7 Diesis
9 Palazzo Maffei; Torre del Gardello; Ristorante Maffei
11 Loggia del Consiglio
12 Palazzo degli Scaligeri
13 Arche Scaligere
17 Scavi Scaligeri
18 Torre dei Lamberti
19 Arco della Costa
20 Casa Mazzanti
22 Main Post Office
24 Casa di Giulietta (Juliet's House)
26 M27
27 Porta Borsari
28 Chiesa di San Lorenzo
30 Castelvecchio
31 Internet Train
33 Banca Popolare di Bergamo
34 Arena Ticket Office
36 Porta Leoni
37 Questura (Police Station)
38 Chiesa di San Fermo
39 Roman Arena
40 Telecom Office
41 Tourist Office
42 Porta Nuova
43 Museo Lapidario Maffeiano
44 Teatro Filarmonico
To Camping Castel San Pietro (400m)
To Porta Vescova (900m)
To Onda Blu Laundrette (1km), A4 (6km) & Venice (120km)
To Tomba di Giulietta & Museo degli Affreschi (500m)
To Bus Station, Train Station (2km) & Verona-Villafranca Airport (16km)
To Basilica di San Zeno Maggiore (800m)
To Hospital (300m)
Adige
Ponte Pietra
Ponte Nuovo
Ponte Navi
Ponte Garibaldi
Ponte Vittoria
Ponte Scaligero
Piazza Duomo
Piazza di Sant' Anastasia
Piazza dei Signori
Piazza delle Erbe
Piazza Viviani
Piazza XIV Novembre
Piazza dell'Isolo
Piazza Brà
Piazza V Veneto
Lungadige Re Teodorico
Lungadige Sanmichele
Lungadige Porta Vittoria
Lungadige B Rubele
Lungadige Panvinio
Lungadige G Matteotti
Via Sottoriva
Via Ponte Pietra
Via Duomo
Via Arche Scaligere
Corso S Anastasia
Via Garibaldi
Via Rosa
Via San Sebastiano
Via Cappello
Via Leoni
Via Stella
Via Mazzini
Via Scala
Corso Porta Borsari
Corso Cavour
Via Roma
Via Nizza
Via Seminario
Via San Vitale
Via G Carducci
Interrato dell'Acqua Morta
Via XX Settembre
Via Redentore
Via S Chiara
Via Fontane di Sopra
Via S Alessio
Via Nino Bixio
Via Prato Santo
Via Rovereto
Via dei Mille
Via G Medici
Via IV Novembre
Viale del Risorgimento
Via XXIV Maggio
Via Carlo Ederle
Via Anfiteatro
Via Frattini
Via G Oberdan
Via A Cantore
Via C Cattaneo
Riva San Lorenzo
Stradone San Fermo
Via Leoncino
0 100 200m
0 100 200yd

heart of the city today. Although the permanent market stalls in its centre detract from its beauty, the square is lined with some of Verona's most sumptuous buildings, including the Baroque **Palazzo Maffei**, at the northern end, with the adjoining 14th-century **Torre del Gardello**. On the eastern side is **Casa Mazzanti**, a former Della Scala family residence. Its fresco-decorated facade stands out.

Separating Piazza delle Erbe from Piazza dei Signori is the **Arco della Costa**, beneath which is suspended a whale's rib. Legend says it will fall on the first 'just' person to walk beneath it. In several centuries, it has never fallen, not even on the various popes who have paraded beneath it. Ascend the nearby 12th-century **Torre dei Lamberti** *(admission €2.10 by elevator, €1.55 on foot, €2.60 with admission to Arche Scaligere; open 9am-6pm Tues-Sun)* for a great view of the city.

Piazza dei Signori The 15th-century **Loggia del Consiglio**, the former city council building at the northern end of this square, is regarded as Verona's finest Renaissance structure. It is attached to the **Palazzo degli Scaligeri**, once the main residence of the Della Scala family.

Through the archway at the far end of the piazza are the **Arche Scaligere** *(admission €2.60 with Torre dei Lamberti; open 9am-6pm Tues-Sun)*, the elaborate tombs of the Della Scala family. You can see them quite well from the outside but if the ticket for the Torre dei Lamberti allows you to wander in and have a closer inspection, why not?

In the courtyard just behind the Arche you can now see some excavation work done on this part of Verona. You enter the **Scavi Scaligeri** *(Scaligeri Excavations; admission depends on the exhibition on show; open 10am-6pm Tues-Sun)*. The excavations are not so exciting as to warrant a big detour, so to make them more attractive the building is used to host international photographic exhibitions.

Churches A combined entrance ticket to all the following churches costs €4.15. Otherwise, admission to each costs €2.10.

North from the Arche Scaligere stands the Gothic **Chiesa di Sant'Anastasia** *(open 9am-6pm Mon-Sat, 1pm-6pm Sun)*, started in 1290 but not completed until the late 15th century. Inside are numerous works of art including, in the sacristy, a lovely fresco by Pisanello of *San Giorgio che Parte per Liberare la Donzella dal Drago* (St George Setting out to Free the Princess from the Dragon).

The 12th-century **cathedral** *(open 10am-5.30pm Mon-Sat, 1.30pm-5.30pm Sun)* combines Romanesque (lower section) and Gothic (upper section) styles and has some intriguing features. Look for the sculpture of Jonah and the Whale on the southern porch and the statues of two of Charlemagne's paladins, Roland and Oliver, on the western porch. In the first chapel of the left aisle is an *Assumption* by Titian, in an altar frame by Jacopo Sansovino.

At the river end of Via Leoni is the **Chiesa di San Fermo** *(open 10am-6pm Mon-Sat, 1pm-6pm Sun)*, which is actually two churches: the Gothic church was built in the 13th century over the original 11th-century Romanesque structure. The **Chiesa di San Lorenzo** *(open 10am-6pm Mon-Sat, 1pm-6pm Sun)* is near the Castelvecchio (see the following section) and the **Basilica di San Zeno Maggiore** (see that section later) is farther to the west.

Castelvecchio South-west from Piazza delle Erbe, on the banks of the River Adige, is the 14th-century fortress of Cangrande II (of the Della Scala family). The fortress was damaged by bombing during WWII and restored in the 1960s. It now houses a **museum** *(☎ 045 59 47 34; admission €3.10; open 9am-6.30pm Tues-Sun)* with a diverse collection of paintings, frescoes, jewellery and medieval artefacts. Among the paintings are works by Pisanello, Giovanni Bellini, Tiepolo, Carpaccio and Veronese. Also of note is a 14th-century equestrian statue of Cangrande I. The **Ponte Scaligero** spanning the River Adige was rebuilt after being destroyed by WWII bombing.

Basilica di San Zeno Maggiore A masterpiece of Romanesque architecture, this church *(open 8.30am-6pm Mon-Sat, 1pm-6pm Sun)* in honour of the city's patron saint was built mainly in the 12th century, although its apse was rebuilt in the 14th century and its bell tower, a relic of an earlier structure on the site, was started in 1045. The basilica's magnificent rose window depicts the Wheel of Fortune. Before going inside, take a look at the sculptures on either side of the main doors. The doors themselves are decorated with bronze reliefs of biblical subjects. The highlight inside is Mantegna's triptych of the *Madonna col Bambino tra Angeli e Santi* (Madonna and Child with Angels and Saints), above the high altar.

Across the River Across Ponte Pietra is a **Roman theatre**, built in the 1st century AD and still used today for concerts and plays. Take the lift at the back of the theatre to the convent above, which houses an interesting collection of Greek and Roman pieces in the **Museo Archeologico** *(admission €2.60; open 9am-6.30pm Tues-Sun Apr-Oct, 9am-3.30pm Tues-Sun Nov-Mar)*. On a hill, high behind the theatre and museum is the **Castel San Pietro**, built by the Austrians on the site of an earlier castle.

City Gates Near the Casa di Giulietta, in Via Leoni, is the **Porta Leoni**, one of the gates to Roman Verona. The other is **Porta Borsari**, at the south-western end of Corso Porta Borsari.

Places to Stay

If you are having problems finding a hotel room, you could try calling the ***Cooperativa Albergatori Veronesi*** *(☎ 045 800 98 44; fax 045 800 93 72)*. They start with two-star hotels and the service is free.

Camping Castel San Pietro *(☎/fax 045 59 20 37, W www.campingcastelsanpietro.com, Via Castel San Pietro 2)* Sites per person/tent/car €4.90/6.20/3.10. Open mid-Jun–Sept. This is not a bad camp site, away from the bustle of the town below. You can get here by bus No 41 or No 95 from the train station. Ask the driver to let you off at the 'camping' or at the first stop along Via Marsala.

Villa Francescati *(☎ 045 59 03 60, fax 045 800 91 27, Salita Fontana del Ferro 15)* B&B in dorm beds €12.40. This beautifully restored HI youth hostel is housed in a 16th-century villa not far from the camp site and should be your first choice of budget lodging. The gardens are gorgeous and they have family rooms too. Meals cost €7.75.

Pensione al Castello *(☎/fax 045 800 44 03, Vicolo Brusco 2a)* Singles/doubles without bath €49.10/72.30, with bath €62/87.80. This is a quiet and simple little hotel in a good spot near the river and castle. Rooms are clean and well maintained, without being spectacular.

Albergo Ciopeta *(☎ 045 800 68 43, fax 045 800 68 43, e ciopeta@iol.it, Vicolo Teatro Filarmonico 2)* Singles/doubles €41.30/62. Just off Piazza Brà, this is a great little place with cosy welcoming rooms, but you'll need to book well in advance.

Albergo Aurora *(☎ 045 59 47 17, fax 045 801 08 60, Piazzetta XIV Novembre 2)* Singles/doubles with bath up to €98.15/108.45. The better rooms in this fairly sprawling hotel are spacious and comfortable, although time is beginning to take its toll. In low season you may snag the odd single without bath for as little as €46.50. The position is about as central as is possible.

Albergo Mazzanti *(☎ 045 800 68 13, fax 045 801 12 62, Via Mazzanti 6)* Singles/doubles up to €67.15/98.15. Just off Piazza dei Signori, this place is just as well located and, if you can get one of the nicer rooms, is probably marginally better value. That said, some of the sleeping cubicles for singles are claustrophobic. In low season prices can reduce to less than half those above for rooms without bath.

Antica Porta Leona *(☎ 045 59 54 99, fax 045 59 52 14, Corticella Leoni 3)* Singles/doubles up to €93/129.10. Located near Juliet's supposed house, this is a reasonable three-star hotel whose rooms are full of character, if somewhat faded.

Albergo Due Torri *(☎ 045 59 50 44 or 045 800 41 30, e duetorri.verona@baglionihotels.com, Piazza di Sant'Anastasia 4)* Singles/doubles up to €268.55/377. Verona's top address is a grand old mansion whose rooms take you back into a long abandoned era of slightly stuffy, studied elegance. Antique wooden furniture dominates the rooms, which at their best are very generous. The place is often booked solid.

Places to Eat

Known for its fresh produce, its crisp Soave (a dry white wine) and boiled meats, Verona offers good eating at reasonable prices. Most places open from about 11am to 3pm and 7.30pm to 10pm. You may be hard pressed being served much after then.

Osteria al Duca *(☎ 045 59 44 74, Via Arche Scaligere 2)* Set menu €13.45. Open 11am-3pm & 6.30pm-midnight Mon-Fri. Housed in the so-called Casa di Romeo (actually the former home of the Montecchis), this place is a long-standing stalwart in central Verona, although its reputation has probably outrun the quality of the cooking. Still, the setting is attractive and the set meal not bad value.

Trattoria Alla Colonna *(☎ 045 59 67 18, Via Pescheria Vecchia 4)* Full meal around €23.25. Open Mon-Sat. For a more genuine traditional dining experience than you are likely to get at the Duca, pop around the corner to this family-run place. The 'column' in the name is a red Verona marble job, smack in the middle of the restaurant, around which huddle the tables. Several polenta dishes are on offer and the wine list isn't bad.

Bottega del Vino *(☎ 045 800 45 35, Vicolo Scudo di Francia 3a)*. Full meal around €36.15. Open Wed-Mon. If wine is your thing then this age-old wine cellar is your place and it happens to serve up some fine food too. The wine list is endless and your choice will be served with all the ceremony you might expect at a highbrow wine-tasting. The cost of your meal can vary wildly depending on your choice of tipple. If nothing else, wander in to this perennially busy dining hall – the frescoes, complemented by shelfloads of ancient bottles, are worth the effort alone.

Ristorante Maffei *(☎ 045 801 00 15, Piazza delle Erbe 38)* Pasta from €7.75, mains from €18.60. The grand Palazzo Maffei makes an elegant setting for this restaurant. Dining in the central courtyard is especially pleasant.

Trattoria all'Isolo *(☎ 045 59 42 91, Piazza dell'Isolo 5a)*. Full meal €18.10. Open Thurs-Tues. Across the river you find yourself in what feels like a more genuine, less touristy Verona. Much the same can be said of this tiny little eatery. Just about anything they do with bigoli is bound to please.

Entertainment

Throughout the year, the city hosts musical and cultural events, culminating in the season of opera and drama from July to September at the Roman Arena. Tickets cost from €16.50 to €154.95 and can be purchased at ***Ente Lirico Arena di Verona*** *(☎ 045 800 51 51, Via Dietro Anfiteatro 6b)*. Otherwise you can buy tickets at nominated travel agents and banks in Verona and around the country. A list of these can be obtained from the theatre or the tourist office. For more information try W www.arena.it.

There is a programme of ballet and opera in winter at the 18th-century ***Teatro Filarmonico*** *(☎ 045 800 28 80, Via dei Mutilati 4)*, just south of Piazza Brà, and Shakespeare is performed at the Roman theatre in summer. Information and tickets for these events are available at the Ente Lirico Arena di Verona (see the previous paragraph for details).

Caffè Antica Osteria al Duomo *(Via Duomo 7)* Open noon-2pm & 7pm-10pm Mon-Sat. This is a cosy tavern with mandolins, balalaikas and other stringed instruments hanging on the wall. Pop in for a drop of *fragolino* (the local sweet strawberry wine).

M27 *(☎ 045 803 42 42, Via G Mazzini 27a)* Open 10am-2am Tues-Sun. If you want something rather more up to date, get down to this angular, modern bar. Young hip Veronese hang out here for morning coffee and evening cocktails, perched on improbable designer stools in a squeaky clean, polished ambience.

The city boasts about a half dozen clubs/discos, all of which open from around 9pm to 4am. For a list (albeit incomplete) of these and other bars, ask for the *Verona di Notte* brochure from the tourist office.

Getting There & Away

Air Verona-Villafranca airport (☎ 045 809 56 66) is 16km outside the town and accessible by regular bus to/from the train station (€4.15, 20 minutes). Flights arrive from all over Italy and some European cities, including Amsterdam, Barcelona, Berlin, Brussels, Cologne, Frankfurt, Helsinki, London, Munich, Paris and Vienna.

Bus The main intercity bus station is in front of the train station, in an area known as Porta Nuova. Although buses serve many big cities, they are generally only a useful option for those needing to reach provincial localities not served by train.

Train Verona has rail links with Milan, Venice, Padua, Mantua, Modena, Florence and Rome. There are also regular trains serving destinations in Austria, Switzerland and Germany (10 daily to/from Munich).

The trip to/from Venice on a regional train (€5.75) takes one hour 35 minutes. It is faster and more expensive on Intercity services.

Car & Motorcycle Verona is at the intersection of the Serenissima A4 (Milan-Venice) and Brennero A22 motorways.

Getting Around

AMT (city transport) bus Nos 11, 12, 13 and 72 (bus Nos 91 or 98 on Sunday and holidays) connect the train station with Piazza Brà and bus No 70 goes to Piazza delle Erbe (tickets cost €0.85 and are valid for an hour). Otherwise, it's a 20-minute walk along Corso Porta Nuova. Day tickets for the buses cost €2.60. Buy tickets before you board the bus from newsagents and tobacconists.

Cars are banned from the city centre in the morning and early afternoon, but you will be allowed in if you are staying at a hotel. There are free car parks at Via Città di Nimes (near the train station) and Porta Vescovo, from where buses run to the city centre.

For a taxi, call ☎ 045 53 26 66.

TREVISO

postcode 31100 • pop 81,240

A small, pleasant city with historical importance as a Roman centre, Treviso is well worth a day trip from Venice (easily accomplished by train) but you could also make a stopover if you are heading north for the Dolomites. People planning to stay overnight should note that there is no decent cheap accommodation in the city.

Treviso claims Luciano Benetton, the clothing manufacturer, as its favourite son. You will find a huge Benetton store in the centre of town but factory outlets around the outskirts of town are the strict preserve of Benetton employees.

Orientation

From the train station head north along Via Roma, (over the canal) past the bus station and across the bridge (the nicely placed McDonald's on the river is an unmistakable landmark) and keep walking straight ahead along Corso del Popolo. At Piazza della Borsa veer left down Via XX Settembre and you arrive in the heart of the city, Piazza dei Signori.

Information

The APT office (☎ 0422 54 76 32) is at Piazzetta Monte di Pietà 8, adjacent to Piazza dei Signori. It opens 9am to 12.30pm and 2.30pm to 6.30pm Monday to Friday, 9.30am to 12.30pm and 3.30pm to 6pm Saturday and Sunday. From October to March the afternoon hours shorten a little. The office sometimes organises free guided tours of the city.

Things to See & Do

The APT promotes Treviso as the *città d'acqua* (city of water) and compares it to Venice. While the River Sile, which weaves through the centre, is quite beautiful in parts, the comparisons are more touching than realistic.

That said, the city is a delight to wander. Piazza dei Signori is dominated by the fine brick **Palazzo dei Trecento**, the one-time seat of city government beneath whose vaults you can now stop for coffee and a bite. The medieval main street is the porticoed Via Calmaggiore, which leads to the **cathedral** *(Piazza del Duomo; open 7.30am-noon & 3.30pm-7pm Mon-Fri, 7.30am-1pm & 3.30pm-8pm Sat-Sun)*, a massive structure whose main source of interest lies in the frescoes inside by Il Pordenone (1484–1539).

Backtrack to Piazza dei Signori and head east (around and behind the Palazzo dei Trecento) and you will soon find yourself in a little warren of lanes that leads to five delightful bridges across the Canal Cagnan. This runs roughly north-south and spills into the River Sile at a particularly pleasant corner where part of the city walls remain intact. Treviso is a comparatively leafy town and this is particularly the case at some points along the canal. You can also see the occasional mill wheel (the one by Vicolo Molinetto still turns). While on the right bank of the canal you might pop into the deconsecrated **Chiesa di Santa Caterina** *(Via di Santa Caterina; admission €1.55; open 9am-noon & 3pm-7pm first Sun of month only)*, decorated with frescoes by Tommaso da Modena (1326–79). Tommaso also left frescoes in the imposing **Chiesa di San Nicolò** *(Via San Nicolò; open 7am-noon & 3.30pm-7pm daily)*, on the other side of town.

In summer, you can take a **boat cruise** *(☎ 0422 78 86 63 or 0422 78 86 71)* on the *Silis* or *Altino* down the Sile to the Venetian lagoon and back. The tours are by reservation only – call or ask at the tourist office.

Places to Stay

Only one hotel deigns central Treviso with its presence.

Albergo Campeol *(☎ 0422 5 66 01, Piazza Ancilotto 4)* Singles/doubles €46.50/77.50. This is a nicely maintained place in a restored building just off Piazza dei Signori and also boasts a good restaurant downstairs, the ***Ristorante alle Beccherie***.

Otherwise a couple of more run-down establishments cluster close to the train station. The remaining 10 or so hotels are well out of the centre, some on the approach roads to town, and thus anything but handy unless you are driving.

Places to Eat

Ristorante al Dante *(☎ 0422 59 18 97, Piazza Garibaldi 6)* Full meal around €15.50. Open Mon-Sat. This is an excellent budget option where you can sidle up to the bar for a host of cicheti or dine at one of the teeny tables. In summer you can sit outside and gaze across to the river. Typically people pop in for bar snacks and prosecco, or perhaps a crisp Friuli white.

Odeon *(☎ 0422 54 48 04, Vicolo Rinaldi 3)* Full meal around €20.65. Open 6.30pm-2am Tues-Sun. In the heart of the old centre, this place is a recent addition to the small circuit of osterias that serve up good traditional Veneto dishes and snacks. Here they do an admirable version of sarde in saor and in summer you can munch outside.

Piola *(☎ 0422 54 02 87, Via Carlo Alberto 11)* Pizzas from around €6.20. Open Tues-Sun. This is a hip little bar-cum-pizzeria, where you can sit outside on a little terrace or bury yourself in the dimly lit innards of the bar with Treviso's night crowd. The pizzas are good and you have a wide choice of toppings.

Shopping

Benetton *(☎ 0422 55 99 11, Piazza dell'Indipendenza 5)* Open 3.30pm-7.30pm Mon, 10am-7.30pm Tues-Sat. For many the call of Benetton, in the heart of town, will be too hard to resist.

Getting There & Away

The bus station is on Lungosile Mattei, near the train station in Piazzale Duca d'Aosta. ACTV buses connect Treviso with Venice and La Marca buses link it to other towns in the province, for example, Conegliano (€2.30, 45 minutes) and Vittorio Veneto (€3.10, one hour 5 minutes).

It often makes better sense to get the train. The journey from Venice (€1.90) takes 25 minutes. Other trains connect the town with Belluno (via Conegliano and Vittorio Veneto), Oderzo, Padua and major cities to the south and west.

By car, take the SS53 for Venice and Padua.

BELLUNO

postcode 32100 • pop 35,230

Belluno is a beautiful little town at the foot of the Dolomites. If you start early enough, you could just about combine it with Treviso in a day trip from Venice, either by train or bus. Better still, hang around for a few days and use it as a base to explore the mountains (see the Trentino-Alto Adige chapter for further information on the Dolomites).

Orientation

Buses arrive at Piazzale della Stazione, in front of the train station. From here take Via Dante (which becomes Via Loreto) and then turn left at the T-junction down Via Matteotti into the central Piazza dei Martiri.

Information

The IAT office (☎ 0437 94 00 83), Piazza dei Martiri 8, produces a feast of information on walking, trekking, skiing and other sporting activities. It opens 9am to 12.30pm and 3pm to 6pm Monday to Saturday, 10am to 12.30pm and 3.30pm to 6.30pm on Sunday (mornings only on Sunday in winter). You should pop in if you're planning to head into the Dolomites.

Things to See & Do

Although no greatly notable monuments await inspection in Belluno, a wander around the compact old town is a pleasant enough experience. The main square (really a broad pedestrian avenue), **Piazza dei Martiri** (Martyrs' Square), takes its name from four partisans hanged here in the dying stages of WWII.

The heart of the old town is formed by **Piazza del Duomo**, dominated on one side by the early-16th-century Renaissance **Cattedrale di San Martino**, the **Palazzo Rosso**, from about the same period, and the **Palazzo dei Vescovi**. The latter's tower is one of three that belonged to the original 12th-century structure, long gone.

For most, the reason for reaching Belluno is as a starting point for activities in the mountains, from summertime **hiking** to **skiing** in winter. Stretching away to the north-west of Belluno is the **Parco Nazionale delle Dolomiti Bellunesi**, a beautiful national park laden with opportunities for those who want some mountain air.

Six Alte **Vie delle Dolomiti** (high altitude walking trails in the Dolomites) pass through the territory surrounding Belluno and along them you will find *rifugi* (mountain huts), on route No 1 in particular, where you can stay at the end of a day's hiking. Route No 1 stretches between Belluno and Lago di Braies.

Places to Stay

Camping Park Nevegal *(☎ 0437 90 81 43, fax 0437 90 81 44, Via Nevegal 347)* Sites per person/tent €6.70/9.30. Open year-round. This camp site has room for about 250 people and lies about 10km from Belluno at Nevegal. Autolinee Dolomiti buses from Belluno run past (€1.80, 20 minutes).

Ostello Imperina *(☎ 0437 6 24 51, Località Le Miniere)* B&B €12.90. Open Apr-Sept. This, the nearest youth hostel, is 35km north-west at Rivamonte Agordino. You can get there on the Agordo bus (€2.60, 50 minutes) from Belluno.

Albergo Taverna *(☎ 0437 2 51 92, Via Cipro 7)* Singles/doubles without bath €15.50/31. This place also has a few nicer doubles with their own bathroom for around €41.30. Equally important is the restaurant, ***La Taverna***, downstairs (see Places to Eat later).

A handful of other hotels dot the town, as well as some B&Bs and *affittacamere* (rooms for rent). B&B amounts to a similar option as the latter but includes breakfast. Plenty more hotels and affittacamere are scattered about the surrounding towns and villages.

Contact the IAT office for details of countryside and mountain accommodation options, including rifugi, which generally open late June to late September.

Places to Eat

La Taverna *(☎ 0437 2 51 92, Via Cipro 7)* Full meal around €23.25. Open Mon-Sat. You can sit at the bar for snacks and prosecco or head on through to the restaurant area, where you will be treated to hearty cooking. Around Christmas they do a local speciality for experienced stomachs only – a snail and eel combo that won't be to everyone's taste!

Getting There & Away

Autolinee Dolomiti buses (☎ 0437 94 12 37) depart from in front of the train station, on the western edge of town, for Agordo, Cortina d'Ampezzo, Feltre and smaller towns in the mountains and south of town.

Trains from Venice (€5.30, one hour 50 minutes) run here via Treviso.

By car you can take the A27 motorway from Venice (Mestre) or follow the state roads via Treviso. The latter can be time-consuming because of heavy traffic.

Friuli-Venezia Giulia

While the Adriatic coast is made up of little more than a series of lagoons and flat wetlands, the Friulian plains and Giulian plateaus lead up to the pine-covered Alps in the north, bordered by the Veneto to the west, Austria to the north and Slovenia to the east.

Roman rule was followed by that of the Visigoths, Attila's Huns, the Lombards and Charlemagne's Franks. The Patriarchate of Aquileia, formed in the second half of the 10th century, unified the local church and remained autonomous for several centuries.

Parts of Friuli went to Venice in 1420 but the easternmost area, including Gorizia, was only briefly touched by its influence. By 1797 the whole region was under the control of Habsburg Austria. Most of Friuli joined Italy in 1866 but it was not until after WWI that Gorizia, Trieste (in a roughly defined area known as the Giulia), Istria and Dalmatia were included – and at what cost. The Latin-Germanic-Slav triangle found its bloodiest expression in the trenches of WWI: Italy's 700,000 dead came from as far afield as Sardinia and Sicily, but a great many of them fell in what would subsequently become Friuli-Venezia Giulia.

After WWII, Italy kept Trieste but was obliged to cede Dalmatia and the Istrian peninsula to Tito's Yugoslavia in 1947. The Iron Curtain passed right through the frontier town of Gorizia. Today, road signs in the area around the town are in Italian and Slovene and you can still stumble across the occasional Slovene monument to Yugoslav partisans along the back lanes of the province. The Slovene community is strong but feels, not without reason, that Rome pays little heed to its needs – for years there has been talk of bilingual education for Italian Slovenes, with little or no result.

Relations between Italy and Slovenia are cordial at best. Each side is critical of the other's treatment of their respective Slovene and Italian minorities. Italy is also miffed that its eastern neighbour tends to turn north towards Austria and Germany in order to expand trade rather than look towards Rome.

West from the frontier, the road signs are in Italian and Friulian. Udine bears the marks of Venetian intervention, with Trieste largely a neoclassical creation of Habsburg Austria.

The region is relatively unexplored, and its cities and towns are worth a few days. You can mix urban culture with nature by heading for the Adriatic beaches, northern ski slopes or forest walking tracks.

Highlights

- Tuck into a buffet lunch in Trieste and follow with a lingering afternoon coffee at Caffè San Marco
- Visit the fine Romanesque basilica at Aquileia
- Behold the Lombard artwork in the pretty town of Cividale del Friuli
- Get away for some skiing and walking in the northern Carniche Alps

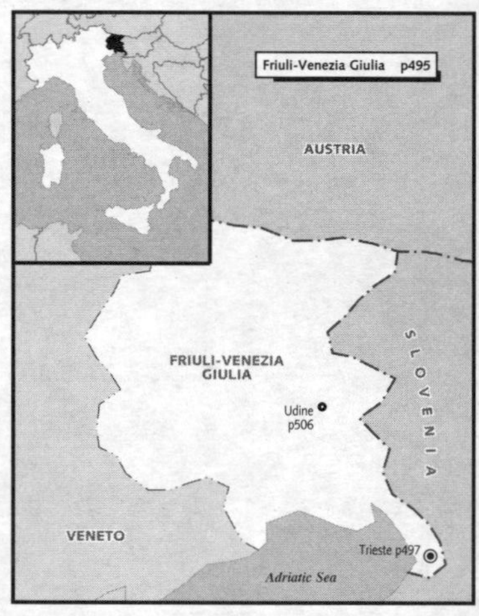

FRIULI-VENEZIA GIULIA

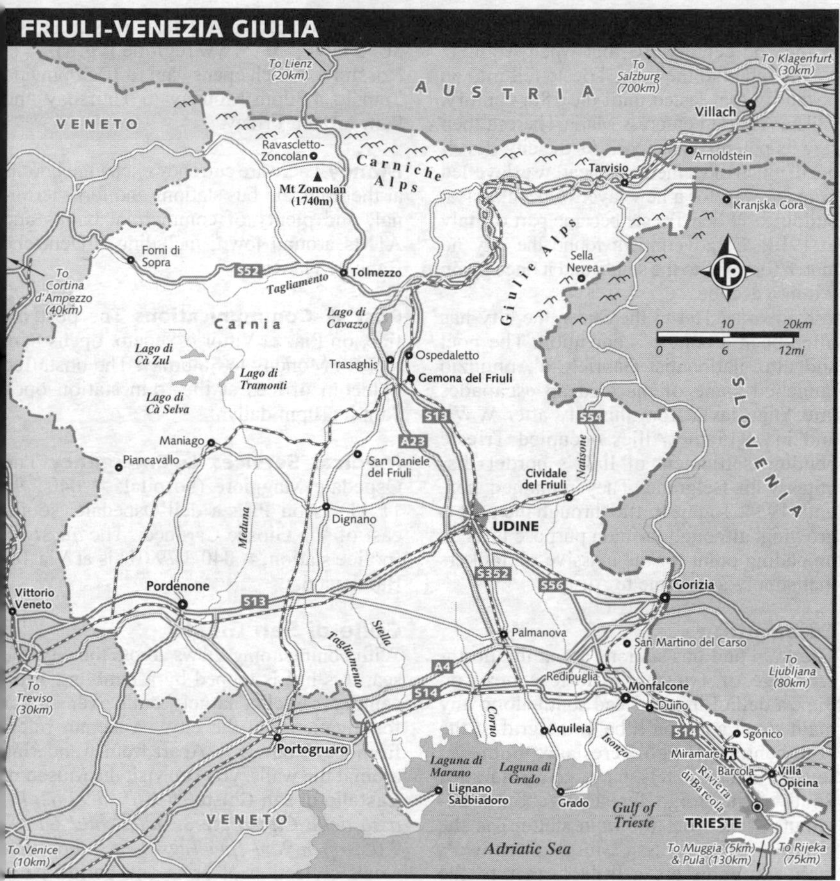

TRIESTE

postcode 34100 • pop 238,000

Sitting snugly between the Adriatic Sea and Slovenia, Trieste is an odd city. The faded grandeur of its largely homogenous architecture is owed entirely to its days as the great southern port of the Austro-Hungarian Empire during the 18th and 19th centuries. The city is a microcosm of one of Western Europe's major preoccupations – migrant pressure from east and south. What could be more incongruous, or more eloquent, than the sight of Croatian shoppers bargaining fiercely with illegal African immigrants hawking their wares in the streets? Czech-born Sigmund Freud came to the seaside town in 1796 to write a paper on the sexual organs of the eel.

Strangely attractive, although hardly strong on specific tourist sights, Trieste is not a bad place to end an Italian tour and embark on a foray into Slovenia and Croatia. The city, including many restaurants and hotels, closes down almost completely in August.

History

Known in antiquity as Tergeste, the fortified settlement was occupied by a succession of Venetian tribes, Gauls and Celts. The city became prominent under the Roman Empire in the 2nd century BC, but when Aquileia was founded to the west, Trieste fell into an obscurity that lasted until the 18th century.

The Austrian empress Maria Theresa then saw its potential as a port. As the city developed, much of its medieval heart was levelled to make way for a new layer of neoclassical buildings. When Trieste became part of Italy in 1918, the government found the city no match for ports to the south, and it once again fell into decline.

Known as Trst to the Slavs, the city has often been a bone of contention. The poet and ultra-nationalist Gabriele d'Annunzio launched some of his madcap escapades into Yugoslavia from this city after WWI, and in 1945 the Allies occupied Trieste pending settlement of Italy's border disputes with Belgrade. They remained here until 1954. Today, traffic through the port is growing, although its main purpose is as an unloading point for the massive oil tankers that supply a pipeline to Austria.

Orientation

The train and bus stations are at the northern edge of Trieste's historic centre, on Piazza della Libertà. Head south along any main street and you'll be in the grid of the 18th-century Borgo Teresiano, home to several budget hotels, bars and restaurants. South of the Borgo Teresiano (about a 20-minute walk from the train station) is the hilltop Castello di San Giusto. The town's main museums are a little farther to the south-west, while the principal shopping boulevards stretch east off Via Giosue Carducci.

Information

Tourist Offices The waterfront APT office (☎ 040 347 83 12, fax 040 347 83 20, ⓔ apt@iol.it), Riva III Novembre 9, opens 9am to 7pm daily. Its counterpart (☎ 040 42 01 82, Ⓦ www.fvgpromo.it) at the train station opens 7.30am to 8.30pm daily. Online try either Ⓦ www.triestetourism.it or www.triestecultura.it.

For information on other places in Friuli-Venezia Giulia, go to the regional tourist information office (☎ 040 36 51 51, fax 040 36 54 96, Ⓦ www.regione.fvg.it), Via Rossini 6, which opens 9am to 12.30pm and 3pm to 4.30pm Monday to Thursday and 9am to 1pm Friday.

Money There are currency exchange booths at the train and bus stations and ferry terminal, and plenty of commercial banks and ATMs around town, including a Deutsche Bank at Via Roma 7.

Post & Communications The post office, on Piazza Vittorio Veneto, opens 8am to 7pm Monday to Saturday. The unstaffed Telecom offices at the train station open 7am to 10pm daily.

Medical Services & Emergency The Ospedale Maggiore (hospital; ☎ 040 399 11 11) is on Piazza dell'Ospedale, south-east of Via Giosue Carducci. The *questura* (police station; ☎ 040 3 79 01) is at Via Tor Bandena 6.

Colle di San Giusto

With commanding views across the city and sea, this hill is topped by a rambling 15th-century **castello**, largely built over earlier fortifications by the city's Venetian rulers from 1470 onwards. Apart from wandering around the walls, you can visit the **Museo di Castello di San Giusto** *(☎ 040 30 93 62, Piazza della Cattedrale 3; adult/child €1.55/1.05; open 9am-1pm Tues-Sun)*. It houses a small collection of arms and period paraphernalia. The castle grounds can be explored from 9am to 6pm (admission €1.05).

The **Basilica di San Giusto**, completed in 1400, is the synthesis of two earlier Christian basilicas, and blends northern Adriatic and Byzantine styles. The interior contains 14th-century frescoes depicting San Justus, the town's patron saint. Down the road, the **Civico Museo di Storia ed Arte** *(Via della Cattedrale 15; adult/child €1.55/1.05; open 9am-1pm Tues & Thurs-Sun, 9am-7pm Wed)* has religious artefacts and Egyptian oddments. The **Orto Lapidario** (Stone Garden), behind the museum, has a collection of bits of classical statues and pottery

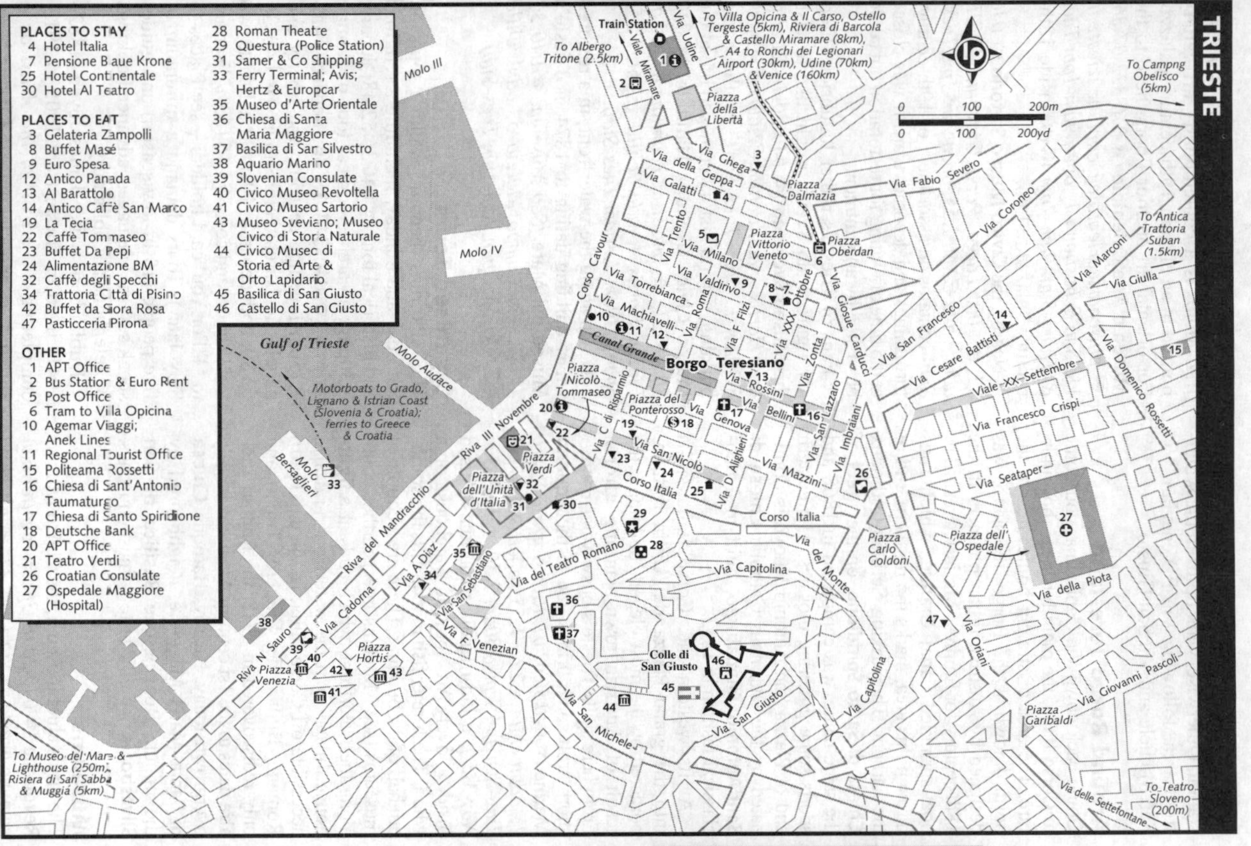

FRIULI-VENEZIA GIULIA

To get here, take bus No 24 from the train station. Otherwise, walk up from the waterfront area, following Via F Venezian, Via San Michele and Via San Giusto.

Around Borgo Teresiano

Going back down Via Capitolina, you come to Corso Italia, the main business thoroughfare. The area of straight boulevards to the north, known as the Borgo Teresiano, was designed by Austrian urban planners in the 18th century for Empress Maria Theresa. The boat-sprinkled **Canal Grande**, which runs through this area, marks the northern end of the harbour. The striking Serbian-Orthodox **Chiesa di Santo Spiridione**, on the street of the same name, was completed in 1868 and sports some glittering mosaics. The eastern end of Piazza San Antonio Nuovo is dominated by the enormous Catholic **Chiesa di Sant'Antonio Taumaturgo**, built in a neoclassical fashion in 1842.

At its western end, Corso Italia spills into the grand **Piazza dell'Unità d'Italia**, bordered by the most elegant buildings, the result of Austrian town-planning efforts. From here spills Trieste's busy waterfront. A short stroll south brings you to the **Aquario Marino** *(☎ 040 30 62 01, Riva Nazario Sauro 1; adult/child €2.60/1.55; open 9am-7pm Tues-Sun Apr-Sept, 8.30am-1.30pm Tues-Sun Nov-Mar)*, a kid-friendly aquarium housed inside a lovely Art Nouveau warehouse on a wharf. The former **fish market** fills the southern half of the building. There are a couple of museums (see Museums later) farther south along the waterfront, which ends at a **lighthouse**. Inland from the waterfront, and also accessible off Corso Italia, is Via del Teatro Romano. Built under Emperor Trajan and only rediscovered in 1938, the **Roman theatre** dates to the 1st century AD but is largely overgrown today. Nearby, Baroque **Chiesa di Santa Maria Maggiore**, neighboured by the minute Romanesque **Basilica di San Silvestro**, is one of Trieste's finest churches.

Museums

The city's chief museum, the **Civico Museo Revoltella** *(☎ 040 30 09 38, ⓔ revoltella@comune.trieste.it, Via Diaz 27; adult/child €6.20/4.15; open 9am-2pm & 4pm-7pm Wed-Mon)*, is a contemporary art gallery housed in an elegant 19th-century palazzo. For oriental art on four floors, head to the **Museo d'Arte Orientale** *(☎ 040 322 07 36, ⓔ museoarteorientale@comune.trieste.it, Via San Sebastiano 1; open 9am-1pm Tues & Thurs-Sun, 9am-7pm Wed)*, inside 18th-century Palazzetto Leo.

Nearby, the **Civico Museo Sartorio** *(☎ 040 31 05 00, Largo Papa Giovanni XXIII; adult/child €2.60/1.55; open 9am-1pm Tues-Sun)* contains an assortment of 19th-century furnishings and decorative art. It was closed at the time of writing for restoration but could be visited by appointment.

Fans of Trieste's rather lugubrious literary figure, Italo Svevo, might like to visit the **Museo Sveviano** *(☎ 040 30 18 21, Piazza Hortis 4; adult/child €2.60/1.55; open 8.30am-1.30pm Tues-Sun)*. In the same building, natural history comes to life at the **Museo Civico di Storia Naturale** *(☎ 040 30 18 21, ⓔ museisci@comune.trieste.it, Piazza Hortis 4; adult/child €2.60/1.55; open 8.30am-1.30pm Tues-Sun)*.

Down along the waterfront, in a restored wharf building dating to 1874, is Trieste's **Museo del Mare** *(Sea Museum; ☎ 040 30 49 87, Via Campo Marzio 5; adult/child €2.60/1.55; open 9am-1pm Tues-Sun)*.

Organised Tours

The APT runs thematic walking tours on Saturday and Sunday, including a religious and historical tour (☎ 040 36 52 48; departs 3.30pm); an archaeological tour of Roman Trieste (☎ 040 347 38 86; departs 4pm/5.15pm low/high season); and liberty and neoclassical architecture tours (☎ 040 36 62 80; both depart at 10am). Each lasts two to 2½ hours and costs €5.15 (50% discount to 'T For You' card holders – see Places to Stay later). Tours demand a minimum of five people (10 in low season) and guides speak several languages; advance bookings by telephone are obligatory.

Dublin-born writer James Joyce (1882–1941) lived in Trieste from 1905 to 1915, completing *A Portrait of the Artist as a Young Man* and kicking off *Ulysses* here.

FRIULI-VENEZIA GIULIA

Risiera di San Sabba

This was once a rice-husking plant at the southern end of Trieste. In 1943, the Germans, with local Fascist help, built a crematorium here and turned it into Italy's only extermination camp. It is believed 20,000 people perished here, including 5000 of Trieste's 6000 Jews. Yugoslav partisans closed it when they liberated the city in 1945, and 20 years later it became a national monument and museum (*☎ 040 82 62 02, Via Valmaura; free; open 9am-6pm Mon-Fri & 9am-1pm Sat & Sun Apr-mid-May, 9am-1pm Tues-Sun mid-May-Oct*). You can get there by bus No 10.

Literary travellers can trail around town in his footsteps with the English-language *Joyce Triestine Itineraries* brochure; the APT office doles it out for free.

Places to Stay

Ask at the APT about 'T For You', a weekend discount deal involving many city hotels.

Camping Obelisco *(☎ 040 21 16 55, fax 040 21 27 44, Strada Nuova per Opicina 47)* Low season sites per person/tent/car €2.85/5.70/2.05, high season €3.60/7.25/2.05. The closest camp site to the city centre is in Villa Opicina and is open year-round. Take tram No 2 or bus No 4 from Piazza Oberdan.

Ostello Tergeste *(☎/fax 040 22 41 02, Viale Miramare 331)* B&B €11.35. Reception opens 7am-10am & noon-midnight daily. Open year-round, this HI hostel is 5km out of town; catch bus No 36.

Pensione Blaue Krone *(☎ 040 63 18 82, fax 040 63 18 82, Via XXX Ottobre 12)* Singles/doubles from €23.25/36.15. 'Simple' sums up this one-star joint; screech down the intercom to get in.

Hotel Al Teatro *(☎ 040 36 62 20, fax 36 65 60, Capo di Piazza 1)* Singles/doubles without bath €43.90/72.30, singles/doubles/triples/quads with bath €62/98/118.80/123.90. One of Trieste's cheapest hotel options peers across at the city's illustrious theatre and opera house.

Hotel Continentale *(☎ 040 63 17 17, fax 040 36 88 16, Via San Nicolò 25)* Singles/doubles €80/111. Its fine location on a quiet pedestrian street in the centre of town makes the Continentale a choice picking.

Hotel Italia *(☎ 040 36 99 00, fax 040 63 05 40, ⓔ hotelitalia@onenet.it, Via della Geppa 15)* Singles/doubles €69.70/90.40. Italia is one of those unstartling, could-be-anywhere-in-the-world places to stay, but it's conveniently close to the train station.

Albergo Tritone *(☎ 040 42 28 11, fax 040 42 29 11, Viale Miramare 133)* Singles/doubles from €46.50/67.15. If you'd prefer to be by the seaside, one-star Tritone is a worthwhile choice on the road to Castello Miramare (bus No 36).

Places to Eat

Restaurants Trieste offers a tantalising taste of Italian tucker.

Al Barattolo *(☎ 040 63 14 80, Piazza San Antonio Nuovo 2)* Pizzas €5.15-7.75. Try this canalside pizzeria with churchly views on Sunday when most other places are shut.

Antico Panada *(☎ 040 347 62 86, Via Rossini 8d)* 1st/2nd courses from €5.15/7.75. Antico Panada dishes up a fantastic self-service buffet lunch for €6.70. Its terrace, smack-bang on the edge of the boat-filled canal, is the icing on the cake.

La Tecia *(☎ 040 36 43 22, Via San Nicolò 10)* 1st/2nd courses €5.15/7.75. With a red brick-topped interior and a pavement terrace on a pedestrianised street, this place gets packed.

Trattoria Città di Pisino *(Via Alberto Boccardi 7c)* Meals around €12.90. The surrounding area is traditional fishers' territory, as some of the street names suggest. This restaurant is good for fish.

Antica Trattoria Suban *(☎ 040 5 43 68, Via Comic 2)* Meals €20.65. One of Trieste's best restaurants has been in business since 1865. Take bus No 6 from the train station.

Buffets Launch your appetite at these lunch counters.

Buffet Da Pepi *(☎ 040 36 68 58, Via Cassa di Risparmio 3)* Meals around €10.35. Duck

Where to Feast on Friulian Fodder

Friulian cuisine has been influenced by many cultures but poverty has contributed the most. One typical dish, *brovada*, sees you eating turnips fermented with the dregs of pressed grapes. Otherwise *gnocchi* (potato, pumpkin or bread dumplings) are popular, as are *cialzons* (a ravioli-gnocchi hybrid stuffed with everything from cheese to chocolate) or sausages and *bolliti* (boiled meats) dished up with *polenta* and *cren*, a rather strong horseradish. *Jota* is a thick soup of beans and sauerkraut.

So exquisitely sweet it almost melts in your mouth is *prosciutti San Daniele*, raw ham sliced off the hind leg of a slaughtered black pig, salted and cured for 12 to 18 months. Locals from San Daniele, the village from which it originates, some 20km north-west of Udine, parade down the streets disguised as hams each year in August to celebrate their prosciutto festival.

Buffets (the local interpretation of a very basic Italian osteria) are the places to munch on all these dishes. Trieste is particularly well endowed with the latter. Wines from the eastern hills of Friuli, stretching from near the city on the Slovene border up into the Alps, are considered the region's tastiest and are best sampled in a *frasca* or *locanda* (an equally rustic, family-run wine bar).

Coffee, the finale to any Friulian feast, can be drunk à la *resentin* (coffee in a cup rinsed with grappa). A *gocciato* or *goccia* is a Triestine espresso or americano with a dash of foamed milk floating dead-centre on top. Stirring in sugar without disturbing the latter is an acquired art.

in here for the most authentic plate of boiled meat and beer you'll down in town – not recommended for those not into the smell (or sight) of meat.

Buffet Masé *(☎ 040 63 94 28, Via Valdirivo 32)* Meals around €10.35. This place has a deliberately Germanic ambience where you can wash down a plate of German sausage with a huge mug of Munich lager – perfect on a freezing winter night.

Buffet da Siora Rosa *(☎ 040 30 14 60, Piazza Hortis 3)* Meals around €10.35. Try the giant gnocchi or *involtini*, light pastry filled with ham and several melted cheeses.

Cafes Triestines take their coffee seriously.

Antico Caffè San Marco *(☎ 040 36 35 38, Via Cesare Battisti 18)* This elegant cafe, rebuilt after WWI, is by far the most atmospheric – a favourite with students, chess players, newspaper readers and anyone in the mood for Austrian-style *kaffeeklatsch* (gossiping with friends over coffee).

Caffè Tommaseo *(☎ 040 36 26 66, Riva III Novembre)* 1st/2nd courses €5.15/11.35. Languishing on the waterfront, this busy cafe – one of Trieste's first – lures tourists in for lunch with a pricey-but-pleasing €18.10 tourist menu.

Pasticceria Pirona *(☎ 040 63 60 46, Largo Barriera Vecchia 12)* James Joyce sought inspiration at this delightful cake shop and cafe, guaranteed to please the sweetest of tooths.

Caffè degli Specchi *(Piazza dell'Unità d'Italia 7)* On the site of an old Greek cafe, Caffè degli Specchi first opened its doors in its current form in 1839. Service is shockingly slow.

Gelateria Zampolli *(☎ 040 36 48 68, Via Ghega 10)* Zampolli might not be historic but its lip-smacking ice cream, concocted in just about every imaginable flavour, is legendary among Triestines.

Self-catering Self-caterers can shop for basic essentials at ***Euro Spesa*** *(Via Valdirivo 13 & 22)* and for dried pasta, pesto, honey and grappa at enticing ***Alimentazione BM*** *(Via San Nicolò 17)*. A daily ***fruit & veg market*** fills Piazza del Ponterosso.

Entertainment

Teatro Verdi *(☎ 040 672 22 98 or 040 672 22 99, W www.teatroverdi-trieste.com, Piazza Verdi 1)* The box office at Trieste's main theatre and opera house opens 9am to noon and 4pm to 7pm daily (6pm to 9pm on performance days).

Politeama Rossetti *(☎ 040 56 72 01, Piazza della Libertà 11)* Trieste's principal stage for drama is currently closed for renovation.

Teatro Sloveno *(☎ 040 63 26 64, Via Petronio 4)* To taste the Slovene side of Trieste life, see what's on at Teatro Sloveno – or rather *Kulturni Dom*, as any Slovenian would say.

Getting There & Away

Air Ronchi dei Legionari international airport (☎ 0481 77 32 25 or 0481 77 32 24), Via Aquileia, is served by direct international flights to/from Munich, London, Belgrade, Istanbul and Moscow, and domestic flights to/from Rome, Milan and Genoa.

Bus National and international buses operate from the bus station (☎ 040 36 70 78 or 040 42 50 20), off Piazza della Libertà at Via Fabio Severo 24. Services include to/from Udine (€4.20), Gorizia (€3.50), Duino (€2.10) and destinations in Slovenia and Croatia such as Ljubljana (€9.85, 2¾ hours, once daily Monday to Saturday), Zagreb (€10.85, five hours, once daily Monday to Saturday) and Dubrovnik (€52.25, 15 hours, once daily).

Train The train station (☎ 147 8 80 88), Piazza della Libertà 8, serves trains to Gorizia, Udine, Venice (€7.90, at least hourly), Rome (€42.85, twice daily) and Naples (€52.65, twice daily). There is one train daily to/from Ljubljana and Budapest.

Car & Motorcycle Trieste is at the end of the A4 (to Venice and Milan) and connects with the A23 to Austria. The S14 follows the coast and connects the city with Venice; it continues into Slovenia, as does the S15. Maggiore National (☎ 040 42 13 23) has an office at the train station; Euro Rent (☎ 040 42 22 89) is at the bus station; Avis (☎ 040 30 08 20), Hertz (☎ 040 322 00 98) and Europcar (☎ 800 01 44 10) are at the ferry terminal.

Boat All ferries use the ferry terminal on Molo Bersaglieri 3. Tickets for year-round boats to/from Corfu, Igoumenitsa and Patras in Greece are sold at Agemar Viaggi (☎ 040 36 40 64 or 040 36 37 37), Via Rossini 2, or direct from ferry operator Anek Lines (☎ 040 322 05 61, **w** www.anek.gr), which has an office in the same building. Agemar also sells tickets for the *C/F Grecia* car ferry that sails twice-weekly to/from Durazzo.

For information and tickets for Ustica Lines ferries to/from Pola in Croatia (€7.75/12.90 single/return, two hours, once daily Tues-Sat) go to Samer & Co Shipping (☎ 040 670 27 11, **e** samer@samer.com, **w** www.samer.com), which has its ticketing office at Piazza dell'Unità d'Italia 7 (4th floor). Tickets are only sold at the terminal a couple of hours before boats depart.

Mid-May to September, Samer also sells tickets for Adriatica motorboats along the coast to/from Grado (€6.45/12.90 single/return), Lignano (€7.25/14.45) and various points along the Istrian coast in Slovenia and Croatia. Tickets are only sold at the terminal 45 minutes before departure.

Getting Around

Buses depart from the bus station to the airport (€2.50, 50 minutes) at least hourly between 5am and 10.30pm daily.

ACT bus No 30 connects the train station with Via Roma and the waterfront, and bus No 24 goes to/from Castello di San Giusto. A single/double journey ticket costs €0.75/0.95. There are services to Miramare (bus No 36) and Villa Opicina (tram No 2 or bus No 4).

Taxi Radio Trieste (☎ 040 30 77 30) operates round the clock.

AROUND TRIESTE

A short trip north-west along the coast takes you to the **Riviera di Barcola**, a busy stretch of coastline guarded by the **Faro della Vittorio**, a sparkling white lighthouse topped by a statue of Vittorio (Victory). Its northern end is crowned with **Castello Miramare** *(☎ 040 22 41 43, 7km north-west of Trieste; adult/chlld €4.15/free; open 9am-7pm Apr-Sept, 9am-6pm Mar & Oct, 9am-5pm Nov-Feb)*, a grandiose, white castle set in fabulous gardens overlooking the sea. Archduke Maximilian of Austria had it built in 1856–60, but he never occupied it. After a brief stint as emperor of Mexico for Napoleon III, he was executed by the Mexicans in 1867. His widow Carlota, who remained at the castle, went mad; it was subsequently rumoured that anyone spending a night at Miramare would come to a bad end. In summer you can see a *suoni e lumi* (sound and light) show recreating all of these events. Take bus No 36 or the train from Trieste. About 5km south of Trieste along the coast is **Muggia**, a pretty fortified fishing village with a 14th-century castle.

Inland, the leggy strip of land between the coast and the Slovenian border, stretching as far north as Monfalcone, is known as **Il Carso** (Carso Heights), a name pertaining to the geological make-up of this white calcerous tableland, pot-holed like cheese with caves and riddled with doline (sink-holes created when caves collapse). Near Villa Opicina (known locally as 'Opicina'), 5km north of Trieste, is the **Grotta Gigante** *(☎ 040 32 73 12; adult/child €6.70/4.65; guided visits hourly 10am-noon & 2pm-4pm Nov-Feb, hourly 10am-4pm Mar & Oct, every 30 minutes 10am-6pm Apr-Sept)*. At 107m high, 130m long and 65m wide, it's said to be the world's largest accessible cave. Coloured globes light up the interior. Take bus No 42 from Trieste's Piazza Oberdan, or tram No 2 – the scenic choice that has covered the 5.2km journey since 1902 – from the same square to Villa Opicina, then bus No 42.

From Opicina, the **Napoleonica** meanders for some 5km north to Prosecco. Some fine panoramas of Trieste can be enjoyed along the trail, the start of which can be picked up from the Obelisco tram No 2 stop. Napoleonic troops supposedly used the path to access Trieste, hence its name.

Carstic flora and fauna can be observed at close quarters at the **Carsiana Giardino Botanico** *(☎ 040 22 95 73; adult/child €2.60/1.55; open 10am-noon Tues-Fri Nov-Mar, 10am-noon Tues-Fri, 10am-1pm & 3pm-7pm Sat & Sun Apr-Oct)*, botanical gardens in Sgónico, which cover 6000 sq metre and shelter some 600 of the 1600 flora species atypical to the limestone Carso.

Carstic folklore and ethnographic tradition comes to life at the **Casa Carsico** *(☎ 040 32 71 24, Rupingrande 31; free; open 11am-12.30pm & 3.30pm-6pm Sun & holidays Apr-Nov)* in the village of Rupingrande, a few kilometres north of Opicina. The traditional Carstic house, restored to its former 19th-century glory, hosts occasional local craft exhibitions. The plateau's most important folk festival, Nozze Carsiche (Carstic Wedding), is held every two years for four days at the end of August in Monrupino's 16th-century fortress, a couple of kilometres south-east of Rupingrande.

Several monuments to soldiers who died in WWI were built in Il Carso during the 1930s. The **Redipuglia memorial** contains the remains of 100,000 dead and is as sobering a reminder of the idiocy of war as any of the WWI monuments littered across Europe. There is a museum and, a couple of kilometres north, an Austro-Hungarian war cemetery. The area is sprinkled with other monuments, including one on **Monte di San Michele**, near San Martino del Carso, the scene of particularly bloody encounters (you can wander through the battlefield today), and the **Sacrario di Olsavia**, north of Gorizia. Redipuglia can be reached by bus (€2.50) or train from Trieste.

With the exception of Villa Opicina and Redipuglia, you'll need your own transport to explore Il Carso.

GORIZIA

postcode 34170 • pop 39,200
elevation 86m

That strangely un-Italian feeling you may have picked up elsewhere in Friuli-Venezia Giulia is no more evident than in Gorizia – right on the frontier of the Latin and Slavic worlds, with a long history of Germanic Austrian tutelage. Most locals speak Italian and Slovenian, and many road signs are in both languages. Austrian-style cafe culture (lots of rustling newspapers) rules and not a few of the GO number plates are from Nova Gorica, that post-WWII creation over the border. Only a short train or bus ride from Trieste or Udine, Gorizia is an interesting and quirky place and a stop worth making. The Colleo area surrounding the town produces some of Italy's finest white wines.

The Rout of Caporetto

The wanton spilling of young blood in the fight for centimetres of ground during WWI was not restricted to the killing fields of France and Russia. From May 1915, Italy decided to join the massacre, in the hope of ending the campaign for independence begun the century before by booting Austria off 'Italian' soil. The price of this folly, to a nation barely 50 years old, was 700,000 dead and more than a million wounded.

The main Italian front stretched from the Alps to the Adriatic Sea through Friuli and the Giulia, and Italy made substantial gains in its first offensive – approaching Gorizia (which did not fall until the following year) and advancing as far as Caporetto in the north (in modern Slovenia).

From then on, typical trench warfare set in, with neither side making much progress. Some of the toughest fighting took place on the Carso plateau between Trieste and Gorizia, and the River Isonzo soon became to the Italians what the Somme was to the Allies in France.

In October 1917, disaster struck when the Austro-Hungarians (with the decisive aid of crack German units) crushed the Italians at Caporetto, pretty much throwing them back to their 1915 starting lines, where they hung on grimly until the collapse of the Central Powers the following year. Italians don't meet their Waterloo, they 'have a Caporetto'.

History

Settled before the arrival of the Romans, the hilltop castle and surrounding town were always on the periphery of someone else's empire – Roman, Holy Roman and, from the early 16th century, that of the Austrian Habsburgs (to whom it became known as the Nice of the Empire). Apart from a brief spell under Venice, Gorizia first came under Italian control after WWI. In the wake of the following world war, Italy and Yugoslavia finally agreed to draw a line through the city in 1947, leaving most of the old city in Italian hands, and spurring Tito's followers to erect the soulless Nova Gorica on the other side.

Orientation & Information

The bus station is on Via IX Agosto, off Corso Italia. The train station is about 1km south-west of the centre on Piazzale Martiri Libertà d'Italia, at the end of Corso Italia.

The APT office (☎ 0481 38 62 22/24/25, fax 0481 38 62 77, ⓔ giubileo11@adriacom.it), Via Roma 5, opens 9am to 1pm and 3pm to 6pm Monday to Friday. The post office straddles the corner of Corso Verdi and Via Oberdan.

Borgo Castello

Gorizia's main sight is its castle *(☎ 0481 53 51 40, Borgo Castello 58; adult/child €4.15/free, €2.60/free when there's no exhibition on; open 9.30am-1pm & 3pm-7.30pm Tues-Sun)*, the original nucleus of the town. It has undergone several transformations and was restored in the 1920s after suffering serious damage in WWI. It makes a pleasant enough excursion and occasional exhibitions are held there.

There is a small **war museum** *(☎ 0481 53 39 26 or 0481 53 03 82, Borgo Castello 36; adult/child €3.10/free; open 10am-7pm Tues-Sun, 10am-6pm winter)* about 50m away downhill, but you will need to understand Italian to benefit from the explanations.

Churches

The most outstanding of Gorizia's churches is **Sant'Ignazio** on Piazza della Vittoria. You can't miss the onion-shaped domes – another sign that you're in *Mitteleuropa*. The little 14th-century **Chiesa di Santo Spirito**, by the castle, is also worth a quick peek. Perhaps more interesting is the 18th-century **synagogue** at Via Ascoli 19.

Places to Stay & Eat

Locanda da Sandro *(☎ 0481 53 32 23, Via Santa Chiara 18)* Singles/doubles €33.55/49.05. Sandro's one-star joint is Gorizia's cheapest place to stay.

Several fine ***trattorias*** are scattered in the old town below the castle. ***Trattoria da Majda*** *(☎ 0481 3 08 71, Via Duca d'Aosta 71–73)* and ***Rosen Bar*** *(☎ 0481 52 27 00, Via Duca d'Aosta 96)* are both well worth a nibble.

FRIULI-VENEZIA GIULIA

Getting There & Away

Trains and buses connect with Trieste and Udine. Buses also run to Nova Gorica, from where you can get buses all over Slovenia.

AQUILEIA

postcode 33051 • pop 3400

Once the fourth city of the Roman Empire, Aquileia was founded in 181 BC. Dubbed the Second Rome within 100 years, the city was a major trading link between the imperial capital and the East. By the beginning of the Christian era, Aquileia was Italy's richest market town and subordinate only to Rome, Milan and Capua. A patriarchate was founded here as early as AD 4 and, in spite of repeated assaults by Huns, Lombards and others, Aquileia's religious importance ensured it a privileged position until as late as the 14th century. The 4th-century mosaics in the town's Romanesque basilica are quite extraordinary.

What is now a small town lies at the eastern end of the Venetian plains. The local dialect is a good measure of the influence that the expanding Venetian republic had on Aquileia.

Things to See

Head straight for the **basilica** *(☎ 0431 9 10 67, ⓔ grmartin@tin.it, Piazza Capitolo; open 8.30am-7pm summer, 9am-12.30pm & 2.30pm-5pm winter)*, largely rebuilt after the 1348 earthquake. The long-hidden floor of the basilica's 4th-century predecessor is a precious and rare pictorial document of Christianity's early days, made up of mosaics depicting episodes in Christ's life, Roman notables and animal scenes. Don't miss out on the basilica's two crypts. The Cripta degli Affreschi boasts some marvellously preserved 12th-century frescoes, while the Cripta degli Scavi (closed at time of writing) reveals the floor mosaics of the 4th-century church. The bell tower was erected in 1030. Sunday mass is celebrated in the basilica at 10.30am.

Scattered remnants of the **Roman town** include ruins of the one-time *porto fluviale* (river port), houses and markets and the *foro romano* (forum) on Via Giulia Augusta. Dozens more finds are displayed in the **Museo Archeologico** *(☎ 0431 9 10 16, Via Roma 1; adult €4.15/free; open 8.30am-7.30pm Tues-Sun)*.

Places to Stay

Camping Aquileia *(☎/fax 0431 91 95 83, ⓦ www.campingaquileia.it, Via Gemina 10)* Sites per person, tent & car €13.45. Open mid-May–mid-Sept. This is the most affordable camp site in the area, north of Aquileia centre near the river-port docks.

Albergo Aquila Nera *(☎ 0431 9 10 45, fax 0431 9 10 45, Piazza Garibaldi 5)* Low season singles/doubles €25.80/41.30, high season €28.40/46.50. Aquileia boasts just a single one-star hotel – Aquila Nera.

Getting There & Away

Aquileia is a 45km trip from both Trieste and Udine. Regular buses from both cities call in on the way to Grado. The S352 road heads north towards Udine and south to Grado.

PALMANOVA

postcode 33057 • pop 5300
elevation 26m

If you flew over it, you'd see what makes this town so special. Built 10km north of Aquileia in 1593 by the Venetians, Palmanova (ⓦ www.palmanova.it) is a fortress in the form of a nine-pointed star. Napoleon and the Austrians made later use of it and to this day the Italian army maintains a garrison here.

From the hexagonal **Piazza Grande**, which sits at the centre of the star, six roads radiate out through the old town to the magnificent defensive walls, the city's real attraction. Head along one of the spokes, Borgo Udine, to uncover several centuries of local history in the **Civico Museo Storico** *(☎ 0432 92 91 06 or 0432 92 21 31, Borgo Udine 4; adult/child €1.05/0.50; open 10am-noon Thurs-Tues)*, inside Palazzo Trevisan. The museum acts as a tourist office and can advise on accommodation and places to eat. It also has the lowdown on some fascinating secret tunnel tours which wind beneath the city walls. Military fiends, for whom Palmanova holds the greatest fascination, should quick-march themselves to the **Museo Storico Militare** *(Borgo Cividale; open 9am-noon & 2pm-4pm Tues-Sat, 9am-noon Sun winter, 9am-noon & 4pm-6pm Tues-Sat, 9am-noon Sun summer)* inside the Porta Cividale, one of three monumental entrances to the fortified town. The military museum traces the history of troops stationed in Palmanova from 1593 through to WWII.

Palmanova is an easy bus ride from Udine.

GRADO

postcode 34073 • pop 9000

About 14km south of Aquileia, Grado is a not unpleasant Adriatic beach resort, spread along a narrow island backed by lagoons. The small medieval centre, criss-crossed by narrow *calli* (lanes), is a bright spot dominated by a Romanesque **basilica** and surrounded by cheery, tumbledown houses.

The APT office (☎ 0431 89 91, fax 0431 89 92 78), Viale Dante Alighieri 72, opens 9am to 1pm and 4pm to 7pm Monday to Saturday. Grado is a day trip by bus from Udine or Trieste, but if you want to stay overnight in summer, book ahead. There are several camp sites and about 90 hotels, many of which close in winter.

Albergo Zuberti *(☎ 0431 8 01 96, 0431 8 55 87, Piazza Carpaccio 31)* Singles with washbasin €25.80, low season singles/doubles with bath €31/38.75, high season €38.75/56.80. Zuberti ranks as one of Grado's cheapest year-round hotels.

LIGNANO

The Lignano area is pure resort, dispensing with the trappings of old-town centres. Lying on the tip of a peninsula facing Laguna di Marano to the north and the Adriatic Sea to the south, **Lignano Sabbiadoro** (postcode 33054, pop 6500) is the main town. The water here and in the neighbouring resorts is about all there is of any inter est. Staff at Lignano Sabbiadoro's APT office (☎ 0431 7 18 21, fax 0431 7 04 49, **W** www.aptlignano.it), Via Latisana 42, can assist with hotel and camp-site reservations.

UDINE

postcode 33100 • pop 99,000
elevation 114m

The region's second-largest city, Udine's topsy-turvy history has left it heir to an oddly mixed Italian, Slavic and Germanic culture. The city lies at the heart of Friuli, and as some inhabitants still speak the local dialect, the town authorities have put up street names in dialect next to the official Italian signs.

The Romans founded Udine as a way-station. By the early 15th century, when it first came under Venetian control, Udine had grown into a substantial city to rival nearby Cividale del Friuli and Aquileia. It is the Venetian influence that most strikes the eye in the town's bright medieval centre. Napoleon's lieutenants briefly took control at the beginning of the 19th century, followed by the Austrians until 1866, when the city joined the Italian kingdom. Udine survived WWII intact, but an earthquake in 1976 caused heavy damage and cost hundreds of lives. The great Renaissance painter Giambattista Tiepolo lived here for many years, leaving a number of works behind, notably in the cathedral.

Orientation

The train station is on Viale Europa Unita at the southern edge of the old city centre. The bus station is opposite the train station, slightly to the east. Walk along Via Roma, through Piazza Repubblica, past the Giardino Giovanni Pascoli, and along Via Carducci for the cathedral. An alternative route from Piazza Repubblica is to veer north-west along Via Dante and continue to Piazza della Libertà. The massive Piazza I Maggio is to the north-east.

Information

Tourist Offices The seemingly disorganised and unhelpful APT office (☎ 0432 29 59 72, fax 0432 50 47 43, **e** arpt1.ud@adriacom.it), Piazza I Maggio 7, opens 9am to 1pm and 3pm to 6pm Monday to Saturday. It has a fair amount of information on the city but practically nothing on the region; try **W** www.regione.fvg.it instead.

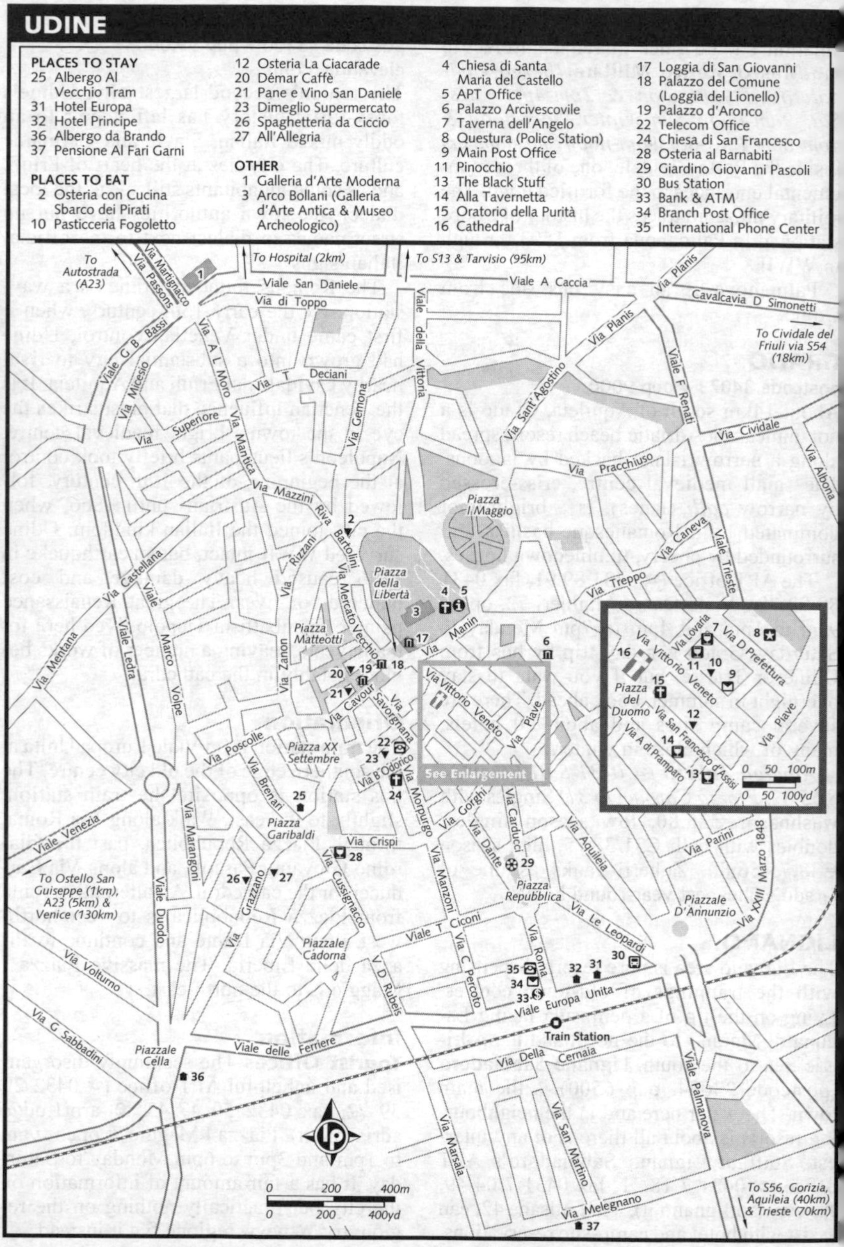

UDINE
PLACES TO STAY
25 Albergo Al Vecchio Tram
31 Hotel Europa
32 Hotel Principe
36 Albergo da Brando
37 Pensione Al Fari Garni
PLACES TO EAT
2 Osteria con Cucina Sbarco dei Pirati
10 Pasticceria Fogoletto
12 Osteria La Ciacarade
20 Démar Caffè
21 Pane e Vino San Daniele
23 Dimeglio Supermercato
26 Spaghetteria da Ciccio
27 All'Allegria
OTHER
1 Galleria d'Arte Moderna
3 Arco Bollani (Galleria d'Arte Antica & Museo Archeologico)
4 Chiesa di Santa Maria del Castello
5 APT Office
6 Palazzo Arcivescovile
7 Taverna dell'Angelo
8 Questura (Police Station)
9 Main Post Office
11 Pinocchio
13 The Black Stuff
14 Alla Tavernetta
15 Oratorio della Purità
16 Cathedral
17 Loggia di San Giovanni
18 Palazzo del Comune (Loggia del Lionello)
19 Palazzo d'Aronco
22 Telecom Office
24 Chiesa di San Francesco
28 Osteria al Barnabiti
29 Giardino Giovanni Pascoli
30 Bus Station
33 Bank & ATM
34 Branch Post Office
35 International Phone Center
To Autostrada (A23)
To Hospital (2km)
To S13 & Tarvisio (95km)
To Cividale del Friuli via S54 (18km)
To Ostello San Guiseppe (1km), A23 (5km) & Venice (130km)
To S56, Gorizia, Aquileia (40km) & Trieste (70km)
Piazza I Maggio
Piazza della Libertà
Piazza Matteotti
Piazza XX Settembre
Piazza Garibaldi
Piazza del Duomo
Piazza Repubblica
Piazzale D'Annunzio
Piazzale Cadorna
Piazzale Cella
Train Station
See Enlargement
0 50 100m
0 50 100yd
0 200 400m
0 200 400yd

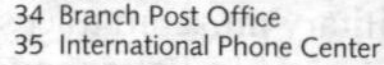

Money There is a bank and ATM opposite the train station at the southern foot of Via Roma, and plenty more on and around Piazza del Duomo.

Post & Communications The main post office, Via Vittorio Veneto 42, opens 8.15am to 7.30pm Monday to Saturday. The branch office, closer to the bus and train stations at Via Roma 25, opens 8.10am to 1.25pm Monday to Saturday.

The Telecom office, Via Savorgnana 15, opens 7am to 10pm daily. You can allegedly speak to great aunt Susy in Senegal for 18 minutes for a mere €8.80 at the International Phone Center (fax 0432 22 89 59), a cut-price place at Via Roma 29, which opens 9.30am to 8.30pm Monday to Saturday.

Medical Services & Emergency For medical attention, go to the Ospedale Santa Maria della Misericordia (☎ 0432 55 21, 0432 55 54 40, Ⓦ www.osp-smm.ud.it), some 2km north of the city centre at Piazza Santa Maria della Misericordia 15. The *questura* (police station; ☎ 0432 59 41 11) is at Via della Prefettura 16.

Piazza della Libertà

A gem of the Renaissance, Piazza della Libertà lies at the heart of the old town, in which most sights of historical interest are clustered. The 15th-century **Palazzo del Comune** (town hall), also known as the Loggia del Lionello after its architect, is a clear reminder of Venetian influence, as is the **Loggia di San Giovanni** opposite, which features a clock with Moorish figures that strike the hours – similar to the Mori of Venice's Torre dell'Orologio.

Castello

The **Arco Bollani** next to the Loggia di San Giovanni was designed by Palladio in 1556 and leads up to the castle, used by the Venetian governors. It now houses the **Galleria d'Arte Antica** *(☎ 0432 50 28 72, Piazzale del Castello; admission €2.05, free Sun morning; open 9.30am-12.30pm & 3pm-6pm Tues-Sun)*, whose extensive collection includes works by Caravaggio, Carpaccio and Tiepolo. The complex includes the **Museo Archeologico**. Also on the hill is 12th-century **Chiesa di Santa Maria del Castello**; the church originally stood within the walls of the medieval castle.

The Cathedral & Around

If you head south down Via Vittorio Veneto from Piazza della Libertà, you'll reach Piazza del Duomo and Udine's 13th-century Romanesque-Gothic **cathedral** with several frescoes by Tiepolo. South across the street is the **Oratorio della Purità**, with a beautiful ceiling painting of the *Assumption* by Tiepolo. Ask in the cathedral if you can get access to the Oratorio.

North-east of Piazza del Duomo is the **Palazzo Arcivescovile** *(Archbishop's Palace; ☎ 0432 2 50 03, Piazza Patriarcato 1; admission €3.60; open 10am-noon & 3.30pm-6.30pm Wed-Sun)*, where Tiepolo completed a remarkable series of frescoes depicting Old Testament scenes in 1726.

South of Piazza del Duomo on Largo Ospedale Vecchio is 13th-century **Chiesa di San Francesco**. Although once one of Udine's most striking churches, it is now used as a gallery and open only when it hosts exhibitions. A tiny ice-skating rink is erected in the square in front of the church in winter.

Galleria d'Arte Moderna

The Galleria d'Arte Moderna *(☎ 0432 29 58 91, Piazzale Diacono 22; adult/child €2.05/free; open 9.30am-12.30pm & 3pm-6pm Tues-Sun)* features a wide selection of well-known 20th-century art and works by modern Friulian artists.

Places to Stay

From cheap to not-so-cheap, Udine has all kinds of accommodation.

Ostello San Giuseppe *(☎/fax 0432 23 29 61, Viale Venezia 281)* B&B €10.35. Udine's hostel is strictly for the budget-conscious.

Albergo da Brando *(☎/fax 0432 50 28 37, Piazzale Cella 16)* Singles/doubles from €12.90/25.80. Dirt-cheap and rock bottom sums up this joint, situated due west of the train station.

Albergo Al Vecchio Tram (☎ *0432 50 25 16, Via Brenari 32)* Singles/doubles €18.10/28.40. A scant notch up the comfort ladder, the Old Tram has decent – if slightly malodorous – rooms.

Pensione Al Fari Garni (☎*/fax 0432 52 21 46, Via Melegnano 41)* Singles/doubles €26.85/37.20. South of the train station in a residential backwater, this place offers a fair enough comfort-price ratio.

Hotel Principe (☎ *0432 50 60 00, fax 0432 50 22 21,* e *hotelprincipe@tin.it, Viale Europa Unita 51)* Singles/doubles €51.65/72.30. Set back off the road in a quiet courtyard, Principe is a friendly mid-range option. Breakfast costs an extra €5.15 per person.

Hotel Europa (☎ *0432 50 87 31, fax 0432 51 26 54, Viale Europa Unita 47)* Singles/doubles €51.65/77.45. Breakfast is included in the rates at this old-world place, which sits cheek-to-cheek with Hotel Principe.

Places to Eat

Don't wait too late to eat out, as the city is generally pretty quiet by 10pm, especially during the week – no Latin excitement in the streets here.

Osteria con Cucina Sbarco dei Pirati (☎ *0432 2 13 30, Riva Bartolini 12)* It might appear to be just another simple bar but step inside and you emerge on a delightful wooden terrace above a stream, crammed with knick-knacks from a bygone era. Cheap fills guaranteed.

Spaghetteria da Ciccio (☎ *0432 50 59 35, Via Grazzano 11)* 1st/2nd courses €5.70/6.20. This one cooks up cheap plates of pasta and pizza laced with atmosphere and charm – another tummy- and eye-pleasing bargain.

Osteria La Ciacarade (☎ *0432 51 02 50, Via San Francesco 6)* Ham hunks hang above the bar, and giant bowls of fresh strawberries and cherries entice you into this absolutely authentic osteria. Wash a hearty meal down with wine from the region.

All'Allegria (☎ *0432 50 59 21, Via Grazzano 18)* About €18.10 per head. This cosy trattoria stays open comparatively late and – despite its endearingly ramshackle, rough 'n' tumble exterior – serves quality local cuisine.

There are several excellent open-air cafes and restaurants on Piazza Matteotti and the pedestrian streets that fan out from this peaceful square.

Pane e Vino San Daniele (Piazzetta Lionello 12) 1st/2nd courses €6.20/11.35, monster-sized salads €5.15-7.75. The fabulous terrace overlooking Palazzo d'Aronco makes this a busy place on sunny days.

Démar Caffè (☎ *0432 50 40 80, Via Rialto 5)* Démar's highly minimalist and contemporary decor lures a trendy crowd.

Pasticceria Fogoletto (Via Vittorio Veneto 36) The Germanic influence is clearly visible in the city's sweets; for great cakes and a coffee, try this place in a building dating from 1392.

Self-caterers can shop at ***Dimeglio Supermercato*** *(Via Bonaldo Stringher)*.

Entertainment

The Black Stuff (☎ *0432 29 78 38, Via Gorghi 3a)* An army of Udine's youth mingles with a fair sprinkling of those more advanced in years at Udine's Irish pub, which is open until 2.30am.

Pinocchio (Via Lovaria 3a) Hip Pinocchio has a sprawling bar with low lights and thumping music.

Taverna dell'Angelo (Via Lovaria 3c) Characterful Angelo pulls pints in a more traditional setting, a couple of doors down from Pinocchio.

Alla Tavernetta (☎ *0432 50 10 66, Via di Prampero)* This cosy tavern offers entertainment in the form of wine tasting for the more refined pleasure-seeker. It serves food, too, for when the munchies bite.

Osteria al Barnabiti (Piazza Garibaldi) Rough-cut around the edges yet oozing charm, this typical osteria offers wine drinkers the quintessential drinking experience, day or night.

Getting There & Away

From the bus station (☎ 0432 50 40 12 or 0432 50 87 62) on Viale Europa Unita there are regular services to/from Trieste (€4.40, 1¼ hours, at least hourly), Lignano Sabbiadoro (€4.40, nine to 11 daily) and Grado (€2.90, 12 daily). SAF (☎ 0432 60 81 11) serves most main centres in the region as well as more distant destinations such as Padova (three hours, twice weekly) and Taranto (€48.05, 15 hours, twice daily). Saita (☎ 0432 51 13 31) operates buses to/from San Candido (six hours, once daily).

Udine is on the main Trieste-Venice train line and services are regular in both directions. There are also direct rail services to/from Milan.

The A23 passes the city to the west and connects the A4 with Austria. The S56 leads to Trieste and the S13 to Austria.

CIVIDALE DEL FRIULI

postcode 33043 • pop 11,000
elevation 138m

A trip to Cividale del Friuli is a must if you make it to Udine. It is one of the most picturesque towns in the region, its small medieval centre managing to survive several devastating earthquakes. The town was founded by Julius Caesar in 50 BC and in AD 6 it became the seat of the first Lombard duchy. About 200 years later, its reputation drew the patriarch of Aquileia to Cividale.

The APT office (☎ 0432 73 14 61, fax 0432 73 13 98, ⓔ a.r.p.t.cividale@regione.fvg.it), Corso Paolino d'Aquileia 10 (near Ponte del Diavolo), has information about Cividale, the Natisone Valley and walks in several parks and the mountains to the north and east.

Cividale is at its most picturesque where the 15th-century **Ponte del Diavolo** (Devil's Bridge) crosses the emerald-green River Natisone. Legend says that the devil himself threw the 22m-high stone bridge into the river. Walk through the cobbled lanes to the **Templetto Longobardo** *(Borgo Brossano; adult/child €2.05/1.05; open 9.30am-12.30pm & 3pm-6.30pm Mon-Sat, 9.30am-1pm & 3pm-5.30pm Sun)*. Also known as the Oratorio di Santa Maria in Valle, this 'little temple' was rebuilt after a 13th-century earthquake and is an exquisite example of Lombard artwork. To the west, the 16th-century **cathedral** is not the most engaging, although the **Museo Cristiano** *(Christian Museum; ☎ 0432 73 11 44, Piazza del Duomo; free; open 9.30am-noon & 3pm-7pm Mon-Sat)* in its annexe stars the Altar of Ratchis, a magnificent example of 8th-century Lombard sculpture.

Albergo Pomo d'Oro *(☎/fax 0432 73 14 89, Piazza San Giovanni 20)* Singles/doubles €41.30/62. This is the cheapest of the three hotels in town.

Trains and buses connect Cividale with Udine and Trieste, or you can drive the 17km from Udine on the S54.

IL CARNIA

North of Udine, the Friulian lowlands gradually give way to Alpine country on the way to Austria. Known generically as Il Carnia, after the people who settled here in around the 4th century BC, the region's prime attractions are walking and skiing – and an agreeable, if only relative, absence of tourists.

The eastern half is characterised by forbidding and rocky bluffs along the valley to **Tarvisio** (postcode 33018, population 5500, elevation 754m). This Alpine resort, 7km short of the Austrian border (heading for Villach) and 11km from Slovenia, is not a bad base for skiing and walking. The town itself is a curiosity. The Saturday market attracts hordes of Austrians; the bargains (everything from alcohol to clothes) must be pretty good because Vienna's visitors are joined by lots of bargain-hunters from as far afield as Budapest, Zagreb and Ljubljana. A few kilometres east are a couple of fairly peaceful lakes, from where you can take forest rambles.

For the more attractive, verdant western half of Il Carnia, head off the main north–south road for Tolmezzo, a small town surrounded by industry. Don't bother stopping but make for the west (Forni di Sopra) or north (Monte Zoncolan, for instance). It's a pretty and comparatively undisturbed area.

Information

There are APT office in the towns of Tarvisio (☎ 0428 21 35, fax 0428 29 72, ⓦ www.tarvisiano.org), Via Roma 10; Forni di Sopra (☎ 0433 88 67 67, fax 0433 88 66 86), Via Cadore 1; Piancavallo (☎ 0434 65 51 91, fax 0434 65 53 54); and Barcis (☎ 0427 7 63 00), Piazza Victor Emanuele II 5.

Activities

There are 18 **skiing** centres across northern Friuli-Venezia Giulia, the most important being (in a rough curve west to east) Piancavallo, Forni di Sopra, Ravascletto-Zoncolan, Sella Nevea and Tarvisio. Decent downhill pistes, best suited to beginners and intermediates, start at about 1700m or higher. Daily, weekly and season ski passes are available, as is a Beyond Borders Skipass that allows skiing forays into neighbouring Kranjska Gora (Slovenia) and Arnoldstein (Austria). A six-day pass costs €50–68.

Those intent on **walking** the region should pick up a copy of *Rifugi Alpini*, a useful guide to *rifugi* (mountain shelters) produced by Udine's APT office. It's in Italian, but you should be able to make out the salient details. Leaflets suggesting various walking routes are also available. Local newsagents sell detailed walking maps.

Little traffic coupled with some splendid panoramas make for invigorating **cycling**. The APT office in Tarvisio has lots of information on itineraries and routes, and produces a series of eight cycling guides to the region, accompanied by maps and detailed trail notes. The latter can also organise guided mountain-bike expeditions.

Places to Stay

Camping Al Pioppi *(☎ 0432 98 03 58, Via Bersaglio 44)* Sites per person/tent/car €4.65/3.60/2.60. This large 8000-sq-metre site, 3.5km north of Gemona del Friuli in Ospedaletto, sports everything from a supermarket and laundrette to ping-pong tables and facilities for disabled travellers.

Most towns have at least a couple of hotels, a surprising number of which are in the one-star bracket. At the height of the season, book ahead. The Udine APT has a full list of the region's accommodation.

Getting There & Away

Tarvisio is connected by train to Udine (1¾ hours, up to 10 daily) and is the most easily accessible town in the region. If you don't have your own transport, you will have to rely on Carnia's infrequent bus service. Drivers heading north from Udine can take the A23 or the S13 – possibly one of the most boring roads in Italy, at least until you pass the chain of supermarkets between Udine and Gemona. The A23 is faster but is a tollway.

Emilia-Romagna & San Marino

Despite its convenient location between the big tourist draws of Tuscany to the south and Lombardy and the Veneto to the north, Emilia-Romagna is largely overlooked by the visiting masses. The regional capital, Bologna, was one of the most important medieval cities; its university is Europe's oldest and turned out the likes of Thomas Becket, Erasmus, Copernicus, Dante and Petrarch. Bologna has also long been regarded as Italy's culinary capital, drawing on produce from the fertile Po Valley (Pianura Padana) and adding tortellini and lasagne to the Italian table. It's a sophisticated city, well worth a visit of several days, and makes a good base for short trips to Ferrara, Modena and Parma, all once important Renaissance towns.

The Adriatic towns of Ravenna, which boasts one of the world's best collections of Byzantine mosaics, and Rimini, with its beaches and nightlife, add to the region's diversity, as does the marshland of the Po Delta (Foci del Po), which Emilia-Romagna shares with the Veneto.

Emilia, which stretches west of Bologna, and Romagna, to the east, were joined on Italian unification. Both former papal states, they each retain their own characteristics: the Emilians are an industrious people and the Romagnoli are known for their entrepreneurial spirit, which finds a special expression in tourism.

Settled by the Etruscans, the area began to prosper after AD 187, when the Romans built the Via Emilia. Apart from a period of Byzantine rule along the Adriatic coast and the medieval experience of the independent *comuni* (communes), the real boom came with the Renaissance, when some of the country's most notable families ruled the various towns – the Farnese in Parma and Piacenza, the Este in Ferrara and Modena and the Bentivoglio in Bologna – and built opulent palaces and courts.

Transport along the Via Emilia (S9) is excellent, and bus connections enable exploration into the mountains and north along the River Po. The region's prosperity means prices are relatively high, but youth hostels enable even budget travellers to see the entire region without too much trouble. However, accommodation can be difficult to find, so book ahead.

Squeezed in between Emilia-Romagna and Le Marche to the south is the tiny independent republic of San Marino, closer to a product of Walt Disney's imagination than a real place (although the views from it are spectacular).

Highlights

- Wander through the historical centre of 'Red' Bologna
- Study Ravenna's spectacular mosaics
- Admire the fine Romanesque cathedral in Modena
- Feast on lasagne, *tortellini*, *prosciutto di Parma*, *parmigiano reggiano* and other specialities of this food-lover's nirvana
- Visit the amazing art collection in Parma's Galleria Nazionale

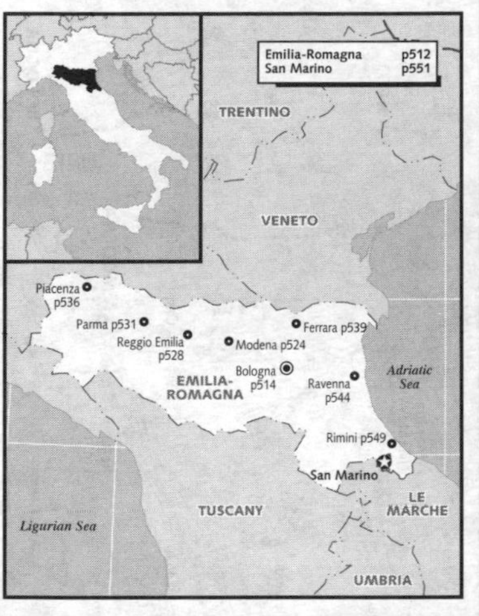

EMILIA-ROMAGNA & SAN MARINO

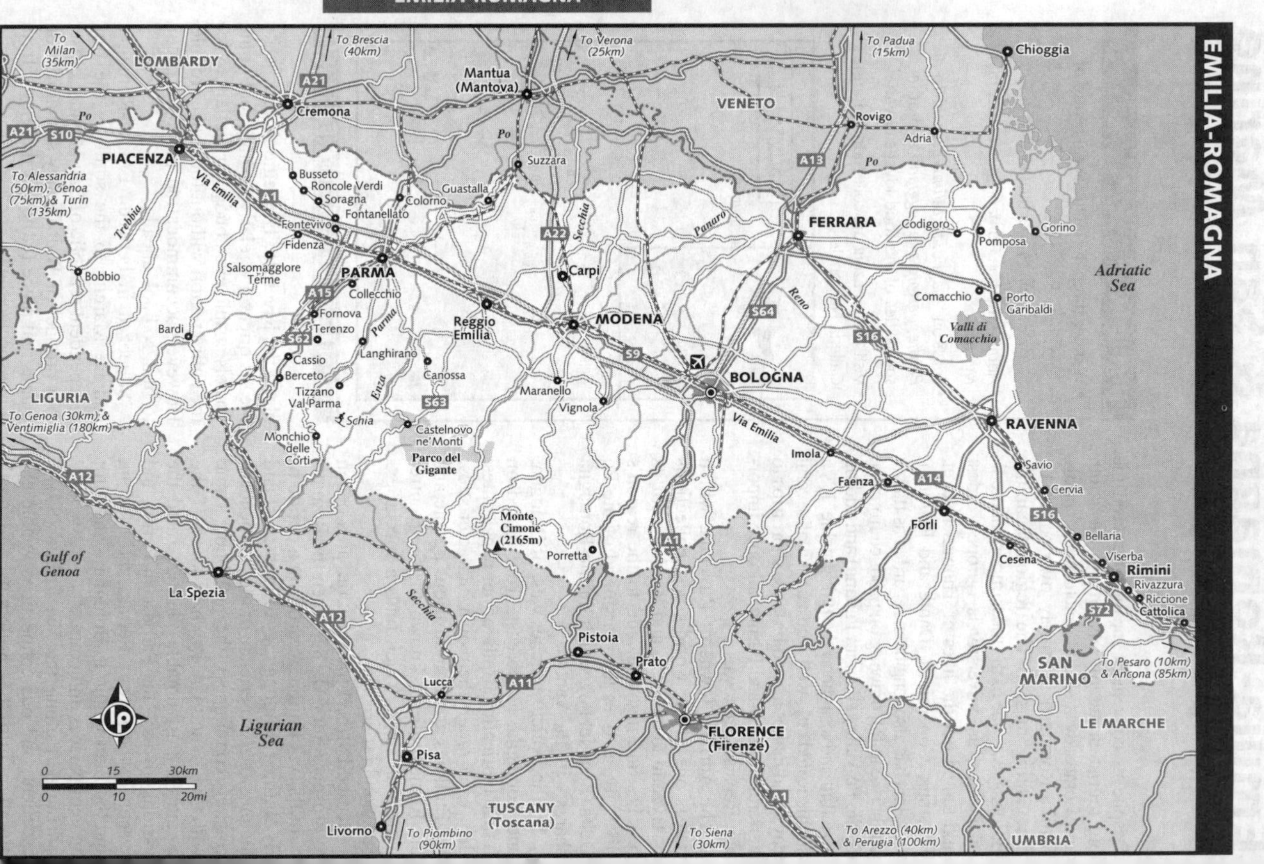
EMILIA-ROMAGNA
To Milan (35km)
LOMBARDY
To Brescia (40km)
A21
Cremona
Mantua (Mantova)
To Verona (25km)
VENETO
To Padua (15km)
Chioggia
Rovigo
Adria
Po
A21
S10
PIACENZA
Via Emilia
To Alessandria (50km), Genoa (75km) & Turin (135km)
Trebbia
Bobbio
Busseto
Roncole Verdi
Soragna
Fontanellato
Fontevivo
Fidenza
Salsomaggiore Terme
A1
Colorno
Guastalla
Suzzara
A22
Secchia
Panaro
A13
FERRARA
Codigoro
Pomposa
Gorino
Adriatic Sea
PARMA
Collecchio
A15
Fornova
Terenzo
S62
Parma
Bardi
Cassio
Berceto
Langhirano
Tizzano Val Parma
Enza
Canossa
S63
Schia
Castelnovo ne'Monti
Monchio delle Corti
Parco del Gigante
LIGURIA
To Genoa (30km) & Ventimiglia (180km)
Carpi
Reggio Emilia
MODENA
S9
Maranello
Vignola
S64
Reno
BOLOGNA
Via Emilia
S16
Comacchio
Porto Garibaldi
Valli di Comacchio
RAVENNA
Imola
Faenza
A14
Forlì
Savio
Cervia
S16
Bellaria
Cesena
Viserba
Rimini
Rivazzura
Riccione
Cattolica
S72
A12
Gulf of Genoa
La Spezia
Monte Cimone (2165m)
Porretta
A1
Secchia
A12
Pistoia
Prato
A11
Lucca
Ligurian Sea
Pisa
FLORENCE (Firenze)
SAN MARINO
To Pesaro (10km) & Ancona (85km)
LE MARCHE
0 15 30km
0 10 20mi
TUSCANY (Toscana)
Livorno
To Piombino (90km)
To Siena (30km)
A1
To Arezzo (40km) & Perugia (100km)
UMBRIA

Bologna

postcode 40100 • pop 382,000

They call it Red Bologna. Until recently a bastion of the Democratici di Sinistra (the democratic party of the left), this elegant, porticoed city really does take on every conceivable hue of red with the changing light of day.

The university is still a source of student agitation, albeit on a smaller scale than in the protest heyday of the 1970s. Together with one of the country's better organised gay communities, the students provide a dynamic air that is missing in smaller Emilian towns. The city administrators chip in with an unstinting arts programme to keep even the most demanding culture-buffs well occupied. This reached its zenith in 2000 when Bologna was a European City of Culture.

History

Bologna started life in the 6th century BC as Felsina, for two centuries the capital of the Etruscan Po Valley territories, until tribes from Gaul took over and renamed it Bononia. They lasted another couple of hundred years before surrendering to the Romans' northward march. As the Western Empire crumbled, Bologna became increasingly exposed to attack from the north, and was sacked and occupied by a succession of Visigoths, Huns, Goths and Lombards.

The city reached its pinnacle as an independent commune and leading European university in the 12th century. Wealth brought a building boom and every well-to-do family left its mark by erecting a tower. There were 180 of them in all, of which 15 still stand. The endless tussle between the papacy and Holy Roman Empire for secular control of the Italian north could not fail to involve Bologna. The city started by siding with the Guelfi (Guelphs), who backed the papacy, against the Ghibellines, but adopted neutrality in the 14th century. Following a popular rebellion against the ruling Bentivoglio family, in which their palace was completely destroyed, the papal troops took Bologna in 1506 and the city remained under papal control until the arrival of Napoleon at the end of the 18th century. In 1860, Bologna joined the newly formed Kingdom of Italy. During heavy fighting in the last months of WWII, up to 40% of Bologna's industrial buildings were destroyed. However, the historic town inside the walls survived and has been carefully preserved. Today, the city is a centre for Italy's high-tech industries and it plays host to numerous trade fairs.

Orientation

It would be a travesty not to explore Bologna on foot, and the compactness of the historic centre leaves few excuses for using buses or taxis. Via dell'Indipendenza leads south from the train and bus stations into Piazza del Nettuno and Piazza Maggiore, the heart of the city. Drivers should follow the *centro* target symbol off the *tangenziale* (ring road). However, much of the centre is off-limits to most traffic and parking can be expensive.

Information

Tourist Offices The main Ufficio Informazioni Turistiche (☎ 051 24 65 41) is on the northern end of Piazza Maggiore in the Palazzo del Podestà. It opens 9am to 7pm Monday to Saturday, 9am to 2pm on Sunday and public holidays. Other offices are at the train station (8.30am to 7.30pm Monday to Saturday) and at the airport (8am to 8pm daily). They all have stacks of information, free maps and brochures, including a list of accommodation possibilities. Check out the Web site at W www.comune.bologna.it and follow the prompts to 'Bologna *turismo*'.

The Centro Servizi per i Turisti (☎ 051 648 75 83 or toll free ☎ 800 85 60 65) is in the same office as the main tourist office and can organise hotel bookings free of charge. Note that Bologna is often booked out due to its active trade fair and convention calendar.

There is a combined ticket for admission to six of the city museums for €6.20 per day and €8.25 for three days. Children up to the age of 14 are admitted free to all museums and there are student and youth discounts. Tickets may be purchased at participating museums or from the tourist office.

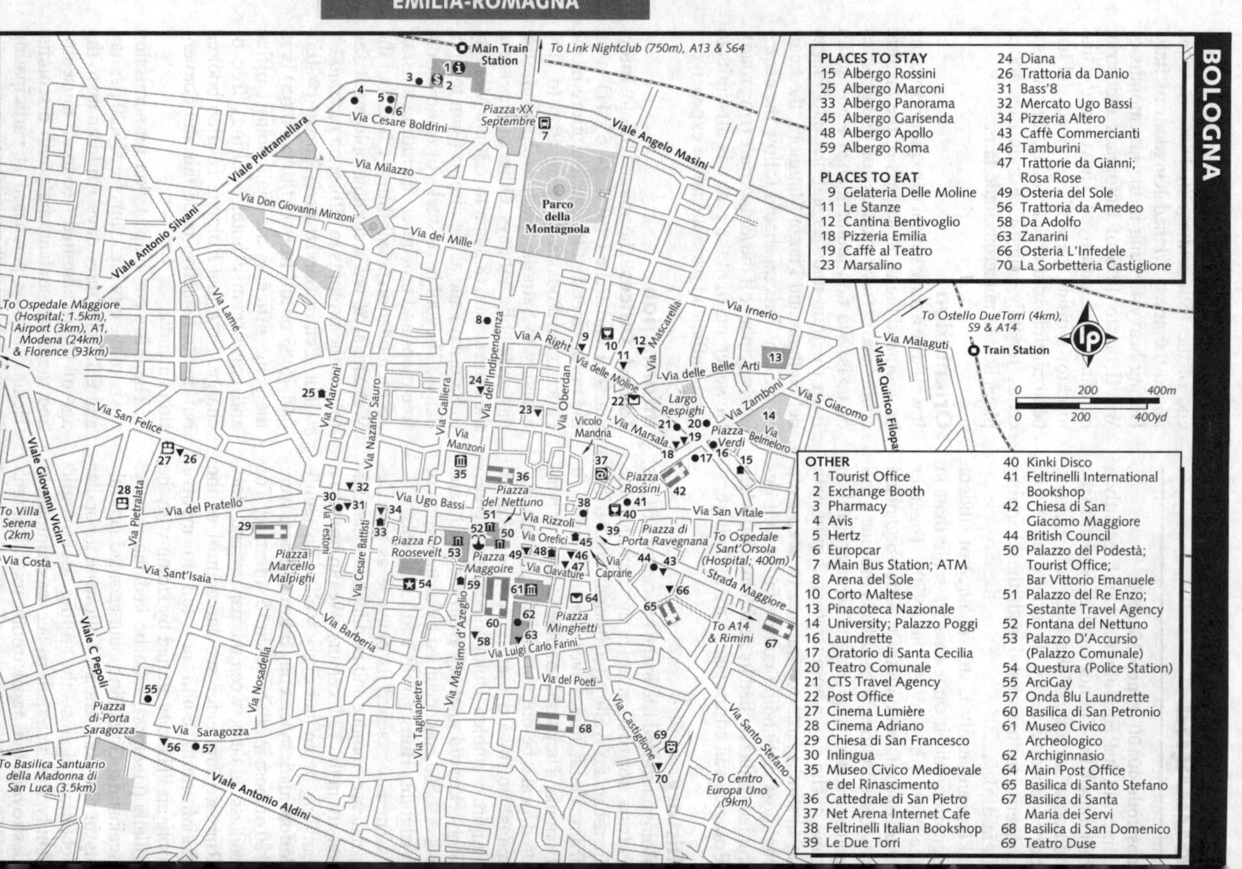
BOLOGNA
EMILIA-ROMAGNA
PLACES TO STAY
15 Albergo Rossini
25 Albergo Marconi
33 Albergo Panorama
45 Albergo Garisenda
48 Albergo Apollo
59 Albergo Roma
PLACES TO EAT
9 Gelateria Delle Moline
11 Le Stanze
12 Cantina Bentivoglio
18 Pizzeria Emilia
19 Caffè al Teatro
23 Marsalino
24 Diana
26 Trattoria da Danio
31 Bass'8
32 Mercato Ugo Bassi
34 Pizzeria Altero
43 Caffè Commercianti
46 Tamburini
47 Trattorie da Gianni; Rosa Rose
49 Osteria del Sole
56 Trattoria da Amedeo
58 Da Adolfo
63 Zanarini
66 Osteria L'Infedele
70 La Sorbetteria Castiglione
OTHER
1 Tourist Office
2 Exchange Booth
3 Pharmacy
4 Avis
5 Hertz
6 Europcar
7 Main Bus Station; ATM
8 Arena del Sole
10 Corto Maltese
13 Pinacoteca Nazionale
14 University; Palazzo Poggi
16 Laundrette
17 Oratorio di Santa Cecilia
20 Teatro Comunale
21 CTS Travel Agency
22 Post Office
27 Cinema Lumière
28 Cinema Adriano
29 Chiesa di San Francesco
30 Inlingua
35 Museo Civico Medioevale e del Rinascimento
36 Cattedrale di San Pietro
37 Net Arena Internet Cafe
38 Feltrinelli Italian Bookshop
39 Le Due Torri
40 Kinki Disco
41 Feltrinelli International Bookshop
42 Chiesa di San Giacomo Maggiore
44 British Council
50 Palazzo del Podestà; Tourist Office; Bar Vittorio Emanuele
51 Palazzo del Re Enzo; Sestante Travel Agency
52 Fontana del Nettuno
53 Palazzo D'Accursio (Palazzo Comunale)
54 Questura (Police Station)
55 ArciGay
57 Onda Blu Laundrette
60 Basilica di San Petronio
61 Museo Civico Archeologico
62 Archiginnasio
64 Main Post Office
65 Basilica di Santo Stefano
67 Basilica di Santa Maria dei Servi
68 Basilica di San Domenico
69 Teatro Duse
0 200 400m
0 200 400yd
Main Train Station
To Link Nightclub (750m), A13 & S64
Piazza XX Settembre
Parco della Montagnola
Viale Angelo Masini
Via Cesare Boldrini
Via Milazzo
Viale Pietramellara
Via Don Giovanni Minzoni
Via dei Mille
Viale Antonio Silvani
Via Lame
To Ospedale Maggiore (Hospital; 1.5km), Airport (3km), A1, Modena (24km) & Florence (93km)
Via San Felice
Via Marconi
Via Nazario Sauro
Via Galliera
Via dell'Indipendenza
Via Oberdan
Via A Righi
Via delle Moline
Via Mascarella
Via Irnerio
Via delle Belle Arti
Largo Respighi
Via Marsala
Vicolo Mandria
Via Zamboni
Via S Giacomo
Via Belmeloro
Piazza Verdi
Viale Quirico Filopa
Via Malaguti
To Ostello DueTorri (4km), S9 & A14
Train Station
Via Manzoni
Piazza del Nettuno
Piazza Rossini
Via San Vitale
To Ospedale Sant'Orsola (Hospital; 400m)
Piazza di Porta Ravegnana
Strada Maggiore
To A14 & Rimini
Via Santo Stefano
To Centro Europa Uno (9km)
Via Castiglione
Via Caprarie
Via Clavature
Via Orefici
Via Rizzoli
Piazza Maggiore
Piazza Minghetti
Via Luigi Carlo Farini
Via del Poeti
Via Ugo Bassi
Piazza FD Roosevelt
Via Massimo d'Azeglio
Via Tagliapietre
Via Cesare Battisti
Via Testoni
Via Barberia
Piazza Marcello Malpighi
Via Nosadella
Viale Antonio Aldini
Via del Pratello
Via Sant'Isaia
Via Saragozza
Via Pietralata
Piazza di Porta Saragozza
Viale C Pepoli
Viale Giovanni Vicini
Via Costa
To Villa Serena (2km)
To Basilica Santuario della Madonna di San Luca (3.5km)

There is a useful pamphlet, *A Guest of Bologna*, compiled by local shopkeepers and hoteliers, available from hotels, shops and the tourist office. You can pick up a copy of the English language monthly magazine *Talk About* (€5.55; W www.talkabout.it) from newsstands, which is full of information and listings.

The tourist office also has details of tours (☎ 051 51 70 70; €12.90) of the city which take place at 10am on Wednesday, Thursday, Saturday and Sunday.

Money You can change currency (commission free) at an exchange booth at the train station, open 7.15am to 8pm daily. The bank at the main bus station has an ATM. Otherwise, there are branches of the major banks with ATM services on Via Rizzoli, the continuation of Via Ugo Bassi, and on Via dell'Indipendenza.

Post & Communications The main post office is on Piazza Minghetti, south-east of Piazza Maggiore. It opens 8.15am to approximately 5.30pm Monday to Friday, 8.15am to 12.20pm on Saturday.

There is an Internet cafe, Net Arena (☎ 051 22 08 50) at Via de' Giudei 3b. Internet access costs €3.10 per hour.

Gay & Lesbian Travellers ArciGay (☎ 051 644 70 54, fax 051 644 6722, e arcigl@iperbole.bolgna.it, W www.gay.it/arcigay), Piazza di Porta Saragozza 2, is the national office for Arcigay and provides information and arranges events.

Medical Services & Emergency There are two hospitals: Ospedale Maggiore (☎ 051 647 81 11) on Via Emilia Ponente, and Ospedale Sant'Orsola (☎ 051 636 31 11) at Via Massarenti 9. There is a 24-hour pharmacy on Piazza Maggiore and the pharmacy at the train station is open to 11pm during the week and to 10pm on Sunday and public holidays. For the Guardia Medica (emergency doctor) service, call ☎ 848 83 18 31 (west Bologna) or ☎ 848 83 28 32 (east Bologna).

The *questura* (police station; ☎ 051 640 11 11) is at Piazza Galileo 7.

Dangers & Annoyances The city is only just starting to have problems with street crime such as bag theft and pickpocketing. The area around the university, particularly Piazza Verdi, is a haunt for drug addicts and can be unpleasant at night.

Other Information The Sestante travel agency (☎ 051 26 61 24) is at Piazza del Nettuno 2, and the CTS (☎ 051 23 75 01) has an office at Largo Respighi 2, east off Piazza Verdi.

Feltrinelli has an Italian bookshop on Piazza Ravegnana 1, near the two leaning towers, and an international one at Via Zamboni 7b.

There is a coin laundrette at Via G Petroni 38, which opens 9am to 9pm daily. There is an Onda Blu laundrette at Via Saragozza 34a/b.

Piazzas Maggiore & Nettuno

At the centre of Bologna's old city, Piazza Maggiore and the adjoining Piazza del Nettuno to the north are lined by some of Bologna's most graceful medieval and Renaissance monuments. The bustling pedestrianised squares are a focal point of city life, with Bolognesi flocking to the cafes and often gathered around the mime artists and buskers who perform on the uneven stone pavement.

Fontana del Nettuno In the area between the two piazzas stands a mighty bronze Neptune, sculpted in 1566 by a Frenchman known to posterity as Giambologna. The four angels represent the winds, and the four sirens – gleefully watching water spouting forth from their breasts – symbolise the continents known at that time.

Palazzo D'Accursio (Palazzo Comunale) Lining the western flank of the two piazzas is the town hall, sporting an immense staircase, attributed to the Renaissance architect, Donato Bramante, and built wide enough for horse-drawn carriages to chauffeur their occupants up to the 1st floor. The left side of the building was the residence of the Accursio family and later home to the

Papal Legate (from the 16th to the 19th centuries). Above the main entrance you'll see a bronze statue of Pope Gregory XIII, a native of Bologna and responsible for the Gregorian calendar. There are two art collections worth visiting. The **Collezioni Comunali** *(☎ 051 20 36 29, Palazzo D'Accursio, Piazza Maggiore 6; admission €4.10; open 10am-6.30pm Tues-Sun)* includes paintings, sculpture and furniture originally in private collections, and has good views over Piazza Maggiore. The magnificent **Museo Morandi** *(☎ 051 20 33 32, Palazzo D'Accursio, Piazza Maggiore 6; admission €4.10; open 10am-6pm Tues-Sun)* contains over 200 paintings, watercolours, drawings and prints covering the Bolognese artist Giorgio Morandi's entire career.

Note the huge panel outside the palazzo covered with photos of Italian partisans killed in the resistance to German occupation. Such displays are common in the cities and towns of Emilia-Romagna, which was a centre of fierce partisan activity.

Palazzo del Re Enzo Across from the Palazzo d'Accursio, this palace is named after King Enzo of Sicily, who was confined here for 20 years from 1249. The palace is open only during exhibitions.

Palazzo del Podestà Beneath this fine example of Renaissance architecture and behind the cafes facing Piazza Maggiore, there is a whispering gallery where the two perpendicular passages intersect. Stand diagonally opposite another person and whisper: the acoustics are amazing. The medieval tower is a feat of engineering as it doesn't rest on the ground but on the pillars of the vault. The palace is open only during exhibitions.

Basilica di San Petronio

Named after the city's patron saint, the basilica is Bologna's largest house of worship *(☎ 051 22 21 12, Piazza Maggiore; free; open 7.15am-1pm & 2pm-6pm daily)*. It was started in 1392 to plans by Antonio di Vincenzo (who was in fact subordinated to Andrea da Faenza) but was never finished.

Originally intended to be larger than the first St Peter's in Rome (the structure destroyed to make way for Rome's present basilica), San Petronio was effectively truncated by the papacy, which decreed it could not be larger than St Peter's and decided that much of the land should be used for a university. If you walk along Via dell'Archiginnasio on the eastern side of the basilica you can see semi-constructed apses poking out oddly from the building and the incomplete facade. Despite the papal intervention, the basilica is the fifth largest in the world and a fantastic example of Gothic architecture.

The central doorway, by Jacopo della Quercia, dates from 1425 and features carvings from the Old and New Testaments, and a beautiful *Madonna and Child*. The chapels inside contain frescoes by Giovanni da Modena and Jacopo di Paolo. A giant sundial, designed by Cassini in 1656, decorates the floor of the eastern aisle.

Museo Civico Archeologico

Just east of the basilica along Via dell' Archiginnasio, the archaeological museum *(☎ 051 23 38 49, Via dell'Archiginnasio 2, entrance on Via de' Museia; admission €4.10; open 9am-6.30pm Tues-Sat, 10am-6.30pm Sun)* has impressive collections of Egyptian and Roman artefacts and one of Italy's best Etruscan displays, featuring two burial chambers unearthed near the city.

Archiginnasio

Site of the city's first university and now its library *(☎ 051 23 64 88, Piazza Galvani 1; free; open 9am-1pm Mon-Sat)*, the Archiginnasio contains an anatomy theatre which was carved entirely from wood in 1647. Note the lecturer's chair with its canopy supported by skinless nude figures. The theatre (as well as many frescoes in the building) was destroyed during WWII (photos on display show the damage) and completely rebuilt. The Sala della Stabat Mater was named after the hymn by Rossini first played here in 1842. It is not always open; ask an attendant.

Museo Civico Medioevale e del Rinascimento

Housed in the Palazzo Ghislardi-Fava, this museum *(☎ 051 20 39 30, Via Manzoni 4;*

admission €4.10; open 9am-6.30pm Tues-Sat, 10am-6.30pm Sun) has a collection of bronze statues and medieval coffin slabs, as well as some armour and a few frescoes by Jacopo della Quercia.

Le Due Torri

The two slender and highly precarious leaning towers that rise above Piazza di Porta Ravegnana are unmistakable landmarks. The taller of the towers is the **Torre degli Asinelli** *(Piazza di Porta Ravegnana; admission €2.60; open 9am-6pm daily in summer, 9am-5pm daily in winter)* at 97.6m. Built by the family of the same name in 1109, it has 498 steps which can be climbed in spite of the 1.3m lean. It affords marvellous views of the city. The Garisenda family was even less cautious with foundations when erecting its tower, originally designed to compete with its neighbour and later sized down to 48m because of its 3.2m lean. It is closed to the public.

University Quarter

North-east of the towers, along Via Zamboni, is the **Chiesa di San Giacomo Maggiore** *(☎ 051 22 59 70, Piazza Rossini; free; open 7am-noon & 3.30-6pm daily)*. Built in the 13th century and remodelled in 1722, the church contains the Cappella Bentivoglio, with frescoes by Lorenzo Costa. Near the church stands the extraordinary **Oratorio di Santa Cecilia** *(☎ 051 22 59 70, Piazza Rossini; free; open 10am-1pm & 3pm-7pm daily in summer, 10am-1pm & 2pm-6pm daily in winter)*, dubbed the Sistine Chapel of Bologna for its impressive cycle of 10 frescoes describing the life of St Cecilia. The decorations, painted by Lorenzo Costa, Amico Aspertini and Francesco Raibolini (known as Il Francia) at the end of the 15th century, have recently been restored. A little farther up the road is the **Teatro Comunale**, where Wagner's works were heard for the first time in Italy.

The university area is worth visiting for the cafes and bars alone. The university has several museums open to the public, mostly in the **Palazzo Poggi** *(☎ 051 209 93 60, Via Zamboni 33)* on the corner of Via Zamboni and Via San Giacomo, details of which can be obtained from the tourist office.

Pinacoteca Nazionale North of the university, the national art gallery *(☎ 051 24 32 22, Via delle Belle Arti 56; admission €4.10; open 9am-2pm Tues-Sat, 9am-1pm Sun)* concentrates on works by Bolognese artists from the 14th century on. The extensive exhibits include several works by Giotto and Raphael's *Ecstasy of St Cecilia*. El Greco and Titian are also represented, but by comparatively little-known works.

Basilica di Santo Stefano

From the two towers, head south-east along Via Santo Stefano, long a residential area for Bologna's wealthy and lined with the elegant facades of their palazzos.

Where the street widens into a pretty triangular piazza, you find yourself before the Basilica di Santo Stefano *(☎ 051 22 32 56, Via Santo Stefano 24; free; open 9am-noon & 3.30pm-6.30pm daily)*, actually a group of four churches (originally there were seven). On the right are the 11th-century Romanesque **Chiesa del Crocefisso** (Crucifix) and the octagonal **Chiesa del Santo Sepolcro** (Holy Sepulchre), whose shape suggests it started life as a baptistry. Crocefisso houses the bones of San Petronio, Bologna's patron saint. The basin in the small courtyard has long been popularly believed to be the one in which Pontius Pilate washed his hands after he condemned Christ to death. In actual fact it is an 8th-century Lombard artefact.

The city's oldest church is **Santi Vitale e Agricola** *(☎ 051 22 05 70, Via San Vitale 50; free; open 8am-noon & 3.30pm-7.30pm daily)*, which incorporates many Roman ruins. The bulk of the building dates from the 5th century, and the tombs of the two saints, 100 years older still, once served as altars in the side aisles (today only one tomb remains). From the **Chiesa della Santa Trinità** you can pass to the modest medieval colonnaded cloister, off which a small **museum** contains a limited collection of paintings and frescoes.

Basilica di San Domenico

The basilica *(☎ 051 640 04 11, Piazza San Domenico 13; free; open 10am-12.30pm & 3pm-5pm Tues-Sat, 3pm-5pm Sun)*, south of the city centre, was erected in the early 16th century to house the remains of San Domenico, the founder of the Dominican order, who had only just opened a convent on the site when he died in 1221.

The **Cappella di San Domenico** contains the saint's elaborate sarcophagus, the reliefs of which illustrate scenes from his life. Designed by Nicolò Pisano in the late 13th century, the chapel was worked on by a host of artists over the following couple of centuries. The angel on the right of the altar was carved by Michelangelo when he was aged 19 and bears a resemblance to *David*, which he sculpted years later. The chapel is also decorated with several paintings of the saint, whose skull lies in a reliquary behind the sarcophagus. Ask an attendant to let you see the small **museum** and the inlaid wood of the choir stalls behind the main altar of the church.

When Mozart spent a month in the city's music academy, he occasionally played the church's organ.

Chiesa di San Francesco

At the western end of Via Ugo Bassi, at Piazza Marcello Malpighi, the Chiesa di San Francesco *(☎ 051 22 17 62, Piazza San Francesco; free; open 6.30am-noon & 3pm-7pm daily)* is fronted by the elaborate tombs of the *glossatori* (law teachers). The church, one of the first in Italy to be built in the French Gothic style, was completed in the 13th century and contains the tomb of Pope Alexander V.

Basilica Santuario della Madonna di San Luca

The hill-top Basilica Santuario della Madonna di San Luca *(☎ 051 614 23 39, Via di San Luca; free; open 7am-12.30pm & 2.30pm-7pm daily in summer, 7am-12.30pm & 2.30-5pm daily in winter)* is visible from most parts of the city. Built in the mid-18th century, it houses a painting of the Virgin Mary, supposedly by San Luca (hence the place's name), which was transported from the Middle East to Bologna in the 12th century.

The sanctuary lies about 4km south-west of the city centre and is connected to the city walls by a long portico with 666 arches, beginning at Porta Saragozza, south-west of the centre. Each April a statue of the Virgin is carried along the portico. Take bus No 20 from the city centre to Villa Spada, from where you can get a Cosepuri minibus to the sanctuary (buy the €2.60 return ticket on the minibus). On a sunny day it is worth getting off at Meloncello and walking the remaining 2km under the arches.

Work

There is no shortage of foreign-language teachers in Bologna. If you want to try your luck, you could start with Inlingua (☎ 051 23 80 22, fax 051 23 70 87), Via Testoni 2, or the British Council (☎ 051 22 51 42, ⓔ info.bologna@britcoun.it), Corte Isolani 8, Strada Maggiore 19.

Special Events

Each summer the city sponsors Bologna Estate, a three-month festival of events involving museums and galleries, the university, and local and national performers. Get programme details from the tourist office. Torri da Estate, another summer programme, takes place at the foot of the modern towers of Kenzo Tange in the Zona Fiera (Fair District) and includes dance performances and discos. Most events are free and a schedule is available at the tourist office.

Places to Stay

Budget hotels in Bologna are in short supply and it is almost impossible to find a single room. The city's busy trade-fair calendar means that hotels are often heavily booked, so always reserve in advance; check with the tourist office to find out when the fairs are on. The city is jammed with expensive hotels catering to business people, but when there are no fairs on some of them offer discounts of up to 50% on doubles.

There are several camp sites within driving distance of the city. Check with the tourist office. You could also ask for student accommodation, but only during university breaks.

Hostels There are a couple of hostels in Bologna.

Ostello Due Torri *(☎/fax 051 50 18 10, Via Viadagola 5)* Beds €11.90, doubles from €13.95 per person. Take bus Nos 93 (Monday to Saturday, daytime) or 21b (evenings) from Via Irnerio or Via Marconi. From there, follow the signs for the hostel.

Centro Europa Uno *(☎/fax 051 625 83 52, Via Emilia 297)* Singles/doubles €12.40/31. Located in San Lazzaro di Savena, about 9km south-east of Bologna, this hostel is open year-round. Bookings are essential. Bus No 94 runs to the hostel from central Bologna.

Hotels Bologna has a good range of hotels.

Albergo Garisenda *(☎ 051 22 43 69, fax 051 22 10 07, Galleria del Leone 1, Via Rizzoli)* Singles/doubles/triples from €41.30/62/82.65. The pick of the city's cheaper hotels has rooms looking out over the leaning towers. But beware the noise from busy Via Rizzoli.

Albergo Apollo *(☎ 051 22 39 55, fax 051 22 39 55, Via Drapperie 5)* Singles/doubles €36.15/51.65, doubles with bath €56.80-77.47. This place is on an attractive and quiet street off Via Rizzoli.

Albergo Marconi *(☎ 051 26 28 32, Via Marconi 22)* Singles/doubles €31/49.05, with bath €38.75/62. The fairly simple rooms on the busy Via Marconi are noisy, but this is a convenient location for the station as plenty of buses pass by.

Albergo Panorama *(☎ 051 22 18 02, fax 051 26 63 60, Via Livraghi 1)* Singles/doubles €43.90/56.80, doubles with bath €72.30. Just south of the central Via Ugo Bassi, this place has airy, spotless rooms, some with views.

Albergo Rossini *(☎ 051 23 77 16, fax 26 80 35, Via dei Bibiena 11)* High season single/doubles €67.15/98.15. Located in the heart of the university area, opposite the Teatro Comunale, this hotel is quirky and friendly, with some newly refurbished rooms. Discounts are offered in low season.

Albergo Roma *(☎ 051 22 63 22, fax 051 23 99 09, e hotelroma@mailbox.dsnet.it, Via Massimo D'Azeglio 9)*. Singles/doubles/triples with bath €84.20/107.40/164.75. The decor is heavy on the floral wallpapers and fabrics, but the upmarket Roma offers superior comfort and an unbeatable location off Piazza Maggiore.

Places to Eat

Some know Bologna as La Grassa (The Fat), and the Bolognesi are indeed serious about food. Just look at the way food, especially pasta and bread are displayed like priceless jewels in shop windows.

The best pasta is *tirata a mano*, hand-stretched and rolled with a wooden pin, not a machine. It is cooked in many ways and eaten with a multitude of sauces. Everyone knows *spaghetti bolognese*, but the Bolognesi call the meat sauce *ragù*. *Mortadella*, known sometimes as Bologna sausage or baloney, hails from the area. The hills nearby produce the Lambrusco red and a full, dry Sauvignon.

Fortunately, it is cheap to eat in Bologna, particularly in the university district north-east of Via Rizzoli. The city has many good bars and osterie, where you can get cheap drinks and snacks. Some serve full meals and rarely levy a cover charge.

Restaurants A busy self-service restaurant, ***Bass'8*** *(Via Ugo Bassi 8)* is particularly popular with lunchtime crowds. Full meals cost from €6.45.

Tamburini *(Via Caprarie 1)* Full meals €5.15-7.75. For a classy version of the self-service genre, head to this place. Apart from selling some of Bologna's finest food products in the deli section, it has a self-service restaurant (open noon to 12.30am daily) where you can taste some of the goodies without having to cook them yourself.

Pizzeria Altero *(Via Ugo Bassi 10)* Pizza slice €0.95-1.15. Open 8am-11pm Mon-Sat. Judging from the crowds that regularly cram into this tiny pizzeria, this is Bologna's best bet for tasty pizza *al taglio* (by the slice).

Pizzeria Emilia *(Via Zamboni 27)* Pizza slice €1.55-2.60. This is a popular student hangout and deservedly so for its filling, tasty pizza slices.

Trattoria da Danio *(☎ 051 55 52 02, Via San Felice 50a)* Price €11.35-12.90, set menu €10.35. This smoky hole is full of locals who look like they're part of the (rather outdated) furniture. They return time and again for delicious pasta, including *tortellini* stuffed with pumpkin, and mains such as grilled veal cutlet.

Trattoria da Amedeo *(☎ 051 58 50 60, Via Saragozza 88)* Pasta €5.15-7.25, mains €6.20-10.85. Traditional home-cooking is the draw here, with tagliatelle bolognese a speciality. There's a bargain lunch menu for €10.35.

Trattoria da Gianni *(☎ 051 22 94 34, Via Clavature 18)* Full meals €25.80. The home-made pasta comes highly recommended, but regardless of what you order, a meal at Gianni's will be a relaxed affair and an experience to remember.

Da Adolfo *(☎ 051 22 64 81, Corte Galluzzi 7)* Pasta €7.75, mains €9.30. Open Mon-Sat. Located in a charming courtyard, behind the Basilica di San Petronio and next to a medieval tower, Adolfo is a very relaxed neighbourhood trattoria.

Diana *(☎ 051 23 13 02, Via dell'Indipendenza 24)* Full meals from €36.15. Open Tues-Sun. Three blocks north of Piazza del Nettuno, Diana is famous for its tortellini and infamous for its slightly patronising white-jacketed waiters.

Osteria L'Infedele *(☎ 0335 669 23 61, Via Gerusalemme 5a)* Meals €5.15-6.20; wine by the glass €2.05. Open from 6.30pm daily. Around the corner from the Basilica di Santo Stefano, L'Infedele is a cosy place to hang out with a glass of wine on a chilly evening or for a light meal; the friendly staff and excellent background jazz music are bonuses.

Cafes & Wine Bars One of the streets mostly frequented by students and young people is Via del Pratello, just off Via Ugo Bassi. It has plenty of cheap bars, *birrerie* (pubs), osterie, and trattorie.

The ***Osteria del Sole*** *(Via Ranocchi 1d)* first opened for business in about 1400 and is the only place left in Bologna that maintains the centuries-old tradition of the osteria as watering hole only. It's also one of Bologna's few early openers, open 8am to 2pm and 7.30pm to 9pm daily, although this is not set in stone. If you want to eat, arm yourself with goodies from the surrounding food shops.

Rosa Rose *(Via Clavature 18)* This place buzzes. It's pleasant for a cocktail or coffee – if you can fight your way to a table amid the throngs of regular locals.

Cantina Bentivoglio *(☎ 051 26 54 16, Via Mascarella 4b)* This bottle-lined cellar is a wine bar with as much atmosphere as you'd want. Thursday sees it transformed into Alhambra Jazz Club for live jazz performances.

Zanarini *(☎ 051 22 27 17, Via Luigi Carlo Farini 2)* Behind the Basilica di San Petronio, Zanarini is one of the city's finest tearooms and specialises in unusual cakes. Some of its past glory is lost, but the grand decor makes a visit worthwhile, if a little expensive.

Caffè Commercianti *(☎ 051 26 65 39, Strada Maggiore 23c)* This cafe is something of a haunt for the city's intelligentsia, apparently inspired by a combination of Umberto Eco and the best martini in town.

Caffè al Teatro *(cnr Largo Respighi & Via Zamboni)* Modestly priced, this place is a relaxing place to hang out, have a drink or a snack. There's plenty of student life at any time of the day.

Marsalino *(☎ 051 23 86 75, Via Marsala 13d)* Just off Via dell' Indipendenza, Marsalino is a tearoom from 4pm, then metamorphoses into a cocktail/wine bar from 6pm and restaurant from 8pm. If you're still around at midnight on Thursdays you can catch its regular stand-up comedy show.

Le Stanze *(☎ 051 22 87 67, Via Borgo San Pietro 1)* Closed Sat morning. The frescoed walls and ceiling of the former chapel of a patrician's palazzo, combined with friendly staff and good music, provide a comfortable ambience for a coffee, aperitif or light meal.

Gelaterias If you're after gelato, try one of the following.

La Sorbetteria Castiglione *(☎ 051 23 32 57, Via Castiglione 44d)* Open Mon-Sun. Reputedly Bologna's best gelateria, with a limited choice of flavours, but made with plenty of love.

Bar Vittorio Emanuele *(Piazza Maggiore)* Next to the tourist office, this is an expensive place to sit and watch the action on Piazza Maggiore, but the gelato is worth it.

Gelateria delle Moline *(Via delle Moline 13b)*. Just off Via dell' Indipendenza, this student hang-out specialises in *focaccia* (flatbread) and gelato sandwiches.

Self-Catering The best place in town to pick up fresh fruit and vegetables is the ***Mercato Ugo Bassi*** *(Via Ugo Bassi 27)*, open Monday to Saturday.

Just east of Piazza Maggiore, the area around Via Drapperie, Via Orefici, Via Pescherie Vecchie and Via Clavature is crammed with speciality food shops including an attractive daily produce ***market***.

Entertainment

The tourist office sometimes has brochures with theatre, cinema and nightlife listings.

Bars, Discos & Clubs Bologna has one of the healthiest night scenes in Italy, bolstered by an active student population and gay community.

Link *(☎ 051 37 09 71, Via Fioravanti 14)* If techno, hip-hop and the very latest music are your thing, head for Link, north of the train station. This former *centro sociale* (social centre) is now housed in a municipal building and is very popular with students.

Kinki *(Via Zamboni 1a)* Cover charge around €15.50. Open Thurs, Fri & Sat nights. This place is a long-time favourite disco that welcomes lesbians and gays.

Villa Serena *(☎ 051 615 67 89, Via della Barca 1)* Admission free. Three floors offer 80s DJ music, film screenings and live music, and a comfortable garden offers relaxed outdoor chilling areas. Things heat up late at night with the hottest dance music in Bologna.

Corto Maltese *(☎ 051 22 97 46, Via del Borgo di San Pietro 9/2a)*. Open until 3am Mon-Thurs, until 4am Fri & Sat. A stylish disco-bar popular with locals, students and foreigners.

Cinemas The public film library promotes the revival of old movies and organises screenings and festivals of old, restored films. Some screenings are part of Bologna's summer festival and are held in open-air venues in Piazza Maggiore and the Palazzo Comunale.

Lumière *(☎ 051 52 35 39, Via Pietralata 55a)* This place shows art-house movies in all languages.

Adriano *(☎ 051 55 51 27, Via San Felice 52)* This cinema shows films in different languages.

Theatre, Opera & Classical Music Check with the tourist office for current programmes and special events. Bologna's cultural life is perennially busy.

Teatro Comunale *(☎ 051 52 99 99, Piazza Verdi)* This theatre is the main venue for opera and concerts, and has a year-round programme.

Arena del Sole *(☎ 051 27 07 90, Via dell' Indipendenza 44)* Modern classics from Chekov to Pirandello are staged here (usually in Italian).

Teatro Dehon *(☎ 051 34 47 72, Via Libia 59)* This place stages Italian productions by Dario Fo and Luigi Chiarelli, and international plays in Italian (by Oscar Wilde, Neil Simon and Agatha Christie).

Teatro Duse *(☎ 051 23 18 36, Via Cartoleria 42)* This theatre has a varied programme, including plays by Pirandello, Moni Ovada, De Filippo and Shakespeare.

Shopping

If you're intending to do any shopping in Bologna, don't come on Thursday as all shops shut for the afternoon. At the weekend there's a flea market at the Parco della Montagnola. The main shopping streets are Via Ugo Bassi, Via Rizzoli, Via Marconi, Via dell'Indipendenza, Via Massimo d'Azeglio, Via Farini and Via San Felice.

Getting There & Away

Air Bologna's Guglielmo Marconi airport (☎ 051 647 96 15), north-west of the city at Borgo Panigale, is serviced by mainly European airlines. There are flights to Rome,

Venice, southern Italy, Pisa, London, Paris and Frankfurt

Bus Services to regional centres such as Ravenna, Ferrara and Modena leave from the depot (☎ 051 29 02 90) opposite Piazza XX Settembre, round the corner from the train station. There are buses to Ancona and Milan, and international buses to London, Paris, Amsterdam, Brussels, Prague and Warsaw.

Train Bologna is a major transport junction for northern Italy and trains from Rome and Milan stop here. Many are Eurostar trains.

Car & Motorcycle The city is linked to Milan, Florence and Rome by the A1 Autostrada del Sole. The A13 heads directly for Ferrara, Padova and Venezia, and the A14 for Rimini and Ravenna. The city is also on the Via Emilia (S9), which connects Milan with the Adriatic coast. The S64 goes to Ferrara.

For car hire, all major companies are represented in the city. Most have offices at the airport. Try Avis (☎ 051 25 50 24) at Via Pietramellara 35, Europcar (☎ 051 24 71 01) at Via G Amendola 12f, and Hertz (☎ 051 25 48 30) at Via G Amendola 16a.

Getting Around

ATC Aerobus connects the city with the airport (€4.10). It leaves from in front of the train station roughly every 15 or 20 minutes from 6.50am to midnight.

Bologna has an efficient bus system, run by ATC, which has information booths at the train station and on Via Marconi at the junction with Via Ugo Bassi and Via Lame. Bus Nos 30 and 21 are among the many connecting the train station with the city centre; not all routes operate on Sunday.

To book a cab call ☎ 051 37 27 27 or 051 53 41 41.

PORRETTA

The tiny thermal spring town of Porretta Terme, known as Porretta, lies about 50km south of Bologna in the Apennines. Traditionally a sleepy resort for people wanting to take advantage of the therapeutic mineral waters, the town has in recent years become a focal point for soul music lovers from across Europe. Each year, during the third weekend in July, the town hosts the **Sweet Soul Music Festival**, a tribute to Otis Redding and a celebration of the Memphis sound. If you happen to be in the region at the time, it really is worth making the trip to Porretta for the festival, held over three nights in the town's Rufus Thomas Park. For information about the festival and about the town itself, contact the APT di Porretta (☎ 0534 2 20 21), Piazza Protche 4.

Trains leave hourly for Porretta from Bologna. The town is also accessible by train from Florence.

Places to Stay & Eat

Hotel Santoli *(☎ 0534 2 32 06, fax 0534 227 44, Via Roma 3)* Singles/doubles €67.15/87.80. This four-star hotel is comfortable and welcoming.

Trattoria Toscana *(☎ 0534 2 22 08, Piazza della Libertà)* Full meal from €12.90. Tuscan and Emilian cuisine are on offer here.

West of Bologna

MODENA

postcode 41100 • pop 180,000

Some 40km north-west of Bologna, Modena was one of a series of Roman garrison towns established along the Via Emilia in the 2nd century BC, in this case on the site of an already existing Etruscan settlement.

Modena remained an obscure little place until it became a free city in the 12th century and passed to the Este family late in the following century. Prosperity finally came when it was chosen as the capital of a much-reduced Este duchy in 1598, after the family had lost Ferrara to the Papal States. Apart from a brief Napoleonic interlude, the Este remained in control until Italian unification.

Modena is home to Italy's favourite tenor, Luciano Pavarotti, and car manufacturers Ferrari, Maserati, Bugatti, Lamborghini and De Tomaso, who all do their bit to make this town one of the most affluent in the country.

Orientation

To get to the centre from the train station in Piazza Dante, head down Viale Crispi and turn right into Corso Vittorio Emanuele II, which leads to the Palazzo Ducale. Walk around the palazzo to Piazza degli Estensi and then straight ahead along Via L C Farini for Via Emilia, the main drag. The cathedral and Piazza Grande are south of Via Emilia, and the bulk of offices, banks, hotels and restaurants are within easy walking distance of the centre.

Information

Tourist Offices The IAT office (☎ 059 20 66 60), Piazza Grande 17, opens 9am to 1pm and 3pm to 7pm Monday to Saturday (closed Wednesday afternoon) and 9am to 12.30pm Sunday. Get information online at W www.comune.modena.it. The IAT has heaps of brochures on Modena and its province, as well as a guide for disabled visitors, *Muoversi nella Città di Modena* – in Italian but with clear symbols indicating access to tourist attractions.

ModenaTur (☎ 059 22 00 22, W www.modenatur.net), Via Scudari 10, is a travel agency that can help with accommodation and tours.

Post & Communications The post office is at Via Emilia 86 and opens 8.15am to 7.15pm. The Telecom office is at Via L C Farini 26 and there's a smaller office at Via dell'Università 23.

Internet access is available in the tourist office (€2.60 for 2 hours).

Medical Services & Emergency You can call an ambulance or locum doctor on ☎ 059 22 22 08. The main hospital (☎ 059 43 72 71/2) is at Piazzale Sant'Agostino, opposite the Palazzo dei Musei. For late night pharmacies, check the *Gazzetta di Modena* newspaper.

The *questura* (police station; ☎ 059 41 04 11) is at Viale delle Rimembranze 12.

Cathedral

Dedicated to Modena's patron saint, San Geminiano, the cathedral *(☎ 059 20 66 60, Piazza Grande; free; open 6.30am-12.30pm & 3.30pm-7pm daily)* was started in 1099 and is one of the finest Romanesque cathedrals in Italy. The facade is adorned with precious bas-reliefs depicting scenes from Genesis by the 12th-century sculptor Wiligelmo. The carvings were a common way to inform the illiterate masses about the Old Testament. Wiligelmo signed his work (to the left of the main door) – a rare practice in those times – as did the building's architect, Lanfranco (in the main apse). Among the many fine carvings are some typical medieval motifs depicting the months and agricultural scenes. Much of Wiligelmo's work has been removed to the **Museo Lapidario del Duomo** *(☎ 059 21 60 78, Via Lanfranco 6; free; open 9.30am-12.30pm & 3.30pm-6.30pm daily)*, adjoining the cathedral.

The Romanesque **Torre Ghirlandina** *(admission €1.05; open 10am-1pm & 3pm-7pm Sun & holidays during Apr-Sept)* was started in 1169 and rises to 87m, culminating in a Gothic spire that has quite a lean.

Palazzo dei Musei

Palazzo dei Musei *(Piazzale Sant'Agostino)* houses several galleries, including the city's art collection and the Biblioteca Estense.

The **Galleria Estense** *(☎ 059 439 57 11, Palazzo dei Musei, Piazzale Sant'Agostino; admission €4.10; open 8.30am-7.30pm Tues-Sun)* features most of the Este family collection and comprises works by Cosme' Tura, Bernini, Guercino, Guido Reni, Velázquez, Correggio and El Greco. The **Biblioteca Estense** *(☎ 059 22 22 48, Palazzo dei Musei, Piazzale Sant'Agostino; admission €4.10; open 9am-7.15pm Mon-Thurs, 9am-1.45pm Fri & Sat; Bible of Borso d'Este on view 9am-1pm Mon-Sat)* has one of Italy's most valuable collections of books, letters and manuscripts, which includes the *Bible of Borso d'Este*, its 1200 pages illustrated by Ferrarese artists and considered the most decorated Bible in existence.

The **Museo Civico del Risorgimento** *(☎ 059 20 01 01, Palazzo dei Musei, Piazzale Sant'Agostino; closed for restoration at time of writing)* is a standard display

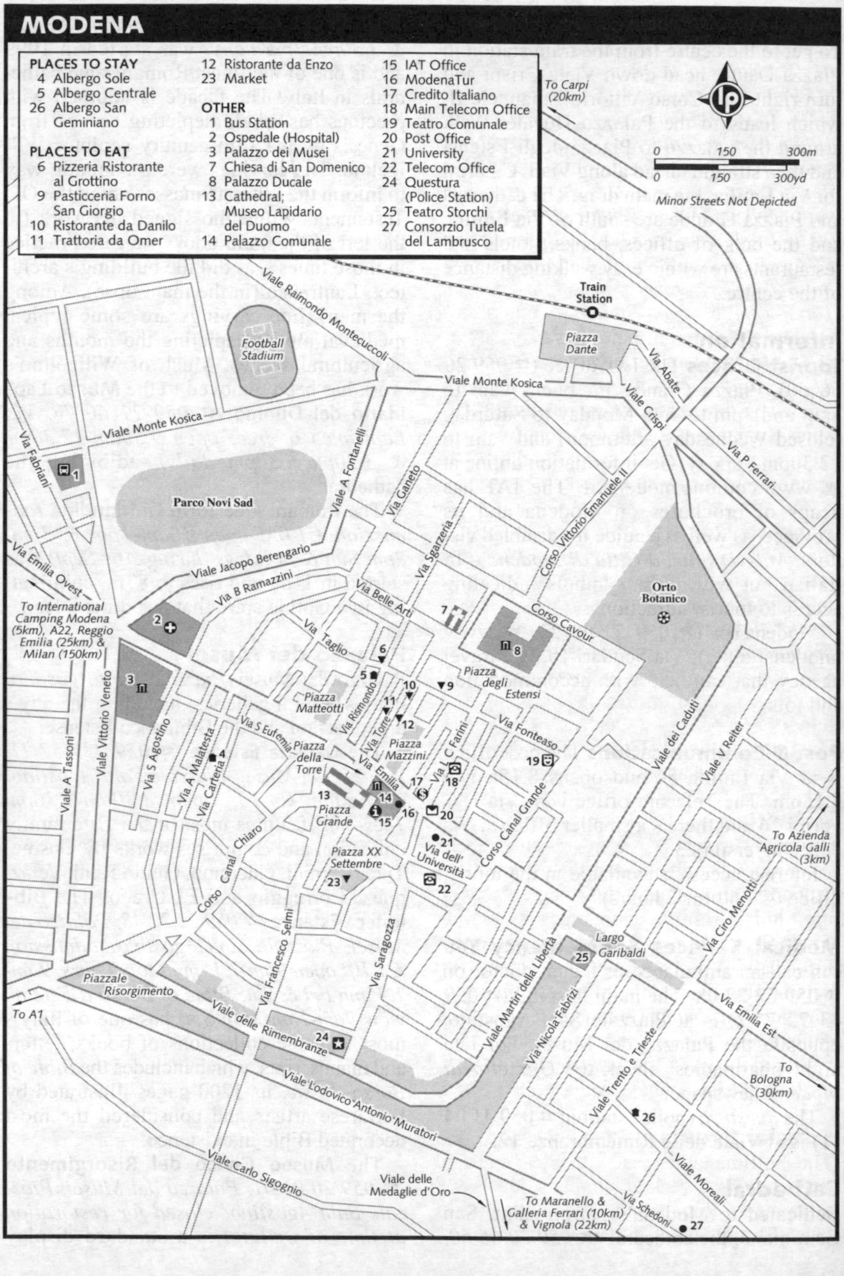

MODENA

PLACES TO STAY
- 4 Albergo Sole
- 5 Albergo Centrale
- 26 Albergo San Geminiano

PLACES TO EAT
- 6 Pizzeria Ristorante al Grottino
- 9 Pasticceria Forno San Giorgio
- 10 Ristorante da Danilo
- 11 Trattoria da Omer
- 12 Ristorante da Enzo
- 23 Market

OTHER
- 1 Bus Station
- 2 Ospedale (Hospital)
- 3 Palazzo dei Musei
- 7 Chiesa di San Domenico
- 8 Palazzo Ducale
- 13 Cathedral; Museo Lapidario del Duomo
- 14 Palazzo Comunale
- 15 IAT Office
- 16 ModenaTur
- 17 Credito Italiano
- 18 Main Telecom Office
- 19 Teatro Comunale
- 20 Post Office
- 21 University
- 22 Telecom Office
- 24 Questura (Police Station)
- 25 Teatro Storchi
- 27 Consorzio Tutela del Lambrusco

0 150 300m
0 150 300yd
Minor Streets Not Depicted

To Carpi (20km)
Train Station
Piazza Dante
Via Abate
Viale Crispi
Via P Ferrari
Viale Monte Kosica
Viale Raimondo Montecuccoli
Football Stadium
Via Fabriani
Parco Novi Sad
Via A Fontanelli
Via Ganeto
Via Sgarzeria
Corso Vittorio Emanuele II
Orto Botanico
Via Emilia Ovest
To International Camping Modena (5km), A22, Reggio Emilia (25km) & Milan (150km)
Viale Jacopo Berengario
Via B Ramazzini
Via Belle Arti
Corso Cavour
Via Taglio
Piazza degli Estensi
Piazza Matteotti
Via Rismondo
Via Torre
Piazza Mazzini
Via LC Farini
Via Fonteaso
Viale dei Caduti
Viale V Reiter
Viale A Tassoni
Viale Vittorio Veneto
Via S Agostino
Via A Malatesta
Via Carteria
Via S Eufemia
Piazza della Torre
Via Emilia
Piazza Grande
Piazza XX Settembre
Via dell' Università
Corso Canal Grande
Corso Canal Chiaro
To Azienda Agricola Galli (3km)
Via Ciro Menotti
Via Francesco Selmi
Via Saragozza
Largo Garibaldi
Piazzale Risorgimento
To A1
Viale delle Rimembranze
Viale Martiri della Libertà
Via Nicola Fabrizi
Viale Trento e Trieste
Via Emilia Est
To Bologna (30km)
Viale Lodovico Antonio Muratori
Viale Carlo Sigognio
Viale delle Medaglie d'Oro
To Maranello & Galleria Ferrari (10km) & Vignola (22km)
Viale Moreali
Via Schedoni

EMILIA-ROMAGNA

chronicling Italian unification. The **Museo Civico Archeologico Etnologico** *(☎ 059 20 01 01, Palazzo dei Musei, Piazzale Sant'Agostino; admission €2.85; open 9am-noon Tues-Fri, 9am-1pm & 4pm-7pm Sat, 10am-1pm & 4pm-7pm Sun)* presents a range of Bronze Age exhibits, as well as items from Africa, Asia, Peru and New Guinea. The **Museo Civico d'Arte** *(☎ 059 20 01 01, Palazzo dei Musei, Piazzale Sant'Agostino; admission €2.85; open 9am-noon Tues-Fri, 9am-1pm & 4pm-7pm Sat, 10am-1pm & 4pm-7pm Sun)* contains a modest collection of paintings.

The **Museo Lapidario Estense** *(☎ 059 22 21 45, Palazzo dei Musei, Piazzale Sant' Agostino; free; open 8am-7pm daily)* contains Roman and medieval stonework, including sarcophagi; it was partly closed for lengthy renovation at the time of writing.

Palazzo Ducale

Started in 1634 for the Este family, this grand Baroque edifice is now home to Modena's **military academy** *(☎ 059 22 56 71, Piazza Roma; admission €5.15; open Army Celebration Day (4 November) & 10am & 11am Sun for guided tours)*, whose cadets wear fuchsia-coloured uniforms (looking like they've stepped off a Quality Street chocolate tin) and are considered Italy's crack soldiers. You need to book a week ahead.

Activities

If you're tiring of soaking up culture, the Apennines south of Modena offer lots of scope for outdoor activities, including walking, horse riding, canoeing and skiing. The IAT office (see Tourist Offices under Information) has stacks of brochures, with details about walking trails and places to stay, including *rifugi* (mountain refuges) and camp sites.

Ask at the IAT office about booking tours of the Maserati and De Tomaso factories.

Special Events

The Settimana Estense, in late June and early July, is a week of banquets, jousts and other early Renaissance fun, with lots of locals flitting about in period costume.

Modena celebrates its great product – balsamic vinegar – with Balsamica, a series of exhibitions, events and tastings from mid-May to early June. See the boxed text 'A Taste Worth Waiting For'.

A Taste Worth Waiting For

Real *aceto balsamico* from Modena is a rare and beautiful thing. Commercial balsamic vinegar, as sold around the world, bears little relation to its upmarket cousin. Balsamic vinegar is made by boiling up vats of must (unfermented grape juice) from Trebbiano vines grown in a delimited area around Modena. The must is then filtered, placed in a large oak barrel, and over many years decanted and transferred into smaller barrels made of different woods, and stored in farmhouse lofts. The summer temperature in these lofts can reach 50°C, so the must condenses as it evaporates. Modena's sharp winters are also essential for the process.

Aceto balsamico tradizionale di Modena is aged for at least 12 years, and *aceto balsamico tradizionale di Modena extravecchio* is aged for at least 25 years. Compared with other vinegars, it is sweet and dense, complex and lingering. The older the vinegar, the thicker and more intensely flavoured it becomes.

Traditionally, balsamic vinegar was made by Modena's noble families, who owned the land and vineyards. This is still the case today. It is very much a boutique industry, with production tightly monitored by a consortium set up to maintain quality and control the quantities produced.

Azienda Agricola Galli (☎ 059 25 10 94, Via Albareto 452), about 3km north of the centre of Modena, is a small family producer of balsamic vinegar. Signora Galli is happy to receive visitors – but call first and try to speak some Italian. Alternatively, ModenaTur (☎ 059 22 00 22, W www.modenatur.net, Via Scudari 10), near the cathedral in the centre of Modena, can arrange a (free) visit to a local producer – English-speaking if you're lucky.

EMILIA-ROMAGNA

Places to Stay

Modena is close enough to Bologna to make it a day trip, although the city does have reasonably cheap accommodation.

International Camping Modena *(☎ 059 33 22 52, Via Cave di Ramo 111)* Cost per person/site €5.60/11.30. Open April-end Sept. This camp site is 5km west of the city in Bruciata. Take bus No 19.

Albergo Sole *(☎ 059 21 42 45, Via Malatesta 45)* Singles/doubles €23.20/41.30. Simple but cheap, this place is west of Piazza Grande.

Albergo San Geminiano *(☎ 059 21 03 03, fax 059 22 04 46, Viale Moreali 41)* Doubles €46.40. Singles/doubles with bath €38.70/61.90. Located south-east of the city centre, this hotel is a little out of the way (a 20-minute stroll into the centre) but good if you have a car as parking is free.

Albergo Centrale *(☎/fax 059 21 88 08, Via Rismondo 55)*. Singles/doubles without bath €38.70/67.10, with bath €67.10/103.20. As its name suggests, the Centrale is well located in the heart of Modena, offering comfortable, if somewhat pricey, rooms.

Places to Eat

Like Bologna and Parma, Modena produces excellent *prosciutto crudo* (cured ham). The city's gastronomic speciality is *zampone* (stuffed pig's trotter). It also produces the bulk of Italy's prized balsamic vinegar, a rich aromatic condiment (see the boxed text 'A Taste Worth Waiting For' earlier). Tortellini is another speciality, as is Lambrusco, one of the more famous Italian sparkling reds, which should be drunk chilled and with everything. The city's Consorzio Tutela del Lambrusco, Via Schedoni 41, can tell you about vineyards and advise on tastings and opening times. The fresh produce ***market*** is just south of Piazza XX Settembre.

Pizzeria Ristorante al Grottino *(☎ 059 22 39 85, Via Taglio 26)* Pizza €3.60-7.75. Open Thurs-Tues. A popular pizza joint, north of Piazza Matteotti, which serves pizza at both lunchtime and dinnertime as well as pasta and mains.

Trattoria da Omer *(☎ 059 21 80 50, Via Torre 33)* Pasta and mains €7.25. Open Mon-Sat. A simple trattoria serving Modenese and traditional Italian pasta and mains.

Ristorante da Enzo *(☎ 059 22 51 77, Via Coltellini 17)* Full meals from €18.10. Open Tues-Sun. This is one of the town's better restaurants, famous for its home-made pasta and various dishes featuring balsamic vinegar.

Ristorante da Danilo *(☎ 059 22 54 98, Via Coltellini 31)* Pasta €5.15-6.20, mains €9.30-15.50. Open Mon-Sat. Comfortable and cosy, Danilo does good home-style cooking, with especially good lasagne

Pasticceria Forno San Giorgio *(☎ 059 22 35 14, Via Taglio 6)* €2.10 for coffee and cake. San Giorgio has been satisfying the sweet tooths of Modena with its cakes and pastries since 1902. A good place for coffee and cake or a snack.

Entertainment

The city's better bars are along Via Emilia, near the cathedral, but check prices as a beer could get costly.

During July and August, outdoor concerts and ballet are staged in Piazza Grande. Posters advertise forthcoming events. Luciano Pavarotti organises *Pavarotti & Friends*, a huge concert featuring the tenor and international stars held at the end of May each year.

Teatro Comunale *(☎ 059 20 00 10, Corso Canal Grande 85)* The opera season is in winter, with most performances at the Teatro Comunale.

Teatro Storchi *(☎ 059 22 32 44, Largo Garibaldi 15)* Check out this theatre for drama. You can also buy tickets at an office in the same building as the IAT office.

Shopping

On the fourth weekend of every month, excluding July and December, a big antiques fair is held in Parco Novi Sad, 500m north-west of the city centre.

Getting There & Around

The bus station is on Via Fabriani. ATCM and other companies connect Modena with most towns in the region and cities including Cremona and Milan.

The main train station is in Piazza Dante. There are services to Bologna, Mantua, Verona, Rome, Parma and Milan.

The city is at the junction of the A1 Autostrada del Sole, which connects Rome with Milan, and the A22, which heads north for Mantua, Verona and the Brenner pass.

ATCM's bus No 7 connects the train station with the bus station and the city centre. For a taxi, call ☎ 059 37 42 42. Bicycles can be hired next to the train station.

AROUND MODENA

Galleria Ferrari

Enzo Ferrari, who died in 1988, reckoned the Modenese possess the rare combination of boldness and hard-headedness needed to build racing cars. His factory is in **Maranello**, 17km south of Modena (regular buses run from Modena), but to visit it you'll have to buy a Ferrari first. The Galleria Ferrari *(☎ 0536 94 32 04, Via Dino Ferrari 43; admission €9.30; open 9.30am-12.30pm & 2.30pm-6pm Tues-Sun)* is the next best thing. Essentially the Ferrari company's museum and historical archive, it boasts one of the largest collections of Ferraris on show in the world, including the vehicle in which Michael Schumacher won the 2000 Formula One world championship, plus a host of memorabilia to satisfy even the most avid Ferrari fan.

Vignola

A lovely medieval village 22km south of Modena, Vignola offers visitors good food and a 14th-century castle, with frescoed rooms. In the spring, the countryside around the town is a mass of cherry blossoms.

Carpi

Once the centre of the Pio family territories, Carpi is an impressive Renaissance town, built using the characteristic local red bricks. It's 20km north of Modena and easily reached by train. Its elegant Palazzo Pio incorporates a medieval castle and dominates one of the biggest squares in Italy, which is closed on one side by a system of ancient porticoes. Visit the 16th-century cathedral and the Romanesque Chiesa di Santa Maria del Castello.

REGGIO EMILIA

postcode 42100 • pop 130,000

Also known as Reggio nell'Emilia, this town started life in the 2nd century BC as a Roman colony along the Via Emilia, which divides it. Nothing remains from those days and much of the present city was built by the Este family during the 400 years it was in control from 1406 on.

Although most of us know the cheese from this area as Parmesan (as in Parma), it is in fact called *parmigiano reggiano*, reflecting the fact that it's produced across both provinces.

Few tourists bother to stop here but Reggio has a pleasant centre and makes a good base for exploring the Apennines to the south.

Information

Tourist Offices The IAT office (☎ 0522 45 11 52), at Piazza Camillo Prampolini 5c, is 1km west of the train station, along Via Emilia San Pietro, and is open from 8.30am to 1pm and 2.30pm to 6pm Monday to Saturday, 9am to noon on Sunday. Get info online at W www.municipio.re.it/turismo.

Post & Communications The post office is at Via Sessi 3 and there's an unstaffed Telecom phone office at Galleria San Rocco 8f. There's an Internet cafe, Qui Qua, at Piazza Fontanesi 4a, open 9am to 9.30pm Monday to Saturday.

Medical Services & Emergency The Ospedale Santa Maria Nuova (hospital; ☎ 0522 29 61 11) is at Viale Risorgimento 80.

The *questura* (police station; ☎ 0522 45 87 11) is at Via Dante Alighieri 6.

Churches

The city's sights are concentrated around Piazza del Monte (formerly Piazza Cesare Battisti), Piazza Camillo Prampolini and Piazza San Prospero. The latter two are separated by the **cathedral** *(☎ 0522 43 37 83, Piazza Prampolini; free; open 7.30am-noon & 3.30pm-7pm daily)*, which was built in the 13th century in the Romanesque style and completely remodelled 300 years later.

The 15th-century **Chiesa di San Prospero** *(☎ 0522 43 46 67, Piazza San Prospero; free; open 7.30am-noon & 3.30pm-7pm daily)*, on the piazza of the same name, is fronted by red marble lions. Its striking octagonal bell tower was built in 1537. The Baroque **Basilica della Ghiara** *(Corso Garibaldi 44; free; open 10am-noon & 4pm-5.30pm Mon-Sat, 10.25am-10.50am & 3.30pm-5.30pm Sun)* houses recently restored frescoes by 17th-century Emilian artists including Ludovico Carracci, Gian Francesco Barbieri (called Il Guercino), Lionello Spada and Alessandro Tiarini.

Palazzo del Municipio

On the southern side of Piazza Camillo Prampolini, the 14th-century town hall contains the **Sala del Tricolore** (☎ 0522 45 61 11, Piazza Prampolini 1), the room where the Italian flag was devised during a conference that established Napoleon's short-lived Cispadane Republic in 1797. It is not open to the public.

Teatro Municipale

On the northern side of Piazza Martiri del VII Luglio, this imposing building could be a royal palace. Built in 1857 as an opera

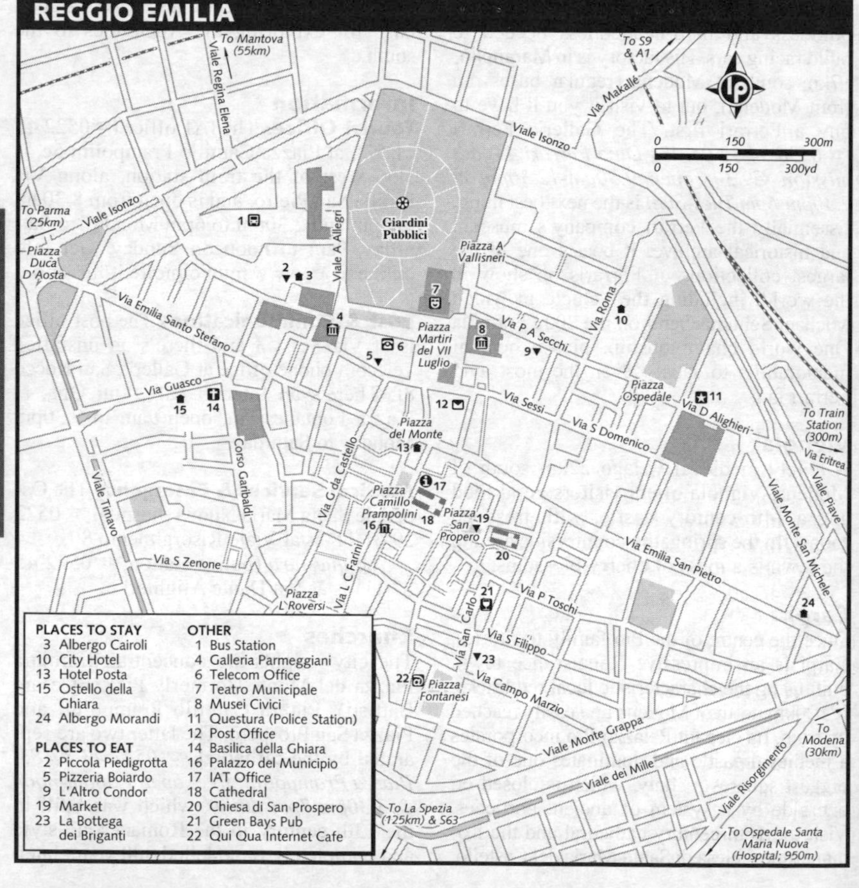

EMILIA-ROMAGNA

house, it is now used for dance, opera and theatre performances.

Museums

North from Piazza del Monte, facing Piazza Martiri del VII Luglio, the **Musei Civici** *(☎ 0522 45 64 77, Via Spallanzani 1; free; open 9am-noon Tues-Fri, 9am-noon & 3pm-7pm Sat, 10am-1pm & 3pm-7pm Sun)* house a collection of 18th-century works of art and archaeological discoveries.

The **Galleria Parmigiani** *(☎ 0522 45 10 54, Corso Cairoli 2; free; open 9am-noon Tues-Fri, 9am-noon & 3pm-6pm Sat, 10am-1pm & 3pm-7pm Sun)* has some worthwhile Italian, Spanish and Flemish canvases, including an El Greco.

Places to Stay & Eat

Ostello della Ghiara *(☎ 0522 45 23 23, Via Guasco 6)* Dorm beds €12.40, family rooms €13.95 per person. Reggio's new hostel, next to the Basilica della Ghiara, is about 1.5km west of the train station, in the city centre off Corso Garibaldi.

Albergo Morandi *(☎ 0522 45 43 97, fax 0522 45 25 70, Via Emilia San Pietro 64)* Singles/doubles with bath €67.15/92.95. All rooms in this three-star hotel near the train station have TVs; parking is available.

Albergo Cairoli *(☎ 0522 45 35 96, fax 0522 45 31 48, Piazza XXV Aprile 2)* Singles/doubles €33.55/46.50, with bathroom, phone and TV €41.30/56.80. Located near the bus station, this two-star hotel is spotless and comfortable. There's free car parking in the square outside the hotel.

City Hotel *(☎ 0522 45 53 76, fax 0522 45 53 79, Via Roma 37)* Singles/doubles €33.55/46.50, with bath €43.90/56.80. Located in a quiet street near the Giardini Pubblici, this place is clean and comfortable. Discounts available for longer stays.

Hotel Posta *(☎ 0522 43 29 44, fax 0522 45 26 02, Piazza del Monte 2)* Singles/doubles €123.95/160.10. For sheer luxury in the centre, try the attractive and historic Hotel Posta.

There is a produce ***market*** each Tuesday and Friday on Piazza San Prospero. Shop at the local *alimentari* (food store) for delicious typical local snacks such as *erbazzone* (herb pie with cheese or bacon) or *gnocco fritto* (fried salted dough – good ones are as light as air!).

Pizzeria Boiardo *(☎ 0522 45 42 35, Galleria Cavour 3f)* Pizzas €4.10-7.75. Open Thurs-Tues. For pizza or straightforward meals, try this pizzeria; the wood-fired oven also burns away at lunch time.

Piccola Piedigrotta *(☎ 0522 43 49 22, Piazza XXV Aprile 1)* Pizzas €3.60-5.15, pasta €5.15. Open Tues-Sun. Next door to Albergo Cairoli, this small pizzeria/trattoria makes tasty pizzas and simple pasta dishes in an informal setting. You can also get dishes to take away.

La Bottega dei Briganti *(☎ 0522 43 66 43, Via San Carlo 14b)* Pasta €60.70, mains €9.30-12.90. Open Mon-Sat. This birreria/osteria has a wonderful conspiratorial atmosphere and a small leafy courtyard. Excellent pasta and risotto dishes are the speciality.

Green Bays Pub *(Via San Carlo 10)* For a post-dinner drink you could retire to the Green Bays Pub, a few paces from La Bottega dei Briganti.

Getting There & Around

ACT buses (☎ 0522 92 76 11) serve the city and region from the bus station in Viale A Allegri. The train station is at the eastern end of town on Piazza Marconi, and plenty of trains serve all stops on the Milan-Bologna line.

The city is on the Via Emilia (S9) and the A1 passes to the north. The S63 is a tortuous but scenic route that takes you south-west across the Parma Apennines to La Spezia on the Ligurian coast.

You are unlikely to need the ACT's city buses. If you are in a blind hurry, you can call a taxi on ☎ 0522 45 25 45.

AROUND REGGIO EMILIA

South-west of the city along the S63, the **Parco del Gigante** national park is spread along the province's share of the Apennines. There are numerous walking trails, well served by rifugi. Climb or walk around the huge limestone rock called the **Pietra di Bismantova**. The tourist office at **Castelnovo ne' Monti** *(☎ 0522 81 04 30, Piazza Martiri* *della Libertà 12b; open 9am-1pm Mon-Sat, 9.30am-12.30pm Sun)* can provide details of activities, hotels, rifugi and camp sites.

The area's main attractions are three medieval castles once owned by Matilda, the countess of Canossa, famed for reconciling the excommunicated Emperor Henry IV with Pope Gregory VII in 1077. The castle of **Canossa** *(☎ 0522 87 71 04, Via del Castello)* built in 940 and rebuilt in the 13th century, is worth a visit – at the time of writing it was closed for restoration. From Canossa, you can see across to the castle of **Rossena** *(☎ 0522 24 20 13, Località Rossena 11; admission €4.10, open 3pm-7pm Sat, 11am-7pm Sun)*, part of which now houses a ***youth hostel*** *(☎ 0522 24 20 09, fax 0522 24 20 13, Via Castello di Rossena)* offering B&B for €12.90–15.50. The other castle, Bianello, is privately owned.

A good base for exploring the Po Valley area north of Reggio Emilia is **Guastalla**, where there's a youth hostel, ***Ostello del Po*** *(☎ 0522 21 92 87, fax 0522 83 92 28, Via Lido Po 11, Guastalla)*. B&B costs €10.35.

Trains and buses run from Reggio Emilia.

EMILIA-ROMAGNA

PARMA

postcode 43100 • pop 200,000

Of the Emilian cities west of Bologna, little Parma is the pick of the crop. Straddling the banks of a Po tributary – the Torrente Parma – this well-off, orderly city should not be missed. The bicycle rules in the squares and cobbled lanes of the old town centre and the surrounding countryside is home not only to parmigiano reggiano (Parmesan) cheese and Parma ham (Italy's best prosciutto), but also to the massive Barilla pasta factory and a variety of castles and walking tracks. The city itself is a little expensive but the budget-conscious can stay at the hostel or camp site.

Verdi and Toscanini composed many of their greatest works here and Stendhal immortalised the city in *La Chartreuse de Parme*.

History

Originally Etruscan, Parma achieved importance as a Roman colony on what would become the Via Emilia. As the Romans' authority dwindled, Parma passed to the Goths and later the Lombards and Franks. In the 11th century, as the conflict between the Holy Roman Empire and the papacy gathered steam, Parma threw in its lot with the former, even furnishing two anti-popes. In the following centuries internal squabbling was largely responsible for the city's turbulent fate, as it fell to the Visconti family, the Sforzas, the French and finally the papacy.

The Farnese family ruled Parma in the pope's name from 1545 to 1731, when the Bourbons took control, making Parma one of the pawns in European power games. Don Philip of Bourbon, son of Spain's Philip V, and his wife Louise Elisabeth, daughter of France's Louis XV, ushered in a period of peace and frenetic cultural activity. From the time of Napoleon's incursions into northern Italy at the beginning of the 19th century, Parma entered a period of instability that ended only with Italian unification. Some 60 years later, the barricades

The Big Cheese

Imitated but never matched, *parmigiano reggiano* (Parmesan) is the king of Italy's cheeses. It has been made in the area around Parma for more than 700 years and is so valuable that it was once quite accepted for wheels of the cheese to be used as currency.

The cheese is made with both the morning and evening milk, which is skimmed, placed in plastic basins, cultured, heated in huge copper vats and then mixed with what appears to be a giant whisk. The cheesemakers delve into the vats – hairy arms and all – to check the consistency of the curd, then lift it out into cheesecloth. Each lump of curd is cut in two, shaped into a wheel form (which also imparts the distinctive parmigiano 'branding' on the rind) and left in brine for over a month before being aged for at least one and often two (or more) years. A consortium checks each cheese for quality before it is sold. The tourist office can suggest parmesan producers to visit but you will need to speak Italian. The cheese is made in the early mornings only.

went up as Parma became the only Emilian city to oppose the infamous march on Rome by Mussolini's blackshirts in 1922.

Orientation

From the train station on Piazzale della Chiesa, head south along Via Verdi for the huge Palazzo della Pilotta. Cross Via Garibaldi for the cathedral area or walk south for Piazza Garibaldi, the main square.

Information

Tourist Offices The extremely helpful IAT office (☎ 0521 21 88 89), Via Melloni 1a, opens 9am to 7pm Monday to Saturday and 9am to 1pm Sunday. Get info online at W http://turismo.comune.parma.it/turismo. InformaGiovani (☎ 0521 21 87 48) in the same building has information for young people and disabled travellers.

Post & Communications The main post office is on Via Melloni, off Via Garibaldi, and opens 8.15am to 7pm Monday to Friday and 8.15am to 12.30pm Saturday. The Telecom office is on Piazza Garibaldi; the telephones are down a flight of stairs in front of the office and are available from 7.30am to

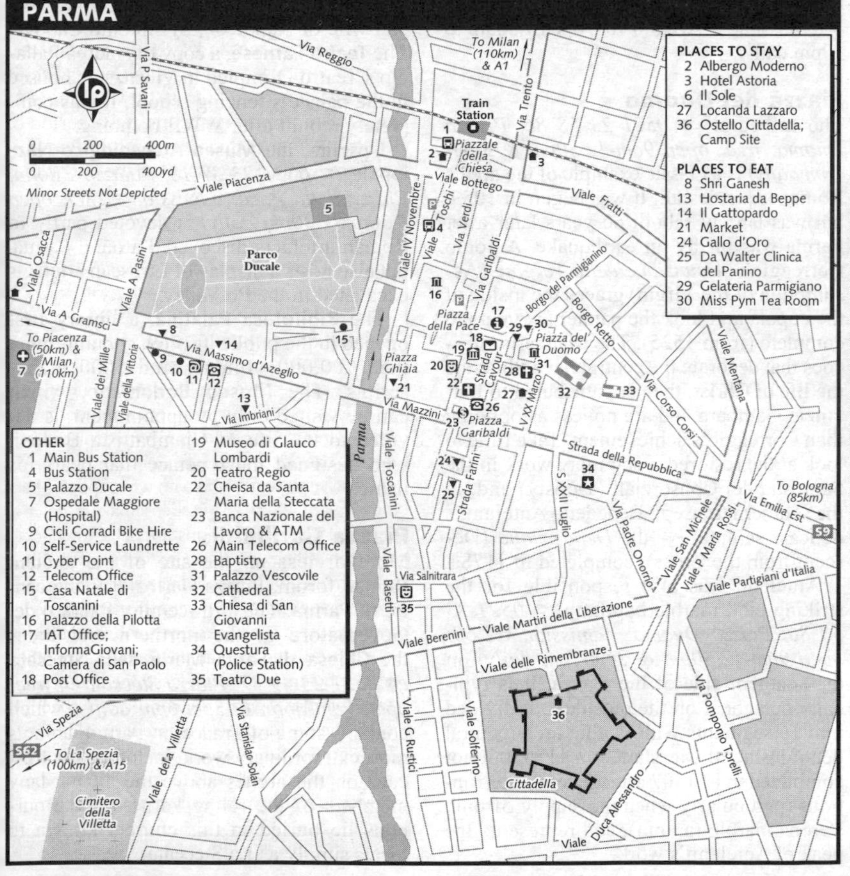

midnight daily. There's another office at Via Massimo d'Azeglio 660. Both are unstaffed.

Cyber Point, at Via Massimo d'Azeglio 72b, offers Internet access from 9.30am to 8pm daily except Friday.

Medical Services & Emergency The Ospedale Maggiore (hospital; ☎ 0521 93 11 11) is at Via Gramsci 14, west of the centre. For a locum doctor at night, call the Guardia Medica (emergency doctor) on ☎ 0521 29 25 55.

The *questura (*police station; ☎ 0521 21 94) is at Borgo della Posta.

Laundry There is a self-service laundrette on Via Massimo d'Azeglio 108, open 7.30am to 10pm daily.

Piazza del Duomo

The **cathedral** *(☎ 0521 23 58 86, Piazza Duomo; free; open 9am-12.30pm & 3pm-7pm daily)* is a classic example of the area's Romanesque design. It was begun in 1059, but was largely rebuilt 60 years later after Parma was hit by an earthquake. Antonio Correggio's *Assunzione della Vergine* (Assumption of the Virgin) graces the inside of the cupola and took the painter six years to complete (from 1525). The Mannerist frescoes that decorate the central nave illustrate the life of Christ; they are attributed to Lattanzio Gambara and are no less astounding than Correggio's achievement. Take time to look at the restored wood inlay work in the Sagrestia dei Consorziali (sacristy) and, in the southern transept, Benedetto Antelami's delicate sculpture – the *Deposizione* (Descent from the Cross), completed in 1178.

Antelami was also responsible for the striking pink marble **baptistry** *(☎ 0521 23 58 86, Piazza Duomo; admission €2.60; open 9am-12.30pm & 3pm-7pm daily)* on the southern side of the piazza. It is typically octagonal on the outside, but divided into 16 segments with Gothic architectural detail inside. It was started in 1196, but not completed until 1307 after several interruptions (particularly when the supply of pink Verona marble ran out), and represents the peak of Antelami's work.

Palazzo della Pilotta

The hulk of this immense palazzo, shattered by WWII air raids, looms over Piazza della Pace. Built for the Farnese family between 1583 and 1622, and supposedly named after the Spanish ball game of pelota which was played within its walls, it now houses several museums and galleries.

The **Galleria Nazionale** *(☎ 0521 23 33 09, Palazzo Pilotta, Piazza della Pace; admission €6.20, includes Teatro Farnese; open 8.30am-2pm daily)* is by far the most important. Its collection includes works by Antonio Correggio, Francesco Parmigianino, Fra Angelico and van Dyck, as well as a sculpture of Empress Marie-Louise, second wife of Napoleon, by Antonio Canova. The **Teatro Farnese**, a copy of Andrea Palladio's Teatro Olimpico in Vicenza, is housed in the palace's fencing school. It was completely rebuilt after WWII bombing.

Upstairs, the **Museo Archeologico Nazionale** *(☎ 0521 23 37 18, Palazzo Pilotta, Piazza della Pace; admission €2.05; open 8.30am-7.30pm daily)* is devoted partly to Roman artefacts discovered around Parma, but also hosts a display of Etruscan artefacts excavated in the Po Valley.

The **Biblioteca Palatina**, a library first opened to the public in 1769, contains more than 700,000 volumes and 5000 manuscripts. The **Museo Bodoniano**, which can be visited only by appointment, is devoted to the life of Giambattista Bodoni, who designed the typeface that bears his name.

Piazza Garibaldi

More or less on the site of the ancient Roman forum, Piazza Garibaldi is the centre of Parma. The 17th-century Palazzo del Governatore at the northern end hides the **Chiesa di Santa Maria della Steccata** *(☎ 0521 23 49 37, Piazza Steccata 9; free; open 9am-noon & 3pm-6pm daily)*, which contains some of Francesco Parmigianino's most extraordinary work, including the frescoes on the arches above the altar. Many members of the ruling Farnese and Bourbons lie buried in this church, known to locals simply as La Steccata.

Chiesa di San Giovanni Evangelista

Just east of the cathedral, this church *(☎ 0521 23 55 92, Piazzale San Giovanni; free; open 9am-noon & 3pm-6pm daily)* and the adjoining convent were built in the early 16th century on the site of a 10th-century church. The ornate Baroque facade was added a century later, and the magnificent decoration on the cupola is by Correggio. Parmigianino's contribution includes the adornment of the chapels. The cloisters open 10am to 1pm and 3.30pm to 6pm daily.

Visit the convent's ancient pharmacy, the **Spezieria di San Giovanni** *(☎ 0521 23 33 09, Borgo Pipa 1; admission €2.05; open 8.30am-2pm daily)*, accessible through a small door on the northern side of the church.

For more Correggio, head for the **Camera di San Paolo** *(☎ 0521 23 33 09, Via Melloni; admission €2.05; open 8.30am-2pm daily)* in the convent of the same name.

Museo di Glauco Lombardi

Waterloo meant different things to different people. While Napoleon headed into miserable exile, his second wife, Marie-Louise of Austria, got off pretty lightly. After her heady few years as Empress of the French, she was left with the dukedom of Parma, Piacenza and Guastalla. She ruled until 1847, with a level of moderation and good sense uncommon for the time.

Several of her belongings, including a portrait of her great husband, ended up in the hands of town notable and collector Glauco Lombardi. An eclectic assortment of Lombardi's artworks and other objects illustrative of life in Parma over the past few centuries now fill the **Museo di Glauco Lombardi** *(☎ 0521 23 37 27, Via Garibaldi 15; admission €4.10; open 10am-3pm Tues-Sat, 9am-1pm Sun)*.

Western Bank

Spread along the western bank of the River Parma (l'Oltretorrente) are the rambling gardens of the **Parco Ducale**, first laid out in 1560 around the Farnese family's **Palazzo Ducale** *(☎ 0521 23 00 23, Parco Ducale; admission €2.60, group visits only, booked in advance; open 9am-noon Mon-Sat)*. The palazzo is now home to the local *carabinieri* (military and civil police). For further details check at the IAT office. The lovely public gardens of the Parco Ducale are open from dawn to dusk, except in summer when you can stroll until midnight.

At the south-eastern corner of the park is the **Casa Natale di Toscanini** *(☎ 0521 28 54 99, Via R Tanzi 13; admission €1.55; open 10am-1pm & 3pm-6pm Tues-Sat, 10am-1pm Sun)*, the birthplace of one of Italy's greatest modern conductors, Arturo Toscanini (1867–1957). His career began almost by accident during a tour in Brazil, when he was asked to take the podium in Rio de Janeiro after the Brazilian conductor had stormed off. In 1908 he joined the New York Metropolitan and from then on split his time between Italy and the USA, where he died. The house contains a small free museum dedicated to Toscanini's life and music.

If in a musical frame of mind, you could visit the tomb of Niccolò Paganini, 2km farther south in the Cimitero della Villetta.

Places to Stay

Cheap accommodation can be difficult to find for most of the year, so bookings are advisable.

Ostello Cittadella *(☎ 0521 96 14 34, Parco Cittadella 5)* Dorm beds €9.30. Open Apr to end-Oct. The city's HI (Hostelling International) youth hostel is atmospherically situated within the walls of the giant former fortress. Take bus Nos 9 or 12 from the train station or city centre and ask the driver for directions. There is a ***camp site*** inside the fortress, run by the same management.

Il Sole *(☎ 0521 99 51 07, Via Gramsci 15d)* Singles/doubles without bath from €25.80/43.90. Basic rooms above a bar and a bit out of the way, but cheap. Take bus No 9 from the train station.

Locanda Lazzaro *(☎ 0521 20 89 44, Via XX Marzo 14)* Singles €33.55, singles/doubles with bath from €38.75/51.65. Garret rooms with views over the Parma rooftops, and an unbeatable position, make Lazzaro one of Parma's best bets. See Places to Eat for details of Lazzaro's restaurant.

***Albergo Moderno** (☎/fax 0521 77 26 47, Via A Cecchi 4)* Singles/doubles with bath €49.05/61.97. This two-star hotel is handy for the train station, but the area is a little unpleasant.

***Hotel Astoria** (☎ 0521 27 27 17, fax 0521 27 27 24, Via Trento 9)* Singles/doubles with bath €82.65/113.60. More upmarket, the Astoria has all the mod cons and is near the train station. Prices include breakfast.

Places to Eat

You won't find it difficult to eat well in Parma. There's a daily produce ***market*** on Piazza Ghiaia, between the river and Piazza Garibaldi. If you're looking for a spot to sip your Campari and read the paper, Piazza Garibaldi is as good as any.

***Gallo d'Oro** (☎ 0521 20 88 46, Borgo della Salina 3)* Full meals €20.65. This is one of Parma's best informal trattorias, serving up consistently good Emilian cuisine, including delicious *affettati* and *salumi* (cured meats and salamis), plus melt-in-the-mouth *tortelli alle erbette* (stuffed with ricotta and herbs) and *tortelli al radicchio* (stuffed with radicchio). Try and save space for some home-made desserts.

***Locanda Lazzaro** (☎ 0521 20 89 44, Via XX Marzo 14)* Full meal €10.35-15.50. This is a real find, with a sumptuous antipasta selection, great pasta and interesting meaty mains as well as vegetarian dishes and crepes.

***Miss Pym** (☎ 0521 20 60 06, Borgo del Parmigiano 5b)* €2.60-3.30. An extensive selection of teas to revive and refresh the weariest of travellers.

***Da Walter Clinica del Panino** (☎ 0521 20 63 09, Borgo Palmia 2d)* €2.60-5.15. Filled rolls, snacks and light meals are on offer here. It's not fancy but it's cheap.

***Gelateria Parmigiano** (☎ 0521 23 84 22, Via Cavour 39b)* Gelati €2.60-5.15. This is one of several tempting gelaterias in the centre.

The western bank is a good place to hunt out restaurants.

***Hostaria da Beppe** (☎ 0521 20 65 08, Via Imbriani 51b)* Pasta €5.15-6.20, mains €6.70-11.90. Open Tues-Sat. For a classier meal in a small spot tucked away from the main streets, search out this restaurant. The house speciality is risotto with *ossobucco* (marrowbone).

***Il Gattopardo** (☎ 0521 28 61 83, Via Massimo d'Azeglio 63a)* Pizza €5.15-7.75. This is one of the city's more popular pizzerias – the pizzas are huge.

***Shri Ganesh** (☎ 0521 20 01 69, Via Massimo d'Azeglio 81)* Mains €7.75, set menus €14.45-18.10. This place serves good Indian grub and is a popular haunt for students.

Entertainment

Parma's opera, concert and theatre season runs from about October to April. Enquire at the IAT office for details of current programmes.

***Teatro Regio** (☎ 0521 21 86 78, Via Garibaldi 16a)* This theatre offers a particularly rich programme of music and opera.

***Teatro Due** (☎ 0521 23 02 42, Via Salnitrara 10)* This theatre presents the city's top drama. In summer the city sponsors outdoor music programmes.

Getting There & Around

TEP (☎ 0521 28 31 78) operates buses throughout the region, including into the Apennines and to Soragna and Busseto (see the Verdi Country section under Around Parma). Services leave from just in front of the train station on Piazzale della Chiesa. Other services run to Mantua and Sabbioneta. Tickets for local travel cost €0.75 and last an hour.

Frequent trains connect Parma to Milan, Bologna, Brescia, La Spezia and Rome.

Parma is just south of the A1 to Milan and east of the A15, which connects the A1 to La Spezia. It is on the Via Emilia (S9), while the S62 provides an alternative route parallel to the A15.

You can park your car at the pay car park in Viale Toschi, and there's plenty of meter parking near the station and along the main roads around the historic centre. Traffic is restricted in the centre itself.

Cicli Corradi, at Via Massimo d'Azeglio 124a, hires bikes for around €10.35 for two days.

AROUND PARMA

Verdi Country

Head north-west of Parma along the Via Emilia (S9) and branch north for Fontevivo and Fontanellato, where you will find one of the more interesting of Parma province's 25 castles. Sitting in a murky moat, the **Rocca Sanvitale di Fontanellato** *(☎ 0521 82 90 55, 10km from Parma; admission €3.60; open 9.30am-12.30pm & 3pm-7pm Tues-Sun in summer, 9.30am-12.30pm & 3pm-5pm Tues-Sun in winter)* was built in the 16th century by the family of the same name, more as a pleasure dome than a military bastion, as the Sanvitale clan was inclined towards more idle pursuits. Parmigianino had a part in the decoration. To see the Parmigianino rooms you have to pay an extra €2.60 for the compulsory guided tour.

Nine kilometres farther north-west is Soragna, the site of the **Rocca Meli Lupi** *(☎ 0524 59 79 64, 28km from Parma; admission by hourly guided tour €6.20; open 9am-11am & 3pm-6pm Tues-Sun in summer, 2.30pm-5pm Tues-Sun in winter)*. It looks more like a stately home than a fortress, but there are Parmigianino works and a display of period furniture. **Casa Natale di Giuseppe Verdi** *(☎ 0524 97 450, Roncole Verdi; admission €3.10; open 9.30am-12.30pm & 2.30pm-5.30pm Tues-Sun Nov-Feb, 9.30am-12.30pm & 3pm-7pm Tues-Sun Mar-Oct)*, site of the humble home where Giuseppe Verdi came into the world, is 10km farther on.

Next stop is **Busseto**, where there is the **Teatro Verdi** *(admission €3.10; open 9.30am-12.30pm & 3pm-7pm Tues-Sun)*. You can also visit a small museum dedicated to Verdi in the run-down Villa Pallavicino and, a few kilometres out of Busseto, his villa at **Sant'Agata**. For more information on the Verdi sights, call Busseto's local tourist office on ☎ 0524 924 87.

TEP buses from Parma run along this route up to six times a day on weekdays.

South into the Apennines

You could take several routes south of Parma to cross the Apennines into north-western Tuscany, stopping at a castle on the way or walking through the hills and around several glacial lakes.

One route roughly follows the Parma river towards Langhirano (a town of 6th-century Lombard origin, now the main production centre of the best quality ham). About 5km short of the town rises the majestic **Castello di Torrechiare** *(☎ 0521 35 52 55, 18km from Parma; admission €2.05; open 8am-3.30pm Tues-Sun Oct-Mar, 8.30am-7pm Tues-Sun Apr-Sept)*, one of many built or rebuilt by Pier Maria Rossi in the 15th century. He romped with his lover Bianca Pellegrino in the Camera d'Oro (Golden Room), where he could look at a map of all his castles on the ceiling.

From Langhirano, follow the road down the western bank of the Parma, crossing the river at Capoponte and proceeding to **Tizzano Val Parma**, a charming Apennines town that offers pleasant walking in summer and skiing in winter (5km farther on at Schia).

Farther south still, the heights around **Monchio delle Corti** offer views to La Spezia on a good day. It's a possible base for exploring some of the 20 glacial lakes that dot the southern corner of the province, bordering Tuscany.

The mountains are in fact riddled with walking and cycling tracks and rifugi. If you'd prefer to be carried, there are several organisations in the province that arrange horse-riding excursions. The IAT office in Parma can point you to some of them. An interesting challenge is to follow the **Romea**, an ancient route for pilgrims heading south to Rome, from Collecchio to Fornovo, Bardone, Terenzo, Cassio and Berceto. All these villages have interesting Romanesque remains. The IAT office in Parma has an excellent walking brochure for this route and can advise on appropriate maps.

Of the other 20 or so castles in the province, **Castello Bardi**, about 60km south-west of Parma (not on the above route), is also worth a mention. Soaring above the surrounding town, it dates from 898, although most of the present structure was built in the 15th century.

Getting There & Away

TEP runs buses from Parma to most destinations throughout the province. On weekdays there are four buses a day to Bardi, for instance, and at least as many to Monchio delle Corti via Langhirano.

At the weekend, the La Spezia-Parma train service guarantees space for transporting bicycles.

PIACENZA

postcode 29100 • pop 105,000

In the north-western corner of Emilia, just short of the Lombardy frontier, Piacenza is another prosperous town generally overlooked by tourists. Its few noteworthy monuments certainly make a stop worthwhile if you're driving past, but an overnight stay is not really recommended as accommodation is both hard to find and expensive. In comparison with the rest of the region, Piacenza is not overly fascinating.

Orientation & Information

The train station is on the eastern edge of town. From here it's a 1km walk to the central square, Piazza dei Cavalli, or you can catch bus Nos 1, 6 or 8.

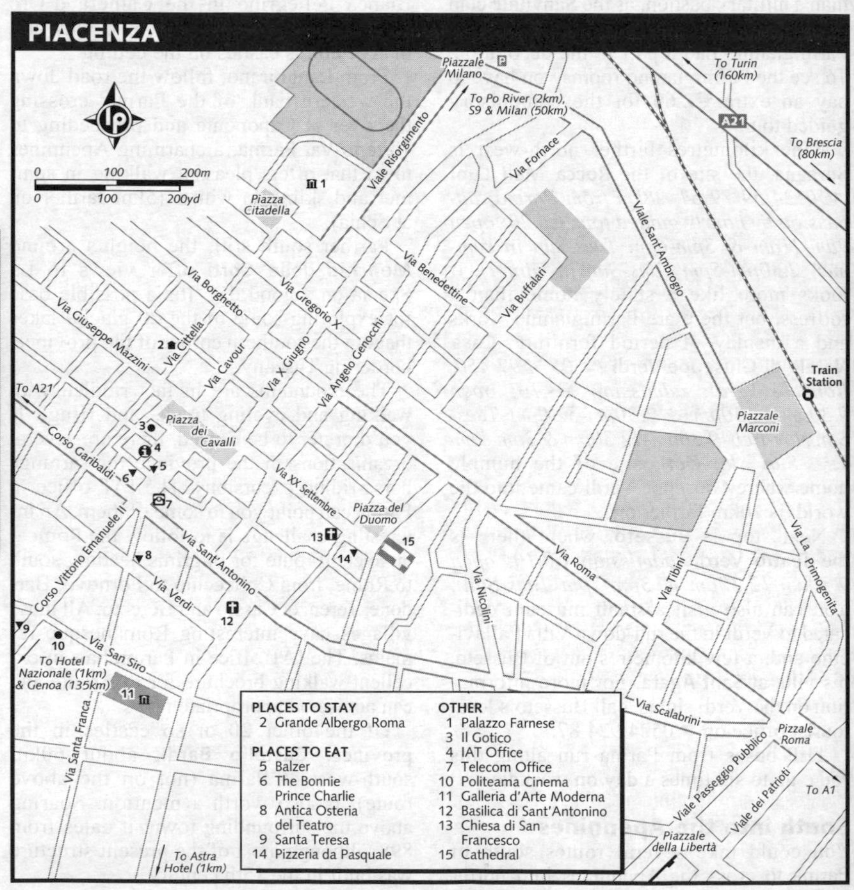

EMILIA-ROMAGNA

The IAT office (☎ 0523 32 93 24), at Piazzetta Mercanti 7, opens 9am to 12.30pm and 3pm to 8pm Tuesday, Wednesday and Friday, and 9am to 12.30pm Saturday.

Things to See

Piazza dei Cavalli is dominated by the impressive brick and marble 13th-century town hall, also known as **Il Gotico**. In front of the building, the two equestrian statues of the Farnese dukes Alessandro and his son Ranuccio, by Francesco Mochi, date from 1625 and are masterpieces of baroque sculpture.

The **cathedral** *(Via XX Settembre; free; open 7.30am-noon & 3pm-7pm daily)* was started in 1122 and is a sombre Romanesque building with frescoes by Guercino. The nearby **Basilica di Sant'Antonino** was built in the 11th century on the site of an earlier church. Its peculiar octagonal tower is claimed to be the oldest of its type in Italy.

The **Palazzo Farnese** *(☎ 0523 32 82 70, Piazza Citadella; €5.15 for all three museums, or €4.10 Museo Civico, €2.05 Museo delle Carrozze, €2.60 Museo Archeologico; open 9am-1pm Tues-Thurs, 9am-1pm & 3pm-6.30pm Fri & Sat, 9.30am-1pm & 3pm-6pm Sun)*, on Piazza Cittadella was started in 1558 but never finished. It houses three little museums, of which the main one, the **Museo Civico**, is home to the Etruscan *Fegato di Piacenza*, a liver fashioned from bronze that was used for divining the future. The other two are devoted to carriages and to Italian unification memorabilia.

A few blocks south of Piazza dei Cavalli, the newly renovated **Galleria d'Arte Moderna** *(☎ 0523 32 07 42, Via San Siro 13; admission €2.60; open 10am-noon & 3pm-5pm daily Mar-Apr, 10am-noon & 3pm-6pm daily May-Sept, 10am-noon & 2pm-4pm daily Oct-Feb)* contains a decent collection of 18th- and 19th-century Italian art and sculpture.

Places to Stay & Eat

Budget accommodation is not one of Piacenza's strong points.

Astra *(☎ 0523 45 43 64, Via Boselli 19)* Singles/doubles without bath €23.25/31. This is your best budget bet – but there's nothing fancy about it and it's about 1km south from the centre of town.

Hotel Nazionale *(☎ 0523 71 20 00, fax 0523 45 60 13, Via Genova 35)* Singles/doubles with bath €67.15/82.65. Located 1km from Piazza dei Cavalli (follow Corso Vittorio Emanuele II which becomes Via Genova), the Nazionale is clean and comfortable – a good mid-range option.

Grande Albergo Roma *(☎ 0523 32 32 01, fax 0523 33 05 48, Via Cittadella 14)* Singles/doubles €129.10/160.10. If for some reason you want to spend big in Piacenza, you could try the Grande Albergo Roma. The rooms have all mod cons, and to entice, they throw in breakfast. But at least it's in the centre of town.

Pizzeria da Pasquale *(☎ 0523 32 46 69, Piazza del Duomo 38)* Pizza €3.60-7.75. Open Fri-Wed. Sit outside on the piazza and enjoy a tasty pizza – even at lunchtime.

Santa Teresa *(☎ 0523 32 57 86, Corso Vittorio Emanuele II 169f)*. Mains €6.20-9.30. Santa Teresa does modestly priced local cuisine.

Antica Osteria del Teatro *(☎ 0523 32 37 77, Via Verdi 16)* Mains from €15.50. Open Tues-Sun lunch. This is one of Piacenza's award-winning dining experiences.

Balzer *(☎ 0523 33 10 41, Piazza dei Cavalli 1.* Open Mon-Sat. This cafe is a popular place for coffee or an aperitif, though the monumental interior is somewhat over the top.

The Bonnie Prince Charlie *(☎ 0523 33 46 85, Vicolo Perestrello 10)* Open daily from 6pm. For an expensive ale or a light meal/snack, you could pretend you're in bonnie England in this pub and restaurant which comes complete with an English telephone booth.

Getting There & Away

The easiest way to get to Piacenza is by train, with direct services from Milan, Turin, Cremona, Bologna and Ancona.

Piacenza is just off the A1 from Milan and the A21 (and S10) from Brescia or Turin. The Via Emilia (S9) runs past Piacenza, passing through the region's main cities on its way to the Adriatic Sea.

East of Bologna

FERRARA

postcode 44100 • pop 150,000

Lucrezia Borgia found that marriage into the Este family brought several disadvantages, not least among them the move to this Po Valley city, just south of the modern frontier with Veneto. Close to the river and wetlands, Ferrara in winter can be cold and grey, shrouded in cloying banks of fog. As she was used to a warmer climate, Lucrezia's feelings were perhaps understandable, but Ferrara (especially on a sunny day) retains much of the austere splendour of its Renaissance heyday, when it was strong enough to keep Rome and Venice at arm's length.

History

The Este dynasty ruled Ferrara from 1260 to 1598, and their political and military prowess was matched by an uninterrupted stream of cultural activity. Petrarch, Titian, Antonio Pisanello and the poets Torquato Tasso and Ludovico Ariosto are just some of the luminaries who spent time here under the patronage of the Este dukes.

When the House of Este fell in 1598, Pope Clement VIII claimed the city and presided over its decline. Ferrara recovered some importance during the Napoleonic period, when it was made chief city of the lower River Po. The local government has carefully restored much of the centre since the end of WWII.

Orientation

The most direct route to the centre from the train station on Piazza Stazione, on the western edge of town, is along Via Cassoli and Via Garibaldi. Alternatively, head north along Via Felisatti and turn right into Viale Cavour, the main street. Turn right again at the Castello Estense (which is impossible to miss) for Piazzetta del Castello. Corso Martiri della Libertà, on the eastern side of the castle, runs into Piazza Cattedrale and Piazza Trento Trieste, the centre of town.

Information

Tourist Offices The main IAT office (☎ 0532 20 93 70, ⓔ infotur@provincia.fe.it), in the main courtyard of the Castello Estense, is open 9am to 1pm and 2pm to 6pm Monday to Sunday. The IAT office has a Web site at Ⓦ www.comune.fe.it.

Post & Communications The post office is at Viale Cavour 27, near the castle. The Telecom office, Largo Castello 30, opens 9am and 12.30pm and 3pm and 7pm daily.

Medical Services & Emergency The Ospedale Sant'Anna (hospital; ☎ 0532 23 61 11) is at Corso della Giovecca 203. For the Guardia Medica (emergency doctor) call ☎ 0532 20 31 31.

The *questura* (police station; ☎ 0532 29 43 11) is at Corso Ercole I d'Este 26.

Castello Estense

The imposing castle *(☎ 0532 29 92 33, Viale Cavour; admission €4.10; open 9.30am-4.45pm Tues-Sun)* in the centre of town was started in 1385 for Nicolò II d'Este, primarily to defend the family from riotous subjects, who at one point rebelled over tax increases. By the middle of the following century, the Este family had begun to expand the fortress. Under Ercole I it became the dynasty's permanent residence.

Although sections are now used as government offices, many of the rooms, including the royal suites, are open for viewing. Highlights are the Sala dei Giganti (Giants' Room) and Salone dei Giochi (Games Salon), with frescoes by Camillo and Sebastiano Filippi; the Cappella di Renée de France; and the dungeon. Here, in 1425, Duke Nicolò III d'Este had his young second wife, Parisina Malatesta, and his son, Ugo, beheaded after discovering they were lovers, providing the inspiration for Robert Browning's *My Last Duchess.*

Palazzo Municipale

Linked to the castle, the town hall once also contained Este family apartments. The grand staircase by Pietro Benvenuti degli Ordani is worth seeing. You may be able to

FERRARA

PLACES TO STAY
1 Estense Camp Site
11 Albergo Annunziata
14 Albergo Centro Storico
19 Albergo Nazionale
21 Casa degli Artisti

PLACES TO EAT
16 Pasticceria Centro Storico
17 Al Brindisi
20 Locanda degli Eventi
24 Pizzeria il Ciclone
25 Trattoria il Mandolino

OTHER
2 Porta degli Angeli
3 Museo d'Arte Moderna e Contemporanea Filippo de Pisis
4 Palazzo dei Diampanti (Pinacoteca Nazionale)
5 Museo del Risorgimento e della Resistenza
6 Questura (Police Station)
7 Post Office
8 Telecom Office; Parking (Foreign Cars)
9 IAT Office
10 Castello Estense
12 Market
13 Bus Station
15 Palazzo Municipale
18 Cathedral
22 Museo della Cattedrale
23 Credito Romagnolo & ATM
26 Casa Romei
27 Monastero del Corpus Domini
28 Palazzina di Marfisa d'Este
29 Ospedale Sant'Anna (Hospital)
30 Palazzo Schifanoia
31 Palazzo di Lodovico il Moro (Museo Archelogico Nazionale)

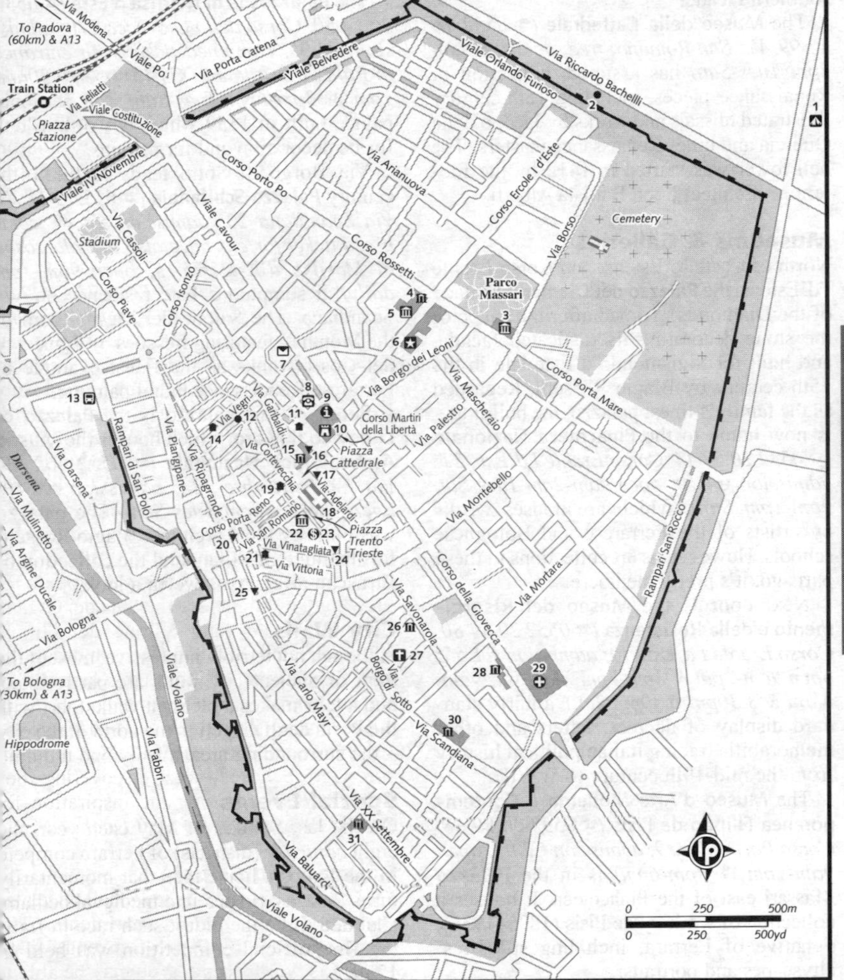

EMILIA-ROMAGNA

see some of the rooms if you turn up between 8am and 1pm Monday to Saturday and ask the porter/attendant.

Cathedral

Consecrated early in the 12th century, the cathedral *(☎ 0532 20 74 49, Via Adelardi 2; free; open 8am-noon & 3pm-7pm daily)* features a mixture of Renaissance and Gothic styles. Note the array of columns along its southern facade.

The **Museo della Cattedrale** *(☎ 0532 76 12 99, Via San Romano; free; open 9.30am-2pm Tues-Sun)* has a superb collection of Renaissance pieces, including 15th-century illustrated missals and works by Jacopo della Quercia and other Renaissance masters. The bell tower was started in 1412 by the Florentine architect Leon Battista Alberti.

Museums & Galleries

North of Castello Estense, on Corso Ercole I d'Este, is the **Palazzo dei Diamanti** (Palace of the Diamonds), named after the shape of the stone decorating its rusticated facade, and built for Sigismondo d'Este late in the 15th century by Biagio Rossetti. Regarded as the family's finest palazzo, the building ~ is now home to the **Pinacoteca Nazionale** *(☎ 0532 20 58 44, Corso Ercole I d'Este 21; admission €4.10; open 9am-2pm Tues-Sat, 9am-1pm Sun)*, which are houses works by artists of the Ferrarese and Bolognese schools. However, as art collections in these parts go, it's pretty mediocre.

Next door is the **Museo del Risorgimento e della Resistenza** *(☎ 0532 20 54 80, Corso Ercole I d'Este 19; admission €1.55; open 9am-2pm & 3pm-7pm Mon-Sat, 9am-noon & 3.30pm-6.30pm Sun)*, a fairly standard display of decrees, letters and other memorabilia tracing Italian political history from the mid-19th century to WWII.

The **Museo d'Arte Moderna e Contemporanea Filippo de Pisis** *(☎ 0532 20 99 88, Corso Porta Mare 9; admission €2.05; open 9am-1pm & 3pm-6pm)* is in the Palazzo Massari east of the Pinacoteca. It houses a collection of work by de Pisis (1896–1956), a native of Ferrara, including still-lifes, cityscapes and portraits.

Lucrezia Borgia spent many of her Fer rara days in what is now the **Casa Rome** *(☎ 0532 24 03 41, Via Savonarola 30 admission €2.05; open 8.30am-7.30pm Tues & Sun)*, a typical Renaissance-styl house. Lucrezia is buried in the nearby **Monastero del Corpus Domini** *(☎ 0532 2 78 25, Via Pergolato 4; open 9.30am-11.30am & 3.30pm-5.30pm Mon-Fri)*, along with several Este family members.

The **Palazzosna di Marfisa d'Este** *(☎ 053 20 74 50, Corso della Giovecca 170; admis sion €2.05, combined ticket with entranc to Palazzo Schifanoia €5.15; open 9.30am-1pm & 3pm-6pm Tues-Sun)* is a patrician palace built in 1559 which is worth a look for its decoration and furnishings.

Via Borgo di Sotto leads to the 14th century **Palazzo Schifanoia** *(☎ 0532 6 41 78, Via Scandiana 23; admission €4.10, combined ticket for entrance also to Palazzosna di Marfisa d'Este €5.15; open 9am-7pm daily)*, a sumptuous Este residence on Via Scandiana. The Salone dei Mesi (Room of the Months), featuring frescoes by Francesco del Cossa, ranks as the finest example of Ferrarese Renaissance mural painting.

South of this palazzo is the **Palazzo di Ludovico il Moro,** which houses the **Museo Archeologico Nazionale** *(☎ 0532 662 99, Via XX Settembre 124; admission €4.10, open 9am-7.30pm Tues-Sun)*. The palazzo was built by local architect Biagio Rossetti for the duke of Milan, and the collection of Etruscan artefacts is worth a look.

City Walls

Although not terribly impressive, most of the 9km of ancient city walls are partly intact and a tour makes a pleasant walk. Start with the Porta degli Angeli in the north of the city – the surrounding area is leafy and tranquil

Special Events

On the last Sunday of May each year, the eight *contrade* (districts) of Ferrara compete in the Palio, a horse race that momentarily turns Piazza Ariostea into medieval bedlam. Claimed to be the oldest such race in Italy, the first official competition was held in 1279.

The Ferrara Buskers' Festival, held late each August, attracts buskers from around the globe, primarily because the city pays travel and accommodation expenses for 20 of the lucky performers. Entry forms are available from the festival organisers (☎ 0532 24 93 37, W www.ferrarabuskers.com).

Places to Stay

Accommodation is usually easy to find, although many hotels close during August.

Estense *(☎/fax 0532 75 23 96, Via Gramicia 76)* €4.13/6.20 per person/site. The city's only camp site is north of the centre and outside the city walls. Take bus Nos 1 or 5 from the train station to Piazzale San Giovanni, then follow the yellow sign.

Casa degli Artisti *(☎ 0532 76 10 38, Via Vittoria 66)* Singles/doubles €18.60/33.10, doubles with bath €46.50. Ferrara's best budget hotel is a few minutes walk south of the cathedral. It's wise to book.

Albergo Centro Storico *(☎/fax 0532 20 97 48, Via Vegri 15)* Singles/doubles €31/46.50. Clean, comfortable, quiet and located in a pretty medieval street – but don't be surprised if you end up sharing your bed with a cat.

Albergo Nazionale *(☎/fax 0532 20 96 04, Corso Porta Reno 32)* Singles/doubles with bath €42/62. This comfortable two-star hotel is perfectly located in the heart of medieval Ferrara, a stone's throw from the cathedral.

Albergo Annunziata *(☎ 0532 20 11 11, fax 0532 20 32 33, Piazza della Repubblica 5)* Doubles from €170. This is well-located luxury – at a price.

Places to Eat

Ferrara's cuisine is typical of the region, incorporating meats and cheeses. One of the local specialities is *cappelacci di zucca*, a pasta pouch filled with pumpkin that looks vaguely like a small, floppy hat.

Pasticceria Centro Storico *(☎ 0532 20 57 85, Corso Martiri della Libertà 16-18)* Coffee and brioche €2.05. Head here for mouthwatering cakes and pastries and very good coffee. The savoury snacks offered free with your aperitif could almost constitute a meal in themselves.

Pizzeria il Ciclone *(☎ 0532 21 02 62, Via Vignatagliata 11)* Pizzas from €5.15. Open Tues-Sun. A bright, friendly pizzeria.

Al Brindisi *(☎ 0532 20 91 42, Via Adelardi 23)* Pasta from €6.20, mains from €7.75, wine by the glass from €3.10. Open Tues-Sun. This osteria-cum-*enoteca* (wine bar), next to the cathedral, dates from 1435 and claims among its past guests Titian and Benvenuto Cellini. The walls are lined with dusty wine bottles, some of which look as old as the place itself.

Locanda degli Eventi *(☎ 0532 76 13 47, Via Carlo Mayr 21)* Pasta €6.20-7.75, mains €9.30-11.90. Open Thurs-Tues. *Tortelli verdi* with vegetables and truffles is one of the house specialities at this typical local trattoria; *scottaditto alle brace* (grilled lamb cutlets) is another.

Trattoria il Mandolino *(☎ 0532 76 00 80, Via Carlo Mayr 83)* Pasta €6.20-7.75, mains €7.75-9.30. Open Wed-Mon lunch. Lasagne so light that it melts in your mouth and *cappelacci di zucca* are two of the treats in store at this shrine of Ferrarese home-cooking.

Getting There & Around

The bus station is at Via Rampari di San Paolo. ACFT buses (0532 59 94 29) operate services within the city and to surrounding towns such as Comacchio, as well as to the Adriatic beaches (some of these leave from the train station).

Frequent bus services run to Bologna, Venice, Ravenna and other towns in the region.

Most traffic is banned from the city centre, but there is a small free parking area for foreigners' cars on Largo Castello. There is parking at the southern end of the centre on Via Bologna and the eastern edge near Piazzale Medaglie d'Oro. ACFT runs bus Nos 1, 2 and 9 from the train station to the city centre. You can hire a bike in the square in front of the station or from Corso Giovecca 21, on the opposite (eastern) side of town.

PO DELTA (FOCI DEL PO)

Considering the incredibly polluted state of the River Po, the Po delta, which straddles Emilia-Romagna and the Veneto, should be an unpleasant place. However, the stretch of coast where the river spills into the Adriatic Ocean is strangely alluring, particularly because the wetlands surrounding its two large lagoons – the Valli di Comacchio in the south and the Valle Bertuzzi in the north – have been designated as nature reserves. The area provides some of Europe's best bird-watching, and after years of neglect by tourist authorities it is now drawing quite a crowd. Despite this, swimming is banned and many beaches have perennial problems with sludge-like algae caused by the dumping of phosphates upstream. Another problem is that the area is plagued by mosquitoes in summer, so be sure to have insect repellent, if not mosquito nets, on hand.

Most towns in the area have tourist offices, although many are open in summer only. The offices produce a wealth of information, including cycling itineraries, walking and horse-riding details, and tips on boat excursions, which are the best way to see the delta.

Things to See & Do

The **Abbazia di Pomposa** *(☎ 0533 71 91 10, Codigoro; admission €2.60; open 8.30am-7pm daily in summer, 8.30am-4pm daily in winter)*, 50km east of Ferrara, is one of the oldest Benedictine abbeys in Italy, with a church dating from the 7th century. It is believed that the monk Guido d'Arezzo invented the musical scale here, and from about 1000 years ago the abbey was one of Italy's supreme cultural centres. Its decline began in the 14th century, and in 1652 the abbey was closed. The church is adorned with frescoes from the 14th-century Rimini school and works by Vitale di Bologna, and it contains a small free museum. The abbey stages a music festival, Musica Pomposa (☎ 0533 72 95 71), each July. Infrequent buses connect Codigoro with Ravenna and Comacchio, but plan carefully or you could end up stranded.

Comacchio is a small fishing village that has one attraction – the Trepponti (Triple Bridge) built in 1635. The city's claim to be a mini-Venice is a trifle exaggerated. The tourist office (☎ 0533 31 01 47) is at Via Buonafede 12.

The delta's main information office (☎ 0544 44 68 66), at **Ca' Vecchia**, a wildlife guardians' centre at Via Fossatone in the Stazione Pineta San Vitale park north of Ravenna, opens 9am to noon and 4pm to 7pm in summer and from 10am to 4pm in winter. It produces a map detailing the types of birds likely to be found in that part of the delta's nature reserve and in the sanctuaries at Punte Alberete and Valle Mandriole. You can pick up the same map at the IAT office in Ravenna (see Information in the Ravenna section later).

Places to Stay

Albergo Luciana *(☎ 0533 71 21 40 Via Roma 66)* Singles/doubles from €20.70/31. This place, in Codigoro, is probably the best place for cheap accommodation in the area.

Getting There & Away

Moving around the area using public transport is difficult. From Ferrara to the Abbazia di Pomposa, for instance, there is virtually nothing. You can get as far as Codigoro, but from there you're on your own. Taxis from Codigoro to Pomposa are hard to come by and cost from €5.15 to €7.75.

RAVENNA

postcode 48100 • pop 90,630

Celebrated for the early Christian and Byzantine mosaics that adorn its churches and monuments, Ravenna was in fact the capital of the Byzantine Empire's western regions during the reign of Emperor Justinian and Empress Theodora.

The city had been the capital of the Western Roman Empire from 402, when the ineffectual Emperor Honorius moved his court from Rome because Ravenna's surrounding malarial swamps made it easier to defend from northern invaders. They, however, simply walked around him and marched into Rome in 410. Honorius was unable, or unwilling, to react, preferring to vegetate in Ravenna until his death in 423. The city finally succumbed 50 years later. The Byzantines arrived in 540 and ruled until the Lombards conquered the city in 752. Venetians controlled Ravenna from

1441 to 1509, when it was incorporated into the Papal States.

Under the Romans, Goths and Byzantines, Ravenna gradually rose to become one of the most splendid cities in the Mediterranean, and its mosaics are matched only by those of Istanbul. In his *Divine Comedy*, Dante described them as a symphony of colour. The city is close to Adriatic beaches, but they are hardly attractive, especially when effluent from the Po is a threat.

Orientation

From the train station, on the eastern edge of town in Piazzale Farini, it's a short walk along Viale Farini and its continuation, Via Diaz, into the central Piazza del Popolo. Nearly everything of interest is within easy walking distance of here. A few of the cheaper hotels are near the train station.

Information

Tourist Offices The IAT office (☎ 0544 3 54 04, W www.turismo.ravenna.it) is at Via Salara 12, off Via Cavour. It opens 8.30am to 7pm Monday to Saturday and 10am to 4pm on Sunday and public holidays. A second office (☎ 0544 45 15 39) at the Mausoleo di Teodorico, Via delle Industrie 14, is open 9.30am to 12.30pm and 3pm to 6pm daily (2.30pm to 5.30pm daily in winter).

Post & Communications The main post office is on Piazza Garibaldi and opens 8.15am to 7.10pm Monday to Friday, 8.15am to 12.50pm Saturday. The Telecom office, at Via G Rasponi 22, opens 8am to 11pm daily.

Medical Services & Emergency The Ospedale Santa Maria delle Croci (hospital; ☎ 0544 28 51 11) is at Via Missiroli 10. The *questura* (police station; ☎ 0544 29 91 11) is some distance from the centre at Via Berlinguer 10–20.

Things to See

A *biglietto cumulativo* (cumulative ticket) allows you into the six main monuments – Basilica di San Vitale, Mausoleo di Galla Placidia, Basilica di Sant'Apollinare Nuovo, Basilica dello Spirito Santo, Museo Arcivescovile, Battistero Neoniano – for €6.20 (March to May, slightly cheaper during the rest of the year). It can be bought at any of the participating monuments. Opening times given are summer times, which tend to be longer than those during the rest of the year. If other prices are listed here, they are for individual entry, but for the main monuments you have to buy the cumulative ticket.

Basilica di San Vitale Set back a little from the street of the same name, and a few minutes walk north-west of the IAT office, the Basilica di San Vitale *(☎ 0544 21 99 38, Via San Vitale; open 9am-7pm daily)* was consecrated in 547 by Archbishop Maximian. Its sombre exterior hides a dazzling internal feast of colour, dominated by the mosaics around the chancel, which was constructed between 521 and 548. The **mosaics** on the side and end walls represent scenes from the Old Testament. To the left, Abraham and the three angels and the sacrifice of Isaac are depicted. On the right are the death of Abel and the offering of Melchizedek. Inside the chancel, the finest mosaics of the series depict the Byzantine Emperor Justinian with San Massimiano and Empress Theodora.

Mausoleo di Galla Placidia In the same grounds as the basilica lies the mausoleum *(☎ 0544 21 99 38, Via San Vitale; open 9am-7pm daily)* erected by Galla Placidia, the half-sister of Emperor Honorius, who initiated construction of many of Ravenna's grandest buildings. The light inside, filtered through the alabaster windows, is dim but good enough to illuminate the city's oldest mosaics.

Museo Nazionale Also near the basilica, this is Ravenna's main museum *(☎ 0544 344 24, Via Flandrini; admission €4.10, not covered by the cumulative ticket; open 8.30am-7.30pm daily)*. Monks began this collection of prehistoric, Roman, Christian and Byzantine artefacts in the 18th century and various items from later periods have been added.

Cathedral, Museo Arcivescovile & Battistero Neoniano The town's cathedral, on Via G Rasponi, was built in 1733 after its 5th-century predecessor was destroyed by an earthquake. The cathedral itself is unremarkable but the small adjoining **Museo Arcivescovile** *(Episcopal Museum; ☎ 0544 21 99 38, Piazza Arcivescovado; admission covered by cumulative ticket; open 9am-7pm daily)* contains an exquisite 6th-century ivory throne of San Maximiano and some beautiful mosaics. More mosaics, of the baptism of Christ and the apostles, can be seen in the neighbouring **Battistero Neoniano** *(☎ 0544 21 99 38, Via Battistero; admission covered by cumulative ticket; open 9am-7pm daily)*. Thought to have started life as a Roman bath-house, it was converted into a baptistry in the 5th century.

Tomba di Dante As Dante indicated in the *Divine Comedy* (much of it written in Ravenna), politics is a dodgy business. Following his exile from Florence in 1302, Dante finally went to live in Ravenna, where he died in 1321. Florence still supplies the oil for the lamp in Dante's tomb, as a perpetual act of penance for having exiled him.

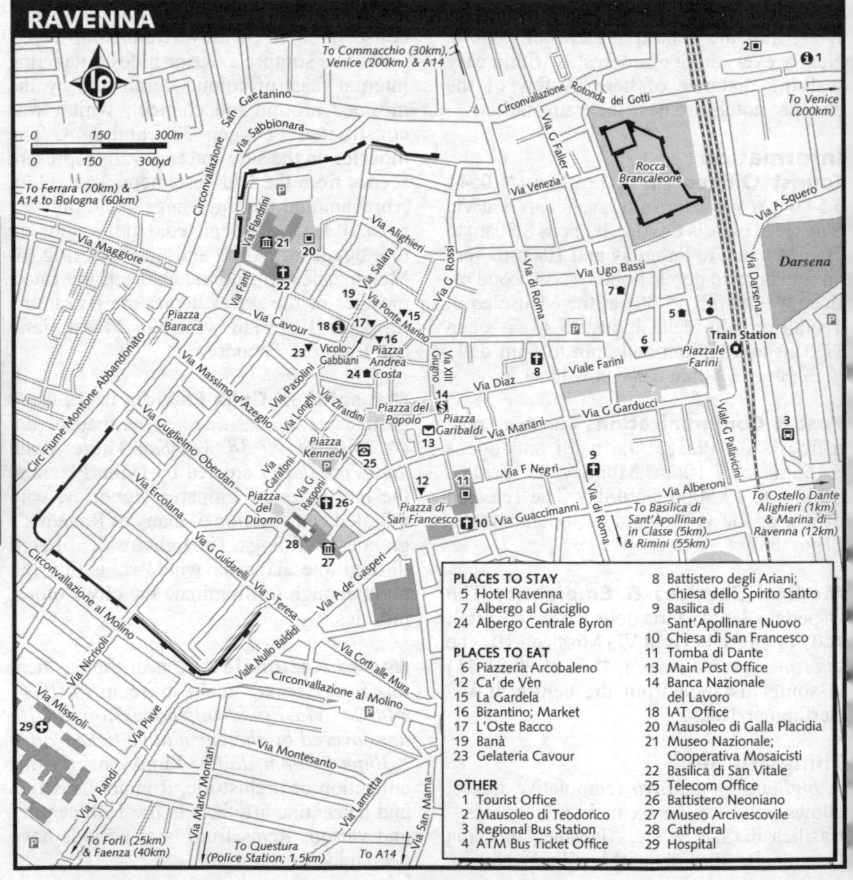

DIANA MAYFIELD

Cividale del Friuli's picturesque medieval centre

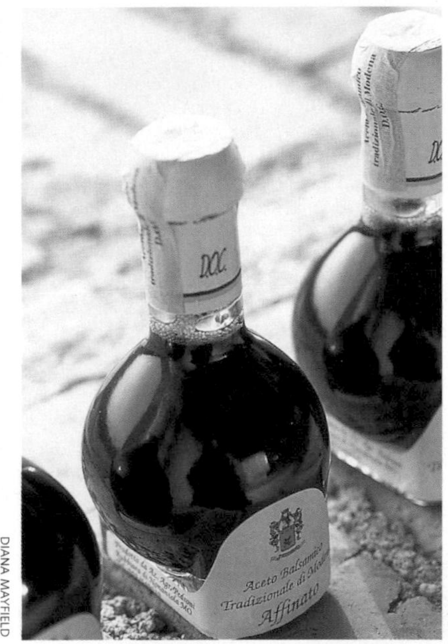

ALAN BENSON

Modena's famous vintage: balsamic vinegar

NEIL SETCHFIELD

Modena's own leaning tower: Torre Ghirlandina

ALAN BENSON

Barrel 1184 of the balsamic?

NEIL SETCHFIELD

Shutting out the light in Modena

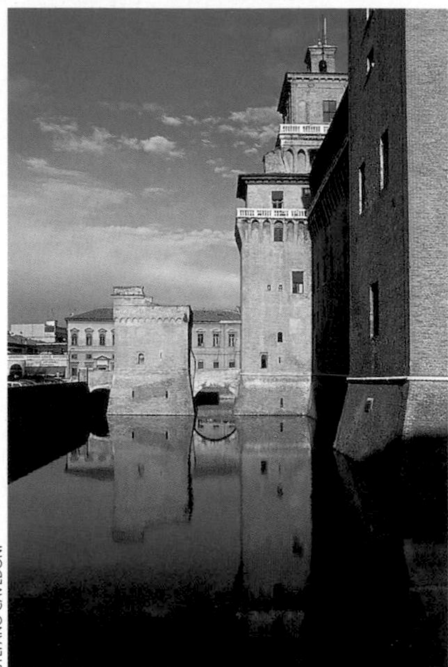

STEFANO CAVEDONI

Ferrara's imposing Castello Estense, begun in 1385

TERESA GAUDIO

The Santuario della Madonna di San Luca, Bologna

NEIL SETCHFIELD

Parma's pink-marble baptistry, completed in 1307

NEIL SETCHFIELD

Bologna, dubbed Red Bologna for its colour...

NEIL SETCHFIELD

...and political leanings

The tomb *(☎ 0544 302 52, Via Dante Alighieri 9; open 9am-noon & 2pm-5pm daily)* is next to the Chiesa di San Francesco. A mound placed over his sarcophagus during WWII, to protect it from air raids, is proudly marked, and the area around the tomb has been declared a *zona di silenzio* (silent zone).

Still on the subject of literary greats, Lord Byron lived in a house on Piazza di San Francesco in 1819.

Other Churches Those appreciative of mosaics will want to visit the **Basilica di Sant'Apollinare Nuovo** *(☎ 0544 21 99 38, Via di Roma; admission covered by cumulative ticket; open 9am-7pm daily)*, originally built by the Goths in the 6th century. The high walls in the nave are covered with mosaics; those on the right depict a procession of 26 martyrs, and those opposite a procession of virgins.

The Gothic **Battistero degli Ariani** *(☎ 0544 344 24, Via degli Ariani; free; open 8.30am-7.30pm daily)* is behind the Chiesa dello Spirito Santo, on Via Diaz.

Five kilometres south-east of the city centre is the **Basilica di Sant'Apollinare in Classe** *(☎ 0544 47 36 43, Via Romea Sud, Classe; admission €2.10; open 8.30am-7.30pm Mon-Sat, 1pm-7pm Sun)*. The basilica was built in the 6th century on the burial site of Ravenna's patron saint, who converted the city to Christianity in the 2nd century; it features a brilliant mosaic over the altar. To get there take bus No 4 or the train to Classe.

Mosaic Courses

The Centro Internazionale di Studi per l' Insegnamento del Mosaico (Cisim) runs a series of two-week mosaic courses between June and September, starting at €476. Contact Cisim (☎ 0544 45 03 44, ⓔ mosaico@racine.ravenna.it), Via M. Monti 32, 48100 Ravenna, or see its Web site at ⓦ www.mosaico.ravenna.it for information.

Places to Stay

The city is an easy day trip from Bologna, but staying overnight is no problem (except in summer) as it has a hostel and a few cheap hotels. The closest camp sites are at Marina di Ravenna on the beach (take ATM bus No 70 or follow the S67 from the town centre).

Camping Piomboni *(☎ 0544 53 02 30, Viale della Pace 421)*. Adult/child/tent site €5.70/4.65/9.30. Convenient to the beach, this a good family camping area.

Campeggio Rivaverde *(☎ 0544 53 04 91, Viale delle Nazioni 301)* Adult/child/tent site €6.20/4.40/10.35. Like Camping Piomboni, this camp site is located on the Marina di Ravenna. Prices drop in the low season.

Ostello Dante Alighieri *(☎ 0544 42 11 64, Via Aurelio Nicolodi 12)*, B&B €12.50, meals €7.50. The HI youth hostel is 1km from the train station towards the beach and is served by bus No 1. It also has family rooms.

Albergo al Giaciglio *(☎/fax 0544 394 03, ⓔ mmambo@racine.ra.it, Via Rocca Brancaleone 42)* Singles/doubles €26/36, singles/doubles with bath €31/47. This simple, family-run hotel is one of the cheaper alternatives around, and also has a decent restaurant.

Hotel Ravenna *(☎ 0544 21 22 04, fax 0544 21 20 77, Viale Maroncelli 12)* Singles/doubles with bath from €41.50/56.90. This place is clean, pleasant and handy for the train station. It also has free parking for guests.

Albergo Centrale Byron *(☎ 0544 334 79, fax 0544 341 14, Via IV Novembre 14)* Singles/doubles with bath €54.30/85.80. Those with looser purse strings could do worse than this central hotel; rooms are clean, comfortable and have all mod cons.

Places to Eat

The city's fresh-produce market **Mercato Coperto**, on Piazza Andrea Costa, north of Piazza del Popolo, is the best bet for budget food.

Bizantino *(Piazza Andrea Costa)* Tourist menus €4.80, €5.90 and €7.25. Open 11.45am-2.45pm Mon-Fri. This self-service restaurant is on the same piazza as the market and offers cheap food and speedy service.

Pizzeria Arcobaleno *(☎ 0544 21 25 36, Viale Farini 34)* Open Mon-Sat. Filling

EMILIA-ROMAGNA

pizza by the slice is on offer near the station to satisfy hungry tourists and travellers.

Al Giaciglio *(☎ 0544 394 03, Via Rocca Brancaleone 42)* Pasta €4.10-4.65, mains €5.15-7.75. Just near the station, and underneath the hotel of the same name, the Giaciglio specialises in Romagnan food, with fresh fish and seafood on Friday and Saturday.

Ca' de Vèn *(Via Corrado Ricci 24)* This attractive enoteca has a good selection of local wines and serves traditional food at reasonable prices in a very nearly medieval atmosphere.

L'Oste Bacco *(☎ 0544 353 63, Via Salara 20)* Pasta/risotto €4.20-7.30, mains €5.20-11.40. Open Wed-Mon. Located in the same street as the tourist office, L'Oste Bacco has an interesting menu. Try the *frittata ai porri dolci* (omelette with leeks) or the *tagliatelle al ragù* (tagliatelle with bolognese sauce).

La Gardela *(☎ 0544 21 71 47, Via Ponte Marino 3)* Full meal €15.50. Open Fri-Wed. An elegant but informal eatery whose specialities include *cappalletti romagnoli al ragù* (hat-shaped pasta with meat sauce).

Banà *(☎ 0544 21 64 64, Vicolo Gabbiani 7)* Full meals from €10.35. Open dinner only Tues-Thurs. If your tastebuds run to something other than Italian, this African eatery serves tasty Moroccan, Eritrean and Senegalese dishes.

Gelateria Cavour *(Corso Cavour 42)* Gelati €1.50-2.60. For a sweet finale, head for Corso Cavour and Gelateria Cavour.

EMILIA-ROMAGNA

Entertainment

Riccardo Muti, director of Milan's La Scala, has close ties with Ravenna and is closely involved each year with the ***Ravenna Festival*** (mid-June to late July) one of Italy's best festivals. World-class performers flood to Ravenna during this time; call ☎ 0544 325 77 or ask at the tourist office about programmes and tickets.

Stars of the jazz scene come to Ravenna at the end of July for ***Ravenna Jazz.***

You can see the mosaics by night (9pm to 11pm) every Friday evening from the end of June until the end of August.

Shopping

To see local artisans constructing mosaics in the traditional way, visit ***Cooperativa Mosaicisti*** *(Via Fiandrini 1)*, next to the Museo Nazionale. It specialises in copies of the city's finer works. Most are for sale.

Getting There & Around

ATM buses (☎ 0544 3 52 88) depart from Piazzale Farini in front of the train station for towns along the coast. Full information is available at the Punto Bus/ATM ticket office on the piazza.

Frequent trains connect the city with Bologna, Ferrara (where you can change for Venice), Faenza, Rimini and the southern coast.

Ravenna is on a branch of the A14 Bologna-Rimini *autostrada* (motorway), and the S16 (Via Adriatica) heads south from Ravenna to Rimini and on down the coast. The main car parks are at the train station and behind the Basilica di San Vitale, but there are several others in town.

Ravenna is easy to cover on foot. To see the city by bicycle, ask about bike hire at the tourist office.

Remembering Il Duce

It might seem a little odd that Italy's great dictator, Benito Mussolini, should have been born and raised in the traditionally left-wing territory of the Romagna. Predappio, a village overloaded with monumental buildings erected by its most infamous son, is also the Fascist leader's final resting place; his remains were buried here in 1957. About 15km south of Forli (a dull town 45km north-west of Rimini along the Via Emilia), Predappio is the scene of pro-Fascist celebrations each year, when the faithful few mark 31 October, the anniversary of the day Mussolini became prime minister in 1922. Many of the young skinheads and older faithful probably forget that their beloved icon, prior to donning the black shirt, started his political life as a card-carrying socialist and journalist who rarely missed a chance to wave the red rag.

AROUND RAVENNA

Bicycle Tour

The Ravenna IAT office (see Tourist Offices under Information in that section) produces a slim brochure detailing a three-day tour beginning and ending in Cervia, on the coast south of the city, which takes you through pine forests and past lagoons in the coastal area up towards the Valli di Comacchio.

Faenza

This Romagnola town has been producing high-grade ceramics for hundreds of years and gave us the word faïence (tin-glazed earthenware). A 30-minute train ride from Ravenna, the **Museo Internazionale delle Ceramiche** *(☎ 0546 212 40, Via Campidori 2; admission €5.20; open 9am-7pm daily in summer)* is worth a visit. There's a tourist office (☎ 0546 2 52 31) at Piazza del Popolo 1.

RIMINI

postcode 47900 • pop 200,000

Originally Umbrian, then Etruscan and Roman, Rimini sits at the centre of the Riviera del Sole and is now inhabited by beach lovers. The city continued to change hands through the Middle Ages, knowing Byzantine, Lombard and papal rule before ending up in the hands of the Malatesta family in the 13th century. At the beginning of the 16th century, Cesare Borgia added the city to his list of short-lived conquests, until it was ruled by Venice and again by the Papal States. Rimini joined the Kingdom of Italy in 1860.

The charming old city centre was badly damaged by 400 bombing raids in WWII, but enough remains to warrant a quick look. The town's main attractions are the beach and its frenetic nightlife; young people flock there every weekend from as far as away as Roma. In summer, Rimini fills with Italian and, increasingly, foreign holiday-makers in search of a scrap of beach and nocturnal fun and games – they have more than 100 discos and clubs to choose from. In spite of all this, it remains a ritual family holiday destination for many Italians.

Orientation

The main train station is on Piazzale Cesare Battisti, on the northern edge of the old city centre. From there, Via Dante becomes Via IV Novembre and leads to Piazza Tre Martiri in the city centre. Corso d'Augusto heads north-west from here to the city's other main square, Piazza Cavour. To get to the beach, walk to the north-western edge of Piazzale Cesare Battisti and turn right into Viale Principe Amedeo di Savoia, which broadens into the Parco di Federico Fellini at the waterfront.

Information

Tourist Offices The IAT office (☎ 0541 513 31, ⓔ infostazione@riminiturismo.it, ⓦ www.riminiturismo.it), at Piazzale Cesare Battisti 1, next to the train station, is open 8.30am to 7pm Monday to Saturday. In summer it opens 8.30am to 2pm on Sunday. There's another office (☎ 0541 5 65 98) at Piazzale Federico Fellini 3, open the same hours. They both provide an array of brochures, including the *Agenda Book*, a useful guide to the city.

Money There are plenty of banks where you can exchange currency. The Banca Nazionale del Lavoro and Cassa di Risparmio di Rimini, both on Corso d' Augusto, have ATMs that accept Visa, MasterCard and several other cards.

Post & Communications The main post office is on Largo Giulio Cesare and opens 8.10am to 5.30pm Monday to Friday and 8.10am to 1pm Saturday. There's a branch on Via Gambalunga.

The Telecom office is at Viale Trieste 1 and opens 8am to 9.30pm.

Medical Services & Emergency The Ospedale Infermi (hospital; ☎ 0541 70 51 11) is at Viale Luigi Settembrini 2, south-east of the city centre along Viale Roma and Viale Ugo Bassi. The Guardia Medica (emergency doctor; ☎ 0541 70 57 57) operates at night and at weekends.

The *questura* (police station; ☎ 0541 35 31 11) is at Corso d'Augusto 192.

Castel Sismondo

Brooding over the south-western corner of the old town, the castle *(☎ 0541 291 92, Piazza Malatesta; admission €7.75; open for exhibitions only, 9am-7pm)*, also known as the Rocca Malatestiana, takes its name from Sigismondo, one of the Malatesta family, who ruled for a couple of centuries until Cesare Borgia took over in 1500. Sigismondo was the worst of a pretty bad lot, condemned to hell by Pope Pius II, who burned an effigy of him in Rome because of his shameful crimes, which included rape, murder, incest, adultery and severe oppression of his people – the usual stuff.

Roman Remains

Evidence of the Roman presence in the city is found in the **Arco di Augusto** (Arch of Augustus), which was built in 27 BC, at the eastern end of Corso d'Augusto. There is also the evocative **Ponte di Tiberio** (Tiberius' Bridge), at the western end of the same thoroughfare, built in the 1st century AD as testimony to the city's importance to the empire. The **Roman amphitheatre**, built in the 2nd century AD, is at the corner of Viale Roma and Via Bastioni Orientali. Archaeologists have recently dug up Piazza Ferrari to get at a Roman villa once owned by a wealthy surgeon. Their explorations have revealed pavement mosaics and the most complete set of ancient surgical instruments ever discovered on a Roman site. There are occasional guided tours (ask at the tourist office) of the site in the summer. The Roman forum lay where Piazza Tre Martiri is today.

Tempio Malatestiano

The temple *(☎ 0541 511 30, Via IV Novembre 35; free; open 8am-12.30pm & 3.30pm-6.30pm Mon-Sat, 9am-1p & 3.30pm-7pm Sun)* of the Malatesta clan is the grandest monument in Rimini. Dedicated to St Francis, the 15th-century church was transformed into a personal chapel for the evil Sigismondo Malatesta and his beloved Isotta degli Atti, and is one of the more significant creations of the Renaissance. Most of the work on the unfinished facade was done by Leon Battista Alberti, one of the period's great architects. A crucifix inside is believed to be the work of Giotto, and the church contains a fresco by Piero della Francesca.

Piazza Cavour

This central piazza is lined with the city's finest palazzos, including the **Palazzo del Municipio**, built in 1562 and rebuilt after being razed during WWII. The Gothic **Palazzo del Podestà** was built in the 14th century and is currently undergoing restoration. The **Teatro Amintore Galli** only went up in 1857 in the feverish years leading to unification.

Beaches

Most of the beaches along the coast are either rented to private companies, which in turn rent space to bathers, or are connected to the many nearby hotels. The average daily charge for a deck chair and umbrella is €9.50 (low season) and €13 (high season). Being the kind of resort it is, many people hire changing facilities and chairs for a week or more. Two deck chairs and an umbrella in the front row with cabin facilities would cost €105 a week! These private areas are probably worth it if you have children. They all have bars and small playgrounds and often organise special activities. Otherwise, head for the public areas of the beach without the umbrellas – there is one near the pier.

The River Po pumps its heavily polluted waters into the Adriatic north of Rimini and this occasionally results in green algae washing onto the shores. Beaches have been closed over summer in the past, so check before you swim.

Sailboards can be hired from Bagno Nettuno on the beach near Piazzale Kennedy, while bicycles can be hired at Piazzale Kennedy.

Theme Parks

Rimini is not just for sun-lovers and socialites; there are numerous theme parks for kids and their suffering parents. You could try **Italia in Miniatura** *(☎ 0541 73 20 04, Via Popilia 239; adult/child over 12 €12.90/9.80, lower prices out of season, children under 12 free; open 9am-sunset*

EMILIA-ROMAGNA

Sat & Sun Oct-Mar, 9am-8pm daily Mar-Sept with late opening until midnight in July & Aug) in Viserba, a fairly ambitious collection of reproductions of, well, bits of Italy, such as the 6600 sq metres given over to 1:5 scale models of some 120 buildings facing Venice's Grand Canal and Piazza San Marco. Take bus No 8 from Rimini's train station.

Fiabilandia *(☎ 0541 37 20 64, Via Cardano, Rivazzura di Rimini; adult/child €13.95/9.80; open 10am-7pm daily Apr-Oct)* is a fantasy park full of weird and wonderful characters. It's not really suitable for very young children. Take bus No 9 from Rimini's train station.

There are also several dolphinariums in the area, including **Delfinario Rimini** *(☎ 0541 5 02 98, Lungomare Tintori 2; adult/child over 3 yrs €7.75/5.15; open Apr-Oct)*, right on the beach at Rimini.

Waterparks in the area include **Aquafàn** *(☎ 0541 60 30 50, Via Pistoia Riccione; adult/child over 5 yrs €18.10/10.35; open 10am-6.30pm daily Jun-Sept)* at Riccione. There are special bus services at 9am and 10.15am from Marina Centro in Rimini but you have to book tickets at a travel agency.

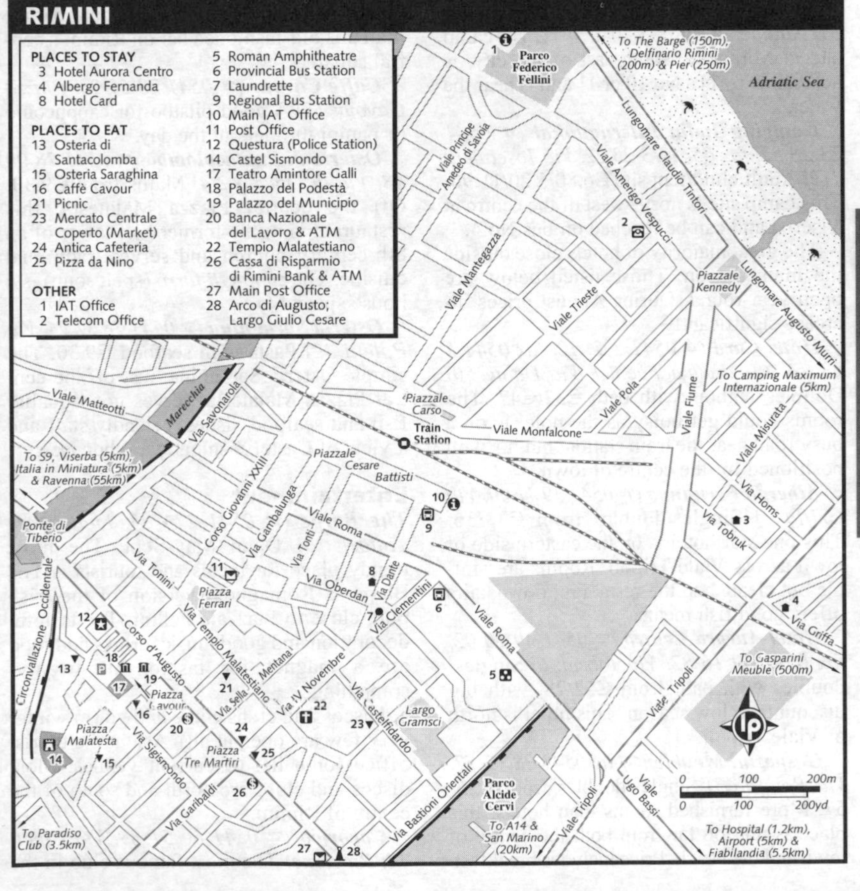

EMILIA-ROMAGNA

Places to Stay

Unless you have booked in advance, accommodation can be difficult to find and very expensive in summer, as proprietors often make full board compulsory. In winter, many of the 1500 hotels close and the city is dead. Your only hope in summer is the touts, sanctioned by the IAT, who frequent intersections on the outskirts of the city and offer rooms at so-called bargain rates, which can be excessive. For booking ahead, ask the IAT office to send you a hotel list. Otherwise, try Adria Hotel Reservation (☎ 0541 39 05 30) or Associazione Albergatori (☎ 0541 5 33 99).

Camping Maximum Internazionale *(☎ 0541 37 26 02, Viale Principe di Piemonte 57)* Adult/child/site €5.70/4.70/11. The camp site at Miramare, south-east of the city, is accessible by bus No 10 or 11 and is near the water.

Camping Italia International *(☎ 0541 73 28 82, fax 0541 73 23 22, Via Toscanelli 112)* Adult/child/tent site €6.80/5.20/11.90. This camp site is north-west of the centre at Viserba and can be reached on bus No 4.

The great majority of hotels close outside the main season. Those listed below are open year-round. During August prices increase significantly.

Hotel Card *(☎ 0541 2 64 12, fax 0541 5 43 74, ⓔ card@adhoc.net, Via Dante 50)* Doubles without/with bath €37/€47. The rooms could get noisy as the hotel is on a busy road near the train station, but it's well positioned for the centre of town.

Albergo Fernanda *(☎ 0541 39 11 00, Via Griffa 2)* Singles/doubles from €33/36. This one-star hotel is on the eastern side of town across Viale Tripoli. Rooms are simple but clean, and the restaurant downstairs offers good fish meals.

Hotel Aurora Centro *(☎ 0541 39 10 02, fax 0541 39 16 82, Via Tobruk 6)* Singles/doubles with bath from €52/78, with big discounts in low season. This hotel is north of Viale Tripoli.

Gasparini Meuble *(☎/fax 0541 38 12 77, Via Boiardo 3)* Singles/doubles from €26/57. More furnished rooms than hotels, this place is not too far from both the centre of town and the beach. Price includes breakfast.

EMILIA-ROMAGNA

Places to Eat

Rimini is not noted for its culinary contribution to the Italian table, and many restaurants offer cheap tourist menus. The **Mercato Centrale Coperto** (produce market) is at Via Castelfidardo.

Picnic *(☎ 0541 75 11 32, Via Tempio Malatestiano 32)* From €15.50 for a full meal. This is one of the better budget deals. Try the *spaghetti allo scoglio* (with seafood).

Pizza da Nino *(Via IV Novembre 9)* Pizza by the slice from €1.55. Tasty, instant, cheap takeaway pizza by the slice.

Antica Cafeteria *(☎ 0541 279 46, Piazza Tre Martiri 47)* There are many worse places to watch the passing people parade than this old-fashioned bar on Rimini's central square.

Caffè Cavour *(☎ 0541 78 51 23, Piazza Cavour 13)* A good pitstop for cappuccino or panini throughout the day.

Osteria di Santacolomba *(☎ 0541 78 00 48, Via di Duccio 2/4)* Mains from €9.30. Off the central Piazza Malatesta, this restaurant is in the former bell tower of an 8th-century church and serves traditional cuisine. The *zuppa di farro* (spelt soup) is a house speciality.

Osteria Saraghina *(☎ 0541 78 37 94, Via Poletti 32)* Pasta with seafood €9.30. The simple Osteria Saraghina, just off the central Piazza Malatesta, serves good quality fish and seafood dishes. Friendly staff and a view of Castel Sismondo are bonuses.

Entertainment

The Barge *(☎ 0541 226 85, Lungomare Tintori 13)* Open May-Sept. The most trendy place for locals and tourists is The Barge, a Romagnola version of the Irish pub, close to Piazzale Fellini. The tasteful decoration and good music, drinks and food are a magnet for fashionable twenty-somethings.

Discos and clubs come and go (in winter very few are open at all). Ask at the tourist office for a list of current venues. Most discos and clubs are north and south of the centre of Rimini.

Cocorico *(☎ 0541 60 51 83, Via Chieti 44, Riccione)* The most famous club in the area is a virtual mecca for Italian teenagers. Underground, techno and house music are played. Go there with 2000 of your closest friends – you'll all fit.

Paradiso Club *(☎ 0541 75 11 32, Via Covignano 260)* Open year-round, Paradiso offers three dance floors, seven bars, a restaurant, shop and billiards tables.

Ask at the IAT office for your type of club and also about the special buses which service the discos.

Getting There & Away

The city's Aeroporto Civile (☎ 0541 71 57 11), Via Flaminia, is served by flights from Rome and Milan.

There are regular buses to towns along the coast, including Riccione (No 11) and Cattolica (Nos 11 and 125). Regular services to San Marino run from Rimini's train station (€8.25 return). There's also a direct bus to Rome.

Trains run frequently down the coast to Ancona, Bari, Lecce and Taranto, and up the line through Bologna and on to Milan and Turin.

You have a choice of the A14 (south into Le Marche or north-west towards Bologna and Milan) or the toll-free but often clogged S16.

Getting Around

TRAM buses operate throughout the city and to the airport. Heading north, bus Nos 10 and 11 pass the station and go through Piazza Tre Martiri, before heading for Piazzale di Federico Fellini. Heading south, bus No 11 runs between the train station and Riccione.

From the end of July to mid-September, TRAM operates special late-night bus services connecting the out-of-town clubs with the city centre, train station and camp sites. The buses run from about 10.30pm to 4.30am, after which you'll have to stay in the clubs or walk.

Taxis (☎ 0541 5 00 20) charge a minimum of €3.60, then €0.95 per kilometre.

If fancy riding around, you can hire bicycles at Piazzale Kennedy, on the waterfront.

San Marino

postcode 47890 • pop 26,000

What did King Arthur say of Camelot in Monty Python's *The Holy Grail*? 'It is a silly place.' Lying 657m above sea level and only 10km from the Adriatic Ocean as the crow flies, the 61-sq-km Repubblica di San Marino seems a little silly as well – one can only speculate as to what Mexico's consul does here! Everybody mocks this place but it's perhaps a little unfair. True, you are unlikely to see a greater density of kitsch souvenir stands in many other tourist centres, but San Marino is not alone in selling kitsch and although there isn't an awful lot to see, the old town is pleasant and the views all around are quite spectacular.

If you're in Rimini, think of it as just another of the beach resort's theme parks. You can take pictures of the republic's soldiers, buy local coinage and send mail

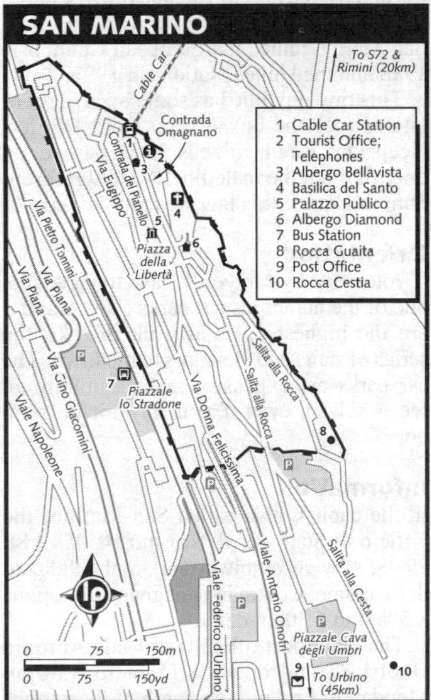

with San Marino stamps. Be warned that at the weekend, especially in summer, central San Marino can be choked with visitors.

History

There are innumerable legends describing the founding of this hilly city-state, including one about a stonecutter who was given the land on top of Monte Titano by a rich Roman woman whose son he had cured. At any rate, the inhabitants of the mountain republic are the inheritors of 1700 years of revolution-free liberty; 'Welcome to the Country of Freedom', the signs proclaim. Everybody has left San Marino well alone. Well almost. Cesare Borgia waltzed in early in the 16th century, but his own demise was just around the corner and his rule was short-lived. In 1739 one Cardinal Giulio Alberoni took over the republic, but the pope backed San Marino's independence and that was that.

During WWII, the republic remained neutral and played host to 100,000 refugees until the Allies marched into the town, in 1944. San Marino joined the European Council in 1988 and the United Nations in 1992.

This tiny republic has some bizarre regulations (see the boxed text 'Gold Diggers Keep Out') and citizenship is passed on only through the male line. A 1999 referendum to change this law was not passed.

Gold Diggers Keep Out

In 1999, the Republic of San Marino introduced measures to stop foreign gold-diggers snatching its supply of rich, elderly men. In the wake of a number of incidences where young foreigners were marrying elderly San Marino residents for their money, regulations were introduced banning female domestic staff aged under 50. A spokesperson for the San Marino congress was reported as saying, 'It's a question of sovereignty and of the measures that a small state takes to protect itself.'

Orientation

If you arrive by car, you'll have to leave it at one of the numerous car parks (Nos 6 and 7 are the highest up) and walk or take the series of stairs and elevators to the town. The car parks are expensive and the minimum fee is €1.20, even if you stay for only an hour.

Information

In the capital, also called San Marino, the Ufficio di Stato per il Turismo (☎ 0549 88 29 98, W www.omniway.sm), in the Palazzo del Turismo, Contrada Omagnano 20, opens 8.30am to 6.30pm daily.

The main post office is at Viale Antonio Onofri 87 and opens 8.15am to 4.30pm Monday to Friday. You can buy the republic's special stamps here. There are telephones at the information offices.

Things to See

The best thing to do is wander along the well-kept city walls and drop in at the two fortresses, **Rocca Guaita** and **Rocca Cestia** *(admission €3.10 for both; open 8am-8pm daily Apr-Sept, 8.50am-5pm daily Oct-Mar)*. Otherwise there are a couple of small **museums** containing ancient weapons, instruments of torture and wax dummies.

Places to Stay & Eat

There are ***camp sites*** signposted off the main road (S72) through the republic from Rimini. San Marino city has quite a few hotels should you decide to stay.

Albergo Bellavista *(☎/fax 0549 99 12 12, Contrada del Pianello 42-44)* Singles/doubles €32/50. This place has simple rooms (some with views) and a good location near the Palazzo Pubblico and the tourist office.

Albergo Diamond *(☎/fax 0549 99 10 03, Contrada del Collegio 50)* Singles/doubles with bath €36/50. Spacious rooms above a large, busy restaurant.

Food is not San Marino's strong point and the best thing about some of the cafes is the views. The city centre is dotted with places offering set meals starting at €15.

Shopping

Nothing is probably the best advice. Liquor stores claim to sell cut-price alcohol, but

SAN MARINO

you would want to be sure about what your poison is worth in Italy before buying here in the belief that you're getting duty-free bargains.

Getting There & Away

Up to nine buses run daily to Rimini. Bonelli (☎ 0541 37 24 32) has a daily service to Urbino. Buses arrive at the parking station in Piazzale Calcigni, better known as Piazzale delle Autocorriere. There are no trains. If you are driving, the S72 leads into the city centre from Rimini. If all the car parks in the city fill up, you are obliged to park near the *funivia* (cable car; ☎ 0549 88 35 90) and catch the latter to the centre (€3.10 return). A trip along the winding roads leading south to Urbino in Le Marche is recommended.

Tuscany (Toscana)

The people of Tuscany can rightly claim to have just about the best of everything – architecture, the country's greatest collection of art, beautiful countryside bathed in soft pink hues and some of Italy's finest fresh produce and best-known wines. It was from Tuscany, about 600 years ago, that the effects of the Renaissance began to ripple out across Europe.

The works of Donatello, Michelangelo, Leonardo da Vinci and other 14th- to 16th-century Tuscan masters remain models for artists worldwide. Tuscan architects – notably Brunelleschi, responsible for the magnificent dome of Florence's cathedral, and Leon Battista Alberti, who designed much of the facade of the Basilica di Santa Maria Novella – have had an enduring influence on the course of architecture.

Dante, Petrarch and Boccaccio planted the seeds for the birth of a unified Italian language with their vigorous literature. Even today the Senesi (Sienese) and the Fiorentini (Florentines) maintain a keen rivalry over who speaks the 'purest' Italian (Italians beyond Tuscany would probably dispute that either can take that accolade, since modern Italian is more than simply a derivative of Tuscan).

Most people are drawn to Tuscany by the artistic splendour of Florence and Siena or to view the Leaning Tower (Torre Pendente) in Pisa. But Tuscany also features some of Italy's most impressive hill towns, including San Gimignano, Volterra, Cortona and Montepulciano.

The Etruscan sites in the south – around Saturnia and Sovana – will take you away from the mainstream tourist itinerary. Southern Tuscany also boasts a handful of pleasant beaches, especially on the Monte Argentario peninsula and on Elba island.

Walkers and nature lovers can enjoy the Apuan Alps (Alpi Apuane), the Garfagnana, the Mugello (north-east of Florence) and the Parco Naturale della Maremma, near Grosseto.

Highlights

- Admire the cathedral and baptistry in the heart of Florence
- Bathe in the ocean of Renaissance art in the Uffizi
- Relax on a beach on the island of Elba
- Meander along the narrow lanes of the glorious medieval city of Siena
- Explore the spectacularly located town of Pitigliano in southern Tuscany
- Tickle your palate with fine Tuscan wines, from Chianti to Montalcino

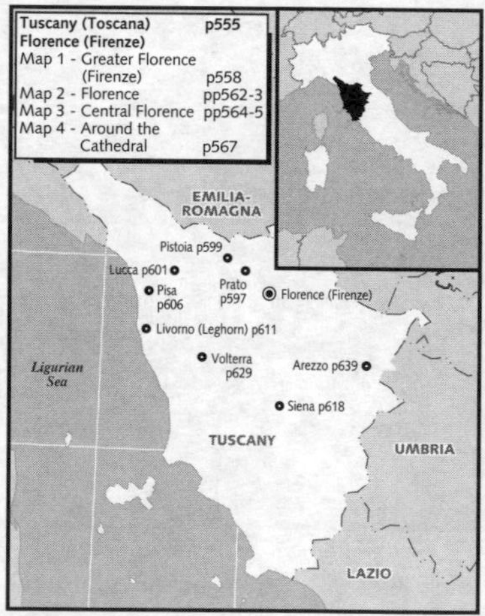

Tuscan cuisine is dominated by unsalted bread and the extra virgin olive oil produced in the region's hills. Bread can feature in every course, even dessert when it is topped with egg yolk and orange rind and sprinkled with a heavy layer of powdered sugar.

You could start a meal with *fettunta* (known elsewhere in Italy as *bruschetta*),

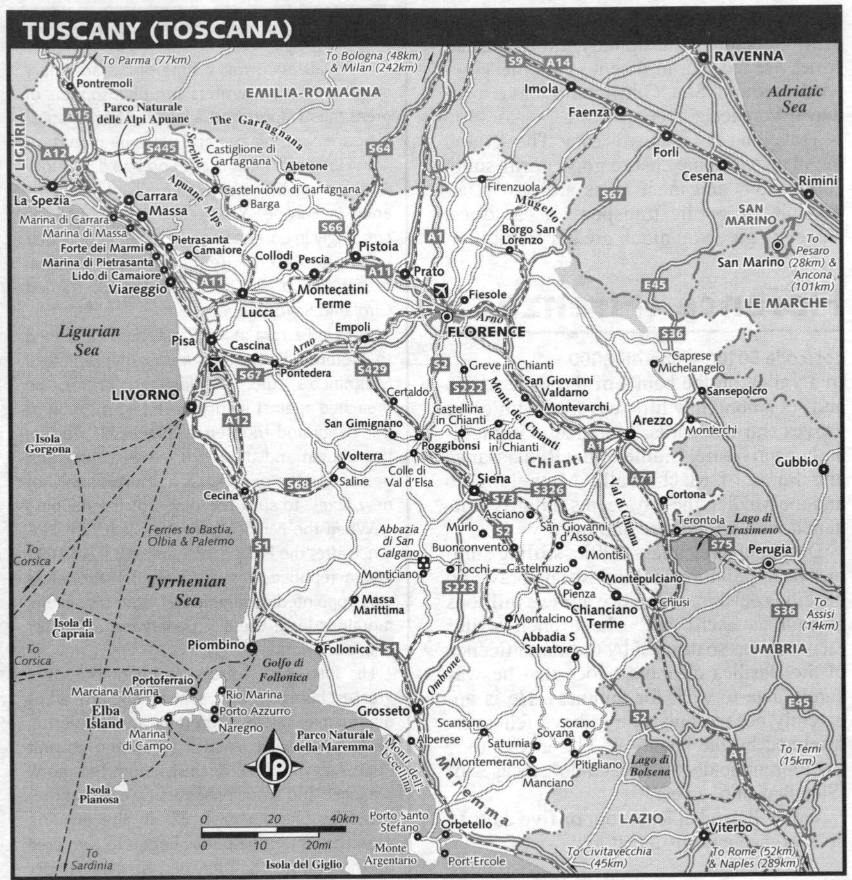

a thick slice of toasted bread rubbed with garlic and soaked with olive oil. Or maybe *crostini* (minced chicken liver canapés).

A light summer dish is *panzanella*, basically a cold mixed salad with breadcrumbs. Tomato, cucumber, red onions and lettuce are tossed into a bowl with stale bread that has been soaked and broken up. Lots of oil, vinegar and basil are mixed in before the dish is chilled.

The winter equivalent is *ribollita*, another example of making use of every last scrap. Basically a vegetable stew, again with bread mixed in, it is a hearty dish for cold winter nights. *Pappa di pomodoro* is a bread and tomato paste served hot.

Although pasta dishes have long been a standard element in local cooking, they are an import from other parts of Italy. Meat and poultry are grilled, roasted or fried and may come simply with a slice of lemon. Game meats figure high on menus and sauces tend to be rich. Seafood is the preserve of the coast. Traditional desserts are simple, such as biscuits flavoured with nuts or spices and served with a glass of the dessert wine *(vin santo)*.

The region's wines are among the country's best known and include Chianti, the *vino nobile* of Montepulciano, and Brunello di Montalcino. Traditionally, most Tuscan wines are red, but in recent years the vineyards around San Gimignano have produced Vernaccia, a crisp white.

Travelling in Tuscany is easy. The A1 and the main train line ensure good north-south connections and most areas are easily accessible by public transport. A car does, however, give you much greater flexibility.

Florence (Firenze)

postcode 50100 • pop 461,000

In a valley on the banks of the River Arno and set among low hills covered with olive groves and vineyards, Florence is immediately captivating. Cradle of the Renaissance and home of Machiavelli, Michelangelo and the Medici, the city seems unfairly burdened with art, culture and history.

Despite the relentless traffic, stifling summer heat, pollution and industrial sprawl on the city's outskirts, Florence attracts millions of tourists each year. The French writer Stendhal was so dazzled by the magnificence of the Basilica di Santa Croce that he was barely able to walk for faintness. He is apparently not the only one to have felt overwhelmed by the beauty of Florence – they say Florentine doctors treat a dozen cases of 'Stendhalismo' a year.

You will need at least four or five days to do Florence any justice at all.

History

Controversy still reigns over who founded Florence. The commonly accepted story holds that Julius Caesar founded Florentia around 30 BC, making it a strategic garrison on the narrowest crossing of the Arno, whose purpose was to control the Via Flaminia linking Rome to northern Italy and Gaul. Archaeological evidence suggests an earlier village may have been founded, perhaps by the Etruscans of Fiesole, as early as 200 BC.

Along with the rest of northern Italy, the city suffered during the barbarian invasions during the Dark Ages. In the early 12th century, it became a free *comune* (town council) and by 1138 was ruled by 12 *priori* (consuls), assisted by the Consiglio di Cento (Council of One Hundred). The council members were drawn mainly from the prosperous merchant class. Agitation among differing factions in

Savonarola

The Renaissance was a time of extraordinary contrasts. Artists, writers and philosophers of great talent flourished against a backdrop of violence, war, plague and extreme poverty.

In Florence, the court of Lorenzo de' Medici was among the most splendid and enlightened in Europe. Yet, in the streets and increasingly in Lorenzo's court itself, people had begun to listen intently to the fanatical preachings of a Dominican monk named Girolamo Savonarola.

Born in Ferrara in 1452, Savonarola moved to Florence in the last years of Lorenzo il Magnifico's rule. An inspired orator, he preached against luxury, greed, corruption of the clergy and the Renaissance itself. To him the Church and the world were corrupt and he accused the ruling class of thinking only 'of new taxes, to suck the blood of the people'.

When the Medici were expelled from Florence after the French invasion of Italy in 1494 and a republic was proclaimed, Savonarola was appointed its legislator. Under his severe, moralistic lead, the city underwent a type of religious reform.

His followers included some of the city's greatest humanist philosophers and artists but his enemies were numerous and powerful. Beside the exiled Medici stood the corrupt Pope Alexander VI, against whom the monk preached and who consequently excommunicated Savonarola in 1497. In the ensuing year, the Florentine public began to turn cold on the evangelistic preacher; he came under attack from the Franciscan monks and began to lose the support of political allies.

After refusing to undergo the challenge of an ordeal by fire, Savonarola was arrested. On 22 May 1498 he was hanged and burned at the stake for heresy, in Piazza della Signoria. His ashes were thrown into the Arno.

the city led to the appointment of a foreign head of state, known as the *podestà*, in 1207.

The first conflicts between two factions, the pro-papal Guelphs (Guelfi) and the pro-imperial Ghibellines (Ghibellini), started in the mid-13th century, with power passing from one to the other for almost a century. The Guelphs eventually formed a government, known as the Primo Popolo, but in 1260 were briefly ousted after Florence was defeated by Ghibelline Siena at the Battle of Montaperti.

If you thought that was complicated, it got worse in the 1290s as the Guelphs split into two factions: the Neri (Blacks) and Bianchi (Whites). When the Bianchi were defeated, Dante was among those driven into exile in 1302. As the nobility lost ground, the Guelph merchant class took control but trouble was never far away. The great plague of 1348 halved the city's population and the government was rocked by growing agitation from the lower classes.

In the late 14th century, Florence was ruled by a caucus of Guelphs under the leadership of the Albizi family. Among the families opposing them were the Medici, whose influence grew as they became the papal bankers.

In the 15th century Cosimo de' Medici emerged as the head of the opposition to the Albizi and eventually became Florence's ruler. His eye for talent and his tact in dealing with artists saw the likes of Alberti, Brunelleschi, Lorenzo Ghiberti, Donatello, Fra Angelico and Fra Filippo Lippi flourish under his patronage. Many of the city's finest buildings are testimony to his tastes.

Cosimo was eventually followed by his grandson, Lorenzo il Magnifico, whose rule (1469–92) ushered in the most glorious period of Florentine civilisation and of the Italian Renaissance. His court fostered a great flowering of art, music and poetry, turning Florence into the cultural capital of Italy. Lorenzo favoured philosophers, but he kept up family tradition by sponsoring artists such as Botticelli and Domenico Ghirlandaio; he also encouraged Leonardo and the young Michelangelo, who was working under Giovanni di Bertoldo, Donatello's pupil.

Not long before Lorenzo's death in 1492, the Medici bank failed and, two years later, the Medici were driven out of Florence. The city fell under the control of Girolamo Savonarola, a Dominican monk, who led a puritanical republic until he fell from public favour and was tried as a heretic and executed in 1498.

After Florence's defeat by the Spanish in 1512, the Medici returned to the city but were once again expelled, this time by Emperor Charles V in 1527. Two years later they had made peace and Charles not only allowed the Medici to return to Florence, but married his daughter to Lorenzo's great-grandson Alessandro de' Medici, whom he made duke of Florence in 1530. Seven years later one of the last truly capable Medici rulers, Cosimo I de Medici, took charge. He became grand duke of Tuscany after Siena fell to Florence in 1569, and died in 1574. The Medici then ruled for another 163 years, during which time they gained control of all of Tuscany.

In 1737 the grand duchy of Tuscany passed to the House of Lorraine, which retained control (apart from a brief interruption under Napoleon from 1799 to 1814) until it was incorporated into the Kingdom of Italy in 1860. Florence became the national capital a year later, but Rome assumed the mantle permanently in 1870.

Florence was badly damaged during WWII by the retreating Germans, who blew up all its bridges except the Ponte Vecchio. Devastating floods ravaged the city in 1966, causing inestimable damage to its buildings and artworks. However, the salvage operation led to the widespread use of modern restoration techniques that have saved artworks throughout the country.

Orientation

Whether you arrive by train, bus or car, the central train station, Santa Maria Novella (Maps 3 & 4), is a good reference point. Budget hotels and pensiones are concentrated around Via Nazionale (Map 3), to the east of Stazione di Santa Maria Novella, and Piazza di Santa Maria Novella (Map 4), to the south. The main route to the city centre

MAP 1 – GREATER FLORENCE (FIRENZE)

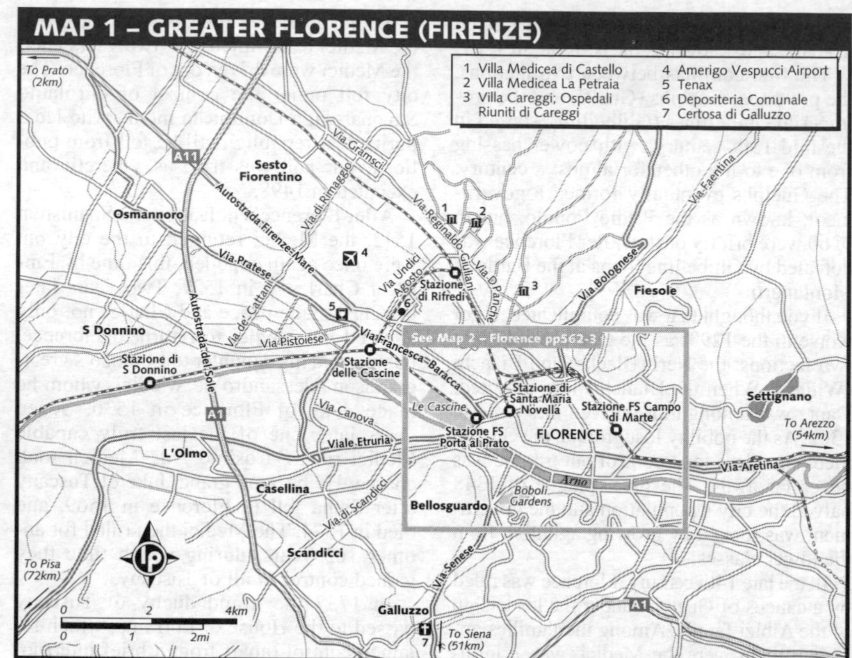

is Via de' Panzani and then Via de' Cerretani, about a 10-minute walk. You'll know you've arrived when you first glimpse the cathedral.

Most of the major sights are in easy walking distance – you can stroll from one end of the city centre to the other in about 30 minutes. From Piazza di San Giovanni next to the cathedral (Map 4), Via Roma leads to Piazza della Repubblica and continues as Via Calimala and Via Por Santa Maria to the Ponte Vecchio.

Take Via de' Calzaiuoli from Piazza del Duomo to get to Piazza della Signoria, the historic seat of government. The Uffizi Gallery is on the piazza's southern edge, near the Arno. Cross the Ponte Vecchio, or the Ponte alle Grazie farther east, to reach Piazzale Michelangelo (Map 2) in the south-east for a view over the city, one of the best vistas in Italy.

You'll find reasonably priced public parking around the imposing Fortezza da Basso, just north of Stazione di Santa Maria Novella and a brisk 10-minute walk to the historic centre along Via Faenza.

Information

Tourist Offices The main APT office (Map 3; ☎ 055 29 08 32, fax 055 276 03 83, **W** www.firenze.turismo.toscana.it) is north of the cathedral at Via Cavour 1r. It opens 8.15am to 7.15pm Monday to Saturday and 8.30am to 1.30pm Sunday from April to October, and 8.15am to 1.30pm Monday to Saturday the rest of the year. The branch at Amerigo Vespucci airport (Map 1; ☎ 055 31 58 74) opens 7.30am to 11.30pm daily.

The Comune di Firenze (Florence's city council) operates a tourist office (Map 3; ☎ 055 21 22 45) at Piazza della Stazione 4. It opens 8.45am to 8pm Monday to Saturday in summer and 9am to 1.45pm Monday to Saturday in winter. It has another office (Map 4; ☎ 055 234 04 44) at Borgo Santa Croce 29r, which opens the same hours.

Inside Stazione di Santa Maria Novella, you can pick up basic information at the Consorzio ITA office (Map 3; ☎ 055 28 28 93). Their main role is to book hotels. The office opens 8.45am to 9pm daily.

The police and tourist offices combine to operate Tourist Help points for the disoriented at the Ponte Vecchio (Map 4) and Piazza della Repubblica (Map 4), open 8.30am to 7pm. From April to October, the APT also offers a special service known as Florence SOS Turista (☎ 055 276 03 82). Tourists needing guidance on matters such as disputes over hotel bills can phone from 10am to 1pm and 3pm to 6pm Monday to Saturday.

One of the handiest commercial maps of the city is the red-covered *Florence* (€5.20), produced by the Touring Club Italiano and scaled at 1:12,500. A cutaway of the centre is scaled at 1:6500.

Money A number of banks are concentrated around Piazza della Repubblica (Map 4). Thomas Cook has a bureau de change (☎ 055 28 97 81) at Lungarno degli Acciaiuoli 6r, near the Ponte Vecchio. It opens 8.30am to 7.30pm Monday to Saturday, and 9.30am to 5pm Sunday. American Express (Map 4; ☎ 055 5 09 81) is at Via Dante Alighieri 22r. It opens 9am to 5.30pm Monday to Friday, and 9.30am to 12.30pm Saturday.

The Red and the Black

Florence has two street-numbering systems: red or brown numbers indicate commercial premises and black or blue numbers denote private residences. When written, black or blue addresses are denoted by the number only, while red or brown addresses usually carry an 'r' for *rosso* (red) after the number. It can be confusing, as the black and blue numbers tend to denote whole buildings, while each red number refers to a commercial premises, several of which may be in the same building. When looking for a specific address, keep your eyes on both sets of numbers – backtracking is sometimes inevitable.

Post & Communications The main post office is on Via Pellicceria, off Piazza della Repubblica (Map 4), and opens 8.15am to 7pm Monday to Friday and 8.15am to 12.30pm Saturday. Fax and telegram services are available.

American Express customers can have their mail forwarded to the American Express office (see under Money earlier).

You will find Telecom phones in an unstaffed office (open 7am to 10pm) near the ATAF information booth outside the Stazione di Santa Maria Novella (Map 3). There is an unstaffed Telecom office (open 7am to 11pm) with national phone books (at the time of writing the Florence one had been stolen) at Via Cavour 21r.

Places to get online are mushrooming in Florence. The cheapest deal in town is at Il Cairo Phone Center (Map 3; ☎ 055 263 83 36), Via de' Macci 90r. If you go at the right time, an hour online costs as little as €1.80. The centre opens 9.30am to 9pm daily. Internet Train (W www.internettrain.it) has 15 branches (and growing!), including Via dell'Oriuolo 40r (Map 4; ☎ 055 263 89 68), Via Guelfa 24a (Map 3; ☎ 055 21 47 94), Via Santa Monaca 6/8r (Map 3; ☎ 055 260 88 80), Via dei Benci 36r (Map 4; ☎ 055 263 85 55) and Borgo San Jacopo 30r (Map 4; ☎ 055 265 79 35). A handy one is in the subterranean pedestrian passage beneath Stazione di Santa Maria Novella. It costs €6.20 (students €5.20) per hour. These places open 10am to midnight daily.

Travel Agencies Sestante has an office (Map 3; ☎ 055 29 43 06) at Via Cavour 56r, where you can book train and air tickets, organise guided tours and so on.

A branch of CTS (Map 3; ☎ 055 28 95 70, W www.cts.it), the national youth-travel organisation, is at Via de' Ginori 25r.

For discounted international rail tickets (if you are under 26), head for the Wasteels office (Map 3; ☎ 055 28 06 83) next to track 16 at Stazione di Santa Maria Novella.

Bookshops The Paperback Exchange (Map 3; ☎ 055 247 81 54), Via Fiesolana 31r, has a vast selection of new and second-hand books in English. Feltrinelli International (Map 4; ☎ 055 21 95 24), Via Cavour 12r, near the APT (Map 3), has a good selection of books in English, French, German, Spanish, Portuguese and Russian. Internazionale Seeber (Map 4; ☎ 055 21 56 97), Via de' Tornabuoni 70r, also has books in those languages, as well as a fine selection of art books.

Gay & Lesbian Travellers Azione Gay e Lesbica Finisterrae (☎/fax 055 67 12 98, W www.azionegayelesbica.it) is at Via Manara 12.

At the Libreria delle Donne (☎ 055 24 03 84), Via Fiesolana 2b, you can get information to tune you into the lesbian scene in Florence.

Laundry The Wash & Dry Laundrette chain (☎ 800 23 11 72) has eight branches across the city. You pay €3.10 for 8kg of washing and €3.10 for drying. They open 8am to 10pm (last wash at 9pm). Addresses shown on the maps include: Via Nazionale 129 (Map 3), Via del Sole 29r (Map 4), Via della Scala 52–54r (Map 3), Via dei Servi 105r (Map 3) and Via de' Serragli 87r (Map 3).

Medical Services The Ospedali Riuniti di Careggi (Map 1; ☎ 055 427 71 11) is the main public hospital and is at Viale Morgagni 85, north of the city centre. There is also the Ospedale di Santa Maria Nuova (Map 4; ☎ 055 2 75 81), Piazza Santa Maria Nuova 1, just east of the cathedral.

The Tourist Medical Service (Map 2; ☎ 055 47 54 11), Via Lorenzo il Magnifico 59, opens 24 hours and doctors speak English, French and German. The APT office has lists of doctors and dentists who speak various languages.

Twenty-four hour pharmacies include: Farmacia Comunale (Map 3; ☎ 055 21 67 61), inside the Stazione di Santa Maria Novella; Molteni (Map 4; ☎ 055 28 94 90), in the city centre at Via de' Calzaiuoli 7r; and All'Insegna del Moro (Map 4; ☎ 055 21 13 43), at Piazza di San Giovanni 28.

The Misericordia di Firenze ambulance station (Map 4; ☎ 055 21 22 22) is at Vicolo degli Adimari 1, just off Piazza del Duomo. They also run a medical attention centre there for tourists, which operates 10am to 7pm Monday to Friday and 9am to 2pm Saturday. If you need a doctor at night or on a public holiday, call the Guardia Medica on ☎ 055 47 78 91.

Queue Jumping

If time is precious and money is not a prime concern, you can skip (or at least shorten) some of the museum queues in Florence by booking ahead. In summer especially, the long and winding queues can mean waits of two to four hours! Watch 'em sweat!

For a €1.55 fee, you can book a ticket to the Uffizi by phoning Firenze Musei (☎ 055 29 48 83). You are given a booking number and agree on the time you want to visit. When you arrive at the gallery, follow the signs to a separate entrance for those with pre-booked tickets, which you pick up and pay for on the spot without queuing. You can book admission to any of the state museums *(musei statali)* this way. They include Palazzo Pitti, Museo del Bargello, Galleria dell'Accademia, Museo Archeologico and Cappelle Medicee. For the Uffizi, you can also buy the ticket in advance at the gallery itself (the booking fee still applies).

If you prefer electronic methods, Weekend a Firenze (W www.weekendafirenze.com) is an online service for booking museums, galleries, shows and tours. For this you pay €5.70 on top of the normal ticket price – book at least three days in advance. You will get an email confirmation that you will have to print out and present at the cashier's desk on the day you go. You can get tickets for the Uffizi, Galleria Palatina, Museo di San Marco, Museo del Bargello, Galleria dell'Accademia, Museo Archeologico, Cappelle Medicee and the Galleria d'Arte Moderna.

Many of the bigger hotels will also book these tickets for you.

When you go to the Uffizi or other sights with prepaid tickets or email confirmation, head for the designated entrance for those with booked tickets and smile smugly at the suffering hordes lining up outside the other entrance.

Emergency The *questura* (police station; Map 2; ☎ 055 4 97 71) is at Via Zara 2. You can report thefts at the foreigners office there. The Polizia Assistenza Turistica (Map 3; ☎ 055 20 39 11) are at Via Pietrapiana 50r (Piazza dei Ciompi). They are a police unit dedicated to dealing with distressed tourists, and have interpreters.

Dangers & Annoyances The most annoying aspect of Florence is the crowds, closely followed by the summer heat. Pickpockets are active in crowds and on buses.

Things to See & Do

Florence is the proverbial chocolate cake. We won't even try to compete with the battalions of literary greats and other important personages who have spilled rivers of ink in the search for an original superlative.

The city is jammed with sights, mostly confined to a small area. Too little space is available in the confines of this book to do them all justice, although we try to steer you through the 'essentials'.

Museums and monuments tend to close on Monday, although due to the hordes of tourists that pour in year-round, quite a few places have made an exception to this rule – the APT has a list of them.

Some sights are state-run or private; others are run by the comune. Many of those run by the latter are secondary on any itinerary but, if you intend to visit the lot, ask about the special *carnet*. It costs €5.20, for which you get an explanatory booklet and discounts of up to 50% on a selection of these sights.

Walking Tours

Here follow a couple of suggested tours of churches, important both architecturally and for the art treasures they contain. The two walks each comprise four churches and you could complete the lot in a day, in morning and afternoon sessions. This works out well, as most churches close for three to four hours in the middle of the day – a handy time to chill out over lunch. The main APT office, at Via Cavour 1r (Map 3), has an updated list of opening hours.

Tour One Start at the **Basilica di Santa Maria Novella (Map 4)** *(☎ 055 21 59 18, Piazza di Santa Maria Novella; admission €2.60; open 9am-5pm Mon-Thurs & Sat, 1pm-5pm Fri, Sun & holidays)*, just south of Stazione di Santa Maria Novella. Begun in the late 13th century as the Florentine base for the Dominican order, the basilica was largely completed by around 1360, but work on its facade and interior continued well into the 15th century. The lower section of the green and white marble facade is transitional from Romanesque to Gothic, while the upper section and the main doorway were designed by Alberti and completed in around 1470. The highlight of the Gothic interior is Masaccio's superb fresco of the *Trinity* (1428), one of the first artworks to use the then newly discovered techniques of perspective and proportion. It is halfway along the northern aisle.

The first chapel to the right of the choir, the **Cappella di Filippo Strozzi**, features lively frescoes by Filippino Lippi depicting the lives of St John the Evangelist and St Philip. Another important work is Domenico Ghirlandaio's series of frescoes behind the main altar, painted with the help of artists who may have included the young Michelangelo. Relating the lives of the Virgin Mary, St John the Baptist (San Giovanni Battista) and others, the frescoes are notable for their depiction of Florentine life in the Renaissance. Brunelleschi's crucifix hangs above the altar in the **Cappella Gondi**, the first chapel on the left of the choir.

The cloisters (entrance on the left of the facade) feature some of the city's best frescoes. The **Chiostro Verde** (Green Cloister) is so named because green is the predominant colour of the fresco cycle by Paolo Uccello. The impressive **Cappellone degli Spagnuoli** (Spanish Chapel) contains frescoes by Andrea di Bonaiuto.

From Piazza di Santa Maria Novella, head east along Via dei Banchi and take the first street on the left, Via del Giglio. Cross Via de' Panzani and continue straight ahead until you reach Piazza Madonna degli Aldobrandini and the Basilica di San Lorenzo. The streets in this area are lined with market stalls specialising in leather goods and knitwear.

MAP 2 – FLORENCE

See Map 3 – Central Florence pp564-5

See Map 4 – Around The Cathedral p567

PLACES TO STAY

- 6 Albergo Torre di Bellosguardo
- 20 Campeggio Michelangelo
- 23 Ostello Villa Camerata & Villa Camerata Campsite

PLACES TO EAT

- 17 Osteria Antica Mescita San Niccolò
- 24 La Bottega del Gelato
- 27 Il Vegetariano

OTHER

- 1 Auditorium Flog
- 2 Museo Stibbert
- 3 Central Park
- 4 Meccanò
- 5 Teatro Comunale
- 7 Porta Romana
- 8 Isolotto
- 9 Fontana del Forcone
- 10 Forte di Belvedere
- 11 Porta San Giorgio
- 12 Museo delle Porcellane
- 13 Swiss Consulate
- 14 Chiesa di San Miniato al Monte
- 15 Chiesa di San Niccolò Oltrarno
- 16 Porta San Miniato
- 18 Porta San Niccolò
- 19 Caffè La Torre
- 21 Azione Gay e Lesbica Finisterrae
- 22 Stadio Comunale
- 25 Tourist Medical Service
- 26 Questura (Police Station)
- 28 Florence By Bike

FLORENCE – MAP 2

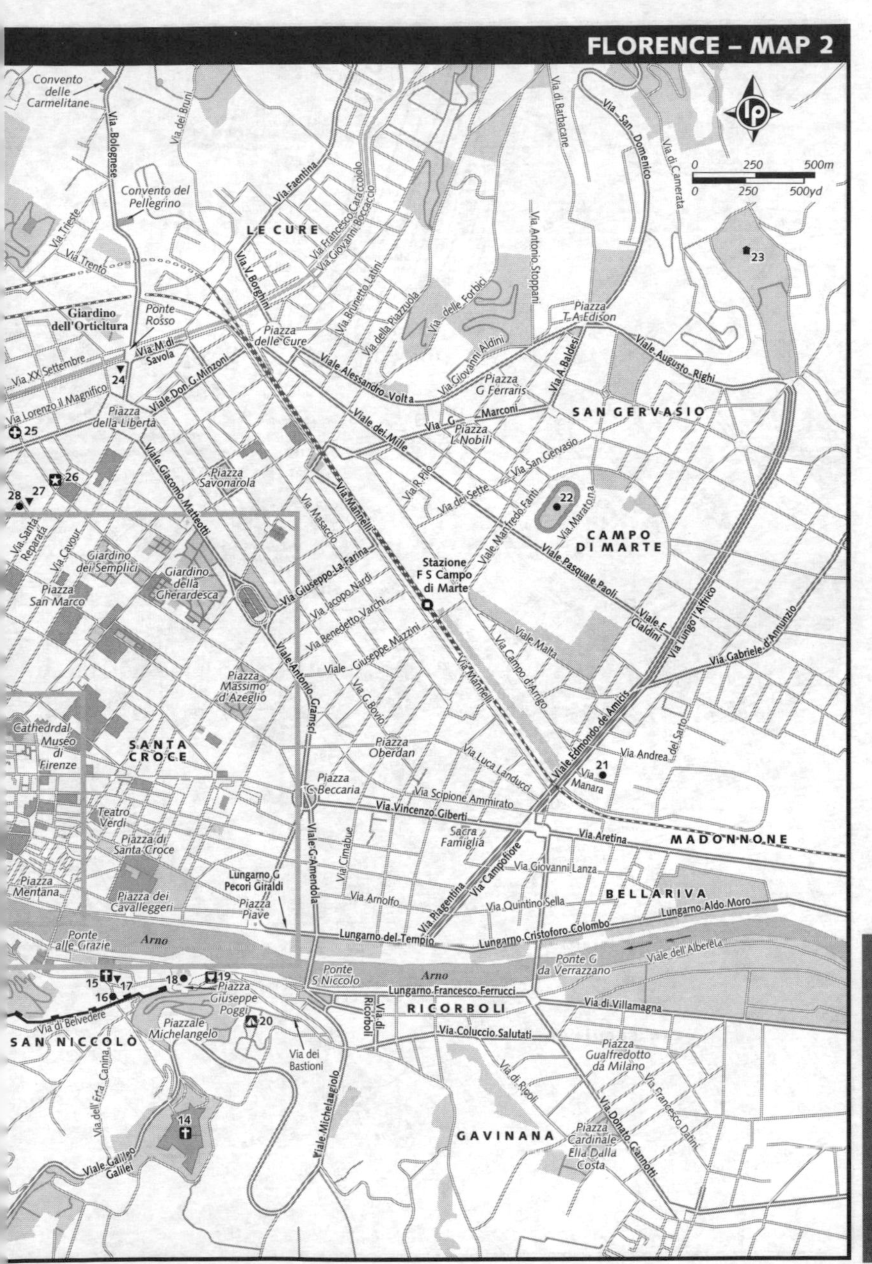

MAP 3 – CENTRAL FLORENCE

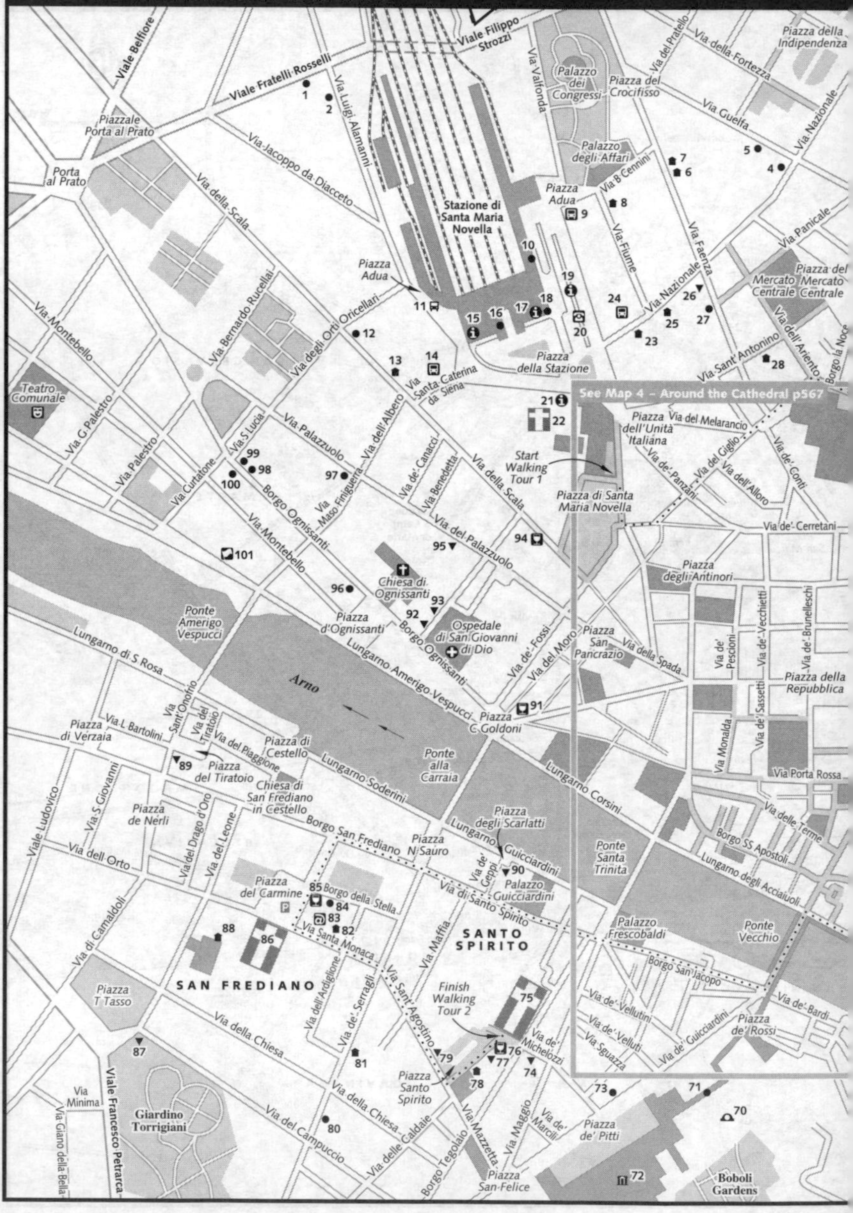

Viale Belfiore
Viale Fratelli Rosselli
Viale Filippo Strozzi
Via Luigi Alamanni
Via Valfonda
Palazzo dei Congressi
Piazza del Crocifisso
Via del Pratello
Via della Fortezza
Piazza della Indipendenza
Via Guelfa
Via Nazionale
Piazzale Porta al Prato
Porta al Prato
Via Jacoppo da Diacceto
Via della Scala
Palazzo degli Affari
Via B Cennini
Piazza Adua
Stazione di Santa Maria Novella
Via Fiume
Via Faenza
Via Panicale
Piazza del Mercato Centrale
Mercato Centrale
Via Bernardo Rucellai
Via degli Orti Oricellari
Via Montebello
Via Sant'Antonino
Via dell'Ariento
Borgo la Noce
Piazza della Stazione
Via Santa Caterina da Siena
Teatro Comunale
Via G Palestro
Via Palestro
Via S Lucia
Via Palazzuolo
Via dell'Albero
Via de' Canacci
Via Benedetta
Via della Scala
Start Walking Tour 1
Piazza di Santa Maria Novella
See Map 4 – Around the Cathedral p567
Piazza dell'Unità Italiana
Via del Melarancio
Via de' Panzani
Via del Giglio
Via dell'Alloro
Via de' Conti
Via de' Cerretani
Via Curtatone
Borgo Ognissanti
Via Maso Finiguerra
Via del Palazzuolo
Chiesa di Ognissanti
Piazza degli Antinori
Piazza d'Ognissanti
Ospedale di San Giovanni di Dio
Via de' Fossi
Via del Moro
Piazza San Pancrazio
Via della Spada
Via de' Pescioni
Via de' Vecchietti
Via de' Brunelleschi
Piazza della Repubblica
Ponte Amerigo Vespucci
Lungarno di S Rosa
Arno
Lungarno Amerigo Vespucci
Piazza C Goldoni
Via de' Sassetti
Via Monalda
Via Porta Rossa
Via Sant'Onofrio
Via del Tiratoio
Piazza di Verzaia
Via L Bartolini
Via del Piaggione
Piazza di Cestello
Piazza del Tiratoio
Lungarno Soderini
Ponte alla Carraia
Lungarno Corsini
Chiesa di San Frediano in Cestello
Via S Giovanni
Via del Drago d'Oro
Via del Leone
Piazza de Nerli
Viale Ludovico
Via dell Orto
Borgo San Frediano
Piazza N Sauro
Piazza degli Scarlatti
Lungarno Guicciardini
Via de' Geppi
Palazzo Guicciardini
Via delle Terme
Borgo SS Apostoli
Lungarno degli Acciaiuoli
Ponte Santa Trinita
Piazza del Carmine
Borgo della Stella
Via di Santo Spirito
Via Santa Monaca
Via Maffia
Santo Spirito
Palazzo Frescobaldi
Ponte Vecchio
Via di Camaldoli
San Frediano
Via dell'Ardiglione
Via de' Serragli
Via Sant'Agostino
Finish Walking Tour 2
Borgo San Jacopo
Via de' Bardi
Piazza T Tasso
Via della Chiesa
Via de' Vellutini
Via de' Velluti
Via Sguazza
Via de' Michelozzi
Via de' Guicciardini
Piazza de' Rossi
Piazza Santo Spirito
Via Minima
Viale Francesco Petrarca
Via Giano della Bella
Giardino Torrigiani
Via del Campuccio
Via delle Caldaie
Borgo Tegolaio
Via Mazzetta
Via Maggio
Via de' Marsili
Piazza de' Pitti
Piazza San Felice
Boboli Gardens

1 2 4 5 6 7 8 9 10 11 12 13 14 15 16 17 18 19 20 21 22 23 24 25 26 27 28 70 71 72 73 74 75 76 77 78 79 80 81 82 83 84 85 86 87 88 89 90 91 92 93 94 95 96 97 98 99 100 101

CENTRAL FLORENCE – MAP 3

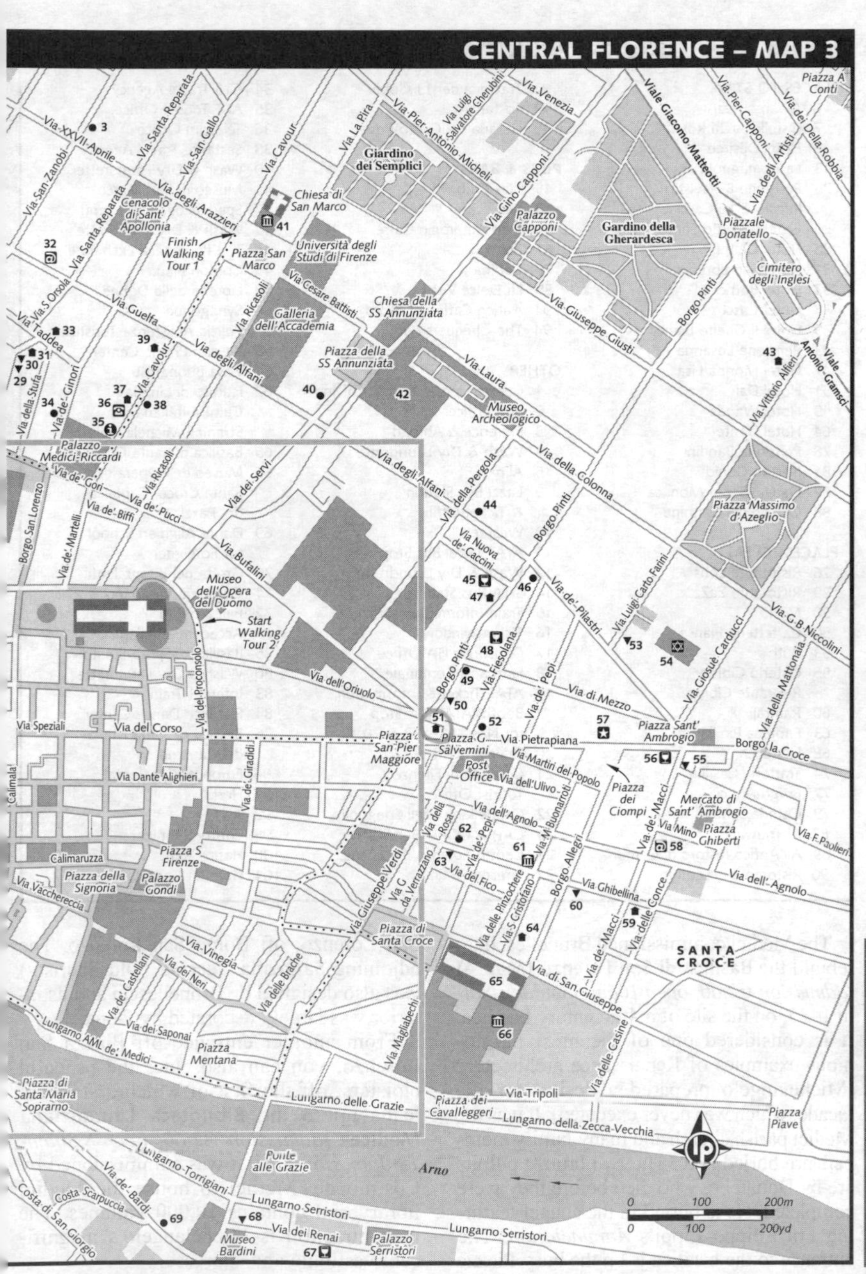
Giardino dei Semplici
Chiesa di San Marco
Cenacolo di Sant' Apollonia
Finish Walking Tour 1
Piazza San Marco
Università degli Studi di Firenze
Palazzo Capponi
Gardino della Gherardesca
Piazzale Donatello
Cimitero degli Inglesi
Galleria dell'Accademia
Chiesa della SS Annunziata
Piazza della SS Annunziata
Museo Archeologico
Palazzo Medici-Riccardi
Piazza Massimo d'Azeglio
Museo dell'Opera del Duomo
Start Walking Tour 2
Piazza San Pier Maggiore
Piazza G Salvemini
Post Office
Piazza Sant' Ambrogio
Piazza dei Ciompi
Mercato di Sant' Ambrogio
Piazza Ghiberti
Piazza S Firenze
Piazza della Signoria
Palazzo Gondi
Piazza di Santa Croce
SANTA CROCE
Piazza Mentana
Piazza di Santa Maria Soprarno
Piazza dei Cavalleggeri
Piazza Piave
Ponte alle Grazie
Arno
Museo Bardini
Palazzo Serristori
Piazza A Conti
Via XXVII Aprile
Via Santa Reparata
Via San Gallo
Via Cavour
Via La Pira
Via Pier Antonio Micheli
Via Luigi Salvatore Cherubini
Via Venezia
Viale Giacomo Matteotti
Via Pier Capponi
Via dei Della Robbia
Via degli Artisti
Via San Zanobi
Via degli Arazzieri
Via Gino Capponi
Via S Orsola
Via Ricasoli
Via Cesare Battisti
Via Guelfa
Via Taddea
Via degli Alfani
Via Giuseppe Giusti
Borgo Pinti
Viale Antonio Gramsci
Via Vittorio Alfieri
Via Laura
Via della Stufa
Via de' Ginori
Via de' Gori
Via dei Servi
Via della Pergola
Via della Colonna
Borgo San Lorenzo
Via de' Biffi
Via de' Pucci
Via de' Martelli
Via Bufalini
Via Nuova de' Caccini
Via Luigi Carlo Farini
Via Giosuè Carducci
Via de' Pilastri
Via G B Niccolini
Via della Mattonaia
Via Fiesolana
Via de' Pepi
Via dell'Oriuolo
Via del Proconsolo
Via di Mezzo
Via Speziali
Via del Corso
Via Pietrapiana
Borgo la Croce
Via Martiri del Popolo
Calimala
Via Dante Alighieri
Via de' Giraldi
Via dell'Ulivo
Via dell'Agnolo
Via M Buonarroti
Via de' Macci
Via Mino
Via F Paolieri
Calimaruzza
Via della Rosa
Via del Fico
Borgo Allegri
Via Vacchereccia
Via Giuseppe Verdi
Via G da Verrazzano
Via delle Pinzochere
Via S Cristofano
Via Ghibellina
Via delle Conce
Via Vinegia
Via dei Neri
Via de' Castellani
Via delle Brache
Via Magliabechi
Via di San Giuseppe
Via delle Casine
Via dei Saponai
Lungarno AML de' Medici
Lungarno delle Grazie
Via Tripoli
Lungarno della Zecca Vecchia
Lungarno Torrigiani
Via de' Bardi
Costa Scarpuccia
Costa di San Giorgio
Lungarno Serristori
Via dei Renai
0 100 200m
0 100 200yd

TUSCANY

MAP 3 – CENTRAL FLORENCE (FIRENZE)

PLACES TO STAY
6 Albergo Azzi
7 Ostello Archi Rossi
8 Hotel Désirée
13 La Romagnola
23 Pensione Bellavista; Pensione Le Cascine
25 Ostello Spirito Santo
28 Hotel Globus
31 Hotel San Lorenzo
33 Hotel Botticelli
37 Hotel Casci
39 Hotel Il Guelfo Bianco
43 Pensione Losanna
47 Hotel Monna Lisa
51 Hotel Dalí
59 Hotel Wanda
64 Hotel Dante
78 Pensione Bandini
81 Istituto Gould
82 Ostello Santa Monaca
88 Ostello del Carmine

PLACES TO EAT
26 Ristorante Lobs
29 Ristorante ZàZà
30 Mario
50 Caffetteria Piansa
53 Ruth's
55 Osterio Cibrèo; Risorante Cibrèo
60 Ramraj
63 Enoteca Pinchiorri
68 I Tarocchi
74 Trattoria Casalinga
77 Borgo Antico
79 Osteria Santo Spirito
87 Al Tranvai
89 All'Antico Ristoro di Cambi
90 Ristorante Beccofino
92 Trattoria dei 13 Gobbi
93 Sostanza
95 Ostaria dei Cento Poveri

PUBS & BARS
45 Jazz Club
48 Rex Caffè
56 Sant'Ambrogio Caffè
67 Zoe
76 Cabiria
85 La Dolce Vita
91 Antico Caffè del Moro
94 The Chequers Pub

OTHER
1 Centro Lingua Italiana Calvino
2 Box Office
3 Florence & Abroad
4 Wash & Dry Laundrette
5 Alinari
9 Lazzi Bus Station & Ticket Office
10 Wasteels
11 ATAF Local Bus Stop
12 Wash & Dry Laundrette
14 SITA Bus Station
15 Train Information Office
16 Ticket windows
17 Consorzio ITA Office
18 Farmacia Comunale
19 ATAF Ticket & Information Booth; ATAF Bus Stop for Nos 7, 13, 62 & 70
20 Telecom Office
21 Comune di Firenze Tourist Office
22 Cappellone degli Spagnoli
24 CAP & COPIT Bus Station
27 Centro Lorenzo de' Medici
32 Internet Train
34 CTS Travel Agency
35 APT Tourist Office
36 Telecom Office
38 Sestante Travel Agency
40 Wash & Dry Laundrette
41 Museo di San Marco
42 Spedale degli Innocenti
44 Wash & Dry Laundrette
46 The Paperback Exchange
49 Cordon Bleu
52 Libreria delle Donne
54 Synagogue
57 Polizia Assistenza Turistica
58 Il Cairo Phone Center
61 Casa Buonarroti
62 Istituto di Lingua e Cultura Italiana per Stranieri Michelangelo
65 Basilica di Santa Croce
66 Museo dell'Opera di Santa Croce; Cappella de' Pazzi
69 Dante Alighieri School for Foreigners
70 Grotta del Buontalenti
71 Corridoio Vasariano
72 Palazzo Pitti
73 Accademia Italiana
75 Basilica di Santo Spirito
80 Wash & Dry Laundrette
83 Internet Train
84 Florence Dance Center
86 Basilica di Santa Maria del Carmine
96 Europcar Car Rental
97 Hertz
98 Avis
99 Thrifty Rentacar
100 Happy Rent
101 German Consulate

The Medici commissioned Brunelleschi to rebuild the **Basilica di San Lorenzo (Map 4)** *(admission €2.60; open 10am-5pm Mon-Sat)* in 1425, on the site of a 4th-century basilica. It is considered one of the most harmonious examples of Renaissance architecture (Michelangelo prepared a design for the facade, which was never executed). It was the Medici parish church and many family members are buried here. The two bronze pulpits are by Donatello, who died before they were completed. He is buried in the chapel featuring Fra Filippo Lippi's *Annunciation*. The entrance to the basilica is on the busy Piazza San Lorenzo, off Borgo San Lorenzo. The adjoining **Sagrestia Vecchia** (Old Sacristy) was also designed by Brunelleschi and its interior was largely decorated by Donatello.

From another entrance off Piazza San Lorenzo, you can also enter the peaceful cloisters, off the first of which a staircase leads up to the **Biblioteca Laurenziana Medicea** *(admission €2.60; open 8.30am-1.30pm Mon-Sat)*. It was commissioned by Cosimo de' Medici to house the Medici library and contains 10,000 volumes. The real attraction is Michelangelo's magnificent vestibule and staircase.

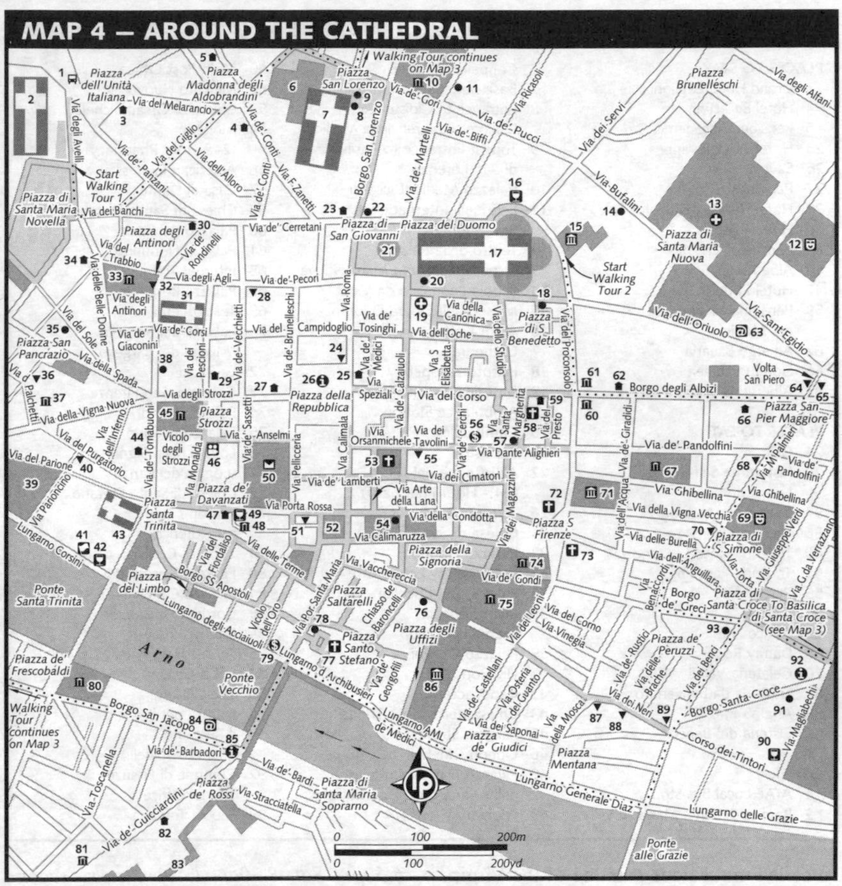

The **Cappelle Medicee (Map 4)** *(☎ 055 238 86 02; admission €5.70; open 8.15am-5pm Tues-Sun, 8.30am-1.50pm holidays)* are entered via Piazza Madonna degli Aldobrandini. The **Cappella dei Principi** (Princes' Chapel), sumptuously decorated with precious marble and semiprecious stones, was the principal burial place of the Medici rulers. The graceful and simple **Sagrestia Nuova** (New Sacristy) was Michelangelo's first architectural work. It contains his beautiful sculptures *Night and Day*, *Dawn and Dusk* and the *Madonna with Child*, which adorn the Medici tombs.

Continue from Piazza San Lorenzo, walking east along Via dei Gori to reach Via Cavour, turn left and walk until you reach Piazza San Marco (Map 3; about 450m), then turn right into Via Cesare Battisti to reach the Piazza della SS Annunziata. Here you'll find the **Chiesa della SS Annunziata** *(free; open 7.30am-12.30pm & 4pm-6.30pm daily)*. The church was established in 1250 by the founders of the Servite order and rebuilt by Michelozzo and others in the mid-15th century. It is dedicated to the Virgin Mary, and in the ornate tabernacle, to your left as you enter the church from the atrium, is a

MAP 4 – AROUND THE CATHEDRAL

PLACES TO STAY
3 Grand Hotel Baglioni
4 Hotel Bellettini
5 Pensione Accademia
23 Hotel San Giovanni
25 Savoy
27 Pendini
29 Hotel Helvetia & Bristol
30 Hotel Abaco
34 Pensione Ferretti
44 Albergo Scoti
47 Hotel Porta Rossa
59 Pensione Maria Luisa de' Medici
62 Albergo Bavaria
66 Hotel Orchidea
82 Albergo la Scaletta

PLACES TO EAT
24 Gilli
28 Ristorante Self-Service Leonardo
32 Cantinetta Antinori
36 Da il Latini
40 Trattoria Coco Lezzone
51 Trattoria Pasquini
55 Perchè No?
64 Il Nilo
65 Antico Noè
68 Danny Rock
70 Gelateria Vivoli
87 Trattoria da Benvenuto
88 Angie's Pub
89 Osteria de' Benci

OTHER
1 ATAF Local Bus Stop
2 Basilica di Santa Maria Novella
6 Cappelle Medicee
7 Basilica di San Lorenzo
8 Entrance to Cloister & Biblioteca Laurenziana Medicea
9 Tourist Entrance to Basilica di San Lorenzo
10 Palazzo Medici-Riccardi
11 Feltrinelli International Bookshop
12 Teatro della Pergola
13 Ospedale di Santa Maria Nuova
14 Scuola Leonardo da Vinci
15 Museo dell'Opera Duomo
16 Astor Caffè
17 Cathedral
18 Istituto Europeo
19 Misericordia di Firenze Ambulance Station
20 Campanile
21 Baptistry
22 All'Insegna del Moro (24 - Hour Pharmacy)
26 Tourist Help Point
31 Chiesa di San Gaetano
33 Palazzo Antinori
35 Wash & Dry Laundrette
37 Palazzo dei Rucellai
38 Internazionale Seeber Bookshop
39 Palazzo Corsini
41 UK Consulate
42 Capocaccia
43 Chiesa della Santa Trinita
45 Palazzo Strozzi
46 Odeon Cinehall
48 Palazzo Davanzati; Museo dell'Antica Casa Fiorentina
49 Loonees
50 Main Post Office
52 Mercato Nuovo
53 Chiesa di Orsanmichele
54 Molteni (24 - Hour Pharmacy)
56 American Express
57 Casa di Dante
58 Chiesa di Santa Margherita
60 Palazzo dei Pazzi
61 Palazzo Nonfinito
63 Internet Train
67 Palazzo Borghese
69 Teatro Verdi
71 Palazzo del Bargello (Museo del Bargello)
72 La Badia
73 Chiesa di San Firenze
74 Palazzo Gondi
75 Palazzo Vecchio
76 Loggia della Signoria (Loggia dei Lanzi)
77 Chiesa di Santo Stefano
78 Walking Tours of Florence
79 Thomas Cook
80 Palazzo Frescobaldi
81 Palazzo Canigiani
83 Corridoio Vasariano
84 Internet Train
85 Tourist Help Point
86 Uffizi Gallery
90 The William
91 Istituto per l'Arte e il Restauro (Palazzo Spinelli)
92 Comune di Firenze Tourist Office
93 Scuola Toscana

so-called miraculous painting of the Virgin. No longer on public view, the painting is attributed to a 14th-century friar and legend says it was completed by an angel. Also of note are frescoes by Andrea del Castagno in the first two chapels on the left of the church, a fresco by Perugino in the fifth chapel, and the frescoes in Michelozzo's atrium, particularly the *Birth of the Virgin* by Andrea del Sarto and the *Visitation* by Jacopo Pontormo.

Head back to Piazza San Marco to the now deconsecrated Dominican convent and Chiesa di San Marco, where you'll find the **Museo di San Marco (Map 3)** *(☎ 055 238 86 08, Piazza San Marco 1; admission €4.15; open 8.30am-1.50pm Tues-Fri, 8.30am-6.50pm Sat, 8.30am-1.50pm every second Mon, 8.30am-6.50pm every second Sun).* The piazza is the centre of the university area. The church was founded in 1299, rebuilt by Michelozzo in 1437 and again remodelled by Giambologna some years later. It features several paintings, but they pale in comparison to the treasures contained in the adjoining convent.

Famous Florentines who called the convent home include the painters Fra Angelico and Fra Bartolommeo, as well as Sant' Antoninus and Girolamo Savonarola (see the boxed text 'Savonarola' earlier). Fra Angelico, who painted the radiant frescoes on the convent walls, and Savonarola were of the same religious order – the latter arriving in Florence almost 30 years after the painter's death in 1455. The convent is a museum of Fra Angelico's works, many of which were moved there in the 1860s. Among the better-known works are the *Deposizione di Cristo* and the *Pala di San Marco*, an altarpiece for the church, paid for by the Medici family. The walls of the upper floor carry some true masterpieces. One of Fra Angelico's most famous works is the *Madonna delle Ombre* (Virgin of the Shadows), to the right of cell No 25.

Tour Two We start at the **Duomo** or **cathedral (Map 4)** *(Cattedrale di Santa Maria del Fiore; ☎ 055 230 28 85 for the cathedral*

Machiavelli's Manoeuvres

Born in 1469 into a poor branch of what had been one of Florence's leading families, Niccolò Machiavelli got off to a bad start. His father was a small-time lawyer whose practice had been all but strangled by the city authorities because he was a debtor.

Young Niccolò missed out on the best schools but could consider himself lucky that his father was at least rich in books. The prospects were not sparkling.

Somehow he managed to swing a post in the city's second chancery at the age of 29 and so embarked on a colourful career as a Florentine public servant. His tasks covered a range of internal dealings in Florence and some aspects of foreign affairs and defence. Our man must have shown early promise, as by 1500 he was in France on his first diplomatic mission. A couple of years later he married Marietta Corsini, with whom he would have five children in the following 12 years.

Impressed by the marshal success of Cesare Borgia and the centralised state of France, Machiavelli came to the conclusion that Florence needed a standing army. The city, like many others across the length and breadth of the Italian peninsula, had a habit of employing mercenaries to fight their wars. The problem with that system was that mercenaries had few reasons to fight and die for anyone. They took their pay and as often as not did their level best to avoid mortal combat. Machiavelli managed to convince his rulers of the advantages of a conscripted militia which he went on to form in 1506. In 1509 he got to try it out on the rebellious city of Pisa, whose fall was in large measure attributed to the troops led by the wily statesman. He was back two years later to dismantle a French-backed schismatic council there. Florence was not Rome's flavour of the month and troops from the Holy See and its allies marched on the city. Machiavelli was now defending not only his hearth but his future – to no avail.

The return to power of the Medici family was a blow for Machiavelli, who was promptly removed from all posts. Suspected of plotting against the Medici, he was even thrown into the dungeon in 1513 and tortured. He maintained his innocence and was freed, but was reduced to penury as he retired to his little property outside Florence.

It was in these years that he produced his greatest writing. *Il Principe* (The Prince) is his classic treatise on the nature of power and its administration. In it he developed his theories not only on politics and power but on history and human behaviour. What was a thoroughly demoralising time for Machiavelli was turned to good account for the generations who came after him. The work and other writings reflect the confusing and corrupt times in which he lived and a desire for strong and just rule in Florence and beyond.

He ached to get back into active public life too, but in this he was never to be truly satisfied. He was commissioned to write an official history of Florence, the *Istorie Fiorentine*, and towards the end of his life he was appointed to a defence commission to improve the city walls and join a papal army in its ultimately futile fight against imperial forces. By the time the latter had sacked Rome in 1527, Florence had again rid itself of the Medici. Machiavelli hoped that he would be restored to a position of dignity, but by now he was suspected almost as much by the Medicis' opponents as he had been years before by the Medici. He died frustrated and, as in his youth, on the brink of poverty, in 1527.

and all attached sights; free; open 10am-5pm Mon-Sat, 10am-3.30pm Thurs, 1pm-3pm Sun, closed during Mass). You will probably have already spotted Brunelleschi's sloping, brown-tiled dome but when you first come upon the cathedral from the crowded streets around the square, you will probably stop momentarily in your tracks, somewhat taken aback by the ordered vivacity of its pink, white and green marble facade (slowly but surely getting an overdue clean).

It was begun in 1296 by the Sienese architect Arnolfo di Cambio and took almost 150 years to complete. The facade was built in the 19th century in Gothic style to replace Arnolfo di Cambio's uncompleted original, which was pulled down in the 16th century. Inside, the cathedral is decorated with frescoes by Vasari and Federico Zuccari and stained-glass windows by Donatello, Andrea del Castagno, Paolo Uccello and Lorenzo Ghiberti.

The cathedral's vast interior, 155m long and 90m wide, and its sparse decoration comes as a surprise after the visually tumultuous facade. The sacristies on each side of the altar feature enamelled terracotta lunettes by Luca della Robbia over their doorways. Lorenzo de' Medici hid in the northern sacristy after his brother, Giuliano, was stabbed and killed by the Pazzi conspirators.

The two frescoes in the northern aisle commemorate the *condottieri* (mercenary leaders) Sir John Hawkwood and Niccolò da Tolentino, who fought for Florence. Paolo Uccello painted the former and Andrea del Castagno the latter. Also in the northern aisle is a painting of Dante, with a depiction of the *Divine Comedy*, by Domenico di Michelino.

A stairway near the main entrance of the cathedral leads to the **crypt** *(admission €2.60; open 10am-5pm Mon-Sat, closed during Mass)*, where excavations have unearthed parts of the 5th-century Basilica di Santa Reparata, which originally stood on the site, and Brunelleschi's tomb.

Brunelleschi won a public competition to design the enormous **dome** *(admission €5.20; open 8.30am-7pm Mon-Fri, 8.30am-5pm Sat)*, the first of its kind since antiquity. Although now severely cracked and under restoration, it remains a remarkable achievement of design. When Michelangelo went to work on St Peter's Basilica (Basilica di San Pietro), he reportedly said: 'I go to build a greater dome, but not a fairer one.' You enter from outside the cathedral.

Giotto designed and began building the graceful **campanile** *(bell tower; admission €5.20; open 8.30am-7.30pm daily Apr-Sept, 9am-5.30pm Oct, 9am-4.30pm daily Nov-Mar)* next to the cathedral in 1334, but died before it was completed. Andrea Pisano and Francesco Talenti continued the work. The first tier of bas-reliefs around the base, carved by Pisano but possibly designed by Giotto, depicts the Creation of Man and the Arts and Industries. Those on the second tier depict the planets, cardinal virtues, the arts and the seven sacraments. The sculptures of the Prophets and Sybils in the niches of the upper storeys are actually copies of works by Donatello and others – the originals are in the Museo dell'Opera del Duomo. The bell tower is 82m high. You can climb to the top but people with a heart condition should not do so.

The Romanesque **baptistry** *(battistero; admission €2.60; open noon-7pm Mon-Sat, 8.30am-2pm Sun)* may have been built as early as the 5th century on the site of a Roman temple. It is one of the oldest buildings in Florence and dedicated, as indeed many baptistries in Italy are, to St John the Baptist. Dante was among those to be baptised here. The present edifice, or at least its facade, dates from about the 11th century.

Stripes of white and green marble bedeck the octagonal structure, which is famous for its gilded bronze doors, particularly the celebrated eastern doors facing the cathedral, the *Gates of Paradise* (Porta del Paradiso) by Lorenzo Ghiberti. The bas-reliefs on its 10 panels depict scenes from the Old Testament.

The southern door, executed by Pisano and completed in 1336, is the oldest. The bas-reliefs on its 28 compartments deal predominantly with the life of St John the Baptist. The northern door is by Ghiberti, who won a public competition in 1401 to design it. The design was based on Pisano's earlier door and its main theme is also St John the Baptist. The *Gates of Paradise*, however, remain his consummate masterpiece. Most of the doors are copies – the original panels are gradually being restored and placed in the Museo dell'Opera del Duomo.

The **Museo dell'Opera del Duomo** *(Piazza del Duomo 9; admission €5.20; open 9am-7.30pm Mon-Sat, 1pm-5pm Sun)*, behind the cathedral, features mostly sculptural treasures from the cathedral. Displays include the equipment used by Brunelleschi to build the dome, as well as his death mask. Perhaps its best piece is Michelangelo's *Pietà*, which he intended for his own tomb. Vasari recorded in his *Lives of the Artists* that, dissatisfied with both the quality of the marble and of his own work, Michelangelo broke up the unfinished sculpture, destroying the arm and left leg of the figure of Christ. A student of Michelangelo later restored the arm and completed the figure of Mary Magdalene.

Five of the original 10 panels from the baptistry's *Gates of Paradise* are also on display.

The collection of sculpture is considered to be the city's second best after that in the Museo del Bargello. Note in particular Donatello's carving of the prophet Habakkuk (taken from the bell tower) and his wooden impression of Mary Magdalene.

After exploring all the cathedral has to offer, walk south from Piazza del Duomo along Via del Proconsolo and turn left into Borgo degli Albizi and the area known as Santa Croce. When you get to Piazza San Pier Maggiore turn right and walk along Via M Palmieri. Continue straight ahead and turn left into Borgo de' Greci, reaching the Franciscan **Basilica di Santa Croce (Map 3)** *(Piazza di Santa Croce; free; open 9.30am-5.30pm Mon-Sat, 3pm-5.30pm Sun Mar-Oct, 9.30am-12.30pm & 3pm-5.30pm Mon-Sat, 3pm-5.30pm Sun Nov-Feb)*. In Savonarola's day, the piazza was used for the execution of heretics, but today it is lined with souvenir shops. Attributed to Arnolfo di Cambio, Santa Croce was started in 1294 on the site of a Franciscan chapel, and the facade and bell tower were added in the 19th century. The three-nave interior of the basilica is grand but austere. The floor is paved with the tombstones of famous Florentines of the past 500 years and monuments to the particularly notable were added along the walls from the mid-16th century.

Along the southern wall (to your right as you enter the church) is Michelangelo's tomb, designed by Vasari, and also a cenotaph dedicated to Dante, who is buried in Ravenna. Farther along you will find a monument to the 18th-century dramatist and poet Vittorio Alfieri by Antonio Canova, along with a monument to Machiavelli and a bas-relief, *Annunciation*, by Donatello.

The Cappella Castellani, in the right transept, is completely covered with frescoes by Agnolo Gaddi. In the Cappella Baroncelli, at the end of the transept, frescoes by his father, Taddeo Gaddi, depict the life of the Virgin. Agnolo Gaddi also painted the frescoes above and behind the altar. Adjoining the sacristy is a corridor by Michelozzo which leads to a Medici chapel, featuring a large altarpiece by Andrea della Robbia. The Bardi and Peruzzi chapels, to the right of the chancel, are completely covered in frescoes by Giotto. In the central chapel of the northern transept (also a Bardi chapel) hangs a wooden crucifix by Donatello.

Brunelleschi designed the serene cloisters just before his death in 1446. His Cappella dei Pazzi, at the end of the first cloister, is a masterpiece of Renaissance architecture. The **Museo dell'Opera di Santa Croce** *(☎ 055 24 46 19, Piazza di Santa Croce 16; admission €4.15; open 10am-7pm Thurs-Tues Mar-Oct, 10am-6pm Thurs-Tues Nov-Feb)*, off the first cloister, features a crucifix by Cimabue, which was badly damaged during the disastrous 1966 flood, when more than 4m of water inundated the Santa Croce area. The crucifix was almost completely destroyed and lost much of its paint. It has been partially restored.

We now head for two churches in the **Oltrarno** ('Over the Arno'). Follow Via dei Benci (Map 4) south from Piazza di Santa Croce to the Arno. Either cross here at the Ponte alle Grazie or follow the river to your right to reach the Ponte Vecchio. Take

Borgo San Jacopo, on your right after you cross Ponte Vecchio, and continue along it as it becomes Via di Santo Spirito (Map 3).

Cross Via de' Serragli and take the first left to reach Piazza del Carmine and the **Basilica di Santa Maria del Carmine (Map 3)**. This 13th-century basilica was nearly destroyed by a fire in the late 18th century. Fortunately the fire spared the magnificent frescoes by Masaccio in the **Cappella Brancacci** *(☎ 055 238 21 95; admission €3.10; open 10am-4.45pm Wed-Mon, 1pm-4.45pm Sun & holidays)*. Considered the painter's finest work, the frescoes had an enormous influence on Florentine art in the 15th century. Masaccio painted them in his early 20s but interrupted the task to go to Rome, where he died aged only 28. The cycle was completed some 60 years later by Filippino Lippi. Earlier frescoes in the cycle were painted by Masolino da Panicale. The frescoes were recently restored and their vibrant colours, combined with Masaccio's vigorous style, create a strong visual impact. Masaccio's work includes *Expulsion of Adam and Eve from Paradise* and *The Tribute Money* on the upper left wall.

From here, head back towards the Ponte Vecchio, but take Via Santa Monica, which runs off the piazza. Cross Via de' Serragli and continue along Via Sant'Agostino until you come to Piazza Santo Spirito and the **Basilica di Santo Spirito (Map 3)** *(free; open 8am-noon & 4pm-6pm Mon, Tues, Thurs & Fri, 4pm-6pm Sat-Sun)*. One of Brunelleschi's last commissions, the church is beautifully planned, with a colonnade of 35 columns and a series of semicircular chapels. The chapels' works of art include a *Madonna and Saints* by Filippino Lippi in the right transept. The piazza outside has developed a somewhat bohemian feel.

Around Piazza della Signoria (Map 4)

The hub of the city's political life through the centuries and surrounded by some of its most celebrated buildings, the piazza has the appearance of an outdoor sculpture gallery. Ammannati's huge Fountain of Neptune sits beside the Palazzo Vecchio and flanking its entrance are copies of Michelangelo's *David* (the original is in the Galleria dell'Accademia) and Donatello's *Marzocco*, the heraldic Florentine lion (the original is in the Museo del Bargello). An equestrian statue of Cosimo I de' Medici by Giambologna stands towards the centre of the piazza. A bronze plaque marks the spot where Savonarola was hanged and burned at the stake in 1498.

The **Loggia della Signoria** was built in the late 14th century as a platform for public ceremonies and eventually became a showcase for sculptures. To the left of the steps is Benvenuto Cellini's magnificent statue of Perseus holding the head of Medusa. To the right is Giambologna's Mannerist *Rape of the Sabine Women*, his final work (now being restored).

Nearby is the **Palazzo Vecchio** *(☎ 055 276 82 24, Piazza della Signoria; admission €6.20; open 9am-11pm Mon & Fri, 9am-7pm Tues, Wed & Sat, 9am-2pm Thurs, Sun & holidays mid-Jun–mid-Sep, 9am-7pm Mon-Wed & Fri, 9am-2pm Thurs, Sun & holidays the rest of the year)*. It was built by Arnolfo di Cambio between 1298 and 1314 and is the traditional seat of the Florentine government. Its **Torre d'Arnolfo** is 94m high and, with its striking crenellations, is as much a symbol of the city as the cathedral.

Created for the Signoria, the highest level of Florentine republican government, Palazzo Vecchio became Cosimo I de' Medici's palace in the mid-16th century, before he moved to the Palazzo Pitti. The Medici commissioned Vasari to reorganise the interior and create a series of sumptuous rooms. Upstairs from Michelozzo's beautiful courtyard, just inside the entrance, are some lavishly decorated apartments. The **Salone dei Cinquecento** was the meeting room of the 'parliament' during Savonarola's time. It was later used for banquets and festivities and features frescoes by Vasari and Michelangelo's *Genio della Vittoria* (Genius of Victory) statue, originally destined for Rome and Pope Julius II's tomb.

Vasari designed the **studiolo** (Francesco I's study) and several Florentine Mannerist artists decorated it. Farther on is the **Cappella dei Gigli**, decorated by Domenico

Ghirlandaio in 1514. You can climb to the battlements that crown the building for fine views across the city.

Uffizi Gallery (Galleria degli Uffizi; Map 4)

Designed and built by Vasari in the second half of the 16th century at the request of Cosimo I de' Medici, the Palazzo degli Uffizi, south of the Palazzo Vecchio, originally housed the city's administrators, judiciary and guilds. It was, in effect, a government office building *(uffizi* means offices).

Vasari also designed the private corridor that links the Palazzo Vecchio and the Palazzo Pitti (Map 3), through the Uffizi and across the Ponte Vecchio. Known as the Corridoio Vasariano, it was long closed to the public but can now be visited occasionally (see Corridoio Vasariano later in the chapter).

Cosimo's successor, Francesco I, commissioned the architect Buontalenti to modify the upper floor of the Palazzo degli Uffizi to house the Medicis' growing art collection. Thus, indirectly, the first steps were taken to turn it into an art gallery.

The Uffizi Gallery houses the family's private collection, bequeathed to Florence in 1743 by the last of the Medici family, Anna Maria Ludovica, on condition that it never leave the city. It is by no means the biggest art gallery around (this is no Louvre) but the Uffizi still houses the world's single greatest collection of Italian and Florentine art.

Sadly, several of its artworks were destroyed and others badly damaged when a car bomb planted by the Mafia exploded outside the gallery's west wing in May 1993. Documents cataloguing the collection were also destroyed.

Partly in response to the bombing, but even more to the gallery's immense popularity (a staggering 1.5 million visitors marched through in 1998, compared with 100,000 in 1950!), restoration and reorganisation will lead to what promoters refer to as the 'Nuovi Uffizi'. The floors below the present gallery have been largely cleared of state archives and, in a project estimated to cost about €57 million, it is hoped to have a much bigger and modernised gallery open by the end of 2004.

The gallery as it stands now is arranged to illustrate the evolving story of Italian and, in particular, Florentine art.

Given the crowds (you can easily find yourself queuing for up to four hours to get to the ticket window), you should consider booking ahead (see the boxed text 'Queue Jumping' earlier in this chapter).

The Gallery Before heading upstairs to the gallery *(☎ 055 238 86 51, Piazza degli Uffizi 6; admission €7.75; open 8.15am-6.50pm Tues-Sun mid-Sept–mid-June, 8.15am-6.50pm Tues-Fri & Sun, 8.15am-10pm Sat mid-June–mid-Sept, ticket office closes 55 mins before gallery)*, visit the restored remains of the 11th-century **Chiesa di San Piero Scheraggio**. The church's apse was incorporated into the structure of the palace but most of the rest of it was destroyed. At the time of writing it was closed, but you can get a fractional idea of the place from what remains on the exterior of the northern wall of the palace.

Upstairs in the gallery proper, the first accessible rooms feature works by Tuscan masters of the 13th and early 14th centuries. Room 2 is dominated by three paintings of the *Madonna in Maestà* by Duccio di Buoninsegna, Cimabue and Giotto. All three were altarpieces in Florentine churches before being placed in the gallery. To look at them in this order is to appreciate the transition from Gothic to the precursor of the Renaissance. Also in the room is Giotto's polyptych *Madonna col Bambino Gesù, Santi e Angeli* (Madonna with Baby Jesus, Saints and Angels).

Room 3 traces the Sienese school of the 14th century. Of particular note is Simone Martini's shimmering *Annunciazione* (Annunciation), considered a masterpiece of the school.

Room 7 features works by painters of the early-15th-century Florentine school, which pioneered the Renaissance. There is one panel (the other two are in Paris' Louvre and London's National Gallery) from Paolo Uccello's striking *La Battaglia di San Romano* (Battle of San Romano). In his efforts to create perspective he directs the lances, horses and soldiers to a central disappearing point. Other works include Piero della Francesca's portraits of *Battista Sforza* and *Federico da Montefeltro*.

Room 9 is devoted largely to Antonio de Pollaiuolo. His series of six virtues is followed by an addition (*Fortezza* – Strength) by Botticelli. The clarity of line and light, and the humanity in the face, set it apart from Pollaiuolo's work and it is a taster for the Botticelli Rooms, Nos 10 to 14 – considered the gallery's most spectacular. Highlights are the *La Nascita di Venere* (Birth of Venus) and *Allegoria della Primavera* (Allegory of Spring). *Calunnia* (Calumny) is a disturbing reflection of Botticelli's loss of faith in human potential that came in later life.

Room 15 features Da Vinci's *Annunciazione*, painted when he was a student of Verrocchio. Perhaps more intriguing is his unfinished *Adorazione dei Magi* (now being restored). Room 16 (blocked off, although you can peer in) contained old maps. Room 17, the Sala dell'Ermafrodito, is closed.

Room 18, known as the Tribuna, houses the celebrated *Medici Venus*, a 1st-century-BC copy of a 4th-century-BC sculpture by the Greek sculptor, Praxiteles. The room also contains portraits of various members of the Medici family.

The great Umbrian painter Perugino, who studied under Piero della Francesca and later became Raphael's master, is represented in Room 19, as is Luca Signorelli. Piero di Cosimo's *Perseo Libera Andromeda* is full of fantastical whimsy with beasts and flying heroes. Room 20 features works from the German Renaissance, including Dürer's *Adorazione dei Magi*. His depictions of Adam and Eve are mirrored by those of Lucas Cranach. Room 21, with a heavily Venetian leaning, has works by Giovanni Bellini and his pupil Giorgione, along with a few by Vittorio Carpaccio.

The star of Room 25 is Michelangelo's dazzling *Tondo Doni*, which depicts the Holy Family. The composition is highly unusual, with Joseph holding Jesus on Mary's shoulder as she twists around to watch him. The colours are so vibrant, the lines so clear, it seems almost photographic. This masterpiece of the High Renaissance leaps out at you as you enter, demanding attention.

In the next room are works by Raphael, including his *Leo X* and *Madonna del Cardellino* (actually a copy as the original is being restored). The former is remarkable for the richness of colour (especially the reds) and detail. Also on display are some works by Andrea del Sarto. Room 27 is dominated by the sometimes disquieting works of Florence's two main Mannerist masters, Pontormo and Rosso Fiorentino.

Room 28 boasts eight Titians, including *Venere d'Urbino* (Venus of Urbino). His presence signals a shift in the weighting to representatives of the Venetian school. Rooms 29 and 30 contain works by comparatively minor painters from northern Italy, but Room 31 is dominated above all by Venice's Paolo Veronese, including his *Sacra Famiglia e Santa Barbara* (Holy Family and St Barbara). In Room 32 it is Tintoretto's turn.

Room 35 comes as a bit of a shock as you are confronted with the enormous and sumptuous canvases of Federico Barocci (1535–1612) of Urbino. Rooms 36 to 37 are part of the exit while the adjoining Room 38 at the moment houses the extraordinary restored *Annunciazione* by Siena's Simone Martini and Lippo Memmi.

For some reason the counting starts at No 41 after this. This room is given over mostly to non-Italian masters such as Rubens, van Dyck and Spain's Diego Velázquez. There are two enormous tableaux by Rubens, sweeping with violence and power, representing the French King Henri IV at the Battle of Ivry and his triumphal march into Paris. The beautifully designed Room 42 (closed at the time of writing), with its exquisite coffered ceiling and splendid dome, is filled with Roman statues.

Caravaggio dominates Room 43 with his play of light and shade (look for *Il Sacrificio d'Isacco*), while Rembrandt features in Room 44. Room 45 takes us back to Venice, with 18th-century works by Canaletto, Guardi, Tiepolo, Crespi and the two Longhi, along with a couple of stray pieces by the Spaniard Goya.

Between Rooms 25 and 34 is an entrance (usually closed) that leads down a staircase into the Corridoio Vasariano.

Corridoio Vasariano (Maps 3 & 4)

When Cosimo I de' Medici's wife bought the Palazzo Pitti and the family moved into their new digs, they wanted to maintain their link – literally – with what from now on would be known as the Palazzo Vecchio. And so Cosimo commissioned Vasari to build an enclosed walkway between the two palaces that would allow the Medicis to wander between the two without having to deal with the public.

The corridor is lined with phalanxes of largely minor art works and has changed considerably over the years. Its present aspect dates to 1923 but it is possible that many of the paintings hung here will be moved to the Nuovi Uffizi (see Uffizi Gallery earlier).

Be that as it may, the corridor was opened to the public in a rather limited fashion in 1999. Let's say right away that, given the difficulty and cost of getting in here, many visitors are likely to be disappointed. To appreciate it at all you will want to have a genuine interest in Florentine history and/or a hunger for relatively obscure art.

You can either join a long (2½-hour) tour *(bookings ☎ 055 265 43 21; €25.80)* that takes in part of the Palazzo Vecchio at the prebooked ticket desk in the Uffizi or a better option for most might be to turn up at 3pm on Wednesdays and Fridays for unguided (but accompanied) visits. For this you buy special tickets for the Uffizi that include the corridor (€9.30). At the appointed time, those with tickets (advisable to book well ahead as only limited numbers may enter) are ushered into the corridor from the Uffizi gallery, where a custodian keeps an eye on visitors as they wander around before returning to the Uffizi.

Around Ponte Santa Trinita

West from the Uffizi is the Ponte Santa Trinita (Map 4), rebuilt after being destroyed by Nazi bombing. Michelangelo is believed to have drawn the original plan but Ammannati built the bridge. North of here is **Via de' Tornabuoni (Map 4)**, one of the city's most fashionable streets, lined with Renaissance mansions and high-class shops including Ferragamo, Gucci and Armani.

The 13th-century **Chiesa di Santa Trinita (Map 4)** *(Piazza Santa Trinita)* features several significant works, including frescoes depicting the life of St Francis of Assisi by Domenico Ghirlandaio in the Cappella Sassetti (in the right transept). The altarpiece of the Annunciation in the fourth chapel of the southern aisle is by Lorenzo Monaco, who was Fra Angelico's master. Monaco also painted the frescoes on the chapel walls.

To the west, the **Palazzo Davanzati (Map 4)** *(Via Porta Rossa 13; closed for restoration at time of writing)* is a well-preserved 14th-century mansion. An antiquarian, Elia Volpi, bought the building in 1904 and had it restored to its former glory. It became the seat of the Museo dell'Antica Casa Fiorentina, which aims to transmit an idea of what life was like in a medieval Florentine mansion. Just past the palace is the **Mercato Nuovo (Map 4)**, a *loggia* (open gallery) built in the mid-16th century to house the city's gold and silver trade, which today is home to souvenir stalls and the leather crowd.

Return to Via de' Tornabuoni and head north for the **Palazzo Strozzi (Map 4)**, one of the most impressive Renaissance palazzos in Florence. Although never completed, the three finished facades in heavy rusticated stone (bulging stone blocks), designed by Benedetto da Maiano, are magnificent. Inside is a grand if somewhat gloomy courtyard. The palazzo is today used for art exhibitions. The beautiful **Palazzo dei Rucellai (Map 4)** *(Via della Vigna Nuova)*, designed by Alberti, is on Via della Vigna Nuova, which branches off to the south-west.

North-west from Ponte Santa Trinita is the 13th-century **Chiesa di Ognissanti (Map 3)** *(open 5pm-7.30pm Mon, Tues & Sat)*. The church was much altered in the 17th century and has a Baroque facade but inside are 15th-century works by Domenico Ghirlandaio and Botticelli. Of interest is Ghirlandaio's fresco above the second altar on the right of the Madonna della Misericordia, protector of the Vespucci family. Amerigo Vespucci, who gave his name to the American continent, is supposed to be the young boy whose head appears between the Madonna and the old man. Ghirlandaio's masterpiece, *Last Supper*, covers most of a wall in the former monastery's refectory.

South of the Cathedral (Map 4)

Take Via de' Calzaiuoli from Piazza del Duomo to reach the **Chiesa di Orsanmichele** *(Via Arte della Lana; free; open 9am-noon & 4pm-6pm, except 1st & last Mon of month)*. Originally a grain market, the church was formed in the 14th century when the arcades of the market building were walled in. Statues of the city guilds' patron saints adorn the exterior. They were commissioned over 200 years and represent the work of many Renaissance artists. Some of the statues are now in the Museo del Bargello but many splendid pieces remain, including *John the Baptist* by Lorenzo Ghiberti and a copy of Donatello's *St George*. The main feature of the interior is the splendid Gothic tabernacle, decorated with coloured marble, by Andrea Orcagna.

North-west is the **Piazza della Repubblica (Map 4)**. Originally the site of a Roman forum, the square was carved out of what had been the heart of the medieval city in the late 19th century. It is now home to Florence's most fashionable and expensive cafes.

If you head east from the piazza and turn left into Via Santa Margherita, you'll find **Casa di Dante** *(☎ 055 21 94 16, Via Santa Margherita 1; admission €2.60; open 10am-6pm Wed-Sat & Mon & 10am-2pm Sun & holidays May-Sept; 10am-4pm Wed-Sat & Mon & 10am-2pm Sun & holidays Oct-Apr)*, which has a small museum tracing Dante's life. Continuing east on Via del Corso will bring you to **Palazzo dei Pazzi**, which is attributed to Brunelleschi and now houses offices. You can wander into the courtyard.

Also known as the Palazzo del Podestà, the **Palazzo del Bargello**, built in 1254, was originally the residence of the chief magistrate after which it became a police station. During its days as a police complex, many people were tortured near the well in the centre of the medieval courtyard. It now houses the **Museo del Bargello** *(☎ 055 238 86 06, Via del Proconsolo 4; admission €4.15; open 8.30am-1.50pm Tues-Sat, also alternating Sun & Mon)* and the most comprehensive collection of Tuscan Renaissance sculpture in Italy. The museum is not to be missed.

Several works by Michelangelo grace the ground floor, notably his drunken *Bacchus* (executed when the artist was aged 22), a marble bust of *Brutus* and a tondo of the *Madonna and Child* with the infant St John. Other works of particular interest are Benvenuto Cellini's rather camp marble *Ganimede* (Ganymede) and *Narciso* (Narcissus), along with Giambologna's *Mercurio Volante* (Winged Mercury). Don't miss Donatello's stunning bronze *David* on the 1st floor, the first free-standing sculpture since antiquity to depict a fully nude man. Among the many other works by Donatello are *San Giorgio* (St George), removed from the facade of the Chiesa di Orsanmichele and replaced with a copy, and the *Marzocco*, which once stood in the Piazza della Signoria and was also replaced with a copy.

Opposite the Palazzo Bargello, **La Badia** *(Via del Proconsolo; open 3pm-6pm Mon)*, built in the 10th century, was the church of a Benedictine monastery. It is worth a visit to see Filippino Lippi's *Appearance of the Virgin to St Bernard*, to the left of the entrance through the Renaissance cloister.

Around Piazza della SS Annunziata

For some it is Florence's most beautiful square. In the university district, the piazza is usually filled with students rather than tourists. Giambologna's equestrian statue of Grand Duke Ferdinando I de' Medici commands the scene. On the south-eastern side of the piazza, **Spedale degli Innocenti (Map 3)** *(☎ 055 249 17 08, Piazza della SS Annunziata 12; admission €2.60; open 8.30am-2pm Thurs-Tues)*, was founded in 1421 as Europe's first orphanage (hence the 'innocents'). Brunelleschi designed the portico, which Andrea della Robbia decorated with terracotta medallions of babies in

JOHN HAY

Michelangelo's *David* could tackle any Goliath.

STAEVEN VALLAK

Giotto designed his intricate bell tower in 1334.

JULIET COOMBE

Statue outside the Basilica di Santo Spirito, Florence

JULIET COOMBE

The modern face of art outside the Pitti Palace

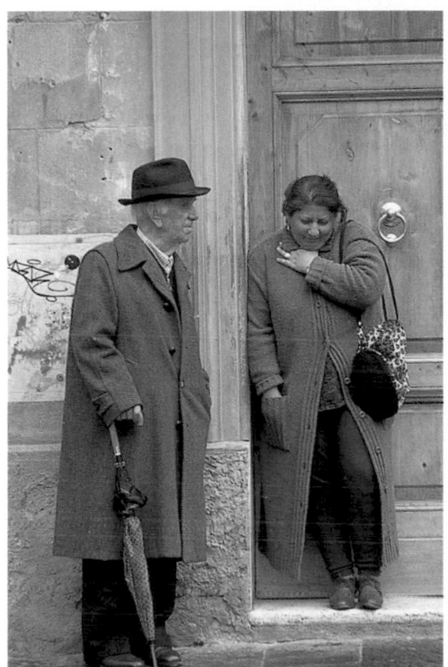

DOUG MCKINLAY

Catching up on the latest gossip in Florence

BETHUNE CARMICHAEL

Siena, one of Italy's most enchanting cities

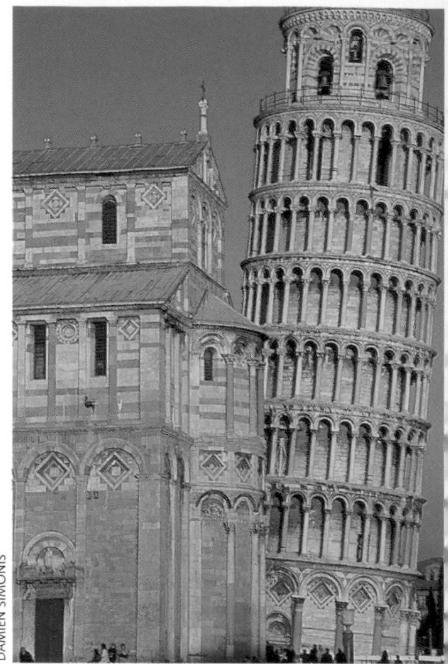
DAMIEN SIMONIS

That building on the right looks wonky...

ALAN BENSON

Visit Norcia for some seriously superior salami.

DAMIEN SIMONIS

Orvieto's cathedral boasts an unusual facade.

DAMIEN SIMONIS

Waiting for the local wine shop to open, Orvieto

swaddling clothes. To the left of the entrance is the small revolving door where unwanted children were left. A good number of people in Florence with surnames such as degli Innocenti, Innocenti and Nocentini can trace their family tree only as far back as the orphanage. A small gallery inside features works by Florentine artists, including Luca della Robbia and Domenico Ghirlandaio. The most striking is Ghirlandaio's *Adorazione dei Magi* at the right end of the hall.

About 200m south-east of the piazza is the **Museo Archeologico (Map 3)** *(☎ 055 2 35 75, Via Colonna 38; admission €4.15; open 2pm-7pm Mon, 8.30am-7pm Tues & Thurs, 8.30am-2pm Wed & Fri-Sun)*. This houses a surprisingly rich collection of finds, including most of the Medici hoard of antiquities. On the 1st floor you can either head left into the ancient Egyptian collection or right into the section on Etruscan and Greco-Roman art.

The former is an impressive collection of sculpture, tablets inscribed with hieroglyphics, various coffins and a remarkable array of everyday objects whose life span has been extraordinary. In the Etruscan section you first pass through two rooms dominated by funeral urns. Particularly noteworthy is the marble *Sarcofago delle Amazzoni* (Amazons' Sarcophagos) from Tarquinia and the alabaster *Sarcofago dell'Obeso* (Sarcophagos of the Fat Man) from Chiusi. Moving on, you come into a hall dedicated to bronze sculptures, ranging from miniatures depicting mythical beasts to the life-size *Arringatore* (Orator).

No tour of Florence is complete without a visit to the **Galleria dell'Accademia (Map 3)** *(☎ 055 238 86 09, Via Ricasoli 60; admission €7.75; open 8.15am-6.50pm Tues-Sun mid-Sept–mid-June, 8.15am-6.50pm Tues-Fri & Sun & 8.15am-10pm Sat mid-June–mid-Sept)*. It houses paintings by Florentine artists spanning the 13th to 16th centuries, but its main draw is Michelangelo's David, carved from a single block of marble when the artist was aged only 29. Originally in the Piazza della Signoria, the colossal statue now stands in an alcove at the end of the main hall on the ground floor.

Heading back towards the cathedral, you will find the extraordinary **Palazzo Medici-Riccardi (Maps 3 & 4)** *(☎ 055 276 03 40, Via Cavour 3; admission €4.15; open 9am-7pm Thurs-Tues)*, just off Piazza San Lorenzo. It is typical of the Florentine Renaissance style and was started by Michelozzo for Cosimo de' Medici in 1444. It served as the Medici residence from 1459 to 1540 and was a prototype for other buildings in the city, such as the Palazzo Pitti. The Riccardi family remodelled it in the 17th century.The chapel upstairs has beautiful frescoes by Benozzo Gozzoli, with regal scenes featuring members of the Medici clan, which are the main attraction here. The Riccardis built the sumptuously decorated Sala di Luca Giordano.

Casa Buonarroti (Map 3)

Michelangelo owned this house *(Via Ghibellina 70; admission €6.20; open 9.30am-1.30pm Wed-Mon)* but never lived in it. Upon his death, the house went to his nephew and eventually became a museum in the mid-1850s. The collection of memorabilia mostly comprises copies of Michelangelo's works and portraits of the master.

To the right of the ticket window is a small archaeological display made up of objects, including some interesting Etruscan pieces, collected by the Buonarroti family down the years. Beyond this room are some paintings done in imitation of Michelangelo's style, along with some fine glazed terracotta pieces by the della Robbia family.

Upstairs you can admire a detailed model of Michelangelo's design for the facade of the Basilica di San Lorenzo – as close as the church came to getting one. There are also a couple of marble bas-reliefs and a crucifix by Michelangelo. Of the reliefs, *Madonna della Scala* (Madonna of the Steps) is thought to be his earliest work.

The Oltrarno

Literally 'Beyond the Arno', the Oltrarno encompasses the part of the city that lies south of the river.

Ponte Vecchio (Map 4) The 14th-century structure has been draped in the glittering wares of jewellery merchants since the time Ferdinando I de' Medici ordered them here to replace the rather malodorous presence of the town butchers who tended to jettison unwanted leftovers into the river. The views of and from the only bridge to survive Nazi explosives in 1944 are every bit as beguiling as you might expect.

Palazzo Pitti (Map 3) Begun in 1458 for the Pitti family, rivals of the Medici, the original nucleus of the palace *(☎ 055 238 86 14)* took up the space encompassing the seven sets of windows on the 2nd and 3rd storeys. Ironically, Cosimo I de' Medici and Eleonora de Toledo acquired the palace in 1549. It remained the official residence of Florence's rulers until 1919, when the Savoy royal family handed it over to the state. Admission to the palace and all galleries and museums *(biglietto cumulativo)* costs €10.35 (€7.75 after 4pm). You can enter them separately; individual prices are included below.

The palace houses five museums. The **Galleria Palatina** *(Palatine Gallery; admission €6.20 including Appartamenti Reali; open 8.15am-6.50pm Tues-Sun)* houses paintings from the 16th to 18th centuries, hung in lavishly decorated rooms. The works were collected mostly by the Medici and their grand ducal successors.

After getting your ticket, you head up a grand staircase to the gallery floor. The first rooms you pass through are a seemingly haphazard mix of sculpture, period furniture and the odd painting.

The gallery proper starts after the **Sala della Musica** (Music Room). The paintings hanging in the succeeding rooms are not in any particular order. Among Tuscan masters you can see work by Fra Filippo Lippi, Sandro Botticelli, Giorgio Vasari and Andrea del Sarto (who is represented in just about every room!). The collection also boasts some important works by other Italian and foreign painters. Foremost among them are those by Raphael, especially in the **Sala di Saturno** (partly under restoration – some of the Raphael paintings were therefore temporarily moved to the Appartamenti Reali). A close second is Titian (especially in the **Sala di Marte**), one of the greatest of the Venetian school. Other important artists represented include Tintoretto, Paolo Veronese, Jose Ribera, Bravo Murillo, Peter Paul Rubens and van Dyck. Caravaggio is represented with the striking *Amore Dormiente* (Love Sleeping) in the **Sala dell'Educazione di Giove**.

From the gallery you can pass into the **Appartamenti Reali**, a series of rather sickeningly furnished and decorated rooms, where the Medici and their successors slept, received guests and generally hung about. The style and division of tasks assigned to each room is reminiscent of Spanish royal palaces, all heavily bedecked with curtains, silk, chandeliers and so on. Each room has a colour theme, ranging from aqua green to deep wine red to dusty mellow yellow.

The other galleries are worth a look if you have plenty of time. The **Galleria d'Arte Moderna** *(Modern Art Gallery; admission €4.15; open 8.15am-1.50pm Tues-Sat, also alternating Sun & Mon)* covers mostly Tuscan works from the 18th to the mid-20th century. The **Museo degli Argenti** *(Silver Museum; admission €2.10; open 8.15am-1.50pm Tues-Sat, also alternating Sun & Mon)*, entered from the garden courtyard, has a collection of glassware, silver and semi-precious stones from the Medici collections. The **Galleria del Costume** *(Costume Gallery; admission €4.15, open 8.30am-1.50pm Tues-Sat, also alternating Sun & Mon)* has high-class clothing from the 18th and 19th centuries, while the **Museo delle Carrozze** *(closed)* contains ducal coaches and the like.

Boboli Gardens (Map 2) Take a break in the palace's Renaissance Boboli Gardens *(Giardino di Boboli; admission €2.10 including Museo delle Porcellane; open 8.15am-8pm daily June-Aug; 8.15am-7pm daily Apr-May & Sept; 8.15am-6pm daily Mar & Oct, 8.15am-5pm daily Nov-Feb)*, which were laid out in the mid-16th century and based on a design by the architect known as Il Tribolo. Buontalenti's noted artificial grotto (Grotta del Buontalenti; Map 3), with a *Venere* (Venus) by Giambologna, is curious. In June, concerts of classical music are sometimes held in the gardens.

Situated inside the garden is the **Museo delle Porcellane (Map 2)** *(closed for renovation at time of writing)*, which houses a varied collection of the fine porcelain gathered over the centuries by the illustrious tenants of Palazzo Pitti, from Cosimo I de' Medici and Eleonora de Toledo onwards. The exhibits include some exquisite Sèvres and Vincennes pieces.

Forte di Belvedere & Piazzale Michelangelo (Map 2)

From the gardens you can reach the Forte di Belvedere *(closed at the time of writing)*. The rambling fortifications were built by Grand Duke Ferdinando I towards the end of the 16th century. From this massive bulwark soldiers could keep watch on four fronts, and indeed it was designed with internal security in mind as much as foreign attack. Set high on a hill, the views across the city are fine.

The walk east along Via di Belvedere and the city walls is a pleasant one and brings you to Piazzale Michelangelo. Where the road changes name to Via dei Bastioni and runs into the tangle of streets and stairs above Porta San Niccolò, follow the stairs up towards the piazzale. The views here are also rewarding and you'll find a couple of places to sit down and have a drink or snack.

Chiesa di San Miniato al Monte (Map 2)

Behind Piazzale Michelangelo, this austere church *(open 8am-7pm daily May-Oct, 8am-12.30pm & 2.30pm-7.30pm daily Nov-Apr)* with its green-and-white marble facade is one of the best examples of the Tuscan Romanesque style. The church was started in the early 11th century and the facade features a mosaic depicting Christ between the Virgin and San Miniato added 200 years later.

Inside you will see 13th- to 15th-century frescoes on the right wall, intricate inlaid marble designs down the length of the nave and a fine Romanesque crypt at the back, below the unusual raised presbytery *(presbiterio)*. The latter boasts a fine marble pulpit replete with intriguing geometrical designs. The sacristy *(sagrestia)*, to the right of the church (they suggest you donate €0.50 to get in), features marvellously bright frescoes. The four figures in the cross vault are the Evangelists.

The Cappella del Cardinale del Portogallo, to the left side of the church, features a tomb by Antonio Rossellino and a ceiling decorated in terracotta by Luca della Robbia. It is possible to wander through the cemetery outside. Some of Michelangelo's battlements remain standing around here too.

Bus No 13 stops nearby.

Certosa del Galluzzo (Map 1)

From Porta Romana (Map 2) at the southern tip of the Oltrarno area, follow Via Senese south about 3km to the village of Galluzzo, which is home to a quite remarkable 14th-century monastery, the Certosa del Galluzzo *(☎ 055 204 92 26; admission by donation; open 9am-noon & 3pm-6pm Tues-Sun May-Oct, 9am-noon & 3pm-5pm Tues-Sun Nov-Apr)*. The Carthusian order of monks once had 50 monasteries in Italy. Of these, only two are now inhabited by monks of that order. The Certosa di Galluzzo passed into Cistercian hands in 1955.

The Certosa can only be visited with a guide (reckon on about 45 minutes). You will first be taken to the Gothic hall of the **Palazzo degli Studi**, now graced by a small collection of art, including five somewhat weathered frescoes by Pontormo. The **Basilica di San Lorenzo**, with 14th-century origins, has a Renaissance exterior. To one side of it is the **Colloquio**, a narrow hall with benches. Here the Carthusian monks were permitted to break their vow of silence once a week, though they got a second chance on Mondays when allowed to leave the monastery grounds for a gentle stroll. You end up in the **Chiostro Grande**, the biggest of the complex's three cloisters. It is flanked by 18 monks' cells and decorated with busts from the della Robbia workshop.

You can take bus No 37 from Stazione di Santa Maria Novella if walking doesn't appeal.

Cycling

At ***Alinari*** **(Map 3)** *(☎ 055 28 05 00, Via Guelfa 85r)*, you can rent a bicycle for

€6.20 for five hours, €10.35 per day or €18.10 per weekend. A mountain bike costs €10.35 for five hours, €15.50 per day or €28.40 for a weekend.

Florence by Bike **(Map 2)** *(☎ 055 48 89 92, W www.florencebybike.it, Via San Zanobi 120/122r)* proposes one half-day city tour by bike (€24.30) and three-day tours, one around the hills near Florence and two separate Chianti tours (each costs €50). You can also hire anything from a standard bicycle for getting around town (up to €10.35 per day) to a scooter (€62 per day).

Florence for Children

The tourist offices have information about child daycare services, courses and special activities for kids (organised for local kids, not tourists, so seek advice on those most suitable for your children). These options might come in handy if you are planning a few days of hectic sightseeing and your children are 'museumed-out'.

There is a small playground in Piazza Massimo d'Azeglio (Map 3), about five to 10 minutes' walk east of the cathedral. Beside the River Arno, about 15 minutes' walk to the west of Stazione di Santa Maria Novella, is a massive public park called Parco delle Cascine (Map 2).

Older children might find the **Museo Stibbert (Map 2)** *(☎ 055 47 55 20, Via Federico Stibbert 26; admission €4.15; open 10am-2pm Mon-Wed, 10am-6pm Fri-Sun)* entertaining. Eye-opening are the life-size figures of horses and their soldierly riders in all manner of suits of armour from Europe and the Middle East. The exhibits also include clothes, furnishings, tapestries and paintings from the 16th to the 19th centuries.

Courses

Florence has more than 30 schools offering courses in Italian language and culture. Numerous other schools offer courses in art, including painting, drawing, sculpture and art history, and several offer cooking courses.

Florence's APT office also has lists of schools and courses, which it will mail on request. You can write in English to individual schools to request information and enrolment forms – letters should be addressed to the *segretaria* (secretary).

Language Courses The cost of language courses in Florence depends on the school, the length of the course (one month is usually the minimum duration) and its intensity. Local authorities sometimes run irregular courses, generally for free and aimed at impecunious migrants, for a couple of hours every week. The APT in Via Cavour has long lists of schools running language courses. The following are among them.

Istituto Europeo *(☎ 055 238 10 71, Piazzale delle Pallottole 1, 50122)* **Map 4** Courses here start at €201.40 for 20 hours (one week). A much better deal is to hang around for four weeks (€459.65).

Istituto di Lingua e Cultura Italiana per Stranieri Michelangelo *(☎ 055 24 09 75, Via Ghibellina 88, 50122)* **Map 3** At this institute you will pay €475.15 for four weeks' tuition but the school will also organise private one-on-one courses, starting at €2189.80 for two weeks. The latter involves six hours per day, Monday to Friday, and lunch with the teacher – so you'd better hope you like your teacher!

Dante Alighieri School for Foreigners *(☎ 055 234 29 84, Via de' Bardi 12, 50125)* **Map 3** This is another well-known school for language and culture classes.

Centro Lingua Italiana Calvino *(☎ 055 28 80 81, Viale Fratelli Rosselli 74, 50123)* **Map 3** You have the option of standard and intensive courses here, the latter totalling 30 hours per week. The problem with this place is the location around the back end of Stazione di Santa Maria Novella – hardly the most romantic little niche of Florence.

Scuola Leonardo da Vinci *(☎ 055 29 44 20, W www.scuolaleonardo.com, Via Bufalini 3, 50122)* **Map 4** Courses offered range from two to 24 weeks, usually averaging four hours' class per day. Basic course costs start at €464.80 for four weeks.

Scuola Toscana *(☎ 055 24 45 83, Via de' Benci 23, 50122)* **Map 4** This school tends to pitch for business customers.

Centro Lorenzo de' Medici *(☎ 055 28 31 42, Via Faenza 43, 50122)* **Map 3** This school is popular with American students wishing to learn Italian. Four hours per day for a month costs €490.65.

Other Courses Many of the schools already listed also offer a programme of courses on art, art history, cooking, music and the like.

Some schools specialise in these sorts of course. Art courses range from one-month summer workshops (costing from €258.25 to more than €516.45) to longer-term professional diploma courses. These can be expensive; some cost more than €3357 per year. Schools will organise accommodation for students, on request and at added cost, either in private apartments or with Italian families. In addition to the following taster, many schools offer courses in applied arts, ceramics, gold work, leather, cinema studies, theatre and fashion. The APT in Via Cavour has exhaustive lists.

Istituto per l'Arte e il Restauro *(☎ 055 24 60 01, Palazzo Spinelli, Borgo Santa Croce 10, 50122)* **Map 4** Here you can learn restoration (anything from paintings to ceramics), interior and graphic design, gilding and marquetry.

Accademia Italiana *(☎ 055 28 46 16, Piazza de' Pitti 15, 50125)* **Map 3** This school offers a wide range of design programmes. They include one-month courses for dilettantes and more rigorous semester courses in painting, graphic arts, fashion design and related fields.

Cordon Bleu *(☎ 055 234 54 68, W www.cordonbleu-it.com, Via di Mezzo 55r, 50123)* **Map 3** This is the place to go to learn some stylish cooking methods.

Florence Dance Center *(☎ 055 28 92 76, Borgo della Stella 23r)* **Map 3** This centre offers a range of courses in classical, jazz and modern dance.

Organised Tours

Walking Tours of Florence *(☎ 055 264 50 33, W www.artviva.com, Piazza Santo Stefano 20)* **Map 4** This company organises walks of the city led by historians (or at least graduates in art history). It does several three-hour walks for €20.65 per person. In addition you can organise all sorts of specific walks to suit your own needs and tastes – at a price.

Special Events

There are a number of festivals in Florence. One of the major ones is the Scoppio del Carro (Explosion of the Cart), in which a cart full of fireworks is exploded in front of the cathedral on Easter Saturday.

The Festa di San Giovanni (St John; Florence's patron saint) on 24 June is celebrated with the lively Calcio Storico medieval football matches played on Piazza di Santa Croce and ending with a firework display over Piazzale Michelangelo.

The Festa delle Rificolone (Festival of the Paper Lanterns), during which a procession of drummers, flag-throwers *(sbandieratori)*, musicians and others in medieval dress winds its way from Piazza di Santa Croce to Piazza della SS Annunziata (Map 3), is to celebrate the eve of Our Lady's supposed birthday on 7 September.

Every two years Florence hosts the Internazionale Antiquariato, an antiques fair attracting exhibitors from across Europe, held at the Palazzo Strozzi, Via de' Tornabuoni (Map 4). The next fair will be in September/October 2003.

The Maggio Musicale Fiorentino in Florence is a major music festival (see Theatre & Classical Music under Entertainment later in the chapter).

Places to Stay

The city has hundreds of hotels in all categories and a good range of alternatives, including hostels and private rooms. There are more than 200 one- and two-star hotels in Florence, so even in the peak season it is generally possible – although not always easy – to find a room.

You are advised to book ahead in summer (from mid-April to October) and for the Easter and Christmas to New Year holiday periods. Frankly, it's not a bad idea at any time.

In addition to the hotels, about 175 houses have been registered as *affittacamere* – basically offering beds in private houses. The authorities are taking it a step further by inviting Florentines looking to make a few euros on the side to enter the 'bed and breakfast' game.

Hotels and pensiones are concentrated in three main areas: near Stazione di Santa Maria Novella, near Piazza di Santa Maria Novella and in the old city between the cathedral and the Arno.

If you arrive at Stazione di Santa Maria Novella without a hotel booking, head for the Consorzio ITA office there (Map 2; ☎ 055 28 28 93, fax 055 247 82 32), open 8.45am to 9pm daily. Using a computer network, they can check room availability and make a booking for a small fee, ranging from €2.30 to €7.75 (for one- to five-star places).

You can also contact the APT for a list of private rooms (affittacamere), where you can sometimes find rooms for about €21 to €26. Most fill with students during the school year (October to June) but are a good option if you are staying for a week or longer.

When you arrive at a hotel, always ask for the full price of a room before putting your bags down. Florentine hotels and pensiones are notorious for their bill-padding, particularly in summer. Some may require up to €5.20 extra for compulsory breakfast and others will charge €1.55 or more for a shower. Contact the APT's Florence SOS Turista (see Tourist Offices earlier) if you have any problems.

Prices listed here are for the high season. Many places, especially at the lower end, offer triples and quads as well as the standard single/double arrangement. If you are travelling in a group of three or four, these bigger rooms are generally the best value.

High season for those hotels that lift their prices starts on 15 April and fizzles out by mid-October (some dip a little in the hot months of July and August). Some hotels have an intermediate stage starting on 1 March. Others don't bother changing prices much at any time of the year.

It follows that low season (mid-October to the end of February, and for some places also March) is the thinnest time for tourists and so the best for getting the cheapest hotel rates.

Hotel Associations

These organisations can book you into member hotels. They usually offer a fair range of possibilities, but rarely drop below two stars.

Associazione Gestori Alloggi Privati (AGAP; ☎/fax 055 28 41 00, W www.agap.it) Piazza San Parco 7. This organisation can get you a room in an affittacamere, which is basically a type of B&B-style accommodation but usually without the breakfast.

Florence Promhotels (☎ 055 57 04 81 or 800 86 60 22, fax 055 58 71 89, W www.promhotels.it) Viale Volta 72.

Family Hotels (incorporating Family Hotels and Sun Ray Hotels; ☎ 199 18 99 99 or 055 33 40 41, fax 055 324 70 58, W www.familyhotels.com) Viale Fratelli Rossi 39r.

In Italia (☎ 800 00 87 77 or 02 272 01 330 in Milan, fax 02 256 40 30, W www.initalia.it). This phone and online booking service operates Italy-wide and is free. You can book hotels, rent cars and organise meetings.

Places to Stay – Budget

Camping There are three camping options in and around Florence.

Campeggio Michelangelo *(☎ 055 681 19 77, fax 055 68 93 48, Viale Michelangelo 80)* **Map 2** Sites per person/tent/car €7.25/ 4.65/4.65. Open Apr-Oct. This is the closest camp site to the city centre, just off Piazzale Michelangelo, south of the River Arno. Take bus No 13 from Stazione di Santa Maria Novella. It's a big and comparatively leafy location and makes a lovely starting point for wanders down into the city (but it's a little painful getting back!).

Villa Camerata *(☎ 055 61 03 00, Viale Augusto Righi 2–4)* **Map 2** Sites per person/tent €5.20/4.65. This camp site is next to the HI (Hostelling International) hostel of the same name (see Hostels next). It has space for 220 people and is well equipped in a congenial, verdant setting but is inconvenient for the city centre. One plus is that it opens year-round, which the others do not.

See Places to Stay & Eat in Fiesole for details of the third camp site, ***Campeggio Panoramico***.

Hostels Florence has a good range of hostels.

Ostello Villa Camerata *(☎ 055 60 14 51,*

fax 055 61 03 00, Viale Augusto Righi 2–4) **Map 2** B&B per person €14.50. Open 7am-9am & 2pm-midnight. This HI hostel is considered one of the most beautiful in Europe. Only members are accepted and the hostel is part of the International Booking Network (IBN), the online booking system for HI (see W www.iyhf.org for more details). Dinner costs €7.75, and there is a bar. Take bus No 17B, which leaves from the right side of Stazione di Santa Maria Novella as you leave the platforms. The trip takes 30 minutes.

Ostello del Carmine *(☎ 055 29 19 74, fax 055 61 03 00, Via del Leone 35)* **Map 3** Dorm beds €11.90. Open 7am-midnight, 15 Mar-31 Oct. HI's other Florence rep is much closer to the action in a fairly soulless new building. The location, in a comparatively untouristy corner of the Oltrarno, lends it a lot of contextual charm.

Ostello Archi Rossi *(☎ 055 29 08 04, fax 055 230 26 01, Via Faenza 94r)* **Map 3** Dorm beds €15, small singles €20.65. This private hostel, particularly popular with a young American set, is close to Stazione di Santa Maria Novella and a reasonable option. It is generally full to the gills.

Ostello Santa Monaca *(☎ 055 26 83 38, fax 055 239 67 04, W www.ostello.it, Via Santa Monaca 6)* **Map 3** Dorm beds €15.50. This hostel is a 15- to 20-minute walk south from Stazione di Santa Maria Novella in the Oltrarno area. You sleep in bunk-bed dorms (price includes the rental of sheets).

Ostello Spirito Santo *(☎ 055 239 82 02, fax 055 239 81 29, Via Nazionale 8)* **Map 3** Dorm beds €23.25. Open July-Oct. This is a religious institution near Stazione di Santa Maria Novella, which offers beds to women and families only. The nuns seem cagey about accepting bookings over the phone – but try in any case. Rooms come with two or three beds so you can avoid the dorm situation. The place is predictably quiet.

Istituto Gould *(☎ 055 21 25 76, fax 055 28 02 74, Via de' Serragli 49)* **Map 3** Dorm beds €19.10-20.15. The bunk beds in rooms of three or four here are small but comfortable enough. Some of the rooms look out over a pleasant garden.

East of Stazione di Santa Maria Novella Many of the hotels in this area are well-run, clean and safe, but there are also a fair number of seedy establishments. The area includes the streets around Piazza della Stazione and east to Via Cavour. If you have nothing booked and don't wish to tramp around town, the area has the advantage of being close to Stazione di Santa Maria Novella. You will find all of these on Map 3.

Pensione Bellavista *(☎ 055 28 45 28, fax 055 28 48 74, Largo Alinari 15)* Singles/doubles €51.65/72.30. Rooms in this hotel at the start of Via Nazionale are small but a bargain if you can manage to book one of the two doubles, which have balconies and a view of the cathedral and Palazzo Vecchio. Breakfast costs €5.20 per head.

Albergo Azzi *(☎/fax 055 21 38 06, Via Faenza 56)* Singles €36.15-46.50, doubles without/with bath €62/72.30. Rooms here are simple and comfortable – ask for one away from the noisy Via Faenza and enjoy breakfast on the hotel's terrace. The helpful management will arrange accommodation for you in other Italian cities.

Hotel Globus *(☎ 055 21 10 62, fax 055 239 62 25, W www.hotelglobus.com, Via Sant'Antonino 24)* Singles/doubles without bath €43.90/69.70, with bath €56.80/85.20. You can snag a single for €33.60 in low season, which is about as cheap as this kind of hotel gets around here. This is a handy little place, with reasonable if unspectacular rooms, and everything is kept spotlessly clean.

Around Piazza di Santa Maria Novella This area is just south of the Stazione di Santa Maria Novella and includes Piazza di Santa Maria Novella, and the streets running south to the Arno and east to Via de' Tornabuoni (Map 4).

Via della Scala (Map 3), which runs north-west off the piazza, is lined with pensiones. It is not the most salubrious part of town, but if you want to find a place to put your head down quickly after arriving, at least you have plenty of choice.

La Romagnola *(☎ 055 21 15 97, Via della Scala 40)* **Map 3** Singles/doubles without bath €24.80/43.40, with bath €28.90/47.50. This place has large, clean rooms and management is helpful. It is one of the few places that has not lifted its prices in several years, making it one of the cheapest deals available.

Pensione Ferretti *(☎ 055 238 13 28, fax 055 21 92 88,* **W** *www.emmeti.it/Hferretti, Via delle Belle Donne 17)* **Map 4** Singles/doubles with bath up to €51.65/82.65. Hidden away on a tiny, quiet intersection, this modest hotel has simple rooms. Frequently prices are lower than the maximum rates and they have some rooms without bath that are a little cheaper still.

Hotel Abaco *(☎/fax 055 238 19 19, Via dei Banchi 1)* **Map 4** Doubles without/with bath €72.30/77.50. This is a simple but well-maintained establishment with no singles, although in low season they will rent a double out for €38.75.

Albergo Scoti *(☎/fax 055 29 21 28, Via de' Tornabuoni 7)* **Map 4** Singles/doubles €38.75/56.80. This hotel, on Florence's posh shopping strip, has a handful of perfectly good rooms without bath.

Between the Cathedral & the Arno This area is a 15-minute walk south from Stazione di Santa Maria Novella in the heart of old Florence.

Hotel San Giovanni *(☎ 055 28 83 85, fax 055 21 35 80,* **W** *www.hotelsangiovanni.com, Via de' Cerretani 2)* **Map 4** Singles/doubles/triples without bath €46.50/62/82.65, doubles/triples with bath €72.30/87.80. Although the stairwell up to the 2nd floor isn't promising, the charming and often spacious rooms in this hotel, many with views of the cathedral, are worth seeking out.

Pensione Maria Luisa de' Medici *(☎/fax 055 28 00 48, Via del Corso 1)* **Map 4** Doubles/triples with bath €58.90/74.40. This hotel is in a mansion dating from the 17th century. The rooms are enormous and cater for families. Indeed some of the bigger rooms can easily sleep four or five people. Prices include breakfast.

Albergo Bavaria *(☎/fax 055 234 03 13, Borgo degli Albizi 26)* **Map 4** Singles/doubles without bath €56.80/72.30, doubles with bath €87.80. This hotel is housed in the fine Palazzo di Ramirez di Montalvo, built around a peaceful courtyard by Ammannati. It's a good bet if you can get a room.

Hotel Orchidea *(☎/fax 055 248 03 46, Borgo degli Albizi 11)* **Map 4** Singles/doubles €38.75/51.65. This is a fine homey old-fashioned pensione in a grand mansion. The rooms are simple but well maintained and it is one of the better deals at this price range.

Hotel Dali *(☎/fax 055 234 07 06,* **W** *www.hoteldali.com, Via dell'Oriuolo 17)* **Map 3** Singles/doubles €36.15/51.65, doubles with bath €67.15. A young, helpful couple, Marco and Samantha, recently took over this place and injected a new spark into what is a simple and pleasant hotel. Try for a room looking over the serene inner courtyard. There is parking.

Santa Croce & East of the Centre Both of these are on Map 3.

Hotel Wanda *(☎ 055 234 44 84, fax 055 24 21 06,* **W** *www.hotelwanda.it, Via Ghibellina 51)* Singles/doubles €51.65/103.30. A somewhat higgledy-piggledy spot close to Piazza di Santa Croce, this hotel has large rooms, many with ceiling frescoes.

Pensione Losanna *(☎/fax 055 24 58 40, Via Vittorio Alfieri 9)* Singles/doubles without bath €36.15/49.10, doubles with bath €64.55. This well-run establishment lies about 400m east of the Museo Archeologico as the crow flies. The lady here runs a tight, if small, ship and the place is frequently full. A couple of rooms can be made up as triples.

Places to Stay – Mid-Range

East of Stazione di Santa Maria Novella Via Fiume in this area is stacked with hotels. It is the slightly upmarket hotel flank of the station. The bulk of the cheaper but frequently not so savoury options is over on the Via della Scala side.

Pensione Le Cascine *(☎ 055 21 10 66, fax 055 21 07 69,* **W** *www.hotellecascine.com, Largo Alinari 15)* **Map 3** Singles/doubles with bath €93/144.60. Near Stazione di Santa Maria Novella, this two-star hotel is

TUSCANY

one of the better choices in an area overburdened with hotels. Its rooms are attractively furnished and some have balconies. Prices include breakfast.

Hotel Désirée *(☎ 055 238 23 82, fax 055 29 14 39, W www.hoteldesiree.com, Via Fiume 20)* **Map 3** Singles/doubles €72.30/103.30. Breakfast per person €5.20. A very personable hotel that offers fine rooms, many of which overlook a tranquil, leafy courtyard at the back. The spick-and-span high-ceilinged rooms are simply but tastefully furnished and have their own bathrooms.

Pensione Accademia *(☎ 055 29 34 51, fax 055 21 97 71, W www.accademiahotel.net, Via Faenza 7)* **Map 4** Single (one only) without bath €77.50, doubles with bath €129.10. This hotel has pleasant rooms with television and incorporates an 18th-century mansion with magnificent stained-glass doors and carved wooden ceilings. Prices include breakfast.

Hotel Bellettini *(☎ 055 21 35 61, fax 055 28 35 51, Via de' Conti 7)* **Map 4** Singles/doubles with bath €82.65/108.45. This is a delightful small hotel with well-furnished rooms – try for one with a view of the Basilica di San Lorenzo. They also have a couple of triples and quads and some slightly cheaper rooms with a bathroom in the corridor.

Hotel San Lorenzo *(☎/fax 055 28 49 25, W www.fionline.it/sanlorenzo, Via Rosina 4)* **Map 3** Singles/doubles €72.30/103.30. This is one of the many small family pensions that dot the city. It has just eight rooms, including one single with shower but a toilet in the corridor. Two of the doubles are likewise without their own toilet and cost €93. The five remaining rooms, some of which are big enough to turn into triples or, at a pinch, quads, come with full bathroom. The place is clean and pleasant enough. In low season a double normally costing €103.30 can come down to €62.

Hotel Casci *(☎ 055 21 16 86, fax 055 239 64 61, W www.hotelcasci.com, Via Cavour 13)* **Map 3** Singles/doubles €93/123.95. The charm of this lower-mid-range hotel is the chance to stay in a 15th-century mansion on one of the city's main streets. The rooms are a little fusty and musty but come equipped with satellite TV, phone, heating and air-con. Look up at the fresco as you scoff your buffet breakfast.

Between the Cathedral & the Arno Both of these places are on Map 4.

Pendini *(☎ 055 21 11 70, fax 055 28 18 07, Via degli Strozzi 2)* Singles/doubles with bath €103.30/144.60. Another excellent choice, Pendini's rooms are furnished with antiques and reproductions. In the off-season they are willing to come down quite a way in price, too.

Hotel Porta Rossa *(☎ 055 28 75 51, fax 055 28 21 79, Via Porta Rossa 19)* Singles €93-123.95, doubles €134.30-165.30. At the time of writing this building was getting some restoration work but was still in operation. The sizeable price differences reflect variations in room size. This is a bit of an old workhorse in central Florence but rooms are not bad in their class.

Santa Croce & East of the Centre Find this on Map 3.

Hotel Dante *(☎ 055 24 17 72, fax 055 234 58 19, W www.hoteldante.it, Via S Cristofano 2)* Singles/doubles €75.90/112.10. Tucked away in a quiet street right by the Basilica di Santa Croce, the rooms here are fine without being spectacular. They all have smallish bathrooms but the real distinguishing feature is that three out of the four rooms on each floor have a kitchen. So if you prefer to eat in rather than out, it's not a problem!

Oltrarno These three choices are all quite central.

Albergo la Scaletta *(☎ 055 28 30 28, fax 055 28 95 62, W www.lascaletta.com, Via de' Guicciardini 13)* **Map 4** Singles/doubles with bath €87.80/123.95. A good choice if you want to stay south of the river, this hotel has a terrace with great views. Some of the rooms looking onto the street cost a little less. Prices include breakfast.

Pensione Bandini *(☎ 055 21 53 08, fax 055 28 27 61, Piazza Santo Spirito 9)* **Map 3** Doubles without/with €96.10/115.70. This is a rattling old pensione overlooking the hippest square in Florence. The rooms are not world class in comfort but the position and old-world atmosphere of the place more than make up for any lack in the mod-cons department.

Hotel Silla *(☎ 055 234 28 88, fax 055 234 14 37,* **W** *www.hotelsilla.it, Via dei Renai 5)* **Map 3** Singles/doubles €108.45/149.80. Set in a charming old palazzo in one of the most attractive and leafy parts of Florence, this hotel offers pleasant and impeccably maintained rooms a stone's throw from the centre.

Places to Stay – Top End

East of Stazione di Santa Maria Novella These are all on Map 3.

Hotel Monna Lisa *(☎ 055 247 97 51, fax 055 247 97 55,* **W** *www.monnalisa.it, Borgo Pinti 27)* Singles/doubles/superior doubles €180.75/273.75/309.90. This hotel is tucked away in a fine Renaissance palazzo. The best rooms are good value and some look out over the private garden where you can enjoy a buffet breakfast in summer.

Hotel Botticelli *(☎ 055 29 09 05, fax 055 29 43 22, Via Taddea 8)* Singles/doubles €118.80/191.10. This charming bijou hotel near the San Lorenzo market is an attractive deal. Rooms, with all mod cons, are elegantly appointed.

Hotel Il Guelfo Bianco *(☎ 055 28 83 30, fax 055 29 52 03,* **W** *www.ilguelfobianco.it, Via Cavour 57r)* Singles/doubles €118.80/165.30. The 29 rooms here are attractively laid out and comfortable. If you are alone, see if you can get the charming single with its own private terrace. A handful of doubles of 'superior' quality, with the best rooftop views, go for €198.85.

Around Piazza di Santa Maria Novella This is on Map 4.

Grand Hotel Baglioni *(☎ 055 2 35 80, fax 055 235 88 95,* **W** *www.hotelbaglioni.it, Piazza dell'Unità Italiana 6)* Singles/doubles €196.25/247.90. Some rooms fall into the 'superior' category and cost an extra €20.10-25.80 per person. All rooms have TV, phone, air-con and heating. The rooftop terrace dining area affords fine views over the city.

Between the Cathedral & the Arno Both of these are on Map 4.

Hotel Helvetia & Bristol *(☎ 055 28 78 14, fax 055 234 67 35,* **W** *www.charminghotels.it, Via dei Pescioni 2)* Singles/doubles €216.90/408. The Web address for this hotel is a big clue: it is one of Florence's most inviting top-level spots, oozing charm and elegance from another era, without being haughty. Prices come down considerably in the low season and the 37 well-appointed rooms are all worthy choices.

Savoy *(☎ 055 2 73 51, fax 055 27 35 88,* **W** *www.rfhotels.com, Piazza della Repubblica 7)* Singles/doubles €387.35/428.65. Recently reopened and completely refurbished and modernised, this stylish jewel in the Forte chain offers spacious living in rooms with a fresh, contemporary feel. Suites come in at €599.10.

Oltrarno This place is on Map 2.

Albergo Torre di Bellosguardo *(☎ 055 229 81 45, fax 055 22 90 08, Via Roti Michelozzi 2,* **e** *torredibellosguardo@dada.it)* Singles/doubles/suites €149.80/253.10/304.70. This is worth considering if only for its position. Long appreciated as a bucolic escape from the simmering heat of summertime Florence, the Bellosguardo hill to the south-west of the city centre offers not only enchanting views but enticing accommodation in what started life as a small castle in the 14th century.

Places to Stay – Rental Accommodation

If you want an apartment in Florence, save your pennies and start looking well before you arrive; they are difficult to come by and can be very expensive. A one-room apartment with kitchenette in the city centre will cost around €517 per month (minimum six months), more for short-term rental. Florence & Abroad (Map 3; ☎ 055 48 70 04, fax 055 49 01 43), Via San Zanobi 58, specialises in short- and medium-term rental accommodation in Florence and the Fiesole area for those with a fairly liberal budget.

Places to Eat

Simplicity and quality describe the cuisine of Tuscany. In a country where the various regional styles and traditions have provided a rich and diverse cuisine, Tuscany is known for its fine cooking. Rich green Tuscan olive oil, fresh fruit and vegetables, tender meat and, of course, the classic wine, Chianti, are the basics of a good meal in Florence.

Meat eaters will sooner or later want to try *bistecca alla fiorentina*, a slab of Florentine steak. It should not cost more than €34 per kilogram, which is usually sufficient for two.

Most eating establishments have a cover charge, which ranges from €0.80 up to €5.20 (!). You usually have to factor in a service charge *(servizio)* of 10% to 15%. Try to avoid the tourist traps in the obvious squares and along the busiest streets in central Florence – seek out the more hidden-away places, some of which appear below.

Places to Eat – Budget

East of Stazione di Santa Maria Novella You can find some popular budget options in this area.

Mario *(☎ 055 21 85 50, Via Rosina 2r)* **Map 3** Mains €3.65-4.65, pasta €3.10-4.15. Open Mon-Sat lunch only. This small bar and trattoria near Piazza del Mercato Centrale is very busy, attracting a mix of foreign strays and local workers.

Ristorante ZàZà *(☎ 055 21 54 11, Piazza del Mercato Centrale 20)* **Map 3** Set lunch menu €12.90. Open Mon-Sat. A few doors down from Mario, this place is so popular that it has spread out into the open. It is the best place on the square for outdoor dining. The menu changes regularly and often sparkles with imaginative dishes.

Il Vegetariano *(☎ 055 47 50 30, Via delle Ruote 30r)* **Map 2** Meal with wine €15.50. Open Tues-Sat (dinner only Sat & Sun). One of the few veggie options in town, this is an unassuming locale with a limited (but changing) menu.

Between the Cathedral & the Arno More budget eateries for Tuscan treats are situated around here.

Ristorante Self-Service Leonardo *(☎ 055 28 44 46, Via de' Pecori 35r)* **Map 4** Mains €3.90. Open 11.45am-2.45pm & 6.45pm-9.45pm Sun-Fri. When it comes to eating a full meal while you pinch pennies, it's hard to beat this refectory-style spot for simply filling an empty tum.

Trattoria Pasquini *(☎ 055 21 89 95, Via Val di Lamona 2r)* **Map 4** Full meals with wine €25.85. Open Thurs-Tues. In this tiny corner they offer a varied menu that includes Tuscan meals such as tripe or bistecca alla fiorentina, and a mix of other national dishes.

Trattoria da Benvenuto *(☎ 055 21 48 33, Via della Mosca 16r)* **Map 4** Full meals €23.25. Open Mon-Sat. Eating here, on the corner of Via dei Neri, is hardly an ambient dining experience, but the food is reliable and modestly priced. Mains include several Florentine favourites, including *lampredotto* (a type of tripe) and bistecca, while the pasta dishes are an interesting mix, including a decent *rigatoni alla siciliana.*

Angie's Pub *(☎ 055 239 82 45, Via dei Neri 35r)* **Map 4** Snacks from €2.10. Open 11am-1am Mon-Thurs, 11am-3am Fri & Sat. Among the great little treasures of Florence is this place, south-east of the Palazzo Vecchio. It offers a vast array of *panini* (bread rolls with filling) and focaccia (flat bread), as well as hamburgers Italian-style, with mozzarella and spinach, and real bagels.

Around Ognissanti This area by the Arno has a couple of good spots.

Da il Latini *(☎ 055 21 09 16, Via dei Palchetti 4)* **Map 4** Mains from €10.35, pasta from €5.20. Open Tues-Sat. This is an attractive trattoria just off Via del Moro and something of a classic for Florentines. The food is largely Tuscan but the dining area has a singularly Spanish touch with all those legs of ham dangling from the ceiling!

Trattoria dei 13 Gobbi *(☎ 055 21 32 04, Via del Porcellana 9r)* **Map 3** Mains from €10.35, pasta from €5.20. Open Tues-Sat. There is a somewhat artificially bucolic scene set inside this trattoria, but in a tasteful fashion. The courtyard at the back and the low ceilings all add atmosphere.

Sostanza *(☎ 055 21 26 91, Via del Porcellana 25r)* **Map 3** Mains from €7.25. Open noon-2pm & 7pm-9.45pm Mon-Fri. This traditional Tuscan eatery is a good spot for bistecca alla fiorentina if you are not fussy about your surroundings. A no-nonsense approach dominates. The minestrone (€5.20) is also good.

Santa Croce & East of the Centre You can get most things at a good price in this area, from snacks to steaks.

Caffetteria Piansa *(☎ 055 234 23 62, Borgo Pinti 18r)* **Map 3** Set lunch €8.30. Open Mon-Sat for lunch only. At this vaulted restaurant, you basically point and choose from a limited number of cheap and tasty dishes. Get in early – it's all over by 2pm.

Osteria de' Benci *(☎ 055 234 49 23, Via de' Benci 13r)* **Map 4** Full meals €23.25. Open Mon-Sat. This is a consistently good bet. They change their menu often and serve up honest slabs of bistecca alla fiorentina. The food is well prepared, the atmosphere cosy and prices moderate.

Antico Noè *(☎ 055 234 08 38, Volta di San Piero 6r)* **Map 4** Panini €3.10, full meals €23.25. Open Tues-Sun. This legendary sandwich bar, just off Piazza San Pier Maggiore, is another option for a light lunch. They have two sections. The sandwich bar is takeaway only and next door they run a cosy restaurant.

Danny Rock *(☎ 055 234 03 07, Via de' Pandolfini 13r)* **Map 4** Meals around €10.35. Open 7pm-3am. This place does not sound promising, but inside is an immensely popular place for pizza, pasta and, perhaps best of all, their *insalatoni* (huge salads; €6.20).

Osteria Cibrèo *(☎ 055 234 11 00, Via de' Macci 114r)* **Map 3** Meals around €21. Open Tues-Sat. This is a true delight to the palate, located next door to the much more expensive restaurant of the same name (see later). They offer no pasta at all but some enticing first courses like *ricotta al ragù* (ricotta cheese in a meat sauce).

Ruth's *(☎ 055 248 08 88, Via Luigi Carto Farini 2a)* **Map 3** Meals around €11. Open 12.30pm-2.30pm & 8pm-10.30pm Sun-Fri. For something a little different, try out this kosher place by the synagogue. You can have a plate of mixed dips with couscous, felafel, filo pastry pie and potato salad, quite filling in itself.

Ramraj *(☎ 055 24 09 99, Via Ghibellina 61r)* **Map 3** Meals €10.35. Open Tues-Sun. Drop in here for takeaway tandoori and other Indian specialities. You can eat at the bench if you want.

Oltrarno Across the river, there are plenty of bargain meals to be eaten.

Borgo Antico *(☎ 055 21 04 37, Piazza Santo Spirito 6r)* **Map 3** Mains €6.20-11.40. This pizzeria and restaurant is a great location in summer, when you can sit at an outside table and enjoy the atmosphere in the piazza. If you decide to go for the expensive menu, which changes daily, you can get some surprisingly good meals. Try the big salads for €6.20.

All'Antico Ristoro di Cambi *(☎ 055 21 71 34, Via Sant'Onofrio 1)* **Map 3** Full meals up to €23.25. Open Mon-Sat. The food here is traditional Tuscan and the bistecca alla fiorentina is succulent. You can eat inside or out on the square.

Al Tranvai *(☎ 055 22 51 97, Piazza Tasso 14r)* **Map 3** Full meals up to €18.10. Open Mon-Fri. If you don't mind eating elbow to elbow with complete (local) strangers, this is a wonderful rustic Tuscan eatery.

Trattoria Casalinga *(☎ 055 21 86 24, Via de' Michelozzi 9r)* **Map 3** Meals around €15.50. Open Mon-Sat. This is a bustling, popular eating place. The food is great and a filling meal of pasta, meat or vegetables plus wine will come in at bargain basement prices. Don't expect to linger over a meal, as there is usually a queue of people waiting for your table.

I Tarocchi *(☎ 055 234 39 12, Via dei Renai 12-14r)* **Map 3** Pizzas & 1st/2nd courses around €5.20. Open Tues-Sat. This is a popular pizzeria/trattoria serving excellent pizzas. The first courses alone are enough to satisfy most people's hunger.

Osteria Antica Mescita San Niccolò *(☎ 055 234 28 36, Via San Niccolò 60r)* **Map 2** Full meals with wine €20.65. Open 7pm-11pm Mon-Sat. This is a fine little eating hideaway where the food is tasty and authentic. Throw in a good bottle from their impressive wine collection and you'll have a great meal.

Places to Eat – Mid-Range

East of Stazione di Santa Maria Novella This place is on Map 3.

Ristorante Lobs *(☎ 055 21 24 78, Via Faenza 75)* Set menu €33.60, mains around €18. Open until 12.30am. This excellent fish restaurant offers a seafood menu, including oysters and Norwegian salmon, and Soave wine from the country's north-east.

Around Piazza di Santa Maria Novella

Ostaria dei Cento Poveri *(☎ 055 21 88 46, Via del Palazzuolo 31r)* **Map 3** Full meals from €25.85. Open 6.30pm-midnight Wed-Mon. A congenial little spot in a not-so-congenial part of town, the 'hostel of the hundred poor people' sits apart from most other places around here as a quality dining option. Tuck in to creative Tuscan food in a down-to-earth setting.

Between the Cathedral & the Arno These are on Map 4.

Trattoria Coco Lezzone *(☎ 055 28 71 78, Via Parioncino 26r)* Full meals with wine up to €41.30. Open Mon-Sat. Ribollita is the house speciality here, but they will do you a genuine bistecca alla fiorentina.

Cantinetta Antinori *(☎ 055 29 22 34, Piazza degli Antinori 3)* Full meals with wine €41.30. Open daily, lunch only Sat & Sun. Feeling posh and flush? This might be the place for you. They offer a reasonable meal accompanied by some fine wines – it is for the latter that most people come here.

Oltrarno These places are on Map 3.

Osteria Santo Spirito *(☎ 055 238 23 83, Piazza Santo Spirito 16r)* Full meals €31. If you prefer a slightly higher quality meal than in the bustling locales across the square, this cosy restaurant is the place. Try the *ravioli burro e salvia* (big ravioli prepared in butter and sage, a Tuscan classic; €7.75).

Ristorante Beccofino *(☎ 055 29 00 76, Piazza degli Scarlatti)* 1st/2nd courses up to €9.30/19.65. Open Tues-Sun. This place is one of a rare breed in this town. The grub is pricey and the surroundings nouvelle chic – no traditional bucolics in here, thank you (and check out the stainless steel, floor-lit loos!).

Places to Eat – Top End

Santa Croce & East of the Centre Find these on Map 3.

Ristorante Cibrèo *(☎ 055 234 11 00, Via de' Macci 118r)* Full meals up to €77.50. Open Tues-Sat. Next door to the fine osteria of the same name, this is the place to come for a special splurge. The decor is much the same as in the osteria, although the table settings are suitably more elegant.

Enoteca Pinchiorri *(☎ 055 24 27 77, Via Ghibellina 87)* Meals €93. Open Tues-Sat. This is one of the city's finest restaurants, noted for its nouvelle cuisine, Italian-style.

Snacks

On the streets between the cathedral and the River Arno harbour are many ***pizzerias*** where you can buy takeaway pizza by the slice for around €1 to €1.50, depending on the weight.

Il Nilo *(Volta di San Piero 9r)* **Map 4** Shawarma & falafel sandwiches up to €3.10. Open 8am-midnight Mon-Sat. Revellers, dropouts and a host of other weird and wonderful beings wander in here in the course of the evening for a takeaway falafel. Some hang about and eat it here, although there's nowhere to sit.

Gelaterias

Gelato can cost anything from €2.10 for a small cup *(coppetta)* to around €5.20 for a massive cone *(cono)*.

Gelateria Vivoli *(☎ 055 29 23 34, Via dell'Isola delle Stinche 7)* **Map 4** Open 9am-1am Tues-Sat. People queue outside this place, near Via Ghibellina, to delight in the gelato widely considered to be the city's best.

Perchè No? *(☎ 055 239 89 69, Via dei Tavolini 19r)* **Map 4** Open Wed-Sun. This gelateria, off Via de' Calzaiuoli, is excellent.

Cafes

Gilli *(☎ 055 21 38 96, Piazza della Repubblica 39r)* **Map 4** Coffee at the bar €0.80, at a table outside €3.10. Open 8am-1am Wed-Sun. This is one of the city's finest cafes and it's reasonably priced if you stand at the bar. The square is actually host to a series of fine historic cafes.

Entertainment

Several publications list the theatrical and musical events and festivals held in the city and surrounding areas. The free bimonthly *Florence Today*, the monthly *Firenze Information*, and *Firenze Avvenimenti*, a monthly brochure distributed by the council, are all available (haphazardly) at the tourist offices. *Firenze Spettacolo*, the city's definitive entertainment publication, is available monthly for €1.55 at bookstalls.

A handy centralised ticket outlet is ***Box Office*** *(Map 3; ☎ 055 21 08 04, Via Luigi Alamanni 39)*.

You can book tickets for the theatre, football matches and other events online through Ticket One (W www.ticketone.it).

Pubs & Bars Florence has a range of drinking establishments.

The Chequers Pub *(☎ 055 28 75 88, Via della Scala 7–9r)* **Map 3** Foreigners hang out here, one of a whole host of UK/Irish-style pubs in Florence.

Astor Caffè *(☎ 055 239 90 00, Piazza del Duomo 5r)* **Map 4** Open 10am-3am. You can take breakfast here if you want but the nocturnal folk gather around at night for loud music and cocktails both inside and out, right by the solemn walls of the cathedral.

Capocaccia *(☎ 055 21 07 51, Lungarno Corsini 12–14r)* **Map 4** Open noon-1am Tues-Sun. The beautiful people of Florence gather here, especially on balmy spring and summer evenings, for a riverside nibble and cocktail before heading on to dinner and clubs.

Loonees *(☎ 055 21 22 49, Via Porta Rossa 15)* **Map 4** Open 8pm-3am. You wouldn't know this place existed if you hadn't been told. Walk into the building and the door is to the left of the staircase. It's a fairly small 'club' – basically just a bar with an expat bent and occasional live music of dubious taste.

The William *(☎ 055 246 98 00, Via Magliabechi 7r)* **Map 4** Open 6pm-2am. This is a loud English-style pub but it has found quite a following among young Florentines in search of a pint of ale rather than Anglos in search of six.

Sant'Ambrogio Caffè *(☎ 055 24 10 35, Piazza Sant'Ambrogio 7r)* **Map 3** Cocktails €5.20. Open 9am-2am Mon-Sat. As well as being a place to get snacks, Sant'Ambrogio Caffè is especially dedicated to the sipping of cocktails. On summer nights they set up tables outside.

Rex Caffè *(☎ 055 248 03 31, Via Fiesolana 25r)* **Map 3** Open 5pm-3am. Another stop on the cocktail circuit, this is a hip place to sip your favourite mixed concoction. Take a martini at the luridly lit central bar or a quiet beer sitting at one of the shadowy metallic tables. Happy hour lasts from 5pm to 9.30pm.

Cabiria *(☎ 055 21 57 32, Piazza Santo Spirito 4r)* **Map 3** Open 11am-2am Wed-Mon. This popular cafe by day converts into a busy music bar by night. In summer the buzz extends on to Piazza Santo Spirito, which itself becomes a stage for an outdoor bar and regular free concerts.

La Dolce Vita *(☎ 055 28 45 95, Piazza del Carmine 6r)* **Map 3** Open to 1am Mon-Thurs, to 3am Fri-Sun. Just a piazza away from Santo Spirito, this place attracts a rather more self-consciously select crowd of self-appointed beautiful types.

Zoe *(☎ 055 24 31 11, Via dei Renai 13r)* **Map 3** Open 3pm-2am Mon-Sat. This bar heaves as its squadrons of punters, mostly young locals, end up spilling out onto the street.

Caffè La Torre *(☎ 055 68 06 43, Lungarno Benvenuto Cellini 65r)* **Map 2** Mixed drinks around €5.20. Open 8.30am-4am. Hang out drinking until the wee hours and listening to all kinds of music from jazz to Latin rhythms.

Live Music Some of the bigger venues are well outside the town centre. Depending on who is playing at these venues, admission costs from nothing to €10.35. Then the drinks will cost you on top of that – at least €5.20 for a beer.

Jazz Club *(☎ 055 247 97 00, Via Nuova de' Caccini 3)* **Map 3** Admission €5.20 (for a year's membership), drinks around €6.20. Open 9.30pm-1am Sun-Thurs, 9.30pm-2am Fri-Sat. This is one of Florence's top jazz venues.

Tenax *(☎ 055 30 81 60, Via Pratese 46)* **Map 1** Admission free-€10.35. Open 10pm-4am Tues-Sun. One of the city's more popular clubs, this place is well out to the north-west of town. It is one of Florence's biggest venues for Italian and international acts. Catch bus Nos 29 or 30 from Stazione di Santa Maria Novella to get there. You'll be looking at a taxi to get home.

Auditorium Flog *(☎ 055 49 04 37, Via M Mercati 24b)* **Map 2** Admission free-€10.35. Open 10pm-4am. Another venue for bands, this place is in the Rifredi area, also north of the centre but a little closer than Tenax. It's not as big (in any sense) as Tenax but has a reasonable stage and dance area. Catch bus Nos 8 or 14 from Stazione di Santa Maria Novella.

Discos & Clubs Both of these can be found on Map 2.

Central Park *(☎ 055 35 35 05, Via Fosso Macinante 2)* Drinks around €7.75. Open 10pm-6am Tues-Sun. This is one of the city's most popular clubs. What music you hear will depend partly on the night, although as you wander from one dance area to another (there are four) you can expect a general range from Latin and pop through to house.

Meccanò *(☎ 055 331 33 71, Viale degli Olmi)* Admission €7.75-10.35. Open 10pm-5am Tues-Sat. Three dance spaces offer house, funk and mainstream commercial music to appeal to a fairly broad range of tastes. Occasionally they put on special theme nights.

Theatre & Classical Music In summer especially, concerts of chamber music are held in churches across the city. Keep an eye out for programmes for the Orchestra da Camera Fiorentina (Florentine Chamber Orchestra), whose performance season runs from March to October.

Teatro Comunale *(☎ 055 2 77 91, Corso Italia 12)* **Map 2** Concerts, opera and dance are performed at various times of the year here, on the northern bank of the Arno. In May and June the theatre hosts Maggio Musicale Fiorentina, an international concert festival. Contact the theatre's box office.

Teatro Verdi *(☎ 055 21 23 20, Via Ghibellina 101)* **Map 4** There are seasons of drama, opera, concerts and dance here from January to April and October to December.

Teatro della Pergola *(☎ 055 247 96 51, Via della Pergola 18)* **Map 4** The Amici della Musica (☎ 055 60 84 20) organise concerts here from January to April and October to December.

Cinemas You have a few choices of venue for seeing films in their original language *(lingua originale)*.

Odeon Cinehall *(☎ 055 21 40 68, Piazza Strozzi)* **Map 4** This is the main location for seeing subtitled films, screened on Mondays and Tuesdays.

Shopping

It is said that Milan has the best clothes and Rome the best shoes, but Florence without doubt has the greatest variety of goods. The main shopping area is between the cathedral and the Arno (Map 4), with boutiques concentrated along Via Roma, Via de' Calzaiuoli and Via Por Santa Maria, leading to the goldsmiths lining the Ponte Vecchio. Window-shop along Via de' Tornabuoni, where the top designers, including Gucci, Saint-Laurent and Pucci, sell their wares.

The open-air market (Monday to Saturday), near Piazza del Mercato Centrale (Map 3), offers leather goods, clothing and jewellery at low prices, but quality varies greatly. You could pick up the bargain of a lifetime, but check the item carefully before paying. It is possible to barter but not if you want to use a credit card. The flea market (Monday to Saturday) at Piazza dei Ciompi (Map 3), off Borgo Allegri near Piazza di Santa Croce, specialises in antiques and bric-a-brac.

Florence is famous for its beautifully patterned paper, which is stocked in the many stationery and speciality shops throughout the city and at the markets.

Getting There & Away

Air Florence is served by two airports: Amerigo Vespucci (Map 1; ☎ 055 37 34 98), 5km north-west of the city centre at Via del Termine 11; and Galileo Galilei (☎ 050 50 07 07; W www.pisa-airport.com), near Pisa and about an hour by train or car from Florence. Amerigo Vespucci caters for domestic and a handful of European flights. Galileo Galilei is one of northern Italy's main international and domestic airports and has regular connections to London, Paris, Munich and major Italian cities.

Bus The SITA bus station (Map 3; ☎ 800 37 37 60 or 055 21 47 21, W www.sita-on-line.it), Via Santa Caterina da Siena 15, is just to the west of Piazza della Stazione. There is a direct, rapid service to/from Siena (€5.70, 1¼ hours) and buses leave here for Poggibonsi, where there are connecting buses for San Gimignano (€5.20, 1½ hours) and Colle di Val d'Elsa, where you change for Volterra (€6.30, 1¼ hours). Direct buses serve Arezzo, Castellina in Chianti, Faenza, Grosseto and other smaller cities throughout Tuscany.

Several bus companies, including CAP (W www.capautolinee.it) and COPIT, operate from Largo Alinari (Map 3; ☎ 055 21 46 37), at the southern end of Via Nazionale, with services to nearby towns including Prato (€1.80, 45 minutes) and Pistoia (€2.60, 50 minutes).

Lazzi (Map 3; ☎ 055 35 10 61, W www.lazzi.it), Piazza Adua 1, next to Stazione di Santa Maria Novella, runs services to Rome, Pistoia and Lucca. Lazzi forms part of the Eurolines network of international bus services. You can, for instance, catch a bus to Barcelona, Paris, Prague or London.

Train Florence is on the Rome-Milan line, which means that most of the trains to/from Rome (€22, two hours), Bologna (€8.80, one hour) and Milan (€21.70, three hours 20 minutes) are Intercities or Eurostar Italia, for which you have to pay a supplement.

There are also regular trains to and from Venice (€18.75, three hours) and Trieste. For Verona you will generally need to change at Bologna. To get to Genoa and Turin, a change at Pisa is necessary.

The train information office (Map 3; open 7am to 9pm) is in the main foyer at Stazione di Santa Maria Novella.

Car & Motorcycle Florence is connected by the A1 to Bologna and Milan in the north and Rome and Naples in the south. The Autostrada del Mare (A11) connects Florence with Prato, Lucca, Pisa and the coast, and a superstrada (no tolls) joins the city to Siena. From the north on the A1, exit at Firenze Nord and then simply follow the bull's-eye 'centro' signs. If approaching from Rome, exit at Firenze Sud.

The more picturesque S67 connects the city with Pisa to the west and Forli and Ravenna to the east.

Getting Around

To/From the Airports The No 62 bus runs approximately every 20 minutes from the Stazione di Santa Maria Novella to Amerigo Vespucci airport. The service from the airport runs from 6.30am to 10.45pm; from Stazione di Santa Maria Novella it runs from 6am to 10.20pm. The trip takes 15 minutes and you buy a normal city bus ticket (€0.80). Alternatively, you can get the faster SITA Navetta (Shuttle) from the airport to the SITA bus station (see Bus under Getting There & Away). It costs €3.10 and runs every 30 minutes from 5.30am to 11pm.

Regular trains leave from platform 5 at Stazione di Santa Maria Novella for Galileo Galilei airport near Pisa. Check your luggage in 15 minutes before the train departs. Services from Florence are roughly hourly from 6.46am to 5pm, with a final service leaving at 11.07pm. From the airport they leave from 8.49am to 6.50pm (7.09pm on Sundays and holidays). The trip takes one hour 30 minutes and costs €4.70.

Bus Azienda Trasporti Area Fiorentina (ATAF) buses service the city centre, Fiesole and other areas on the city's periphery. For information, call ☎ 800 42 45 00.

You'll find several main bus stops for most routes around the Stazione di Santa Maria Novella (Map 3). Some of the most useful lines operate from a stop just outside the south-eastern exit of Stazione di Santa Maria Novella below Piazza Adua. Buses leaving from here include:

No 7 For Fiesole.
No 13 For Piazzale Michelangelo.
No 62 For Amerigo Vespucci airport.
No 70 For the cathedral and the Uffizi (night bus)

A network of dinky little electric *bussini* (minibuses) operates around the centre of town. They can be handy for those getting tired of walking around or needing to backtrack right across town. Only Linea D operates from 8am to 9.20pm daily. The others run from 8am to 8.20pm Monday to Saturday. You can get a map of the routes, published by ATAF, from tourist offices.

Tickets for both the buses and bussini cost €0.75 for 60 minutes and €1.30 for three hours. A 24-hour ticket costs €3.10. A four-ticket set *(biglietto multiplo)* for night buses (valid for one hour each) costs €3. You are supposed to stamp these in the machine when you get on your first bus. If you are hanging around Florence longer, you might want to invest in a monthly ticket *(mensile)* at €28.50 (€18.60 for students). Yearly *(annuale)* tickets are also available. If you just hop on the bus without a ticket between 9pm and 6am, you can get one for €1.55 (double the normal price).

There is a special 30-day ticket for using the bussini (lines A to D) only. It costs €12.90.

Car & Motorcycle Traffic is restricted in the city centre. A no-parking regime (except for residents) rules from 7.30am to 6.30pm Monday to Friday. Non-residents may only stop in the centre to drop off or pick up luggage from hotels or park in hotel or public garages (the latter will cost you a fortune).

There are several major car parks and numerous smaller parking areas around the fringes of the city centre. If you are planning to spend the day in Florence, your best option is to park at the Fortezza da Basso (Map 2), which costs €1.05 per hour.

If your car is towed away, call ☎ 055 41 57 81 for the Depositeria Comunale (car pound; Map 1) at Via Olmatello, which is way out on the city limits. You will have to pay around €46.50 to recover it plus whatever fine you are charged. Fines vary depending on the offence.

A bunch of car rental agencies cluster together in the Borgo Ognissanti area. Among the biggies, Avis (Map 3; ☎ 199 10 01 33) is at Borgo Ognissanti 128r; Europcar (Map 3; ☎ 800 82 80 50) is at Borgo Ognissanti 53r; and Hertz (Map 3; ☎ 199 11 22 11) is at Via Maso Finiguerra 33r. Thrifty Car Rental (Map 3; ☎ 055 28 71 61), Borgo Ognissanti 134r, and Happy Rent (Map 3; ☎ 055 239 96 96), Borgo Ognissanti 153r, are a couple of local competitors. Their rates are similar, with small cars starting at €62 per day. Happy Rent also rents out motorbikes and scooters.

Alinari (Map 3), Via Guelfa 85r, rents out motorcycles for up to €92.95 per day and scooters for up to €41.30 per day. In summer it also sets up shop at several camp sites – check at the APT for details.

Taxi Taxis can be found outside Stazione di Santa Maria Novella and several other ranks around town. Alternatively, you can call ☎ 055 42 42, 055 47 98, 055 44 99 or 055 43 90. The basic charge is €0.75, on top of which you pay €1.35 per kilometre within the city limits (€2.35 per kilometre beyond). You are charged at the rate of €0.10 every 20 seconds while stationary. There is a night-time surcharge (from 10pm to 6am) of €3.75. On public holidays you pay an extra €1.65 (not if you are already paying the night surcharge). Each piece of luggage costs €0.55.

AROUND FLORENCE

Fiesole

Perched in hills about 8km north-east of Florence, between the valleys of the Arno and Mugnone rivers, Fiesole has attracted the likes of Boccaccio, Carducci, Giovanni Dupré, Marcel Proust, Gertrude Stein and Frank Lloyd Wright, all drawn by the lush olive groves and valleys – not to mention the spectacular view of Florence. Fiesole was founded in the 7th century BC by the Etruscans and long remained the most important city in northern Etruria. It is well worth visiting for the views and is a fabulous spot for a picnic and short walk.

Staff at the APT in Florence (see Tourist Offices under Florence earlier in this chapter) or in Fiesole (☎ 055 59 87 20), Piazza Mino da Fiesole 36, can assist with information about the town and can advise on accommodation, walks and any other activities.

Things to See & Do Opposite the tourist office in Piazza Mino da Fiesole, the centre of this small town, is the **cathedral**, started in the 11th century and altered in the 13th century, although a 19th-century renovation has eradicated many earlier features. Behind it is the **Museo Bandini** *(☎ 055 5 94 77, Via Duprè; admission €6.20, including Zona Archeologica; open 10am-7pm daily May-Oct, 9am-5pm Wed-Sun Nov-Apr)*, featuring an impressive collection of early Tuscan Renaissance works, including Taddeo Gaddi's *Annunciation* and Petrarch's beautifully illustrated *Triumphs*.

Opposite the entrance to the museum, the **Zona Archeologica** *(☎ 055 5 94 77, Via Portigiana; admission €6.20, including Museo Bandini; open 9.30am-7pm Wed-Mon May-Oct, 9.30am-5pm Wed-Mon Nov-Apr)* features a 1st-century-BC Roman theatre, which is used from June to August for the Estate Fiesolana, a series of concerts and performances. Also in the complex are a small Etruscan temple and Roman baths, which date from the same period as the theatre. The small archaeological museum is worth a look, as it includes exhibits from the Bronze Age to the Roman period.

If you are planning a picnic or just want a refreshing walk, head uphill along the main street from Piazza Mino da Fiesole to Via Corsica. Take Via Pelagaccio, which eventually becomes a dirt track as it weaves around the mountain overlooking Florence and winds back into Fiesole.

Places to Stay & Eat The APT advises that you camp in designated areas.

Campeggio Panoramico *(☎ 055 59 90 69, fax 055 5 91 86, Via Peramonda 1, Fiesole)* Sites per person/tent & car €7.75/12.90. To get to this camp site, which (as the name suggests) offers some great views, take bus No 70 from Piazza Mino da Fiesole. It is a big rambling site and in summer has the advantage of being just a little cooler than down in Florence itself. Bungalows are also available.

The city has eight mostly expensive hotels and a handful of affittacamere and *agriturismo* (farm accommodation) rooms. The APT in Florence has details.

Villa Sorriso *(☎ 055 5 90 27, fax 055 597 80 75, Via Gramsci 21)* Singles/doubles €36.15/59.40. Villa 'Smile' is the cheapest joint in town. It has heating and air-con, and is perfectly acceptable.

Bencistà *(☎/fax 055 5 91 63, Via Benedetto da Maiano 4)* Doubles from €154.95 with half-board. This hotel is about 1km from Fiesole, just off the road to Florence. It is an old villa and from its terrace there is a magnificent view of Florence. It might bust the budget but for one or two days it's worth it. Ask for, erm, a room with a view.

There are several eateries right on Piazza Mino da Fiesole that are perfectly all right. There are much finer options available, however.

Trattoria Cave di Maiano *(☎ 055 5 91 33, Via Cave di Maiano 16, Fiesole)* Full meals €25.80. Open daily, closed Mon lunch. This is a fine spot for traditional meat dishes and is a favourite with Florentines. In summer you can sit outside in the garden. Getting here without a car is a little tricky as the restaurant is actually in Maiano, a *frazione* (division) of Fiesole, and off the bus routes. You could try getting a taxi from central Fiesole.

Getting There & Away Fiesole is easily reached from Florence. ATAF bus No 7 from the Stazione di Santa Maria Novella in Florence connects with Piazza Mino da Fiesole. If you are driving, find your way to Piazza della Libertà in Florence and follow the signs to Fiesole.

The Medici Villas

The Medicis built several opulent villas in the countryside around Florence as their wealth and prosperity grew during the 15th and 16th centuries. Most of the villas are now enclosed by the city's suburbs and industrial sprawl, and are easily reached by taking ATAF buses from Stazione di Santa Maria Novella.

One of the finest of the Medici villas, **Villa Medicea La Petraia** *(☎ 055 45 26 91, Via della Petraia 40; admission €2.05, including Villa Medicea di Castello; open 8.15am-8pm daily Jun-Aug, closes earlier in other months and on 2nd & 3rd Mon of the month year-round)*, is about 3.5km north of the city. Commissioned by Cardinal Ferdinando de' Medici in 1576, this former castle was converted by Buontalenti and features a magnificent garden. ATAF bus No 28 from Stazione di Santa Maria Novella runs here.

Further north of the city is the former summer home of Lorenzo il Magnifico, **Villa Medicea di Castello** *(☎ 055 45 47 91, Via di Castello 47, admission €2.05 including Villa Medicea La Petraia; open 8.15am-8pm daily Jun-Aug, closes earlier in other months and on 2nd & 3rd Mon of the month year-round)*. You can visit the park only. Again, take bus No 28.

Access to **Villa Careggi** *(☎ 055 427 97 55, Viale Pieraccini 17; free; open 9am-6pm Mon-Fri, 9am-noon Sat)*, where Lorenzo il Magnifico breathed his last in 1492, is limited as it is used as administrative offices for the local hospital. Groups must book ahead. ATAF bus No 14 (which you can pick up in Florence at Piazza Beccaria, the cathedral or Stazione di Santa Maria Novella) runs past.

Another Medici getaway was the **Villa di Poggio a Caiano** *(☎ 055 87 70 12, Piazza dei Medici 12; admission to villa €2.05 by guided tours only, grounds free; tours every hour 9.30am-6.30pm daily Jun–mid-Sep, 9.30am-5.30pm daily mid-Sep–May)*. About 15km from Florence on the road to Pistoia, the building is set in magnificent sprawling gardens. Its interior is sumptuously decorated in frescoes and furnished much as it was early in the 20th century when it was a royal residence of the Savoys. The easiest way to get there without your own transport is with the COPIT bus service (€3.50 return, 27 minutes) running between Florence and Pistoia – there is a bus stop right outside the villa.

The Mugello

The area north-east of Florence leading up to Firenzuola, near the border with Emilia-Romagna, is known as the Mugello and features some of the most traditional villages in Tuscany. The River Sieve winds up a valley that is one of Tuscany's premier wine areas.

Start with the APT office in Florence or contact the Comunità Montana del Mugello (☎ 055 849 53 46, fax 055 845 62 88), Via P Togliatti 45, Borgo San Lorenzo.

Promo Mugello (☎ 055 845 87 42, fax 055 849 57 72), Piazza Martin Luther King 5–6, Borgo San Lorenzo, can help with hotel information and bookings.

The Medici originated from the Mugello and held extensive property in the area. Several Medici family castles, villas and palaces dot the area, some of which are open to the public. Others can be visited with a guide. The APT office in Florence has information. Otherwise contact the Associazione Turismo Ambiente (☎ 055 845 87 93), Piazza Dante 29, Borgo San Lorenzo.

If you're interested in a wineries tour, there is a so-called *strada del vino* (wine road) mapped out, which will take you through the areas producing Chianti Rufino and Colli Fiorentini. Again, the Florence APT office has details. Also ask about the various walking trails through the Mugello.

Northern & Western Tuscany

PRATO

postcode 59100 • pop 171,100

Virtually enclosed in the urban and industrial sprawl of Florence, 17km to the north-west, Prato is one of Italy's main textile centres. Founded by the Ligurians, the city fell to the Etruscans and later the Romans and by the 11th century was an important centre for wool production. It is worth visiting on your way to the more picturesque cities of Pistoia, Lucca and Pisa.

Orientation

The old city centre is small and surrounded by the city wall. The main train station (Prato Stazione Centrale), on Piazza della Stazione, is east of the city centre.

Information

The APT office (☎ 0574 2 41 12, **e** apt@prato.turismo.toscana.it) is at Via B Cairoli 48–52, two blocks east of the central Piazza del Comune. It opens 9am to 1.30pm and 2pm to 7pm (2.30pm to 6pm in winter) Monday to Saturday. If you plan to see all the sights, it's probably worth investing in a *biglietto cumulativo* (combined ticket), which costs €5.15. Ask at the APT office for details.

The main post office is at Via Arcivescovo Martini 8.

For medical emergencies, the hospital (☎ 0574 43 41) is on Piazza dell'Ospedale, south-west of Piazza del Comune. The *questura* (police station; ☎ 0574 55 55) is well out of the centre at Via Cino 10, but operates a small station at Via B Cairoli 29.

Museo di Pittura Murale

This museum *(☎ 0574 44 05 01, Piazza San Domenico; adult/child €5.15/3.10; open 10am-6pm Mon & Wed-Sat, 10am-1pm Sun & holidays)* houses the small but impressive collection of largely Tuscan paintings, transferred from the Palazzo Pretorio as it undergoes a long restoration. Among the artists represented here are Filippo Lippi and Vasari. There's also a collection of 14th- to 17th-century frescoes and graffiti. The museum is reached through the cloisters of the Chiesa di San Domenico.

Cattedrale di Santo Stefano

Along Via G Mazzoni from Piazza del Comune is Piazza del Duomo and the 12th-century Cattedrale di Santo Stefano *(☎ 0574 2 62 34, Piazza del Duomo; free; open 7am-12.30pm & 3.30pm-7pm Mon-Sat, 7am-1pm & 3.30pm-8pm Sun)*. The rather simple Pisan-Romanesque facade features a lunette by Andrea della Robbia and the white and green marble banding you will undoubtedly see elsewhere in Tuscany (Siena, Pistoia, Lucca). The most extraordinary element, however, is the oddly protruding **Pulpito della Sacra Cintola**, jutting out over the piazza on the right-hand side of the main entrance. The eroded panels of the pulpit, designed by Donatello and Michelozzo in the 1430s, are in the **Museo dell'Opera del Duomo** *(☎ 0574 2 93 39, Piazza del Duomo 49; adult/child €5.15/3.10; open 9.30am-12.30pm & 3pm-6.30pm Mon & Wed-Sat, 9.30am-12.30pm Sun)*. The pulpit was expressly added so that the *sacra cintola* (sacred girdle) could be displayed to the people five times a year (Easter, 1 May, 15 August, 8 September and 25 December). It is believed the girdle (or belt) was given to St Thomas by the Virgin and brought to the city from Jerusalem after the Second Crusade. In medieval times, great importance was attached to such holy relics, but just how many girdles did Mary have? Another, declared the real thing in 1953 by the Orthodox Patriarch of Antioch, is stored in the Syrian city of Homs.

Among the magnificent frescoes inside the church, look for those behind the high altar by Filippo Lippi, depicting the martyrdom of St John the Baptist and St Stephen, and Agnolo Gaddi's *Legend of the Holy Girdle* in the chapel to the left of the entrance.

Chiesa di Santa Maria delle Carceri

Built by Giuliano da Sangallo towards the end of the 15th century, the interior of this church *(☎ 0574 2 79 33, Piazza Santa Maria delle Carceri; free; open 7am-noon*

& 4pm-7pm) is considered a Renaissance masterpiece, with a frieze and medallions of the Evangelists by the workshop of Andrea della Robbia.

Also on the same piazza is the **Castello dell'Imperatore** *(☎ 0574 3 82 07, Piazza Santa Maria delle Carceri; admission €2.05; open Mon-Sun 10am-7pm May-Sept; 10am-4pm Nov-Feb; 10am-5pm Mar & Apr)*, built in the 13th century by the Holy Roman Emperor Frederick II.

Places to Stay & Eat

Albergo Il Giglio *(☎ 0574 3 70 49, fax 0574 60 43 51, Piazza San Marco 14)* Singles/doubles without bath €38.75/54.25, with bath €54.25/67.15. This comfortable and popular place has been run by the same family since 1969 (they also own Albergo Roma), so they must be doing something right.

Albergo Roma *(☎ 0574 3 17 77, fax 0574 60 43 51, Via G Caradori 1)* Doubles with bath €55.25. All 12 rooms at this one-star hotel are doubles but they may discount for singles in the low season. Ask for a room at the back, as the hotel overlooks a busy road.

Hotel Flora *(☎ 0574 3 35 21, fax 0574 4 02 89, e hotelflora@texnet.it, Via B Cairoli 31)* Singles/doubles up to €87.80/134.30. Rooms at the Flora have all the mod-cons but it still has a certain charm to it. The tiny rooftop restaurant serves excellent food.

Ristorante Lo Scoglio *(☎ 0574 2 27 60, Via Verdi 42)* Meals around €20.65, pizzas from €5.15. Open Tues-Sun. Lo Scoglio is a pleasant spot for a meal. The menu is wide-ranging, offering up everything from pizza to fresh fish.

Ristorante Baghino *(☎ 0574 2 79 20, Via dell'Accademia 9)* Meals €18.05-20.65. Open Mon-Sat. This place is in much the same vein as Lo Scoglio with classier deco.

There is a ***produce market*** *(Piazza Lippi)*, from 8am to 1pm Monday to Saturday.

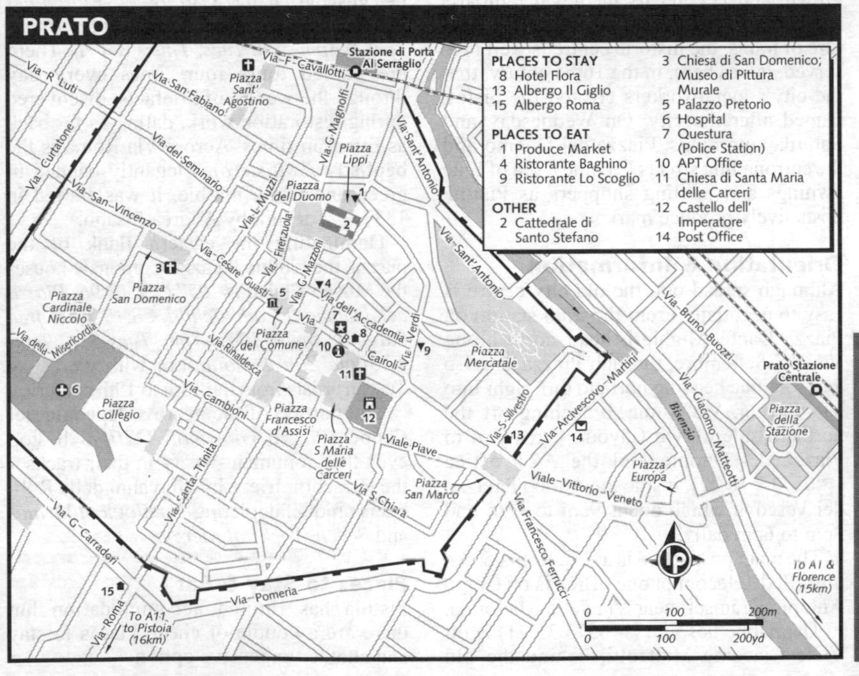

Getting There & Around

CAP and Lazzi buses operate regular services to Florence (€1.80, 45 minutes, every 15 minutes) from in front of the main train station. Prato is on the Florence-Bologna and Florence-Lucca train lines. Sample fares and destinations include to Florence (€1.35, 25 minutes, every 10 minutes), Bologna (€4.25, one hour, 20 daily), Lucca (€3.60, 55 minutes, 20 daily) and Pistoia (€1.35, 15 minutes, every half hour).

By car, take the A1 from Florence and exit at Calenzano, or take the A11 and exit at Prato.

Several buses, including No 5, connect the main train station with the cathedral (€0.75).

PISTOIA

postcode 51100 • pop 90,200

A pleasant city at the foot of the Apennines only 45 minutes north-west of Florence by train, Pistoia deserves a lot more attention than it normally gets. Although the city has grown well beyond its medieval ramparts and is now a world centre for the manufacture of trains, the historic centre is well preserved. It was here, in the 16th century, that the city's metalworkers created the pistol, named after the city. On Wednesday and Saturday mornings, Piazza del Duomo and the surrounding streets become a sea of blue awnings and jostling shoppers as Pistoia hosts lively produce markets.

Orientation & Information

Although spread out, the old city centre is easy to negotiate. From the train station on Piazza Dante Alighieri, head north along Via XX Settembre, through Piazza Treviso and continue heading north to turn right into Via Cavour. Via Roma, branching off the northern side of Via Cavour, takes you to Piazza del Duomo and the APT office (☎ 0573 2 16 22), inside the Antico Palazzo dei Vescovi, which opens 9am to 1pm and 3pm to 6pm daily.

The main post office is at Via Roma 5. An unstaffed Telecom phone office is on Corso Antonio Gramsci, near Via della Madonna.

The public hospital (☎ 0573 35 21) is on Viale Giacomo Matteotti, behind the old Ospedale del Ceppo. The *questura* (police station; ☎ 0573 2 67 05) is out of the centre at Via Macallé 23. If you need a doctor fast, call ☎ 0573 36 36.

Piazza del Duomo

Much of Pistoia's visual wealth is concentrated on this central square. The Pisan-Romanesque facade of the **Cattedrale di San Zeno** *(☎ 0573 2 50 95, Piazza del Duomo; free; open 8.30am-12.30pm & 3.30pm-7pm)* boasts a lunette of the Madonna and Child by Andrea della Robbia, who also made the terracotta tiles that line the barrel vault of the main porch. Inside, in the Cappella di San Jacopo, is the remarkable silver **Altarpiece of San Giacomo**. It was begun in the 13th century, with artisans adding to it over the ensuing two centuries until Brunelleschi contributed the final touch, the two half-figures on the left side.

The venerable building between the cathedral and Via Roma is the **Antico Palazzo dei Vescovi** *(☎ 0573 36 92 72, Piazza del Duomo 4; admission €3.60; open 10am-1pm & 3pm-5pm Tues, Thurs & Fri)*. There are guided tours four times every day through the wealth of artefacts, discovered during restoration work, dating as far back as Etruscan times. Across Via Roma is the **baptistry** *(battistero)*. Elegantly banded in green and white marble, it was started in 1337 to a design by Andrea Pisano.

Dominating the eastern flank of the piazza, the Gothic Palazzo Comunale houses the **Museo Civico** *(☎ 0573 37 12 96, Piazza del Duomo 1; adult/child €3.10/1.55, free Sat pm; open 10am-7pm Tues-Sat, 9am-12.30pm Sun & holidays)*, with works by Tuscan artists from the 13th to 19th centuries.

The portico of the nearby **Ospedale del Ceppo** *(Piazza Giovanni XXIII)* will stop even the monument-weary in their tracks – the terracotta frieze by Giovanni della Robbia is unique, depicting *Theological Virtues* and *Seven Works of Mercy*.

Places to Stay & Eat

Pistoia has limited accommodation but there are a couple of cheap places to stay and another expensive option.

TUSCANY

Hotel Firenze *(☎/fax 0573 2 31 41, Via Curtatone e Montanara 42)* Singles/doubles without bath €31/54.25, singles/doubles with bath €36.15/62. Breakfast is an extra €5.15. The rooms here are large and simple, and it has got a great central location, which is a bonus.

Albergo Autisti *(☎ 0573 2 17 71, Via le Antonio Pacinotti 89)* Singles/doubles without bath €20.65/36.15, doubles with bath €41.30. You can pick up a pokey room at Albergo Autisti. The doubles with bathroom are slightly better, but they're often full with long-term lodgers.

Hotel Leon Bianco *(☎ 0573 2 66 74, fax 0573 2 67 04, Via Panciatichi 2,* **W** *www.promonet.it/leonbianco)* Singles/doubles €62/87.80, buffet breakfast €7.75. This hotel has immaculate large rooms, all with private bathroom, and if you have your own transport, they can organise free parking for you in the town centre. Prices come down by 10% in winter.

Trattoria dell'Abbondanza *(☎ 0573 36 80 37, Via dell'Abbondanza)* Meals about €12.90. Open Thurs-Tues. This little trattoria down a quiet passageway off Piazza Spirito Santo has a menu that changes daily

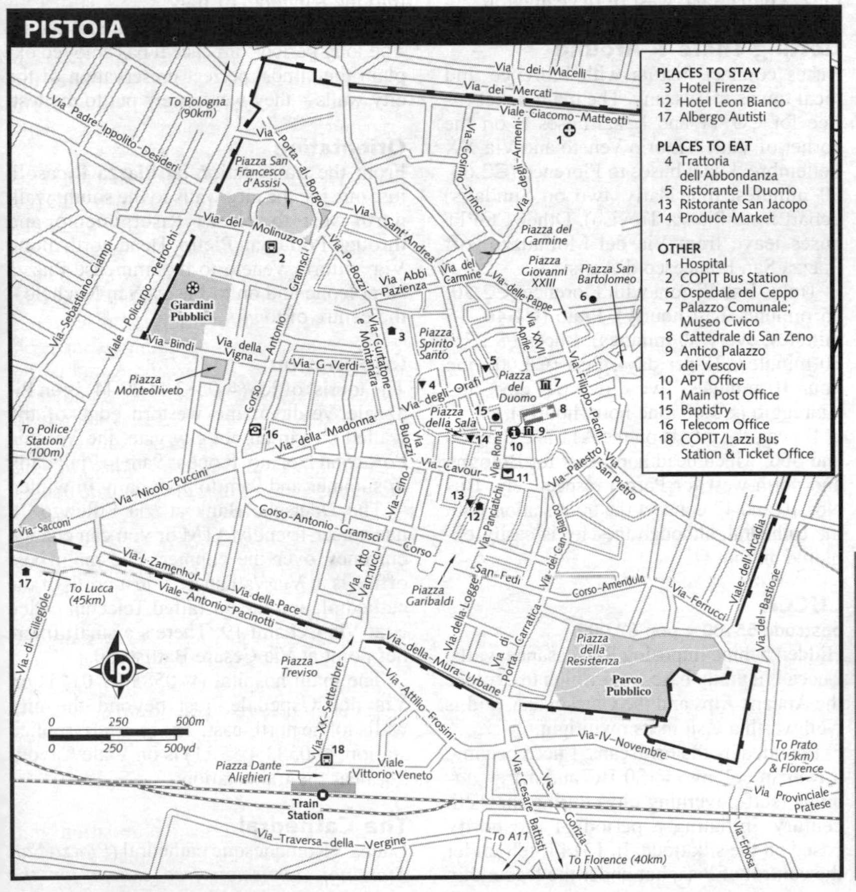

but there's usually a good selection of soups and pasta.

Ristorante San Jacopo *(☎ 0573 2 77 86, Via Crispi 15)* Meals €20.65. This place serves great Tuscan dishes – house specialities include *baccalà alla Livornese* (salted cod) and *pappardelle alle lepre* (wide flat pasta ribbons with stewed hare, red wine and tomato sauce).

Ristorante El Duomo *(☎ 0573 3 19 48, Via Bracciolini 5)* Mains €5.15. Open noon-3pm. This is a cheap self-service buffet-style place with a daily fare of pasta and salad.

A ***produce market*** is open most days on Piazza della Sala, west of the cathedral.

Getting There & Around

Buses connect Pistoia with Florence and local towns in Tuscany. The main ticket office for COPIT and Lazzi buses is on the corner of Viale Vittorio Veneto and Via XX Settembre. Lazzi buses to Florence (€2.60, 50 minutes, nine daily, two on Sundays) depart from Piazza Treviso). Other COPIT buses leave from Via del Molinuzzo, off Piazza San Francesco d'Assisi.

Trains link Pistoia with Florence (€2.30, 45 minutes, half hourly), Prato (€1.40, 15 minutes, every 30 minutes), Lucca (€2.75, 50 minutes, 25 per day), Pisa (€3.60, one hour 10 minutes, five direct per day) and Viareggio (€3.60, one hour, hourly).

By car, the city is on the A11 and the S64 and S66, which head north-east for Bologna and north-west for Parma respectively. Bus Nos 10 and 12 connect the train station with the cathedral, although the city is easily explored on foot.

LUCCA

postcode 55100 • pop 87,000

Hidden behind imposing Renaissance walls, Lucca is a pretty base from which to explore the Apuane Alps and the Garfagnana, and is well worth a visit in its own right.

Founded by the Etruscans, Lucca became a Roman colony in 180 BC and a free *comune* (self-governing city) during the 12th century, initiating a period of prosperity based on the silk trade. In 1314 it fell under the control of Pisa, but under the leadership of local adventurer Castruccio Castracani degli Anterminelli, the city regained its independence and began to amass territories in western Tuscany. Castruccio died in 1325, but Lucca remained an independent republic for almost 500 years.

Napoleon ended all this in 1805. He created the principality of Lucca and, unswerving in his innate sense of democratic values, placed one of the seemingly countless members of his family in need of an Italian fiefdom (this time his sister Elisa) in control. Twelve years later, the city became a Bourbon duchy, before being incorporated into the Kingdom of Italy.

Lucca remains a strong agricultural centre. The long periods of peace it has enjoyed explain the almost perfect preservation of the city walls – they were rarely put to the test.

Orientation

From the train station on Piazza Ricasoli, just outside the city walls to the south, walk north-west to Piazza Risorgimento and through Porta San Pietro. Head north along Via Vittorio Veneto to the immense Piazza Napoleone and on to Piazza San Michele – the centre of town.

Information

The tourist office (☎ 0583 44 29 44) is on Piazzale Verdi, at the western edge of the walled city in an old city gate, the Vecchia Porta San Donato. It opens 9am to 7pm daily in summer and 9am to 3pm daily in winter.

The Deutsche Bank at Via Fillungo 76 has a user-friendly ATM or you can change currency over the counter. The main post office is at Via Vallisneri 2, just north of the cathedral, and the unstaffed Telecom office is at Via Cenami 19. There's a small Internet point at Via Cesare Battisti 60.

The main hospital (☎ 0583 97 01) is on Via dell'Ospedale, just beyond the city walls to the north-east. The *questura* (police station; ☎ 0583 4 55 11) is on Viale Cavour 38, near the train station.

The Cathedral

Lucca's Romanesque cathedral *(Piazza San Martino; admission free except for the*

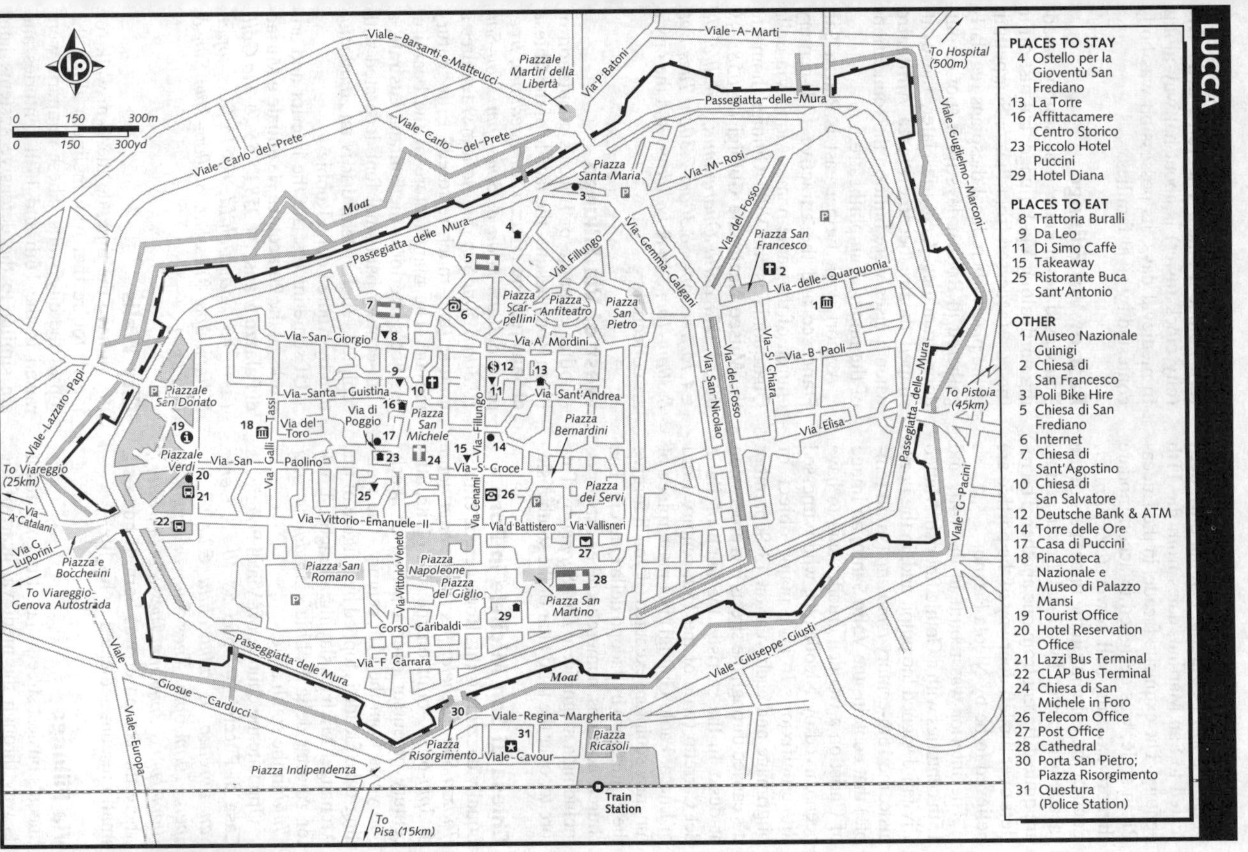
LUCCA
PLACES TO STAY
4 Ostello per la Gioventù San Frediano
13 La Torre
16 Affittacamere Centro Storico
23 Piccolo Hotel Puccini
29 Hotel Diana
PLACES TO EAT
8 Trattoria Buralli
9 Da Leo
11 Di Simo Caffè
15 Takeaway
25 Ristorante Buca Sant'Antonio
OTHER
1 Museo Nazionale Guinigi
2 Chiesa di San Francesco
3 Poli Bike Hire
5 Chiesa di San Frediano
6 Internet
7 Chiesa di Sant'Agostino
10 Chiesa di San Salvatore
12 Deutsche Bank & ATM
14 Torre delle Ore
17 Casa di Puccini
18 Pinacoteca Nazionale e Museo di Palazzo Mansi
19 Tourist Office
20 Hotel Reservation Office
21 Lazzi Bus Terminal
22 CLAP Bus Terminal
24 Chiesa di San Michele in Foro
26 Telecom Office
27 Post Office
28 Cathedral
30 Porta San Pietro; Piazza Risorgimento
31 Questura (Police Station)

sacristy which costs €1.55; open 9.30am-5.45pm Sun-Fri, 9.30am-6.45pm Sat), dedicated to San Martino, dates from the 11th century. The exquisite facade, in the Lucca-Pisan style, was designed to accommodate the pre-existing bell tower *(campanile)*. Each of the columns in the upper part of the facade was carved by a local artisan and all are quite different from one another. The reliefs over the left doorway of the portico are believed to be by Nicola Pisano.

The interior was rebuilt in the 14th and 15th centuries with a Gothic flourish. Matteo Civitali designed the pulpit and, in the north aisle, the 15th-century *tempietto* (small temple) that contains the **Volto Santo**, an image of Christ on a wooden crucifix said to have been carved by Nicodemus, who witnessed the crucifixion. It is a major object of pilgrimage and each year on 13 September it's carried through the streets in a procession at dusk. In the sacristy, the tomb of Ilaria del Carretto (wife of the 15th-century Lord of Lucca, Paolo Guinigi) is a masterpiece of funerary sculpture executed (if you'll forgive the expression) by Jacopo della Quercia. The church contains numerous other artworks, including a magnificent *Last Supper* by Tintoretto, over the third altar of the south aisle.

Chiesa di San Michele in Foro

Equally dazzling is this Romanesque church *(Piazza San Michele; free; open 8am-noon & 3pm-6pm)*, built on the site of its 8th-century precursor over a period of nearly 300 years from the 11th century. The wedding-cake facade is topped by a figure of the Archangel Michael slaying a dragon. Look for Andrea della Robbia's *Madonna and Child* in the south aisle.

Opposite the church, off Via di Poggio, is **Casa di Puccini** *(☎ 0583 58 40 28, Corte San Lorenzo 9; adult/child €2.60/1.55; open 10am-6pm Tues-Sun in summer, 10am-1pm & 3pm-6pm Tues-Sun in winter)*, where the composer was born. It houses a small museum dedicated to his life.

Via Fillungo

Lucca's busiest street, Via Fillungo, threads its way through the medieval heart of the old city and is lined with fascinating, centuries-old buildings. The **Torre delle Ore** (city clock tower) is about halfway along. In medieval days, its possession was hotly contested by rival families.

East of Via Fillungo

You would never know it by simply parading north along Via Fillungo, but just off to the east (accessed from Piazza Scarpellini) is the place where local thespians regularly gathered in Roman days for a spot of outdoor dramatics. Centuries later, the oval-shaped theatre became **Piazza Anfiteatro** when houses were built on the foundations of the imperial amphitheatre.

A short walk farther east is **Piazza San Francesco** and the attractive 13th-century church of the same name. Along Via della Quarquonia is the Villa Guinigi, home to the **Museo Nazionale Guinigi** *(☎ 0583 49 60 33, Via della Quarquonia; adult/child €4.15/free; open 8.30am-7.30pm Tues-Sat, 8.30am-1pm Sun & holidays)* and the city's art collection.

West of Via Fillungo

Another example of Lucca's adaptation of Pisan Romanesque, the facade of the **Chiesa di San Frediano** *(Piazza San Frediano; free; open 8.30am-noon & 3pm-5pm Mon-Sat, 10.30am-5pm Sun and holidays)* features a unique (and much-restored) 13th-century mosaic. The main feature of the beautiful basilica's interior is the **Fontana Lustrale**, a 12th-century baptismal font decorated with sculpted reliefs. Behind it is an *Annunciation* by Andrea della Robbia.

Of some interest are the interior and artworks of the **Pinacoteca Nazionale e Museo di Palazzo Mansi** *(☎ 0583 5 55 70, Via Galli Tassi 43; adult/child €4.15/free; open 8.30am-7pm Tues-Sat, 8.30am-1pm Sun & holidays)*.

City Walls

If you have the time, do the 4km walk (or jog if you're that way inclined) along the top of the city walls. These ramparts were raised in the 16th and 17th centuries and are similar to the defensive systems later developed by the French military engineer Vauban.

Courses

Centro Koinè *(☎ 0583 49 30 40, fax 0583 49 16 89, e koinelu@tin.it, Via A Mordini 60)* The school offers Italian courses for foreigners. A two-week summer course costs €346, while month-long courses, available year-round, cost €488. The school can also arrange accommodation.

Places to Stay

It is always advisable to book ahead, but if you're in a spot try the city's hotel association, the ***Sindacato Lucchese Albergatori*** *(☎ 0583 49 41 81, Via Fillungo 121)*. If they fail, there is another ***hotel reservation office*** *(☎ 0583 31 22 62, Piazzale Verdi 1)*, although this was closed at the time of writing.

Ostello per la Gioventù San Frediano *(☎/fax 0583 46 99 57, Via della Cavallerizza 12)* Dorm beds from €15. Reception open 7am-10am & 3.30pm-11.30pm. This newly opened, HI-affiliated hostel occupies a vast former schoolhouse behind the Chiesa di San Frediano. With 148 beds, a sweeping staircase and voluminous ceilings, space isn't an issue but an HI card is obligatory. There's also a bar and Internet access.

La Torre *(☎/fax 0583 95 70 44, Piazza del Carmine 11)* Singles/doubles without bath €31/36.15, double with bath €51.65. This is a great little spot with original rooms close to the Piazza Anfiteatro. Breakfast should be included in the price and there's a kitchen for guests' use.

Affittacamere Centro Storico *(☎/fax 0583 49 07 48, Corte Portici 16)* Doubles without bath €46.50, doubles with bath €67.15. This place is a good budget option smack in the heart of town. There's no curfew (as you are given your own front-door key) but newcomers are not accepted after 8pm. In slack periods, they may discount for singles.

Hotel Diana *(☎ 0583 49 22 02, fax 0583 46 77 95, e info@albergodiana.com, w www.albergodiana.com, Via del Molinetto 11)* Singles/doubles without bath €33.55/46.50, doubles with bath up to €62. Nine slightly chintzy rooms are available at this family-run two-star hotel. There's a pleasant six-room annexe just around the corner, but rooms there are pricier.

Piccolo Hotel Puccini *(☎ 0583 5 54 21, fax 0583 5 34 87, e info@hotelpuccini.com, w www.hotelpuccini.com, Via di Poggio 9)* Singles/doubles with bath €51.65/74.90. If you can afford the extra, this smart but cosy three-star hotel is one of Lucca's better deals.

Places to Eat

Lucca boasts a good selection of relatively cheap trattorias.

Ristorante Buca Sant'Antonio *(☎ 0583 5 58 81, Via della Cervia 3)* Meals €31. Open Tues-Sun. Lucca's classiest restaurant is expensive but well worth splashing out for. The menu includes such treats as veal and guinea-fowl, but do book ahead.

Trattoria Buralli *(☎ 0583 95 06 11, Piazza Sant'Agostino 9)* Set menu from €9.30. Open Thurs-Tues. The tourist menu at this trattoria is simple but filling and incorporates Luccanese specialities such as *zuppa di faro* (barley soup). Their fried chicken is also a wonder.

Da Leo *(☎ 0583 49 22 36, Via Tegrimi 1)* Main courses about €8.25. Open Mon-Sat. A popular, noisy trattoria, Da Leo is always a good bet. In summer, the shaded outside seating is a bonus and an excellent little corner for people-watching.

Di Simo Caffè *(Via Fillungo 58)* This is a grand bar and gelateria serving local specialities such as *buccellato* cakes.

For pizza by the slice, go to the small ***takeaway*** *(Via Fillungo 5)*.

Getting There & Away

CLAP buses (☎ 0583 58 78 97) serve the region, including destinations in the Garfagnana such as Castelnuovo (€3.10, 1½ hours, every two hours). Lazzi (☎ 0583 58 48 77) operates hourly buses to Florence (€4.45, 1½ hours), Pistoia (€3, 35 minutes) and Pisa (€1.85, 45 minutes). There are about seven services every day to La Spezia (€4.70, three hours), Marina di Carrara (€3.20, two hours) and Marina di Massa (€3.20, two hours), Both companies operate from Piazzale Verdi.

Lucca is on the Florence-Pisa-Viareggio train line and there are also services into the Garfagnana. Sample fares include to Pisa (€1.85, 25 minutes, 24 daily) and Florence (€4.05, 1½ hours, 20 daily).

By car, the A11 passes to the south of the city, connecting it with Pisa and Viareggio. The S12, which becomes the S445 at Barga, links the city with the Garfagnana.

Getting Around

Most cars are banned from the city centre, although tourists are allowed to drive into the walled city and park in the residents' spaces (yellow lines) if they have a permit from one of the hotels. There are paid parking areas in piazzas Santa Maria, San Donato, Ex Caserma Mazzini and Ex Caserma Lorenzini, and along Corso Garibaldi.

CLAP buses connect the train station, Piazza del Giglio (near Piazza Napoleone) and Piazzale Verdi, but it is just as easy, and more pleasurable, to walk. Bikes, including tandems, can be hired from Poli (☎ 0583 49 37 87) at Piazza Santa Maria 41 from €2 an hour.

For a taxi, call ☎ 0583 49 49 89.

THE GARFAGNANA

The heart of the Garfagnana is in the valley formed by the River Serchio and its tributaries. This is an excellent area for walking, horse riding and a host of other outdoor pursuits, and the region is well geared for tourism. Staff at the tourist offices in Lucca or Pisa can advise. The most useful organisation in the Garfagnana is Consorzio Garfagnana Turistica (☎ 0583 64 44 73), at the Comunità Montana, Via Vittorio Emanuele 9, in Castelnuovo di Garfagnana. Pro Loco tourist offices in several smaller villages can help with details on hotels and *rifugi* (mountain huts).

Walkers should pick up a copy of *Garfagnana Trekking*, which details a 10-day walk. Another booklet, *Garfagnana a Cavallo*, details guided horse treks that can cost €10.35 per hour or €46.50 per day. Details of these and other aspects of the mountains, including agriturismo accommodation, are available from the Azienda Agrituristica La Garfagnana (☎ 0583 6 87 05), Località Prade 25, in Castiglione di Garfagnana.

Apuane Alps

This mountain range is bordered on one side by the stretch of coastline known as the Versilia Riviera and on the other by the vast valley of the Garfagnana. Altitudes are relatively low, in comparison with the Alps farther north, but the Apuane Alps are certainly not lacking in great walking possibilities: some trails afford spectacular views to the coastline and the Ligurian Sea. The landscape in some areas has been utterly destroyed by marble mining, an industry that has exploited these mountains since Roman times. No environmental laws have been in place to prevent mining companies from literally removing entire peaks in some places. But, in the end, the extent of interference in the natural landscape has created a new environment with a certain aesthetic appeal. You'll find a good network of marked walking trails and several rifugi in the Apuane Alps. The 1:25,000 *Carta dei Sentieri e Rifugi,* published by Multigraphic of Florence, is a good map.

You can get information from the Comunità Montana in Castiglione di Garfagnana.

MASSA & CARRARA

These two towns in the northern reaches of Tuscany don't really warrant a visit unless you're interested in seeing Italy's famous marble quarries. Massa is the administrative centre of the province and is rather unattractive, although the beachfront extension, Marina di Massa, is popular with holidaying Italians. You might wonder why, if you happen to stumble onto the overpopulated shores.

Carrara, however, is quite picturesque. At the foothills of the Apuane Alps, the town appears to be dominated by snow-capped mountains, an illusion created by limestone formations and the vast quarries that virtually cover the hills. The texture and purity of Carrara's white marble is unrivalled and was chosen by Michelangelo for many of his masterpieces. He often travelled to the quarries to personally select blocks of the stone.

The APT has offices at Marina di Massa (☎ 0585 24 00 63), Viale Vespucci 24, and in Carrara (☎ 0585 84 44 03), Via Settembre XX.

Ostello Apuano *(☎ 0585 78 00 34, fax 0585 77 42 66, ⓔ ostelloapuano@hotmail.com, Via delle Pinete 237, Partaccia)* Dorm beds €7.75, open mid-Apr–Sept. This is a youth hostel on the coast at Partaccia, 3km from Carrara train station (catch the bus marked via Avenza Mare if you don't want to walk).

Both Massa and Carrara are accessible from the A12 and the S1 Via Aurelia; signs direct you to the quarries and other attractions, such as museums.

PISA

postcode 56100 • pop 98,000

Once, if briefly, a maritime power to rival Genoa and Venice, Pisa now draws its fame from an architectural project gone terribly wrong: its Leaning Tower *(Torre Pendente)*. But the city offers quite a deal more. Indeed, the tower is only one element of the trio of Romanesque beauties astride the green carpet of the Campo dei Miracoli – along with Piazza San Marco in Venice one of Italy's most memorable squares.

Pisa has a centuries-old tradition as a university town and even today is full of young students. A perhaps unexpectedly beautiful city, it really deserves more than the usual one-day stopover planned by the average tourist.

History

Possibly of Greek origin, Pisa became an important naval base under Rome and remained a significant port for many centuries. The city's so-called Golden Days began late in the 9th century when it became an independent maritime republic and a rival of Genoa and Venice. The good times rolled on into the 12th and 13th centuries, by which time Pisa controlled Corsica, Sardinia and most of the mainland coast as far south as Civitavecchia. The majority of the city's finest buildings date from this period, as well as the distinctive Pisan-Romanesque architectural style.

Pisa's support for the Ghibellines during the tussles between the Holy Roman Emperor and the pope brought the city into conflict with its mostly Guelph Tuscan neighbours, including Siena, Lucca and Florence. The real blow, however, came when Genoa's fleet inflicted a devastating defeat on Pisa at the Battle of Meloria in 1284. The city fell to Florence in 1406 and the Medici encouraged great artistic, literary and scientific endeavour and re-established Pisa's university. The city's most famous son, Galileo Galilei, later taught at the university.

Orientation

By train you'll arrive at Stazione Pisa Centrale, on Piazza della Stazione at the southern edge of the town. The main intercity bus station is on Piazza Vittorio Emanuele II, a short walk north along Viale Gramsci. The medieval centre is about a 15-minute walk north, across the River Arno, and Campo dei Miracoli (aka Piazza del Duomo) is about another 10-minute walk north-west. It is quicker to catch a city bus from outside the station (see Getting Around later).

Information

Tourist Offices The main APT office (☎ 050 56 04 64, ⓔ info@pisa.turismo.toscana.it) is in a little cube of a building just outside the city walls. It opens 9am to 6pm Monday to Saturday (9.30am to noon and 3pm to 5.30pm in the low season) and 10.30am to 4.30pm on Sunday. The office at the train station (☎ 050 4 22 91) keeps longer hours (9am to 7pm Monday to Saturday, and 9.30am to 3.30pm on Sunday) but has little more than a map and a list of hotels – the most useful items for late-night arrivals, however.

Money Try to avoid the currency-exchange booths near the cathedral. Change currency at banks along Corso Italia or at Stazione Pisa Centrale.

Post & Communications The main post office is on Piazza Vittorio Emanuele II. You'll find phones scattered throughout the town. Internet Planet (☎ 050 83 07 02), at Piazza Cavallotti 3–4, charges €3 an hour for Internet access.

Laundry Clean all those smelly socks at Onda Blu self-service laundrette, Via San Francesco 8a.

Medical Services & Emergency The hospital (☎ 050 99 21 11) is a complex at Via Roma 67. The Farmacia Nuova Fantoni (pharmacy), Lungarno Mediceo 51, is open 24 hours. The *questura* (police station; ☎ 050 58 35 11) is on Via Mario Lalli.

Campo dei Miracoli

The Pisans can justly claim that the Campo dei Miracoli is one of the most beautiful squares in the world. Set among its sprawling lawns is surely one of the most extraordinary concentrations of Romanesque splendour – the cathedral, the baptistry and the Leaning Tower. On any day, the piazza is teeming with people – students studying or at play, tourists wandering and local workers eating lunch.

A staggered pricing system operates for tickets to enter one or more of the monuments and museums in and around the

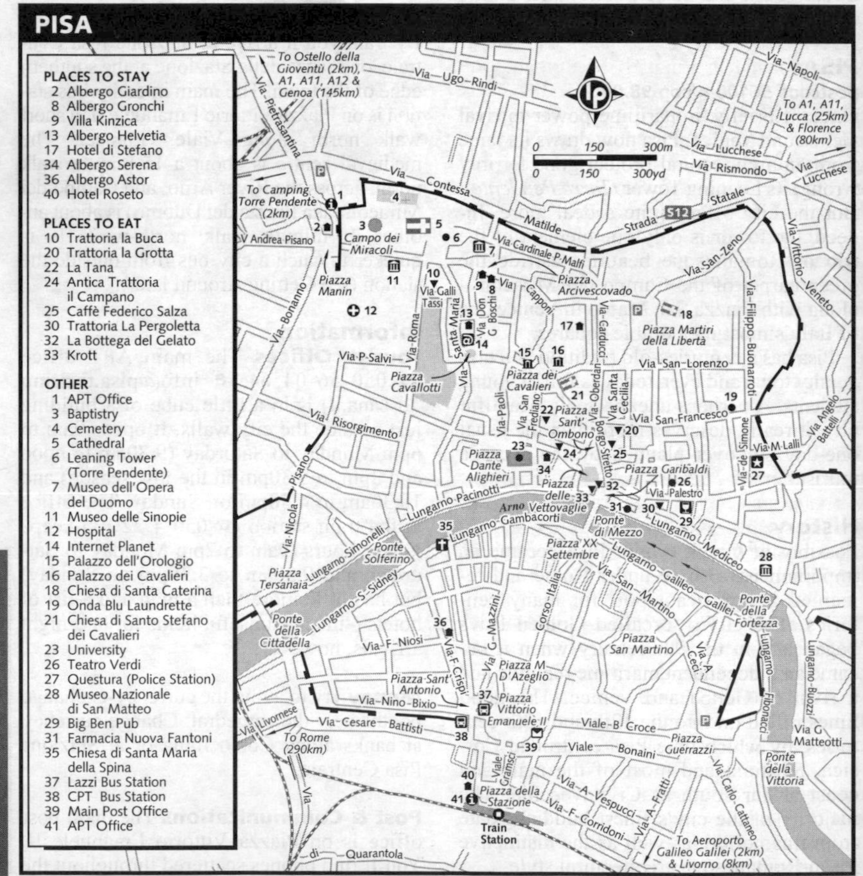

square. €6.20 admits you to two monuments or museums and €8.25 to four – the two museums, the baptistry and the cemetery *(cimitero)*. The cathedral itself is not included and costs an extra €1.55. At the time of writing, the Leaning Tower remained closed to visitors.

Opening times are complex. In some cases there are summer, autumn and winter times. What follows below gives the summer and winter 'extremes'.

The Cathedral The majesty of Pisa's cathedral *(☎ 050 56 05 47; admission €1.55; open 10am-7.40pm Mon-Sat, 1pm-7.40pm Sun in summer, 10am-12.45pm & 3pm-4.45pm Mon-Sat, 3pm-4.45pm Sun in winter)* made it a model for Romanesque churches throughout Tuscany and even on Sardinia. Begun in 1064, it is covered inside and out with the alternating bands of the (now somewhat faded) dark green and cream marble that were to become characteristic of the Pisan-Romanesque style.

The main facade is a sight to behold, adorned as it is with four tiers of columns. The huge interior is lined with 68 columns in classical style. The bronze doors of the transept, facing the Leaning Tower, are by Bonanno Pisano. The 16th-century bronze doors of the main entrance were designed by the school of Giambologna to replace the wooden originals, destroyed in a fire in 1596. The interior was also greatly redecorated after this devastating fire. Important works to survive the blaze include Giovanni Pisano's early-14th-century pulpit and an apse mosaic of *Christ in Majesty* completed by Cimabue in 1302.

The Leaning Tower (Torre Pendente) Welcome to one of the world's great cock-ups. The cathedral's bell tower *(campanile)* was in trouble from the start. Its architect, Bonanno Pisano, managed to complete only three tiers before the tower started to lean on the southern side. The problem is generally believed to have been caused by shifting soil and the 'leaning tower' continued to lean by an average of 1mm every year. In the past, several solutions to stop the lean were tried without success and occasionally with some opposition: the controversial Italian art historian, Vittorio Sgarbi, once said it would be 'better to see it fall and remember it leaning than see it straightened by mistake'.

In 1998 a plan was approved to wrap cables around the third storey and attach them to A-frames on the northern side. This held the tower in place while workers removed small portions of soil on the northern side to create a counter subsidence. It seems to have done the trick: the operation has taken 40cm out of the famous lean and experts say that the tower is safe for at least the next 300 years. The lean is now 4.1m off the perpendicular (at one stage it was 5m) but more importantly the slippage that caused the tower to lean in the first place has finally been arrested.

Galileo is sometimes claimed to have climbed the tower's 294 steps to experiment with gravity and it soon may be possible to follow in his footsteps. The tower, which has been closed since 1990 for rescue operations, is set to open to the public (call ☎ 050 56 05 47 for the latest update).

The Baptistry (Battistero) The unusual round baptistry *(☎ 050 56 05 47; admission part of €6.20 or €8.25 combined ticket; open 8am-7.40pm daily in summer, 9am-4.40pm daily in winter)* was started in 1153 by Diotisalvi, remodelled and continued by Nicola and Giovanni Pisano more than a century later, and finally completed in the 14th century – which explains the mix of architectural styles. The lower level of arcades is in the Pisan-Romanesque style and the pinnacled upper section and dome are Gothic. Inside, the beautiful pulpit was carved by Nicola Pisano and signed in 1260, and the white marble font was carved by Guido da Como in 1246. The acoustics beneath the dome are quite remarkable too.

The Cemetery (Cimitero) Behind the white wall to the north of the cathedral, this exquisite cemetery *(☎ 050 56 05 47; admission part of €6.20 or €8.25 combined ticket; open 8am-7.40pm in summer, 9am-4.40pm in winter)* is said to contain soil that was shipped from Calvary during the crusades. Many precious frescoes in the cloisters were badly damaged or destroyed during WWII Allied bombing raids. Among those saved were the *Triumph of Death* and *Last Judgement*, attributed to an anonymous 14th-century painter known as 'The Master of the Triumph of Death'.

The Museo delle Sinopie This museum *(☎ 050 56 05 47; admission part of €6.20 or €8.25 combined ticket; open 8am-7.40pm daily in summer, 9am-4.40pm daily in winter)* houses reddish-brown sketches drawn onto walls as the base for frescoes, discovered in the cemetery after the WWII bombing raids. The *sinopie* have been restored and provide a fascinating insight into the process of creating a fresco, although they are really only worth visiting if you have a particular interest in the subject.

The Museo dell'Opera del Duomo Near the Leaning Tower, this museum *(☎ 050 56 05 47, Piazza Arcivescovado 8; admission part of €6.20 or €8.25 combined ticket; open 8am-7.20pm daily in summer, 9am-4.20pm daily in winter)* features many artworks from the cathedral, tower and baptistry, including a magnificent ivory carving of the *Madonna and Crucifix* by Giovanni Pisano. Another highlight is the bust known as the *Madonna del Colloquio*, by the same artist, taken from the exterior of the baptistry.

The City

From Campo dei Miracoli, head south along Via Santa Maria and turn left at Piazza Cavallotti for the splendid **Piazza dei Cavalieri**, remodelled by Vasari in the 16th century. The **Palazzo dell'Orologio**, on the northern side of the piazza, occupies the site of a tower where, in 1288, Count Ugolino della Gherardesca, along with his sons and grandsons, were starved to death on suspicion of having helped the Genovese enemy at the Battle of Meloria. The incident was recorded in Dante's *Inferno*. The **Palazzo dei Cavalieri**, on the north-eastern side of the piazza, was redesigned by Vasari and features remarkable graffiti decoration. The piazza and palazzo are named for the Knights of Santo Stefano, a religious and military order founded by Cosimo de' Medici. Their church, **Santo Stefano dei Cavalieri**, was also designed by Vasari. The **Chiesa di Santa Caterina**, north of Via San Lorenzo on Piazza Martiri della Libertà, is a fine example of Pisan-Gothic architecture and contains works by Nino Pisano.

Wander south to the area around **Borgo Stretto**, the city's medieval heart. East along the waterfront boulevard, the Lungarno Mediceo, is the **Museo Nazionale di San Matteo** *(☎ 050 54 18 65, Piazza San Matteo; adult/child €4.15/free; open 9am-7pm Tues-Sat, 9am-2pm Sun)*, a fine gallery. It features works by Giovanni and Nicola Pisano, Masaccio and Donatello. Bring along some form of ID if you want to enter.

Cross the Ponte di Mezzo and head west to reach **the Chiesa di Santa Maria della Spina** *(☎ 055 321 54 46, Lungarno Gambacorti; admission €1.05; open 11am-1.30pm & 2.30pm-6pm Tues-Fri, 11am-1.30pm & 2.30pm-8pm Sat & Sun in summer, 10am-2pm Tues-Sun in winter)*. It was built in the early 14th century to house a thorn from Christ's crown.

Special Events

The Palio delle Quattro Antiche Repubbliche Marinare (Regatta of the Four Ancient Maritime Republics) sees a procession of boats and a race between the four historical maritime rivals – Pisa, Venice, Amalfi and Genoa. The event rotates between the four towns: Pisa in 2002, Venice in 2003, Genoa in 2004, Amalfi in 2005. Although usually held in June, it has been known to be delayed as late as September.

Other cultural and historical events include the Gioco del Ponte, a festival of traditional costume held on the last Sunday in June. On 17 June, the River Arno comes to life with the Regata Storica di San Ranieri, a rowing competition commemorating the city's patron saint.

Places to Stay

Pisa has a reasonable number of budget hotels for a small town, but many double as residences for students during the school year, so it can be difficult to find a cheap room.

Camping Torre Pendente *(☎ 050 56 17 04, fax 050 56 17 34, W www.camping toscana.it/torrependente, Via delle Cascine 86)* Sites per person/tent €6.45/5.65. This large camp site, about 2km west of the cathedral, has a supermarket, restaurant, a small pool and money exchange facilities.

Ostello della Gioventù *(☎/fax 050 89 06 22, Via Pietrasantina 15)* Bed in quad €11.90. Reception open after 6pm, midnight curfew. This rambling hostel, on the bank of a rather dirty stream, is a long hike north-west of the cathedral. Take bus No 3 from the town centre (walking the 2km from Campo dei Miracoli is a huge pain).

Albergo Serena *(☎/fax 050 58 08 09, e serena.pisa@csinfo.it, Via D Cavalca 45)* Singles/doubles up to €25.80/38.75. This place, just off Piazza Dante Alighieri, has simple rooms with an eclectic range of furniture and will give a discount for longer stays.

Albergo Helvetia *(☎ 050 55 30 84, Via Don Gaetano Boschi 31)* Singles/doubles without bath €28.40/38.75, doubles with bath €51.65. Albergo Helvetia, south of the cathedral, has pleasant rooms but the communal areas are a little soulless.

Hotel di Stefano *(☎ 050 55 35 59, fax 050 55 60 38, e hds@csinfo.it, W www.hoteldistefano.pisa.it, Via Sant'Apollonia 35)* Singles/doubles with bath up to €56.80/69.70, without bath €36.15/49.05 without bath). This place, near Via Carducci, has good modern rooms and a small private bar. You can glimpse the Leaning Tower from the hotel's roof terrace.

Albergo Gronchi *(☎ 050 56 18 23, Piazza Arcivescovado 1)* Singles/doubles €17.05/32. This place is a steal for its position alone. The rooms are slightly tatty but appealing nonetheless and the staff are friendly.

Albergo Giardino *(☎ 050 56 21 01, fax 050 831 03 92, e giardino@csinfo.it, Piazza Manin 1)* Singles/doubles with bath and breakfast €61.95/92.95. Albergo Giardino, just west of Campo dei Miracoli, has been given a thorough overhaul and the rooms are sparkling. Breakfast is served on a lovely terrace.

Villa Kinzica *(☎ 050 56 04 19, fax 050 55 12 04, Piazza Arcivescovado 2)* Singles/doubles with bath €67.15/92.95. One of Pisa's more attractive options, Villa Kinzica has bags of character and views of the Leaning Tower. Prices include breakfast.

Hotel Roseto *(☎/fax 050 4 25 96, e hotelroseto@csinfo.it, Via Mascagni 24)* Singles without bath €36.15, singles/doubles with bath €46.50/61.95. Near Stazione Pisa Centrale, this place has comfortable rooms and a small garden.

Albergo Astor *(☎ 050 4 45 51, fax 050 2 60 01, Via Manzoni 22)* Doubles from €38.75. This two-star hotel, near Via Francesco Crispi, has a variety of comfortable modern rooms and a helpful, English-speaking receptionist.

Places to Eat

Being a university town, Pisa has a good range of eating places. Head for the area north of the river around Borgo Stretto and the university.

La Tana *(☎ 050 58 05 40, Via San Frediano 6)* Meals from €9.30. Open Mon-Sat. With friendly service and affordable prices, it's not surprising that La Tana is so popular with students and professors from the nearby university. The food, mainly pizza and pasta, is served up on rustic wooden tables and you can snuggle down in the booths.

Antica Trattoria il Campano *(☎ 050 58 05 85, Vicolo Santa Margherita)* Full meals €2.05. Open Thurs-Tues. This place is in an old tower near Piazza Sant'Ombono and has loads of atmosphere and an adventurous Tuscan menu.

Trattoria La Pergoletta *(☎ 050 54 24 58, Via delle Belle Torri 38)* Meals €20.65. Open Tues-Sun. This is a wonderful sprawling place, tucked away out of sight just north of the river.

Trattoria La Grotta *(☎ 050 57 81 05, Via San Francesco 103)* Meals €18.10. Open Mon-Sat. As the name suggests, La Grotta is suitably cavernous and serves up good portions of Tuscan fare.

***Trattoria La Buca** (☎ 050 56 06 60, Galli Tassi 6)* Meals €12.90, pizzas from €4.15. Open Sat-Thurs. This is a friendly, popular trattoria, although its location near the Campo di Miracoli makes it a bit of a tourist trap. The tables in the rear garden are fun.

***Krott** (☎ 050 58 05 80, Lungarno Pacinotti 2)* This is a wonderfully exuberant spot for coffee, gelato, a cocktail or some fine focaccia.

***Caffè Federico Salza** (☎ 050 58 02 44, Borgo Stretto 46)* There's a tantalising selection of cakes, gelati and chocolates at this bar, one of the city's finest. Prices inside are one-third of those charged if you eat at the tables outside.

***La Bottega del Gelato** (Piazza Garibaldi)* For great ice cream, head for this place near the river and join the back of the queue.

There is an open-air ***food market*** on Piazza delle Vettovaglie, off Borgo Stretto.

Entertainment

The APT office has a list of discos and events in the city.

***Big Ben Pub** (☎ 050 58 11 58, Via Palestro 11)* Open 6pm-2am. Big Ben is one of a handful of UK-style pubs that have sprung up in Pisa which can be quite pleasant if you're in the mood for a soothing pint.

***Teatro Verdi** (☎ 050 94 11 11, Via Palestro 40)* Opera and ballet are staged at this theatre from September to November.

Getting There & Away

Air The city's Aeroporto Galileo Galilei (☎ 050 50 07 07), about 2km south of the city centre, is Tuscany's main international airport and handles flights to major cities in Europe. Alitalia and other major airlines are based there.

Bus Lazzi (☎ 050 4 62 88), Piazza Vittorio Emanuele II, operates hourly services to Lucca (€1.85, 45 minutes) and Florence (€5.80, two hours). Change at Lucca for services to Prato, Pistoia, Massa and Carrara. CPT (☎ 050 50 55 11), Piazza Sant'Antonio, has 10 services per day to Volterra (€4.90, two hours) and half-hourly services to Livorno (€2.05, 50 minutes).

Train Pisa is connected to Florence and is also on the Rome-La Spezia train line, with frequent services running in all directions. Sample destinations and fares include to Florence (€4.50, one hour 10 minutes, 40 per day), Rome (€13.95–23.75, three to four hours, 19 daily), Livorno (€1.35, 15 minutes, hourly), Pistoia (€3.60, one hour 10 minutes, five direct daily) and Lucca (€1.85, 25 minutes, 24 per day).

Car & Motorcycle Pisa is close to the A12, which connects Parma to Livorno and is being extended south to Rome, although that may yet take some years to complete. The city is also close to the A11 (tollway) and S67 to Florence, while the north-south S1, the Via Aurelia, connects the city with La Spezia and Rome.

Getting Around

To get to the airport, take a train from the station (€1, five minutes, 13 per day), or the CPT city bus No 3, which passes through the city centre on its way to the airport (€0.75). For a taxi, call ☎ 050 54 16 00.

To get from the station to the cathedral, take CPT bus No 4 (€0.75) or walk the 1.5km.

Large car parks abound in Pisa. The one just north-west of the cathedral is perfect for day-trippers.

Trattoria La Buca (see Places to Eat earlier in this section) hires out bicycles.

LIVORNO (LEGHORN)

postcode 57100 • pop 173,000

Tuscany's second-largest city, Livorno is the perfect antidote for those who get too carried away with the region's many beauty spots. This place was hammered in WWII and is frankly a bit of a dump. One good reason for coming is to hop on a boat for Sardinia or Corsica and leave again.

Orientation & Information

From the main train station on Piazza Dante, east of the city centre, walk west along Viale Carducci, Via de Larderel and then Via Grande into the central Piazza Grande. The main APT office (☎ 0586 89 81 11) is at Piazza Cavour 6 (2nd floor) to

TUSCANY

the south, and opens 9am to 1pm Monday to Saturday. A smaller APT office (☎ 0586 89 53 20), near the main ferry terminal at the entrance of the Stazione Marittima, opens mornings and afternoons in summer only.

The main post office is at Via Cairoli 46 and the unstaffed Telecom office, at Largo Duomo 14, opens 8am to 9.45pm daily.

The hospital (☎ 0586 22 31 11) is at Viale Alfieri 36, near the main train station. The *questura* (police station; ☎ 0586 23 51 11) is in the Palazzo del Governo, Piazza Unità d'Italia.

Things to See

The city does have a few worthy sights. The **Fortezza Nuova**, in the area known as Piccola Venezia (oh please!) because of its small canals, was built for the Medici in the late 16th century. Close to the waterfront is the city's other fort, the **Fortezza Vecchia**, built 60 years earlier on the site of an 11th-century building.

At the **Museo di Storia Naturale del Mediterraneo** *(☎ 0586 80 22 94, Via Roma 234; admission €2.60; open 9am-1pm & 3pm-6pm Tues-Sun)* you can see the 20m-long skeleton of 'Annie', a common whale,

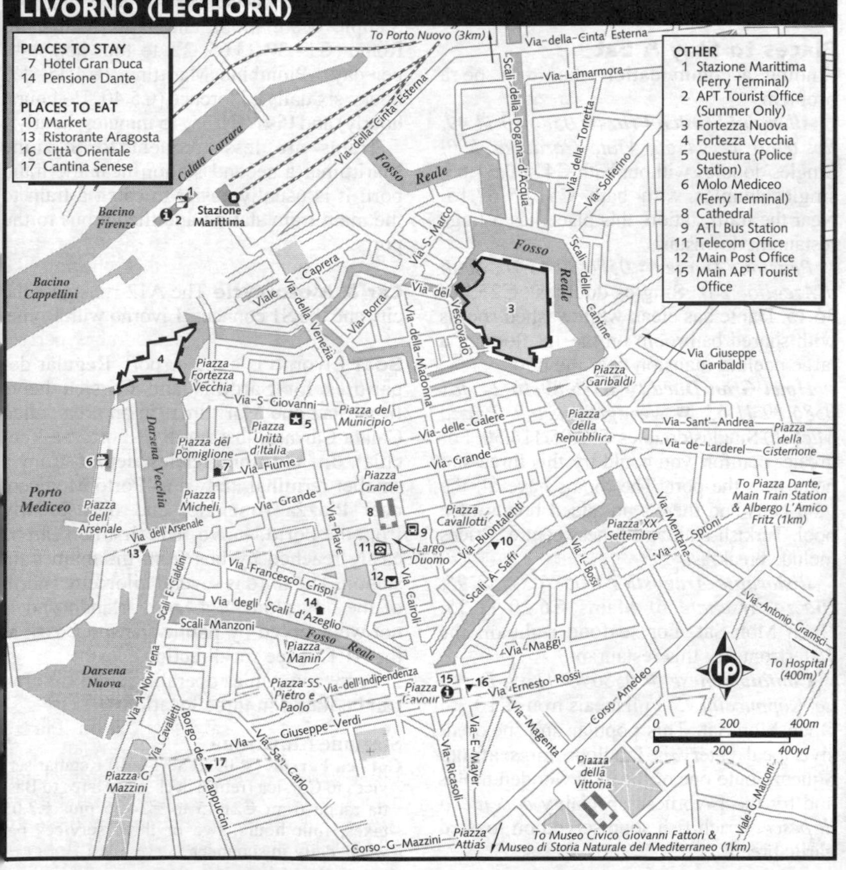

which dominates the *sala del mare* (sea room). Other specimens of Mediterranean creatures are also on display at this fine museum.

If you still have time to kill, about the only other museum worth your while is the **Museo Civico Giovanni Fattori** *(☎ 0586 80 80 01, Via San Jacopo in Acquaviva 65; admission €4.15; open 9am-1pm Tues-Sun)* It's in a pretty park at Via San Jacopo 65 and features works by the 19th-century Livorno-based movement led by the artist Giovanni Fattori. The gallery often has temporary exhibitions (phone for details). The city's unspectacular **cathedral** is just off Piazza Grande.

Places to Stay & Eat

Finding accommodation shouldn't be a problem.

Albergo L'Amico Fritz *(☎ 0586 40 11 49, fax 0586 42 94 66, Viale Carducci 180)* Singles/doubles without bath €41.30/51.65, singles/doubles with bath €51.65/67.15. Near the train station, this place has a large restaurant downstairs.

Pensione Dante *(☎ 0586 89 43 70, Scali d'Azeglio 28)* Singles/doubles €25.80/36.15. Dante has clean whitewashed rooms with shared bathroom on the 1st floor of a large peeling mansion near the port.

Hotel Gran Duca *(☎ 0586 89 10 24, fax 0586 89 11 53, W www.granduca.it, Piazza Micheli)* Singles/doubles €92.95/118.50. For greater comfort you could try this three-star hotel near the port. The rooms have all the mod cons and there's an added bonus of a pool, Turkish bath and fitness centre. Prices include breakfast.

Ristorante Aragosta *(☎ 0586 89 53 95, Piazza Arsenale 6)* Mains €6.20-11.35. Open Mon-Sat. For seafood right on the waterfront, try this restaurant.

Cantina Senese *(☎ 0586 89 02 39, Borgo dei Cappuccini 95)* Full meals from €10.35. Open Mon-Sat. This popular and inexpensive local eatery is fabulous for seafood. Squeeze onto one of the long wooden tables and try the Livornese speciality *cacciucco di pesce*, a rich fish soup served on toasted garlic bread.

Città Orientale *(☎ 0586 88 82 66, Via Ginori 23)* Meals from €10.35. For a bit of variety, you could try this Chinese restaurant.

For produce, the ***market*** is on Via Buontalenti and the area around Piazza XX Settembre is great for bars and cafes.

Getting There and Away

Bus ATL buses (☎ 0586 88 42 62) depart from Largo Duomo for Cecina (€2.60, one hour, every half hour), Piombino (€5.65, 2¼ hours, nine daily) and Pisa (€2.05, 45 minutes, hourly).

Train Livorno is on the Rome-La Spezia line and is also connected to Florence and Pisa. Sample destinations and fares include to Rome (€14.30-23.65, 2¾ to four hours, 12 per day), Piombino Marittima (€4.45, 1½ hours, six daily), Florence (€5.40, 1½ hours, hourly) and Pisa (€1.35, 15 minutes, hourly).

Trains are less frequent to Stazione Marittima, a second station near the main port. It is usually easier to catch a train to the main train station and then a bus to the ports.

Car & Motorcycle The A12 runs past the city and the S1 connects Livorno with Rome.

Boat Livorno is a major port. Regular departures for Sardinia and Corsica leave from Stazione Marittima (in an area called Calata Carrara, just north of Fortezza Vecchia). In addition, ferries depart from a smaller terminal known as Porto Mediceo, near Piazza Arsenale, and occasionally from the Porto Nuovo. The first two can be easily reached by bus from the main train station. The third is several kilometres north of the city along Via Sant'Orlando and is not well served by public transport. Ask at the APT office for directions.

Ferry companies operating from Livorno can be found in three locations:

Stazione Marittima

Corsica Ferries (☎ 0586 88 13 80) Regular services to Corsica (return deck-class fares to Bastia range from €21.45 to €34.35 plus €2.05 taxes, four hours, two or three services per week, daily in summer).

TUSCANY

Corsica Marittima (☎ 0586 21 11 01) High speed ferries to Corsica Bastia (one-way deck-class fares range from €18.10 to €27.40, two hours). A regular service goes to Corsica Porto Vecchio (one-way deck-class fares from €27.90 to €31, 10 hours).

Sardinia Ferries (☎ 0586 88 13 80) Regular services to Sardinia (return deck-class fares to Golfo Aranci, near Olbia, range from €31 to €47.45 – the latter fare on summer weekends only).

Moby Lines (☎ 0586 82 68 23/4/5) Services to Corsica (return fares to Bastia range from €15 to €27.35 depending on season, four hours) and Sardinia (return fares to Olbia range from €21.15 to €46.50, 10 hours).

Porto Mediceo

Toremar (☎ 0586 89 61 13) Services to Isola di Capraia (€10.35, 2½ hours, twice daily except Wednesday and Saturday when there is only one service daily).

Porto Nuovo

Lloyd Sardegna Compagnia di Navigazione Marittima (☎ 0565 22 23 00) At Varco Galvani-Calata, with ferries to Olbia (Sardinia).

Grandi Navi Veloci (☎ 0586 40 98 04) At Varco Galvani, with boats to Palermo in Sicily (one-way seats range from €54.25 to €85.20).

Getting Around

To get from the main train station to Piazza Arsenale and the Porto Mediceo, take ATL bus No 1. To reach Stazione Marittima take bus No 7. Both these buses and several others pass through Piazza Grande and tickets cost €0.75.

ELBA ISLAND (ISOLA D'ELBA)

postcode 57307 • pop 29,400

Napoleon should have considered himself lucky to be exiled to such a pretty spot. He arrived in May 1814 and lasted a year. He just had to have another shot at imperial greatness. Well, he met his Waterloo and the rest is history.

Nowadays people willingly allow themselves to be marooned here, to the tune of more than one million tourists every year. They come to swim in its glorious blue waters, lie on the beaches, eat fine food and generally loll about.

Don't come in August (the best thing any sensible being can do in August anywhere in Europe is fly to another hemisphere or stay at home and wait for better days), as it gets unpleasantly crowded.

Elba is growing in popularity among walkers. Its mountainous terrain can provide some tough treks, although there are better places to walk in Tuscany.

Just 28km long and 19km across at its widest point, Elba is well equipped for tourists, with plenty of hotels and camp sites. The main towns are Portoferraio on the northern side and Marina di Campo in the south.

Prior to the advent of tourism, its main industry was iron-ore mining. The hordes have only arrived in recent years, so the island is not (as yet) overdeveloped. Which is not to say the people of Elba haven't learned a few tricks of the trade – don't expect to eat well *and* cheaply here. Also, in the height of summer most hotels operate a half-board policy – you pay an all-in price per person for room, breakfast and lunch or dinner. This may or may not suit, but is rarely a terribly attractive deal. It is another reason to stay away in high summer (from mid-July to the end of August).

Orientation & Information

Most ferries arrive at Portoferraio, Elba's capital and main transport hub. Ferries from Piombino travel less frequently to Rio Marina, Porto Azzurro and Marina di Campo. The main APT office (☎ 0565 91 46 71), Calata Italia 26, Portoferraio, opens 8am to 8pm Monday to Saturday, 8am to 2pm on Sunday Easter to October. The ***Associazione Albergatori Isola d'Elba** (☎ 0565 91 55 55, Calata Italia 20)* will find you a room. Book ahead in summer.

A summer tourist medical service operates at: Portoferraio (☎ 0565 92 61 11), at the public hospital, Località San Rocco; Marina di Campo (☎ 0565 97 60 61), Piazza Dante Alighieri 3; Rio Marina (☎ 0565 96 24 07), Via Principe Amadeo; Marciana Marina (☎ 0565 90 44 36), Viale Regina Margherita; and Capoliveri (☎ 0565 96 89 95), Via Soprana.

Walkers should pick up the leaflet *Elba, un anno di Sport* from the tourist office, which lists walking and cycling trails and details each itinerary. For more information about walking, contact Il Genio del Bosco – Centro Trekking Isola d'Elba (☎ 0565 93 08 37) at Portoferraio. The Comunità Montana (☎ 0565 93 81 11), at Viale Manzoni 4, has contour maps of the island, with paths clearly marked.

Getting There & Away

Unless you have your own boat, the best way to get to Elba is by ferry from Piombino, or from Livorno via the island of Capraia. If you arrive in Piombino by train, get the connecting train to the port. Several companies (Moby Lines, Toremar and Elba Ferries) run ferries and have offices at Piombino and Portoferraio. Unless it is the middle of August, you shouldn't have any trouble buying a ticket at the port. Generally you pay €5.15 per person or €26.10 for a small car and driver (other passengers extra), and a port tax of €0.50. All lines offer a special deal on certain runs (indicated in timetables). The ferry trip takes an hour.

Elba Ferries has a faster catamaran, which carries cars and makes the trip in 25 minutes. Prices are from €6.20 per person, €28.15 for a small car and €0.50 port tax.

The island has a small airport (☎ 0565 97 60 11) just outside Marina di Campo, with flights to Pisa, Florence and Rome and some other European destinations including Munich and Berne.

Getting Around

Bus The island's bus company, ATL (☎ 0565 91 43 92), runs regular services between the main towns. From Portoferraio (the terminal is right by the port), for instance, you can reach all of the main towns, including Marciana Marina, Marina di Campo, Capoliveri and Porto Azzurro, as well as smaller resorts and beaches such as Sant'Andrea, Cavo and Fetovaia for about €1.80. Ask at the tourist office for an updated timetable.

Car, Motorcycle & Bicycle The best way to get around Elba is to hire a mountain bike, scooter or motorcycle. In the high season mountain bikes start at €10.35 per day and €51.65 for one week; mopeds (50cc) are from €18.10 to €25.80 per day; motorbikes start at about €51.65 per day. Two Wheels Network (TWN; ☎ 0565 91 46 66), Viale Elba 32, Portoferraio (branches at Marciana Marina, Marina di Campo, Porto Azzurro and several other locations) is one of several car-rental outlets. Happy Rent (☎ 0565 91 46 65), Viale Elba 5, is another.

Portoferraio

The new part of Portoferraio encompasses the port and is of little interest, so head up to the old town, enclosed by a medieval wall. Here you'll encounter the **Villa dei Mulini** *(☎ 0565 91 58 46, Piazzale Napoleone; admission €3.10, including Villa Napoleonica di San Martino; open 9am-7pm Mon & Wed-Sat, 9am-1pm Sun & holidays)*, one of the residences where Napoleon mooched about. It features a splendid terraced garden and his library.

The ticket also allows you admission to the **Villa Napoleonica di San Martino** *(☎ 0565 91 46 88; admission €3.10, including Villa dei Mulini; open 9am-7pm Tues-Sat, 9am-1pm Sun & holidays)*, Napoleon's summer residence, set in hills about 5km south-west of the town. The villa houses a modest collection of Napoleonic paraphernalia and also hosts an annual exhibition based on a Napoleonic theme.

Places to Stay & Eat The closest camp sites are about 4km west of town and are easily found.

Campeggio La Sorgente *(☎/fax 0565 91 71 39, Località Acquaviva)* Low season sites per adult/child/tent €6.70/5.15/6.20, high season sites per adult/child/tent €11.35/7.75/9.30. There are plenty of quiet and shaded sites at this camp site and there are also bungalows for rent.

Acquaviva *(☎/fax 0565 91 55 92)* Low season sites per adult/child/tent €5.65/4.15/6.20, high season sites per adult/child/tent €10.35/8.50/9.30. Right on the beach with its own shop, bar and restaurant, Acquaviva's a pleasant spot.

Ape Elbana *(☎/fax 0565 91 42 45, ⓔ apelbana@elba2000.it, Salita de' Medici 2)* Singles/doubles with bath from €41.30/61.95. This place is in the old town, with bags of charm and large sunny rooms. Prices include breakfast.

Villa Ombrosa *(☎ 0565 91 43 63, fax 0565 91 56 72, Via De Gasperi 3)* Low season singles/doubles with bath from €39.75/64.05, high season singles/doubles with bath €49.05/77.45. This hotel has a great location overlooking the sea and Spiaggia delle Ghiaie, but the grey plastic furniture is a bit of a disappointment. They may insist that you take half-board, which is OK as their restaurant serves good Tuscan dishes.

Emanuel *(☎ 0565 93 90 03, Località Enfola)* Set menu from €23.65. Out on a headland a few kilometres west of town, Emanuel has been serving up consistently good Elban dishes for years – probably the best way to go is the set menu *(menù di degustazione)*, which gives you a rounded experience of the local cuisine.

Stella Marina *(☎ 0565 91 59 83, Banchina Alto Fondale)* Meals from €15.50. This popular seafood restaurant is literally on the docks, and you can pick your choice of crustacean out of a glass tank before it's cooked up for you.

Marciana Marina

Almost 20km west of Portoferraio, Marciana Marina is slightly less popular with tourists and is fronted by some pleasant pebble beaches. It makes a fine base for the island's best walking trails too. The inland villages of **Marciana** and **Poggio**, the latter particularly charming, are easily visited. From Marciana, you can take a funicular to the summit of Monte Capanne, from where you can see across Elba and as far as Corsica to the west.

Casa Lupi *(☎/fax 0565 9 91 43, Località Ontanelli)* Singles/doubles €41.30/67.15. In Marciana Marina, one of the cheapest hotels is Casa Lupi, about half a kilometre inland on the road to Marciana, with good views. Prices include breakfast.

Hotel Marinella *(☎ 0565 9 90 18, fax 0565 99 68 95, Viale Margherita)* Singles/doubles €77.45/118.50. The three-star Marinella is on the sea promenade in the centre of town and has a garden with a pool and tennis courts. Try and snaffle a room with a sea view if you can.

Pensione Monte Capanne *(☎/fax 0565 9 90 83, Poggio)* Singles/doubles €25.80/51.65, half-board per person €46.50. If it all gets too warm for you down on the coast, chill out a little at this place, with wonderful views, up in Poggio. The price depends on the time of year, and they may insist on half-board.

Osteria del Piano *(☎ 0565 90 72 92, Via Provinciale 24)* Meals €20.65. About halfway between Portoferraio and Marciana Marina, on the road just outside Procchio, is the unassuming Osteria del Piano. Looks aren't everything. Here they make all their own pasta and serve up some astonishing concoctions, such as black-and-white spaghetti in a lobster sauce. It's not dirt cheap, but you get what you pay for.

Marina di Campo

Elba's second-largest town is Marina di Campo, on the Golfo di Campo to the island's south. The beaches are not bad at all (although if you venture farther west you will find a few less crowded ones). There are many camp sites around the town and along the coastline.

Albergo Thomas *(☎ 0565 97 77 32, fax 0565 97 68 70, Viale degli Etruschi 32)* Doubles from €67.15. This three-star hotel is one of the more affordable in the town centre and may give a discount in the low season – a standard story around here.

Porto Azzurro & Capoliveri

Dominated by its fort, built in 1603 by Philip III of Spain and now a prison, Porto Azzurro is a pleasant resort town close to some excellent beaches.

Albergo Villa Italia *(☎/fax 0565 9 51 19, Viale Italia 41)* Singles/doubles €41.30/64.55. This place is clean and friendly but it's on a noisy road away from the waterfront.

Ristorante Cutty Sark *(☎ 0565 95 78 21, Piazza del Mercato 25)* Meals €31. If you can loosen the purse strings a little around dinnertime, try the Cutty Sark. The *ravioloni* *alla Cutty Sark* are big ravioli filled with courgettes (zucchini) and shrimp meat and bathed in a shrimp and tomato sauce. You also get to wrestle with seafood critters to extract those slivers of extra flesh.

From Porto Azzurro, take a short trip south to Capoliveri, one of the island's little hilltop surprise packets. Wander its narrow streets and enjoy the giddy views before trying out one of the nearby beaches – Barabarca, accessible only by a steep track that winds down a cliff, and Zuccale, more easily accessible and perfect for families. The beach of Naregno is a pleasant spot, if your scene is a hotel literally on the beachfront.

Central Tuscany

IL CHIANTI

The hills and valleys spreading out between Florence and Siena are known as Il Chianti. Home to some of the country's best-marketed wines, they don't call it Chiantishire for nothing. In some of the small-town tourist offices, they just assume everyone who wanders in speaks English! Of the wines, Chianti Classico is the most well known. It is a blend of white and red grapes and sold under the Gallo Nero (Black Cockerel) symbol.

The Monti del Chianti, which rise into the Apennines, form Il Chianti's eastern boundary and comprise some of Tuscany's loveliest countryside. Il Chianti is divided between the provinces of Florence and Siena, into the areas known as Chianti Fiorentino and Chianti Sienese.

Now Il Chianti is indeed very pleasant – lots of rolling hills, olive groves and vineyards. Among them stand the many castles of Florentine and Sienese warlords, and Romanesque churches known as *pievi*. But perhaps the hype has been just a trifle overdone. In other areas of Tuscany, there is plenty of more spectacular country to be seen (around Pitigliano or up in the Apuane Alps, for instance). Not that we want to put you off, but the Tuscan countryside by no means begins and ends in Il Chianti.

You can get around by bus, but your own wheels make exploration a lot easier. You might like to do it by bicycle or even on foot. You could take a few days to travel along the state road S222, known as the Strada Chiantigiana, which runs between Florence and Siena.

Budget accommodation is not the area's strong point, and you'll need to book well ahead, since it is a popular area for tourists year-round.

Virtually every tourist office in Tuscany has good information, but the best is at Radda in Chianti. The tourist office there also has a Web site (see under Chianti Sienese later in this section).

Chianti Fiorentino

About 20km south of Florence on the Chiantigiana is **Greve in Chianti**, the first good base for exploring the area. You can get there easily from Florence on a SITA bus. The unusual, triangular Piazza Matteotti is the old centre of the town. An interesting provincial version of a Florentine piazza, it is surrounded by porticoes.

The tourist office (☎ 055 854 52 43), at Via L Cini 1, 500m east of the piazza, opens 9.30am to 1pm daily in summer. Afternoon hours are more erratic (nothing on Sunday and closed at 3pm on Wednesday, otherwise a safe bet is 2.30pm to 5pm). It can provide maps and information in several languages, including English.

If you're looking for a place to stay, there are a couple of choices.

***Giovanni da Verrazzano** (☎ 055 85 31 89, fax 055 85 36 48, e verrazzano@ftbcc.tin.it, Piazza Matteotti 28)* Singles/doubles €72.30/82.65. A central and pleasant three-star hotel with ten rooms, this place also has a good restaurant.

***Del Chianti** (☎/fax 055 85 37 63, w www.albergodelchianti.it, Piazza Matteotti 86)* Singles/doubles €77.45/92.95. Another three-star hotel well located in Greve's central piazza, Del Chianti has a pool and garden and 16 good rooms.

Montefioralle This ancient castle-village is only 2km west of Greve. It's worth the walk, particularly to see its church of Santo Stefano, with its precious medieval paintings.

TUSCANY

From Montefioralle, follow the dirt road for a few hundred metres, then turn off to the right to reach the simple **Pieve di San Cresci**. From here, it's possible to descend directly to Greve.

Nearby, in a magnificent setting of olive groves and vineyards, is the evocative **Badia di Passignano**, founded in 1049 by Benedictine monks of the Vallombrosan order. The abbey is a massive towered castle encircled by cypresses.

The abbey's **Chiesa di San Michele** *(☎ 055 807 16 22; admission by appointment only; open weekends)* has early-17th-century frescoes by the artist known as Passignano (so called because he was born here). In the refectory, there's a *Last Supper* painted by Domenico and Davide Ghirlandaio in 1476. Take a look at the huge medieval chimney in the kitchen. Food and drinks are available in the tiny village surrounding the abbey.

Travelling south along the Chiantigiana, you will pass the medieval village of Panzano; after about 1km, turn off for the Chiesa di San Leolino at **Pieve di Panzano**. Built in the 10th century, it was rebuilt in Romanesque style in the 13th century and a portico was added in the 16th century. Inside, there is a 14th-century triptych.

Chianti Sienese

Castellina in Chianti This is one of the best organised towns for tourists, with lots of hotels and restaurants. Its tourist office (☎ 0577 74 02 01) is at the central Piazza del Comune 1 and opens 10am to 1pm and 3.30pm to 7.30pm Monday to Saturday, and 10am to 1pm on Sunday.

You might prefer to head east to **Radda in Chianti**, which has retained much of its charm despite the tourist influx. It is also handy for many of Chianti's most beautiful spots. The tourist office (☎ 0577 73 84 94), at Piazza Ferrucci 1, is very helpful. It has loads of information about places to stay and eat in Chianti, as well as things to see and do, including suggestions for independent walking tours or tours to local wineries, where you can try the local wines before enjoying a traditional lunch. The tourist office has a Web site at **W** www.chiantinet.it and an email address at **e** proradda@chiantinet.it.

For cooking courses in this area, you could consider ***Posere le Rose*** *(☎ 055 29 45 11)*, in the village of Poggio San Polo, about 10km from Radda. One week costs €619.75 (excluding accommodation).

One of the cheapest forms of accommodation in the region is a room in a private house.

Da Giovannino *(☎/fax 0577 73 80 56, Via Roma 6–8)* Singles/doubles €41.30/51.65. This place is a real family house in the centre of Radda.

The Radda tourist office can provide details about apartments and the numerous farms and wineries offering accommodation. Prices start at around €51.65 for a double.

Getting Around

Buses connect Florence and Siena, passing through Castellina and Radda, as well as other small towns.

SIENA

postcode 53100 • pop 59,200

Siena is without doubt one of Italy's most enchanting cities. Its medieval centre is bristling with majestic Gothic buildings, such as the Palazzo Pubblico on Il Campo (Piazza del Campo), Siena's main square, and a wealth of artwork is contained in its numerous churches and small museums. Like Florence, Siena offers an incredible concentration of things to see, which simply can't be appreciated in a day trip. A few days at least are needed to get to know the place and its treasures.

Siena also makes a good base from which to explore central Tuscany, in particular the medieval towns of San Gimignano and Volterra. Note, however, that it can be difficult to find budget accommodation in Siena unless you book ahead. In August and during the city's famous twice-yearly festival, Il Palio, it is impossible to find any accommodation without a reservation.

History

According to legend, Siena was founded by the son of Remus, and the symbol of the wolf feeding the twins Romulus and Remus is as ubiquitous in Siena as in Rome. In reality the city was probably of Etruscan origin, although it wasn't until the 1st century BC, when the Romans established a military colony there called Sena Julia, that it began to grow into a proper town.

In the 12th century, Siena's wealth, size and power grew with its involvement in commerce, banking and trade. Consequently, its rivalry with neighbouring Florence also grew, leading to numerous wars during the first half of the 13th century between Guelph Florence and Ghibelline Siena. Siena defeated Florence at the Battle of Montaperti in 1260, but it was a short-lived victory. Only 10 years later, the Tuscan Ghibellines were defeated by Charles of Anjou and for almost a century Siena was allied to Florence, the chief town of the Tuscan Guelph League (supporters of the pope).

During this period, Siena reached its peak under the rule of the Council of Nine, a group dominated by the middle class. Many of the fine buildings in the Sienese-Gothic style, which give the city its striking appearance, were constructed under the direction of the Council, including the cathedral, the Palazzo Pubblico and Il Campo. The Sienese school of painting had its origins at this time with

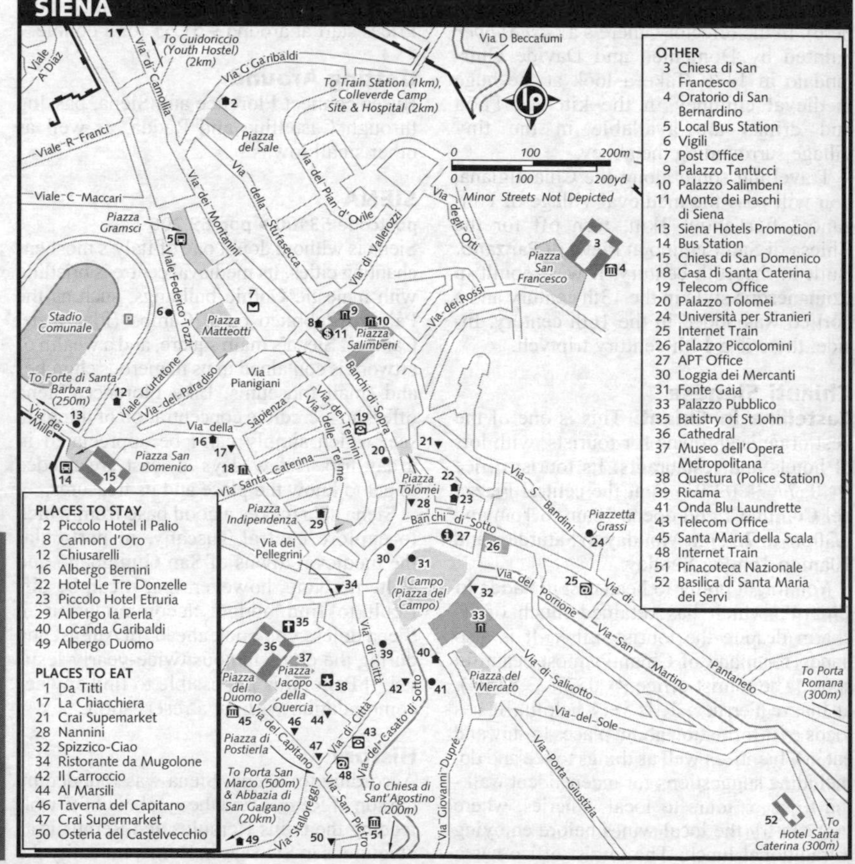

Guido da Siena and reached its peak in the early 14th century with the works of artists including Duccio di Buoninsegna, Simone Martini and Pietro and Ambrogio Lorenzetti.

A plague outbreak in 1348 killed two-thirds of the city's 100,000 inhabitants and led to a period of decline for Siena.

The plague also put an end to an ambitious plan to dramatically enlarge the cathedral. At the end of the 14th century, Siena came under the control of Milan's Visconti family, followed in the next century by the autocratic patrician Pandolfo Petrucci. Under Petrucci the city's fortunes improved, but the Holy Roman Emperor Charles V conquered Siena in 1555 after a two-year siege that left thousands dead. Consequently, the city was handed over to Cosimo I de' Medici, who barred the inhabitants from operating banks and thus curtailed Siena's power for good.

Siena was home to Santa Caterina, one of Italy's most famous saints. But saints don't make money. Siena today relies for its prosperity on tourism and the success of its Monte dei Paschi di Siena bank, founded in 1472 and now one of the city's largest employers.

Orientation

Historic Siena, still largely surrounded by its medieval walls, is small and easily tackled on foot, although the way streets swirl around Il Campo in semicircles may confuse you. At the city's heart is the gently sloping square, around which curve its main streets: Banchi di Sopra, Via di Città and Banchi di Sotto. By bus you will arrive at Piazza San Domenico, which affords a panoramic view of the city. Walk east along Via della Sapienza and turn right into Banchi di Sopra to reach Il Campo.

From the train station, you will need to catch a bus to Piazza Matteotti. Walk south-east out of the piazza on Via Pianigiani to reach Banchi di Sopra, turn right and follow it to Il Campo. Drivers should note that streets within the walls are blocked to normal traffic – even if you are staying at a hotel in the centre of town, you will be required to leave your car in a car park after dropping off your bags.

Of the eight city gates through which you can enter Siena, probably the best is Porta San Marco, south-west of the city centre, as it has a well-signposted route to the centre.

Information

Tourist Offices The APT office (☎ 0577 28 05 51, fax 0577 28 10 41, e aptsiena@siena.turismo.toscana.it, w www.siena.turismo.toscana.it) is at Piazza del Campo 56 and opens 8.30am to 7.30pm Monday to Saturday and 9am to 3pm on Sunday in summer. For the rest of the year, the hours are 8.30am to 1.30pm and 3.30pm to 6.30pm Monday to Friday, 8.30am to noon on Saturday. Enquire here about combined tickets for the sights, as offers vary throughout the year.

Money There are several banks near Il Campo. The main branch of the Monte dei Paschi di Siena bank, with an automatic currency exchange service, is at Banchi di Sopra 9.

Post & Communications The main post office is at Piazza Matteotti 1. There are unstaffed Telecom offices at Via dei Termini 40 and Via di Città 113. For Internet access, Internet Train has two branches (one at Via di Pantaneto 5 and the other at Via di Città 121) and does good student discounts.

Laundry At the self-service laundry Onda Blu, Via del Casato di Sotto 17, you can wash and dry 6.5kg for €5.15.

Medical Services & Emergency The public hospital (☎ 0577 58 51 11) is on Viale Bracci, just north of Siena at Le Scotte.

The *questura* (police station; ☎ 0577 20 11 11) is on Via del Castoro, between the cathedral and Via di Città. It is open 24 hours.

Il Campo

This magnificent, shell-shaped, slanting square has been the city's civic centre since it was laid out by the Council of Nine in the mid-14th century. Tourists gather in the square to take a break from sightseeing – backpackers lounge on the pavement in the square's centre, while the more well-heeled drink expensive coffees or beers at the outdoor cafes around the periphery.

The square's paving is divided into nine sectors, representing the members of the Council of Nine. In the upper part of the square is the 15th-century **Fonte Gaia** (Gay Fountain). The fountain's panels are reproductions – the originals, by Jacopo della Quercia, can be seen in the Palazzo Pubblico.

Palazzo Pubblico At the lowest point of the piazza, this impressive building is also known as the Palazzo Comunale *(town hall; ☎ 0577 29 22 63, Piazza del Campo; adult/student €6.20/3.60, including Museo Civico; open 10am-11pm Mon-Sat, 9am-1.30pm Sun July & Aug; it opens as early as 6.30pm at other times of the year)*. Its graceful bell tower, the **Torre del Mangia** *(☎ 0577 29 22 63; admission €5.15; open 10am-7pm summer, 10am-4pm winter)*, is 102m high and dates from 1297.

The lower level of its facade features a characteristic Sienese-Gothic arcade. Inside is the **Museo Civico**, based on a series of rooms with frescoes by artists of the Sienese school. Of particular note is Simone Martini's famous *Maestà* in the Sala del Mappamondo. Completed and signed in 1315, it features the Madonna beneath a canopy, surrounded by saints and angels. It is one of the most important works of the Sienese school. In the Sala dei Nove is Ambrogio Lorenzetti's fresco series depicting *Allegories of Good and Bad Government*, which are among the most significant to survive from the Middle Ages. There is also a chapel with frescoes by Taddeo di Bartolo.

The Cathedral

Although it has some Romanesque elements, the cathedral *(☎ 0577 4 73 21, Piazza del Duomo; free; open 7.30am-7.30pm daily Mar 14-Oct, 7.30am-1pm & 2.30pm-5pm daily Nov–mid-Mar)* is one of Italy's great Gothic churches. Begun in 1196, it was largely completed by 1215, although work continued on features such as the apse and dome well into the 13th century. Work then began on changing, enlarging and embellishing the structure. The magnificent facade of white, green and red polychrome marble was begun by Pisano, who completed only the lower section, and was finished towards the end of the 14th century. The mosaics in the gables were added in the 19th century. The statues of philosophers and prophets by Giovanni Pisano above the lower section are copies, the originals being preserved in the adjacent Museo dell'Opera Metropolitana.

In 1339 the city's leaders launched a plan to enlarge the cathedral and create one of Italy's largest churches. Known as the Nuovo Duomo (New Cathedral), the remains of this unrealised project can be seen on Piazza Jacopo della Quercia, at the eastern side of the cathedral. The plan was to build an immense new nave; the present church would have become the transept. The plague of 1348 put a stop to this ambitious plan.

The cathedral's interior is rich with artworks and warrants an hour or more of your time. Its most precious feature is the inlaid marble floor, decorated with 56 panels depicting historical and biblical subjects. The earliest panels are the graffiti designs in simple black and white marble, dating from the mid-14th century. The latest panels were completed in the 16th century. The most valuable are kept covered and revealed to the public only from 7 to 22 August annually.

The beautiful pulpit was carved in marble and porphyry by Nicola Pisano. Other artworks include a bronze statue of St John the Baptist by Donatello, in the northern transept.

Through a door from the northern aisle is another of the cathedral's great treasures, the **Libreria Piccolomini** *(☎ 0577 4 73 21, inside the cathedral; admission €1.55 or included in the €7.25 combined ticket for the Baptistry of St John, Museo dell'Opera Metropolitana & Oratorio di San Bernadino; open 9am-7.30pm daily mid-Mar–Oct, 10am-1pm & 2.30pm-5pm daily Nov–mid-Mar)* which Pope Pius III (pope in 1503) built to house the books of his uncle, Enea Silvio Piccolomini, who was Pope Pius II. The walls of the small hall are covered by an impressive series of frescoes by Bernardino Pinturicchio, depicting events in the life of Piccolomini. In the centre of the hall is a group of statues known as the *Three Graces*, a 3rd-century-AD Roman copy of an earlier Hellenistic work.

Museo dell'Opera Metropolitana

This museum *(☎ 0577 28 30 48, Piazza del Duomo 8; admission €5.15, or included in the €7.25 combined ticket for the Libreria Piccolomini, Baptistry of St John & Oratorio di San Bernadino; open 9am-7.30pm mid-Mar–Sept, 9am-6pm Oct, 9am-1.30pm Nov–mid-Mar)* is next to the cathedral, in what would have been the southern aisle of the nave of the Nuovo Duomo. Its great artworks formerly adorned the cathedral, including the 12 statues of prophets and philosophers by Giovanni Pisano that decorated the facade. However, the museum's main draw is Duccio di Buoninsegna's striking early-14th-century *Maestà*, painted on both sides as a screen for the cathedral's high altar. The front and back have now been separated and the panels depicting the Story of the Passion hang opposite the *Maestà.* It is interesting to compare Buoninsegna's work with Martini's slightly later *Maestà* in the Palazzo Pubblico. Other artists represented in the museum are Ambrogio Lorenzetti, Simone Martini and Taddeo di Bartolo. The collection also includes tapestries and manuscripts.

Baptistry of St John

Behind the cathedral and down a flight of stairs is the baptistry *(Battistero di San Giovanni, Piazza San Giovanni; admission €2.05, or included in the €7.25 combined ticket for the Libreria Piccolomini, Museo dell'Opera Metropolitana & Oratorio di San Bernadino; open 9am-7.30pm daily mid-Mar–Sept, 9am-6pm daily Oct, 10am-1pm & 2.30pm-5pm daily Nov–mid-Mar).*

The baptistry's Gothic facade is unfinished but its interior is heavily decorated with frescoes. The real attraction is a marble font by Jacopo della Quercia, decorated with bronze panels in relief, which depict the life of St John the Baptist, by artists including Lorenzo Ghiberti *(Baptism of Christ* and *St John in Prison)* and Donatello *(Herod's Feast).*

Santa Maria della Scala

On the south-western side of Piazza del Duomo, this former pilgrims' hospital *(☎ 0577 22 48 11, Piazza del Duomo 2; adult/student €5.15/3.10; open 10am-6pm daily in summer, 10.30am-4.30pm daily in winter)* has frescoes by Domenico di Bartolo in the main ward. The building also has a collection of Roman and Etruscan remains.

Pinacoteca Nazionale

The gallery of the 15th-century Palazzo Buonsignori *(☎ 0577 28 11 61, Via San Pietro 29; adult/student €4.15/2.05; open 8.30am-1.30pm Mon, 8.15am-7.15pm Tues-Sat, 8.15am-1.15pm Sun & holidays)*, a short walk south-east of the cathedral, houses numerous masterpieces by Sienese artists. Look for Duccio di Buoninsegna's *Madonna dei Francescani*, the *Madonna col Bambino* (Madonna with Child) by Simone Martini, and a series of Madonnas by Ambrogio Lorenzetti.

Chiesa di San Domenico

This imposing Gothic church *(☎ 0577 28 90 81, Piazza San Domenico; free; open 7.30am-1pm & 3pm-6.30pm daily)* was started in the early 13th century but has been much altered over the centuries. It is known for its association with Santa Caterina di Siena, who took her vows in its Cappella delle Volte. In the chapel is a portrait of the saint painted during her lifetime. In the **Cappella di Santa Caterina**, on the southern side of the church, are frescoes by Sodoma depicting events in the saint's life. Santa Caterina di Siena died in Rome and her body is preserved there in the Chiesa di Santa Maria Sopra Minerva. In line with the bizarre practice of collecting relics of dead saints, her head was given back to Siena. It is contained in a tabernacle on the altar of the Cappella di Santa Caterina.

Off Via della Sapienza is the **Casa di Santa Caterina** *(☎ 0577 4 41 77, Costa di Sant'Antonio; free; open 9am-12.30pm & 3.30pm-6pm daily in summer, 9am-12.30pm & 2.30pm-6pm daily in winter)*, the house where Santa Caterina was born. The rooms of the house were converted into small chapels in the 15th century and are decorated with frescoes and paintings by Sienese artists, including Sodoma.

Il Palio

This spectacular event, held twice yearly on 2 July and 16 August, in honour of the Virgin Mary, dates from the Middle Ages and features a series of colourful pageants, a wild horse race around Il Campo, and much eating, drinking and celebrating in the streets.

Ten of Siena's 17 *contrade* (town districts) compete for the coveted *palio* (a silk banner). Each of the contrade has its own traditions, symbol and colours plus its own church and palio museum. The centuries-old local rivalries make the festival very much an event for the Sienese, although the horse race and pageantry continue to attract larger crowds of tourists.

On festival days, Il Campo becomes a racetrack, with a ring of packed dirt around its perimeter serving as the course. From about 5pm representatives of each contrada parade in historical costume, each bearing their individual banners.

The race is run at 7.45pm in July and 7pm in August. For not much more than one exhilarating minute, the 10 horses and their bareback riders tear three times around Il Campo with a speed and violence that make your hair stand on end.

Even if a horse loses its rider, it is still eligible to win, and since many riders fall each year, it is the horses in the end who are the focus of the event. There is only one rule: riders are not to interfere with the reins of other horses. The Sienese place incredible demands on the national TV network, RAI, for rights to televise the event.

Book well in advance if you want to stay in Siena at this time and join the crowds in the centre of Il Campo at least four hours before the start, or even earlier, if you want a place on the barrier lining the track. If you can't find a good vantage point, don't despair – the race is televised live and then repeated throughout the evening on TV.

If you happen to be in town in the few days immediately preceding the race, you may get to see the jockeys and horses trying out in Il Campo – almost as good as the real thing.

Other Churches & Palazzos

From the **Loggia dei Mercanti**, north-west of Il Campo, take Banchi di Sotto to the east for the **Palazzo Piccolomini** *(☎ 0577 24 71 45, Banchi di Sotto 52; free; open 9am-1pm Mon-Sat)*, the city's finest Renaissance palazzo. It houses the city's archives and a small museum but was closed at the time of writing. Farther east are the 13th-century **Basilica di Santa Maria dei Servi**, with a fresco by Pietro Lorenzetti, and the 14th-century **Porta Romana**.

Return to the Loggia dei Mercanti and head north along Banchi di Sopra and past Piazza Tolomei, dominated by the 13th-century **Palazzo Tolomei**. Farther along there's Piazza Salimbeni, featuring the **Palazzo Tantucci** to the north, the Gothic **Palazzo Salimbeni** to the east, the head office of the Monte dei Paschi di Siena bank and the Renaissance **Palazzo Spannocchi**. North-east of here, along Via dei Rossi, is the **Chiesa di San Francesco**.

Also worth investigating when they are open are the **Oratorio di San Bernardino** *(☎ 0577 28 30 48, Piazza San Francesco; admission €2.05 or included in the €7.25 combined ticket for the Libreria Piccolomini, Museo dell'Opera Metropolitana & Baptistry of St John; open 10.30am-1.30pm & 3pm-5.30pm mid-Mar–Oct)*, with its small museum of religious artworks, and the **Chiesa di Sant'Agostino** *(☎ 0577 38 57 86, Prato di Sant'Agostino; admission €1.55; open 10.30am-1.30pm & 3pm-5.30pm daily mid-Mar–Oct)*.

West along Via del Paradiso from Piazza Matteotti is Piazza San Domenico, from where you can see the massive **Forte di Santa Barbara**, built for Cosimo I de' Medici.

Courses

Language Siena's ***Università per Stranieri*** *(University for Foreigners; ☎ 0577 24 01 15, fax 0577 28 10 30, Piazzetta Grassi 2)* is open year-round and the only requirement for enrolment is a high-school graduation/pass certificate. The four-week summer courses have no entry requirements. There are several areas of study and courses cost €568.10 for 10 weeks. Brochures can be obtained by making a request to the secretary of the university, or from the Istituto Italiano di Cultura in your city (see also Useful Organisations in the Facts for the Visitor chapter). The university's Web site is at W www.unistrasi.it.

Non-EU students are usually required to obtain a study visa in their own country; it is important to check with an Italian consulate. See under Visas & Documents in the Facts for the Visitor chapter for more details.

Music The ***Accademia Musicale Chigiana*** *(☎ 0577 4 61 52, fax 0577 28 81 24, Via di Città 89)* offers classical music courses every summer, as well as seminars and concerts performed by visiting musicians, teachers and students as part of the Settimana Musicale Senese. Classes are offered for most classical instruments and range from €144.60 to €619.75.

The ***Associazione Siena Jazz*** *(☎ 0577 27 14 01, fax 0577 28 14 04, Via Vallerozzi 77)* offers courses in jazz which start at €196.25. It's one of Europe's foremost institutions of its type.

Organised Tours

The *Treno Natura* is a great way to see the stunning scenery of the Crete Senese, south of Siena. The train line extends in a ring from Siena, through Asciano, across to the Val d'Orcia and the Stazione di Monte Antico, before heading back towards Siena. The line, which opened in the 19th century, was closed in 1994 and trains now run exclusively for tourists. Trains run on some Sundays during May, June, September and the first half of October. There are usually three per day, stopping at Asciano and Monte Antico, and there are connecting trains from Florence. Tickets cost €12.90. Check at the Siena APT office or at Siena's train station for precise details or call ☎ 0577 20 74 13.

Special Events

The Accademia Musicale Chigiana holds the Settimana Musicale Senese each July, as well as the Estate Musicale Chigiana in July, August and September. Concerts in these series are frequently held at the Abbazia di San Galgano (an imposing former abbey about 20km south-west of the city) and at Sant'Antimo, near Montalcino. Concerts are also held year-round. For information, call ☎ 0577 4 61 52. See also the Abbazia di San Galgano section later in this chapter.

The city hosts Siena Jazz, an international festival each July and August, with concerts at the Fortezza Medici, as well as various sites throughout the city. For details, call ☎ 0577 27 14 01.

The Festa di Santa Cecilia, a series of concerts and exhibitions, also takes place in Siena in honour of the patron saint of musicians.

Places to Stay

Siena offers a good range of accommodation, but budget hotels generally fill quickly, so it is always advisable to book in advance if you want to pay less than about €67.15 for a double. Forget about finding a room during Il Palio unless you have a booking. For help in finding a room, contact the APT or ***Siena Hotels Promotion*** *(☎ 0577 28 80 84, fax 0577 28 02 90, e info@hotelsiena.com, Piazza San Domenico)*. The latter opens 9am to 8pm Monday to Saturday in summer and 9am to 7pm in winter.

If you are having trouble finding a hotel room, don't despair. The APT office has a list of about 120 affittacamere in town. Agriturismo is well organised around Siena and the APT office has a list of establishments that rent rooms by the week or month.

Colleverde *(☎ 0577 28 00 44, fax 0577 33 32 98, Strada di Scacciapensieri 47)* Sites per adult/child €7.75/5.15 (tent pitch included). Open late Mar-early Nov. This camp site is 2km north of the historical centre (take bus No 3 from Piazza Gramsci).

Guidoriccio *(☎ 0577 5 22 12, Via Fiorentina 89, Località Stellino)* B&B €15. Full meals €8.25. The non-HI youth hostel is about 2km north-west of the city centre. Take bus No 3 from Piazza Gramsci. If driving, leave the city by Via Vittorio Emanuele II, which is an extension of Via di Camollia.

Hotel Le Tre Donzelle *(☎ 0577 28 03 58, fax 0577 22 39 33, Via delle Donzelle 5)*

Singles/doubles without bath €31/43.90, doubles with bath €56.80. This place is off Banchi di Sotto, north of Il Campo. The rooms are clean and simple and the shared bathrooms are spotless. Even the 1am curfew is fairly relaxed. It is popular, so make reservations.

Piccolo Hotel Etruria *(☎ 0577 28 80 88, fax 0577 28 84 61, Via delle Donzelle 3)* Singles/doubles with bath €41.30/67.15. This place has pleasant, large rooms with all the mod cons and the 12.30am curfew shouldn't be too much of a drawback.

Locanda Garibaldi *(☎ 0577 28 42 04, Via Giovanni Dupré 18)* Doubles €61.95. Locanda Garibaldi, just south of Il Campo, is above a restaurant so can get a bit noisy. The communal areas are dark and interesting but the seven bedrooms are big and bright.

Albergo Bernini *(☎/fax 0577 28 90 47, Via della Sapienza 15)* Doubles with/without bath €77.45/61/95. This friendly, family-run hotel has a wonderful roof terrace with views across to the cathedral and the Basilica de San Domenico. All nine rooms are doubles so it's not such a great deal for solo travellers. There's a midnight curfew and they do discounts in the low season.

Albergo La Perla *(☎ 0577 4 71 44, Via delle Terme 25)* Singles/doubles with shower €46.50/61.95. In spite of the grotty entrance, this place has clean rooms but the en-suite bathrooms are not for the claustrophobic – fine for a night or two but a bit depressing for longer stays.

Piccolo Hotel il Palio *(☎ 0577 28 11 31, fax 0577 28 11 42, Piazza del Sale 19)* Singles/doubles with bath €67.15/82.65. This hotel is a good 15-minute walk from Il Campo on a quiet piazza, so it's slightly out of the way. The rooms are cosy, many with open rafter ceilings, and have a farmhouse feel.

Cannon d'Oro *(☎ 0577 4 43 21, fax 0577 28 08 68, Via dei Montanini 28)* Singles/doubles €69.70/80, less €23.25 in winter. Breakfast €6.20. The rooms at this two-star hotel are clean and bright and all have private bathrooms.

Albergo Duomo *(☎ 0577 28 90 88, fax 0577 4 30 43, Via Stalloreggi 38)* Singles/doubles €103.30/129.10. In a fairly imposing building, a short walk from the cathedral, Albergo Duomo has lovely rooms, many with country views.

Chiusarelli *(☎ 0577 28 05 62, fax 0577 27 11 77, Viale Curtatone 15)* Singles/doubles €67.15/98.15. Just off Piazza San Domenico, the rooms here are pleasant and there's a good restaurant downstairs. It's also very quiet, except Sundays – the back of the hotel overlooks the football stadium.

Hotel Santa Caterina *(☎ 0577 22 11 05, fax 0577 27 10 87, Via Enea Silvio Piccolomini 7)* Singles/doubles with bath up to €95.55/129.10. This place is small and friendly with good service but it's a little out of the way.

Places to Eat

The Sienese claim that most Tuscan cuisine has its origins in Siena and that the locals are still using methods introduced to the area by the Etruscans, namely simple cooking methods and the use of herbs. Among the city's many traditional dishes are soups such as ribollita; *panzanella* (a summer salad of soaked bread, basil, onion and tomatoes); *papardelle con la lepre* (pasta with hare); and the succulent steaks of the Chianina, cooked over a charcoal grill. Bread is made without salt, as throughout Tuscany. *Panforte*, a rich cake of almonds, honey and candied melon or citrus fruit, has its origins in the city – it was created as sustenance for the crusaders to the Holy Land.

Restaurants You'll find Sienese specialities on the menu at most of the following restaurants.

Spizzico-Ciao *(☎ 0577 4 01 87, Piazza del Campo 77)* Full meals less than €10.35. Open Wed-Mon. This cheap self-service restaurant has a first-rate position on Il Campo, which more than compensates for the nasty strip lighting.

Il Carroccio *(☎ 0577 4 11 65, Via Casato di Sotto 32)* Pasta €5.15, mains €11.35. Open Thurs-Tues. South of Il Campo, this place has excellent pasta. Try the *pici*, a kind of thick spaghetti, followed by the *friselle di pollo ai zucchini* (bite-sized juicy chicken bits with courgette), all served in fine rustic surroundings.

Taverna del Capitano *(☎ 0577 28 80 94, Via del Capitano 8)* Full meals about €18.10. Open Wed-Mon. This is a good little spot for local food with friendly service. Specialities include *zuppa di faro* (barley soup) and *ossobuco al tegame* (veal stew). The tables outdoors are pleasant in summer.

Osteria del Castelvecchio *(☎ 0577 4 95 86, Via Castelvecchio 65)* Mains from €6.20. Open Wed-Mon. Expensive but highly regarded by locals is Osteria del Castelvecchio, where the menu changes daily. It is also a good spot for veggies, with at least four vegetarian dishes on offer daily.

La Chiacchiera *(☎ 0577 28 06 31, Costa di Sant'Antonio 4)* Pasta from €3.60, full meals about €18.10. Open Wed-Mon. Off Via Santa Caterina, this restaurant is tiny (only 40 covers) but has a great menu of local specialities. The wooden tables on a quiet pedestrian street make this a good lunch venue.

Al Marsili *(☎ 0577 4 71 54, Via del Castoro 3)* Meals from €23.25. Open Tues-Sun. This is one of the city's better-known restaurants and booking is essential. The vaulted dining rooms are smart and the menu features lots of meaty mains and fruity desserts.

Ristorante da Mugolone *(☎ 0577 28 32 35, Via dei Pelligrini 8)* Meals €20.65. Open Fri-Wed. This is another excellent Sienese restaurant dishing up local specialities.

About a 10-minute walk north of Il Campo, in a less frenetic neighbourhood, are several trattorias.

Da Titti *(☎ 0577 4 80 87, Via di Camollia 193)* Full meals with wine €15.50. Open Sun-Fri. This is a no-frills establishment with big wooden benches and standard Tuscan fare.

Self-Catering There are ***Crai*** supermarkets scattered around the town centre, including one at Via di Città 152–156 and another on Via Cecco Angiolieri.

Nannini *(Banchi di Sopra 22)* Nannini is one of the city's finest cafes and cake shops.

Shopping

Ricama *(☎ 0577 28 83 38, Via di Città 61)* This shop promotes the crafts of Siena, in particular embroidery, and is worth a visit.

Getting There & Away

Bus From Piazza Gramsci, regular Tra-in buses leave for Florence (€5.65, 1¼ hours, every half hour), San Gimignano (€4.45, one hour, half hourly, change at Poggibonsi) and Colle di Val d'Elsa (€2.15, half an hour, half hourly, for connections to Volterra). Daily Sena buses also leave from Piazza Gramsci for Rome (€13.95, three hours, every two hours). Buses to Perugia (€7.25, 1½ hours, twice daily, once on Sunday), Montalcino (€2.75, 1¼ hours, seven daily), Montepulciano (€4.15, 1½ hours, five daily) and other destinations in the Crete Senese and Chianti area leave from Piazza Stazione. The Tra-in and Sena offices operate from offices underneath Piazza Gramsci.

Train Siena is not on a major train line, so from Rome it is necessary to change at Chiusi and from Florence at Empoli, making buses a better alternative. Trains arrive at Piazza F Rosselli, north of the city centre. Sample fares and prices include to Certaldo (€1.90, 40 minutes, hourly), Chiusi (€4.45, 1½ hours, hourly), Empoli (€3.60, one hour, hourly) and Grosseto (€5.35, 1½ hours, six daily).

Car & Motorcycle From Florence take the S2 (the *superstrada* which goes direct to Siena). Alternatively, take the S222, also known as the Chiantigiana, which meanders its way through the hills of Chianti. From the Florence-Siena superstrada, take the San Marco exit and follow the 'centro' signs.

Getting Around

Tra-in operates city bus services from a base on Piazza Gramsci. From the train station, catch bus No 3, 9 or 10 (€0.75) to Piazza Gramsci, about a 10-minute walk from Il Campo. No cars, apart from those of residents, are allowed in the city centre. There are large car parks at the Stadio Comunale and around the Fortezza Medici;

both are just north of Piazza San Domenico. Technically, it is necessary to get a special permit to enter the city by car just to drop off your luggage at your hotel. This can be obtained from the *vigili* (traffic police) on Viale Federico Tozzi, but only if you have a hotel booking. Otherwise, phone your hotel for advice. For a taxi, call ☎ 0577 4 92 22 or, after 9pm, ☎ 0577 28 93 50.

SAN GIMIGNANO

postcode 53037 • pop 7100

As you crest the hill coming from the east, the 13 towers of this walled town look like a medieval Manhattan. And when you arrive you might feel half of Manhattan's population has moved in. Within easy reach of both Siena and Florence, San Gimignano is quite a tourist magnet. Come in the dead of winter, preferably when it's raining, to indulge your imagination a little. In summer most of your attention will probably be focused on dodging fellow visitors.

There is a reason for all this, of course. The towers were symbols of the power and wealth of the city's medieval families and once numbered 72. San Gimignano delle Belle Torri (meaning 'of the Fine Towers') is surrounded by lush and productive land and the setting is altogether enchanting.

Originally an Etruscan village, the town later took its name from the bishop of Modena, San Gimignano, who is said to have saved the city from the barbarians. It became a comune in 1199, but fought a lot with neighbouring Volterra. Internal battles between the Ardinghelli (Guelph) and Salvucci (Ghibelline) families over the next two centuries caused deep divisions. Most towers were built during this period – in the 13th century, one *podestà* (town chief) forbade the building of towers higher than his (51m). In 1348 the plague wiped out much of the population and weakened the power of its nobles, leading to the town's submission to Florence in 1353. Today, not even the plague would dent the summer swarms!

Orientation

The manicured gardens of Piazzale dei Martiri di Montemaggio, at the southern end of the town, are outside the medieval wall and next to the main gate, the Porta San Giovanni. From the gate, Via San Giovanni heads north to Piazza della Cisterna and the connecting Piazza del Duomo, in the city centre. The other major thoroughfare, Via San Matteo, leaves Piazza del Duomo for the main northern gate, Porta San Matteo.

Information

The Associazione Pro Loco (☎ 0577 94 00 08, ⓔ prolocsg@tin.it) is at Piazza del Duomo 1, on the left as you approach the cathedral. It opens 9am to 1pm and 3pm to 7pm daily (to 6pm in winter).

The post office is at Piazza delle Erbe 8, on the northern side of the cathedral.

Things to See

If you are planning to see all the sights, buy the €10.35 ticket, which allows admission to most of San Gimignano's museums and the Collegiata, from the ticket offices of any of the city's sights.

Start in the triangular Piazza della Cisterna, named after the 13th-century cistern in its centre. The piazza is lined with houses and towers dating from the 13th and 14th centuries. In the adjoining Piazza del Duomo, the cathedral (known as the Collegiata) looks across to the late-13th-century **Palazzo del Podestà** and its tower, the **Torre della Rognosa**. The Palazzo del Popolo, left of the cathedral, still operates as the town hall.

Collegiata Up a flight of steps from the piazza is the town's Romanesque **cathedral** *(☎ 0577 94 22 26, Piazza del Duomo; adult/child €3.10/1.55; open 9.30am-7.30pm Mon-Fri, 9.30am-5pm Sat & 1pm-5pm Sun Apr-Oct; 9.30am-5pm Mon-Sat & 1pm-5pm Sun Nov-Mar)*, its simple facade belying the remarkable frescoes covering the walls of its interior. There are five main cycles. On the left wall as you enter are scenes from the Old Testament by Bartolo di Fredi, dating from around 1367. To the right are New Testament scenes by Barna da Siena, which were completed in 1381. On the inside wall of the facade, as well as an adjoining wall, Taddeo di Bartolo probably scared the

TUSCANY

daylights out of pious locals with his gruesome depiction of the Last Judgement (1393). In the **Cappella di Santa Fina** are beautiful frescoes by Domenico Ghirlandaio depicting events in the life of the saint.

Palazzo del Popolo From the internal courtyard, climb the stairs to the **Museo Civico** *(☎ 0577 94 00 08, Piazza del Duomo; adult/child €3.60/2.60; open 9.30am-7.30pm daily Mar-Oct, 10am-5.30pm daily Nov-Feb)*, which features paintings from the Sienese and Florentine schools of the 12th to 15th centuries. Dante addressed the locals in 1299 in the Sala del Consiglio, urging them to support the Guelphs' cause. The room contains an early-14th-century fresco of the *Maestà* by Lippo Memmi. Climb up the palazzo's **Torre Grossa** for a spectacular view of the town and surrounding countryside.

Other Things to See The **Rocca**, a short walk to the west of Piazza del Duomo, is the atmospheric ruin of the town's fortress from where you have great views across the valley.

At the northern end of the town is the **Chiesa di Sant'Agostino** *(Piazza Sant'Agostino; free; open 7am-noon & 3pm-7pm daily in summer, 7am-noon & 3pm-6pm daily in winter)*. Its main attraction is the fresco cycle by Benozzo Gozzoli in the apse, depicting the life of Sant'Agostino.

More grisly is the **Museo della Tortura** *(☎ 0577 94 22 43, Via del Castello 1/3; admission €7.75 – note this museum is not included in the combined ticket; open 10am-7pm daily Oct-June, 10am-midnight daily July-Sept)*, filled with a horrifying assortment of skull splitters, tongue cutters and thumbscrews dating from the 15th to 18th centuries (although some exhibits are replicas). There's even an electric chair from Alabama.

Places to Stay

San Gimignano has only a handful of hotels, with eye-popping prices. Coming to the rescue are, apart from the hostel and a camp site, numerous affittacamere at reasonable prices. The tourist office will provide details, but will not make bookings. The Cooperativa Hotels Promotion (☎ 0577 94 08 09) on Via San Giovanni, just inside the gate of the same name, can place you in a hotel. It will make arrangements months in advance and charges a €1.55 fee.

Il Boschetto di Piemma *(☎ 0577 94 03 52, fax 0577 94 19 82, Santa Lucia)* Sites per person/tent €4.65/4.65. Open Easter-15 Oct. This camp site is at Santa Lucia, 2km south of the Porta San Giovanni. There's a supermarket, swimming pool and lots of shade under oak trees. Buses leave from Piazzale dei Martiri di Montemaggio.

Ostello della Gioventù *(☎ 0577 94 19 91, fax 0558 05 01 04, e info@franchostel.it, Via delle Fonti 1)* B&B €15.50. The non-HI hostel is at the northern edge of town inside the city walls. It has great views and is famous for its excellent breakfast.

Hotel La Cisterna *(☎ 0577 94 03 28, fax 0577 94 20 80, e lacisterna@iol.it, Piazza della Cisterna 24)* Singles/doubles from €64.55/95.55. This place is on the magnificent Piazza della Cisterna. Ask for a room in the medieval section, with a view across the valley. Prices include breakfast.

Places to Eat

Il Castello *(☎ 0577 94 08 78, Via del Castello 20)* Pasta from €5.15. Open Thurs-Tues. This osteria stays open till midnight and it's a good spot to sample some local wines.

Trattoria La Mangiatoia *(☎ 0577 94 15 28, Via Mainardi 5)* Full meals €23.65-25.80. Open Wed-Mon. This is one of the town's better restaurants serving traditional Tuscan dishes.

Le Vecchie Mura *(☎ 0577 94 02 70, Via Piandornella 15)* Meals €18.05. Open Wed-Mon, evenings only. This is a wonderful spot, especially if you can snap up a table on the terrace on a warm summer's night. The food competes with the view (of rolling green hills) and you should definitely book ahead if you don't want to queue.

Locanda Sant'Agostino *(☎ 0577 94 31 41, Piazza Sant'Agostino 15)* Bruschettas from €5.15. Open Tues-Sun. This is a pleasant spot for a relatively quiet drink and a choice of 49 bruschettas.

Gelateria di Piazza *(Piazza della Cisterna 4)*. This is the place for gelati in San Gimignano. Among other flavours, you can try an ice cream made from Vernaccia, the local wine.

A ***produce market*** is held on Thursday morning on Piazza della Cisterna and Piazza del Duomo.

Getting There and Around

San Gimignano is accessible from Florence (€5.15, one hour 40 minutes, hourly) and Siena (€4.45, 1½ hours, half-hourly) by regular Tra-in buses, but you'll probably need to change at Poggibonsi. For Rome and areas such as Perugia and Assisi, you need to get to Siena first. There's also a service to Volterra (€4.15, 1½ hours, four daily) but you have to change in Colle di Val d'Elsa. Bus timetables are available from the Pro Loco office. Buses arrive in Piazzale dei Martiri di Montemaggio at the Porto San Giovanni. The closest train station is in Poggibonsi.

To reach San Gimignano by car, take the S68 from Colle di Val d'Elsa, which is on the S2 between Florence and Siena, and follow the signs. There's a large car park outside the Porta San Giovanni.

VOLTERRA

postcode 56048 • pop 13,400

The Etruscan settlement of Velathri was an important trading centre and remained so under the Romans, who renamed it Volaterrae. A long period of conflict with Florence started in the 12th century and ended when the Medici took possession of the city in the 15th century.

Perched high on a rocky plateau, 10km south-west of San Gimignano, the town's well-preserved medieval ramparts give Volterra a forbidding air but the gentle Tuscan countryside rolling out for miles around provides the perfect contrast. The city has long had a strong alabaster industry, a legacy from the Etruscans.

Orientation & Information

Driving and parking inside the walled town are more or less prohibited. Park in one of the designated parking areas and enter the nearest city gate – all the main streets lead to the central Piazza dei Priori.

The tourist office (☎ 0588 8 72 57), at Piazza dei Priori 20, opens 10am to 1pm and 2pm to 6pm. The post office faces it on the northern side of the square. Next door is the *questura* (police station) in the Palazzo Pretorio.

Piazza dei Priori

Piazza dei Priori is surrounded by austere medieval mansions. The 13th-century **Palazzo dei Priori** *(Piazza dei Priori; admission €1.05; open 10am-1pm & 2pm-6pm Sat & Sun)* is the oldest seat of local government in Tuscany and is believed to have been a model for Florence's Palazzo Vecchio. Look out for a fresco of the *Crocifissione* (Crucifixion) by Piero Francesco Fiorentino as you walk up the stairs. Other frescoes and paintings can be seen in the magnificent cross-vaulted council hall and a small antechamber on the 1st floor, where you get a bird's-eye view of the piazza below. The **Palazzo Pretorio**, also dating from the 13th century, is dominated by the Torre del Porcellino (Piglet's Tower), so named because of the wild boar sculpted on its upper section.

Behind the Palazzo dei Priori, along Via Turazza, is the **cathedral** *(Piazza San Giovanni; free; open 8am-12.30pm & 3pm-6pm daily)*, built in the 12th and 13th centuries. Highlights inside include a small fresco by Benozzo Gozzoli, the *Adoration of the Magi*, behind a nativity group in the oratory at the beginning of the left aisle. The 15th-century tabernacle on the high altar is by Mino da Fiesole. Next door is the **Museo Diocesano d'Arte Sacra** *(☎ 0588 8 62 90, Palazzo Vescovile, Via Roma 13; admission €6.20 including the Pinacoteca Comunale & Museo Etrusco Guaranacci; open 9.30am-1pm & 3pm-6pm daily in summer, 9am-1pm daily Nov–mid-Mar)*. It's worth a peek for its collection of ecclesiastical vestments and gold reliquaries and works by Andrea della Robbia and Rosso Fiorentino. Opposite the cathedral, the 13th-century **baptistry** features a font by Andrea Sansovino.

The **Pinacoteca Comunale** *(☎ 0588 8 75 80, Palazzo Minucci Solaini, Via dei Sarti 1;*

admission €6.20, including the Museo Etrusco Guaranacci & Museo Diocesano d'Arte Sacra; open 9am-7pm daily in summer, 9am-2pm daily in winter) houses a modest collection of local art.

Museo Etrusco Guaranacci

All the exhibits at this fascinating Etruscan museum *(☎ 0588 8 63 47, Via Don Minzoni 15; admission €6.20, including the Pinacoteca Comunale & Museo Diocesano d'Arte Sacra; open 9am-7pm daily in summer, 9am-2pm daily in winter)* were unearthed locally, including a vast collection of some 600 funerary urns carved from alabaster, tufa and other materials. The urns are displayed according to the subjects depicted on their bas-reliefs and the period from which they date. The best examples (those dating from later periods) are on the 2nd and 3rd floors. Most significant is the **Ombra della Sera** sculpture, a strange, elongated nude figure that would fit in well in any museum of modern art, and the urn of the **Sposi**, featuring an elderly couple, their faces depicted in portrait fashion rather than the stylised method usually employed.

Fortezza Medicea & Parco Archeologico

Further along Via Don Minzoni is the entrance to the Fortezza Medicea, built in the 14th century and altered by Lorenzo il Magnifico and now used as a prison.

Near the fort is the pleasant Parco Archeologico, whose archaeological remains have suffered with the passage of time. Little has survived, but it's a good place for a picnic.

Other Things to See

On the city's northern edge is a **Roman theatre**, a well-preserved complex that includes a Roman bath.

The **Balze**, a deep ravine created by erosion, about a 2km walk north-west of the city centre, has claimed several churches

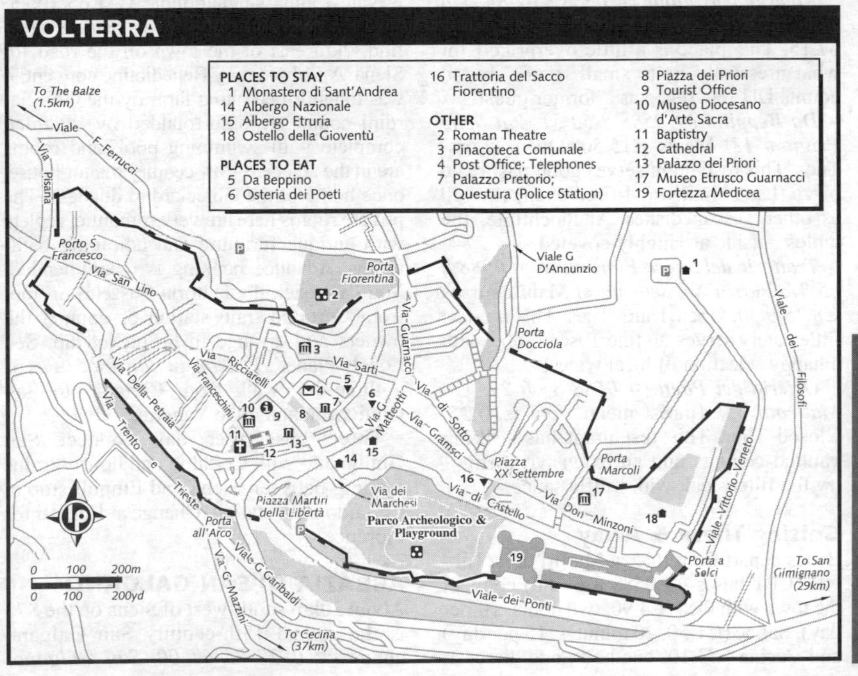

TUSCANY

since the Middle Ages, the buildings having fallen into its deep gullies. A 14th-century monastery is perched close to the precipice and is in danger of toppling into the ravine.

Places to Stay & Eat

Ostello della Gioventù *(☎/fax 0577 8 55 77, Via del Poggetto 3)* Dorm beds from €10.35, meals €8.80. Reception opens at 5.30pm. Large and airy, this privately run hostel near the Museo Etrusco Guaranacci is the best deal around but don't expect much of the food.

Monastero di Sant'Andrea *(☎ 0588 8 60 28, fax 0588 9 07 91, Viale Vittorio Veneto)* Doubles without/with bath €28.90/35.10. This is a wonderfully peaceful place with vaulted ceilings and 60 large, clean rooms.

Albergo Etruria *(☎/fax 0588 8 73 77, Via Giacomo Matteotti 32)* Singles/doubles with bath 46.50/67.15. There are the remains of an Etruscan wall inside this hotel and fine views from the roof garden.

Albergo Nazionale *(☎ 0588 8 62 84, Via dei Marchesi 11)* Singles/doubles €49.05/67.15. This place is a little overpriced for what are really quite small rooms, but it counts DH Lawrence as a former guest.

Da Beppino *(☎ 0588 8 60 51, Via delle Prigioni 13)* Meals €15.50. Open Thurs-Tues. This restaurant serves good pasta and pizza (baked in a wood-fired oven) as well as other Tuscan dishes. At lunchtime, the tables outside are highly coveted.

Trattoria del Sacco Fiorentino *(☎ 0588 8 85 37, Piazza XX Settembre)* Main courses €8.25-9.30. Open Thurs-Tues. This modest little eatery serves up fine Tuscan food with a happy selection of local wines.

Osteria dei Poeti *(☎ 0588 8 60 29, Via Matteotti 55)* Tourist menu from €10.35. Closed Thur. This restaurant has striking vaulted ceilings and an extensive menu – try the fillet steak with truffle sauce.

Getting There & Away

Buses depart from Piazza Martiri della Libertà. CPT buses (☎ 0588 8 61 86) connect the town with Pisa (€4.90, two hours, 10 per day), Saline (€1.50, 20 minutes, 15 per day) and Cecina (€3.10, one hour, one direct at 1.45pm, otherwise daily with connections at Saline); timetables are available from the tourist office. For San Gimignano (€4.15, 1½ hours, four daily), Siena (€4.25, 1½ hours, four daily) and Florence (€6.20, two hours, four daily), you need to change at Colle di Val d'Elsa.

From the small train station in Saline, 9km to the south-west (bus from Volterra), you can get a train to Cecina, from where you can catch trains on the Rome-Pisa line. By car, take the S68 which runs between Cecina and Colle di Val d'Elsa.

CERTALDO

Located in the Val d'Elsa, in a strategic position between Florence, Siena (40km by train) and San Gimignano, this small medieval town is definitely worth a visit. Giovanni Boccaccio, one of the fathers of the Italian language, was born here in 1313.

Fattoria Bassetto *(☎/fax 0571 66 83 42, e bassetto@dedalo.com)* Dorm bed €19.65, private rooms single/double €51.65/70.25, minimum stay two nights. This place is a real find, 2km east of the town on the road for Siena. A 14th-century Benedictine convent, it was transformed into a farm by the Guicciardini counts. It is surrounded by a garden complete with swimming pool, and rooms are in the adjacent 19th-century manor house, once home of the Guicciardini duchess. The private rooms here are very romantic, replete with antique furniture and adjoining bathrooms. Advance booking is recommended. You can reach the Fattoria Bassetto on foot from Certaldo train station or contact the owners and arrange to be picked up. See Lonely Planet's *Walking in Italy* for details of a three-day walk from Certaldo to San Gimignano and on to Volterra.

Three buses per day connect San Gimignano with Certaldo and hourly trains running between Siena and Empoli stop at Certaldo train station. Change at Empoli for Florence.

ABBAZIA DI SAN GALGANO

About 20km south-west of Siena on the S73 is the ruined 13th-century San Galgano abbey *(☎ 0577 75 67 00, San Galgano;*

TUSCANY

free; open 8am-7.30pm daily), one of the country's finest Gothic buildings in its day and now a very atmospheric ruin. A former Cistercian abbey, its monks were among Tuscany's most powerful, forming the judiciary and acting as accountants for the communes of Volterra and Siena. They presided over disputes between the cities, played a significant role in the construction of the cathedral in Siena and built themselves an opulent church.

By the 16th century, the monks' wealth and importance had declined and the church had deteriorated to the point of ruin. The walls remain standing but the roof collapsed long ago. The abbey is definitely worth a diversion if you are driving, but visiting by public transport is quite difficult. The best option is the bus service between Siena and Massa Marittima, a little farther south-west. The Accademia Musicale Chigiana in Siena sponsors concerts at the abbey during summer. See Special Events in the earlier Siena section.

On a hill overlooking the abbey is the tiny, round Romanesque **Cappella di Monte Siepi**. Inside are badly preserved frescoes by Ambrogio Lorenzetti, which depict the life of San Galgano, a local soldier who had a vision of St Michael on this site. A real-life 'sword in the stone' is under glass in the floor of the chapel, put there, legend has it, by San Galgano.

If you have your own transport, drive via Monticiano towards the S223. Stop off at **Tocchi**, a tiny village with a restored castle nearby.

Posto di Ristoro a Tocchi *(☎/fax 0577 75 71 26, Località Tocchi)* B&B from €23.25. Meals around €18.05. You can enjoy an excellent meal of fresh local produce at Posto di Ristoro a Tocchi, and they also have a few simple rooms if you want to spend the night.

You can also get here on the Tra-in bus which travels between Siena and Monticiano. Continue across the valley towards **Murlo**, an interesting medieval fortified village. This was once an important Etruscan settlement and experts claim that DNA tests show the locals to be close descendants of these ancient people.

LE CRETE

South-east of Siena, this area of rolling clay hills is a feast of classic Tuscan images – bare ridges topped by a solitary cypress tree flanking a medieval farmhouse, four hills silhouetted one against the other as they fade off into the misty distance. If you have the funds to spare, hire a car in Florence or Siena and spend a few days exploring Le Crete. Another option is the *Treno Natura,* a tourist train which runs from Siena through Asciano and along the Val d'Orcia (see Organised Tours in the Siena section earlier for details).

Apart from the scenery, one of the main attractions in the area is the **Abbazia di Monte Oliveto Maggiore** *(☎ 0577 70 76 11; free; open 9.15am-noon & 3.30pm-6pm daily in summer, 9.15am-noon & 3.30pm-5pm daily in winter)*, a 14th-century Olivetan monastery, famous for the frescoes by Signorelli and Sodoma that decorate its Great Cloister. The frescoes illustrate events in the life of the rather severe St Benedict.

The fresco cycle begins with Sodoma's work on the eastern wall (immediately to the right of the entrance into the church from the cloisters) and continues along the southern wall of the cloisters. The nine frescoes by Signorelli line the western side of the cloisters and Sodoma picks up again on the northern wall. Note the decorations on the pillars between some of Sodoma's frescoes – they are among the earliest examples of 'grotesque' art, copied from decorations found in the then newly excavated Domus Aurea created by Nero in Rome. It is possible to stay at the monastery from Easter to the end of September. They don't take bookings, so it's a case of first in best dressed.

From the monastery, if you have your own transport, head for **San Giovanni d'Asso**, where there's an interesting 11th-century church with a Lombard-Tuscan facade and a picturesque *borghetto* (historic centre) with the remains of a castle. Continue on to Montisi and Castelmuzio. Along a side road just outside Castelmuzio is the **Pieve di Santo Stefano in Cennano**, an abandoned 13th-century church. Ask for the key at the adjacent farm buildings. Two kilometres past

Castelmuzio on the road to Pienza is the uninhabited 14th-century Olivetan monastery of **Sant'Anna in Camprena**.

The route south from Abbazia di Monte Oliveto Maggiore runs almost entirely along a high ridge, with great views of Le Crete.

MONTALCINO

postcode 53024 • pop 5100

A pretty town, perched high above the Orcia valley, Montalcino is best known for its wine, the Brunello. Produced only in the vineyards surrounding the town, Brunello is said to be one of Italy's best red wines and has gained considerable international fame. There are plenty of *enoteche* (wine cellars) around the town where you can taste and buy Brunello, as well as the other local wine, the Rosso di Montalcino, although you'll pay a minimum of €12.90 for a Brunello.

The tourist information office (☎ 0577 84 93 31) at Costa Municipio 1, just off Piazza del Popolo (the main square), opens 10am to 1pm and 2pm to 5.40pm daily.

Inside a former monastery, off Piazza Sant'Agostino, is the **Museo Civico e Diocesano d'Arte Sacra** *(☎ 0577 84 60 14, Via Ricasoli; admission €4.15; open 10am-6pm Tues-Sun Apr-Oct, 10am-1pm & 2pm-5pm winter)* with some interesting work by Andrea di Bartolo, Sano di Pietro and others. There's also a fine collection of painted wooden sculptures.

Dominating the town is the 14th-century **Rocca** *(Fortress; ☎ 0577 84 92 11, Piazzale Fortezza; free; open 9am-1pm & 2.30pm-8pm Tues-Sun)*. Within the fortifications is an *enoteca* (wine bar), where you can sample and buy the local wines. Buy a €2.60 ticket at the bar, which allows you to walk up onto the Rocca's ramparts for magnificent views.

Places to Stay & Eat

There are plenty of places to stay in Montalcino and the surrounding countryside, including hotels, apartments and agriturismo.

Il Giardino *(☎/fax 0577 84 82 57, Piazza Cavour 4)* Singles/doubles €41.30/51.65. This two-star hotel occupies an old building overlooking Piazza Cavour. All 10 rooms are doubles and the decoration has a distinct 1970s-feel to it. The owner, a wine buff, stocks an impressive cellar.

Hotel Il Giglio *(☎ 0577 84 86 66, fax 0577 84 81 67, e hotelgiglio@tin.it, Via S Saloni 5)* Singles/doubles €46.50/67.15. Il Giglio is a very comfortable hotel with pretty rooms and a restaurant downstairs. For cheaper rooms, the owner runs a small 'dependence' just a few doors up on the same street.

Trattoria Sciame *(☎ 0577 84 80 17, Via Ricasoli 9)* Full meals about €18.05. Open Wed-Mon. This place serves good home-made pasta dishes but it's small and popular so get there early.

Taverna Il Grappolo Blu *(☎ 0577 84 71 50, Scale di Via Moglio 1)* Meals about €20.65. Open Sat-Thurs. The chef here does ingenious things with local ingredients – try the succulent *coniglio al brunello* (rabbit cooked in Brunello wine).

Getting There & Away

Montalcino is accessible from Siena by regular Tra-in buses (€2.75, one hour 20 minutes, nine daily). By car, follow the S2 south from Siena and take the turn off to Montalcino before you reach San Quirico d'Orcia.

SANT'ANTIMO

Set in a broad valley, just below the village of Castelnuovo dell'Abate, the 12th-century **Abbazia di San Antimo** *(☎ 0577 83 56 59, Castelnuovo dell'Abate; free; open 10.30am-12.30pm & 3pm-6.30pm Mon-Sat, 9am-10.30am & 3pm-6pm Sun & holidays)* is strikingly beautiful. It is best to visit this superb Romanesque church in the morning, when the sun shines through the east windows to create an almost surreal atmosphere. Built in pale stone, the church's exterior is simple, but there are numerous fascinating architectural and decorative features, particularly the stone carvings of the bell tower and the apse windows, which include a *Madonna and Child* and the various fantastic animals typical of the Romanesque style. The interior of the church is in pale travertine stone. Take the time to study the capitals of the columns lining the nave, including one representing

Daniel in the lion's den (second on the right as you enter). There is a 13th-century wooden statue of the Madonna in the right aisle and above the altar is a painted wooden crucifix, also dating from the 13th century. Behind the altar, in the ambulatory, there are traces of frescoes. The bases and capitals of some of the columns are of alabaster, which creates a stunning effect when the morning sun shines through the apse windows.

Ask the attendant to let you into the sacristy, where there are monochrome frescoes depicting the life of St Benedict. The sacristy is in what is known as the Carolingian Chapel, which probably dates back to the 8th century. The 9th-century crypt beneath the chapel is closed to the public, but you can get a murky glimpse of it through the small round window at the base of the exterior of the chapel's apse.

Four buses per day connect Montalcino with the village of Castelnuovo dell'Abate (€1.05, 15 minutes). From here, it's an easy walk to the church.

MONTEPULCIANO

postcode 53045 • pop 5300

Set atop a narrow ridge of volcanic rock, Montepulciano combines Tuscany's superb countryside with some of the region's finest wines. This medieval town is the perfect place to spend a few quiet days. The hordes that swamp other Sienese hill towns thankfully don't seem to make it here in such stifling numbers, which means you'll have a fairly free run of the town's steep winding streets. Stop by the various enoteche to sample the local wines.

Orientation & Information

However you arrive, you will probably end up at the Porta al Prato on the town's northern edge. From here, buses take you through the town to Piazza Grande. The 1km walk is extremely steep but well worth the exercise.

The Pro Loco office (☎ 0578 75 73 41), Via di Gracciano nel Corso 59, opens 9.30am to 12.30pm and 3pm to 8pm daily in summer, 9.30am to 12.30pm and 3pm to 6pm daily in winter, and can help with accommodation.

Things to See

Most of the main sights are clustered around Piazza Grande, although the town's streets provide a wealth of palazzos, fine buildings and churches (unfortunately, the sheer number of churches and dearth of priests means that many remain locked up).

To the left as you enter the **Porta al Prato**, designed by the Florentine Antonio da Sangallo the Elder, you'll see the 18th-century **Chiesa di San Bernardo** *(Piazza Savonarola, usually closed)*. Look out for the **Colonna del Marzocca**, a splendid stone lion on top of a column at the upper end of Piazza Savonarola. Erected in 1511 to confirm Montepulciano's allegiance to Florence, the original is in the Museo Civico and what you see is a 1856 copy. Several palazzos line the Via di Gracciano nel Corso, including the **Palazzo Bucelli** *(Via di Gracciano nel Corso 73)*, whose facade features Etruscan and Latin inscriptions and reliefs. Sangallo also designed the **Palazzo Cocconi** opposite at No. 70.

Continuing up Via di Gracciano nel Corso, you'll find Michelozzo's **Chiesa di Sant' Agostino** *(Piazza Michelozzo; free; open 9am-noon & 3pm-6pm daily)* with its lunette above the entrance holding a terracotta Madonna and Child, John the Baptist and St Augustine. Opposite, a medieval **tower house** is topped by the town clock and the bizarre figure of **Pulcinella** (Punch of Punch & Judy fame), which strikes the hours.

Continue up the hill and take the first left past the Loggia di Mercato for Via del Poggiolo, which eventually becomes Via Ricci. In the Gothic Palazzo Neri-Orselli is the **Museo Civico** *(☎ 0578 71 73 00, Via Ricci 10; adult/child €4.15/2.60; open 10am-7pm daily in summer, 10am-1pm & 3pm-6pm daily in winter)*. The small collection features terracotta reliefs by the della Robbia family and some Gothic and Renaissance paintings.

Piazza Grande marks the highest point of the town and features the austere **Palazzo Comunale** *(☎ 0578 71 22 43, Piazza Grande 1; free; open 9.30am-12.30pm Mon-Sat, plus 3.30pm-5.30pm Mon & Wed)*, a 13th-century Gothic building remodelled in the 15th century by Michelozzo. From the top of the

14th-century tower, on a clear day, you can see the Monti Sibillini to the east and the Gran Sasso to the south-east. Opposite is the impressive **Palazzo Contucci** and it's wine cellar **Cantine Contucci** *(☎ 0578 75 70 06, Palazzo Contucci, Piazza Grande; free, phone ahead for guided tours; open 8am-12.30pm & 2.30pm-6.30pm daily)*, where you can sample some local wines.

The 16th-century **cathedral** *(Piazza Grande; free; open 9am-noon & 4pm-6pm daily)* has an unfinished facade. There is a lovely triptych above the high altar, depicting the Assumption, by Taddeo da Bartolo.

Outside the town wall, about 1km from the Porta al Prato, is the pilgrimage **Chiesa di San Biagio** *(Via di San Biagio; free; open 9am-12.30pm & 3pm-7pm daily in summer, 9am-12.30pm & 3pm-6pm daily in winter)*, a fine Renaissance church built by Antonio da Sangallo the Elder and consecrated in 1529 by the Medici Pope Clement VII.

Places to Stay & Eat

Il Cittano *(☎ 0578 75 73 35, Vicolo della Via Nuova 2)* Singles/doubles €20.65/36.15. Montepulciano's cheapest accommodation consists of just two doubles and one single room above a restaurant. It's a bit dark and pokey and often full.

Bellavista *(☎ 0578 75 73 48 or 0347 823 23 14, ⓔ bellavista@bccmp.com, Via Ricci 25)* Doubles €43.90. The seven double rooms in this house have fantastic views – try to get one of the west-facing rooms at the back. No-one else lives here, so phone ahead in order to be met and given a key.

Il Riccio *(☎/fax 0578 75 77 13, Via Talosa 21, ⓔ info@ilriccio.net, ⓦ www.ilriccio.net)* Singles/doubles €56.80/77.45. This gorgeous but tiny hotel (five rooms only) occupies an ancient 13th-century palazzo just off Piazza Grande. The communal areas are good and there's a very pretty porticoed courtyard.

Albergo Il Marzocco *(☎ 0578 75 72 62, fax 0578 75 75 30, Piazza Savonarola 18)* Singles/doubles with bath from €56.80/82.65. This 16th-century building has been run as a hotel by the same family for 100 years. The rooms are large and there are some interesting antiques dotted about the place. Try and bag a room with a balcony.

Caffè Poliziano *(☎ 0578 75 86 15, Via di Voltaia nel Corso 27)* Montepulciano's oldest cafe (1868) is wonderfully elegant but not at all pretentious, and the cakes are superb.

Trattoria Diva e Maceo *(☎ 0578 71 69 51, Via di Gracciano nel Corso 90)* Meals €15.50. Open Wed-Mon. An honest trattoria and a favourite with locals, Diva e Maceo also has a good selection of local wines.

Il Cantuccio *(☎ 0578 75 78 70, Via delle Cantin 1)* Meals €18.05. Tucked down an alley off Via di Gracciano nel Corso, Il Cantuccio is another popular eatery dishing up traditional Tuscan mains and pasta (including *pici*, fresh pasta).

La Grotta *(☎ 0578 757479, Località San Biagio)* Meals €41.30. Open Thurs-Tues. Opposite the church of San Bagio, La Grotta is probably Montepulciano's best restaurant. Inside, the dining is suitably elegant while the tables in the garden are tempting for a summer lunch.

Borgo Buio *(☎ 0578 71 74 97, Via Borgo Buio 10)* Meals €25.80. This osteria, just off Via di Gracciano nel Corso, is a good place to sample local wines. It also does rather pricey meals.

Getting There & Around

Tra-in runs five services daily between Montepulciano and Siena (€4.15, 1½ hours) via Pienza. Regular LFE buses connect with Chiusi (€1.90, 50 minutes, half hourly).

The most convenient train station is at Chiusi-Chianciano Terme, 10km south-east, on the main Rome-Florence line. Buses for Montepulciano meet each train, so it is the best way to get there from Florence or Rome. Stazione di Montepulciano, about 5km to the north-east, has very infrequent services.

By car, exit the A1 at Chianciano Terme and follow the SS166 for the 18km trip to Montepulciano. Most cars are banned from the town centre and there are car parks near the Porta al Prato. Small town buses weave their way from here to Piazza Grande.

Southern Tuscany

MAREMMA & ETRUSCAN SITES

The area known as the Maremma extends along the Tuscan coast from just north of Grosseto to the southern border with Lazio, incorporating the Parco Naturale della Maremma (also known as Parco dell' Uccellina) and Monte Argentario. It also extends inland to the extraordinary hill towns of Sovana, Sorana and Pitigliano.

Information

Grosseto is the main town in the Maremma area but is of little interest. Its helpful APT office (☎ 0564 41 43 03) is at Via Fucini 43c, a block from the train station. Information about the Parco Naturale della Maremma can be obtained there or at the Centro Visite del Parco Alberese (☎ 0564 40 70 98) on the northern edge of the park, which opens 9am to sunset daily (from 7am to sunset from mid-June to the end of September). The ***Associazione Albergatori** (☎ 0564 2 63 15)*, next door to the APT office at Via Fucini 43, can help you find a bed in the province.

The individual towns in the area each have small tourist offices that open daily during summer only.

Parco Naturale della Maremma

Definitely the main attraction in the area, the park *(☎ 0564 40 70 98; adult/child €7.75/5.15 including bus transport from Alberese to the park entrance)* incorporates the Monti dell'Uccellina and a magnificent stretch of unspoiled coastline. Admission to the park is limited and cars must be left in designated parking areas. Certain areas can be visited only on particular days and excursions into the park are always limited to set itineraries. Depending on your chosen route, you may see plenty of native animals (including deer, wild boar, foxes and hawks). Certain routes also provide access to the sea. You must buy tickets at the visitor centre in Alberese. There are no shelters, bars and so on within the park, so make sure you carry water and are properly dressed. Cycling is an option (if you bring your own). The park gets crowded in summer, especially at weekends.

Etruscan Sites

If you're heading inland by car, stop off briefly at **Manciano**, a former Sienese fortress, and **Montemerano**, a picturesque walled medieval town, where you can buy outstanding Tuscan olive oil at La Piaggia, an agriturismo establishment. Visit the town's Chiesa di San Giorgio, which is decorated with 15th-century frescoes of the Sienese School. **Saturnia** is more famous for its sulphur spring and baths at Terme di Saturnia, but its Etruscan remains, including part of the town wall, are worth a diversion. A tomb at Sede di Carlo, just north-east of the town, is one of the area's best preserved. Bring along a bathing costume and take advantage of the curative waters at the thermal baths.

Sovana This pretty little town has more than its fair share of important Etruscan sites and historical monuments. There's an information office (☎ 0564 61 40 74) in the Palazzetto dell'Archivio on the Piazza del Pretorio.

Pope Gregory VII was born here. Medieval mansions and the remains of a fortress belonging to his family are at the eastern end of the town. The **Chiesa di Santa Maria** *(☎ 0564 61 65 32, Piazza del Pretorio; free; open 10am-6pm daily Feb-Dec, Sat & Sun only in Jan)* is a starkly simple Romanesque church featuring a magnificent 9th-century ciborium in white marble, one of the last remaining pre-Romanesque works left in Tuscany. Inside the church, there are also some early Renaissance frescoes.

Walk east along Via del Duomo to reach the imposing Gothic-Romanesque **cathedral** *(☎ 0564 61 65 32, Via del Duomo; free; open 10am-1pm & 2.30pm-7pm daily in summer, 10am-1pm & 2.30pm-5pm daily in winter)*. The original construction dates back to the 9th century, although it was largely rebuilt in the 12th and 13th centuries. Of particular note are the marble portal and the capitals of the columns that divide the interior into three naves. Several of the capitals feature biblical scenes and are thought to be the work of the Lombard school, dating from the 11th century.

About 1km to the south of the town are a number of Etruscan tombs, the most important being the **Tomba Ildebranda** *(☎ 0564 61 40 74, Parque Archeologico; admission €5.15; open 10am-1pm & 3pm-7pm daily in summer, 10am-1pm & 3pm-6pm daily in winter)*, the only surviving temple-style tomb. The area is famous for the spectacular *vie cave*, narrow walkways which were carved like mini-gorges into the rock. The walkways continue for 1km and date from Etruscan times. Other tombs and several necropolises in the area are also worth a visit.

If you'd like to stay in Sovana, there are several good options.

Hotel Etrusca *(☎ 0564 61 61 83, fax 0564 61 41 93, Piazza Pretorio 16)* Singles/doubles with bath €41.30/72.30. Open Feb-Dec. This three-star hotel has simple but attractive rooms with stripped wooden floors and a good restaurant downstairs.

Albergo Scilla *(☎ 0564 61 65 31, fax 0564 61 43 29, Via R Siviero 1–3)* Singles/doubles €61.95/77.45. Just off the piazza, this recently renovated hotel is a little expensive but the rooms are very comfortable, with fabulous wrought-iron beds, and mosaics in the bathrooms. It also has a good restaurant.

Camere di Roberto *(☎ 0564 61 40 73, Via del Pretoria 8)* Singles/doubles €38.75/51.65. This house has five immaculate double rooms. Make inquiries at ***Bar della Taverna*** in Piazza del Pretorio.

Sorano High on a rocky spur, this small medieval town has largely retained its original form. Its houses seem to huddle together in an effort not to shove one another off their precarious perch. There's a small tourist office (☎ 0546 63 30 99) on Piazza Busati. The town's main attraction is the newly renovated **Fortezza Orsini** *(☎ 0564 63 37 67, Via San Marco; admission €1.55; open 10am-1pm & 3pm-7pm daily Apr-Sept, 10am-5pm Fri-Sun Oct-Mar)*.

You could also climb up **Masso Leopoldino** for a spectacular view of the surrounding countryside. The gate is open at the same times as the castle.

A few kilometres out of Sorano, on the road to Sovana, is the **Necropoli di San Rocco**, an Etruscan burial area.

Pitigliano The visual impact of this town goes one better again than Sorano. It seems to grow out of a high rocky outcrop that rises from a deep gorge. The tourist office (☎ 0564 61 44 33), at Via Roma 6, on the corner of Piazza della Repubblica, has erratic opening hours.

The town itself is a pleasant stopover – its offerings include the 13th-century **Palazzo Orsini** *(☎ 0564 61 44 19, Piazza Fortezza Orsini 25; adult/child €2.60/1.55; open 10am-1pm & 3pm-7pm Tues-Sun in summer, 10am-1pm & 3pm-5pm Tues-Sun in winter)* and an imposing 16th-century aqueduct. There's a small museum in the palazzo. The town's cathedral dates from the Middle Ages, but its facade is Baroque and its interior has been modernised. It is interesting to wander the town's narrow medieval streets, particularly in the area known as the **Ghetto**, once home to a large Jewish population. You can visit a small but richly adorned **synagogue** *(☎ 0564 61 63 96, Vicolo Manin; free; open 10am-1pm & 3pm-6pm daily May-Oct)*, which was practically rebuilt from scratch in 1995 after the original fell into disrepair with the demise of Pitigliano's Jewish community at the end of WWII.

Albergo Guastini *(☎ 0564 61 60 65, fax 0564 61 66 52, Piazza Petruccioli 4)* Singles/doubles with bath €38.75/67.15. The Guastini is very friendly and welcoming. Perched on the edge of the cliff face, the views are marvellous but parties of noisy school children can be bothersome in the low season.

Osteria Il Tufo Allegro *(☎ 0564 61 61 92, Vico della Costituzione 2)* Full meals €23.25, including wine & dessert. Just off Via Roma, this is the *numero uno* place to eat in town. The aromas emanating from the kitchen into the street should be enough to draw you into the cavernous chamber, carved out of the tufa-rock foundations.

Getting Around

Rama buses leave from the train station at Grosseto for Pitigliano (€4.80, two hours, five per day) by way of Manciano. Infrequent Rama buses also connect Pitigliano with Sorano (€1.55, 15 minutes, seven daily) and Sovana (€1.55, 30 minutes, two per day). If you have the funds, hire a car in Grosseto, or even in Rome, and explore the area for a few days.

MONTE ARGENTARIO

Situated on an isthmus some 120km northwest of Rome, **Orbetello** is a pleasant place, popular with Romans at weekends. The Pro Loco office (☎ 0564 86 04 47, e info@comune.ortobello.gr.it), Piazza della Repubblica 1, opens 10am to 12.30pm and 4pm to 8pm daily.

Orbetello's main attraction is its **cathedral** *(Piazza della Repubblica; free; open 9am-noon & 3pm-6pm daily)*, which has retained its 14th-century Gothic facade despite being remodelled in the Spanish style in the 16th century. Other reminders of the Spanish garrison that was stationed in the city include the fort and city wall, parts of which are the original Etruscan wall. Another attraction is the increasingly popular Monte Argentario and its two harbour towns, Port'Ercole and Porto Santo Stefano, both crammed with equally expensive-looking yachts and people.

Around the Peninsula

Monte Argentario is popular with holidaying Romans but not many tourists go there. **Porto Santo Stefano** and **Port'Ercole** are resort towns for the wealthy, but Port'Ercole, in a picturesque position between two forts, retains some of its fishing-village character. The main tourist office (☎ 0564 81 42 08) is in Porto Santo Stefano, in the Monte dei Paschi di Siena building, at Corso Umberto 55. It opens 9am to 1pm and 4pm to 6pm Monday to Saturday.

For a pleasant drive, follow the signs to Il Telegrafo, one of the highest mountains in the region, and turn off at the **Convento dei Frati Passionisti**, a church and convent which has sensational views across to the mainland.

There are plenty of good beaches, usually of the pebbly or rocky (rather than sandy) variety. One of the most popular is the long strip of **Feniglia**, between Orbetello and Port'Ercole. Near Port'Ercole the beach is serviced, which means it's clean but cluttered with deck chairs and umbrellas for hire. As you move farther away the beach becomes less crowded but unfortunately it also gets dirtier.

Places to Stay

Accommodation on the peninsula is generally expensive.

***Camping Feniglia** (☎ 0564 83 10 90, fax 0564 86 73 35, Località Feniglia)* Sites per person/tent €7.75/10.35. Near Port'Ercole, this camp site is on the northern fringe at the Feniglia beach, just 50m from the sea.

***Pensione Weekend** (☎/fax 0564 81 25 80, Via Martiri d'Ungheria 3)* Doubles with bath from €51.65. In Porto Santo Stefano, the Weekend is central and the owner speaks English, German and French. Try and wangle room 19, with its own terrace and wonderful sea views.

***Albergo Belvedere** (☎/fax 0564 81 26 34, Via del Fortino 51)* High season singles/doubles €67.15/87.80. This is a luxurious complex overlooking the water with its own private beach. Prices include breakfast.

Cheaper accommodation can be found in Orbetello.

***La Perla** (☎ 0564 86 35 46, fax 0564 86 52 10, Via Etruria 2)* Singles/doubles with bath €36.15/61.95. This one-star hotel is above a popular cafe in Orbetello with functional but slightly soulless rooms.

Places to Eat

There is a good selection of restaurants in Porto Santo Stefano but at weekends freshly caught fish is hard to come by – there are simply too many people eating their way through the peninsula then!

***Il Veliero** (☎ 0564 81 22 26, Strada Panoramica 149)* Meals around €25.80. This excellent restaurant high above the town has great views.

***Trattoria Da Siro** (☎ 0564 81 25 38, Corso Umberto 104)* Full meals €25.80. Open Tues-Sun. This place is just off the waterfront and is also good for seafood.

***I Due Pini** (☎ 0564 81 40 12, Località La Soda)* Full meals €25.80. I Due Pini is just outside the port and is a good bet for fresh seafood.

Lo Sfizio (☎ 0564 81 25 92, Lungomare dei Navigatori 26) Pizzas from €5.15. Open Wed-Mon. Here you can have cheap bruschetta, pizza or seafood.

Getting There & Away

Rama buses connect most towns on the Monte Argentario with downtown Orbetello (€1.35, 15 minutes, 28 daily) and continue to the train station; and Grosseto (€3.05, one hour, five daily). By car, follow the signs to Monte Argentario from the S1, which connects Grosseto with Rome.

Eastern Tuscany

AREZZO

postcode 52100 • pop 91,700

Heavily bombed during WWII, Arezzo is not the prettiest city in Tuscany. That said, the small medieval centre packs some inspiring highlights. The sloping Piazza Grande and the Romanesque jewel that is Pieve di Santa Maria are lesser known, perhaps, than the frescoes by Piero della Francesca in the Chiesa di San Francesco. It is well worth a visit, easily accomplished as a day trip from Florence.

An important Etruscan town, Arezzo was later absorbed into the Roman Empire. A free republic from the 10th century, it supported the Ghibelline cause in the awful battles between pope and emperor and was eventually subjugated by Florence in 1384. Sons of whom Arezzo can be justly proud include the poet Petrarch, the writer Pietro Aretino and Giorgio Vasari, most famous for his *Lives of the Artists*.

A widely known antiques fair is held on Piazza Grande and the surrounding streets on the first Sunday of every month, which means accommodation can be difficult to find unless you book well ahead.

Orientation & Information

From the train station on the southern edge of the walled city, walk north-east along Via Guido Monaco to the garden piazza of the same name. The old city is to the north-east and the modern part to the south-east along Via Roma.

The APT office (☎/fax 0575 2 08 39), near the train station on Piazza della Repubblica, opens 9am to 1pm and 3pm to 7pm Monday to Saturday and 9am to 1pm Sunday in summer.

The post office is at Via Guido Monaco 34. The hospital is outside the city walls on Via A de Gasperi. The *questura* (police station; ☎ 0575 2 36 00) is on Via Fra Guittone.

Chiesa di San Francesco

The apse of this 14th-century church *(☎ 0575 2 06 30, Piazza San Francesco; free; open 8.30am-noon & 2.30pm-6.30pm)* houses one of the greatest works of Italian art, Piero della Francesca's fresco cycle of the *Legend of the True Cross*. This masterpiece, painted between 1452 and 1456, relates the story of Christ's death in 10 episodes. The frescoes were badly damaged by damp and have recently been restored. You can see the frescoes quite clearly from the church's altar, but if you want to take a closer look, join a guided tour for €5.15. You must, however, call to book the day before your visit (☎ 0575 90 04 04). Groups of about 15 people are taken in on this basis .

Pieve di Santa Maria

This 12th-century church *(☎ 0575 2 26 29, Corso Italia; free; open 8am-1pm & 3pm-6.30pm daily)* has a magnificent Romanesque arcaded facade reminiscent of the cathedral at Pisa (but without the glorious marble facing). Each column is of a different design. Over the central doorway are carved reliefs representing the months. The 14th-century bell tower, with its 40 windows, is something of an emblem for the city. The stark interior of the church shows a Gothic influence, the only colour coming from the polyptych by Pietro Lorenzetti on the raised sanctuary at the rear of the church.

Piazza Grande & Around

The high end of this lumpy sloping piazza is lined by the porticoes of the **Palazzo delle Logge Vasariane**, completed in 1573. The

Palazzo della Fraternità dei Laici, on the western flank, dates from 1375. It was started in the Gothic style and finished after the onset of the Renaissance. Via dei Pileati leads to **Casa di Petrarca** *(☎ 0575 2 47 00, Via dell'Orto 28; free)*, the former home of the poet, which contains a small museum and the Accademia Petrarca. The building was closed for restoration at the time of writing but check at the APT office to see if it has re-opened.

The Cathedral

At the top of the hill is the cathedral *(☎ 0575 2 39 91, Via Ricasoli; free; open 7am-12.30pm & 3pm-6.30pm daily)*, started in the 13th century and not completed until the 15th century. The Gothic interior houses several artworks of note, including a fresco of Mary Magdalene by Piero della Francesca.

Chiesa di San Domenico & Around

It is worth the walk to the **Chiesa di San Domenico** *(☎ 0575 2 29 06, Piazza San Domenico; free; open 9am-7pm daily)* to see the crucifix painted by Cimabue, which hangs above the main altar. South-west, the **Casa di Vasari** *(☎ 0575 40 90 40, Via XX*

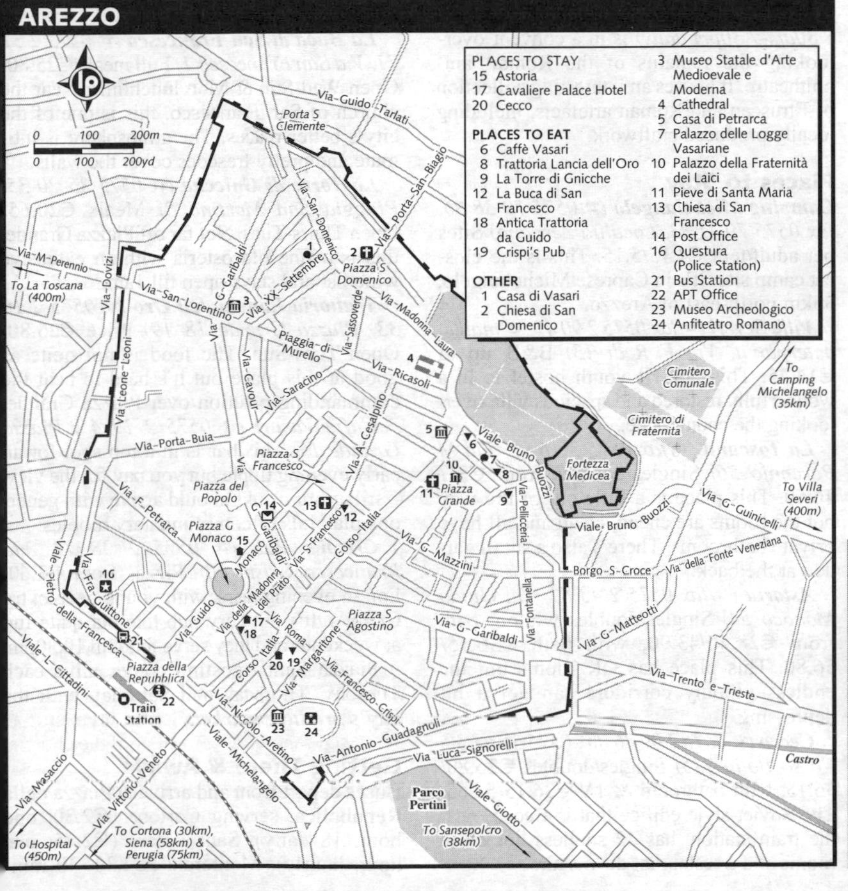

TUSCANY

Settembre 55; free; open 8.30am-7.30pm Mon & Wed-Sat, 8.30am-1pm Sun) was built and sumptuously decorated by the architect himself. Down the hill, the **Museo Statale d'Arte Medioevale e Moderna** *(☎ 0575 40 90 50, Via San Lorentino 8; admission €4.15, free to EU citizens under 18; open 8.30am-7.30pm Tues-Sun)* houses works by local artists, including Luca Signorelli and Vasari, which span the 13th to 18th centuries.

Museo Archeologico & Roman Amphitheatre

East of the train station, the museum *(☎ 0575 2 08 82, Via Margaritone 10; admission €4.15, free to EU citizens under 18; open 8.30am-7.30pm daily)* is in a convent overlooking the remains of the Roman amphitheatre. It houses an interesting collection of Etruscan and Roman artefacts, including locally produced craftwork.

Places to Stay

Camping Michelangelo *(☎ 0575 79 38 86, fax 0575 79 11 83, Località Zenzano)* Sites per adult/tent €4.15/5.15. This is the closest camp site. It's in Caprese Michelangelo, 35km north-east of Arezzo.

Villa Severi *(☎/fax 0575 2 90 47, ⓔ mail@peterpan.it, Via F Redi 13)* B&B up to €14.45. This non-HI youth hostel is in a wonderfully restored and spacious villa overlooking the countryside.

La Toscana *(☎/fax 0575 2 16 92, Via M Perennio 56)* Singles/doubles from €31/46.50. This place is a little out of the way but the rooms are cheap, clean and all have private bathrooms. There's also a small garden at the back.

Astoria *(☎/fax 0575 2 43 61, Via Guido Monaco 54)* Singles/doubles without bath from €28.40/43.90, with bath €36.15/56.80. This place has OK rooms but the endless gloomy corridors can get a bit depressing.

Cecco *(☎ 0575 2 09 86, fax 0575 35 67 30, Corso Italia 215)* Singles/doubles €25.80/36.15, with bathroom & TV €36.15/51.65. The Soviet-style edifice that is Cecco, near the train station, has 42 soulless but clean rooms and a restaurant downstairs.

Cavaliere Palace Hotel *(☎ 0575 2 68 36, fax 0575 2 19 25, ⓔ info@cavalierehotels.com, Ⓦ www.cavalierehotels.com, Via della Madonna del Prato 83)* Singles/doubles €82.65/123.95. This place is between the train station and the old centre, near Piazza Guido Monaco. Since it changed hands, it has transformed into a very plush (and pricey) option.

Places to Eat & Drink

Antica Trattoria da Guido *(☎ 0575 2 37 60, Via della Madonna del Prato 85)* Full meals €15.50. Open Mon-Sat. This is one of the best-value trattorias in town. Here you'll eat excellent, home-style food.

La Buca di San Francesco *(☎ 0575 2 32 71, Via San Francesco 1)* Full meals €25.80. Open Wed-Sun & Mon lunchtime. Near the church of San Francesco, this is one of the city's better places. The atmosphere is intimate and pretty frescoes cover the walls.

La Torre di Gnicche *(☎ 0575 35 20 35, Piaggia San Martino 8)* Meals €20.65. Open Thurs-Tues. Not far off Piazza Grande, this is a fine old osteria with an extensive wine list and stays open till 1am.

Trattoria Lancia dell'Oro *(☎ 0575 2 10 33, Piazza Grande 18–19)* Price €25.80. Open Tues-Sun. The food is not quite as good at this place but it's hard to beat the commanding position over Piazza Grande.

Caffè Vasari *(☎ 0575 2 19 45, Piazza Grande 15)* This bar is in a top spot for an early evening tipple but you pay for the view – still, your drinks should arrive with generous platefuls of complimentary nibbles.

Crispi's Pub *(☎ 0575 2 28 73, Via Francesco Crispi 10)*. Pizzas from €3.60. For an evening drink with young people, try Crispi's. It's not very pub-like but quite fun at weekends and they serve food till 10.30pm.

Piazza Sant'Agostino comes alive each Tuesday, Thursday and Saturday with the city's ***produce market***.

Getting There & Away

Buses depart from and arrive at Piazza della Repubblica, serving Cortona (€2.30, one hour, 18 daily), Sansepolcro (€2.75, one hour, hourly), Monterchi (€2.30, 40 minutes, 11 daily), Siena (€4.15, 1½ hours, three daily), Florence (€5.10, 2½ hours, five daily) and other local towns. The city is also on the Florence-Rome train line with regular services to Rome (€11.20–17.70, 2½ hours, 14 per day) and Florence (€4.45, one hour 20 minutes, hourly). Arezzo is a few kilometres east of the A1 and the S73 heads east to Sansepolcro.

SANSEPOLCRO

Along with Arezzo and nearby Monterchi, Sansepolcro is an important stop on an itinerary of Piero della Francesca's work. Both Monterchi and Sansepolcro are easy day trips from Arezzo. Visit the town of **Monterchi** to see the artist's famous fresco **Madonna del Parto** (a pregnant Madonna). It was removed from its original home in the local cemetery for restoration and is currently on display in a former **primary school** *(☎ 0575 7 07 13, Via della Reglia 1; adult/child €2.60/free; open 9am-1pm & 2pm-7pm Tues-Sun Apr-Oct, 9am-1pm & 2pm-6pm Tues-Sun Nov-Mar).*

Sansepolcro is the birthplace of Piero della Francesca. He left the town when quite young and returned in his 1970s to work on his treatises, which include *On Perspective in Painting*.

The small tourist office (☎ 0575 74 05 36), at Piazza Garibaldi 2, can assist with local information. The itinerary of della Francesca's work takes in other towns in Tuscany, Umbria and Le Marche, including Rimini, Urbino, Perugia and Florence.

The **Museo Civico** *(☎ 0575 73 22 18, Via Aggiunti 65; adult/child €5.15/2.60; open 9am-1.30pm & 2.30pm-7.30pm daily June-Sept, 9.30am-1pm & 3.20pm-6pm daily Oct-May)*, in the former town hall, is the pride of Sansepolcro and features Piero della Francesca's Renaissance masterpiece, *Resurrection*.

If you need to stay, there are several hotels.

Orfeo *(☎ 0575 74 20 61, fax 0575 74 22 87, Viale A Diaz 12)* Singles/doubles €25.80/46.50. This is a budget place to stay just outside the city walls, but the floor-to-ceiling pink decor can be a bit overwhelming.

Albergo Fiorentino *(☎ 0575 74 03 50, fax 0575 74 03 70, W www.emmeti.it, Via L Pacioli 60)* High season singles/doubles with bath €41.30/61.95. This is a very friendly and central hotel. The rooms are comfortable and breakfast is included.

SITA buses link Arezzo with Sansepolcro (€2.75, one hour, hourly) and the town is on the Terni-Perugia train line, with 12 services daily to Perugia (€3.80, 1½ hours).

CORTONA

postcode 52044 • pop 22,500

Set on the side of a hill covered with olive groves, Cortona offers stunning views across the Tuscan countryside and has changed little since the Middle Ages. It was a small settlement when the Etruscans moved in during the 8th century BC. It later became a Roman town. In the late 14th century, it attracted the likes of Fra Angelico, who lived and worked in the town for about 10 years. Luca Signorelli and the artist known as Pietro da Cortona were born here. The city is small enough to be easily seen in a couple of hours, but it's much more atmospheric to spend at least one night here.

Each year, on the first Sunday in June, the town hosts the *Archidado* games – a crossbow competition. Among other festivities, contestants from the city's traditional neighbourhoods dress up in medieval garb to compete for the *Verretta d'oro* (golden arrow).

Orientation & Information

Piazzale Garibaldi, on the southern edge of the walled city, is where buses arrive. It has a large car park and also offers some of the most sensational views in the city across to Lago di Trasimeno. From the piazzale, walk straight up Via Nazionale to Piazza della Repubblica, the centre of town. The town's streets are disconcertingly steep at times but every twist and turn brings new delights.

The APT office (☎ 0575 63 03 52), at Via Nazionale 42, opens 9am to 1pm and 3pm to 7pm Monday to Saturday, 9am to 1pm on Sunday, from May to September. The rest of the year, it shuts at 6pm during the week and on Saturday and Sunday afternoons.

Sensory Tracks travel agency, at Vicolo del Precipizio 2, has two computers with Internet access.

Things to See

Start in Piazza della Repubblica with the crenellated **Palazzo Comunale**, which was renovated in the 16th century. To the north is the attractive Piazza Signorelli, which featured briefly in Roberto Benigni's film *Life is Beautiful*. Dominating the north side of the piazza is the 13th-century **Palazzo Casali**, whose facade was added in the 17th century. Inside is the **Museo dell'Accademia Etrusca** *(☎ 0575 63 04 15, Piazza Signorelli 9; admission €4.15; open 10am-7pm Tues-Sun Apr-Oct, 10am-5pm Tues-Sun Nov-Mar)*, which displays substantial local Etruscan finds, including an elaborate 5th-century-BC oil lamp.

Little is left of the Romanesque character of the **cathedral**, north-west of Piazza Signorelli. It was completely rebuilt late in the Renaissance and again in the 18th century. Opposite is the **Museo Diocesano** *(☎ 0575 6 28 30, Piazza del Duomo 1; adult/child €4.15/1.05; open 9.30am-1pm Tues-Sun year-round, plus 3.30pm-7pm Tues-Sun Apr-Sept, 3.30pm-6pm Tues-Sun Oct, 3.30pm-5pm Tues-Sun Nov-Mar)* in the former church of Gesù. Its fine collection includes works by Luca Signorelli and a beautiful *Annunciation* by Fra Angelico.

At the eastern edge of the city centre is the **Chiesa di Santa Margherita** *(☎ 0575 60 31 16, Piazza Santa Margherita; free; open 7.30am-noon & 3pm-7pm daily)*, which features the Gothic tomb of Santa Margherita. Farther up the hill is the 16th-century **Fortezza** *(☎ 0575 60 37 93; adult/child €2.60/1.55; open 10am-6pm daily Apr-Sept)*, built for the Medici by Laparelli, who designed the fortress city of Valletta in Malta.

Places to Stay & Eat

Ostello San Marco *(☎/fax 0575 60 13 92, ⓔ ostellocortona@libero.it, Via Maffei 57)* B&B €10.35, meals €7.75. Open 15 Mar-15 Oct. A short walk east of Piazzale Garibaldi, this HI hostel is in a former monastery. The vaulted common room is enormously atmospheric and most meals surprisingly good.

Betania *(☎ 0575 6 28 29, fax 0575 60 42 99, Via Severini 50)* Singles/doubles from €20.65/31. This place is part of a monastery, so it's very quiet and there's a large garden.

Albergo Italia *(☎ 0575 63 02 54, fax 0575 60 57 63, Via Ghibellina 5)* High season singles/doubles with bath up to €59.40/87.80. This three-star hotel, just off Piazza della Repubblica, is in an old palazzo. Rooms have all the modern trimmings but still retain a traditional charm with cross-beamed ceilings and tiled floors.

Piazza della Repubblica hosts a ***produce market*** each Saturday, and several ***grocery shops*** dot the area.

Trattoria Dardano *(☎ 0575 60 19 44, Via Dardano 24)* Full meals around €15.50. Open Thurs-Tues. This place is just one of half a dozen no-nonsense trattorias that line Via Dardano. Try the *ravioli al burro e salvia* (butter and sage ravioli).

Ristorante Tonino *(☎ 0575 63 03 33, Piazza Garibaldi 1)* Meals about €25.80. This restaurant specialises in antipasto; also try the Florentine steak in black pepper sauce.

Getting There & Around

For bicycle and scooter hire, try Axofidis (☎/fax 0575 60 42 44) at Piazza Signorelli 26. Bikes start from €7.75 per day and scooters from €31.

From Piazzale Garibaldi, regular LFI buses connect the city with Arezzo (€2.30, one hour, 18 per day). The city is served by two train stations, both on the main Rome-Florence line. Camucia-Cortona, 6km away in the valley below Cortona, is more convenient for trains to Arezzo (€1.85, 20 minutes, hourly) and Florence (€6.30, two hours, hourly), while Terontola, about 5km to the south of Camucia-Cortona, is the best bet for trains to Rome (€9, two hours 10 minutes, every two hours) and Perugia (€3.25, 40 minutes, 16 per day).

Half-hourly shuttle buses connect Cortona's Piazzale Garibaldi with the stations at Camucia (€0.95, 15 minutes) and Terontola (€1.45, 20 minutes). The APT office has schedules and sells tickets. By car, the city is on the north-south S71 that runs to Arezzo and it is close to the S75 that connects Perugia to the A1.

Umbria & Le Marche

Dotted with splendid medieval hill towns, and offering a chance to flee from the madding crowds to isolated valleys or mountains, the regions of Umbria and Le Marche need to be explored rather than simply visited. Umbria certainly offers some star attractions – the beautifully preserved medieval town of Perugia, St Francis' home town of Assisi and the extraordinary cathedral in Orvieto. The main attraction of Le Marche is Urbino, home of the painter Raphael and Duca Federico da Montefeltro, who gathered the cream of Renaissance Italy's artists together to decorate his palace. But in both regions there are a host of smaller, lesser-known towns and villages, and plenty of opportunities for nature lovers, walkers and mountain bikers to escape from the standard tourist attractions and get some exercise. This is also prime hang-gliding territory.

Both Umbria and Le Marche were devastated by the 1997 earthquakes, which affected around 48 towns, including Nocera Umbra (one of the worst affected areas), Foligno, Bevagna, Montefalco, Assisi, Spello and many small mountain villages. Thirteen people were killed and over 100,000 were left homeless. There was much criticism that the damage to the cultural patrimony (especially at Assisi) took precedence over the devastation that the populace suffered. By the time Assisi's basilica reopened at the end of 1999 (after a US$37million operation), more than 3000 villagers had spent a third winter in makeshift accommodation.

Although a few sights still remain closed for repair, most have now re-opened and tourism, which virtually ground to a halt after the earthquakes, has since returned to normal levels.

Highlights

- Take in some mellow jazz in beautiful Perugia during the Umbria Jazz festival
- Tuck into some typical Umbrian cuisine laced with *tartufi neri* (black truffles)
- Get a sore neck admiring the magnificent frescoes by Giotto and others in the Basilica di San Francesco in Assisi
- Amble around the streets of Orvieto and check out the magnificent cathedral
- Watch a concert, play or dance performance under the stars at Spoleto's Teatro Romano during the Spoleto Festival
- Explore the splendid Renaissance town of Urbino
- If the timing is right, attend a concert at the Arena Sferisterio in Macerata

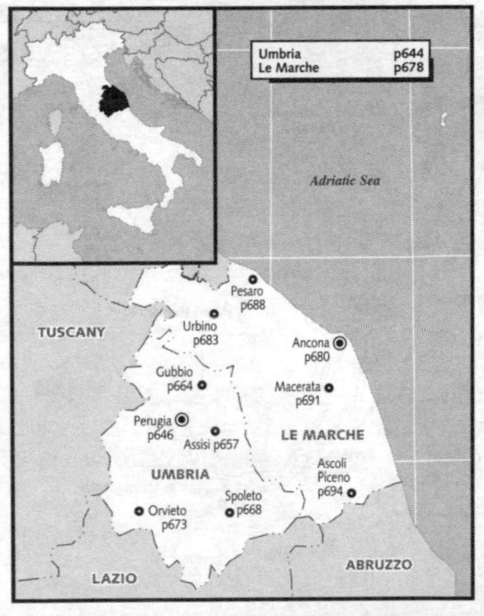

Umbria

One of the few landlocked Italian regions, Umbria likes to think of itself as *Il cuore verde dell'Italia* (Italy's green heart). In spring the countryside is splashed with the red, pink, yellow, purple and blue of wild flowers, and in summer it explodes with the vibrant yellow of the sunflowers harvested to make cooking oil. The rolling mountains

UMBRIA

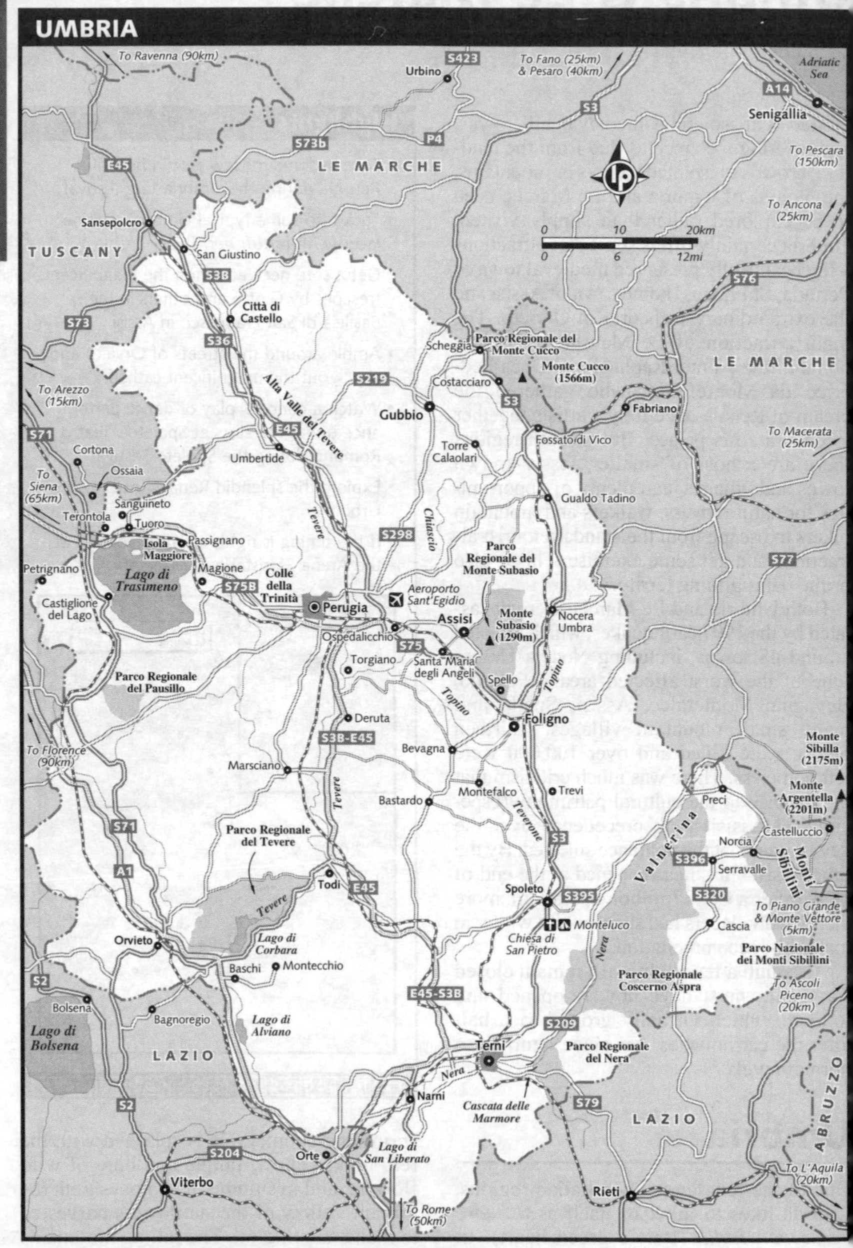

To Ravenna (90km)
Urbino
S423
To Fano (25km) & Pesaro (40km)
Adriatic Sea
A14
Senigallia
S3
S73b
P4
To Pescara (150km)
LE MARCHE
E45
To Ancona (25km)
0
10
20km
0
6
12mi
Sansepolcro
TUSCANY
San Giustino
S38
S76
Città di Castello
S73
S36
Scheggia
Parco Regionale del Monte Cucco
Monte Cucco (1566m)
LE MARCHE
To Arezzo (15km)
Alta Valle del Tevere
S219
Costacciaro
S3
Gubbio
Fabriano
E45
Fossato di Vico
To Macerata (25km)
S71
Cortona
Umbertide
Torre Calaolari
To Siena (65km)
Ossaia
Sanguineto
Gualdo Tadino
Terontola
Tuoro
Tevere
Chiascio
Isola Maggiore
Passignano
S298
Parco Regionale del Monte Subasio
S77
Petrignano
Lago di Trasimeno
Magione
Colle della Trinità
Castiglione del Lago
S75B
Perugia
Aeroporto Sant'Egidio
Assisi
Monte Subasio (1290m)
Nocera Umbra
Ospedalicchio
S75
Torgiano
Santa Maria degli Angeli
Spello
Parco Regionale del Pausillo
Topino
Topino
Deruta
Foligno
S3B-E45
To Florence (90km)
Bevagna
Monte Sibilla (2175m)
Marsciano
Montefalco
Trevi
Bastardo
Preci
Monte Argentella (2201m)
Tevere
Teverone
Castelluccio
S71
Parco Regionale del Tevere
S3
Norcia
Valnerina
Monti Sibillini
S396
Serravalle
A1
Todi
E45
Spoleto
S395
S320
Tevere
To Piano Grande & Monte Vettore (5km)
Monteluco
Cascia
Orvieto
Lago di Corbara
Chiesa di San Pietro
Nera
Parco Nazionale dei Monti Sibillini
Baschi
Montecchio
S2
Parco Regionale Coscerno Aspra
E45-S3B
To Ascoli Piceno (20km)
Bolsena
Bagnoregio
Lago di Alviano
S209
Lago di Bolsena
LAZIO
Terni
Parco Regionale del Nera
Nera
ABRUZZO
S2
Narni
Cascata delle Marmore
S79
LAZIO
Lago di San Liberato
S204
Orte
To L'Aquila (20km)
Viterbo
Rieti
To Rome (50km)

of the Apennines in the north and east descend into hills, many capped by medieval towns, and eventually flatten out into lush valleys along the River Tiber. With the exception of the industrial blight around Terni in the south, most towns are unspoiled and have preserved their medieval centres.

The Romans named Umbria after the Umbrii, the Iron Age tribe who occupied the region. The Roman naturalist Pliny the Elder described the Umbrii as the oldest tribe in Italy but little more is known about them. The Etruscans later settled the western bank of the Tiber, founding the towns of Perugia and Orvieto, and eventually creating 12 powerful city-states.

The Saracen invasions of the 5th and 6th centuries ended Roman rule and caused the Umbrians to retreat to the hill towns, leading to the growth of fortified medieval cities such as Gubbio and Todi. Domination by the Goths, the Lombards and various ruling families, as well as centuries of Guelph-Ghibelline rivalry (see Humanism under History in the Facts about Italy chapter), led to a long decline that left Umbria ripe for papal rule from the early 16th century.

St Francis (1182–1226) was born in Assisi, in the east of the region, and after his death the town was transformed by the construction of Basilica di San Francesco, with its superb frescoes.

Perugia, a short distance to the west and the region's capital, is a stunning city that enjoys a lively nightlife fired by the city's Università per Stranieri (University for Foreigners). Spoleto's internationally renowned arts festival, the beauty of the Valnerina area in Umbria's south-east, and the Italian peninsula's largest lake, Lago di Trasimeno, are all powerful attractions.

Umbrian cuisine is simple: most dishes contain only three or four ingredients. *Tartufo* (a type of truffle) is used in sauces, pasta and rice dishes. Umbria's *porcini* (a type of mushroom) are truly delicious; they can be added to pasta or rice, but are best eaten as 'steaks' – an experience not to be missed. Among the best known of the local pastas is *strangozzi*, which looks a little like heavy, square-sided spaghetti. Orvieto's golden wines are popular throughout Italy. Look out for the Sagrantino of Montefalco, a heavy wine that goes down particularly nicely in the cooler months.

Umbria offers many possibilities for *agriturismo* (holidays in farm accommodation). Several organisations can suggest destinations and the APT office in each town has a list of farms. Extensive bus routes, state train services and the private Ferrovia Centrale Umbra (Umbrian Central Railway) make most areas of the region easily accessible.

PERUGIA

postcode 06100 • pop 150,000

One of Italy's best-preserved medieval hill towns, Perugia has a lively and bloody past. The Umbrii tribe inhabited the surrounding area and controlled land stretching from present-day Tuscany into Le Marche, but it was the Etruscans who founded the city, which reached its zenith in the 6th century BC. It fell to the Romans in 310 BC and was given the name Perusia. During the Middle Ages the city was racked by the internal feuding of the Baglioni and Oddi families and violent wars against its neighbours. In the mid-13th century Perugia was home to the Flagellants, a curious sect who whipped themselves as a religious penance. In 1538 the city was incorporated into the Papal States under Pope Paul III, remaining under papal control for almost three centuries.

Perugia has a strong artistic and cultural tradition. It was home in the 15th century to fresco painters Bernardino Pinturicchio and his master Pietro Vannucci (known as Perugino), who was to teach Raphael, and also attracted the great Tuscan masters Fra Angelico and Piero della Francesca. The Università per Stranieri, established in 1925, offers courses in Italian and attracts thousands of students from all over the world.

The town is also the home of the best-known version of *baci*, the mouth-watering chocolate-coated hazelnuts made in Perugia.

Orientation

If you arrive at Perugia's main train station, Stazione Fontivegge, you'll find yourself a few kilometres downhill from the historic centre, so unless you fancy a steep,

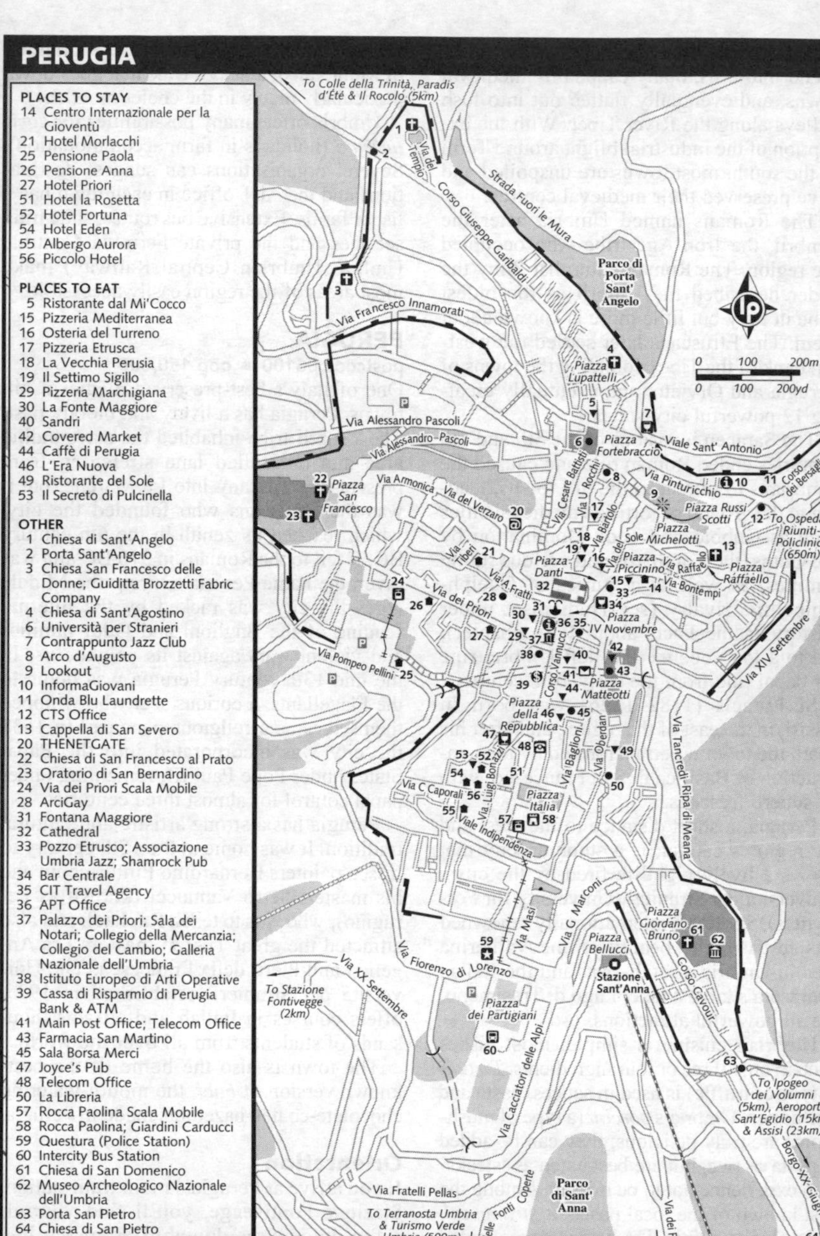
PERUGIA
PLACES TO STAY
14 Centro Internazionale per la Gioventù
21 Hotel Morlacchi
25 Pensione Paola
26 Pensione Anna
27 Hotel Priori
51 Hotel la Rosetta
52 Hotel Fortuna
54 Hotel Eden
55 Albergo Aurora
56 Piccolo Hotel
PLACES TO EAT
5 Ristorante dal Mi'Cocco
15 Pizzeria Mediterranea
16 Osteria del Turreno
17 Pizzeria Etrusca
18 La Vecchia Perusia
19 Il Settimo Sigillo
29 Pizzeria Marchigiana
30 La Fonte Maggiore
40 Sandri
42 Covered Market
44 Caffè di Perugia
46 L'Era Nuova
49 Ristorante del Sole
53 Il Secreto di Pulcinella
OTHER
1 Chiesa di Sant'Angelo
2 Porta Sant'Angelo
3 Chiesa San Francesco delle Donne; Guiditta Brozzetti Fabric Company
4 Chiesa di Sant'Agostino
6 Università per Stranieri
7 Contrappunto Jazz Club
8 Arco d'Augusto
9 Lookout
10 InformaGiovani
11 Onda Blu Laundrette
12 CTS Office
13 Cappella di San Severo
20 THENETGATE
22 Chiesa di San Francesco al Prato
23 Oratorio di San Bernardino
24 Via dei Priori Scala Mobile
28 ArciGay
31 Fontana Maggiore
32 Cathedral
33 Pozzo Etrusco; Associazione Umbria Jazz; Shamrock Pub
34 Bar Centrale
35 CIT Travel Agency
36 APT Office
37 Palazzo dei Priori; Sala dei Notari; Collegio della Mercanzia; Collegio del Cambio; Galleria Nazionale dell'Umbria
38 Istituto Europeo di Arti Operative
39 Cassa di Risparmio di Perugia Bank & ATM
41 Main Post Office; Telecom Office
43 Farmacia San Martino
45 Sala Borsa Merci
47 Joyce's Pub
48 Telecom Office
50 La Libreria
57 Rocca Paolina Scala Mobile
58 Rocca Paolina; Giardini Carducci
59 Questura (Police Station)
60 Intercity Bus Station
61 Chiesa di San Domenico
62 Museo Archeologico Nazionale dell'Umbria
63 Porta San Pietro
64 Chiesa di San Pietro
To Colle della Trinità, Paradis d'Été & Il Rocolo (5km)
Via del Tempio
Strada Fuori le Mura
Corso Giuseppe Garibaldi
Parco di Porta Sant' Angelo
Via Francesco Innamorati
Piazza Lupattelli
0 100 200m
0 100 200yd
Via Alessandro Pascoli
Piazza Fortebraccio
Viale Sant' Antonio
Via Pinturicchio
Corso dei Bersaglieri
Piazza San Francesco
Via Armonica
Via del Verzaro
Via Cesare Battisti
Via U Rocchi
Via Bartolo
Piazza Russi Scotti
To Ospedale Riuniti-Policlinico (650m)
Piazza Michelotti
Via del Sole
Via Tiberi
Via A. Fratti
Piazza Danti
Piazza Piccinino
Via Raffaello
Via Bontempi
Piazza Raffaello
Via dei Priori
Piazza IV Novembre
Via XIV Settembre
Via Pompeo Pellini
Corso Vannucci
Piazza Matteotti
Piazza della Repubblica
Via Baglioni
Via Oberdan
Via Tancredi Ripa di Meana
Via C Caporali
Via Luigi Bonazzi
Piazza Italia
Viale Indipendenza
Via Masi
Via G Marconi
Piazza Giordano Bruno
Piazza Bellucci
Stazione Sant'Anna
Corso Cavour
Via Fiorenzo di Lorenzo
Via XX Settembre
To Stazione Fontivegge (2km)
Piazza dei Partigiani
Via Cacciatori delle Alpi
To Ipogeo dei Volumni (5km), Aeroporto Sant'Egidio (15km) & Assisi (23km)
Borgo XX Giugno
Parco di Sant' Anna
Via Fratelli Pellas
To Terranosta Umbria & Turismo Verde Umbria (500m)
Via delle Fonti Coperte
Via dei Filosofi
To Agriturist Umbria (1km)

fume-filled climb, it's best to catch a bus. Drivers should follow the Centro signs and park in one of the well-signposted car parks, then take a *scala mobile* (escalator) up to the city centre (for more details see Getting Around later in this section).

Old Perugia's main strip, Corso Vannucci (named after Perugino), runs south to north from Piazza Italia through Piazza della Repubblica and finally ends in the heart of the old city at Piazza IV Novembre, bounded by the cathedral and the Palazzo dei Priori. City buses will drop you off at Piazza dei Partigiani, from where you can take a scala mobile up to Piazza Italia.

Information

Tourist Offices The APT office (☎ 075 572 33 27) is in the Palazzo dei Priori, Piazza IV Novembre 3, opposite the cathedral, and opens 8.30am to 1.30pm and 3.30pm to 6.30pm Monday to Saturday and 9am to 1pm Sunday. The monthly publication *Viva Perugia – What, Where, When* (€0.50 from newsstands) lists all events and useful information. InformaGiovani (☎ 075 572 06 46), Via Idalia 1 (off Via Pinturicchio), can help young travellers and students and provides information on culture, education and work opportunities.

Money The currency exchange booth at Stazione Fontivegge is open from 7.30am to 8.30pm daily. Corso Vannucci is lined with banks, all of which have ATMs; the Cassa di Risparmio di Perugia (Savings Bank of Perugia) at No 39 also has a currency exchange machine.

Post & Communications The main post office is on Piazza Matteotti and opens 8.10am to 6pm Monday to Saturday.

There is a Telecom office in the post office and another on Piazza della Repubblica; both open 8am to 10pm daily. The Telecom office is staffed from 9am to 1pm and 4pm to 7pm on weekdays. You can access the Internet at Thenetgate, Via Cesare Battisti 19.

Travel Agencies The CIT travel agency (☎ 075 572 60 61) is at Corso Vannucci 2, while CTS (☎ 075 572 70 50), specialising in budget and student travel, is at Via del Roscetto 21. It will sell ISIC cards to foreigners studying at the university, even to those on short courses

Bookshops La Libreria bookshop, Via Oberdan 52, stocks a selection of English-language books.

Gay & Lesbian Perugia For information on gay events, try ArciGay (☎ 075 572 31 75), Via A Fratti 18.

Laundry You can do your laundry at the Onda Blu coin laundrette at Corso dei Bersaglieri 4, on the corner of Via Pinturicchio. It opens 9am to 10pm daily.

Medical Services & Emergency The Ospedale Riuniti-Policlinico (hospital; ☎ 075 57 81) is on Viale Bonacci Brunamonti, north-east of the city centre. To find a doctor at night, on Sunday or on public holidays, call ☎ 075 3 40 24. The Farmacia San Martino (pharmacy) at Piazza Matteotti 26 is open 24 hours.

The *questura* (police station; ☎ 075 5 06 21) is on Piazza dei Partigiani, down the scala mobile that starts in the Rocca Paolina at Piazza Italia.

Around Piazza IV Novembre

The imposing facades identify Piazza IV Novembre as the old city's main square. Indeed, in the case of the austere **cathedral** *(☎ 075 572 38 32, Piazza IV Novembre; free; open 8am-noon & 4pm-sunset)*, size is everything. Started in 1345 and completed in 1430 (although its red-and-white marble facade was never finished), the Gothic giant offers comparatively little to enthuse over inside. Galeazzo Alessi's magnificent 16th-century doorway, facing the Fontana Maggiore in the square, is an exception to the rule. If you happen to be around on 30 July, grab a pew for the annual unveiling of the city's prized relic: the Virgin Mary's wedding ring, which is locked away in 15 boxes fitted inside each other for added security.

…gned the **Fontana Mag-** …untain) in 1278, but it was … and Giovanni Pisano to exe- …n. The bas-relief statues repre- s… es from the Old Testament and the 12 …ths of the year. A female figure on the upper basin (facing Corso Vannucci) bears fruit representing fertility, the city's symbol. Hardly surprising, then, that she is called Perugia.

Most eye-catching of all in the square is the 13th-century **Palazzo dei Priori**. Long the seat of secular power in Perugia, it still houses the municipal offices. Annexed to these is the **Galleria Nazionale dell'Umbria** *(☎ 075 574 12 47, Corso Vannucci 19; adults/under-18s €6.20/free including science museum; open 8.30am-7.30pm daily)*, a collection of paintings mostly by Umbrian artists, including Pinturicchio, Perugino and Fra Angelico.

The vaulted **Sala dei Notari** *(Notaries' Hall; ☎ 075 577 23 39, Palazzo dei Priori, Piazza IV Novembre 3; free; open 9am-1pm & 3pm-7pm Tues-Sun year-round plus Mon June-Sept)*, on the 1st floor of the palazzo, was built in 1296 for the city council. Its walls are decorated with colourful frescoes (with charming depictions of animals) by various anonymous artists. To reach it, climb the flight of steps from Piazza IV Novembre.

In the Corso Vannucci side of the palazzo is the **Collegio della Mercanzia** *(Merchants' Guild; ☎ 075 573 03 66, Corso Vannucci 15; admission €1.05; open 9am-1pm & 2.30pm-5.30pm Mon-Sat & 9am-1pm Sun & holidays Mar-Oct; 8am-2pm Tues, Thurs & Fri, 8am-4.30pm Wed & Sat & 9am-1pm Sun & holidays Nov-Feb)*. This was the seat of the city's powerful Renaissance-era merchants who formed one of several *arti* (guilds) that still exist today (though their power is a shadow of what it was). Reflecting their one-time prestige is the impressive early-15th-century carved-wood panelling inside. Look at the designs closely and it will be hard to escape the impression that they were influenced by Islamic artistry – possibly imported from the Orient via Venice. A few doors up in the same building is the **Collegio del Cambio** *(Exchange Guild; ☎ 075 572 85 99, Corso Vannucci 25; admission €2.60; open 9am-12.30pm & 2.30pm-5.30pm Tues-Sun, 9am-12.30pm Sun Mar-Oct; 8am-2pm Tues-Sat, 9am-12.30pm Sun & holidays Nov-Feb)*, constructed in 1450 for another guild, the city's moneychangers, and decorated with magnificent frescoes by Perugino. A combined ticket for both guilds costs €3.10.

West of Corso Vannucci

Head west along Via dei Priori to reach Piazza San Francesco. The 15th-century **Oratorio di San Bernardino** has a facade decorated with bas-reliefs by the early Renaissance sculptor Agostino di Duccio. Next to it is the ruined **Chiesa di San Francesco al Prato**, destroyed over the centuries by various natural disasters. It is used as an atmospheric location for concerts.

Towards the Università per Stranieri

You can venture down into the 3rd-century-BC **Pozzo Etrusco** *(Etruscan Well; ☎ 075 573 36 69, Piazza Danti 18; adult/child €1.80/1.05, includes Cappella di San Severo; open 10.30am-1.30pm & 2.30pm-6.30pm daily Apr-Sept; 10.30am-1.30pm daily, 2.30pm-4.30pm Mon-Fri & 2.30pm-5.30pm Sat & Sun Oct-Mar)*. From here take Via del Sole to the **Cappella di San Severo** *(☎ 075 573 38 64, Piazza Raffaello; admission €1.80, includes Pozzo Etrusco; open same hours as Pozzo Etrusco)*, decorated with Raphael's *Trinity with Saints* (thought by many to be his first fresco) and frescoes by Perugino. Frankly, unless you are desperate to see what *might* be Raphael's first fresco or happen to be an aficionado of large, brown, wet, dank holes in the ground, your €1.80 would probably be better spent on an ice cream.

From the cappella, walk back to Piazza Michelotti and turn north into the small Piazza Rossi Scotti, from where you can enjoy a lovely view across the countryside. Take the steps down to Piazza Fortebraccio and the Università per Stranieri, housed in the Baroque Palazzo Gallenga. To the south-east is the **Arco d'Augusto**, one of the ancient city gates. Its lower section is Etruscan, dating from the 3rd century BC;

the upper part is Roman and bears the inscription 'Augusta Perusia'. The loggia on top dates from the Renaissance.

Around Corso Giuseppe Garibaldi

North along Corso Giuseppe Garibaldi is the **Chiesa di Sant'Agostino** *(Piazza Lupattelli; free; open 8am-noon & 4pm-sunset daily)*, with a beautiful 16th-century choir by sculptor and architect Baccio d'Agnolo. Small signs forlornly mark the places where artworks once hung before they were carried off to France by Napoleon and his men. Farther north along the same thoroughfare, Via del Tempio branches off to the Romanesque **Chiesa di Sant'Angelo** *(☎ 075 57 22 64, Via Sant'Angelo; free; open 9.30am-noon & 3.30pm-sunset daily)*, said to stand on the site of an ancient temple. The columns inside the round church were taken from earlier buildings. Corso Giuseppe Garibaldi continues through the 14th-century wall by way of the **Porta Sant'Angelo**. A 10-minute walk south of the gate along Via Zefferino Faina takes you to the former Chiesa di San Francesco delle Donne and the headquarters of the **Giuditta Brozzetti fabric company** *(☎ 075 4 02 36, fax 075 500 24 92, W www.brozzetti.com, Via T Berardi 5; open 9am-1pm & 3pm-6pm Mon-Fri)*, where you can buy hand-woven linens produced using traditional techniques.

South of the Centre

At the southern end of Corso Vannucci are the tiny **Giardini Carducci**, with lovely views of the countryside. The gardens stand atop a once-massive 16th century fortress, now known as the **Rocca Paolina**, built by Pope Paul III and standing over a medieval quarter formerly inhabited by some of the city's most powerful families. Destroyed by the Perugini after Italian unification, the ruins remain a symbol of defiance against oppression. A series of scala mobili run through the Rocca and you can wander around inside the ruins, which are often used for exhibitions.

Along Corso Cavour, the early-14th-century **Chiesa di San Domenico** *(☎ 075 573 15 68, Piazza Giordano Bruno; free; open 8am-noon & 4pm-sunset daily)* is the city's largest church. Sadly, its Romanesque interior, lightened by the immense stained-glass windows, was replaced by austere Gothic fittings in the 16th century. Pope Benedict XI, who died after eating poisoned figs in 1325, lies buried here. The adjoining convent is the home of the **Museo Archeologico Nazionale dell'Umbria** *(☎ 075 57 27 14, Piazza Giordano Bruno 10; admission €2.05, free to EU citizens under 18; open 8.30am-7.30pm daily)*, which has an excellent collection of Etruscan pieces and a section on prehistory.

Continuing along Corso Cavour, you come to the **Porta San Pietro**. Keep going along Borgo XX Giugno to reach the 10th-century **Chiesa di San Pietro** *(☎ 075 3 47 70, Borgo XX Giugno; free; open 8am-noon & 4pm-sunset)*, entered through a frescoed doorway in the first courtyard. The interior is an incredible mix of gilt and marble and contains a *Pietà* by Perugino.

About 5km south-east of the city, at Ponte San Giovanni, is the **Ipogeo dei Volumni** *(☎ 075 39 33 29, Via Assisana; admission €2.05, free to EU citizens under 18; open 9am-1pm & 3.30pm-6.30pm daily Sept-June, 9am-12.30pm & 4.30pm-7pm daily July-Aug)*, a 2nd-century-BC Etruscan burial site discovered in 1840. An underground chamber contains a series of recesses holding the funerary urns of the Volumnio family. Unless you're a big fan of the Etruscans, you'll probably find the tombs at Cerveteri or Tarquinia in Lazio more interesting. Visits are limited to five people at a time, so there can be delays. Take the ASP bus from Piazza Italia to Ponte San Giovanni and walk west from there.

Courses

The list of courses available to locals and foreigners in and around Perugia could constitute a book in itself. You can learn Italian, take up ceramics, study music or spend a month cooking. The tourist office has details of all available courses.

Università per Stranieri *(☎ 075 5 74 61, W www.unistrapg.it, Palazzo Gallenga, Piazza Fortebraccio 4, Perugia 06122)* Italy's foremost academic institution for foreigners offers courses in language, literature, history, art and other subjects. It runs a series of degree courses as well as one-, two- and three-month intensive courses. The basic language course costs €232.40 per month.

Istituto Europea di Arti Operative *(☎ 075 6 50 22, Via dei Priori 14)* This arts' institute runs courses in fashion, graphic design, industrial and interior design, drawing and painting.

To study in Perugia, you may need to apply for a student visa in your country of residence before arriving in Italy. See Visas & Documents in the Facts for the Visitor chapter for more details.

Special Events

The Umbria Jazz festival attracts international performers for 10 days each July, usually around the middle of the month. Check with the tourist office for details. Tickets cost from €7.75 to €25.80 and can be bought in advance from Associazione Umbria Jazz (☎ 075 573 24 32, fax 0175 572 26 56, ⓔ umbriajazz@tin.it), Piazza Danti 28, or from Sala Borsa Merci (☎ 075 573 02 71), Via Mazzini 9. See the Web site at ⓦ www.umbriajazz.com for information.

The Guarda Dove Vai (Watch Where You're Going) festival, held during August, features theatre, music and cinema. Ask at the tourist office for a programme.

Places to Stay

Perugia has a good selection of reasonably priced hotels, but if you arrive unannounced during the Umbria Jazz festival or in August, expect problems. The tourist office can provide a complete hotel listing.

For agriturismo throughout Umbria, try ***Agriturist Umbria*** *(☎ 075 3 20 28, Via Savonarola 38)*; ***Terranostra Umbria*** *(☎ 075 500 95 59), Via Campo di Marte 10)*; or ***Turismo Verde Umbria*** *(☎ 075 500 29 53)*, Via Campo di Marte 14.

About 10 religious institutions and orders offer accommodation in Perugia. Generally, rates are cheap and a stay must last at least two days. They have a curfew of 9pm (10pm in summer). The tourist office can provide a list.

Camping The city has two camp sites, both in Colle della Trinità, 5km north-west of the city and reached by taking bus No 9 from Piazza Italia (ask the driver to drop you off at the Superal supermarket, from where it's a 300m walk to the camp sites).

Paradis d'Été *(☎ 075 517 31 21, fax 075 517 60 56, Via del Mercato 29/A, Colle della Trinità)* Sites per person/tent €5.15/4.15. Open year-round. This camp site has 50 well-shaded sites with good facilities and a swimming pool.

Il Rocolo *(☎/fax 075 517 85 50, ⓔ jnlagu@tin.it, Str Fontana 1/n, Loc. Colle della Trinità)* Sites per person/tent up to €4.65/3.85. Open 15 June to 15 Sept. Il Rocolo has over 100 sites with a bit of shade and all the standard facilities.

Hostels There's a non-HI (Hostelling International) hostel in town for those on a mid-range budget.

Centro Internazionale per la Gioventù *(☎/fax 075 572 28 80, ⓔ ostello@ostello.perugia.it, ⓦ www.ostello.perugia.it, Via Bontempi 13)* Beds €10.35, sheets €1.05. Open mid-Jan–mid-Dec. The common room has a fresco-decorated ceiling and the views from the terrace are fantastic. The large kitchen is another bonus but the midnight curfew is strictly enforced and thoroughly frustrating.

Pensiones & Hotels Visitors have more than 50 hotels to choose from in Perugia.

Pensione Anna *(☎/fax 075 573 63 04, ⓔ annahotel@hotmail.com, Via dei Priori 48)* Singles/doubles without bath up to €25.80/41.30, with bath up to €36.15/51.65. This fabulous little pensione, on the 2nd floor of a 17th-century town house, has jovial owners and is brimming with interesting antiques.

Pensione Paola *(☎ 075 572 38 16, Via della Canapina 5)* Singles/doubles €25.80/38.75. This modern house is five minutes from the town centre, down the scala mobile from Via dei Priori. There are eight rooms with shared bath and you have use of the kitchen.

Piccolo Hotel *(☎ 075 572 29 87, Via Luigi Bonazzi 25)* Doubles with bath €41.30. Just off Corso Vannucci, the Piccolo

Hotel only has doubles, two of which have private balconies – OK, but nothing special.

Albergo Aurora *(☎/fax 075 572 48 19, Viale Indipendenza 21)* Singles without bath €28.40, doubles with bath €51.65. This two-star hotel has doubles and a couple of singles, but these overlook a fume-ridden garage. It's OK but not really a first choice.

Hotel Eden *(☎ 075 572 81 02, fax 075 572 03 42, Via C Caporali 9)* Singles/doubles €31/51.65. This place has 12 bright, clean rooms and it's quiet and central. Breakfast costs extra.

Hotel Morlacchi *(☎ 075 572 03 19, fax 075 573 50 84, Via Tiberi 2,* e *morlacchi@tiscalinet.it)* Singles/doubles/triples with bath €38.75/56.80/67.15. This friendly, family-run two-star hotel is an understandably popular choice, so phone ahead for reservations.

Hotel Priori *(☎ 075 572 33 78, fax 075 572 32 13, Via Vermiglioli 3,* e *hotelpriori@perugia.com)* Singles/doubles with bath €51.65/72.30, triples/quads €98.15/118.80. This pleasant hotel, another two-star, is in a great location. The rooms are large and breakfast is served on a lovely terrace.

Hotel Fortuna *(☎ 075 572 28 45, fax 075 573 50 40, Via Luigi Bonazzi 19,* e *fortuna@umbriahotels.com)* Singles/doubles up to €77.45/110.50. This hotel has rooms with all the trimmings. It's very comfortable and there is even the odd fresco dotted about the place – there's free Internet access as well. In low season, prices drop by €15.50.

Hotel la Rosetta *(☎/fax 075 572 08 41, Piazza Italia 19,* e *larosetta@perugiaonline.com)* Singles/doubles €74.90/113.60. This is one of Perugia's better hotels with exquisite individually designed rooms.

Rental Accommodation If you are planning to study in Perugia, the Università per Stranieri will organise accommodation costing from €206.60 to €413.15 per month, depending on your needs. The weekly *Cerco e Trovo* (€1.05 at newsstands) lists all available rental accommodation and the tourist office can help you find holiday houses and *affittacamere* (rooms rented on a weekly or monthly basis).

Places to Eat

Restaurants Being a student city, Perugia offers many budget eating options.

Pizzeria Marchigiana *(Via dei Priori 3)* For great pizza by the slice, this pizzeria is just west of Corso Vannucci.

Pizzeria Etrusca *(☎ 075 572 07 62, Via Ulisse Rocchi 31)* Pizzas from €3.10. Etrusca is a popular student haunt; try their *cuscino*, a closed pizza stuffed with sausage, ham and mozzarella.

L'Era Nuova *(☎ 075 572 65 11, Via Baldo 6)* Pizzas €3.10-5.16. Open Thurs-Tues. This is a good spot for a sit-down pizza.

Osteria del Turreno *(☎ 075 572 19 76, Piazza Danti 16)* Price €7.75. Open Sun-Fri. For a cheap and filling meal, try this osteria overlooking the cathedral.

Ristorante dal Mi'Cocco *(☎ 075 573 25 11, Corso Giuseppe Garibaldi 12)* Set menu €12.90. Open Tues-Sun. This place, popular with students, serves up local specialities on rustic tables with bright-red checked covers. The menu changes daily, so basically you eat what you're given.

Il Secreto di Pulcinella *(☎ 075 573 62 84, Via Larga 8)* Meals €12.90. Open Tues-Sun. This popular place is a classic Neapolitan-style pizzeria.

Pizzeria Mediterranea *(☎ 075 572 63 12, Piazza Piccinino 11/12)* Pizzas from €4.15. Open Wed-Mon. Very trendy and in a good location, Mediterranea can get fairly busy at times so be prepared to queue.

Il Settimo Sigillo *(☎ 075 572 43 06, Via Ulisse Rocchi 1)* Meals €15.50. Open evenings only Tues-Sun. This medieval-themed restaurant has loopy decor, with cages, suits of armour and even a dragon dangling from the ceiling. It's almost a bar (with a long list of cocktails), but it's a fun place for a meal as well.

La Vecchia Perusia *(☎ 075 572 59 00, Via Ulisse Rocchi 9)* Full meals €20.65. A little more upmarket than the others, La Vecchia Perusia serves fine local cuisine. It can fill quickly, so be prepared to wait.

Ristorante del Sole *(☎ 075 573 50 31, Via della Rupe 1)* Full meals with wine around €23.25. Open Tues-Sun. Ristorante del Sole is a popular spot. It's actually down a side alley and, if you aren't dazzled by the views, you'll probably want to just roll around in the antipasto and dessert displays. The food tastes as good as it looks, but expect to pay for it.

Cafes & Bars Bask in Perugia's lively atmosphere while supping coffee and scoffing gelato.

Sandri *(Corso Vannucci 32)* This is the city's finest cafe. It retains a medieval air, and prices are more-or-less reasonable.

Caffè di Perugia *(Via Mazzini 10)* Claiming to be a 'meeting point of infinite art and intriguing flavours', this cafe has a cheerful Art Deco interior and does a great cappuccino.

Bar Centrale *(Piazza IV Novembre 35)* With its smoky, studenty interior, umbrella-shaded outside seats and views to the cathedral, this bar has it all.

La Fonte Maggiore *(Via della Gabbia 3)* Come here for the best gelato in town.

Self-Catering There is a ***covered market*** down the stairs from Piazza Matteotti, open 7am to 1.30pm Monday to Saturday, where you can buy fresh produce, bread, cheese and meat.

Entertainment

You don't have to wander very far in search of Perugia's nightlife. Just stroll down to Piazza IV Novembre in the early evening and you'll find the entire city's student population lolling on the steps of the cathedral, chatting, strumming guitars and keeping a general eye out for the action. Although if you *do* fancy a pint or two, there are a few good pubs to try.

Shamrock Pub *(☎ 075 573 66 25, Piazza Danti 18)* Open 6pm-2am. For late-night drinks, sample a Guinness at the Shamrock, down an appropriately dank but atmospheric alley off Piazza Danti.

Joyce's Pub *(☎ 075 573 46 95, Via Luigi Bonazzi 15)* Open noon-3pm Mon-Fri and 7.30pm-2.30am daily. Another Irish pub, Joyce's is a little less murky than the Shamrock. It does tasty bar snacks and there's usually sport showing on the TV.

Contrappunto Jazz Club *(☎ 075 573 36 67, Via Scortici 4)* Open 7pm-2am. This is one of Perugia's best clubs, and regularly features top-notch Italian and international jazz musicians. The beer garden is a blessing on summer evenings.

Keep an eye on the notice boards at the Università per Stranieri, as the university often organises free concerts and excursions.

Getting There & Away

Air Aeroporto Sant'Egidio (☎ 075 59 21 41), 15km east of the city, has flights to/from Milan and Palermo and some international services.

Bus Buses leave from Piazza dei Partigiani (take the scala mobile from Piazza Italia). The Perugia-Rome service is operated by Sulga (☎ 075 500 96 41); there are roughly five buses daily (€14.45, 2½ hours) in each direction and three continue on to Fiumicino airport (€18.10, 3¾ hours). Sulga also operates the Perugia-Florence service (€10.35, two hours), which runs daily in each direction, leaving Perugia at 7.15am and Florence at 6.40pm. Buses also depart from Piazza dei Partigiani for Siena (€7.25, 1½ hours, twice daily, once on Sunday) and cities throughout Umbria, including Assisi (€2.60, 50 minutes, 10 daily), Gubbio (€3.80, one hour 10 minutes, nine daily), Orvieto (€6.20, two hours, at 2pm Mon-Sat) and Spoleto (€5.35, 1½ hours, at 2pm and 3.45pm Mon-Fri, at 2pm only on Sat).

Current bus routes, company details and timetables are listed in the monthly booklet *Viva Perugia – What, Where, When* (€0.50), available from the APT office or at newsstands.

Train The main train station, Stazione Fontivegge (☎ 075 500 74 67), is on Piazza Vittorio Veneto, a few kilometres west of the city centre and easily accessible by frequent buses from Piazza Italia. There are one or two daily direct services to Rome (€10.10-18.45, two to 2½ hours), but otherwise change at Terontola (€3.25, 40 minutes, every two hours) or Foligno (€2.15, 40 minutes, hourly). Trains to Florence run about every two hours (€7.90, two hours). Other destinations and fares include Assisi (€1.55, 20 minutes, hourly), Spello (€1.95, 30 minutes, hourly) and Arezzo (€3.80, one hour 10 minutes, every two hours).

The private Ferrovia Centrale Umbra railway (☎ 075 572 39 47) runs from Stazione Sant'Anna on Piazzale Bellucci and serves Deruta (€1.30, 20 minutes, seven daily), Sansepolcro (€3.80, one hour 20 minutes, 12 per day), Terni (€4.25, 1½ hours, hourly) and Todi (€2.80, one hour, hourly).

Car & Motorcycle From Rome, leave the A1 at the Orte exit and follow the signs for Terni. Once there, take the S3b-E45 for Perugia. From the north, exit the A1 at Valdichiana and take dual carriageway S75b for Perugia. The S75 to the east connects the city with Assisi.

For car hire, the Hertz office (☎ 075 500 24 39) is at Stazione Fontivegge.

Getting Around

From Stazione Fontivegge, catch any bus heading for Piazza Italia (including Nos 6, 7, 9 and 11) to get to the centre. Tickets (€0.75) must be bought from a small kiosk in front of the station entrance before you board and validated in the machine as you enter.

An airbus connects Piazza Italia with Aeroporto Sant'Egidio (€2.60, 30 minutes, three per day) to coincide with flights.

If you arrive in Perugia by car, following the Centro signs along the winding roads up the hill will bring you to Piazza Italia. You can leave your car here in a metered parking spot (€1.55), either on the piazza or on the hill immediately preceding it. You are only allowed to stay for one hour, but on Sunday parking is free all day.

The remainder of the city centre is largely closed to normal, nonresident traffic, although tourists may drive to their hotels. Scala mobili to large car parks include the one on Via dei Priori (open from 6.45am to 12.30am) that leads to the car parks in Piazza della Cupa and Viale Pompeo Pellini, and the series of scala mobili that descend through the Rocca Paolina to Piazza dei Partigiani. The supervised car park here costs €0.75 for the first hour and €1.05 per hour thereafter, and is open from 6.15am to 1am. If you intend to use the car park a lot, buy an *abbonamento* (unlimited parking ticket pass; cost per day/week €8.25/43.65, from the ticket office at the car park) for tourists.

If you park illegally and return to find your car gone, chances are it has been towed away. Call the Deposito Veicoli Rimossi (☎ 075 577 53 75) to check; be prepared to pay around €103.30 to retrieve your car.

For a taxi, call ☎ 075 500 48 88.

LAGO DI TRASIMENO

The fourth-largest lake in Italy, Lago di Trasimeno is not a bad location for swimming, fishing and other water sports, but is hardly comparable with the country's northern lakes. The only blemish is the *autostrada* (motorway) running along its northern shore.

In 217 BC this area witnessed one of the bloodiest battles in Roman history as Hannibal's Carthaginians ambushed and near-annihilated Roman army troops led by Consul Flaminius, killing 15,000 soldiers. The battlefield extended from Cortona and Ossaia (Place of Bones), in Tuscany, to the small town of Sanguineto (The Bloody), just north of the lake.

Passignano (or Passignano sul Trasimeno) is the most popular spot for holidaying Italians, so book accommodation in advance for the summer months. More enticing is **Castiglione del Lago**, up on a chalky promontory on the lake's western side, dotted with olive trees and dominated by a 14th-century fortress.

Information

In Passignano, the Pro-Loco office (☎ 075 82 76 35), Via Roma 25, can provide details of accommodation and water sports. It's open from 10am to noon and 3pm to 6pm Monday to Saturday, 10am to noon Sunday. In Castiglione del Lago, the APT office (☎ 075 965 24 84), Piazza Mazzini 10, opens 8.30am to 1pm and 3.30pm to 7pm Monday to Saturday and 9am to 1pm Sunday. Staff can advise on the many agriturismo options and good walking tracks in the area.

Things to See & Do

Water sports, walking and horse riding are the main reasons to visit the lake. The scenery is agreeable but hardly Umbria's best. Castiglione del Lago's attractions include the **Palazzo della Corgna** *(☎ 075 965 82 10, Piazza Gramsci; admission €2.60, includes entrance to Rocca del Leone; open 10am-1pm & 4pm-7.30pm daily in summer, 9.30am-4.30pm weekends only in winter)*, an ancient ducal palace housing an important series of 16th-century frescoes by Giovanni Antonio Pandolfi and Salvio Salvini. A covered passageway connects the palace with the 13th-century **Rocca del Leone**, a pentagon-shaped fortress and an excellent example of medieval military architecture. Seen from the lake rearing up on a rocky promontory, it cuts a striking pose.

The lake's main inhabited island, **Isola Maggiore**, near Passignano, was reputedly a favourite with St Francis. The hill-top **Chiesa di San Michele Arcangelo** contains a *Crucifixion* by master painter Bartolomeo Caporalimaster. The island is famed for its lace and embroidery production and you can see examples in the **Museo del Merlotto** *(Lace Museum; ☎ 075 825 42 33, Via Gugliemi, near the port, Isola Maggiore; admission €2.60; open 10am-1pm & 2.30pm-6pm daily)*.

Ask at one of the tourist offices for *Tourist Itineraries in the Trasimeno District*, a booklet of walking and horse-riding tracks. Horse-riding centres include the ***Maneggio Oasi*** *(☎ 0337 65 37 95, Localitá Orto, in Castiglione del Lago)* and the ***Poggio del Belveduto*** *(☎ 075 82 90 76 in Passignano)*. You'll find other riding centres around the lake.

Places to Stay & Eat

Passignano There are various places to stay around Passignano.

Kursaal *(☎ 075 82 80 85, fax 075 82 71 82, e kursaalcamp@libero.it, w www.camping.it/umbria/kursaal, Viale Europa 41)* Sites per person/tent €6.20/8.25. Open Apr-Oct. This camp site is on the lake shore but there's not much privacy. There's also a hotel and swimming pool here.

Pensione del Pescatore *(☎ 075 829 60 63, fax 075 82 92 01, Via San Bernardino 5)* High season singles/doubles €28.40/43.90. This family-run pensione has 11 simple but appealing rooms above a charming local trattoria.

Castiglione del Lago Choose between lakeside or town centre.

Listro *(☎/fax 075 95 11 93, Via Lungolago)* Sites per person/tent €4.15/4.15. Open Apr-Sept. This camp site is on the lake shore, with about 100 pitches, various leisure activities (including table tennis and volleyball) and facilities for the disabled.

Albergo Fazzuoli *(☎ 075 95 11 19, fax 075 95 11 12, Piazza Marconi 11)* Singles/doubles up to €36.15/54.25. This is about the cheapest hotel you'll find in town but it's outside the historic centre and lacks character.

Hotel Milagro *(☎ 075 95 11 57, fax 075 95 19 24)* Singles/doubles €51.65/82.65. Open Apr-Oct. The Milagro is very central and top floor rooms have magnificent lake views. There's also a good restaurant downstairs.

Pizzeria Come Te Pare *(☎ 075 95 10 68, Via V Emanuele 80)* Pizza slices €0.75, whole pizzas from €3.10. Great food is served by the slice at this tiny place. The *pizza porcini* is a dream.

Isola Maggiore Camping is forbidden on the island.

Hotel Da Sauro *(☎ 075 82 61 68, fax 075 82 51 30)* Singles/doubles €31/56.80. This family-run establishment has just 10 rooms in a rustic stone building at the northern end of the village. The restaurant downstairs is very popular so expect a lot of noise at mealtimes.

Getting There & Around

Buses connect Perugia with Passignano (€2.60, one hour, five daily) and Castiglione del Lago (€4.15, one hour 20 minutes, eight daily). Passignano is also served by regular trains from Perugia (€1.95, 25 minutes, hourly) via Terontola (€1.30, 10 minutes, hourly), making it the most accessible part of the lake.

Castiglione del Lago is on the Florence-Rome train line, but the Intercity trains don't stop here and local trains are slow and stop at every station.

APM (☎ 075 82 71 57) operates a regular ferry service between the main towns. The company has information offices on the waterfront at each town, where you can pick up a timetable. The return trip to Isola Maggiore from Passignano costs €5.15 and takes 20 minutes each way. Hourly ferries connect Passignano with Castiglione del Lago (€6.70 return, one hour).

DERUTA

postcode 06053 • pop 7400

About 15km south of Perugia, on the S3b-E45 to Terni, Deruta is famed for its richly coloured and intensely patterned pottery. The Etruscans and Romans worked the clay around Deruta but it was not until the majolica glazing technique, with its bright blue and yellow metallic oxides, was imported from Majorca in the 15th century that the ceramics industry took off.

There is not much else to Deruta, but it is probably the place to buy ceramics as prices are lower than in Perugia and other towns. Watch out for low-quality, mass-produced stuff as you browse through the large showrooms in town.

APM buses connect the town with Perugia (€1.95, 30 minutes, six daily) and it has a handful of hotels.

TODI

postcode 06059 • pop 17,000

Originally an Etruscan frontier settlement, Todi ended up as a prosperous *comune* in the early Middle Ages – a prosperity reflected in the grandness of its central Piazza del Popolo.

Set atop a craggy hill, Todi seems to have ignored the 21st century, notwithstanding the growing stream of tourists, and getting there by public transport can be quite a slog.

The Pro Loco del Tuderte (☎ 075 894 34 56), at Piazza del Popolo 38, opens 9am to 1pm and 4pm to 7pm (3.30pm to 6.30pm winter) Monday to Saturday and 9.30am to 12.30pm Sunday. There are public telephones in the Pro Loco office and Internet access at Piazza Umberto 1° 17. The Banco Populare di Todi, Piazza del Popolo 27, has a user-friendly ATM.

Things to See

The 13th-century **Palazzo del Capitano** *(☎ 075 895 62 16, Piazza del Popolo; admission €3.10; open 10.30am-1pm & 2pm-6pm daily)* features an elegant triple window and houses the city's recently restored *pinacoteca* (picture gallery) and archaeological museum. Also facing the square are the 13th-century **Palazzo del Popolo** and the gloomy **Palazzo dei Priori**.

The **cathedral** *(☎ 075 894 30 41, Piazza del Popolo; free; open 8.30am-12.30pm & 2.30pm-6.30pm daily)*, at the north-western end of the square, has a magnificent rose window and intricately decorated doorway. The 8th-century crypt is worth visiting for the inlaid wooden stalls in the chancel. Wander through Todi's medieval labyrinth and popping into some of the other churches, including the lofty **Tempio di San Fortunato** *(Piazza Umberto 1°; free; open 9.30am-12.30pm & 3pm-6pm daily)*, with frescoes by Masolino da Panicale and the tomb of San Jacopone, Todi's beloved patron saint. Just outside the city walls is the late Renaissance **Chiesa di Santa Maria della Consolazione**, designed by Donato Bramante in 1508 but not completed until 99 years later.

Special Events

The Todi Festival, held for 10 days each July/August, is a mixture of classical and jazz concerts, theatre, ballet and cinema.

Places to Stay & Eat

If you are planning to stay overnight, expect to spend a wedge of money on accommodation. For details of agriturismo opportunities, contact ***Agritop-Umbria*** *(☎ 075 894 26 27, Via Paolo Rolli 3).*

Casa per Ferie L Crispoliti *(☎/fax 075 894 53 37, ⓔ info@crispolitiferie.it, Ⓦ www.crispolitiferie.it, Via Cesia 96)* Singles/doubles €31/51.65. This is the best bet for affordable accommodation within the city walls. It's a huge converted Augustine monastery that dates from the 14th century, although it has since been thoroughly modernised.

Hotel Tuder *(☎ 075 894 21 84, fax 075 894 39 52, ⓔ hoteltuder@libero.it, Via*

Maesta dei Lombardi 13) High season singles/doubles from €46.50/77.45. The Tuder is a functional three-star hotel where they've clearly made an effort, but the result is a bit soulless. It's also about 2km east of the historic centre.

Villa Luisa *(☎ 075 894 85 71, fax 075 894 84 72, Via A Cortesi 147)* Singles/doubles €51.65/77.45. Again, this place is well out of the city walls but it's set in its own park-like grounds with a swimming pool.

Ristorante Umbria *(☎ 075 89 43 90, Via Santa Bonaventura 13)* Price €25.80. This restaurant, behind the Pro Loco office, is reasonably expensive but worth it for the view from the terrace over the countryside.

Ristorante Cavour *(☎ 075 894 37 30, Corso Cavour 21)* Full meals about €15.50. If you'd prefer a pizza or pasta (and good views if you snaffle the right tables), try the Cavour.

Getting There & Away

APM buses from Perugia (€4.75, 1½ hours, seven per day) terminate in Piazza Jacopone, just south of Piazza del Popolo. Other buses may terminate in Piazza Consolazione (from here take city bus A or B or walk uphill 2km to the centre). There is one daily service to Orvieto (€4.15, 1½ hours) at 5.50am, which returns at 1.55pm.

Todi is on the Ferrovia Centrale Umbra train line but the train station is inconveniently located 3km east of the town centre in the valley below. City bus C runs there (€0.60, 20 minutes). By road, Todi is easily reached on the S3b-E45, which runs between Perugia and Terni.

ASSISI

postcode 06081 • pop 25,000

Despite the millions of tourists and pilgrims it attracts every year, the home town of St Francis remains a beautiful and tranquil refuge. Since Roman times, its inhabitants have been aware of the visual impact of their city, perched halfway up Monte Subasio (1290m). From the valley, its pink and white marble buildings shimmer in the sunlight.

St Francis was born here in 1182 and his spirit hovers over every aspect of the city's life. He renounced his father's wealth in his late teens to pursue a life of chastity and poverty, founding the order of mendicant friars known as the *Frati Minori* (Order of Minors; they became known as the Franciscans after St Francis' death), which attracted a huge following in Europe. With one of his disciples, St Clare (Santa Chiara), born in 1193, St Francis co-founded the Franciscans' female *Ordine delle Clarisse* (Order of the Poor Clares).

The Basilica di San Francesco is the city's, and possibly Umbria's, main draw. Don't be put off by the prospect of huge crowds, but do check before coming to Assisi that your trip doesn't coincide with a religious celebration, when hotels are likely to be booked out.

Orientation

Piazza del Comune is the centre of Assisi. At the north-western edge of this square, Via San Paolo and Via Portica both eventually lead to the Basilica di San Francesco. Via Portica also leads to the Porta San Pietro and the Piazzale dell'Unità d'Italia, where most intercity buses stop, although APM buses from smaller towns in the area terminate at Piazza Matteotti. The train station is 4km south-west of the city in Santa Maria degli Angeli (use the shuttle bus).

Information

Tourist Offices The APT office (☎ 075 81 25 34, ⓔ info@iat.assisi.pg.it), on Via S Croce, opens 8am to 2pm and 3.30pm to 6.30pm Monday to Friday, 9am to 1pm and 3.30pm to 6.30pm Saturday and 9am to 1pm Sunday. It has all the information you'll need on hotels, sights and events. There is a small branch office (☎ 075 81 67 66) just outside Porta Nuova, open from Easter to November.

Money The Cassa di Risparmio di Perugia in Piazza del Comune has an ATM and currency exchange machine.

Post & Communications There are post offices just inside Porta San Pietro and next to Porta Nuova. They are open 8.10am to 6.25pm Monday to Friday and 8.10am to 1pm at the weekend.

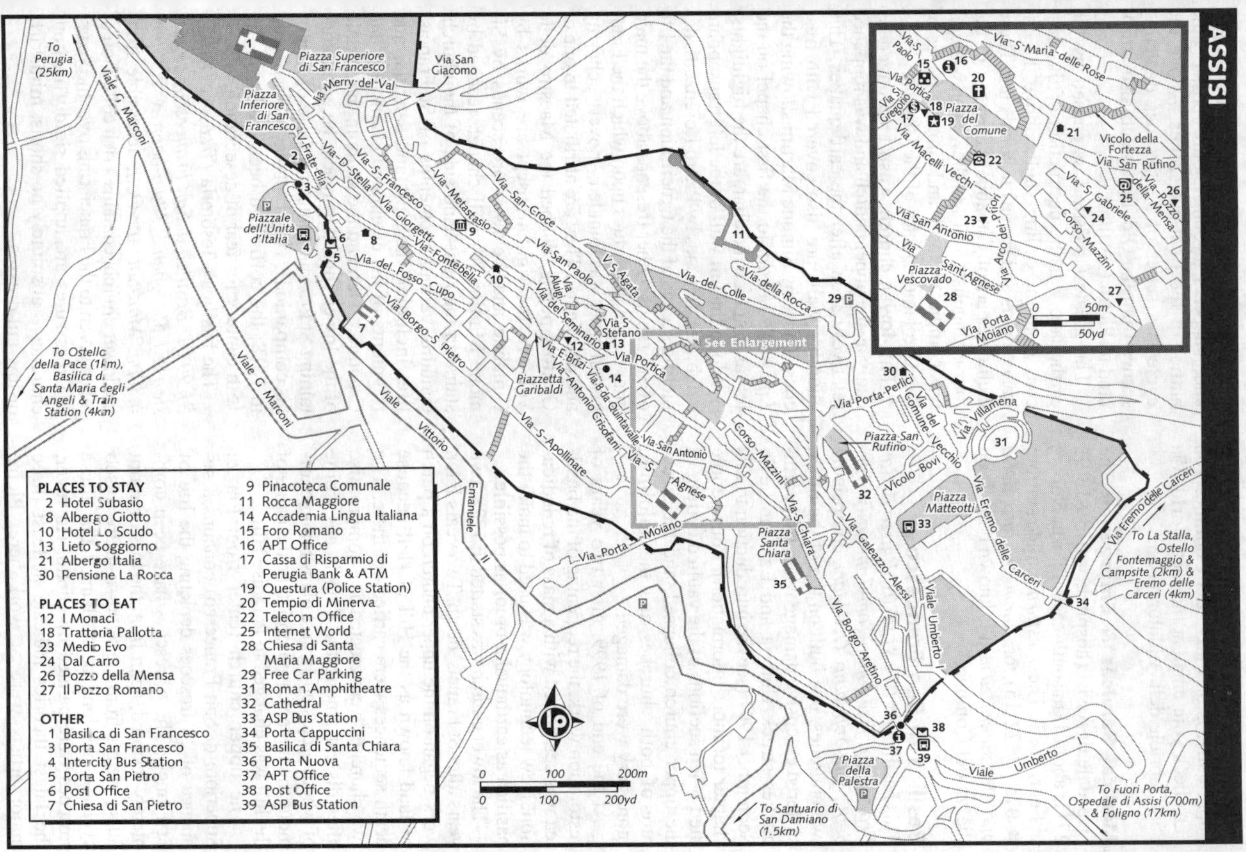
ASSISI
PLACES TO STAY
2 Hotel Subasio
8 Albergo Giotto
10 Hotel Lo Scudo
13 Lieto Soggiorno
21 Albergo Italia
30 Pensione La Rocca
PLACES TO EAT
12 I Monaci
18 Trattoria Pallotta
23 Medio Evo
24 Dal Carro
26 Pozzo della Mensa
27 Il Pozzo Romano
OTHER
1 Basilica di San Francesco
3 Porta San Francesco
4 Intercity Bus Station
5 Porta San Pietro
6 Post Office
7 Chiesa di San Pietro
9 Pinacoteca Comunale
11 Rocca Maggiore
14 Accademia Lingua Italiana
15 Foro Romano
16 APT Office
17 Cassa di Risparmio di Perugia Bank & ATM
19 Questura (Police Station)
20 Tempio di Minerva
22 Telecom Office
25 Internet World
28 Chiesa di Santa Maria Maggiore
29 Free Car Parking
31 Roman Amphitheatre
32 Cathedral
33 ASP Bus Station
34 Porta Cappuccini
35 Basilica di Santa Chiara
36 Porta Nuova
37 APT Office
38 Post Office
39 ASP Bus Station
To Perugia (25km)
To Ostello della Pace (1km), Basilica di Santa Maria degli Angeli & Train Station (4km)
To Santuario di San Damiano (1.5km)
To Fuori Porta, Ospedale di Assisi (700m) & Foligno (17km)
To La Stalla, Ostello Fontemaggio & Campsite (2km) & Eremo delle Carceri (4km)
Piazza Superiore di San Francesco
Piazza Inferiore di San Francesco
Piazzale dell'Unità d'Italia
Piazzetta Garibaldi
Piazza San Rufino
Piazza Matteotti
Piazza Santa Chiara
Piazza della Palestra
Piazza del Comune
Piazza Vescovado
Via San Giacomo
Via Merry del Val
Viale G Marconi
Viale Vittorio Emanuele II
Viale Umberto I
Via Eremo delle Carceri
Via Porta Perlici
Via Villamena
Via del Comune Vecchio
Vicolo Bovi
Corso Mazzini
Via S Chiara
Via Galeazzo Alessi
Via Borgo Aretino
Via Porta Moiano
Via S Apollinare
Via Borgo S Pietro
Via del Fosso Cupo
Via Fontebella
Via Giorgetti
Via D Stella
V Frate Elia
Via S Francesco
Via Metastasio
Via San Croce
Via San Paolo
V S Agata
Via del Colle
Via della Rocca
Via Aluigi
Via del Seminario
Via S Stefano
Via Portica
Via E Brizi
Via 8 da Quintavalle
Via Antonio Crisofani
Via San Antonio
Via S Agnese
Via S Paolo
Via S Gregorio
Via S Maria delle Rose
Vicolo della Fortezza
Via San Rufino
Via Pozzo della Mensa
Via S Gabriele
Via Macelli Vecchi
Via Arco dei Priori
Via Sant'Agnese
See Enlargement
0 50m
0 50yd
0 100 200m
0 100 200yd

The Telecom office, open from 8am to 10pm daily, is on Piazza del Comune. You can check your email at Internet World, Via San Gabriele dell'Addolorata 25.

Medical Services & Emergency The Ospedale di Assisi (hospital; ☎ 075 813 92 27) is about 1km south-east of Porta Nuova, in Fuori Porta. The *questura* (police station; ☎ 075 81 22 15), or *commissariato della pubblica sicurezza* as it is known here, is on Piazza del Comune.

Basilica di San Francesco

This basilica *(☎ 075 81 90 01, Piazza di San Francesco; free; open 7am-7pm daily Apr-Sept, 7am-5pm daily Oct-Mar)*, comprising two churches, one built on top of the other, suffered extensive damage when two earthquakes struck Umbria and Le Marche in September 1997 (see the introduction to this chapter for more information). Four people died when sections of the vaulted ceiling of the upper church collapsed, and the structure of both churches and the adjoining monastery were damaged.

At the end of 1999, after two years of restoration work, the reopening of the basilica was celebrated with a mass of rededication. New technology was used to make the basilica as earthquake-proof as possible.

The lower church was started in 1228, two years after St Francis' death. Two years later, work began on the upper church on a patch of land known as the Hill of Hell because death sentences were carried out there. The two churches were erected as a compromise after dissent among the Franciscans, some of whom protested against plans for an enormous monument. Appropriately, the name of the hill was changed to Paradise Hill.

The **upper church** (enter from Piazza Superiore di San Francesco) contains a sequence of 28 frescoes depicting the life of St Francis. These frescoes have been completely restored, apart from the loss of about 30 sq metres from the 5200-sq-metre fresco cycle. It has long been claimed that these frescoes were painted by Giotto. However, the latest theories indicate at least three major artists were at work here: Pietro Cavallini, an (as yet) unidentified colleague and, it appears, a young Giotto – possibly the author of the final six scenes. Above the cycle is a series of 32 frescoes depicting scenes from the Old Testament, also attributed to Pietro Cavallini.

The greatest artistic loss caused by the earthquake was the destruction of the frescoes from the ceiling vaults above the entrance doors and above the papal altar. These included part of Cimabue's frescoes of the four evangelists – St Matthew (San Matteo) was completely lost – and Giotto's fresco of San Girolamo, Doctor of the Church.

The **lower church** wasn't damaged as badly as the upper church and was reopened relatively soon after the earthquakes. This church's walls are also covered with frescoes. Those by Simone Martini showing the *Life of St Martin*, in the first chapel on the left as you face the altar, are the highlights.

Along the left wall of the left transept are celebrated frescoes by Pietro Lorenzetti, depicting scenes of the Crucifixion and the life of St Francis. Other frescoes above the main altar depict the virtues upon which the Franciscan order was founded – poverty, chastity and obedience. They are attributed to one of Giotto's pupils, dubbed the Maestro delle Vele. In the right transept are works by Cimabue and, below, more scenes by Simone Martini. A small chapel, reached by stairs on the right-hand side of the church, contains various mementos of St Francis' life, including his shirt and sandals, and fragments of his celebrated *Canticle of the Creatures*. Descend the stairs in the middle of the lower church to reach the crypt containing St Francis' tomb and those of four of his companions. The crypt was rediscovered in 1818; the coffin had been hidden in the 15th century for fear of desecration.

The basilica's **Tesoreria** *(Treasury; ☎ 075 81 90 01, Basilica di San Francesco; admission €1.55; open 9.30am-noon & 2.30pm-6.30pm Mon-Sat Apr-Oct)*, accessible from the lower church, contains a rich collection of relics given to the Franciscans over the years.

Dress rules are applied rigidly in both churches – absolutely no shorts, miniskirts or low-cut dresses.

St Francis of Assisi

Of all the Catholic saints, one of the best known and most loved is St Francis (San Francesco). Born in Assisi in 1182, the son of Pietro di Bernardone, a wealthy cloth merchant, St Francis' early years were a sharp contrast to the humble life that he became so famous for. A witty and reckless youth, he showed little aptitude for study, preferring instead to hang out with the other wealthy young men of Assisi, feasting, singing and squandering his father's money.

During a skirmish with the rival city of Perugia, Francis (aged about 20) was captured and held prisoner for a year. Laid low by an illness (probably contracted in a Perugian jail), he started to regret his idle youth and on recovery decided to become a knight, before a voice in a dream told him to go back to Assisi.

On his return, Francis took up an increasingly nomadic and eccentric lifestyle – embracing lepers, talking to crosses and once, during a pilgrimage to Rome, switching clothes with a beggar and fasting on the steps of St Peter's Basilica. But when he impulsively sold a large stock of his father's cloth to raise money to rebuild the church of St Damian, Bernardone's patience finally snapped. Fleeing his father's wrath, Francis hid in a cave, emerging a month later dirty, emaciated and the laughing stock of Assisi, who thought him a madman and pelted him with mud and stones as he walked through town.

Exasperated, his father disinherited him (probably to his son's delight) and dragged him before the city council, whereupon Francis pointed out that since he had entered the service of God he was no longer under civil jurisdiction. Stripping off his clothes and handing them to his father, Francis set forth into the hills behind Assisi, where he renounced all worldly goods, flung himself into charitable works and improvised hymns of praise.

It wasn't long before Francis started to build up a following and the foundations of the Franciscan order were established. In 1212 he co-founded a second order for women, called the Poor Clares. He continued with charitable works throughout his life and went on to preach in market places throughout Italy. In 1224, he received the stigmata on the hill at La Verna but by now the years of unremitting toil had taken their toll on his body. Weakened, exhausted and practically blind, St Francis died on the dirt floor of a small hut in Assisi on 3 October 1226 at the age of 44.

Other Things to See

From the basilica, take Via San Francesco back to Piazza del Comune, once the site of a partially-excavated **Foro Romano** *(Roman Forum; ☎ 075 81 30 53, entrance Via Portica; admission €2.05; open 10am-1pm & 3pm-7pm (2pm-5pm in winter) daily)*. The **Tempio di Minerva**, facing the same square, is now a church but retains its impressive pillared facade. Wander into some of the shops on the piazza, which open their basements to reveal Roman ruins. The city's **Pinacoteca Comunale** *(☎ 075 81 20 33, Via San Francesco 10; adult/child €2.05/1.55; open 10am-1pm & 3pm-7pm daily in summer, 10am-1pm & 3pm-5pm daily in winter)* displays Umbrian Renaissance art and frescoes from Giotto's school.

Off Via San Antonio is Piazza Vescovado and the Romanesque **Chiesa di Santa Maria Maggiore**, formerly the city's cathedral, with an interesting rose window. South of Piazza del Comune, along Corso Mazzini and Via Santa Chiara, is the pink and white 13th-century Romanesque **Basilica di Santa Chiara** *(☎ 075 81 22 82, Piazza Santa Chiara; free; open 7am-noon & 2pm-7pm daily)*, with a deteriorating but nonetheless striking facade. The body of Santa Chiara is in the crypt. If you believe in talking crosses, cast a glance at the Byzantine crucifix that is said to have told St Francis to re-establish the moral foundations of the Church. At the time of writing, part of the Basilica di Santa Chiara remains closed for repairs to earthquake damage.

North-east of the Basilica di Santa Chiara, the 13th-century Romanesque **cathedral** (*☎ 075 81 60 16, Piazza San Rufino; free; open 7am-noon & 2pm-7pm daily*), remodelled by Galeazzo Alessi in the 16th century, contains the font at which St Francis was baptised. The facade is festooned with grotesque figures and fantastic animals.

Dominating the city is the massive 14th-century **Rocca Maggiore** (*☎ 075 81 52 92, Via della Rocca; admission €2.60; open 10am-sunset daily*), a hill fortress offering fabulous views over the valley and across to Perugia. Most of the fortress is closed for a long restoration that will eventually see it converted into an immense art gallery.

A 30-minute walk south from Porta Nuova, the **Santuario di San Damiano** (*☎ 075 81 22 73; free; open 10am-12.30pm & 2pm-6pm daily in summer, 10am-12.30pm & 2pm-4pm daily in winter*) was built on the spot where the crucifix spoke to St Francis and where he wrote his *Canticle of the Creatures*. The convent on this pleasant, bucolic site was founded by St Clare.

About 4km east of the city, reached via the Porta Cappuccini, is the **Eremo delle Carceri** (*☎ 075 81 23 01; free; open 6.30am-7.15pm daily Easter-Nov, 6.30am-5.30pm daily in winter*), to which St Francis retreated after hearing the word of God. The *carceri* (prisons) are the caves that functioned as hermits' retreats for St Francis and his followers. Apart from a few fences and tourist paths, everything has remained as it was in St Francis' time, and a few Franciscans live here.

In the valley south-west of the city, near the train station, the imposing **Basilica di Santa Maria degli Angeli** (*☎ 075 8 05 11, Santa Maria degli Angeli; free; open 6.30am-8pm daily*) was built around the first Franciscan monastery. St Francis died in its **Cappella del Transito** on 3 October 1226.

Activities

Local bookstores sell maps (€7.75) of walks on nearby Monte Subasio, produced by the Club Alpino Italiano (CAI). None of them are too demanding and the smattering of religious shrines and camp sites could make for an enjoyable two-day excursion.

Courses

Some people may favour Assisi over Perugia as a place to live and learn Italian.

Accademia Lingua Italiana (*☎/fax 075 81 52 81, W www.krenet.it/alia/, Via Giotto 5*) The Accademia runs a variety of language and culture courses and can arrange accommodation.

Special Events

The Festa di San Francesco falls on 3 and 4 October and is the main religious event of the city's calendar. Easter week is celebrated with processions and performances. The Ars Nova Musica festival, held from late August to mid-September, features local and national performers. The colourful Festa di Calendimaggio celebrates the coming of spring in perky medieval fashion and is normally held over several days at the end of the first week of May.

Places to Stay

Assisi is well-appointed for tourists but in peak periods, such as Easter, August and September, and the Festa di San Francesco, you will need to book accommodation well in advance. Even outside these times, many of the hotels will often be full. The APT office has a complete list of private rooms, religious institutions (of which there are 17), flats and agriturismo options in and around Assisi. Otherwise, keep an eye out for *camere* (rooms for rent) signs as you wander the streets. If you fail to find anything in Assisi itself, consider staying in Santa Maria degli Angeli, 4km south-west of Assisi – this way you are near the train station and a half-hourly shuttle bus runs to the city centre.

Ostello Fontemaggio (*☎ 075 81 36 36, fax 075 81 37 49, Via Eremo delle Carceri*) Dorm beds €13.95. To reach this non-HI hostel, just east of town at Fontemaggio, walk about 2km uphill along Via Eremo delle Carceri. There's also a camp site.

Ostello della Pace (*☎/fax 075 81 67 67, Via Valecchie 171*) B&B €12.90, family rooms €15.50. Open 1 Mar-10 Jan. Assisi's HI youth hostel is spotless and has great pillows. It's on the shuttle-bus route between Santa Maria degli Angeli and Assisi.

Pensione La Rocca *(☎/fax 075 81 22 84, Via Porta Perlici 27)* Singles/doubles €31/38.75. All 24 rooms at this popular one-star hotel have private baths, but try and nab one with sweeping views of the valley.

Albergo Italia *(☎ 075 81 26 25, fax 075 804 37 49, Vicolo della Fortezza)* Singles without bath €14.45, singles/doubles with bath €23.25/35.65. This place is just off Piazza del Comune in a great location, but was undergoing renovation at the time of writing, so expect prices to shoot up.

Lieto Soggiorno *(☎ 075 81 61 91, Via A Fortini 26)* Singles/doubles without bath from €23.25/38.75, doubles with bath €49.05. This quiet, family-run two star is a short walk west of Piazza del Comune.

Hotel Lo Scudo *(☎/fax 075 81 31 96, Via San Francesco 3)* Singles/doubles with bath and shower up to €33.55/49.05. Lo Scudo is close to the Basilica di San Francesco and has eight simple but decent rooms.

Albergo Giotto *(☎ 075 81 22 09, fax 075 81 64 79, Via Fontebella 41)* Singles/doubles €85.20/130.15. This large three-star hotel, with modern but tasteful decor, has private parking and offers 30% discounts in winter.

Hotel Subasio *(☎ 075 81 22 06, fax 075 81 66 91, W www.umbria.org/hotel/subasio, Via Frate Elia 2)* Singles/doubles €103.30/160.10. The Subasio is a truly gorgeous but pricey hotel, so it's best for splash-out occasions only. All the rooms are furnished in Florentine Renaissance style, and distinguished former guests include Greta Garbo and Charlie Chaplin.

Places to Eat

Assisi offers a good selection of traditional Italian and Umbrian delicacies.

I Monaci *(☎ 075 81 25 12, Scaletta del Metastasio)* Pizzas from €4.15. Open Wed-Mon. This restaurant, halfway up a flight of steps leading off Piazzetta Garibaldi, has tasty pizza and other standard Italian fare for very reasonable prices.

Il Pozzo Romano *(☎ 075 81 30 57, Via Sant'Agnese 8)* Pizzas €3.60. Open Fri-Wed. If pennies are everything, try this pizzeria.

La Stalla *(☎ 075 81 36 36, Via Eremo Caceri 8)* Meals €15.50. Open Tues-Sun. This restaurant is in the same complex as the camp site at Fontemaggio. You can have filling meals under an arbour.

Dal Carro *(☎ 075 81 33 07, Vicolo dei Nepis 2)* Price €12.90, pizzas from €4.15. Open Thurs-Tues. Off Corso Mazzini, Dal Carro is a good bet – the *strangozzi alla norcina* (pasta with a black truffle sauce) is a marvel and so is the homemade tiramisù.

Trattoria Pallotta *(☎ 075 81 26 49, Vicolo della Volta Pinta 2, off Piazza del Comune)* Set meals with wine from €13.95. Open Wed-Mon. Having moved from a better spot on Via Rufino, Pallotta has lost some of its character but it still churns out good Italian fare.

Pozzo della Mensa *(☎ 075 815 52 36, Via Pozzo della Mensa 11)* Full meals €20.65. Open Thurs-Tues. This place specialises in Umbrian dishes. It's charming, fairly laid-back and has a good vegetarian option.

Medio Evo *(☎ 075 81 30 68, Via Arco dei Priori 4)* Meals €25.80. Open Thurs-Tues. This is one of Assisi's better restaurants, serving traditional Umbrian dishes in fabulous vaulted 13th-century surroundings.

Getting There & Away

APM buses connect Assisi with Perugia (€2.60, 50 minutes, 10 per day) and other local towns, leaving from the bus station on Piazza Matteotti. Most APM buses also stop on Largo Properzio, just outside the Porta Nuova. Piazzale dell'Unità d'Italia is the terminus for SULGA buses (☎ 075 500 96 41) for Rome (€16.55, three hours, three daily), Florence (€11.65, 2¾ hours, one per day at 6.45am, returning at 5pm) and other major cities.

Although Assisi's train station is 4km away at Santa Maria degli Angeli, the train is still the best way to get to many places as the services are more frequent than the buses. It is on the Foligno-Terontola line with regular services to Perugia (€1.55, 30 minutes, hourly). Change at Terontola for Florence (€9, 2 hours, ten daily) and at Foligno for Rome (€11.20, two hours, 11 daily).

To reach Assisi from Perugia by road, take the S75, exit at Ospedalicchio and follow the signs.

Getting Around

A shuttle bus (€0.60) operates every half-hour between Piazza Matteotti and the train station. Normal traffic is subject to restrictions in the city centre and daytime parking is all but banned. If you object to paying for one of the several car parks dotted around the city walls (and connected to the centre by orange shuttle buses), head for Via della Rocca, the road that leads up to Rocca Maggiore. There are no restrictions beyond the P (parking) sign. This leaves you a fairly short, if steep, walk to the cathedral and Piazza del Comune.

SPELLO

postcode 06038 • pop 7600

Spello's proximity to Perugia and Assisi makes it well worth a brief trip. Emperor Augustus developed much of the land in the valley, but the Roman ruins are some distance from the town and your time could be better spent wandering Spello's narrow cobbled streets.

The Pro Loco office (☎ 0742 30 10 09), at Piazza Matteotti 3, opens 9.30am to 12.30pm and 3.30pm to 5.30pm. They can provide you with a list of accommodation and they have maps of walks in the surrounding area, including an 8km walk across the hills to Assisi.

The Augustan **Porta Venere** leads to the gloomy **Chiesa di Sant'Andrea** *(Piazza Matteotti; free; open 8am-7pm daily)* where you can admire a fresco by Bernardino Pinturicchio. A few doors down is the 12th-century **Chiesa di Santa Maria Maggiore** *(Piazza Matteotti; free; open 8.30am-12.30pm & 3pm-7pm daily in summer, 8.30am-12.30pm & 3pm-6pm daily in winter)* and the town's real treat, Pinturicchio's beautiful frescoes in the Cappella Baglioni. Also of note is the Cappella's exquisite floor (dating from 1566) made of tiles from Deruta.

The people of Spello celebrate the feast of Corpus Domini in June (the date changes each year) by skilfully decorating stretches of the main street with fresh flowers in colourful designs. If you want to enjoy it, come on the Saturday evening before the Sunday procession to see the floral fantasies being laid out (from about 8.30pm) and participate in the festive atmosphere. The Corpus procession begins at 11am Sunday, but the crowds can make it a stifling event.

Hotels are expensive and there are cheaper options in Assisi and Perugia.

Residence La Terraza *(Affittacamere Merulli; ☎/fax 0742 65 11 84, fax 0742 65 12 27, Via Belvedere 39)* Singles/doubles €31/41.30, mini apartments €51.65. This quiet affittacamere has simple rooms surrounding a pretty garden. The apartments, equipped with kitchen and en-suite bath, are worth the extra splurge.

Il Cacciatore *(☎ 0742 65 11 41, fax 0742 30 16 03, Via Giulia 42)* Singles/doubles with bath €43.90/67.15. This place has a great restaurant (closed Monday) with a large terrace, perfect for a summer lunch. The rooms are large and traditional.

Hotel Palazzo Bocci *(☎ 0742 30 10 21, fax 0742 30 14 64, ⓔ bocci@bcsnet.it, Via Cavour 17)* Singles/doubles from €67.10/113.60. This exquisite 18th-century hotel is a classy alternative complete with walled garden and frescoes in the sitting room.

APM buses connect Spello with Perugia (€2.90, one hour, five daily) and Foligno (€0.60, 15 minutes, nine daily), and there are also connections to Assisi (€1.30, 15 minutes, six daily, Monday to Saturday). Trains are a better option, with almost hourly connections linking Spello with Perugia (€2, 30 minutes), Assisi (€1.10, 10 minutes) and Foligno (€0.80, 15 minutes). Spello is on the S75 between Perugia and Foligno.

AROUND SPELLO

Those with time (and, better still, their own wheels) could do worse than undertaking a few excursions in the area south-west of Spello. **Bevagna**, about 8km south-west of Foligno (through which you'll pass if you're on public transport), is a charming, medieval hamlet with a couple of Romanesque churches on the central Piazza Silvestri. It comes to life in the last week of June for the Mercato delle Gaite, a bit of a medieval lark where olde-worlde taverns open up and medieval-era handicrafts are brought back to life. The town also boasts a few remnants of its Roman days, including some impressive mosaics at the site of the former Roman hot baths.

Seven kilometres to the south-east, **Montefalco** is also known as the Ringhiera dell'Umbria (Balcony of Umbria) for its expansive views. Again, the town is a pleasant medieval backwater graced with several churches. The deconsecrated Chiesa di San Francesco now serves as an overpriced art gallery. Don't leave here without trying the local Sagrantino wine.

GUBBIO

postcode 06024 • pop 32,000

Hitched onto the steep slopes of Monte Ingino and overlooking a picturesque valley, the centuries-old palazzos of Gubbio exude a warm ochre glow in the late afternoon sunlight. It doesn't require a great deal of imagination to feel that you have stepped back into the Middle Ages while meandering along the town's quiet, treeless lanes and peering into some of the city's many fine ceramic shops.

Gubbio is famous for its Eugubian Tables, which date from 300 to 100 BC and constitute the best existing example of ancient Umbrian script. An important ally of the Roman Empire and a key stop on the Via Flaminia, the town declined during the Saracen invasions. In the 14th century it fell into the hands of the Montefeltro family of Urbino and was later incorporated into the Papal States.

Like many hill towns from Tuscany to Le Marche, Gubbio has taken on the feel of a museum. Despite this, it's well worth losing yourself within the city's labyrinth for a day or so.

Orientation

The city is small and easy to explore. The immense traffic circle known as Piazza Quaranta Martiri, at the base of the hill, is where buses to the city terminate, and it also has a large car park. The square was named in honour of 40 local people who were killed by the Nazis in 1944 in reprisal for partisan activities. From here it is a short, if somewhat steep, walk up Via della Repubblica to the main square, Piazza Grande, also known as the Piazza della Signoria. Corso Garibaldi and Piazza Oderisi are to your right as you head up the hill.

Information

The APT office (☎ 075 922 06 93), on Piazza Oderisi, opens 8.15am to 1.45pm and 3.30pm to 6.30pm (3pm to 6pm winter) Monday to Friday, 9am to 1pm Saturday and 9.30am to 12.30pm Sunday. You can also get information at Easy Gubbio, Via della Repubblica 13, near Piazza Quaranta Martiri.

The main post office, Via Cairoli 11, is open from 8.10am to 5pm Monday to Saturday. The Telecom office is at Easy Gubbio.

The Ospedale Civile (hospital; ☎ 075 9 23 91) is on Piazza Quaranta Martiri. The *questura* (police station), or *pretura* as it is known here, is at Via XX Settembre 97.

Chiesa di San Francesco

Perugia's Fra Bevignate is said to have designed this church *(Piazza Quaranta Martiri; free; open 7.15am-noon & 3.30pm-7.30pm daily)*. It features impressive frescoes by a local artist, Ottaviano Nelli. Wander into the **Chiostro della Pace** (Cloister of Peace) in the adjoining convent to view some ancient mosaics.

Piazza Grande

Gubbio's most impressive buildings look out over Piazza Grande, dominated above all by the 14th-century **Palazzo dei Consoli**, attributed to Gattapone. The crenellated facade and tower can be seen from all over the town. The building houses the **Museo Civico** *(☎ 075 927 42 98, Piazza Grande; adults/under-25s €3.60/2.05 including gallery; open 10am-1pm & 3pm-6pm daily Apr-Sept, 10am-1pm & 2pm-5pm daily Oct-Mar)*. This displays the Eugubian Tables, discovered in 1444 near the Teatro Romano (Roman Theatre) south-west of Piazza Quaranta Martiri (See Other Things to See). The seven bronze tablets are the main source for research into the ancient Umbrian language. Upstairs is a picture gallery featuring works from the Gubbian school. Across the square is the **Palazzo Pretorio**, built along similar lines to its grander counterpart and now the city's town hall.

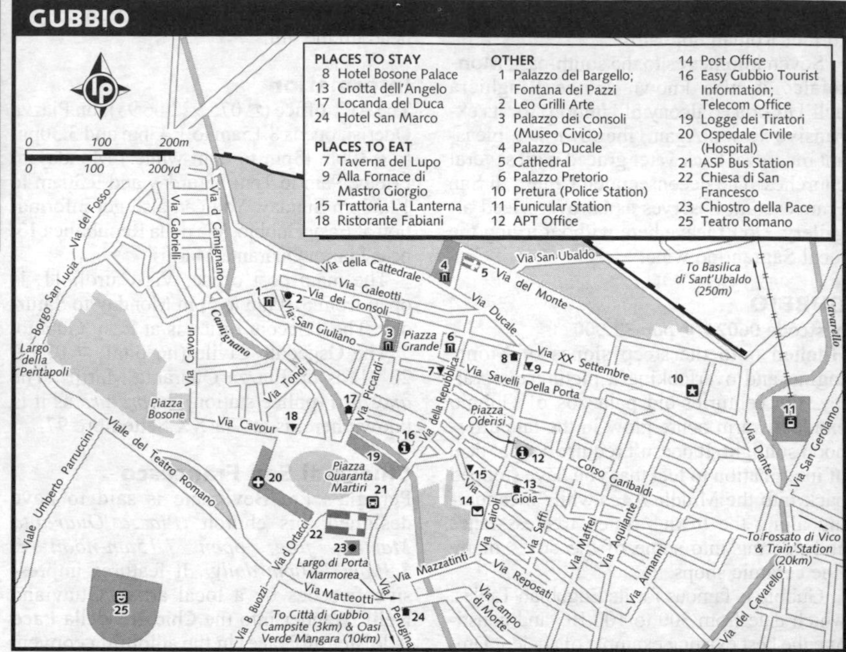

Cathedral & Palazzo Ducale

Via Ducale leads up to the 13th-century pink cathedral *(Via Federico da Montefeltro; donations welcome; open 9am-7pm Mon-Sat, 9am-1pm Sun)*, a plain beast with a fine 12th-century stained-glass window, a fresco attributed to Bernardino Pinturicchio and not much else. Opposite the cathedral, the 15th century **Palazzo Ducale** *(☎ 075 927 58 72, Via Federico da Montefeltro; adult/child €2.05/free; open 8.30am-7.30pm Tues-Sun)* was built by the Montefeltro family as a scaled-down version of their grand palazzo in Urbino, and its walls hide an impressive Renaissance courtyard.

Other Things to See

From Piazza Grande, Via dei Consoli leads west to the 13th-century **Palazzo del Bargello**, the city's medieval police station and prison. In front of it is the **Fontana dei Pazzi** (Fountain of Lunatics), so named because of a belief that if you walk around it three times, you will go mad – on summer weekends the number of tourists carrying out this ritual is indeed cause for concern about their collective sanity.

South-west of Piazza Quaranta Martiri, off Viale del Teatro Romano, are the overgrown remains of a 1st-century-AD **Teatro Romano** *(☎ 075 922 09 22; free; open 8.30am-7.30pm daily Apr-Sept, 8am-1.30pm daily Oct-Mar)*. Most of what you see is reconstructed.

From Via San Gerolamo you can ride the curious birdcage funicular (€4.65 return, 10 minutes) to the **Basilica di Sant'Ubaldo**, an uninspiring church that houses the three huge 'candles' used during the Corsa dei Ceri (see Special Events) and the preserved body of Sant'Ubaldo himself in a glass coffin above the altar.

Special Events

The Corsa dei Ceri (Candles Race) is held each year on 15 May to commemorate the city's patron saint, Sant'Ubaldo. The event starts at 5.30am and involves three teams, each carrying a *cero* (these 'candles' are massive wooden pillars weighing about 400kg, each bearing a statue of a 'rival' saint) and racing through the city's streets. This is one of Italy's liveliest festivals and warrants inclusion in your itinerary, but be wary if you have small children as the crowd gets excited and scuffles between the supporters of the three teams are common.

Also in May, on the last Sunday of the month, there's the annual Palio della Balestra, an archery competition involving medieval crossbows, in which Gubbio competes with its neighbour, Borgo San Sepolchro.

Shopping

Leo Grilli Arte *(☎ 075 922 22 72, Via dei Consoli 78)* Open 9.30am-1pm and 3pm-7pm Tues-Sun. In the Middle Ages, ceramics were one of Gubbio's main sources of income and there are some fabulous contemporary samples on display in this crumbly 15th-century mansion.

Places to Stay

Many locals rent rooms to tourists, so ask at the APT office about affittacamere.

Città di Gubbio *(☎/fax 075 927 20 37, Loc. Ortoguidone)* High season sites per person/tent €7.75/8.25. Open Apr-Sept. For camping, try this site in Ortoguidone, a southern suburb of Gubbio, about 3km south of Piazza Quaranta Martiri along the S298 (Via Perugina).

Locanda del Duca *(☎/fax 075 927 77 53, Via Piccardi 1)* Singles/doubles/triples from €33.60/43.90/54.20. One of the cheapest hotels in town, Locanda del Duca has just seven rooms, all with pleasant polished wood interiors.

Grotta dell'Angelo *(☎ 075 927 17 47, fax 075 927 34 38, ⓔ grottadellangelo@jumpy.it, Via Gioia 47)* Singles/doubles from €31/46.50. Closed 7 Jan-7 Feb. Clean, simple and welcoming, this two-star hotel has modern rooms and a charming garden restaurant.

Hotel San Marco *(☎ 075 922 02 34, fax 075 927 37 16, ⓔ info@hotelsanmarcogubbio.com, ⓦ www.hotelsanmarcogubbio.com, Via Perugina 5)* Singles/doubles up to €56.80/82.60. There are 60 rooms in this large converted monastery, so it's a bit too spacious to be cosy. Many of the rooms have traditional cross-beamed ceilings, a few have private balconies and there's a pleasant garden.

Hotel Bosone Palace *(☎ 075 922 06 88, fax 075 922 05 52, Via XX Settembre 22)* Low season singles/doubles €62/82.65, high season from €72.30/98.15. This chic three-star hotel has 17th-century frescoes in the breakfast room and benefits from its central position.

Oasi Verde Mengara *(☎ 075 92 01 56, fax 075 92 00 49, ⓔ mengara@tin.it, ⓦ www.gubbio.com/oasiverdemengara, Loc. Mengara Vallingegno 1)* Half-board up to €43.90 per person. Just 10km south of the city is the agriturismo Oasi Verde Mengara. Its fine restaurant is open to the public and you can eat a memorable and very filling meal for around €15.50. They also organise horse-riding (€12.90 per hour). Oasi Verdi Mengara is easily accessible from Gubbio using the regular APM bus to Perugia, which stops right outside (ask the driver to tell you when to get off).

Places to Eat

Lose yourself in Gubbio's labyrinthine streets and sample some of the nosh on offer.

Ristorante Fabiani *(☎ 075 927 46 39, Piazza Quaranta Martiri 26)* Meals around €15.50. Open Wed-Mon. This place is a large traditional trattoria with garden seating.

Trattoria La Lanterna *(☎ 075 927 66 94, Via Gioia 23)* Meals around €15.50. Open Fri-Wed. Here, where local specialities are on hand, many meals feature delicious *tartufi* (truffles).

Alla Fornace di Mastro Giorgio *(☎ 075 922 18 36, Via Mastro Giorgio 2)* Mains from €15.50. Open Wed-Mon. One of the better restaurants in town, this is also one of the more expensive, with dining in elegant surroundings.

Taverna del Lupo *(☎ 075 927 43 68, Via Ansidei 21)* Set meals from €18.80. Open Tues-Sun. Stylish, yet not too extravagant, this restaurant serves up good food with impeccable service.

Getting There & Around

APM buses run to Perugia (€3.80, one hour 10 minutes, 10 daily), Gualdo Tadino (€2.25, 50 minutes, 10 daily) and Umbertide (€2.60, 50 minutes, three daily) and the company operates a service to Rome (€14.45, four hours) leaving daily at 5.50am. Buses depart from Piazza Quaranta Martiri. You can buy tickets at Easy Gubbio, Via della Repubblica 13.

The closest train station is at Fossato di Vico, about 20km south-east of the city. Trains run from Fossato to Rome (€10.10, 2½ hours, eight daily), Ancona (€4.20, one hour 20 minutes, nine daily), and Foligno (€2.40, 40 minutes, roughly hourly) where you can pick up connections to Arezzo, Perugia and Florence. Hourly APM buses connect the station with Gubbio (€1.95, 30 minutes), although there are delays between train and bus connections of anything between five minutes and an hour.

By car or motorcycle, take the S298 from Perugia or the S76 from Ancona, and follow the signs. Parking in the large car park in Piazza Quaranta Martiri costs €0.50 per hour.

Walking is the best way to get around, but ASP buses connect Piazza Quaranta Martiri with the funicular station and most main sights.

AROUND GUBBIO

Parco Regionale del Monte Cucco

East of Gubbio, this park is a haven for outdoor activities and is dotted with caves, many of which can be explored. It is well set up for walkers, rock climbers and horse riders, and has many hotels and *rifugi* (mountain huts). **Costacciaro**, accessible by bus from Gubbio (€1.95, 30 minutes) via Scheggia or Fossato di Vico, is a good base for exploring the area and is the starting point for a walk to the summit of Monte Cucco (1566m).

The Centro Escursionistico Naturalistico Speleologico (☎ 075 917 04 00, Ⓦ www.infoservice.it/ass/cens), Via Galeazzi 5 in Costacciaro, can help with information about exploring local caves, walking and mountain-bike routes. Club Alpino Italiano (CAI) produces a walking map, *Carta dei Sentieri Massiccio del Monte Cucco*, for sale in local bookshops and newsagents (€4.65). Those interested in horse riding should try the Campeggio Rio Verde camp site (☎ 075 917 01 38), 3km west of Costacciaro. They charge €12.90 per hour, but horses are only available for hire during July and August. Many agriturismo establishments in the area can also arrange horse riding; the APT office in Gubbio has further details. It is possible to hire mountain bikes at the Coop Arte e Natura (☎ 075 917 07 40), Via Stazione 2, in the village of Fossato di Vico, about 8km south-east of Costacciaro.

Alte Valle del Tevere

The northernmost reaches of Umbria, clamped in between Tuscany and Le Marche and known as the Alta Valle del Tevere (Upper Tiber Valley), hardly constitute the region's showcase, but there are a few odds and ends to keep you occupied. Among the more interesting spots are **Città di Castello**, which was a powerful centre during the Renaissance, **Umbertide**, with a couple of castles and dominated by a 14th-century fortress (closed to the public), and **San Giustino**, whose centre is graced by the Castello Bufalini. The area is connected with Perugia by the private Ferrovia Centrale Umbra railway and the occasional bus. SITA buses also connect the valley with nearby Arezzo in Tuscany and then on to Florence. The best way to see the area is by car or motorcycle.

SPOLETO

postcode 06049 • pop 37,360

Each June and July, this otherwise quiet town takes centre stage for an international parade of drama, music, opera and dance (see Special Events later).

If you plan to visit Spoleto during the festival, book accommodation and tickets months in advance. When the festival ends, Spoleto goes back to sleep, but it's nonetheless an enchanting town to spend a day or two exploring.

Orientation

The old part of the city is about 1km south of the main train station – take the orange shuttle bus marked A, B or C for Piazza della Libertà in the centre, where you'll find the tourist office and the Roman-era theatre. Piazza del Mercato, a short walk north-east of Piazza della Libertà, marks the engaging heart of old Spoleto. Between here and Piazza del Duomo you'll find the bulk of the city's monuments and some fine shops.

Information

Tourist Offices The APT office (☎ 0743 22 03 11), Piazza della Libertà 7, has lots of information about the town. It opens 9am to 1pm and 4pm to 7pm Monday to Friday in summer, 9am to 1pm and 3.30pm to 6.30pm Monday to Friday in winter and 10am to 1pm and 4pm to 7pm Saturday year-round.

Post & Communications The main post office faces Piazza della Libertà, although the entrance is off Viale Giacomo Matteotti. It opens 8.15am to 7pm Monday to Saturday.

The main Telecom office is at Via A Saffi 5, opens 8am to 10pm daily. There's an Internet terminal at *A Tuta Birra*, a pub at Via di Fontesecca 7.

Medical Services & Emergency The casualty section of the Ospedale di Madonna di Loreto (hospital; ☎ 0743 21 01) is on Via Madonna di Loreto, west of Porta San Matteo. For an ambulance, call ☎ 0743 4 48 88. The *questura* (police station; ☎ 0743 4 03 24) is on Viale Trento e Trieste, a block south of the train station.

Roman Spoleto

Make your first stop the **Teatro Romano** *(☎ 0743 22 32 77, Via S Agata; adult/child €2.05/1, includes museum; open 9am-7pm daily)* on the western edge of Piazza della Libertà. The 1st-century theatre has been rebuilt many times and is currently used for performances during the summer. Have a quick look at the ceramics collection in the **Museo Archeologico** next to the theatre.

East of Piazza della Libertà, around Piazza Fontana, are more Roman remains, including the **Arco di Druso e Germanico** (Arch of Drusus and Germanicus; sons of the Emperor Tiberius), which marks the entrance to the old forum. The excavated **Casa Romana** *(Roman house; ☎ 0743 437 07, Via di Visiale; adult/child €2.05/1; open 10am-1pm & 3pm-6pm Wed-Mon)* dates from the 1st century.

The city boasts an **Anfiteatro Romano** (Roman Amphitheatre), one of the country's largest. Unfortunately it is within military barracks and closed to the public. Wander along Via dell'Anfiteatro, off Piazza Garibaldi, in search of a glimpse.

Churches

A short walk north through Piazza del Municipio takes you to the 12th-century **Chiesa di Sant'Eufemia** *(☎ 0743 23 10 22, Via A. Saffi; adult/child €3.10/1.55 including Museo Diocesano next door; open 10am-12.30pm & 3.30pm-7pm daily in summer, 10am-12.30pm & 3.30pm-6pm daily in winter)*. Set within the grounds of the Archbishop's palazzo, it is notable for its *matronei* – galleries set high above the main body of the church to segregate the female congregation. Artists from the 15th-century Sienese school left behind some striking frescoes.

From here, it is a quick stroll north-east to the **cathedral** *(☎ 0743 443 07, Piazza del Duomo; free; open 7.30am-12.30pm & 3pm-6pm daily in summer, 7.30am-12.30pm & 3pm-5pm daily in winter)*, consecrated in 1198 and remodelled in the 17th century. The Romanesque facade is fronted by a striking Renaissance porch. In the 11th century, huge blocks of stone salvaged from Roman buildings were put to good use in the construction of the rather sombre bell tower. Inside, the first chapel to the right of the nave was decorated by Bernardino Pinturicchio, and Annibale Carracci completed an impressive fresco in the right transept. The frescoes in the domed apse were executed by Filippo Lippi and his assistants. Lippi died before completing the work and Lorenzo de Medici travelled to Spoleto from Florence and ordered Lippi's son, Filippino, to build a mausoleum for the artist. This now stands in the

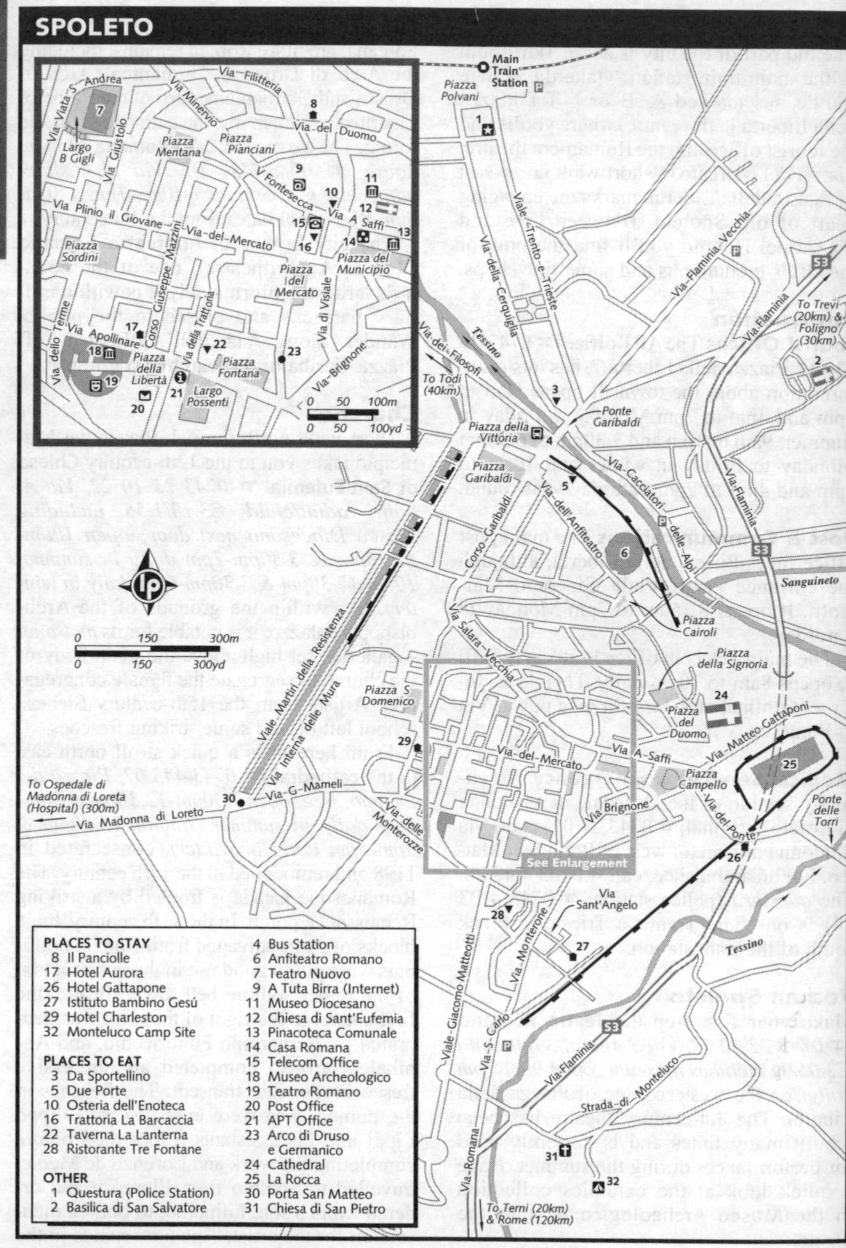
SPOLETO
Main Train Station
Piazza Polvani
Via Filitteria
Via Viata S Andrea
Via Minervio
Largo B Gigli
Via Giustolo
Piazza Mentana
Piazza Pianciani
Via del Duomo
Fontesecca
Via A Saffi
Via Plinio il Giovane
Via del Mercato
Piazza Sordini
Corso Giuseppe Mazzini
Piazza del Mercato
Piazza del Municipio
Via di Visiale
Via della Trattoria
Via dello Terme
Via Apollinare
Piazza della Libertà
Piazza Fontana
Largo Possenti
Via Brignone
0 50 100m
0 50 100yd
Viale Trento e Trieste
Via della Cerquiglia
Via Flaminia Vecchia
Via Flaminia
To Trevi (20km) & Foligno (30km)
Tessino
Via dei Filosofi
To Todi (40km)
Ponte Garibaldi
Piazza della Vittoria
Piazza Garibaldi
Via Cacciatori delle Alpi
Via dell'Anfiteatro
Corso Garibaldi
Via Salara Vecchia
Sanguineto
Piazza Cairoli
Piazza della Signoria
Piazza del Duomo
Via Matteo Gattaponi
Piazza S Domenico
Viale Martiri della Resistenza
Via Interna delle Mura
0 150 300m
0 150 300yd
Via del Mercato
Via A Saffi
Piazza Campello
Via Brignone
Via del Ponte
Ponte delle Torri
To Ospedale di Madonna di Loreta (Hospital) (300m)
Via Madonna di Loreto
Via G Mameli
Via delle Monterozze
See Enlargement
Via Sant'Angelo
Via Monterone
Viale Giacomo Matteotti
Via S Carlo
Via Flaminia
Strada di Monteluco
Via Romana
To Terni (20km) & Rome (120km)
PLACES TO STAY
8 Il Panciolle
17 Hotel Aurora
26 Hotel Gattapone
27 Istituto Bambino Gesú
29 Hotel Charleston
32 Monteluco Camp Site
PLACES TO EAT
3 Da Sportellino
5 Due Porte
10 Osteria dell'Enoteca
16 Trattoria La Barcaccia
22 Taverna La Lanterna
28 Ristorante Tre Fontane
OTHER
1 Questura (Police Station)
2 Basilica di San Salvatore
4 Bus Station
6 Anfiteatro Romano
7 Teatro Nuovo
9 A Tuta Birra (Internet)
11 Museo Diocesano
12 Chiesa di Sant'Eufemia
13 Pinacoteca Comunale
14 Casa Romana
15 Telecom Office
18 Museo Archeologico
19 Teatro Romano
20 Post Office
21 APT Office
23 Arco di Druso e Germanico
24 Cathedral
25 La Rocca
30 Porta San Matteo
31 Chiesa di San Pietro

right transept of the cathedral. No 8 on Piazza del Duomo is the house where composer Gian Carlo Menotti stays when in town. The spectacular closing concert of the Spoleto Festival is held on the piazza.

Other Things to See

Inside the town hall on Piazza del Municipio is the **Pinacoteca Comunale** *(☎ 0743 21 82 70, Via A Saffi; adult/child €2.05/1; open 10am-1pm and 4pm-7pm Tues-Sun, guided tour only)*. It is a sumptuous building, with some impressive works by Umbrian artists.

Dominating the city is the **Rocca** *(☎ 0743 437 07, Piazza Campello, adult/child €4.65/ 3.60; open 10am-6pm daily by guided tour only, reservations essential)*, a former papal fortress that until 1982 was a high-security prison housing such notables as Pope John Paul II's attempted assassin, Ali Agca.

Along Via del Ponte is the **Ponte delle Torri**, erected in the 14th century on the foundations of a Roman aqueduct. The bridge is named after the towers on the far side.

If you feel like a walk, cross the bridge and follow the lower path, Strada di Monteluco, to reach the **Chiesa di San Pietro** *(☎ 0743 448 82, Loc. San Pietro; free; open 9.30am-11am & 3.30pm-6.30pm daily)*. The 13th-century facade, the church's main attraction, is liberally bedecked with sculpted animals.

Special Events

The Italian-American composer Gian Carlo Menotti conceived the Festival dei Due Mondi (Festival of Two Worlds) in 1958. Now known simply as the Spoleto Festival, it has given the city a worldwide reputation and brought great wealth to the small population, which basks in its reflected glory. However, the festival is not what it once was. For the past decade or so, there have been severe funding crises, affecting both the quality and quantity of events. While ticket prices continue to creep up, cutting-edge performances, for which the festival gained its reputation, are now rarely seen. Moreover, in recent years ongoing squabbles between the local authorities and the festival organisers have resulted in threats to relocate the festival.

Events at the festival, held over three weeks from late June to mid-July, range from opera and theatre to ballet and art exhibitions. Tickets cost from €5.15 to €103.30, depending on the performance and whether you want luxury seats or standing room, and generally sell out by March or April. There are usually several free concerts in various churches.

For information, call ☎ 0743 4 47 00, fax 0743 4 05 46, or write to The Box Office, Piazza della Libertà 12, 06049 Spoleto, Italy. You can find further details and book tickets online at W www.spoletofestival.it.

Places to Stay

The city is well served by cheap hotels, affittacamere, hostels and camp sites, although if you're coming for the festival you will need to book a room months in advance.

Monteluco *(☎/fax 0743 22 03 58, Loc. San Pietro)* High season site per person/tent €4.10/4.10. Open Apr-Sept. This leafy, quiet camp site is just behind the Chiesa di San Pietro, in easy walking distance of the town centre.

There are also agriturismo options around Spoleto. The APT office has a booklet with the details.

Istituto Bambino Gesù *(☎ 0743 402 32, Via Sant'Angelo 4)* Singles/doubles €25.80/ 51.65 with breakfast. The nuns at this religious institution, just off Via Monterone, are incredibly welcoming and the convent itself is very attractive. What's more, the perfect silence means you're guaranteed to sleep like a log.

Hotel Aurora *(☎ 0743 22 03 15, fax 0743 22 18 85, e info@hotelauroraspoleto.it, W www.hotelauroraspoleto.it, Via Apollinare 3)* Low season singles/doubles from €41.30/46.50, high season €59.40/75.40. Just off Piazza della Libertà, the Aurora is very central. Some rooms have pleasant balconies and breakfast is excellent.

Il Panciolle *(☎/fax 0743 456 77, Via del Duomo 3)* Singles/doubles with bath from €36.15/51.65. This very sweet, comfortable hotel near the cathedral has its own restaurant downstairs and is a reliable bet.

Charleston (☎ *0743 22 02 52, fax* ... *12 44,* e *info@hotelcharleston.it,* w *www.hotelcharleston.it, Piazza Collicola 10)* Low season singles/doubles €31/62, high season €67.15/103.30. The Charleston has a relaxing chalet feel with an open fireplace in the hall and wood-panelled rooms. It's very agreeable and there's a great little terrace outside for breakfast.

Hotel Gattapone *(☎ 0743 22 34 47, fax 0743 22 34 48, Via del Ponte 6)* Singles/doubles from €103.30/134.30 to €118.80/154.95. For rooms overlooking the Ponte delle Torri, this place is in a top location and the interiors are suitably chic.

Places to Eat

Spoleto is one of Umbria's main centres for the *tartufo nero* (black truffle), used in a variety of dishes. Trying them can be a costly exercise – so check the price before digging in.

Taverna la Lanterna *(☎ 0743 498 15, Via della Trattoria 6)* Full meals about €12.90. Open Thurs-Tues. A great place in the town centre is La Lanterna, serving a variety of Umbrian pasta dishes with liberal sprinklings of tartufi and good vegetarian options.

Osteria dell'Enoteca *(☎ 0743 22 04 84, Via A Saffi 7)* Tourist menu €10.30. Open Wed-Mon. A small but good value spot, Osteria dell'Enoteca's set menus incorporate local ingredients. You can also buy some typical Umbrian wine and food products here.

Trattoria la Barcaccia *(☎ 0743 22 11 71, Piazza Fratelli Bandiera 2)* Tourist menu €15.50. Open Wed-Mon. The *strangozzi al tartufo* (pasta with truffles) is the house speciality at this restaurant but, at the time of writing, the veranda looked straight onto a building site.

Ristorante Tre Fontane *(☎ 0743 22 15 44, Via Egio 15)* Pizzas from €3.60. Open Thurs-Tues. This is a great spot for pizza in an informal but pleasant garden dining area.

There are a couple of good restaurants to be found outside the old town.

Due Porte *(☎ 0743 403 99, Piazza della Vittoria 14)* Set meals with wine €12.90, pasta from €3.60. Open Mon-Sat. This is a very informal but wonderfully affordable trattoria just off Piazza della Vittoria.

Da Sportellino *(☎ 0743 452 30, Via della Cerquiglia 4)* Main courses from €7.75. Open Fri-Wed. This friendly, traditional trattoria has lots of tables for two and is just a couple of minutes' walk north of the city walls.

Getting There & Around

Most Società Spoletina di Imprese Trasporti (SSIT) buses (☎ 0743 21 22 11) depart from Piazza della Vittoria and some also make a stop at the train station to pick up passengers. Buses to Perugia (€5.15, one hour) leave daily at 6.20am and 7.10am. There are also services to Bastardo (€2.60, 40 minutes, five daily), Norcia (€4.15, one hour, six daily) and dozens of other small towns. Buses to Monteluco run only in summer (€0.60, 15 minutes, every two hours).

Trains from the main station (☎ 0743 485 16), Piazza Polvani, connect with Rome (€6.80-13.20, one to 2½ hours, hourly), Ancona (€7.75, two hours, 10 daily), Perugia (€3.40, one hour, hourly) and Assisi (€2.40, 30 minutes, hourly).

The city is easily explored on foot, though local buses weave through the streets. Orange shuttle buses A, B and C run between the train station, Piazza Garibaldi and Piazza della Libertà (€0.60).

THE VALNERINA

Incorporating most of the lower eastern parts of Umbria, along the River Nera, the Valnerina is a beautiful area. Stretching north-east to the barren summit of Monte Sibilla (2175m) in neighbouring Le Marche, it makes for great walking territory. It also has a couple of hang-gliding schools in one of the best areas of Europe to learn.

If you plan to spend a few quiet days wandering the valley, the pretty medieval village of Preci is a good place to stay.

Agli Scacchi *(☎/fax 0743 9 92 21, Q.re Scacchi 12, Preci)* Singles/doubles from €25.80/41.30, half-board from €36.15 per person. This small but pleasant two-star hotel is in the pretty medieval village of Preci.

The area is criss-crossed by walking trails and you might try to pick up a copy of the aptly titled *20 Sentieri Ragionati in Valnerina* (20 Well-Thought-Out Routes in Valnerina; in Italian), available for free from local tourist offices in the region.

If you are driving, the APT Valnerina-Cascia (☎ 0743 711 47), Piazza Garibaldi 1, in Cascia, is a good place to go for information. Tourist bodies in Umbria and Le Marche have erected road signs identifying suggested itineraries.

Getting There & Away

Spoleto is the best point from which to head into the Valnerina. Spoleto's SSIT bus company (☎ 0743 21 22 11) operates buses from Piazza Stazione to the terminal at Via della Stazione in Norcia (€4.15, one hour, six daily), from where connecting buses run along the Valnerina to Preci (€1.95, 40 minutes, Monday to Saturday at 1.25pm) and Cascia (€1.95, 30 minutes, nine daily). Getting to Castelluccio is not so easy, as there are only two services from Norcia, both on Thursday at 6.25am and 1.30pm (€2.60, 50 minutes).

The S395 from Spoleto and the S209 from Terni join with the S320 and then the S396, which passes through Norcia. The area is also accessible from Ascoli Piceno in Le Marche.

Norcia

This fortified medieval village is the valley's main town and a transport hub of sorts. Like the rest of the Valnerina, Norcia has suffered from earthquakes over the centuries; several buildings were damaged in 1997. For tourist information, visit the Casa del Parco (☎ 0743 81 70 90) at Via Solferino 22, open 9.30am to 12.30pm and 3pm to 6pm Monday to Friday, and 9.30am to 12.30pm and 3.30pm to 6.30pm on Saturday and Sunday.

Activities The Casa del Parco has information on walking and other activities in the surrounding area. Hang-gliders should aim for Castelluccio (for more details see Around Norcia).

Places to Stay & Eat Norcia produces what is considered to be the country's best salami and is a stronghold of the elusive black truffle.

Da Benito *(☎ 0743 81 66 70, fax 0743 82 42 42, Via Marconi 5)* High season singles/doubles up to €36.15/51.65. This is a friendly one-star hotel with eight modest rooms above a family-run restaurant within the city walls.

Hotel Grotta Azzura *(☎ 0743 81 65 13, fax 0743 81 73 42, ⓔ info-booking@bianconi.com, Ⓦ www.bianconi.com, Via Alfieri 12)* High season singles/doubles €72.30/82.65. In the low season, prices literally halve at this hotel, an 18th-century palazzo with suits of armour in the reception. Downstairs, a vast medieval-style banquet hall with stuffed boars' heads adorning the walls, is one of Norcia's better restaurants.

Around Norcia

If you have a car, don't miss the opportunity to visit the vast **Piano Grande**, a high plateau east of Norcia, under Monte Vettore (2476m). It becomes a sea of colour as flowers bloom in early spring.

Perched above the Piano Grande is the tiny, hilltop village of **Castelluccio**, famous for its lentils and *pecorino* and *ricotta* cheeses.

You can camp just about anywhere on the Piano Grande, but if you want to stay in town overnight, Castelluccio does have one hotel.

Albergo Sibilla *(☎ 0743 87 01 13, Via Piano Grande 2)* Singles/doubles from €25.80/41.30. This hotel has just 11 rooms, so try to bag one with a view. There's a good restaurant downstairs.

The area forms part of the **Parco Nazionale dei Monti Sibillini**, where you can indulge several outdoor whims. Before going off into the Monti Sibillini, at least buy Kompass map No 666 (scale 1:50,000) of walking trails, available from the Casa del Parco in Norcia.

If you want to learn hang-gliding, contact Pro Delta (☎ 0743 82 11 56), Via delle Fate 3, in Castelluccio; it opens in summer only. Another school is Fly Castelluccio, but the office (☎ 0736 25 56 30) is based at Via

Iannella 32, Ascoli Piceno, in the neighbouring region of Le Marche. A beginners course of five days will cost about €361.50.

This is also mountain-bike territory. To hire bikes you could try the Associazione Pian Grande (☎ 0743 81 72 79, 0743 81 70 22), Pian Grande di Castelluccio di Norcia, which is open mostly in the afternoons from Easter to October. They can also arrange horse riding.

TERNI

postcode 05100 • pop 110,484

Terni is a major industrial city, virtually obliterated in WWII bombing raids and subsequently rebuilt. San Valentino was born here and was bishop of Terni until his martyrdom in AD 269. If you're using public transport, you might need to pass through here on the way to the Valnerina, Norcia and the Monti Sibillini.

Terni's IAT office (☎ 0744 42 30 47, e info@iat.terni.it) is south of the main train station and just west of Piazza C Tacito at Viale Cesare Battisti 7, near Largo Don Minzoni. It opens 9am to 1pm and 3.30pm to 6.30pm Monday to Thursday, 9am to 1pm Friday.

At Easter, Terni's theatres, churches and streets are given over to the Gospel and Soul Festival, a spin-off of the Umbria Jazz festival (see Special Events under Perugia earlier in this chapter), which attracts international performers. Ask at the tourist office or the main Umbria Jazz office in Perugia.

If you arrive in Terni by train and need to get to the bus station on Piazza Europa, or vice versa, catch local bus No 1 or 2.

Cascata delle Marmore

About 6km east of Terni, this waterfall was created by the Romans in 290 BC when they diverted the Velino river into the River Nera. These days the waterfall provides hydroelectric power and its flow is confined to certain times of the day. It is worth catching a bus to see it, particularly to witness the arrival of the water after it has been switched on. The falls operate on weekends year-round, usually for an hour or so before noon and again for a couple of hours in the late afternoon and early evening. They also flow for a few hours (usually afternoons around 4pm) on weekdays from mid-March to the end of August. Ask at the Terni tourist office for the exact times that the water is turned on. The water is illuminated in the course of a sound-and-light show. Whenever the waterfall is switched on, the S79 road connecting Terni with Rieti resembles a car park as drivers stop to gawk at the spectacle. Local bus No 24 runs from the bus station on Piazza Europa to the falls. A number of short walking tracks around the falls allow you to get close up.

ORVIETO

postcode 05018 • pop 21,600

The phalanxes of high-season tourists who crowd into Orvieto are drawn first and foremost by the magnificent cathedral, one of Italy's finest Gothic buildings. The town rests on top of a craggy cliff, pretty much in the same spot as its precursor, the Etruscan League city of Velsina. Although medieval Orvieto is the magnet, Etruscan tombs and the city's underground chambers testify to the area's antiquity.

Orientation

Trains pull in at Orvieto Scalo, the modern, downhill extension of the town. From here you can catch bus No 1 up to the old town or board the funicular to Piazza Cahen. From the funicular and bus station, walk straight along Corso Cavour, turning left into Via del Duomo to reach the cathedral. There's plenty of parking space in Piazza Cahen and in several designated areas outside the old city walls.

Information

The APT office (☎ 0763 34 17 72, e info@iat.orvieto.tr.it), Piazza del Duomo 24, opens 8.15am to 1.50pm and 4pm to 7pm Monday to Friday, 10am to 1pm and 4pm to 7pm Saturday, and 10am to noon and 4pm to 6pm Sunday.

If you plan to spend more than a day in Orvieto, and to see absolutely everything the town has to offer, consider buying the Orvieto Unica card (€10.30), which entitles you

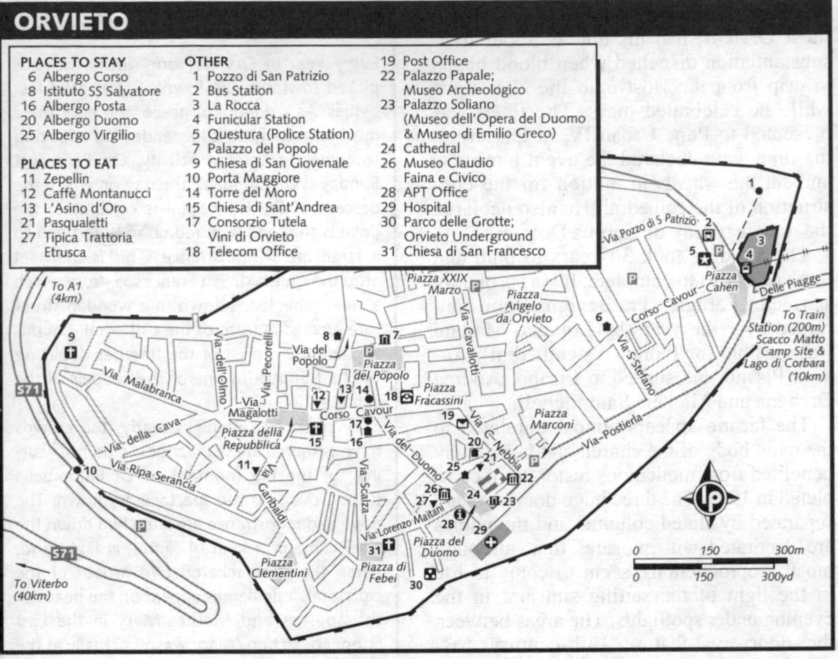

to five hours' free car parking at the train station or a return trip on the funicular and city buses, plus admission (only once) to the Cappella di San Brizio in the cathedral, the Museo Claudio Faina e Civico, the Torre del Moro (Moor's Tower) and Orvieto Underground in Parco delle Grotte (for details of all these attractions see Around the Cathedral and Other Things to See later). The card is valid for one year.

There are several banks, all with Visa and MasterCard-friendly ATMs, on Piazza della Repubblica.

The post office is on Via Cesare Nebbia, off Corso Cavour, and opens 8.10am to 6pm Monday to Saturday. There is an unstaffed Telecom office at Corso Cavour 119 and an Internet terminal at Caffè Montanucci (see Places to Eat for details).

The hospital (☎ 0763 30 91) is on Piazza del Duomo. In a medical emergency, call ☎ 0763 34 02 44. The *questura* (police station; ☎ 0763 34 47 93) is on Piazza Cahen.

The Cathedral

Little can prepare you for the visual feast that is the cathedral *(☎ 0763 34 11 67, Piazza del Duomo; free; open 7.30am-12.45pm daily year-round plus 2.30pm-7.15pm daily Apr-Sept, 2.30pm-6.15pm daily Mar & Oct & 2.30pm-5.15pm daily Nov-Feb)*. Started in 1290, this remarkable edifice was originally planned in the Romanesque style but, as work proceeded and architects changed, Gothic features were incorporated into the structure. The black-and-white marble banding of the main body of the church, reminiscent of other great churches you may already have seen in Tuscan cities such as Siena and Pisa, is overshadowed by the rich rainbow colours of the facade. A harmonious blend of mosaic and sculpture, plain stone and dazzling colour, it has been likened to a giant outdoor altar screen.

Pope Urban IV ordered that the cathedral be built, following the so-called Miracle of Bolsena in 1263. A Bohemian priest who was passing through the town of Bolsena (near Orvieto) had his doubts about transubstantiation dispelled when blood began to drip from the Host onto the altar linen while he celebrated mass. The linen was presented to Pope Urban IV, in Orvieto at the time, who declared the event a miracle and set the wheels in motion for the construction of the cathedral. He also declared the new feast day of Corpus Domini.

The building took 30 years to plan and three centuries to complete. It was probably started by Perugia's Fra Bevignate and continued over the years by Lorenzo Maitani (responsible for Florence's cathedral), Andrea Pisano, his son Nino Pisano, Andrea Orcagna and Michele Sammichelli.

The **facade** appears almost unrelated to the main body of the church and has greatly benefited from meticulous restoration, completed in 1995. The three huge doorways are separated by fluted columns and the gables are decorated with mosaics that, although mostly reproductions, seem to come to life in the light of the setting sun and in the evening under spotlights. The areas between the doorways feature 14th-century bas-reliefs of scriptural scenes by Maitani and his pupils, while the rose window is by Andrea Orcagna. The great bronze doors, the work of Emilio Greco, were added in the 1960s.

After the splendour of the exterior, the interior may at first be a disappointment. Brace yourself, however: reopened in late 1996 after years of painstaking restoration, Luca Signorelli's fresco cycle *The Last Judgement* shimmers with life. Look for it to the right of the altar in the **Cappella di San Brizio** *(admission €1.55; open 10am-12.45pm daily year-round, plus 2.30pm-7.15pm daily Apr-Sept, 2.30pm-6.15pm daily Mar & Oct & 2.30pm-5.15pm Mon-Sat & 2.30pm-5.45pm Sun Nov-Feb; closed during Mass)*. Signorelli began work on the series in 1499, and Michelangelo is said to have taken inspiration from it when he began the Sistine Chapel fresco of the same subject 40 years later. Indeed, to some, Michelangelo's masterpiece runs a close second to Signorelli's work. Not to be ignored in the chapel are ceiling frescoes by Fra Angelico.

The Dove Has Landed

Every year in Orvieto, one 'lucky' dove is picked to star in the town's Pentecostal festivities. As a symbol of peace, the poor thing must wonder how it has ended up in such a supremely disturbing activity. On Pentecost Sunday (Whit Sunday), the day on which the descent of the Holy Spirit is celebrated, the dove is strapped with red ribbons and tied to a large metal monstrance. This is then set atop the Chiesa di San Francesco, from which a steel cable loops down to a wooden structure erected in front of the cathedral. On this is painted a replica of the frescoes depicting the Last Supper in one of the chapels of the cathedral.

By noon everything is ready; the crowds have gathered in the Piazza del Duomo, waiting for the big moment of La Palombella ('The Dove'), as the spectacle is known. The dove and monstrance are launched down the steel cable in a kind of flightless flight and, when the straitjacketed bird arrives at the cathedral, little flames appear on the heads of the apostles and Mother Mary in the Last Supper depiction (Mary wasn't actually at the supper but, for the purposes of the feast day, this anomaly is overlooked), and a salvo of mortars is let off.

Assuming our little winged friend survives without a heart attack (which it usually doesn't), it is solemnly handed over to the bishop in the Palazzo Soliano. After much officious speech-making, the bishop then gives the bird to a newly wed couple who are instructed to look after the creature for the remainder of its (hopefully less traumatic) life.

The people of Orvieto have celebrated Pentecost Sunday in this manner since at least 1404. In the old days, the whole thing was done inside the cathedral. Then in 1846 it was decided to hold the event outdoors, out of respect for the Roman Lateran Council's stipulations forbidding the use of fireworks or flares inside churches. That edict was issued in 1725, so one can only speculate as to why the church authorities of Orvieto delayed its application by a mere 121 years!

The **Cappella del Corporale** *(free; open 7.30am-12.45pm & 2.30pm-7.15pm daily in summer, shorter hours daily in winter; closed during Mass)* houses the blood-stained altar linen, preserved in a silver reliquary decorated by artists of the Sienese school. The walls feature frescoes depicting the miracle, painted by Ugolino di Prete Ilario.

Around the Cathedral

Next to the cathedral is the **Museo dell'Opera del Duomo** *(☎ 0763 34 24 77, Palazzo Soliano, Piazza del Duomo)*, which houses a clutter of religious relics from the cathedral, as well as Etruscan antiquities and works by artists such as Simone Martini and the three Pisanos: Andrea, Nino and Giovanni. The museum has been closed for restoration for ages but telephone or check at the APT office to see if it has reopened.

Museo di Emilio Greco *(☎ 0763 34 46 05, Palazzo Soliano, Piazza del Duomo; adult/child €2.60/1.55; open 10.30am-1pm & 2pm-6.30pm Tues-Sun Apr-Sept, 10.30am-1pm & 2pm-5.30pm Tues-Sun Oct-Mar)* displays a collection of modern pieces donated by the creator of the cathedral's bronze doors. A €4.15 combined ticket includes admission to the Pozzo di San Patrizio (see Other Things to See later).

Around the corner, you can see Etruscan antiquities in the **Museo Archeologico** *(☎ 0763 34 10 39, Palazzo Papale, Piazza del Duomo; admission €2.05; open 8.30am-7.30pm daily)*

In the unlikely event that your thirst for Etruscan widgets isn't quenched, try the **Museo Claudio Faina e Civico** *(☎ 0763 34 15 11, Piazza del Duomo 29; adult/child €4.15/2.60; open 9.30am-6pm daily Apr-Sept, 10am-5pm Tues-Sun Oct-Mar)* opposite the cathedral. Most of the stuff in here was found near Piazza Cahen in tombs dating back to the 6th century BC.

Other Things to See

Head north-west along Via del Duomo to Corso Cavour and you'll see the stout **Torre del Moro** *(Moor's Tower; ☎ 0763 34 45 67, Corso Cavour; adult/child €2.60/1.80; open 10am-8pm daily May-Aug, 10am-7pm daily Mar, Apr, Sept & Oct, 10.30am-1pm & 2.30pm-5pm daily Nov-Feb)*. Climb all 250 steps for sweeping, pigeon-eye views of the city. Back on ground level, continue west to Piazza della Repubblica, where you'll stumble upon the 12th-century **Chiesa di Sant'Andrea** *(Piazza della Repubblica; free; open 8.30am-12.30pm & 3.30pm-7.30pm daily)* and its curious decagonal bell tower. As with many Italian churches, it was built over a Roman structure, which itself incorporated an earlier Etruscan building. You can see the ancient foundations in the crypt. The piazza, once Orvieto's Roman forum, is at the heart of what remains of the medieval city.

North of Corso Cavour, the 12th-century Romanesque-Gothic **Palazzo del Capitano del Popolo** presides over the piazza of the same name. At the north-western end of town is the 11th-century **Chiesa di San Giovenale** *(Piazza Giovenale; free; open 8am-12.30pm & 3.30pm-6pm daily)*, its interior brightened by 13th- and 14th-century frescoes.

Standing watch at the town's easternmost tip is the 14th-century **La Rocca**, part of which is now a public garden. To the north of the fortress, the **Pozzo di San Patrizio** *(St Patrick's Well; ☎ 0763 34 37 68, Viale Sangallo; adult/child €3.10/2.05; open 10am-6.45pm daily Apr-Sept, 10am-5.45pm daily Oct-Mar)* is a well, which was sunk in 1527 on the orders of Pope Clement VII. More than 60m deep, it is lined by two spiral staircases for water-bearing mules.

For a trip back in time, **Orvieto Underground** *(☎ 0763 34 48 91, Parco delle Grotte; admission €5.15; open 11am-6pm daily)* is a fascinating tour of the city's underground caves which date from Etruscan times and were used throughout the medieval period when, among other things, they housed pigeons. The caves were still in use well into last century: the cool air meant that food could be safely stored before the advent of the fridge. They even doubled up as air-raid shelters in WWII. Tours leave from in front of the APT office on Piazza del Duomo at 11am, 12.15pm, 4pm and 5.15pm.

Special Events

Umbria Jazz Winter first took place in Orvieto in 1994 and is now well established on the global jazz calendar, attracting top international and Italian artists. It takes place from the end of December to early January. Ask at the APT office for a programme. See Special Events in the Perugia section earlier in this chapter for details.

Places to Stay

You should have no trouble getting a room here during most of the year, but it is always a good idea to book ahead if you're planning to come over New Year, during the Umbria Jazz Winter, in summer or at the weekend.

Scacco Matto *(☎ 0744 95 01 63, fax 0744 95 03 73, Lago di Cobra)* Sites per person/tent €4.15/4.65. The closest camp sites are about 10km east of the town, on Lago di Corbara near Baschi. Scacco Matto is tiny (just 12 pitches) and fairly basic but it stays open year-round.

Istituto SS Salvatore *(☎/fax 0763 34 29 10, ⓔ istitutosansalvatore@tiscalinet.it, Ⓦ www.argoweb.it/orvieto/ospitalita/case.uk.html, Via del Popolo 1)* Singles/doubles €31/51.65. The nuns prefer it if you stay a minimum of two nights at this simple but spotless religious hostel. There's a 10pm curfew.

Albergo Posta *(☎/fax 0763 34 19 09, Via L Signorelli 18)* Singles/doubles without bath €25.80/38.75, with bath €36.15/49.05. Rooms in this stolid 16th-century building are simple but have a quirky edge and the owners are friendly and helpful.

Albergo Corso *(☎/fax 0763 34 20 20, ⓔ hotelcorso@libero.it, Ⓦ www.argoweb.it/hotel_corso, Corso Cavour 343)* Singles/doubles with bath up to €56.80/77.45. This attractive three-star hotel near Piazza Cahen has 16 bright air-conditioned rooms all with private bath.

Albergo Duomo *(☎ 0763 34 18 87, fax 0763 39 49 73, ⓔ hotelduomo@tiscalinet.it, Ⓦ www.argoweb.it/hotel_duomo, Via di Maurizio 7)* Singles/doubles €51.65/82.65. Since its recent revamp, Albergo Duomo has become really rather swish; the rooms are very comfortable and a handful have views to the cathedral.

Albergo Virgilio *(☎ 0763 34 18 82, fax 0763 34 37 97, Piazza del Duomo 5)* High season single/doubles with bath €61.95/85.20. This three-star hotel has an unrivalled position on Piazza del Duomo but reception could do with smiling a bit more often.

Places to Eat

Look out for local dishes with tartufo and porcini.

Caffè Montanucci *(☎ 0763 34 12 61, Corso Cavour 21)* Hot dishes from €3.60. Open Thurs-Tues. This is a good place for a sandwich or pasta. They also make their own chocolates, which shouldn't be missed.

L'Asino d'Oro *(☎ 0763 34 44 06, Vicolo del Popolo 9)* Main courses around €7.75. Open Tues-Sun Apr-mid Oct and during the Jazz Festival. Despite its modest appearance, the food at this place is superb. Meals are served outside on wooden tables under an arbour and the menu changes daily.

Tipica Trattoria Etrusca *(☎ 0763 34 40 16, Via Lorenzo Maitani 10)* Mains from €7.75. Open Tues-Sun. This is a good trattoria just 100m from the cathedral. The chef's specialities include *coniglio all' Etrusca* (Etruscan-style rabbit cooked in aromatic herbs), fava beans and local dishes made with tartufo and porcini.

Ristorante Zeppelin *(☎ 0763 34 14 47, Via G Garibaldi 28)* Full meals €20.65-25.80. Open daily except Sunday evening. This natty place has a cool 1920s' atmosphere, jazz on the stereo and serves traditional Umbrian food with a creative twist.

Pasqualetti *(☎ 0763 34 10 34, Piazza del Duomo 14)* This gelateria serves mouth-watering ice-cream and there are plenty of tables on the piazza so you can gaze at the magnificent cathedral while you gobble.

Getting There & Away

Buses depart from the station on Piazza Cahen and make a stop to pick up passengers at the train station as well. COTRAL buses connect the city with Viterbo in Lazio (€2.80, 1½ hours, seven daily) and Bagnoregio (€1.55, one hour, seven daily). ATC buses (☎ 0763 34 22 65) run to Baschi (€1.75, 40 minutes, seven daily), Bolsena

(€2.60, 40 minutes, twice daily), Perugia (€8.70, two hours, one daily at 5.45am) and Todi (€4.15, one hour, at 1.55pm returning at 5.50am). SIRA (☎ 0763 417 30 053) runs a daily service to Rome at 8.10am, and at 7.10am on Sunday (€4.65, 1½ hours).

Trains run to Rome (€6.80, 1 hour 20 minutes, hourly) and Florence (€9.30, 2¼ hours, every two hours); change at Terontola for Perugia (€5.90, 1¼ hours, every two hours). The city is on the A1, and the S71 heads north to Lago di Trasimeno.

Getting Around

A century-old funicular connects Piazza Cahen with the train station, with carriages leaving every 15 minutes from 7.15am to 8.30pm daily (€0.65 or €0.85 including the bus from Piazza Cahen to Piazza del Duomo). Bus No 1 also runs up to the old town from the train station (€0.65). Once in Orvieto, the easiest way to see the city is on foot, although ATC bus A connects Piazza Cahen with Piazza del Duomo and bus B runs to Piazza della Repubblica.

AROUND ORVIETO

The Etruscans produced wine in the district, the Romans continued the tradition, and today the Orvieto Classico wines are among the country's most popular. There are 17 vineyards to visit in the area, but unfortunately one unlucky person can't quaff the produce – you need a car to reach the vineyards, as ATC bus services to most small towns nearby are irregular at best.

Grab a copy of the free pamphlet *Andar per Vigne* (in Italian) from the APT office or pop into the Consorzio Tutela Vini di Orvieto (☎ 0763 34 37 90), Corso Cavour 36 in Orvieto for details of its driving tour of the local vineyards.

Le Marche

Characterised by undulating countryside and peppered with quiet and seemingly untouched medieval towns and villages, Le Marche forms a narrow and little-travelled band between the Apennines and the Adriatic Sea. Now that Tuscany has overpriced itself and Umbria is well on the road to doing the same, Le Marche is becoming increasingly popular with Italians and foreigners intent on buying old farmhouses for renovation. Most visitors come for the Renaissance splendour of Urbino or to catch a ferry from Ancona, but the rest of the region deserves at least a few days exploration.

In the south-west, the treeless Monti Sibillini form an impressive and, in parts, forbidding stretch of the Apennines, with plenty to keep even the most die-hard walker busy for days. Unfortunately, much of the coastline has been overdeveloped, with rows of characterless seaside hotels and beaches swamped with umbrellas. It's not all doom-and-gloom – some of the nooks and crannies outside Ancona and around Senigallia and Pesaro are among the best the Adriatic has to offer.

The small hill towns, however, are the region's most enchanting feature. Urbino and Macerata are the best known, but the countryside is littered with little towns and villages, often crowned by an ancient castle or medieval monastery. In the south, Ascoli Piceno boasts a historic centre of elegant squares and several grand monuments in a web of narrow, cobbled lanes.

The Piceni, one of Italy's earliest tribes, were the first inhabitants of the area, which later fell under Roman control. The region prospered in the Middle Ages and boomed during the 15th and 16th centuries, when the powerful Montefeltro family ruled Urbino. Le Marche attracted great Renaissance architects and painters, and Urbino gave the world the genius of Raphael and Donato Bramante.

Local cuisine draws inspiration from two sources. Inland mountain dishes comprise fish, beef, lamb, mushrooms and *tartufi* (truffles). Nearer the sea, sole and prawns resembling lobsters are popular. *Brodetto* is a tempting fish stew common along the coast, while *vincisgrassi*, a rich lasagne with meat sauce, chicken livers and tartufo nero, is popular inland. The region produces a small amount of wine, with one of the best drops being Vernaccia di Serrapetrona, a sparkling red.

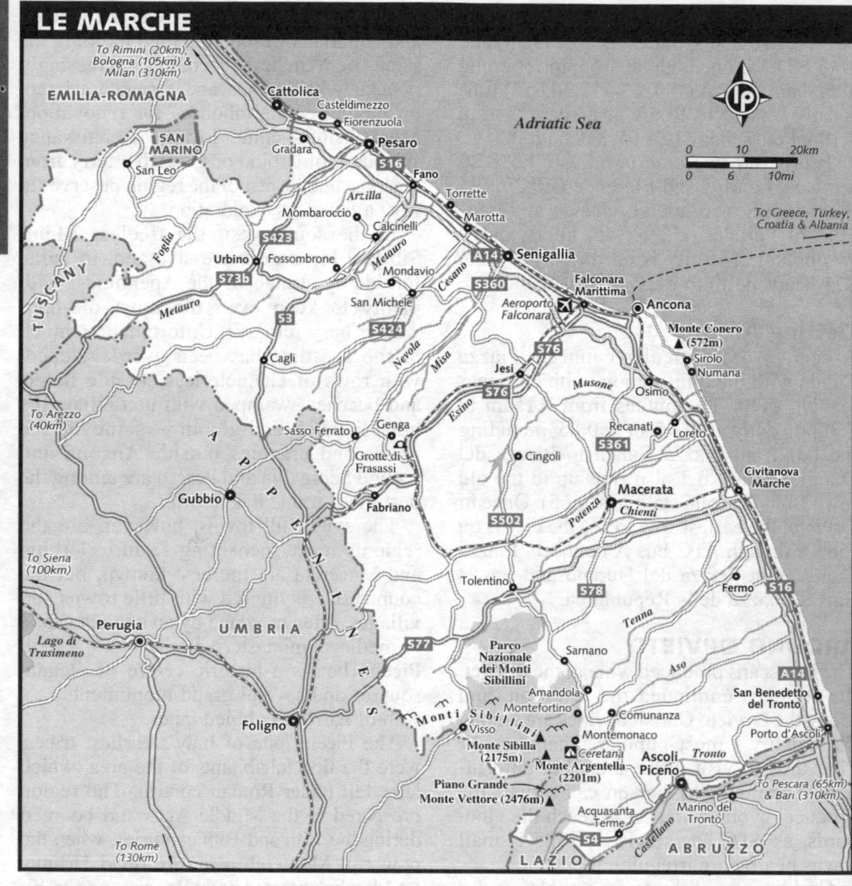

The A14 and S16 (Via Adriatica) hug the coastline, while the inland roads are good and provide easy access to all towns. Inland bus services are frequent and regular trains ply the coast on the Bologna-Lecce line.

ANCONA

postcode 60100 • pop 100,000

Most people visit Ancona in order to head off elsewhere, namely by ferry to Greece, Turkey, Croatia or Albania (although the Albania services mostly remained suspended at the time of writing). A major point of trade with the east since the Middle Ages, Ancona remains the mid-Adriatic's largest port, doing a healthy business in tourists as well as road freight. The old centre was heavily bombed in WWII but it still has a few faded gems to offer the listless voyager waiting for a boat.

Orientation

All trains arrive at the main station on Piazza Nello e Carlo Rosselli and some continue 1.5km north to the ferry terminal. From Largo Dogana, near the ferry terminal, walk uphill south-east to the central Piazza Roma and east to the city's grand

Piazza Cavour. There are several hotels near Piazza Roma and a cluster around the main train station. What remains of the old town stretches in an arc around the waterfront.

Information

Tourist Offices The main APT office (☎ 071 35 89 91, fax 071 358 99 29, ⓔ info.apt@regione.marche.it) is inconveniently placed at the eastern end of town at Via Thaon de Revel 4. In summer it opens 9am to 2pm and 3pm to 6pm Monday to Friday, 9am to 1pm and 3pm to 6pm Saturday, and 9am to 1pm Sunday; opening hours are shorter during the winter. There's a branch office at the ferry terminal (☎ 071 20 11 83), which opens 8am to 8pm Tuesday to Saturday and 2pm to 8pm on Sunday and Monday from 1 June to 15 September. There is a useful Web site at ⓦ www.comune.ancona.it.

Money There are currency exchange booths at the main train station and ferry terminal (where there is also an ATM that accepts Visa and MasterCard), but rates are not especially good.

Post & Communications The main post office is on Largo XXIV Maggio and opens 8.15am to 7pm Monday to Saturday. There is a branch office on the corner of Via Ciriaco Pizzecolli and Via della Catena.

The main Telecom office is opposite the main train station and opens 8am to 9.45pm daily. There is another office, open the same hours, at Piazza Roma 26. For email, try Internet Point at Corso Carlo Alberto 82.

Medical Services & Emergency In a medical emergency, call ☎ 071 20 20 95. The Ospedale Generale Regionale Umberto I (hospital; ☎ 071 59 61) is at Largo Cappelli 1. The Farmacia Centrale, on the corner of Corso Giuseppe Mazzini and Via Gramsci, has an emergency night service.

The *questura* (police station; ☎ 071 2 28 81) is at Via Giovanni Gervasoni 19, south of the city centre.

Other Information CTS (☎ 071 207 09 63) has an office at Via XXIX Settembre 4/c. There's a laundrette at Corso Carlo Alberto 76.

Piazza del Plebiscito

This elegant piazza was medieval Ancona's main square, which has since been overtaken by grander, if less atmospheric, piazzas in the modern town. **La Prefettura**, the former police station, is in a 15th-century palace dominating the piazza and is noted for its beautiful courtyard. At its eastern end stands the Baroque **Chiesa di San Domenico** *(Piazza del Plebiscito; free; open 7.15am-12.30pm & 4pm-7pm daily)*, containing the superb *Crucifixion* by Titian and *Annunciation* by Guercino. Near the church is the 13th-century city gate, the **Arco di Garola** (Garola's Arch), also known as Porta San Pietro. Most of the buildings overlooking the piazza went up in the 18th century, largely replacing their medieval precursors.

Museums & Churches

From La Prefettura, head north along Via Ciriaco Pizzecolli through the old city's ramparts to Palazzo Bosdari, which houses the **Pinacoteca Comunale** and **Galleria d'Arte Moderna** *(☎ 071 222 50 45, Via Ciriaco Pizzecolli 17; adult/under 20s €2.60/free; open 9am-7pm Tues-Sat, 9am-1pm Mon, 3pm-7pm Sun)*. The gallery displays works spanning some six centuries, including pieces by Guercino, Carlo Crivelli and Lorenzo Lotto. Search out Titian's *Madonna and Saints.*

A bit farther north along Via Ciriaco Pizzecolli and off to the right is **Chiesa di San Francesco delle Scale**, noteworthy for its 15th-century Venetian-Gothic doorway by Orsini. Beyond the church is Vanvitelli's **Chiesa del Gesù** (Church of Jesus), which is nearly always closed. Nearby is the economics faculty of the city's 13th-century university in the **Palazzo degli Anziani**.

The **Museo Archeologico Nazionale delle Marche** *(☎ 071 20 26 02, Via Ferretti 1; adult/child €4.15/free; open 8.30am-7.30pm Tues-Sun in summer)* is in the Palazzo Ferretti, which was restored twice last century, once after WWII bombing and again after an earthquake in 1972. It includes impressive

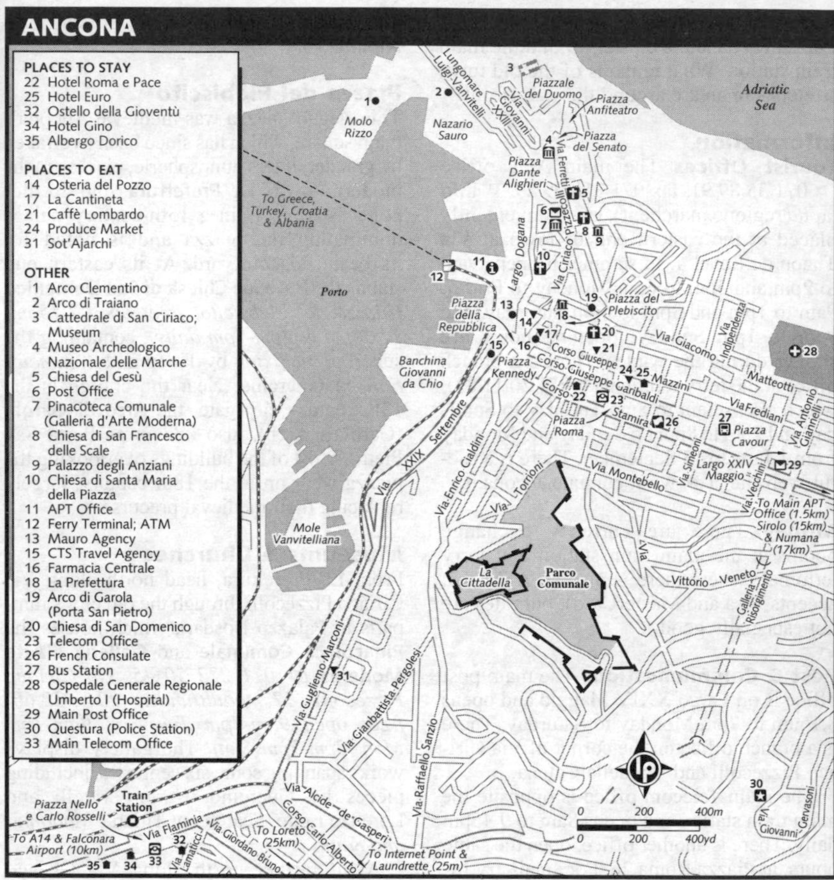

collections of Greek vases and artefacts from the Iron Age as well as Celtic and Roman remnants.

Cattedrale di San Ciriaco

Via Giovanni XXIII leads up Monte Guasco to Piazzale del Duomo where there are sweeping views of the city and the port. Here, the Romanesque cathedral *(☎ 071 20 03 91, Piazzale del Duomo; free; open 8.30am-noon & 3pm-7pm daily)* was built on the site of a Roman temple and has Byzantine and Gothic features. The small **museum** *(☎ 071 5 26 88, Piazzale del Duomo 9; free, donations welcome; open 5pm-7pm daily in summer, book at other times)* by the church holds the 4th-century sarcophagus of Flavius Gorgonius, a masterpiece of early Christian art.

Waterfront

North of Piazza Dante Alighieri, along the esplanade Lungomare Luigi Vanvitelli, is the **Arco di Traiano** (Trojan's Arch), erected in 115 BC. Vanvitelli's **Arco Clementino** (Clementine's Arch), dedicated to Pope Clement XII, is farther on, near Molo Rizzo. South of Piazza Dante Alighieri, you'll find the small Piazza Santa Maria and the disused, tumbledown **Chiesa di Santa Maria della Piazza**, which retains scraps of 5th- and 6th-century pavement mosaics. Heading southwest along Via XXIX Settembre, the large building seemingly marooned in the port is the **Mole Vanvitelliana**. A former quarantine area, it now stages exhibitions throughout the year. Call ☎ 071 207 23 48 for details.

Places to Stay

There are several hotels handy for the train station, in addition to the city centre options.

Ostello della Gioventù *(☎/fax 071 4 22 57, ⓔ aigancona@tiscalinet.it, ⓦ www.hostels-aig.org/shop-uk/ancona.htm, Via Lamaticci 7)* B&B €11.90. Closed 11pm-4.30pm. Ancona's HI-youth hostel has clean and sunny dorms in a rather ugly-looking building a block from the train station.

Hotel Gino *(☎/fax 071 421 79, ⓔ hotel.gino@tiscalinet.it, Via Flaminia 4)* Singles/doubles without bath €15.50/31, with bath €25.80/46.50. This two-star hotel is nothing special but it's friendly, affordable and convenient for the train station.

Albergo Dorico *(☎/fax 071 4 27 61, Via Flaminia 8)* Singles/doubles without bath €23.25/31, with bath €31/41.30. Another functional two-star hotel close to the train station, the Dorico has simple rooms.

Hotel Euro *(☎ 0389 6702392, Corso Giuseppe Mazzini 42)* Singles/doubles €20.65/36.15. This small but central one-star hotel, on the 2nd floor of a large building on Corso Mazzini, will do at a pinch.

Hotel Roma e Pace *(☎ 071 20 20 07, fax 207 47 36, Via Leopardi 1)* Singles/doubles €56.80/92.95. The rooms at this elegant three-star hotel in the city centre have all mod cons and there's a good restaurant downstairs. Prices include breakfast.

Places to Eat

Sample Ancona's seafood specialities in a selection of eateries.

Osteria del Pozzo *(☎ 071 207 39 96, Via Bonda 2)* Meals around €15.50. This small place is just off Piazza del Plebiscito and serves good, reasonably priced food.

La Cantineta *(☎ 071 20 11 07, Via Gramsci 1/c)* Two course set menu €9.80. This is a popular, simple trattoria near the old town centre but the clientele are predominantly male.

Sot'Ajarchi *(☎ 071 20 24 41, Via Gugliemo Marconi 93)* Full meals about €25.80. Open Mon-Sat. For seafood (Ancona is a port after all), try this place with its bright checked tablecloths, generous portions and extensive wine list. The house speciality, *scampi alla buzara*, is a wonder.

Caffè Lombardo *(Corso Giuseppe Mazzini 59)* Sandwiches from €2.60. This is a pleasant spot for salads and light lunches, with tables spilling out onto the street. Service can be a bit slow at peak periods.

The ***produce market*** *(Corso Giuseppe Mazzini 130)* sells fresh fruit, vegetables and other food.

Getting There & Away

Air Scheduled flights from London, Rome, Milan and Turin, as well as the odd charter flight (most of them from Russia and the Ukraine), land at Falconara airport (☎ 071 2 82 71), 10km west of Ancona. In summer there are also flights to Olbia on Sardinia.

Bus Most provincial and regional buses depart from Piazza Cavour. COTRAN (☎ 071 20 27 66) and Reni (☎ 071 804 65 04) run buses to provincial towns such as Loreto (€1.70, one hour, five per day), Recanati (€1.90, 1¼ hours, five per day), Osimo (€1.30, 40 minutes, half-hourly), Sirolo (€1.25, 35 minutes, hourly) and Numana (€1.25, 40 minutes, hourly). Other companies run buses to Macerata (€2.60, 1½ hours, ten daily), Senigallia (€1.50, 35 minutes, four daily) and Pesaro (€2.95, 1 hour 20 minutes, four daily) – the last two are run by Bucci. Bucci (☎ 071 79 22 737) also has a service to Urbino (€5.15, 2½ hours) at 2pm Monday to Saturday.

Train Ancona is on the Bologna-Lecce line and regular services link it with Milan (from €19.35, 5½ hours, every two hours), Turin (from €24.65, 6½ hours, four direct daily), Rome (from €13.20, 3¾ hours, every two hours), Bologna (from €10.10, 2¾ hours, 20 daily), Lecce (from €24.65, seven hours, eight daily) and most main stops in between, such as Pesaro (€5.35, 50 minutes, hourly) Senigallia (€1.75, 25 minutes, hourly) and Fano (€4.05, 40 minutes, hourly). For information, call ☎ 147 88 80 88.

Car & Motorcycle Ancona is on the A14, which links Bologna with Bari. The S16 coastal road runs parallel to the autostrada and is a more pleasant (toll-free) alternative. The S76 connects Ancona with Perugia and Rome.

Boat Ferry operators have booths at the ferry terminal. Timetables are subject to change, prices fluctuate with the season, and some lines come and go – check at the APT office or at the terminal. Most lines offer discounts on return fares, and the boats are generally roll-on, roll-off car ferries. There is a €2.60 port tax added to fares to Albania and Croatia and €5.15 for Greece. Prices listed here are for one-way deck class in the high season:

Adriatica (☎ 071 20 49 15) Adriatica runs two ferries a week to Split (€41.30, eight hours) and Durrës (services mostly suspended; €80.05, 18 hours).

Anek (☎ 071 207 23 46) This company runs daily ferries to Igoumenitsa (15 hours) and Patras (21 hours) from €48.05 per person and €60.45 for a car.

Jadrolinija (☎ 071 20 43 05 or 071 207 14 65) This operator runs three services a week to Zadar (from €41.30, eight hours) and Split (€44.95, 10 hours) in Croatia.

Minoan Lines (☎ 071 20 17 08) This company operates about six ferries a week to Patras (€64.05). Most services stop during the winter.

Blue Star Ferries – Strintzis Lines (☎ 071 207 10 68) This operator runs a daily service to Patras (20 hours) and Igoumenitsa (15 hours) from €41.30.

Superfast Ferries (☎ 071 207 02 40 or 071 20 20 33) Superfast operates a daily ferry to Patras, departing at 5pm and taking 19 hours (€55.80). It charges €71.80 for a small car and offers a 30% discount on a return booking.

Other companies that operate in summer include SNAV CroaziaJet (☎ 071 207 61 16) and the SEM Maritime Company, both of which have services to Croatia.

Getting Around

Conerobus' service J runs roughly every hour from the train station to the airport, from 6.05am to 8.30pm Monday to Saturday and seven times a day on Sunday (€1.10, 25 to 45 minutes). The bus labelled 'Ancona-Aeroporto' does the trip during August and on Sunday and public holidays.

There are about six Conerobus services, including No 1/4 which connects the main train station with the ferry terminal and Piazza Cavour (€0.65) – look for the bus stop with the big sign displaying Centro and Porto.

For a taxi, call ☎ 071 4 33 21.

AROUND ANCONA

Loreto

The story goes that angels transferred the house of the Virgin Mary from Palestine to this spot towards the end of the 13th century. Why the angels should have done such a thing is unclear (some link this 'miracle' to the pillaging of the Holy Land that occurred during the crusades), but a church was soon built over the site and later expanded to become today's **Santuario della Santa Casa** *(☎ 071 97 01 04, 071 97 68 37, Piazza della Madonna; free; open 6.15am-12.30pm & 2.30pm-8pm daily)*, an important site for pilgrims. Restoration began in 1468 and additions have been made ever since. The house itself, whatever its origin, is beneath the dome inside the sanctuary. Loreto lies about 28km south of Ancona and can be reached easily by bus. Loreto train station (Bologna-Lecce line) is a few kilometres away, but shuttle buses connect it with the town centre.

Beaches

If you are hanging about Ancona for any length of time, head about 20km south along the coast road (take a bus from Piazza Cavour) for **Sirolo** and **Numana**, below Monte Conero. These beaches are among the more appealing on the Adriatic coastline, although they fill up in summer.

URBINO

postcode 61029 • pop 6000

Urbino is the jewel of Le Marche and one of the best-preserved and most beautiful hill towns in Italy. It enjoyed a period of great splendour under the Montefeltro family from the 12th century onwards, and reached its zenith under Duca Federico da Montefeltro, who hired some of the greatest Renaissance artists and architects to construct and decorate his palace and other parts of the town. The architects Donato Bramante, who was born in Urbino, and Francesco di Giorgio Martini were among his favourites. Painters in particularly good grace with the duke included Piero della Francesca, who developed his theories on mathematical perspective in Urbino, Paolo Uccello, Justus of Ghent and Giovanni Santi (the father of Raffaello d'Urbino, the great Raphael, who was born in the city).

After Duca Federico lost his right eye and broke his nose in a tournament, he insisted on being portrayed only in profile. The most famous result of this caprice was executed in 1466 by Piero della Francesca and hangs in the Galleria degli Uffizi in Florence.

The town can be a pain to reach by public transport, but should not be missed. The area to the north, particularly the winding road to San Marino and on into Emilia-Romagna, is a treat and there are plenty of hotels in the small towns along the way.

Orientation

Buses arrive at Piazza Mercatale at the walled city's western edge. From there it's a short walk up Via G Mazzini to Piazza della Repubblica and then back south along Via Vittorio Veneto for Piazza Duca Federico and the sprawling Piazza del Rinascimento. Drivers are most likely to arrive at Piazzale Roma at the city's northern edge, where cars can be parked free of charge. Via Raffaello connects Piazzale Roma with Piazza della Repubblica.

Information

The IAT office (☎ 0722 26 13, fax 0722 24 41), Piazza Duca Federico 35, opens 9am to

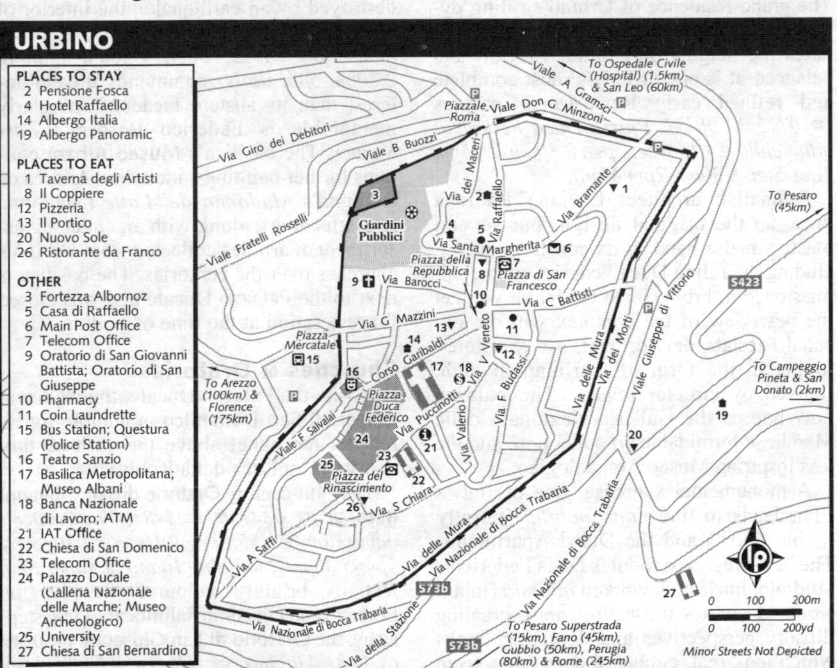

1pm Monday to Saturday. From May to September, it also opens 3pm to 6pm and from 9am to 1pm on Sunday morning.

There are several banks around town. The Banca Nazionale di Lavoro, on Via Vittorio Veneto, has an ATM.

The main post office is at Via Bramante 18. It opens 8.30am to 6.30pm Monday to Saturday. The Telecom office, at Via Puccinotti 4, opens 8am to 10pm daily. There's another office, open the same hours, at Piazza di San Francesco 1. Il Portico bookshop and cafe also has Internet access (see Places to Eat for details).

First aid (☎ 0722 30 12 72) is available at the Ospedale Civile (hospital; ☎ 0722 30 11) on Via Bonconte da Montefeltro, 1.5km north of the city centre. There is a pharmacy at Piazza della Repubblica 9. The *questura* (police station; ☎ 0722 35 181) is on Piazza Mercatale.

Palazzo Ducale

The grand residence of Urbino's ruling dynasty was completed in 1482 and still dominates the heights of Urbino. Elegant and balanced, it is one of Italy's most complete and refined early Renaissance palaces *(☎ 0722 32 90 57, Piazza Duca Federico; adult/child €4.15/free; open 8.30am-7.15pm Tues-Sun, 8.30am-2pm Mon)*.

Dalmatian architect Luciano Laurana drew up the original design, but several masters had a hand in its construction, including the ruling Duca Federico who commissioned it. From Corso Garibaldi you get the best view of the complex with its unusual **Facciata dei Torricini**, a three storey loggia in the form of a triumphal arch, flanked by circular towers. The palazzo now houses the Galleria Nazionale delle Marche, a formidable art collection, and the less inspiring Museo Archeologico.

A monumental staircase, one of Italy's first, leads to the *piano nobile* (literally 'noble floor') and the Ducal Apartments. The best-preserved room is Duca Federico's **Studiolo**. Intricately worked *intarsia* (inlaid wood) decorates the entire room, creating illusory perspectives and depicting books which look real, cupboard doors that seem to be hanging open and even a letter that appears to be lying in a desk drawer.

Among the paintings in the **Galleria Nazionale delle Marche**, look out for Piero della Francesca's masterpiece, *The Flagellation*, and *The Ideal City*, long held to be by Piero but now attributed to Laurana. Another highlight is the remarkable portrait of Federico and his son Guidobaldo, attributed to the Spanish artist Pedro Berruguete. The art collection, which continues on the 2nd floor, also features several works, including a large number of drawings, by the Urbino artist Federico Barocci. The mildly interesting **Museo Archeologico**, on the far side of the Cortile d'Onore (Courtyard of Honour), is worth a look – you may as well, since admission is included in the ticket.

Basilica Metropolitana

Rebuilt in the early 19th century in neoclassical style after Francesco di Giorgio Martini's original Renaissance building was destroyed by an earthquake, the interior of Urbino's basilica *(Piazza Duca Federico; admission €1.55; open 9.30am-noon & 2.30pm-6pm daily)* commands greater interest than its austere facade. Particularly memorable is Federico Barocci's *Last Supper*. The basilica's **Museo Albani** contains further paintings, including Andrea da Bologna's *Madonna del Latte* (Madonna Breastfeeding), along with an engaging assortment of articles collected from Urbino's churches over the centuries. The basilica is next to the Palazzo Ducale and was closed for restoration at the time of writing.

Churches & Oratories

Opposite the Palazzo Ducale, the medieval **Chiesa di San Domenico** is notable for its lunette, the panel above the 15th-century doorway, by Luca della Robbia.

The 14th-century **Oratorio di San Giovanni Battista** *(☎ 0347 671 11 81, Via Barocci; admission €1.55; open 10am-12.30pm & 3pm-5.30pm Mon-Sat, 10am-12.30pm Sun)* features brightly coloured frescoes by Lorenzo and Giacomo Salimbeni. A few steps away, the **Oratorio di San Giuseppe** *(☎ 0347 61 11 81, Via Barocci; admission €1.55; open*

10am-12.30pm & 3pm-5.30pm Mon-Sat, 10am-12.30pm Sun) boasts a stucco *Nativity* by Federico Brandani.

The **Chiesa di San Bernardino** *(☎ 0722 32 05 39, Viale Giuseppe di Vittorio; free; open 8am-6pm daily)*, 2km south-east of the city walls, houses the mausoleum of the Dukes of Urbino, designed by Donato Bramante and Francesco di Giorgio Martini.

Casa di Raffaello

If you want to see where Raphael first saw the light of day, head to the north of the Piazza della Repubblica where you'll find the house of his birth *(☎ 0722 32 01 05, Via Raffaello 57; admission €2.60; open 9am-1pm & 3pm-7pm Mon-Sat, 10am-1pm Sunday, in spring & summer, mornings only Nov-early Mar)*. It was here, in this stolid 15th-century building, that Raphael spent the first 16 years of his life. On the first floor is possibly one of Raphael's first frescoes, a Madonna with child. You can also see the house's original kitchen, restored to appear as it would have looked in Raphael's time.

Courses

Università di Urbino *(☎ 0722 30 52 50, fax 0722 30 52 87, e corstran@uniurb.it, Via Saffi 2, Urbino 61029)* The university offers an intensive course in language and culture for foreigners during August at a cost of €380 and it can arrange accommodation for €210 for the month. You can get details and make a booking from March to 19 July by writing to the Segreteria dell' Università.

Places to Stay

The IAT office holds a full list of private rooms.

Campeggio Pineta *(☎ 0722 47 10, fax 0722 4734, Via San Donato, Loc. Cesane)* Sites per person/tent up to €5.15/10.85. Urbino's only camp site is 2km east of the city in San Donato and has all the standard facilities.

Penslone Fosca *(☎/fax 0722 32 96 22, Via Raffaello 61)* Singles/doubles €20.65/33.55. This charming but tiny pensione, on the top floor of an ancient building, just up from the Casa di Raffaello, has simple but appealing rooms with shared bath.

Albergo Panoramic *(☎ 0722 26 00, Via Nazionale 192)* Singles/doubles up to €31/41.30. Albergo Panoramic is to the east of the city walls, but it's awkward to reach without your own transport.

Albergo Italia *(☎ 0722 27 01, fax 0722 32 26 64, W www.albergo-italia-urbino.it, Corso Garibaldi 32)* Singles/doubles from €67.15/113.60. This place enjoys a good position behind the Palazzo Ducale and has recently undergone extensive renovations.

Hotel Raffaello *(☎ 0722 47 84, fax 0722 32 85 40, Via Santa Margherita 40)* Singles/doubles €77.45/103.30. Despite the rather austere marbled entrance, the three-star Raffaello has comfortable rooms and serves a good breakfast.

Places to Eat

Don't miss the *strozzapreti al pesto*, available in most restaurants. These worm-like shreds of pasta were designed to choke priests – sounds horrid but they're delicious. There are numerous ***bars*** around Piazza della Repubblica and near the Palazzo Ducale that sell good *panini* (filled rolls). Try the ***pizzeria*** *(Via Vittorio Veneto 19)* for takeaway pizza by the slice.

Nuovo Sole *(☎ 0722 32 87 78, Via Nazionale 73)* Meals from €12.90. Just east of the city walls, this affordable Chinese restaurant makes a good change for those who can't face another plate of pasta.

Il Portico *(☎ 0722 27 22, Via G Mazzini 7)* Snacks from €1.55. Open Mon-Sat. For *bruschetta*, salads and light meals, try Il Portico, which is both a bookshop and osteria.

Ristorante da Franco *(☎ 0722 24 92, Via del Poggio 1)* Lunch less than €10.35. Open Mon-Sat. This place is just off Piazza Rinascimento next to the university. Lunch is a good deal at its self-service section.

Taverna degli Artisti *(☎ 0722 26 76, Via Bramante 52)* Meals around €15.50. Closed Tues winter. This restaurant serves good pasta and meat dishes. Their giant pizzas, served on huge wooden slabs, are big enough to feed an army.

Il Coppiere *(☎ 0722 32 23 26, Via Santa Margherita 1)* Meals €25.80. This 1st-floor restaurant has elegant dining.

Entertainment

The arts come alive in Urbino during the summer season. La Festa del Duca (The Festival of Dukes) takes place on the third Sunday in August. The town's streets become the setting for a costume procession and the re-enactment of a tournament on horseback in celebration of the splendid era of Duca Federico.

Teatro Sanzio *(☎ 0722 22 81, Corso Garibaldi)* hosts an occasional play or concert, particularly from July-Sept. Pick up a brochure at the IAT office.

Getting There & Around

The Pesaro-based company Soget (☎ 0721 37 13 18) runs up to 10 services daily between Urbino and Pesaro (€1.90, 55 minutes). Bucci (☎ 0721 3 24 01) runs two buses per day to Rome (€18.10, five hours) at 6am and 4pm, has one service to Ancona (€5.15, 2½ hours) at 4.40pm and goes to Arezzo (€5.15, 2 hours 40 minutes) at 7am.

Take the bus to Pesaro to pick up trains (see Pesaro Getting There & Around later in this chapter for details).

An autostrada and the S423 connect Urbino with Pesaro, and the S73b connects the town with the S3 for Rome.

Most motor vehicles are banned from the walled city. Taxis (☎ 0722 25 50) and shuttle buses operate from Piazza della Repubblica and Piazza Mercatale. There are car parks outside the city gates. Note that there's no parking on Piazzale Roma on Saturday morning as it's market day.

AROUND URBINO

San Leo

Machiavelli, who knew a thing or two about such matters, thought the fortress of San Leo, about 60km north-west of Urbino, 'quite impregnable'. He was probably right – it is difficult to see how the walls, perched defiantly on a high outcrop of stone, could be assailed.

Part of the Montefeltro duchy, San Leo was first fortified by the Romans, who erected a temple to Jupiter here. The temple was later replaced by the 12th-century **cathedral**, and nearby you can also admire the pre-Romanesque **pieve**, an 11th-century basilica. The Papal States converted the fortress into a prison and the Fascists used it as an aircraft-spotting post during WWII.

Without your own transport, San Leo is a little difficult to reach. Although it is in Le Marche, the most reliable bus route is actually from Rimini, in Emilia-Romagna.

PESARO

postcode 61100 • pop 90,000

Like other resort towns on the Adriatic Sea, Pesaro offers an expanse of beach, the remains of a medieval centre and not much else. In mid-summer you can't move for the crowds, and out of season the waterfront has a sad air about it – maybe it's all the tacky concrete hotel blocks boarded up for the winter. It is, however, a handy transport junction and the best place to get a bus for Urbino, an hour's drive inland.

Orientation

The train station is south-west of the centre, away from the beach. From the station, walk along Viale del Risorgimento, through Piazza Lazzarini and continue to Piazza del Popolo, the town's main square. Via Rossini takes you to Piazzale della Libertà and the waterfront.

Information

Tourist Offices The IAT office (☎ 0721 6 93 41, ⓔ pesaro@regione.marche.it, Ⓦ www.comune.pesaro.ps.it), on Piazzale della Libertà, opens 9am to 1pm and 3.30pm to 7pm daily July to September, and 9am to 1pm Monday to Friday (also 3.30pm to 6.30pm on Tuesday and Thursday) October to June.

Money There are plenty of banks around town. The Banca Nazionale del Lavoro on Piazza del Popolo has an ATM.

Post & Communications The main post office is on Piazza del Popolo and opens from 8.15am to 7.40pm Monday to Saturday.

The Telecom office is on Piazza Matteotti, south-east of Piazza del Popolo, and is open from 7am to 11pm daily in summer (the hours are reduced in the low season).

There is free Internet access at the Biblioteca Centrale Comunale (☎ 0721 38 74 96), Via Rossini 37, but you must make a reservation in person the day before you want to use it.

Laundry There's an Onda Blu laundrette at Piazzale I Maggio 12.

Medical Services & Emergency In a medical emergency try *pronto soccorso* (casualty) on ☎ 0721 3 29 57. The Ospedale San Salvatore (hospital; ☎ 0721 36 11) is on Piazzale Albani.

The *questura* (police station; ☎ 0721 38 61 11) is at Via Giordano Bruno 5.

Things to See

The 15th-century **Palazzo Ducale**, dominating Piazza del Popolo, housed the ruling Della Rovere family. Today it houses bureaucracy and is closed to the public. The splendid windows that grace its facade are by Domenico Rosselli.

Head north-west along Corso XI Settembre for Via Toschi Mosca and the town's combined **Musei Civici**, **Museo delle Ceramiche** and **Pinacoteca** *(☎ 0721 38 75 41, Piazza Toschi Mosca 29; adults/under-25s €2.60/free; open 9.30am-12.30pm Tues-Sun year-round, plus 4pm-7pm Thurs & Sun Sept-Jun, 5pm-8pm Wed & Fri-Sun, 5pm-11pm Tues & Thurs July & Aug)*. The production of ceramics has long been a speciality of Pesaro and the museum has a worthy collection, while the pinacoteca's prize is Giovanni Bellini's magnificent altarpiece depicting the *Coronation of the Virgin*.

In 1792 the composer Rossini was born in what is now known as the **Casa Natale di Rossini** *(☎ 0721 38 73 57, Via Rossini 34; adults/under-25s €2.60/free; open 9.30am-12.30pm Tues-Sun & 4pm-7pm Thurs-Sun)*. Here, a small museum contains various personal effects and his spinet. You can purchase a joint ticket for the Musei Civici and the Casa Natale di Rossini for €4.15.

Rossini fans may also want to visit the Conservatorio di Musica, which includes the **Museo Rossini** *(also called Tempietto Rossiniano; ☎ 0721 3 00 53, Piazza Olivieri, off Via Branca; guided tours only – phone ahead or contact the tourist office)*.

The **Chiesa di Sant'Agostino** *(Corso XI Settembre; free; open 8am-7pm daily)* features intricate 15th-century inlaid-wood choir stalls. The modest **Museo Oliveriano** *(☎ 0721 333 44, Via Mazza 97; free; open 4pm-7pm Mon-Sat July & Aug, 9.30am-12.30pm Mon-Sat the rest of the year on request)* contains archaeological finds from the area, including a child's tomb from the Iron Age, complete with miniature utensils such as eating implements. Apply for admission at the adjoining **library**, which has a collection of ancient coins, manuscripts and medals.

Places to Stay

The town's hotel association, the Associazione Pesarese di Albergatori (☎ 0721 6 79 59), has an office at Viale G Marconi 57/1 and will help you find a room. The IAT office has a lengthy list of apartments, although most are more expensive than hotels. Many hotels close from October to April and the camp sites may well do the same. If you can, go to the IAT office when you first arrive to find out what's open.

The closest camp sites are about 5km south of the town centre at Fossosejore on the coast.

Marinella *(☎/fax 0721 5 57 95, Loc. Fossosejore)* Sites per person/tent up to €6.70/13.15. Open Apr-Sept. This camp site is on the S16. You can get here from Pesaro on one of the regular AMI buses to Fossosejore.

Norina *(☎ 0721 5 57 92, fax 0721 5 51 65, Via Marina Ardizia 181, Loc. Fossosejore)* Sites per person/tent up to €6.20/11.90. Open Apr–mid-Oct. This place is close to the Marinella camp site.

Hotel Athena *(☎ 0721 3 01 14, fax 0721 3 38 78, Viale Pola 18)* Singles/doubles from €25.80/36.15. On a leafy street at the north-west end of town, the Athena is a good two-star choice. The conservatory-style entrance, filled with potted plants, is welcoming and the rooms are clean and bright.

Hotel Holiday *(☎ 0721 3 48 51, fax 0721 37 03 10, Viale Trento 159)* Low season singles/doubles €20.65/36.15, high season €36.15/51.65. It seems that the concrete hotel block is standard issue in Pesaro and the Holiday is no exception. Although it lacks charm, all rooms have private balconies and fairly large bathrooms.

Hotel Excelsior *(☎ 0721 3 27 20, fax 0721 3 55 02, Lungomare Nazario Sauro)* Full board high season singles/doubles starting at €58.65/100.20. The Excelsior is right on the beach and it's got a swimming pool, but otherwise there's not much to distinguish it from the rest of Pesaro's 50-odd three-star hotels.

Places to Eat

This resort town offers up a few tasty options.

Ristorante C'Era Una Volta *(☎ 0721 3 09 11, Via Cattaneo 26)* Pizzas from €2.60. This is a good pizzeria with a great atmosphere – diners share long wooden tables and are watched over by a tank of piranha.

Polo *(☎ 0721 37 59 02, Viale Trieste 231)* Full meals €12.90-18.10. Polo's a fairly hip

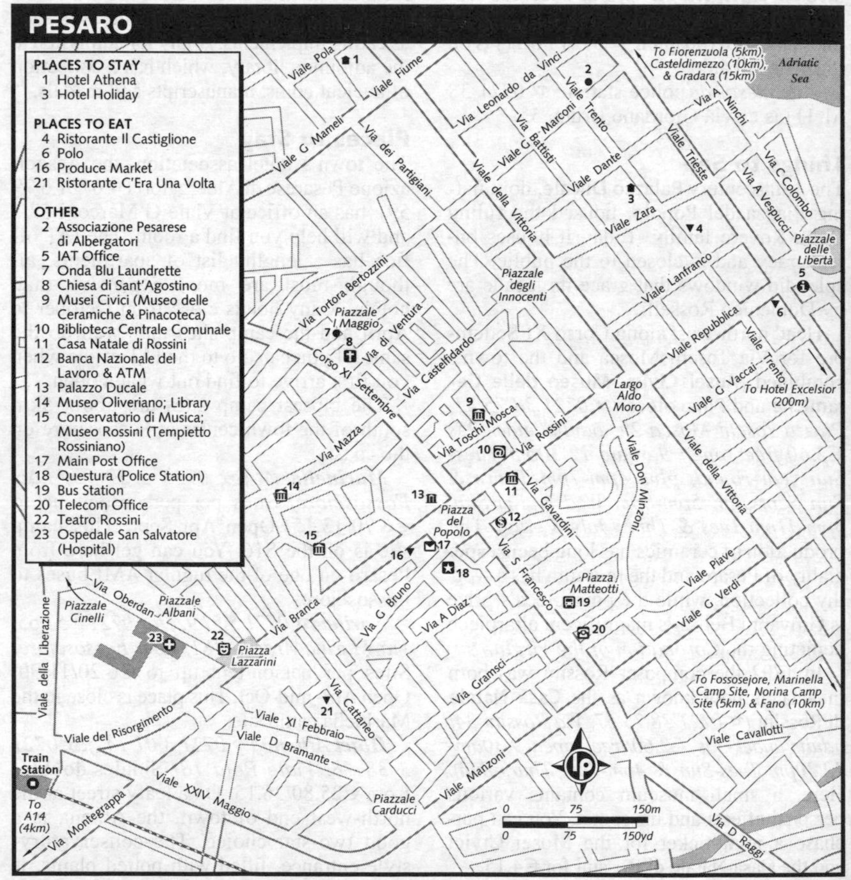

and popular establishment which serves a good mix of Italian and international food (and an extraordinary variety of grappa). The pleasant balcony-seating is perfect for watching the world go by.

Ristorante Il Castiglione *(☎ 0721 6 49 34, Viale Trento 149)* Meals about €31. Open Tues-Sun. If you're prepared to part with the euros, try this swish place which has the air of a small castle set in rambling gardens. Fresh fish is a speciality.

There are food shops and a ***produce market*** on Via Branca, behind the post office.

Entertainment

In honour of Rossini, the town hosts a series of concerts each August at the ***Teatro Rossini*** *(☎ 0721 6 93 59, Piazza Lazzarini).*

Getting There & Around

The main bus station is on Piazza Matteotti. AMI buses (☎ 0721 28 91 45 or 0721 37 48 62) connect Pesaro with Cattolica (€1.10, 45 minutes, hourly), Fossosejore (€0.60, 15 minutes, half-hourly), and most small towns in the region. Bucci (☎ 0721 3 24 01) operates a service to Ancona (€2.95, 1 hour 20 minutes, four daily) and to Rome at 6am daily (€19.35, 4 hours 40 minutes). Buses make the return journey from Rome at 4pm. Soget (☎ 0721 37 13 18) runs up to 10 buses daily to Urbino (€1.90, 55 minutes).

Pesaro is on the Bologna-Lecce train line and you can reach Rome (€15.45, four hours) by changing trains at Falconara Marittima, just before Ancona. There are hourly services to Ancona (€5.35, 50 minutes), Rimini (€2.25, 30 minutes) and Bologna (€7.25, two hours). Catch the Ancona-bound train for Fano (€1.30, 10 minutes) and Senigallia (€2.20, 25 minutes). By car, Pesaro is on the A14 and the S16.

AMI buses connect the train station with Piazza Matteotti, including bus Nos 1, 3, 4, 5, CD and CS. For a taxi in the centre, call ☎ 0721 3 14 30; at the train station, call ☎ 0721 3 11 11.

AROUND PESARO

If you want slightly more secluded beaches than the Pesaro waterfront, take the Strada Panoramica Adriatica coast road heading north from Pesaro to Cattolica in Emilia-Romagna. The walled, hilltop town of **Gradara** boasts an impressive 14th-century castle. The smaller fishing towns of **Casteldimezzo** and **Fiorenzuola** are appealing and quieter, even during the summer. Fighting in WWII was heavy around here, as the Allies struggled to break the Germans' Gothic Line, which ran from Pesaro to La Spezia on Italy's western coast. Two kilometres east of Gradara, there is a **British war cemetery** *(just off the S16; open all the time).*

Regular AMI buses link Pesaro with Casteldimezzo (€1.10, 30 minutes, five daily), Fiorenzuola (€0.85, 25 minutes, five daily) and Gradara (€1.10, one hour, hourly).

FANO

postcode 61032 • pop 30,000

Only 12km south-east of Pesaro, Fano is a fairly sedate beach resort that nevertheless fills up in the summer rush. The IAT office (☎ 0721 80 35 34, e iat.fano@regione.marche.it) is at Viale Cesare Battisti 10. The ancient Roman village took its name from the Fanum, the Temple of Fortune, and its pleasant historic centre retains several reminders of its Roman and medieval past. A **triumphal arch** built in AD 2 for Augustus still stands despite losing part of its masonry to surrounding buildings over the centuries. Sections of the Roman and medieval **walls** also remain. There is a **museum** *(adult/child €2.60/1.55)* with works produced by local artists over the centuries within the 16th-century **Corte Malatestiano** *(☎ 0721 80 07 50, Piazza XX Settembre; free; open 8.30am-12.30pm & 5pm-7pm Tues-Sun in summer, 8am-1pm Tues-Sun in winter).*

Places to Stay

Cheap accommodation is in short supply along this stretch of coastline, making Pesaro a more economical base, although try picking up the accommodation list from the IAT office. Five camp sites at the southern end of Fano's seashore all charge much the same prices.

Fano *(☎/fax 0721 80 26 52, Loc. Metaurilla)* Sites per person/tent up to €5.75/9.70.

Open mid-Apr–mid-Sept. This shady camp site has tennis courts, a bar and a restaurant right on the beachfront. It also offers accommodation in bungalows.

Getting There and Away

Regular AMI buses connect Fano with Pesaro (€0.85, 25 minutes, half-hourly). The town is also on the Bologna–Lecce train line, with hourly trains to Pesaro (€1.30, 10 minutes) and Ancona (€4.05, 40 minutes).

AROUND FANO

If you're staying for a while, a couple of excursions inland are worth considering. **Mondavio** is a charming Renaissance town about 35km south of Fano. Buses run from Fano (€1.70, one hour, five daily). If driving, take the S16 south to Marotta, from where you head inland to San Michele; Mondavio is a few kilometres to the north.

Some 21km south-west of Fano is **Mombaroccio**, a pleasant 15th-century hill town. The main attraction is the view from the old castle walls. Take the S3 west from Fano and turn north at Calcinelli or catch one of the five daily buses from Pesaro (€1.30, 45 minutes).

SENIGALLIA

postcode 60019 • pop 30,000

Senigallia's aptly named **Spiaggia di Velluto** (Velvet Beach) is reputedly one of the best *lidos* (bathing beaches) on the Adriatic coast.

The IAT office (☎ 071 792 27 25, ⓔ iat.senigallia@regione.marche.it), at Piazzale Morandi 2, is between the beach and the train station and opens 9am to 1pm and 3.30pm to 6.30pm Monday to Saturday. In summer it is also open on Sunday mornings.

Apart from sun, sea and sand, the main draw is the **Rocca Roveresca** *(☎ 071 632 58, Piazza del Duca; admission €2.05; open 8.30am-7.30pm Tues-Sun)*, whose four stout, crenellated towers make it hard to miss. Built for Duca Federico da Montefeltro's son-in-law, its plush Renaissance interior makes a visit well worthwhile if you have a spare hour or two.

Places to Stay

If you're having trouble finding a room, which in summer would come as no surprise, try the ***Associazione Alberghi e Turismo*** *(☎ 071 6 53 43, Viale IV Novembre 2).*

Spiaggia di Velluto *(☎/fax 071 648 73, Lungomare Leonardo da Vinci)* High season sites per person/tent from €4.40/13.45. This camp site is about 3km south of Senigallia, right on the beach.

Liana *(☎ 071 6 52 06, fax 071 792 17 50, Lungomare Leonardo da Vinci 54)* High season sites per person/tent from €4.65/13.45. This camp site, just north of Spiaggia di Velluto, has slightly better facilities.

Albergo Eleonora *(☎ 071 792 73 73, fax 071 65 94 82, Lungomare G Marconi 2)* Low season singles/doubles from €20.65/41.30, compulsory full board in Aug €46.50 per person. This fairly anonymous red high-rise is on the waterfront, close to the train station. It's friendly, open year-round, and has a handy bar and restaurant downstairs.

Getting There & Away

All buses stop at the main train station which is in the town centre on Via Rafaele Sanzio. Bucci buses operate along the S16 coastal road to Ancona (€1.50, 35 minutes, 25 daily), Fano (€1.50, 30 minutes, five daily) and Pesaro (€1.70, 50 minutes, four daily). Plenty of trains also service the same stretch.

GROTTE DI FRASASSI

In September 1971 a team of climbers stumbled across an aperture in the hill country around Genga, about 50km south-west of Ancona, and decided to drop in. What they found were the biggest known caves in Europe, containing a spectacle of stalactites and stalagmites, some of them 1.4 million years old.

Three years later they were opened to the public, with a 1.5km-long trail carefully laid through five chambers. **Ancona Abyss**, the first chamber, is almost 200m high, 180m wide and 120m long, and could easily accommodate Milan's cathedral.

Tour groups are taken through the caves every couple of hours. Tours last about an hour and cost €10.35. The ticket area and car park are just outside San Vittore Terme, and the entrance to the caves is 600m farther west. For €25.80, you can get rigged up in caving gear to explore the remaining chambers, while for €36.15 you can have a more challenging experience that lasts for three hours and involves passing across 30m chasms and crawling on your hands and knees along narrow passages and tunnels. A certain degree of know-how or just sheer bravado is required for this latter tour. It also has to be booked well in advance by calling the Consorzio Grotte di Frasassi (☎ 0732 9 00 80). Should you need to stay overnight nearby, there are a couple of hotels in San Vittore Terme and Genga.

To reach the caves from Ancona, take the S76 or catch the train for Genga (€2.95, 45 minutes, four daily), about 2km from the caves' ticket area; a shuttle bus runs from the train station in summer.

MACERATA

postcode 62100 • pop 42,000

This bustling provincial capital is one of Italy's better kept secrets. Situated atop a rise between the Potenza river valley to the north and the River Chienti in the south, Macerata was established in the 10th century. It is as impressive as many Umbrian and Tuscan hill towns but lacks the tourists, and makes a good base for exploring the surrounding countryside – some of the region's most picturesque.

Orientation

Piazza della Libertà is the focal point of the medieval city, contained within the 14th-century walls above the sprawl of the more modern development. Buses arrive at the huge Giardini Diaz, which is a stone's throw from the Porta Romana (the main gate) and the IAT office. A shuttle bus links the train station, which is south of the city centre, to Piazza della Libertà.

There is parking virtually right around the walls and you may even find a space on one of the main squares inside the old city.

Information

The IAT office (☎ 0733 23 48 07), Piazza della Libertà 12, opens 9am to 1pm and 3pm to 7pm Monday to Saturday in summer, 9am to 1pm and 3pm to 6pm in winter, and 9am to 1pm on Sunday year-round.

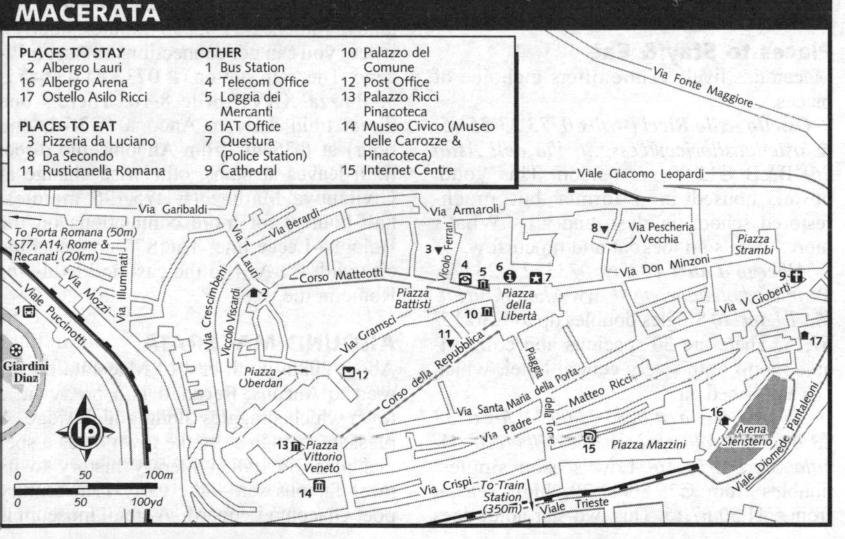

The post office is at Piazza Oberdan 1–3 and opens 8am to 7pm Monday to Saturday. The Telecom office at Galleria del Commercio 33 opens 8am to 7pm daily. There's an Internet centre (☎ 0733 26 44 04) at Piazza Mazzini 52.

Things to See

Piazza della Libertà is adorned with one of the city's finest buildings, the 16th-century Renaissance open-air **Loggia dei Mercanti**, built by the Farnese pope, Paul III. In the courtyard of the **Palazzo del Comune** are archaeological remains from Helvia Recina, a Roman town 5km north of Macerata, which was destroyed by the Goths.

Corso della Repubblica, the main boulevard where locals take their late-afternoon strolls, spills into Piazza Vittorio Veneto. Here, in the same building, you will find the **Museo Civico**, the **Museo delle Carrozze** and the **Pinacoteca** *(☎ 0733 25 63 61, Piazza Vittorio Veneto; free; open 9am-1pm & 5pm-7.30pm Tues-Sat, 5pm-7.30pm Mon, 9am-1pm Sun)*. The latter has a good collection of early Renaissance works, including a 15th-century *Madonna* by Carlo Crivelli.

The rather ordinary Baroque **cathedral** is unfinished and worth visiting only if you have time to spare.

Places to Stay & Eat

Macerata's lively centre offers a choice of places.

Ostello Asilo Ricci *(☎/fax 0733 23 25 15, ⓔ ostelloasiloricci@cssg.it, Via dell'Asilo 36)* B&B €12.90 per person. This youth hostel, housed in a former but much-restored school, is clean and airy. What's more, there's no lockout and no curfew.

Albergo Lauri *(☎/fax 0733 23 23 76, ⓔ info@hotellauri.it, ⓦ www.hotellauri.it, Via T Lauri 6)* Singles/doubles up to €36.15/67.15. There are 30 spacious and comfortable rooms at this very central hotel, which has a polished air.

Albergo Arena *(☎ 0733 23 09 31, fax 0733 23 60 59, ⓔ albergoarenamc@libero.it, Vicolo Sferisterio 16)* Low season singles/doubles from €25.80/41.30, high season from €41.30/67.15. This two-star hotel does a great breakfast (included in the price). The rooms are clean, with all the mod cons of a more expensive hotel, yet it manages to retain an intimate feel.

Several pizzerias, such as ***Rusticanella Romana*** *(Corso della Repubblica 13)* and ***Pizzeria da Luciano*** *(☎ 0733 26 01 29, Vicolo Ferrari 12)*, serve quick takeaway food.

Da Secondo *(☎ 0733 26 09 12, Via Pescheria Vecchia 26)* Full meals about €25.80. Open Tues-Sun. This is one of the better restaurants in town, with dining on a shaded terrace.

Entertainment

The Stagione Lirica (Lyric Festival) is one of Italy's most prestigious musical events, attracting big operatic names to the superb open-air Arena Sferisterio, off Piazza Mazzini, between 15 July and 15 August every year. At the same time, the private Palazzo Ricci Pinacoteca, in the street of the same name, organises a national exhibition of 20th-century Italian art.

Getting There & Away

Several bus companies operate services to Rome (€17.55, four hours, three daily), Ancona (€2.60, 1½ hours, ten daily), Foligno (€3.60, two hours, two daily) and Civitanova Marche (€1.05, 50 minutes, hourly), where you can get connections to Ascoli Piceno. The train station (☎ 0733 24 03 54) is at Piazza XXV Aprile 8/10. There's one direct train daily to Ancona (€3.70, one hour) at 6.35am (from Ancona, the direct train leaves at 8am), otherwise change at Civitanova Marche (€1.75, 25 minutes, half-hourly) for more connections on the Bologna-Lecce line. The S77 connects the city with the A14 to the east and roads for Rome in the west.

AROUND MACERATA

About 20km north-east of Macerata on the road to Ancona, **Recanati** is a pretty little town which straggles along a high ridge. A pleasant enough stop, the town owes a special place in Italian literary history to its most famous son – the early-19th-century poet Giacomo Leopardi. A small museum is

Giacomo Leopardi

'The most solid pleasure in this life is the empty pleasure of illusion.'

Born in Recanati of well-to-do parents, Giacomo Leopardi (1798–1837) became the greatest romantic poet to emerge from Italy. Plagued throughout his life by solitude and sickness (he referred to himself as a 'walking sepulchre'), Leopardi poured his anxiety, pain and fleeting moments of joy into his lyrical, despair-filled poetry. Leopardi was steeped in a classical education from a precocious age and his verse, however much it belongs to the stormy age of the Romantics, remains firmly planted in the disciplined framework of classicism. The pick of his work is the *Canti*, first published between 1824 and 1835, and now a standard element of Italian literary education.

dedicated to his life in the Palazzo Leopardi. Hourly buses connect Macerata with Recanati (€1.30, one hour).

ASCOLI PICENO

postcode 63100 • pop 55,000

Legend has it that a woodpecker was responsible for the founding of this southern Le Marche town by leading the prehistoric first settlers to the site. The extensive old centre is bounded by the River Tronto to the north and the Castellano river to the south and east, and is dominated by nearby mountains leading into the Apennines. The city is among the region's most interesting after Urbino and deserves more attention than it gets.

Woodpecker stories aside, Ascoli Piceno was probably settled by the Piceni tribe in the 6th century BC. The salt trade eventually brought the city into contact with the Romans, to whom it fell after clamorous defeats in the battlefield in 268 BC. By the 6th century AD, the Goths and then the Lombards had come to supplant the Romans. The city flourished in the Middle Ages, despite being ransacked by the troops of Holy Roman Emperor Frederick II after a long siege in 1242.

Orientation

The old town and its modern extension are separated by the Castellano river. The train station is in the new town, east of the river. From the station, head west across Ponte Maggiore, along Corso Vittorio Emanuele and past the cathedral. Any of the narrow cobbled lanes to the north of Via XX Settembre will eventually take you to Piazza del Popolo, the heart of the medieval city.

Information

The IAT office (☎ 0736 25 30 45), at Piazza del Popolo 17, opens 8.30am to 1.30pm and 3pm to 7pm Monday to Friday, 9am to 1pm and 3pm to 7pm Saturday, and 9am to 1pm Sunday.

The main post office is on Via Crispi. It opens 8.15am to 7.40pm Monday to Saturday.

For Internet access, visit the centre at Piazza della Viola 14.

The Telecom office is on Corso Vittorio Emanuele and is open from 9am to 1pm Monday to Friday.

The Ospedale Generale Mazzoni (hospital; ☎ 0736 35 81) is in Monticello, a newly built area 4km to the east of town. The *questura* (police station; ☎ 0736 355 111) is at Viale della Repubblica 8.

Piazza del Popolo

The heart of medieval Ascoli and the town's forum in Roman times, Piazza del Popolo is dominated on the western side by the 13th-century **Palazzo dei Capitani del Popolo**. The seat of Ascoli's rulers, it was burned to the ground in 1535 during a bitter local feud and rebuilt 10 years later. The statue of Pope Paul III above the main entrance was erected in recognition of his efforts to bring peace to the town. The building's colourful history did not end there, as it was the headquarters for the local branch of the Fascists from 1938 and became the seat of the partisan Comitato di Liberazione in 1945. It is now used for council meetings and the occasional exhibition (ask at the IAT office for details).

Closing off the piazza to the north, **Chiesa di San Francesco** (*☎ 0736 25 94 46,*

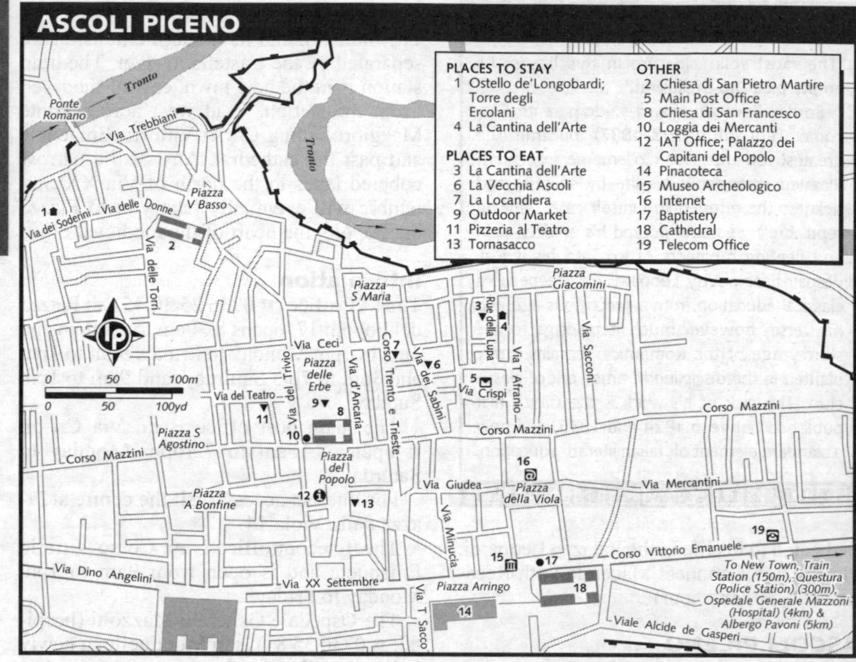

Piazza del Popolo; free; open 7am-12.30pm & 3.30pm-8pm daily) was started in 1262 and features a 15th-century wooden crucifix and 16th-century works by Cola dell'Amatrice. Virtually annexed to the church is the **Loggia dei Mercanti**. It looks suspiciously Tuscan, but was in fact built by Lombard masons in the 16th century. Merchants hawk their wares there to this day.

Pinacoteca

The second-largest art gallery in Le Marche is inside the 17th-century Palazzo Comunale on Piazza Arringo, south-east of Piazza del Popolo. The Pinacoteca *(☎ 0736 29 82 13, Piazza Arringo; adult/child €3.10/1.55; open 9am-1pm daily plus 3pm-7pm in summer)* boasts 400 works, including paintings by van Dyck, Titian, Carlo Crivelli and even Turner. Among the prints and drawings is an etching by Rembrandt. The gallery was founded in 1861 with works taken from churches and religious orders that were suppressed in the wake of Italian unification. Across Piazza Arringo, the **Museo Archeologico** *(☎ 0736 25 35 62, Piazza Arringo; adults/under-18s €2.05/free; open 8.30am-7.30pm Tues-Sun)* has a collection of implements used by the ancient Piceni tribe.

The Cathedral

Standing on the eastern flank of Piazza Arringo, Ascoli's cathedral *(☎ 0736 25 97 74, Piazza Arringo; free; open 7am-12.30pm & 4pm-8pm daily)* is a lavish example of Baroque excess, embellished in what some connoisseurs consider to be a less than tasteful manner. In compensation for the overkill, you will encounter what is possibly Carlo Crivelli's best work, *Virgin and Saints*, in the **Cappella del Sacramento**. The baptistery next to the cathedral, something of a traffic barrier today, has remained unchanged since it was constructed in the 11th century.

Vecchio Quartiere

The town's Old Quarter stretches from Corso Mazzini (the main thoroughfare, or *decumanus*, of the Roman-era settlement) to the River Tronto. Its main street is the picturesque Via delle Torri, which eventually becomes Via Solestà. This is a perfect spot to put away the guidebooks and just wander where your whims take you. Worth watching for on the curiously named Via delle Donne (Women Street) is the 14th-century **Chiesa di San Pietro Martire** (*☎ 0736 25 52 14, Piazza V Basso; free; open 7.30am-12.30pm & 3.30pm-7pm daily*), dedicated to the saint who founded the Dominican community at Ascoli. The chunky Gothic structure houses the Reliquario della Santa Spina, containing what is said to be a thorn from Christ's crown of thorns. This church is one of about a dozen in Ascoli dating to at least the 15th century.

The 40m-high **Torre degli Ercolani** on Via dei Soderini, west of the Chiesa di San Pietro Martire, is the tallest of the town's medieval towers. Abutting it is the **Palazzetto Longobardo**, a 12th-century Lombard-Romanesque defensive position and now a youth hostel (see Places to Stay for details). Just to the north is the well-preserved **Ponte Romano**, a single-arched Roman bridge.

Special Events

The town's big festival is Quintana, a medieval pageant held on the first Sunday of every August. Hundreds of locals dressed in traditional costume fill the town centre for jousting, parades and other medieval doings. Between October and February, the city also comes alive with shows, concerts and opera during the city's Stagione Lirica.

Places to Stay

Don't forget to book ahead during festival times.

Ostello de'Longobardi (*☎ 0736 25 90 07, fax 0736 25 91 91,* **W** *www.hostels-aig.org/shop-uk/ascoli_piceno.htm, Via dei Soderini 26*) B&B €10.35. An HI-card is obligatory at this hostel inside a 12th-century castle, but thankfully there's no curfew. It's certainly not the cleanest of places, and the hot water system is decidedly dodgy, but as far as youth hostels go, they don't get much more atmospheric than this.

La Cantina dell'Arte (*☎ 0736 25 11 35, fax 0736 25 51 91, Rua della Lupa 8*) Singles/doubles €25.80/36.15. The rooms here are simple but clean and all have private bath. The owners also run a very cheap restaurant opposite.

Albergo Pavoni (*☎/fax 0736 34 25 75, Via Navicella 135/b*) Singles/doubles €25.80/41.30 with bath. This place is 5km out of town in Marino del Tronto. Take bus No 3 from Piazza Arringo. Rooms with shared bath are cheaper and prices come down in the low season.

Places to Eat

Ascoli is responsible for a delicious idea for a starter. *Olive all'ascolana* are olives stuffed with meat and deep-fried.

La Cantina dell'Arte (*☎ 0736 25 56 20, Rua della Lupa 5*) Full meals €7.75. Open Mon-Sat. For a really cheap meal, try this restaurant; the service is lightning and the decor's fun, with copper pans and musical instruments covering the walls.

La Locandiera (*☎ 0736 26 25 09, Via Goldoni 2*) Full meals €15.50. Open Tues-Sat. This friendly trattoria, with vaulted brick ceilings, is popular with locals and good value for money.

La Vecchia Ascoli (*☎ 0736 25 11 44, Via dei Sabini 10*) Full meals around €15.50. Open Tues-Sun. Try this place for abundant helpings of good local cuisine.

Pizzeria al Teatro (*☎ 0736 25 35 49, Via del Teatro 3*) Pizzas from €3.10, mains from €5.15. Open Tues-Sun. This place has a good garden restaurant and is well positioned to catch the theatre crowd.

Tornasacco (*☎ 0736 25 41 51, Piazza del Popolo 36*) Full meals around €23.25. A spiffy establishment in the heart of town, Tornasacco specialises in olive all'ascolana.

There is an ***outdoor market*** on Piazza delle Erbe, near Piazza del Popolo, every morning except Sunday.

Getting There & Away

Buses leave from Piazzale della Stazione, in front of the train station, which is in the new part of town on the eastern side of the Castellano river. Start (☎ 0736 34 22 43) runs four buses daily to Rome (€10.85, three hours). In Rome, Start buses leave from Viale Castro Pretorio 84, near Stazione Termini. Mazzuca (☎ 0736 40 22 67) serves Montemonaco (€2.60, 1½ hours, three daily), Amandola (€2.20, 1 hour 10 minutes, three daily) and other towns near the Monti Sibillini range. At 6.30am daily, Amadio (☎ 0736 34 23 40) runs a service to Florence (€22.70, 6¼ hours) via Perugia (€13.45, 4¼ hours) and Siena (€20.15, 5½ hours).

A spur train line connects Ascoli Piceno hourly with Porto d'Ascoli (€1.70, 35 minutes) and San Benedetto del Tronto (€2.20, 40 minutes), both of which are on the Bologna-Lecce line. From San Benedetto there are half-hourly trains to Ancona (€4.15, 1 hour 10 minutes).

The S4 connects Ascoli Piceno with Rome and the Adriatic coastline.

MONTI SIBILLINI

Rising bare and forbidding in the lower south-west of Le Marche, and reaching into neighbouring Umbria, the stark Monti Sibillini range is one of the most beautiful stretches of the Apennines. Dotted with caves and lined with walking trails, the mountains are also the scene of more energetic sporting activities such as hang-gliding and horse riding. The range is littered with rifugi and offers reasonable skiing in winter.

Amandola makes a good centre from which to explore the area, but lacks cheap accommodation. It is one of the prettiest villages in Le Marche. Just south is **Montefortino**, a good base for accessing Montemonaco, at the base of Monte Sibilla, a place for serious walkers.

Montemonaco is an out-of-the-way town and not easily reached by public transport, although you'll be surprised by the number of tourists in summer. Many are there for the Gola dell'Infernaccio (Gorge of Hell), one of the easiest and most spectacular walks in Le Marche.

To reach the range, take the S4 from Ascoli Piceno and follow the signs. Buses connect the area with Ascoli Piceno and various cities throughout Le Marche. See also The Valnerina in the Umbria section earlier in this chapter for details about hang-gliding and how to get to the mountains from Umbria.

Information

If approaching from the north along the S78 from Ancona, stop at the IAT office (☎ 0733 65 71 44) at Largo Ricciardi 1 in Sarnano. It sometimes has limited walking and climbing information. The CAI publishes a detailed guide to the mountains (in Italian), complete with maps: *Parco Nazionale dei Sibillini – Le Più Belle Escursioni*, by Alberico Alesi and Maurizio Calibani.

Places to Stay

There is a camp site just south of Montefortino at Ceretana.

Montespino *(☎/fax 0736 85 92 38, Loc. Ceretana)* Sites per person/tent €3.60/6.20. Open 1 June-30 Sept. There are over 100 sites here, and good services including restaurant and supermarket.

Montemonaco offers accommodation at good rates.

Albergo Sibilla *(☎ 0736 85 61 44, Via Roma 52)* Low/high season per person €38.75/43.90. This friendly, family-run place has 10 rooms, all with private bath. Prices include breakfast.

Rifugio della Montagna *(☎/fax 0736 85 63 27, Loc. Foce)* Per person without breakfast €20.65, more than 2 nights €18.10 per night. This pleasant place is just outside Montemonaco but it's not a typical mountain refuge as its name would suggest. There's also a good restaurant here that caters for vegetarians.

Abruzzo & Molise

Abruzzo, along with neighbouring Molise, is one of the few areas of Italy to be spared the influx of mass tourism. Although neither region is as rich in artistic and cultural heritage as their more illustrious neighbours, there is still plenty to explore, especially in Abruzzo.

Until administratively divided in 1963, Abruzzo and Molise were known as the Abruzzi, a term still commonly used to describe the two. The earthquake-prone region was particularly hard-hit in 1915, when a massive jolt left 30,000 people dead.

Highlights

- Trek beneath Corno Grande of the Gran Sasso d'Italia, the Apennines' highest peak
- Come close to a wolf or two at Civitella Alfedena in the Parco Nazionale d'Abruzzo
- Squirm like the snakes in Cocullo's Processione dei Serpari (Snake Charmers Procession)
- Savour the Roman Ruins and rural setting of Saepinum

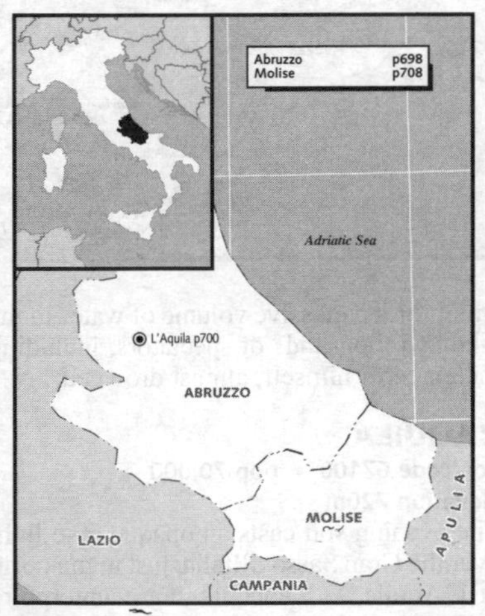

Abruzzo

The wild beauty of Abruzzo's mountain terrain is captivating – the bald, craggy peaks of Gran Sasso d'Italia are capped by the Corno Grande (2914m), the highest mountain in the Apennines, and have perilous drops of up to 1000m. Farther south, wolves and bears still roam (protected) in the forests of the Parco Nazionale d'Abruzzo.

The region isn't just for nature-lovers. The medieval towns of L'Aquila and Sulmona are well worth visiting and the countryside is speckled with an array of castles and isolated, hilltop *borghi* (cluttered towns and villages little changed over hundreds of years).

In antiquity, Abruzzo was famed for its witches, wizards and snake-charmers – members of a tribe known as the Marsi, who lived around modern-day Avezzano. Even today, snakes feature in a bizarre annual religious festival in the mountain village of Cocullo, near Sulmona.

Traditionally Abruzzo is grazing territory and its sheep farmers still play an important role in the local economy. A key agricultural area is the Piana del Fucino (Fucino Plain), east of Avezzano, which was created by draining the vast Lago Fucino in the late 19th century. Prince Torlonia undertook the project, on the condition that he would have title to the land, and completed it during the Fascist period. It was not until the 1950s that the Italian government took over the plain and parcelled out the land to local peasants.

Torlonia's efforts were not a first. The ancient Romans had a shot at draining the lake in what proved a remarkable, yet disastrous, feat of engineering. Under the orders of Emperor Claudius, the Romans built a tunnel about 10km long to drain the lake into a neighbouring valley. Unfortunately, when the outlet tunnel was opened, it proved too

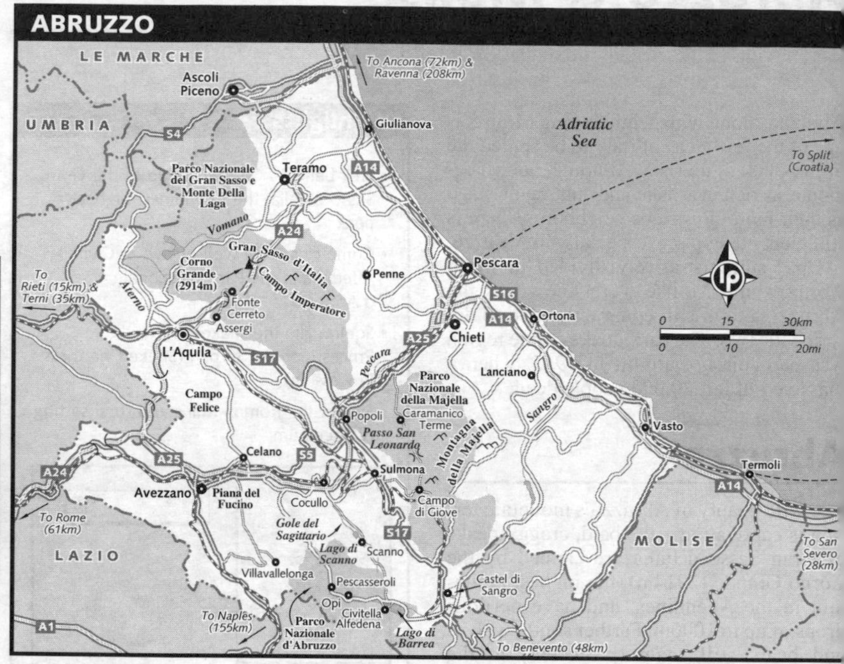

small for the massive volume of water in the lake and thousands of spectators, including the emperor himself, almost drowned.

L'AQUILA

postcode 67100 • pop 70,000
elevation 720m

The evening sun casts an opaque rose light over the Gran Sasso d'Italia, just to the north of L'Aquila – an encouraging counterpoint to the somewhat gloomy regional capital.

Despite repeated earthquakes, the medieval core of the city remains an interesting place to explore, but L'Aquila's curious beginnings are perhaps more intriguing still. Emperor Frederick II founded the city in 1240 by, it is said, drawing together the citizens of 99 villages. Whether true or not, the number 99 became the city's symbol. The citizens of L'Aquila (meaning 'The Eagle' – a reference to the eagle in the imperial coat of arms) established 99 churches and 99 piazzas, as well as a fountain with (almost) 99 spouts. Earthquakes, particularly one in 1703, have destroyed most of the churches and piazzas but the medieval fountain survives. As does the town hall bell, which chimes 99 times every evening.

L'Aquila's people have a rebellious spirit but have frequently backed the wrong horse. The Swabian King Manfred sacked the city in 1266 because the people sided with the pope against him. Then it endured a 13-month siege by the Aragonese for supporting the House of Anjou in the fight for mastery of the Kingdom of Naples. L'Aquila rose against Spanish rule twice in the 16th and 17th centuries and both times the city was crushed. The 1703 earthquake all but finished L'Aquila off. Revolt finally proved fruitful when, in 1860, the city was made regional capital for its efforts towards national unity.

Orientation

L'Aquila's train station is west and downhill from the old centre. Bus No 79 will take you into town. Get off in Corso Federico II, the continuation of the elegant old main boulevard, Corso Vittorio Emanuele. The intercity bus station is on Piazza Battaglione Alpini L'Aquila, from where it's a short walk down Corso Vittorio Emanuele to the Piazza del Duomo and the heart of town.

Information

Tourist Offices The main IAT office (☎ 0862 41 08 08) is at Piazza Santa Maria Paganica 5. It opens 8am to 1pm and 3pm to 6pm daily April to September, 8am to 1pm and 3pm to 6pm Monday to Saturday and 8am to 1pm Sunday October to March. There's a smaller office (☎ 0862 2 23 06) at Via XX Settembre 8 which observes similar hours. For advance planning, check out W www.laquila.com.

The Centro Turistico Gran Sasso (☎ 0862 2 21 47), Corso Vittorio Emanuele 49, operates as a travel agency with a hotel reservation service. Run by the municipality, it's another source of information about both the town and outdoor activities in the Gran Sasso range.

Post & Communications The main post office is on Piazza del Duomo. There's a private telephone office at Via Patini 48.

You can log on at Centro Multimediale e Pub, Via Cimino 51, open 5pm to midnight Tuesday to Saturday, at or Internet Games, Via dell'Arcivescovado 13, open 8.30am to 1am Monday to Saturday, 4pm to 1am Sunday.

Medical Services & Emergency The Ospedale San Salvatore (hospital; ☎ 0862 36 81) is north-west of the town centre in Localita Coppito. The *questura* (police station; ☎ 0862 43 01) is at Via Strinella 2, also well out of the centre.

Castle

This massive edifice of steep, blanched battlements sunk deep into a now-empty moat is L'Aquila's most impressive monument. Looking out to the Gran Sasso d'Italia, it was built by the Spanish to overawe the locals after they'd abortively rebelled. Within is the **Museo Nazionale d'Abruzzo** *(☎ 0862 63 31, Castello Cinquecentesco; admission €4.15; open 9am-7pm Tues-Sun)*, home to a collection of mainly local religious artworks. Its main draw, however, is the skeleton of a mammoth, found near the town in the early 1950s.

Churches

The **Basilica di San Bernardino** *(☎ 0862 2 22 55, Piazza San Bernardino; free; open 6.30am-11.45am & 3.30pm-7.30pm daily in summer, 6.30am-11.45am & 3.30pm-6.30pm daily in winter)* is fronted by a magnificent three-tiered, cream-coloured classical facade. Within, peer up at the exquisite Baroque ceiling in gilded woodwork and savour the intricately detailed relief decoration of San Bernardino's mausoleum, the work of local artisan Silvestro dell'Aquila. San Bernardino, originally of Siena, spent his last years in L'Aquila, where he died.

The Romanesque **Basilica di Santa Maria di Collemaggio** *(☎ 0349 732 50 07 – ask for Don Valeriano, Viale di Collemaggio; free; open 8.30am-1pm & 3pm-8pm Mon-Fri,*

La Perdonanza

Tempted by the thought of a little extra indulgence in L'Aquila? It's not the kind you might imagine and you'll have to time your visit finely if you want to take advantage.

L'Aquila's *festa* (festival) par excellence goes back to 1294 and the day when Celestine V, on his inauguration as pope in the Basilica di Santa Maria di Collemaggio, established La Perdonanza (the forgiveness or pardoning). Since that time, every evening of 28th August, the Porta Santa (Holy Door) of the church where he lies buried – the only pope not to lie within St Peter's in Rome – is swung open. The faithful stream through in their thousands for the next 24 hours, confident that all who cross its threshold will be absolved of their sins.

Nowadays La Perdonanza is as much a lay as a spiritual celebration and the whole town gives itself over to partying throughout the week leading up to the opening of the portal.

ABRUZZO

8.30am-8pm Sat & Sun), south-east of the centre, has an equally imposing facade – its rose windows encased by a quilt pattern of pink and white marble. The basilica was built at the instigation of a hermit, Pietro da Morrone, who was elected pope at the age of 80 in 1294. Pietro took the name Celestine V, but this unworldly and trusting man was no match for the machinations of courtiers and politicians and he was eventually forced to abdicate. His successor, Pope Boniface VIII, saw Celestine as a threat and threw him into prison, where he died. As founder of the Celestine order, he was canonised seven years later and his tomb lies inside the basilica. By contrast to these two splendid basilicas, L'Aquila's **cathedral**, shattered more than once by earthquakes, can boast only an unexceptional neoclassical facade.

Casa Museo Signorini Corsi

This museum *(☎ 0862 41 09 00, Via Patin 42; admission €3.10/2.10; open 4pm-7pm Tues-Fri, 10am-1pm & 4pm-7pm Sat & Sun)* occupies the Palazzo Signorini Corsi, ancestral home of the Corsi family, who bequeathed all of their considerable collection to the town. It houses a particularly fin small collection of religious art (more stimulating than that within the Museo Nazionale d'Abruzzo – see under Castle earlier – if you have to choose) and period furniture.

Fontana delle 99 Cannelle

A symbol of the city, the 'Fountain of the 99 Spouts' was constructed in the late 13th century. No-one knows where the water originates but it was the town's lifeblood until well into the 20th century. Count the various stone faces, gargoyles and the like – they don't seem to add up to the magic number!

JANE SMITH

How many spouts are there again?

Places to Stay

The nearest camp site is in Fonte Cerreto, about 12km north of town (see the following Parco Nazionale del Gran Sasso e Monti della Laga section).

Locanda Orazi *(☎ 0862 41 28 89, Via Roma 175)* Singles/doubles without bath €20.70/31. This, the only cheap place in town, is often fully occupied by students during the academic year.

Hotel Duomo *(☎ 0862 41 08 93, fax 0862 41 30 58, Via Dragonetti 6)* Singles/doubles with bath, telephone & TV €49.10/77.50. A pleasant place and pick of the mid-range hotels.

Hotel Castello *(☎ 0862 41 91 47, fax 0862 41 91 40, ⓔ hotel.Castello@worldtel.it, Piazza Battaglione Alpini L'Aquila)* Singles/doubles/triples/quads €51.65/77.50/98.15/108.50. This three-star place has similar facilities to Hotel Duomo.

Places to Eat

Traditional local dishes include *maccheroni alla chitarra*, thick macaroni which is cut by feeding the pasta through a contraption with strings that apparently reminded someone of a guitar. Lamb *(agnello)* also makes a regular appearance, either roasted or grilled. Fresh produce is sold in the ***market*** *(Piazza del Duomo)*, which is held most days .

La Perla Nera *(☎ 0862 41 34 79, Piazza Palazzo)* Open Mon-Sat. A great little place which does calzone and a variety of original pizzas at €1.30 a slice.

Trattoria San Biagio *(☎ 0862 2 21 39, Piazza San Biagio 4) Menu* €15.50, full meal around €18.10. Open Mon-Sat. Popular – just see the way the locals flock in at lunchtime – and over 150 years history as a restaurant, San Biagio is something of a local institution.

Trattoria del Giaguaro *(☎ 0862 2 40 01, Piazza Santa Maria Paganica 4)*. Open all day Wed-Sun & lunchtime Mon. This place, although lacking the antiquity of San Bagio, makes another good choice for a medium-priced meal.

Ristorante Renato *(☎ 0862 2 55 96, Via dell'Indipendenza 9)* Full meals about €18.10. Open Mon-Sat. Ristorante Renato is a good place for regional cuisine, especially lamb dishes.

Trattoria San Biagio *(☎ 0862 2 21 39, Piazza San Biagio 4)* Tourist *menu* €15.50, full meals around €18.10. Open Mon-Sat. Popular – just see the way the locals flock in at lunchtime – and over 150 years as a restaurant, San Biagio is something of a local institution that excels in regional cuisine.

Cafes, Bars & Pasticcerias If you fancy a lighter bite, try one of the options listed below.

Gran Caffè Eden *(☎ 0862 2 62 26, Corso Vittorio Emanuele 92)* One of the more elegant bars along Corso Vittorio Emanuele, it also does a bargain *menu* for €7.75.

Torrone Sorelle Nurzia *(Corso Vittorio Emanuele 38)*. This elegant parlour specialises in a chocolate variety of *torrone*, a scrumptious nougat confection.

ABRUZZO

Pasticceria Fratelli Nurzia *(Piazza del Duomo 50–51)* Torrone Sorelle Nurzia's competition and a breakaway from the same family business, which goes back to 1835.

Entertainment

An annual season of weekly concerts is held between October and May by, among others, the Società Aquilana dei Concerti (☎ 0862 41 41 61 for reservations). If you're in town during the summer, ask about the special open-air concert, ballet and drama performances. Staff at the IAT offices can provide information.

Getting There & Away

ARPA buses (☎ 0862 41 28 08 or 06 442 33 928 in Rome) run to Rome's Stazione Tiburtina (€9.30). They also connect the city with Avezzano (€4.50, frequent), Sulmona (€5.10, seven daily) and Pescara (€7.25, five daily) via the *autostrada* (motorway). All leave from the bus station on Piazza Battaglione Alpini L'Aquila.

By train, the town is accessible from Rome via Sulmona or Terni, and from Pescara via Sulmona. Buses Nos 30 and 79C regularly link the train station and town centre.

PARCO NAZIONALE DEL GRAN SASSO E MONTI DELLA LAGA

The bulk of the 150,000 hectares of this, one of Italy's newest national parks, lies within Abruzzo, but it also spills over into Lazio and Le Marche. From the rocky limestone and dolomite peaks of the Gran Sasso d'Italia to the more gentle rounded sandstone summits of the Monti della Laga to the north, it's stimulating trekking terrain.

Check out Ⓦ www.gransassolagapark.it for more details.

The Abruzzo park office (☎ 0862 6 05 21, Via del Convento 1) is in Assergi, some 10km north-east of L'Aquila. Open 10.30am to 1pm and 4pm to 6pm Monday to Friday, it carries information and a park map in English. For walking, pick up the IGN map *Parco Nazionale del Gran Sasso* (€7.75) at 1:25,000.

A funicular railway leaves **Fonte Cerreto** every 30 minutes for **Campo Imperatore** (2117m), where there are walking trails and a small, but popular, ski area.

The park has a network of *rifugi* (mountain huts) for walkers. Hotel accommodation is limited and expensive but there is a camp site and a hostel.

Camping Funivia del Gran Sasso *(☎ 0862 60 61 63)* €4.65/5.70/1 per person/tent/car. Open mid-May–mid-Sept. At Fonte Cerreto and handy as a base for walking, this is also the nearest camp site to L'Aquila.

Ostello Campo Imperatore *(☎/fax 0862 40 00 11)* €15.50 per person. In Campo Imperatore, this hostel offers by far the cheapest accommodation in rooms for two or four.

From L'Aquila, take bus No 6 (€0.80, seven daily) from Via Castello to the funicular at Fonte Cerreto.

SULMONA

postcode 67039 • pop 25,000
elevation 400m

Sulmona, birthplace of the classical poet Ovid, whose statue stands proud in the main square, is an understated but charming little town, hemmed in by mountains. The medieval centre is a joy to wander, and the town is well placed to serve as a base for touring southern Abruzzo.

Its modern claim to fame is the *confetti* industry – the making of elaborate flower-shaped arrangements of sugar almonds, a must at traditional Italian weddings. Check out the shops along Corso Ovidio; this edible foliage in a whole range of designs makes an original, easily transported and inexpensive gift for the folks back home.

Orientation & Information

The town's main street, Corso Ovidio, runs from the Via Communale, a small park beside Piazzale Tresca, to the vast Piazza Garibaldi, a five-minute walk. It's closed to traffic outside business hours.

Sulmona's friendly IAT office (☎/fax 0864 5 32 76), Corso Ovidio 208, opens 9am to 1pm and 4 to 7pm daily (shorter hours in winter).

To check your email, log on at Elmar Technology, Via Barbato 9, which charges

€2.60 per hour. It's open 9.30am to 1.15pm and 4pm to 8.15pm Monday to Saturday

Things to See

The **Palazzo dell'Annunziata** *(Corso Ovidio)* is a harmonious blend of Gothic and Renaissance. Note the beautifully carved frieze halfway up the facade. The building houses a small **municipal museum** *(☎ 0864 21 02 16, Corso Ovidio; free; open 9.30am-1pm & 4pm-9pm daily)*. Beside the palazzo is a Baroque church of the same name, rebuilt after the 1703 earthquake, while on Piazza XX Settembre beside Corso Ovidio is a statue of Ovid, local boy made good (see the boxed text).

Piazza Garibaldi is the scene of a colourful market every Wednesday and Saturday morning. In one corner is the austere Renaissance **Fontana del Vecchio** (Fountain of the Old One) and the medieval **aqueduct**, which borders the piazza on two sides. The most interesting feature of the **Chiesa di San Martino**, also on the piazza, is its Gothic entrance. On the adjacent Piazza del Carmine, the Romanesque portal is all that remains of **Chiesa di San Francesco della Scarpa**, destroyed in the 1703 earthquake.

Ovid

The Augustan poet, considered by some as being second only to Virgil, has a mixed, and not altogether flattering, reputation. Born in Sulmona in 43 BC and sent at an early age to Rome to study rhetoric and make himself a comfortable career in politics, Ovid preferred to write poetry instead. His early erotic verse, such as *Amores* and *Ars Amatoria* (The Art of Love), gained him quick popularity in Roman high society. Possibly his most ambitious work was the *Metamorphosis*, a kind of extended cover version of a whole gamut of Greek myths which culminated in descriptions of Caesar's transformation into a star and the apotheosis of Augustus, ruler at the time. This last piece of sycophancy did not stop the emperor from banishing him to the Black Sea in AD 8. He died in Tomi, in modern Romania, 10 years later.

In Sulmona, sweet-making becomes art. Fabbrica Confetti Pelino, largest of the sugared-almond manufacturers, houses the **Museo dell'Arte Confettiera** *(☎ 0864 21 00 47, Via Stazione Introdacqua 55; free; open 8.30am-12.30pm & 3.30pm-6.30pm Mon-Sat)*. A 15-minute walk from Porta Napoli (signposted), at the southern end of Corso Ovidio, it's a must for every candy cruncher.

Places to Stay & Eat

Hotel Traffico *(☎ 380 72 44 816, Via degli Agghiacciati 17)* Singles/doubles with bath €20.70/41.35. Just off Corso Ovidio, Hotel Traffico represents good value in its category.

Hotel Italia *(☎/fax 0864 5 23 08, Piazza Salvatore Tommasi 3)* Singles/doubles with bath €28.40/46.50. Just west of central Piazza XX Settembre, this lovely building with marble columns is full of fading character (though increasingly in need of a good lick of paint).

Ristorante Mafalda *(☎ 0864 3 45 38, Via Solimo 20)* Full meal €15.50-18.10. Open Mon-Sat. Some 50m east of Corso Ovidio, it has a pleasant summertime garden and an equally agreeable indoor vaulted dining room. Try their *cabritto con formaggio pecorino e uova* (kid – the goat kind – prepared with strong cheese and egg).

Ristorante Italia *(☎ 0864 3 30 70, Piazza XX Settembre 23)* Full meal €15.50-18.10. Open Tues-Sun. This is another excellent choice, where the service is positively motherly and the menu adventurous.

Gran Caffé *(Piazza XX Settembre)* is popular with locals, young and old. Take to heart these wise words, painted above the bar, from *Ars Amatoria* (The Art of Love) by Ovid, whose statue you see through the cafe window: *Et Venus in vinis ignis in igne fuit* ('Love is to wine as flames are to fire').

Getting There & Away

ARPA buses (☎ 0864 20 19 33) leave from a confusing variety of points, including the Via Communale, the train station and beneath the Ponte Capograssi. To find out which stop you need, ask when you buy your ticket from the tobacconist at Piazza XX Settembre 18, the official sales point.

Buses link Sulmona to L'Aquila (€5.20, seven daily), Pescara (€5.20, seven daily), Naples (€11.40, five daily), Scanno (€2.60, 10 daily) and other nearby towns.

The train station is about 2km downhill from the historic centre, and the half-hourly bus No A runs between the two. Regular trains link the town with Rome and Pescara.

AROUND SULMONA

Skiing

Some modest ski slopes lie east of Sulmona. About 18km of tortuous driving brings you to **Campo di Giove**, around which you'll find 15km of downhill runs and also some cross-country trails. It is the first in a series of small ski areas (the next is at Passo San Leonardo, about 10km north of Campo di Giove) leading up into the Montagna della Majella and the Parco Nazionale della Majella.

Parco Nazionale della Majella

This 75,000-hectare national park stretches like a rough-cut diamond to the east of Sulmona. Within it are Monte Amaro (2795m), the second highest summit in the Apennines, and over 25 other peaks which exceed 2000m. For walking, consult the visitors centre (☎ 085 92 23 43) at Caramanico Terme (700m), where there's also a small nature museum (☎ 085 92 23 43).

Cocullo

The tiny mountain village of Cocullo only warrants a visit on one day of the year – the first Thursday in May, when its inhabitants celebrate the feast day of San Domenico in a truly original and weird fashion. A statue of the saint is draped with jewels and banknotes donated by pilgrims and festooned with live snakes. It's borne in procession through the village, accompanied by villagers, also bedecked with wriggling reptiles. The festival, which has distant pagan origins, is known as the Processione dei Serpari (Snake Charmers' Procession).

Cocullo has no accommodation but is accessible by ARPA bus from Sulmona and Scanno. Plan to arrive in the village early on the day of the festival as it attracts huge crowds. Festivities start around 10am, the procession begins at noon and the fun continues throughout the afternoon.

Ask at the tourist office in Sulmona or Scanno for details on buses to Cocullo, as the usual scant services are increased for the event.

Scanno

This village (1050m) was assaulted by various photographers after WWII and made into an example of traditionalism in the modern world. As a result, Scanno has become something of a minor tourist mecca for Italians. The handful of elderly women who still skittle about in traditional costume must, you can't help thinking, take some affront at having become tourist 'sights'.

Scanno was long a centre of wool production, and for centuries an exclusive supplier to the Franciscan order. Today the cheerfully jumbled medieval village is surrounded by an outcrop of uninspired modern 'suburbia', much of which is given over to hotel space.

Scanno is well worth the effort. The drive south from Sulmona through the Gole del Sagittario (Sagittarius Gorges) and past the peaceful Lago di Scanno is delightful, while south of Scanno the road, scarcely less impressive, takes you right into Parco Nazionale d'Abruzzo. Above the village, a chair lift leads to a small ski area.

The IAT office (☎ 0864 7 43 17), Piazza Santa Maria della Valle 12, is on the edge of the medieval town centre.

Places to Stay & Eat There are plenty of hotels, one camp site and some interesting places to eat.

Camping I Lupi *(☎ 0864 74 01 00)* Sites per person/tent/car €4.20/4.70/2.10. Open year-round. This camp site is attractively sited near the Lago di Scanno.

Pensione Nilde *(☎/fax 0864 7 43 59, Viale del Lago 101)* Singles €18.10-25.85, doubles €36.15-46.50, all with bath. Compulsory full board in Aug €46.50 per person . Scanno's cheapest option is on a rise overlooking the old town.

Pensione Grotta dei Colombi *(☎/fax 0864 7 43 93, Viale dei Caduti 64)* Doubles with bathroom €41.35. Half-board €35.15, compulsory full board in Aug €38.75. Deep in the medieval city, its worth staying at this friendly hotel for the food alone.

Albergo Margherita *(☎/fax 0864 7 43 53, Via Domenico Tanturri 100)* Singles/doubles with bath €30.00-49.10, compulsory full board in Aug €38.75-51.65. This hotel, on the southern side of town, is an easy walk from the medieval quarter.

Hotel Vittoria *(☎ 0864 7 43 98, fax 0864 74 71 79, ⓔ hotelvittoria@hotmail.com, Via Domenico di Rienzo 46)* Singles/doubles/triples with bath €41.35/67.15/87.80. Hotel Vittoria is a rather more upmarket option which also offers fine views over the old town.

Ristorante La Porta *(☎ 0864 74 72 80, Via Cioria 31)* Full meal €13.00-15.50. Open Wed-Mon. In the shadow of Porta della Croce, the old city gate on the southern side of the medieval quarter, this friendly place makes its own pasta, changes its menu daily and also serves pizza in the evenings.

Trattoria Lo Sgabello *(☎ 0864 74 74 76, Via dei Pescatori 45)* Full meal €15.50-23.25. Trattoria Lo Sgabello is a reliable medium range option.

Ristorante Gli Archetti *(☎ 0864 7 46 45, Via Silla 8)* Full meal around €26.00. Open Wed-Mon. Within the medieval town, its door, plastered with stickers from Italian gastronomic magazines, bears witness to the quality of its cuisine.

Getting There & Away ARPA buses connect Scanno with Sulmona. An Autolinee Schiappa bus leaves Stazione Tiburtina in Rome for Scanno three times a day. Departure times are noon, 3pm and 5.30pm.

PARCO NAZIONALE D'ABRUZZO

Established in 1923 with a former royal hunting reserve as its nucleus, the Parco Nazionale d'Abruzzo now incorporates 110,000 hectares of the Apennines, ringed by an external protected area of 150,000 hectares. Along with neighbouring Parco Nazionale della Majella, this park is the last refuge of the Marsican brown bear and Apennine wolf, two native species now being actively re-introduced. At the last count there were around 100 bears and 40 to 50 wolves roaming wild. The park is also home to over 500 indigenous Abruzzo chamois – their kids welcome prey for the few golden eagles, wildcat and lynx.

The park receives over two million visitors each year and its villages seethe with tourists at the height of summer. Its forests and meadows are perfect for both family excursions and long-distance walks, and you'll find that you can be almost alone only a few hundred metres from the highway. Pick up a copy of the excellent *Discovering the Abruzzo National Park* (€7.75), which describes eight half- and full-day walks plus eight shorter (about one hour) nature trails. Supplement this with the park's *Carta Turistica* (€5.20) at 1:50,000, where walking routes and rifugi are also highlighted, and you're ready to go. You can buy both at the Uffici di Zona (Park Information Office) in Pescasseroli and Civitella Alfedena. (Note that two of the most popular trails, Valle di Rose and Monte Amazo, can only be undertaken in a group led by a park guide in high summer.)

The most convenient base is the town of **Pescasseroli** (elevation 1167m), in the centre of the park. The Ufficio di Zona (☎ 0863 9 19 55), Via Consultore 1, opens 9am to noon and 3pm to 7pm daily. The IAT office (☎ 0863 91 04 61), at Via Piave 2, opens 9am to 1pm and 4pm to 7pm Monday to Saturday plus Sunday in high season. The park's **Centro di Visita** *(☎ 0863 91 04 05, Viale Santa Lucia; admission €5.20; open 10am-1pm & 3pm-7pm daily)* has a small natural history museum and zoo, where you can see at least one of the park's major species up close, including a wolf, a Marsican brown bear and a lynx.

Smaller **Civitella Alfedena** (elevation 1121m), on the park's eastern edge and poised above Lago di Barrea, lies closer to the park's most spectacular scenery. Less touristy than Pescasseroli, the village has a combined park information and visitors centre, the ***Centro Lupo*** *(Wolf Centre; ☎ 0864 89 01 41, admission free to information centre or €2.60 to wolf museum; open 10am-1pm & 3pm-7pm daily)*. At the small wolf museum, you can look over the open-air corral behind

ABRUZZO

the centre, where a few wolves prowl in semi-captivity. In a smaller enclosure lurks a little family of three lynx. There's also a small IAT office (☎ 0349 213 23 94), which opens the same hours as the Centro Lupo.

Places to Stay

Free-camping is forbidden in the park but there are several camp sites, open 15 June to 15 September.

Campeggio dell'Orso *(☎ 0863 9 19 55)* Sites per person/tent/car €3.10/3.10/2/10. About 1km south of Pescasseroli, this camp site also has a ***rifugi*** (€5.20 per bed), bookable directly or through the Pescasseroli Ufficio di Zona.

Campeggio Wolf *(☎ 0864 89 03 60, Via Nazionale)* Sites per person/tent/car from €1.85/1.85/1.55 to €4.40/3.65/3.10. This camp site is conveniently situated in the heart of Civitella Alfedena.

Hotel Cristiana *(☎ 0863 91 07 95, Via Collachi 3)* Rooms €31.00-41.35. Half-board €33.60-38.75 per person. A little outside Pescasseroli, Hotel Cristiana, if rather too self-consciously rustic, is a good base for exploring the park.

Albergo La Torre *(☎/fax 0864 89 01 21, Via Castello 3)* Rooms per person with bath €15.50 (€24.80 in August), half-board €28.40-38.75. Open year-round. In Civitella Alfedena, this homely walkers' favourite also has a good restaurant serving primarily hearty local cuisine (count on around €18 for a full meal).

Getting There & Away

Pescasseroli, Civitella Alfadena and other villages in the park are linked by five daily ARPA buses to Avezzano (and from there to L'Aquila) and to Castel di Sangro (with onward travel to Sulmona by bus or train). Between mid-June and mid-September, a daily Roma Tiburtina bus runs between Rome and both villages.

PESCARA

postcode 65100 • pop 127,200

A heavily developed summertime resort and commercial centre, Pescara's only real permanent attraction is its beach – and even that's nothing to write home about. However, travellers to Abruzzo are likely to pass through since it's also the main regional transport hub.

Jazz fans should go out of their way to take in the annual jazz festival (☎ 085 37 41 98 for information and reservations), which pulls in top-rank international musicians. It's held in the second half of July at the Teatro D'Annunzio.

Orientation & Information

From the FS train and intercity bus stations on Piazzale della Repubblica, the beach is just a short walk north-east down Corso Umberto I.

The IAT office (☎ 085 429 00 212) is at Via Nicola Fabrizi 171. It opens 9am to 1pm and 4pm to 7pm daily except Sunday afternoon in summer, and 9am to 1pm Monday to Saturday in winter. In the peak summer months another information booth normally opens at the train station.

Things to See

If you've a little time on your hands, fill it with a visit to the ***Museo Ittico*** *(☎ 085 428 35 16, Via Raffaele Paolucci; admission €1.55, open 9am-1pm Wed, Fri & Sat, 9am-1pm & 4.30pm-6.30pm Tues & Thurs)*, a fishery museum on the waterfront.

Places to Stay & Eat

Pensione Planet *(☎ 085 421 16 57, Via Piave 142)* Singles/doubles with bath €25.90/46.50. This recently upgraded hotel offers good value for its price.

Hotel Natale *(☎ 085 422 28 85, Via del Circuito 175)* Singles/doubles/triples/quads with bath €31.00/46.50/64.60/77.50. A good budget choice with more creature comforts, it also has a couple of doubles without bath for €36.20.

Hotel Alba *(☎ 085 38 91 45, fax 085 29 21 63, Via Michelangelo Forti 14)* Singles/doubles with bath €49.10/72.30 including breakfast. This place is near the train station, has decent rooms – and gets cheaper the longer you stay.

Pinguino *(☎ 085 6 28 69, Corso Manthonè 36)* Full meal €13-18. Across the

ABRUZZO

River Pescara, this reasonably priced restaurant also functions as a pizzeria.

Cantina di Jooz *(☎ 085 451 88 00, Via delle Caserme 61)* Full meal around €23. This is a more expensive option for a more subtle cuisine.

Getting There & Away

Bus ARPA buses (☎ 085 421 50 99) leave from the train station on Piazzale della Repubblica for L'Aquila (€7.25, 2 hours, 9 daily), Sulmona (€4.65, 1¼ hours, 6 daily) and many other destinations in Abruzzo. ARPA also runs to Naples, (Piazza Garibaldi; €16, 4½ hours, 3 daily) and Rome (Stazione Tiburtina; €14.50, 2¾ hours, 2 daily). Buses by Di Febo-Capuani (☎ 085 421 18 91) and Di Fonzo (☎ 085 421 18 91) also serve the latter. Timetables are posted at the ARPA ticket office (☎ 085 421 50 99) on the piazza.

Train Pescara is on the main train line along the Adriatic coast and is easily accessible for towns such as Bologna, Ancona, Foggia and points farther south, as well as L'Aquila, Sulmona and Rome.

Car & Motorcycle Heading north or south along the coast, you can choose between the A14 and the often busy S16, which hugs the coast more closely. Both the A25 and S5 lead towards Rome, L'Aquila and Sulmona.

Boat The high-speed catamaran Aldebaran (passengers only) runs four times weekly to Croatia's Dalmatian islands of Vis and Hvar and on to Split (Spavato; from €150, about 6 hours) between mid-June and late September. For information and reservations, contact Agencia Sanmar (☎ 085 451 08 73) whose office is at the port.

Molise

Hived off from Abruzzo, its bigger northern sibling, in 1963, Molise is a small, hilly and rather undistinguished region. A kind of cultural bridge from north to south, it has a low ranking on the tourist trail.

Largely rural and repeatedly shaken by devastating earthquakes, its towns are prosaic and of little interest. In fact, the traveller moving north to south will notice, perhaps for the first time, those great clumps of hideous concrete blocks that too often pass for a kind of standard in modern Mediterranean 'architecture', whether in southern Italy, Spain, Morocco or Egypt.

It's not all bad news. You can wander through the Roman provincial town ruins of Saepinum, south-west of Campobasso, and there are good walking opportunities in the Monti del Matese. Excavations in Isernia have unearthed what is believed to be the oldest village in Europe, and the small beach resort of Termoli is a jumping-off point for the Isole Tremiti, bunched together off the coast of northern Apulia (see Apulia in the Apulia, Basilicata & Calabria chapter).

CAMPOBASSO

postcode 86100 • pop 51,000
elevation 701m

Molise's regional capital, Campobasso, predominantly modern and basically unappealing, nevertheless makes a good base for exploring nearby Saepinum. The national *carabinieri* (military police) training school is here, as is a high-security prison.

The EPT office (☎ 0874 41 56 62), Piazza della Vittoria 14, opens 8am to 2pm Monday to Saturday. To reach it from the train station, turn left into Via Cavour, right into Via Gazzani and left again into Corso Vittorio Emanuele.

You can kill a couple of hours wandering up into the older part of town to take a look at the Romanesque churches of **San Bartolomeo** (13th century) and **San Giorgio** (12th century). The castle, striking from a distance, is less impressive close up. More worthwhile is the **Museo Samnitico** *(Samnite Museum; ☎ 0874 41 22 65, Via Chiarizia 12; free, open 9am-1pm & 3pm-7pm Tues-Sun)* which displays items, not only from the Samnite period, from local sites.

Campobasso is connected by bus to Termoli, Isernia and Pescara. Local trains run to Isernia (9 daily), Benevento (5 daily) and Termoli (7 daily). Long distance ones serve

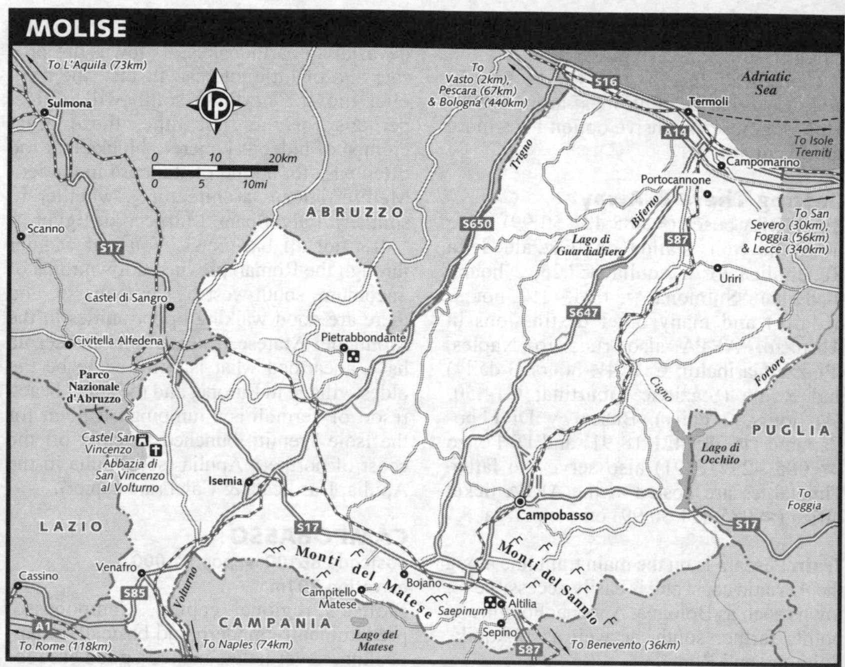

Rome (€17.50, 3½ hours, four daily) and Naples (€9.00, three hours, three daily).

AROUND CAMPOBASSO

One of Italy's least visited Roman ruins, **Saepinum** *(free)*, though a tough destination if you're without wheels, more than merits the effort. An unimportant provincial town, it survived into the 9th century before being sacked by Arab invaders. The well preserved ruins include much of the town walls and bastion towers in reticulated stone, a temple, a triumphal arch and the foundations of numerous houses. They survive amid small farm buildings, tasteful two-storey stone constructions that blend wonderfully with the classical remains. You're free to wander at will.

To reach Saepinum by public transport, take one of the infrequent provincial buses from Campobasso which pass by the hamlet of Altilia, right beside the site, or to Sepino, a 3km walk away.

The **Monti del Matese**, south-west of Campobasso, offer good walking in summer and adequate skiing in winter. Take a bus from Campobasso to Campitello Matese or a train from Campobasso or Isernia to Bojano (Boiano). From either point trails lead into the mountains.

Campitello Matese (elevation 1430m) is a small winter and summer sports resort where, according to season, you can hire mountain bikes (€3.70 per hour) or ski equipment from Galeassi Sport (☎ 0874 78 41 80). Around this upland valley, there's some fine walking through pine and beech woods and above the tree line.

The resort has several hotels, but there's nothing cheap about them.

Rifugio Jezza *(☎ 0874 78 41 88)* Full board around €42 per person. Open year-round. The pick of the possibilities, this friendly, family-run place with considerable character (it started life as a WWII mountain refuge) is considerably less spartan than its name might imply. Accommodation is in cosy double rooms with full facilities and the restaurant serves up filling local fare (€13-15.50 for a full meal).

Albergo Kristiana *(☎/fax 0874 78 41 37)* B&B rooms €52-62. Open Dec-Apr & June-Sept. At the entrance to the resort, Albergo Kristiana has a sauna, swimming pool and other sports facilities.

In season, Autolinee Micone (☎ 0874 78 01 20) buses run four times daily to Bojano and Campobasso.

ISERNIA

In 1979 evidence was discovered here of a village thought to be up to 700,000 years old, possibly the most ancient settlement in Europe. Excavations continue and stone tools discovered at the site are on display at the town's small **Museo Santa Maria delle Monache** *(☎ 0865 41 51 79, Corso Marcelli 48; admission €2.10; open 8.30am-7.30pm daily)*. From the train station it's a good 20-minute walk; head left along Corso Garibaldi and continue under the cathedral arch into the old quarter.

A new **Museo Paleontologico** *(☎ 0865 41 35 26)*, at the site of the excavations and some 2km from the station, is due to be inaugurated in 2002.

Isernia's EPT office (☎ 0865 39 92) is on the 6th floor of the Palazzo della Regione, Via Farinacci 9, a 200m walk from the train station (turn left into Corso Garibaldi and right into Via Farinacci). It opens 8am to 2pm Monday to Saturday.

Hotel Sayonara *(☎ 0865 5 09 92, fax 0865 41 59 19, ⓔ info@sayonara.it, Via G Berta 131)* B&B rooms with bath €41.35-56.85. To reach this conveniently central hotel, go straight (north) from the train station, turn right onto Via Berta and follow it for four blocks.

Isernia is easily reached by bus from Campobasso and Termoli, and by train from Sulmona, Pescara and Campobasso.

AROUND ISERNIA

Just outside **Pietrabbondante**, about 30km north-east of Isernia, are the remains of a pre-Roman village, including a Greek-style theatre. It was originally settled by the Samnites, who controlled the area before Roman domination. Three buses a day connect Isernia and Pietrabbondante.

Near Castel San Vincenzo, about 25km north-west of Isernia, is the **Abbazia di San Vincenzo al Volturno** *(free)*. This Benedictine abbey was one of the foremost monastic and cultural centres in 9th-century Europe before it fell prey to the familiar devastating combination of earthquake and Arab raiders. After centuries, the contemplative life has been resumed, bizarrely in the persons of a community of American nuns from Connecticut. But they're not what draws the visitor (and they certainly don't want to see you); within the remains of the original abbey complex, itself well documented by interpretative panels in Italian and English, and deep down in the crypt, is a cycle of magnificently preserved Byzantine frescoes. The site opens 9am to noon plus 3pm to 5pm daily in summer, and weekends only during the rest of the year. To confirm times, ring ☎ 0328 342 23 93 or the Isernia tourist office (see Isernia earlier). Buses run between Isernia and Castel San Vincenzo, a 1km walk from the site.

TERMOLI

More low-key than some of its northern rivals, Termoli makes a relaxing if unexciting beach stop. The tiny medieval *borgo* (village) will keep you occupied for a wee while with its 12th-century **cathedral** and 13th-century Swabian **castle**, built by Frederick II. Termoli is also a year-round jumping-off point for the Isole Tremiti. The town is filled with holidaymakers in summer and accommodation, especially for the budget conscious, is tight. Things don't improve in winter as much of Termoli simply shuts down.

The APT office (☎ 0875 70 67 54) is tucked away around the back of Piazza Bega, 100m east of the train station along Corso Umberto I. It opens 8am to noon, Monday to Saturday.

Places to Stay & Eat

Cala Saracena *(☎/fax 0875 5 21 93, SS Europa 2, 174)* Site for two people, tent & car €24.30. Open June–mid-Sept. There are camping facilities at Cala Saracena on the S16 Adriatica to Pescara road (also known as Europa 2). It can be reached by local bus from the train station.

Pensione Villa Ida *(☎ 0875 70 66 66, Via Mario Milano 27)* Singles/doubles/triples/quads with bath and air-con €38.75/51.65/69.75/82.80. Open Easter-Nov. A short 150m walk from the train station and two blocks from the sea, it represents good value in all but the highest season. Full board is compulsory in August. Breakfast included.

Hotel Meridiano *(☎ 0875 70 59 46, fax 0875 70 26 96, Lungomare Cristoforo Colombo 524)* Singles/doubles with bath €56.85/67.25. This place is reasonably priced for a hotel that overlooks the beach.

Da Antonio *(☎ 0875 70 51 58, Corso Umberto I 59)* Full meal around €21. Da Antonio is a good choice for a reasonable fish meal and some rough house wine.

Getting There & Away

Bus The intercity bus station is beside Via Martiri della Resistenza. SATI buses (☎ 08 74 9 47 38) link Termoli to Campobasso (hourly) and Pescara (three daily). Cerella (☎ 0873 39 11 68) has two early morning buses daily to/from Isernia and is one of several companies to serve Rome and Naples.

Train Termoli is on the main Bologna-Lecce train line along the Adriatic coast.

Car & Motorcycle Termoli is on the A14 and S16 which follow the coast north to Pescara and beyond and south to Bari. The S87 links Termoli with the Campobasso area overlooking the Cigno river valley.

Boat Termoli is the only port with a year-round daily ferry service to the Isole Tremiti (see Apulia in the Apulia, Basilicata & Calabria chapter). The service is operated by Adriatica Navigazione (☎ 0875 70 53 41) and leaves Termoli at 9am; it sets back from the Isole Tremiti at 2.30pm. Between June and August, Navigazione Libera del Golfo and Navigargano both operate services as well, so sailings are much more frequent. Buy your ticket at each company's kiosk at the ferry terminal. The fare is €14.50 return by boat or about €28.50 return for the faster hydrofoil or hydrojet trip.

ALBANIAN TOWNS

Several villages to the south of Termoli form an Albanian enclave dating back to the 15th century. These include Campomarino, Portocannone, Ururi and Montecilfone. Although the inhabitants shrugged off their Orthodox religion in the 18th century, locals still use – as their first language – a version of Albanian incomprehensible to outsiders. All can be reached by bus from Termoli.

Campania

Presided over by Naples, the only true metropolis in the Mezzogiorno (literally 'midday', the evocative name for Italy's south), Campania has most things a traveller might want. As well as a chaotic city, it is also blessed with some of Italy's most dramatic coastline, a sprinkling of magical islands and a rich heritage set in ancient ruins.

In the shadow of Mt Vesuvius (Vesuvio; 1277m) lie the ruins of Pompeii and Herculaneum, Roman cities buried by the volcano and so preserved for posterity. Both are a short excursion south-east of Naples. There's plenty more to explore, including the Campi Flegrei to the west of town with their reminder of the world celebrated in the writings of Homer and Virgil and, to the south-east, the Greek temples of Paestum, among the best preserved in the world.

Many writers have waxed lyrical about the natural beauty of the Amalfi Coast and the islands out in the Gulf of Naples, particularly Capri.

Travel inland to Caserta for the sumptuous Palazzo Reale of the Spanish Bourbons, set in magnificent gardens and modelled on Versailles.

Campania is alive with myth and legend. Stories tell how sirens (sea nymphs) lured sailors to their deaths off Sorrento; how islands in the Gulf of Naples were the domain of mermaids; and how Lago d'Averno (Lake Avernus), in the Campi Flegrei, was believed, in ancient times, to be the entrance to the underworld. Ulysses, Aeneas and other characters of classical storytelling and history have also left their mark, real or imagined, hereabouts.

Naples is the most densely populated area of Campania, although the city itself started life humbly, first as a Greek settlement, then as a pleasure resort for Rome's high society. Little touched by Vesuvius' eruption in AD 79, which wiped out Pompeii and neighbouring towns, Naples also survived several Saracen assaults. It was an independent city-state until southern Italy came under the sway of the Normans in the mid-12th century. The short-lived kingdom of the Normans, with its capital in Palermo (Sicily), changed hands and dimensions regularly but always comprised the bulk of southern Italy, including all of Campania. Under Spanish Bourbon rule in the 18th century, Naples was one of Europe's great capitals.

Campanian cooking is simple – its greatest contribution to world cuisine is the pizza.

Highlights

- Marvel at the famous *Toro Farnese*, just one of the Greco-Roman wonders in Naples' Museo Archeologico Nazionale
- Peer into the shimmering waters of Capri's Grotta Azzurra
- See how the Romans lived at perfectly preserved Pompeii
- Gaze down at the sparkling Amalfi Coast from hill-top Ravello
- Munch a *pizza margherita* in downtown Naples

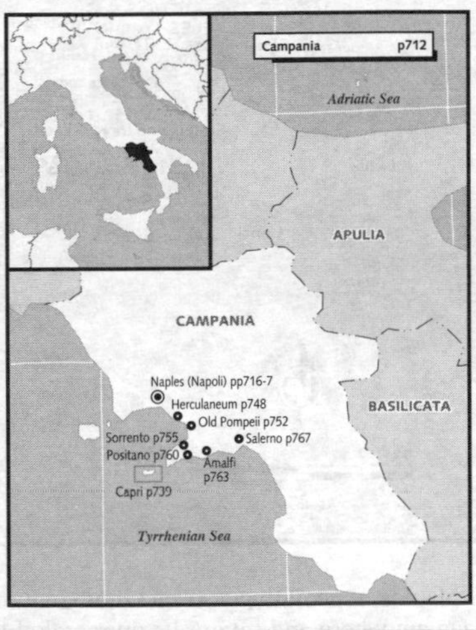

CAMPANIA

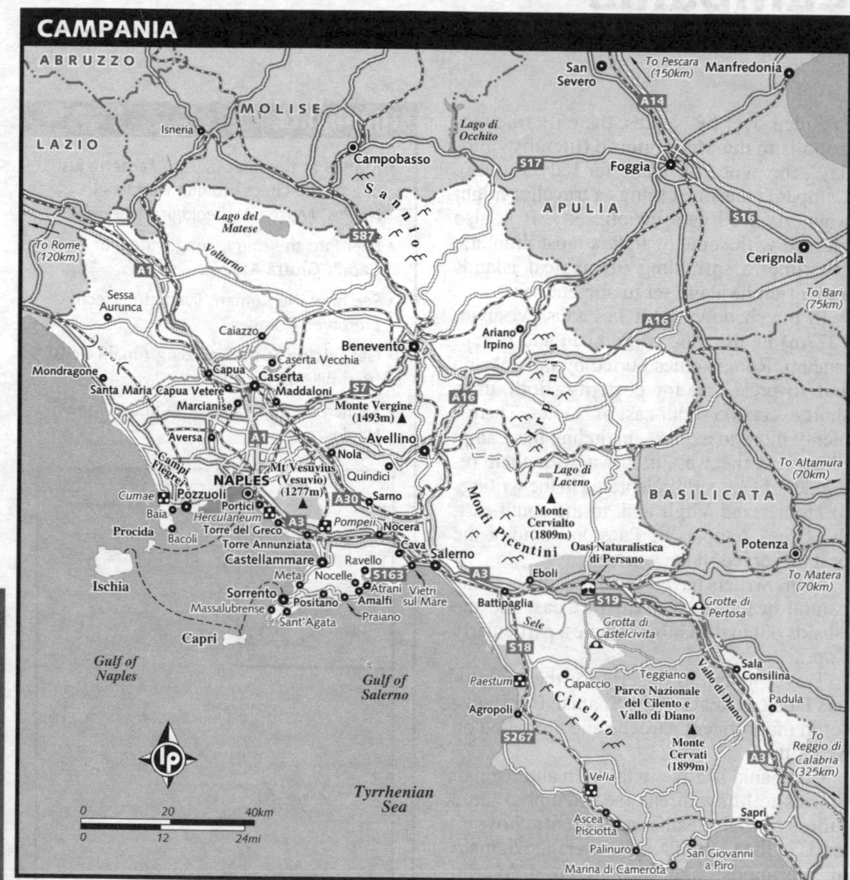

In Naples especially, you can get a quick pizza anywhere and savour its unmistakable, rich, tomato sauce. Campania also produces some decent wines, including the popular white Falanghina and various tipples under the Greco di Tufo name. *Limoncello*, a bright-yellow, sweetish, lemon liqueur with a hidden kick, is a regional speciality. Produced along the Amalfi Coast, around Sorrento and on Capri and the other Gulf of Naples islands, it's best sipped chilled – and in moderation.

Naples, on the main train line south from Rome, is a regional transport hub. Most places of interest in Campania are accessible by train, which is an advantage as tracking down buses can be tiresome.

For the more adventurous and energetic the mountains of the Amalfi Coast and the Penisola Sorrentina have some good walking terrain.

Naples (Napoli)

postcode 80100 • pop 1,050,000

Someone who has seen Naples, said Goethe, can never be sad. The third-largest city in Italy, Naples defies description. *Cook's*

Tourist's Handbook of 1884 declared: 'Naples is an ill-built, ill-paved, ill-lighted, ill-drained, ill-watched, ill-governed and ill-ventilated city.' Naples has since made big strides forward but, to many, the observations of over a century ago retain a grain of truth. There is, however, another side to the coin. After all the carping, *Cook's* concludes that the city 'is, perhaps, the loveliest spot in Europe'.

Raucous, polluted, unruly, anarchic, deafening and with so many of its majestic historical buildings grubby and crumbling, Naples has at least as much in common with Casablanca in Morocco or Egypt's Alexandria on the other side of the Mediterranean as with fellow Mediterranean ports such as Genoa, Marseilles or Barcelona. And, like the cities on the other side of the pond, it's glued together by the sheer zest and vitality of its inhabitants.

Beautifully positioned on the bay, Naples has a little – and often a lot – of everything. The old centre, once the heart of ancient Neapolis and now bristling with ancient churches, a medieval university and countless eateries and cafes, pulsates to the beat of noisy street markets and their clientele, swarms of people buzzing around on Vespas and the general chaos of a city at work.

Nothing is orderly and regulation is observed with absolute discretion. Traffic lights are routinely ignored, as are one-way signs and just about every other road rule. When it became mandatory in Italy to wear seatbelts, it was in Naples that someone thought up the idea of wearing a T-shirt with an imprint of a seatbelt sash. It's not unusual to see a whole family aboard a single Vespa or children careening about on mopeds.

Naples is the centre of a booming counterfeit clothes racket and the base for much of Italy's contraband cigarette smuggling. This alternative industry involves the Camorra (Naples' brand of the Mafia) whose other specialities are bank hold-ups, controlling the local fruit and vegetable markets, prostitution and the massive *toto nero* (illegal football pools).

After the election in 1993 of the proactive, left-wing mayor Antonio Bassolino, there were huge and successful efforts to clean up the city, reopen many churches, museums and monuments that had been off-limits to the public for decades, and make tourist areas safer with a prominent police presence. But now, while his party, the Partido Democratico de la Sinistra (PDS) remains in power, he himself has been elevated (some would say booted upstairs) to president of the Campania region. It remains to be seen whether the political will and dynamism he imparted have roots deep enough to outlive him.

History

Soon after founding Cumae in 1000 BC, colonists from Rhodes established a settlement on the western side of Mt Vesuvius. Many centuries later, Phoenician traders from present day Lebanon and Greeks from Athens were attracted by the splendour of the coast and so expanded the settlement, christening it Neapolis (New City). It thrived as a centre of Greek culture and later, under Roman rule, became a favourite of emperors Pompey, Caesar and Tiberius.

After successive waves of invasion by the wild Goths and a couple of spells associated with Byzantium, Naples remained an independent dukedom for about 400 years until captured by the Normans in 1139. They, in turn, were replaced by the German Hohenstaufens, whose Swabian dynasty lasted until 1266 and gave the city many new institutions, including its university. After the defeat and death of Manfred, king of Sicily, at the battle of Benevento in 1266, Charles I of Anjou took control of the Kingdom of Sicily and turned Naples into its de facto capital. Following a period of disorder, the Angevins were succeeded in 1442 by the Spanish house of Aragón, under whom the city came to prosper. Alfonso I of Aragón, in particular, introduced new laws and a more modern concept of justice and also promoted the arts and sciences.

In 1503 Naples and the Kingdom of Sicily were absorbed by Spain, which sent viceroys to rule as virtual dictators. Despite their heavy-handed rule, Naples flourished artistically and acquired much of its splendour during this period. Indeed, it continued to flower when the Spanish Bourbons re-established Naples as capital of the Kingdom of the Two Sicilies in 1734 (which encompassed part of the Italian peninsula and Sicily from the mid-15th to mid-19th centuries). Aside from a Napoleonic interlude under Joachim Murat (1806 to 1815), the Bourbons remained until unseated by Garibaldi and the Kingdom of Italy in 1860, when Naples was a serious but unsuccessful contender for capital of the new nation.

The city was heavily damaged during more than 100 bombing raids in WWII and marks can still be seen on many monuments. The Allies subsequently presided over a fairly disastrous period of transition from war to peace – many observers have since attributed the initial boom in the city's organised crime, at least in part, to members of the occupying forces. A severe earthquake in 1980 and the dormant, but not extinct, Vesuvius looming to the east, remind Neapolitans of their city's vulnerability.

Orientation

Naples stretches along the waterfront and is divided into *quartieri* (districts; normally a street sign bears the name of both street and district). Stazione Centrale and the bus station are off Piazza Garibaldi, east of Spaccanapoli, the ancient heart of Naples. Piazza Garibaldi and its side streets form an enormous, unwelcoming transport terminus and street market. The area is distinctly seedy. Quite a few of the cheaper hotels, some of which double as brothels, are here.

A wide shopping street, Corso Umberto I, skirts the southern edge of Spaccanapoli, aligned south-west from Piazza Garibaldi to Piazza Bovio. From here Via A Depretis runs to the huge Piazza Municipio, dominated by the unmistakable Castel Nuovo. From the waterfront behind the castle, ferries sail to the bay islands, Palermo and other long-distance destinations.

The Palazzo Reale (the former royal palace), next to the castle, dominates Piazza Trento e Trieste. Naples' main street, Via Toledo, leads north from the square, briefly becomes Via Roma, passes alongside Piazza Dante, on the western boundary of Spaccanapoli, then undergoes three more name changes before reaching the Parco di Capodimonte, north of the centre.

The extensions of two of Naples' more original streets, Via San Biagio dei Librai (which becomes Via B Croce at its western end) and Via dei Tribunali, eventually meet Via Roma. Much of Naples' street life, artisans and a host of good, cheap restaurants can be found in this area. Via San Biagio dei Librai is part of an almost straight run from near Stazione Centrale through Spaccanapoli to the foot of the hill-top Vomero district.

To the south and west extend broad boulevards and majestic squares leading to Santa Lucia and chic Mergellina. Above it all sits Naples' upper-middle class in the relative calm of Vomero, a natural balcony with grand views across the city and bay to Vesuvius.

To get your head round the city's geography, head up on foot or by funicular railway to Largo San Martino (see Vomero later) and enjoy the panoramic view.

Information

Tourist Offices Naples has several tourist offices that share a common Web site: **W** www.aziendaturismonapoli.com. Each office stocks *Qui Napoli*, a free, information-packed monthly listings brochure that includes details of opening hours for museums and other places to see. Here too you can pick up a reasonable city map plus guides to some of the city's major monuments. All, unless they're overwhelmed with visitors, will telephone hotels on your behalf at no cost but, as they make clear, the responsibility for the reservation is yours alone.

The EPT office (☎ 081 20 66 66) at Stazione Centrale opens 9am to 7.30pm Monday to Saturday and 9am to 1.30pm Sunday. The main EPT office (☎ 081 40 53 11), Piazza dei Martiri 58, opens 8.30am to 2.30pm Monday to Friday. There are branch offices at the Mergellina train station and the airport.

There's a particularly helpful AAST office (☎ 081 552 33 28) on Piazza del Gesù Nuovo, south-east of Piazza Dante, which

CAMPANIA

opens 9am to 8pm Monday to Saturday and 9am to 3pm Sunday.

The student travel centre, CTS (☎ 081 552 79 60), is at Via Mezzocannone 25.

Money American Express is represented by Every Tour (☎ 081 551 85 64), Piazza Municipio 5–6. This travel agency also changes money and acts as agent for Western Union.

Post & Communications The main post office is at Piazza Matteotti, off Via A Diaz, in a grand, Fascist-era building worth a visit in its own right. It opens 8.15am to 7pm Monday to Saturday.

The main Telecom office is at Via A Depretis 40 and opens 9.30am to 1pm and 2pm to 5.30pm Monday to Friday. There are plenty of other places in town to phone from as well.

Your best bet for the Internet, both for ease of access (there are 35 computers) and price (a bargain €1.55 per hour), is friendly Multimedia (☎ 081 29 84 12, W www.viasapienza43.com). It's on the 1st floor of Via Sapienza 43 (entrance from the courtyard) and opens 9.30am to 9.30pm daily. If you're a late-night emailer, try Internetbar (☎ 081 29 52 37), Piazza Bellini 74. It opens 9am to 2am Monday to Saturday and 8pm to 2am Sunday, and charges €2.60 per half-hour. Right on Piazza Garibaldi (at No 73), Internet Café di Napoli (☎ 081 553 50 19), which opens 9am to 9pm Monday to Saturday, logs you on for €1.55/2.60 per half-hour/hour.

Laundry My Beautiful Laundrette, Via Montesanto 2, is that rarity in Italy – a true laundrette where you can load your own wash and not pay the earth. It costs €3.10 for up to 6kg and the same to dry your wash, and it opens 9am to 8.30pm Monday to Saturday. There is also has an Internet point (€2.60 per hour) so you can soap and surf simultaneously.

Medical Services For an ambulance, call either the Pan-European emergency number, ☎ 112, or ☎ 081 752 06 96. Each district has a Guardia Medica with a doctor on duty at night and weekends. Their phone numbers are listed in *Qui Napoli*. The Ospedale Loreto-Mare (hospital; ☎ 081 254 27 01), Via Amerigo Vespucci, is on the seafront. The pharmacy at Stazione Centrale opens 8am to 8pm daily.

Emergency The *questura* (police station; ☎ 081 794 11 11) is at Via Medina 75, off Via A Diaz. It has an office for foreigners where you can report thefts and other misdemeanours. To report a stolen car, call ☎ 081 794 14 35.

Dangers & Annoyances Petty crime is a big problem in Naples. For some tips on how to reduce the risk of being a victim, see the Dangers & Annoyances section in the Facts for the Visitor chapter. Be especially vigilant for moped bandits and pickpockets on crowded transport.

Car and motorcycle theft is also rife, so think twice before bringing a vehicle into town.

Travellers should be careful walking alone in the streets at night, particularly near Stazione Centrale and Piazza Dante. Never venture into the dark side streets at night unless you are in a group. The area west of Via Toledo and as far north as Piazza Carità, though safe enough during the day, can be threatening after dark.

Take care when crossing roads. There are few functioning traffic lights and pedestrian crossings, and Neapolitans rarely stop anyway. When facing a green light they drive with caution, believing that those facing the red light will not stop. Vehicles and pedestrians simply slip around each other in a kind of unwritten code of road 'courtesy' that can be a little unnerving at first. But don't dither; within a couple of days, you'll probably be dodging and weaving like a true-born Neapolitan. However, it could take a lifetime to master the elaborate code that dictates when you show annoyance and how far up the irritation scale you go. Similarly, the subtle courtesies of when to cede and when to push on can't be picked up in a short visit.

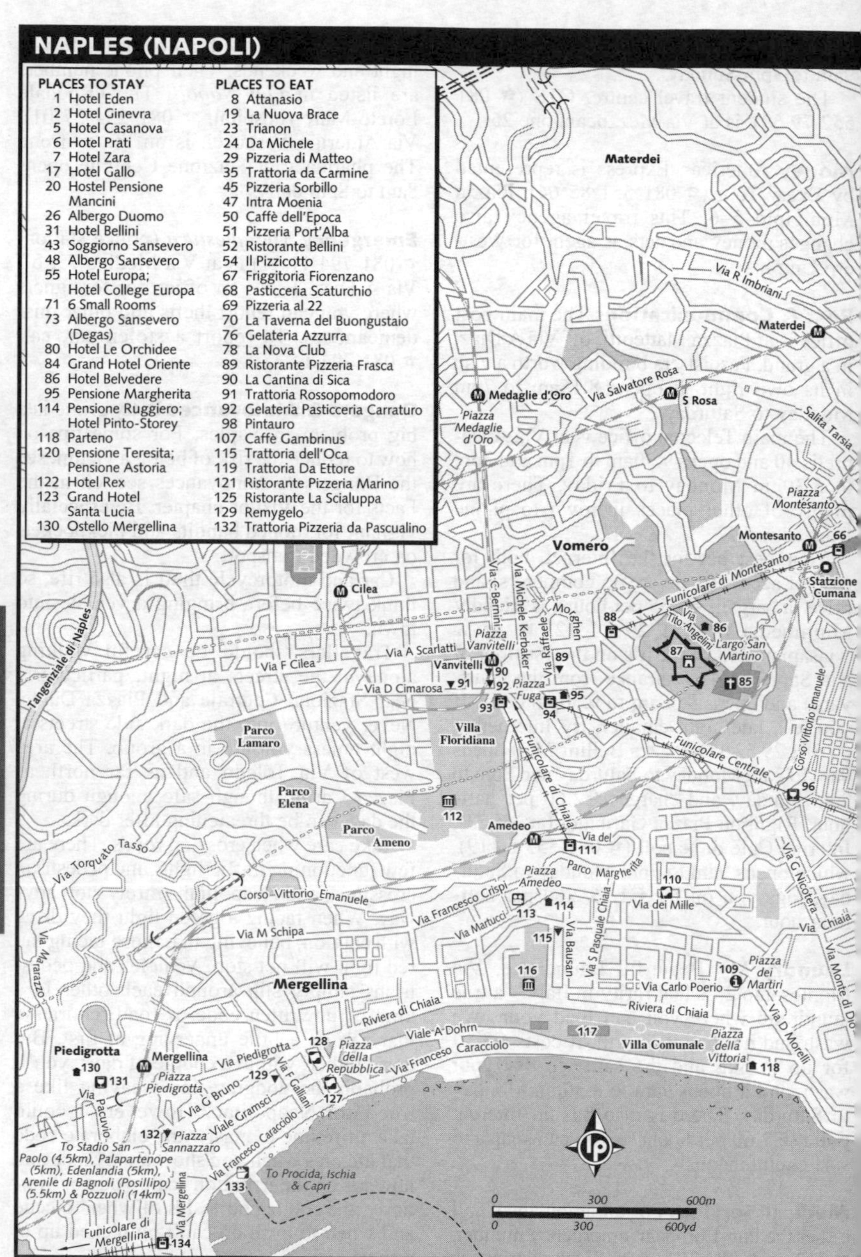
NAPLES (NAPOLI)
PLACES TO STAY
1 Hotel Eden
2 Hotel Ginevra
5 Hotel Casanova
6 Hotel Prati
7 Hotel Zara
17 Hotel Gallo
20 Hostel Pensione Mancini
26 Albergo Duomo
31 Hotel Bellini
43 Soggiorno Sansevero
48 Albergo Sansevero
55 Hotel Europa; Hotel College Europa
71 6 Small Rooms
73 Albergo Sansevero (Degas)
80 Hotel Le Orchidee
84 Grand Hotel Oriente
86 Hotel Belvedere
95 Pensione Margherita
114 Pensione Ruggiero; Hotel Pinto-Storey
118 Parteno
120 Pensione Teresita; Pensione Astoria
122 Hotel Rex
123 Grand Hotel Santa Lucia
130 Ostello Mergellina
PLACES TO EAT
8 Attanasio
19 La Nuova Brace
23 Trianon
24 Da Michele
29 Pizzeria di Matteo
35 Trattoria da Carmine
45 Pizzeria Sorbillo
47 Intra Moenia
50 Caffè dell'Epoca
51 Pizzeria Port'Alba
52 Ristorante Bellini
54 Il Pizzicotto
67 Friggitoria Fiorenzano
68 Pasticceria Scaturchio
69 Pizzeria al 22
70 La Taverna del Buongustaio
76 Gelateria Azzurra
78 La Nova Club
89 Ristorante Pizzeria Frasca
90 La Cantina di Sica
91 Trattoria Rossopomodoro
92 Gelateria Pasticceria Carraturo
98 Pintauro
107 Caffè Gambrinus
115 Trattoria dell'Oca
119 Trattoria Da Ettore
121 Ristorante Pizzeria Marino
125 Ristorante La Scialuppa
129 Remygelo
132 Trattoria Pizzeria da Pascualino
Materdei
Via R Imbriani
Materdei
Medaglie d'Oro
Via Salvatore Rosa
S Rosa
Piazza Medaglie d'Oro
Salita Tarsia
Piazza Montesanto
Montesanto
66
Vomero
Statzione Cumana
Funicolare di Montesanto
Cilea
Via C Bernini
Via Michele Kerbaker
Via Raffaele Morghen
Via Tito Angelini
Largo San Martino
Piazza Vanvitelli
Vanvitelli
Via A Scarlatti
Via F Cilea
Via D Cimarosa
Tangenziale di Naples
Piazza Fuga
Villa Floridiana
Parco Lamaro
Parco Elena
Parco Ameno
Funicolare di Chiaia
Funicolare Centrale
Corso Vittorio Emanuele
Amedeo
Via del Parco Margherita
Piazza Amedeo
Via Torquato Tasso
Corso Vittorio Emanuele
Via Francesco Crispi
Via Martucci
Via Bausan
Via S Pasquale Chiaia
Via dei Mille
Via G Nicotera
Via Chiaia
Via Monte di Dio
Via M Schipa
Via Mataraazzo
Mergellina
Piazza dei Martiri
Via Carlo Poerio
Riviera di Chiaia
Riviera di Chiaia
Viale A Dohrn
Villa Comunale
Piazza della Vittoria
Via D Morelli
Piedigrotta
Mergellina
Via Piedigrotta
Piazza della Repubblica
Via Francesco Caracciolo
Piazza Piedigrotta
Via Pacuvio
Via G Bruno
Via F Galliani
Viale Gramsci
Via Francesco Caracciolo
Piazza Sannazzaro
To Stadio San Paolo (4.5km), Palapartenope (5km), Edenlandia (5km), Arenile di Bagnoli (Posillipo) (5.5km) & Pozzuoli (14km)
To Procida, Ischia & Capri
Funicolare di Mergellina
Via Mergellina
0 300 600m
0 300 600yd

CAMPANIA

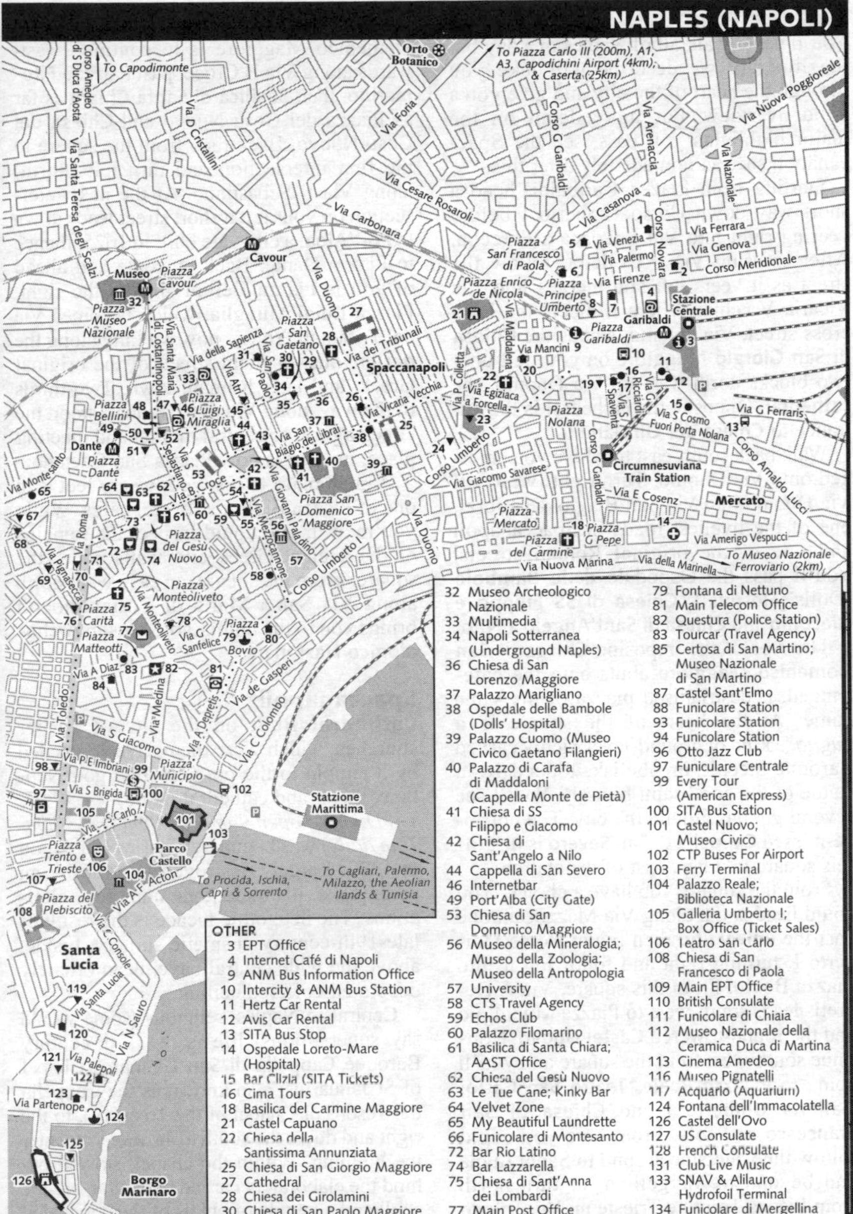
NAPLES (NAPOLI)
Orto Botanico
To Piazza Carlo III (200m), A1, A3, Capodichini Airport (4km), & Caserta (25km)
To Capodimonte
Stazione Centrale
Piazza Garibaldi
Spaccanapoli
Circumvesuviana Train Station
Mercato
Statzione Marittima
Parco Castello
Santa Lucia
Borgo Marinaro
To Museo Nazionale Ferroviario (2km)
To Procida, Ischia, Capri & Sorrento
To Cagliari, Palermo, Milazzo, the Aeolian Ilands & Tunisia
OTHER
3 EPT Office
4 Internet Café di Napoli
9 ANM Bus Information Office
10 Intercity & ANM Bus Station
11 Hertz Car Rental
12 Avis Car Rental
13 SITA Bus Stop
14 Ospedale Loreto-Mare (Hospital)
15 Bar Cizia (SITA Tickets)
16 Cima Tours
18 Basilica del Carmine Maggiore
21 Castel Capuano
22 Chiesa della Santissima Annunziata
25 Chiesa di San Giorgio Maggiore
27 Cathedral
28 Chiesa dei Girolamini
30 Chiesa di San Paolo Maggiore
32 Museo Archeologico Nazionale
33 Multimedia
34 Napoli Sotterranea (Underground Naples)
36 Chiesa di San Lorenzo Maggiore
37 Palazzo Marigliano
38 Ospedale delle Bambole (Dolls' Hospital)
39 Palazzo Cuomo (Museo Civico Gaetano Filangieri)
40 Palazzo di Carafa di Maddaloni (Cappella Monte di Pietà)
41 Chiesa di SS Filippo e Giacomo
42 Chiesa di Sant'Angelo a Nilo
44 Cappella di San Severo
46 Internetbar
49 Port'Alba (City Gate)
53 Chiesa di San Domenico Maggiore
56 Museo della Mineralogia; Museo della Zoologia; Museo della Antropologia
57 University
58 CTS Travel Agency
59 Echos Club
60 Palazzo Filomarino
61 Basilica di Santa Chiara; AAST Office
62 Chiesa del Gesù Nuovo
63 Le Tue Cane; Kinky Bar
64 Velvet Zone
65 My Beautiful Laundrette
66 Funicolare di Montesanto
72 Bar Rio Latino
74 Bar Lazzarella
75 Chiesa di Sant'Anna dei Lombardi
77 Main Post Office
79 Fontana di Nettuno
81 Main Telecom Office
82 Questura (Police Station)
83 Tourcar (Travel Agency)
85 Certosa di San Martino; Museo Nazionale di San Martino
87 Castel Sant'Elmo
88 Funicolare Station
93 Funicolare Station
94 Funicolare Station
96 Otto Jazz Club
97 Funiculare Centrale
99 Every Tour (American Express)
100 SITA Bus Station
101 Castel Nuovo; Museo Civico
102 CTP Buses For Airport
103 Ferry Terminal
104 Palazzo Reale; Biblioteca Nazionale
105 Galleria Umberto I; Box Office (Ticket Sales)
106 Teatro San Carlo
108 Chiesa di San Francesco di Paola
109 Main EPT Office
110 British Consulate
111 Funicolare di Chiaia
112 Museo Nazionale della Ceramica Duca di Martina
113 Cinema Amedeo
116 Museo Pignatelli
117 Acquario (Aquarium)
124 Fontana dell'Immacolatella
126 Castel dell'Ovo
127 US Consulate
128 French Consulate
131 Club Live Music
133 SNAV & Alilauro Hydrofoil Terminal
134 Funicolare di Mergellina

Walking Tour

You'll never walk all of Naples in a day but the itinerary we describe will take you through the heart of the city and give you a good overview. For more detail on the major highlights you pass, see the Spaccanapoli section immediately after this.

Starting from Piazza Garibaldi, head a short way down Corso Umberto I before veering right into Via Egiziaca a Forcella. After crossing Via P Colletta, follow the street as it veers left and merges into Via Vicaria Vecchia. Where it meets the busy cross street, Via Duomo, stands the **Chiesa di San Giorgio Maggiore** on your left and, two blocks north-west up Via Duomo, the **cathedral**. Opposite the cathedral is the entrance to **Chiesa dei Girolamini**.

Walk back south-east to where you emerged onto Via Duomo. Turn right (west) off Via Duomo into Via San Biagio dei Librai, one of the liveliest roads in Spaccanapoli and one of the original Roman streets. You'll pass the **Ospedale delle Bambole** (Dolls' Hospital), **Chiesa di SS Filippo e Giacomo** and **Chiesa di Sant'Angelo a Nilo**.

The rear of the imposing **Chiesa di San Domenico Maggiore** abuts onto the cafe-fringed, pedestrianised piazza of the same name. At the heart of the square is a *guglia*, a kind of ground-level, richly carved Baroque steeple or obelisk, topped by a statue of the good saint himself. You'll see several guglias around the city. The not-to-be-missed **Cappella di San Severo** is just off this square in a lane east of the church.

From the square, you have a choice. You could head south along Via Mezzocannone past the **university**, then rejoin Corso Umberto I, turning right and following it into Piazza Bovio. From this square, Via A Depretis leads south-west to Piazza Municipio and the round-towered **Castel Nuovo**. Continue south-west from the square and you'll come to **Palazzo Reale**, **Teatro San Carlo**, **Galleria Umberto I** and **Chiesa di San Francesco di Paola**. From here you could follow the waterside around to Santa Lucia and beyond to Mergellina, or turn north from Piazza Trento e Trieste up Via Toledo back into the heart of Spaccanapoli.

The other option from Piazza San Domenico Maggiore is to continue westwards along Via B Croce, past **Palazzo Filomarino**, then **Basilica di Santa Chiara** as far as Piazza del Gesù Nuovo and **Chiesa del Gesù Nuovo**. Backtrack from the square to the first intersection and turn left (north) along Via S Sebastiano. At the next intersection on your left a short street leads down to **Port'Alba**, a city gate built in 1625, thence to Piazza Dante. Back on route and ahead of you is Piazza Bellini and, to the right, Piazza Luigi Miraglia, which becomes Via dei Tribunali. You're now walking along the **decumanus**, or main street, of the original Greek, and later Roman, town. Two-thirds of the way along Via dei Tribunali stood the Greek **agora**, or central market and meeting place, in what is now Piazza San Gaetano.

A great place to rest your weary feet is in one of Piazza Bellini's several cafes. While you're at it, you could inspect the remains of the ancient Greek city walls under the square. From the square, an easy walk north along Via Santa Maria di Costantinopoli brings you to the unmissable **Museo Archeologico Nazionale**.

Spaccanapoli

Cathedral Built on the site of earlier churches, which were themselves preceded by a temple to the pre-Christian god Neptune, this grand cathedral *(☎ 081 44 90 97, Via Duomo; open 9am-12.30pm & 4.30pm-7pm daily)* was begun by Charles I of Anjou in 1272. Largely destroyed in 1456 by an earthquake, it's undergone numerous alterations. The neogothic facade is the result of late-19th-century cosmetic surgery. Inside, above the wide central nave, is an ornately decorated coffered ceiling.

Central to Naples' religious (some would say superstitious) life is the 17th-century Baroque **Cappella di San Gennaro** (Chapel of St Januarius; also known as the Cappella del Tesoro or Chapel of the Treasury), to the right and down the south aisle after you enter the building. Within the chapel, stowed behind the elaborately carved high altar, are the skull and a couple of phials of the congealed blood of San Gennaro, the city's patron saint.

He was martyred at Pozzuoli, west of Naples, in AD 305 and tradition holds that these phials of his blood liquefied when his body was transferred back to Naples. Three times a year, thousands gather here to pray for a miracle – that the blood will again liquefy and save Naples from any potential disaster. The saint is said to have saved the city from calamity on numerous occasions – although the miracle unspectacularly failed to occur in 1941 when Vesuvius erupted. For further details of the festival see Special Events later.

The next chapel eastwards contains an urn with the saint's bones, cupboards full of femurs, tibias and fibulas and a stash of other relics. Below the high altar is the **Cappella Carafa**, also known as the Crypt of San Gennaro, a Renaissance chapel built to house the saint's relics.

Halfway down the north aisle and beyond the mainly 17th-century **Basilica di Santa Restituta** is the so-called 'archaeological zone' *(admission €2.60; open 9am-noon & 4.30pm-7.30pm Mon-Sat, 9am-1pm Sun)*. The tunnels lead you deep into the remains of the site's original Greek and Roman buildings. Here too is the **baptistry**, the oldest in western Europe, with its remarkably fresh 4th-century mosaics.

Around the Cathedral Opposite the cathedral is the entrance to **Chiesa dei Girolamini** *(also called San Filippo Neri; open 9.30am-12.30pm daily 2pm-5.30pm Mon-Sat)*, a rich Baroque church with two facades. The more imposing 18th-century facade, facing Via dei Tribunali, is now closed. A small picture gallery in the adjoining convent features works from the 16th to 18th centuries.

Duck around the corner into Via dei Tribunali and, to the left in Piazza San Gaetano, you'll come across **Chiesa di San Lorenzo Maggiore** *(Via dei Tribunali 316; admission to the church free, to excavations €0.80; open 9am-1pm & 3.30pm-5.30pm daily in winter, 9am-1pm & 4pm-6.30pm daily in summer)*. The interior of the church, begun by Provençal architects under the Franciscans in the 13th century, is French Gothic. Catherine of Austria, who died in 1323, is buried here and her mosaic-covered tomb is among the most eye-catching of the church's adornments. You can pass through to the cloisters of the neighbouring convent, where Petrarch stayed in 1345. Beneath the complex are some fascinating excavations of the original Greco-Roman city.

Across Via dei Tribunali is **Chiesa di San Paolo Maggiore** *(Piazza San Gaetano; open 9am-1pm daily)*. It was built in the late 16th century on the site of a Roman temple and the opulent interior houses the tomb of San Gaetano. For details of Napoli Sotterranea (Underground Naples; entrance just beside the church), see Organised Tours later.

While you're in the area check out **Chiesa di San Giorgio Maggiore** *(Via Duomo; open 8.30am-noon daily, 5pm-7pm Mon-Sat)*. It's situated where Via San Biagio dei Librai meets Via Duomo and is worth a quick look for its classical and relatively austere – by Neapolitan standards – interior.

Across the road is the 15th-century **Palazzo Cuomo**, built by Tuscan artists. The building was moved several metres in 1881 when the street was widened. It now contains the **Museo Civico Gaetano Filangieri** *(☎ 081 20 31 75, Via Duomo)*, closed at the time of writing.

Via San Biagio dei Librai Take a quick look at the **Ospedale delle Bambole** *(Via San Biagio dei Librai 81)*. This 'dolls' hospital' looks a mite macabre, with little heads piled up in the windows, but there can't be many places like it anywhere for buying or repairing dolls. This street and its continuation, Via B Croce, the parallel Via dei Tribunali to the north and the labyrinth of side alleys, are thronged with artisans of all kinds. You'll find not only goldsmiths and other jewellers, but makers of the famously elaborate Neapolitan *presepi* (nativity scenes).

At No 39, two blocks west of the dolls' hospital, is **Palazzo Marigliano**, behind whose grubby facade is a magnificent Renaissance entrance hall. Carrying on westwards you pass **Palazzo di Carafa di Maddaloni** and **Chiesa di SS Filippo e Giacomo** with their contrasting Baroque and classical styles.

Chiesa di Sant'Angelo a Nilo *(entrance on Vico Donnaromita 15; open 8.30am-noon & 5pm-7pm Mon-Sat)* sits square beside Via San Biagio dei Librai, its recently renovated facade benignly presided over by a quartet of tubby gilt cherubs. Built in 1385 and remodelled in the 18th century, it contains the monumental Renaissance tomb of one Cardinal Brancaccio, to which Donatello contributed.

Where Via San Biagio dei Librai becomes Via B Croce, in the piazza bearing its name, stands the Gothic **Chiesa di San Domenico Maggiore** *(Piazza San Domenico Maggiore 8a; open 8am-noon & 4.15pm-7pm daily)*, which was completed in 1324 by the Dominican order and much favoured by the Aragonese nobility.

The church's interior, a cross between Baroque and 19th-century neogothic, features some fine examples of Renaissance sculpture. In the sacristy are 45 coffins of the princes of Aragón and other nobles.

The deceptive simplicity of **Cappella di San Severo** *(Via de Sanctis 19; admission €4.20; open 10am-7pm Mon & Wed-Sat, 10am-1pm Sun May-Oct, 10am-5pm Mon & Wed-Sat, 10am-1pm Sun Nov-April)*, on a narrow lane east of the church, is a dazzling contrast to the treasure chest of sculpture inside. Giuseppe Sanmartino's *Cristo Velato* (Veiled Christ), for instance, still confounds experts, who cannot agree on how he created the apparently translucent veil. Also baffling is Corradini's *Pudicizia* (Modesty), which makes no attempt to hide the erotic. Also known as the Cappella di Santa Maria della Pietà dei Sangro, the chapel is the tomb of the princes of Sangro di San Severo.

Around Piazza del Gesù Nuovo From Piazza San Domenico Maggiore Via B continues west, following the course of the old Roman main street. Croce, Italy's foremost philosopher and historian in the first half of the 20th century, lived and died in **Palazzo Filomarino**, a grand Renaissance building on the right at No 12 just before you reach Via S Sebastiano.

Across Via S Sebastiano is **Basilica di Santa Chiara** *(Via B Croce; open 7am-12.30pm & 4pm-7pm daily)*, one of Naples' principal medieval monuments, and its adjacent convent. Built by the Angevins in the 14th century, it suffered from subsequent earthquakes and Baroque alterations. Since WWII, when incendiary bombs burned out the church and destroyed many works of art, it has been returned more or less to its original spare Gothic appearance. Note the magnificent 14th-century tombs at the eastern end. Within the **nuns' cloisters** *(admission €3.10; open 9.30am-1pm & 2.30pm-5.30pm Mon-Sat, 9.30am-1pm Sun)*, behind the church, is a long parapet entirely covered in decorative ceramic tiles, depicting landscapes and scenes from the nuns' lives. There is also a small museum.

A few steps west, Piazza del Gesù Nuovo opens before you with its ornate free-standing guglia. The 16th-century **Chiesa del Gesù Nuovo** *(Piazza del Gesù Nuovo; open 6.30am-1pm & 4pm-7pm)*, on the northern side of the piazza, is one of the city's greatest examples of Renaissance architecture. Note particularly the lozenge-shaped rustication of its 15th-century facade. The interior was redecorated in Neapolitan Baroque style after a fire in 1639.

The 15th-century **Chiesa di Sant'Anna dei Lombardi** *(Piazza Monteoliveto; open 8.30am-12.30pm Tues-Sat)*, south-west of Piazza del Gesù Nuovo, features fine Renaissance sculpture, including a superb terracotta *Pietà* (1492) by Guido Mazzoni.

Around Piazza del Carmine On the waterfront in Piazza del Carmine, the **Basilica del Carmine Maggiore** was the scene of the 1647 Neapolitan Revolution led by Masa-niello. Each year on 16 July a fireworks display celebrates the festival of the Madonna by simulating the *incendio del campanile* (the burning of the bell tower).

Museo Archeologico Nazionale

The archaeological treasures of Naples' principal museum *(☎ 848 80 02 88, Piazza Museo Nazionale; admission €6.20; open 9am-7.30pm Wed-Mon)* form one of the most comprehensive collections of Greco-Roman artefacts in the world. You could easily lose yourself in here for several

CAMPANIA

hours. Originally a cavalry barracks and later the seat of the city's university, the museum was established by Charles of Bourbon in the late 18th century to house the rich collection of antiquities he had inherited from his mother, Elizabeth Farnese, as well as the treasures that had been discovered at Pompeii and Herculaneum. It also contains the Borgia collection of Etruscan and Egyptian relics.

To avoid getting lost in its rambling galleries – irritatingly numbered in Roman numerals – invest €5.20 in the bilingual *guida di orientamento* or, to concentrate upon the highlights, €3.60 for an audioguide in English.

Many items from the Farnese collection of classical sculpture, including the famous *Toro Farnese* (Farnese Bull), are displayed on the ground floor. Sculpted in the early 3rd century AD, the *Toro Farnese*, probably a Roman copy of a Greek original, is an enormous group of figures depicting the death of Dirce, Queen of Thebes, who in Greek mythology was tied to a bull and torn apart over rocks. Carved from a single block of marble, it was later restored by Michelangelo.

On the mezzanine floor are mosaics, mostly from Pompeii, including the *Battle of Alexander*, the best-known depiction of the great Macedonian emperor. It once paved the floor in the Casa del Fauno at Pompeii and is just one of a series of remarkably detailed and lifelike pieces depicting animals, scenes from daily life, musicians and even Plato with his students.

The 1st floor is largely devoted to a treasure trove of discoveries from Pompeii, Herculaneum, Stabiae and Cumae. Items range from huge murals and frescoes to a pair of gladiator helmets, household items, ceramics, glassware – even eggcups. Galleries 86 and 87 house an extraordinary collection of vases of mixed origins, many carefully reassembled from fragments. In the basement is a smaller Egyptian collection.

The **Gabinetto Segreto** (Secret Room), recently opened to the public after decades of being accessible only to the seriously scientific and ardently archaeological, displays a variety of erotic statues including an intriguing one of Pan up to no good with a nanny goat and nine paintings depicting erotic positions, which served as a catalogue or menu for brothel clients. To gain entry (at no extra cost), don your dirty mac and ask sotto voce at the desk beside the cloakroom for a time to join a group visit.

South of Spaccanapoli

Castel Nuovo When Charles I of Anjou took over Naples and the Swabians' Sicilian kingdom, he found himself in control not only of his new southern Italian acquisitions, but also of possessions in Tuscany, northern Italy and Provence (France). It made sense to base the new dynasty in Naples, rather than Palermo on the island of Sicily, and Charles launched an ambitious construction programme to expand the port and city walls. His plans included converting a Franciscan convent into the castle that still stands in Piazza Municipio. Also called the Maschio Angioino, its crenellated round towers make it one of the most striking buildings in Naples.

The 'New Castle' was erected in three years from 1279 but what you see today was the result of renovations by the Aragonese two centuries later, as well as a meticulous restoration effort in the last century. The heavy grey stone that dominates the castle was imported from Mallorca. The two-storey Renaissance triumphal arch at the entrance, the Torre della Guardia commem orates the triumphal entry of Alfonso I of Aragón into Naples in 1443.

Spread across several halls on three floors is the **Museo Civico** *(☎ 081 795 20 03; admission €5.20; open 9am-7pm Mon-Sat)*. The 14th- and 15th-century frescoes and sculptures on the ground floor are of most interest. The other two floors display paintings, either by Neapolitan artists or with Naples or Campania as subjects, covering the 17th to the early 20th centuries.

North-east of the Castel Nuovo on Piazza Bovio is the **Fontana di Nettuno**, dating from 1601. Gianlorenzo Bernini sculpted this fountain's sea creatures and Naccherini the figure of Neptune.

Piazza Trento e Trieste One of Naples' more elegant squares, Piazza Trento e Trieste is fronted on the north-eastern side by Italy's largest opera house, the sumptuous **Teatro San Carlo** *(☎ 081 797 21 11, Via San Carlo 98; admission €2.60)*, famed for its perfect acoustics. Tours are conducted at 2pm, 2.30pm, 3pm and 3.30pm Saturday and Sunday. Locals proudly boast that it was built in 1737 – 40 years before Milan's La Scala. True in a way; but San Carlo, nowadays home to one of Italy's oldest ballet schools, was destroyed by fire in 1816 and later restored. Across Via S Carlo is one of the four entrances to the imposing glass atrium of the **Galleria Umberto I**, opened in 1900.

Palazzo Reale Facing the grand Piazza del Plebiscito, this magnificent palace *(☎ 081 794 40 21, entrance on Piazza Trento e Trieste; admission €4.20; 9am-8pm Thurs-Tues, last tickets 7pm)*, built around 1600, was completely renovated in 1841 and suffered extensive damage during WWII. The statues of the eight most important kings of Naples were inserted into niches in the facade in 1888.

From the courtyard, a huge double staircase leads to the royal apartments, which house the **Museo del Palazzo Reale**, a rich collection of furnishings, porcelain, tapestries, statues and paintings.

The palace has also, since 1925, been home to the **Biblioteca Nazionale** *(☎ 081 40 12 73; admission free; open 9am-7.30pm Mon-Fri, 9am-1.30pm Sat)*, which includes the vast Farnese collection brought to Naples by Charles of Bourbon, with at least 2000 papyruses discovered at Herculaneum and fragments of a 5th-century Coptic Bible. Bring ID as they check it as a security measure.

Chiesa di San Francesco di Paola, at the eastern end of Piazza del Plebiscito, was begun by Ferdinand I in 1817 to celebrate the restoration of his kingdom after the Napoleonic interlude. Flanked by semicircular colonnades, the church is based on the Pantheon and is a popular wedding spot.

Santa Lucia

Castel dell'Ovo The so-called Castle of the Egg *(☎ 081 240 00 55, Borgo Marinaro; admission free; open 9am-6pm Mon-Fri, 9am-1pm Sat-Sun)* is on the small rocky island off Santa Lucia, known as Borgo Marinaro and connected to Via Partenope by a bridge. Built in the 12th century by the Normans on the site of a Roman villa, the castle became a key fortress in the defence of Campania. You can wander through the island's small lanes, which are mostly occupied by restaurants.

The **Fontana dell'Immacolatella**, at the end of Via Partenope, dates from the 17th century and features statues by Bernini and Naccherini.

Mergellina

West of Santa Lucia, Via Partenope spills into Piazza della Vittoria, marking the beginning of the Riviera di Chiaia. This boulevard runs beside **Villa Comunale**, a large park marked off on its seaward side by Via Francesco Caracciolo. Within the park, is the city's **acquario** *(aquarium; ☎ 081 583 31 11, Villa Comunale; admission €1.60; open 9am-6pm Mon-Sat & 10am-6pm Sun in summer, 9am-5pm Mon-Sat & 9am-2pm Sun in winter)*. Founded in the late 19th century by German naturalist Anton Dohrn, this is Europe's oldest aquarium. Its 30 tanks contain some 200 species of sea life exclusively from the Gulf of Naples.

Close by is **Museo Pignatelli** *(☎ 081 761 23 56, Riviera di Chiaia 200; admission €2.10; open 8.30am-7.30pm Tues-Sun)*, an old patrician residence containing mostly 19th-century furnishings, china and other nick-nacks. A pavilion set in the villa's gardens houses a coach museum.

Vomero

Visible from all over the city, Vomero (**vom**-e-ro) hill is a serene and well-to-do residential quarter that rises above the chaos of the great metropolis below. Three funicular railways connect the two (see Getting Around later for more details).

Castel Sant'Elmo Commanding spectacular views across the city and bay, this austere, star-shaped castle *(☎ 081 578 40 30, Via Tito Angelini; admission €1.30; open 10am-6pm Tues-Sun)* was built under Spanish viceregal rule in 1538. Impressive though it is, the castle has seen little real action, serving more often than not as a prison. Admission times and cost can vary when the castle is the venue for a temporary exhibition.

Certosa di San Martino Barely 100m from the castle lies this Carthusian monastery, established in the 14th century and rebuilt in the 17th century in Neapolitan Baroque style. It houses the **Museo Nazionale di San Martino** *(☎ 081 578 17 69, Via Tito Angelini; admission €5.70; open 8.30am-7.30pm Tues-Sun)*, which features a section on naval history, an area dedicated to the history of the Kingdom of Naples and an extensive art collection. Of particular interest is the Sezione Presepiale, several rooms devoted to a collection of Neapolitan presepi, elaborate nativity scenes carved in the 18th and 19th centuries. Not all of the monastery is open to the public but you can enjoy the tranquil Baroque Chiostro Grande, or Main Cloister, whose manicured gardens are ringed by elegant porticoes.

Adjacent is the monastery's church, with exquisite marblework and a good number of frescoes and paintings, particularly by 17th-century Neapolitan artists. There is a magnificent view from the terraced gardens and – for absolutely free – from Largo San Martino, the square outside its main entrance.

Villa Floridiana In a city decidedly short of green space, this public park *(admission free; open 9am-1 hr before sunset Tues-Sun)*, where you can actually hear birds sing, is a tonic, spreading down the slopes from Via D Cimarosa in Vomero to Mergellina. The stately home at its lower, southern end was built in 1817 by Ferdinand I for his wife, the Duchess of Floridia. Today it contains the **Museo Nazionale della Ceramica Duca di Martina** *(☎ 081 578 84 18; admission €2.60; open 9am-12.30pm Tues-Sun)*, which has an extensive collection of European, Chinese and Japanese china, ivory, enamels and Italian majolica.

Capodimonte

Palazzo Reale di Capodimonte Work on a new palace for Charles of Bourbon started in 1738 and took almost a century to complete. On the northern edge of the city, the distinctive pinky-orange and grey palace is set in extensive parklands that

Voracious Collecting, Farnese Style

It was Cardinal Alessandro Farnese who founded the Farnese collection. On becoming Pope Paul III in 1534, he began by gathering art treasures for the Vatican, then turned his attention to embellishing the family seat, Palazzo Farnese, in Rome. Through papal influence, the Farnese family monopolised excavations around the city. In 1540 the *Toro Farnese* (Farnese Bull) was discovered near the Terme di Caracalla and installed in the gardens of Palazzo Farnese. It remained there until 1787, when it was moved to Naples' Museo Archeologico Nazionale, now the home of other famous Farnese treasures such as *Venere Callipigia* and *Ercole a riposo*.

This particular pope's vow of celibacy didn't prevent him from fathering four children. One of the most interesting paintings at the Palazzo Reale di Capodimonte is an unfinished portrait by Titian of Paul III with his two grandsons – Ottavio, who became the Duke of Parma and Piacenza, and Gran Cardinale Alessandro, who later became a serious collector in his own right. Alessandro continued the collection, commissioning works from Michelangelo, El Greco and other contemporary painters of renown.

The collection was transferred to Capodimonte from the Farnese family's power base in Parma and Piacenza in 1759. Many paintings were sold off in the 19th century, when the entire remaining collection was transferred to what is now the Museo Archeologico Nazionale. The paintings were returned to Capodimonte in 1957.

CAMPANIA

were once aristocratic hunting grounds. Extensively restored during the last decade, the palace houses the **Museo e Gallerie di Capodimonte** *(☎ 081 749 91 11, Parco di Capodimonte; admission €7.25 or €6.20 after 2pm; open 8.30am-7.30pm Tues-Sun)*, which displays the important Farnese collection (see the boxed text 'Voracious Collecting, Farnese Style'). The paintings hang in the royal galleries on the 1st floor and are divided into periods and schools; there are informative panels in each room in both Italian and English. The extensive collection boasts works by, among many others, Bellini, Botticelli, Caravaggio, Correggio, Masaccio and Titian. One of its most famous paintings is Masaccio's *Crocifissione* (Crucifixion). Other highlights are Bellini's *Trasfigurazione* (Transfiguration), and nine canvases by Titian.

Also on the 1st floor are the **royal apartments** with an extensive collection of armour, ivories, bronzes, porcelain and majolica (including a whole room covered in porcelain decoration), tapestries and other works of art.

The 2nd-floor galleries display work by Neapolitan artists from the 13th to 19th centuries.

Admission to the glorious park surrounding the palace is free. It opens from 8am to one hour before sunset daily.

Catacombe di San Gennaro The catacombs *(☎ 081 741 10 71, Via di Capodimonte 16; admission €2.60)* are just below the palace – enter from Via di Capodimonte. Guided tours are conducted at 9.30am, 10.15am, 11am and 11.45am. Dating from the 2nd century, the catacombs are quite different from Rome's dark, claustrophobic warrens. Here, you'll find a mix of tombs, corridors and broad vestibules held up by columns and arches and decorated with early Christian frescoes and mosaics, now much dilapidated. Tradition has it that San Gennaro was originally buried here.

Naples for Children

Kids of all ages will enjoy visiting Naples' various castles. They will also have fun at the aquarium (see under Mergellina earlier) and older children may appreciate the archaeological museum (see Museo Archeologico Nazionale earlier).

Within the university are three museums *(☎ 081 547 31 11, Via Mezzocannone 8; admission to each €0.60, families €1.10; open 9am-1pm daily)*, which older children might appreciate. **Museo della Mineralogia**, between Via B Croce and Corso Umberto I, features minerals, meteorites and quartz crystals collected from the Vesuvius region. **Museo della Zoologia** is the most child-friendly of the three while **Museo della Antropologia**, across the courtyard, is also worth peeking into.

Edenlandia *(☎ 081 239 40 902)* is a traditional funfair with over 200 attractions. Take the Ferrovia Cumana from Stazione Cumana, westbound, and get off at Edenlandia station.

East, out of town and stretching along the waterfront is **Museo Nazionale Ferroviario** *(☎ 081 47 20 03, Corso San Giovanni a Teduccio, Portici; admission free; open 9am-2pm Mon-Sat)*, Europe's largest railway museum. Take an FS train from Stazione Centrale to Pietrarsa-San Giorgio a Cremano.

Organised Tours

Cima Tours *(☎/fax 081 20 10 52, ⓔ cimatour@tin.it, Piazza Garibaldi 114)* and ***Tourcar*** *(☎ 081 552 04 29, Piazza Matteotti 1)* organise excursions to the Gulf of Naples islands, the Amalfi Coast and Pompeii, Herculanium and Vesuvius. A half-day tour to Pompeii costs about €38, including admission costs.

Napoli Sotterranea *(Underground Naples; ☎/fax 081 29 69 44, ⓦ www.napolisotterranea.com, Piazza San Gaetano 68)* Admission €5.20. Open noon-4pm Mon-Fri, 10am-6pm Sat-Sun. For something completely different, dip underground for a guided tour that takes you 40m below the city to explore the network of passages and caves – originally hewn by the Greeks to extract the soft tufa stone for construction, extended by the Romans as water conduits, clogged up with illegally dumped refuse over centuries, serving as air raid shelters in WWII – and nowadays source of a fascinating 1¼-hour visit.

Special Events

Naples' main festivals honour San Gennaro. On the first Sunday in May, on 19 September and on 16 December each year, thousands gather in the cathedral for the Festa di San Gennaro to pray that the saint's blood, held in two phials, will liquefy: a miracle said to save the city from potential disasters. Get there very early as police turn back the crowds once the cathedral is full. See also the Cathedral section earlier.

Other important festivals are the Madonna del Carmine held on 16 July in Piazza del Carmine, which culminates in a fireworks display and the Madonna di Piedigrotta (5 to 12 September). At Christmas, thousands of elaborate nativity scenes are erected around the city.

Neapolis Rock Festival, held at the height of summer, attracts international topliners and looks like becoming an annual event. It's held west of town, down by the beach at Arenile di Bagnoli (see Bars, Discos & Clubs under Entertainment later).

Places to Stay

At the budget end of the spectrum, Naples can be cheap, compared to the north of the country, although most of the modest hotels, (which are safe in themselves) are clustered near Stazione Centrale in a decidedly unsavoury area. Staff at tourist offices will recommend hotels and even call on your behalf, if they're not under pressure. Parry the hawkers who may harass you around the station – they are on commission and often pushing less reputable establishments. Some of the cheapest hotels double as brothels.

While room prices should always be read as a guide rather than gospel truth in Italy, this is even more the case in Naples. The following prices are a fair indication. Unfortunately some hotels only have doubles and often are not willing to offer lower prices for solo travellers. The closest camp sites are in Pozzuoli to the west and Pompeii to the east – see those sections later in this chapter.

Hostels There is one youth hostel in Naples.

Ostello Mergellina *(☎ 081 761 23 46, fax 081 761 23 91, Salita della Grotta 23)* B&B per person dorms/doubles €12.90/15.50. 12.30am curfew, open year-round. This HI (Hostelling International) hostel in Mergellina is modern, safe and has laundry facilities. There's a maximum stay of three nights in July and August. Take the Metropolitana from Stazione Centrale (platform 4, direction Pozzuoli) to Mergellina and follow signs.

Pensiones & Hotels – Around Stazione Centrale Although much of the area is dubious, all the places we list are clean, safe and reliable.

Hostel Pensione Mancini *(☎ 081 553 67 31, fax 081 554 66 75, W www.mds.it/mancini, Via Mancini 33)* Dorm beds/singles/doubles without bath €14.50/20.70/38.70, doubles/triples/quads with bath €33.60/46.50/56.80. You're a little squashed for space but that's the only downside to this small, highly recommended, welcoming place run by a young Polish-Italian couple. If, as may well happen, others have beaten you to a bed here, you can always try the following option.

Hotel Eden *(☎/fax 081 28 56 90, e hotel_eden_napoli@libero.it, Corso Novara 9)* Singles/doubles/triples/quads €21.70/34.80/46.50/55.80. This hotel represents very good value for money as all 45 rooms have a bathroom.

Weekend Fun

The atmosphere is somewhat more relaxed in Naples at the weekend, with great street jazz and in places such as pedestrianised Via A Scarlatti in Vomero there's a release from the tyranny of the traffic. You can also join the hundreds of strollers, skaters, bikers, scooters, and joggers on Via Francesco Caracciolo, closed to traffic between 10am and 1pm on Sunday (try any other time and you'll be road kill), in this celebration of what shoreside Naples could be like if it were car free.

CAMPANIA

Hotel Zara *(☎ 081 28 71 25, fax 081 26 82 87, ⓔ hotelzar@tin.it, Via Firenze 81, 2nd floor)* Singles/doubles/triples without bath €20.70/36.20/51.70, doubles/triples with bath €46.50/62. Rooms are spick and span and the service is caring. It's a tranquil haven from the bustle of the surrounding streets.

Hotel Ginevra *(☎/fax 081 28 32 10, ⓔ hginevra@tin.it, Via Genova 116)* Singles/doubles/triples/quads without bath €23.25/36.20/51.70/64.60, with bath €38.75/46.50/69.75/77.50. This is a hyperfriendly, family hotel and longtime travellers' favourite.

Hotel Casanova *(☎ 081 26 82 87, fax 081 26 97 92, Corso G Garibaldi 333)* Singles/doubles without bath €19.25/38.25, singles/doubles/triples/quads with bath €25.40/49.60/62/72.30. Here's another small concern, owned by the same family as Hotel Zara. In summer, the small roof terrace is a delight. Use the safer Corso G Garibaldi entrance rather than the main one on Via Venezia.

Hotel Gallo *(☎ 081 20 05 12, fax 081 20 18 49, Via S Spaventa 11)* Singles/doubles/triples with bath €57/82.75/108.50. Rooms are clean, comfortable and freshly decorated and the price includes breakfast.

Hotel Prati *(☎ 081 26 88 98, fax 081 554 18 02, ⓦ www.hotelprati.it, Via C Rosaroll 4)* High season singles/doubles €98.65/121.40, low season singles/doubles €72.30/93. With an attractive roof garden, private garage and rooms with full facilities, this three-star hotel is one of the best in its category.

Pensiones & Hotels – Around Spaccanapoli Many hotels in this area are near Piazza Dante, which you can reach by bus No R2 from Stazione Centrale. Alternatively, Piazza Dante is under five minutes' walk from Montesanto or Piazza Cavour Metropolitana stations – the nearest until its own, at the time of writing under noisy construction, is completed.

6 Small Rooms *(☎ 081 790 13 78, ⓦ www.at6smallrooms.com, Via Diodata Lioy 18)*. B&B in dorm beds €15.50. Established in late 1999 on the top floor of a venerable old building, 6 Small Rooms, run by Jenny, a cheery Australian, has quickly become a backpackers' favourite. There's free use of the kitchen to cook up rich fare from nearby street markets – or a brimming evening pasta plate is available for €3.10 if you can't face a hot stove. There are also a couple of rooms for 3/4 people at €18.10 per person.

Hotel Europa and ***Hotel College Europa*** *(☎ 081 551 72 54, fax 081 552 22 12, Via Mezzocannone 109c)* Singles/doubles without bath at Hotel Europa €36.25/46.50, singles/doubles with bath at Hotel College Europa €62/97. Above Cinema Astra, these two hotels on adjacent floors and with a common owner are in the heart of the university quarter.

Hotel Bellini *(☎ 081 45 69 96, fax 081 29 22 56, Via San Paolo 44)* Singles/doubles with bath €41.40/67.20. Tucked away in the heart of Spaccanapoli is this welcoming hotel, run by the delightful Antonio Riccardi for over 30 years. All rooms have TV, phone, fridge and – an asset in this city – wall safe. There's also secure parking (€13.00 per night).

Hotel Le Orchidee *(☎ 081 551 07 21, fax 081 251 40 88, Corso Umberto I 7)* Singles/doubles with bath €62/72.30, air-con supplement €15.50. Just outside the rabbit warren of Spaccanapoli with some rooms overlooking the bay, this place is also well positioned for the ferry terminal.

Albergo Duomo *(☎ 081 26 59 88, ⓔ egraziano@infoblue.com, Via Duomo 228)*. High season doubles/triples/quads €62/77.50/97, low season singles/doubles €52/67.50/87. Just down from the cathedral, this is a friendly place with freshly and eccentrically decorated rooms in warm pink with sky blue bathrooms.

Just a euro or two up the ladder are three mid-range hotels (listed in the following three paragraphs) under the same ownership that represent excellent value for money. All three have the same airy decor and simple, tasteful wicker furniture. Each occupies a slice of a charming historical building. Because they're protected buildings, the owners can't erect a sign outside so you'll need to look carefully. Doubles with bath and breakfast at all three places cost from €72.30 to €97 and each has a couple of rooms without bath for €62 to €72.30.

Albergo Sansevero *(☎ 081 21 09 07, Via Santa Maria di Costantinopoli 101)* Look for the two fine marble pillars flanking the courtyard entrance as you head north from Piazza Bellini.

Albergo Sansevero (Degas) *(☎ 081 551 12 76, Piazza del Gesù Nuovo 53)* This hotel is so called because the building once belonged to Edgar Degas, the French impressionist painter and sculptor. Enter the courtyard opposite Caffè Novocento and take the lift to the third floor.

Soggiorno Sansevero *(☎ 081 551 57 42, Piazza San Domenico Maggiore 9)* You'll find this place on the eastern side of the semi-pedestrianised piazza.

Grand Hotel Oriente *(☎ 081 551 21 33, fax 081 551 49 15, W www.oriente.it, Via A Diaz 44)* Singles/doubles €144.60/206.60. For the looser wallet, this ranks among the city's finest hotels. Breakfast is included.

Pensiones & Hotels – Mergellina, Vomero & Santa Lucia In Santa Lucia, near or on the waterfront, are a number of worthwhile options.

Pensione Teresita *(☎ 081 764 01 05, Via Santa Lucia 90)* Singles/doubles without bath €23.25/36.20. On the second floor and run by an old couple, Pensione Teresita is like stepping into your grandparents' home. At this price you can't expect much in the line of comfort but their rooms, all with washbasin and bidet, are clean and acceptable. Directly below you'll find ***Pensione Astoria*** *(☎ 081 764 99 03)*, where prices are maintained in tandem with Teresita and facilities are much the same.

Hotel Rex *(☎ 081 764 93 89, fax 081 764 92 27, W www.hotel-rex.it, Via Palepoli 12)* Singles/doubles €87.80/103.30, air-con supplement €7.75. For a little more comfort (and a hike in price), head to Hotel Rex where breakfast, included in the price, is served in your room.

Grand Hotel Santa Lucia *(☎ 081 764 06 66, fax 081 764 85 80, W www.santalucia.it, Via Partenope 46)* Singles €154.40-206.10, doubles €195.70-309.40. This hotel overlooks the marina and Borgo Marinaro. Breakfast is included in the price and facilities include – something still rare in Italy – a nonsmoking floor.

Parteno *(☎ 081 245 20 95, fax 081 247 13 03, W www.parteno.it, Via Partenope 1)* Singles/doubles/triples with bath €103.30/129.20/155. Also in the top-end range on the seafront but much more intimate and with comparable views, this place is highly recommended. Its six rooms are exquisitely furnished and prices include breakfast. Internet access and use of the nearby gym and sauna are both free and the charming young owners speak excellent English.

You'll find more options up the hill in Vomero, all easily accessible by funicular.

Pensione Margherita *(☎/fax 081 556 70 44, Via D Cimarosa 29)* Singles/doubles/triples with bath €31/56.90/80.10. This place is just a few doors from the funicular station in Vomero.

Hotel Belvedere *(☎ 081 578 81 69, fax 081 578 54 17, Via Tito Angelini 51–59)* Singles/doubles with bath €72.30/98.20, with bath and view €98.20/134.30. Right beside the Certosa di San Martino monastery at Naples' highest point, Hotel Belvedere has magnificent sweeping vistas of the city and bay.

In Mergellina, within an attractive late-19th-century building and a stone's throw from Amedeo Metro station, are two good places to lay your head.

Pensione Ruggiero *(☎/fax 081 66 35 36, Via Martucci 72, 3rd floor)* Singles/doubles with bath €62/82.70. Rooms are clean and bright and the friendly young owners are welcoming.

Hotel Pinto-Storey *(☎ 081 68 12 60, fax 081 66 75 36, e pintostorey@campnet.it, Via Martucci 72, 4th–5th floor)* Singles/doubles/triples with bath €72.30/113.70/142.10. Facilities are fine and rooms are cosily furnished although the welcome can be frosty.

Places to Eat

Neapolitan street food is among Italy's best. The pizza topped with mozzarella cheese and fresh tomato sauce is standard fare, as is the related *calzone*, a puffed up version with the topping becoming a filling instead. *Misto di frittura* – deep-fried potato, aubergine (eggplant) and courgette (zucchini) flowers – tempts from tiny stalls in tiny streets, as does mozzarella in *carozza* –deep-fried in bread. Seafood, particularly clams and mussels, is a speciality (although it is best to avoid uncooked shellfish as the bay is very polluted).

Restaurants – Spaccanapoli & Stazione Centrale This area has an array of pizzerias and a couple of spots for seafood.

Trattoria da Carmine *(☎ 081 29 43 83, Via dei Tribunali 330)* Full meal €7-10. Open lunch time only. One of dozens of small family trattorias in this area, it serves good value pasta and main dishes and the drinks come cheap.

The Perfect Pizza

Naples and Rome vie for pizza supremacy. Yet the two products could scarcely be more different. Pizzas in Naples have a soft doughy base while your true Roman pizza usually has a very thin crust. The only consensus is that both are delicious.

Neapolitans regard their version as the authentic one – after all, they will argue, their forefathers actually invented pizza in the 18th century. Pizzerias in Naples serving the 'real thing' have a sign on the door, *la vera pizza napolitana* (the real Neapolitan pizza). It's not just for show – to merit the seal of approval a pizza maker has to conform to strict requirements. For a Margherita, named after Queen Margherita (1851–1926, wife of King Umberto of Savoy), the cheese must be mozzarella (preferably made from buffalo milk), the olive oil extra virgin and the salt from the sea. Rolling pins are banned (the dough must be tossed by hand) and the pizza has to be cooked in a wood-fired oven at a temperature of between 215°C and 250°C.

Do your own research. For about the best pizza in Naples, head for Da Michele near Stazione Centrale. In Rome, try Pizzeria Remo in Testaccio (see the relevant Places to Eat sections). Buon appetito!

Da Michele *(☎ 081 553 92 04, Via Cesare Sersale 1)* Pizzas €5-7. Da Michele serves Naples' best pizza, which is quite an achievement! There are only two types: *margherita* (mozzarella and tomato) or *marinara* (mozzarella and garlic). It's always crowded – make sure you get a numbered ticket and be prepared to wait.

Pizzeria Sorbillo *(☎ 081 44 66 43, Via Tribunali 32)*. Pizzas €2-5. Here is a serious rival to Da Michele. There are now 21 members of the Sorbillo family, three generations of them, all in the pizza business in Italy or the US. Try the *capriciosa* (€5), liberally sprinkled with ham, artichoke and small, slimy mushrooms that burst with flavour. Immensely popular (be prepared to queue; it's well worth it), it also does takeaways.

Pizzeria di Matteo *(Via dei Tribunali 94)* Pizzas from €2.60. This is another excellent option for pizza that also does takeaway. Try the pizza lasagne with ricotta and the misto di frittura.

Il Pizzicotto *(☎ 081 551 62 91, Via Mezzocannone 129)* Pasta around €3, mains from €3.50. Tight for space, bright and friendly, Il Pizzicotto is a popular student eatery. Its lunch-time three-course menu (€9.30) is excellent value.

Trianon *(☎ 081 553 94 26, Via P Colletta 42–46)* Pizzas €2.80-5.70. For fine pizzas, topped with contemporary social history, Trianon – on the dough since 1923 – was for years a favourite with Italian celebrities such as film director Vittorio de Sica, comic actor Totò and other local luminaries.

La Nuova Brace *(☎ 081 26 12 60, Via S Spaventa 14–16)* Full meal €15.50-21. Open Mon-Sat. Handy for Piazza Garibaldi and Stazione Centrale, this place is a recommended no-nonsense eatery that does a good tourist menu for a bargain €8.30.

Ristorante Bellini *(☎/fax 081 45 97 74, Via Santa Maria di Costantinopoli 79–80)* Full meal from €21. Open noon-3pm daily & 7.30pm-1am Mon-Sat. A popular restaurant where seafood is the house speciality.

Try the *linguine al cartoccio* (pasta strands and shellfish, steamed together; €10.40). If you're pushed for time, grab a mini pizza (€1.10) from their street-side stall.

Pizzeria Port'Alba *(☎ 081 45 97 13, Via Port'Alba 18)*. Open Thurs-Tues. Just around the corner from Ristorante Bellini and founded in 1830, this is one of Naples' oldest and most characterful pizzerias.

La Nova Club *(☎ 081 551 48 94, Via Santa Maria La Nova 9)* Full meal around €21. Open lunch time Mon-Fri, dinner Sat. This place offers excellent food at reasonable prices – you can even tell the waiter your upper limit and he will help you order accordingly.

La Taverna del Buongustaio *(☎ 081 551 26 26, Vico Basilico Puoti 8)* Full meal €10-13. Tucked away off the western side of Via Toledo, this simple place has become something of a local celebrity. Nevertheless, it remains good value and has excellent seafood (try the grilled calamari).

Pizzeria al 22 *(☎ 081 552 27 26, Via Pignasecca 22)* Pizza from €2.50. Off Piazza Carità, this place is handy if you fancy a takeaway pizza.

Restaurants – Santa Lucia You tumble over restaurants in Borgo Marinaro where you pay for the view and ambience as much as for the food. All are very popular.

Ristorante La Scialuppa *(☎ 081 764 53 33, Via Lucilliana)* Full meal €25-31. Open Tues-Sun. A fairly reasonable option, you can eat on the terrace of this restaurant overhanging the marina and sample the *frittura de paranza* (deep fried fish and seafood; €10).

Ristorante Pizzeria Marino *(☎ 081 764 02 80, Via Santa Lucia 118–120)* Full meal €18. Open Tues-Sun. Long established and popular with locals, this typical Neapolitan restaurant/pizzeria does a huge antipasto (starter) spread and good pizzas.

Trattorla Da Ettore *(☎ 081 764 04 98, Via Santa Lucia 56)* Pizzas €3.50-5.50. Open Mon-Sat. Farther along from Marino is Da Ettore, which serves delicious *pagnotiello*, a sort of calzone stuffed with mozzarella, ham and mushrooms (€4.75).

Restaurants – Mergellina & Vomero If you're out of the centre there are good options for eating out in the following areas.

Trattoria dell'Oca *(☎ 081 41 48 65, Via Santa Teresa a Chiaia 11)* Full meal €15.50-18.50. Open Mon-Sat Sept-July. You'll enjoy the ochre walls and wooden tables of this snug place, just south of Piazza Amedeo. The cooking (Luca the cook changes the menu every month) is as appealing as the decor.

La Cantina di Sica *(☎ 081 556 75 20, Via C Bernini 17)* Full meal from €18. Open Tues-Sun. In Vomero, this trattoria with its high, vaulted roof serves excellent Neapolitan dishes. The spaghetti *alle vongole e pomodorini* (with clams and cherry tomatoes) and the *pasta genovese* are superb.

Ristorante Pizzeria Frasca *(☎ 081 556 51 98, Via Raffaele Morghen 12)* Pizza & pasta from €4.25. Open Wed-Mon. Also in Vomero, and less stylish than Trattoria dell' Oca, Frasca has a pleasant garden for alfresco dining in summer and also does home/hotel deliveries.

Trattoria Rossopomodoro *(☎ 081 556 81 69, Via D Cimarosa 144)* Full meal €13-26. The giant cans of tomato painted on the walls might not be Andy Warhol but they're bright and cheerful, like the place itself. The daily menu (pasta, main course and salad) is a bargain at €9.30.

Trattoria Pizzeria da Pasqualino *(☎ 081 68 15 24, Piazza Sannazzaro 77–79)*. Full meal around €18. Open Wed-Mon. This trattoria in Mergellina, with its bustling terrace, is the first of the eateries you meet as you enter the square from the Ostello Mergellina. You can go for anything from a plate of chips to a full pigout. People drive from miles around to pick up one of the takeaway pizzas.

Cafes If you're after a snack or a caffeine fix drop in on a Neopolitan cafe.

Intra Moenia *(☎ 081 29 07 20, Piazza Bellini 70)* Arty, literary, left-leaning with a mixed gay and hetero clientele, Intra Moenia, established in one of the city's more beautiful piazzas, is also one of its more interesting cafes. It has a small bookshop and publishing house too.

***Caffè dell'Epoca** (☎ 081 29 17 22, Via Santa Maria di Costantinopoli 81–82).* Open Mon-Sat. Virtually across the road from Intra Moenia, this stylish cafe has been serving its fare since 1886.

***Gambrinus** (☎ 081 41 41 33, Via Chiaia 12)* Even more venerable, Naples' oldest and most stylish cafe remains the haunt of artists, intellectuals and musicians – including, recently, saxophonist and ex-president of the US, Bill Clinton. It's the perfect place for a restorative coffee and pastry after a visit to the Palazzo Reale.

Gelaterias & Pasticcerias You have to search diligently for anything other than a great ice cream in Naples. For particularly saliva-inducing ones, stop by ***Gelateria Azzurra** (☎ 081 552 34 88, Piazza Carità 4).*

***Remygelo** (☎ 081 66 73 04, Via F Galliani 29a)* In Mergellina, Remygelo draws the sweet-toothed from all over the city – all prepared to go out of their way to pick up a tub or two of ice cream or some figure-wrecking pastries.

Popular ***Gelateria Pasticceria Carraturo*** has five outlets around town including, up in Vomero, one at Via Bernini 9–11.

***Attanasio** (☎ 081 28 56 75, Vico Ferroviario 2–4)* Convenient for a snack if you're passing through Stazione Centrale, this place is deservedly famous throughout Italy for its *sfogliatelle* – the great Neapolitan pastry, a vaguely sweet ricotta-filled number that tastes best straight from the oven.

***Pintauro** (☎ 081 41 73 39, Via Toledo 275)* You can smell the sfogliatelle, served fresh from the oven throughout the day, as you approach.

***Pasticceria Scaturchio** (☎/fax 081 551 38 50, Via Portamedina alla Pignasecca 22–24)*. In business since 1903, a bar and gelateria on the side, commissioned for weddings, baptisms and other celebrations, this pasticceria has become something of a landmark in the *centro storico* (old city).

Snacks Typical of the modest food shops and stalls you'll find throughout the Spaccanapoli area, ***Friggitoria Fiorenzano** (Piazza Montesanto)* sells deep-fried vegetables for €0.15 a piece – the aubergine slices and courgette (zucchini) flowers are especially good.

Entertainment

The monthly *Qui Napoli* and local newspapers are the best guides to what's on when. You can buy tickets for most sporting and cultural events at Box Office (☎ 081 551 91 88), Galleria Umberto I 15–16. Ask here or at the tourist office about what is happening during your stay.

Each May the city authorities organise Maggio dei Monumenti, a month of concerts and cultural activities in various museums and monuments around town. Most of these are free. From May until September there are open-air concerts in various locations. Ask at the tourist offices for details.

Cinema Finding undubbed films in English is not easy but you might have luck at ***Cinema Amedeo** (Via Martucci 69)*. It's something of an art-house place showing lots of classics.

Theatre & Classical Music There are year-round performances of opera, ballet and concerts at ***Teatro San Carlo** (☎ 081 797 21 11, Via San Carlo 98)*. Unfortunately for visitors, most tickets are sold on a seasonal, subscription basis and relatively few are left over for individual purchase. These start at around €13 then spiral steeply upwards, always selling like hot sfogliatelle.

Bars, Discos & Clubs Young, hip Neapolitans tend to loaf around their cars and mopeds licking on a gelato before moving on lateish to jazz joints or trendy (some might say tacky) clubs. Some of the smarter clubs charge hefty admission or membership fees (up to €40). For late night action in the heart of the city, head for Piazza del Gesù Nuovo, Piazza San Domenico Maggiore and the areas immediately to their north and south.

***Bar Rio Latino** (☎ 081 420 32 99, Calata Trinità Maggiore 49)* Open 9pm-at least 2am Mon-Sat. This Neapolitan newcomer has a large dancing area and throbs to a south American beat.

Bar Lazzarella *(☎ 081 551 00 05, Calata Trinità Maggiore 7–8)* You can sit on the terrace here, opposite Bar Rio Latino, with a small beer (€1.60) and watch the night time crowds drift by.

Echos Club *(☎ 338 229 20 87, Vico San Geronimo 24)* Open Wed-Sun. First obligatory drink €5.20 minimum charge. In an underground cellar, this laid back place usually has live music with an international flavour. It has recently promoted groups from, for example, Turkey, Ireland and the Balkans.

On Via Cisterna dell'Olio, there are three great clubs which, if you've stamina and money in your pocket, you can manage in a single night.

Operating from cellars which abut each other, neighbouring ***Le Tue Cane*** *(Via Cisterna dell'Olio 14–15)* and ***Kinky Bar*** *(☎ 081 552 15 71, Via Cisterna dell'Olio 21)* both attract a lively, in-the-know crowd and both are at their most active during the university year. Kinky Bar mainly blares out reggae; Le Tue Cane is more versatile.

Velvet Zone *(Via Cisterna dell'Olio 11)* Admission including first drink €5.20. Open 10pm-6am. You'll hear an eclectic mix of hip hop, rock, techno, pop and more here.

Club Live Music *(☎ 081 28 52 27, Salita della Grotta 10)* In Mergellina, just downhill from the youth hostel and burrowed into the hillside, this club lives up to its name, though on occasion the music's canned. It heats up early for Naples and a queue usually starts forming by 9.30pm.

Elsewhere in town there are a couple more places worth checking out.

Otto Jazz Club *(Piazzetta Cariati 23)*, west of Piazza Trento e Trieste, is a long established place that primarily features Neapolitan jazz.

Biggest of the venues for live music concerts is ***Palapartenope*** *(☎ 081 570 68 06, Via Barbagallo 115)*. Seating over 8000, it pulls in both Italian and international acts.

In summer, consider heading out of town for the relative evening cool of the beach.

Arenile di Bagnoli *(☎ 081 230 30 50, Via Nuova Bagnoli 10, Posillipo)* Admission €10.50. Open 10pm-5am May-Sept. This huge complex has several bars and cabanas where you can dance. It's also the venue for the annual Neapolis Rock Festival (see Special Events earlier).

Spectator Sports

Poor old Napoli, the local football team! The most revered institution in town after San Gennaro, they yo-yo from season to season between Serie A and Serie B, the Italian first and second divisions, never comfortable in either. At the end of the 2000–2001 season, the squad tumbled yet again down to Serie B. Home matches are played at the Stadio San Paolo, Piazzale Vincenzo Tecchio in the western suburb of Mostra d'Oltremare, usually on Sunday. Call ☎ 081 593 40 01 for details. Tickets if the opposition's any good are very hard to come by unless you're prepared to pay scalpers' prices. Take the Metropolitana to Campi Flegrei. See also the boxed text 'Goooooooooaaaaaaaaaallllllll!' in the Facts for the Visitor chapter.

Shopping

They say you can buy anything in Naples and you can see why after even a short wander around the city centre. From designer stores to improvised stalls with goods straight off the back of a truck, Naples certainly seems to have it all.

In particular, Naples is renowned for its gold and Christmas items such as presepi and *pastori* (shepherds). The nativity scenes can take on huge proportions, becoming fantastic models of the whole of Bethlehem. Most artisans are in Spaccanapoli, in particular along Via dei Tribunali, Via B Croce and the side streets and lanes. Many goldsmiths and *gioiellerie* (jewellery shops) are clustered around Via San Biagio dei Librai. Be warned, some inflate prices for tourists.

If you like old dolls, head for ***Ospedale delle Bambole*** (see Via San Biagio dei Librai under Spaccanapoli earlier).

The city's more exclusive shops are in Santa Lucia, behind Piazza del Plebiscito, along Via Chiaia to Piazza dei Martiri and down towards the waterfront. Young people shop along Via Roma and Via Toledo.

Street markets, where you can buy just about everything, are scattered across the city centre, including Piazza Garibaldi and along Via Pignasecca, off Piazza Carità.

Getting There & Away

Air Capodichino airport (☎ 081 789 62 59, ☎ 848 88 87 77 for flight information), about 8km north-east of the city centre, is southern Italy's main airport, linking Naples with most Italian and several major European cities.

Airlines represented in Naples include:

Alitalia (☎ 081 709 33 33 or 848 86 56 42 for international flights) Internal flights and international connections via Rome and Milan.
Air France (☎ 081 88 44 66) Daily to Paris.
British Airways (☎ 081 789 62 59 or 848 81 22 66 for information and reservations) Daily to London (Gatwick).
Go (☎ 848 88 77 66) Regular flights to London (Stansted).

Bus Most buses for Italian and some European cities leave from Piazza Garibaldi in front of Stazione Centrale. Check destinations carefully or ask around because there are no signs. Regular buses serve, for example, Caserta, Benevento and Avellino from here. See those towns for more information.

Maco (☎ 080 310 51 85) has two buses to Bari. Miccolis (☎ 099 735 37 54) has buses to Taranto, Lecce and Brindisi, while CLP (☎ 081 531 17 07) has four buses to Foggia.

The exception is the predominant local company SITA (☎ 081 552 21 76, **W** www.sita-on-line.it). You can buy tickets and catch SITA buses either from the main office on Via Pisanelli (near Piazza Municipio) or from Via G Ferraris, near Stazione Centrale (tickets at Bar Clizia, Corso Arnaldo Lucci 173).

Within Campania, SITA runs buses to Pompeii, Ercolano, Sorrento, other towns on the Amalfi Coast and Salerno (by motorway). Casting wider, it also links Naples with Bari and Potenza and operates a service to Germany.

Train Naples is the hub for the south and many trains originating in the north pass through Rome and terminate here. For information, ring ☎ 848 88 08 88. The city is served by regionale, diretto, Intercity and the superfast Eurostar trains. They arrive and depart from Stazione Centrale (☎ 081 554 31 88) or Stazione Garibaldi (on the lower level). There are up to 30 trains daily to/from Rome.

The Ferrovia Cumana and the Circumflegrea (☎ 081 551 33 28), based at Stazione Cumana in Piazza Montesanto, 500m south-west of Piazza Dante, operate services to Pozzuoli and Cuma every 20 minutes. Giranapoli tickets (see Tickets under Getting Around later) are not valid as far as Pozzuoli.

The Circumvesuviana (☎ 081 772 24 44), on Corso G Garibaldi about 400m south-west of Stazione Centrale (take the underpass from Stazione Centrale), operates trains to Sorrento via Ercolano, Pompeii and other towns along the coast. There are about 40 trains daily running between 5am and 10.30pm (reduced services on Sunday) and the standard fare, whatever your destination, is €2.60.

Car & Motorcycle Naples is on the major north–south Autostrada del Sole, numbered A1 (north to Rome and Milan) and A3 (south to Salerno and Reggio di Calabria). The A30 rings Naples to the north-east, while the A16 heads north-east to Bari.

When approaching the city, the motorways meet the Tangenziale di Napoli, a major ring road around the city. The ring road hugs the city's northern fringe, meeting the A1 for Rome and the A2 to Capodichino airport in the east and continues towards Campi Flegrei and Pozzuoli and to the west.

Boat Ferries and hydrofoils leave for Capri, Sorrento, Ischia, Procida and Forio from Molo Beverello in front of the Castel Nuovo.

Longer distance ferries for Palermo, Cagliari, Milazzo, the Aeolian Islands (Isole Eolie) and Tunisia leave from the Stazione Marittima, next to the Molo Beverello.

Alilauro and SNAV also operate hydrofoils to Ischia, Procida and Capri from Mergellina.

Qui Napoli lists current timetables for Gulf of Naples services.

Tickets for shorter journeys can be bought at the ticket booths on Molo Beverello and at Margellina. For longer journeys, try the offices of the ferry companies or travel agents.

A list of the routes serviced follows. The fares quoted are for a one-way journey. The reduction for a return journey isn't significant.

Alilauro (☎ 081 552 28 38) Operates hydrofoils to Ischia (€11.40), Sorrento (€13) and Forio (€12.40).

Caremar (☎ 081 551 38 82) Serves Capri (ferry €5.10, hydrofoil €10.40), Ischia (hydrofoil €9.10) and Procida (hydrofoil €7.50).

Linee Lauro (☎ 081 551 33 52) Linked with Alilauro and has ferries to Ischia (€5.70) and a year-round run at least weekly to Tunis (deck class €62-97; an airline-style seat – *poltrona* – €67.25-98.20; bed in shared cabin €72.30-124). It also has direct runs to/from Sardinia and Corsica in summer. Fares for both destinations are: deck class €28.50-36.25; bed in shared cabin €36.25-72.30.

Navigazione Libera del Golfo (NLG; ☎ 081 552 72 09) Runs hydrofoils to/from Capri (€10.40) year-round and to/from Amalfi (€14.50; summer only).

Siremar (☎ 091 690 25 55) Part of the Tirrenia group, Siremar operates boats to the Aeolian Islands and Milazzo (€36.15-40.80). The service is up to six times a week in summer, dropping to half as many in the low season.

SNAV (☎ 199 12 31 99) Runs hydrofoils to Capri (€10.40), Procida (€8.80) and Ischia (€10.40). In summer there are daily services to the Aeolian Islands. SNAV also operates Sicilia Jet (poltrona €51.65-77.50), which foams down the coast daily to Palermo between mid-April and September.

Tirrenia (☎ 199 12 31 99) Has a weekly boat to/from Calgiari (deck class €21.50-40.30; shared cabin €30.50-55.30) and one to/from Palermo (deck class €30.25-39.80; shared cabin €35.20-51.20). The service increases to twice weekly in summer. From Palermo and Cagliari there are connections to Tunisia, directly or via Trapani (Sicily).

Getting Around

To/From The Airport For the airport, there are two possibilities: ANM (Ⓦ www.anm.it) bus No 14 (€0.65, 30 minutes, every 15 minutes) from Piazza Garibaldi or CLP's airport bus (☎ 081 251 41 57; €1.55, 20 minutes, at least hourly) from Piazza Municipio. The same buses run to the city centre from outside the airport arrivals area.

A taxi in either direction will set you back about €21. Make sure the meter has been activated.

Tickets You can buy 'Giranapoli' tickets at stations, ANM booths and tobacconists. A ticket costs €0.80 and is valid for 90 minutes of unlimited travel by bus, tram, Metropolitana, funicular, Ferrovia Cumana or Circumflegrea. A daily tourist ticket is good value at €2.35. These tickets are not valid to Pompeii or Ercolano on the Circumvesuviana train line.

Bus & Tram Most city ANM buses operating in the central area depart from and terminate in Piazza Garibaldi, where bus stops are appallingly signed. The city produces one rather vague bus map and it is difficult to find decent information. If it baffles you, ask at the ANM information office at the western end of the square.

There are four frequent routes (R1, R2, R3 and R4) that connect to other (less frequent) buses running out of the centre. Useful services include:

R1 From Piazza Medaglie d'Oro to Piazza Carità, Piazza Dante and Piazza Bovio.

R2 From Stazione Centrale, along Corso Umberto I, to Piazza Bovio, Piazza Municipio and Piazza Trento e Trieste.

R3 From Mergellina along the Riviera di Chiaia to Piazza Municipio, Piazza Bovio, Piazza Dante and Piazza Carità.

Nos 14 & 14R From Piazza Garibaldi to the airport and the north of the city.

No 24 From the Parco Castello and Piazza Trento e Trieste along Via Toledo, Via Roma to Capodimonte.

No 110 From Stazione Centrale to the Museo Archeologico Nazionale, past Capodimonte and farther north.

No 137R From Piazza Dante north to Capodimonte, farther north and then back to Piazza Dante.

No 401 A night bus operates from midnight to 5am (hourly departures on the hour), from Stazione Centrale through the city centre to the Riviera di Chiaia and on to Pozzuoli, returning to Stazione Centrale.

CAMPANIA

Trams No 1 and 1B operate from east of Stazione Centrale, through Piazza Garibaldi, the city centre and along the waterfront to Riviera di Chiaia. Tram No 2B travels from Piazza Garibaldi to the city centre along Corso G Garibaldi.

Train The Metropolitana (Underground Railway) is, in fact, mostly above ground. The main line runs from Gianturco, just east of Stazione Centrale, with stops at Piazza Garibaldi (for Stazione Centrale), Piazza Cavour, Montesanto, Piazza Amedeo, Mergellina, Piazza Leopardi, Campi Flegrei, Cavaleggeri d'Aosta, Bagnoli and Pozzuoli. A second line, the Metropolitana Collinare, runs north from Piazza Vanvitelli to Piazza Medaglie d'Oro and seven stops beyond. A fair amount of the city's heart will remain a dusty construction site until the completion of an extension, linking Piazza Garibaldi, the cathedral, Piazzas Bovio, Carità and Dante, the Museo Archeologico Nazionale and Piazza Vanvitelli.

Funicular Railway Three of Naples' four funicular railways connect downtown with Vomero. The Funicolare Centrale ascends from Via Toledo to Piazza Fuga. The Funicolare di Chiaia travels from Via del Parco Margherita to Via D Cimarosa, while the Funicolare di Montesanto climbs from Piazza Montesanto to Via Raffaele Morghen. The fourth, Funicolare di Mergellina, connects the waterfront at Via Mergellina with Via Manzoni. Giranapoli tickets are valid for one trip only on the funicular railways.

Car & Motorcycle The constant honk of impatient motorists, the blue lights of ambulances and police cars flashing, the car behind a constant 10cm from your rear end, one-way streets and traffic lights that the more individualistic locals don't bother to observe – forget driving in town unless you have a death wish. Park your car at one of the several car parks, most of which are staffed, and walk around the city centre.

In addition to the anarchic driving, car theft is a major problem in Naples. See also Dangers & Annoyances under Information earlier in this chapter.

Both Avis (☎ 199 10 01 33) and Hertz (☎ 199 11 22 11) have offices at the airport and near the Stazione Centrale: Avis at Corso Arnaldo Lucci 203 and Hertz at Piazza Garibaldi 91b. Or try the national company Maggiore (☎ 848 86 70 67), which has branches within both the station and the airport.

It's impossible to hire a moped in Naples because of the high incidence of theft.

Taxi Official taxis are white, metered and bear the Naples symbol on their front doors. They generally ignore kerb-side arm wavers. There are taxi stands at most of the city's main piazzas or you can call one of the five taxi cooperatives such as Napoli (☎ 081 556 44 44) or Consortaxi (☎ 081 552 52 52). There's also a baffling range of supplements: €2.10 flag fee, €1.60 extra on Sundays and holidays, €2.10 more between 10pm and 7am, €0.80 for a radio taxi, €2.60 for an airport run, €0.60 per piece of luggage in the boot (trunk) and €1.10 for transporting a small animal (so leave the gerbil at home). Because of traffic delays, even a short trip may cost up to €13.

Taxi drivers may tell you that the meter's kaput. However, you can, and should insist, that they switch it on – you might find that it miraculously works again, especially if you begin to jot down the driver's name and number, inscribed on the photo ID they all display.

Around Naples

CAMPI FLEGREI

The area west of Naples is called the Campi Flegrei (Phlegraean – 'Fiery' – Fields), a classical term for the volcanic activity that has made it one of the globe's most geologically unstable areas. It was partly through the Campi Flegrei, which include the long-settled towns of Pozzuoli, Baia and Cuma that Greek civilisation arrived in Italy. Homer believed the area to be the entrance to Hades, fiery Hell, and Virgil wrote of it

CAMPANIA

in *The Aeneid*. St Paul also briefly put in and found time to give a sermon. Now part of suburban Naples, it retains several reminders of the ancient Greeks and Romans. Easily accessible by public transport or car, it makes a worthwhile half-day visit.

Pozzuoli

Now a largely uninspiring suburb south-west of Naples, Pozzuoli is enlivened by some impressive Roman ruins. Established by the Greeks in 530 BC and renamed Puteoli (Little Wells) by the Romans, it was once one of the Mediterranean's most important ports. And it's here that the actress Sofia Loren was born...

The helpful tourist office (☎ 081 526 66 39), Piazza Matteoti 1a, is beside the Porta Napoli gate. Core hours are 9am to 3.30pm, Monday to Friday. Ask for the brochure, *Welcome to Campi Flegrei*.

Just east of the port, you can gaze down upon the **Tempio di Serapide** (Temple of Serapis), so named because a statue of the Egyptian god Serapis was found among its ruins. In fact, it was the town market with, archaeologists reckon, skilfully designed toilets at either side of the eastern apse. It has been badly damaged over the centuries by the seismic activity known as bradyseism (slow earthquake), which raises and lowers the ground level over long periods. The church of Santa Maria delle Grazie, some 400m away, is sinking at a rate of about 2cm a year because of this.

Head north-east along Via Rosini to the substantial ruins of the 1st-century-AD **Anfiteatro Flavio** *(Via Rosini; admission €2.10, open 8.30am-2 hrs before sunset daily)*. Italy's third largest amphitheatre, with seating for over 20,000 spectators, it could be flooded, like many amphitheatres, for mock naval battles.

Continue north-east up Via Rosini, which becomes Via Solfatara and leads to the desolate **Solfatara Crater** *(☎ 081 526 23 41, Via Solfatara 161; admission €4.15; open 9am-1 hr before sunset daily)* after about 2km. You can catch any city bus heading uphill. Known to the Romans as the Forum Vulcani (home of the god of fire), its acrid steam, sulphurous waters and mineral-rich mud were famed as a health cure from classical times until the 20th century. With the whiff of brimstone in your nostrils, pass beside the pool of glooping mud as steam jets squirt and burp from the ground. The entire crater is a layer of rock supported by the steam pressure beneath.

Pozzuoli has several camp sites, the nearest ones to Naples (the alternative is those in Pompeii, east of the city). They're much of a muchness and full to the gills in summer. One that stands out from the usual tented villages is ***Camping Vulcano Solfatara*** *(☎ 081 526 74 13, fax 081 526 34 82, ⓔ solfatara@iol.it, Via Solfatara 161)* Sites per person/tent/car €8.80/5.20/5.70. Open Apr-Oct. Green, shaded and 750m from the Pozzuoli Metropolitana station, it's just beyond sniffing distance from the Solfatara Crater.

Baia & Cuma

About 7km west of Pozzuoli is **Baia**, once a fashionable Roman bathing resort, its extensive remains are now submerged some 100m from the shore. At weekends between April and September, you can view them from the *Cymba*, a glass-bottomed boat (€7.75). Year-round, however, you can see the elaborate Nymphaeum, dredged up and reassembled in the small **Museo Archeologico dei Campi Flegrei** *(☎ 081 523 37 97, Via Castello; admission €2.10; open 9am-1 hr before sunset Tues-Sun)*. The vast castle that houses the museum was constructed, like many a Neapolitan coastal fortification, in the late 15th century by the house of Aragón as a defence against possible French invasion. It served as a military orphanage during most of the 20th century.

Cuma (known to the Greeks as Cumae) some 10km north-west of Pozzuoli, was the earliest Greek colony on the Italian mainland. If Sybil the oracle, one of the ancient world's greatest prophetesses, speaks to you, you should pay a visit to the **Antro della Sibilla Cumana** (Cave of the Cumaean Sybil) within the **Acropoli di Cuma** *(☎ 081 854 30 60, Via Montecuma; admission €2.10; open 9am-2hrs before sunset daily)*.

There's plenty of ancient history – or myth – hereabouts. Inland and 5km from Pozzuoli is the **Lago d'Averno** (Lake Avernus), one of three crater lakes and the mythical entrance to the underworld where Aeneas descended to meet his father and a good spot for a picnic!

Getting There & Away

Train Ferrovia Cumana serves Pozzuoli, Baia and Cuma while the Metropolitana runs as far as Pozzuoli. For details of both, see the Naples Getting Around section.

Car & Motorcycle Take the Tangenziale ring road and hop off at the Pozzuoli exit. Less swiftly, more scenically and infinitely more frustratingly, take Via Francesco Caracciolo along the Naples waterfront to Posillipo, then on to Pozzuoli.

Boat There are frequent car and passenger ferries from Pozzuoli to the islands of Ischia and Procida, run by a variety of companies. Typical prices are €2.35 to Procida and €4.90 to Ischia – more if you take the hydrofoil option.

CASERTA

postcode 81100 • pop 71,000

Probably founded in the 8th century by the Lombards on the site of a Roman emplacement atop Monte Tifata, Caserta, a mere 22km north of Naples, spread onto the plains below from the 12th century onwards. The construction of the Bourbons' grand palace assured the town a grandeur it would otherwise never have known.

Caserta's EPT tourist office (☎ 0823 32 11 37) is in the Palazzo Reale.

Palazzo Reale

This splendid palace *(☎ 0823 44 74 47; admission €6.20; open 9am-7pm Tues-Sun)*, also known as the Reggia di Caserta, is, after Pompeii, Italy's most visited historical site. Work started in 1752 after Charles III of Bourbon, ruler of Naples, decided to build himself a palace that would emulate Versailles. Neapolitan Luigi Vanvitelli was commissioned for the job and established his reputation as one of the leading architects of the time after working on the palace.

The building, with a facade stretching 250m and with 1200 rooms, 1790 windows and 34 staircases, is of massive proportions. You enter by Vanvitelli's immense staircase and follow a route through the royal apartments, most richly decorated with tapestries, furniture, mirrors and crystal. Beyond the library is a room containing a vast collection of presepi, composed of hundreds of hand-carved characters. A walk in the elegant landscaped **grounds** is a must. They're open 8.30am to two hours before sunset (last entry one hour before closing) daily. Since they're some 3km long, you might want to take the special bus to the far end (€0.80 return), which is marked by a waterfall and the fountain of Diana, then stroll back. In greater style, you can also clip-clop your way along the wide alleys in a pony and trap. Also at the far end, is the **Giardino Inglese** (English Garden) with its intricate pathways, exotic plants, little lakes and fake Roman ruins – all very much the taste of the day at the time it was laid out.

Your ticket gives entry to the royal apartments, grounds, Giardino Inglese (tours every half-hour), and a museum of local archaeological finds (open 8.30am to 12.30pm). Within the palace there's also the recently inaugurated **Mostra Terrea Motus** (admission €3.70) illustrating the 1980 earthquake that devastated the region. At the end of all this, you can restore your energy in the palace's cafeteria and restaurant.

There's a good guidebook, *The Royal Palace of Caserta and the Old Town*, which the persistent vendors will thrust upon you. It's worth giving in.

Getting There & Away

CPTC buses connect Caserta with Naples (Piazza Garibaldi) about every 30 minutes between 8am and 8pm. Some Benevento services also stop in Caserta. The town is on the main train line between Rome and Naples. Both bus and train stations are near the Palazzo Reale entrance, which is signposted from each. If you're driving, follow the signs for 'Reggia'.

JOHN HAY

The Parco Nazionale d'Abruzzo is home to the Marsican brown bear and the Apennine wolf.

ALAN BENSON

Charming Sulmona, birthplace of the poet Ovid

JOHN HAY

Abbazia di San Vincenzo al Volturno, near Isernia

JENNY JONES

A statue looks to Amalfi's cathedral for inspiration.

RUSSELL MOUNTFORD

A brake pad's dream on the Isle of Capri

JENNY JONES

Picturesque Positano perches on the Amalfi coast.

JONATHAN SMITH

The Aragonese Castello d'Ischia at Ischia Ponte

JONATHAN SMITH

Capri: popular but none the poorer for it

AROUND CASERTA

About 10km to the north-east of Caserta (take a CPTC bus) lies **Caserta Vecchia**, the original medieval hill town, which includes the remains of a 9th-century castle and a 13th-century cathedral.

The modern city of **Santa Maria Capua Vetere** (ancient Capua), about 12km west of Caserta, was populated by the Etruscans, the Samnites and later the Romans. The ruins include a 1st-century-AD **amphitheatre** *(☎ 0823 79 88 64; open 9am-5.30pm Tues-Sun)*. The largest in Italy after the Colosseum in Rome, it had its own gladiator school; the famous gladiators' revolt led by Spartacus originated here. There are also remains of the **Arco d'Adriano** (Hadrian's Arch), under which passed the Via Appia and a **Mithraic temple**. Most of the artefacts from the area are now in the **Museo Provinciale Campano** *(☎ 0823 96 14 02, Via Roma 68; open 9am-1.30pm Tues-Sun)* in the modern town of Capua. A combined ticket (€2.60) gives admission to the museum and all three monuments.

Regular CPTC buses run from the Caserta train station to Santa Maria Capua Vetere.

BENEVENTO

postcode 82100 • pop 65,000

A provincial capital about 60km north-east of Naples, Benevento is on Via Appia (S7). After a period as a Lombard duchy, when it controlled much of southern Italy, the town was transferred to the control of the papacy in the 11th century and remained mostly under papal rule until 1860. The tourist office (☎ 0824 31 99 11) is at Via Sala 31.

Things to See

The town was heavily bombed in WWII and the Romanesque **cathedral** with its elaborate facade had to be largely rebuilt. South-west of the cathedral is a restored Roman theatre dating from Hadrian's time. The **Arco di Traiano** (Trajan's Arch), built in AD 114, commemorates the opening of the Via Traiana. The **obelisk** in Piazza Matteotti is a reminder of the Napoleonic invasion of Italy. **Chiesa di Santa Sofia**, near the piazza, adjoins what was once a Benedictine abbey. Founded in AD 762, its main entrance dates from the 12th century. The abbey contains the **Museo del Sannio** *(☎ 0824 2 18 18, Piazza Santa Sofia; admission €2.60; open 9am-1pm Tues-Sun)*, which houses remnants of a temple dedicated to Isis, dating from AD 88, along with a gallery of mainly medieval paintings.

Places to Stay

Albergo Genova *(☎ 0824 42 926, Via Principe di Napoli 103)* Singles/doubles

The Battle of Benevento

In 1250, Emperor Frederick II died in Apulia, leaving his southern Italian kingdom to his son Conrad. For the next eight years Conrad fought the papacy for control of the kingdom until Manfred, also Frederick's son but from the wrong side of the blanket, asserted his control over the entire kingdom.

Rome, however, was not idle and in 1265 reached an agreement with Charles I of Anjou, entitling the Frenchman to the kingdom in the name of the Church in exchange for the removal of Manfred and his Swabians.

Manfred assembled an army to meet the threat and on 25 February 1265 was lying in wait for the French on the Grandella plain north of Benevento. Charles had hoped to take the city by surprise and gain control of the road to Naples but, with his 30,000 troops exhausted by the long march, he decided to stay put. Manfred, with only half that number of men, calculated that his only chance was to attack, abandoning his favourable, defensive position.

At dawn the following day, Manfred's Saracen archers and German cavalry stormed Charles' camp but when the French cavalry entered the fight, things began to go awry. As Manfred, seeing his chances of victory fade, charged into the melee, he was abandoned by many of the more prudent or pusillanimous of his barons. With a handful of diehards, he pressed on. Every one of them fell. Manfred was 34, and with him passed the short, but illustrious, Swabian line.

without bathroom €15.55/25.90. This is an economical, basic place close to the train station.

Getting There & Away

FBN (trains ☎ 0824 32 07 56, buses ☎ 0824 32 07 64) operates from Naples (Stazione Centrale; both €4, 1½ hours, frequent). The Vallegaudina line runs direct trains to/from Naples while FS is slower since you have to change trains in Caserta. FS has direct trains to/from Rome while buses also link Benevento with Rome and Campobasso. Benevento is on the S7 (the Via Appia) and close to the A16.

AVELLINO & AROUND

About 50km east of Naples is the largely modern town of Avellino). The EPT office (☎ 0825 747 31) is at Via Due Principati 5. A day trip from Naples is the best idea as accommodation options are poor.

The mountainous area south-west of Avellino, particularly around the towns of Quindici and Sarno, was the scene of horrific mud slides in 1998, in which over 130 people died. The immediate cause was excessive rainfall sluicing down an already geologically unstable area but irresponsible deforestation and unauthorised building on the surrounding hills also contributed to the disaster.

The area's main attraction is the vertiginous summit of **Monte Vergine** and the **sanctuary** devoted to the Virgin Mary, north of the city. A young pilgrim, Guglielmo di Vercelli, erected a church here in the 12th century and so began a tradition of pilgrimage that continues to the present day. His remains were finally laid to rest in the crypt of the modern basilica in 1807.

From the summit (1493m) you can see Naples on a clear day and the twisting drive up from Avellino is quite thrilling. In winter, there's limited skiing at Lago di Laceno, about 30km south-east of Avellino.

Avellino is connected to Naples by buses running every 20 minutes. There are daily buses from Avellino to the summit of Monte Vergine and the sanctuary in summer.

CAMPANIA

Gulf of Naples (Golfo di Napoli)

CAPRI

postcode (Capri) 80073 (Anacapri) 80071
pop 13,000

Despite the boatloads of tourists (up to 5000 daily) who pour onto the Marina Grande and restaurants that boast *würstl* (German sausages), real English butter and Maxwell House coffee, Capri remains an enchanting island haven in the Gulf of Naples. Breathtaking caves, luxuriant vegetation and the charming narrow lanes of its small towns have attracted visitors for centuries. The best time to visit is spring or October, once the summer crowds have ebbed away.

History

Already inhabited in the Palaeolithic age, Capri was subsequently occupied by the Greeks. The Romans, for their part, had taste; Emperor Augustus made the island his private playground and Tiberius retired there in AD 27. Augustus is believed to have founded the world's first palaeontological museum, in the Villa Augustus, to house fossils and Stone Age artefacts unearthed by his workers.

Tiberius, a victim of Tacitus' pen, has gone down in history as something of a porn king on the island, although there is little evidence to back the lurid claims concerning the emperor's orgies. The mud stuck, however, and until modern times his name has been equated by the islanders with evil. When the eccentric Swedish doctor Axel Munthe first began picking about the ruins of Roman palaces and villas on the island in the late 19th century, locals would observe that it was all '*roba di Timberio*' – Tiberius' stuff.

Throughout history, the people of Capri and Anacapri have been at loggerheads and are always ready to trot out their respective patron saints to ward off the *malocchio* (evil eye) of their rivals.

Orientation

About 5km from the mainland at its nearest point, Capri is a mere 6km long and 2.7km

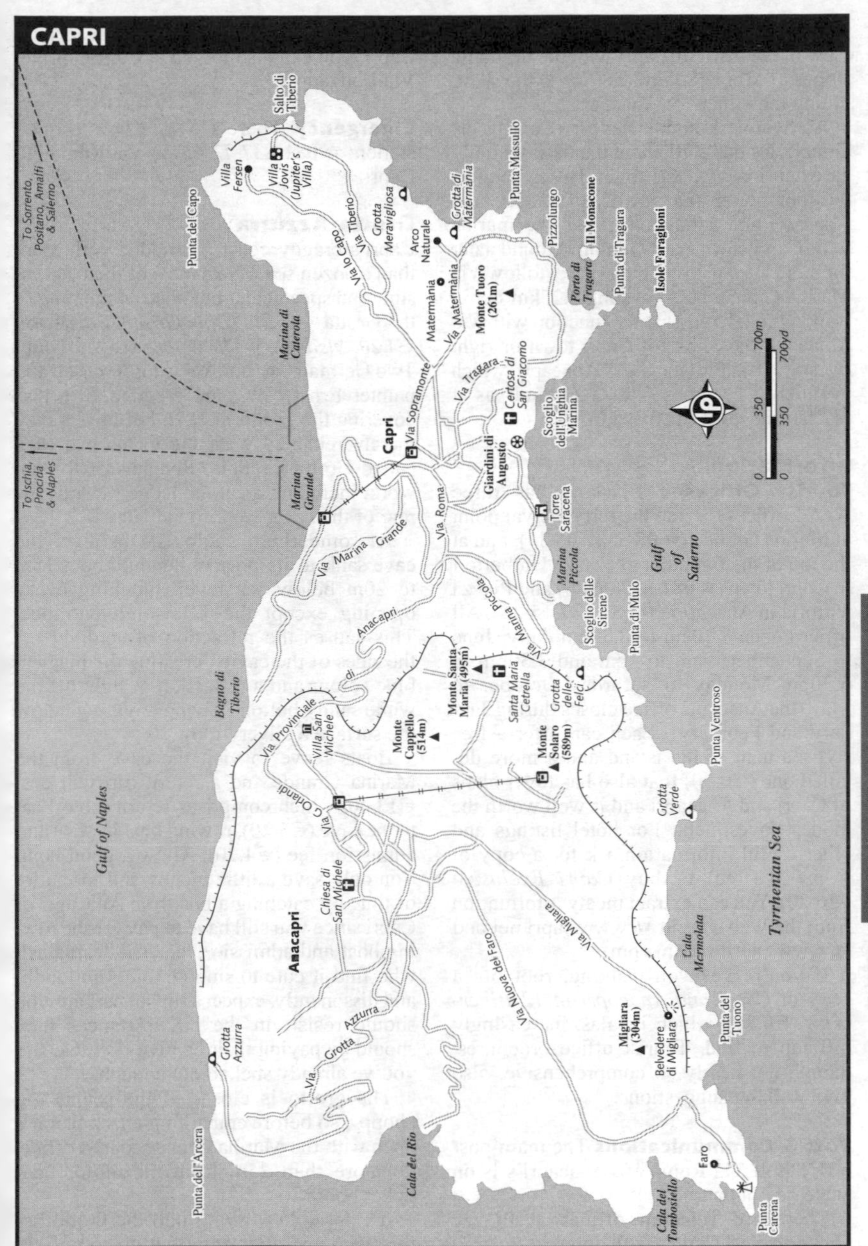
CAPRI
To Sorrento, Positano, Amalfi & Salerno
To Ischia, Procida & Naples
Punta del Capo
Villa Fersen
Villa Jovis (Jupiter's Villa)
Salto di Tiberio
Via Tiberio
Via lo Capo
Grotta Meravigliosa
Arco Naturale
Grotta di Matermània
Punta Massullo
Matermània
Via Matermània
Monte Tuoro (261m)
Pizzolungo
Il Monacone
Porto di Tragara
Punta di Tragara
Isole Faraglioni
Marina di Caterola
Via Sopramonte
Via Tragara
Certosa di San Giacomo
Scoglio dell'Unghia Marina
Capri
Marina Grande
Via Roma
Giardini di Augusto
Torre Saracena
Via Marina Grande
Marina Piccola
Via Marina Piccola
Gulf of Salerno
Scoglio delle Sirene
Punta di Mulo
Bagno di Tiberio
Via Provinciale di Anacapri
Villa San Michele
Monte Cappello (514m)
Monte Santa Maria (495m)
Santa Maria Cetrella
Grotta delle Felci
Monte Solaro (589m)
Punta Ventroso
Via G Orlandi
Gulf of Naples
Chiesa di San Michele
Anacapri
Grotta Verde
Via Migliara
Via Nuova del Faro
Tyrrhenian Sea
Cala Mernolata
Grotta Azzurra
Via Grotta Azzurra
Migliara (304m)
Belvedere di Migliara
Punta del Tuono
Punta dell'Arcera
Cala del Rio
Faro
Cala del Tombosiello
Punta Carena
0 350 700m
0 350 700yd
lp

CAMPANIA

wide. As you approach, you get a lovely view of the town of Capri with the dramatic slopes of Monte Solaro (589m) to the west, hiding the village of Anacapri.

All hydrofoils and ferries arrive at Marina Grande, a small settlement that is essentially an extension of Capri town. Buses connect the port with the towns of Capri and Anacapri and a funicular links the marina with Capri town (see Getting Around later for more information). Otherwise, follow Via Marina Grande for a twisting 2.25km uphill walk. Turn left (east) at the junction with Via Roma for the centre of Capri town or right (west) for Via Provinciale di Anacapri, which eventually becomes Via G Orlandi as it reaches the town of Anacapri.

Information

Tourist Offices The island has three AAST offices: beside the ferry arrival point at Marina Grande (☎ 081 837 06 34), and at the top of the funicular at Piazza Umberto I in Capri town (☎ 081 837 06 86) and Piazza Vittoria in Anacapri (☎ 081 837 15 24). All offices open 8.30am to 8.30pm daily, June to September; 9am to 1pm and 3.30pm to 6.30pm Monday to Saturday October to May (the Anacapri office closes during January and February). Each can offer a free stylised map of the island and a more detailed one (€0.80) that also has town plans of Capri and Anacapri and is well worth the modest investment. For hotel listings and other useful information ask for a copy of *Capri È* (free) or buy *Capri Exclusive* (€6.20). You can extract meaty information from the Web sites at Ⓦ www.capri.net and Ⓦ www.capritourism.com.

If you're keen on walking, root out a copy of *Capri and Anacapri in 12 Itineraries* (€0.80), which is, alas, increasingly difficult to find. Tourist office brochures, though not nearly so comprehensive, also give walking suggestions.

Post & Communications The main post office is at Via Roma 50. Anacapri's is on Viale de Tommaso.

There are Telecom offices at Piazza Umberto I in Capri (with Internet access) and at Piazza Vittoria 4, in Anacapri. In Capri, you can also log on at CapriOnLine, Via Longano 37.

Emergency There's a *questura* (police station; ☎ 081 837 72 45) at Via Roma 70, Capri.

Grotta Azzurra

Capri's craggy coast is studded with more than a dozen sea caves, most of them accessible and spectacular but none as stunning as the Grotta Azzurra *(Blue Grotto; admission €4.20; visits 9am-1hr before sunset daily)*. Two Germans, writer Augustus Kopisch and painter Ernst Fries, are credited with discovering the grotto in 1826 but in fact they merely renamed what the locals had long called Grotta Gradola. Remains of Roman work, including a carved ledge towards the rear of the cave, were found later.

At some time, geologists believe, the cave sank to its present height, about 15m to 20m below sea level, blocking every opening except the 1.3m-high entrance. This causes the refraction of sunlight off the sides of the cavity, creating the magical blue colour and a reflection of light off the white sandy bottom, giving anything below the surface a silvery glow.

Boats leave to visit the cave from the Marina Grande and a return trip will cost €13.40, which comprises return motorboat to the cave (€5.20), rowing boat in (€4) and admission fee (€4.20). Allow a good hour. You only save a little money and lose a lot of time by catching a bus from Anacapri or Capri since you still have to pay for the rowing boat and admission fee. The 'captains', who find it cute to sing *O Sole Mio* loudly and dissonantly, expect a tip but perhaps you should resist: in the circumstances they should be paying their captive clientele and you've already shelled out enough.

The grotto is closed if the sea is too choppy, so before embarking check that it's open with the Marina Grande tourist office, no more than 25m from the motor boat ticket booth.

It's possible to swim into the grotto before 9am and after 5pm, but do so only in company and if the sea is completely calm. Because of tidal flows through the small entrance, it can be quite dangerous but locals, despite their fear of the dragons and witches believed to inhabit the cave, have swum in it for centuries.

Capri Town

From Piazza Umberto I in the centre of Capri, you can contentedly while away an afternoon wandering through the narrow lanes. In the square itself is the 17th-century **Chiesa di Santo Stefano**. Note the pair of languidly reclining patricians in the chapel to the south of the main altar and the well preserved Roman tiling in the northern one. Beside the latter is a reliquary with some saintly bone that reputedly saved Capri from the plague in the 19th century.

Head down Via D Birago or Via V Emanuele, for **Certosa di San Giacomo** *(☎ 081 837 62 18, Viale Certosa; admission free; open 9am-2pm Tues-Sun)*, a rather stark 14th-century Carthusian monastery with cloisters and a painted chapel. The nearby **Giardini di Augusto** (Gardens of Augustus) are altogether more colourful and command a good view of the **Isole Faraglioni**, the rock stacks along the southern coast.

The **Museo del Centro Caprese i Cerio** *(☎ 081 837 66 81, Piazzetta Cerio 5; admission free; open 10am-2pm Tues-Sat)*, has a library of books and journals about the island and a collection of Neolithic and Palaeolithic fossils found locally.

Villa Jovis & Around

East of the town centre, a comfortable hour's walk along Via Tiberio leads to the one-time residence of Emperor Tiberius, Villa Jovis *(Jupiter's Villa, also known as the Palazzo di Tiberio; ☎ 081 837 06 34, Via Tiberio; admission €2.10; open 9am-1 hr before sunset daily)*. The largest and best preserved of the island's Roman villas, in its heyday it was a vast complex which included imperial quarters, entertainment areas, baths, grand halls, gardens and woodland.

The stairway behind the villa leads to **Salto di Tiberio** (Tiberius' Leap), a cliff from where, says the story, Tiberius had out-of-favour subjects pitched into the sea.

A pleasant walk down Via Matermania leads to the **Arco Naturale**, a rock arch formed by the pounding sea. Doubling back to the first crossroads, you can turn left to drop down a long series of steps and follow the path south, then west, back into town enjoying good views of Punta di Tragara and Isole Faraglioni on the way.

Anacapri & Around

Many visitors are lured to **Villa San Michele** above all by the words of one of its most troubled inhabitants, Dr Axel Munthe. The house he built on the ruined site of a Roman villa remains immortalised in his book *The Story of San Michele*. The villa *(☎ 081 837 14 01, Viale Axel Munthe; admission €4.20; open 9am-6pm daily May-Sept, 10.30am-3.30pm daily Nov-Feb, 9.30am-4.30pm daily March, April & Oct)*, a short walk north of Piazza Vittoria, houses Roman sculptures from the period of Tiberius' rule. The pathway behind offers superb views over Capri. The (often closed) stairway of 800 steps leading from the town was the only link between Anacapri and the rest of the island until the mountain road was built in the 1950s.

From Piazza Vittoria, you can take a chair lift (€5.20) to the top of Monte Solaro where, on a (rare) clear day, you can see for miles. It runs from 9.30am to sunset daily, March to October and 10.30am to 3pm daily, November to February. From Anacapri, a bus runs to Faro, a less crowded spot that boasts one of Italy's tallest lighthouses.

Activities

If you fancy scuba diving, contact **Sercomar** *(☎ 081 837 87 81, Via Colombo 64, Marina Grande)*. **Bagni Le Sirene** *(☎ 081 837 69 70, Marina Piccola)* hires out canoes and motorised dinghies and can take you water-skiing. For sailboards and catamarans, contact **Banana Sport** *(☎ 081 837 51 88, Via Marina Grande 12)*.

The main places to swim are at Bagno di Tiberio, a small inlet west of Marina Grande, where the emperor himself dipped; a rocky area at Marina Piccola; at Faro; off concrete ledges at the Grotta Azzurra (only before 9am or after 5pm); and farther west of the grotto below the restaurants. There are no private beaches on the island and the best areas can only be reached by hired boat.

Special Events

The main secular festival is from 1 to 6 January, when local folk groups perform in Piazza Diaz, Anacapri, and in Capri's Piazza Umberto I.

Places to Stay

Hotel space is at a premium during the summer and many places close in winter. There are few really cheap rooms at any time of the year. Beware of the compulsory breakfast in summer.

During the summer months and occasionally in winter, hundreds of young people flock to Capri to party on Friday and Saturday nights, usually around Piazza Umberto I. So, if you want peace and quiet at night, avoid this area!

Camping is forbidden and offenders are either prosecuted or 'asked' to relocate to a hotel. You might want to enquire at the tourist office about renting a room in a private home.

Marina Grande Views are the main pull for staying in this area.

Belvedere e Tre Re *(☎ 081 837 03 45, fax 081 837 88 22, Via Marina Grande 238)* Doubles with bathroom €67.20-113.70. This place, under five minutes' walk from the port, has good views.

Italia *(☎ 081 837 06 02, fax 081 837 03 78, Via Marina Grande 204)* Singles €46.50-80.10, doubles €56.90-100.80. Up the hill beyond Belvedere e Tre Re, the views here are even better and the quality is pretty much the same. All rooms have a bathroom.

Capri You'll not have trouble finding somewhere luxurious to lay your head in Capri.

Albergo Stella Maris *(☎ 081 837 04 52, fax 081 837 86 62, Via Roma 27)* Singles €15.50-31, doubles €62-72.30, triples €77.50-82.70. Open year-round. Stella Maris is right in the noisy heart of town, opposite the bus station and just off Piazza Umberto I.

Albergo Esperia *(☎ 081 837 02 62, fax 081 837 09 33, Via Sopramonte 41)* Doubles €97-129.20. Open year-round. A guard of honour of diminutive lions and cherubs leads you up the steps into this charming, recently renovated 19th-century villa. Tranquil and intimate, most rooms enjoy spectacular views and all have bathroom and air-con. It also has a small restaurant.

Pensione La Reginella *(☎ 081 837 05 00, fax 081 837 68 29, e falcopaolo@interfere.it, Via Matermania 36)* Singles €41.40-56.90, doubles €82.70-113.70. Up the hill and east of Albergo Esperia, vistas here are just as breathtaking, the prices, less so. All rooms have bathroom and there's also a restaurant.

Albergo La Vega *(☎ 081 837 04 81, fax 081 837 03 42, Via Occhio Marino 10).* Singles €93-144.70, doubles €144.70-217. Upmarket La Vega has a spectacular view from the hotel pool.

Grand Hotel Quisisiana *(☎ 081 837 07 88, fax 081 837 60 80, w www.quisi.com)* Singles/doubles from €217/273.70 May-Sept, singles/doubles from €175.60/227.25 Oct-April. At the tip-top end of the spectrum, this prestigious hotel, set in its gracious garden, started life as a sanatorium in the mid-19th century.

Anacapri Anacapri and its hotels virtually close during the winter.

Loreley *(☎ 081 837 14 40, fax 081 837 13 99, e loreley@mbox.caprinet.it, Via G Orlandi 16)* Singles €46.50-62, doubles €87.80-98.20. Open Mar-Nov. Loreley offers one of Capri's better hotel deals. Some rooms have views across to Naples.

Places to Eat

Food is generally good and reasonably priced (although watch out for inflated cover and service charges). *Insalata caprese*, a delicious salad of fresh tomato, basil and mozzarella with olive oil dribbled over, has its origins here. Look out too for caprese cheese, a cross between mozzarella and ricotta.

Capri There is a range of good eating options in Capri.

Ristorante Settanni *(☎ 081 837 01 05, Via Longano 5)* Pasta from €4.20, full meal €15-23. Open Fri-Wed mid-Mar–Jan. This friendly place, tucked away from the crowds up an alley, has a good view over the bay.

La Cisterna *(☎ 081 837 56 20, Via M Serafina 5)* Pizza €2.60-5.20, full meal €13-23. Family-run La Cisterna is one of several cosy restaurants in the lanes off Piazza Umberto I.

Da Giorgio *(☎ 081 837 0898, Via Roma 34)* Full meals from €20. Here's *yet another* place with a great panorama.

Ristorante Moscardino *(☎ 081 837 06 87, Via Roma 28)* Tourist menu €15, full meal €15-31. A stone's throw from Da Giorgio, this place also does a tempting light lunch special of pasta and a fish dish for €7.25.

La Capannina *(☎ 081 837 07 32, Via Le Botteghe 12)* Full meal €30-46. Open mid-Mar–mid-Nov. For something very special, visit La Capannina, one of the island's longest established and best traditional restaurants.

Ristorante le Grottelle *(☎ 081 837 57 19, Via Arco Naturale 13)* Pasta €4-7.75, mains from €9. Open Apr-Oct. Le Grottelle is tucked inside a couple of small caves 200m before the Arco Naturale (see Villa Jarvis & Around earlier).

Locals do their fruit and vegetable shopping at the ***mercatino*** (indeed a *very* small market) underneath the Capri bus station. ***Sfizi di Pane*** *(Via Le Botteghe 15)* has a rich selection of local breads and cakes. For a midday snack, pop into ***Raffaele Buonacore*** *(Via Vittorio Emanuele 35)*. It does tasty takeaway pizzas, savoury tarts and cold cuts, all to be chased down by a dollop of their scrummy ice cream.

Anacapri The western side of the island also has a number of restaurants.

Il Solitario *(☎ 081 837 13 82, Via G Orlandi 96)* Pasta from €4, mains from €8. The leafy garden enhances the pleasure of eating here.

La Giara *(☎ 081 837 38 60, Via G Orlandi 67)* Pizzas from €4. The pizzas are good here and a full menu is also on offer.

Trattoria Il Saraceno *(☎ 081 837 20 99, Via Trento e Trieste 18)* Full meal from €12. Try the *ravioli caprese* (€4.50) and a drop or two of the proprietor's own wine.

Pizzeria Materita *(☎ 081 837 33 75, Via G Orlandi 140)* and ***Mamma Giovanna*** *(☎ 081 837 20 57, Via Boffe 3–5)* are a couple of cheap and cheerful places facing onto Piazza Diaz.

Entertainment

Capri There's no shortage of watering holes in town. ***Guarracino*** *(Via Castello 7)* is among the more pleasant spots for a drink. By contrast, nightlife on the island is a bit thin. In Capri, try discos ***Musmé*** *(Via Camerelle 61b)*, ***Number Two*** *(Via Camerelle 1)*, a short stroll away down the street, or ***Baraonda*** *(Via Roma 6)*.

Anacapri Sit around in one of the cafes on Piazza Diaz or shoot pool at ***Bar Materita*** *(Via G Orlandi 140)*. For nightlife, the discos ***Zeus*** *(Via G Orlandi 103)* and ***Underground*** *(Via G Orlandi 259)* might get your blood rushing.

Shopping

Everywhere on the island you'll spot ceramic tiles illustrating street names, numbers and romantic scenes.

Massimo Goderecci *(Via P Serafino Cimino 8, Capri)*, just off Piazza Umberto I, takes credit for most types of ceramic tiles and will bake you one for about €50.

The island is famous for its perfume and limoncello. The former smells like lemons and the latter tastes like sweet lemon vodka. Visit ***Limoncello Capri*** *(Via Capodimonte 27, Anacapri)* and taste the liqueur. The perfumeries are everywhere.

If your ship has come home, you might like to pick up a little number from one of the designer shops on Via Cammarelle, Capri, which is like walking into a page from *Vogue* magazine.

Getting There & Away

See Getting There & Away under Naples (earlier) and Sorrento (later) for details of year-round ferries and hydrofoils. In summer, there's also a service to/from Salerno (€13), Positano (€11.40), Amalfi (€10-12.40).

Getting Around

There is no vehicle hire service on the island and roads wide enough for a car are few. Between March and October, you can only bring a vehicle to the island if it's either registered outside Italy or hired at an international airport – but you'd be pretty irresponsible if you did since buses are regular and taxis plentiful.

The best way to get around is by SIPPIC bus (☎ 081 837 04 20). A ticket costs €0.95 on the main routes between Marina Grande (departing from Via Marina Grande, just west of the pier), Capri, Anacapri, Grotta Azzurra and Faro. Buses run between Capri and Anacapri until past midnight. A funicular links Marina Grande with Capri. It is swifter than the bus and costs €0.95.

From Marina Grande a taxi ride costs around €10 to Capri and about €14 to Anacapri – the open-topped 1950s Fiats are very inviting. For a taxi in Capri, call ☎ 081 837 05 43 and in Anacapri, call ☎ 081 837 11 75.

ISCHIA

postcode 80077 • pop 18,200

Ischia manages to retain some sense of its past despite being the largest and most developed of the islands in the Gulf of Naples and a major tourist destination. Away from its few towns, people still work the land as if they'd never seen a tourist – itself an improbable proposition. Although nowadays Ischia is especially loved by Germans, it was the Greeks who first colonised the island in the 8th century BC, calling it Pithecusa. Largely volcanic, it's noted for its thermal springs and in summer is frequented as much for the curative powers of its waters and mud as for its beaches.

The main centres are the touristy towns of Ischia and Ischia Porto, Casamicciola Terme, Forio and Lacco Ameno, all fairly unattractive and overcrowded compared to picturesque Ischia Ponte, Serrara, Fontana, Barano d'Ischia and Sant'Angelo. Sant' Angelo is, in addition, tranquil; no cars are allowed in town. Reasonable hotel prices and camping opportunities make the island affordable and its size means you might just be able to get away from the August crowds.

Orientation

Ferries dock at Ischia Porto, the main tourist centre. It's about a half-hour walk from the pier to Ischia Ponte, an attractive older centre, off which lies an islet with a picturesque Aragonese castle complex on it.

Information

Tourist Offices The tourist office (☎ 081 507 42 31) on Via Iasolino (Banchina Porto Salvo) at the main port opens 9am to 2pm and 4pm to 8pm daily in summer. Off-season hours are shorter and you may find it closed on Sunday. It has little to offer and you'll find its Web site (W www.ischiaonline.it) more informative.

Things to See & Do

In Ischia Ponte you'll find the remains of **Castello d'Ischia** *(☎ 081 99 28 34; admission €6.20; open 9.30am-1hr before sunset daily Apr-Oct)*. Within this Aragonese castle complex on an islet, joined to the mainland by a causeway, are a 14th-century cathedral, several smaller churches and a weapons museum, admission to which is optional and costs an extra €2.60.

Keen gardeners, and indeed anyone who loves plants, should visit **La Mortella** *(☎ 081 98 62 20, Via F Calese 35, Forio; admission €6.20; open 9am-7pm Tues, Thurs, Sat & Sun Apr-Nov)*. Here in one of Italy's finest landscaped gardens thrive over 300 species from all over the world. The gardens were established by Sir William Walton, the late British composer, and his wife, who made La Mortella their home in 1949.

A fairly strenuous uphill walk (about 1½ hours) from the village of Fontana brings you to the top of **Monte Epomeo** (788m), the island's highest point, with superb views of the Gulf of Naples.

Among the better beaches is Lido dei Maronti, south of Barano. If you're interested in diving, **Gator Sub** *(☎ 081 90 08 93, Casamicciola Terme)*, **Ischia Diving Center**

(☎ 081 98 50 08, Ischia Porto) and **Roja Diving Center** *(☎ 338 762 01 45, Sant' Angelo)*, all have equipment for hire and run courses.

Organised Tours

Ischia Direct Tours *(☎ 081 99 12 15, W www.ischiadirecttours.com, Via Porto 5–9)* Between April and October, this company offers a three-hour tour of the island with an English speaking guide for €77 (one to four people) or €112 (five to 14 persons). If you're only on the island for the day, this compares quite favourably with the cost of hiring a vehicle.

Places to Stay

Few hotels open in winter and prices in those that do normally drop considerably. In summer, call the tourist office in advance to establish room availability. During the peak period, watch for the compulsory breakfast or half-board and extra charge for the showers.

Camping There are three camp sites on the island.

Mirage *(☎/fax 081 99 05 51, Lido dei Maronti 37)* Sites per person/tent €7.25/8.30. Open year-round. This is perhaps the best-placed camp site, on the beach south of Barano.

Camping Internazionale *(☎ 081 99 14 49, fax 081 99 14 72, Via Foschini)* Sites per person/tent/car €6.20/8.30/7.25. Open May-Sept. Not far from Ischia Porto, this camp site is handy for the ferry terminal.

Eurocamping dei Pini *(☎ 081 98 20 69, fax 081 98 41 20, Via delle Ginestre 28)* Sites per person/tent €7.75/7.75, bungalows for 2/3/4 people €51.70/67.20/77.50. Open year-round. This camp site is also near Ischia Porto and offers a bungalow option.

Hostels There's one hostel on Ischia – and it must be one of the best there is.

Il Gabbiano *(☎/fax 081 90 94 22, SS Forio-Panza 162, Forio)* B&B €15.50. This hostel boasts a pool, nearby beach and bedrooms sleeping two, four or six, all with balconies and great sea views.

Hotels There are two budget places less than five minutes walk from the ferry terminal.

Locanda Sul Mare *(☎/fax 081 98 14 70, Via Iasolino 90)* June-Aug singles/doubles €28.50/51.65, March-May & Sept-Nov singles/doubles €13/25.90. Closed Dec-Feb. This agreeably eccentric place, handy for the port, is a bargain, in or out of season. Rooms have bathrooms.

Albergo Macrí *(☎/fax 081 99 26 03, Via Iasolino 96)* July-Sept singles/doubles/triples €33.10/60/75, Oct-June singles/doubles/triples €24.80/49.10/67.20. Open year-round. Just beyond Locanda Sul Mare down a blind alley, this place offers more comfort for your greater outlay. The rooms have bathrooms.

Villa Antonio *(☎ 081 98 26 60, fax 081 98 39 41, Via San Giuseppe della Croce 77)* Singles/doubles €49.10/77.50. Open Apr-Sept. This place, a 20-minute walk from the port, is a good option. Rooms have bathroom and fridge. Price includes breakfast.

Conchiglia *(☎/fax 081 99 92 70, Via Chiaia delle Rose)* July-Aug B&B per person €41.32, Sept-June B&B per person €33.60. In Sant'Angelo, friendly Conchiglia, perched over the water, also has a good restaurant (full meal around €23.25). The rooms have bathrooms.

Casa Francesco *(☎ 081 99 91 50, Via Nazario Sauro 42)* Doubles €62. Also in Sant'Angelo, Casa Francesco is across a small causeway leading to the tip of the promontory. The rooms have bathrooms and breakfast is included.

Da Franceschina *(☎/fax 081 99 01 09, Via Corrado Buono 51)* Singles/doubles €30/46.50. Open Easter-Oct. This place is in Barano. Half-board is compulsory in August.

Places to Eat

Cicco e Domingo *(Via Luigi Mazzella 80)* Full meal €15-20. In Ischia Porto, this is a pleasant trattoria offering pasta and seafood dishes.

Pirozzi *(☎ 081 99 11 21, Via Seminario 26)* Pizzas €2.60-7.25. Mains €4.20-7.75. This place is in Ischia Ponte.

Lo Scoglio *(☎ 081 99 95 29, Sant'Angelo)* Full meals around €20. Open Apr-Nov. For a delicious seafood meal try Lo Scoglio, overlooking a small cove where the pedestrian zone begins.

Getting There & Away

See the Naples Getting There & Away section earlier in the chapter for details. You can catch ferries direct to Capri (€11.40) and Procida (€1.90) from Ischia.

Getting Around

The main bus station is at Ischia Porto. There are two principle lines: the CS (Circo Sinistra; Left Circle) and CD (Circo Destra; Right Circle), which circle the island in opposite directions, passing through each town and leaving every 30 minutes. Buses (single journey €0.95) pass near all hotels and camp sites. Taxis and micro-taxis (Ape three-wheelers) are also available.

You can do this small island a favour by not bringing your car. If you want to hire a car or scooter for a day, there are plenty of rental firms. Fratelli del Franco (☎ 081 99 13 34), Via A De Luca 133, in addition to hiring out cars (from €28.40 per day) and mopeds (€15-21), also has mountain bikes (around €10 per day). You can't take a rented vehicle off the island.

CAMPANIA

PROCIDA

postcode 80077 • pop 10,400 (double in summer)

The pastel pinks, whites and yellows of Procida's tiny cubic houses, cluttered along the waterfront, make for a colourful introduction to the island. The beauty of the Gulf of Naples' smallest island is immediately apparent. With only five hotels and six camp sites, it's attractive for backpackers, particularly during high summer when the other islands are crowded.

Orientation & Information

Marina Grande is the hop-off point for ferries and hydrofoils and forms most of the tourist showcase. Procida's information office (☎ 081 810 19 68) opens 9am to 2pm and 4pm to 7.20pm (oh yes!) Monday to Saturday. You'll find it on Via Roma, as you tumble off the ferry, right by the ticket office.

Things to See & Do

The best way to explore the island is on foot – a complete circumnavigation will take you less than four hours – or by bike (see Getting There & Around later). However, the island's narrow roads can be clogged with cars – one of the island's few drawbacks.

The 16th-century **Palazzo Reale d'Avalos**, more recently used as a prison, dominates the island but is now all but abandoned. More interesting is **Abbazia San Michele Arcangelo** *(☎ 081 896 76 12, Via Terra Murata 89; open 9.45am-12.45pm daily year-round, 3pm-6pm daily May-Oct, 3pm-5pm daily Nov-Apr)*, about a 1km uphill walk from Marina Grande. Within the complex are its church (admission free), a small museum with some arresting naive ex-voto paintings (admission €1.55) and a honeycomb of catacombs.

You have to be up and about fairly early to visit the **nature reserve** *(admission free; open 8.30am-noon Mon-Sat, last entry 10am)* on the tiny satellite island of Vivara. Linked to Procida by a bridge, it's an excellent place for bird-watching or strolling. Then, perhaps, walk or catch a bus to Chiaolella for lunch. The **Procida Diving Centre** *(☎ 081 896 83 85)* hires out boats and diving equipment and will organise boat tours around the island.

Special Events

On Good Friday in Procida there's a colourful procession of the Misteri – life-size tableaux of plaster and papier mâché illustrating, with considerable artistic licence, events leading to Christ's crucifixion. Men process in blue tunics with white hoods over their heads while many of the young girls are dressed as the Madonna Addolorata.

Places to Stay & Eat

Camp sites are dotted around the island. Typical prices are €7.75 per site plus €4.50 to €7.75 per person. On the eastern side of the island, try ***Vivara*** *(☎ 081 896 92 42, Via IV Novembre)* or, on the same road, ***La Caravella*** *(☎ 081 896 92 30, Via IV Novembre)*. Near the better beaches of Ciraccio on the western side are ***Privato Lubrano*** *(☎ 081 896 94 01, Via Salette 14)* and its neighbour ***Graziella*** *(☎ 081 896 77 47, Via Salette 15)*.

There are only a few hotels on Procida. Both the following two hotels are in Marina di Chiaolella.

Hotel Riviera *(☎/fax 081 896 71 97, Via G da Procida 36)* Singles/doubles with bath €31/62. Open Apr-Oct. Prices are reasonable (and include breakfast), August excepted when half-board is compulsory at €62 per person.

Crescenzo *(☎ 081 896 72 55, fax 081 810 12 60, Via Marina di Chiaolella 33)* Singles/doubles €62/72.30. Open year-round. This place has a very pleasant fish restaurant overlooking the small harbour. Rooms have bathrooms and the price includes breakfast.

Hotel Casa Gentile *(☎ 081 896 77 99, fax 081 896 90 11, Via Marina Corricella 88)* Singles/doubles with bath €51.70/97. This is a friendly hotel that serves up delicious home cooking.

La Rosa dei Venti *(☎/fax 081 896 83 85, W www.vacanzeaprocida.it/frameres01.htm, Via Vincenzo Rinaldi 32)*. Cottages €20.70-31. Open Mar-Oct. This is a cluster of self-contained cottages that sleep up to six people. Set in a large garden on a cliff top overlooking the sea, the charge depends on the season and how many people you pack in.

There are several good restaurants along the waterfront near the port, including ***L'Approdo***, serving fresh seafood and pizzas at reasonable prices, and ***Il Cantinone*** where a full meal costs around €15.

Getting There & Around

Procida is linked by boat and hydrofoil to Ischia (€1.90, 45 minutes), Pozzuoli and Naples. See the Naples and Campi Flegrei Getting There & Away sections earlier in the chapter for more details.

SEPSA runs a limited bus service (flat fare €0.75), with four lines radiating from Marina Grande. Bus No L1 connects the port and Chiaolella. The small open micro-taxis can be hired for two to three hours for about €18, depending on your bargaining prowess. You can hire boats from Barcheggiando (☎ 081 810 19 34) and local fishermen may be willing to take you out for between €5 and €10 per person, depending on the size of your group.

Perhaps the best – and certainly the most ecologically friendly – way to move around the island is by bike. **Associazione Azione Verde** (☎ 081 896 73 95 or 034 701 57 188) will rent you one for €6.20/13/18.25 per day/three days/week.

South of Naples

HERCULANEUM & ERCOLANO

Twelve kilometres south-east of Naples, modern Ercolano is a congested, tangled suburb of the city. Classical Herculaneum by contrast was a peaceful fishing and port town of about 4000 and something of a resort for wealthy Romans and Campanians. According to legend, Herculaneum was a Greek settlement founded by Hercules. Whatever the truth of this, it later passed to the Samnites before becoming a Roman town in 89 BC.

History

The fate of Herculaneum paralleled that of nearby Pompeii. Destroyed by an earthquake in AD 63, it was completely submerged in the AD 79 eruption of Mt Vesuvius. The difference was that Herculaneum was buried by a river of volcanic mud, not the lapilli (burning fragments of pumice stone) and ash that rained on Pompeii. The mud helped preserve it for posterity. The town was rediscovered in 1709 and amateur excavations were carried out intermittently until 1874, with many finds being carted off to Naples to decorate the houses of the well-to-do or to end up in museums. Serious archaeological work began in 1927 and excavation continues today.

Orientation & Information

Modern Ercolano's main street, Via IV Novembre, leads from the Circumvesuviana train station, at the town's eastern edge, to Piazza Scavi and the main ticket office for the excavations – an easy 10-minute walk.

There is a tourist office (☎/fax 081 788 12 43), Via IV Novembre 84, open 9am to 2pm Monday to Saturday, but it has little more to offer than a brochure with an inadequate map of the ruined city.

On sale at the bookshop beside the exit point at Herculaneum are two useful guidebooks in English translation: *Pompeii, Herculaneum & Vesuvius* (€6.20), published by Edizioni Kina, and the more academic *Herculaneum: A Reasoned Archaeological Itinerary* (€10.35), by Mario Pagano, the site's director of archaeology

The site itself is disgracefully inadequate in its signing and the tourist-office map is scarcely more illuminating.

The Ruins

At the ruins *(☎ 081 739 09 63; admission €8.30; open 8.30am-1 hr before sunset daily)* be prepared for some of the houses to be closed, although an attendant may be around to open them. You can buy a combined ticket, valid for three days, giving entry to Herculaneum, Pompeii and three minor sites for €13.50.

Beside the main entrance and ticket office you may be gently assailed by guides – if you do take one on, make sure both of you understand what kind of fee or 'gift' is expected at the end.

Follow the path running above and around the site, then descend through a short tunnel to emerge beside the **Terme Suburbane** (Suburban Baths) in the site's southernmost corner. These baths make a great introduction to the site with their deep pools, stucco friezes and bas reliefs looking down upon marble floors and wall cladding.

The site is divided into 11 *insulae* (islands) carved up in a classic Roman grid pattern. The two main streets, Decumano Massimo and Decumano Inferiore, are crossed by Cardo III, IV and V.

Casa d'Argo (Argus House) is a well preserved example of a Roman noble family's house, complete with a porticoed garden and *triclinium* (dining area).

The most extraordinary mosaic to have survived intact is in the *nyphaeum* (fountain and bath) of **Casa di Nettuno ed Anfitrite**

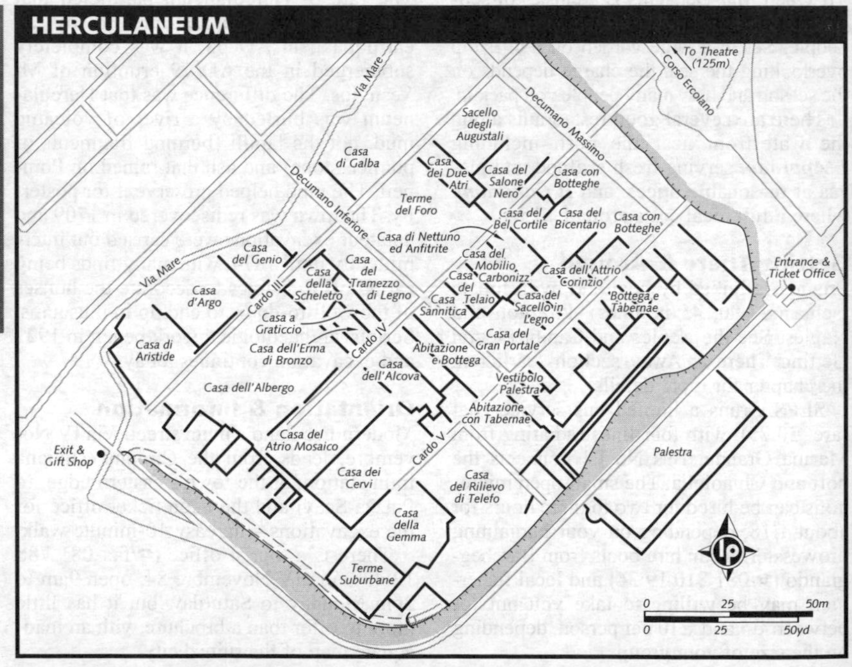

(House of Neptune & Amphitrite) on Cardo IV. The warm colours in which the two deities are depicted hint at how lavish the interior of other well-to-do households must have been. For more fine mosaics, make your way to another of the city's public baths, **Terme del Foro** (Central Baths), with its separate sections for men and women. The floor mosaics in the latter are in pristine condition. While women passed from the *apodyterium* (changing rooms; note the finely executed naked figure of Triton adorning the mosaic floor) through the *tepidarium* (warm room) to the *caldarium* (steam bath), men had the added bracing option of the *frigidarium* – a cold bath. You can still see the benches where bathers sat and the wall shelves for clothing.

Casa del Atrio Mosaico (House of the Mosaic Atrium; closed at the time of writing), an impressive mansion on Cardo IV, also has extensive floor mosaics – time and nature have left the floor buckled and uneven.

Behind it, and accessible from Cardo V, **Casa dei Cervi** (House of the Deer) is probably the most imposing of the nobles' dwellings. The two-storey villa, built around a central courtyard, contains murals and still-life paintings. In the courtyard is a diminutive pair of marble deer assailed by dogs and an engaging statue of a drunken Hercules peeing.

On the corner of the Decumano Inferiore and Cardo V is **Casa del Gran Portale**, named after the elegant brick Corinthian columns that flank its main entrance. Inside are some well preserved wall-paintings.

Sacello degli Augustali, in its time a school, retains a pair of lively, well preserved murals.

Off the main street, Decumanus Massimo, is **Casa del Bicentenario** (Bicentenary House), so named because it was excavated 200 years after digging at Herculaneum first began. A crucifix found in an upstairs room is evidence that there might have been Christians in the town before AD 79.

North-west of the ruins and along Corso Ercolano are the remains of a **theatre**, dating from the Augustan period.

Places to Stay & Eat

You'll do better staying in Naples or Pompeii and making the easy rail journey to Herculaneum than staying in Ercolano.

I Moschettieri *(☎ 081 777 48 61, Via IV Novembre 90–92)* Snacks from €3.10. This spruce quick-service place, at the crossroads just before the train station, stands out for its cheerful service and wide range of tasty snacks.

Getting There & Away

By far the easiest way to get from central Naples or Sorrento to Ercolano (and also to Pompeii, which many visitors cover in the same day) is by the Circumvesuviana train (€2.60; see Getting There & Away under Naples earlier and Sorrento later). Otherwise, SITA buses plying the Naples-Pompeii route stop at Ercolano. By car, take the A3 from Naples, exit at Ercolano Portico and follow the signs to car parks near the site's entrance.

MT VESUVIUS (VESUVIO)

This active volcano dominates the landscape, looming ominously over Naples. After the last eruption in 1944, its plume of smoke, long a reminder of the peril, disappeared. This may have eased the minds of some, but living in the shadow of Vesuvius is as secure as staying on the fault line in Los Angeles – scientists consider more eruptions a sure thing.

Vesuvius' name is probably derived from the Greek *besubios* or *besbios*, meaning 'fire'. The volcano erupted with such ferocity on 24 August AD 79 that it all but destroyed the towns of Pompeii and Herculaneum and pushed the coastline out several kilometres. Subsequent years have witnessed regular displays of the mountain's wrath, the more destructive being those of 1631, 1794 (when the town of Torre del Greco was destroyed), 1906 and, most recently, 1944, when poverty-stricken Naples was struggling back onto its feet under Allied occupation.

Trasporti Vesuviani (☎ 081 559 31 73) buses run from Ercolano train station to Vesuvius car park (€3.10 return), from where it's a 1.5km walk (allow 30 to 45 minutes) to the summit area (admission €4.65) and the rim of the crater. From April to October buses leave Ercolano at 9am, 10.10am, 11.30am, 1.10pm and 2.10pm, and the two last returning buses leave at 3.30pm and 6pm. The rest of the year buses depart from Ercolano at 10.10am, 11.30am and 12.40pm. Don't miss the last bus back at 3pm or you're in for a cold, spooky night – unless Vesuvius chooses the occasion to blow its top. All services leave Pompeii 30 minutes earlier. By car, exit the A3 at Ercolano Portico and follow signs for Parco Nazionale de Vesuvio.

Watch out for a pair of scams. Readers have reported independent bus owners in Ercolano lying about public transport times and charging up to €20 per person to get you up and down. And the little old couple who thrust walking sticks at visitors to help them on the push to the summit aren't doing it for charity, as they will make very clear when you descend.

Pack a sweater since it can be chilly up top, even in summer. Sunglasses are useful against the swirling ash and trainers or walking shoes are more practical than sandals or flip-flops (thongs).

On the winding route up to the crest, check out **Museo dell'Osservatorio Vesuviano** *(Museum of the Vesuvian Observatory; ☎ 081 777 71 49)*. Currently a rather dry exhibition, open weekend mornings only, it's due to be transformed into a multimedia interpretative centre with high-tech simulations. For further information check out 🆆 www.osve.unina.it or 🆆 www.parks.it.

CAMPANIA

POMPEII

postcode 80045 • pop 25,700

Pompeii, which receives over 1.5 million visitors annually, is Italy's most popular tourist attraction. Ever since Pliny the Younger wrote his moving letters to Tacitus describing the eruption of Vesuvius that buried Pompeii in AD 79 (see the boxed text 'Ashes, Fire & Brimstone'), the city has been the stuff of books, scholarly and frivolous, and a perfect subject for the big screen. Offering the richest insight into the daily life of the Romans, most of it is open to the public and requires at least three or four hours to visit.

History

Founded in the 7th century BC by the Campanian Oscans on a prehistoric lava flow of Vesuvius, Pompeii eventually fell to the Greeks and later, in the 5th century BC, came under the influence of the Samnites. It became a Roman colony in 80 BC and prospered as a major port and trading town, adorned with grand temples, villas and palaces, until it was devastated by an earthquake in AD 63. Pompeii had been largely rebuilt when Vesuvius, overshadowing the town to the north, erupted in AD 79 and buried it under a layer of lapilli.

Although the town was completely covered by the shower of ash, only about 2000 of its 20,000 inhabitants are believed to have perished. Later, Emperor Titus considered rebuilding the city and the Roman Emperor Severus (193–211) plundered it a little, but Pompeii gradually receded from the public eye.

The Pompeii area was wholly abandoned during the period of Saracen raids and its remains were further shaken by subsequent earthquakes. In 1594, the architect Domenico Fontana stumbled across the ruins during the construction of a canal. Though the discovery was recorded, substantial excavation was not conducted until 1748, in the time of Charles of Bourbon, who was interested above all in retrieving items of artistic value. Credit for most of the major discoveries belongs to Giuseppe Fiorelli, who worked under the auspices of the Italian government from 1860.

Most of the ancient city has been uncovered yet work continues and significant finds are still being made; in 2000, for example, road works on the nearby A3 revealed a whole frescoed leisure area. Many of the most spectacular mosaics and murals have been removed to the Museo Archeologico Nazionale in Naples and other museums around the world.

Pompeii has suffered in recent decades from overtourism and underfunding and the deterioration is alarming. Archaeologists warn that many of its treasures are in grave danger of being lost forever. The inclusion of the site on Unesco's World Heritage List, in the late 1990s, coincided with a new Italian law enabling Pompeii to manage its own money and generate income. Perhaps private sector contributions may guarantee that Pompeii is conserved properly – something that government funds alone cannot hope to do.

Orientation

The Circumvesuviana drops you at Pompei-Scavi-Villa dei Misteri station, beside the main Porta Marina entrance. By car, signs – and energetic touts – direct you from the A3 to the *scavi* (excavations) and car parks. There are several camp sites, hotels and restaurants in the vicinity, although the choice is better in the adjacent modern town of Pompeii.

Information

There are two tourist offices: one in modern Pompeii at Via Sacra 1 and the other just outside the excavations at Piazza Porta Marina Inferiore 12, near the Porta Marina entrance. Both share a central telephone line (☎ 081 850 72 55 or toll free 800 01 33 50) and open 8am to 3pm Monday to Saturday (8am to 8pm in summer). At either, you can

Ashes, Fire & Brimstone

One of the most vivid accounts of the eruption of Vesuvius is by Pliny the Younger, writing to the historian Tacitus. In it Pliny describes how his uncle, Pliny the Elder, renowned as an early naturalist, met his death:

'He embraced his terrified friend, cheered and encouraged him and, thinking he could calm the latter's fears by showing his own composure, gave orders that he was to be carried to the bathroom. After his bath he lay down and dined; he was quite cheerful, or at any rate pretended he was, which was no less courageous.

Meanwhile on Mount Vesuvius broad sheets of fire and leaping flames blazed at several points, their bright glare emphasised by the darkness of the night. My uncle tried to allay the fears of his companions by repeatedly declaring that these were nothing but bonfires left by the peasants in their terror, or else empty houses on fire in the districts they had abandoned. Then he went to rest and certainly slept, for as he was a stout man his breathing was rather loud and heavy and could be heard by people coming and going outside his door. By this time the courtyard leading to his room was full of ashes mixed with pumice stones so that its level had risen; if he had stayed in the room any longer he would never have got out. He was wakened and came out to join Pomponianus and the rest of the household who had sat up all night. They debated whether to stay indoors or take their chance in the open, for the buildings were now shaking with violent shocks and seemed to be swaying to and fro as if torn from their foundations. Outside on the other hand, there was the danger of falling pumice stones, even though these were light and porous; however, after comparing the risks they chose the latter. As a protection against falling objects they put pillows on their heads tied down with cloths.

Elsewhere there was daylight by this time but they were still in darkness, blacker and denser than any ordinary night, which they relieved by lighting torches and various kinds of lamp. My uncle decided to go down to the shore and investigate on the spot the possibility of escape by sea but he found the waves still wild and dangerous. They spread a sheet on the ground for him to lie down and he repeatedly asked for cold water to drink. Then the flames and smell of sulphur, giving warning of the approaching fire, drove his companions to flight and roused him to stand up. He stood leaning on two slaves and then suddenly collapsed, I imagine because the dense fumes choked his breathing by blocking his windpipe, which was constitutionally weak and narrow and often inflamed. When daylight returned on the 26th – two days after he had last been seen – his body was found intact, uninjured and still fully clothed as though he were in sleep rather than in death.'

CAMPANIA

pick up a map of the excavations with text in English.

A good guidebook is a real asset since it's easy to miss important sites. Among the best is *Pompeii, Herculaneum & Vesuvius* (€6.20) published by Edizioni Kina.

The Ruins

The Porta Marina is nowadays the principle entrance to the ruins *(admission €8.30; open 8.30am-7.30pm daily, last entry 6pm, Apr-Oct; 8.30am-5pm daily, last entry 3.30pm, Nov-Mar)*. You can buy a combined ticket, valid for three days, giving entry to Herculaneum, Pompeii and three minor sites. The original town was encircled by a wall punctuated by towers and eight gates. The south-western sea gate, **Porta Marina**, was considerably closer to the water before the eruption. Immediately as you enter you see on the right the remains of an imperial villa with lengthy porticoes. The **antiquarium** above it contains remnants gathered from the city and, in one room, body casts formed by hollows left in the hardened tufa (soft porous rock) by decayed corpses, depicting their final moments of horror.

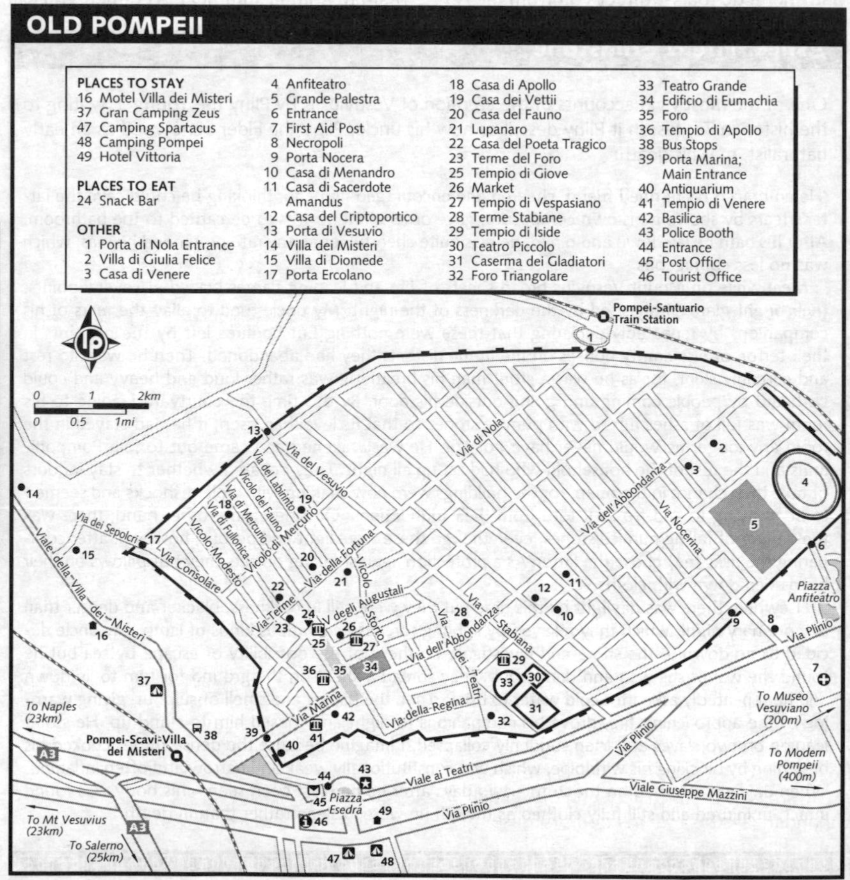

Farther along Via Marina, on the left, you pass the striking **Tempio di Apollo** (Temple of Apollo), built originally by the Samnites in the Doric style, and then enter the **foro** (forum), the centre of the city's life. To the right, opposite Tempio di Apollo, is the **basilica**, the city's law courts and exchange. Dating back to the 2nd century BC, it was one of Pompeii's greatest buildings. Among the fenced-off ruins to the left as you enter, are more gruesome body casts.

The various buildings around the foro include **Tempio di Giove** (Temple of Jupiter), one of whose two flanking triumphal arches remains, the **market**, where you can see the remains of a series of shops, and the **Edificio di Eumachia**, which features an imposing marble doorway.

Taking the street to the right of the Edificio di Eumachia, Via dell'Abbondanza, wander along and turn right into Via dei Teatri and enter the **Foro Triangolare**, which is surrounded by the remains of a Doric colonnade. To your left is the entrance to **Teatro Grande**, originally built in the 2nd century AD and capable of seating 5000 spectators. Adjoining it is the more recent **Teatro Piccolo**, also known as the Odeon. The **Caserma dei Gladiatori** (Gladiators' Barracks), behind the theatres, is surrounded by a portico of about 70 columns.

From the pre-Roman **Tempio di Iside** (Temple of Isis), rebuilt after the AD 63 earthquake and dedicated to the Egyptian goddess, return to Via dell'Abbondanza, which intersects with Via Stabiana. **Terme Stabiane** is a large baths complex with many rooms, some featuring original tiling and murals. Several body casts are located here. Farther along Via dell'Abbondanza are the newer excavations where an attempt has been made in some buildings to keep frescoes (now behind glass) and artefacts in their original positions. Look for **Casa del Criptoportico, Casa di Sacerdote Amandus** (House of the Priest Amandus) and **Casa di Menandro** (House of Menander), all well preserved.

Towards the north-eastern end of Via dell' Abbondanza, **Casa di Venere** (House of Venus) has a remarkable fresco of the goddess standing in her conch shell. In the next block is the so-called **Villa di Giulia Felice**, a rambling affair that includes a private residence, public bath, various shops and an inn. Behind it lies the **anfiteatro**, the oldest such Roman amphitheatre known and, at one time, capable of holding an audience of 12,000. The nearby **Grande Palestra** is an athletics field with an impressive portico and, at its centre, the remains of a swimming pool.

Return along Via dell'Abbondanza and turn right into Via Stabiana (which becomes Via del Vesuvio) to see some of Pompeii's grandest houses. Turn left into Via della Fortuna to meet, on your right, **Casa del Fauno** (House of the Faun) which featured a magnificent mosaic, which is now in Naples' Museo Archeologico Nazionale. A couple of blocks farther along Via della Fortuna is **Casa del Poeta Tragico** (House of the Tragic Poet), with some decent mosaics still *in situ*. Nearby **Casa dei Vettii**, on Vicolo di Mercurio, sports some well preserved paintings and statues. Across the road from Casa del Fauno, along Vicolo Storto, was the **Lupanaro**, a brothel with eye-opening murals. A good place for Pompeii's rakes to head for after the Lupanaro was probably the **Terme del Foro** (Forum Baths), a short walk away on Via Terme.

From the Terme del Foro you can continue to the end of Via Terme and turn right into Via Consolare, which takes you out of the town through Porta Ercolano at Pompeii's north-western edge. Once past the gate, you pass Villa di Diomede, then turn right and you'll come to **Villa dei Misteri**, one of the most complete structures left standing in Pompeii. The Dionysiac Frieze, the most important frescoes still on the site, spans the walls of the large dining room. One of the largest paintings from the ancient world, it depicts the initiation of a bride-to-be into the cult of Dionysus, the Greek god of wine.

Museo Vesuviano, Via San Bartolomeo, south-east of the excavations, contains an interesting array of artefacts.

Organised Tours

The tourist offices warn against the dozens of unauthorised guides who swoop at tourists, charging exorbitant prices for brief and generally inaccurate tours. Authorised guides wear identification tags and belong to one of three cooperatives: ***Asso Touring*** *(☎ 081 850 88 55)*, ***Casting*** *(☎ 081 850 07 49)* and ***Gata*** *(☎ 081 861 56 61)*. A typical price for a two-hour tour, whether you're alone, a couple or in a group of up to 25, is around €90. Be wary if visiting out-of-the-way ruins unless you're in a group.

Places to Stay

Pompeii is best visited on a day trip from Naples, Sorrento or Salerno as, apart from the excavations, there is little else to see. It has three camp sites, all open year-round.

Gran Camping Zeus *(☎ 081 861 53 20, fax 081 861 75 36, e campingzeus@uniserv.uniplan.it, Viale della Villa dei Misteri 1)* Sites per person/tent/car €3.65/3.10/2.60 (€4.65/4.13/3.65 Jul-Sept). Rooms cost from €36.15. Readers report that the approach can be seedy after dark.

Camping Spartacus *(☎ 081 536 95 19, fax 081 862 40 78, e spartacus@uniserv.uniplan.it, Via Plinio 117)* Sites per person/tent/car €5.20/1.55/1.55.

Camping Pompei *(☎ 081 862 28 82, fax 081 850 27 72, Via Plinio)* Sites per person/tent/car €4.65/5.20/2.60 (€3.65/3.65/1.55 Nov-Apr). Bungalows costs from €36.15 and rooms from €57. Camping Pompei is right beside Spartacus.

There are some 25 hotels around the ruins and in the nearby modern town.

Motel Villa dei Misteri *(☎ 081 861 35 93, fax 081 862 29 83, Via Villa dei Misteri 11)* Doubles/triples €46.50/62. With its own pool and a good restaurant, as reasonably priced as the rooms are, this place is much more intimate than the name 'motel' might suggest. Rooms have bathrooms and air-con.

Hotel Vittoria *(☎ 081 536 90 23, fax 081 536 73 95, w www.pompeihotelvittoria.com, Piazza Porta Marina)* Singles/doubles €41.35/72.30. Hotel Vittoria, occupying a charming old building, speaks style and couldn't be handier for the ruins. Overrun at midday by visitors lunching in its four restaurants, it's a pleasant place to relax once the hordes have retreated. Rooms have bathrooms and the price includes breakfast.

CAMPANIA

Places to Eat

There's a snack bar within the ruins. If you want something more substantial, rest your feet in the restaurant of Hotel Vittoria or Motel Villa dei Misteri. Alternatively, head for modern Pompeii, where busy Via Roma, the continuation of Via Plinio, has several options.

Á Dó Giardiniello *(Via Roma 89)* Pizzas around €5. This place is a no-nonsense pizzeria with prices to match.

Getting There & Away

Bus SITA (see Getting There & Away under Naples earlier in this chapter) operates regular bus services between Naples and Pompeii, while CSTP (see Getting There & Away under Salerno later) runs buses from Salerno. Marozzi (see Getting There & Away under Rome in the Rome & Lazio chapter) offers services between Pompeii and Rome. Buses arrive and depart from the bus stops opposite the Circumvesuviana Pompei-Scavi-Villa dei Misteri train station.

Train From Naples, take the Circumvesuviana train (€2.60) for Sorrento and get off at Pompei-Scavi-Villa dei Misteri station.

Car & Motorcycle Take the A3 from Naples, a trip of about 23km, otherwise you could spend hours weaving through narrow streets and traffic snarls. Use the Pompeii exit and follow signs to Pompei Scavi. Car parks are clearly marked and vigorously touted.

SORRENTO

postcode 80067 • pop 19,500

According to ancient Greek legend, the Sorrento area was known as the Temple of the Sirens. Sailors of antiquity were powerless to resist the beautiful song of these maidens-cum-monsters who would lure them and their ships to their doom on the reefs. Homer's Ulysses escaped the sirens' deadly lure by having his oarsmen plug their ears and by strapping himself to the mast of his ship as he sailed past the fatal place.

Today's visitors to Sorrento have less to fear and in the high season this unashamed resort town is bursting with holidaymakers, predominantly from Britain and Germany. However, there is still enough southern Italian charm to make a stay here enjoyable and it is handy for Capri (15 minutes away) and the Amalfi Coast. The road to Pompeii is pretty in parts, but has unfortunately been spoiled by expanding residential and industrial sprawl.

Orientation

Piazza Tasso, bisected by Sorrento's main street, Corso Italia, is the centre of town, having supplanted Piazza Angelina Lauro as its nucleus. It's about a 300m walk northwest of the train station, along Corso Italia. If you arrive at Marina Piccola, where ferries and hydrofoils dock, you walk south along Via Marina Piccola, then climb about 200 steps to reach the piazza. Corso Italia becomes the S145 on the way east to Naples and, heading west, changes its name to Via Capo.

Information

The AAST office (☎ 081 807 40 33), Via Luigi de Maio 35, is within the Circolo dei Forestieri (Foreigners' Club), an office and restaurant complex. The AAST opens 8.45am to 2.30pm and 3.30pm to 6.30pm Monday to Saturday.

American Express is represented by Acampora Travel (☎ 081 807 23 63, fax 081 807 20 33), Piazza Angelina Lauro 12. Deutsche Bank nearby has an ATM.

The post office is at Corso Italia 210 and the Telecom office at Piazza Tasso 37.

For medical emergencies, contact the Ospedale Civile (☎ 081 533 11 11). It's set back from Corso Italia, west of Piazza Tasso.

Computers hum at Blu Blu Internet Cafe (☎ 081 807 48 54) at Via Fuorimura 20d, just off Piazza Tasso. It opens 10.30am to 1.30pm and 4.30pm to 1am daily – although it was firmly closed one Sunday when we called by to check it out. Internet

Point, Traversia Pietà 23, is another, smaller option, which opens 3pm to 8.30pm daily.

Things to See & Do

The gleaming white and understated – by Italian standards – main facade of the **cathedral** on Corso Italia gives no hint of the exuberance within. There's a particularly striking crucifixion above the main altar. Its triple tiered bell tower rests on an archway into which three classical columns and a number of other fragments have been set.

Within the 18th-century **Palazzo Correale**, which has some interesting murals, is **Museo Correale** *(☎ 081 878 18 46, Via Correale; admission €5.20; open 9am-2pm Wed-Mon)*, which contains a small collection of 17th- and 18th-century Neapolitan art and a disparate assortment of Greek and Roman artefacts. The gardens offer views of the bay and steps lead down to the shore.

Views up and down the coast from **Villa Comunale park** are breathtaking – and equally impressive from the gardens of the beautiful, if modest, cloister of **Chiesa di San Francesco**, just beside the park.

Corso Italia is closed to traffic between 10am and 1pm and 7pm to 7am. It makes a pleasant stroll but you take your life in your hands if you jaywalk outside these hours.

For a **beach**, head for Marina Grande, a 15-minute walk west from Piazza Tasso, which has small strips of sand. The jetties nearby, with ubiquitous umbrellas and deck chairs, will cost up to €13 a day. **Bagni Regina Giovanna**, a 20-minute walk west along Via Capo (or take the bus for Massalubrense), is more picturesque, set among the ruins of the Roman Villa Pollio Felix. To the east is a small beach at Marinella. See below for boat-hiring information.

Organised Tours

Sic Sic *(☎ 081 807 22 83, Marina Piccola)* Open May-Oct. This company hires out a variety of boats (starting at around €18 an hour) and organises boat cruises.

Goldentours International *(☎ 081 878 10 42, Corso Italia 38e)* This outfit offers tours to the Amalfi Coast, Pompeii, Capri and other destinations.

Special Events

The Sorrento Film Festival, regarded as the most important in the country for Italian-produced cinema, is held annually, usually in November.

The city's patron saint, Sant'Antonio, is remembered on 5 February each year with processions and huge markets. The saint is credited with having saved Sorrento during WWII when Salerno and Naples were heavily bombed.

Places to Stay

Most accommodation is in the town centre or clustered along Via Capo, west of the centre (most accommodation here has views over the bay). To reach this area, catch a SITA bus for Sant'Agata or Massalubrense from the train station. Book early for the summer season.

Camping There are a couple of camp sites just west of town. They're an easy walk from the centre and SITA buses pass by so transport is pretty easy.

Camping Nube d'Argento *(☎ 081 878 13 44, fax 081 807 34 50, W www.nubedargento.com, Via Capo 21)* Sites per person/tent/car €6.75/5.16/3.10, July-Aug €8.30/7.75/3.65, bungalows for 2/3/4/6 people €62/72.30/87.80/108.50. Open Mar-Dec. The beach is 200m away and there's also a pool at the camp site.

Campogaio-Santa Fortunata *(☎ 081 807 35 79, fax 081 807 35 990, Via Capo 41)* Sites per person/tent/car €8.30/6.20/4.20 in Aug. Open Apr-Sept. Sites cost 20% less from April to July and in September.

Hostels The only hostel in Sorrento is centrally located.

Ostello delle Sirene *(☎/fax 081 877 13 71, Via degli Aranci 160)* Dorm beds €13, high season singles/doubles €46.50/51.70, low season singles/doubles €38.75/44. Open year-round. This private hostel is handy for bus and train stations and all prices include breakfast.

Hotels There is a range of hotels in Sorrento, central to town or along the coast.

Hotel City *(☎/fax 081 877 22 10, ⓔ hotel_city@libero.it, Corso Italia 221)* Singles/doubles/triples/quads €38.75/64.60/87.80/103.30. A clean and friendly place, its only downside is the intrusive traffic noise from the street. Rooms have bathroom, the price includes breakfast and Internet access for guests costs €2.60 per half-hour.

Albergo Nice *(☎ 081 878 16 50, fax 081 878 30 86, Corso Italia 257)* Single/doubles €51.65/75. Open Mar-Nov. Another decent place in the heart of town, it too has as its sole disadvantage the traffic noise. Rooms have bathrooms and air-con.

Pensione Linda *(☎/fax 081 878 29 16, Via degli Aranci 125)* Singles €26-36.20, doubles €41.40-72.30. For old fashioned courtesy and caring service at pensione prices, this place is superb value for money. Prices vary according to season and rooms have bathrooms.

Hotel Loreley et Londres *(☎ 081 807 31 87, fax 081 532 90 01, Via Califano 12)* High season doubles €103.30, low season doubles €82.65. Open Mar-Nov. In addition to its other attributes, it has stirring views over the Bay of Naples. The rooms have bathrooms.

Just west of town on Via Capo are a whole string of hotels, each offering great views of the bay.

Hotel Elios *(☎ 081 878 18 12, Via Capo 33)* Singles/doubles with bath €23.25/41.35, with balcony €25.85/46.50. Open Easter-Oct. For no-frills, budget-end accommodation with stunning views, Elios makes a good choice.

Hotel Désirée *(☎/fax 081 878 15 63, Via Capo 31b)* Singles/doubles/triples/quads €51.65/82.65/98.15/113.65. Open Apr-Dec. The welcome is especially warm at Hotel Désirée where the friendly owners readily dispense tourist lore and information. There's a pleasant roof terrace and a lift (elevator) takes you down to the beach below. Rooms have bathrooms and prices include breakfast.

Hotel La Tonnarella *(☎ 081 878 11 53, fax 081 878 21 69, ⓔ pippo@syrene.it, Via Capo 31).* Rooms without/with sea view €118.80/€129.15. Open Mar-Oct. La Tonnarella is a cosy place, tastefully decorated with antique tiles and prints but the service can be offhand. It too has its own lift for beach access.

Grand Hotel Excelsior Vittoria *(☎ 081 807 10 44, fax 081 877 12 06, Ⓦ www.exvitt.it, Piazza Tasso 34)* Singles/doubles/triples from €191.10/232.40/281.47. To sense Sorrento's former glory, visit this venerable old hotel and its extensive, carefully tended gardens, once the site of a villa belonging to Emperor Augustus. The main entrance is on Piazza Tasso.

Places to Eat

Self Service Angelina Lauro *(☎ 081 807 40 97, Piazza Angelina Lauro 39–40)* Pasta and mains from €2.60. Open Wed-Mon. One of several economical snack places ringing the square, this also functions as a cafe and bar. Vegetarians will welcome its wide buffet range of non-meat dishes.

Red Lion *(☎/fax 081 807 30 89, Via Marziale 25)* Set menu €7.75. Though little more authentically Italian than its name, the Red Lion is an economical eatery, popular with the hostel crowd, where you can pick up a pizza and a pint of ale for €4.70.

Pizzeria Gastronomia *(Via degli Aranci)* Pizzas from €2.75. This place is bang opposite Pensione Linda and handy for the hostel too.

Osteria la Stalla *(☎ 081 807 41 45, Via Pietà 30)* Full meal €13-18. Open dinner only Thurs-Tues. In a converted stable, this is one of the rare restaurants in Italy to offer an optional gluten-free menu. In summer, meals are served in its delightful garden.

Ristorante Sant'Antonino *(☎ 081 877 12 00, Via Santa Maria delle Grazie 6)* Pizza €4.20-6.20, full meal €13-18, menus €13, €15.50 and €21.75. This restaurant offers good-value budget eating in the heart of town. Choose either the first-floor terrace or cosy interior.

Circulo dei Forestieri *(Foreigners' Club; ☎ 081 877 32 63, fax 081 877 30 12, Via Luigi de Maio 35)* Although the last place to meet the locals, Circulo dei Forestieri enjoys one of Sorrento's most spectacular views. Drop by for a lunch-time snack (11.30am to 3pm) or dinner (7pm to 11pm) – or just sip a drink on its broad terrace.

La Fenice *(☎ 081 878 16 52, Via degli Aranci 11)* Full meal €13-26. Open Tues-Sun. Green is the dominant colour at this restaurant with its agreeable covered patio and fresh flowers on every table. The menu suits all tastes and budgets.

O'Parrucchiano *(☎ 081 878 13 21, Corso Italia 67)* Full meal €13-15.50. Open Thurs-Tues. Dining here is like being in some vast conservatory, amid the flowers and fronds of vegetation. Although this is a tour-group favourite and caters on an almost industrial scale, don't be put off. The food is good and the service cheerful and attentive.

Ristorante il Buco *(☎ 081 878 23 54, Rampa Marina Piccola 5)* Full meal €26-36. Beside the gate that once provided Sorrento's only access to its port, Il Buco, within what was once a monastic wine cellar, offers subtle cuisine, attractively presented. Browse the photos of old Sorrento around the walls – and don't let the excruciatingly bland piped music (this excellent place's only downside) set you chewing the tablecloth.

CAMPANIA

Entertainment

Music & Theatre Outdoor concerts are held during the summer months in the cloisters of Chiesa di San Francesco.

Teatro Tasso *(☎ 081 807 55 25, Piazza San Antonino)* If you thrill to the *Sound of Music*, you might enjoy *Sorrento Musical* which plays here at 9.30pm Monday to Saturday, March to October. It's a pot pourri of Neapolitan songs, including a sing-along with *O Sole Mio* and *Torna a Sorrento*, plus many other less-overworked Neapolitan numbers. Admission costs €20.75.

Bars & Clubs The terrace of the ***Circulo dei Forestieri*** (see Places to Eat earlier) has nightly live music with dancing (though you're unlikely to find yourself snuggling up to a Sorrentino here) and also reasonably priced drinks.

Bollicine *(☎ 081 878 46 16, Via dell' Accademia 9)* Open 7pm-1am year-round, noon-3pm July-Sept. You can sample Campanian and other wines by the glass here over a plate of local specialities, cheeses or cold meats.

For locals, whether perched at the bar or on the terrace, ***Fauno Bar***, watching over Piazza Tasso, is, *the* late evening place to see, be seen and be heard.

Feim *(☎ 081 807 46 80, Piazza San Antonino 2)* Open to 2.30am Mon-Fri, to 4am Sat & Sun, May-Sept, Tues-Sun, Oct-Apr. Below ground, and decorated with a cinema theme, Feim is new but looks likely to stay. Its sandwiches and panini all have film star names: devour a Kidman, Cruise or Gibson. There's music nightly and live groups at weekends. Friday is Latino night.

Filou Club *(☎ 081 878 20 83, Via Pietà 12)* Open Thurs-Tues. Less wild (though the funky pre-midnight canned music can raise the heartbeat), this popular piano bar, where the ivories are tickled until 4am, makes a great place to round off a night on the town.

Shopping

Shoppers will enjoy browsing the small, nominally pedestrian alleys north of Corso Italia and west of Piazza Tasso. Look out for the local embroidery and lace and, peculiar to Sorrento, the elaborate marquetry, compositions of inlaid wood.

Rummage through the three floors of ***Coin Casa*** *(Piazza Tasso)*. It's a quirky treasure trove of cheerful household goods, items ranging from the mundane to the downright wacky.

Getting There & Away

SITA buses serve the Amalfi Coast, Naples and Sant'Agata, leaving from outside the Circumvesuviana train station. Buy tickets at the station bar or from shops bearing the blue SITA sign. At least 12 buses a day run between Sorrento and Amalfi, looping around Positano.

Circumvesuviana trains run every half-hour to/from Naples via Pompeii and Ercolano (a standard €2.60 to each).

Linee Marittime Partenopee (☎ 081 807 18 12) runs up to 10 hydrofoils daily to/from Capri and at least six to/from Naples, while Caremar (☎ 081 807 30 77) has one hydrofoil and three fast ferry sailings daily to/from Capri. A one-way hydrofoil fare is €7.75 while the ferry costs €6.20.

Getting Around

Sorrento Rentacar (☎ 081 878 13 86), Corso Italia 210a, is one of several rental companies which hire out scooters and cars. For a taxi call ☎ 081 878 22 04.

Amalfi Coast (Costiera Amalfitana)

This 50km stretch of coastline running from Sorrento to Salerno is one of Europe's most beautiful. A narrow asphalt ribbon winds along cliffs that drop to crystal-clear blue waters and passes through the beautiful towns of Positano and Amalfi, with the no less stunning hillside village of Ravello a short detour off it. In summer, the coast is jam-packed with wealthy tourists, prices are inflated and finding a room is next to impossible; you're much better off coming during spring and autumn. The Amalfi Coast all but shuts down in winter but you can still find places to stay. The area is also famous for its ceramics.

When planning your itinerary, you'll find W www.amalficoast.it a useful Web source.

Walking

In the hills that tumble to the sea are dozens of small paths and stairways connecting the coastal towns with mountainside villages. Lonely Planet's *Walking in Italy* has a chapter featuring the best walks around the Amalfi Coast and Sorrento peninsula. *Landscapes of Sorrento and the Amalfi Coast* by Julian Tippett in the Sunflower series (about €15.50 locally) has clear descriptions of over 60 walks in the area. The most reliable map to walk by is the Club Alpino Italiano's *Monti Lattari, Peninsola Sorrentina, Costiera Amalfitana: Carta dei Sentieri* (€7.75) at 1:30,000.

Getting There & Away

Bus SITA operates a service along the S163 between Sorrento and Salerno with buses leaving about every hour. Buses also connect Rome and the Amalfi Coast, terminating in Salerno (see Getting There & Away in the Rome chapter for details).

Train From Naples, you can either take the Circumvesuviana to Sorrento or an FS train to Salerno, then continue along the Amalfi Coast, either eastwards or westwards, by SITA bus.

Car & Motorcycle The coastal road is breathtakingly beautiful, if a little hairy at times, as buses manoeuvre past each other on narrow sections. In summer, it becomes a 50km traffic jam and can take hours to navigate as the hordes flock to the coast. From Naples, take the A3. Just after Pompeii, branch off for Castellammare and follow signs for Sorrento. At Meta, you can continue to Sorrento or, if your destination's farther east, bypass the town by taking a short cut over the hills, thus saving yourself a good 30 minutes. To join the coastal road from Salerno, follow signs for Vietri sul Mare or Amalfi.

Boat Linee Marittime Partenopee (☎ 081 807 18 12) operates year-round ferries and hydrofoils between Sorrento and both Naples and Capri. Caremar (☎ 081 807 30 77) also serves the Sorrento-Capri route. Otherwise, most other routes operate only in summer, when a variety of companies operate hydrofoils between Sorrento, Amalfi, Positano and Capri. (See also Getting There & Away under Naples earlier in this chapter.)

POSITANO

Positano is the most picturesque of the coastal towns and some might think the most precious, with its cute houses and expensive shops.

Orientation

Positano is split in two by a cliff which bears the Torre Trasita (tower). West of this is the smaller, less crowded Spiaggia del Fornillo beach area and the less expensive side of town; east is Spiaggia Grande, backing up to the town centre.

Navigating is easy, if steep. Via G Marconi, part of the S163 Amalfitana, forms a huge hairpin around and above the town, which cascades down to the sea. From it, quieter, one-way Viale Pasitea makes a second, lower loop, ribboning off Via G Marconi from the west towards the town centre then climbing back up as Via Cristoforo Colombo to rejoin Via G Marconi and the S163.

Information

The small APT office (☎ 089 87 50 67), Via del Saracino 4, at the foot of the Chiesa di Santa Maria Assunta steps, opens 8am to 2pm Monday to Saturday plus 3.30pm to 8pm in July and August.

On Via dei Mulini, both Banco di Napoli and its near neighbour, Banca dei Paschi di Siena, have ATMs.

Both the post office and *caserma* – the station of the *carabinieri* (police; ☎ 089 87 50 11) are at the junction of Via G Marconi and Viale Pasitea.

Things to See & Do

Positano's main sight is **Chiesa di Santa Maria Assunta** *(Piazza Flavio Gioia)*, its ceramic dome gleaming under the sun. Inside, regular classical lines are broken by pillars and pilasters topped by gilded Ionic capitals while winged cherubs peek from above every arch. Above the main altar is a 13th-century Byzantine Black Madonna and Child.

Boating isn't cheap. Head for the 'To Rent' signs on Spiaggia Grande and expect to pay from €10 an hour for a rowing boat or €20 for a small motor boat, both cheaper by the half or full day.

For **diving** enthusiasts, Centro Sub Costiera Amalfitana (☎ 089 81 21 48) operates from Spiaggia del Fornillo.

Lovers of **classical music** may want to make their visit coincide with Positano's 'Summer Music', an annual international chamber music festival held at the end of August/early September.

Hiring a chair and umbrella on the fenced-off areas of the **beaches** costs around €12 per day but the crowded public areas are free.

If you're a keen walker and reasonably fit, set aside a day for the classic Sentiero degli Dei (Path of the Gods; five to 5½ hours). It follows the steep, well-defined paths linking Positano and Praiano, from where you can catch a bus back along the coastal road. See also Around Positano later.

CAMPANIA

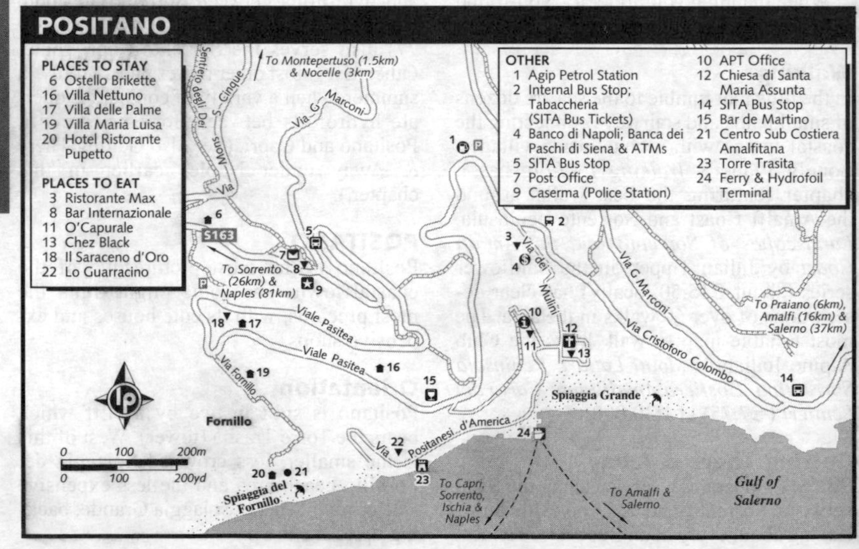

For staggering views with much less input, stroll the Via Positanesi d'America, the cliff-side path which links the two beaches, and reward yourself with a cold drink on the terrace of Hotel Ristorante Pupetto.

Places to Stay

Positano has several one-star hotels, which are usually booked well in advance for summer. Ask at the APT office about rooms in private houses, which are generally expensive, or apartments.

Ostello Brikette *(☎ 089 87 58 57, W www.brikette.com, Via G Marconi 358)* Dorm beds €18.10, one double with bath €57. Open Apr-Nov. Run by the two Annas, this little jewel is friendly, clean as a pin, full of character and, to crown it all, enjoys a staggering view of the bay.

All of the following hotels have rooms with bathrooms.

Villa Maria Luisa *(☎/fax 089 87 50 23, Via Fornillo 42)* Singles/doubles €36.20/62. Open Mar-Nov. The pick of the less expensive hotels, this one's larger doubles have their own balconies and there's a small terrace with magnificent views of the bay.

Villa delle Palme *(☎/fax 089 87 51 62, Viale Pasitea 252)* Doubles €82.65. Open Mar-Dec. The owners also run the excellent Saraceno d'Oro restaurant, just below (see Places to Eat). The price includes breakfast.

Villa Nettuno *(☎ 089 87 54 01, Viale Pasitea 208)* High season doubles €67.20-77.50, low season doubles €62-72.30. Most rooms have pleasant balconies or open onto a communal terrace.

Hotel Ristorante Pupetto *(☎ 089 87 50 87, fax 089 81 15 17, e pupetto@starnet.it, Via Fornillo 37)* High season singles/doubles from €77.50/134.30, low season singles/doubles from €67.20/113.70. Open late-Mar–Dec. Right beside Spiaggia del Fornillo, all its rooms, from which you can just about tumble onto the beach, have sea views and the price includes breakfast. You can also eat at their restaurant (see the following section).

Places to Eat

Most restaurants are overpriced for the food they serve and many close over winter, making a brief reappearance for Christmas and New Year.

Il Saraceno d'Oro *(☎ 089 81 20 50, Viale Pasitea 254)* Pizzas mostly €5.25, full meal €15-25. With fresh cut flowers on each table, good food and attentive service, this family restaurant, popular with the locals, scores on all counts.

Lo Guarracino *(☎ 089 87 57 94, Via Positanesi d'America)* Pasta from €4.25. Eat and savour the panorama from Lo Guarracino, on the cliffside path connecting the two beaches.

O'Capurale *(☎ 089 87 53 74, Via Regina Giovanna)* Pasta from €4.25. Near the main beach, this restaurant serves primarily local dishes.

Chez Black *(☎ 089 87 50 36, Via del Brigantino 19)* Pasta €7.75, full meal €23-35. Overlooking the beach at Spiaggia Grande, here's a popular, recommended spot specialising in seafood. Try the *spaghetti a la Black* cooked in cuttlefish ink and, for a blowout, the mixed seafood grill (€23.25).

Ristorante Max *(☎/fax 089 87 50 56, Via dei Mulini 22)* Full meal €25-35. In much the same price bracket and also specialising in things pulled from the sea, this newcomer to the Positano gastronomic range offers elegant, intimate dining within a contemporary art gallery.

For good value fish and seafood with the briny almost at your feet, dine on the vast terrace of ***Hotel Ristorante Pupetto*** (see Places to Stay), where restaurant prices are much more reasonable than its hotel rates.

The terrace of ***Bar de Martino*** *(Viale Pasitea 170)*, with its commanding views of town and sea, makes a great place for a relaxing drink.

Getting There & Around

To take a SITA bus (services to Amalfi, Sorrento and intervening towns) at the top (northern end) of Viale Pasitea, buy your ticket at Bar Internazionale, just opposite the stop. For the easternmost bus stop, get it in town from the tabaccheria at the top of Via dei Mulini. If you forget – and it's happened to many a traveller – you're in for a long descent and climb back up.

Positano is a snakes-and-ladders town. If your knees can take a steep ascent or drop, there are dozens of narrow alleys and stairways that make walking relatively easy and joyously traffic-free.

A small orange bus follows the lower ring road every half-hour, passing along Viale Pasitea, Via Cristoforo Colombo and Via G Marconi. Stops are clearly marked and you buy your ticket (€0.80) on board. It passes by both SITA bus stops.

Between Easter and October, ferries link Positano with Capri, Naples and other towns along the Amalfi coast.

AROUND POSITANO

Nocelle (450m) is a tiny, still relatively isolated village west of Positano. It's accessible by road or, more interestingly, by a short walking track from the end of Positano's Via Mons S Clinque. Before heading back, have lunch at ***Trattoria Santa Croce*** *(☎ 089 81 12 60)* and enjoy, as you eat, the panoramic views from its terrace. In summer, the place is open for both lunch and dinner; at other times of the year it's best to phone and check in advance. Buses link Nocelle and Positano, running roughly every half-hour in summer.

The coastal town of **Praiano** is less scenic than Amalfi but has more budget accommodation options, including the only camp site on the Amalfi Coast.

Along the coastal road east of Praiano, ***La Tranquillità*** *(☎ 089 87 40 84, fax 089 87 47 79, ⓔ contraq@contraqpraiano.com)* has camp sites (€13 per site and per person) and bungalows (about €36 per person) and also a pensione (€62 per person for half-board). The complex has a restaurant and the SITA bus stops outside.

AMALFI

postcode 84011 • pop 10,150

At its peak in the 11th century, Amalfi, which in those days had a population of around 70,000, was a supreme naval power and a bitter enemy of the northern maritime republics, Pisa and Genoa. Its navigation tables, the *Tavole Amalfitane*, formed the world's first maritime code and governed all shipping in the Mediterranean for centuries.

The town was founded in the 9th century. Through its connections with the Orient, the city, so it claims, introduced to Italy such modern wonders as paper, coffee and carpets. Nowadays one of Italy's most popular small resorts, Amalfi still bears reminders of its seafaring and trading heyday.

Orientation

Most of Amalfi's hotels and restaurants are around Piazza Duomo or along Via Lorenzo d'Amalfi and its continuation, Via Capuano, which snakes north from the cathedral.

Information

Three places that you might need to visit cluster together on Corso Repubbliche Marinare, parallel to the waterfront. The AST office (☎ 089 87 11 07) at No 19 opens 8.30am to 1.30pm and 3pm to 5.15pm Monday to Friday, 8.30am to 12.30pm Saturday. It's flanked by the post office and Deutsche Bank, which has an ATM.

Things to See

The **Duomo Sant'Andrea** makes an imposing sight at the top of its sweeping flight of stairs. Dating in part from the early 10th century, its ornate facade has been rebuilt twice, most recently at the end of the 19th century. Although the building is a hybrid, the Arabic-Norman style of Sicily predominates, particularly in the two-tone masonry and bell tower. The interior is mainly Baroque and the altar features some fine statues together with 12th- and 13th-century mosaics.

The adjoining 13th-century **Chiostro del Paradiso** *(admission €2.10; open 9am-1pm & 3pm-7pm daily)* was built in Arabic style to house the tombs of prominent citizens.

The small, one-room **Museo Civico** *(☎ 089 87 10 66, Piazza Municipio; admission free; open 8am-2pm Mon-Fri)*, behind Corso Republicche Marinare in the town hall building, contains the *Tavole Amalfitane* and other historical documents. Ask at the window halfway up the entry stairs for a guide sheet in English. The former republic's restored **Arsenale** *(Via Matteo Camera; admission free; open 9am-8pm daily Easter-Sept)* is the only ship-building depot of its kind in Italy.

CAMPANIA

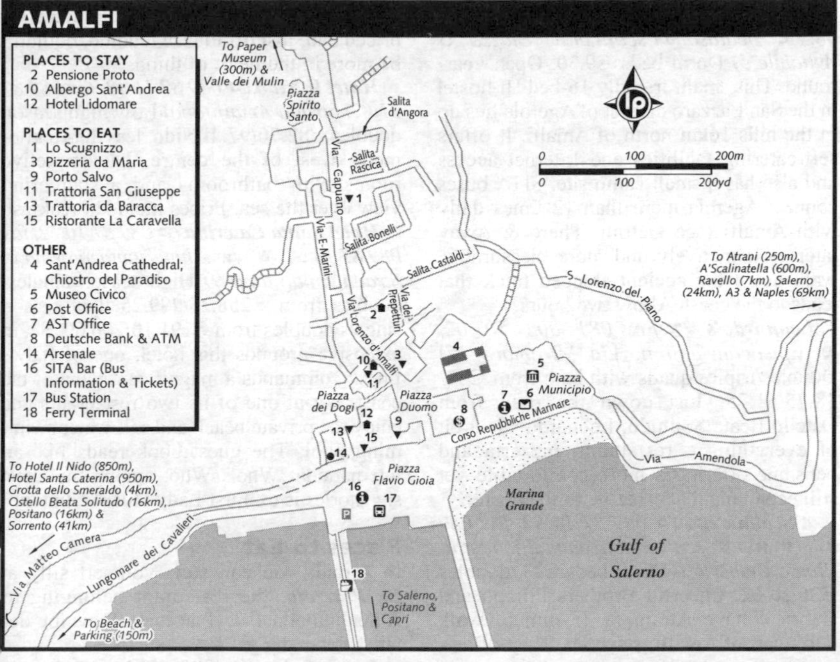

Up in Valle dei Mulini, an easy walk from town, is a **paper museum** *(☎ 0328 318 86 26, Via delle Cartiere; admission €3.10; open 9am-1pm & 3pm-7pm Tues-Sun)*, set up in a paper mill dating back to the 13th century.

The ceramics shops that you'll see mostly clustered around Piazza Duomo, reflect Amalfi's traditional promotion of this craft.

In Conca dei Marini, about 4km along the coast towards Positano, is the **Grotta dello Smeraldo** *(admission €5.20; open 9am-4pm daily)*, a grotto so-called for the emerald colour of its sandy floor. Though less spectacular than Capri's Grotta Azzurra, it's well worth a visit. SITA buses pass by but it's more fun to take one of the boats that run frequently from Amalfi in season (€5.20 return; allow about 1½ hours).

Walking

The paths and stairways which thread the hills behind Amalfi and up to Ravello make for grand walking. For useful guidebooks, see the Walking section at the beginning of the Amalfi Coast section.

Boating

In summer, you can hire boats in the Marina Grande area, at Spiaggia Santa Croce and at Grotta dello Smeraldo.

Special Events

On 24 December and 6 January, skin divers make their traditional pilgrimage to the ceramic crib in Grotta dello Smeraldo (see Things to See & Do earlier).

The Regatta of the Four Ancient Maritime Republics, which rotates between Amalfi, Venice, Pisa and Genoa, is held on the first Sunday in June. Amalfi's turn comes round again in 2005.

Places to Stay

The first three following options are outside Amalfi.

Ostello Beata Solitudo *(☎/fax 081 802 50 48,* ⓔ *beatasol@tiscalinet.it, Piazza G Avitabile 5)* Dorm beds €9.30. Open year-round. This small, friendly 16-bed HI hostel in the San Lazzaro district of Agerola lies up in the hills 16km north of Amalfi. It offers self-catering facilities and Internet access and also has a small camp site. SITA buses connect Agerola more than 12 times daily with Amalfi (see Getting There & Away later). Alternatively and more pleasurably, walk down the ancient stepped track that leads to the coast. Allow two hours.

Leonardo's *(☎/fax 081 802 50 02,* ⓔ *v.pisacane@tin.it, Via Miramare 17)* Doubles/triples/quads with bath from €31/38.75/51.75. Just down the road from Ostello Beata Solitudo, Leonardo's is a bit of everything – restaurant, pizzeria and pensione offering a more comfortable yet still economical alternative to the hostel.

A'Scalinatella *(☎ 089 87 14 92, fax 089 87 19 30,* ⓔ *scalinatella@amalficoast.it, Piazza Umberto I)* Dorm beds €13, doubles €36.20-62. Cheerful Brothers Filippo and Gabriele have Atrani, a 15-minute walk north-east of Amalfi, sewn up. They offer a variety of good value accommodation, all of which has self-catering facilities. The pair are also a mine of information about local walking possibilities. Dorm bed prices rise to €18.10 in high season but include breakfast.

Within Amalfi you'll find more accommodation.

Pensione Proto *(☎ 089 873 61 80, fax 089 87 10 03, Salita dei Curiali 4)* High season doubles/triples without bath €64.60/72.30, with bath €75/95.60. This is a clean, reliable family hotel.

Hotel Lidomare *(☎ 089 87 13 32, fax 089 87 13 94,* ⓔ *lidomare@amalficoast.it, Largo Duchi Piccolomini 9)* Low/high season rooms with bath €72.30/87.80. The spacious rooms in this one-time ducal residence are elegantly furnished with antique pieces – down to the grand piano and map prints in the breakfast room. This is another cosy family hotel, strongly recommended, where the price includes breakfast.

Albergo Sant'Andrea *(☎ 089 87 11 45, Via Santolo Camera)* Singles/doubles €36.20/54.25. This place is moderately priced and, just off Piazza Duomo, couldn't be more in the heart of things.

Hotel Il Nido *(☎ 089 87 11 48, fax 089 87 21 03, Strada Amalfitana)* Low/high season doubles €82.70/97. Il Nido, less than a kilometre west of the centre, has attractive rooms with bathrooms and a staggering view over the sea. Prices include breakfast.

Hotel Santa Caterina *(☎ 089 87 10 12, fax 089 87 13 51,* ⓦ *www. hotelsantacatarina.it, Strada Amalfitana 9)* High season singles/doubles from €258.25/289.25, low season singles/doubles from €191.10/206.60. Set in extensive grounds this hotel, one of Italy's finest, commands a magnificent view of the coast. Eat at one of its two restaurants and enjoy the private beach and salt-water swimming pool. The guest book reads like an international Who's Who; among the latest signatories is ex-First Lady Hilary Clinton.

Places to Eat

In Atrani, you can stuff yourself silly at ***La Piazzeta***, the restaurant belonging to A'Scalinatella (see Places to Stay for details) for under €10.

Porto Salvo *(☎ 089 87 24 45, Piazza Duomo)* Pizzas from €2.10. In the south-western corner of the square and primarily a takeaway place, Porto Salvo does fantastic pizza, panini and *panozzo* (pizza stuffed with mozzarella and tomatoes) by the slice. You can also enjoy lunch at their outside tables for no extra charge.

Pizzeria da Maria *(☎ 089 87 18 80, Via Lorenzo d'Amalfi 16)* Pizzas €4-9.50, full meal around €25. This cavernous place, as much restaurant as pizza joint, is a tour-group favourite – and with good reason. Evenings are much quieter.

Trattoria San Giuseppe *(☎ 089 87 26 40, Salita Ruggiero II 4)* Pizzas €3.75-7.25, full meal €18-28. Open Fri-Wed. You have to wriggle your way through the alleyways to reach this trattoria, clearly signed from Via Lorenzo d'Amalfi. Its rich family cuisine is well worth the navigating.

Trattoria da Baracca *(☎ 089 87 12 85, Piazza dei Dogi)* Full meal €15.50-20.70. Open Thurs-Tues. If you disregard the naff tourist-ensnaring fishing nets above your head, you can eat quite comfortably here.

Ristorante La Caravella *(☎/fax 089 87 10 29, Via Matteo Camera 12)* Full meal €35-45. Open Wed-Mon. Among Amalfi's finest restaurants, La Caravella offers intimacy, fine fare and attentive service.

For great pastries, drop in at ***Lo Scugnizzo*** *(Via Capuano 16)*.

Getting There & Away

SITA buses run from Piazza Flavio Gioia to Sorrento (€2.50, more than 12 daily) via Positano (€1.20) and also to Salerno (€1.70, at least hourly), Agerola (€1.20, more than 12 daily) and Naples (€3.20, eight daily, various routes). You can buy tickets and check current schedules at SITA Bar.

Between Easter and mid-September there are daily ferry sailings to Salerno (€3.10), Naples (€14.50), Positano (€4.50) and the islands of Capri (€10-12.40) and Ischia (hydrofoil; €32.10 return).

RAVELLO

postcode 84010 • pop 2510
elevation 350m

Ravello, overlooking the Gulf of Salerno, sits like a natural balcony from where you can peer down on Amalfi and the nearby towns of Minori and Maiori. The 7km drive from Amalfi up the Valle del Dragone passes through the soaring mountains and deep ravines that characterise the area – watch the hairpin turns! From Ravello, you can continue inland across the mountains to link up with the A3 to Naples and Salerno near Nocera.

Ravello's helpful tourist office (☎ 089 85 79 77), Piazza Duomo 10, opens 8am to 8pm Monday to Saturday in summer and 8am to 7pm the rest of the year.

Things to See & Do

The **cathedral** *(Piazza Duomo)* dates from the 11th century and features an impressive marble pulpit with six lions crouched at its base. The free museum in the crypt contains religious artefacts.

Overlooking the piazza is **Villa Rufolo**. Its last resident was the German composer Wagner, who wrote the third act of *Parsifal* there. The villa was built in the 13th century for the wealthy Rufolos and was home to several popes as well as Charles I of Anjou. From the terraces there is a magnificent view over the gulf. The villa's **gardens** *(☎ 800 21 32 89; admission €3.10; open 9am-6pm daily)* are the inspirational setting for the town's impressive programme of classical music (see Special Events later).

Some way east of Piazza Duomo is the 20th-century **Villa Cimbrone** set in beautiful gardens.

You can also visit the city's vineyards: the small **Casa Vinicola Caruso** *(Via della Marra)*, **Vini Episcopio** *(Hotel Palumbo, Via Toro)* or **Vini Sammarco** *(Via Nazionale)*. If you prefer a tincture of the hard stuff, visit **Giardini di Ravello**, *(beside Vini Sammarco, Via Nazionale)*, or **Profumi di Ravello** *(Via Trinità)* where limoncello, the local lemon liqueur, is produced. Whatever tickles your palate, don't forget that it's a hairy, hairpin ride back to the coast.

Special Events

Ravello's programme of classical music begins in March and continues until late October. It reaches its crescendo in the **Festivale Musicale di Ravello**, held in the second half of July, when international orchestras and special guests play a repertoire that always features Wagner. Tickets start at €20 and can go as high as €130 for some performances. For information and reservations, contact the Ravello Concert Society (☎ 089 85 81 49, fax 089 85 82 49, Ⓦ www.rcs.amalficoast.it). The concerts are held in the gardens of the Villa Rufolo (see earlier).

Ravello's patron saint, San Pantaleon, is recalled with fun and fireworks in late July.

Places to Stay & Eat

Book well ahead for summer – especially if you're planning a visit during the Festivale Musicale in July.

Hotel Toro *(☎/fax 089 85 72 11, Via Wagner 3)* Singles/doubles from €47.50/71.25. Open Easter-Nov. It's a very pleasant place although the clang of the cathedral bells, just over the wall, may disturb your beauty

CAMPANIA

sleep. Rooms have bathroom and prices include breakfast.

Parsifal *(☎ 089 85 71 44, fax 089 85 79 72,* ⓔ *hparsifa@tin.it, Via d'Anna 5)* Singles/doubles €62/98.20. Half-board (obligatory Jun-Sept) €77.50 per person. This delightful hotel is in a former convent, parts of which date back to the 13th century. Enjoy its fine restaurant and views. Rooms have bathrooms and prices include breakfast.

Albergo Ristorante Garden *(☎ 089 85 72 26, fax 089 85 81 10, Via Boccaccio 4)* Low/high season rooms €67.20/75. Open mid-March–late Oct. This welcoming place also has magnificent vistas of the coastline. Hilary Clinton may have recently stayed at the swish Hotel Santa Caterina (see Amalfi earlier) but in her time and prime, Jacqueline Kennedy passed by here, as the photo of the owner, then a girl, with the Kennedy kids and a yellowing letter from the White House attest. Rooms have bathrooms and the price includes breakfast.

Cumpà Cosimo *(☎ 089 85 71 56, Via Roma 44–46)* Full meal €20-25. A magnificent, intimate, almost self-sufficient place. Meat comes fresh from the family butchers shop. Vegetables and fruit in season, even the house wine, are likewise from their own land.

Ristorante Palazzo della Marra *(☎ 089 85 83 02, Via della Marra 7)* Full meal €28-31. You may possibly enjoy the best meal of your trip here. There's usually a tourist menu or you can splash out a la carte.

If you're pushed for time or simply want to chew on a pizza, drop in at ***Take Away Pizza*** *(☎ 089 85 76 05, 41 Viale Parco della Rimembranza)*.

Getting There & Away

SITA operates about 15 buses daily between Ravello and Amalfi. By car, turn left (north) about 2km east of Amalfi. Vehicles, thank the Lord and local authorities, are not permitted in Ravello's town centre but there's plenty of space in supervised car parks on the perimeter.

FROM AMALFI TO SALERNO

The 20km drive to Salerno, although marginally less exciting than the 16km stretch westwards to Positano, is both exhilarating and dotted with a series of little towns, each worth a brief look around and each a potential base.

Atrani, just round a headland, is a pretty extension of Amalfi with a little beach. Farther on are the towns of **Minori** and **Maiori**. Although lacking much of the charm of their better-known partners up the road, both have plenty of hotels and Maiori has a fairly decent-sized beach. Perhaps most attractive is the fishing village of **Cetara**. Shortly before you reach Salerno, you pass through **Vietri sul Mare**, set on a rise commanding views over its larger neighbour and a good place to buy local ceramics. The town has plenty of workshops and showrooms and there are some good buys if you shop around.

SALERNO

postcode 84100 • pop 150,000

After the pretty-pretty little towns of the Amalfi Coast, the urban sweep of Salerno along its bay might come as a shock. Salerno is one of southern Italy's many victims of earth tremors and even landslides. To compound things, it was also left in tatters by the heavy fighting that followed the 1943 landings of the American 5th Army, just to the south of the city. With the exception of a charming, tumbledown medieval quarter and a pleasant seafront promenade, the city today is unexciting, although there have been successful efforts to smarten it up. It is, however, an important transport junction and an excellent base for exploring the Amalfi Coast to the west and Paestum and the Costiera Cilentana to the south-east.

Originally an Etruscan and later a Roman colony, Salerno flourished with the arrival of the Normans in the 11th century. Robert Guiscard made it the capital of his dukedom in 1076 and under his patronage the Scuola Medica Salernitana was renowned as one of medieval Europe's greatest medical institutes.

Orientation

The train station is on Piazza Vittorio Veneto, at the eastern end of town. Most

CAMPANIA

intercity buses stop here and there are a number of hotels nearby. Salerno's main shopping strip, the car-free Corso Vittorio Emanuele, leads off north-west to the medieval part of town. Running parallel is Corso Garibaldi, which becomes Via Roma as it heads out of the city for the Amalfi Coast. Tree-lined Lungomare Trieste, on the waterfront, changes its name to Lungomare Marconi at the massive Piazza della Concordia on its way out of town, south-east towards Paestum.

Information

The EPT office (☎ 089 23 14 32) is near the train station on Piazza Vittorio Veneto. It opens 9am to 8pm (generally closing around 1.30pm for an hour) Monday to Saturday. Ask the laid back *ragazzi* (lads) – so laid back they're almost falling off their seats – for a copy of *Memo*, a fortnightly listing of what's on. Check out their Web site (W www.salernocity.com) too.

There's an ATM inside the train station. You'll find several banks with ATMs on Corso Vittorio Emanuele.

The main post office is at Corso Garibaldi 203. The Telecom office is at Corso Garibaldi 31.

Check your electronic post at Interlanguage Point, Corso Vittorio Emanuele 14, 1st floor. Right under Albergo Santa Rosa (see Places to Stay later), it opens 9am to 1pm and 3.30pm to 9pm Monday to Saturday. Alternatively, log on at Mailbox, Via Diaz.

Ospedale Ruggi d'Aragona (☎ 089 67 11 11) is at Via San Leonardo. The *questura* (police station; ☎ 089 61 31 11) is at Piazza Amendola.

Cathedral

The city's cathedral *(Piazza Alfano; open 7am-noon & 4pm-7.30pm daily)*, built by the Normans under Robert Guiscard in the 11th century and remodelled in the 18th

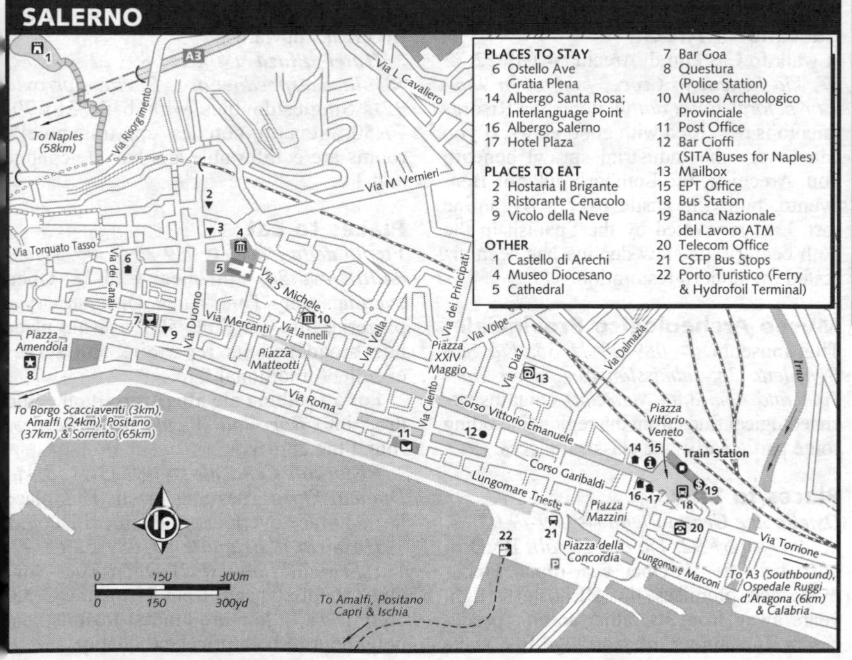

CAMPANIA

century, sustained severe damage in the 1980 earthquake. It's dedicated to San Matteo (St Matthew), whose remains were reputedly brought to the city in 954 and buried in the crypt. It's flanked by a Romanesque bell tower and preceded by a courtyard in polychrome stone. With its 28 slender recycled Roman columns, most of them plundered from Paestum, it has a decidedly Moorish air.

The Cappella delle Crociate (Chapel of the Crusades), so called because crusaders' weapons were blessed here, has the 11th-century Pope Gregory VII interred under the altar. The 12th-century mosaic and sculptural decoration on the left side of the central nave has a naive charm.

Next door on the northern side of the cathedral is **Museo Diocesano** *(☎ 089 23 13 87, Largo del Plebiscito 12; free; open 9am-6pm daily)*, which has a modest collection of artworks including items from the Norman period and a few fragments of Lombard sculpture.

Castello di Arechi

A walk to Castello di Arechi *(☎ 089 22 72 37, Via Benedetto Croce; free; open 9am-1 hr before sunset daily)* along Via Risorgimento is rewarded with good views, if you can ignore the industrial sprawl beneath you. Arechi II, the Lombard duke of Benevento, built the castle over a Byzantine fort. Last renovated by the Spanish in the 16th century, its slow decline has been arrested by modern restoration.

Museo Archeologico Provinciale

This museum *(☎ 089 23 11 35, Via San Benedetto 28; admission free; open 9am-1pm and 4pm-8pm Mon-Sat)* contains archaeological finds from the region, including some particularly fine classical pieces.

Places to Stay

Ostello Ave Gratia Plena *(☎ 089 79 02 51, fax 089 40 57 92, Via dei Canali)* B&B in dorm beds €9.20. Open year-round. Occupying new premises, this HI hostel is light years away from its rather scruffy predecessor. In summer, they arrange free visits to Pompeii, Amalfi and Capri for you if necessary.

Borgo Scacciaventi *(☎/fax 089 46 66 31, Piazza San Francesco 1)* B&B in dorm beds €11.40. Open Apr-Sept. This too is an HI hostel, it's huge (220 beds) and wonderfully located in a restored 16th-century convent in the small village of Cava de' Tirreni, 3km east of Vietri sul Mare. Take bus No 4 or 9 from Salerno train station.

Albergo Santa Rosa *(☎/fax 089 22 53 46, ⓔ alb.srosa@fiscalinet.it, Corso Vittorio Emanuele 14, 2nd floor)* Singles/doubles without bath €23.25/33.60, with bath €33.60/51.70. Here's a friendly place offering good value for money at the budget end of the scale.

Albergo Salerno *(☎ 089 22 42 11, fax 089 22 44 32, ⓔ paviansas@tiscalinet.it, Via G Vicinanza 42, 5th floor)*, Singles/doubles without bath, €33.60/41.40, with bath €44/54.25. This is another budget option, also a stone's throw from the bus and train stations. Disregard the scruffy entrance patio; things improve as the antique lift creaks upwards.

Hotel Plaza *(☎/fax 089 22 44 77, ⓔ plaza@speednet.org, Piazza Ferrovia 42)*, Singles/doubles with bath €51.70/77.50. Several notches up, this hotel's rooms are comfortable and have telephone and TV.

Places to Eat

Vicolo della Neve *(☎ 089 22 57 05, Vicolo della Neve 24)* Full meal €15-25. Open evenings only Thurs-Tues. Once strictly a pizzeria, this venerable 500-year-old place has broadened its repertoire and serves excellent traditional fare.

For a soothing ale afterwards, you could drop into ***Bar Goa*** *(Vicolo della Neve 5)* round the corner.

Ristorante Cenacolo *(☎ 089 23 88 18, Via Duomo)* Open Tues-Sun lunch. This place has a terrace overlooking Piazza al Duomo.

Hostaria il Brigante *(☎ 089 22 65 92, Via Fratelli Linguiti 2)* Open Tues-Sun. Only about 20 paces from Ristorante Cenacolo, it's a little more modest than its near neighbour in both price and quality.

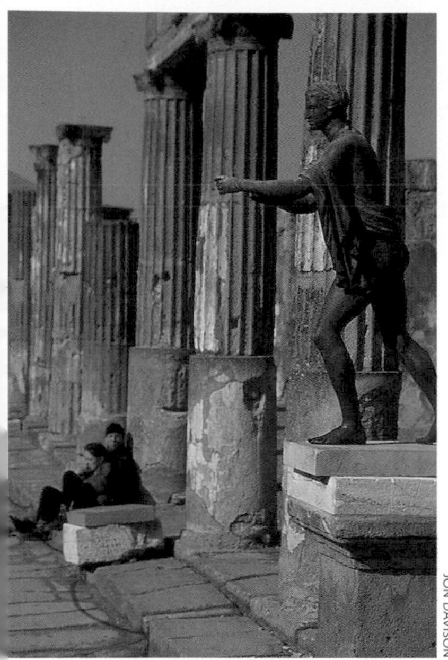
JON DAVISON

Statue frozen in time amdist the ruins of Pompeii

JON DAVISON

Ancient art preserved on internal walls, Pompeii

RUSSELL MOUNTFORD

Eerily empty – Pompeii's Teatro Grande

JON DAVISON

Clear and present danger: Mt Vesuvius

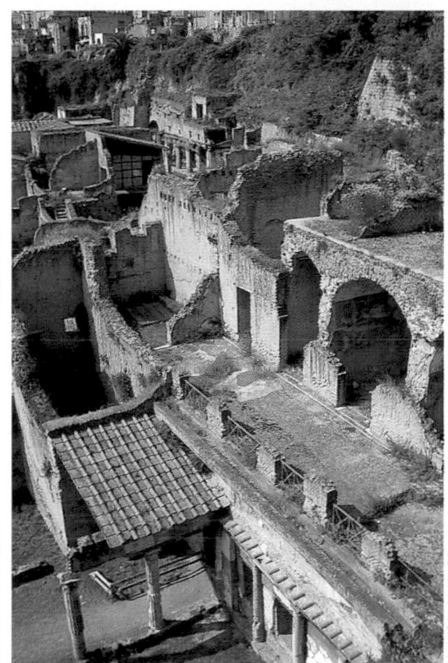
JONATHAN SMITH

A herculean task: unveiling Herculaneum.

BILL WASSMAN

Nothing to do all day but smile, smile, smile...

DAMIEN SIMONIS

Watching the tides of Mar Piccolo in Taranto

SALLY WEBB

The popular seaside town of Vieste

OLIVER STREWE

The strangely shaped *trulli* houses of the Itria Valley

DAMIEN SIMONIS

Elaborate pinnacles atop the conical *trulli* houses

Getting There & Away

Bus Most SITA buses (☎ 089 40 51 45) set out from Piazza Vittorio Veneto, beside the train station. Those that follow the Amalfi Coast leave about every hour. The exception is its Naples service, which departs every 25 minutes from outside Bar Cioffi (where you buy your ticket) at Corso Garibaldi 134.

CSTP operates bus Nos 4 and 41 to Pompeii from Piazza Vittorio Veneto. Its services to Paestum (catch the bus for Sapri) and other towns along the southern coast run from Piazza della Concordia.

Buonotourist runs an express weekday service to Rome's Fiumicino airport, departing from Piazza della Concordia. It also passes by the EUR-Fermi Metropolitana stop in Rome. However, if Rome rather than the airport is your destination, it probably makes more sense to take the train.

Train Salerno is a major stop between Rome, Naples and Reggio di Calabria and is served by all types of trains. It also has good train links with both inland towns and the Adriatic coast.

Car & Motorcycle Salerno is on the A3 between Naples and Reggio di Calabria, which is toll free from Salerno southwards.

Boat Ferries run from Salerno's Porto Turistico to Capri, Positano and Amalfi from April to October and to Ischia in high summer only. Hydrofoils to these destinations also run in summer only. Contact the tourist office for current schedules.

Getting Around

Walking is the most sensible option if you're remaining in the heart of Salerno but plenty of local buses run from the train through the town centre.

PAESTUM

The image of three Greek temples bursting from fields of wild flowers lingers on the retina and in itself makes the trek to this archaeological site well worth the effort. The trio are among the best preserved monuments of the ancient Greek world, remnants of Magna Graecia (Greater Greece), as the Greeks called their colonies in southern Italy and Sicily. The small town nearby is close to some of Italy's better beaches and just south of where US forces landed in 1943.

Paestum, or Poseidonia as the city was originally called in honour of Poseidon, the Greek god of the sea, was founded in the 6th century BC by Greek settlers and fell under Roman control in 273 BC, becoming an important trading port. The town, hit by the successive blows of the retreat of the Roman Empire, periodic outbreaks of malaria and savage raids by the Saracens, was gradually and understandably abandoned. Its temples were rediscovered in the late 18th century by road builders – who proceeded to plough their way right through the ruins. The hapless director of works, one engineer R Petrilli, was prosecuted for having desecrated the national heritage. However, the road of which he was so proud did little to alter the state of the surrounding area, which remained full of malarial swamps, teeming with snakes and scorpions, until well into the 20th century.

Such days are long past and the site, these days a Unesco World Heritage Site, is easily covered on foot. The tourist office (☎ 0828 81 10 16) at Via Magnia Grecia 887, just beside the museum, has a free multilingual brochure, nice and glossy but not too informative, about the temples. For more depth and detail – perhaps too much more for the day visitor – buy the English version of *Poseidonea Paestum* (€11.90) by E Greco, I d'Ambrosio and D Theodorescu.

The most economical way to enjoy Paestum is to buy a combined entrance ticket (€6), covering both temples and museum.

The Ruins

At the ruins *(admission €4.15; open 9am-1 hr before sunset daily)*, the first temple you meet on entering the site from the northern end, near the tourist office, is the 6th-century-BC **Tempio di Cerere** (Temple of Ceres). Smallest of the three, it served for a time as a Christian church.

As you head south, you can pick out the basic outline of the large rectangular **forum**, heart of the ancient city. Among the partially

CAMPANIA

standing buildings are the vast domestic housing area, an Italic temple, the Greek theatre, the Bouleuterion (where the Roman senate met), and, farther south, the amphitheatre – through which that infamous road was ploughed.

Tempio di Nettuno (Temple of Neptune), dating from about 450 BC, is the largest and best preserved of the three temples; only parts of its inside walls and roof are missing. Almost next door, the so-called **basilica** (in fact, a temple to the goddess Hera) is Paestum's oldest surviving monument. Dating from the middle of the 6th century BC and with nine columns across and 18 along the sides, it's indeed a majestic building. Just to its east, you can, with but a touch of imagination, make out remains of the temple's sacrificial altar.

In its time, the city was ringed by an impressive 4.7km of walls, subsequently built and rebuilt by both Lucanians and Romans. The most intact section is south of the ruins themselves.

Tickets are sold at the main entry point or, during winter, from the museum.

Museo di Paestum

This well appointed museum *(☎ 0828 81 10 23; admission €4.15; open 9am-7pm daily)*, just east of the site, houses a collection of much weathered metopes (bas-relief friezes), including 33 of the original 36 from Tempio di Argive Hera (Temple of Argive Hera), 9km north of Paestum, of which virtually nothing else remains. Other highlights from Paestum and neighbouring sites include some striking tomb paintings, their original colours scarcely faded; terracotta votive offerings; eight giant copper urns and some fine Attic amphoras and urns. The ground floor displays artefacts from the Greek occupation while upstairs is primarily devoted to the Roman period.

Places to Stay & Eat

Paestum is a short trip from Salerno, which offers a better range of accommodation. There are more than 20 camp sites in the area, including ones barely a kilometre from the ruins and right beside the beach.

Camping Villaggio dei Pini *(☎ 0828 81 10 30, Via Torre)* Two people & site €15.50-28.40. This is one of the very few camp sites to remain open year-round. The price varies according to season and bungalows are also available.

See under Agropoli later for details of the nearest HI hostel.

Albergo Villa Rita *(☎/fax 0828 81 10 81, ⓔ hotelvillarita@tiscalinet.com, Zona Archeologico 5)* High season singles/doubles €62/77.50, low season singles/doubles €57/67.20. Open Mar-Oct. In its own grounds, conveniently close to the ruins and with its own swimming pool, this is a peaceful place compared to the coastal alternatives in high summer. Prices include breakfast and rooms have bathrooms.

There are a few cafes and snack bars and a couple of restaurants along Via Magnia Grecia, which slices between the temples and the museum. For something more special at prices to suit every budget, just outside the southern walls you'll find another option.

Ristorante Nettuno *(☎/fax 0828 81 10 28, Via Principe di Piemonte – aka Via Nettuno)* Full meal €13-35. Open Tues-Sun lunch time only (lunch and dinner daily July-Aug). Founded in 1929, this delightfully appointed restaurant integrates elements of one of the original city gates. Go for the *crespolini*, small pancakes filled with mozarella cheese, made with milk from the buffalo farm just down the road. Then move on to the fresh fish, Ristorante Nettuno's speciality.

Getting There & Away

CSTP buses run hourly from Salerno's Piazza della Concordia to Paestum and on to Agropoli.

Paestum is on the train line from Naples through Salerno to Reggio di Calabria. Most trains stop at Stazione di Capaccio, nearer the new town (about 6km from the site) and less frequently at Stazione di Paestum, less than 1km from the temples. Trains are less frequent than CSTP buses.

You could take the A3 from Salerno and exit for the S18 at Battipaglia. Better, however, and altogether more pleasant is the

Litoranea, the minor road that hugs the coast. From the A3, take the earlier exit for Pontecagnano and follow signs for Agropoli and Paestum, which is 36km from Salerno.

PARCO NAZIONALE DEL CILENTO E VALLO DI DIANO

Parco Nazionale del Cilento e Vallo di Diano occupies the area south-east of Salerno up to the regional borders with Basilicata and Calabria. The World Wide Fund for Nature has a wildlife sanctuary, **Oasi Naturalistica di Persano**, about 20km north-east of Paestum on the River Sele. Mainly wetlands, it's home to a wide variety of birds, both resident and seasonal. The sanctuary (☎ 0828 97 46 84) opens September to April and signs direct you there from the S18.

Grotte di Pertosa *(☎ 0975 39 70 37; short tour €5.20, long tour €7.75; open 9am-7pm daily in summer, 9am-4pm daily in winter)*, 40km east of Paestum, were discovered in the late 19th century. The tour takes you through 1700m of caves bristling with stalagmites and stalactites. A SITA bus leaves at about 9am from Salerno's Piazza della Concordia; another will take you back in the afternoon. By car, take the A3 southbound from Salerno. The caves are 9km from the Petina exit.

About 20km farther down the A3 towards Calabria, the pretty medieval hill town of **Teggiano** makes a pleasant stop. Just beneath the village of Padula, up on the escarpment 10km farther south, is **Certosa di San Lorenzo** *(☎ 0975 77 74 5; admission €4.25; open 9am 7.30pm daily)* which merits a detour. Also known as Certosa di Padula, this vast monastery has had a turbulent history. Begun in the 14th century and much modified over the centuries, it was abandoned in the 19th century, then suffered further degradation as a children's holiday home and also as a concentration camp. Many of the monks who lived here were from wealthy aristocratic families and no expense was spared in its construction – as the restored elaborate chapels, huge central courtyard and wood panelled library reveal.

US readers might find **Museo Joe Petrosino** *(☎ 0328 459 05 09, Via Guiseppe Petrosino; admission free; open 10am-1pm & 3-6pm daily mid-Mar–Sept)* particularly interesting. Up in Padula, the unexceptional village house where this early fighter against the US mafia was born contains a small museum recording *'la vita e morte di un detective'* who was gunned down in 1909 by the leader of the local clan as he returned to his native country.

Lamanna buses run from Salerno to Padula and (less frequently) to Teggiano.

COSTIERA CILENTANA (CILENTO COAST)

South-east of the Gulf of Salerno, the coastal plains begin to give way to more rugged territory, a foretaste of what lies farther on in the stark hills and mountains of Basilicata and the more heavily wooded peaks of Calabria. This southernmost tract of the Campania littoral lends itself little to summer seaside frolics (with some exceptions), although snorkellers will appreciate some of the rocky points. Despite an irregular splattering of camp sites and holiday accommodation, the beaches are not as popular as those farther north-west or south-east into Basilicata and Calabria. CSTP buses leave Salerno for Sapri, on the regional boundary between Campania and Basilicata. Trains heading south from Salerno also stop at most towns on the Costiera Cilentana. By car, take the S18 which connects Agropoli with Velia via the inland route, or the S267, which hugs the coast.

Agropoli

This modern coastal town south of Paestum has a small, ramshackle medieval core, perched on a high promontory overlooking the sea and topped by a crumbling old castle. Agropoli is a rewarding stop and can be a good base for travel to the temples at Paestum and also to the clean, sandy beaches to the north-west.

Camping Torino *(☎/fax 0828 81 18 51, Via Litoranea Linora)* Sites per person/tent €7.75/17.50. Open Mar-Sept. About 6km north of Agropoli along the Litoranea road, this camp site beside the beach is a short drive from Paestum. It also has bungalows sleeping four or six which cost from €51.25 with a one week minimum stay in July and August.

Ostello La Lanterna *(☎/fax 0974 83 83 64, ⓔ lanterna@cilento.it, Via Lanterna 8)* B&B dorms/doubles per person €9.80/10.30. Open mid-Mar–Oct. At Agropoli's northern extremity, this friendly HI hostel is a home from home.

Hotel Carola *(☎ 0974 82 30 05, fax 0974 82 64 25, Via Pisacane 1)* Singles/doubles €51.75/67.25. You'll find Hotel Carola near the harbour on the western side of town.

Ristorante U'Sghiz *(☎ 0974 82 45 82, Piazza Umberto I)* Pizza from €3.25, full meals from €13. Beside the church and just off the main square of the old town, here's a restaurant with attitude, flourishing under new ownership.

Velia

The ruins of the Greek settlement of Elea, founded in the mid-6th century BC and later a popular spot for wealthy Romans, are worth a visit if you have the time. Considerably smaller than Paestum, its ruins are in a far worse state.

The closest town with accommodation is Ascea, which has several camp sites and hotels.

Camping Alba *(☎ 0974 97 23 31, Piana di Velia)* Site & up to 5 people around €36.15. This place, near Marina di Ascea, is close to the sea and a few kilometres from the main town.

Albergo Elea *(☎/fax 0974 97 15 77, Via Elea 69)* Singles/doubles €26/38.75. Prices at this hotel, which is conveniently near the water, are negotiable other than in summer. In August full board is compulsory and costs €51.65.

The train station for Ascea is at Marina di Ascea. To get to the ruins from there, wait for a local bus to Castellamare di Velia.

South to Sapri

From Ascea to Sapri, a dowdy seaside town a few kilometres short of Basilicata, the road climbs, dips and curves its way through country that, while not Italy's prettiest, is rarely dull and at times spectacular. The beaches along this part of the coast are good and the water usually crystal clear.

Pisciotta, 12km south-east of Ascea, is an attractive medieval village that clings to the mountainside.

Agriturismo San Carlo *(☎/fax 0974 97 61 77, Via Noce 8)* Bed & full board from €36.20. Agriturismo San Carlo is a bargain place to stay and eat. It also produces a remarkable olive oil from the unique local Pisciotta olive trees. The price rises to €51.65 in August.

Another 25km or so farther on are some striking white sandy **beaches** south-east of the resort town of Palinuro (in and around which are camp sites and several hotels). A little farther still, where the road turns steeply inland to pass through San Giovanni a Piro, is Marina di Camerota, which has a small medieval centre. From there, it's another 25km to Sapri. If you get this far you should really make the effort to continue the short distance into Basilicata (see Maratea under Tyrrhenian Coast in the Apulia, Basilicata & Calabria chapter).

CAMPANIA

Apulia, Basilicata & Calabria

A good number of visitors to Italy, drawn by the beauty of the Amalfi Coast and Capri, summon up the gumption to proceed south of Rome to Naples but few venture much beyond the boundaries of Campania. Those who do are rewarded.

These southern regions are Italy's poorest but also the least populated – a decided advantage for travellers wanting to get off the beaten tourist track for a while. Accommodation and food are often more affordable than in other parts of the country and foreign travellers are a definite minority – a welcome change. Above all, it is the dramatic and varied natural beauty – including some of Italy's most spectacular coastline – that will leave its impression, as will the warm welcome of the hospitable southern Italians.

While you won't find the sumptuous artistic treasures of Rome or Florence, the Mezzogiorno beyond Campania nevertheless retains many reminders of the march past of several civilisations since the Greeks first established the colonies of Magna Graecia along the coast of Calabria, Basilicata and Apulia.

Of the three, Apulia came out best from the eras of Norman, Swabian, Angevin and Spanish rule, each of which left a diverse heritage of churches, fortresses and other monuments. Those same rulers pretty much left Basilicata and Calabria to their own devices, thus all too often allowing petty local overlords to maintain a violent grip on their territories. Great strides towards improving living standards have been made since the end of WWII, especially in Apulia but much remains to be done.

Highlights

- Visit Apulia's Romanesque cathedrals, in particular Trani, Ruvo di Puglia and Barletta
- Travel the *trulli*-dotted countryside around Alberobello
- Savour Lecce's elegant Baroque architecture, then head down Penisola Salentina to the tip of Italy's heel
- While away a couple of days on Vieste's beaches after exploring the Promontorio del Gargano
- Pick your way through Matera with its *sassi* (cave dwellings) and churches hewn from the rocks
- Walk in Calabria's Sila Massif mountain range
- Take an evening stroll along Reggio di Calabria's new shorefront promenade as the lights of Sicily twinkle across the water

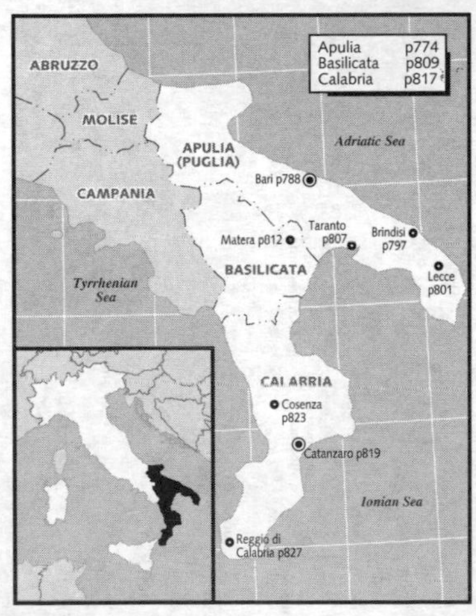

Apulia (Puglia)

The 'spur' and 'heel' of Italy's boot, Apulia is bordered by two seas, the Adriatic to the east and the Ionian (marked on this map as the Golfo di Taranto) to the south.

Apulia's strategic position as the peninsula's maritime gateway to the east made it a

APULIA

APULIA (PUGLIA)

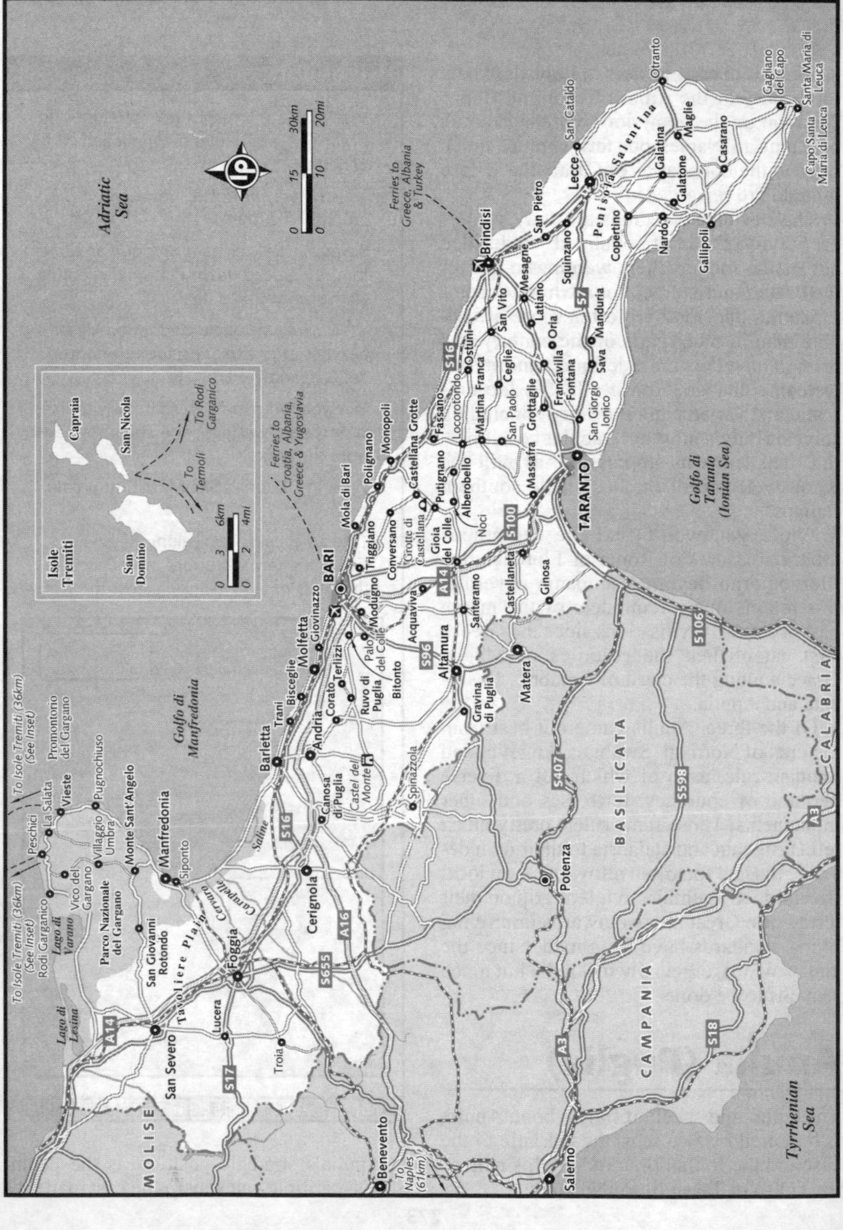

Adriatic Sea
Golfo di Manfredonia
Golfo di Taranto (Ionian Sea)
Tyrrhenian Sea
Isole Tremiti
San Domino
San Nicola
Capraia
To Termoli
To Rodi Garganico
Ferries to Croatia, Albania, Greece & Yugoslavia
Ferries to Greece, Albania & Turkey
To Isole Tremiti (36km) (See Inset)
To Naples (61km)
MOLISE
CAMPANIA
BASILICATA
CALABRIA
Penisola Salentina
Promontorio del Gargano
Parco Nazionale del Gargano
Tavoliere Plain
Lago di Lesina
Lago di Varano
San Severo
Foggia
Lucera
Troia
Benevento
Salerno
Potenza
Matera
Manfredonia
Siponto
Monte Sant'Angelo
San Giovanni Rotondo
Rodi Garganico
Peschici
Vieste
Pugnochiuso
Cerignola
Canosa di Puglia
Castel del Monte
Spinazzola
Barletta
Trani
Andria
Bisceglie
Molfetta
Corato
Giovinazzo
Ruvo di Puglia
Terlizzi
Bitonto
Palo del Colle
Modugno
BARI
Triggiano
Mola di Bari
Polignano
Monopoli
Conversano
Acquaviva
Altamura
Gravina di Puglia
Santeramo
Gioia del Colle
Grotte di Castellana
Castellana Grotte
Putignano
Noci
Alberobello
Locorotondo
Fassano
Martina Franca
Ostuni
Castellaneta
Ginosa
Massafra
TARANTO
Grottaglie
San Paolo
Ceglie
Francavilla Fontana
San Giorgio Ionico
Sava
Manduria
Oria
Latiano
San Vito
Mesagne
Brindisi
San Pietro
Squinzano
Lecce
San Cataldo
Copertino
Nardò
Galatone
Galatina
Maglie
Otranto
Casarano
Gallipoli
Gagliano del Capo
Santa Maria di Leuca
Capo Santa Maria di Leuca

APULIA

major thoroughfare and a target for colonisers and invaders. Today it is a gateway for illegal immigrants from the Balkans, Turkey, the Middle East and Africa.

The ancient Greeks founded Magna Graecia, a string of settlements along the Ionian coast, including Taranto, settled by Spartan exiles. Brindisi marks the end of the Roman Via Appia which, completed around 190 BC, ran all the way from Rome to the Adriatic coast; the Norman legacy is seen in magnificent Romanesque churches across the region; Foggia and its province were favoured by the great Swabian king, Frederick II, several of whose castles remain; and Lecce, richly Baroque, bears the architectural mark of its Spanish colonisers.

Highlights include the sanctuary dedicated to St Michael the Archangel (San Michele Arcangelo) at Monte Sant'Angelo; the *trulli* (conical-roofed stone houses) of Alberobello; and the extraordinary floor mosaic in Otranto's cathedral. Natural wonders include the offshore, unspoiled Isole Tremiti, the ancient Foresta Umbra on the Promontorio del Gargano, and the pleasant beaches of the Penisola Salentina (Salentine Peninsula) at the tip of the heel.

Intensive efforts to crank up industry, improve communications and education, and spur economic growth over the past 30 years have made Apulia the richest of Italy's southern regions but high unemployment remains a grinding problem. This may have had a hand in the growth of Mafia-style organised crime run by the Sacra Corona Unità in the south and La Rosa in the north.

To explore Apulia, you need your own transport or lots of time, since many sights are in or near small towns and villages that are ill-served by public transport. For the energetic, Apulia, which is mostly flat, makes ideal cycling territory.

FOGGIA

postcode 71100 • pop 154,890

Sitting amid the patchwork landscape of the broad Tavoliere Plain, Foggia, an important transport junction, is an agreeable enough place that, nevertheless, has little to hold the traveller for long. In the 12th century, the town was one of the Swabian king Frederick II's favourite cities but it later declined under the rule of the Spanish house of Aragon. Like much of Apulia, Foggia has been a frequent victim of earthquakes, and what was left

A Taste of Apulia

Apulia is a food and wine lover's paradise – no matter how hard you try, it's difficult to eat badly here. One reason is that the fresh produce is of such high quality. Indeed, many of the basic elements of the Italian kitchen originate from Apulia – a huge proportion of Italy's fish is caught off the extensive Apulian coast, 70% of the country's olive oil is produced here and the region provides 80% of Europe's pasta.

Tomatoes, broccoli, chicory, fennel, figs, melons, cherries and grapes are just some of the choice fruits and vegetables that you'll find, often sold at bargain prices on roadside stalls. Almonds, grown near Ruvo di Puglia, are used in many traditional cakes and pastries.

Like their Greek forbears, the folk of Apulia eat a lot of *agnello* (lamb) and *capretto* (kid). The meat is usually roasted or grilled with aromatic herbs, or served in tomato-based sauces.

Fish and seafood are abundant and better priced than in other parts of Italy. Raw fish (such as anchovies or baby squid) marinated in olive oil and lemon juice is not uncommon. *Cozze* (mussels) are prepared in a variety of ways. One recipe from the Bari area, *tiella alla barese*, has mussels baked with rice and potatoes.

You'll find *orecchiette* (small ear-shaped pasta, sometimes called 'strascinati') in most places, often served with vegetable toppings. Other common Apulian pastas are *cavatelli* and *capunti*.

Many quality wines are produced on the Penisola Salentina (the Salice Salentino is one of the best reds), in the trulli area around Locorotondo (home to a particularly pleasing dry white of the same name), and in the plains around Foggia and Lucera. Some of Italy's best rosé wines hail from Apulia and perfectly complement the local cuisine.

standing of the old city centre was efficiently flattened under Allied bombardment in WWII. The town's location makes it a possible launch pad for excursions to the forest and beaches of the Promontorio del Gargano and to two small towns to the west that are worth visiting: Troia, for its beautiful Puglian-Romanesque cathedral, and Lucera, for its Swabian-Angevin castle.

Orientation

Train and bus stations face Piazza Vittorio Veneto, on the northern rim of the town. Viale XXIV Maggio leads south into Piazza Cavour. On or around the Viale are several hotels, restaurants and smart shops, as well as the post and telephone offices. From Piazza Cavour, Via Lanza leads to Corso Vittorio Emanuele II and what remains of the old quarter.

Information

Tourist Offices The APT office (☎ 0881 72 31 41), on the 1st floor at Via Senatore Emilio Perrone 17, is a good 20-minute walk from the train station. From Piazza Cavour (see Orientation), head south along Corso P Giannone. Take the third turning left into Via Cirillo and go straight on until Piazzale Apulia – Via Perrone is on the right. The office opens 8.30am to 1.30pm Monday to Friday.

Post & Communications The post office is on Viale XXIV Maggio. There's a Telecom office (open 8am to 9pm daily) at Via Piave 29, just west of Viale XXIV Maggio.

Things to See

The **cathedral** *(☎ 0881 77 34 82, off Corso Vittorio Emanuele; opens unpredictably)* is Foggia's only noteworthy sight. Built in the 12th century, the lower section remains true to the original Romanesque style. The top half, exuberantly Baroque, was grafted on after an earthquake. Most of the cathedral's treasures were lost in the quake but you can see a Byzantine icon preserved in a chapel inside the church. Legend has it that in the 11th century shepherds discovered the icon lying in a pond over which burned three flames. These flames are now the symbol of the city.

The **Museo Civico** *(☎ 0881 72 62 45, Piazza Nigri; free; open 9am-1pm Sun-Fri plus 5pm-7pm Tues & Thurs)* houses province-wide archaeological finds, including relics from the Roman and medieval town of Siponto, outside Manfredonia. Three portals in the side of the building, one featuring two suspended eagles, are all that remain of Frederick II's palazzo. To get there, take Via Arpi to the right (northwards) off Corso Vittorio Emanuele.

Places to Stay & Eat

***Albergo Venezia** (☎ 0881 77 09 03, fax 0881 77 09 04, Via Piave 40)* Singles/doubles/triples with bath and air-con €41.40/51.70/67.20. Near the station, this recently upgraded hotel represents good value for money.

***Hotel Europa** (☎ 0881 72 10 57, fax 0881 72 02 28, ⓔ hoteleuropafg@tin.it, Via Monfalcone 52)* Singles/doubles from €57/82.70. A tad more upmarket than Hotel Venezia and a block nearer the station, this is a reliable if unspectacular mid-range hotel. Prices include breakfast.

***Hotel Cicolella** (☎ 0881 56 61 11, fax 0881 77 89 84, ⓔ hotel-cicolella@isnet.it, Viale XXIV Maggio 60)* Singles/doubles from €90.40/144.70 Smartest and longest established of Foggia's limited top-end alternatives, it's a delightful blend of old-world charm spiced with contemporary efficiency.

There are several trattorias in the side streets west of Viale XXIV Maggio.

***Ristorante Margutta** (☎ 0881 70 80 60, Via Piave 33)* Tourist menu €13, full meals €21-26. This is a friendly family restaurant that specialises in fish dishes and offers a small but select menu.

***Ristorante L'Angolo Preferito** (☎ 0881 60 85 90, Via Trieste 21)* Full meals €15-21. It's more modest – and offers slightly more modest prices – than Ristorante Margutta.

Fill up on fresh produce from the animated ***street market*** on Via Giuseppe Rosati, running south-west from Piazza Cavour. Directly opposite the station is ***Pizza e Panini***, which serves exactly that.

Getting There & Around

Bus Buses depart from Piazzale Vittorio Veneto, in front of the train station, for towns throughout the province of Foggia.

SITA (☎ 0881 77 31 17) runs buses to Vieste on the Promontorio del Gargano (€4.70, 2¾ hours, five daily) via Manfredonia (€2.10, 50 minutes). It also serves Monte Sant'Angelo (€2.60, 1½ hours, seven daily), San Giovanni Rotondo (€2.60, one hour, frequent), Lucera (€1.60, 30 minutes, eight daily) and Campobasso in Molise (€5.70, 1½ hours, two daily).

Ferrovie del Gargano (☎ 0881 72 51 88) runs buses to Manfredonia (€1.85, 45 minutes, frequent), Troia (€1.55, 50 minutes, frequent) and Barletta (€4.15, two hours, 11 daily). Tickets for both companies are available from the tobacconist at the train station or the bar opposite on Viale XXIV Maggio.

CLP (☎ 081 531 17 06 in Naples) runs six direct *autostrada* (motorway) buses daily (€8.80), connecting Foggia with Naples – they're a faster option than the train. Buy your ticket on board.

Train There's a frequent service from Foggia to Bari and on to Brindisi and Lecce. Northwards, up to 10 trains daily head for Pescara, Ancona (€31, 3½ hours) and Bologna (€47.60, 5½ hours), from where three trains daily continue to Milan (€61.60, 7½ hours).

Car & Motorcycle Take the S16 south for Bari or north for the Adriatic coast, Termoli and Pescara. The Bologna-Bari A14 also passes Foggia. For Naples, take the S655, which links with the east–west A16.

LUCERA

postcode 71036 • pop 37,030
elevation 219m

Less than 20km west of Foggia (and a more pleasant place to spend the night), Lucera has the distinction of having been re-created as an Arab city by Frederick II.

Surrounded, like Foggia, by the flat plains of the Tavoliere, the site was first settled in the 4th century BC by the Romans, who named it Luceria Augusta. The fall of the Empire meant decay for the town but Frederick II resuscitated it in the 13th century. Arab bandits had become a growing problem in Sicily, so Frederick decided to remove the thorn from his side by relocating all of them to Apulia. Some 20,000 were despatched to Lucera, where the emperor allowed them to build mosques and practise Islam freely. From the Arabs of Lucera, he recruited his famous Saracen bodyguard, who accompanied him on his journeys between castles and even to the Crusades against their fellow Saracens.

The French occupiers replaced many of the town's mosques with Gothic churches when Charles I of Anjou conquered Lucera in 1269, and in 1300 his successor, Charles II, had all the Arabs slaughtered.

Things to See

The imposing **castle** was built by Frederick II in 1233. Charles II of Anjou added its external walls, which form a pentagon guarded by 24 towers. The remains stand in the north-eastern corner of the enclosure. Excavations have also revealed the remains of Roman buildings. The **cathedral**, in the centre of the old town, was begun by Charles II in 1300 and is considered the best example of Angevin architecture in southern Italy. The Gothic **Chiesa di San Francesco** was also erected by the prolific Charles II. On the eastern outskirts of town is a poorly maintained 1st-century-BC **Roman amphitheatre** *(free; open 7am-1pm & 2pm-dusk daily)*.

Lucera has a small **museum** *(☎ 0881 54 70 41, Via de Nicastri 36; admission €0.80; open 9am-1pm & 4pm-7pm Tues-Sun)*. In addition to the usual small-town displays of Roman votive offerings, altars, columns and capitals, Lucera's museum has the added interest of 13th-century Arab ceramics and a few Ming vessels which the Arabs imported from China.

Places to Stay

Hotel La Balconata 2 *(☎/fax 0881 52 09 98, W www.labalconata.it, Via Ferrovia 17)* Singles/doubles with bath and air-con

APULIA

€33.60/54.25. This is a pleasant enough modern establishment with a cavernous restaurant and private garage. Prices include breakfast.

The hotel also owns and acts as reception for the more characterful ***Albergo Al Passetto*** *(Piazza del Popolo, just within the old city gate)*, where singles/doubles with bath cost €26/46.50 including breakfast.

Getting There & Away

Lucera is easily accessible from Foggia by SITA buses (€1.60, 30 minutes, eight daily), which terminate in Piazza del Popolo.

TROIA

The village of Troia, 18km south of Lucera, has nothing to do with the Troy of legend. However, its beautiful Puglian-Romanesque **cathedral** *(Piazza Episcopio)* definitely merits the hardly strenuous effort of getting there. Set into the main facade is a splendid 13th-century rose window, while beneath it is a pair of richly wrought 12th-century bronze portals. Gargoyles and other creatures adorn the exterior, and there are hints of Oriental influence – look particularly for the geometric designs across the top of the eastern wall. Once inside, seek out the superbly sculpted pulpit.

Albergo Alba d'Oro *(☎ 0881 97 09 40, Viale Kennedy 28)* Singles/doubles with bath €26/41.40. It's a simple, pleasant place, on the way out of town heading towards Foggia, offering good-value rooms,.

Regular Ferrovie del Gargano buses link Troia and Foggia.

MANFREDONIA

postcode 71043 • pop 57,870

Founded by the Swabian king Manfred, Frederick II's illegitimate son, this port town has little to attract tourists other than as a transport junction on the way to the Promontorio del Gargano. Intercity buses and trains both terminate in central Piazza Marconi. From there, semi-pedestrianised Corso Manfredi leads to Piazza del Popolo after 300m and to the IAT office (☎ 0884 58 19 98), at No 11, which opens 8.30am to 1.30pm Monday to Friday.

Things to See

At the far end of Corso Manfredi is the town's majestic **castle** *(admission €2.10; open 8.30am-1.30pm & 3.30pm-7.30pm daily except 1st and 3rd Mon of month)*. The building was started by Manfred and completed by Charles of Anjou. Within it, the **Museo Archeologico Nazionale del Gargano** displays local finds.

About 2km south of town is **Siponto**, an important port from Roman to medieval times, when it was abandoned in favour of Manfredonia because of earthquakes and malaria. Apart from the **beaches**, the only thing of interest is the distinctly Byzantine-looking 11th-century Romanesque **Chiesa di Santa Maria di Siponto**.

Places to Stay & Eat

Hotel Sipontum *(☎/fax 0884 54 29 16, Viale di Vittorio 229)* Singles/doubles with bath €26/41.40. The hotel is no more sophisticated than you'd expect at such a rate but the rooms are more than OK and the price is nice.

There are four ***camp sites*** south of town.

Ristorante Coppolarossa *(☎ 0884 58 25 22, Via dei Celestini 13)* Full meals €18-26. Just off Corso Manfredi, this friendly, warmly recommended family concern offers a lightning service rarely encountered in Italy. Position yourself adroitly and you can watch Dad in the kitchen rustling up your next course. Go for the seafood buffet (€6.20) as a starter, followed by fresh fish.

Getting There & Away

Regular trains and both SITA and Ferrovie del Gargano buses connect Manfredonia with Foggia, while SITA has seven buses daily to/from Vieste (1¾ hours). There are also several buses daily to/from Monte Sant'Angelo. Get tickets and timetable information from Bar Impero on Piazza Marconi, from where all services leave.

PROMONTORIO DEL GARGANO (GARGANO PROMONTORY)

Limestone mountains, ancient forests and beautiful beaches adorn the 'spur' of the Italian boot, much of it within the Parco Nazionale del Gargano. With two important religious sanctuaries, the Promontorio del Gargano has for centuries been an important pilgrim destination. Nowadays, it's a popular tourist playground, its beach resorts, especially around Vieste and Peschici, developing rapidly to accommodate the annual influx of sun-and-fun seekers.

Foresta Umbra

The ancient beeches and oaks of the **Foresta Umbra**, in the promontory's mountainous interior, make up one of Italy's last remaining original forests. Walkers and mountain bikers will find plenty of well-marked trails and there are several picnic areas.

At the Villaggio Umbra, in the heart of the forest (see the Apulia map at the beginning of this chapter), there's a small **museum and nature centre** *(☎ 0884 56 09 44; admission €1.10; open 8am-7pm daily June-Sept)*, which includes a re-creation of a woodcutters' and charcoal burners' camp.

From Vieste, ***Viaggi Kelian*** *(☎ 0884 70 23 44, Via Firenze 3)* organise guided walks (€18.10) and mountain-bike rides (€18.10-23.25) through the forest. Prices include equipment hire and transport. ***Agenzia Sol*** *(☎ 0884 70 15 58, Via Trepiccioni 5)* can also arrange trekking and biking excursions. In Monte Sant'Angelo, the ***Associazione Guidi Ufficiali del Parco Nazionale del Gargano*** *(☎ 0884 56 789 11, Via San Antonio Abate 121)* organises guided walks and tours in the forest and throughout the peninsula.

Monte Sant'Angelo

postcode 71037 • pop 14,250
elevation 840m

For centuries, this isolated mountain town overlooking the south coast of the Gargano has been the last stop on a gruelling pilgrimage. The object of devotion is the Santuario di San Michele. Here, in AD 490, St Michael the Archangel is said to have appeared in a grotto before the Bishop of Siponto. The legend goes that a local man who had lost his prize bull eventually found it at the entrance to a cave. Unable to budge the animal, he fired an arrow at it. But – would you believe it? – the arrow reversed itself in midair and sped back to its launcher, who went straight to his bishop to tell the tale. St Michael later appeared to the bishop at the grotto, ordering him to consecrate a Christian altar there in place of a pagan shrine.

During the Middle Ages, the sanctuary marked the end of the pilgrims' Route of the Angel, which began in Normandy and passed through Rome. In AD 999, Holy Roman Emperor Otto III made a pilgrimage to the sanctuary to pray that prophecies of the end of world in the year 1000 would not be fulfilled. The sanctuary's fame grew after the widely predicted apocalypse proved to be a damp squib.

Things to See Like so many great pilgrimage destinations, the **Santuario di San Michele** *(free; open 6.30am-7pm daily in summer, shorter hours in winter)* has become big tourist business. A flight of stone steps leads down to the grotto. As you descend, note the graffiti on the walls, some of it the work of 17th-century pilgrims. St Michael is said to have left a footprint in stone inside the grotto, so it became customary for pilgrims to carve outlines of their feet and hands and leave accompanying messages.

Finely etched Byzantine bronze and silver doors open into the grotto itself. Inside, a 16th-century statue of the archangel covers the site of his footprint. To its left is an imposing marble bishop's chair resting on two lions, while behind the main altar is a small fountain of legendary 'healing' waters, now sealed.

Once outside, head down the short flight of steps opposite the sanctuary to the **Tomba di Rotari** *(admission €0.60)*, which is, in fact, not a tomb but a 12th-century baptistry. Notice the deep basin sunk into the floor for total immersion, US Southern Baptist style. You enter the baptistry through the facade of the **Chiesa di San Pietro**, with its intricate rose window, all that remains of the church, which was destroyed by a 19th-century earthquake. The Romanesque portal of the adjacent 11th-century **Chiesa di Santa Maria Maggiore** has some fine bas-reliefs. Within are some well-preserved medieval frescoes.

The serpentine alleyways and jumbled houses of this town are perfect for a little aimless ambling. Commanding the highest point is a Norman **castle** *(admission €1.55; open 8am-7pm daily in summer, shorter hours in winter)* with Swabian and Aragonese additions. Take time too to head for the **belvedere**, a specially situated building that gives visitors sweeping views of the coast.

Places to Stay & Eat You're better off elsewhere. Surprisingly in a place that teems with visitors, there are only a couple of hotels.

Rotary Hotel *(☎/fax 0884 56 21 46, Via Pulsano)* Singles/doubles from €41.40/62. This comfortable, if charmless, three-star place is 1km downhill from the historic centre. Prices include breakfast.

By contrast, there are plenty of takeaways and trattorias, especially on Via Reale Basilica.

Ristorante San Michele *(☎ 0884 56 56 95, Via Reale Basilica 59)* In addition to the a la carte selection, they do a neat four-course tourist menu for €13.

La Jalantuúmene *(☎/fax 0884 56 54 84, Piazza de Galganis 5)* Full meals €26-31. Open daily Apr-Sept, closed Tues Oct-Mar & all of Jan. It serves excellent fare, accompanied by a long, select wine list. In summer, tables spill into a picturesque square.

Don't leave town without tasting the local sweets, *ostie ripiene* (literally, 'stuffed hosts'; two wafers like the hosts used at Mass with a filling of caramelised almonds).

Getting There & Away Monte Sant' Angelo is accessible by SITA bus from Foggia, Manfredonia, Vieste and San Giovanni Rotondo.

San Giovanni Rotondo

When Padre Pio (1887–1968), an ailing Capuchin priest in need of a cooler climate, arrived in 1916, San Giovanni Rotondo was a tiny, isolated medieval village in the heart of the Gargano. Pio soon gained a reputation as a mystic and miracle-worker for the way he literally came out smelling of roses; for the stigmata which appeared on his hands; and for his reputed wrestling with the devil, who

Modern-day saint: Padre Pio

appeared before him sometimes in the guise of a black cat, sometimes as a naked woman.

San Giovanni Rotondo, too, underwent something of a miraculous transformation, expanding well beyond its original limits. These days, the good Padre upstages even the archangel St Michael, who is reputed to have appeared farther down the road (see Monte Sant'Angelo earlier). Beatified in May 1999, he annually pulls in over seven million pilgrims, who roll up to pay homage to the priest (and euros to the tacky souvenir shops).

The tomb of Padre Pio, venerated like any senior saint of old, lies in the modern **sanctuary** *(free; open 5.30am-7.30pm daily)*, within which is his **cell** *(open 7.30am-noon & 3.30pm-6pm daily)*. The sanctuary is at the heart of a vast complex that also includes the Home for the Relief of Suffering, one of Italy's premier hospitals, established by Pio, and a new church, still under construction, which will seat over 7000 faithful.

If you want to stay, there are more than 20 hotels, although many are fully booked in advance by pilgrims.

SITA buses run five times daily to/from Monte Sant'Angelo and over ten daily serve both Manfredonia and Foggia.

Vieste

postcode 71019 • pop 13,800

The most popular seaside resort on the promontory and the best equipped with tourist facilities, Vieste is a bright little place. The better beaches are to the south, between Vieste and Pugnochiuso, and to the north towards Peschici, particularly in the area known as La Salata. There are several camp sites along both stretches of coastline.

Orientation & Information From Piazzale Manzoni, where intercity buses terminate, a 10-minute walk east along Via XXIV Maggio, which becomes Corso Fazzini, brings you to the old town and the attractive promenade of the Marina Piccola. The IAT office (☎ 0884 70 88 06) is on Piazza Kennedy, at the south end of the Marina. It's open 8.30am to 1pm and 3.30pm to 8pm Monday to Saturday (8.30am to 9.30pm plus Sunday morning June to September). The post office is on Piazza Vittorio Veneto, where there are also several public telephones.

Things to See & Do The old town, with its whitewashed houses and winding medieval streets, offers a couple of sights of interest, although tourists come here for the beaches rather than the history. The **cathedral** is Puglian-Romanesque but underwent alterations in the 18th century.

Head down to the **Chianca Amara** *(Bitter Stone; Via Cimagliaon)*, on which thousands of citizens were beheaded when the Turks sacked Vieste in the 16th century. Nearby, at the town's highest point, is a **castle**, built by Frederick II, now occupied by the military and closed to the public.

The **Museo Malacologico** *(Mollusc Museum; ☎ 0884 70 55 12, Via Pola 8; free; open 9.30am-noon & 5pm-8.30pm daily)* contains a huge collection of seashells from all over the world.

At the port, ***Centro Ormeggi e Sub*** *(☎ 0884 70 79 83; open May-Sept; ask for Catrina from Canada)* does diving courses in English and rents out sail and motor boats.

If you're just after a beach and don't have your own transport, **Spiaggia del Castello** is just south of town.

Places to Stay Most of Vieste's many hotels and pensiones are scattered along the beach-front roads north and south of town. Camp sites (as many as 80) abound, particularly along Lungomare E Mattei to the south.

Campeggio Capo Vieste *(☎ 0884 70 63 26, fax 0884 70 59 93, Litoranea Vieste Peschici Km 8)* Sites per person/tent/car from €2.90/5.20/2.60. Open Apr-Oct. At La Salata, between Vieste and Peschici, this camp site is accessible by Ferrovie del Gargano bus.

Villaggio Baia di Campi *(☎/fax 0884 70 00 00)* Sites per person/tent/car €5.70/6.75/2.60. Here's another good camping option, near Pugnochiuso on the coast road between Vieste and Mattinata.

There's no lack of accommodation with character, albeit at something of a price.

Pensione al Centro Storico *(☎/fax 0884 70 70 30, ⓔ cstorico@viesteonline.it, Via Mafrolla 32)* Singles €20.70/36.20, doubles €36.20/62 according to season, all with bath. Open Easter-Oct. In a former convent in the old quarter, this place has large, high-ceilinged rooms. The terrace, where breakfast (included) is served, offers magnificent views over the port.

Hotel Seggio *(☎ 0884 70 81 23, fax 0884 70 87 27, ⓔ hotel.seggio@tiscalinet.it, Via Vieste 7)* Doubles €67-85.30, triples €69.75-98.20, quads €82.70-113.70, all with bath and air-con; compulsory full board in Aug €77.50 per person. Open Apr-Oct. Occupying a renovated 17th-century palazzo, this hotel has a private pool, beach and sunbathing terraces.

Albergo Punta San Francesco *(☎ 0884 70 14 22, fax 0884 70 14 24, ⓔ scalanim@tiscalinet.it, Via San Francesco 2)* Singles €31-44, doubles €41.35-62. Open year-round. This place occupies a one-time olive oil factory. Rooms have bathroom and air-con and prices include breakfast.

Vela Velo *(☎ 0884 70 63 03, fax 0884 70 14 62, ⓔ velavelo@viesteonline.it, Lungomare Europa 19)* Low season singles/doubles/triples/quads with bath €20.65/31/41.30/46.50, high season doubles/triples/quads €77.45/103.30/118.80. Open Easter–mid-Oct. Recommended Vela Velo ('Sail and Cycle'), on the shoreside road 600m north of the old town, is an environmentally and client-friendly place. Prices include access to a private beach, free mountain-bike use and breakfast. The hotel also runs a windsurfing school.

Places to Eat ***Il Fornaio*** *(Via Fazzini 1)* This place, near the entrance to the old town, serves tasty pizza by the slice.

Chianca Amara *(Via Cimaglia 4)* Here's another snacky place selling typical local cakes and pastries.

Sapori di Mare *(☎ 0884 70 79 79, Via Judeca 30)* Open Jun-Sept. At the end of Via Cimaglia, this is a panoramic spot for a fish dinner or just a cool drink while savouring the glorious view of sea and coastline.

Osteria degli Angeli *(☎ 0884 70 11 12, Via Celestino V 50)* Full meals €15-20. Open late May-end Sept. Near the cathedral, this is a friendly restaurant offering fine cooking. Try their delicious *troccoli dell'angeli* (pasta speciality with prawns).

Enoteca Vesta *(☎ 0884 70 64 11, Via Duomo 14)* Full meals €20-28. Enoteca Vesta offers intimate dining in a small natural cave. Choose liberally from their magnificent selection of Apulian wines.

La Ripa *(☎ 0884 70 80 48, Via Cimaglia 16)* Full meals about €25. Open Mar-Oct, evenings only. Candlelit, and renowned for its fresh, live seafood, this place, dating mostly from the 16th century, is a mini-museum of objects collected by the owner over the years.

Getting There & Around SITA buses run between Vieste and Foggia (€4.75, 2¾ hours, five daily) via Manfredonia, while the Ferrovie del Gargano bus and train network connects the town with Peschici, Rodi Garganico and other towns on the promontory. Buses terminate in Piazzale Manzoni and timetables are posted outside the town hall nearby. Services connecting coastal towns are frequent in summer and almost non-existent at other times of the year.

Vieste's port is just north of the old town, about a five-minute walk from the IAT office. In summer, several companies with ticket offices at the port, including Adriatica and Motonave, run boats to the Isole Tremiti. There's at least one boat daily from May to September and a return trip costs €23.25.

Between July and September, the *Moby Dick*, normally a fishing vessel, runs three-hour boat trips (€18.50), calling in at some of the sea caves that pock the coastline.

Agenzia SOL *(☎ 0884 70 15 58, e sol@solvieste.it)*, at Via Trepiccioni 5, 100m from the tourist office, sells bus and boat tickets and can provide information on walking and cycling opportunities plus car and boat hire. They also rent mountain bikes from €2.60/18.40/51.70 per hour/day/week.

Peschici

On a rocky outcrop above a sparkling bay, Peschici, though a fast-developing resort, remains relatively unspoiled.

Its whitewashed houses reminiscent of villages of the Greek islands, Peschici has cobbled alleyways with suggestive names – Vico Purgatorio (Purgatory Lane), Via Malconsiglio and Via Buonconsiglio (Bad Advice and Good Advice Streets). Their origins are anyone's guess; Vico Stretto (Narrow Lane) is more straightforward.

Peschici's sandy beaches and hotels fill up in summer, so book well in advance.

Orientation & Information The medieval and more interesting part of town clings to the cliff top at the point of the bay, while the newer parts extend inland and around the bay. In winter, buses terminate beside Chiesa di San Antonio. For the rest of the year, the terminal is beside the sports ground, uphill from the town's main street, Corso Garibaldi. Turn right into the Corso and walk straight ahead to reach the old town.

Your best source of information, in the absence of a tourist office, is Agrifolio Tour (☎ 0884 96 27 21), on Piazza Sant'Antonio 3, a private travel agency that can arrange hotel reservations and sell train, boat and bus tickets.

Places to Stay & Eat Numerous camp sites dot the coast east and west of Peschici.

Baia San Nicola *(☎/fax 0884 96 42 31)* Sites for two people tent & car €14.75-21.20. Open mid-May–mid-Oct. This camp site is 2km out of town on the road towards Vieste.

Camping Parco degli Ulivi *(☎ 0884 96 34 04, fax 0884 96 33 90)* This is a shaded site with pool and private beach a few kilometres west on the road to Rodi Garganico.

Peschici has several hotels and pensiones but prices are usually on the expensive side and many insist upon a minimum of half-board.

Locanda al Castello *(☎ 0884 96 40 38, Piazza Castello 29)* Singles/doubles with bath €26/57. Open year-round. This pleasant family place is situated right by the cliffs and is definitely the pick of the old quarter, with fine sea views. Prices include breakfast. It also runs a decent restaurant (full meals about €13) and neighbouring pizzeria (evenings only).

Hotel Timiana *(☎/fax 0884 96 43 21, Viale Libeta 73)* Full board per person €36.15-67.15 according to season. Open mid-Apr–mid-Sept. Up several notches, Hotel Timiana, set amid mature pines, has its own pool and offers a free shuttle bus to the beach, 800m away. The restaurant alone merits a visit.

Ristorante La Taverna *(☎ 0884 96 41 97, Traversa di Via Castello 6)* Full meals €18-21. Just off Via Castello, in the heart of the old town, this is a cosy, characterful place.

Ristorante Vecchia Peschici *(Via Roma 31)* Meals around €18. Here you can have an excellent meal on the terrace overlooking the sea.

Getting There & Away Ferrovie del Gargano serves Peschici. It runs buses to/from Vieste (seven daily) and has five trains daily to/from San Severo (with connections to/from Foggia) via Rodi Garganico. From April to September, boats (daily from June) leave Peschici's port for the Isole Tremiti. For information and tickets, go to Agrifoglio Tour (see Orientation & Information earlier) or CTM Compagnia de Navigazione (☎ 0884 96 42 34) on Corso Umberto I.

ISOLE TREMITI

This small archipelago 36km north of the Promontorio del Gargano has three main islands: San Domino, San Nicola and Capraia. A convict station until the 1930s, the islands are now a popular summer day trip from the mainland. Out of season, most tourist facilities close down and the few permanent residents resume their quiet, isolated lives.

Legend says that Diomedes, a Greek hero of the Trojan War, was buried here. A rare species of bird (the Diomedee) found on the islands are said to be his faithful warriors who continue to lament his death with their mournful cries. Early in the 11th century, Benedictine monks founded the Abbazia e Chiesa di Santa Maria (Abbey of St Maria) on San Nicola. The Bourbon King Ferdinand IV used the abbey as a jail, a tradition continued by the Fascists, who sent political exiles to the islands in the 1920s and 1930s.

Easily defensible, San Nicola was always the administrative and residential centre of the islands, while the lusher San Domino was used to grow crops. Nowadays, pirates are no longer a threat and most of the islands' accommodation and other facilities are on San Domino.

Your boat will arrive at either San Domino or San Nicola. Don't panic if you think you have been dropped off on the wrong island; small boats regularly make the brief crossing (€1 one way).

Things to See & Do

San Nicola Within the abbey complex is the **Abbazia e Chiesa di Santa Maria**, which features an 11th-century floor mosaic, a painted wooden Byzantine crucifix brought to the island in AD 747 and a black Madonna, probably transported here from Constantinople in the Middle Ages.

San Domino San Domino has the islands' only sandy beach, which becomes extremely crowded in summer. However, there are several small coves where you can swim off the rocks.

If you're feeling energetic, a walking track around the island starts at the far end of San Domino village, beyond Pensione Nassa. Alternatively, you could hire a bicycle from

IBIS Cicli at Piazzetta San Domino. Motorised rubber dinghies are available for hire at the port for about €67 per day (go to the Il Piràta bar). Boats (€7.50) leave from San Domino's small port to visit the island's sea caves.

Places to Stay & Eat

In summer, you need to reserve well in advance. Out of season, phone to check that your chosen hotel is open. In the high season, most hotels insist on full board – no bad idea, since eating options are limited.

Al Faro *(☎/fax 0882 46 34 24, Via della Cantina Sperimentale, San Domino)* Doubles €44, compulsory half-board in Aug €56.90 per person. Al Faro is on San Domino.

Hotel Gabbiano *(☎/fax 0882 46 34 10, San Domino)* Per person €38.75-49.25. Open year-round. This hotel has pleasant rooms and a terrace restaurant overlooking San Nicola.

Getting There & Away

See Getting There & Away under the Peschici and Vieste sections earlier in the chapter, and under the Termoli (Molise) section in the Abruzzo & Molise chapter.

TRANI

postcode 70059 • pop 55,000

A vigorous face-lift and a magnificent portside cathedral have made Trani one of those little jewels that turn up where you least expect to find them. Some 40km north-west along the coast from Bari, such a compact and easily manageable town makes a good base for exploring this part of Apulia, including Barletta, Molfetta and the Castel del Monte.

Trani was important in the Middle Ages – the modern world's earliest written maritime code, the *Ordinamenta Maris*, was drawn up here in 1063 – and was at its height during the reign of Frederick II.

Orientation

The train station is on Piazza XX Settembre, which is also the point of departure for most provincial buses. From it, Via Cavour leads through tree-lined Piazza della Repubblica, the main square, to Piazza Plebiscito and the public gardens. Turn left for the small harbour and the cathedral, spectacularly located on a rise at its northern end.

Information

The IAT office (☎ 0883 58 88 30) is on the 1st floor of Palazzo Palmieri in Piazza Trieste, about 200m south of the cathedral. It opens 8.30am to 1.30pm Monday to Friday, plus 3.00pm to 5.30pm Tuesday and Thursday.

Cathedral

Started in 1097 on the site of a Byzantine church, the cathedral *(open 8am-noon & 5pm-8pm daily)*, dedicated to St Nicholas the Pilgrim, was not completed until the 13th century. Its simple but imposing facade is decorated with blind arches. The original bronze doors of the main portal (now on display inside the church for conservation reasons) were cast by Barisano da Trani, an accomplished 12th-century artisan who also cast the bronze doors of the cathedral at Ravello and the side doors of the cathedral at Monreale.

The grand interior of the cathedral was recently restored to its original Norman simplicity. Near the main altar, take a look at the remains of a 12th-century floor mosaic, similar in style to the one at Otranto. Below the church is the crypt, a forest of ancient columns, where the bones of St Nicholas are kept beneath the altar.

The crypt opens onto the Byzantine Chiesa di Santa Maria della Scala with its **Madonna Dolorata**, a life-size statue of the Madonna dressed in black velvet, a dagger protruding from her heart. Down another flight of stairs is the **Ipogèo San Leucio**, a chamber believed to date from the 6th century.

Castle

The spiritual and the secular each powerfully announce their presence in Trani; some 200m north of the cathedral, the vast 13th-century castle *(☎ 0883 50 66 03, Via Lionelli; admission €2.10; open 8am-7pm daily)* sits squat. Built by Frederick II, then altered by the Angevins, it served until recently as a prison – fittingly so given its uncompromisingly forbidding exterior.

Around the Port

There are several interesting palazzos and churches around the port area. The 15th-century Gothic **Palazzo Caccetta** and nearby 12th-century **Chiesa di Ognissanti** (All Saints' Church) are both on Via Ognissanti, close to the cathedral. The Templars built the church as part of a hospital complex for knights injured in the crusades. From a different era, the 18th-century **Palazzo Palumbo-Quercia**, facing Piazza Quercia on the south side of the harbour, is also worth searching out.

Places to Stay

Albergo Lucy *(☎ 0883 48 10 22, Piazza Plebiscito 11)* Rooms €41.50. This modest place is Trani's most economical option.

Hotel Capirro *(☎/fax 0883 58 95 82, Via Corato)* Singles/doubles/triples with bath €26/46.50/62. About 3km south of town (accessible by the blue bus for Corato from the station), this vast, tacky-at-the-edges hostelry is popular with Italian coach parties but the price is right. The dining room can accommodate over 200 and the food, prepared on an institutional scale, is hearty.

Hotel Regia *(☎ 0883 58 44 44, fax 0883 50 65 95, Piazza Duomo 2)* Singles/doubles/triples/quads €77.50/108.50/146.20/184. Occupying the 18th-century Palazzo Filisio, just across the road from the cathedral, this is the pick of the top-end hotels. Rooms are elegant and there's also a good restaurant.

Places to Eat

Ristorante La Nicchia *(☎ 0883 48 20 20, Via S Gervasio 69)* Meals around €15. Close to the station, this place serves up some very decent fare.

Pizza l'Ancora *(☎ 0347 803 46 18, Via Banchina al Porto 10)* Pizzas from €3. Open Thurs-Tues plus Wed lunch. Enjoy your pizza or pasta on the terrace overlooking the harbour or in the pleasant high-ceilinged interior of this popular waterfront venue.

Pizzeria Al Faro *(☎ 0883 48 72 55, Via Statuti Marittimi 48)* Full meals from €13. Open Thurs-Tues. This is a good choice for a plentiful snack or *tavola calda* (cheap pre-prepared meal) – try their seafood pizza.

La Darsena *(☎ 0883 48 73 33, Via Statuti Marittimi 98)* Full meals from €20. Open Tues-Sun. Occupying part of the Palazzo Palumbo-Quercia (see Around the Port earlier), this stylish trattoria is *the* harbourside place for fish and seafood.

There's a ***produce market*** on Monday to Saturday mornings at Piazza della Libertà, about 150m north of Piazza della Repubblica.

Getting There & Away

STP buses (☎ 0883 49 18 00) connect Trani with points along the coast and inland, including Barletta, Andria and Altamura. Timetables and tickets are available at Bar Desirée, opposite the train station in Piazza XX Settembre, and at the STP office.

At least one early morning bus from Trani leaves in time to connect with the 8.30am summertime service from Andria to Castel del Monte (see that section later in this chapter). The first return run to Andria leaves the castle at 3pm, while the second – and last – heads back at 5pm. Check with the tourist office for updated times.

Trani is on the main train line between Bari and Foggia and is easily reached from towns along the coast.

The S16 runs through Trani, linking it to Bari and Foggia, or you can hook up with the A14 Bologna-Bari autostrada.

AROUND TRANI

Barletta

About 13km north-west along the coast from Trani, Barletta is more faithful to the stereotype of a grubby neglected port town. Even so, it merits a quick visit for its cathedral, castle and the so-called Colossus, a Roman-era bronze statue in the town centre.

Orientation & Information From the train station, go down Via Giannone and through the municipal gardens. Turn right along Corso Garibaldi to reach Barletta's centre. From the bus station on Via Manfredi, walk to Piazza Plebiscito and turn right to meet Corso Vittorio Emanuele.

The IAT office (☎ 0883 33 13 31) is at Corso Garibaldi 208.

Things to See The 12th-century Puglian-Romanesque **cathedral** *(Corso Garibaldi; open during church services)* is among the region's better-preserved examples of this architectural style and has recently been restored. It has an impressive canopy over the high altar.

The imposing waterside **castle** *(☎ 0883 57 83 20, Piazza Corvi; admission €2.60; open 9am-1pm & 3pm-5pm Tues-Sun)*, one of Italy's largest, was initially built by the Normans, then rebuilt by Frederick II and fortified by Charles II of Anjou. Whisper sotto voce in the cannon room, impressive in itself, and enjoy its strange stereophonic echo. Enjoy too the display of Sicilian puppets and the castle's art collection, which includes over 90 works by Barletta's famous son, Giuseppe De Nittis, who was strongly influenced by the French Impressionists.

Back in the town centre, just off Corso Garibaldi on Corso Vittorio Emanuele, is the **Colossus**, a chubby bronze Roman statue over 5m tall, believed to be of Emperor Valentinian I. It was plundered during the sacking of Constantinople in 1203 and snapped up by Barletta after the ship carrying it sank off the Apulian coast. Green with verdigris, it stands stolidly before the 12th-century **Basilica del Santo Sepolcro** (not usually open to the public). Originally Romanesque, this church subsequently underwent Gothic and Baroque face-lifts.

Special Events The main event on the town's calendar is the *Disfida* (Challenge) of Barletta, held annually on the last Sunday in July. One of Italy's best-known medieval pageants, it re-enacts a duel between 13 Italian and 13 French knights on 13 February 1503, when the town was besieged by the French. The Italians won and the chivalrous French decamped.

Getting There & Away From the bus station on Via Manfredi, Ferrovie del Gargano buses link Barletta with Foggia (€4.15, two hours, 11 daily); there are regular STP buses to Trani and Molfetta; SITA serves Manfredonia and Bari; and Ferrotramviaria goes to Andria.

Barletta is on both the Bari-Foggia FS coastal train line and the Bari-Nord train line. It's easily accessible from Trani and other points along the coast, as well as inland towns.

Castel del Monte

Castel del Monte *(admission €3.10; open 10am-7.30pm daily Mar-Sept, 9am-6.30pm daily Oct-Feb)*, rising like a royal crown from a hilltop, is one of Apulia's most prominent landmarks, visible for miles around. It is in the Murge, a long limestone plateau stretching west and south of Bari.

Nowadays a UNESCO World Heritage site, the stronghold was built by Frederick II (see the boxed text 'The Castle that Frederick Built'), probably for his own pleasure and to his own design, in the mid-13th century. Just why is the subject of many theories, from the mathematical (because of the octagons and recurring multiples of eight which feature in the castle's design) to the astronomical and metaphysical. What's sure is that the castle's most bellicose use was as a hunting lodge – in Frederick's day, the surrounding country was heavily forested and teeming with game. The absence of a moat or other system of defence suggests that it was not built primarily to withstand attack.

The castle is built on an octagonal base, each corner equipped with an octagonal tower. Completely restored, its interconnecting rooms have decorative marble columns and fireplaces, and the doorways and windows are framed in corallite stone, which once covered the entire lower floor.

The car park (€2.60 per vehicle) is over 1km from the castle entrance. A free shuttle bus runs between the two.

Getting There & Away Without wheels, travelling to Castel del Monte is a pain. The least difficult way is via Andria. From June to October, the first of two daily buses leaves Piazza Municipio in Andria for the castle at 8.30am Monday to Saturday, returning at 3pm. Andria is within easy reach

The Castle that Frederick Built

Legend has it that during the construction of Castel del Monte, Frederick II dispatched one of his courtiers to Apulia to check progress. However, the courtier was distracted in Melfi, Basilicata, where he fell in love with a beautiful woman 'whose eyes caused him to forget Castel del Monte and his sovereign'. He dallied in Melfi until a messenger from Naples arrived with orders for him to submit his report at once. Rather than admit that he'd been negligent in his duty, the courtier told Frederick that the castle was 'a total failure, neither beautiful nor practical' and that the architect was 'an imposter'. The architect, hearing of Frederick's anger at the courtier's assessment, threw himself to his death from one of the castle's towers rather than face his emperor's wrath. When news of the architect's death reached Frederick, he set out for Castel del Monte with the dishonest courtier. Seeing the magnificent building and again enraged, this time at the death of its architect, Frederick hauled the courtier up one of the towers and threw him, in turn, to his death.

Castel del Monte

of Trani by bus, or of Bari via the Bari-Nord train. The Andria-Spinazzola bus (several per day) passes close to the castle – ask the driver to let you off. See also the Getting There & Away sections under Trani and Bari.

BARI

postcode 70100 • pop 450,000

Unless you are planning to catch a ferry to Greece, Bari won't rank high on your destination list – but it does offer a handful of interesting sights and can make a good base for exploring neighbouring towns such as Ruvo di Puglia, Molfetta, Bitonto, Altamura and even Alberobello and the trulli area.

Capital of Apulia and the south's most important city after Naples, Bari can be a frenetic sort of place with choking peak-hour traffic. Once an important Byzantine town, it continued to flourish under the Normans and later under Frederick II. And while Bari may be a long way from the North Pole, it's here that San Nicola di Myra, better known as Father Christmas, was finally laid to rest. His remains, embalmed in manna, a liquid said to have miraculous powers, were stolen from what is now present-day Turkey in 1087. They were interred in Bari's Basilica di San Nicola, built especially for the purpose, which remains an important place of pilgrimage.

Occupied by the Allies during WWII, the port city endured heavy German bombing.

Orientation

Bari is easy to negotiate. Orient yourself from Piazza Aldo Moro in the newer, 19th-century section of the city; on or around it are as many as four different train stations. From the square, it's about 1km northwards to Bari Vecchia, the old town.

The newer part of Bari is on a grid plan. Any of the streets heading north from Piazza Aldo Moro (pedestrianised Via Sparano da Bari is a relatively calm option) will take you to Corso Vittorio Emanuele II, separating old and new cities, and on to the ferry terminal. Wide, elegant Corso Cavour is the main shopping strip.

Information

Tourist Offices The IAT office (☎ 080 540 11 11) is at Via Bozzi 45, about ten minutes' walk from the main train station. Officially open 10am to noon, it's usually staffed throughout the day. You'll find this place more useful than the APT headquarters

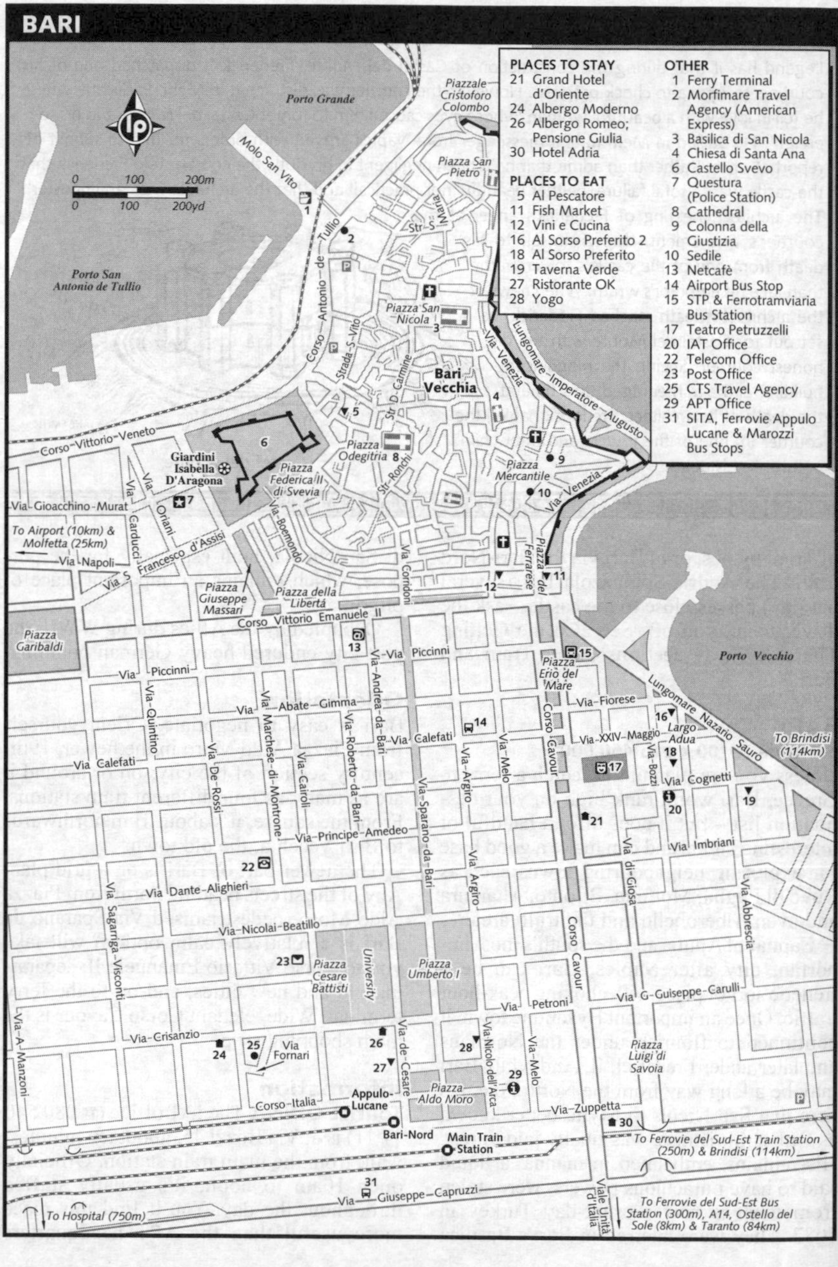

BARI

PLACES TO STAY
21 Grand Hotel d'Oriente
24 Albergo Moderno
26 Albergo Romeo; Pensione Giulia
30 Hotel Adria

PLACES TO EAT
5 Al Pescatore
11 Fish Market
12 Vini e Cucina
16 Al Sorso Preferito 2
18 Al Sorso Preferito
19 Taverna Verde
27 Ristorante OK
28 Yogo

OTHER
1 Ferry Terminal
2 Morfimare Travel Agency (American Express)
3 Basilica di San Nicola
4 Chiesa di Santa Ana
6 Castello Svevo
7 Questura (Police Station)
8 Cathedral
9 Colonna della Giustizia
10 Sedile
13 Netcafè
14 Airport Bus Stop
15 STP & Ferrotramviaria Bus Station
17 Teatro Petruzzelli
20 IAT Office
22 Telecom Office
23 Post Office
25 CTS Travel Agency
29 APT Office
31 SITA, Ferrovie Appulo Lucane & Marozzi Bus Stops

0 100 200m
0 100 200yd

Porto Grande
Porto San Antonio de Tullio
Molo San Vito
Piazzale Cristoforo Colombo
Piazza San Pietro
Str-S Marta
Corso Antonio de Tullio
Strada S Vito
Piazza San Nicola
Bari Vecchia
Str-D Carmine
Via Venezia
Lungomare Imperatore Augusto
Corso Vittorio Veneto
Giardini Isabella D'Aragona
Piazza Federica II di Svevia
Piazza Odegitria
Str-Ronchi
Piazza Mercantile
Via Gioacchino Murat
Via Carducci
Via Oriani
To Airport (10km) & Molfetta (25km)
Via Napoli
Via S Francesco d'Assisi
Via Boemondo
Via Cordoni
Piazza del Ferrarese
Piazza Giuseppe Massari
Piazza della Libertà
Corso Vittorio Emanuele II
Piazza Garibaldi
Via Piccinni
Porto Vecchio
Piazza Erio del Mare
Via Fiorese
Lungomare Nazario Sauro
Via Quintino
Via Abate Gimma
Via Marchese di Montrone
Via Roberto da Bari
Via Andrea da Bari
Via Calefati
Via Argiro
Via Melo
Corso Cavour
Via XXIV Maggio
Largo Adua
To Brindisi (114km)
Via De Rossi
Via Cairoli
Via Sparano da Bari
Via Bozzi
Via Cognetti
Via Principe Amedeo
Via Imbriani
Via di Giosa
Via Abbrescia
Via Dante Alighieri
Via Nicolai Beatillo
Via Sagarriga Visconti
Piazza Cesare Battisti
University
Piazza Umberto I
Via G Guiseppe Carulli
Via Petroni
Via Crisanzio
Via Fornari
Via de Cesare
Via Nicolò dell'Arca
Piazza Luigi di Savoia
Via A Manzoni
Piazza Aldo Moro
Corso Italia
Appulo-Lucane
Via Zuppetta
Bari-Nord
Main Train Station
To Ferrovie del Sud-Est Train Station (250m) & Brindisi (114km)
Via Giuseppe Capruzzi
Viale Unità d'Italia
To Hospital (750m)
To Ferrovie del Sud-Est Bus Station (300m), A14, Ostello del Sole (8km) & Taranto (84km)

APULIA

(☎ 080 524 23 61) at Piazza Aldo Moro 33a (1st floor).

Money There are plenty of banks, including one with an ATM at the station. While there's a currency exchange booth at the ferry terminal, you may well find that exchange rates are better in town. American Express's representative is Morfimare travel agency (☎ 080 578 98 11) at Corso Antonio de Tullio 36–40.

Post & Communications The main post office is on Piazza Cesare Battisti.

There's a Telecom office at Via Marchese di Montrone 123, open 8am to 10pm daily.

Netcafè, on Via Andrea da Bari 11, opens 8.30am to 11pm daily, and charges €2.10/3.70 per half-hour/hour to use the Internet.

Travel Agencies CTS (☎ 080 521 32 44), good for student travel and discount flights, is at Via Fornari 7.

Medical Services & Emergency There is a *pronto soccorso* (casualty) at Ospedale Consorziale Policlinico (hospital; ☎ 080 547 31 11), Piazza Giulio Cesare, about 750m south-west of the main train station.

The *questura* (police station; ☎ 080 529 11 11) is at Via G Murat, near the castle.

Dangers & Annoyances Bari has a reputation as a drug and crime centre – this means a high rate of petty crime. Don't leave anything in your car, don't display valuable jewellery, wear a moneybelt and avoid carrying a bag. Don't overdo the paranoia but be particularly careful when visiting the historic centre (Bari Vecchia) and avoid it altogether at night.

Bari Vecchia

Squeezed into the tight, uneven alleyways of Bari's old quarter are some 40 churches and more than 120 little shrines dedicated both to the Madonna and to a veritable heavenly choir of saints, great and small.

The city's main churches, the **Basilica di San Nicola** *(☎ 080 521 12 05, Piazza San Nicola)* and the **cathedral** *(Piazza Odegitria)*, are discussed in the boxed text 'A Little Romanesque Tour of Apulia' later.

You could start your exploration of Bari Vecchia at Piazza del Ferrarese. Walk north to Piazza Mercantile, a cacophony of jack hammers and in the throes of frenetic rehabilitation when we last passed through. In the piazza is the **Sedile**, the medieval headquarters of Bari's Council of Nobles. Set aside in the square's north-east corner is the **Colonna della Giustizia** (Column of Justice), to which, says tradition, debtors were tied. Make a morning visit to coincide with the piazza's fresh produce market and the lively fish market alongside Piazza del Ferrarese.

Then head north-west past the small Chiesa di Santa Ana to the Basilica di San Nicola. A brief walk south via Strada D Carmine – both street and monument signing are all but non-existent – brings you to the cathedral, from where the Castello Svevo is a well-flung stone's throw west.

Castello Svevo

Just beyond the perimeter of Bari Vecchia broods the so-called Swabian Castle *(Piazza Isabella d'Aragona; admission €2.10; open 8.30am-7.30pm, Tues-Sun)*. Its stones relate four levels of history. A Norman structure was built over the ruins of a Roman fort (currently being excavated). Frederick II then incorporated parts of the Norman castle into his own design, including two towers that still stand. The bastions with corner towers overhanging the moat were added in the 16th century during Spanish rule. Inside you'll find the **Gipsoteca**, a collection of plaster copies of Romanesque monumental decoration from throughout the region. Most of the castle is, however, closed to the public.

Special Events

Bari's big annual event is the Festa di San Nicola (Festival of St Nicola), celebrated on the closest May weekend to the 2nd and 3rd of May. On Saturday evening a procession with participants dressed in Norman costume leaves the castle for the Basilica di San Nicola, where they re-enact the delivery of St Nicholas' bones to the Dominican friars. The next day, with a statue of the saint in pride of place, a fleet of boats sets sail along the coast.

Places to Stay

Ostello del Sole *(☎ 080 549 11 75, fax 080 549 12 02, Strada Adriatica 78)* Dorm bed €13, bed in double room €15.50, meals €7.75. Open year-round. To reach this new HI (Hostelling International) youth hostel, take bus No 12 from the main train station.

Hotel Adria *(☎ 080 524 66 99, fax 080 521 32 07, ⓔ hoadria@tin.it, Via Zuppetta 10)* Singles/doubles with bath €36.20/57. Heading for its first century as a hotel and truly the star of the cheaper range, Hotel Adria's comfort quotient is considerably higher than you'd expect at such a price. The restaurant also deserves a mention.

Albergo Romeo *(☎ 080 523 72 53, Via Crisanzio 12)* Singles/doubles/triples/quads with bath €36.20/59.50/72.30/97. An easy walk from the station brings you to this comfortable but undistinguished albergo.

Pensione Giulia *(☎/fax 080 521 82 71, Via Crisanzio 12)* Singles/doubles/triples €36.20/46.50/62, with bath €41.40/62/77.50. On the 1st floor, above Albergo Romeo, this place has more of a family atmosphere. Prices include breakfast.

Albergo Moderno *(☎ 080 521 33 13, fax 080 521 47 18, Via Crisanzio 60)* Singles/doubles with bath €41.40/64.60. Albergo Moderno offers trim, airy rooms, all with air-con, in a cheery, welcoming building.

Grand Hotel d'Oriente *(☎ 080 524 40 11, fax 080 524 39 14, Corso Cavour 32)* Singles/doubles/triples €67.20/103.30/137. A lovely, mature, truly grand hotel whose prices, proportionately high, nevertheless represent good value for money. Prices include breakfast.

Places to Eat

Vini e Cucina *(☎ 338 212 03 91, Strada Vallisa 23)* Full meals around €10. It's difficult to eat more economically in Bari. And meals don't come much more basic than in this bustling, cheap and cheerful barrel-vaulted-tunnel of a place, its tablecloths (of paper) the only concession to sophistication. Great fun!

Ristorante OK *(☎ 080 521 69 97, Via de Cesare 19)* Full meals around €10. Prices here are OK indeed, competing with those of Vini e Cucina. You can grab a sandwich, a snack or a full-scale meal but, when it comes to atmosphere, the plastic and neon can't hold a candle to its rival.

Taverna Verde *(☎ 080 554 08 70, Largo Adua 19)* Full meals €15-18. Open Mon-Sat. Low-ceilinged and stylish, this justifiably popular place pulls in a largely professional clientele. Its fine pasta and main dishes are very reasonably priced.

Al Sorso Preferito *(☎ 080 523 57 47, Via de Nicolò 42)* Full meals around €18. Open Wed-Mon. Prices and quality are much the same as the Taverna Verde's at this roomy old hotel with loads of character. A block away is its sister restaurant, ***Al Sorso Preferito 2*** *(☎ 080 524 00 22)*, open Tuesday to Sunday.

Al Pescatore *(☎ 080 523 70 39, Piazza Federico di Svevia 6-8)* Full meals around €25. Al Pescatore specialises in seafood and grilled fish. The grilled squid in particular is memorable.

Yogo *(☎ 0347 807 20 77, Via Nicolo dell'Arca 5)* Chill out with their great frozen yoghurt.

If you're self-catering or stocking up for a ferry journey, pass by the ***fish market*** *(Piazza Mercantile)* and the ***open-air market*** *(Piazza del Ferrarese)*.

Getting There & Away

Air Bari's airport (☎ 080 583 52 04), 10km west of the city centre, services domestic flights to/from Bologna, Catania (Sicily), Florence, Milan, Palermo, Rome and Venice. The Ferrovia Bari-Nord train line runs right by. An Alitalia airport bus leaves the main train station, calling by the airline's office at Via Calefati 37, about 80 minutes before most flight departures. To get aboard you need to show your plane ticket.

Bus Intercity buses leave from several locations around town.

From Via Giuseppe Capruzzi, on the southern side of the main train station, SITA buses (☎ 080 579 01 11) cover local destinations. Here also is the departure point for

Ferrovie Appulo-Lucane buses (☎ 080 542 65 52) serving Altamura, Gravina di Puglia and Matera, plus Marozzi buses (☎ 080 552 00 53) for Rome and other long distance destinations.

Piazza Eroi del Mare is the terminal for STP buses (☎ 080 555 93 05) serving Andria (€3.35, seven daily), Barletta (€3.35, frequent), Molfetta (€1.80, frequent), Trani (€3.35, one hour, frequent) and Margherita di Savoia (€4.40, 1¼ hours, nine daily). Ferrotramviaria buses (☎ 080 523 22 02) also leave from here for Andria, Barletta and Ruvo di Puglia.

Ferrovie del Sud-Est (FSE) buses (☎ 080 542 65 52) leave from Largo Ciaia, south of Piazza Aldo Moro, for Brindisi (€6.20, 2½ hours, four daily) and Taranto (€4.65, 1½ hours, six daily). They run frequently to Alberobello (€3.10, 1½ hours), Grotte di Castellana (€2.10, one hour; also FSE trains), Locorotondo (€3.65, 1¼ hours), Martina Franca (€3.65, 1½ hours), Polignano (€2, 45 minutes) and Ostuni (€4.15, two hours).

In summer, enterprising locals often organise private buses to ferry tourists directly from Bari to Castel del Monte (see the Around Trani section per person) – check with the tourist office.

Train Like buses, a whole network of train lines connects Bari with the wider world.

From the main train station (☎ 848 88 80 88), national FS trains go to Milan (€44, 8½ hours) and Rome (€26.20, five hours). There are frequent services to cities across Apulia, including Foggia (€6.20, 1½ hours), Brindisi (€5.70, 1¼ hours), Lecce (€11.10, 2¼ hours) and Taranto (€9.20, 1¼ hours).

Of the private train services, the Ferrovia Bari-Nord line connects the city with the airport (€0.80, at least 20 daily), continuing to Bitonto, Andria and Barletta.

The Ferrovie Appulo–Lucane line (☎ 080 572 52 10) links Bari with Altamura (€2.75), Matera (€3.60, 10 trains and six buses daily), Gravina (€3.20) and Potenza (€6.25, four trains and one bus daily).

FSE trains (☎ 080 546 21 11) head for Alberobello, Castellana, Locorotondo, Martina Franca and Taranto, leaving from the station in Via Oberdan – cross under the train tracks south of Piazza Luigi di Savoia and head east along Via Giuseppe Capruzzi for about half a kilometre.

Car & Motorcycle Bari is on the A14 autostrada, which heads north-west to Foggia, south to Taranto and connects with the A16 to Naples at Canosa di Puglia. Exit at Bari-Nord to reach the centre of town.

Boat Unlike ferry traffic to/from Brindisi, it's busy year-round in Bari, especially to Greece but also to Albania and Yugoslavia. All boat companies have offices at the ferry terminal, accessible from the main train station by bus Nos 20 and 22. Fares to Greece from Bari are generally more expensive than from Brindisi; the trip takes much the same time. Once you have bought your ticket and paid the embarkation tax (€5.20 per person/car to Greece or Yugoslavia, €2.60 per person/car to Albania), you get a boarding card, which must be stamped by the police at the ferry terminal.

The main companies and the routes they served at the time of writing are listed. We quote single fares and, where there's a seasonal variation, the high summer one. Tariffs can be as much as one third cheaper outside the peak period of mid-July to late August. Bicycles normally travel free.

Adriatica (☎ 080 523 58 25, Ⓦ www.adriatica.it) To/from Durrës (Durazzo; eight hours) in Albania. Deck class €59.40; *poltrona* (airline-type seat) €64.60; cabin berth from €82.70; car €97. Daily departure at 11pm year-round.

Superfast (☎ 080 528 28 28, Ⓦ www.superfast.com) To Igoumenitsa (9½ hours) and Patras (Patrassa; 15½ hours) in Greece. Deck class €42.40; poltrona €56.90; dorm bed €67.70; cabin berth from €84.70. Daily departure at 8pm year-round. Superfast is the only company that accepts Eurail, Eurodomino and Inter-Rail passes (you have to pay only port taxes and a high season supplement, if applicable).

Ventouris Ferries (☎ 080 521 76 09, Ⓦ www.ventouris.gr) To Igoumenitsa, Patras and Corfu. Deck class €45.50; poltrona €56.30; cabin berth from €92.45; car €56.30. Regular ferries. Also daily ferries to/from Durrës (Albania).

Montenegro Lines (☎ 080 578 98 27; reservations via Morfimare travel agency – see Money earlier in this section). To Bar in Montenegro (Yugoslavia). Deck class €38.75; cabin berth €57; car €64.60. Six ferries per week.

Poseidon Lines (☎ 080 578 98 30; reservations via Morfimare travel agency – see Money earlier in this section) To/from Igoumenitsa. Deck class €44 (students €35.20); cabin berth €90.40 (students €72.30); car €57. Four ferries per week.

Getting Around

Central Bari is quite compact – a 15-minute walk will take you from Piazza Aldo Moro to the old town. Useful city buses are Nos 20 and 22 from Piazza Aldo Moro to the ferry terminal and No 12 from the FS train station to the youth hostel. A single journey costs €0.80 and a day pass is €1.90.

Street parking is hell. There's a large free parking area just south of the main port entrance and a paying multistorey car park between the main and Ferrovie del Sud-Est train stations.

THE TRULLI AREA

Trulli are circular, conical-roofed whitewashed houses built of stone without a single trowelful of mortar. Their roofs, topped with pinnacles, are tiled with concentric rows of grey slate and often painted with astrological or religious symbols. Their origin is obscure but few of these solid-looking constructions date back more than a couple of centuries.

The trulli area is in the Itria Valley and extends from Conversano and Gioia del Colle in the west to Ostuni and Martina Franca in the east. The greatest concentration of trulli houses is in and around Alberobello.

A Little Romanesque Tour of Apulia

Of over 15 significant Romanesque religious buildings in Apulia, only nine have been preserved in the original style. These include the cathedrals at Bari, Altamura, Barletta, Bitonto, Molfetta, Ruvo di Puglia and Trani. Although considered to be merely a church, the Basilica di San Nicola in Bari, of exceptional architectural value, served as a model for many of the churches built in the Puglian-Romanesque style.

With careful planning, you can make your way to all of them on day trips from Bari, although the town of Trani is worth a stop in its own right. To visit all, it's best to hire a car for two or three days. This way you can also take in a couple of less important Romanesque churches in the province – and build in a trip to Castel del Monte, the stunning octagonal castle of Frederick II of Swabia, about 40km west of Bari (see Around Trani for details).

Begin in **Bari** with the 12th-century Basilica di San Nicola, built on the ruins of a Byzantine palazzo to house the reputedly miracle-working bones of St Nicholas, stolen by Bari sailors from their resting place in Myra (in what is now Turkey). The basilica has a stark, imposing facade, simply decorated with blind arches and mullioned windows and flanked by two bell towers. On the north side, look for the Lion's Doorway with its beautiful sculptures and bas-reliefs depicting chivalric scenes. Inside, below the richly gilded 17th-century ceiling, are a splendid 12th-century altar canopy and bishop's chair, known as the throne of Elias. The remains of St Nicholas are down in the crypt.

Bari's cathedral, from the same era, was built on the remains of a Byzantine original. Although retaining its elegant Romanesque shape and bell tower, it's been much altered over the centuries.

The cathedrals of Bitonto, Ruvo di Puglia and Molfetta lie west of Bari and can be easily reached by public transport. **Trani** and **Barletta** are farther along the coast; Trani makes the better base (see the Trani and Around Trani sections for more details of each). If you have time, fit in too the cathedrals in **Conversano** and **Palo del Colle**.

The cathedral of **Bitonto** is a particularly stunning example of Puglian-Romanesque architecture. Built in the late 12th century on the model of the Basilica di San Nicola in Bari, it is dedicated to St Valentine. Note the carved animals and plants that decorate the capitals on the side walls. Nearby is

Grotte di Castellana

These spectacular limestone caves *(☎ toll free 800 21 39 76 or 080 499 82 11, Piazzale Anelli; open 8.30am-7pm daily, tours on the hour)*, 40km south-east of Bari, are Italy's longest natural subterranean network. The interlinked galleries, with their breathtaking stalactite and stalagmite formations, were first explored in the 1930s by the speleologist Franco Anelli; today's visitors can follow his route in a guided group. After trudging down 265 steps (or taking the elevator) to a huge cavern known as La Grave, you pass through a series of caves, culminating in the magnificent **Grotta Bianca**.

There are two tours: a 1km, 50-minute trip (€7.75) that does not include the Grotta Bianca; and the full 3km, two-hour trip (€13) that does. Visit too the recently inaugurated **Museo Speleologico Franco Annelli** *(admission €2.60; open 9am-noon & 3pm-6pm daily)*.

By rail, head for Castella Grotte station on the FSE Bari-Taranto train line, from where the caves are a 2km walk.

Alberobello

Much of this pretty town exists for tourism these days but, with a couple of quarters sprouting trulli like fields of mushrooms, it's a place to be seen. Although it's a UNESCO World Heritage site, many of its trulli are now souvenir and wine shops, boutiques and restaurants.

The IAT office (☎ 080 432 51 71) is in the Casa d'Amore, just off car-free Piazza del Popolo, the main square. It opens 8.30am to 1.30pm and 4pm to 7.30pm daily (shorter hours Monday to Saturday in winter).

A Little Romanesque Tour of Apulia

the 17th-century Chiesa di Purgatorio. Above its main door are sinners burning in purgatory, flanked by two large figures of Death dancing with delight at their fate. You can get to Bitonto from Bari on the private Bari-Nord train line. From the station, walk directly ahead along Via Matteotti for about 1km to the medieval part of town. You'll see an Angevin tower and signs direct you to the cathedral.

The graceful cathedral in **Ruvo di Puglia** has a striking facade with a fine rose window and three portals. The delicately carved central portal features columns supported by griffins, resting on (now very worn) lions, themselves supported by squashed human figures. Ruvo too is on the Bari-Nord train line. Otherwise you can take a Ferrotramviaria bus from Bari's Piazza Eroi del Mare (approximately every half hour daily, except Sunday), which arrives at Cortugno, just off Ruvo's main piazza. The same bus also goes to Bitonto, Andria and Barletta.

Molfetta is worth a stop not only for its impressively simple cathedral but also for its largely abandoned, tumbledown medieval centre. Known as the Duomo Vecchio, the cathedral, started in 1150, was completed at the end of the 13th century. Its stark, undecorated white facade is flanked by two bell towers. The interior is a mix of Romanesque, Byzantine and even Islamic architecture. The Borgo Vecchio, the medieval quarter behind the cathedral, is crumbling although parts are being restored. Molfetta is on the main Bari-Foggia train line, about 20 minutes from Bari. From the station, ask for directions to Via Dante and *il porto* (the port), near which you'll find the cathedral on Via Chiesa Vecchia.

Altamura is about 45 minutes south-west of Bari and easily accessible on the Appulo-Lucane train line (see the Bari Getting There & Away section). Its 13th-century cathedral, constructed during the reign of Frederick II, was badly damaged by an earthquake in 1316. It later suffered some unfortunate Baroque renovations, when the elegant medieval main portal and rose window were moved from their original position to what had been the apse. The cathedral is in the old town's main street, Via Federico II di Svevia. Ferrovie Appulo-Lucane buses also connect Bari and Altamura, arriving in Piazza Santa Teresa. From the piazza, turn right and walk to Piazza Unità d'Italia.

You can check your emails (€5.20 per hour) at the single computer of Emmegi, Via Ten, just off Piazza del Popolo behind the Palazzo Municipio.

Within the quarter of **Rione Monti**, on the south side of town, over 1000 trulli, many converted into souvenir shops and the like, cascade down the hillside. To its east, on the other side of Via Indipendenza, is **Rione Aia Piccola**. It's much less commercialised, with a respectable 400 trulli, most of which are still used as family dwellings.

In the modern part of town, the 16th-century **Trullo Sovrano** *(☎ 080 432 54 82, Piazza Sacramento; admission €1.30; open 10am-1pm & 3pm-6pm daily)* has been converted into a small museum.

Places to Stay & Eat Accommodation ranges from camp sites to the trulli themselves.

Camping dei Trulli *(☎ 080 432 36 99)* Sites for two people tent & car €18.10-28.50. This camp site is just out of town on Via Castellana Grotte.

Hotel Lanzillotta *(☎ 080 432 15 11, fax 080 432 53 55, Piazza Ferdinando IV 31)* Singles/doubles with bath €36.20/51.70. Just off the central Piazza del Popolo, this hotel boasts what must be Italy's slowest lift (elevator). The slow haul apart, it represents excellent value – as does its three-course dinner of local specialities for €13. Prices include buffet breakfast.

Hotel dei Trulli *(☎ 080 432 35 55, fax 080 432 35 60, e htrulli@inmedia.it, Via Cadore 28)* Rooms €144.60 with breakfast, half-board per person €98.15. At the southern extremity of Rione Monti, this, the town's top hotel, is a complex of self-contained trulli set in a wonderful shady garden of pine, juniper and cypress – a far cry from the deprived lives of the original trulli dwellers.

You can even rent a trullo. Prices vary hugely according to season, starting from around €62 per day and €205 per week. For details online, see W www.alberobellonline.it or contact the IAT office.

Ristorante Trullo d'Oro *(☎/fax 080 432 18 20, Via Felice Cavallotti 27)* Full meals €20-25. The food, though pleasant enough, isn't quite up to the tasteful decor and intimacy of this converted trullo.

Getting There & Away The easiest way to get to Alberobello is on the FSE Bari-Taranto train line. From the station, walk straight ahead along Via Mazzini, which becomes Via Garibaldi, to reach Piazza del Popolo.

Locorotondo

Locorotondo, perched on a hill above the Valle dei Trulli and on the FSE Bari–Taranto train line, is completely circular. In addition to the charm of its rambling streets and alleys, it offers a couple of fine restaurants.

U'Curdunn *(☎/fax 0804 31 70 70, Via Dura 19)* Full meals €15-20. Open Tues-Sun. Beneath the shadow of the parish church, this intimate place prides itself on its use of local produce.

La Taverna del Duca *(Via Papatodero 3)* Meals around €15. Open Tues-Sun. Also in the old town, this place serves home-style, delicious, hearty local food.

Martina Franca

Founded in the 10th century by refugees fleeing the Arab invasion of Taranto, Martina Franca flourished from the 14th century, when it was granted tax exemptions (*franchigie*, hence the name Franca) by Philip of Anjou.

The town is at the edge of the trulli area and you'll see few of these conical constructions. There's also a well-maintained old quarter with some fine examples of Baroque architecture.

Information The tourist office (☎ 080 480 57 02, Piazza Roma 34–35) occupies a couple of rooms within the Palazzo Ducale.

Things to See Passing under the Baroque Arco di Sant'Antonio at the western end of pedestrianised Piazza XX Settembre, you emerge into Piazza Roma, flanked by the 17th-century **Palazzo Ducale**, a vast edifice now used as municipal offices.

From the piazza, follow Corso Vittorio Emanuele into Piazza Plebiscito, at the heart of the historic centre and dominated by the exuberant Baroque facade of the 18th-century **Chiesa di San Martino**, its centrepiece the good St Martin himself, sharing his cloak with an underclad beggar.

Special Events In the second half of July and early August, the town stages its annual Festival della Valle d'Itria, a feast for opera lovers. For information and tickets, contact the Centro Artistico Musicale Paolo Grassi (☎ 080 480 51 00, fax 080 480 51 20), in the Palazzo Ducale.

Places to Stay & Eat The cheapest accommodation options, both with acceptable restaurants, are a little south of town on the road to Taranto. FSE buses running between Taranto and Martina Franca pass by each place.

Hotel Da Luigi *(☎/fax 080 485 60 66, Via Taranto 172)* Singles/doubles with bath €31/46.50. The preferred option, this hotel is 2km from Martina Franca.

La Cremaillere *(☎ 080 449 00 52, Via Taranto)* Rooms with bath €36.20. Near San Paolo and 5.5km beyond Da Luigi, this is a run-down sort of place where you get what you pay for.

One of the best options is in Martina Franca itself.

Park Hotel San Michele *(☎ 080 480 70 53, fax 080 480 88 95, ⓔ info@parkhotelsm.it, Viale Carella 9)* Singles/doubles/triples/quads with bath and air-con €64.60/87.80/103.50/114. This friendly, cosy place is set in a leafy garden with a pool. Prices include breakfast.

Trattoria La Tavernetta *(☎ 080 430 63 23, Corso Vittorio Emanuele 30)* Full meals from €15. This trattoria serves decent food at acceptable prices.

Rosticceria Ricci *(☎ 080 480 55 34, Piazza Plebiscito 10–12)* Count on around €13 for a platter of local roast meats accompanied by a salad and wine.

Villaggio In *(☎ 080 480 59 11, Via Arco Grassi 8)*. Full meals around €18. This is a decidedly classy joint where you can dine downstairs then clamber up to the roof bar, which often has live music at weekends.

Getting There & Around Take the FSE train from Bari or Taranto. FSE buses also connect Martina Franca with Taranto, Alberobello, Castellana Grotte and Bari, arriving in Piazza Crispi, off Corso Italia.

Local buses connect the FSE train station, down on the plain, with Piazza XX Settembre.

Ostuni

This stunning town of stark, whitewashed buildings is set on three hills east of Martina Franca and about 40km north-west of Brindisi. The seemingly disordered tangle of narrow cobblestone streets, many little more than arched stairways between the houses, recalls a North African Arab *medina*. Rising above it all in sombre brown stone is the 15th-century Gothic **cathedral**. Its distinctive cupolas, covered in green, yellow and white slate tiles, signal like a beacon among the surrounding buildings.

Orientation & Information From Piazza della Libertà, where new town meets old, take Via Cattedrale uphill to the cathedral. From the tiny piazza in front of the cathedral, turn right for a view across the olive groves to the Adriatic – or turn left to get agreeably lost in Ostuni's whitewashed lanes.

Ostuni's APT office (☎ 0831 30 12 68) is at Corso Giuseppe Mazzini 8, just off Piazza della Libertà. It opens 8.30am to 1.30pm and 3pm to 6pm Monday to Friday.

Places to Stay & Eat Ostuni makes an easy day trip from Brindisi or Bari but, if you want to stay, there are a couple of relatively inexpensive options.

Albergo Tre Torri *(☎/fax 0831 33 11 14, Corso Vittorio Emanuele 298)*. Singles/doubles €32.60/44, with bath €36.20/49.10. It's on the main boulevard as you enter the new town from the south.

Hotel Orchidea Nera *(☎ 0831 30 13 66, Via Mazzini)* Singles/doubles €28.50/36.20, with bath from €36.20/46.50. The decor of this slightly wacky place leans towards the kitsch but the prices are right; their huge, high-ceilinged doubles with views over plain and sea are especially good value at €62.

There are several excellent eating places in the old town.

Osteria del Tempo Perso *(☎ 0831 30 33 20, Gaetano Tanzarella Vitale 47)* Full meals around €25. This osteria prepares magnificent local food in a pair of delightful rustic salons, one the converted village bakery. Face the cathedral's south wall, turn right through an archway into Largo Giuseppe Spennati and follow signs to the restaurant.

Getting There & Around Società Trasporti Pubblici (STP) buses run between Ostuni and Brindisi about every two hours, arriving in Piazza Italia in the newer part of Ostuni. They also connect the town with Martina Franca. Trains run more regularly to/from Lecce (via Brindisi) and Bari. An intermittent local bus runs between station and town, 2.5km away.

You can rent a bike – the ideal way to explore the quiet backroads linking the trulli villages – from Hotel Orchidea Nera (see Places to Stay & Eat later) or Alba Travel Agency, Largo Biancheri 3.

BRINDISI

postcode 72100 • pop 96,000

When we last visited Brindisi, the town was, to put it charitably, in a state of flux. Some boats were still leaving from the old port while most were using the new Costa Morena terminal across the harbour. No regular bus service had been scheduled to take passengers the 7km from the train station to Costa Morena, thus leaving visitors at the mercy of Brindisi's taxi drivers, many of whom have yet to discover the meter. To compound things, the tourist office had just changed premises, had no maps of town and staff took over five minutes to produce their new telephone number. Things can only improve.

Travellers associate Brindisi with waiting. The major embarkation point for ferries between Italy and Greece, it swarms with people in transit. What's more, there's not much to do here other than wait. Most backpackers gather at the train station, at the ferry terminal or in pedestrianised Piazza Cairoli or Piazza del Popolo.

Settled in ancient times and occupied by Rome in 3 BC, Brindisi is a natural safe harbour that prospered under the Romans and retained its importance until after the crusades. Invasion, plague and earthquake brought about decline but today it is a busy merchant and passenger port with, if you care to linger, a small historic heart.

Orientation

The new port is east of town, across the Seno di Levante at Costa Morena, in a bleak industrial wilderness.

The old port is about 1km from the train station along Corso Umberto I, which leads into Corso Garibaldi. There are numerous takeaway food outlets and places to eat along the route, as well as a bewildering array of ferry companies and travel agencies.

Information

Tourist Office The APT office (☎ 0831 52 30 72) is at Viale Regina Margherita 44. It opens 8.30am to 2pm and 3.30pm to 7pm Monday to Friday, 8.30am to 1pm Saturday. Don't go in with great expectations...

Money Corsos Umberto I and Garibaldi bristle with currency exchange offices, and good old-fashioned banks also abound.

Post & Communications The main post office is on Piazza Vittoria.

The only public email access in this medium-sized town and major port is an Internet Point at Photocenter, Corso Umberto I 114.

Medical Services The Ospedale Generale Antonio di Summa (hospital; ☎ 0831 51 05 10) is on Piazza Antonio di Summa, west of the train station.

Dangers & Annoyances At the height of summer, Brindisi is a thieves' paradise – so valuables should be carried in a money belt and nothing of the remotest interest should be left unattended in your car. Women are advised not to walk through the town alone at night.

In general, the safest strategy is to deal directly with a ferry company. In particular, if you have a Eurail or Inter-Rail pass, go directly to the town or port office of Hellenic Mediterranean Lines (see Getting There & Away later), the only company here which accepts them. Readers report that some other less scrupulous travel agents will assure you that your pass is invalid or that the quota's full in order to sell you a full-price ticket.

Brindisi is extremely busy in summer, so if you arrive by car allow extra time for the eternal traffic jam around the port.

Things to See

For the Romans, as for travellers today, Brindisi was the end of the line or, more specifically, of the Via Appia, which stretched cross country from Rome. For centuries, two great **columns** marked the end of the imperial highway. One was presented to the town of Lecce back in 1666 as thanks to San Oronzo, that town's patron saint, for having relieved Brindisi of the plague. The other has been hauled away for repairs so only a pair of pedestals remain. Tradition has it that the Roman poet Virgil died in a house near here after returning from a voyage to Greece.

In the small historic quarter, the modest **cathedral** *(Piazza del Duomo)* was originally

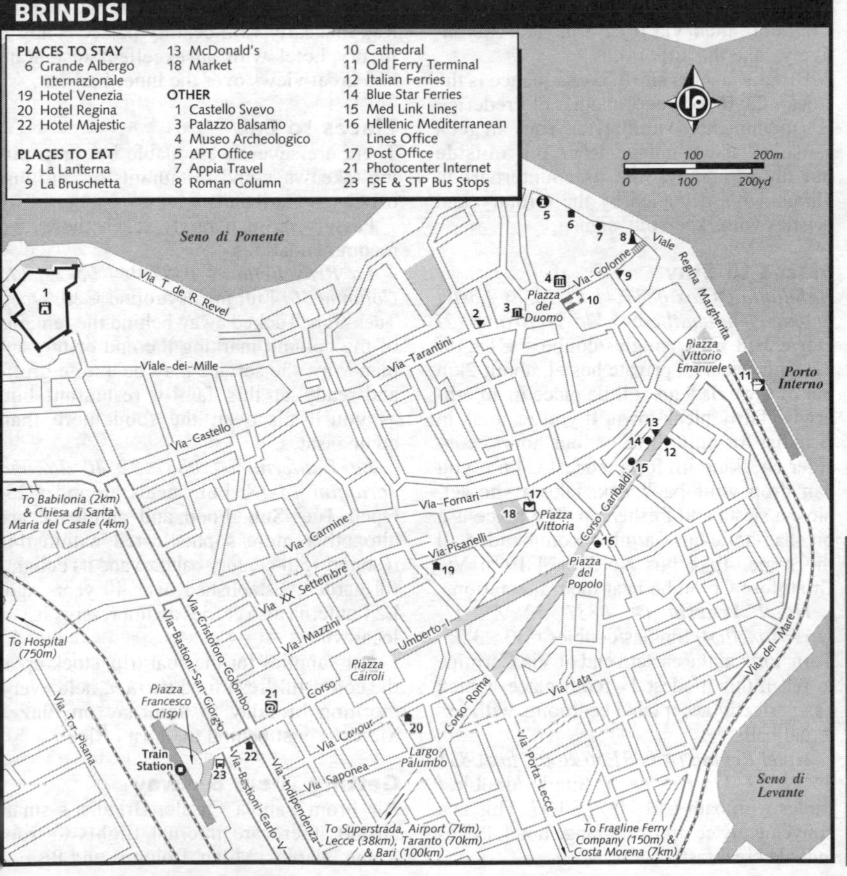

APULIA

built in the 11th century but substantially remodelled about 700 years later. Abutting it on the north side is the small **Museo Archeologico** *(☎ 0831 22 14 01, Piazza del Duomo 8; free; open 9am-1pm & 3pm-7pm Mon-Fri, mornings only Sat & Sun)*. Across the tranquil square is **Palazzo Balsamo**, which has a fine loggia.

The town's main sight is the **Chiesa di Santa Maria del Casale**, 4km north of the centre towards the airport. Built by Prince Philip of Taranto around 1300, this originally Romanesque church has both Gothic and Byzantine touches. To get there, follow Via Provinciale San Vito round the Seno di Ponente bay. The road becomes first Via E Ciciriello, then Via R de Simone. Alternatively, take the airport bus.

Brindisi's other site of consequence is the stocky **Castello Svevo**, another of Frederick II's monuments to militarism. You can get a sense of its grandeur from the outside but unfortunately, like its counterpart in Taranto, it's occupied by the military and bristles with 'keep out' signs.

Places to Stay

Babilonia *(☎/fax 0831 41 31 23, ⓔ hostel brindisi@hotmail.com, Via N Brandi 2)* Dorm bed €12, singles/doubles €18.10/31. This cheerful private hostel, about 2km out of town, is a great little place in an otherwise fairly bleak town. If you're stuck in Brindisi for only three or four hours, consider checking in; for a modest €4.65, you can drop your backpack, take a shower, have a siesta and freshen up. The place is a bit shambolic but warmly recommended all the same. Take bus No 3 or 4 from Via Cristoforo Colombo near the train station.

Hotel Venezia *(☎ 0831 52 75 11, Via Pisanelli 4)* Singles/doubles €13/23.25. Turn north at the eastern end of Via Carmine to reach this modest 11-room place, which has perfectly acceptable bedrooms with external bath.

Hotel Regina *(☎ 0831 56 20 01, fax 0831 56 38 83, Via Cavour 5)* Singles/doubles/triples with bath €51.70/77.50/97. This is a conveniently central, mid-range hotel. Prices include breakfast.

There are two top-end hotels, quite different in character from each other.

Hotel Majestic *(☎ 0831 59 79 41, fax 0831 52 40 71, ⓔ reception@hotel-majestic.net, Corso Umberto I 151)* Singles/doubles with bath €82.70/108.50. Convenient for the train station, it's altogether more comfortable than the dreary concrete exterior would suggest and a particularly good deal at weekends, when rates fall by 20%.

Grande Albergo Internazionale *(☎ 0831 52 34 73, fax 0831 52 34 76, ⓔ gh.internazionale@libero.net, Viale Regina Margherita 23)* Singles/doubles with bath from €85.20/103.30. Built for English merchants on their way to and from Bombay and the Raj, this early 19th-century palace is now a luxury hotel with an excellent restaurant and great views over the inner harbour.

Places to Eat

There are several reasonable but uninspiring takeaways and restaurants on and just off Corso Garibaldi.

Passers through rarely reach these two recommendations.

La Bruschetta *(☎ 0347 464 05 22, Via Colonne 30)* Full meals around €20. Open Tues-Sun. Tucked away behind the remains of the column marking the end of the Appian Way, the service may be a mite gruff-and-ready at this family restaurant but, as you'll discover, the food more than compensates.

La Lanterna *(☎ 0831 22 40 26, Via Tarantini 14-18)* Full meals around €25. Open Tues-Sun. Food and ambience are altogether more sophisticated within this restored 15th-century palazzo and its delightful garden. Established over 40 years ago, La Lanterna also carries an impressive list of local wines.

For supplies for the boat trip, stock up at the colourful fresh food ***market***, held every morning Monday to Saturday on Piazza Mercato, just behind the post office.

Getting There & Away

Air From Papola Casale, Brindisi's small airport, there are internal flights to/from Rome, Naples, Milan, Bologna and Pisa.

Bus STP buses connect Brindisi with Ostuni and towns throughout the Penisola Salentina. Most leave from Via Bastioni Carlo V, in front of the train station. FSE buses serving local towns also leave from here.

Marozzi runs to Rome (Stazione Tiburtina; €30–32.60, nine hours, four daily), leaving from Viale Arno. Appia Travel (☎ 0831 52 16 84), on the waterfront at Viale Regina Margherita 8–9, sells tickets.

Train Brindisi is on the main FS train line. It has regular local services to Bari (€5.70), Lecce (€2.35) and Taranto (€3.35). Other destinations include Bologna (€39.25, 8¼ hours), Milan (€48.10, 9½ hours), Naples (€23.40, 6¼ hours) and Rome (€32.10, six hours).

Car & Motorcycle For the new ferry terminal, follow signs for Costa Morena from the autostrada. Allow plenty of time to board your ferry.

Boat Ferries, all of which take vehicles and have snack bars or restaurants, leave Brindisi for Greek destinations including Corfu (10 to 15 hours), Igoumenitsa (nine to 12 hours), Patras (15 to 20 hours) and the Ionian Islands. From Patras there is a bus to Athens. Boats also service Albania (daily) and Turkey (seasonal).

Most ferry companies operate only in summer. All have offices at Costa Morena (the new port), and the major ones also have offices in town. There's a €10.40 port tax. Fares generally increase by up to 40% on peak travel days in July and August (we list low season, one-way fares).

Hellenic Mediterranean Lines (☎ 0831 52 85 31, Town Office at Corso Garibaldi 8) To Corfu, Igoumenitsa and Patras (Apr-Oct) and the Ionian Islands (July & Aug). Deck class €26.35; poltrona €37.20; bed in shared cabin €49.05. The largest and most reliable of the lines, Hellenic Mediterranean accepts Eurail and InterRail passes, entitling you to travel free in deck class (paying a €15 supplement during Jul & Aug). If you intend to use your pass, it is recommended that you reserve in advance in high summer. Out of season, go to the town office since the port one may not be staffed outside high season.

Blue Star Ferries (☎ 0831 54 81 15, Town Office on Corso Garibaldi) To/from Igoumenitsa, mostly via Corfu. Deck class from €30; cabin berth from €64.60. Daily sailings year-round. To/from Patras. Deck class €30; poltrona €40; cabin berth €57.30. Daily sailings Apr-Sept, three times weekly Oct-Mar.

Fragline (☎ 0831 54 85 40, Town Office at Via Spalato 31) To Corfu and Igoumenitsa. Deck class €21.70; poltrona €31; cabin berth €40.30. Ferries from Apr-Sept.

Italian Ferries (☎ 0831 59 08 40, Town Office at Corso Garibaldi 96–98) To/from Vlore (Valona; in Albania). Fares €67.25. Daily ferries.

Med Link Lines (☎ 0831 52 76 67, Town Office on Corso Garibaldi) To Greece and to Cesme (Turkey; bi-weekly car ferry, summer only). Deck class €51.75; poltrona €62; cabin berth €98.25.

Check in at least two hours before departure or you risk losing your reservation (a strong possibility in the high season).

At the time of writing, Hellenic Mediterranean Line's fares for vehicles to Greece were €6.75 to €20.15 for motorcycles, €25 to €47.75 for cars and €70.75 to €107 for minibuses and caravans. Bicycles are usually carried free. Several companies offer travellers with camper vans the option of paying deck class and sleeping in their vehicles on the open deck.

Getting Around

A free minibus operated by Il Servicio Portabagagli – this may well be an interim measure – transports travellers who already have a boat ticket between the old ferry terminal and the new one at Costa Morena. At the time of writing, the only other way to cover the 7km of road from train station to terminal was to take a long walk or a taxi, which should set you back between €13 and €15.50.

LECCE

postcode 73100 • pop 100,150

Baroque architecture too often tumbles over the top but never in Lecce. Here, the style is so refined and particular to the city that the Italians call it *barocco leccese* (Lecce Baroque). The local stone actually encourages extravagance; it's particularly malleable yet soon after being quarried it hardens, making it the perfect building and sculpting material.

A centre of learning, Lecce recalls Montpellier in France or Salamanca in Spain, fellow university towns with deep roots, style, grace – and plenty of student cafes and bars. Convenient for both the Adriatic and Ionian Seas, the town makes an agreeable base for exploring the Penisola Salentina.

History

The original settlement was overrun in the 3rd century BC by the Romans, who named it Lupiae. From this period are the remains of an imposing amphitheatre, in Piazza Sant' Oronzo, and a Roman theatre. Ruled in turn by Byzantines, Normans and Swabians, the city came into its own between the 16th and 18th centuries, when it was embellished with splendid religious buildings and secular palaces.

Orientation

The train station is about 1km south-west of Lecce's historic centre. The town centre's twin main squares are Piazza Sant'Oronzo and Piazza del Duomo, linked by pedestrian Corso Vittorio Emanuele. From the station, walk straight ahead along Viale Oronzo Quarta, which becomes Via B Cairoli, then bear left into Viale Paladini.

Information

Tourist Offices The APT office (☎ 0832 24 80 92) is at Corso Vittorio Emanuele 24. It opens 10.30am to 1pm Monday to Friday, and 5pm to 7.30pm Wednesday and Friday.

There's a CTS travel agency, offering youth fare bargains, at Via G Palmieri 89.

Money You'll find several banks on and around Piazza Sant'Oronzo.

Post & Communications The main post office is on Piazza Libertini, just east of Lecce's castle. There is a Telecom office at Via Oberdan 13.

Chatwin Netcafe (☎ 0832 27 78 59), at Via Isabella Castriota 8, occupies an 18th-century palazzo and is much more than another log-on local. Named after Bruce Chatwin, the travel writer who died tragically young, this friendly place lays on a selection of the international press, good coffee and a travel library – including a number of Lonely Planet titles. It opens 4pm to at least midnight Tuesday to Sunday (and also from around 10am to 1pm in summer) and charges €2.60 an hour.

Medical Services Ospedale Vito Fazzi (hospital; ☎ 0832 66 11 11) is on Via San Cesario, 2km south of the centre on the road to Gallipoli.

Basilica della Santa Croce

Little can prepare you for the opulence of the most celebrated example of Lecce Baroque *(Via Umberto I; open 8am-1pm & 5pm-7pm daily)*. Throughout the 16th and 17th centuries, a team of artists worked to decorate the building and its extraordinarily ornate facade, divided by a broad balcony supported by 13 caryatids and fantastic figures. The interior is more conventionally Renaissance and definitely deserves a look if you can recover from the impact of the exterior. Giuseppe Zimbalo also left his mark in the former Convento dei Celestini just north of the basilica, which is nowadays the **Palazzo del Governo**, the headquarters of local government.

Piazza del Duomo

Although it fails to rival the splendour of the Basilica della Santa Croce, the Baroque feast continues in Piazza del Duomo. The almost unassuming 12th-century **cathedral** *(☎ 0832 30 85 57; open 7am-9pm daily)* was completely restored in Baroque style by Giuseppe Zimbalo, who was also responsible for the 70m-high **bell tower**. Also in the piazza is the 15th-century **Palazzo Vescovile** (Episcopal Palace), reconstructed in 1632, with a beautiful 1st-floor loggia. On the western side of the square is the **Seminario** *(seminary; open 9am-noon Mon, Tues & Thurs)*, designed by Giuseppe Cino and completed in 1709. Its elegant facade features two levels of windows balanced by a fine portal.

LECCE

PLACES TO STAY
- 19 Hotel Risorgimento
- 31 Centro Storico B&B
- 36 Grand Hotel
- 37 Hotel Cappello

PLACES TO EAT
- 4 Caffè Paisiello
- 7 Asian Shop Center
- 10 Dolomiti
- 11 Ristorante da Guido e Figli
- 14 Market
- 16 Caffè Alvino
- 20 Lu Laurieddhu
- 23 Valentina
- 34 La Capannina

OTHER
- 1 Chiesa di SS Nicolò e Cataldo
- 2 Porta Napoli
- 3 STP Bus Station
- 5 CTS Travel Agency
- 6 Chatwin Netcafe
- 8 Palazzo del Governo (Convento dei Celestini)
- 9 Basilica della Santa Croce
- 12 Telecom Office
- 13 Post Office
- 15 Castle
- 17 Colonna di Sant'Oronzo
- 18 Roman Amphitheatre
- 21 Chiesa di Sant'Irene
- 22 APT Office
- 24 Chiesa di Santa Chiara
- 25 Roman Theatre
- 26 Cathedral
- 27 Palazzo Vescovile
- 28 Seminario
- 29 Porto Rudiae
- 30 Chiesa del Rosario
- 32 Chiesa di San Matteo
- 33 FSE Bus Station
- 35 Museo Provinciale
- 38 Local Buses to Centre

Churches & Other Sights

Peek into the patios of the old quarter, richly decorated with scrolls of sculpted masonry, both geometric and floral, each one a private delight.

On Corso Vittorio Emanuele, the interior of 17th-century **Chiesa di Sant'Irene** *(open 8am-11am & 4pm-6pm Mon-Sat)* boasts a magnificent pair of mirror-image Baroque altarpieces, squaring up to each other across the transept and outshining the relatively subdued main reredos. Other Baroque churches of interest include the last work of Giuseppe Zimbalo, **Chiesa del Rosario** *(Via G Libertini)*; the **Santa Chiara** *(Piazza Vittorio Emanuele)*, its every niche a swirl of twisting columns and ornate statuary; and, 200m to its south, the **Chiesa di San Matteo** *(Piazza Vittorio Emanuele)*. The **Chiesa di SS Nicolò e Cataldo** *(Via San Nicola, along from the Porta Napoli gate)* was built by the Normans in 1180 and rebuilt in 1716 by the prolific Cino, who retained the Romanesque rose window and portal.

Roman Remains

Well below the level of Piazza Sant'Oronzo is the 2nd-century-AD **Roman amphitheatre**, discovered in the 1930s. Nearby rises the **Colonna di Sant'Oronzo**, one of the two columns that marked the end of the Via Appia at Brindisi. Donated to the city by the burghers of Brindisi in thanks to Lecce's patron saint for relieving the town of the plague in 1666, it was subsequently topped by a disproportionately small statue of the good St Oronzo himself.

Within the small **Roman theatre** *(☎ 0832 24 61 09, Via Ammirati; admission €2.60; open 10am-1pm daily)*, also uncovered in the 1930s, is an equally small museum, with some wonderfully preserved frescoes and mosaics, transferred from local sites.

Museo Provinciale

The museum *(☎ 0832 24 70 25, Viale Gallipoli; free)* is still undergoing extensive renovations. Sad, that, since it has an impressive collection of Roman artefacts and treasures from later periods, including, in particular, some fine glasswork from Murano.

Places to Stay

Camping Torre Rinalda *(☎ 0832 38 21 62, fax 0832 38 21 65, Litoranea Salentina 73)* Sites for up to 3 people, tent & car €17.10-33.10. Near the sea at Torre Rinalda, this camp site's accessible from Lecce by STP bus.

Centro Storico B&B *(☎/fax 0832 24 27 27, ⓔ bed_breakfast.lecce@libero.it, Via Vignes 2b)* Singles/doubles with bath €23.25/41.35. Newly established in a 16th-century palazzo, it's a place with considerable character and comfort. Rooms have TV, fridge, air-con and private balcony – a real bargain.

Hotel Cappello *(☎ 0832 30 88 81, fax 0832 30 15 35, Via Montegrappa 4)* Singles/doubles with bath €27.40/44. A short walk from the station and offering both street and off-road parking (€5 per night), this hotel is great value for money.

Grand Hotel *(☎ 0832 30 94 05, fax 0832 30 98 91, Viale Oronzo Quarta 28)* Singles/doubles/triples with bath €41.40/77.50/103.30. Here's an excellent medium-range choice, cosy and welcoming with delightful early-20th-century decor. Prices include breakfast.

Hotel Risorgimento *(☎ 0832 24 21 25, fax 0832 24 55 71, Via Imperatore Augusto 19)* Singles/doubles/triples with bath €46.50/82.70/98.20. Hotel Risorgimento is a good medium-range hotel with very pleasant bedrooms. Prices include breakfast.

Places to Eat

Eating in Lecce is a pleasure and needn't be expensive.

Ristorante Da Guido e Figli *(☎ 0832 30 58 68, Via XXV Luglio 14)* Full meals €13-16. The antipasto buffet (€4.20) at this deep cavern of a place, with its discrete, vaulted dining areas, makes a great start to a great meal.

La Capannina *(☎ 0832 30 41 59, Via B Cairoli 13)* Tourist menu €9.30, full meals €13-16. Open Tues-Sun. A friendly, family place with another great antipasto buffet of over 20 items. Warmly recommended.

Dolomiti *(☎ 0832 24 63 84, Viale A Costa 5)* Brash Dolomiti reckons it's all things to all people, billing itself as pizzeria, rosticceria, restaurant – even 'tearoom'. What's certain is that it's great for a last, late-night drink and that its €8.30 daily menu is one of Lecce's best bargains.

Lu Laurieddhu *(☎ 0832 24 70 81, Corso Vittorio Emanuele 48)* Pizzas €2.60-5.20, full meals from €10. This is a cheerful, moderately priced establishment with a relaxing garden dining area.

Asian Shop Center *(☎ 0832 24 07 24, Via Principe di Savoia 35)* Dishes from €2.60. Open 7pm-11.30pm. Fancy something exotic after all that pasta? The Asian Shop Center is that rarity in southern Italy – a genuine Indian takeaway.

There are many fine cafes to chose from around town.

Caffè Alvino *(Piazza Sant'Oronzo 30)* You know where you are in this place as they dust a large capital 'A' for Alvino on the froth of your cappuccino. It's a good place to sample *rustica*, a tasty local confection of puff pastry, mozzarella cheese and tomato.

Caffè Paisiello *(☎ 0832 30 14 04, Via G Palmieri 72)* Open Thurs-Tues. Sample its pastries or ice cream as you sip your chosen drink.

Valentina *(Via Petronelli 3)* This delicatessen has a rich selection of quality pastas, cheeses and local specialities.

There is a ***fresh produce market*** every morning Monday to Saturday on Piazza Libertini.

Getting There & Away

STP buses (☎ 0832 30 28 73) connect Lecce with towns throughout the Penisola Salentina, including Galatina and Santa Maria di Leuca, leaving from Via Adua.

FSE buses (☎ 0832 34 76 34) for towns including Gallipoli (€2.10, one hour, four daily), Otranto (€2.10, one hour, two daily) and Taranto (€4.65, two hours, frequent) leave from Via Torre del Parco.

There are frequent trains to Bari (€6.75, 1¾ hours) via Brindisi (€2.40, 40 minutes), and daily services to/from Rome (€32, seven hours) and Bologna (€46.30, 8½ hours). For Naples (€25.75, six hours), change in Caserta. FSE trains also depart from the main station for Taranto, Bari, Otranto, Gallipoli and Martina Franca.

Brindisi is 30 minutes away from Lecce by motorway and the S7 leads to Taranto.

Getting Around

The historic centre of Lecce is easily and better seen on foot. Bus Nos 1, 2 and 4 run from the train station to Viale Marconi. Ask the driver to drop you near Piazza Sant'Oronzo.

AROUND LECCE

The small town of **Galatina**, 18km south of Lecce, was a Greek colony up until the Middle Ages, and the Greek language and customs were sustained until the early 20th century. It is almost the only place where the ritual of tarantulism – a frenzied dance meant to rid the body of the poison from a tarantula bite – is still practised. The tarantella folk dance evolved from it and, each year on the feast day of St Peter and St Paul (29 June), the ritual is performed at the (now deconsecrated) church dedicated to the saints.

The town's gem is its late-14th-century **Basilica di Santa Caterina d'Alessandria** *(open 7am-noon & 4.30pm-8pm daily in summer, 7am-noon & 3.30pm-6pm daily in winter)*, one of Apulia's rare examples of Gothic architecture. The earlier Romanesque facade has three intricate portals and a lovely rose window. But hold your breath for the interior: its five naves and Gothic pointed arches are almost entirely covered in frescoes – scenes from the Old and New Testaments and the lives of the Madonna and Santa Caterina d'Alessandria. Some of them are thought to be by Giotto's pupils, recalling frescoes at the Basilica di San Francesco in Assisi. And don't omit the 15th-century cloister, also frescoed and attached to the church.

STP buses run between Galatina and Lecce.

OTRANTO

Otranto, Italy's easternmost port and long a base of Byzantine power was, in its time, a major point of departure for merchants, pilgrims and crusaders heading for the Orient and the Holy Land. In 1480 the Turks, in a brief incursion, massacred the inhabitants at what is known as the Sack of Otranto.

Otranto makes a good place for a coastal tour of the Penisola Salentina. This is much easier if you've got your own transport but local bus companies manage to link all the towns on the peninsula. The town, charming out of season, gets overrun in high summer, primarily with Italian holiday-makers.

The tourist office (☎ 0836 80 14 36) is on Piazza Castello, facing the castle.

Things to See

First built by the Normans in the 11th century and subsequently subjected to a face-lift or two, the magnificent Romanesque **cathedral** *(open 8am-noon & 3pm-7pm daily in summer, 8am-noon & 3pm-5pm daily in winter)* is a forest of slender pillars and carved capitals. The walls bear well-preserved Byzantine frescoes, while underfoot is a vast restored 12th-century floor mosaic occupying the whole of the nave. Depicting the tree of life and other scenes of myth and legend, both Christian and pagan, it's a vibrant masterpiece. Rex Arturis (King Arthur as he is more commonly known nowadays) is depicted on horseback near the top of the tree.

In the chapel to the right of the altar is a bizarre sight. Its walls are lined with glass cases packed tight with skulls and bones, the remains of the victims (said to be 800) of the Sack of Otranto.

Just south of the cathedral is a small **diocesan museum** *(open 10am-noon & 4pm-8pm daily in summer, 10am-noon & 3pm-6pm daily in winter)*.

Within tiny **Chiesa di San Pietro** are more vivid Byzantine frescoes. If, as is probable, you find the church closed, call by the guardian's house at Piazza del Populo 1, some 30m away.

The Aragonese **castle** *(Piazza Castello; free except when there's an exhibition; open 9am-1pm Mon-Fri)*, at the eastern edge of town beside the port, is typical of the squat, thick-walled forts you'll find in coastal towns throughout Apulia. Built in the late 15th century after the Turkish massacre, it is characterised by cylindrical towers that widen towards the base.

Places to Stay & Eat

There are several camp sites in or near Otranto and a dozen or so hotels in the area.

Hydrusa *(☎ 0836 80 12 55, Via del Porto)* Sites per person/tent/car €5.20/6.75/1.10. This camp site near the port is fairly basic but, wow, what a price.

Hotel Bellavista *(☎/fax 0836 80 10 58, Via Vittorio Emanuele 18)* Singles/doubles from €46.50/62, in Aug from €72.30/93. Only the promenade separates this pleasant hotel, just outside the old city boundary, from the seashore. Prices include breakfast.

La Duchesca *(☎ 0836 80 12 04, Piazza Castello)* Pizzas from €2.50. This is a bright place for a simple meal or a drink, on the square with the castle looming before you.

Getting There & Away

Otranto can be reached from Lecce by FSE train or bus. A Marozzi bus runs daily to/from Rome via Lecce and Brindisi.

Between July and mid-September, a hydrofoil (€44 to €54.25) scuds across the Adriatic to Corfu (Greece) in 2¾ hours. For both hydrofoil and Marozzi bus information and reservations, go to Ellade Viaggi (☎ 0836 80 15 78, W www.elladeviaggi.it) at the port.

AROUND OTRANTO

The road south from Otranto takes you along a wild coastline. The land here is rocky, and when the wind is up you can see why it is largely treeless. This is no Costa Azzura or Amalfi Coast but it gives you a feeling rare in Italy – that of being well off the beaten tourist track. Many of the towns here started life as Greek settlements and a few of the older folk still speak Greek. There are few monuments to be seen but the occasional solitary tower appears, facing out to sea. When you reach **Santa Maria di Leuca**, you've hit the bottom of the heel of Italy and the dividing line between the Adriatic and Ionian Seas. Here, as in other small Salentine towns, summer sees an influx of Italians in search of seaside relaxation. The Ionian side of Penisola Salentina in particular is spattered with reasonable beaches. There are few cheap hotels in the area but camp sites abound along the coast.

GALLIPOLI

postcode 73014 • pop 20,500

Jutting into the Ionian Sea 39km south-west of Lecce, the picturesque old town of Gallipoli is actually an island connected to the mainland and modern city by a bridge. An important fishing centre, it has a history of strong-willed independence, being the last Salentine settlement to succumb to the Normans in the 11th century. The IAT office (☎ 0833 26 25 29) is at Piazza Imbriani 8, within the old town, just over the bridge.

The entrance to the medieval island-town is guarded by an Angevin **castle**. Just opposite, below the ramp leading to the island, is a fish market that makes up in variety for its small size. Treat yourself to a dozen raw sea urchins, split for you on the spot, for €2.60.

At the heart of the old town is the 17th-century Baroque **cathedral** *(☎ 0833 26 19 87, Via Antonietta de Pace; open only during services)*, adorned with paintings by local artists. A little farther west, the small **Museo Civico** *(☎ 0833 26 42 24, Via Antonietta de Pace)* was closed for renovations at the time of writing. It contains a mixed bag of ancient artefacts, paintings and other odds and ends. The old quarter's main pleasure, however, is simply to wander its maze of narrow lanes or take a walk around the perimeter with the sea constantly in sight.

Back over the bridge and just in the modern part of town is the **Fontana Antica**. Reconstructed in the 16th century from a Greek original, its much-weathered sculptured figures tell a steamy tale of incest and bestiality.

Hotel Al Pescatore *(☎/fax 0833 26 36 56, Riviera Colombo 39)* Singles/doubles/triples €44/67.20/82.70, compulsory half-board in Aug €67.20 per person. The pick of the old town hotels, Al Pescatore has 16 spacious, modern rooms, some with views of the port. Prices include breakfast. It also runs a good restaurant, specialising in the freshest of fresh fish, where a full meal costs €12-20. The decor has a marine theme but relatively tastefully so – not a limply hung fishing net or plastic lobster in sight.

Trattoria La Tonnara *(☎ 0833 26 10 58, Via Garibaldi 7)* Full meals €15-20. Near the cathedral, La Tonnara is one of several restaurants in the old town where you can eat well. In addition to the a la carte menu, it does pizzas over wood (in the evenings only).

FSE buses and trains link Gallipoli to Lecce.

TARANTO

postcode 74100 • pop 245,000

In an ideally protected location, the port of Taranto has always looked to the sea. Founded in the 7th century BC by exiles from Sparta, Taras, as it was then known, became one of the wealthiest and most important colonies of Magna Graecia. At the height of its power, the city was home to some 300,000 people. The Romans, who conquered it in the 3rd century BC, changed its name to Tarentum, yet Greek laws and customs were maintained.

Taranto is Italy's second most important naval port after La Spezia, and during WWII the bulk of the nation's fleet was bottled up there by the British. One of the city's more esoteric claims to fame is that it is alleged to be the point where the first cat landed on European shores.

Orientation

Taranto neatly splits into three. The old town is on a tiny island, lodged between the port and train station to the north-west and the new city to the south-east. The more expensive hotels, APT office and banks are in the grid-patterned new city.

The drive into the centre of town from the state highway, particularly approaching from the east, is a long, dull one. Simply follow the familiar *centro* signs; Lungomare Vittorio Emanuele III makes a good point of reference.

Information

Tourist Office Taranto's APT office (☎ 099 453 23 92) is at Corso Umberto I 113. It opens 9am to 1pm and 5pm to 7pm Monday to Friday (4.30pm to 6.30pm winter), 9am to noon on Saturday.

Post & Communications The main post office is on Lungomare Vittorio Emanuele III. If you need to make a phonecall, there's a Telecom office on Via d'Aquino.

You can log on at Chiocciolin@ (☎/fax 099 453 80 51, Corso Umberto I 85), open 9am to 1pm and 4.30pm to 9pm Tuesday to Saturday and Monday afternoon.

Medical Services Ospedale S Annunziata (hospital; ☎ 099 458 51 11) is on Via Bruno. Follow Lungomare Vittorio Emanuele III and turn left at Via de Noto. The Polizia Municipale headquarters (☎ 099 732 32 04) are on Piazza Dante 6.

Dangers & Annoyances You need to stay alert in Taranto, particularly in the old town, which can be dodgy after dark.

Città Vecchia

Taranto's old town is seriously run-down and dilapidated. Large areas are like a ghost town, with windows shuttered tightly and doors bricked up. Only the washing flapping in the breeze confirms that the occasional house is still occupied. Some efforts have been made to renovate the town's once splendid palazzos and churches, though too often measures seem limited to simply sticking up an informative plaque. The **Castello Aragonese**, at the island's southern extreme, an interesting enough structure completed in 1492, is occupied by the Italian navy and inaccessible to visitors.

The 11th-century **cathedral** *(Via del Duomo)* is one of Apulia's oldest Romanesque buildings. Remodelled in the 18th century, its three-nave interior is divided by 16 ancient marble columns supporting Romanesque and Byzantine capitals. Its fine Baroque Cappella di San Cataldo is decorated with frescoes and inlaid marble. The whole cathedral is dedicated to San Cataldo, Taranto's patron saint.

Visit Via Cariati's **fish markets**, where all the rich variety of the morning's catch is on display. Taranto has been famous since antiquity for what it draws from the sea, in particular its shellfish and its gorgeously fleshy oysters.

Museo Nazionale

Taranto's archaeological museum *(☎ 099 458 17 15, Corso Vittorio Emanuele II; free; open 8.30am-7.30pm daily)*, one of the most important in Italy, temporarily occupies the Palazzo Pantaleo in the old town. Here, a significant selection of the extensive collection is on display until renovations on its Piazza Garibaldi premises are complete.

Special Events

Le Feste di Pasqua (Holy Week) in Taranto is a time of high emotion, as in many Italian towns. On Holy Thursday there is the Procession of the Addolorata and on Good Friday there is the Procession of the Mysteries, when statues representing the Passion of Christ are carried around the town.

Places to Stay

Hotel Sorrentino *(☎ 099 470 74 56, Piazza Fontana 7)* Singles/doubles €18.10/25.90, with bath €23.25/36.20. At the northern end of the island, this is a reliable budget place.

Hotel Pisani *(☎ 099 453 40 87, fax 099 470 75 93, Via Cavour 43)* Singles/doubles €20.70/38.75, with bath €23.75/45.50. Safe and set back down a quiet side road in the new city, this is another value-for-money budget option.

Hotel Plaza *(☎ 099 459 07 75, fax 099 459 06 75, Via d'Aquino 46)* Singles/doubles with bath and air-con €62/82.70. Also in the new city, Hotel Plaza ranks among the best of the medium-range places.

Places to Eat

Birreria *(☎ 099 459 37 58, Via d'Aquino 27)* Meals €2.50-15. Here you can pick from self-service, pizza or the full menu.

Trattoria da Mimmo *(☎ 099 459 37 33, Via Giovinazzi 18)* Full meals around €13. Open Thurs-Tues. It serves up good food at very reasonable prices.

Trattoria al Gatto Rosso *(☎ 099 452 98 75, Via Cavour 2)* Full meals around €13. Open Tues-Sun. This is another popular no-nonsense place to dine.

Ristorante Gambrinus *(☎ 099 471 65 52, Via Fontana 61)* Mains €6.20-9.30. Open Thurs-Tues. This bustling restaurant is strongly recommended. With the fish markets only a cast away, how can you go wrong? Its terrace overlooks the port, and it serves the freshest fish and seafood at moderate prices. Go for the house menu at €15.50, including as much wine as you want to knock back.

Ristorante al Gambero *(☎ 099 471 11 90, Piazzale Democrate)* Full meals around €25. Also overlooking the port, and the old city too, Al Gambero, its walls bedecked with certificates of merit, offers fish and seafood as fresh as Ristorante Gambrinus but in more elegant surroundings.

There's a ***fresh produce market*** every Monday to Saturday morning on Piazza Castello, just west of the Canale Navigabile.

Getting There & Around

FSE buses connect Taranto with Martina Franca and Bari (leaving from Piazza Castello), as well as Ostuni (leaving from Via Magnaghi, in the east of the new city) and smaller towns in the area. Infrequent SITA buses leave from Piazza Castello for Matera (stopping at Castellaneta) and Metaponto. Chiruzzi buses also serve Metaponto. STP and FSE buses connect Taranto with Lecce.

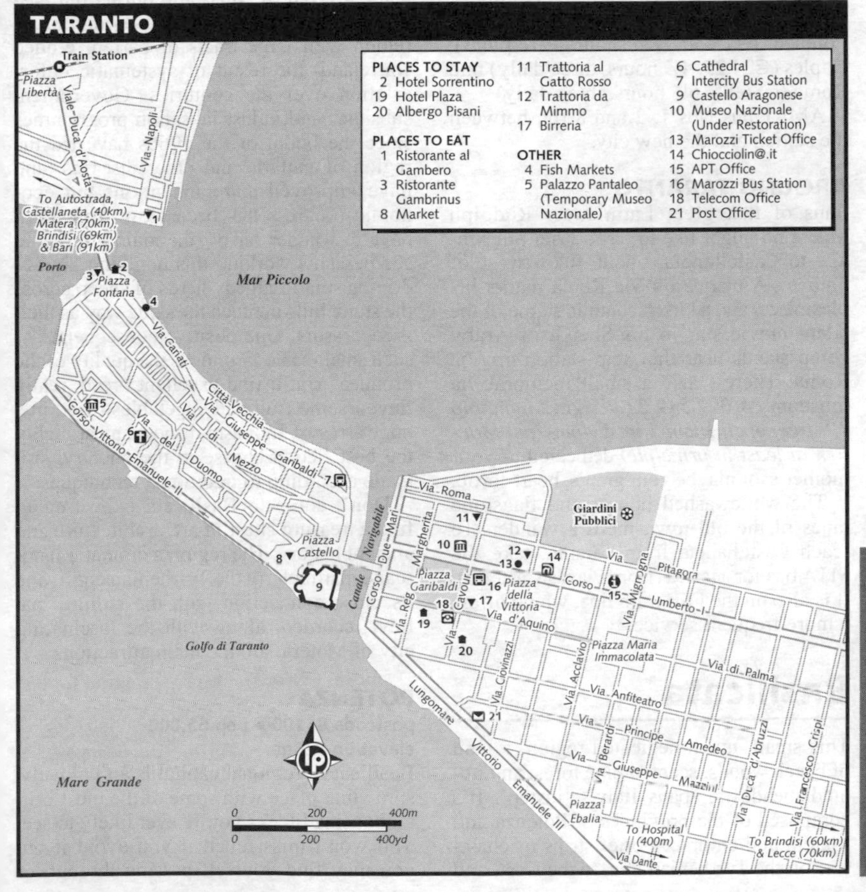

APULIA

Marozzi (☎ 099 459 40 89) has express services to/from Rome's Stazione Tiburtina (€33.60, six hours, three daily), leaving from Via Cavour. Marino Autolinee does a through-the-night run to Turin (€44) via Milan (€37.75). Autolinee Miccolis runs three buses daily to/from Naples (€13.45, four hours) via Potenza (€7.25, two hours) and Salerno (€11.90, 3¼ hours). The ticket office for all three companies is at Corso Umberto I 67.

Trains (both FS and FSE) connect Taranto with Brindisi (€3.40, 1¼ hours, seven daily), Bari (€5.70, 1¼ hours, frequent), Martina Franca (€2.25, 45 minutes, three daily) and Alberobello, as well as Potenza (€15.39, 2¼ hours, frequent), Naples (€24.25, 4½ hours, three daily) and Rome (€36.85, 6½ hours, three daily).

AMAT bus Nos 1, 2 and 8 run between the station and the new city.

AROUND TARANTO

Fans of that great Latin lover Rudolph Valentino might like to pay a brief pilgrimage to **Castellaneta**, about 40km west of Taranto. A plaque on Via Roma marks his birthplace, and a kitsch ceramic statue of the silent movie star in his Sheikh of Araby getup stands near the Agip station on Via Roma. There's also a small memorabilia **museum** *(☎ 099 849 23 98, Via Municipio 19; free; open 10am-1pm & 4pm-7pm Mon-Fri, at least in principle)* dedicated to your mother's, or maybe your gran's, heart-throb.

The whitewashed houses and flagstone lanes of the old town merit a wander. To reach Castellaneta from Taranto, take the SITA bus for Matera (from Piazza Castello). It is also on the FSE train line, which offers a more frequent service.

Basilicata

This small, much-neglected region, a land of beech woods, scented pine forest and upland meadows, spans Italy's 'instep'. It's composed of the provinces of Potenza and Matera and embraces brief strips of coastline on the Tyrrhenian Sea, to the west, and the Ionian Sea, off its eastern shore. Basilicata, while no longer the desolate, malaria-ridden land of poverty-stricken peasants so powerfully described by Carlo Levi in his novel *Christ Stopped at Eboli*, retains a strong sense of isolation and remains one of Italy's poorest regions. Oil from the mountainous area south of Potenza – the biggest reservoir of its kind in mainland Western Europe – recently came on stream. While Basilicata will never be Italy's Kuwait, there's every hope that revenue generated here will help to turn the region's fortunes.

Known to the Romans as Lucania (a name revived by Mussolini during the Fascist period), Basilicata is a mountainous region with large tracts of barren, eroded wasteland, the result of systematic deforestation over the centuries. Government subsidies and industrialisation programmes since the boom of the 1960s have rid the region of malaria and other diseases, and have improved communications but economic progress has been slow. You don't have to wander far off the main arteries to see peasants working this ungiving land or driving small raggedy herds of sheep across the stony hills in much the same way as their predecessors. One positive consequence of such small-scale farming is the quality of the produce. You'll find excellent bread, really flavoursome fruit and vegetables (used in a huge array of antipasto dishes) and arguably the best ricotta cheese in the country, still made according to traditional techniques.

Don't come to Basilicata expecting to find a treasure chest of art, architecture and ancient history. The region's dramatic landscape, particularly the Tyrrhenian coast, and its close connection with the culture that Levi recorded, along with the fascinating city of Matera, are the main attractions.

POTENZA

postcode 85100 • pop 65,000
elevation 825m

Basilicata's regional capital is an unlovely, sprawling place with some of the most brutal housing blocks you're ever likely to see. You won't miss much if you avoid it but you may find yourself passing through or

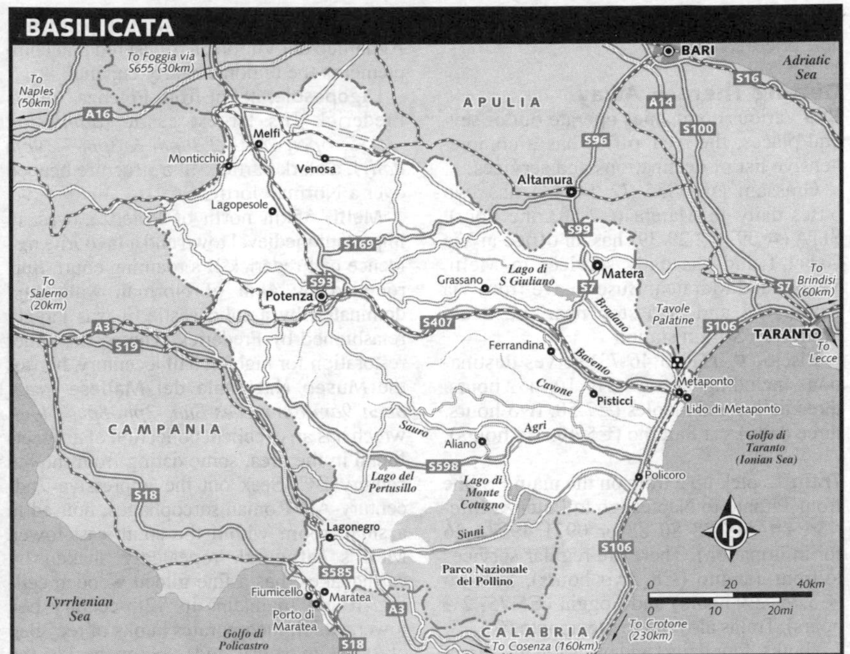

even overnighting here. Badly damaged in repeated earthquakes, Potenza has lost most of its medieval buildings. Its altitude makes the town cloyingly hot in summer and it can be bitterly cold in winter.

The centre of town straggles east to west across a high ridge. To the south lie the main FS and Ferrovie Appulo-Lucane train stations, connected to the centre by local buses.

Information

The APT office (☎/fax 0971 27 44 85), at Via Cavour 15, opens 8am to 2pm Monday to Friday, plus 4pm to 7pm Tuesday and Thursday.

The post office is on Via IV Novembre. You can find telephones outside the neighbouring INPS building.

Things to See

In the old centre of town a couple of modest churches remain, plus the **cathedral**, originally erected in the 12th century but rebuilt in the 18th. Elegant Via Pretoria, flanked by a boutique or two worthy of Milan, makes a pleasant traffic-free stroll. North of the town centre is the **Museo Archeologico Provinciale** (*☎ 0971 44 48 33, Via Ciccotti; free; open 9am-1pm Tues-Sun plus 4pm-7pm Tues-Fri*), which houses a collection of artefacts discovered in the region.

Places to Stay & Eat

Pensione Europa (*☎ 0971 3 40 14, Via Giacinto Albini 3*) Singles/doubles €15.50/26, doubles with bath €31. The welcome's fairly frosty but visitors don't check in here, the cheapest place in town, primarily for the smiles.

Grande Albergo Potenza (*☎/fax 0971 41 02 20, e albergo@libero.it. Corso 18 Agosto 46*) Singles/doubles with bath €72.50/98.25. This quality hotel adds a much-needed touch of style to the town.

Monticchio (*☎ 0971 2 48 80, Via Caserma Lucana 30*) Meals about €10. Open Mon-

Sat. Call in here for a tasty meal at a reasonable price.

Getting There & Away

Bus Various companies operate out of several places; the APT office has a comprehensive list of destinations and services.

Grassani (☎ 0835 72 14 43) has two buses daily to Matera (€2.50, one hour). SITA (☎ 0971 2 29 39) has an office at Via Gabet 1 and has daily services to Melfi, Venosa and Maratea. Buses leave from Via Appia 185 and also stop near the Scalo Inferiore FS train station.

Liscio (☎ 0971 5 46 73) serves destinations including Rome (€17.10, 4½ hours, three daily) and Naples (€7.50, two hours, three daily) via Salerno (€5.40, 1½ hours).

Train To pick up a train on the main FS line from Taranto to Naples, go to Potenza Inferiore (☎ 848 88 80 88 or 0971 49 72 26 for information). There are regular services to/from Taranto (€8, two hours), Salerno (€5.75, 2¼ hours) and Foggia (€5.75, 2½ hours). Trains also run to Metaponto (€5.75, 1¾ hours, four daily) and occasionally direct to Naples. To get to Matera (€3.35, one hour, frequent), change to a FAL bus at Ferrandina on the Metaponto line. For Bari (€6.25, three hours, three daily), use the Ferrovie Appulo–Lucane (☎ 0971 41 15 61) at the Potenza Superiore station.

Car & Motorcycle Potenza is connected to Salerno in the west by the A3, also called the E45 (take the signed E847 branch east near Sicignano). Metaponto lies south-east along the S407. For Matera, take the S407 and then turn north onto the S7 at Ferrandina.

NORTH OF POTENZA

The fast S93 highway, which sweeps northwards from Potenza, has drawn all but sparse local traffic from the old road, making the latter an ideal cycle route for exploring Basilicata's northern treasures.

The area is one of green valleys flanked by rolling hills. It's dotted with several interesting sites which, alas, are time consuming to explore without your own wheels. Here is the home of Basilicata's best wine, Aglianico del Vulture, a robust red that complements the region's hearty cuisine.

Lagopesole, 28km from Potenza, boasts Frederick II's largest castle *(admission €1.55; open 9am-12.30pm & 3pm-7.30pm daily)*, a stark barrack-like structure heaped over a Norman fortress.

Melfi, 55km north of Potenza, was an important medieval town and a favourite residence of Frederick II's roaming court. Surrounded by 4km of Norman walls and dominated by a solid castle, it was largely refashioned by Frederick. The castle, under restoration for nigh on half a century, houses the **Museo Nazionale del Malfese** *(free; open 9am-8pm Tues-Sun, 2pm-8pm Mon)*, which has an excellent collection of artefacts found in the area, some dating from the 8th century BC. Seek out the impressive 2nd-century-AD Roman sarcophagus, housed in a small room within the south-east tower. Melfi's **cathedral**, repeatedly shaken by earthquakes, has a fine gilded wooden ceiling. It still maintains its 12th-century bell tower, which incorporates hunks of recycled classical masonry and, up top beside the bells, a handsome pair of griffons, symbol of the town, picked out in darker stone.

Some 15km south-west of Melfi, the lakes at **Monticchio** are a popular summer recreation spot.

Venosa, about 20km east of Melfi, was once a thriving Roman colony, the birthplace of the Roman poet Quintus Horatius Flaccus, better known in English simply as Horace. At the north-eastern end of town, you can wander around the sparse remains of the original **Roman settlement** *(free; open 9am-1 hr before sunset Wed-Mon)*, which includes a bath complex and an amphitheatre. Next to the ruins – which are well documented in both Italian and English in a way that puts both Pompeii and Herculaneum to shame – is the **Abbazia della Santissima Trinità**, the most impressive Norman legacy in Basilicata. Within the complex are the abbey palazzo and a pair of churches, one never completed.

Venosa's 15th-century Aragonese castle, entered from Piazza Umberto I, the town's

Living in Matera's Sassi

Carlo Levi, the painter and writer, quotes his sister's reactions when passing through Matera on her way to visit him in Aliano, where he was exiled from 1935 to 1936 as punishment for his criticism of the Fascist regime. Describing the stone dwellings of Sasso Caveoso and Sasso Barisano as 'a schoolboy's idea of Dante's Inferno', she went on to say:

> The houses were open on account of the heat, and as I went by I could see into the caves, whose only light came in through the front doors. Some of them had no entrance but a trapdoor and ladder. In these dark holes with walls cut out of the earth I saw a few pieces of miserable furniture, beds, and some ragged clothes hanging up to dry. On the floor lay dogs, sheep, goats, and pigs. Most families have just one cave to live in and there they sleep all together; men, women, children, and animals. This is how twenty thousand people live.

She depicted children suffering from trachoma or:

> with the wizened faces of old men, their bodies reduced by starvation almost to skeletons, their heads crawling with lice and covered with scabs. Most of them had enormous, dilated stomachs, and faces yellow and worn with malaria.

main square, contains a small **archaeological museum** *(☎ 0972 3 60 95; open 9am-8pm Wed-Mon, 3pm-8pm Tues)*.

Hotel Orazio *(☎ 0972 3 11 35, fax 0972 3 14 64, Corso Vittorio Emanuele 142)* Singles/doubles with bath €36.20/49.10. Here you'll get high-ceilinged, graciously decorated rooms and an old-fashioned courtesy from the pair of grandmotherly ladies who run the hotel – anywhere else in Italy, you'd be paying half as much again. Highly recommended.

Melfi and Venosa can both be reached by bus from Potenza (see the Potenza Getting There & Away section earlier).

MATERA

postcode 75100 • pop 57,000
elevation 405m

Matera evokes powerful images of a poor, peasant culture, which first began to hew the city's famous cave houses in medieval times or earlier. Now a Unesco world heritage site, Matera was a troglodyte city of 20,000 until well after WWII, where people and animals slept together and where, despite an infant mortality rate of over 50%, a typical family cave sheltered an average of six children. Its famous *sassi* – buildings of tufa stone, half constructed, half-bored into the rock lining the twin ravines that slice through Matera – were home to more than 50% of the populace until the local government built new residential areas in the late 1950s and forcefully relocated the sassis' inhabitants.

The most striking account of how these people lived is given in Carlo Levi's *Christ Stopped at Eboli*. It took half a century and vast amounts of development money to eradicate malaria and starvation in Basilicata. Today people are returning to live in the sassi – but now it's a trend rather than a necessity.

Orientation

A short walk down Via Roma from the train and bus stations off Piazza Matteotti brings you to Piazza Vittorio Veneto, the pedestrianised heart of town. The two sassi ravines open up to its east and south-east.

Information

Tourist Offices The APT office (☎ 0835 33 19 83) is at Via De Viti De Marco 9, off Via Roma. It opens 9am to 1pm Monday to Saturday plus 4pm to 6.30pm Monday to Thursday. There are also three information kiosks run by the Comune di Matera (☎ 0835 24 12 60) on Via Madonna delle Virtù (in the sassi),

Piazza Matteotti and Via Lucana. Staffed only in summer, they're usually open 9.30am to 12.30pm and from about 4pm to 7pm daily.

The tourist offices can put you in contact with groups that provide guides to the sassi. Itinera (☎ 0835 26 32 59, ⓔ arttur@tin.it) organises guided tours in English. Another such organisation is Cooperativa Amici del Turista (☎ 338 599 67 14, Via Fiorentini 28–30, Ⓦ www.materaturistica.it). You will also probably be approached in the street by unofficial guides of unproven quality.

It's easy enough to find your own way around. Arm yourself with the map *Matera: Percorsi Turistici* (€1.30), which describes in English four well-signposted itineraries. It's also explicit enough to allow you to roam off-route. To be more fully documented, pick up a copy of the excellent multilingual *Sassi e Secoli* (Stones and Centuries; €13) by R Giura Longo. Both are available from Libreria dell'Arco, Via Ridola 37.

Post & Communications The main post office is on Via del Corso and the Telecom office is immediately to its west.

For Internet access, the vast Biblioteca Provinciale on Piazza Vittorio Veneto,

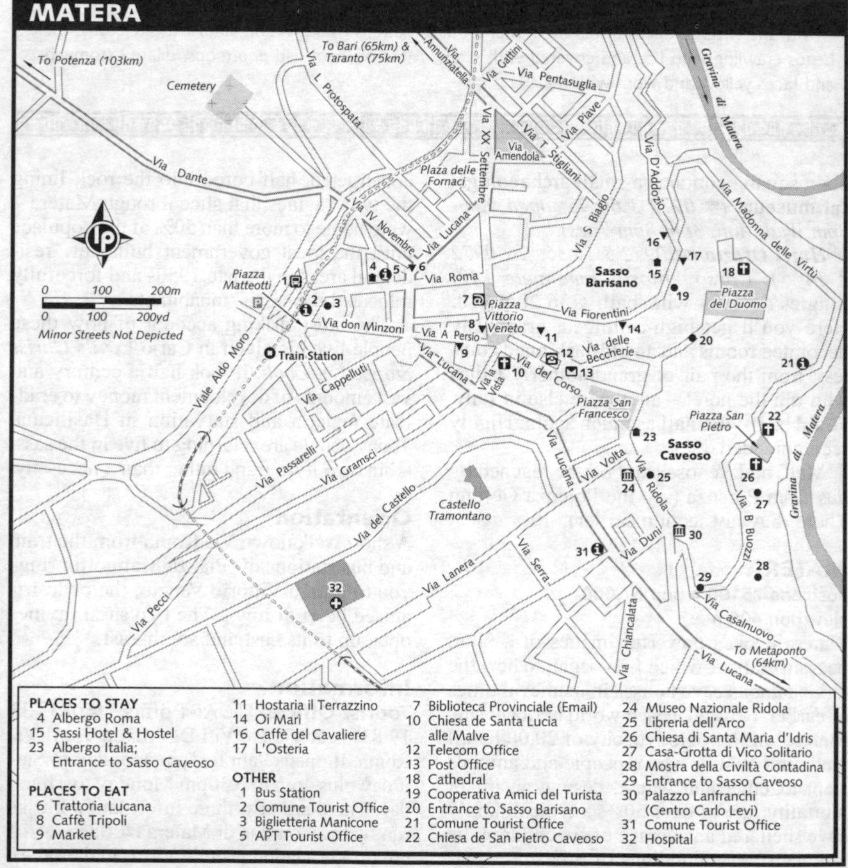

open 8.30am to 6.30pm Monday to Friday and 8.30am to 1.30pm Saturday, has one computer that operates with a Telecom phone card.

Medical Services The public hospital (☎ 0835 24 32 12) is on Via Lanera, south of the city centre. Alternatively, ring the Guardia Medica (☎ 0835 24 35 38).

The Sassi

The two Sassi areas, **Barisano** and **Caveoso**, had no electricity, running water or sewerage system until well into the 20th century. The oldest sassi are at the top of the ravine and the dwellings in the lower sections of the ravine, which seem the oldest, were in fact established this century. As space ran out in the 1920s, the population started moving into hand-hewn or natural caves.

The sassi zones are accessible from several points around the centre of Matera. There is an entrance just off Piazza Vittorio Veneto. Alternatively, take Via delle Beccherie to Piazza del Duomo and follow the tourist itinerary signs to enter either Barisano or Caveoso. Sasso Caveoso is also accessible from Via Ridola by the stairs next to Albergo Italia.

Caveoso is the more picturesque of the two sassi. Highlights include the **Chiesa de San Pietro Caveoso** *(Piazza San Pietro, Sasso Caveoso)*, plus the rock churches of **Santa Maria d'Idris** and **Santa Lucia alle Malve**, both with well-preserved Byzantine frescoes.

A couple of sassi have been refurnished as they were when the last inhabitants occupied them. There's the **Mostra della Civiltà Contadina** *(off Via B Buozzi; admission €0.60)*, and – better and well worth the extra fee – the **Casa-Grotta di Vico Solitario** *(off Via B Buozzi; admission €1.10)*, which has a guide sheet in English.

More and more of the sassi are being renovated and used as restaurants, gift shops and the like. In the outlying rock churches, the self-appointed guardians insist upon declaiming an automaton spiel in severely fractured English – and expect a backhander for this dubious service.

Town Centre

Recent excavations in Piazza Vittorio Veneto have yielded some remarkable discoveries. Beneath the square lie yet more ruins of Byzantine Matera, including a rock church with frescoes, a castle, a large cistern and numerous houses. You can gaze down from the piazza and visit part of the complex.

The relatively sedate exterior of the 13th-century Puglian-Romanesque **cathedral** *(Piazza del Duomo)* ill-prepares you for the neo-Baroque excess within, a clumsy 19th-century aberration. Do take in the graphic primitive representation of the fire of hell in the upper panel of the Byzantine fresco beside the south entrance and visit the small side chapel carved from the rock.

The **Museo Nazionale Ridola** *(☎ 0835 31 00 58, Via Ridola 24; admission €1.30; open 9am-8pm Tues-Sun, 2pm-8pm Mon)* occupies the 17th-century convent of Santa Chiara and has a collection of primarily prehistoric and classical artefacts. A little south, on Piazzetta Pascoli, is the **Centro Carlo Levi** *(☎ 0835 31 42 35, Palazzo Lanfranchi)*. It houses paintings by Levi, including an enormous mural depicting peasant life in Matera. It was closed for extensive renovation at the time of writing.

Special Events

Matera celebrates the feast day of Santa Maria della Bruna (the city's patron saint) on 2 July. The high point of the festival is a colourful procession from the cathedral when a statue of the Madonna is carried along in the *carro trionfale*, a cart ornately decorated in papier maché. When the procession ends (and once the statue has been removed), it's time for the *assalto al carro*, when the crowd descends on the cart and its contents and tears them to pieces in order to take away what the faithful regard as precious relics.

Places to Stay

Albergo Roma *(☎/fax 0835 33 39 12, Via Roma 62)* Singles/doubles €20.70/31. Here is good accommodation for the budget traveller. However, you may find it closed as renovations are planned.

Sassi Hotel *(☎ 0835 33 10 09, fax 0835 33 37 33, Via San Giovanni Vecchio 89)* Singles/doubles with bath from €41.40/62. Cascading down the hillside, the rooms here offer great views of Sasso Barisano. Prices include breakfast. On the bottom level is a small **hostel** (dorm beds €15.50). The Sassi is unique, friendly and warmly recommended, whichever accommodation you choose.

Albergo Italia *(☎ 0835 33 35 61, fax 0835 33 00 87, e info@albergo-italia.com, Via Ridola 5)* Singles/doubles/triples/quads with bath €79/97/113.70/129.20. This is a pleasant hotel overlooking Sasso Caveoso.

Places to Eat

L'Osteria *(☎ 0835 33 33 95, Via Fiorentini 58)* Full meals from €13. Rustic and intimate (there are only six tables), this simple osteria offers 1st-class family cuisine and friendly service. Typical of the hearty fare is their *capunti e flageoli*, white beans and pasta the shape of cowrie shells simmered in a pork stock to make you drool.

Trattoria Lucana *(☎ 0835 33 61 17, Via Lucana 48)* Full meals €15-18. Open Mon-Sat. Though it serves a mean meat dish or two, this trattoria has an excellent selection of vegetarian options. Kick off with the all-veggie *antipasto della casa* then get into your stride with their *orecchiette alla materana* (fresh ear-shaped pasta with a tomato, aubergine and courgette sauce).

Hostaria il Terrazzino *(☎/fax 0835 33 25 03, Vico San Giuseppe 7)* Pizzas €2.25-5.50, full meals €15-18. Open Wed-Mon. Eat on the terrace with a tumbling view down over Sasso Barisano, or beneath the soft shapes of their cave. The Hostaria's signposted from Piazza Vittorio Veneto.

Oi Marí *(☎ 0835 34 61 21, Via Fiorentini 66)* Full meals around €15. At this stylish restaurant in the old quarter, the food's as fine as the ambience.

To eat in a renovated sasso, visit ***Caffè del Cavaliere*** *(off Via Fiorentini in Sasso Barisano)*, a bar/cafe serving cakes and light meals.

Caffè Tripoli *(Piazza Vittorio Veneto 17)* There's nowhere more central for a kick of coffee and a delicious pastry or two.

There's a small daily ***fresh produce market*** just south of Piazza Vittorio Veneto on Via A Persio.

Getting There & Away

Bus The bus station is just north of Piazza Matteotti, near the train station. SITA buses (☎ 0835 33 28 62) connect Matera with Taranto (€4.40, 1½ hours, six daily) and Metaponto (€2.70, one hour, up to five daily), as well as many small towns in the province. Grassani (☎ 0835 72 14 43) has two buses per day to Potenza.

Marozzi (Rome ☎ 06 225 21 47) runs three buses daily between Rome and Matera. A joint SITA/Marozzi service leaves at 10.35pm for the northern cities of Siena, Florence and Pisa via Potenza. Advance booking is essential.

Buy your ticket for all services except Grassani (pay on the bus) at Biglietteria Manicone (☎ 0835 33 28 62), Piazza Matteotti 3–4.

Train Ferrovie Appulo-Lucane (FAL; ☎ 0835 33 28 61) runs regular trains (€3.70, 1½ hours, at least 12 daily) and buses (four to six daily) to/from Bari. For Potenza, take a FAL bus to Ferrandina and connect with an FS train, or go to Altamura to link up with FAL's Bari-Potenza run.

Car & Motorcycle Matera's narrow alleys and steep contours are no place for a vehicle. It's better to leave your car north of the Sassi area and continue on foot. Central Piazza Vittorio Veneto is pedestrianised.

ALIANO

Not one of Italy's – or even Basilicata's – great tourist stopovers, this tiny hilltop village south-west of Matera might attract those who have read Carlo Levi's *Christ Stopped at Eboli* and have their own transport. When he was exiled to Basilicata between 1935 and 1936 for his opposition to Fascism, Levi lived for a time in Aliano. In the novel, he called the town Gagliano and little has changed since he was interned here. The landscape is still as he described it – an 'endless sweep of clay, with the white dots of villages, stretching out as far as the invisible sea' – and you are just as likely to see the locals riding a donkey as driving a car.

Wander to the edge of the old village to see the house where he stayed. Two museums have been established in the town, one devoted to Levi (who is buried in Aliano) and another to the peasant tradition of the area.

Aliano is accessible by SITA bus from Matera, with a change in Pisticci Scalo.

METAPONTO

Founded by Greek colonisers between the 8th and 7th centuries BC, the city of Metaponto prospered as a commercial and grain-producing centre. One of its most famous residents was Pythagoras, who established a school here after being banished from Crotone (in what is now Calabria) towards the end of the 6th century BC.

After Pythagoras died, his house and school were incorporated into a Temple of Hera. The remains of the temple – 15 columns and sections of pavement – are known as the Tavole Palatine (Palatine Tables), since knights, or paladins, are said to have gathered there before heading to the crusades.

Overtaken politically and economically by Rome, Metaponto met its end as a result of the Second Punic War. Hannibal had made it his headquarters after Rome retook Tarentum (Taranto) in 207 BC, and he is said to have relocated the town's population to spare it the fate of the people of Tarentum, who were sold into slavery by the Romans for backing the Carthaginians.

Modern Metaponto's only real attraction is a sandy beach, Lido di Metaponto, that attracts loads of summer holiday-makers. It's about 3km east of the train station.

Things to See

From the train station, go straight ahead for half a kilometre to a roundabout. To your right (east) is the **Parco Archeologico** *(about 1.5km; free)* and to the left, the **Museo Archeologico Nazionale** *(600m; ☎ 0835 74 53 27, Via Aristea 21; admission €2.60; open 9am-8pm Tues-Sun, Mon 9am-2pm)*. In the park, the site of ancient Metapontum, you can see what little remains of a **Greek theatre** and the Doric **Tempio di Apollo Licio**. The museum houses artefacts from Metapontum and other sites. If it's at home (it's often on tour), the accompanying exhibition on wine, *Il Vino di Dionisiò*, is fun to visit.

For the most memorable reminder of this ancient city-state, the **Tavole Palatine**, follow the slip road for Taranto onto the S106. The temple ruins are north, just off the highway, behind the old Antiquarium that used to house the museum.

Places to Stay

At Lido di Metaponto on the coast, there are several camp sites but virtually nothing opens in winter.

Camping Magna Grecia *(☎ 0835 74 18 55, Via Lido)* Sites per person €3.65-7.75, per tent €4.15-7.75, per car €2.35-3.10 according to season. Open Apr-Oct. This camp site, an easy 800m from the sea, has its own pool.

Hotel Kennedy *(☎/fax 0835 74 19 60, ⓔ hrkennedy@bernalda.net, Viale Ionio 1)* Singles/doubles from €43.90/59.40. Rooms have air-con and prices include breakfast.

Getting There & Away

SITA buses run to Metaponto from Matera and from Taranto's Piazza Castello. The town is on the Taranto-Reggio di Calabria line, and trains connect with Potenza, Salerno and occasionally Naples. The station is 3km west of the Lido di Metaponto. If you don't want to walk, wait for one of the regular SITA or Chiruzzi buses to pass by on the way to the beach.

AROUND METAPONTO

If you get as far as Metaponto, consider continuing about 17km south-west along the coast to **Policoro**, originally the Greek settlement of Eraclea. The ruins are not much more complete than those of Metapontum itself but its **museum** *(☎ 0835 97 21 54, Via Colombo 8; admission €2.60; open 9am-8pm Wed-Mon, 2pm-8pm Tues)* is worth the visit alone – it has a fabulous display of artefacts excavated in the area, including two complete tombs with skeletons surrounded by the objects and jewellery with which they were buried.

SITA buses run down the coast from Metaponto to Policoro but are frequent only in summer.

TYRRHENIAN COAST (COSTA TIRRENICA)

Basilicata's Tyrrhenian coast is short (about 20km) but sweet. The S18 threads its way between craggy mountains on the inland side and, to the west, cliffs that drop away to the sea. This makes for one of the prettiest drives on the whole Tyrrhenian coast – but one that peters out virtually as soon as you leave Basilicata in either direction.

About halfway between the Campanian and Calabrian borders, and a short, steep ride up from the coast, lies the small town of **Maratea**. Watched over by a 22m-tall statue of Christ at the Santuario di San Biagio, Maratea has been done no harm by tourism. The high part of town, as so often along the south Tyrrhenian coast, forms the historic core. The new town has spread out below, although so far it's unobtrusive.

Maratea is the administrative centre of a series of coastal villages, the prettiest of which are **Fiumicello** and **Porto di Maratea**, which has plenty of bars and restaurants, and buzzes until the early hours in summer. Most of the accommodation is down in these coastal settlements and each has at least one small, protected beach.

Centro Sub Maratea *(☎ 0973 87 00 13, Via Santa Caterina 28, Maratea)* does diving courses for all levels, while ***Maratea Mare Service*** *(☎ 0973 87 69 76, based in Porto di Maratea)* rents boats.

The APT office for the area (☎ 0973 87 69 08) is at Piazza Gesù 40 in Fiumicello. It opens 8am to 2pm and 3pm to 9pm daily in summer. Hours are reduced in winter.

Albergo Fiorella *(☎ 0973 87 65 14, fax 0973 87 69 21, Via Santa Veneri 21)* Singles/doubles €31/46.50, with bath €36.15/51.70. One of the cheapest places to stay is the fairly simple Albergo Fiorella in Fiumicello.

Villa degli Aranci *(☎/fax 0973 87 63 44, Via Profiti 7)* Singles/doubles with bath €67.20/82.70, compulsory half-board in summer €77.50 per person . Also in Fiumicello, this place is more attractive than Albergo Fiorella.

SITA buses link Maratea to Potenza. They also run up the coast to Sapri in Campania and south to Praia a Mare in Calabria. Local buses connect the coastal towns and Maratea train station with the old centre of Maratea, running frequently in summer. Some trains on the Rome-Reggio di Calabria line stop at Maratea train station, below the town. Local trains run infrequently between Praia a Mare, Maratea's various coastal settlements and Sapri.

Calabria

With some of the country's better beaches and a brooding, mountainous interior, the toe of the Italian boot represents for many travellers little more than a train ride down the Tyrrhenian coast on the way to/from Sicily. Although it may not loom large on the average visitor's list of Italian destinations, Calabria is worth a little exploration. The beaches are among the cleanest in Italy, and lovers of ancient history can explore the sparse reminders of the civilisation of Magna Graecia. The disadvantages are the spread of ugly holiday villages along parts of the Ionian and Tyrrhenian coasts, and sometimes having to settle for pebbles rather than sand. Along the roads heading inland, you'll encounter some magnificent natural beauty and, every now and then, picturesque medieval villages huddled on hill tops.

Sparsely inhabited in Palaeolithic times, the area was first settled by Greeks from Sicily, who founded a colony at what is now Reggio di Calabria. The process of colonisation spread along the Ionian coast, with Sibari and Crotone the most important settlements. Siding with Hannibal against Rome turned out to be a mistake and, with the general's retreat to Carthage in 202 BC, the cities of Magna Graecia came under Rome's permanent sway. Later, as Rome declined, the Byzantines took superficial control. Their ineffectual rule and the

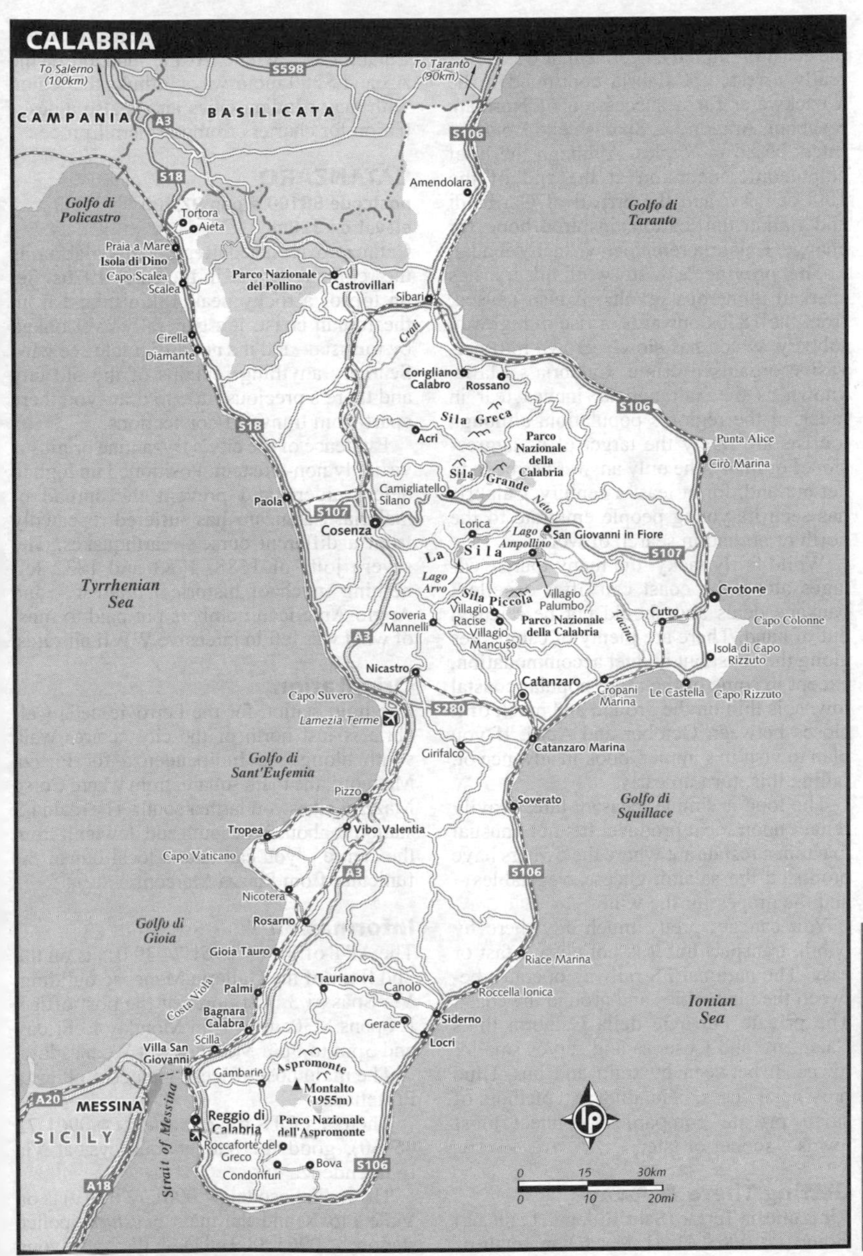
CALABRIA
To Salerno (100km)
To Taranto (90km)
CAMPANIA
BASILICATA
S598
A3
S106
S18
Golfo di Policastro
Tortora
Aieta
Praia a Mare
Isola di Dino
Capo Scalea
Scalea
Parco Nazionale del Pollino
Castrovillari
Amendolara
Golfo di Taranto
Sibari
Crati
Cirella
Diamante
Corigliano Calabro
Rossano
Sila Greca
Acri
Parco Nazionale della Calabria
Punta Alice
Cirò Marina
Sila Grande
Neto
Camigliatello Silano
Paola
S107
Cosenza
Lorica
Lago Ampollino
San Giovanni in Fiore
La Sila
Lago Arvo
Tyrrhenian Sea
Sila Piccola
Villagio Palumbo
Crotone
Soveria Mannelli
Villagio Racise
Villagio Mancuso
Parco Nazionale della Calabria
Tacina
Cutro
Capo Colonne
Isola di Capo Rizzuto
Nicastro
Catanzaro
Cropani Marina
Le Castella
Capo Rizzuto
Capo Suvero
Lamezia Terme
S280
Girifalco
Catanzaro Marina
Golfo di Sant'Eufemia
Pizzo
Soverato
Golfo di Squillace
Tropea
Vibo Valentia
Capo Vaticano
Nicotera
Golfo di Gioia
Rosarno
Gioia Tauro
Riace Marina
Palmi
Taurianova
Canolo
Roccella Ionica
Costa Viola
Bagnara Calabra
Gerace
Siderno
Ionian Sea
Locri
Scilla
Villa San Giovanni
Gambarie
Aspromonte
Montalto (1955m)
A20
MESSINA
Strait of Messina
Reggio di Calabria
Parco Nazionale dell'Aspromonte
SICILY
Roccaforte del Greco
Bova
Condonfuri
A18
0 15 30km
0 10 20mi

CALABRIA

appearance of Saracen (Arab) raiders off the coast prompted a decline that was never really arrested; Calabria continued to be a backwater for a succession of Norman, Swabian, Aragonese, Spanish and Bourbon rulers based in Naples. Although the brief Napoleonic incursion at the end of the 18th century, and the arrival of Garibaldi and Italian unification, inspired hope for change, Calabria remained virtually feudal.

The province's history of misery has sparked numerous revolts. It also caused, from the 1870s onwards, a rise in highway robbery, which has slowly grown into pervasive organised crime. Calabria's Mafia, known as the 'ndrangheta, incites fear in much of the region's population, although tourists are rarely the target of its aggression. For many, the only answer has been to get out and, for at least a century, Calabria has seen its young people emigrate to the north or abroad in search of work.

While fairly tacky, the many tourist villages along the coast can offer excellent package deals and should not be rejected out of hand. There are plenty of camp sites along the coast but budget accommodation, except in some of the more popular coastal towns, is thin on the ground and much of it closes between October and April. If you plan to visit in summer, book in advance or, failing this, turn up early.

The food is simple, peasant fare, heavily reliant upon local produce. It's not unusual to eat in a restaurant where the owners have produced the salami, cheese, vegetables – and the grapes for the wine.

You can get pretty much anywhere by public transport but it is not always fast or easy. The national FS railway operates between the main cities and around the coast. The private Ferrovie della Calabria links Catanzaro and Cosenza and serves smaller towns in between by train and bus. Blue provincial buses, belonging to a plethora of small private companies, connect most towns – sooner or later.

Getting There & Away

Air Lamezia Terme (Sant'Eufemia Lamezia) airport (☎ 0968 41 41 11), 63km south of Cosenza and 36km west of Catanzaro, serves Calabria as a whole. At the junction of the A3 and S280 motorways, it links the region with major Italian cities and is also a destination for charters from northern Europe.

CATANZARO

postcode 88100 • pop 97,100
elevation 320m

Catanzaro replaced Reggio di Calabria as the regional capital in the early 1970s. Set on top of a rocky peak 13km inland from the Ionian coast, it's generally overlooked by tourists – and it's not difficult to see why. Scarcely anything remains of the old city and there's precious little to draw you there apart from transport connections.

Evidence of the city's Byzantine origins is virtually non-existent. Positioned up high to deter raiders and prevent the spread of malaria, Catanzaro has suffered repeatedly from a different curse – earthquakes. The severe jolts of 1688, 1783 and 1832 left nothing much of historical interest – and Anglo-American bombers put paid to most of what was left in intensive WWII air raids.

Orientation

The train station for the Ferrovie della Calabria is just north of the city centre. Walk south along Via Indipendenza for Piazza Matteotti, the main square, from where Corso Mazzini takes you farther south. The main FS station is about 2km south and downhill from the centre – you can take a local bus or the funicular from Piazza Marconi.

Information

The APT office (☎ 0961 74 39 01) is on the 2nd floor of the Galleria Mancuso building, Via Spasari 3, just north of the post office. It opens 8.30am to 1pm Monday to Friday and 3pm to 5pm Monday and Wednesday.

The main post office is located on Piazza Prefettura.

There's a CTS travel agency (☎ 0961 72 45 30), good for budget journeys, at Via Indipendenza 26.

The main hospital (☎ 0961 72 67 19) is on Viale Pio X and the main *questura* (police station; ☎ 0961 88 91 11) on Piazza Cavour.

Things to See

Don't budget in too much time. The **cathedral** was almost completely rebuilt after the last war and is quite ordinary. Nearby, the **Chiesa di San Domenico** (also known as the Chiesa del Rosario) contains several attractive Renaissance paintings by comparative unknowns but you'll be lucky to find it open. More impressive, at least externally, is the Baroque **Basilica dell'Immacolata** with its marble-clad columns.

The city's **Museo Comunale** is just inside the Villa Trieste, a pleasant garden worth a stroll in its own right. When it reopens (they've been renovating it for years), the museum will display a large collection of coins and some local archaeological finds.

Catanzaro Marina, also known as Catanzaro Lido, 12km away down on the coast, is the city's access to the sea and one of the Ionian coast's major resorts. Although heavily developed, it's less tacky than many others and the beaches stretching off in both directions are among the best on this coast.

Places to Stay & Eat

Catanzaro has few hotels and they are generally expensive.

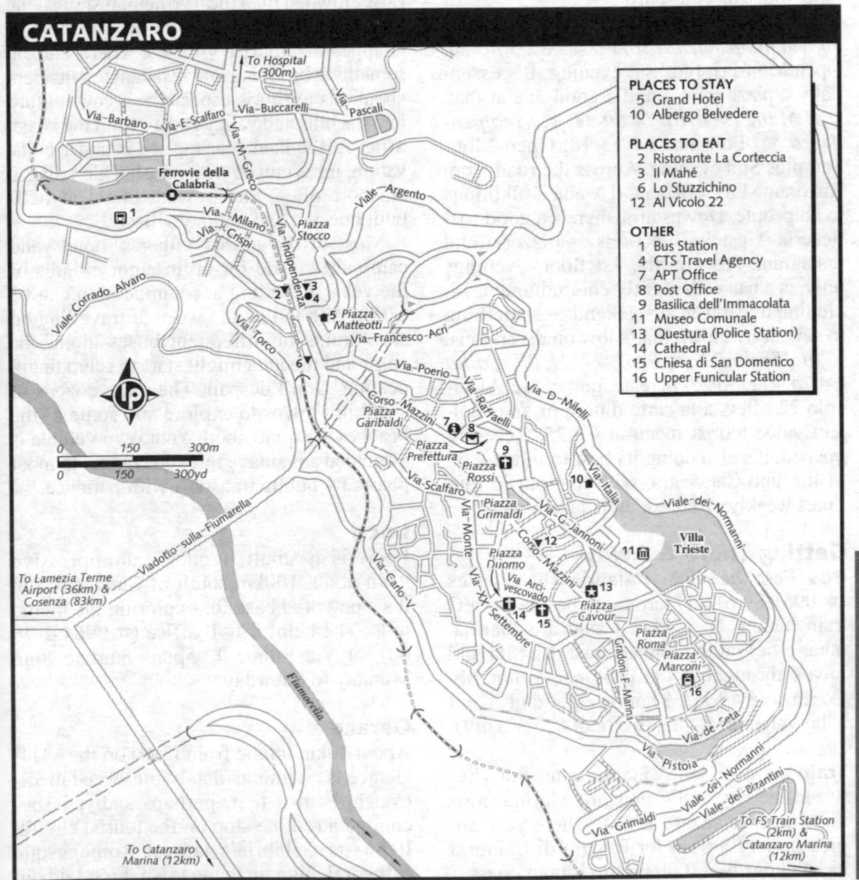

Albergo Belvedere *(☎/fax 0961 72 05 91, Via Italia 33)* Singles/doubles €23.25/41.40, singles/doubles/triples with bath €31/51.70/69.75. You get what you pay for at this pleasant stopover. Ask for a room with a view.

Grand Hotel *(☎ 0961 70 12 56, fax 0961 74 16 21, Piazza Matteotti)* Singles/doubles with bath €64.60/90.40. Rooms are bland but comfortable, and you couldn't be more central. Prices include breakfast.

Lo Stuzzichino *(☎/fax 0961 72 44 87, Piazza Matteotti 5)* Full meals from €8, pasta from €2.25. A self-service, no nonsense, plonk-it-on-the-plate joint that offers excellent value for your euro.

Ristorante La Corteccia *(☎ 0961 74 61 30, Via Indipendenza 30)* Pizzas €2.50-6.50. Open Mon-Fri, plus Sat evening. It's essentially a pizza joint – and a good one at that.

Il Mahé *(☎ 0961 74 60 34, Via Indipendenza 55)* Full meals €13-18. Open Mon-Sat, plus Sun evening. Across the road from Ristorante La Corteccia, Il Mahé is all things to all people. Downstairs, there's a good rosticceria. Upstairs functions as pizzeria and restaurant. Also on the 1st floor, evenings only, is a bar with nightly entertainment, including live music at weekends – something to savour in a town that's low on diversions.

Al Vicolo 22 *(☎ 0961 72 21 00, Salita Corso Mazzini 22)* In restaurant mode, Al Vicolo 22 offers a la carte dining or an excellent value tourist menu at €7.25. Recently opened, it's also doing its best to inject a bit of life into Catanzaro, with live music four times weekly; Wednesday is jazz night.

Getting There & Away

Bus Ferrovie della Calabria (FC) buses (☎ 0961 89 61 11) terminate beside the FC train station. They serve Catanzaro Marina, other cities on the Ionian coast, La Sila and towns throughout the province – notably Cosenza (€4.15, 1½ hours, eight daily) and Vibo Valentia (€4.65, two hours, four daily).

Train Ferrovie della Calabria runs trains between the city and Catanzaro Marina (also known as Catanzaro Lido), where you can pick up an FS train for Reggio di Calabria or head north-east along the Ionian coast.

From the Catanzaro city FS station, trains connect with Lamezia Terme, Reggio di Calabria and Cosenza, as well as Naples, Rome, Milan and Turin.

Getting Around

Catanzaro's funicular railway (tickets €0.55) rises from the FS train station to Piazza Marconi near the city centre. Otherwise, take city bus Nos 11, 12, 40 or 41. The Circolare Lido bus connects the city centre, the FS train station and Catanzaro Marina.

IONIAN COAST

Less crowded than the Tyrrhenian shores, the Ionian coast nevertheless has its fair share of unappealing tourist villages. There can be something brooding and resistant to outsiders about this territory, especially if you venture into the hills and valleys away from the coast. Much of the land near the sea is under cultivation, interspersed with ramshackle villages or, more often, the growing blight of half-built housing and holiday villas.

Most of the tourist villages, hotels and camp sites close for up to eight months of the year, so finding accommodation can be tricky. Add to that the woes of travelling on slow trains or infrequent buses along the coast and the area might start to seem unappealing. Don't despair. There are dozens of small hill towns to explore and some of the beaches are quite good. Your own vehicle is a decided advantage but you *can* get to most places by public transport with patience.

Locri

Locri is a small, modern, unimpressive town about 100km south of Catanzaro but it's a potential base for exploring the inland hills. The helpful IAT office (☎ 0964 2 96 00), at Via Fiume 1, opens 8am to 8pm Monday to Saturday.

Gerace

About 10km inland from Locri on the S111, Gerace is an immaculately preserved medieval hill town that, perhaps sadly, is becoming a routine stop on the tourist circuit. It boasts Calabria's largest Romanesque **cathedral**, high up in the town. First laid out in 1045, later alterations have robbed it of none of its majesty.

Ristorante a Squella *(☎ 0964 35 69 36, Viale della Resistenza 8)* Meals about €13. This is an excellent traditional restaurant.

Farther inland is **Canolo**, a small hamlet seemingly untouched by the 20th century. Buses connect Gerace with Locri.

Isola di Capo Rizzuto

postcode 88841 • pop 12,687

The area around Isola di Capo Rizzuto, 40km north-east of Catanzaro Marina, offers some of the best camping along the Ionian coast. There are around 15 camp sites near this small town.

La Fattoria *(☎ 0962 79 11 65, fax 0962 95 78 95, Via del Faro).* Sites cost €2.10-8.30 & per person €3.62-7.25. This place opens June to September.

Pensione L'Aragonese *(☎/fax 0962 79 50 13, Via Discesa Marina)* Singles/doubles with bath €36.20/62. This place at Le Castella, about 10km south-west of Isola, has a decent restaurant overlooking an Aragonese castle, currently under restoration and linked to the mainland by a short causeway.

At the northern tip of this zone, whose shore is a protected marine reserve, is **Capo Colonne**, marking the site of the Greek fortress complex of Hera Lacinia. Only a solitary column belonging to a Doric temple remains to testify to the spot's former splendour.

Crotone

postcode 88900 • pop 59,550

About 10km north of Isola di Capo Rizzuto, Crotone was founded by the Greeks in 710 BC and reached its zenith in the following century, when it virtually controlled all of Magna Graecia. In more recent times, it has regained influence as one of the region's heavyweight industrial centres and ports.

The APT office (☎ 0962 2 31 85) is at Via Torino 148. It opens 8.30am to 1pm Monday to Saturday and 3pm to 7pm Monday and Wednesday.

The town's **Museo Archeologico Statale** *(☎ 0962 2 30 82, Via Risorgimento 120; admission €2.10; open 9am-7.30pm daily except 1st and 3rd Mon of month)* is one of Calabria's better museums. Nearby is a restored 16th-century **castle** *(☎ 0962 92 15 35, Via Risorgimento; admission €2.10; open 9am-1pm & 4.30pm-7pm Tues-Sun).* Typical of the cylindrically towered fortresses erected by the Aragonese in southern Italy's main coastal cities, it nowadays houses a small **museum**.

Albergo Italia *(☎/fax 0962 2 39 10, Piazza Vittoria 12)* Singles/doubles with bath €23.25/46.50. Open year-round. This place has comfortable enough rooms and is the cheapest of Crotone's few accommodation options.

North of Crotone

The coastline from Crotone to Basilicata is the region's least developed, partly because the beaches are not terribly good. Public transport is generally irregular, although the coast road is decent and is gradually being upgraded.

Cirò Marina About 30km north of Crotone, Cirò Marina is a decent-sized town with plenty of hotel rooms and good beaches marred only by the ugly offshore concrete breakwaters.

Punta Alice *(☎ 0962 3 11 60)* A couple of kilometres north of the town, this is a pleasant camp site.

Hotel Atena *(☎ 0962 3 18 21, Piazza Municipio)* Singles/doubles with bath 33.60/46.50, compulsory full board in Aug €57 per person. Plastic and chipboard are the dominant materials but the beds are comfortable and a bargain outside peak season.

Rossano Rossano, 56km north-west of Cirò, is really two towns – Lido Sant'Angelo, a standard beach resort and coastal extension of the modern plains town of Rossano Scalo, and the altogether more interesting original hill town itself, 6km inland.

The transformation over such a short climb is remarkable. The snaking road takes you through green countryside to the tranquil and picturesque old town, once an important Italian link in the Byzantine Empire's chain.

Various reminders of Rossano's ties to the ancient city of Constantinople remain. In the central aisle of the **cathedral** is a 9th-century Byzantine fresco of the Madonna and Child, nowadays encased within an ornate polychrome Baroque structure. For more proof, visit the **Museo Diocesano** *(☎ 0983 52 52 63; admission €1.10; open, in principle, 10am-noon & 5pm-7pm Mon-Sat)* next door, which houses a precious 6th-century codex containing the gospels of St Matthew and St Mark in Greek. If it's closed, ask at Cooperativa Neilos, beside the phone kiosk.

Hotel Scigliano *(☎/fax 0983 51 18 46, ⓔ hscigliano@hotelscigliano.it, Viale Margherita 257)* Singles/doubles/triples/quads €51.70/82.70/98.20/108.50, €10.50 extra in July-Aug. Down in the modern town and a shortish walk from the station, this hotel also runs a good restaurant. Prices include breakfast.

Ancient Minorities

Possibly Calabria's richest testament to the era of Magna Graecia can be found not in the sparse ruins of abandoned ancient settlements along the coast but in the hill towns east of Reggio di Calabria – for in the towns of Bova, Condofuri and Roccaforte del Greco (most easily reached from the coastal road), you can still hear the older folk speaking Greek as their native tongue. It is not, say some experts, a dialect of modern Greek but rather a descendant of the ancient language of Pythagoras. Sceptics claim it is the Greek of the much later Byzantine empire. Even so, it is remarkable to think that this linguistic time capsule has survived for so many hundreds of years.

More numerous, and more recently arrived, are the Albanians, who began fleeing Muslim persecution in the mid-15th century. You'll find them mostly in small towns scattered about the Piana di Sibari, 50km south of the border with Basilicata on the Ionian coast. Not only have they preserved their language but in many cases they remain faithful to the Greek Orthodox rite in this bastion of Catholicism.

Camping Torino *(☎ 0983 51 00 80)*. This camp site is at Marina di Rossano.

Rossano is on the Taranto-Reggio di Calabria train line. From the town, the S177 makes a pretty drive across La Sila to Cosenza.

Sibari About 4km south of Sibari are the **remains** *(free; open 9am-1 hr before sunset daily)* – 90% of them beneath reclaimed farmland and bisected by the highway – of what was once the seat of the ancient Sybarites, the people of the brief-lived Greek city state renowned for its wealth and love of comfort. It was destroyed by a jealous Crotone in the 6th century BC, and excavations since the 1960s have brought only a glimmer of its glory to light. The small **Museo Archeologico della Sibaritide** *(admission €2.07; open 9am-7.30pm daily)* is 7km from the site by road and can't compare with the riches within similar museums at Metaponto and Policoro farther north.

COSENZA

postcode 87100 • pop 83,900
elevation 238m

Cosenza, as you approach, appears to be a dismal array of cheek-by-jowl concrete high-rises, and indeed the majority of the town is quite without charm. So its medieval core, seated at the confluence of two rivers, the Crati and Busento, comes as an all-the-more-unexpected pleasure, with its narrow *vicoletti* (alleys), some no more than steep stairways, winding past elegant (if much decayed) mansions.

A university town since 1968, Cosenza – or rather its heart – is the most attractive of Calabria's three provincial capitals. What's more, it's a transportation hub and a gateway into the mountains of La Sila and on across to the Ionian coast.

Orientation

The main drag, Corso Mazzini, runs south from Piazza Fera (near the bus station) and intersects Viale Trieste before meeting Piazza dei Bruzi. What little there is of accommodation, food, banks and tourist assistance is all within about a 10-minute

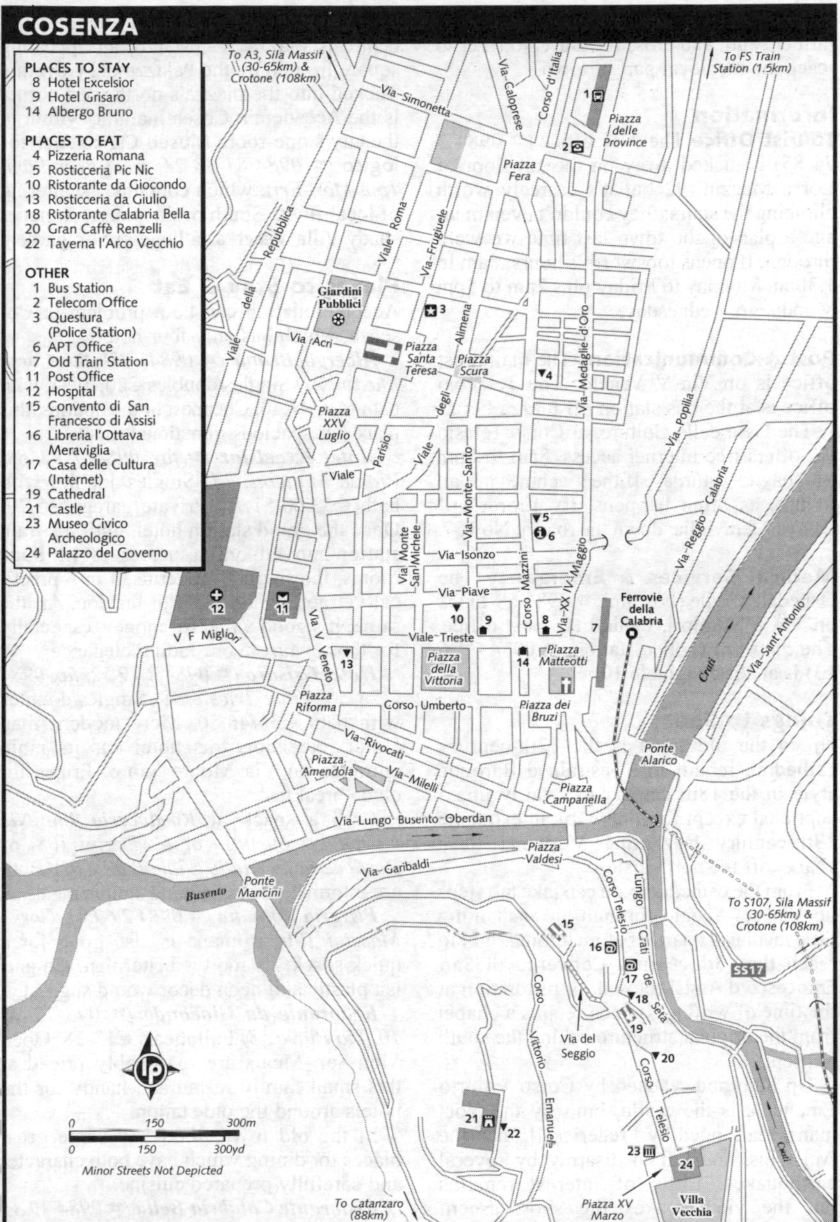

COSENZA

PLACES TO STAY
8 Hotel Excelsior
9 Hotel Grisaro
14 Albergo Bruno

PLACES TO EAT
4 Pizzeria Romana
5 Rosticceria Pic Nic
10 Ristorante da Giocondo
13 Rosticceria da Giulio
18 Ristorante Calabria Bella
20 Gran Caffè Renzelli
22 Taverna l'Arco Vecchio

OTHER
1 Bus Station
2 Telecom Office
3 Questura (Police Station)
6 APT Office
7 Old Train Station
11 Post Office
12 Hospital
15 Convento di San Francesco di Assisi
16 Libreria l'Ottava Meraviglia
17 Casa delle Cultura (Internet)
19 Cathedral
21 Castle
23 Museo Civico Archeologico
24 Palazzo del Governo

walking radius of this intersection. Head farther south and cross the Busento river to reach the medieval part of town.

Information

Tourist Office The APT office (☎ 0984 2 74 85) is tucked away on the 1st floor of Corso Mazzini 92 but it's scarcely worth climbing the stairs; they couldn't even manage a plan of the town last time we were through. It opens jobsworth's hours, 8am to 1.30pm Monday to Friday plus 2pm to 5pm Monday to Wednesday.

Post & Communications The main post office is on Via V Veneto. The Telecom office is at the bus station off Piazza Fera.

The Casa delle Culture, at Corso Telesio 98, offers free internet access, 8am to 8pm Monday to Saturday. If the machines are all in use, as often happens, try Libreria l' Ottava Meraviglia, down the road at No 157.

Medical Services & Emergency The Ospedale Civile (hospital; ☎ 0984 68 11) is on Via F Migliori, behind the post office. The *questura* (police station; ☎ 0984 7 26 13) is at Via Frugiuele 10.

Things to See

Up in the old town is the 12th-century **cathedral**, rebuilt in a restrained Baroque style in the 18th century. It's fairly unexceptional except for a copy of an exquisite 13th-century Byzantine Madonna in a chapel off the north aisle.

From the cathedral, you can take the steps up Via del Seggio through an enchanting little medieval quarter before turning right to reach the 13th-century **Convento di San Francesco d'Assisi** (closed for restoration at the time of writing), which retains a chapel from the original structure behind the south transept.

Up high and reached by Corso Vittorio Emanuele is the **castle**, built by the Normans, rearranged by Frederick II, then the Angevins, and left in disarray by several earthquakes. Little of interest remains but the view makes the short ascent worthwhile.

At the southern edge of the old city centre is Piazza XV Marzo, an appealing square fronted by the Palazzo del Governo. Tucked into the piazza's north-west corner is the Accademia Cosentina and, within it, the city's one-room **Museo Civico Archeologico** *(☎ 0984 81 33 24; free; open 9am-1pm Mon-Fri)*, which contains a scattering of local finds. South of the piazza stretches shady **Villa Vecchia**, a huge public garden.

Places to Stay & Eat

Accommodation can be a problem in Cosenza, which has only four hotels.

Albergo Bruno *(☎ 0984 7 38 89, Corso Mazzini 27)* Singles/doubles €20.70/31, with bath €26/41.40. Cheapest of the options, this place has spacious, functional rooms.

Hotel Excelsior *(☎/fax 0984 7 43 83, Piazza Matteotti 14)* Singles/doubles with bath €33.60/51.70. Private garage €5.20. Once the grand station hotel, until the train station moved on, it preserves its huge rooms, thoroughly modernised in a practical yet not always tasteful fashion. All the same, it's good value for money, especially for those who savour fading elegance.

Hotel Grisaro *(☎ 0984 2 79 52, fax 0984 2 78 38, Viale Trieste 38)* Singles/doubles with bath €31/46.50. More modern than Hotel Excelsior, this hotel has its main entrance on Via Monte Santo. Prices include breakfast.

Grab a snack at ***Rosticceria Pic Nic*** *(☎ 0984 2 69 08, Corso Mazzini 108)* or ***Rosticceria da Giulio*** *(Viale Trieste 81)*. Both are informal places offering simple meals.

Pizzeria Romana *(☎ 0984 2 69 91, Corso Mazzini 190)* Romana is also good for a quick snack; its food is better than the garish plastic and neon decor would suggest.

Ristorante da Giocondo *(☎ 0984 2 98 10, Via Piave 53)* Full meals €13-18. Open Mon-Sat. Meals are reasonably priced at this small family restaurant, handy for the hotels around the old station.

In the old town, there are some great places for dining which have both character and carefully prepared cuisine.

Ristorante Calabria Bella *(☎ 0984 79 35 31, Piazza Duomo)* Full meals €18-21.

Intimate and much patronised by discerning locals, this place has the youngest waiters that you ever did see.

***Taverna l'Arco Vecchio** (☎ 0984 7 25 64, Piazza Archi di Ciaccio 21)* Tourist menu €18, full meals €18-23. Open Mon-Sat. Similar in style to the Calabria Bella, it has attractive, low-ceilinged rooms

***Gran Caffè Renzelli** (☎ 0984 2 68 14, Corso Telesio 46)* This venerable cafe, which bakes its own deliciously gooey cakes and desserts, has been run by the same family for five generations. Sink your teeth into their *torroncino torrefacto*, a confection of sugar, spices and hazelnuts, or *varchiglia alla monocale* (chocolate and almond cake).

Getting There & Around

Bus The city's main bus station is just north-east of Piazza Fera. Services leave for Catanzaro, Paola and towns throughout La Sila. Autolinie Preite has half a dozen buses daily along the north Tyrrhenian coast as far as Praia a Mare, while Romano does two runs daily to/from Crotone.

Amaco bus Nos 15, 16 and 28 link the town and Stazione Nuova, the FS train station.

Train The national FS Stazione Nuova is about 2km north-east of the city centre. Trains go to Reggio di Calabria, Salerno, Naples and Rome, as well as most destinations around the Calabrian coast. The Ferrovie della Calabria line, which has its terminal beside the old FS station, serves La Sila and other small towns around Cosenza.

Car & Motorcycle Cosenza is off the A3 autostrada. The S107 connects the city with Crotone and the Ionian coast, across La Sila.

Taxi For a taxi, call ☎ 0984 2 88 77.

LA SILA

Though less spectacular than many of the mountain ranges farther up the peninsula, La Sila (the Sila Massif) is still impressive and offers good walking. The highest peaks, many covered in thick forest, reach 2000m. Here the dominant tree is the Corsican pine, tall and found in Italy only in Calabria and on the slopes of Mt Etna (Sicily). There is some winter skiing in the central Sila Grande, over 7000 hectares of which are national park. The other two areas are the Sila Greca, north of the Grande, and the Sila Piccola to the south. Sadly, there are few *rifugi* (mountain huts) and camping in the national parks is forbidden.

The main towns are Camigliatello Silano and San Giovanni in Fiore, both accessible by Ferrovie della Calabria buses (about 10 daily) along the S107, which links Cosenza and Crotone, or by the twice-daily train running between Cosenza and San Giovanni in Fiore. You will find accommodation in various towns throughout La Sila and at several tourist resorts, including Villaggio Palumbo and Villaggio Mancuso. Skiers can use lifts around Camigliatello Silano and near Lorica, on Lago Arvo.

Information

Unfortunately, the tourist offices can help with little more than vague maps and accommodation lists. Most brochures are in Italian.

Camigliatello Silano

Ordinary enough in summer, Camigliatello looks quite cute under snow. It is a popular local skiing resort but won't host any international competitions. A few lifts operate on Monte Curcio, about 3km to the south.

The forests of La Sila yield a wondrous variety of wild mushrooms, both edible and poisonous. Sniff around Antica Salumeria Campanaro, Piazza Misasi 5; it's a temple to things fungoid, an emporium of rich odours, fine meats, cheeses, pickles and wines, rivalled in richness, if not in size, by its neighbour, La Casa del Fungho.

The town has about 15 hotels, a couple of which are listed here.

***Hotel Miramonti** (☎ 0984 57 90 67, fax 0984 57 90 66, ⓔ haquila@fitad.it, Via Forgitelle 87)* Singles/doubles with bath €26/36.25. Up in the heart of the village, it offers impeccable accommodation at budget prices.

***Hotel Aquila & Edelweiss** (☎ 0984 57 80 44, fax 0984 57 87 53, Viale Stazione 11)*

Singles/doubles with bath €41.50/62. This three-star hotel, wood-panelled, cosy and welcoming behind a rather stark facade, also runs a good restaurant specialising in Calabrian cuisine.

San Giovanni in Fiore

Although this is the biggest town in La Sila, it really has little to recommend it. The provincial accommodation guide lists a lot of hotels here but most are scattered around the nearby small villages – some as far away as Lorica, 20km to the west.

Lorica

A peaceful little spot on Lago Arvo, amid thick woods, Lorica is a minor ski resort, with a lift operating nearby. There are several camp sites in the area.

Villagio Turistico Lago Arvo *(☎/fax 0984 53 70 60, Passo della Cornacchia)* Low season sites per person €3.70, high season €5.20, bungalows from €26. Here's a true bargain in a scenically delightful area.

Camping Lorica *(☎ 0984 53 70 18)*, with sites at €5.75 per person, is beside the lake.

Albergo La Trota *(☎ 0984 53 71 66, fax 0984 53 71 67, Via Nazionale)* has doubles (€41.35) and compulsory full board in August (€44).

Villaggio Palumbo

About 10km south of San Giovanni in Fiore, this is a tourist village resort (☎ 0962 49 30 17) on Lago Ampollino. There are two similar ventures farther south on the road to Catanzaro: **Villagio Racise** and **Villaggio Mancuso**. All offer weekend package deals including food and accommodation and are set up for outdoor activities such as cross-country skiing and horse riding.

Soveria Mannelli

Set in woodlands, this HI hostel is within striking distance of La Sila.

La Pineta *(☎/fax 0968 66 60 79, Bivio Bonacci)* Dorm bed €10.90. La Pineta is on the S19 inland Catanzaro-Cosenza road, 43km north of Catanzaro. It's 4km from the nearest train station but buses running between Cosenza and Catanzaro can drop you nearby.

REGGIO DI CALABRIA

postcode 89100 • pop 179,800

As you gaze across the strait from Reggio's smart new pedestrian promenade to the twinkling lights of Messina in Sicily, you can almost feel romance in the air. And indeed the part of town near the waterfront, where you're most likely to find yourself, has its charm. But it's backed by hectares of concrete slum tenements. Rocked repeatedly by earthquakes, the last most devastating time in 1908, this once-proud ancient Greek city has plenty of other woes, including organised crime. You may notice an awful lot of *carabinieri* and Alpine soldiers (Italy's elite troops) in the streets. Wander up to Piazza Castello, where heavily armed guards surround the law courts, and you begin to gauge the depth of the problem.

Orientation

Stazione Centrale, the main train station, is at the southern edge of town on Piazza Garibaldi, where most buses also terminate. Walk north along Corso Giuseppe Garibaldi, the city's main street, for the APT office and other services. The *corso* has long been a kind of de facto pedestrian zone in the evening, as streams of locals parade in the ritual *passeggiata* (evening stroll). Nowadays, however, it faces strong competition from the new promenade running parallel to it along the shoreline.

Information

The APT office has branches at the train station (☎ 0965 2 71 20) and airport (☎ 0965 64 32 91). In town, the head office (☎ 0965 2 11 71) is on the 1st floor at Via Roma 3, and there's a branch (☎ 0965 89 20 12 or toll free 800 23 40 69) at Corso Garibaldi 329 in the Teatro Comunale building. Stated opening hours, not always rigorously observed, are 8am to 8pm Monday to Saturday.

The main post office is at Via Miraglia 14, near Piazza Italia.

The Ospedale Riuniti (hospital; ☎ 0965 39 71 11) is on Via Melacrino. The most

CALABRIA

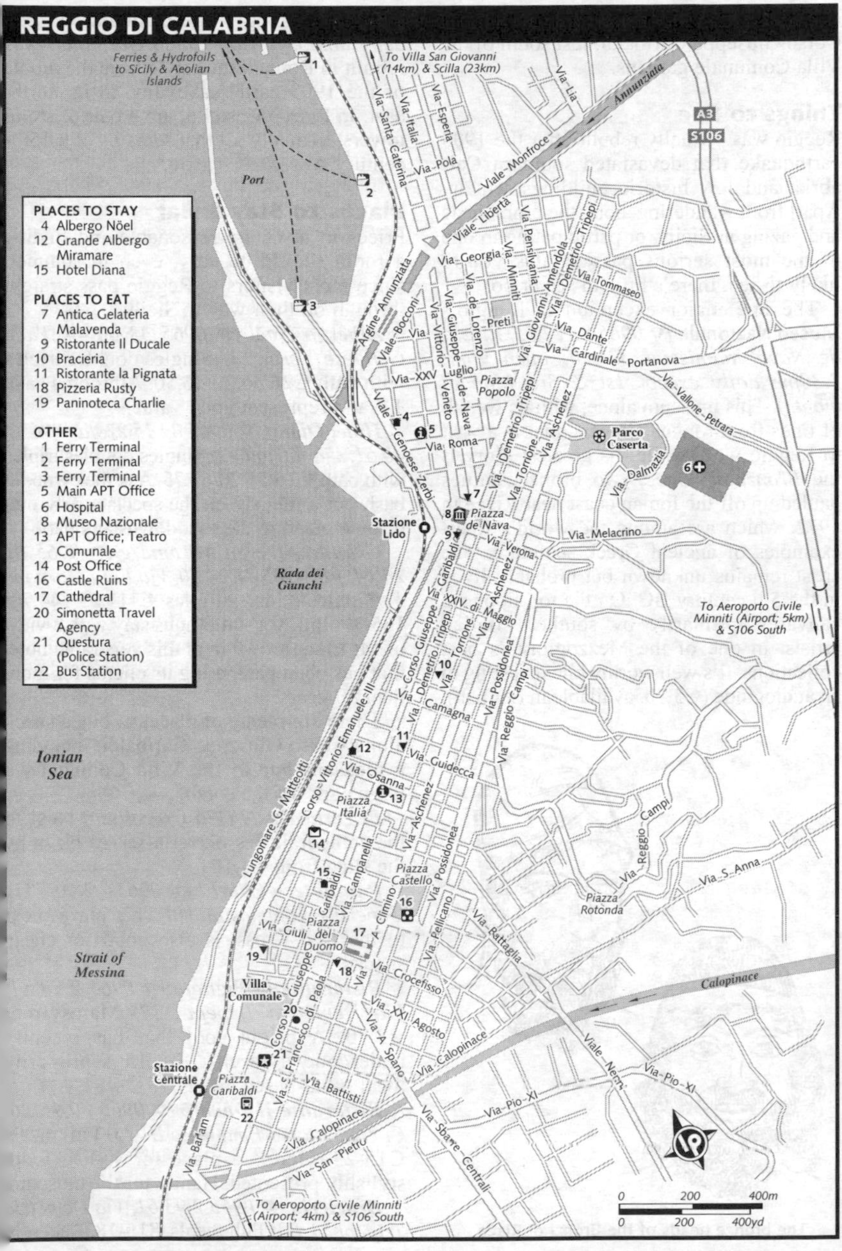

REGGIO DI CALABRIA

PLACES TO STAY
- 4 Albergo Nöel
- 12 Grande Albergo Miramare
- 15 Hotel Diana

PLACES TO EAT
- 7 Antica Gelateria Malavenda
- 9 Ristorante Il Ducale
- 10 Bracieria
- 11 Ristorante la Pignata
- 18 Pizzeria Rusty
- 19 Paninoteca Charlie

OTHER
- 1 Ferry Terminal
- 2 Ferry Terminal
- 3 Ferry Terminal
- 5 Main APT Office
- 6 Hospital
- 8 Museo Nazionale
- 13 APT Office; Teatro Comunale
- 14 Post Office
- 16 Castle Ruins
- 17 Cathedral
- 20 Simonetta Travel Agency
- 21 Questura (Police Station)
- 22 Bus Station

central police station (☎ 0965 41 11) is on Corso Giuseppe Garibaldi, just south of the Villa Comunale gardens.

Things to See

Reggio was virtually rebuilt after the 1908 earthquake that devastated southern Calabria, and few historic buildings remain. Apart from wandering along the promenade and gazing at Sicily, or participating in one of the most serious passeggiatas you're likely to see, there's little to see or do.

The one major exception is Reggio's **Museo Nazionale** *(☎ 0965 81 22 55, Piazza de Nava; admission €4.20; open 9am-7.30pm daily except 1st & 3rd Mon of month)*. This museum alone, with its wealth of finds from Magna Graecia, makes a visit to Reggio worthwhile. Its greatest glory is the *Bronzi di Riace*, two bronze statues hauled up off the Ionian coast near Riace in 1972, which are among the world's finest examples of ancient Greek sculpture. The artist remains unknown but probably lived in the 5th century BC. On the top floor are canvases, primarily by southern Italian artists, in one of the Mezzogiorno's best collections. It's well worthwhile investing in an audioguide (€3.70, available in English).

The bronze heads of the Bronzi di Riace

The gleaming white **cathedral** *(Piazza del Duomo, just off Corso Garibaldi)* was rebuilt in Romanesque style from the rubble of the 1908 earthquake. Just to its north-east, in Piazza Castello, are a pair of stolid towers, virtually all that remains of a 15th-century Aragonese **castle**.

Places to Stay & Eat

Prices in town are reasonable and finding a room should be easy, even in summer, since most visitors to Reggio pass straight through on their way to Sicily.

Albergo Noël *(☎ 0965 33 00 44, Viale Genoese Zerbi 13)* Singles/doubles/triples with bath €26/36.20/46.50. All rooms have TV and represent good value.

Hotel Diana *(☎ 0965 89 15 22, fax 0965 2 40 61, Via Vitrioli 12)* Singles/doubles/triples with bath €26/51.70/69.75. Ask the owner to bash out a melody on the spectacularly out-of-tune piano in the vast downstairs patio.

Grande Albergo Miramare *(☎ 0965 81 24 44, fax 0965 81 24 50, Via Fata Morgana 1)* Singles/doubles/triples €111.25/144.70/165.30. Enjoy a sumptuous stay with a view of Mt Etna thrown in at this venerable hotel that has been pampering its clients for more than 80 years.

There are plenty of places to buy a snack along Corso Giuseppe Garibaldi, including a pleasant ***bar*** in the Villa Comunale, a large park off the corso.

Pizzeria Rusty *(Via Crocefisso)* Next to the cathedral, this pizzeria serves pizza by the slice from €1.10.

Paninoteca Charlie *(☎ 0965 2 28 05, Via Generale Tommasini 10)* This place, next to the Red Cross, is also good for cheap snacks.

Ristorante la Pignata *(☎ 0965 2 78 41, Via Demetrio Tripepi 122)* Mains from €3.70. A bright spot that has recently undergone a facelift, it offers primarily local pasta-based dishes.

Ristorante Il Ducale *(☎ 0965 89 15 20, Corso Vittorio Emanuele III 13)* Full meals €15-23. Here's a place for stylish food, stylishly presented. Handy for the museum.

Bracieria *(☎ 0965 2 93 61, Via Demetrio Tripepi 81-83)* Full meals €15-18. Recently opened, its relaxed rustic setting (sip your drink from an earthenware pot) is popular with the young set. Unbeatable in town for grilled meat and fish.

Antica Gelateria Malavenda *(☎ 0965 89 14 49, cnr Via Romeo & Via Giovanni Amendola)* For the town's richest ice cream, you can't surpass this long-established Reggio favourite, which has been filling the tubs for over 100 years.

Getting There & Away

Air Aeroporto Civile Minniti (☎ 0965 64 05 17), the city's airport, is at Ravagnese, about 6km to the south. Alitalia and/or Air One fly to/from Rome, Milan and Bergamo, and the occasional charter flight drops by. Alitalia is represented by Simonetta travel agency (☎ 0965 33 14 44) at Corso Giuseppe Garibaldi 521.

Bus Most buses terminate at Piazza Garibaldi, in front of Stazione Centrale. Several different companies operate to towns in Calabria and beyond. ATAM (☎ 0965 62 01 29 or toll free ☎ 800 43 33 10) serves the Aspromonte Massif, with regular bus No 127 to Gambarie (1½ hours, three daily). Salzone (☎ 0965 75 15 86) has buses to Scilla about every 1½ hours. Lirosi (☎ 0965 5 75 52) has three daily runs to Rome and three to Catanzaro.

Train Trains stop at Stazione Centrale (☎ 848 88 80 88 for information) and less frequently at Stazione Lido, near the museum. Reggio is the terminus for daily trains to/from Milan (four), Turin (four), Florence (three), Rome (six), Venice (two) and Naples (two). For a wider choice, change at Paola (15+ daily). Regional services run daily to Catanzaro (six), Sapri (four) and, less frequently, to Cosenza, Taranto, Nicotera and Bari.

Car & Motorcycle The A3 ends at Reggio di Calabria. If you are continuing farther south, the S106 hugs the coast round the 'toe', then heads north along the Ionian Sea.

Boat Boats for Messina leave from the port (just north of Stazione Lido). In high season, SNAV (☎ 0965 2 96 58) has up to 20 hydrofoils per day (€2.90 one way). In low season, there may be as few as two sailings. Some boats continue to the Aeolian Islands.

The FS national railway (☎ 848 88 80 88) runs a dozen big hydrofoils every day to/from Messina (€4.20 return). Meridiano (☎ 0965 81 04 14) and Navigazione Generale Italiana (NGI; ☎ 335 842 77 84) each run up to 12 car ferries daily on this route. Prices for cars are single/return €7.75/€11.40 (passengers don't pay extra), and for foot passengers €1.60/3.

Ferries for cars and foot passengers cross to Messina around the clock from Villa San Giovanni, 20 minutes farther north along the rail line. Both Caronte (☎ 0965 79 31 31) and Tourist Shipping (☎ 0965 75 14 13) run regular ferries throughout the year; medium-sized car one way/return €17.10/30.50 valid 60 days (passengers don't pay extra), motorcycles €5.20 each way. The crossing takes 20 to 30 minutes, departing every 15 to 20 minutes.

Getting Around

Orange local buses run by ATAM (see Getting There & Away) cover most of the city. For the port, take bus Nos 13 or 125 from Piazza Garibaldi outside the station. The Porto-Aeroporto bus runs from the port via Piazza Garibaldi to the airport and vice-versa (€0.55 per trip or €0.80 for up to 90 minutes of travel). Buy tickets at ATAM offices, tobacconists or newsstands.

ASPROMONTE MASSIF

Inland from Reggio di Calabria rises the Aspromonte massif. Its highest peak, **Montalto** (1955m), is dominated by a huge bronze statue of Christ and offers sweeping views across to Sicily.

The Montalto area, now a national park, has some walking trails, albeit not quite as spectacular or demanding as those in La Sila.

To reach the Aspromonte's main town of Gambarie, take ATAM city bus No 127 from Reggio di Calabria (1½ hours, three daily). Most of the roads inland from Reggio eventually hit the main S183 road that runs north to the town.

TYRRHENIAN COAST (COSTA TIRRENICA)

The region's western seashore is a mixture of the good, the bad and the ugly. Certain stretches are crammed with tacky package resorts that attract holidaying Italians by the thousand each summer. But there are several small towns that are pleasant to stay in and the odd cove with a protected sandy beach.

The journey along the Costa Viola, from Rosarno to Scilla and on towards Reggio di Calabria, is one of Italy's great coastal drives, with breathtaking views of Sicily.

For information about the coast, try the main APT office in Reggio di Calabria. If you're coming from the north, the one in Cosenza might be able to rustle up a brochure or two. They'll probably recommend that you stay at one of the tourist villages – don't be immediately put off. Many offer excellent value and all have private beaches, generally some of the best on the coast. Most, however, require a minimum stay of one week in high season.

Out of season, most hotels, camp sites and tourist villages close. In summer many of the hotels are full, although you should have an easier time with the camp sites.

Most coastal towns are on the main train line between Reggio and Naples, and the S18 road hugs the coast for much of the way. The A3 from Reggio di Calabria to Salerno runs farther inland.

Scilla

After the urban confusion of Reggio and Villa San Giovanni, the S18 brings you to a striking stretch of Calabria's coastline. The highlands of the Aspromonte extend right to the coast and the views from the cliffs across to Sicily fuel the imagination.

Coming from the north, the drive is even better (especially if you take it slowly on the S18). Arching around its beach, the first of any consequence north of Reggio, is the picturesque town of Scilla. Its northern end is dominated by the rock associated with Scylla, the mythical six-headed sea monster who drowned sailors as they tried to navigate the Strait of Messina (and if she didn't get them, Charybdis, across in Sicily, would). Just north of the small port is a narrow alley that is worth strolling along, where fisherfolk's houses front the water.

***Pensione le Sirene** (☎ 0965 75 40 19, Via Nazionale 55)* Singles/doubles with bath €23.80/41.40. Ask for one of the rooms with a view of the beach and on to Sicily. This pensione also has a large terrace, which offers the same views and is ideal for observing the evening passeggiatta along the promenade.

Promontorio di Tropea

The Promontorio di Tropea, 50km north of Scilla, is like a bunion on the 'bridge' of Italy's foot. Stretching from Nicotera in the south to Pizzo at the northern end, it boasts Calabria's best sandy beaches and aquamarine seas.

Nicotera is dominated by its own medieval castle.

***Sayonara Club** (☎ 0963 8 19 44, fax 0963 8 11 36, ⓔ sayonara@sayonara.it)* Low season sites per person/tent/car from €2.60/2.60/2.60, high season €11.40/11.40/2.60, bungalows €31-114. Open May-Oct. This tourist village, where prices vary hugely – and typically – according to season, is down at sea level at the southern extremity of Nicotera Marina.

About 20km north-west of Nicotera at **Capo Vaticano** are dozens of tourist villages and hotels, most of which are open from May to October and impose a full-board arrangement and, frequently, a one-week minimum stay in high season.

***Hotel Residence Costa Azzurra** (☎ 0963 66 31 09, fax 0963 66 39 56, ⓔ costazzura@virgilio.net)* Full board per person €40.80-68.20 according to season. This is a smallish, family-run hotel.

***Hotel Villaggio Stromboli** (☎ 0963 66 90 93, fax 0963 66 92 56, ⓔ hotel.stromboli@tiscalinet.it)* Low season villas from €36.15, high season from €92.96, full board per person €38.73/64.55. This stylish, above average holiday village, 4km north-east of Capo Vaticano, remains open year-round.

Around 10km north-east of Capo Vaticano, **Tropea** is a picturesque little town perched high above the coast. Probably the prettiest spot on Calabria's Tyrrhenian coast, it has several long sandy beaches within walking distance of town. There is a Pro Loco office (☎ 0963 6 14 75) on Piazza Ercole, in the centre of the old town. It opens 9.30am to 12.30pm and 5pm to 8pm daily except Sunday afternoon. Most of the 10 or so hotels are in the higher price bracket and many close for winter.

Hotel Virgilio *(☎ 0963 6 19 78, fax 0963 6 23 20, Viale Tondo 27)* Singles/doubles/triples/quads with bath from €33.55/50.60/69.75/74.90 (nearly double in Aug). Open year-round. This pleasant family hotel is a bargain outside the peak holiday period.

Ristorante Pizzeria L'Arca *(Largo San Giuseppe)* Open Apr-Oct. This place, 100m from the tourist office, does just about the best fish soup on the promontory.

About 8km south of Pizzo, up high and slightly inland, is the long-established town of **Vibo Valentia**, good for a brief roam and a useful transport hub. The APT office (☎ 0963 4 20 08) on Via Forgiari, just off the main Corso Vittorio Emanuele (behind the Galleria Vecchia), opens 8am to 12.30pm Monday to Friday. Above the town is its castle, built by the Normans and later extended and reinforced by both Frederick II and the Anjevins. From it, there's a sweeping panorama of coast, inland hills and, on a clear day, the volcanic island of Stromboli. It houses an excellent small **museum** *(☎ 0963 4 33 50; admission €2.10; open 9am-8pm daily)*, which has a wealth of well-displayed and -documented (in Italian) artefacts from Hipponion, the original Greek settlement, and Roman Valentia, which superseded it. You'll find Roman votive offerings by the ton and a coin collection big enough to make a numismatist faint.

A coastal railway runs around the promontory from Rosarno and Nicotera to Vibo Marina and Pizzo. SAV buses also connect most resorts with Tropea and Pizzo.

Pizzo

In the bars of Pizzo, you will find possibly Italy's best *tartufo*, a type of chocolate ice-cream ball.

Inside the town's 16th-century Chiesa Matrice di San Giorgio, on Via Marconi, lies the tomb of Joachim Murat, king of Naples from 1808 until 1815, when he was defeated by the Austrians and the Bourbons were restored to the Neapolitan throne. Although he was the architect of various enlightened reforms, the locals preferred the Bourbon devil they had known and showed no great concern when Murat was imprisoned and executed here.

Just north of town, almost on the beach, the tiny **Chiesa di Piedigrotta** was literally carved into the tufa rock by Neapolitan shipwreck survivors in the 17th century. The church was later added to (the statue of Fidel Castro kneeling before a medallion of Pope John XXIII is an obvious recent addition) but the place is crumbling away and there is no move afoot to stop the rot.

Wander through Piazza della Repubblica, at the heart of the picturesque old centre of Pizzo, before settling in at of one of the square's many ***Bar Gelateria*** terraces for a cold drink or ice-cream fix. Immediately to its south is the bijou **Castello Murat**, built by the Aragonese in the 15th century. You can't get in but there's a great seascape from the balconies that flank it.

For a typical seafood meal, ***La Nave***, in a rusting boat on the waterfront south of town, has plentiful main courses from €10.

Paola

The 80km of coast from Pizzo northwards to Paola is mostly overdeveloped and ugly. Paola is the main train hub for Cosenza, about 25km inland, and is a large, comparatively nondescript place. Watched over by a crumbling castle, its main attraction is the **Santuario di San Francesco di Paola** *(☎ 0982 58 25 18; free; open 6am-12.30pm & 2pm-6pm daily)*. The saint lived and died in Paola in the 15th century, and the sanctuary that he and his followers carved out of the bare rock has for centuries been the object of pilgrimage. You can wander through the spartan chambers but there is precious little to see. More interesting is the pleasant cloister of the monastery (still in use today), planted with roses and surrounded by naive wall paintings depicting the saint's – truly incredible – miracles. The original church contains an ornate reliquary of the saint. Also within the complex is a modern basilica, built to mark the second millennium, with a huge pair of rich, glowing stained-glass panels set in the ceiling's acres of stained woodwork.

There are several hotels near the station but it might be preferable to stay in towns farther north along the coast.

Diamante to Praia a Mare

Diamante and Cirella mark the southern end of a largely uninterrupted stretch of wide, grey pebbly beach that continues for about 30km to Praia a Mare, just short of Calabria's regional boundary with Basilicata. Although popular with the locals, it is for the most part uninspiring. Backed by rows of camp sites and growing development projects, the coast lacks much of the scenic splendour to the north in Basilicata or indeed south towards Reggio di Calabria.

Il Fortino *(☎ 0985 8 60 85, Via Vittorio Veneto)* In Cirella, this is one of several camp sites along the coast.

If you're finding the coast a little flat, head for the hills and old Scalea (not the modern holiday development stretching along the plain). About 15km south of Praia, it's one of the more eye-catching towns along the northern coast. Climb the stairway lanes past the muddle of tumble-down houses, or stop in Piazza de Palma for a beer at the Tarì Bar.

Praia a Mare

A couple of kilometres short of the border with Basilicata, Praia a Mare is a modern and not terribly appealing town built to serve Italian holiday-makers. At least the surrounding landscape takes a more dramatic tone here, with the S18 coastal highway climbing away behind the town up into Basilicata. The **Isola di Dino**, just off the coast south of town, has an expansive grey beach and an easily accessible **sea cave**, every bit as impressive as Capri's better-known Grotta Azzurra.

La Mantinera *(☎ 0985 77 90 23, fax 0985 77 90 09, ⓔ mantinera@labnet.it)* Sites for 2 people, car & tent €12.95-33.55, according to season. Open mid-Apr–Sept. This tourist village at the southern end of town in the Fiuzzi area, although 300m from the beach, offers above-average camping facilities. It also has bungalows on offer (€232.40-1110.40 per week).

As an alternative place to stay, consider Maratea, across the regional frontier in Basilicata (see Maratea in the earlier section on Basilicata's Tyrrhenian Coast), which has considerably more charm.

Autolinee Preite operates five or six buses daily in each direction between Cosenza and Praia a Mare. SITA goes north to Maratea.

Aieta & Tortora

The hill villages of **Aieta** and **Tortora**, about 12km and 6km inland, respectively, from Praia, belong to another world. Infrequent local buses serve both villages. The towns are precariously perched upon ridges that must have been hard going before asphalt days. Aieta is higher than Tortora and the journey constitutes much of the reward for going there. When you arrive, walk up to the 16th-century **Palazzo Spinello** at the end of the road and take a look into the ravine behind it.

Sicily (Sicilia)

Sicily represents the very essence of Italy: history and passion, beauty and destruction, awe-inspiring artworks and architecture, fabulous food, fiery volcanoes, stunning beaches, chaos and organised crime. It is a place of contrasts, from the crumbling grandeur of the capital, Palermo, to the upmarket glitz of the tourist resort of Taormina. There are Greek ruins at Syracuse, Agrigento, Selinunte and Segesta, and the volcanic Aeolian Islands off Sicily's northern coast have a wild beauty matched only by the spectacular Mt Etna on the island's eastern coast. If you thought religion and tradition were no longer a part of daily life, experiencing the Easter festivities on the island will probably change your mind. Particularly worth seeing are the Procession of the Mysteries at Trapani and the Byzantine Easter rites at Piana degli Albanesi near Palermo, when women in colourful 15th-century costume give out Easter eggs to the public.

Sicily is the largest island in the Mediterranean and its strategic location made it a prize for successive waves of invaders. As well as Greek temples, there are Roman ruins, Norman churches and castles, Arab and Byzantine domes and splendid Baroque churches and palazzos.

History

It is believed that the earliest settlers on Sicily were the Sicanians, Elymians and Siculians, who came from various points around the southern Mediterranean; they were followed by the Phoenicians. Greek colonisation began in the 8th century BC with the foundation of Naxos. The cities of Syracuse, Catania, Messina and Agrigento grew and still dominate the island. By 210 BC, Sicily was under Roman control, with power eventually passing to the Byzantines and then to the Arabs, who had settled in by AD 903, cultivating oranges and lemons there for the first time.

Norman conquest of the island began in 1060, when Roger I of Hauteville captured

Highlights

- Marvel at the mosaics of the Cappella Palatina and those of the spectacular Monreale cathedral
- Visit the Parco Archeologico in Syracuse, the ancient Greek city that once rivalled Athens
- Wander through the remains of Greek temples in the Valley of the Temples near Agrigento
- Gorge yourself on sweet, ricotta-filled *cannoli* or just sip a refreshing coffee or lemon *granita*
- Climb Stromboli at night (with a guide, of course)
- Visit the Egadi Islands during the *mattanza*, the traditional annual tuna catch
- Take in the view of Mt Etna from the Teatro Greco in Taormina
- Experience the Easter rituals of the *Misteri* in Trapani

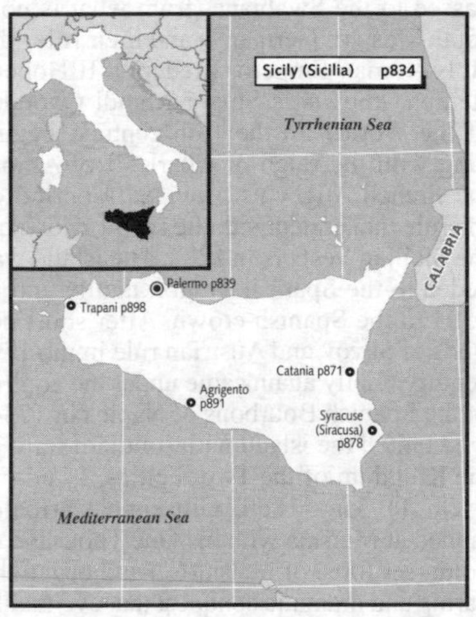

Messina. Mastery of Sicily subsequently passed to the Swabians (from what is now south-western Germany) and their ruler the Holy Roman Emperor Frederick II Hohenstaufen, known as Stupor Mundi (Wonder of the World). In the 13th century, beginning with the reign of Charles I of Anjou, the French Angevins provided a period of misrule that ended with the revolt known as the Sicilian Vespers in 1282. The island was ceded to the Spanish Aragon family and in 1503 to the Spanish crown. After short periods of Savoy and Austrian rule in the 18th century, Sicily again came under the control of the Spanish Bourbons of Naples in 1734, who united the island with southern Italy in the Kingdom of the Two Sicilies.

On 11 May 1860, Giuseppe Garibaldi landed at Marsala with his One Thousand (a volunteer force of 'redshirts') and began the daring and dramatic conquest that eventually set the seal on the unification of Italy. Life did not greatly improve for the people and between 1871 and 1914 more than one million Sicilians emigrated, mainly to the USA.

In 1943, some 140,000 Allied troops under General Dwight Eisenhower landed on south-eastern Sicily. Initially blocked by dogged Italian and German resistance, Eisenhower's field commanders entered Messina within six weeks, after heavy fighting had devastated many parts of the island. The Allied occupation lasted until early 1944. In 1948 Sicily became a semi-autonomous region and, unlike other such regions in Italy, it has its own parliament and legislative powers.

The Mafia

Sicilians feel offended that the image of their proud island abroad is one portrayed in blood. There is no need to fear that you will be caught in the crossfire of a gang war while on Sicily. The 'men of honour' have little interest in foreign tourists. Nonetheless, the Mafia – or Cosa Nostra, as the Sicilian Mafia is known – is alive and well.

The overt presence of the Italian army in Sicily (you'll see armed soldiers at 'strategic' spots here and there) has done little to dent the Mafia's activities. However, since the arrest of the Sicilian 'godfather' Salvatore ('Toto') Riina in 1993 and his successor, Giovanni 'The Pig' Brusca, in 1996, Mafia *pentiti* (turncoats) have continued to blow the whistle on fellow felons, politicians, businessmen and others, right up to former prime minister Giulio Andreotti. At two separate trials in 1997, Andreotti stood accused of supporting the Sicilian Mafia, helping fix court cases and ordering, or consenting to, the murder of an investigative journalist.

Some fear the pentiti are inventing confessions to settle private scores, but there must be something in it otherwise the Cosa Nostra would not be 'discouraging' pentiti by bumping off their relatives. Tommaso Buscetta, the most famous *pentito* of them all, has lost at least 33 relatives, his wife and three sons included. There were more than 1000 pentiti in 1997 waiting to give evidence in return for immunity or leniency and protection. However, evidence has surfaced that some pentiti have been continuing their criminal activities while under state protection – which has thrown the witness protection programme into confusion.

With the Andreotti trial, in a sense the prosecution didn't just have the ex-PM in the dock but also the course of Italian history over the previous 50 years. Considering that the country was only beginning to recover from the widespread revelations of the *Tangentopoli* scandal (the institutionalisation of kick-backs and bribes that had been the country's *modus operandi* since WWII), many commentators felt that the country could not stomach the possibility of the charges being proven. On 23 October 1999, Andreotti was cleared of all charges against him and walked out of the courtroom a free man – despite the fact that most Italians believe he is anything but clean. There is a common belief and acceptance that the Mafia and the establishment are intertwined, and that this partnership is part and parcel of Italy's political system. As the Italian author Luigi Barzini once wrote: 'The phenomenon has deep roots in history, in the character of the Sicilians, in local habits. Its origins disappear down the dim vistas of the centuries.'

Orientation & Information

Although some industry has developed and tourism is a fast-growing sector, the island's economy is still largely agricultural and the people remain strongly connected to the land. Along the eastern coast especially, there is mile upon mile of citrus groves.

The coastal landscape ranges from rugged and windswept shores to long stretches of sandy beach, while rolling hills, mountains and dry plateaus dominate the interior. The climate brings mild weather in winter, but summer is relentlessly hot and the beaches swarm with holiday-makers. The best times to visit are spring and autumn, when it is warm enough for the beach but not too hot for sightseeing.

Sicilian food is spicy and sweet – no doubt part of the island's long contact with Arab colonisers. The focus along the coast is on seafood, notably swordfish, and fresh produce. Some say fruit and vegetables taste better on Sicily. The cakes and pastries can be works of art, but are very sweet. Try the *cassata*, a rich cake filled with ricotta and candied fruits (there is also cassata ice cream); *cannoli*, tubes of pastry filled with cream, ricotta or chocolate; and *dolci di mandorle*, the many varieties of almond cakes and pastries. Like the Spaniards, Sicilians have a penchant for marzipan, which they make just as well as their Iberian cousins. Then there is *granita*, a drink of crushed ice flavoured with lemon, strawberry or coffee, to name a few flavours – perfect on a hot Sicilian day.

Dangers & Annoyances

Sicilians are generally welcoming and sociable, but women might find the local men a little too friendly. Female tourists should take a hint from local women and avoid walking around at night alone in the bigger cities such as Palermo, Catania and Messina. Exercise caution elsewhere too.

You won't have to worry about confronting the Godfather but petty criminals abound, especially in the bigger centres. Pickpockets and motorcycle-mounted snatch thieves are the worst – the latter love handbags and small day-packs. If you have to carry one of these items, keep a firm hold on it. Don't wear jewellery and keep all your valuables in a money belt or in your hotel.

Car theft is a problem in Palermo, so using private, guarded car parks is advisable.

Shopping

As in Spain and Portugal, the Arabs brought a rich tradition of ceramic production to Sicily. Although the modern products are directed at tourists, they are evocative of the island, as souvenirs go. Simple designs with base colours of blue and yellow best reflect the ceramics' artisanal roots; more luridly decorated plates, vases, pots and bowls can be found all over the island. Or you could go for a ceramic *trinacria*, a face surrounded by three legs representing the three-pointed island. Major ceramics centres include Caltagirone and Santo Stefano di Camastra.

Since the 18th century, Sicily's *carretti* (carts) have been a byword for the island. Used for transport until the arrival of the motorcar, the wooden carts were lovingly sculpted and bedecked with brightly coloured illustrations of mythic events, local characters or even family histories. You'd be lucky to see one in action now, but they are occasionally hauled out as tourist attractions. For the ultimate in memento kitsch, however, you could always buy one of the models on sale in virtually every souvenir shop.

Getting There & Away

Air Flights from all over mainland Italy and from major European cities land at Palermo and Catania. Palermo's airport, renamed Falcone-Borsellino after the two anti-Mafia judges assassinated in the city in 1992, is at Punta Raisi, about 32km west of the city, while Catania's airport, Fontanarossa, is 7km south. Buses run from both airports into the respective city centres. See Getting There & Away and Getting Around under Palermo and Catania later for further details. To obtain information on flights to/from Sicily, contact Sestante or Alitalia offices.

Bus Direct bus services between Rome and Sicily are operated by several companies, including SAIS (☎ 091 616 60 28, **W** www.saisautolinee.it or www.saistrasporti.it), Via P Balsamo 20, Palermo, and Segesta (☎ 091 616 90 39 or 091 616 79 19, **W** www.segesta.palermo2000.com), Via P Balsamo 26, Palermo. In Rome, the buses leave from Stazione Tiburtina.

The Segesta bus runs from Rome direct to Messina (€25.80 one way), Palermo (€33.55) and on to Trapani (€36.15), which leaves Rome at 9.30pm daily, arrives in Messina at 6am, Palermo at 9.20am and Trapani at noon.

SAIS runs two services between Rome (leaving 8pm and 10pm daily) and Catania, continuing to Agrigento. You have to change at Messina to continue to Palermo. The 8pm bus arrives at Messina at 4.30am, Catania at 6.15am and Agrigento at 9.30am. In Catania the bus connects with others to Syracuse, Ragusa and Enna. Going the other way, there are two services departing Agrigento at 5pm and 6.15pm (the connecting buses from Palermo depart at 5pm and 7pm). The 5pm service from Agrigento departs Catania at 8pm, Messina at 9.30pm, and arrives in Rome at 6.30am the following day. One-way tickets from Rome to any of these destinations in Sicily cost €38.75.

In Rome, you can get tickets and information at the Eurojet agency (☎ 06 474 28 01) in Piazza della Repubblica 54, or go to the bus station at Piazzale Tiburtina. Booking is obligatory. See Getting There & Away under Palermo later and Rome for more details.

Train Direct trains run from Milan, Florence, Rome, Naples and Reggio di Calabria to Messina and on to Palermo, Catania and other provincial capitals – the trains are transported from the mainland by ferry from Villa San Giovanni. Be prepared for long delays on Intercity trains on this route. Ticket prices depend on distance travelled. For example, one-way 2nd-class fares on Intercity trains are: Rome-Palermo €67.15 (11 hours, four daily); Rome-Catania €62 (9½ hours, three daily); Milan-Palermo €77.45

(19 hours, one daily); Milan-Catania €77.45 (17 hours, two daily).

For train information, call ☎ 147 88 80 88 (7am to 9pm) or go to the information office at any train station.

Boat Regular car/passenger ferries cross the strait between Villa San Giovanni (Calabria) and Messina. Hydrofoils run by the railways and snappier jobs run by SNAV connect Messina directly with Reggio di Calabria. See Messina in this chapter and the Reggio di Calabria section (in the Apulia, Basilicata & Calabria chapter) for details.

Sicily is also accessible by ferry from Genoa, Livorno, Naples and Cagliari, and from Malta and Tunisia. The main company servicing the Mediterranean is Tirrenia (W www.forti.it/tirrenia/Inglese/index.html) and its services to/from Sicily include Palermo-Cagliari, Palermo-Naples, Trapani-Cagliari and Trapani-Tunisia.

Grandi Navi Veloci, run by the Grimaldi group, has more upmarket and luxury ferries from Livorno (three per week) and Genoa (daily) to Palermo. For information check the Web site W www.grimaldi.it or call the relevant office (Livorno ☎ 058 640 98 94, Genoa ☎ 010 58 93 31, Palermo ☎ 091 58 74 04).

Ustica Lines runs summer ferries from Trapani to Naples via Ustica and from Trapani to Pantelleria.

SNAV (Naples ☎ 081 761 23 48, Palermo ☎ 091 58 60 66) run a summer ferry between Palermo and Naples (four hours). See Getting There & Away under Palermo for details.

Ferry prices are determined by the season and jump considerably in summer (Tirrenia's high season varies according to destination, but is generally from July to September). Timetables can change dramatically each year. Tirrenia publishes an annual booklet listing all routes and prices, which is available at Tirrenia offices and agencies.

In summer, all routes are busy and unless you book several weeks in advance you may literally miss the boat. Tickets can be booked through the company concerned or at travel agencies throughout Italy. Offices and telephone numbers for the ferry companies are listed in the Getting There & Away sections for the relevant cities.

The following is a guide to fares, based on high-season travel at the time of writing. For an airline-type seat, fares were: Genoa–Palermo on Grandi Navi Veloci €106.50 (20 hours), Naples-Palermo on Tirrenia €40.50 (11 hours), Palermo-Cagliari on Tirrenia €37.70 (14 hours) and Trapani-Tunisia on Tirrenia €51 (11 hours). For a 2nd-class cabin (shared with up to three other people and usually segregated by gender) fares are: Genoa-Palermo on Grandi Navi Veloci €106.50, Naples-Palermo on Tirrenia €51.50, Palermo-Cagliari on Tirrenia €51.50 and Trapani-Tunisia on Tirrenia €63.

Fares for cars vary according to the size of the vehicle. High-season charges for the Palermo-Cagliari route range from €78 to €93.

There are also ferry and hydrofoil services, mainly operated by Siremar (☎ 091 749 31 11, W www.siremar.it), from Sicily to the small groups of islands off the coast (Aeolian Islands, Egadi Islands, Isole Pelagie, Pantelleria and Ustica). See the relevant Getting There & Away sections in this chapter for details.

Getting Around

Bus The best mode of public transport on Sicily is the bus. Numerous companies run services connecting the main towns around the coast, including Messina, Catania, Syracuse, Agrigento, Trapani and Palermo. Services also connect these cities with the smaller towns along the coast and in the interior. The companies with the most extensive networks are SAIS and AST. See the Getting There & Away and Getting Around sections for each town.

Train The coastal train service between Messina and Palermo and between Messina and Syracuse is efficient, and the run between Palermo and Agrigento is also generally OK. However, train services to other places in the interior can be infrequent and slow, and it is best to do some research before deciding between train and bus. The service from Noto to Ragusa, for instance, is picturesque but very slow.

Car & Motorcycle There is no substitute for the freedom your own vehicle can give you, especially for getting to places not well served by public transport. Roads are generally good and *autostrade* (motorways) connect most major cities. It is possible to hitchhike on Sicily, but don't expect a ride in a hurry. Single women should not hitch-hike under any circumstances.

Palermo

postcode 91100 • pop 730,000

At one time an Arab emirate and the seat of a Norman kingdom, and in its heyday regarded as the grandest city in Europe, Palermo today is in a remarkable state of decay. It was heavily bombed in WWII and has been much neglected since. It is noted now more for the Mafia trials of the 1980s, the assassinations in 1992 of Giovanni Falcone and Paolo Borsellino, the top anti-Mafia judges, and the upsurge in gangland killings in the mid-1990s.

Beneath the grime, enough evidence of its golden days remains for Palermo to be a compelling city to visit, if only as a crossroads between east and west. Cultural cross-fertilisation finds expression in the city's architectural mix, obvious in such monuments as the adjacent churches of La Martorana and San Cataldo.

Palermo's superb position by the sea at the foot of Monte Pellegrino, with the fertile Conca d'Oro valley behind it, has long made it a rich prize for Sicily's colonisers. Around the 8th century BC, the Phoenicians established the town of Ziz (meaning 'flower') here, on the site of a prehistoric village. It remained a relatively minor town under Roman, and later Byzantine, domination and it was not until AD 831, when it was conquered by the Arabs, that the city truly flourished and became a jewel of the Islamic world.

Things only improved when the Normans took control in 1072. The centre of Roger I of Hauteville's kingdom, Palermo was hailed as one of the most magnificent and cultured cities of 12th-century Europe. After Roger's death, the monarchy passed to his son Roger II but foundered shortly afterwards, eventually passing to the German Hohenstaufens from Swabia and the Holy Roman Emperor Frederick II, still remembered as one of Sicily's most enlightened rulers. After his death, Palermo and all of Sicily passed to the French Anjou family, themselves later deposed following the Sicilian Vespers revolt in 1282, which started in Palermo. By then eclipsed by Naples, Palermo sank into a long, slow decline.

Orientation

Palermo is a large but manageable city. The main streets of the historical centre are Via Roma and Via Maqueda. These extend from the train station in the south to Piazza Castelnuovo, a vast square in the northern, modern part of town and a 20-minute walk from the train station. Around the train station are most of the cheaper pensiones and hotels. It's a grimy and chaotic area, but behind the decaying palazzos lining the main streets is a fascinating maze of narrow lanes and tiny piazzas where you will find markets and trattorias and, unfortunately, get an even better idea of just how dilapidated Palermo is.

The area around Piazza Castelnuovo seems a world away, with its malls, outdoor cafes and designer shops. Intersecting Via Maqueda and Via Roma are Corso Vittorio Emanuele and Via Cavour, the main thoroughfares to the port and the ferry terminal (about a 10-minute walk east of Via Roma).

Information

Tourist Offices The main APT office (☎ 091 58 61 22 or 091 58 38 47) is at Piazza Castelnuovo 35. It was under renovation at the time of writing, but you could still fight your way through the scaffolding. It has a hotel list for Palermo and its province, and will give limited assistance to tourists looking for accommodation. It also has brochures on major sights and attractions in and around Palermo. The office opens 8.30am to 2pm and 2.30pm to 6pm Monday to Friday plus

PALERMO

PLACES TO STAY
- 6 Grand Hotel et Des Palmes
- 7 Hotel Petit
- 15 Hotel Joli
- 16 Hotel Tonic
- 17 Hotel Elite; Hotel Boston-Madonia
- 23 Massimo Plaza Hotel
- 36 Hotel Moderno
- 39 Grande Albergo Sole
- 41 Centrale Palace Hotel
- 46 Hotel Confort
- 50 Hotel Letizia
- 59 Hotel Corona
- 60 Hotel Sicilia; Hotel Alessandra
- 61 Hotel del Centro; Albergo Concordia
- 68 Albergo Vittoria
- 69 Albergo Orientale

PLACES TO EAT
- 5 Antico Caffè
- 9 Hostaria Al Duar
- 20 Charleston
- 24 Dal Pompiere
- 28 Panineria e Pizzeria Fabrizio
- 34 Da Pina
- 35 Vucciria Market
- 45 Da Ciccio
- 47 Antica Focacceria di San Francesco
- 51 La Cambusa
- 53 Il Crudo e Il Cotto
- 54 Osteria dei Vespri
- 55 Il Massimo dei Sapori; Trattoria Da Massimo
- 70 Bar Gastronomia Aiello Vittorio

OTHER
- 1 CTS Travel Agency
- 2 Sestante Travel Agency
- 3 APT Office
- 4 Teatro Politeama Garibaldi
- 8 Pietro Barbaro (SNAV Agents)
- 10 Ruggieri & Figli (American Express)
- 11 Ferry Terminal
- 12 Tirrenia
- 13 Siremar
- 14 Grandi Navi Veloci
- 18 Record Viaggi Travel Agency
- 19 Monte dei Paschi di Siena (Bank)
- 21 Telecom Office
- 22 Teatro Massimo
- 25 Opera dei Pupi
- 26 British Consulate
- 27 Museo Archeologico Regionale
- 29 Feltrinelli Bookshop
- 30 Post Office
- 31 Banca Nazionale del Lavoro
- 32 Chiesa di San Domenico
- 33 I Grilli Giù
- 37 Teatro Biondo
- 38 Chiesa di San Matteo
- 40 Quattro Canti
- 42 Chiesa di San Giuseppe dei Teatini
- 43 Fontana Pretoria
- 44 Chiesa di Santa Caterina
- 48 Oratorio di San Lorenzo
- 49 Chiesa di San Francesco d'Assisi
- 52 Palazzo Chiaramonte-Steri
- 56 La Martorana
- 57 Palazzo del Municipio
- 58 Chiesa di San Cataldo
- 62 Chiesa della SS Trinità
- 63 Lo Spasimo
- 64 Telecom Office
- 65 Urban Bus Station
- 66 Intercity Bus Station
- 67 La Cascio Night Pharmacy
- 71 Chiesa del Gesù
- 72 Cathedral
- 73 Questura (Police Station)
- 74 Porta Nuova
- 75 Palazzo dei Normanni (& Cappella Palatina)
- 76 Chiesa di San Giovanni degli Eremiti
- 77 AST Bus Station
- 78 Ospedale Civico (Hospital)

Raised from Rubble

Moves are afoot to do something about the decrepit state of Palermo's historical centre and many monuments have been or are being restored. The area around Via Alloro, for instance, is literally being raised from the rubble – it was bombed intensively during WWII due to its proximity to the port – and is worth exploring. Known as the Kalsa, this area was founded in the late 10th century and is one of the oldest quarters of Palermo.

(at least in high season) 8.30am to 2pm Saturday. There is a branch office at the train station (☎ 091 616 59 14), open the same times as the main office, and another at the Falcone-Borsellino airport (☎ 091 59 16 98), open 8am to midnight daily.

There is also a tourist information booth in the middle of Piazza Castelnuovo, with enthusiastic, multilingual staff who can answer most tourist queries. Other booths are located at major places of tourist interest around the city, including: the ferry terminal; Via Cavour, near Teatro Massimo; Piazza Marina; Piazza Bellini, near Palazzo del Municipio; Piazza della Vittoria; Piazza Giulio Cesare, in front of the station. They all distribute a good tourist map and have information on current events. They open 9am to 2pm and 3pm to 8pm Monday to Thursday, 8.30am to 8.30pm Friday and Saturday, 9am to 1pm and 3pm to 7pm Sunday.

Money The currency exchange booth at the train station is open 8am to 8pm daily, and there's another at the airport (Banca di Sicilia). Banks are generally open 8.30am to 1.15pm. Several have ATMs, including Banca Nazionale del Lavoro, Via Roma 297, and Monte dei Paschi di Siena, off Via S Oliva. American Express (Amex) is represented by Ruggieri & Figli (☎ 091 58 71 44), Via E Amari 40.

Post & Communications You can't miss the main post office at Via Roma 322 – it's a huge salmon-pink and grey Fascist edifice. It opens 8.30am to 7pm (8.30am to 1.30pm on Saturday) and has fax services.

There is a Telecom office virtually opposite the train station on Piazza G Cesare. It opens 8am to 9.30pm daily. Another Telecom office is on Piazzale Ungheria.

Travel Agencies Sestante (☎ 091 58 63 33), where you can book train, ferry and air tickets, is at Via della Libertà 12. There is a CTS travel agency (☎ 091 611 07 13 or 091 32 57 52) at Via N Garzilli 28/G. A bit more convenient is Record Viaggi (☎ 091 611 09 10), Via Mariano Stabile 168 (between Via R Settimo and Via Roma).

Bookshops & Newsstands Feltrinelli (☎ 091 58 77 85), Via Maqueda 395, has a foreign-language section that includes English. Several newsstands around Piazza Giuseppe Verdi and in Via Roma sell foreign newspapers.

Medical Services & Emergency The Ospedale Civico (hospital; ☎ 091 666 22 07) is on Via Carmelo Lazzaro. Ring for an ambulance on ☎ 091 30 66 44. There is an all-night pharmacy, Lo Cascio (☎ 091 616 21 17), at Via Roma 1 near the train station.

The *questura* (police station; ☎ 091 21 01 11) is on Piazza della Vittoria.

Dangers & Annoyances A strong police presence in Palermo's historic centre has helped reduce petty crime – but not eradicate it totally. Take the usual precautions; avoid wearing ostentatious jewellery or carrying a bag that could be snatched and keep your valuables in a money belt.

Until a few years ago, few locals would venture into the area between the Vucciria market and the port. It's now being cleaned up and is much safer than it once was, but it's still not advisable to wander down the backstreets at night. Women should be careful about walking alone in the historic centre at night; if you must, stick to the main streets, which are busy and well lit. Watch out for pickpockets and bag snatchers around the main intercity bus station on Via Balsamo and in the city's side streets.

Quattro Canti

The busy intersection of Corso Vittorio Emanuele and Via Maqueda marks the Quattro Canti (Four Corners), the centre of the oldest part of town. A 17th-century Spanish Baroque facade decorated with a fountain and a statue sits on each corner. They were shrouded in restorers' scaffolding at the time of writing. On the south-western corner is the Baroque **Chiesa di San Giuseppe dei Teatini** *(☎ 091 33 12 39, Piazza Pretoria; admission free; open 7.30am-noon & 6pm-8pm daily)*, its interior bursting with marble.

Piazza Pretoria

This piazza hosts the eye-catching **Fontana Pretoria**, created by Florentine sculptors in the 16th century. At the time of its unveiling, the shocked populace named it the Fountain of Shame because of its nude figures. Take time to study the numerous figures that decorate its every corner. (At the time of writing the 'shameful' figures were veiled in canvas and scaffolding as a long restoration was coming to an end.)

Closing off the eastern side of the piazza is the Baroque **Chiesa di Santa Caterina** (closed for restoration at the time of writing). The **Palazzo del Municipio**, also known as the Palazzo delle Aquile because of the eagles that guard each corner of the roof, stands on the southern side of the square.

Chiesa di San Matteo

On the northern side of Corso Vittorio Emanuele, just before it crosses Via Roma, this Baroque church *(☎ 091 33 48 33, Corso Vittorio Emanuele; admission free; open 9am-5pm Mon-Sat, 10am-11am Sun)* has a richly decorated (but badly dilapidated) interior. The four statues in the pilasters of the dome represent the Virtues and were carved by Giacomo Serpotta in 1728.

La Martorana

Also known as the Chiesa di Santa Maria dell'Ammiraglio, La Martorana *(☎ 091 616 16 92, Piazza Bellini 3; admission free; open 8.30am-1pm & 3.30pm-5.30pm Mon-Sat, 8am-1pm Sun)*, a few steps south of Piazza Pretoria, is one of Palermo's most famous churches. The original 12th-century structure – a Greek cross – has been much altered, but the church retains its Arab-Norman bell tower. The Greek cross part of the church is richly decorated with stunning Byzantine mosaics, while the Baroque additions are covered with frescoes. Totally in keeping with the decoration, the Greek-Catholic eastern rite Mass (not to be confused with the Greek Orthodox Mass) is still celebrated here. Try to time your visit to avoid the many weddings celebrated in the church.

Chiesa di San Cataldo

Next to La Martorana is this tiny, simple church *(Piazza Bellini 3; admission free; open 9am-3.30pm Mon-Fri, 9am-12.30pm Sat, 9am-1pm Sun)* dating from the period of the Norman domination of Sicily. Its battlements and red domes are another fusion of Arab and Norman styles.

Cathedral

Despite its hotchpotch of styles, Palermo's cathedral *(☎ 091 33 43 76, Corso Vittorio Emanuele; admission free; open 7am-7pm Mon-Sat, 8am-1.30pm & 4pm-7pm Sun)*, south-west of the Quattro Canti along Corso Vittorio Emanuele, is certainly grand.

Built in the late 12th century, the cathedral has been modified many times since, most disastrously in the 18th century when the dome was added, spoiling the architectural harmony of the building. In the same period the interior was restored. Although the only part conserved in purely original Norman style is the apse, the church remains an impressive example of Norman architecture. Arab influences in some of the geometric decoration are unmistakable, and the graceful Gothic towers distract the eye from that dome. The interior of the church is fairly boring compared to the outside. It contains royal tombs, and among those interred in porphyry (a reddish-purple rock) sarcophagi are Roger II, Henry VI of Hohenstaufen, Constance de Hauteville and Frederick II of Hohenstaufen. The ashes of Santa Rosalia, patron saint of Palermo, are contained in a silver urn in the sixth chapel on the right (as you face the altar).

Palazzo dei Normanni

Across Piazza della Vittoria and the gardens is the Palazzo dei Normanni, also known as the Palazzo Reale (Royal Palace). Built by the Arabs in the 9th century, it was extended by the Normans and restructured by the Hohenstaufens. It is now the seat of Sicily's regional government.

The most famous part of the palace is the **Cappella Palatina** *(☎ 091 705 48 79, Palazzo dei Normanni, enter from Piazza dell'Indipendenza; admission free; open 9am-noon & 3pm-5pm Mon-Fri, 9am-noon Sat, 9am-10am & noon-1pm Sun)*. This magnificent example of Arab-Norman artistic genius was built during the reign of Roger II and decorated with Byzantine mosaics. The chapel is undoubtedly Palermo's most extraordinary treasure (disregarding Monreale – see Around Palermo later in this chapter), a breathtaking example of art at its most exalted. Enjoyment of the chapel is spoiled only by the look-and-get-out attitude of some of its guardians – though in fairness, the place does get pretty packed. The mosaics alone, rivalled only by those of Ravenna and Istanbul, make the chapel an absolute must on any tourist itinerary.

While the mosaics demonstrate the Byzantine influence on Palermitan art, the geometric tile designs are a clear reminder of Arab input. The carved wooden ceiling is a classic example of intricate, Arab-style stalactite design. On Sunday the chapel is overrun by tour groups, so it's better to visit on another day, if possible.

The **Sala di Ruggero** (King Roger's Room), upstairs from the Cappella Palatina, is also worth visiting. You can see the room as part of a guided tour of the **Palazzo Reale** *(☎ 091 705 43 17, enter from Piazza dell' Indipendenza; admission free; regular guided tours according to demand)*. The former king's bedroom is decorated with superb 12th-century mosaics, featuring secular images of animals. The tour also includes a look at the Sicilian parliamentary assembly when parliament is not in session. The whole exercise becomes a nightmare, though, if you have to share your tour with hundreds of noisy school children.

Next to the palazzo is the **Porta Nuova**, built to celebrate the arrival of Charles V in Palermo in 1535.

Chiesa di San Giovanni degli Eremiti

South of the palazzo, you can find a tranquil refuge from the chaos outside in this simple **church** *(Church of St John of the Hermits; ☎ 091 651 50 19, Via dei Benedettini; admission €4.15 or €7.75 for a two-day cumulative ticket to the cloisters at Monreale, La Zisa and La Cuba; open 9am-1pm & 3pm-7pm Mon-Sat, 9am to 12.30pm Sun & holidays)*. The building is another example of the Sicilian Arab-Norman architectural mix. Built under Roger II, it is topped by five red domes and set in a pretty, atmospheric garden with cloisters. The bare interior of the now deconsecrated church features some badly deteriorated frescoes.

Museo Archeologico Regionale & Around

A block north of the main post office is the Museo Archeologico Regionale *(☎ 091 611 68 05, Via Roma; admission €4.15; open 9am-1.50pm Mon & Sat, 9am-1.50pm & 3pm-6.30pm Tues-Fri, 9am to 12.30pm Sun & public holidays)*. To enter, turn left onto Via Bara all'Olivella and onto Piazza Olivella. The museum holds a collection of Greek metopes from Selinunte, the Hellenistic *Bronze Ram of Syracuse* and finds from archaeological sites throughout the island. Although there is not a lot to see apart from the metopes, the museum is definitely worth a visit.

About 200m south is the **Chiesa di San Domenico** *(☎ 091 58 48 72, Piazza San Domenico; admission free; open 9am-11.30am Mon-Fri, 5pm-7pm Sat & Sun)* just off Via Roma. The grand 17th-century structure houses the tombs of many important Sicilians and a wealth of paintings.

Towards Piazza Marina

Plunge into the streets heading towards the waterfront from the intersection of Corso Vittorio Emanuele and Via Roma and you'll find a few more architectural gems. The

Oratorio di San Lorenzo *(Via dell'Immacolatella; admission free; open 9am-noon Mon-Sat)* is decorated with stuccoes by Giacomo Serpotta (his greatest work). Caravaggio's last known piece, a Nativity, once hung over the altar. It was stolen in 1969 and has never been recovered.

Next door, the 13th-century **Chiesa di San Francesco d'Assisi** *(☎ 091 616 28 19, Piazza San Francesco; free; open 8am-5pm Mon-Sat)* features a fine rose window and Gothic portal, which have survived numerous restorations and restructuring.

Palazzo Chiaramonte-Steri

This imposing 14th-century palazzo *(☎ 091 33 41 39, Piazza Marina; open for exhibitions only)* boasts an imposing facade that served as a model for many other buildings on Sicily. The island's Grand Parliament sat here in the 16th century and, for many years, so did the Holy Office of the Inquisition. The palazzo is open during exhibitions.

Galleria Regionale della Sicilia

Sicily's most important art gallery, the Galleria Regionale della Sicilia *(Via Alloro; admission €4.15; open 9am-1.30pm & 3pm-7.30pm Tues & Thurs, 9.30am-12.30pm Sat & Sun)* is housed in the imposing Catalan-Gothic Palazzo Abatellis, which was built from 1490 to 1495 for the praetor of Palermo, Francesco Abatellis. The building was badly damaged during WWII but has been substantially restored. It houses an impressive collection of work, most notably sculptures and paintings dating from the 14th to the 16th centuries. The ground floor is devoted to sculpture, beginning with a remarkable 12th-century Arabic door frame and a painting of *Madonna con Santi* (Madonna with Saints) by Tommaso de Vigilia. In Room 2, the palace's former chapel, is the magnificent fresco *Trionfo della Morte* (Triumph of Death), which has been attributed by some scholars to Pisanello. Death is a mounted archer piercing the wealthy and smug while the miserable – tellingly represented by a painter and his pupil – pray for release. Room 4 houses the gallery's most famous piece, the exquisite white marble bust of *Eleonora d'Aragona* by Francesco Laurana.

The 2nd floor is devoted primarily to Sicilian paintings, including Antonello da Messina's well-known panel of the *Annunziata* (Annunciated Virgin). A number of Flemish panels are also on show, perhaps to illustrate the influence of the Dutch school on Sicilian art; the most important of these is the *Malvagna* triptych by Jan Gossaert.

Lo Spasimo & Around

South of Piazza Marina, across Via Alloro, this complex of buildings includes the **Chiesa di Santa Maria dello Spasimo** *(☎ 091 616 14 86, Via Spasimo; admission free; open 9am-midnight daily)*, a typical example of the late-Gothic style, although it was actually built during the Renaissance. Building work on the church extended as far as the walls and the soaring apse, but it has stood for centuries without a roof and its interior is host to a couple of tall *Ailanthus altissima* (Tree-of-heaven) trees. Restored and opened to the public in 1995, the complex is an atmospheric venue for concerts, performances and exhibitions. It's sensational to visit at night.

Across a vast piazza from Lo Spasimo is the **Chiesa della SS Trinità** *(Chiesa della Magione; ☎ 091 617 05 96, Via Magione 44; admission free; open 9.30am-6.30pm daily)*, a fine Norman church dating from 1193.

Catacombe dei Cappuccini

For centuries, Sicilians of a certain social standing who didn't want to be forgotten on their death were embalmed by Capuchin monks. The catacombs *(☎ 091 21 21 17, Via Cappuccini 1; admission €1.30; open 9am-noon & 3pm-5pm daily)* in the Capuchin convent on Piazza Cappuccino, west of the city centre, contain the mummified bodies and skeletons of some 8000 Palermitans who died between the 17th and 19th centuries. Although time has been unkind to most (some are just skeletons with suits on), a few are remarkably intact. Rosalia Lombardi, who died at the age of two, has auburn hair tied in a yellow bow, and looks as though she could be sleeping – even if she is rather pallid.

La Zisa

In the same area as the catacombs is the 12th-century Arab-Norman castle, the **Castello della Zisa** *(☎ 091 652 02 69, Piazza Guglielmo il Buono; admission €2.60 or €7.75 with a two-day cumulative ticket to the cloisters at Monreale, San Giovanni degli Eremiti and La Cuba; open 9am-6.30pm Mon-Sat, 9am-1pm Sun).* The name derives from the Arabic *el aziz*, which translates as 'the Splendid'. The once-magnificent palace was built for William I and completed by William II, who used it as a seasonal residence. After long years of neglect, it was purchased by the government who undertook substantial restoration on it. Today it houses a museum of Arabic crafts of which the main features are the superbly crafted screens and a gorgeous 12th-century bronze basin. Take bus No 124 from Piazza Ruggero Settimo.

La Cuba

William II planned an enormous park, which was to incorporate the castles of La Zisa and La Cuba *(☎ 091 59 02 99, Corso Calatafimi 100; admission €2.05 or €7.75 with a two-day cumulative ticket to the cloisters at Monreale, San Giovanni degli Eremiti and La Zisa; open 9am-6.30pm Mon-Sat, 9am-1pm Sun)* This castle was built in 1180. In the 14th century, Giovanni Boccaccio used it as the setting for a story of his *Decameron*; two centuries later it was used as a leper colony before being converted into an army barracks. There's not much to see today.

Teatro Massimo

Overlooking Piazza Giuseppe Verdi, the proud and haughty 19th-century Teatro Massimo *(☎ 091 605 31 11, Piazza Verdi 9; guided tours €2.60; open 10am-4pm Tues-Sun)* finally reopened in 1997 following a 20-year restoration programme. Building first commenced in 1875 when the original square was levelled to make way for Giovanni Battista Basile's masterpiece, which was eventually completed in 1897 by his son Ernesto. The monumental structure was the pride of Sicily when it first opened (with a performance of Verdi's *Falstaff*) and it boasts one of the largest stages in the world. The engineering was cutting edge in its day, with a complex system of pulleys able to lift the painted ceiling panels that ventilated the theatre.

High society and illustrious personages failed to prevent it from falling into disrepair less than 100 years after it opened. When it closed in 1973, few could have imagined that it would be 24 years before its doors were opened to the public once again. Palermo's former mayor Leoluca Orlando made its restoration a priority of his term in office and today it has been returned to its previous lustre.

If you can't see a performance there, take a guided tour (in English, French, German and Italian); they take place approximately every 30 minutes, except when there are rehearsals in progress.

Markets

Palermo's historical ties with the Arab world and its proximity to North Africa are reflected in the noisy street life of the city's ancient centre and nowhere is this more evident than in its markets.

Several markets are spread through the tangle of lanes and alleys of central Palermo. The most famous is the **Vucciria**, winding south from the Chiesa di San Domenico. Here you can purchase anything your taste buds desire (and several items they may recoil at – slippery tripe for one) as well as a host of off-the-back-of-a-lorry-style bargains. This is another place where it is a bad idea to carry bags or purses; keep your cash in a money belt.

Places to Stay

You should have little trouble finding a room in Palermo at whatever price you choose. Staff at the tourist office will make recommendations and might help with bookings (if they're in a good mood).

Places to Stay – Budget

Camping To reach this recommendation, catch bus No 616 from Piazza A de Gasperi (which can be reached by bus No 101 from the train station).

***Trinacria** (☎/fax 091 53 05 90, Via Barcarello 25, Sferracavallo)* Sites per adult/child €4.15/3.35, 2-person bungalows €41.50-51.65. Palermo's best camp site is by the sea at Sferracavallo, an area noted for its fish restaurants.

Hotels Head for Via Maqueda or Via Roma, between the train station and Quattro Canti, for the bulk of the cheap rooms, some of which are in old apartment buildings.

Albergo Orientale (☎/fax 091 616 57 27, Via Maqueda 26) Singles/doubles without bath €25.80/41.50, singles/doubles with bath €31/51.65. Near the train station, this hotel is located in an old and dilapidated building with a once-grand courtyard. The somewhat unique managers provide coupons for a free breakfast at the bar across the road and discounts on meals at a nearby trattoria. Car parking costs €7.75 per day.

***Albergo Vittoria** (☎/fax 091 616 24 37, Via Maqueda 8)* Singles/doubles €20.65/31. Probably best as a last resort, the Vittoria has spartan rooms with toilets (but not showers) in them.

***Hotel del Centro** (☎ 091 617 03 76, fax 091 617 36 54, ⓔ hoteldelcentro@libero.it, Ⓦ www.hoteldelcentro.it, Via Roma 72)* Singles/doubles without bath €25.80/36.15, singles/doubles with bath €36.15/49.05. Formerly the rather run-down Albergo Piccadilly, this hotel (on the 2nd floor) has recently had a makeover. You could eat off the floor of the communal bathrooms they're so clean, and the management are friendly and helpful. Proximity to the station is a bonus.

***Albergo Concordia** (☎ 091 617 15 14, ☎ 091 58 86 14, Via Roma 72)* Singles without bath €18.10, singles/doubles with bath €23.25/41.50. The rooms may be basic, but this hotel, on the 4th floor of the same building as Hotel del Centro, is good value.

***Hotel Corona** (☎ 091 616 23 40, no fax, Via Roma 118)* Singles €18.10, doubles with bath €36.15. This pensione is in dire need of renovation but is clean and comfortable nonetheless. All rooms face onto the internal courtyard so the noise of traffic on Via Roma is blocked out. It might be harder to block out the noise of the eccentric signora who runs the place with an iron fist and is prone to scream and yell at guests!

***Hotel Sicilia** (☎ 091 616 84 60, fax 091 616 36 06, Via Divisi 99)* Singles/doubles €38.75/62. This is a good upper-end-of-budget choice, with rooms containing TV and telephone. Be aware that it can be noisy. The hotel is on the 4th floor.

***Hotel Alessandra** (☎ 091 617 39 58, fax 091 616 51 80, Ⓦ www.cot.it, Via Divisi 99)* Singles/doubles €31/51.65. A security-conscious place, on the 2nd floor of the same building as Hotel Sicilia, the Alessandra has simple, pleasant rooms. Parking costs €5.15 per day and Internet access €2.60 for 30 minutes.

***Hotel Petit** (☎/fax 091 32 36 16, Via P di Belmonte 84)* Singles €23.25, doubles with bath €36.15. Near Piazza Castelnuovo, this tiny hotel lives up to its name. If you can get one of its rooms, though, you'll find it pleasant and comfortable.

***Hotel Letizia** (☎/fax 091 58 91 10, ⓔ hotel-letizia@neomedie.it, Ⓦ www.hotelletizia.com, Via dei Bottai 30)* Singles/doubles without bath €31/46.50, singles/doubles with bath €38.75/51.65. One of the few accommodation options down near Piazza Marina, this attractive hotel is just off the piazza (where you can park your car for free). It's a clean, friendly, family-run place.

***Hotel Confort** (☎ 091 33 17 41, Via Roma 188)* Singles/doubles without bath €23.25/40.30, singles/doubles with bath €31/46.50. Near Corso Vittorio Emanuele, this hotel is agreeable and clean.

Places to Stay – Mid-Range

***Hotel Moderno** (☎ 091 58 86 83, fax 091 58 86 83, Via Roma 276)* Singles/doubles/triples with bath €43.90/59.40/77.50. This is one of the best mid-range choices in Palermo. The rooms are attractive, with TV and telephone, and get cheaper (per head) the more of you there are.

***Hotel Elite** (☎ 091 32 93 18, fax 091 58 86 14, Via Mariano Stabile 136)* Singles/doubles with bath €46.50/67.15. This place isn't particularly special but it does have clean rooms (with TV and telephone) and is close to Piazza Castelnuovo.

Hotel Boston-Madonia *(☎ 091 58 02 34, fax 091 33 53 64, Via Mariano Stabile 136)* Singles/doubles with bath €46.50/67.15. If you can ignore the rather gruff man on reception, you'll find simple, clean rooms. Prices include breakfast.

Hotel Tonic *(☎ 091 58 17 54, fax 091 58 55 60, e hoteltonic@hoteltonic.com, w www.hoteltonic.com, Via Mariano Stabile 126)* Singles/doubles with bath €72.30/92.95. This hotel has had a tasteful makeover, and its rooms are extremely nice and spotlessly clean. All have air-conditioning, TV and telephone.

Hotel Joli *(☎ 091 611 117 65, fax 091 611 117 66, e info@hoteljoli.com, w www.hoteljoli.com, Via Michele Amari 11)* Singles/doubles up to €67.15/103.30. This delightfully renovated hotel, not far from Piazza Ruggero Settimo, is one of Palermo's best deals. It has spotless, comfortable rooms, all with air-con, TV and telephone. Parking is available in the street outside the hotel or in a nearby garage.

Massimo Plaza Hotel *(☎ 091 32 56 57, fax 091 32 57 11, e booking@massimoplazahotel.com, w www.massimoplazahotel.com, Via Maqueda 437)* Singles/doubles €98.15/134.30. Scoring 10 out of 10 for position (directly opposite the Teatro Massimo) and 11 out of 10 for quality and value for money, this intimate hotel is Palermo's best mid-range deal. Prices include breakfast.

Places to Stay – Top End

Grande Albergo Sole *(☎ 091 604 11 11, fax 091 611 01 82, Corso Vittorio Emanuele 291)* Singles/doubles €87.80/118.80. You'll need your sunglasses to cope with the bright yellow foyer of this upmarket hotel; fortunately they seem to have run out of paint so the elegant bedrooms are decorated in more sombre shades.

Grand Hotel et Des Palmes *(☎ 091 58 39 33, fax 091 33 15 45, e des-palmes@thi.it, w www.thi.it, Via Roma 398)* Singles/doubles €118.80/175.60, including breakfast. This four-star hotel at the Piazza Castelnuovo end of town has a sense of slightly faded splendour about it, but is still one of the ritziest hotels in town. Rooms are large and comfortable (although beware of the overpriced singles facing onto noisy Via Roma) with antique furniture and all services. The staff are noted for their professionalism and discretion.

Centrale Palace Hotel *(☎ 091 33 66 66, fax 091 33 48 81, Corso Vittorio Emanuele 327)* Singles/doubles/triples €136.85/196.25/260.80, including breakfast. This renovated 18th-century palazzo is one of Palermo's most elegant hotels, with luxurious rooms overlooking the entrance atrium. As far as position goes, you can't do much better.

Places to Eat

With more than 300 officially listed restaurants and eateries to choose from in the city and surrounding area, you should have little trouble finding something to suit the tightest budget.

Palermo's cuisine takes advantage of the fresh produce of the sea and the fertile Conca d'Oro valley. One of its most famous dishes is the tasty *pasta con le sarde*, with sardines, fennel, peppers, capers and pine nuts. Swordfish is served here sliced into huge steaks. A reflection of Sicilia's proximity to North Africa is the presence on menus of couscous, basically a bowl of steamed semolina with a sauce.

Palermitans are late eaters and restaurants rarely open for dinner before 8pm.

Places to Eat – Budget

Bar Gastronomia Aiello Vittorio *(Via Maqueda 33)* Pizzas from €1.55, meals from €2.05. One of many *tavola calda* (literally 'hot table') places where you can get pizza slices, *calzone* or choose a really decent plate of vegetables (such as *caponata* – aubergines, celery, capers and olives cooked with a rich tomato sauce) from an abundant *antipasto* display.

Dal Pompiere *(☎ 091 32 52 82, Via Bara all'Olivella 107)* Antipasto €4.15, pasta €4.15. This place, just up the road from the Opera dei Pupi puppet theatre, serves simple but filling fare for lunch, with a couple of pasta choices, pizza slices and a great antipasto buffet.

Antica Focacceria di San Francesco *(☎ 091 32 02 64,* W *www.anticafocacceriasfrancesco.it, Via A Paternostro 58)* Pasta €4.15, salads €4.15-6.20, vegetable side dishes €3.10. Open 10.30am-midnight daily. This atmospheric place is one of the city's oldest eating houses and worth seeking out; it also serves calzone, pizza slices and similar snacks. Thanks to restrictions due to mad cow disease, you probably won't be able to try an age-old Palermitan snack – a *panino* (filled roll) with *milza* (veal innards) and ricotta cheese – but the caponata (a vegetable starter served with olives, anchovies and capers) or pasta con le sarde dishes are worth the trip anyway.

Da Pina *(Via Cassari 69)* Full meals around €12.90. Open lunch only Mon-Sun. Down near Piazza Marina, 70-year-old Pina has been whipping up delicious fish meals for decades. You take a look at the daily catch on display and decide what you'll eat. Cheap, delicious and a Palermo experience not to be missed – but don't expect anything but Italian (or Sicilian) spoken here.

Panineria e Pizzeria Fabrizio *(☎ 0349 463 52 49, Via Trabia 33-35)* Pizzas €2.60-3.60, panini €1.05. These two eateries are next door to each other and serve delicious pizzas or hearty filled *focaccia* (flatbread) and panini.

Da Ciccio *(☎ 091 32 91 43, Via Firenze 6)* Meals from €15.50. Open Mon-Sat. This is one of Palermo's best-loved cheaper eating places. Dive into the delicious antipasto selection, then move onto *maccheroni con le sarde* followed by roast swordfish and you won't go wrong. You'll find it just off Via Roma 178.

Il Massimo dei Sapori *(☎ 091 616 75 20, Via Dicesa dei Giudici 22)* Pizzas from €1.05, pasta from €2.60. A new place in the centre of town, this *rosticceria/focacceria* serves cheap, tasty pizza, grills and pasta dishes. There's a restaurant, ***Trattoria Da Massimo***, next door if you want something more substantial.

Hostaria Al Duar *(☎ 0347 701 78 48, Via Ammiraglio Gravina 31A)* Set menus €9.30-12.40. Al Duar does a kind of Italo-Arab cuisine, worth a try if you feel like couscous and other typical North African dishes. It's in the first street south of Via E Amari.

La Cambusa *(☎ 091 58 45 74, Piazza Marina 16)* Full meals €15.50. A place packed with locals is always a good sign, so you should eat well here. There's an excellent antipasto spread plus typical Sicilian favourites. Sometimes it has a set, all-inclusive seafood menu for €18.10.

Pizzeria Trattoria Mistral *(☎ 091 637 22 85, Via Bordonaro 30, Vergine Maria)* There are plenty of pizzerias in Palermo, but if you want the best, head straight for Mistral, even though it is slightly out of town in Vergine Maria. Pizzaiolo Ron Garofolo is the European champion pizza maker; taste his creations and you'll understand why. He's made pizza for the pope, and can even make a gluten-free pizza if that's what you want. And the best recommendation of all – if Ron goes away on holiday, word gets out in Palermo, and people don't go there until he's back.

Places to Eat – Mid-Range & Top End

Most of the posher restaurants are on the outskirts of Palermo or in nearby towns. The locals head for Mondello to eat seafood.

Il Crudo e Il Cotto *(☎ 091 616 92 61, Piazza Marina 45a)* Pasta €4.15-6.20, mains €5.15-10.35. Open Wed-Mon. On Piazza Marina near the port, this small trattoria is eternally popular. The *farfalle* (butterfly-shaped) pasta with *radicchio* and the *grigliata di pesce* (mixed grilled fish) are not to be missed.

Osteria dei Vespri *(☎ 091 617 16 31, Piazza Santa Croce dei Vespri 8)* Full meals from €25.80. Self-styled as an *enoteca con cucina* (wine cellar with kitchen), this pleasant eatery is in a small piazza off Via Roma, past Chiesa di Santa Anna, and has excellent food and atmosphere. Outside tables along with meat and seafood cooked on an outdoor barbecue are summer attractions.

Al Delfino *(☎ 091 53 02 82, Via Torretta 80, Sferracavallo)* Full meal €20.65. Probably the best place for fish in Palermo, by the sea at Sferracavallo (take the road to the airport then follow the signs for Mondello). Its popularity means that the turnover of produce is huge, so you can be guaranteed the freshest fish available. You don't order, the food just comes – first antipasti of fried calamari, marinated prawns, sardine *involtini* (stuffed rolls) and other delights, then spaghetti with *vongole* (clams), risotto with prawns and another pasta dish, then for main course, delicious grilled whole fish. It's an experience more than a meal!

Charleston *(☎ 091 32 13 66, Piazzale Ungheria 30)* Full meals around €51.65. Charleston is one of Palermo's classiest, most formal restaurants. Its main establishment is in Palermo, not far from Teatro Massimo, but in summer it generally closes and its Mondello branch *(☎ 091 45 01 71, Viale Regina Elena)*, with outdoor eating, takes over.

Cafes & Bars

On Via Principe di Belmonte (which is closed to traffic between Via Ruggero Settimo and Via Roma), there are numerous cafes with outdoor tables where you can linger over breakfast or lunch. If you want to spend less, buy a panino in one of the many bars along Via Roma.

Antico Caffè *(☎ 091 58 32 31, Via P di Belmonte 111)* This cafe has shady outdoor tables and cakes that are so beautiful they should be works of art. The gelato is pretty popular too.

Self-Catering

The ***Vucciria market*** is held Monday to Saturday in the narrow streets between Via Roma, Piazza San Domenico and Corso Vittorio Emanuele. Here you can buy fresh fruit and vegetables, meat, cheese and seafood. Or you can just watch as huge, freshly caught swordfish and tuna are sliced up and sold in minutes. Numerous stalls sell steaming-hot boiled octopus. Although the best known, the Vucciria is far from the only such market around town.

For other grocery supplies, try the ***Standa supermarket*** *(Via della Libertà 30)*.

Entertainment

Theatre The daily paper *Il Giornale di Sicilia* has a listing of what's on. Tourist information booths also have programmes and listings.

Teatro Massimo *(☎ 091 605 31 11, Piazza Verdi 9)* Ernesto Basile's Art Nouveau masterpiece, restored to its former glory, stages opera, ballet and music concerts.

Teatro Politeama Garibaldi (☎ 091 605 32 49, Piazza Ruggero Settimo) This is the main venue for opera and ballet.

Teatro Biondo *(☎ 091 743 43 41, Via Roma)* If your Italian is up to it, you can see plays at Teatro Biondo.

Opera dei Pupi South of Via Cavour, puppet theatre is performed by the Cuticchio family at ***Opera dei Pupi*** *(☎ 091 32 34 00, Via Bara all'Olivella 52)*. It is an enchanting experience and something of a Sicilian speciality. It's a good break for young kids and the elaborate old puppets will endear themselves to adults too. Shows are generally staged at 5.30pm at weekends. Tickets cost €5.15 (children €2.60). At No 40 in the same street is one of several artisans who makes and repairs the puppets.

Bars Rub shoulders with the Palermo *bene* (smart set) in the bars around town.

I Grilli Giù *(☎ 091 58 47 47, Piazza Cavalieri di Malta 11)* This is a popular cocktail bar (and restaurant), north-east of the Vucciria market, where you can sip a cocktail and listen to the latest DJ sounds.

La Cuba *(Viale F Scaduto)* This bar is in the middle of Villa Sperlinga and gets packed to bursting. Not to be confused with the castle of the same name, this is an Arabic folly converted into a super-trendy (and pricey) early-evening or late-night bar. Sunday brunch is good but avoid the food at other times.

Getting There & Away

Air Falcone-Borsellino airport is at Punta Raisi, 32km west of Palermo. For 24-hour information about domestic flights, call Alitalia on ☎ 8488 6 56 43, and for international flights, call ☎ 8488 6 56 42. Alitalia has an office (☎ 091 601 93 33) at Via della Libertà 39. At any time of year, it's usually possible to get charter flights between

Palermo and major European cities such as London – shop around.

Bus The main Intercity bus station is around Via P Balsamo, to the north of the train station. See Getting There & Away at the beginning of this chapter for details of Segesta and SAIS main services. In addition to those, SAIS Trasporti runs services twice daily to Cefalù. SAIS Autolinee (☎ 091 616 60 28) also services Catania (more than 15 daily), Enna (six daily), Piazza Armerina (four daily), Messina (via Catania, every two hours). Interbus runs to Syracuse (six daily). For Marsala, go to Salemi (☎ 091 617 54 11), Via Rosario Gregorio 44. Between them, Cuffaro (☎ 091 616 15 10) and Camilleri (☎ 091 616 59 14) have about 10 buses daily to Agrigento.

AST (☎ 091 680 00 11), away from the main terminal on the corner between Viale delle Scienze and Via Brasa 31, near Piazza dell'Indipendenza and the university, runs four daily buses to Ragusa. It also operates services to Corleone, Cefalù, Palazzo Adriano and Montelepre.

Numerous other companies service points throughout Sicily and most have offices in the Via Paolo Balsamo area. Their addresses and telephone numbers, as well as destinations, are listed in the *Agenda*, available at the APT office.

Train Regular trains leave from the train station for Milazzo, Messina, Catania, Trapani, Syracuse and Agrigento, as well as nearby towns such as Cefalù. There are also Intercity trains to Reggio di Calabria, Naples and Rome. Train timetable information is available in English at the station. There is a Transalpino office inside the station, as well as left-luggage and bathing facilities.

Car & Motorcycle Palermo is accessible by *autostrada* from Messina (only partially completed) and from Catania via Enna (this route is quicker). Trapani and Marsala are also easily accessible from Palermo by autostrada, while Agrigento and Palermo are linked by a good state road through the interior of the island.

To rent a car, try Avis (☎ 091 58 69 40), which has an office at Via Francesco Crispi 115 near the port, as well as an office at the airport (☎ 091 59 16 84). Europcar has offices at the train station (☎ 091 616 50 50) and the airport (☎ 091 59 12 27). All major rental companies are represented in Palermo. Look in the telephone directory under '*autonoleggio*'.

Boat Ferries leave from Molo Vittorio Veneto, off Via Francesco Crispi, for Cagliari (Sardinia), Naples, Livorno and Genoa (see Getting There & Away at the beginning of this chapter for further details).

The Tirrenia office (☎ 199 12 31 99 or 091 602 11 11, **W** www.tirrenia.it) is at the port in Palazzina Stella Maris, Calata Marinai d'Italia.

Siremar (☎ 091 690 25 55 or 091 58 24 03, **W** http://siremar.gestelnet.it) runs ferries and hydrofoils to Ustica; its office is at Via Francesco Crispi 118.

SNAV's main office is in Naples (☎ 081 761 23 48). It is represented in Palermo by the Pietro Barbaro agency (☎ 091 58 60 66) at Via P di Belmonte 55. It runs a summer-only hydrofoil service to the Aeolian Islands. SNAV also operates a daily ferry service between Palermo and Naples from April to October. Tickets cost €49.60 each way (€62 in July, August and September).

Grandi Navi Veloci (☎ 091 58 79 39, **W** www.grimaldi.it), part of the Grimaldi Group, at the port in Calata Marinai d'Italia, runs ferries from Palermo to Genoa (daily) and Livorno (three weekly).

The *deposito bagagli* (left luggage) at Stazione Marittima opens 7am to 8pm daily.

Getting Around

To/From the Airport Taxis to the airport cost upwards of €36.15. The cheaper option is to catch one of the regular blue buses run by Prestìa e Comandè (☎ 091 58 04 57), which leave from outside the train station, in front of Hotel Elena, roughly every hour from 5am to around 10.45pm. Buses run from the airport to the train station from 7.30am to 12.30am (or until the arrival of the last flight). The timetable is posted at the bus stop outside the train station, to your right as you leave the station. Buses also stop on Piazza Ruggero Settimo, in front of Teatro Politeama Garibaldi. The trip takes about 45 minutes and costs €4.65.

Bus Palermo's city buses (AMAT, ☎ 091 35 01 11, W www.amat.pa.it) are efficient and regular, and most stop in front of the train station. Tickets must be purchased before you get on the bus and are available from tobacconists or the booths at the terminal. They cost €0.75 and are valid for 90 minutes. A day pass is €2.60.

There are two small buses that operate in the narrow streets of the *centro storico* and can be useful if you are moving between tourist sights and your feet need a rest. Other useful routes are:

No 101 From the train station along Via Roma to Piazza Ruggero Settimo, then along Via della Libertà, past the Giardino Inglese to Piazza A de Gasperi, from where there are connecting buses to Mondello and Sferracavallo.

No 107 From the train station along Via Roma to Piazza Ruggero Settimo, and on to the Giardino Inglese, up Via della Libertà to Piazza A de Gasperi and the stadium.

No 109 From the train station to Piazza dell' Indipendenza, from where there are connecting buses to Monreale and the Convento dei Cappuccini.

No 124 From Piazza Ruggero Settimo (Teatro Politeama) to the Castello della Zisa.

No 139 From the train station to the port and Vergine Maria.

No 327 From Piazza dell'Indipendenza to the Convento dei Cappuccini.

No 389 From Piazza dell'Indipendenza to Monreale.

No 603 From Piazza A de Gasperi (stadium) to Mondello.

No 628 From Piazza A de Gasperi to Sferracavallo–Isola delle Femmine.

No 812 From near Piazza Don Sturzo (Teatro Politeama) to Monte Pellegrino.

No 833 From Piazza Don Sturzo to Mondello, along the coast (summer only).

Metropolitana Palermo's metro system won't be of much use to most people as its 10 stations radiating out from the train station are a good hike from any destinations of tourist interest. There is talk of expanding the system to Falcone-Borsellino airport, which would be useful. A single trip ticket costs €0.75. The €2.60 day passes for the bus system can also be used on the metro.

Car & Motorcycle If you have dealt with Rome or Naples in your own vehicle, Palermo will present no difficulties. Theft of and from vehicles is a problem, however, and you are advised to use one of the attended car parks around town if your hotel has no parking space. You'll be looking at €7.75 to €10.35 for 24 hours. Some hotels have small car parks, but they are often full; check with your hotel proprietor.

AROUND PALERMO

There are beaches north-west of the city at Mondello and Sferracavallo, but if you're really into spending some time by the sea, you'd be better off heading farther afield, to Scopello (see Golfo di Castellammare under North-Western Sicily later) for example. **Mondello** is popular with Palermitans, who crowd the beachfront Viale Regina Elena for the evening stroll. There are numerous seafood restaurants and snack stalls along the avenue. For bus information, see the Palermo Getting Around section earlier.

Between Palermo and Mondello is Monte Pellegrino and the **Santuario di Santa Rosalia** *(☎ 091 54 03 26, Monte Pellegrino; admission free; open 7am-7pm daily)*. Palermo's patron saint, Santa Rosalia, lived as a hermit in a cave on the mountain, now the site of a 17th-century shrine. The water, which is channelled from the roof of the cave into a large font, is said to have miraculous powers. Whatever your beliefs, this is a fascinating place to visit, but remember that it is a shrine, not a tourist haunt. See the Palermo Getting Around section for bus details. The road to the sanctuary suffers from landslides and is often closed for repairs.

On the northern side of Monte Pellegrino, at Addaura, is the **Grotta dell'Addaura** *(admission free; open only by prior arrangement with Soprintendeza Archeologica ☎ 091 696 13 199)*, where several cave drawings from the Palaeolithic period have survived.

Monreale

An absolute must is a visit to **Monreale Cathedral** *(☎ 091 640 44 13; admission free; open 8am-noon & 3.30pm-6pm daily)* The town is about 8km south-west of Palermo and accessible by frequent city buses (see Getting Around under Palermo for details).

The magnificent 12th-century Norman cathedral was built for William II. It is said he did not want to be inferior to his grandfather, Roger, who was responsible for the cathedral in Cefalù and the Cappella Palatina in Palermo. Considered the finest example of Norman architecture in Sicily, the cathedral in fact incorporates Norman, Arab, Byzantine and classical elements and, despite renovations over the centuries, remains substantially intact. The central doorway has bronze doors by Bonanno Pisano and the northern door is by Barisano da Trani. Although the exterior is both graceful and elegant, nothing can quite prepare you for the dazzling interior, one of the most impressive creations of the Italian Middle Ages and one of the most beautiful to be found anywhere in the world.

The walls of the aisles, sanctuary and apses are entirely covered in magnificent gilded mosaics. The artists were local and Venetian mosaicists, but the influence of the Byzantine style is all-pervasive. Completed in 1184 after only ten years' work, the mosaics are the apogee of Norman-Arabic art, an articulate and fitting tribute to the grandeur of Sicilian culture at the time.

In the central apse is the dominating half-figure of Christ *Pantokrator* (all-powerful) giving benediction, and below him the Virgin Mary and child, bearing the legend *Panacronatas* (all-chaste). Beneath them again are the ranks of saints, each identified by name (look out for St Thomas à Becket between Silvester and Laurence; he was canonised in 1173, just before the mosaics were started). The side apses are dedicated to the martyrdoms of St Paul (cast) and St Peter (west), whereas the central nave is a pictorial history of the early books of the Bible, beginning with the Creation.

Outside the cathedral is the entrance to the **cloisters** *(admission €4.15 or €7.75 with a 2-day cumulative ticket to La Cuba, San Giovanni degli Eremiti and La Zisa; open 9am-7pm Mon-Sat, 9am-1pm Sun)*, which were part of a Benedictine abbey once attached to the church. There are 228 twin columns with polychrome ornamentation. Each of the Romanesque capitals is different, depicting plants, animals and fantastic motifs. The capital of the 19th column on the west aisle depicts William II offering the cathedral to the Madonna.

Solunto

About 17km east of Palermo are the remains of the Hellenistic-Roman town of Solunto *(☎ 091 90 45 57; admission €3.10; open 9am-4.30pm Mon-Sat, 9am-12.30pm Sun)*. Although the ancient city is only partially excavated, what has been brought to light is well worth the trip. Founded in the 4th century BC on the site of an earlier Phoenician settlement, Solunto was built in a particularly panoramic position on Monte Catalfano, overlooking the sea. Wander along the main street and take detours up the steep, paved side streets to explore the ruined houses, some of which still sport their original mosaic floors. Take particular note of the theatre and the House of Leda (if you can find it), which has an interesting floor mosaic.

To get there, take the train from Palermo to the Santa Flavia-Solunto-Porticello stop and ask for directions. It's about a half-hour uphill walk.

Ustica

Almost 60km north of Palermo lies the lonely island of Ustica. In 1980, a passenger jet crashed near the island in mysterious circumstances, leaving 81 people dead. Investigators suspect the military was involved and a dozen Italian airforce officers stand accused of a cover-up.

Ustica is otherwise a tranquil place with around 1000 inhabitants, most living in the mural-bedecked village of the same name. The best months to visit are June and September. Staying here in August is sheer lunacy. Parts of the rocky coast have been declared a *riserva marina* (marine reserve) and the limpid waters, kept sparkling clean by an Atlantic current through the Straits of

Gibraltar, are ideal for diving and underwater photography.

There is an APT office (☎ 091 844 94 56) for the marine reserve on Piazza Umberto I, part of an interlocking series of squares in the centre of the village. It opens 8am to 1pm and 4pm to 6pm Monday to Friday, 8am to 2pm Saturday and Sunday (to 9pm during summer). Staff can advise on dive centres around the island.

For medical emergencies, contact *pronto soccorso* (casualty) on ☎ 091 844 92 48. For police, call the *carabinieri* (military police with civic duties) on ☎ 091 844 90 49.

Activities Among the most rewarding dive sites are the Secca Colombara to the north of the island and the Scoglio del Medico to the west. Note that Zone A of the riserva marina, taking in a good stretch of the western coast north of Punta dello Spalmatore, is protected. Fishing, diving and even swimming are forbidden in the area without permission. The riserva's information office can organise seawatch diving excursions into the zone. The only dive hire outlet, Ailara Rosalia (☎ 091 844 91 62), Banchina Barresi, operates in summer. Otherwise, bring your own gear.

You can also hire a boat and cruise around the island, visiting its many grottoes and tiny beaches. Hotel Ariston (☎ 091 844 90 42), Via della Vittoria 5, organises boat trips and diving (it also rents motorcycles) or you could try Scubaland (☎ 091 844 92 16), Via Petriera 7, to hire a boat or dinghy.

Places to Stay & Eat There are eight hotels and several *affittacamere* (rooms for rent) on Ustica.

Pensione Clelia *(☎ 091 844 90 39, fax 091 844 94 59, ⓔ clelia@telegest.it, Via Magazzino 7)* High season singles/doubles up to €33.55/62. Half-board up to €59.90. This decent little hotel also has a good ***restaurant***.

Hotel Ariston *(☎ 091 844 90 42, fax 091 844 93 35, Via della Vittoria 5)* Singles/doubles from €31/46.50. A slightly cheaper option, with clean, comfortable rooms.

Getting There & Around Siremar operates a car ferry daily (two hours 20 minutes) year-round. From June to September there are at least two Siremar hydrofoils a day from Palermo (one hour 15 minutes). One-way passenger fares are €16 (hydrofoil) and €10.85 (ferry) in the high season. The Siremar office (☎ 091 874 93 111, W www.siremar.it) is at Piazza Capitano Longo 9, in the centre of Ustica.

During the summer you can also pick up the Trapani-Favignana-Ustica-Naples hydrofoil, run by Ustica Lines three days perweek. The journey from Naples to Ustica takes four hours and costs €64.55 one way.

Orange minibuses run around the island from the village, or you can hire a moped at Hotel Ariston in town.

Northern Coast

PARCO NATURALE REGIONALE DELLE MADONIE

This 40,000 hectare park, between Palermo and Cefalù, incorporates the Madonie mountain range and some of the highest mountains on Sicily after Mt Etna. The highest peak in the range is Pizzo Carbonara at 1979m. Instituted in 1989 by the Region of Sicily, the park also takes in several small towns and villages and plenty of farms and vineyards. It is an inhabited area, rather than simply a nature reserve – so you can combine walking with visits to some of the more interesting towns in the park, such as Geraci Siculo, Petralia Soprana and Petralia Sottana. In winter it is the only place in Sicily, other than Etna, where you can ski.

There are information offices of the Ente Parco delle Madonie (the body responsible for the park) in Petralia Sottana (☎ 0921 68 40 11) and Isnello (☎ 0921 66 27 95), with information about the park and several one-day walks, as well as transport and accommodation.

There are several *rifugi* (mountain huts) in the park.

Rifugio Ostello della Gioventù *(☎ 0921 4 99 95, Piano della Battaglia, Località Mandria Marcate)* Singles/doubles €15.50/36.15. Not quite a youth hostel in the proper sense, this rifugio caters to all visitors. It is located at Mandria Marcate.

Madonie *(☎ 0921 64 11 06, Corso Paolo Agliata 81, Petralia Sottana)* Singles/doubles €51.65/72.30. This small hotel, at Petralia Sottana, offers country comfort.

If you're looking for something with a little more character, there are excellent agriturismo-style establishments in the area.

Tenuta Gangivecchio *(☎ 0921 68 91 91, fax 0921 68 91 91, Contrada Gangi Vecchia)* Half-board €56.80. This place, run by the Tornabene family, is in a former Benedictine convent, dating from the 14th century, just out of the town of Gangi towards the interior of Sicily. Children under 10 aren't accepted at Easter or New Year.

Fulgy Barone d'Aspermont *(☎ 0921 67 41 28, fax 0921 67 41 28, Contrada Ogliastro)* Half-board from €51.65. This place is close to San Mauro Castelverde and Cefalù. It has accommodation in small apartments with kitchens.

Transport could be a problem in the Madonie unless you have a car. The towns within the park are serviced by SAIS and AST buses from Palermo, but if you want to reach some of the more secluded parts of the park, you might find that hitching a ride is the only option.

CEFALÙ

Just over an hour by train or bus from Palermo, Cefalù is an attractive beachside village which has become the premier destination on the Tyrrhenian coast. Its popularity is reflected in the number of tour buses that hit town daily during summer and the near-exorbitant prices of everything, including restaurants. Still, the town's location on the sea, backed up against the towering crag known simply as La Rocca (The Rock), plus its relatively unspoiled medieval streets and historic sights, make for a relaxing day trip from the capital – or a place to pass a few (rather pricey) days.

From the train station, turn right into Via Moro to reach Via Matteotti and the old town. If you are heading for the beach, turn left and walk along Via Gramsci, which becomes Via V Martoglio. The AAST office (☎ 0921 42 10 50, **W** www.cefalu-tour.pa.it) is at Corso Ruggero 77 and opens 8am to 2.30pm Monday to Friday, 9am to 1pm Saturday.

Things to See & Do

Roger II built the superb **Duomo di Cefalù** *(☎ 0921 92 20 21, Piazza del Duomo; admission free; open 8am-noon & 3.30pm-7pm daily)* in the 12th century to fulfil a vow to God after his fleet was saved during a violent storm off Cefalù. The twin pyramid towers of the cathedral stand out over the town centre, but the real beauty is inside. A towering figure of Christ Pantocrator in the apse is the focal point of the elaborate Byzantine mosaics – you'll have to go to Monreale or the Cappella Palatina to see anything finer. The columns of the twin aisles support Arab-style pointed arches and have beautiful capitals.

Off Piazza del Duomo is the private **Museo Mandralisca** *(☎ 0921 42 15 47, Via Mandralisca 13; admission €4.15; open 9am-7pm daily)*. Its collection includes Greek ceramics and Arab pottery, as well as paintings, notably the *Portrait of an Unknown Man* by Antonello da Messina.

From the old town's main street, Via Matteotti, look for the sign pointing uphill to the **Tempio di Diana** *(always open)* and the straggly remains of a set of fortified walls built during the Byzantine period. The main attraction of making the 30-minute climb is the panoramic view.

Places to Stay & Eat

There are several camp sites in the area, with readers particularly recommending Costa Ponente Internazionale, situated about 4km west of Cefalù at Contrada Ogliastrillo. Catch the bus from the train station heading for La Spisa.

Costa Ponente Internazionale *(☎ 0921 42 00 85, Località Contrada Ogliastrillo)* High season adults/tent €5.95/11.90. This site is shady, has a pool and is one of the best maintained sites in Italy.

If you want to stay in town, there are a few options.

Locanda Cangelosi *(☎ 0921 42 15 91, Via Umberto I 26)* Singles/doubles €18.10/36.15.

This small hotel is the only really cheap option in town, but with limited rooms you'll have to book in advance.

La Giara *(☎ 0921 42 15 62, fax 0921 42 25 18, Via Veterani 40)* High season singles/doubles €49.05/77.45. The recently refurbished La Giara has decent rooms; it is uphill from the beach and off Corso Ruggero.

Baia del Capitano *(☎ 0921 42 00 05, fax 0921 42 01 63, Contrada Mazzaformo)* High season singles/doubles €64.55/98.15. Delightfully situated in an olive grove near the beach at Mazzaforno, a few kilometres out of town towards Palermo, the Baia del Capitano offers a good standard of accommodation.

You won't have trouble finding a place to eat – there are dozens of restaurants and several bars along Via Vittorio Emanuele – but the food can be surprisingly mundane and the ubiquitous tourist menus unimaginative.

Trattoria La Botte *(☎ 0921 42 43 15, Via Veterani 6)* Full meals around €15.50. This eatery is just off Corso Ruggero; its pasta con le sarde is particularly good.

L'Antica Corte *(☎ 0921 42 32 28, Corso Ruggero 193)* Full meals from €20.65. This is one of the better restaurants in town, and the prices reflect it.

Getting There & Away

SAIS buses leave Palermo for Cefalù twice daily, arriving at Cefalù's train station.

Trains from Palermo leave every 30 minutes (€2.40). From mid-June to September, hydrofoils link Cefalù with the Aeolian Islands (€15.50 one way, twice daily).

TINDARI

At Capo Tindari, farther along the coast towards Milazzo, are the **ruins** of ancient Tyndaris *(☎ 0941 36 90 23; admission €2.05; open 9am-1 hr before sunset daily)*, a Greek settlement founded on a rocky promontory in 396 BC. It was later occupied by the Romans and destroyed by Arab invaders. Today, a Greek theatre, Roman buildings (including a house and public baths) and fragments of the city's ramparts remain. A museum houses a collection of Hellenistic statues as well as Greek and Roman pottery.

Nearby is the **Santuario della Madonna Nera** *(open 8am-noon & 3pm-7pm daily)*. Built in the 1960s to hold a statue of a black Madonna revered since Byzantine times, the religious sanctuary is a place of pilgrimage. From the Oliveri beach you can reach the Laghetti di Marinello Riserva Naturale, visible from the square in front of the sanctuary.

Nearby, in Patti, are the remains of a Roman villa *(☎ 0941 36 15 93; admission €2.05; open 9am-1hr before sunset daily)*, well worth visiting if you're passing through.

To get to Tindari, catch a train to Patti (6km away on the Palermo-Messina line) and then a bus to the site from outside the station (€1.30, three daily, with increased services in summer).

MILAZZO

This is not the prettiest sight on Sicily, but it has its share of Baroque churches and palaces. Most people aiming for the Aeolian Islands pass through here. The APT office (☎ 090 922 28 65), Piazza C Duilio 10, is behind Via Crispi. All the ferry company offices are directly opposite the port, along Via Rizzo.

If you've got an hour or two to spare, you could head to the pretty northern end of town for a peek at the 16th-century Spanish **castle** *(☎ 090 922 12 91, Via Impallomeni; admission free; guided tours on the hour 10am-noon & 3pm-5pm Tues-Sun Sept-May, 10am-noon & 5pm-7pm Tues-Sun June-Aug)*.

There are several hotels near the port if you get stuck for the night.

Central *(☎ 090 928 10 43, Via del Sole 8)* Singles/doubles up to €25.80/46.50. Basic accommodation but, as its name suggests, it's central.

For a hearty, delicious and cheap meal, try the ***Bar-Pasticceria-Rosticceria*** *(☎ 090 928 18 13, Via Pescheria 40)*, which serves pasta and vegetable dishes from €2.05. For the best *pasta al forno* (oven-baked pasta) outside a real Italian home kitchen, head to this place. It's situated about 400m north of the port, near the tourist office.

Milazzo is easy to reach by bus or train from Palermo and Messina. See Getting

There & Away in the Messina section later. Intercity buses terminate on Piazza della Repubblica, a five-minute walk back along Via Crispi to the port. The train station is a little farther away, on Piazza Marconi, connected to the port by AST buses.

Aeolian Islands (Isole Eolie)

The seven islands of this volcanic archipelago stretching north of Milazzo offer: the developed tourist resort of Lipari; rugged Vulcano; the fertile vineyards of Salina; the understated jet-set haunt of Panarea; the spectacular scenery of Stromboli and its fiercely active volcano; and the solitude of outlying Filicudi and Alicudi. Also known as the Lipari Islands, the Aeolians have been inhabited since the Neolithic era, when people travelled there for the valuable volcanic glass, obsidian.

The ancient Greeks believed the islands were the home of Aeolus, the god of the wind, and Homer wrote of them in his *Odyssey*. Characterised by their rich colours and volcanic activity, the rugged coastlines are at times lashed by violent seas. As attractive as all this may appear to the modern traveller, the Aeolian Islands have traditionally made for a difficult living environment. From the 1930s to the 1950s many inhabitants migrated to Australia (often referred to here as the eighth Aeolian Island), virtually abandoning the outer islands and leaving behind only a small contingent on the others.

Cinema fans might like to see Nanni Moretti's *Caro Diario* (Dear Diary). Part of this quirky film is set in the islands and Moretti captures their essence well. Massimo Troisi's last film *Il Postino* was shot on the island of Salina. While you are there, look out for the distinctive murals depicting local scenes by Brescian artist Armando Pacchiani which seem to crop up in the most unlikely places.

You will need to book accommodation well in advance in the July/August high season. The best time to come is in May and early June or late September and October. Ferries and hydrofoils operate year-round, but winter services are much reduced and sometimes cancelled – to the outer islands at any rate – due to heavy seas.

Getting There & Away

Ferries and hydrofoils leave regularly from Milazzo. All the ticket offices are along Via L Rizzo, at the port. You have to purchase your tickets at the port ticket offices before boarding; telephone bookings are not accepted unless they are done weeks in advance. All the following prices were one-way high-season fares at the time of writing.

Both SNAV and Siremar run hydrofoils (€10.05) to Lipari and on to the other islands. SNAV hydrofoils also connect the islands with Messina (€16) and Reggio di Calabria (€17, one service daily, year-round), as well as Naples and Palermo (summer only).

Siremar runs car ferries from Milazzo to the islands for just over half the price of the hydrofoil (passengers €7.50, small cars €24), but they are slower and less regular. NGI Traghetti runs a limited car-ferry service for around the same rates.

Siremar also runs ferries from Lipari to Naples (three per week).

Regular hydrofoil and ferry services operate between the islands, but they can be disrupted to the outer islands by heavy seas. Lipari's two ports are separated by the citadel – hydrofoils arrive at and depart from Marina Corta, while ferries service Marina Lunga. Siremar and SNAV have ticket offices in the same building at Marina Corta. Siremar also has a ticket office at Marina Lunga. Full timetable information is available at all offices. On the other islands, ticket offices are at or close to the docks.

Examples of one-way fares and sailing times from Lipari are:

Panarea
 Hydrofoil: €6.70, 30 minutes
 Ferry: €3.85, one hour
Stromboli
 Hydrofoil: €13.15, 50 minutes
 Ferry: €7.75, 2¾ hours

Alicudi
Hydrofoil: €13.95, 1½ hours
Ferry: €9.05, 3¼ hours

LIPARI

postcode 98050 • pop 11,000

The largest and most developed of the islands, Lipari is also the most popular with tourists. The main town, of the same name, is typically Mediterranean, with pastel-coloured houses huddled around its two harbours. A thriving exporter of obsidian in ancient times, it is now a centre for mining pumice stone (another volcanic product). It's the best-equipped base for exploring the archipelago.

Orientation

Lipari's two harbours, Marina Lunga and Marina Corta, are on either side of the cliff-top citadel, which is surrounded by 16th-century walls. The town centre extends between them. The main street, Corso Vittorio Emanuele, runs roughly north-south to the west of the castle. From Marina Corta, walk to the right across the piazza to Via Garibaldi and follow the 'centro' signs for Corso Vittorio Emanuele.

Information

Tourist Offices The AAST office (☎ 090 988 00 95) is at Corso Vittorio Emanuele 202. It is the main tourist office for the archipelago, although offices open on Stromboli, Vulcano and Salina in summer. Staff here will assist with accommodation, which is useful in the busy summer months. Pick up a free copy of *Ospitalità in blu*, which contains details of accommodation and services on all the islands. The office opens 8am to 2pm and 4pm to 7.30pm Monday to Saturday, 8am to 2pm on Sunday and holidays in the high season. In the low season, it's open 8am to 2pm and 4pm to 6.30pm Monday to Saturday.

Money There are several banks in Lipari, including the Banca del Sud on Corso Vittorio Emanuele. You should have no trouble using Visa, MasterCard or Eurocheque cards for cash advances. Outside banking hours, exchange facilities can be found at the post office and several travel agencies.

Note that banking facilities on the other islands are limited.

Post & Communications The post office (☎ 090 981 13 79) is at Corso Vittorio Emanuele 207, near the AAST office, and opens 8.30am to 6.30pm Monday to Friday and 8.30am to 1pm on Saturday. Public telephones can be found throughout the town. There's an Internet point (☎ 090 981 42 28) at Corso Vittorio Emanuele 53.

Medical Services For medical emergencies, contact the hospital (☎ 090 9 88 51) or *pronto soccorso* (casualty; ☎ 090 988 52 67). Both are on Via Sant'Anna.

Things to See & Do

After the mercenary Barbarossa rampaged through the town in 1544, the Spaniards rebuilt and fortified Lipari in the **citadel** *(open 9am-7pm daily)* at the top of the small cliff between the town's harbours. These fortifications are still pretty much intact. Contained within their walls is the Baroque **cathedral** *(open 9am-1pm & 4pm-7pm daily)*, built in 1654 to replace the Norman church that Barbarossa destroyed. The only part of the original structure to survive the raids was the 12th-century Benedictine cloisters *(€0.50, open 9am-1pm & 4pm-7pm daily)*.

The southern part of the citadel contains viewable **archaeological ruins**, some dating back to the 17th to 14th centuries BC. These have yielded many of the exhibits now in the **Museo Archeologico Eoliano** *(☎ 090 988 01 74, Castello di Lipari; admission €4.15; open 9am-1.30pm & 3pm-7pm Mon-Sat, 9am-1pm Sun)*. This fabulous museum boasts a superb collection which traces the volcanic and human history of the islands. There are good labels giving overviews of each period and, although the collection is extensive, it is manageable. It is divided into three sections: an archaeological section devoted to artefacts found on Lipari, from the Neolithic and Bronze Ages to the Roman era (including pottery, flints and cutting tools); a classical section with finds from Lipari's necropolis (including urns, vases, jewellery and the most complete collection of sensational miniature Greek theatrical masks in the world); and a section on finds from the other islands.

It is worth exploring the island, in particular for views of Salina, Alicudi and Filicudi from the rugged, windy cliffs of Lipari's north-western corner. Sunbathers and swimmers head for **Canneto**, a few kilometres north of Lipari town. The beach is accessible by a track just north of Canneto. Farther north are the pumice mines of **Pomiciazzo** and **Porticello**, where there is another beach. The village of **Quattropani** and the lookout known as **Quattrocchi**, south of **Pianoconte**, are good spots to drink in the views.

Scuba diving is popular in the Aeolian Islands. Contact Diving Center La Gorgonia (☎ 090 981 20 60), Salita San Giuseppe, Marina Corta. For information on sailing courses, contact the Centro Nautico Eoliano

Easter Mysteries

Dinner on Good Friday in Lipari was a hurried affair; the clock was counting down the minutes until the Venerdì Santo parade – *I Misteri* – passed through the centre of town. The watching crowds came to a standstill as the parade departed from the cathedral in the citadel. It was standing room only on the main street, Corso Vittorio Emanuele, and the benefits of my height (at least compared to 99% of Italians) became immediately apparent.

First came two lines of children, making a racket with those whirly-clacker things that spin round and round.

Then came the 14 Stations of the Cross, represented by almost life-size models (carried by four men each) of Christ crowned with thorns, carrying the cross, being nailed to it, lying dead in the Virgin Mary's arms (the classic *pietà*) and the deposition, with Christ's body encased in a glass coffin.

In charge of it all was a man dressed in a crimson robe, a man I recognised. Earlier that day he'd been in the cathedral, dressed in blue overalls and overseeing the work of dozens of Liparese women, who were decorating the floats with flowers. I'd noticed him because his mobile phone had rung – loudly, several times, and with a tune that sounded suspiciously like Waltzing Matilda. This was clearly a man on a mission. When he waved his arms, the procession moved on; when he gestured to stop or slow down, the processionists toed the line like clockwork.

The men carrying the heavy floats were clearly under strain – there was regular shoulder-swapping going on. Alongside them in controlled, obedient lines walked women dressed in black carrying candles – the mourning mothers of Christ, perhaps. They were followed by men dressed almost like nuns, wearing blue robes under white tunics, complete with white veils. And at the end, after the model of Christ on the cross, the Pietà, and the Deposed Christ, came the local bishop, shielded and identified by the crimson canopy above his head, which was supported by four canopy bearers.

The local law enforcement officials, the heads of the Polizia, the *carabinieri* (military police with civic duties), the *vigili del fuoco* (fire brigade) and the *vigili urbani* (traffic police) marched in full dress uniform and solemn silence behind the procession. They were followed by a badly out-of-tune semi-military band, with an inordinate number of oboes producing a rich, bleating wail, and a single tenor saxophonist who quite clearly had not had time to practise before setting out on this journey.

As each part of the procession went past, the spectators – without exception – crossed themselves. At the end, they solemnly fell into line and followed the shuffling processionists down to the port, then eventually back up to the cathedral.

It was all there: religion, atmosphere, colour and beauty – the stuff that makes Sicily, well, Sicily. And accompanied all the time by that all-pervasive, mournful music, which sounded just like – no, it couldn't have been – the theme tune to the Godfather.

(☎ 090 981 26 91), also at Salita San Giuseppe, Marina Corta, or ask at the AAST office.

Viking (☎ 090 981 25 84), Vico Himera 3 (with ticket booths at both Marina Corta and the ferry port), conducts boat tours of all the islands from March to October, including one to Stromboli by night (€25.80) to see the Sciara del Fuoco (Trail of Fire). There are also tours to Alicudi and Filicudi (€25.80), and to the other islands.

Places to Stay

Lipari provides plenty of options for a comfortable stay, from budget level to luxurious. However, prices soar in summer, particularly in August. In peak season, if all else fails, AAST staff will billet new arrivals in private homes on the island. Don't reject offers by touts when you arrive, as they usually have decent rooms in private houses.

To rent an apartment, contact the AAST office for a list of establishments.

Places to Stay – Budget

The island's only camp site is at Canneto, about 2km out of Lipari town and accessible by bus from the Esso service station at Marina Lunga.

Baia Unci *(☎ 090 981 19 09, fax 090 981 17 15, Marina Garibaldi, Località Canneto)* Low season adult/tent €5.70/7.25, high season adult/tent €7.75/13.95. Open 15 Mar-15 Oct. Sites at Baia Unci are underneath shady eucalypts.

The various affittacamere operators renting furnished rooms are a good deal, as you can usually have use of a kitchen (for a small extra charge).

Diana Brown *(☎ 090 981 25 84, fax 090 981 32 13, e dbrown@netnet.it, Vico Himera 3)* Doubles with bath €25.80-62 depending on the season. Diana Brown's spotless, comfortable rooms (all with air-con, fridge and kettle; use of kitchen and washing machine extra) are close to Marina Corta, just off Corso Vittorio Emanuele. South African-born Diana is a fount of local information. She also operates a book exchange (leave one, take as many as you like) and, together with her husband Salvatore, runs Viking, a company which organises boat trips (see Things to See & Do).

Casa Vittorio *(☎ 090 981 15 23, e casavittorio@netnet.it, Vico Sparviero 15)* Doubles with bath €31-62. These comfortable furnished rooms are off Via Garibaldi near Marina Corta. You'll find the owner (unless he finds you first) at Via Garibaldi 78, on the way from Marina Corta to the town centre. There are two terraces with views.

Enzo il Negro *(☎ 090 981 24 73, fax 090 981 31 63, e enzoilnegro@libero.it, Via Garibaldi 29)* Low season per person €31, high season per person €38.75. This place has spotless, comfortable digs. All rooms have bath, air-conditioning, a fridge and balcony, and there is a large terrace.

Places to Stay – Mid-Range

Pensione Neri *(☎ 090 981 14 13, fax 090 981 36 42, e htlneri@netnet.it, Via G Marconi 43)* Low/high season doubles with bath €62/€124. A lovely old renovated villa is the setting for this small hotel off Corso Vittorio Emanuele. Breakfast is included – and if you have to catch an early ferry, they'll provide brekky for you to take away.

Hotel Oriente *(☎ 090 981 14 93, fax 090 988 01 98, e hoteloriente@netnet.it, Via G Marconi 35)* Low season singles/doubles with bath €28.40/51.65, high season singles/doubles with bath €59.40/98.15. Next to Pensione Neri, this hotel has a bar, garden and very comfortable rooms – great value in low season, dearer in high season. Rooms have air-con and prices include breakfast.

Costa Residence Vacanze *(☎ 090 988 07 40, fax 090 981 11 66, e costaresidence@netnet.it, Località San Leonardo 7)* Low season apartments sleeping 2/4 from €29.92/51.65 per day, high season €147.70/221.55. These self-catering apartments with one or two bedrooms are a good option for families.

Places to Stay – Top End

Villa Meligunis *(☎ 090 981 24 26, fax 090 988 01 49, e villa meligunis@netnet.it, Via Marte 7)* Low/high season doubles €113.60/175.60 including breakfast, high season half-board €108.45 per person. Villa Meligunis is Lipari's top hotel, on a hill overlooking

Marina Corta; if it's complete luxury you want, this is your place.

Carasco *(☎ 090 981 16 05, fax 090 981 18 28, ⓔ carasco@tin.it, Porto Delle Genti)* Low/high season half-board €62/100. The Carasco's got the works – private swimming jetty, lovely pool and terrace, a decent restaurant – but it could do with some updating, and minimum stays are imposed in high season. It's the big yellow building as far to the left as you can go from Marina Corta (a bit of a hike) – just follow the signs.

Places to Eat

Try pasta prepared with the island's excellent capers and be prepared to spend big to eat the day's sea catch, particularly swordfish. The waters of the archipelago abound in fish, including tuna, mullet, cuttlefish and sole, all of which end up on restaurant tables at the end of the day. The local wine is the sweet, white Malvasia, but most restaurants also offer a good selection of Sicilian tipples.

Although prices go up in the high season, you can still eat cheaply by sticking to the pizzerias along Corso Vittorio Emanuele.

Il Galeone *(☎ 090 981 16 43, Corso Vittorio Emanuele 222)* Pizzas €4.65-6.20. Good pizzas are the staple here, although the set lunch (around €12.90) is good value if you've got an appetite.

Da Bartolo *(☎ 090 981 17 00, Via Garibaldi 53)* Full meals €18.10. This eatery is one of the island's better trattorias and a good choice for seafood. Tucked away around a corner is its wood-fired oven which produces delicious bread for the restaurant as well as excellent pizzas.

A Sfiziusa *(☎ 090 981 12 16, Via Roma 29)* Pasta €5.15-6.20, mains €6.70-10.35. This unassuming, cosy trattoria produces typical Aeolian cuisine, based on fish and seafood.

Kasbah *(Via Maurolico 25)* Wine by the glass €2.60, cocktails €3.60, pasta up to €4.15, pizzas €4.15-6.70, fish mains €10.35-20.65. Open Mar-Oct, evenings only, until 3am in summer. Boasting the most attractive decor and atmosphere of any of Lipari's eateries, the Kasbah, with its North African theme, is a relaxing place for an aperitif or after-dinner drink and an excellent place for a really good meal. Try the linguine with *bottarga* (dried pressed fish roe), almonds and fennel or the spaghetti with lobster. The whole fish served *alla eoliane* (with capers, olives and tomatoes) is delicious but expensive. Wine buffs note: the wine list features over 100 different Sicilian wines.

People with access to a kitchen can shop for supplies at the ***grocery shops*** and ***SISA supermarket*** along Corso Vittorio Emanuele.

If you fancy a late-night drink, ***Bar La Precchia*** *(☎ 090 981 13 03, Corso Vittorio Emanuele 191)* is a friendly place. In summer it's open until 3am and often has live music.

Getting There & Around

See Getting There & Away under the Aeolian Islands earlier for more details.

Urso buses (☎ 090 981 12 62) leave from the Esso service station at Marina Lunga for Canneto (nine daily, more frequently in summer), Porticello (seven daily) and Quattropani (at least nine daily). The company also offers special sightseeing trips around the island at 9.30am, 11.30am and 5pm daily. The AAST office has timetables.

Boats and scooters are available for hire from Roberto Foti (☎ 090 981 23 52), Via F Crispi 31, to the right as you leave Marina Lunga, and several other establishments (the tourist office has a list). A moped costs €5.15 for the first hour, €2.60 for subsequent hours, with discounts for rentals of a few days or more. A four-seater motorised rubber dinghy costs from €51.65 daily and a 14-seater from €258.25.

VULCANO

postcode 98050 • pop 800

Just south of Lipari and the first port of call for ferries and hydrofoils from Milazzo, Vulcano is known for its therapeutic mud baths and hot springs. To the ancients, the island of Thermessa, Terasia or Hierà – as Vulcano was variously known – must have inspired a good deal of respect, if not downright fear. Not only did the god of fire, Vulcan, have his workshop here, but Aeolus, the god of the wind, also swirled about.

Of Vulcano's three volcanoes, the oldest lies on the island's southern tip and was already extinct in ancient times. The youngest, Vulcanello, next to the mud baths at the island's north-eastern end, rose from the sea in the 2nd century BC, according to Pliny. The only active volcano, Gran Cratere, has a number of fumaroles; its broad, smoking crater broods over the port. A tranquil place, Gran Cratere hasn't blown for more than four centuries, but you'll notice on arrival the all-pervading stench of sulphurous gases.

Orientation & Information

Boats dock at the Porto di Levante. To the right, as you face the island, is the small Vulcanello peninsula. All facilities are concentrated between the Porto di Levante and the Porto di Ponente, where you will find the Spiaggia Sabbia Nera (Black Sand Beach), the only smooth, sandy beach on the islands.

A tourist office (☎ 090 985 20 28) at Porto di Levante opens from June to October.

The Guardia Medica can be contacted on ☎ 090 985 22 20.

Things to See & Do

Climbing **Gran Cratere** is the main attraction. Follow the signs south along Via Provinciale out of town. A track is then signposted off the road. Take the left fork and head up – about an hour's scramble. The views from the top are reward enough for the sweat. The walk is best done early in the day when the trail is mostly in the shade. If you want to do the walk with a guide, contact the Gruppo Nazionale Vulcanologia Marcello Carapessa (☎ 090 985 25 28).

Even if you don't need a skin cure, a wallow in the hot, sulphurous mud pool of **Laghetto di Fanghi** can be a relaxing way to pass the time, if slightly offensive to the nose (don't wear your best bathing costume, as you'll never get the smell out). It's next to Vulcanello, so when you've had enough you can hop into the water at the adjacent beach where underwater hot springs create a natural Jacuzzi effect. Paddle boats are usually available for hire on the beach.

Various operators organise boat trips around the island (around €12.90) and to Stromboli (approximately eight hours return) for €25.80. Bus tours are also organised if enough people are interested; ask at the port.

Viking (☎ 090 981 25 84), based in Lipari, offers a boat trip around the island for around €12.90 per person.

Places to Stay & Eat

The mud baths pong – remember this when choosing rooms nearby.

Pensione Agostino *(☎ 090 985 23 42, Via Favaloro 1)* Low/high season doubles with bath €31/62. This place is close to the mud baths.

La Giara *(☎ 090 985 22 29, fax 090 985 24 51, Via Provinciale 18)* Low season singles/doubles with bath €29.95/40.30, high season singles/doubles with bath €56.80/98.15. Towards the Gran Cratere, these furnished rooms are pleasant. A few singles with shared bath are available at discounted rates.

Sea House Residence *(☎ 090 985 22 19, fax 090 985 21 43, Porto di Levante)* Low season apartments sleeping 2/4 €58.35/71.25, high season €116.70/142.55. Close to the mud baths, Sea House is a complex of self-contained apartments (which sleep up to five people) in a garden setting.

Hotel Arcipelago *(☎ 090 985 20 02, fax 090 985 21 54, Località Vulcanello)* Low season singles/doubles €41.30/62, high season singles/doubles €62/103.30, low/high season half-board €77.45/113.60 per person. This three-star hotel has a beautiful position on the northern coast of Vulcano.

Vulcano has a couple of places where you can get a decent meal.

Da Maurizio *(☎ 090 985 24 26, Via Porto di Levante)* Full meals from €15.50. This down-to-earth trattoria serves ubiquitous Sicilian dishes.

Da Vincenzino *(☎ 090 985 20 16, Via Porto di Levante)* Full meals from €15.50. Fish is – not surprisingly – the main attraction at this eatery.

Getting There & Away

Vulcano is an intermediate stop between Milazzo and Lipari and a good number of vessels go both ways throughout the day.

SALINA

postcode 98050 • pop 850

Just north-west of Lipari, Salina is the most fertile of the islands and consists of two extinct volcanoes, Monte dei Porri and Monte Fossa delle Felci. Its high coastal cliffs are topped with vineyards, where most of the islands' Malvasia wine is produced.

Orientation & Information

Boats dock at Santa Marina Salina, where you will find most accommodation, or at Rinella, a fishing hamlet on the southern coast. The other main villages on the island are Malfa, on the northern coast, and Leni, slightly inland from Rinella.

In summer, AAST booths operate at Rinella, Malfa and Santa Marina Salina; the rest of the year, contact the Lipari bureau. For medical assistance, call ☎ 090 984 40 05. For the police, phone ☎ 090 984 30 19.

Things to See & Do

If you are feeling energetic, you could climb the **Fossa delle Felci** volcano and visit the **riserva naturale** (nature reserve). From Santa Marina Salina, head for Lingua, a small village 3km south, from where paths lead up the mountain.

The **Santuario della Madonna del Terzito** at Valdichiesa, just south of Malfa, is a place of pilgrimage, particularly around the Feast of the Assumption on 15 August.

Rinella is a popular spot for spear-gun fishing. For information, contact the AAST booths. Boats are available for hire from June to August at Nautica Levante (☎ 090 984 30 83), Via Risorgimento, Santa Marina Salina.

Don't miss a trip to the beach at Pollara, the setting for much of Massimo Troisi's last film, *Il Postino*. The climb down is a bit tricky but the beach itself with its backdrop of cliffs is absolutely unbeatable.

Places to Stay & Eat

Camping Tre Pini *(☎ 090 980 91 55, Frazione Rinella-Leni)* Sites per person/tent €6.20/12.90. Right on the beach at Rinella, this camp site is well-equipped and even has a small trattoria.

Pensione Mamma Santina *(☎ 090 984 30 54, fax 090 984 30 51, e mammasantina@ctonline.it, Via Sanità 40)* Half-board per person €46.50-77.45 depending on season. A family atmosphere, spotless rooms and great views are the features of this pensione in Santa Marina Salina. Head for Via Risorgimento (the narrow main street) and walk north for a few hundred metres. The pensione is uphill along a winding lane to your left. The trattoria is worth the trip alone.

Hotel L'Ariana *(☎ 090 980 90 75, fax 090 980 92 50, e lariana@netnet.it, w www.hotelariana.it, Via Rotabile 11)* Low/high season singles without bath €18.10/31, low season singles/doubles with bath €25.80/46.50, high season singles/doubles with bath €46.50/87.80. A late-19th-century villa overlooking the sea at Rinella is the setting for this lovely little hotel. It has terraces, a bar and restaurant, with good deals on half/full board in summer.

There are several restaurants clustered around the docks at Santa Marina Salina.

Portobello *(☎ 090 984 31 25, Via Bianchi 1)* Full meals €20.65. Without doubt the best restaurant in town, where you can tuck into the daily catch for reasonable prices.

Il Gambero *(☎ 090 984 30 49, Località Lingua, Santa Marina Salina)* Full meals from €20.65. Fish is the star attraction at this popular eatery.

Getting There & Around

Hydrofoils and ferries service Santa Marina Salina and Rinella. You'll find ticket offices in both places.

Regular buses run from Santa Marina Salina to Malfa and Lingua and from Malfa to Leni and Rinella. Timetables are posted at the ports. Motorcycles are available for hire from Antonio Bongiorno (☎ 090 984 34 09), Via Risorgimento 240, Santa Marina Salina. A Vespa costs from €25.80 per day and a moped from €20.65 per day – less if you hire for longer periods.

PANAREA

postcode 98050 • pop 320

Easily the most picturesque of the Aeolian Islands, tiny Panarea is 3km long and 2km wide. Boats dock at San Pietro, where you'll find most of the accommodation.

After wandering around San Pietro, head south to Punta Milazzese, about a half-hour walk (there is a small beach along the way), to see the **Bronze Age village**, made up of 23 huts, which was discovered in 1948. Pottery found at the site is now in the museum at Lipari. Hire a boat at the port to explore the coves and beaches of the island, which are otherwise inaccessible.

Locanda Rodà *(☎ 090 98 30 06, fax 090 98 32 12, Via San Pietro)* Low season singles/doubles with bath €25.80/41.30, high season singles/doubles with bath €51.65/77.45. This place, uphill from the port and left, is as close as you'll come to a cheap hotel on Panarea. It has a well-priced pizzeria/trattoria.

La Sirena *(☎ 090 98 30 12, fax 090 988 00 69, ⓔ studiobarca@netnet.it, Via Drautt 4)* Low/high season doubles with bath €62/85.20. These very nice furnished rooms, on the way to the Bronze Age village, have the added advantage of a pleasant trattoria.

Trattoria da Pina *(☎ 090 98 30 32, Via Drautt)* Meals up to €20.65. Simple home-cooked food and a terrace overlooking the sea are the attractions of Da Pina.

Hydrofoils and the occasional ferry link the island with Stromboli to the north and Salina (and on to Lipari and Milazzo) to the south.

STROMBOLI

postcode 98050 • pop 500

Stromboli's almost constant explosions of fiery molten rock make an unforgettable spectacle at night. Lava flow is confined to the Sciara del Fuoco (Trail of Fire) on the volcano's north-western flank, leaving the villages of San Bartolo, San Vincenzo and Scari (which merge into one town) to the east and Ginostra to the south quite safe. Some 5000 people lived on the island until the massive eruption of 1930, when most took fright and left. Permanent residents now number about 500. The volcano's most recent eruption was in March 1996 and, although minor, left several people injured.

Stromboli, the most captivating of the islands, is inconveniently placed and boat services are prone to disruption. There's a fair choice of accommodation and a stay is more than recommended.

Orientation & Information

Boats arrive at Scari/San Vincenzo, downhill from the town. Accommodation is a short walk up the Scalo Scari to Via Roma, or, if you plan to head straight for the crater, follow the road along the waterfront (see the following section for details).

A tourist office, situated under the Ossidiana Hotel on Via Roma, is open in summer. The post office is on Via Roma and the one bank, on Via Nunziante at Ficogrande, is open June to September only.

Climbing the Volcano

From the port, follow the road along the waterfront, continuing straight past the beach at Ficogrande. Once past the village the path heads uphill, deviating after about 20 minutes to a bar/pizzeria and observatory. Alternatively, follow it through a slightly confusing section of reeds until it starts to ascend to the crater. About halfway up is a good view of the Sciara del Fuoco, although in daylight the glow of the molten lava is imperceptible. The path eventually becomes quite steep and rocky. Note the warning signs at the summit and do not go too close to the edge of the crater. The round trip from the village should take about four hours. Take plenty of drinking water and wet-weather clothing, as conditions are unpredictable. Volcano climbs should only be done with authorised guides. See Lonely Planet's *Walking in Italy* for more detailed descriptions of walks on Stromboli.

The climb is a totally different experience at night, when darkness throws the molten lava of the Sciara del Fuoco and the volcanic explosions into dramatic relief. There are several groups who organise climbs or boat trips to view the Sciara del Fuoco at night.

Alpine Guides *(☎ 090 98 62 63, just off Piazza San Vincenzo; about €18.10 per person)* Experienced guides take groups of 10 people or more to the crater at 4.30pm daily and return at 11.30pm; this depends on weather conditions and whether a group can be formed. Contact the office around noon to make a booking. For the night climb, you will need: heavy shoes; clothing for cold, wet weather; a torch (flashlight); food; and a good supply of water.

Società Navigazione Pippo *(☎ 090 98 61 35, Via Roma 47; around €12.90 per person)* The boat *Pippo* takes visitors for a 2½-hour gander at the Sciara del Fuoco from the sea. It leaves at 10pm from the port and at 10.10pm from Ficogrande. The same company also runs two daytime trips, leaving at 10am and 3pm.

Viking *(☎ 090 981 25 84, based on Lipari; €25.80 per person)* Boat trips start in Lipari at 2.30pm and depart from the Stromboli ferry port for the Sciara del Fuoco at 8pm.

Water Sports

Make your way to the beach of rocks and black volcanic sand at Ficogrande to swim and sunbathe. If you feel more energetic, contact ***La Sirenetta Diving Center*** *(☎ 090 98 60 25 or 0347 353 47 14, La Sirenetta Park Hotel, Via Marina 33)*, which offers diving courses and accompanied dives.

Places to Stay & Eat

There's nothing much in the dirt cheap bracket on Stromboli.

Casa del Sole *(☎/fax 090 98 60 17, Via Soldato Cincotta)* Low season singles/doubles €12.90/25.80, high season singles/doubles €20.65/41.30. Off the road to the volcano, before you reach Ficogrande, Casa del Sole is one of the cheapest options on the island and is popular with young travellers. Prices include use of the kitchen.

You'll also find a few affittacamere, charging from €25.80 to €31 per person in the high season.

Locanda Stella *(☎ 090 98 60 00, Via Fabio Filzi 14)* Doubles €51.65, with bath €56.80. You'll be lucky to get a room at this tiny place.

Barbablù *(☎ 090 98 61 18, fax 090 98 63 23, e barbablu@hpc.it, Via Vittorio Emanuele 17)* Low season doubles/triples with bath €92.95/118.80, high season doubles/triples with bath €118.80/216.90. A cross between a pensione and an affittacamere, this place has pleasant furnished rooms.

Hotel Villaggio Stromboli *(☎ 090 98 60 18, fax 090 98 62 58, e villagiostromboli@netnet.it, Via Regina Elena)* Low season singles/doubles with bath €33.55/46.50, high season singles/doubles with bath €82.65/134.30. This place is on the beach front and has a terrace bar/restaurant.

Park Hotel La Sirenetta *(☎ 090 98 60 25, fax 090 98 61 24, e lasirenetta@netnet.it, Via Marina 33)* Low season singles/doubles with bath €51.65/92.95, high season singles/doubles with bath €98.15/206.60. This hotel is perfectly sited on the beach at Ficogrande in front of Strombolicchio, a towering rock rising out of the sea at San Vincenzo. It has a swimming pool, a panoramic terrace with a restaurant (with reputedly one of the best chefs on the island). Luxury – at a price.

You won't find anything very cheap, but a few places offer reasonably priced meals.

Punta Lena *(☎ 090 98 62 04, Lungomare)* Full meals from €18.10. This place is on the waterfront, heading away from the port towards the volcano, and has a terrace overlooking the sea.

Ai Gecchi *(☎ 090 98 62 13, Vico Salina 12)* Full meals from €23.25. Follow the white geckos spray-painted on the ground to get to this restaurant in a small street off Via Roma. The fish is excellent and the octopus salad especially good.

The ***pizzeria*** at the observatory, about 20 minutes' walk up the lower slope of the volcano, is also reasonable.

Getting There & Away

Ticket offices for SNAV and Siremar are at the port. Bear in mind the cost and the distance if you're considering a day visit (which in any case will rob you of the opportunity to climb the volcano at night). Heavy seas can cause cancellation of ferry and hydrofoil services – so you could get stuck overnight.

FILICUDI & ALICUDI

postcode 98050 • pop 400

You will need a strong desire to get away from it all to stay on either of these islands west of Lipari. Facilities are limited (severely so on Alicudi) and boats can be cancelled due to heavy seas, even in summer.

Filicudi is the larger of the two and its attractions include **Grotta del Bue Marino** (Grotto of the Monk Seal) and **La Canna** rock pinnacle, about 1km off the island towards Alicudi. On Capo Graziano, south of the port, are the remains of a **prehistoric village** dating from 1800 BC. Boats are available for hire if you want to explore the grotto and scuba-diving courses are available in summer. While on the island, walk up Monte Filo dell'Arpa to see the **crater** of the extinct Montagnola volcano and the **Timpone delle Femmine**, huge fissures where women are said to have taken refuge during pirate raids.

The island has two hotels, both of which serve meals and offer half-board options, a good idea as the island's restaurant possibilities are limited.

La Canna *(☎ 090 988 99 56, fax 090 988 99 66, ⓔ vianast@tin.it, Via Rosa 43)* Low season singles/doubles €23.25/41.30, high season singles/doubles €36.15/72.30, half-board per person up to €62 . Just uphill from the port, La Canna has good facilities and pleasant rooms.

Phenicusa *(☎ 090 988 99 46 or 090 988 99 55, fax 090 988 99 55, Via Porto)* Low season singles/doubles €23.25/46.50, high season singles/doubles€36.15/67.15, half-board up to €64.55 per person. Open June-Sept.

Isolated Alicudi is the farthest from Lipari and the least developed of the Aeolian group. There is only one hotel and restaurant.

Ericusa *(☎ 090 988 99 02, Via Regina Elena, Località Perciato)* Doubles €62, half-board up to €59.40 per person. Open June-Sept. This place is open during the summer months and booking is strongly advised.

Eastern Coast

MESSINA

postcode 98050 • pop 268,000

For most, Messina is the point of arrival on Sicily and you could hardly imagine a less auspicious introduction. Devastated many times over the centuries, the modern city is pretty much bereft of any hint of its past. Known to the ancient Greeks as Zankle (Sickle) for its beautiful, curved harbour, Messina grew into a splendid city as a Greek colony and later thrived under Roman, Byzantine and Norman rule. Since the 18th century, Messina has been something of a disaster area – hit first by plague, then cholera and finally by earthquakes, including the massive 1908 jolt that all but destroyed the city and killed more than 80,000 people in the region. The city had barely been rebuilt when it was flattened by bombing during WWII.

If you're stuck in Messina, don't despair. The city centre, with its wide avenues, is a pleasant place to wander around, and there remain a couple of vestiges of happier days.

Orientation

The train station is on Piazza della Repubblica, at the southern end of the long waterfront. FS car and truck ferries also arrive here. The main intercity bus station is outside the train station, to the left on the piazza. To get to the city centre from Piazza della Repubblica, walk either straight across the piazza and directly ahead along Via I Settembre to the Piazza del Duomo or turn left into Via La Farina and take the first right into Via Cannazzaro to reach Piazza Cairoli.

Those coming by hydrofoil from Reggio di Calabria arrive about 1km north of the city on Corso Vittorio Emanuele II, while drivers on the private car ferry from Villa San Giovanni land a few kilometres farther along, just north of the trade-fair area (Fiera).

Information

Tourist Offices The AAPIT office (☎ 090 67 42 36) is at Via Calabria 301, 100m to the right as you leave the train station. It opens 8.30am to 6pm Monday to Saturday. The less well-informed city tourist office (☎ 090 292 32 92) is at Piazza Cairoli 45. It is ostensibly open the same hours as the AAPIT office but seems to close on a whim.

Money There are numerous banks in the city centre – most with ATMs – and a currency exchange booth at the timetable information office at the train station.

Post & Communications The main post office is on Piazza Antonello, on Corso Cavour near the cathedral. It opens 8.30am to 6.30pm Monday to Saturday.

There is a Telecom office on Corso Cavour, near Via Cannazzaro.

Travel Agencies There's a CTS travel agency (☎ 090 292 67 61) at Via Ugo Bassi 93.

Medical Services & Emergency The Ospedale Piemonte (hospital; ☎ 090 22 22 11) is on Viale Europa; at night, call ☎ 090 67 50 48. A booklet, available at the tourist office, lists pharmacies open at night on a rotation basis.

The *questura* (police station; ☎ 090 36 61) is at Via Placida 2.

Things to See & Do

The Norman **cathedral** *(Piazza del Duomo; admission free; open 7.30am-11.45am & 3.30pm-6pm daily)*, built in the 12th century, was almost completely destroyed by the combined effects of the 1908 earthquake and WWII bombing. Rebuilt virtually from scratch, its fine 15th-century doorway is one of the few original elements. The clock tower houses what is thought to be the world's largest astronomical clock, which strikes at noon.

On Piazza del Duomo is the **Fontana di Orione**, an elegant 16th-century work by Giovanni Angelo Montorsoli. Nearby (off Via Garibaldi) is the 12th-century **Chiesa della Santissima Annunziata dei Catalani** *(☎ 090 35 71 15, Piazza Catalani; admission free; open 8am-noon & 4pm-6.30pm daily)*, a jewel of Arab-Norman construction. In front of it is a monument to Don John of Austria, who beat the Turks at the Battle of Lepanto in 1571. Farther north, where Via Garibaldi spills into Piazza dell'Unità d'Italia, is Messina's other great fountain, the 16th-century **Fontana del Nettuno**.

The **Museo Regionale** *(☎ 090 36 12 92, Viale della Libertà 465; admission €4.15; open 9am-1.30pm Tues-Sat, 4pm-6.30pm Tues, Thurs & Sat, 9am-12.30pm Sun)* is a long walk along Viale della Libertà or you can take bus No 8 from the train station. It houses works of art, including the *Virgin and Child with Saints* by Antonello da Messina (born here in 1430) and two masterpieces by Caravaggio – *Adorazione dei Pastori* and *Resurrezione di Lazzaro*.

If you have your own transport, the drive north along the coast from Messina to Capo Peloro and then round to the east is pretty, and there are some reasonable **beaches** between the cape and Acquarone. Where the coast road meets the A20 heading for Milazzo, take the tollway, as the S113 can be incredibly congested from this point.

Places to Stay & Eat

The first two hotels below are convenient for the train station.

Touring *(☎/fax 090 293 88 51, Via N Scotto 17)* Singles/doubles €20.65/36.15, singles/doubles with bath €36.15/62. The rooms without baths here are fairly basic, but those with private facilities are decent.

Mirage *(☎ 090 293 88 44, no fax, Via N Scotto 3)* Singles/doubles €20.65/36.15, doubles with bath €50.60. Simple but clean rooms are on offer at this hotel.

Hotel Cairoli *(☎/fax 090 67 37 55, Viale San Martino 63)* Singles/doubles with bath €44.40/72.30. Hotel Cairoli offers a higher standard of accommodation than the cheaper alternatives; breakfast is included in the price.

Eating cheaply won't be a problem in Messina.

Self-Service *(Via dei Mille 12)* Meals from €2.60. This cafeteria-style lunch spot is popular with locals in a hurry.

Astral *(☎ 090 77 10 87, Via XXVII Luglio 71)* Full meals around €5.15. Just off Piazza Ciaroli, Astral serves up surprisingly good if basic food on plastic plates.

Sacha *(☎ 090 292 29 50, Via Nicola Fabrizi 15)* Full meals from €15.50, pizzas from €4.65. Hospitality is in the blood for Sacha Del Bono, whose parents run a hotel on Lipari; the Aeolian influence is evident in a couple of dishes but there's always pizza to enjoy if you prefer.

Il Cenacolo *(☎ 090 69 10 03, Via dei Mille 277a)* Full meals from €18.10. Il Cenacolo refers to the Last Supper – hopefully it won't be your last, but it's guaranteed to be a good one either way at this large popular eatery.

Getting There & Away

Bus Interbus (☎ 090 66 17 54) runs a regular service (approximately every hour, last bus leaves at 8pm) to Taormina (€2.60 one way), Catania and Catania's airport (both €5.40 one way). The company's office and bus station are at Piazza della Repubblica 6, to the left as you leave the train station. There is a direct connection to Rome (see Getting There & Away at the beginning of this chapter). Giuntabus (☎ 090 67 37 82) runs a service to Milazzo (for ferries and hydrofoils to the Aeolian Islands, 50 minutes) roughly every hour from Via Terranova 8, on the corner of Viale San Martino.

Train Regular trains connect Messina with Catania, Taormina, Syracuse, Palermo and Milazzo, but buses are generally faster. The train stations for Milazzo and Taormina are inconveniently located some distance from the city centre.

Car & Motorcycle If you arrive in Messina by FS ferry with a vehicle (see the following section), it is simple to make your way out of town. For Palermo (or Milazzo and the Aeolian Islands), turn right from the docks and follow Via Garibaldi along the waterfront. After about 1km, turn left into Viale Boccetta and follow the green *autostrada* (tollway) signs for Palermo. To reach Taormina and Syracuse, turn left from the docks into Via La Farina and follow the autostrada signs for Catania.

If you arrive by private ferry, turn right along Viale della Libertà for Palermo and Milazzo and left for Taormina and Catania – follow the green autostrada signs. You can also take the S113 (busy in summer).

Boat The FS railway runs car ferries to Villa San Giovanni, about 10km north of Reggio di Calabria, from next to the train station. The private Caronte company does the same run from docks a few kilometres up the waterfront, just north of the Fiera (trade-fair centre), and services are more frequent. It costs €15.50 one way to take a small car with Caronte (FS prices are similar). The trip takes about 20 minutes, with departures around the clock.

There are also big FS hydrofoils to Reggio di Calabria (€2.60 one way). SNAV (☎ 090 36 40 44) runs up to 20 hydrofoils on weekdays to Reggio di Calabria (15 minutes, €2.85 one way). In summer SNAV hydrofoils also connect Messina with the Aeolian Islands (Lipari €16 one way).

SOUTH TO TAORMINA

Those driving the Messina-Taormina route should consider a brief excursion into the foothills of the Monti Peloritani. Head for **Savoca**, 4km of winding road inland from the grey pebble beaches of Santa Teresa di Riva, which takes you through lemon and almond groves to a quiet village with a few medieval churches. You might recognise it – the famous Sicilian wedding scene from *The Godfather* was filmed here. Of interest is a Capuchin monastery, containing **catacombs** *(☎ 0942 76 12 45, ☎ 0942 76 13 88; admission free, but donation expected; open 9am-1pm & 4pm-7pm daily May-Sept, 9am-1pm & 3pm-5pm daily Oct-Apr)*. Some eerie-looking skeletons in raggedy 18th-century rig are all that remain of local nobles who paid good money for this kind of 'immortality'. AST buses run between Savoca and Santa Teresa di Riva.

TAORMINA

postcode 98039 • pop 11,000

Spectacularly located on a terrace of Monte Tauro, dominating the sea and with views westwards to Mt Etna, Taormina is easily Sicily's most picturesque town. From its foundation by the Siculians, Taormina remained a favourite destination for the long line of conquerors who followed. Under the Greeks, who moved in after Naxos was destroyed during colonial wars in the 5th century BC, Taormina flourished. It later came under Roman dominion and eventually became the capital of Byzantine Sicily, a period of grandeur that ended abruptly in AD 902 when the town was destroyed by Arab invaders. Taormina remained an important centre of art and trade throughout the subsequent Norman, Spanish and French rules.

Long ago discovered by the European jet set, Taormina is an expensive and touristy town. It is well served by hotels, pensiones and eating places, but some travellers might find the glitz and kitsch a little overwhelming. It would be a shame to miss this place, though, as its magnificent setting, the Teatro Greco and nearby beaches remain as seductive as they were for the likes of Goethe and DH Lawrence.

Orientation

The train station (Taormina-Giardini) is at the bottom of Monte Tauro. You'll need to hop on an Interbus to the bus station (for local and intercity services – where you'll arrive anyway if you catch the bus from Messina) on Via Pirandello. A short walk uphill from there brings you to the old city entrance and Corso Umberto I, which traverses the town.

Information

Tourist Offices The AAST office (☎ 0942 2 32 43, W www.taormina-ol.it) is in Palazzo Corvaja, just off Corso Umberto I, near Largo Santa Caterina. It opens 8am to 2pm and 4pm to 7pm Monday to Saturday.

Money There are several banks in Taormina, mostly along Corso Umberto I; all have ATMs. You'll also find currency exchange places along the same street. Check on commissions. Amex is represented by La Duca Viaggi (☎ 0942 62 52 55), Via Don Bosco 39.

Post & Communications The main post office is on Piazza Sant'Antonio, just outside the Porta Catania, at the far end of Corso Umberto I from the AAST office. There are public telephones in the Avis office (☎ 0942 2 30 41), Via San Pancrazio 7, to your right off Via Pirandello at the entrance to the old town.

Medical & Emergency Services There is a free night-time medical service in summer for tourists (☎ 0942 62 54 19) on Piazza San Francesco di Paola. The Ospedale San Vincenzo (hospital; ☎ 0942 537 45) is on Piazza San Vincenzo, just outside the Porta Catania. Call the same number for an ambulance.

The police can be contacted on ☎ 0942 2 38 88 or 113.

Things to See & Do

At the end of Via Teatro Greco, off Corso Umberto I, you'll find the 3rd-century-BC **Teatro Greco** *(☎ 0942 2 32 20, Via Teatro Greco; admission €4.15; open 9am-7pm daily May-Aug, 9am-6.30pm daily Apr & Sept, 9am-5pm daily Mar & Oct, 9am-4pm daily Nov-Feb)*. Later expanded and remodelled by the Romans, what you see is pretty much a Roman structure, despite its name. In the final years of the empire, the amphitheatre was given over solely to gladiatoral combat – obviously a mighty draw at the box office. The structure has been much tampered with over the centuries – the family of the Spanish Costanza d'Aragona built its home in the 12th century over part of the theatre (to the right as you face the stage). However, it remains a most atmospheric place. Film buffs might note that Woody Allen filmed the Greek chorus scenes here for his film *Mighty Aphrodite*. The view of Mt Etna and the sea through what was once the stage area is breathtaking. Concerts are held in summer.

From the theatre, wander down to the beautiful Parco Duchi di Cesarò, more commonly referred to as the **villa comunale** *(Via Bagnoli Croci; admission free; open 9am-7pm daily in summer, 9am-4.30pm daily in winter)*. Take a picnic and enjoy the best panorama in town as well as some stunning plants and flowers – for free. In summer the gardens stay open until midnight.

Back in the town centre is the **Odeon**, a small Roman theatre, badly preserved and partly covered by the adjoining church of Santa Caterina. It was discovered and excavated in the late 19th century and is believed to have been erected on the site of a Greek temple of Apollo. Taormina's **cathedral** *(Piazza del Duomo; admission free; open 8am-noon & 4pm-7pm daily)* was built in the early 15th century.

There are several mansions in Taormina, including **Palazzo Corvaja**. Begun by the Arabs as a defence tower in the 11th century, it was extended several times and includes halls dating from the 14th and 15th centuries. **Palazzo Duca di Santo Stefano**, at the other end of town, is an important example of Sicilian Gothic architecture, with a fanciful mix of Arab and Norman styles. **Badia Vecchia** (Old Abbey), nearby, is a 14th-century Gothic building, again with Norman-Arab elements.

Just wandering along the main drag, Corso Umberto I, you can see a smattering of stately old buildings, some dating from the 15th century.

The peak of **Monte Tauro** is adorned by the lonely, windswept ruins of the town's **medieval castle**, 3km from the town centre along the road to Castelmola (see Around Taormina later) or accessible by climbing the linking stairs. The views are great.

You can reach the beaches at **Isola Bella** and **Mazzarò** directly under Taormina by cable car from Via Pirandello. It costs €2.60 return and runs from 8.30am to 1.30am in summer (8.30am to 8.15pm in winter). Both beaches are largely taken up by private operators (a space with deckchairs and umbrella costs up to €12.90 per day), but there is some space for free bathing. An Interbus service also connects the beaches with the upper town.

Organised Tours

Several companies run organised excursions.

***CST** (☎ 0942 62 60 88, Corso Umberto I 99)* Destinations include Mt Etna (€24), Etna at sunset (€52), Agrigento (€37), Syracuse (€34) and Lipari & Vulcano (€44). Prices exclude admission to museums and archaeological sites at the destinations. One of the more interesting tours is a four-wheel-drive tour to Etna's central crater (€52).

***SAT** (☎ 0942 2 46 53, W www.sat-group.it, Corso Umberto I 73)* This company also runs tours to Mt Etna, Agrigento, Syracuse and other destinations.

Special Events

Films, theatrical events and music concerts are organised throughout the summer during Taormina Arte, a yearly arts festival. Contact Taormina Arte (☎ 0942 2 11 42, W www.taormina-arte.com), Corso Umberto I 19, for details, programmes and bookings.

The Raduno del Costume e del Carretto Siciliano, featuring parades of traditional Sicilian carts and folkloric groups, is usually held in autumn – ask at the AAST office for details.

Places to Stay

Taormina has plenty of accommodation, but in summer you should book in advance as rooms fill rapidly, particularly during August (a good time to stay away). In winter you can sometimes get prices brought down a tad.

***Campeggio San Leo** (☎ 0942 2 46 58, Via Nazionale, Località San Leo)* Adults €4.15. Kids go free at this camp site near the beach at Capo Taormina.

There are numerous private rooms in Taormina and the tourist office has a full list.

***Il Leone** (☎/fax 0942 2 38 78, Via Bagnoli Croci 127)* Per person €23.25. Near the villa comunale gardens, this place is a real find, as some rooms have terraces with spectacular sea views. Prices include breakfast.

***Pensione Svizzera** (☎ 0942 2 37 90, fax 0942 62 59 06, e svizzera@tao.it, Via Pirandello 26)* Low season singles/doubles with bath from €36.15/46.50, high season singles/doubles with bath up to €51.65/85.20. Open Mar-Nov. Downhill from the town centre on the way to the bus station, this pretty pink building has simple, pleasant rooms. Prices include buffet breakfast.

***Pensione Inn Piero** (☎ 0942 2 31 39, Via Pirandello 20)* Singles/doubles with bath up to €51.65/72.30. Inn Piero has comfortable rooms; prices are slightly reduced in low season.

***Pensione Villa Gaia** (☎/fax 0942 2 31 85, Via Fazzello 34)* Low season singles/doubles from €36.15/51.65, high season singles/doubles up to €56.80/87.80. Closed in winter. Set amid its own pretty gardens, just off Corso Umberto near the cathedral, the Villa Gaia is an excellent choice, and not badly priced – for Taormina.

***Villa Fiorita** (☎ 0942 2 41 22, fax 0942 62 59 67, Via Pirandello 39)* Doubles from €103.30. This is one of Taormina's nicer mid-range hotels (but being Taormina, the prices are still steep). It is well-furnished and comfortable, with a garden, swimming pool, terraces and rooms with sea views. Prices include breakfast.

Hotel Villa Belvedere *(☎ 0942 2 37 91, fax 0942 62 61 17, ⓔ info@villabelvedere.it, Via Bagnoli Croci 79)* Singles/doubles up to €98.15/153.90. You're heading upmarket here, as this extremely nice hotel has a swimming pool and private garden. Some rooms (all with full services) have views of Mt Etna; all are delightful.

Grand Hotel Timeo *(☎ 0942 2 38 01, fax 0942 62 85 01, ⓔ framon@framon-hotels.it, Via Teatro Greco 59)* Low season singles/doubles €134.30/175.60, high season singles/doubles €175.60/222.10. So you've just inherited a fortune and want the complete luxury deal? Then head for the five-star Timeo, whose front garden spills down a series of terraces to meet the villa comunale and whose back garden is comprised of Taormina's Teatro Greco. Can't do better than that!

Villa Caterina *(☎/fax 0942 2 47 09, Via Nazionale 155)* Per person €41.30. If you want to stay near the beach at Mazzarò, Villa Caterina is a good choice.

Places to Eat

Those on a tight budget will be limited in their choice of eating places. Be aware that many of the cafes on Corso Umberto I charge extortionately in the high season, and that quite a few restaurants close in winter.

Myosotis *(☎ 0942 2 43 42, Corso Umberto I 113)* Pizzas €2.60. For a quick takeaway, you could do worse than Myosotis. It also has *arancini* (breaded rice balls stuffed with meat sauce and peas then fried – the superior Sicilian version of the Italian *suppli*) and panini for around €2.60.

Shelter *(☎ 0942 2 40 34, Via Fratelli Bandiera 10)* Pizzas €5.15/6.20. Open 11am to 3.30pm and 6pm to midnight, Shelter is a good spot for a lunchtime pizza or snack.

Mamma Rosa *(☎ 0942 2 43 61, Via Naumachia 10)* Pizzas €4.65-6.70, mains €6.20-11.35. An excellent antipasto buffet, good pizza and tasty main dishes (both meat and fish) make Mamma Rosa a good bet.

La Piazzetta *(☎ 0942 62 63 17, Via Paladini 5)* Full meals from €15.50. For an excellent meal in lovely surroundings, head for this attractive eatery in a tiny piazza downhill from Corso Umberto I.

Il Baccanale *(☎ 0942 62 53 90, Piazzetta Filea)* Full meals from €18.10. Off Via Giovanni di Giovanni, this is a popular restaurant, moderately priced by Taormina standards.

Antica Trattoria la Botte *(☎ 0942 2 41 98, Piazza Santa Domenica 4)* Antipasto €7.75, pasta €6.20-9.30. Open Tues-Sun. The antipasto buffet is so good at this eatery that you can get away with only eating one course – and still be full at the end of it.

Vicolo Stretto *(☎ 0942 2 38 49, Vicolo Stretto 6)* Full meals from €25.80. Open Tues-Sun. Atmospherically located in Taormina's narrowest street (off Corso Umberto I), this delightful eatery's special dishes are couscous *alla Trapanese* (served with a type of fish sauce) and ravioli with *bresaola* (dry-cured beef) and saffron.

Arco Rosso-Da Micio *(☎ 0942 2 45 14, Via Naumachia 7)* A low-key place for a quiet drink, just off Corso Umberto I. The owner makes his own wine (it's a bit rough but full of character) and there are several Italian and international beers on tap or in bottles.

Bam Bar *(Via di Giovanni 45)* Sicilian granita €2.05, toasted sandwiches €3.10. The pretty Bam Bar is a reasonably priced and very pleasant place for a coffee, cocktail or snack.

There are several gourmet grocery shops along Corso Umberto I, where prices are high. Alternatively, try the side streets between Via Teatro Greco and the villa comunale, where you can buy picnic supplies at several grocery and pastry shops. There is a ***Standa supermarket*** *(Via Apollo Arcageta)* just up from the post office.

Getting There & Around

Bus The bus is the easiest means of reaching Taormina. Interbus (☎ 0942 62 53 01) services leave for Messina (€3.10, 1½ hours) and Catania (about the same) at least hourly from about 6am to 7pm.

Train There are also regular trains, but the awkward location of Taormina's station is a strong disincentive. If you arrive this way, catch an Interbus service up to the town. They run roughly every 30 to 90 minutes (much less frequently on Sunday).

Car & Motorcycle Taormina is on the A18 tollway and the S114 between Messina and Catania. Parking can be a problem in Taormina, particularly during the summer. The Lumbi car park is open 24 hours daily and there is a shuttle service to the centre from Porta Messina.

There are several car rental agencies in Taormina, including Avis, Hertz and Maggiore. California (☎ 0942 2 37 69), Via Bagnoli Croci 86, hires out cars and motorcycles at reasonable prices. A small car will cost between €232.40 and €273.70 per week. A Vespa costs around €36.15 per day.

AROUND TAORMINA

Panorama fanatics should head 5km up the hill to **Castelmola**, literally the high point of the area, with a ruined castle and sweeping views of, well, everything. Several buses run from Taormina.

There is an **archaeological park** *(☎ 0942 5 10 10, Località Giardini-Naxos; admission €2.05; open 9am-7pm daily in summer, 9am-5pm daily in winter)* south of Taormina at Giardini-Naxos (follow the 'scavi' signs), the site of the first Greek settlement on Sicily. Founded in 735 BC, it was destroyed by Dionysius, the tyrant of Syracuse, in 403 BC. There is not a lot to see, but the park is a pleasant green refuge. Regular buses leave from the Taormina bus station on Via Pirandello for Giardini-Naxos. Giardini's AAST office (☎ 0942 5 10 10) is at Via Tysandros 76e.

A relatively short drive (Interbus services from Taormina €4.65 return, departing 9.30am and 11.30am Monday to Friday only, returning at 2.20pm and 3.20pm) gets you to the **Gole Alcantara**, a series of modest lava gorges on the river of the same name, a few kilometres short of Francavilla. You could stop in here on your way to Mt Etna. There is lift access to the gorges (€2.05) and you can hire wading boots, which you'll need if you want to do anything more than peer into the gorges. It is also possible to reach the gorges by the stairs on the main road 200m uphill from the lift entrance. It is forbidden to enter the gorges from around November to May because of the risk of unexpected floods.

CATANIA

postcode 95100 • pop 376,000

Catania's crumbling appearance, chaotic traffic and reputation as a major crime centre may make it seem an intimidating and uninviting place on arrival (the ugly location of the train and bus stations doesn't help), but the city merits the benefit of the doubt. You may end up using it as a base for visiting Mt Etna, so take the time to look around its grand, if poorly maintained, Baroque palaces and churches. It is well served by hotels and the food is good and cheap.

A busy industrial and commercial port town, Catania has an unfortunate history. Situated at the foot of Mt Etna, it was partially destroyed in a massive eruption in 1669 and, as reconstruction began, was shaken to the ground in 1693 by an earthquake that devastated much of south-eastern Sicily. The 18th-century project to rebuild the city in Grand Baroque style was largely overseen by the architects Giovanni Vaccarini and Stefano Ittar.

Orientation

The main train station and intercity bus terminal are near the port at Piazza Giovanni XXIII. From here, Corso Martiri della Libertà heads west towards the city centre, about a 15-minute walk (1km). Follow the road to Piazza della Repubblica and continue along Corso Sicilia to Via Etnea, the main thoroughfare running north off Piazza del Duomo. Most sights are concentrated around and west of Piazza del Duomo, while the commercial centre of Catania is farther north around Via Pacini and Via Umberto I.

Information

Tourist Offices The APT office (☎ 095 730 62 22 or 095 730 62 11, **W** www.apt.catania.it) is at Via Cimarosa 10–12. It opens 9am to 7pm Monday to Saturday. There are branches at the train station (☎ 095 730 62 55), on platform No 1, open roughly the same hours;

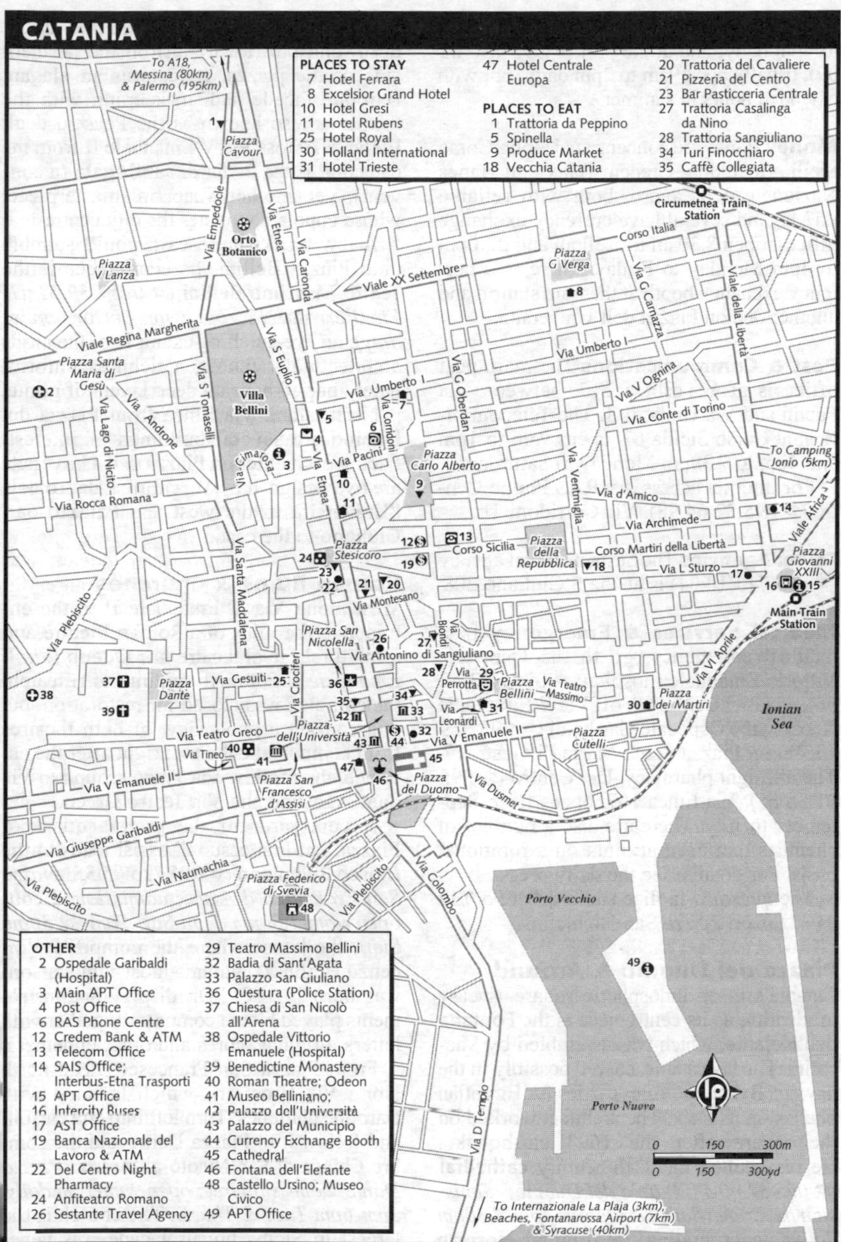
CATANIA
PLACES TO STAY
7 Hotel Ferrara
8 Excelsior Grand Hotel
10 Hotel Gresi
11 Hotel Rubens
25 Hotel Royal
30 Holland International
31 Hotel Trieste
47 Hotel Centrale Europa
PLACES TO EAT
1 Trattoria da Peppino
5 Spinella
9 Produce Market
18 Vecchia Catania
20 Trattoria del Cavaliere
21 Pizzeria del Centro
23 Bar Pasticceria Centrale
27 Trattoria Casalinga da Nino
28 Trattoria Sangiuliano
34 Turi Finocchiaro
35 Caffè Collegiata
OTHER
2 Ospedale Garibaldi (Hospital)
3 Main APT Office
4 Post Office
6 RAS Phone Centre
12 Credem Bank & ATM
13 Telecom Office
14 SAIS Office; Interbus-Etna Trasporti
15 APT Office
16 Intercity Buses
17 AST Office
19 Banca Nazionale del Lavoro & ATM
22 Del Centro Night Pharmacy
24 Anfiteatro Romano
26 Sestante Travel Agency
29 Teatro Massimo Bellini
32 Badia di Sant'Agata
33 Palazzo San Giuliano
36 Questura (Police Station)
37 Chiesa di San Nicolò all'Arena
38 Ospedale Vittorio Emanuele (Hospital)
39 Benedictine Monastery
40 Roman Theatre; Odeon
41 Museo Belliniano;
42 Palazzo dell'Università
43 Palazzo del Municipio
44 Currency Exchange Booth
45 Cathedral
46 Fontana dell'Elefante
48 Castello Ursino; Museo Civico
49 APT Office
To A18, Messina (80km) & Palermo (195km)
Piazza Cavour
Via Empedocle
Via Etnea
Via Caronda
Orto Botanico
Piazza V Lanza
Viale XX Settembre
Circumetnea Train Station
Corso Italia
Piazza G Verga
Via G Carnazza
Viale della Libertà
Viale Regina Margherita
Via S Euplio
Via Umberto I
Piazza Santa Maria di Gesù
Via S Tomaselli
Villa Bellini
Via Androne
Via Lago di Nicito
Via Cimarosa
Via Corridoni
Via G Oberdan
Via V Ognina
Via Conte di Torino
Via Pacini
Piazza Carlo Alberto
Via Ventimiglia
To Camping Jonio (5km)
Via Rocca Romana
Via d'Amico
Via Archimede
Viale Africa
Piazza Stesicoro
Corso Sicilia
Piazza della Repubblica
Corso Martiri della Libertà
Via L Sturzo
Piazza Giovanni XXIII
Main Train Station
Via Santa Maddalena
Via Montesano
Via Plebiscito
Via Biondi
Piazza San Nicolella
Via Antonino di Sangiuliano
Via Gesuiti
Piazza Dante
Via Crociferi
Via Perrotta
Piazza Bellini
Via Teatro Massimo
Via VI Aprile
Piazza dei Martiri
Ionian Sea
Via Teatro Greco
Piazza dell'Università
Via Leonardi
Via V Emanuele II
Piazza Cutelli
Via Tineo
Piazza San Francesco d'Assisi
Piazza del Duomo
Via Dusmet
Via Giuseppe Garibaldi
Via Naumachia
Via Plebiscito
Piazza Federico di Svevia
Via Colombo
Porto Vecchio
Porto Nuovo
Via D Tempio
0 150 300m
0 150 300yd
To Internazionale La Plaja (3km), Beaches, Fontanarossa Airport (7km) & Syracuse (40km)

at the airport (☎ 095 730 62 66), open 8am to 9pm daily; and at the port (☎ 095 730 62 09), usually open 9am to 2pm daily, but with extended hours in summer.

Money Banks are concentrated along Corso Sicilia (including Credem Bank and Banca Nazionale del Lavoro, both with reliable ATMs) and several have currency exchange offices, open 8.30am to 1.30pm and 2.30pm to 4pm Monday to Friday. There is a currency exchange booth at the train station and another one on Piazza dell'Università.

Post & Communications The main post office is at Via Etnea 215, between Via Pacini and Via Umberto I. The Telecom office, at Corso Sicilia 67, opens 9am to 1pm and 4pm to 7.30pm Monday to Saturday.

For Internet access, try RAS Phone Centre (☎ 095 32 64 98), Via Corridoni 1b.

Travel Agencies The Sestante travel agency (☎ 095 715 10 04) is at Via S Giuliano 208.

Medical Services & Emergency In a medical emergency, go to the Ospedale Vittorio Emanuele (hospital; ☎ 095 743 52 56), Via Plebiscito 268, off Via V Emanuele II, or try the Ospedale Garibaldi (☎ 095 759 43 71) on Piazza Santa Maria di Gesù 5/7. The all-night pharmacy, Del Centro (☎ 095 31 36 85), Via Etnea 107, opens from September to July. There are also a number of chemists that open at night on a rotational basis. For details, see the daily press.

The *questura* (police station; ☎ 095 736 71 11) is on Piazza San Nicolella.

Piazza del Duomo & Around

Catania's most atmospheric square is easy to identify, as its centrepiece is the **Fontana dell'Elefante**, which was assembled by Vaccarini. The lava statue, carved possibly in the days of Byzantine rule, carries an Egyptian obelisk on its back. The architect worked on the square after the 1693 earthquake. He remodelled the 11th-century **cathedral** *(☎ 095 32 00 44, Piazza del Duomo; admission free; open 8am-12.30pm & 4pm-7.30pm daily)*, incorporating the original Norman apses and transept, and designed the **Palazzo del Municipio** (town hall) on the northern side of the piazza. It features an elegant Baroque facade and, in keeping with the theme, is also known as the Palazzo degli Elefanti. Across Via V Emanuele II from the cathedral is the **Badia di Sant'Agata** (a convent), yet another Vaccarini masterpiece, whose cupola dominates the city centre.

A few blocks north-east, you'll stumble onto Piazza Bellini. Its centrepiece is the **Teatro Massimo Bellini** *(☎ 095 730 61 11, Via Perrotta 12; open for performances only)*, an eye-catching example of the city's architectural richness, a richness unfortunately buried beneath deep layers of grime.

North along Via Etnea from Piazza del Duomo are several buildings of interest. Facing each other on Piazza dell'Università are two designed by Vaccarini, **Palazzo dell'Università** to the west and **Palazzo San Giuliano** to the east.

Roman Ruins & Churches

West along Via V Emanuele II is the entrance to the ruins of a **Roman theatre** and a small rehearsal theatre, the **Odeon** *(Via V Emanuele II 266)*. At the time of research, the complex was closed for restoration, but you can get a good view of both theatres from behind; take the first right after the entrance, then follow Via Tineo around to Via Sant'Agostino and Via Teatro Greco.

A courtyard off the pretty square of Piazza San Francesco d'Assisi leads to the **Museo Belliniano** *(☎ 095 715 05 35, Piazza San Francesco d'Assisi; admission €2.60; open 9am-1.30pm Mon-Sat, 9am-12.30pm Sun)*, the house where the composer Vincenzo Bellini (Catania's most famous son) was born in 1801. On display are instruments played by the composer together with letters, original scores and other ephemera.

From Piazza San Francesco, head north along Via Crociferi, which is lined with Baroque churches. Turn left into Via Gesuiti and follow it to Piazza Dante and the sombre **Chiesa di San Nicolò all'Arena** *(Piazza Dante; admission free; open 9am-1pm daily, 3pm-6pm Tues & Thurs)*. The church is the largest in Sicily, but its facade was never completed. Next to the church is an 18th-century **Benedictine monastery**, the biggest in Europe after that of Mafra in Portugal. It is now part of the university and is slowly being restored. Wander in for a look at the cloisters – the beauty is faded, but it's there.

North of Piazza del Duomo, more left-overs from Roman days include a modest **anfiteatro** (amphitheatre) on Piazza Stesicoro. For relief from the madding crowd, continue north along Via Etnea and cut in to the left behind the post office for the lovely **Villa Bellini gardens**, named in memory of Bellini.

Castello Ursino

This grim-looking moated **fortress** *(☎ 095 34 58 30, Piazza Federico di Svevia; admission free; open 8.30am-1pm Mon-Sat, 9am-12.30pm Sun)* was built in the 13th century by Frederick II, one of the great castle-builders of the Middle Ages. It's in an equally grim neighbourhood (where you'll feel safer travelling in pairs or groups) south-west of Piazza del Duomo, just over the train line. The castle was once on a cliff top overlooking the sea; following the earthquake of 1693, the whole area to the south was reclaimed and the castle became landlocked. The **Museo Civico** inside contains finds from the Roman era up to the 18th century.

Special Events

Catania celebrates the feast of its patron saint Agata from 3 to 5 February. During this period, one million Catanians and tourists follow as the *Fercolo* (a silver reliquary bust of the saint covered in marvellous jewels) is carried along the main street of the city. There are also spectacular fireworks during the celebrations.

In July the city hosts three festivals: Catania Musica Estate (classical music), Settimana Barocca (a week of Baroque concerts, pageants and other performances) and Etna Jazz. The APT offices have details and programmes of all events.

Places to Stay – Budget

Camping facilities are available on the outskirts of the city.

Internazionale La Plaja *(☎ 095 34 08 80, fax 095 34 83 40, Viale Kennedy 47)* Adult/child/tent €6.20/2.60/9.80. Open year-round, this camp site has a private sandy beach, and is on the way out of the city towards Syracuse (take bus No 527 from Piazza Borsellino).

Camping Jonio *(☎ 095 49 11 39, fax 095 49 22 77, Via Villini a Mare 2)* Adult/tent €5.40/11.90. This place is about 5km out of the city, close to a beautiful rocky beach. To get there, catch bus No 334 from Via Etnea.

Budget hotels are located around the centre and if you are low on money Catania is a good place to hole up. There are several places with rock-bottom prices.

Hotel Trieste *(☎ 095 32 71 05, Via Leonardi 24)* Singles/doubles €15.50/36.15. No-frills is the order of the day in this simple hotel near Piazza Bellini, an area full of bars and pubs. The entrance is a bit seedy, but the hotel is OK.

Holland International *(☎ 095 53 36 05, fax 095 746 58 92, Via V Emanuele II 8)* Doubles up to €33.55, with bath up to €41.30. Just off Piazza dei Martiri, this place is super-convenient for the train station, although it hasn't got much else going for it.

Hotel Rubens *(☎ 095 31 70 73, fax 095 715 17 13, Via Etnea 196)* Singles/doubles without bath €22.20/31, singles/doubles with bath €28.40/40.30. Tucked away at the back of a courtyard off Via Etnea, Hotel Rubens offers half-decent accommodation.

Hotel Ferrara *(☎ 095 31 60 00, fax 095 31 30 60, Via Umberto I 66)* Singles/doubles without bath €23.25/36.15, singles/doubles with bath €33.55/43.90. Well positioned on Via Umberto, the Ferrara's rooms have TV and telephone and are a cut above most hotels in this price range.

Hotel Gresi *(☎ 095 32 37 09, fax 095 715 30 45, Via Pacini 28)* Singles/doubles with bath €33.55/46.50. Not far from the tourist office and just off Via Etnea, the Gresi is central but is a little timeworn.

Places to Stay – Mid-Range & Top End

Hotel Centrale Europa *(☎ 095 31 13 09, fax 095 31 75 31, Via Vittorio Emanuele II 167)* Singles/doubles with bath €43.90/62. The best mid-range hotel in Catania, the Centrale Europa has spotless, elegant rooms, some looking over Piazza del Duomo (although traffic noise might be a problem). Breakfast is included.

Hotel Royal *(☎ 095 31 34 48, fax 095 32 56 11, Via Antonino di Sangiuliano 337)* Singles/doubles with bath €51.65/77.45. This hotel is on the corner with Via dei Crociferi near beautiful Baroque churches. It closes for certain holiday periods, so check first.

Excelsior Grand Hotel *(☎ 095 747 61 11, fax 095 53 70 14, ⓔ excelsior-catania@thi.it, Piazza G Verga 39)* Low season singles/doubles from €93/145, high season singles/doubles up to €145/197, suites €192-308 depending on season. Catania's five-star jewel is the newly renovated Excelsior, in a Fascist building on Piazza Verga. You might need to remortgage your house to stay here, but this is sheer luxury. Note that this hotel's high season is April to June and September to October.

Places to Eat

Don't miss the savoury *arancini*, the superior Sicilian version of the lesser Italian *suppli* (breaded rice balls filled with *ragù* and peas, then fried), *cartocciate* (focaccia stuffed with ham, mozzarella, olives and tomato) or baked onions, available for around €1.30 apiece from a tavola calda, found all over town; or stop at a pasticceria to try the mouthwatering Sicilian sweets. ***Bar Pasticceria Centrale*** *(Via Etnea 121)* on the corner of Piazza Stesicoro, does delicious cannoli and farther north towards Via Umberto I ***Spinella*** *(☎ 095 32 72 47, Via Etnea 300)*, near the corner of Via Umberto I, is probably Catania's most famous pasticceria; one taste of its produce – especially the ricotta-filled cannoli – will tell you why.

Eating out can be pleasant and inexpensive in Catania. Students head for the area around Via Teatro Massimo, where there are several sandwich bars and 'pubs'. The area between here and the cathedral is littered with small restaurants and trattorias, but some open only for lunch.

Pizzeria del Centro *(☎ 095 31 14 29, Via Montesano 11)* Pizzas €2.05-4.15. This tiny hole-in-the-wall churns out divine pizza. Perch on a stool inside or take way.

Trattoria da Peppino *(☎ 095 43 06 20, Via Empedocle 35)* Meals around €15.50. Good, basic antipasti and pasta are the staples here.

Trattoria del Cavaliere *(☎ 095 31 04 91, Via Paternò 11)* Pasta €4.15-7.75, mains €5.15-12.90. Open Thurs-Tues. Close to Piazza Stesicoro, this friendly place with a rustic theme serves up excellent Sicilian (and traditional Italian) pasta dishes, as well as grilled fish and meat. But the abundant antipasto might finish you off before you get that far.

Trattoria Casalinga Da Nino *(☎ 095 31 13 19, Via Biondi 19)* Full meals from €12.90. It's not fancy but the home-made food is as good as its name ('Home cooking by Nino') suggests.

Trattoria Sangiuliano *(☎ 095 31 34 28, Via Antonino di Sangiuliano 207)* Full meals from €20.65. Open Wed-Mon. This classy restaurant is a step up from your basic eatery, serving fish, the whole fish and nothing but fish.

Turi Finocchiaro *(☎ 095 715 35 73, Via Euplio Reina 13)* Full meals from €15.50. Simultaneously a restaurant, meeting place and pizzeria, Turi Finocchiaro has been around for years and is as popular as ever. The courtyard is a nice place to chill out on a hot evening.

Vecchia Catania *(☎ 095 53 35 00, Via Ventimiglia 317)* Full meals from €18.10. Open Wed-Mon. Pizzas and traditional Catanese cooking are the drawcard here (if you don't count the atmospheric murals of scenes of old Catania).

There are several decent cafes along Via Etnea, especially down the Piazza del Duomo end. Try ***Caffè Collegiata*** *(Via della Collegiata 3)*, in the basement of an elegant Art Nouveau building, a popular student hangout. ***Nievski Pub*** *(☎ 095 715 12 84, Scalinata Alessi 15)* is a good place to mingle with Catania's alternative crowd – there are also terminals for Internet access.

Every morning except Sunday, Piazza Carlo Alberto is flooded by the chaos of a ***produce market***, known locally as La Fiera, but not dissimilar to a middle-eastern kasbah. You can pick up supplies of bread, cheese, salami, fresh fruit and all manner of odds and ends. The other major fresh produce market is ***La Pescheria***, off Piazza del Duomo, selling fresh fish. It opens until 2pm from Monday to Saturday and is well worth a visit.

Getting There & Around

Air Catania's airport, Fontanarossa, is 7km south-west of the city centre and services domestic and European flights (the latter all via Rome or Milan). Meridiana flies between London and Catania. In summer you may be able to dig up the odd direct charter flight to London or Paris. Take the special Alibus (€2.30) from outside the train station.

Bus Intercity buses terminate in the area around Piazza Giovanni XXIII, in front of the train station. SAIS (☎ 095 53 62 01 or 095 53 61 68), Via d'Amico 181–187, serves Syracuse, Palermo (€10.35, two hours 40 minutes via autostrada) and Agrigento. It also has a service to Rome (€38.75 one way) leaving at 8pm. AST (☎ 095 746 10 96 or 095 53 17 56), Via L Sturzo 232, also services these destinations and many smaller provincial towns around Catania, including Nicolosi, the cable car on Mt Etna and Noto. Interbus-Etna Trasporti (☎ 095 53 27 16 or 095 746 13 33), at the same address as SAIS, runs buses to Piazza Armerina, Taormina, Messina, Enna, Ragusa, Gela and Rome.

Many of the more useful AMT city buses (☎ 095 736 01 11) terminate in front of the train station. These include: Alibus (station-airport); Nos 1–4 and 1–6 (station-Via Etnea); and Nos 4–7 and 4–6 (station-Piazza del Duomo). Buy a daily ticket for €1.80. In summer, a special service (D) runs from Piazza G Verga to the sandy beaches. Bus No 334 from Via Etnea takes you to the Riviera dei Ciclopi and the beautiful Norman castle at Acicastello (admission is free).

Train Frequent trains connect Catania with Messina and Syracuse (both 1½ hours) and there are less frequent services to Palermo (3¼ hours), Enna (1¾ hours) and Agrigento (an agonisingly slow four hours). The private Circumetnea train line circles Mt Etna, stopping at the towns and villages on the volcano's slopes. See Getting There & Away under Mt Enta later.

Car & Motorcycle Catania can be easily reached from Messina on the A18 and from Palermo on the A19. From the A18, signs for the centre of Catania will bring you to Via Etnea. Some words of warning: there are complicated one-way systems around the city, the narrow streets get terribly clogged with traffic and parking is a problem.

MT ETNA

Dominating the landscape in eastern Sicily between Taormina and Catania, Mt Etna (3350m) is Europe's largest live volcano and one of the world's most active. Eruptions occur frequently, both from the four live craters at the summit (one, the Bocca Nuova, was formed in 1968) and on the slopes of the volcano, which is littered with fissures and old craters.

The volcano's most devastating eruption occurred in 1669 and lasted 122 days. A huge river of lava poured down its southern slope, engulfing a good part of Catania and dramatically altering the landscape. In 1971, an eruption destroyed the observatory at the summit, and another in 1983 finished off the old cable car and tourist centre (you can see where the lava flow stopped on that occasion). Nine people died in an explosion at the south-eastern crater in 1979, and two died and 10 were injured in an explosion at the crater in 1987. In 1992 a stream of lava pouring from a fissure in its south-eastern slope threatened to engulf the town of Zafferana Etnea. The town was saved, but not before one family lost their home and others much of their farmland. In September 1999 Etna roared once more, spitting ash into the skies above and releasing rivulets of molten rock down the northern side. Etna's most recent eruption occurred in 2001, when lava flows and falls of ash forced the closure of one resort. Visitors should be aware that volcanic activity can disrupt services in the area.

The volcano's unpredictability means people are no longer allowed to climb to the craters. A rope marks the point where it becomes unsafe and you are not allowed to go any further.

The Etna Sud APT office (☎ 095 91 63 56) is at Rifugio Sapienza and opens daily. You can also try the local tourist office in Nicolosi (☎ 095 91 15 05) at Via Garibaldi 63. On the northern side of the volcano, the APT office (☎ 095 64 73 52) is at Piano Provenzana. There is also a Pro Loco tourist centre (☎ 095 64 30 94) at Piazza Annunziata 7 in Linguaglossa. All have information about skiing and excursions to the craters. The APT offices in Catania also have information.

There are several groups that organise tours up towards the craters, involving both trekking and 4WD vehicles with a vulcanologist or alpine guide. They include: Gruppo Guide Alpine Etna Sud (☎ 095 791 47 55); Gruppo Guide Alpine Etna Nord (☎ 095 64 78 33 or 095 64 34 30 or 0337 95 61 24); NeT Natura e Turismo (☎ 095 33 35 43, ⓔ natetur@tin.it).

To the Craters

South With a daily bus link from Catania via Nicolosi, the southern side of the volcano presents the easier option for an ascent towards the craters. From Rifugio Sapienza, the closest the surfaced road comes to the summit, a cable car (☎ 095 91 41 41 or 095 91 11 58) climbs to 2500m. It operates 9am to 4pm year-round, 9am to 5pm in summer (€19.65 return). In summer, 4WD vehicles then take you through the eerie lava-scape to the 2900m level or you can walk up (around 1½ hours one way). You are not allowed to go past the 2900m point to get closer to the craters. The price for cable car, 4WD and mountain guide was €37.20 return at the time of writing.

In winter you can ski down (snow permitting) but there is no transport beyond the cable car. There are four ski lifts and five runs in the area. A day ski pass costs €18.60, including use of the cable car.

Some tourists make the long climb from Rifugio Sapienza to the roped-off limit (3½ to four hours on a track winding up under the cable car and then following the same road used by the minibuses).

North Several ski lifts run at Piano Provenzana, snow permitting (a day ski pass costs up to €15.50). From the lifts, you're looking at about an hour's walk to come close to the top – a difficult proposition in winter when there's heavy snow. Enquire about the feasibility of the walk at the Etna Nord APT or the Linguaglossa Pro Loco about hiring a guide or going with an organised group. In winter, most people visit Etna to ski.

In summer, the ski lifts don't operate but 4WDs make the same journey, and then it's about an hour's scramble up to the highest point. You can't go all the way to the craters as it's unsafe, and it is best to do the trek with a guide. At Piano Provenzana, Le Betulle/STAR (☎ 095 64 34 30) charges around €36.15 for the three-hour return trip to 3100m with a 4WD and guide.

Places to Stay

Accommodation around Etna is scant; you're probably better off in Catania. You could try the following, but be sure to book in advance in summer.

Etna Camping *(☎ 095 91 43 09, fax 095 791 51 86, Via Goethe)* Sites per adult/tent €4.15/7.75. This camp site, based in Nicolosi, is about as close as campers will get to Etna. Well shaded, cool and with a pool, it also has a particularly nice quiet area for tents under pine trees.

Rifugio Sapienza *(☎/fax 095 91 10 62, Piazzale Funivia)* Singles €12.90-18.10. Right next to the cable-car station, this refuge fills up fast, both in winter and summer.

Etna Garden Park *(☎ 095 791 46 86, fax 095 791 47 01, Via della Quercia, Nicolosi)* Dorm beds €12.90, family rooms per person €12.50 , doubles with bath €46.50. This establishment is an HI-affiliated (Hostelling International) hostel (with dorms and family rooms) and a hotel; it's open year-round.

Hotel Corsaro *(☎ 095 91 41 22, fax 095 780 10 24)* Singles/doubles with bath €54.25/77.45. This hotel is at Rifugio Sapienza on the southern side, 200m from the cable car.

Rifugio Nord-Est *(☎ 095 64 79 22, Via Mareneve, Piano Provenzana)* Beds up to

€20.65. This hostel-like rifugio at Piano Provenzana, a small ski resort on the northern side of Etna, has simple accommodation.

There are small hotels at Piano Provenzana and in some of the towns along the Circumetnea train line, including Linguaglossa and Randazzo. For details, contact the APT office at Etna Nord.

Getting There & Away

Having your own transport will make life much easier around Mt Etna, but there are some public transport options. The easiest approach is from the south.

South An AST bus (☎ 095 746 10 96 or 095 53 17 56) departs from the car park in front of the main train station in Catania at 8.15am for Rifugio Sapienza via Nicolosi. It returns from the rifugio at 4.30pm. The return ticket costs €5.15. The AST office (☎ 095 91 15 05), at Via Etnea 32 in Nicolosi, opens 8am to 2pm Monday to Saturday. You can also drive this route (take Via Etnea north out of town and follow the signs for Nicolosi and Etna).

North SAIS and FCE buses connect Linguaglossa with Fiumefreddo on the coast (from where other SAIS buses run north to Taormina and Messina and south to Catania). Unless the FCE puts on a winter ski-season or summer bus to Piano Provenzana, your only chance from Linguaglossa is your thumb. If driving, follow the signs for Piano Provenzana out of Linguaglossa.

Around the Mountain Another option is to circle Mt Etna on the private Circumetnea train line. It starts in Catania at the train station at Corso delle Province 13, opposite Corso Italia. Go to the ticket office (☎ 095 37 48 42) for information. Catch bus No 628, 448 or 401 from the main train station in Catania to Corso delle Province, or use the Metropolitana to Borgo. The line runs around the mountain from Catania to the coastal town of Riposto, passing through numerous towns and villages on its slopes, including Linguaglossa. You can reach Riposto (or neighbouring Giarre) from Taormina by train or bus if you want to make the trip from that end.

Catania-Riposto is about a 3½ hour trip, but you needn't go that far. If you're leaving from Catania, consider finishing the trip at Randazzo (2 hours), a small medieval town noted for the fact that it has consistently escaped destruction despite its proximity to the summit. Randazzo is mildly interesting itself, with a couple of churches to punctuate a brief stroll along a few quiet streets, some lined with Aragonese apartments. A good example of lava architecture are the walls of the Norman cathedral of Santa Maria, while the church of Santa Maria della Volta preserves a squat 14th-century *campanile* (bell tower).

SAIS buses connect Randazzo with Taormina/Giardini-Naxos; there are two services daily.

South-Eastern Sicily

SYRACUSE (SIRACUSA)

postcode 96100 • pop 126,000

Once a powerful Greek city rivalling Athens, Syracuse is one of the highlights of a visit to Sicily. The city was founded in 734 BC by colonists from Corinth, who established their settlement on the island of Ortigia. Ruled by a succession of tyrants from the 5th century BC, Syracuse became a dominant sea power in the Mediterranean, prompting Athens to attack it in 413 BC. In one of history's great maritime battles, the Athenian fleet was sent to the bottom of the sea.

Syracuse reached its zenith under the rule of the tyrant Dionysius and attracted luminaries from all around, Plato among them. He apparently so bored Dionysius with his diatribes that the tyrant tried to sell the philosopher as a slave.

The Romans marched into Syracuse in 212 BC, but the city remained important and enlightened under the new administration. Less sensitive handling came from the barbarians in the 5th century AD, later succeeded by the Byzantine empire. Syracuse's

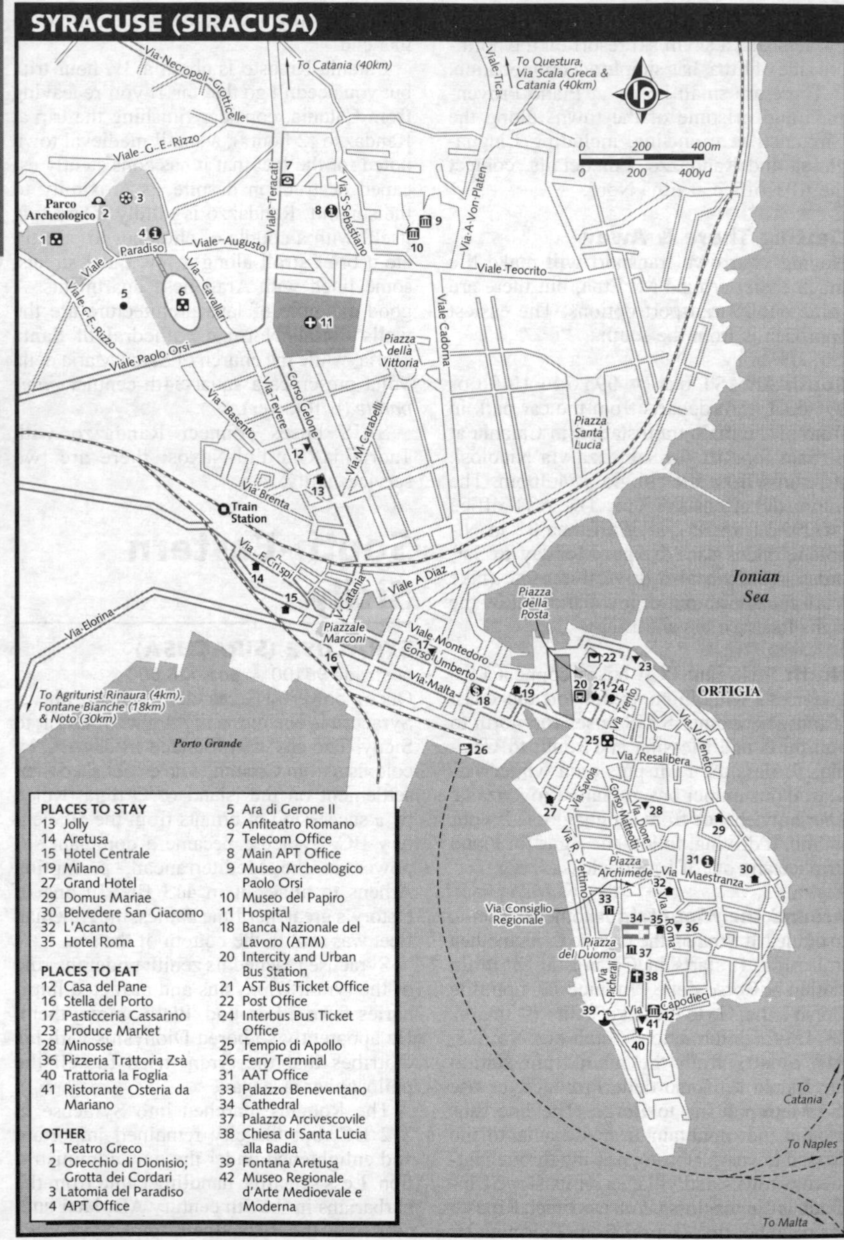

PLACES TO STAY
13 Jolly
14 Aretusa
15 Hotel Centrale
19 Milano
27 Grand Hotel
29 Domus Mariae
30 Belvedere San Giacomo
32 L'Acanto
35 Hotel Roma

PLACES TO EAT
12 Casa del Pane
16 Stella del Porto
17 Pasticceria Cassarino
23 Produce Market
28 Minosse
36 Pizzeria Trattoria Zsà
40 Trattoria la Foglia
41 Ristorante Osteria da Mariano

OTHER
1 Teatro Greco
2 Orecchio di Dionisio; Grotta dei Cordari
3 Latomia del Paradiso
4 APT Office
5 Ara di Gerone II
6 Anfiteatro Romano
7 Telecom Office
8 Main APT Office
9 Museo Archeologico Paolo Orsi
10 Museo del Papiro
11 Hospital
18 Banca Nazionale del Lavoro (ATM)
20 Intercity and Urban Bus Station
21 AST Bus Ticket Office
22 Post Office
24 Interbus Bus Ticket Office
25 Tempio di Apollo
26 Ferry Terminal
31 AAT Office
33 Palazzo Beneventano
34 Cathedral
37 Palazzo Arcivescovile
38 Chiesa di Santa Lucia alla Badia
39 Fontana Aretusa
42 Museo Regionale d'Arte Medioevale e Moderna

fate followed that of much of the island, witnessing the arrival of the Arabs, Normans, Swabians, French and Spaniards over the centuries.

The Greek mathematician Archimedes was born here and the apostle Paul converted the city to the Christian faith.

Orientation

The main sights of Syracuse are in two areas: on the island of Ortigia and 2km across town in the Parco Archeologico della Neapolis (archaeological zone). From the train station, walk east along Via F Crispi to Piazzale Marconi. Heading straight through the piazza to Corso Umberto will bring you to Ortigia, about 1km away. Alternatively, turn left from Piazzale Marconi into Via Catania, cross the train line and follow the busy shopping street, Corso Gelone, to Viale Paolo Orsi and the Parco Archeologico. If you arrive by bus, you'll be dropped in or near Piazza della Posta in Ortigia. Most accommodation is in the newer part of town, to the west, while the better eating places are in Ortigia.

Information

Tourist Offices The main APT office (☎ 0931 48 12 00, W www.apt-siracusa.it), Via S Sebastiano 43, opens 8.30am to 1.30pm and 3.30pm to 6pm Monday to Friday. In summer it sometimes also opens on Saturday and Sunday. There's also a branch office at the Parco Archeologico.

The AAT office (☎ 0931 46 42 55, W www.flashcom.it/aatsr), on Ortigia at Via Maestranza 33, deals specifically with Syracuse and is probably the most convenient office to pick up a map and hotel list. It opens 8.30am to 1.30pm and 2.30pm to 5.30pm Monday to Friday, 8.30am to 1.30pm Saturday.

Money Numerous banks (all with ATMs) line Corso Umberto, including the Banca Nazionale del Lavoro at No 29. There are others on Corso Gelone. The rates at the train station currency exchange booth are generally poor.

Post & Communications The post office is on Piazza della Posta, to your left as you cross the bridge to Ortigia. It opens 8.30am to 6.30pm Monday to Friday and 8.30am to 1pm on Saturday.

The Telecom office, Viale Teracati 46, is open 8.30am to 7.30pm Monday to Saturday.

Medical Services & Emergency The public hospital is at Via Testaferrata 1. For medical emergencies, ring ☎ 0931 6 85 55.

The *questura* (police station; ☎ 0931 46 35 66 or 0931 40 21 11) is on Via Scala Greca, some distance north of the centre of town.

Ortigia

The island of Ortigia is the spiritual and physical heart of the city. Its buildings are predominantly medieval, with some Baroque palaces and churches. The 7th-century **cathedral** *(Piazza del Duomo; admission free; open 8am-noon & 4pm-7pm daily)* was built on top of a Greek temple dedicated to Athena, incorporating most of the original columns of the temple in its three-aisled structure. The cathedral is a melting pot of architectural styles. Rebuilt after various earthquakes, it has a Gothic-Catalan ceiling, Baroque facade and Baroque chapels and altars. The towers on the left side of the church's exterior were built by the Saracens, who used the building as a mosque. Some of the columns on the left side have shifted on their bases, the result of an earthquake in 1545; also lost during that earthquake were mosaics that adorned the church. Another earthquake in 1693 resulted in the collapse of the facade; the great stylist of Sicilian Baroque, Andrea Palma, is responsible for the impressive facade we see today.

Piazza del Duomo, once the site of the Greek acropolis, is lined with Baroque palazzos, including **Palazzo Beneventano** and **Palazzo Arcivescovile** (Archbishop's Palace), and is one of the finest Baroque squares in Italy. At the southern end is the **Chiesa di Santa Lucia alla Badia**, dedicated to St Lucy, the city's patron saint, who was martyred at Syracuse during the reign of the Roman Emperor Diocletian. The church's Baroque facade is decorated wi[illegible] a wrought-iron balustra[illegible]

Walk down Via Picherali to the waterfront to find **Fontana Aretusa**, a natural freshwater spring only metres from the sea. Legend has it that the goddess Artemis transformed her beautiful handmaiden Aretusa into the spring to protect her from the unwelcome attention of the river god Alpheus. Undeterred, Alpheus jumped into the pool. Now populated by ducks, grey mullets and papyrus plants, the fountain is a popular spot for Syracusans during their evening constitutional.

At the entrance to Ortigia lies **Tempio di Apollo** *(Temple of Apollo; Piazza Pancali)* Little remains of the 6th-century-BC Doric structure, apart from the bases of a few columns.

Museo Regionale d'Arte Medioevale e Moderna

Located in a 13th-century palace, this museum *(☎ 0931 6 96 17, Palazzo Bellomo, Via Capodieci 14; admission €4.15; open 9am-1.30pm Tues-Sun, 9am-1.30pm & 3pm-7pm Wed)* has a sizeable collection of sculpture and paintings, dating from the Middle Ages up to the 20th century. Highlights include a beautiful *Annunciazione* (Annunciation) by Antonello da Messina (1474) and *La Sepoltura di Santa Lucia* (The Burial of St Lucy) by Caravaggio (1609).

Parco Archeologico della Neapolis

For the classicist, Syracuse's treasures at the Neapolis archaeological park *(☎ 0931 6 62 06, Viale Paradisa; admission €4.15; open 9am-2hrs before sunset daily)* are summed up in one image – that of the sparkling white, 5th-century-BC **Teatro Greco** (Greek Theatre), completely hewn out of the rock. A masterpiece of classical architecture, the ancient theatre could seat 16,000 people. When the Romans took Syracuse, they altered the theatre in order to stage gladiatorial combats there.

[illegible]ear the theatre is **Latomia del Paradiso** (Garden [illegible] Paradise), which was a former [illegible] run by the Greeks along [illegible] prison, where cap- [illegible] subterranean tunnels for building projects. Most of the area remained covered by a 'roof' of earth, which collapsed during the 1693 earthquake. After this, the garden of citrus and magnolia trees was created.

In the garden is **Orecchio di Dionisio** (Ear of Dionysius), an ear-shaped grotto 23m high and 65m deep. It was named by Caravaggio who, during a visit in the 17th century, was much impressed by its extraordinary acoustics. Caravaggio mused that the tyrant must have taken advantage of them to overhear the whispered conversations of his prisoners. Next to it is the now-closed **Grotta dei Cordari** (Ropemakers' Cave), so named because it was used by ropemakers to practise their craft.

Back outside this area and opposite the APT office you'll find the entrance to the 2nd-century-AD **Anfiteatro Romano**. The amphitheatre was used for gladiatoral combats and horse races. Roman punters used to park their chariots in the area between the amphitheatre and Viale Paolo Orsi. The Spaniards, little interested in archaeology, largely destroyed the site in the 16th century, using it as a quarry to build the city walls of Ortygia. West of the amphitheatre is the 3rd-century-BC **Ara di Gerone II**

Cumulative Tickets

It's a little-known fact that there are three cumulative tickets which make seeing the sights in Syracuse a fraction cheaper. You should be able to buy the tickets at the participating sight, so check with the relative ticket offices. Each ticket is valid for two days, prices are for adults/concessions:

€5.15/2.60 Museo Archeologico Paolo Orsi & Museo Regionale d'Arte Medioevale e Moderna
€6.20/3.10 Museo Archeologico Paolo Orsi & Parco Archeologico della Neapolis
€7.75/3.85 Museo Archeologico Paolo Orsi, Museo Regionale d'Arte Medioevale e Moderna & Parco Archeologico della Neapolis

(Altar of Hieron II). The monolithic sacrificial altar was a kind of giant abattoir where 450 oxen could be killed at one time.

To get here, catch a bus (No 1 and several others) from Riva della Posta on Ortigia.

Museo Archeologico Paolo Orsi

Located in the grounds of Villa Landolina, about 500m east of the Parco Archeologico, is the Museo Archeologico Paolo Orsi *(☎ 0931 46 40 22, Viale Teocrito; admission €4.15; open 9am-1pm Tues, Thurs & Sun, 9am-1pm & 3.30pm-7.30pm Wed, Fri & Sat, 3.30pm-7pm Mon)*. It contains the best-organised and most interesting archaeological collection in Sicily (and is one of the most extensive archaeological collections in Europe) and certainly merits a visit. It is divided into three sections: Section A deals with proto and prehistoric Sicily, Section B has an excellent collection from the ancient Greek colonies of Megara Hyblea and Syracuse itself and Section C looks at Syracusan sub-colonies such as Eloro, as well as several Hellenised indigenous towns, and Agrigento and Gela. The opening hours are all over the place and often get extended in summer; check with one of the tourist offices.

Museo del Papiro

The collection of this small museum *(☎ 0931 6 16 16, Viale Teocrito 66; closed for restoration at the time of writing)* includes papyrus documents and products. The plant grows in abundance around the Ciane river, near Syracuse, and was used to make paper in the 18th century.

Special Events

Since 1914, Syracuse has hosted a festival of Greek classical drama in May and June. Until 2000, these took place only on even-numbered years; at the time of research this had been changed to become an annual event. Performances are given in the Teatro Greco and prices range from around €12.90 for a non-reserved seat to €31 for reserved seating close to the stage. Tickets are available from the APT office or at a booth at the theatre entrance. You can call for information on ☎ 0931 6 74 15 or toll free 800 90 70 80.

The Festa di Santa Lucia, on 13 December, is celebrated with a procession where a silver statue of the saint is carried through the streets.

Places to Stay – Budget

Camping Catch bus Nos 21 or 22 from Corso Umberto to these camp sites.

Agriturist Rinaura *(☎ 0931 72 12 24, SP115, Località Rinaura)* Sites per adult/child/tent €4.50/2.60/4.50. About 4km west of the city, this camp site has a children's playground and is equipped for disabled campers. Prices include electricity and car space. In addition to the two buses above, No 24 will also get you there.

Fontane Bianche *(☎ 0931 79 03 33, Località Fontane Bianche)* Sites per adult/tent €6/4.50. Open May-Oct. This camp site is about 18km south-west of Syracuse, at the beach of the same name. It is slightly more expensive than Agriturist Rinaura, but they don't charge for children.

Hotels The first two mid-range hotels listed here are handy for the train station.

Hotel Centrale *(☎ 0931 605 28, fax 0931 6 11 75, Corso Umberto 141)* Singles/doubles €20/26, doubles with bath €39. Hotel Centrale has small, basic rooms.

Aretusa *(☎/fax 0931 2 42 11, Via Francesco Crispi 75)* Singles/doubles €24/37, with bath €26/42. This two-star hotel has comfortable rooms.

Milano *(☎ 0931 6 69 81, Corso Umberto 10)* Singles/doubles without bath €19/37, singles/doubles with bath €37/66. About the only things going for this spartan, no-frills hotel is that it is a stone's throw from Ortigia and is also within easy access of the archaeological area. Don't expect a warm welcome from the grumpy proprietors.

Bed & Breakfast B&B is becoming increasingly popular in Syracuse, which is good news for travellers.

L'Acanto *(☎/fax 0931 46 11 29, e lacanto@tiscalinet.it, Via Roma 15)* Singles/doubles with bath €4[illegible]

SICILY

The family-run L'Acanto has delightful rooms with TV and air-conditioning off a pretty courtyard.

Belvedere San Giacomo *(☎ 0931 6 90 05, fax 0931 46 11 29, ⓔ beb@supereva.it, Via Maestranza 111)* Singles/doubles €36.15/ 51.65. Run by the same people as L'Acanto, these rooms are also very pleasant but bathrooms are shared.

Places to Stay – Mid-Range & Top End

Domus Mariae *(☎ 0931 2 48 54, fax 0931 2 48 58, ⓔ htldomus@sistemia.it, Via V Veneto 76)* Singles/doubles €93/130. This restored former school for nuns on Ortigia has been transformed into an elegant, comfortable hotel which is good value for the price. Some rooms have sea views (and cost more than the others). There's free parking outside.

Hotel Roma *(☎ 0931 46 56 26, fax 0931 46 55 35, Via Minerva 10)* Singles/doubles €150/235. Almost attached to the town's cathedral, Hotel Roma has *the* best position in Ortigia and is a superb luxury hotel to boot – with prices that reflect it.

Jolly *(☎ 0931 46 11 11, fax 0931 46 11 26, Corso Gelone 45)* Singles/doubles up to €119/150. The rather characterless Jolly is still a good choice, as it's near both the train station and the Parco Archeologico. The rooms are fully serviced and soundproofed.

Grand Hotel *(☎ 0931 46 46 00, fax 0931 46 46 11, Viale Mazzini 12)* Singles/doubles €123.95/180.75. The restored Grand, on Ortigia, has top-class rooms.

Places to Eat

Casa del Pane *(Corso Gelone 65)* As its name suggests, this place does excellent takeaway focaccia and pizza for snacks on the run or light lunches.

Pasticceria Cassarino *(☎ 0931 6 80 46, Corso Umberto 86)* If you've not had your fill of Sicilian sweets such as *cannoli di ricotta* and *cassata* (cake stuffed with [illegible]tta and candied fruit), make a bee-line [illegible]ria Cassarino.

[illegible] *(☎ 0931 6 05 82, Via* [illegible]12.90. In the new [illegible] is a simple trattoria with a small menu concentrating on seafood. Try the *pesce spada* (spaghetti with swordfish).

Trattoria la Foglia *(☎ 0931 6 62 33, Via Capodieci 21)* Full meals from €20.65. Here the eccentric owner/chef and her vegetarian husband serve whatever seafood and vegetables are fresh that day and bake their own bread. The *tagliolini pesce* (seafood pasta) is especially tasty and the ambience is delightful with cute and colourful decor.

Ristorante Osteria da Mariano *(☎ 0931 6 74 44, Vicolo Zuccalà 9)* Full meals from €18.10. Open Wed-Mon. This restaurant, tucked away in an alleyway south of the cathedral on Ortigia, serves very good traditional Sicilian fare.

Pizzeria Trattoria Zsà *(☎ 0931 2 22 04, Via Roma 73)* Pizzas €3.10-7.25. Pizzas – 65 different varieties – fly out of the oven here but there's also a good selection of starters and mains.

Minosse *(☎ 0931 6 63 66, Via Mirabella 6; closed Mon)* Pasta €6.20-7.75, mains from €10.35. Open Tues-Sun. The *linguine all Visetti* (pasta with prawns and sweet cherry tomatoes) is a signature dish at this popular restaurant.

In the streets near the post office, there's a ***produce market*** until 1pm Monday to Saturday. There are several grocery shops and supermarkets along Corso Gelone.

Getting There & Away

Bus Unless you're coming from Catania or Messina, you'll find buses faster and more convenient than trains. Interbus services (☎ 0931 6 67 10) leave from Riva della Posta or near their office at Via Trieste 28. They connect with Catania and its airport, Palermo (€10.35, 3½ hours), Enna and surrounding small towns, including Noto. Interbus also has a daily service to Rome, leaving Syracuse at 7.45am and connecting with the Rome bus at Catania. A single ticket costs €36.15 (€31 for people under 26 and over 60).

AST buses (☎ 0931 46 48 20) leave for Catania, Piazza Armerina, Noto, Modica and Ragusa from their office at Riva della Posta 9/11.

Train More than a dozen trains depart daily for Messina (three hours) via Catania (1½ hours). Some go on to Rome, Turin, Milan and other long-distance destinations. There is only one direct connection to Palermo, leaving at 6.40am and taking five hours. If you miss this one, you'll have to go to Catania and wait for a connection. There are several slow trains to Modica and Ragusa.

Car & Motorcycle By car, if arriving from the north, you will enter Syracuse on Via Scala Greca. To reach the centre of the city, turn left at Viale Teracati and follow it around to the south; it eventually becomes Corso Gelone. There is ongoing confusion over the *superstrada* (super-highway) connection between Catania, Syracuse and towns such as Noto farther along the coast. An autostrada is supposed to connect the towns but starts and ends virtually in the middle of nowhere some kilometres out of Syracuse. You'll need to follow the (green) signs to find it.

Getting Around

Only a few kilometres separate the Parco Archeologico and Ortigia, so it's possible to walk. Otherwise, bus Nos 1 and 2 make the trip from Piazza della Posta.

NOTO

postcode 96017 • pop 23,000

Flattened by the 1693 earthquake, picturesque Noto was rebuilt in Grand Baroque style by its noble families. The warm gold and rose hues of the local stone tone down the heavily embellished palaces and churches. However, many of Noto's most important buildings are in a state of extreme disrepair – the result of decades of neglect and plenty of minor earth tremors. The town was shocked in early 1996 when the dome and roof of its splendid Baroque cathedral collapsed – apparently local authorities knew that the roof was cracked, but nothing was done. Fortunately, the church was empty at the time. The absence of the dome has dramatically altered the town's skyscape, since the original designers of Baroque Noto had taken particular account of the town's visual impact as a whole. Major works are in progress to stabilise the church and eventually fix the roof; whether the dome will be replaced is unknown.

Noto is also good for your tastebuds and particularly renowned for its cakes and pastries. Be aware that accommodation is a problem.

Orientation & Information

Intercity buses drop you in the Porta Reale, which is at the beginning of Corso Vittorio Emanuele, the town's main street. You can get a map at the APT office (☎ 0931 57 37 79) on Piazza XVI Maggio. It opens 8am to 2pm and 3.30pm to 7pm Monday to Saturday.

The public hospital is on Via dei Mille, on the way out of town towards Noto Antica. In a medical emergency, call ☎ 0931 57 12 25.

The travel agency Allakatakka (☎ 0931 83 50 05), at Corso Vittorio Emanuele 47, wears various hats including tour guide and renter of bikes and scooters.

Things to See & Do

The collapse of the cathedral dome revealed that previous restoration work done on the city's monuments had been very superficial – a significant problem, since the local white *tufo* stone is very soft and, as a building material, requires constant maintenance. The situation is so bad that several buildings remain standing only because they're held up by wooden supports. Lots of money has been allocated in the past, only to remain unspent or to evaporate into the ether. However, it seems that the authorities are now serious and numerous projects are under way to restore the cathedral and other important buildings in the city centre. There has also been a move to have Noto added to Unesco's World Heritage List.

Most of the important monuments line Corso Vittorio Emanuele. Overlooking Piazza XVI Maggio are the **Chiesa di San Domenico** and the adjacent **Dominican convent**, both designed by Rosario Gagliardi, a Sicilian architect who made a big contribution to the town's reconstruction. Back towards the Porta Reale is **Palazzo**

(Palazzo Nicolaci; ☎ 0931 83 50 05, Via Corrado Nicolaci; admission €3.10; open 9.30am-1pm & 4pm-7pm Tues-Sun), noted for the grotesque figures on its facade which support an iron ballustrade. Of note inside are richly coloured brocade wall coverings and frescoed ceilings. Once the home of the princes of Villadorata, the building is now partly used as municipal offices and houses the public library.

On the third Sunday in May, Corso Vittorio Emanuele is transformed into a sea of flowers for the **Infiorata**, a festival to welcome the spring. Each of the palazzo's richly sculpted balconies is decorated differently for the celebration, sporting a veritable menagerie of centaurs, horses, lions, sirens and tragic masks.

The **cathedral** stands at the top of a sweeping staircase overlooking Piazza Municipio. The facade (likely to be shrouded in scaffolding for years) is imposing, but less extravagant than most of Noto's other Baroque monuments. Next to the cathedral is **Palazzo Landolina**, now abandoned, but belonging to the Sant'Alfano, Noto's oldest noble family. Across the piazza is **Palazzo Ducezio**, the town hall.

Farther along Corso Vittorio Emanuele are the **Chiesa del Santissimo Salvatore** *(Corso Vittorio Emanuele; admission free; open 8am-noon & 4pm-7pm daily)* and an adjoining **monastery**. The interior of the church is the most impressive in Noto. The monastery was reserved for the daughters of local nobility. The fountain suspended on a wall next to the monastery was left there after Noto's streets were lowered in 1840 to facilitate the movement of carriages.

If you are interested in taking home a few pieces of Sicilian ceramics, ***All'Angolo*** *(cnr Piazza dell'Immacolata & Corso Vittorio Emanuele)* has an excellent selection of pieces from Caltagirone and Santo Stefano di Camastra.

[illegible]ces to Stay

[illegible] ***Noto*** *(☎/fax 0931 57 15 34, [illegible]tin.it, Via F Bandiera 1)* [illegible]22.20. This hostel [illegible] of Noto.

There are only a handful of hotels, all of which are down by the sea at Noto Marina, a 15-minute drive or bus trip (buses run only in summer). The other option is renting a room from one of several affittacamere establishments.

Camere Belvedere *(☎ 0931 57 38 20, Piazza Perelli-Cippo 1)* Singles/doubles with bath €29/50. This new establishment rents pleasant furnished rooms.

La Suma Sumalia *(☎/fax 0931 89 42 92, ⓔ sumasumalia@digtec.com, SS287 Contrada San Giovanni)* About 1.5km west of the centre of Noto (past the hospital), this new affittacamere operation is a good choice.

Albergo Korsal *(☎/fax 0931 81 21 19, Località Noto Marina)* Singles/doubles with bath €31/50. This simple hotel at Noto Marina has few frills but is clean and comfortable.

President *(☎ 0931 81 25 43, fax 0931 81 25 78, Località Falconara)* Singles/doubles with bath €65/100. This three-star hotel has top-quality rooms at reasonable prices.

Places to Eat

The people of Noto are serious about their food, so take time to enjoy a meal and follow it up with a visit to one of the town's excellent bars/pasticcerias.

Caffè Sicilia *(☎ 0931 83 50 13, Corso Vittorio Emanuele 125)* & ***Corrado Costanzo*** *(☎ 0931 83 52 43, Via Silvio Spaventa 9)* Round the corner from each other, these places are neck and neck when it comes to the best gelato and cakes in Noto. Both make superb *dolci di mandorle* (almond cakes and sweets), real cassata cake and *torrone* (nougat), as well as heavenly gelati and granita – try Caffè Sicilia's almond and cinnamon gelato or the one made with *fragolini* (tiny wild strawberries).

Trattoria del Carmine *(☎ 0931 83 87 05, Via Ducezio 9)* Full meals from €12.90. This place serves excellent home-style meals. Try the *coniglio alla stimpirata* (rabbit in local sauces).

Ristorante Neas *(☎ 0931 57 35 38, Via Rocco Pirri 30)* Pasta €6.20-9.30, mains €6.20-12.90. You'll find a high standard of both food and service at this place, which opens up its lovely terrace in summer. Try the linguine *allo scoglio* (with mixed seafood), or the legendary fish soup.

Getting There & Away

Noto is easily accessible by AST and Interbus buses from Catania and Syracuse. There are two trips (45 minutes) daily leaving Syracuse at around 7am and 1.30pm (the bus continues on to Gela). Buses run frequently between Noto and Noto Marina from June to August only.

RAGUSA & RAGUSA IBLA

postcode 97100 • pop 68,000

This prosperous provincial capital is virtually two towns in one: Ragusa Ibla, a curious cocktail of medieval and Baroque, and the 18th-century 'new' town, simply known as Ragusa.

Orientation & Information

The lower town, Ibla, has most of the sights but transport and accommodation are in the newer upper town. The train station is on Piazza del Popolo and the intercity bus station is on the adjacent Piazza Gramsci. From the train station, turn left and head along Viale Tenente Lena, across the bridge (Ponte Nuovo) and straight ahead along Via Roma to reach Corso Italia, the upper town's main street. Turn right on Corso Italia and follow it to the stairs to Ibla or follow the winding road to the lower town.

The tourist office (☎ 0932 62 14 21), at Via Capitano Bocchieri 33 in Palazzo La Rocca, opens 9am to 1.30pm Monday to Saturday (also open 4pm to 6pm Tuesday) and has heaps of information.

The Ospedale Civile (hospital; ☎ 0932 62 39 46 for the Guardia Medica) is across Piazza del Popolo from the train station. For an ambulance, call ☎ 0932 62 14 10.

Things to See & Do

The stairs linking the upper and lower towns are next to the **Chiesa di Santa Maria delle Scale** *(Via XXIV Maggio; open 10am-1pm & 4pm-6pm daily)*. The church, rebuilt after the 1693 earthquake, retains parts of the original 15th-century structure, including the campanile and doorway. Take in the panoramic view of Ibla before heading down the stairs.

The impressive **Basilica di San Giorgio** *(☎ 0932 22 00 85, Piazza del Duomo; admission free; open 10am-1pm & 4pm-6pm daily)*, at the top of a flight of stairs, dominates Ibla. Designed by Rosario Gagliardi and built in the late 18th century, it has the boisterous, 'wedding-cake' appearance of High Baroque.

Follow Corso XXV Aprile downhill, past the **Chiesa di San Giuseppe** *(Piazza Pola; admission free; open 10am-1pm & 4pm-6pm daily)*, which also exhibits the genius of Gagliardi, until you reach the **Giardino Ibleo**, the town's pleasant public gardens, a good place for a picnic.

In the upper town, visit the early-18th-century **cathedral** *(Piazza San Giovanni; free; open 10am-1pm & 4pm-6pm daily)* off Corso Italia and the **Museo Archeologico Ibleo** *(☎ 0932 62 29 63, Via Natalelli; admission €2.05; open 9am-1.30pm & 4pm-7.30pm Mon-Sat)* off Via Roma.

Places to Stay & Eat

All of Ragusa's accommodation is in the upper town. There are no budget hotels.

Hotel San Giovanni *(☎ 0932 62 10 13, fax 0932 62 12 94, Via Traspontino 3)* Singles/doubles without bath €24/37, singles/doubles with bath €31/52. To get here from Piazza del Popolo, head down Viale Leonardo da Vinci, turn left at Via Ingegnere Migliorisi and follow it to the footbridge.

Hotel Rafael *(☎ 0932 65 40 80, fax 0932 65 34 18, Corso Italia 40)* Singles/doubles with bath €47/68. This is a pleasant establishment near Piazza Matteotti offering comfortable rooms.

Hotel Montreal *(☎ 0932 62 11 33, fax 0932 62 10 26, Corso Italia 70)* Singles/doubles with bath €47/68. Rooms in this hotel are very comfortable if somewhat characterless, but it's a friendly place. Prices include breakfast. Parking in the off-street garage costs €5.50.

Trattoria la Bettola *(☎ 0932 65 33 77, Largo Camerina 7)* Full meals from €15.50. Downhill to the left off Piazza del [illegible] this small trattoria do[illegible]

U Saracinù *(☎ 0932 24 69 76, Via del Convento 9)* Tourist menu €12.90, full meals around €20.60. Also off Piazza del Duomo in Ragusa Ilba, this is a popular local eatery.

Al Bocconcino *(☎ 0932 65 14 05, Corso Vittorio Veneto 96)* Pasta from €3.10. Delicious and cheap *cucina Ragusana* (Ragusanese cuisine) is on offer at this small trattoria in the upper town, a block from both the Hotel Rafael and Hotel Montreal. The pasta, broccoli and ricotta soup is exceptionally good.

There is a ***Standa supermarket*** *(Via Roma 187)* near the bridge.

Getting There & Around

Ragusa is accessible by not-so-regular trains from Syracuse, Noto and Agrigento. Buses are better. Etna Trasporti (☎ 0932 62 34 40), a subsidiary of SAIS (information and tickets at Gran Bar Puglisi, Via Dante 94, opposite the train station), runs eight buses per day to Catania.

AST (☎ 0932 68 18 18) serves Palermo (four buses per day) and runs more regularly to Noto and Syracuse (seven daily). An AST timetable is posted at the spot on Piazza Gramsci where AST and SAIS buses stop.

City bus Nos 1 and 3 run from Piazza del Popolo in the upper town to Piazza Pola and the gardens in the lower town of Ragusa Ibla. It's only a 10-minute walk down to Ragusa Ibla, but it will take you at least 30 minutes to ascend.

MODICA

About 10km south-east of Ragusa, Modica seems to be a close cousin. It has the same sun-bleached colour and is also divided into two sections: Modica Alta (High Modica) and, you guessed it, Modica Bassa (Low Modica).

The highlight is the **Chiesa di San Giorgio** *(Corso San Giorgio; admission free; open 8am-noon & 4pm-7pm daily)* in the [illegible] part of town (local buses run by from [illegible]), easily one of the most ex[illegible] churches in the prov[illegible] sweeps up to a [illegible] Rosario Gagliardi in the early 18th century – it looks as if it was meant to be a tower. There are regular AST buses from Ragusa.

Central & South-Western Sicily

ENNA

postcode 94100 • pop 29,000

High on a commanding ridge in the sun-scorched centre of Sicily, Enna is somewhat isolated from the main tourist route around the coast. Known since Greek times as the 'umbilicus' of Sicily, the journey itself is rewarding, from whichever direction you approach. The exercise becomes more tempting still if combined with an excursion to nearby Piazza Armerina for the extraordinary mosaics of the Villa Romana (see Piazza Armerina later in this section).

Enna, 931m above sea level, has been an ideal defensive position and lookout post since prehistoric times. First settled by the Sicani, Enna later became Greek, submitting to the tyranny of Syracuse in 307 BC and thereafter falling into Carthaginian and Roman hands. In Byzantine times it became a fortress and one of the main bulwarks against the Arabs, who nonetheless managed to capture the town in 859. Today it is an important agricultural and mining centre.

Orientation

The principal road into the town is Via Pergusa, which eventually links with Via Roma, the main street of historic Enna. The intercity bus station is on Viale Diaz. To get to the town centre, turn right from the station and follow Viale Diaz to Corso Sicilia, turn right again and follow it to Via Sant'Agata to the left, which heads down to Via Roma.

Information

The AAPIT office (☎ 0935 52 82 28) is at Via Roma 413. The staff are helpful and have maps and information on the city and province. The office opens 9am to 1pm and 3pm to 7pm Monday to Saturday. There is also an AAST office (☎ 0935 50 08 75), next to Albergo Sicilia in nearby Piazza Colajanni 6, which has information mainly on the city itself (much of it about 15 years out-of-date) and opens 8am to 2pm daily.

The post office is at Via Volta 1, just off Piazza Garibaldi. Public telephones are scattered around the town or you can try Albergo Sicilia.

There are several banks on Piazza VI Dicembre, a short walk downhill from the AAPIT office.

For medical assistance, go to the Ospedale Civile Umberto I (hospital) on Via Trieste or call ☎ 0935 4 51 11. Out of hours, the Guardia Medica is on ☎ 0935 50 08 96.

Castello di Lombardia

Enna's most visible monument is the medieval castle *(☎ 0935 50 09 62, Piazza Mazzini; admission free; open 9am-1pm & 3pm-5pm daily)* which crowns the town's highest point at the eastern end. Built by the Swabians and altered by Frederick III of Aragon, it was one of the most important defensive structures in medieval Sicily. It retains six of its original 20 towers and the views of the surrounding countryside are spectacular – you can make out Mt Etna in the distant north-east. Closer and across the valley rises the town of Calascibetta, erected by the Arabs in the 9th century. It forms the northern sentinel over a valley which now contains the Palermo-Catania A19 and railway. The castle is now part-theatre.

Other Things to See & Do

Back along Via Roma, the 14th-century **cathedral** retains its Gothic apse and transept despite remodelling in the 15th and 16th centuries. Behind it is the **Museo Alessi** *(☎ 0935 50 31 65, Via Roma; admission €2.60; open 8am-8pm daily)*, which houses the contents of the cathedral's treasury.

Across Via Roma, the **Museo Archeologico** *(Museo Varisano; ☎ 0935 52 81 00, Palazzo Varisano, Piazza Mazzini; admission €2.05; open 9am-6.30pm daily)* has a small collection of ancient artefacts found in the area.

On Piazza Vittorio Emanuele, the most impressive element of the **Chiesa di San Francesco** *(Piazza Vittorio Emanuele; admission free; open 8am-noon & 4pm-7pm daily)* is its 15th-century campanile, adorned with fine Gothic windows. The tower once formed part of the city's defence system.

From the church, wander over to the new part of town and the chunky **Torre di Federico** *(Tower of Frederick II; Via Torre di Federico)* in the villa comunale, also part of the town's old defence system. The octagonal tower, standing 24m high, was once linked by a secret passage to the castle. At the time of writing, it was closed indefinitely for restoration.

For a pleasant evening stroll, head for Piazza Francesco Crispi and wander along Viale Marconi to enjoy the view.

Special Events

During Holy Week at Easter, Enna is the setting for colourful, traditional celebrations. On Good Friday, thousands of people wearing hoods and capes of different colours participate in a solemn procession to the cathedral.

Places to Stay & Eat

There is no cheap accommodation, so be prepared. Enna itself has only one hotel.

Albergo Sicilia *(☎/fax 0935 50 08 54, Piazza N Colajanni 7)* Singles/doubles €56.80/87.80. Even though it's virtually cornered the market, given the lack of competition, recent renovations make this hotel is a very pleasant place to stay. Prices include breakfast.

For other options, catch city bus No 5 from Piazza Vittorio Emanuele to Lago di Pergusa (a small, touristy lake with beaches about 10km south).

Miralago *(☎/fax 0935 54 12 72, Contrada Staglio, Pergusa)* Singles/doubles with bath €31/41.30. The cheapest option at Pergusa, this is the first place you pass on the right before entering the town proper along Via Nazionale.

Ristorante-Pizzeria Tiffany *(☎ 0935 50 13 68, Via Roma 467)* Pizzas from €4.15, pasta from €4.65. A pleasant eatery that also does pizza in a wood-fired oven [illegible] lunchtime and has a good [illegible]

L'Ariston *(☎ 0935 2 60 38, Via Roma 353)* Full meals around €2.60. This is one of Enna's better restaurants.

Ristorante Centrale *(☎ 0935 50 09 63, Piazza VI Dicembre 9)* Full meals €20.65. This place serves traditional Sicilian food, with a menu that changes daily.

There is a morning ***market*** Monday to Saturday on Via Mercato Sant'Antonio, where you can find fresh produce.

Getting There & Away

SAIS buses (☎ 0935 50 09 02) connect Enna with Catania (and on to Rome), Palermo and Syracuse. It is possible to reach Agrigento via Caltanissetta. Buses terminate on Viale Diaz. Regular SAIS buses also run to Piazza Armerina. Don't take a train – the station is miles away at the foot of the mountain-top town.

PIAZZA ARMERINA

A pleasant town less than an hour by bus or car from Enna, Piazza Armerina boasts an interesting Baroque **cathedral**. This self-proclaimed *città dei mosaici* (city of mosaics) is the nearest town to the wonderful treasure that lies in the Villa Romana del Casale, a Roman villa some 5km away.

The AAST office (☎ 0935 68 02 01) is at Via Cavour 15, in the town centre, uphill along Via Umberto I or Via Garibaldi from the intercity bus stops. It opens 8am to 2pm Monday to Saturday. Get the brochure on the villa here; it explains the layout of the ruins and the mosaics and is often unavailable at the site. SAIS buses connect Enna and Piazza Armerina (about 10 per day). There is also a daily AST bus from Syracuse.

Villa Romana del Casale

Built between the end of the 3rd and mid-4th century, the villa *(☎ 0935 68 00 36, ☎ 0935 68 73 02, just outside Piazza Armerina; admission €4.15; open 8am-1hr before sunset* [illegible]) was probably the home or hunting [illegible] Roman dignitary. Buried under [illegible]tury flood, it remained [illegible] its magnificent [illegible]

Covering about 3500 sq metres, the villa was designed in line with the lie of the hill on which it stands, creating three main areas. The mosaics cover almost its entire floor and are considered unique for their narrative style of composition, range of subject and variety of colour – many of them clearly influenced by African themes.

The villa is well organised to cope with hordes of tourists and, by following the raised walkways, you will see all the main areas. The most captivating of the mosaics include the erotic depictions in what was probably a private apartment on the northern side of the great peristyle (colonnaded garden). The *Little Hunt*, one of the richest mosaics in terms of colour and action, is in the largest room. Next door is the villa's most famous piece, illustrating 10 girls clad in what must have been the world's earliest bikinis.

The eastern side of the peristyle opens onto a long corridor, its floor paved with the astonishing mosaic of the *Great Hunt*, depicting the chase for exotic wild animals. On the other side of the corridor is a series of apartments, whose floor illustrations reproduce scenes from Homer, as well as mythical subjects such as Arion playing the lyre on a dolphin's back, and Eros and Pan wrestling. There is also a lively circus scene.

Three ATAN buses (☎ 0935 68 22 72) leave for the villa from Piazza Senatore Marescalchi in Piazza Armerina at 9am, 10am, 11am, 4pm, 5pm and 6pm May to September. Buses leave the villa for Piazza Armerina at 9.30am, 10.30am, 11.30am, 4.30pm, 5.30pm and 6.30pm. If you have a car, you will be charged €1.05 to park outside the entrance.

Places to Stay & Eat

There are several places to stay in and around Piazza Armerina.

Villa Romana *(☎/fax 0935 68 29 11, Via A de Gasperi 18)* Singles/doubles with bath up to €51.65/77.45. This is about the cheapest accommodation in town.

Hotel Mosaici *(☎/fax 0935 68 54 53, Contrada Paratore 11)* Singles/doubles with bath €33.55/43.90. This hotel is 3km out of Piazza Armerina on the way to the Roman villa.

Azienda Agriturista Savoca *(☎ 0337 88 90 52, fax 0935 68 30 78, Località C da Polleri, Piazza Armerina)* Doubles with bath from €41.30. This place is 3km out of Piazza Armerina, on the road to Mirabella. Ask for a room in the older building in preference to the newer rooms under the swimming pool. Prices include breakfast.

Restaurants near the Roman villa tend to be fairly touristy and are best avoided.

Totò *(☎ 0935 68 01 53, Via Mazzini 29)* Full meals from €12.90. This is a typical Sicilian restaurant, in the heart of Piazza Armerina.

Del Teatro *(☎ 0935 8 56 62, Piazza del Teatro 1)* Full meals from €15.50. Del Teatro is close to Piazza Armerina's splendid Teatro Garibaldi.

MORGANTINA

About 16km north-east of Piazza Armerina, just beyond the town of Aidone, the remains of what started life as a rich Siculian town have been unearthed. What you see of its *agora* (marketplace), theatre and other buildings owes more to subsequent Greek occupation than to the Siculians, however. That the remains are not more spectacular is largely the fault of the Romans, who destroyed the town in 211 BC. Set in pleasant country with wide views to Mt Etna, the Morgantina site *(☎ 0935 873 84, Località Morgantina; admission €3.10; open 8am-1 hr before sunset daily)* is an easy detour if you have your own transport, but a difficult proposition without.

AGRIGENTO

postcode 92100 • pop 55,000

This pleasant medieval town, set high on a hill, overlooks both the Mediterranean and the spectacular Valley of the Temples (Valle dei Templi), a significant ancient Greek site. Founded in 582 BC by settlers from Gela, themselves originally from Rhodes, the town became powerful in the 5th century BC and most of the temples date from then. The Greek poet Pindar described the town as 'the most beautiful of those inhabited by mortals'.

Sacked and destroyed by the Carthaginians in 406 BC, Akragas, as it was known, was conquered and rebuilt by the Romans in the 3rd century BC. The newcomers renamed the town Agrigentum and it continued to prosper under Byzantine and Arab rule. On the road between Agrigento and Porto Empedocle is Caos, where the playwright Luigi Pirandello (1867–1936) was born.

The Greek temples are the obvious reason to come to Agrigento but don't overlook the town itself.

Orientation

Intercity buses arrive on Piazza Rosselli and the train station is slightly south on Piazza Marconi. Lying between the two is the green oasis of Piazzale Aldo Moro, at the eastern end of Via Atenea, the main street of the medieval town. Frequent city buses run to Valley of the Temples below the town. See the Getting Around section.

Information

Tourist Offices There are three tourist offices in Agrigento, all of which are spectacularly disorganised. The provincial tourist office, the Uffico Relazioni con il Pubblico (☎ 0922 40 10 50), is at Piazzale Aldo Moro 1 (inside the Provincia offices). It opens 8am to 2pm and 3pm to 7pm Monday to Friday, 8am to 2pm Saturday. It also operates a toll-free line (☎ 800 23 68 37) for tourist information about Agrigento and its province.

The AAST office (☎ 0922 2 04 54, e aastagrigento@oasi.net, w www.aastagrigento.oasi.net), Via Cesare Battisti 15, opens 9am to 2pm Monday to Friday. It also opens 4pm to 7pm June to September. This office claims to provide information on the town of Agrigento but it's not evident exactly what form that information takes, although they do claim to help tourists with hotel reservations.

The third office is the comune-run information kiosk (no tel) in the centre of Piazzale Aldo Moro, open 9am to 1pm and 3pm to 7pm. About the only thing that's worth picking up here is the cute fold-out map they produce.

Money Banks generally open 8.30am to 1.30pm (larger banks also open 3pm to

4pm) and the Monte dei Paschi di Siena at Piazza Vittorio Emanuele 1 has an ATM. Out of hours, there's a currency exchange booth at the post office and another at the train station – watch the rates.

Post & Communications The post office, on Piazza Vittorio Emanuele, opens 8.30am to 6.30pm Monday to Friday and 8.30am to 12.30pm on Saturday.

There is a Telecom office at Via A de Gasperi 25, open 9am to 7pm Monday to Friday.

Medical Services & Emergency The Azienda Ospedaliera San Giovanni di Dio (hospital; ☎ 0922 49 21 11) is on Via Rupe Atenea 1. For an ambulance, call ☎ 0922 40 13 44.

The *questura* (police station; ☎ 0922 46 61 11 or 113) is at Piazza Vittorio Emanuele 2.

Valley of the Temples (Valle dei Templi)

The five main Doric temples along the 'valley' (actually a ridge) were built around the 5th century BC and are in various states of ruin, due to earthquakes and vandalism.

The area *(☎ 0922 261 91; admission €2.05; open 8.30am-1hr before sunset daily)* is divided into two sections. East of Via dei Templi are the most spectacular temples. The first you will come to is **Tempio di Ercole** (Temple of Hercules), built towards the end of the 6th century BC and believed to be the oldest of the temples. Eight of its 38 columns have been raised and you can wander around the remains of the rest. The magnificent **Tempio della Concordia** (Temple of Concord) is the only one to survive relatively intact. Built around 440 BC, it was transformed into a Christian church in the 6th century AD. Its name is taken from a Roman inscription found nearby. The **Tempio di Giunone** (Temple of Juno) stands high on the edge of the ridge, a five-minute walk to the east. Part of its colonnade remains and there is an impressive sacrificial altar. This section of the valley is open to 9pm.

Across Via dei Templi is what remains of the massive **Tempio di Giove** (Temple of Jupiter), actually never completed. Now totally in ruins, it covered an area 112m by 56m, with columns 20m high. Between the columns stood *telamoni* (colossal statues), one of which was reconstructed and is now in the Museo Archeologico. A copy lies on the ground among the ruins, giving an idea of the immense size of the structure. Work began on the temple around 480 BC and it was probably destroyed during the Carthaginian invasion in 406 BC. The nearby **Tempio di Castore e Polluce** (Temple of Castor and Pollux) was partly reconstructed in the 19th century, although probably using pieces from other constructions. All the temples are lit up at night.

The **Museo Archeologico** *(☎ 0922 40 15 65 or 0922 49 72 21, Via dei Templi, Contrada San Nicola; admission €4.15; open 9am-1pm Sun-Tues, 2pm-6pm Wed-Sat)*, just north of the temples, has a collection of artefacts from the area worth inspecting. Check on opening hours – they change according to the season.

Just opposite the museum, the **Quartiere Ellenistico-Romano** (Hellenistic-Roman quarter) constituted part of urban Agrigento. Some of its structures date from the 4th century BC, while others were built as late as the 5th century AD.

Casa Natale di Pirandello

West of the temples is the country house in Caos where author and playwright Luigi Pirandello was born. It is now a small museum *(☎ 0922 51 11 02, S115, Contrada Caos; admission €2.05; open 8.30am-7.30pm daily)*. Take bus No 1 from the station. The house is just short of Porto Empedocle and overlooks the sea.

Medieval Agrigento

Roaming around the town's narrow, winding streets is relaxing after a day among the temples. The **Chiesa di Santa Maria dei Greci** *(Salita Santa Maria dei Greci; admission free; open 8am-noon & 3pm-6pm Mon-Sat)*, uphill from Piazza Lena (at the end of Via Atenea), is an 11th-century Norman church built on the site of a 5th-century-BC Greek temple. Note the remains of the wooden Nor-

man ceiling and some Byzantine frescoes. If the church is closed, check with the custodian at Salita Santa Maria dei Greci 1, who'll open the doors for you (with a tip expected).

A not-so-relaxing walk farther uphill is to the fragile-looking **cathedral** *(Via Duomo; admission free; open 9am-noon & 4pm-7pm daily)*. Built in the year 1000, it has been restructured many times, and is dedicated to the Norman San Gerlando. The unfinished campanile was erected in the 15th century and the panelled ceiling inside dates from the 17th century.

Back towards Piazza Vittorio Emanuele, the **Monastero del Santo Spirito** was founded by Cistercian nuns at the end of the 13th century. Giacomo Serpotta is responsible for the stuccoes in the chapel. There is a small ethnographic **museum** *(☎ 0922 59 03 71, Via Foderà; admission free; open 9am-1pm & 4pm-7pm Mon-Sat)* above the old church. You can buy cakes and pastries from the nuns. See the Places to Eat section later.

Special Events

Agrigento's big annual shindig is the Sagra del Mandorlo in Fiore (Festival of the Almond Blossom), a folk festival set on the first Sunday in February in the Valley of the Temples.

Places to Stay

You can camp by the sea at San Leone, a few kilometres south of Agrigento. Take bus No 2 or 2/ from Agrigento or drive down Via dei Templi, continue along Viale Emporium towards the sea and turn left at Lungomare Akragas.

Camping Nettuno *(☎ 0922 41 62 68, Contrada Le Dune)* Adult/tent €4.15/4.65. Open year-round. This camp site is good value, especially for families as it's free for kids.

Camping Internazlonale *(☎ 0922 41 61 21, Contrada Le Dune)* Adult/child/tent €5.15/3.10/5.15. Open year-round, this camp site has good facilities, including a bar.

Hotel Bella Napoli *(☎ 0922 2 04 35, fax 0922 2 04 35, Piazza Lena 6)* Singles/doubles with bath €25.80/41.30. This place is uphill off Via Bac Bac. It has clean, basic rooms, and is one of the best deals in town.

Hotel Belvedere *(☎/fax 0922 2 00 51, Via San Vito 20)* Singles/doubles €31/38.75, with bath €41.30/56.80. This hotel is in the newer part of town, uphill from Piazza Vittorio Emanuele. The plumbing could do with some attention, but some rooms do indeed have beautiful views.

Hotel Concordia *(☎/fax 0922 59 62 66, Piazza San Francesco 11)* Singles/doubles €25.80/41.30. Just off Via Atenea, this is probably the best-positioned hotel in Agrigento if being in the *centro storico* (historic centre) is what you want. It offers good discounts out of season.

Most of Agrigento's better hotels are out of town around the Valley of the Temples or near the sea.

Hotel della Valle *(☎ 0922 2 69 66, fax 0922 2 64 12, Via dei Templi)* Singles/doubles up to €103.30/134.30. This place has lovely rooms with full services, a pool and gardens.

Hotel Costazzurra *(☎ 0922 41 12 22, fax 0922 41 40 40, e reception@hotelcostazzurra.it, Via delle Viole 2, San Leone)* Singles/doubles with bath €67.15/87.80. Located in San Leone, down by the beach (about 3km away from the Valley of the Temples), this family-run hotel also has a very nice restaurant. Half-board arrangements probably work out cheaper in summer.

Hotel Kaos *(☎ 0922 59 86 22, fax 0922 59 87 70, Contrada Pirandello)* Singles/doubles up to €113.60/154.95. This large resort complex in a restored villa is by the sea, about 2km from the temples.

Places to Eat

Manhattan *(Salita Santa Maria degli Angeli)* Pizzas from €4.15. Open Mon-Sat. If it's a pizza or light lunch you're after, the Manhattan pizzeria, in a steep street off Via Atenea, is a good choice.

Monastero del Santo Spirito *(Via Foderà)* For the best pastries, and just for the experience, go to the end of Via Foderà. The nuns in this convent have been baking heavenly *dolce di mandorle* (almond cakes and pastries) to a secret recipe for centuries. You can buy a small tray of them for €3.35. Press the door bell (to the right of the entrance to the convent/museum) and say 'Vorrei comprare qualche dolce' – and see how you go.

Black Horse *(☎ 0922 2 32 23, Via Celauro 8)* Set menu from €7.75. Just off Via Atenea, the Black Horse serves tasty, reasonably priced meals, with a good-value tourist menu.

Ambasciata di Sicilia *(☎ 0922 2 05 26, Via Giambertoni 2)* Full meals from €18.10. Typical Sicilian fare is on offer here in a cosy, attractive basement with a spectacular terrace for open-air dining.

Kalos *(☎ 0922 2 63 89, Via Salita Filino 1)* Full meals around €25.80. Heading up the price scale, but still offering traditional Sicilian food, is Kalos.

Trattoria Concordia *(☎ 0922 2 26 68, Via Porcello 8)* Pasta from €6.20, fish mains from €9.30. For what it is (your bog-standard trattoria) Concordia is expensive. If you feel like fish, it's an OK choice, especially as – despite what the menu says – they're unlikely to have anything else.

Trattoria-Pizzeria Kokalo's *(☎ 0922 60 64 27, Viale C Magazzeni 3)* Pizzas from €5.15. East of the temples, this trattoria-pizzeria dishes up (allegedly) the area's best pizza.

The daily ***produce market*** is held on Piazza San Francesco.

Getting There & Away

Bus For most destinations, bus is the easiest way to get to and from Agrigento. The intercity bus station is on Piazza Rosselli, just off Piazza Vittorio Emanuele, and timetables for most services are posted in Bar Sprint on the piazza. The AAST tourist office also has timetables.

Cuffaro (☎ 0922 41 82 31) and Camilleri (☎ 0922 47 27 98) both run buses to Palermo (between them, there are 10 daily). SAIS buses serve Rome, Catania, and Caltanissetta. Information about SAIS buses (☎ 0922 59 52 60) can be obtained at Via Ragazzi del '99 12.

Train Trains run to Palermo (two hours), Catania (3½ hours) and Enna. For Palermo, the train is fine, if a little slow. For anywhere else you should consider the bus.

Car & Motorcycle Agrigento is easily accessible by road from all of Sicily's main towns. The S189 links the town with Palermo, while the S115 runs along the coast, north-west towards Sciacca and south-east for Gela and eventually Syracuse. For Enna, take the S640 via Caltanissetta. There is plenty of parking on Piazza Vittorio Emanuele in the centre.

Getting Around

City buses run down to the Valley of the Temples from in front of the train station. Take bus No 1, 1/, 2, 2/ (every 30 minutes) or 3 and get off at either the museum or farther downhill at Piazzale dei Templi.

The Green Line (Linea Verde) bus runs every hour from the train station to the cathedral, for those who prefer not to make the uphill walk. Tickets cost €0.50 and are valid for 1½ hours.

ERACLEA MINOA

A colony within a colony, Eraclea Minoa *(☎ 0922 84 60 05; admission €2.05; open 9am-1 hr before sunset daily)* lies about halfway between Agrigento and Selinunte to the west, on top of a wild bluff overlooking a splendid, sandy beach and the magnificent Capo Bianco cliff. Founded by Selinunte in the 6th century BC, the ruins are comparatively scanty and the 4th-century theatre's seating has been covered in moulded plastic to protect the crumbling remains.

You can also visit the **Riserva Naturale del Fiume Platani**. Buses between Sciacca and Agrigento will drop you at the turn-off, from where it's a 4km walk. In summer, buses go from Cattolica Eraclea (which can be reached from Agrigento and Sciacca) to the site.

Eraclea Minoa Village *(☎ 0922 84 73 10, Località Eraclea Minoa)* Adults/tent €3.10/5.15. Open 15 June-15 Sep. This camp site is not particularly exciting but the turquoise blue waters in front of it are among the island's most attractive.

ISOLE PELAGIE (PELAGIC ISLANDS)

postcode 92010 • pop 5000

Some 240km south of Agrigento, this tiny archipelago lies farther from mainland Sicily than Malta, and in many respects has more in common with nearby Tunisia or Libya than Italy. Indeed, Libya's Colonel Gaddafi is so convinced of this that he launched a couple of wobbly missiles its way in 1987. Of the three islands, which rise on the African continental shelf, only Lampedusa is of any interest. Linosa has nothing to offer and Lampione is little more than an uninhabited pimple on the sometimes rather tempestuous surface of the Canale di Sicilia, the stretch of the Mediterranean Sea separating Africa from Sicily.

Lampedusa, a rocky, sparsely covered and (in winter) wind-whipped place, is becoming increasingly popular with Italians looking for an early tan, and the water is enticingly warm. Of the several beaches on the southern side of the 11km-long island, the best known is Isola dei Conigli (Rabbit Island), where Caretta-Caretta turtles lay their eggs between June and August. These timid creatures generally only come in when no-one's about.

There are several dive rental outlets; for more information, ask at the Pro Loco office (☎ 0922 97 14 77) at Piazza Comm-Brignone 12 (closed at the time of writing). Orange minibuses run hourly from near the Pro Loco to the beach or you could hire a Vespa from one of several outlets around town (look for the *autonoleggio* signs).

Places to Stay

Cheap accommodation can be hard to find. The little pensiones are often full in summer and closed in winter.

Albergo Le Pelagie *(☎ 0922 97 02 11, fax 0922 97 10 45, Via Bonfiglio 11)* Singles/doubles with bath €56.80/92.95. This place is off Via Roma, a 30-minute walk west along the waterfront from the port (alternatively, ring when you get to the port and they will come and pick you up). Like most places, Le Pelagie makes at least half-board compulsory in summer (€77.45 per person).

Getting There & Away

A Siremar ferry leaves Porto Empedocle (7km south-west of Agrigento) at midnight daily year-round. It takes six hours to reach Linosa and another two to reach Lampedusa; the one-way fare to the latter is €34. You can buy tickets at the Siremar booth (☎ 0922 63 66 83) at the port. Orange buses from Agrigento arrive at Piazza Italia, from where it's a quick walk down Via Quattro Novembre to the port entrance (the last bus from Porto Empedocle leaves for Agrigento at about 9pm). Boats from Lampedusa (and Linosa) leave daily (10.15am from Lampedusa). Trips can be cancelled due to bad weather, especially in winter. There are also flights between Lampedusa and Palermo.

SCIACCA

postcode 92019 • pop 40,000

Sciacca started life as a Roman settlement but only really took off with the arrival of the Arabs. The Normans fortified this prosperous farming town, which later came to be ruled alternately by local feuding families. Today a bustling fishing port, the centre of town has a few monuments worthy of a quick look, including the **cathedral**, which was erected by the Normans in the 12th century, the peculiar 15th-century **Steripinto** building, the neogothic **Palazzo San Giacomo** and the ruins of a **castello** dominating the town.

The time to come is February, when the townsfolk let their hair down for Carnevale. The AAST office (☎ 0925 2 27 44) is at Corso Vittorio Emanuele 84.

Paloma Blanca *(☎/fax 0925 2 51 30, Via Figuli 5)* Singles/doubles €31/46.50. This place is on the eastern side of town and has decent, if unexciting, rooms.

Buses for Palermo leave from Viale della Vittoria (tickets at No 22). Others, run by the Lumia company, serve Trapani, Agrigento and destinations between, leaving from Via Agatocle.

SELINUNTE

The ancient Greek city of Selinus, founded in the 7th century BC, was long a prosperous and powerful city, but its standing rivalry with Segesta to the north was to be its undoing. In 409 BC, the latter called in a powerful ally, Carthage, whose troops destroyed Selinunte. The city later recovered under the Siracusans and then Carthaginians, but in 250 BC its citizens delivered the *coup de grace* to prevent it passing to the Romans. What they left standing, mainly temples, was finished off by an earthquake in the Middle Ages.

Things to See

One of the more captivating ancient sites in Italy, Selinunte *(☎ 094 4 62 51; admission €4.15; open 9am-1 hr before sunset daily)* once fairly bristled with temples. They are known today simply by the letters A to G, O and M. Five are huddled together in the acropolis at the western end of the site, accessible by road from the ticket office, or on foot across the depression known as the Gorgo di Cottone – once Selinunte's harbour. Of particular note is **Temple C** – several of the metopes in Palermo's archaeological museum came from this temple, and there is also a reconstruction of the temple's clay roof at the museum.

Temple E, reconstructed in 1958 amid much criticism, stands out for its recently acquired completeness. Built in the 5th century BC, it is the first of three temples you'll come to at the eastern end of the site. The more outstanding metopes in Palermo's archaeological museum came from this temple. The northernmost **Temple G** was built in the 6th century BC and, although never completed, was one of the largest in the Greek world. Today it is a massive pile of rubble, but evocative nonetheless.

The ticket office shuts one hour before closing time. There is an information office (☎ 094 4 62 51) just outside the entrance to the site, open 8am to 8pm Monday to Saturday, 9am to noon and 3pm to 6pm Sunday and holidays.

Places to Stay & Eat

Selinunte is close to the village of Marinella di Selinunte, where you can find accommodation.

Il Maggiolino *(☎/fax 0924 4 60 44, ⓔ magiol@potin.it, Località Marinella di Selinunte)* Person/tent/car €4.15/2.60/2.60. This is one of a couple of camp sites in the area. It is located on the SS115, as you come into Selinunte.

Pensione Costa d'Avorio *(☎ 0924 4 62 07, Via Stazione 10, Marinella di Selinunte)* Singles/doubles without bath from €20.65/36.15, singles/doubles with bath from €25.80/43.90. This has good rooms for the price and a good trattoria to boot.

Hotel Garzia *(☎ 0924 4 66 60, fax 0924 4 61 96, Via Pigafetta 6)* Singles/doubles €41.30/67.15. This hotel overlooks the sea and has nice rooms.

Hotel Alceste *(☎ 0924 4 61 84, fax 0924 4 61 43, Via Alceste 23, Marinella di Selinunte)* Singles/doubles with bath up to €54.25/69.70. This place has some of the more up-market rooms around.

There are some pleasant little restaurants along the beachfront.

Lido Azzurro *(Lungomare Marinella di Selinunte)* Full meals from €15.50. Also known as Baffo's, this eatery serves good pizzas, pasta and fresh seafood virtually beside the water's edge.

Getting There & Away

Regular AST buses link Selinunte and Marinella di Selinunte to Castelvetrano (€0.75), which can be reached by bus from Agrigento, Mazara del Vallo, Marsala and Trapani. Very slow trains also run from Palermo and Trapani to Castelvetrano. The tourist office has timetables.

North-Western Sicily

MARSALA

postcode 91025 • pop 80,000

Best known for its sweet dessert wines, Marsala is a surprisingly pleasant town, with an interesting historic centre. If you have a car, it's a good alternative to Trapani as a base for exploring Sicily's north-west. Founded as Lilybaeon on Cape Lilibeo by Carthaginians who had fled nearby Mozia (or Motya) after its destruction by Syracuse, the city was eventually conquered by the Arabs, who renamed it Marsa Allah (Port of God). It was at Marsala that Garibaldi landed with his One Thousand in 1860.

Information

Marsala's APT office (☎ 0923 71 40 97) is at Via XI Maggio 100, just off Piazza della Repubblica, in the centre of town. It opens 9am to 2pm and 3pm to 8pm Monday to Saturday. An APT information kiosk next to the Museo Baglio Anselmi, Lungomare Boeo, opens 8am to 2pm and 4pm to 8pm Tuesday to Sunday (mornings only on Monday) June until September.

The public hospital (☎ 0923 71 60 31) is on Piazza San Francesco, just west of the city centre. For a medical emergency, call ☎ 0923 95 14 10.

The *questura* (police station; ☎ 0923 92 43 71) is at Via San Giovanni Bosco 26.

Things to See & Do

Visit the **cathedral** on Piazza della Repubblica, built in the 17th and 18th centuries, and its **Museo degli Arazzi** *(☎ 0923 71 29 03, Via Garaffa 57; admission €1.05; open 9am-1pm & 4pm-6pm Tues-Sun)*. In the museum are eight 16th-century Flemish tapestries, woven for the Spanish King Philip II and depicting scenes from the war of Titus against the Jews.

On the seafront is the **Museo Archeologico Regionale Baglio Anselmi** *(☎ 0923 95 25 35, Lungomare Boeo; admission €2.10; open 9am-2pm Mon, Tues & Thurs, 9am-2pm & 4pm-7pm Wed, Fri & Sat, 9am-2pm & 4pm-6.30pm Sun)*. To get there, follow Via XI Maggio to Piazza della Vittoria and turn left along Via N Sauro. Well worth a visit, the museum houses a partly reconstructed Carthaginian warship, which may have seen action in the First Punic War. It was found off the coast north of Marsala in 1971. Other exhibits include amphoras and artefacts discovered in and around Marsala.

North of the museum, along Viale Vittorio Veneto, is the partly excavated **Insula Romana**, which was a 3rd-century-AD Roman house. East is the magnificent **Cine Impero**, originally a cinema but now a cultural centre, built in monumental Fascist style.

Pay a visit to Marsala's open-air **market**, open every morning Monday to Saturday, in a piazza off Piazza dell'Addolorata next to the *comune* (municipal offices). In this small, lively marketplace, you'll likely be serenaded by a fruit vendor.

Tipplers should head to **Florio** *(☎ 0923 78 11 11, Lungomare Florio; open 9am-noon & 2.30pm-5pm Mon-Thurs, 9am-noon Fri)* on the road to Mazara del Vallo (bus No 16 from Piazza del Popolo). This is the place to buy the cream of Marsala's wines. Florio opens its doors to visitors to explain the process of making Marsala and to give you a taste of the goods. Pellegrino, Rallo, Mavis and Intorcia are four of the other producers in the same area, and all have an *enoteca* (wine bar) where you can select a bottle or two (usually open from about 9am to 12.30pm). Booking is recommended; ask the tourist office. For free tasting, try the enotecas Luminario or La Ruota, both at Lungomare Boeo 36.

If you're travelling with small children, they might enjoy the small playground on Piazza della Vittoria, at the end of Via XI Maggio.

How Sweet it Is

Marsala wine was 'discovered' by Englishman John Woodhouse who, after landing in the city in 1773 and tasting the local product, decided it should be marketed throughout Europe. His first competitor was Benjamin Ingham, who established his own factory in the town and began exporting the wine to the USA and Australia.

One particularly interesting figure in the Marsala-making trade was Ingham's nephew, Joseph Whitaker. He bought the island of San Pantaleo, where the ancient city of Mothia was based, and built a villa there (now a museum – see 'Between Marsala and Trapani' later in this chapter). Whitaker was responsible for renewing interest in the archaeological site of Mothia and for the few excavations carried out.

Special Events

Marsala's most important annual religious event is the Processione del Giovedì Santo (Holy Thursday Procession). A tradition dating back centuries, the procession of actors depicts the events leading up to Christ's crucifixion. Many children participate in the procession, dressed in colourfu costumes as saints.

Places to Stay & Eat

Garden *(☎/fax 0923 98 23 20, Via Gambin 36)* Singles/doubles €33.55/49.05. The Garden is a good hotel, near the train station.

Hotel Cap 3000 *(☎ 0923 98 90 55, fax 0923 98 96 34, Via Trapani 161)* Singles doubles with bath €46.50/72.30. Rooms in this hotel are comfortable with telephone and TV, but it's outside the historical centre on the road to Trapani.

Baglio Vajarassa *(0923 96 86 28 Contrada Spagnola 176)* High season singles doubles €31/46.50. This agriturismo/mano house, 6km north of Marsala near Mothia is the most interesting accommodatio option – if you have your own wheels Prices include a hearty lunch.

Trattoria Garibaldi *(☎ 0923 95 30 06 Piazza dell'Addolorata 5)* Full meals abou €18.10. This place is a reliable trattoria specialising in fish.

Trattoria Alfayer *(☎ 0923 71 30 30, Lungomare Boeo 38)* Full meals €15.50 Hearty food, good prices.

Getting There & Away

Buses head for Marsala from Trapani (AS or Lumia, €2.30, 1 hour, eight daily), Agrigento (Lumia, 3½ hours, four daily) an Palermo (Salemi, €6.70, 2½ hours). Palerm buses arrive at Piazza del Popolo, off Vi Mazzini, in the centre of town. All othe buses stop on Piazza Pizzo. The Agrigent buses generally stop at Castelvetrano, fro where you can get another to Selinunte.

Trains serve Marsala from Trapani an Palermo, although from the latter you hav to change at Alcamo.

MARTIN LLADO

A colourful fishing boat, Giardini-Naxos, Sicily

IONAS KALTENBACH

Kids stuff – a colourful clothing store on Lipari

IONAS KALTENBACH

The weathered facade of a Strombolian house

BETH-UNE CARMICHAEL

Typical Norman architecture, south of Monreale

DAMIEN SIMONIS

All dressed up and nowhere to go on Sicily

BETHUNE CARMICHAEL

The stark ruins of the once-powerful Selinunte

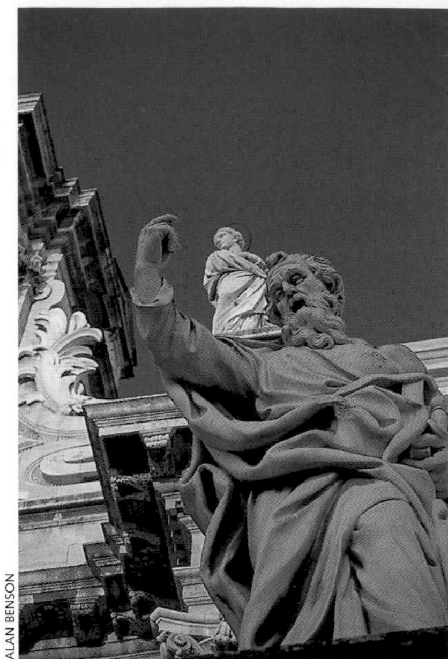
ALAN BENSON

Syracuse's 7th-century cathedral on Ortigia

BETHUNE CARMICHAEL

Calm waters: the ancient harbour town of Cefalù

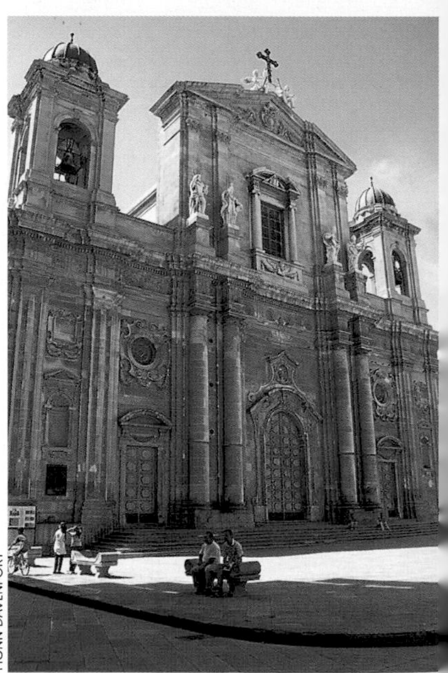
FIONN DAVENPORT

Marsala's cathedral dominates the main square.

Between June and September, Sandokan (☎ 0923 71 20 60 or 0923 95 34 34) runs a boat service from Molo Dogana to the Egadi Islands.

BETWEEN MARSALA & TRAPANI

The site of ancient **Mothia** (also known as Motya or Mozia), on the island of San Pantaleo in the Stagnone lagoon, is about 11km north along the scenic coast from Marsala. The island and lagoon form part of the **Riserva Naturale di Stagnone**, a noted wetlands area with a large population of water birds. Mozia was the site of one of the most important Phoenician settlements in the Mediterranean, coveted for its strategic position and eventually destroyed by Dionysius the Elder, tyrant of Syracuse, in 379 BC. The island is accessible by a ferry (€2.60 return) which operates 9am to 1pm and 3pm to around 6pm or 7pm, mornings only in winter. A local bus (No 4, direction Birgi) runs between Marsala's Piazza del Popolo and the ferry landing.

Today, it is the island's picturesque position in the saltpans, dotted with windmills and piles of salt, that attracts visitors. Little remains of the city of Mothia, but it is interesting to follow the path around the island to the various excavations, including the ancient port and dry dock. Note the submerged road at the port, which connects the island to the mainland. The island is home to the **Whitaker Museum** *(☎ 0923 71 25 98; admission €2.60; 9am-1pm & 3pm-6.30pm daily Mar-Sept, 9am-1pm daily Oct-Feb)*. Its main treasure is *Il Giovinetto di Mozia*, a 5th-century-BC Phoenician sculpture of a young boy.

At Nubia, 5km south of Trapani, is the **Museo delle Saline** *(☎ 0923 86 74 42; admission free; open 9am-1pm & 3pm-7pm daily)*, housed in a 17th-century salt mill. Exhibits demonstrate how the salt is extracted; water is pumped into the saltpan via a windmill then left to evaporate in the summer sun.

TRAPANI

postcode 91100 • pop 72,000

Although not one of Sicily's top attractions, Trapani is a comfortable base from which to explore the north-west. From the ancient Greek city of Segesta and the medieval town of Erice to the beaches of the Golfo di Castellammare, the Riserva Naturale dello Zingaro and the Egadi Islands, this small corner is a smorgasbord of Sicily's main delights.

A Carthaginian and later a Roman city, Trapani thrived as a trading centre under Arab and Norman rule and, after the arrival of the Spanish, enjoyed a period as western Sicily's most important town. Since then, slow decline has reduced it to a coastal backwater, kept afloat by moderate sea traffic and some fishing. A handful of Baroque churches and piazzas warrant some exploration and the town's Easter celebrations are a high point of the year.

I Misteri

Sicily's most venerated Easter procession is a four-day festival of extraordinary religious fervour. Since the 17th century, the ordinary citizens of Trapani – represented by 20 traditional *maestranze* or guilds – have begun the celebration of the Passion of Christ on the Tuesday before Easter Sunday. The festival beings with the procession of a remarkable, life-sized wooden statue of the Virgin Mary.

Over the course of the next three evenings, processions make their way through the old quarter and port to a temporary chapel in Piazza Lucatelli specially erected for the celebrations, where the icons are stored overnight. Each statue is carried on the shoulders of the town's men and is accompanied by barefooted women and a local band, which plays dirges to the slow, steady beat of a drum.

The high point of the celebration is on Friday afternoon, when the 20 guilds emerge from the Chiesa del Purgatorio and descend the steps of the church carrying each of the statues to begin the 1km-long all night procession up to Via Giovan Battista Fardella and back to the church the following morning. The massive crowds that gather to witness the slow march often reach a peak of delirious fervour. If you're not around at Easter, you can always see the figures in Chiesa del Purgatorio, where they are stored throughout the year.

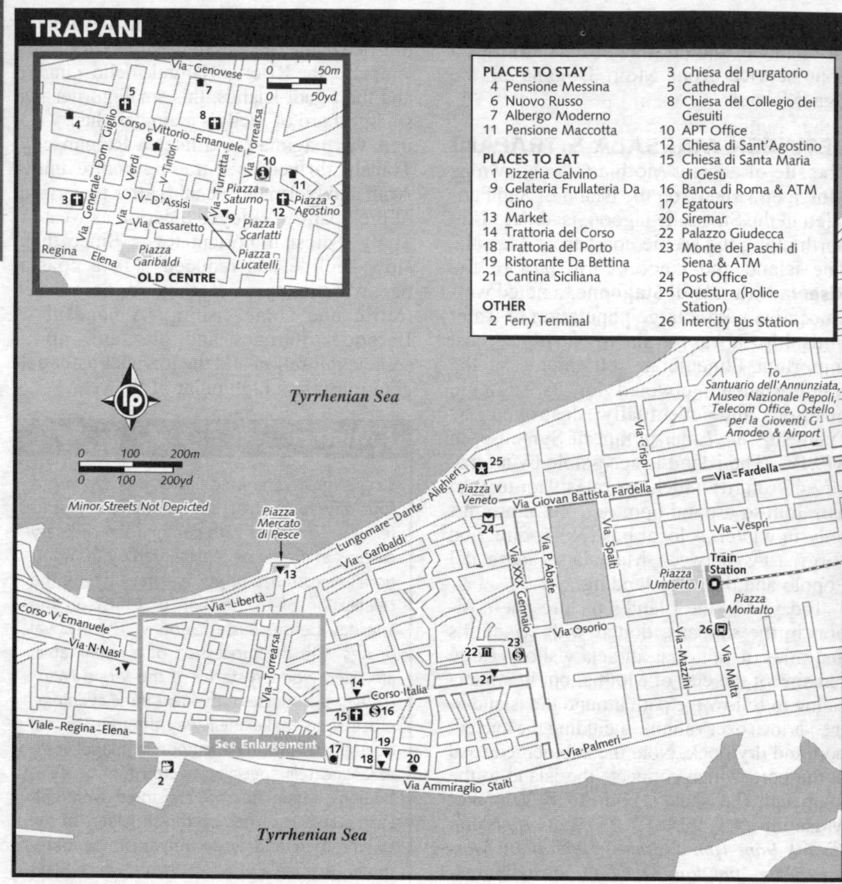

Orientation

The main bus station is on Piazza Montalto, with the train station around the corner on Piazza Umberto I. The cheaper hotels are in the heart of the old centre, about 500m west. Make for Piazza Scarlatti down Corso Italia. The narrow streets of the old part of town can be a nightmare to negotiate if you're driving, so head for the port and park near there.

Information

Tourist Offices The well-organised APT office (☎ 0923 2 90 00, e apttp@mail.cinet.it, w www.apt.trapani.it) on Piazza Saturno, off Piazza Scarlatti, gets the prize for most hard-working tourist office in Italy. It opens 8am to 8pm Monday to Saturday and 9am to noon on Sunday.

Post & Communications The main post office is on Piazza V Veneto and opens 8.20am to 7pm Monday to Saturday. The Telecom office is at Via Agostino Pepoli 47.

Money There are several banks in the town. The Banca di Roma, on Corso Italia, and Monte dei Paschi di Siena, at Via XXX Gennaio 80, have ATMs.

Medical Services & Emergency The Ospedale Sant'Antonio Abate (hospital; ☎ 0923 80 91 11) is on Via Cosenza, some distance from the centre of town. Dial the same number for an ambulance, or dial *pronto soccorso* (casualty) on ☎ 0923 80 94 50. For the Guardia Medica, Piazza Generale Scio 1, call ☎ 0923 2 96 29.

The *questura* (police station; ☎ 0923 59 81 11) is on Via Virgilio, off Piazza V Veneto.

Things to See

The 16th-century **Palazzo della Giudecca** on Via Giudecca, with its distinctive facade, stands out among the general decay of the old and run-down Jewish quarter. Cross Corso Italia and walk west to reach the **Chiesa di Santa Maria di Gesù** on Via San Pietro, whose exterior has both Gothic and Renaissance features. The 14th-century **Chiesa di Sant'Agostino** *(Piazza Saturno; open 8am-noon & 3.30pm-7pm daily)* is worth a look for its fine Gothic rose window and portal. Continue along Corso Vittorio Emanuele, noting the 17th-century town hall and **Chiesa del Collegio dei Gesuiti**, before reaching the **cathedral**, with its Baroque facade and iced-Christmas-cake-style stuccoed interior. Off the corso, south along Via Generale Dom Giglio, **Chiesa del Purgatorio** *(☎ 0923 56 28 82, Via D'Assisi; admission free; open 4pm-6.30pm daily)* houses the Misteri, 18th-century life-size wooden figures depicting Christ's Passion. On Good Friday, they are carried in procession (see the boxed text 'I Misteri' earlier).

Trapani's major sight is the 14th-century **Santuario dell'Annunziata** *(☎ 0923 53 91 84, Via Conte Agostino Pepoli; admission free; open 7am-noon & 4pm-7pm daily)*, some way from the centre on Via A Pepoli. Remodelled in Baroque style in the 17th century, it retains its original Gothic rose window and doorway. The Cappella della Madonna, behind the high altar, contains the venerated *Madonna di Trapani*, carved, it's thought, by Nino Pisano.

Adjacent to the Santuario dell'Annunziata, in a former Carmelite monastery, is the **Museo Nazionale Pepoli** *(☎ 0923 55 32 69, Via Conte Agostino Pepoli 2000; admission €3.10; open 9am-1.30pm Mon, Wed, Fri & Sat, 9am-1.30pm & 3pm-6.30pm Tues & Thurs, 9am-12.30pm Sun)*. It has an archaeological collection, statues and coral carvings.

Places to Stay

Ostello per la Gioventù G Amodeo *(☎ 0923 55 29 64, fax 0923 55 29 64, Strada Provinciale Trapani-Erice, Contrada Raganzili)* B&B €11.90. Open year-round. This hostel is a few kilometres up the winding road from Trapani to Erice.

Pensione Messina *(☎ 0923 2 11 98, Corso Vittorio Emanuele 71)* Singles/doubles €15.50/31. This small hotel has very basic rooms. Redeeming features are that the building dates from the 17th century and that this is Trapani's cheapest hotel.

Pensione Maccotta *(☎ 0923 2 84 18, fax 0923 43 76 93, Via degli Argentieri 4)* Singles/doubles without bath €20.65/41.30, singles/doubles with bath €25.80/51.65. Located near Piazza S Agostino, this small place is probably the most centrally located in Trapani. Its simple rooms are of a good standard.

Albergo Moderno *(☎ 0923 2 12 47, fax 0923 2 33 48, Via Genovese 20)* Singles/doubles with bath €23.25/34.60. The not-so-modern Moderno has rather basic rooms.

Nuovo Russo *(☎ 0923 2 21 66, fax 0923 2 66 23, Via Tintori 4)* Singles/doubles with bath €36.15/62. More upmarket than the other options, the Nuovo Russo has very clean, simple rooms, some of which are classics of the 1950s, and friendly management.

Places to Eat

Sicily's Arab heritage and Trapani's unique position on the sea route to Tunisia has made couscous (or cuscus/kuscus as they spell it here) something of a speciality, particularly when served with a fish sauce that includes tomatoes, garlic and parsley.

Gelateria Frullateria Da Gino *(Piazza Lucatelli 2)* Open Tues-Sun. The word on the streets of Trapani is that Gino's does the best ice cream in town, and if the hordes of young Trapanese spilling out of its doors is anything to go by, the word is right.

Pizzeria Calvino *(Via N Nasi 77)* Pizzas from €3.10. You can't get a much better recommendation than being told this place (towards the port off Corso Vittorio Emanuele) is the town's favourite takeaway pizza and pasta place.

Trattoria del Porto *(☎ 0923 54 78 22, Via Ammiraglio Staiti 45)* Meals €18.10. This place, on the southern waterfront, is popular with locals and serves reliably good meals. It's also known as Da Felice.

Ristorante Da Bettina *(☎ 0923 2 48 00, Via San Cristoforo 5–7)* Full meals from €15.50. Open Tues-Sun. It's not often that a restaurant in a port area is one of the best in town; in this case it is. Don't miss the kuscus (sic) with fish.

Cantina Siciliana *(☎ 0923 2 86 73, Via Giudecca 52)* Full meals €15.50. You'll eat well at this popular restaurant opposite the Palazzo Giudecca.

Trattoria del Corso *(☎ 0923 2 34 75, Corso Italia 91)* Pasta €6.20-7.75, mains €5.15-7.75. *Spaghetti con i ricci* (with the rich insides of spiky sea anemones) is one of the specialities here. Fish mains tend to be more expensive than meat ones.

An open-air ***market*** is held every Monday to Saturday morning on Piazza Mercato di Pesce, on the northern waterfront. The area around Piazza Lucatelli is a pleasant place for a sandwich and coffee.

Getting There & Around

Air Trapani has a small airport, 16km out of town at Birgi. AST buses leave from Piazza Montalto to coincide with flights. Segesta (☎ 091 34 20 55) has a daily bus for the island's main airport, Falcone-Borsellino, at Punta Raisi. Its timetable changes regularly, so check with the APT office.

Bus Segesta (☎ 091 34 20 55) runs express buses (around eight daily) connecting Trapani with Palermo. Lumia (☎ 0923 2 17 54) serves Agrigento (four daily). All intercity buses use Piazza Montalto, from where AST (☎ 0923 232 22) buses serve Erice (approximately every hour), Castellammare del Golfo (four per day), Castelvetrano (seven daily), Marsala and Mazara del Vallo (four daily), and San Vito lo Capo (six daily). Autoservizi Tarantola runs a bus service to Segesta and Calatafimi (six per day Monday to Friday, two on Sunday).

The APT office has updated timetables of all bus routes.

A free bus (No 11) does a circular trip through Trapani, leaving from the bus station and stopping at the train station on the return leg.

Train Trains connect Trapani to Palermo (note that some trains run via Marsala and are therefore slow), Castelvetrano and Marsala. For Segesta, you can either get off at Segesta Tempio (one train per day), from where you'll have to walk 3km to the temple, or Calatafimi (many) on the way to Palermo. The stations are roughly equidistant from the ancient Greek site.

Boat Siremar runs ferries and hydrofoils to the Egadi Islands. The high-season one-way fare to Favignana (the main island) and also to Levanzo is €5.20 on the hydrofoil (20 minutes). The journey to Marettimo costs €11.70. Tickets are cheaper on the slower car ferries. Siremar's ticket office (☎ 0923 54 54 55, ⓔ siremar@gestelnet.it, ⓦ www.siremar.it) is at Via Ammiraglio Staiti 61. The same company runs a daily ferry to Pantelleria at midnight June to September (with a reduced service the rest of the year). The high-season fare for the six-hour trip is €20.40. The boat returns (usually) at noon, reaching Trapani at 4.45pm.

Ustica Lines (☎ 0923 2 22 00) runs regular hydrofoils to the Egadi Islands (€6), as well as a service from Naples to Trapani (€80 one way), via Ustica (€60) and the Egadi Islands (€73). It also has a ferry to Pantelleria (€31). Get tickets at Egatours, Via Ammiraglio Staiti 13, or directly at the Ustica Lines embarkation point.

Tirrenia runs weekly ferries to Tunisia from Trapani, leaving at 10am on Monday. Tickets for the eight-hour trip cost €51 for an airline-type seat and €63.30 for a bed in a 2nd-class cabin in the high season. The return boat leaves Tunisia at 9pm. There is also a weekly Tirrenia service to Cagliari, leaving at 9pm on Tuesday. Tickets cost €37.70 for an airline-style seat and €51.20

for a bed in a 2nd-class cabin. Tickets can be purchased at Salvo Viaggi (☎ 0923 54 54 11), Corso Italia 48, or directly from the ferry terminal (☎ 0923 54 54 33 or call centre 199 12 31 99).

ERICE

postcode 91016 • pop 29,000

This dramatic medieval town, 750m above the sea, is about 40 minutes from Trapani by bus and should not be missed on any account. Settled by the Elymians, an ancient mountain people who also founded Segesta, it was an important religious site associated with the goddess of fertility – first the Carthaginian Astarte, then the Greek Aphrodite and finally the Roman Venus. It has unfortunately become a bit of a tourist trap (watch out for exorbitant charges for food and drinks), but manages to maintain a relatively authentic medieval atmosphere.

The tourist office (☎ 0923 86 93 88) is at Viale Conte Pepoli 56. It opens 9am to 1pm Monday to Friday. An additional tourist information booth at the car park in Piazza Grammatico, just outside the Porta Trapani entrance, operates 9am to 5pm Saturday, 9am to 3pm Sunday and 9am to 4pm Monday. Both provide maps and information on the town.

Things to See

The triangular-shaped town is best explored by pottering around its narrow streets and peeking through the doorways into courtyards. On the hilltop is the Norman **Castello di Venere** *(Castle of Venus; Via Castello di Venere; admission free; open 8am-7pm daily)*, built in the 12th and 13th centuries over an ancient temple of Venus. Not much more than a ruin, the castle is upstaged by the panoramic vistas north-east to San Vito lo Capo and Monte Cofano and west to Trapani.

Of the several churches and other monuments in the small, quiet town, the 14th-century **Chiesa Matrice** *(Via V Carvini; admission free; open 10am-1pm & 3pm-6pm daily)*, just inside Porta Trapani, is probably the most interesting by virtue of its separate campanile with mullioned windows. The interior of the church was remodelled in neogothic style in the 19th century (with heavy use of royal-icing-like stucco) but the 15th-century side chapels were conserved.

Places to Stay & Eat

Unless you're staying at the youth hostel, don't stay overnight if you can help it – tourism has got the better of hotel room rates in Erice.

Ostello della Gioventù CSI *(☎/fax 0923 55 29 64, Viale delle Pinete)* Beds €15.50. Open mid-Jun–late-Sep. This hostel is about 1km out of Erice, off the road to Trapani.

Edelweiss *(☎ 0923 86 94 20, fax 0923 86 91 58, Cortile Vincenzo 5)* Singles/doubles €62/82.65. This is about as cheap as it gets in Erice!

Moderno *(☎ 0923 86 93 00, fax 0923 86 91 39, via Vittorio Emanuele 63)* Singles/doubles with bath €77.45/113.60. One of the more upmarket choices in upmarket Erice, the Moderno has all the comforts you'd want in a three-star hotel, and is ideally located in the centre of the medieval town.

Erice has some delicious cafes to while away a few hours.

Caffè Maria *(☎ 0923 86 96 96, Via Vittorio Emanuele 4)*. Regardless of the length of your stay in Erice – hours or days – you *cannot* leave without a visit to this place. The cannoli here are to die for. If you go to the actual *pasticceria* (pastry shop) a few doors down, you might get a glimpse of the pastry cooks at work.

Pasticceria Michele *(☎ 0923 86 96 72, Via Vittorio Emanuele 10–12)* This is a superb but pricey place for a coffee and a pastry.

Ristorante La Pentolaccia *(☎ 0923 86 98 99, Via G Guarnotta 17)* Pasta from €6.20. This atmospheric but touristy restaurant is in a 16th-century former monastery.

Getting There & Away

There are regular AST buses (hourly in summer) to Trapani (Piazza Montalto).

SEGESTA

The ancient Elymians must have been great aesthetes if their choice of sites for cities is any indication. Along with Erice and Entella, they founded Segesta on and around Monte

Barbaro. The Greeks later took over and it is to them that we owe the two outstanding survivors: the theatre high up on the mountain with commanding views out to sea (how did spectators concentrate on the show with such a backdrop?) and the temple.

The city was in constant conflict with Selinunte in the south and this rivalry led it to seek assistance from a succession of allies, including Carthage, Athens, Syracuse and the Romans, and eventually Selinunte was destroyed. Time has done to Segesta what violence inflicted on Selinunte, and little remains save the theatre and the never-completed Doric **temple** *(☎ 0924 95 23 56; admission €4.15; open 9am-4pm daily Nov-Mar, 9am-7pm daily Apr-Aug)*, the latter dating from around 430 BC and remarkably well preserved. The Hellenistic **theatre** is also in a fair state of repair and the only structure inside the old city walls to have survived intact. Nearby are ruins of a castle and church built in the Middle Ages. A shuttle bus runs every 30 minutes from the entrance 1.5km uphill to the theatre and costs an additional €1.05. If you've got the energy, walk up instead – the views are magical.

During July and August of every odd-numbered year (alternating with Syracuse), performances of Greek plays are staged in the theatre. For information, contact the APT office in Trapani.

Segesta is accessible by Autoservizi Tarantola bus (☎ 0924 3 10 20) from Piazza Malta in Trapani (at 8am, 10am, noon, 2pm, 5pm and 7.30pm, €4.15 return) or from Palermo (Piazza Marina) at 7.50am and 2pm. Otherwise catch an infrequent train from Trapani or Palermo to Segesta Tempio; the site is then a 20-minute walk away.

GOLFO DI CASTELLAMMARE

Saved from development and road projects by local protests, the tranquil and wildly beautiful **Riserva Naturale dello Zingaro** *(☎ 0924 54 11 97; admission free; open 7am-9pm daily May-Aug, 7am-6pm daily Sept-Apr)* is the star attraction on the gulf. A stroll up the coast between San Vito lo Capo and the little fishing village of Scopello will take about four hours along a clearly marked track. There are also several trails inland, which are detailed on maps available for a small fee at the information offices at the park's two entrances (near Scopello and near San Vito lo Capo). **Punta della Capreria** is a pebble beach in a tiny cove about 1km from the Scopello entrance to the park.

Once home to tuna fishers, **Scopello** now mainly hosts tourists – although its sleepy village atmosphere remains unspoiled. Its port is interesting to visit, with an abandoned *tonnara* (tuna processing plant) and *faraglione* (rock towers rising out of the sea).

There are numerous camp sites in the area, all of which have good facilities.

International Camping Soleado *(☎ 0923 97 21 66, fax 0923 97 21 66, Via del Secco 40, San Vito lo Capo)* Adult/child/tent €5.15/3.60/6.70.

Camping La Fata *(☎ 0923 97 21 33, fax 0923 97 21 33, Via Piersanti Mattarella, San Vito lo Capo)* €5.15 per person.

Camping Baia di Guidaloca *(☎ 0924 54 12 62, fax 0924 3 04 43, Località Guidaloca, Castellammare del Golfo)* Adult/child/tent €5.40/2.85/5.15. This is a well-equipped camp site, located near a lovely swimming hole (the Cala Bianca) and on the bus route between Scopello and Castellammare del Golfo.

There are numerous pensiones and hotels at touristy **San Vito lo Capo** and at **Castellammare del Golfo**, a busy coastal town with an interesting medieval core 10km south-east of Scopello. The APT office at Trapani has a full list.

Punta Nord Est *(☎ 0924 305 11, Via Leonardo da Vinci 67, Castellammare del Golfo)* High season singles/doubles up to €62/92.95. This well-equipped hotel in busy Castellammare del Golfo has comfortable rooms, a bar, restaurant and TV and phones in all rooms, but you'll probably do better in Scopello.

Pensione Tranchina *(☎ 0924 54 10 99, fax 0924 54 10 99, Via Diaz 7, Scopello)* Singles/doubles with bath up to €41.30/62. This is an excellent small hotel, with comfortable rooms. The hotel is a good choice; it also has a restaurant which serves whatever fish is fresh that day – but unless you're a hotel guest, you'll need to make a booking to eat there.

AST buses run to San Vito lo Capo and Castellammare del Golfo from Trapani's Piazza Malta. From Castellammare, it is possible to catch a bus to Scopello. There is no road through the Zingaro park.

EGADI ISLANDS (ISOLE EGADI)

For centuries the Egadi islanders have lived from tuna fishing. Nowadays tourism looks set to be the main earner – even the *mattanza*, the almost ritual slaughtering of tuna, is becoming a spectator sport (see the boxed text 'La Mattanza'). Made up of three islands, the archipelago is only a short hop from Trapani.

Favignana

Windswept Monte Santa Caterina dominates the otherwise flat main island of Favignana. It is pleasant to explore, with plenty of rocky coves and crystal-clear water. Wander around the tonnara at the port. It was closed at the end of the 1970s due to the general crisis in the local tuna fishing industry. A lack of funding has blocked plans to turn the building into a complex which would include a school and art and craft shops.

There is a Pro Loco office (☎ 0923 92 16 47) at Piazza Matrice 8 in Favignana town, which opens 9am to 12.30pm and 4pm to 8pm Monday to Saturday plus 9.30am to 12.30pm on Sunday from June to September. You'll find dive hire outlets and bicycles for rent around town and the small harbour.

Places to Stay & Eat There's plenty of accommodation on Favignana, although during the period of the mattanza and in August you'll have trouble finding a bed without a booking. Many local people rent out rooms. The cheapest option is to pitch a tent.

Miramare *(☎ 0923 92 13 30, fax 0923 92 22 00, W www.egadi.com/miramare, Località Costicella)* Adult/child €12.40/5.70. This place is a well-equipped camp site with a decent campers' kitchen and good bathrooms.

Albergo Bouganville *(☎ 0923 92 20 33, fax 0923 92 26 49, Via Cimabue 10)* High season singles/doubles €28.40/51.65. Out of high season, prices for decent rooms at this small hotel drop by about 10–15%. There's also a decent restaurant attached.

Albergo Egadi *(☎ 0923 92 12 32, Via Colombo 17)* Singles/doubles €25.80/51.65, half-board €56.80. This place is just off Favignana town's main piazza and has comfortable rooms. It has an acclaimed restaurant, where you'll eat one of your best meals in Italy at a very reasonable price.

La Mattanza

A centuries-old tradition, the Egadi Islands' *mattanza* (the ritual slaughter of tuna) survives despite the ever-decreasing number of tuna fish swimming in the local waters each year. For centuries, schools of tuna have used the waters around western Sicily as a mating ground. Locals can recall the golden days of the islands' fishing industry, when it wasn't uncommon to catch giant breeding tuna of between 200 and 300kg. Fish that size are rare these days due to worldwide overfishing of tuna, and the annual catch is increasingly smaller. However, even though the islands' fishing industry is in severe crisis as a result, the tradition of the mattanza goes on.

Now that the slaughter of tuna can no longer support the islands' economy, it is reinventing itself as a tourist attraction. From around 20 May to 10 June, tourists flock to the Egadi Islands to witness the event. For a fee you can join the fishers in their boats and watch them catching the tuna at close hand – note that you'll need a strong stomach. This is no ordinary fishing expedition: the fishers organise their boats and nets in a complex formation designed to channel the tuna into a series of enclosures that culminate in the *camera della morte* (chamber of death). Once enough tuna are imprisoned there, the fishers close in and the mattanza begins (the word is derived from the Spanish word for killing). It is a bloody affair – up to eight or more fishers at a time will sink huge hooks into a tuna and drag it aboard. Anyone who has seen Rossellini's classic *Stromboli* will no doubt recall the famous mattanza scene.

Levanzo

This island, 4km north of Favignana, is known for its beaches and for the **Grotta del Genovese**, a cave with walls bearing Palaeolithic etchings of bison and deer and a series of fascinating figures dating from the Neolithic period. The figures of women and men were 'painted' using animal fat and carbon. Interestingly, there is also a representation of a tuna fish – indicating that tuna fishing in the Egadi Islands is indeed an ancient tradition. If you have the time, this is an experience not to be missed. You can go to the cave on your own following the path that crosses the island. Alternatively, contact the custodian of the cave (☎ 0923 92 40 32); he does guided tours (€12.90) for small groups.

Accommodation options are limited as Levanzo has only two pensiones.

Paradiso *(☎ 0923 92 40 80, Via Lungomare)* Singles/doubles with bath €23.25/43.90. Paradiso is on the seafront. It has a restaurant where you'll eat very well for around €20.65 per head.

Marettimo

The most distant of the islands is also the least modern. A few hundred people live mostly in the tiny village on the eastern coast and there are no roads. You can go with fishing boats along the coast or follow mule tracks into the scenic hills. But its beaches are the island's main drawcards.

There are no hotels on Marettimo, but you should be able to dig up a room with the locals.

Getting There & Away

Ferries and hydrofoils run between the islands and to Trapani. See the Trapani section for more details.

PANTELLERIA

Known to the Carthaginians as Cossyra, the island fell to the Romans in 217 BC and five centuries later to the Arabs. The Arab presence lives on in the names of various localities. Pantelleria is a curious place that lies closer to Tunisia than Sicily. It has sea and sunshine and a mountainous, volcanic interior, with thermal springs and remnants of several ancient settlements, such as Mursia, a few kilometres south of the main town. Giorgio Armani, Michelle Pfeiffer, Isabella Rossellini and Sting have all sought out the island's magic.

There is a small tourist office (☎ 0923 91 18 38) on Piazza Cavour, open Monday to Saturday June to September. The island has a Web site W www.pantelleria.it.

There is nothing cheap here, especially in summer, when it is best to book ahead.

Albergo Miryam *(☎ 0923 91 13 74, fax 0923 91 17 77, Corso Umberto I)* Low season singles/doubles with bath €38.75/62, high season singles/doubles with bath €54.25/77.45. High prices, but probably your best bet in summer.

You can also rent *dammusi*, the characteristic domed houses of the island.

Siremar boats go to Trapani (see Getting There & Around under Trapani) and Alilauro's summer season Trapani-Tunisia boat generally calls in at Pantelleria on the way.

Sardinia (Sardegna)

The second largest island in the Mediterranean, Sardinia has always been considered an isolated land. Even today, its people and culture maintain a separate identity from the mainland, which they call *il continente* (the continent).

The island is dotted with some 7000 *nuraghi*, the conical megalithic stone fortresses that are the only remnants of the island's first inhabitants, the Nuraghic people. This sheep-rearing race lived in separate communities led by warrior-kings and their culture flourished from around 1800 BC.

Sardinia's coast was visited by Greeks and Phoenicians, first as traders then as invaders, and the island was colonised by the Romans. They were followed in turn by the Pisans, Genoese, Spanish, Austrians and, finally, the Royal House of Savoy, the future kings of a united Italy. In 1948 Sardinia became a semi-autonomous region.

Despite the succession of invaders and colonisers, it is often said that the Sardinians (known as the Sardi) were never really conquered, but simply retreated into the hills. The Romans were prompted to call the island's central-eastern mountains the Barbagia (from the Latin word for barbarian) because of the uncompromising lifestyle of the warrior-shepherds, who never abandoned their Nuraghic customs. Even today, the Sardi of the interior speak an ancient Latin-based dialect and proudly maintain traditional customs and costume. Until the late 1980s, many of the island's shepherds spent long periods in almost complete isolation, living in traditional conical shelters of stone and wood called *pinnettas*. These days the shepherds reach their sheep by 4WD and sometimes walkers are given permission to use the shelters as refuges.

As described by DH Lawrence, Sardinia's 'savage, dark-bushed, sky-exposed land' has incredibly beautiful gorges and highlands and kilometres of unspoiled coastline with salt lakes and herons. Hunters have always been active in Sardinia, but some wildlife remains, notably the wild pig, the golden and Bonelli's eagles, the peregrine falcon, pink flamingoes, the Sardinian deer and a

Highlights

- Visit the ancient Su Nuraxi fortress at Barumini
- Swim at the sand-duned beaches along the unspoiled Costa Verde
- Make the challenging descent into the magnificent Gola di Gorropu
- Explore the coast between Cala Gonone and Santa Maria Navarrese, with its numerous isolated coves and beaches accessible only on foot or by boat
- Feast on a traditional meal of *porcheddu* (roast suckling pig) washed down with some good Sardinian wine
- Take a ferry to the lively island of La Maddalena and go walking in the nearby nature reserve of Caprera
- Climb to the hidden, mountain-top ruins at Tiscali

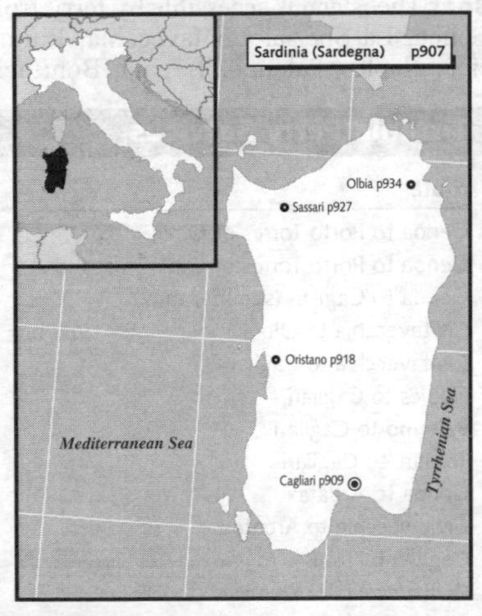

SARDINIA

colony of griffon vultures on the west coast. Miniature horses are raised on the Giara di Gesturi plain in the south-west. Unfortunately, the famous colony of Mediterranean monk seals previously found at the Grotta del Bue Marino, near Cala Gonone, has not been sighted for some years.

The island offers visitors a wide range of attractions, from spectacular beaches and archaeological treasures to the isolated interior, perfect for the more adventurous traveller. If you do venture into the interior, you will find the people extremely gracious and hospitable, although you might find it difficult to make initial contact. Try to avoid coming to the island in July and August, when the weather is very hot and the beaches are overcrowded. Warm weather generally continues from April to October.

Getting There & Away

Air The airports at Cagliari, Olbia, Alghero and Arbatax-Tortoli link Sardinia with major Italian and European cities.

Boat The island is accessible by ferry from Genoa, La Spezia, Civitavecchia, Fiumicino, Naples, Palermo, Trapani, Bonifacio (Corsica) and Tunisia, as well as Toulon and Marseille in France. The departure points in Sardinia are Olbia, Golfo Aranci, Palau and Porto Torres in the north, Arbatax on the east coast and Cagliari in the south.

The main ferry company is Tirrenia. See the boxed text 'Tirrenia Ferry Services' for details of routes and prices.

Ferrovie dello Stato (FS, the Italian state railway) runs a slightly cheaper ferry service between Civitavecchia and Golfo Aranci. Other companies include Moby Lines, which runs ferries from Livorno to Olbia as well as between Sardinia and Corsica, and Sardinia Ferries, operating from Livorno or Civitavecchia to Golfo Aranci. Brochures detailing Moby Lines, Sardinia Ferries and Tirrenia services are available at most travel agencies. Note that timetables change dramatically every year and that prices fluctuate according to the season. During the low season, the frequency of some services is reduced.

Addresses and telephone numbers for Tirrenia's offices in Sardinia are listed throughout this chapter. Nationwide offices include Via Bissolati 41, Rome; Stazione Marittima, Civitavecchia; and Stazione

Tirrenia Ferry Services

route	fares	duration
Genoa to Porto Torres or Olbia	€43/53.20/68	13 hours
Genoa to Porto Torres or Olbia (fast ferry)	€71/92	6 hours
Genoa to Cagliari (summer only)	€53/68/85.30	20 hours
Civitavecchia to Olbia	€23/33/41	8 hours
Civitavecchia to Cagliari	€40/50/66	14½ hours
Naples to Cagliari	€41/56/73	16 hours
Palermo to Cagliari	€38/51/67	13½ hours
Trapani to Cagliari	€38/51/67	11½ hours
Genoa to Arbatax	€44/57/71	19 hours
Civitavecchia to Arbatax	€34/43/53	10½ hours
Cagliari to Tunis	€59/73/100	11½ hours
Civitavecchia or Fiumicino to Olbia or Golfo Aranci (fast ferry, summer only)	€45/60	4 hours

Fares listed are for a air-line style seat *(poltrona)* in a 2nd-class cabin, a bed in a 2nd-class cabin and a bed in a 1st-class cabin. Services run year-round unless specified otherwise.

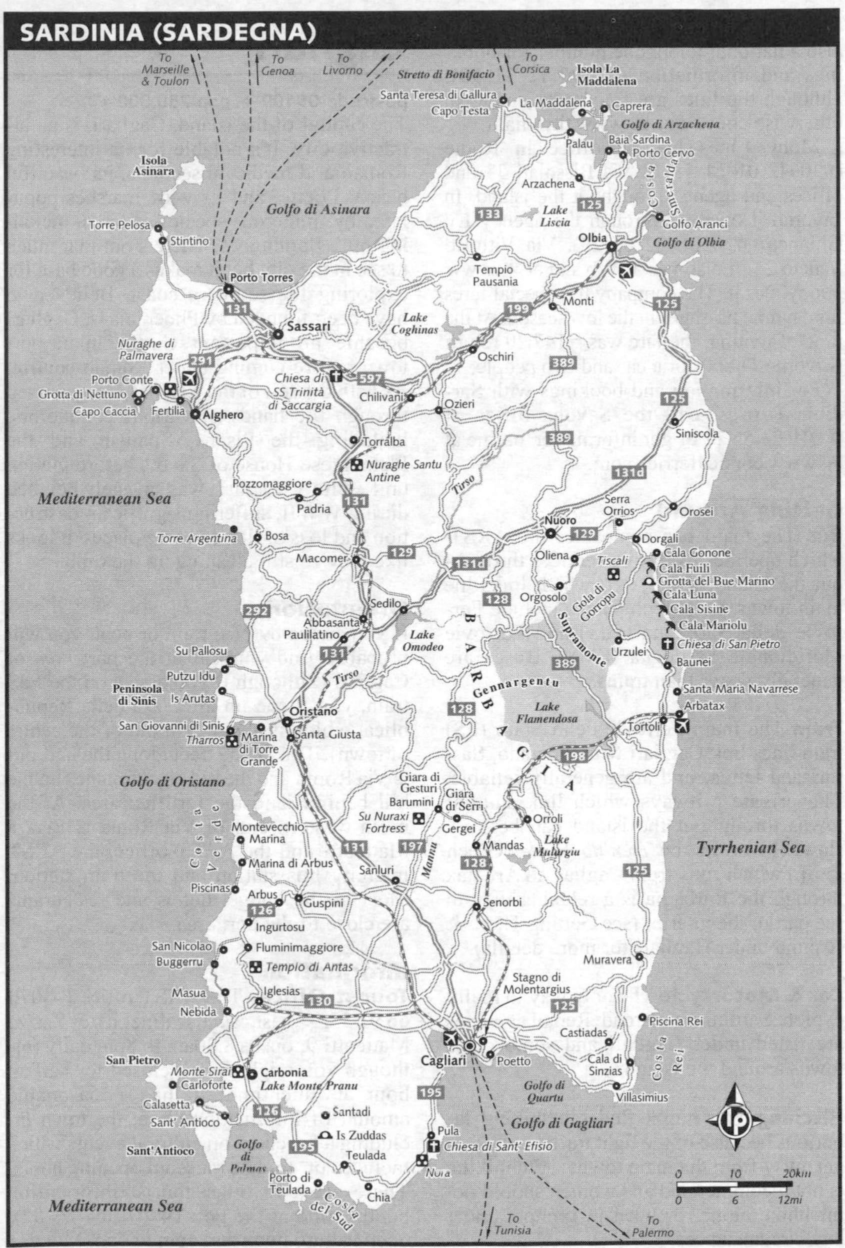
SARDINIA (SARDEGNA)
To Marseille & Toulon
To Genoa
To Livorno
Stretto di Bonifacio
To Corsica
Isola La Maddalena
Santa Teresa di Gallura
Capo Testa
La Maddalena
Caprera
Golfo di Arzachena
Palau
Baia Sardina
Porto Cervo
Arzachena
Costa Smeralda
Isola Asinara
Golfo di Asinara
Lake Liscia
Golfo Aranci
Golfo di Olbia
Olbia
Torre Pelosa
Stintino
Tempio Pausania
Porto Torres
Monti
Sassari
Lake Coghinas
Nuraghe di Palmavera
Oschiri
Porto Conte
Chiesa di SS Trinità di Saccargia
Grotta di Nettuno
Capo Caccia
Fertilia
Alghero
Chilivani
Ozieri
Siniscola
Torralba
Nuraghe Santu Antine
Tirso
Pozzomaggiore
Padria
Mediterranean Sea
Serra Orrios
Orosei
Nuoro
Torre Argentina
Bosa
Dorgali
Cala Gonone
Macomer
Oliena
Tiscali
Cala Fuili
Grotta del Bue Marino
Cala Luna
Cala Sisine
Cala Mariolu
Orgosolo
Gola di Gorropu
Supramonte
Sedilo
Abbasanta
Paulilatino
Lake Omodeo
BARBAGIA
Urzulei
Chiesa di San Pietro
Baunei
Su Pallosu
Putzu Idu
Gennargentu
Santa Maria Navarrese
Peninsola di Sinis
Is Arutas
Arbatax
Lake Flamendosa
Oristano
San Giovanni di Sinis
Tortolì
Tharros
Marina di Torre Grande
Santa Giusta
Giara di Gesturi
Golfo di Oristano
Giara di Serri
Barumini
Su Nuraxi Fortress
Gergei
Orroli
Costa Verde
Montevecchio
Marina
Mandas
Lake Mulargia
Tyrrhenian Sea
Marina di Arbus
Mannu
Sanluri
Piscinas
Arbus
Guspini
Senorbi
Ingurtosu
San Nicolao
Fluminimaggiore
Buggerru
Tempio di Antas
Muravera
Stagno di Molentargius
Masua
Iglesias
Nebida
Piscina Rei
Castiadas
Costa Rei
San Pietro
Cagliari
Poetto
Cala di Sinzias
Monte Sirai
Carbonia
Carloforte
Lake Monte Pranu
Golfo di Quartu
Villasimius
Calasetta
Santadi
Sant' Antioco
Golfo di Gagliari
Is Zuddas
Pula
Sant'Antioco
Golfo di Palmas
Chiesa di Sant' Efisio
Teulada
Nora
Porto di Teulada
Chia
Costa del Sud
Mediterranean Sea
To Tunisia
To Palermo
0 10 20km
0 6 12mi
133 125 131 199 291 597 389 131d 129 292 128 198 197 126 130 195

SARDINIA

Marittima Ponte Colombo, Genoa. There is also a national telephone number for bookings and information (☎ 199 12 31 99), although the lines are frequently engaged; otherwise check out W www.tirrenia.it.

Moby Lines has an office in Rome (☎ 0642 01 14 55) at Via Bissolati 33 and offices and agents throughout the island. In Livorno it operates through the agency LV Ghianda (☎ 0586 82 68 23), Via Vittorio Veneto 24. It also has a Web site at W www.mobylines.it. The company has special fares for daytime passages in the low season. At the time of writing, the fare was €147.20 return (Livorno-Olbia) for a car and two people.

For information and bookings with Sardinia Ferries, call the Savona office at ☎ 019 21 55 11 or get information online at W www.corsicaferries.com.

Getting Around

Bus The main bus companies are ARST, which operates extensive services throughout the island; and PANI, which links the main towns. Other companies include Ferrovie della Sardegna (FdS) and Ferrovie Meridionale Sardegna (FMS). Buses are generally faster than trains.

Train The main Ferrovie dello Stato (FS) train lines link Cagliari with Oristano, Sassari and Olbia, and are generally reliable. The private railways which link smaller towns throughout the island can be very slow. However, the *Trenino Verde* (Green Train) which runs from Cagliari to Arbatax through the Barbagia is a relaxing way to see part of the interior (see Getting There & Around under Cagliari for more details).

Car & Motorcycle The only way to really explore Sardinia is by road. Rental agencies are listed under Cagliari and some other towns around the island.

Hitching You might find hitchhiking laborious because of the light traffic once you get away from the main towns. Hitchhiking is not recommended and women should not hitchhike alone, or even in groups, under any circumstances.

Cagliari

postcode 09100 • pop 250,000

The capital of the island, Cagliari, is an attractive city. It's notable for its interesting Roman and medieval sections, its beautiful beach, Poetto, and its wide marshes populated by numerous species of birds, including pink flamingoes. There's not that much to see in the city but it makes a good base for exploring the southern coast. Believed to have been founded by Phoenicians, Cagliari became an important Carthaginian port town before coming under Roman control. As with the rest of the island, the city passed through the hands of various conquerors, including the Pisans, Spanish and the Piemontese House of Savoy, before joining unified Italy. Cagliari was savagely bombed during WWII, suffering significant destruction and loss of life. In some places, it looks like they're still cleaning up the rubble.

Orientation

If you arrive by bus, train or boat, you will probably find yourself at the port area of Cagliari (although if you arrive on the FdS train, you'll end up in Piazza della Repubblica, which is about 2km out of the centre of town). The main street along the harbour is Via Roma and the old city stretches up the hill behind it to the fortified area. At the north-western end of Via Roma is Piazza Matteotti and the AAST office, the ARST intercity bus station and the train station. Most of the budget hotels and restaurants are close to the port area.

Information

Tourist Offices The AAST office (☎ 070 66 92 55, e aast.ca@tiscalinet.it), at Piazza Matteotti 9, opens 8.30am to 8pm daily (although you might find it closed for half an hour at lunchtime). It has a reasonable amount of information about the town including a brochure on cultural events which includes up-to-date museum opening hours. There are two other tourist information booths: one at the port (☎ 070 66 83 52), open 9am to noon and 4pm to 7pm Monday

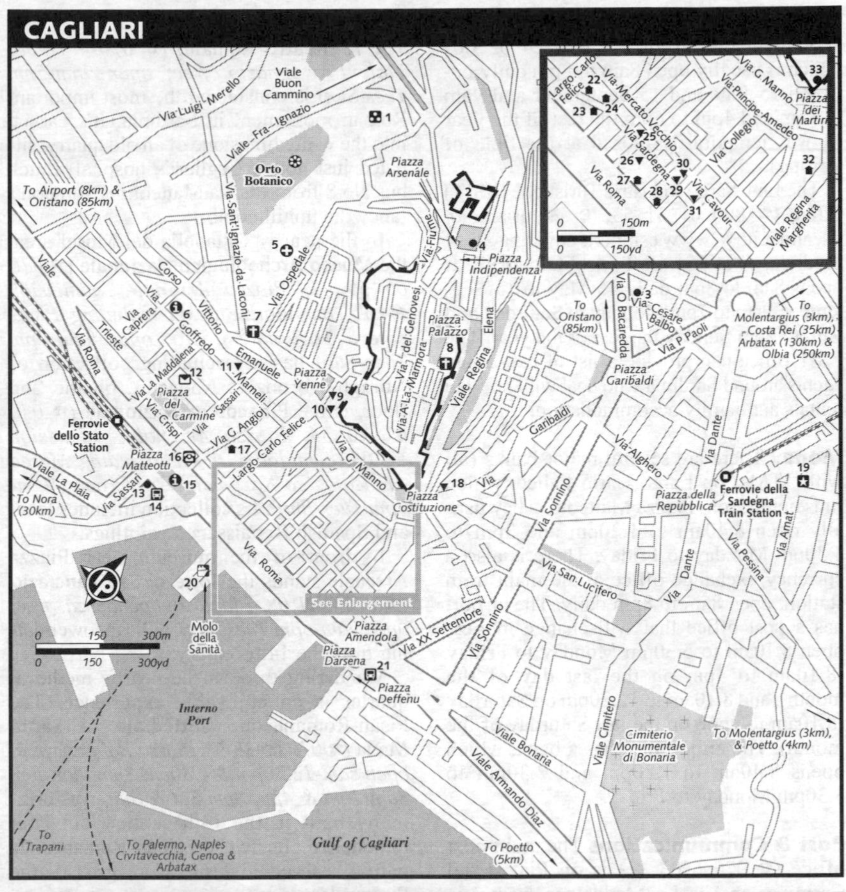

CAGLIARI

PLACES TO STAY
17 Hotel Quattro Mori
22 Albergo Palmas
23 Hotel Italia
24 Albergo La Perla
27 Pensione Vittoria
28 Locanda Miramare
32 Hotel Regina Margherita

PLACES TO EAT
9 Forum Café
10 L'Isola del Gelato
11 Ristorante Il Corso
18 Antico Caffè
25 Ristorante al Porto
26 Trattoria Ci Pensa Cannas
29 Trattoria Gennargentu
30 Antica Hostaria
31 Trattoria Lillicu

OTHER
1 Anfiteatro Romano
2 Cittadella dei Musei (Museo Archeologico Nazionale; Pinacoteca Nazionale)
3 CTS Travel Agency
4 Torre di San Pancrazio
5 Hospital
6 ESIT Office
7 Chiesa di San Michele
8 Cattedrale di Santa Maria
12 Post Office
13 Hertz
14 ARST Bus Station
15 AAST Office
16 Telecom Office
19 Questura (Police Station)
20 Ferry Terminal
21 PANI Bus Station
33 Bastione di San Remy

to Saturday (mornings only Sunday), and another at the airport (☎ 070 24 02 00) which is usually open 8am to 8pm daily between 15 June and 15 September and 9am to 1pm and 4pm to 6pm the rest of the year (it was temporarily closed at the time of writing).

The Ente Sardo Industrie Turistiche (ESIT) office (☎ 800 01 31 53, ⓔ esiturismo@tiscalinet.it, ⓦ www.esit.net), covering all of Sardinia, is at Via Goffredo Mameli 97. It opens 8am to 8pm daily 15 May to 15 September, 9am to 7pm Monday to Saturday and 9am to 2pm Sunday the rest of the year. The ESIT office can provide a list of real-estate agents around Sardinia who deal with holiday rentals and family accommodation.

Money There are several major banks (all with ATMs) on Largo Carlo Felice, which runs uphill from Piazza Matteotti. They usually open 8.40am to 1.20pm and 3pm to 4.30pm Monday to Friday. There is also a currency exchange office at the main train station, open 8am to 8pm daily. The airport has a post office that will change money, open 8.10am to 5.30pm Monday to Friday (8.10am to 4pm on the last day of the month), and 8.10am to 12.20pm on Saturday (8.10am to noon on the last Saturday of the month). The airport also has a bank, which opens 8.40am to 1.20pm and 2.30pm to 3.30pm Monday to Friday.

Post & Communications The main post office (☎ 070 6 03 11) is on Piazza del Carmine, up Via La Maddalena from Via Roma. It's open 8am to 6.30pm Monday to Friday and 8am to 1.20pm on Saturday. You can also change money there. The Telecom office at Via G Angioj, off Piazza Matteotti, is open 8am to 10pm daily.

Travel Agencies There is a CTS office (☎ 070 48 82 60) at Via Cesare Balbo 4.

Medical Services & Emergency Ospedale Civile (hospital; ☎ 070 609 22 67) is on Via Ospedale.

To report thefts, go to the *questura* (police station; ☎ 070 6 02 71) at Via Amat 9.

Things to See

The **Anfiteatro Romano** *(☎ 070 4 11 08, Viale Fra Ignazio; free; open 9am-5pm Tues-Sun)* is considered the most important Roman monument in Sardinia. It's carved into the white limestone of an old quarry, situated just above Cagliari's hospital. Catch bus No 8 from Piazza Matteotti if you don't fancy the uphill climb.

In the nearby Cittadella dei Musei area, the **Museo Archeologico Nazionale** *(☎ 070 65 59 11, Piazza Arsenale; admission €4.15, cumulative ticket including Pinacoteca Nazionale €5.15; open 9am-7pm Tues-Sun)* has a fascinating collection of Nuraghic bronzes. Above it, on the 2nd floor, is the **Pinacoteca Nazionale** *(☎ 070 67 40 54, Piazza Arsenale; admission €2.05, cumulative ticket including Museo Archeologico Nazionale €5.15; open 9am-7pm Tues-Sun)*. Its collection includes local and Spanish Renaissance paintings.

In front of the museum near Piazza Arsenale stands the **Torre di San Pancrazio** *(☎ 070 4 11 08, Piazza Indipendenza; free; open 9am-5pm Tues-Sun)*, a Pisan tower dating from the 14th century.

Wandering through the nearby medieval quarter is an enjoyable experience. The Pisan-Romanesque **Cattedrale di Santa Maria** *(☎ 070 66 38 37, Piazza Palazzo; free; open 8am-12.30pm & 4.30pm-8pm Mon-Fri, 8am-1pm & 4pm-8pm Sat & Sun)* was originally built in the 13th century but later remodelled. Its two precious Romanesque pulpits, carved in 1160, were gifts of the Pisan rulers.

There is a good view of the city and harbour from the **Bastione di San Remy** *(Piazza Costituzione)*, which once formed part of the old city's fortifications.

The **Orto Botanico** *(Botanical Garden; ☎ 070 675 35 01, Viale Sant'Ignazio da Laconi 11; admission €0.50; open 8am-1.30pm & 3pm-6.30pm daily Apr-Sept, 8am-1.30pm daily Oct-Mar)*, not far from the Anfiteatro Romano, is a lovely spot for a quiet rest.

You can spend a day at Poetto beach, east of the centre, where several small bars have outside tables. Alternatively, amble over to the Stagno di Molentargius, just west of

Poetto, to see the pink flamingoes on the salt lake.

Special Events

The Festival of Sant'Efisio is held annually from 1 May. It's a colourful occasion, which mixes the secular and the religious. The highlight is when an effigy of the saint is carried in procession to the small church of Sant'Efisio in the nearby town of Nora.

Places to Stay

There are numerous budget hotels in the old city near the port and main train station.

Locanda Miramare *(☎/fax 070 66 40 21, Via Roma 59)* Singles/doubles €31/38.75, with bath €43.90/46.50. This one-star hotel has simple rooms looking over the port.

Albergo Palmas *(☎/fax 070 65 16 79, Via Sardegna 14)* Singles/doubles €20.65/31, doubles with shower €36.15. This family-run hotel is tucked away in a little lane behind Via Roma. The 'bathroom' is actually a shower-stall plonked unceremoniously in the corner, but rooms are fresh and clean.

Albergo La Perla *(☎ 070 66 94 46, Via Sardegna 18)* Singles/doubles €28.40/36.15. Virtually next door to Albergo Palmas, La Perla offers accommodation of a similar standard.

Pensione Vittoria *(☎ 070 65 79 70, fax 070 66 79 70, Via Roma 75)* Singles/doubles €33.55/49.05, with bath €38.75/56.80. This is a pleasant establishment offering clean, simple rooms a stone's throw from the port. Be aware that it's a bit of a climb to the 3rd floor and the lift doesn't always work.

Hotel Quattro Mori *(☎ 070 66 85 35, fax 070 66 60 87, Via G Angioj 27)* Singles/doubles €25.80/46.50, with bath €41.30/62. The Quattro Mori, just off Largo Carlo Felice, has good rooms and friendly staff.

Hotel Italia *(☎ 070 66 04 10, fax 070 65 02 40, Via Sardegna 31)* Singles/doubles €59.40/82.65. The three-star Italia classes itself as a grandish hotel and the comfortable rooms are equipped with all mod cons, but the place itself is very drab and in desperate need of an overhaul. Try to get a room overlooking Via Sardegna – they're brighter and better.

Hotel Regina Margherita *(☎ 070 67 03 42, fax 070 66 83 25, Viale Regina Margherita)* Singles/doubles with bath €116.20/149.75. What was built to resemble a Renaissance castle looks more like a bomb shelter from the outside, but the rooms are pleasant and functional with all mod cons.

Places to Eat

There are several reasonably priced trattorias in the area behind Via Roma, particularly around Via Cavour and Via Sardegna.

Trattoria Gennargentu *(☎ 070 67 20 21, Via Sardegna 60c)* Full meals from €18.10. It's packed to the brim most nights of the week with hungry locals wanting a fix of good Sardinian pasta and seafood.

Trattoria Ci Pensa Cannas *(☎ 070 66 78 15, Via Sardegna 37)* Pasta €3.10-4.65, mains €5.15-15.50. This is very much a locals' haunt, with grilled fish and meats keeping them running back for more.

Ristorante al Porto *(☎ 070 66 31 31, Via Sardegna 44)* Pasta from €6.20, mains from €7.75, fish dishes more expensive. Fish, fish and more fish is the order of the day here. Try the spaghetti *all'aragosta* (with lobster) or the famous Sardinian spaghetti *alla bottarga* (with dried tuna roe).

Antica Hostaria *(☎ 070 66 58 70, Via Cavour 60)* Full meals from €18.10. Open Mon-Sat. A cut above the rest of the local eateries in this area, the elegant and friendly Antica Hostaria is the place for a splurge. You *can* spend €28.90 on Chateaubriand, but stick to the pasta and grills and you won't break the bank.

Trattoria Lillicu *(☎ 070 65 29 70, Via Sardegna 78)* Antipasto €5.15, pasta €6.70. If you only have one meal in Cagliari, make sure it's at Lillicu. Settle down at your marble-topped table and tuck into excellent seafood antipasti such as deep-fried whitebait (in the lightest of batters) and *sardine al agrodolce* (in a sweet-and-sour oniony sauce); be sure to follow it with spaghetti *ai ricci* (with sea urchin flesh) or spaghetti alla bottarga.

Ristorante Il Corso *(☎ 070 66 26 90, Corso Vittorio Emanuele 78)* Full meals from €15.50. Located near Piazza Yenne, this family-run eatery is informal and atmospheric and serves up reliably good food. Fish features prominently on the menu.

Forum Café *(☎ 070 65 19 80, Piazza Yenne 23)* Cappuccino €0.95, *panini* (filled rolls) €1.55-2.60, meals from €5.15. This bar/cafe also offers a changing daily menu of good, wholesome food.

L'Isola del Gelato *(☎ 070 65 98 24, Piazza Yenne 35)* Gelato €1.05-1.55. For the best ice cream in Cagliari bar none, and decor out of the Flintstones, this gelateria is the place – try the rich'n'creamy mousse varieties.

Sardinian Food

Sardinia's cuisine is as varied as its history. Everything is based on what is local, practical and cost-effective. Along the coast, most dishes feature seafood and there are many variations of fish soup or stew such as *brodetto* and *burrida*. Another speciality is *bottarga* – dried, pressed tuna roe – which is served finely grated over piping hot spaghetti. Traditional pasta dishes tend to be on the heavy side and include *culingiones*, delicious parcels of pasta filled with potato and wild mint.

Inland you will find *porcheddu* (roast sucking pig flavoured with herbs and wood-roasted whole on a spit), kid goat with olives and even lamb trotters in garlic sauce. The preferred bread throughout the island is the crisp and paper-thin *pane carasau*, also called *carta musica*, often sprinkled with oil and salt. The shepherds would carry it with them for weeks at a time. When soaked, pane carasau becomes malleable like large sheets of pasta; topped with tomato, egg and *pecorino* (the ever-present ewe's milk cheese), it becomes *pane frattau*, a cheap and protein-filled meal.

Pecorino reaches its greatest heights in Sardinia, and you will rarely find Parmesan here. *Pecorino sardo* is a semi-cooked, nutty-flavoured cheese sold at different ages.

L'Antico Caffè *(☎ 070 65 82 06, Piazza Costituzione 10-11)* Pasta from €4.65, salads from €3.60, crepes from €4.15. Is it a bar, a cafe, a gelateria, a cocktail bar or a tearoom? Actually, it's all of the above and transforms itself into a French-style bistro if you fancy something more substantial.

If you want to buy picnic supplies, head for ***Via Sardegna***, where there are several good grocers and green grocers as well as a bakery *(forno)*.

Getting There & Around

Air Cagliari's airport is 8km north-west of the city at Elmas. ARST buses leave regularly from Piazza Matteotti to coincide with flights (€0.75). There's an Alitalia office at the airport (☎ 070 24 00 79), otherwise contact the Alitalia central office on ☎ 848 86 56 41 for the cost of a local call. Meridiana is another airline with an office at the airport (☎ 070 24 01 69).

Bus ARST buses leave from the bus station (☎ 070 409 83 24 or toll free 800 86 50 42 if you are in Sardinia) on Piazza Matteotti for nearby towns, including Pula, the Costa del Sud and Teulada, south-west of Cagliari, as well as Villasimius and the Costa Rei to the east. PANI buses leave from farther along Via Roma on Piazza Darsena for towns such as Sassari, Nuoro, Oristano and Porto Torres. The PANI ticket office (☎ 070 65 23 26) is at Piazza Darsena 4.

CTM (☎ 070 2 09 11) runs the local transport network within Cagliari. Tickets (available from the booth in Piazza Matteotti or from newsstands) cost €0.75 for 90 minutes or €2.05 for a day. To avoid the uphill climb to the Anfiteatro Romano, take bus No 8. If you want to head for the beach at Poetto, take bus PF or PQ from Piazza Matteotti.

A tourist trolley car, *Il Trenino Turistico*, does a round trip of all of Cagliari's main sights, departing from Largo Carlo Felice at Piazza Yenne. Tickets are €5.15/2.60 per adult/child and can be bought on board.

Train Regular trains leave for Oristano, Sassari, Porto Torres and Olbia. The private FdS train station is on Piazza della Repubblica.

For information about the Trenino Verde, which runs along a scenic route between Cagliari and Arbatax, contact the ESIT office (see Tourist Offices earlier) or FdS directly (☎ 070 58 02 46). The most interesting and scenic section of the route is between Mandas and Arbatax.

Car & Motorcycle If you want to hire a car or motorcycle, try Hertz (☎ 070 66 81 05), Piazza Matteotti 1, or Avis (☎ 070 66 81 28), inside the train station on Via Roma. Scooters, cars and minibuses (with drivers) can be hired from Autonoleggio Cara (☎ 070 66 34 71, W http://web.tiscali.it/carasnc), who will deliver the vehicle to your hotel.

Travel Service Giuseppe Lodde (☎ 0340 223 66 01, fax 070 27 45 63, e travelservice@tin.it) offers airport transfers and organised trips by private vehicle with driver into hard-to-reach places in the centre of the island.

Boat Ferries arrive at the port just off Via Roma. Bookings for Tirrenia can be made at the ferry terminal in the port area (☎ 070 66 60 65). The office opens 8.30am to 6pm Monday to Friday (8.30am to 7pm for the line to Sicily) and 8.30am to noon and 3.30pm until the boat sails on Saturday. Ferries connect Cagliari with Palermo, Trapani, Naples, Civitavecchia and Genoa, as well as Tunisia (via Trapani). See Getting There & Away at the beginning of this chapter for further information.

You can leave your luggage at the port for free as long as you are taking a ferry out the same day.

AROUND CAGLIARI

Costa Rei

There are good beaches on the largely undeveloped Costa Rei which can be visited on day trips from Cagliari. The area is dotted with camp sites and (generally expensive) hotels.

Villasimius is the most developed town in this area and makes a comfortable base for exploring the attractive coastline.

Albergo Stella d'Oro *(☎ 070 79 12 55, fax 070 79 26 32, Via Vittorio Emanuele 25)* Singles/doubles with bath €31/51.65. It's a comfortable two-star hotel but note that half-board is obligatory in August (€80.05 per person).

Camping Spiaggia del Riso *(☎ 070 79 10 52, fax 070 79 71 50, Località Spiaggia del Riso)* Adult/child €9.80/6.20. This camp site is on the beach.

Camping Garden Cala Sinzias *(☎ 070 99 50 37, fax 070 99 50 82, Località Cala di Sinzias)* Sites per adult/child/tent €6.20/5.15/8.80. This place is on the coast near Castiadas, but be warned that prices soar in July and August.

Camping Piscina Rei *(☎ 070 99 10 89, fax 070 99 10 96, Località Piscina Rei)* Sites per adult/child/tent €5.05/3.95/12.15. This is a well-priced camp site, north of Costa Rei not far from Muravera.

Slightly farther along the coast west of Villasimius is another place to stay.

Hotel Cormoran *(☎ 070 79 81 01, fax 070 79 81 31, Località Campus)* Low season singles/doubles with bath from €77.45/154.95, high season full board €201.40. This is a really lovely resort hotel with a private sandy beach.

For full details on camping and other accommodation along the coast, contact the tourist office at Cagliari. Regular daily ARST buses connect Cagliari with Villasimius and places along the Costa Rei, including camp sites.

Nora

Founded in the 9th century BC by the Phoenicians, on the coast south-west of Cagliari, Nora was considered important for its strategic position and eventually came under Roman control. The ruins of the city extend into the sea and offer evidence of both civilisations, including temples, houses, a Roman theatre and baths. To get to the ruins *(☎ 070 920 91 38, Pula; admission €2.60; open 9am-7pm daily)*, take an ARST bus from Cagliari to Pula, then a local bus (Autolinee Murgia) to Nora (only three daily).

Costa del Sud

The small town of **Chia** marks the start of the beautiful Costa del Sud, which is protected from further development by special ordinances – private homes can be built only in certain zones. The area includes the town of **Teulada** and its port **Porto di Teulada**. Regular ARST buses connect Cagliari with Chia and about eight per day continue on to Teulada.

If you have a car, you can make a detour to the **Is Zuddas caves** *(☎ 0781 95 57 41, 6km south of Santadi; admission €5.15, guided tours only; open 9am-noon & 2.30pm-6pm daily Apr-Sept, shorter hours the rest of the year)* on the road to Teulada. The series of caves has interesting stalagmite and stalactite formations.

Another deviation could include the remains of the Phoenician/Carthaginian city on **Monte Sirai** *(☎ 070 66 50 37, Monte Sirai, Carbonia; admission €1.55; open 9am-7pm Tues-Sun)* just out of Carbonia. This 7th-century-BC fort town commanded a view for miles around. The site is still being excavated.

Places to Stay & Eat There are various camp sites and a few hotels in the area.

Camping Comunale Porto Tramatzu *(☎ 070 928 30 27, fax 070 928 30 28, Località Porto Tramatzu)* Sites per adult/child/tent €6.70/5.95/6.70. Open Apr-Oct. This camp site is by the sea (just past Porto di Teulada) and has a supermarket, bar, pizzeria and restaurant. To get there by public transport, take the ARST Cagliari-Teulada bus, get off at Porto di Teulada and then walk the short distance from the port (signs will point you in the right direction).

Hotel & Ristorante Sebera *(☎ 070 927 08 76, fax 070 927 00 20, Via San Francesco 8, Teulada)* Per person €25.80-41.30 depending on the season, full board €46.50-62. This pleasant establishment is in the town of Teulada, 7km from the sea, in the central piazza where buses stop.

Grand Hotel Baia delle Ginestre *(☎ 070 927 30 05 or 0342 90 47 77 in winter, fax 070 927 30 09, Località Portu Malu)* Doubles with bath up to €185.90, high season half-board up to €144.60 per person per day. This large hotel complex (apartments are also available) about halfway between Chia and Teulada rather blights the coastline. Service and comforts are four-star but prices skyrocket in high season.

At Porto di Teulada there is a very pleasant ***bar/trattoria***, open April to September, which specialises in fresh seafood. You can enjoy lunch in the small courtyard for around €25.80.

Southern Sardinia

SANT'ANTIOCO & SAN PIETRO

These islands, off the south-western coast of Sardinia, have sandy beaches and quiet coves, as well as the pleasant towns of Calasetta (Sant'Antioco) and Carloforte (San Pietro), both with whitewashed or pastel-coloured houses lining narrow streets. The town of Sant'Antioco is more developed.

Information

The Pro Loco office (☎ 0781 8 20 31 or 0781 84 00 32) in the town of Sant'Antioco is at Via Roma 41, and opens 10am to noon and 5pm to 7pm Monday to Saturday (also on Sunday in high season). It can provide information and advice on accommodation, including apartments for rent. You can request information by writing (in English) to the Associazione Turistica Pro Loco, 09017 Sant'Antioco.

There is a very helpful Pro Loco office in Calasetta (☎ 0781 8 85 34, **W** www.prolococalasetta.it), open 10am to noon and 3.30pm to 6.30pm Monday to Saturday. In high season, the office is also open on Sunday. Centro Sub Calasetta (☎ 0368 328 52 98, **e** mapusced@tin.it), at Viale Colombo 13, organises scuba courses and accompanied dives.

San Pietro has a separate tourist office (☎ 0781 85 40 09) at Carloforte in Corso Tagliafico 1, opposite the port.

Places to Stay

In Sant'Antioco, there's a camp site and a couple of hotels.

Campeggio Tonnara *(☎ 0781 80 90 58, fax 0781 80 90 36, Località Calasapone CP 83, Sant'Antioco)* Sites per adult/child/tent

€7.25/3.60/8.25. Open Apr-Sept. Located by the sea, this camp site is away from the town and accessible on the orange FMS buses that service both islands.

Hotel Moderno *(☎ 0781 8 31 05, fax 0781 84 02 52, Via Nazionale 82)* Singles/doubles with bath €36.15/54.25, half-board up to €54.25 per person. The clean and central Moderno is popular so unless it's low season you'll need to book well in advance.

Hotel del Corso *(☎ 0781 80 02 65, fax 0781 8 23 78,* W *www.hoteldelcorso.it, Corso Vittorio Emanuele 32)* High season singles/doubles with bath €46.50/82.65. With pleasant rooms located above the bar of the same name, Hotel del Corso is clean, comfortable and welcoming. It also has a lovely roof terrace.

In Calasetta, there's also one camp site but there's more choice in the hotel category.

Camping Le Saline *(☎ 0781 8 86 15, fax 0781 8 84 89, Località Le Saline)* has sites per adult/child/tent for €7.75/4.65/7.75.

Fjby Hotel *(☎ 0781 8 84 44,* e *htl.fjby@tiscalinet.it, Via Solferino 83)* High season singles/doubles with bath €46.50/72.30, half-board/full board per person up to €62/72.30. This pleasant establishment is the best choice in the town of Calasetta and is open year-round.

Hotel Luci del Faro *(☎ 0781 81 00 89, fax 0781 81 00 91,* e *hotel.lucidelfaro@tiscalinet.it, Località Manglabarche)* High season single/doubles €62/82.65, low season half-board/full board from €67.15/77.45, rising to €98.15/108.45 in Aug. Open Mar-Dec. For beachside luxury or a romantic getaway in a beautiful, windswept location, you can't do better than this resort hotel. The management can organise transfers from Cagliari if you are without private transport, and run a shuttle bus to various beaches on the island.

In Carloforte on San Pietro, choices are limited and there's no camp site.

Hieracon Hotel *(☎ 0781 85 40 28, fax 0781 85 48 93, Corso Cavour 62a)* Singles/doubles €41.30/67.15, high season half-board per person €62, high season apartments sleeping 4 up to €103.30 per night. Conveniently located by the port, this place also has apartments good for groups and longer stays.

Places to Eat

In Sant'Antioco, there are several good trattorias and restaurants.

Il Cantuccio *(Viale Trento)* Pizzas from €5.15. Near Piazza Repubblica, big pizzas (and other dishes) are the speciality here.

There is a ***Coop*** supermarket in the town of Sant'Antioco on the corner of the Lungomare and Via Eleonora d'Arborea.

Calasetta offers some pleasant choices for a bite to eat.

L'Anfora *(☎ 0781 8 85 42, Via Roma 10)* Pizzas from €5.15, full meals about €15.50. This is one of Calasetta's most popular pizzeria-restaurants.

Da Pasqualino *(☎ 0781 8 84 73, Via Roma 99)*. Full meals around €15.50, fish meals from €25.80. the speciality here is good Sardinian home cooking with an emphasis on fish.

Ristorante L'Approdo *(☎ 0781 8 83 75, Viale Regina Margherita 1)* Full meals from €12.90. With a lovely terrace overlooking the port, this restaurant is one of Calasetta's most popular, but closes out of season.

In Carloforte you can try a couple of restaurants.

Barone Rosso *(Via XX Settembre 26)* Panini from €1.80. This is a good place for a snack or a sandwich.

Hieracon Hotel *(☎ 0781 85 40 28, Corso Cavour 62a)* Full meals from €15.50. For a hotel restaurant, the Hieracon is better than most, with good home cooking.

Pick up supplies at the ***Mercato Super Crai*** *(Via Diaz)*.

Getting There & Around

Sant'Antioco is connected to the mainland by a land bridge and is accessible by FMS bus from Cagliari and Iglesias. Regular ferries connect Calasetta and Carloforte (person/car €1.55/4.15, 30 minutes, every hour in summer and every two or three hours in winter).

Orange FMS buses link the small towns on Sant'Antioco and the camp site, and isolated groups of houses on San Pietro.

In the town of Sant'Antioco, you can hire scooters/mountain bikes for around €28.40/12.90 per day from Euromoto (☎ 0781 84 09 07), Via Nazionale 57, and make your own tour of the island. In Carloforte, Viracarruggi (☎ 0368 305 55 54), Corso Cavour 28, has scooters/mountain bikes for €28.40/10.35 per day. Both outlets also hire motorised rubber dinghies for around €103.30 per day.

For boat hire, contact Cantiere Sifredi (☎ 0781 85 44 37) or ask in the shop Boutique Mare at the port at Carloforte. Prices range from about €51.65 to €154.95 per day, depending on the size of the boat.

IGLESIAS

This mining centre, slightly inland from Sardinia's south-western coast, is left off most tourist itineraries but it's well worth a stopover. Iglesias is in a zone rich in minerals, including lead, zinc and some silver and gold, and its mining history extends back to Roman and Carthaginian times. From the 13th century, it was occupied by the Pisans, who called it Argentaria (Place of Silver) after the rich silver deposits discovered there during that period. However, it was the Spanish Aragons who left a greater mark on the town in the form of Spanish-style buildings and architectural features.

The tourist office (☎ 0781 4 17 95), located in the public library in the centre of town on Via Gramsci 9/11, opens 9am to 1pm and 4pm to 6.30pm.

Things to See

The **cathedral** *(Piazza Municipio; open 7am-1pm & 4pm-8.30pm daily)*, opposite the municipal offices, dates from the period of Pisan domination and was built in Romanesque-Gothic style. Nearby, on Piazza San Francesco, is the Gothic **Chiesa di San Francesco**. Above the old town, along Via Campidano, there are the remains of Pisan towers and fortified walls.

Places to Stay & Eat

Hotel Ristorante Leon d'Oro *(☎ 0781 3 35 55, fax 0781 3 35 30, Corso Colombo 72)* Singles/doubles €56.80/82.65. This has decent, comfortable rooms and a good restaurant (meals from €15.50) underneath to boot.

Artu *(☎ 0781 2 24 92, fax 0781 3 24 49, Piazza Quintino Sella 15)* Singles/doubles with bath €49.05/74.90. This hotel is east of the old part of town; follow the signs from Via Gramsci.

There are numerous pastry shops, takeaways and grocery shops in the shopping area around Via Martini and Via Azuni, a short walk from Piazza del Duomo.

Bar Capocabana *(Via Gramsci 4)* This is a friendly place for a drink and a snack – try the delicious *pizzette* (little pizzas), stuffed with tomato, anchovies and capers.

Gazebo Medievale *(☎ 0781 3 08 71, Via Musio 21)* Meals from €20.65. Off Via Corso Matteotti, this elegant restaurant is one of Iglesias' best.

Getting There & Away

The bus station is on Via Oristano, off Via XX Settembre, south-east of the old town, and tickets can be purchased at Sulcis Agenzia Viaggi, Via Roma 52 (parallel to Via Oristano). Regular FMS buses link Iglesias with Cagliari, Carbonia, Sant'Antioco and Calasetta. Two FMS buses per day head for Arbus, from where you can pick up connections to the Costa Verde. Iglesias is also accessible by train from Cagliari, Carbonia and Oristano; the train station is on Via Garibaldi, a 15-minute walk along Via Matteotti from the town centre.

AROUND IGLESIAS

The Phoenician-Roman **Tempio di Antas** is about 15km north of Iglesias towards Fluminimaggiore. Set in a wide, picturesque valley, the small temple was dedicated to a god of fertility and hunting by the Phoenicians, while the Romans dedicated it to a local Nuraghic divinity. Six columns remain standing. Those without their own transport can take the FMS bus from Iglesias for Fluminimaggiore and get off just after the village of Sant'Angelo. The temple is then a 3km walk along a dirt road. For information on current opening hours and prices, contact the local Pro Loco office (☎ 0781 58 10 40).

Western Sardinia

COSTA VERDE

This magnificent stretch of coastline remains almost entirely unspoiled, despite the fact that much of the area has been extensively mined. Former mining towns such as Buggerru, Masua and Nebida are now seeking to make their fortunes as small coastal resorts.

The Costa Verde starts just north of Buggerru at Capo Pecora and continues to Montevecchio Marina. Laws have been passed to protect much of the coastline from development and the area remains a paradise for lovers of secluded beaches. Discreet campers will find that they can free-camp in the area without any hassle. The isolation of much of the coast makes it difficult, but not impossible, for people to reach without their own transport.

Costa Verde Trekking *(☎ 0360 21 45 91, ⓔ cciro@tin.it)*, based at Scivu near Arbus, organises economically priced camping and walking holidays in the area.

Buggerru

This is a good place to make your base. It doesn't have any hotels as yet, but there is space set aside for camping by the waterfront and you can free-camp along the coast to the south of the town. Many residents rent out rooms and apartments and, by asking at one of Buggerru's bars or supermarkets, you will easily find a bed for the night (although most will be booked out in August). FMS buses run to Buggerru from Iglesias. You can contact the Pro Loco office on ☎ 0781 5 45 22.

San Nicolao

North of Buggerru, this is a long, sandy beach and, unlike many other public beaches in Italy, it's clean. In addition, the rows of deck chairs and umbrellas characteristic of the private beaches in other parts of the country are missing. San Nicolao is accessible by FMS bus from Iglesias.

Piscinas

In the heart of the Costa Verde, at the mouth of the Piscinas river, this magnificent unspoiled beach is backed by a vast protected area of 100m-high sand dunes, which support a rich variety of wildlife. An organised parking area for camper vans has been established behind the dune area, just off the road from Ingurtosu, about 2km from the sea, and is due to open in the summer of 2000. Camping is strictly prohibited on the beach and in the sand dunes.

Le Dune *(☎ 070 97 71 30, fax 070 97 72 30, Via Bau 1)* Low season half-board/full board per person €62/72.30, high season €134.30/144.60. The only building in the area, set right on the beach, Le Dune is an atmospheric, comfortable three-star hotel. It offers excellent food and can organise guided tours to the island's most important archaeological sites, as well as to the nearby mining village of Montevecchio.

To reach Piscinas from Guspini (Pro Loco ☎ 070 9 76 01), take the road for Ingurtosu, then take the dirt road to the right where you see the sign for the hotel Le Dune. The distance from the turn-off to the sea is (a very rocky) 7km, but if you're on foot the walk is interesting as you'll pass the ruins of the numerous mines which once operated in the valley. ARST buses run a twice-daily service between Guspini and Ingurtosu, at 6.30am and 2.05pm – ask the driver where to get off. ARST buses also run from Cagliari and Oristano to Guspini. The hotel will pick you up from the port or the airport in Cagliari if you can spare the €82.65 fare (a public taxi will probably cost you more).

Marina di Arbus Marina di Arbus, also known as Gutturu Flumini, is several kilometres north and is more developed. The Pro Loco can be contacted on ☎ 070 975 91 23.

Accommodation possibilities are a little limited.

Camping Costa Verde *(☎/fax 070 97 70 09, Località Marina di Arbus)* Sites per adult/child/tent €7.25/5.95/6.20. This well-equipped camp site right is near the water.

Getting to Marina di Arbus is not simple by public transport. You will need to catch an ARST bus from Oristano or an FMS bus from Iglesias to Arbus. From Arbus, catch a bus from Via della Repubblica to Marina di Arbus, operational in summer only, at 7.30am and 2.20pm, returning to Arbus in the evening. Alternatively, if you have your own transport, take the very windy but sealed road from Guspini towards Piccalinna and Marina di Arbus.

ORISTANO

postcode 09170 • pop 32,000

Originally inhabited by the Nuraghic people, the area around what is now Oristano was colonised by the Phoenicians, who established the port town of Tharros, later controlled by the Carthaginians and then the Romans.

Oristano is believed to have been founded sometime in the 7th century AD by the people of Tharros, who abandoned their ancient town, probably to escape raids by Moorish pirates. Oristano grew to prominence in the 14th century, particularly during the rule of Eleonora d'Arborea, who opposed the Spanish occupation of the island and drew up a body of laws known as the *Carta de Logu*, a progressive legal code which was eventually enforced throughout the island. The code is also considered important because it

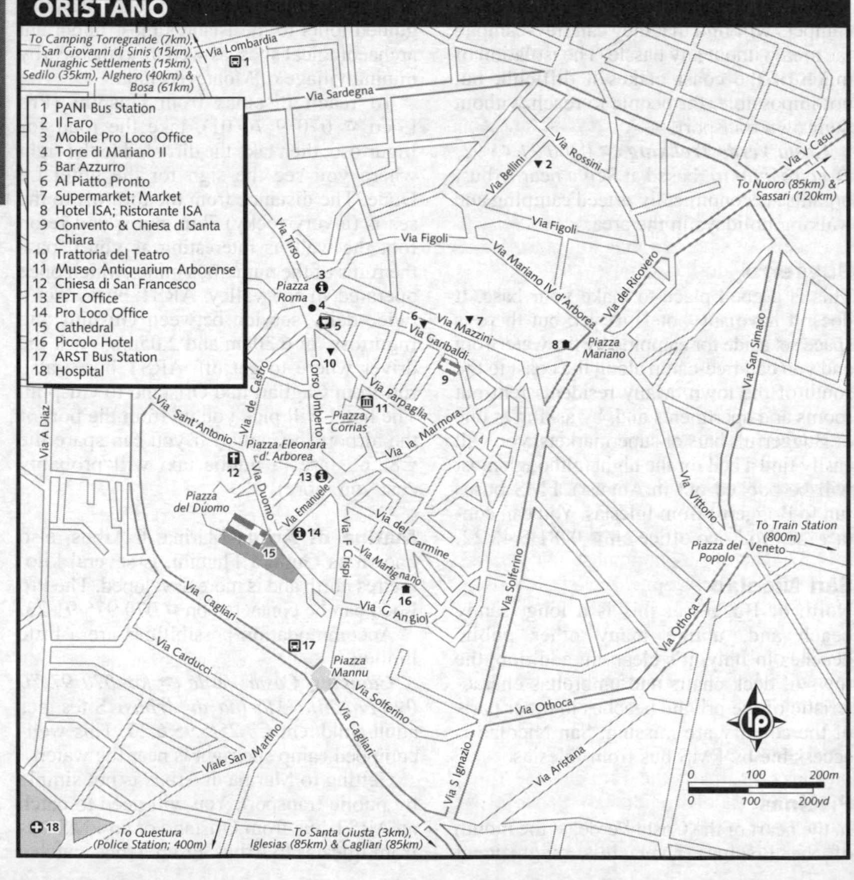

acts as a record of the ancient Sardinian language in which it was written.

Orientation

A good point from which to orient yourself is Piazza Roma, not far from the PANI bus station (off Via Tirso in Via Lombardia) and about 500m from the ARST bus station (in Via Cagliari, just off Piazza Mannu). The train station is about 1.6km away in Piazza Ungheria. To reach Piazza Roma from the station, follow Via Vittorio Veneto to Piazza Mariano and then take Via Mazzini.

Information

Tourist Offices The EPT office (☎ 0783 3 68 31) at Piazza Eleonora d'Arborea 19 opens 8am to 2pm and 4pm to 7pm Monday to Thursday and 8am to 2pm Friday. It has loads of information on the town and the province and will advise on accommodation and transport. There is a Pro Loco office (☎ 0783 7 06 21), Via Emanuele 8, open 9am to noon and 4.30pm to 7.30pm Monday to Friday and 9am to noon on Saturday. Pro Loco operates a mobile tourist office in Piazza Roma during summer.

Post & Communications The main post office is on Via Liguria, north-west of Piazza Roma along Via Tirso, and opens 8.15am to 7.30pm Monday to Saturday. There are Telecom public telephones throughout the town.

Medical Services & Emergency For an ambulance, call ☎ 0783 31 72 13. The Guardia Medica can be contacted on 0783 7 43 33. There is a public hospital (☎ 0783 31 71) at Via Fondazione Rockefeller, along Viale San Martino from Piazza Mannu.

The *questura* (police station; ☎ 0783 21 21 21) is at Via Beatrice d'Arborea 2, behind the playing fields not far from the hospital.

Things to See

On Piazza Roma is the 13th-century **Torre di Mariano II** (Torre di San Cristoforo). From here, walk along Corso Umberto until you get to **Piazza Eleonora d'Arborea**, where you will find a 19th-century statue of Oristano's heroine. The neoclassical **Chiesa di San Francesco** *(Via Sant'Antonio; free; open 7am-noon & 4pm-7pm Mon-Sun)* is adjacent. Of note inside the church are a 15th-century polychrome wooden crucifix, a 14th-century marble statue of Saint Basil by Nino Pisano and a 16th-century polyptych by Pietro Cavaro.

Follow Via Eleonora d'Arborea or Via Duomo to reach the **cathedral** *(☎ 0783 7 15 82, Piazza del Duomo; free; open 7am-noon & 4pm-7.15pm Mon-Sat, 8am-1pm Sun)*, built in the 13th century but completely remodelled in the 18th century. It has a Baroque bell tower, topped by a multicoloured dome.

Also of interest is the 14th-century **Convento & Chiesa di Santa Chiara**, between Via Parpaglia and Via Garibaldi.

The **Museo Antiquarium Arborense** *(☎ 0783 7 44 33 or 0783 79 12 62, Via Parpaglia; admission €2.05; open 9am-8pm daily)* in Palazzo Parpaglia on Piazza Corrias in the heart of the town contains interesting finds from the ancient Phoenician port of Tharros. The entrance fee includes a guided tour of the museum in English and entrance to some of the town's monuments, including the Torre di Mariano II (also part of the guided tour).

About 3km south of Oristano at Santa Giusta, and easily accessible by local ARST buses, is the **Basilica di Santa Giusta**. Built in around 1100, the church is Romanesque with Pisan and Lombard influences.

Special Events

The most important festival in Oristano is the colourful Sa Sartiglia, held on the last Sunday of carnival (late February or early March) and repeated on Shrove Tuesday. Probably one of the island's most beautiful festive events, the Sartiglia had its origins in a military contest performed by the knights of the Second Crusade. It developed into a festival during the period of Spanish domination and now involves masked, costumed riders who parade through the town before participating in a tournament, where they must pierce the centre of a silver star with their swords while riding at full speed.

Places to Stay

Oristano is not exactly bursting with hotels and there are no budget options.

Camping Torregrande *(☎/fax 0783 2 22 28, Località Marina di Torre Grande)* Sites per adult/child/tent €5.15/3.10/6.70. Open June-Sept. The camp site, at Marina di Torre Grande, is about 7km west of Oristano (regular ARST buses connect the two towns – see Getting There & Around later). It gets really booked up during August.

Piccolo Hotel *(☎ 0783 7 15 00, Via Martignano 19)* Singles/doubles €25.80/51.65. This is Oristano's cheapest deal, with clean rooms in a central position near Piazza Eleonora d'Arborea.

Hotel ISA *(☎/fax 0783 36 01 01, Piazza Mariano 50)* Singles/doubles with bath €43.90/72.30. Comfortable, spotless rooms are on offer here. At the time of writing, half the hotel had been very nicely renovated and a name change was planned.

Agriturismo (accommodation on a working farm) is very well organised in the province, with half-board in a double room costing around €31 per person. It is organised by the ***Consorzio Agriturismo di Sardinia*** *(☎ 0783 7 39 54, fax 0783 7 39 24).*

Places to Eat

Bar Azzurro *(Piazza Roma 73)* Cappuccino and *cornetto* (croissant) €1.60. This bar-cum-pasticceria is *the* place to go for breakfast. Try the to-die-for savoury pizzette filled with tomato and anchovies, ham or spinach.

Al Piatto Pronto *(☎ 0783 7 31 37, Via Mazzini 21)* Meals/snacks from €4.15. Near Piazza Roma, this place does ready-cooked snacks and pre-prepared dishes which make perfect picnic fare.

Trattoria del Teatro *(☎ 0783 7 16 72, Via Parpaglia 11)* Seafood antipasto €6.20, pasta from €7.75. Open Mon-Sat. A good selection of local wine, a cosy, comfortable setting and some of the best *antipasto misto del mare* (mixed seafood appetiser) make this an eatery to seek out.

Ristorante ISA *(☎ 0783 7 15 00, Piazza Mariano 50)* Full meals from €18.10. Tucked away within the Hotel ISA, this restaurant serves excellent food and is well priced. Try the warming and filling *minestre di verdure* (vegetable soup); fish is also good.

Il Faro *(☎ 0783 7 00 02, Via Bellini 25)* Full meals from €36.15. Open Mon-Sat. Il Faro is considered one of Oristano's better restaurants; it's certainly one of the town's more expensive places.

There's a ***supermarket*** and covered ***market*** at Via Mazzini 54.

Getting There & Around

The terminal for ARST buses, which service the province, is on Via Cagliari. Regular buses head for Marina di Torre Grande, Putzu Idu and Su Pallosu; during summer they also serve San Giovanni di Sinis and the ruins of Tharros. Four buses daily leave for Bosa.

The PANI bus station is on Via Lombardia, next to the Blu Bar at No 30 (where you can check timetables). There are connections to Cagliari, Sassari and Nuoro.

Oristano is accessible by train from Cagliari, Sassari and Olbia.

The city is easy to negotiate on foot, although urban bus No 2 Circolare Destra (clockwise) or Sinistra (anticlockwise) is handy for getting around. Small buses will also take you into the historic centre of town.

AROUND ORISTANO

Penisola di Sinis

Just west of Oristano is the **Penisola di Sinis** (Sinis Peninsula), with some lovely sandy beaches (which have been awarded a coveted Blue Flag for cleanliness by the EU), the opportunity to see lots of flamingoes and the ruins of the ancient Phoenician port of Tharros. If you have the time, spend a few days relaxing here. There are only a couple of hotels, but rooms are available for rent and several farms participate in the local agriturismo programme. Check at the EPT tourist office in Oristano for details.

At the village of **San Giovanni di Sinis** is the 6th-century Byzantine church of the same name, where mass is still celebrated. Nearby, in a tiny village of pastel-coloured houses, is the tiny church of **San Salvatore**, built over a pagan temple.

Tharros Located just outside San Giovanni di Sinis at the southernmost end of the peninsula, Tharros was originally a Phoenician and later a Roman port town. The important ruins *(☎ 0783 37 00 19, Località San Giovanni di Sinis, Cabras; admission €4.15; open 9am-8pm daily in summer, 9am-5pm daily in winter)*, discovered in 1851 by an English archaeologist, yielded significant treasures and are well worth a visit.

San Giovanni and Tharros can be reached from Oristano by regular ARST buses during summer.

Putzu Idu & Su Pallosu At the northern end of the Sinis Peninsula are the villages of Putzu Idu and Su Pallosu, both offering peaceful surroundings and lovely beaches. Between the two villages are marshes which are home to hundreds of pink flamingoes, as well as other water birds. The loveliest beach on the peninsula is nearby at **Is Arutas**.

If you want to stay in Putzu Idu, try the following option.

Da Cesare *(☎ 0783 5 20 95, fax 0783 5 20 15, Vico S'Architteddu)* Singles/doubles around €62/77.45. Half-board €85.20 (obligatory in high season). When the sun doesn't shine, Da Cesare seems windswept and lonely; when it's hot and beachy, you're in the thick of the action. You can get good meals at the hotel ***restaurant***.

About 1km away is the smaller, quieter village of Su Pallosu.

Hotel Su Pallosu *(☎ 0783 5 80 21, fax 0783 5 80 05, Via Sa Marigosa 2)* Singles/doubles €38.75/56.80. The hotel has simple, clean rooms, all with bath, and special deals on half-board (from €33.55) at certain times of the year. Its ***restaurant*** is recommended.

Both villages and the beach of Is Arutas are accessible by the ARST bus from Oristano.

Sedilo

Those who want to experience Sardinia's wilder side should see the Sa Ardia in **Sedilo**. This spectacular festival is held on 6 and 7 July in honour of San Costantino. It features a fascinating, and at times dangerous, ritualised horse race, run just out of town around the country church of **San Costantino**. Thousands of spectators witness the event, with some firing guns (only blanks are used) into the ground and air to excite the horses. Needless to say, there are injuries every year. The race starts at 6pm on 6 July and is rerun the following morning at about 7am. Information about the event is available at the EPT tourist office in Oristano. Sedilo is about 50km north-east of Oristano, near Abbasanta and Lago Omodeo.

Nuraghic Settlements

On the S131 north of Oristano, a few kilometres before Paulilatino, you will find the important Nuraghic **Pozzo Sacro di Santa Cristina** *(Sacred Well of St Christina; ☎ 0785 5 54 38, Località Paulilatino; admission €2.05; open 8.30am-9pm daily in winter, 8.30am-11pm daily in summer)*, a fascinating old well and Nuraghic village. Farther along the S131, just south of Abbasanta, there's the **Nuraghe Losa** *(☎ 0785 5 48 23, Località Losa; free; open 8am-7pm daily)*, one of the tallest and best-conserved *nuraghe* (see the boxed text 'Homes Made of Stone' later) in Sardinia.

BOSA

The only town of the Nuoro province on the west coast, Bosa is fast becoming a popular tourist destination, but it is yet to show signs of becoming touristy. The town's historic centre has a pleasant architectural balance which is uncommon in Sardinia. For local information, try the town council (☎ 0785 37 31 14 or 0785 37 34 10) or go to SWS travel agency (☎ 0785 37 43 91), Corso Vittorio Emanuele 45, which also offers a ticket-booking service.

A medical service for tourists is available in summer only at Bosa Marina at ☎ 0785 37 46 15. The Guardia Medica is at the hospital (☎ 0785 37 31 07).

Things to See & Do

Bosa has a fascinating town centre with lovely little squares and elegant Baroque churches. The imposing medieval **castle** was built in 1112 by the Malaspina, a noble Tuscan family, to control the valley of the

SARDINIA

River Temo. The Temo, with its 8km of navigable waters, made a local tanning industry possible. Also of interest is the Romanesque **church** of San Pietro Extramuros, 2km from the old bridge on the south bank of the Temo.

The coastline between Bosa and Alghero is stunning, with rugged cliffs dropping down to unspoiled beaches. The beaches here are often busy on summer weekends but the area remains a paradise for **walkers** in all seasons. However, the only way to really explore it is by car or motorcycle. Don't leave anything in your car: thieves patrol the coast looking for easy targets such as unattended cars loaded with luggage.

Also near Bosa is one of the last habitats of the griffon vulture. It is quite an experience if you are lucky enough to spot one of these huge birds whose wingspan can reach 2m.

Places to Stay & Eat

There are hotels in Bosa and at nearby Bosa Marina, an anonymous, modern resort town at the mouth of the River Temo.

Hotel Perry Clan *(☎ 0785 37 30 74, fax 0785 37 52 63, Via Alghero 3)* Singles/doubles with bath €25.80/41.30. Close to the centre of town, the Perry Clan has functional rooms and a decent restaurant.

Hotel Mannu *(☎ 0785 37 53 06, fax 0785 37 53 08, Via Alghero 28)* High season singles/doubles €41.30/62. Seafood meals €25.80. This hotel has clean, modern rooms and a good restaurant.

All hotels in Bosa can organise guided tours and boat and bicycle rental, as well as a shuttle service to the best beaches on the rocky coastline.

Tatore *(☎ 0785 37 31 04, Piazza IV Novembre 13b)* serves full meals for about €31.

Ristorante Borgo Sant'Ignazio *(☎ 0785 37 46 62, Via Sant'Ignazio 33)* Pasta €5.15-7.25, full meals from €15.50. Open daily in summer, Tues-Sun afternoon in winter. Tucked away in the medieval quarter of Sas Costas, this eatery does excellent, well-priced dishes. Try the *culinzones e calameda*, home-made ravioli stuffed with ricotta and mushrooms and served in a rich meat sauce.

Getting There & Away

Regular ARST buses link Bosa with Sassari and Oristano, arriving at and departing from Piazza Zanetti. There is a daily bus connection to Alghero, Porto Torres and Olbia, the latter coinciding with the Civitavecchia ferry.

Central Sardinia

AROUND BARUMINI

There are innumerable Nuraghic sites on the island, but some of the most interesting are in the interior and are often very difficult to reach without your own transport. The most important is the **Su Nuraxi** fortress *(☎ 0337 81 30 87, 070 936 81 28, Via Tuili, Barumini; admission €4.15; open 9am-7pm daily in summer, 9am-5pm daily in winter)*, 1km west of Barumini and about 60km north of Cagliari. This vast Nuraghic complex consists of a well-preserved castle, made up of several conical towers, and the ruins of its surrounding village.

On a day trip you will probably spend most of your time travelling if you use public transport. A better option than spending hours trying to juggle bus timetables is to stay overnight in the nearby town of **Gergei** (10km east of Barumini).

Hotel Dedoni *(☎/fax 0782 80 80 60, Via Marconi 50, Gergei)* Singles/doubles €28.40/41.30, half-board/full board per person from €38.75/46.50. This delightful hotel offers a very high standard of accommodation (rooms are simple but well appointed, all with bathrooms) and traditional food at reasonable prices. The management organises day trips and overnight excursions in the area (mainly for groups and only by prior reservation), which can incorporate horse riding, cycling and travel on the Trenino Verde. They will also pick you up from Cagliari (around €62) or Olbia (around €129).

Although Gergei itself is pretty anonymous, it is a perfect base from which to explore the Su Nuraxi site and the nearby plain of **Giara di Gesturi**, inhabited by wild ponies. North of Gergei is the **Giara di Serri**, a high-plain area which, like the Giara di Gesturi, is a great place for walking and experiencing the daily life of the local sheep farmers who abound in the area.

Also in this area is the Nuraghic sanctuary of **Santa Vittoria di Serri**, less well known than Su Nuraxi but certainly worth visiting. Of particular interest in this ancient complex is the *recinto delle feste*, a large enclosure lined with small rooms where, it is believed, cult objects and other goods were displayed and sold.

East of Gergei, not far from Orroli, in a lovely, isolated position on the ridge of the Flumendosa gorge, stands the imposing **Nuraghe Arrubiu** *(☎ Cooperativa Is Janas 0782 84 72 69, 0330 43 55 51, Località Orroli; admission €3.60; open 9am-1pm & 3pm-8pm daily in summer, 9am-5pm daily in winter)*. Recently restored, this obscure Nuraghic fortress is an unusual red thanks to the lichen that has colonised the outside.

A few kilometres south of Barumini, off the road to Cagliari, are the spiky ruins of a 12th-century castle, protruding from a hill at **Las Plássas**.

There is an ARST bus from Cagliari to Barumini, but to return you will need to catch an FdS bus to Sanluri and then an ARST bus to Cagliari. FdS buses also serve Gergei. To avoid being stranded, check the latest bus timetables at the Cagliari AAST tourist office. The Trenino Verde, which runs between Cagliari and Arbatax, passes nearby at Mandas. The section between Mandas and Arbatax is the most scenic part of the railway, so it might be worthwhile catching the train there if you have the time.

Homes Made Of Stone

Among the most dominant features of Sardinia's landscape are the 7000 or so *nuraghi* dotted around the island. Dating from 1500 to 400 BC, these truncated conical structures were made out of huge basalt blocks taken from extinct volcanoes. The towers were used for shelter and for guarding the surrounding territory. The name *nuraghe* derives from the Sardinian word *nurra*, which means 'heap' or 'mound'. Very little is known about the identity of the Nuraghic people. Judging by their buildings, they were well organised and possessed remarkable engineering skills, but they appear to have left no written word.

Northern Sardinia

ALGHERO

postcode 07041 • pop 40,000

On the island's north-western coast, in the area known as the Coral Riviera, Alghero is one of the most popular tourist resorts in Sardinia. The Catalan Aragonese won the town from Genoa in 1354 and even today the locals speak a dialect strongly linked to the Catalan language. Alghero is a very pretty – albeit touristy – town and a good base from where to explore the magnificent coastline that links it to Bosa to the south and the famous Grotta di Nettuno nearby (see Around Alghero later in this chapter).

Orientation

Alghero's historic centre is on a small promontory jutting into the sea, with the new town stretching out behind it and along the coast to the north. Intercity buses arrive in Via Catalogna, next to a small park just outside the historic centre. The train station is about 1km north, on Via Don Minzoni, and connected to the centre by a regular bus service.

The old town and most hotels and restaurants are in the area west of the AAST office.

Information

Tourist Offices The AAST office (☎ 079 97 90 54) is at Piazza Porta Terra 9, near the port and just across the gardens from the bus station. It opens 8am to 1pm Monday to Saturday. They have maps of the town and can help you find a hotel.

Post & Communications The main post office is at Via XX Settembre 108. Public phones are on Via Vittorio Emanuele, on the other side of the park from the AAST office.

Medical Services During the summer there is a tourist medical service (☎ 079 93 05 33) on Piazza Venezia Giulia in Fertilia, just west of Alghero. It opens 9am to 12.30pm and 4.30pm to 7.30pm, although for emergencies you can telephone 24 hours. Otherwise go to the Ospedale Civile (hospital; ☎ 079 99 62 33) on Via Don Minzoni.

Things to See

Wander through the narrow streets of the old town and around the port. The most interesting church is the **Chiesa di San Francesco** *(Via Carlo Alberto; open 8am-noon & 4pm-7pm daily)*. The **cathedral** has been ruined by constant remodelling (it was undergoing major renovations at the time of writing and looks likely to be closed for years), but its bell tower remains a fine example of Gothic-Catalan architecture.

There are three defensive towers in the town; you can look at them from the outside but you can't get into them. The **Torre del Portal**, on Piazza Porta Terra, was furnished with a drawbridge and moat and was one of the two entrances to the walled town. The **Torre de l'Esperò Reial** was one of the bastions of Alghero's fortified wall. The octagonal **Torre de Sant Jaume**, also known as the Torre dei Cani (Dogs' Tower), was used as a pound for stray dogs.

Special Events

In summer Alghero stages the Estate Musicale Algherese in the cloisters of the Chiesa di San Francesco. A festival, complete with firework display, is held annually on 15 August for the Feast of the Assumption.

Places to Stay

It is virtually impossible to find a room in August unless you book months in advance. At other times of the year, you shouldn't have too much trouble, but booking ahead is a good idea.

Camping Calik *(☎/fax 079 93 01 11, Località Fertilia, Strada Statale 127 bis, Km 41)* Mid-season sites per adult/child/tent €9.30/5.70/4.15, high season €11.90/7.25/8.25. Open Jun-Sept. This camp site is not far from the airport in Fertilia, about 6km north of town.

Ostello dei Giuliani *(☎ 079 93 03 53, Via Zara 1)* B&B from €7.75, hot water €2.05. Open year-round. This HI (Hostelling International) hostel is in Fertilia; there are only 25 beds so book early. Food is available (meals €7.75). To get there, take the hourly bus AF from Via Catalogna to Fertilia.

Hotel San Francesco *(☎/fax 079 98 03 30, ⓔ hotsfran@tin.it, Via Ambrogio Machin 2)* Singles/doubles with bath from €38.75/62. A popular hotel located in the heart of the old town.

Pensione Normandie *(☎/fax 079 97 53 02, Via Enrico Mattei 6)* Singles/doubles €23.25/43.90. Rooms are shabby but large and the hotel is a fair way out of the centre but it's still Alghero's cheapest deal. To get there, follow Via Cagliari (which becomes Viale Giovanni XXIII).

La Margherita *(☎ 079 97 90 06, fax 079 97 64 17, Via Sassari 70)* Low season singles/doubles with bath from €41.30/67.15, high season up to €62/98.15. Rather run-down rooms and fairly disorganised staff are the features here, but it's well positioned and reasonably well priced.

Hotel Catalunya *(☎ 079 95 31 72, fax 079 95 31 77, Via Catalogna 20)* Singles/doubles with bath from €56.80/87.80. The four-star Catalunya is a bit of a garish blight on the landscape (you can't miss its multicoloured upper storey) near the Bastione della Maddalena and the public gardens. Despite this, rooms are attractive and comfortable – and there are a lot of them, so it's a good place to try if everything else is booked out.

Places to Eat

Caffè Costantino *(Piazza Civica)* This is an atmospheric spot to sit down and enjoy a beer or a cappuccino.

Polli Arrosto/Pizze al Taglio *(☎ 097 97 43 77, Via Simon 14)* Pizza slices €1.05, half chickens €3.10. As its name suggests, this place does pizza *al taglio* (by the slice) and roasted chicken.

Al Vecchio Mulino *(☎ 079 97 72 54, Via Don De Roma 3)* Pizzas €3.60-6.70, pasta €5.15-8.25, mains €7.25-12.90. This attractive trattoria has an atmospheric vaulted ceiling. *Gamberoni alla griglia* (grilled prawns) and *cozze alla marinara* (clams with white wine, garlic and onion) are house specialities.

Posada del Mar *(☎ 079 97 95 79, Vicolo Adami 29)* Pasta €6.70/10.35, mains from €10.35. Excellent (but pricey) fish dishes are the attraction here. Try the *orato al cartoccio* (fish served in a foil parcel) or scampi with cherry tomatoes and courgettes.

Mabroux *(☎ 079 97 00 00, Via Santa Barbara)* Set menu (four courses) €20.70. Located in a tiny *vicolo* (alley) between the cathedral and the sea wall, this is one of Alghero's best finds – a true mamma's kitchen where the menu is limited and you pay €20.70 for the best fish-based dinner in town. Be sure to book.

Da Ninetto *(☎ 079 97 80 62, Via Gioberti 4)* Full meals from €20.70. The house speciality here is *aragosta all'Algherese* (lobster, Alghero-style) and they do fish well, but there are also staples such as lasagne.

Salumeria del Centro *(☎ 079 97 58 14, Via Simon 2)* Pick up typical Sardinian gourmet treats – wine, grappa, sausage, bottarga, cheese and sweets – to take home as souvenirs or eat on a gourmet picnic.

There are numerous supermarkets, including ***Mura*** in Via Lamarmora, and plenty of gelaterias dotted about the old town to satisfy any sweet cravings.

Getting There & Away

The airport, inland from Fertilia, has domestic flights from major cities throughout Italy. Regular buses leave from the corner of Via Vittorio Emanuele and Via Cagliari to coincide with flights.

Intercity buses terminate in Via Catalogna, next to the public park. ARST buses leave for Sassari and Porto Torres, and FdS buses serve Sassari as well. There is a special service to Olbia, leaving at 8pm, to coincide with the 10pm ferry departure. FdS also runs a service between Alghero and Bosa. Regular buses leave for Capo Caccia and Porto Conte. Timetables are posted in the ticket office (☎ 079 95 01 79), near a bar beside the bus stop area, in Via Catalogna. They are also posted outside the tourist office.

Alghero is on the local FdS railway line, which links it with Sassari and the main FS Cagliari–Oristano–Olbia line. Trains run to Sassari about ten times per day Monday to Saturday (less frequently on Sunday and public holidays).

Getting Around

Urban bus No AF runs hourly between Alghero and Fertilia from 7am to 9.40pm. The more regular A0 goes only as far as the Spiaggia di Maria Pia. Some FdS buses run between the port and the train station, a distance of about 1km, also serviced by urban bus Nos AP or AF.

If you want to hire a bicycle or motorcycle to explore, Cicloexpress (☎ 079 98 69 50), Via Garibaldi Porto, has bicycles/mountain bikes/mopeds/scooters from €7.75/10.35/18.10/31 per day. Velosport (☎ 079 97 71 82), Via Vittorio Veneto 90, is another option; its prices are slightly lower.

AROUND ALGHERO

There are good beaches north of Alghero, including the **Spiaggia di San Giovanni** and the **Spiaggia di Maria Pia**, easily accessible on the Alghero-Fertilia bus.

The **Grotta di Nettuno** *(Neptune's Cave; ☎ 079 94 65 40, Località Capo Caccia; adults/under-12s €7.75/4.15; hourly tours 8am-7pm daily in summer, 9am-2pm daily in winter)* is on Capo Caccia, west of Alghero. The easiest way to see the cave is by taking a boat from Alghero's port. There are regular trips operated by various companies; tickets cost €9.30 including admission to the cave (call NaviSarda ☎ 079 95 06 03 for information). You can also reach the Grotta di Nettuno by road (via Fertilia). The SFS bus departs from Via Catalogna in Alghero (€3.60 return). If you arrive by road, you descend to the cave by a staircase carved into the rock (remember you have to make the arduous 650-step climb on the way back). Given that you still have to pay to enter the cave, it's probably more relaxing (and cheaper) to take the boat (the round trip takes about three hours).

If you have your own means of transport, explore the Capo Caccia area and visit the **Nuraghe di Palmavera** *(☎ 079 95 32 00, SS127 bis (Strada Fertilia-Capo Caccia); admission €2.05, including hourly guided tour €3.60; open 9am-7pm daily Apr-Oct,*

9.30am-4pm daily Nov-Mar), about 10km out of Alghero on the road to Porto Conte. You can also visit the **Necropoli di Anghelu Ruju** *(Cooperativa SILT; ☎ 079 95 32 00, Alghero-Porto Torres road; admission €2.05 or €3.60 with guided tour; open 9am-7pm daily)*. This necropolis is quite hard to find – use the Tenuta Sella e Mosca vineyards as your landmark; the entrance is on the left just before the vineyards, coming from Alghero. Information on both the Nuraghe di Palmavera and the necropolis can be found on the Cooperativa SILT Web site at W http://web.tiscalinet.it/coopsilt. A cumulative ticket for €3.60 (admission only) or €6.20 (with guided tour) gives admission to both sites.

SARDINIA

SASSARI

postcode 07100 • pop 120,000

The capital of Sardinia's largest province and the island's second-largest city after Cagliari, Sassari is probably the one place in Sardinia that you should aim to miss. One of its few redeeming features is the Cavalcata Sarda, one of the island's most important festivals, which takes place in May.

Orientation

Sassari has a compact centre concentrated around its cathedral, but most services are in the busy newer part of town in the area around the vast 18th-century Piazza Italia. Most intercity buses stop in the central Corso Margherita di Savoia, opposite Emiciclo Garibaldi, before reaching the main bus station in Via XXV Aprile, south of the train station. To reach Piazza Italia from the bus stop in the city centre, head up Via Brigata Sassari to Piazza Castello and turn right.

The train station is about 10-minutes' walk from the centre. From the station, head north to Piazza Sant'Antonio and then follow Corso Vittorio Emanuele to Piazza Castello.

Information

Tourist Offices The AAST head office is at Via Umberto 72 (☎ 079 23 17 77, fax 079 23 75 85) and opens 9am to 1pm and 4pm to 6pm Monday to Friday. There is usually also an information office at Via Roma 62 near the Museo Sanna but it was closed at the time of writing. There is an EPT office at Fertilia airport (☎/fax 079 93 51 24).

Money You can exchange travellers cheques and obtain cash advances on Visa and MasterCard at Banca Commerciale Italiana in Piazza Italia.

Post & Communications The main post office is at Via Brigata Sassari 13, just off Piazza Castello. There are Telecom pay phones throughout the town, including a bank of them outside the post office.

Medical Services & Emergency The Ospedale Civile (hospital; ☎ 079 206 10 00) is on Via E De Nicola, off Viale Italia. For emergencies (☎ 079 206 16 21), enter by the Viale Italia entrance and follow the sign *pronto soccorso* (casualty).

The *questura* (police station; ☎ 079 283 55 00) is at Viale Coppino 1.

Things to See

Sassari's **cathedral** *(Piazza del Duomo; open 7am-noon & 4pm-7pm daily)* is in the old town. Built in Romanesque style in the 13th century, it was remodelled and given a Baroque facade in the 17th century. Also worth a look is the **Chiesa di Santa Maria di Betlem** *(Viale Coppino; open 7am-noon & 4pm-7pm daily)* near the station. It has a 13th-century facade and lovely 14th-century cloisters.

Museo Sanna *(☎ 079 21 06 24, Via Roma 64; admission €2.05; open 9am-8pm Tues-Sun)* is of considerable interest for its Nuraghic collection, as well as its display of traditional costumes.

Special Events

The Cavalcata Sarda (Sardinian Cavalcade) is generally held on the penultimate Sunday in May (although the day can change from year to year). It attracts participants from all over the island, who dress in traditional costume and take part in a large and quite colourful parade, followed by equestrian competitions, to mark a victory of the Saracens in 1000. It's well worth visiting Sassari during the festival.

I Candelieri (The Candlesticks) is held on 14 August at Sassari. It features town representatives in medieval costume carrying huge wooden columns through the town. The celebrations are held in order to honour a vow made by farmers and craftsmen in 1652 for deliverance from a plague.

Places to Stay

Hotels and pensiones are not abundant in Sassari and if you plan to arrive in high summer or for the Cavalcata it is advisable to book a room in advance.

Hotel Giusy *(☎ 079 23 33 27, fax 079 23 94 90, Piazza Sant'Antonio 21)* Singles/doubles with bath €28.40/38.75. This place has decent accommodation and is close to the station.

Hotel Leonardo da Vinci *(☎ 079 28 07 44, fax 079 285 72 33, Via Roma 79)* Singles/doubles with bath up to €67.15. Here you'll find quality rooms in an up-market hotel which is about as central as it gets in Sassari. Prices include breakfast.

Hotel Carlo Felice *(☎ 079 27 14 40, fax 079 27 14 42, e carlofelice@tiscalinet.it, Via Carlo Felice 43)* Singles/doubles

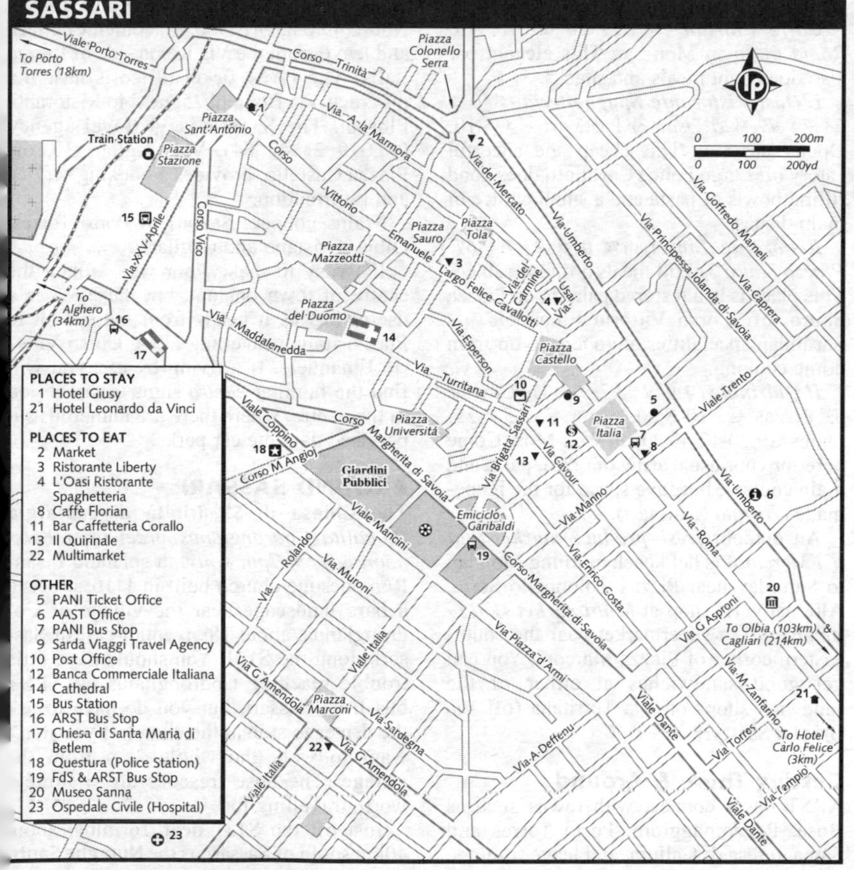

€56.80/82.65. On the outskirts of Sassari (connected to the centre by Via Roma but OK only if you have private transport), the Carlo Felice is a functional hotel (part of the Best Western group) with comfortable if characterless rooms.

Places to Eat

Strangely for Sardinia, eating well in Sassari is harder than it looks. There are several bars around the main squares, but few decent, well-priced restaurants.

Bar Caffetteria Corallo *(☎ 079 23 31 58, Via Cavour 2)* Panini from €2.05, drinks from €1.05. A friendly place for a quick refuelling, right in the centre of town.

Caffè Florian *(☎ 079 20 03 40, Via Roma 6)* Open Mon-Sat. This elegant bar also does light meals and snacks.

L'Oasi Ristorante Spaghetteria *(☎ 079 23 74 99, Via Usai 7)* Pasta from €3.10. Open Tues-Sun. This cheap and cheerful eatery off Largo Felice Cavallotti does good filling bowls of pasta and a small choice of main dishes.

Ristorante Liberty *(☎ 079 23 63 61, Piazza Sauro 3)* Full meals around €20.65. This place is in a restored palazzo on Piazza Sauro, off Corso Vittorio Emanuele. Its Sardinian specialities are one step up from home cooking.

Il Quirinale *(☎ 079 23 23 63, Via Cavour 3)* Pizzas €3.10-6.20, pasta €5.15-7.25, mains €9.30-12.40. Open Wed-Mon. Come here for your usual array of pizza, pasta and main courses, but save space for the home-made *crostata* (fruit tart).

An outdoor ***fresh-produce market*** *(Via del Mercato)* is held each morning Monday to Saturday near Piazza Colonnello Serra. Alternatively, shop at ***Multimarket*** *(Via G Amendola)*, a supermarket near the south-eastern corner of Piazza Marconi. You can get good sandwiches at either of the sandwich shops on Via Turritana (off Via Brigata Sassari).

Getting There & Around

ARST buses connect with towns such as Bosa, Pozzomaggiore, Porto Torres and Santa Teresa di Gallura, and leave from the southern end of Via XXV Aprile, at the corner with Piazza Santa Maria di Betlem. Services also connect with flights to Fertilia airport. ARST buses also stop on Corso Margherita di Savoia, opposite Emiciclo Garibaldi. Tickets are available from some central bars and at the ARST office (☎ 079 263 92 20) at Emiciclo Garibaldi, where you can also get timetable information.

FdS (☎ 079 24 13 01) buses run to Tempio Pausania, Alghero, Fertilia, Bosa, Olbia and Palau. You can check timetables at the company's ticket office (shared with ARST) at Emiciclo Garibaldi.

PANI (☎ 079 23 69 83) long-distance buses connect Sassari with Porto Torres, Nuoro, Olbia, Oristano, Macomer, Cagliari, and leave from the Via Roma side of Piazza Italia. The PANI ticket office is near the piazza at Via Bellieni 25, next to Ristorante Florian. The Sarda Viaggi travel agency (☎ 079 23 47 84), Via Cagliari 30, off Piazza Castello, provides a booking service and information.

Trains connect Sassari to Porto Torres, Olbia, Oristano and Cagliari.

It's easy to make your way around the centre of town on foot, but the No 8 is a useful bus as it heads from the station to Piazza Italia, travelling along Corso Vittorio Emanuele. If arriving by car, you will find the familiar *centro* signs to direct you to the centre, where there are numerous supervised daytime car parks.

AROUND SASSARI

The **Chiesa di SS Trinità di Saccargia** *(Località Codrongianus; free; open 8am-noon & 4pm-7pm daily)*, a splendid Pisan-Romanesque church built in 1116, is set in a bare landscape near the village of Codrongianus, about 18km south-east of Sassari along the S131. You should have little trouble reaching Codrongianus by ARST bus from Sassari, but you do have to ask the driver to stop at the church if you don't want to walk the whole 2km from the village. The apse frescoes are definitely worth travelling for.

Just off the S131 near Torralba, about 40km south of Sassari, is the **Nuraghe Santu**

DOUG MCKINLAY

Sardinia's precious, protected Costa del Sud

ALAN BENSON

Traditional dress is common in eastern Sardinia.

FRANCES LINZEE GORDON

Tranquil waters hide a busy past: the River Temo made Bosa's tanning industry possible.

DOUG MCKINLAY

The bright bell tower of Alghero's cathedral

DOUG MCKINLAY

The local tipple in production: Sardinian vines

DOUG MCKINLAY

Looking out to sea: Alghero's port

DOUG MCKINLAY

Boats moored along the Costa Verde, Sardinia

DOUG MCKINLAY

Mural calling for Sardinian independence, Orgosolo

Antine *(Cooperativa La Pintadera; ☎ 079 84 72 96 or 079 84 72 96, Via Carlo Felice; admission €2.05, €2.60 including museum, €4.15 including guided tour in Italian; open 9am-8pm daily, guided tours hourly)*. Said to be the most beautiful nuraghe in Sardinia, it is well worth a visit. It can be reached from Sassari on the ARST bus heading for Padria, which stops at Torralba.

PORTO TORRES

This port town and major petrochemical centre has three main attractions other than the ferry: a megalithic altar (4500 BC), 6km out of town on the road to Sassari, the only example of its kind on Sardinia; a well-preserved Roman bridge (1st century BC) and Roman thermal baths; and the Pisan-Romanesque **Basilica di San Gavino** dating from the 11th century. To the north-west is the fast-developing beach resort of Stintino, a former fishing village which has managed to retain some of its atmosphere.

The town's main street is Corso Vittorio Emanuele, which is directly in front of you as you face away from the port. The tourist office (☎ 079 51 50 00), Piazza XX Settembre 2, is open 8.30am to 12.30pm and 3.30pm to 5.30pm Monday to Friday between June and mid-September. In April and the second half of September, it's only open in the morning.

Places to Stay & Eat

You may find it necessary to spend the night in Porto Torres.

Albergo Royal *(☎ 079 50 22 78, Via Sebastiano Satta 8)* Singles/doubles with bath €36.15/56.80. Decent accommodation and prices that drop significantly out of season.

Hotel Elisa *(☎/fax 079 51 32 60, Via Mare 2)* Singles/doubles with bath €43.90/67.15. The rooms are fine but it's the position that wins points here – any closer to the port and you'd be in the water.

There are numerous places where you can buy snacks and pizza by the slice, most of which are near the port.

Smile Café *(Corso Vittorio Emanuele 24)* This place does excellent sandwiches and panini – with a smile.

Poldiavolo *(☎ 079 50 18 78, Piazza XX Settembre 7)* Full meals from €12.90, pizzas from €4.15. For a simple meal, try this restaurant opposite the Banco di Sardegna and just near the tourist office.

Getting There & Away

Regular ARST buses connect Porto Torres with Sassari and Stintino. The bus station is on Piazzale Colombo at the port and the ticket office is at the Acciaro Bar, Corso Vittorio Emanuele 38. Regular trains connect Porto Torres with Sassari. A new train station has been built about 2km to the west of the port.

Tirrenia runs daily ferries to Genoa (three per day in summer). Its office (☎ 079 51 41 07) is in the ferry terminal at the port. Grimandi-Grandi Navi Veloci also runs a daily ferry to Genoa in summer (departure 9.30am, arrival 7pm). The French line SNCM runs four or five ferries per month to Toulon and Marseille, some via Bastia in Corsica, from the end of March to September. The agent for SNCM and Grimaldi in Porto Torres is Agenzia Paglietti/Petertours (☎ 079 51 44 77, fax 079 51 40 63), Corso Vittorio Emanuele 19.

STINTINO

A picturesque fishing village turned tourist resort, Stintino is very crowded in summer. A few kilometres north of the town at Torre Pelosa, facing Isola Asinara, is a magnificent sandy beach, the **Spiaggia La Pelosa**, with gorgeous white sand and that aquamarine water for which Sardinia is famous. In recent years, however, it has been badly eroded by storms.

Albergo Silvestrino *(☎ 079 52 30 07, fax 079 52 34 73, Via Sassari 14)* Singles/doubles with bath €46.50/77.45, low/high season half-board €67.15/87.80. Open Feb-Dec. The three-star Silvestrino offers attractive rooms in the centre of the village.

Hotel Lina *(☎ 079 52 30 71, fax 079 52 31 92, Via Lepanto 38)* Doubles €43.90-56.80 depending on the season. Located opposite the village's small port, this hotel is the best deal as far as centrality is concerned.

Lu Fanali *(☎ 079 52 30 54, Lungomare Cristoforo Colombo)* Pizzas €4.15-5.70, mains around €10.35. This snack bar/pizzeria/gelateria has a lovely big terrace overlooking the sea. Fish and seafood are the things to order here – especially the calamari, which is cooked in about eight different ways.

Stintino is accessible from Porto Torres by ARST bus (five daily in summer).

SANTA TERESA DI GALLURA

Together with Palau, about 20km to the east, this seaside resort is an affordable alternative to the jet-set hangouts on the Costa Smeralda. It is a very pleasant spot to pass a few relaxing days, especially if the magnificent coves, rock pools and small beaches of nearby Capo Testa appeal. From the town, you can see across the Stretto di Bonifacio to Corsica and catch one of the regular ferries which make the crossing to Corsica's southern tip.

SARDINIA

Information

Santa Teresa's AAST office (☎ 0789 75 41 27, fax 0789 75 41 85, ⓔ aaststg@tiscalinet.it, ⓦ www.regione.sardegna.it/aaststg) is in the town centre at Piazza Vittorio Emanuele 24. It opens 8.30am to 1pm and 3.30 to 8pm daily June to August, and 8.30am to 1pm and 3.30pm to 6.30pm Monday to Friday and 8.30am to 1pm on Saturday from October to May. The helpful staff can provide loads of information and may assist in finding accommodation. They have a booklet of hotels and camping options in town which includes a list of estate agents for apartment and villa rentals. You can ring/email ahead for information on hotels, as well as rooms and apartments for rent.

You can exchange money daily at the port or at the bank on Piazza V Emanuele.

For medical attention, go to the Guardia Medica (☎ 0789 75 40 79) on Via Carlo Felice, on the corner of Via Eleonora d'Arborea, a short walk from the town centre.

Things to See & Do

The main reason for a visit to this area is to spend time on the beach. There is the small **Spiaggia Rena Bianca** next to the town but it is recommended that you head for **Capo Testa**, a small cape connected to the mainland by an isthmus, about 5km west of Santa Teresa. There are lovely little beaches on either side of the cape, as well as a large sheltered rock pool. The road ends just below the lighthouse; the path to the right leads to the rock pool and the path to the left leads to a small cove and sandy beach. The cape is actually a military zone, but you'll only have problems if you try to get to the lighthouse.

Motorised rubber boats for up to six people are available for hire at Santa Teresa's port from €77.45 to €129.10 per day. **GULP Immobiliare** *(☎ 0789 75 56 89, ⓦ www.gulpimmobiliare.it, Via Nazionale 58)* rents apartments and villas as well as cars, which are handy for exploring the area. **Global Information** *(☎ 0789 75 50 80, Via Maria Teresa 40)* rents *motorini* (scooters) as well as cars. In low season scooters cost €15.50 per day rising to €31 in high season. **Sardinya Auto e Moto Noleggio** *(☎ 0789 75 42 47, Via del Porto 43)* at the port also hires cars and scooters.

Places to Stay

Santa Teresa offers extensive accommodation possibilities, including rooms and apartments for rent (contact the AAST office or GULP Immobiliare). It's advisable to book if you plan to arrive during late July or August.

You'll find all the camping facilities are out of town.

La Liccia *(☎/fax 0789 75 51 90, Strada Provinciale per Castelsardo, Km 66)* Sites per adult/child/tent up to €10.60/6.70/15. Open mid-June–Sept. This camp site is about 6km from Santa Teresa towards Palau, 400m from the beach.

Albergo Da Cecco *(☎ 0789 75 42 20, fax 0789 75 56 34, ⓔ hoteldacecco@tiscalinet.it, Via Po 3)* Singles/doubles with bath up to €46.50/62. Pleasant rooms near the centre of town are on offer at Da Cecco. To get there, take Via XX Settembre from the AAST office and turn right at Via Po.

Hotel al Porto *(☎ 0789 75 41 54, Via del Porto 20)* Low season singles/doubles with bath from €25.80/41.30, high season €31/51.65. Slightly out of the town centre down at the port (but within walking distance), this hotel is of the old-fashioned variety – time worn furnishings, saggy beds and gruff but friendly owners. Take the road to the port and turn left at the bottom.

Moderno *(☎ 0789 75 42 33, fax 0789 75 92 05, Via Umberto 39)* Low season singles/doubles with bath €38.75/72.30, high season €51.65/87.80. Just down from the main piazza, the Moderno offers clean, comfortable three-star accommodation.

Grade Hotel Corallaro *(☎ 0789 75 54 75, fax 0789 75 54 31, e info@hotelcorallaro.it, Località Rena Bianca)* Just out of the centre of town, the Corallaro is Santa Teresa's smartest hotel and offers luxurious four-star accommodation with all mod cons. Worth it if you want to splurge.

Places to Eat

There are plenty of good bars and sandwich shops where you can buy sandwiches.

Poldo's Pub *(☎ 0789 75 58 60, Via Garibaldi 4)* Open from 6pm Tues-Sun. This place fancies itself as a disco bar as well as a sandwich pitstop. Go there for a drink and a snack and decide for yourself.

Pasticceria Magnon *(☎ 0789 75 50 60, Via Magnon 26)* Open Tues-Sun. For takeaway cakes and pastries, head straight for Magnon, Santa Teresa's award-winning pasticceria.

Papè Satan *(Via Larmorama 20–22)* Pizzas from €5.15. For a taste of real Neapolitan pizza, you can't go past Papè Satan. His *margherita* with a thick, soft, doughy crust is as devilishly good as his name suggests.

Azzurra *(☎ 0789 75 47 89, Via del Porto 19)* Full meals from €15.50. Just up from the port, Azzurra does excellent pasta (try the home-made tagliatelle *alla curduiola* with fresh tomatoes, rocket, pecorino and heaps of pungent garlic) and is also popular for its seafood and pizzas.

La Torre *(☎ 0789 75 46 00, Via del Mare 36)* Seafood meals €20.65. Typical Sardinian fare is on offer here with an emphasis on fish and seafood.

If visiting Capo Testa, try ***Trattoria Bocche di Bonifacio*** *(☎ 0789 75 42 02, Località Capo Testa)*, whose speciality is seafood. Full meals from €20.65.

Getting There & Away

Regular ARST buses connect Santa Teresa with Olbia, Golfo Aranci and Palau, arriving in Via Eleonora d'Arborea, a short walk to the centre. There are also four buses daily to Sassari. Tickets can be purchased at the Bar Baby on Via Lu Pultani, running perpendicular to Via Nazionale, near the bus stop.

Ferry services to Corsica are run by two companies, Moby Lines (☎ 0789 75 14 49) and Saremar (☎ 0789 75 41 56); both have small offices at the port. Together, the two companies run between seven and 14 services daily, depending on the season.

PALAU & LA MADDALENA

Close to the Costa Smeralda, Palau is little more than a conglomeration of expensive hotels and private apartment blocks and is not as nice as Santa Teresa.

Just off the coast there are two islands which are much more interesting: **La Maddalena**, site of a US navy base, and **Caprera**, which was given to the hero of Italian unification, Giuseppe Garibaldi, by Vittorio Emanuele II. Garibaldi spent his last years there and it is possible to visit his house, now the **Museo Garibaldino** *(admission €2.05; open 9am-1.30pm daily, closed for renovation at the time of writing)*. Most of the island is a nature reserve, which means that camping is forbidden; however, it offers wonderful walking opportunities. The two islands are connected by a narrow causeway over which vehicles can pass.

La Maddalena has an attractive main town, several good beaches and is popular with campers. Its drawback is its disaffected youth whose presence in the central streets can't be ignored.

Information

Palau's tourist office (☎/fax 0789 70 95 70) is at Via Nazionale 96. It opens 8am to 1pm and 4pm to 7pm Monday to Saturday. From June to September, it also opens the same hours on Sunday. It has little in the way of tourist information, but staff can assist with accommodation, including apartments and rooms for rent.

SARDINIA

La Maddalena's tourist office (☎ 0789 73 63 21, fax 0789 73 66 55) is at Piazza Barone de Geneys, about 400m from the port (turn left as you get off the ferry and keep walking/driving until you see a pink building with a big yellow 'i'). It opens 8.30am to 1pm and 4.30pm to 5.30pm Monday to Friday, 8.30am to 1pm Saturday. In July and August, it usually opens on Sunday as well.

Places to Stay

Camping Capo d'Orso *(☎ 0789 70 20 07, fax 0789 70 20 06, Località Le Saline)* High season sites per adult/child/tent €5.70/4.15/18.10. Open May-Sept. This popular, well-equipped camp site is just east of Palau by the seaside on the cape of the same name. It's expensive in July and August but in low season prices are significantly reduced.

There are numerous hotels and rooms for rent in Palau, but you should book ahead for July and August.

Hotel Serra *(☎ 0789 70 95 19, fax 0789 70 97 13, Via Nazionale 17)* Singles/doubles without €28.40/41.30, with bath €31/43.90. This hotel is Palau's cheapest deal with adequate rooms in the centre of town.

La Roccia *(☎/fax 0789 70 95 28, Via dei Mille 15)* Singles/doubles €46.50/67.15. Single rooms are overpriced at this three-star hotel, but accommodation is clean and comfortable.

Hotel Palau *(☎ 0789 70 84 68, Via Baragge)* June & Sept singles/doubles from €82.65/123.95, July & Aug €118.80/185.90. Open June-Sept. If you're looking for luxury accommodation, the four-star Hotel Palau will suit you.

On La Maddalena there are several options.

Villaggio Camping La Maddalena *(☎ 0789 72 80 51, fax 0789 72 77 76, Località Moneta)* Sites per adult/child €11.35/5.15, bungalows (sleeping 4) from €36.15 per day. Open June–mid-Oct. This good camping ground, located at Moneta, is accessible by local bus to Caprera from the port of La Maddalena.

Campeggio Abbatoggia *(☎ 0789 73 91 73, Località Abbatoggia)* Sites per adult/child/tent €10.35/5.70/2.60. This place is at Lo Strangolato, near a lovely beach. It's reasonably cheap and accessible by local bus.

In the town of La Maddalena, there are a couple of OK hotels.

Hotel Il Gabbiano *(☎ 0789 72 25 07, fax 0789 72 24 56, Via Giulio Cesare 20)* Rooms with bath up to €59.40. One of the most central of La Maddalena's hotels, with decent rooms (if rather hefty prices).

Hotel Giuseppe Garibaldi *(☎ 0789 73 73 14, fax 0789 73 73 26, ⓔ htlgaribaldi@tiscalinet.it, Via Lamarmora)* Singles/doubles up to €77.45/123.95. This place has clean, comfortable, functional rooms – but they're nothing special. Look for the modern orange brick building up behind the seafront (bear left as you leave the port and follow the signs).

Places to Eat

In Palau, there are several decent places to eat.

La Capannaccia *(☎ 0789 70 40 14, SS Paula-Santa Teresa Km 5)* Pizzas from €4.15, full meals from €15.50. It's 5km out of Palau (on the road to Santa Teresa) but this huge pizzeria really pulls in the crowds. When it's full, it's noisy and fun and it's always good value.

Da Robertino *(☎ 0789 70 96 10, Via Nazionale 22)* Full meals around €23.25. Good home cooking is the hallmark of this reliable, family-run trattoria.

La Taverna *(☎ 0789 70 92 89, Via Rossini)* Full meals around €36.15. This is a top-of-the-range eatery, located off Via Nazionale, where you can eat excellent seafood and fish.

On La Maddalena, you've got several choices, although you're unlikely to find the meal of your trip here.

Pappa e Ciccia *(Via Garibaldi 42)* Pizza slices €1.30-2.05, *focaccia* (flatbread) from €1.05. This is one of several fast-food/takeaway joints on the road parallel to the seafront.

Ristorante La Terrazza *(☎ 0789 73 53 05, Via Villa Glori)* Meals from €18.10. Open Mon-Sat. This is a good choice if you want something a little more upmarket. The special *cena alla Sarda* (four courses for

€25.80) is a full meal comprising local dishes and produce.

You can buy supplies at the ***Minimarket da Gemma*** *(Via Nazionale 66)*.

Getting There & Around

Palau is easily accessible by ARST bus from Sassari, Santa Teresa di Gallura and Olbia. Turmotravel (☎ 0789 2 14 87) operates a service to the airport at Olbia (five daily). FdS operates a year-round bus service to Tempio Pausania and Sassari (three daily mid-June to mid-September). Autoservizi Caramelli (☎ 0789 70 94 95) buses also run to Porto Torres and connect Palau with places along the Costa Smeralda, including Baia Sardinia and Porto Cervo. All buses stop at Palau's small port. Timetables are posted inside the ferry terminal at the port; the tourist office also has timetables.

Traghetti Isole Sarde (TRIS; ☎ 199 13 30 01, W www.tris.it) ferries connect Palau with Genoa and La Spezia. Linee Lauro operates to Naples three days per week from April to January. Contact the Bulciolu agency in Palau (☎ 0789 70 95 05), Via Fonte Vecchia 11, for more details.

Car ferries (operated by TRIS ferries and by Saremar) make the short crossing between Palau and La Maddalena every 20 minutes during summer, and about every half hour in the off season. One-way tickets cost €2.30 per person (€1.55 in low season) and €4.90 for a small car. Ferries generally operate from 8.15am until 7.15pm.

Once on the island, you can catch one of the blue local buses which leave from the port every hour or so (more frequently in summer). The buses to Nido d'Aquila and Panoramica make good round trips of the island; the Panoramica bus goes to the island's best beaches. Buses for Caprera also leave from the port. Alternatively, hire bikes or scooters from Nicol Sport (☎ 0789 73 75 94), Via Aldo Moro 18, on the seafront just to the left of the car-ferry dock.

COSTA SMERALDA

For the average tourist, the Costa Smeralda (Emerald Coast) is out of reach. There are no hotels of less than three stars, which means that prices for a double room start at around €103.30 per night. The coast was purchased in 1962 by a group of international investors led by Prince Karim Aga Khan and was basically developed from scratch. Its resorts include Baia Sardinia, Liscia di Vacca and Porto Cervo, all bearing a stronger resemblance to Disneyland than traditional seaside towns. The coastline is certainly beautiful but it is not the real Sardinia and unless you have money to burn, or very rich friends with an apartment, it's better to spend the day on one of its beaches and continue your journey.

Those who would like to stay on the Costa Smeralda can obtain information about accommodation from the tourist office at Arzachena (☎ 0789 8 26 24, fax 0789 8 10 90), Via Paolo Dettori 43 (inside the ERSAT building). It opens 8am to 2pm and 3pm to 6.30pm Monday to Friday (closed Monday afternoons in low season) and 8am to 1pm Saturday.

The coast is accessible by ARST, FdS and Autoservizi Caramelli buses from Palau and Olbia.

OLBIA

postcode 07026 • pop 43,000

This busy port and industrial centre will very likely be the first glimpse of Sardinia for many tourists. It is a major port for ferries arriving from Civitavecchia, Genoa and Livorno and, while it's not particularly unpleasant, it's not particularly interesting either and is best passed through quickly.

Orientation

If arriving by ferry, you will find yourself at a well-organised port complete with a new ferry terminal and a local bus (No 3) to take you into the centre of town (only about 1km). Trains run from the station to the port to coincide with ferry departures. Intercity buses terminate at the end of Corso Umberto. Head east along Corso Umberto to reach the town centre. The train station is close by on Via Pala, off Piazza Risorgimento.

Information

Tourist Offices The AAST office (☎ 0789 2 14 53, fax 0789 2 22 21) is at Via C Piro 1,

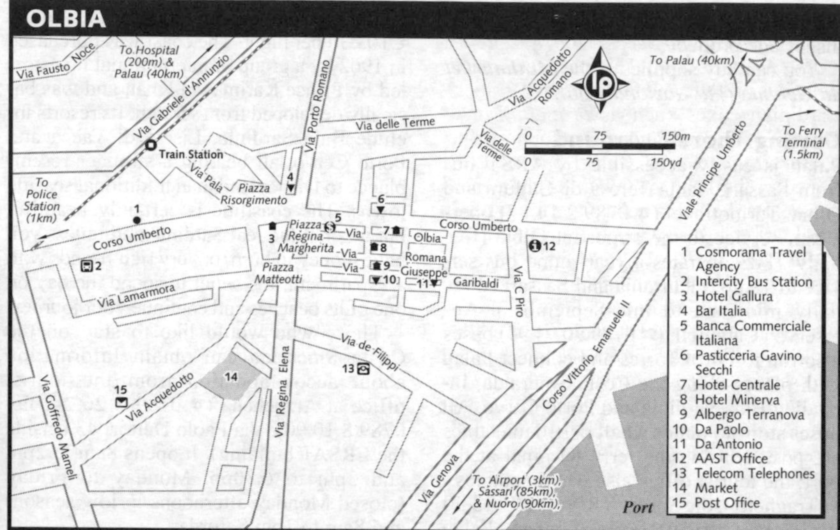

just off Corso Umberto. It opens 8.30am to 1pm and 4pm to 6pm Monday to Friday, 8.30am to 1pm Saturday (the hours are sometimes extended in high season). The staff are very keen to help and will advise (in English) on places to stay and eat locally. They can also provide information about accommodation and places to visit throughout Sardinia.

Money There are three major banks on Corso Umberto, including the Banca Commerciale Italiana at No 191, which does cash advances on both Visa and MasterCard.

Post & Communications The main post office is on Via Acquedotto, off Piazza Matteotti, and there is a row of Telecom pay phones on Via de Filippi.

Medical Services & Emergency The Ospedale Civile (hospital; ☎ 0789 55 22 00) is on Viale Aldo Moro, about a 15-minute walk north of the centre along Via Porto Romano and Via Gabriele d'Annunzio. The police station, called the *commissariato* (☎ 0789 2 20 81), is at Via Piemonte 5–7.

Places to Stay

Albergo Terranova *(☎ 0789 2 23 95, fax 0789 2 72 55, e htlterranova@tiscalinet.it, Via Giuseppe Garibaldi 6)* Low season singles/doubles from €36.15/49.05, high season €67.15/98.15. You might not want to fork out the high season rates, but you can't get a much better-positioned hotel in Olbia than the Terranova.

Hotel Minerva *(☎/fax 0789 2 11 90, Via Mazzini 7)* Singles/doubles €25.80/36.15, with bath €33.55/51.65. This hotel is as equally well positioned as Albergo Terranova but is considerably cheaper (and less fancy).

Hotel Gallura *(☎ 0789 2 46 48, fax 0789 2 46 29, Corso Umberto 145)* Singles/doubles with bath from €51.65/72.30. This is a pleasant hotel located just west of Piazza Regina Margherita; its excellent restaurant is a bonus.

Hotel Centrale *(☎ 0789 2 30 17, fax 0789 2 64 64, Corso Umberto 85)* Singles/doubles with bath €62/82.65. The name must come from its central position. This hotel offers comfortable, clean accommodation, with some rooms looking over Corso Umberto.

Places to Eat

Pasticceria Gavino Secchi *(☎ 0789 2 21 78, Corso Umberto 144)* This pasticceria does delicious pizzette and fabulous sweet, sticky Sardinian cakes such as *arancini*, small clusters of almonds, honey and orange rind.

Bar Italia *(Corso Umberto 138)* Positioned in the heart of Olbia, on the central square, Bar Italia is a good place for a speedy breakfast, a leisurely lunch or an aperitif.

Da Paolo *(☎ 0789 2 16 75, Via Giuseppe Garibaldi 18)* Full meals from €18.10. Open Mon-Sun afternoon. Typical Sardinian fare is on offer at Da Paolo. Its muralled interior is almost a bit too twee but the food and service more than make up for it. Try the *culingiones*, a fat pasta parcel filled with potato, cheese and herbs, or the *crespelle* (crepes) with ricotta and artichokes.

Da Antonio *(☎ 0789 2 13 35, Via Giuseppe Garibaldi 48)* Pizzas from €5.15. Tasty pizza is the highlight here and it's served at both lunch and dinner.

If you want to stock up on food supplies, head for the Mercato Civico on Via Acquedotto.

Getting There & Away

Olbia's airport, a few kilometres south-east of the town, has flights to and from Italy's main cities. To get to the airport, take city bus No 8. Contact the local transport company ASPO (☎ 0789 2 13 17 or 0789 2 13 26) for information.

ARST buses depart from both the port (coinciding with ferry arrivals) and the bus station in the centre for Arzachena and the resorts of the Costa Smeralda, Palau, Santa Teresa di Gallura, Sassari and Nuoro.

There are some train connections to the major towns, including Sassari, Cagliari and Oristano.

In the high season, the crossing to Civitavecchia is made by Tirrenia ferries (eight hours, daily) and the fast service (four hours, departing at 8.30am; six hours, departing at midnight). The company has an office at the ferry terminal (☎ 0789 20 71 06 or 0789 20 71 07). This is an extremely busy route and it is very important to book at least three weeks in advance during the summer months, particularly if you want to take a car.

Ferries run by Moby Lines connect Olbia with Livorno three times per day in the high season. The company has an office at the ferry terminal (☎ 0789 2 79 27). You can book ferry travel on both Tirrenia and Moby Lines at Cosmorama Travel Agency (☎ 0789 2 85 33), Corso Umberto 17.

If you are taking a car on a ferry, you will find clear signs directing you to the port and to your point of embarkation. From the town centre, head for Viale Principe Umberto and then Viale Isola Bianca to reach the ferry terminal.

GOLFO ARANCI

Golfo Aranci is a ferry terminal on the promontory north-east of Olbia where FS ferries from Civitavecchia dock. You can catch a train directly to Olbia, or take an ARST bus to Olbia, Palau or Santa Teresa di Gallura. It's possible to buy a ticket in Rome (at Stazione Termini or any Sestante office) which covers the cost of the train trip to Civitavecchia, the ferry crossing and the train to Olbia. Sardinia Ferries link Golfo Aranci with Livorno (day and night services) and Civitavecchia (three daytime services including two fast runs) from April to September. For booking and information, call the Livorno office on ☎ 0586 88 13 80, Golfo Aranci on ☎ 0789 4 69 10 or 0789 4 68 25 or Civitavecchia on ☎ 0766 50 07 14. Sometimes there are special prices for two people and a car on daytime trips.

Eastern Sardinia

Nuoro province, about halfway up the east coast of Sardinia, encompasses the area known as the Barbagia. It has unspoiled, isolated beaches, spectacular gorges and great walking routes, as well as important Nuraghic sites. More than in any other part of Sardinia, this is where you'll be able to get a real sense of the island's traditional culture. Though tourism in the area is increasing, the people remain strongly tied to traditions swept aside by tourism in other parts of the island. Shepherds still tend their flocks in remote areas of the province, often living alone in stone or wooden shacks and having little contact with the outside world. It is common to see older women in the traditional black, ankle-length dresses of the area, their heads covered by Spanish-style black, fringed shawls. It's best to visit the area in spring when patron saint feast days are frequent. On these occasions, the young people dress in beautifully embroidered traditional costumes and perform ancient folk dances.

The locals remain fairly aloof and it is important when visiting the smaller, more remote towns to behave respectfully. If you manage to befriend a local, you'll find them incredibly hospitable and helpful.

Larger towns in the area are accessible by bus, but a car is a necessity to explore the smaller villages and the mountains. A surprisingly cheap way to explore parts of the area is by walking with an organised guide.

Nuoro is the provincial capital and gateway to the enchanting coastline around Cala Gonone, Baunei and Urzulei's dramatic highlands and gorges and the Gennargentu and Supramonte mountain ranges.

If you are travelling by car in eastern Sardinia, you will need a detailed road map of the area. One of the best is published by the Istituto Geografico de Agostini. The various tourist offices have maps which detail the locations of the main sights.

NUORO

postcode 08100 • pop 40,000

There is not a lot to see and do in Nuoro, but it is a good starting point for an exploration of the Barbagia. The old centre of town is around Piazza delle Grazie, Corso Garibaldi and Via Italia, near the tourist office. From Piazza delle Grazie, walk along Via IV Novembre and Via Dante. ARST buses terminate in Via Lucania, near the train station. The station is about a 20-minute walk from Piazza delle Grazie along Via La Marmora (turn left as you leave the station).

Information

The EPT office (☎ 0784 3 00 83) is at Piazza Italia 19. It opens 9am to 1pm Monday to Friday and also 4pm to 6.30pm Tuesday and Wednesday. It is also open on Saturday and Sunday in summer.

The main post office is on Piazza Crispi, between Corso Garibaldi and Piazza Dante, and there is a Telecom office at Via Brigata Sassari 6.

Things to See

While in town, you might as well take a look at the neoclassical **Cattedrale di Santa Maria della Neve** *(Piazza Santa Maria della Neve; open 8am-noon & 4pm-7pm daily)* and the monument and square dedicated to the local poet Sebastiano Satta. Up the hill behind the cathedral is the **Museo della Vita e delle Tradizioni Popolari Sardi** *(Museum of the Life and Traditions of the Sardinian People; ☎ 0784 24 29 00, Via Antonio Mereu 56; admission €2.60; open 9am-1pm & 3pm-7pm daily Oct–mid-June, 9am-8pm daily mid-June–Sept)*. It's well worth a visit, housing as it does a superb collection of traditional costumes (many of which are still used during local festivals), jewellery, masks, textiles and musical instruments.

Special Events

At the end of August, the Festa del Redentore is held in Nuoro. This folk festival and parade is attended by thousands of people from all over the island, who dress in traditional regional costume.

Places to Stay

There are no real budget options.

Mini Hotel *(☎ 0784 3 31 59, Via Brofferio 13)* Singles/doubles with bath €32/43.90. This pleasant hotel is – as its name suggests – a small place. It is off Via Roma, near Piazza Sebastiano Satta.

Hotel Grillo *(☎ 0784 3 86 78, fax 0784 320 05, Via Monsignor Melas 14)* Singles/doubles with bath €47.50/63, half-board €56.80. From the outside this hotel is pretty ugly, but inside the rooms are pleasant.

Places to Eat

Caffè Venezia *(☎ 0784 3 00 26, Via B Sassari 1)* Fruit juice €1.30, panini from €1.55. Located diagonally opposite the tourist office on the corner of Piazza Italia, this is as good a place as any for a snack or light meal.

Pizzeria-Trattoria Il Rifugio *(☎ 0784 23 23 55, Vico del Pozzo 4)* Pizzas from €4.65. This place is in a narrow street parallel to Via La Marmora in the old centre near Le Grazie. The pizzas are tasty and filling.

To pick up supplies, shop at the ***Emanuela market*** *(Via Isonzo)*, off Via Trieste just near Piazza Italia, or at the great little ***grocery shop*** *(Corso Garibaldi 168)* and the ***cheese shop*** next door.

Getting There & Away

ARST (☎ 0784 29 41 73) buses connect Nuoro with Cagliari (one daily), Olbia (six daily) and Sassari (one daily), as well as towns throughout the province, including Oliena (hourly), Orgosolo (10 daily), Dorgali and Cala Gonone (seven daily) and Baunei (two daily). PANI buses head for Cagliari, Sassari and Oristano. The train reaches Macomer and Bosa on the west coast, where there are connections with the main north-south line.

OLIENA

The value of visiting Oliena, or Orgosolo farther south, is to get a better idea of how locals live in Sardinia's interior. Neither town offers much in the way of tourist facilities or sights, although both, in their own way, provide an alternative travel experience.

Oliena is about 12km south-east of Nuoro and is easily accessible by regular ARST bus. For the more adventurous, it is a place from which to set out on a walking exploration of the Supramonte area to the south, to **Tiscali**, or to various isolated Nuraghic sites. Remember that there are very few clearly marked trails and that the area is full of goat tracks, so orientation is a serious problem; it is probably more sensible to go with a guide on an organised trek. There are several groups based in Oliena and Dorgali which organise guided walks; most hotels in the area also have guides who work for them (see the boxed text 'Discovering the Barbagia' later).

On the morning of Easter Sunday, S'Incontru, a traditional festival dating back to the time of Spanish domination, takes place. In separate processions, the women of the town carry a statue of the Madonna and the men carry a statue of Christ on the cross. They meet in Oliena's main piazza and the place goes crazy, as every man and boy in town greets the *incontru* (meeting of the statues) by shooting a gun into the air.

Places to Stay & Eat

Accommodation options are limited.

Ci Kappa *(☎/fax 0784 28 87 33, Via Martin Luther King 2)* Singles/doubles €31/43.90, half-board €38.75. This is at the cheaper end of the scale and becomes good value when you do the half-board option, as it has a very good pizzeria-restaurant.

Hotel Su Gologone *(☎ 0784 28 75 12, fax 0784 28 76 68, e gologone@tin.it, Località Su Gologone)* Low season singles/doubles €87.80/129.10, high season half-board up to €113.60, full board up to €134.30. A few kilometres east of town, at the beginning of the beautiful Lainitto valley, is the four-star Su Gologone. This stunning hotel is in an exquisite setting and is a particularly good option for people wanting to explore the area, as it organises guided tours, walks and even horse-riding expeditions. It has its own swimming pool, supplied by an impressive underground spring. The ***restaurant*** serves excellent traditional local dishes and is justifiably renowned throughout the island.

ORGOSOLO

About 18km farther south and reached from Nuoro on an ARST bus, Orgosolo is famous for its tradition of *banditismo* (banditry), but this isn't a subject you will find the locals willing to discuss openly. This tradition was immortalised by the 1963 Italian film *The Bandits of Orgosolo*. One of the town's more notorious *banditi* was released from prison in 1992 and acted as an unofficial negotiator in the much-publicised kidnapping of the son of a Costa Smeralda hotelier (and a relative of the Aga Khan). The child was eventually released in the countryside close to the town.

Orgosolo is also interesting for the series of leftist and nationalistic murals which

SARDINIA

Discovering the Barbagia

There are several groups based in or around Oliena and Dorgali which organise guided treks to various parts of the Supramonte. Most of these excursions are half- or full-day treks. In some cases, the organisers include a packed lunch, sometimes lunch at a local agriturismo organisation is arranged and sometimes you can have a traditional lunch cooked by local shepherds. Most groups will pick you up (and drop you off) at your accommodation in Cala Gonone, Dorgali or Oliena.

There are several **Nuraghic sites** in the area and these form the destinations of many organised treks. The most famous of these is the archaeological area of **Tiscali**. It is touted as a Nuraghic site and indeed pre-Nuraghic and Nuraghic artefacts have been found here, but archaeologists now think the (badly preserved) remnants of the stone huts actually date from the medieval period. It is believed that Nuraghic ruins lie beneath the visible remnants, but excavations have only just commenced so it will be some years before the truth about Tiscali comes out.

Regardless of its exact archaeological origins, however, Tiscali and its huge *dolina* (once an enclosed cave whose roof fell in around 50,000 years ago) is incredibly atmospheric, and a trek there is highly recommended (except for the vertiginous). After a short four-wheel drive through the beautiful Valle di Lainitto, you start the trek uphill. About an hour later, and having passed through the so-called secret passage (which explains the positioning of the settlement in a protected, easily defensible place), you peer into the dolina from above, then descend into the chasm. The views on the way up are simply breathtaking. Once in the **dolina** *(admission €2.60; open 9am-7pm daily May-Sept, 9am-5pm daily in winter)*, you have to pay a fee to the guardians of the site, which includes a talk by an Italian-speaking guide and a pamphlet (in English) about the chasm.

You *can* reach Tiscali on your own, but it is not recommended if you are inexperienced. The intrepid can get maps and directions from the tourist office in Dorgali (a longer, but less steep, walk than the approach from the Valle di Lainitto).

Other Nuraghic sites in the area include **Serra Orrios** and **Nuraghe Mannu**. Both can be reached easily if you have private transport. See Nuraghic Sites under Cala Gonone, Dorgali & Around later.

Another trekking possibility is to explore the spectacular **Gola di Gorropu** (Gorropu Gorge), about 15km south of Dorgali. To get right into the gorge, you'll need to hire a guide, or to go on an organised trek, since you'll need ropes and harnesses to descend some sections of the gorge. However, it's possible to walk into the gorge from its northern entrance for about 1km before it becomes impossible to proceed.

To get to the entrance by car, go south from Dorgali along the road for Urzulei for a couple of kilometres. After the turn-off to the left for Cala Gonone, there is a dirt road to the right, which

decorate the facades of many of its buildings. The brainchild of a local art teacher, Francesco del Casino, a native of Siena who has lived in Orgosolo for many years, the murals started appearing in 1973. Generally designed by him, they have been painted by local students as well as other artists. The murals originally reflected fairly extreme political views on a range of international issues, such as the war in Vietnam, apartheid in South Africa and the Palestinian question, but they now deal mainly with domestic social issues.

Places to Stay & Eat

Petit Hotel *(☎/fax 0784 40 20 09, Via Mannu)* Singles/doubles with bath €23.25/33.55. This small family-run hotel is a good choice.

A local group organises **lunches** in the countryside just outside town, where you can enjoy one of Sardinia's most traditional dishes, *porcheddu* (roast sucking pig flavoured with herbs and wood-roasted whole on a spit). The travel agency ***Avitur*** *(☎ 0789 5 32 30), Corso Umberto 142b, Olbia)*, organises guided trips by bus from Olbia to Orgosolo, including the lunch, for around

Discovering the Barbagia

heads for the Hotel Sant'Elene (see Places to Stay & Eat under Dorgali, Cala Gonone & Around later). Follow this into the valley for about 8km (don't head uphill for the hotel) and you'll get to a small bridge. Here you'll have to park the car and continue on foot. Walk for about an hour and a half to reach two small lakes and the entrance to the gorge – one of the most spectacular and romantic landscapes in Sardinia. The huge boulders scattered around the entrance to the gorge are a reminder that nature can be harsh as well as beautiful in Sardinia. Allow a full day for the expedition, which will give you time for the walk, a picnic and a swim in the lakes.

If you're on foot, but want to explore the gorge, you could stay at the Hotel Sant'Elene and walk to its entrance from there. Ask at the Dorgali tourist office for information.

Both Coop Ghivine (see below) and Società Gorropu (see Baunei, Urzulei & Around later) organise treks into the Gola di Gorropu.

For longer walks in the Barbagia (up to three days or even a week, where overnight stays involve either camping or accommodation in agriturismo locations), contact the groups in advance. One popular three-day walk is through the Gola di Gorropu to the beach at Cala Luna.

The tourist offices at Oliena and Dorgali have lists of the groups that organise excursions, but beware that not all guides speak English. (For longer, pre-organised treks, interpreters are usually involved.)

Trekking organisers include: ***Sardegna Nascosta*** *(☎ 0784 28 85 50, Via Masiloghi 35)*; ***Centro Escursioni*** *(☎ 0347 824 95 17, Rifugio Sa Oche, Località Lanaitto Oliena, just out of Oliena)*; and ***Barbagia Insolita*** *(☎ 0784 28 60 05 or 0348 391 49 60, W www.barbagiainsolita.it, Corso Vittorio Emanuele 48, Oliena)*. They all organise pretty similar excursions; Barbagia Insolita, for example, has a half-day trek to the Nuraghic site at Tiscali (€31); they also do full-day treks which include packed lunch or lunch with shepherds in the mountains (€51.65). You can choose between demanding or more manageable walks to places including Tiscali, the Gola di Gorropu, Monte Corrasi and the Codula di Luna valley.

The Dorgali-based ***Coop Ghivine*** *(☎ 0336 32 69 57, fax 0784 967 21, e ghivine@tiscalinet.it, W www.ghivine@tiscalinet.it, Via Lamarmora 69e)* is one of the most professional groups in the area and organises guided walks in the Supramonte, treks to the Gola di Gorropu or the Codula di Luna, and even horse trekking if you prefer.

Most hotels in the area also have guides who work for them and take groups of guests on guided walks. For example, Trekking Su Gologone, based at the Hotel Su Gologone (see Places to Stay & Eat under Oliena earlier), organises a variety of treks and gentler walks combined with 4WD tours.

€41.30 per head. Otherwise you can arrange to attend a lunch by contacting the organisers in Orgosolo directly on ☎ 0784 40 20 71. The cost for lunch only is €15.50 per head. (Note that these lunches are generally only for large groups; individual travellers must join a pre-planned trip, but they are organised frequently in summer.)

DORGALI, CALA GONONE & AROUND

The fast-developing seaside resort of **Cala Gonone** is an excellent base from which to explore the coves along the coastline, as well as the Nuraghic sites and rugged terrain inland. There is a Pro Loco office (☎ 0784 9 36 96) on Viale del Bue Marino, where you can pick up maps, a list of hotels and information to help you explore the area. It has rather sporadic opening hours, but is generally open from May to September. More reliable and open throughout winter is CeST (☎ 0784 92 01 49, e cestgal@tin.it, W www.calagonone.com), Viale Colombo 8, which has heaps of information about small towns in the heart of Sardinia, including advice on local festivals and events. The office opens 9am to 1pm Monday to Friday; it also opens 5pm to 7pm Monday to Friday from May to September and the same hours on Saturday and Sunday in July and August.

There is also a very helpful tourist office (☎/fax 0784 9 62 43, W www.dorgali.it), Via Lamarmora 108, in the nearby town of **Dorgali**, through which you will pass on your way to Cala Gonone. It opens 9am to 1pm and 3.30pm to 7pm Monday to Friday. It is also open on Saturday and Sunday (approximately the same hours) from July to September. Dorgali is a pretty town which still has a very traditional feel, with plenty of the older women still wearing traditional costume. It has a small **archaeological museum** *(☎ 0784 9 61 13, Via Lamarmora; admission €2.05; open 9am-1pm & 4pm-7pm daily May-Sept, other months by request only)* which contains finds from Nuraghic and other sites in the area.

Nuraghic Sites

Villaggio Nuragico Nuraghe Mannu *(admission €2.60; guided tours hourly 9am-11am & 3pm-5pm daily May; 9am-11am & 4pm-7pm daily June-Aug; 10am-noon & 3pm-5pm daily Sept; closed Oct-Mar)* is just off the road that connects Dorgali with Cala Gonone. As the road descends (after you have passed through the tunnel), there is a signpost clearly marked to the left just after the first hairpin bend. Archaeologists have found evidence that the site was active from the Bronze Age up to the Roman period. Recent excavations have defined the remains of a single Nuraghic tower as well as foundations of Roman buildings.

Villaggio Nuragico Serra Orrios *(admission €3.10; guided tours hourly 9am-noon & 2pm-4pm daily Oct-Mar; 9am-noon & 3pm-5pm daily Apr-June & Sept; 9am-noon & 4pm-6pm daily July-Aug)* can be reached from Dorgali by taking the road to Nuoro and Oliena. Go past the Oliena turn-off (to the left 4km out of Dorgali) and continue towards the S129. About 2km before the S129 (if you hit that road, you've gone too far) is an unpaved road with a sign to Nuraghe Serra Orrios. Park your car; it's about a 600m walk to the site. The settlement is interesting because of the remains of two small temples and the complex urban structure, involving what appear to be blocks of streets. Around 70 huts are visible, in which it is believed around 300 people lived. There is evidence that its inhabitants were involved in cattle breeding, agriculture, and arts and crafts (including wool spinning and weaving and pottery).

For information on all these Nuraghic sites, contact the Dorgali tourist office (☎ 0784 9 62 43). Note that opening times do vary so it is wise to check before setting out.

Coves & Caves

From Cala Gonone's small port, you can catch a boat to the spectacular entrance of the **Grotta del Bue Marino** (Cave of the Monk Seal), where a guide will take you on a 1km walk to see vast caves with stalagmites, stalactites and lakes. The caves were one of the last habitats of the rare monk seal which has not been sighted for some years. The return boat trip costs €6.70 (high season) or €5.70 (low season) and admission to the caves costs €5.15.

There are also boats to the beautiful **Cala Luna** (between €8.25 and €13.95 return, depending on the season). This stunning, isolated cove is accessible only on foot or by boat. The journey can be combined with a trip to the Grotta for €10.35 to €16 return, depending on the season. In July and August the beach is crowded with sunbathers and camping is forbidden. At other times it is deserted and you can ask for permission to camp near the only building in the area, the restaurant Su Neulagi (☎ 0784 9 33 92). Boats also head along the coast to beaches at **Cala Sisine** (from €12.40 to €14.45 return, depending on the season) and **Cala Mariolu** (from €15.50 to €21.70).

There are various operators who do these boat trips; all are based at the port of Cala Gonone. For information on all boat trips contact the Nuovo Consorzio Trasporti Marittimi (☎ 0784 9 33 05, fax 0784 9 33 02) Via Vespucci, Cala Gonone.

Another cave well worth seeing is the **Grotta Ispinigolo** *(☎ Dorgali Tourist Office*

0784 9 62 43, Località Ispingolo; admission €5.15; open Apr-Sept; guided visits hourly 9am-noon & 3pm-5pm daily May & June; 9am-1pm & 3pm-6pm daily July & Aug; 9am-noon & 3pm-6pm daily Sept) It's located about 5km out of Dorgali off the road to Orosei. Turn right onto a paved road following the signs; the cave is 2km from the turn-off. A well-organised guided itinerary takes you down (280 steps) into the cave, a feature of which is a 38m-high column, formed when a stalactite and a stalagmite joined thousands of years ago. Archaeologists believe the cave was used as a shelter for prehistoric humans, and Phoenician necklaces were found here (they are now in the archaeological museum in Dorgali).

Walking Trails

There is a walking track along the coast linking Cala Gonone and Cala Luna. The track starts at Cala Fuili, which is about 3.5km from Cala Gonone. It's then about 4km between the two coves on rocky terrain but with breathtaking coastal views, and the walk takes about 1½ hours one way. You can organise with the boat operators at Cala Gonone either to be dropped off at Cala Luna and walk back to Cala Gonone or to be picked up at Cala Luna at a specified time.

The **Codula di Luna** is a long valley stretching from Cala Luna to the S125 Orientale Sarda, a road near Urzulei. You can walk from Teletotes (signposted off the S125) through the Codula di Luna (about 3½ hours one way). Ask at the Cala Gonone or Dorgali tourist offices for information.

The Dorgali tourist office has information about other trails in the area, including how to reach the archaeological remains at Tiscali, although most locals advise to undertake this trail only with a guide (see the boxed text 'Discovering the Barbagia' earlier).

Other Activities

For boat/dinghy hire or charter cruises, there are plenty of options at the port. **Cielomar** *(☎ 0784 92 00 14, Piazzale Porto)* at Cala Gonone's port rents four-person dinghies for around €98.15 per day.

For diving courses, contact **Dimensione Mare** *(☎ 0784 9 67 66, W www.calagonone.com/dimensionemare, on Viale Colombo, Cala Gonone)*.

Places to Stay & Eat

Free-camping is strictly forbidden in the area.

Camping Cala Gonone *(☎ 0784 9 31 65, fax 0784 9 32 55, W www.campingcalagonone.it, Via Collodi 1)* Sites including tent per adult/child up to €14.45/8.25, low/high season bungalows sleeping four €62/103.30. Open Jun-Oct. This is one of Sardinia's best camp sites, with excellent sports facilities including a nice pool. It also offers caravans (with shared facilities) and bungalows and chalets with bathrooms.

Piccolo Hotel *(☎ 0784 9 32 32, fax 0784 9 42 93, Via Cristoforo Colombo)* High season singles/doubles with bath up to €31/51.15. This hotel is near the port and has very pleasant rooms.

Hotel La Plaia *(☎/fax 0784 9 31 06, Via Collodi)* Singles €33.55-49.05, doubles €49.05-69.70. All mod cons and very comfortable rooms are the features of this three-star hotel.

Pop Hotel *(☎ 0784 9 31 85, fax 0784 9 31 58, Via Marco Polo)* Singles/doubles from €46.50/77.45, half-board/full board €56.80/67.15. Conveniently located right at the port, Pop Hotel has good accommodation and an attractive, inexpensive restaurant.

Hotel Sant'Elene *(☎ 0784 9 45 72, fax 0784 9 53 85, Località Sant'Elene)* Singles/doubles €25.80/56.80, half-board from €49.05. Just out of Dorgali, at the start of the road to Gola di Gorropu, is Hotel Sant' Elene, which boasts spotless rooms and an excellent restaurant with a reasonably priced tourist menu.

Due Chiacchiere *(☎ 0784 9 33 86, Via Acquadolce 13)* Pizzas from €5.15, full meals from €15.50. This pizzeria-restaurant overlooks the sea near the port in Cala Gonone.

Ristorante Il Pescatore *(☎ 0784 9 31 74, Via Marco Polo)* Full meals from €20.65. Fish and seafood are the house specials at this restaurant just near the port.

El Bocadillo *(☎ 0338 580 33 29, Via Colombo 8)* Panini €1.55-2.60. One street back from the port, this groovy bar/cafe does excellent coffee and great sandwiches and rolls.

Getting There & Away

Six daily ARST buses run from Nuoro to Cala Gonone via Oliena and Dorgali. There is only one daily run to Tortoli (inland of Arbatax) leaving from Dorgali at around 3pm. The bus stop in Dorgali is on Via La Marmora, in front of the post office.

BAUNEI, URZULEI & AROUND

These small villages on the S125 between Dorgali and Arbatax provide a good base for exploring the spectacular Gola di Gorropu (Gorropu Gorge, near Urzulei) and the high plain known as the Golgo (near Baunei).

Baunei and Urzulei are accessible by ARST bus from Olbia, Nuoro, Dorgali and Cagliari, but it is easier to reach them from Tortoli and Arbatax. Santa Maria Navarrese can be reached by ARST bus from Tortoli. However, to really explore this area, it is best to have your own transport.

The Golgo

This beautiful area has an almost magical atmosphere and is one of the many places on Sardinia where you can see evidence of the ancient Nuraghic civilisation. The rustic **Chiesa di San Pietro** has been a place of pilgrimage for centuries. It stands isolated in the countryside and is surrounded by a wall lined with pilgrims' shelters. Nearby are some Nuraghic *betili*, conical sacred stones that were carved to indicate feminine forms.

To get to the high plain and church from Baunei, you need to take a very steep road, which winds uphill to the north of the town centre; the road is not served by public transport. A sign indicates San Pietro, but you'll probably need to ask for directions. It's about 8km to the church.

On the way to the high plain, 1km before the church uphill on the left, is a restaurant, ***Golgo*** *(☎ 0782 61 06 75, 0337 81 18 28, Località Golgo)*, designed to blend into its natural surroundings and open Easter to end-September. Meals cost from €23.25. You can request to camp here if you want to explore the area (approximately €6.20 per person per night). The restaurant serves filling, traditional-style Sardinian meals.

Farther north, about 300m before you reach the church of San Pietro, a road to the left leads to a group of low buildings (visible from the road). This is the base of ***Cooperativa Goloritzé*** *(☎ 0782 61 05 99, e goloritze@tiscalinet.it)*, a well-organised excursion company run by young locals that offers guided treks in the area – on foot, on horseback or, if you prefer, by donkey. They can organise pick-ups at Baunei. Their programme includes a day on horseback exploring the Golgo high plain (€36.15 per person), a two-day walk from Golgo to Cala Sisine (from €77.45 per person), a three-day guided horseback trek (€232.40) and a one-week walk from the Lanaittu Valley near Oliena to Santa Maria Navarrese (€573.25 per person). You can either camp or stay in local hotels. If you like the idea of a rustic lunch at a traditional shepherd's hut, they can organise it for €18.10 per head.

From the church, a trail continues on for around 10km to Cala Sisine; otherwise head back to Golgo and take the walking trail down to the sea at Cala Goloritzé (one hour). The beauty of the scenery will take your breath away.

For inexpensive and efficient guided tours and walking in the Urzulei area, call ***Società Gorropu*** *(☎ 0782 64 92 82 or 0347 423 36 50, e francescomurru@virgilio.it)*, a group of expert young guides based at Sa Domu Es'Orcu, a bar-restaurant on the S125 near Urzulei. They can help you make the exciting descent into the Gola di Gorropu or explore the area's fascinating underground caves and rivers. They also organise treks of other parts of the Barbagia. See also the boxed text 'Discovering the Barbagia' earlier.

Places to Stay & Eat There are no hotels at Baunei, but there is one near Urzulei.

Albergo Silana *(☎ 0784 9 51 20, 7km north of Urzulei on the SS125)* Singles/doubles without bath €18.10/31, with bath €20.65/36.15. Rooms are basic but there's not a lot of choice in this area.

If you want to stay in either Baunei or Urzulei, it is possible to rent rooms in private homes – ask the Società Gorropu guides for information. This is an excellent way to get a feel for the real Sardinia. Expect to pay around €12.90 to €15.50 per night.

For a good meal at Urzulei, try ***Ristorante La Ruota*** *(☎ 0782 64 90 94, Via San Giorgio 14)*. Traditional Sardinian meals start from €15.50.

Santa Maria Navarrese

On the coast, 10km south of Baunei, is the small and pleasant seaside town of **Santa Maria Navarrese**. This family-style holiday resort was developed in the 1970s around an ancient church and a medieval tower. The town has a small tourist port and a very long sandy beach dotted with rocky outcrops. Unlike many beaches in Italy, this one is quite undeveloped – although there are a few bars and restaurants.

Albergo Santa Maria *(☎ 0782 61 53 15, fax 0782 61 53 96, ⓔ albergosantamaria@tiscalinet.it, Via Plammas 30)* Low season singles/doubles €41.30/67.15, high season €46.50/77.45. Open early April-Oct. The staff are particularly friendly and helpful in this charming hotel, which boasts, among other things, a private section of the beach, and a van and boat to shuttle the guests to the beginning and end of walks, or to secluded beaches in the area. There are good deals on half-board arrangements.

ARBATAX

If you're planning to explore the Barbagia, this small port town, not far from Baunei towards Cagliari, is probably the most convenient place to arrive by ferry. Tirrenia ferries dock here from Civitavecchia twice weekly, as do the fast ferries from Fiumicino in summer (mid-July to early September). If you're heading north to Baunei, Cala Gonone, Dorgali or Nuoro, you will need to catch an ARST bus or walk 4km to Tortoli, where you can catch the direct once-daily ARST bus for Nuoro (via Lanusei). It's best to check at the tourist offices in Dorgali or Nuoro for up-to-date information. Buses leave from Arbatax for Cagliari two or three times per day, but don't necessarily coincide with ferry arrivals. Another, more extravagant, option would be to catch the Trenino Verde to Cagliari (see Getting There & Around under Cagliari earlier).

For accommodation, try ***Il Gabbiano*** *(☎ 0782 62 35 12, Località Porto Frailis, a few km from Arbatax)*, a small, intimate family-run hotel. Comfortable singles/doubles with bath cost €41.30/51.65.

SARDINIA

Language

Italian is a Romance language related to French, Spanish, Portuguese and Romanian. The Romance languages belong to the Indo-European group of languages, which includes English. Indeed, as English and Italian share common roots in Latin, you will recognise many Italian words.

Modern literary Italian began to develop in the 13th and 14th centuries, predominantly through the works of Dante, Petrarch and Boccaccio, who wrote chiefly in the Florentine dialect. The language drew on its Latin heritage and many dialects to develop into the standard Italian of today. Although many dialects are spoken in everyday conversation, standard Italian is the national language of schools, media and literature and is understood throughout the country.

There are 58 million speakers of Italian in Italy; 500,000 in Switzerland, where Italian is one of the official languages; and 1.5 million speakers in France, Slovenia and Croatia. As a result of migration, Italian is also spoken in the USA, Argentina, Brazil and Australia.

Visitors to Italy with more than the most fundamental grasp of the language need to be aware that many older Italians still expect to be addressed by the third person formal, that is, *lei* instead of *tu*. Also, it is not considered polite to use the greeting *ciao* when addressing strangers, unless they use it first; it's better to say *buon giorno* (or *buona sera*, as the case may be) and *arrivederci* (or the more polite form, *arrivederla)*. We have used the formal address for most of the phrases in this guide. Use of the informal address is indicated by (inf). Italian also has both masculine and feminine forms (they usually ending in 'o' and 'a' respectively). Where both forms are given in this guide, they are separated by a slash, the masculine form first.

If you'd like a more comprehensive guide to the language, get a copy of Lonely Planet's *Italian phrasebook*.

Pronunciation

Italian pronunciation isn't very difficult to master once you learn a few easy rules. Although some of the more clipped vowels and stress on double letters require careful practice for English speakers, it is easy enough to make yourself understood.

Vowels

Vowels are generally more clipped than in English:

a as in 'art', eg, *caro* (dear); sometimes short, eg, *amico/a* (m/f) (friend)
e as in 'tell', eg, *mettere* (to put)
i as in 'inn', eg, *inizio* (start)
o as in 'dot', eg, *donna* (woman); as in 'port', eg, *dormire* (to sleep)
u as the 'oo' in 'book', eg, *puro* (pure)

Consonants

The pronunciation of many Italian consonants is similar to that of their English counterparts. Pronunciation of some consonants depends on certain rules:

c as the 'k' in 'kit' before **a**, **o** and **u**; as the 'ch' in 'choose' before **e** and **i**
ch as the 'k' in 'kit'
g as the 'g' in 'get' before **a**, **o**, **u** and **h**; as the 'j' in 'jet' before **e** and **i**
gli as the 'lli' in 'million'
gn as the 'ny' in 'canyon'
h always silent
r a rolled 'rr' sound
sc as the 'sh' in 'sheep' before **e** and **i**; as 'sk' before **a**, **o**, **u** and **h**
z as the 'ts' in 'lights', except at the beginning of a word, when it's as the 'ds' in 'suds'

Note that when **ci**, **gi** and **sci** are followed by **a**, **o** or **u**, the 'i' is not pronounced unless the accent falls on the 'i'. Thus the name 'Giovanni' is pronounced 'joh-**vahn**-nee'.

Word Stress

A double consonant is pronounced as a longer, more forceful sound than a single consonant.

Stress generally falls on the second-last syllable, as in *spa-**ghet**-ti*. When a word has an accent, the stress falls on that syllable, as in *cit-**tà*** (city).

Greetings & Civilities

Hello.	*Buongiorno.* *Ciao.* (inf)
Goodbye.	*Arrivederci.* *Ciao.* (inf)
Yes.	*Sì.*
No.	*No.*
Please.	*Per favore/Per piacere.*
Thank you.	*Grazie.*
That's fine/ You're welcome.	*Prego.*
Excuse me.	*Mi scusi.*
Sorry (forgive me).	*Mi scusi/Mi perdoni.*

Small Talk

What's your name?	*Come si chiama?* *Come ti chiami?* (inf)
My name is ...	*Mi chiamo ...*
Where are you from?	*Di dov'è?* *Di dove sei?* (inf)
I'm from ...	*Sono di ...*
I (don't) like ...	*(Non) Mi piace ...*
Just a minute.	*Un momento.*

Language Difficulties

Please write it down.	*Può scriverlo, per favore?*
Can you show me (on the map)?	*Può mostrarmelo (sulla carta/pianta)?*
I understand.	*Capisco.*
I don't understand.	*Non capisco.*
Do you speak English?	*Parla inglese?* *Parli inglese?* (inf)
Does anyone here speak English?	*C'è qualcuno che parla inglese?*
How do you say ... in Italian?	*Come si dice ... in italiano?*
What does ... mean?	*Che vuole dire ...?*

Paperwork

name	*nome*
nationality	*nazionalità*
date of birth	*data di nascita*
place of birth	*luogo di nascita*
sex (gender)	*sesso*
passport	*passaporto*
visa	*visto*

Getting Around

What time does the ... leave/arrive?	*A che ora parte/ arriva ...?*
aeroplane	*l'aereo*
boat	*la barca*
(city) bus	*l'autobus*
(intercity) bus	*il pullman*
train	*il treno*
I'd like a ... ticket.	*Vorrei un biglietto ...*
one-way	*di solo andata*
return	*di andata e ritorno*
1st class	*di prima classe*
2nd class	*di seconda classe*
I want to go to ...	*Voglio andare a ...*
The train has been cancelled/delayed.	*Il treno è soppresso/ in ritardo.*
the first	*il primo*
the last	*l'ultimo*
platform number	*binario numero*
ticket office	*biglietteria*
timetable	*orario*
train station	*stazione*
I'd like to hire a ...	*Vorrei noleggiare ...*
bicycle	*una bicicletta*
car	*una macchina*
motorcycle	*una motocicletta*

Directions

Where is ...?	*Dov'è ...?*
Go straight ahead.	*Si va sempre diritto.* *Vai sempre diritto.* (inf)
Turn left.	*Giri a sinistra.*
Turn right.	*Giri a destra.*
at the next corner	*al prossimo angolo*
at the traffic lights	*al semaforo*
behind	*dietro*
in front of	*davanti*
far	*lontano*
near	*vicino*
opposite	*di fronte a*

Signs

Ingresso/ Entrata	**Entrance**
Uscita	**Exit**
Informazione	**Information**
Aperto	**Open**
Chiuso	**Closed**
Proibito/ Vietato	**Prohibited**
Camere Libere	**Rooms Available**
Completo	**Full/No Vacancies**
Polizia/ Carabinieri	**Police**
Questura	**Police Station**
Gabinetti/Bagni	**Toilets**
Uomini	**Men**
Donne	**Women**

Around Town

I'm looking for ... — *Cerco ...*
- a bank — *un banco*
- the church — *la chiesa*
- the city centre — *il centro (città)*
- the ... embassy — *l'ambasciata di ...*
- my hotel — *il mio albergo*
- the market — *il mercato*
- the museum — *il museo*
- the post office — *la posta*
- a public toilet — *un gabinetto/ bagno pubblico*
- the telephone centre — *il centro telefonico*
- the tourist office — *l'ufficio di turismo/ d'informazione*

I want to change ... — *Voglio cambiare ...*
- money — *del denaro*
- travellers cheques — *degli assegni per viaggiatori*

beach — *la spiaggia*
bridge — *il ponte*
castle — *il castello*
cathedral — *il duomo/la cattedrale*
church — *la chiesa*
island — *l'isola*
main square — *la piazza principale*
market — *il mercato*
old city — *il centro storico*
palace — *il palazzo*
ruins — *le rovine*
sea — *il mare*
square — *la piazza*
tower — *la torre*

Accommodation

I'm looking for a ... — *Cerco ...*
- guesthouse — *una pensione*
- hotel — *un albergo*
- youth hostel — *un ostello per la gioventù*

Where is a cheap hotel? — *Dov'è un albergo che costa poco?*
What is the address? — *Cos'è l'indirizzo?*
Could you write the address, please? — *Può scrivere l'indirizzo, per favore?*
Do you have any rooms available? — *Ha camere libere?*

I'd like (a) ... — *Vorrei ...*
- bed — *un letto*
- single room — *una camera singola*
- double room — *una camera matrimoniale*
- room with two beds — *una camera doppia*
- room with a bathroom — *una camera con bagno*
- to share a dorm — *un letto in dormitorio*

How much is it ...? — *Quanto costa ...?*
- per night — *per la notte*
- per person — *per ciascuno*

May I see it? — *Posso vederla?*
Where is the bathroom? — *Dov'è il bagno?*
I'm/We're leaving today. — *Parto/Partiamo oggi.*

Shopping

I'd like to buy ... — *Vorrei comprare ...*
How much is it? — *Quanto costa?*
I don't like it. — *Non mi piace.*

May I look at it?	*Posso dare un'occhiata?*
I'm just looking.	*Sto solo guardando.*
It's cheap.	*Non è caro/a.*
It's too expensive.	*È troppo caro/a.*
I'll take it.	*Lo/La compro.*
Do you accept ...?	*Accettate ...?*
credit cards	*carte di credito*
travellers cheques	*assegni per viaggiatori*
more	*più*
less	*meno*
smaller	*più piccolo/a* (m/f)
bigger	*più grande*

Time & Dates

What time is it?	*Che ore sono?*
It's (8 o'clock).	*Sono (le otto).*
in the morning	*di mattina*
in the afternoon	*di pomeriggio*
in the evening	*di sera*
When?	*Quando?*
today	*oggi*
tomorrow	*domani*
yesterday	*ieri*
Monday	*lunedì*
Tuesday	*martedì*
Wednesday	*mercoledì*
Thursday	*giovedì*
Friday	*venerdì*
Saturday	*sabato*
Sunday	*domenica*
January	*gennaio*
February	*febbraio*
March	*marzo*
April	*aprile*
May	*maggio*
June	*giugno*
July	*luglio*
August	*agosto*
September	*settembre*
October	*ottobre*
November	*novembre*
December	*dicembre*

Emergencies

Help!	*Aiuto!*
Call ...!	*Chiami ...!* *Chiama ...!* (inf)
a doctor	*un dottore/ un medico*
the police	*la polizia*
There's been an accident	*C'è stato un incidente!*
I'm lost.	*Mi sono perso/a.*
Go away!	*Lasciami in pace!* *Vai via!* (inf)

Numbers

0	*zero*
1	*uno*
2	*due*
3	*tre*
4	*quattro*
5	*cinque*
6	*sei*
7	*sette*
8	*otto*
9	*nove*
10	*dieci*
11	*undici*
12	*dodici*
13	*tredici*
14	*quattordici*
15	*quindici*
16	*sedici*
17	*diciassette*
18	*diciotto*
19	*diciannove*
20	*venti*
21	*ventuno*
22	*ventidue*
30	*trenta*
40	*quaranta*
50	*cinquanta*
60	*sessanta*
70	*settanta*
80	*ottanta*
90	*novanta*
100	*cento*
1000	*mille*
2000	*due mila*
one million	*un milione*

Health

I'm ill.	*Mi sento male.*
It hurts here.	*Mi fa male qui.*
I'm ...	*Sono ...*
asthmatic	*asmatico/a*
diabetic	*diabetico/a*
epileptic	*epilettico/a*
I'm allergic ...	*Sono allergico/a ...*
to antibiotics	*agli antibiotici*
to penicillin	*alla penicillina*
antiseptic	*antisettico*
aspirin	*aspirina*
condoms	*preservativi*
contraceptive	*anticoncezionale*
diarrhoea	*diarrea*
medicine	*medicina*
sunblock cream	*crema/latte solare (per protezione)*
tampons	*tamponi*

FOOD

Basics

breakfast	*prima colazione*
lunch	*pranzo*
dinner	*cena*
restaurant	*ristorante*
grocery store	*un alimentari*
What is this?	*(Che) cos'è?*
I'd like the set lunch.	*Vorrei il menù turistico.*
Is service included in the bill?	*È compreso il servizio?*
I'm a vegetarian.	*Sono vegetariano/a.*

Menu

This glossary is intended as a brief guide to some of the basics and by no means covers all of the dishes you're likely to encounter in Italy. Names and ingredients of dishes often vary from region to region, and even pizza toppings can change. Most travellers to Italy will already be well acquainted with the various Italian pastas, which include spaghetti, fettucine, penne, rigatoni, gnocchi, lasagne, tortellini and ravioli. The names are the same in Italy and no further definitions are given here.

Useful Words

affumicato	smoked
al dente	firm (as all good pasta should be)
alla brace	cooked over hot coals
alla griglia	grilled
arrosto	roasted
ben cotto	well done (cooked)
bollito	boiled
cameriere/a	waiter/waitress
coltello	knife
conto	bill/cheque
cotto	cooked
crudo	raw
cucchiaino	teaspoon
cucchiaio	spoon
forchetta	fork
fritto	fried
menù	menu
piatto	plate
ristorante	restaurant

Staples

aceto	vinegar
burro	butter
formaggio	cheese
limone	lemon
marmellata	jam
miele	honey
olio	oil
olive	olives
pane	bread
pane integrale	wholemeal bread
panna	cream
pepe	pepper
peperoncino	chilli
polenta	cooked cornmeal
riso	rice
risotto	rice cooked with wine and stock
sale	salt
uovo/uova	egg/eggs
zucchero	sugar

Meat, Fish & Seafood

acciughe	anchovies
agnello	lamb
aragosta	lobster
bistecca	steak
calamari	squid

capretto	kid (goat)
coniglio	rabbit
cotoletta	cutlet or thin cut of meat, usually crumbed and fried
cozze	mussels
dentice	dentex (type of fish)
fegato	liver
gamberi	prawns
granchio	crab
lumaca	snail
manzo	beef
merluzzo	cod
ostriche	oysters
pesce spada	swordfish
pollo	chicken
polpo	octopus
salsiccia	sausage
sarde	sardines
seppia	cuttlefish
sgombro	mackerel
sogliola	sole
tacchino	turkey
tonno	tuna
trippa	tripe
vitello	veal
vongole	clams

Vegetables

asparagi	asparagus
carciofi	artichokes
carote	carrots
cavolo/verza	cabbage
cicoria	chicory
cipolla	onion
fagiolini	string beans
melanzane	aubergines
patate	potatoes
peperoni	peppers
piselli	peas
spinaci	spinach

Fruit

arance	oranges
banane	bananas
ciliegie	cherries
fragole	strawberries
mele	apples
pere	pears
pesche	peaches
uva	grapes

Soups & Antipasti

brodo – broth
carpaccio – very fine slices of raw meat
insalata caprese – sliced tomatoes with mozzarella and basil
insalata di mare – seafood, generally crustaceans
minestrina in brodo – pasta in broth
minestrone – vegetable soup
olive ascolane – stuffed, deep-fried olives
prosciutto e melone – cured ham with melon
stracciatella – egg in broth

Pasta Sauces

alla matriciana – tomato and bacon
al ragù – meat sauce (bolognese)
arrabbiata – tomato and chilli
carbonara – egg, bacon and black pepper
napoletana – tomato and basil
panna – cream, prosciutto and sometimes peas
pesto – basil, garlic and oil, often with pine nuts
vongole – clams, garlic, oil and sometimes with tomato

Pizzas

All pizzas listed have a tomato (and sometimes mozzarella) base.

capricciosa – olives, prosciutto, mushrooms and artichokes
frutti di mare – seafood
funghi – mushrooms
margherita – oregano
napoletana – anchovies
pugliese – tomato, mozzarella and onions
quattro formaggi – with four types of cheese
quattro stagioni – like a capricciosa, but sometimes with egg
verdura – mixed vegetables; usually courgette (zucchini) and aubergine (eggplant), sometimes carrot and spinach

Glossary

AAST – Azienda Autonoma di Soggiorno e Turismo; local tourist office
abbazia – abbey
ACI – Automobile Club Italiano; Italian Automobile Association
affittacamere – rooms for rent
affresco – the painting method in which watercolour paint is applied to wet plaster
agriturismo – tourist accommodation on working farms
AIG – Associazione Italiana Alberghi per la Gioventù; Italian Youth Hostel Association
albergo (s), **alberghi** (pl) – hotel (up to five stars)
alimentari – grocery shop
aliscafo (s), **aliscafi** (pl) – hydrofoil
Alleanza Nazionale – National Alliance; neo-Fascist political party
al taglio –by the slice
alto – high
ambasciata – embassy
ambulanza – ambulance
anfiteatro – amphitheatre
antipasto (s), **antipasti** (pl) – starter, appetiser
APT – Azienda di Promozione Turistica; provincial tourist office
ASL – Azienda Sanitaria Locale; Provincial Health Agency
autonoleggio – car hire
autostrada (s), **autostrade** (pl) – motorway (highway)

bambino (s), **bambini** (pl) – child
bancomat – ATM
battistero – baptistry
bene – well, good; the smart set
benzina – petrol
benzina senza piombo – unleaded petrol
bianco – white
biglietto – ticket
biglietto chilometrico – kilometric card; train pass
biglietto cumulativo – a ticket that allows entrance to a number of associated sights
bivacchi – unattended mountain hut
borgo (s), **borghi** (pl) – cluttered towns and villages, little changed over hundreds of years
Brigate Rosse (BR) – Red Brigades (terrorist group)
bruschetta – toasted bread with various toppings

cambio – exchange office
camera – room
campanile – bell tower
campo – field
cappella – chapel
carabinieri – police with military and civil duties
carnevale – carnival period between Epiphany and Lent
carretti – carts
carta – menu
carta d'identità – identity card
carta geografica – map
carta telefonica – phonecard
casa – house
castello – castle
cattedrale – cathedral
cena – evening meal
centro – city centre
centro storico – historic centre
chiesa (s), **chiese** (pl) – church
chiostro – cloister; covered walkway, usually enclosed by columns, around a quadrangle
cicheti – snacks
cima – summit
CIT – Compagnia Italiana di Turismo; Italy's national travel agency
città – town, city
colazione – breakfast
colle – hill
colonna – column
comune – equivalent to a municipality or county; town or city council; historically, a self-governing town or city
consolato – consulate
contrada – district
coperto – cover charge in restaurants
corso – main street

CTS – Centro Turistico Studentesco e Giovanile; Centre for Student and Youth Tourists
cuccetta – couchette
cupola – dome

Democrazia Cristiana (DC) – Christian Democrats; political party
Democratici di Sinistra (DS) – Left Democrats; political party
deposito bagagli – left luggage
diretto – direct; slow train
duomo – cathedral

ENIT – Ente Nazionale per il Turismo; Italian Tourist Board
enoteca – wine bar
EPT – Ente Provinciale per Il Turismo; local tourist bureau
ES – Eurostar; very fast train
espresso – express mail; express train; short black coffee
estiva – summer

farmacia – pharmacy
fermo posta – poste restante
ferramenta – hardware store
ferrovia – train station
festa – feast day; holiday
Feste di Pasqua – Holy Week
fiume – river
focaccia – flatbread
fontana – fountain
forno – bakery
foro – forum
Forza Italia – Go Italy; political party
francobollo – postage stamp
frazione – small area
fresco – see affresco
FS – Ferrovie dello Stato; State Railways
funicolare – funicular railway
funivia – cable car

gabinetto – toilets, WC
garni – B&Bs
gasauto or **GPL** – liquid petroleum gas (LPG)
gasolio – diesel
gelato – ice cream
gelaterie – ice-cream parlours
gettoni – telephone tokens
giardino (s), **giardini** (pl) – gardens
golfo – gulf
granita – drink of crushed ice flavoured with lemon, strawberry, coffee and so on
grotta – cave
guardia forestale – forest ranger

HI – Hostelling International

IAT – Informazioni e Assistenza ai Turisti; local tourist office
IC – Intercity; fast train
IDP – International Driving Permit
interregionale – long-distance train that stops frequently
inverno – winter
isola – island
IVA – Imposta di Valore Aggiunto; value-added tax of around 19%

lago – lake
largo – (small) square
lavanderia – laundrette
Lega Nord – Northern League; federalist political party
lido – beach
lingua originale – original language
locanda – inn, small hotel
loggia – covered area on the side of a building; porch; lodge
lo sci – downhill skiing
lungomare – seafront road, promenade

mar or **mare** – sea
mercato – market
Metropolitana – the Rome and Naples underground transport systems
Mezzogiorno – literally midday; name for the south of Italy
MM – Metropolitana Milano; Milan's underground transport system
monte – mountain
motorini – scooters
motoscafo – motorboat
municipio – town hall
musico – musician

Natale – Christmas
nave (s), **navi** (pl) – large ferry, ship
necropoli – (ancient) cemetery, burial site
nuraghi – megalithic stone fortresses (on Sardinia)

oggetti smarriti – lost property
ospedale – hospital
ostello per la gioventù – youth hostel
osteria – a snack bar; cheap restaurant
Pagine Gialle – Yellow Pages; phone directory
palazzo (s) **palazzi** (pl) – mansion, palace; large building of any type, including an apartment block
palio – contest
panetteria – bakery
panino (s), **panini** (pl) – bread roll with filling
paninoteche – cafes
parco – park
passeggiata – traditional evening stroll
pasticceria – cake shop
patrician – a member of the hereditary aristocracy of ancient Rome
Partito Comunista Italiano (PCI) – Italian Communist Party; political party
pellicola – film
pensione – small hotel, often offering board
percorino – hard, spicy cheese made from ewe's milk
permesso di lavoro – work permit
permesso di soggiorno – permit to stay in Italy for a nominated period
piazza – square
piazzale – (large) open square
pietà – literally pity or compassion; sculpture, drawing or painting of the dead Christ supported by the Madonna
pinacoteca – art gallery
pizzeria – pizza restaurant
polenta – cooked cornmeal
polizia – police
Polo per le Libertà – Freedom Alliance; right-wing political coalition
poltrona – airline-type chair on a ferry
ponte – bridge
pontile – jetty
porta – gate, door
portico – portico; covered walkway, usually attached to the outside of buildings
porto – port
posta – post office
Partito Rifondazione Comunista (PRC) – Refounded Communist Party; political party
primo (s), **primi** (pl) – first; starter (meal)
presepio – nativity scene
pronto soccorso – first aid; casualty ward
Partito Socialista Italiano (PSI) – Italian Socialist Party; political party
passeggiata – tradtional evening stroll

quartieri – districts
questura – police station

reale – royal
regionale – slow local train
rifugio (s), **rifugi** (pl) – mountain huts; accommodation in the Alps
riserva marina – marine reserve
riva – river bank
rocca – fortress
ronda – roundabout
rosticceria – shop selling roast meats

sala – room, hall
salumeria – delicatessen
santuario – sanctuary
sassi – stone houses built in two ravines in Matera (in Basilicata)
scala mobile – escalator, moving staircase
scalinata – staircase
sci alpinismo – ski mountaineering
sci di fondo – cross-country skiing
servizio – service charge in restaurants
sestiere – city section (in Venice)
Settimana Bianca – White Week; skiing package
soccorso alpino – mountain rescue
soccorso stradale – highway rescue
sovrintendenza – supervisor
spiaggia – beach
stazione – station
stazione di servizio – petrol or service station
stazione marittime – ferry terminal
strada – street, road
strada provinciale – main road; sometimes just a country lane
strada statale – main road; often multilane and toll free
superstrada – expressway; highway with divided lanes
supplemento – supplement; payable on a fast train

tabaccheria – tobacconist's shop
tavola calda – literally 'hot table'; pre-prepared meat, pasta and vegetable selection, often self-service
teatro – theatre
tempio – temple
tempietto – small temple
terme – thermal baths
tesoro – treasury
torre – tower
torrente – stream
traghetto (s), **traghetti** (pl) – small ferry
tramezzino – sandwich
trattoria – cheap restaurant
treno – train

ufficio postale – post office
ufficio stranieri – foreigners bureau
uffizi – offices
Ulivo – Olive Tree Alliance; centre-left political coalition

vaporetto – small passenger boat/ferry (in Venice)
via – street, road
viale – avenue
vico – alley, alleyway
vigili del fuoco – fire brigade
vigili urbani – traffic police, local police
villa – town house or country house; also the park surrounding the house

Zona Rimozione – Vehicle Removal Zone

Acknowledgements

Many thanks to the travellers who used the last edition and wrote to us with helpful hints, useful advice and interesting anecdotes:

A Bowler, Aaron Cuthbertson, Adam Schreck, AE Beare, Aileen Bracken, Alan Lambert, Alejandro Salgo, Alex Lee, Alice Twain, Alison Buchanan, Amanda Kapp, Ana Eloisa Soto Canino, Andrea Besnard, Andrea Jerzyna, Andrew Aspinall, Andrew Jenkinson, Andrew Keeley, Andrew Kirkwood, Andrew Land, Andrew Leckonby, Andrew Wolton, Andy Rumsey, Andy Semmler, Andy Sparrow, Anette Munthe, Anke Snoeck, Anne L Barton, Anne McCoy, Anneke van Luxemburg, Annette Satterfiled, Anthony Alps, Asa Bergstrom, B Ballard, BJ Pitts, BP Sutton, Barry Slicock, Baylor Lancaster, Belinda Howard, Bethan Lewis, Betty Bridgens, Betty Teltscher, Bill & Ann Stoughton, Bill Kerr, Blair O'Connar, Bogdan Siewierski, Bonny Vrielink, Brian & Carol Little, Bridget Fox, Brie Back, Brodie Woodland, Buzz Cavalier, Cameron Bush, Carly Jassy, Carmel Sexton, Carol Skilton, Carole Bennett, Catherine Boreal, Cathy Vertzyas, Catriona Kealy, Catriona Mackechnie, Charity Pitton, Charlie Clancy, Chia Teck Wee, Christine Barbour, Christine Kent, Christine Themar, Christine Wichert, Ciara O'Mahony, Claire Duffy, Claire Duiker, Clyde and Elva Slonaker, Colette Baron, D Collins, Dale Stevens, Dan Minor, Danielle Brand, David & Merryn Thomas, David Deutscher, David Fuller, David Giannoni, David John Pitts, Debbie Coleman, Deborah Marchant, Derek Simpson, Diana James, Don & Helen Burns, Don Bennett, Donald Cooper, Dorothy Graham, Elaine Brewitt, Elaine Koh, Elena Grant, Elitza Naumova, Elizabeth Finch, Elizabeth R Macaulay, Emma Beechey, Emma Wright, Enrico Buselli, Espen Lauritzen, Eugene Chow, Ewan Girvan, F Blackwood, Felicity Steen, Fiona Wilson, Francesco Diodato, GG Dakin, Gabriel Garnier, Gabriele Marsch, Gabrielle Mathieu, Gail Lefever, Gaynor Carruthers, George Prince, Gerard Wilkie, Gloria Miller, Graciela Juarez, Graeme M. Morland, Gregoire Le Divillec, Gretchen Reinhart, H Pedersen, Harald Horvei, Hardy Weinrebe, Harris Hwang, Helen Russell, Helen Wilms, Helene Eichholz, Hilary & Ian Potts, Hugh Finsten, Ian & Jan Scott, J Hamson, J Hayes, J Noel Burke, James Balding, James Parkhurst, Jan M Pennington, Jan Swart, Jan Zielinski, Jane Alston, Jane Darvall, Janet & Allan Warman, Jennifer Cohen, Jennifer Kochan, Jenny Geoghegan, Jerry Azevedo, Jerry Peek, Joanna Lincolne, Jody Steyls, John and Cynthia Miles, John H Sergeant, John V Lennon, Jonathan Hiller, Jorg Bienzeisler, Jorge Calasaus, Josephine Vanheems, Joy Gilmour, Judith Brookes, Judith O'Brien, Judy Danielson, Julia Tobey, Julie Fenwick, Julie Furber, Jussi Hyttinen, KW Chapman, Kat Wrobel, Kate Belton, Kate Overheu, Ken Steele, Kevin McIntyre, Kieran Briggs, Kim Graham, Kim Van Bussel, Kristin Pedroja, Kylie Cox, Kylie Jeans, Laura Brewer, Laura Crippa, Laura Cusick, Laura Pratt, Laurie Stott, Lenie Vaan Drafer, Lin Qiu, Lorenzo Ferrari, Louisa Prest, Louise Mozzanica, Lucy Botta, Lyman Lee, M McAllister, M Soroko, Majorie Douglass, Makota Hosoya, Marg Ewin, Margaret Nankivell, Margaret Oshea, Marguerite Wells, Marilyn Flax, Mark & Sany Lane, Mark Sternfeld, Marloes Wesselingh, Martha Bird, Martin Schiefelbusch, Mary Armstrong, Mary Kate Libonate, Mary Marmery, Mary Richards, MaryAnne Nelson, Marzia Beltrami, Masami Heiser, Matevz Zgaga, Matt Dawson, Matt Paradise, Maurik Van Haagen, Max Miller, Melissa Anderson, Menno F Chang, Michael Berg, Michael Glass, Michael Levine, Michael Power, Michael Travis, Michaela Newell, Michele Esposito, Michelle Flanagan, Michelle Flieler, Michelle Kidd, Mie Bogo Thaysen, Miguel Guglielminpietro, Mike Appleyard, Miranda Alagich, Mirjam de Koningh, Monika Perendyk, Morgan Dye, Mrjam van der Gugten, Myriam Alexowitz, Natalie Moss, Natasha Markovic, Nathan Dhillon, Neil Cropper, Nidhi Sharma, Nigel A Lee, Nobi Hyakutake, Orly Gal, PA Lekhi, Pablo Iveli, Paddy Murray, Pamela Hagedorn, Patrice Meunier, Patti Ryan, Paul Falvo, Paul Graalman, Paul Levatino, Paul McKernan, Paul W Gioffi, Peter Feldchen, Peter Kunkel, Peter Maher, Peter Strazzabosco, Phil Vernon, Philip Scheir, Philippa Haselgrove, Philippe Glorenec, Preecha Preedaanuntasuk, RF

Parsons, RA Zambardino, Rachel Curtis, Rachel Yapp, Reinhard Goettert, Renato Losio, Richard Adams, Rins Spinhoven, Rob Hale, Robert M Herbst, Robyn Forrester, Roger Tjong, Ron & Marisol Gagliano, Rosemary Dunne-Smith, Ross Crawford, Roy Atkins, Roy Pyne, Ruth Vander Zee, Ryan & Peter Olwagen, Ryan Flagg, Ryoko Kawamura, Sally & Phil Laing, Sandeep Puthran, Sarah Simpson-Goff, Saskia Cornes, Scott Hilberg, Scott Warren, Sean Murphy, Seth Nagel, Shai Grandt, Sharda Ugra, Shari Posey, Sharon Pitardi, Sheila McGrath, Shelley Porfiri, Sigrid Schwarz, Simon Maughan, Skye Cardinal, Sophie Mccarthy, Stephen Iacono, Steve Moore, Steven Stuart, Stuart Moore, Stuart Waddington, Sue Boorman, Sue Walker, Sui-Linn White, Susan Ball, Susan Hansell, Susan Karunaratne, Susan Kirinich, Susana Fortini, Suzanne Goulet, Suzanne Kocher, Tammy Sanderman, Terence Tam, Terry Casstevens, Terry Gray, Thng Hui Hong, Tim Manning, Tom Hall, Tom Splain, Tom Walker, Tony De Curtis, Tony Weston, Travers Grant, Trish Ramsay, Uri Sadeh, Vince Dimasi, Virginia Saffioti, Wan-Cheng Wong, Wayne Mulholland, Will Hegman

LONELY PLANET

ON THE ROAD

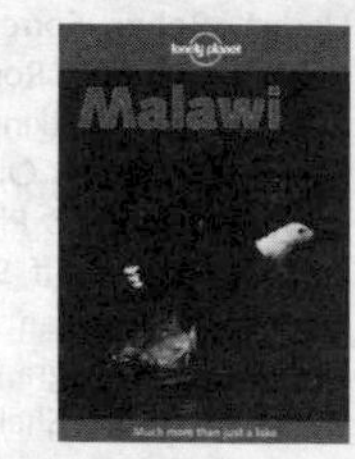

Travel Guides explore cities, regions and countries, and supply information on transport, restaurants and accommodation, covering all budgets. They come with reliable, easy-to-use maps, practical advice, cultural and historical facts and a rundown on attractions both on and off the beaten track. There are over 200 titles in this classic series, covering nearly every country in the world.

Lonely Planet Upgrades extend the shelf life of existing travel guides by detailing any changes that may affect travel in a region since a book has been published. Upgrades can be downloaded for free from **www.lonelyplanet.com/upgrades**

For travellers with more time than money, **Shoestring** guides offer dependable, first-hand information with hundreds of detailed maps, plus insider tips for stretching money as far as possible. Covering entire continents in most cases, the six-volume shoestring guides are known around the world as 'backpackers bibles'.

For the discerning short-term visitor, **Condensed** guides highlight the best a destination has to offer in a full-colour, pocket-sized format designed for quick access. They include everything from top sights and walking tours to opinionated reviews of where to eat, stay, shop and have fun.

CitySync lets travellers use their Palm™ or Visor™ hand-held computers to guide them through a city with handy tips on transport, history, cultural life, major sights, and shopping and entertainment options. It can also quickly search and sort hundreds of reviews of hotels, restaurants and attractions, and pinpoint their location on scrollable street maps. CitySync can be downloaded from **www.citysync.com**

MAPS & ATLASES

Lonely Planet's **City Maps** feature downtown and metropolitan maps, as well as transit routes and walking tours. The maps come complete with an index of streets, a listing of sights and a plastic coat for extra durability.

Road Atlases are an essential navigation tool for serious travellers. Cross-referenced with the guidebooks, they also feature distance and climate charts and a complete site index.

LONELY PLANET

ESSENTIALS

Read This First books help new travellers to hit the road with confidence. These invaluable predeparture guides give step-by-step advice on preparing for a trip, budgeting, arranging a visa, planning an itinerary and staying safe while still getting off the beaten track.

Healthy Travel pocket guides offer a regional rundown on disease hot spots and practical advice on predeparture health measures, staying well on the road and what to do in emergencies. The guides come with a user-friendly design and helpful diagrams and tables.

Lonely Planet's **Phrasebooks** cover the essential words and phrases travellers need when they're strangers in a strange land. They come in a pocket-sized format with colour tabs for quick reference, extensive vocabulary lists, easy-to-follow pronunciation keys and two-way dictionaries.

Miffed by blurry photos of the Taj Mahal? Tired of the classic 'top of the head cut off' shot? **Travel Photography: A Guide to Taking Better Pictures** will help you turn ordinary holiday snaps into striking images and give you the know-how to capture every scene, from frenetic festivals to peaceful beach sunrises.

Lonely Planet's **Travel Journal** is a lightweight but sturdy travel diary for jotting down all those on-the-road observations and significant travel moments. It comes with a handy time-zone wheel, a world map and useful travel information.

Lonely Planet's eKno is an all-in-one communication service developed especially for travellers. It offers low-cost international calls and free email and voicemail so that you can keep in touch while on the road. Check it out on **www.ekno.lonelyplanet.com**

FOOD & RESTAURANT GUIDES

Lonely Planet's **Out to Eat** guides recommend the brightest and best places to eat and drink in top international cities. These gourmet companions are arranged by neighbourhood, packed with dependable maps, garnished with scene-setting photos and served with quirky features.

For people who live to eat, drink and travel, **World Food** guides explore the culinary culture of each country. Entertaining and adventurous, each guide is packed with detail on staples and specialities, regional cuisine and local markets, as well as sumptuous recipes, comprehensive culinary dictionaries and lavish photos good enough to eat.

OUTDOOR GUIDES

For those who believe the best way to see the world is on foot, Lonely Planet's **Walking Guides** detail everything from family strolls to difficult treks, with 'when to go and how to do it' advice supplemented by reliable maps and essential travel information.

Cycling Guides map a destination's best bike tours, long and short, in day-by-day detail. They contain all the information a cyclist needs, including advice on bike maintenance, places to eat and stay, innovative maps with detailed cues to the rides, and elevation charts.

The **Watching Wildlife** series is perfect for travellers who want authoritative information but don't want to tote a heavy field guide. Packed with advice on where, when and how to view a region's wildlife, each title features photos of over 300 species and contains engaging comments on the local flora and fauna.

With underwater colour photos throughout, **Pisces Books** explore the world's best diving and snorkelling areas. Each book contains listings of diving services and dive resorts, detailed information on depth, visibility and difficulty of dives, and a roundup of the marine life you're likely to see through your mask.

LONELY PLANET

OFF THE ROAD

Journeys, the travel literature series written by renowned travel authors, capture the spirit of a place or illuminate a culture with a journalist's attention to detail and a novelist's flair for words. These are tales to soak up while you're actually on the road or dip into as an at-home armchair indulgence.

The range of lavishly illustrated **Pictorial** books is just the ticket for both travellers and dreamers. Off-beat tales and vivid photographs bring the adventure of travel to your doorstep long before the journey begins and long after it is over.

Lonely Planet **Videos** encourage the same independent, tough-minded approach as the guidebooks. Currently airing throughout the world, this award-winning series features innovative footage and an original soundtrack.

Yes, we know, work is tough, so do a little bit of deskside dreaming with the spiral-bound Lonely Planet **Diary** or a Lonely Planet **Wall Calendar**, filled with great photos from around the world.

TRAVELLERS NETWORK

Lonely Planet Online. Lonely Planet's award-winning Web site has insider information on hundreds of destinations, from Amsterdam to Zimbabwe, complete with interactive maps and relevant links. The site also offers the latest travel news, recent reports from travellers on the road, guidebook upgrades, a travel links site, an online book-buying option and a lively traveller's bulletin board. It can be viewed at **www.lonelyplanet.com** or AOL keyword: lp.

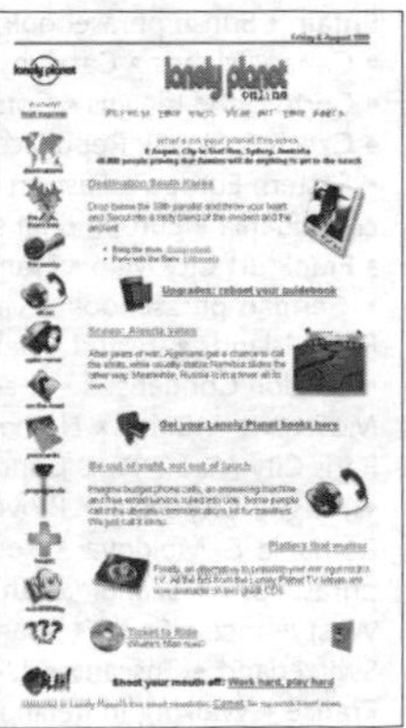

Planet Talk is a quarterly print newsletter, full of gossip, advice, anecdotes and author articles. It provides an antidote to the being-at-home blues and lets you plan and dream for the next trip. Contact the nearest Lonely Planet office for your free copy.

Comet, the free Lonely Planet newsletter, comes via email once a month. It's loaded with travel news, advice, dispatches from authors, travel competitions and letters from readers. To subscribe, click on the Comet subscription link on the front page of the Web site.

Lonely Planet Guides by Region

Lonely Planet is known worldwide for publishing practical, reliable and no-nonsense travel information in our guides and on our Web site. The Lonely Planet list covers just about every accessible part of the world. Currently there are 16 series: Travel guides, Shoestring guides, Condensed guides, Phrasebooks, Read This First, Healthy Travel, Walking guides, Cycling guides, Watching Wildlife guides, Pisces Diving & Snorkeling guides, City Maps, Road Atlases, Out to Eat, World Food, Journeys travel literature and Pictorials.

AFRICA Africa on a shoestring • Botswana • Cairo • Cairo City Map • Cape Town • Cape Town City Map • East Africa • Egypt • Egyptian Arabic phrasebook • Ethiopia, Eritrea & Djibouti • Ethiopian Amharic phrasebook • The Gambia & Senegal • Healthy Travel Africa • Kenya • Malawi • Morocco • Moroccan Arabic phrasebook • Mozambique • Namibia • Read This First: Africa • South Africa, Lesotho & Swaziland • Southern Africa • Southern Africa Road Atlas • Swahili phrasebook • Tanzania, Zanzibar & Pemba • Trekking in East Africa • Tunisia • Watching Wildlife East Africa • Watching Wildlife Southern Africa • West Africa • World Food Morocco • Zambia • Zimbabwe, Botswana & Namibia
Travel Literature: Mali Blues: Traveling to an African Beat • The Rainbird: A Central African Journey • Songs to an African Sunset: A Zimbabwean Story

AUSTRALIA & THE PACIFIC Aboriginal Australia & the Torres Strait Islands •Auckland • Australia • Australian phrasebook • Australia Road Atlas • Cycling Australia • Cycling New Zealand • Fiji • Fijian phrasebook • Healthy Travel Australia, NZ & the Pacific • Islands of Australia's Great Barrier Reef • Melbourne • Melbourne City Map • Micronesia • New Caledonia • New South Wales • New Zealand • Northern Territory • Outback Australia • Out to Eat – Melbourne • Out to Eat – Sydney • Papua New Guinea • Pidgin phrasebook • Queensland • Rarotonga & the Cook Islands • Samoa • Solomon Islands • South Australia • South Pacific • South Pacific phrasebook • Sydney • Sydney City Map • Sydney Condensed • Tahiti & French Polynesia • Tasmania • Tonga • Tramping in New Zealand • Vanuatu • Victoria • Walking in Australia • Watching Wildlife Australia • Western Australia
Travel Literature: Islands in the Clouds: Travels in the Highlands of New Guinea • Kiwi Tracks: A New Zealand Journey • Sean & David's Long Drive

CENTRAL AMERICA & THE CARIBBEAN Bahamas, Turks & Caicos • Baja California • Belize, Guatemala & Yucatán • Bermuda • Central America on a shoestring • Costa Rica • Costa Rica Spanish phrasebook • Cuba • Cycling Cuba • Dominican Republic & Haiti • Eastern Caribbean • Guatemala • Havana • Healthy Travel Central & South America • Jamaica • Mexico • Mexico City • Panama • Puerto Rico • Read This First: Central & South America • Virgin Islands • World Food Caribbean • World Food Mexico • Yucatán
Travel Literature: Green Dreams: Travels in Central America

EUROPE Amsterdam • Amsterdam City Map • Amsterdam Condensed • Andalucía • Athens • Austria • Baltic States phrasebook • Barcelona • Barcelona City Map • Belgium & Luxembourg • Berlin • Berlin City Map • Britain • British phrasebook • Brussels, Bruges & Antwerp • Brussels City Map • Budapest • Budapest City Map • Canary Islands • Catalunya & the Costa Brava • Central Europe • Central Europe phrasebook • Copenhagen • Corfu & the Ionians • Corsica • Crete • Crete Condensed • Croatia • Cycling Britain • Cycling France • Cyprus • Czech & Slovak Republics • Czech phrasebook • Denmark • Dublin • Dublin City Map • Dublin Condensed • Eastern Europe • Eastern Europe phrasebook • Edinburgh • Edinburgh City Map • England • Estonia, Latvia & Lithuania • Europe on a shoestring • Europe phrasebook • Finland • Florence • Florence City Map • France • Frankfurt City Map • Frankfurt Condensed • French phrasebook • Georgia, Armenia & Azerbaijan • Germany • German phrasebook • Greece • Greek Islands • Greek phrasebook • Hungary • Iceland, Greenland & the Faroe Islands • Ireland • Italian phrasebook • Italy • Kraków • Lisbon • The Loire • London • London City Map • London Condensed • Madrid • Madrid City Map • Malta • Mediterranean Europe • Milan, Turin & Genoa • Moscow • Munich • Netherlands • Normandy • Norway • Out to Eat – London • Out to Eat – Paris • Paris • Paris City Map • Paris Condensed • Poland • Polish phrasebook • Portugal • Portuguese phrasebook • Prague • Prague City Map • Provence & the Côte d'Azur • Read This First: Europe • Rhodes & the Dodecanese • Romania & Moldova • Rome • Rome City Map • Rome Condensed • Russia, Ukraine & Belarus • Russian phrasebook • Scandinavian & Baltic Europe • Scandinavian phrasebook • Scotland • Sicily • Slovenia • South-West France • Spain • Spanish phrasebook • Stockholm • St Petersburg • St Petersburg City Map • Sweden • Switzerland • Tuscany • Ukrainian phrasebook • Venice • Vienna • Wales • Walking in Britain • Walking in France • Walking in Ireland • Walking in Italy • Walking in Scotland • Walking in Spain • Walking in Switzerland • Western Europe • World Food France • World Food Greece • World Food Ireland • World Food Italy • World Food Spain **Travel Literature:** After Yugoslavia • Love and War in the Apennines • The Olive Grove: Travels in Greece • On the Shores of the Mediterranean • Round Ireland in Low Gear • A Small Place in Italy

Lonely Planet Mail Order

Lonely Planet products are distributed worldwide. They are also available by mail order from Lonely Planet, so if you have difficulty finding a title please write to us. North and South American residents should write to 150 Linden St, Oakland, CA 94607, USA; European and African residents should write to 10a Spring Place, London NW5 3BH, UK; and residents of other countries to Locked Bag 1, Footscray, Victoria 3011, Australia.

INDIAN SUBCONTINENT & THE INDIAN OCEAN Bangladesh • Bengali phrasebook • Bhutan • Delhi • Goa • Healthy Travel Asia & India • Hindi & Urdu phrasebook • India • India & Bangladesh City Map • Indian Himalaya • Karakoram Highway • Kathmandu City Map • Kerala • Madagascar • Maldives • Mauritius, Réunion & Seychelles • Mumbai (Bombay) • Nepal • Nepali phrasebook • North India • Pakistan • Rajasthan • Read This First: Asia & India • South India • Sri Lanka • Sri Lanka phrasebook • Tibet • Tibetan phrasebook • Trekking in the Indian Himalaya • Trekking in the Karakoram & Hindukush • Trekking in the Nepal Himalaya • World Food India **Travel Literature:** The Age of Kali: Indian Travels and Encounters • Hello Goodnight: A Life of Goa • In Rajasthan • Maverick in Madagascar • A Season in Heaven: True Tales from the Road to Kathmandu • Shopping for Buddhas • A Short Walk in the Hindu Kush • Slowly Down the Ganges

MIDDLE EAST & CENTRAL ASIA Bahrain, Kuwait & Qatar • Central Asia • Central Asia phrasebook • Dubai • Farsi (Persian) phrasebook • Hebrew phrasebook • Iran • Israel & the Palestinian Territories • Istanbul • Istanbul City Map • Istanbul to Cairo • Istanbul to Kathmandu • Jerusalem • Jerusalem City Map • Jordan • Lebanon • Middle East • Oman & the United Arab Emirates • Syria • Turkey • Turkish phrasebook • World Food Turkey • Yemen **Travel Literature:** Black on Black: Iran Revisited • Breaking Ranks: Turbulent Travels in the Promised Land • The Gates of Damascus • Kingdom of the Film Stars: Journey into Jordan

NORTH AMERICA Alaska • Boston • Boston City Map • Boston Condensed • British Columbia • California & Nevada • California Condensed • Canada • Chicago • Chicago City Map • Chicago Condensed • Florida • Georgia & the Carolinas • Great Lakes • Hawaii • Hiking in Alaska • Hiking in the USA • Honolulu & Oahu City Map • Las Vegas • Los Angeles • Los Angeles City Map • Louisiana & the Deep South • Miami • Miami City Map • Montreal • New England • New Orleans • New Orleans City Map • New York City • New York City City Map • New York City Condensed • New York, New Jersey & Pennsylvania • Oahu • Out to Eat – San Francisco • Pacific Northwest • Rocky Mountains • San Diego & Tijuana • San Francisco • San Francisco City Map • Seattle • Seattle City Map • Southwest • Texas • Toronto • USA • USA phrasebook • Vancouver • Vancouver City Map • Virginia & the Capital Region • Washington, DC • Washington, DC City Map • World Food New Orleans **Travel Literature**: Caught Inside: A Surfer's Year on the California Coast • Drive Thru America

NORTH-EAST ASIA Beijing • Beijing City Map • Cantonese phrasebook • China • Hiking in Japan • Hong Kong & Macau • Hong Kong City Map • Hong Kong Condensed • Japan • Japanese phrasebook • Korea • Korean phrasebook • Kyoto • Mandarin phrasebook • Mongolia • Mongolian phrasebook • Seoul • Shanghai • South-West China • Taiwan • Tokyo • Tokyo Condensed • World Food Hong Kong • World Food Japan **Travel Literature:** In Xanadu: A Quest • Lost Japan

SOUTH AMERICA Argentina, Uruguay & Paraguay • Bolivia • Brazil • Brazilian phrasebook • Buenos Aires • Buenos Aires City Map • Chile & Easter Island • Colombia • Ecuador & the Galapagos Islands • Healthy Travel Central & South America • Latin American Spanish phrasebook • Peru • Quechua phrasebook • Read This First: Central & South America • Rio de Janeiro • Rio de Janeiro City Map • Santiago de Chile • South America on a shoestring • Trekking in the Patagonian Andes • Venezuela **Travel Literature**: Full Circle: A South American Journey

SOUTH-EAST ASIA Bali & Lombok • Bangkok • Bangkok City Map • Burmese phrasebook • Cambodia • Cycling Vietnam, Laos & Cambodia • East Timor phrasebook • Hanoi • Healthy Travel Asia & India • Hill Tribes phrasebook • Ho Chi Minh City (Saigon) • Indonesia • Indonesian phrasebook • Indonesia's Eastern Islands • Java • Lao phrasebook • Laos • Malay phrasebook • Malaysia, Singapore & Brunei • Myanmar (Burma) • Philippines • Pilipino (Tagalog) phrasebook • Read This First: Asia & India • Singapore • Singapore City Map • South-East Asia on a shoestring • South-East Asia phrasebook • Thailand • Thailand's Islands & Beaches • Thailand, Vietnam, Laos & Cambodia Road Atlas • Thai phrasebook • Vietnam • Vietnamese phrasebook • World Food Indonesia • World Food Thailand • World Food Vietnam

ALSO AVAILABLE: Antarctica • The Arctic • The Blue Man: Tales of Travel, Love and Coffee • Brief Encounters: Stories of Love, Sex & Travel • Buddhist Stupas in Asia: The Shape of Perfection • Chasing Rickshaws • The Last Grain Race • Lonely Planet ... On the Edge: Adventurous Escapades from Around the World • Lonely Planet Unpacked • Lonely Planet Unpacked Again • Not the Only Planet: Science Fiction Travel Stories • Ports of Call: A Journey by Sea • Sacred India • Travel Photography: A Guide to Taking Better Pictures • Travel with Children • Tuvalu: Portrait of an Island Nation

LONELY PLANET

You already know that Lonely Planet produces more than this one guidebook, but you might not be aware of the other products we have on this region. Here is a selection of titles that you may want to check out as well:

Europe on a shoestring
ISBN 1 86450 150 2
US$24.99 • UK£14.99

Mediterrean Europe
ISBN 1 86450 154 5
US$27.99 • UK£15.99

Read This First: Europe
ISBN 1 86450 136 7
US$14.99 • UK£8.99

Tuscany
ISBN 1 86450 357 2
US$17.99 • UK£10.99

Milan, Turin & Genoa
ISBN 1 86450 362 9
US$14.99 • UK£8.99

Italian phrasebook
ISBN 0 86442 456 6
US$5.95 • UK£3.99

Rome
ISBN 1 86450 311 4
US$15.99 • UK£9.99

Venice
ISBN 1 86450 321 1
US$15.99 • UK£8.99

Florence
ISBN 1 74059 030 9
US$17.99 • UK£8.99

Walking in Italy
ISBN 0 86442 542 2
US$17.95 • UK£11.99

World Food Italy
ISBN 1 86450 022 0
US$12.95 • UK£7.99

Rome Condensed
ISBN 1 86450 360 2
US$11.99 • UK£5.99

Available wherever books are sold

Index

Text

A

Abbazia di Monte Oliveto Maggiore 631
Abbazia di Pomposa 542
Abbazia di San Galgano 630–1
Abbazia di San Vincenzo al Volturno 709
Abbazia e Chiesa di Santa Maria 783
Abruzzo 697–707, **698**
accommodation 127–30
Acqui Terme 302
activities, *see* individual entries
Aeolian Islands 855–64
  getting there & away 855–6
Agrigento 889–93, **891**
agriturismo 128–9
Agropoli 771–2
AIDS, *see* HIV/AIDS
Aieta 832
air travel 146–51, 159
  Africa 151
  Asia 151
  Australia 150–1
  Canada 150
  continental Europe 148–9
  New Zealand 151
  UK & Ireland 147–8
  USA 149–50
  within Italy 159
Alagna Valsesia 332
Alassio 304
Alatri 271
Alba 328–9
Albanian Towns 710
Albenga 303–4
Alberobello 793–4
Alberti, Leon Battista 78
Alghero 923–5
Aliano 814–15
Alicudi 863–4
Alpe di Siusi 424–5
Alps 43
Altamura 793
Alte Valle del Tevere 666
Alto Adige 417–32
Amalfi 762–5, **763**
Amalfi Coast 759–72

Bold indicates maps.

Amandola 696
Anagni 271
Ancona 678–82, **680**
Aosta 334–8, **335**
Appenines 43
Apricale 309
Apuane Alps 43, 604
Apulia 773–808, **774**
Aquileia 504
Arbatax 943
architecture 66–84
Arezzo 638–41, **639**
Armeno 388
Arona 387
Arquà Petrarca 479
art 66–84
Art Nouveau 83
Ascea 772
Ascoli Piceno 693–6, **694**
Aspromonte Massif 829
Assisi 656–62, **657**
Asti 330–1
Avellino 738
Avigliana 326

B

Babylonian Captivity 32
Badia di Passignano 617
Baia 735–6
Bajardo 309
Balbo, Cesare 36
Balzi Rossi 310
Barbagia 935–6, 938–9
Bard 339
Bari 787–92, **788**
Barletta 785–6, 792
Barolo 330
Baroque 80–1
bars 140
Basilica di San Marco, *see* St Mark's Basilica
Basilica di San Pietro, *see* St Peter's Basilica
Basilica di Santa Caterina d'Alessandria 803
Basilicata 808–16, **809**
Baunei 942–3
Bay of Naples, *see* Gulf of Naples
Bella (Borromean Islands) 386
Bellagio 394

Belluno 492–3
Benevento 737–8
Bergamo 369–74, **370**
Berlusconi 41–3
Bernini 80
Bevagna 662
bicycle travel 166–7, *see also* cycling
  buying a bicycle 167
  rental 167
Bitonto 792
boat travel 157, 167–8
  Sardinia 906–8
  Sicily 837
  within Italy 167–8
Bologna 513–22, **514**
Bolzano 417–20, **418**
books 103–5, *see also* literature
Bordighera 308–9
Borromean Islands 386–7
Bosa 921–2
Bozen, *see* Bolzano
Bramante 77
Brenta Dolomites 409–13
Brenta Riviera 473
Brescia 374–7, **375**
Brigate Rosse 40–1
Brindisi 796–9
Brissago 387
Brunate 390
Brunelleschi 77
Brunico 431
Brusson 342
Buggerru 917
bus travel 151–3, 159–60
  continental Europe 152
  passes 151–2
  UK 152
  within Italy 159–60
business hours 120–1
Busseto 535
Byzantine 70–2

C

Ca' Vecchia 542
Cagliari 908–913
Cala Gonone 939–942
Cala Luna 940
Cala Mariol 940
Cala Sisine 940
Calabria 816–32, **817**

Camigliatello Silano 825–6
Camogli 291–2
Camorra 63
Campania 711–72, **712**
camper vans 156–7
Campi Flegrei 734–6
Campitello Matese 708
Campo di Dentro 431
Campo di Giove 704
Campo Imperatore 702
Campobasso 707–8
Campomarino 710
Canazei 415–16
CanevaWorld 396
Cannero Riviera 387
Cannobio 387
Canossa 530
Capella Sol LeWitt-David Tremlett 330
Capo Vaticano 830
Capoliveri 615–16
Cappella di Monte Siepi 631
Cappella Sistina, *see* Sistine Chapel
Capraia 783
Capri 738–44, **739**
car travel 153–7, 162–6
  buying a car 156, 166
  driving licence 92, 162
  organisations 166
  parking 164
  petrol 164
  rental 156, 164–5
  road rules 163–4
Caravaggio, *see* da Caravaggio, Michelangelo Merisi
Carpi 527
Carrara 604–5
Carsiana Giardino Botanico 502
Casa Natale di Giuseppe Verdi 535
Cascata delle Marmore 672
Caserta 736
Caserta Vecchia 737
Castel del Monte 786–7
Castel Savoia 339
Castel Vittorio 308
Casteldimezzo 689
Castellaneta 808
Castelli Romani 270
Castellina in Chianti 617
Castello Bard 535
Castello di Fénis 338
Castello di Manta 328
Castello di San Pierre 339
Castello di Sarre 339
Castello di Torrechiare 535
Castello di Verrès 338–9
Castello d'Issogne 339
Castello Miramare 501–2
Castellucci 671
Castelmola 870
Castelnovo ne' Monti 529
Castiglione del Lago 653
catacombs 226–7
Catania 870–5, **871**
Catanzaro 818–20, **819**
cathedrals, *see* individual entries
Catholicism, *see* religion
Cavour, Count Caillo Benso di 36–7
Cefalù 853–4
Ceriana 309
Certaldo 630
Certosa di Pavia 368
Certosa di San Lorenzo 771
Cerveteri 262–3
Cervo 304
Champoluc 342
Chia 913–14
Chiesa di San Michele 617
Chiesa di SS Trinità di Saccargia 928
children, travel with 116–17
churches, *see* individual entries
Cicero 52
Cilento Coast, *see* Costiera Cilentana
cinema 57–60
Cinque Terre 295–7
Cinzano 329–30
Cirella 832
Cirò Marina 821
Città di Castello 666
city-states 29–30
Cividale del Friuli 509
Civita di Bagnoregio 268
Civitavecchia 264–5
Civitella Alfedena 705
classical music 56–7
climate 45
clubs 140–1
Cocullo 704
Codula di Luna 941
coffee 139
Colli Euganei 479
Colosseum 188–189
Comacchio 542
Como 390–3, **391**
comunes, *see* city-states
conservation, *see* environmental considerations
consulates 92–4
Convento dei Frati Passionisti 637
Conversano 792
Corniglia 296
Cortina d'Ampezzo 427–30
Cortona 641–2
Corvara 426–7
Cosa Nostra 62–3
Cosenza 822–5, **823**
Costa del Sud 913–14
Costa Rei 913
Costa Smeralda 933
Costa Tirrenica, *see* Tyrrhenian Coast
Costa Verde 917–18
Costacciaro 666
Costiera Amalfitana, *see* Amalfi Coast
Costiera Cilentana 771–2
Counter-Reformation 34–5
Courmayeur 339–41
courses 125
Cremona 377–80, **378**
Crissolo 328
Crotone 821
cultural considerations 60–2, 88–9
Cuma 735–6
Cuneo 326–7
custom regulations 94
cybercafes, *see* Internet
cycling 124–6, 143

D

da Caravaggio, Michelangelo Merisi 81, 212
da Vinci, Leonardo 51–2, 79
Dante Alighieri 53
Deruta 655
Desenzano del Garda 396
design 363–5
Diamante 832
disabled travellers 115–16
discos 140–1
documents 90–2
Dolceacqua 308
Dolomites 43, *see also* Brenta Dolomites, Gruppo di Sella and Sesto Dolomites
  skiing 405–6
  walking 404–5
Domodossola 332–4
Donatello 78
Dorgali 939–42
drinks 138–40

Cinzano 329
Marsala wine 896
martini 330
Dronero 327
Duomo 569–71
drugs 119
duty free, *see* custom regulations

E

earthquakes 44
ecology 46
economy 49–50
education 51
Egadi Islands 903–4
Elba Island 613–16
electricity 107–8
email 102–3
embassies 92–4
Emerald Coast, *see* Costa Smeralda
emergencies 100
Emilia-Romagna 511–51, **512**
Enlightenment 35
Enna 886–8
entertainment 140–1
environmental considerations 46, 88–9
Eraclea Minoa 893
Ercolano 747–9
Erice 901
Este 479
Etruscan sites 262–4, 635–7
Etruscans 17
EUR 228
euro 94–5

F

Facism 38–9
Faenza 547
Fano 689–90
Faro della Vittorio 501
fashion 364
fauna 47–8
Favignana 903
fax services 102
Fellini, Federico 59
Feniglia 637
Ferrara 538–4, **539**
ferries, *see* boat travel
festivals, *see* special events
Fiesolc 594–5
Filicudi 863–4

Bold indicates maps.

film 105, *see also* cinema
Finale Ligure 302–3
Fiorenzuola 689
Firenze, *see* Florence
Fiumicello 816
flora 46–7
Florence 556–93, **558**, **562–5**, **567**
accommodation 581–7
Duomo 569–71
entertainment 590–1
food 587–90
getting around 592–4
getting there & away 592
information 558–61
Ponte Vecchio 577–8
Uffizi Gallery 573–5
walking tours 561–2
Foci del Po, *see* Po Delta
Foggia 775–7
Fonte Cerreto 702
food 130–8
staples 132–5
regional variations 135–7
football 142–3
Forcella Lerosa 428
Foresta Umbra 779
Foro Romano, *see* Roman Forum
Forte di Exilles 326
Friuli-Venezia Giulia 494–510, **495**
Futurism 84

G

Galatina 803
Galilei, Galileo 52
Galleria degli Uffizi, *see* Uffizi Gallery
Galleria Ferrari 527
Gallipoli 805
Gardaland 396
Gardone Riviera 396–7
Garfagnana, The 604
Gargano Promontory, *see* Promontorio del Gargano
Gargnano 398
Garibaldi, Giuseppe 36
gay travellers 115
Genoa 276–290, **277**, **280–1**
accommodation 286–7
entertainment 288–9
food 287–8
getting around 290
getting there & away 289–90
information 278–9

geography 43
geology 43–4
Gerace 820–1
Gergei 922
Ghibellines 28
Giara di Gesturi 922
Giara di Serri 922
Gioia del Colle 792
gladiators 189
Gola di Gorropu 938
Gole Alcantara 870
Golfo Aranci 935–6
Golfo di Castellammare 902–3
Golfo di Napoli, *see* Gulf of Naples
Golgo, The 942–3
Gorizia 502–4
Gothic 74–6
government 48–9
Grado 505
Gran Paradiso 334
Great Schism 32
Gressoney-St-Jean 342
Greve in Chianti 616
Grotta del Bue Marino 940
Grotta dell'Addaura 850
Grotta di Nettuno 925
Grotta Gigante 502
Grotta Ispinigolo 940–1
Grotte di Castellana 793
Grotte di Frasassi 690–1
Grotte di Pertosa 771
Gruppo di Sella 416–17
Guastalla 530
Gubbio 663–6, **664**
Guelphs 28
Gulf of Naples 738–47

H

Hadrian, Emperor 24
health 108–14
HIV/AIDS 112
Herculaneum 747–9, **748**
hiking, *see* walking
history 16–43
hitching 167
HIV/AIDS 112
Holy Roman Empire 28–30
Holy Shroud 317
Humanism 31–2

I

Iglesias 916
Il Carnia 509–10
Il Carso 502
Il Chianti 616–17

Imperia 304–5
Inquisition 34
insurance
  health 108
  travel 91–2
Internet
  access 102–3
  resources 103
Ionian Coast 820–2
Is Arutas 921
Is Zuddas 914
Ischia 744–6
Iseo 400
Isernia 709
Isola Comacina 393
Isola dei Pescatori (Borromean Islands) 386
Isola d'Elba, *see* Elba Island
Isola di Capo Rizzuto 821
Isola Maggiore 654
Isola San Giulio 388
Isolabona 308
Isole Borromee, *see* Borromean Islands
Isole Egadi, *see* Egadi Islands
Isole Eolie, *see* Aeolian Islands
Isole Pelagie 893–94
Isole Pontine 272–3
Isole Tremiti 783–4
itineraries 85–6
Itria Valley 792

J

Julius Caesar 21–22

L

La Maddalena 931–3
La Morra 330
La Rosa 63–4
La Sila 825–6
La Spezia 297–300, **298**
Ladin 426
Lago di Bolsena 269
Lago di Bracciano 269
Lago di Braies 431
Lago di Como 389–95
Lago di Garda 395–9
Lago di Laceno 738
Lago di Nemi 270
Lago di Sennes 428
Lago di Tovel 411
Lago di Trasimeno 653–5
Lago d'Iseo 399–400
Lago d'Orta 388–9
Lago Maggiore 384–8
Lagopesole 810
Langhirano 535
language 64, 944–9
L'Aquila 698–702, **700**
Las Plássas 923
laundry 108
Lazio 259–7, **260**
Le Crete 631–2
Le Marche 677–96, **678**
Leaning Tower 607
Lecce 799–803, **801**
Leghorn, *see* Livorno
Leonardo da Vinci, *see* da Vinci, Leonardo
Leopardi, Giacomo 693
Lerici 300–1
lesbian travellers 115
Levanzo 904
Lignano 505
Liguria 274–310, **275**
Lipari 856–9
literature 52–6
Livorno 610–13, **611**
local transport 168
Locorotondo 794
Locri 820
Lombard Italy 27
Lombardy 343–400
Loreto 682
Lorica 826
Lovers' Lane, *see* Via dell' Amore
Lucca 600–604, **601**
Lucera 777–8
lumache, *see* snails

M

Macerata 691–2, **691**
Machiavelli 569
Madonna di Campiglio 412–13
Madre (Borromean Islands) 386
Mafia 62–3
  Sicily 834–5
magazines 105–7
Malè 413–14
Malinverni 484
Manarola 296
Manciano 635
Manfredonia 778
Mantua (Mantova) 380–3, **381**
maps 87
Maranello 527
Maratea 816
Marciana Marina 615
Marcus Aurelius, Emperor 24
Maremma 635–7
Marettimo 904
Marina di Arbus 917
Marina di Camerota 772
Marina di Campo 615
Marone 400
Marsala 895–7
Marsican bear 47, 705
Martina Franca 792
Massa 604–5
Masso Leopoldino 636
Matera 811–14, **812**
Mattanza, La 903
Matterhorn 334, 341
Mazzini, Giuseppe 36
Medici Villas 595
Medicis 33
Melfi 810
Merano 420–2
Messina 864–6
Michelangelo Buonarroti 79, 220–1
Milan 344–67, **346**, **348–9**, **350**, **365**
  accommodation 356–8
  cathedral 352
  entertainment 361–3
  fashion 364
  food 358–61
  getting around 366–7
  getting there & away 365–6
  information 346–51
  La Scala 353
  shopping 363–4
Milazzo 854–6
Modena 522–7, **524**
Modica 886
Molfetta 793
Molise 707–10, **708**
Molveno 410–12
Mombaroccio 690
Monchio delle Corti 535
Mondavio 690
Mondello 850
money 94–9
  ATMs 96
  costs 97–8
  credit cards 96
  taxes 98
  tipping 98
  travellers cheques 95–6
Monreale 851
Monselice 479
Montagnana 479–80
Montalcino 632
Montalto 829
Monte Argentario 637–8

Monte di San Michele 502
Monte Isola 400
Monte Rosa 334
Monte Rossa 43
Monte Sant'Angelo 779–80
Monte Sibillini 696
Monte Sirai 914
Monte Vergine 738
Montecilfone 710
Montefalco 663
Montefioralle 616
Montefortino 696
Montemerano 635
Montemonaco 696
Montepulciano 633–4
Monterosso 295
Monti del Chianti 616
Monti del Matese 708
Monti Peloritani 866
Monticchio 810
Monviso 328
Morgantina 889
mosaics, *see* art
Mothia 897
motor racing 141–2
motorcycle travel 153–7, 162–6
  buying a motorcycle 166
  driving licence 162
  organisations 166
  parking 164
  petrol 164
  rental 156, 165–6
  road rules 163–4
Mt Blanc 43, 334
Mt Etna 875–7
Mt Vesuvius 749–50
Mugello, The 595–6
Muggia 502
Museo delle Saline 897
Museo Joe Petrosino 771
Museo Martini di Storia dell' Enologia 330
Museo Regionale della Fauna Alpina 342
music 56–7
Mussolini, Benito 38–9

N

Naples 712–34, **716–17**
  accommodation 725–7
  entertainment 730–1
  food 727–30
  getting around 733–5
  getting there & away 732–3
  information 714–15
  Spaccanapoli 718–20
  walking tour 718
Napoleon 35–6
national parks 48, *see* individual entries
Necropoli di Anghelu Ruju 926
Necropoli di San Rocco 636
Nemi 270
Neoclassicism 81–3
Nervi 290
'ndrangheta 63
newspapers 105–7
Nicotera 830
Nocelle 762
Noli 302
Nora 913
Norcia 671
Noto 883–5
Nubia 897
Numana 682
Nuoro 936–7
Nuraghe Arrubiu 923
Nuraghe di Palmavera 925
Nuraghe Losa 921
Nuraghe Mannu 938
Nuraghe Santu Antine 928–9
Nuraghic sites 921, 922–3, 925, 928–9, 938–40

O

Oasi Naturalistica di Persano 771
Olbia 933–5, **934**
Oliena 937
Omegna 388
opera 141
Orbetello 637
Orgosolo 937–9
Oristano 918–20, **918**
Orta San Giulio 388–90
Orvieto 672–7, **673**
Ostia Antica 261
Ostuni 792, 795–6
Otranto 803–4
Oulx 326
Ovid 53, 703

P

Padre Pio 780
Padua (Padova) 473–9, **475**
Paestum 769–71
painting, *see* art
Palatine 186–188
Palau 931–3
Palazzo Farnese 268
Palermo 838–50, **839**
  accommodation 844–6
  entertainment 848
  food 846–8
  getting around 849–50
  getting there & away 848–9
Palestrina 270–1
Palinuro 772
Palio, Il 622
Palmanova 504–5
Palo del Colle 792
Panarea 861–2
Pantelleria 904
Pantheon 211
Paola 831–2
Papal States 27
Parco dei Mostri 268
Parco del Gigante 529–30
Parco Naturale Adamello-Brenta 400, 411
Parco Naturale della Maremma 635
Parco Naturale dello Sciliar 424–5
Parco Naturale di Fanes-Sennes-Braies 416
Parco Naturale Regionale delle Madonie 852–3
Parco Nazionale d'Abruzzo 705–6
Parco Nazionale dei Monti Sibillini 671
Parco Nazionale del Cilento e Vallo di Diano 771
Parco Nazionale del Circeo 271
Parco Nazionale del Gran Paradiso 341–2
Parco Nazionale del Gran Sasso e Monti della Laga 702
Parco Nazionale della Majella 704
Parco Nazionale delle Incisioni Rupestri 400
Parco Nazionale dello Stelvio 400, 422–3
Parco Regionale del Monte Cucco 666
Parma 530–4, **531**
Parmesan 530
Passignano 653
Passo Ghimbegna 309
pasta 132–3
Pavia 367–9, **368**
Peio Terme 414

Bold indicates maps.

Pelagic Islands, *see* Isole Pelagie
Pella 388
Penisola di Sinis 920–1
people 50–1
Permesso di Soggiorno 91
Perugia 645–53, **646**
Pesaro 686–9, **688**
Pescara 706–7
Pescasseroli 705
Peschici 782–3
philosophy 51–2
photography & video 107
Piacenza 536–7, **536**
Piano Grande 671
Piedmont 310–32, **311**
  walking 312
Pietra di Bismantova 529
Pietrabbondante 709
Pieve di Panzano 617
Pieve di San Cresci 617
Pieve di Santo Stefano in Cennan 631
Pigna 308
Pinzolo 412–13
Pisa 605–10, **606**
  Leaning Tower 607
Piscinas 917
Pisciotta 772
Pistoia 598–600, **599**
Pitigliano 636
pizza 132
Pizzo 831
Plan de Corones 431
Po Delta 541–2
Po Valley 43
police 119–20
Policoro 815
politics 48–9
pollution 46, 118
Pompeii 750–4, **752**
Ponte Vecchio 577–8
pop music 57
population 50–1
Port'Ercole 637
Porto Azzurro 615–16
Porto di Maratea 816
Porto Santo Stefano 637
Porto Torres 929
Porto Venere 300
Portocannon 710
Portoferraio 614–15
Portofino 293
Positano 759–62, **760**
postal services 99–100
Potenza 808–10
Pozzo Sacro di Santa Cristina 921
Pozzuoli 735
Praia a Mare 832
Praiano 762
Prato 596–8, **597**
Procida 746–7
Promontorio del Gargano 778–83
Promontorio di Tropea 830–1
public holidays 121
pubs 140
Puglia, *see* Apulia
Putzu Idu 921

R

Ra Stua 428
Radda in Chianti 617
Radio 106
Ragusa 885–6
Ragusa Ibla 885–6
Rapallo 294
Raphael 79
Ravello 765–6
Ravenna 542–6, **544**
Recanati 692–3
Recco 291
Red Brigades, *see* Brigate Rosse
Reggio di Calabria 826–9, **827**
Reggio Emilia 527–9, **528**
religion 63–4
Renaissance 32–4, 76–8
Rimini 547–51, **549**
Riomaggiore 296–7
Riserva Naturale del Fiume Platani 893
Riserva Naturale di Stagnone 897
Risorgimento 35, *see also* Unification
Riva del Garda 398–9
Riva di Solto 400
Riviera di Barcola 501
Riviera di Levante 291–301
Riviera di Ponente 301–10
Rocca Meli Lupi 535
Rocca Sanvitale di Fontanellato 535
Roman Forum 184–6
Romanesque 72–4
Romans 18–27
  Empire 20–7
  Republic 18–20
Rome 170–259, **179**, **185**, **187**, **193–208**, **256**
  accommodation 229–38
  Ara Pacis 223
  Aventine Hill 192, 209
  Basilica di San Giovanni in Laterano 191–2
  Caelian Hill 192
  Capitoline Hill 180–2
  Castel Sant'Angelo 222
  catacombs 226–7
  Colosseum 188–9
  Domus Aurea 189–90
  entertainment 248–52
  Esquiline Hill 190–1
  EUR 228
  food 238–48
  getting around 256–9
  getting there & away 254–256
  Gianicolo 227–8
  Imperial Forums 183
  information 173–7
  Jewish Ghetto 209
  Palatine 186–8
  Palazzo Altemps 210–11
  Palazzo Massimo alle Terme 225
  Pantheon 211
  Piazza del Popolo 212
  Piazza di Campo de' Fiori 210
  Piazza Navona 210
  Piazza Venezia 182–3
  Quirinale 224–5
  Roman Forum 184–6
  St Peter's Basilica 215, **216**
  San Lorenzo Fuori-le-Mura 225
  San Paolo Fuori-le-Mura 225
  shopping 252–4
  Sistine Chapel 222
  Spanish Steps 212
  Terme di Diocleziano 225
  Trastevere 209–10
  Trevi Fountain 211–12
  Vatican 213–22
  Via Appia Antica 226–7
  Via Vittorio Veneto 224
  Villa Borghese 223–4
  Villa Doria Pamphilj 227–8
  walking tour 178–80
Rossano 821–2
Rossena 530
Rossiglione 302
rugby union 143
Ruvo di Puglia 793

S

Sabbioneta 383–4
Sacra Corona Unita 63–4
Sacra di San Michele 326
Sacrario di Olsavia 502
Sacro Monte 388
Saepinum 708
safety 117–19
St Francis of Assisi 659
St Mark's Basilica 444–5
St Peter's Basilica 215, **216**
Salerno 766–9, **767**
Salina 861
Salò 396
Saluzzo 327–8
San Benedetto Po 384
San Domino 783–4
San Fruttuoso 293–4
San Gimignano 626–8
San Giovanni d'Asso 631
San Giovanni di Sinis 920
San Giovanni in Fiore 826
San Giovanni Rotondo 780
San Giustino 666
San Leo 686
San Marino 551–3, **551**
San Martino di Castrozza 414–15
San Maurizio 390
San Nicola 783
San Nicolao 917
San Pietro 914–16
San Remo 305–308, **306**
San Salvatore 920
Sansepolcro 641
Santa Margherita 292–3
Santa Maria Capua Vetere 737
Santa Maria di Leuca 804
Santa Maria Navarrese 943
Santa Teresa di Gallura 930–1
Santa Teresa di Riva 866
Santa Vittoria di Serri 923
Sant'Agata 535
Sant'Antimo 632–3
Sant'Antioco 914–16
Santuario della Santa Casa 682
Santuario di San Romedio 411
Santuario di Santa Rosalia 850
Sapri 772
Sardinia (Sardegna) 905–43, **907**

Bold indicates maps.

- getting around 908
- getting there & away 906–8

Sarnico 400
Sassari 926–8, **927**
Sassello 302
Sassi, The 813
Saturnia 635
Savoca 866
Savona 301–2
Savonesi Apennines 302
Scanno 704
Sciacca 894
science 51–2
Scilla 830
sculpture, *see* art
sea travel, *see* boat travel
Sedilo 921
Segesta 901–2
Selinunte 894–5
Senigallia 690
senior travellers 116
Serra Orrios 938
Sesto Dolomites 431–2
Sestriere 326
shopping 144–5
Shroud of Turin, *see* Holy Shroud
Sibari 822
Sicily (Sicilia) 833–904, **834**
- getting around 837–8
- getting there & away 836–7
- Mafia 834–5

Siena 617–26, **618**
Siracusa, *see* Syracuse
Sirmione 395–6
Sirolo 682
Sistine Chapel 222
skiing 124, 143–4
- Campo di Grove 704
- Dolomites 405–6

snails 329
soccer, *see* football
Solunto 851
Sorano 636
Sorrento 754–9, **755**
Sovana 635–6
Soveria Mannelli 826
Spanish Steps 212
Spartacus 21
special events 121–3
Spello 662
Sperlonga 271–272
Spiaggia di Maria Pia 925
Spiaggia di San Giovanni 925
Spoleto 666–70, **668**
sport 141–4
Stintino 929–30
Stresa 384–6
Stromboli 862-3
Su Nuraxi 922
Su Pallosu 921
Sulmona 702–4
Sulzano 400
Susa 326
Syracuse 877–83, **878**

T

Taggia 308
Tangentopoli 41
Taormina 866–70
Taranto 805–8, **807**
Tarquinia 263–4
Tarvisio 509
taxi 168
Teggiano 771
telephone services 100–2
Tempio di Antas 916
Termoli 709–10
Terni 672
terrorism 40–1
Teulada 914
Tharros 921
theatre 141
time 107
Tindari 854
Titian 79
Tivoli 261–2
Tizzano Val Parma 535
Tocchi 631
Todi 655–6
toilets 108
Tomba Ildebranda 636
Torino, *see* Turin
Torre Pendente, *see* Leaning Tower
Tortora 832
Toscana, *see* Tuscany
tourist offices 89–90
tours 157–8, 168–9
Trafoi 422
train travel 153, 160–2, **161**
- continental Europe 153
- costs 162
- discounts 154–5
- passes 154–5, 160
- UK 153
- underground 168
- within Italy 160–2

Trani 784–5, 792
Trapani 897–901, **898**
Tre Cime di Lavaredo 431
trekking, *see* walking

Tremezzo 393–4
Trent 406–9, **407**
Trentino 406–17,
Trentino-Alto Adige 401–32, **402–3**
Trevi Fountain 211–12
Treviso 490–1
Trieste 495–501, **497**
Triora 308
Troia 778
Trulli Area 792–6
tuna 48
Turin 312–25, **314–15**
  accommodation 320–1
  entertainment 323–4
  food 321–3
  getting around 325–6
  getting there & away 325
  Holy Shroud 317
  information 313–16
Tuscany 554–642, **555**
Tusculum 270
TV 106–7
Tyrrhenian Coast 816–18, 830–2

U

Udine 505–9, **506**
Uffizi Gallery 573–5
Umbertide 666
Umbria 643–77, **644**
Unification 36–7
Urbino 682–6, **683**
Ururi 710
Urzulei 942–3
Ustica 851–3

V

Val Badia 425–7
Val Brembana 374
Val d'Ayas 342
Val de Gotres 428
Val di Fassa 415
Val di Genova 413
Val di Gressoney 342
Val di Magra 301
Val di Non 413
Val di Solda 422–3
Val di Sole 413–14
Val Fiscalina 431
Val Gardena 423–4
Val Martello 423
Val Pusteria 431–2
Val Salata 428
Val Seriana 374
Valentino, Rudolph 808
Valle Argentina 308
Valle Bertuzzi 542
Valle Camonica 400
Valle d'Aosta 332–42, **333**
Valle del Biois 415–16
Valle di Landro 431
Valle di Peio 413–14
Valle di Susa 325–6
Valle Gesso 327
Valle Intemelia 309
Valle Maira 327
Valle Nervia 308
Valle Stura 327
Valley of the Temples 890
Valli di Comacchio 542
Valnerina 670–2
Valtellina 374
Valtournenche 341
Valzoldana 430–1
Varallo 331–2
Varenna 394–5
Vatican 213–22
  Castel Sant'Angelo 222
  St Peter's Basilica 215
  Sistine Chapel 222
  Vatican Museums 218–21
Velia 772
Veneto 433–493, **434**
Venice (Venezia) 433–73, **440–1**, **446–7**, **455**
  accommodation 461–5
  Cannaregio 454–6
  Castello 456–7
  Chioggia 459
  Dorsoduro 451–2
  entertainment 469–70
  food 465–468
  getting around 471–3
  getting there & away 470–1
  information 438–43
  islands 457–9
  San Marco 444–51
  San Polo 452–4
  St Mark's Basilica 444–5
Venosa 810
Ventimiglia 309–10
Verbania 387
Vernazza 295–6
Verona 484–90, **486**
Via dell'Amore 296
Vibo Valentia 831
Vicenza 480–4, **481**
video, *see* photography & video
Vieste 780–2
Vignola 527
Villa Adriana 261–2
Villa Aldobrandini 270
Villa Careggi 595
Villa Cinzano 330
Villa d'Este 262
Villa di Poggio a Caiano 595
Villa Foscari 473
Villa Godi-Valmarana, *see* Malinverni
Villa Grimaldi Fassio 290
Villa Hanbury 310
Villa Kunkler 479
Villa Lante 268
Villa Medicea di Castello 595
Villa Medicea La Petraia 595
Villa Pallavicini 290
Villa Pisani 473
Villaggio Nuragico Nuraghe Mannu 940
Villaggio Nuragico Serra Orrios 940
Villaggio Palumbo 826
Virgil 53, 380
visas 90–2
Viterbo 265–8, **267**
volcanoes 44
  Mt Etna 875–7
  Mt Vesuvius 749–50
  Stromboli 862–3
Volterra 628–30, **629**
Vulcano 859–60

W

walking 123–4
  Dolomites 404–5
  Piedmont 312
water 138
water sports 124
weights & measures 108
wine 138–40
women travellers 114–15
  health 113–14
work 125–7
work permits 91, *see also* Permesso di Soggiorno

Z

Zone 400

Boxed text

Acque Alte 436
Alpine Coral Reef, An 404
Ancient Minorities 822
Ashes, Fire & Brimstone 751
Battle of Benevento, The 737
Battle of the Oranges 331
Big Cheese, The 530
Birds, Bears & Tree Trunks 411
Borgia Family, The 33
Bury the Dead 285
Caffè Society 139
Caravaggio Crawl 212
Castle that Frederick Built, The 787
Chaste & Royal Poet, The 380
Cheap Bus & Train Tickets 259
Chocolate 322
Cumulative Tickets 880
Discounts on Admission 442
Discovering the Barbagia 938–9
Dove Has Landed, The 674
Earthquakes & Volcanoes 44
Easter Mysteries 857
Eating alla Romana 238
Eating Ethnic 244
Emergency Numbers 100
Endangered Species 47
Family Walk from Rifugio Malga Ra Stua to Forcella Lerosa 428
Fashion 364, **365**
Free Wheelers 165
Gastronomic Orgasms 410
Genius of Genoa, The 279
Get the Gear 405
Giacomo Leopardi 693
Gladiators 189
Gold Diggers Keep Out 552
Goooooooooaaaaaaaaaallllllll! 143
Hay Baths 408
Historical Cafes 361
Homes Made Of Stone 923
How Sweet it Is 896
How to Buy Tickets 362
I Misteri 897
Iceman Cometh, The 16
Il Palio 622
Information Dial-Up 347
Italian Bar, The 140
La Mattanza 903
La Perdonanza 699
Ladin Tradition, The 426
Landmark Trust 129
Little Romanesque Tour of Apulia, A 792–3
Living in Matera's Sassi 811
Lovely Lumache 329
Lovers' Lane 296
Machiavelli's Manoeuvres 569
Making his Mark 450
Martini & Rossi 330
Money Savers (Cremona) 379
Money Saver (La Spezia) 297
Money Saver (Turin) 318
Mummy's Boys 61
Mushroom Magic 328
Nero Rules, OK? 171
Ocean Blue 284
Ovid 703
Perfect Pizza, The 728
Prices Quoted 95
Queue Jumping 560
Rail Passes & Discount Tickets 154–5
Raised from Rubble 840
Red and the Black, The 559
Remembering Il Duce 546
Risiera di San Sabba 499
Rock Varieties 43
Roman Underworld 227
Rout of Caporetto, The 503
St Francis of Assisi 659
Saint of the World, A 355
Sardinian Food 912
Saving Venice 438
Savonarola 556
Scenic Loop 309
Spartacus the Dimply One 21
Special Shopping Species, A 119
Splash Out 389
Stars of the Screen 58
Stray Flock 64
Street by Any Other Name, A 437
Taking Music to New Heights 406
Taking Your Mobile Phone 101
Taste of Apulia, A 775
Taste Worth Waiting For, A 525
Tickets Please 482
Tirrenia Ferry Services 906
Tremezzo Trivia 394
Turin's Holy Shroud 317
Venice in a Nutshell 444
Voracious Collecting, Farnese Style 723
Weather, The 405
Weekend Fun 725
What a Cow! 336
Where to Feast on Friulian Fodder 500

MAP LEGEND

BOUNDARIES

International
Provincial
Regional

HYDROGRAPHY

Coastline, Lake
River, Creek
Canal
Swamp

ROUTES & TRANSPORT

Freeway
(under construction)
Highway
Major Road
Minor Road
Unsealed Road
City Freeway
City Highway
City Road

City Street, Lane
Pedestrian Mall
Tunnel
Train Route & Station
Metro & Station
Cable Car or Chair Lift
Walking Track
Walking Tour
Ferry Route

AREA FEATURES

Building
Urban Area
Park, Gardens
Cemetery
Market
Beach, Desert

MAP SYMBOLS

ROME National Capital
MILAN Provincial Capital
La Spezia City
Varazze Town
Arenzano Village

Point of Interest

Place to Stay
Camp Site
Caravan Park
Hut or Chalet

Place to Eat
Pub or Bar

Airport
Ancient or City Wall
Archaeological Site
Bank
Beach
Cable Car or Funicular
Castle or Fort
Cave or Grotto
Cathedral, Church
Cliff or Escarpment
Embassy or Consulate
Hospital
Lookout
Monument
Mountain or Hill

Mountain Range
Museum
National Park
Parking
Pass
Petrol Station
Police Station
Post Office
Stately Home
Synagogue
Telephone
Temple
Tomb
Tourist Information
Zoo

Note: not all symbols displayed above appear in this book

LONELY PLANET OFFICES

Australia
Locked Bag 1, Footscray, Victoria 3011
☎ 03 8379 8000 fax 03 8379 8111
email: talk2us@lonelyplanet.com.au

USA
150 Linden St, Oakland, CA 94607
☎ 510 893 8555 TOLL FREE: 800 275 8555
fax 510 893 8572
email: info@lonelyplanet.com

UK
10a Spring Place, London NW5 3BH
☎ 020 7428 4800 fax 020 7428 4828
email: go@lonelyplanet.co.uk

France
1 rue du Dahomey, 75011 Paris
☎ 01 55 25 33 00 fax 01 55 25 33 01
email: bip@lonelyplanet.fr
www.lonelyplanet.fr

World Wide Web: www.lonelyplanet.com *or* AOL keyword: lp
Lonely Planet Images: lpi@lonelyplanet.com.au